CAMBRIDGE LIBR

MW00862055

Books of enduring scholarly value

British and Irish History, Nineteenth Century

This series comprises contemporary or near-contemporary accounts of the political, economic and social history of the British Isles during the nineteenth century. It includes material on international diplomacy and trade, labour relations and the women's movement, developments in education and social welfare, religious emancipation, the justice system, and special events including the Great Exhibition of 1851.

Dictionary of Political Economy

Sir Robert Harry Inglis Palgrave (1827–1919) began his career in country banking, but through assiduous self-education became a leading figure in economic circles. In 1877, he was made an editor of *The Economist* and formulated plans with other experts to further the general understanding of economics. The most significant result of these plans was the present work. Similar books had already been published in Europe, but a work in English was long overdue. Concerned less with abstract theory and more with practical and historical issues, Palgrave gathered a distinguished group of international contributors, and the three volumes originally appeared in 1894, 1896 and 1899. A landmark in publishing, the work made the discipline of economics accessible to educated adults for the first time. Volume 2, covering F to M, includes entries on free trade, gilds, income tax, labour, and Malthus.

Dictionary of
Political Economy

VOLUME 2

EDITED BY R.H. INGLIS PALGRAVE

CAMBRIDGE
UNIVERSITY PRESS

CAMBRIDGE
UNIVERSITY PRESS

University Printing House, Cambridge, CB2 8BS, United Kingdom

Cambridge University Press is part of the University of Cambridge.
It furthers the University's mission by disseminating knowledge in the pursuit of
education, learning and research at the highest international levels of excellence.

www.cambridge.org
Information on this title: www.cambridge.org/9781108080385

© in this compilation Cambridge University Press 2015

This edition first published 1896
This digitally printed version 2015

ISBN 978-1-108-08038-5 Paperback

This book reproduces the text of the original edition. The content and language reflect
the beliefs, practices and terminology of their time, and have not been updated.

Cambridge University Press wishes to make clear that the book, unless originally published
by Cambridge, is not being republished by, in association or collaboration with,
or with the endorsement or approval of, the original publisher or its successors in title.

AND truly as we look for greater knowledge of human things and a riper judgment in the old man than in the young, because of his experience and of the number and variety of the things which he has seen and heard and thought of ; so in like manner from our age, if it but knew its own strength and chose to essay and exert it, much more might fairly be expected than from the ancient times, inasmuch as it is a more advanced age of the world, and stored and stocked with infinite experiments and observations.— BACON, *Novum Organum* (Ellis and Spedding's edition, 1858), vol. iv. p. 82 (translation).

. . . So far is it from being true, as some would seem to suppose, that economic science has done its work, and thus become obsolete for practical purposes, an object of mere historical curiosity, it belongs, on the contrary, to a class of sciences whose work can never be completed, never at least so long as human beings continue to progress ; for the most important portion of the data from which it reasons is human character and human institutions, and everything consequently which affects that character or those institutions must create new problems for economic science.—CAIRNES, *The Character and Logical Method of Political Economy*, 2nd edition, lecture i., introductory, p. 22.

DICTIONARY OF POLITICAL ECONOMY

DICTIONARY

OF

POLITICAL ECONOMY

EDITED BY

R. H. INGLIS PALGRAVE, F.R.S.

Ore trahit quodcumque potest atque addit acervo.

VOL. II.

F—M

London

MACMILLAN AND CO., Ltd.

NEW YORK: THE MACMILLAN CO.

1896

INTRODUCTION TO VOLUME II.

THE remarks made by way of introduction to the first volume of this work, both as to the method followed and the general plan, may be usefully continued here.

The work has been carried on upon the lines previously proposed, with the assistance which the experience thus gained has given. The great desire of the Editor has been to assist the student to understand the existing position of economic thought. To do this effectively, the past also has had to be investigated, and the many lessons which it contains brought again before the mind. In this reference attention may particularly be drawn to the article on the Historical School of Economists, and the articles on the French, German, and Italian Schools of Economics, which the present volume contains. It has been encouraging to the Editor to be assured that the histories of the Dutch and the English schools, which appeared in the first volume, have been found of value by other economists, and he sincerely trusts that the histories specified above will also be serviceable in a similar manner.

The better knowledge of economic teaching in other countries, which has extended itself among us of recent years, is, of itself, one proof of the more fruitful attention given to the study. In every branch of science it is always advantageous to know how a subject has been regarded by those who have examined it from other points of view than our own. This is especially the case with such a study as economics. The ruling modes of thought and of training, the very conditions of society, all tend to cause differences in the way of regarding social questions. Familiar instances of this are found in the fiscal arrangements of different countries, the modes of levying taxation, the laws regulating labour, and many other matters. For instance, large sums are raised by methods of taxation in France— e.g. the Octroi duties—which would never be borne in this country. Here they would be considered to shackle trade and to oppress the working classes; there they are regarded as an equitable mode of collecting the sums needed for local administration.

Again, there are always some differences of treatment, some differences of surroundings, which colour and shape with their special influences the work of students in other lands. The sketch of the French school shows what progress economic thought had made in France before the end of the 18th century; the improvements in fiscal legislation, which were effected by successive ministers, influenced by the teaching of the *Économistes*, and exemplified by Turgot.

In Germany, the attention given to "cameral science," even in the mediæval period, gave early economic study a different and more practical turn from that followed in any other country of Europe. It will be new to many of our readers to learn that a Zollverein for the empire was proposed in the Imperial Diet of 1522-23. But the most brilliant period in German economic thought is found in the present century. The influence of the great leaders of the German mind—of Fichte, Hegel, and Kant—was slow to develop itself in economics, but it has leavened all the subsequent literature of the subject.

Of the historical articles the one on the Italian school will probably contain most that is new to English readers. The political subdivision of Italy, carried on for centuries and perpetuated to a comparatively recent period, had its counterpart in the prolific wealth of Italian economic literature. The number of small principalities and independent states with the most dissimilar forms of government—from free-trade Tuscany, the great commercial republics of Venice and Genoa, to the militant mediævalism of Naples, with almost every intermediate form of political association—had the result of enriching Italian economic literature with the works of many writers who had continual opportunities of recording the effect of the different systems pursued.

The works of the writers noticed throughout the volume are widely unlike in character. Some are the labours of practised scholars with a perfect command of the vocabulary they employ, enforcing the broad views which wider experience enables them to express. Others have been the jottings down of hard-working but comparatively uneducated men, full of practical common sense and of shrewd observation, but sometimes exhibiting a deficiency in dialectic skill which prevents them from setting forth the truths they desire to inculcate to fullest advantage. Again, the history of science has often to record periods of abatement in energy, but after a time of quiescence the vigour of a living study invariably revives.

Besides the historical articles and those describing the works of economic writers, the side of pure theory has also received due attention. Thus, to select merely the subject of Method, the volume contains articles on Graphical Method, Historical Method, and Inductive Method, Logic and Political Economy, and Method of Political Economy, Mathematical Method, and many other articles on similar subjects, and the Laws of Political Economy, giving a full explanation of this difficult and often debated expression. Under the heading of Labour Exchange will be found illustrations of the Labour Notes issued by associations under the influence of Owen and Place. This phase of an earlier movement, designed to bring all labour to a parity of value, is now almost forgotten. But in its time it bore an important part among the passing influences on current thought.

I desire again to express my best thanks for many valuable suggestions, much kind help and useful information most liberally supplied. This has been to me a source of constant pleasure and a great advantage to the work; especially I desire to record that this volume has greatly benefited both as to its form and its substance through the special help of Dr. Bonar, Mr. Henry Higgs, Mr. E. Schuster, and Mr. H. R. Tedder. Only the Editor can know the value of this assistance.

Considerable progress has been made with Vol. III.

R. H. INGLIS PALGRAVE.

BELTON, NEAR GREAT YARMOUTH,
Midsummer 1896.

TABLE OF CONTENTS OF VOL. II.

PLATES

The numbers immediately following the headings of the Articles are those of the pages on which the Articles will be found. BIOGRAPHIES *in small capitals.*

DICTIONARY OF POLITICAL ECONOMY

F'S, THE THREE

Fixity of Tenure, p. 1; Fair Rent, p. 1; Free Sale, p. 2.

The "Three F's" is a cant term to express three things desired by some tenants of agricultural land—fixity of tenure, a fair rent, and freedom of sale of the tenant's interest in the land. The first two are closely connected, for the tenant would derive no benefit from fixity of tenure if the landlord was free to demand whatever rent he pleased; nor would the tenant derive benefit from the ascertaining of a fair rent if he might at any moment receive notice to quit. Fixity of tenure at a fair rent, or, to put the same thing in other words, a fair rent with the assurance that while circumstances continue the same it will not be raised, is the really desirable thing. Nor would this be hard to secure if the tenant always did his duty by the land and the landlord always did his duty by the tenant.

FIXITY OF TENURE.—It is clear that the cultivator will cease to cultivate unless he has some assurance of reaping the fruits of his labour. But the possible degrees of assurance are many. The cultivator who is not a proprietor must pay for the use of the land and must give up the land when he can pay no longer. Subject to this liability, however, he may be protected from disturbance either by law or by custom. Under Roman law the person who held land in virtue of a contract of EMPHYTEUSIS (*q.v.*) was absolutely irremovable so long as he paid his rent and did not commit waste. A lessee for a term of years is protected by English law so long as he fulfils the covenants of his lease. If there is no evidence to the contrary, our courts assume that every contract for the letting of agricultural land is for a year at least, so as to ensure the harvest to the tenant who has sown it. Under the Irish Land Act of 1881 the Irish tenant has fixity of·tenure so long as he pays the rent determined either by a judgment of the land court or by an agreement made with his landlord to avoid the necessity of litigation. The

Crofters Act of 1887 contains similar provisions for the benefit of a class of agricultural tenants in Scotland. Legal fixity of tenure is also enjoyed by certain classes of cultivators in our Indian empire.

But the same result has frequently been brought about by custom. The mediæval villein was originally a slave cultivating the soil for his lord. But the services due from the villein were gradually fixed by custom, and then the villein acquired fixity of tenure. In England a further step was taken when these services were commuted for money. In the case of the metayers, who form so large a class in several European countries, the share of the produce due to the landlord came to be fixed at one-half or two-thirds of the whole; and subject to this claim of the landlord, the METAYER (*q.v.*) was secured in his holding by custom. Even in modern England the apparent insecurity of tenancies from year to year has been mitigated by the feeling general among all good landlords that a satisfactory tenant should not be displaced merely in order to get a higher rent from a newcomer.

FAIR RENT.—Few vaguer terms than "fair rent" can be found in the whole range of economics. Some limitation to the demand for rent is an indispensable condition of fixity of tenure. Such a limitation may be the result either of custom or of law. In those societies where custom has created fixity of tenure, custom has determined the landlord's claim whether for service, for produce, or for a money rent. But the ascertainment of rent by custom has not proceeded from any abstract notion of farmers. Experience has settled how much the cultivator can afford to give, one year with another. But when the rent is to be settled by judicial award, some guiding principle must be sought and is extremely hard to find. If the fair rent be taken to mean the economic rent, the surplus due to the natural advantages of the land, the amount of this surplus in the case of any particular farm, is something which eludes inquiry. But if the landlord or his pre-

B

decessors in title have expended capital on the improvement of the land, the fair rent must be something different from the economic rent. It must include, over and above the economic rent, an allowance for the. return upon the capital invested in the soil in so far as the effects of that investment are not exhausted. The ascertainment of the fair rent would thus involve two additional inquiries, one almost hopeless, viz. how much the landlord and his predecessors in title have expended in improving the land, the other quite hopeless, viz. what additional value the land at this moment possesses as the result of that expenditure. But, if the law neglects these considerations and adopts the principle that a fair rent is that which allows a fair subsistence to the cultivator, new difficulties arise. In the first place, the standard of living differs much in different districts and in different classes. In the second place, it is well known that one man will thrive on the farm on which another man starves. In the third place, it is unlikely that the cultivator to whom a fair subsistence is secured by law will exert himself to produce anything over and above that fair subsistence. He is not likely to labour in order that there may be a surplus for the landlord. He is more likely to reduce his exertions to providing for himself and to trust that the next judicial award will lessen his rent in consequence. Lastly, the holding may be so small that under no circumstances could it support a family. In such a case the tenant will derive much of his income from other sources, and it will be doubly difficult to say how much his holding should contribute to his maintenance. These difficulties may explain the fact that in the Irish Land Act of 1881 and in the Scotch Crofters Act of 1887 no precise instructions were laid down for the guidance of the courts entrusted with the determination of fair rents. The actual process of determination has unquestionably been very summary, and the result is at best a rough compromise between the claims of the landlord and of the tenant. Only urgent necessity can justify the state in undertaking such a hopeless task as the ascertainment of "fair rents." So long as the settlement of rents by competition does not occasion any violent social disturbance, competition should be left to take its course (see FAIR PRICE ; FAIR RENTS).

FREE SALE.—Wherever the first and second F's have been accepted, the third F follows as a matter of course. For the tenant who enjoys fixity of tenure at a fair rent has an interest in the land which approaches nearly to ownership, which has an appreciable value in the market, and which he should be allowed to sell whenever he wishes to part with it. It is for the landlord's advantage that the tenant should have this power of sale. For it is a strong incentive to the tenant to labour for the improvement of his holding, and thus to augment the landlord's security. It is only just, however, that the landlord should have the right of objecting upon definite grounds to a person who wishes to purchase the tenant's interest and to take his place. Otherwise the landlord might occasionally be forced to accept a man who would let the holding dilapidate and fall into arrear with his rent. Such cases however are rare. Recent experience in Ireland shows that with fixity of tenure and judicial rents the tenant's interest in the land has become extremely valuable. The man who is willing to pay the high price demanded for the tenant-right is probably anxious to make the most of the farm when he gets it. In conclusion, it may be said that when the principle of the three F's has been fully admitted, the tenant is economically, although not legally, part owner of his holding. Economically, although not legally, there is a divided ownership. In countries which have only attained a low stage of economic development, where all economic relations are settled by custom, and where the mass of mankind have no distinct idea of " getting on," divided ownership of land may continue for many hundreds of years. Divided ownership was a lasting phenomenon in mediæval Europe. It is likely to survive a long time in India. But in modern Europe and especially in the United Kingdom it is not likely to last. The farmer who has secured the three F's will wish to take another step and to become full owner of the land. The landlord who has been obliged to yield the three F's will feel that he retains no more than a rent-charge on his land and a rent-charge of a highly precarious nature. The landlord will be willing to sell and the farmer will be eager to buy. When arrangements for sale are based on mutual agreement they are far more likely to be satisfactory to both parties than when resulting from the influence of legal rules. In the classic country of the three F's, in Ireland, where these have been so long demanded and at last so fully conceded, they are gradually losing their importance as one large estate after another is bought by the tenants. The Land Act of 1881 was followed by the Ashbourne Act of 1885, and the Purchase of Land (Ireland) Act of 1891.

[In *Cobden Club Essays*, "Systems of Land Tenure in various Countries."—J. S. Mill, *Political Economy*, and Speeches on the Irish Question.—J. Boyd Kinnear, *Principles of Property in Land*.—O'Connor Morris, *The Land Question in Ireland*.—Baden-Powell, *Land Systems of British India*.]

F. C. M.

FABBRONI, GIOVANNI (1752-1822), born in Florence of noble parentage. He devoted his time to natural science, political economy, and foreign languages, and attained high position under the government of the Grand Duke Leopold of Tuscany. When Tuscany was annexed to the first empire of France, Fabbroni was appointed deputy in the Paris legislative assembly for Pisa, and baron of the empire. When Napoleon I. fell Fabbroni retired to Tuscany, and became honorary professor at the university of Pisa. He wrote on agriculture, technology, chemistry, physics, and mathematics, and his writings are read with interest to the present day. He was greatly esteemed at home and abroad : Jefferson dedicated to him a house in far Virginia ; Cuvier honoured him with an historical eulogium.

A complete catalogue of Fabbroni's works is in his "Life" by Andrew Mustoxidi inserted in the *Biography of Tipaldo* (vol. i. p. 337 *et seq.*). In economics he supported Leopold's liberal reforms, especially free trade in corn, which he discussed in different polemical writings, and with more energy in his *Dei provvedimenti annonari* (1804, 2nd ed., 1817) ; here he examines and refutes the various systems of restricting commerce in corn, and concludes in favour of full liberty. In his treatise *Della prosperità nazionale, dell' equilibrio del commercio e dell' istituzione delle -dogane* (1789), published under the name of VALENTINO FORONDA, he opposes custom-houses as they "are contrary to the principle of fraternity which ought to be the ensign of all nations," and violate the rights of property and liberty. No foreign commerce ought to be feared ; because "it requires fourfold the advantages of our nation to cover the risks and commission, carriage, and the like." Thus, in his treatise *Dei premi d'incoraggiamento che si retribuiscono alle mercature, dei privilegi esclusivi che si accordano alle manifatture, e della libertà che si concede al commercio dei grani*, he opposes any interference with the natural development of commerce. In another treatise, he opposed (1791) the retrograde views of the *Sentimento imparziale per la Toscana*, by Biffi Tolomei. Fabbroni supports the theory of free-trade, gathering together all the arguments of contemporary writers : he sets out the respect due to property and liberty, describing the natural conditions through which national industries succeed in home markets ; the advantage accruing to all classes from the increase of rent of land, which causes a demand for manufactures—an idea derived from the physiocratic doctrine as to the products of land,—which doctrine Fabbroni, however, does not accept in its entirety.

[*Scritti di pubblica economia* del cavaliere Giovanni Fabbroni (Firenze), 1847-1848 (in the *Raccolta degli economisti toscani*, 4 vols.).] A. B.

FACE VALUE, or nominal value, is the value mentioned on the face of a security as distinguished from the market value. The face value of securities passing by delivery determines the amount of the government stamp, and generally also of the broker's commission. Thus the stamp duty on £1000 Egyptian state domain bonds is the same as on £1000 Honduras bonds, though the market value of the former is (1893) about £1030, while the market value of the latter is only about £75. The face value generally represents the amount at which the security is repayable or redeemable, but this is not always the case. There are some debentures which are repayable at a higher amount than the amount represented by the face value, and instances also occur of securities being redeemable at a discount. E. S.

FACTOR (Scots law). A paid commercial agent, remunerated by commission, entrusted with the possession, apparent ownership, management, and disposal of the employer's property and the management of all the principal's affairs in the place where he resides, or in a particular department. He is in point of law a person distinct from his principal. Factorship or "factory," is express or implied, special (*i.e.* limited to a particular department), or general, or both special and general, his commission in the last case conferring on him both general powers and special powers, which would not otherwise have been included. He must act personally, as a rule ; he must remit, according to the principal's directions, all money received by him in the course of the factory business. The employer is bound by all engagements contracted by the factor within his powers ; by the common law of Scotland, which in this respect differs from that of England, as well as by the FACTORS ACTS (*q.v.*) he can pledge the goods of his principal ; and the risk of goods in the factor's hand is, as a rule, with the employer. Third parties deal with the factor as with a principal, unless he expressly deals as a factor for a disclosed principal, not one resident abroad. Factory endures, unless recalled, or terminated in terms of the commission, or superseded, during the life of the employer, and thereafter for unfinished transactions or those entered into in ignorance of the death of the principal.

[See Bell's *Commentaries*, i. 506. Also a steward, a law-agent who manages the letting of farms and other landed estate business. See also JUDICIAL FACTORS.] A. D.

FACTOR (English law). See FACTORS' ACTS.

FACTORIES. The East India Company early established stations in the east for their trade with Persia, Japan, and especially India and the Islands. The first was built at Acheen, in Sumatra, 1602, and within forty years was followed by factories at Bantam, Surat, Agra, Banda, Masulipatam, Jaccatra (Batavia), Scinde, Hooghly, and many other places. Some, *e.g.* Fort St. George (Madras) and Surat, were fortified. These factories were houses containing resident traders—merchants, factors, and writers—the foreign agents of English traders, whether of individual "interlopers" or of a company. These gave their employers much trouble by private trading, perhaps because of their low salaries. Factors received only £20 yearly. Against factories are urged their expensiveness, the patronage enjoyed by the directors, the collisions they occasioned with the Portuguese and Dutch merchants, who feared competition ; for them it is argued that they systematised, extended, and gave continuity to the company's trade, that merchants without permanent stations and forts could not have resisted Dutch opposition (Mill's *British India*, 1840, vol. i. p. 105-106 and note). The success of the system seems to justify it. The factories became governmental centres and led to territorial acquisitions.

[Bruce's *Annals*, 1810.—Elphinstone, *Rise of British Power in the East*, 1887.] E. G. P.

FACTORS' ACTS. The Factors' Act 1889 (52 & 53 Vict. c. 45), which consolidates and repeals the previous acts dealing with similar subject matter, is a partial application to English law of the celebrated French maxim, "En fait de meubles possession vaut titre." The present act is the outcome of a long struggle between the mercantile community on the one hand and the principles of common law on the other. The general rule of the common law as of the civil law was *Nemo dat quod non habet*, and it was held that the mere fact that a person was in possession of goods, or documents of title to goods, did not enable him to bind his principal by disposing of the goods or documents in contravention of his instructions with respect to them. The merchants and bankers contended that, in the interests of commerce, if a person was put or left in possession of goods or documents of title, he ought, as regards innocent third parties dealing with him in the ordinary course of business, to be treated as the owner of the goods. The object mainly contemplated by legal rules is to guard against fraud, the object mainly contemplated by mercantile usages is to guard against the risks of insolvency. The legislature has effected a compromise between the legal and mercantile contentions, but in doing so has in each enactment given more and more weight to the mercantile opinion. The first Factors' Act was passed in 1823 (4 Geo. IV. c. 83), the second in 1825 (6 Geo. IV. c. 94), and the third in 1842 (5 & 6 Vict. c. 39). The object of these three acts was to validate sales and pledges made by factors and other mercantile agents of the same class who were entrusted by their principals with either goods or the documents of title to goods. The Factors' Act 1877 (40 & 41 Vict. c. 39) made a new departure by putting the seller who was left in possession of the documents of title, and the buyer who obtained the documents without paying the price, on the same footing as factors.

The present act, after defining the terms "mercantile agent," and "document of title to goods," enacts that when a mercantile agent is with the consent of the owner in possession of goods or documents, any sale pledge or other disposition made by him in the ordinary course of business shall be as effectual as if it were authorised by the owner of the goods, provided that the person with whom he deals has no notice of the agent's want of authority (§ 2). If, however, the goods are pledged for an antecedent debt or liability, the pledgee acquires no better title than the pledger had at the time of the pledge (§ 4). Protection is then given to *bona-fide* exchanges of goods or documents, and to the lien of consignees, when the consignor is not the owner of the goods (§§ 5 and 7). Some important alterations in the law of sale are next effected. Henceforth if the seller is left in possession either of the goods themselves or of the documents of title to them, any sale or pledge by him to a transferee in good faith and without notice binds the original buyer, and in like manner, if the buyer of goods obtains possession either of the goods or documents without having paid for them, any sub-sale or pledge by him binds the original seller (§§ 8 and 9). Finally when any document of title is lawfully transferred to a holder for value, the seller's lien or right of stoppage is defeated to the same extent as it would be defeated by the transfer of a bill of lading which by common law is treated as a quasi-negotiable instrument (§ 10).

The misappropriation of goods or documents by factors or other agents is made penal by §§ 77-79 of the 24 & 25 Vict. c. 96. The Factors' Act 1889 applies to England and Ireland, and operates on transactions subsequent to the 1st January 1890. Its provisions are now applied to Scotland by the Factors (Scotland) Act 1890. M. D. C.

FACTORY ACTS. Under this general title is commonly included the whole of that very exceptional code of laws for the regulation of labour in this country, which, springing up about the beginning of the present century, and gradually extending, now covers almost the whole area of industrial production. The title is, however, no longer either logically or even conventionally accurate. For, firstly, the designation "factory" is applied by statute in a manner constantly varying and often inconsistent ; and secondly, under that general designation are popularly included other establishments engaged in production, as workshops, which are not technically factories.

England is the original home of factory legislation. Previous to the first Factory Act (1802) no precisely similar enactments are known to have existed in any country. Statutes in restraint of slave labour there had been, both in ancient and modern times, and in constraint of free labour : as *e.g.* the celebrated Statute of Apprentices (5 Eliz. c. 4), of which Prof. Jevons says, in *The State in Relation to Labour*, p. 35 (1882), "The hours of labour were prescribed, not, as in our factory acts, by way of limitation, but by imposition" ; but up to that time the regulation of voluntary work had been chiefly undertaken, where it was undertaken at all, by associations of the nature of the Roman colleges (*Collegia Opificum*) and mediæval gilds, either with or without the direct cognisance of the State. About the end of the last century, however, the GILDS(*q.v.*) having fallen into decay, and the pressure of competitive industry having been enormously increased by the introduction of new methods of industry and the great extension of British trade, public attention began to be drawn to the hardships endured by workers in factories, and some supervision of them was demanded. At first this attention was concentrated on the new type of factories exclusively, and principally on juvenile labour employed there. (On juvenile employment, see CHILDREN'S LABOUR.) The first Factory Act (42 Geo. III. c. 73), was further restricted in application by being mainly confined to apprenticed, pauper, labour, and absolutely confined to cotton and woollen mills. It was amended from time to time by subsequent ones, 59 Geo. III. c. 66 ; 60 Geo. III. c. 5 ; 6 Geo. IV. c. 63 ; 10 Geo. IV. c. 51 ; 10 Geo. IV. c. 63, all of which were repealed, however, by 1 & 2 Will. IV. c. 39 ; which was itself repealed by 3 & 4 Will. IV. c. 103. In this last act a notable advance was made in the principle of factory legislation. It no longer applied exclusively to cotton and woollen mills, but to "any cotton, woollen, worsted, hemp, flax, tow, linen, or silk mill or factory, wherein steam or water or any other mechanical power is, or shall be, used to propel or work the machinery," . . . and it included within its operation, not only apprentices, but all children up to the age of thirteen years and over eight, and others (in subsequent acts denominated "young persons") between the ages of thirteen and eighteen, for all of whom special hours of work were enacted, and, in particular, night work prohibited. This important act was amended and much improved by 7 & 8 Vict. c. 15 ; and these two statutes constitute together the foundation of the laws at present in force, not alone for the special classes of factories to which they had then exclusive reference, but for all others. By the last-named an elaborate set of regulations was provided for the conduct of factories (still confined to "textile" factories), and female operatives above the age of eighteen years (thereafter called "women") were for the first time put upon the same footing as "young persons." A department of factory inspection was constituted, having a central office in London ; and the well-being of the workpeople was aimed at by many minute regulations and in many thoughtful ways.

With the enactment of this statute (1844) the first stage in the progress of English factory legislation may be said to have been accomplished ; that stage, namely, which brought the textile industries under some sort of efficient control. For the next twenty years the energy of factory reformers was principally expended in securing the advantages thus gained and perfecting the system of inspection now fully introduced. To this season belongs, too, the successful conclusion of the long controversy of the Ten Hours' Bill. The demand for a day's work of ten hours, or sixty a week, began as early as before the passing of the act of 1833, which fixed them at forty-eight per week or nine per day, for children from nine to thirteen, and at twelve per day or sixty-nine per week for "young persons" from thirteen to eighteen. By the Factory Act of 1844 these hours were altered to six and a half per day for children between eight and thirteen (not nine and thirteen as formerly), and twelve per day and nine on Saturday for young persons and women (now first included). The object of the agitators was to reduce this number by five hours per week. Such a consummation was apparently achieved by the enactment of 10 Vict. c. 29, fixing them at fifty-eight per week, which, with the shorter time on Saturday, was the equivalent of ten hours' work per day. But in this statute there was a fatal defect. It was not exactly provided when the hard-won ten hours were to be taken—between the extreme limits of 5.30 A.M. and 8.30 P.M.—so that opportunities were offered for evasion, which were only too freely embraced. The remedy was supplied by the Factory Act of 1850, 13 & 14 Vict. c. 54, which definitely introduced the normal working day of twelve hours ; six to six, or seven to seven, with one and a half out for meals ; thus slightly increasing the full number of working hours per week by two, whilst securing that these should not be exceeded. A subsequent Factory Act (1874) made ample compensation to operatives for any disappointment experienced in this result by reducing the hours in textile factories to fifty-six and a half a week, at which they still remain. During this period (from 1844 to 1864) several valuable new measures were added also to the statute book, some of an amending kind, others distinctly widening the scope of legislation. The first of these was the Print Works Act (8 & 9 Vict. c. 29), applying the principles of the factory acts to print works, as therein defined. This was a very ill-conceived and ill-drawn statute, which was afterwards repealed, and those works were brought under the provisions of 33 & 34 Vict. c. 62. In 1853 and 1856 again further acts relating to factories were passed : the first for the purpose of clearing up some debatable points connected with employment ; the latter relating to the fencing of machinery : and in 1860 was passed "An Act to place the employment of women, young persons, and children in bleaching works and dyeing works under the regulation of the Factories Acts" (23 & 24 Vict. c. 78), followed by three amending acts, since repealed, and by the Lace Works Act (24 & 25 Vict. c. 117). But in the meanwhile the same impulse which had produced these laws had been active also in other directions, and had produced substantial results. As early as 1788 some protection had been afforded to chimney-sweeping boys, and this was extended by other legislation in 1834 and 1840 respectively. In the same year (1840) was issued the first of the great Commissions on the employments of the people, popularly known as the Children's Employment Commissions, one of whose earliest results was the passing of a Mines Act (5 & 6 Vict. c. 99), enlarged and improved (1860) by a subsequent act (23 & 24 Vict. c. 151). Three years later (1863) bakeries were brought under a much-needed supervision by the Bakehouse Act (26 & 27 Vict. c. 40); and in 1864 a whole batch of other industries followed, whose inclusion commences a fresh chapter in the history of English factory legislation.

The Factory Act of 1864, which followed on an early report of the second great Commission of inquiry into the occupations of the people, introduced some startling innovations. Hitherto it had been held, either directly or by inference, that the proper arena of factory legislation was specially the textile industries, or, at most, these and a few others closely related to them ; and it had been assumed at all events as a matter of course that *manufacture* was their peculiar sphere. In this view the Print Works Act, and the Bleaching and Dyeing, and Lace Works Acts, had been regarded rather as affiliated than belonging to the Factory Acts, as the Bakehouse Act is to this day. From the Factory Act of 1864 must be dated an entirely new conception of that sphere and this arena. This Act (27 & 28 Vict. c. 48) brought under inspection, not merely several new manufactures in no way connected with textile industry, but certain *employments* as well ; and this it did no longer by affiliation, but distinctly by inclusion, thereby formally abandoning the earlier presumptions of what constituted a factory and the proper subjects of factory legislation. The included manufactures were : (*a*) the manufacture of earthenware, "except bricks and tiles not being ornamental tiles"; (*b*) the manufacture of lucifer matches ; (*c*) the manufacture of percussion caps; (*d*) the manufacture of cartridges. The *employments* were : (*e*) the "employment" of paper staining ; (*f*) the "employment" of fustian cutting. It is clear that the statutory conception of the term factory had hereby undergone a great transformation, and clear also that the present could but be regarded as an instalment of more and larger changes of a like kind to follow. These industries, some of them at least, were not new, the first being possibly the oldest manufacture in the world ; nor were they all carried on by novel methods, whether of greatly congregated labour or by means of labour-saving machinery. The operation of fustian cutting, for instance, was a purely manual occupation, largely pursued in the work-people's own houses ; it formed in fact a typical "home industry." Nor was the above presumption falsified by the event. Three years afterwards (1867) the Factory Acts Extension Act (30 & 31 Vict. c. 103), passed the legislature, whereby a still greater number and variety of fresh industries were brought in. Under the comprehensive terms of this statute the designation "factory" obtained a very wide significance indeed. First, it included all previous definitions not specially mentioned in the act; and next some thirty new and specially-mentioned ones. But it included also "*any premises* whether adjoining or separate, in the same occupation, situate in the same city, town, parish, or place, and constituting one trade establishment in or within the precincts of which fifty or more persons are employed in any manufacturing process," this last expression being further defined to mean "any manual labour exercised by way of trade or for purposes of gain, in or incidental to the making any article, or in, or incidental to, the altering, repairing, finishing, or otherwise adapting for sale any article"—than which it would be difficult to devise more inclusive terms. To all appearance it only remained now to legislate for the places where under fifty persons were employed in manual labour to cover the whole field of industrial production. This task was undertaken accordingly, within the same year, by the Workshop Regulation Act (30 & 31 Vict. c. 106), the preamble distinctly stating this to be its object. A set of similar, not the same, provisions were enacted for workshops as for factories, and the new term defined. "Workshop" meant any place, not a factory or bake-house, where any handicraft was carried on, *in which any child, young person, or woman was employed* and "to which or over which the employer of the persons working therein has the right of access or control" ; so that work-shops employing only adult men were, unlike factories, exempt, and places to which work was taken home to be done were likewise unregulated. With the enactment of these two statutes factory legislation in England theoretically reached the highest point of efficiency that it has yet touched.

But in practice this efficiency was not so apparent. The administration of the Workshop Act had been confided to local authorities, and these almost universally refused or failed to put the law in operation. After three years of unsuccessful trial it was handed over to the inspectors of factories, and seven years afterwards (1878) the two acts were incorporated under the title "Factory and Workshop Act" (41 Vict. c. 16). Unfortunately, whilst so incorporated, the purely artificial distinctions between factories and workshops were retained, whence arises much of the confusion which still encumbers the treatment of this subject, and constantly thwarts the best endeavours of legislators to remove. Repeated inquiries, by parliamentary committees and otherwise, have but succeeded hitherto in making those inconsistencies more apparent, and the remedies applied of demonstrating the impossibility of fixing a complicated mass of legal regulations on a sound basis by means so empiric as those adopted. The act of 1878 deals with five classes of works :—Textile factories, non-textile factories, workshops, workshops in which neither children nor young persons are employed, domestic workshops. By its definitions a "factory" is a place in which machinery is moved by the aid of steam, water, or other mechanical power, and factories are divided into two classes, textile factories and non-textile factories ; the words textile factories and non-textile factories being now first used in an act of parliament. The definition of a textile factory remains the same as under former acts, and the regulations affecting them continue the same, as to hours of work and meals, education of children, limewashing, holidays, etc. The term "non-textile factory" applies to the occupations enumerated in the acts of 1864 and 1867 respectively, whether having mechanical power or not, and includes in addition all unnamed occupations in which such power is used. This definition releases from the special factory regulations all those occupations which were factories under the Factory Act 1867 by reason of fifty persons being employed, and in which mechanical power is not used, which therefore become workshops. The works which are specially named as non-textile factories under the act of 1867 are :—Blast furnaces, copper mills, iron mills, foundries. The manufacture of machinery, of any article of metal, or of india-rubber or gutta-percha, by the aid of mechanical power. Paper manufacture, glass manufacture, tobacco manufacture, letterpress printing, bookbinding. All unnamed occupations in which power is not used, except those specially named in the acts of 1864 and 1867, are workshops as above. In these the hours of work and meals, the sanitary condition, and education, are as strictly provided for as in factories, but unless circumstances satisfy the secretary of state that they are required, registers, and certificates of fitness for young persons and children, obligatory in factories, will not be compulsory. The next class of works, to which fewer regulations apply, are the workshops in which none but women above the age of eighteen are employed. In these workshops the actual time of work and of meals must be the same as in non-textile factories, but with more elasticity of arrangement, and the sanitary condition is to be cared for by the sanitary authority. The last class of works is designated "domestic workshops." These exist where work is carried on in a private house, room, or place, in which the only persons

employed are members of the same family dwelling there. In them the actual hours of work and meals for children and young persons must be the same as in non-textile factories, but with more elasticity of arrangement ; the education of children is on the same plan, and the sanitary condition is cared for by the medical officer of health. The employment of women in domestic workshops is unrestricted. But the act exempts even from such regulations as apply to domestic workshops, and leaves altogether free from this act certain occupations of a light character when carried on in a dwelling-house by the family dwelling there, viz. :—Strawplait making, pillow-lace making, glove making, or others of a like nature to which a secretary of state may extend the exemption. It also exempts from the regulations as to hours of labour and meals, flax scutch mills in which women only are employed intermittently, and for not more than six months in the year. It also exempts any handicraft which is exercised in a dwelling-house by the family dwelling there, at irregular intervals, and does not furnish the whole or principal means of living to the family. Quarries are brought under inspection by this act, either as factories or workshops ; and *pit banks*, that is, all parts of a metalliferous mine not subject to the provisions of the Metalliferous Mines' Act.

Since this act has been in operation another important Factory Act (54 & 55 Vict. c. 75) has been passed (1891), in addition to several minor ones. In the act of 1891 some disposition is shown to return to the method of inspection under the Workshop Act, which placed the administration of the law in the hands of local authorities. In both of them a decided retrogression is shown from the strong position occupied by the dual acts of 1867. This is principally apparent in the multiplication of different classes of protected places and the multiplication of authorities having legal cognisance of them. In the meanwhile several cognate acts have also found a place in our statute book ; dealing with shop labour, with the injection of steam in cotton factories, the abuses of the Truck system, the protection of children employed in theatres, with bakehouses, white-lead works, etc. ; most or all of which are conventionally understood as being included under the general designation factories, and are either wholly or in part under the jurisdiction of the inspectors. Nor has this tendency to spread the utility of factory legislation by the fiction of conceiving of almost any and every occupation as carried on in a factory, reached its probable limit yet, and it is not easy to predict at what point it will do so. The continuous success that has hitherto waited on all these experiments is a strong practical argument in their favour, and the inconveniences which have resulted are not so distinctly of the kind that enlists general sympathy as to call for any very strong protest against them. Only it should surely not be beyond the bounds of legislative capacity to retain what is good in the present arrangement while eliminating what is faulty, —to secure that a reasonable and consistent technology should replace the present unreasonable one, and a real, not nominal, harmony pervade the whole body of law.

The history of factory legislation abroad is to a large extent but a repetition of the story that has now been told. In other countries, as in England, the pressure of competition, and the novel circumstances brought about by greatly subdivided labour and the increasing use of machinery, have necessitated some counter impulse to neutralise the worst evils which have everywhere been found to accompany the advantages of this great industrial change. In other countries, too, the counter impulse has been usually supplied from the central power of the state. As was also natural the example of this country has been, in a great number of instances, closely followed at first, England being the country that not only had earliest made trial of the new experiment of the factory system itself, but on its greatest scale. Thus foreign factory acts have followed pretty closely the lines of English ones, commencing with partial legislation for only textile fabrics, and proceeding afterwards to other industries. But this rule is not universal. In some countries where remedial measures were late in being adopted, the course pursued has been of a more logical kind, and our more palpable errors have been avoided. Partly on account, no doubt, of the useful object-lesson which they provided ; partly, also, from a greater freedom from that tyranny of precedent and mere words, which is so marked a national characteristic here, they have in many cases kept themselves much clearer of inconsistencies and contradictions.

Prussia was the first country of Europe to adopt the principle of the English factory acts, in a law dated the 9th of March 1839, imposing certain restrictions on the employment of young persons and children in textile manufacture. Other states of Germany followed intermittently : Bavaria in 1840, Saxony not till 1861, the North German Confederation in 1869. There is now a general law of a comprehensive kind, embracing the whole German empire. France was but little behind Prussia. The first factory act was enacted there in 1841. Sweden was comparatively early in the field (1846) ; Norway much later (1860). Austria promulgated her first factory act in 1859 ; but Hungary not till 1872. Only quite recently have Belgium and Holland moved in the matter, but much has been done of late by these countries to make up for lost time. In Switzerland a few cantons led the way in 1862 ; others have followed since ; and factory legislation is now

general. Neither in Italy nor Spain has much been accomplished, but Portugal since 1888 has entered heartily on the path of regulation. In Russia there has been a factory act in force since 1881. The United States of America have no general system, but different states provide for their requirements by different laws, while a few are still without any. In India there is a factory act, but a very inefficient one from our point of view. In the civilised parts of Australia one of a very comprehensive kind is in operation, and an extremely stringent one has been in force in New Zealand since 1873.

[George Jarvis Notcutt, *The Factory and Workshop Acts* (Stevens and Sons, 1874).—Alexander Redgrave, C.B., *The Factory and Workshop Acts*, 4th ed. (Shaw and Sons, 1891).—Ernst Edler von Plener, *The English Factory Legislation* (Chapman and Hall, 1873).—R. Whately Cooke-Taylor, *The Modern Factory System* and *Introduction to a History of the Factory System* (Bentley and Son, 1886, and Kegan Paul and Co., 1891).—Victorine Jeans, *Factory Act Legislation* (1892) ; being the Cobden Club Prize Essay for 1891, and describing legislation from 1850. —W. Stanley Jevons, *The State in Relation to Labour* (English Citizen Series, 1882).—Karl Marx, *Capital*, English translation (1887).—Edwin Hodder, *Life of Lord Shaftesbury* (Cassell and Co., 1886).—Philip Grant, *History of Factory Legislation* (1866).—" Alfred," *History of the Factory Movement* (1857) ; down to the passing of the Ten Hours' Bill.]   w. c. t.

FACTORY LAWS IN THE UNITED STATES. The regulation of factory labour in the United States is not a subject of federal, but of state legislation. Consequently there is no uniformity in laws of this character. Some states have progressed much farther than the rest, and are much more active in the execution of the laws. Massachusetts on the whole has taken the lead, while New York, Ohio, New Jersey, and Pennsylvania have advanced in the same direction. In Massachusetts the first law regulating the hours of labour was passed in 1874, making ten hours a legal day for women and children. This was followed by the act of 1877, which provided for the guarding of belting, shafting, gearing, etc., in factories. Members of the state police are detailed to act as inspectors. The act of 1886 provides for weekly payment to operatives employed by corporations. By other legislations night labour is forbidden for women and children, and the time of meal hours is governed. There are numerous other provisions, similar, however, in most respects to factory legislation in England. In 1892 a further reduction of hours, to 58 per week, was made. As yet no attempt has been made in any American state to regulate the hours of male adults. In a few of the states women are employed as inspectors. The labour laws of Massachusetts may be found in the *Annual Report of the Bureau of Labour of Massachusetts* for 1890.   D. R. D.

FACTORY SYSTEM. "The term Factory System designates in technology," says Dr. Ure (*Philosophy of Manufactures*, pp. 13, 14), "the combined operation of many orders of workpeople, adult and young, in tending with assiduous skill a series of productive machines continuously impelled by a central power." It includes, he continues, "such organisations as cotton, flax, silk, and wool mills, and also certain engineering works," but it excludes "those in which the mechanisms do not form a connective series, and are not dependent on one prime mover," . . . such as "iron-works, dye-works, soap-works, brass foundries, etc." "Some authors indeed," says Dr. Ure, "have comprehended under the title factory all extensive establishments wherein a number of people co-operate towards a common purpose of art, and would therefore rank breweries, distilleries, as well as the workshops of carpenters, turners, coopers, etc., under the factory system. But I conceive that this title in its strictest sense involves the idea of a vast automaton, composed of various mechanical and intellectual organs, acting in uninterrupted concert, for the production of a common object, all of them being subordinated to a self-regulated moving force." "If," he concludes, "the marshalling of human beings in systematic order for any technical enterprise were allowed to constitute a factory, this term might embrace every department of civil and military engineering—a latitude of application quite inadmissible." It has been shown already (see FACTORY ACTS) that many of the work-places enumerated by Dr. Ure as "quite inadmissible," have, nevertheless, been since included in the statutory term "factory," and many others under the cognate term "workshop." Moreover his definition is inconsistent with itself, and too recondite for ordinary use. "An automaton composed of various mechanical and intellectual organs, acting in uninterrupted concert," is a definition of the factory system which, even if technically correct, would be of little practical use. A more recent writer, Hon. Carroll D. Wright, special agent of the U. S. government, who some years ago conducted an elaborate investigation into the origin and working of the factory system in America and this country, approaches much nearer a proper conception of the subject (*Report on the Factory System of the United States*, Washington, 1884). "A factory is an establishment where several workmen are collected for the purpose of obtaining greater and cheaper conveniences for labour than they could procure individually at their homes, for producing results by their combined efforts which they could not accomplish separately and for preventing the loss occasioned by carrying articles from place to place during the several processes necessary to complete their manufacture. The principle of a factory is that each labourer, working separately, is controlled by some associating principle which directs his producing powers to effect a common result, which it is the object of all collectively to obtain."

The factory system is therefore a system of production carried on in establishments such as these, and a factory must be defined to be an *establishment*, as laid down by Mr. Wright; not a series of productive operations, which appeared to be the idea of Dr. Ure. It is a concrete fact, a *place* of definite and assured bounds. In such places, then, a mode of industry is carried on that differs, and differs even greatly, from what is carried on in other places. Now wherein does that difference consist? Not exclusively in those facilities of manufacture; some of which Mr. Wright has pointed out; certainly not—economically considered—in the circumstance of a greater or less quantity of machinery being used there, or no machinery at all, nor because of any manner of setting or not setting such machinery in motion (which is the distinction of the current Factory Acts). The difference in the social relation resides in the part allotted to labour under it, and in the purely economical relation in the amount, not the nature, of the product. Under a system of manufacture not so carried on the labourer is master of the industry; he is the prime mover in the enterprise; the active centre of the productive act. In manufacture carried on by factory methods he is this no longer. Where machinery is employed, his duty is principally to keep that going, to feed it, clean it, connect it with some exterior motor, and remove the manufactured commodity from it; or where machinery is not employed, he replaces it. He is then but a portion of the producing organism; whose component subdivisions are partly animate and partly inanimate, and whose initiative is supplied from outside; and in this case he is but an adjunct in the general result. He must go altogether with that method of production or withdraw altogether from it; he cannot choose his time or place of work within it, or choose or venture anything. Such is the position of the labourer towards the system; his attitude towards the product has undergone a great change too. Formerly this relation was intimate. He had actually made it, or part of it; an appreciable quantity of his own personality, of his "labour force," had passed into it; it was *of*, even if not *belonging* to him. It is both of and belonging to the system now. A similar transformation marks his position towards the producer. This also under the smaller system of production was intimate, and is so no longer; the great combinations of labour characteristic of the new method, and the great capitals requisite in manœuvring them, rendering each individual human instrument of comparatively small account. The organism is the supreme object of concern, and hence the relation of the worker to the producer tends to be as remote and impersonal as his relation to the system and the product.

But although machinery, automatic or otherwise, is no necessary feature of the factory system, it was, undoubtedly, the great spread of mechanical invention, and its application to purposes of industry, that fostered its modern growth; just as it was, undoubtedly, the application of the motive power of steam which conferred upon it its most characteristic new form. That the already existent factory system would have continued to spread had these events not occurred is practically certain in view of the industrial history of the time, but no less certain that it would not have spread so rapidly and so much; and it is a natural subject of interest, therefore, at this stage of development —when it begins already to show some signs of entering on a new phase—to inquire what are the most conspicuous economic results that have proceeded from it thus far. The most conspicuous of all results is the immensely increased production of which it has been the instrument; but this is one so patent, and which has been so often the theme of eulogy, that it does not seem necessary to descant upon it here. It will be more to the purpose in such an undertaking as the present to consider to what extent the human agents of production have been affected, and through them the economic position and prospects of the community at large.

It may be said at once, then, that many dismal prophecies which accompanied the unusual development of modern factory labour during its initial period have not been hitherto fulfilled. The factory population has not become less moral during that period, but more moral; not less religious, but more religious. The criminal statistics of factory districts may be appealed to with confidence on the first head; and on the second we have the conclusive evidence accumulated by Sir Edward BAINES (q.v.) in a remarkable pamphlet published in 1843, called The Social, Educational, and Religious State of the Manufacturing Districts, with Statistical Returns (Simpkin and Marshall), wherein it is shown that in the four typical manufacturing counties of Lancashire, Yorkshire, Cheshire, and Derbyshire, the proportion of sittings in church and chapel to the population was much greater than in—for instance— London, and the proportionate advance in the provision of new sittings during the typical factory period 1801 to 1841 far more rapid. It has not become less intellectual but more intellectual. For, first, the Factory Acts and Elementary Education Acts have secured better instruction; and, next, it is clear from the quantity and quality of literature circulating in factory districts that opportunities of intellectual culture are more appreciated now than formerly. Moreover, it was actually owing to the opportunities afforded by the factory system that the first trial of compulsory education was made in this country through the preliminary medium of the half-time system. Its effect on public sanitation has been good. The large spaces and highly-organised conditions required for the successful prosecution of factory labour might, in any case, have been expected to secure this, and it is further provided for by statute. A physical deterioration has been assumed among the operative population, but this remains to be proved. It is an assertion easily made and readily believed; but is in direct opposition to the opinion of some of the most acute and unprejudiced observers, like Mr. Carroll Wright, and M. Louis Reybaud, the well-known French statistician, who have minutely investigated the facts. Or, if that deterioration be allowed in the case of male operatives compared with the race of domestic manufacturers whom they superseded, the same should not be lightly assumed to apply to women. No one familiar with the textile industries of the north of England can have failed to notice the robust type of women employed there, presenting an especially striking contrast with the equivalent class among sempstresses, domestic servants, or the female population of agricultural districts. Mr. Wright declares the women factory workers in France and Germany to be far superior in physique to those who are employed in workshops, and holds the same to be true both of America and England. Neither, it appears, is it the case that the children of these women are degenerate when compared with the children of others at work at other occupations, or compared with children of wholly unemployed mothers (of the same class), or that infant mortality is higher in factory districts than elsewhere. Mr. Cooke-Taylor has even gone the length of arguing that the opposite is true (see Transactions of the National Association for the Promotion of Social Science, 1874 and 1882; Fortnightly Review, May 1875; Contemporary Review, September 1882; Modern Factory System, pp. 408, 423), and has produced a long array of statistics in support of the contention. As for the further question— more social than economic—of the degree in which family life has been affected by the factory system; that is again of wider import than appears at first sight. It is allowed that the arena of productive labour, especially in the greater industries, has been largely transferred from the home to the factory; but is that necessarily an evil? Is it not even what some of our philanthropists are crying out loudly for at the present time? It is true, too, that the factory system fosters independence of character among the young, and has a tendency to break down the old organisation of the domestic circle.

But independence of character may be a gain, not a loss, when not pushed to illegitimate excess ; and all modern experience is in favour of limiting the power of parents over their off-spring. We have probably not yet seen all that the factory system portends in this connection, just as we have not yet seen the ultimate lineaments of that system itself ; the present is a time of rapid transition in labour relations, and it may be well to wait for further readjustments before pronouncing hastily on this and some kindred points.

Some of the more apparent results may, nevertheless, be indicated. How has the factory system affected the relations between capital and labour ; and what is its attitude towards the consumer ? We have noticed its effect on the relations between employer and employed : it has diminished the intimacy that formerly subsisted between these partners in production. It is much to be feared that its action in the mass has followed the same course as its action in individual instances. It is alleged that capital has not become more, but less, careful of the interests of labour, that labour is not more, but less, careful of the interests of capital ; and that even in disputes between the two the aim of each side is sometimes openly proclaimed to be the ruin of the other ; what is more apparent, in almost every dispute, is the utter indifference of both to the welfare of the consumer. This was not so always. The gilds and mediæval trade societies, whether of masters or men or both combined, were as careful to make rules against bad workmanship as against bad workers or harsh masters ; they were not formally constituted on a purely selfish basis. These are not exclusively the results of the factory system ; they are determined by the fierce competition that rages throughout all modern industry ; but it must be said of it, at least, that it has never done anything of its own instance to moderate this struggle, while much in its methods inevitably tends to aggravate it.

There is one result, though but an indirect one, which must be set unequivocally to the credit of the modern factory system, and which will remain long after the present form of it has passed into that oblivion which is likely to be its final home. It was the originator of the Factory Acts. By concentrating the evils of competitive industry, it drew public attention to the cruelties of which that vast influence for good was capable, and caused to be set in motion a body of laws of exceptional humanity, whose purpose is to counteract them. The political economy of the future has no worthier task before it than the harmonising those laws with its own principles, the defining their proper sphere of influence, and the guiding their free extension towards just and legitimate ends.

[Andrew Ure, M.D., *The Philosophy of Manufactures* (Bohn's ed., 1861).—Charles Babbage, *Economy of Machinery and Manufactures*, 4th ed. (Murray, 1846).—"Alfred," *History of the Factory Movement* (Simpkin and Marshall, 1857). —Karl Marx, *Capital ; A Critical Analysis of Capitalist Production*, vols. i. and ii., English translation (Swan Sonnenschein, 1887).—R. Whately Cooke-Taylor, *Introduction to a History of the Factory System* (Bentley and Son, 1886) ; *The Modern Factory System* (Kegan Paul and Co., 1891).—Carroll D. Wright, *Report of the Factory System of the United States* (Washington, Government Printing Office, 1884).]   w. c. t.

FACTS. In political economy all true theory depends on facts. But the dependence is not always of the same sort. It may be immediate or through a chain of deduction. Thus when Carey maintains that settlers in a new country cultivate the worse lands first, he depends upon comparatively direct evidence ; whereas a critic of Carey's theory brings to bear deductively more general facts of human nature when he humorously doubts whether a settler, having a choice between two equally accessible pieces of land, would reject the better as being too good for the "likes of" him. When the two sets of facts, the general and the special, are consilient, there is the strongest evidence (Mill's *Logic*, bk. iii. ch. xi., bk. vi. ch. ix. x.) When they seem to conflict, care is required to interpret fact by theory and to correct theory by fact. The danger of resting exclusively on abstract reasoning has been shown under the head of DOCTRINAIRE. The converse fallacy, to which the "practical man" is liable, may be noticed here.

"Facts by themselves are silent," says Prof. Marshall (*Principles of Economics*, bk. i. ch. v. § 2) ; "they teach nothing until they are interpreted by reason." They are often only "half facts" : for instance, the local variations of wages adduced as a fact proving that there is little competitive mobility among the working-classes ; the explanation of the fact being that there is a difference of efficiency between the working-classes in the compared districts (*id.* bk. vii. ch. iv. § 1). The reckless use of facts is well exemplified in the controversies about free trade. Many instances of blindly following the suggestion of facts are contained in Taussig's *Tariff History of the United States*. The same facts have been used to prove that raising the tariff increases and that it diminishes prosperity. "One disputant ascribes to a recent lowering of the tariff a result which another says was part of the effect of a raising of the tariff that occurred some years before" (Marshall, *Present Position of Economics*, p. 43). "The most reckless and treacherous of all theorists is he who professes to let facts and figures speak for themselves, who keeps in the background the part he has played, perhaps unconsciously, in selecting and grouping them" (*id.* p. 44). Much the same view as to the need of combining facts with theory is presented by Dr. Sidgwick in his

Scope and Method of Economic Science, Professor Wagner in a communication to the *Quarterly Journal of Economics*, October 1886, and other high authorities living and dead—pre-eminently Mill in his *Logic* and *Unsettled Questions*. A lively statement of the truth here emphasised is contained in Lunt's *Economic Science* (Questions of the Day), 1888.

[Consult also Keynes, *Scope and Methods of Political Economy*.]   F. Y. E.

FAILURE. See BANKRUPTCY.

FAIR PRICE. The word "fair," when used in reference to economic matters, has rarely a scientific meaning. On the assumption that a fair price is one just both for buyer and seller, the proper definition is that it is that price at which the same quantity of a commodity is offered for sale and demanded. It must be observed, however, that the term is in practice never used in this signification. Indeed, it is chiefly met with in discussions on questions relating to land ; where it is generally used, not in consonance with, but in contradistinction to, the above definition. The received and now statutory term "fair rent," is perhaps responsible for this use of the term, and in the case of rent of land, as of land itself, there is a possible scientific meaning attachable to the phrase which is not the meaning commonly associated with it. In fact, fair price has come to be applied exclusively to those commodities in which, through some form of monopoly, it is thought that one party to the bargain of exchange has an advantage over the other if the laws of supply and demand are left to work out the price without interference. Thus when it is said that public bodies ought to be allowed to acquire land compulsorily for a fair price, the meaning conveyed is that a computation based on the market value of the land is too high and therefore unfair. A fair wage, it may be noticed, is merely a fair price for labour, and is generally used without reference to the state of trade or of the labour market, but on the assumption that without some interference with the contract for the hire of labour the wage paid will be too small for the proper sustenance of the workman. Such a term, however, is not properly economic (see JUSTUM PRETIUM).   M. G. D.

FAIR RENTS. Fair rent, like the similar expressions "fair wages," "fair price" (JUSTUM PRETIUM, *q.v.*), is used to convey an ethical judgment on an economic fact. Applied in a primitive community, it means the customary or usual rent of land, especially when held by a member of the group (Maine, *Village Communities*, p. 187). Again, like fair wages or price, it implies the idea of an amount that will allow the person interested to live—the rent under which a tenant "can live and thrive." The development of economic science brought about the identification of fair rent

with competitive or Ricardian rent as paid by a capitalist farmer,—the surplus remaining after expenses of production, ordinary profit included, have been satisfied. Lastly, Mill and his leading disciple Cairnes were led from their study of the Irish land question to separate competitive from fair rent in the case of cottier tenants, and to regard the latter as being equivalent to "economic" rent, from which under the pressure of demand the actual rents paid by the cultivators were likely to diverge. "Economic rent," says Cairnes, "is no other than the fair valuation rent of the good landlord. The fair valuation rent of the popular platform admits, in short, of being reduced to strictly scientific expression" (*Essays in Political Economy*, p. 205). Where competition fails to secure justice the intervention of an external authority becomes necessary. According to Mill rent paid by a capitalist . . . may safely be abandoned to competition ; rent paid by labourers cannot. . . . Peasant rents ought never to be arbitrary . . . either by custom or law it is comparatively necessary that they should be fixed" (*Principles*, bk. ii. ch. 10, § 1).

The Report of the Bessborough Commission in 1881 (C. 2779) accepts this view, arguing that there is no "freedom of contract" between landlord and tenant (p. 21) and recommends that fair rents should be fixed "by a constituted authority" (p. 19), and proceeds "to negative the idea that such rent means what in England is known as a full or fair commercial rent, but in Ireland as a rack-rent" (p. 23).

The Irish Land Act of 1881, avowedly based on the Report of the Bessborough Commission, is in fact the legislative enactment of Cairnes's theory as to Irish land rents. It creates a tribunal for the fixing of fair rents, a term which is not further defined, and lays down that the court, "after hearing the parties and having regard to the interest of the landlord and tenant respectively, and considering all the circumstances of the case, holding, and district, may determine what is such fair rent" (44 & 45 Vict. c. 49, § 8).

This measure, which became law on 22nd August 1881, applied to yearly tenancies only ; and pastoral holdings over £50 valuation, were excluded from its operation. By an act of 1887 (50 & 51 Vict. c. 33) leaseholders for less than 99 years were admitted to the privilege of having a fair rent fixed.

During the ten years ending 22nd August 1891, fair rents have been fixed or arranged in 277,160 cases, affecting 8,316,878 acres, being over two fifths of the area of Ireland. In these the former rents come to £5,739,153 : 3s., the new judicial or fair rents £4,548,147 : 2 : 8, showing a reduction of £1,191,006 : 0 : 4 or 20·7 per cent. Fuller details are given in the following table.

Table showing the Operation of the Irish Land Acts 1881 and 1887, for the ten years ending 22nd August 1891.

Method of Settlement.	Number of Cases.	Area Affected.	Tenement Valuation.	Former Rents.	Judicial Rents.	Percentage Reduction.
		Acres R. P.	£ s. d.	£ s. d.	£ s. d.	
Rents fixed by Chief and Sub-Commissions (yearly tenancies)	124,451	3,641,428 3 27 19/24	1,824,080 2 10	2,378,293 16 5½	1,875,021 19 5	21·2
Rents fixed by Chief and Sub-Commissions (leaseholds) *four* years ending August 22nd 1891	20,883	1,212,604 3 18 17/20	756,164 10 4½	1,048,756 15 9¾	786,322 18 9¼	25·0
Rents fixed by Civil Bill Courts (yearly tenancies)	12,078	306,534 1 22½	145,589 12 8	194,295 10 10½	149,502 7 5½	23·0
Rents fixed by Civil Bill Courts (leaseholds) *four* years ending August 22nd 1891 . . .	1,622	69,233 0 18½	45,700 13 7	63,707 13 4½	45,851 16 1	28·0
Fixed by Court Valuers . .	1,306	55,856 2 38½	26,740 12 5½	36,451 19 8	29,441 3 5	19·4
Fixed by Agreements, registered with Commissions . . .	109,753	2,845,165 2 4 23/24	1,573,101 5 2¾	1,892,978 17 0½	1,559,188 19 3	17·6
Fixed by Agreements, registered on Civil Bill Court . . .	7,030	182,866 1 11½	94,802 17 0	121,566 16 0	100,623 0 7	17·2
Arbitration under Commissions .	35	2,719 1 39	1,880 0 0	2,567 5 8½	1,854 17 8	27·7
Arbitration under Civil Bill Courts	2	469 1 24	352 10 0	544 8 1	340 0 0	37·5
Total	277,160	8,316,878 3 5⅗	4,468,412 4 1¾	5,739,153 3 0	4,548,147 2 8	20·7

Under the Act of 1886 (49 & 50 Vict. c. 29) a commission has been appointed to fix fair rents for the crofters in six northern Scotch counties (see F's, THE THREE).

[H. S. Maine, *Village Communities*, Lecture VI.—J. E. Cairnes, "Political Economy and Land" in *Essays in Political Economy* (1873). For the details of fair rents in Ireland and Scotland, the successive *Reports* of the Irish Land Commission and the Crofters Commission.] C. F. B.

FAIR TRADE. A term recently brought into use in antithesis to FREE TRADE (*q.v.*) and applied to commerce on which no restriction is imposed by either party or on which equal restrictions are imposed by both. The fair trader regards reciprocity as being essential for fair exchange, and looks on the English system as "one-sided free trade." In consequence of trade depression the Fair Trade League was founded in 1881 to advocate (1) the use of retaliatory duties against countries that tax British exports, and (2) the closer fiscal union of Great Britain and the colonies. The germ of fair trade ideas is to be found in the work of TORRENS (*q.v.*) entitled *The Budget.*

[T. H. Farrer, *Free Trade versus Fair Trade* (4th ed.), 1887.—C. J. Fuchs, *Handelspolitik Englands*, Leipzig, 1893, pp. 157-172 (see RETALIATION), and the publications of the Fair Trade League.] C. F. B.

FAIRS AND MARKETS, THE DEVELOPMENT OF. Before discussing the history and development of fairs and markets in this country, it will be useful to define the meaning of the terms according to the law. "A market, viewed in its strictly legal aspect, may be defined as an authorised public concourse of buyers and sellers of commodities, meeting at a place, more or less strictly limited or defined, at an appointed time." "A market right is a franchise or privilege to hold a market: to this is generally attached the right to levy tolls and other dues." "A fair has been described as a larger market. Thus in Comyns' *Digest* we have the following definition. 'Every fair is a market—not *è contra* therefore when any statute speaks of a fair, a market should also be comprehended.'" "The specific difference between a fair and a market appears to be that a fair is held less frequently, it generally extends over a longer continuous period, and is of a more miscellaneous character than a market." The above definitions are taken from the final Report of the Royal Commission on Market Rights and Tolls (1887-1891). A few comments will serve to explain these definitions. "A market is a public concourse." Therefore a private meeting of traders—as for instance in many so-called corn-markets—is not a market at all; nor are the auction-marts, which are now so frequent throughout the country for the sale of cattle, in any proper sense of the term cattle-markets. "The place of meeting must be more or less strictly limited or defined." The owner of an English market has exclusive possession for market purposes of an area—it may be a manor, or it may be a township—and within that area he is entitled to shift his market from place to place; beyond the limits of the area he cannot move. "The meeting must be at an appointed time." Market days are fixed either by the terms of the grant which creates the market or by length of usage; and the general law is that a change of the day without the consent of the crown will forfeit the right to hold the market. "A market right is a franchise." A franchise is a royal prerogative and is one of those *jura regalia* which the king, if he think fit, can grant to a subject. No English subject therefore can hold a market unless he can show a grant of this monopoly by letters-patent or such long enjoyment of the right that it will be presumed that a grant was made to him at an early period and has since been lost. "The right to levy toll and other dues" is not a necessary incident of a market. Free markets exist in many places in England, as for instance at Chippenham in Wiltshire. The right to keep standard weights and measures, to hold a market court, and to sentence offenders to fine or pillory, were parts of the privileges of market-owners in the past. Markets are seldom held less frequently than once a week ; fairs are seldom held more frequently than three or four times a year. It seems tolerably certain that in origin fairs and markets are distinct. The fair is a holiday or "wake" or festival of a saint, which is incidentally utilised by the itinerant trader for purposes of gain. The name is probably derived from the Latin *feria* (a holiday), and a fair in Brittany at the present day would show us with tolerable accuracy what an English fair was before the Reformation. A market, on the other hand, comes into existence for the express purposes of trade. The Latin name (*nundinæ*) shows that under the Romans a market was usually held once in their nine-day week. From these considerations we can understand why we find in England what are called "pleasure fairs," while such a thing as a "pleasure market" is unknown.

Fairs.—Dealing in the first instance with fairs, it would appear that before the Norman Conquest the ownership of a fair was not a matter of great value. It is observed in an antiquarian report forming the first volume of the proceedings of the royal commission of 1887 that "there are only two notices of fairs in Domesday Book, namely, the mention of the third part of a fair at 'Aspella' in Suffolk and of the *forum annuale* held by the Earl of Moretain at 'Matele' in Cornwall ;" and that "even in these instances there is no estimate of annual value, as is usual where markets are described."

The trade of England developed rapidly after the Norman Conquest and under the Plantagenet kings, and its development took a shape which led to the great development of fairs in the direction of trade. It was a natural result of the kingdom of England and duchy of Normandy being in the same hands that trade across the English Channel should become larger, and in Plantagenet times this connection with Europe increased still further, not only on account of the extended possessions of our kings in France, but also by reason of the genius for commerce which more than one of them displayed. For such a foreign trade, at a time when the means of communication were imperfect, the system of fairs was a godsend. The

fixed dates at which the fairs were held enabled the merchant or dealer to arrange his circuit with certainty ; and thus, at a fair, merchandise would be found which was necessarily absent from the weekly market; or, as the late Professor Rogers expresses it, the fair was "a market in which goods which could not be found in the ordinary town market would be procurable, and in which there would be a wider market for ordinary goods." The same writer gives us a picture of the great fair of Stourbridge near Cambridge, which it is impossible to read without wonder at the present day. The day of the proclamation of the fair was 4th September. On 8th September the fair was opened and lasted for three weeks. "The temporary wooden buildings were commenced by custom on St. Bartholomew's Day, 24th August, and the builders of these houses were allowed to destroy corn grown on the spot with impunity if it were not cleared before that time. The space allotted to the fair, about half a square mile, was divided into streets which were named sometimes by nations, and in each of these streets some special trade was carried on, the principal being foreign spices and fruits, ironmongery, fish, metal goods, cloth, wool, leather, and latterly books." At this fair, as we learn, there would be found traders from the Levant, from Genoa, and from Venice, "war-horses and jennets from Spain, and iron from Seville."

For securing merchants and their goods from robbery and violence we find that from the earliest times a special "peace" was enforced which in course of time came to afford protection to all minor offenders who could find sanctuary within the limits of the fair. A quotation from the Scottish *Leges Quattuor Burgorum* will illustrate this practice.

"This is the ordinance of the peace of fairs in a royal burgh on the hither side of the water of Forth, to wit ; That from the time when the peace of the fair is proclaimed, no man be taken nor attached within the time of that fair, either in coming to the fair or in passing thence or in sojourning in the fair itself; unless he has broken the peace of the fair, or unless he be an outlaw of the Lord King or the King's traitor, or such a misdoer as the peace of Holy Church ought not to save. And if he be such a misdoer, or have broken the peace of the fair, he shall be attached securely until the mort of that fair, and there he shall stand for his right, and justice shall be done in the matter whereof he has been charged."

During the continuance of the fair, then, the ordinary executive and judicial officers of the place were ousted of their jurisdiction and were replaced by the officials of the owners of the fair. In the court of PIE-POWDER (*q.v.*) (pieds poudrés) the "dusty-feet" or travelling dealers found a substitute for the ordinary courts of law. There is nothing strange in the lord of the fair thus usurping the position of the ordinary magistrate ; for no principle is more firmly fixed in old English law than the doctrine that ownership of land carries with it the right to hold courts of justice within its limits ; and of this doctrine the court of "pie-powder" forms a typical illustration.

The legislation of Edward I. and Edward III. did very much to make the conduct of trade more easy, to prevent the encroachments of middlemen, and to substitute for the special privileges and usages of particular districts a general system of trade for the whole country. Slight reflection will show that the more secure and definite ordinary commerce becomes, the less are periodical fairs required. If the single trader can readily go through the country from day to day, there is no necessity for his customers to come together at stated intervals to meet him. The development of the craft-gilds operated upon the fortunes of fairs from another side. And thus they have long ceased in England to be of importance for trade purposes. Pleasure fairs have also sunk very low. An act of the present reign, reciting that they are often the cause of "grievous immorality," gives power to the Home Secretary to abolish any fair with the consent of the owner. The country would probably suffer very little if all purely pleasure fairs were done away with.

Markets.—Markets, so far as we can judge, were far more numerous and valuable than fairs during the period before the Norman Conquest. The century which followed the taking of the Domesday Survey was a period of remarkable development in town life. The town-gilds, which were one of the outcomes of this development, had for their business "the framing and enforcing a sort of market law—seeing to the weights and measures in use, taking measures for securing and evidencing by their trade-marks the quality of goods exported from the town." The town-gild was in many cases the authority which fixed the Assize of Bread and Beer (*q.v.*), that is to say "the sliding scale by which their values were adjusted as corn varied in price."

The accession of Edward I. is a crucial period in the history of markets. Finding that during his father's reign the rich nobles had in many places usurped the royal rights and abused them for the oppression of the poor, he sent commissioners throughout the country, to inquire in every "hundred" of each shire what were the king's lands and the king's rights there. The results of this remarkable inquiry were recorded in rolls called the Hundred Rolls (*q.v.*), and of these rolls those which relate to seven of the counties still survive. They show by their extraordinary detail how special jurisdictions and special exemptions were spread like network over the country, which must have been most prejudicial to the interests of trade. It was these varieties of local usage, and the abuses

they engendered, which Edward I. had to meet by statutes which should apply to the whole realm. Two or three illustrations may show the nature of the evils he had to remedy ; their extent may be appreciated when we remember that during the period of seventy-four years, which preceded the commencement of Edward's reign, John and Henry III. had made grants of about 1500 new markets and fairs. The first instance comes from the county of Berkshire, and records that "the burgesses of Wallingford were not accustomed to take toll save only of merchants, but now, contrary to their ancient franchise, they take toll of the men of the country who buy corn and other victuals for their household supplies." In Derbyshire "the masters of the hospital of Yeveley appropriate and attach to themselves men of the royal borough of Assheburn—whereby the king loses toll and passage. And the same masters have made themselves of late a seal for stamping gallons and bushels without warrant, whereas the men of the borough used to have the seal." In Devonshire "the jurors say that the prior of Frompton has toll in his manor of Norham, and that of late only, and takes toll of the men of the said borough wrongfully, to the great damage of the borough, by what warrant they know not." This great survey, or inquisition, was followed by the series of trials of *Quo Warranto*, in which the king tested "by what warrant" the markets were held which were in private hands, and enforced uniformity of practice as a condition of continued enjoyment of the franchise.

The management of markets in Scotland during this period took a different course. Large tracts of country were granted by the crown to various towns as areas within which the "burghs" should have the monopoly of buying and selling. Thus "the royal borough of Rutherglen had by charter rights of taking toll and exclusive dealing over the district where Glasgow afterwards rose."

After the time of the Edwards grants of new markets become much rarer. The decay of the manorial system, and the social changes indicated by the Statute of Labourers and the rising of the villeins give a sufficient explanation of this fact. The demand for grants of letters-patent for new markets steadily decreased during succeeding centuries, until the following result is arrived at, as recorded in the final report of the commission of 1887 : "Between the years 1700 and 1846 we have in England and Wales, exclusive of the metropolis, only twenty-four markets created during 147 years ; while during the forty-six years of this present century only eleven grants have been made. Two of these were grants of markets in the metropolis ; three extended existing rights ; and in three of the remaining instances no markets are now in existence." But while royal grants were becoming obsolete, a system was springing up of creating new markets by private acts of parliament, by special local acts, and by general legislation.

In 1847 the "Markets and Fairs Clauses Act" for the first time codified the "provisions usually contained in acts of parliament authorising the construction or regulation of markets and fairs." But the provisions of this act only apply to markets created by act of parliament after the year 1847, and thus the scope of a very useful act was much limited.

The Public Health Act of 1875 for the first time gave urban sanitary authorities—i.e. boroughs, improvement act districts, and local government districts, conditional powers to establish markets. Under this act local authorities may establish markets if they do not interfere with markets already existing; may acquire existing markets by purchase or lease; may provide buildings for the convenient use of the market; may make bye-laws for their regulation; and take rents and tolls for their use. For carrying out these objects the sanction of the local government board must be obtained by the local authority.

There appear to be at the present day some 769 markets in England and Wales, exclusive of the metropolis. Of these 261 are in boroughs, 266 in other urban districts, and 242 in rural sanitary districts. Of the markets held in the boroughs, 216 out of 261 belong to the local authority, of the markets recorded in rural sanitary districts, 142 out of 242 belong to private persons, 18 to trading companies, 24 to bodies of persons other than trading companies, and 8 only to local authorities, while in 10 instances the market rights are questionable, and in no fewer than 40 instances the markets are not held. Thus, speaking broadly, large markets are now in the hands of local authorities and small markets in the hands of private persons. Under the existing law local authorities have no compulsory powers of purchasing markets within their districts which are in private hands. It is not easy to ascertain how far markets are remunerative at the present day. A selection of 40 markets made in the final report of the commission of 1887 shows that on a capital expenditure of over two and a half millions, a return is made of very nearly 6 per cent in tolls and other incomings. The nine markets belonging to the corporation of London on an expenditure of over 3 millions obtain a revenue of nearly 4 per cent.

The accommodation provided by private market owners is often merely an open space, or open street. There are still many cattle markets in England which are held in the streets. Many private owners lease their markets to persons who make a business of taking tolls on hire and making a living out of the difference between the rent they pay and the tolls they collect. In the south of England even local authorities are found to lease their markets in this way. Markets are a decaying institution in the south of England, but flourish in the northern counties.

The majority of the commissioners of the 1887 commission recommended the abolition of market monopolies upon payment of compensation. A strong minority preferred the compulsory transfer of all markets to local authorities.

(See further MEDIÆVAL FAIRS ON THE CONTINENT.)

[First Report of Royal Commission on Market Rights and Tolls by Mr. Charles Elton, Q.C., M.P., and Mr. B. F. C. Costelloe.—Final Report of the Royal Commission. — Cunningham, Growth of English Industry and Commerce.—Thorold Rogers, A History of Agriculture and Prices in England. —Sir F. Palgrave, The Merchant and the Friar.]

FAJARDO or FAXARDO, COUNT DIEGO DE SAAVEDRA FAXARDO (1584-1648), knight of the Order of St. James, Spanish historian and political philosopher, was descended from a noble family of Murcia, being the son of Peter de Saavedra and Fabiana Faxardo. He became doctor of laws in the university of Salamanca, and in 1606, as secretary of the viceroy of Naples, Cardinal Gaspar Borgia, commenced a distinguished career in foreign diplomacy, which involved a residence of thirty-four years in Italy, Switzerland, and Germany. He died at Madrid, a member of the council for the government of the Indies. His works were widely read, not only in their original tongue, but also in Latin, Italian, French, and English translations, but neither these, nor any Spanish edition subsequent to the first, have the reputation of being faithful reproductions of the original. The English translation of his most important work, Idea de un Principe, published by Sir J. A. Astry in 1700 under the title of The Royal Politician, is from the fourth edition (Valencia, 1660). In this book, "under the awkward arrangement of a hundred ingenious emblems, with mottoes that are generally well-chosen and pointed, he has given a hundred essays on the education of a prince; his relations with his ministers and subjects, his duties as the head of a state in its internal and external relations, and his duties to himself in old age and in preparation for death" (Ticknor's History of Spanish Literature, iii. 215,216).

Idea de un Principe politico cristiano, representada en cien empresas, Münster, 1640, in 4to. See also Obras politicas y historicas, of Faxardo. Antwerp, 1677-78 and Madrid, 1789-90. C. A. F.

Faxardo represented Philip IV. of Spain at the Congress of Münster, which laid the foundation of the treaty of peace of 1648.

His Idea de un Principe politico Cristiano (Idea of a Wise and Christian Prince), written in his leisure moments during his German embassies, and dedicated to the Prince Royal of

Spain, is full of sound and judicious counsel on all matters of state, but rather oddly divided under one hundred mottoes or *empresas*. The author's reflections on economic questions are mostly to be found under the *empresas* LXVI., LXVII., and LXIX. He advocates exemption from taxation for all goods of first necessity consumed by the labouring classes, and holds agriculture to be the principal wealth of a country and the richest mine it can possess. The cost of coinage is the only item that should be added to the intrinsic value of money. Fajardo, however, shares the opinion prevailing in his time that export duties are always borne by the foreign purchaser.

Frequently printed and reprinted, the *Idea de un Príncipe político cristiano* was translated into Italian (Venice, 1648), into French (Paris, 1668), and anonymously in Latin under the title of *Symbola christiana politica* (Brussels, 1649). It is included in Rivadeneyra's *Biblioteca de Autores Españoles* (Madrid, 1853, vol. xxv.) E. Ca.

FALDAGE originally appears to have been the same as faldsoke, viz. the right of a feudal lord to compel his tenants to fold their sheep at night in his fold on his demesne lands, so that his lands might have the benefit of the manure. The term, however, afterwards came to be applied to the money payment for which tenants generally commuted this service.

[Cowell, *Interpreter of Words and Terms*, London, 1701.—Ducange, *Glossarium Mediæ et Infimæ Latinitatis*, Paris, 1733.—Martin, *Record Interpreter*, London, 1892.] A. H.

FALD-SILVER. A customary manorial payment on sheep (see FALDAGE); Vinogradoff (*Villainage in England*, p. 291) considers it an original, not a commuted payment. E. G. P.

FALLACIES may be defined as "apparent evidence which is not real evidence" (Mill, *Logic*, bk. v. ch. i. § 1). Logicians from Aristotle downwards have made it their business to class and label fallacies. The species termed by the schoolmen *a dicto secundum quid ad dictum simpliciter* comprehends many of the bad arguments in political economy; if with Mill we include under this head all cases "where a principle true *in the abstract*, that is all modifying causes being supposed absent, is reasoned on as if it were true absolutely" (see DOCTRINAIRE). A signal instance is the omission of the condition of *time*. It is not true that prices, profits, wages, etc. "always find," but that they "are always finding" their level (Mill, *loc. cit.*) Mill places under this head several economical errors which might also be referred to the fallacy of *composition and division*, that is using a term collectively in one part of an argument and distributively in another. This sort of confusion affects many of the popular errors which economic science has dispelled. Thus, at the root of the mercantile theory lies the fallacy that an increase

of money is good for the community, because it is good for the individual. The inflation school of currency commit the same mistake. Many popular fallacies relating to wages fall under the same head. The notion of "making work" by breaking things is plausible only as long as attention is confined to the interest of the particular man who may thus obtain a job. Prof. Marshall well observes of an argument in favour of short hours of work : "It rests on the fallacy that all trades will gain by the general adoption of a mode of action which has been proved to enable one trade under certain conditions to gain at the expense of others" (*Principles of Economics*, p. 734). A similar fallacy affects some of the arguments which are used in defence of trades unions (Cairnes, *Leading Principles*). Prof. Marshall's words are equally applicable to the prejudices which maintain protection. Nor are free-traders free from the fallacy of *composition and division*, when they ignore the distinction between the interest of any particular nation and of all nations collectively. List maintains that Adam Smith has only proved free-trade to be advantageous in the latter sense. Another fallacy often exemplified in economic arguments is *ignoratio elenchi*, not understanding the thesis which you controvert. Refuting the Malthusian theory by showing that in fact population has not outstripped subsistence is an instance of this fallacy (Mill, *loc. cit.*) It would be possible to include other economic fallacies under other scholastic headings. But it may be doubted whether a minute chart, so to speak, of the paths of error is of much practical use. What is required is rather a broad indication which, occurring in the course of one's reasoning, may prevent taking a wrong step. As a danger-signal of this sort may be offered the warning that in political economy a great many mistakes have arisen from treating, as fixed, quantities which are variable. Thus DE QUINCEY (*q.v.*) misses the true theory of value by assuming that the demand for a commodity is a fixed quantity independent of its price. A predetermined fund for purchasing commodities, is hardly less tenable than a similarly-fixed *wage-fund*. The "iron law" that wages tend to sink to the point of bare subsistence is an instance of the same fallacy which has probably affected every theory of distribution down to recent times. It is well shown by Prof. Marshall that the different economic factors "mutually determine one another" (*Principles*, bk. vii. ch. ii.). Some theories about the rent of ability become insignificant when it is reflected that the margin from which, as base line, the surplus remuneration of any calling is measured, is itself a variable depending on that remuneration (*id. sub voce* "Quasi-Rent"). In economics "all things," or at least most things, "are in flux."

[Effective refutations of economic fallacies are given by Bastiat (*q.v.*). Bentham's *Fallacies* may also be referred to. Of the writers on logic who have treated of fallacies Mill and Whately are particularly suggestive.]   F. Y. E.

FALLATI, JOHANNES (1809-1855), German statistician and economist, was born at Hamburg, where his father, originally of Rovigo (Venetia), was a merchant. Educated at Tübingen and Heidelberg, he was appointed in 1838 professor of political history and statistics at the former university. In 1839 he travelled in England, inquiring into English statistical societies and other institutions. In 1848 he became a member of the Würtemberg parliament, and under-secretary for commerce in the short-lived Frankfurt imperial assembly, 1848, 1849. On its dissolution he returned to an academic career, becoming in 1850 university librarian at Tübingen. From 1844 to 1855, the date of his death, he was joint-editor of the quarterly *Zeitschrift für die gesammte Staatswissenschaft*. During his brief political career Fallati planned and embodied legislative organisation in four directions, viz. the imperial consulate, inland navigation, marine measurement, and—his most cherished idea—an imperial statistical bureau. He also prosecuted inquiry in the question of emigration. To a winning personality and many-sided culture he united clear and practical method.

Works, economic and statistical :—*Die statistischen Vereine der Engländer*, Tübingen, 1840.—*Ueber die sogenannte materielle Tendenz der Gegenwart*, Tübingen, 1842.—*Einleitung in die Wissenschaft der Statistik*, Tübingen, 1843. In the *Deutsche Vierteljahrsschrift*, "Ueber die Haupterscheinungsformen der Sucht, schnell und mühelos reich zu werden, im Gegensatze des Mittelalters uud der neueren Zeit," 1840. 3tes Heft. In the *Zeitschrift f. Staatsw.* : on Social Origins, i. (1844) ; on Association as a Moral Force, i. (1844) ; on English Working Men's Clubs and Institutes ; on Free Trade in Land ; and on German Blue Books, ii. (1845) ; on Agriculture and Technology at the Congresses of Italian Scientists, iii. iv. (1846-47) ; on Progress in Practical Statistics ; and on modes of Statistical Inquiry in England, France, and Belgium, iii. ; on Dearth and Famine Policy in Belgium ; Belgian Excise ; Belgian Census ; Statistics in Sicily, Denmark, and Schleswig-Holstein ; and Socialism and Communism, iv. ; on Statistics at the Lübeck Germanist (Philoteuton) Conference, v. (1848) ; on the Evolution of Law in Savage and Barbarous Tribes ; a proposed Inland Navigation Law ; and Administrative Statistics in Germany, vii. (1850) ; on Trade Combinations in France, viii. (1851) ; on Statistics of Area and Population in British India ; and Administrative Statistics in Norway, ix. (1852) ; on the Statistical Congress at Brussels, ix. (1853).   C. A. F.

FALSA DEMONSTRATIO NON NOCET. A wrong description in a will of an heir or legatee does not invalidate a disposition if there is no doubt as to the identity of the person whom the testator had in his mind. (*Inst.* 2, 20, 30 ; *Dig.* 28, 5, 49, 3.)   E. A. W.

FAMILISTÈRE, the name given by GODIN (*q.v.*) to the settlement which he founded at Guise, Aisne, France, in 1846. The word is reminiscent of the *Phalanstère* of FOURIER, by whom Godin was much influenced.

The Familistère is now a co-operative joint-stock company, possessing iron works as well at Guise as at Laeken in Belgium. A full description of it has already been given under the title CITÉ OUVRIÈRE, *supra*. An excellent and authoritative account, with maps, charts, and details respecting the nature, organisation, and march of the society, is *Le Familistère de Guise, Association du Capital et du Travail, et son fondateur, J. B. A. Godin. Étude faite au nom de la Société du Familistère de Guise, Dequenne et Cie., par F. Bernardot, Membre du Conseil de Gérance*, Guise, 1889.

[Godin, *Solutions Sociales.*—Urbain Guérin, *Monographie de l' Usine et du Familistère de Guise*, 1885.—*Les Ouvriers des deux Mondes*, 1892.—E. V. Neale, *Associated Homes*, 1880.—E. O. Greening, *Co-op. Traveller Abroad*, 1888.] H. H.

FAMILY BUDGET, the balance sheet of receipts and expenses of a family. Such a record is of prime importance in studying the consumption of wealth. It shows directly the standard of comfort and the real wages of the industrial classes, and is particularly useful in estimating the incidence of taxation, constructing weighted index numbers, and judging the various effects of movements of prices. It also brings to light subsidiary sources of income, where these exist, and generally lays bare to the eye of the statistician the whole economic life of the family concerned. The budget should, under ordinary circumstances, cover a whole year, to eliminate, so far as possible, the effect of disturbances due to the influence of climate and season, and to include clothing and other expenses which do not often recur. Budgets were compiled by writers like David DAVIES and Sir F. EDEN in the last century, but their modern history dates from 1855, when important works were published by DUCPÉTIAUX and Le Play. The last-named writer (see LE PLAY) devoted his life to the collection of budgets and founded in 1856 the *Société Internationale d'Économie Sociale* at Paris, which still carries the work on. Among recent writers on the subject may be mentioned Sargant, Dudley Baxter, L. Levi, Engel, Ballin, Schnapper-Arndt, Grüber, Cheysson, U. Guérin, Hector Denis, V. Brants, L. Bodio, the Countess Pasolini, Landolt, etc. Budgets are now frequently found in official publications (*e.g.* Consular Reports, Blue-Books, Reports of American Labour Bureaus). The subject has also received attention from the International Institute of Statistics, whose *Bulletins* should be consulted.

[See especially F. le Play, *Les Ouvriers Européens*, Paris, 1855.—*Les Ouvriers des deux Mondes* and *La Réforme Sociale*, published periodically at Paris.—*La Science Sociale*, Paris.—*Sixth and Seventh Reports of Commissioner of Labour*, Washington, 1891.—*Les Budgets Comparés des Cent Monographies de Famille* par Cheysson et Toqué, Rome, 1890.—*Labour Statistics. Returns of Expenditure by Working Men*, London, 1889, c. 5861.—*Journal, Royal Stat. Soc.*, June 1893.]

H. H.

FAMILY, JOINT (see JOINT FAMILY).

FAMINE.

Economic Study of, p. 19 ; Social Conditions Predisposing to, p. 19 ; Price of Corn as a Symptom of, p. 21 ; Natural Remedies, p. 22 ; Remedial Action by the State, p. 22.

Famines constitute for the economist a study in what may be called the pathology of wants, and their satisfaction ; in them he sees the conditions of some of the greater deviations from that average capacity on the part of production and purveyance to meet consumption, in which economic equilibrium consists. Under certain conditions these deviations find to some extent an index in the fluctuations of price, and hence famine, or scarcity of food, the term being extended only by analogy to other kinds of scarcity (see COTTON FAMINE), has at times been used interchangeably with *dearth* (*dear*-th),—the latter word giving in terms of price that which *scarcity* expresses under the aspect of supply and *famine* under that of felt want or demand. It is more usual, however, to apply the several names to denote different degrees in this kind of economic disturbance. Thorold ROGERS, for example, limited *dearth* to mean a famine in which the rise in the price of wheat is only from 50 to 100 per cent, reserving *scarcity* for those famines in which the increase extends to over twice the average price (*Industrial and Commercial Hist. of England*, p. 59).

A disproportionate intensity of demand for the more important kinds of food in general, as compared with the supply, is here measured in one kind in particular,—the kind which has constituted the staple food of all classes of English people for a good many centuries. For the whole of Great Britain a more comprehensive measure by means of corn averages would be required ; for Ireland and some parts of Europe it would be necessary to include potatoes in the computation ; and for some Asiatic countries the price of rice would afford a truer index of the presence or absence of famine.

Social Conditions Predisposing to Famine.—As M. A. Legoyt has said : in France *famines* have gradually been replaced by *disettes*, and to-day only *chertés* are known.

The causes of present immunity from famine in some countries must be sought, not in milder seasons, nor altogether in that wars are fewer and less barbarous, but in the removal of many circumstances which enhanced the effects of bad seasons, of wars, and other positive checks to life. It is true that modern civilisation tends to develop certain predisposing conditions in the growth of cities and the extension of international division of labour ; but through the progress of economic organisation, famine, if it be still a possible disaster, is rendered infinitely less probable. In past ages long immunity from famine rarely happened in Europe. The producer of corn was hampered by his own rudimentary methods of agriculture, by game-laws, and often by heavy taxation, by foreign military service or civil strife. The merchant was impeded by undeveloped communication and transport, by irregularity in international trade, and by a system of state-restriction in the interest of the consumer. The latter was much in ignorance as to the state of the general food-supply,—either was, or imagined himself to be, the victim of the merchant's engrossing and withholding his food, and was prone to panic. Money was scarce ; the machinery of credit undeveloped ; the money-lender oppressive. Under such circumstances, the introduction of one of the exciting causes of famine—sterile seasons, war, vermin, or pestilence—would be far more quickly and more intensely felt than at a stage of more advanced civilisation.

TOOKE expressed his amazement that parliamentary and other inquiries into the high and low prices between 1793 and 1815 did not assign as the principal cause the varying character of the seasons (*Hist. Prices*, I. iii. § 5). Adam SMITH was convinced that nothing but the waste of war and the fault of the seasons—especially the latter—had ever created a dearth, the violence of well-intentioned governments however converting dearth into famine (*Wealth of Nations*, IV. v.).

To the English economist the narrow margin of surplus corn in the home supply, prior to regular importation on a large scale, and in the absence of any regulated storage of grain, made an absolute deficiency of corn a matter of more than hypothetical interest.

England seldom had a surplus of three months' provision (DAVENANT reckoned it in his time at four to five months' stock) at the new harvest. While the national food supply stood foremost among political questions, economic opinion was divided on the crucial point as to the effective power of either a free or a regulated trade to induce, prevent, or remedy famine.

French economists of the last two centuries, concerned directly with a country of greater area and fertility, were more disposed to see in famines the result of merely partial deficiencies in crops in which collectively there was never a deficit. France commanded, even with an ordinary yield.

an overflowing abundance of the means of subsist-ence,[1] and was both self-sufficing and the feeder of her neighbours. A good harvest meant a store sufficient for three years (cp. the allusions to Boisguilbert, Vauban, Richelieu, De Boislisle, Delamare, and Herbert, in Biollay, *Etudes écono-miques sur le 18me siècle*, 1885). The years of famine during the 17th and 18th centuries—there were forty-one in all—were imputed to commercial speculation, to "the malice of some merchants and regrators" (Delamare, pp. 1007 ; 954 ; 707), to the stupidity and brutality of the people (Boisguilbert, vi.), to changes in currency and disordered finances (Forbonnais, *Recherches et considérations sur les finances*, ii.), to the intrigues of officials (Saint-Simon, *Memoires*, ed. Chéruel, v. p. 332), then to those of ministers, finally to those of the king (Biollay, p. 11), and, by Turgot, to the restrictions on inland trade (*Lettres sur les grains*, pp. 27, 109). Necker was slightly more cautious :—*je sçais bien qu'un vuide réel n'existe presque jamais*, etc. (*Sur la législation et le com-merce des grains*, i. xiii.).[2] And Colbert, a century earlier, by frequently keeping himself informed as to local harvests, was constrained to admit that the great disorder in the finances was due quite as much to the general sterility, involving "an infinity of scarcity and need," which had prevailed in France since the death of Henry IV. (1610-1662), as to official abuses and the exhaustion from long wars (Colbert, *Lettres*, etc., ed. Clément, ii. 5, 8, 10, 19, etc.). Yet in much more recent times Cherbuliez took as the starting-point of his arguments against the interference of the state in the corn-trade the hypothesis of an actually adequate supply (*d'un approvisionnement réellement suffisant*) (*Dict. de l'Econ. politique, s.v.* "Disette").

It is contended that India is self-sufficing taken as a whole (Walford), and that her great famines, which are always partial, are, if not wholly preventible, certainly in great measure to be palliated and kept within the limits of a mere dearth. The chief predisposing conditions are local density of population, in conjunction with anti-migratory instincts, disafforestation (till the middle of this century), (see FORESTS), rigidity in taxation of land, absence of diversity of industry, 92 per cent of the population being engaged in agriculture, insufficient irrigation and imperfectly developed means of transport. Storage of surplus grain in pits is largely practised both by cultiva-tors and by merchants, so that the crops of one year are never the only resource.

Famines, however, in India and elsewhere, bear this generic likeness to sorrow, that they come not single spies but in battalions. The seven lean kine which came up out of a seven times shrunken Nile have replicas in every history. The great famines in India have usually been the result of drought continued over two or three years. The record of French famines exhibits, besides shorter periods, series of bad harvests as follows :—

1043-49	1475-77	1692-94
1138-44	1528-34	1708-10
1338-47	1572-74	1788-95
1415-19	1625-31	1811-13
1430-39	1660-63	(*Legoyt*).

The law of the recurrence of famines has occupied economists intermittently from Petty downward, but first took shape as an inchoate scientific hypothesis in the researches made by Hyde Clarke and Jevons. (*Investigations in Currency*, vi.-viii.).

There does not seem to be *conclusive* evidence that a famine ever ensued in Europe in mediæval or modern times solely from what have here been called predisposing conditions. The only doubtful cases in English history seem to be (1) the famine of 1124, spoken of by Simeon of Durham as *magna per Angliam fames*, when the dead lay about un-buried in city, village, and cross-road, and to which Penkethman assigns as the immediate cause, the dearth occasioned "by means of changing the coine" (*Artachthos*, 1765); (2) the "great penury" of 1248, "by reason of embasing the coin." There was peace in the former year, civil war in the latter; no mention is made of failure of crops, but it is probable that they were at least deficient.

However necessary a physical or social dis-turbance of abnormal intensity be to bring about strain and distress amounting to a famine, it is equally certain that men have in many instances so shaped their physical and social environment, "either by blundering, by intention, or even by the zeal of them who govern" (Bandini), as to go far to bring themselves within hailing distance of hunger. Earlier generations are liable to render the land they live in worse adapted for the require-ments of their successors by exhausting its resources (Sidgwick, *Principles of Political Economy*, i. iv.). William Rufus is said to have taxed the land so heavily that agriculture was discouraged and famines ensued. There were four in his short reign (Walford). The TAILLE (*q.v.*) crushed the French peasant, whilst the noble was exempted. Rome, both in ancient and modern times, ruined Italian agriculture to indulge itself in cheap bread (Mommsen, *Hist. of Rome*, ii. 394-395 ; Galiani, *Dialogues sur le commerce des blés*). In 1295 and again in 1390 the export of wool was checked through our anxiety to secure coin at staple towns ; the slender capital of the period was not "turned" and men famished (Penkethman ; Knyghton). Fearful that corn might be exported in the famine of 1438-39, the government refused to take the more positive remedy of relaxing the restraints on inland water-carriage. Commerce, it is true, "recognising neither king nor country," will go on exporting grain, while the people are famish-ing, as in England, 1586, 1595, and 1709 (see speeches of Queen Elizabeth and Queen Anne) ; and *Parliamentary Hist.*, vi. 802) ; Tudor kings, by issuing base money, have made famine "endemic" (Th. Rogers) ; and under a republic depreciated *assignats* may intimidate the farmer from bringing corn to a hungry town (Thiers, *Hist. de la Révolu-tion*, iii. 93, etc.). Neglect of reservoirs have been a potent factor in enabling a scarcity of crops to dissolve Ceylon villages. Over-population may, as in the great Irish famine, be suffered to precipi-tate unchecked the action of the law of diminish-

---

[1] In the famine 1528-34, owing to heat and vermin, the harvest barely furnished enough grain for sowing (Delamare ; cp. Legoyt).
[2] He would not admit that restrictions had ever occasioned *disette* or *cherté*, ii. cp. vi.

ing returns (Cairnes, *Fragments on Ireland*). The result of a relatively rigid law assessing wages, and a relatively elastic assize of bread, "necessarily brought want and starvation to the labourers" when corn grew suddenly dear (Denton, *England in the 15th century*, p. 96). Dependence on a staple commodity is in itself a risk. And ignorance generally, rendering man weak in wielding natural forces, strong in hatred of his neighbour and superstitious as to cause and remedy, is a predisposing condition implied in all the rest, constituting at times well-nigh an efficient and sufficient cause of famine (cp. Hazzi, p. 15 ; Leland, *Etruscan Roman Remains*, i. x. ; King, *Italian Valleys*, p. 132).

On the other hand a country predisposed by physical conditions to scarcity, as *e.g.* Holland, may by effective organisation and enterprise have remained a stranger to national famishment (cp. Blanqui, *History of Political Economy*, p. 314).

Price of Corn as a Symptom of Famine.—That scarcity in the supply of corn (where corn is the staple food) is dearth in terms of price, is a truism. Observation, however, has shown that the price does not rise in the same ratio as the supply falls short. In an article used as a prime necessity of life the elasticity of demand is at a minimum, while the demand itself is habitually at a maximum. Thus when the supply is checked consumption is reduced reluctantly, creating the purveyor's opportunity and then the producer's. The intensity of demand has moreover ever been rendered the more stubborn at the rumour of a scarcity of bread, "by emotions against which reason is of no avail, and out of which populations are not to be educated" (Dupin, cp. Biollay, p. 22). "There arises a sort of general scramble for the scanty and waning stock" (Fullarton, *infra*, c. v. ; Necker, *op. cit.* i. xiii.), which DAVENANT (*q.v.*) formulated by the famous law called after Gregory KING.

In considering this formula it must be borne in mind that fertile years beget confidence and check dearth ; a bad year accelerates alarm in the next. The famine of 1390 was preceded by years of such plenty that it was believed a five years' stock might have been accumulated and the price rose not much (*non nimis excessivum*, Knyghton).

The maintenance of a heavy outlay for bread in times of scarcity involves a redistribution in the demand for other commodities. "Famine depreciates all but food" (F. Newman, *Lectures*, p. 85) ; but this must be accepted with reservations. "Fancy" foods will depreciate (Roscher, 61), although in a siege famine they may command a fancy price at the outset (Labouchere, *Diary of Besieged Resident in Paris*), but there will be an appreciation in the price of all the "surrogates" of the staple article of food, partly because they are scarce from the same cause, partly owing to increased demand. "Men," as Locke put it, "would not rob themselves of all other conveniences of life by paying all their money for wheat, when oats, that are cheaper, though with some inconveniences, would supply that defect" (*Several Papers on Money*, 1696, p. 48). If all kinds of corn have been deficient, grass, especially in a wet famine, and roots may be abundant, and dairy produce and mutton not much affected, although the cost of fattening cattle

will tell on beef before long. If the course of prices be traced in Thorold Rogers's tables during *e.g.* the chief famine of the fifteenth century, 1438, it will be seen that oxen rose in price in about the same proportion as corn, but not till the year after ; wool, wine, and salt fish rose also, but pigs and sheep did not. Again, in the famine 1647-49, 1648 being the dearest year for corn ; butter and candles rose in years 1 and 2, then fell ; sugar and beef rose in all three years, sheep first fell, but shot up in year 3.

Disturbances and readjustments such as these are but the upper layer in the basket. The poor, when corn rises out of reach, betake themselves to inferior food, unless, indeed, by habitually living on something cheaper than corn, they have no such resource left them. Herein is another limitation to the sufficiency of the price of corn as a criterion of plenty or dearth. In the reign of Edward II. when the purchasing power of the people had been brought very low by the wars of Edward I., and a series of unproductive harvests supervened, wheat often entered in very moderate proportion into the loaf of the great bulk of the population, chestnuts, acorns, and fern-roots being substituted (Denton, p. 91). Waster, in *Piers Plowman* (W. Langland, c. 1332-1400) when gripped by Hunger, is glad to eat the horses' beans ; bark has been much sought after both in European and Chinese famines, nor has exception been taken to dogs, cats, and vermin, dead bodies and living children, while the newly-imprisoned thief has found prompt sepulture in the stomachs of famished captives (cp. the accounts of English chroniclers in the writings by Farr and Walford referred to below).

Finally, excessive mortality, both through want and "famine fever," and other want-engendered illnesses (as well as at the hand of the enemy in case of war), constitutes a slackening in demand and a consequent modification in the movement of price, which is hardly a positive symptom of the cessation of famine. The excess over the average annual deaths in Ireland during 1846-47 amounted, taken together, to 216,716, of which 208,617 were the result of famine fever. Nevertheless 9395 died of starvation in the two years following, when prices had abated, wheat being cheaper than for sixty-seven years past, viz. 38s. 6d. (cp. Walker, *Wages Question*, p. 111).

The harrying of Northumbria by William the Conqueror in 1068, leaving a few survivors "to live like beasts of the field" and surrender themselves as slaves (Stubbs, *Hist.*, i. 78), the Black Death, 1349, when cattle roamed loose and corn rotted in its abundance, and "there were small prices for everything," yet the survivors feared to touch the plague-infected food (Knyghton), are instances of dislocation in the equation of supply and demand not easily interpreted by readings of price. DEPOPULATION itself, as a symptom of famine, is significant enough (*v. sub voce*). Mediæval towns have cast the beggar and the "casual" out of their gates in time of scarcity (Villani, Voigt, Wachsmuth, cited by Roscher). Famine, as checking population, has been held a necessary condition of internal peace in China, (Malthus, *Essay*), and has been tolerated as a chronic easing-off of demand in modern Europe.

Cantillon commented on the poor dying of "la misère, comme nous le voyons journellement en France." The peasant of southern Italy emigrates from sheer destitution (Nitti, *Rev. d'Ec. Polit.*, July 1892) ; and the history of industrial centres tells of chronic misery which has suffered, out of 21,000 infants, only 300 to survive their fifth year (cp. Schönberg's *Handbuch der polit Oekonomie*, i. 689, n. on "Starvation Diseases"). Histories, such as Malthus desiderated, of the nations viewed as mostly poor people, will, with him, look on years of plenty as "interrupting causes, obscuring" the normal working of the great ultimate check to population.

Natural Remedies to Famine.—In the natural course of things "while the earth remaineth, seed time and harvest . . . shall not cease," the heat of war dies out, the recuperative recoil characterising the springs of human energy after mishap asserts itself markedly in obliterating the traces of famine (cp. Malthus, *Essay*, ii. xiii.) and by natural selection the predisposing conditions are re-adjusted. Dupont de Nemours's saying, *Ce qu'on l'appelle cherté est l'unique remède à la cherté*, is applicable both to the extended operations of the cultivator and the merchant, encouraged by the high price of corn, and also to restricted consumption. Demand for bread may suffer some contraction without entailing suffering. Penkethman even assigns wasteful "use of the creature" as a cause of famine (*e.g.* in London in 1369).

Nor is corn the staple food it once was. Tooke was careful to omit the labourers from that "agricultural interest" which derived benefit from scarcity. The wages of labour do not rise in full proportion to the advance in the price of provisions (i. 2). In a long famine they do rise especially, Thorold Rogers found, in the case of the worst paid kind of labour, as for instance, the wages of women and threshers of oats (*Econ. Interpretation of Hist.* i. 16, 17). The rise, after 1315 and 1621, was 10 per cent.

Theoretically the collector and redistributor of the annual supply of corn should, by steadying the fluctuating price of corn, be both a preventive and remedial force with regard to scarcity. But his aim being to produce profit rather than plenty, and often short-sighted at that, his power also, where publicity was small, being very great, he has been wholly mistrusted by the consumer as a "dearth-desiring Hoorder" (see FORESTALLERS, cp. Proverbs xi. 26).

Importation of German corn, as a remedy in time of famine, is mentioned in connection with the scarcity of 1258, and often subsequently. Knyghton accounts for the cheapness of corn at London, as compared with his native town of Leicester, through the number of grain-ships meeting in the Thames. Davenant, while estimating that the variety of soil and elevation in our corn-fields rendered us the less liable to more than local dearth, deemed us only "safe because we have everywhere the sea to friend." In modern times the advent of Russia to the international corn-market (in the French famine 1778 ; South Russia in 1816-17), and of America in the middle of this century, more recently of Australia and India, minimised the chances of serious famine in Great Britain.

Remedial Action by the State.—This may briefly be analysed as follows :—

1. Subvention of the corn trade, viz.—(*a*) Regulated collection and distribution of corn in public granaries. Burke could point to the farmer's rick-yard and barn as the only British granary, but English economists have winced at Holland, with her well-stocked "conservatories," retailing to us our own grain (Davenant. Cp. *Britannia Languens* and Sir W. Raleigh, p. 303, etc. "a dearth of only one year in any other part of Europe enriches Holland for seven years" (*Observations upon Trade*). (*b*) Purchase of foreign corn, the drain of bullion to effect which, was often a source of financial anxiety (Fullarton). (*c*) Restriction of export of corn. (*d*) Suspension of duties on Imports. (*e*) Bounties on imports of corn. (*f*) Suspension of bounties on exports, "a peculiarly English policy," pursued since the 15th century (Cunningham, *Growth of English Industry*, etc., Modern Times, p. 372).

2. Subvention of the producer by advance of loans, as in recent Indian and Russian famines. A developed banking system may herein replace the state (Fullarton, Roscher).

3. Economising the supply of corn by prohibiting the use of barley in brewing and distilling, or that of flour for hair powder ; or the sale of bread before it is stale.

4. Compulsory lowering of the price of corn and bread.

5. Relief works and gratuitous distribution.

6. Publication of corn statistics.

[Besides the works mentioned, see :—Burke, *Thoughts and Details on Scarcity*, 1795.—Davenant, *Essay upon the probable Methods of making a People gainers in the Balance of Trade*, § iii. 1699.—Farr, *Journal of the Statistical Society*, June 1846.—Fullarton, *On the Regulation of Currencies*, 1844, cp. vi.—J. E. Thorold Rogers, *History of Agriculture and Prices.*—Walford, *Journal of the Statist. Soc.*, Sept. 1878 ; Mar. 1879.—Danvers, F. C., *A Century of Famines*, 1877.—Hunter, Sir W. W., *The Indian Empire*, 1878, etc.—Short, Th., M.D., *General Chronological History of the Air, Weather, Seasons, Meteors*, etc., 1749.—Fleury, *Famines, misères*, etc., 1849.—Legoyt, *Journal de la Soc. de Statistique*, vol. i. (1860).—Von Hazzi, *Betrachtungen über Theuerung und Noth*, 1818.—Von Koch-Sternfeld, *Versuch über Nahrung und Unterhalt*, 1805.—Roscher, *Ueber Kornhandel, und Theuerungs-politik*, 1852.—Bandini, *Discorso sopra la Maremma di Siena*, 1775.—Issaïew, *Revue d'economie politique*, July 1892.—Bernouilli, *Populationstatistik*, 1841, pp. 365 *et seq.* On physiological effects of hunger.—Luciani, *Fisiologia del digiuno*, and other authors cited by Lebrecht, "*Il Malthusismo*" (1893), p. 71, note.]

C. A. F.

FARMER-GENERAL. From early times it was the custom in France to farm out a tax to a contractor, who having advanced a fixed sum to the government, collected and pocketed the tax which he had bought. In 1697 the indirect taxes, customs, excise, *octroi*, taxes on wine, salt, tobacco, oil, and manufactures, were collectively leased to a body of financiers, thenceforward distinguished by the name of farmers - general (*fermiers généraux*), to show that their powers of collection were general, and not confined to one particular tax. These farmers, sixty in number, were appointed by the king for periods of six years, and they paid an agreed sum in advance year by year. Their selection was largely governed by court favour, and the coveted contracts were often awarded to needy favourites who found wealthy financiers willing to surreptitiously share the transaction. The privileges of the farmers yielded to the government—

In 1697	37 millions of francs.
1743	64 ,, ,,
1763	90 ,, ,,
1786	112 ,, ,,
1789	180 ,, ,,

There can be no doubt that the farmers' profits were, as Adam Smith says, "exorbit-ant" (*W. of N.*, bk. v. ch. ii.), and the cost of collection "wasteful and expensive." The amount taken out of the pockets of the people was thus out of all proportion to the amount received by the state (see especially Necker's remarks upon this subject, *De l'Administration des Finances*). Moreover, the taxes, grievous in themselves, were collected harshly. Domiciliary visits, the seizure of goods suspected to be smuggled, and the efforts to capture smugglers who were, if caught, sent to the galleys or the gibbet, caused frequent personal collisions be-tween the agents of the farmers and the public, often resulting in bloodshed. "Those who con-sider the blood of the people as nothing," says Adam Smith indignantly, "in comparison with the revenue of the prince, may, perhaps, approve of this method of levying taxes." The osten-tatious luxury in which the farmers lived accentuated the popular anger against them, though their riches were sometimes antecedent to their contracts ; and though some of them made a noble use of their wealth, e.g. Beaujon, who founded a hospital, Helvetius, Dupin, and Lavoisier. The Convention prosecuted the farmers-general as enemies of the people, and thirty-five of them, including Lavoisier, were guillotined. The Constituent Assembly abolished the system of farming-out the national revenues. The farmers-general have thus a history of less than a hundred years.

The disfavour in which they were held is best illustrated by a story told of Voltaire, who once gave a dinner at which the talk fell upon the exploits of famous robbers. When each guest had recounted some notorious exploit, Voltaire was pressed for a story in turn. "There was once upon a time," he began, "a farmer-general . . . " ; then after mock hesita-tion, "I forget the rest !"

[Most French writers on finance refer to this subject. Sully scolded the farmers as vigorously as Turgot, and Necker criticised them sharply. On disadvantages of the system, see Adam Smith, *loc. cit.*, COST OF COLLECTION OF TAXES ; FARMING OF TAXES ; TAXATION, INDIRECT. On the other hand, it is contended that the necessary defects of the system are not considerable. J. B. Say thought the French post office might have been farmed out with advantage, and better managed by men of business who were not state officials, maximum rates being fixed by the government (*Cours Complet d'Écon. Pol.*, ii. 413). The money order department of the English post office has only ceased to be farmed out within the last five or six years (1893). Comp. PUBLICANI.]   H. H.

FARMERS' ORGANISATIONS IN THE UNITED STATES.

Order of Patrons of Husbandry, p. 23 ; National Farmers' Alliance and Industrial Union, p. 24 ; Farmers' Organisations in the North and West, p. 24 ; Coloured Farmers' National Alliance and Co-operative Union, p. 25 ; Other Organisations, p. 25 ; General Principles and Present Demands, p. 25 ; Ocala-Indianapolis Demands, p. 25 ; Business Feat-ures, p. 26 ; Political Action, p. 26.

The Order of the Patrons of Husbandry.—The first great farmers' organisation in the United States was a secret society founded December 1867, under the name "Order of the Patrons of Husbandry," but more familiarly known as "The Grange" ; not an accurate designation, as the word "grange" is a term applied to one of the units of the order, as for example the local grange, the state grange, etc. (see GRANGERS). The aim of the Patrons of Husbandry was to bring the farmers into closer relation with one another, and thus to lessen the disadvantages of the isolation in the farmer's life, Social intercourse was emphasised and the educa-tional features, including courses of reading and study, were made prominent ; and it was sought to render life on a farm more attractive, especi-ally to the sons and daughters of farmers. Economic purposes were from the earliest days leading features in the activity of the order, and for a time a large measure of success in dis-tributive co-operation was achieved. The farmers sought to meet combination with combination.

A movement among the farmers to correct railway abuses had begun before the Patrons of Husbandry became a great power, and this order naturally enough joined in the struggle, and soon became the chief factor on the side opposed to railway corporations. Stringent laws were passed to regulate railways, railway commissions began to be created in various states, and this movement continued until now we have such commissions in most of the states of the union, and also a federal commission, called the Inter-State Commerce Commission. These laws were not always wisely conceived, the railway corporations rallied their forces, and finally a reaction began, which among other things weakened the Patrons of Husbandry. The order spread rapidly until 1874, when it claimed a half-million members, and then began to decline in numbers and influence. One evil in the order was the presence of professional politicians and other designing persons slightly or not at all connected with agriculture, who attempted to use it for selfish ends. Membership was accordingly restricted in that year and limited to persons actually engaged in agriculture, and a few others, such as editors of agricultural periodicals and country mechanics who could reasonably be supposed to be in active sympathy with agricultural interests. The reaction following the meeting of 1874 continued for a long time, but recently the order began to grow again, stimulated no doubt by other powerful organisations, and it now claims to have organised 26,500 sub-granges, with an aggregate membership of 1,325,000. Deducting one-half of this number for extinct granges, gives a conservative estimate of 662,500 as the present membership. For a long time the political influence of the Patrons of Husbandry had been so slight as to attract little attention, although it has doubtless had some influence on legislation, even in recent years. The members of the order have for the most part acted with one or other of the two great parties, the Republican and the Democratic, and it is now the most conservative of the farmers' organisations of the United States. Its influence is chiefly social and educational, and it furnishes an excuse for annual gatherings of farmers' families, in which amusement is as prominent a feature as speech-making.

The National Farmers' Alliance and Industrial Union.—The Order of the Patrons of Husbandry is called the mother of the Farmers' Alliance, and it has undoubtedly, directly and indirectly, had great influence upon all the other farmers' organisations which have in recent years come into existence. The farmers turned from the grange to organise more radical orders, and these began to exist at about the same time in various parts of the south and west. Their purposes were similar, their platforms all having a striking resemblance to one another, owing to the similar conditions out of which they grew ; and the various organisations coming into closer connection produced the present "farmers' movement."

The National Farmers' Alliance and Industrial Union is at present the greatest farmers' organisation in the United States, and is perhaps the most powerful organisation of farmers known to history. It and the Patrons of Husbandry are to be remembered as the two chief farmers' organisations which have thus far arisen in America. The National Farmers' Alliance and Industrial Union may be traced back to a local society in Lampasas County, Texas. The precise date of its birth is a matter of dispute, but it was somewhere between the years 1870 and 1875. The Local Texas Farmers' Alliance was organised to protect the farmers against cattle thieves and "land-sharks," that is speculators in land, especially dishonest speculators and land thieves. The scope of the local society was enlarged, and in 1879 the Texas State Alliance was formed, one year later it received a charter from the state. This grew and united with other societies. There had arisen an order in Louisiana called the Farmers' Union with similar aims. This was the first larger order absorbed. The two consolidated in January 1887, at Waco, Texas, and took the name National Farmers' Alliance and Co-operative Union. As this society grew, it came in contact with the National Agricultural Wheel, which was founded in Arkansas in 1882, and was at first a local body. It grew rapidly and had membership in most of the southern states in 1887, and claimed a half-million members. Its avowed purposes were so similar to those of the National Farmers' Alliance and Co-operative Union that a plan of fusion was arranged at Meridian, Miss., in 1888, and having been ratified by three-fourths of the local organisations of both societies, the Union was declared in force 13th September 1889, and the new order became known as the Farmers' and Labourers' Union of America.

Farmers' Organisations in the North and West.—The organisations just mentioned operated chiefly in the southern states of the union, but similar bodies in the north and west had begun to make themselves known, of which the most important was the National Farmers' Alliance, sometimes called the Northern Alliance as the other society is occasionally, though now with less propriety, called the Southern Alliance. The National Farmers' Alliance grew from a local society established in 1880 to a national body organised in 1887 and claiming, in 1889, a membership of nearly 400,000. This was a non-secret order, whereas the National Farmers' Alliance and Co-operative Union was a secret order with grips and passwords, but the purposes of the two organisations were the same. Still another society with like aims was founded in 1883 in Southern Illinois. This was the Farmers' Mutual Benefit Association. It soon acquired a membership in Missouri, Kentucky, and Kansas, as well as Illinois, becoming a national organisation in 1887. A fruitless attempt to unite these orders was made in St. Louis in December 1889. Personal ambitions, sectional animosities, the race question, and the question of secrecy or non-secrecy seem all to have had more or less influence in preventing a fusion ; nevertheless they came into closer relationship with one another, and have since then been acting together in the pursuit of their aims.

The Knights of Labour were represented by delegates at St. Louis, and thus were brought together urban mechanics, employés chiefly, and farmers, not employés, but in so far as they did not cultivate their farms alone, employers rather than employés. Thus began a strange and probably hitherto unknown combination of industrial classes for political aims. A platform was agreed upon, acceptable to all, and this platform embodied what is known as the "St. Louis demands." In anticipation of fusion with the Northern Alliance the name of the Farmers' and Labourers' Union of America was changed at St. Louis to National Farmers' Alliance and Industrial Union. This is the body almost invariably meant when the Farmers' Alliance or The Alliance is mentioned in the press, and it has in fact extended its membership into states in which the National Farmers' Alliance was formerly strong, and appears nearly to have absorbed the latter.

The Coloured Farmers' National Alliance and Co-operative Union. — Only one other prominent farmers' organisation remains to be mentioned, and this is the Coloured Farmers' National Alliance and Co-operative Union. All who know the south in the United States will at once understand the difficulties in the way of common action of whites and blacks in a single society. A coloured alliance was established in Houston County, Texas, in 1886, and in 1888 it became a national body with the above-mentioned name. In 1891, it claimed a membership of considerably over a million, and representation in thirty states. It held a meeting in Ocala, Florida, in December 1890, at the same time when the National Farmers' Alliance and Industrial Union met; friendly greetings were interchanged, and it virtually agreed to act with the organisations of the white farmers for the attainment of the "St. Louis demands." The Farmers' Mutual Benefit Association also held a meeting at the same time and place, and appears to have come nearer to the other organisations present.

Other Organisations.—Other organisations are heard of here and there, as the National Farmers' League, the Farmers' National Congress, and the Supreme Association of the Patrons of Industry of North America—not the Patrons of Husbandry already mentioned—but all these are of minor importance. The Citizens' Alliance (Mrs. Annie L. Diggs, Washington, D.C., Secretary; Noah Allen, President) may be mentioned as an attempt to organise professional and business people in the cities, and thus to enable them to act with the farmers' organisations.

General Principles and Present Demands.—All the farmers' organisations have a statement of general principles similar to that of the Alliance, in which expression is given to feelings of fraternity and general goodwill to mankind, a determination to promote the education of the farmers is avowed, and sectional prejudice is condemned. The immediate demands of the

Alliance are stated in the platform adopted at St. Louis, which was endorsed by the Knights of Labour. As amended at Ocala in 1890, and at Indianapolis in 1891, the platform reads as follows :—

Ocala-Indianapolis Demands :

1. (a) We demand the abolition of national banks.

(b) We demand that the government shall establish sub-treasuries in the several states which shall issue money direct to the people at a low rate of tax, not to exceed 2 per cent per annum on non-perishable farm products, and also upon real estate, with proper limitations upon the quantity of land and amount of money.

(c) We demand that the amount of the circulating medium be speedily increased to not less than $50 per capita (say £10).

2. We demand that Congress shall pass such laws as will effectually prevent the dealing in futures of all agricultural and mechanical productions ; providing a stringent system of procedure in trials that will secure prompt conviction, and imposing such penalties as shall secure the most perfect compliance with the law.

3. We condemn the silver bill recently passed by Congress, and demand in lieu thereof the free and unlimited coinage of silver. [The Silver Bill condemned was that of 14th July 1890, providing for the purchase of 4,500,000 ounces of silver bullion per month.]

4. We demand the passage of laws prohibiting alien ownership of land, and that Congress take prompt action to devise some plan to obtain all lands now owned by aliens and foreign syndicates ; and that all lands now held by railroads and other corporations in excess of such as is actually used and needed by them be reclaimed by the government, and held for actual settlers only.

5. Believing in the doctrine of equal rights to all, special privileges to none, we demand—

(a) That our national legislation shall be so framed in the future as not to build up one industry at the expense of another.

(b) We further demand a removal of the existing heavy tariff tax from the necessities of life, that the poor of our land must have.

(c) We further demand a just and equitable system of graduated tax on incomes.

(d) We believe that the money of the country should be kept as much as possible in the hands of the people, and hence we demand that all national and state revenues shall be limited to the necessary expenses of the government economically and honestly administered.

6. We demand the most rigid, honest, and just state and national governmental control and supervision of the means of public communication and transportation, and if this control and supervision does not remove the

abuse now existing, we demand the government ownership of such means of communication and transportation.

7. We demand that the Congress of the United States submit an amendment to the Constitution providing for the election of United States senators by direct vote of the people of each state.

Demand No. 6 was substituted for the St. Louis demand for complete ownership and operation of the means of communication and transportation. At a meeting of representatives of farmers' organisations and other organisations, most prominent among which were the Knights of Labour, the original St. Louis demand for complete ownership and operation was adopted as a platform for independent political action.

The following tabular statement gives some leading facts touching the different farmers' organisations mentioned :—

	Patrons of Husbandry	Southern Alliance[1]	Northern Alliance	Mutual Benefit Association	Coloured Alliance
Date of Organisation	1867	1870-1875	1880	1883	1886
Character of Ritual	Secret	Secret	Non-Secret	Secret	Secret
Estimated Membership[2] 1892	662,500	3,000,000	200,000	150,000 [claimed membership in 1890]	1,250,000
Demands.					
Free Coinage of Silver	*	*	*	*	*
Abolition of National Banks	*	*	*	*	*
Establishment of Sub-Treasuries		*		*	*
Prohibition of Alien Ownership of land	*	*	*	*	*
Government Ownership of Railways		*	*	*	
Tariff Revision	*	*	*	*	*

An asterisk (*) indicates that the "demand" appears in the platform of the particular body designated.

Business Features.—The Alliance has made various efforts in business, all of which have been, to a greater or less extent, co-operative. Co-operation in buying and selling has been the chief of these, but mutual insurance has been a prominent feature. "Alliance Exchanges" have transacted business amounting to many millions of dollars ; and although these appear to have failed frequently or sus-

pended, the claim is made that the gains to the farmers can be counted by the million. The abolition of the middleman is one of the goals of the Alliance.

Political Action.—The different farmers' organisations claim to be non-partisan, but the Alliance avows a willingness to use parties as "a method" of attaining their ends. At first there was an evident desire to work through the old parties, but the feeling that independent political action is a necessity has grown. A "third party," composed for the most part of members of the alliance, has made itself prominent in the country, and in 1890 astonished the politicians by capturing two states and gaining important positions in others ; while in some southern states the alliance seemed to have gained control of the democratic party. In that year the alliance had nine members, chosen as "third party" candidates, in the House of Representatives, and claimed twenty-six members elected as democrats. There were also two members in the senate.

The Knights of Labour and the farmers' organisations are not in so many words committed to a third party, but the third party was formed by delegates from these organisations, and the same men are prominent in both. The members of the organisations appear to have liberty to vote as they please, but these organisations are the recruiting grounds of the "third party."

The meeting at St. Louis, February 22-24, 1892, already alluded to, adopted a platform called "The Second Declaration of American Independence" of the "Confederated Industrial Organisations of America." The preamble begins with these words : "This, the first great labour conference of the United States, and of the world, representing all divisions of urban and rural organised industry, assembled in national congress, invoking upon its action the blessing and protection of Almighty God, puts forth to and for the producers of the nation this declaration of union and independence."

The platform resembles closely that of the Alliance already given, except that a "land plank" is added which reads as follows :—"The land, including all the natural resources of wealth, is the heritage of all the people, and should not be monopolised for speculative purposes, and alien ownership of land should be prohibited.

"All land now held by railroads and other corporations in excess of their actual needs, and all lands now owned by aliens, should be reclaimed by the government and held for actual settlers only."

A demand for a Postal Savings Bank is added, and the incorporation of the telegraph and telephone as part of the postal system is specially mentioned as a desirable reform. The whole platform is described as a "three-fold

---

[1] This is the main body, familiarly known as the Alliance or Farmers' Alliance.

[2] These estimates are not vouched for by the writer of this article.

contention of industry," for it is divided into three parts, viz. money, land, and transportation, but the money part is most emphasised. A convention to nominate candidates for the political campaign of 1892 met at Omaha, Nebraska, in July. This movement was inaugurated and carried on chiefly by members of the Farmers' Alliance, though others were invited to co-operate. In order to attract various classes of voters the name "People's Party," used in the campaign of 1890, was adopted as a national party name. In the general election which took place in November 1892, General Weaver, the party's candidate for president, received a popular vote of about a million and a quarter, and obtained twenty-two votes in the electoral college. The party has eight members in the present (1893) House of Representatives and three in the Senate. The most prominent of the representatives is Mr. Jeremiah Simpson of Kansas, and the senator most frequently mentioned is Mr. W. A. Peffer of the same state—the state indeed in which the Alliance has secured its greatest victories. Immediately after the election an effort was made to repress the partisan tendencies of the Alliance, but without avail.

Peculiarities.—It must be remembered by English readers that the American farmer is a proprietor, but that means a peasant rather than a European landlord. The American farmer dreads becoming a tenant, and the fear that he may become one is a partial explanation of the farmers' movement. He has heard much of rack-rented Irish tenants, and he sees something of rack-renting in his own country. The farming and peasant class is regarded by conservatives as a bulwark against revolutionary tendencies, but the American farmer appears to have become revolutionary, and his organisations have joined hands with the Knights of Labour. Perhaps to the economist the most remarkable peculiarity is that already mentioned, viz. the combination of organisations of landowners with organisations of wage-earning mechanics.

Causes.—It would require a treatment of recent American economic history to explain the causes of the present American farmers' movement. The contraction of the currency at the close of the civil war, lowering the price of land, and raising the value of mortgages, is one cause ; another is the extension of the means of communication and transportation, increasing the supply of available agricultural land, and lowering the prices of agricultural products. The American railway system, which has entrusted the ownership and operation of railways to private corporations, whatever may be its advantages, has been productive of grave abuses ; and these have had something to do with the discontent of the farmers. Great fortunes and urban luxury, of which the farmer

hears much and of which he catches glimpses, may be also mentioned as a general cause.

The Future.—An estimate of the future farmers' organisations is so difficult that a wise man will be extremely careful in making one. The past would seem on the one hand to justify the belief that large political results ought not to be anticipated in the near future ; on the other, that if the present organisations disappear, they will be succeeded by others. A clearer, fuller, more scientifically elaborated economic "platform" would also seem to be a condition of permanence as a political factor, but this may come as the result of continued discussion.

[Nothing like an accurate account of the farmers' organisations of the United States has appeared. They are mentioned in their connection with the labour movement in Ely's *Labour Movement in America* (New York, 1886). Mr. N. A. Dunning, who is connected with the Farmers' Alliance, has edited *The Farmers' Alliance History and Agricultural Digest* (Washington, D.C., 1891). This contains historical sketches of the principal farmers' organisations, and a number of essays upon topics connected with their demands or activity. Senator Peffer explains his monetary ideas in *The Farmers' Side* (New York, 1891). Annual reports of the various bodies are important but difficult to obtain. The periodical literature is vast. It is said that over 1000 newspapers now advocate the platform of the Alliance. The principal of these is the official organ of the Alliance, *The National Economist*, published in Washington, D.C. The *National Economist* has issued considerable pamphlet literature of importance as hand-books, tracts, etc. American magazines contain many articles about the Farmers' Alliance. Various numbers of the *Arena* for 1892 may be mentioned as containing articles favourable to the Alliance. The "Farmers' Alliance," by W. A. Peffer, in the *Cosmopolitan* for April 1891, gives a historical view. A more critical sketch is that which appears in the *Political Science Quarterly* for June 1891, by Frank M. Drew, entitled "The Present Farmers' Movement."]

R. T. E.

FARMING. This word has come to signify in general the cultivation of land, and a farm a portion of land cultivated as one holding. But it is derived from a Saxon word signifying provisions, and was originally applied to the rent reserved for the use of land by a tenant, which in early times was in the form of a portion of the produce. When in money it was called "*alba firma*," meaning silver. So in Scotland "a victual rent" is still used to express a rent consisting of a certain quantity of grain, though that is now converted into its current equivalent in money as ascertained by the FIARS PRICES. For the purpose of the present article farming will be understood to be the system of letting land for cultivation to a tenant, who finds the whole of the capital, and pays the rent reserved to the landlord, whether as a definite quantity of produce or as money. Where the landlord finds part of the capital, and receives a share of the produce, the arrangement follows the METAYER SYSTEM (*q.v.*).

The cultivation of land by interposition of a tenant belongs almost necessarily to a somewhat advanced stage of social organisation, and to conditions in which large domains are held by one individual. In the earliest times the land of a tribe was held in common, and after separate property began to be recognised, the several portions were only such as one family could cultivate. With the division of labour, however, there occasionally occurred cases in which it was convenient that the owner should follow some different pursuit, and then the land might be for a consideration handed over to the temporary occupation of another. Such an arrangement was called by the Romans *precarium* whenever it endured only at the pleasure of the owner. The term *locatio* was applied when the land was let for a definite period. But the large estates acquired by Roman magnates towards the close of the republic and under the empire were chiefly cultivated by slaves working under the stern discipline of a steward, himself generally also a slave.

During the middle ages the aggregation of land in large estates under the Feudal System (see FEUDALISM) gave rise to various methods of holding. Part of the extensive grants from the crown were by subinfeudation transferred to smaller owners,—for military service, for certain dues payable on occasion of the lord's exigencies, and occasionally for some small annual rent in money or kind. But the chief lords, as well as the subordinate tenants, drew the main part of their subsistence and revenues from the domain or "demesne" lands which they retained in their own occupation. The cultivation of these lands was carried on partly by dependents who were wholly maintained by their lord, partly by means of services reserved from bondsmen, or peasants, who received a grant of so much land as sufficed to maintain them, subject to the obligation of giving the services necessary to cultivate the lord's domain lands. This system continued to prevail generally on the continent till it was put an end to in France by the revolution, in Germany by the land reforms of Stein and Hardenberg. In England the same system gave rise to the copyhold tenures, in which the services, which abroad were indefinite and arbitrary and therefore oppressive, came gradually to be restricted by the courts to fixed amounts and periods. But early in the Plantagenet period there began to grow up a system of farming out land to tenants for fixed rents in money or kind. The records of certain manors show that this arrangement had become general by the middle of the 14th century. The statute book bears similar testimony. The pestilence known as

the BLACK DEATH (*q.v.*) had about that period swept off half the labouring population, and the immense rise of wages which followed, and which the statutes of labourers (23 & 25 Edw. III. an. 1346-49) (see LABOUR STATUTES) were passed to repress, prove that there existed a large body of free labourers unconnected with any special lands, but ready to give their services to whatever masters offered the highest wages. Up to this time the food grains were the main objects of culture, but the growing of wool, for which England became specially famous, gradually took a leading place in husbandry. The consequence was that less labour was required in agriculture, and small farms were consolidated into large. The statute book shows that by the beginning of the reign of Henry VII. the depopulation caused by this system had advanced to a degree which endangered the safety of the realm. The statute 4 Hen. VII. c. 16 (1487) states that in the Isle of Wight the practice of landlords throwing small arable farms into large pastoral ones, in order to obtain the higher profits yielded by wool, had proceeded to such an extent that the population was seriously diminished, and the island left without adequate defence against an invader, and it was therefore ordained that no one tenant should hold a farm exceeding the value of ten marks a year, though tenants who might be thus evicted from possession were declared to be entitled to compensation for improvements they had made or buildings they had erected. Although this statute applied only to the Isle of Wight, as being the part of the realm most exposed to invasion, there is no doubt that the greater part of England was in the same economic position. The mischiefs arising from the consolidation of small arable farms into large sheepwalks were some of the most prominent popular grievances during the whole period of the Tudor dynasty.

In Scotland also, half a century earlier than the last cited statute, an act of parliament (1449, c. 18) was passed for assuring to tenant farmers (puir pepil that labouris the grund), holding under leases for definite terms, security against eviction by a purchaser of the land, which shows that this system of tenure must already have become general in that country.

The simultaneous rise of the practice in both North and South Britain excludes some explanations which otherwise might have appeared to account plausibly for its prevalence in place of the continental systems of cultivation by forced labour. The immunity of England from foreign invasion cannot be accepted as a reason, for Scotland was harried by incessant inroads of her English neighbours. Neither could the richness of English soil, and the wealth produced by exportation of corn and wool, explain the result, for Scotland was comparatively a desert, and grew barely enough for her own consumption. But the one point of resemblance between the two countries was that in both the great owners of estates were of Norman descent, while the bulk of the labouring population was, in the lowland districts, Celtic-Saxon. To the proud and warlike Norman personal superintendence of agricultural operations was distasteful if not degrading, and he willingly assented to an arrangement by which the whole risk and trouble were devolved on a tenant, from whom he drew a fixed annual rent in produce or cash. On the side of the labourer, the sturdy Saxon independence preferred the payment of rent for an assured possession of what he could on that condition call his own to the rendering of personal services on his lord's domains. The idiosyncrasies of both races thus, under great divergencies of actual conditions, combined to establish the system of farming of land to tenants. In England land seems to have been from the first, as it still continues to be generally, let from year to year. In Scotland the caution of the race, or the extreme poverty of the soil, which refused its returns except to a long preliminary process of reclamation, made leases for long terms the rule. This we see was the case in the 15th century, and it continues in Scotland to this day. The customary length is nineteen years; it is not known why this particular number has been adopted. Of late years the uncertainty of prices has tended to the introduction of shorter terms.

Under the system of farming land the landlord as a general rule places the land in a position for cultivation and supplies the necessary apparatus affixed to the soil. Thus he reclaims the land from waste, drains it, removes boulders, forms fences and roads, and in addition erects a dwelling-house for the tenant, as well as stables, barns, cattle-sheds, and all the other buildings requisite for stock and grain. The outlay demanded under these heads is of course variable, but in almost all cases it is very large, and probably in most cases equals or even exceeds, and often in a series of years greatly exceeds, the original fee-simple value of the land. In general also the landlord is at the expense of upholding all these improvements and structures. But these general rules are subject to occasional exceptions. Thus under the cottier system which formerly prevailed in Ireland, the tenant made the reclamations and erected the humble structures required for his habitation and stock. Not unfrequently, however, the landlord gave wood, stones, or slate to aid him. In Scotland a great deal of land has been reclaimed under what are known as "improving leases," these being for a duration varying between thirty and fifty years. During the first decade the tenant probably sits rent free—he will pay a small sum during the second, and a gradually-increasing one afterwards, under the condition that he brings the land under cultivation and erects suitable buildings on it. In this system the absence or smallness of rent is the consideration for the improvements, so that in this form they are paid for by the landlord.

After this expenditure of capital on the part of the owner of the land, the application of capital in the charges of cultivation is under the farming system made wholly by the tenant. The purposes to which it is applied are the purchase of horses and implements, of seed and manures, of live stock, and the payment of wages till returns come in. The amount invested by a tenant for these purposes varies between £5 and £15 per acre. Probably £7 or £8 is now an average, but all good farmers agree that it should not be less than £10. Under metayage most of this capital, except that required for wages, would be supplied by the landlord. Hence it appears that the farming of land has the effect of drawing in additional capital; it thus contributes to improved cultivation, while at the same time it tends to the maintenance of large estates. On the other hand a cultivator who has capital generally prefers to rent land instead of buying it, because as a tenant he obtains the use of his landlord's capital, which has been expended in the purchase of the soil, in draining and fencing, and in erection of buildings, and for all this the rent which he pays amounts to only a very low rate of interest. In this way the tendency is to promote the holding of large farms. In point of fact it is not till a tenant-farmer has made his fortune and intends to retire that he ever thinks of buying land; up to that time he usually invests his increase of capital in renting more land.

As a means of thus attracting capital to the cultivation of the soil the tenant-farming system has no doubt contributed materially to the fact that cultivation is on the whole better in Great Britain than in any other country; as, also, possession of capital implies comfort and some degree of education, it has elevated the position of the cultivators. The relation between landlord and tenant has in general been friendly and often accompanied with much personal regard. Nor, though really commercial in character, has it usually been conducted on strict legal rules. Landlords being often wealthy men have been easy in regard to the period of payment of rents, and liberal in accepting less than the full amount due when bad years occurred. Tenants, though holding only from year to year, have often retained the same farm for several generations, and in reliance on this usage have often expended a great deal of money in improvements which strictly belonged to the province of the owner of the soil. In Scotland, where leases in writing and for definite terms are almost universal, this reliance on usage has not been the rule, and it has been common to submit each farm at the end of the lease to public competition. But even then many tenants have, at the cost of a moderate rise in rent—balanced frequently by the landlord executing further improvements—remained for life in the same holding; while in the exaction of the stipulated rent the same liberality, or laxity, has been shown as in England. Yet this very liberality has had a tendency to raise rents, since a sanguine man will offer more if he has some hope that in the event of losses he will not be severely pressed.

This easy-going arrangement went well on the whole not only in the periods of prosperity in the beginning of the present century, and again during 1850-70, but even during the agricultural depression which existed 1815-25, and again in 1833-40. When, however, a series of bad seasons set in from 1869, followed by severe falls in prices of corn dating from 1875, and of meat from 1884, all combined with a material rise in wages, some new influences were felt in the relation of landlord and tenant. A good many estates had changed hands, and the purchasers being generally commercial men, were inclined to take a strictly legal view of the liabilities of their tenants. Further, the extension of the franchise not only gave votes to the smaller tenants, but strengthened the general radical feeling in favour of tenants against landlords, and the Irish land legislation suggested some parallel changes in the laws of Great Britain. Under such motives the two successive AGRICULTURAL HOLDINGS ACTS (*q.v.*) were passed. But the social and personal effects of the depression have been much more vital. On nearly all estates very considerable changes of the tenantry have taken place. In a good many, leases or other written agreements have been introduced; a more commercial spirit has arisen; better agricultural education begins to make its way; more capital is invested alike on the landlord's and tenant's parts; and as a necessary consequence stricter calculations are made as to the profits and security of such investments. There is indeed an infinite variety in the degree in which such a spirit affects landlords and tenants; there are still many estates in which it is not felt at all, but such is undoubtedly the direction in which, with more or less rapidity, the mutual relations are moving.

One tolerably definite change may be said to be almost universally in progress. As a general rule it has been found that the largest holdings have felt the depression most severely, and that rents have been most regularly paid, and with least claim for reduction, on the smaller. One reason for this is that the smaller can be more closely superintended, another is that the tenant's capital consists partly of his own labour and that of his family, on which he does not expect full or at least regular payment of interest. Hence the process of consolidating small farms into large has been checked, and the reverse process of letting land in small farms or in allotments has made considerable way. The subdivision of large farms into small farms would undoubtedly proceed more rapidly were it not that it demands an outlay of landlords' capital in providing dwellinghouses and other buildings which the rents at present current would hardly repay. The same cause prevents any subdivision by tenants themselves. Where, as in Ireland, they erect their own buildings, and these are so inexpensive as to be within the means of an ordinary labourer, a tendency to subdivision among different members of the family at once develops itself, and is with difficulty kept within reasonable bounds by the landlord. No such tendency occurs where the outlay of capital required for such a purpose is considerable.

These considerations explain the rapid growth of "allotments," which, speaking generally, involve no outlay of capital in buildings, and the comparatively slow progress of "small holdings," which as a rule require erection of buildings and fences. The fact that cultivation on the small scale of allotments pays well, even at the present very low rate of prices, is shown by an important paper in the *Economic Journal* for March and June 1893 (see ALLOTMENT; SMALL HOLDINGS ACT).

The question whether farming is best conducted by leases for fixed periods, or by agreement from year to year, has been viewed differently in Scotland and in England. Strange as it seems, the latter has tended in practice to a more continuous possession by the same tenant and his descendants. On estates belonging to old families a tenant is seldom removed, and the rent is generally moderate. Thus cultivation proceeds on the assumption that there will be no disturbance, and this, if verified, is unquestionably the system on which the best farming can exist and the best returns be obtained. But where a fixed determination of the lease impends, and there is uncertainty of its renewal, the tenant takes as much out of the land as possible, and hence whoever succeeds him (or he himself, should he ultimately obtain a renewal) has to spend two or three years in bringing the farm again into condition. Some landlords have endeavoured to remedy this mischief by a clause in the lease declaring that it shall continue in force until three or more years' notice has been given. Leases for lives were at one time common, especially on estates belonging to corporations and in Ireland, but they combine the disadvantages of a certainty of expiry with an uncertainty of time, and hence are unfavourable to good culture. They are seldom now adopted.

Certain conditions or rules of rotation of crops

and other methods of culture used to be universally found in written leases or in estate regulations. They are necessary to prevent bad farming when either knowledge or inclination to adopt good farming is absent. But the advance of scientific knowledge and the general recognition that only good farming can pay has tended to make these rules less strictly insisted on, and even to disappear altogether.

RENT, whatever be its theoretical definition, is, in the practice of farming, the surplus of produce after paying the expenses of cultivation and interest on the tenant's capital. It is really fixed by the tenant, for although in England it may be nominally fixed by the landlord, yet it depends on the tenant's acceptance of the farm at such rate. In Scotland farms are almost universally let by tender, and therefore the rent is directly fixed by the tenant. The rate of interest which a tenant generally looks for on his own capital is 10 per cent, or it may be viewed as 5 per cent of interest and 5 per cent as remuneration for his personal exertions. The INCOME TAX Acts assume that a tenant's profits in England are equal to half the rent and in Scotland to one-third of the rent, but the fall in rents (following on the fall in gross value of returns) has altered this proportion, and on average it may be assumed that the tenant's profits are expected to be about equal to, or even more than, the rent he covenants to pay. In computing the profit to be retained by himself, a tenant does not in general include the farm produce (milk, potatoes, etc.) consumed in his own household, nor the dwelling-house, so that the actual interest he expects to make on his capital is nearer 12 than 10 per cent. This refers to the making of new bargains; with falling prices the actual profits have often been much less, or have disappeared. Rates and tithes, till the recent change in the Tithe Act, were in England generally paid by the tenant, in Scotland by the landlord—under recent legislation partly by each,—but in either case they form a deduction ultimately from the rent and not from tenants' profits.

The rent paid for farms is in the United Kingdom almost always in cash. In Scotland the practice long prevailed of paying in kind, i.e. the rent was fixed at so many "bolls" (four to six bushels) of the different grains grown in the district, commuted each year for money at the rates fixed as the FIARS PRICES. Some poultry were often added, known as "kain hens." This arrangement met equitably the case of fluctuations in prices, but not of fluctuations in crop; if the price rose in consequence of a bad crop the tenant whose crop was bad suffered, he had less to sell and more rent to pay; while with a large crop and low prices the landlord suffered by the fall of rent while the tenant, though his crop might be good, made no better profit. But when free trade rendered prices in a great degree independent of the home crop, there ceased to be any compensatory influence at all, a low price might coincide with a bad crop; consequently the system of grain rents has now almost entirely died out. A further reason for its cessation is that grain is now only a part of the produce, the production of meat having become a material source of revenue and the price of meat varying only within narrower limits; but, these variations occurring from market to market, its value could not be taken as any safe indication of the profits of the year. It may happen that store cattle are cheap while beef is dear, which gives good returns to the feeders while the rearer of young cattle is impoverished; or the reverse may occur and the breeder may make profits while the feeder buys so dear that he loses. These complications appear to render impracticable the suggestion which has sometimes been made recently that rents should vary in accordance with varying prices of produce.

Legislation has not very materially interfered with farming in Great Britain. In the Tudor period laws were enacted with the purpose of preventing the consolidation of small holdings and the laying down of land to grass. We have no definite record how far they proved effectual, but the fact of reiterated enactments and complaints seems to indicate that they did not attain their object. The influence of modern land legislation in Ireland and the Highlands of Scotland is yet hardly clear. In the rest of Scotland and in England the only compulsory enactments have been those giving compensation to tenants for the unexhausted value of manures and feeding stuffs, and giving to tenants the right to kill ground game. Neither have yielded much satisfaction to the parties concerned. The compensation is frequently more than balanced by claims made by the landlord for dilapidations or bad farming, which are quite legitimate but probably would not have been urged had there not been claims for compensation put forward by the tenant. If the Acts were more onerous than they have been found to be the result would have been that landlords would have refused to let farms, and have cultivated them by means of bailiffs. So also with regard to game, any compulsory provision is evaded by the tenant being made to understand that exercise of his legal rights will be followed by notice to quit. It is probably only the recent depression in agriculture—leading on the one hand to a difficulty in finding tenants at all, and on the other making existing tenants dependent on the kindness of the landlords—which has prevented these compulsory statutes from greatly diminishing the prevalence of the system of farming.

It is not easy to forecast the direction which farming may take in the future. The influence which developed it in the past,—the desire to maintain large estates in land,—with all the social and political position which they implied, has in a great measure passed away, and more and more every year land is coming to be viewed and dealt with as a commercial commodity. The dominating question will therefore be whether land yields the best return to capital when cultivated by an owner or a tenant. The rent usually given by a tenant is little more than interest on buildings, drainage, and fences, so that he virtually gets the land for nothing. The position of tenant, therefore, with rents on their present basis, is undeniably an advantageous one. New purchasers of land, however, and old landowners who take a commercial view of it as an investment, may come to think that the tenant's profits might as well go into their own pockets. There would be the charges of a competent bailiff to come off, but an intelligent and thoroughly educated agent would probably grow better crops and make better profits than the tenant-farmer with his present education is able to do. But any alteration in this direction involves the possession of capital by the landlord, and there must be a considerable transfer of land from impoverished to wealthy owners before this can become the general case.

[Mommsen, *History of Rome*, bk. iii. cap. xii. —Thorold Rogers, *History of Agriculture and Prices.*—Prothero, *Pioneers and Progress of English Farming.*—Shaw-Lefevre, *Agrarian Tenures.* —Boyd Kinnear, *Principles of Property in Land.* —Pell on the "Making of the Land in England," *Journal Royal Agric. Soc.*, 2nd series, vol. xxiii. p. 355.—J. Caird, *The Landed Interest*, 4th ed. 1880.]   J. B. K.

FARM, OF THE COUNTIES. The revenue received by the crown in composition for its ancient claims on the land. The old payments in kind, *feorm-fultum* made to the king by the tenants of demesne lands, were commuted in Norman times for money rents (*Dialogus*, i. 8). These rents, together with the profits arising from the king's claims on the land, were termed collectively the *ferm*, or farm, of the county. The collection of this farm was usually entrusted to the sheriff or some other accountant, who was called the farmer, and was made absolutely responsible for the whole farm due to the crown. In some cases, however, the collector was called the *custos* or bailiff of the crown, and, as such, was only responsible for as much of the farm as he actually received. In the revenue rolls of the exchequer the farm includes the following items: (1) The *corpus comitatus* or rents, which remained the same from year to year and were charged with certain fixed payments ; (2) The *remanens firmæ post terras datas*, or remainder of the farm, after the value of the lands granted away from the body of the county had been deducted ; (3) The *crementum* or INCREMENTUM chiefly arising from new tracts of land being brought into

cultivation ; (4) The *proficuum*, including any profits arising from the king's territorial jurisdiction. There was formerly an important record preserved in the exchequer called the *Rotulus Exactorius*, which contained the details of all the farms of England as they appeared in the Pipe Rolls, and this list was posted up to date from Michaelmas to Michaelmas. This record, however, no longer exists. The *Red Book of the Exchequer* contains several lists of farms ; and in the nearly related MS. Hargrave 313, a unique table is preserved of the farms of England as they appear in the Pipe Rolls from the year 1154 to the end of the reign of Henry III. In later times it was usual for the crown to grant fee-farms, or long leases of land at low rents, to corporations and others, who answered severally for the same as farmers. In this way also a large area of forest land was brought under cultivation before the reign of James I., but most of these *assart-rents* (see ESSART) were resumed by the crown in the reign of Charles I.   A. E. S.

FARMING OF TAXES. The collection of revenue has always proved a problem to governments, especially in early times before the growth of efficient administrative machinery, or in states of very large extent. An obvious method of solving the problem has been to entrust the difficult and invidious task to private individuals or companies, who pay a fixed sum to the government and take any surplus they can make from the taxpayers as their own profits. The two states in which this system of farming the taxes has been most extensively adopted are ancient Rome and France under the old régime.

As the dominions of Rome grew, the privilege of extorting contributions from the provincials was sold by the censors for a period of years to PUBLICANI (*q.v.*), most of whom belonged to the equestrian order. Their profits were enormous, especially when Asia fell under Roman rule, and the equestrian capitalists became a very influential body in the state from the days of C. Gracchus. As the *publicani* had to give security to the state, and this was often beyond the wealth of any individual, it was usual for them to form associations among themselves and to share the profits. Sometimes a company only contracted for a particular branch of the revenue, sometimes it collected the whole payments of a particular province. A provincial governor could never have an interest in the companies of *publicani*, and this rule had the effect of excluding the senatorial class. The actual collection of the taxes was entrusted to subordinate agents.

In France it was only the indirect taxes which were farmed (see FARMER-GENERAL). The practice originated in the constant pressure of pecuniary needs upon the French government, which compelled it to anticipate its revenue, and thus threw it into the hands of financiers. By the 18th century nearly all the taxes were farmed by a single company, the *ferme générale*. This consisted of sixty capitalists, who were nominated by the king, and were under the management of the controller-general. They paid a fixed sum for the right of collecting the *gabelle*, the *traites*, the *entrées de Paris*, and for managing the tobacco monopoly. The lease was made for six years, and the controller received a *pot de vin* of 300,000 francs, which was, however, refused by Turgot and Necker. The position of *fermier-général* was eagerly sought after, and the kings had always a long list of candidates for vacancies. The chief defects of the system arose from the tyranny of local agents, who were often ill paid, and from the action of the king. In appointing the *fermiers* he often saddled them with obligations to pay considerable sums to courtiers and favourites. These charges, called *croupes* and *pensions*, compelled the government to lease the taxes at a lower rate than would otherwise have been obtainable.

In England, the system of farming the revenue was adopted in Anglo-Saxon and Norman times, when the sheriffs paid a composition (*ferm* or *firma*), for the various dues which they had to collect from their shires. It was a great object of the towns to free themselves from the sheriff's control and to pay their contributions direct to the crown. The acquisition of this privilege, or *firma burgi*, marks the beginning of municipal independence. In the 12th century the collection of the DANEGELD (*q.v.*) was farmed by the government to the sheriffs, but after Henry II.'s reign the practice of farming the taxes gradually disappeared. This was due partly to royal jealousy of the power of the sheriffs, and partly to the rise of the new system of taxing personal property.   R. L.

FARMING TAXES, PRINCIPLE OF. The system of letting out the collection of taxes to contractors at a fixed rent, as opposed to direct levy by state officials (REGIE, *q.v.*), marks a low stage of financial development. It is naturally employed where a skilled administrative staff has not been formed, and where private capitalists are ready to undertake the work. Farming has been in most cases limited to taxes on commodities—the Roman direct taxes were for a time an exception (Mommsen, *Hist. Rome*, vol. iii. p. 115)—and may be given either by delegating the collection of the tax, or bestowing a monopoly of the taxed product. The most conspicuous examples of this form of collection in ancient times are found in the Roman state, where powerful companies, *societates vectigales*, were formed for the purpose. France from the 16th to the 18th century is the chief modern instance (see FARMER GENERAL). Under the *ancien régime* the salt monopoly (GABELLE, *q.v.*), the *aides* or drink duties, and the tobacco monopoly were farmed

out. At present the system is limited to cases in which taxation is raised through monopoly of the taxed article—as tobacco in Italy—or to indirect taxes for local purposes (OCTROI, *q.v.*).

The objections to farming taxes are weighty and easily perceived. Politically, it interposes a privileged body between the ruler and his subjects, and leads to the enactment of oppressive revenue laws, which are harshly applied (*Ubi publicanus est, ibi aut jus publicum vanum aut libertatem sociis nullam esse*, Livy, xlv. ch. 18). Economically, it reduces the income of the state by the profits—generally exorbitant —obtained by the farmers. The early financial theorists protested against its use. Montesquieu (*Esprit des Lois*, bk. xiii. chs. 19, 20), while admitting that it is "sometimes desirable to give new taxes in farm," strongly approves of direct collection by the state as good for both sovereign and subjects. Justi is still stronger, "the farmer is the leech of the people," *Natur und Wesen der Staaten*, p. 451, ed. 1771. Adam Smith declares that "the best and most frugal way of levying a tax can never be by farm"; the great capital required for farming the revenue practically excludes competition, which is replaced by combination, "even a bad sovereign feels more compassion for his people than can ever be expected from the farmers of his revenue"; the permanent interests of ruler and people are in harmony, while those of farmer and taxpayer are opposed (*Wealth of Nations*, bk. v. ch. ii. art. 4, ed. Nicholson, p. 383).

The intense hostility that the farmers of revenue excited both at Rome and in France supports these strictures (see PUBLICANI). Collection by public officials is the only proper course in a well-organised state. Farming is, however, admissible when the public economy is imperfect, and the chief source of revenue is from the domain. To entrust the collection of dues on commodities to persons whose self-interest will secure strict supervision, and whose profits will be but a part of the larger return obtained by their efforts, is under such conditions the most economical mode. Wide-spread official corruption may also justify the employment of farming, which, however, is plainly a transitional step to be superseded by means of deeper reforms.

[In addition to quotations in text, the leading German writers on *Finanzwissenschaft*, viz. Roscher, bk. ii. ch. vi. § 67, 2nd ed. 1886,—G. Cohn, § 385, 1889.—A. Wagner, vol. ii. pp. 746-752, 2nd ed. 1890), also Bastable, *Public Finance*, 1892, pp. 656, 657.]   C. F. B.

FARR, WILLIAM (1808-1887). Born at Kenley, Shropshire, died in London. He was educated for the medical profession, but exchanged it to enter, in 1838, the department of the registrar-general of births, deaths, and marriages. His knowledge of statistical science, and lucid and original style of study and composition were early recognised by his superiors in office ; and, although he did not advance beyond the post of Deputy-Registrar-General, his talents and force of character made him, throughout his long public service, the most prominent man, in general estimation, of that section of the official hierarchy to which was confided not only the registration, study, and analysis of the three leading events in the lifetime of the population, but also the very important duties of the census enumerations. Dr. Farr's literary activity was very considerable, and was directed, with much earnestness and consistency, to the scientific analysis of subjects having a real practical bearing on social economy, sanitation, and the prevention of cholera and other specific diseases. Dr. Farr's contributions to the mathematical and statistical improvement of the theory of vital statistics and their tabulation were also important. Some were treatises from the medical, others from the mathematical or economical point of view, and all were remarkable for clear insight, and for novelty of conception. To Dr. Farr also belongs the credit of instituting a proper nosology, or classification according to diseases, of those dying at each age, and also of doing much to aid the labours of actuaries by the calculation of life tables based on reasonably accurate returns of the mortality according to the most modern facts revealed by the census enumerations of the whole population of England and Wales. His first essay on this subject dates from 1843, when he published his *English Life Table No. 1*, to be followed in 1853 by the *English Life Table No. 2*, and in 1864 by a more elaborate work, the *English Life Table No. 3* (often called Farr's Tables), which contains many tabulated values of annuities, and auxiliary tables for the calculation of all sorts of ordinary life contingencies, with an excellent introduction. The results are still largely used by actuaries when an approximation is desired to the most modern available experience of the duration of life amongst the general public of all classes in this country. Dr. Farr also wrote many able papers upon provident funds for widows and children of the civil servants of the state as a whole, and for single departments, such as the post-office. He was also partial to the study of centralising schemes, such as the purchase of railways by the state, government insurance of capital sums and survivorship annuities, and mutual cattle insurance associations for agriculturists. A vast number of reports on subjects more or less cognate with those above indicated were contributed by him to the various periodical publications and blue-books of the registrar-general and census commissioners, and to the transactions of English and foreign societies with which he was connected. It may be said with truth that no English statistician was ever

before so cosmopolitan, or so appreciated abroad as Dr. Farr. His genuine goodness of disposition, as well as his scientific attainments, made him a *persona grata* at the many international statistical congresses held at London and on the Continent, which he punctually attended as one of the English delegates. The effectual manner in which he played a leading part in the organisation of the congress of which Prince Albert was the president in London is still an agreeable reminiscence with the one or two still surviving secretaries of sections. At the Royal Statistical Society Dr. Farr was equally esteemed. He took, for a long period of years, a great share in its management, contributed many valuable papers, and filled with credit the post of president from 1871 to 1873.

Some illustrations of the style and scope of Dr. Farr's views and conclusions respecting his work and his important studies in the domain of vital statistics, a subject with which his name and public services will long continue to be honourably associated, will be found in his book under that title, named below.

In 1885 the Sanitary Institute of Great Britain reprinted, under the editorship of Mr. Noel A. Humphreys, of the registrar-general's office, a selection from Dr. Farr's works above mentioned, in some instances in rather an abridged form. This was issued by subscription as a memorial volume under the title of *Vital Statistics*, London, 1885, 8vo, pp. xxiv + 563. It contains also an appreciative and interesting sketch of Dr. Farr's life, by Mr. Humphreys.

Among Dr. Farr's principal works are :— "Report upon the Mortality of Lunatics" (*Stat. Soc. Journal*, 1841).—"The Influence of Scarcities and of the High Prices of Wheat on the Mortality of the People of England" (*Stat. Soc. Journal*, 1846).—"Statistics of Civil Service of England, with Observations on Funds for Children and Orphans" (*Stat. Soc. Journal*, 1849). —"Influence of Elevation on Fatality of Cholera" (*Id.* 1852).—"Formules adoptées en Angleterre pour l'inscription des naissances," etc. (*Congrès Internat. de Stat.*, 1853).—*Report on Internat. Stat. Congress*, Paris, 1855.—*Report on Nomenclature and Stat. Classification of Diseases*, 1856.—*Report on Internat. Stat. Congress of Vienna*, 1857.—"On the Pay of Ministers of the Crown," *Stat. Soc. Journal*, 1857.—*Rapport sur la statistique de la G. Bretagne*, 1858.—*Tables relative to the state of the British Army in Russia*, 1854-56, published 1859.—*Reports on the Vienna Int. Stat. Congress*, 1861.—"Recent Improvements in Health of Brit. Army" (*Brit. Assoc.*, 1861).—*English Life Table No. 3*, large 8vo, clv. + 605 pp., London, 1864.—"Address as President of Section F" (*Brit. Assoc.*, Bath, 1864). — "On Infant Mortality" (*Stat. Soc. Journal*, 1865).—"Mortality of Children in Principal States of Europe" (*Id.*, 1866).— "Statistik von Gross Britannien' (*Congrès Intern. de Stat.*, 1865) —"Statistique de la Grande Bretagne" (*Id.* 1867-69).—"International Coinage" (*Brit. Assoc.*, 1869).—"On the Question of

Metric Weights and Measures " (*Intern. Stat. Congress*, 1870). —"Inaugural Addresses as President of the Stat. Soc. 1871 and 1872.—"On the Valuation of Railways, Telegraphs," etc. (*Stat. Soc. Journal*, 1876).—"Étude sur la mortalité en Angleterre" (*Annales de démographie*, 1877).—"Some Doctrines of Population" (*Brit. Assoc.*, 1877).—"Éloge de Samuel Brown" (*Congrès Intern. de Stat.*, 1878), [cf. art. on Farr by Prof. V. John in *Handwörterb. der Staatswissenschaften*.] F. H.

FARTHING. Originally the name given to the fourth part of a silver penny (fourth-ing). First struck as a separate coin in reign of Henry I. The coinage of silver farthings was continued until the reign of Queen Mary. Copper farthings were introduced in 1613 during the reign of James I., and were coined until 1860, when the present bronze coinage was adopted. The bronze farthing weighs 43·75 grains, and is legal tender to the amount of one shilling. F. E. A.

FASHION, ECONOMIC INFLUENCE OF. Fashion, when taken in its more general sense as the mode in which a civilised society is satisfying its various wants, or more specifically that of dress, conveys the idea of a more or less incessant tendency to *change*. The French recognise this quality of variableness with greater emphasis than the English, *mode* being defined by them as taste that is essentially mobile and transient. For us fashion is current usage ; for them "usage is long fashion." Fashion cannot claim to include all such changes in habits and modes of life as are due to fresh discoveries and improvements in taste and comfort as such, or are consequent on change in physical or social environment. These may all involve corresponding changes in fashion, but when eliminated they will leave a residuum of variableness in wants not accounted for, but which, together with the complementary fact of a general conformity to that variableness, make up the phenomenon of fashion properly so called. For the economist it is one of the causes producing disturbing fluctuations in demand and supply, and therefore requiring "a more careful investigation than those causes whose action is more constant and more undeviating" (H. Fawcett, *A Manual of Political Economy*, 1876, p. 84). Under present economic conditions fashion, or any given fashion, comes to be both for consumer and purveyor an element on the one hand of complication, on the other of simplification. The field for the selective play of the consumer's choice is so great that purveyance is rendered very speculative. On the other hand, where his choice settles, demand is certain, at least for a brief period, to be both prompt and extensive, though of uncertain duration. "Changes of fashion are often due to the steady deterioration in the quality of articles which sets in the moment they become open to the fierce and unscrupulous competition of the market" (Foxwell, *Irregularity of Employment*, p. 69).

Fashion in Consumption.—In this connection the economic historian has to trace how "custom in wants, locally homogeneous and temporarily stable, has become fashion distributed in space and transient in time" (V. Schäffle, *Das gesellschaftliche System der menschlichen Wirthschaft*, Tübingen, 1873, pt. iii. sect. iii. The phenomenon of fashion, rooted as it is in elemental instincts and tendencies, is absent from no society or social epoch. "Every epoch has colours and contours which it prefers, forms which it affects, symbols which it venerates " (H. Havard, *L'art à travers les mœurs*, Paris, 1884), ebullitions of sentiment, whims, and fantasies to indulge in. Every nation, while it differs from others in geographical conditions, in political and social constitution, has also its own passing ideas to express. Every individual modifies this sentiment of the day according to his own individuality. The *essential* elements of fashion are present in all societies (cp. Darwin, *Descent of Man*, II., p. 383 ; Westermarck, *The History of Human Marriage*, London, 1891, pp. 165-186 and 274).

As an element in present-day consumption of wealth, fashion may be ranked, not so much as a class of wants under either necessaries, comforts, or luxuries, but rather as a co-efficient of any of these, a want *in* wants, *i.e.* a factor affecting a want already categorised under one of these three heads. Thus it may enter even into necessaries, there being no one commodity, unless pure air and pure water be considered as relative exceptions, which admits of being produced in one *mode* only. The essential elements in food may be taken in a variety of products, some of which, such as "Vienna bread," may be sold at a "satiety price" and yet be fairly viewed as a fashionable taste. In comforts, and still more in luxuries, fashion is a co-efficient of higher power. There is more scope for change because there is a wider field for choice. Fashion in such wants has been ranked as one of the four principles of luxury (Baudrillart, *Histoire du Luxe*, Paris, 1878, i. p. 5 *et seq.*), and as the outcome expressed in unreal needs of refined sensuality, opinion, or caprice (J. B. Say, *Traité d'Économie Politique*, Paris, 1841, bk. iii. ch. iv.). At the same time it has been claimed for fashion and by the same national temperament, that love of change and mobility of taste, of which fashion is an apparently inevitable expression, constitute the mighty incentive or *primum mobile* of all progress, and if wisely cultivated, would banish *ennui* and social strife (Baudrillart, *op. cit.* i. p. 10 ; Fourier, *Le Nouveau Monde Industriel*, Paris, 1845, § 1, notices 1 and 2 on "La Passion Papillonne"). Berkeley expresses the same idea in the *Querist* (Query 20) when he asks "whether the creating of wants be not the likeliest way to produce industry in a people?" (Nos. 10-14, 18, 102, 140, 141, 144, 406, may also be consulted.)

As a want in wants, fashion may be considered as influencing—(a) the quality (or kinds) of wealth consumed ; (b) the relative quantities of the different kinds of wealth consumed ; (c) the rapidity of consumption.

(a) As expressing desire for change, as well as for distinction, fashion will prompt to departures in the direction of *contrast*. Changes in dress abound with illustrations of this tendency. Further, as an expression of the effort after social equalisation, fashion, in diffusing itself outwards and downwards, involves deterioration in quality through adulteration, reproduction in coarser material, and more coarsely finished production. When every woman wishes to wear silk, cotton admixture is lavishly used, even in a proportion of 9 to 1. Again, as expressing the drift of some epochal idea, fashion selects some class of materials, forms, and colours in preference to others ; deserting, for instance, the perukes, powder, and the gay hues of a courtly, conventional, and aristocratic *régime* for the simpler modes of a phase of social upheaval and democratic ideals.

(b) Thus also fashion affects the relative quantities of goods in demand. Ribbon is always to some extent in request, but consumed in far greater quantities when fashionable wear. Further illustration is needless.

(c) In enumerating the causes governing the rate at which wealth is consumed, Storch distinguished, beside nature and use, opinion, which destroys the value of wealth independently of matter (*Cours d'économie politique*, St. Petersburg, 1815, IV. vii. cp. I.). This truth, expressed more picturesquely by Shakspeare, "the fashion wears out more apparel than the man," is dealt with by some economists, notably by J. B. Say, who asserts that fashion, by its privilege of condemning what is still fresh, and perhaps comfortable and pretty as well, as worthless, impoverishes the state both in what it consumes and in what it does not consume,—an epigram limited in application through the redistribution and prolonged consumption of whilom fashionable goods in the second-hand trade. Nevertheless the effect of fashion on very many is to throw a glamour over certain products irrespective of beauty, convenience or fitness, and which, as it fades, causes the same product to be the more hastily superseded in proportion as those qualities are absent.

These constitute to a greater or less extent limitations to the nature and rapidity of changes in fashion. Beauty and fitness combined may limit the mode of dress in one age and climate to draping and swathing the body, in another to close-fitting raiment. Hygienic principles, where accepted, proscribe some tastes potentially or actually in fashion. The love of comfort and convenience may, and in Germany does, tend to diminish the love of change in fashion (*vide* Carl Junghans, *Der Fortschritt des Zollvereins*, Leipzig, 1848, pp. 27-58). Economy may either prolong or proscribe a mode. Custom and routine, whether or not coinciding with convenience, may greatly circumscribe change, as in uniforms and special "costumes." Finally philanthropy and patriotism, morality and religion, have all been brought to bear as regulative principles on excessive instability or wantonness in tastes. Fashion on the other hand has often rendered such principles yeoman's service by investing them, as *their* co-efficient, with a constraining power exceeding that conferred by reason.

Viewed from the standpoint of the budget, changes of fashion, increasing some values and lowering others, have been considered as cancelling each other in the national income (Roscher, *Principles of Political Economy*, New York, 1878, § ccviii.). Modern production, on the "mass-pattern," and "ready-made" system renders it cheapest to buy what is in fashion. Yet Locke struck the true key-note when he wrote, "Things of fashion will be had, . . . whatever rates they cost, and the rather because they are dear" (*Some Considerations of the Consequences of the Lowering of Interest*, etc. 1692, pp. 93, 94 ; and H. S. Foxwell, *Irregularity of Employment*, etc., 1886, pp. 36, 37 ; cp. also a contrast in this respect alleged between French and German ladies, Junghans, *op. cit.*, pp. 57, 58).

Fashion in Production and Distribution.— The anxious purveyor to fashionable whims is as ancient a figure in history as fashion itself (cp. *e.g.* Plautus, *Epidicus*, ii. 2 ; *Aulularia*, iii. 10). Were the record of industrial and commercial statistics of longer standing, there might be many such instances preserved as that in the *Limburger Chronik*, which describes in A.D. 1380 the failure year by year of tailors who competed unsuccessfully in ministering to the swift changes of fashion. As affecting modern trade and industry, fashion is now considered, not merely under the special question of overproduction or "gluts," but in connection with the more generic subject of trade risks, fluctuations of industry, or variations in production. The great expansion of variableness in demand has involved the extension of principles once governing the production of articles of luxury only, to all forms and modes of supply. More or less, every maker and every purveyor, even of necessaries, has now to study both to supply what people want and to win them to want what he supplies. Like everything else in the struggle for life, success, *i.e.* survival, is a feat of adjustment in midst of fluctuating conditions. Failure is the result of miscalculation, of maladjustment.

Even owners and cultivators of land are not exempt from this species of risk. Viticulture, sericulture, the cultivation of the finer sorts of garden produce, and the conducting of ostrich farms, are liable to be affected by changes in fashion. The value *e.g.* of the ostrich feathers imported into this country had declined between 1880 and 1889 in the proportion of 5 : 2 ; the weight in that of $2\frac{1}{2}$: 2.

In the tactics of the manufacturer the symptoms (1) of indecision in vacillating demand raise the problem : What can I "bring out" to attract ? (2) of a favourable turn : How long will it last ? What can I do to get, or keep, ahead in the race ? Can I devise developments ? (3) of a recoil : Can I turn out what is now in demand with such plant, machinery, and hands as I have ? In such an attitude he has to confront demand with its co-efficient fashion, and armed with "money, wits, and perseverance," compass the capture of the lucky *conjunctur*. "Wits" he partly embodies in superiority of machinery, of designing, *i.e.* in the faculty of taking a lead in designs that "sell," of dyeing and finishing, and finally in that fine commercial *flair* which leads to "hits" rather than to "misses." By it he lays his hand upon the pulse of taste, and, divining the symptoms, is able in some degree to eliminate from his business that "aleatory" element which dominates else the amount of his reward (cp. Leroy Beaulieu, *La Répartition des Richesses*, pp. 299, 302). The importance of such augury was expressly admitted by a Lyonnese manufacturer (*v.* "Report by Mr. Dyce to the Board of Trade on Foreign Schools of Design," 1840, cp. *Edinburgh Review*, vol. xc. 1849, p. 481). "That something, which in the world of fashion is only an indefinite sentiment, in fact, a mere predisposition, we endeavour to render palpable, to give it a strongly-pronounced character and assign it a name. Therefore it is that with us fashion is so paramount : the objects of industry, the commencement of a season, exactly chime in with, and anticipate, the predispositions of society." Others who are content to follow rather than lead fashions, watch the inception of a taste, estimate the rate of its diffusion, and anticipate its final stage in mass-production. Exact estimates of the effect of fashion on the career of an industrial centre or firm are complicated for *entrepreneurs* as well as for laymen, by demand being a plurality of effects, and by the "intermixture of causes" in trade fluctuations. Of nineteen merchants and manufacturers who gave evidence before the Commission of Inquiry into the Depression of Trade and Industry, 1886—an inquiry which negatively absolved fashion as a cause of that specific depression—one (a German in Scotland) stated that adaptation to demand and avoiding large stocks were sufficient to meet changes. Another confirmed this, the adjustment being possible " in the great majority of cases " without change of machinery,

an exception being the recent preference of worsteds (combed yarns or "serges," etc.) to woollens (carded yarns or cloth). All, in one way or another, while not clearly distinguishing between the grounds of change in taste, admitted that such changes, especially in the silk and lace trades, were "one of the greatest difficulties " they had to contend with, and had occurred, perhaps, with greater frequency and rapidity in late years. Bradford, Paisley, and Coventry in Great Britain, St. Etienne and Lyons in France, may be cited from a long list of centres, the industrial careers of which have experienced fluctuations peculiarly aggravated, if not created, by changes of fashion. In the words of a Yorkshire mill-owner, "in the crinoline days Bradford dress goods from English wools were in great demand. When ladies preferred clinging fabrics (cashmeres, etc.) the advantage went to the 'soft goods' of France, which now are largely made in Bradford. When mohairs and alpacas were in fashion, Bradford, by its yarns, got the advantage. When braids are fashionable, Bradford benefits. When calico prints were much in fashion, Bradford suffered ; on the other hand it obtained advantage from the demand for *mousselines de laine*." If these and other towns and firms are to-day surviving in the fight, it is in consequence of adjustment to new tastes and of substituting many-sidedness for over-concentration. As the demand for the pseudo-Indian or Paisley shawl died out, which till about 1850 gave occupation to one-third of the Paisley town population, several industries —thread, starch, engineering, shipbuilding— were developed instead. "Trade is on a broader basis and less liable to severe fluctuations." Coventry has ceased to concentrate itself on ribbons, and realised locally unprecedented fortunes in cycles, besides developing other trades. Lister's spin thread when plush and velvet is "sluggish," and with superlative machinery, skill, and invention, weather every storm, even the blast of McKinley tariffs.

Adjustment to, and creation of, new demand in the business of the modern "purveyor" is in conformity to the democratic nature of to-day's fashions. Dress, for instance, was at one time imposed from above. Now the sovereign people's tastes have to be besieged simultaneously and *en bloc* by the shop-window, the stage, the park and race-course, by advertisement, daily paper, and fashion journal—this last organ coming to birth with the French Revolution. Royalty can only suggest, not lead, the fashion. Just as the highest class of dressmakers will equip their customers completely, so the modern "Grands Magasins " cater for the million from head to foot. And always rigidity is avoided by the purchase of lighter stocks, smaller quantities.

The interests of the wage-earner are affected

by fashion in a precisely parallel manner. New demands, if within the range of his skill, mean more work. Rigidity, whether by over-specialisation, want of technical versatility, or any accidents of combination, is fraught with danger. When the ribbon trade was slack at St. Etienne the workmen were reported to be in the habit of getting taken on in the other industries of that centre (v. M. de Lanessan's Report; Depression of Trade Commissioners' Report, 1886). The Coventry ribbon weavers with domestic looms fared very badly, especially after the French treaty (1860). Fashion was more responsible for the poverty occasioned by the decay of the Irish cottage industry of embroidery muslin (*Journal Statist. Soc.*, xxiv. 515-517, cp. De Laveleye, *Le Luxe*, Verviers, 1887, p. 70). A sudden cessation of employment is not alone disastrous, a slowly-decaying industry bringing with it degradation in skill and reduced wages. "East-End" industries, such as artificial flower-making, trimmings, *e.g.* fringes, etc., and fur-sewing, especially where there is no alternative occupation, suffer more sudden fluctuations, the London season—a political quantity with a co-efficient of fashion —greatly aggravating the precariousness of maintenance (v. Miss Collet on "Women's Work" in Booth's *Life and Labour*. See also CUSTOM; DEMAND; HABIT).

[Beside the works referred to, there are brief allusions to the effects of fashion in Cantillon, *Essai sur la Nature du Commerce*, 1755, ch. xiv., xv.—Malthus, *Essay on Population*, bk. iii. c. 13. —M'Culloch, *Principles of Political Economy.*— H. Sidgwick, *Principles of Political Economy*, bks. i. ch. iv. and ii. ch. 11.—Walker, *The Wages Question*, ch. xi.—A. Marshall, *Principles of Economics*, 2nd ed.; vol. i. pp. 144-145, 161, 167-168, 448.— Herrmann, *Staatswirthschaftliche Untersuchungen*, München, 1870, pp. 98-100.—De Molinari's art. "Mode," in Guillaumin's *Dictionnaire de l'Économie Politique*, 1853, is, of course, more comprehensive; still more so is J. Lessing's *Der Modeteufel*, Berlin, 1884. For the philosophy of fashion see J. von Falke, *Zur Cultur und Kunst*, Wien, 1878, "Costüm und Mode"; and F. Kleinwächter, *Zur Philosophie der Mode*, Berlin, 1880.—H. Spencer, *Principles of Sociology*, II. pt. iv. ch. 11. For influence of fashion on demand for gold or silver as currency see Giffen, *The Case against Bi-metallism*, p. 220.] C. A. F.

FASTNYNGSEED. A doubtful term connected with certain ploughing work due from the holder of a full carucate on a manor.

[Vinogradoff, *Villainage in England*, 1892, p. 282, with reference to the *Ely Inquisition*.]

E. G. P.

FATHERS, THE; THEIR ECONOMIC TEACHING AND INFLUENCE. The history of Christian teaching, as expressed by the Fathers, concerning material goods and the proper conduct of life in relation to them, falls into three periods—(1) that of the Primitive Church; (2)

that of the third century; (3) that of Post-Constantinian times.

(1) The church of the first two centuries was marked by a fraternal sympathy in face of the hostile world, and by a belief in the approaching end of the dispensation. Accordingly there was a liberality of charity among its members which amounted almost to a common enjoyment of possessions, so that Tertullian (160-240) boasted, "We Christians have all things in common except wives"; and earthly possessions were treated with indifference except so far as they contributed to actual sustenance. It was scarcely necessary to enforce the duty of almsgiving; but, when it was referred to, the rule was laid down that relief should be given to every suppliant. Clement of Alexandria (*d.* 220) warns his readers not to attempt to discriminate; "for by being fastidious and setting thyself to try who are fit for thy benevolence and who not, it is possible thou mayest neglect some who are the friends of God." But as this charity was practically restricted to the necessary relief of the brethren, whose desert was sufficiently guaranteed by their avowal of Christianity, it could hardly have had any baneful effects. Moreover the Christian teachers constantly exhorted their followers to labour industriously at their several callings, that they "might have enough for themselves and for the poor, and not be a burden to the church"; and this attitude towards labour certainly helped to remove the stigma which the institution of slavery had put upon it. Wealth was recognised as a gift of God to be rightly employed. Tertullian explained that the Christians were "no Brahmans or Indian gymnosophists, no wild men of the woods, and separatists from life"; and it was only among Gnostics and some of the Judæo-Christian communities that there was any rejection on principle of private property.

(2) The ascetic Montanist movement at the end of the 2nd and beginning of the 3rd century, though itself unsuccessful, seems to have affected Christian thought by suggesting a "double ethic,"—the idea of the diverse duties of perfect and of ordinary Christians. Renunciation of earthly property became with Origen (185-253), and S. Cyprian (200-258), a counsel of perfection in the same way as celibacy. Almsgiving, also, was spoken of by the writers of the period as itself sin-atoning; and the treatise of Cyprian *On Good Works and Alms* had great influence on the subsequent doctrine and practice of the church.

(3) The situation in the post-Constantinian period was fundamentally changed by the adoption of Christianity as the state religion. The church now included multitudes whose moral standard was low, and with deepening distress among the poorer part of the population the sphere of its duties became more extensive.

Accordingly increasing stress needed to be laid on the duty of almsgiving; and to overcome the reluctance of their hearers, the great preachers—such as among the Greeks, S. Basil (329-379) and S. Chrysostom (347-407); among the Latins, S. Ambrose (340-397) and S. Augustine (354-430)—were led to use extremely forcible language as to the wrongfulness of a selfish use of wealth. Thus S. Basil, in a frequently quoted passage, puts into the mouth of the hard-hearted the question, "Whom do I injure, if I keep what is my own?" and replies, "Tell me then what is thine own? Whence didst thou obtain it, and bring it into the world? The rich are just like one who has taken his place in the theatre, and crowds all who come in later, as if the playhouse, which is for all, were for him only. For they first take possession for themselves alone of what is common to all, and then lay claim to it as property, because they obtained it first. If each would only take as much as he needs to satisfy his necessary requirements, where then would be the rich, and where the poor?" Expressions almost verbally identical, and apparently calling in question the rights of property, fell also from S. Ambrose. But such language is to be explained, partly as rhetorical exaggeration; partly as due to the idea that voluntary surrender of property was the duty of every Christian who would be perfect; and partly as due to another idea which now made its appearance—that the natural and original order was one of communism, and that private property first arose from sin. But this original order Christians were to aim at restoring only by self-abnegation; and the Fathers did not intend to imply, nor were they understood to imply, that the compulsory abolition of private property would be justifiable. The case is parallel with that of slavery. Slavery also was held by the Fathers to be a departure from natural equality produced by sin. But though the Fathers regarded manumission as a work well-pleasing to God, and endeavoured to mitigate the lot of the slave, they never attacked slavery as an institution. Similarly S. Chrysostom describes the happy society which would be constituted if all the Christians in Constantinople would only agree to live in common; but he meant by this rather a distant ideal than a practical proposal. It is clear, however, that the duty of giving all one had to the poor *was* taught as a means of perfection; and that this teaching, while it led to much noble self-sacrifice, led also to an indiscriminate distribution of doles, which must have had a pauperising effect. A more excellent way of charity was taken by the establishment of hospitals for the sick, which made their first appearance in the 4th century. The contempt for earthly goods, pushed frequently to the point of asceticism, had

already led some of the Fathers, such as Tertullian and S. Jerome, to condemn trade,—especially foreign trade; and even S. Augustine spoke of trade as itself evil since it turned men from seeking God. Teaching such as this encouraged the early anchorite and monastic movements. But the more sober judgment of the church, as expressed by Leo the Great (390-461), held that trade was good or bad according to the way in which it was carried on. The conditions on which trade was justifiable were as yet hardly analysed; but the idea that buyer and seller should abide by the "just price" of every commodity had even thus early made its appearance (see JUSTUM PRETIUM).

Of more immediate effect was the teaching of the Fathers who with one voice reprobated the taking of usury, i.e. of all payment for the use of money. It is abundantly clear that the Fathers themselves condemned the practice absolutely,—whether the payment was small or great, and whether it was taken from rich or poor. But it is almost equally clear that, although borrowing for the purpose of business investment was not at all unknown, loans were far more commonly contracted by the poor to help them through seasons of distress; and it was in their character as the administrators of charity that the problem was brought before the rulers of the church. Thus Pope Gregory the Great (544-604) felt himself obliged on more than one occasion to make advances without interest out of church funds to farmers who were constrained to pay their taxes before selling their crops, and were having recourse to usurers. The Council of Nicæa (325) forbad the practice of usury to the clergy; and it was doubtless due to the influence of the church that the Code of Justinian (529) limited the rates of interest which could lawfully be taken by laymen.

Christian teaching had, however, a wide economic influence outside its bearing on the personal employment of wealth. This is seen in its condemnation of infanticide; its suppression of the gladiatorial shows; its consecration of Sundays and festivals as days of rest; and above all in its effect upon slavery. Mr. Lecky has thus summed it up, "Christianity supplied a new order of relations in which the distinction of classes was unknown. It imparted a moral dignity to the servile classes; and it gave an unexampled impetus to the movement of enfranchisement." In all these ways it contributed immeasurably to the gradual elevation by which slavery slowly passed into mediæval serfdom.

[The above is based chiefly on the excellent work of Gerhard Uhlhorn, *Christian Charity in the Ancient Church*, Eng. trans. 1883, especially bk. ii. chs. ii. vi.; bk. iii. ch. iii.—Lecky, *History of European Morals*, 1869, ch. iv. gives an impressive account of the practical consequences

of Christian teaching, especially in relation to slavery; and Milman's chapter on "Christian Jurisprudence," in vol. i. of his *History of Latin Christianity*, 1854, should also be consulted.—F. X. Funk, *Geschichte des kirchlichen Zinsverbotes*, 1876, furnishes the best statement of the views of the Fathers on usury. The very suggestive criticism of the economic ideas of the Fathers in K. Knies, *Politische Oekonomie vom geschichtlichen Standpunkte*, 1853 (2nd ed. 1883, pp. 113-120) is the source of most of the later expressions of opinion on the subject by professed economists.]
W. J. A.

FAUCHER, JULIUS (1820-1878) was descended from French Huguenot exiles. He studied philosophy at Berlin, and there resided during the greater part of his life. As a journalist, lecturer, publicist, politician, and delegate in different capacities, he impressed himself upon his age mainly as an opponent of protection and collectivism. In 1846 he founded the first free-trade association at Berlin with Prince Smith, E. Wiss, and others. When the paper he edited was suppressed, he joined the staff of the *Morning Star* in London, and became Cobden's secretary. In 1863 he founded, and for fourteen years edited, the Liberal economic journal entitled the *Vierteljahrschrift für Volkswirthschaft und Kulturgeschichte*. He laboured also for the unification of fiscal and commercial legislation in Germany, and founded for the promotion of inland navigation the *Verein für Fluss- und Kanal-schiffahrt*.

He wrote (*a*) separate works, *Die Vereinigung von Sparkasse und Hypothekenbank, und der Anschluss eines Häuserbauvereins als socialökonomische Aufgabe unserer Zeit, insbesondere der Bestrebungen für das Wohl der arbeitenden Klassen*, Berlin, 1845, 8vo.—*In der Bankfrage gegen Gustav Julius*, Berlin, 1846, 8vo.—*The Russian Agrarian Legislation of 1861* (being No. 7 of the "Systems of Land Tenure in Different Countries," published under the sanction of the Cobden Club), London, 1870, 8vo.—*Ein Winter in Italien*, etc., Magdeburg, 1876, 8vo.—*Vergleichende Culturbilder aus den vier europäischen Millionenstädten*, Hannover, 1877, 8vo. — *Streifzüge durch die Küsten und Inseln des Archipels, und des ionischen Meeres*, Berlin, 1878, 8vo.—(*b*) Articles in the *Vierteljahrschrift :* 1863—" Die Baumwollennoth," " Staats- und Kommunal-budgets," "Geschichte, Statistik und Volkswirthschaft," "Zur Frage der besten Heeresverfassung." 1864—" Oesterreich und die Handelsfreiheit." 1865 —" Die Bewegung für Wohnungsreform " (pt. ii. 1866). 1866—"Sachsen am Scheidewege." 1867—" Die zehnte Gruppe auf der Pariser Ausstellung" (workmen's dwellings), " Die Hypothekennoth in Norddeutschland." 1868—"Währung und Preise." 1869 — " Vom Wegezoll und seinem möglichen Ersatze," " Ueber Hausbau - Unternehmung im Geiste der Zeit," " Gedanken über die Herkunft der Sprache" (continued in subsequent numbers). 1871 — " Auf kosmopolitischer Fahrt." 1874 — " Ueber die wirthschaftliche Zukunft des osmanischen Reiches," " Ein Rückblick auf die Geschichte des lebenden Geschlechts aus örtlichen und persönlichen Perspektiven." 1875—" Kurze Wechselziele zur Vorbeugung der Handelskrisen," " Die handelspolitische Grenzzollfrage vor dem 16ten Kongresse der deutschen Volkswirthe in München," " Die handelspolitische Grenzzollfrage vor dem deutschen Reichstage," "Die warnende Dynamit explosion in Bremerhaven." 1876—"Der Plan einer Erwerbung sämtlicher Eisenbahnen in Deutschland durch das Reich."
C. A. F.

FAUCHER, LÉON (1803-1854), born at Limoges, died at Paris. A man of action rather than a thinker, at once a politician and an economist, he led a varied life. His first occupation was that of a teacher in the humblest sphere, but his essentially energetic temperament soon drew him into more active pursuits. The revolution of 1830 had scarcely terminated before he joined the *Temps*, a paper belonging to Jacques Coste, and he remained working on it, side by side with Dussard, up to 1833. He then joined the *Constitutionnel*, and also worked on the *Bien public*, a short-lived journal, and finally, in 1834, on the *Courrier Français*, of which he became chief editor in 1839. It was at this time that he published his work *De la réforme des prisons*, 8vo, 1838, and soon afterwards *L'Union du midi*, which, to checkmate the German Zollverein, proposed a customs association between France, Belgium, Switzerland, and Spain, 1837-1842, in 8vo. Faucher was, after 1834, a constant contributor to the *Revue des deux mondes ;* his sober and exact style, contrasting with his impulsive ideas, rendered him popular with the readers of that journal. He read, in 1843, his *Recherches sur l'or et sur l'argent* before the Academy of moral and political sciences, and entered it in 1849. Meanwhile he commenced publishing, in 1845, his *Études sur l'Angleterre*, 2 vols. 8vo, a very interesting work which, though now of course out of date, may still be read with pleasure. The city of Reims elected him, in 1846, to a seat in the chamber of deputies, where he urged, but in vain, the issue by the bank of France and the departmental banks of notes of 100 francs (£4), a step in the direction of progress which was not taken till 1848. Meanwhile Faucher turned with increasing force towards those occupations for which he had a special taste. He was one of the most active movers in the free-trade campaign in France of 1846-47— which was itself a preparation for the campaign against socialism. Two works of his, *Du système de Louis Blanc, ou le travail, l'association, et l'impôt*, 1 vol. 16mo, and *Du droit au travail*, 1 vol. 8vo, testify to his labours in this direction. He became a representative of the people successively at the constituent and legislative assemblies. After this time politics, and for a moment, during the period of transition, finance, absorbed him. He discussed questions connected with the budget and the income-tax, which last he opposed. Unfortunately also he gradually gave up economics for politics. Thus, in November 1849 he opposed the abolition of the law for the restriction of combinations among workmen, and in June 1851 he abstained from voting on Sainte-Beuve's resolution in favour of commercial liberty. On the 20th December 1848 the president of the republic placed in his hands the portfolio of public works, an office which he exchanged, the 29th of the same month, for the ministry of the interior. His unwonted intervention in the elections compelled him to quit office after a stormy sitting of the assembly, in which he defended a bad cause with a courage worthy of better things. He was intrusted again, on the 16th April 1851, with the office of minister of the interior only to be deprived of it on the 26th October following. His bias towards absolute government had led the man who was seeking power to imagine that he would find in Léon Faucher a useful ally in the government which arose after the *coup d'état* of the 2nd December. But Léon Faucher, when appointed on the consultative commissions which the prince-president joined in the character of a protector, entered his protest against him with a rather noisy indignation, and then retired into private life, devoting himself to economic work in the *Revue des deux mondes*, the *Journal des économistes*, and other similar publications. If something was wanting in Léon Faucher's character, his honourable disinterestedness was at all events highly appreciated by all parties.   A. C. f.

FAUQUIER, FRANCIS (1704?-1768), author of *An Essay on Ways and Means of raising money for the support of the present war without increasing the public debts*, 1756, was Lieutenant-Governor of Virginia from 1758 to 1768, and in that capacity is said to have written to Mr. Pitt about 1760 warning him against a project of taxing the colonies.

His *Essay* maintains that the poor cannot themselves pay any tax, since taxes levied from them necessarily raise the price of labour, and thus ultimately fall on the consumer, or "man of fortune who lives on his income." To the "consumer," therefore, the best tax would be that which is subject to the fewest deductions before reaching the exchequer, and this, Fauquier thought, would be a tax on houses roughly proportioned to their value. To the 2nd edition, 1756, he added a postscript in which he declared that his only object was to recommend the plan of raising sufficient revenue to meet expenses instead of contracting debt, and proposed a graduated capitation tax as a possible substitute for the house tax (see DECKER).

[*Dictionary of National Biography*, vol. xviii. p. 249.]   E. C.

FAVOURED, MOST, NATION CLAUSE. See MOST FAVOURED NATION CLAUSE.

FAVRE, ANTOINE, also FABER and FAURE (1587-1624), chief president of the senate of Savoy, the father of the French grammarian Vaugelas, and friend of St. Francis of Sales, was one of the most distinguished writers of his time on Roman law and jurisprudence.

Besides other miscellaneous writings, such as a tragedy (*Les Gordiens*), and sacred poetry, he wrote a short treatise, *De variis nummariorum debitorum solutionibus* (Lyons, 1598, and Nürnberg, 1622), which, according to Michaud's *Biographie Universelle*, was directed against the more liberal views of Dumoulin (MOLINAEUS, *q.v.*) on usury and interest.   E. CA.

FAWCETT, HENRY (1833-1884), was born at Salisbury, and died at Cambridge. He was educated at King's College School and at Cambridge, where he migrated from Peterhouse to Trinity Hall. He graduated seventh wrangler in 1856, and was elected to a fellowship at Trinity Hall in the same year. In 1858 he was suddenly deprived of his eyesight by an accidental shot from his father's gun, but the infliction of this, perhaps the most serious and disheartening of all physical calamities, did not cause him to swerve from the intention to enter public life which had been formed in early boyhood. He deliberately set himself to smoke and to improve his taste for music, because these occupations would help him to pass his time independently of the attentions of other persons. He walked, rode, skated, and fished, and throughout his public career he eagerly promoted any promising scheme for the encouragement of habits of self-reliance and means of self-support on the part of the blind. After his accident he returned to Cambridge, where he resided for some time. In 1863 he published a *Manual of Political Economy*, which commanded a wide sale, and was re-issued in successive editions, until at the time of his death it had reached a sixth. In the same year (that of 1863) he was elected professor of political economy, and he continued to hold this appointment throughout his life, re-publishing in the form of books more than one course of the lectures which he had delivered from the chair. In 1867 he married Miss Millicent Garrett, and in 1877 he was for some little while a candidate for the mastership of Trinity Hall, finally withdrawing, together with the present Master (1893), in favour of Sir Henry Maine. Meanwhile he had, after standing and then withdrawing as a candidate for the parliamentary representation of Southwark in 1860, and contesting Cambridge and Brighton unsuccessfully in 1863, been elected for the latter constituency at the general election of 1865, and had entered Parliament as an advanced liberal. In the House he adopted an independent attitude on more than one occasion. He supported Mill in the proposed extension of the suffrage to women; he advocated the inclusion of the agricultural labourers within the range of the Factory Acts ; he pressed for the abolition of religious tests in the Universities in 1870 ; he separated from the Birmingham League on the question of national education, and he was largely instrumental in defeating Mr. Gladstone's Irish University Bill in 1874. But it was as "member for India," as he came to be called, that he especially won a reputation, and it was in this capacity that he occupied the most distinctive position. He devoted considerable attention to the study and improvement of Indian finance, which he regarded as the key to the successful and useful government of India. He maintained that India was a manifestly poor country, associated in partnership with a rich country like England, and that in the terms and regulations of this partnership there should be the most scrupulous avoidance of anything that savoured of meanness or injustice. The account-keeping should be at once strict and clear, and the budget, instead of being discussed at the fag-end of the session, should be introduced at an earlier period and carefully examined, and, if need be, severely criticised. But, while the finances of India required this vigilant watchfulness, the Indians themselves were unrepresented in Parliament, and the government officials were, not unnaturally, inclined to resent unpleasant inquiries. Fawcett, however, overcame official opposition, and secured the full investigation of these matters before parliamentary committees. He wrote some articles on the subject for the monthly magazines, in which he showed that the revenue of the Indian government was inelastic, while its expenditure was elastic and increasing. The revenue derived from the land tax was settled in perpetuity in some districts, and for long periods in others. The revenue derived from the cultivation of opium as a government monopoly, or from taxes on its exportation, was precarious. The salt tax was imposed on a prime necessity of Indian life, and the other sources of revenue were inconsiderable. But the expenditure was continually growing. The cost of the civil service and of the army was increasing, the burden of the interest of the debt, which had to be remitted to England, was rendered heavier by the fall in exchange, and the execution of expensive works of irrigation and railway construction, and there was no surplus to meet such recurring emergencies as a famine. The practical sagacity and sober common sense with which Fawcett addressed himself to the consideration of these questions of finance, which his training as an economist fitted him to handle, the generous hatred of injustice and oppression which led him to insist on the strictest equity in the relations of England to India, the appreciation of plain simple principles, which inclined him to interest the public in a few broad considerations of

importance, and the resolute independence with which he persevered in his inquiries, were perhaps the most conspicuous features of his character, and they revealed themselves also in his attitude on other questions of political interest and in his writings on economic matters. He opposed the extension of the Factory Acts to adult women for fear of undermining their independence, and he urged the preservation of commons in the interest of the neglected agricultural labourer. In the election of 1874 he was defeated at Brighton, but was almost immediately selected as a candidate for Hackney. He was successfully returned, and occupied this seat, in spite of differences, frankly confessed and courageously adhered to, with sections of his constituents, until his death. In 1880, on the formation of Mr. Gladstone's ministry, he was offered, and accepted, the post of Postmaster-General, when he introduced some changes of practical convenience, and some reforms designed to elicit and render easier the thrift of the poor. His administration was allowed on all sides to be most successful, and to afford evidence of the possession of practical qualities of a high order. "He regarded the post-office," writes his biographer, "as an engine for diffusing knowledge, expanding trade, increasing prosperity, encouraging family correspondence, and facilitating thrift." In 1882 he was attacked by an illness which aroused a remarkable amount of public sympathy. From this illness he eventually recovered, but in 1884 he succumbed rapidly to the effects of a chill. After his death Mr. Gladstone, writing to his father, declared that there had been no public man of our days whose remarkable qualities had been more fully recognised by his fellow-countrymen, and more deeply embedded in their memories. These qualities were, as it has been already attempted to show, largely of a practical order, and he cannot be said to have contributed much to the development of economic theory, though his powers of exposition were considerable. His love of independence and abhorrence of pauperism were shown in two little books— one on the *Economic Position of the British Labourer*, and the other on *Pauperism*, and he strenuously opposed any scheme of social reform which promised, by invoking the power and resources of the state, to endanger individual initiative and discourage private experiments. This spirit was also shown in the new chapter on State Socialism, which he added to the sixth edition of his *Manual*. He was, in fact, a faithful disciple of that school of economic thought which inclined in the direction of emphasising individual liberty and limiting the interference of the state, although he was willing enough that the state should endeavour to elicit thrift and self-help through the medium of the post-office, or protect the interests of those who could not defend themselves—such as children who needed education, or agricultural labourers who were deprived of commons. His *Manual* was in the main, and it was intended to be, an abridgment of Mill's larger work, but he added materials of his own on such practical subjects as Co-operation and the Poor Law. His *Free Trade and Protection* was also, together with apt and recent illustrations drawn from the practice and facts of commerce, an exposition of orthodox theory. A biography of him has been written by Mr. Leslie Stephen under the title *Life of Henry Fawcett* (1885). From this biography the appended list of his books is taken—

A Manual of Political Economy, 1863 (sixth edition, 1883).—*The Economic Position of the British Labourer,* 1865.—*Pauperism : its Causes and Remedies,* 1871.—*Essays and Lectures on Social and Political Subjects,* by Professor and Mrs. Fawcett, 1872.—*Speeches on some Current Political Questions,* 1873.—*Free Trade and Protection,* 1878.—*Indian Finance,* 1880. See also L. L. Price's *Short History of Political Economy in England.*   L. L. P.

FAXARDO. See FAJARDO.

FEALTY. It was the peculiar characteristic of the feudal system that the political position of individuals was determined by their relation to the land. The man who held land of another was for some purposes his subject, or at least his dependent. The tenant became his lord's man (Lat. *homo*) ; did homage to him, and took an oath of fealty (fidelity) to him. On this principle, only those who held directly from the crown should have taken an oath of fealty to the king, whilst their sub-tenants should have taken the oath of fealty only to them. In some countries this was the case. But in England William I. at the great council of Salisbury compelled all landed men to take an oath of fealty to him. The obligation of this oath would override that of fealty to an immediate lord, if the two happened to conflict. An oath of fealty is still technically due from a freehold tenant to his lord, if any lord can be found ; but it is never exacted (see FREEHOLD, HISTORICAL ; FREEHOLD, LEGAL).   F. C. M.

FEDERAL CO-OPERATION. The federal principle is to be traced, in one form or other, in most of the organisations of any importance which make up the British co-operative movement. Its development has not been primarily due to any school of theory, but to considerations of economy and stability. Obviously, if the co-operative movement was to consist of anything more than a number of local societies, with no common policy, centre, or organisation, some federal arrangement would be necessary,—either that, or something in the nature of an amalgamation. The co-operators hold—and it would seem that experience justifies the opinion—that the combination of autonomy for purely local purposes, and federation for general purposes, is the best working form of constitution. It gives at once a large measure of liberty, together with all the advantages and economies to be derived from mutual organisation. The federal theory of government adopted by the co-operators is based simply on expediency and experience. As the movement has grown, so it has become advisable to provide, not for the supersession of local effort by any form of central administration, but for the better co-ordinating and more effective interaction, for the common benefit of local effort and organisation. But though federalism has been of spontaneous growth, the massing of local effort and resources for common purposes has inevitably had a stimulating effect, in its turn, on the movement as a whole. The federal embodiments tend to become propagandist bodies ; their advice and help is sought by the weaker members of the associated groups, and they increasingly focus the opinions of the main body on matters affecting their social and political interest.

The Co-operative Union, to which most of the societies are attached, provides a sort of consultative and advising executive for the movement, and organises an annual congress, attended by delegates from the united societies. It is largely due to the influence of the union that such extraordinary uniformity characterises the constitution and methods of the societies. No pains are spared in devising the very best rules, as a guide to local effort ; and the Industrial and Provident Societies Act, 1876, of which the union is the parent, forms the legislative basis for these rules. An amended act, promoted by the Co-operative Union, was passed in 1893. The functions of the executive of the union, which is known as the central board, are declared to be to act as (*a*) a board of legal and general advice in all matters relating to the business and interest of societies as co-operative associations ; (*b*) a statistical bureau, collecting and collating for the free use of societies every kind of information likely to be of service to them ; (*c*) a propagandist agency for the dissemination of principles of co-operation throughout both Great Britain and Ireland, and afterwards to the world at large. No society is admitted to the union unless its management is of a representative character, nor unless it agrees to accept the general principles enunciated by the union in favour of the promotion and practice of truthfulness, justice, and economy in production and exchange. The name of Mr. Vansittart NEALE will always be associated with the Co-operative Union, of which he was secretary for many years, and to which he devoted infinite labour. The present secretary is Mr. J. C. Gray ; the headquarters of the union are at City Buildings, Corporation Street, Manchester. There are some co-operative societies unaffiliated to the union, but the majority recognise the advantages which it offers, and subscribe to its funds, take part in the election of its executive, and send their delegates to the annual congresses.

The two co-operative wholesale societies—one of which embraces England and Wales, the other Scotland—are in many ways the most remarkable and powerful workmen's organisations in the world. Both are due to federal developments. The two federations are, in the first place, wholesale agents for the supply of their constituents, the retail stores. The capital is accumulated in precisely the same way as in the stores, which are conducted on what is known as the Rochdale system. Thus a society, on applying for membership, has to take up so many shares—not less than three £5 shares for every twenty members, or fractional part of twenty—on which it pays, on admission, not less than one shilling on each share. These shares are transferable only—that is to say, they may not be withdrawn, but only disposed of to some other society within the federation. No dividends on purchases or interest on capital (which is fixed at 5 per cent) can be withdrawn until such time as the shares are fully paid up. The usual plan is to allow the dividends and interest to accumulate until this shareholding qualification is reached. But the object of the wholesale societies is not to make profit, but to effect economies for their constituents by direct and effective purchasing. Their operations are conducted on such a gigantic scale that they are enabled to command the best terms to be had in the market ; and with their fleet of half-a-dozen steamers, their buyers in different parts of the world, and their system of cash trading, they are practically independent of the middleman. At the end of 1891 there were 966 societies, comprising 751,269 members embraced by the English federation, with a share capital of £473,956, and loans and deposits amounting to £900,752, whilst the sales for the year stood at £8,766,430. The Scottish society's share and loan capital at the same date amounted to £671,108, and its trade for the year was £2,828,036. These two federations, though distinct in their constitution, work together in many ways in making their purchases ; so that the combined influence of the British co-operators is brought to bear upon the markets of the world. The federal agencies have many advantages not possessed by the ordinary trader. They are practically free from bad debts, as the societies are only allowed the briefest credit ; their dealings are not speculative, inasmuch as their constituents provide an assured market whose demands can be foreseen with practical certainty from year to year ; and their expenses for travelling and advertisements are very small. The cost of management is also extremely low. The constitution of the societies is on the basis of membership, not of stock.

The societies composing "the wholesale" may nominate one representative for every 500 of its members, to represent them at the general or branch meetings, which are held quarterly. These meetings examine the balance sheet, and discuss the proposals submitted by the directors of the society, who in their turn are elected by the retail societies. In addition to acting as wholesale purchasers, both the English and Scottish wholesale societies have started manufacturing on a considerable scale, the branches of industry selected being those for which there is the most constant and regular demand—such, for instance, as boots, ready-made clothes, furniture, flour, soap, and so on.

The federal principle has also been adopted for many years in the co-operative flour-mills, many of which exist in the northern and midland counties. There is no need to enter into details as to these bodies, which are conducted on the same basis as that of the co-operative wholesale societies, a fixed rate of interest being paid on capital, whilst the savings effected after paying working expenses and depreciation are returned to the shareholders' societies in proportion to the amount of their purchases. These mills, however, form a highly important part in the economy of co-operation ; and they have served more than once to break up flour rings ; whilst their influence on the prices of bread affects others besides co-operators.

The Co-operative Insurance Company is another federal association which has been promoted, for fire and life insurance, amongst co-operators. The Co-operative Newspaper Society conducts a weekly paper, the *Co-operative News*, its shares being subscribed for the most part by co-operative societies, though there are a certain number of individual members. A good many co-operative productive societies are conducted partly on a federal, and partly on an individual basis, the capital being found, and the direction provided, by co-operative societies and individual co-operators as well.

Something must be said upon the controversy as to the merits or demerits of co-operative production conducted upon the federal principle. The main arguments of the anti-federalists are based upon the fact that under the federal system the consumer and not the producer receives the first consideration—manufacture is carried on, not for the benefit of the workman but for the use of those whom he serves, though now in the Scottish Wholesale Society the workers receive a share in the profits. This school would be appeased in part if the workmen were allowed to share in the profits and management with the consumers; and various schemes have been put forward with the view of detaching the productive departments from the co-operative wholesale societies, and placing them under the directorship of the workmen employed. It is claimed also that under the federal system there is an absence of that spontaneity and scope for free development which alone can call forth the spirit and energy which must be the inspiration of co-operative production. On the other hand, the federalists point to what has been attained by their system, and to the comparatively scanty results of co-operative production carried on independently of the consumer. A considerable section of this school contend that co-operation is not concerned with profit-making, though the dividend is a feature of all the societies, but with a system of production and distribution based upon use. They hold, however, that good wages, good hours, good surroundings, and general conditions of work are on the whole more advantageous to the workmen than a problematical share in more or less speculative profits. As to management, they take the line that it is impossible for the workmen to hold the balance true in matters of workshop administration ; and it must be confessed that a study of the history of co-operative production bears out this fact (see papers on "Co-operative Production" in *Co-operative News*, by Benjamin Jones). Though an award based upon the achievements of the two schools is by no means conclusive as to their merits, yet the controversy is coming to turn more and more on results, and the increased attention paid to the interests of labour by the federated societies may perhaps in time satisfy those who claim—and rightly claim— that the interests of the workman-consumer can never be served by depreciating the value of labour. It is, however, evident that experiments will continue to be freely tried in conducting co-operation on a basis in which federalism plays no part, and in which the consumer does nothing more than trade with the workmen associated in production.

[See *Co-operative Wholesale Society's Annuals*, published at Balloon Street, Manchester ; and *Reports of Annual Congress of the Co-operative Union*, City Buildings, Corporation Street, Manchester.]

v. n.

FEDERATION, COMMERCIAL, as applied to the British empire, aims at establishing closer and more favourable trade relations between the colonies and the mother land than those which now prevail. When Great Britain, commencing in 1846, adopted the principle of free trade, she finally abandoned the right which she had previously exercised of directly regulating the commercial relations of the colonies. Those colonies had up to that time enjoyed advantages over foreign countries in British markets for many of their products, and in return they had often submitted to trade restrictions imposed by the imperial parliament. They were now to receive no better and no worse commercial treatment than foreign countries ; they were on the other hand to be left quite free to frame such trade policies as seemed to themselves best, without reference to other interests than their own. The result has been the adoption of extremely divergent systems in different parts of the empire. While the United Kingdom has followed out the principle of free trade, imposing duties for revenue alone, several of the most important self-governing colonies have adopted tariffs intended not only to produce revenues, but to artificially develop local industries by shutting out the products of other countries and even those of Britain itself.

In thus having no fiscal system common to all its parts, the British empire occupies a position peculiar among all the nations of the world. The fact is accounted for in part by the extremely anomalous composition of the empire. "In it we find communities existing under widely different conditions, some with vast populations concentrated in a small space, while others have their inhabitants thinly scattered over immense areas. Some with wealth which lends itself readily to direct taxation, others which can only collect revenue easily at the ports ; some chiefly engaged in manufacture, others in the production of food and raw material ; some with capital and cheap labour in such abundance that they can cheerfully face any competitors, others under severe pressure from the competition of commercially hostile neighbours more rich and numerous than themselves" (*Imperial Federation*, Parkin, p. 279).

It seems not unreasonable to suppose that this very variety of condition might have been turned to account in forming a common system. But no serious effort was made to check the tendency to commercial separation on account of two false assumptions on the part of political thinkers of the last generation. The first of these was that all other nations would soon follow the example of Great Britain in the adoption of free trade : the second, that the growth of the great colonies must inevitably result in their separation from the empire. The persistent advance of protective systems abroad has turned attention to commercial federation as a means of maintaining industrial prosperity : the growing belief that the empire can and should be held together has led to its consideration as helpful to the maintenance of political union.

All known precedents lead us to associate the idea of commercial federation with that of political federation. In the existing federal systems with which we are familiar, such as those of the United States, Germany, Switzerland, Austria-Hungary, and Canada, freedom of internal trade has been the result, even where it has not been the fundamental condition, of political unity. In the system which has been proposed for the Australasian colonies one of the chief objects aimed at is the same freedom of internal trade. Free commercial intercourse, indeed, seems one of the most distinctive marks of national unity. It appeals directly to the masses, and gives at once a sense of mutual interest and mutual benefit. A common flag and common appliances for defence may mean more in times of danger : under the normal conditions of peace, the unhindered movement of commerce has the greater significance as a mark of common national life. The tendency, therefore, to look to commercial unity as a bond of national unity is natural and reasonable. Different methods have been suggested by which a greater or less degree of commercial unity may be attained.

1. By general adoption throughout the whole extent of the empire of the system of free trade as it prevails in Great Britain. The existence of high tariffs in many of the colonies, and especially of those imposed on great numbers of articles in order to give protection of local industries, certainly tends to weaken the sense of community of interest which is the strongest of national bonds. Earl Grey has pointed out (*Commercial Policy of the British Colonies, 1892*), that a feeling of annoyance has not unnaturally been caused among the merchants and manufacturers of the United Kingdom by finding the products of British industry prevented from competing on equal terms with similar goods produced in the colonies, while at the same time narrow feelings of commercial jealousy have been fostered in the colonies. He continues : "It is not only between this country and the colonies but between the different colonies with each other that feelings of animosity have been excited by the measures adopted in pursuance of the policy of protection. A few years ago bitter, and just, complaints were made in Tasmania of the conduct of their neighbours in Victoria in imposing duties on the fruits of Tasmania to protect their own growers from their competition. There have been disputes of the same nature between Victoria and New South Wales, and between New South Wales and Queensland, and quite lately threats at least of a tariff war between Canada and Newfoundland. In this manner it is to be feared that feelings far from favourable to the maintenance of a firm union of all parts of the empire must have been created both in this country and in the colonies."

The federation of the Australian colonies, the amalgamation of Newfoundland with the Dominion, will put an end to the conflict of interests between these colonies ; it is not so easy to find a solution as complete where the interests of the United Kingdom and the colonies in the same way are opposed to each other. Purely protective tariffs could be removed ; to do the same with ordinary tariffs, often necessarily high, would not be easy. Even the United Kingdom would suffer considerable loss of revenue if the duties were remitted on the tea, coffee, and one or two other articles subject to duty imported from India, Ceylon, and other parts of the empire. But the chief difficulty would occur in the colonies, which, great and small, depend chiefly upon import duties for their public revenues. In most cases the bulk of these imports come from the United Kingdom or from other colonies. Inter-imperial freedom of trade would therefore leave a very large amount of necessary revenue to be raised by direct taxation. To such taxation the objection felt in most of the colonies is so decisive as to render impracticable its substitution for import duties. Complete freedom of trade within the empire, therefore, such as exists between the different parts of the United Kingdom, of Canada, of the United States, or of Germany, is at present admitted to be impossible. Still the abolition of protective duties throughout the colonies, and the limitation to a few articles of import duties imposed for revenue alone, would be a great advance towards commercial union. The desire, felt as strongly in many of the colonies as in foreign countries, to build up manufacturing industries, and the belief that this can best be done by protective tariffs, are the chief obstacles to the adoption of this policy. There are indications, not as yet entirely decisive, that in the colonies, as in the United States, faith in the protective system of developing industries is giving way. Should this change of public opinion go on, the prospects of commercial union by means of greater freedom of trade will be improved.

2. A system of preferential tariffs has been proposed in order to secure some measure of commercial federation while recognising existing differences of policy. Under this system, while each self-governing division of the empire would be left as free as before to choose between a tariff for protection or one merely for revenue purposes, it would be bound to make a fixed discrimination in favour of countries within the empire as against countries without it. The advocates of preferential tariffs for the empire claim that by them several important results would be secured. The preference given to colonial products in the home market would, it is believed, tend to direct emigration towards countries under the British flag, thus retaining as citizens great numbers of emigrants who now go away to add to the strength of foreign nations. This increased colonial population, with its greater productive power, would gradually make the empire almost entirely independent of other countries for supplies of food and raw material of manufacture : it would also furnish a large, friendly, and constantly increasing market for the output of British manufactures. The immense extent of the national territory and the variety of its produc-

tions are facts which are relied upon to give weight to these arguments for preferential tariffs. The undeveloped or half developed areas under the British flag in every zone produce almost every kind of food, every raw material of manufacture, every article of use and luxury. The sufficient application of labour and capital, it is argued, is all that is necessary to bring production up to the level of national consumption. The overflowing population of the United Kingdom and its superabundant capital would thus find the necessary outlet within the empire, and the colonies in these respects would receive what they most need. It is even asserted that if the resources of the empire were fully developed there would be no need to draw upon other parts of the world for any article of commerce, and that within a measurable time the supply of her colonies and dependencies would furnish full occupation for the factories of the United Kingdom.

Another argument has had much weight. The belief of the early advocates of free trade that all nations would be led to adopt that system having proved fallacious, it is now claimed that preferential tariffs within the empire will prove the best means of obtaining better trade relations with foreign protective countries. At present, for instance, the United Kingdom continues to give free admittance to American products, although the United States show an increasing tendency to impose duties for the express purpose of keeping out British and other goods, and so securing the home market for the home manufacturer. Cut off by a preferential tariff from free access to what is his best market, the American, it is said, would be glad to make concessions in order to regain his old privileges. In this case a preferential tariff would be a temporary expedient for coercing protective nations into a greater or an absolute freedom of trade.

Some of the difficulties in the way of adopting a preferential tariff are obvious. The United Kingdom still depends upon foreign countries for more than 75 per cent of its imports : these would be taxed to favour countries which furnish less than 25 per cent. Granting that the empire can produce within itself all that it requires, a lengthened period must elapse before it actually does so, and there still remains the doubt whether natural conditions would allow the products to be supplied as cheaply by places within the empire as by places without it. Sir Rawson Rawson has pointed out (*Analysis of the Maritime Trade of the United Kingdom*) as an important consideration, "the inconvenience, expense, and intolerable delay that would be imposed upon commerce by the revival in England, and the universal adoption elsewhere, not only of a duty upon every article, but of a discriminating duty upon every article, which would necessitate the revival of the system of

certificates of origin. . . . Its re-imposition here and its universal introduction into every part of the empire, considering the immense increase of trade at the present day, would strike a blow at the freedom of commerce which would go far to counteract any advantage arising from the proposed difference in the rate of duty."

3. A plan for preferential tariffs within the empire was submitted to the colonial conference of 1887 by Mr. Hoffmeyer, one of the representatives from Cape Colony. Mr. Hoffmeyer, in proposing that on all produce imported into the United Kingdom and the colonies from foreign countries a small fixed duty should be levied over and above any duty which like imports had to pay when coming from British countries, added the important condition that the revenues derived from this additional duty should be paid into a common fund for national defence. Such a plan, he said, would "establish a feeling on the part of the colonies that whilst they were paying for the defence of the empire they were at the same time enjoying in British markets and inter-colonial markets certain advantages which foreigners did not enjoy. That would establish a connecting link between the colonies mutually as well as between the colonies and the empire also, such as is not at present in existence, and which might further develop by and by into a most powerful bond of union" (*Proceedings Col. Conference, 1887*, vol. i.). Mr. Hoffmeyer estimated that an additional duty of 2 per cent on all imports of foreign produce would give a revenue of £7,000,000, a sum which would materially lessen the burden of taxation for defence. Under existing circumstances this method would apparently bear heavily upon the mother country. Whereas more than 75 per cent of the imports of the United Kingdom are from foreign countries and therefore liable to the additional duty, the imports of the colonies are chiefly from the United Kingdom or from other parts of the empire, and therefore not in the same way liable. In the case of South Africa only about 10 per cent of the whole imports would pay the duty ; in Australia 15 per cent or 20 per cent ; in Canada 35 per cent or 40 per cent. The distribution of the tax would therefore not be at all in proportion to the whole volume of trade to be protected.

The fairness of the impost might be destroyed in another way. A section of the empire might adopt tariffs practically prohibitive of products from other sections. To these latter it would be no advantage that still higher duties were nominally charged on foreign products. It is to be noted, too, that the value of the additional duty as a means of raising revenue for defence would diminish in exact proportion to the attainment of the other object of preferential tariffs, viz. the self-dependence of the empire for exports and imports.

The difficulties, therefore, which confront any plan hitherto suggested, for the commercial federation of the empire, are many and great. On the other hand, if the stringent methods of protection adopted by foreign communities are maintained, there is no doubt that the minds of producers, traders, and statesmen alike will be turned more and more to seek within the empire the free commercial intercourse which is denied without. The gradual formation of a strong political bond may lead to the gradual assimilation of commercial systems. Prof. Nicholson says (*Britannic Confederation*, page 95): "Nothing is more common than to speak of the complicated tariffs and the vested interests of the newest colonies as insuperable obstacles to any general fiscal reform. As a matter of historical fact, however, in much less than a century the commercial policy of the British empire has passed, speaking broadly, from the extreme of central regulation to the extreme of non-interference, and there is, *primâ facie*, no reason why a reaction should not occur if such a course is shown to be to the mutual advantage of the colonies and the mother country." The confederation of groups of colonies like those of Australia and of South Africa, carrying with it, as confederation has already done in Canada, entire freedom of commercial intercourse between the different provinces, will do much to reduce the existing complexity of tariffs. Any inclination towards free trade in the protective colonies, even to the extent of lessening the number of articles taxed, would render much easier the task of arranging these tariffs on a basis of mutual advantage throughout the empire. The attitude of foreign nations on trade questions will probably go far to determine the strength of the forces which make for or against commercial federation.

[See Sir Rawson Rawson's *Synopsis of the Tariffs and Trade of the British Empire.—Sequel to the same.—Analysis of the Maritime Trade of the United Kingdom 1869 to 1889.—Analysis of the Maritime Trade of the United Kingdom 1889 to 1891, with special reference to the proposals for the establishment of a Zollverein.*—G. W. Medley (Cobden Club, 1892), *The Fiscal Federation of the Empire.* To *Britannic Confederation 1892*, Prof. J. S. Nicholson contributes an article on "Tariffs and International Commerce," and Mr. G. G. Chisholm one on "The commerce of the British Empire." *Blue book, No. C. 5091*, fully reports the discussions of the colonial conference of 1887 on Mr. Hoffmeyer's scheme for an Imperial Zollverein. G. R. Parkin's *Imperial Federation the problem of National Unity*, gives a chapter to Trade and Fiscal Policy. H. O. Arnold-Forster, M.P., edits *Tables published by the London Chamber of Commerce.* Much leaflet and pamphlet literature has been published by the United Empire Trade League, a body "formed for the purpose of promoting mutually advantageous trading relations between all parts of the British empire upon a preferential basis." The same may be said of the Fair Trade League, "formed to agitate for such fiscal readjustment as shall prevent the products of foreign states, which refuse to deal with the United Kingdom in fair trade, from unduly competing in British markets with the products of home labour : and to promote, by means of the bond of commercial union between the mother country and her colonies and dependencies, an extension of trade with our own empire." The publications of the Imperial Federation League discuss impartially the merits of free trade and of preferential trade as offering each a possible basis of commercial federation. Articles touching upon the question have been numerous in most of the leading magazines during the last few years.]   G. R. P.

FEE. (*a*) In English law the term *fee* means an estate of inheritance as distinguished from a lesser estate, but in feudal law it was used to denote that which was the "subject of tenure" as opposed to the *alod* or hereditary estate, for which the owner rendered no service to a superior (see FEOD ; Challis on *Real Property*, London, 1885).

(*b*) Payments made by suitors in courts of justice or to the steward of a manor. The former are regulated by ancient usage or by rules of court, the latter are regulated entirely by custom (see Scriven on *Copyholds*, London, 1882).   J. E. C. M.

FEE (Scots law). The right of a tenant or "feuar" of land under the feudal system of tenure : also reversion and remainder. The rules of law relating to fee are based on the principle that the fee can never be *in pendente*, for the superior, or lord, is always entitled to have a vassal.

[For the fee in the case of an heir of entail, see ENTAIL (Scotland). See Bell's *Principles of the Law of Scotland*, §§ 1713-1715.]   A. D.

FEE SIMPLE. An estate "descendible to the heirs generally, that is, simply, without restraint to the heirs of the body or the like" (*Co. Litt.*, 1 b). It is the greatest estate or interest which the law of England permits any subject to enjoy in land. In theory the ultimate ownership belongs to the crown. Williams (in *Principles of the Law of Real Property*, London, 1892, p. 54), says, "A small occasional quit-rent, with its accompanying relief, suit of the court baron, if any such exists, an oath of fealty never exacted, are now, it appears, the ordinary incidents of modern socage tenure" (see Stephens, *Commentaries*, bk. ii. pt. i. ch. iii. ; Digby's *History of the Law of Real Property*, Oxford, 1884 ; Williams, on *Real Property*, London, 1892). The owner of a fee simple has full power of leasing or alienating it, and on his death it descends to the heir of the last person who acquired the estate otherwise than by descent.   J. E. C. M.

FEELING OF VALUE. See VALUE.

FEE TAIL. Land is held in fee tail if, according to the intention of the original grant, it passes, on the death of any individual owner, to one of the descendants of the original donee. Land may be held in "tail general" or in "tail special." In the first case the grant is made to the use of "A and the heirs of his body," and the land descends to the next heir of the original donee according to the rules regulating the intestate succession to land held in fee simple (see HEIR); it therefore passes to females in default of males of the same degree. Gifts in "tail special" occur much less frequently than gifts in tail general, the least rare instance being a gift to the use of "A and the heirs *male* of his body," in which case female heirs are excluded. If the tenant in tail is in possession he can, by the execution and enrolment of a disentailing deed, convert the fee tail into a FEE SIMPLE (*q.v.*), and thus becomes absolute owner of the land. If, however, the land is in the possession of a tenant for life on the death of whom it would pass to the tenant in tail, the latter cannot bar the entail except with the concurrence of the former, who for that purpose is called the "protector" of the entail. In the case of large family estates the land is generally held by a tenant for life under the provisions of a settlement, the tenant in tail being entitled to succeed on his death; and it is usual, as soon as the tenant in tail attains his majority, to "resettle the estates" by barring the entail, giving the former tenant in tail an estate for life and making his next heir tenant in tail in remainder. It is one of the commonplaces of popular oratory to say that the free movement of land is hindered by "the law of entail"; but, as shown above, entailed land, if not forming part of a family settlement, can always be brought under the absolute control of the owner; settlements, not entails, impose fetters on land. But even these fetters can easily be broken through, as under the provisions of the Settled Land Acts the tenant for life has, subject to certain excepted parts, the power to sell any part of the settled land at his discretion; and as regards the excepted parts (mansion-house, heirlooms, etc.), he can do so subject to the consent of the court. [For further particulars see ENTAIL, LAW OF.]

E. S.

FELDAGE, see FALDAGE.

FELT, JOSEPH B. (1789-1869), was born in Salem, Massachusetts, and was educated for the Congregational ministry, from which he early retired. Throughout his life he engaged in antiquarian researches of a historical and statistical nature. To the economist the most important of his writings are: *Historical Account of Massachusetts Currency*, Boston, 1839, pp. 259; and the contributions to *Collections of the American Statistical Association*, vol. i., Boston, 1847, containing especially *Statistics of Taxation in Massachusetts*, pp. 221-596. (See Memoir by Henry M. Dexter in *Mass. Hist. Soc. Proc.*, 1875-76, pp. 113-117.)

D. R. D.

FEMALE LABOUR. The introduction of machinery and the growth of the factory system have effected considerable changes in the conditions of female labour during the present century in every country where these causes have operated. Women in the poorer classes had been accustomed to add to the family income by casual work, and by spinning or weaving for manufacturers in their own homes. Much light is thrown on the conditions of working women in England, towards the end of the 18th century, by Sir F. Eden (*The State of the Poor*, 1797), but he does not always make it quite clear whether the women actually worked at the factory or at home. Home work was the rule, and of one village Eden remarks that "employment for labourers' wives and children is much wanted; they are oftener seen basking in the sun in summer, and shivering over a stolen wood fire in winter, than in any profitable exertions of industry." The use of machinery made it economically necessary for female labour to be employed at the factory itself, and a long uninterrupted working day was enforced instead of work at irregular intervals varied by household occupations. The increased demand for female labour in the factory was accompanied by a diminished need for their services at home. The questions of economic interest which the history of the employment of women should explain are (1) the extent to which they compete with men; (2) the effect of such competition on the wages of men in the same trade; (3) the effect of the economic independence of women on the rate of wages of men in the same class, and hence on the income of the family; (4) the effect of the employment of married women in factories on the well-being of the family. The first point is the only one on which we have statistics of any general value. The regulation of factories and workshops in which women and children work (*vide* FACTORY ACTS) has made it possible to obtain returns of the numbers of males and females in such factories in the United Kingdom.

Year.	Cotton Manufacture.		Woollen Manufacture.	
	Girls under 13 to every 100 boys under 13.	Women and girls above 13 to every 100 men and boys above 13.	Girls under 13 to every 100 boys under 13.	Women and girls above 13 to every 100 men and boys above 13.
1850	57	138	66	65
1856	71	148	78	72
1861	77	156	78	74
1868	86	159	77	98
1870	87	162	69	99
1874	98	168	65	104
1878	117	169	82	111
1885	108	163	79	107

Year.	Worsted Manufacture.		Flax Manufacture.	
	Girls under 13 to every 100 boys under 13.	Women and girls above 13 to every 100 men and boys above 13.	Girls under 13 to every 100 boys under 13.	Women and girls above 13 to every 100 men and boys above 13.
1850	135	209	96	230
1856	133	204	111	250
1861	111	188	142	260
1868	126	208	102	253
1870	111	164	172	230
1874	110	164	147	250
1878	112	177	150	257
1885	111	158	151	251

The increase in the proportion of women to men in the cotton and woollen manufactures has not involved a diminution in the number of men employed. The men and women in the same trade rarely do exactly the same kind of work. The effect of female labour on men's wages and the extent to which they have actually superseded men's labour are extremely difficult to ascertain. The time rate of wages, if the piece rate is not given, affords but a small basis for comparison. Women are paid in printing-offices in England and Scotland at a lower rate than men, and their cheapness is often their chief recommendation, but the difference is not so great as appears on the surface, as some of the heavy work done by the men themselves is done for the women. The history of the cigar trade in East London affords examples of the acceptance by women of low rates which had been rejected by men already employed, who were in consequence thrown out of employment. Work requiring neither muscular strength nor long training would naturally be remunerated at a low rate, whether done by men or women, and much of the work in which women have superseded men is of this nature. Speaking of women's labour in the 15th century, Thorold Rogers remarks "that women's work, when of what we may call an unskilled kind, was equally well paid with that of men," and in the present century there is much ground for believing that inequality in the rate of payment is most frequently to be found when women compete with men in work requiring training and education. But of the 3¼ million females entered in the census of 1881 as industrially employed, more than 2¼ millions were employed in domestic service, dressmaking, nursing, and teaching, and of the 590,624 engaged in the textile manufactures, large numbers were employed on work never done by men. There is not sufficient evidence to enable us to form any judgment as to the effect of married female labour on the wage of the husband. Jevons, in his article on "Married Women in Factories," has drawn attention to the social effects of such

labour, and to the great infant mortality in manufacturing districts, which he traces to the employment of mothers in factories (see FEMALES AND CHILDREN, EARNINGS OF, and FACTORY ACTS).

[*Royal Labour Commission.—The Employment of Women*, 6894, xxiii. 1893-94.—W. S. Jevons, *Married Women in Factories*.]   C. E. C.

FEMALES AND CHILDREN, EARNINGS OF. Previous to the growth of the factory system the earnings of women were principally gained by irregular work done at home for employers. Women also worked in the fields, but rarely for long periods, as such work made it necessary for them to leave their homes; it was more highly paid than those industries which were carried on by married women in their leisure hours. Adam Smith, in speaking of the domestic industries, says that "in most parts of Scotland she is a good spinner who can earn 20d. a week." Sir F. Eden (*State of the Poor*, 1797) gives the earnings of spinners in different parts of England: in Cumberland they earned from 4d. to 6d. a day; at Wirksworth by worsted-spinning 5½d to 6d. a day, and by cotton-spinning 3s. to 5s. a week; at South Tawton, in Devonshire, by serge-spinning 6d. to 7d. a day; at Colchester, children of eight or nine years of age spun for 2d. or 3d. a day, and women weavers earned 5s. to 5s. 6d. a week. At Leicester, women worsted-spinners earned 4d. to 8d. a day, and at Kilworth 6d. to 10d., children from twelve to fourteen earning 6d. a day; at Kirkby Lonsdale, Underbarrow, Southam, Inkborough, and Sheffield the women earned 4d. to 8d. a day. Whereas the spinners at the last-mentioned town earned about 6d. a day, washerwomen earned 1s. a day and victuals. The earnings of lacemakers in Bedfordshire and Buckinghamshire ranged from 6d. to 1s. a day, a few women in Leighton Buzzard earning as much as 1s. to 1s. 3d. In Northamptonshire, the lacemakers by hard work earned 1d. to 1½d. an hour, the earnings ranging from 6d. to 1s. 2d. a day, but the ordinary earnings being about 8d. to 10d. a day. At Dunstable, the straw plaiters earned from 6s. to 12s., children earning from 2s. to 4s. a week. The total earnings in the factories were higher. At Carlisle, women in the stamperies earned 3s. to 12s. a week; at Manchester in the cotton trade from 6s. to 12s., 8s. being the average; at Birmingham in button-making, when in full work, 7s. to 10s. a week. In some cases, however, the wages in cotton mills and other factories are put at a very low rate, leaving it also somewhat doubtful whether the women worked the whole week at the factory. Thus, Eden says, that at Newark "women and children" earned 1s. to 5s. a week in the cotton thread mill; at Northampton 2s. to 5s.; but at Settle children eight to fourteen years of age earned from 1s. to 5s. or 6s. in the cotton works. Children under ten earned 2s. 6d. a week for attending the machines at Frome, 2s. to 3s. in winding silk at Coventry, 1s. to 2s. 6d. in the silk and cotton mills at Derby, 2s. to 4s. at Manchester. In 1816 the average earnings of 316 children under ten years of age employed in twenty-four cotton factories in Preston were 2s. to 3s. 3d., the hours worked being $12\frac{1}{2}$ to $13\frac{1}{3}$ on ordinary days, and 9 hours on Saturdays. In some silk mills in Cheshire in 1816, of the people employed, fifty-four children under ten years earned from 1s. 6d. to 4s. a week, 129 young persons between ten and eighteen earned from 3s. to 8s. 6d., and of 114 men and women, the men earned from 9s. to 15s., and the women from 4s. 6d. to 9s. In 1832-33 the wages of women and children in cotton mills in Glasgow and Manchester were obtained with more exactitude.

Statement of the ages and wages of persons employed in cotton mills in Glasgow and its neighbourhood in 1832:

Ages.	Males.	Weekly Wages.
9 to 10	128	*1s. 3d. to 3s.*
10 to 12	361	*2s. to 4s.*
12 to 14	417	*2s. 9d. to 6s.*
14 to 16	274	*3s. 6d. to 7s.*
16 to 18	214	*4s. 3d. to 9s. 6d.*
18 to 21	143	*6s. to 20s.*
21 and upwards	1050	*9s. 1d. to 35s.*

Ages.	Females.	Weekly Wages.
9 to 10	114	*1s. 3½d. to 4s.*
10 to 12	463	*2s. to 4s.*
12 to 14	479	*2s. 9d. to 6s. 6d.*
14 to 16	419	*3s. 6d. to 7s. 6d.*
16 to 18	520	*4s. 3d. to 7s. 6d.*
18 to 21	581	*5s. to 20s.*[1]
21 and upwards	1411	*6s. 6d. to 20s.*[1]

Statement of the ages and wages of persons employed in weaving mills in Glasgow and its neighbourhood in 1832:

Ages.	Males.	Weekly Wages.
9 to 10	1	*1s. 6d.*
10 to 12	31	*1s. 9d. to 4s. 6d.*
12 to 14	38	*3s. to 6s.*
14 to 16	60	*3s. to 10s.*
16 to 18	36	*6s. 8d. to 12s.*
18 to 21	56	*7s. to 25s.*
21 and upwards	760	*16s. to 24s.*

Ages.	Females.	Weekly Wages.
9 to 10	9	*2s. to 3s. 6d.*
10 to 12	66	*2s. 6d. to 7s. 6d.*
12 to 14	220	*3s. to 7s. 6d.*
14 to 16	447	*4s. 10d. to 9s.*
16 to 18	538	*6s. 1½d. to 10s. 2½d.*
18 to 21	826	*7s. to 10s. 0½d.*
21 and upwards	1235	*7s. to 9s. 9½d.*

Average weekly earnings of persons employed in forty-three cotton mills in Manchester in 1833:

Ages.	Males.	Average Weekly Wages.
9 to 10	498	*2s. 9¾d.*
10 to 12	819	*3s. 8d.*
12 to 14	1021	*5s. 0½d.*
14 to 16	853	*6s. 5½d.*
16 to 18	708	*8s. 2¾d.*
18 to 21	758	*10s. 4d.*
21 and upwards	3632	*22s. 5¾d.*

Ages.	Females.	Average Weekly Wages.
9 to 10	290	*2s. 11½d.*
10 to 12	538	*3s. 9¼d.*
12 to 14	761	*4s. 10½d.*
14 to 16	797	*6s. 4¾d.*
16 to 18	1068	*8s. 0½d.*
18 to 21	1582	*8s. 11d.*
21 and upwards	3910	*9s. 6½d.*

The tables of wages in the textile and other trades issued by the statistical department of the board of trade are the most general and comprehensive. The changes in machinery and methods of production make it in any case difficult to trace the rise or fall of payments for different kinds of work. Few statistics are given as to the numbers who only earn the minimum, and of those who earn the maximum wage. The range of wages earned by women above eighteen, generally in the textile trades lies between 7s. 6d. and 16s., and the same range is found in factories in other trades, the hours worked being $56\frac{1}{2}$ per week.

The nominal wages of women employed in field labour have varied but little. In 1610 the Rutland magistrates assessed the wages of a female reaper at 6d. a day. In 1651 the Essex magistrates fixed the wages for the county, giving women in the harvest-field 1s. 2d., in the hay-field 10d. a day. In 1682 the magistrates at Bury St. Edmund's fixed the wages of women haymakers at 6d., and of women reapers at 1s. In 1684 the Warwick magistrates fixed their wages at 4d. for haymaking and 8d. for reaping. In 1725 the Lancashire magistrates fixed them at 7d. for haymaking and 10d. for reaping. In 1796 women's wages in parts of Cumberland amounted to 10d. a day and victuals, the men being paid the same sum but presumably eating more food. The statistics of time wages in agricultural occupations for 1860 and 1870 give a minimum of 2s. 6d. or 3s., except in the north-western counties, where the minimum was 4s. in 1860, and 6s. in 1870. The maximum in the different counties varies, being about 6s. in the eastern, south-western, and midland counties, about 9s. in the south-eastern, and ranging from 9s. to 11s., or even higher in the north-western and northern counties, and in Yorkshire. The higher wages earned in these latter counties are partly due to the superior physique of the women.

The majority of women are employed in occupations and under conditions which make

[1] Probably forewomen.

it impossible to measure with any exactness the real wages earned. Domestic service in its different branches employs more than one and a half million who receive a large part of their wages in food and lodging of the most diverse kinds (*vide* FACTORY ACTS).

[*Parliamentary Papers, Labour Statistics*, 1887.—*Reports of Royal Commissions on employment in Factories*, 1832, 1841-43, 1862-66, 1874-1876,—*Reports of Inquiries into employment of Women and Children in Agriculture*, 1867-71.— *Reports of Select Committee of House of Lords on Sweating*, 1888-90.—*Reports of Royal Labour Commission*, 1891.—*Annual Reports of the Massachusetts Bureau of Statistics of Labour.*—C. D. Wright (Washington), *Report on Working Women in Great Cities.*—Miss de Graffenried, *Child Labour* (Boston, U.S.).—*Labour and Life of the People*, vol. i. (East London) edited by Charles Booth.— *The Women's Year Book.*—*Journal of the Women's Protective and Provident League.*]   C. E. C.

FÉNELON, FRANÇOIS DE SALIGNAC DE LA MOTHE (1651-1715), born at the Château de Fénelon (Perigord), and died at Cambrai. He was the author of *Télémaque*, in which very decided communistic ideas are to be found; (*Bétique*, bks. vii. and *Salente*, bks. x. and xvii.), which have led the socialists to claim the writer as on their side. Strongly-pronounced views on commercial freedom are also to be found in the *Conseils de Narbal à Télémaque*, bk. iii. These, like the communistic ideas, cease to be surprising when the reader remembers that the book is a classical romance, written (1699) not for the public, but for the moral education of the Duke of Burgundy. Fénelon expressed his opinions more decidedly when passing judgment on the policy of Louis XIV. The letter which this eminent writer addressed to the monarch (dated about 1691-1694), the instructions which he gave to the king's grandson, the Duke of Burgundy, and finally many passages in *Télémaque*, for none of which Fénelon sought publicity, show how great a mind his was. Yet Fénelon was not free from the prejudices of his age in matters of politics and religion, Augustan age though that age might be called. Fénelon was appointed tutor of the Duke of Burgundy in 1689, and archbishop of Cambrai in 1695. He was from 1693 a member of the French academy.   A. C. f.

FEOD OR FEUD. Land granted to be held of the grantor or donor as opposed to land (ALOD) which a man could call his own either personally or as a member of a group or tribe. Alodial land disappeared and the words *feod feudum*, came to be applied to an estate of inheritance as opposed to an estate for life (see FEE).

[Digby, *History of the Law of Real Property*, Oxford, 1884, pp. 31, 71. See also p. 31 for the various suggested etymologies of the word. Sir H. Maine, in *Early Law and Custom*, 1883, p. 338, discusses the history of the feud.]   J. E. C. M.

FEODARY. A book or roll containing lists of knights' fees showing the liabilities of the tenants in respect of military service and scutage, and serving as an assessment for any system of taxation which has the knight's fee for its basis. The best known and most important feodaries are the "The Red Book" and "Small Black Book" of the exchequer, the *Liber Feodorum* or "Testa de Nevill," "Kirby's Quest," and the "Book of Aids." Of these the "Testa de Nevill" or "Book of Fees" is the most perfect specimen: it was compiled probably in the latter part of the reign of Edward I. and contains the result of an inquisition held during the last years of Henry III. and the first of Edward I., giving a detailed list of knights' fees, crown livings, widows and heiresses whose hands were in the gift of the crown, together with the scutages, aids, etc. payable by each tenant. The "Red Book" contains a list of all the scutages levied between 1156 and 1212, and the result of the inquisition held in 1166 on account of the marriage of Henry II.'s daughter; the latter is also contained in the "Black Book"; both books contain, besides, a large amount of miscellaneous matter more or less closely connected with the exchequer. "Kirby's Quest" and the "Book of Aids" contain the results of similar inquisitions held in 1296 and 1356 respectively. DOMESDAY BOOK, the earliest known survey of the country, differs from the above-mentioned works in having for its unit the hide instead of the knight's fee. These books are not merely of historical and antiquarian interest; they afford the student of economics an excellent means of determining the distribution of wealth and population in mediæval England (see KNIGHT'S FEE).   A. E. S.

FEOFFMENT. The term applied to the conveyance of a fee, *i.e.* an estate of inheritance, by the livery or handing over of the seizin (*i.e.* feudal possession) of the land. It was the usual method of transferring fees in feudal times, and though it still survives it is rarely used.

[H. W. Challis, *Law of Real Property*, London, 1885.]   J. E. C. M.

FEORMFULTUM. A term of Anglo-Saxon times of doubtful meaning. It sometimes applies to contributions in kind paid to the sheriff for the maintenance of the king and his household, corresponding to the later purveyance. Sometimes it seems to refer to the rent paid to the sheriffs for the occupation of unbooked folkland.

[Stubbs' *Select Charters.*]   R. L.

FERDEL OR FERLING. A fourth part of a virgate, and, speaking generally, a sixteenth part of a hide. But as the hide contained a varying number both of virgates and of acres, the ferdel cannot be considered as a fixed quantity, though the normal ferdel was probably 7½ acres. The holder of a ferdel was reckoned among the lower classes of villeins, and seems not to have contributed an ox to the common plough-team.

[Vinogradoff, *Villainage in England*, 1892, pp. 148, 256.] E. G. P.

FERGUSON, ADAM, LL.D. (1723-1818), began life as an army chaplain, but in 1757 became librarian to the faculty of advocates at Edinburgh. In 1759 he was appointed professor of natural philosophy at Edinburgh university, from which chair he was transferred in 1764 to that of moral philosophy, which he occupied till 1785. While he ranks rather as an historian and a philosopher than an economist, Ferguson has a fair claim to the latter title through the *Essay on the History of Civil Society* (Edinburgh, 1767, 7th ed., 1814), and the *Institutes of Moral Philosophy for the use of students in the College of Edinburgh* (Edinburgh, 1769). The first-named work consists of an inquiry into the development of civilisation from the savage state : the influence of MONTESQUIEU is clearly seen in this as well as in his other writings. The style is diffuse and ornamental. Ferguson's views in pt. iv. § 1, on the advantages and disadvantages of individuals being confined to one particular employment, are entirely in accordance with those of Adam SMITH. Though this work was published nine years before the *Wealth of Nations*, it is not certain that Ferguson's ideas may not have been influenced by Smith, for the two philosophers were on intimate terms, and Ferguson entertained a high admiration for his friend. Several German writers, notably Karl MARX, referring particularly to the division of labour, consider Smith, but scarcely on sufficient grounds, as the pupil of Ferguson. In his *Institutes of Moral Philosophy*, which are written in a terse aphoristic manner, Ferguson deals with "arts and commerce" (pt. i. ch. i. § 9); here he admits his obligations to Joseph HARRIS (*q.v.*), to whom both he and Smith owe considerably, unless, indeed, Ferguson was acquainted with CANTILLON. He has, in the same work, a more important part (vii.) on "politics," subdivided into "public economy" and "political law." The former treats, among other subjects, of taxation, in respect to which he lays down the following six maxims : "(1) that the exigencies of the state must be provided for at any hazard or expense to the subject ; (2) that in levying taxes no subject be unnecessarily burdened ; (3) that the security of the subject, or that of his property, be not impaired ; (4) that no useful branch of trade be unnecessarily burdened ; (5) that taxes least felt as grievances be preferred ; (6) that the least burdensome method of collecting taxes be chosen." Of these the 2nd, 3rd, 5th, and 6th convey some of the ideas included in Smith's 2nd, 3rd, and 4th canons, though the latter in every case cover far more ground. There is

nothing in Ferguson corresponding to Adam Smith's first maxim. But Ferguson's examination into the expediency, or otherwise, of the various kinds of taxes, divided into capitation, assessment, customs, and excise, might almost have been the text of Smith's arguments on these methods of taxation. Pt. i. ch. i. § 7 of the *Institutes* deals with population, the laws of increase being set out, in some respects, as by Malthus thirty years later. In his *Principles of Moral and Political Science* (Edinburgh, 1792) —a revision of his own lectures—pt. ii. ch. vi. he treats of such economic questions as population, wealth, revenue, liberty, "judicature," and executive power. Here also he repeats his maxims on taxation, omitting the 4th and 6th but adding, "No tax should be laid on in such a manner as to drain the source from which it is derived." He does not mention Smith's canons.

With Ferguson political economy is only incidental, and not yet dissociated from "politics" ; his views, without being entirely original, are considerably in advance of his predecessors', and more generally consonant with those of Adam Smith. In his opinions on mankind may be seen the dawn of what is now known as SOCIOLOGY. In his philosophical system, while being, on the whole, a pupil of Reid, Ferguson introduced a new theory by maintaining that the principle of perfection was of more importance than the principles of self-conservation and sociability, though he admits the influence of these latter, which had till then been held sufficient to explain human morality. Cousin considers that he was the first Scotch moralist to understand the true destiny of man. Ferguson also wrote an important *History of the Progress and Termination of the Roman Republic* (London, 1783).

[Small, J., *Biographical Sketch of A. Ferguson*, Edin., 1864.—*Encyclopædia Britannica*, suppl. to 4th, 5th, and 6th editions, art. "Ferguson," 1824. —Hasbach, *Untersuchungen über Adam Smith und die Entwicklung der Politischen Ökonomie*, Leipzig, 1891.—Cousin, V., *Cours d'histoire de la philosophie morale au 18me siècle ;* 2de partie, Ecole Ecossaise, Paris, 1839-42.—Carlyle, Alex., *Autobiography*, Edinburgh and London, 1860.— Cockburn, Lord, *Memorials of his Time*, Edin., 1856.—Burton, J. H., *Life and Correspondence of David Hume*, Edin., 1846.] R. H. H.

FERM OR FIRMA. The composition paid by the sheriffs in Anglo-Saxon and Norman times, for the domain and other revenues due from their shire (see FARMING OF TAXES).

[Cp. the title of Madox's well-known *Firma Burgi*.] R. L.

FERRARI, JACOPO (living in 1600), born at Rovigo. Though a friar and a theologian, he maintained that payment of interest on money lent was justifiable. After giving a description of the different modes of operation then practised by the bank of St. Ambrogio at Milan, he proved their lawfulness, and opposed and argued against the well-known objection of theologians, *pecunia non potest parere fructum nisi ratione lucri cessantis vel damni emergentis*, as it was referable to money in its primary use; in its secondary use it is a class of merchandise on which it is right to ask an interest for lawful transactions (see CANON LAW).

Digressio resolutoria in contractus usitatos a Banco S. Ambrosii ciuitatis Mediolani, per Fratrem Jacobum Ferrarium, Rhodiginum, in conuentu S. Mariae gratiarum Mediolani, Ordinis Praedicatorum sectorem primum Mediolani, 1623.

A. B.

FERRETTI, JULIUS (fl. 1500), a jurisconsult, born at Ravenna, who applied himself to subjects referring to the revenue. Like his contemporaries Francis Lucano and John Batacchio,—mentioned by Ricca-Salerno in his *Storia delle Dottrine Finanziarie in Italia*,—he considered that taxes should be for revenue only.

He wrote, *De Gabellis.—Quaestiones et decisiones utiles et quotidianae in materia vectigalium et gabellarum tam in terra quam in mari*, Venetiis, 1547.—*In civitate Campaniae* (Fabris), 1547, 8vo.

A. B.

FERRIES (Scotland). As in England, ferries are *inter regalia*, that is, they belong to the Crown, unless granted away. In that case the grantee must keep sufficient boats running in order to meet the requirements of the public, and the rates charged, if not specified in the grant, are regulated by the justices of the peace. Rights of ferry must not be evaded or competed with. Public ferries are under the administration of the local authorities, or of bodies constituted by special acts.　　A. D.

FERRONI, PIETRO (19th century), an abbot of Florence, was the author of—

Rapporto sopra una lettera sulla libertà del commercio dei viveri di Monsignor Antonio Scarpelli (6 Giugno, 1804).—In *Atti della R. Accademia dei Georgofili* (vol. v. Firenze, 1804).

A. B.

FEU (Scotland). Land held under the Scottish form of the feudal tenure, copyhold in form, freehold in substance, though subject to seizure (after declaratory action) for failure to "pay the canon," or meet the stipulated annual payments to the immediate superior. The feu is, in effect, land held under conditions of fixity of tenure for an indefinite period, fixed rent, and free sale or subletting, subject always to the conditions of the original grant. The tenant of a feu is called the "feuar," or in popular language, or even in legal narrative, the "proprietor"; the lord or granter, who receives a fee-farm rent, as also certain incidents or "casualties," is called the superior, and his rent the feu-duty. He in his turn may have superiors over him, and so on up to the Crown.

A. D.

FEUD. See FEOD.

FEUDALISM, ITS ECONOMIC CHARACTERISTICS. It is difficult to state with precision the economic characteristics of feudalism; partly because the term itself is used very loosely, and partly because the conditions which it is commonly employed to denote did not long remain absolutely unchanged in any country, and were not altogether identical in any two. For the present purpose it will be allowable to use "feudalism" for the whole complex of social relations in Western Europe from about the 10th to about the 15th century. "Feudalism" must, indeed, in the strict sense of the term, be defined as an organisation resting on a peculiar system of land-tenure—a system in which ownership was divided between tenants and lords, and in which the connection as to land was accompanied by a close personal tie between lord and tenant, involving mutual rights and duties. The economic features of mediæval life were many of them the results of this system of land-tenure; but it would be pedantic to confine our attention here to those which could be definitely connected with it.

I. Early feudal society was (1) almost exclusively agricultural, and (2) the population was divided into two great rural classes, the lords of the soil (from the king and the great vassals down to the pettiest *seigneur* or manorial lord), and the cultivators of the soil. The husbandmen were able to spend only part of their time—as a rule, perhaps, less than half—on the cultivation of their own holdings; the rest of their time was devoted to labour upon the demesne of their lords. In the later feudal centuries these labour services were, in whole or in part, commuted for money payments: a change which, if we may judge from modern experience in eastern Europe, must have led to a great increase of production both on the servile holdings to which the tenants were now able to give the whole of their labour, and on the demesnes which could be better cultivated by hired labourers than by unwilling serfs. (3) Those lords, lay or clerical, who held many estates were obliged to devise methods by which the net produce could be forwarded to them; but with this exception each MANOR or Seigneurie (*q.v.*) formed a self-dependent economic unit, scarcely connected by exchange with the outside world. (4) Such exchanges as went on, and such dues as needed to be rendered, within or without the rural group, were arranged in what later economists have called a *Naturalwirthschaft* as opposed to a *Geldwirthschaft;* payments in kind or in services being the rule instead of payments in money. (5) Social relations were also marked by a high degree of fixity. Labour dues must, at some period, have become limited; but once the limitation was made, it remained for centuries unchanged; and, again, after labour was exchanged for money, the payments rapidly became well-nigh unalterable. There was but little movement from place to place on the part of the vast majority of the people ; ascription to the soil being not only a legal rule but a social custom. Population, moreover, increased so slowly that there was little difficulty in finding room for additional members in each manor. The forces which are now summed up in the term " competition "were not, indeed, altogether absent ; but they were so much weaker than they are now, and they moved within such narrow limits, that they may almost be regarded as non-existent.

II. In a feudal kingdom sovereignty tended to disappear in suzerainty. But the king, besides being the supreme over-lord, was himself the immediate lord of great estates. The royal court was normally maintained by the proceeds of the royal manors. In time of war the overlord called upon his vassals for personal service. (1) Thus neither for the ordinary nor for the extraordinary needs of government was taxation resorted to unless as an exceptional occurrence,—a marked contrast alike to the financial system of the later Roman empire and to the habitual reliance on taxation of modern states. (2) Taxation being something exceptional, it was held to require the express consent of those to be burdened. Herein appeared the motive which led to the establishment of parliamentary assemblies, and the feudal organisation furnishes the key to their early constitution.

III. In the later feudal centuries trade and industry sprang up in the towns. In the absence of strong government, and under existing conditions as to communication and transportation, it was natural that the towns should not only be the centres of, but should secure control over, this new activity, and that they should seek to regulate it in their own interest. Thus, side by side with a manorial-economy, sprang up a town-economy ; both to be superseded in later times by a territorial and a national economy. Under the sheltering care of municipalities and guilds arose a middle class, a *bourgeoisie*, by the side of, and after a time in a sense *between*, the two classes previously existing ; and it is this class which has been the peculiar representative and champion of modern ideas in economic and constitutional matters.

[On the history of feudalism in Europe the most generally accepted authority of late has been G. Waitz, *Deutsche Verfassungsgeschichte* (last ed. 1880 *seq.*) This should, however, now be compared with Fustel de Coulanges, *Histoire des Institutions Politiques de l'ancienne France* (1889 *seq.*). For England the standard authority is Stubbs's *Constitutional History* (1873 *seq.*), a summary of whose conclusions as generally accepted in 1887 will be found in the essay on " Feudalism," in *Constitutional Essays*, ed. Wakeman and Hassall. Much information of the details of mediæval life will be found in the writings of Thorold Rogers, either in the *History of Agri-*

culture and Prices (vols. i. ii. 1866 ; vols. iii. and iv. 1882), or, in a more popular form, in *Six Centuries of Work and Wages* (1884). For Germany, Inama-Sternegg, *Deutsche Wirthschaftsgeschichte* (vol. i. 1879, vol. ii. 1891). On mediæval labour-rents light is thrown by Richard Jones in his *Essay on the Distribution of Wealth* (1831). The work of most vital importance for understanding the inner life of mediæval society is *English Village Community* by F. Seebohm (3rd ed. 1884). An endeavour is made to trace English agricultural development in Ashley, *Economic History*, (pt. i. 1888 ; pt. ii. 1893 ; in Amer. ed. vols. i. and ii.)].

W. J. A.

[See FORESTS, MEDIÆVAL ; KNIGHT SERVICE.]

FIARS PRICES (Scotland). In the month of February every year the sheriff of every county in Scotland fixes, with the aid of a jury, the average local or "fiars" price of the different kinds of grain. The prices so fixed serve to regulate the money equivalent of all payments in grain, clerical stipends, grain-rents, or of payments stipulated to be in grain sold at fiars prices, or the price of grain stipulated to be delivered without any price having been fixed.

[See Connell, *On Tithes.*—A. Smith, *W. of N.*, I. xi. p. 84, l, ed. M'Culloch.—*Add. Report of Lanarkshire Commissioners of Supply on Fiars of Grain*, 1817.—J. H. Maclean, *Fiar Prices and Produce Rents*, 1825.] A. D.

FIAT MONEY. A colloquial term in the United States applied to paper money issued by the government as money, but not supported by coin, bullion, or any promise of redemption. It circulates because the government wills it. The advocates of this money are in extreme opposition to the HARD MONEY or bullion party. D. R. D.

FIBONACCI (*filius-Bonacci*), LEONARDO PISANO (12th and 13th centuries), the mathematician of Pisa, chiefly famous for having introduced Arabic numerals from Barbary into Italy at the commencement of the 13th century, contributed materials to the history of currency and of commerce in his work on arithmetic, entitled : *Incipit Liber Abbaci compositus a Leonardo filio Bonacci Pisano in anno 1202.* In it an account is given of the various coins and their values, as well as of the different weights and measures used, when he wrote, at the principal cities of Italy. Extracts from it are given by Targioni Tozzetti (*Relazioni d'alcuni viaggi fatti in diverse parti della Toscana*, ed. 2 ; vol. ii. pp. 62-65, Firenze, 1768). C. A. F.

FICHTE, JOHANN GOTTLIEB (1762-1814). Fichte, though of the first importance as a philosopher, cannot be called an economist. Yet through his philosophy he has indirectly exercised great influence on economists, his system giving in outline the theory of development worked out by Hegel, and applied by certain of Hegel's followers to economic history and theory (see HEGEL, LASSALLE, MARX, PROUDHON). Yet the direct influence of Fichte, through his writings on social and political questions, has been much less strong than might have been expected from the power of the writer and the brilliancy of his theories.

Fichte himself had two social ideals. (*a*) He looked forward to a condition of human society when the state and the coercion of laws would not be needed ; as regards the remote future, he is what is now called an anarchist, of the type of William GODWIN (*q.v.*). (*b*) But he sees that men have, strictly speaking, no rights without the state, and conceives that they must necessarily pass through a stage of development in which the state and the laws shall educate them. He has, therefore, a proximate ideal, an ideal state. The best state is to him a "closed state"; it is not merely to have its separate nationality and laws, but it is to be separate in its industry and wealth. It is not to be merely "protected" against its neighbours' competition; it is to have a cordon drawn round it, and, with a few jealously-watched exceptions, it is to have no trade and hardly any intercourse with the foreigner.

The cordon once drawn, the guardians of the state can, he thinks, regulate production and trading, prices and wages. They can introduce a *Landes-geld* or peculiar national currency, valueless abroad ; and they can control its value by controlling its quantity. Thus in all departments of economical life there would be hope of introducing constancy, security, and the maintenance of the chief right of man, the right to labour. Fichte means by right to labour the same sort of exclusive privilege as was secured by the old gilds to their members ; and he regards this as the most important form of property. Private property in the ordinary sense of the word, family life, and even accumulation of fortunes, are not excluded ; and the advantages of family life are clearly recognised. Fichte is a socialist but not a communist ; and he does not try to regulate consumption.

The fire of enthusiasm always present in Fichte's writings is not wanting in the *Closed State ;* but the *Characteristics,* and *Vocation of Man,* are better examples of his best manner.

Collected works ed. by J. H. Fichte, Berlin, 1845-46 (8 vols.). There are passages of economic interest scattered up and down in nearly all these volumes. *Der Geschlossene Handels-Staat* (1800) was an appendix to the *Naturrecht* (1796). Both are contained in vol. iii. of works.

The *Characteristics of the Present Age, The Vocation of Man,* and other of the more popular works of Fichte were translated into English (with much spirit) by the late Sir William Smith (Chapman, 1848, etc.). The translator published also a *Memoir* of Fichte that went through two editions. Fichte's chief philosophical treatise is *Wissenschaftslehre* (1794), vol. i. of works.

[Gustav Schmoller, *Litteraturgeschichte der Staats- und Social-wissenschaften* (Leipzig), 1888.— J. B. Meyer, *Fichte, Lassalle, und der Sozialismus,* 1878.—Ferd. Lassalle, *Die Philosophie Fichtes*

und die Bedeutung des deutschen Volksgeistes, Festrede, May 1862 ; also the article *Fichte* in the *Handwörterbuch der Staatswissenschaften,* by Dr. Karl Diehl ; also Bonar's *Philosophy and Political Economy* (1892), bk. iv. ch. ii.] J. B.

FICTITIOUS EXAMPLES. See EXAMPLES.

FICTITIOUS PAYEE. By § 7 (3) of the Bills of Exchange Act, 1882, which by virtue of §§ 73 and 89 applies *mutatis mutandis* to cheques and promissory notes, when the payee of a bill is a fictitious or non-existing person the bill may be treated as payable to bearer. This provision has been held to apply to the case of a forged bill, when the name of a real person was inserted as payee, but the bill was never negotiated, or intended to be payable, to him ; see Bank of England *v.* Vagliano (1891), 1 App. Cas. 107 ; and see the whole subject discussed in an article on that case in *Law Quarterly Review,* vol. vii. p. 216. In France the insertion of a fictitious payee constitutes a *supposition de nom,* and makes the bill void in hands of any party with notice of the fact. Most of the continental codes contain similar provisions. M. D. C.

FIDEICOMMISSUM. A legacy by way of informal request instead of formal command, thus differing from the strict *legatum.* The fulfilment of the request at first depended entirely on the good faith of the person to whom it was made, but it subsequently became legally enforceable on any one who succeeded to property of the testator. The advantage of *fideicommissa* was, that being originally outside the law, they were not subject to the restricted rules applicable to *legata.* Thus many kinds of bequest were valid as *fideicommissa,* though invalid as *legata.* In course of time, however, the differences between these two forms of legacy disappeared, the law relating to them being assimilated. The idea of vesting property in one person in the confidence that he will allow another to have the benefit of it is common to the fideicommissum and the trust of English law. Indeed some writers suppose that the existence of fideicommissa suggested to mediæval chancellors the enforcement of uses and trusts. But the analogy is only of a general kind. A fideicommissum is simply a form of bequest requesting a transfer of property to be made by some one after the testator's death, whereas a trust is much more freely enacted and may be of much wider extent.

The notion of a double estate, legal and equitable, which belongs to trusts, being derived from the separation between common law and equitable jurisdiction, is foreign to fideicommissa. From the fideicommissum of Roman law a form of family settlement was evolved in France and some other continental countries by which the property affected by it was made inalienable in accordance with feudal ideas (see MAJORAT). E. A. W.

FIDES, Bona, Mala. These terms are frequently used in connection with the acquisition of property, a person acquiring the property of another *bona fide*, *i.e.* not knowing of his defective title, being sometimes in a more favourable legal position than one acquiring *mala fide*, *i.e.* knowing that he has no right. Thus according to Roman law only a person who comes *bona fide* into possession of the property of another can acquire ownership of it by usucapion, and in English law only a *bona fide* holder of a bill of exchange for value, not a *mala fide* holder, can recover on it. (See Bona Fide.) E. A. W.

FIDUCIARY. A person entrusted with the management of property or business transactions on behalf of another person or other persons is said to stand in a fiduciary relation to the owner or owners of the property, or the person or persons on whose behalf the business is transacted. The more usual instances of fiduciary relations are those between trustees and beneficiaries,—principals and agents,—directors and shareholders. The nature of the responsibility varies according to the character of the relation, but the rule that a person standing in a fiduciary position must not, in the absence of special authority, derive any direct or indirect profit from his position, is common to all cases. E. S.

FIELDING, Henry (1707-1754), playwright, novelist, and essayist, was made a justice of the peace "for the County of Middlesex and for the City and Liberty of Westminster," by the whigs, in return for his anti-jacobite journalistic writings. Some results of his magisterial experience took shape in two essays, which are not without interest to the economist from the historical point of view—*An Enquiry into the Causes of the late Increase of Robbers, etc., with some Proposals for Remedying this Growing Evil*, London, 1751 ; and *A Proposal for Making an Effectual Provision for the Poor, for amending their morals, and for rendering them useful members of the society. To which is added a Plan of the Buildings Proposed, with proper Elevations*, London, 1753.

"*The history of Jonathan Wild the Great*," says Mr. Leslie Stephen in his biographical essay, "is a powerful illustration of the facts which were going on under Fielding's nose." He was compelled to "set a thief to catch a thief," for "London at this period, and for long afterwards, was without any proper system of police. Although the population was close upon a million, the organisation for such purposes was still that of a country village. . . The weakness of the police, in fact, made it convenient for private persons to come to terms as best they could with the criminal classes," by means of advertisements promising silence if restoration of stolen property were made.

Fielding attributes the increase of theft (1) to the growth of luxury introduced by trade (and of which as such he approves), through which the working classes had become unsettled, idle, extravagant, and addicted to drunkenness and gambling ; (2) to the abuse or neglect of the laws for the regulation of the poor. Neither the receivers of stolen goods nor the thieves were prosecuted with vigour, the tortuous mazes of London buildings favoured escape, conviction was difficult, pardons were frequent, and executions made festive, not solemn, as in Holland, but "a day of glory" for the criminal.

In the second essay Fielding insists—(1) that work should be provided for the poor ; and (2) that the poor should be compelled to work. He descants on the burthen and nuisance they had become, gives an early instance of "slumming," and pointed out that there was no street in Westminster "which doth not swarm all day with beggars and all night with thieves," that open insults by day were frequent and depredations in the suburban parishes of nightly occurrence. He planned, with full regulations, a county workhouse and house of correction to contain at least 5000, to which vagrants and thieves should be sent, and to which the unemployed might go. There instruction should be given in "manufactures and mysteries," and a labourers' registry kept. In support of his principles, he quotes from Sir Josiah Child, "the great Mr. Law," and "Sir William Petyt." C. A. F.

FIELD SYSTEMS. The prevailing agricultural system, in the middle ages, of England as well as of many European countries. The enclosure acts of the 18th and 19th centuries finally put an end to it in most parts of England, but a few relics may yet be found. Open-fields and town-fields are names often given to lands cultivated under this "three-field" system. One of the three fields was left fallow each year, while the other two were under crops. In some cases a simpler two-field system existed. The open-fields were divided into strips, generally of an acre or some fraction of an acre, varying in breadth, but usually, except where the irregularity of the land prevented it, a furlong in length ; evidently the shape was dictated by the necessities of ploughing. Balks of unploughed turf separated the strips, and across the ends ran a common way, sometimes a path, sometimes a strip, the last to be ploughed. The cultivators, whether freeholders, villeins, or copyholders, held a varying number of strips in each field ; the demesne land of the lord of the manor, and probably even the church lands, were similarly scattered in strips in each field ; the tenants paid rent, in early times chiefly in produce and in labour on the lord's strips, in the later middle ages and since, chiefly in money. Ploughing, sowing, reaping, carting, felling wood, washing sheep, repairing hedges, were among the commonest services performed by the tenants. These would come under the head of week-work, usually the labour of three days a week from the ordinary serfs ; other services, not fixed in time or amount, were called boon-work. In addition to their holdings in the fields the cultivators had grazing rights on the common pasture land which was never divided into strips like the arable, and also, as soon as hay-harvest was over, on the lands temporarily enclosed for hay by the several tenants. "Lammas meadows" (see LAMMAS LANDS) still recall this old right, which points to the common ownership originally existing in the village community. Another evidence of this is the communal or manorial rule, enforced by the township or manor courts, by which common cultivation was made compulsory. The same crops must be grown by all, the same fields cultivated and left fallow in the same order. Individual ownership was *practically* established, but there was no individual freedom of action. Economically, the system was wasteful, tending to keep the standard of farming at the level of the worst farmer, giving scope for endless quarrels, and preventing the adoption of improved methods and implements. The holdings being scattered, the farmhouses could not stand in the midst of the farms, but were placed side by side in the village street. The normal holding of the better class of villein, if in the complexity of classes and holdings anything can be called normal, may be taken to have been 30 acres,—a virgate or yardland ; such a tenant usually owned two oxen, and combined with other tenants to form the common plough-team. Others held a half-virgate,—bovate or oxgang, and contributed one ox to the team, while others again of the lowest class of villein had little or no share in the common fields and owned no ox, but held a hut with a small plot of garden. All gradations are found between these classes, and some villeins even held more than a full virgate. The co-operative plough-team, like the compulsory common cultivation, calls to mind the common ownership of earlier times.

The chief points which are still controversial are, the origin of the scattered holdings and of the services and rents of the peasants. But the latter, though intrinsically the more important, cannot be considered here. With regard to the former, Seebohm argues that the strips were apportioned to the co-owners of the plough-team in a certain rotation, and in proportion to the number of oxen owned by each. Vinogradoff, contesting Seebohm's explanation of the problem by coaration, mentions the fact that in central Russia the strips are intermixed although the plough is drawn by one horse, and argues that the large landholders, who must have owned beasts enough for at least one full team of eight oxen, would under this theory have had compact holdings, which was not the case ; and that very many instances are found of small

teams of four oxen owned by two peasants, which under the system of distribution by coaration would have given the strips alternately to two tenants,—an arrangement which seems not to be found. Vinogradoff explains the intermixed strips by the desire to divide the land fairly ; on the ground that, as due allowance for the uneven quality and irregular conformation of the land was nearly impossible, the plan of dividing good, bad, and indifferent land alike equally among the claimants, would be the most natural resource.

[Nasse, *Geschichte der mittelalterlichen Feldgemeinschaft in England*, 1869.—Thorold Rogers, *Six Centuries of Work and Wages*, 1884.— Seebohm, *English Village Community*, 1883.— Vinogradoff, *Villainage in England*, 1892.]

E. G. P.

FIERI FACIAS, WRIT OF. This writ, commonly called *fi. fa.*, is the one most frequently used for the purpose of enforcing judgments for the recovery of money claims. It directs the sheriff to "cause to be made" (*fieri facias*) the sum of the judgment debt by sale of so much of the debtor's goods as are required for that purpose. The sheriff's officer must be careful not to seize more goods than are required, and not to seize goods which are not the debtor's property. It sometimes happens that goods seized by the sheriff are claimed by the debtor as his property as well as by some other person ; in such a case the sheriff may have the rights of the parties ascertained by a procedure known by the technical name of Interpleader. Formerly the sheriff was unable to take possession of anything beyond "goods and chattels" in the strict sense, but a statute passed in the beginning of the present reign (1 & 2 Vict. c. 110) enables him to seize money, banknotes, bills of exchange, bonds, and other securities for money, and to enforce such securities in the judgment debtor's place.

E. S.

FIFTEENTHS AND TENTHS. The expedient of raising money by means of a tax on personal property is said to have been first tried in England in the time of Henry II. (reigned 1154-1189), who raised money for a crusade by means of the *Saladin tenth*. Whether this was the first occasion or not is a disputed point ; it is, however, certain that as soon as subsidies began to be granted by parliament, these subsidies took the form of a tax on personal property. The amount levied was some definite fraction of the value of each person's movables ; the inhabitants of cities, boroughs, and ancient demesnes being taxed somewhat more heavily than the rest of the country. In the reign of Edward I. (reigned 1272-1307), the usual grant became a *fifteenth and tenth ;* that is to say, a tenth of the value of all movables was to be collected from the inhabitants of cities, boroughs, and ancient demesnes, and a fifteenth from every one else. At first a special assessment was made for each grant, but in the year 1334, when a *fifteenth and tenth* was granted to Edward I., a great inquisition was held, the tax being assessed with much care, extraordinary pains being taken to secure an accurate result, and after this date a *fifteenth and tenth* was a technical expression, and meant that each district was to contribute the amount fixed by the great assessment of 1334. When, owing to changes in the distribution of wealth, the burden of taxation was no longer fairly distributed by the assessment of 1334, the balance was restored by allowing a drawback of £4000, and in later years of £6000, on each *fifteenth and tenth*, in favour of waste and impoverished places ; but no new assessment was made till the reign of Henry VII. (reigned 1485-1509). The whole system of taxation was altered during the commonwealth, and *fifteenths and tenths* were levied for the last time in 1626. The accounts of the assessment and collection of these subsidies, extending as they do from the reign of Henry III. to the end of the reign of Charles I., form a class of documents of great importance in economic and general history.

[Stubbs, *Constitutional History of England*, vol. ii., Oxford, 1883.— Blackstone's *Commentaries on the Laws of England*, vol. i., London, 1862.—*Second and Third Reports of the Deputy-Keeper of the Public Records*, appendix ii.—Dowell, *History of Taxation*, 2nd ed., 1888.]　A. E. S.

FILANGIERI, GAETANO (1752-1788), was born at Naples. His parents, nobles, intended him for a military career, which he soon abandoned to study law and philosophy, with a strong belief in the high future of science, and a desire to discover a new system for the good of mankind. He was the king's chamberlain, and passed his youth at court. During that time he supported the reforms which the Minister Tanucci introduced in the juridical administration (1774), and published, in 1780, the two first volumes of his great work, *La Scienza della Legislazione*, and soon after (1783) the 3rd and 4th vols., which, if they brought him honours both at home and abroad, brought him enemies also. He married, and removed to Cava, where he published (1785) three volumes more, and was appointed a member of the supreme treasury council by Ferdinand IV. His impaired health and zealous work in his new office obliged him to retire to the country at Vico Equense, to recover his strength. But in vain : he died suddenly, aged 36, leaving a lasting fame.

Filangieri was one of the most important writers on economics in the latter years of the last century. He did not, as he himself declares, create new systems, or any new theory ; he had a considerable acquaintance with the economical studies of his time, but it is strange he knew nothing about Smith, whom he never refers to. However, he followed no leader, standing between the physiocratic and mercantile theories. He was a zealous partisan of free-trade and the SINGLE TAX, while he believed in the BALANCE OF TRADE ; so that he may be termed eclectic, but not in the same sense as his fellow-citizen GALIANI. Filangieri is a connecting link between MERCANTILISM and FREE-TRADE; he sustains the principle of the balance of trade, but he argues for a system of liberty both for exportation and importation, tempered only by the opinion that laws ought to be different in countries differently circumstanced ; his works are thus the prelude to a historical system of social legislation. In this aspect Cossa (*Introduzione allo studio dell' Economia Politica*) justly classes him among the authors who accept the new liberal theory without giving up entirely the ancient ones, physiocratic and mercantile.

La Scienza della Legislazione, Venezia, 1822, vol. ii. The 1st ed. is of 1780, and another at Genoa, 1798.—See especially lib. ii. *Delle Leggi Politiche ed Economiche*, reprinted by Custodi in his *Collezione P. Mod.* vol. xxxii.—*Parere presentato al Re sulla proposizione di un affitto sessennale del così detto Tavogliere delle Puglie*, Napoli, 1788.—*Estratto dell' opera* [*William*] *Playfair sul Debito Nazionale*, Napoli, 1788. Playfair's work is *An Essay on the National Debt*, London, 1787. Filangieri, in sending his work to the Marquis Tommasi, explains that he owed to Playfair his opinions against establishing a national debt, to meet the extraordinary requirements of the state.　A. B.

FILIUCCI, VINCENZO (18th century), a Jesuit, born at Siena, who summed up with intelligence the oft-repeated theological considerations about the determination of price, and discussed usury and exchange operations, faithfully keeping to the canon law. The first part of his volume treats of the theory of price, and is interesting to the economical student.

Moralium quæstionum de christianis officiis et casibus conscientiæ, auctore Vincentio Filiuccio, Lugduni, 1622.　A. B.

FINAL DEGREE OF UTILITY is the expression used by Jevons for the DEGREE OF UTILITY (*q.v.*) of the last increment of any commodity secured, or the next increment expected or desired. The increments being regarded as infinitesimal, the degree of utility is not supposed to vary from the last possessed to the next expected. It will be obvious, after a study of the article on DEGREE OF UTILITY, that it is the *final* degree of utility of various commodities that interests us commercially, not, for instance, their initial or average degrees of utility. That is to say (Fig. 1), if a is a small unit of the commodity A, and b a small unit of the commodity B, and q_a the quantity of A I possess, and q_b the quantity of B I possess, then, in considering the equivalence of a and b I do not ask whether A or B has the greater initial degree of utility, *i.e.* I do not compare the lines Oa and Ob, nor do I inquire which has the greater average degree of utility, *i.e.* I do not compare the height of the rectangle on base Oz which shall equal the area $aOxa'$, with the height of the rectangle on base Oy which shall equal the area $bOyb'$, but I compare the length xa' with the length yb', and ask what are the relative rates at which increments of A and B will *now add* to my satisfaction. If xa' is twice the length of yb', then (since a and b are supposed to be small units, throughout the consumption of which the decline in the curves aa', bb' may be neglected) it is obvious that $2b$ will be equivalent to a, since either increment will yield an equal area of satisfaction.

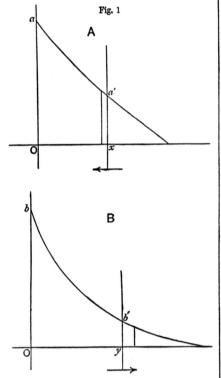

Fig. 1

A

B

Now suppose (Fig. 2) that some other possessor of the commodities A and B, either because he possesses them in different proportions, or because his tastes and wants are different, finds that the relative final utilities of the small units a and b are not the same for him (2) as they are for me (1). Say that for him $3b$ is the equivalent of a, clearly the conditions for a mutually advantageous exchange exist. Let δ be greater than 2 and less than 3, so that $\delta - 2$ and $3 - \delta$ are both positive. Now suppose (1) exchanges with (2), giving him a and receiving from him δb. Then, (1) receives δb in exchange for a (worth $2b$ to him) and benefits to the extent of $(\delta - 2)\, b$, and by the same transaction (2) has received a (worth $3b$ to him)

in exchange for δb, and has benefited to the extent of $(3 - \delta)\, b$. The result of this exchange will be a movement of all the verticals that indicate the amount of each commodity possessed by each exchanger, in the directions indicated

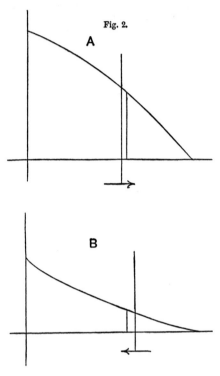

Fig. 2

A

B

by the arrow-heads ; and this again will (as is obvious from inspection of the figures) tend to reduce the difference between the ratio of equivalence between a and b in the case of the two exchangers. The process of exchange will go on (δ not necessarily remaining constant) until the ratio of equivalence between a and b coincides for the two exchangers, the last exchange bringing about an equilibrium in accordance with that ratio. Such a ratio of equilibrium is a limiting ratio of exchange ; that is to say, exchange constantly tends to approach such a ratio, and would cease were such a ratio actually arrived at.

Hence follows Jevons's fundamental theorem: "The ratio of exchange of any two commodities will be the reciprocal of the ratio of the final degrees of utility of the quantities of commodities available for consumption after the exchange is completed."

The final degree of utility of a commodity is thus seen to be the same as its exchange value, and a precise relation is established between EXCHANGE VALUE (*q.v.*) and VALUE IN USE (*q.v.*), the former being the differential coefficient of the latter.

The subject is worked out in an elementary and expository manner in Wicksteed's *Alphabet of Economic Science*, where Jevons is closely followed, but the term "marginal usefulness" is substituted for "final degree of utility."

The conceptions of "degree of utility" and "final degree of utility" lie at the heart of the mathematical method of political economy, and their complete history would almost coincide with the history of mathematical economics. Incidentally the idea has been struck from time to time by sundry mathematicians, and it has been worked out independently by economists no fewer than four or five times. COURNOT (1838), DUPUIT (1844), GOSSEN (1853), and JEVONS (1862 and 1871), successively discovered and taught the theory, each one in ignorance of the work of his predecessors. In 1871 the Austrian Menger, and in 1874 the Swiss Walras (working on the basis laid down by Cournot), adopted essentially the same central conception, and since then the theory has not again sunk into oblivion. Many writers in Germany, Holland, Denmark, France, Italy, and England are now engaged in developing it. See the bibliographies and lists of writers in the appendix to Jevons's *Theory of Political Economy*, 3rd ed., and the Preface to Walras's *Théorie de la Monnaie*, 1886.

[Jevons's "final degree of utility" is the *Grenznutzen* of the Austrian school, Gossen's *Werth der letzten Atome*, and Walras's *rareté* (see VALUE).]

P. H. W.

FINANCES, PUBLIC. See BUDGET, THE ; DIRECT TAXATION ; DEBTS, PUBLIC ; FLOATING DEBT ; INDIRECT TAXATION ; TAXATION, Articles on.

FINANCES.

General Principles of, p. 61 ; of United Kingdom, p. 65—
I. Imperial Finance, p. 65, (*a*) Revenue, p. 65, (*b*) Expenditure, p. 66 ; II. Local Finance, p. 66. Colonial and Indian, p. 67. Belgium, p. 68. France, p. 68. Germany, p. 71. Netherlands, p. 75. United States, p. 77—I. Revenue, p. 77, (*a*) Import Duties, p. 77, (*b*) Internal Revenue, p. 78 ; (*c*) Other Sources of Revenue, p. 78 ; II. Expenditure, p. 78 ; III. Debt, p. 79 ; State and Local Finance, p. 80 ; (*a*) Debts, p. 80 ; (*b*) Revenue and Expenditure, p. 80.

[The details of the taxation in each country must of necessity, in a work like the present, become rapidly out of date, but the examples of the methods of finance given will remain of service to the student of economics by showing him the manner in which the public revenue is raised in the countries cited, which have been selected as important instances of different methods.]

GENERAL PRINCIPLES. The word "finance," originally applied to the payment of a fine (*financia, finatio*), has by a series of changes come now to denote dealings with wealth or capital, most frequently, however, in respect to the management of public or state wealth. Public finance is in fact state housekeeping or "political economy" in the earlier sense of that term, which, according to Adam Smith (*Wealth of Nations*, bk. iv. ch. i. note), "considered as a branch of the science of a statesman or legislator, proposes two distinct objects," the second of which is "to supply the state or commonwealth with a revenue sufficient for the public services." It is accordingly concerned with the best methods of raising and applying the revenue of the state, with the administration of public property and debts, and finally with the systems of accountability and control. The forms and mode of financial organisation, and the principles on which it may best be carried on, have been gradually developed with the progress of political life and the growth of economic knowledge. The earliest societies show the direct levy of commodities and services from the members by the ruler. This simple method of supplying public wants after a time proves inadequate, and more complicated forms come into use. The sovereign obtains property sufficient to enable him to discharge the state services, or, as it was said, "to live of his own" (see DOMAINE), with the power of imposing taxes on extraordinary occasions. As the use of money in transactions becomes more general, the revenue is collected in the shape of coin, which is then expended for the public needs. It is regarded as the duty of the sovereign to accumulate treasure as a safeguard against emergencies, and the administrative arrangements for collection are improved and centralised. The sources of revenue are widened by the employment of various forms both of DIRECT TAXATION and INDIRECT TAXATION, the private or peculiar receipts from state property sink into a position of less importance, while on the other hand the forms of outlay expand with the increasing duties of the state. A further factor is introduced in the establishment of CREDIT, which allows of the substitution of borrowing (see DEBTS, PUBLIC) for the older plan of keeping a treasure. Credit also, by its use, as a medium of exchange, facilitates the collection and disbursement of the public receipts, which are readily managed through the banking system. Parallel with this movement is the application of a better and fuller method of AUDIT, and the greater power obtained by the people over finance, until, under the modern representative system, complete control has been given to the legislature over the appropriations for expenditure and the taxes laid for the obtaining of revenue. This stage, only reached by the most progressive nations within the last century, marks the highest type of financial organisation as yet known. The ruder and less developed forms still survive in backward countries, but their position only shows the course which progress has taken, and does not aid in the explanation of the best system of finance.

Theories on the subject of finance are of comparatively recent origin. At first the financier's sole idea was to take possession of whatever articles were nearest to hand. The ulterior consequences of his action did not seem to need any consideration ; therefore both in ancient and mediæval societies visible and accessible wealth formed the chief object on which the initial weight of the public burdens fell. Even high administrative organisation—as in imperial Rome—did not secure any wiser policy in the substantive methods of finance. Fiscal science took its rise with the need for increased outlay caused by the formation of the modern European system. "Statecraft," as understood by the rulers of the 16th and 17th centuries, included the management of national resources in the public interest. It therefore, more especially under the influence of the ideas of the MERCANTILE SYSTEM, sought to adjust financial rules in a way calculated to stimulate the growth of wealth. Not only the direct but the indirect effects of the fiscal policy adopted were taken, however mistakenly, into account. Thus in the *De Republica* of BODIN, certain kinds of taxation are preferred, and the rule of taxing according to "faculty" or "ability" is stated (bk. vi. ch. ii.). Modern maxims of finance in a crude form appear in the German writers of the 17th century on the subject of "the treasury," and in a more developed shape in the CAMERALISTIC SCIENCE of the succeeding one. The expediency of retaining, and the proper management of state property, the distribution of taxation, and the limits of its amount, the principle of public expenditure, and finally the questions of public treasures and debts are treated in his *Staatswirthschaft* (2nd ed. 1758), and his *System des Finanzwesens* (1761) by JUSTI who systematised the cameralist doctrines.

But the great source of financial principles in the scientific form has been POLITICAL ECONOMY (*q.v.*) as expounded by Adam SMITH (*q.v.*) and his successors, and either included, as in England, in the usual text-books of the science, or, as mostly in Germany, considered in a distinct department with the title *Finanzwissenschaft*. In the midst of much difference of opinion and dispute on controverted points some general principles may be found that have commanded widespread acceptance, or at least enable the opposed views to be realised and defined. Taking the several departments of finance in what seems their natural order, public expenditure first presents itself. The broad rule on this head is admittedly that of "economy." No expenditure should be undertaken unless for an adequate object, and the utility to be gained should be carefully balanced against the disutility or cost of the service. Not only must the total state outlay be weighed against the total sacrifice involved in the raising of revenue, but a due proportion between the several wants to be satisfied must be also observed. The "necessary" functions

of the state should be met before what J. S. Mill (*Principles*, bk. v. ch. i. § 1) calls the "optional" ones receive attention. "Defence," to adopt a phrase otherwise used by Adam Smith, is prior to "opulence," and therefore expenditure for security comes before that for the encouragement of industry or the improvement of art. The rule of "economy," or perhaps better, "maximum utility," holds in respect to each class of outlay. There are limits beyond which even the most necessary object cannot be wisely pursued ; and most disputes as to particular cases of expenditure,—*e.g.* the recurring one as to the sufficiency of the English army and navy—turns on the question of the observance or breach of this rule, which in practice only admits of a rough empirical application. The expediency of increasing or reducing state action may theoretically be regarded as coming under the same comprehensive canon. It should be carried up to and not pushed beyond the point at which the distribution between public and private activities produces the maximum advantage. In this respect the doctrine of FINAL DEGREE OF UTILITY (*q.v.*), promulgated by JEVONS (*q.v.*), and Menger has been employed by Mazzola (*Finanza Pubblica*, Rome, 1890), Viti de Marco (*Economia Finanziaria*, Rome, 1888), and others, but owing to the complications of the factors, it seems as yet impossible to get any definite results. On the lower plane of practice the prudence and insight of the statesman form the only guarantee for successful treatment. Other laws of expenditure are those laid down by Prof. Wagner (*Finanzwissenschaft*, vol. i. pp. 76-83, 3rd ed. 1883) as (1) the law of increase in state functions with the progress of society, and (2) the preference of prevention to repression in modern state-action. These, however, are bare generalisations from the specific experience of Germany (and in a less degree other states) during the present century rather than fundamental laws of financial policy.

Of the two great classes into which the public receipts are divided, the older, "drawn from some fund which peculiarly belongs to the sovereign" (*Wealth of Nations*, bk. v. ch. ii. 1st paragraph), may consist of lands or industrial property. The weight of authority represented in Adam Smith's dictum that "the revenue which, in any civilised monarchy, the crown derives from the crown lands . . . in reality costs more to the society than perhaps any other equal revenue which the crown enjoys" (*Wealth of Nations*, bk. v. ch. ii. part 1), favours the sale of public lands, in European countries at all events, and is opposed to fresh purchases. Any exceptions, *e.g.* the case of FORESTS (*q.v.*), are made not on financial grounds, but for reasons of public policy. As a necessary result the revenue derived from this source is quite insignificant. The question of retention or appropriation of rent by the use of taxation is treated under LAND NATIONALISATION (*q.v.*) (see also SINGLE TAX.)

Though the industrial receipts of the state are not declining as much as those from the DOMAINE (*q.v.*), yet up to the present the field of public enterprise is a limited one, being confined to the means of communication and transport (see POST OFFICE; RAILWAYS, STATE; TELEGRAPHS), certain municipal services, as waterworks, gasworks, and tramways, and lastly industries monopolised for the purpose of securing revenue (MONOPOLIES, *q.v.*). The contribution from this source is comparatively small owing to the great disparity between net and gross receipts. Any considerable gain, as in the instances of the English post office, and (till quite lately) the Prussian railways, is in fact a covert form of TAXATION (*q.v.*). The relatively small yield of the quasi-private or "peculiar" sources of revenue, together with the increasing expenditure for public purposes, compels recourse to a larger extent to the agency of TAXATION.

The nature and general features of TAXATION, its just division, and its real pressure on those affected, as well as the technical rules for its convenient and economical levy, belong to the articles assigned to that head (TAXATION; TAXATION, EQUALITY OF; TAXATION, INCIDENCE OF; TAXATION, MAXIMS OF, *q.v.*). There are, however, some financial principles applicable to the subject of revenue as a whole, which may best be considered here.

One very important rule has been expressed by the word "sufficiency," *i.e.* the public revenue should be large enough to meet the public wants (Wagner, *Finanzwissenschaft*, vol. ii. p. 307, 2nd ed.). No methods of taxation or fiscal management generally—no matter how perfect in other respects—are financially sound unless they provide funds sufficient to meet all usual expenses, and thus obviate the creation of a DEFICIT (*q.v.*). Productivity is therefore one of the essential qualities of a good tax system, and the net amount produced is a most material element in determining the imposition or remission of a tax. As a corollary from the principles on which the foregoing rule is based, it may be said that excessive revenue is not desirable. A large surplus leads to waste and profusion. As Prof. Adams (*Public Debts*, pp. 81, 82) remarks, "The full realisation of self-government requires a delicate adjustment of budgetary machinery, but surplus revenue acts as a weight which throws that machinery out of balance." Thus the ideal system is one in which receipts and outlay are completely balanced, provision for repaying debt being regarded as normal expenditure.

Closely connected with the rule of "sufficiency" is that of "elasticity." Adjustment of revenue in accordance with changes in expenditure should always be within easy reach. Were this not so it would be impossible, owing to the fluctuating nature of public expenditure, to secure the desired balance. For this purpose the best expedient is the general INCOME TAX (*q.v.*) at a movable rate, as in England. The return from such a tax can be predicted within narrow limits, and the yield "begins almost at once" (Blunden, *Econ. Journal*, vol. ii. p. 642). Increase of duty on lightly-taxed articles in general consumption supplies the best substitute for, or (where a large increase in revenue is wanted) the best auxiliary to, the income tax. Abnormal pressure that cannot be easily met by state agencies must be discharged for the time by borrowing (see DEBTS, PUBLIC) which is practically a distribution of the burden over a longer period.

In addition to these requirements of financial policy, it is further desirable that the rules of "generality" and "equality" should be as far as possible observed. The former—flagrantly violated in the case of the privileged classes in France under the *ancien régime*—prescribes that all citizens should contribute to the public services. "Every privilege that tends to exemption from that contribution is" says Vauban, "unjust and abusive" (*Dîme Royale*, ed. Daire, p. 48). The latter rule, though admitting of various interpretations (see TAXATION, MAXIMS OF), lays down that: "The subjects of every state ought to contribute towards the support of the government as nearly as possible in proportion to their respective abilities" (Adam Smith, *Wealth of Nations*, ed. Nicholson, p. 347). Quite apart from ethical or political reasons, it is financially advantageous to secure the contributions of all citizens, and to avoid placing an undue burden—or even what may plausibly be regarded as such—on any individual or class.

Given the foregoing general principles as guiding rules in organising a financial system, it becomes a question of art to duly apply them in the most effective way. First it must be decided whether a SINGLE TAX (*q.v.*) will obtain the needed amount, and if so what form it should take; whether on land, on Revenue, or on Capital (see TAXATION). As, however, both theorists and practical men are agreed in favouring the use of more than one tax or form of tax, the selection and combination of the most suitable classes of imposts have to be considered. To what extent INDIRECT TAXATION (*q.v.*) should be employed; how it should be counterbalanced by DIRECT TAXATION (*q.v.*), and the supplementing of these main categories of revenue by other taxes, are the most important points for notice. At first, and even now to a great degree, indirect taxation in the shape of duties on commodities (CONSUMPTION, TAXES ON, *q.v.*) was the prevailing method. Imported goods were subject to

CUSTOMS DUTIES (*q.v.*), and the European monarchies generally employed the EXCISE (*q.v.*). Customs and excise combined furnish by far the largest part of the revenue of the UNITED KINGDOM (FINANCES OF), of the UNITED STATES (FINANCES OF), and of most other countries. In the first-named they are confined to a very small number of articles, but being laid exclusively for revenue, their yield is high. Elsewhere the inclusion of a much greater number does not give any substantial increase in the return, partly because customs duties are arranged with the design of giving PROTECTION (*q.v.*) to native industry, partly in consequence of the limited consumption of minor articles, the DEMAND (*q.v.*) for which is besides more elastic, and therefore easily reduced by taxation. Good policy, moreover, requires the freedom from taxation of certain classes of articles. Thus taxes on raw materials, and on absolutely necessary articles of food, are not levied in England ; as the former would hamper industry, and the latter trench on the MINIMUM OF SUBSISTENCE (*q.v.*). Articles of luxury, particularly if hurtful, have since the time of Bodin been regarded as specially suitable objects for fiscal treatment, as the almost universal heavy taxation of alcohol and tobacco bears witness. Co-ordination between the excise and customs is desirable in order to avoid diversion of the course of industry or disturbance of the natural movements of consumption. The use of protective import duties or excises unbalanced by corresponding customs is equally a violation of this condition. Nor should articles for which substitutes free from duty are obtainable be subjected to taxation, and the actual duties imposed should be suitably arranged in respect to objects of interchangeable use, as *e.g.* beers, wines, and spirits, or tea, coffee, and cocoa.

Direct taxation is gradually taking a large place in the financial system. The English INCOME TAX (*q.v.*), at first extraordinary and exceptional, has become in practice permanent. The DEATH DUTIES have been increased and are much more productive. The extended use of the income tax on the continent, as in Prussia and the other German states, and in Holland, with in many cases a progressive form (see PROGRESSIVE TAXATION) are instances of the same tendency. Taxes on property, as in Switzerland, the "state" taxation of the American Union, and quite recently in Prussia, may be further cited. On the whole it appears that both income and realised wealth, especially when passing by succession, are being made to bear a greater proportion of the increased public expenditure of modern societies. By this change a partial shifting of the burden involved in supporting the state from the consumers of ordinary commodities to the recipients of the higher grades of income and the holders of realised wealth is being gradually produced.

Some other kinds of contribution are employed by the financier. By the agency of stamps, various legal and commercial transactions are charged. Of the same character are the fees for legal formalities, and more generally for services rendered by the public departments, which in some degree differ from taxes, since they are paid for service done. In their case the rates of charge have to be fixed on other than purely financial grounds.

·In the working of finance it is difficult and indeed practically impossible to avoid excess of expenditure over income in periods of great pressure. Hence the growth of Public Debts (see DEBTS, PUBLIC), and the need of providing for their support and ultimate discharge (see AMORTISATION ; SINKING FUND).

The systematic treatment of national finance is facilitated by the exhibition of its true position at definite intervals, and its consideration by the legislature. This is secured by the BUDGET (*q.v.*), round which has gathered a mass of conventional rules as in England, or strict legal enactments as in France, designed to secure publicity and responsibility. A thorough system of audit, verifying both the reality of alleged expenditure and its conformity to the legalised appropriations, is an additional and valuable guarantee for the sound management of the public finances.

Lastly the existence of a complementary system connected with the numerous local bodies both urban and rural must be noticed. Each of the several heads touched on above—expenditure, revenue, indebtedness, and administration —has its counterpart, though with instructive differences in LOCAL FINANCE (*q.v.*). But it is the reciprocal action of the tax system that requires to have special emphasis placed on it. When estimating the legitimacy of outlay, the distribution and proper forms of taxation, the weight of public debt, or any similar questions, it is absolutely necessary to take both general and local finance into account. Otherwise a true judgment on such points will be impossible, as some elements essential for its attainment will have been omitted.

[The literature of finance is quite overwhelming in amount. Nearly all text-books of political economy deal more or less with financial questions. There is also a mass of special works. In addition to those quoted in the text or given in the various articles referred to, the following manuals may be mentioned. M'Culloch, *Taxation and the Funding System*, 1845, 3rd ed. (revised) 1863.—Thorold Rogers, art. "Finance" in 9th edition of *Encyclopædia Britannica*.—P. Leroy-Beaulieu, *Traité de la Science des Finances*, 2 vols., Paris (5th ed.), 1892.—W. Roscher, *Finanzwissenschaft*, the 4th vol. of his *System der Volkswirthschaft*, 3rd ed., Stuttgart, 1889.—G. Cohn, *Finanzwissenschaft*, (now in course of translation into English), Stuttgart, 1889.—C. F. Bastable, *Public Finance*, 1892. Among brief introductory text-books the most convenient are L. Cossa, *Scienza delle Finanze*, 6th ed. 1893, the 3rd ed. translated into English under title *Taxation*, New York, 1888.—G. Ricca-Salerno, *Scienza delle Finanze*, Florence, 1888.—K. J. Eheberg, *Grundriss der Finanz-wissenschaft*, 3rd ed. Leipzig, 1891.]   C. F. B.

UNITED KINGDOM. In the articles on the BUDGET; EXCISE; and FINANCE, GENERAL PRINCIPLES OF, reference has been made to the historical development of the British financial system. Those on IMPORT DUTIES and the MERCANTILE SYSTEM explain its connection with the industrial development of the nation. The purpose of this article is to state broadly existing facts, and the principles on which the finance of the United Kingdom is at present based.

I. IMPERIAL FINANCE.

The following table indicates the growth of the resources of the kingdom since the beginning of modern finance—the time of the corn law repeal. It should be compared with the general growth of the nation's wealth—*e.g.* with the IMPORTS and EXPORTS. Some have thought that no limit existed to the buoyancy of the revenue of the country, but the last decade in this series has not borne out that promise : there has certainly been a check.

	Revenue.	Expenditure.
1842	£46,965,630	£50,945,169
1847	51,546,264	54,502,948
1852	53,210,071	50,792,512
1857	72,787,965	76,042,570 [1]
1862	69,674,479	72,086,485
1867	69,434,568	66,780,396
1872	74,708,314	71,490,020
1877	78,565,036	78,125,228
1882	83,955,229	83,605,503
1887	90,772,758	89,996,752
1892	90,994,786	89,927,773

[1] War expenditure.

a. Revenue.

The revenue may be classified concisely under the heads :

	Yield in 1892.	Per cent of whole.
Customs . . .	£19,736,000	22
Inland Revenue—		
Excise . . .	25,610,000	28
Stamps (which include succession duties, etc. . .	13,700,000	15½
Land Tax, etc. .	1,484,000	1¾
Property and Income Tax .	13,810,000	15½
Postal and Telegraphic	12,630,000	13¾
Crown Lands . .	430,000	½
Interest and Miscellaneous . . .	2,594,786	3
	£90,994,786	100

Though the actual receipt of this revenue is, of course, not so simple as might appear from this table, it is immeasurably more so than in any foreign country of which we are aware. Taking the heads in order, we may bring out a few further details.

The customs (import) duties are raised on about seven chief articles :

Tea	which gave in 1892	£3,418,162
Coffee	,, ,,	177,206
Spirits	,, ,,	4,427,904
Wines	,, ,,	1,291,052
Tobacco, etc.	,, ,,	9,948,810
Currants, etc.	,, ,,	346,941
Miscellaneous	,, ,,	418,234

The process by which this purely revenue tariff has been attained will be found sketched in the articles on COMMERCE ; FREE TRADE ; and IMPORT DUTIES. For about twenty years it has remained much the same ; and has produced annually about £20,000,000. A slight increase of the tobacco duties and some re-adjustment of those on wines have been the chief changes in that period.

The excise revenue has also remained fairly constant, varying from £25,000,000 to £27,000,000 for many years past. The chief items in 1892 were—

Spirits .	. .	£15,284,067
Beer .	. .	9,445,893
Railway Tax	.	310,325

The spirit and other licenses, which up to 1889 produced £3,500,000 for general revenue, were in that year, all but a small portion, handed over to the local authorities. It is only since 1881 that an excise duty has been levied direct on beer—previously it was imposed on the materials used in brewing.

"Stamps" include death duties,—an important item of revenue, which, owing to changes introduced in 1894, will produce a considerably increased yearly sum. The property and income taxes and the inhabited house duties are amongst the most important items in the national taxation. The income tax is at once the most convenient and the most notoriously unfair. Originally imposed as a temporary expedient, it has become one of the chief engines in the hands of the chancellor of the exchequer. A penny in the pound on the income tax produces a sum which may now be put at £2,500,000, but tends to increase with the wealth of the country and the care taken in collecting the tax. The principle of the tax is excellent, but, as levied, it excites a good deal of grumbling and invites evasion. If it were arranged on a scientific basis, it would be more satisfactory and productive. The main burdens on houses and land belong to local finance.

The revenues of the postal and telegraph services are the other large items in the public revenue. They are rather to be considered as returns for services rendered. The net revenue on this account, after deducting expenses, has averaged considerably over £3,000,000 for five years past: this profit is obtained almost entirely on the inland post.

The incidence of the above taxation, which is an important point for the financier, will be found on examination to be in a marked degree heaviest on the middle classes, *i.e.* persons of moderate means: it bears much more lightly on the working classes and the very wealthy.

Before passing to expenditure, it is well to explain that the term CONSOLIDATED FUND (*q.v.*), originally used in its proper sense, has, owing to the great changes in the raising of revenue, come to be practically a term earmarking that expenditure which was originally assigned to the fund—notably, the charges of debt and the salaries of the judges.

b. Expenditure.

The expenditure may be classified under the heads—

Charges of Debt .	£25,200,000	in 1892	or	28%
Civil Administration, Pensions, etc.	} 12,789,681	„	„	14%
Education . .	6,216,956	„	„	7%
Naval and Military	33,312,571	„	„	37%
Collection of Revenue	2,691,948	„	„	3%
Postal, etc., Services	9,316,617	„	„	11%
	£89,927,773			100

The article on DEBTS, PUBLIC, gives a sufficient view of the history of the English debt. The chief points for the financier to consider are the weight of its burthen and the permanency of its charge. Dr. Giffen, some years ago (*Essays in Finance*), pointed out that it would not require an insupportable effort to pay off, in a few years, a burthen which is less than half the national income. But English financiers have preferred more gradual measures. In ten years the annual charge has been diminished about £4,000,000, the great factor in this diminution being Mr. Goschen's conversion in 1888. Taking debt as the cost of past wars, and our naval and military expenditure as the cost of insurance against the future, we have the enormous sum of £58,500,000 annually as the result of national jealousies—a sum much higher than the charges of ordinary administration. Of the fighting expenditure the army takes over £17,000,000, as against £14,150,000 for the navy, in 1892; but the recent "naval defence fund" of £1,428,751 does something to equalise the expenditure. This fighting expenditure is one of the most anxious subjects with which the chancellor of the exchequer has to deal, the economy of British administration in this respect having been seriously impugned. Of civil administration the chief items on the estimates for 1892-93 were—

Public Works and Buildings	£1,685,215
Civil Departments . .	1,984,483
The Law Courts . . .	826,658
Irish Police, etc. . .	1,482,416
Prisons, etc. . . .	1,701,460
Diplomatic Service, etc. .	419,747
Colonial grants in aid . .	152,783

From this it will be seen that the administration as a rule is fairly economical. Special attention may be called to the small expenditure in connection with the colonial empire: most of the British colonies are altogether self-supporting.

On the other items we need only remark that education is an annually increasing charge—it has practically doubled in ten years—and that the cost of collection of revenue is moderate. The control of this expenditure is secured by the audit department and by the annual investigation of the public accounts committee appointed by the House of Commons.

A word may be given to the actual financing of the United Kingdom. Although a large balance is kept in the exchequer, it is constantly necessary to borrow in advance of revenue for short terms, in order to meet the regular demands of expenditure. This necessarily gives rise to EXCHEQUER BILLS, etc.

II. LOCAL FINANCE.

A few years ago Mr. Goschen described the local finance of the United Kingdom as a complete chaos. The chief sources of receipt for the purposes of local expenditure are the rates on houses and property, reimbursements for gas and water supplied, and various tolls and dues in markets and otherwise. Some of these last, *e.g.* the toll on fish coming into Billingsgate Market, are objectionable as being practically an *octroi* on food.

The total receipts of local authorities for 1890-91, exclusive of loans from or under the control of the central government, were £52,373,537, of which more than half, £27,828,236, was from rates; the amount of government contributions was £7,190,241.

The expenditure of these sums fell under the following chief heads. It is impossible to give a complete view:—

Poor Relief in the Parishes . .	£8,646,944
Municipalities—Police and General Administration	30,995,188
Counties —Police and General Administration	3,972,102
School Boards, etc. . . .	6,003,672
Highway Boards, etc. . . .	2,421,783
Harbour, Pilotage, etc. . . .	3,827,110

These amounts include loans.

The average annual current expenditure on local purposes comes to more than half that of the general government, so that the total burthen of public expenditure on the people of

Great Britain is at present about £140,000,000. (For further details see LOCAL FINANCE.)

[The great parliamentary return 366 and 366-1 of 1868-69, often called *Chisholm's Analysis.*—The *Statistical Abstract of the United Kingdom.* —Reports of the Public Accounts Committee, etc., etc.]   C. A. H.

COLONIAL AND INDIAN. Finance is a wide term, somewhat indefinitely used ; and in a short article it will not be possible to do more than indicate briefly the basis on which the finances rest in the British possessions. The general objects of the public expenditure of all these possessions are much the same : civil and judicial administration requires a considerable fund ; public works are usually the most important item apart from this ; services for the public benefit, such as post offices and railways, in some cases form a large item. In many colonies and India the charge for debt is heavy. The point of view from which it is most interesting to examine the finances of each possession is that of the method of raising the revenues ; and the different methods in vogue lend themselves to a rough classification.

(1) Import duties have a very decided preponderance in Malta, Ceylon, Natal, the West African colonies, the West Indian colonies, Newfoundland, and Canada.

This appears from the following figures :—

	Total Revenue, 1892.	Revenue from Customs.
Canada (Dom.) . .	$36,921,872	$20,501,059
Newfoundland . .	1,883,790	1,731,892
Jamaica . . .	£714,434	£303,657
West African Colonies	384,869	328,680
Ceylon	Rs.18,509,186	Rs.4,385,636
Queensland . .	£3,473,716	£1,145,660

This method of raising revenue was usually the easiest, and adopted first (see IMPORT DUTIES) in colonies where great natural resources have not recently been developed, the customs revenue still remains the mainstay of the financier, and in most temporary emergencies the resource is an addition to the customs duties, often merely to the *ad valorem* duties. In the West Indian colonies there have been several recent proposals to lighten the customs dues and replace them to that extent by direct taxation ; but these proposals have had little success.

(2) In several of the colonies, while the customs revenue forms a very important item, there are others which run it close in point of yield. Such are almost all the Australian colonies, the Cape, the Mauritius, Falkland Islands, and Fiji. The competing items vary so much that it would be difficult to make a classification which was not cumbrous. Excise and liquor licenses in some cases, and land revenue of different kinds in others, are the chief sources. Indeed it is true of many colonies in our first group that excise is an important item.

(3) In a few colonies, the chief of which are the Australian, land and royalties on minerals and timber contribute a substantial amount to the annual revenue ; in the Falkland Islands the rental of crown lands produces nearly half ; in India the land revenue is the mainstay of the finances, producing, in 1892-93, nearly 25,000,000 out of 88,000,000 rupees, and more if the indirect sources of revenue from land, as timber royalties, etc., be included.

(4) Revenue from public works, generally railways, swells the total considerably in many colonies. Natal is perhaps the best instance, where under this head the accounts have £665,335 out of a total of £1,392,455 in 1891-2. But the item requires careful scrutiny in all cases, in the light of the corresponding expenditure under the other side of the account, and very often of the charge of debt. It may be said generally that in no place at present is there a net revenue from such works.

The most satisfactory form of revenue is doubtless that derived from land. It is on this ground that Strachey (*Finances of India*, ch. i.) claims that India is one of the least heavily burdened countries in the world. It is a good policy to keep the land as far as possible in the hands of the state or under some sort of state control, and in her colonies, England, applying traditions from her own history, has only slowly realised this. Most colonial governments have parted with the freehold of the land, and have sold, or granted, rather than rented it ; afterwards, when fresh need of revenue has arisen, they have had recourse to taxation.

Various methods of raising revenue in the British possessions have of late years been the object of attack in this country—notably the opium and salt revenues of India, and the paddy tax in Ceylon. For the controversies which have raged round the import duties, see article on IMPORT DUTIES. Tonnage dues are generally disappearing. Besides the customs, the most thoroughly established methods of raising revenue are by excise, spirit and still licenses, stamps, and taxes on land and houses,— all of which are very general.

An important factor in the finance of all countries is their public debt ; in nearly all the colonies the debt has been contracted for works of public improvement, which should eventually not only pay the charges of debt, but yield a revenue beyond ; in the case of the crown colonies the debts will be repaid within a limited period, leaving the colonists with valuable assets in the completed works for which the loans were raised. In some of the more important colonies, especially the Australian, the charge for debt is large even in proportion to revenue and population ; in the smaller colonies it has been kept comparatively light.

In India, Mauritius, the eastern colonies, and some others, the presence of a silver currency has introduced special difficulties of finance.

The control of finance is entirely in the hands of the local government in colonies with responsible government; in the other colonies it is supervised generally, and in the crown colonies very carefully, by the imperial colonial office. C. A. H.

BELGIUM. (Amounts in francs converted as 25 = £1), According to the twenty-second volume of the *Annuaire Statistique de la Belgique*, published by the ministry of the interior, the total actual receipts of the state in 1889 were subdivided as follows :—

	Millions of Francs.	£
Taxation (a) . . .	170	6,800,000
Péages (tolls) (b) . .	148	5,920,000
Income of State Property .	17	680,000
Reimbursements . . .	3	120,000
	338	£13,520,000
Extraordinary and Special Resources . . .	49	1,960,000
	387	£15,480,000

(a) Taxation.—The principal items are—

	Millions of Francs.	£
Contribution foncière (on real property)	24	960,000
Contribution personnelle .	19	760,000
Patentes (Trade Licenses) .	6	240,000
Customs	27	1,080,000
Excise [1]	41	1,640,000
Registration, Stamps, etc. .	30	1,200,000
Donation and Death Duties .	18	720,000

(b) *Péages* (tolls) comprise the gross proceeds of the State

	Millions of Francs.	£
Railway	132	5,220,000
Post Office . . .	97	3,880,000
Telegraphs	36	1,440,000

The extraordinary receipts consisted mainly in the proceeds of a public loan (forty-four millions of francs or £1,760,000).

For the same year the actual expenditure was—

	Millions of Francs.	£
Interest on Public Debt .	98	3,920,000
Dotations (Civil List) . .	5	200,000
Ministry of Foreign Affairs .	3	120,000
Ministry of Agriculture, Industry and Public Works	16	640,000
Ministry of Railways, Post and Telegraph . .	94	3,760,000
Ministry of Finance . .	15	600,000
Ministry of War . . .	51	2,040,000
Ministry of the Interior and Public Instruction (the latter 16 millions, £640,000)	22	880,000
Ministry of Justice (includes 5 millions for religious endowment) . . .	16	640,000
Sundries	2	80,000
	322	£12,880,000
Special Services . .	51	2,040,000
	373	£14,920,000

[1] Includes Foreign wines 3 (£120,000), alcohol 24 (£960,000), beer and vinegar 9 (£360,000), sugar 4 millions of francs (£160,000).

Special services include public works executed at the expense of the state ; thus, in 1889, 15 millions of francs (£600,000) were spent on railways, and 11 millions (£440,000) on the forts erected in the valley of the Meuse.

The subdivision of administrative functions between the different ministries is not exactly the same as in France ; the separate ministry of railways was created in 1884, and is justified by the fact that the Belgian state owns the greater part of the railway lines—3250 kilometers, or say 2000 miles against 1276 kilometers, or 800 miles worked by companies in 1890.

The Belgian financial system has much the same basis as the French system (see below). Taxation, however, is much lighter, since the net proceeds of the state railways ought to be deducted and the amount paid per head in taxation is not one-half of what it is in France. State monopolies, such as the French *Régie* of tobacco, do not exist in Belgium ; there is no tax on the income derived from dividends of shares, securities, etc., and the custom duties are generally arranged with a purely fiscal aim.

Belgian finance presents one particular feature. Since 1859, the *octrois* or municipal duties on consumption levied at the entrance of the towns (see OCTROI) have been suppressed, and a special fund, called the *Fonds Communal*, instituted to compensate the loss to the municipalities. This fund is provided for by a fixed percentage on the proceeds of the postal receipts and of certain excise or custom duties (sugar, coffee, alcohol, wine, and beer). This distinct attribution to local purposes of a specified part of the general national revenue constitutes an exceptional departure from the leading principles in Belgian and also French finance.

The Belgian public debt amounts to about 2000 millions of francs (say £80,000,000 sterling).

[Apart from official publications such as the *Annuaire Statistique* already mentioned, the *Moniteur Belge*, and the *Comptes Généraux de l'Administration des Finances*, much information concerning Belgian finance will be found scattered over M. P. Leroy-Beaulieu's *Traité de la Science des Finances*, and also occasionally in the French official *Bulletin de Statistique*. For the period 1830-70, a general sketch was published in the *Patria Belgica* (vol. ii. *Belgique Politique et Sociale*, pp. 865 - 903), Brussels, 1873. The English reader may also be referred to Messrs. Le Hardy de Beaulieu, and Couvreur's (both some time vice-presidents and members of the Belgian chamber of representatives) contributions to the *Correspondence relating to the Budgets* published by the Cobden Club.]   E. Ca.

FRANCE (Amounts in francs converted as 25 = £1). Practically it is only since the time of Napoleon I. (first consul 1799, proclaimed emperor 1804), that regular estimates of receipts and expenditure have been yearly prepared ; and only since the restoration of the Bourbons (1814), that these have been submitted to the effective preliminary approval of the French parliament. The *Budget des Voies et Moyens* (ways and means) is drawn up by the minister of finance ; the *Budget des Dépenses* (expenditure) by each minister for his own department ; it is divided into chapters, corresponding to each particular branch of the service, and since 1871 each chapter must be voted separately. The vote opens a *crédit* (supply) to the minister, who is now no longer allowed, as under the second empire, to effect transfers (*virements*) from one chapter to another. In case of need, *additional credits* are granted after the vote of the *budget;* these sometimes reach a considerable amount (15 millions sterling in 1885), and are a permanent cause of instability in the financial equilibrium. The whole of the expenditure and receipts must be voted yearly, and first by the lower chamber.

RECEIPTS.—In the financial bill for 1893, (*Projet de loi portant fixation du budget général de l'Exercice 1893*), the total estimates amount to 3299 millions of francs (£131,960,000). The main elements of this revenue are given as follows in millions of francs and round numbers :—

	francs	£
Direct taxation . . .	495 mill.	19,800,000
Indirect taxation . . .	2044 „	81,760,000
State monopolies and manu-factures . . .	625 „	25,000,000
State Property . . .	46 „	1,840,000
	3210 mill.	128,400,000

The words "direct" and "indirect taxation," are of course used in their French administrative and purely empirical sense, without regard to the ultimate incidence of the tax itself. Direct taxation includes, for instance, taxes on clubs, royalties paid by mines and collieries, and the *contribution des Patentes*, or "trade licences."

The principal direct taxes are the—

		francs	£
Contribution foncière (Tax on real property) . .	Buildings	77 mill.	3,080,000
	Land	119 „	4,760,000
Contribution personnelle et mobilière (personal taxes and on house-rent)		87 „	3,480,000
Doors and windows . . .		56 „	2,240,000
Patentes (trade licences). .		121 „	4,840,000

It may perhaps be as well to notice here parenthetically that these four direct contributions provide indirectly the means for local expenditure. To the principal of these are added *centimes additionnels*, or an additional percentage, the greatest part of which is handed over to the local authorities, departmental or municipal. The former may be considered as having no other revenue, and their share of the *centimes additionnels* amounts annually to 162 millions of francs (£6,480,000). The municipalities' share amounts to 174 millions(£6,960,000); and in towns, the OCTROI (*q.v.*) or municipal duties on consumption make up the bulk of communal financial resources.

The legislature at the time of the outbreak of the great revolution was eager to follow the teachings of the PHYSIOCRATS and to repeal indirect taxation. But necessity compelled the reversal of their plan, and direct taxation now scarcely provides one-sixth of the receipts, whilst indirect taxation, under which head are included stamp and registration duties, provides about two-thirds.

The revenue derived from indirect taxation may be summarised thus :

	francs.	£
1. Registration duties .	540 mill.	say £21,600,000

The principal branches of these duties yield—

	francs.	£
Registration on transfer of property	164 mill.	6,560,000
Death duties	194 „	7,760,000
Duties on donations (mostly marriage settlements) .	22 „	880,000
Transfer of joint-stock shares .	42 „	1,680,000
Fixed duties on judicial acts .	42 „	1,680,000
Ad Valorem „ „ „	10 „	400,000
2. Stamps (on commercial bills and cheques 27 mill. of francs (£1,080,000) . .	163 „	say 6,520,000
3. Tax of 4 per cent on the dividends of joint-stock shares and bonds . .	70 „	say 2,800,000

[The interest on the French national debt, mortgages, private loans, and commercial profits of private partnerships remain (1893) free.]

	francs	£
4. Customs . . . . (Of this 446 mill. (£17,840,000) on imports)	492 mill.	19,680,000
5. Sugar	196 „	7,840,000
Other " Contributions in-directes," or excise .	582 mill.	23,280,000
Alcohol	356 mill.	14,240,000
Wine and cider	79 „	3,160,000
Beer	17 „	680,000

It is now proposed to take off state duties on the so-called hygienic drinks—wine, cider, and beer. Salt pays to the customs and excise together 33 millions of francs (£1,320,000). The *Contributions Indirectes* also comprise the duties on transport and communications by rail, the latter 46 millions of francs (£1,840,000).

In the next division of the budget of receipts, appear the gross proceeds of state monopolies and state manufactures for a total amount of 625 millions of francs (£25,000,000), subdivided in the following way :—

	francs	francs	£
Matches . . .	26 mill.		
Tobacco . . .	372 „	407 mill.	16,280,000
Gunpowder . .	9 „		
Post Office . . .	163 „		
Telegraphs . . .	36 „	208 „	8,320,000
Telephones . .	9 „		
Net revenue of railway lines belonging to the state . .	8 „		320,000

The working expenses or cost of production come in under sundry headings in the *Budget des Dépenses* (expenditure). The net revenue of the post and telegraphs is generally taken at about 50 millions of francs (£2,000,000) ; and tobacco is calculated to yield net about 300 millions (£12,000,000).

Of the 46 millions of francs (£1,840,000) derived from the state property, more than one half, 28 millions (£1,120,000), are derived from forests owned by the state. The present property of the state plays thus a very secondary part in French finance, but towards the middle of the next century it will vastly increase, as between 1950 and 1960, the *concessions* of most of the railway companies will expire, and their lines and buildings become the property of the state. About 40,000 kilometres (25,000 miles) are worked at the present time, and will necessarily yield a considerable revenue to the nation.

EXPENDITURE.—The following table gives the amount of the *crédits* or supplies granted to the different ministries :—

		francs		£
Ministry of finance	. . .	1526 mill.		61,040,000
1276 millions or £51,040,000, for interest of the national debt				
Ministry of justice and religious worship—				
Justice	.	35 mill.	£1,400,000	
Religious worship	.	44 ,,	£1,760,000	
		79	,,	3,160,000
Ministry of foreign affairs	. .	16	,,	640,000
Ministry of the interior	. .	68	,,	2,720,000
Ministry of war	. . .	645	,,	25,800,000
Ministry of the navy and colonies		320	,,	12,800,000
(Navy 247 millions or £9,880,000 ; colonies 73 millions or £2,920,000)				
Ministry of public instruction and fine arts	. . . .	192	,,	7,680,000
(Public instruction 184 millions £7,360,000, and arts 8 millions £320,000)				
Ministry of commerce and industry		180	,,	7,200,000
Ministry of agriculture	. .	42	,,	1,680,000
Ministry of public works	. .	215	,,	8,600,000
Total expenditure		3283	,,	£131,320,000

The difference between the totals of receipts and expenditure, 16 millions of francs (£640,000), goes to balance the budget of Algeria.

In appearance, the budget of 1893 is thus brought into a state of strict equilibrium ; but even assuming that the actual receipts will reach the amount of estimates, about 100 millions of francs (4 millions sterling), mostly subsidies to railways under the form of a guarantee of a minimum rate of interest on capital invested, are not comprised in the general budget. Although the principle of the *universality* of the budget of expenditure, namely that it ought to comprise the whole of the foreseen expenses, has been constantly acknowledged in theory, it has been in fact often disregarded, sometimes under the pressure of real necessity, sometimes under various pretences to disguise the unsound state of national finance. The creation of *extraordinary budgets* and funds (*caisses*), supposed to deal with temporary and special expenditure, has then been the expedient resorted to. The creation of the *Compte de Liquidation* immediately after the disastrous war of 1870, when France had to pay an enormous war indemnity and to recon-

struct the whole of its military establishment, was no doubt perfectly justified. But, principally since 1882, the institution of such funds has had for its object the concealment of real deficiencies, over 28 millions sterling in 1883, incurred on account of public works undertaken on a gigantic scale, and rather premature reductions of taxation. However, within the last few years there has been a steady and laudable tendency towards financial honesty ; and as stated above, the financial bill for 1893, as presented by the minister of finance, only included about 100 millions of francs (£4,000,000) of expenditure not provided for by the ordinary budget.

It cannot be said that any definite method has been adopted towards assessing taxation so as to divide its burden between property and income. Only about 40 millions of francs (£1,600,000) are levied directly on what may be called luxuries, but affluence is indirectly, though effectively, reached through the duty on house-rent.

No such thing exists as a general income-tax on the English model ; professional incomes contribute through the operation of the *patentes*, (trade licences), and the income derived from securities other than the national debt or mortgage, through the tax of 4 per cent on the dividends of *valeurs mobilières* (transferable securities), but other incomes generally escape taxation. After the events of 1870-71, 750 millions of francs, 30 million sterling, of new taxes were suddenly wanted, and the aim of the government was to find out the line of least resistance, a circumstance which explains, and more or less excuses, the absence of methodical foresight. Whenever the necessity of levying an increased amount of taxation occurs, the want is felt of a form of tax, such as the English income-tax, which can be easily adjusted to the exigencies of the moment. New taxes are devised almost at hap-hazard, sometimes according to the crotchets of influential members of the lower house, who unhappily too often and too freely indulge their initiative power in financial matters. In France, customs-duties, it is well known, are as much a protectionist as a fiscal machinery.

After the Franco-German war, a large annual provision (200 millions of francs or 8 million sterling) was carefully made for the paying off of the national debt ; but for several years scarcely any other reduction has been made except the paying off of annual quotas of the terminable debt, *rente amortissable*, instituted in 1878 when the extensive scheme of public works known as the *plan Freycinet* was launched. This terminable debt scarcely represents one-eighth of the national liabilities. Some, however, contend that since, at the expiration of the *concessions* of the railway companies already mentioned, the net proceeds of these lines will cover the interest on consolidated debt, any other form of financial redemption can be dispensed with.

No special quota of the general revenue is reserved for local expenditure, although the state largely contributes to several of its branches.

To conclude, a summary view of the state of French finance is here given :

	francs	£
Budget (1893)	3,348 mill.	133,920,000
Public debt	32,000 ,,	1,280,000,000
General taxation . . .	2,800 ,,	112,000,000
Local taxation . . .	690 ,,	27,600,000

In 1869, the last normal year before the war, the parallel figures were :

	francs	£
Budget of expenditure . .	2,014 mill.	80,560,000
Public debt	12,000 ,,	480,000,000

[A clear and handy summary of the budget of 1893 is given in M. Bidoire's *Tableau résumé du Budget de 1893* (Paris, 1892). For general works see the *Dictionnaire des Finances* (Paris, 1888) published under the direction of M. Léon Say.— The *Nouveau Dictionnaire d'Économie Politique* (1892).—Paul Leroy Beaulieu, *Traité de la Science des Finances* (5th edition, 1892).—René Stourm, *Le Budget.*—Félix Faure, *Les Budgets contemporains.*—Ch. Sudre, *Les Finances de la France au XIXᵉ Siècle.*—Richard de Kaufmann, *Les Finances de la France* (translated from the German into French).—Henri Germain, *Discours Parlementaires sur les Finances.*—D'Audiffret, *Système financier de la France.*—Boileau, *Fortune Publique et Finances de la France.* For modern times.— Esquirol de Parieu, *Traité des Impôts,* 4 vols., Paris, 1877.—K. J. von Hock, *Die Finanzverwaltung Frankreichs,* 1887 (translated into French under the title *L'Administration financière de la France,* 1859).—Ad. Wagner, *Finanzwissenschaft,* vol. iii.—The *Bulletin de Statistique,* published by the ministry of finance, is a rich source of statistical data, and the English reader will find a great quantity of condensed and well-digested information on French finance in Professor Bastable's *Public Finance* (1892).

For French finance prior to the Revolution of 1789 see Fromenteau, *Le Secret des Finances,* 1851. — Moreau de Beaumont, *Mémoires Concernant les Impositions et droits en Europe et en France,* 5 vols., 1768-1789.—Le Febvre de Bellande, *Dictionnaire Général des Aides,* Paris, 1760.—Necker, *De l'Administration des Finances,* 3 vols., 1784.—Clamagéran, *Histoire de l'Impôt en France,* 3 vols., 1867-76.—René Stourm, *Les Finances de l'ancien Régime* (1885); and an article under the same title in the *Nouveau Dictionnaire d'Économie Politique.*—Bouchard, *Le Système Financier de l'ancien Régime* (1891). —3 vols. in the *Encyclopédie Méthodique* (1784-1787).—Vuitry, *Études sur le Régime Financier de la France avant 1789* (from the 11th to the 15th century).—Jacqueton, *Documents relatifs à l'histoire financière en France (1449-1523).*— Forbonnais, *Recherches et Considérations sur les Finances de la France depuis 1598 jusqu'en 1721* (Bâle, 1758), and the bibliography published by M. Stourm in the *Annales de l'École des Sciences Politiques* (15th July 1886 and 1887).] E. Ca.

GERMAN EMPIRE and PRUSSIA (Amounts in marks converted as 20 = £1). In Germany the functions of government are partly performed by the confederation of all the individual states, the German empire, and partly belong to these individual states themselves. These are (Elsass-Lothringen included), twenty-six in number and extremely different in size, ranging between 30,000,000 and only 39,000 inhabitants. Besides, there exists in Germany as elsewhere the local finance connected with the cities and country districts which defray their expenses independently.

I. THE FINANCES OF THE EMPIRE.—The chief expenditure is that for the army and navy, the organisation of which belongs to the confederation, not to the particular states. The Bavarian army only has in time of peace its separate financial administration ; but the money spent by the Bavarian government on its army is paid to it in a lump from the exchequer of the empire. Among other expenses are those of the foreign office, including diplomatic service, the high court of judicature, to which under certain conditions appeals lie from the courts of the individual states both in civil and criminal cases, and the imperial home department. Among the expenses of the latter department are those for the economic interests of the country, such as the subvention of mercantile shipping, and workmen's insurance, etc. The fiscal year runs, as in England, from 1st April to 31st March. The amount of the expenditure is voted yearly by the federal council and the parliament. Among the expenditure a distinction is made between recurring and exceptional items. Among the last named, a further distinction has been made for some years between "exceptional expenditure of the ordinary budget," and "exceptional expenditure of the extraordinary budget." The expenditure of the former description is that which, like the recurring expenditure, is defrayed out of the ordinary revenue, while, on the other hand, the "exceptional expenditure of the extraordinary budget" is raised by loans or from special funds. In reality the whole difference between recurring and exceptional expenditure is very slight, because though the special occasion calling for any particular exceptional expenditure does not recur in every year, the total amount even of this class of expenditure does not vary much from year to year. The consolidated debt of the empire is £94,000,000.

For the fiscal year 1894-1895 the following expenses of the Empire have been voted :—

(The statement does not include the expenditure for the postal service—which is deducted from the revenue under the same head—see p. 73—nor the part of the expenditure for pensions derived from the income of the Invalid Fund.)

Expenses, Empire of Germany.

| Item of Expenditure. | Recurring. | Exceptional. | | Total. |
		Ordinary Budget.	Extra-ordinary Budget.	
	£	£	£	£
Chancellor's office and Imperial Diet and Foreign office . .	544,000	238,000	..	782,000
Home Department .	1,360,000	215,000	1,036,000	2,611,000
Army	24,001,000	1,917,000	4,636,000	30,554,000
Navy	2,535,000	950,000	212,000	3,697,000
Administration of Justice	103,000	50,000	..	153,000
Finance Department .	254,000	8,000	..	262,000
Railway Department .	17,000	..	630,000	647,000
Imperial Debt Service .	3,587,000	..	..	3,587,000
Audit Department	32 000	..	..	32,000
Pensions, etc. (chiefly Military, but not including pensions derived from Income of Invalid Fund) .	2,428,000	..	..	2,428,000
	£34,861,000	£3,378,000	£6,514,000	£44,753,000

The means adopted by the empire to raise this amount are the following:—

1. *Revenue arising from the property of the state.*

(*a*) The empire reserved out of the French war indemnity several large sums which produce interest. If necessary, besides the interest, the principal itself is gradually applied to certain objects which have to be carried out by the state. The largest of these reserved capitals is the "Invalidenfond." At its foundation it was appropriated only to the payment of pensions to the invalids and the widows of the soldiers who fell in the French war. Afterwards some further payments for military pensions were assigned to it. The amount of the fund originally was £28,050,000; up to 30th June 1891 (the date of the last report published), £4,900,000 of this capital, had been spent besides the interest; the amount remaining was therefore £23,150,000.

(*b*) The empire is the proprietor of the railways in Alsace-Lorraine (Elsass-Lothringen); their original purchase-money, together with the sum afterwards spent on them, was upwards of £25,000,000. The net revenue arising to the exchequer is estimated for 1893-94 at £1,037,500, and nearly as high for 1894-95.

(*c*) The empire takes the revenue arising from the post and telegraphs outside of Bavaria and Wurtemberg, which for 1894-95 is estimated at £989,000.

(*d*) The empire owns a printing-office which works both for the public and for private customers; the net revenue is estimated at £58,600, and for 1894-95, £68,300.

2. *Customs.* The whole territory of Germany is included in one customs-frontier with the exception of some inconsiderable parts of Baden, Prussia, and Hamburg; on the other hand Luxemburg, though not belonging to the confederation, is also within this same frontier.

But the customs revenue does not entirely fall to the empire. Since 1878, according to the Franken-stein-clause (so called after the name of the deputy who moved it in the Reichstag), the empire only takes yearly from the customs revenue, together with the duty on home-grown tobacco, £6,500,000, the whole surplus being distributed among the individual states. The total customs revenue for 1893-94 is estimated at £17,056,100, and for 1894-95 at £17,485,000.

3. *Excise.*

(*a*) The salt duty, being 6 marks on every cwt. of salt produced in the empire and destined for human consumption within the country, brings about £2,137,000 for 1894-95. The duty on foreign salt imported is naturally included in the customs revenue, and is between £100,000 and £150,000; hence the salt duty in Germany amounts to about 11d. per head of the population.

(*b*) The sugar duty is 18s. for every two cwts. of sugar produced and consumed within the country, the sugar reserved for export remaining duty free, and even receiving a bounty. This latter is now—for raw sugar 1s. 3d. for every two cwts., for candy 2s., for other refined sorts 1s. 8d. These bounties and the drawbacks on confectionery exported amount to £525,000. The estimated net revenue to the empire for 1894-95 after deduction of this sum is £3,770,000.

(*c*) Tobacco, if grown within the empire, is taxed at £2 : 5s. for every two cwts. of dried produce; the amount of the tax is estimated for 1894-95 at £554,000. But the exchequer of the empire does not receive this sum, because the internal tax on tobacco, as far as, together with the surplus of the customs duties, it is above £6,500,000 yearly, is distributed among the individual states. The revenue from imported tobacco, which is much larger than that derived from home-grown tobacco, is included in the customs revenues. It was in 1891-92 more than £2,150,000. Great alterations in the tobacco duty were contemplated (November 1893); and the tax on the raw produce of the country was to be abolished, the customs duty reduced, and the product ready for consumption taxed at the manufacturer's, but this scheme has been dropped for the present.

(*d*) The beer duty is raised as a federal duty in the northern part of the empire only; whilst in Bavaria, Wurtemberg, Baden, and Elsass-Lothringen the beer taxes are a revenue of the individual state, levied according to its separate legislation. The federal duty is laid on the malt, or the substitutes for malt, when brought to the brewery; it is 4s. for two cwts. on all descriptions of grain, and for substitutes in proportion. The beer coming from the southern states to those in which the empire receives the tax on production has to pay an import-duty to the empire. The beer duty and this internal import-duty are estimated, in the revenue of the empire for 1894-95, at £1,243,000.

(e) The duty on spirits has been levied since 1st October 1887, throughout the whole empire. It consists of two parts—of a tax on the production of spirits, and of a tax on consumption. For the purposes of the tax on production three classes of distilleries are distinguished: 1st, such as employ grain as material, and are at the same time part of agricultural undertakings (called agricultural distilleries); 2nd, such as employ sugar or sacchariferous materials; 3rd, such as employ grain but are not altogether part of agricultural undertakings (called industrial distilleries). The tax on the production of the first class of works is levied on the space which the mash fills in the fermenting vats; it is 1s. 4d. for every hectoliter of the contents of the tub. In the second class, if sugar or similar substances—e.g. fruits—form the materials, the substances employed are to be taxed according to their weight and kind. The industrial distilleries, finally, pay an addition of £1 per hectoliter on the tax on consumption. The smaller establishments among all the classes are allowed some reduction on the normal rate of the duties. The amount of the duty on consumption is fixed in the following manner. For a quantity of 4½ liter per head of the population in northern Germany, and of 3 liter per head of the population in the south, the tax on consumption is 6d. the liter; for any excess in the consumption of the country the duty is 8½d. the liter. The total quantity allowed to be produced at the lower rate is allotted to the individual distilleries according to their size.

Of these different duties on spirits only the tax on production remains to the empire. The tax on consumption and the tax on the ready-made produce in the industrial distilleries are distributed to the individual states according to the number of their inhabitants. For 1894-95 the taxes on spirits remaining to the empire were estimated at £899,000, those to be distributed among the states at £5,005,000.

4. *Stamp duties.*

(a) A tax on bills of exchange of 6d. for every £50 drawn; but amounts below £50 are taxed somewhat lower. The revenue is estimated for 1894-95 at £379,000.

(b) A tax on playing-cards, estimated for 1894-95 at £62,800.

(c) Taxes on—1st, the issue of stock exchange securities; 2nd, on every sale of such securities. The former duty is estimated for 1894-95 at £221,000, the latter at £552,000. These sums are to be distributed among the individual states. An act passed in 1894 imposes a higher *ad valorem* scale.

(d) A tax on public and private lotteries, producing in 1894-95 £452,000. This tax also does not accrue to the empire, but is divided among the states according to their population.

(e) A statistical duty on the goods exported and imported, levied with the receipt of the declarations relating to the quantities, the origin, and destination of the goods. It produces for 1894-95 £34,000.

5. Share of profits from the imperial bank, and tax from other banks of issue, amounting, according to the estimate for 1894-95, to £362,000.

6. *Contributions by the Individual States.* There can never be a deficit in the imperial budget because any excess of expenditure over the imperial taxes is covered by these contributions which are called matricular contributions, and are distributed among the states in proportion to their respective populations, additional contributions being imposed on those states which have a separate postal administration, and also on those in which no federal beer duty is levied. The total amount of these contributions, as fixed for 1894-1895, is £19,875,000, but this sum is of course subject to a deduction of £17,772,000, being the amount of the above-mentioned duties and taxes collected by or on behalf of the empire for the benefit of the individual states. The matricular contributions form an element of uncertainty in the state budgets, and a bill has in consequence been brought forward by the imperial government providing that the amount of matricular contributions shall in future be at least £2,000,000 below the amount of taxes and duties collected for the individual states, and that any deficiency thus caused must be covered by imperial taxation. It is very doubtful whether this proposal will be carried through.

For the fiscal year 1894-1895 the following revenue of the empire has been voted:—

Revenue—Empire of Germany.

Item of Revenue.	Amount.
Balance from last year . . .	£69,000
Revenue from State property (not including revenue from Invalid Fund, and deducting extraordinary expenses incurred in respect of Postal Department)	2,207,000
Customs	17,485,000
Excise	13,612,000
Stamps	1,702,000
Revenue from Imperial Bank, etc. .	362,000
Sale of land	70,000
Miscellaneous Revenue . . .	629,000
Matricular Contributions . £19,875,000	
Less amounts payable to individual States . . 17,772,000	2,103,000
	38,239,000
Revenue raised by loans and from special funds	6,514,000
	£44,753,000

II. The expenditure of the individual states for their own purposes is about equal to the expenditure of the empire for federal purposes. Thus the Prussian expenditure for 1894-1895—as shown below (after deduction of the amount required for the service of the public debt which must be set off against the revenue from state property) amounted to about £22,000,000 (= 50 per cent of the expenditure of the empire), the Prussian population representing about 60 per cent of the whole population of Germany, and similarly Bavaria (having a population of about 11 per cent, of the whole German population) spends a yearly sum amounting (after deduction of the interest on the railway debt, which is about equal to the income from the railways) to £5,100,000 (= 11½ per cent of the imperial expenditure).

Prussian Expenditure, 1894-95.

Civil List Recurring Expenditure . .	£786,000
Houses of Parliament	69,000
Chief Government Department and Audit Department	130,000
Foreign Affairs	26,000
Financial Administration, Inland Revenue Department, and Provincial Government	3,509,000
Public Works, etc.	1,084,000
Trade Department (including subventions to technical education and technical industry)	231,000
Administration of Justice (after deduction of Court fees)	1,550,000
Home Department (including Local Government Expenditure, Prisons, and Police)	2,099,000
Agricultural Department	669,000
Education : (Elementary and Higher as well as University) and Public Worship	5,138,000
Pensions and Miscellaneous . .	3,841,000
Service of Public Debt . . .	14,101,000
Exceptional Expenditure . . .	2,893,000
	36,076,000
Contribution to Empire	12,399,000
	£48,475,000

Prussian Revenue, 1894-95.

Government Lands and Forests . .		£2,636,000
,, Mines and Smelting Works .		814,000
,, Railways . . .		18,372,000
,, Lottery . . .		488,000
,, Bank (Seehandlung) .		94,000
Taxes—		
Direct	£8,827,000	
Indirect	1,982,000	22,404,000
		10,809,000
Miscellaneous Revenue (including Return of Taxes collected by Empire) . .		11,752,000
To be raised by the issue of a Loan . .		3,510,000
		£48,475,000

The indirect taxes in the German states which do not levy a state duty on beer are of no great importance. A wine duty exists in some of the southern states, and in Saxony and Baden a duty on meat. As to the direct taxes they are of two kinds : taxes on property or income levied at the source (objective taxes), and personal income-tax. In the southern states, especially in Bavaria and Wurtemberg,

objective taxation prevails, whilst in the northern states, as Prussia, Saxony, the personal income tax is of greater importance. Baden and Hesse are between these extremes.

A complete system of objective taxes comprises : (1) a land tax ; (2) a house tax ; (3) a tax on trades ; (4) a tax on income from stocks and shares ; (5) a tax on wages and salaries. All these five taxes are to be found in Bavaria and Wurtemberg ; the tax on wages and salaries is not levied in Baden and Hesse ; while Saxony has only a so-called land tax ; Prussia has the three first named objective taxes, but they have been repealed as from the 1st April 1895. In Bavaria, of the direct taxes for 1892 or 1893, the land tax is estimated as £575,000, the house tax £262,500, the tax on trades £325,000, the tax on loans £208,330, that on wages and salaries £100,000. In Prussia up to this date the land tax produces about £2,000,000, the house tax £1,825,000, the tax on trades £1,125,000.

The income-tax in Prussia has lately been rearranged by the law of 24th June 1891. Incomes under £45 are free. The rate on small incomes is below 1 per cent ; for incomes of £150, 2 per cent ; for incomes of £400, about 3 per cent ; and incomes of £5000 and above pay 4 per cent. The produce of the tax is about £6,250,000. In Saxony £15 is the limit of exemption and the rate does not rise higher than 3 per cent. The produce of the tax for 1893 is estimated at £962,500. In Baden the income-tax has been during recent years 2 per cent on the estimated income. But an abatement is allowed for smaller incomes, only those of £1500 and upwards paying the full tax. The produce of the tax thus assessed was about £200,000. In 1894 the percentage to be levied from the higher incomes has been increased.

A new personal tax, viz. a tax of $\frac{1}{10}$th per cent of the capital value of each taxpayer's real and personal property has been introduced in Prussia as from the 1st April 1895 ; its produce is estimated at £1,750,000. Persons of small means are exempt, and real property situate outside of Prussia is not included in the assessment.

III. Of great importance also is the local finance. In Prussia the parish rates in 1884 were £8,600,000, and the district rates £1,150,000. Among the expenses of the parishes the most considerable are those for the poor, for the roads and for education. In Prussia, 1883-84, out of a total of £18,550,000 the expenditure on roads was £2,500,000 (13 per cent), for the poor £2,450,000 (13 per cent), for education £4,250,000 (23 per cent). Part of these expenses is covered by revenue from property and by profitable undertakings, as gas and water works. In Baden the net value of the property of the parishes was estimated, 1st January 1887, at £15,500,000. In Prussia in the rural districts the parishes cover 20 per cent of their expenses in this way, in the towns 11·6 per cent. The taxation is chiefly a direct one, consisting of an addition to the taxes assessed and levied by the state for its purposes. In the towns of the southern states indirect taxes of some importance exist, such as additions to the state taxes on consumption—the wine, beer, meat duties—and an octroi duty on various necessaries and conveniences brought to the town—coal, flour, meat, fish, etc. In Bavaria, 1878, the direct local taxes were £850,000, the indirect taxes in the twelve largest towns £250,000. In Baden, 1888, the direct taxes of the communes not considered as towns were £466,666, those of the towns nearly £175,000, together £637,500, the indirect taxes in the towns only £450,000 to £500,000. In Prussia the towns raised in 1883-84 local taxes per head of the population 12s. 4d., the rural districts 5s. 10d.; in Baden the towns, 16s. 9d., the rural districts, 7s. In Baden in 1889 the direct local taxes add on average 50 per cent to the corresponding state taxes.

In Prussia the system now existing will be altered from 1895. The land-tax, house-tax, and tax on trades will be handed over entirely to the parishes, the state reserving to itself out of the existing direct taxes only the income-tax and the new property tax, the income-tax remaining still further subject to additions for the local purposes.

[Gustav Cohn, *System der Finanzwissenschaft*, Stuttgart, 1889, bk. iii. pp. 532-669.—Schönberg, *Handbuch der politischen Oekonomie*, vol. iii., Tübingen, 1891.—Laband, *Staatsrecht des deutschen Reichs*, Freiburg, 1888-91, vol. i. 379 *seq.*, ii. 42 *seq.*, 839-1037.—G. Meyer, *Lehrbuch des deutschen Staatsrechts*, Leipzig, 1885, p. 616-632—v. Mayr, art. "Reichsfinanzen" in *Handwörterbuch der Staatswissenschaften*, vol. v., Jena, 1893, pp. 384-403.—Rönne, *Staatsrecht des preussischen Monarchie*, vol. i., Leipzig, 1881, p. 590 *seq.*; iv., Leipzig, 1884, p. 737 *seq.*—Stockar von Neuforn, *Handbuch der gesammten Finanzverwaltung im Königreich Bayern*, 3rd ed. by T. Hock, 3 vols., Bamberg, 1881-1885.—Riecke, Der wurttembergische Staatshaushalt, in *Jahrbuch für Gesetzgebung, Verwaltung und Volkswirtschaft*, vol. vii., Leipzig, 1883, p. 193-230.—Philippovich, *Der badische Finanzhaushalt in den Jahren 1868-1889*, Freiburg, 1889.—Zeller, *Handbuch der Verfassung und Verwaltung im Grossherzogthum Hessen*, Darmstadt, 1885-86, i. 78-118, ii. 343-422.—Löbe, *Der Staatshaushalt des Königreichs Sachsens*, Leipzig, 1889.—Eheberg, art. Gemeindefinanzen in *Handwörterbuch der Staatswissenschaften*, vol. iii., Jena, 1892, pp. 760-785. —Schanz, *Finanz-Archiv*, Stuttgart, appearing since 1884.]   **E. L.**

THE NETHERLANDS. (Amounts converted at 12 guilders = £1.) The finances of the Netherlands are in a sound condition. Whilst forty-five years ago, in 1850, with a population of barely 3,000,000 and a budget of about

£6,000,000 sterling, the capital of the national debt amounted to over £100,000,000 sterling with an annual interest-charge of £3,000,000 ; nowadays, with a population of about 4,700,000 and a budget of almost double the amount of 1850, the capital of the national debt is only £92,000,000 with about £2,700,000 annual interest-charge. The exact figures of the national debt are—

	Nominal Capital.	Annual Interest.
1850	£102,637,700	£3,020,155
1893	£92,267,000	£2,683,600

From 1850 until 1892 inclusive, a total amount of £23,905,585 has been expended on amortisation of debt. In the latter years, however, the debt has increased again, namely by a total amount of £16,145,600. But against this increase of debt stands expenditure on remunerative public works for an amount vastly superior. Between 1860-1892 the expenditure for building railroads alone amounted to £25,278,750.

Again, whilst formerly the East India colony, namely Java, contributed a rather important amount to the revenue of the Netherlands, since 1877 this contribution has ceased entirely. From 1850-1877 these contributions amounted in all to £48,975,600. It was, in fact, these contributions which, from 1850 until the middle of 1870, enabled the government to amortise the debt for such an important amount (it may be useful to add that for a large amount the debt had been contracted previously in behalf of the colonies also) devoting at the same time very large sums to public works.

At first, when these colonial contributions to the revenue of the Netherlands had to be given up this caused some embarrassment, the more so as about the same time there was a considerable increase in the expenditure principally for public schools. The consequence was that for some years after 1880 the expenditure was not entirely covered by the revenue. But within a few years, by raising new taxes and other measures, the situation was modified and there was an end to the deficits. The cessation of the colonial contribution arose partly from the increase of expenditure in Java to which the war with Atchin contributed, but most of all from a change in the colonial policy of the government, the colonies being nowadays governed only for their own benefit, no tribute whatever being exacted from them on behalf of the Netherlands ; more than this, the expenditure made by the Netherlands indirectly on behalf of the colonies (part of the home-charges) is not even repaid from the revenue of the colonies.

The fiscal system, however, had for many years been in serious want of some reform. This was not undertaken until quite recently, namely under the last government—finance-minister M. Pierson—which came into power in 1891, but the government having again been turned out of power early in 1894, this reform was interrupted. Unfortunately the financial result of the property tax, levied since May 1893, has been somewhat disappointing. It was expected to bring in £716,666, but the proceeds were not higher than £566,666 the first year.

The revenue for 1894 is derived from the following sources :—

Direct taxes	Land tax . . .	£981,450
	Personal tax . .	967,583
	Droit de patente (till 1st May 1894) . .	121,333
	Tax on incomes not arising from property (after 1st May 1894) . .	255,583
	Property tax . .	566,666
Indirect taxes	Excise . . .	3,495,833
	Registration duties .	370,833
	Succession duties .	966,000
	Stamps, etc. . .	302,916
	Import duties . .	480,104
Domains		194,583
Post and telegraphs . .		744,416
Railways		329,166
Other items . . .		912,176

Total £10,688,642

The land tax is levied on the ratable yearly value of land and houses ; the state levies 6 per cent on the net rateable rent from land not built upon, and 5·2 per cent on the gross rateable rent from houses.

The personal tax, a tax on expenditure, is calculated principally on the letting value of the dwelling occupied, the value of the furniture, and the number of servants. There is a universal agreement that this tax needs revision.

Real property, besides being subject to the land tax, is also subject to the property tax. The object of this tax is to levy a percentage on the income from property, but the percentage is computed not on the income itself, but on the capital value of the property. The tax is slightly progressive. For every 1000 guilders (£83 : 6 : 8) above 10,000 (£833 : 6 : 8) the tax is 1·25 guilders, but if the property amounts to more than 200,000 guilders, (£16,666 : 13 : 4) 2 guilders per 1000 are paid on the surplus.

On 1st May 1894 the *droit de patente*, or tax on occupations, was replaced by a tax on business profits, and on all incomes from labour, assessed in such a manner that, in connection with the property tax, it will have the effect of a general income tax. This tax also is slightly progressive ; for the incomes below 8200 guilders per annum, it is 2 per cent, for higher amounts 3·20 per cent on the surplus is added. The property tax being levied at the rate of 1¼ and 2 per mille on the capital, the tax on business profits is 36 per cent less than the tax on incomes derived from property only

—on the hypothesis adopted by the government that the income from property averages 4 per cent. Property up to 13,000 guilders (£1083 : 6 : 8) is free from property tax, and income up to 650 guilders (£54 : 3 : 4) from the tax on profits and wages.

The succession duties are not progressive ; they differ according to the degree of relationship between the deceased and his successors. From parents to children the duty is 1·38 per cent ; husband and wife pay the same amount, if they inherit one from the other, when there are descendants from their union ; if parents inherit from their children, the duty is 4·14 per cent ; between brothers and sisters, or between husband and wife, if there are no descendants, it is 5·52 per cent ; between uncle and niece, or inversely, 8·28 per cent ; and between all others 13·8 per cent. In so far as the property inherited consists of stock, bonds, stock-exchange securities and other interest-bearing securities, there is levied, besides the succession duties referred to, a special succession duty, varying from 0·345 to 2·76 per cent. The total amount of the succession duties rises in this way from 1·725 per cent in the first degree of relationship, to 16·56 per cent from distant relatives or strangers.

The excise on spirits is high, £5 : 5s. on every hectoliter (22 gallons) ; from spirits alone a revenue of £2,166,000 annually is raised. The fiscal law concerning the sugar duties gives a bounty to the producers.

The Netherlands are a free-trade country, food and raw produce enter without duty, manufactured goods generally pay 5 per cent of the declared value. Measures are under consideration for securing that the proper percentage is really paid.

The railroads are leased to private companies ; the rents which they pay form the greater portion of the receipts under this head. The miscellaneous receipts include various payments to the treasury which are distributed over the several departments : repayments, reimbursements, legal fees, etc. ; and also (a) £62,500 payment by the Netherlands Bank for the right of issue of banknotes, which payment depends from the amount of the bank's profits of the year ; (b) £154,500 reimbursement by the colonial treasury for interest on debt—£3,806,250—contracted in 1883 by the home government on behalf of the East Indian colonies.

The expenditure for 1894 is divided as in the following table :—

Civil list		£67,000
Parliament		55,625
Foreign affairs		65,410
Justice		452,681
Home Office		1,069,717
Carry forward .		£1,710,433

Brought forward . £1,710,433
Marine 1,301,761
National debt 2,910,719
Finances 1,595,904
War 1,856,560
"Waterstaat," commerce and industry 1,837,337
Colonies 113,434
Unforeseen 4,166

Total . £11,330,314

The item finances includes: (a) £714,288 payment by the government treasury to the municipal governments on account of the personal tax in virtue of an arrangement that was made in 1865 when the municipal excise-taxes were abolished ; (b) £164,280 payments to the clergy of the Reformed, Roman Catholic, and Jewish churches by the state ; (c) £125,671 pensions ; and further, the expenditure of collecting revenue and the general expenditure of the department of the treasury and also of administration of debt.

The item Waterstaat includes the expenditure for post and telegraphs, amounting to £710,000 ; and the expenditure on embankments and other defence against the sea's encroachments, on canals and rivers, and also almost annually a certain amount of expenditure for remunerative public works.

It will be observed that the total of the expenditure for 1894 is

£11,330,314
Against total revenue 10,688,642

Leaving a deficit of £641,672

But the expenditure includes this year disbursements for remunerative public works for a total amount of £221,750, and besides it is calculated that the credits opened in the budget for general expenditure exceed regularly the real expenditure for an amount of, at least, £250,000. Deducting these two items, the deficit is reduced to about £180,000. This deficit is the consequence of the proceeds of the property tax not having been as high as it was expected they would be. Towards meeting this the finance-minister in the late government proposed some modifications in the mode of levying the import-duties, which are said to produce at least £150,000 less than ought to be the case in consequence of frauds in the declaration of values.

The provinces and the communes have separate financial arrangements. The expenditure of the provinces was in 1891 £373,908, and that of all the communes £5,948,833 for the same year. For the greater part this expenditure is covered by taxation : the payment of the treasury to the communes on account of the personal tax, additional cents on the state taxes, and other taxes. It is only in so far as the expenditure relates to permanent improvements of public works and the building of public schools that it is covered by loans.

The budget of the East Indian colonies shows for 1894 a total expenditure of £11,591,600 against an income of £10,427,630, but the expenditure includes an item of £1,115,750 for remunerative public works.

[Annual Reports on Dutch finance in *Consular Series*.—Fiscal reform in Holland, in the *Economic Journal*, 1893 ; *Bescheiden betreffende de geldmiddelen*.—G. M. Boissevain, *Die neueste Steuerreform in den Niederlander im Anschluss an die Finanzgeschichte des Landes seit der Verfassungsrevision im Jahre 1848*, Aus den "Finanzarchiv," herausg. von G. Schanz.] H. B. G.

THE UNITED STATES. NATIONAL FINANCE. (The $ converted as 5=£1 in this statement.)

I. REVENUE—(a) *Import Duties.*—The main source of national revenue has always been from the customs. The first tariff of import duties was enacted immediately after the formation of the government under the present constitution in 1789. At first chiefly a revenue measure, with increasing rates to yield larger revenues, the tariff gradually became a system of avowed protection to American industry. The rates varied with the successive domination of political parties, but the yield increased steadily from decade to decade. At the outbreak of the civil war the rates were largely augmented, the largest revenue under the war rates being $216,000,000 (*£43,200,000*) in 1872. The crisis of 1873 reduced the revenue to $130,000,000 (*£26,000,000*) in 1877, and it was not until 1882 that the preceding greatest yield was reached and even slightly exceeded. Since the civil war there have been several changes, generally in the direction of higher protective duties, which diminished the revenue for several years at a time. The tariff of 1883 reduced the revenue from $220,000,000 (*£44,000,000*) in 1882 to $181,000,000 (*£36,200,000*) in 1885 ; the tariff of 1890 reduced the revenue from $230,000,000 (*£46,000,000*) in 1890 to $177,000,000 (*£35,400,000*) in 1892.

Almost 1500 separate classes of dutiable articles figure in the tariffs of 1883 and 1890. Tea, coffee, and since 1890 sugar, are not taxed. The duties are levied almost exclusively on raw materials and on products which are also grown or manufactured in the United States. The sugar planters were recompensed for the removal of the duty on sugar in the law of 1890 by the grant of a bounty. The recent overwhelming defeat of the Republican party will bring with it a recasting of the protective system in the direction of a revenue tariff. The chief non-dutiable imports in 1891 were as follows :—

	Millions of Dollars.	
Coffee . . .	96	£19,200,000
Hides and Skins .	30	6,000,000
Chemicals and Drugs .	32	6,400,000
Raw silk . . .	18	3,600,000

	Millions of Dollars.	
Tea . . .	14	£2,800,000
Fruits . . .	10	2,000,000
Sugar . . .	97	19,400,000

(Duty taken off during year)

The duties collected on the chief articles were :—

	Millions of Dollars	
Raw Wool . . .	7	£1,400,000
Wool manufactures .	35	7,000,000
Silk manufactures .	19	3,800,000
Iron and Steel manufactures . .	18	3,600,000
Tobacco and Tobacco manufactures . .	16	3,200,000
Cotton manufactures .	15	3,000,000
Flax, Hemp and Jute manufactures . .	10	2,000,000
Liquors . . .	9	1,800,000

(b) *Internal Revenue.* — The present system of so-called internal revenue taxes is an outgrowth of the civil war. They were tried for a few years during the last decade of the 18th century, and again during the war with England of 1812. Of the comprehensive system of taxation adopted during the civil war most of the burdensome taxes were repealed before 1872, and many of the others were reduced or repealed in 1883 and 1890. The only taxes now left are those on distilled and fermented liquors, on tobacco and tobacco manufactures, and on bank circulation. The tax on national banks is not technically included in the so-called internal revenue. In addition to these taxes the law of 1886 imposed a tax of 2 cents (1d.) a pound on the manufacture and sale of oleomargarine, together with so-called "special taxes" of from $48 (£9 : 15s.) to $600 (£120) a year on manufacturers and dealers in oleomargarine. The law of 1890 imposed a prohibitory tax of $10 (£2) a pound on all opium manufactured in the United States.

The maximum yield of the internal revenue, when it included an immense complex of all imaginable taxes, direct and indirect, was in 1866, $309,000,000 (£61,800,000). The reductions of 1872 and prior to that year decreased the revenue in 1874 to $102,000,000 (£20,400,000). The reductions of 1883 diminished the revenue from $146,000,000 (£29,200,000) in 1882 to $112,000,000 (£22,400,000) in 1885 ; notwithstanding the reductions of 1890 the revenue increased from $140,000,000 in 1890 to $154,000,000 (£30,800,000) in 1892.

The income from internal revenue during 1892 was as follows :—

Distilled spirits .	$91,309,983	£18,261,996
Fermented liquors .	30,037,452	6,007,490
Manufactured tobacco	31,000,493	6,200,098
Oleomargarine .	1,266,326	253,265
Miscellaneous .	243,288	48,657

The cost of collection was 2·8 per cent.

(c) *Other Sources of Revenue.* — The customs and internal revenue form the great bulk of the entire receipts of the national government, amounting in 1892 to $331,000,000 (£66,200,000) out of $425,000,000 (£85,000,000). The proportion is even larger than it appears, because the postal service, which is almost self sustaining, is counted on both sides of the balance sheet, the receipts and expenditures for the post office being $71,000,000 (£14,200,000,). The policy of the national government is to reduce postal rates rather than to make profits. In 1892 the deficiency in postal revenues was $4,000,000 (£800,000). Moreover, the budget of the district of Columbia, in which the city of Washington lies, is included in the federal budget. The receipts from this alone in 1892 amounted to almost $3,000,000 (£600,000).

The remaining $20,000,000 (£4,000,000) of revenue were derived from sales of public lands, fees, profits of coinage, sinking fund for Pacific railways, tax on national banks, and a number of minor miscellaneous sources. The profits on coinage were very much swollen between 1878 and 1891, owing to the difference between the market price and the mint price of the silver dollars issued under the Bland bill, amounting in some years to 25 to 30 per cent of the entire amount coined. Under the Bland bill 378,166,793 silver dollars were coined between 1878 and 1891, on which the seignorage, or profit, to the government was $71,952,392 (£14,390,478). This was one cause of the large surplus in the treasury. During the sixties the government loaned the Central and Union Pacific Railway Companies about $64,000,000 (£12,800,000). The law of 1878 provided for a sinking fund and gradual repayment of the debt. During 1892 the revenues from this source were about two and three quarter millions of dollars (£550,000). The *tax on national banks*—½ of 1 per cent on the circulation—is all that remains of the comprehensive system of bank taxation during the civil war. The *immigrant fund* is composed of a tax of fifty cents on each immigrant, since 1882 ; and the *tax on sealskins* is paid by the corporation to which the Alaska seal fisheries are farmed out.

II. EXPENDITURE. —The striking features in the national expenditure during recent years have been the increased outlay for naval construction, the immense growth of the pension list, and the decrease of the interest charge for the public debt. From the end of the civil war to 1880 the amount of *pensions* to the survivors of the civil war or their families varied annually from twenty to thirty-five millions of dollars (£4,000,000 to £7,000,000). In 1880 the classes were enlarged and the pensions jumped to $56,000,000, (£11,200,000). For the next eight years they varied from fifty to seventy millions of dollars, (£10,000,000 to £14,000,000).

In 1889 the old law was more liberally construed, and in 1890 a new "dependent pension" law was enacted. As a consequence the pensions grew enormously, to $88,000,000 (£17,600,000) in 1889, to $107,000,000 (£21,400,000) in 1890, to $124,000,000 (£24,800,000) in 1891, and to $135,000,000 (£27,000,000) in 1892. For 1893 they are estimated at $158,000,000 (£31,600,000), and for 1894 at $166,000,000 (£33,200,000), unless, as is probable, the new Democratic administration will reform both the law and

REVENUE FOR 1892.

	$	£
From customs	177,452,964.15	35,490,593
From internal revenue	153,971,072.57	30,794,214
From profits on coinage, bullion deposits, and assays	2,020,512.39	404,102
From sales of public lands	3,261,875.58	652,375
From fees—consular, letters patent, and land	3,130,437.06	626,088
From sinking-fund for Pacific railways	1,828,771.46	365,754
From tax on national banks	1,261,338.11	252,268
From customs fees, fines, penalties, and forfeitures	909,249.66	181,849
From repayment of interest by Pacific railways	962,437.67	192,488
From sales of Indian lands	847,813.23	169,563
From Soldiers' Home, permanent fund	194,385.45	38,877
From tax on sealskins	46,749.23	9,350
From immigrant fund	330,128.65	66,026
From sales of Government property	236,498.38	47,299
From deposits for surveying public lands	149,966.21	29,994
From sales of ordnance material	101,242.35	20,249
From sales of condemned naval vessels	31,854.12	6,370
From sale of old custom-house, Milwaukee, Wis.	64,000.00	12,800
From sale of land, Brooklyn navy-yard	593,860.33	118,772
From Smithsonian fund	200,000.00	40,000
From navy pension and navy hospital funds, &c.	1,118,155.25	223,631
From depredations on public lands	61,623.85	12,325
From the District of Columbia	2,967,044.71	593,409
From proceeds District of Columbia ten-year funding bonds	2,412,744.00	482,549
From miscellaneous sources	783,059.83	156,612
From postal service	70,930,475.98	14,186,095
Total receipts	425,868,260.22	85,173,652

The expenditure for 1892 was—

	$	£
For the civil establishment, including foreign intercourse, public buildings, collecting the revenues, deficiency in postal revenues, rebate of tax on tobacco, refund of direct taxes, French spoliation claims, district of Columbia, and other miscellaneous expenses	99,841,988.61	19,968,397
For the military establishment, including rivers and harbours, forts, arsenals, and sea-coast defences	46,895,456.30	9,379,091
For the naval establishment, including construction of new vessels, machinery, armament, equipment, and improvement at navy-yards	29,174,138.98	5,834,827
For Indian service	11,150,577.67	2,230,115
For pensions	134,583,052.79	26,916,610
For interest on the public debt	23,378,116.23	4,675,623
For postal service	70,930,475.98	14,186,095
Total expenditure	415,953,806.56	83,190,761
Leaving a surplus of	9,914,453.66	1,982,890

the execution of the law. On the other hand, the *interest charge* on the public debt has diminished in almost the same proportion that the pension outlay has increased. The interest charge in 1867 was $143,781,592 (£28,756,318; in 1892 $23,378,116 (£4,675,623). The burdens resulting from the civil war have thus remained about unchanged.

A new source of expenditure, due to the law of 1890, is the *sugar bounty*, paid as a compensation to the planters for the removal of the import duty on sugar. In 1892 the bounty amounted to $7,342,077 (£1,468,415).

The exact figures of receipts and expenditures for the fiscal year, 1892, are herewith appended.

III. THE DEBT. — *The funded debt* at the close of the civil war consisted of $1,258,000 (£251,600), 6 per cent bonds issued to aid the Pacific railways, and of other 5 per cent and 6 per cent bonds issued chiefly during the war. The total funded debt amounted to $1,109,568,191 (£221,913,638). In addition to this there was a large unfunded debt, funded during the next few years, which brought the total debt to a sum exceeding $2,800,000,000 (£560,000,000). The two great refunding acts were those of 1870 and 1881. In 1870 the interest bearing debt consisted almost entirely of $1,934,696,750 (£386,939,350) 5 per cent and 6 per cent bonds. After the act of 1881, all the 6 per cent bonds were redeemed in 1882 (except the $64,523,512 (£12,904,702) Pacific railway bonds which are still outstanding); the 5 per cents were converted into 3½ per cents, then into 3 per cents, and finally redeemed in 1887; the 4½ per cents were redeemed in 1891, but $25,412,200 (£5,082,440) were continued at 2 per cent; the 3 per cent navy pension bonds were redeemed in 1891. The present interest bearing debt (January 1893) is as follows :—

2 per cent bonds, Redeemable at option of U.S.	$25,364,500	£5,072,900
4 per cent bonds Redeemable July 1, 1907	559,594,150	111,918,830
Refunding Certificates, 4 per cent	75,010	15,002
	$585,033,660	£117,006,732

In addition to this the outstanding debt on which interest has ceased since maturity is $2,357,755 (£471,551).

THE UNFUNDED DEBT.—The debt bearing no interest is—

Legal tender notes (greenbacks)	$346,681,016	£69,336,203
Old Demand notes	55,647	11,129
National Bank notes, Redemption Account	22,771,492	4,554,298
Fractional Currency (nominally outstanding)	6,903,463	1,380,692
	$376,411,618	£75,282,322

In addition to this the outstanding certificates and notes, issued on deposits of coin and purchases of silver are—

Gold Certificates (acts of 1863 and 1882)	$136,375,589	£27,275,118
Silver Certificates (act of 1878)	328,146,509	65,629,302
Currency Certificates (act of 1872)	15,030,000	3,006,000
Treasury notes (act of 1890)	127,946,489	25,589,298
	$607,498,582	£121,499,716

The aggregate debt is thus : $1,571,301,615 (£314,260,323); against which the treasury holds in cash (money and bullion) $607,498,582 (£121,499,716); making a net debt of $963,803,033 (£192,760,606).

STATE AND LOCAL FINANCE.

(a) *Debts.*—In addition to the national debt there are three kinds of debt ; state, county, and municipal debts. The *state debts* arose chiefly in the period 1830-1840, and were contracted for public works. During the past two decades the commonwealths have been diminishing their debts very quickly, and a considerable number are now entirely out of debt. Some still have a nominal debt, consisting of their own state bonds invested in so-called trust funds, the interest of which is devoted to education and other purposes. These states also are virtually out of debt. The few debts of any importance which still exist are found in the southern states, as a result of the civil war and reconstruction period. According to the census of 1890, the net debt of the states and territories, or the debt over and above all resources, was $132,336,689 (£26,467,338) as against $204,500,674 (£40,900,135) in 1880. The debt less sinking fund alone in 1890 was $223,107,883 (£44,621,576), of which

$150,194,322 (£30,038,864) was owed by the southern states.

The *county debt* has somewhat increased, owing chiefly to the number of new counties. The county gross debt in 1890 was $145,693,840 (£29,138,768), as against $125,621,455 (£25,124,291) in 1880. The county net debt in 1890 was $115,224,885 (£23,044,977).

The *municipal debt* has slightly decreased. Any extravagant increase has been rendered impossible by the provisions in most of the state constitutions which limit local debts to a certain percentage—varying from 5 to 15 per cent—of the assessed valuation of property. The debts can thus never increase faster than the wealth of the country. The gross municipal debt in 1890 was $745,949,786 (£149,189,957) as against $695,494,741 (£139,098,948) in 1880. But the sinking fund had increased from $115,158,742 (£23,031,748) in 1880 to $147,181,191 (£29,436,238), and the other available resources had increased from $79,185,040 (£15,837,008) in 1880 to $143,394,655 (£28,678,931) in 1890. So that the net debt is lower in 1890 than in 1880. The annual interest charge on combined state and local funded debts in 1890 was $65,541,776 (£13,108,355 or 5·29 per cent, as against $68,935,807 (£13,787,161), or 6·17 per cent in 1880.

(b) *Revenue and Expenditure.* —Owing to the separation of governmental functions, the expenses of the states are far less than those of the municipalities or the national government. The state expenses are mainly for education, charity, salaries of state officers, and militia. In the southern states we must add pensions, and in a few states expenses for public works, like the Erie Canal in New York. In the municipalities the expenses are far greater. The six largest states of the Union spent in 1890 $28,859,010 (£5,771,802), while New York city alone spent $48,937,694 (£9,787,538) in ordinary expenditures. In 1890 the 100 largest cities, containing about two-thirds of the urban population, had $234,626,655 (£46,925,331) ordinary expenditures.

The state and local revenues are derived chiefly from taxation. Some of the states obtain a slight revenue from land sales. In Texas this forms an important source of revenue. Many of the municipalities own their water works, and a few own gas and electric light works ; but except in Philadelphia, and one or two other cities, there is no attempt made to derive net revenues therefrom.

The system of taxation is based almost everywhere on the general property tax. In the southern states, and to a less extent in three or four northern and western states, we also find a comprehensive system of "license" or "privilege taxes" on most occupations. Income and stamp taxes are found in a few cases, but the receipts are everywhere insignificant except in Pennsylvania, where the stamp taxes yield a fair revenue. Collateral inheritance taxes are found in a few of the eastern states, and a direct succession tax exists in New York. Special and general taxes on private corporations abound.

While the great tax is the general property tax, personal property has to a great extent slipped out of the assessment lists, and the tax falls principally on real estate. Thus in New York state personalty pays less than 10 per cent, and realty more than 90 per cent. The system, moreover, is greatly confused by the lack of uniformity in the different state tax laws. In some states debts are exempted, in others not ; in some states mortgages are exempted, in others not. Real estate is generally taxed where it is situated ; but personalty is taxed sometimes where it is situated, sometimes where the owner resides, sometimes in both places, and often in neither place. During recent years the difficulty of reaching personalty has led to a variety of new plans. These are as follows :—

1. *To enforce the personal property tax by more vigorous measures.* The so-called *listing system* requires every tax-payer to make a complete list of every article of his personalty under oath. This plan is much favoured by the farmers and has been introduced in several states. But it has not been very successful.

2. *To reach intangible personalty by a system of registration.* This has been adopted by Connecticut. Any one owning securities may have them registered in the treasurer's office, and by paying the "investment tax" will then be exempt from other taxation on the securities. This has been fairly successful ; but is, of course, only a partial solution.

3. *To reach mortgages by declaring them to be realty, not personality, for purposes of taxation.* This plan has been adopted in California, Oregon, Massachusetts, and Michigan. In these states mortgages do not follow the person of the holder according to the rule, *mobilia personam sequuntur*, but are taxable where the land is situate. The landowner is taxed on the value of the land less the mortgage ; the owner of the mortgage is taxed on the value of the mortgage.

4. *To abolish the personal property tax and put the whole weight on real estate.* This plan is favoured chiefly by the followers of Henry George, who desires all taxes to be put on land values. It was tried in Hyattsville, Maryland, but was pronounced unconstitutional.

5. *To abolish the personal property tax, and to substitute for it the income tax.* This is a plan favoured by a few writers and officials. But the income taxes already existing, as in Massachusetts, Virginia, etc., are mere farces, and there is no likelihood of their being extended.

6. *To abolish the personal property tax and to replace it by state taxation of corporations and inheritances, leaving the real estate tax to the local divisions.* To this plan many of the states are gravitating. The general tax on corporations has been most fully developed in Pennsylvania and New York, but exists in whole or in part in many other states. Collateral inheritance taxes are found in several states, and the direct tax on successions to personalty has recently been introduced in New York. No satisfactory solution of the tax problems can be expected until joint measures are adopted by the commonwealths to regulate inter-state relations, and thus avoid double taxation. For most of the difficulties are referable to this source.

To state the entire burden of taxation resting on the American people is difficult. It depends on whether we include the fees from postal service, waterworks, licences, etc., among taxes. They certainly represent a charge upon the people. The figures of the eleventh census for the total ordinary receipts of the states and local divisions are not yet published ; and the figures of the tenth census are of little value because of the failure to separate ordinary from extraordinary revenues. According to a recent census bulletin the ordinary receipts of 100 principal cities in 1890 were $215,000,000 (*£43,000,000*). As these cities include two-thirds of the urban population, it is safe to assume that the total city and town receipts in the United States in 1890 amounted to $320,000,000 (*£64,000,000*). The receipts of the federal government were $426,000,000 (*£85,200,000*). The commonwealth and county ordinary receipts were probably between $100,000,000 (*£20,000,000*), and $150,000,000 (*£30,000,000*). This would give a total of about $1,000,000,000 (*£200,000,000*) representing the annual burden resting on the people.

The incidence of these charges is likewise difficult to determine. The bulk of the federal taxation would, however, rest on the consumer ; while the bulk of the local and state taxation would rest on the owners of real estate. In so far as local taxation is composed of the tax on personalty and license taxes, it would be subject to the general laws affecting the taxation of profits. For these points, with especial reference to American conditions, see Seligman, *The Shifting and Incidence of Taxation* (1892).

[Annual reports of the secretary of the treasury, Washington. Annual and biennial reports of the state treasurers, auditors, and comptrollers, and of the city comptrollers. Seligman, *Finance Statistics of the American Commonwealth* (1889). —Ely, *Taxation in American States and Cities.* (1887).—Seligman, "The General Property Tax," and "The Taxation of Corporations," in *Political Science Quarterly*, vol. v. (also separately).— Adams, *Public Debts* (1888).—Rosewater, *Special*

Assessments (*Columbia College Studies in History, Economics, and Public Law*, vol. ii., No. 3, 1893).

Among the reports of special commissioners on taxation may be mentioned those of New York (First and Second Reports, 1871-1872), Massachusetts (1875), West Virginia (1884), Illinois (1886), Connecticut (1887), Maryland (1888), Pennsylvania (1889), Maine (1890), Boston (1889 and 1891), New York (1893).]   E. R. A. S.

FINE. 1. A payment to be made by way of punishment for an offence.

2. A payment to be made to a feudal lord on the alienation of land,—such payments still occur in the case of copyhold lands or freehold lands held of a manor.

3. A proceeding which, similarly to the proceeding by RECOVERY (*q.v.*), was formerly used for the purpose of barring an entail (see FEE TAIL) The act for the abolition of fines and recoveries (1833), which enables tenants in tail to recover the entail by the execution and enrolment of a disentailing deed, has abolished this procedure.   E. S.

FINENESS OF COINS. The amount of pure or "fine" metal contained in a coin is expressed either by means of the ancient "carat pound" system or by the more modern millesimal method.

The *carat pound system* consists in recording the alloy as being so much better or worse than standard, and is founded on an ideal unit, the carat pound, which is divided into 24 parts called carats. British standard gold contains 22 carats of gold and 2 carats of copper or other alloying metal in every 24 parts. The carat is further subdivided into 4 "carat grains," and the carat grain into 8 parts, the smallest division of the carat scale being thus $\frac{1}{8}$th of a carat grain, or the $\frac{1}{768}$th part of the carat pound. In order to attain a still greater degree of minuteness, the eighth part of a carat grain is further subdivided into $7\frac{1}{2}$ parts, or "excess grains." Each of these final divisions is thus the $\frac{1}{5760}$th of the carat pound, and, as the troy pound also contains 5760 grains, each "excess grain" of gold beyond the last eighth in the assay report is reported as an "excess grain of gold in the troy pound."

Snelling, writing in 1766, says, in his *Doctrine of Gold and Silver Computations*, that, "by the word silver we understand not only the metal so called, pure and unmixed, but also when in a mass with copper ; and if but one half, two-thirds, or any other proportional part of it be silver, yet the whole bears that name. The same is to be understood of gold, when by itself or in a mass with silver and copper together, or with either of them alone." . . . "This is the reason that inquiries are not made what quantity of fine gold or fine silver is contained in any mixture, which seems to be the most natural inquiry, but how much standard it holds." . . . "The assay master, in reporting

the result of an assay, does not give the absolute fineness or the quantity of fine silver or fine gold present, but only the relative quantity or fineness, that is, how much the mixture is more or less than standard. In the case of gold of 20 carats fine (20 parts of pure gold in 24 parts $^{car.}$ of the alloy) the assayer puts down Wo ij., [which means *worse* (than 22) by 2 carats], and if it is 23 carats $3\frac{1}{2}$ grains fine, he puts down $^{car.\ gr.}$ Br j. iij. ob," [which means *better* (than 22) by 1 carat $3\frac{1}{2}$ grains]. The sign *ob* represents an obolus or half a carat grain. In modern times, however, the final division has been $\frac{1}{10}$ of a carat grain. The carat pound system was in use at the royal mint till so recently as the year 1882, when the *millesimal method* of expressing the fineness of the precious metals was adopted. According to this system the metal is considered as being divided into 1000 parts, the proportion of fine to alloy metal being expressed in thousandths. Thus sterling standard gold, which was formerly referred to as containing 22 carats fine and 2 carats alloy, becomes "916·6 fine," and sterling standard silver is reported by the assayer as "925 fine."

Prior to the reign of Henry III. the only gold coins in use in England were pieces of pure metal known as byzants (coming originally from Byzantium), and florences (originally struck in Florence). The coins struck by Henry III. were also of pure gold. In the reign of Edward III. the standard was altered to 23 carats $3\frac{1}{2}$ grains fine and $\frac{1}{2}$ a grain of alloy. It was again reduced by Henry VIII. to 20 carats of gold and 4 of alloy. In his reign, however, crowns were coined of the standard of 22 carats of gold and 2 of alloy. This standard, known as "crown gold," was, in the reign of Charles II., finally adopted by act of parliament as the sole standard, and it has not since been altered.

The present standard of fineness for silver coins, 11 oz. 2 dwts. of silver and 18 dwts. of alloy (925 fine), was probably first introduced by the Saxons, but it has been subject to many changes. Henry VIII. greatly debased it, reducing it first to 10 ozs. silver and 2 ozs. alloy, and subsequently to 4 ozs. silver and 8 ozs. alloy. Edward VI. at first still further debased the silver coinage by reducing the silver to 3 ozs. only in the 12. Towards the end of this reign, however, the standard was slightly improved, and Elizabeth, in the second year of her reign, restored the fineness to its original standard, which has been maintained without alteration from that time to the present day.

The following list gives the fineness, expressed millesimally, of the standard coins of the principal countries of the world :—

(The coins which form the standard of value in France, Belgium, Italy, and Switzerland, will be found recorded under the head of the Latin Union.)

Country.	Gold Coins.	Silver Coins.	Fineness.
Argentine Republic . .	5 Pesos (dollars)	..	900
Austria-Hungary	Ducat	..	986
	8 florins (20 frs.)	..	900
		2 florins	900
Brazil .	20,000 Reis	..	917
British India .	Mohur	..	916·6
		Rupee	916·6
Bulgaria . .	..	5 Leys (frs.)	900
Chile . . .	10 Pesos (dollars)	..	900
Colombia . .	20 Pesos	..	900
Egypt . .	Egyptian Pound	..	875
		20 Piastres	833·3
Germany . .	20 Marks	..	900
Great Britain .	Sovereign	..	916·6
Greece . .	100 Drachmas	..	900
		5 drachmas (frs.)	900
Holland . .	Ducat	..	983
	10 florins	..	900
		Rixdaler	945
Japan . .	20 Yen (dollars)	..	900
		1 Yen (dollar)	900
"Latin Union" { France, Italy, Belgium, Switzerland }	20 francs	..	900
		5 francs	900
Mexico . .	10 Pesos (dollars)	..	875
		1 Peso (dollar)	902·7
Persia . .	Thoman	..	900
Peru . . .	10 Sols (dollars)	..	900
		1 Sol (dollar)	900
Portugal . .	2 Milreis	..	916·6
		500 Reis	916·6
Roumania . .	20 Leys (frs.)	..	900
		5 Leys (frs.)	900
Russia . .	Imperial	..	900
		Rouble	900
Scandinavia .	20 Crowns	..	900
Sweden		Crown	800
Norway			
Denmark			
Servia . .	20 Dinars (frs.)	..	900
		5 Dinars (frs.)	900
Spain . . .	Alfonso (20 frs.)	..	900
		5 pesetas (frs.)	900
Turkey . .	500 Piastres	..	916·6
		20 Piastres	880
United States .	Eagle	..	900
		Dollar	900
Venezuela . .	100 Bolivars	..	900
		5 Bolivars	900
Zanzibar . .	5 dollars	..	900
		Dollar	900

See ASSAY ; MINT.   W. R.-A.

FINESCHI, F. VINCENZO (18th century), a Dominican, was keeper of the records in the convent of S. Maria Novella at Florence, and wrote on early famines in that city.

Istoria compendiata di alcune antiche carestie e dovizie di grano occorse in Firenze, cavate da un Diario MS. in cartapecora del secolo XIV. Firenze, Pietro Gaetano Viviani, 1767.   A. B.

FINLAISON, JOHN (1783-1860), born and educated in Scotland, a civil servant and statistician of ability almost amounting to genius. He studied for the Scotch bar, but gave up the law and was employed by the admiralty from 1805 to 1822. In this service he effected a great saving by the reform of the system of accounts, and invented a system of digesting and indexing the admiralty records and correspondence—which had been almost inaccessible for want of arrangement—so perfect that it still continues in use, and has been adopted by several foreign governments. He also drew up an account of the French forces, 1811, the first navy list, 1814, and a register of all the officers in the navy, with their antecedents, for the use of the department. From 1822 to 1851 he was employed by the treasury as actuary and principal accountant of the check department of the national debt office, and his investigations into the subject of life annuities, which were being granted at a price much below their value, saved, it has been estimated, £3,000,000 to the country. In addition to the immense amount of labour entailed by his official work he was mainly instrumental in establishing pensions for widows and orphans in the civil departments of the navy, 1812 to 1819. His close study of the principles of life assurance, his most original work, carried on during these years, led to his help being sought in the formation of many friendly and assurance societies, which would not otherwise have been placed upon a sound footing. In connection with the compensation to slave-owners at the emancipation of slaves, 1833, he made computations of the duration of slave and creole life ; in 1835 to 1837 he drew up reports for the ecclesiastical commissioners on church leases, church rates, and other similar subjects ; and he was consulted on the system of registering births, marriages, and deaths established in 1837. From 1847 until his death he was president of the institute of actuaries ; yet, in spite of such appreciation his incredible industry and invariable uprightness did not always save him from calumny and neglect.

Finlaison wrote a continuation of Sir R. Yorke's *Naval History* down to 1780.

[*Assurance Magazine*, April 1862, gives the fullest account.—Southwood Smith's *Philosophy of Health.* — Walford's *Insurance Cyclopædia*, vol. iii. — *Dictionary of National Biography*.— *Times*, 23rd April 1860.—For Finlaison's views on the organisation and management of insurance societies, see his *Evidence before the Select Committee on Assurance Associations*, 1853.]

E. G. P.

FIORENTINO, NICOLA, a Neapolitan, wrote (18th cent.) on the utility and importance of agriculture, and against protective duties, especially in an agricultural nation, where town industries ought not to be encouraged more than country ones, as foreign competition compels manufacturers to improve, and supplies the funds needed by agriculture.

Riflessioni sul Regno di Napoli, di Nicola Fiorentino, Napoli, presso de Bonis, 1794.

A. B.

FIRE INSURANCE. See INSURANCE.

FIRM. "Partners are called collectively a firm. . . . Commercial men and accountants are apt to look upon a firm . . . as a body distinct from the members composing it. Hence in keeping the partnership accounts the *firm* is made debtor to each partner for what he brings into the common stock, and each partner is made debtor to the *firm* for all he takes out of the stock. . . . In taking partnership accounts and in administering partnership assets, courts have to some extent adopted the mercantile view, and actions may now be brought by or against partners in the name of their firms ; but speaking generally the firm as such has no legal recognition. The law, ignoring the firm, looks to the partners composing it. Any change amongst them destroys the identity of the firm ; what is called the property of the firm is their property ; and what are called the debts and liabilities of the firm are their debts and their liabilities. In point of law a partner may be the debtor or the creditor of his co-partners, but he cannot be either debtor or creditor of the firm of which he is himself a member " (Lindley on *Partnership*, 5th ed. pp. 110, 111).

In addition to the difference between the mercantile and legal conception of a firm pointed out as above by Lord Justice Lindley, there is a difference as to the use of the term between lawyers and traders which must be borne in mind. While to a lawyer the word "firm" is the collective designation of partners trading together (see Partnership Act, 1890, § 4), laymen generally employ it for the purpose of describing the name under which a business is carried on, and which in legal language is called the "firm name" (Partnership Act, 1890, *ibid.*) Thus in ordinary language we may speak of the firm of a single trader while, according to legal terminology, there can be no firm, unless two persons at least are trading together. The word "firm" in Scotland and the German word *firma* is used in the sense of trade-name, both in legal and mercantile language ("the firm of a trader is the name under which he trades, and which he uses for his signature in the course of his business"—German Mercantile Code, § 15). The French word *raison sociale* only applies to partnerships ; and in Italian there are two distinct words—*ditta*, which is the trade name of a person trading without any partners, and *ragione sociale*, which is used in the case of partnerships.

It would be a great convenience for bankers and traders generally if there were a public register of firms (in the sense of trade names) as in other countries, it being often most difficult to find out who carries on business under a given name—a circumstance which has frequently been taken advantage of for fraudulent purposes. A register of firms is more necessary in this country than on the continent (where it generally exists), because there is much greater freedom here than elsewhere in the choice of trade names, inasmuch as traders may at their option carry on business under their own names or under those of other persons, or under entirely fictitious names, subject to the one condition only that they do not interfere with any existing

right. The question as to the circumstances under which the use of a firm name is deemed an interference with existing rights is too complicated to be discussed in this place ; the following recent cases throw light on the subject : Levy *v.* Walker, 10 Chancery Division, 436 ; Gray *v.* Smith, 43 Chancery Division, 208 ; Thynne *v.* Shore, 45 Chancery Division, 577) (see PARTNERSHIP, STYLE, TRADE NAME). According to Scotch law a partnership forms a separate legal person like a corporation.

E. S.

FIRMIN, THOMAS (1632-1697), son of Henry Firmin and Prudence his wife, was born at Ipswich. He started business with a capital of £100, and twenty years later (1676) he is said to have been worth £9000. His philanthropic schemes are of some importance in the economic history of England for the light they throw upon the condition of the working classes at the end of the 17th century. After the Fire of London, Firmin built a warehouse for storing corn and coal, to be supplied to the poor at reasonable rates,—a scheme which recalls the practice of the city companies during the 15th and 16th centuries. His most important undertaking, however, was his "workhouse" which he built in Little Britain for the employment of the poor in the linen manufacture. The broad outlines of this scheme were suggested by a similar one which had been tried by B. GOUGE in the parish of St. Sepulchre. Two years later (1678) Firmin unfolded his plans for dealing with poverty in his pamphlet, *Some Proposals for the employment of the Poor and for the prevention of Idleness and the consequence thereof, Begging, etc., in a letter to a Friend by T. F.*, London, 4to, 2nd edition, 1681, 8vo, reprinted in 1787 in a collection of pamphlets on the poor.

Firmin's proposals were (1) to set up in every parish a school "in the nature of a workhouse" in which the children of the poor should be taught spinning, weaving, silk-winding, stocking-knitting, etc.; (2) to provide home work of the same kind for poor women ; (3) to erect workhouses for the reception of the aged poor ; (4) in addition to the churchwardens, to appoint "fathers of the poor" in every parish to administer poor relief. In his own "workhouse" the children began work at 5 or 6 years of age. He found that they had to work 16 hours a day to earn 6d., and instead of recreation two hours were spent on their "education." Firmin was of opinion that "poor children that must be put out to poor trades, where they must work hard and fare hardly," should not be fed with white bread or taught farther than was necessary for such trades. He supplemented the miserable earnings of those employed in his workhouse, sometimes from 1600 to 1700 in number, with gifts of food and clothes. His scheme involved him in heavy losses. In 1690 it was taken up by the patentees of the linen manufacture, who appointed him overseer. But they were unsuccessful and unable even to pay Firmin his promised salary. He therefore took up the cause again and is said to have made it "bear its own charges." According to his partner he might have left an estate of at least £20,000, if he had not bestowed so much upon public and private charities. These reduced it to one-sixth of that amount. In addition to his "workhouse," Firmin took great interest in the releif of poor debtors and other philanthropic schemes.

[Full details of Firmin's life are given in the *Dictionary of National Biography*. There is an interesting account of his workhouse in *The Life of Mr. Thomas Firmin, late citizen of London. Written by one of his most intimate acquaintance. With a sermon on Luke x. 36, 37. Preached on the occasion of his death.* London, 1698, reprinted 1791, 12mo. *Vide* also M'Culloch's *Literature of Pol. Econ.*—Eden's *State of the Poor*, vol. i.]
W. A. S. H.

FIRST-FRUITS AND TENTHS. At the time when the papal authority was at its height, the popes laid on the clergy the taxes known as first-fruits and tenths. The first-fruits were the first year's income of a benefice paid by the new incumbent. They were also known as ANNATES (Lat. *annus* a year). The tenths were 10 per cent of the income of the benefice paid in subsequent years. After Henry VIII. had quarrelled with the pope, the first-fruits and tenths payable by the English clergy were transferred to the crown by an act of 1534. The annual produce of these taxes then amounted to £14,000. It was expended on secular objects until the reign of Queen Anne, who was persuaded by Gilbert Burnet, the celebrated bishop of Salisbury, to devote it to the augmentation of poor livings. An act of 1703 empowered the queen to incorporate the persons whom she should appoint to be trustees of the fund, and relieved them from the restraints imposed by the statute of mortmain, thus enabling them to receive gifts of land. The tenths and first-fruits continue to be levied upon the ancient valuation, so that their proceeds have not increased. Since 1703 the fund has been augmented by parliamentary grants and by private liberality, but it is still known as Queen Anne's Bounty. F. C. M.

FISCAL SYSTEMS. See TAXATION.

FISC, a name sometimes given in modern states to the national as well as to the private royal treasury, though derived from the Latin *fiscus*, which was originally the Roman treasury under imperial control, as distinct from the *ærarium* or state-chest under control of the senate. (See FISCUS.) In the feudal language of the middle ages the domain of the crown was sometimes called *fiscus regius*.

[Madvig, *l'Etat Romain*, transl. Morel, tome 4.—Smith, *Dictionary of Greek and Roman Antiquities.*—Wright, *Universal Pronouncing Dictionary.*]
E. G. P.

FISCUS. The treasury of the Roman emperor. Under Augustus and the early emperors the administration was divided between the senate, representing the *populus*, and the emperor. Consequently there were two treasuries, the *Ærarium Populi*, an institution of the free republic, and the *Fiscus Cæsaris*, established by Augustus. When the empire grew into an autocratic form of government, the *Fiscus Cæsaris* became the only treasury of the Roman state. E. A. W.

FISH-SILVER, probably a commuted payment for fish due in feudal times to the lord of the manor. Seebohm (*English Village Community*, pp. 44, 58), has mention of a "fish-penny" and a "fish-fee."

[Vinogradoff, *Villainage in England*, 1892, p. 291.] E. G. P.

FITZHERBERT, SIR ANTHONY (1470-1538), was a son of Ralph Fitzherbert of Norbury, Derbyshire, and of Elizabeth, daughter of John Marshall of Upton, Leicestershire (Nichols, *Leicestershire*, IV. ii. 957). According to Anthony Wood he went to Oxford, and then to Gray's Inn ; 18th November 1510 he was called to the degree of sergeant-at-law, 24th November 1516 was appointed king's sergeant, and in 1516 became a justice in the court of Common Pleas. From 1509 to 1512 he was Recorder of Coventry, when pressure of work forced him to resign that post (*Coventry Leet Book*, ff. 304 b, 309,311). Anthony Wood states that he was knighted about 1516, but gives no authority, and the earliest mention of *Sir A.* Fitzherbert seems to be in a State Paper of February 1522, and is not found again until the close of 1524, after which he is more commonly described as a knight. From 1509 to his death frequent mention is made in the State Papers of his appointment to serve on commissions of the peace, and of gaol delivery, for the northern and midland circuits, as well as on special commissions, and it is from these papers that the outline of his career must be drawn.

In 1514 he was sent as commissioner to Ireland together with Dr. Denton, dean of Lichfield, and Sir Ralph Egerton, to attempt a settlement of affairs, a work which seemed at the time so successfully accomplished that the commissioners received Henry VIII.'s hearty thanks on their return in the autumn. In June 1529 Fitzherbert formed a member of the commission appointed "to hear and determine causes moved before the king in Chancery, and committed to them by Thomas, Cardinal of York" (*Letters and Papers Hen. VIII.*, iv. iii. 2502), while on 1st December 1529 he signed the articles preferred against Wolsey by the Lords, one indictment in which was that Wolsey had "removed into Chancery indictments against his officers for taking 12d. in the pound for probation of wills, and rebuking Mr. Justice Fitzherbert" (*Letters and Papers Hen. VIII.* iv. iii. 2713). Fitzherbert was among the judges who attended Anne Boleyn's coronation on 1st June 1533 (*ib.* vi. 263), and in July Cromwell addressed a letter to him concerning "the title of Antony Stydolffe, my ward," which he fears "may be prejudicial to me," and requires Fitzherbert "to stay the trial till he has further knowledge" (*ib.* vi. 380). In November of the same year he is mentioned as a member of the Council at Ludlow with a yearly fee of £10. In June 1535 he sat on the tribunal by which Bishop Fisher and three Charterhouse monks were tried and convicted of high treason (*ib.* viii. p. 350), and in July took part in the trial of Sir Thomas More. Again on 13th May 1536 Sir Anthony was one of those who received a mandate to return all indictments found against Anne Boleyn and Lord Rocheford (*ib.* x. p. 361). He was written to about the Northern Rebellion, and was at Warrington in February 1537 for the trial of cases connected with it, while about the same time he took part in the business connected with the surrender of the monasteries of Whalley and Furness. His activity in the North was so great that he was "highly commended for his diligence" by Sussex, who wrote to Cromwell that "he cannot be spared from hence."—We hear of him next on the king's Council in Wales (*ib.* xii. ii. 321), but shortly after, while still in active service as a judge, he died 27th May 1538, and was buried at Norbury.

Fitzherbert married 1st, Dorothy, daughter of Sir Henry Willoughby of Woolaton, Notts.; 2nd, Matilda, daughter and co-heiress of Richard Cotton of Hempstall Ridware, Staffs., by whom he had five sons and five daughters, according to an epitaph preserved in the Le Neve collection (Harl. MSS. 3609). Although Fitzherbert did not enter into possession of the manor of Norbury until the death of his brother John in 1531, he certainly held land in the counties of Stafford, Warwick, Oxford and Northampton acquired by purchase and through his wife from 1503 onwards (unpublished family papers). From the notices scattered through the State Papers, Fitzherbert seems to have been a man of weight in practical matters, but he is best known to us as a legal writer. His chief works are (1) *La Graunde Abridgement*, first published by Pynson in 1514, an attempt to systematise existing law in the form of a digest of the year-books; (2) *La Novelle natura breuium* (1534); (3) *L'office et auctoryté des Justyces de peas*, first published by R. Redman in 1538, who also issued a translation of it known as the *Newe Boke of Justices of the peas* by A. F. K. That part which treats of

"l'office de visconts bailiffes escheators constables, coroners" appeared later as a separate tract (Middleton, 1545 ; R. Crompton, 1583); (4) *Diuersite de courtes et lour jurisdictions et alia necessaria.* (Redman, 1523 ; Pynson, 1526, though Coke, *Institutes*, iv. c. ix. ascribes it to 21 Hen. VIII.) But beside these and possibly other legal writings, two works on agriculture are generally, and probably with reason, ascribed to Fitzherbert.

(1) *The Boke of Husbandrie* (Pynson, 1523 ; Treuerys, 1525 ? ; Berthelet, 1532, 1534, 1546, 1548 ; Walle, 1555 ? ; M. Marshe, 1560 ? ; Awdeley, 1562, 1576 ; White, 1598 ; Bathurst and Newbery, 1767 ; Trübner, 1882) was a practical manual for the working farmer, and the numerous editions through which it passed during the 16th century afford some evidence of the estimation in which it was held, and of the need it supplied. It is generally considered the earliest treatise in English on agriculture, if we except the translation of Walter of Henley's *Husbandry*, attributed to Grosseteste.

(2) *The Boke of surueyinge and improuements* (Pynson, 1523 ; Berthelet, 1539, 1546, 1567 ; Marshe, 1587 ; Bathurst and Newbery, 1767) was a more technical work, based upon the statute *Extenta Manerii*, and written for the benefit of lords of manors. It describes how the survey of a manor should be taken, how its resources might be increased, and in what relations lord and tenants stand to one another. The stress laid on the advantages of enclosures, the minute directions concerning the management of sheep, the warning against the raising of rents, the incidental notices marking an increase in general prosperity, and the plea for the abolition of the still existing evil of villainage are interesting points on which a student of Tudor times may learn much from Fitzherbert, while a comparison between his experience and the practice of the 13th century, as described by Walter of Henley, is of value.

Some writers have maintained that these works on agriculture were not written by Sir Anthony Fitzherbert, but by his brother John, though the latter is not known to have written anything else. It is said that Sir Anthony's professional engagements could not have allowed him to "exercise husbandry forty years" as alleged in the *Boke of Husbandrie.* Fitzherbert as a judge must, however, have had much leisure time, which he may well have given to agricultural pursuits ; and family papers show that he added considerably to his landed possessions. The difficulty presented by a comparison of his age with the date of publication of the *Boke of Husbandrie* (1523) is lessened when we remember that Fitzherbert himself merely says that he has been "an householder this forty years and more." It is Berthelet, the printer, who says that he had "exercised husbandry forty years." The fact that he is called "mayster" instead of "Sir Anthony" in the printer's note also seems an objection of little weight. It is not known exactly when he was knighted, it was certainly before February 1522, but since, as already noticed, the State Papers, with one exception use the title "Mr." until the close of 1524, and frequently afterwards, it is not surprising to find that a printer does the same when the title "Sir" would have been more correct.

The technical character of the *Boke of Surueyinge* points to its authorship by a man intimately acquainted with the law, while various indications in the *Boke of Husbandrie* show that the writer was something more than a farmer; he was clearly a country gentleman who could make experiments, and a man of scholarly tastes who could quote the Scriptures and the Fathers as readily as the statute book.

Professor Skeat, who has discussed the matter fully in the introduction to his edition of the *Boke of Husbandrie*, may safely be followed in his conclusion that Sir Anthony Fitzherbert was the author of these books, until more convincing arguments to the contrary are forthcoming.
[Copy of brass on tomb, Brit. Mus. Harl. MSS. 3609.—Wood's *Athenæ Oxon.* (Bliss).—Nichols's *Leicestershire*, iv. pt. ii.—Douthwaite's *Gray's Inn.—Notes and Queries*, 6th ser. ii. iii. iv.—Ames's *Typogr. Antiq.* (Dibdin), ii. iii. iv.—Dugdale's *Orig. Jurid.—Letters and Papers For. and Dom. of the reign of Hen. VIII.*—Skeat's *Introduction to the Boke of Husbandry* (Trübner, 1882). —*Coventry Leet Book* (Town Clerk's Office, Coventry).]
E. A. M.

FIVE-FRANC PIECE. Standard gold as well as silver coin of the countries forming the "Latin" Monetary Union (France, Belgium, Italy, Switzerland, and Greece). *Gold*: weight, 24·89 grains; fineness, 900; value in gold (916·6 fine at £3 : 17 : 10½ an ounce), 3s. 11½d. *Silver*: weight, 385·81 grains; fineness, 900; value in silver (925 fine at 5s. 6d. an ounce), 4s. 3½d.
F. E. A.

FIVE-POUND PIECE. English standard gold coin, provided for in the first schedule to the Coinage Act, 1870, but not actually coined for circulation until 1887, on the occasion of the jubilee of Queen Victoria; weight, 616·37 grains; fineness, 916·6; value in gold francs, 126·1 francs. A further issue of these coins, bearing a new effigy of the queen, was made during the year 1893.
F. E. A.

FIX, THÉODORE (1800-1846) born at Soleure (Switzerland), died at Paris. He migrated at an early age into France, where he first carried on the profession of a land surveyor, and then occupied himself with translating German works into French. This last-mentioned employment led to his forming a taste for economic science. He obeyed this call and founded, in July 1833, the *Revue mensuelle d'économie politique*, which was the forerunner of the *Journal des économistes*. Fix's

review, however, was very coldly received by the public—though he had the assistance of Buret, Blanqui, Rossi, Sismondi, and others. This periodical came to an end at the close of the year 1836. Fix then worked on several journals, the *Siècle*, the *Quotidienne*, the *Constitutionnel*, and especially on the *Journal des économistes*. In 1840 his essay, called *Un mémoire sur l'association des douanes allemandes*, won him a prize from the Academy of the moral and political sciences. After this, Fix, though never elected a member of the Institute, was employed in working on the report on the progress of sciences since the Revolution—a work which the Institute had undertaken. Finally, in March 1846, but a few months before his death, Fix completed and sent to the printer his *Observations sur l'état des classes ouvrières*, 1 vol. 8vo, a very solid and well-written monograph, full both of common-sense and of learning, and distinguished by a high standard of enlightened intelligence. It may be read at the present day with pleasure.
[See also J. A. Blanqui, *Histoire de l'économie politique en Europe, depuis les anciens jusqu'à nos jours*.]
A. C. f.

FIXED AND FLOATING CAPITAL. Adam Smith drew a distinction between capital which yielded a profit without passing from one owner to another, and capital which did not. This distinction—which is really one between food and fuel for the support of labour and all other kinds—was modified by Ricardo into one between "goods of slow consumption" and those which "require to be frequently reproduced"; a discrimination which does not, on the face of it, profess to be scientific, and about the usefulness of which he himself was dubious. Mill, following the same train of thought, formulated the recognised classical division between fixed and circulating capital in these terms: "Capital which fulfils the whole of its office, in the production of which it is engaged, by a single use, is called circulating capital; capital which exists in any durable shape, and the return to which is spread over a period of corresponding duration, is called fixed capital." According to these definitions fixed capital is practically invested capital, and comprehends machinery, houses, public works, railways, canals, improvements to land, and anything productive which exists in a durable shape. Circulating capital, on the other hand, comprehends raw material, metals and minerals, the actual produce of land, and all that is set aside for the sustenance of labourers. Money can hardly be placed in either class; it is generally placed in the latter, although it does not fall within Mill's definition. The term "circulating" is not a very happy designation for this sort of capital; because by hypothesis it does not circulate, but is, on the contrary, consumed in a single use. The term "floating capital" seems to be better adapted in describing the class of commodities in question.

There are two other divisions of capital, both of which ought to be noticed, as they run on lines very nearly similar to that which discriminates between fixed and floating capital. One is that between capital which directly sustains labourers, called wage - capital, and capital which only indirectly aids labourers, called auxiliary capital. The only practical difference between wage-capital and floating capital is that the latter includes raw material, which is classed as auxiliary. The other division of capital is that into specialised and non-specialised capital. Fixed capital, with the exception of houses, is generally properly to be classed as specialised ; but the line of demarcation between these last-mentioned classes of capital is not to be defined with accuracy, any more than that between specialised and non-specialised labour. There is little to choose between these three classifications of capital ; but that which forms the subject of the present article has come down from the earlier English economists, and is the most commonly employed.

The progress of industry is, speaking generally, marked by the increasing ratio which fixed capital bears to floating. Fixed capital really represents the saving, or foresight, which is of the essence of the creation of nearly every form of capital. On pasture and agriculture there is comparatively little fixed capital employed, though this gradually increases ; but in all other industries the tendency to increase the quantity of fixed capital is very great. The most striking result of this progress is, that the proportion of industries which exist for the purpose of constructing fixed capital — i.e. making raw material (floating capital) into machinery—constantly increases. It is this, along with other causes springing essentially from the same source, that produces the phenomenon of the slow depletion of rural districts and growth of towns and large villages. There is therefore, while the process is going on, a gradual but continuous displacement of labour which in normal periods passes unnoticed and creates little disturbance. A sudden conversion of floating into fixed capital on a large scale, however, has always a very serious effect, at least temporarily, on labour ; and this at many periods has caused new machinery to be unpopular with the working classes. There are two ways in which a conversion such as that mentioned affects labour. If a large quantity of capital is withdrawn from agriculture, and invested in machinery on permanent works, (the illustration given by Professor Fawcett, *Manual of Political Economy*, ch. iv.), there is not the same quantity of the annual return from the converted capital available for consumption. It must be remarked that this result can only be temporary. In the long run, floating capital is increased by the growth of fixed capital, but at a much slower rate, and it is liable to great fluctuations, as it depends on the continued existence and success of the industries in which the fixed capital is invested. The other manner in which labour is affected by a great conversion of floating capital is this : such a change means in effect the specialisation of a quantity of capital, and as specialised capital generally employs specialised labour, the workmen have to learn to change their business if they want to get employment. The demand for skilled labour increases suddenly, and the unskilled man suffers.

A country which possesses a great stock of fixed capital has the main element of financial strength, and the chief contributor to national credit. It may be observed, however, that when a country comes to be the scene of a war, its loss, and the consequent distress of its inhabitants, are greater where much fixed capital exists. The destruction of a harvest is the destruction of a year's agricultural income ; the breaking-up of machinery and works is a breach made in national capital.

[Adam Smith, *Wealth of Nations*, bk. ii. ch. i. —Mill's *Principles*, and *Unsettled Questions in Political Economy*, essays iii. and v.—Marshall's *Principles of Economics.*—Marx, *Das Kapital.*— Cairnes, *Leading Principles.*] M. G. D.

FIXED INCOMES do not afford a constant benefit to the recipients when the value of money changes. Incomes may be thus classified according to the degree in which they are affected by a change in the value of money (Jevons, *Currency and Finance*, p. 96). (1) Incomes derived from funds, annuities, mortgages, etc., where the whole loss or gain consequent on depreciation or appreciation falls upon the holder. (2) Incomes made up of "fixed charges established by law or custom or convenience, such as the fees of lawyers, physicians, etc." The increase of business consequent on a virtual reduction of charge may here make some compensation, as in the case of traffic increasing with the diminution of tolls. (3) Incomes "entirely independent of the value of gold," such as those of manufacturers, merchants, artisans, etc. ; from which class, however, must be excepted salaries and wages which, though not fixed, are slow to move.

To correct the evils incident to the fixity of incomes—the loss to the recipient in case of depreciation, to the community in case of appreciation—is one of the objects proposed by schemes designed to obviate the change in the value of money, as CORN RENTS, and tabular standards. (For these see INDEX NUMBERS.) F. Y. E.

FIXTURES. The older law, both of England and Scotland, allowed no exception to the maxim that whatever was fixed to the soil went with it. Accordingly, every object, even though originally movable in character, that had once been fixed to land or to a building, became a part of that land or building, and could not be removed at the will of the person who had fixed it. It thus became a fixture, the property of the landlord in the same sense as the rest of the land or building. But between things fixed to the soil, so as to render the premises complete and ensure the appropriate use of them ; things difficult to move on account of their weight; and things temporarily attached for convenience' sake, with no intention of transferring the property in them, it became difficult to· distinguish, and the maxim was unduly harsh in its operation. The early rules of law remain on the whole in force in questions between heirs-at-law and personal representatives, except in particular cases where such objects as mirrors, pictures, tapestries, and the like have been held not to have been fixtures, and between personal creditors and mortgagees. As between lessors and lessees, however, there has been a considerable relaxation of the older rules ; and the rule seems now clear in England, not quite so clear in Scotland, that fixtures put up for trade purposes or for domestic use may, as against the lessor, be removed by the lessee, or severed from the tenement, and that they thereupon regain their character as movables and as the personal property of the lessee ; provided that what he so does he must do during the term or during the continuance of his possession as tenant, and that the tenement is not to be injured or impaired in its use by the removal. Such fixtures are called "Tenants' Fixtures," while those which must remain attached to the Freehold are called "Landlords' Fixtures." This relaxation was not effectively extended to agricultural tenancies until the passing of the Agricultural Holdings Act of 1883, by which it was provided that agricultural fixtures or buildings, for which the tenant was not entitled to compensation under the act, or which he was not bound by his agreement to put up, or had not put up instead of some fixture or building belonging to the landlord, might be removed by the tenant before the end of his tenancy, on condition that he had paid his rent, etc. ; that no avoidable damage was done ; that any actual damage was made good, and that notice was given and an option given to the landlord to purchase the fixtures or buildings at a valuation. A. D.

FLEETWOOD, WILLIAM (1656-1723),—the first English collector of statistics of prices,—became fellow of King's College, Cambridge ; gained reputation as a preacher with strong Whig sympathies, and was appointed successively canon of Windsor (1702), bishop of St. Asaph (1708), and bishop of Ely (1714).

In 1707 Fleetwood published anonymously his *Chronicon Preciosum ; or an Account of English Money, the Price of Corn and other Commodities for the last 600 years ; in a Letter to a Student in the University of Oxford.* The question had been presented to him how far the statutes of a certain college (founded between 1440 and 1460), which vacated a Fellowship if the Fellow had an estate in land of inheritance, or a perpetual pension, of five pounds per annum, were binding in conscience. Fleetwood answered that this rule must be interpreted according to the changed value of money ; and the purpose of his book was to determine what that change had been. He concluded that "£5 two hundred and sixty years ago, was equivalent to £28 or £30 now." But his treatise took a wider range ; it brought together all the information he could find on the values of money and the prices of commodities during the Middle Ages in England ; and it is still well worth consulting. His figures were taken almost exclusively from chronicles ; but he clearly foretold such inquiries as those of Mr. Thorold Rogers. "The Gentlemen of each University," he remarked, "will have it in their Hands to make what Amendments they shall see good, out of their old *Rolls* and *Bursars' Accounts;* which I look upon as the most sure Guides in Enquiries of this Nature ; because our General Histories do mostly give us the Prices of Things which are *Extraordinary,* either for *Cheapness* or for *Dearness.* Whereas the *College Accounts* deliver faithfully the *ordinary* and *common* Price of most Commodities and Provisions."

Fleetwood's sermons frequently dealt with subjects of current interest. Thus in 1694 he preached a *Sermon against Clipping* before the Lord Mayor at Guildhall Chapel, wherein he considered "First, The Use and Necessity of Money to the carrying on the Trade and Commerce of the World ; Secondly, the Mischiefs of corrupting and debasing Money, the Coining of bad Metal, or the clipping and stealing from good ; Thirdly, the Reasonableness and Justice of the Laws which punish such Offenders. So also he published in 1720 (during the South Sea Panic) a *Sermon,* preached some years before to a City congregation, *On the Justice of Paying Debts.*

A Complete Collection of the Sermons, Tracts, and Pieces of all kinds that were written by . . . Dr. William Fleetwood, was published by subscription in 1737. W. J. A.

FLETCHER, ANDREW (1655-1716), of Saltoun, published a remarkable discussion of pauperism in Scotland at the end of the 17th century (*vide* the *Second Discourse,* etc. in *Two Discourses concerning the affairs of Scotland,* Edinburgh, 1698 ; reprinted in Fletcher's *Political Works,* London, 1737, 8vo). He points out that the bad seasons of 1695-1698 were a special cause of poverty, but he attributes its origin to the church, "which encouraged setting slaves at liberty." . . . "Provisions by hospitals, almshouses, and the contributions of churches or parishes, have by experience been found to increase the numbers of those that live by them. And the liberty every idle and lazy person has of burdening the society in which he lives, with his maintenance, has increased the numbers to the weakening and impoverishing of it : for he needs only to say that he cannot get work, and then he must be maintained by charity" [p. 129]. Then, regarding "not names, but thir̦̦s," Fletcher expresses the opinion that slavery is preferable to a bad system of workhouses. While he does not defend "any of those bad and cruel regulations about slaves," he "proceeds to explain under what conditions they might be both good and useful, as well as I think they are necessary in a well-regulated government." According to his scheme the master is not to have power over the slave's life, or for mutilation or torture. The slave, his wife and children, are to be provided with clothes, food, and lodging, to be educated at the master's expense, and to have Sunday holidays. Except in matters relating to their duty as servants they are to be under the protection of the law and not subject to the will of their masters. They are not to possess property, and they may be sold, *i.e.* Fletcher explains, their services may be alienated without their consent. He proposes to compel "every man of a certain estate" to take a proportionate number of vagabonds on those conditions and to set them to work. Under such a system he maintains that they would be better off than those who "having a power to possess all things, are very often in want of everything."

[A full life of Fletcher is given in the *Dictionary of National Biography*, vol. xix.]   W. A. S. H.

FLEYLAND is satisfactorily explained by Vinogradoff (*Villainage in England*, p. 170) as land held by the villein tenure of agricultural work (*ad furcam et flagellum, i.e.* by pitchfork and flail), not by payment of rent.   E. G. P.

FLOATING CHARGE is the name given to the general charge of the undertaking of a company frequently given in favour of debenture holders (see DEBENTURE ; DEBENTURE STOCK). The expression "*floating* charge" implies that it does not attach to any specific property but to all the property held by the company at any particular moment subject to the company's right to dispose of it in the ordinary course of their business. It is only in case of default or liquidation proceedings that the charge becomes effective. A receiver may then be appointed who takes possession of all the assets, and the general creditors will be shut out. A floating charge, like all other mortgages, ought to be registered in the company's register of charges (Comp. Act, 1862-73), but as the omission to register does not entail any consequences except the payment of certain penalties by the parties responsible for the omission (Wright *v.* Horton, 12 Appeal Cases, 371), the creditors of a company

can never know whether, in the case of a winding up, their claims will not be frustrated by debenture holders, the legislature having given additional facilities for the creation of secret charges by declaring that the Bill of Sale Act of 1882 (see BILL OF SALE) does not apply to the debentures of a company. Up to recent times creditors who were secured by a specific mortgage of any part of a company's property were comparatively safe, but the ingenuity of company lawyers has found a new method of defeating their claims, as well as those of unsecured creditors, by inserting an additional clause in debentures by which the company undertakes "not to create any mortgage or charge in priority" to the debentures in question.   E. S.

FLOATING DEBT. The expression "Floating Debt" in state finance is used as equivalent to "unfunded" and opposed to "funded debt." The floating debt of a state is generally intended to be repaid within a comparatively short period, but it may also be raised in that form in order to be converted into funded debt at a subsequent period. A part of the floating debt of the United Kingdom consists of temporary advances required for the supply services in anticipation of revenue payable at a later period within the same financial year, but it also happens that expenditure is incurred for objects for which an addition to the funded debt does not seem justified, but which cannot conveniently be raised out of one year's revenue, and in such cases the creation of a floating debt repayable within a fixed number of years is a useful expedient. Thus for instance the Naval Defence Act 1889 provides that the sums required for the purpose of building certain vessels may be raised by the creation of floating debt repayable within seven years.

A good recent instance of the creation of floating debt, subsequently converted into funded debt, was the issue of exchequer bonds, for the purpose of paying off holders of consols who were unwilling to convert under Mr. Goschen's Act ; their bonds were afterwards, through the operation of the National Debt (Conversion of Exchequer Bonds) Act 1892, exchanged against a charge in favour of the holders which now forms part of the funded debt. The effect of the operation will be seen by comparing on the table given below the respective amounts of funded and unfunded debt for 1892 and 1893.

The floating debt consists of advances made by the Bank of England, exchequer bonds repayable within a fixed number of years, interest being payable at fixed intervals in the meantime, and treasury bills repayable at much shorter periods and issued at a discount in the same way as mercantile bills. Terminable annuities are also in a certain sense part of the floating debt ; they are partly used like exchequer bonds for the purpose of spreading expenditure over a number of years, and partly also for the purpose of paying off funded debt. As the National Debt is to a great extent held by public bodies, a conversion of funded into unfunded debt for the purpose of ultimate repayment can always be easily arranged if the state of the finances allows such an operation. The proportion of the floating to the funded debt is shown in the following table, which has been extracted from the last annual report of the Public Debt Commissioners :—

Year.	Funded debt.	Capital value of terminable annuities.	Unfunded debt.
	£	£	£
1836	760,295,000	60,698,000	30,083,000
1843	774,859,000	48,112,000	18,684,000
1853	764,541,000	31,862,000	17,743,000
1863	787,423,000	18,074,000	16,495,000
1873	727,374,000	47,019,000	4,829,100
1883	712,699,000	27,571,000	14,185,000
1892	577,945,000	64,422,000	35,313,000
1893	589,533,082	60,761,000	20,748,000

The annual interest charge on the unfunded debt in 1893-94 was £486,000.

The disadvantage of a floating debt, especially in the shape of short treasury bills which have frequently to be renewed, is that in a moment of financial crisis it might be difficult to find new takers, when current bills fall due ; but when it is remembered that a considerable part of the amount granted by parliament for the service of the debt is used for the repayment of capital, and that, in case of necessity the commissioners, instead of purchasing consols, may use the sinking fund for the repayment of treasury bills, this risk in view of the comparative smallness of the amount does not seem a serious one.

The expression floating debt is also used in the case of large mercantile and industrial undertakings, more especially in the case of railways, to distinguish trade debts and debts borrowed from banks for temporary purposes from debts incurred by the issue of DEBENTURES (q.v.) or DEBENTURE STOCK (q.v.). The priorities as between the debenture-holders and the other creditors depend on the special circumstances of each case and the law of the country in which the debtor's undertaking is situate.

[As to the theoretical aspects of the subject of floating debt in state finance, see Roscher, Finanzwissenschaft, § 143.]   E. S.

FLOATING POLICY (Marine Insurance). A floating policy is a policy which designates the subject matter insured in general terms, and leaves the name of the ship, the particular subject matter, and the value of it to be defined by subsequent declarations. The

declarations may be made by indorsement on the policy or in other customary manner, but the general rule is that they must be made in order of shipment and with reasonable diligence. When a declaration of value is not made until after notice of loss, the policy must be treated as an open, and not as valued policy, as regards the subject matter of that declaration.

[See Arnould's Marine Insurance, ed. 6, p. 337.]   M. D. C.

FLOREZ ESTRADA, ALVARO (1765-1853), entered early the financial administration of Spain, and was appointed in 1798 procurador general de las Asturias. As such he contributed powerfully to the organisation of the resistance to Napoleon, and was promoted, in 1813, asistente in Seville : his jurisdiction extended over the whole of Andaluzia. During the troubled reign of Ferdinand VII. he was twice obliged to take shelter in England, where he devoted himself to the study of political economy. After the establishment of the constitutional monarchy during the minority of Queen Isabella, he returned to Spain and was appointed a member of the senate, over which he presided. In 1851 he was elected a corresponding member of the French Académie des Sciences morales et politiques.

Florez Estrada is considered the most distinguished Spanish economist of the first half of this century. He published in 1814, in Madrid, his Examen imparcial de las disensiones de America, in which he advocated the emancipation of the Spanish colonies of the New World. Later on, he wrote a pamphlet entitled Efectos producidos en Europa por la Baja en el producto de las minas de plata (London, 1824), on the effects of the reduced production of the silver mines and his Examen de la Crisis Comercial de la Inglatierra, translated into French under the title : Réflexions sur la Détresse Commerciale de la Grande Bretagne (Paris, 1826). But his principal work is his treatise of political economy, of which different editions were issued in London (1828), Paris (1831), and Madrid (1841 and 1848), sometimes under the title of Tratado and sometimes of Curso de Economía Política. A French translation under the appropriate heading of Cours Éclectique d'Économie Politique appeared in Paris and London in 1833 (3 vols. 8vo). In fact, Florez Estrada was not, and expressly disclaims being, an original writer, whilst he candidly confesses his obligations to Ricardo, M'Culloch, and James Mill. But he is by no means their undiscriminating follower, and, for instance, freely criticises some of their views on the advantages of a paper currency. He insists on the necessity of what is now called a high standard of life for the working classes; "nations cannot prosper if the working classes are not active, intelligent, and industrious ; this is impossible if their wages are not high enough to secure them a comfortable and agreeable life" (p. 375, edit. 1831). The most original part is to be found in the chapters concerning taxation. They are written from the point of view of an experienced and enlightened Spanish official, who ascribes the decay of his country to its defective financial and economic government and to the undue and excessive imposition of taxes on consumption. He energetically rejects the policy of meeting current expenses by public loans, and recommends the introduction into Spain of a moderate land-tax, leaving untouched the profits derived from investments in the improvement of land.

E. Ca.

FLORIDA-BLANCA, José Moñino, Count of (1728-1808), appointed in 1766 *fiscal* and in the following year member of the council of Castile, was sent on a mission to Rome to obtain from the Pope the suppression of the order of the Jesuits. As a reward for his success Charles III. of Spain gave him, in 1773, the title of count of Florida-Blanca and appointed him, in 1776, minister of state and later on of grace and justice. After his disgrace under Charles IV. in 1792, he retired to a convent in Murcia, his native place, where he remained until the rising against Napoleon, when his popularity caused him to be put at the head of the national government as president of the supreme governing *junta*. He died shortly afterwards.

Before his elevation to the ministry he had already made known his reforming tendencies on the question of the supply of corn for Madrid, and by his protest against the privileges of the Mesta (*q.v.*) or right of passage allowed to herds of cattle (*Respuesta fiscal . . . contra los ganaderos trashumantes*, 1770).

As a minister, he distinguished himself by his unification of the Spanish import tariff, which was different in the different kingdoms of the monarchy, and by raising the revenue derived from customs from 60 to 130 millions of reales (£600,000 to £1,300,000), although he had lowered the taxes on raw materials and machinery. He also reduced the *alcavala* or tax on every sale from 14 to about 6 per cent, and remitted it on all sales of goods by the manufacturer himself (see Alcavala). He built about 600 miles of new roads, improved the sea-ports, and gave an active impulse to irrigation. At the same time he took stringent measures for the repression of beggary and vagrancy by the establishment of the *fondo pio beneficial* or poor fund for the endowment of hospitals and orphanages, to be supplied by a fixed charge on all ecclesiastical benefices.

In the *Memorial* presented in 1788 to Charles III., Florida-Blanca sets forth the result of his endeavours and his views for the future. Some of the latter are rather striking; he intends to put down the excess of entails by submitting henceforth their creation to the royal approba-

tion, and by authorising the municipal *junta* to sell for building purposes any unoccupied land in the neighbourhood of towns. On the other hand he is willing to declare the life owner of an entailed estate full owner of the value of all the improvements he has effected in the way of irrigating, planting, or clearing unbroken fields.

The *Memorial* has been published, with most other works of Florida-Blanca, in Rivadeneyra's *Biblioteca de Autores Españoles*, vol. 59 (Madrid, 1867), and has been given in French in Muriel's translation of Coxe's work on Spain under the house of Bourbon (*L'Espagne sous les rois de la maison de Bourbon*, vol. vi. p. 257.)

E. Ca.

FLORIN.

Florin, History of the English Gold, p. 92; Florin, English (Gold and Silver), p. 92; Florin, Austrian, p. 93; Florin, Dutch, p. 93.

FLORIN, HISTORY OF THE ENGLISH GOLD. A gold coin of the reign of Edward III., so called from a Florentine coin, the *florino*, first issued in 1252, which derived its name from the fact of its having upon it a lily (*fiore*, flower). The English coin was sometimes called a florence; it was, however, equal in weight to two of the Italian coins. The issue of florins authorised by parliament of 1343 and made current by proclamation dated 27th January (o.s.) of the same year, was the second attempt since the 9th century to introduce a gold coinage into England, the first attempt, Henry III.'s gold pennies, having failed. The florins were to be current at 6s., to weigh 108 grains, to be of the same fineness as the Florentine coin, 23 carats, $3\frac{1}{2}$ grains of gold to $\frac{1}{2}$ grain of alloy, and to be made and current equally in England and in Flanders, for the facilitation of trade. Half and quarter florins were issued at the same time. In 1344, however, it having been found that they had been overvalued in proportion to silver, the florins were, according to Kenyon, made "no longer current without the consent of the receiver, but they were to be considered as bullion and taken according to their value as such," and a coinage of Nobles took their place. Thus they were not called in but demonetised, and left to take their place as bullion. Only two specimens of the English florin, two of the half, and three of the quarter florin are extant.

[Kenyon, *Gold Coins of England*, 1884.]

E. G. P.

FLORIN (ENGLISH), *Gold*. A coin struck in the reign of Edward III. and issued at the rate of 6s. sterling. There was only one coinage of these pieces, the exact date of which is uncertain, but it was either in 1343 or 1344. Weight, 115·25 grains; fineness, 994·8. Value in gold (916·6 fine at £3 : 17 : 10½ an ounce), £1 : 0 : 3.

Silver. Token coin of the nominal value of 2s., and legal tender to the amount of £2. First struck in the year 1849; weight, 174·54 grains; fineness, 925. Value in silver francs (900 fine), 2·32 francs.

[Henfrey's *English Coins*, 1885.—Ruding's *Annals of the Coinage*.]   F. E. A.

FLORIN (AUSTRIAN), OR GULDEN. Silver standard coin, 900 fine, weighing 190·53 grains. Also double florins of proportionate weight and same fineness. Value of the florin in silver (925 fine at 5s. 6d. an ounce), 2s. 1½d. ; in silver francs (900 fine), 2·47 francs.

Austrian florins were last coined in 1892. On the 2nd of August of that year, a law was passed establishing a gold standard and a new metallic currency, with a gold crown, of the weight of ·3387 grammes of gold nine-tenths fine, as the unit of value. The crown is divided into 100 hellers.

The coins of the new "crown system," which were first struck in 1893, are as follows :—

STANDARD COINS.

	Grammes.	Fine.	Sterling value (gold 916·6 fine, at £3 : 17 : 10½ an oz.).
Gold—Twenty crowns	6·775	900	16/8
Ten crowns	3·387	900	8/4

SUBSIDIARY COINS.

	Grammes.	Fine.	Nominal value in sterling.
Silver—Crowns . .	5·000	835	10d.
Nickel—Twenty hellers	4·000	..	2d.
Ten hellers .	3·000	..	1d.
Bronze—Two hellers .	3·333	..	0·2
Hellers . .	1·666	..	0·1

It will be seen that the smallest standard coin is the ten-crown piece ; the silver, nickel, and bronze pieces being merely tokens. The crown is equal in value to half of the florin of the former currency.   F. E. A.

FLORIN (DUTCH), OR GULDEN. Silver standard coin, 945 fine, weighing 154·32 grains, and divided into 100 cents. The 50 cent piece is 945 fine and proportionate in weight. The 25, 10, and 5 cent pieces, 645 fine, are tokens only. Value of the florin in silver (925 fine at 5s. 6d. an ounce), 1s. 9½d. ; in francs (900 fine), 2·1 francs.   F. E. A.

FLOTSAM AND JETSAM. These legal terms may be defined as follows—*flotsam* comprehends all floating articles which once formed part of a wreck or of her cargo ; *jetsam* comprehends all things cast overboard (Fr. *jetter*) in a storm or shipwreck. Under the common law the crown became proprietor of all flotsam and jetsam. But the right to flotsam and jetsam was frequently conferred by the crown upon the owners of manors abutting on the sea. The right whether of the crown or of the lord of the manor is now limited by the right of the original owner to reclaim his property within a

year. (See Stephen's *Commentaries*, vol. ii. pp. 552-555.)   F. C. M.

FLOW OF CAPITAL. It may be said that of the three agents of production known to classical economics capital is the one pre-eminently distinguished by mobility. Land is immovable, labour is movable, but frequently with difficulty and under disadvantages ; nor does it necessarily tend to become more easily transferred, in spite of the increasing knowledge of the labourers and the spread of means of conveyance, because these elements are to a large extent counterbalanced by the highly-specialised character which modern labour tends to assume. Capital, however, since the early hunter of the text-books took to canoe-building, has become continuously more movable, and is now extremely sensitive to the exigencies of supply and demand ; so that, notwithstanding the enormous quantity of capital invested in such a way as to preclude the possibility of immediate conversion, the flow of capital is far more continuous, whether between different trades, districts, or countries, than formerly. The flow of capital may be examined under three phases : (1) international, (2) local, and (3) industrial. The first of these terms designates the migration of capital from one country to another ; the second the same migration from one district to another within the same country ; and the third the transference of capital from one trade or industry to another. All these movements are greatly facilitated by a well-organised system of banking.

1. *International.* — As capital, like labour, finds its most natural employment at home, it is only where there is capital relatively to spare in a country that any appreciable portion of it goes abroad. Moreover, as it is only free capital that can be sent out of the country, the flow of capital from one country to another is determined chiefly by the amount of capital of this sort. When free capital exists in any great quantity, as it does in England, it competes against itself so as to lower the rate of interest at home ; and the low rate of interest encourages the owners of such capital to attempt to gain a higher rate by investing where capital is more scarce.

2. *Local.*—The movements of capital within a country differ chiefly from the international movements in this that the rate of interest plays no part in them, as it may be assumed that it is the same throughout the whole country. Probably the most important attraction to capital that we find in a country such as England is the discovery of fields of minerals hitherto unwrought. It would be difficult to trace the gradual changes in the locality which capital seems to favour ; the establishment of an industry, once fairly begun, almost always has the effect of drawing other industries related to and depending upon it, into

the immediate neighbourhood. Railways are great factors in the local flow of capital. A railway established between two large centres of industry must necessarily pass through the intervening country, and it encourages men to set up factories or other industrial undertakings near it, which in time attract capital. Lancashire and the West Riding of Yorkshire, and, in a minor degree, Lanarkshire, have come to possess the enormous amount of fixed capital they can lay claim to from such causes as these. On the other hand foreign tariffs may cause a flow of capital in the home country, though this is more properly industrial than local. Protracted struggles between employers and labourers are also credited with a certain quantity of force in driving capital from the locality in which they occur.

3. *Industrial.* — This is the form of the movement of capital which causes the greatest disorganisation of labour, and the most acute hardship, though it is, according to some, most generally beneficial in the end. The introduction of machinery and the comparative depletion of the rural districts are phenomena traceable to it, as they involve the conversion of floating capital into fixed.

Foreign tariffs and inventions assist the natural forces of supply and demand to promote the flow of capital from one trade to another. Capital will flow readily into those channels where for the time being the price gives an extra profit because of great demand; but where the transference is necessitated by over-production of some commodity, there cannot fail to be a temporary loss, and a permanent loss to the individual capitalist. The withdrawal of agricultural capital in England during the last two decades must have involved those whose capital was formerly invested in land in very serious loss ; and similarly the transference of capital from the sugar industry to others cannot be effected without severe loss, and is not due to the large profits to be made elsewhere, but to the diminution of profits in the refining trade, owing to foreign bounties.

[Walker's *Political Economy*, pt. ii. ch. iii.— *Wealth of Nations*, bk. ii. ch. i.—Mill's *Principles of Political Economy ;* and *Unsettled Questions in Political Economy*, Essays 3 and 5.— Cairnes's *Leading Principles.*—Marshall's *Principles of Economics.*—Marx's *Capital.*] M. G. D.

F. O. B. An abbreviation for *free on board.* Goods shipped from one country to another are generally sold either *f. o. b.,*—in which case the purchaser must pay freight and insurance ; *c. and f.,*—cost and freight, in which case the vendor has to pay the freight ; or *c. i. f.,*—cost, insurance, freight, in which case the vendor has to pay both insurance and freight.   E. S.

FŒNUS NAUTICUM. The requirements of maritime commerce induced the Romans to adopt from Greece a peculiar kind of contract of loan. This originally consisted in borrowing a sum of money to be taken by sea to a particular place for the purpose of buying merchandise there, the condition on which the contract depended being that, if the money was lost on the voyage by accidental perils of the sea, the borrower should not be bound to repay the lender. Money lent on such terms is called *trajecticia pecunia*, because of its being carried over the sea (*quia trans mare vehitur*). Subsequently the contract was extended, so that *trajecticia pecunia* included money lent to buy goods for export to a port agreed on, the repayment of the loan depending on the safe arrival of the goods there. Such goods were frequently pledged to the lender as security for the debt, but this was not necessary. Loans made for the purpose of repairing a ship, or for paying the crew their wages, were also brought under the same rule, the condition of repayment being the safe arrival of the ship at the port of destination. As in this contract the risk of accidental loss was on the lender, not on the borrower, as in ordinary cases, he was allowed to charge more than the ordinary legal rate of interest on money loans. The maximum rate of interest on account of *trajecticia pecunia* was fixed by Justinian at 12 per cent. The technical term for interest on such a loan is *fœnus nauticum* (see BOTTOMRY). It was treated as innocent even by the CANON LAW.   E. A. W.

FOLKES, MARTIN (died 1754), wrote *Tables of English Gold and Silver Coins, with their Weights, Intrinsic Values,* etc., London, 1745.

" A new and much improved edition of these valuable tables, illustrated with numerous plates of coins, edited by Dr. Andrew Gifford, was published in London, 1763." M'Culloch's *Lit. Pol. Ec.*

FOLKLAND was the surplus land which was not distributed to the free or dependent village communities when the English tribes conquered and settled in Britain. It must be carefully distinguished from the common lands which belonged to a community, but were not distributed among individuals (see ALOD). The folkland was regarded as the property of the tribe, and after the union of the tribes to the nation, it could be alienated to individuals by *boc* or charter granted by the king and his witan (see BOCLAND). It could also be let out to individuals on payment of a rent usually in kind, and these rents were collected by the sheriffs and formed part of the royal revenue. The above view has been held by all the chief authorities on the early constitutional history of England. But Prof. Vinogradoff, in an article in the *English Historical Review* for January 1893, has argued, with great force, that folkland does not mean the land of the folk, but land held by folkright, *i.e.* that it is the same as what the older authorities call alod or ethel (see FEORMFULTUM).

[Stubbs's *Constitutional History*, i.—Kemble, *Saxons in England*.]

R. L.

FONFRÈDE, HENRI (1788-1840), the son of a well-known Girondist member of the convention, was one of the most active journalistic writers of France during the first half of this century. His articles and essays, scattered in five or six different Bordeaux and Paris newspapers, were collected after his death and published in ten volumes (*Œuvres de Henri Fonfrède*, Paris and Bordeaux, 1844-48). The volumes seven and eight, entitled *Questions d'Économie Publique*, contain his economic writings, and one of them, *Le Système Prohibitif*, a luminous and incisive plea in favour of free trade, was republished as a pamphlet in 1846 by the *Association pour la Liberté des Échanges*. Fonfrède, very independent in his views, remained throughout his life a steady opponent of the conversion of public debts ("there is no more reason for a *maximum* price of 100 francs for public stock than for the same *maximum* price for coffee"—vi. p. 227), of sinking funds ("is it not mere folly to pay off in order to borrow, and to borrow in order to pay off?" *Système Prohib.*, p. 61), of Algerian colonisation, of commercial and administrative centralisation in Paris, and of government measures proposed to facilitate the raising of money on landed securities ("Every attempt to render land more fluid is an intense political and economic mistake. Land must be made easy to divide, not easy to mobilise."—vii. p. 231). E. CA.

FONTANELLI, CARLO (died 1886, at Florence), was professor of political economy at the Scuola di Scienze Sociali in Florence. Author of—

Manuale popolare di Economia sociale, Firenze, 1870, 2nd ed. 1881; *Gli scioperi*, Napoli, 1874-75.

A. B.

FONTEYRAUD, ALCIDE (1822-1849), born in the island of Mauritius, died at Paris. He became at a very early age a teacher in the higher commercial school under Blanqui, whose pupil he had been. Political economy soon absorbed him, and after March 1845 he was placed on the staff of the *Journal des économistes*. In January 1846, the *Revue britannique* published an article by him entitled "La ligue anglaise" (Anti-corn law league), which brought him into the notice he so well deserved. After this Messrs. Guillaumin entrusted him with annotating and preparing for publication the works of David Ricardo (vol. xiii. *Collection des Principaux Économistes*), which appeared in 1847. Fonteyraud was enabled, through his perfect knowledge of the English language, to translate the works of that economist, which up to that time had never appeared in French, and also to revise the translation made by Constancio. Fonteyraud wrote at the commencement of this volume, which is occupied entirely with the works of Ricardo and notes made on them by J. B. Say and others, a brilliant and interesting notice of the great English economist, who up to that time had been but little understood on the continent. He also translated the *Definitions in Political Economy* by Malthus. He finally wrote for the collection *Encyclopédie des connaissances utiles, Principes d'économie politique* (8vo, 1849). L. Wolowski had no hesitation in endorsing the opinions expressed in this volume. Fonteyraud was removed by cholera at the age of twenty-seven years from the study of that science to which, had it not been for his premature death, he would doubtless have rendered signal services. His principal works were collected by Joseph Garnier and published with a notice from the pen of that writer, under the title of *Mélanges d'économie politique*, 1 vol. 8vo, 1853.

A. C. F.

FOOD-RENTS existed in Anglo-Saxon and earlier manorial times side by side with rents in labour and in money. They were included under the general name of *gafol*, tribute, which comprised other payments of produce besides actual food ; and they were payable by freemen as well as serfs, in contradistinction to the labour services known as week-work which were usually a mark of villein status. The food-rents paid to the lord of the manor may be connected in origin with the FEORM-FULTUM and the later PURVEYANCE (*q.v.*), payable for the use of the king and his court ; they may perhaps be considered as taxes or exactions rather than as economic rents. Owing to the frequent absence of the lord these rents would be commuted for money earlier than labour rents, which could be paid just as conveniently in the lord's absence as during his residence on the manor ; and it is pretty certain that the free tenants who paid rents in kind did become money-paying tenants earlier than the serfs who owed week-work as well as produce. The commutation was general by the 14th century, but the dates of the stages of the process cannot be exactly given as payments in kind are found mixed, apparently without system, with original and commuted money payments in most statements of manorial services and rent drawn up before that time. The commonest articles of food paid by the tenants were poultry and eggs, but oats, barley, malt, ale, sheep, pigs, meat, loaves, honey, occur often ; evidently the manorial household expected to be provisioned by the tenants, and it was not uncommon for a definite part of the estate, the lands, for instance, of a monastic house, to undertake such provisioning for a week, a fortnight, or some other fixed time. The growing need for money helped to put an end to such rents as well as to labour dues.

[Seebohm, *English Village Community*, 1883.— Vinogradoff, *Villainage in England*, 1892.]

E. G. P.

FOOD, TAXES ON. These were common in

the 18th century, in the form of duties on flour, bread, and meat (*Wealth of Nations*, bk. v. ch. ii. pt. ii. art. iv.). They have now disappeared as general internal taxes, the last instance being the Italian Grist Tax (see MACINATO). They still exist as CUSTOMS DUTIES (see also CORN LAWS), and also make a part of local taxation in France and Italy (see OCTROI ; SALT DUTIES). In theory they may be treated as one division of taxes on necessaries. The general discussion of their effect belongs to TAXATION (*q.v.*).   C. F. B.

FORBONNAIS, FRANÇOIS VÉRON DE (1722-1800), born at Mans, died at Paris. Though he never occupied any official position or received any appointment equal to his merits, Forbonnais exercised a great influence over his contemporaries. He came of a respectable business family, and began life in retail trade ; he then travelled for five years, and afterwards improved his knowledge of affairs by studying the workings of business on a large scale at Nantes for the same period of time. By 1752 he considered his economic education sufficiently advanced to justify him in preparing a memorial on the position of public affairs which he then presented to the controller-general of Finance, an office filled at that time by J. B. de Machault, a financier of high ability. Through an unfortunate accident his memorial was not read, and its author became discouraged. Forbonnais then resolved to address himself directly to the public, and he printed a great number of works of which we can only mention the most important. These are *Considérations sur les finances d'Espagne*, 1753, 1 vol. 12mo ; *Éléments du commerce*, 1754 and 1796, 2 vols. 12mo ; *Recherches et considérations sur les finances de France depuis 1595 jusqu'en 1721 ;* Bâle, 2 vols. 4to, and Liège, 6 vols. 12mo, 1750 ; *Principes et observations économiques*, 1767, 2 vols. 12mo (reproduced in Guillaumin's collection of the principal economists) ; and finally *Observations succinctes sur l'émission de deux milliards d'assignats* 1790, 1 vol. in 12mo. Forbonnais was never able to free himself from the errors of the mercantile system, and shows himself favourable to the theory of the balance of trade. Besides this he was a protectionist, although he considered that the rate of duty, beyond which no branch of industry had any rights to existence at the cost of the consumer, should be limited to 15 per cent. How many ministers in our own days would be excused by the supporters of free trade if they would only restrict their demands to this scale ! Forbonnais, however, showed himself in other respects so sound an economist and financier, and so distinctly opposed to all crotchets, that he has left behind him a well-deserved reputation. His works are read and quoted even at the present day. He was consulted by all the influential politicians,

and by all the great administrators of his time. Silhouette placed him at the head of his office in 1759 ; Forbonnais had at that time filled the office of inspector-general of the mint for three years. Causes which were entirely honourable to himself caused disagreements between him and Madame de Pompadour, and he was sent to reside in exile on his estates. One of his unquestioned merits consists in having endeavoured to apportion the incidence of public taxation equally among all classes. Forbonnais did not solicit office in 1789, contenting himself with writing many detached papers, still in manuscript, on economic subjects. He controverted the doctrines of the physiocrats, but, it must be admitted, without seriously impugning their arguments. Forbonnais was admitted to the Institute in 1794 and died six years after, leaving behind him the reputation of a man conscientious and sincere, whose judgment was of the highest delicacy, who was an indefatigable worker of a frank and vigorous temperament.   A. C. f.

FORCED CURRENCY usually implies two attributes : it must be received as legal tender ; it need not be cashed on presentation. As Prof. Walker points out, the character of force may exist even in the absence of the first attribute,—for instance, money "may not be made legal tender, but all remedy at law may be taken away from creditors who refuse to receive it." It is argued that the silver currency of India is in this position at the present time (1894).

For other incidents, and for examples of forced currency, see INCONVERTIBLE CURRENCY.
                                                F. Y. E.

FORCED LABOUR, COMMON CHARACTERISTICS OF. In the articles on CONSCRIPTION ; CORVÉE ; ENFRANCHISEMENT ; IMPRESSMENT ; MANOR ; SERF ; SLAVERY, will be found details relating to the principal ways in which forced labour has come into prominence at various stages in the history of society. Here it is proposed only to deal with the common characteristics of these systems of labour. One classification may divide the subject into two branches. Forced labour may be either an industrial phenomenon or a financial one. Slavery and the kindred institution of serfdom arise in the relations between individuals ; corvée and conscription, and all other methods by which the state exacts unpaid labour from the citizen, are, apart from political considerations, rather in the nature of financial expedients. Similar economic disadvantages are found in both these classes, although the second is to some extent free from the moral stigma attached to the first class. An important disadvantage is that the labour is more inefficient than paid labour, and less susceptible of control and organisation. The labourer naturally treats the doing of the work, and not the efficiency of it, as the main thing that concerns him, and any relaxation in the method of compulsion employed may result in the labourer's abandoning his task altogether. The *Report of the Poor Law Commissioners of 1834*, ch. iv., shows how difficult it was found to compel the paupers to work on the roads by way of task work. Many authorities have insisted upon the greater cost of slave labour as compared with free, and the necessity of supervision and management entailed by its use. Even in the case of the forced labour exacted from jurymen, the quality of the work is found to be inferior, in spite of the fact that an effort is made to impress the juror with a sense not only of the responsibility but also of the dignity of his position. Where, however, a moderate degree of labour is demanded for purposes of obvious public advantage from fairly enlightened citizens the system may succeed. In the early history of the Canadian colonies the statute labour exacted for the repair and construction of roads was willingly contributed, and men were even found ready to work beyond the time demanded of them. It need scarcely be pointed out that these conditions are not likely to be often discovered in any ordinary industrial system based upon forced labour.

Forced labour has been employed in many countries for penal purposes ; and in England it is frequently used in the administration of the poor law as a test of real destitution. Secondary effects have been supposed to be produced in this way on the labour market, and it has been alleged that the wages of unskilled labour have been depressed by the competition of prisons in the same trade ; for the questions arising hence see PRISON LABOUR; WORKHOUSES. C. G. C.

FORCED LABOUR, instances of. Egypt affords in the Great Pyramid the earliest example of the employment of such labour. According to Herodotus (bk. ii. ch. 124), Cheops "closed the temples, and forbade the Egyptians to offer sacrifice, compelling them instead to labour, one and all, in his service . . . 100,000 men laboured constantly, and were relieved every three months by a fresh lot. It took ten years' oppression of the people to make the causeway for the conveyance of the stones. . . . The Pyramid itself was twenty years in building." But if we accept the conjecture of Mr. W. M. Flinders Petrie (*The Pyramids and Temples of Gizeh*, 1885), that the work of transport of the stones had only to be performed each year during the three months of inundation, when the land was under water and the inhabitants were necessarily almost idle, the hardship of thus requisitioning the labour of the people in a great measure disappears.

Coming to modern times, we find in the CORVÉE (*q.v.*) the general application of forced labour to the construction and maintenance of roads. In England, statute labour, as it was called, finally disappeared in 1835, but in France the *corvée*, in its modified form of PRESTATION (*q.v.*), still exists as an effective working system. The municipal council having, in exercise of the law of 21st May 1836, voted three days' *prestation*, every inhabitant of the commune between the ages of eighteen and sixty who has elected to work in lieu of making a money payment, is called on to attend at a convenient period fixed by the prefect. The work, usually breaking and carrying stone, may be performed by the day or piece, the latter method being favoured by the authorities as giving more satisfactory results. The money payment, which may be substituted for *prestation en nature*, is fixed annually by the departmental assemblies, and is always below the real value of a day's work. But the peasants for the most part prefer to give their labour rather than their money, 65 per cent of the total value (57,000,000 frs.— say £2,280,000) of the three days' *prestation* in 1888 being acquitted *en nature*. The proportion thus acquitted has, however, steadily decreased from 81 per cent, the average for the decade 1837-46. It is estimated that one-tenth of the cost of the work is saved by the system of *prestation* as compared with the employment of contractors. The system is often attacked as a survival of the hated *corvée*, but in 1888 sixty-seven of the departmental assemblies were in favour of its maintenance (Say et Chailley, *Nouveau Dictionnaire d'Économie Politique*, 1891).

If we except the system of *prestation* now existing in France, we must turn to Egypt for the last as well as the first chapter in the history of forced labour. From the earliest time it is probable that the irrigation canals were made and kept in repair by the forced unpaid labour of the Egyptian people. Theoretically speaking, there was no great objection to this, for the very life of the country has always depended on the maintenance of the means of irrigation. Until the present century the land yielded only one crop a year, sown as the Nile water receded in November, and requiring little attention till reaped in April. The agricultural labourer had little to do at other seasons, and could not be better employed than in clearing out the canals leading to his fields and repairing the Nile embankments which defended him from inundation. Therefore, though it cannot be supposed that the burden of the *corvée* was fairly apportioned, or that the rich took their just share with the poor, the evil was not a very crying one. But the introduction of cotton and sugar-cane cultivation caused an important change. These crops require to be moderately watered all round the year, and for their culture a system of summer canals had to be dug, so deep as to take in water at the lowest Nile. These canals were yearly choked with the mud deposit of the Nile flood, and for miles of their course had to be cleared, the depth of silt being as great as from 6 to 10 feet. For this purpose, the *corvée* was annually called out, and as the Khedive and other large proprietors generally evaded their liability to furnish men, the burden of the work, which was far heavier than any previously required, fell on the poor, and this at a period of the year when their time had become valuable to themselves. Thousands of persons were forced to work for five or six months in the year, without pay or any provision of food, without proper tools, often far away from their homes, and on canals from which they could themselves derive no advantage. In the years 1878, 1879, and 1880, it is estimated that 188,000 men were summoned to the works. In 1883, the *corvée* was equivalent to an army of 202,650 men working for 100 days. This was the last year of the old *régime*, for in 1884 the irrigation service was placed in the hands of English engineers. Partly owing to improved methods of regulating the Nile waters, whereby the quantity of silt was diminished, and partly to the expenditure of £73,461 in payment for work done by contract, the *corvée* in 1884 was reduced to the equivalent of 165,000 men for 100 days, and in 1885, with an outlay of £116,535, a further reduction to 125,936 men was effected. Part of this last-mentioned sum was provided under a scheme, whereby the *corvéables* in certain districts were allowed to redeem themselves by a money payment. An immense increase in the cotton cultivated in these villages followed.

The evils of the *corvée* system, and the great economic advantages that would ensue from its abolition, were so strongly recognised by the new Ministry of Public Works that in 1885 they proposed that a sum of £250,000 net, which had been decreed for the reduction of the land tax, should be applied instead in abolishing the *corvée* as far as possible, such an application being considered as really the best method of relieving the burdens on land. It was estimated that the whole work of clearing the canals would cost, by contract, about £400,000 a year, so that a moderate *corvée* would still be necessary after expending the available sum. The proposal was adopted ; the numbers employed were reduced to 95,093 in 1886, 87,120 in 1887, and 58,788 in 1888. The beneficial effects of the change were so apparent that the total abolition of the *corvée* was at once generally demanded. A further sum of £150,000 was required, and in December 1889 the National Assembly, although composed almost entirely of landlords, without a dissentient voice passed a measure imposing a special tax on land to raise that amount. The new tax was, as a matter of fact, never levied,

the needful fund being eventually provided out of savings from conversion of debt.

In 1890 the *corvée* in Egypt, as a regular system of forced labour for the execution of public works, thus ceased to exist. A large annual levy of men, it is true, is still made to guard and, in the event of a breach, to repair the Nile banks during the season of flood ; but every fellah feels a direct interest in this duty, and the obligation to perform it is not a hardship at all comparable to the tremendous labour of clearing the canals, to say nothing of the hundred and one illegitimate objects for which the *corvée*, now suppressed, was formerly employed (Milner's *England in Egypt*, 1892.—Blue Books, Egypt, 1886-91.—Sir C. Scott Moncrieff's *Irrigation Reports*, 1884-88).

The Suez Canal having been projected at a time when the *corvée* was in full operation in Egypt, it is not surprising that forced labour should have been largely employed in its construction. By a contract entered into with M. de Lesseps in July 1856, the Viceroy, Mohammed-Saïd Pasha, engaged that workmen should be supplied by the Egyptian government, on the demand of the chief engineers of the canal, at wages to be fixed according to the average rate paid in the country by private individuals. The wages actually paid being, however, far below the market value of the work, the arrangement was very economical as far as the company was concerned, and between 20,000 and 30,000 men (at one time 80,000) were pressed into the service. This compulsory employment of the natives gave rise to remonstrances in the English House of Commons, based on humanitarian grounds, and partly on this account and partly because the men were withdrawn from cultivating his own lands, the successor to Saïd Pasha, Ismaïl, was anxious to retire from the obligation of finding forced labour for the company. Consequently, by diplomatic note of 6th April 1863, the Porte, "seeing in the stipulations for the providing of workmen a contravention of the laws under which the Ottoman Empire is governed," declared its opposition to the continuance of the works. This determination was a great blow to the company, which now had to engage European labour as well as the voluntary services of the natives. The result was to more than treble the cost of excavation. As compensation for the loss entailed by the withdrawal of the forced labour, the Egyptian government, on the award of the Emperor of the French acting as arbitrator, paid the company 38,000,000 frs. (say £1,520,000). It may be added that the note of the Porte did not prevent the Viceroy from continuing the long-established custom of employing forced labour without pay in the cultivation of the vice-regal lands, and that the gross abuses arising under this system only came to an end when, under the British occupation, the lands themselves passed from the control of the Viceroy (Percy Fitzgerald, *The Great Canal at Suez*, 1876).

The history of forced labour in Egypt illustrates in a striking manner the theoretical justification of the system, its economical advantages when legitimately used, and the economic loss arising from its abuse. It is capable of defence on the same grounds as compulsory military service, when used for purposes with which the vital interests of the nation are bound up. Where money is scarce, it may be less burdensome than taxation to effect the same objects, and certainly is so where the labourers subject to it would otherwise be idle. But the system becomes oppressive and economically wasteful when the burden falls on a busy population, and the service entails the removal of the labourer, especially for a lengthened period, from his own proper work. Generally speaking, a man's labour in his own fields and at his own direction is economically more valuable than the same labour applied to objects in which his interest is less direct and in which he is under official control. There is no doubt that where forced labour, even for indispensable public works, involves a considerable interruption of the natural course of industry, it is in the long run more costly than taxation to ensure the same purposes [see CORVÉE; PRESTATION].   F. A.

FORD, SIR EDWARD (1605-1670), proposed the issue of exchequer bills in *Experimented Proposals how the King may have Money to pay and maintain his Fleets with ease to his People*, etc., London, 1666, 8vo, reprinted in the *Harleian Misc.*, 1744 (vol. iv.) and 1808 (vol. vii. 8vo, and vol. iv. 4to). He also published *A Demonstration that Farthings are as necessary as bread for most of the People; And that Farthings of an intrinsic value are useless and deceitful*. n.d. and *A design for bringing a navigable river from Rickmanswort in Hartfordshire to St. Gyles in the fields*, etc., London, 1641, 4to. Sir W. Roberts published in the same year an *Answer to Mr. Ford's book entitled a Designe*, etc. and both pamphlets were reprinted in 1720.

[Full details of Ford's life are given in the *Dictionary of National Biography*.] W. A. S. H.

FORECLOSURE. The extinguishment by the decree of a court of an equity of redemption (see EQUITY OF REDEMPTION).   J. E. C. M.

FOREIGN DIVIDENDS is a term correlative to FOREIGN INVESTMENTS (*q.v.*). By a dividend something more than mere interest is implied: it may be held to cover some special risk as well as what are constructively earnings of management (cp. Professor Marshall's *Economics of Industry*, VI. vi. § 4 *seq.* on net and gross interest). Under "foreign," in this connection, we include every dividend earned by members of a community in places external to the community. We include the interest on private investments abroad as well as that on shares of public companies and government loans. In the case of England we should in-

clude dividends accruing from the colonies as well as those accruing from foreign countries. There is no country in which such dividends are so important as England. This fact goes a long way towards explaining our excess of imports (cp. article on COMMERCE). In 1891, when the excess of imports was £126,327,546, the amounts due to us from abroad were from £75,000,000 to £85,000,000.

A little consideration will show that all such dividends must eventually be paid by means of the importation of commodities. They are distributed by the agency of banks and financial houses, which are placed in funds by bills of exchange. The fact that importers have these bills to sell implies that they have to pay for commodities coming from abroad; or, to put it perhaps more accurately, parties abroad who have to pay interest on borrowed capital can only pay it by shipping bullion or commodities, and they use the ordinary methods of adjusting mercantile accounts. There is no real difference between the bill of exchange used for these payments and that used for settling ordinary debts between merchants. In the latter case the bills practically pass from importers to exporters or *vice versa*. In the case of dividend payments they pass from the importers to the bankers, as representative of the sources of invested capital. The actual payments are by commodities, of which bullion is only a small fraction. On an average of three years, ending with 1891, the annual importation of bullion and specie was £33,584,788, its exportation £29,171,497. In that year the dividends receivable on the foreign investments of England may safely be placed at least at £75,000,000. This is sufficient to prove our point.

Mr. Phipson's book, *The Redemption of Labour*, vol. ii., seeks to draw a distinction between true and spurious dividends. The reasoning in that work is undermined with fallacies, and the conclusions cannot be accepted. Nevertheless, one point of some value is suggested, viz.: that the majority of payments received from abroad are raised by taxation and not earned as dividends proper. This is a distinction which hardly concerns the receiving country; although there is no doubt that the objects of British colonial loans are more and more scrutinised as each issue is made, since there is a very definite sense amongst investors that productive expenditure of the loan is a guarantee of their dividends.   O. A. H.

FOREIGN EXCHANGES, see EXCHANGES, FOREIGN.

FOREIGN INVESTMENTS. In this connection we use "foreign" in its original sense as meaning outside the territorial area which, for the time being, is under discussion. Probably few countries are without some investment of capital outside their own limits. We do not include capital taken out of the country by the settler, which is his own property; that becomes part of the capital of the community to which it is transferred. The term indicates capital belonging to persons resident in any given territory but employed by other persons outside that territory; and it includes, of course, the acknowledgments for capital which has been so employed, and forms a debt from those who enjoyed its use to the lenders. Thus the debts of foreign states, as well as the capital of companies operating abroad, and capital lent by individuals to persons at work abroad, form the sum total of foreign investments.

No country in the world has such a mass of such investments as the United Kingdom—whether in its own dependencies or in foreign countries, usually so called. The following table gives some idea of their amount :—

Colonial Government Securities .	£225,000,000
Foreign Stocks and Bonds . .	525,000,000
Railways in British Possessions .	75,000,000
„ India . . .	65,000,000
„ America . .	120,500,000
„ Foreign Countries .	127,500,000
Banks Operating Abroad . .	50,000,000
Foreign Breweries . . .	3,500,000
Colonial and Foreign Corporation Stocks	20,000,000
Gas Companies Operating Abroad	6,500,000
Iron Companies Operating Abroad	500,000
Land and Mortgage Companies .	100,000,000
Tea Companies . . .	2,500,000
Telegraph Companies . .	10,000,000
Waterworks Companies Operating Abroad	3,000,000
Tramway Companies Operating Abroad	4,000,000
Mines—Colonial and Foreign .	30,000,000
Miscellaneous Companies—Colonial and Foreign	30,000,000
Bank Deposits, say . .	50,000,000
Private Investments . .	250,000,000
Total .	£1,698,000,000

The amounts above given with the exception of the amount of the private investments, are arrived at from the stock exchange daily list for the beginning of January 1893, by estimating what proportion of each class of security is held in this country. For this purpose the best expert information has been sought. The proportion varies in several cases. About seven-eighths of the colonial stocks are held in Great Britain; of some foreign stocks hardly any, but on the whole range of those quoted in London it has been thought safe to estimate three-fourths as held here; of American railways, beyond the gold bonds, in spite of occasional bouts of speculation, but a small proportion is held in England, although more than we were at first inclined to think. As a general rule. it may be stated that from two-thirds to three-fourths of the other classes of securities quoted on the London stock exchange are held in this country. Only a small proportion

of bank deposits in the colonies and elsewhere is taken as belonging to this country; the majority probably belongs to *bona fide* colonists or is not actually invested.

To private investments we have less guide. We know generally that large sums are invested in the management of estates and the conduct of businesses, and by way of mortgage and otherwise, throughout all the colonies as well as in foreign countries. We have Mr. Lubbock's estimate of West Indian property alone, almost all of which is held in England, as over £30,000,000. Mr. Giffen placed the amount of foreign investments which escaped income tax in 1885 at £500,000,000. It is clear that this figure includes many public companies, but he speaks of "immense investment in private channels." It is highly probable that the amount is not less than the aggregate of banking deposits, land companies, and miscellaneous companies, and that half of Mr. Giffen's figure, above quoted, is a very modest computation.

In his *Growth of Capital*, from which we quote, Mr. Giffen speaks of the foreign investments of Great Britain in 1885 as being £1,300,000,000, but his detailed estimate of the income of the nation derived from public sources abroad, above £85,000,000, implies a higher figure, for at fifteen years' purchase this would give nearly £1,300,000,000 for public investment alone, and twenty years' purchase is the rate he elsewhere adopts for capitalising this income. However, capitalising the £85,000,000 at fifteen years' purchase, and adding £200,000,000 for private investments, we should make the amount of foreign investments in 1885 to be over £1,475,000,000. Consequently our figure of £1,700,000,000 for 1892 may be considered moderate, showing an increase of only £225,000,000 in seven years. This figure gives the same annual rate of increase as that adopted by Mr. Giffen in another part of his book, and we should have expected a higher proportionate rate.

Interesting statistics as to the growth of foreign indebtedness to England will be found in *Fenn on the Funds*. The editor states that between 1862 and 1872 the external borrowings of foreign states quadrupled, and that the mass of these loans was raised in London or Paris; and some index to the growth of the obligation is found in the capital amounts of foreign securities quoted in successive decades in the stock exchange, viz. :—

January 1862 .	.	£143,930,000
„ 1872 .	.	600,000,000
„ 1882 .	.	830,000,000

Similarly, Mr. Giffen computes that between 1865 and 1875 miscellaneous foreign investments increased fourfold, and he makes the increase in those which pay income-tax between 1875 and 1885 at least £320,000,000, explaining that, in the latter decade, the actual new issues of colonial and foreign government loans, municipal loans, and railways, amounted to £361,800,000. It is hardly wise to give more than such indications of growth. To approximate to an accurate proportion of the annual increase in the past it would be necessary to have figures for many years back made up exactly on the same principle. These hardly exist, except, perhaps, in Mr. Giffen's hands, but we may accept, as a minimum, that some £30,000,000 a year are invested abroad.

In our estimate above, of course, no notice has been taken of lost capital, which has a very large place in the history of foreign investment. We have regarded only that which has at least the potentiality of a dividend. We reckon that it is fair to compute the interest at $4\frac{1}{2}$ per cent on the average. This would give an annual produce of £76,500,000, a figure which comes curiously near to the £75,000,000 assumed in the article on COMMERCE (q.v.) as the proportion of the excess of imports represented by the interest on capital invested abroad. (See also INVESTMENTS.)

[See Giffen's *Growth of Capital*, 1889, pp. 26, 27, 40, 41 app.—Burdett's *Official Intelligencer*, iv. p. 13.—*Investor's Monthly Manual*, etc.]

C. A. H.

FOREIGN LABOUR. International migration of labour on a large scale is a marked characteristic of the present day. This movement was never contemplated by the older writers on political economy. Capital and labour alike were believed to be extremely tenacious of their native soil and averse to transplantation into foreign lands. But in our time capital and labour display a wonderful mobility, and the economic situation has in some instances been gravely affected by the transfer of vast bodies of producing agents from one country to another. The figures in the Blue-Book on the Emigration and Immigration of Foreigners (1888-89) show how large an amount of labour is now migratory in character. By reason of the proportions it has attained, various states have of late taken steps to regulate the immigrant labour-market, and in some instances have imposed on it harsh and inhospitable restraints. The evidence contained in the blue-book above referred to and the mass of material collected by the Committee of the House of Lords on the Sweating System (cp. Blue-Book on Sweating System, 1888-89) supply much useful information regarding the amount of immigrant labour and its effect on domestic industry. For further details see *Labour and Life of the People*, London (East), edited by Mr. Charles Booth, 1889.

It is not proposed here to investigate the number of aliens that arrive in this country, as that subject will be more fitly considered under the head of IMMIGRATION (q.v.).

The better class of immigrant only crosses this country on the way to other lands. Large bodies of aliens arrive every year, for example, *en route* for America. But the poorest and worst type of foreigner remains here, either permanently or for a considerable period.

The trades which these foreign workmen chiefly undertake are baking, boot and shoe making, cabinetmaking, tailoring, and also such minor industries as cigar-making, fur-cap making, and ostrich-feather cleaning. Moreover, fifty thousand aliens—including lascars and Asiatics in the Indian trade—are said to be working in vessels that fly the British flag, and to be in demand as being more sober and amenable to discipline than Englishmen (see Mr. Glover's paper before Statistical Society, March 1892, "Tonnage Statistics of the Decade 1880-1890"). And a considerable number of Germans are engaged as domestic servants. To appreciate the economic situation, it will be necessary to see in what branches of the principal industries foreign and domestic labour come into contact.

Baking.—No trustworthy statistics exist at present regarding the number either of natives or aliens employed in the provinces, but in London the master bakers are estimated at three thousand, and the operatives at ten thousand or more, one half of the masters and fully that proportion of the men being Germans. The evidence given before the Royal Commission of Labour, Group C, 12th August 1892, showed that in many cases the foreign immigrant was boarded and lodged by a fellow-countryman and taught the trade, until, by thrift and perseverance, he himself became a small master. The better class of immigrant works in bakeries where "Vienna" bread is made, earns good wages, and holds aloof from trade societies. A lower type of alien supplies foreigners and Jews in East London, and often belongs to the Amalgamated Union of Bakers and Confectioners. Few foreigners, if any, compete in the wholesale business, nor does foreign competition seem to have seriously affected wages throughout the trade.

Boot and Shoe making.—In the boot and shoe trade of East London 25 per cent of those engaged are stated to be foreigners, and in number over ten thousand persons. No statistics are available as to the proportion of aliens now at work in other parts of the kingdom.

In the machine-sewn trade, the greater portion of what is known as "finishing" is in the metropolis monopolised by foreign workmen. For details see Mr. Booth's book above cited, pp. 274 *seq.* Mr. David F. Schloss, an authority on the subject, maintains that the unskilled labour of the "sweated" Jews in the "finishing" department leads to a considerable increase of employment on the part of a large body of well-paid and skilled English workers.

The boot clickers and closers, for example, the tanners and others employed in the leather trade, are all Englishmen in receipt of fairly good wages and subject to reasonable hours of work.

In the class of goods known as "sew-rounds," *i.e.* fancy shoes and slippers, the better class of work is almost entirely in English hands, but the inferior work is made chiefly by Jewish work-people. Speaking generally it is alleged that, within the last ten or fifteen years, foreign Jews have gradually secured the commoner class of work in which native workmen generally learnt their trade. Further allegations appear, in the Emigration and Immigration Blue-Book above referred to, to the effect that we are being injured in our foreign markets by the stuff produced by this cheap labour, a great portion of it being made of cardboard and composition. The statistics of the exports of boots and shoes from this country do not, however, bear out this contention.

Cabinetmaking. — It is said that of 23,000 persons employed in this trade in London 4000 are foreigners. Here there can be little doubt that the pressure of foreign immigration has not yet become acute. Although the average wages earned by the alien are somewhat lower than those of domestic labour, yet he has not imported into this industry a standard of life or of work economically degrading (for details, cp. Booth, p. 360 *seq.*)

Tailoring. — The ready-made clothing trade is very largely adopted by the immigrants, and Mr. Burnett, the labour correspondent of the Board of Trade, contemplates the time when this department will be entirely in their hands (cp. his Report on Sweating System, 1887). Eighteen or twenty thousand of them are stated by this authority to be employed in the manufacture of cheap clothing or "slops" in East London. Nor is the increase of foreign employment in the tailoring trade confined to London only ; it is proceeding likewise in Birmingham, Leeds, Manchester, Newcastle-on-Tyne, and Glasgow. The majority of these aliens are Russian, German, or Polish Jews, working, for the most part, under a Jewish contractor. Conflicting views prevail as to the extent to which this trade has been invaded by foreigners, and, in the absence of any recent census returns, all statements on this head must be received with caution. There is also a conflict of opinion whether the immigrants engaged in the cheap clothing business compete with English labour or not, some competent observers alleging that they chiefly compete with one another, and that if they compete at all with native workers it is in a trade which they themselves have created. The best opinion seems to be that, as regards the supply of ready-made clothing to wholesale houses, the actual competition lies between the staff of the Jewish contractor and domestic female labour employed in provincial factories. These factories, however, make little headway against the particular industry of "coat-making," a department of wholesale business which the Jewish operative practically monopolises. In this branch we find no contractors on a large scale, but a multitude of small masters who avail themselves of the necessities of the immigrant "greener"—as the alien is termed on his first arrival—to secure from him a day's work of indefinite duration at merely nominal wages. The social surroundings of these operatives are often deplorable, and the prices at which work is taken are constantly reduced by the fact that the alien hands have little desire or capacity for labour or trade combination, with a standard of life that admits of an enormous amount of toil under the worst possible conditions (cp. Booth's work, *supra*, p. 224 *seq.*).

We have now cleared the ground for the consideration of the attitude of economists towards foreign labour. The subject naturally falls into two branches.

a. First, the competition between native workers and foreigners, who work for a fair wage, with abilities equal and a social status not inferior to those whom they displace.

b. Next we are confronted with cheap labour supplied by aliens, who arrive in a more or less impoverished condition, and whose standard of existence is very low.

As to the class of competitors under head *a*, there can be no objection consistently raised, from an economic point of view, by those who are in favour of commercial freedom. Mr. Fawcett, in his treatise on *Free Trade and Protection*, 3rd ed., deprecates any attempt to restrict this class of worker. Where no moral disadvantage can result from the settlement amongst us of such workmen, an employer would undoubtedly be justified in making use of their services. To interfere with the importation of such labour would be opposed to all the best instincts of free trade. Can any distinction be drawn economically between the competition of labour and the competition of the products of labour ? Why should freedom to buy and sell be denied to those who have labour to dispose of ? Moreover, the denial of such a right would injuriously affect not only the parties immediately concerned, but also the public who purchase the industrial product.

Again the foreigner is often engaged on account of his superior qualifications, and not only because he is willing to sell his services at a cheaper rate. Thus German scientific men are secured by some of our large manufacturers, and so are German clerks, owing to their linguistic attainments ; while German bakers, whose knowledge of the processes of fermentation often exceeds that of Englishmen, readily find employment in English houses. Skilled mechanics from France and Italy have invaded some of our textile industries. So far from any valid objection lying against the importation of such workers, it is probable that they give a distinct spur and impetus to the advance of education in this country.

As an exception, however, to the general rule of non-interference, take the instance of labourers imported under contract to perform certain services in a foreign country. Here it has been argued that the native workman is injuriously affected, because the immigrant may be ignorant of the conditions prevailing in the labour market he is about to enter. Advantage may be taken of his ignorance to extort terms unfair both to him and to domestic labour. The government of the United States has passed a law to prevent contracts of this nature being enforced. Such action must not be viewed as an attempt to restrict immigration, but as an endeavour to protect the alien against the consequences of his own heedlessness, and to provide that the native worker shall not thereby suffer loss.

Passing on to head *b*, what attitude should the economist assume towards any attempt to fetter the introduction of cheap labour ? The advocates of *laissez-faire* base their attitude of non-intervention on the ground that "natural liberty" conduces best to the production of wealth. The business of the employer, they say, is to buy his labour in the cheapest market. If, by engaging Russian or Polish Jews, he lowers the cost of production, he ought to have full liberty to do so. Government should interfere as little as possible with the distribution of wealth resulting from free competition, because any such interference must tend to impair aggregate production more than it could increase the utility of the produce by a better distribution (cp. Sidgwick, *Principles of Political Economy*, 2nd ed. bk. iii. ch. ii., where this view of the question is stated). Enlightened self-interest on the part of the consumer will lead him to demand the commodities that are most useful to society, while self-interest will induce the producer to turn out these commodities at the least cost.

Setting aside for the moment the question of free competition and the alleged right of the consumer to secure at all hazards the cheapest article, a less sordid argument may be advanced in favour of non-interference with existing industrial conditions. The argument, it is true, only applies to one branch of trade, but it may be regarded as a representative one. A large section of the tailoring industry has, within the last thirty years, been transformed from a retail to a wholesale business. This transformation has rendered it impossible for the English journeyman tailor, apart altogether from the question of price, to compete with the contractor for orders from wholesale houses. The

organisers of Jewish labour in the metropolis are able to meet the demand of these houses—coming into competition, it is true, with provincial factories in certain directions, but, so far as the wholesale coat manufacture is concerned, supplying a want that under existing circumstances could not be otherwise satisfied, as pointed out in Mr. Booth's book, p. 235 *seq.* In connection with this aspect of the case attention should be paid to the enormous volume of export trade in ready-made clothing that has gradually been developed under the present system. The total export of the country under the head of "apparel and slops" has doubled itself within the last twenty years, and as regards the port of London, is 2½ times what it was. In 1868 the exports of these articles from the United Kingdom were £2,313,000, and from London only, £1,233,000. In 1888 the figures are : from the United Kingdom £4,658,000, from London only, £3,091,000. Now it may be taken for granted that, in default of her supply of cheap foreign labour, England, under prevailing industrial conditions, would be unable to keep up this export trade, and legislation by way of restriction upon immigration would simply have the result, to use the words of Mr. David F. Schloss, "of making a gift of our exports of 'slop' clothes to Germany, which already carries on a considerable foreign trade in these articles, and which, while her protective system excludes English material from the German market, would be only too ready to supplant us in all markets of the world by the substitution for English goods of garments made in Germany, by German cheap labour, and of German cloth." Is it better, in fine, to buy cheap clothes from the Continent or to make them here cheap, and export the surplus that you do not need ? Unless you forbid both the entry of cheap goods and cheap labour you will be in a worse plight than now, for, if you only forbid cheap labour, you may throw the cheap goods trade into other hands.

Let us now examine the position from another standpoint, whether the free competition of cheap immigrant labour with native workers may not diminish the volume of that aggregate industrial production to which all economists rightly attach so much importance. Mr. Gunton discusses in *Wealth and Progress*, 1887, ch. viii., at some detail, the action of wages on productive power. His conclusions, which should perhaps for the present be accepted with reserve until the question is more thoroughly considered, are that high wages in the long-run mean cheap products and low wages dear products. That high wages conduce to large consumption and large consumption introduces a more extensive use of capital with improved methods of production, and as a consequence always reduces prices. In a comparative table that deals with Great Britain and the principal continental countries, Mr. Gunton shows that wages are 84 per cent higher, the use of steam 117 per cent greater, and the cost of productive power 37 per cent less in England than on the average in continental countries. Moreover, this writer contends that a considerable amount of the social advance noticeable in Great Britain is due to her short-time industrial policy, and he enforces this proposition by a further table showing that in England—despite of shorter hours of toil—the increase in the average wages has been greater than in any nation of the Continent. Should these conclusions be sound, they will go far to sustain objections that have been made against the influx of cheap labour on the ground of its tending to impair the productive power of the community. May not the economist condemn the foreign colony in our midst as forming a barrier against the advance of a more productive industrial system ? (cp. Mr. David A. Wells, *Practical Economics*, New York, 1885). As an example of the way in which high-class machinery brings in its train high wages for operatives, reference is made by that writer to the action of certain English shoe-manufacturers, who have introduced American machinery, and who find that it pays them better to work these machines at wages which are at least double those paid to the shoemaker under the old hand-system. So also it appears that in Nottingham the introduction of more complex and costly machines for lace-making has, while economising labour, augmented wages to the extent of over 100 per cent.

From this aspect the influx of cheap foreign labour may be deemed to have had an evil effect in retarding the advent of more favourable conditions of production.

In justice to the impoverished immigrant, it is but fair to state that there is nothing definite to show that he tends directly to become a burden on the community. Even in Whitechapel—the portion of the metropolis where they chiefly reside—the number of aliens in receipt of parochial aid is infinitesimal. There is, however, evidence from certain localities, such as Hackney and Shoreditch, of an increase of pauperism due to the crowding out of English labour by foreign immigration. Moreover, the industrial position of the small Jew workshops tends to that irregularity of work which is by far the most serious trial under which the people of London suffer ; for the smaller the capital involved, and the less the permanent fixed charge for working a business, the better suited is it for irregular employment. The man who engages only two or three others in a workshop or in his own house, as is frequently the case with the petty Jew master, can, if work fails, send them all adrift to pick up a precarious living, but a large factory cannot stop at all without serious loss.

In attempting to estimate the effect of the influx of needy aliens on the social and moral condition of domestic workers, the following points present themselves.

The evidence contained in the blue-books above referred to shows that a large proportion of the Russian and Polish immigrants are exceedingly poor when they reach this country. Their mode of life here is wretched in the extreme, their houses being in a most insanitary state and their food of a scanty nature. They are generally an inoffensive race, moral in their habits, and capable of hard work in spite of an inferior physique. They are very industrious, toiling for long hours at low wages, and maintaining existence on much less than an English workman. Such are their characteristics, and we find it stated by the committee of the House of Commons that, in those trades which they follow, there has been, in consequence of their competition, a marked fall in wages and a tendency to reduce still lower than at present the social and material condition of our own poor.

It is alleged, moreover, that the lowest class of alien labourer exhibits an incapacity for, or an aversion to, anything in the shape of trade organisation. His early training, his social surroundings and subservient position, render the German, Russian, or Polish Jew generally unfitted for free combination, and he forms a serious obstacle to the onward march of labour in the industries affected by his immigration. Now increased combination amongst the workers stands first among the needs of the time. Trades unions have undoubtedly put the English workman on a better footing as regards his employers. In many cases they have raised the standard of comfort and increased the efficiency of the labourer. And it is claimed for them that their moral effects have been as surprising as their economical. To all this these aliens are for the most part indifferent, and they constitute an inert mass that bars the progress of reform in the inferior grades of the trades concerned.

It should be stated, however, that recent efforts to organise the Jewish aliens at work in the boot trade have met with some success, and two Jewish branches of the National Union of Boot and Shoe Operatives, viz. the "London City" and "London East," are now established in the metropolis.

To sum up the situation regarding foreign labour in this country, we arrive at the following conclusions. That against the better class of workmen, who take fair wages and compete on an equal footing with domestic labour, no valid objection exists. That, as regards the wholesale coat-industry, it cannot be justly demurred to on the ground of its competing with native produce, but lies open to the reproach of barring the path of industrial reform. That in the retail tailoring department the immigrants do injuriously affect the earnings of both English men and women. That in the lower class of boot and shoe making, the immigrants have appropriated work formerly executed by native operatives, but that it is open to doubt whether the aggregate domestic industry has suffered. That in cabinetmaking and the other minor trades in which they are found, the foreigners have not exercised any appreciable effect. That while there are grave objections from both an economic and social point of view to any large influx of impecunious aliens, the amount of immigration that has hitherto taken place does not call for any immediate action of a restrictive character.

[The bibliography of foreign labour is exceedingly scanty.

The evidence given before the Royal Commission of Labour (1891-92) and that contained in the blue book on *Emigration and Immigration of Foreigners* (1888-89), and on *The Sweating System* (1888-89) will repay careful perusal.— In Mr. Charles Booth's *Labour and Life of the People*, London, East (1889), the bearing of foreign labour upon certain selected trades is examined. Interesting details again are given in the *Report on the Sweating System*, 1887, compiled by Mr. Burnett. —Fawcett, in *Free Trade and Protection*, briefly alludes to imported labour, and so does Mr. Sidgwick in his *Principles of Political Economy*, pt. iii.—Mr. Gunton's *Wealth and Progress*, 1887, and Mr. David A. Wells's *Practical Economics*, New York, 1885, present many economic questions connected with the subject in a new light.

For an interesting account of the attitude of our colonies towards foreign labour, reference should be made to Dilke, *Problems of Greater Britain*, (1890). For American views cp. Report of Bureau of Statistics of Labour for the State of New York (1885). Also Report of the Bureau of Industrial Statistics . . . for State of Pennsylvania (1884), part iii. Industrial Statistics, and First Biennial Report of the Bureau of Labour Statistics of California, 1883-84.

Alien Immigration. Reports to the Board of Trade on Alien Immigration, Burnett and Schloss [c. 7113], 1893.] **S. N. F.**

FOREIGN LAW IN ENGLISH COURTS. There are many occasions on which English courts have to consider foreign law. This may occur with reference (1) to questions of personal status ; (2) to contracts ; (3) to questions as to the devolution of property after death ; (4) to questions relating to real property situate outside of England.

(1) Questions as to personal status (legitimacy, majority, guardianship, marriage and divorce) depend upon the DOMICILE (*q.v.*) of the person concerned, but this is subject to the condition that the "status" described in a certain way in a foreign country is really the same as the "status" described in the same way in England. Thus "a marriage which is not that of one

man and one woman, to the exclusion of all others, though it may pass by the name of a marriage, is not the status which the English law contemplates when dealing with the subject of marriage" (Sir Charles Butt in Brinkley *v.* Attorney-General, 15 Probate Division, on p. 79).

(2) The question what law governs a contract is frequently one of great difficulty. The general rule is that the law of the place where the contract is made ought to prevail in the absence of circumstances indicating a different intention (in *re* Missouri Steamship Co., 42 Ch. D. 321-326). As regards contracts of affreightment the well-known case of Lloyd *v.* Guibert (L. R. L. and B. 115) has established the rule that any questions relating to sea damage and its incidents are, subject to any contrary agreement between the parties, governed by the law of the country to which the ship belongs (see *The August* [91] Probate, 328).

(3) The devolution of personal property on death is regulated by the law of the testator's or intestate's DOMICILE (*q.v.*) at the time of his death ; on the other hand the devolution of real property is regulated by the law of the country in which it is situate. Thus an English court, in dealing with the personal property left by a domiciled Scotchman, will have to consider the claims of his wife and children before having regard to the dispositions made by his will, as, according to Scotch law, these rights to a share of the residuary estate cannot be defeated by any testamentary dispositions.

(4) The law of the country where real property is situate must be considered in any questions as to priorities of mortgages, transmutation of possession, and rights of execution creditors. English courts have of course no direct jurisdiction as to foreign land, but by their control over the person of a defendant residing within the jurisdiction, they may indirectly obtain the same results as would have been obtained directly by a judgment affecting the land (Penn *v.* Lord Baltimore, i. Vesey, sr. 444). When an English court has to decide any point according to foreign law, "the opinions of experts who in their profession are acquainted with such law are the only admissible evidence thereof" (Stephen, *Digest of the Law of Evidence*, art. 49). It should be borne in mind that the provisions of the foreign law are considered with the sole object of ascertaining the mutual rights of the parties, but that as regards the remedies for the enforcement of such rights English law must always prevail, *e.g.* a contract for personal services could according to some systems of foreign law be specifically enforced, but nothing beyond damages could be obtained in an English court in respect of such a contract. It must also be pointed out that an English court "will

not enforce a contract against the public policy of this country, wherever it may be made" (Rousillon v. Rousillon, 14 Ch. D. 351, 369). For this reason a contract in restraint of trade, though it may be governed by French law and be valid according to French law, will, if void according to English law, not be enforced by an English court (see RESTRAINT OF TRADE).

[Von Bar, *International Law*, translated by Gillespie, 2nd ed. 1892.—Foote, *Private International Jurisprudence*, 1890.—Westlake, *International Law*, 3rd ed. 1890.—Nelson, *Cases in Private International Law*, 1889.]   E. S.

FOREIGN TRADE, REGULATIONS OF. See TRADE, FOREIGN REGULATIONS of.

FOREIGN TRADERS AND THEIR RIGHTS, HISTORY OF.—In England, as in every other country during the middle ages, the position of the adventurous foreign trader landing on her shores was precarious. As a stranger he was without rights in the view of the ordinary law of the country unless particularly protected by royal license. Such licenses were granted in some cases to individuals, in others to the subjects of certain sovereigns or the inhabitants of certain cities or countries. Of the former nature was the general treaty entered into by Offa and Charles the Great (797) providing that the subjects of each should be held worthy of justice. Still later we find licenses granted with the apparent desire of encouraging foreign merchants, and even of foreign settlers. Thus John granted foreign merchants protection in coming and going both for themselves and for their wares, while among the provisions of the Magna Carta there are two (cc. 41, 42), which deal with their safe conduct and their necessary freedom from *mala tolta*. Under Henry I. colonies of Flemish weavers appear to have been settled in different parts of the land. Toward the end of the 11th and beginning of the 12th centuries two definite policies with reference to the treatment of foreign merchants had gradually developed themselves. The king and the nobles on the one hand saw that it was to the advantage of the kingdom to be brought into connection with the industries and activities of foreign nations. It is possible that they were assisted to the perception of this by the benefits obviously accruing to themselves. On the other hand the English traders resented the intrusion of their foreign rivals within the country. As a matter of fact at one time much of the internal trade of the country seemed likely to slip out of native and into foreign hands. As the towns grew in size and power it was only natural that these views should find more forcible expression. During the struggle between Henry III. and Simon de Montfort, the cause of the towns was warmly espoused by the latter, who, seeing farther into the future, urged that the nation should strive to make itself self-supporting by wearing cloth wrought within the country, and staying its exports of wool to Flanders. After the victory of the royalists the towns suffered a period of reverse.

During this period, extending with intermissions from 1272 to 1376, the foreign trader was treated with all possible consideration and even encouragement. The period may be divided into two parts, during the earlier of which (viz. in the reign of Edward I.) foreign traders were encouraged without any particular attempt being made to encourage the trade and industry of the country itself. No doubt Edward was partly actuated by hostility to the towns, and especially to London, on account of the opposition encountered from them both by his father and himself. Their complaints and requests were alike set aside. Their main demands were these (1) That the foreign traders should dwell in the house of a citizen. (2) That retail trade should be prohibited to them. (3) That their term of residence should be limited to forty days. These points, except the last, were refused by Edward I., who definitely supported the foreigners and assured them security. The Carta Mercatoria (1303) is practically a judgment in favour of the foreign traders on all counts. During the weak rule of Edward II. the towns were able to reassert themselves and to obtain acknowledgment of their claims. But when Edward III. began his effective reign the position changed. During this, the second, part of the period referred to, security and free rights etc. are guaranteed to the foreigners, but at the same time the policy of the king in encouraging home industry by prohibition on the export of wool and the import of foreign cloth, and by the settlement of foreign weavers in England who might instruct the English by their skill and example, averted the evil consequences which had seemed likely to ensue from the position which the foreign merchants had held and endeavoured to retain. England was ceasing to be merely a buyer of foreign goods and a source of supply for the wool required in foreign industries.

With the next period (1376-1461) a reaction in favour of the exclusive policy of the towns set in. In 1376 Edward III. made his peace with them by virtually affirming their demands in the points mentioned above, a course in which he is followed by his successors. The Lancastrians could ill afford to alienate popular support. In addition to legislation (as for instance 18 H. VI. c. 4) in the directions indicated, they added one provision of great interest in view of the later trade policy. Under Henry IV. (5 H. IV. c. 7), it was ordained that merchant strangers must spend what they obtain from the sale of the goods they bring on English goods of export. They are to export wares and not gold. Under Henry VI. (18 H. VI. c. 4) the foreign merchant was compelled to reside with an official host, who was responsible for his employing his receipts in purchasing English commodities. (Jones, *Pol. Econ.*, ed. Whewell, p. 310.)

Gradually much of the legislation with regard to merchant strangers became obsolete in practice. It was frequently re-enacted but difficult to maintain. The real danger against which it was aimed had passed by. Not only had English industry become strong but the enterprises of the staplers and the merchant adventurers (see ADVENTURERS, MERCHANT; STAPLE) had enabled the English to carry the war, as it were, into the country of the foreigners. They were pressing on to take their rightful share in the commerce of the world. From these and other causes the struggle of the later period under Richard III. and the early Tudors is not so much a struggle against the foreign trade in the more strict sense of the word, but against the intrusion of the stranger into the domain of industry.

[Schanz, *Engl. Handelspolitik.*—Macpherson, *Annals of Commerce;—Statutes at Large.*—Rymer's *Fœdera.*] E. C. K. G.

FORESHORE. That part of the shore which lies between ordinary and low water mark, that is to say, between high and low water mark at the time of neap tide. Till the reign of Queen Elizabeth no distinction seems to have been made between foreshore and seashore above high-water mark. About 1568 a certain Thomas Digges wrote a treatise entitled *Proof of the Queen's Interest in lands left by the Sea and the salt shores thereof*, in which he maintained the crown's right, in virtue of the royal prerogative, to all the foreshore; a right which could not be alienated except by express grant. On this theory the crown lawyers acted till the beginning of the 18th century, when the claims of the crown were gradually allowed to die. They were revived in 1830, when Hall published his *Essay on the rights of the Crown and the Privileges of the Subject in the Seashores of the Realm*. The law at present seems to be that foreshore may be parcel of an estate or manor, that title to it may be shown by prescription, and that possession or enjoyment for sixty years displaces whatever rights the crown may have.

[S. A. Moore, *History and Law of the Foreshore and Seashore*, London, 1888.] A. E. S.

FORESTALL. In the stock-exchange sense this verb, which is practically obsolete and is seldom used, is almost synonymous with the verb to bull, meaning the act of speculation for the rise. A speculator, or band of speculators, may foresee a rise in the price of certain securities or commodities. The operation begins by the quiet buying up of such securities or commodities in order to forestall the rise which is expected to take place, in consequence of the buying of the operators, backed up or not, as the case may be, by favouring events. A forestaller in this sense is simply a BULL (*q.v.*),

but opinion is divided as to the fairness of his operations. A. E.

FORESTALLERS AND REGRATORS. Together with regrating and engrossing, this signified the undue intervention of a middleman between the producer and consumer. Forestallers, regrators, and engrossers were viewed with disfavour, and their practices prohibited, because they were regarded as raising the price of commodities without adding to their value. In the act of 1551-52 (5 & 6 Edw. VI.), they are defined in the following terms: forestallers as "persons buying goods or victuals on their way to a market or port, or contracting to buy the same before actually brought for sale, or endeavouring by these or other means to enhance the price or prevent the supply"; regrators as "persons buying corn or other victuals, and reselling the same in the same market-place or in any other fair or market within four miles"; engrossers as "any buying corn growing, or any other corn, grain, butter, cheese, fish, or other dead victual, with intent to resell the same again." With regard to the foregoing definitions, the last names while describing the practice of the time, incorrectly restricts, so far as earlier times were concerned, the action of the engrosser to dealing with certain commodities. Regrating must be taken as the complete action embracing both forestalling and engrossing, which were particular stages in the action; but it is doubtful if any very definite discrimination was shown so far as the 13th and 14th centuries, in the use of the three terms. The practice they signify was condemned both because it might lead to monopoly, which was combated in its many forms, and because it resulted in unrighteous gains and enhancement of price. E. C. K. G.

Numerous English, Scotch, and Irish statutes have imposed heavy punishments on these offences, partly generally, partly in so far as they affect particular commodities (victuals, wines, cattle, butter and cheese, etc.), one of the earliest being the Statute of the Pillory of Henry III. (51 Hen. III. § 6—A.D. 1266), but they did not prove effectual, and some of the later English acts were, in 1772, repealed by 12 Geo. III. c. 71. As the older acts remained in force, and the judges, moreover, held that forestalling was an offence at common law as well as by statute, prosecutions continued down to 1800, in which year a person who, in the corn-market, bought wheat at 41s. and resold it to another dealer at 43s., was tried before Lord Kenyon and a jury (R. v. Rusby—Peake, Additional Nisi Prius Cases, 189). The judge refers to Adam Smith's observations on the subject, and holds that if that author "had lived to hear the evidence of to-day" he "would have seen whether such an offence exists and whether it is to be dreaded." It appears, however, that already in that case the judges were divided in opinion, and that no subsequent prosecutions took place. In 1844 "the offences of forestalling, regrating, and engrossing" were abolished by 7 & 8 Vict. c. 24, and cannot now form the subject of a prosecution in any part of the United Kingdom.

[*Statutes of the Realm.*—Macpherson, *Annals.* —Account of practice in Ashley's *Economic History.*—Cunningham, *Growth of English Industry and Commerce.*—Girdler, *Observns. on Forestalling, Regrating, and Ingrossing* (1800).—Dugald Stewart, *Political Economy.*—Stephen, *History of the Criminal Law*, iii. p. 200, and for a list of the repealed statutes, see 7 & 8 Vict. c. 24, § 2.] R. S.

FORESTS.

Forests have influenced the economic condition of countries and of their inhabitants in such widely different manners that it is desirable to indicate some of the leading branches of this subject.

As the hunting-grounds of monarchs and great nobles they were, during early and mediæval times, the occasion of severe and oppressive laws which lingered long in Europe, and vestiges of which may even now be traced at the present time. The article on FOREST, MEDIÆVAL, describes this part of the subject.

On the other hand the influence of forests on the climate of a country is very great. The article on FORESTS, ECONOMIC INFLUENCE OF, deals with this part of the question.

Forests, whether on hills or plains, are believed to promote the deposition of moisture from the atmosphere ; and they are certainly most beneficial in preventing the rapid evaporation of what is deposited. Vast areas of the globe, in both tropical and temperate zones, have been rendered more or less sterile through the destruction of these forests, being hence exposed to destructive floods in the rainy season and to excessive droughts in the dry.

As an illustration of this, reference may be made to the remarks of Gibbon (*Decline and Fall*, vol. i.) on the extent of woodland in Germany, temp. Cæsar and Tacitus, and its striking effect on the climate, which supported reindeer and elks. He draws an ingenious analogy with Canada on the same parallels as London but icebound and forest-covered, and argues that clearing the soil will enable the sun to penetrate it and fertilise it.

FORESTS, MEDIÆVAL (English forests as typical of mediæval forests generally).

The DIALOGUS DE SCACCARIO (i. 12) defines the king's forest as "a safe mansion for wild beasts ; not of any sort, but bred in the woods ; not in any places, but particular and proper ones for this purpose ; whence it is called forest, by changing the letter E into O, as *ferest :* that is, a station for wild beasts." The king has not a forest in every county, but "only in the wooded ones, where there are the best coverts and most fertile feedings for the beasts : neither does it matter to whom the woods belong, whether to the king or the nobles of the kingdom ; for the beasts are at their liberty to range uncontrolled over every part of them" (ed. Madox, p. 29).

According to Manwood, there are four chief properties of a forest—vert, venison, particular laws, and proper officers, but he quotes Coke as giving eight—soil, covert, laws, courts, judges, officers, game, bounds (4 *Inst.* 289).

Forest Courts. Under the Norman kings these seem to have been held by the foresters or keepers. In later times there were three forest courts, the court of Attachments, the Swanimote, and the Justice Seat.

I. *The Court of Attachments* is so called because it was held *ad videndum attachiamenta.* The Charter of the Forest (1217) provided that it should be held every forty days, and therefore it is sometimes called the Forty Days' Court. Before the charter, it was held very often at the will of the chief forest officers, and was called the Woodmote, in Shropshire, the Woodplea Court. At this court, which only dealt with injuries to vert or venison, the foresters brought attachments to the verderers who enrolled them. Cases were also referred from this court to the Swanimote.

Attachments in the Forest were of three kinds. 1. By goods and chattels. 2. By the body with pledges and mainprise. 3. By the body without pledges.

II. *The Swanimote.* The pleas in this court were called pleas of the forest, and the verderers were the proper judges. Before the Charter of the Forest the chief wardens and foresters held it at any time, and oppressed the people greatly by compelling them to attend it. By the Charter of the Forest (c. 8) it was to be held only three times in the year. 1. Fifteen days before Michaelmas, when the agistors of the king's woods met to take agistments. 2. About St. Martin's Day in winter, when they received pannage. In these two courts only the foresters, verderers, and agistors had jurisdiction. 3. Fifteen days before St. John Baptist's Day, when the agistors met to fawn the deer. The foresters and verderers only had jurisdiction in this court. But by the Ordinance of the Forest, 1 (34 Edw. I.), presentments of offences in vert and venison were to be made at the next Swanimote before the foresters, verderers, regarders, agistors, and other forest officers. In early times it appears that all freeholders living in the forest, and the four men and reeve of every village, had to be present to hold inquisitions and serve on juries on pain of amercement by the chief warden. Among the offences inquired into at this court, besides offences in vert and venison, were those of narrowing church-ways in the forest, digging for mines without licence, extortions by forest officers. The regarders presented what mastiffs were kept in the forest unexpeditated. Offenders indicted in the Swanimote in the words, " Quod sunt communes malefactores de venatione Domini Regis in foresta," might be outlawed.

III. *The Justice Seat* was held every third year (4 *Inst.* 291), after forty days' notice by the sheriff's proclamation. A jury of twenty-four, twenty, or eighteen was chosen from the freeholders and others in court, and the rolls of offences, sealed with the verderer's seal at the Court of Attachments and Swanimote, were presented.

Forest Officers.—Besides the *Custos totius Forestœ* (mentioned Stat. 1 Edw. III. cap. 3) and the *Supervisor Forestariorum*, there were six classes of forest officers, — stewards, verderers, foresters, regarders, agistors, woodwards. No one could hold more than one office at a time. By the Ordinance of the Forest, 34 Edw. I. c. 3 (1306), forest officers were exempt from attending assizes, juries, and inquests, without the forest.

Verderers were judicial officers of the king's forest chosen *in pleno comitatu* by his writ to the sheriff *de viridario eligendo*, and sworn. They were judges in the Swanimote, and directors of the other forest officers. They reviewed and enrolled attachments and presentments of trespass in vert and venison, and held inquisitions "by the four townships nearest to the forest" (Assize of the Forest, art. 7). The verderers, of whom there were usually four, were esquires or men of good estate.

Foresters were officers sworn to preserve vert and venison. They attached offenders and presented them at the forest courts. Foresters were appointed by the king's letters patent and held office sometimes for life, sometimes during pleasure. In some cases they paid fee-farm rents to the king, and a man might be a forester in fee *in jure uxoris*. That a woman might be a forester, but had to appoint a deputy, is shown by the sheriff's return to a writ of summons to the Justice Seat in Pickering Forest 8 Edw. III. (4 *Inst.* 310). Foresters might pursue offenders with fresh pursuit within their view out of the forest, but might not wound, beat, or kill them there as in some cases it was lawful (Stat. 21 Edw. I. of trespassers in parks, etc.) for them to do within the forest. They had the right of topping trees in another man's ground for browse (Assize of Pickering, 8 Edw. III., fo. 19). Those holding land in the forest paid yearly to the foresters at their scotale 5s. or one sheep or lamb, and when the forest and officers had been in existence time out of mind, the foresters were entitled by prescription to 1½d. a day, or to all windfall wood, shoulders and skin of deer, etc. They could neither hawk nor hunt nor license others to do so. Every forester had to appear at the Justice Seat and present his horn on his knees to the chief justice in eyre, who delivered it to the marshall. It was returned to the forester on payment of a fine of 6s. 8d.

Regarders were instituted by the Assize of the Forest, (c. 4) 1184. They were twelve knights who viewed and inquired into offences in vert and venison, concealments and defaults of other forest officers. They were appointed (1) by the king's letters patent or by the justice in eyre, for life, or in fee (4 *Inst.* 291). (2) On the king's writ to the sheriff to summon a *regard* of the forest. Vacancies by death were filled by the sheriff's election in the county court. In this case the office was held during the king's pleasure. (3) The chief justice in eyre appointed a substitute for a regarder to attend the Swanimote, *pro hac vice tantum*. It was necessary thus to keep up the number because the twelve had to agree concerning offences.

Regards, formerly called *visitatio memorum*, were held once in three years without a new writ, by regarders, foresters, and woodwards (Assize of the Forest, c. 10). The regarders appointed as many foresters for this as they thought fit. They surveyed wastes, assarts, and purprestures, and entered them on a roll. This they brought to the Court of Attachments on the Swanimote, when it was sealed and signed and was presented at the next Justice Seat. Woods within the forest metes but not part of the forest were out of regard.

Agistors were four officers appointed by letters patent. They took the beasts to pasture in the forest, presented trespasses done by cattle, looked after the demesne woods and lands enclosed, and received the cattle and payments of those living in the forest who had common in the unenclosed ground there. The king's demesne woods and lands were agisted by his foresters, verderers, and agistors, who met at the Swanimotes for this purpose, and to receive the money (Charter of the Forest, c. 8). The verderers' rolls of the Swanimote, on which the foresters' and verderers' agistments were enrolled, was the king's record to charge the agistors with the receipt, and they alone were answerable for it. (Assize of Pickering, 8 Edw. III., fo. 7, 8, 9.) They brought to the Justice Seat an account of the money received for pannage. The agistors, foresters, and verderers certified the chief justice in eyre when it was time to agist the king's demesne woods and lands, and he directed a commission to them to be returned at the next Justice Seat.

Agistment is the pasture or herbage of any ground, or the money taken for it. It is of two kinds. (1) Herbage—of woods, lands, and pastures. (2) Pannage—of woods alone, *i.e.* the mast of trees. The time of agistment in the king's demesne woods and lands for herbage, for commonable beasts, was from the Swanimote fifteen days before St. John the Baptist's Day until Holy Rood Day (14th September). (Charter of the Forest, c. 8). This was the fence month. The agistment for pannage, which might be for beasts not commonable (swine and hogs), lasted for forty days from the Swanimote fifteen days before Michaelmas until about St. Martin's Day.

Woodwards were officers who had the care of the woods and vert and presented offences at the Court of Attachments. If a subject had wood in the forest and his woodward did not appear at the justice seat to present his hatchet to the chief justice, his wood was seized to the king until he replevied it and paid a fine. If not replevied in a year, it remained in the king's hands for ever. An owner who appointed a woodward where there was not one before was fineable (Assize of Pickering, 8 Edw. III. fo. 8).

Assart, Purpresture, and Waste:

Assart. To assart "is to destroy any covert by the rooting it up and to make it plain ground" (Manwood). The word comes from the French *assartir* (*essarter*, Coke) or from the Latin *exuro* or possibly from *ad sero*, it being sometimes spelt *assertare*. The *Dialogus de Scaccario* (I. 13) says, "What you find called *occasiones* by Isidorus are generally said to be *estrepement;* that is, when the woods and brambles of the forest are occasionally cut down for food and coverts ; after the cutting down of which, and the roots pulled up, the land is turned up and cultivated. But if the woods were cut down in such a manner that scarcely the stock of an oak, or any other tree, remained standing in those parts where they had been cutting, and five could be found cut down together in one place, they looked upon it as waste" (Madox, p. 29). Forest land might not be assarted without the king's warrant, and land thus wrongfully assarted was seized into the king's hands and was redeemable by a fine. If this was not paid by the owner or his heir, the king continued to hold the land for ever. The fine for assarting was not fixed by the forest laws, but was levied at the discretion of the king or chief justice in eyre, usually according to the number and value of the acres assarted. A man found making assart or purpresture, if in the king's woods, was committed for the first offence without bail until he paid the fine to the king, if in the woods of a subject, he was bailable for the two first offences (see *State of Realm*, i. 243).

Restold, sheriff of Oxfordshire, in the reign of Henry I. owed seven pounds ten shillings "for the king's woods, which are so destroyed that no village can pay the farm for them." Robert, Earl of Leicester, "once on the eve of a visitation of the woods, generally called a survey, made every three years, procured the king's writ to be free from those sums of money that were demanded out of his land for waste, putting in the number arising out of them, which, being carried and read in public at the exchequer, all were amazed and astonished, saying does not this earl weaken our liberty" (*Dialogus*, i. 2; Madox, p. 28). Whole counties are found in the Pipe Rolls, *in misericordia pro foresta.* Wood rents paid for forest land, converted by the king's license into pasture, were not included in the farm of the crown lands on account of the fluctuation in their value.

Purpresture is thus described by the *Dialogus* (ii. 10): "It sometimes happens through the sheriff's negligence, or his officers', or by a long continuance of war, whereby those who lived near the estates appropriated to the crown, usurped part of them, and annexed them to their own possessions. But when the itinerant justices, by the oath of lawful men, discovered them, they rated them separately from the ferme of the county, and delivered them to the sheriff to be answered for separately; and these are called purprestures or seizures; which, when they are discovered, are taken as was said, from the possessors of them, and hence fall to the treasury. But if he from whom the seizure is taken committed the fact, he shall at the same time be punished by a very heavy fine, unless the king thinks proper to forgive it him; if he did not commit the fact, but is his heir, the recalling of the estate is held sufficient punishment" (Madox, p. 45). No man might enclose any ground in the forest to the hurt of the deer, and if he had a license to enclose he might not do it with a high hedge and ditch or a high paling, for this was against the Assize of the Forest (c. 10). A man might not build a house on his own free land in the forest without license, and a house so built was to be pulled down before a certain day, or a yearly rent paid to the king for it (Assize of Lancaster, 12 Edw. III., fo. 6). By the Assize of Clarendon c. 7 (1166) gaols might be built out of the king's woods.

Waste. "To fell or cut down any woods which grow scattering, or any thick covert in the forest, though on a man's own inheritance, yet if done without license of the chief justice in eyre, or view of the foresters, 'tis *waste*" (Manwood).

The wood or place wasted was seized into the king's hand until the owner or his heir paid a fine assessed by the chief justice in eyre according to the number and value of the acres wasted (Assize of Pickering, 8 Edw. III., fol. 22).

Purvieu was certain territory, adjoining the forest, bounded with unmovable boundaries and known by matter of record only. It was once forest-land and disafforested by the perambulations made in 1218.

Forest Beasts. A forest was not a privileged place for all wild beasts and fowls, but only for those of the forest, chase, and warren. The beasts of the forest were, the hart, hind, and hare, and later, the boar and the wolf. But wolves were almost destroyed by Edgar, and no care was afterwards taken to preserve them. As late as Edward I.'s time there were many wolves in England, for, in 1281, Peter Corbet was commissioned to destroy them in Gloucestershire, Worcestershire, Herefordshire, Shropshire, and Staffordshire: "Lupos cum hominibus, canibus, et ingeniis suis capiat et destruat modis omnibus quibus viderit expedire" (Rymer, i. 591).

Beasts of the chase were the buck, doe, and fox, and formerly the marten and roe. Those of the warren were the hare, cony, pheasant, and partridge. The difference between beasts of the forest and of the chase is that forest beasts frequent woods and coverts, and those of the chase are field beasts. Each had its season, and there are many interesting terms in this connection. The so-called laws of Canute established the king's right to have forest "wherever I shall wish to have it." From this time until the granting of the Forest Charter in 1217, the king issued a commission under the great seal declaring his will to make a forest in any place, and commanding that a perambulation be made. When this is returned and certified the king is entitled to the forest by matter of record. A writ was then issued to the sheriff commanding him to proclaim through the county that the king had appointed such ground to be a forest, and that no one might hunt there after a certain day. But this made it only a chase until the king appointed the officers.

Strictly speaking, only the king could hold a forest, because he alone had power to appoint a justice in eyre of the forest. Forests were granted to subjects by letters patent, and all the officers remained except the justice in eyre.

A *Park* equally with a chase is a place of privilege for wild beasts of venery, and also for other wild beasts that are beasts of the forest and of the chase. It must be enclosed, and if open might be seized into the king's hands as a free chase. Parks were held by subjects by license to impark. The monastery of St. Albans appears to have had a park in the vill adjoining (Dom. i. 135 b). Domesday mentions sixteen subjects who held parks. From Edward I. most great men had parks and chases, and the Patent Rolls contain many licenses to impark.

A *Chase* is a harbour for wild beasts, usually smaller than a forest and not having so many liberties, and larger and with a greater diversity of beasts than a park. The officers were keepers and woodwards. A chase differs from a forest in that it may be in the hands of a subject, and from a park in that it is not enclosed.

A *Warren* is a franchise or place privileged either by prescription or by a grant from the king to keep beasts and fowls of warren. A free warren may be open without being seized.

Offenders in parks, chases, and warrens were punishable at common law, and by stat. 21 Edw. III. *De Malefactoribus in parcis et chaceis*, etc.

Haia is a hedge, sometimes a park or enclosure. Beasts were caught by driving them into a hedged or paled part of a wood or forest called a *haia*. The haias mentioned in Domesday were chiefly in Worcestershire, Herefordshire, Shropshire, and Cheshire. They occur in the Pipe Rolls as royal preserves. Edward III. had a chapel in his haia of Kingesle.

Names and Extent.—The woods mentioned in Saxon charters are generally very small and only in a few counties, but in early Saxon times the whole country between Tyne and Tees was a vast forest, the home of wild beasts. Only four forests are mentioned as such in Domesday besides the New Forest. These are Windsor Forest in Berkshire, Gravelinges Forest in Wiltshire, Winburne Forest in Dorsetshire, and Hucheuuode or Whichwood Forest in Oxfordshire. Neither Middlesex nor Essex forests are mentioned, though they must have existed, but *Forestarius de silva regis* occurs under Writtle in Essex (ii. 5 b). There are evident notices of forest land in Worcestershire, a forest is alluded to under Langebridge Hundred, Gloucestershire, and another in Herefordshire, but not by name (i. 179 b. 181, 184, 186). The forest of Dean is evidently alluded to under Dene (i. 167 b.), and under the lands of William de Ow in Wigheiete, Gloucestershire occurs this entry : "Alestan tenuit T. R. E. nunc est jussu Regis in foresta sua." In making the New Forest, William I. afforested portions of manors which were already woods. At least 17,000 acres were afforested in Hampshire between the reign of Edward the Confessor and the Domesday survey. Most of this land appears to have been on the borders of an older forest called by several writers Ytene. Names of parts of the forest ending in "ham," "ton," and "tune" show that they were sites of manors or villages. The royal demesnes in the reign of William I. are usually said to have consisted of 1422 manors, 30 chases, 781 parks, and 67 forests, but this is probably inaccurate (Stubbs, i. 403). From a passage in Abingdon cartulary, William seems to have extended the limits of Windsor Forest by four hides from Winckefeld towards Wildeshoram. Forests were probably at their greatest extent in John's reign, and until this time the whole of Cornwall, one of the least wooded counties, was under forest laws. The whole of Essex seems to have been afforested by John (Rot. de Oblatis, p. 102). The largest forest in England began to be destroyed when ironworks were established on a large scale in Sussex in the thirteenth century. Coke says that the newest forest in England is Hampton Court forest, made by act of parliament 31 Henry VIII. c. 5 (4 *Inst.* 301).

The forests of England are contemporary with the royal demesne, and both are supposed to have had their origin in the folc-land, but this view is rather shaken by the recent researches of Professor Vinogradoff (*Eng. Hist. Rev.* viij. 1). Gradually, as the king became looked on as more fully representative of the nation, the folc-land disappeared before the *terra regis* which we find in Domesday. The forests, a source of pleasure as well as of wealth, were considered as especially a royal possession. Among the Anglo-Saxons there were two chases, the higher reserved for the king, and the lower enjoyed by the holder of the land.

A great industry of the Anglo-Saxons was keeping pigs, and woodland was very valuable not only for deer, for fuel, and for wood for building, but chiefly for the support of pigs. A "wood of so many pigs," is a frequent entry in Domesday. In Ine's laws (A.D. 690) the worth of a tree is estimated by the number of swine that can stand under it. These laws forbade the felling and burning of trees, and imposed a fine of 60s. for burning a log in a wood, lest in this way woods should be destroyed. By Cnut's laws, cutting brushwood in the king's forest is forbidden, and the fine for destroying a tree which the beasts eat is 20s. Even in Henry I.'s time, Herbert Losinga, Bishop of Norwich, refused to give fuel from a wood at Thorpe to the sick, and preferred to give money, saying, "Tu vero custodi *sylvam sanctæ* Trinitatis sicut vis custodiri a sancta Trinitate " (Epis. viij.). Forests were sometimes waste land, *terra non lucrabilis*, often mentioned in the Pipe Rolls, and the preservation of game included, besides deer, boars, wolves, otters, and water-fowl, the fishing of rivers and coursing in great plains. An ancient privilege of the citizens of London confirmed by charter of Henry I. was coursing in Middlesex, Wiltshire and Surrey. In the so-called laws of Edward the Confessor, now known to be dated about 1217 (Liebermann, *Leges Anglorum*), public as well as royal rights were protected ; any one claiming a private fishery or preserve for wild fowl without royal charter was fined by the jurors of the hundred, and a mill or weir made on a river was removed and the trespasser fined. The fence of the great rivers was removed by Magna Carta, cc. 47. By the forest laws attributed to Cnut, which are now known to be forgeries (Stubbs, *Select Charters*, 156 ; Liebermann, *Instituta Cnuti*, ed. R. Hist. Soc., p. 90), four thanes were appointed in every province to administer justice, and received a yearly salary of two hundred silver shillings. Under them were four inferior thanes (lesthegenes) who had the care of vert and venison, at a salary of sixty silver shillings, and under each of these were two men who watched at night and did the more servile work, receiving fifteen silver shillings yearly. They were all provided with horses and arms. Those of the two lower classes were tried for offences by the superior thanes, who were answerable only to the king. Harts, bisons, hares, and rabbits were enclosed, and the service of enclosing and stalling was imposed on the villeins and burghers. All men were allowed to shoot wolves and foxes outside the enclosure, and every two villeins had to keep a dog. Domesday mentions a class of royal huntsmen who seem to have all been English, and to have passed into the service of William, and an elaborate establishment of the Royal Hunt is given in the *Constitutio Domus Regis* in the red book of the exchequer, which is now known to be as old as Henry I.'s time. After the Conquest all the remaining unenclosed folc-land was reserved to the crown, and the crown-land was further increased by the property of those who had fought in defence of England at Hastings.

William I. introduced the idea that hunting was the pastime of kings, to be followed simply for their pleasure and rigorously kept from their subjects.

In making the New Forest, villages and churches were destroyed with the one purpose of promoting the king's pleasure. Entries in Domesday show how the properties of individuals dwindled under the king whose fatherly affection was greater for the "tall deer" than for his people. The nature of the Conqueror's forest laws is known from later notices and from the complaints of chroniclers. "His great men bewailed it, and the poor men murmured thereat ; but he was so obdurate that he recked not of the hatred of them all ; but they must wholly follow the king's will, if they would live or have property, land, or even his peace." (*A. S. Chron.*, Rolls Series, p. 190). Under William II. these laws were probably enforced with increased severity, the greatest sufferers naturally being Englishmen who still kept some of their old property. Fifty such men were charged with breaking the Conqueror's forest laws, and proved their innocence by ordeal. William I. first attached the punishment of mutilation to offences against the forest laws : William II. punished such offences with death, even when the offenders were Normans of high rank and his own relations. But it must be remembered that William I. substituted mutilation for capital punishment in every case ; in the forest laws it took the place of the fine imposed by Cnut and led the way to the still heavier penalty.

In the charter granted by Henry I. early in his reign, he says that by common consent of his barons he has kept the forests in his own hand as his father had them. He probably issued forest laws of great severity and extended their jurisdiction within all franchises, so keeping to himself the right of hunting throughout the kingdom. So greatly did he care for the deer for the sake of the delights of hunting, that he scarcely made a distinction between the slaying of deer and the slaying of men (William of Newburgh, i. 3.).

Stephen came to the throne anxious to conciliate the barons and full of concessions. He promised that he would not keep other men's woods in his hands "as King Henry had done, who every year impleaded them if they took venison in their own woods, or if they destroyed or lessened them for their own needs." In the charter granted at his first great council he promised to restore to the churches and the nation the forests added by Henry I., retaining those held by William I. and William II. He did not keep his promise (Stubbs, i. 403). But that it should have been made at such a time, and accepted by the barons, shows that in this direction the crown was becoming stronger ; for the forests made by William II. which Henry

I. had given up are now added to those of William I. In the unsettled times of Henry I. and Stephen encroachments and trespasses were made in the king's forests.

From the accession of Henry II. the administration of the forests occupies a very important and clearly-defined position, side by side with the common law. Early in his reign he appointed justices who visited the forests when the justices itinerant were on circuit. The general visitation of 1166, after the council of Clarendon, when two justices visited the whole country, was followed the next year by a survey of the forests, and this again by a circuit of the shires. Again in 1175 Henry himself held a great visitation of the forests at Nottingham, and in spite of the expostulations of the justiciary, he exacted large fines for the destruction of vert and venison which he had himself authorised in the war. Just before this, he had hanged four knights at Lichfield for the murder of a forester. The assize of Woodstock (A.D. 1184) is the first forest code now extant. The punishments were probably not quite so severe as those enforced by Henry I. The archbishops, bishops, earls, barons, knights, free tenants, and all other men were to attend the court of the forest justice at the summons of the chief forester (art. 11). This was enforced by Richard I., and repealed by the great charter (art. 44), and the charter of the forest (art. 2). By the connivance of the legate, Hugo Pierleoni, even the clergy, whom the common law could not touch, were to be subject to the law of the forests ; the foresters were strictly enjoined not to hesitate to lay hands on them if they found them trespassing (art. 9). No one was to cut his own wood in the king's forest except for fuel, and even this, subject to the view of the forester (art. 3). Every one twelve years of age living within the forest bounds was to swear to the king's peace (art. 13).

In 1198, when Geoffrey Fitz-Peter succeeded Hubert Walter as justiciar, one of his first measures was to hold a visitation of the forests. He enlarged the assize of Woodstock, and attendance at the session of the forest justice, required by article 11, was enforced as rigorously as attendance at the shire and hundred courts. Fitz-Peter, however, was equally severe in other branches of the administration.

Forest Charter. The first forest charter is that of Henry III., issued by the earl marshall on 6th November 1217. Formerly a charter of John dated 1216 was cited on the authority of Matthew Paris, but this is really the charter of 1217 (Stubbs, i. 403). In a recently discovered charter of liberties, supposed to be a French forgery of 1216, references to the forests occur which seem to anticipate the charter of 1217 (*Eng. Hist. Rev.*, April 1894). All the forests made by Richard I. and John were to be at once disafforested (c. 3), but those of Henry II. only if they were to the damage of the owners of the woods afforested (c. 1). No one was to lose life or limb for offences in venison, but to be heavily fined. If he could not pay this fine he was to be imprisoned for a year and a day, and then in default of sureties was to be banished (art. 10). An archbishop, bishop, earl, or baron, going through the forest, was to be free to take two beasts by view of the forester. If he was not present they were to cause a horn to be blown that they might not seem to be stealing the king's deer (c. 11). Only foresters in fee were to take tolls. Thus some of the abuses pressing most heavily on the people were removed, and this charter was to the forest administration very much what the great charter was to the constitution at large. In both cases tyranny led to a definition and assurance of liberties, thus making them more secure for the future than they would otherwise have been. In 1218, the year following the issue of the charter, a perambulation of the forests was held to determine their extent for all time. By an ordinance of the same year, Henry III. was restricted from making grants in perpetuity until he should be of age, and in 1227, when he attained his majority, this ordinance was said to invalidate all former grants unless they were now renewed on payment. At the parliament of Oxford the barons had again to seek redress against the encroachments of the king, who had re-afforested woods and lands disafforested by perambulation (art. 7), and had given warrens in forests disafforested by charter (c. 9).

In 1299, when Edward I. was in urgent need of money for the French war, he confirmed the great charter and the charter of the forest in return for a grant of one-eighth from the barons and knights. In the case of the forests, the phrase "salvo jure coronæ nostræ" was inserted, but a second confirmation was demanded and granted two months after without this clause. In consequence of delay in carrying out disafforestations under the charter of the forest, twenty articles called "Articuli super Cartas" were passed the next year by the first complete parliament since 1296. Infringements of the charters were to be inquired into, and severe measures taken with regard to forest administration. A perambulation was held in 1301, and Edward confirmed the charters again at the parliament of Lincoln. In 1305, Clement V. granted him absolution from his oath, and this he only used to evade the forest articles which he had been compelled to grant in 1299 and 1301. The people still complained of the oppressions of forest officers. Their grievances were (1) Accusations and indictments were not made by lawful inquests, but by command of one or two foresters or verderers in order to extort money. (2) The great number of forest officers who were obliged to live near the forest, and to sell the wood and deer for their means of livelihood. These complaints were met in 1306 by the ordinance of the forest. One of its six articles provided that no forest officer was to take part in any assize, jury, or inquest without the forest (c. 3).

From the reign of Edward III. the hold of the crown on the forests became gradually weaker. Elizabeth and James I. alienated much of the forest territory, letting it on lease or in fee-farm, and great dissatisfaction was caused in 1641 by the attempts of Charles I. to reclaim this land. The king's title was found by inquisition, but by a jury acting under prejudiced direction. The Earl of Holland held a court as chief justice in eyre of the forests almost every year, though the

old custom had been once in three years. The royal forests in Essex were so enlarged that they were said to include the whole county as in John's time. The Earl of Salisbury was nearly ruined by the loss of his estate near the New Forest. The boundaries of Rockingham Forest were extended from six to sixty miles, and enormous fines imposed on the trespassers. Thus the Earl of Salisbury was fined £2000, the Earl of Westmoreland, £19,000, and Sir Charles Hatton, £12,000. It is probable, however, that these fines were not exacted in full. The king obtained Richmond Park by depriving many of his subjects both of their freehold lands and their rights of common, but they probably received compensation. In 1641 the Act for the Limitation of the Forests determined for ever the extent of the royal forests according to their boundaries in 20 James I.

[*Dialogus de Scaccario*, ed. Madox, 1768.— Manwood's *Forest Laws*, ed. Nelson, 1717.— Stubbs, *Const. Hist.* i., *Select Charters.*—Ellis, *Int. to Domesday*, i.—Freeman, *Norman Conquest.*— Hall, *Court Life under the Plantagenets.*—Pearson, *Hist. Maps of England.*—Lappenberg (trans. Thorpe), *Hist. of England under the A. S. Kings.* —Cowell, *Interpreter.*—*Statutes of the Realm* (2nd edition) for Charters and Statutes of the Forest after 1215.—Gardiner, *Select Documents of the Puritan Revolution.*] M. T. M.

FOREST, BEASTS OF. See FOREST, MEDIÆVAL, p. 110.

FOREST CHARTER. See FOREST, MEDIÆVAL, p. 112.

FOREST, COURTS OF. See FOREST, MEDIÆVAL, p. 108.

FOREST, NAMES AND EXTENT OF. See FOREST, MEDIÆVAL, p. 111.

FOREST, OFFICERS OF. See FOREST, MEDIÆVAL, p. 108.

FORESTERS. See FOREST, MEDIÆVAL, p. 109.

FORESTS, ECONOMIC ASPECTS OF. History shows that, except in arctic regions, there was once a natural covering of woodlands over the greater part of the globe. In the writings of Tacitus and Cæsar distinct evidence is given of the general distribution and character of these woodlands throughout France, Germany, and Britain ; and in those parts of the world, such as the backwoods of America and the jungles of Burma, where increase in the population is only now gradually necessitating the clearance of the primeval forests in order to permit of the extension of arable and pasture land, the same processes may at the present day be seen as took place centuries ago in the more civilised and settled portions of the globe.

In many of the countries of Europe the processes by which the present ratio of woodland to total area has been attained are clearly traceable. To detail them or to examine into their causes is beyond the scope of this article. According to the Board of Agriculture's *Returns* for 1892, the utilisation of the soil is as follows throughout most of the European countries :—

Country.	Latest data available for.	Total Area (acres), incl. Lakes, Rivers, etc.	Total Acreage (approximate) under			
			Corn Crops.	Grass and Clover.	All other Crops.	Woodlands.
United Kingdom . . .	1892	77,642,099	9,328,701	27,533,326	10,440,571	3,005,670
Germany	1890	133,441,960	34,358,023	19,082,667	11,549,871	34,353,743
France	1889	130,557,281	36,467,561	14,349,836	39,238,183	20,740,914
Russia in Europe (excl. Poland)	1887	1,244,367,351	161,953,560	176,522,484	126,045,863	425,564,842
Austria	1889	74,106,022	17,432,393	19,994,555	8,018,873	24,105,213
Hungary	1890	79,617,286	20,287,664	6,471,773	2,841,572	22,552,646
Sweden	1889	100,243,794	4,034,063	7,806,332	537,086	43,914,810
Italy	1883	70,787,236	19,712,099	..	7,704,681	10,266,310
Denmark	1888	9,352,761	3,029,404	3,720,146	300,574	559,256
Holland	1887	7,821,243	1,376,790	3,004,933	556,098	562,009
Belgium	1880	7,275,916	2,390,357	1,523,699	747,015	1,208,875

If we compare the most civilised countries of Europe, the following ratios will exhibit themselves :—

Country.	Percentage of Total Area under		
	Forest.	Tillage.	Pasturage.
United Kingdom .	3¼	25¼	35½
France . . .	16	50	14
Germany . . .	26	48	20
Austria and Hungary	30	38	26

The proportion in which woodlands should be retained for climatic, national-economic considerations can never be stated in anything like an authoritative manner. Thanks to our insular position, and more particularly to the beneficial influence exerted on the climate of Britain by the Gulf Stream, the woodland area has with impunity been restricted to so low a ratio as would undoubtedly have entailed agricultural disaster in the interior of the continent of Europe. It is not merely the proportion of woodland to the total area that must be taken into account, but also the manner in which it is distributed over the surface of the country. Thus British India, with a total area of 894,059 square miles, has, according to the *Review of Forest Administration* for 1890-91, state forests aggregating 112,608 square miles or 13 per cent of the whole, without reckoning the unclassed jungles covering many thousands of square miles throughout the thinly-populated provinces of Burma and Assam ; but as these are not equally distributed over the length and breadth of the land, certain portions of Bengal, Madras, and Upper Burma are in particular now and again liable to famine when the southwest monsoon fails to deposit the normal quantities of moisture in any year.

In Britain the clearance of the forests was throughout the middle ages not only unchecked but directly encouraged, so that as early as the reign of Henry VII. the woodlands covered only about one-third of the total area ; in Ireland, too, so late as the 17th century the policy of clearance of forests was urged on by James I., Charles I., and Cromwell. On the continent, on the other hand, legal action was taken as early as the beginning of the 14th century to restrict clearance of woodlands. Thus in Germany in 1304 the first edict was issued forbidding fresh clearances in a part of Alsace, and ordering land to be replanted which had been cleared without permission. Similar edicts were issued in France by Charles IX. and Henry IV. in the 16th century, and a more stringent law on the subject was the celebrated *ordonnance des forêts* of 1669. At the time of the revolution this was practically set aside by a decree of 1790, but the impetus thus given to excessive clearance was so soon productive of evil results that a prohibition had to be issued from the consulate prohibiting further clearances. At the present day all circumstances relative to the clearance of woodland are provided for in the *code forestier*, framed for the better administration of the national, communal, and private forests.

The Climatic Influence of Forests is discussed by Humboldt, who in the *Aspects of Nature* laments that the wants and restless activity of man "gradually despoil the face of the earth of the refreshing shades which still rejoice the eye in Northern and Middle Europe, and which, even more than any historic documents, prove the recent date and youth of our civilisation." The subject was never studied seriously until 1867, when observations were begun by Prof. E. Ebermayer of Munich, of which the first results were published in 1873 in his celebrated work *Die physicalischen Einwirkungen des Waldes auf Luft und Boden*. Since then, however, more extended observations conducted throughout Germany, France, and Switzerland have in many ways caused his deductions to be modified. The best *résumé* of the work accomplished in this direction is to be found in Prof. R. Weber's *Die Aufgaben der Forstwirthschaft*, forming the opening portion of Prof. J. Lorey's *Handbuch der Forstwissenschaft*, 1886, from which the following results are taken.

1. *As regards Atmospheric Temperature.* The average results of observations made during ten years (1875-85) in different kinds of forest at heights varying from 10 to 3000 feet above the sea-level, and at latitudes between 47½° to 55½° N., showed that in general the mean atmospheric temperature in woodlands is cooler than in the open, as shown in the following table :—

Temperature of Woodland Air, compared with that of Air in the Open.		
In ° Fahr.	At 5 feet above the ground.	In the Tree-crown.
Spring . . .	1·24° cooler	0·57° cooler
Summer . . .	2·55° ,,	1·47° ,,
Autumn . . .	1·13° ,,	0·41° ,,
Winter . . .	0·61° ,,	0·03° warmer
Annual Average of all recorded Observations.	1·044° cooler	0·414° cooler

The annual average temperature in woods growing in closed canopy is found to be lower than in the open, although the crowns of the trees are on the whole a little warmer in winter. The difference is greatest in summer, least in winter, and about midway between these extremes in spring and autumn ; but the mean annual difference seldom amounts to over 1° Fahr. near the ground, and to scarcely ½° in the crown. The prevention of insolation of the soil during the long hot days of summer, and the rapid transpiration of the foliage, exert greater influence on the atmospheric temperature than can be ascribed to shelter from wind and decrease of nocturnal radiation.

Observations made in southern Germany established the fact that in the forests it is cooler during the day, and warmer during the night than in the open. During the day the shade afforded by the crowns of the trees keeps the air cool, whilst the leafy canopy interferes with the radiation of warmth during the night. These equalising influences are naturally strongest during spring, summer, and autumn, when foliage is most abundant, whilst in winter the coniferous woods with evergreen canopy are milder than deciduous forests. Owing to these differences in temperature, beneficial currents of air set in between the woodlands and the open country, in the same manner as land and sea breezes are formed. During the day the cooler and moister air of the forest flows out to the open, to take the place of the heated air ascending ; at night a current sets in from the open, cooled by radiation, towards the forest. The immediate action of forests is, therefore, to modify the daily maxima and minima of atmospheric temperature, hence it may be deduced that a comparison of the absolute extremes of temperature during the year must exhibit the sum total of the influence exerted by woodlands on atmospheric temperature. As extremes of temperature are bad alike for man and beast, and for agricultural operations, this modifying effect can sometimes be of immense importance from a national-economic point of view, for many places that were once fertile are now little better than barren wastes in consequence of the reckless denudation of forest. The German observations yielded the following results on this point :—

Average difference of temperature in the forest and in the open at 5 feet above the ground.	
Exhibited by maxima of July	Exhibited by minima of January
6·82° Fahr. cooler in forest	2·05° Fahr. warmer in forest

In making these observations it was found that geographical position, exposure to winds, and the nature of the forest exerted modifying influences to a certain, and often not inconsiderable extent.

2. *As regards soil temperature*, observations in southern Germany gave the following results :—

Average soil temperature in the forest compared with that in the open.
− = cooler by. + = warmer by.

In ° Fahr.	At surface	At 1 ft. depth	At 2 ft depth	At 3 ft. depth	At 4 ft. depth
Spring	− 4·08°	− 3·08°	− 3·24°	− 2·79°	− 2·32°
Summer	− 6·10°	− 6·71°	− 7·07°	− 6·86°	− 6·53°
Autumn	− 1·85°	− 2·16°	− 3·04°	− 3·26°	− 3·58°
Winter........	− 0·23°	+ 0·43°	− 0·45°	− 0·22°	− 0·34°
Annual average	− 3·15°	− 2·88°	− 3·45°	− 3·28°	− 3·19°

Thus the mean annual temperature of the soil in woods is at all these depths of observation cooler than in the open. The differences are greatest in summer, least in winter, and about the mean in spring and autumn. In countries with warm summers this reduction of soil temperature over large areas by means of woods has a decidedly beneficial tendency.

3. *As regards the Degree of Atmospheric Humidity.*—Observations throughout Germany and Switzerland have shown that as regards the *absolute humidity of the air*, forests have no appreciable climatic effect, although they of course exert very great influence on its *relative humidity*. Taking all the observations together, the results arrived at show that the mean annual relative humidity of woodland air is from 3½ to 10 per cent greater than that of air in the open, but that the difference varies greatly according to the season of the year, being greatest in summer and autumn and least in winter and spring.

4. *As regards the Precipitation of Aqueous Vapour.*—As has above been stated, woodland air is cooler than that in the open, whilst the trees themselves are also cooler, especially in summer, hence when a current of air is wafted from the open into the forest its temperature falls and it approaches nearer to the point of saturation, *i.e.* its relative humidity increases. If it were already near the point of saturation, the formation of dew must take place. Woodlands, therefore, act as condensers of atmospheric moisture, and decrease the absolute humidity of the air whilst increasing its relative humidity ; at the same time they also add to the humidity of the air by transpiration. Very

careful observations made for the purpose have as yet failed to establish the actual effect of forests in the precipitation of dew and rainfall. Corrections of such various sorts have to be made for the correlation of readings at different points in the forest and in the open, as to make the deductions open to serious objections. Thus readings at 192 points of observation in Germany, corrected as carefully as possible with reference to causes of difference, lead to no other trustworthy inference than that at high altitudes large extents of woodland must considerably increase the local rainfall. But as nearly one-fourth of the rainfall is actually intercepted by the crowns and stems of the trees, forest growth offers great mechanical advantages in preventing the scouring and washing away of soil in mountainous tracts. Although it is a generally accepted dictum that rainfall is greater near large forests than in the open under similar physical conditions, this has not yet been proved by scientific observers. But owing to their lower temperature, their greater relative humidity, and the mechanical obstruction they offer to currents of air, forests certainly act as condensers of aqueous vapour, though their influence in this respect is much greater in mountainous tracts than on plains.

5. *As regards Evaporation of Soil-moisture.* —Observations made in Germany and Austria during ten years (1875-85) proved that, even in the vicinity of the forest, evaporation in the open was considerably greater than within the woods. The results are as follows :—

	Water evaporated.
In the Open	20·9 inches
In the Forest	9·5 ,,
Lower in forest than the open by	11·4 inches
Evaporation in forest expressed in the percentage of that in the open . . .	46 %.

The practical importance of this will be at once seen when it is recollected that the mineral food-supplies can only be taken up from the soil by the rootlets of plants when presented in the form of *soluble* salts.

6. *As regards the Feeding of Streams and the Protection of the Soil.* The action of forests is to retain in the soil a large proportion of the rainfall, which, by percolation to the lower layers and the subsoil, tends to feed the streams perennially, and to maintain a constant supply of moisture. That the mechanical action of rain in regard to washing away soil on steep slopes is interfered with by the crowns and stems of trees, has already been noted. But by the decomposition of dead foliage, etc., to form *humus* or mould, a strongly hygroscopic admixture is conveyed to the upper layer of the soil, thereby enabling it to imbibe and retain moisture with sponge-like capacity, and

giving the latter time to percolate instead of running off rapidly on sloping ground. The evaporating action of sun and wind is counteracted by the leaf-canopy, which also prevents radiation of warmth at night. When large tracts of country are denuded of forest, increase of temperature during the days of summer, rapid radiation of warmth by night, diminished dew-formation in spring and summer, and unchecked evaporation of moisture (through insolation and the free play of winds), must be the inevitable results. Such consequences, involving serious agricultural disasters, might easily be pointed out in many parts of continental Europe, Western Asia, and India ; references may, however, be made on these matters to the articles in the *National Review,* "Forest Science," July 1889, p. 691, and the *Edinburgh Review,* "The Penury of Russia," January 1893. The latter instance is a terrible object-lesson regarding the indiscriminate clearing of woodlands ; in the nine years ending in 1887 a decrease of no less than 101,861,668 acres took place in the area returned as woodlands, a great deal of which has simply become waste land. Forests tend to break the violence of the rainfall, retain temporarily a large proportion on the stem and branches, from which it trickles to the ground, bind the soil by means of their roots and the humus layer formed by the dead foliage, and imbibe and retain the moisture till it can gradually percolate to the lower strata for the maintenance of the beneficial perennial streams. In the alpine districts of southern Europe "ban-forests" are subject to special laws, being retained as protection against landslips, avalanches, etc.

7. *As regards General Hygienic Effect on the Atmosphere.*—Whilst fresh clearance of forest tracts, especially in tropical and sub-tropical countries, induces fever and ague, the re-planting of feverish localities, like the Campagna di Roma and the Tuscan marshes, has improved their climate. But these effects are more likely due to the degree of direct insolation, freely accorded in the one case, and counteracted in the other, than to any hygienic property inherent in tree-growth. In the latter case the evaporation of stagnating soil-moisture owing to the transpiration through the foliage would of itself go far to remove causes of insalubrity.

Ebermayer's experiments showed that woodland air had most ozone in winter, which proves that the amount of ozone it retains can not be due to any chemical action of the foliage, for even the evergreen conifers only transpire during the winter period of rest. But as in the decomposition of the carbonic acid of the air by tree-foliage from spring to autumn, the carbon is absorbed and oxygen set free, and as during the period of active vegetation the hours of sunlight far outnumber those of darkness—when oxygen is imbibed by the foliage, and carbon set free—it follows that, apart from their invaluable æsthetic influence, the planting of trees in towns and cities decidedly tends towards the purification of the air from its excess of carbonic acid ; trees and forests act like filters in fact.

The Monetary Value of Forests and of Forest Produce.—In actuarial calculations affecting woodlands a somewhat lower rate of interest must be adopted than is obtainable on ordinary investments, owing mainly to the social prestige which usually accompanies large wooded estates with good shooting, and also to the fact that timber and forest produce have hitherto steadily appreciated in value whilst other commodities have relatively depreciated ; this matter is well stated in Prof. G. Heyer's *Einleitung zur Waldwerthrechnung*, 1883, pp. 3-16. What rates of interest should be fixed on for a comparison of the *rentability* of the agricultural or the sylvicultural utilisation of any soil depends on varying local conditions. Considering the much longer period elapsing between the formation and the realisation of timber crops, and the greater dangers to which they are meanwhile exposed from wind, fire, insects, etc., a higher rate of interest might naturally be looked for ; but in most civilised countries, as a matter of fact, woodlands are practically confined to tracts which, either from poverty of soil or other physical causes, are unsuited for agricultural occupation, or pay better under timber. According to Heyer, whilst the ordinary rate of interest was from 4 to 4½ per cent throughout Germany, the rate of interest for calculations relating to agricultural soils was 2 to 3 per cent, and that prescribed for sylvicultural calculations in the state forests was from 2½ to 3 per cent. The economic importance of the *steady appreciation in the market value of forest produce* is a feature that deserves attention, for this is bound to be accentuated in the future, seeing that whilst population and demands for timber, etc., are constantly increasing, the woodland area, and therefore the possibility of satisfying these demands easily, are constantly decreasing throughout the whole world.

Prof. K. Gayer, in his rectorial address before the university of Munich in 1889, *Der Wald im Wechsel der Zeiten*, page 15, states that the 34½ millions of acres of woodland in Germany annually produce about 60,000,000 cubic méters of timber and fuel, and yield annually about £20,000,000 to £22,500,000, which at 2 per cent would make their capital value about £1,000,000,000. And, according to Weber, *op. cit.* page 85, it was found in 1875 that no less than 583,000 persons were engaged in industries directly dependent on the timber trade, in addition to £4,150,000 being annually disbursed for various manipulations before the

produce reached the buyer, and without reckoning costs of transport thereafter.

The most valuable forests in the British empire are undoubtedly those of India, which yielded a gross income of 14,967,135 rupees during the year 1890-91. Even accepting 2 per cent as the rate of interest obtained, this would make their capital value about 750,000,000 rupees ; but it is probably more.

Even the 3,005,670 acres of woodland in the United Kingdom represent a very considerable capital. Taking the average period of rotation of the timber crops at 90 years, the rental of the land at 5s. per acre per annum, the cost of planting, etc., at £2 an acre, and the rate of interest at which the landowner is content to work as 2½ per cent, their actual cost at the present moment (treating them as ranging normally up to 90 years) would amount to $(3,005,670 \times £2 : 5s.) \ 1 \cdot 025^{45} = £20,544,571$. But the timber and minor forest produce of home growth is entirely inadequate to supply the demands existing in Britain, as may be seen from the following statement showing the quantities of the chief imports during 1892, and the countries whence they were obtained :—

IMPORTS Wood and Timber.	Loads of 50 cb. ft.	Value £ Stg.
Hewn (in the round or square)		
From Russia . . .	329,636	517,599
„ Sweden and Norway . . .	782,677	1,051,715
„ Germany . .	288,614	688,087
„ United States .	165,488	669,104
„ British East India	34,897	372,443
„ British North America . .	194,654	919,470
„ other countries .	673,174	687,428
Total . .	2,469,140	£4,905,846
Split or sawn, planed or dressed.		
From Russia . . .	1,316,258	2,726,113
„ Sweden and Norway . . .	2,046,167	4,224,391
„ United States .	407,854	1,133,771
„ British North America . .	1,212,877	2,811,059
„ other countries .	111,153	284,807
Total . .	5,094,309	£11,180,141
Staves of all dimensions	136,063	593,539
Totals for timber alone .	7,699,512	£16,679,526
Minor produce.		
Pulp of wood for paper .	Tons 190,938	981,025
Rosin	Cwt. 1,681,393	384,050
Bark for tanners and dyers	Cwt. 380,337	158,105
Total value of imports .	....	£18,202,706
EXPORTS Wood and Timber.	Loads.	Value £ Stg.
Sawn or split, planed or dressed . .	20,935	72,860
Excess value of imports over exports . .	....	£18,129,846

These do not include the imports of mahogany, cutch, gambier, caoutchouc, gutta-percha, etc., amounting to nearly £5,000,000 more.

It would of course be a physical impossibility to produce the greater part of these imports in Britain, but there is no climatic reason why, at any rate, a considerable portion of the following timber should not be home grown :—

Imported from Russia, Sweden, Norway, and Germany.		
Timber in the rough .	Loads 1,400,927	£2,257,401
Converted timber . .	,, 3,362,425	6,950,504
Total . .	Loads 4,763,352	£9,207,905

Before enumerating the more important literature touching on the economic aspects of forests, special and prominent mention must be given to the very masterly and complete short treatise on the history of forestry, and the national-economic importance of forests and of forest-produce, which is comprised in the three articles on *Forsten*, contributed by Prof. M. Endres of Tübingen to the *Handwörterbuch der Staatswissenchaften*, edited by Conrad, Elster, Lexis and Löening, 1889-1894. [Rau, *Lehrbuch der Polit. Oekonomie*, article "Forstwirthschaft," by Wagner-Nasse.—Schönberg, *Handbuch der Polit. Oekonomie*, art, "Forstwirthschaft," by J. v. Helferich.—Lorey, *Handbuch der Forstwissenschaft*, 1886, art, "Forstpolitik," by J. Lehr.—*Encyclopædia Britannica*, art, "Forests." —W. Schlich, *Manual of Forestry*, 1887, vol. i. pp. 13-96.—*Nineteenth Century*, art, "Woodlands," July 1891.—*Edinburgh Review*, art, "The Penury of Russia," January 1893.—J. Nisbet, *British Forest Trees*, 1893, Preface and Introduction.— Roscher, *Nationalökonomie des Ackerbaues*, etc., bk. iii. ch. iii.—*Ein nationalökonomisches Hauptprinzip der Forstwirthschaft*, 9th ed., 1878.—B. E. Fernon, *Forest Influences*, U.S.A., 1893.— Professor Isaac Bayley Balfour, *Address on Forestry at the British Association*, § D. (Biology), Oxford, 9th August 1894.] J. N.

FORETHOUGHT. Forethought may be defined as that species of imagination which enables a man to realise at any given time his probable wants in the future. What is not immediately present to the senses cannot excite intense fear or desire unless it be vividly realised by the imagination. Without forethought, therefore, it would be impossible for a man to deny himself now in order that he might enjoy hereafter. He might desire riches as the means of instant enjoyment; but he would not accumulate riches as the means either of enjoyment or of production in the future. Thus forethought is the necessary condition of all saving, and therefore of the formation of capital.

The degree of forethought possessed by any race or individual is determined by causes too numerous and too obscure for complete enumeration. Among the more obvious of these causes is climate. In some countries the climate is so benign as to provide the means of life and of pleasure almost without any assistance from man, in others the climate is so rigorous that, with the most pinching parsimony, only a bare existence can be gained. In neither case can we expect much forethought from the inhabitants. In the one case they are comfortable without forethought, in the other case no forethought could make them comfortable. Moreover a luxurious climate relaxes, and a frozen climate benumbs the intellectual powers. It is in the intermediate climates that man can do most to better his condition and has most mental energy to conceive and to desire improvement.

Another influence which affects forethought is religion. Some religions have stimulated, others have repressed the natural instinct to enjoy the present which so often operates against forethought. It is true that the ascetic temper which condemns pleasure condemns also the pursuit of riches. Yet no communities have developed a higher degree of forethought than Scotland and New England, where an austere religion has been all but universally accepted. In such communities the enjoyment of the passing hour is doubly difficult, and the mind even of the ordinary man is forced to direct itself upon the future. A third influence is government. Men will not deny themselves in order to attain a remote object unless they have fair grounds for hoping that their self-denial will bear fruit. Such grounds they can have only under a tolerably good government. A government which takes an undue proportion of the national means to fill its treasury, or which permits its servants to practise extortion, or which fails to defend public order against foreign assailants or domestic criminals, or which maintains the thoughtless in comfort at the charge of the provident—still more a government which commits many of these faults—will effectually weaken forethought, and may in time reduce the richest country to penury. On the other hand a good and orderly government will stimulate forethought to such an extent as to cause a steady accumulation of capital. Another influence is education. In so far as education weakens the force of momentary appetite, and strengthens the reflective and imaginative powers, it tends to increase forethought.

Yet another influence affecting forethought is the opportunity for safe and profitable investment of savings. The motives to save are stronger where savings can be not merely hoarded but so employed as to produce an immediate return. In this way the modern development of joint-stock companies has done much to diffuse forethought. But where forethought is general the accumulation of capital will gradually lower the rate of interest and profit obtainable. Whether this process will ultimately weaken forethought by lessening its returns is a question which we are hardly in a position to solve. We have not sufficient materials for judging the effect of a very low rate of interest continued for a very long time. As yet the rate even in the richest countries appears sufficient to stimulate forethought. A certain amount of saving has always been prompted by the need of a reserve fund against old age, sickness, or other calamity, and has therefore been independent of the attraction of interest, indeed where the rate of interest is low more must be saved for these purposes and for the benefit of children, to produce the same income. But such saving as is prompted by the desire to better one's condition, to increase one's income, must be discouraged as the future return to a given exertion of immediate self-denial becomes less and less. Saving of this kind was narrowly restricted in those states of society in which there were few modes of safe and lucrative investment. Much that would now be saved was then spent upon stately houses, large retinues, massive plate, and gay clothing. It is at all events possible that, as investments become less profitable, the taste for unproductive expenditure may become stronger. Taking mankind as a whole, it may safely be said that they are deficient in forethought. Yet there are many individuals whose forethought is excessive. Forethought is not, like truth or justice, a virtue of which one cannot have too much. It is a faculty which needs to be balanced by other faculties. Men defective in a healthy power of enjoyment or constitutionally timid or stunted in feeling by early privation do frequently over-estimate the future in comparison with the present, and persevere in this error until they are ready to descend into the grave. In such men the habit of looking to the future has become a disease fatal to happiness and pernicious to their higher nature. Nay, it sometimes goes so far as to defeat its own object, the accumulation of riches. For the miser will deny himself the recreation and even the food needful to his full efficiency as a producer. The firm and tranquil temper which can duly balance the future with the present may not always tend to the greatest individual accumulation, but it is most conducive to the general well-being.

[Adam Smith, *Wealth of Nations*, bk. ii. ch. iii., Of the Accumulation of Capital.—Mill, *Principles of Political Economy*, bk. i. ch. xi. ; On the Law of the Increase of Capital.—Marshall, *Principles of Economics*, bk. iv. ch. vii., On the Growth of Wealth.—Bagehot, *Economic Studies.*]

F. C. M.

FORFEITURE is the loss of property or of rights in consequence of some act or omission on the part of the owner of the property or of the person in whom the right was vested. Forfeiture of leasehold property in consequence of a breach of covenant on the part of the lessor is now comparatively rare, as recent legislation enables the lessee in most cases to remedy the breach before the lessor can enforce his right (see ENTRY, RIGHT OF). Forfeiture may occur through the non-observance of a condition imposed by the will or settlement under which property is held (e.g. when property is given over to a third person in the event of the tenant for life, remarrying, or changing his religion or his name, or becoming a bankrupt, etc.). E. S.

Formerly, when a man was convicted of treason or felony, he forfeited all his property both real and personal. By a barbarous legal fiction his blood was said to be corrupted so that descent could not be traced through him, and upon his execution his children had no claim to his land. It therefore escheated to the lord in cases of felony and to the crown in cases of treason. It was thus that the demesne of the crown was so often enlarged when great landowners suffered for treason. The personal property, whether of the traitor or of the felon, passed to the crown immediately upon his conviction. This aggravation of punishment was objectionable on many grounds. If the felon or traitor actually suffered death, any further punishment was unnecessary. Forfeiture of property in such a case bore most hardly on the innocent widow and children. If the punishment of death were remitted there was the further inconvenience of taking away a man's livelihood and adding to his temptations as soon as he was set at large. Lastly the penalty of forfeiture acted as a temptation to rulers to seek the conviction of a wealthy accused person. For these reasons it had often been condemned by theoretical writers before it was abolished by the act 33 & 34 Vict. c. 23. Under this act, however, a person convicted of felony and sentenced to twelve months' imprisonment or upwards is still liable to forfeit any office under the crown, any ecclesiastical benefice, any place in a corporation, or any pension which he may hold.

Another case of forfeiture occurs when the lessee of land breaks a covenant in his lease to which a proviso for re-entry is attached. In such a case the lessor could formerly sue on the covenant without more ado. But by the Conveyancing and Law of Property Act of 1881 (44 & 45 Vict. c. 41) he must now serve on the lessee a notice specifying the particular breach complained of, and require him to remedy the breach or make compensation. Only if the lessee fails to comply within a reasonable time can he enforce his right of re-entry, and even then the court has full discretion to grant the lessee relief on reasonable terms. These provisions do not apply to the breach of a covenant against underletting, or to the case of non-payment of rent. Indeed they are only intended to protect the lessee against forfeiture in cases where it is an excessive penalty, and thus to increase his reasonable security.

Under the feudal land law a freehold tenant might forfeit his land by certain breaches of the conditions on which he held it.

Smugglers are still liable to forfeiture of the goods smuggled, in addition to other penalties.

The Post Office Savings Bank regulations decree the forfeiture of deposits in other savings banks which are concealed at the time the Post Office account is opened, in spite of the depositor's declaration to the contrary. Partial forfeiture to the National Debt Commissioners under this rule are of constant occurrence.

[Sir James Stephen's *History of the Criminal Law of England*, vol. i. pp. 487-489.—Goodeve, *Modern Law of Real Property.*—Williams, *Law of Real Property.*—Woodfall, *Law of Landlord and Tenant.*— *The Conveyancing and Law of Property Act*, 1881, ed. Clark and Brett or ed. Wolstenholme.] **F. C. M.**

FORGED TRANSFER. The risk to which buyers of shares, stock, or debentures transferable by deed of transfer were formerly exposed, owing to the possibility of the vendor's signature on the transfer being forged, has been considerably reduced by the Forged Transfer Acts of 1891 and 1892. These acts enable companies and local authorities to make compensation to persons to whom certificates have been issued in pursuance of such forged transfers, and have already been very widely adopted. It must, however, be borne in mind that the adoption of the acts is purely voluntary, and that in the case of companies who refuse to recognise the rights of defrauded purchasers, the old state of things continues. **E. S.**

FORGERY. "There is," says Mr. Justice Stephen (*History of the Criminal Law*, vol. iii. p. 186), "no statutory definition of forgery. The common law definition is making a false document with intent to defraud." Making includes, not merely the composition of an entire document, but also altering a document or signing it in the name of another person. Intent to defraud is presumed to exist if at the time of making there was in existence a specific person capable of being defrauded thereby. There are as many kinds of forgery as there are instruments which can be forged. Forgery was a misdemeanour at common law.

The first severe statute directed against forgery is the 5 Eliz. c. 14. In the 18th century the use of paper money and the increase of trade gave an impetus to forgery which it was sought to counteract by statutes making many forms of forgery capital. The law was mitigated by the Act 11 Geo. IV. and 1 Will. IV. c. 66, and again by the Act 7 Will. IV. and 1 Vict. c. 84, but forgery of the great seal remained treason and capital until 1861, in which year the statute law relating to forgery was consolidated by the Forgery Act 1861 (24 & 25 Vict. c. 98). Forgery of the great seal, of securities in the public funds, of bank-notes, bills of exchange, wills, and certain other documents, is punishable by penal servitude for life. Other kinds of forgery are punishable with maximum terms of fourteen and seventeen years' penal servitude respectively. Forgery of a trade mark makes the offender liable to two years' imprisonment with hard labour. The making or possessing of instruments or paper for forging bank-notes is also severely punished. In general the uttering of a forged document, *i.e.* the offering or disposing of a forged document knowing it to be forged, is punishable as severely as the act of forging. The scope of forgery increases with the multiplication of documents consequent on the advance of civilisation, and the progress of science perhaps affords as many new expedients to the forger as safeguards to the public. These considerations may perhaps justify the great severity of even the modern law of forgery.

[For the present state of the law of forgery see Stephen, *Digest of the Criminal Law*, Arts. 355-366, and for its development see Stephen, *History of the Criminal Law*, vol. iii. pp. 180-188.] **F. C. M.**

FORMALEONI, VINCENZO (18th cent.), a man of much learning, born and lived at Venice.

Saggio sulla Nautica dei Veneziani, con una illustrazione di alcune carte idrografiche della Biblioteca di S. Marco in Venezia, dimostranti l'Isole Antille prima della scoperta di Cristoforo Colombo, Venezia, 1785 (translated into French by Chev. Dr. Hénier, Venise, 1788).—*Storia filosofica e politica della Navigazione, del commercio e delle colonie degli antichi, nel Mar Nero*, Venezia, 1788 (id. id., Venise, 1791). **A. B.**

FORMARIAGE, DROIT DE. This was a feudal right of the French lords to exact a payment from a female serf when she married either a freeman or the serf of another lord. **R. L.**

FORONDA, VALENTIN DE. In his *Miscelánea* (Madrid, 1787), in his *Cartas sobre los asuntos mas exquisitos de la economía política*. (Letters on the most interesting questions of Political Economy) (Madrid, 1794), and in his *Cartas sobre la policía* (Letters on Policy). (Madrid, 1801). Foronda was one of the first to popularise the new economic ideas in Spain. He advocates commercial and industrial *laissez-faire*, and opposed all measures contrary to free trade, "the pole star which ought always to be kept in sight."

[Colmeiro's *Biblioteca de los Economistas Españoles*, p. 87.] **E. Ca.**

FORONDA, VALENTINO—name used by **FABBRONI, GIOVANNI**, in publishing his letters: *Della prosperità nazionale, dell' equilibrio del commercio e dell' istituzione delle dogane*, Firenze, Tofani, 1789. (*v.* T. I° of the *Scritti di Pubblica Economia di Giovanni Fabbroni*, pp.83-110). **A. B.**

FORSTER, NATHANIEL, D.D. (1726 or 1727-1790), rector of All Saints, Colchester.

Besides some sermons and a pamphlet on Wilkes, he wrote *An Enquiry into the causes of the Present High Price of Provisions*, 1767, and an *Answer to Sir John Dalrymple's pamphlet upon the Exportation of Wool*, 1783. Perhaps the best parts of the *Enquiry* are the arguments against breeding horses instead of oxen for farm work, and an explanation of the effect of enclosures upon the price of pigs, poultry, and eggs. The economic arguments are weakened by his neglect of the rate of wages, and by his treatment of wealth and money as synonymous. In his pamphlet on wool he strongly objects to the exportation of raw wool, on account of home manufactures, which, he argues, would in consequence rise in price and be undersold by foreign goods.

[*European Magazine*, vol. xvii., 320.—*Dictionary of National Biography*.—M'Culloch, *Literature of Political Economy*.] E. G. P.

FORTI, E., was, from 1875 to 1878, editor of the *Giornale degli Economisti*, at Padua, and a strong supporter of the "socialists of the chair."

L' Azione economica del Parlamento, dal 23 Nov. 1874 al 20 Giugno 1875, e dal 15 Nov. 1875 al 26 Luglio 1876.—*Giorn. degli Economisti*, Padova, 1875 e 1876. A. B.

FORTREY, SAMUEL (1622-1681), author of *England's Interest and Improvement consisting in the increase of the Store and Trade of this Kingdom*, Cambridge, 1663, was gentleman of the chamber to Charles II., clerk of the deliveries of the ordnance in the Tower, and a bailiff in the Corporation of the Great Level. He belonged to a family of Flemish refugees, who had settled as merchants in London. In his tract he writes in favour of immigration, inclosure, and a reform of the coinage, and urges that the king should set the fashion of preferring English-made goods to foreign manufactures, which should further be discouraged by high import duties. Subsequent mercantilist writers very frequently quoted an account which Fortrey says he obtained from a "particular not long since delivered in to the king of France." This gives a detailed list of the English imports into France, and the French exports to England, making the total value of the imports from England £1,000,000, and that of the exports to England £2,600,000. Fortrey and his followers concluded that this showed that England lost £1,600,000 a year by her trade with France. The tract was reprinted in 1673, 1713, 1744, in Whitworth's *Tracts on Trade and Commerce*, 1778, and in Lord Overstone's *Select Tracts* (vol. on "Commerce") 1856.

[*Dictionary of National Biography*.] E. C.

FORTUNATO, NICOLO (living at Naples in end of 18th century), was one of those writers who, after studying carefully the evils then afflicting the kingdom of Naples, and the true sources of its wealth, pointed out the proper remedies and the way in which to put theory into practice. According to him economics are a part of philosophy, and may be divided between public economy (proper to a prince), and private (proper to families), which is limited to individuals. Fortunato dwelt on the true sources of public wealth, pointing out England as the example in this, the principles of economic science being well known there, and practised by the encouragement of agriculture, by permitting free exports of produce, by keeping the carrying trade to the national shipping, etc. He criticised the system of taxation then maintained in the kingdom of Naples, and proposed an equitable basis of custom-house duties, the abolition of internal tolls, and a uniform assessment for the taxes. He showed the necessity of a census of the population, and supported—like Gianni and Neri in Tuscany, though less fortunate than they, as they saw their ideas put into practice —the free export of corn.

Riflessioni intorno al commercio antico e moderno del Regno di Napoli, di Nicola Fortunato, Napoli, 1760. A. B.

FORTUNE, E. F. THOMAS, stockbroker, author of *Epitome of the Stocks and Public Funds*, 1796, which ran to seventeen editions; of *A Concise and Authentic History of the Bank of England, with Dissertations on Metals and Coin, Bank Notes and Bills of Exchange*, 1797 (translated into French 1798? a third edition issued in 1802) intended to defend the bank against adverse rumours caused by a temporary stoppage of cash payments ordered by government and sanctioned by parliament; and of *National Life Annuities, comprising all the Tables and every necessary information contained in the act of Parliament for granting the same*, 1808.

[*Brit. Mus. Catalogue.*—*Biographical Dictionary of Living Authors*, 1816.] E. G. P.

FOSSOMBRONI, VITTORIO, Count (about 1800), professor in the university of Pavia.

Idee sui vincoli commerciali. Lettera d' un professore dell' Universita di Pavia (1 Giugno 1804). (*v.* Fabroni's *Scritti*, etc., pp. 336-417.) A. B.

FOSTER, JOHN LESLIE (*d.* 1842), grandson of Anthony Foster, lord chief baron of Ireland, was an Irish judge, and member of parliament on the Tory side for Dublin University 1807-1812, for Yarmouth, Isle of Wight, 1816, for Armagh 1818-1820, for Louth 1824, 1826. He spoke frequently (see Hansard under above years) chiefly on Irish subjects, such as Catholic Relief, Irish Grand Juries, and the Irish Insurrection Bill. He wrote an *Essay on the Principle of Commercial Exchanges, more particularly on the Relations between England and Ireland*, 1804. Through an argument against the old theory that the wealth of a nation is proportionate to the excess of its exports over its imports, in which he shows that the balance of debt is distinct from the balance of trade, he proceeds to a discussion of the financial relations then subsisting between England and Ireland ; he describes, in an original way, the loss suffered by Ireland through remittances to absentees and the interest of her debt payable in England, which caused an increase of imports and a decrease of exports ; and he concludes with an argument to show that the rate of exchange does not depend on the balance of debt but on the cost of transmitting specie, and with a description of the monetary evils caused by bank restriction. The first chapter treats of the general principles governing the balance of trade, showing that foreign expenditure and other international financial relations help to produce the balance of *debt* of which the balance of *trade* forms only a part, if the larger part ; that the balance of trade, whether favourable or unfavourable, can never be permanent, as the varying value of the circulating medium, which is here treated on the same footing as any other commodity, will always restore the equilibrium. The old theory that the wealth of a nation is proportionate to the excess of exports over imports is replaced by an argument to show that such excess is a loss to the nation, being the payment without return for foreign expenditure. The following proposition sums up the argument : " If the exports to all the world could be added to the amount of specie exported, they would be found equal to the amount of imports and of foreign expenditure." The rest of the essay is devoted to the financial relations of Ireland with England, and deals less with general principles than with existing facts. Ireland's foreign expenditure is shown to be a loss to her : remittances to absentees cause industry, but, the produce of this industry being exported without return, Ireland, though not being ruined, cannot accumulate capital but spends her savings on the absentees ; while the raising of Irish loans in England interferes, by introducing an unnatural supply of specie into Ireland, with the natural relation between exports and imports and specie. Irish imports are increased and exports diminished in proportion to the balance of debt. The effects of bank restriction are then adversely discussed, and the rates of exchange explained as depending on the cost of transmitting specie, not, as hitherto generally believed, on the balance of debt. In the case of Ireland the rate of exchange is unfavourable, owing to English trade regulations which increase the cost of transmission, though the balance of debt is favourable. The essay closes with a detailed view of the causes of and the remedies for the excessive issue of paper money in Ireland, shows that only inconvertible paper can be issued in excess, and recommends the regulation of the issue by law. The whole essay is distinguished by clearness of style, by lucid reasoning, and by enlightened views.

[*Times*, July 13, 1842.—See M'Culloch's *Literature of Political Economy* for notice of remarks on Irish absentees.] E. G. P.

FOSTERLAND. Land set apart to provide a sustenance for a particular person or persons. [COWEL's *Interpreter.*] A. E. S.

FOTHER. See MEASURES AND WEIGHTS.

FOUAGE, or **FEUAGE,** the French equivalent of our hearth-tax. The most famous, though not the earliest, imposition of this tax was under Charles V., when it provoked numerous revolts, and Charles was induced to abolish it on his deathbed. But the *fouage* remained a provincial impost in Brittany, and the extraordinary injustice of its assessment was the great subject of discussion at the meeting of estates of Brittany in 1788, where, according to some writers, the Revolution really began. [For the *fouage* in Brittany, see Bertrand de Moleville, *Mémoires Particuliers*, i. p. 36.] R. L.

FOUCQUET, NICOLAS (1615-1680), began public life under the auspices of Richelieu, and, after the death of the Cardinal, continued to enjoy the protection of his successor Mazarin, and was created Marquis of Belle Isle. He was successively made minister of state, superintendent of finance, and general attorney in the parliament of Paris ; finally he was arrested in 1661 on a charge of embezzlement. The question of his culpability is doubtful : he had incurred the persistent aversion of Louis XIV., acting under the hostile influence of Colbert, and was sentenced to the confiscation of all his property and to perpetual banishment, which the king "commuted" into perpetual confinement. Foucquet died in 1680, after fifteen years' captivity, during which he composed several works of piety and the *Défenses de M. Foucquet* (15 vols. 1665-1667). Some of his old friends, among others La Fontaine and Madame de Sévigné, remained faithful to him until the end.

The study of his trial is interesting on account of the light it sheds on the management, and also the mismanagement, of French finance under Louis XIV.

[Chéruel, *Mémoires sur la vie publique et privée de Foucquet* 2 vols.—Pierre Clément, *Histoire de Colbert.—Nicolas Foucquet* (2 vols. 1890) by M. Lair, who has printed several unpublished documents on this subject. A very complete account, based on M. Lair's book, will be found in the *Revue des Deux Mondes* (1st and 15th December 1890).] E. CA.

FOUNDLING HOSPITALS. These institutions illustrate the dangers of attempting to gratify charitable impulses without due regard to consequences. Foundling hospitals relieve after more or less of inquiry, and with more or less of restriction, children whose parents cannot or will not support them. Sometimes they are voluntary institutions, sometimes maintained and directed by the state, sometimes they receive only illegitimate children, as is the case with the Foundling Hospital in London, sometimes children born in wedlock as well. Their object is threefold, viz. (1) that child-murder and exposure may be prevented, as being without excuse; (2) that a better training and education may be given to the children than would be given by the parents; (3) that a retreat may be found for the victims of seduction. What are their effects?

Malthus has pointed out the excessive mortality which the system occasions. He found that in the Maison des Enfants Trouvés at St. Petersburg, in spite of every precaution, the number of deaths was almost incredibly high. At the London Foundling Hospital, in the middle of the last century, the system was adopted of taking all comers; as a result, in a little less than four years 14,934 were received, of whom but 4400 lived to be apprenticed; and, as a further result, large numbers died whilst being carried to the hospital from every part of England by unscrupulous contractors. The same writer has shown that they infallibly give encouragement to vice. Not only do they remove one of the most powerful motives to conduct, viz. a dread of public opinion, but they also guarantee an escape from the responsibilities of paternity; thus marriage is discouraged and illicit unions are encouraged. Lastly, they help to lower wages, "by artificially increasing the number of apprentices," for "the demand for labour among the legitimate part of the society must be proportionally diminished, the difficulty of supporting a family increased, and the best encouragement to marriage removed." In answer to the argument that they diminish exposure and infanticide, Malthus remarks, "An occasional child-murder from false shame is saved at a very high price, if it can only be done by the sacrifice of some of the best and most useful feelings of the human heart, in a great part of the nation."

These criticisms on a system of foundling hospitals are borne out by a consideration of the history of these institutions in England and France. The London Foundling Hospital was established in 1741 by Captain Coram for the "maintenance and education of exposed and deserted young children." At first admission was restricted owing to want of funds, but by a resolution of parliament, 5th April 1756, the maintenance of the hospital was undertaken by the nation, and the gates were thrown open to receive all children who should be offered. On the first day 117 were admitted, in the next three years and ten months no fewer than 14,934, at the end of which time parliament withdrew its subsidy. The present practice of the hospital is to admit only illegitimate children, under one year old, who are not paupers, are the first-born of their mothers, and whose fathers are unknown or not, from whatever cause, liable for their maintenance. A total of 504 children is received, of whom the younger are put out to nurse in the country, and 330 are educated in the hospital itself.

France differs from England, fundamentally, in the fact that desertion is not an offence in that country, unless it be accompanied by injury or risk to the child. By the decree of 18th January 1811, every *arrondissement* was to contain a *hospice* for foundlings, and to every *hospice* was to be attached one of the famous *tours* for their reception. In these *tours* any child might be placed without risk of identification, and become henceforward the ward of the state. As a result, in 1833 no fewer than 136,943 children were maintained at the public expense, which led to successive acts of the legislature reducing the number of *tours*, and the facilities for desertion, till in 1858 the figure stood at 76,520. The *tours* are now abolished, but all children are received à *bureau ouvert* without restriction.

[The criticisms of Malthus may be seen in his *Principles of Population.*—The *History of the London Foundling Hospital* has been written by Brownlow (1858).—The various provisions, etc., for *Enfants Trouvés* in France are set forth in *Régime et Législation de l'Assistance Publique et Privée en France*, by Léon Béquet, *Die Armengesetzgebung Frankreichs*, by the Freiherr v. Reitzenstein (Schmoller's *Staats - und socialwissenschaftliche Forschungen*, vi. 4), and *Législation Charitable*, by A. de Watteville.]   L. R. P.

FOURIER, CHARLES (1772-1837) born at Besançon, died at Paris. He was one of the best-known French socialists, the founder of the school which takes its name from him (*École fouriériste sociétaire ou phalanstérienne*). Personally he was mild and sympathetic, possessing a singularly rich vein of imagination. His father was a linen-draper, and he himself was ruined when the city of Lyons was besieged by Chalier in October 1793. He had joined, like Jacquard, the army of the Count de Precy, who defended that city against the Convention. Fourier was fortunate enough to escape the scaffold, but he had to enlist, and passed two years under the colours. Having retired from active service, he started in life afresh in 1799, at Marseilles, as a commercial traveller attached to a house of business, and after that time was never out of employment, though this might be in a very humble capacity, living in the most quiet manner, his only amusements being the dreams on which the doctrines of his school were based. Fourier's disposition was gentle and conciliatory, and though his system might call up a smile, it never provoked hostility either before or after his death. Fourier commenced thinking out his system as early as 1799, but it was not till 1808 that his first work, a single volume in 8vo, appeared, entitled *Théorie des quatre mouvements et des destinées générales* (2nd ed. 1841). This contains what he proudly called his discovery. He sets forth in this that our planet is destined to exist for 80,000 years, of which 40,000 are occupied with ascending, and 40,000 equally with descending vibrations. The first 5000 years are occupied with the movement upwards out of chaos. They contain seven successive periods of retrogression : (a) the series of confusion (shadowing—happiness) ; (b) the savage state ; (c) the patriarchal ; (d) barbarism—of progress ; (e) civilisation (that in which we live) ; (f) garantisme (a state in which we are under protection) ; finally (g) series merely sketched out (the twilight of happiness). The 35,000 years which follow are designated "the ascending harmonies." They contain nine periods : first, the series of simple combinations (the dawn of happiness) ; then seven composite ascending series ; finally, one entitled "First septigenesic creation, advancing to perfection." The world will then enter (in 35,000 or 38,000 years) into the apogee of happiness. This is to last about 8000 years. After this the descending period (40,000 years) is to commence, which is to be passed through in an order symmetrically corresponding with the ascending period. Then the author, with a boldness of conception which disdains to indicate the course of the investigations which led him to this marvellous discovery, foresees, in an epoch comparatively nearer to our own, that is to say about 10,000 years distant, the advent of a "Northern Crown" (resembling the ring of Saturn) which, "through the influence of this crown, will usher in the disinfecting the oceans, and the perfuming them by means of the boreal fluid and an aromatic dew." This blessed result will last about 40,000 years, for the author, whose exactness is most conscientious, lets us know that all these figures respecting periods are based on the division of the whole into eighths. It is true that when the 40,000 years of the ascending period are added to the 40,000 years of the descending period, the 8000 years which form "a central or amphiharmonic period," and occupy the very centre of the existence of the earth, are omitted. It is indeed sad that this should be the case, for this period, 8000 years of perfect felicity, is the apogee of happiness. But all will desire to know what the four Movements are which Fourier indicates. These are "the social, the animal, the organic, and the material." Ten years later Fourier perceived that he had omitted one, which he describes as "the Aromatic," that is to say, "the system of the distribution of the aromas which sway men and animals, and form the germs of winds and epidemics, governing the sexual relations of the stars, and furnishing the specific characters of the different species." It should not be forgotten that Fourier regards the stars as having a life of their own. They are born and die. The moon is a dead planet, a corpse. Our own planet, as has been seen, will live for 80,000 years (more or less, within an eighth) and then will die. Fourier explains the way the stars come into existence in a note. A star may be generated : (1) Self-generated from a simple star through its north and south poles ; (2) from another star through the contrasting poles ; (3) from intermediaries, as the tuberose comes into existence from three aromas (Terre-sud, Herschell-nord, and Soleil-sud). To return to our poor planet which has to wait 38,000 years for complete happiness. The most eminent disciples of Fourier (V. Considérant, H. Renaud, and Hennequin, for example) have not followed him in his description of the future of the universe. They have contented themselves with accepting the organisation of society heralded by their leader. What is this organisation of society? Fourier starts from the position that neither passions nor inclinations are evil in themselves. What renders them so is the medium through which they develop. In a complete condition of harmony—it is thus that Fourier designates the final end to be attained—every passion will contribute its share to the general good, a prosperity so perfect that those who are the most difficult to please will be satisfied a hundredfold. In his system there is no appeal to self-devotion, but to the most unrestrained desires, to the most unbridled passions. Men and women are to be classified in accordance with their inclinations. Fourier expects to raise work from mere drudgery, as it is under our miserable state of civilisation, to being pleasant and attractive. To attain this he would have for the motive-power, not a sense of duty, nor even self-interest, but the passions. If every one only works as his fancy and his inclinations lead him all will be well. In order to reach this result he divides the workers into series and groups, and utilises their defects. Even their vices become, when arranged in harmony, useful stimulants. It would be somewhat tedious to follow Fourier through all the details of an organisation of society which, while most original, yet unfortunately panders to the physical appetites in a manner which renders his writings sometimes of dubious propriety. He extends the idea of the family in a singular manner. Thus a woman was to be allowed several husbands—a spouse, a father to her children, and a favourite, besides mere possessors—under different titles and with different rights, but all variable, according to taste or caprice. The man also is not in these matters bound to a very strict life. According to Fourier this liberty of love is to make an end to the vice and the hypocrisy of our civilisation. But would not this condition of things be itself a state of vice? According to our socialist this would not be the case, for in the state of harmony that which is vice to us becomes virtue, and *vice versa*. As will be seen, Fourier has treated morality in the same easy-going style that he has treated natural science. From the point of view of an economist and an administrator, Fourier organises the *Phalange*, which was to take the place of the *Commune*. The *Phalange* has for its centre (dwelling, workshop, school, town hall, and everything else) the *Phalanstery*, in which a life in common is carried on under certain rules which recall those of our early monasteries. The workers of each phalange, divided into series, groups, or sub-groups, according to their inclinations, are to go out to work as soldiers go out to drill. The individual disappears, and is replaced by the groups. Thanks to this marvellous organisation which through its perfection foresees everything, and provides for every want, prosperity replaces poverty, cheerfulness replaces all cares and troubles, good order and morality, as interpreted by Fourier, vice and crime. The chief of each phalange is entitled the *Unarque ;* three or four phalanges when united are placed under the charge of a *Duarque*, twelve phalanges under that of *Triarque*, and thus onwards to *Tetrarques, Pentarques, Exarques*, up to the *Omniarque* who governs the entire system of the phalanges (Fourier makes their number 2,985,984, neither more nor less). The omniarch is the sole ruler of our globe, and decides to live at Constantinople, which is to become the capital city of this world. He has to look after all these dignitaries, both small and great, the elected commissioners, etc. etc. The group or sub-group ought to be composed of at least nine persons ; the series includes from twenty-four to thirty-two groups or sub-groups. The number of the series of each phalange is not fixed. In this happy community there are neither to be courts of justice nor judges. How could these be needed since every error or crime, as we might term it, is a useful motive power. There is to be a division of profits in each phalange, as profits are to reach the consumer by means of exchanges, and not through any authoritative distribution. Capital is to be preserved in this stage, and the profits in the phalanges to go by shares. The division was to be between capital four-twelfths, labour five-twelfths, and ability three-twelfths. But how can consumption regulate production in this medium in which there is nothing to direct any one to useful labour except his instincts, his feelings, or his passions ? Fourier has omitted to inform us. One has to feel that in working through all this detail our author has never troubled himself about any crisis, whether caused by Man or Nature. All that we have stated and a vast deal more is to be found with but few exceptions in the work he wrote when launching his scheme, which bears the title of the *Théorie des quatre mouvements*.

[Fourier, however, went into more circumstantial details in other works, as *Le traité de l'association domestique agricole ou attraction industrielle*, 2 vols. 8vo, 1822 ; reprinted in 1841-43 in 4 volumes under the title of *Théorie de l'unité universelle, Le nouveau monde industriel et sociétaire* etc., 1 vol. 8vo, 1829. Two other editions have followed, the last (the 3rd) in 1848.—*Pièges et charlatanisme des sectes de Saint Simon et d'Owen*, 8vo, 1831, and finally *La fausse industrie morcelée, répugnante, mensongère, et l'antidote l'industrie naturelle, combinée, attrayante, véridique*, etc., 1835-36, 1 vol. of 840 pages. Periodical journals were also established to spread a knowledge of the societary doctrine. (1) *Le Phalanstère*, 1832-34, which became (2) *La Phalange*, 1835-1843, transformed after the death of Fourier into (3) *La démocratie pacifique*. This was the best known of all. It was suppressed by the *coup d'état* of 2nd December 1851. Fourier has been followed by many disciples both in France and in other countries, and a larger number still have adopted his ideas of social organisation. The best known of these is M. Victor Considérant, still vigorous at the age of eighty-five (written in 1893), hardy mountaineer as he is. All of Fourier's disciples have followed peaceful methods of propagating their ideas, and like their master, have lived generally respected. Attempts to establish phalansteries have been made at various times, but without success. At Condé-sur-Vesgres, and in 1832-33 at the expense of MM. Baudet-Dudlary and Devay brothers, who were disciples of the school, at Citeaux, in the buildings of the old abbey (a good choice so far). This last effort, under the guidance and at the expense of the brothers Young, was made in Algeria, l'Union du Sig, which afterwards was transformed into an ordinary business enterprise. In Texas, the colony was under the management of M. Victor Considérant. The FAMILISTÈRE (*q.v.*) at Guise borrows part of its regulations from Fourier. But these appear to be based on those laws which Fourier in his turn had borrowed from that natural organisation which political economy describes, see Ch. Gide's "Charles Fourier" in Guillaumin's *Petite Bibliothèque Écon. ;* also J. S. Mill's *Principles of Pol. Econ.*, vol. i. bk. ii. chap. i. §§ 3, 4.] A. C. f.

"Communism," Professor H. Sidgwick remarks (*Principles of Pol. Econ.*, bk. iii. ch. vii.), "is generally regarded as an extreme form of socialism, in which the most thoroughgoing antagonism to the institution of private property is manifested. . . . The proposal to organise society on a communistic plan, so as to distribute the annual produce of the labour and capital of the community either in equal shares, or in shares varying not according to the deserts, but according to the needs of the recipient, is one of which the serious interest has now passed away ; though a generation ago it had not a few adherents, and was supported with earnestness and ability by more than one competent writer."

FOURPENCE OR GROAT. The first English silver coin of greater value than the penny ; called a groat or grosse because of its size.

Reign.	Year.	Weight grains.	Fineness.	Value. In silver 925 fine at 5/6 an ounce.	Value. In silver francs 900 fine.
				d.	franc
Edward III.	*1351*	72	925	10	·96
Henry IV.	*1412*	60	„	$8\frac{1}{4}$	·80
Edward IV.	*1464*	48	„	$6\frac{1}{2}$	·64
Henry VIII.	*1527*	42·5	„	$5\frac{3}{4}$	·57
Do.	*1543*	40	„	$5\frac{1}{2}$	·53
Mary	*1553*	32	„	$4\frac{1}{2}$	·43
Elizabeth	*1601*	31	„	$4\frac{1}{4}$	·41
Charles II.	*1663*	Discontinued			
Victoria	*1836*	Recommenced			
Do.	*1836*	29·09	925	4	·39
Do.	*1856*	Again discontinued			
Do.	*1888*	Struck for use in the Colony of British Guiana only			
Do.	*1891*	Special coinage bearing the inscription "British Guiana and West Indies."			

Groats struck in the reign of Victoria bear the word "Fourpence" on the reverse. The coinage of Maundy fourpences was not discontinued in 1663, but these coins have been struck each year from that date till the present time (1893). F. E. A.

FRACHETTA, Girolamo (16th century), a statesman who, writing on financial matters, in reference to the duties of a ruler, considers it incumbent on him "to maintain abundance." He argued that for this purpose the nobility should bear their share of the public burdens, contributing, proportionately to their wealth, to the taxes paid by the common people.

Il Principe, di Girolamo Frachetta, 1597, Venetia. 2ª ediz. riveduta et in molti luochi ampliata dall' autore medesimo, Venetia, 1599. 3ª ediz. 1647. A. B.

FRACTIONAL CURRENCY. In countries using metallic currency, a considerable supply of small change is required in order to carry on the daily transactions of retail trade. This want is generally met by the use of token coins, authorised by law to be received as equal to a certain fraction of the standard of value, although not actually worth so much. Such coins are usually legal tender for comparatively small sums only (*e.g.* British silver coins are not legal tender for a greater sum than 40s.), and are occasionally limited in number to so many per head of the population. Fractional coins need not necessarily be mere tokens, and, indeed, are not always such; but in view of the fact that they are only required for convenience in conducting small transactions within the country of their issue, and are not used internationally, there does not appear to be sufficient reason for losing the profit which accrues on the issue of tokens (see Billon). F. E. A.

FRANC, History of. The origin of this name, as applied to a coin, is derived from the striking of a gold coin in 1360, on which was represented the king, John II., *the Good*, on horseback, with the legend Johannes Dei gracia Francorum Rex. These *francs à cheval*, as they were called, disappear after the middle of the 15th century. The *franc d'argent* from the first was equivalent to the *livre tournois*, and was worth twenty sous. French writers use the terms *francs* and *livres* almost without distinction, except that usage prescribed the use of *francs* only for even sums. It was possible to say either quatre francs or quatre livres, but not to say quatre francs cinq sols (now sous), the correct phrase being quatre livres cinq sols. The modern franc is the unit of the decimal coinage of France and the Latin Union. R. L.

FRANC, Coin. The unit of value, as well as the money of account, in the countries forming the Latin monetary union is, in France, Belgium, and Switzerland, called the franc. In Italy it bears the name lire, and in Greece drachma. The franc is divided into 100 centimes, the lire into 100 centesimi, and the drachma into 100 lepta.

The franc may consist of either 4·98 grains of gold 900 fine, or 77·16 grains of silver of the same fineness; the ratio between gold and silver being thus taken at $15\frac{1}{2}:1$.

The value of the gold franc in sterling (gold ($916\dot{6}$ fine at £3 : 17 : $10\frac{1}{2}$ an oz.), 9·52d. That of the silver franc is in English standard silver (925 fine at 5s. 6d. an oz.) 10·32d.; but with silver at the price of $34\frac{1}{2}$d. per ounce (August 1893) the melting value of a standard silver franc is slightly less than $5\frac{1}{2}$d.

There is no *standard* French coin of the value of one franc, the silver coin bearing that name being a token composed of silver 835 fine, and of the value only of ·93 of a standard silver franc.

The smallest standard coin in gold, and the only one in silver, is of the value of five francs. F. E. A.

FRANCE, Bank of. See Banks.

FRANCFIEF, Droit de. This was a payment made by a Roturier (*q.v.*) on acquiring lands previously held by a noble. The payment was originally made to the immediate lord, but in the 14th century it was claimed by the crown, and henceforth forms part of the domain revenue. The *droit de francfief* was of great importance in emphasising and maintaining the rigid division of classes in France.

[De Tocqueville, *L'Ancien Régime.*] R. L.

FRANCHI, Carlo (end of 18th century), a Neapolitan lawyer. There had been much discussion in the kingdom of Naples about redeeming the *arrendamenti*—that is, the public income, which had formerly been given to the creditors of the state. This transaction—which would now be termed a conversion of the public debt—had been proposed already by Pompeo Neri in Tuscany, and steps had been taken towards it in the kingdom of Naples by the institution of a council (*Giunta per la ricompera degli arrendamenti,* 1751), which proposed to reduce the interest to 4 per cent, or to pay off the money lent, principal and interest, with 7 per cent. The latter proposal was accepted, but many difficulties arose about the redemption of taxes; for, as the creditors had received these as their absolute property, they denied the right to take them back. Legal proceedings followed; and it was only in 1753 that the tribunal pronounced a judgment in favour of the government. During this BROGGIA proposed redemption at the current price, which was below the original one. On the other hand, Franchi strenuously defended the creditors in a memoir which Cossa thinks superior for its style to that of Broggia (*Introduzione allo studio dell' Economia Politica,* 1892, p. 251).

[*Memoria da umiliarsi a S. Maestà, in nome dei consegnatari dell' arrendamento dei Sali di Puglia,* 1750.]   A. B.

FRANCHISE. (*a*) Any privilege granted by the crown to exercise a right not otherwise exercisable by a subject, *e.g.* the right to have a forest or the right of manorial jurisdiction. The most conspicuous franchise in modern times is the right to hold a market (see MARKET). Franchises are termed "incorporeal hereditaments." (*b*) The right to vote at parliamentary elections. The parliamentary franchise in the United Kingdom has been simplified by the Representation of the People Act of 1884, but is still very complicated. The great bulk of the population vote as householders or lodgers in boroughs or counties. In England a person not otherwise disqualified is entitled to be put on the register as voter in respect of the household franchise:

(1) If he has for twelve calendar months before 31st July in the year in which he claims to be placed on the list, been a resident occupier, as owner or tenant, or by virtue of any office or employment of any dwelling-house within the borough or county for which he claims a vote;

(2) If the premises so occupied have been rated to the poor rate during the time of such occupation;

(3) If the rates payable up to the preceding 5th January have been paid before 20th July of the same year.

Any person not otherwise disqualified is in England entitled to be placed on the register as a lodger if he has for twelve calendar months before the 31st July resided in lodgings in the same house within the borough or county for which he claims a vote, such lodgings being, if occupied by the claimant alone, of the yearly value of £10 (if let unfurnished), and if occupied by the claimant jointly with others, of a yearly value equal to £10 for each lodger (if let unfurnished).

The household and lodger qualifications in Scotland and Ireland are of a similar nature.

Besides this franchise which depends on residence, there is one which depends on occupation of any land or house or part of a house of a clear yearly value of not less than £10—within the borough or county. The conditions as to time of occupation and payment of rates are similar to those to which the household franchise is subject. In English and Scotch boroughs residence within seven miles of the borough is a further condition, but in counties throughout the United Kingdom and in Irish boroughs no condition as to residence is attached to the occupation franchise.

Another kind of franchise is the property franchise, which depends on the ownership of land irrespectively of occupation or residence. The land in respect of which the right is available may be freehold, copyhold, or leasehold; but as regards the last mentioned kind of property the original length of the lease must have been at least fourteen years in Ireland, nineteen years in Scotland, and twenty years in England. The conditions as to yearly value vary between £2 and £5 in the case of freeholds; between £5 and £10 in the case of long leases, and between £20 and £50 in the case of short leases. The ownership of a rent-charge does not, since 1884, entitle to a vote, and in the case of joint tenants only one is now entitled to be placed on the register. In this way two easy methods of creating faggot votes have ceased to be available.

In addition to these general franchises some special franchises exist, viz. the franchise of the freemen or burgesses in certain ancient boroughs, and the university franchise.

In all cases the franchise is confined to adult men who are British subjects. Peers and certain public officers are disqualified, as well as convicts and persons in receipt of parochial relief other than surgical or medical assistance. Persons guilty of certain offences under the Corrupt Practices Act may be disenfranchised for a period which varies according to the nature of the offence.

There are substantial reasons for the agitation for a removal of the numerous anomalies connected with the parliamentary franchise, and much can be said for the principle embodied in the maxim "one man one vote." The usual argument that the present system gives a certain preponderance to property and education which it would be undesirable to remove, is open to many objections. As regards property it will be seen that only landed property is favoured, and only such landed property as happens to be situated in districts in which the owner does not reside. As regards education it is very doubtful whether it has any advantage under the present system. Considering how long education has been compulsory, it is now time for the "illiterate voter" to be removed from the register. As a general rule men belonging to the educated classes become householders much later in life than uneducated persons, and if they carry on any profession or business, it depends on merely accidental circumstances whether they have one vote or several votes or none at all. A barrister, not otherwise qualified, who has chambers in Lincoln's Inn and resides in Kensington, has two votes ; one who resides in Richmond has only one vote ; and one who during the summer months has lodgings in Richmond and during the winter months lodges in Kensington can take no part in parliamentary elections. A small tradesman may have a vote in respect of his place of business, and if he has shops in several districts, may have a number of votes, but the manager of a large joint-stock company has no similar privilege. A country banker not otherwise qualified, whose residence is within the borough in which his bank is situated, has one vote ; if he lives outside the borough but less than seven miles away from it he has two, if more than seven miles one. Similar instances showing that electoral power does not depend on education may be easily multiplied, and prove that the demand for further reform is not unreasonable. But the maxim "one vote one value" is closely connected with "one man one vote" and the consideration of this would take us beyond the limits to which this notice must be confined.

The qualifications for the franchise in continental countries vary considerably. In several countries the upper house is elective as well as the lower house, and the voters for the first-named chamber are taken from a more limited sphere than those for the other house: this was the plan adopted by Mr. Gladstone in his Home Rule Bill of 1893. By the new Belgian Constitution universal franchise is recognised, but certain classes of voters are to have a larger voting power. The German Reichstag is elected by universal suffrage—every male person having attained the age of twenty five has a vote—but in the individual German states the franchise varies. In Prussia the voters are divided into three classes according to the taxes which they pay ; each class elects an equal number of electors, and a majority of the chosen electors elect the members. As the first class is naturally much less numerous than the second, and the second less numerous than the third, a considerable advantage is given to the wealthier classes.

[Anson, *Law and Custom of the Constitution*, vol. i. pp. 89-112.] E. S.

FRANCIS, JOHN (1810-1886), entered the service of the bank of England 1833, became chief accountant 1870, retired 1875. Francis was author of the works named below, which form rather anecdotic than historical contributions to the analysis of the economic "anatomy" of the middle of the 19th century. In (a) the writer introduces his main inquiry by a sketch of the history of interest and banking ; in (b) he gives an outline of financial history and speculation, and describes the establishment and growth of the royal and stock exchanges ; (c) is both historical and statistical ; (d) includes a history of the practice of life assurance from Roman times, with some account of the origins of statistical science and of the modern application of the theory of probabilities to vital statistics.

(a) *History of the Bank of England ; its Times and Traditions*, London, 1848.—(b) *Chronicles and Characters of the Stock Exchange*, London, 1849.—(c) *A History of the English Railway ; its social Relations and Revelations, 1820-1845*, London, 1851.—(d) *Annals, Anecdotes, and Legends : a Chronicle of Life Assurance*, London, 1853.
O. A. F.

FRANCIS, PHILIP (1740-1818). Francis, son of the translator of Horace, was born at Dublin, educated in England first by his father, and then (1753-56) at St. Paul's school ; went from school to a clerkship in a government office ; was private secretary to General Bligh in the expedition to Cherbourg, 1758, and secretary of the embassy to Portugal, 1760. In 1762, Townshend procured him a clerkship in the war office, and he then began his career as a political writer. *The Letters of Junius*, which appeared 1769 to 1772, are now generally acknowledged to be his. In 1773 he went to India as member of the council of Bengal, and distinguished himself by persistent opposition to Warren Hastings. Returning in 1780, he represented Yarmouth (Isle of Wight), and sided with the opposition. He took a keen interest, if not an active part, in politics, even to the latest years of his life.

If we except the few remarks in the first Letter of Junius (*To the Printer of the Public Advertiser*, 21st January 1769), on the Public Debt, and Public Lotteries, there is little or nothing of economics in the famous *Letters*. Francis appears as an economist first (a) in a *Letter to Sir James Steuart on the Indian Currency*, dated Calcutta, 20th November 1776, and published in vol. v. of *Steuart's Collected Works*, ed. 1805, pp. 121-133. "On the 30th August 1771, Warren Hastings ordered that rupees of the eleventh, twelfth, and fifteenth years of Shah-Alam should pass on an equality with those of the nineteenth, and that thereafter all future issues should bear this date" (Mr. F. C. Harrison in *Econ. Journal*, 1893, p. 53). Steuart had communicated his opinion on this measure to the council ; and Francis defends the decision of the council. In 1810 (b) Francis published his *Reflections on the Abundance of Paper in Circulation, and the Scarcity of Specie*, with the motto, "*Ad tempora quibus nec vitia nostra nec remedia pati possumus perventum est.*" He writes before the report of the bullion committee (June 1810).

He describes the disease ; there is hardly any gold coin in the country ; it has all gone to pay our foreign creditors. Indeed there is hardly any silver coin. "There is none other than that of Birmingham for common change, and lately a few dollars. . . . They are all alike birds of passage. A lame dollar [slow to fly] will be as much a curiosity as a woodcock in August, for the dollars go just like the guineas" (p. 23). In spite of bank notes, we are falling into bankruptcy and beggary.

Where is the remedy ? There is none but a change of regimen. We must stop our foreign expenses, and give up useless wars like that in defence of Portugal (26, 27), and dismiss our present ministers, under whom "peace is not to be had with honour and security" (28).

He fortifies his position by quotations from Locke, from Sir John Moore's dispatches, and from a speech of his own on "the exorbitant paper circulation," delivered in the House of Commons, 31st March 1806. "Though it has been long in print, I see no reason to suspect that anybody has hitherto perused it but myself" (p. 41). It is worth noting, that in the said speech he had quoted from his old correspondent Steuart, on French Finance (p. 42). J. B.

The work of PINTO (q.v.) on *Circulation and Credit* was translated in 1774 by "Rev. S. Baggs," a pseudonym for Philip Francis, who feared by using his own name to offend Lord North and the ministry, and therefore borrowed his cousin's (M'Culloch, *Catalogue of the Library of a Political Economist*, 1862, p. 280. M'Culloch's authority is Joseph Parker).

FRANKALMOIGN, or *libera eleemosyna*, was applied, not to clerical tenure in general, but to a particular kind of it. A tenant held land in frankalmoign, when he was bound to say masses for the donor and his family, but was freed from the ordinary incidents of lay tenure. Frankalmoign corresponds somewhat to lay tenure by serjeanty, and both were maintained by the statute of 1660, which abolished feudal incidents (Kenelm Digby, *Hist. of Law of Real Property*, 1884). (See FREEHOLD.) R. L.

FRANKLIN, BENJAMIN (1706-1790), was a son of Josiah Franklin, a tallow chandler of Boston, Massachusetts. He was apprenticed to the printing business at the age of thirteen, but, restless and ambitious, he sought, in 1723, against his father's will, his fortunes in Philadelphia. In 1729 he established a newspaper, and soon became a leading spirit in colonial affairs. From 1736 to 1749 he was clerk to the General Assembly ; in 1737 he was appointed postmaster of Philadelphia, and in 1753 postmaster-general of the colonies. In 1754 he drew up a plan of union of the colonies, which, however, was not ratified. He was repeatedly engaged in diplomatic service, especially in France, both before and during the revolution of 1789.

Throughout his life Franklin contributed to newspapers essays on moral, philosophical, and political topics. Indolent, though fond of public affairs, he never devoted himself earnestly or persistently to any one department of knowledge, or he would undoubtedly have made a marked name in literature. On the subjects of commerce and money he displayed considerable originality. In 1729 he wrote *A Modest Inquiry into the Nature and Necessity of a Paper Currency*, in which he favoured an issue of paper money based upon land—a contribution to the landbank controversy of the period. The security of these bills would constantly improve as the increase of population would cause the land to rise in value. This first essay was followed by many others.

Although he confused capital and money he understood quite clearly the essential uses of the latter : "Money as a currency has an additional value by so much time and labour as it saves in the exchange of commodities." When he emphasised the advantages of a paper currency he had in mind paper money which was "well founded." In the latter part of his life he opposed the bill favoured by Congress authorising the first issue of bills of credit, and afterwards urged the substitution of loans. He favoured freedom of trade, deplored the evils of the mercantile system, and declared that industry is stimulated afresh when a country has to an inconvenient degree parted with its gold and silver. In the judgment of Dugald Stewart, "the expressions *laissez-faire* and *pas trop gouverner* are indebted chiefly for their extensive circulation to the short and luminous comments of Franklin, which had so extraordinary an influence on public opinion both in the old and new world." The circulation of his views on trade and industry was largely aided by the publication of *Richard's Almanac*, beginning in 1732. He reflected with more than usual acuteness upon the laws of population, and perceived that population was limited by definite checks ; see *Observations concerning the Increase of Mankind, Peopling of Countries*, etc., 1751. He was the first to estimate that the population of the American colonies doubled every twenty years. He condemned the English poor laws, and denounced any imitation of them by the colonies. In *Reflections on the Augmentation of Wages* he discriminated between cheap and low-priced labour, showing that high wages may be cheap labour.

Franklin was influenced by the writings of the French economists, which had considerable circulation in America, and in 1769 he followed the physiocratic doctrine of the unproductiveness of manufactures in *Positions to be Examined Concerning National Wealth*. His economic writings are conveniently collected in *Works of Benjamin Franklin* (Spark's ed.), Boston, 1836, vol. ii. pp. 253-521, annotated by Willard Phillips; or may be found in the several volumes of the last and best edition (edited by J. Bigelow, New York, 1887, 10 vols.), by consulting the index. A bibliography of his numerous writings is found in *Life of Benjamin Franklin*, by John Bigelow, Philadelphia, 1874, vol. iii. pp. 491-512.

D. R. D.

FRANKPLEDGE. There being no police system among the Anglo-Saxons, its place was supplied by the *frithborh*, or mutual responsibility. Every freeman had to have a *borh*, who was responsible for producing him if he was charged of crime, and whose property could be seized if the accused failed to appear. Under the Normans this practice grew into the more highly-organised frankpledge. The whole community was divided into bodies of ten men, who were responsible for bringing to justice any of their members. The visits of the sheriff to the hundred courts to see that this system was kept up were called the view of frankpledge.

R. L.

FRAUD. English judges have always been loth to bind themselves down to any hard and fast definition of fraud, lest the restless ingenuity of the dishonest should evade the wholesome restraint of the law. Fraud may be described roughly as any deceit practised by one person on another to the prejudice or intended prejudice of the latter. If the guilty party relies on a fraudulent transaction (for instance, a fictitious sale to defraud an execution-creditor), the transaction may be set aside though no one has been actually prejudiced, but if one person sets up fraud as a ground of relief against another, he must show that he was in fact deceived and prejudiced by the fraud. It consists essentially in a false representation, or its equivalent by active concealment as opposed to a mere non-disclosure of material facts. The false representation may be made by means of conduct as well as by words, written or spoken; and it is not necessary that any particular person should be contemplated as the victim of the fraud. For instance, if two persons agree to draw and accept fictitious bills of exchange, in order to defraud the acceptors' creditors in bankruptcy, whoever they may be, the transaction is a fraud.

It was formerly thought that there was a distinction between "legal" and "moral" fraud, and that a man might be guilty of legal fraud if he made a false representation, to the detriment of some other person, without reasonable grounds for believing his representation to be true. But it is now finally settled that there is no *tertium quid* between good faith on the one hand, and bad faith or fraud on the other. It is not essential that the person making the false representation should know it to be false. A reckless false statement, made without regard to its truth or falsehood, may amount to a fraud, for if a man asserts that he knows a thing to be true without knowing whether it is true or false, he is simply telling a lie. It is of course necessary that the false statement should be believed and acted upon by the person to whose detriment it operates. A lie, known to be such, does not come within the legal scope of fraud. It is at most an attempt to defraud. It follows from what has been already said that there may be various untrue representations which do not constitute frauds. The contract of sale may be taken as affording a good illustration. First, a representation made by the seller may form part of the contract, and amount to a warranty. In that case the false to the truth of it whether he believed it to be true or not. Secondly, the representation may be a mere expression of opinion or commendation by the seller of his wares. In that case it is inoperative, for the rule is, *simplex commendatio non obligat*. Thirdly, the representation may constitute part of the description of the thing sold. In that case the seller's knowledge is immaterial, for if the representation be not true, the parties were never at one as to the subject matter of the contract. Fourthly, the representation may be false and fraudulent. In that case, even if the representation only goes to part of the consideration, the whole transaction may be vitiated thereby.

A contract induced by fraud is voidable, not void. It is in the option of the party defrauded, when he finds out the fraud, either to affirm the transaction, holding the guilty party to the truth of his statements, and claiming compensation if necessary, or to set up fraud. If the contract has not been performed, the party guilty of the fraud cannot enforce it. If the contract has been performed, wholly or in part, the party defrauded may still repudiate the contract, unless it has become impossible to restore the parties to the position in which they would have been if the contract had not been made, or unless the rights of innocent third parties have intervened. If restitution be impossible, the party defrauded is driven to his remedy by action for damages, in respect of the injury he has suffered. Formerly this action was known as the "action of deceit," but it is now commonly described as an action for false and fraudulent representations.

Various specific frauds are punished by the criminal law, and it is to be noted that any combination of two or more persons to defraud the public, or a third person, constitutes an indictable conspiracy.

[Anson on *Contracts*, 5th ed. (1888).—Pollock on *Contracts*, 5th ed. (1889).—Stephen's *Digest of the Criminal Law*, 3rd ed. (1883).] M. D. C.

FRAUDS, THE STATUTE OF. This statute, 29 Charles II. c. 3, is entitled in the statutes at large "an act for prevention of frauds and perjuries." It was passed in the year 1678, as explained in the preamble, "for the prevention of many fraudulent practices, which are commonly endeavoured to be upheld by perjury and subornation of perjury." It guards against these evils by providing for certain important transactions an obligatory form consisting of a writing and signature. But a brief analysis is necessary for the proper understanding of the statute.

The statute consists of twenty-five short sections roughly drafted and arranged in a very loose order. It deals with the following subjects :—(1) contracts ; (2) leases ; (3) creations and assignments of trusts ; (4) wills ; (5) judgments.

1. *Contracts.*—The sections relating to contracts are : § 4 requires a memorandum in writing signed by the party who is to be made liable, or by the agent of such party, for any contract of the five following kinds :—

(*a*) Promise by an executor or administrator to make good out of his own estate damages recoverable out of the estate of the deceased.

(*b*) Promise amounting to guarantee or undertaking to go surety.

(*c*) Promise made upon consideration of marriage (explained not to mean a promise of marriage).

(*d*) Agreement for sale of real property or of any interest therein.

(*e*) Agreement not to be performed within the space of a year from the making thereof.

§ 17 requires for a contract for the sale of goods for the price of £10 or upwards, either

(*a*) part acceptance of goods sold, or

(*b*) payment of earnest or part payment of price, or

(*c*) a memorandum in writing made and signed by *both* parties to the contract or by their agents.

Lord Justice Brett in the case of Britain v. Rossiter, and Lord Blackburn in the case of Maddison v. Alderson, have laid down that the effect of failure to comply with the provisions of either of these sections, in a case to which they are applicable, is not to prevent the formation of a contract, but to render proof of the contract inadmissible. But these sections cannot be correctly understood without reference to text-books on contract, and to the reported cases, amounting to many hundreds, which elucidate them. Their utility has been the subject of the most contradictory opinions by experts. Their intent was to ensure proper evidence of important contracts. The objections to these sections are briefly as follows :—

(*a*) "Restrictions on contracts so wide and general as are prescribed by this act are peculiar to the English law and the American, which has derived them from the English" (Leake, *Papers of Juridical Society*, vol. i. No. 14).

(*b*) As the existence of these restrictions is not generally known to men of business, the statute has introduced insecurity into business transactions. Thus a verbal contract for the sale of goods over the value of £10, where there has not been part payment of the price or part acceptance of the goods, cannot be enforced because of the statute, although of frequent occurrence in business. Although it has hindered the perpetration of fraud through a feigned contract established by perjury, it has enabled dishonest men to elude agreements which they were morally bound to keep.

(*c*) The evils against which these sections were originally directed have been much lessened since parties were allowed to be witnesses in their own causes. (See 14 & 15 Vict. c. 99, § 2, etc.)

(*d*) These sections being roughly drafted have "introduced great confusion and uncertainty into the law of contract," so that "it is universally admitted that no enactment of any legislature ever became the subject of so much litigation" (Leake).

The 17th section appears to have fallen practically into disuse. Mr. Justice Stephen says that he has hardly ever been called upon to decide a case under it, and is informed that in some large towns mercantile men repudiate it in practice.

2. *Leases.*—The sections relating to leases are §§ 1, 2, and 3. They require (*a*) that every lease shall be in writing signed by the parties or their agents, except leases not exceeding the term of three years, and in which the rent reserved to the landlord amounts to at least two-thirds of the full improved value of the property demised. A lease which fails to comply with this requirement creates only a tenancy at will.

(*b*) That every assignment, grant, or surrender of a leasehold interest shall be in writing signed by the parties or their agents.

In cases where the statute of frauds requires a writing for the creation or assignment of a leasehold interest, the Act 8 & 9 Vict. c. 106 requires a deed. But a lease invalid for non-compliance with these statutes may yet be valid as an agreement to grant a lease. Such agreements come under the provision of § 4 respecting agreements for the sale of interests in land.

(3) *Creations and Assignments of Trusts.*—The sections relating to trusts are—

§ 7 requires that every creation of a trust in real estate shall be proved by some writing signed by the party creating the trust or by his last will in writing.

§ 8 excepts from the operation of the statute trusts arising not from the act of any party, but from an implication of law in case of certain transactions.

§ 9 requires that every assignment of a trust, not in real estate only, shall be in writing signed by the party assigning, or by his last will in writing.

§§ 10 and 11 enact that real estate held upon trust for any person shall be regarded as forming part of that person's assets both in his own hands and in those of his heir.

These sections continue in force, but have not occasioned much criticism.

4. *Wills.*—The sections relating to wills are no longer in force. They provided as follows :—

§ 5 required every will of real estate to be in writing signed by the testator or by some other person in his presence, and by his express direction, and attested and subscribed by three or four credible witnesses.

§ 6 provided that no will of real estate should be revoked otherwise than by (*a*) a subsequent will or codicil or some other writing executed as above, or by (*b*) burning, tearing, or obliterating by the testator, or in his presence by his direction.

§§ 19, 20, 21 imposed restrictions on the validity of nuncupative wills (wills made by word of mouth).

§ 22 rendered null and void the alteration, by word of mouth only, of a written will of personal property.

§ 23 made an exception for the nuncupative will of a soldier on service or sailor at sea.

§§ 24 and 25 do not call for notice here.

The above were the first enactments which imposed an obligatory form upon wills. The objections to such a requirement made in the case of contracts certainly do not apply in the case of wills. But this part of the statute of frauds has been wholly superseded by the Wills Act, 1 Vict. c. 26, which requires every will other than that of a soldier on service or a sailor at sea to be in writing signed by the testator and attested by two witnesses, and requires for the revocation of a will either a writing executed with these forms or the destroying of the will by the testator or in his presence and by his direction.

5. *Judgments.*—The sections relating to judgments—

§§ 13, 14, 15 provide that a judgment as against purchasers, *bona fide*, of real estate, liable under the judgment, shall take effect only from the time when the judgment is signed. Formerly judgments had taken effect as against such purchasers from the first day of the term wherein they were entered, or some other time prior to the one thus fixed. Now no judgment affects any land until such land shall have been actually delivered in execution in pursuance of the judgment, 27 & 28 Vict. c. 112.

§ 16 provides that a writ of execution against goods shall take effect only from the time when the writ is delivered to the sheriff for execution. Formerly such writs took effect against such purchasers from the first day of the term in which they were issued. Now they do not take effect until the goods have been actually seized, 19 & 20 Vict. c. 97.

[For further information respecting the statute of frauds, consult text of statute and the following authorities :—Pollock, *Principles of Contract.*—Leake, *Digest of the Law of Contract.*—Williams on *Personal Property ;* Williams on *Real Property*, and the cases referred to in these works. For general criticism of the statute consult No. 14 in the first volume of *Papers of the Juridical Society* (by Mr. Leake), and an article on "Section Seventeen of the Statute of Frauds," contributed by Mr. Justice Stephen and Sir Frederick Pollock to the *Law Quarterly Review*, January 1885.] F. C. M.

FRAUDULENT CONVEYANCE. These words are generally used with reference to conveyances pronounced to be void by the statutes 13 Elizabeth c. 5, and 27 Elizabeth c. 4. The first-named act avoids, as against *creditors*, all conveyances of landed estates and goods for the purpose of "delaying, hindering, or defrauding" such creditors, unless made on valuable consideration to any person not having any notice of such fraud. As the Bankruptcy Act 1883, subjects all voluntary settlements within ten years of a bankruptcy to the possibility of being declared void, it is seldom necessary to have recourse to the act of Elizabeth, but this may be necessary in cases where property has been given away by an insolvent debtor without being settled, or when the voluntary conveyance was more than ten years old at the date of the bankruptcy. The act of the 27th year of Elizabeth is applicable to *real* property only, and was intended to meet the case of a vendor who, previously to conveying land to a purchaser for value, had fraudulently conveyed it to another person, who by virtue of his priority had acquired the whole property ; but judicial interpretation has extended its scope, and until 1893 all voluntary conveyances of land were void as between the original donee and a subsequent purchaser for value. The Voluntary Conveyances Act of 1893 has repealed this extension of the act of Elizabeth, and the operation of the act will in future be confined to such voluntary conveyances as are fraudulent in the real sense of the word. E. S.

FRAUDULENT PREFERENCE (IN BANKRUPTCY). The main object of the bankruptcy laws is to secure the equal distribution of the debtor's assets amongst his various creditors. From the time when the trustee's title accrues, the debtor is no longer free to select the order in which he will pay his debts. Under § 43 of the Bankruptcy Act 1883, the title of the trustee relates back to the earliest act of bankruptcy within three months of the petition, and this provision is supplemented by § 48, which enacts that "every conveyance or transfer of property or charge thereon made, every obligation incurred, every payment made, and every judicial proceeding taken or suffered by any person unable to pay his debts as they become due from his own money, in favour of any creditor, or in trust for any creditor, *with a view of giving such creditor a preference over the other creditors*" shall, if the debtor be adjudged bankrupt on a petition presented within three months of the date of the transaction in question, be deemed fraudulent and void as against the trustee. Under the act of 1869 the transaction was protected if the creditor acted in good faith and without notice of any act of bankruptcy. The present act disallows the exception. The only question for consideration is the motive of the debtor in making the transfer or payment.

Fraudulent preference in bankruptcy must be distinguished from fraudulent conveyance under the statute 13 Elizabeth, c. 5. The act of Elizabeth operates whether there be a bankruptcy or not,—it contains no provision as to time, and its general scope is somewhat different. It strikes at collusive transactions by which creditors may be defeated or delayed, but does not prohibit the honest preference of one creditor over another.   M. D. C.

FREE BANKING is the term applied in the United States to a system under which (1) banking powers are granted to all applicants under certain prescribed conditions, and (2) bank-notes issued under such authority are protected by a deposit of security held by the government which establishes the system. The earlier banks in the United States, whether established by congress or by the state legislatures, were organised under special charters. Various expedients were resorted to for the prevention of unsound issues, with various degrees of success, but without arriving at any generally acceptable method. The suspension of specie payments in May 1837, and the extraordinary confusion of the paper currency which ensued, finally brought the general discontent to a climax in New York, and the legislature of that state, in June 1838, passed an act for the free organisation of banks issuing a secured currency. Under this act, as amended and revised, any group of persons proposing to form a banking association, and contributing a capital in no case less than $25,000, say £5000, can be incorporated with full banking powers, subject to uniform regulations as to the conduct of their business, its supervision by the state, and their corporate liabilities and duties. Individual bankers and firms, who use the name "bank," are also required to conform to the system, although they may remain unincorporated. The right of issue is given to any association or individual coming under the system. The notes are prepared and registered by a public officer, are delivered to the issuing bank only after the deposit of security of a prescribed kind and amount, and must be signed by the officers of the bank before issue. Banks organised upon such a system are called free banks.

Free banking does not imply, then, an unrestricted management of the business, or complete liberty in the issue of notes. Such a system is called free because the right to organise, upon compliance with fixed conditions, is extended to all, free from any requirement of special legislation. It is not essential that there should be any engagement by the state to make the notes good, if the security, of which the state is trustee, proves insufficient. Neither does the deposit of security for the ultimate payment of the notes answer the question as to proper provision for daily redemption. As the provision for secured notes gave promise of insuring the ultimate solvency of bank notes, it settled the one banking question as to which the public were most sensitive, and enabled the legislature to renounce the task of deciding upon applications for special charters. The system adopted by New York was copied by many other states before the civil war, but in some cases with relaxations which impaired its safety. In 1861 the New York free banks, having on deposit stocks of the United States and other solid securities, met the strain of war with success. In several states, where the law was less rigid, many free banks went down, and their notes, secured in some cases chiefly by bonds of seceded states and others in low credit, caused heavy losses to the holders. Two years later congress adopted the free banking system on a great scale, by a law providing for national banks, to be organised on application under a general act, and to issue notes with United States bonds as the only admissible security. In 1865 congress laid a tax of ten per cent on all bank notes other than national, thus excluding from the field all issues authorised by the states. Several of the states, however, still retain their laws as to circulation, although these have been entirely dormant since 1866. Free banking under the national system was for some years seriously limited, by the provision that the aggregate of notes issued by all the national banks should not exceed $300,000,000, afterwards $354,000,000 (say £60,000,000, and £70,800,000) although the organisation of banks was still free to all. The act of 1875, for resuming specie payments, removed the limit of aggregate circulation, and thus completely established free banking under the national government. The rapid rise in price of United States bonds, and the low return yielded by an investment in them, have since put a new check upon the system ; and if the use of bank-notes is to continue, the alternative may soon be presented, of either finding for deposit by national banks some other security than United States bonds, or removing the prohibitory tax upon issues authorised by the states. In the latter case free banking would be likely to be adopted by the states more widely than before, and with provisions exhibiting great variety of detail, unless some arrangement should be devised for the regulation of local issues by national authority upon a common plan.

[*Report of the Comptroller of the Currency* (United States), 1876.—*Public Statutes of Massachusetts,* 1880.—*Revised Statutes of New York,* 1889.—C. F. Dunbar, *Chapters on the Theory and History of Banking; and Laws of the United States relating to Currency, Finance, and Banking from 1789 to 1891.*—Andrews, *Institutes of Economics,* 1889, pt. iii.]   C.F.D.

FREE BENCH. A widow's dower out of lands held by customary tenure for customary estates of inheritance. It is generally one-third for life, but varies from a portion of the profits to the whole inheritance. The right to free bench does not arise until the death of the husband, and therefore it only affects land of which he was donor at the time of his death (Challis, on *Real Property,* London, 1885).

                                                   J. E. C. M.

FREE COINAGE. In its fullest sense a right enjoyed by all persons to bring gold or silver bullion, or both, to a mint and to receive it back in the form of coin, no deduction being made to defray the expenses of manufacture, alloy metal, etc. The conversion at a mint of bullion belonging to a private holder into coin at a fixed charge, as till lately in Austria, may however be considered *free* when compared with such a system as that in force in this country in regard to the silver currency. For in this latter case the government purchases bullion at the market price, always issuing it at a circulating value of 5s. 6d. per troy ounce of standard metal.

In this country until towards the end of the 17th century, any person was permitted to bring bullion, both gold and silver, to the mint and receive it back in the form of coin, less a certain deduction which was paid to the king as a SEIGNORAGE (*q.v.*), or was employed to defray the expenses of the mint, see BRASSAGE. In 1666 perfect freedom of coinage for both metals was established. An "Act for encouraging of Coynage" (18 Chas. II. c. v.) was passed whereby it was enacted that "Whatsoever person or persons, Native or Foreigner, Alien or Stranger, shall from and after the twentieth day of December, one thousand six hundred sixty and six, bring any Foreign Coyn, Plate or Bullion of Gold or Silver, in Mass, Molten or Allayed, or any sort of Manufacture of Gold or Silver into His Majesties Mint or Mints within the Kingdom of England, to be there melted down and Coyned into the current Coyns of this Kingdom, shall have the same there Assayed, Melted down and Coyned with all convenient speed, without any defalcation, diminution, or charge for the Assaying

Coynage or waste in Coynage." This important change was proposed in consequence of the great scarcity of currency owing to the common practice of melting and exporting coins, and the act was to remain in force for a period of seven years only. It was, however, renewed at seven-year intervals without intermission until 1768, and then made perpetual. The continuing acts make frequent reference to the desirability of renewing the grant to the king of rates, duties, and impositions "upon the importation of Wines, Vinegar, Cyder, Beer, Brandy, and Strong Waters," which were set aside for the maintenance of the mints, lest "this Kingdom be deprived for the future of so great a good as it hath for so many years last past enjoyed." It is clear, from the currency literature of the period, especially that published towards the end of the 17th century, that this latter opinion was far from being universally held. Sir Dudley NORTH, for example, writes in 1691, in reference to the melting of newly-coined money by private persons, "Thus the Nation hath been abused and made to pay for the twisting of Straw for Asses to eat," and the imposition of a charge sufficient to defray the expenses of the mint has been advocated by Adam SMITH, J. S. MILL, RICARDO, and many other economists of note.

The free coinage of silver was suspended in 1798, in consequence of the low price of bullion, and finally abolished in 1816, when our present currency was introduced, although the right was then reserved to the king to authorise the receipt of silver for coinage at the mint, subject to a deduction on account of seignorage of 4s. from every pound weight of sixty-six shillings. This right has, however, never been exercised.

When in 1869 the chancellor of the exchequer, Mr. Lowe, afterwards Lord Sherbrooke, proposed to meet the expenses of coinage by deducting one grain of gold from the weight of each sovereign issued, the subject of free coinage was exhaustively discussed in parliament and the press, and it is curious to note that, whereas two centuries previously free coinage had been adopted "for the encouragement of the bringing of Gold and Silver into the Realm," the main argument urged against Mr. Lowe's proposal was that it would have a disastrous effect on British commerce by interfering with the free use of the sovereign in commercial transactions abroad.

In no other country is the coinage of gold as absolutely free as it is in England, but in the United States all charges have been abolished since 1875, except that for the alloying metal. In France, and the other States forming the "Latin" Union, the charge imposed amounts to 6·70 fr. per kilog. of gold of standard 900 (value 3,100 fr.) or 0·216 per cent; in Germany it is 0·215 per cent, or nearly the same ; and the Japanese mint imposes a charge of 0·7 per cent.

Free coinage of silver, even in the more restricted sense, has now been generally abolished. Up to June, 1893, silver was coined for private persons at the Indian mints at a charge of 2·1 per cent, but this liberty was then withdrawn. No European State undertakes the coinage of silver except on government account, and the same is the case in the United States, where the law requiring the purchase by the government of a definite quantity of the metal has now been repealed. In Mexico the export of uncoined silver bullion is prohibited ; all silver intended for export must, therefore, pass through one of the mints, where a coinage charge amounting to 4·41 per cent, is imposed. Most of the Central and South American states impose a charge for the coinage of silver, which amounts, in Peru, to as much as 9·86 per cent.

[*Report of the Royal Commission on International Coinage*, 1868, p. 320.—*The Times* and other newspapers, Aug. to Oct. 1869.—S. Dana Horton, *The Silver Pound*, 1887.—Lord Liverpool's *Letter to the King on the Coins of the Realm*, 1805.—*The Gold Coinage Controversy*, 1869 (privately printed by the Bank of England).—"Seigneurage and Mint Charges," by J. B. Martin, *Journ. Inst. Bankers*, vol. v. (1884), p. 171.]   E. R.

The Bank of England is bound by law to purchase at the rate of £3 : 17 : 9 an ounce any gold bullion of the legal standard brought to it by the public for sale. Private persons may likewise bring bullion to the mint, and receive back the full amount (at £3 : 17 : 10½ an ounce) converted into coin, free of any charge for loss or manufacture ; but as there may be considerable delay, the public prefer to sell their bullion to the bank and receive their value at once (see article on Mint, *Ency. Brit.*, 9th ed., vol. xvi. p. 485). The payment to the bank thus does not represent any charge on the coinage, but only remuneration for trouble and loss of time.

FREEDOM IN THE MIDDLE AGES. Though there was not an absolutely fixed line in the middle ages between those who were possessed of freedom, and those who were not, yet the division between these two classes was for many purposes very distinctly marked. The following article on the FREEDOM OF THE CITY OF LONDON will serve as an example of the rights and privileges conferred by obtaining freedom in a city. For other branches of the subject see articles on ENFRANCHISEMENT, FREEMAN, FREE TOWNS, SERF, SERFDOM, SERVITUDE, and VILLEIN.

FREEDOM OF THE CITY OF LONDON. The right to share in the duties and privileges of citizenship in London seems in the earliest times to have been extended to all holders of tenements, who were in SCOT AND LOT (*q.v.*), and who were therefore called upon to contribute

to common civic burdens and to fill leet offices. Even to-day "inhabitancy as a householder is still termed the common law qualification of burghers, and the scot and lot householder, when admitted a freeman, remains the only true and efficient citizen for *all* civic purposes" (Norton, *Commentaries*, pp. 100, 101), although others have in later times been admitted with certain qualifications to the enjoyment of some of his rights. After the grant of a corporation, *temp.* Richard I. (1189-1199), *enrolment* into the civic freedom was required of all freemen. Norton suggests that this step was taken "very soon after, if not immediately upon, the foundation of the corporation itself," and that enrolment took place in the hustings court, urging that such admissions are referred to as common in the reigns of Edward I. (1272-1307) and Edward II. (1307-1327). It would seem, however, that the practice of enrolment can be definitely traced to the year 1275, when it was provided that the names of apprentices and of all who wished to buy the freedom should be inscribed "in papirio camere gildaulæ" (Brit. Mus. *Cott. MSS.*, *Otho*, B iii. transcribed in *Add. MSS.*, 5444, f. 90 ; Brandon, *Inquiry into the Freedom of the City of London*, p. 15). In that same year the methods of acquiring the freedom would seem to correspond to those in vogue to-day. It is stated in the MS. above quoted that there are three ways, (1) by birth ; (2) by apprenticeship, and that for a term of not less than seven years—an interesting and possibly the earliest notice of this custom of London ; (3) by taking it up "before the mayor and other aldermen in the chamber of the city." In Edward II.'s reign a mercantile qualification becomes an important feature. By a charter of 12 Edw. II. inhabitants and others, being of any certain mystery or trade, might be admitted into the freedom only "by surety of six honest and sufficient men of the mystery or trade that he shall be of, who is so to be admitted," and that in the hustings courts. If, however, they were strangers and not of some certain mystery, they could not be admitted into the freedom without the assent of the commonalty ; "saving always, that concerning apprentices the ancient manner and form of the said city be observed" (Cp. Birch, *Hist. Charters*, p. 47). Somewhat later it was ordained that no one should be admitted into the freedom of the city, unless the wardens of a company gave their consent and certified that he was a member of their body (Brandon, p. 19, quoting *Liber Dunthorne*, f. 101 b). This restriction remained in force until by a resolution of common council, 17th March 1835, it was decided to confer freedom on certain terms through the city chamberlain irrespective of the great trading companies (Minutes of Common Council, 17th March 1835).

(1) The most ordinary form of acquiring

freedom was by serving an apprenticeship to a freeman, free both of a company and of the city, until an act of common council (9th March 1836) sanctioned the binding of apprentices to freemen of the City who had not taken up the freedom of any company (Minutes). The term of service in London was for seven years until 1889, when it was reduced to four years (Act of Common Council, 14th March 1889). While, however, apprenticeship for a varying term of years (until 5 Eliz. c. 4, fixed the minimum at seven)—came in most English towns to be the one method by which citizenship was acquired, in London, although very usual, it never became the sole qualification.

(2) Freedom by patrimony has, as shown above, conferred civic freedom from early times ; all children male and female of a freeman born after his admission can claim their freedom at the age of twenty-one years.

(3) Freedom by redemption or purchase. This is possible (a) where the apprenticeship indentures have, for some good reason, been only imperfectly executed ; (b) where persons, not aliens, are admitted by grace and favour ; (c) where the presentment is by the chamberlain, or some person entitled by grant to confer freedom (Reports, 1837, xxv. p. 61). The commission on municipal corporations issued a report in 1835 which excluded London, a subject which was dealt with in a special report issued in 183. In this the important resolution and the a s of common council (17th March 1835 ; 9th March 1836) are left out of account, and an additional case of freedom by redemption is quoted as possible, though not very common ; (d) this was where an individual, entitled to admission through one company, desired to be admitted through another. The majority of cases by redemption are simple purchases, the buyers being presented to the Court of Aldermen and admitted upon the payment of certain fees (Pulling, Customs, p. 64), though the consent of the Court of Common Council is required in the case of aliens. And to-day, practically any one can buy the freedom, although such a purchase does not confer all the privileges of citizenship (City of London Directory, 1893).

Females may obtain the freedom by patrimony or by apprenticeship, taking an oath, similar to that of a freeman, as a "free sister." As such they may take male apprentices and enjoy various privileges, though these are suspended by marriage. Widows of freemen are deemed free by courtesy during the period of widowhood (Reports, 1837, xxv. 61, 63).

The fines payable on admission seem to have been very arbitrary, and to have varied considerably at different times, the exact sum being fixed at the discretion of the aldermen and chamberlain (Brandon, p. 20).

From early times exceptional privileges have been granted by the crown to the citizens of London in a series of charters, while ancient customs have been confirmed or amended by city ordinances (Charter, 15 Edw. III. ; Norton, p. 364) ; in case of necessity these are recorded "by the mouth of the recorder" before the king's justices without the intervention of a jury (Charter, 2 Edw. IV. ; Birch, p. 76). For a detailed account of the privileges, careful examination of many documents is essential, and it may be sufficient to indicate such as are noticed by the chief authorities on the subject, and which have dealt with the trade and government of the city. The right to engage in retail trade could be enjoyed by all freemen whether resident or not, and by them alone, until an act of common council in 1856 admitted all, whether free of the city or not, to retail trade. On the question of wholesale trade there has been much difference of opinion. It would seem that though strangers, i.e. non-freemen, might engage in wholesale trade, they might deal only with freemen and not with other strangers ; the commissioners of 1837 stated however that, though not enforced, wholesale trading should, strictly speaking, be limited to freemen. Freemen have always been held exempt from all tolls and customs held by the crown throughout the country when Henry I.'s charter was granted, non-resident freemen being merely free from city tolls and port dues. They were free from impressment as soldiers or sailors (Charter, 15 Edw. II.), nor could they be forced to plead without the city. The right to share in the government of the city, directly or indirectly, has also from early times been restricted to freemen ; they alone can enjoy appointments in the gift of the common council, though this rule is suspended in the case of barristers (Reports, 1837, xxv. 38) ; and the highest civic officials, e.g. lord mayor, sheriffs, etc., even to-day must be liverymen of some company. For centuries the freemen paying scot and bearing lot elected the members of the common council, the aldermen, and ward officers, until, indeed, by 30 Vict. c. 1, the right was extended to occupiers and lodgers who were not freemen of the corporation (Norton, pp. 244, 251). By a civic ordinance of 49 Edw. III., the trading companies were empowered to nominate a certain number of freemen to vote in the elections of lord mayor, sheriffs, corporation officials, and parliamentary representatives, and from these the mayor selected the voters (Norton, p. 245). But by ordinance of 15 Edw. IV. the nomination was left entirely in the hands of the companies, the members of which, then and for long afterwards, were all traders and therefore almost necessarily householders. They were directed to send some of their more important members to take part in elections, attired in a distinctive dress or livery. And from this dates the appearance of the livery men as a superior class within the companies, to whom was entrusted the elective franchise in the common hall; this they exercised until 11 Geo. II. c. 18 extended it to liverymen, free of the city, but not necessarily residents (Norton, 107). And this remains to-day the qualification of electors to corporate offices in common hall (*ib.* 251); the number of liverymen thus qualified was 7603 in 1893 (*City of London Directory*, 198). The various reform bills of this century have extended the parliamentary franchise to others than freemen, although a liveryman and freeman of London by birth or servitude, and residing within twenty-five miles, can still claim a vote.

The right to benefit by certain charities, and of appointment to certain civic offices, and to the election of certain municipal and parliamentary representatives, are perhaps the most obvious and the most important of those which may be enjoyed by freemen and liverymen to-day, although the ancient "custom" still holds good where it has not been expressly given up.

[Norton, G., *Commentaries, etc., on London* (1869). —Pulling, A., *Laws, Customs, etc., of London* (1854).—Brandon, W., *Enquiry into the Freedom of City of London* (1850).—Extracts (*Brit. Mus.*, 6425, cc. 19).—Austin, E., *Law Relating to Apprentices* (1890).—Birch, W. de Gray, *Historical Documents and Charters, etc., of London* (1887).—Bohun, W., *Privilegia Londini* (1702).—Welch, C., *Leaves from History of Gilds, etc., in Newbery House Magazine* (1892, 1893).—Merewether, H. A., and Stephens, A. J., *History of Boroughs and Municipal Corporations.—Second Report of Commissioners appointed to enquire into Municipal Corporations in England and Wales* (1837, xxv.). Also *Reports*, 1854, vi.—*Acts and Minutes of Court of Common Council.—Liber Albus.—City of London Directory* (1893).] E. A. M.

FREE ENTERPRISE. See LAISSEZ-FAIRE.

FREEHOLD, HISTORICAL. The term "freehold" we owe to the mediæval law of real property. It is used to describe such tenures as were considered worthy of a freeman. According to the theory of feudalism the political and civil rights of the individual depended on his relation to the land. In a feudal society developed according to strict logic the freeholder alone would have been a freeman, and only the freeman would have been a freeholder. But in no European country, least of all in England, was the feudal principle worked out to all its logical consequences. Only the freeman could be a freeholder. But even in the feudal period freemen frequently held land by tenures other than freehold, by tenures technically regarded as base or servile.

The term "freehold" appears to have come into use about the end of the eleventh or the beginning of the twelfth century. "Some time before the reign of Henry II., but apparently not so early as Domesday, the expression *liberum tenementum* was introduced to designate land held by a freeman by a free tenure" (Kenelm

Digby, *History of the Law of Real Property*, p. 49). But the thing had been developed long before the name had been found for it.

Some characteristics are common to all freehold tenures. (1) The indefinite duration of the freeholder's interest in his land. An estate to a man for his life (a life estate), an estate to a man and his descendants (estate tail), an estate to a man and his heirs (fee simple estate) are all freehold estates. They are likely to differ much in point of duration. But they are all alike in this that the moment of determination is uncertain. A lease of land for 999 years does not give a freehold estate to the lessee. It is not likely that this consideration would have led any free man to prefer an estate for life to an estate for 999 years. But when the theory of freehold tenures grew up, long leases were unknown and leases of whatever duration were uncommon. (2) The obligation of fealty. The freehold tenant did homage to the lord for his land and took an oath of fealty. (3) The liability to forfeiture and escheat. Upon the tenant's failure to perform any of the conditions on which he received his land, he incurred the penalty of forfeiture and his land might be resumed by the lord. Upon the failure of the tenant's line either for want of heirs or through corruption of blood consequent upon his conviction for felony the land reverted to the lord in virtue of his right of escheat (see FORFEITURE). (4) Suit of court. The tenant was bound to appear as an assessor in the lord's feudal court of justice, and for some purposes to submit himself to the jurisdiction of that court.

In general the services which the various classes of freehold tenants had to render to their lords were only such as appeared consistent with the dignity of a free man. But they differed so much in character that they must be considered separately with reference to each species of freehold tenure.

I. Tenure by chivalry or by knight service. On this tenure land was held by the military tenants of the crown and also by the military tenants of earls and barons. Its distinguishing characteristic was the obligation to render military service, if called upon, for forty days in each year, with a number of fully-armed horsemen proportioned to the size of the estate. From the time of Henry II. onwards this obligation was frequently commuted for a money payment known as scutage (shield-money). But this tenure involved other burthensome obligations. The principal were as follows:—

(*a*) The liability to aids or payments made to the lord upon certain important occasions, the knighting of his eldest son, the marriage of his eldest daughter, or the ransoming of his person from captivity. (*b*) The liability to reliefs or payments made to the lord by the heirs of deceased tenants upon coming into their estates. (c) Wardship or the right of the lord to administer the estate during the minority of his tenant without having to render any account when the tenant came of age. (d) Marriage, or the right of the lord to choose a husband for a female tenant who was his ward, and to receive a payment from the favoured suitor. Those burthens were regulated by Magna Charta in the year 1215. But they remained so onerous that under James I. it was proposed to commute them for a permanent revenue to be settled on the crown. Under Charles II. they were so commuted by the act for the abolition of military tenures (12 Car. ii. c. 24).

II. Tenure by grand sergeantry. On this tenure land was held direct from the crown for service rendered in person to the king, such as carrying the royal banner when he went to war. This tenure still exists, but is extremely rare and of no consequence save as a legal curiosity.

III. Tenure by free or common socage. The etymology of the term "socage" is doubtful. It has been derived from an English word "soc," a privilege, as in the phrase "sac and soc," and from a French word "soc," meaning a plough-share. "Sochemanni" form one class of the population as enumerated in Domesday Book, and are probably the representatives of the class of free landed proprietors other than thegns or churchmen previous to the Norman Conquest. Persons holding land by socage tenure were free from some of the most oppressive burthens incidental to military tenure. They owed no military service for their land although they were liable, as were all freemen, to serve in the national militia when necessary. They were accordingly exempt from scutage, the money payment in lieu of military service. They were exempt from the annoyances incidental to wardship and marriage. For the lawful guardian of a minor holding land by this tenure was not his lord, but the nearest of kin not capable of inheriting the land. And such a guardian was not allowed to make any profit by the marriage of his ward. The tenant in socage was obliged to make certain money payments, aids, reliefs, rent, etc., or to render his lord certain agricultural services strictly defined beforehand. On account of the advantageous character of socage tenure it was provided by the act 12 Car. ii. c. 24, that all land formerly held on military tenure should thenceforwards be held on socage tenure. Thus by far the greater part of the land of England is now held in socage. In the course of time the burthens of socage tenure have become almost nominal. For by the statute *Quia Emptores* of 1290 (18 Ed. I. c. 1) sub-infeudation was forbidden. Thenceforwards any person taking a transfer of freehold lands stepped into the place of his predecessor and became liable only to those obligations

to which his predecessor had been liable. Thus the freeholder of to-day has to make only such feudal payments for his land as had been settled before the year 1290 and these have become nominal in consequence of the fall in the value of money and the rise in the value of land. As society became more settled the lord lost his motive for exacting the oath of fealty, which has long since become obsolete. The feudal courts having dwindled to mere forms, the obligation to suit and service now means nothing. Corruption of blood and escheat of lands upon the tenant's conviction for felony are no longer enforced by law. The enlarged power of testamentary disposition has made escheat for lack of heirs to the tenant a very rare occurrence. Finally, the rights of the lord having lost all their value have in many cases been allowed to fall into utter desuetude. The record of them has frequently perished. Thus many freeholders cannot be shown to have any lord under the crown, and the freeholder has come to regard himself, and is regarded by others, as full proprietor of his land.

Socage tenure, being a product of customary law, has sometimes assumed peculiar forms. In one form, known as petty sergeantry, the tenant held his land of the king on condition of rendering him every year some object of use in war, such as a pair of gilt spurs. Other forms, known as burgage tenure and gavelkind tenure, are distinguished by peculiar rules of succession, when the tenant dies intestate (see DESCENT OF PROPERTY).

It remains to mention a free tenure of land so distinct from those which have been mentioned as hardly to admit of being classed with them. This is FRANKALMOIGN or free alms (Lat. *libera eleemosyna*). On this tenure land was and is held by ecclesiastical corporations. The service rendered for land thus held was spiritual, consisting simply in prayer and performance of the rites of religion. The holders paid no rent in money or in kind. They were not subject to aids or reliefs. They were not subject (being corporations and therefore immortal) to escheat or forfeiture. They were not capable of military service. Thus their tenure approached more nearly than any other tenure recognised by English law to a full ownership.

[For further information see FREEHOLD (Legal) and the articles therein referred to.

Goodeve, *The Law of Real Property.*—Williams, *The Law of Real Property.*—Kenelm Digby, *History of the Law of Real Property.*—Pollock, *Land Laws.*—Hallam, *History of the Middle Ages.* —Stubbs, *Constitutional History of England.*]

F. C. M.

FREEHOLD, LEGAL. A freehold tenure of land meant formerly a tenure which obliged the tenant only to such services as were worthy of a freeman (see FREEHOLD, HISTORI-

CAL). In course of time these services have either wholly disappeared or have become insignificant. A quit-rent of nominal amount is still payable in some cases to the lord of the manor, and when an heir succeeds to the freehold he has to pay a relief amounting to one year's value of this quit-rent. Where a manor is still existent the freeholder is still bound to attend the court baron held by the lord. But the court baron is practically never held. An oath of fealty to the lord, where there is a lord, is still due in theory but in practice is never exacted. In short the freeholder has practically the full enjoyment of his land unencumbered by any real duties towards a lord. He therefore approaches much more nearly than a leaseholder or a copyholder to the character of an absolute owner.

But the interest of a freeholder in his land differs in extent accordingly ; as it is (1) an estate for life ; (2) an estate in tail ; (3) an estate in fee simple. (For the nature and peculiarities of these different estates, see ESTATE.) If a man have an estate in tail or in fee simple, he has an interest in the land which extends beyond his own life. This interest descends to his heirs according to the peculiar rules governing the devolution of real estate (see DESCENT OF PROPERTY). In many cases a family settlement (see ESTATE) provides for the creation of life estates or estates tail in remainder, which come into possession as the preceding life estate or estate tail expires. But the power of thus controlling the devolution of the land is restricted by law (see PERPETUITIES).

Owing to the gradual enfranchisement of copyhold land (see COPYHOLD), an increasing proportion of the land of England is held as freehold, and at no distant date the whole will be so held (see also LEASEHOLD).   F. C. M.

FREE LIST is a term arising out of the prevalence of unwieldy tariffs of import duties in foreign countries and many British colonies. It denotes the schedule of commodities exempted from payment of duty on the importation into any given country.   C. A. H.

FREEMAN. Modern conceptions of the distinction between freedom and non-freedom can be applied only with caution to ancient and mediæval history. As applied to the middle ages they are particularly misleading ; for the most characteristic feature of the social conditions of the time was the existence of the intermediate position now commonly spoken of as SERFDOM (q.v.). Thus, under the later Roman empire, the large class of coloni were distinctly free by condition, with all the civil rights of other freemen, and even the power of suing their masters ; they were nevertheless bound to the soil, and subject to burdensome duties from which they could not escape. A law of the fifth century distinguishes " the bond of colonate," nexus colonarius, from " the condition of

slavery," conditio servitutis ; and yet another, somewhat earlier, remarks that " though the coloni are of course free by condition, they must be looked upon as the slaves of the land on which they are born." Moreover the slave proper, during this period, by no means obtained that independence towards his former master, when he received manumission, which was gained by a modern freedman. He remained in close dependence upon him, usually as the cultivator of a holding on very onerous terms.

The question of the condition of the rural population in England in the earlier Saxon centuries is still undecided. But it is generally agreed that the position of the cultivators of the soil for at least two centuries before the Norman Conquest was substantially the same as that of the villeins and cotters after that event. If these cultivators were as a class identical with the ceorls, as is almost certain, they were doubtless technically free, though held in strict economic subjection, and bound to labour two or three days every week, and in busy seasons almost every day, for the lord of whom they held their land. Hence the Domesday survey, while it registers only some 12,000 persons (= heads of households) as freemen, liberi homines, and 23,000 as SOCMEN (q.v.) (persons, in all probability, in much the same position)—the " free men " being almost exclusively in Norfolk and Suffolk ; and on the other hand notices 25,000 as slaves, servi ; gives about 200,000 as falling into the classes of VILLEINS and COTTIERS (q.v.), whose status between that of the LIBER HOMO and that of the SERVUS (q.v.) it leaves undetermined.

The introduction of the feudal jurisprudence after the Norman Conquest led to a greater importance being attached to the nature of tenure ; and for the next four centuries the questions of tenure and personal condition almost inextricably confused. The class of "free tenants," LIBERE TENENTES (q.v.), which grew so rapidly after the 11th century, was practically coextensive with that of " free men." But as to what exactly constituted free tenure the courts did not maintain a consistent doctrine. A very widely spread idea was that inability to give a daughter in marriage, or to sell an ox or a horse without the lord's consent, was a certain mark of servile tenure. On the other hand, exemption from the more laborious dues known as WEEK-WORK (q.v.) was frequently regarded as constituting free tenure ; and villeins relieved from these obligations tended to rise to the class of freeholders. It is possible that in their desire to place the whole population in one of the two classes of free and non-free, the lawyers of the 13th and 14th centuries came at last to deny freedom to persons in a position which in Saxon times would have been regarded as free. But this more rigid application of mutually exclusive terms did not necessarily involve any material degradation of the class in question, and was not inconsistent with a material elevation.

The legal identification of villeinage with non-freedom was probably beneficial to the class of chattel slaves which certainly existed in the 11th century. The servile stigma, attached to so large a part of the nation, ceased to involve any peculiar disabilities even in the case of the descendants of actual slaves, who became merged in the class of customary holders and copyholders. Slavery had long been forgotten when, in 1772, Lord Mansfield declared, in the case of the negro Sommerset, that slavery could not exist in England,—"a decision which did more credit to the hearts of the judges than to their knowledge of history."—The terms "freedom," and "franchise," were also applied to the possession of the rights of a burgher, and to membership of the city companies.

[For the Roman colonate see Fustel de Coulanges, *Recherches sur quelques problèmes d'histoire* (1885), espec. pp. 98 *seq.* The best introduction to the discussion on Saxon ranks will be found in note iii. to ch. viii. in Hallam's *Middle Ages.* For post-Saxon conditions in England the most important treatises, from very different points of view, are F. Seebohm, *English Village Community* (1883), espec. pp. 86 *seq.*, and P. Vinogradoff, *Villainage in England,* 1892 (summing-up pp. 217 *seq.*), whereon see also the criticism by Seebohm in *Eng. Hist. Rev.,* July 1892; by Ashley in *Econ. Rev.,* April 1893; and by Leadam in *Pol. Sci. Qu.,* Dec. 1893. On the disappearance of slavery, cp. Freeman, *Norman Conquest,* v. p. 140. Reference may also be made to Sommerset's case in Broom's *Constitutional Law,* where the historical and juristic aspect of slavery is discussed with much learning.] W. J. A.

FREE TOWNS. In the article on mediæval cities (see CITY, MEDIÆVAL), it was pointed out that, though they had many features in common, in whatever part of western, southern, and central Europe they were established, yet their powers and privileges differed greatly according to their surrounding circumstances. In England and France, the growing predominance of the monarchical *régime* tended inevitably to curtail the rights of civic self-government, and it was only in those countries where the traditions of the old Roman empire were still strong, or the power of the new monarchical principle weak, that *free cities,* in the sense of more or less self-governing communities, were really established. They may be defined as cities possessing independent governments of their own, each virtually forming a state by itself; many were republics. It is, therefore, in Italy, Spain, the Netherlands, Germany, and Switzerland, that we find the historic examples of true civic liberty, though even in these cases the prestige of a feudal aris-

tocracy, or hereditary oligarchy, or again the rise of a loose federation, or the proximity of an imperial suzerainty tended inevitably to modify the primitive features of that liberty. Italy is the historic ground of the free cities of the middle ages. There, owing to the weakness of the imperial sovereignty, whether emanating from Constantinople or Germany, the towns, especially in the northern portion of the peninsula, were able to raise themselves to the proud position of independent states, not only exercising complete control over their internal affairs, but waging war, making peace, and entering into alliances with each other, like the city-states of ancient Greece and Italy. Inland, Milan, Florence, Verona, and other cities contended with each other for empire over the fertile plains of Lombardy; while on the seaboard, Pisa, Genoa, and Venice raised themselves into great sea-powers in the east and west Mediterranean waters; and lesser cities, like Naples and Amalfi, scattered on the Italian coasts, followed their example with greater or less success. The enterprise and energy of all these cities alike was largely due to the fact that the fierce feudal aristocracy, that had sprung from the loins of barbaric invaders, had with its absorption into the civic life instilled the spirit of war into the workshop. The territory originally subjected, after the disruption of the Roman empire, to the count or bishop of these cities, had been reduced by concessions to the rural nobility, but after a while the cities began to reassert their sovereignty. Sometimes they besieged the strongholds of the nobility, sometimes they purchased feudal suzerainties, and finally by the 12th century there could hardly be found a single nobleman, except the marquis of Montferrat, and some noble families like those of Este and Malaspina, who had not given in their submission. The rural nobility, having lost its power outside the cities, strove to recover it inside, and by the erection of strongholds within the cities established a basis of further political and military operations. Hence a fierce belligerency at home and abroad is the chief feature of Italian republicanism; resulting in a striking development of the arts of war alongside those of peace, a development in some towns crowned with the laurels of an art and literature that recalled the palmy days of ancient Athens and Rome. Among the Lombard cities, Milan was most conspicuous for its wealth and wide-reaching power. By its warlike policy, shown in its ruthless conquest of neighbouring towns, like Lodi and Como, it drew on it the resentment of the imperial power in the person of Frederick Barbarossa, who in 1158 reduced the city, and handed it over to the vengeance of its enemies. He then proceeded to restore the imperial authority over the other towns of Lombardy, but his savage treatment led to a general insurrection in which for a time local feuds were forgotten. After the victory of Legnano in 1176, the Lombard republics regained their independence, but the rivalry between the imperial and papal powers, taken up by their respective partisans the Ghibelines and Guelfs, introduced a new element of contention into the already stormy politics of northern Italy. Leagues were formed again and again between different cities on the new lines of cleavage, and, as was natural in a state war, under the cover of great principles various self-seeking tyrannies were established. During the 13th century there were four great groups of city-states to be found in northern Italy. The first included the cities of central Lombardy, Milan, Cremona, Pavia, Brescia, Bergamo, Parma, Piacenza, Mantua, Lodi, Alessandria, and others less known. The second group consisted of Verona, Vicenza, Padua, and Treviso. Another group was composed of the cities in Romagna, Bologna, Modena, Imola, Faenza, Ferrara, and others less important. The fourth cluster comprehended the whole of Tuscany, headed by Florence and Pisa. Sometimes the Ghibeline faction, sometimes the Guelf faction got the upper hand, and, according to the rise and fall of each, fresh wars and fresh alliances were entered into. We have an interesting account of the condition of Milan in 1288, from Galvaneus Flamma, a Milanese writer. The inhabitants are reckoned at 200,000, and the private houses at 13,000; the nobility alone dwelt in 60 streets, 8000 gentlemen or heavy cavalry might be mustered from the city and its district, and 240,000 men capable of bearing arms. In the district were 150 castles with their adjoining villages. The wealth and enterprise of the Milanese was astonishing, as was shown especially in the construction of the canal from the Tesino to the city, and the architectural splendour of the buildings. Their military ardour and commercial activity were equally conspicuous. The government of Milan and of the other Italian city-states was subject to continual change. In most of them the magistrates, elected after they threw off the rule, in the 10th and 11th centuries, of the count or imperial official or bishop, were styled in Roman fashion consuls. They were chosen annually, and generally from the ranks of the nobility; and they formed the responsible civil and military executive. There were besides legislative and deliberative councils. A council of trust and secrecy, consisting of a small number of persons, formed the advisers of the consuls; but the decision of high state affairs, such as treaties of alliance and declarations of war, the choice of consuls and ambassadors, rested with the general council of a more or less democratic type. About the end of the 12th century, as a result of the imperial intervention of Frederick Barbarossa, the custom arose in many cities of appointing, as a kind of temporary dictator, a citizen of some neighbouring state, though invariably a man of noble birth. He was called *podestà*, and held office for a year, though re-eligible. He received a fixed salary, and was compelled to remain in the city after expiration of office for answering charges brought against him. He could neither marry a native of the city nor have any relation resident in the city, nor even—so great was the fear of his being involved in the feuds and factions of the city—eat or drink in the house of any citizen. He was regarded as the highest arbitrator in all disputes, and sometimes superseded the consuls and commanded in war. There was great need of such an arbitrator in the Italian cities, where there were continual quarrels between the various noble families, and between them and the commonalty. The latter, composed of the artisans, were generally arranged into companies according to their occupations; and these fraternal guild associations were set over against the alliances of the nobility. The quarrels between social classes were further intermingled with the quarrels between political partisans, looking to the German emperor or the pope as their respective heads; while both kinds of quarrel were further embittered by personal outrages such as we read of in Dante and Shakespeare. Whoever conquered in these intestine conflicts, the state suffered from the merciless revenge of the conquering party, till at last the cities of Italy, like those of ancient Greece, were glad to be controlled by the strong though often cruel hand of some one family which established a quasi-hereditary despotism. At Milan, first the Torriani and then the Visconti raised themselves to power, and the latter gradually extended their sway over central Lombardy, overthrowing the reigning nobility in surrounding cities, and finally forming alliances with the French monarchy which in turn invaded and conquered north Italy. The history of the Tuscan is similar to that of the Lombard cities. Florence played the part of Milan. There too there was originally a more or less democratic constitution. The population was divided into fourteen companies or *arts*, the seven greater arts each electing a council of its own, with a chief magistrate or consul for civil jurisdiction, and a *gonfalonière* for military affairs. Criminal justice was administered by a *podestà* and a *capitano del populo*. But gradually, after many trials of various constitutions, political power became centred in the hands of some powerful family, till at last, in the 15th century, the famous Medici ruled supreme.

While Milan and Florence were gradually asserting their supremacy over the territory of northern and central Italy, three maritime cities, Pisa, Genoa, and Venice, were pushing their conquests over the Mediterranean Sea. It was these Italian cities that, after the general disturbance of Europe caused by the irruption of the various tribes of barbarians and the devastating conquests of the Mohammedans, first succeeded in reviving the commerce of the Mediterranean world. As early as the age of Charlemagne, they had begun to carry on trade with the Greek cities, and imported to their own countries the rich commodities of Asia. In the 10th century the Venetians had formed a connection with Alexandria in Egypt, and the inhabitants of Amalfi and Pisa had also extended their trade to the same port. Later on, the crusades had poured riches into the laps of Venice, Genoa, and Pisa alike. These cities provided the necessary transports, and received enormous sums for their services as carriers. The crusaders also contracted with them for military stores and provisions, and the fleets of these cities kept on the coast, while the armies advanced by land, and during that advance sought every opportunity of promoting their commercial interests. Charters were granted to them, whereby they soon secured most extensive privileges in various settlements made by the crusaders in Asia. The property of entire suburbs in some, and of large streets in others, was vested in them, and the right of appointing their own magistrates assigned. When the crusaders seized Constantinople, the Venetians secured a part of it, and also part of the Peloponnesus in Greece and some of the islands of the Archipelago. With the conquest of many important maritime points in the eastern Mediterranean, trade with Asia revived. The Italian cities not only imported Indian commodities, but established manufactures of delicate fabrics in their own country, especially of silk. Silk weavers were kidnapped from the east of Europe, and settled in Italy, and silk stuffs gradually spread through Europe. The sugar-cane, indigenous in the east, was likewise imported into and cultivated in the west, whence it was eventually transported to America. After the decline of Pisa, partly owing to the rivalry of Genoa and the growing power of Florence, which conquered it early in the 15th century, Genoa contended with Venice for the commercial supremacy of the Mediterranean. Genoa had more especially command of the western Mediterranean and the northern part of the Archipelago and the Bosphorus. Caffa, a famous seaport on the Black Sea, and the port of Azov on the mouth of the Don, belonged to the Genoese, and served as *entrepôts* for their overland commerce with China and the Indies. Smyrna in Asia Minor, and the suburbs of Pera and Galatz at Constantinople, and the isles of Scio and Tenedos were ceded to them by the Greek emperors, and at one time they had the kings of Cyprus as their tributaries. Venice, starting from a more secure position in the lagunes of the northern Adriatic, pushed its conquests on the adjoining coasts of Dalmatia,

Albania, Greece, and the Morea, and gradually secured settlements in Corfu, Cephalonia, and Crete. Genoa and Venice inevitably came into collision in the 14th century ; and in the war of Chioggia, 1376-82, the famous Genoese admiral Peter Doria nearly succeeded in capturing Venice, which was only saved by the courage and energy of the Venetian admiral Vittorio Pisani. After this victory, Venice more and more secured her ascendency on the Syrian and Egyptian coasts, and the consequent trade with the east, till the discovery of the new sea route by the Cape of Good Hope handed over the oriental trade to the Portuguese and Dutch. The Italian traders naturally proceeded to find markets in western, central, and northern Europe, and to exchange their own commodities with those of other European countries. They were allowed the most extensive immunities in France in the 13th century, even greater than those granted to native inhabitants. As the Lombards, a name generally given to the Italian merchants, engrossed the chief trade of Europe, they became the chief bankers of Europe. By the church their money-lending was denounced as sinful and criminal, and, as a consequence, the interest charged was all the higher on account of the insecurity of their dealings, reaching even to 20 per cent. The chief northern mart for Italian goods was at Bruges. The sea voyage from the Mediterranean to the Baltic being of too prolonged a nature to be carried on in one summer, it was necessary to find some entrepôt or halfway centre for trade, and this was placed at Bruges. Here they exchanged the wool of England, the linen of the Netherlands, the furs, fish, and hemp of the Baltic for the silks, and spices, and silver of the south. The great galiasses, in which they carried their goods were the wonder of the north. At the beginning of the 13th century Bruges was famed as the greatest emporium of northern Europe, and the Hanseatic league of the Baltic cities established also their centre there, while Ghent and Ypres looked to it as their most powerful ally in their struggles with feudalism. For two centuries Bruges held its place, but the gradual closing of its channels, side by side with the increase of the size of trading ships, finally gave the supremacy to Antwerp. During the 15th and 16th centuries Antwerp surpassed all the ports of Europe in its commerce, and in 1568 its population reached 103,000 ; a civic population only exceeded by that of Paris. Its supremacy was destined in the following centuries to pass to London.

In Spain, although the cities, owing to the strength of the feudal nobility and the growth of the monarchy, never reached the complete independence of the Italian and German towns ; yet in very early times, owing to the exigencies of the struggle with the Moors, the towns of Castile and Aragon were invested with very important privileges or charters, on the condition of protecting their country. They had the right of appointing their own magistrates and common councils, which exercised civil and criminal jurisdiction over the inhabitants not only of the towns but also of extensive areas round them. They were bound in turn to pay certain sums and provide a certain force of armed men, horse and foot. Toledo, Saragossa, Valladolid, and others, became noted for their splendid enterprise. Barcelona, as a seaport, attained a special height of prosperity and power, and vied with the Italian cities on the seaboard in trade with Alexandria and the east. Its maritime laws are among the earliest mercantile jurisprudence of modern times, and were adopted by the Italian states. With other Spanish cities it secured special privileges in France, similar to those of the Italian towns; and Spanish silk and woollen goods, and the spices, drugs, and perfumes, imported from the east, spread far and wide in Spanish bottoms. See Prescott (*Ferdinand and Isabella*), vol. i. pp. 64-68.

Since the beginning of the 10th century, towns had been growing up in northern, southern, and western Germany, especially where the sea or rivers formed the easiest and safest means of communication, or where the traditions of Roman colonies had been handed down through the times of barbaric invasion. Lübeck, Hamburg, Bremen, and Frankfort, Cologne, Treves, Mainz, Strasburg, Worms, Speyer, Nuremberg, Ulm, Regensburg and Augsburg, and others gradually became places of importance, resting on the protection of imperial authority, and ready to fight for further privileges with the ecclesiastical or feudal oligarchy. During the 11th and 12th centuries these powers more and more extended under imperial encouragement, and towards the end of the latter century we find them electing councils of citizens, and in the following century appointing their own magistrates. The growing weakness of the empire naturally led to greater independence, and when, towards the end of the 13th century, the Hapsburg family succeeded to the imperial throne, we find the cities taking their place in the diet side by side with the feudal and ecclesiastical princes. In their struggle for freedom the cities found it necessary to form alliances. In the north there arose, about 1241, the famous HANSEATIC LEAGUE (*q.v.*), initiated by the cities of Lübeck and Hamburg. Their example was followed in 1255 by sixty cities forming the League of the Rhine. In 1370 this league was extended for a time by the adhesion of the cities of Swabia, while farther south the Swiss cities of Lucerne, Zurich, Glarus, Zug, and Berne joined with the three famous cantons of Uri, Schwyz, and Unterwalden in winning republican independ-

ence. Each of these German and Swiss towns formed rallying centres for the victims of feudal oppression, and kept alive the spirit of civic and industrial freedom.

[Adam Smith, *Wealth of Nations*, bk. iii. ch. iii. and iv.—Anderson, *Commercial History.*—Bryce, *Holy Roman Empire.*—Freeman, *Essays*, vol. ii.—Gibbon, *Roman Empire.*—Guizot, *Civilization of Europe.*—Hallam, *Middle Ages.*—Koch, *History of Europe.*—Marshall, *Political Economy.*—Motley, *The Rise of the Dutch Republic.*—Prescott, *Ferdinand and Isabella, Charles V.*—Sismondi, *Fall of Roman Empire, Histoire des Républiques Italiennes du Moyen Age.*—Zimmern, *Hanse Towns.*—*Ency. Brit.*, 9th ed., art. on "Hanseatic League" by R. Lodge.]   A. K. C.

FREE TRADE, THEORY OF. The term "free trade," or freedom of trade, at first used somewhat vaguely to denote absence of restraint in general, has now acquired a definite specialised sense. To MISSELDEN (*q.v.*), 1622, it meant "the free export of bullion"; to the opponents of the ADVENTURERS, MERCHANT (*q.v.*) "the abolition of the monopoly held by that body"; in the time of Sir Walter Scott "free-traders" meant smugglers (see *Guy Mannering*), at the opening of the 18th century, and in 1782 in Ireland, "the right to export freely." Adam Smith's authority, and the direction given by him to economic thought, have caused its limitation to that system of commercial policy which draws no distinction between domestic and foreign commodities, and, therefore, neither imposes additional burdens on the latter nor grants any special favours to the former. Free trade in this now well-established sense does not require the removal of all duties on commodities; it only insists that they shall be levied exclusively for revenue, not at all for PROTECTION (*q.v.*). "Our object," said Cobden, "is not to take away the queen's officers from the custom-house, but to take those officers away who sit at the receipt of custom to take tithe and toll for the benefit of particular classes" (*Speeches*, pop. ed. p. 41).

Free trade as a practical policy is based on the economic theory of INTERNATIONAL TRADE (*q.v.*), which explains the nature of the benefits obtained through foreign commerce, and shows that it is only carried on so long as it yields a gain to those concerned. But "if," as Cairnes urges, "nations only engage in trade when an advantage arises from their doing so, any interference with their free action in trading can only have the effect of debarring them from an advantage" (*Leading Prin.*, pt. iii. ch. iv. § 1). Foreign trade is a particular form or species of EXCHANGE (*q.v.*), and its utility is therefore at a maximum when impediments to its action are completely removed. The free trade doctrine thus rests on the most elementary economic facts, and is so simple as almost to appear trivial. The operation of free trade is negative; by removing obstacles it affords room for the working of the normal and beneficent forces of commerce.

Again, free trade—to slightly change the point of view—has a reactive effect on production. DIVISION OF LABOUR (*q.v.*) only becomes possible by means of exchange, which permits each industrial group to confine its efforts to the most profitable employment, and to satisfy its various wants by exchange with other bodies. Elaborate and efficient production almost necessarily implies a developed system of trade. This is particularly true where specialisation of industry is due to local advantages. "The territorial division of labour," which forms no small part of the general movement, is in great measure dependent on facilities for foreign commerce, and is therefore promoted by the establishment of free trade. Each country can devote itself to those forms of production in which it has a comparative advantage (see INTERNATIONAL TRADE), and obtain from foreigners all other commodities. Individuals "find it for their interest to employ their industry in a way in which they have some advantage over their neighbours"; and, as Adam Smith proceeds to observe, "what is prudence in the conduct of every private family can scarce be folly in that of a great kingdom" (*Wealth of Nations*, ed. Nicholson, p. 185). Thus regarded, free trade appears to be an obvious dictate of common sense rather than the product of refined and difficult theory, a circumstance which accounts for the somewhat scornful tone that many advocates of commercial liberty have used towards opponents. There are, however, some complicating conditions which render the argument from division of labour harder to follow in foreign than in domestic trade. The individual producer has little difficulty in perceiving that a special line of work is more profitable to him than the attempt to directly supply all his wants by his own exertions. To the nation the first effect of foreign trade seems to be the displacement of so much home industry, with resulting loss to the supplanted producers. Hence the necessity for showing that an "imported commodity is always paid for directly or indirectly with the produce of our own industry," and "that the alternative is not between employing our own people and foreigners, but between employing one class and another of our own people" (Mill, *Principles*, bk. v. ch. x. § 1). Imported goods must undoubtedly be paid for, and, normally speaking, be paid for by the export of native products; but some power of analysis is needed to realise this truth amidst the complications of trade. Adam Smith meets the difficulty by insisting that "the general industry of the society never can exceed what the capital of the society can employ" (*Wealth of Nations*, p. 183), and that therefore regulations of commerce can only divert a part of that capital into an artificial direction. The individual is, however,

able to determine the most profitable direction for the employment of his capital far better than the "statesman or lawgiver"; and he is urged to so use it by the stimulus of self-interest. Mill's "first fundamental proposition," viz. "that industry is limited by capital," with its corollary, that "demand for commodities is not a demand for labour," serves the same purpose (*Principles*, bk. v. ch. x. § 1). The optimistic doctrine of the *Wealth of Nations*, with its belief in the guidance of "an invisible hand" (bk. iv. ch. ii.), is replaced by the Ricardian theory of foreign trade, which assumes both the domestic mobility and the international immobility of labour and capital (cp. Bagehot, *Economic Studies*, p. 67), but either suffices as a basis for the free-trade position. Nor is it essentially altered by modern developments of the theory of WAGES (*q.v.*). Even if capital is not the sole limit to industry, and if efficiency in work is also to be taken into account; still as free trade tends to increase general efficiency, it follows that the "produce theory" of wages gives quite as valid a support to the policy of freedom. This general argument is strengthened by reference to the statistics of trade, and by consideration of the elements that make up international indebtedness (see COMMERCE), from which it appears that imports and exports stand in a definite relation to each other. The intervention of MONEY (*q.v.*), a potent cause of economic fallacies, further obscures the case; but the cardinal principle, that foreign like domestic trade is fundamentally barter in which goods are exchanged for goods, throws light on this side of the question. It is shown that a permanently favourable BALANCE OF TRADE (*q.v.*) is an impossibility, and even were it attainable, that it would not be advantageous, since the undue accumulation of the precious metals means the locking up of what would otherwise be productive capital.

By the analysis and exposure of the fallacies connected with (1) the sources of employment, and (2) the nature of the circulating medium, the argument for freedom of trade as a general rule has become a part of practical economics, and has been largely accepted by the educated public, and even recognised as the ultimate goal by such representative protectionists as LIST and CAREY. But its admission in the vague shape of an "abstract principle" or "theory" has not hindered the existence of widespread dissent to its reduction to "practice," a hostility not wholly due to ignorance and the influence of particular interests. Exceptions to free trade may be urged either on the ground of special economic conditions or by appealing to wider considerations than those relating to material wealth. Cases of both kinds are to be found in the *Wealth of Nations* (bk. iv. ch. ii.). Of the former the most important is that of temporary protection in order to encourage the development of infant industries, which, feeble at first, will ultimately become self-supporting. This case requires the balancing of present against future advantage : immediate gain is to be sacrificed for a larger one at a later time. Such a policy applied to manufactures in general is the "industrial protective system" of List, regarded by him as suited for a particular stage of economic development. Its validity—with, however, stringent limitations—is conceded by Mill (loc. cit.), and more unreservedly by Prof. Sidgwick (Pol. Economy, bk. iii. ch. v. § 1), and Roscher (System, vol. iii. § 138). Adam Smith's contention that individual enterprise is a better guide for industry than the dictates of governments, seems, as he himself held, to be fully applicable here. The difficulties in selecting the industries to be encouraged, and the amount of protection required by each, have been justly dwelt on by free traders (see especially Wise, Industrial Freedom, pt. iv. ch. ii. and app. ii.) who have further asked without much result for evidence of the successful use of protection for this purpose. Thus, while it is theoretically possible that the temporary protection of a particular industry might yield a surplus of advantage, it is plain that the discovery of such an instance will be much rarer than the injurious employment of the same instrument in unsuitable cases (see BOUNTIES).

Protection may also be sought on like grounds, for older industries become for the moment unprofitable through a temporary disturbance in trade conditions (Sidgwick, Pol. Econ., bk. iii. ch. v. § i.), and should be tried by the same tests.

The foregoing argument has some affinity with the plea that diversity of industry is economically beneficial, especially in a new country, and therefore deserving of encouragement. The advantages of the "home market" as affording a steady demand, and saving the cost of transport, have been unduly emphasised by protectionists with curious disregard of the fact that cost of carriage is a natural protection to the home producer, and only overcome by the greater benefit of foreign trade. Experience, besides, does not confirm the belief that fluctuations are less frequent in a limited market, nor does it show that diversity of industry is incompatible with complete freedom of trade.

In like manner the possibility of enlarging the national market by causing immigration of labour and capital, or of hindering its contraction by checking their efflux, has been alleged as a good reason for the use of protection, and the claim has been theoretically admitted by some economists (e.g. Prof. Sidgwick, Pol. Econ., bk. iii. ch. v. § 3). Unless, however, in the case of a country possessing the sole or chief market for a commodity, it is hard to see how the imposition of duties will even tend to draw in labour, as the cost of living will almost certainly be higher,

while the investment of foreign capital will depend on the prospect of a high return, which is not likely to be increased by the adoption of protection.

A much more plausible argument for departing from the free-trade rule is that based on the idea of preserving national resources. A country's mineral stores form a stock which is being gradually worked out, and it may be held that protective duties on imports will act as a check to their too rapid use (cp. Jevons, Coal Question, Preface). Again, as Carey urges, food - exporting countries may exhaust the fertility of their soil—or to take a further step in refinement of the doctrine—may find the MARGIN OF CULTIVATION (q.v.) pushed to a lower point. Thus the community experiences the same effects that would follow from an increased population at home (cp. S. N. Patten, Economic Basis of Protection, pp. 47, 48). On the other hand, the gain to the landowners, and therefore to the revenue of the society from an increase in rent must be taken into account as well as the cheaper terms on which imports are obtained under free trade ; and on the balance it is probable that even in so peculiar a case the advantage would be on the side of freedom.

On the border between economic and political exceptions is the proposal to make freedom of trade dependent on reciprocity. If based on the belief that trade to be advantageous must be free on both sides, the idea is clearly fallacious, but where it simply aims at removing foreign protective duties and thus securing wider freedom of trade in the future, it "may be good policy," as Adam Smith (Wealth of Nations, p. 190) asserts, since "the recovery of a great foreign market will more than compensate the transitory inconvenience" of retaliation. Here, however, as in respect to infant industries, the probability of success is much smaller than that of failure, owing to the inevitable irritation produced in foreign countries by retaliation, which leads to increase rather than reduction of protective duties.

All the preceding cases have often been supported on non-economic grounds, but chief stress has been laid on the economic gain to be sooner or later derived. Different in kind is the preference of national security to increase of wealth, which formed the strongest argument in support of the CORN LAWS and the NAVIGATION LAWS, and which actually won for the latter the favourable judgment of Adam Smith (bk. iv. ch. ii.), and of J. S. Mill, who, however, approved of their repeal. In such instances the question is one for the statesman rather than the practical economist, but in making a calculation the economic loss, though not of itself decisive, should never be dropped out of sight, as opulence is one of the chief elements of political and military power.

Social protective duties (*sociale Schutzzölle*) have been advocated in order to hinder the degradation of labour, in consequence of the pressure of foreign competitors working under inferior conditions of life, and in countries with stringent FACTORY LAWS (see also FACTORY ACTS) the plea has in certain cases an apparent force. In its more extreme form, as in the United States, where protection against the "pauper labour" of Europe is a popular cry with the opponents of free trade, it is only a repetition of the fallacy already noticed that free trade reduces the amount of employment, and it also erroneously assumes that with unrestricted commerce wages will everywhere fall to the lowest existing level, though it is obvious that IMMIGRATION of poorly-paid foreign labour, which is the real cause of lowered wages, may happen under, and even be stimulated by, the most rigid protection.

On the whole it does not appear that the various exceptions suggested to the broad canon of free trade have much practical weight, at least in the present stage of social development, though they suggest some interesting qualifications of economic theory. Some of them are connected with the possible evils that accompany extended division of labour—evils not sufficiently recognised by the older English writers, but nevertheless of serious social import. They further bring out the varying consequences that follow from the action of industrial effort according as it is placed under the law of INCREASING RETURNS or under the law of DIMINISHING RETURNS, and show, as Mill had briefly noticed (*Principles*, bk. v. ch. x. § 1), that agricultural and manufacturing communities are not affected in the same way by free trade. The "infant industry" argument gains its force from the consideration of time ; it appeals to the future as against the present. The real nature of national interest, and its possible divergence from the individual interests of producers and consumers, have been brought into stronger relief, without, however, invalidating the proposition that in the main the interest of the community is served by the widest freedom.

The result then is that the practical policy of free trade is a sound deduction from established economic doctrines, and that any proposed exception must be clearly made out by its advocates, on whom the burden of proof rests, and who are bound not merely to adduce special circumstances that appear to favour the claim, but to take into account all the surrounding conditions, and to give due weight to each. Submitted to such a test, the most plausible cases for interference with the normal course of trade turn out to be theoretical subtleties, not practicable or advisable expedients.

[The literature of the subject is too extensive for adequate notice. Adam Smith, *Wealth of Nations*, bk. iv., is the source of the most effective free-trade arguments. The petition of the merchants of London, 1820 (in *Wealth of Nations*, ed. M'Culloch, note 15), drawn up by Thos. Tooke (Tooke and Newmarch, *History of Prices*, vol. vi. p. 335), summarised them most concisely.—F. Bastiat, *Sophismes Économiques*, Œuvres, tomes iv. and v., contain the most brilliant exposure of popular fallacies.—W. G. Sumner, *Protectionism*, New York, 1883, and B. R. Wise, *Industrial Freedom*, 1892, deal with the latest phases of the controversy. See also references given above, and for writers who have opposed, see articles on A. A. COURNOT ; and PROTECTION.] C. F. B.

FREE TRADE, EARLY HISTORY OF. The free-trade agitation of the 19th century, itself only one phase of the growth of the competitive system, was the last though not the final stage of a great movement extending over several centuries. As we may expect, therefore, the expression "free trade" has different meanings at different periods in the economic history of the country. The foreign merchants of the middle ages who desired to obtain a footing in England on a free-trade basis, meant by this expression that, subject to the payment of the usual customs, they should be allowed to exercise their calling in English ports and mart towns without let or hindrance ; that they should not be subjected to unreasonable exactions ; that their ships and goods should not be arrested without due cause, etc. The English "free trader" of the latter part of the 16th century wished to see the revival of the regulations of the STAPLE system, and the withdrawal of the privileges of exclusive trading companies, such as the Merchant Adventurers. In the 17th century he meant the broadening of the basis of the companies, so that all who desired might obtain admission on easy terms. There were also some writers, such as Roger COKE (*q.v.*), who clearly perceived the advantages of free importation, of the repeal of the navigation acts, and of the acts restricting certain trades, such as the cattle and woollen trades of Ireland, and who advocated the more enlightened policy of the Dutch in the regulation of commerce. The free trader of the 18th century advocated the removal or reduction of duties on imports and exports, but at this time he seldom belonged to the commercial classes. It is impossible, therefore, to understand the significance of the various phases of the free-trade movement, apart from the general economic conditions which prevailed when each phase became prominent. From the standpoint of to-day, for example, the elaborate regulations of Edward III.'s great Ordinance of the Staples appear unwise and oppressive. But the experiment of dispensing with staple towns had been tried and had led to bad results. In the policy he adopted with regard to foreign merchants, he was singularly favourable to their claims ; and many of his statutes were intended to give security to traders, to repress lawlessness, to provide means of settling disputes, or to place the collection of customs on a satisfactory basis. These elaborate regulations, so far from being a restraint on trade, were frequently the means which made trade possible. Moreover it does not appear to have been difficult to obtain exemption from the staple acts when it could be shown that such a course was advantageous, and throughout the middle ages there were numerous bodies of merchants, such as the Hanse merchants, the merchants of Florence, Venice, etc., who enjoyed such privileges. So also, the elaborate commercial treaties of the 14th and 15th centuries have been too hastily condemned by some writers. If they had been arbitrarily imposed by governments on unwilling communities where there had formerly been free exchange of commodities, and where there were all the conditions requisite for peaceful and uninterrupted commerce, they would have been an unwarrantable interference with the course of trade. But these assumptions would be incorrect. Though unwise regulations were frequently adopted, the effect of the commercial treaties was to assimilate the conditions of different countries and communities, to build up the fabric of international law, and to extend trade far beyond the limits which would have been possible in a state of perfect freedom. With the growth of capital and industry, the rise of a manufacturing class, and the development of a national foreign trade which took place in the 15th century, the prevailing hostility to foreigners became more strongly marked. The demand arose for the encouragement of native commerce, and the protection of English industries. The reign of Edward IV. is full of acts of parliament passed with this object, and from this time onwards we can note the gradual development of the great protective system which was not overthrown till our own day. The privileges enjoyed by foreign merchants were restricted. Those of the Hanse merchants, who attained their greatest influence in England in the 15th century, were suspended by Edward VI., and after a partial renewal under Mary and Elizabeth, were finally withdrawn by the latter. English trading companies were incorporated, protective tariffs imposed, corn laws and navigation acts were passed, and the country was apparently getting deeper and deeper into a narrow national policy. We cannot here discuss the question how far the mercantile system achieved the objects which its advocates had in view (vide ENGLISH EARLY ECONOMIC HISTORY; HANSEATIC LEAGUE; MERCANTILE SYSTEM; NAVIGATION ACTS). The period which saw its growth saw also the growth of the forces which led to its final overthrow. Throughout their history the policy of confining the foreign trade of the country to exclusive trading companies was subjected to much hostile criticism. It was assailed in Parliament, and in the works of economic writers. The regulations of some of the companies were modified to meet the claims of outsiders; Cromwell tried the experiment of a free and open trade with the East Indies; privileges were granted to bodies of merchants in contravention of the charters of the companies; in a great debate at the committee on trade in 1657, only two persons were favourable to the Merchants Adventurers, while all the other members were for the free merchants. There were many men like Ralph GARDINER (q.v.), who were willing to suffer much in the struggle against monopoly; and after the revolution of 1655, few of the old companies are of great practical importance except the EAST INDIA COMPANY (q.v.), which itself was reorganised on a national basis. With the 18th century the movement for the removal or reduction of duties on imports and exports becomes important. It can best be traced in the history of the commercial treaties of the period and the negotiations which led up to them, e.g. the METHUEN TREATY with Portugal (1703), the Treaty of Utrecht (1713), the commercial clauses of which were drafted by Arthur Moore, and W. PITT'S commercial treaty with France (1786). In the first we have a typical treaty framed on the principles of the mercantile system. "The Methuen Treaty" said Fox in 1786, "had justly been considered as the commercial idol of England." The eighth and ninth clauses of the Treaty of Utrecht raised a storm amongst the commercial classes, for they were an attempt to move in the direction of free trade with France. It was found impossible to carry them, though the principles they embodied were most ably advocated chiefly by Arthur Moore in Parliament, and by Defoe in Mercator. Pitt's treaty, avowedly an attempt to carry into effect the teaching of Adam Smith, was passed without serious opposition,—"No great manufacturing body of men" said Pitt, "had taken alarm,"— and during the short period of its operation before the outbreak of the war with France it was very successful. Many other illustrations of the growth of free-trade principles during the 18th century may be given, such as Walpole's commercial and colonial policy, Pitt's Irish propositions, etc. The principal obstacle in their way was the bitter hostility of the commercial classes. But there can scarcely be any doubt that but for the French revolutionary war, and the difficulties into which it plunged the country, Pitt would have anticipated by fifty years the later free-trade movement.

W. A. S. H.

Free trade principles were early maintained in France by the economists, being a natural deduction from their principle of *laissez-faire* and a necessary corollary to their doctrine that freedom in exchange, an absolutely unshackled use of the wealth of individuals, could not be dissociated from the full enjoyment of the rights of private property (see DUPONT DE NEMOURS, ECONOMISTES, EPHEMERIDES, PHYSIOCRATS, QUESNAY, and TURGOT).

FREE TRADE,— MODERN HISTORY OF. The history of the modern movement in favour of free trade practically begins with the year 1786, when Pitt concluded a commercial treaty with France which abolished many of the protective duties between the two countries. Ten years before, however, a great impetus had been given to free-trade doctrines by the publication of Adam Smith's *Wealth of Nations*. Yet the protective system was so interwoven with our commercial policy at home and abroad, that no really successful assault could be made upon it until nearly forty years after the passing of Pitt's French treaty. With the appointment of WILLIAM HUSKISSON (*q.v.*) as president of the board of trade in 1823, a complete change came over the commercial policy of England, and the bulwarks of protection began to give way. In the session of 1823 Huskisson carried his Reciprocity of Duties Bill, a measure which largely modified the effects of the NAVIGATION ACTS (*q.v.*), by freeing English and foreign shipping. He next reduced the duty on raw and spun silk, and lowered the import and export duty on wool. The right of free emigration was restored to artisans, and the laws controlling the combinations of either masters or workmen were repealed. "These were the beginnings of free trade ; but a further development of political liberty was essential to the triumph of that generous and fruitful policy" (Lord Farnborough's *Constitutional History of England*, vol. ii.).

Various efforts to regulate the price of corn by act of parliament were made in 1773, 1791, 1804, 1815, and 1822 ; but in consequence of the ill effects of such legislation in 1825-26— years of severe commercial panic—the privy council was authorised to issue orders to suspend the operation of the acts, and to permit the importation of foreign corn under circumstances of necessity. Grave doubts now arose as to the soundness of a protective policy and the beneficial operation of the corn laws ; and during the brief administration of George Canning in 1827, that brilliant and progressive statesman carried resolutions in the House of Commons pointing to a more liberal policy. A relief bill based on the resolutions passed the Lower House, but owing to Canning's death and the opposition of the Duke of Wellington in the Lords, the measure was lost. In 1828, when the Duke had assumed office, with Peel and Huskisson among his colleagues, the duties on foreign corn were regulated in accordance with a new sliding scale. By an act passed on the 15th of July the import duty on wheat was to be 25s. 8d. per quarter when the average price in England was under 62s. ; 24s. 8d. when from 62s. to 63s. ; and so to be gradually reduced to 1s. when the average price was 73s. and upwards.

Catholic emancipation and parliamentary reform now absorbed public attention for some years, and nothing further was done to remedy the grievance of the corn laws. The abundant harvest of 1835 came as a slight relief by making bread cheaper for the people, and the year 1836 witnessed no direct action in parliament on free-trade questions. But early in 1837, in consequence of the deficient harvest in the previous autumn, followed by a commercial collapse, an anti-corn law association was formed in London. On the committee were twenty-two members of parliament, including George Grote the historian, J. Silk Buckingham, founder of the *Athenæum*, T. S. Duncombe, Joseph Brotherton, W. Clay, Joseph Hume, J. A. Roebuck, Colonel Perronet Thompson, and Sir W. Molesworth. Three popular writers and poets—Thomas Campbell, Ebenezer Elliott, and William Howitt—were also upon the committee. In the House of Commons, Mr. Clay endeavoured to procure a modification of the corn laws. He moved the adoption of a fixed impost of 10s. per quarter on wheat, in lieu of the sliding scale of duties, but his resolution was lost by 223 votes to 89. In September 1838, Dr. (afterwards Sir John) Bowring addressed a meeting of fiscal reformers at Manchester, which had been hastily called together by Mr. A. Prentice. A proposition to form an anti-corn law association was welcomed with enthusiasm. A preliminary meeting, attended by seven earnest reformers, was held on the 24th of September, and on the 13th of October there was published in the *Manchester Times* a list of thirty-eight gentlemen, as a "Provisional Committee of the Manchester Anti-Corn Law Association." The name of John Bright appeared in this first list, and that of Richard Cobden in the second list, issued a week later. A young medical student named Paulton delivered eloquent lectures in various towns on the advantages of free trade, and Lancashire was soon stirred to action. On the motion of Mr. Cobden, the Manchester chamber of commerce petitioned parliament against the corn laws. The free-trade organisation assumed a larger character in 1839, and became formally known as the National Anti-Corn Law League. A journal entitled the *Anti-Corn Law Circular* was established to advocate the movement. Mr. C. P. Villiers, one of the earliest pioneers of the advancing cause (still living, 1895), now took the lead in parliament, and annually brought forward his resolution in favour of free trade. In March 1839 his motion for a committee on the corn laws was rejected by

342 to 195, and in 1840 by 300 to 177. Lord Fitzwilliam's resolutions in the House of Lords condemnatory of the corn laws were rejected in 1839 by 224 votes to 24, and in 1840 by 194 to 42. During the debate in the Lords on 14th March 1839, the premier, Lord Melbourne, said, "To leave the whole agricultural interest without protection, I declare before God I think it the wildest and maddest scheme that has ever entered into the imagination of man to conceive." In the session of 1840, 763 petitions, with 775,840 signatures, were presented to the House of Commons against the obnoxious laws. In the session of 1841 ministers proposed a fixed duty of 8s., but no measure was brought in owing to the dissolution. Sir Robert PEEL (*q.v.*) came into power in September, and in the ensuing winter there was such terrible distress in all the great centres of population that a conviction gained ground of the absolute necessity for some change in the restrictive laws which pressed so heavily upon the community.

Early in 1842 Mr. Bright stepped into the front rank of the repealers, and created much effect by his earnest eloquence. With Cobden, Villiers, and Wilson, he was instrumental in forming many provincial branches of the league. The government was now moved to action, and in the session of 1842 Peel carried his new sliding scale. By this, there was to be 20s. duty when the price was at 51s., decreasing to 12s. at 60s., and 1s. at 73s.; the duty was not to exceed 20s. when the price fell below 51s. An amendment in favour of a fixed duty, proposed by Lord John Russell in the Commons, was rejected by 349 to 226, and a similar amendment proposed by Lord Melbourne in the Upper House was lost by 207 to 71; an amendment in favour of total repeal proposed by Mr. Villiers in the Commons was rejected by 393 to 90, and a similar amendment brought forward by Lord Brougham in the Peers was lost by 109 to 5. The second reading of the Sliding-scale Bill in the Lords was carried by 119 to 17. To meet the growing deficit in the revenue, which had now become very serious, Peel brought in a bill for the imposition of an income tax of 7d. in the pound, to be levied for three years. But in order to alleviate the new burden, he either partially or wholly abolished the duties on numerous important articles, such as drugs, butter, eggs, cheese, lard, dye-woods, cattle, sheep, pigs, and salted meat. The Manchester Free Trade Hall, built by the repealers on the site of the Peterloo massacre, was opened 30th January 1843. At the inaugural meeting subscriptions of £40,600 to the league fund were announced. In February, the House of Commons was invited by Lord Howick to discuss the question of free trade on a side issue, when his lordship moved for a committee to inquire

into the distress of the country. During the debate a strange scene occurred. After a powerful speech by Mr. Cobden in favour of repeal, Sir Robert Peel rose, and in his excitement indirectly insinuated that Mr. Cobden was inclined to favour his assassination. The unhappy incident arose out of a misinterpretation put upon certain words by Mr. Cobden. The premier's overwrought feelings were further intensified by the attempt upon himself which had resulted in the death of his secretary Mr. Drummond. The affair passed over, and Lord Howick's motion was rejected by 306 to 191 votes. Votes of sympathy with Mr. Cobden were passed at various public meetings. In the spring of 1843 the league held a series of demonstrations in Drury Lane Theatre. Lords Russell and Monteagle brought forward motions in parliament to inquire into the effects of Peel's sliding scale, but they were rejected in the Commons and Lords respectively by 244 votes to 145, and 200 to 78. Mr. Villiers's motion for total repeal was rejected this year by 381 to 125, but in the minority were several prominent and ex-official whigs. The council of the league distributed, in 1843, tracts and publications, etc., to the number of 9,026,000. It was also determined now to raise a fund of £100,000 to further the objects of the league. In March 1844 Mr. Cobden moved for a committee of the House of Commons to inquire into the effects of protective duties on agricultural tenants and labourers, but he was defeated by 224 to 133. Mr. Villiers's annual motion was subsequently brought forward and lost by 328 to 124, but Mr. Bright predicted that either Sir Robert Peel would abolish the corn laws or his government would be overthrown. At a great meeting held in Covent Garden Theatre, Mr. Cobden announced that they would petition the existing House of Commons no more, but would memorialise the Queen direct in favour of the immediate dissolution of parliament.

Sir Robert Peel brought forward the Budget for 1845 on the 14th of February. There was a surplus of £3,409,000, which he proposed to devote to the reduction of the sugar duty, the abolition of the duty on glass, cotton, wool, and on the importation of Baltic staves. He also proposed to abolish the duty on all those articles which merely yielded nominal amounts, a step which would sweep away 430 articles from the tariff. The budget was not thorough enough for the friends of the league, who complained that it took away with one hand what it gave with the other. On the 7th of March Mr. Cobden moved for a select committee to inquire into the causes and extent of the existing agricultural distress, and into the effects of legislative protection upon the interests of landowners, tenant farmers, and farm labourers. The motion was lost by 213 to 121.

Early in May a great bazaar in connection with the league was held in Covent Garden Theatre. On the 26th of May, Lord John Russell brought forward eight resolutions in parliament in the hope of forcing on the question, and shortly afterwards Mr. Villiers repeated, for the last time, his annual motion for the abolition of the corn laws. On this occasion Mr. Bright said that Sir Robert Peel knew well enough what the country wanted, and he ought to do it, being the only statesman competent for the task. The premier brushed aside Lord John Russell's resolutions, and, in replying to the motion of Mr. Villiers, said that he could not see his way to apply the principle of free trade completely to agriculture and the total abolition of the corn laws. But there were signs of wavering and perplexity in the premier's mind. When the House rose on the 8th of August there were grave apprehensions as to the approaching harvest, and it was felt that the question of the continuance of the corn laws was mainly dependent upon the variations of the barometer. That which actually occurred was worse than the anticipation. The harvest was deficient in Great Britain, while in Ireland the potato crop, the staple sustenance of the population, failed entirely. Terrible suffering ensued, and at a mass meeting at Manchester on the 28th of October, Mr. Cobden called on Sir Robert Peel to save the country, which was menaced by famine. The cabinet met frequently, being much discomposed at the aspect of affairs ; but even in this narrow circle there were strong differences of opinion as to the measures required. On the 22nd of November Lord John Russell issued a manifesto to the electors of the City of London declaring for the abolition of the corn laws. "Let us unite," wrote his lordship, "to put an end to a system which has been proved to be the blight of commerce, the bane of agriculture, the source of bitter divisions among classes, the cause of penury, fever, mortality, and crime among the people." This address precipitated matters, and it was followed by similar declarations from Lord Morpeth at Leeds, and Mr. (afterwards Lord) Macaulay at Edinburgh. The cabinet met on 25th November, and the crisis was now felt to be most urgent. The ministerial discussions lasted for several days. At length the Duke of Wellington gave way, and on the 3rd of December the *Times* made the startling announcement—received in many quarters with incredulity—that the abolition of the corn laws had been resolved upon, and that parliament was to meet at once to consider the question. As Lord Stanley, however, and some other ministers absolutely declined to support complete abolition, the premier resigned. Lord John Russell endeavoured to form a government, but his negotiations fell through, and Peel was recalled. Foreseeing that he could carry aboli-

tion through the combined efforts of his own friends and the whigs and free-traders, he consented to resume office, and Lord Stanley was replaced in the government by Mr. Gladstone.

Meanwhile, the anti-corn law league did not relax its efforts. An important meeting was held at Manchester on 23rd December, when it was resolved to raise a fund of £250,000 for the purpose of promoting free-trade principles in the existing emergency. Upwards of £60,000 was subscribed in the room in an hour and a half—the largest sum ever subscribed in the same space of time for any cause. On the 27th of January 1846 Peel brought forward his measure for the abolition of the corn laws before a crowded House of Commons. Prolonged debates took place at each stage of the bill, but eventually, on the 16th of May, the third reading was carried by a majority of 98 in a house of 556. The list of 327 members who voted in favour of the bill included 104 conservatives, and 223 whigs and liberals ; the minority of 229, with the exception of seven votes, was composed exclusively of conservatives. Partly through the arguments and influence of the Duke of Wellington, the House of Lords passed the second reading of the bill by a majority of 47 votes, and the measure became law on the 25th of June. On the same day the Peel ministry fell upon the Irish Coercion Bill. The premier, in his speech on leaving office, delivered on the 29th, reviewed the course and policy of his government, paid a warm tribute to Mr. Cobden, and closed with these memorable words—"It may be that I shall leave a name sometimes remembered with expressions of goodwill in the abodes of those whose lot it is to labour, and to earn their daily bread by the sweat of their brow, when they shall recruit their exhausted strength with abundant and untaxed food, the sweeter because it is no longer leavened by a sense of injustice." The measure for abolishing the corn laws provided that from the passing of the act, and until the 1st of February 1849, the maximum duty would be 10s., exigible when the price was under 48s., and it was to fall a shilling with every shilling of rise in the price till the latter reached 53s. or upwards, when the duty was to remain at the minimum of 4s. The duties on barley and oats would undergo an alteration proportionally the same ; while all grain from British colonies was to be admitted free of duty, and maize or Indian corn was to be admitted, immediately after the passing of the act, at a nominal duty. Other articles in the tariff, under the heads of articles of food, agriculture, manufacture, etc., were dealt with to the number of several hundreds, in the way of duties repealed or reduced. The duty on corn was to cease altogether in 1849, with the exception of a registration duty of 1s. a quarter, which was ultimately abolished in 1869.

The Anti-Corn Law League was dissolved on the 2nd of July 1846, its work having been practically accomplished. It had a temporary revival, however, in 1852, when there was some fear that the brief administration of Lord Derby would return to a protectionist policy. After the abolition of the corn laws other restrictions upon the freedom of trade were gradually removed. The navigation laws were repealed in 1849, and in 1853 Mr. Gladstone greatly relieved the tariff by the reduction or total remission of imposts on 133 articles. Further steps in abolishing protective impediments were taken in 1860, 1869, 1874, etc. The policy of free trade in the United Kingdom has been justified by its effects on the prosperity of the country ; for just as the free-trade system has enabled us to take the utmost possible advantage of periods of prosperity, so it has enabled us to meet phases of reaction and adversity with less strain on our resources than any of the protected countries. The British tariff is now virtually one for revenue only, and under this system we have secured a great expansion of both home and foreign trade. As the tendency of all our recent financial legislation has been towards the general abolition and diminution of duties in order to liberate trade, our commerce has shown in consequence a remarkable elasticity, and a gratifying power of recuperation in periods of depression.

[*History of the Anti-Corn Law League*, by Archibald Prentice, 2 vols. 1853.—*Free Trade and Protection*, by Henry Fawcett, 1878.—*Free Trade v. Fair Trade*, by Sir Thomas H. Farrer, 1885.—*Life of Richard Cobden*, by John Morley, 2 vols. 1881.—*Life and Speeches of John Bright*, by G. Barnett Smith, 2 vols. 1881.—*History of the Free Trade Movement in England*, by Augustus Mongredien, 1881.] G. B. S.

FREGIER, A. (1789 ; died soon after 1850), an official of the prefecture of the department of the Seine, was from 1824 to 1830 secretary of the *Conseil de Préfecture*, and from 1830 to 1843 head of the *Bureau du Domaine* (state property) in Paris. He wrote principally on subjects connected with the dangerous classes in large towns :—*Des Classes Dangereuses dans les grandes Villes* (Paris, 2 vols. 1839-40), and *Histoire de l'Administration de la Police à Paris depuis Philippe Auguste* (Paris, 2 vols. 1850). His pamphlet, *Solution Nouvelle du Problème de la Misère* (Paris, 1851), is in favour of a *minimum* rate of wages, to be fixed by the local authorities according to the cost of food and lodgings, coupled with an interdiction of employing *married* women in factories (p. 37), and of erecting new factories in large towns (p. 44). These rules were only to be applied to manufacturers employing more than twenty workmen. E. Ca.

FREIGHT is the reward paid by the owner of goods to the shipowner for the service of transporting merchandise from the agreed place of shipment to the agreed place of delivery. It accrues usually under written contracts called charter-parties or bills of lading. When an entire ship is hired for service a charter-party is made. When a part cargo is laden in what is called a "liner," a "berth" ship, or sometimes, a "general cargo" ship, no charter-party is made between the owner of the goods and the shipowner, but a bill of lading is issued to each shipper for his own parcel of goods, and the cost of freight as well as all the other conditions of the contract are set forth therein. In the latter class of cases freight is generally prepaid, the payment being made in exchange for the bill of lading. In the former class—where a charter-party is drawn up, and the whole ship is hired, the method of payment varies very much. Sometimes the freight is paid partly in advance at the time of shipment, but most frequently it is paid at the time and place of delivery. If in either case the goods are not delivered at the agreed port of destination, and the freight has not been paid in advance, no freight becomes due, no matter what portion of the voyage may have been accomplished. By the laws of some Continental States what is called "distance freight" is due to the ship when an accident prevents the vessel carrying the goods to the agreed destination, except in the case of total loss ; but English law does not recognise any freight to be due which the charter-party makes payable at the port of destination on due delivery of the goods until the goods are so delivered. In the absence, however, of express stipulation to the contrary, freight, once prepaid in accordance with the terms of either charter-party or bill of lading, is not recoverable from the shipowner if, through the occurrence of some sea peril, the vessel fails to make delivery at the port of destination. The theory in this case is, that such prepayment of freight is added to the value of the goods shipped, and that the insurable interest in the amount prepaid vests in the owner of the goods, the value of which is enhanced by this prepayment. The shipowner has no insurable interest in prepaid freight. It is not, in fact, at sea-risk, from the fact that it is paid. The shipowner has it, and no sea peril makes him liable to return the money if the goods are not delivered. The incidents of freight no longer attach to the money so paid.

The word "freight" covers a good many variations, such as chartered freight, bill-of-lading freight, owners' freight, charterers' freight, lump-sum freight, and dead freight, indicating various contract relations to the thing itself. Lump-sum freight means an agreed amount for a voyage, irrespective of the number of tons delivered, so that, unless otherwise provided, the lump sum is payable at destination, even although part of the cargo may have been lost from sea perils during the voyage. Dead freight is money due to the shipowner in respect of goods agreed to be shipped but not shipped by the person who has failed to make the shipment according to his contract to do so. It may also be observed that the word freight has a more exclusive significance between the shipowner and an underwriter in a policy of insurance than it has between the shipowner and the owner of the goods under charter-parties and bills of lading.

When freight is payable on right delivery at the agreed port of destination, the shipowner is entitled to payment even if the goods are delivered in a damaged condition. Whether the owner is responsible for not making delivery in the like good order and condition to that in which he received the goods depends on whether the damage results from sea perils or some other cause, from liability for which the shipowner is exempted by the terms of the charter or bill of lading. But the right to recover freight on the goods delivered is not affected by some of them being damaged.

Many disputes occur as to where freight is payable. It has been held that the captain should deliver the goods first and claim payment afterwards. This, however, conflicts with two important conditions. The first results from the common-law dictum, which gives the carrier a lien for freight on the goods he carries. Obviously, his lien lasts so long as the goods are in his custody, and cannot be exercised after they have passed into the premises or possession of the person by whom the freight is payable. To be available against him, payment before getting possession is essential. The second results from a condition now frequently inserted in charter-parties, by which the charterer stipulates that after the cargo is once shipped his liability under the contract shall absolutely cease, and that the shipowner shall look to, in other words, exercise his lien on, the cargo to secure payment of the agreed freight; so that if he fails to do so, and, from any cause cannot, after delivery, get the freight from the receiver of the goods, he shall have no right to come back on the original charterer and enforce payment against him under the charter. In business language this is called the "cesser-clause." The shipowner, therefore, has lien both by common law and by special contract, and, in consideration of the latter, generally gives specific release from liability to the original charterer, after he has once shipped the cargo on which the shipowner's lien for freight is to accrue. In consequence of these two conditions it has been held that the master should deliver and the consignee receive the goods at the ship's side, and that on such delivery the master ceases to be responsible for the goods, and to have any

lien, so that he is justified in refusing to proceed with the delivery unless the freight is paid. These considerations secure that delivery and freight payment are, as nearly as possible, coincident, and have the effect of preventing shipowners from making bad debts on the one hand, and, on the other, of saving charterers from paying freight twice over, both being equally objectionable. In practice they work easily although this description makes them look rather elaborate.

Freight has become, in recent years, an object of greatly increased interest to the inhabitants of the United Kingdom. Half a century ago we could generally feed ourselves by the productions of our own country. Since then the population has increased more than 40 per cent. And the economic condition of the larger population is so much improved that the scale of consumption is much larger than in former times. It is doubtful whether half the commodities consumed now are produced here, and it is certain that of our daily bread, barely one-third is grown at home. The carriage of these vast supplies of food, in addition to the raw materials for our manufactures, makes the question of freight of interest to every inhabitant of the kingdom. Our food cannot come here without sea-carriage; this cannot be provided without the payment of adequate freights. It is, therefore, matter of common interest to inquire—what must freight cover? what items do really enter into its cost? and what has the payment called freight to provide?

In the first place, freight has to provide for the building, maintenance, depreciation, and ultimate loss of the ship itself. If freight were not adequate for all these purposes, sea-carrying would not be continued as a trade. No capitalist would invest money in the building or buying of ships unless he expected on the ultimate loss or sale of the vessel to find his original capital in hand, plus something more than 3 per cent interest for the time of the investment, otherwise the money had better have been put into consols or railway debentures. No one invests in very troublesome and precarious trades but for the hope that at the end of the adventure they would find not the capital only, but interest at a higher rate than that yielded by investments which give no trouble, and are practically without risk.

In the second place, a ship is only a tool; a tool moreover which demands the constant employment of labour for its use. It must be prepared and outfitted for every voyage. To the outfit of stores and provisions nearly every trade makes contributions. To load cargo, docks and harbours are necessary; their cost must largely be provided out of freight. Captains, mates, engineers, firemen, and seamen, all must be paid wages, and fed while at sea. The light and pilotage services round our coasts are also paid for out of freight, these being special charges on shipping. When the vessel comes back with her cargo, the same charges have all to be paid again. Freight therefore may be said in one sense to be a very large employer of labour. Large classes of labourers on shore as well as the seamen afloat, live out of it, and freight must be sufficient to bear the cost of all these charges.

The students of economic facts will be prepared to hear that great changes have taken place with regard to all these elements in the cost of freight in late years. Ships were formerly built of wood, then of iron, now almost exclusively of steel. They were propelled by sails ; steam propulsion, excepting in the very long trade voyages, is rapidly superseding the use of sails. To build wooden ships we had to depend on timber imported from other countries. For iron and steel ships, the raw material in unlimited quantities lies under our feet in the iron and coal measures. The cost of shipbuilding, therefore, is much less than in former times. The cost of maintenance is probably about the same. The depreciation is also not less. It used to be thought that the iron structures would last indefinitely. But the vicissitudes of climate and other things have modified this opinion. It has also been found in recent years that changes in requirements of size, type, and speed have rendered many vessels useless, in an economic sense, long before they were worn out. To cover inevitable outlays on surveys, on new boilers in the case of steamships, and the risks and depreciation between old and new, something like 10 per cent on the original cost must be set aside annually to secure the replacement of the capital with reasonable interest. This, of course, must also be borne by freight, and from all recent experience is an increasing rather than a diminishing charge. Much loss has taught the lesson that a ship is like property held on a short lease for which a large premium has been paid, necessitating the cost being extinguished by the time the lease runs out.

It is probable that the costs of navigation have decreased. Wages are higher both for seamen and on shore ; but so much steam is used to economise labour, that in spite of higher pay to the men actually employed, it is probable that this item in the cost of freight is less than formerly. Insurance is probably cheaper, in·most cases it certainly is so.

None of these items, however, are so changed as to explain the largely reduced cost of freight. Limiting our view to the last twenty-five years, which mark the time within which steam began to be used for ordinary cargo-carrying, the reduction is very large. It is difficult to state it in figures. The short-voyage trades necessarily show the least reduction because freight on these includes the labour of loading and unloading, of light and harbour dues, etc., so frequently ; and these items are higher than formerly. But in the long-voyage trades, reductions to far less than half the former rates of freight are quite common. If the comparison be extended to fifty years ago, many freights would be found one-third or one-fourth of what they were then. They still fluctuate much, with variations in crops, and seasons, and are affected sometimes by wars and famines ; but apart altogether from such exceptional causes, the permanent level of freight is lower in the proportion stated. Two causes have led to this : (1) The shortened time of voyages by the use of steam. Coasting voyages which frequently occupied a month now occupy less than a week. Mediterranean voyages that used to occupy five or six months are now completed in two. Indian voyages, via the Cape, by sailing ships, which frequently occupied ten, eleven, and twelve months, are now frequently performed by cargo steamers in three, and seldom exceed four months. (2) The greatly increased size of the vessels. Cargoes of 3000 tons are as common now as those of 1000 tons before the use of steam ; and cargoes of 4000 to 6000 tons are becoming frequent. These larger bulks can be carried at greatly reduced rates. The large steam vessels of to-day can make profits out of rates of freight on which either the small steamships or the large sailing ships of former times would have made large losses. These two are the chief factors in this great reduction in the cost of freight. Steam has saved time, and the growth of business has made it economically possible to carry in larger bulks.

We have recently been passing through a remarkable revolution in all that related to freight. The material of the vessels, the method of propulsion, the speed, the size, have all changed, and all have conduced to the reduction in the cost of freight already mentioned.

The economic effects of this change are very considerable already, but are probably more far-reaching than anything apparent yet. Men used to live where their food was grown, and were limited in their numbers to the local means of subsistence. Cheapened freight has made maritime distance of very small account so that millions of human beings in these islands are living thousands of miles away from the localities in which their daily bread is grown, without any sense of risk or insecurity. Indeed, they are better off than their fathers, who had to live on what was locally grown, whether it was a bad crop or a good one ; but now, if the local crop is either bad or short, it makes very little difference in the price though a great difference to the grower, so cheap and good and constant is the over sea supply. Cheapened freight, therefore, may be said to have modified the operation of the Malthusian law in an important degree, for the time at all events, by bringing the surplus food production of the most distant countries to our markets, at constantly decreasing prices, 38,000,000 of people in these islands, being now fed with far cheaper, and generally better bread, than half the number formerly.

This would be an important matter if it affected our own state only. But other states are following in our steps, and in spite of duties more or less prohibitory, find it impossible to keep out of their ports the cheaply produced grain of distant lands, carried by English steamers at little more than nominal freight. There is no record of these transactions between foreign states in our board of trade and navigation returns ; but the quantities of food carried under our flag to Germany, Holland, France, Belgium, Norway, Sweden, Spain, and Italy are very large indeed. When the sea freight has come to be less in many cases than the cost of inland transport from one part to another part of the same kingdom, it is easy to see how large coast populations begin to draw on the over-sea supplies, which are found cheaper than the home-grown food.

Whether such a state of affairs will last it is impossible to say. Will men go to live where the food is grown ? or will they continue to depend on cheap freight for bringing the treasures of other climes to consumers here. This is a new state of things, and one of the very remarkable effects of cheap ocean carriage. It is only necessary to allude to one other fact connected with freight. Though so much cheaper than in earlier years, the transactions are so large as to have furnished economists with one of the chief factors in making up the difference between the apparent value of our imports and exports. Fifteen years ago there was much concern at the growing gulf between these two values. We were reminded of the dividends the United Kingdom had to receive from abroad as partly explaining the difference, but they were not an adequate explanation. All further anxiety on the matter was disposed of when it was shown that the import value included the freight, and had to be reduced by the amount thereof, also that the export value, in most cases, also required that the freight should be added, because both freights were earned so largely by the English flag, *i.e.* by Englishmen working in English ships, and constituted as real an export value as any other item of export that appeared in the trade returns. It was happily called "an invisible export," the value of which being duly deducted from imports and added to exports, explained the manner in which the apparent excess of imports was paid for.   J. G.

FREIGHT, DEAD, and other terms. See FREIGHT.

FREIGHT IS THE MOTHER OF WAGES. This maxim, which means that unless a ship earns freight the sailors are not entitled to wages, has ceased to be applicable in the United Kingdom since 1854, by the Merchant Shipping Act of that year, providing by § 183 that "no right to wages shall be dependent on the earning of freight," subject, however, to the reservation that a sailor's claim is to be barred if it can be proved "that he has not exerted himself to the utmost to save the ship, cargo, and stores." Any attempted modification of this provision by private agreement is wholly inoperative (see § 182). Previously to the statutory abrogation of the old rule, the Courts had already engrafted many exceptions on it, and it was never applied to the master of a ship (see Hawkins v. Twizell, 25 Law Journal (Q. B.) 160) ; but it seems strange that a rule so inhuman and unjust should have been allowed to remain law for such a long period.

According to French and Italian law a sailor was not entitled to wages in case of capture or total loss of the ship and goods (Code de Commerce, § 258 [unamended] ; Codice di Commercio, § 235), but as regards France this rule was, in 1885, altered in favour of the sailors ; and in the case of loss of freight for other reasons, the codes of both countries always upheld the sailors' claims in the absence of express stipulations to the contrary.

According to German law, a sailor belonging to a ship which has been lost is entitled, not only to the wages earned up to the date of the loss, but also to the expenses incurred in returning to the port from which the vessel started on its voyage.

[As to the present state of English law on the subject, see Maclachlan, *Law of Merchant Shipping*, 4th ed. 1892. — Abbott, *Law of Merchant Ships and Seamen*, 13th ed., 1892 (see also the report of Cutter v. Powell in Smith's *Leading Cases*).]   E. S.

FRENCH SCHOOL OF POLITICAL ECONOMY.

Period I., p. 154 ; Period II., p. 156 ; Period III., p. 157 ; Period IV., p. 158.

A survey of the French school, from its commencement to the present time, will show that it has passed through four successive phases, which are clearly marked off one from the other, and form the natural subdivisions of this article.

PERIOD I. (1615-1803).

During this first period, which may be termed the period of the foundation of economic science, France may assuredly be said to have taken a more important part than any other country. With the increasing interest felt by economists in the history of economic doctrines, and with the greater amount of study they bestow upon the older authors, more and more ample justice is paid by them to the great services rendered in the past by the French school. It might be said that nowhere else has political economy had a larger number of precursors. It is now generally agreed that it was in France that political economy first saw the light and even received its name ; for the first book bearing the title of *Économie Politique* is that by Antoine de MONTCHRÉTIEN, *Traicté d'Économie politique*, 1615. (This fact is specially admitted by Cossa, on page 61 of his *Introduction to the study of Political Economy*, English translation). Unfortunately the title of Montchrétien's book is practically the only portion that has deserved to survive, but that was certainly a beginning. What, however, may be held to be the first systematic treatise on political economy is the *Essai sur la Nature du Commerce*, by Richard CANTILLON, which, although not published till 1755, was obviously written before 1734, since that was the year of his death. In this work nearly all the subject-matter of modern political economy is dealt with in a most clear and definite manner. A new edition has just appeared, with a preface by Mr. Higgs, who, in the *Quarterly Journal of Economics* (July 1892), writes that "good reasons might be given for regarding him as the father of political economy without putting any strained interpretation upon the phrase."

Questions concerning money and taxation greatly attracted the attention of the early French economists, probably by way of re-action against the debasement of the coinage habitually practised by the kings of France, and against the unjust privileges in respect to taxation which characterised the old régime. Thus, long antecedent to Antoine de Mont-chrétien, deep in the middle ages, just half way through the 14th century, Nicolas ORESME, bishop of Lisieux, the tutor of Charles V., wrote a treatise entitled *Tractatus de Origine, Natura, Jure, et Mutationibus Monetarum*, of which Professor Ingram has been able to say that it "contains a theory of money which is almost entirely correct according to the views of the 19th century" (Ingram, *History of Political Economy*, p. 36). In this Bishop Oresme protests boldly against the alterations in the value of money made by the king—these he terms a "fraudulent act" (*actio fraudulenta*). In the same way two centuries later, during the time of the serious rise in prices which characterised this epoch, BODIN was the first to give the scientific explanation of the causes which led to this, in a memorandum written in 1568, showing that the enormous importation of gold and silver in Europe depreciated the value both of the precious metals and of the money. Finally BOISGUILBERT, in the *Détail de la France* (1692), made this bold statement respecting money : "It is very certain that money is not a value in itself, and that its quantity adds nothing to the wealth of a

country." With regard to taxation, those writers whom we have just mentioned, Bodin and Boisguilbert, both insisted that taxation should be proportional, and that the exemptions in favour of the nobility and clergy should be suppressed. We must join with these the illustrious Marshal VAUBAN, who in *La Dîme Royale* (1707) proposed the abolition of all the existing taxes, and the replacing them by one single tax "charged proportionally on all who possessed an income." In writing on these subjects Vauban was the first to employ statis-tical documents ; these had been collected by himself, and are almost the only ones we possess referring to that epoch.

A short time before the date of the PHYSIO-CRATS, a man who is perhaps best known to us by the encomium pronounced by TURGOT on him, Vincent de GOURNAY (who died in 1759), drew up the programme of the "liberal school." To him also has been attributed that famous saying *laisser-faire, laisser-passer*. Whether this is true or false, it is certain that it was he who promulgated the view that, since private interests concurred with public interests, the best thing, from the point of view of the ad-vantage of the public, was to let every one follow his own way in life.

Full justice, too, is nowadays awarded to the genius of QUESNAY and to the merits of his disciples MERCIER DE LA RIVIÈRE ; DUPONT DE NEMOURS ; LE TRÔSNE ; TURGOT (see all these), that illustrious body of men who first bore the name of ECONOMISTES, and were in the main much in advance of their time. Universal tribute is paid to their praiseworthy endea-vours to form a vast synthesis of economic facts, and to their skill in deducing from a few principles a large concourse of individual items of knowledge, the very characteristic of the formation of a new science. Although they did much to make plain the notion of wealth, still it was not "wealth" but the "natural order of society" that they regarded as the subject of the new science ; perhaps, in-deed, their conception was more correct than that of Adam SMITH. There is no need here to analyse the physiocratic system, for that will be treated of in a special article in this Dic-tionary. All that is required here is to assign to the physiocrats their place in the history of the French schools (see EPHEMERIDES ; PHYSIO-CRATS).

Great indeed was their influence over Europe: every one knows their relations with the Mar-grave of Baden (whose correspondence with MIRABEAU and Dupont has lately been pub-lished) (see KARL FRIEDRICH) ; with Leopold, Grand Duke of Tuscany, afterwards Emperor of Austria ; with Gustavus III. of Sweden ; with Stanislaus, King of Poland ; and even with the Empress Catherine of Russia. Moreover, these relations were not purely literary, but also had a beneficial influence over the laws of the countries above mentioned. In France, their influence on legislation might have been expected to have been even greater, seeing that one of the most illustrious of their number, Turgot, was minister of state. As a matter of fact, in his edicts with regard to the abolition of the restrictions on the movement of grain, of the exclusive trade corporations and of forced labour, Turgot did not fail to apply in all their integrity the principles of the physiocrats. However, most of these reforms came to nothing—perhaps because he applied these principles too hastily, or as a philosopher rather than as a statesman ; or because the resistance to them was too powerful for the weak hands of Louis XVI. to overcome.

The Catholic school has bitterly reproached the physiocrats for having by their teaching prepared the way for the French Revolution ; it might be more correct to say that had these doctrines been applied, there would have been no necessity for the revolution. The influence of the physiocrats has been less powerful in the sphere of science than in the region of legislation, partly because the glory of Adam Smith caused them to be forgotten, partly because even in France their successors have treated them with excessive disdain. But their influence over Adam Smith, and through him, indirectly, upon the general evolution of the science, cannot be gainsaid, though even now not sufficient light has been thrown upon it. The classical school, at its first introduction, encountered two important opponents— both heretics in the opinion of those who held to the doctrines of the school—the first one, FORBONNAIS (*Principes Économiques*, 1767), who defended the protectionist system, the other the philosopher CONDILLAC, who in his book on *Le Commerce et le Gouvernement* (1770) criticised several of the doctrines of the physiocrats, notably that on value, as to which he develops for the first time a psychological theory closely approaching the one so celebrated at the present day under the name of the theory of "FINAL UTILITY."

A place amongst the founders of political economy must be reserved for Jean Baptiste SAY, not indeed on account of the originality or depth of his ideas, but simply because he was the author of the first really popular work on political economy. His *Traité d'Économie politique* (1803), which was wonderfully well arranged and lucid, was translated into many languages, and thus made the new science accessible to all classes of society. Nor was he simply a mere populariser ; he gave economic science its present form and its definitions ;— from his categories, his vocabulary (*e.g.* the term "ENTREPRENEUR," which has been borrowed by most other languages), and his great divisions of the science, has been con-

structed the scale it was henceforward to work by. The classifications which he planned, the impress he stamped on the science has been reproduced in every text-book published during this century.

PERIOD II. (1803-1848).

In this second period the series of economists received a strange interruption. During more than forty years economic science in France underwent an almost total eclipse. From Jean Baptiste Say's work (1803), which we have just referred to, up to DUNOYER'S publication (in 1845) of his book on *La Liberté du Travail*, no economist can be mentioned who created a school. No doubt there were several works of some merit, but they dealt rather with subjects bordering on political economy than with the science itself. Amongst these are the treatises of DESTUTT DE TRACY (1823) and of Joseph DROZ (1829), which were strictly speaking the writings of a philosopher and a moralist ; the *Systèmes de Culture* of Hippolyte PASSY (1846), which treated of rural economy ; COURNOT'S even more important work, *Recherches sur les principes mathématiques de la théorie des richesses* (1838), which is an early instance of the application of mathematics to political economy,[1] and VILLERME'S *Tableau de l'état physique et moral des ouvriers* (1840) ; this last is an excellent statistical study. There was a sudden break in the series of great didactic works, while contemporaneously it continued in England. No account can be taken here of STORCH (*Cours d'Économie politique*, 1815, and *Considérations sur la nature du revenu national*, 1824), since his work lay outside France ; of ROSSI (*Cours d'Économie politique*, 1840), since he was an Italian ; or of SISMONDI (*Nouveaux principes d'économie politique*, 1819), since he was a Swiss ; indeed the latter could in no case be counted as an economist of the classical school, inasmuch as he was their vigorous opponent.

In truth, if the classical economists disappeared from sight in the period now under review, the reason was that they were replaced by their foes, the socialists. The period is filled with the names of Saint-SIMON, FOURIER, PROUDHON, Louis BLANC, and of such writers, less known than they deserve, as BAZARD, ENFANTIN, LEROUX, BUCHEZ, VIDAL, and CABET. These men attracted general attention and drew the thoughts of all men towards them. It is the fashion nowadays, especially with

---

[1] Cournot "taught that it is necessary to face the difficulty of regarding the various elements of an economic problem—not as determining one another in a chain of causation, A determining B, B determining C, and so on—but as all mutually determining one another. Nature's action is complex, and nothing is gained in the long run by pretending that it is simple, and trying to describe it in a series of elementary propositions." [Marshall, *Principles of Economics*, vol. i., in his preface to the first edition bears a high tribute to the ability of Cournot . . . "Cournot's genius must give a new mental activity to everyone who passes through his hands," p. xv. Macmillan, 2nd ed., 1891.]

socialists of the German school, notwithstanding their obligations to it, to turn this socialism, which they term "utopian," into ridicule. But in my opinion, when the history of socialism and of its first beginnings receives the same amount of attention as the history and origins of political economy have received, the French school will be found to have taken, in the creation of contemporary socialism, a share equal, or even superior, to that which it had in the formation of economic science. No doubt there was much that was utopian in the exuberant blossoming of ideas that characterised this period ; but many of them have borne fruit and have taken their place in what is now called scientific socialism. The notion that man, as a member of society, has functions to fulfil rather than rights to exercise (in direct opposition to the revolutionary programme of the "Rights of Man"), forms the basis of the teachings of Saint-Simon. In the writings of his follower, Bazard (*Doctrine de Saint-Simon*, 1828-29), there is a perfectly clear exposition both of the social question of the present day, i.e. the separation of the labourer from the instruments of his labour, and of the solution proposed by the collectivist school, i.e. the nationalisation of the instruments of production. Again, never have the advantages of co-operative association for purposes of consumption been analysed with more precision, and never have the disadvantages of the increase of "middlemen" been more vigorously assailed, than in the works of Fourier (*Association Domestique Agricole*, 1822). The theory of the "Iron Law" (*loi d'airain*), and the proposition destined to become so terrible a weapon in the hands of the Marxists, namely, that wealth is the product of the *labour of others*, are plainly set forth in Vidal's *Répartition des Richesses* (1846). In 1831, twelve years before the Rochdale Pioneers, Buchez founded the first co-operative society for production, as a means of social transformation, and suggested as the aim of the working classes that system of *collective saving* in the shape of a reserve fund, in preference to the method of individual saving, which is the characteristic feature of trades unions. Of the unreadable writings of Leroux but one word survives ; yet it, the term *solidarity*, shines out as a guiding star. Proudhon's confused and vehement reasonings (*Qu'est-ce que la Propriété?* 1840 ;—*Système des Contradictions Économiques ou Philosophie de la Misère*, 1848) have been, perhaps, of little special value to the doctrine of socialism ; but they have rendered a very real service to economic science by obliging it to examine and to consolidate the foundations of political economy, which till then had been regarded as unshakable. The *Système*, however, is memorable as having called forth Karl Marx's taunting reply *La Misère de la Philosophie*.

Auguste Comte, also, should not be counted as a socialist, but at any rate he must be placed amongst the opponents of the economists ; they have never forgiven him for the contempt he poured on them and for his assertion of the absolute uselessness and irrationality of endeavouring to make political economy an independent science. Perhaps Mr. Ingram goes a little too far in saying that Comte, the founder of sociology, was also the founder of the historical school of political economy.

Never has France, and Paris in particular, shone more brightly in the world, or exerted more influence over the socialistic movement, than in the period which ended in the Revolution of 1848, an event, indeed, that nearly set all Europe in a blaze. That influence spread on the one side to America, where communities were founded after the fashion of Fourier's phalanstery, and in the other direction to Russia, exiles from which country, the future chiefs of anarchism (e.g. Herzen and Bakounine), came to Paris for instruction.

PERIOD III. (1848-1878).

This third period is in striking contrast to its predecessor. The socialists vanish from the scene and are not again spoken of; never before has any school of thought seemed smitten by so sudden a death. The following passage occurred in the article on the "Socialists" in the *Dictionnaire d'Économie politique* which appeared in 1853 : "When we state that socialism, at any rate in its recent shape, is altogether extinguished, there is no fear of our assertion being falsified either by the course of time or by future events." A sufficient explanation of the phenomenon lies in the failure of the revolution of 1848 and its replacement by the second empire.

On the other hand, the classical school of economists, who had never been heard of during the second period, sprang up on every side. This fresh movement had already been begun by Charles Dunoyer's book in 1845, but the liberal and optimistic traditions of the French school were first renewed, with remarkable energy, by Frédéric Bastiat in his *Harmonies Économiques*, published in 1850, the year of his death. The final triumph of the orthodox and liberal school was effected by many authors. Mention may be made of the numerous writings of M. Michel Chevalier, the series of which had commenced in the preceding period with his *Cours d'Économie politique* (1842-1844), and comprised *La Monnaie* (1850), *Le Système protecteur* (1853), and *La Baisse probable de l'Or* (1859). In 1852 and 1853, MM. Coquelin and Garnier issued the *Dictionnaire d'Économie politique ;* in 1855 came M. de Molinari's *Cours d'Économie politique ;* in 1857 M. Baudrillart's *Manuel ;* in 1858 M. Courcelle Seneuil's *Traité d'Économie politique ;* in 1861 M. Frédéric

PASSY'S *Leçons d'Économie politique;* and in 1867 M. Levasseur's *Précis d'Économie politique.* Indeed, all those liberal ideas which had been proscribed by Napoleon III. appear to have taken refuge in political economy, and to have breathed into it a new life.

The opinions of the economists of this period do not differ materially from the tenets of the "MANCHESTER SCHOOL," *i.e.* free trade, distrust of state interference, and monometallism. However, Stanley JEVONS observes that the French school is less dogmatic in its ways than the English school, and with reference to "the doctrine of wages," for example, he observes, that the true doctrine may be more or less clearly traced through the writings of a succession of great French economists, from Condillac, Baudeau, and Le Trôsne, through J. B. Say, Destutt de Tracy, Storch, and others, down to Bastiat and Courcelle-Seneuil . . . "The truth is with the French school."

Indeed, in the hands of the French school political economy becomes a natural rather than a deductive science. In spite of their disinclination to acknowledge their debt, French economists have remained faithful to the traditions left them by the physiocrats. They frequently take a delight in contrasting the generous and idealistic spirit of their school with the egoism and mercantile tendency of the English school. Perhaps this contrast is less real than they suppose it to be. As a matter of fact their egoism is as great as that of the Manchester school, the difference being that their temperament is light-hearted, whereas that of the English economists may be regarded as sombre; in short, the latter are pessimists, the former are optimists. OPTIMISM, indeed, has been the characteristic feature of the French school ever since the days of the physiocrats even to our own time ; the fullest expression of this is found in Bastiat. It may be defined as a belief in a natural order which regulates human society, and, though not exempt from certain disorders, is still, human nature being as it is, the best possible. Moreover, this natural order of things is capable of indefinite improvement through the unfettered action of liberty and of competition. Beyond this lies the conviction that no attempt to modify the machinery of the system should be made, and that all that is necessary is the removal of the obstacles that might impede its due working.

And if this school in a general way rejects the English theories respecting rent, wages, and population, this arises from the idea (*idée a priori*) that the discouraging consequences of these theories enhance the difficulty of the justification of the existing social order.

During this period there were but two dissentient economists. The first of these, WOLOWSKI, indeed, separated himself from the school only on a question of detail, *i.e.* bimetallism,

which he warmly advocated in his *Liberté des Banques* (1864), and in his *L'or et l'argent* (1870). The other was LE PLAY, who wrote *Ouvriers Européens* (1855), and *La Réforme Sociale* (1864), and founded a school,—the first, indeed, to branch off from the parent stock. Still, Le Play, and his followers in a marked degree, continued to adhere to the liberal school in their distrust of state interference, and in their apologies for the "essential principles" of our present social organisation, including competition. Le Play, however, abandons the optimistic standpoint and the deductive method ; he desires a "reform," and strives to find the elements of such a reform in the observation of facts, especially in the study of the family life of the working classes.

During this period the influence of the economists was so great that it could not fail to penetrate into the sphere of legislation. It is well known that Michel Chevalier negotiated, together with COBDEN, the famous treaty of commerce of 1860 between France and England, which inaugurated an era of modified free trade not only for France but also for the rest of Europe.

Protection was believed to be as completely stamped out as socialism. The conviction of this double victory contributed largely to the maintenance of the proud self-confidence of the orthodox school. Credit may also be given them for the law of 1864, which abolished the penalties attaching to the right of combination between workmen. In accordance with their principles the economists had always admitted that combination was "the natural, regular, and legitimate means of resistance afforded to the working classes by the system of free competition" (*Dictionnaire d'Économie politique, sub voce* "Coalition "). They had also no small share in the development of the French railway system (the conventions of 1859) and of joint-stock companies (the Act of 1867), and in the formation of the great international exhibitions of 1855 and 1867, in which important parts were played by Michel Chevalier and Le Play. Further, Le Play endeavoured to procure the enactment of a measure granting freedom of disposition of property by will, at least up to a certain point ; but in spite of the support of Napoleon III., the bill failed to pass through the Chamber, for it was in too flagrant contradiction with the "principles of '89."

In this period the liberal French school reached its apogee, but it was also approaching the commencement of its decline, or at any rate, the end of its uncontested supremacy. The conflict between the liberal school and its rivals occupies the fourth and last period, on which we are about to enter.

PERIOD IV. (1878-1892).

The date from which this last period should

be reckoned is necessarily to some extent undetermined; the year 1878 has been chosen, since it marks an important event that we shall presently discuss, that is to say, the rupture between university education and the orthodox school.

During the time we are now considering, most of the leading economists of the preceding period still bore on high the banner of the liberal school, MM. de Molinari, Frédéric Passy, and Levasseur. Michel Chevalier, Baudrillart, and Courcelle-Seneuil have gone, but their places have been filled by MM. Leroy-Beaulieu, Block, Léon Say, and De Foville, and taking all in all, the liberal school contains as many men of high ability as ever it did. This school is in exclusive occupation of the benches of the Institute and of the professorial chairs at the various schools of Paris. The venerable *Journal des Économistes* has received as companions the *Économiste français* (1873), edited by M. Paul Leroy-Beaulieu, and the *Monde Économique* (1891), edited by M. Beauregard, Professor in the Faculty of Law at Paris; both of these organs uphold the same cause. A new *Dictionnaire d'Économie politique* (1890-1892) has appeared under the care of MM. Léon Say and Chailley; it is written in the same spirit as the former one. To all outward appearance, therefore, things would seem to be as they were; but in reality there have been great changes. The liberal school has lost the public ear and the legislative support that it possessed in the preceding period. It is hated by the working classes, who upbraid it for its quietism; by the agriculturists and manufacturers, who have never forgiven it for free trade; by the Catholics, who regard it as the embodiment of the principles of the Revolution, and whom the very name of liberalism irritates; and, last of all, by the radicals, who are hastening on towards state socialism. From every side rival schools are rising, all of which are preparing for the conflict by starting their own "Reviews."

Le Play's school, which grew in importance after the disasters of 1870, is now detaching from the main body a constantly-increasing band of recruits. In all parts of France it is forming groups which are termed *Unions de la Paix Sociale*, and in 1881 it founded a fortnightly review, the *Réforme Sociale*, which abstains from all theoretical subjects, but is one of the best publications for the discussion of all questions relating to economic legislation. Its chief representative in France was M. Claudio JANNET, Professor at the Roman Catholic University of Paris, whose most important work is *Le Socialisme d'État et la Réforme Sociale*. For all this, Le Play's school is a rival rather than an enemy of the liberal school, with which it preserves very friendly relations; indeed, it is almost as liberal, but its apologies are made less for things as they are than for things as they were.

But by the side of Le Play's followers another Roman Catholic school has risen, of a far more pronounced religious character, which is the representative of what we have now agreed to call Catholic socialism, in spite of its energetic repudiation of the epithet "socialistic." It is very bitter, as vehement indeed as the socialists themselves, in its criticisms of the economic organisation of the present day, especially of *laisser-faire* and competition, and is much inclined to fall back upon the state, which it terms the "Minister of God." Its organ is *L'Association Catholique*, a monthly review that was founded in 1876, and its most eloquent spokesman is the Comte de Mun, a member of the Chamber of Deputies. Further information on the subject may be found in M. Urbain Guérin's *L'Évolution Sociale* (1891).

Again, a new lease of life had been taken by the socialist school after the termination of the Paris Commune of 1871, and around this revolution, which by no means deserved the distinction, a great "socialist legend" grew up, its two chief apostles being Jules Guesde and Lafargue, Karl Marx's son-in-law, who has of late become a member of the Chamber of Deputies. These two represent collectivism of the Marxist variety. M. Benoit MALON, the editor of the *Revue Socialiste* (started in 1885) and author of a number of books, the chief of which is *Socialisme Intégral* (1890-1892), clings more closely to the traditions of the socialism of the French species, which is less materialistic and holds that the matter of "filling one's belly" does not exhaust the whole social question.

In 1878 the event occurred that I here referred to as the starting-point of a new period, namely, the institution, at all the universities in France, strictly speaking, in their faculties of law, of professorial chairs or lectureships of political economy, which duly appear on the official schedule of education and examination. Till then political economy had been taught only in the special schools at Paris, and at the Collège de France. Instruction in this subject was given entirely by a small number of economists, all of the same school, sometimes of the same family, and lecturing in the same city. Naturally, therefore, the teaching of political economy became a sort of monopoly and received that restricted and almost sectarian tendency which has thrown it into discredit. When in the year 1825 Jean Baptiste Say wrote in the preface to the *Traité d'Économie politique*—"Nowadays political economy is taught wherever knowledge is valued. It has already had professors in the universities of Germany, Scotland, and Italy";[1] little did he think that as far as regards French universities his

---

[1] In speaking of Scotland Say was thinking, no doubt, of Adam Smith, Dugald Stewart, etc. The "chair" of Edinburgh is of later date (established in 1871).

wish would take more than half a century to realise.

The new professors of political economy in the faculties of law did not all of them secede from the orthodox school; for instance, M. JOURDAN (who died in 1891) and M. Villey still adhered to the principles of the liberal school, but in some instances the rupture was immediate. This was especially the case with M. Cauwès, who lectured on political economy in the faculty of law at Paris, and who occasioned much commotion by the publication in this very year, 1878, of his *Cours d'Économie politique*. The cause of irritation lay in his avowing the same scepticism as De LAVELEYE with regard to natural laws, and his inculcation of LIST's theories on the question of protection. In 1887 one of the new professors took the lead in founding the *Revue d'Économie politique*, which received the support of all the professors in the various faculties of law, and of a large number of professors at foreign universities, particularly in Germany, who till then had received practically no hearing in France. The aim which the founders of this organ had in view was not exactly to form a new school, but merely, to use their own words, "to open out a neutral territory on which both doctrines and facts might be studied and compared with one another." As a matter of fact, they are being more and more drawn into the sphere of attraction of the historical school, and also of state socialism.

Further details on this last period may be found in the writer's article on "The Economic School in France," in the *Political Science Quarterly* (vol. v. No. 4).

Our survey would be incomplete if we failed to mention a large number of publications that propagate either socialistic ideas or protectionist principles; such notions are not confined to special organs, but are set forth in a whole host of political newspapers. To these might be added purely literary works, such as those of Zola, Cladel, and Rosny, which resemble the writings of George Sand and Eugène Sue half a century ago, in spreading socialistic ideas far and wide.

Naturally enough legislation has been affected by this change of front by the French school. The treaties of commerce which were negotiated between 1860 and 1870, under the auspices of the free trade school, have now been denounced by French lawgivers, and an exceedingly protectionist customs tariff has been imposed. Concurrently with this large numbers of bills, most clearly marked with state socialism, have been laid before parliament, sometimes by private members, sometimes by the government. One bill, which has become law, limits the hours of labour for children and women. Others purpose a great superannuation fund for workmen; to grant certain privileges to workmen's syndicates, such as the dispensing of the giving of securities in competing for public works; other proposals forbid employers, under severe penalties, to dismiss any workman on the ground that he is a member of a union; to compel contractors for the execution of public works to introduce profit-sharing; another subjects the companies which work the coal mines to the rigorous supervision of delegates elected by workmen; to relieve the distributive co-operative societies from the payment of income-tax and the charges for trade licences, etc. etc.

In this historical sketch of the French school we must not omit a reference to a special branch of political economy, in which this school has perhaps most successfully displayed its characteristic qualities—precision, order, and clearness, that is in treatises relating to finance and taxation. M. de Parieu's *Traité des Impôts* (1862) and M. Paul Leroy-Beaulieu's *Traité de la Science des Finances*; R. Stourm, *Le Budget;* Léon Say, *La Solution démocratique de la question des impôts;—Le Dictionnaire des Finances;* have deservedly attained the position of classical works throughout Europe.   C. G.

FRENCH TREATY OF 1860. See COMMERCIAL TREATIES.

FRICTION IN ECONOMICS. In economic investigation, according to the classical view of it, abstraction is made from the mass of general human motives; and the effect of a selected few, or, as some have held, only *one*, of them is traced out first of all. One by one thereafter the elements, from which abstraction was made at the beginning, are restored to their place, and the conjoint effects of the conjoined causes are traced out with so much of accuracy as the case allows. But the degree of accuracy is not high, economic factors occurring as a rule in the midst of a very complex plurality of causes.

The disturbing effects of causes that are not economic, on the action of the causes that are strictly so called, may be regarded as an "economic friction."

Examples may be drawn not only from distribution and exchange but from production itself, especially if "laws of population" are to be included under that head. Not only the customs, but the vices, follies, and mistakes of men are accountable for economic friction. Economic tendencies, too, may be counteracted deliberately and advisedly by principles of morality, statesmanship, art, religion, or pedagogics. The favourite example of economic friction is perhaps taxation. If it be true (see Thorold Rogers, *Local Taxation*, Cobden Club pamphlet, 1886, p. 12), that taxes tend to stay where they are put, instead of being shifted where economic principles by themselves would have carried them at once, this is an undoubted case of economic friction. There is least of such friction perhaps in the distribution of currency, and in the movements of capital on a great scale in modern business (see Bagehot's *Lombard Street*). There is probably most of it in wages and salaries, even in modern business, and in the agricultural rents and.burdens of all backward countries and backward districts of advanced countries. Marshall's view of "long and short periods" (*Principles of Economics*, 1890, *passim*) would seem to involve that over a long period, in the major sense of "long," friction might be neglected. Some such conclusion is also implied in the view of Loria and others that in all history economical causes are supreme over all others. [Cp. Keynes, *Scope and Method of Pol. Econ.*, ch. iv. pp. 124 *seq.*, 1891 ; Loria, *La Constitution Sociale* (1893).]　　J. B.

Economic friction may further be described as the opposition encountered by the movements of capital and the inability of labour to meet readily the demand for work ; and generally by all the circumstances which prevent economic forces from bringing about their natural effects the instant they come into operation. It is, for instance, matter of common observation that, though prices are affected by changes in supply and demand, they are not necessarily altered by these changes at once ; and even when the effect on price can be detected, it is often not instantaneous, but gradual. The causes of friction are various, chief among them being the want of accurate knowledge. In the case of the demand for and supply of labour, this is an exceedingly important consideration, as also is the frequent immobility of labour. In the friction which affects the price of goods, want of knowledge often increases the delay experienced before matters are adjusted to meet new conditions. CUSTOM and HABIT, also, are factors in producing economic friction ; prices, especially of valuable articles, where competition is restricted, do not move readily, no matter what change there may have been in the conditions of production or in the state of supply and demand. It is due, no doubt, to habit, or prejudice, that the effect of a new tax, or of the remission of an old one, though matters of universal knowledge, do not always reach the persons intended. The salesman and the manufacturer cannot always pass on an indirect tax to the consumer ; nor can the owner of property always exact the full amount of a new rate from his tenant.

　　　　　　　　　　　　　　　　M. G. D.

FRIEDRICH, MARGRAVE KARL. See KARL FRIEDRICH.

FRIENDLY SOCIETIES. Friendly societies may be defined as insurance societies based on mutual principles : they are the means by which small tradesmen and the working class provide against sickness, old age, and the expenses of burial. They may possibly be traced to the gilds of the middle ages, or, at any rate, the disappearance of the gilds nearly coincides with the rise of friendly societies ; but practically they first became popular and important in this country at the beginning of the present century. The early history of friendly societies is a melancholy record of failures. They were constantly dissolved or becoming insolvent, through mismanagement, dishonesty, or other irregularity on the part of officers and members. So late as 1882 there were in workhouses in England no fewer than 3913 persons who had been members of friendly societies which had disappeared. But gradually a reform took place which may be summarised by saying that a system of premiums was substituted for a system of levies. These words call for explanation. A society on the levy system looks to its annual income to cover its annual expenditure, and any deficit is made up by a levy or contribution among its members. Now as the benefits of a society are mainly prospective, and as, therefore, the charges are lighter at first than after some years, this system clearly is not likely to secure permanence. On the premium system the probable charges in the future are calculated, and the annual payments scaled accordingly. The sheet anchor of this system is the valuation, which is made at intervals, generally of five years, and consists of an elaborate review of present position and liabilities of a society. It might be thought that the collection of averages of longevity and periods of sickness would by this time be sufficiently large to give an almost infallible guide ; but, as a matter of fact, the circumstances vary widely in different cases. The prospects of a society depend on a vast number of conditions, as the habits of a population, the character of an occupation, etc.; so much so that it is the actual experience of the society which gives the best clue to its future. On the results of such a valuation the table of premiums is constructed and revised from time to time.

The simplest form of friendly society is that in which each member pays a weekly sum, and in return is supported during sickness, whilst at the end of every year the funds of the society, less a sum for a reserve fund, are divided amongst the members. Such a society clearly lacks most of the elements of permanence, but at the same time it serves a valuable purpose as an educator in habits of thrift. The ordinary "village club" goes a step farther, and aims at extending its advantages over a longer period. There is no division of funds yearly, and hence a greater stability, but this is often purchased at a considerable cost. The very permanence of the club invites a ruinous competition on the part of other clubs, with the result that premiums are lowered below the point required for solvency, whilst young men tend to form clubs of their own, thus breaking the succession which is essential to the continuance of a club: again, greater opportunities are given for dishonesty on the part of officers. It is not necessary to dwell on the various kinds of object, etc., which distinguish village clubs, some of which tend to become savings-banks rather than friendly societies. The difficulties in the way of the success of such clubs are partly met by county clubs. Of these the area is the county, and the management is generally in the hands of the clergy, magistrates, and others, with rules and premiums carefully framed to guarantee solvency. But these advantages entail considerable sacrifices. There is far less of the social element, which has a high educational value in the village clubs; the area is too large for any common interest in the management, and therefore there is none of the political training which self-governing societies give; it is too large also to ensure that thorough supervision by neighbours, which is essential in all cases of persons drawing sick allowances, to prevent malingering. As a result county clubs are not able to offer sufficient advantages to their members to compete with other clubs. The difficulty of finding an area sufficiently small to insure good supervision, neighbourly relations, and self-government, and yet large enough to secure good business capacity at the head of affairs, and sound general principles, is met by the affiliated orders, the largest of which are the Foresters and the Manchester Unity of Oddfellows. The unit here is the lodge, which may consist of any number of members, is generally on a local basis, has its own officers, rules, etc., is independent both of control and of support. Above the lodge comes the district, a geographical grouping of lodges, and above the district the order, which comprises a general committee of management, elected by the various districts and lodges, officers of the order, etc. The relations between the order and the lodges differ in different societies. In some cases the order formulates principles, tables of premiums, etc., in others it takes certain business, e.g. life insurance or pensions, and treats it as a central rather than a local matter; in all cases it is ready with advice in the formation and management of a lodge, and the fact of such a body with large experience bringing pressure to bear on ill-managed lodges, being ready with friendly help in times of stress, and having an indirect control does much to promote sound management. In some cases the name of friendly society is applied to companies which for a fixed payment, weekly or monthly guarantee a sum in the event of death, and are commonly known as "Collecting Societies." They differ from friendly societies in the following points: (1) They give no relief in sickness; (2) they have no common bond of union amongst the insured; (3) they have paid collectors and a hierarchy

of officers, as agents and inspectors, but no self-government. In them, it has been said, "the officials are everything, the members are nothing." But although these societies do not fulfil the objects of friendly societies, we must be careful to avoid underrating their usefulness.

The history of the laws affecting friendly societies illustrates the attitude of government in this country towards combined independent effort. The original Friendly Societies' Act of 1793 (33 Geo. III. c. 54) was of a permissive kind. It granted certain advantages to such societies as had exhibited their rules at quarter sessions and had them approved. In 1829 by 10 Geo. IV. c. 56 the justices were supplemented by a barrister-at-law appointed for the purpose, to whom all societies seeking registration were to exhibit their rules for approval. In 1846 by 9 & 10 Vict. c. 27 the barrister was given the title of Registrar of Friendly Societies, and the justices were relieved of their duties in registration. In 1850 (13 & 14 Vict. c. 113) an attempt was made to give some certificate of solvency, but the distinction between "certified" and "registered" societies was abolished in 1855. In 1875 an act was passed (38 & 39 Vict. c. 60) as the result of a commission of inquiry which, with some amendments, is still law. By this act the definition of a friendly society is made as wide as possible, registration is facilitated, and the powers of the registrar are enlarged. The registrar can not only refuse to register, suspend, or cancel registration, but, at the request of the members of a society, he can interfere in its management, can order an examination of its affairs, and, if he think fit, dissolve it. He can also act as arbitrator in disputes between a society and its individual members. But his powers and his sphere of activity are strictly limited. The fact is still often overlooked, but should always be borne in mind, that registration is no guarantee of the soundness of a society. It ensures publicity and publicity only. It does not even imply that the tables, etc., of a society are after an approved model—the government have always declined the responsibility of putting out such a model. In the case of registered societies the government insists that certain rules should be carried out, that e.g. the management should be separated from the benefit branch, that annual returns and quinquennial valuations by skilled persons should be sent to the registrar, and failure to comply with these rules renders the officers of a society liable to prosecution, and the society itself to have its registration suspended or cancelled. Indirectly this cannot but operate strongly in favour of sound management, but the limitations of the central office may be gathered from the statement of the late chief registrar that he held himself precluded from communicating to a member of a society the fact of its insolvency, and from taking any step to publish the fact. Briefly, the advantages of registration to a society are these :—It can hold property, can sue and be sued, can proceed against fraudulent officers summarily, has a first claim upon the estates of deceased officers, can invest in government securities, can be easily and cheaply dissolved, is exempt from certain, now inconsiderable, stamp-duties. Against these privileges must be set the following restrictions :—The rules must be according to an authorised pattern, must approximate *i.e.* to a prescribed type, the field of investment is narrowly limited, elaborate returns must be made to the chief office. The habit of registration is *growing*, the number of accurate returns increases steadily, the total number of societies now registered is in England and Wales some 24,500, in Scotland 900, in Ireland 400, but it is impossible to say what proportion this forms of the whole. The relations of the state to friendly societies in this country have been of a uniformly permissive character. The state has never insisted upon registration, or upon uniformity of management, premiums, etc., among the registered societies, and it has given up the attempt to guarantee their solvency. It has assisted them in a variety of ways. It has always been ready to advise as to management, to facilitate procedure in prosecutions for fraud. It has given exemptions from taxation and pecuniary aid in the form of a rate of interest above the normal, but these have gradually lost importance. The chief assistance which it has given of late years has been the conduct of a rival institution in the annuity or insurance branch of the post-office, the development of which is strongly urged in some quarters. In France and Germany the action of the state has been far more extended. The tendency in France is to interfere with independent societies by legislation, in Germany to take over the whole business of insurance against sickness, funeral expenses, etc., and constitute a department of the administration to conduct it.

[Hardwick, *History of Friendly Societies.*— Wilkinson, Rev. J. F., *The Friendly Society Movement*, 1876. — Bärnreither, J. M., *English Associations of Working Men*, English ed., 1889. —Ludlow, J. M., and Lloyd Jones, *Progress of the Working Class*, 1867.—Neison, F. G. P., *The Manchester Unity of Oddfellows*, 1869.— *Chief Registrar of Friendly Societies, Reports of*, 1857-91.—Pratt, *Laws Relating to Friendly Societies*, 11th ed., by Brabrook, 1888.—*Royal Commission on Friendly Societies, Report of*, 1874. —*Select Committee H.C. on Friendly Societies, Report of*, 1888.— *Select Committee H. C. on National Provident Insurance*, 1886.] L. R. P.

FRIENDLY SOCIETIES, THEIR NUMBERS AND CONSTITUTION. The statement of the successive enactments affecting friendly societies contained in the previous article shows that, however they may have varied in detail, the main principles

of legislation have never been departed from since 1793. Thus there has been for exactly one hundred years a recognition by the state of these voluntary bodies as worthy of encouragement, and in some sort of protection ; but there has never yet been any attempt to restrain the free association of citizens for the purpose of mutual aid. The suggestion has often been made—why should societies be allowed to exist if they will not comply with certain conditions ? but the wisdom of the legislature has always hitherto consistently rejected it. Hence registration has always implied the granting of facilities and privileges upon certain easy conditions, rather than the imposing restrictions and penalties ; and the swing of the pendulum from one side to the other has been marked by an increase or diminution respectively in the number of societies registered. The act of 1793 was purely enabling ; that of 1819 restrictive ; that of 1829, and still more that of 1834, enabling ; that of 1846, and still more that of 1850, restrictive ; that of 1855 enabling, and that of 1875 somewhat restrictive. Under the enabling acts, registrations have been numerous ; under the restricting acts they have been few. There is no doubt, however, that the formation of friendly societies goes on irrespectively of legislation ; and that unregistered friendly societies abound during the periods of restriction. The Friendly Society Commissioners in 1874 stated that unregistered societies were in England probably nearly co-extensive with, in Scotland far more powerful than, the registered bodies. In the county of Middlesex alone nearly 1000 societies were enrolled within a very few years after the passing of the act of 1793, and the number in some other counties was almost as great. Altogether, between 1793 and 1855 as many as 26,034 societies had been enrolled. The act of the last-mentioned year provided for making annual returns to the registrar, and directed him to make an annual report to parliament. It was then ascertained that more than 800 of these societies had been dissolved, and that more than 700 were not for the purpose of assuring sick pay. Of the remaining 24,500 societies, nearly 3000 could not be found, leaving about 21,500 societies as presumably still in existence. An attempt was made to ascertain how long the various societies had been established ; but only 3073 answered the question. Of these it appeared that more than 100 had existed for many years before the act of 1793, and that as many as 20 societies claimed to be centenarians by the middle of the 19th century.

Of the 21,500 societies, about 2800 were in Middlesex ; 2045 in Lancashire ; 993 in Staffordshire ; 979 in Yorkshire ; 874 in Warwickshire ; 752 in Surrey ; 681 in Devon ; and 642 in Kent. They are thus found to have been distributed among the manufacturing and agricultural districts; and in fact to have over-spread the country, and to have met the wants of all classes of its working population.

A considerable number of the societies which existed before 1793, and took advantage of the act of that year to enrol their rules, are still in existence. They have in general only a small number of members; indeed, it was not unusual in the early days of friendly societies to limit the number. This was of great advantage in maintaining the friendly feeling which it was one of the main purposes of these societies to encourage among their members; and it gave rise to a sentiment very common among them, that the benefit of sick pay and even of funeral money should not be claimed except in case of necessity. By this means, many societies whose contributions would not have been sufficient to provide the benefits, as a matter of insurance, were able not only to meet all claims which the members cared to make upon them, but also to accumulate funds from year to year. In some of these societies members would introduce their sons, and the society would continue from generation to generation among members of the same families. This is particularly marked in the very interesting group of societies founded among the Huguenot settlers. Some of them were formed by a number of persons coming from the same town or village, as the society of Lintot, which originally consisted wholly of persons deriving their family origin from Lintot, and still contains many members who can trace their descent back to the original settlers from that district. Those excellent, laborious, and thrifty men, who created new industries for us, and gave the British work-man many valuable lessons, were largely pioneers in the good work of establishing friendly societies also.

In the twenty years from 1855 to 1875 as many as 21,875 societies were registered, or an average of 1094 per annum. Some allowance has to be made, however, for duplicate registra-tions; when a society sent up for registration a complete set of rules, it was not always easy to ascertain whether the society had been previously registered or not. Under the act of 1855 all branches of societies were registered as separate societies. The act of 1875 has made a clear distinction between them, and contains various provisions against duplicate registry. Under that act, from 1876 to 1892, 4240 societies and 7995 branches have been registered, being an average of 249 societies and 470 branches each year. There is thus a certain diminution in the new registrations, which becomes more significant when closely looked into; for a large proportion of the registrations of new societies are such as are exempt from the obligation of making a quinquennial valuation, the onerous but most beneficial provision which the act of 1875 introduced. Many are dividing societies;

others are juvenile societies; and from both these classes valuations are not required. A dividing society, as it does not seek to accumu-late funds, but to distribute them, does not look forward to the future, but contents itself with provision for the wants of the immediate present. A juvenile society, which consists wholly of members above three and under twenty-one years of age, is a mere resting-place on the way to membership of an adult society, and ought not to be permitted to accumulate funds, though many juvenile societies show a strong tendency to do so.

The efforts of the registrar have been directed, since the passing of the Act of 1875, to the gradual enforcement of its provisions relating to valuation, without bearing with undue severity on the societies. For this purpose, it has been necessary, after fair warning, to suspend and ultimately to cancel the registration of many societies, and to take proceedings against others and recover penalties. The result of these measures has been, that in each period of five years the number of valuations received and the number of grants of dispensation from valuation added together, have tended more nearly to reach the total number of registered societies known to be in existence. The results of the valuations have been such as to excite serious anxiety in the friends of the societies. Of 14,988 valuations, only 3122 showed a sur-plus; the aggregate of such surpluses amounting to £1,781,319, while 11,866 showed a de-ficiency; the aggregate of such deficiencies amounting to £10,734,515. This statement must not be misunderstood. It does not mean that it is necessary to raise more than ten millions of hard cash to make friendly societies solvent. It means that each society must materially diminish the benefits it promises to its members, and materially increase the con-tributions it exacts from them, besides raising a certain sum in cash, in order to make both ends meet. Assuming that the 11,866 societies in question had something more than 3,000,000 members, a contribution of £1 from each mem-ber, would raise about one-third of the deficiency, leaving the other two-thirds to be met by reduc-tion of benefits and increase of contributions. It must be remembered, moreover, that the valuations themselves are mere estimates, founded on a great variety of hypotheses as to the liability to sickness and mortality and the rate of interest, and that a valuer who wishes to make things pleasant for a society may adjust his hypothesis to that view; while another may exaggerate the valuation deficiency by omitting to take into account favourable considerations that are essential to the true view of the society's position.

The societies with branches, commonly called the affiliated orders, though showing very con-siderable deficiencies, appear to be in a somewhat better position than the independent societies, in which latter term, however, are included many societies which are really branches of affiliated orders, but have done nothing since the act of 1875 was passed to constitute themselves legally so. The registered branches were 11,242 ; and of these 2281 showed surpluses amounting to £874,679 ; and 8961 showed deficiencies amounting to £6,716,838. The societies registered as independent were 3717, of which 827 showed surpluses amounting to £658,252 and 2890 deficiencies amounting to £3,901,435. The collecting societies are not included in these figures. In speaking of branches, commonly called courts, lodges, or tents, it should be understood that as yet no arrangement exists by which the insurances effected by each branch are guaranteed by the central bodies of the orders, and that therefore for financial purposes they are in the same position as the independent societies. This is almost universally true as regards the insurance of sick pay. For insurance of funeral money, branches are grouped into districts. In the largest and most progressive of the orders, the Manchester Unity of Oddfellows, which has made during many years past heroic efforts to secure the solvency of all its branches, an arrangement exists by which a lodge in distress may seek help from the district to which it belongs, and a district in distress may seek help from the central body of the Order. The Ancient Order of Foresters, the Loyal Order of Ancient Shepherds, Ashton Unity, with many smaller orders, are also making strenuous exertions to reduce the deficiencies shown by the valuations of their courts and lodges. These bodies possess great advantages in their annual meetings for conference and discussion. Many of their members have acquired influential positions in municipal life, largely through the knowledge of affairs and the capacity to rule which have been acquired and developed by the means of these meetings. To be the chief of an organisation having 600,000 members, and to be called upon to preside over meetings constituted of their delegates, picked men from all parts of the country, is a distinction that is much coveted and an honour that is highly prized.

According to the latest available information, there are 10,426 independent societies on the register, and the returns that have been received from these show that they have 2,133,710 members and £9,289,361 funds. There are 16,400 branches, and the returns received show 1,727,809 members, and £12,121,202 funds. Together, these give 26,826 societies and branches, 22,313 of which made returns, giving 3,861,519 members and £21,410,563 funds. According to a recent estimate, the annual income and expenditure of the independent societies is—

Contributions of members	£1,707,000	Benefits to members	£1,596,000
Interests, fines, and other receipts	410,000	Expenses	195,000
		Annual Saving	326,000
	£2,117,000		£2,117,000

For the branches of affiliated orders—

		Benefits to members	£2,681,000
Contributions	£3,024,000	Expenses	449,000
Other receipts	531,000	Annual Saving	425,000
	£3,555,000		£3,555,000

Together:—

Contributions	£4,731,000	Benefits	£4,277,000
Other receipts	941,000	Expenses	644,000
		Saving	751,000
	£5,672,000		£5,672,000

From another point of view it appears that while the average contribution per member in an independent society, assuring both sick pay and funeral money is about £1, in a branch it rises to about £1 : 11s., which seems to show that the affiliated orders are seeking to raise their contributions more nearly to the amount required to meet the benefits assured, and perhaps that they are able in general to exact larger contributions and give greater benefits than the independent societies. Of the £1 : 11s., about 4s. goes for management, or about 12½ per cent, which is a moderate proportion considering the number of small transactions involved, and it implies that in general the officers receive a very low rate of remuneration. If it be assumed that the £1 : 11s. represents from one to one-and-a-half week's income of the member, it must be admitted that he obtains a considerable benefit by way of insurance at a sacrifice of a comparatively small portion of his revenue.

The relation of friendly societies to provisions for old age is a matter that has recently received much consideration. Statistics have been sought of the number of paupers who have been members of friendly societies, with a view to throw discredit on the societies by implying that they have failed in their purpose of preventing pauperism. The result is very small, when compared either with the whole number of paupers or with the whole number of members of friendly societies, and the inference drawn is not a sound one. The primary object of a friendly society is not the preventing pauperism in old age, but the providing relief to a man generally able to work, yet momentarily prevented from doing so by sickness. Some societies, it is true, have tables under which a definite annuity in old age can be purchased ; and where that is the case, such tables are required by law to be certified by an actuary ; hence these societies are in general well able to fulfil their contracts, and their members are not those who are found in workhouses. The other societies, which do not pretend to assure against old age, do not affect to provide against pauperism, and are therefore liable to no reproach if their members become paupers. Many societies, however, without insuring old-age pay, insure sick pay throughout the whole of life ; and by a lax interpretation, inspired by a benevolent sentiment, promise their members what is in effect a pension, though usually very small in amount. Such societies actually pay this pension under the name of permanent sick pay, until it is claimed by so many members, and so persistently, that the funds will not support the burden ; and it is these societies which swell the number of failures. Sounder views on this point are being entertained by the leaders of friendly society opinion.

The collecting societies are 39 in number, and from the returns of thirty-five of them it appears that they had 3,318,942 members, and only £2,289,858 funds. Twenty-nine of these societies had been valued ; and of these 14 showed surpluses amounting in the aggregate to £248,388, and 15 showed deficiencies amounting in the aggregate to £116,242. It would seem, therefore, that the financial condition of these societies, as shown by valuation, is better than that of the ordinary friendly society of either class ; although the amount of capital they possess per member is much less, being only 13s. 9d., as against £5 : 11s. The reason is that the collecting societies insure only a small sum at death, and charge a premium much in excess of that necessary to cover the risk ; while the ordinary friendly society insures sick pay in addition, and too often charges an inadequate premium. The enormous membership of the collecting societies consists largely of infants, who in many cases are insured at the time of birth. The rates of premium charged are high enough to allow of an inordinate expenditure, approaching and sometimes exceeding 50 per cent, so that a member pays away 1d. to the officers and collectors for their remuneration for every 1d. he invests for his own benefit. It is true, in this as in so many other matters, that the poorer a man is the more he has to pay for what he wants. Whether it will ever be practicable to organise a system of small insurance for the poor, in which a closer relation shall subsist between the amount contributed and the amount received, it is difficult to say ; the collection of small sums periodically is necessarily a costly affair, and until the working classes can be persuaded to dispense with the services of the collector they must be prepared to pay him for the work he does. On the present system, the pay is so high that a collecting-book is a valuable commodity and is often passed from hand to hand for a considerable sum.

The privileges granted to friendly societies by the existing Acts may be briefly summed up as follows :—

1. The right to hold land.

2. The summary remedy in case of misapplication of funds.

3. Priority of claim on estates of deceased or bankrupt officers.

4. Transfer of stock by direction of the chief registrar.

5. Exemption from stamp duty on all documents of the society.

6. Permission to admit persons under twenty-one years of age as members.

7. Reduction of the fee for certificates of birth and death.

8. Power to invest with the National Debt Commissioners.

9. Admission of trustees to copyhold property at a single fine.

10. Discharge of mortgages by endorsed receipt without reconveyance.

11. Power to call officers to account and recover property from them.

12. Power to settle disputes in the manner the rules provide.

13. Power to insure the funeral expenses of members' wives and children.

14. Power to members to nominate for sums at death up to £100.

15. Power to pay sums under £100 without administration.

16. The services of a public auditor at a fixed scale of fees.

17. The recording of its documents in the office of the registrar.

In order to restrict these privileges to societies whose members are mainly of the working class, it is enacted that no society shall insure more than £200 on a death or other event, or more than £50 by way of annuity. In fact, these limits are rarely reached. Several wealthy and prosperous mutual assurance societies were originally established as friendly societies, but by an act passed in 1854, they were discharged from the provision of the Friendly Societies Acts, except so far as relates to the registration of trustees, which still takes place with regard to some of them, and is the only relic of their original constitution.

E. W. B.

FRITH-GILDS, see Gilds.

FRUGALITY, see Thrift.

FUGÆ WARRANT (Scotland). A warrant to apprehend a debtor, foreigner or native, who meditates or is reasonably believed to meditate flight from Scotland. It is granted by a magistrate, usually the sheriff ; the creditor applies for the warrant, giving upon oath or affirmation his claim of debt, which may be even a contingent debt, and his grounds for believing that the debtor means to fly from the country ; the magistrate makes inquiry into the facts ; he may then grant a warrant to arrest the debtor for examination ; and this may be followed by a warrant to commit the debtor to prison until he finds security to appear in court. The creditor is liable in damages if his statements are unfounded. The sheriff's warrant may be executed in any Scottish county, if backed, but has no force outside Scotland.   A. D.

FUGGERS. A well-known German merchant family, and an interesting example of hereditary enterprise and success. They came originally from Suabia; at least as early as the 14th century they settled at Augsburg. The first known by name, Hans Fugger, was a poor weaver. His descendants became traders as well as artisans, Ulrich carrying on trade early in the 16th century in the Baltic and the Mediterranean, and Jacob importing goods direct from India instead of by way of Venice. A little later they added banking to their other undertakings, though hitherto none but Jews and Lombards had traded in money; Alexander (died 1560) even set up counting-houses in India and Venezuela. Their willingness to lend immense sums of money to the emperors Frederick III. and the impecunious Maximilian, to Charles V. and to Philip II. of Spain, fixed the family fortunes. Lands and mines, first given as security, were retained in full ownership when the loans were not repaid. To estates titles were added; by marriage and purchase new lands were continually acquired; at the same time the family trade was kept up. "Rich as a Fugger" became a proverb. With liberality proportioned to their wealth they were foremost in public spirit; they were founders of religious and charitable institutions, they were patrons of art and learning; one collected antiquities, another brought together a fine library of books and MSS. Some branches of the family are still in existence.

[Von Stetten, *Geschichte der adelichen Geschlechter in der freien Reichs-Stadt Augsburg.*— Say et Chailley, *Dictionnaire d'Économie Politique.* Genealogy in Hübner's *Gen. Tabellen der Reichs-Gräflichen Familien.*—Portraits in *Pinacotheca Fuggerorum S. R. I. comitum ac baronum in Kierchperg* (Kirchberg) *et Weissenhorn*, by Custos and L. and W. Kilian, 1754.—Coins in Kull's book, *Die Münzen des gräflichen und fürstlichen Hauses Fugger*, 1882.—The mining operations of the Fuggers are described in Jacob, *On the Precious Metals*, i. 276.] E. G. P.

FULLARTON, JOHN (*c.* 1780-1849), writer on currency. After having been an assistant surgeon in Bengal from 1802 to 1813, Fullarton became partner in a bank at Calcutta; and, having there acquired a fortune, retired to England. He contributed some articles to the *Quarterly Review* at the time of the reform. But he is principally remembered for his book on *The Regulation of Currencies* (1844), a work "of exceeding ability" in Prof. Walker's words.

An uncompromising assailant of the CURRENCY PRINCIPLE (*q.v.*), Fullarton maintains the impossibility of over-issuing a convertible currency (ch. v.). "The self-regulating principle of a convertible currency operates in every such case with the precision of clock-work" (*Ibid.*). Mill places Fullarton with Tooke as one of "the most prominent representatives" of the

"counter-theory," which is the extreme opposite of the currency principle; quotes an important passage from him, and adds: "I believe that the theory grounded by Mr. Fullarton upon this fact [the action of the country bankers] contains a large portion of truth, and is far nearer to being the expression of the whole truth than any form whatever of the currency theory" (*Political Economy*, bk. iii. ch. xxiv. §§ 1, 2) Prof. Walker strikes the balance of judgment less favourably to Fullarton's views (*Money*, p. 426 *et seq.*). For a very unfavourable estimate of Fullarton's book see Col. Torrens, *Principles and Practical Operation of Sir Robt. Peel's Bill of 1844 explained and defended against the objections of Tooke, Fullarton, and Wilson* (1848).

Besides the main thesis of Fullarton's work, there are in it important minor contributions to monetary science. Thus at p. 23 (ed. 1845) he attributed to an inconvertible currency much the same defects as Mill afterwards did (*Pol. Econ.*, bk. iii. ch. xiii.); with this additional remark as to the supposed possibility of regulating the paper currency by the price of bullion: "it is quite a mistake to suppose that the market prices of the precious metals would observe the same range of fluctuation, when those metals should be reduced to a common footing with other commodities, which they observe when constituting the circulating medium of a country"; in proof of which he adduces the fluctuations in the price of gold during "the hundred days." Many other interesting historical allusions occur.

On the regulation of Currencies, being an examination of the principles on which it is proposed to restrict within certain fixed limits the future issues on credit of the Bank of England and of the other banking establishments throughout the country, 1st ed. 1844, 2nd ed. 1845.

[Mill, *Political Economy*, bk. iii. ch. xxiv.— Walker, *Money*, *sub voce* Fullarton.—Wagner, *Beiträge zur Lehre von den Banken*, ch. v.— *Athenæum*, 3rd Nov. 1849, *Economist*, 28th Sept. 1844].

See also CURRENCY PRINCIPLE. F. Y. E.

FUMAGE. See HEARTH TAX.

FUNCTIONS. When two quantities are so selected that any variation in one is attended with some variation in the other, the latter is said to be a function of the former; and is called the dependent variable—dependent on the other variable which is called independent. In symbols: $y = f(x)$, where y is the dependent, and x the independent variable. For the symbol f some other letter, usually of cognate sound, as ϕ or ψ, is often used. The following are particular examples; $y = a + bx$; $y = a + bx + cx^2$; $y = a + \log (b + cx)$; where a, b, c are *constants*. One of the most important properties of a function is the rate at which it increases or decreases as the independent variable is increased. This rate is measured by another function which is called the derived function, or differential co-efficient: in symbols $f'(x)$ or $\dfrac{dy}{dx}$. Thus, if y, the original function is $\log(a+bx)$; it is found that the derived function is $\dfrac{b}{a+bx}$, supposing that "natural" (or Napierian) logarithms are used; otherwise the expression in the text must be multiplied by a certain constant. Whence it appears that the rate at which y increases with an increase of x is less for larger values of x. A derived function has its own derivee, called, with reference to the primary function, the second derived function or second differential co-efficient. Thus, in symbols $f''(x)$, or $\dfrac{d_2 y}{dx^2}$ the second differential of $\log(a+bx)$ is $\dfrac{-b^2}{(a+bx)^2}$; denoting that the rate of increase measured by the first differential diminishes at a rate which is slower for larger values of x. This notation and conception is extended to the case of two (or more) independent variables. The symbols $z = f(x, y)$ denote that any variation in either of the independent variables x or y is attended with some variation in the dependent variable z. The rate of variation due to change in each variable may be separately measured. The measure is called the differential co-efficient with respect to either x or y as the case may be; in symbols $\dfrac{df(xy)}{dx}$ and $\dfrac{df(xy)}{dy}$; or more shortly $\dfrac{df}{dx}$ and $\dfrac{df}{dy}$. An important inquiry with respect to any function is: what are the values of the independent variables for which the dependent variable is a maximum or minimum. The solution of this problem, in the case of a function of a single variable, is given by the equation $f'(x)\left[\text{or } \dfrac{dy}{dx}\right] = 0.$[1] Thus the value of x, for which the function $\log(a+bx) - cx$ is a maximum, is found by equating to zero the first differential of that function namely, $\dfrac{b}{a+bx} - c$.[2] Whence the value of x is found to be $\dfrac{b-ac}{bc}$. In the case of two (and *mutatis mutandis* more) independent variables there are two simultaneous equations of the form $\dfrac{df}{dx} = 0 \dfrac{df}{dy} = 0$, to determine the values of x and y for which z the independent variable is a maximum or minimum.

These mathematical principles have important applications to political economy. The propositions in virtue of which economics may claim to be an exact science, involve the ideas of a function and its variation. The Law of

DIMINISHING RETURNS (*q.v.*) may be thus stated: $y = f(x)$, where x is the amount of outlay (on a given portion of land), y is the corresponding return, and f is such a function that f' continually decreases as x increases: or, in other words f'' is always negative. The logarithm, as has been shown above, is such a function; and, accordingly, this simple function was used by Malthus to express the relation between increasing population and subsistence; for such is the import of his statement, that the one increases in arithmetical, the other in geometrical, progression. The vain disputes to which this dictum has given rise illustrate the advantage of using the general language of symbols. A similar notation may be employed to represent the analogous Law of Diminishing Utility (see UTILITY). The Law of INCREASING RETURNS (*q.v.*) might be represented by a function, like $a + bx + cx^2$, whose first differential, $a + b + 2cx$, continually increases with the increase of x. It has been well said that every theory in economics may be regarded as the solution of a problem in the calculus of maxima and minima: to obtain the greatest satisfaction with the least effort and sacrifice being the aim of the economic man. The language of that calculus is the mother tongue of abstract economics. The simplest economic problem, the case of one commodity x being exchanged against another y in a perfect market, is governed by the principle that each party seeks to maximise his advantage considered as a function of the amount which he obtains of one commodity, and parts with of the other. The equations which determine the position of maximum are given by Jevons (*Theory of Political Economy*, ch. iv.; cp. Marshall, *Principles of Economics*, 2nd ed. Mathematical Appendix, note xii. *sub finem*). Especially where the number of variables is considerable the use of functions is required; since in that case geometrical illustration is not available. The difficult theory which Prof. Marshall formulates as the Law of SUBSTITUTION (*Principles of Economics*, passages referred to in Index, *sub voce*) is perhaps most easily deduced by regarding the profit of the entrepreneur as a function of the amounts of each agent of production which he employs. Say $z = f(x_1, x_2, x_3 \text{ etc.})$ The condition that z should be a maximum gives the equations $\dfrac{df}{dx_1} = 0$; $\dfrac{df}{dx_2} = 0$, etc. This is the equivalent of the proposition that "the tendency of every one to select the best means for obtaining his own ends . . . would have caused each several kind of labour or machinery, or other agent of production to be used for each several purpose until its further use was no longer remunerative; the employment of each several agent in each branch of production would have been extended until full advantage has been taken of its special fitness for the work" (*Prin-*

---

[1] To discriminate a maximum from a minimum, a second condition is required; and is afforded by the *sign* of the second differential co-efficient.

[2] See note 1.

ciples of Economics, 2nd ed. p. 559, cp. Mathematical Appendix, note xiv.). Still more generally we may regard the "net advantages" of the economic man as a function of two sets of variables, corresponding to his efforts and sacrifices, and his consumption. The position of equilibrium is then determined by two sets of equations of the form,

$$\frac{df}{dx_1}=0 \quad \frac{df}{dx_2}=0, \text{ etc}$$
$$\frac{df}{dy_1}=0 \quad \frac{df}{dy_2}=0, \text{ etc.}$$

In the light of such general theories the dispute whether normal or natural value is determined by utility or cost of production appears nugatory. You might as well ask whether, when two unknown quantities, x and y, are determined by two simultaneous equations, x or y contributes more to the solution.

[A knowledge of the theory of functions sufficient for the economist is afforded by the introduction to the second edition of Prof. Walras's *Éléments d'Economie Politique Pure.*—Pantaleoni, *Econ. Pura;* and by Mr. Wicksteed's *Alphabet of Economic Science.*] F. Y. E.

FUNDED DEBT. This expression was originally used as a description of debt, the service of which was secured by a special fund (*e.g.* the produce of a certain tax) but gradually the meaning acquired by the term was that of debt raised for permanent purposes and either repayable at a distant date or not repayable at any definite date. The funded debt of the United Kingdom belongs to the latter class but the government have the right to redeem after a fixed period ; *e.g.* the local loans stock is redeemable from 1912, the new consols (Goschen's) from 1923. This does not, however, prevent a gradual reduction of the funded debt before the periods named ; this is accomplished in the following way. A fixed yearly sum, 25 millions since 1889, is applied to the service of the debt, and any amount not required for payment of interest is used by the National Debt Commissioners for the purchase and subsequent extinction of parts of the funded debt. Another mode of reducing the debt is the conversion of consols into TERMINABLE ANNUITIES (*q.v.*). The funded debts of foreign countries are frequently repayable at fixed dates either gradually, by yearly purchases or drawings, the funds being supplied by a regular sinking fund, or by simultaneous repayment of the whole issue. The consolidation of the funded debt of a country into one stock is convenient for many reasons. [For unfunded debt, see FLOATING DEBT. For general history, see NATIONAL DEBT.] E. S.

FUND, SINKING. See SINKING FUND.

FUNDING SYSTEM. This expression, which properly denotes the system of creating FUNDED DEBT, came to refer specially to a particular abuse of the system. (See NATIONAL DEBT.) C. A. H.

FUNDS, THE PUBLIC. See DEBTS, PUBLIC.

FUNGIBLES—a term borrowed by the mediæval economists from the Roman lawyers, *res quæ mutuâ vice funguntur* (are interchangeable). By both it is opposed to CONSUMPTIBLES (*q.v.*), but whereas in law fungibles are those things which, when borrowed, have to be returned not *in specie*, but *in genere*, in economics the term is employed to denote things of which the use is prolonged, as, *e.g.*, a house. For these interest was permissible, whereas to exact interest for the former was to sell a thing and also to charge for its use, consequently it was unjust. Money was classed as a *consumptible*, and usury declared to be wrong (see CANON LAW).

[Thomas Aquinas, *Summ. Theol. Secunda Secundæ*, lxxviii.—Ashley, *Economic History*, vol. i. ch. iii.—Böhm-Bawerk, *Kapital und Kapitalzins.* —Block, *Les Progrès de la Science Economique*, vol. ii. p. 332 (for a revival of the controversy by Pothier and Turgot).] L. R. P.

FUOCO, FRANCESCO, who died at Naples, 1841, passed his life under the pressure of want, a long exile, and even the necessity of selling some of his works, for which other and ignorant persons got the credit. He possessed above any of his contemporaries a keen spirit, apt to study, suited to economic investigation ; but never enjoyed the comfort of seeing his works valued in their true light. To SCIALOJA (1840) and MOHL (1844) is due the honour of reviving his fame by their eulogies ; Professor Ricca-Salerno (*Storia delle Dottrine Finanziarie in Italia*, Roma, 1881), and T. Fornari (*Delle Teorie economiche nelle Prov. Napoletane dal 1735 al 1830*, Milano, 1888) wrote later and at greater length on his theories.

Fuoco treated all the most important theories of economic science. The *theory of method* in his opinion should be positive, using mathematical formulæ. The *theory of value* he analyses with a peculiar insight, supporting in general the doctrine which bases the value of things on their utility, and derives the measure of value from the comparison of quantity and quality. He was the first in Italy to acknowledge the importance of Ricardo's theory of rent,—which he fully supports, particularly fixing attention on the rent derived through *situation*. He wrote on population, industry, and other social matters, arguing as a final thesis that moral and economic principles are reducible to a common basis. He also discussed coinage and bank questions, especially in one of those works (*La magia del credito svelata*) which he sold under the burden of want, to Giuseppe de Welz of Como, who published it under his own name. Fuoco had written this work to support the financial policy of the minister Medici. In this work he proved, with great brilliancy, that credit multiplies capital—a thesis which was afterwards considered from another side and with a more severe logic by Francesco Ferrara, the greatest economist of our modern days in Italy (see *Biblioteca dell' Economista*, ii. S. vol. vi., Torino, 1857, Introduzione).

[*Saggio sui mezzi da moltiplicare prontamente le ricchezze della Sicilia* (G. de Welz), Parigi, Stamperia Firmin Didot, 1822.—*Comento di comento, ossia lettere critiche del Sig. F. N. sul Saggio del Sig. G. de Welz riprodotto dal Sig. Dr. in medicina*, Giuseppe Indelicato, Napoli, Stamp. Francese, 1823.—*La magia del credito svelata*, Napoli, Stamperia Francese, 1824, 2 vols. (G. de Welz).—*Saggi economici*, Pisa, Stamp. Nistri, 1825-27, 2 vols.—*Introduzione allo studio della Economia industriale, o principî di Economia civile applicati all' uso delle forze*, Napoli, Stamp. Trani, 1829.—*Le Banche e l'Industria*, Napoli, Stamp. Severino, 1834.]   A. B.

FÜRSTENAU, KARL GOTTFRIED (1734-1803), a theologian and lecturer on economics, Hebrew, general literature, and logic in the University of Rinteln (East Prussia), his native town, where in 1786 he became *primarius* of the Faculty of Philosophy. In 1779 was published, at Cassel, his *Apologie des physiocratischen Systems*, highly esteemed by his contemporaries. Fürstenau, although a firm adherent of the doctrine of the physiocrats, did not conceal his opinion that it was impossible to apply its practical conclusions in old countries, organised on an antagonistic basis.

E. Ca.

FUSTEL DE COULANGES, NUMA DENIS (1830-1889). The aim of the most important works of M. Fustel de Coulanges is to establish a bridge over the obscure gap which separates the institutions of Roman Gaul from those of mediæval France ; in particular, he has very carefully worked out a theory of the origin of feudalism and the manor, which is in many respects worthy of study even by those who differ from the results at which he arrives.

Though not the first published of the author's works, the *Recherches sur quelques problèmes d'histoire* is in many ways the first in order. It consists of four essays entitled *Le colonat Romain, Du régime des terres en Germanie, De la marche Germanique*, and *L'organisation judiciaire dans le royaume des Francs*. The first three essays are directly connected with the third volume of the *Histoire des institutions politiques de l'ancienne France*, which has for sub-title *L'alleu et le domaine rural*, and may be treated of with that work. Together they contain the author's theory of the manor, and demand a fuller treatment than his other work, inasmuch as they deal with questions which touch economics more nearly.

The starting-point of the history of the manor is to be found, according to M. Fustel de Coulanges, in the institutions of the Roman empire. The system then existing was one of complete private ownership of land with certain peculiar characteristics. The country was divided into estates or "domains," each normally under one proprietor, who had full powers of alienation and bequest. Each estate was, as a rule, compact, and possessed a name by which it was known and which adhered to it. One proprietor might own many such estates not contiguous. But the estate in itself remained an organised unit never divided and rarely uniting with another to form a new unit. The cultivation of such an estate in the later empire was carried on partly by slave labour employed upon land retained in the owner's own possession. But side by side with this another system had grown up. Certain slaves were allowed as a privilege to become tenants-at-will of parts of the estate, paying for their land partly at any rate in services performed on the remaining land. The tenure, legally speaking, was of course wholly at the will of the owner, but the action of the officers of the Roman treasury began to give it a species of stability. From the end of the 3rd century the names of slaves holding under this tenure were noted in the surveys made for the purpose of taxation, and this action did something to make this kind of tenure more permanent. The freed slaves of the owner probably occupied a similar position on the estate. But in addition to these servile cultivators, there was another class, the "coloni," *i.e.* free cultivators attached to the estate and incapable of quitting it, paying for their land in services and rent, both being fixed for each estate by local custom. The management of this system was in the hands of officers who looked after the collection of rents, and directed the employment of the labour of the tenants on the part of the estate reserved to the owner. For the estate was divided into two parts, the part let out to the free or semi-servile cultivators, and the part retained in the owners' hands. In the same way on each estate there was the "villa" for the proprietor, and the barracks ("ergastula") where the real slaves were housed, and elsewhere the separate dwellings of the other cultivators. This seems to have been the state of things in France, as in other parts of the Roman empire at the time of the German invasions. In the first two volumes of the series the character of the invasion is discussed, and there and in several essays the author deals with the character of landed property in Germany before the invasion. His conclusion on the latter point is that there is no ground for supposing that any common ownership of land existed in Germany outside the limits of the family. This conclusion is perhaps not unassailable, but the author's attack on Maurer's well-known theory of the mark community in the essay entitled "Le problème des origines de la propriété foncière" (*Revue des Questions Historiques*, April 1889) certainly makes out a formidable indictment against that scholar's theory.

The character of the estate has been described as it existed just before the German invasion. But during the period of conquest and after the conquest is complete the estate can be discovered existing in the same form. The method of cultivation is the same. The estate retains its old name and often its old owner. The new German settlers added, in fact, nothing to the land system they found, and took nothing from it. The manor sprang not from a Teutonic mark community, but from a Roman "domain" under the influence of Roman law and custom. The "Saltus Buritanus" noticed in the essay on the Roman colonies is to all intents and purposes a manor existing in the time of the Emperor Trajan in a province of Africa out of the reach of Teutonic influence. Nor can this estate have been a solitary instance. In one point the theory is open to criticism. It accounts for the existence of the manor court, as will be seen on reference to the chapter on "L'immunité" in the fifth volume of the *Histoire des Institutions;* but it does not account for the peculiar system of cultivation known as the THREE-FIELD SYSTEM (*q.v.*), which is so closely associated with the MANOR in many countries. No allusion to this point occurs indeed in the volumes whose argument has been summarised above.

The fourth and fifth volumes of the series deal with problems of politics and government; in the volume entitled *La Monarchie Franque* the author lays down that during the rule of the Merovingian dynasty the dominant power in the state was the king. He succeeded in fact to the position of the Roman emperor. There was no popular assembly to oppose him, and only the elements of a nobility. The Roman bureaucracy, which remained after the fall of the empire, became his instruments of government. The administration of justice was carried on by the king's officers, and there are only traces to be noticed of the growth of local jurisdictions. Even the financial system remained almost unaltered. The invading Germans had expelled the Roman governors but not their method of government; and there is no authority for tracing to their influence either the popular assemblies of later times or the military system known as feudalism. The history of the origin and growth of feudalism is the subject of the last volume of the series. The sources of this, according to the author, are three in number. In the first place he considers the history of the subordination of land; that is to say, the custom of holding land belonging not to the holder but to a superior. This he traces to the Roman custom of holding land "precariously," *i.e.* not in full property but at the will of the real owner, who permitted what was in the eye of the law an usurpation; this tenure gradually grew to be for the life of the tenant, and was on his death

renewed for his heir on his making a formal request for its continuance. Hence sprang the early form of the "fief." The second source is the relation of patron and client, a relation common to Rome, Gaul, and Germany, which familiarised men's minds with the notion of "fealty." It only needed local independence to complete the scheme of a non-military feudalism. This was supplied by the "immunities" which the Merovingian kings not unfrequently granted. A lord who received such a grant became possessed of full power over his lands. The king's officers could not enter; justice was administered solely by the lord; and the local independence of the district and its complete subjection to its owner followed. The military character of the services rendered was only one phase of the militarism of the period. But military service, historically speaking, is of later growth than feudalism.

The concluding volume of the series deals with the complete establishment of feudalism, and traces the gradual fall of the Merovingian kings before the new organisation of society which they had allowed to grow up. The crown lost its power of legislation, its power of taxation, and its control over the army; and with these the administrative system inherited from the Roman empire also disappeared. With Pepin a new form of monarchy based upon feudalism begins.

Something must be said of the method of study which led the author to his conclusions. The only evidence he accepted is documentary evidence, and to the study of this evidence he brought an unrivalled knowledge of the documents and of their language. Few scholars have ever approached him in knowledge of the variations in meaning through which a word in mediæval Latin may pass. In particular his study of the word "marca" in the essay referred to above is well worth notice. That all his conclusions will stand the test of criticism is hardly to be expected, but the publication of his books has certainly been an epoch in the history of mediæval scholarship.

His life was passed in teaching, first as professor at Strasbourg, and afterwards in similar posts at Paris.

La cité Antique, 1864.—*Histoire des Institutions de l'ancienne France,* vol. i.— *La Gaule Romaine,* 1891; vol. ii., *L'invasion Germanique,* 1891. [First published in one volume in 1875; reprinted, 1877; now republished with large additions.]—Vol. iii. *La Monarchie Franque,* 1888.—Vol. iv. *L'alleu et le domaine rural pendant l'époque Mérovingienne,* 1889.—Vol. v. *Les origines du système féodal,* 1890.—Vol. vi. *Les transformations de la royauté pendant l'époque Carolingienne,* 1892. [Vols. i. ii. v. and vi. were published after the author's death, under the editorship of M. Camille Jullian].—*Recherches sur quelques problèmes d'histoire,* 1885.—*Nouvelles recherches sur quelques problèmes d'histoire,* 1893.

—*Questions Historiques*, 1893. [These two volumes contain reprints of the more important articles contributed by the author to the *Revue des deux Mondes ;* the *Revue des questions historiques; the Revue historique de droit Français et Etranger,* and other periodicals. Among them are essays on the law of property in ancient Greece, on Polybius, on the island of Chios, and other classical subjects, and an essay on the origin of property in land (translated into English by Margaret Ashley, 1891,—Sonnenschein).]

C. G. C.

FUTURE GOODS AND SERVICES. Terms that have acquired a technical meaning and importance in recent economic theory ; primarily in that of the AUSTRIAN SCHOOL, and particularly in the writings of v. Böhm-Bawerk, where they connote differentiations of economic phenomena in time ; secondarily, in the writings of American economists, where they have begun to connote also the dynamic phases of economic phenomena, for which "time" is a mere abstraction. Future goods and future services must be carefully distinguished from certain other economic factors with which they are often confounded, and they must then be observed in their relations to the phenomena of subjective value, of objective value in exchange and distribution, of consumption and production.

In this article the term "goods" always means those concrete physical objects that render what Böhm-Bawerk has called "material services" through redistributions of matter and energy. "Services" are useful actions, efforts, or changes that are immaterial, personal, or social in character. The same laws govern the values of future goods and future services, and it is therefore quite unnecessary to treat them separately, except when it is desired to emphasise the fact that services are often more transient in useful action than goods. But this is by no means always true. Certain immaterial utilities, *e.g.* legal rights, may endure through periods of time compared to which the economic life of a vast majority of material goods is insignificant. (See also GOODS, CLASSIFICATION OF ; GOODS, ECONOMIC.)

Future goods and services are not identical with Menger's category : "goods of the second order," *i.e.* instruments of production. Not only do future goods include prospective consumers' goods, but producers' goods now existing are not future goods, though frequently so called. Strictly speaking, they are present equivalents of future goods. In accurate analysis we must remember the possibilities of cross-classification. Future goods may be primary—*i.e.* consumers' goods, or secondary—*i.e.* producers' goods. Consumers' goods or producers' goods may be present or future.

Future goods comprise all economic goods not now existent or complete, but which, it is practically certain, will be existent and ready for use at any designated future time. They include all goods in process of production which will doubtless be finished and put in market. As communities provide more adequately for their future, future goods become an increasingly important economic category. They become "as much objects of economical dealing as present goods." They are produced, valued, bought, and sold.

In the market, future goods are of less value than present goods of like kind and number. According to the theory that derives market or objective value from subjective valuations, we have to seek the reason for this phenomenon in the lower marginal utility of future goods. Marginal utility, in turn, is not an ultimate fact, and Böhm-Bawerk names three co-operating causes of the relatively low marginal utility of future goods. These are (1) the better provision for future want ; *i.e.* the reasonable assurance that future want will be more adequately met by supply than present want ; (2) men's usual under-estimation of the future ; (3) the technical superiority of present goods. The second cause is resolved into three factors ; namely (*a*) imperfect imagination of future conditions, (*b*) weakness of will, attributable in part no doubt to imperfect imagination, (*c*) the uncertainty of life. The technical superiority of present goods is the group of circumstances : (*a*) that a surplus of consumers' goods enables men to spend time in making such producers' goods as tools and machinery ; (*b*) that these in turn co-ordinate natural energies in useful ways, enormously multiplying productive power ; and (*c*) that as these processes take time, the sooner they are begun the greater the gain. It is obvious that human progress tends to correct the under-estimation of the future, and therefore to emphasise the relative importance of (1) and (3) as permanent causes of the under-valuation of future goods. In the view of the present writer, Böhm-Bawerk has not sufficiently developed the underlying connection of the better provision for future want with the technical superiority of present goods, and has therefore failed to discover the ultimate and permanent economic cause of the under-valuation of future goods, and consequently the true cause of interest, in the relatively low cost of production of future, the relatively high cost of production of present, goods. This phase of the question will be referred to again.

The unequal values of present and future goods affect two great classes of transactions. One is the exchange of future consumers' goods, FUNGIBLES, for present CONSUMERS' GOODS, and the agio takes the form of loan interest. The other is the exchange of consumers' goods for producers' goods of various ranks—mills, machinery, tools, materials in all stages of production, and of labour, both skilled and unskilled. In transactions of this latter kind producers' goods are equivalents of future consumers' goods and must be valued in terms of such. The dealers are capitalist-undertakers, and the differential value of the present goods which they are constantly exchanging for future goods, though essentially the same thing as interest, is merged with such other elements as gains of speculation, rent of ability, wages of superintendence, etc., in the gross profits of production.

The economic phenomenon here described has found expression in the ambiguous formula that "the value of means of production lags behind the value of finished products." The intended meaning is that the value of means of production equals the value of the future finished products which they will bring forth, and is therefore less than the value of present finished products of like kind and number. In the modern world the phenomena have become exceedingly complicated through a double use of innumerable kinds of goods, which, at any moment, may be devoted to consumption or to the furtherance of production. Since cattle exactly alike will not sell in the same market for different prices simply because some of them are to be kept for breeding and others butchered for beef, the formula quoted above seems to be contradicted. The Austrian reconciliation is through recourse to the doctrine that the value of the whole stock of any commodity which admits of different uses is determined by the marginal use. If there are nine possible uses, present and future, for 500 pieces of goods, in groups of 100 pieces each, only five uses can be actually chosen, and these will be the five of highest utility. The lowest utility of these five will determine the value of the entire 500 pieces. Let this be a utility of present consumption. Then, since the utilities realisable in the future are greater, the pieces devoted to future use may undergo a present discounting of their future value, and yet sell at the same price per piece as the pieces devoted to present use. This explanation is consistent with the intended meaning of the formula that "the value of means of production lags behind the value of finished products" on one condition only, namely, that the future value of finished products to be obtained by means of 100 units of present goods used productively shall be greater than the present value of 100 units of exactly similar goods now used in consumption. The mere "ripening" of the value of so many units of goods productively employed until their future value exactly equals the present value of goods of like kind and number, consumed in present time, does not at all satisfy the conditions of this problem. The alternative is exactly that kind of productivity of capital which Böhm-Bawerk has stoutly denied. Economists generally have not followed him in rejecting the productivity theory of interest, and it would seem that his own "positive" theory, so far from being incon-sistent with it, is in fact built upon it in a disguised form. Capital invested in productive means must be not only "technically" productive of "more goods," but economically productive of "more value" to realise the following combination, which the modern industrial world does actually present, namely, (a) goods available indifferently for consumption or production ; (b) selling for either purpose for the same price in the same market ; but (c), if used productively, equal in value now only to the present value of the consumers' goods that they will make available at the end of a production period ; yet (d) of less value now as producers' goods than are present consumers' goods, equal in quality and quantity to the future consumers' goods to be brought forth by these given producers' goods at the end of the given production period.

These phenomena of the unequal values of present and future goods affect all the phenomena of distribution. All shares in distribution must be reckoned in terms of present values. This is a principle of fundamental importance, unrecognised in earlier discussions, which compels us now to correct many of the classical formulas. All co-operating parties or factors in production who take their shares in future goods will get, in the normal course of things, at the end of their waiting, a greater quantity of goods of any given kind than can be obtained by those whose needs or desires must be met immediately. Those who can take their pay wholly or in part in producers' goods will in the long run have more to show for their labour than those who must get consumers' goods at once. This, as Böhm-Bawerk says, is the true secret of the dependence of the labourer on the capitalist. It is also the element of truth in the WAGES-FUND doctrine. To the extent that a labouring population is employed on distant results, but is unable to take its pay in the ownership of future goods, must its wages be limited by disposable present goods, the free or remuneratory capital of the English economists. The value of these is the means of measurement of what Professor Clark has called pure capital, since the fund of available value invested in producers' goods must always be measured in terms of present goods. Wages can never exceed the concrete free capital of the older nomenclature except as labourers become capitalists and take part of their reward in the pure capital invested in productive instruments, or in materials in process of advancement towards future consumers' goods. If then, denying the wages-fund doctrine, we affirm that wages are drawn from product and measured by product, we must add that to the extent that our modern production is capitalistic in its methods, wages are drawn from capitalised product and are measured only by product in terms of capital.

So far our account of future goods has adhered rather closely, though not strictly, to the Austrian exposition. The relation of future goods to the theory of consumption and to cost of production has been worked out chiefly by American writers. Professor Patten, who was among the first to point out the importance of present and future in wage theories, has given attention chiefly to the phenomena of consumption. In a discussion of Marshall's doctrine of consumers' rent he denies the possibility of consumers' surplus from producers' goods. For example, we cannot get consumers' surplus from ploughs and from wheat produced by means of ploughs. The value of the ploughs is "imputed" to them by the future consumers' goods, wheat, etc., and their value, in turn, must be converted into the value of present wheat, which alone, therefore, yields a true consumers' surplus.

Of greater importance, however, is Professor Patten's theory of the dynamic action of changes in consumption itself. These affect all values, subjective and objective, and react on production and distribution. Consumption is governed in its evolution by (a) the psychological law that a harmonious combination of many moderate but varied pleasures will make up a larger total of subjective utility than will a few intense pleasures, and (b) the objective fact that, because of diminishing returns on the one hand and the variety of nature's resources on the other, it costs less to enlarge a harmonious group of many moderate pleasures than to intensify a few. The consumption of a progressive community is a progressive adjustment to these conditions. Irrespective of increasing population, it becomes more varied, and the uses of particular kinds of goods are multiplied as they enter into new combinations. Therefore, we have no right to conclude that if future goods of any given kind are more abundant than present goods of like kind, they must be less valuable per unit. Demand for just these goods may increase as fast as supply, or faster, and the ground disappears on which rested the criticism of productivity theories of interest.

Professor J. B. Clark develops this thought even farther. He denies that in one important class of cases—the very class most often appealed to in the Austrian argument—there is any comparison whatever between present goods and future goods of like *kind*. When men save, they are either postponing the consumption of wealth or they are for ever renouncing consumption and converting wealth for all time into producers' goods. The latter only is permanent capitalisation. Postponement of enjoyment, as in provision for future travel, or for an education of culture merely, or for old age, is temporary capitalisation to be followed by decapitalisation. In permanent capitalisa-tion we certainly do not compare present goods with future goods of like kind only, if any changes in consumption or in methods of production are contemplated, and, in fact, changes of both kinds always are contemplated, and capitalisation would not occur if they were not. Much less do we compare present and future goods of like kind when we merely postpone enjoyment. When the time for consumption comes, we shall have changed subjectively, and the conditions of life will have changed objectively. Our consumption will not be the same that it would be to-day, and, in fact, we do not expect or wish it to be. We deliberately exchange a group of pleasures that we could enjoy now for a different group that we can enjoy only in the future. Therefore the unequal values of present and future goods of like kind and number cannot be explained by subjective comparisons in the mind of the same individual.

If these conclusions are accepted, it follows that the value of future goods is always determined by comparisons of present goods of one kind with future goods of another kind, and that the difference in value per unit between present and future goods of the same kind is a resultant of many such comparisons by different persons. It is, in short, a phenomenon of objective or market value only. The under-estimation of the future disappears from our list of causes of interest, and we have left the purely objective fact that present goods are strictly limited in quantity, while, owing to the technical superiority, or productive potentiality, of present goods, and the progressive development of invention, future goods are relatively abundant. The value of future goods is determined, like any other value in any actual market, solely by the demand for and the supply of concrete goods.

If this is true, the relative quantities of present and future goods ought to be explained in terms of their cost of production. Like all commodities continuously produced, they should be found to have a normal as well as a market value. Cairnes showed that wages are not a cost, but that they correspond to and repay a cost, and but for the cost would fall to zero. In like manner, interest is not a cost, but it corresponds to and repays a cost, and but for the cost would wholly disappear. The attempt to show these relations has been made by the present writer. Future goods being always in relatively abundant supply, for reasons already given, he affirms that their conversion into present goods can always be hastened if desired, thus increasing the relative supply of present goods and diminishing their relative value. But hastened production is more costly than production at a usual or normal rate. It involves overtime or intensified labour, which is labour of diminishing return. This is the whole significance of the "fatal lapse of time between the beginning and the end of the lengthy capitalist process" that Böhm-Bawerk speaks of. The process can be shortened, but shortening is costly. This extra cost, therefore, normally prevents the lowering of value of present as compared with the value of future goods which otherwise would be possible through an abnormal acceleration of production. The abnormal cost of hastened production is the normal measure of the difference in value between present and future goods and the normal measure of interest.

[For details of the views here presented consult *Capital and Interest,* and *The Positive Theory of Capital,* by Dr. E. v. Böhm-Bawerk, translated by Wm. Smart. A sketch is given in *Quart. Jour. of Econ.,* April 1889, by J. Bonar.—Francis A. Walker, "Dr. Böhm-Bawerk's Theory of Interest," in *Quarterly Journal of Economics,* vol. vi. No. 4, July 1892.—Simon N. Patten, "The Dynamic Theory of Economics." — President Walker's "Theory of Distribution," in *Quarterly Journal of Economics,* vol. iv.—No. 1, October 1889.— "Cost and Expense," in *Annals of the American Academy of Political and Social Science,* vol. iii. No. 6, May 1893.—John B. Clark, "Capital and its Earnings," in *Publications of the American Economic Association,* vol. iii. No. 2, May 1888. — and "Distribution as Determined by a Law of Rent," in *Quarterly Journal of Economics,* vol. v. No. 3, April 1891. — F. H. Giddings, three articles in the *Quarterly Journal of Economics,* namely, "The Cost of Production of Capital," vol. iii. No. 4, July 1889 ; "The Theory of Capital, vol. iv. No. 2, January 1890, and "The Growth of Capital and Cause of Interest," vol. v. No. 2, January 1891. The important remark of Professor Clark, that the same individual does not exchange present for future goods of like kind, is from his paper in the *Yale Review,* November 1893.—Consult also the writings of the English economists, John Rae, N. W. Senior, J. S. Mill, Jevons, Sidgwick, and Marshall ; the Italian economist Loria and the German Dietzel for criticisms ; and of the Austrians, Menger, Sax, and Wieser.] F. H. G.

FUTURES. Dealings in "futures" take place in almost every large market. On the London Stock Exchange, transactions are for a settling day, fixed, or to be fixed (see SETTLING DAY), and a large proportion of the bargains are made in the expectation, on one side at least, of their outset by a future transaction (see also OPTIONS, PUT AND CALL). In many kinds of commodities bargains also are made for delivery at future dates, whether delivery may ultimately be taken, or the right thereto be sold. In the United States, dealings in "futures" are the chief feature in the wheat trade. In London, "futures" in silver, tea, coffee, sugar, and wheat are largely dealt in through the London Produce Clearing House, which guarantees to buyers and sellers the due performance of the contracts, bargains being made for delivery at any time up to six months, against a deposit of 5 per cent of the value (see MARGIN). The power to purchase "futures" is sometimes an important part of a manufacturer's arrangements, enabling him safely to take extensive contracts by ensuring a continued supply of raw material at a definite price. On the other hand, a large proportion of such dealings is purely gambling, and upon this ground their suppression by law has been advocated. Besides these objections upon moral grounds, it has been urged that the sale of "futures" has a direct effect upon prices, equal to that of a large increase of supply, and has, in the case of wheat at least, caused a prolonged depression of price beyond the minimum cost of production. (On this last point see *Commercial Gambling the Principal Cause of Depression in Agriculture and Trade,* by C. W. Smith, 1893.) R. W. B.

FUTURES IN COTTON will supply an example of dealing in "futures." The term is applied to contracts made for future delivery of cotton, transactions of this nature forming by far the larger proportion of business done in the Liverpool market ; a fact which is self-evident when we reflect that almost every bale of American cotton imported into Liverpool is hedged by a sale of distant futures, whilst spinners also find this a convenient method of covering forward orders taken for yarns ; and speculators, it is needless to add, resort almost entirely to this mode of doing business, involving, as it does, no outlay of capital beyond a margin to be agreed upon at time of contract, or a payment of weekly differences as customary by the rules of the cotton association.

The "future" market is also largely used for "straddling" purposes between Liverpool and New York, when the difference in price between the two markets is such as to permit of a commission being earned by a simultaneous purchase and sale.

Differences, unless otherwise stipulated at time of contract, are settled weekly, through the medium of the cotton CLEARING (q.v.), the price of settlement being struck each Monday at 1.45 P.M. and payment exacted on the Thursday following, and some idea of the magnitude of the business may be formed from the fact that in a single week as much as £308,000 has passed through the clearinghouse for differences incurred during that short period only. R. C. B.

FYRD was the Anglo-Saxon militia. There was very little taxation before the Norman Conquest, because most of the expenses were defrayed by local obligation. Every freeman was subject to the *trinoda necessitas, i.e.* service at his own expense when summoned by the king (*fyrdung*), the repair of fortifications (*burhbot*), and the repair of bridges (*brdbot*). R. L.

GABELLE. This term, originally applied to any tax upon commodities, was gradually limited to the tax upon salt, perhaps the most odious and inequitable impost in France. Not only did the state reserve to itself the monopoly of the trade in salt, but it actually compelled the purchase of a minimum amount for every individual over eight years of age. This was called the *sel du devoir*. Originally the tax was uniform throughout France, but as time went on the most extraordinary inequalities grew up. The country was divided into five groups of provinces according to the price at which salt was sold by the GRENIERS À SEL (*q.v.*). These were (1) the *pays de grandes gabelles*, where the price was 62 francs the quintal ; (2) the *pays de petites gabelles*, where the price was 33 francs 12 sous ; (3) the *pays de salines*, where it sold for 21 francs 12 sous, and the tax was levied on the extraction of salt from the salt marshes ; (4) the *pays redimés*, which had purchased exemption in 1549 ; (5) the *pays exempts*, which were exempted from the tax by the terms of their union with the monarchy. Many individuals received the privilege of being on the list of *franc-salé*, which included all hospitals, religious communities, and magistrates. The inevitable result of these inequalities was to give rise to a regular smuggling trade, and this in turn to a harsh and expensive system of police, often assisted by the troops. Necker says, "Thousands of men, attracted by the prospect of easy gain, devote themselves to a commerce contrary to the laws. Agriculture is abandoned for a career which promises greater and more speedy returns, and children are trained under the eyes of their parents to forget their duties to the state." The fact was that ever since 1548 the *gabelle*, like the other indirect taxes, had been farmed out to speculative companies. The net revenue from the *gabelle* is reckoned by Necker at 54,000,000 francs. The tax was condemned by all advocates of reform, from Vauban to Turgot, but it was not abolished until 1790. The Gabelle had the effect of seriously diminishing the consumption of salt, which was only half as much per head in the *pays de grandes gabelles* as in the exempted provinces.

[A. Smith, *W. of N.*, bk. v. ch. ii.—Gasquet, *Précis des Institutions Politiques de l'ancienne France.*—Necker, *Compte Rendu.*—Clamagéran, *Histoire de l'Impôt en France.* (See also SALT TAX ; INDIRECT TAXATION.)]   R. L.

GABLATORES, servile tenants, who paid rent either in money or kind in lieu of actual service. Such rent, *gafol* or *gablum*, occurs frequently in Domesday ; seven gablatores are mentioned on the manor of Cheddar, part of the *terra regis* in Somerset, as paying seventeen shillings yearly to the king. By the 14th century such commutation was becoming general,

and led to the formation of a class of tenants at money rents (see GEBUR).

[Cunningham, *Growth of English Industry and Commerce, Early and Middle Ages*, 1890, p. 160.—Round, *Danegeld and the Finance of Domesday*, in *Domesday Studies*, 1888, vol. i.]   E. G. P.

GAËTA, DUKE OF, MARTIN MICHEL CHARLES GAUDIN (1756-1841), born at Saint Denis (Seine), died at Paris. He was placed at the age of seventeen in the office of the ministry of finance. In 1791 he was appointed one of the six commissioners of the national treasury. He resigned office on the breaking out of the Reign of Terror, and refused the portfolio of finance under the Directory, contenting himself with being the general commissioner of the post office, but accepted it after the 18th Brumaire from the hands of the First Consul. He continued to hold this office up to the fall of the empire, and during the Hundred Days. He assisted in the reorganisation of the administration of the system of finance. In this reorganisation the system of the *ancien régime* was taken for a model, of which he was, unfortunately, only too faithful a follower. For he thus recalled to life that spirit of bureaucracy which, while painstaking and order-loving, as we freely admit, was over-exact to a fault, treating the people as if they were children, incapable of understanding and managing their own interests, and especially of foreseeing what would serve those interests best. Absolutely honest and unassuming, acting always with the most perfect good faith, he earned and deserved the respect of the government of the Restoration, which appointed him (he was deputy for the department of the Aisne from 1815 to 1819) governor of the Bank of France in 1820, a post which he held till 1834. He declined a seat in the chamber of peers.   A. C. f.

"He was," writes Napoleon from St. Helena, "an honest and orderly administrator, who knew how to be on good terms with his inferiors and to progress with a demure but steady step. Everything he did and projected from the beginning, he maintained and perfected during fifteen years of a wise administration." In his *Mémoires relatifs à la Révolution, à l'Empire et à la Restauration* (Paris, 2 vols. 1826), Gaëta himself explained the principle which guided him throughout life in the following terms :—"The spirit of order is the first desideratum in financial administration : it applies to everything and embraces both men and things."

In his *Notice Historique sur les Finances de la France* (1818), published to defend his financial administration against attacks from the more ardent among the Legitimists, the Duke of Gaëta states that when he first entered the ministry, the treasury only possessed in cash the miserable sum of 177,000 francs (say

£7080). "The *Assemblée Constituante*, with the best possible intentions, had decreed the ruin of our finances on the day when sacrificing true principles and the warnings of experience to vain abstractions, it had decreed the suppression of all taxes on consumption." In a note (p. 3) he adds that "indirect taxation is one of the *necessary* elements of a system of finance, capable of adaptation to all circumstances and to all wants." He adds (pp. 225 *et seq.*) that on principle and from the first day he assumed office he pursued two main objects : "first, to improve and consolidate (the national) credit by looking carefully after the interests of the creditors of the state ; and second, to bring the ordinary revenue to the necessary level by taxes on consumption." . . . He also successfully organised the system of collecting the taxes and the execution of the general land survey (*Cadastre*) by the law of the 15th of September 1807,which is due to him, following in this the principle of the law of September 1791 (see CADASTRAL SURVEY). Gaudin ranks as the author of the modern system of French financial administration, acting on the opinion he had expressed in his *Notice historique* (p. 6) that, at the time of the outbreak of the revolution, the national assembly "might easily have *ameliorated* the older system instead of *destroying* it." The italics are his own.

Apart from the above mentioned works, the Duke of Gaëta published ; *Observations et éclaircissements sur le paragraphe concernant les finances dans l'Exposé de la situation du Royaume présenté à la Chambre des Pairs* (1814).—*Opinion préliminaire sur les Finances* (1815).—*Mémoire sur le Cadastre* (1817).—*Aperçu théorique sur les Emprunts, suivi de quelques observations . . . sur l'ouvrage de M. Ganilh* (1817).—*Observations sur la proposition faite de réduire le crédit pour les travaux du Cadastre* (1820).—*Considérations sur la Dette publique de France, sur l'emprunt et sur l'amortissement* (1828).—*Considération sur l'Exposé des Motifs de la Loi du 17 Mai 1837 portant création d'un fonds extraordinaire pour les Travaux Publics* (1837).—*Des Conséquences du rejet par la Chambre des Pairs du projet de loi concernant la Conversion de la rente 5 per cent* (1840). [See also *Essai sur la Vie et l'Administration du duc de Gaëte, ministre des Finances de l'Empire*, by Aug. Portalis (Paris, 1842).] E. CA.

GAFOL, GABEL, or GABLE, "payments in kind or in money, in labour, service in the field defined or undefined" (Gneist, *English Constitution*, translation, 1886, 1, 4). It was the least servile of the incidents of serfdom, paid by the GEBUR or villein, less fully by the cottier (Seebohm, *Village Community*, 1884, 141, 142). Vinogradoff (*Villainage in England*, 1891, 184) considers *gafol* to be an original, not a commuted payment, "the old Saxon rent in money or in kind," but admits exceptions, as in Kent (cp. GAVELKIND), where it may be unconnected with any base or villein service (p. 187). The

word occurs in combination, *e.g.* gafol-earth, *i.e.*ploughing over and above the week-work, gafol-ale, etc. Seebohm (pp. 318-327) attempts to trace it to the dues paid by the Roman *coloni*. [Kemble, *Saxons in England*, vol. i. ch. xi.— Round, *Domesday Studies*, vol. i. p. 132, and *Eng. Hist. Review*, January 1887, p. 103.— Stevenson, *Eng. Hist. Review*, April 1887, p. 336.] E. G. P.

GAINAGE or WAINAGE. The oxen, horses, ploughs, and other instruments used in carrying on the work of a farm. [Cowel's *Interpreter*, ed. 1727, arts. "Gainagium" and "Gainage."] A. E. S.

GAITO, GIOVANNI DOMENICO (at Naples in 17th century) ; wrote a comprehensive treatise on transactions of credit, in which, like other writers, especially the Roman Sigismondo Scaccia, without openly endeavouring to modify the ideas of theologians and jurists, he proved the lawfulness of interest on money. It is interesting to observe the effort made in it to overcome the prejudice, existing at that time, to consider money as being an unfruitful property, without, however, venturing to oppose this opinion openly. *Tractatus absolutissimus de credito*, Venetiis, 1626. A. B.

GALANTI, GIUSEPPE M. (1743-1799), born at Campobasso in one of the Neapolitan states on the south-east coast, of which in 1781 he wrote a description. His father destined him for the bar, which he gave up early to study literature and rural matters closely, a choice fostered in him by GENOVESI, whom he greatly admired, and on whose death in 1772 he composed *Elogio storico del Sig. Abate Genovesi*.

Galanti was invited by the government in 1786 to write the *Descrizione geografica e politica della Sicilia*, Napoli (translated into French and German, abridged in English). In this work, much esteemed at the time, Galanti expresses his opinions on the means proper to improve the national wealth. Following many Neapolitan writers before him, he, though eclectic, supports mercantilism. In his *Testamento forense*, Venezia, 1806, based on the arguments of Delfico, he supported the abolition of the feudal system on which the crown estates were still carried on at that date, maintaining that the general prosperity would have been more increased by selling or farming them, and agriculture improved by the consequent adoption of better methods. Galanti was a supporter of the single tax on land, admitting indirect taxes only when really needed and not weighing unduly on goods of first necessity ; he deplored the existence of privileged classes, exempted from the payment of taxes, for taxes ought to be paid proportionately to property. Writing on population, he developed such sound principles as to be justly considered by Prof. Fornari, *Delle teorie economiche nelle Prov. Napoletane*, vol. ii., the forerunner of Malthus. A. B.

GALDI, MATTEO (18th century) a Neapolitan jurist. In his lifetime the laws regulating the property in land were much discussed. He was of opinion that these should be as liberal as possible, and that in order to attain the greatest public prosperity, the number of proprietors should be as large as possible in every nation. Every legal institution which tended to prevent the free distribution of a great part of the territory of a nation should be abrogated.

Analisi ragionata del Codice Ferdinandino . . . Napoli, 1790.   A. B.

GALE, AND HANGING GALE. An expression used in Ireland for an instalment of rent. Gale day is the day on which rent is payable. The word is connected with *Gabellum*, gavel (see GAFOL). The "hanging gale" is the half-year's rent in respect to which the tenants on many estates were allowed to remain in arrear.
                                                  O. F. B.

GALEON. The Spanish name of the ships *flotas y galeones* engaged in the officially authorised trade between Spain and America. Charles V. in 1526 and again Philip II. in 1561 decreed that the whole of this trade was to be monopolised by these *galeones* sailing every year or eighteen months and under military convoy from Seville to Carthagena and Portobello or Porto Rico and Vera Cruz. Occasionally a few ships, *navios de registro*, obtained licenses to sail by themselves or from other Spanish ports, but with such delays and formalities that these licenses were almost useless. In America the goods imported from Spain were sold at fairs and at previously fixed prices, which left profits ranging from 100 to 500 per cent. On their journey home, the *galeones* were also bound to unload their cargoes of precious metals in Seville (from 1717, Cadiz). The whole system resulted in an enormous premium to smuggling, and lasted until the middle of the 18th century, when it had greatly declined in importance.

[Colmeiro, *Historica de la Economia Politica en España*, ii. pp. 401-421.]   E. CA.

GALIANI, FERDINANDO (1728 - 1787), born at Chieti, south-east coast of Italy. He lived at Naples and became an ecclesiastic and eventually a monsignore. From his youth upwards he showed high intellectual power, and reached high office, being a member of the supreme board of trade at Naples. In 1759 he was appointed secretary to the Neapolitan embassy at Paris, and soon after an envoy. He went to London, where he lived a long time and published his *Dialogues sur le commerce des blés*, Londres (Paris), 1770, which made him known throughout Europe, and drew forth vigorous replies. In 1773 he was recalled to Naples, and employed in high public office, which he filled to the entire satisfaction of the king.

The writings of Galiani were highly useful, especially his work *Sui doveri dei principi neutrali verso i principi belligerenti*, published during the Seven Years' War, during which the kingdom of Naples stood neutral. He investigated, with much originality, the fundamental problems of economic science, opening the way to its future progress. In his able work, *Della Moneta* (anonymous 1750, 2nd ed. with his name, 1780), he analysed the phenomenon of value, forming a theory which may have a little in common in its details with the other systems known in his time, but differing essentially from them in its theory of the basis of value. Galiani placed this in the concrete utility of single quantities of wealth—a utility which, according to him, is determined by the different degrees of demand ; he remarks on the influence of time and the reciprocal influence of demand on value, which, in its turn, influences the former. This theory of the limit of utility forms a complete and regular system in which the several elements are first ascertained and then reduced to one alone. This element is neither labour nor rarity, separately considered, nor even utility itself. According to Galiani, the law regarding normal value is a mixture of several elements, all tending to give the idea of utility in its widest sense, and differently distinguished in degree and demand. Galiani's system has nothing in common with that of Locke and Cantillon, then generally accepted. It anticipates the theories of Jevons and Menger. In the work, *Della Moneta*, he defends charging interest. The chapter on the course of exchange, though imbued with *mercantilist* opinions, and showing some inconsistencies in the remarks on international trade, has great merits. His eight dialogues, *Dialoghi sul commercio dei grani* were translated into French by Diderot, January 1770, and are the most brilliant writings published up to that time in support of practical economics. The author declares himself in them the follower of no school ; according to him in the corn trade the only system to be followed is to follow none. As he wrote subsequently in his *Corrispondenza*, the dialogues were never completed, he having intended to add one more (IX.), which was never published. Pecchio, *Storia dell' Econ. pubbl. in Italia*, Lugano, 1819, pp. 95-96, has given copious extracts and a short analysis of the dialogues. In the *Dialoghi*, Galiani does not speak of agriculture as the sole basis of wealth, as the physiocrats do, because several states have territories quite insufficient for their requirements. He praises the edict of 1764, which established free trade in corn in France, but he does not do this through an absolute conviction of the correctness of the theory. Every nation, every age, requires, according to him, different laws ; it is absurd to resolve the problems of economical legislation by reference to abstract and absolute principle, because consideration must be had of an indefinite quantity which cannot be determined,—that is man, who may be entirely modified by habits. Many objections were raised to these opinions, and all the *économistes* opposed Galiani. Further, the French government gave MORELLET the task of refuting him. The attempt was published three years later.

In the history of economic doctrines, Galiani has the great merit to have remarked in the 2nd edition of *Della Moneta* (1780) on the great importance of the work of Antonio SERRA, *Breve trattato delle cause che possono fare abbondare i regni d'oro e d'argento dove non sono miniere,* Napoli, 1613, which every one had unjustly forgotten.   A. B.

GALITZIN, DIMITRI, Prince (1730-1803). From 1765 to 1772 he was Russian ambassador in Paris, where he met on friendly terms QUESNAY and other members of the school of the PHYSIOCRATS. On leaving Paris he occupied the Russian embassy in the Netherlands, and retired to Germany, where he died, after the outbreak of the French Revolution.

To vindicate the memory of his former friends, Galitzin published, in 1796, at Brunswick, a book entitled *De l'Esprit des Économistes ou les Économistes justifiés d'avoir posé par leurs principes les bases de la Révolution française* (The spirit of the Economists, or the Economists not guilty of having laid, by means of their principles, the foundation of the French Revolution).   E. Ca.

GALLATIN, ALBERT (1761-1849), an American statesman and writer, was born at Geneva in Switzerland, and emigrated to the United States in 1780. He was active in the state (Pennsylvania) and federal legislatures from 1789 to 1801, and became secretary of the treasury in 1801. He served in that capacity with distinguished success until 1813. In 1814 he took a leading part in negotiating the treaty of Ghent, by which the war between the United States and Great Britain was brought to an end. From 1816 to 1823 he was minister to France, and in 1826-27, minister to England. In the later years of his life he was president of a bank in New York, where he died. His character was singularly pure and noble, and his career marked by unfailing public spirit combined with rare good sense.

Gallatin's official writings on economic and financial subjects are voluminous, consisting of his reports as secretary of the treasury, and of other state papers and speeches. All are marked by sound judgment and perfect accuracy of statement, and are material of high value on the industrial and financial history of the United States. The same qualities appear in his un-official writings, a list of the more important of which is subjoined. In the two pamphlets on currency and banking, published in 1831 and 1841, he gave sketches of the currency history of the country, which are the best sources of information on that period ; and he urged strongly the maintenance of specie payments. It is noteworthy that the function and importance of deposit banking as virtually supplying currency received adequate recognition at his hands. In the memorial which he drew up in 1832 on behalf of a free-trade convention, he presented with force the argument in favour of free trade, showing in his treatment of the subject signs of the influence of the Ricardian school.

Gallatin's life has been fully written by Mr. Henry Adams (*Life of Gallatin*, Philadelphia,

1879). The same author edited at the same time three volumes of Gallatin's works, the third of which contains most of those enumerated below, and gives also a complete list of all Gallatin's public and private writings. The more important of his unofficial writings are :—*A Sketch of the Finances of the United States*, New York, 1796. —*Views of the Public Debt, Receipts, and Expenditures of the United States*, Philadelphia, 1800.—*Considerations on the Currency and Banking Systems of the United States*, Philadelphia, 1831.—*Memorial of the Free Trade Convention*, New York, 1832.—*Suggestions on the Banks and Currency of the several United States, in reference principally to the suspension of specie payments*, New York, 1841.   F. W. T.

GAMBRINI, FRANCESCO (early 19th century), born at Asti in Piedmont.

In his work, *Delle Leggi Frumentarie in Italia*, 1819, Gambrini defended free trade in corn and free trade in general, opposing the system of protection to manufactures by forbidding the export of raw materials and imposing heavy duties on the import of manufactured articles. Nevertheless he considered a protective system justified if it prepared domestic manufactures against a time when they could compete with foreign countries. *Osservazioni sulla proibita estrazione della seta greggia dal Piemonte* (*Racc. di opere di Econ. Pol. di Aut. Piem.*, p. 144).   A. B.

GAME LAWS. These laws are an artificial arrangement for the purpose of securing to owners of land the game on their estates, which, by the common law, is not, while living, capable of being property. In this respect the common law is founded on the civil or Roman law. In the view of Roman lawyers, wild or undomesticated animals were *res nullius*, the property of no one, until killed or captured, when they became the property of the captor, no matter on whose land they might have been taken (Inst. II. 2). If they were caught and confined they became property only so long as they were in actual detention, but if they recovered their liberty they again became *res nullius*. Even if tamed, animals *feræ naturæ* were the subject of property so long only as they were either on the owner's estate, or retained an *animus revertendi* to it, and if that did not exist, they became subject to the right of appropriation as if wild. These rules were carried still further by the Anglo-Saxons, whose presumption in favour of equality of rights led to the prohibition of keeping wild animals in confinement for purposes of pleasure, because by so doing they were abstracted from the common right of all to kill them. But the Norman love of sport, and their introduction of the feudal principle, gave a new development to these doctrines. Game continued to be in law not a subject of property, but the right to pursue it became a privilege vested only in the landowner, and pre-eminently in the sovereign as lord paramount. In particular the right to confine animals of chase within certain bounds was limited to the sovereign and to those private individuals on whom he bestowed the right—by grant of privilege of a "forest," in which the forest laws prevailed ; of a "chase," where game might be preserved, but without protection of the forest laws ; or a "park," in which game might be confined by a fence. The "forest laws" were a code established by the arbitrary decree of the Conqueror and his immediate successors, which inflicted fines, mutilation, and death on all who might hunt within the limits in which it applied. The severity of this code caused deep murmuring, and it was restrained both by the Great Charter and by the *Charta de Foresta* (1217). (See FORESTS, MEDIÆVAL.)

A series of game laws gradually took the place of this code of privilege, and these were consolidated by the Night and Day Poaching Acts, 9 Geo. IV. c. 69, 1 & 2 Will. IV. c. 32, and 2 & 3 Will. IV. c. 68, which now form the principal enactments framed for preservation of game. These still proceed on the basis that game is not property, and therefore the taking of it alive is not theft. But they convert trespass, which by itself is not criminal, but only gives room for a civil action for damages, into a criminal offence, if it is for the purpose of taking game. The offence during day is punishable only by fine, but the taking of game by night is punishable by imprisonment with hard labour for three months, six months, and two years, or even penal servitude for seven years for a first, second, and third offence. There are further penalties for aggravation by resistance, etc., and the 7 & 8 Vict. c. 29 applies the rule to highways. The game thus protected by night are hares, pheasants, partridges, grouse, heath or moor game, black game (these two latter are the same), and bustards. The Day Act applies, in addition to these, to deer, roe, woodcock, snipes, quails, landrails, wild ducks, and conies. The 25 & 26 Vict. c. 114 entitles policemen to apprehend and search any person suspected of having game in his possession. In addition to these restraints it was formerly unlawful for any one to kill game, even on his own ground, unless he were possessed in England of an estate of £100 a year (22 & 23 Car. II. c. 25), and in Scotland of a "ploughgate" of land. But the necessity of a qualification was abolished by 1 Will. IV. c. 32, and in its place was substituted the requirement to take out a licence. The present statute is the 23 & 24 Vict. c. 90. The 11 & 12 Vict. c. 29 relieved occupiers of this obligation as regards the killing of hares, and as regards both hares and rabbits the Ground Game Act, 1880, declares that the tenant of lands shall have a right of killing which he cannot contract himself out of. There is also a close time appointed by 13 Geo. III. c. 54, during which the killing and selling of game is illegal.

Such are the leading provisions which constitute the code of game laws. As there is no moral question involved in their principle, whatever may arise out of their exercise, the policy must be judged on grounds of expedience and public advantage. Two arguments may be stated in their favour. In the first place they adapt to modern conditions ancient rules of law which have ceased to be applicable. In a sparsely-inhabited country the doctrine that wild animals are no man's property is reasonable. But when every inch of ground has its owner, and every plant is private property, it is pedantic to affirm that animals which live and die on private land, and are wholly fed on private property, become public because they have the power of flying or leaping over the fences which separate one private property from another. Common sense would suggest that they should be recognised as part of the property of the landowner on whose territory they are for the moment, and that their being taken by another person is as much stealing as the appropriation of a sheep or turkey. But in the second place there is the plea in favour of the game laws that by encouraging sport they encourage the residence of owners on their estates ; the advantage of which to the community cannot be disputed. But these arguments are met by others of undeniable force. Human nature has not confined the love of sport to the breasts of landowners, or of rich men who can hire their rights. It exists as deeply in the hearts of poor men ; and no enactments can convince them that its indulgence is a crime. Further, the excessive preservation of game, which the game laws foster, makes poaching a very profitable pursuit. At the same time the valuable animals thus multiplied are somewhat in the position of a shopkeeper's goods exposed outside his door instead of within his window : they are not in a place of safe custody, watched over by regular attendants, so that the temptation to take them is enhanced by apparent negligence and the prospect of carrying them off without detection. It is against public policy to foster in this manner temptations to crime, and most of all to offences which are artificially created by law. The impolicy is heightened by the fact that those yielding to the temptation are often brought into situations where in self-defence they commit murder or are themselves murdered.

The economic effects of preservation of game have been often exaggerated on both sides. The advocates of the system urge that a large amount of food is produced and a great deal of employment given. The opponents insist that crops are destroyed, land thrown out of cultivation in order to form preserves, and agricultural employment diminished. Excluding deer forests from view for the present, the mischiefs on both sides have been practically much reduced in amount by the effect of recent agricultural depression. This fact has given to tenants in general an increased power of making their own conditions, among which moderation in the preservation of game is not one of the least essential. There are probably not now many farms in which any considerable amount of damage to crops arises from game. The actual preserves are mostly within parks, partly grazed by cattle and sheep; and in woods, which under present circumstances return as much profit from timber as the land would if under cultivation. Nor can any reasonable person think it desirable that sylvan scenery should be utterly abolished in England, even if a small addition to the supply of human food were thereby attained. The number of keepers is also not greatly less than the number of agricultural labourers would be.

The case of deer forests (which are really treeless tracts of mountain heath) is, however, peculiar in its circumstances. If the deer were limited to the higher ranges, in which culture is unprofitable, the small number of sheep and cattle which they would displace would be scarcely worth computation. But of late years rich strangers have offered tempting rents for immense ranges of country, including a proportion of fertile glens, with the view of driving out the existing population on the pretence that their presence frightens the deer away. The pretence is unfounded, for deer soon become reconciled to the sight of those who do not molest them. But even if it were true it would be contrary to sound national policy to allow a wide district to be depopulated for the sake of yielding sport to a rich man. A royal commission has lately investigated the extent of land suitable for crofter holdings or common pasture, but the figures in its report do not distinguish between forests and lands at present in cultivation or pasture.

[Rich. Griffiths Welford, *The Influences of the Game Laws*, 1846 (Extracts from Evidence before House of Commons Committee, Speech of Bright, etc.).—Shaw Lefevre, *Freedom of Land*, 1880.—*Report of Highlands and Islands Commission*, 1892.] J. B. K.

GAMING CONTRACTS. A gaming or wagering contract "is one by which two persons professing to hold opposite views touching a future uncertain event mutually agree that, dependent upon that event, one shall receive from the other, and the other shall pay or hand over to him, a sum of money or other stake; neither of the contracting parties having any other interest in that contract than the sum or stake he will so win or lose, there being no other real consideration for the making of such contract by either of the parties." (Justice Hawkins in Carlill *v.* Carbolic Smoke Ball Company (1892) Queen's Bench 484). Contracts of this description are declared to be null and void by an act passed during the present reign (8 & 9 Vict. c. 109, p. 18). Notwithstanding this act it was held that a betting agent who had paid the amount due by his principal on the loss of a bet was entitled to recover the same from the latter (Read *v.* Anderson, 10 Queen's Bench Division 100; 13 Queen's Bench Division 779), but this indirect recognition of betting transactions has lately been set aside by the Gaming Act of 1892, which enacts that no action shall be brought to recover any sum of money paid in respect of any gaming or wagering contract. The subject of gaming contracts has recently been discussed with reference to the "missing word competitions" organised by certain newspapers, which were held to be illegal, as the result did not depend on skill and judgment but upon mere chance (Barclay *v.* Pearson—1893—2 Chancery 154). The principle of the statute against gaming and wagering contracts was, to a certain extent, already recognised by the statute of 14 Geo. III. c. 48, which forbids the insurance of a life in which the insurer has no interest, and which is still in force.

Much discussion has taken place both in England and abroad on the question whether certain time bargains on the stock exchange and in the produce markets are to be considered as partaking of the nature of wagers, and the result of the decisions seems to be that a contract is not enforceable where it can be proved that it was not the intention of the parties to deliver or receive a certain quantity of securities or produce at a certain price, but that the payment of the difference between the price at which the bargain was made and the market price at the time fixed for the completion of the bargain was the sole object of the transaction; in the absence of such proof the parties must be presumed to have intended a real sale (Grizewood *v.* Blane, 11 Common Bench 526; Thacker *v.* Hardy, 4 Queen's Bench Division 685—see also the decision of the German *Reichsoberhandelsgericht*, vol. 6, p. 224, and of the German *Reichsgericht Entsch. in Civilsachen*, vol. 12, p. 16, and vol. 30, p. 214).

In France time bargains entered upon in the ordinary way are not considered gaming contracts unless an agreement in writing between the parties proves the contrary (see the decision of the Court of Appeal at Dijon, dated 18th May 1891, reported *Dalloz Recueil périodique*, 1891, II. 384) (cp. also LOTTERIES). E. S.

GANGS, AGRICULTURAL, also called "public gangs," are to be distinguished from "private gangs," organised by the farmer himself who employs them, and superintended by one of his own men who works with them. The public gangs are engaged by an independent gang-master, who makes his own terms with the women or boys who compose them, and sees a certain amount of agricultural work executed for a farmer, who pays by the piece. The system is to be found throughout the Fen district. In 1865 it existed in the counties of

Cambridgeshire, Huntingdonshire, Lincolnshire, Nottinghamshire, Norfolk, and Suffolk, and was the direct result of the enclosure of wild land without providing an adequate number of cottages for resident cultivators. This enclosure went on with great rapidity in the two last decades of the reign of George III., and, combined with the unreformed poor law, which rated the parish rather than, as now, the union of parishes, and therefore discouraged landowners from keeping cottages, lest, as was said, they should become "nests for beggars' brats," made it necessary for occupiers of land to look elsewhere for the labour they needed. The Poor Law Union Chargeability Act (1865) altered the condition of affairs to a certain extent, but the expenses of cottage-building and repair have partially replaced the evil then removed. The moral evils to which these gangs led, particularly in a part of England which, being exceptionally free from fences or hedges, admitted of a strict look-out being kept by the culprits against observation, and the physical ruin caused to the employees, were so great that in 1865 Lord Shaftesbury, supported by the then Bishop of Lincoln (Dr. Jackson) and Earl Granville, carried an address from the House of Lords to the Queen for including agricultural child-labourers in the scope of inquiry by the children's labour commission appointed in 1862, and then sitting. They reported in 1867 that under the public gang system the payment of children according to their age and abilities, and the adjustments of work to their powers, were studied to a great nicety. There were, however, many children employed far too young, and the distances they had to travel on foot led to appalling cruelty. The preponderance of evidence as to a well-regulated system, however, showed that the exercise was good for the health of the elder children, and many medical men said the same also of the effect on the women. On the other hand the gross immorality and general coarsening of character, the obscenity and uncleanliness grafted on the young women by the irregularity and vagrancy of the life, were testified to almost universally by labourers, farmers, and ministers of the Gospel. The report of the commissioners startled the public with its revelations. The result was the passing, 20th August 1867, of an act which forbade the employment of any child under eight years old, of any female in the same gang with males, and of any female under a male gang-master unless a female licensed to act as gang-mistress were also present. Gang-masters must be licensed by two justices, and may not hold a liquor license. The distances to be travelled on foot by the gang are to be fixed by the justices, and each license must be renewed every six months. These enactments have been made more stringent by the Education Act 1870, which forbids the employment of any child under the age of ten, or under fourteen without a certificate of school proficiency. The work done with the gang varies with the different months, and ceases during harvest time. It consists principally of weeding, picking twitch, singling turnips, gathering stones, spreading manure, setting potatoes, selecting seeds. The advantages of the system are the training of the young to agricultural work, the securing of occasional extra hands for the farmer, and of extra wages for the cottage home, and in the case of the boys at any rate, the healthy effect of outdoor exercise. What disadvantages remain since the regulation by the act of 1867 are the usual mischiefs arising from the herding of twenty to thirty children together, and their possible subjection to an excessive amount of labour where it is the interest of their employer to "drive" them too fast; the danger to women's health in particular, from cold and exposure, and strain, and the harm arising to their homes by their absence; and possibly the discouragement of adult male labour by the competition of the gangs. Happily the general improvement in education and refinement among agricultural labourers' families is gradually causing all women, except widows who have no breadwinner, to refuse such labour, the conditions of which are quite unlike the annual hiring of whole families to work together, as in Northumberland. When, however, the justices really exercise their right of choice, and appoint as gang-master only a man who is at once skilled in the treatment of land, firm in command, and gentle in discipline, gangs seem to form a basis for just that technical training which is needed in our rural districts. The Education Acts wisely prevent parents from withdrawing their sons from school till they have learnt to read and write. The literary education thus being guarded, the state may possibly find in the gang system the nucleus of a technical education which, bringing in a little to the home, would not be unpopular. It is far otherwise with the employment of the future wives and mothers of England in labour which unfits them for domesticity. There are at present (1894) in the county of Norfolk alone 21 licensed gang-masters and 14 gang-mistresses.

[For much valuable evidence, see *Children's Employment Commission*, sixth report, 1867; for the debate in the House of Lords, *Hansard*, vol. clxxix. p. 174; for the history, Hodder's *Life of Lord Shaftesbury;* and for references Fred Clifford's *Agricultural Look-out*, p. 296.—Thorold Rogers, *Six Centuries of Work and Wages*, p. 511.—Prothero's *Pioneers of English Farming*, p. 225, comp. "Sachsengängerei " in *Jahrb. für Gesetzgebung*. — Kebbel, *Agricultural Labourer*. For private gangs, see *Children's Employment Commission*, appendix part ii., Fourth Report, 1870.]

H. L. W.

GANILH, CHARLES (1758-1836), a French economist and financial writer, was born in Allanche (Cantal) and moved early to Paris. During the period of the Revolution and the subsequent rule of Napoleon he held various public offices.

He was a mercantilist with considerable modifications, due no doubt largely to his extensive acquaintance with the economic literature of his own time, of which he wrote a history, probably his most important work. Among his writings were : *Essai sur les revenus des peuples depuis l'antiquité* (1806). — *Des systèmes d'Économie politique* (1809).—*Réflexions sur le budget de 1814* (1814) ; *Théorie de l'économie politique, fondée sur les faits recueillis en France et en Angleterre*, etc. (1815). — *Considérations générales sur la situation financière de la France en 1815* (1815).—*Considérations générales sur la situation financière de la France en 1816* (1816). —*De la législation, de l'administration et de la Comptabilite des finances de la France depuis la restauration* (1817). E. C. K. G.

Ganilh also wrote a *Dictionnaire analytique d'Économie politique*, published at Paris and Brussels 1826. This work is very restricted both in its range of subjects and in its method. *Exportations* has only two pages allotted to it, while *Demande* and *Offre*, which form two separate articles, have scarcely more than one page between them. Perhaps the main use of the volume to the modern reader is to remind him of the subjects most under public notice at the time when it was written. M'Culloch refers to this book slightingly in his *Literature of Political Economy*.

GARBLED COIN. A term used by bankers to indicate coins which have been sorted out from those in general use. To "garble" coin means to select from a number of coins those pieces which are required for a particular purpose, such as, for instance, to melt into bullion or to send to a mint for recoinage. F. E. A.

GARDINER, OR GARDNER, RALPH (*b.* 1625), son of Devereux Gardiner of Newcastle-on-Tyne. His father appears to have been an attorney, but failing in this profession, he became writing master at Queen Elizabeth's Grammar School, Newcastle. In 1650, Ralph Gardiner was established as a brewer at North Shields, and so infringed the monopoly of the Company of Brewers and Bakers of Newcastle. He maintained that the charters which conferred their privileges were contrary to the statute-law of the kingdom, and therefore of no authority. Throughout his life he carried on a struggle with the companies in defence of this principle. In 1650-51 the bakers and brewers warned him to cease brewing and brought several actions against him. Gardiner, however, took no notice of them, and in August 1652 he was arrested, "actions being laid for nine hundred pounds, when twenty pound could not be recovered, and he kept lockt up in a prison, from all comforts, in a tower above 36 foot high." His bail was at first accepted, but afterwards refused, and he was not allowed to defend his own cause. In February 1653 he escaped from prison ; in the following August he was again arrested by the constables of Newcastle corporation, but rescued by the sailors. Shortly afterwards he was imprisoned, and on 29th Sept. 1653 he addressed to parliament a petition which was referred (5th Oct.) to the committee on trade, and (18th Oct.) ordered to be taken into consideration on 15th Nov. The mayor and burgesses of Newcastle, however, asked for a delay of fourteen days, which was granted ; but on 18th Nov. many of the witnesses were examined. On the application of Samuel Hartlib, solicitor to the corporation, proceedings were deferred until the 13th Dec. Unfortunately for Gardiner, Cromwell dismissed the long parliament on 12th Dec., and so his case was not heard. He was at this time still in gaol, but shortly afterwards appears to have regained his freedom. On 15th Dec. 1656 a committee of the common council was appointed to consider his charges against the corporation. A certain Ralph Gardiner, hanged at York for coining on 30th March 1661, has been identified with the subject of this notice. But there can be no foundation for the charge, for Gardiner was still carrying on his business in 1662-63.

Gardiner published *Englands Grievance Discovered in relation to the Coal Trade ; the tyrannical oppression of the Magistrates of Newcastle ; their Charters and Grants ; the several Tryals, Depositions, and Judgments obtained against them*, etc., London 1655, 4to. Much of this work was written in prison. It contains much useful information on the Newcastle coal trade and the conservatorship of the Tyne ; but it is chiefly valuable as a record of the relations between the exclusive corporations of the 17th century and the private trader. *The Plea and Defence of the Magistrates of Newcastle against the allegations of Ralph Gardiner*, as exhibited by him before Parliament in 1653, published in 1848 in vol. iii. of Richardson's Reprints of Rare Tracts. *Englands Grievance*, etc. was republished in 1796, and again, at North Shields, in 1849, when a life of Gardiner and copious notes were added.

[Life of Gardiner in the North Shields edition of *Englands Grievance.*—*Memoirs of Ambrose Barnes* (Surtees Society), pp. 215, 369.]

W. A. S. H.

GARELLI DELLA MOREA, GIUSTO EMANUELE (died 1893), an economist and jurisconsult, and professor at the university of Turin; an able writer, well known in Italy for his school compendiums. He supported liberal principles and the theories of the classical economists.

His most important works are *Principii di Economia Politica*, Roma, 1881, 2nd ed.—*Scienza delle Finanze*, Torino, 1888. A. B.

GARFIELD, JAMES ABRAM (1831-1881) was born in Orange, Ohio. He entered political life in which he rapidly advanced, and was elected president of the United States in 1880 ; he was assassinated while in office. His speeches, which reflect the economic opinions of the Republican party between the Civil War and

1880, have been collected : *The Works of James Abram Garfield*, edited by Burke A. Hinsdale, 2 vols., Boston, 1882. Garfield had a special interest in the success of the ninth (1870) census, for which see his *Speeches*, 6th April and 16th December 1869. He also contributed an article on the "Census" to the first edition of *Johnson's New Universal Encyclopædia ;* republished in *The Works*, etc., vol. ii. pp. 185-217. The same subject, *The American Census*, is treated in a paper read before the American Soc. Sci. Assoc., published in *Transactions*, No. 2, 1870, pp. 31-55, also more exhaustively in *Report of the Committee on the Ninth Census*, House of Rep. 41st Cong. 2nd Sess., 18th January 1870, pp. 120.   D. R. D.

GARNIER, COMTE GERMAIN (1754-1821), was born at Auxerre and died at Paris. Up to the date of the revolution he had given no sign of being the economist he afterwards became. An Anacreontic poet, he was well known through his society verses, some of which are among the classics of that order of poetry. It was not till 1790 that he began life in earnest. He declared himself a warm supporter of the monarchy, and in that character won the confidence of Louis XVI., who offered him office, which he declined to accept. After the 10th August 1792 he emigrated to Switzerland, and did not return to France till 1795. A year later he published his *Abrégé des principes de l'économie politique*, 1 vol. 12mo, a work which, considering its date, is not without merit. His adhesion to the *coup d'état* of the 18th Brumaire gained him the prefecture of the departments of Seine and Oise, a post which he exchanged in 1804 for a seat in the senate ; and he was president of that body from 1809-1811. We need not dwell on other official posts which he held ; these, though lucrative, were rather dignified than laborious. It may be mentioned that he employed the time which they left at his disposal in his favourite studies of economics and finance. He was thus led to publish in 1805 his translation of Adam Smith's *Wealth of Nations*, 5 vols. 8vo, the best in the French language. It should be added that a second edition of this translation appeared in 1822, 6 vols. in 8vo, one volume being notes, the object of which is to refute Adam Smith from the point of view of the physiocrats. A third edition was published by Guillaumin, under the care of Adolphe Blanqui and of Eugène Buret, 2 vols. gr. in 8vo, 1843. Garnier's feelings of gratitude towards the imperial regime did not hinder him from voting in 1814 for the deposition of Napoleon I. This led to his being appointed a peer of France by Louis XVIII. He held aloof during the Hundred Days, and was, in consequence, appointed a minister and a member of the council of state as soon as the king returned to France. The empire had made him a count ; the restoration made him

a marquis. Justice to the memory of Garnier requires us to remember that he defended free trade in corn, and the freedom of the press in the chamber of peers. The other works of Garnier did not rise to the level of his translation of Adam Smith ; though interesting, considering the time when they were written, they did not maintain the reputation which that work had won for him. The following are the titles of the most important : *Théorie des banques d'escompte*, 1806, pamphlet, 8vo, and a *Histoire de la monnaie*, tracing this subject from the earliest ages to the time of Charlemagne, 2 vols. 8vo, 1818. This last work was composed by putting together various papers read at the Institute in 1817 and 1818. As a peer of France, he wrote several reports, ephemeral in character, dealing with subjects of the day.   A. C. f.

GARNIER, JOSEPH (1813-1881), was born at Beuil (*Alpes maritimes*) and died at Paris. Sprung from a family engaged in agriculture, who were comfortably off, he made his way to Paris a short time before the revolution of 1830. He was on the point of entering the banking house of Jacques Laffitte, when, being warmly received by Adolphe Blanqui, who had just taken in hand the direction of the *Superior School of Commerce*, founded in 1820, he determined to enter that model institution, in which he was successively pupil, secretary to the governing body, assistant master, and finally professor. His energy led him to seek a wider field, and he became a contributor in 1835 to the *National*, managed at that time by Armand Carrel, and the scientific bulletin of that journal was entrusted to him. He also contributed, between 1835 and 1839, to the *Dictionnaire du commerce et des marchandises*, published by Guillaumin. He continued his contributions to this work, which became in 1861 the *Dictionnaire universel du commerce et de la navigation*. He attended regularly the lectures of Blanqui in the *Conservatoire des arts et métiers*, and reproduced the course with the assistance of Ad. Blaise (of the Vosges) between November 1836 and August 1838. They formed three volumes 8vo of a collection the fourth volume of which was entirely from the pen of his fellow-labourer. After this he established in 1838 a technical school of trade and manufactures. He had, however, no special aptitude for this work, and on it he expended, fruitlessly, six years of his life. The failure of this effort weighed heavily, from a pecuniary point of view, on the years which followed. But Garnier set himself with courage and determination to wipe out all traces of this unsuccessful step. He returned to his favourite occupations, and in November 1842 founded, with the assistance of other rising economists, the *Société d'économie politique*. In 1843 Garnier commenced a course of lectures on political economy at the

Athénée (rue de Valois), an institution similar in character to the existing polytechnic and philotechnic associations in France. After this date the productions of Garnier's pen were numerous. These works were of various forms, some being his own individual productions, while some were written in concert with others ; but all of them equally were devoted to the explanation of the theory or the practical application of political economy. He edited the *Annuaire de l'économie politique et de la statistique*, which had been established by Messrs. Guillaumin in 1844, from that year till 1855. In 1845 he became the principal editor of the *Journal des économistes* (established in 1842), which post he did not quit till 1855, resuming it in 1866 and retaining it thenceforward till his death. In 1853 he undertook the management of the *Nouveau journal des connaissances utiles*, but gave it up in 1860. We have thus described the principal works which Garnier undertook in connection with others in the course of his busy literary life. We will now revert to those which are exclusively personal to himself. He published, in 1845, the 1st edition of his *Éléments d'économie politique*, the title of which, after the 4th edition in 1860, was altered to the *Traité d'économie politique*, now in its 9th edition (1889). This work alone would have made the name of Garnier famous. It forms in reality an encyclopædia of economic science ; methodical order and deep knowledge of the subject being alike conspicuous in it. And it should be added that the author has shown a perfect power of appreciating those opinions which are opposed to his scientific convictions. Garnier grafted on this treatise other works more or less distinctly connected with it. Thus he wrote his work *Du principe de la population* (1857), the 2nd edition of which appeared in 1885 after the writer's death ; *Les éléments des finances* (1858), which was developed, after the 2nd edition (1862), into *Le traité des finances*, the 4th edition having been published in 1883, also after his death ; followed by *L'Abrégé des éléments de l'économie politique* (1859), a very succinct compendium of his great treatise. This had reached in 1884 its 6th edition. His last work was *Notes et petits traités* (1865), a collection containing among other things the 3rd edition of his *Éléments de statistique*.

It was Garnier to whom Guillaumin entrusted in 1845 the work of annotating his edition of the *Principles of Population* by Malthus. In 1848 Garnier also collected in one volume all the speeches made and the opinions expressed on the subject of the *Droit au travail*, a point of doctrine dear to the socialists. Garnier was able to prove, by a simple and impartial reproduction of the opposite opinions expressed concerning it, that there was no sound basis for this doctrine. Besides these works his *Traité complet d'arithmétique théorique et pratique*, the foundation of which was laid when he commenced work in the school of Blanqui, bears testimony to his constant desire to be of service, in however humble a manner, to the cause of commercial teaching. This work reached its 4th edition in 1887. In 1846 a professorship of political economy was established for him at the *École des ponts et chaussées*. He held this till his death, as he did also the similar professorships at the *École supérieure de commerce*, at the *École commerciale de l'Avenue Trudaine*, and at the *Collège Chaptal*, etc. Garnier's reputation was European. Several of his writings, especially his most important work, his *Treatise*, were translated into Italian, Spanish, and into Russian, and are employed as the basis of economic teaching. He became, 24th May 1873, a member of the Institute (*Académie des sciences morales et politiques*), in succession to Baron Charles Dupin, and in 1876 the department in which he was born elected him a senator. During the last year of his life he became, by seniority, the president of the *Société d'économie politique* without giving up the duties of permanent secretary, an office which he had held since its establishment in 1845.
A. C. f.

GARNISHEE. When a judgment recovered by a creditor against a debtor remains unsatisfied and a debt is due to the debtor from a third party, the creditor can obtain an order from the court requiring the third party to show cause why he should not pay the debt to the creditor. The third party is called the "garnishee" and the order a "garnishee order."

[*Rules of the Supreme Court*, Order, xlv., in the *Annual Practice*, London, 1894.] J. E. C. M.

GARRATI, MARTINO (c. 15th century), born at Lodi, near Milan. He studied under Bartolo da Sassoferrato, the ablest jurisconsult of his time (1313-1359), and was the best lawyer and scholar among his pupils. He wrote on "Money." Cossa gives the date as 1438.

M. Garrati's dissertation was printed with similar treatises in the compilation *De Monetis*, made by M. Boyss (1574), and R. Budelius (1591), and by G. Tesauro (1609).

"All these writers begin by showing a lively appreciation of the intrinsic value (*bonitas intrinseca*) of coins, which leads to an energetic description of the economic disasters involved in their debasement, and to urgent protests against such practices addressed to the heads of states. But after all they are sure that the value of coins is attached to them by arbitrary enactment (*valor impositus*), and end by defending in cases of necessity a resort to the device of debasing the currency."—Luigi Cossa, *An Introduction to the Study of Political Economy*, 1893, tr. by Louis Dyer, M.A., p. 170. A. B.

GARVE, CHRISTIAN (1742-1798), was appointed in 1768 extraordinary professor of philosophy in Leipsic ; owing to his bad health he resigned this office in 1772, and retired to Breslau, his native town, where he resided until the time of his death.

Garve published in 1794-96 the first good German translation of Adam Smith's *Wealth of Nations*, besides several other translations, viz. of Cicero, *De Officiis*, Macfarlane's *Inquiries concerning the Poor*, Aristotle's *Politics*, and Paley's *Moral and Political Philosophy*. He was very fond of translating, and used to say that his own thoughts were only excited when he commented on the thoughts of other writers.

Garve's original (economic) writings comprise various essays on the character of the German peasantry and their relation towards the landlords (*Ueber den Charakter der Bauern und ihr Verhältniss gegen die Gutsherren*, Breslau, 1786), on the relation between moral philosophy and politics (*Abhandlung über die Verbindung der Moral mit der Politik*, 1788), on literary, moral, and social subjects (*Versuche über verschiedene Gegenstände aus der Moral, der Litteratur und dem gesellschaftlichen Leben*, Breslau, 1792-1802), and descriptive contributions on the spirit, character, and government of Frederick II. (*Fragmente zur Schilderung des Geistes, des Charakters und der Regierung Friedrichs II.*, 1788-91).

Garve was a great admirer of Scotch philosophy and Scotch philosophers ; he declares HUTCHESON to be a really great philosopher, and FERGUSON's and SMITH's books to be "real masterpieces" ; still, in accordance with his own views " on the practical dangers of all general maxims," he states his opinion that several of Smith's generalisations only apply to England and France. A man of a quiet and evenly-balanced temper, Garve was adverse to all sudden reforms ; for the improvement of the condition of the German peasantry, he expected more from the better and higher education of the landlords than from sweeping state measures. He distinguishes three stages of industrial development : in the first, all men are equally unskilled, and on nearly the same low level ; in the second, great local differences arise from the fact that progress is always due to individuals ; in the third and higher stage, the tendency is again in favour of equality.

On the subject of trade, Garve expresses the opinion that a completely developed and firmly established trade tends to foster superior morality, because it leaves less room for suspicion and overreaching, as all goods are then exchanged in large quantities and by men thoroughly acquainted with each other's business.

Many of Garve's views are to be found in the introductions which he wrote for his translations ; his original compositions supply useful historical information on the state of Germany towards the close of the last century.

[Roscher, *Geschichte der Nat. Oekonomik in Deutschland*, pp. 603-608.]   E. CA.

GASKELL, P. (19th century), author of

Artisans and Machinery, London, 8vo, 1836, a reprint with some additions of *The Manufacturing Population of England*, London, 8vo, 1833, by the same author. It contains an interesting and apparently trustworthy account of the physical and social condition of the cotton operatives. The writer, as a medical man, speaks with some authority, but is hardly to be followed in his indignation at the regulation of child labour by the FACTORY ACT 1833, or in his prophecy that the time was rapidly approaching when the labour of men would be almost entirely superseded by machinery.

[*The Manufacturing Population of England* is referred to in Plener's *English Factory Legislation*, Eng. trans. London, 1873, 8vo, p. 12 note.]
H. E. E.

GASPARIN, ADRIEN ETIENNE PIERRE, Count of (1783-1862), began life as a soldier, but abandoned the military service in consequence of a wound he received in 1806, and devoted himself to the cultivation of his extensive landed property in the neighbourhood of Avignon. Under Louis Philippe he was successively made a prefect, minister of the interior, and minister of agriculture ; in 1850 he organised, as director, the *Institut Agronomique* of Versailles which was suppressed by the second empire. His principal works are— *Des petites Propriétés considérées dans leurs rapports avec l'Agriculture et le sort des ouvriers* (Paris, 1821) ; *Recueil de Mémoires d'Agriculture et d'Économie Rurale*, Paris, 1829-41, 3 vols., the first volume being a handbook for the owners of property farmed at a rent, the second on *Métayage*, and the third on the introduction of silkworms into Europe,—the *Coup d'œil sur l'Agriculture en Sicile* (1832), and his *Cours d'Agriculture* (5 vols. 1843-49). The last volume of his *Cours d'Agriculture* gives the substance of his views, opinions, and experiences, embracing both theoretical questions, such as the theory of rent of Ricardo, which he attempts to complete, and purely practical questions, such as the calculation of the cost of production in agriculture, the yield of manures, methods of agricultural book-keeping, etc.

M. de Gasparin is one of the most distinguished modern French agriculturists ; his opinions are those of a practical man, looking carefully and objectively at every aspect of a question. Thus, on small and large properties, he writes : " If we have to pronounce on the advisability of large or small properties in a country, let us first remember that, like all other industries, agriculture wants capital, and that the size of an estate must everywhere be proportionate to the average available capital of the tenants (*Cours d'Agriculture*, v. p. 253)."

He considers FARMING as superior to MÉTAYAGE, because "the exact and complete distinction between the interests of the landowner and of the farmer affords the powerful stimulus which has brought cultivation to its degree of perfection. The proprietor is obliged steadily to ameliorate the value of his estate in order to maintain or raise his rent at the expiration of the lease, and the farmer, impelled by competition to pay the highest possible rent, . . . makes use of the largest possible circulating capital and the more advanced methods to secure a profit in his undertaking (*Cours d'Agriculture,* v. p. 302)." Still Gasparin had stated in his *Recueil de Mémoires* (ii. p. 105) that "métayage is not an arbitrary arrangement independent of social conditions, but a necessary contract, wherever the rural population is not in possession of capital," and in his *Cours d'Agriculture,* (v. p. 324) he points out that under this system "both the owner and the tenant have an inheritance to transmit to their family, the former his land, the second his tenure. . . . Inferior to farming as a system of cultivation, *métayage* is superior in many other respects."

Strongly impressed with the importance of the cultivator being sufficiently paid, M. de Gasparin insisted, in his first publication (*Des petites Propriétés*), on the advantage of high agricultural wages : "In countries where the peasant is well fed, high wages are only high in appearance ; their high rate is compensated by the strength and energy of the worker" (p. 9).   E. Ca.

GASPARINO, BARTOLOMEO (17th century), a Bolognese theologian.

Gasparino wrote on the measures by which the government in the pontifical states sought to regulate the corn trade. He devoted the first part of his work to the theory of price, and collected the doctrines of the canonists on the JUSTUM PRETIUM. The altered circumstances of the times induced him to adopt different principles. According to him, price is founded on utility, as well as on supply ; therefore he declares the *legitimate price* to be an untrue price when established without considering such circumstances, and when it is not regulated in such a manner as to bring prosperity both to buyer and seller, replacing to the latter the cost of production.

De legitimo et naturali rerum venalium pretio præsertim circa frumenta, Forolivii, 1634.
                        A. B.

GASSER, SIMON PETER (1676-1745). After having studied at Leipsic and Halle, he lectured on law at Halle, and was called by King Frederick William I. of Prussia to the first chair of economy founded in the Prussian dominions, at the university of Halle, in 1727. It is known how intensely the king was devoted to the economic development of his states, according to the methods of the mercantilists. Gasser's purely practical tendencies, and his disinclination to theory, were in strict concordance with the king's personal aims. His writings on law are all in Latin, but he published in German his introduction to the economic, political, and cameralistic sciences (*Einleitung zu den oekonomischen, politischen, und Kameralwissenschaften,* 1729), although he never went beyond the first part, in which he successively deals with state domains, royal dues, taxes, cattle-breeding and rights of pasture, minor agriculture, peasant services and dues, forestry, etc. The book is dedicated to king Frederick William I., "the great *Œconomus,* and still greater soldier."

Gasser is at heart a matter-of-fact man of his time, with no anticipation of a still remote future. The revenue derived from the state domains and royal dues was to cover the civil expenditure ; taxation proper, the military expenses. He deems the voting of taxes by assemblies quite useless, as the existing services are well acquainted with what the land can bear, and are better able to remonstrate in case of need. Still he is no blind admirer of the king's favourite *Plus* (bonus) policy, as he knows "things which cannot be estimated in money."

He observes of theoretical rules, that in their application a great deal always depends on personal skill and ability, and judiciously lays stress on the fact that the various parts of the kingdom being very unequally developed, each must be dealt with according to the level it has reached. His clear practical insight also leads him to take a discriminating view of the relative merits and demerits of extensive and intensive agriculture : tillage with oxen is cheapest and safest in some places and with horses in others. He has a strong bias in favour of large family estates and trusts (*fideicommissa*) (see FIDEICOMMISSUM), and although he confesses that the peasantry were heavily burdened, he objects to a policy of alleviation of their burdens, and prefers to leave things as they were.

[Roscher, *Gesch. der Nat. Oek. in Deutschland,* pp. 371-376.]   E. Ca.

GAUDIN, MARTIN MICHEL CHARLES. See GAËTA, DUKE OF.

GAUGER, the name by which the exciseman was some years ago not unfrequently known, is a term of considerable antiquity. It occurs in 5 & 6 Edw. VI. ch. 16, and again in 12 Car. II. c. 23 ; so that it was legally recognised as an official title : it was used as such in the old form of commission to officers of excise. It is obviously derived from the duty of gauging or measuring casks of wine or spirits which was first established by 27 Edw. III. (1352). It is found in Scott *passim,* and was used by Burns, but it appears to have fallen into disuse since the passing of the Act 12 Vict. c. 1.
                        C. A. H.

GAUTIER, JULES (1781-1858), was born at Bordeaux and died at Paris. He began life in trade, and became a deputy for the Gironde in 1823. He was one of those who signed the "address of the 221 " at the breaking out of the revolution of 1830. He became a peer of France in 1832, and sub-governor of the Bank of France in 1833. He was minister of finance for some months (from the 31st March to the 11th May

1839), and finally became a senator in 1852. He was the author of a considerable number of official reports, but the work which won him his greatest reputation as a liberal economic thinker—liberal, considering the period when he lived—is his book *Des banques et des institutions de crédit en Amérique et en Europe*, 1839, 1 vol. large 8vo. "A system of free competition is no doubt more favourable than any other to the progress of trade. The absence of every fetter and restraint, absolute liberty in fact, marks the soil in which commerce grows the quickest and flourishes the best. It is especially to prudent self-interest that recourse must be had to avoid the dangers with which the course of credit is beset." It was a deputy-governor of the Bank of France who wrote these sentences, and during the time when he held that office.   A. C. f.

GAVELKIND. Before the Norman Conquest this term was applied to lands which paid GAFOL or rent, either in money or in kind. The Norman Conquest generally introduced feudal tenures into England. But in some parts of the country land is still held by the customs of gavelkind. In the county of Kent this survival of old customs is the rule, and land is held to be gavel-kind unless it can be proved either that it was never subject to this tenure, or that it has been disgavelled by custom or otherwise. Outside Kent this tenure is a rare exception. The chief peculiarities of gavelkind are as follows :—(1) if the holder died intestate his lands passed to all his sons as co-heirs, without any preference for the eldest ; (2) the tenant can alienate at the age of fifteen ; (3) estates were deviseable by will at a date when other lands are not subject to testamentary disposition ; (4) lands never escheated on conviction of felony.

[Elton, *Tenures of Kent.*—Digby, *History of the Law of Real Property.*]   R. L.

GAZETTE. Announcements of an official nature are, in England, made in the *London Gazette ;* in Scotland, in the *Edinburgh Gazette ;* in Ireland, in the *Dublin Gazette.* Such announcements are evidence as to any matters in which the crown or the government is concerned (see King *v.* Holt, 5 Term Reports, 436), but in the absence of express statutory provisions, they are not in themselves evidence of matters concerning private interests only. As to the dissolution of partnerships, etc., the Partnership Act, 1890, provides (§ 36) that "an advertisement in the *London Gazette* as to a firm whose principal place of business is in England or Wales, in the *Edinburgh Gazette* as to a firm whose principal place of business is in Scotland, and in the *Dublin Gazette* as to a firm whose principal place of business is in Ireland, shall be notice as to persons who had not dealings with the firm before the date of the dissolution or change so advertised."

As to the bankruptcy proceedings in England, it is enacted by the Bankruptcy Act 1883, § 132, that "the production of a copy of the *London Gazette* containing any notice of a receiving order, or of an order adjudging a debtor bankrupt, shall be conclusive evidence in all legal proceedings of the order having been duly made, and of its date."   E. S.

GEBUR (modern *boor*), an Anglo-Saxon term for a villein. The *Rectitudines Singularum Personarum*, of the 10th century, describes him as doing service, week-work, and paying rent (*gafol* or *gablum*). Vinogradoff thinks that in Norman times the word was inexactly used and becoming obsolete (see GABLATORES).

[Seebohm, *English Village Community.*—Kemble, *Saxons in England*, vol. i.—Vinogradoff, *Villainage in England.*]   E. G. P.

GEE, JOSHUA, a merchant, known only by his writings on commerce and manufactures, published 1725-50. In these he expressed a keen anxiety to see the government of Great Britain, in the face of decaying agriculture, declining woollen industry, and Gallicised tastes, intervene more actively to foster and regulate trade and manufacture ; that this kingdom is capable of raising within itself, and its colonies, materials for employing all our poor in those manufactures, which we now import from such of our neighbours who refuse the admission of ours. Influenced by Petty, he gave a descriptive analysis of England's foreign trade and also an historical sketch of legislation affecting wool. He proposed that the export of wool be absolutely prohibited, but in a second pamphlet expressed a preference, in order to prevent over-production and increase of smuggling, for a limited export regulated by a system of local registration. A reply, in general terms, may be read in Defoe's *A Plan of the English Commerce*, pt. ii., with some account of the commodities each country we trade with take from us, and what we take from them, with observations on the balance.

Gee was no mercantilist of the somewhat mythical sort who were supposed to care only for the retention and increase of bullion as such. His great solicitude was to see agriculture and manufactures occupying with profit all the available manual stock in England, a considerable part of which in his day was infesting town and country as beggars and vagabonds. He held this could be at least more promptly and efficiently brought about by protective legislation. The *specific* motive for immediate legislation lay he thought in the fact of Louis XIV. having compelled "The wearing of French manufactures" in France, "which before used to be supplied from England, and turned the trade so much against us"; also in the effect produced by the peace between England and France early in the 18th century, namely, a great influx of English into France, and a consequent diffusion of taste for French fashions and French goods in England.

Gee was a contributor to the *British Merchant*, and is the author of the following :—

The Trade and Navigation of Great Britain considered ; showing that the surest way for a nation to increase in riches is to prevent the importation of such foreign commodities as may be raised at home, London, 1729, 8vo.—*An Impartial Enquiry into the Importance and Present State of the Woollen Manufactures of Great Britain, as likewise the Improvements they are capable of receiving*, Lincoln and London, 1742, 8vo.—*The Grazier's Advocate, or Free Thoughts of Wool and the Woollen Trade*, London, 1742, 8vo.

C. A. F.

GEIJER, ERIC GUSTAV (1783-1847), an eminent Swedish historian and poet ; appointed professor of history at the university of Upsala in 1817. His principal writings are *Annals of the Kingdom of Sweden* (*Svea Rikes Häfder*, Upsala, 1825), and *History of the Swedish People* (*Svenska Folkets Historia*, Örebrö, 1832) ; neither of them brought down to his own time. The latter has been translated into English by J. H. Turner (London, 1845). Geijer wrote besides many political and philosophical essays, especially in the *Litteratur-bladet*, a monthly journal edited by himself (1838-39). A series of articles in this journal, on *The Poor-laws and their Bearing on Society*, have been reprinted in English, and published separately (Stockholm, 1840). The "chief purport" of the treatise "is to vindicate the freedom of labour." Geijer traces the causes of the growth of poverty from ancient times, and deals especially with the poor laws of Sweden, but poverty in England is also discussed, and the Poor Law of 1834 is favourably criticised.

[Turner, Introduction to *History of the Swedes*, translated by J. H. Turner, London, 1845 ; Geijer, *Minnen*, Upsala, 1834.]   R. H. H.

GEMELLI, FRANCESCO (1700), a Piedmontese eclectic writer.

He considered agriculture the most important industry in every country. He agreed with FILANGIERI in theory ; he did not go far enough to follow him in complete free trade, though he was willing to admit free trade in corn at home, and to allow a perfect free trade in corn to avoid famine in Europe ; but, since an agreement on this point is not probable, he thinks that every sovereign should study the peculiar conditions of his own state. Hence he praises the reforms in Tuscany since it has access to the open sea ; he praises the policy followed in England, because the price of corn there is regularly higher than elsewhere.

Rifiorimento della Sardegna, proposto nel miglioramento di sua agricoltura, Turin, 1776.

A. B.

GÉNÉRALITÉ. In 1551 the French king, Henri II., appointed sixteen *trésoriers généraux* to supervise the collection of taxes throughout the kingdom. The district assigned to each of these officials was called a *généralité*. When Richelieu set himself in the 17th century to

break down the traditional independence of the provinces, he made use of the *généralités* as the administrative districts of his intendants. Henceforward, until the creation of departments in 1790, the district thus designated was the chief unit of local administration, and when the states-general were summoned for the last time in 1788, the deputies were elected from each *généralité*, instead of from the *bailliage* or *sénéchaussée*. In the 18th century France contained twenty-six *généralités*, and there were also seven intendancies in provinces which had been added to France since the time of Richelieu.

[Gasquet, *Précis des institutions politiques et sociales de l'ancienne France.*]   R. L.

GENOA, BANK OF. See BANKS.

GENOVESI, ANTONIO (1712-1769), born near Salerno and died at Naples, took holy orders in 1736. In 1741 he taught metaphysics at the university of Naples. He was intimately acquainted with Bartolomeo Intieri, who induced him to follow BROGGIA and GALIANI in the study of economics ; and when, in 1754, by the advice of Intieri and with funds liberally supplied by him, the teaching of economics, then termed mechanics and commerce, was established at Naples, Genovesi was called to the chair. He was "the most distinguished and the most moderate of all Italian mercantilists. . . . Commerce was for him not an end only, but also a means by which the products of industry at large were brought to the right market. He, moreover, distinguished between useful commerce which exported manufactured goods and brought back in return raw material, and harmful commerce which exported raw material and imported foreign goods ; he also insisted that useful commerce calls rather for liberty than for protection, while upon harmful commerce the strictest embargo should be laid, or at least it should as far as possible be bound hand and foot " (Cossa, *Introduction to Pol. Ec.*, translation, p. 235).

These ideas, neither new nor original even in his time, were maintained by Genovesi in many of his works, and brought together, but without any systematic order, in his *Lezioni di Commercio ossia di Economia Civile* (Napoli, 1765, e. ii. ediz. 1768-70, 2 vols.). Though the *Lezioni* do not form a regular treatise, they contain the author's opinions on the mercantilist system and the most important principles of economics, which he terms *Civile* "*la scienza che abbraccia le regole per rendere la sottoposta nazione popolata, potente, saggia, polita*" (the science which embraces the laws which make a nation populous, powerful, wise, and cultured), limiting thus the science to the increase of population and the production of wealth.

As to population, Genovesi follows the mistaken principle of his times, exaggerating the advantage of a large population, proposing that government should encourage marriages by granting privileges and honours. He says that the population ought not only to be numerous but supplied with comforts, and he sees the relation between population and means of subsistence or production of wealth.

As a writer he is a mercantilist, though he does not regard money as the only form of riches; he says that the wealth of a nation is quite apart from the quantity of money treasured up.

He derives the idea of value from demand, distinguishing different degrees of demand according to their abstract importance in several categories, maintaining that a thing which satisfies a want repeatedly has a higher value than what satisfies only a few wants or the same only sometimes (*puo soddisfare ad un bisogno più volte, ha maggior prezzo che non quella, la quale o non puo soddisfare che pochi bisogni o al medesimo qualche volta*). What is able to satisfy a great want is of more value than what satisfies a small want (*una cosa fatta a soddisfare il maggior bisogno si apprezza più che quella la quale non è fatta che a soddisfare ad un minore*); and further he asserts that the quality of things influences the value. Graziani (*Storia della teoria del valore in Italia*, Milano, 1889, p. 108) justly remarks that in this Genovesi approaches the important question which GALIANI answered : namely, why do luxuries generally cost more than necessaries ? In this he is obliged to have recourse to the element of scarcity, a line of argument which he does not know how to reconcile with those previously mentioned. Genovesi's want of originality is obvious, as F. Ferrara has shown (*Bibl. dell' Econo.*, 1ª. S. vol. iii. Introduz.) in contradistinction to the exaggerated opinion which Bianchini held respecting him (*La scienza del ben vivere sociale*), since the SOCIALISTS OF THE CHAIR persist, erroneously, in considering him as a precursor of their opinions. This tendency is also attributed to Genovesi, as well as to BECCARIA, VERRI, and ROMAGNOSI by the French socialist B. MALON ; which is a further example of the errors of the socialists in their historical criticism of political economy.

"According to Gobbi the Neapolitans FORTUNATO (1760), Strongoli (1783), and VENTURI (1798), belonged to Genovesi's school, and then there was also ZANON of Udine (*Lettere*, 1756-67), Todeschi of Ferrara (*Opere*, 1784) and Marcello Marchesini of Istria (*Saggio d'Econ. Pol.*, Napoli, 1793)."—Cossa, *Introduction to Pol. Ec.*, translation, p. 236.

Besides his philosophical works, Genovesi wrote : *Ragionamento intorno all' agricoltura, con applicazione al Regno di Napoli* 1769 (Scrittori classici italiani di Ec. Pol. Custodi, p. ii. vol. ix.).—*Altro Ragionamento*, ed. (ibid.).—*Ragionamento sul commercio in generale* 1750 (id. vol. x.).—*Ragionamento sulle manifatture* (ibid.).—*Ragionamento sullo spirito della Pubblica Economia* (ibid.).—*Digressioni Economiche* (ibid.).

[For the works of Ferrara, see A. Bertolini, *La Vita e il Pensiero di Francesco Ferrara*, 1895.]　　　A. B.

GENTLEMAN, TOBIAS (fl. 1614), was "a fisherman's son by the sea-side and spent his youthful time at sea about fisher affairs." He published *England's Way to win Wealth, and to employ Ships and Marriners*, etc. London, 1614, 8vo, Reprinted in the *Harleian Miscellany* (1809), vol. viii. This pamphlet was the result of a conference between the author and John Keymor, whose *Observation made upon the Dutch Fishing about the year 1601*, was printed from the original manuscript, for Sir Edward Ford, in 1664. *England's Way*, etc. evidently owes much to Keymor's investigations. It contains a good description of Dutch fishing in English waters and of the ports on the east coast. The author urges the importance of developing the herring fishery, and attributes the prosperity of the Dutch to their activity in this respect. His tract is frequently quoted with approval by 17th century writers, *e.g.* MALYNES, who gives an abridgment of it (*Lex Mercatoria*, c. xlvii.).　　　W. A. S. H.

GENTZ, FRIEDRICH VON (1764-1832), an eminent German publicist, was born at Breslau. His father was an official of the mint there ; through his mother he was connected with the family of the minister Ancillon. He studied at the Joachimsthal Gymnasium at Berlin, to which city his father had been transferred, and afterwards at Königsberg, where he came under the influence of KANT. In 1786 he was appointed secretary of the general directory, and afterwards became Kriegsrath. His life at Berlin seems to have been for some time a dissipated and aimless one ; an illness led him to change his course and follow more serious pursuits ; and the outbreak of the French Revolution still further awakened his intellectual activity. He was an ardent admirer and well-wisher of the Revolution till repelled by its excesses, when he became its determined opponent, and a warm advocate of the English constitutional system. This change in his opinions is indicated by his translation—a masterpiece in its kind—of Burke's *Reflections* and of the anti-revolutionary writings of Mallet du Pan and Mounier. He discussed political events and handled financial questions with great ability in several journals—amongst others in the *Neue Deutsche Monatschrift*, a periodical which he founded, and for some years conducted. He also published in 1797 a German version of D'IVERNOIS' work on French financial administration, and in 1801 (in French) an *Essai sur l'état actuel de l'administration des finances et de la richesse nationale de la Grande Bretagne*. The economic views in favour of free industry, which he had learned from Adam Smith, are exhibited in his letter (1797) on the accession of Frederick William III., which is said to have offended the king and hindered Gentz's promotion. He was believed to be in the pay of the British Government, as he warmly applauded their policy ; but there can be no doubt that the writings by which he earned their gifts expressed his genuine convictions. What made such pecuniary aid almost necessary to him was the extremely expensive and wasteful management of his private affairs, which kept him in difficulties all his life. He had domestic troubles, due, it is said, chiefly to his own conduct ; and, such advancement as was suitable to his powers being no longer open to him in Prussia, he left that country in 1802, and, after residing some months in Dresden, where he entered into relations with Metternich, went in the same year to Vienna, where he became a member of the imperial council. Before settling finally in Austria he paid a visit to England, made the personal acquaintance of Pitt and other leading politicians there, and obtained a regular pension from the British government. We cannot here follow in detail the course of his general political action, which is indissolubly connected with the history of Germany. Up to 1812 he fought, as a literary volunteer, side by side with STEIN as a relentless enemy of Napoleon and his system, and an earnest and uncompromising advocate of German independence. He drew up a number of vigorous and telling memoirs directed against the oppressive policy of France, which, however, for a long time failed to rouse the energies of the Austrian court or to impress upon it the necessity of joint action with Prussia. All through the course of the wars with Napoleon, and in the negotiations which followed them, his ready and powerful pen was in frequent requisition, and all the most important state-papers of the allies were his work. After the peace he exercised much influence on the internal politics of Austria; his tendencies then became retrograde, and he contradicted the principles of his earlier years. He seems to have been affrighted by the growth of revolutionary ideas, and especially by the excesses of democratic journalism; and devoted himself to the support of existing governments, and the maintenance of the restored states-system of Europe. He was employed to draw up the protocols at many congresses of princes and ministers, and became the favoured and richly-rewarded champion of reigning powers, and a resolute antagonist of the spirit of the age. But he felt that this spirit would be too strong for all opposing forces, and towards the end of his career endeavoured to reconcile the principles of legitimacy with the dogma of the sovereignty of the people. To the end he remained true to the liberal economic doctrines he had imbibed from the *Wealth of Nations*.

[Editions of selected writings of Gentz have been published by W. Weich, 5 vols. 1836-38, and by G. Schlesier, 5 vols. 1838-40. His Correspondence with Johannes v. Müller and others has been edited by Prokesch-Osten, Schlesier, and Mendelssohn-Bartholdy. The last-named has also published a biography of Gentz, 1867. In addition to such of his writings as have been already named may be mentioned his *Politische Parodien*, 1799; *Ueber den Ursprung und Charakter des Kriegs gegen die französische Rev.*, 1801; and *Fragmente aus der Geschichte des politischen Gleichgewichts in Europa*, 1804; which last, for the glowing patriotism which it breathes, has been compared to Fichte's *Reden an die deutsche Nation*.] J. K. I.

GEOGRAPHY, COMMERCIAL (CONNECTED WITH GREAT BRITAIN). During the 19th century the world has been passing through an economic revolution utterly without precedent. In spite of the commercial enterprise shown by various European nations in bringing distant countries into touch with each other, up to the end of the 18th century and even during the earlier part of the 19th century each country remained for the most part self-sufficing as regards the chief necessities of existence. The wants of the great mass of slowly expanding populations were supplied through the medium of a vast number of local markets, serving as depôts for the corn and raw material for clothing produced in the surrounding districts. Agriculture and home industries of every description were carried on side by side; it was only the finer species of manufactured articles that found an outlet in foreign markets. Prices varied largely in different districts, according to the varying supplies of the local market. Proximity to a sea-coast, or navigable river, or canal, enlarged the area of supply, but, as a rule, each locality produced what it required for ordinary consumption, and the growth of population was necessarily limited by the enormous difficulty, in the existing state of communications, of drawing its food supplies from a distance. Foreign goods, such as the precious metals, tea, sugar, tobacco, spices, wine, silks, and muslins, which might bear the cost of expensive transport, formed part of the market wares of every European country which had distant commercial dealings, but such foreign products formed but a small portion of the local trade compared with the indigenous products. Even in the United Kingdom, where there were greater facilities for internal movement than in the rest of Europe, land-transport met with almost insurmountable obstacles. A broad-wheeled waggon drawn by eight horses, and attended by two men, took three weeks to carry four tons of goods between London and Edinburgh (*Wealth of Nations*, bk. i. ch. iii.), while a coach took a week or more to go the same distance. Under such conditions, prevailing even in the most progressive countries, stationariness of production and population alike remained the prevailing feature of the economic world. During the present century the ever-increasing application of steam-power to industry has tended more and more to transform the old condition of things; by facilitating the transport of the heavier agricultural products it has brought the interior of every country into touch with the coast, and therefore extended the whole range of commercial dealings. Chicago, for instance, at a distance of 4000 miles, is now much nearer to London than Edinburgh was sixty years ago, and the carriage of a quarter of wheat from Delhi to Liverpool costs now only a little more than half a sovereign. The local market for all the ordinary necessities of life has more and more become part and parcel of the world's market. The poorest British household may now find its wants satisfied by every quarter of the globe. Its flour may have come from India, its meat from Canada or New Zealand, and the raw material of its clothes from America or Australia.

In effecting this great economic revolution Great Britain has been the chief agency. Her prolonged struggle with the naval and military forces of Europe, organised by the genius of Napoleon, left her burdened with an enormous national debt, but it left her mistress of the seas, able to appropriate the results of the commercial enterprise of Europe, and to augment it with an energy all her own. Without the risk of any European rivalry, she was allowed a free hand in consolidating her Indian Empire, developing her Canadian colony, founding new settlements in Australia and New Zealand, and paving the way for an African protectorate. During the last seventy years she has made good use of her great mineral resources—coal and iron—to establish markets in every quarter of the world. The area of the British Empire, including dependencies, colonies, and spheres of influence, is now estimated by Mr. J. Scott Keltie at about 10,000,000 square miles, very nearly one-fifth of the whole land area of the globe. It is nearly three times the size of Europe, one and a half million square miles larger than the whole of the Russian empire in Europe and Asia, ten times the size of the German empire at home and abroad ; 8 million square miles more than the whole of the French dominions, and just about a million less than the area of Africa. This immense territory is inhabited by something like 350,000,000 souls, embracing almost every type of humanity, about the same population as that of all Europe, and constituting from one-fourth to one-fifth of the population of the world. Its products are of infinite variety, and the only supplies which at present its population must draw largely from foreign countries are corn and cotton. The trade of the empire is valued at about £1,200,000,000, or just one half of the trade of all other civilised countries put together. Of this total the trade of the United Kingdom is £740,000,000, while £460,000,000 is to be credited to the empire beyond our shores. Of these £460,000,000, about £170,000,000 belong to the 7,000,000 odd square miles of colonies proper, with a population of about 10,000,000, mostly whites ; and £290,000,000 to the tropical and sub-tropical possessions covering an area of only about 2,700,000 square miles, but with a population of 300,000,000, chiefly coloured. In order to protect the carriage of commodities that circulate between the most distant portions of this widely-scattered empire, Great Britain has found it necessary to hold certain points of vantage along the main sea-routes. Along the quickest route to our Indian empire are to be found the strongly-fortified stations of Gibraltar,

Malta, and Aden, the latter garrisoned by Indian troops. The magnitude of our commercial interests in this direction is proved by the fact that the transit trade of Malta amounts to nearly £50,000,000, and that, out of the total number of ships (3389) that passed through the Suez Canal in 1890, 2522 were British, the gross tonnage being respectively 9,749,129, and 7,438,682. The danger to which these interests are exposed from the hostility of Russia or the rivalry of France, has been held to justify the occupation of Cyprus and Egypt.

In India and Ceylon, British shipping has the protection of Bombay and Trincomalee, and in a lesser degree of Kurrachee, Colombo, and Calcutta ; and it is proposed to add Rangoon to the number of fortified stations. Farther east, Singapore commands the entrance to the Chinese seas, while in those seas Hong-Kong forms the central stronghold of British power. If we take the alternative route to the east round Africa, a similar series of fortified stations at convenient distances from each other is to be seen,—Sierra Leone, St. Helena, Cape Town, and Mauritius. The importance of Cape Town to British commerce cannot be over-estimated. It has been calculated by Lord Brassey that £90,000,000 of commerce centres at or passes this point every year, including £20,000,000 of outward trade to Australia, £13,000,000 to the Cape itself, and portions of the Indian, Chinese, and other eastern trade. But if, as might well happen in the event of a European war, the Suez Canal were to be closed, at least £150,000,000, and possibly £200,000,000 of British trade would be forced to go round the Cape. At the converging points of the two great eastern routes we find the important Australasian stations of King George's Sound, Thursday Island, Melbourne, Sydney, and Auckland. Going westward across the Atlantic we find fortified stations in Halifax, Bermuda, St. Lucia, and Jamaica, and farther south the Falkland Islands, lying on the route round Cape Horn. In the Pacific, Esquimault and Vancouver are destined to form the basis of protection for the new route opened up to the east by the completion of the Canadian Pacific railway, while the Fiji Islands, supplied by nature with excellent harbours, lie across the path of ships sailing either from British Columbia or round South America to the Antipodes.

The existence of these well-selected stations on all the chief lines of communication is the greatest element of strength in the naval supremacy of Great Britain, and upon their safety in time of war would depend the preservation of British commerce. From these stations would have to be drawn those supplies of coal without which no modern fleet can keep the sea for more than a few weeks. And inasmuch as Great Britain has, in all the ports of the world directly under the control of its government, adopted the policy of free-trade, and is favoured by no differential tariffs, even where its self-governing colonies have adopted a protective system, it may fairly claim, while guarding its own commerce, to be guarding that of the world at large.

To appreciate the absolute dependence of Great Britain on its commercial relations with the rest of the world, we have only to look at the economic features of its existence. Fifty years ago one-third of its working population consisted of agricultural labourers and one-third of artisans. Now only an eighth are agricultural labourers, and three-fourths are artisans. As a consequence of this change, Great Britain can no longer feed itself. She has now (1894) to draw about three-quarters of her supplies of corn and flour from abroad. The United States, Canada, India, Russia, and even Australia and New Zealand, send her people corn, maize, and rice. It is the same with her meat supplies. It has been calculated that the quantity of meat food at any time in the United Kingdom is only sufficient for three months. Hundreds of thousands of live cattle and many hundred thousands of tons of meat have to be imported into the country every year from across the sea, the United States, Canada, South America, Australia and New Zealand; even the home supply of eggs, butter, and cheese has to be supplemented from abroad; while the ordinary comforts of every breakfast-table—tea, coffee, cocoa, and sugar, are entirely supplied from each of the four great continents. For these articles of daily existence alone Great Britain has to pay over £150,000,000 to the rest of the world, and if she were cut off from the outside world for even a few days, every household would feel the pressure of a sudden rise in prices. But not merely does Great Britain depend for its daily food on foreign supplies; it largely depends on the same source for its daily wage. With the exception of coal and iron, the raw material of British industry comes chiefly from abroad. Wool is imported to the value of over £26,000,000 from Australia, New Zealand, Africa, and South America; cotton to the value of £40,000,000 from America, India, and Egypt; wood to the value of £14,000,000 from Canada, Russia, Scandinavia, and Honduras; and flax, hemp, and jute, to the value of £10,000,000, from Russia, India, and other countries. But it is not sufficient for Great Britain to import food and the raw material of her industries; she has to have access to markets for her manufactured products. Nearly one half of the British exports consists of more or less manufactured fabrics. The export of cotton manufactures reaches £70,000,000, of woollen manufactures £24,000,000, and of linen and jute £8,000,000; of metals, hardware, and cutlery the exports amount to about £38,000,000, and of machinery to over £15,000,000.

The trade of the United Kingdom itself, excluding exports of foreign and colonial produce, may (1893) be divided into four great portions:—

	Imports.	Exports.
	£	£
With Europe	181,000,000	84,000,000
,, United States . .	97,000,000	32,000,000
,, British Possessions .	96,000,000	87,000,000
,, Other foreign countries	46,000,000	60,000,000
	420,000,000	263,000,000

Great Britain's export trade with Europe is to a very great extent made up of woollen, cotton, and linen manufactures, metals—especially iron and copper—coal, and machinery. To a lesser degree she sends leather, hardware, and chemicals. On the other hand her European imports show every possible variety. She takes corn from Russia, Germany, Austria, and Roumania; cattle and meat from Belgium, Holland, Denmark, and Germany; butter, poultry, and eggs, from Belgium, Denmark, Sweden, France, and Italy; cheese and milk from Switzerland. From France, Germany, Italy, Spain, and Portugal she takes sugar, wine, oil, and fruit; of the raw material of industry she imports flax, hemp, and wool from Belgium and Russia, timber from Norway, Sweden, Germany, and Russia; lead and iron from Belgium and Spain; of manufactured fabrics she takes silk and woollen from France, Belgium, and the Netherlands.

The commerce between Great Britain and the United States is much less varied in nature than that between Great Britain and Europe. It is almost entirely the exchange of manufactured articles for food or the raw material of industry. The United States sent Great Britain, in 1890, corn and cotton to the value respectively of about £20,000,000 and £31,000,000 and meat (dead and alive) to the value of about £22,000,000. She took in exchange iron, cotton, linen, woollen, flax, hemp, and jute manufactures. The only articles of food she takes from Great Britain are delicacies such as biscuits, pickles, sauces, and marmalade, though she imports sugar and tea from British possessions. The total export and import trade of the United States now amounts to about £300,000,000 sterling, of which about £130,000,000 is with the United Kingdom.

But the trade between the United Kingdom and the United States, though far exceeding the proportions of that between the United Kingdom and any one foreign country, is itself largely surpassed by that between Great Britain and the British empire, amounting to over £180,000,000. At the head of the list stands British India. Great Britain finds there her largest market for cotton goods and yarn, of which the average import amounts to over £20,000,000.

Iron, copper, and machinery make up another £7,000,000, out of the total value of British imports of about £33,000,000. From India Great Britain takes in exchange cotton, jute, seeds, tea, coffee, rice, and indigo. In 1891 one-fifth of the foreign wheat came from India, and of the tea, which used to come almost entirely from China, more than two-thirds came in 1890 from India and .Ceylon. Of the total trade of India more than half is with the United Kingdom. The total trade of Ceylon is £10,000,000, and the British share is about £3,000,000. The chief exports, besides tea, are coffee, cinchona, plumbago, and cocoa-nut products.

The trade of Straits Settlements—consisting of Singapore, Penang, and Malacca—is largely a transit trade, but there is also a considerable local trade in the exchange of tin, spices, cutch, gambier, gutta-percha, with the cotton and iron goods of the United Kingdom. The total trade amounts to about £60,000,000 sterling annually, but of this England's share is only between £8,000,000 and £9,000,000. The total number of vessels that cleared at the ports during 1890, exclusive of native craft, was 8110, with a tonnage of 4,859,720 tons. Hong-Kong is the farthest point east in the British Empire, and is the great centre of British commerce with China and Japan. Its trade amounts to about £6,000,000 and of that about £4,000,000 is with Great Britain. The trade of Hong Kong, like that of Singapore, is chiefly a transit trade carried on by over 4000 vessels and over 24,000 junks.

The commercial intercourse of China is mainly with the United Kingdom and the British colonies, and is carried on through the twenty-three trading ports of the Empire. The exports to and imports from Great Britain amounted in 1890 to over £11,000,000, the former being chiefly made up of tea and silk, and the latter of cotton and woollen goods. The import of cotton goods from Bombay is rapidly growing, while that of Indian opium is falling off, though it still remains, next to cotton, the chief import, valued at about £6,000,000. The trade of Japan is of a somewhat similar character to that of China, but its exports are rather more varied. It takes over £4,000,000 of cotton and woollen fabrics, iron, and machinery from Great Britain, but it only exports to it about £1,000,000. Its chief export trade is with North America, and is likely to increase with the development of the sea route to Vancouver.

Turning south, we come to the tropical British dependency of North Borneo, administered by a chartered company. Its chief products are sago, rice, gums, coffee, pepper, gambier, gutta-percha, tapioca, and tobacco. Adjacent to it on the north-west are the sultanate of Brunei and the district of Sarawak, which, in addition to their specially tropical products, are said to be rich in minerals, especially coal. Off the coast of Borneo lies the little island of Labuan, which seems likely to become an important naval station in the East Indian Archipelago. Last among our purely tropical settlements in the eastern seas must be mentioned New Guinea, with its still undeveloped resources, waiting the help of coloured labour.

Passing across the Pacific we find many islands belonging to the British empire, but at present of no great commercial value. There is a small trade in copra, guano, sugar, and fruit, and there is likely to be a great increase of transit trade, when the new sea-route between Van-couver and Australia and New Zealand is more frequented by steamships. In view of the probability of Central America being pierced some day by a canal, our West India possessions are admirably placed for sharing in the transit trade that would spring up. Though, owing to the competition of the beet-sugar of Europe, these islands are not as valuable as they used to be, yet they have lately made a fresh start in experimenting with cocoa, cinchona, tea, and fibres, and their trade with the United States and Canada in fruit is rapidly developing. The total trade of British West India amounts to about £12,000,000, and half of it is with Great Britain. On the South American continent there is only one piece of country under the British flag—British Guiana, and it is the only part of South America secure against disorder. Its trade, similar to that of the West Indies, amounts to about three and a half millions sterling — two millions with the mother country. With the whole of South America the trade of Great Britain was in 1890 about £40,000,000, but recent disturbances have greatly reduced its value. The chief exports are animal products and wheat, in exchange for cottons, woollens, iron, and machinery.

We come last to the three great colonial settlements of the British empire in the proper sense of the term—Canada, Australasia, and South Africa. Canada covers an area of three and a half million square miles, but the northern portions of it can hardly be regarded as habitable by people of European extraction. Its population is about 5,000,000, and since the opening up of the western portions it has been rapidly growing, swollen as it is by an annual addition of about 80,000 to 100,000 emigrants. Its total trade has now reached the amount of £43,000,000, Great Britain and the United States sharing in it about equally. Its chief exports are timber, cattle, sheep, agricultural produce, fish, and minerals. Its imports consist largely of manufactured articles, of which it took in 1890 from Great Britain about £6,000,000. Off the coast of Canada is the oldest British colony, Newfoundland. It has only one industry of any commercial value, and that is fishing. Its exports are almost entirely marine produce, amounting to over £1,000,000 sterling. Compared with Canada, the commercial development of Australasia has been remarkably rapid. With a population of only 3,600,000 it has a trade of £126,000;000 of which about £50,000,000 is with the United Kingdom. The British imports into Australasia embrace nearly every article of home manufacture, iron (wrought and unwrought), hardware, cutlery, woollen goods, apparel and haberdashery, cotton goods, machinery, paper, and beer. In exchange Australasia exports gold, wool, meat, wheat, hides, sugar, cotton, butter, and wine. Australasia has become the great supplier of wool for the great textile industries of England and Scotland. Of the total imports of wool into the United Kingdom in 1890 amounting to 633,028,131 lbs., 418,771,604 lbs. came from Australasia.

Africa, though on its northern shores for centuries past taking an important share in the commerce of the Mediterranean, is still for the most part undeveloped. Settlements had been made by various European nations along its western and eastern coasts, but only of late years has any attempt been made to open up its interior. In the scramble that has ensued Great Britain has secured nearly all that portion which seems suited for European colonisation. We have now the whole region round the middle and lower Niger. We have four colonies on the Gold and West Coasts with a trade of about two and a half millions, all the great region south of the Zambesi with the exception of the Transvaal and the Orange Free State, and an extensive territory along the east coast that gives us access to the great lake system. We "protect" Zanzibar, and we occupy Egypt. The total trade of the continent is estimated at £90,000,000 sterling, and Britain's share at £40,000,000. Of this trade the most important portion is that of the territories along the Mediterranean shore. The exports and imports of Egypt amount to about £20,000,000 ; the export of cotton and cotton seed together amounts to about £8,000,000 ; wheat, rice, beans, sugar, and wool making up the other chief commodities. The trade of Tunis, Algeria, and Morocco makes up another £20,000,000, cereals, wine, wool, sheep, and cattle being the chief exports. Thus nearly half the commerce of Africa is through Mediterranean ports ; of the remaining £40,000,000 to £50,000,000 of trade, £30,000,000 belong to Africa south of the Zambesi—gold, diamonds, wool, hides, ostrich feathers, and sugar being the chief exports. The rest of the trade on the east and west coasts may be roughly estimated at £10,000,000. Great Britain's share in the whole of African commerce may be estimated at about 45 per cent, France comes next with 26 per cent, while Germany, Portugal, Spain, Turkey, Russia, and other countries share the rest between them. Of all this vast commerce circulating between

every country in the world, England is the centre. Not merely does she pass through her ports a much larger proportion of that commerce than any other country, but her ships carry more commerce than those of all the other countries of the world put together. She has also supplied most of the capital for developing railway communications in India, Canada, South Africa, and Australasia, and thereby actually brought vast territories into touch with commercial enterprise. England has no doubt had great natural advantages to start with. Her climate has facilitated continuous work, her soil has given her mineral wealth, and her insular position has safeguarded her, but it is the intelligence, energy, and courage of her people that have won for her a commercial supremacy unique in the world's history (see COMMERCE, BRITISH and COMMERCE).

[Lord Brassey's *Naval Annual.*—Cotton, J. S., and Payne, E. T., *Colonies and Dependencies*, in English Citizen Series.—Dilke, Sir C. W., *Problems of Greater Britain.*—Keltie, J. S., *Applied Geography.*—Mahan, Capt. A. T., *The influence of sea power upon History* and *The influence of sea power upon French Revolution and Empire.*—Parkin, G. R., *Imperial Federation.*—Payne, E. J., *History of European Colonies.*—Lucas, *Hist. Geography of the British Colonies*, 1887, etc.—Gonner, *Commercial Geography.*—Reclus, E., *Geographie Universelle.*—Seeley, Prof. J., *Expansion of England.*—*Statesman's Year Book.*—Strachey, Sir J., *India.*—G. G. Chisholm, *Commercial Geography*, 3rd ed., 1892.—Zehden, *Commercial Geography*, tr. F. Muirhead, 1888.]   A. K. C.

GEOMETRICAL RATIO OR PROGRESSION. Three or more quantities are in geometrical progression when, as in cases of sums of money at compound interest, each after the first is equal to the preceding one multiplied by some constant factor. For example, 1, 3, 9, 27, when the constant factor or "common ratio," as it is called, is 3, and 100, 101, $102\frac{1}{100}$, $103\frac{301}{10000}$, when the common ratio is $1\frac{1}{100}$, are in geometrical progression. Malthus, who maintained that food could only be increased in an ARITHMETICAL RATIO (*q.v.*), observed that since any number of pairs of human beings can each have as many children as one pair, the population of a country, if it were regulated by procreative power alone, would be multiplied in each successive equal interval of time by a constant factor, or, to put it more shortly, would "increase in a geometrical ratio." The point of Malthus's comparison of the two ratios lies in the fact that if food could only be increased in an arithmetical progression, the addition which could be made to its production in a given period would never grow, while if population increased in a geometrical progression, the addition which would be made to the number of mouths in the same period would constantly be growing. For eighty years after Malthus first wrote, the population of Great

Britain continued to grow in a geometrical progression, the censuses showing that, roughly speaking, it multiplied itself by $1\frac{12}{100}$ every ten years.

[Todhunter's *Algebra*.—Malthus, *Essay on the Principle of Population*, bk. i. ch. i. and elsewhere throughout. Though Malthus was doubtless the first to apply the phrase "arithmetical progression" to the increase of food, he was not, of course, the first to apply the phrase "geometrical progression" to the growth of population. It is *e.g.* suggested by the opening of the article on population in the *Encyclopédie*, and is actually used by Voltaire (*Dictionnaire philosophique* in *Œuvres complètes*, vol. xx., p. 253).]   E. C.

GÉRANDO, JOSEPH MARIA, Baron de (1772-1842), was born at Lyons and died at Paris. His life, especially in his youth, was full of dramatic incidents. He was on the eve of taking orders when the massacres of September 1792 deterred him from this step. He retired to Lyons and sided against the Convention when that city was besieged in 1793. Wounded, imprisoned, and condemned to death, he still contrived to escape and to find a refuge in Savoy. He returned to France after the amnesty, and joined the army as a private (*chasseur à cheval*). While he was in garrison at Colmar he competed (in 1799) for a prize offered by the Institute. He gained the prize; and the jury, astonished that a common soldier should have won such a distinction, begged, with success, that he might be transferred to Paris. He rapidly rose to high position ; he became secretary-general in the office of the ministry of the interior. In this post he remained eight years ; he then became a counsellor of state—a dignity of which the Restoration did not deprive him—and in 1830 a peer of France. In 1819 and 1820 he had given a course of lectures on administrative law. Moral science was the study which he preferred. In 1806 he had been elected to the Academy of moral and political science ; and when, in 1832, this section of the Institute, which had been suppressed in 1816, was reconstituted, he was restored to the position in it he had formerly held. We shall pass by his philosophical works, and even those connected with the moral sciences, and shall refer only to the one of them which deals with political economy, that entitled *De la bienfaisance publique*, 4 vols. 8vo, 1839, a powerful book, dealing with a wide range of subjects but somewhat diffuse, the writer having covered too much ground in his work. There was no question that he was competent to deal with these subjects, having administered the Blind Asylum for thirty-five years. He had also taken part in many charitable associations, for savings, mutual help, etc., in which his assistance had been very valuable.

His other works of the same class were : *Tableau des sociétés et des institutions religieuses, charitables et de bien public de Londres*, 1 vol. 12mo, 1824.—*Le visiteur des pauvres*, 1820-1837. Of this there have been several editions, and the work received the *prix Montyon* from the French Academy.—*De l'éducation des sourds-muets de naissance*, 2 vols. 8vo, 1827, and finally *Des progrès de l'industrie dans leur rapport avec le bien-être, physique et moral, de la classe ouvrière*, which received a prize from the *Société industrielle* of Mulhouse, 1841-45, and has gone through several editions.   A. C. f.

GERMAN SCHOOL OF POLITICAL ECONOMY. "Political economy in Germany up to the present time has been a foreign science. . . . It was imported from England and France as a ready-made commodity, and the German professors and those who taught it remained no more than scholars." This oft-quoted expression from Karl MARX's *Das Kapital* (vol. i. appendix) is on the whole justified, if applied to the period since Adam SMITH, but does not correctly apply to pre-Smithian times, when the economic precepts termed collectively "the cameral sciences" (see CAMERALISTIC SCIENCE) formed a distinct doctrine not till later affected by any foreign influence.

The "cameral sciences" (from *camera*, chamber, in particular the chamber in which the revenue and expenditure of the sovereign were administered) had a wider scope than the political, or "national" economy (*Volkswirthschaftslehre*) of the present day. In the narrower sense, as cameral science proper, the study comprised merely the financial administration just mentioned ; in its wider sense it embraced not only the doctrines relating to the administrative measures for the public welfare, but also the technical side of production, *e.g.* agriculture, mining, technology, commerce, etc. The immediate object of the cameral sciences was to educate a competent staff of state officials. When absolute government was supplanted by English constitutional ideas the cameral sciences retreated in their turn before political economy as represented by Adam Smith. Survivals of them exist nevertheless in Germany up to the present day. Established as it was by the Golden Bull of 1356, territorial sovereignty in Germany did not attain to full development till after the peace of Westphalia (1648). Hence it was only since this last date that cameral science came forward as an independent body of doctrine. In more ancient times it is treated as a supplement to jurisprudence.

Hence also it results that the history of political economy in Germany falls into three main sections :—I. the period before the end of the Thirty Years' War ; II. the interval between the Thirty Years' War and Adam Smith ; III. from Adam Smith up to the present day.

I. *The period before the end of the Thirty Years' War* (1648). — Germany during the middle ages presents a state of affairs resembling that of other European countries. It is only among the exponents of CANON LAW that we meet with disquisitions on economic relations. The standpoint corresponds to the theological basis of the main doctrine. Natural economics are more pleasing in the sight of God than economics based on money. The encroachments of the latter are to be opposed by severe usury laws (see INTEREST). Germany has no teacher in this line who overtops his fellows, as, for example, France has in her Bishop ORESME (died 1382).

With the approach of modern times and the victorious advance of monetary economics, a change also took place in theory. The Humanists (see HUMANISM), as adherents of absolute government copied from classic ideals, discussed the means by which that system of government, as opposed to the feudal organisation of society, could be established, putting forward views akin to the mercantilism of a later age (see MERCANTILE SYSTEM). This holds good for the *Institutio principis christiani* of Erasmus, translated under the title of *Unterweisung eines frummen und christlichen Fürsten* (1521), which is the first independent work on these matters. It is dedicated to Charles V. and culminates in the advice that a sovereign should follow a thrifty régime, and, in the event of his needing a tribute, should in the first place levy it on the goods of foreign merchants. There can be no doubt that this work was a material incentive to the scheme brought forward in the imperial diet in the winter of 1522-23 for consolidating the imperial customs. It proposed to encircle the empire, including the Netherlands but excluding Switzerland, with a customs line and a duty of 4 per cent *ad valorem* on imports and exports. The project was defeated through the opposition of the mercantile interest in the imperial towns.

The reformers, especially LUTHER, contribute with more or less discursiveness to the discussion of the economic situation, without, however, showing any marked originality. They hold a kind of middle position between the standpoint of canon law and that of the mercantilism of territorial sovereignty.

A somewhat lively literary controversy, chiefly conducted by jurists, arose towards the middle of the 16th century respecting the currency. The question whether coins should be minted at their full nominal value, or at less than their full nominal value in metal, was the apple of discord in a semi-official paper war, which became celebrated, between the two branches, Ernestian and Albertian, of the princely house of Saxony (1530). The reign of the most remarkable territorial sovereign of his time, the Elector Augustus of Saxony (1553-86), soon after gave occasion for several more important economic works, notably Von OSSA'S *Prudentia regnativa* (written 1556, published

1607). More than a century later (1717) it was republished by THOMASIUS and made the basis of his economic lectures.

Special mention under this period may further be made of OBRECHT, professor of law at Strassburg, with his posthumous work (1617) entitled *Fünff unterschiedliche* secreta politica *von Anstellung und Vermehrung guter Policey*, etc., in which he urges the necessity of a fund of money (*ærarium sanctum*) for the sovereign, and proposes to connect with it a system of fire insurance. He also discusses a special institution to provide for children (*ærarium liberorum*) on almost modern insurance principles. The names of the chief originator of the so-called "*Hausvæter* literature" of rural economy — T. Colerus (*Œconomia ruralis et domestica*, 1591-1605), of the jurist T. Bornitz (*De rerum sufficientia in republica et civitate procuranda*, 1625), and of the professor of law at Tübingen and subsequently at Ingolstadt, Chr. BESOLD (*De ærario*, 1620), also deserve mention, the two latter being more or less encyclopædic in treatment. A transition between this and the next period is afforded by K. KLOCK, whose book *De contributionibus* (1634), written during the Thirty Years' War, contains a detailed and rather advanced theory of taxation, in which some attempt is made to construct a progressive system.

II. *The period between the Thirty Years' War and Adam Smith* (1648-1790).—Seldom has it ever befallen a nation to experience an overthrow, both in its internal and external relations, similar to that which Germany sustained between 1618 and 1648. Prosperity was annihilated and the nation lacerated to death. The lead in politics and culture was henceforward, for centuries, surrendered to the western states of Europe. It was no easy task which confronted territorial sovereignty, the principle of which had, since the peace of Westphalia, been made one of the essential parts of the imperial constitution. The land laid waste had to be brought into cultivation again, and, for this purpose, had to be re-populated, and the state debt incurred by the war to be liquidated. Scientific skill was called in to help. The theory of administration or cameral science, which at that period was attaining its full development, thus became on one side a theory of agriculture; on another, a policy of population; on a third, a science of state revenue, or finance. And hence there grew up the composite title under which, from the beginning of the 18th century, these subjects were taught at the universities, viz. "economic, police, and especially cameral science" (*Oekonomische Polizei- und* (besondere) *Cameral-wissenschaft*).

The science split into two "confessions," corresponding to the religious dualism of the empire. There was a Catholic branch, grouping itself around the house of the Hapsburgs ; and a Protestant branch, the central force of which gradually developed together with the growing ascendency of the Hohenzollerns.

In the Catholic group the sectarian character is less prominent. It starts with J. J. BECHER (*q.v.*), whose brilliant work, *Politischer Discurs von den eigentlichen Ursachen des Auf- und Abnehmens der Reiche, Städte und Republiken*, etc. (1668), might even to-day be read with profit. Dedicated, in the second edition, to the emperor, Leopold I., it maintains that "*die volkreiche und nahrhafte Gemeine*," a populous and well nourished community, should be the aim of territorial administrative policy. Without the means of subsistence there is no population ; the converse also holds good that without an adequate population there can be no proper means of subsistence, since human beings are dependent on each other. Hence the states-man has impartially to keep in view both these poles on which the welfare of the state turns. In so doing he must guard against the three cardinal foes of well-being, namely *monopolium* (monopolies) ; *polypolium* (industrial anarchy); and *propolium* (usurious forestalling). Becher's proposals for preventive organisation border more or less on socialism. He detested mer-chants who imported from abroad goods that may also be produced at home, and abused them roundly as the real "propolists." On the other hand. men of business who invested their capital in the promotion of native industry seemed to him the "pillars" of society. The whole political system ought to be based on true religion (Catholicism). Nevertheless the clergy has to stand within, and not without, the state, and must be subject to civil law. The development of Becher's ideas is continued by F. W. HORNECK's *Oesterreich über alles wann es nur will* (1684). One proposition in it has become celebrated, viz. "it were better to give two thalers for a commodity and keep them in the country, than to give only one which leaves the country." Horneck attaches cardinal importance to the industrial inde-pendence of his country, and especially with regard to France. To compass this he would prohibit in general all foreign manufactures, and do this without waiting till all the corre-sponding industries were started in the country, inasmuch as they would at once spring up out of the earth. The third of this group was W. von SCHRÖDER, author of a book dedicated to the Emperor Leopold, *Fürstliche Schatz- und Rent-Kammer* (1686). Here highest import-ance is ascribed to the financial interest of the ruler, which ultimately coincides with the national interest. The sentence, "that the wealth or the poverty of the country is caused, not by import and export of money, but by the equilibrium of manufacture" (cp. lix.), is characteristic of the writer's standpoint. This

being so, Schröder should not be termed, as he is by many, *e.g.* by ROSCHER, a strict mercan-tilist in the sense of confounding wealth with metallic money. There is in fact no "strict" mercantilist in this sense amongst the German cameralists.[1]

The Protestant section presents a richer, if not exactly a more important, literature. At the head stands V. L. von SECKENDORFF (*q.v.*), whose work *Der teutsche Fürstenstaat* (1655) is written in a strictly Lutheran spirit. The Protestant disposition comes out yet more keenly in the later work *Der Christenstaat* (1685), which seeks to show "what things in church and state are Christian and right, and what can be reformed according to the principles of Christianity" (*i.e.* of Protest-antism). Seckendorff had set himself the task of initiating young statesmen into the theory and art of government. His *Fürstenstaat* is, therefore, essentially didactic in character. The leading idea is the coincidence between the interest of sovereign and people, whom he wished to see as numerous as possible. "The greatest treasure of the country consists in numbers of well-nourished people." After he had spent the chief part of his life in the service of the Dukes of Gotha, he was appointed chancellor of the newly-founded university of Halle in the service of the Elector of Branden-burg, but died in the same year (1692). In the reign of the Great Elector of Brandenburg, Frederick William the Great (1640-1688), a violent paper controversy took place concerning the excise. It was opened by the work *Entdeckte Goldgrube in der Accise*, by Chr. Teutophilus (pseudonym for Tenzel), 1685. In it the Great Elector is extolled for keeping on foot a standing army (*miles perpetuus*) for the maintenance of his Protestant supremacy, for which the "sweet-tempered, gently-flowing excise" was a far more fitting fiscal means than the "violent levy." This advice, as we know, was not unheeded by the prince.

Cameral studies underwent an important development during the reign of king Frederick William I. of Prussia (1713-1740). Although

---

[1] The statement that "wealth is money" I have come across but once in the economic literature of Germany, viz. in the second of the three pamphlets concerned with the currency controversy between the two branches of the ruling house of Saxony mentioned above (1530). (See pp. 66 and 70 of the new edition prepared by W. Lotz, Leipzig, 1893.) This little tract, put together merely for controversial purposes, *Das Münz-Belangende Antwort und Bericht*, etc., is justly stigmatised by Roscher as being "strikingly ill-written" and "sophistical," and can in no case rank as represent-ing a prevailing tendency of thought. It is much more common, in cameralistic literature, to find sentences apparently postulating identity between wealth and population. Yet it would again be incorrect to regard this view as especially characteristic of cameralism. On closer inspection the two notions, wealth and popula-tion, are found to be distinct, while they are related as reciprocally cause and effect. The wealth or well-being of the nation consists in the equilibrium, conditioned by progress, of both elements.   A. O.

no friend to the university system, he held that in connection with his reorganisation of the Prussian civil service the establishment of cameralistic chairs was necessary. The professorship at Halle university was given to GASSER, till then professor of law, while that at Frankfurt on the Oder was bestowed on Dithmar the historian (1727). From the date of the latter's book, *Einleitung in die Oekonomische Polizei- und Cameralwissenschaft* (1731), the division of subjects indicated by its title remained unchanged till the time of SONNENFELS. Dithmar also was the first to start an economic journal in Germany under the title *Oekonomische Fama* (from 1729).

From this date also specialised treatises began to appear. J. R. von ROHR (1688-1742) set forth "economic" science, i.e. the theory of rural economy, in his *Compendiöse Haushaltungsbibliothek*. Through his work *Silvicultura œconomica* (1713), H. C. von Carlowitz became the father of the economics of forestry. P. T. MARPERGER (1656-1730) achieved in his own writings an entire literature of commerce. The theory of population found its classic representative in T. P. SÜSSMILCH (*q.v.*), whose famous work, *Die göttliche Ordnung in den Veränderungen des menschlichen Geschlechts* (1742), which appeared in the reign of Frederick the Great (1740-1786), may be looked upon as the programme of that monarch as regards the politics of population. Süssmilch takes as his text the scriptural injunction, "Be fruitful and multiply." The king considered it as "un axiome certain, que le nombre des peuples fait la richesse des États."

Two side channels, one philosophical and one statistical, now flow parallel to the main stream of the Protestant branch of cameral science.

At the head of the former stands LEIBNITZ, who, in his *Bedenken von Aufrichtung einer Societät in Deutschland zur Aufnahme der Künste und Wissenschaften* (1669), expresses opinions in essential agreement with Becher's economic ideas. G. MORHOF, professor at Kiel, reviving the old Greek division of practical philosophy into ethics, politics, and economics, in his large work, *Polyhistor* (1688 and 1692), treated comprehensively of the literature and history of the last-named subject. Chr. THOMASIUS of Halle, in his popular philosophical lectures, dealt fully with economic matters, taking as his basis the writings of Ossa and Seckendorff. Political economy is specially appreciated by Chr. WOLFF, at first in his *Vernünftige Gedanken vom gesellschaftlichen Leben der Menschen* (1721), and then in his *Œconomica methodo scientifico pertractata* (1754), the standpoint being throughout a moderate mercantilism.

The statistical parallel line takes its origin in the writings of the father of the history of German law, H. CONRING (*q.v.*) of Helmstedt (d. 1681). It is continued by G. SCHMEIZEL

(d. 1747), who included in his university lectures at Jena and Halle a *collegium politico-statisticum*, and received further development from his pupil, G. ACHENWALL (*q.v.*, d. 1772) at Göttingen, and gained for him, though inappropriately, the sobriquet of a "father of statistics." He was followed at Göttingen by A. SCHLÖZER, the author of the well-known definition, "Statistics are stationary history, and history is continuous statistics." In contrast to the English "political arithmeticians," such as PETTY, GRAUNT, HALLEY, and others, the chief strength of his method lies not in the figures "Zahlen," but in the description in words "Wortbeschreibung." This "Staatenzustandskunde" (science of the condition of states), in its geographical aspects—is further developed by BÜSCHING (d. 1793).

It was, thus that matters stood in Germany when foreign science began to exercise an influence on cameral science, which till then had moved entirely within its own national limits. The movement began in the work of the diplomatist and friend of Frederick the Great, T. F. von Bielfeld — *Institutions politiques* (1760 ; German edition entitled *Lehrbegriff der Staatskunst*, 1761). This, though destitute of originality, was an epoch-making book for Germany, inasmuch as it dealt with matters entirely outside the range of the cameral sciences of that day, and, as it was written in French, is exclusively based on French economic works. For the first time the German reading public became acquainted with such authors as VAUBAN, MELON, DUTOT, FORBONNAIS, etc. From that time the influence of foreign writings on cameralistic literature became permanent.

The merit of having united into one systematic whole the collected antecedent tendencies of the Catholic and Protestant sections as well as of the later foreign influences, belongs to J. H. G. von JUSTI (d. 1771). Justi had been in the employ both of Austria and of Prussia, as well as for a time in that of Hanover (Göttingen). The earliest of his principal works is *Staatswirthschaft* (1st ed. 1750) ; his later writings are but more comprehensive expositions of it. Justi follows in general the divisions of Dithmar, but he establishes the science of trade or commerce, as a separate sub-division to be detached from the science of political administration. To Justi can be traced the scheme, which was subsequently carried out in various places, of establishing in the German universities, not only separate chairs, but entire faculties of political economy, with six or seven professors. His saying that a state can never be over-peopled is well known. In political philosophy his model is MONTESQUIEU, with whose preference for the English constitution he is in sympathy. English economic literature, on the other hand, was almost entirely unknown to him. It was reserved for a British citizen, Sir J. STEUART (*q. r.*), a partisan of the house of Stuart, to introduce a knowledge of it into Germany. He fled to the Continent after the battle of Culloden (1746), and for a time enjoyed the hospitality of the courts of Baden and Wurtemberg. During this period Steuart composed the celebrated *Inquiry*, etc., the English edition appearing in 1767, the German translation (in two versions), 1769. The work made a great stir, but its influence was soon weakened by the intrusion of the doctrines of the French Physiocrats.

The system of the physiocrats could find no soil so favourable as that of Germany. What proved its special attraction in that country was its metaphysical element. At many of the smaller German universities, some of which are now closed, the chair of philosophy was united to that of the cameral sciences. QUESNAY'S theories, professing to form a philosophical system based on economics, were in striking correspondence to this arrangement. Great enthusiasm arose for the *science nouvelle*, which became known chiefly through the *Éphémérides du citoyen*, published from 1767 onwards (see ÉPHÉMÉRIDES).

At the head of its adherents stood A. SCHLETTWEIN (*q.v.*), formerly *Privatdocent* at Jena, and in 1763 taken into the service of the Margrave Carl FRIEDRICH of Baden. Both these men entered on the experiment of introducing the IMPÔT UNIQUE (*q.v.*) into some villages of Baden (see MIRABEAU, V. R., Marquis de). The margrave, moreover, was the author of the celebrated *Abrégé des principes d'économie politique*, which was revised by DU PONT and Quesnay, and appeared in the issue for 1772 of the *Éphémérides du citoyen*. Schlettwein's zeal was equalled by that of the state secretary of Basle, Isaak ISELIN (*q.v.*) whose periodical, *Ephemeriden der Menschheit* was started in 1776 as a pendant to the Parisian organ similarly named. A prominent position among German economists belongs to the professor of military construction at Kassel, J. MAUVILLON (*q.v.*) of French descent. In his *Sammlung von Aufsätzen über Gegenstände aus der Staatskunst, Staatswirthschaft und neuesten Staatengeschichte*, published in 1776, occurs the first use of the terms "physiocrat" and physiocratic system," which were derived from the word "physiocratie," chosen by Du Pont as the title of a collection of essays published by him ; Mauvillon challenged any opponents to a public contest. The glove was taken up by more than one, the first to respond being the Kassel professor, C. W. Dohm, in an article which appeared in the *Deutsches Museum* for 1778, entitled *Ueber das physiokratische System*, followed in 1780 by Von PFEIFER's *Der Anti-physiokrat*, etc. On behalf of the system then appeared K. F. FÜRSTENAU *Versuch einer Apologie des physiokratischen Systems* (1779) ; E. SPRINGER *Ueber das physiokratische System* (1780) ; also

Mauvillon's own *Physiokratische Briefe an den Herrn Professor Dohm* (1780). A middle position was taken up by G. A. WILL, *Versuch über die Physiokratie, deren Geschichte, Literatur, Inhalt und Werth* (1782). The contest, which was conducted in the most chivalrous manner, had no favourable issue for the system. Its fall was brought about less by the arguments of its opponents than by the rapidly increasing preponderance of the doctrine of Adam Smith.

Specially noteworthy among the opponents of the Physiocrats is J. von SONNENFELS (*q.v.*), professor of financial and political science at Vienna from 1763. He borrowed his arguments from Quesnay's vehement French opponent, FORBONNAIS, and entered the lists more especially against the IMPÔT UNIQUE. The belief in the desirability of the maximum increase of population, which had been, by the teaching of the Physiocrats, thrust more into the background, emerges with renewed energy in Sonnenfels. The measure of the population in a state is set, not by the means of subsistence, but by the opportunities for employment. The increase of the latter is accordingly the duty of the statesman. Sonnenfels distinguished two kinds of balance in trade, the "numerical," or monetary, balance, and "the balance of advantage," *i.e.* the balance of employment. The one can be active while the other is passive. If *e.g.* Austria and Portugal exchange linen to the value of £2,500,000 for diamonds to the value of only £2,000,000, the numerical balance is unfavourable to Austria, but the balance of advantage is favourable. To Sonnenfels also is due a new classification of economic subjects, indicated already in the title of his principal work—*Grundsätze der Polizei, Handlung und Finanz* (Principles of Police, Commerce, and Finance, 1st ed. 1765). The science of police was to detach the branch dealing with the measures for the public welfare, and to confine itself to the doctrines relating to the maintenance of the public safety. The former should be included in the science of commerce, by which arrangement that science is made to embrace approximately the same subjects which in our days are dealt with by political economy. What was hitherto cameral science proper became the science of finance. This is essentially the classification as now used in the German universities.

Towards the end of the 18th century political economy in Germany becomes a chaos first cleared in the 19th century by the victorious advance of the doctrines of Adam Smith. Original thinkers like Justus MÖSER went their own way, but without producing any abiding influence. Others, such as J. BECKMANN of Göttingen (*q.v.*), JUNG-STILLING of Heidelberg (subsequently of Marburg), kept firm to the old cameralistic pattern, setting forth the doctrine in its completeness, *i.e.* inclusive of technical methods of production, such as the theory of rural economy, forestry, mining, technology, and trade, and for this purpose compiling countless text-books. Others again followed Sonnenfels. The remainder were divided into adherents of the Physiocrats, and adherents of Adam Smith. The teaching of the latter in particular made irresistible progress through its popularisation in the translated treatises of the French writer J. B. SAY.

Cameral science, nevertheless, as already stated, has even at the present day not disappeared from Germany. In the south German states the cameralistic career is still a separate career in the state service, and for the preparation of its candidates the universities of Munich and Tübingen have special independent economic faculties; while elsewhere the subjects in question come under the jurisdiction of the faculties of philosophy or jurisprudence. The technological branches moreover are studied at polytechnical academies, as well as at special schools for agriculture, forestry, mining, and commerce. Modern political economy in Germany shows, however, still many traces of its past. Even though the epigonous attempt of Th. SCHMALZ, professor at Berlin, to infuse new life into cameral science by infusing physiocratic doctrine into it failed (Encyclopädie der Kameralwissenschaft, 2nd ed. 1819), yet the manuals of RAU of Heidelberg (d. 1870) stand with one foot in the old cameral science and the other in Adam Smith's doctrine. This also holds good as to BAUMSTARK of Greifswald (d. 1889), who has been called "the last of the cameralists" (Kameralistische Encyclopädie, 1835). At the present time, however, during the 19th century, the Smith-Say tendency has prevailed in academic chairs and in the opinion of the public at large, and accordingly Karl Marx's assertion, quoted at the introduction to this article, respecting this period is, upon the whole, correct. During quite recent years political economy in Germany and Austria has taken an independent flight, and has exercised a most powerful influence over modern thought in other countries.

[Julius Kautz, Die geschichtliche Entwicklung der National-Oekonomik und ihrer Literatur, Wien, 1860. — Wilhelm Roscher, Geschichte der National-Oekonomik in Deutschland, München, 1874.—Gustav Marchet, Studien über die Entwicklung der Verwaltungslehre in Deutschland von der zweiten Hälfte des 17 bis zum Ende des 18 Jahrhunderts, München, 1885. Also the other standard works on the history of political economy.] A. O.

III. The period from Adam Smith to the present day (1790-1895).—Though the Wealth of Nations was translated[1] into German by Johann Friedrich Schiller (not the poet) as soon as it appeared, its influence in Germany and Austria was very inconsiderable till the end

[1] This translation is in 2 vols. Vol. i. 1776; ii. 1778.

of the century. The most enlightened university of the day was that of Göttingen in Hanover; and the Göttinger Gelehrten Anzeigen (10th March and 5th April 1777), while it declared the book to be of great value, pronounced against its chief conclusions, especially in regard to economic policy. The statesmen of the time, when they troubled themselves about economic principles at all, inclined to the PHYSIOCRATS, till the shock of the French Revolution discredited everything French. But in 1817 Adam MÜLLER, whose bias was against Adam SMITH, speaks of him notwithstanding as "the greatest writer of all times in political economy"; and Müller nine years before had written against him in the tone of one who recognises the great and increasing power of his opponent. Under Adam Smith he says, "the science of national economy was no longer directed to a speculative examination of the resources of the state, but to a continual increase of the same in practice." In fact the man and the book were in Germany identified with the active pursuit of wealth rather as an end than as a means. The condition of things described in FICHTE's Closed State (1800), the eager competition for material riches all the world over, is regarded as Smith's ideal and aim. GARVE, the popular philosopher, had popularised Adam Smith by presenting the public with a new translation (1794), and the Scottish economist was already creating a school in Germany. He had become to economics what KANT was to philosophy. The Prussian statesmen of the war of liberation were his followers to a great extent in finance. Many professors were with him. Professor Christian Jakob KRAUS of Königsberg (1753-1807) carried his devotion even to the copying of literary peculiarities. Professor Georg SARTORIUS of Göttingen (1766-1828) departed from his master mainly in the matter of economic policy; he insisted on a number of exceptions to the principle of "natural liberty." Professor August Ferdinand LÜDER (1760-1819) at first contented himself with discursive illustration of Smith's doctrines from books of travel and statistics, with too little regard to the facts of his own country, but fell by degrees into a scepticism which was as exaggerated as his earlier faith. HUFELAND (1760-1817), LOTZ (1771-1838), SODEN (1754-1831), and JAKOB (1759-1827), were little more than intelligent popularisers. As Garve's economics were connected with the philosophy of WOLFF, the economics of Jakob were connected with the philosophy of KANT, of which he was an ardent defender. The influence of FICHTE and HEGEL on the progress of economics was slow to reveal itself.

The melancholy which accompanied the political depression of Germany in the early years of the 19th century, and which is shown not only by Fichte's *Closed State* but by such books as *Der gesunkene Menschenwerth* (anon. 1804), gave place to a manlier spirit after the war of liberation ; there is an improved tone even in economics. The text-book of RAU, the Heidelberg professor (1792-1870), showed an activity of mind which was above mere reproduction of English writings, while the said writings, not only of Smith but of his successors, were really better known and better utilised than before. So important was Rau's *Lehrbuch* (1826) that it may be said to have held the field in spite of much criticism till Professor Adolf Wagner in our own time attempted to re-edit it, and then found he must re-write it. The features characteristic of German economics in its early period are not altogether absent in Rau. Economic books were largely written for the practical statesmen of Germany and not for the economic students, or even the statesmen of the world in general. Rau's book is partly written, like the old *kameralistische Lehrbücher*, for working politicians and diplomatists. But it contains also theoretical economics of a wider range ; and its criticisms of the past are largely founded on really economic arguments, not as in what is called the "romantic" school largely on appeals to sentiment. At the same time it seems hardly fair to attach the name romantic to the works of men like Adam MÜLLER (1779-1829), when we consider that the romantic school in literature is on the whole in sympathy with the ideas of the French Revolution, and this "romantic school" in economics is in reaction against them.

From the peace of 1815 we may trace three lines of development in German economics, the theoretical, the historical, and the socialistic, though the lines sometimes cross each other. After Rau on the field of theory the work of Von THÜNEN (1780-1850) is most important. In *Der isolirte Staat* (1826) Von Thünen published investigations on the theory of rent substantially at one with the theory of RICARDO, but worked out independently. His conception is not, as the title might suggest, that of an ideal state, but of a theoretical simplification of the conditions of inquiry. The effect is shown, theoretically, of the distance of equally fertile zones of land from the town as their centre, when all outside influences are conceived to be removed. The influence of situation on rent is thus presented in a figure which shows how nearly the abstract method may approach the pictorial. Von Thünen himself attached even more importance to his theory of natural wages, described by him mathematically as the square root of ap where a is the necessaries of life and p the product of capital and labour. Wages are not simply necessaries, but should increase with the product. Von Thünen is sometimes claimed as a socialist, but his attitude was rather that of a landowner,

who was very advanced in his social programme, but could not altogether forget his own order.

HERMANN (1795-1868), the Bavarian minister, was in one respect more worthy than even Von Thünen to rank beside the great English and French economists. His *Staatswirthschaftliche Untersuchungen* (1832) cover all branches of purely economic theory, and there is hardly any part of the subject on which he has not left fruitful suggestion. Like Von Thünen, he showed how a practical man could reason abstractly, though it may perhaps be a sign of a practical bent that in his book he devotes most space to production. He makes a clear distinction between matters technical and matters economical. He dwells on "subjective" aspects of goods and wealth that were afterwards brought into prominence by the Austrian school. The distinction of consumer's capital from productive capital, and joint action from collective action, the analysis of the various elements in cost, and of employer's profits, and the relation of cost to price and to value, are very characteristic. The second half of his book is indeed largely a treatise on value, as was said of the *whole* of Ricardo's. There is perhaps no single German economic work that leaves on its readers so deep an impression of strength as Hermann's ; and yet it would be hard to say in what particular his work effected a profound change in economic speculation. Until recently, when Professor Marshall has paid him due recognition, Hermann's name was little known by English economists, BANFIELD being in this respect a notable exception.

Since Hermann, there has no doubt been much theoretical work done in Germany, but it has as a rule taken the shape of monographs, as of MANGOLDT on *Unternehmergewinn*, Schäffle on *Ausschlieszende Absatzverhältnisse*, or else it has occurred incidentally in the course of a treatise perhaps headed *Volkswirthschaftslehre*, but containing more of history, statistics, and politics than of abstract reasoning. In Austria, on the contrary, excellent theoretical work of the old type is being done, and it began in a reaction against the German historical school of political economy. Between this historical school and the theoretical we may take men like LIST as occupying a midway position. After NEBENIUS (1784-1857), List (1789-1846) has the chief merit of persuading the states, and sections of states, to adopt free trade within their borders and a uniform tariff outwards,—to institute in other words a customs union (ZOLLVEREIN). Baden, and more effectively Prussia, led the way ; and between 1828 and 1852 the Zollverein had drawn nearly all the minor states into its fold.

This movement is in many ways to be compared with the English agitation against the corn laws and for free trade. Yet the Zollverein secured only what England had possessed for some centuries, and the United Kingdom since 1707 and 1800 ; there was to be free trade within, and a uniformity in the protective duties against the foreigner. List was a powerful advocate of both domestic free trade and protection against the foreigner. He agreed with COBDEN and BRIGHT in desiring that "political economy should descend from the studies of the learned, from the chairs of the professors, from the cabinets of the statesmen, into the counting-houses of the men of business, the offices of public servants, the dwellings of the landowners, the county meetings of the agriculturists, — to become the common property of all educated citizens" (National-System). But this must not be the ruling political economy, which deals with the whole world, as if the universal peace had been already established. Till political strife has ceased, it will be needful for political economy to be national and not cosmopolitan. A protective system will develop the "productive powers" of each several nation, and fit it better for the ultimate state of brotherhood and peace and universal free trade. Political economy should be much more the study of these productive forces than, as hitherto, the study of exchange and value. Like A. COMTE, List had his law of the three stages, and he made some show of justifying it from history.

List was, however, not a good representative of the rising historical school. The historical school, of which the main position is that all economical doctrine is relative to the particular epochs in which it appears, and has nothing in it permanent or true for all times, was better represented by SCHÖN, HILDEBRAND, Schäffle, ROSCHER, and Knies. Whether it can claim descent from SAVIGNY and the jurists, or only from Gervinus and the historians, is a question which need not be decided here. It is discussed by Prof. C. Menger (Methode der Socialwissenschaften, 1883, bk. iv. ch. iii.) (see HISTORICAL SCHOOL).

Since the time of Hermann some of the best work done in Germany, even in theory, has been done by adherents of this school, and this shows the elasticity of their chief principle. Schäffle has written on Exclusive rights of Sale (1867), L. von STEIN on finance and administration (1860), Knies on money (1873 seq.). Very significant too is the presence in such a book as Roscher's Political Economy of the old economic discussions of capital, wages, profits, rent, and taxation. Even the extreme section treat the theory of the currency and money as comparatively fixed and permanent, and the Malthusian law of population is so treated on the whole by Roscher, RÜMELIN, and Wagner. There are in fact at least three groups, which may be called a right, a left,

and a centre. Roscher and Schäffle, belonging to the right, use deduction freely ; RÖSLER, HELD, NASSE, less often ; Schmoller and Brentano would fain avoid it altogether, though (like Thorold ROGERS in our own country) they are not able to preserve complete consistency. As was said above (article A. COMTE and ENGLISH EARLY ECONOMIC HISTORY), the historical economists are really historians who have studied economics rather than economists pur sang ; and this appears especially in the left and centre, — in the historical work of Schmoller, Ochenkowsky, and Nasse.

The difficulty of preserving the threefold classification of German economists appears when we come to deal with the SOCIALISTS OF THE CHAIR. Such a prominent writer as Professor Adolf Wagner or Professor Cohn or Professor Rümelin might find a place among either the socialists or the historical economists. The same might be said of LANGE, who has written the best book on John S. MILL yet published, Mill being known in Germany much better by his Logic than by his Political Economy. Wagner's work, besides his discussions of taxation and finance, owes much of its value to his constant sense of the bearings of law and philosophy on economical questions. He does not go so far as Schäffle and others in claiming that economics itself should be an ethical science; and his recent commendations of Marshall's Principles would show that he is not far from the purely theoretical point of view. In fact the division into three schools is logically defective, though practically convenient. It may serve to point out (1) the men, comparatively few in Germany, who have confined themselves mainly to abstract theory ; (2) the men who, without entirely abandoning theory, have looked more to concrete economic facts, especially of past ages ; and (3) the men who use both history and theory to support a political scheme—the active intervention of the state in economic movements. Instead of being exclusive, the principles of the three classes are tenable together.

SOCIALISM, as representing not only a conflict of doctrine with doctrine in universities and in the book mart, but almost necessarily a struggle with the government of the day, has had a much more exciting history than orthodox and historical economics. Fichte, who was, with reservations, a socialist (see FICHTE), contrived to avoid this political conflict ; and his philosophical successors were even farther from danger. But the Hegelians of the left,—MARX, LASSALLE, Engels, more particularly,—took an active part in political agitation on the side of socialism ; and their combination of political and intellectual audacity made them a formidable power.

As the school of abstract theory drew inspiration from Adam Smith and his followers, the socialists were inspired by the writings of OWEN and READ, THOMPSON and GRAY, but not to the same extent. The influence of the French revolution of 1848, and of the corresponding movements in Germany, was probably much greater ; and the intellectual armoury of the socialists was furnished very largely by Ricardo, already known to the Germans in BAUMSTARK's translation (1837).

Karl MARX, in his *Manifest* (1848) and *Lohnarbeit* (1849), maintained the doctrine that wages are, and must be, simply the cost price of living, and—though this is more clearly brought out in the *Kapital* (1867)— that the gains of capital are due to a production by the labourer for which no wages are paid. That wages mean bare necessaries, and value is cost price, are doctrines that may be drawn from Ricardo with a fair appearance of reason. On this foundation Marx raises his doctrine of surplus value : it means that under threat of starvation workmen produce for the employer more than is enough for their maintenance, but this extra-product goes not to them but to him as the master of the situation. Without the imposing apparatus of illustration from English bluebooks with which *Das Kapital* is provided, Marx would not have made so strong an impression on economists. His contemporary, RODBERTUS (1805-75) had the advantage in power of hard reasoning. Like Von Thünen, he talked like Ricardo, with little or no knowledge of the English writer. He had the disadvantage of being averse to active political agitation, and not disinclined to political compromise. On the other hand, his doctrines on the subject of wages, the normal working day, and capital, are so like those of Marx that the question of priority has been often debated. The famous "iron law," so often identified with German socialism, is strictly speaking the formula of neither Marx nor Rodbertus but of LASSALLE, the gifted and scholarly but too rhetorical and impulsive agitator (1825-64). Lassalle organised the German socialists into a formidable political party ; and it is he who is to be specially credited with the creation of state socialism (see SOCIALISM), in its modern form. He threw scorn on SCHULZE-DELITSCH, and his attempt to regenerate society by means of co-operation ; but only because he desired co-operation to be subsidised and promoted by the state itself.

The "socialists of the chair," who become noticeable, name and thing, especially after the Austro-Prussian war, are described by one of themselves, Professor Nasse, as owing something of their influence as moderate state socialists to the success of the Prussian bureaucracy at a time when it was a political necessity ; and traces of the connection are readily to be seen.

The economists of the present generation may perhaps be better classed under six than under three heads. There are (1) the "Epigoni" or successors of the old classical school, including such men as Karl Braun, Treitschke, Max Wirth, as earlier they included PRINCE SMITH and MICHAELIS. They are usually identified with the MANCHESTER SCHOOL of English politicians. They are still of considerable weight in the journals and on the platforms of the country as well as in parliament.

There are (2) the men of what has been called the "theoretical renaissance," among whom Philippovich and the mathematical economists Launhardt, Auspitz, and Lieben are to be reckoned. They are more or less closely associated with the Austrians (see AUSTRIAN SCHOOL). We can hardly count Dühring and other revivers or transplanters of CAREY's doctrines, among them ; but Dietzel, though a keen critic of the Austrians, must have a place.

(3) In the third place we have the historical school with its various groups ; and (4) fourth the socialists of the chair, among whom Wagner and Schmoller, and (earlier) Held, are to be included. Schäffle must have a place, though his recent writings against social democracy have accentuated the difference between his very moderate state socialism and socialism pure and simple. Samter, though sometimes reckoned *Katheder-Socialist*, is almost to be reckoned among the socialists pure and simple. The latter (5) have Bebel and Liebknecht for their chief political champions. Even with his pen Bebel is by no means a mean adversary. Engels, though living in England, is to be reckoned as of this school, and is in many respects the most powerful writer in it, though Kautsky is not far behind him. The description of the organisation of the party, and the history of its various congresses and journals, belong rather to politics than to economics. The repressive law of October 1878, which lasted above ten years, gave socialism the benefit of persecution. The social democrats of Germany polled 1,700,000 votes in 1893, and returned forty-three members to the Reichstag. The insurance laws of 1883 (sickness), 1884 (accidents), and 1889 (old age) showed that the government had determined to outbid their opponents. It is well known too that Bismarck, who was then in power, had not disdained to learn something from Lassalle. (6) The Christian socialists, under Döllinger, Bishop Ketteler of Mainz and Canon Moufang of Mainz, as Roman Catholics, and latterly Todt, Stöcker, and other Protestants, have no claim to independent economic doctrine ; but as social reformers they have, like the socialists of the chair, rivalled the social democrats or socialists pure and simple, and they have contributed to socialistic politics the new element of religion.

The chief associations and journals connected more or less with economics may be mentioned briefly. The free traders have their "economic congress " (*Volkswirthschaftlicher Kongress*) and Economic Society founded in 1858 ; and they have done much to remove feudal obstructions and keep the extreme protectionists in check. Something more positive was wanted, however ; and in 1872 Schmoller convened a meeting at Eisenach, which issued in the institution of the union for social politics (*Verein für Sozial-politik*) (1873). The union may justly claim a share in the making of the insurance laws ; and it has from the first acted in avowed rivalry with the social democrats. It meets for discussion once a year, publishes transactions, and is in many ways like the economic section of the British Association with the addition of a directly practical aim. It has included such men as Nasse, Roscher, Held, Knapp, Mithoff, Conrad, Engel the statistician, Brentano, Wagner, Philippovich, Schönberg, and Miaskowski.

The leading economic journals of Germany represent very clearly the state of economics in that country. The *Jahrbücher für National-ökonomie und Statistik* (edited by Conrad, and frequently called " Conrad's *Jahrbücher* ") admits chiefly theoretical, statistical, and descriptive articles without respect of schools. The *Jahrbuch für Gesetzgebung* (" Schmoller's *Jahrbuch* ") is more closely allied with law and history. The *Vierteljahrsschrift für Volkswirthschaft und Kulturgeschichte* is the organ of the free traders ; the *Archiv für Soziale Gesetzgebung und Statistik* (Berlin), edited by Braun, deals chiefly with social reform, and also the *Sozial-politisches Wochenblatt*, formerly brought out by the same editor. The new *Zeitschrift für Sozial-und Wirthschafts-geschichte* (Freiburg), is the organ of the purely historical economists. Some of Professor Oncken's best historical work has appeared there. The *Zeitschrift für die gesammte Staatswissenschaft* (Tübingen) is edited by Fricker, Schäffle, and Schönberg, and is fairly catholic. The most temperate and valuable of the socialistic periodicals is *Die Neue Zeit* (Stuttgart). Good economical writing is frequently to be found in the *Preussische Jahrbücher* and *Göttingische Gelehrten Anzeigen*, while it occasionally happens, though more seldom than in England or America, that important articles on economic subjects find their way into journals that are printed for the general reader. In Germany, more than elsewhere, the writing of elaborate articles on economical or social topics has come to be regarded as a kind of condition precedent of a government appointment ; and the result is a tendency towards over-production of such articles (see BOUNTIES).

The production of books on economical subjects goes on also without ceasing ; but as yet economic theory, if not neglected altogether, is treated by most writers very eclectically, and economics may be more truly described as being in a state of transition in Germany than

in England or America. This is shown not only by the minute divisions of schools, which recall the political particularism of old Germany, but by the variety of points of view adopted in such a collection of economical treatises as Schönberg's *Handbuch* (1882) or in such a work as the *Handwörterbuch der Staatswissenschaften*, completed 1894 under the editorship of Conrad, Elster, Lexis, and Loening.

It ought to be added that among the valuable monographs published in Germany in the present generation, not a few, like those of Lange, Hasbach, Walcker, and Leser, deal with English economists ; and the intercourse between English and German economists was probably never so close as it is now. This is the more welcome as the conditions of life in the two countries are tending to become more and more similar, and the same problems will face the thinkers and legislators in both of them. The influence on economical speculation of the condition of the particular country where it is carried on is always considerable. It is not by accident that the weight of economic opinion in Germany is in favour of Malthus and in France against him. The success, too, or failure of particular social schemes, as cooperative banking, or labour colonies, has helped to influence the views of the learned concerning theoretical possibilities. The same kind of lesson has been taught by the changes in currency. The adoption of a gold standard, after the war of 1870, has led to an active discussion of questions of currency ; and the effects that followed the change have made German economists cautious in their theoretical decisions on the subject of the standard. A commission is now sitting (1894) which may perhaps bring about a thorough sifting of opinion in the matter, such as was effected two years ago in Austria (1892) by the great currency commission. It remains to be said that the change, so far as it introduced a uniform coinage throughout the German empire, is admitted on all hands to have been a valuable reform.

[Held (Adolf), *Principienstreit in der National-ökonomie*, 1872 (from *Preussische Jahrbücher*, July 1872).—Cohn (Gustav), *Fortnightly Review*, Sept. 1873, " Political Economy in Germany " [written with too evident a bias], and *History of Political Economy* (pub. by American Acad. of Pol. Science, 1894).—Roscher (Wilhelm), *National-ökonomik in Deutschland* (1874) (an English summary is given by Ingram, *History of Pol. Econ.*, 1888, pp. 184 *seq.*)—Cliffe Leslie, T. E., *Fortnightly Review*, July 1875, a review of Roscher, reprinted in *Essays in Political and Moral Philosophy*, 1879, pp. 167 *seq.*, under the title " The History of German Political Economy."—Contzen (Heinrich), *Geschichte der Literatur und Bedeutung der Nationalökonomie oder Volkswirthschaftslehre*, 1881 (2nd ed.) [somewhat didactic].—Resch (Peter), *Geschichte der deutschen Nationalökonomie im* 19*ten Jahrhunderte* (1889) [too meagre].—Eisenhart (Hugo), *Geschichte der Nationalökonomik*, 2nd ed., 1891 [the best general history]. — Nasse (Erwin), *Quarterly Journal of Economics* (Harvard) i. (1886), 498 *seq.*—Cossa (Luigi), *Introduction to the Study of Pol. Econ.* (Eng. transl., 1893), pp. 399 *seq.*—Rae John), *Contemporary Socialism* (2nd ed., 1891) "The Economic Movement in Germany."—Dawson (W. H.), *German Socialism and Ferdinand Lassalle*, a biographical history of German socialistic movements during this century, 1888, and *Germany and the Germans*, 1894.—Schmoller (Gustav), *Zur Litteraturgeschichte der Staats- und Socialwissenschaften* (1888) (On Fichte, List, Carey, Stein, etc., down to Hertzka and Menger). —Hasbach (Wilhelm), *Economic Journal*, i. 509 *seq.* (Sept. 1891), "Recent Contributions to Economic History in Germany."—Philippovich (Eugen), *Quarterly Journal of Economics*, v. pp. 220 *seq.* (January 1891), "The Verein für Sozialpolitik." A good account of the new insurance laws is in the *Forum* for October 1889, by Prof. Taussig : who also gives a good account of the theory of wages as it has developed in Germany since Hermann, *Quarterly Journal of Economics*, Oct. 1894. In the *Edinburgh Review* for Sept. 1828, there is an article by M'Culloch headed "Prussian Political Economy ; " but it is a mere review of a French translation of Schmalz's *Political Economy*, and notes the free-trade doctrines of that physiocratic Epigonos, without any general survey of his contemporaries. For other remarks on modern German school, especially on Wagner, see Marshall's, *Principles of Economics*, 3rd ed. vol. i.] J.B.

GERSON, JEAN CHARLIER DE (1363-1429), of the village of Gerson near Rheims, the famous chancellor of the university of Paris, contributed in the wide range of his written sermons and tractates to the theological economics of scholasticism. He is especially interesting as one who by his breadth of view and eminent gifts of piety and statesmanship, was drawn in opposite directions when dealing with economic ethics, now upholding the scholastic theories of "divine and natural law" (see JUS DIVINUM, HUMANUM, NATURALE), now driven to compromise by the teaching of experience ; forced to conclude that the former might, because of the hardness of men's hearts, never be so imperative as not to permit the advisableness, and sanction the validity, of some less absolute code of civil rules. Thus in his sermon *De reddendo debito* he approves of the assize of "wine and bread and the like," inasmuch as no amount of sermons, or multiplication of preachers would ever be sufficient to correct the fraudulent and excessive prices demanded by self-perjuring tradesmen. Again Usury is repeatedly and utterly condemned by him as contrary to divine and natural law, essentially bad and not to be made good. Yet he admitted its contingent benefits, approved of a legal (low) rate of usury as likely to check abuse of it, and at the council of Constance, when a sweeping measure to abolish usury was called

for, he quashed the motion by demanding that a distinction between a fair and a usurious contract should first be made out.

The *Tractatus de Contractibus, de Venditione, et Emptione* contains essentially his contribution to the analysis of EXCHANGE together with his chief disquisition on usury. In it he describes the various forms of contract, and defines it as a kind of mutual justice and a legitimate exchange of property, not to be condemned because the bargain may incline to the relatively greater advantage now of buyer, now of seller. He discusses also the function of the state in relation to contracts, recognising its right to modify them, but resenting multiplication of statutes and penalties as an intolerable yoke. Against usury he adduces the usual arguments, scriptural and classical. He also endeavours to prove that, since to use money is to consume it, none but the owner of it can use it. Hence the "iniquity of the usurer" in receiving back what has ceased to be his, and more into the bargain, or rather "out of the bargain." And generally it is rather the mutual injustice imputed to lending on interest that moved Gerson. Taking advantage of the credulity of the buyer, or the urgency of his need, is to him usurious business equally with receiving money *ultra sortem* (*i.e.* as interest). And in the "accidental" circumstance of a *commutativa justitia* attending lending at interest he saw grounds for mitigating his condemnation. The loan might avert ruin or crime in the case of the borrower. Hence it might be tolerated, "lest a worse thing befall us." In all cases the decision lay between the "dual tribunal of intrinsic and extrinsic conscience, the one of the church, the other of secular politics."

[Charlier de Gersonii, *Opera*, Parisiis, 1606, esp. vol. ii.—Funk, *Geschichte des kirchlichen Zinsverbotes*, Tübingen (Universitätsschriften), 1876.]

C. A. F.

GHENT, HENRY OF (1217 ?-93), schoolman, born in that city at the commencement of the 13th century, was the son or descendant of a tailor. He was educated at Tournai, where he was a canon in 1267, and archdeacon in 1278. He was known as "Doctor Solemnis," and besides many theological and metaphysical works, is believed to have written *Quodlibetum de Mercimoniis et Negotiationibus*, of which the only copy in MS. was formerly in the abbey of St. Val Sainte Marie near Valenciennes (Val. Andreæ, *Bibliotheca Belgica*, London, 1643, p. 345). This book is now lost, but Cossa considers that the author appears to have shown in it "a somewhat juster understanding of commerce, its lawfulness and utility, than most of his contemporaries" (Cossa, *Introduction*, etc., 2nd ed. Eng. Translation, p. 147).

[F. Huet, *Recherches sur Henri de Gand*, 1838. —B. Hauréau, *De la Philosophie Scolastique*, t. ii.—*Histoire Littéraire de la France*, t. xxii.,

1842, pp. 144-203.—F. Ehrle, *Recherches critiques sur Henri de Gand*, 1887.—N. de Pauw, *Dernières découvertes concernant Henri de Gand*, 1889.]

H. R. T.

GHETTI, LUDOVICO, was one of the humanist philosophers who flourished in Florence and Tuscany during the 15th century. Ghetti applied himself to finance, aud the system of taxation, a problem much discussed at that time in Florence, where very different methods had been tried.

"Savonarola, the Christian reformer, was in favour of the rating of real property ; Guicciardini gives a scheme for levying taxes on a sliding or proportionate scale" (Cossa, *Introduction to Pol. Econ.*, translation, p. 156). Ghetti advocated the IMPÔT UNIQUE (*q.v.*).

[For the history of the influence of the humanists on political economy, see Cossa, *Introduction to Pol. Econ.*, translation. p. 157.—And for fuller detail, Toniolo, E., *Scolastica ed umanismo nelle dottrine economiche al tempo del risorgimento in Toscana*, Pisa, 1887.]

A. B.

GIANNI, FRANCESCO MARIA (1728-1821) born at Florence. His works on economics do not mark any progress in science, but his great reputation rests on his sagacious co-operation in the great economic reforms of Leopold II. of Tuscany. In carrying these out, perhaps assisted by a study of the works of BANDINI, he advocated free trade in corn. This step, proposed after 1756, led on to complete free trade in grain and food in Tuscany (1767).

In his *Meditazione sulla teoria e sulla pratica delle Imposizioni e Tasse pubbliche*, Gianni considers custom-houses as means to obtain the equilibrium and sometimes a surplus on the balance of international trade ; but when he speaks of the grain trade, with a singular contradiction he evinces himself a regular free-trader. Firm in his opinions, after having triumphed in the liberal reforms of 1767, he opposed by several *Memorie* the edict of 1792, which deprived Tuscany of its free government.

He maintains that liberty alone can produce prosperity, and trade needs no restraints to enable it to thrive, as clearly shown in Tuscany during twenty-four years.

Gianni did not write a treatise on this question ; even in his *Memorie Speciali*, which deal with the subject, he never discusses theory as FABRONI did, but his arguments are supported by facts, which render them far more convincing.

[Gianni's *Memorie*, his speeches, and other writings are carefully collected in the *Raccolte degli Economisti toscani* (Firenze, 1847-49, 4 vols.) which contain Gianni's and Fabroni's works.]

A. B.

GIBBONS, JAMES SLOAN (19th century), was born in Wilmington, Delaware, in 1810. He was a merchant in Philadelphia, and removed to New York in 1835, where he became identified with banking interests. He wrote *Banks of New York, their Dealers, the Clearing House, and the Panic of 1857*, New York, 1859 (reprinted 1870), pp. 399. Gibbons gives in this a detailed and vivid description of the administration of banks, and discusses the causes of the panic of 1857, attributing it to the expansion of bank credit. He also wrote *The public Debt of the United States : its Organisation ; its Liquidation ; Administration of the Treasury ; the Financial System*, New York, 1867, pp. xii. 276, in which he condemns the loose administration of the national finances, and the heavy taxes upon labour.

D. R. D.

GIFT in its modern sense means a voluntary transfer of property. According to Roman law an agreement to make a gift may be a valid contract, but English law does not enforce promises of that nature unless made by deed under seal. On the other hand English law does not restrict the power to deal with property by way of gift, while Roman law and some modern systems of law contain such restrictions. According to French law a person leaving on his decease one child or other descendant may not dispose of more than one-half of his property by way of gift, and if he leaves two children or other descendants his gifts may not exceed one-third (if three or more, one-fourth) of his property (*Code Civil*, art. 913). An English donor need not consider the claims of his family, but the law to a certain extent protects his creditors, inasmuch as it allows gifts to be set aside in certain cases, either by virtue of the provisions of the Bankruptcy Act or under one of the statutes of Elizabeth against voluntary conveyances (see LEGISLATION, ELIZABETHAN ; DONATIO MORTIS CAUSA).

E. S.

GIGINTA, MIGUEL DE (16th century), a canon of the church of Elna in Spain, and author of several works on the treatment of the poor : *Tratado de Remedio de Pobres* (A Treatise on the Remedy for Poverty), Coïmbra, 1579 ; *Exhortacion á la Compasion de los Pobres*, Madrid, and Saragossa, 1584 ; *Cadena de Oro del Remedio de los Pobres* (A Golden Chain of the Remedy, etc.), Perpignan, 1584 ; and *Atalaya de Caridad* (A Watchtower of Charity), Saragossa, 1587. In a *Memorial* approved by the cortes of Madrid in 1586, and inserted by Don Firmin Iglesias in his *Beneficencia en España* (Madrid, 1876, vol. ii. p. 1169, Appendix ix.), Giginta insists upon the necessity of establishing *Casas de Misericordia* (Houses of Mercy) to be kept distinct from hospitals for the sick. The test of labour was to be applied under penalty of a diminution in the allowance of food. As the stubborn poor will thus be impelled to leave the house, the author hopes that charitable persons will deny all help to such vagrants, and reserve their alms for the well-conducted poor duly appointed by the house to collect alms at the gates of churches, or market-places, etc. The houses of mercy were thus to be supported by pious donations and foundations. The cortes petitioned King Philip in favour of this scheme, but with scanty success.

[Iglesias, *Beneficencia en España* (vol. i. p. 256).—Colmeiro, *Historia de la Economía Política en España* (vol. ii. p. 37).]   E. Ca.

GILBART, JAMES WILLIAM (1794-1863), was of Cornish descent, though born in London. He was at first in a London bank, until it stopped payment in 1825 ; in 1827 he went as manager, first to the Kilkenny, and afterwards to the Waterford branch of the Provincial Bank of Ireland. On the formation of the London and Westminster Bank in 1834, Gilbart became its manager. He did much to secure the successful establishment of joint-stock banks. In 1836 the Bank of England procured an injunction against his bank " prohibiting their accepting any bills drawn at less than six months after date." Gilbart evaded the difficulty by inducing the country banks corresponding with the London and Westminster to draw bills upon it "without acceptance." Gilbart also gave evidence before various parliamentary committees, and secured the insertion of a clause in the renewal of the Bank Charter Act in 1844, granting to joint-stock banks the power "to sue and be sued by their public officers," and also the right of accepting bills at less than six months' date. He became F.R.S. in 1846. Much of his leisure was devoted to the promotion of literary and scientific institutions among the middle and working classes. He was the author of several useful works on banking—the principal treatises being devoted to familiarising the public with the methods and advantages of banks. He also wrote on logic. He bequeathed a sum of £1250 to King's College as an endowment for an annual course of lectures on banking. The *Gilbart Lectures* were commenced in 1872, and are continued to the present time.

Gilbart's works, besides some essays, are (the dates applying in all cases to the first edition) : *A Practical Treatise on Banking*, 1827.—*History and Principles of Banking*, 1834.—*History of Banking in Ireland*, 1836.—*History of Banking in America*, 1837.—*An Inquiry into the Causes of the Pressure on the Money Market in 1839,* 1840.—*The London Bankers,* 1845.—*Lectures on the History and Principles of Ancient Commerce*, 1847.—*Logic for the Million*, 1851.—*Elements of Banking*, 1852.—*The Laws of the Currency*, 1855.—*The Moral and Religious Duties of Public Companies*, 1856.—*Logic of Banking*, 1859.—*Social Effects of the Reformation*, 1860. An edition of Gilbart's works was issued after his death, London, 6 vols. 1865, but it does not include all the above-mentioned works.

[*Dictionary of National Biography* ; Biographical Notice prefixed to the collection of Gilbart's works, 1865.]   R. H. H.

GILBERT, THOMAS (1720-98), son of Thomas Gilbert of Cotton, Staffordshire ; barrister in 1744 ; land agent to Lord Gower,

M.P. for Newcastle-under-Lyne, 1763-68 ; and Lichfield, 1768-95, wrote on Poor Law Reform ; promoter of GILBERT'S ACT (*q.v.*).

GILBERT'S ACT. The act 22 Geo. III. c. 83, for the better relief and employment of the poor, was commonly known as Gilbert's Act, from the name of its proposer, who represented Lichfield in parliament. The preamble states that the sufferings and distress of the poor are great from two causes, viz. (1) the incapacity of overseers, who misapply funds and favour litigation ; (2) the want of proper regulation and management of workhouses. To remedy these evils it makes the following changes in the law. The provisions of 9 Geo. I., which had allowed of the union of small parishes for certain purposes, are extended. Parishes, not more than ten miles apart may combine together, when two-thirds of the ratepayers assessed at £5 and upwards desire it, may build a common workhouse, and borrow money on joint credit. In all such cases, the church-wardens and overseers are released from the duty (imposed by 14 Car. II. c. 12) of relieving the poor, but continue to be responsible for the collection of the rate. The relief of the poor is entrusted to three persons nominated by the justices of the peace, viz. the guardian, who represents his parish at the monthly board, and may be paid up to £10 yearly ; the governor, who is charged with the management and discipline of the workhouse ; the visitor, who inspects the workhouse, checks accounts, and is generally charged with supervision. In all parishes, whether incorporated or not, the workhouse is to be used only for the aged, sick, and infirm. Able-bodied labourers are to be found work, and the wages they earn to go towards their maintenance. In any case in which the guardians refuse relief, an appeal may lie to the justices.

The act was repealed by the act 34 & 35 Vict. c. 116. It was avowedly an experiment, and contained the germs of much good and much evil. Under the former head we may put (1) the enlargement of the area of administration, a principle made general in 1834 ; (2) the attempt to improve the status of administrators ; (3) the permission to board out children. Under the second (1) the large powers given to the justices, which were soon abused ; (2) the granting of relief in aid of wages, which developed into the allowance system (see ALLOWANCE SYSTEM) ; (3) the practical abolition of the workhouse-test imposed by 9 Geo. I. In 1834, when the POOR LAW was remodelled, there were 67 incorporations under this act containing 924 parishes ; in 1853, 14 containing 203.

[Nicholls, *History of Poor Law*, vol. ii. ch. xi. —Aschrott, *The English Poor-Law System* (Engl. trans.) pt. i. § 5.—Fowle, *The Poor Law*, English Citizen series.]   L. R. P.

GILDS.

Early History, p. 209; Religious Gilds, p. 210; The Gild Merchant, p. 210; Craft Gilds, p. 211; Gilds of Newcastle-upon-Tyne, p. 213; Gild System in Spain, p. 213.

Early History.—Mediæval gilds were voluntary associations established for mutual assistance. Various theories have been advanced concerning their origin. Some writers, especially Coote and Lambert, regard them as a continuation of the Roman *collegia* and *sodalitates*. There are certainly striking analogies between Roman and Germanic fraternities, but there is little evidence to prove their unbroken continuity of existence.

A more prevalent theory derives gilds wholly or in part from the early Germanic or Scandinavian sacrificial banquets, or drinking bouts. Brentano, Hegel, Wilda, and others, ascribe considerable influence to this heathen element. Sacrifice and banquet are indeed two of the earliest meanings of gild; but when a word has a variety of meanings, and may therefore refer to different things, those things have not necessarily an historical connection. It matters little whether the earliest signification of gild is sacrifice, expiation, penalty, feast, or payment; the solution of the question of verbal derivation does not necessarily affect the origin of gild in the sense of fraternity or society. The heathen sacrificial carousals lack two of the most essential elements of the later institution, namely, corporate solidarity, or permanent association, and the spirit of fraternal co-operation or Christian brotherhood. This last conception included a mixture of worldly and religious ideals—the support of the body and the salvation of the soul.

Another theory has recently been advanced by Dr. Pappenheim. He ascribes the origin of Germanic gilds to the northern "foster-brotherhood," or "sworn-brotherhood,"—an artificial bond of union generally between two persons, sometimes between more than two. After the performance of peculiar ceremonies, such as the intermingling of their blood in the earth, the contracting parties grasped hands, and each took the oath of brotherhood, swearing to avenge any injury done to the other. We cannot here state all the objections to this view (see Hegel, *Städte,* i. 250-253). It will suffice to say that the foster-brotherhood seems to have been unknown to the Franks and the Anglo-Saxons, the nations in which mediæval gilds first appear; and hence Dr. Pappenheim's conclusions, if tenable at all, apply only to Denmark or Scandinavia.

No theory on this subject can be satisfactory which wholly ignores the influence of the Christian church. Imbued with the idea of the brotherhood of man, the church naturally fostered the early growth of gilds, and tried to make them displace or absorb the old heathen banquets. While conceding the influence of

Christianity upon the early development of gilds, we must not, however, ascribe their origin to this source. The work of the church was directive rather than creative. Gilds were a natural growth of civilisation, a natural manifestation of the associative spirit which is inherent in mankind. The same needs produce similar associations in different ages. While all such associations have striking resemblances, those of each age have peculiarities which indicate a spontaneous growth. It is not necessary to seek the germ of gilds in any antecedent age or institution. When the old kin-bond—the *maegth* or *sippe*—was dissolving, and the state was still undeveloped, individuals naturally united for mutual help.

The earliest references to gilds are found in the Carolingian capitularies of 779 and 789, and in the enactments made by the synod of Nantes, early in the 9th century, which last are repeated in the ecclesiastical ordinances of Hincmar of Rheims (A.D. 852). There are also vague references to sworn associations of some sort in the capitularies of 805 and 821. The Carolingians, like the Roman emperors, seem to have regarded such unions as dangerous to the state. The gilds of Norway, Denmark, and Sweden are first mentioned in the 11th, 12th, and 13th centuries respectively; those of France and the Netherlands in the 11th. In England they are not clearly referred to before the second half of the 9th century, though many writers believe that they were already in existence in the reign of Ine. We have little information concerning Anglo-Saxon gilds before the 11th century. To the first half of that century belong the statutes of the fraternities of Cambridge, Abbotsbury, and Exeter—the oldest gild ordinances of Europe. The object of the thanes' gild at Cambridge was to provide for the payment of the *wergeld,* in case a member killed any one, and to afford help in blood-feuds. In Orcy's gild at Abbotsbury, and in the brotherhood at Exeter, the religious element is more prominent, the chief object of the brethren's solicitude being the salvation of their souls. The fraternity at Exeter also extended assistance in case of conflagration. Feasting, prayers for the dead, attendance at funerals of members, the solemn entrance oath, fines for neglect of duty and for unseemly behaviour, contributions to a common purse, mutual assistance in distress, the gild-hall, periodical meetings—in short, all the characteristic features of later gilds already appear in the statutes of the Anglo-Saxon fraternities. Continental historians have made conjectural data concerning Anglo-Saxon gilds the basis of important deductions regarding the origin of municipal government throughout western Europe. Hence it is important clearly to sum up all that is known concerning this whole subject. The following three propositions seem incontrovertible. (1) In the second half of the Anglo-Saxon period the gild is a well-known institution, but its prevalence has been greatly exaggerated. (2) There is no evidence to show that there was any organic or official connection between gilds and municipal government, much less that the latter emanated from the former. (3) There is no trace of the existence of either craft or merchant gilds before the Norman Conquest. Commerce and industry were not yet sufficiently developed to call for the creation of such associations.

It is difficult to classify gilds. We have already indicated the three chief classes: religious or benevolent, merchant, and craft or artisan gilds. Those thus far specifically mentioned belong to the first category. The last two categories, which do not become prominent anywhere in Europe until the 12th century, had, like all gilds, a religious tinge, but their aims were primarily worldly. They are, furthermore, distinguished from religious fraternities by being generally confined to a particular occupation or class of persons. We must now examine the later history of religious gilds, and then pass to the other two categories.

Religious Gilds.—After the Norman Conquest religious gilds multiplied in England. They were particularly numerous in the boroughs. Their ordinances and customs were similar to those of the above-mentioned Anglo-Saxon fraternities. The brethren were aided in old age, sickness, and poverty, often also in cases of loss by robbery, shipwreck, and conflagration,—for example, the gild of St. Katherine, Aldersgate, assisted any member if he "falle in poverte, or be aneantised thorwz (through) elde or thorw fyr oder water, theves or syknesse." Alms were often given even to non-gildsmen; lights were supported at certain altars; feasts and processions were held periodically; attendance at funerals of brethren, and at masses for the dead, was required. Some such functions appear in the ordinances of all kinds of gilds, but they are especially prominent in those of the religious brotherhoods. Some of these fraternities came to be closely connected with the municipal government; but, as a rule, they were simply private societies with a limited sphere of activity. They played an important rôle in the social life of England, especially as eleemosynary institutions, down to the time of their suppression in 1547. Religious gilds also flourished on the continent throughout the middle ages, and closely resembled those of England.

The Gild Merchant.—Students of political science are particularly interested in merchant and craft fraternities. The gild merchant came into existence in England soon after the Norman Conquest, as a result of the increasing importance of trade. Whether it was of indigenous growth or a transplantation from Nor-

mandy, it is difficult to determine. Until clear evidence of foreign influence is forthcoming, it may be safer to regard it simply as a new application of the old gild principle. But this new application may have been stimulated by continental example. The evidence seems to indicate the pre-existence of the gild merchant in Normandy, though it is not mentioned anywhere on the continent before the 11th century. It spread rapidly in England, being regarded by the townsmen as one of their most important chartered privileges; in the reign of John it was a well-known institution common to many English boroughs. But in some prominent towns it did not exist, notable examples of its absence are found in London, Colchester, Norwich, and the Cinque Ports. The smaller the town in which it existed the more conspicuous was the rôle it played. Its chief function was to regulate the trade monopoly conveyed to the borough by the royal grant of *gilda mercatoria*. The gildsman had the right to trade freely in the town, and to impose payments and restrictions upon others who desired to exercise that privilege. The ordinances of the fraternity thus aim to protect the brethren from the commercial competition of strangers or non-gildsmen. More freedom of trade was allowed at all times in the selling of goods by wholesale; and also in retail dealings during the time of markets and fairs. The ordinances were enforced by an alderman with the assistance of two or more deputies, or by one or two masters, wardens, or keepers. At the *morwenspeches*, or periodical meetings of the society, there was feasting and merrymaking, new ordinances were made, members admitted, officers elected, and other business transacted.

Many writers assert that the gild merchant and the borough were identical, and that the former was the basis of the whole municipal constitution. But the records in the local archives show clearly that gild and borough, gildsmen and burgesses, were originally distinct conceptions; and they continued to be discriminated in most towns throughout the middle ages. Admission to the society was not restricted to burgesses; nor did the brethren form an aristocratic body controlling the whole municipal government. No good evidence has, moreover, been advanced to prove that this or any other kind of gild was the germ of the burghal constitution. On the other hand, the gild merchant was certainly an official organ or department of the borough administration; and its influence upon the economic and corporative growth of English municipalities was considerable.

The early relations of the craftsmen and their fraternities to the gild merchant are not clearly indicated in the meagre sources at our disposal. Many artisans seem to have been admitted to the mercantile fraternity. They bought raw material and sold the manufactured commodity ; hence they were regarded as merchants ; no sharp line of demarcation was drawn between the two classes in the 12th and 13th centuries. Separate societies of craftsmen were formed in England soon after the gild merchant ; but at first they were few in number and of much less importance than the general mercantile fraternity. The origin of the former is not to be attributed to the latter ; there was seemingly no organic connection between the two classes of gilds, though many artisans probably belonged both to their own craft fraternity and to the gild merchant, and the latter, owing to its great power in the town, seems to have exercised some sort of supervision over the craftsmen and their societies. When any single body of artisans, such as the weavers or tanners, received from the king the right to have a gild, they secured the monopoly of working and trading in their branch of industry. Thus, with every creation of a craft fraternity the gild merchant was weakened, and its sphere of activity was diminished, though the new bodies were subsidiary to the older and larger fraternity. The greater the commercial and industrial prosperity of a town, the more rapidly did this process of subdivision into craft gilds proceed, keeping pace with the increased division of labour. In the smaller towns, in which agriculture continued a prominent element, few or no craft gilds were formed ; and hence the old gild merchant remained longest intact and powerful in that class of boroughs. The period of the three Edwards constitutes an important epoch in the history of industry and gilds. With the rapid development and specialisation of industry, particularly under Edward III., craft fraternities multiplied and grew in power, many master craftsmen became wealthy employers of labour, dealing extensively in the wares which they produced. The class of dealers or merchants, as distinguished from trading artisans, also greatly increased, and established separate fraternities. When these various unions of dealers and of craftsmen embraced all the trades and branches of production in the town, little or no vitality remained in the old gild merchant ; it was deprived of its independent sphere of activity. In short, the function of guarding and supervising the trade monopoly had become split up into various fragments, the aggregate of the crafts superseding the old gild merchant. A natural process of elimination, the absorption of its powers by other bodies, had rendered the old organisation superfluous. This transference of authority from the ancient general gild merchant to a number of distinct bodies, and the consequent disintegration and decay of the former, was a gradual spontaneous movement, which, generally speaking, may be assigned to the 14th

and 15th centuries, the very period in which the craft gilds attained the zenith of their power. As the present writer's views on this subject appear to have been misinterpreted, it may be well to add that the gild merchant did not give birth to craft fraternities or have anything to do with their origin ; nor did it delegate its authority to them. The development was one of slow displacement, or natural growth and decay, due to the play of economic forces. The history of the English gild merchant is mainly of antiquarian interest. In some places it long survived either as a religious fraternity, shorn of its old functions, or as a periodical feast, or as a vague term applied to the whole municipal corporation. In most towns the name and organisation disappeared toward the close of the middle ages, and the institution was represented by the aggregate of the crafts. The mediæval gild merchant played a less important rôle on the continent than in England. On the continent it occupies a less prominent place in the town charters and in the municipal polity, and generally corresponds to the later fraternities of English dealers, established either for foreign commerce or to regulate a particular part of the local trade monopoly. Its place in the civic government was in such cases similar to that of many later craft associations.

Craft Gilds.—The bond of union in a craft gild was at first that of common occupation ; a craft fraternity comprised all the artisans in a single branch of industry in a particular town. In the 15th and 16th centuries "mistery" and "company" were the most common names for craft societies, though the old term "gild" continued to be used. Craft gilds first appear in England and on the continent early in the 12th century. Their origin was similar to that of the gild merchant ; it was occasioned by the expansion of trade and industry, which increased the number of artisans. In banding together for mutual protection they simply followed a natural tendency of the age. It is not necessary to elaborate any more profound theory regarding the origin of these societies. As the trade of England continued to expand in the 13th century their number increased. In the 14th they were fully developed and in a flourishing condition ; by that time each branch of industry in every large town had its gild.

The members elected officers who were most commonly called wardens. The chief function of the latter was to supervise the quality of the wares produced, so as to secure honest and excellent workmanship. Hence the hours of labour and the terms of admission to the society, including apprenticeship, were regulated. Members were also expected to make periodical payments to a common fund, and to participate in certain common religious observances, festivities, and pageants. But the regulation of industry was always paramount to social and religious aims ; the chief object of the fraternity was to supervise the processes of manufacture and the monopoly of working and dealing in a particular branch of industry. The organisation and the aims of the craft societies of the continent were similar to those of England.

There was at no time a general struggle in England between the gild merchant and the craft gilds, though in a few towns there may have been some friction between merchants and artisans. There was no conflict in England like that between these two classes in Scotland in the 16th century. Nor is there any close parallel in England to the great continental revolution of the 13th and 14th centuries, by which the crafts threw off the yoke of patrician government and secured more independence in the management of their own affairs and some participation in the civic administration—in certain cases even a monopoly of the latter, the civic constitution being remodelled with the craft fraternities as a basis. Such a conflict was easily avoided in a country where royalty was potent enough to suppress local dissensions and to exact obedience from the towns, and where borough government was mainly democratic until the 15th century. True, there were popular uprisings in England ; but they were generally class conflicts between the poor and the rich, the crafts as such seldom taking part in these tumults. While many continental municipalities were drifting from an aristocratic to a more democratic *régime* in the 14th century, those of England were drifting in the reverse direction, toward oligarchy, toward government by a close " select body." As a rule the craft gilds obtained no paramount influence in the boroughs of England, but continued to be subordinate to the town government. Whatever power they did secure, whether as potent subsidiary organs of the municipal polity for the regulation of trade, or as the chief or sole medium for the acquisition of citizenship, or as integral parts of the common council, was, generally speaking, the logical sequence of a gradual economic development, and not the outgrowth of a revolutionary movement by which oppressed craftsmen endeavoured to throw off the yoke of an arrogant patrician gild merchant.

With the expansion of commerce and industry in the 14th century, though the organisation of most crafts was not greatly changed, two new kinds of fraternities appeared, and in the 15th century they became more prominent, namely, the merchants' and the journeymen's companies. The misteries or companies of merchants traded in one or more kinds of wares. They were pre-eminently dealers, who sold what others produced. They are not, however, to be confused with the old gild merchant, which originally comprised both merchants and artisans, and had the whole monopoly of trade in the town. The company of merchants was, in most cases, simply one of the many craft unions, or misteries, which superseded the gild merchant.

The appearance of journeymen, or yeomen, fraternities marks a differentiation or cleft within the ranks of some particular class of artisans, a conflict or divergence of interests between employers, or master artisans, and workmen,—an organised struggle which foreshadows modern strikes. The journeymen combined to protect their special interests—rates of wages, etc. But in most cases the new English fraternities, after struggling a while for complete independence, seem to have become subsidiary and affiliated organs of the older craft gilds. The movement assumed large proportions on the continent, and probably was wide-spread in England, though the published sources give us little information concerning the subject.

One more phenomenon in connection with the organisation of crafts is of considerable interest, namely, their tendency to amalgamate, which is occasionally visible in the 15th century, and still more frequently in the 16th and 17th. Several fraternities—old gilds or new companies—with their respective cognate or heterogeneous branches of industry and trade, were fused into one body. In some towns all the crafts were thus consolidated into a single fraternity ; in this case a body was reproduced which regulated the whole trade monopoly of the borough, and hence bore some resemblance to the old gild merchant. It is interesting to observe that already in the 14th century a similar tendency toward the union of crafts is visible in some continental cities, notably in the Netherlands and in Westphalia.

A notable feature in the history of gilds during the Tudor period was the policy of the crown to bring them under public or national control. Laws were passed, for example in 1503, requiring new ordinances of crafts to be approved by the justices of assizes ; and the authority of the companies to fix the prices of wares was thus restricted. The statute of 5 Elizabeth, c. 4, also curtailed their jurisdiction over journeymen and apprentices.

The statute of 1547 (1 Edward VI.) did not suppress the craft fraternities. They were expressly excepted from its general operation. Such portions of their revenues as were devoted to definite religious observances were, however, appropriated by the crown. The revenues confiscated were those used for " the finding, maintenance, or sustentation of any priest or of any anniversary, or obit, lamp, light, or other such things." Professor Ashley aptly calls this "the disendowment of the religion of the misteries." Thus Edward VI.'s statute marks no break of continuity in the life of the companies or craft fraternities. But signs of decay had already begun to appear even before the Reformation, and these multiplied in the 16th and 17th centuries. The old gild organisation was breaking down under the action of new economic forces ; its dissolution was due especially to the appearance of new industries, organised on a more modern basis, and to the extension of the domestic system of manufacture. The companies gradually lost control over the regulation of industry, though they still retained their old monopoly in the 17th century, and in many cases even in the 18th. The mediæval form of association was incompatible with the new ideas of individual liberty and free competition, with the separation of capital and industry, employers and workmen, and with the introduction of the factory system and mechanical improvements.

In the second half of the 18th century many craft fraternities still survived, but their usefulness had disappeared. Oblivious of their duties to the community, and intent only on self-interest, they had become an unmitigated evil. "They were," as Dr. Held aptly remarks, "ruins which hindered the building of new edifices ; the old stones could not even be used in the new structures." There seems to be no evidence of lineal descent or organic connection between them and trades unions. The privileges of the old fraternities were not formally abolished until 1835 ; and the substantial remains or spectral forms of some are still visible in other towns besides London.

[Wilda, *Gildenwesen*, 1831.—Fortuyn, *De gildarum historia*, 1834, especially for Holland.—Pappenheim, *Alt-dänische Schutzgilden*, 1885.—Hegel, *Städte und Gilden der germanischen Völker*, 1891.—Toulmin Smith, *English Gilds*, with Brentano's introductory essay on *The History and Development of Gilds*, 1870.—Von Ochenkowski, *Englands wirthschaftliche Entwickelung*, 1879.—Gross, *Gild Merchant*, 1890.—Ashley's *Economic History*, bks. i.-ii. 1888-93, contains the best general account of English craft gilds. The following works are also useful : W. Cunningham, *Growth of English Industry and Commerce*, 1890-1892.—Walford, *Gilds*, 1888.—Salvioni, *Gilde Inglesi*, 1883.—Seligman, *Mediæval Guilds*, 1887.—Lambert, *Two Thousand Years of Gild Life*, 1891.—Levasseur, *Histoire des classes ouvrières en France*, 1859. There is a bibliography of German gilds in Schönberg's *Handbuch der politischen Oeconomie*, vol. ii. 3rd ed. 1890, and a bibliography of French gilds in *Parliamentary Papers*, 1884, vol. xxxix. pt. v. p. 390. See also CORPORATIONS OF ARTS AND TRADES, especially for continental gilds.—A. Doren, *Untersuchungen zur Geschichte der Kaufmannsgilden*, 1893.] C. Gr.

GILDS OF NEWCASTLE-UPON-TYNE. At Newcastle the ancient gilds have survived probably more distinctly than in most other cities of England. Three of the most important of them, the Merchant Adventurers, the Hoastmen, and the Masters and Mariners, have a cor-

porate existence under royal charters. The Merchant Adventurers claim to represent the merchant gild granted to Newcastle by King John in 1215. They received their charter of incorporation in 1546 from Edward VI. under the name of the Merchant Adventurers of Newcastle-upon-Tyne, and the benefit of the charter is confined in express terms to merchants inhabiting Newcastle-upon-Tyne, who then belonged to the Society of Merchant Venturers in the parts of Brabant beyond the seas—a title by which the London Company of the Merchant Adventurers of England, who had branches at Newcastle, Yarmouth, and other maritime towns, were then known. Both before and after receiving the charter, they controlled, as a merchant gild, the foreign and domestic trade of the town. They were subdivided into three distinct fellowships : the drapers or merchants of woollen cloth, the mercers or merchants of silk, and the boothmen or merchants of corn. The Hoastmen, a gild for loading and disposing of coal and stones, were incorporated 1600 by Queen Elizabeth. The Masters and Mariners were incorporated 1536 by King Henry VIII.

Of the other existing gilds, about twenty-nine in number, two or three claim a corporate existence under early charters from the crown, but most of them are unincorporated fraternities constituted by ordinances granted to them by the borough corporation of Newcastle-upon-Tyne. In most of the companies the members no longer follow the trades or occupations designated, and in none of them do the companies exercise any control or influence over these trades or crafts ; they principally exist to administer the property they have inherited or acquired. The stewards of the companies are the statutory representatives of the freemen of Newcastle, in whom the exclusive right of grazing the town moor, locally called the "eatage," is still vested.

[Some information as to these gilds may be found in Walker and Richardson's *Armorial Bearings of the Incorporated Companies of Newcastle-upon-Tyne*, 1824.—Brand's *History of Newcastle*, 1789.—Brown's *Short Account of the Customs and Franchises of the Freemen of Newcastle*, 1823.—Gibson's *Newcastle-upon-Tyne Improvement Acts*, 1881, and in *Extracts from the Records of the Merchant Adventurers of Newcastle-upon-Tyne*, published by the Surtees Society in 1895.—Mackenzie's *History of Newcastle*, 1827.—Walford on *Gilds*, 1888, which contains a chapter on Newcastle gilds.]

GILD SYSTEM IN SPAIN. GREMIOS or CRAFT-GILDS arose in Spain during the middle ages under the influence of the same causes as in the rest of Europe. Each separate kingdom of the Spanish monarchy had its own separate laws on the subject, but in all it was strictly kept in hand by the royal prerogative. In Barcelona alone, the *gremios* were exclusively subordinate to the municipal authorities, even in matter of statutes and legislation, and the royal judges had no jurisdiction over them.

The first opposition against the exclusiveness of the *gremios* arose in Aragon towards the end of the 17th century, but the general opinion remained favourable to their existence for a century more, notwithstanding the striking abuses to which they had given rise. Thus in 1763 the five *Gremios Mayores* of Madrid (silk-weavers, clothiers, hosiers, grocers, and jewellers) succeeded in farming the royal revenue and in founding a privileged company, trading with its own vessels and owning factories in different parts of Spain. The *Gremios* preserved a legal standing up to 1834, although in 1775 CAMPOMANES (*q.v.*) had already proposed their reform in his *Discurso sobre la Educacion Popular*, and, ten years later, JOVELLANOS (*q.v.*) advocated their suppression in his report on the liberty of industry (*Informe sobre la libertad de las Artes*) submitted to the general council of commerce.

[Colmeiro, *Historia de la Economía Política en España*, vol. ii. pp. 237-251. For the regulations of the *Gremios Mayores* see LARRUGA, *Memorias Políticas* (1787), vol. i. pp. 105-169 and 283-314.]

E. CA.

GIOGALLI, SIMONE (17th century), though not an economist, holds a distinguished place in the history of economic doctrine in Italy. He was a clever Venetian merchant, highly esteemed for a memoir presented to the board of enquiry for trade of the Venetian republic.

When consulted as to the causes of the falling away of the trade of Venice, once so prosperous, and the remedies for this, Giogalli presented the paper mentioned above (*Scrittura inedita di Simone Giogalli, negoziante veneto del sec. xvii.* Venezia, 1856), containing principles of economic liberty. Giogalli's ideas certainly do not go beyond the narrow boundaries of his republic, but his aim was to foster the commerce of Venice through liberty, in order to establish competition with other markets. However far this was from an international free trade, it is remarkable considering that monopoly, privileges, and heavy taxes were then the basis of national economic government.

A. B.

GIOJA, MELCHIORRE (1767-1829), born at Piacenza, died at Milan, studied first theology, then mathematics, economics, and statistics, to which last he applied himself steadily. The political vicissitudes towards the end of the last and the beginning of the present century involved his life : he was imprisoned several times, held and lost various positions, including that of director of the statistical office at Milan under the French ; and on returning to that city after a short exile his writings were his sole means of support.

Gioja's works are on public economy, statistics, morals, education, and logic. "He could work hard, and his knowledge was extensive. Analysis was his strong point, but not criticism, where he showed himself captious and unbridled. Not a few of Gioja's observations are equally subtle and original, particularly in his theory of the association of labour of various kinds ; but once get him with one of his tabulated statements in hand, and he is the very genius of pedantry " (Cossa, *Introduction to Pol. Econ.*, translation, p. 488). Gioja's greatest work, *Nuovo prospetto delle scienze economiche* (serie i. "Teoria." Milano, 1815-17, vols. i.-iv.) sums up what had been written on *economics, finance, and administration* : he opposed the price fixed for bread by authority (*calmieri*), and favoured large properties ; he preferred the arts to agriculture, great manufactures to small ones, great merchants to small merchants, and large towns to small ones.

But while Gioja partly adopted the teaching of the English economists, he contributed to hinder the progress of economic science by a narrow harsh system of protection and government interference, in support of which he wrote *Discorso popolare sulle manifatture nazionali e tariffe daziarie dei commestibili ed il caro prezzo del vitto*, Milano, 1802.

Still he deserves praise for his acute observations on the theory of *associazione dei travagli*. He studies there all the advantages derived from these, justly considering them a cause of improvement in production. He also initiated with CUSTODI and ROMAGNOSI the *Annali universali di Statistica* (1824-1871), continued by Sacchi, which form one of the best collections of economic, statistical, and social studies which Italy can boast of. Among the many works of this author, besides the numerous writings in the *Annali* and his economic papers of local interest may be noted :— *Del merito e delle ricompense*, etc., Milano, 1818.—*Filosofia della Statistica*, Milano, 1826.—*Indole, estensione e vantaggi della Statistica*, Milano, 1809. —*Logica Statistica*, Milano, 1808.—*Tavole Statistiche*, etc., Milano, 1808.

A. B.

GIRARDIN, ÉMILE DE (1806-1886), born and died at Paris, was a man who carried everything to extremes. An unscrupulous speculator, an original and impartial thinker, a devoted friend, active in business, eminent as a man of letters, and constantly seeking notoriety, he loved discussion above all things, though it should only end in paradox. He was proud, rash, brave, and chivalrous. The natural son of Alexander Comte de Girardin, he accepted his lot in life with courage, almost glorying in it. He was appointed inspector-general of the *Beaux Arts* in 1828. Two years later he founded the journal *Le Voleur* afterwards *La Mode*. After the revolution of 1830 he warmly took up the cause of cheap periodical literature. This of all the acts of his life was the one which brought him the best deserved reputation.

He proposed to Casimir Périer to apply that system to the *Moniteur universel*, then the official journal, and to reduce its price to one sou. The minister refused, with a smile of contempt—he was not far-sighted enough to perceive what a force the cheap press might become. Girardin, repulsed by him, founded the *Journal des connaissances utiles* at the price of four frs. a year. This obtained 130,000 subscribers. He next became the champion of savings banks, freely spending his own money, though he was then not wealthy, to encourage them. Next he established the *Musée des familles*, a periodical which was a formidable competitor to the *Magasin pittoresque*. After founding other periodicals, he plunged into such speculations as the mines of Saint Bérain. After this Girardin commenced his first important attempt to establish a cheap daily paper. On the 1st July 1836, *La Presse* appeared, a journal costing forty frs. a year, while all the other great newspapers were charging eighty frs. Success attended this bold enterprise. It brought on, however, a duel with Armand Carrel, in which Girardin had the misfortune to kill his opponent. He made a vow never to fight a duel again, this last had been his fourth, and, whatsoever the provocation, kept his oath. In 1834 he became a deputy, and retained his seat till 1848. He professed at that time to belong to no political party, and to be attached to no form of government, declaring himself on different occasions in favour of absolute liberty. The revolution of 1848 came on, and notwithstanding all that he had said he took up a side, warmly professing confidence in the new order of things. But this state of feeling did not last long. He was annoyed at not being elected a member of the constituent assembly, and was embittered by an illegal imprisonment which he suffered. He sacrificed his political sympathies to his personal animosity against General Cavaignac. He took an active part in the presidential elections of the 10th December 1848 in favour of Louis Napoléon Bonaparte, who knew his character so little that he omitted to appoint him one of his ministers—ministerial position being at this time the height of Girardin's ambition. The unsteadiness of his principles and the force of public opinion drove him into isolation—the undisciplined character of his mind retained him in that condition. At last a district of the department of the *Bas-Rhin* sent him to parliament only a short time before its violent dispersion. The second of December drove him into exile, whence he speedily returned, connected himself again with *La Presse*, left it, returned to it, quitted it again, then bought the newspaper *La Liberté*. His fertile pen revived the prosperity of that journal. Shortly after this Girardin got into favour at court and was named a senator, unhappily in time to urge his country into the war of 1870 so fatal for France. He then founded the paper *La France*, supported the government of Thiers, and energetically attacked Marshal MacMahon. The last ten years of his life were scarcely less active than those which had preceded, but the public paid no further attention to him.

Among the great mass of his works a good many

were concerned with political economy, the following being the more important : *De l'instruction publique en France*, 1838.—*De la liberté du commerce et de la protection de l'industrie.* Letters exchanged between Ad. Blanqui and Émile de Girardin, Paris, 1846-47, 8vo.—*L'abolition de la misère par l'élévation des salaires*, 1850, 8vo.—*L'Impôt*, 8vo, 1853. In this last work he declared himself in favour of a single tax, which he proposes to make the basis of an insurance against those risks which disturb owners in the enjoyment of their possessions.—*Questions administratives et financières*, 1858. A. C. f.

GIUSTINIANI, D. BERNARDO, was a priest (17th century). He is known in connection with a dispute as to lawful and unlawful forms of exchange. The application of the then existing theories of the canonists on usury led to difficulties in the new contracts entered into by dealers in the different kinds of exchange. According to the canonists, profit on exchange was lawful, provided it was real and did not conceal usury. The *cambio colla rincorsa*, as it was called, which Padre Giustiniani opposed, was practised in order to conceal usury. He describes it thus : "Titius, an inhabitant of Genoa, requires 1000 scudi, and asks Cajo, a money-lender, to supply them ; saying to him, 'Arrange this for me on bills on Piacenza.' This is done as follows :—Cajo writes to his agent in Piacenza telling him to pay the sum to himself, crediting himself and debiting Titius, and after computing the charge to remit the debt and credit to Genoa—and thus it is done." In this manner money was borrowed in the kingdom of Naples, and as much as 30 per cent per annum paid. Giustiniani shows clearly that all this is merely a semblance of an exchange operation entered into to conceal a loan of money on usury. Some money-lenders even told him that they did not really send letters of exchange, but only made notes in their books. Starting from the principle, prevalent in those days, that usurious loans of money are wrong, Giustiniani's reasoning is sound. *Breve trattato delle continuationi dei Cambi*, Genoa, 1619.

[Gobbi, *L'economia politica negli Scrittori italiani del Secolo XVI.-XVII.*, Milan, Hoepli, 1889.] U. R.

GLANVILL, RANULF (died 1190, at the siege of Acre), sheriff, judge, and chief justiciar, 1180, under Henry II. He fought for the king against the Scots in the rebellion of 1174 ; in 1185 he took the cross, which perhaps accounts for his being deprived of the justiciarship on the accession of Richard I. He took a large part in carrying out Henry's legal and judicial reforms, especially in organising the *Curia Regis* —the later king's bench. A collection of the laws of England was drawn up by him (Hoveden, end of 1180), and he wrote a treatise, *De Legibus et Consuetudinibus Regni Angliæ*, which "deals principally with procedure or the mode of enforcing legal rights, but incidentally also with the rights themselves" (Digby, *Real Property*, 68). Incidentally therefore, apart from the invaluable information concerning the legal practice of the time, much light is thrown upon the tenure of land through all classes, and upon the status, both legal and economic, of the serfs. If his account is too much coloured by legal theory and maxims of the Roman law, giving no hint of the variety of rights and customs ascertained by historical research, Glanvill remains valuable as the earliest writer who has left any definite description of the land economy of his time.

[Roger of Hoveden (Stubbs), ii. Pref. xxii. and iii. Pref. xxiii.—Kate Norgate, *Angevin Kings*, ii. 279 and notes.—Extracts in Stubbs's *Select Charters*, and Digby's *Hist. of the Law of Real Property*.] E. G. P.

GLEBE LAND. Church land. The endowments of the church have consisted mainly of land from very early times : to each parish church belonged a number of pieces of land varying in size and position according to the nature of the soil and the manner of cultivation, and these have been added to by more recent gifts. The word glebe, which meant simply farm, has become restricted in meaning, and now means land belonging to a parish church, which the parson may farm himself or let for a short term of years, forming, with tithes, etc, the endowment of the church.

[Jacob's *Law Lexicon*.—T. M. Dale, *Clergyman's Legal Handbook*, London, 1858.—Canon Isaac Taylor in *Domesday Studies*, London, 1888.] A. E. S.

GLOCK or GLOCKE, see KLOCK, KASPAR.

GLUT is a name (cp. glutton) given to abundance by those who, for any reason good or bad, look on it as pernicious.

An unusual abundance of a particular commodity often reduces its price so much that it is injurious to the interests of those who produce the commodity for sale, *i.e.* in order to exchange it for other commodities. These persons accordingly say that there is a glut, or that the market is glutted, whenever there is so much of the commodity they sell that it cannot be disposed of at prices fairly remunerative to them. Purchasers on the other hand merely say that the commodity is plentiful and cheap.

Ricardo (Principles, ch. xxi., in *Works*, p. 176) following J. B. Say (*Traité*, L. i. ch. xv.) and James Mill (*Commerce Defended*, p. 81) denies the possibility of a "universal glut"—a glut, that is, of all commodities taken together simultaneously. Malthus, following Sismondi (*Nouveaux Principes*, L. iv. ch. iv.) holds in his *Political Economy* (p. 353 ff.) that a "general glut" is possible, and in his *Definitions* (p. 247) he says "a glut is said to be general when either from superabundance of supply or diminution of demand, a considerable mass of commodities falls below the elementary costs of production." [For a discussion of this question see DÉBOUCHÉS, THÉORIE DES ; OVER-PRODUCTION.] E. C.

GODFREY, MICHAEL (d. 1695), brother of Sir Edmundbury Godfrey, was a financier and closely connected with Paterson in the formation of the Bank of England, of which he became the first deputy-governor in 1694. Macaulay states that he was one of the ablest, most upright, and opulent of the merchant princes of London of his day. He appears also to have been connected with Heathcote and PATERSON in their opposition to the monopoly possessed by the East India Company. Godfrey was killed in the trenches before Namur, whither he had been sent to the king in reference to money matters. His death caused a fall of two per cent in the price of bank stock. He was author of *A short account of the Bank of England*, London, 1694. The formation of the bank called forth strong opposition, and this tract of twelve pages was written in its defence, pointing out the advantages to be derived from it, especially as regards the lowering of the rate of interest throughout the country, and answering the objections made by its opponents. These, according to Godfrey, were chiefly goldsmiths and others who foresaw that their exorbitant gains were likely to be reduced.

[Thorold Rogers, *The first nine years of the Bank of England*, Oxford, 1887.—Macaulay, *History of England*.—Saxe-Bannister, *Writings of William Paterson*, 1859, vol. ii.] R. H. H.

GODIN, JEAN BAPTISTE ANDRÉ (1817-1888), was born at Esquéhéries, Aisne, France, and died at Guise, Aisne, after a life of beneficent activity as a captain of industry. The son of an artisan, he was but poorly educated, and in his twelfth year left school to join his father in the ironworks. At seventeen he started on a tour of France as a journeyman. The industrial revolution and the ideas of FOURIER and SAINT SIMON combined to dissatisfy him with the wages system as he saw it, and he determined that if ever he rose to be an employer of labour he would endeavour to raise the level of the workman's life and make it more pleasant and less laborious. In 1837 he returned to his native village, and after his marriage in 1840 opened a small factory for apparatus for heating, with one or two assistants. Employing the process of casting for portions of stoves, etc., not hitherto made in that way, he soon succeeded in increasing his business, until in 1846 he employed some thirty hands, and found the lack of communication at Esquéhéries becoming a serious drawback. He therefore removed his factory to Guise, on the river Oise. At the time of Godin's death in 1888 the annual output of his works exceeded in value four millions of francs (£160,000), of which nearly one half was paid out for wages to upwards of one thousand workpeople.

Godin proved a model employer. His constant solicitude for the comfort of his workmen, with whom he kept in the closest touch as their colleague rather than their master, exhibited itself in his encouragement of benefit and insurance and co-operative societies, his establishment of free schools, nurseries, libraries, theatres, clubs, etc. in his social palace or FAMILISTÈRE, founded in 1859, and in the gradual introduction of a system of profit-sharing, developing through industrial partnership into a co-operative company on a broad basis, which should continue to work smoothly even after its founders had personally passed away. This well-built and well-organised CITÉ OUVRIÈRE offers many collective facilities for comfort and enjoyment rarely within the reach of individual workmen elsewhere ; and the solidarity of its members in their social and industrial relations constitutes a guarantee of continued stability.

After the revolution of 1848 Godin subscribed £4000 (at that time the third of his fortune) towards the ill-starred expedition of Considérant to form a Fourierist community in Texas. The failure of this expedition was in some sense a disillusion to Godin. With his more practical intelligence he laid the plans of his own *Familistère*, and successfully carried them out. In 1870 he was elected *conseiller-général* by the republican party, and as president of the municipal commission of Guise, during the military occupation of that town by the Germans, he inspired it to refuse to pay any contribution to the victorious army—a refusal which the Germans were unable to overcome. In 1871 Godin was elected deputy for his department, and remained a member of the Chamber till 1876, when he withdrew from practical politics to devote the rest of his life to the management of the *Familistère*, the publication of its journal, *Le Devoir*, and the elaboration of his industrial and political ideas in the writings mentioned below. In 1882 he was created a knight of the legion of honour. In 1886 he married his second wife, who had for twenty-five years acted as his secretary, and has since edited his posthumous work, *La République du Travail et la Réforme Parlementaire*, 1889.

The other principal writings of Godin are : *Solutions Sociales*, 1871.—*La Richesse au Service du Peuple.*—*Les Socialistes et les Droits du Travail.*—*La Politique du Travail et la Politique des Priviléges.*—*La Souveraineté et les Droits du Peuple.*—*Mutualité Sociale*, 1880.—*Le Gouvernement : ce qu'il a été, ce qu'il doit être*, 1883. In these works he exhibits the bold and original qualities which distinguished him as a man of affairs, but shows the limitations of an untrained mind. He proposed the abolition of inheritance by intestacy, except by direct descent, and graduated death-duties rising from 1 per cent on £80 or less to 50 per cent on

£200,000, the state devoting the proceeds to the payment of its expenses, to the exclusion of all other forms of taxation. By this means he considered all members of the community would be provided with equality of opportunity. He urged peace between nations, and between the industrial classes of a nation, the latter result to be attained by the legal association of masters and men into groups of common interest.

[See the articles CITÉ OUVRIÈRE and FAMILISTÈRE, and the works there referred to.] H. H.

GODWIN, WILLIAM (1756-1836), author of *Enquiry concerning Political Justice*, London, 1793, 4to, the 2nd edition with material alterations, 1796, 8vo. The great doctrine of the treatise was declared by Godwin himself, *Thoughts on Dr. Parr's Spital Sermon*, 1801, to be the perfectibility of man. The characters of men are blanks, which their external circumstances, and, above all, political institutions, fill in. Justice is a general appellation for all human duty. Government is an evil, but necessary ; "it finds our rights invaded, and substitutes an invasion less mischievous for one that is more so." It is perpetuated "by the infantine and uninstructed confidence of the many "; but its action should be circumscribed within narrow limits. Society can only declare and interpret, it cannot enact. Private property in the labour of others is unjust, but is not therefore to be violently uprooted. Still, the goal must be complete equality of conditions. In treating of the benefits of a system of equality, Godwin is confronted with the objection from the principle of population. His answer is the conjecture of Franklin that "mind will one day become omnipotent over matter." The speculations of Godwin — in the essay on "Avarice and Profusion " in *The Enquirer*, 1797, 8vo—provoked the *Essay on Population* (see MALTHUS). In the *Thoughts on Dr. Parr's Spital Sermon*, pp. 54-77 are devoted to the essay, but, at that time, the main proposition of the argument appeared to Godwin "no less conclusive than new." He only complained of the limitation of the checks to misery and vice, so that the inclusion of the prudential checks, in later editions of the essay, may be in part due to Godwin. As time went on, however, and the views of the essay became more generally adopted, the attitude of Godwin grew more hostile, until in 1820 he published his work *Of Population*, which had taken two years in writing, and which purports to be a complete refutation of the essay.

[Godwin's argument will be found ably criticised in Mr. Bonar's *Malthus*, London, 1885, pp. 364-371; see also *William Godwin*, etc., by C. Kegan Paul, 2 vols. 1876 ; and the article in the *Dictionary of National Biography*, vol. xxii. p. 64, by Leslie Stephen.] H. E. E.

In his *Enquirer*, a series of essays (1797), there is an essay on "Riches and Poverty" (pt. ii. essay i.), in which amongst other things Godwin maintains that one evil result of poverty is the absence of leisure entailed on the poor man. He looks forward to a time when the economy of resources, better division of labour, and better division of wealth, will make it unnecessary for any one to give more than one-tenth or even one-twentieth part of the labour now bestowed on the earning of a livelihood (cp. MORE, OWEN).

Another essay, on "Avarice and Profusion," deals with the question of luxury in the manner of Tolstoi. If the rich would relieve the poor, they must *share* their labour, not by inventing new luxuries set the poor new tasks. Human wants need to be diminished rather than increased. Equality is always Godwin's chief aspiration. A third essay, on "Beggars," is adverse to indiscriminate charity as creating professional beggars, "the most abject thing upon the face of the earth"; but the course of the author's reflections on this matter does not run smooth. He insists that our feelings of humanity demand some indulgence.

Anarchism has never, on the whole, been so consistently, so patiently and so peaceably worked out into its details as in Godwin's *Political Justice* (1793). The use of violence in any form, even in penal laws, is absolutely condemned. The spread of intellectual enlightenment is to work the whole change. War is treated as due to the too limited intercourse between individual citizens of one nation and those of another, governments and diplomatists having too much power (cp. COBDEN).

Yet Godwin's allusions to the economists are not complimentary. He refers to the famous example of division of labour in the *Wealth of Nations* (pin-making), only to sneer at it; "The division of labour, as it has been developed by commercial writers, is the offspring of avarice" (*Pol. Justice*, vii. viii.).

At a later period of his life, when Malthus seemed to have convinced even Godwin's friends, the *Essay on Population* naturally became the object of Godwin's special enmity. With the aid of his friend Booth, he attacked its principles and its figures with all the force he could muster. The geometrical and arithmetical ratios are rejected. The increase in the American population is declared to be exceptional. He sums up his reasoning in three arguments:— (1) Population in many states is not increasing at all; (2) every new improvement enables the two ratios to start at par; (3) the excess must begin with the infants, and infants need comparatively little food and give us fair warning. Positively he contends that in all cases where there is excess the cause lies in political institutions (Godwin, *Population*, 1820, pp. 485 *seq.*). He was too sanguine in believing he had routed his opponent; many admirers of the *Political Justice* and *Caleb Williams*, will regret that the author of these remarkable books should have written so much that was of little merit.

J. B.

GOGEL, ISAAC JAN ALEXANDER (1765-1821), born at Vugt (North Brabant), member of a business house at Amsterdam, played a great part in the revolutionary and French period of 1795-1815, being a warm adherent of the patriotic (anti-Orangist) party. He was the head of the department of finance, first from 1798-1801, then under the Pensionary Schimmelpenninck (1805), under King Louis Napoleon (1806-1808), and the French government (1810-1813), when he was also a member of the French *Conseil d'État*. After the restoration he undertook a manufactory of blue at Overveen near Haarlem, and lived there until his death (1821). He was an economist especially in a practical sense. The present Dutch system of taxes is to a large extent his work. His ideas on this subject may be learned best by studying that system itself as it existed in the years 1805-1810, and his work: *Memoriën en Correspondentiën betrekkelijk den Staat van 's Rijks geldmiddelen* (Memorials and Correspondence on the State of the Finances of the Kingdom), written by the order of King William I., first published 1844, by the author's son. His principles are these: Taxes should be proportional to the wealth of the contributors, and to the measure of protection they stand in need of. Direct taxes are to be preferred to indirect, the latter being only allowable for fiscal ends, and to draw contributions from the less wealthy classes. Yet he is an opponent of an income-tax because he does not believe in the possibility of obtaining the necessary information. The mode of levying ought to be simple, the laws clear; he recommends few functionaries, centralisation, and special judges.

When a director of the Amsterdam loan-bank (1801), he proposed the creation of a general bank of issue and deposit, intended to be a private concern under government control. This plan was strongly opposed, but a few years later (in 1814) it became the basis of the charter granted to the Netherland Bank.

Gogel was a staunch adherent to the rule of *laissez-faire* in matters of trade and commerce. He disapproved of duties on articles of export, *e.g.* tobacco, in opposition to the Emperor Napoleon I., and vigorously opposed a measure proposed by Louis Napoleon containing a new regulation of gilds (1808). A. F. v. L.

GOLD

Gold as consumed in Industry, p. 218; Gold as Standard, p. 220; Gold Bullion, as a Commodity at the Mints, p. 224; Gold, Distribution and Production of, p. 225; Gold Certificates, p. 226; Gold Notes, p. 226; Gold Points in Foreign Exchanges, p. 226.

GOLD, AS CONSUMED IN INDUSTRY. Gold was probably employed for ornament before it came into use as money, although in the earliest records the monetary use is mentioned as much as the other. Its application to ornamental purposes was probably very ancient. There are instances of its having been applied to industrial purposes among savages who were unacquainted with iron and other metals. Its employment in the arts, so far as our records go, appears to have originated in the east, probably in India. It is now chiefly used for watch-cases, chains, rings, and other articles of jewellery ; for plate and similar ornaments ; for gilding, as gold-leaf and wire ; in dentistry, etc., etc.

It is very difficult to form an estimate of the amount used for purposes other than coinage ; and in all serious calculations of this quantity no opinion is expressed as to the requirements of Asia. A very great deal of gold is undoubtedly consumed in the arts in India, more, probably, indeed, than in any other single country. Mr. S. Pixley estimated very tentatively, in giving evidence before the Gold and Silver Commission in 1886, that £5,000,000 of gold were annually exported to India for this purpose alone ; but as the total annual imports of gold into India are now less than that sum, there is doubtless some over-estimate here.

As regards former centuries, JACOB has endeavoured to arrive at an approximate idea of the proportion of the precious metals applied to industrial uses ; but we have no means of judging how far he was correct, even for the time when he wrote. He considered that the proportion of the precious metals (gold and silver) applied to purposes other than coin was one-tenth of the whole quantity produced in the 16th century, and one-fifth in the 17th ; while he concludes that in the 110 years, 1700-1810, " the quantity of gold and silver which was converted into other objects than coin amounted to two-thirds of that which was left in Europe, after the part which was conveyed to Asia is subtracted from the total produce of the mines." But Jacob's estimate of the quantity of gold annually consumed in industry about 1830 is undoubtedly much too high, although he was at considerable pains to make careful inquiries. A better estimate is that of A. von HUMBOLDT, who supposes the European consumption in 1824 to have been about 9200 kilogrammes.

The only official inquiries on this subject are those instituted in recent years by the director of the United States mint. In that country a return is now annually furnished by the state and by private firms of the amount of gold used for industrial purposes. A certain quantity, estimated during the last four or five years at $3,500,000 (£700,000), is then added as the amount of coin melted down by jewellers and others for repairs and similar requirements. The whole amount appears by these returns

to have increased considerably of late years, from about $11,000,000 (£2,200,000) in 1880 to over $19,000,000 (£3,800,000) in 1892. But these estimates are considered by English statisticians to be too high.

For the civilised world—i.e. Europe and the United States—the best estimates are undoubtedly those of the late Dr. A. SOETBEER. These are based on careful computations, and are deduced mainly from official returns of the quantities stamped by government in each country, these quantities being subjected to various corrections, and estimates being made of the amount which escapes stamping, or which is old material melted down, etc. His estimates are, for the period 1831-40, about 18,000 kilogrammes annually, and, in 1871-80, about 84,000 kilogrammes annually, while he puts the whole quantity of gold used in industry during the period 1831-1880 at 2,070,000 kilogrammes. These are the net quantities—i.e. a deduction has been made on account of old material re-melted, but gold melted from coin is included. For 1883 he considers the gross consumption to have been 110,000 kilogrammes, less 20,000 kilogrammes for old material, or 90,000 kilogrammes net. Since then the requirements have still further increased, and the net consumption, following Soetbeer's calculations, must be put, in 1890, at between 100,000 and 120,000 kilogrammes. It is impossible to say how much of this represents coin melted down. In making the above calculations Soetbeer accepts the estimate of the director of the United States mint for that country. English economists generally hold Soetbeer's figures to be slightly too high, this being possibly due to his incorporation of the American values.

As regards the quantities consumed in different countries, Soetbeer gives the following (annual average, about the year 1885) :—

	Gross Use.	£ mill.	Subtract for old Material.	Net Use.	£ mill.
	kg.		per cent.	kg.	
United States .	21,700	2·71	10	19,500	2·44
Great Britain .	20,000	2·50	15	17,000	2·12
France . .	21,000	2·62	20	16,800	2·10
Germany . .	15,000	1·87	20	12,000	1·50
Switzerland .	15,000	1·87	30	10,500	1·31
Holland and Belgium . .	3,200	·40	20	2,500	·31
Austria-Hungary	2,800	·35	15	2,400	·30
Italy . . .	6,000	·75	25	4,500	·56
Russia . .	3,000	·38	20	2,400	·30
Other countries (Europe) .	2,300	·29	..	2,000	·25
Total .	110,000	13·75	..	89,600	11·20

No opinion can be given of the stock of gold actually in existence in a form other than bullion or coin.

A point still to be considered is, what proportion do these quantities bear to the whole amount of gold annually produced ? According to Soetbeer's estimates of production and consumption, the amount used in industry and the arts, old material being deducted, for each decade from 1831 to 1880 was

	Total Production.	£ mill.	Industrial Use.	£ mill.	Per cent.
	kg.		kg.		
1831-40	203,000	25·4	180,000	22·5	=89
1841-50	548,000	68·5	200,000	25·0	=38
1851-60	2,018,000	252·2	280,000	35·0	=14
1861-70	1,885,000	235·6	570,000	71·3	=30
1871-80	1,703,000	212·9	840,000	105·0	=49

The proportion for 1883 was 60 per cent of the quantity produced, and in 1889 57-68 per cent.

It would thus appear that about 60 per cent of the gold annually produced is at the present time devoted to purposes other than coinage in Europe and the United States.

[W. Jacob, *History of the Precious Metals*, 2 vols., London, 1831.—A. Soetbeer, (1) *Verwendung des Goldes und Silbers*, in *Conrad's Jahrbücher für National-ökonomie und Statistik*, Neue Folge, band iii., Jena, 1881; (2) *Edelmetallgewinnung und Verwendung, 1881-90*, ib. dritte Folge, band i., 1891; (3) *Materialien zur Erläuterung und Beurteilung der wirtschaftlichen Edelmetallverhältnisse*, 2nd ed., Berlin, 1886 (translated for the use of the Gold and Silver Commission)—*Annual Reports of the Director of the United States Mint*, Washington.—*Reports and Evidence of the Gold and Silver Commission*, London, 1887-1888; *Parl. Papers*, Nos. C., 5099, 5248, 5512.—Dr. S. M'C. Lindsay, *Preisbewegung der Edelmetalle seit, 1850*, Jena, 1893.]   R. H. H.

GOLD AS STANDARD. In history gold appears first as a valuable commodity. Thus in the new world the Peruvians, at the time of the Spanish invasion, valued, used, and treasured the metal, but do not appear to have employed it as a medium of exchange. Rare and highly esteemed, portable, durable, readily divisible, homogeneous, and easily worked, it soon came into use independently among many nations, and at early stages of civilisation, as a medium of exchange, to facilitate the process of barter. Thus the Mexicans used quills of gold dust for this purpose at the time of Cortes. And in the old world, among the Anglo-Saxons of the 9th century, rings of gold, the chief treasure of the kings, seem to have served as a medium of exchange, and by weight as a rough measure of value (Beowulf). These two functions of the metal are not in fact easily separated. The next great stage in the adaptation of the metal as an exact measure of value was the introduction of coinage—an invention which appears to have had a single origin to the east of the Mediterranean, and was adopted by different peoples at different chronological epochs, though at nearly the same stage of economic development. Among the Greeks its progress may be traced almost from its beginnings by extant coins.

Uncoined gold may be a measure of value, but it can hardly be a standard. A measure of value may be said to become a standard when recognised and defined by law, when legal payments are estimated in legal units appointed for that purpose. Thus oxen may be said to be recognised in some Germanic codes as a standard of value, side by side with gold and silver coins. When a piece of gold received the stamp of a king or a city it was thereby effectively declared to be such a unit.

It is unnecessary to enter on the barren discussion whether value can really be measured. Accurately or inaccurately, it is measured in millions of daily transactions, and the attempt to devise an accurate standard measure begins almost with the beginning of history. The definition of value "as power in exchange," though it leaves much to be desired in lucidity and theoretical completeness, may be accepted for the purposes of discussion. The object whose power in exchange is most nearly constant with all persons and at all times will make the best standard measure of value.

Since very early times gold coins have been used as a standard of value, but gold itself can hardly be said to serve as a standard of value until mint regulations have been devised to secure that the value of gold coins shall exactly conform to the value of the gold contained in them. The necessary regulations are these: (1) Gold coins of a certain stamp may only deviate within narrow and fixed limits from a well-known standard of weight and fineness (see REMEDY). To secure this end, means must be taken to withdraw periodically from circulation coins that have become light through wear and tear. (2) All who bring gold bullion to the mint must have the right to receive in return an equivalent in the form of coins. If the coinage of gold is not *free*, the action of the government may tend to a restriction of the coinage, and *pro tanto* raise its value above bullion level. The custom of coining for government profit, usual in ancient and mediæval times, and not altogether unknown in our own, tends to this result. Again, if coinage is not *gratuitous*, there is a margin of possible variation between the value of gold as bullion, and the same *plus* the charge for seigniorage (see SEIGNIORAGE). (3) Exportation and melting of coins must be permitted without restriction. Otherwise the supply of coins may from time to time exceed the needs of the community, and the value of the coins will fall below bullion level.

If the government of any country enacts that gold coins issued under the above conditions shall be unlimited legal tender in payment of debts contracted in the terms of the customary measure of value, gold is in that country a standard of value. Given these conditions, gold will be the sole standard of value, if the issue of other legal tenders is so regulated and limited that their value shall always conform to the value of the gold coins, of which they represent a definite multiple or fraction.

If both gold and silver are freely coined, and are unlimited legal tender in payment of all debts, at a fixed rate, a certain number of silver units being treated as equivalent to one gold unit, we have a joint or bimetallic standard of value. Gold is still a standard, so long as it circulates in the country at all on these terms, but it is a standard jointly with the other metal : the two standards are inseparable so long as the system works. This system, with all the conditions necessary to the maintenance of a joint standard, was in force in France from 1803-1874. A similar system is of high antiquity. It would appear that coins of gold and silver circulated at a fixed rate in Greek cities : the rate being 12½ to 1. Philip of Macedon seems to have made both his gold and his silver coins full legal tender, at this fixed rate, and his gold coins had a wide circulation even outside the Macedonian empire. Under the Roman republic and early empire gold and silver coins circulated at a fixed rate, the unit of value being the silver DENARIUS, or the SESTERTIUS (money of account). Under Constantine the gold SOLIDUS became the chief unit of value ; the denarius a subordinate unit. But we do not know enough about the mint regulations of the Greek and Roman states to say with any certainty whether gold or silver was the standard ; or, if there was a true joint standard. It seems more probable that neither metal was the standard, but that the coins were a joint standard at a fixed rate, circulating at a price considerably above their bullion value.

Professor Soetbeer's researches appear to make it probable that the ratio of 12½ to 1, as between silver and gold coins, was preserved throughout the Græco-Roman period by the custom of mint artificers and mint authorities ; but we know nothing about the market for bullion. (See Mommsen, *Hist. of Rome*, on these points.)

Throughout the middle ages, and indeed till recent times, silver coins were the standard generally in Europe. The position of gold was undefined and anomalous.

Under another system, sometimes known as unrated BIMETALLISM, both gold and silver are freely coined and circulate at no fixed rate. It naturally results that one metal is by consent though not by law adopted as the standard of value, the relative value of the other metal being settled by private agreement for each case. This is not a true bimetallic system, the conditions of legal tender being confused ; and may arise from circumstances such as existed in England between 1660 and 1717, when guineas of the nominal value of 20s. were freely coined, and also silver coins 20 shillings

to the pound, the pound (money of account) being the unit of value. This system aimed at rated bimetallism—a guinea = a pound. But the silver coins were so overrated, mainly owing to their worn and clipped condition, that no one would give guineas at the legal rate,—guineas were accepted at a rate varying from 22s. to 30s. The standard of value, as is theoretically possible in a bimetallic community, was in effect a single metal—silver : or perhaps it would be more correct to say the silver coins,—which were also unlimited legal tender.

When the treasury in 1698 fixed 21s. 6d. as the highest rate at which guineas would be accepted by government in payment of taxes, a step was taken in the direction of true bimetallism, which was rendered possible by the recoinage of the silver currency in the latter years of the reign of. William III. The last step was taken in 1717 (Newton's Reform), when guineas were made full and unlimited legal tender at 21s. This rate (about 15¼ to 1) was above the market rate, and occasioned a great influx of gold to the mint ; the silver coinage having returned to its silver value. Nevertheless the bimetallic standard was maintained without serious difficulty until 1775, when a limit was placed for legal tender of silver coins by tale. In 1797 the Bank suspended gold payments, and the country was for some twenty years confined to the use of inconvertible paper. In 1816, with a view to the return to cash payments, gold was established as the sole unlimited legal tender and standard. The free coinage of silver, which had been suspended since 1798, was no longer permitted, and the legal tender of silver was limited to 40s.

The study of monetary science has led in the last two centuries to the adoption of mint regulations and improvements in coinage without which a true metallic standard cannot exist. The influence of Lord LIVERPOOL (father and son, *q.v.*) led to the adoption by this country in 1816 of gold as the sole standard. Since 1872 the chief countries of the civilised world have followed the example of England. It is important therefore to be able to observe and estimate any variations in the value of gold ; and for this purpose it is necessary that the laws and circumstances which affect its value should be clearly understood.

The value of gold depends on interaction of demand and supply. Demand for gold is (a) demand for currency ; (b) demand for the arts (see GOLD AS CONSUMED IN INDUSTRY) ; (c) demand for hoarding, which tends theoretically to vary inversely with the value of gold—a smaller hoard of dearer metal being equivalent to a larger hoard of the cheaper (see HOARDING). Alterations in the legal standard of any country will affect this demand in so far as they increase the amount of gold required for daily use in that country, which need not necessarily be the case.

If the value of gold falls or rises, more or less gold will be required to do the same work as currency. (*d*) Demand for banking reserves. This demand is to a certain extent alternative to the demand for currency (see RESERVES, BANKING).

The existence of an effective bimetallic area of considerable extent tends to keep the value of gold in all civilised countries at a bimetallic level. During the period 1803-1873, if gold appreciated in relation to silver, the demand for silver in France increased, and gold was exported. Similarly during the period of enormous gold production in California and Australia, 1850-1865, France was taking gold and exporting silver, and thus no serious deviation in the proportion between the values of the two metals from the standard of $15\frac{1}{2}$ to 1 was felt. 1853-1860 France coined £155,000,000 sterling in gold, and meanwhile exported great quantities of silver, especially to the east.

Of changes in the demand for gold the most important are those that may arise from alterations in the standard of any country. When Germany in 1872 adopted a gold standard, she at once proceeded to sell silver coins and buy gold for coinage. Between 1872 and 1878 inclusive, about £80,000,000 sterling of gold were coined in Germany. Austria - Hungary prepared for the adoption of a gold standard by the accumulation of a reserve of some £30,000,000 sterling, and Italy secured about £20,000,000 for the same purpose. Between 1873 and 1881 the United States coined nearly £100,000,000 ; which may be taken approximately as the additional demand due to the adoption of a gold standard by that country in 1878.

It will thus be seen that every country, by altering its mint regulations, has power to alter the metallic standard of value *pro tanto* in every other country using a metallic standard ; and from this point of view the contention of those who desire to make currency arrangements a matter of international agreement may be accepted.

The demand for gold and silver as currency has until recent times been alternative. If more silver was used as currency, less gold, and *vice versa*. Recent changes have interfered with this substitution. The international measure of value, gold, has been more and more isolated ; silver has been becoming a commodity like other commodities ; any increase of supply of gold or any diminution of supply acts with full force upon the standard of value ; there is no longer a question of the proportion of any new demand or supply to the total stock of gold and silver, but of its proportion to the total stock of gold alone.

This general change in the currency of the civilised world has been rendered possible partly by the enormous increase in the pro-duction of gold during the last forty years, partly by the extension of the banking system, and the greater use of banking facilities, which enable a given amount of metallic currency to effect the exchange of a much greater amount of commodities. Gold, the international standard of value, still circulates in considerable quantities ; but it chiefly serves as a reserve to support the fiduciary currency and the book-entry transactions which to a large extent replace it in ordinary use. But this system has its disadvantages. Any sudden demand on the available supply of gold may remove in one country or in many the support on which the fiduciary currency rests. Promises to pay may cease to be current ; gold may be eagerly appropriated and jealously held ; hence follow temporary fluctuations in the standard of value through increased demand, which disturb for a time all commercial relations.

On the side of supply the value of gold depends, primarily, on the stock in existence. The stock in existence can hardly be estimated at less than £1,000,000,000 sterling ; it may well be more. Annual additions have little power to affect the value of so large a stock. But a great increase in production, extended over a long period, as has been the case since 1850, may considerably affect the value.

Some writers on economics have assumed that the value of gold depends solely on cost of production. Others have boldly stated that gold is always produced at a loss. It is probably true that some gold is always produced at a loss. The question with regard to gold is not one of the margin of profitable production, but of unprofitable production. When alluvial gold deposits are being worked this margin is very low. Many claims are worked at a loss under the incentive of gains secured in others. When gold is found in the quartz, at present the chief source of gold production, much capital is wasted in sinking shafts and erecting machinery for unprofitable mines. But no mine will long continue to be worked that does not produce enough to pay current expenses. Circumstances vary, and fluctuations are great. It is, however, certain that gold may continue to be worked below the marginal cost of production.

Such are the conditions that affect the value of gold—the most general and international standard of value. Under these complicated influences it would be surprising if the value of gold remained stable over long periods of time For short periods this value has great stability owing to the high proportion that the total stock of gold bears to any possible sudden changes in the amount demanded or supplied. An exception may perhaps be made in cases where inflated credit is suddenly shaken. The fall in prices that then occurs, accompanied by an exceptional demand for gold, is in one aspect the result of a sudden and temporary variation in the standard.

But over long periods great changes have taken place in the value of gold. These changes have been on the whole in the direction of depreciation, but there have been long periods of progressive appreciation. Such changes are very difficult to measure. No certain and unalterable test of value can be applied. The price of wheat, and the money wages of unskilled labour, are useful tests, but leave much to be desired on the score of accuracy. But such questions, however interesting, have only academic importance in so far as they relate to remote periods. The attempt to estimate the fluctuations of gold within a lifetime or a generation is one that must be made, and has often been made. It involves the most important consequences for trade and social relations.

An appreciating standard of value benefits the creditor at the expense of the debtor. A depreciating standard benefits the debtor at the expense of the creditor. It is often argued that if instability is unavoidable, it is better that the debtor should gain than that the creditor should. The masters of industry and commerce are debtors on a large scale. If the money values of their commodities are constantly rising by small increments, trade and industry are affected by a constant stimulus, such as is believed to have affected them between 1850 and 1866, and to have been succeeded, about 1875, by a continuous and progressive depression in all countries that use the gold standard. The burden of government debt is also increased by a rise in the value of gold. The social effects are more obscure though not less certain than those which appear in industry, trade, and taxation. To estimate such changes in the standard the following tests may be applied. The prices of commodities may be studied. If a general rise of prices, lasting over a considerable period, can be substantiated, a fall in the standard may be suspected. If a similar fall in prices appears, then a rise in the standard may be suggested as a possible explanation. But we must see if there be not some general cause or causes affecting commodities that will account for such fluctuations.

The wages earned by labour at different times may also be compared, especially those of unskilled labour. But here the changes affecting efficiency, supply, and demand are more obscure, and their results very difficult to estimate.

Finally, we may observe the causes affecting the supply of, and demand for, the metal or metals established as the standard of value. If two or all of these tests give a similar result, we may consider the change of the standard as sufficiently proved ; but it cannot be measured accurately.

To take the recent period 1850 - 1893 : Throughout this period the supply of gold has been largely in excess of all known previous epochs. But that increase was largest in the decade 1851-1860. Again in the period 1851-1866 no great new demand for gold coinage arose, except in France ; which liberated a corresponding amount of silver for use as currency elsewhere. The increased demand for currency must in great measure have been met by the constant extension of banking facilities.

A study of the general prices of commodities by means of index-numbers establishes for the period 1850-1870 a considerable rise. Comparing the depressed year 1850 with the depressed year 1869 by means of Mr. Sauerbeck's figures, we get a rise of prices of about 27 per cent, and other methods (those of Dr. Giffen, Prof. Soetbeer, Mr. Inglis Palgrave, the *Economist*), give very similar results, though the exact proportion is differently estimated. And this in a period when improvements in methods of production, and transport, and exploitation of new countries might have been expected to cause a general fall in prices.

A general rise in money wages between 1850 and 1869 can hardly be denied. Thus the fact of a fall in the standard of value between 1850 and 1870 seems proved ; and 20 per cent is the most moderate estimate that can be accepted.

On the other hand, between 1870 and 1893, although the production of gold was still very great, it was less than in the previous twenty years. Great new demands on the stock of gold for currency were made by Germany, the United States, Italy, and Austria - Hungary. The consumption of gold for the arts increased, and has been very roughly estimated by Professor Soetbeer at 11½ millions sterling, nearly one half of the total annual production. The hoards of gold for war treasure by the great continental nations grew. The demand for gold in India (a new demand, specially important in the decade 1860-1870) continued, and absorbed, in the years 1870-1893, nearly £70,000,000. The bulk of trade over the whole world increased steadily, and a larger proportion of it was conducted on a gold basis.

The general prices of commodities which had previously risen showed during this period a considerable net fall ; bringing them lower than they had been in 1850. The general level of wages was probably lower in 1893 than in 1870 ; though the fact of the fall, and especially its amount, is not so certain as the fall in commodities. This case is more uncertain than the other. The circumstances of demand and supply lead us to expect a rise in the standard ; though, considering the great and continuous production of gold, it could not, on this ground alone, be certainly affirmed. The fall in commodities is a certain fact. But some such fall might have been anticipated from the continued improvement of machinery, methods, and transport, and the development of new agricultural areas. And the wages of labour have not fallen in anything like the same proportion. The estimates of the appreciation of gold since 1873 and the corresponding depreciation of commodities have varied so much that it is hardly practicable to include them here—especially as at the present time (1895) the process appears to continue. Any estimate of this description must be very uncertain.

[This subject is so closely connected with that of bimetallism that a general reference may be made to the list given above under that head. The Report of the Indian Currency Committee, 1893, is the most valuable recent contribution to the literature of the subject. The following works may also be mentioned : Adolph Soetbeer, *Edelmetallproduktion und Werthverhältniss zwischen Gold und Silber*, 1493-1875, in Petermann's *Geographische Mittheilungen*, Gotha, 1879.—Dana Horton, *The Silver Pound*, London, 1887.—Del Mar, *A History of the Precious Metals*, London, 1880.—*A History of Money in Ancient Countries*, London, 1885.] S. M. L.

GOLD BULLION, AS A COMMODITY AT THE MINTS (see PRECIOUS METALS for bullion as an article of commerce, and GOLD AS CONSUMED IN INDUSTRY for use under that head). So many interesting and peculiar phenomena in the gold bullion trade, and so large a part of the status which it holds in relation to the standard of value, are due to the position in which gold stands at the mints of the world that, without trespassing upon its position in commerce and industry, or without touching upon the metallurgical and mechanical processes through which it passes before it appears clothed with the stamp of authority, a word may be said upon the treatment it receives as a commodity at the hands of the world's coining establishments.

All the mints of the civilised world are open to-day to this commodity in unlimited quantities at a fixed rate or price determined by law. The minor regulations differ in different countries, but the peculiar economic fact—an unlimited demand at a fixed and known rate—holds good for all alike. In England the royal mint, according to the act of 1870, must receive gold bullion when sent in parcels of not less than £100 nominal value. The master of the mint may refuse to receive, assay, or coin it if the standard value of the whole of the bullion is less than its gross weight, requiring a portion of it to be refined in order to bring it to standard fineness ; and if the assay reports show that any of the ingots are brittle or contain iridium they will be returned to the depositor. For purposes of convenience it is customary to require intending depositors to give the deputy master of the mint two days' notice, and to furnish in duplicate forms, supplied at the mint, a statement of the mark and assay report on each ingot, and the name of the assayer on whose assay they purchased it. The ingots are then weighed by the proper officer of the mint, and a statement of their weights is added to each copy of the aforesaid forms, one of which is kept by the mint and depositor respectively. If the report of the mint's assayer differs from that furnished by the depositor, and is disputed by the latter, the consulting assayer of the mint makes a new assay, and his decision is final. When these conditions are complied with, and the bullion found to be 916·6, or eleven-twelfths fine, the full mint rate, £3 : 17 : 10½ per ounce, is paid without making any charge for coinage, but notice is not sent to the depositor, nor is the money actually paid, until the coinage of the bullion is completed.[1] This causes, therefore, a loss of time and interest on the value of the deposit to the depositor. He consequently prefers to take his bullion to the Bank of England, where he always receives its value immediately upon announcement of the results of the bank's assay, at a rate of £3 : 17 : 9, or 1½d. per ounce less than the mint rate. Thus as a matter of fact the English mint has in recent years dealt solely with the Bank of England for its gold bullion. When the Bank has a large stock in hand it requests the mint to take it and resume coinage of gold, and likewise when the mint desires to commence coinage of gold it sends notice to the Bank, which immediately furnishes or procures the bullion. The Coinage Act of 1870 in England has been modified in one particular by the Coinage Act of 1891, whereby light-weight coins, within the limits of reasonable wear and tear prescribed by law, will be received at the mint at their face value, whereas formerly they were dealt with merely as bullion and received according to weight. The injustice whereby the last holder had to bear the whole cost of loss by wear during the entire life of the coin has thus been removed, and the cost of recoinage is now charged to mint account. An exactly similar relation to that existing between the English mint and the Bank of England exists in Germany between the German mints and the Reichsbank. The present regulations governing the gold coinage of Germany are to be found in the order of the chancellor of June 8, 1875, and the Reichsbank law of

[1] England is the only country in which the price for gold is not quoted for the weight of the fine metal but for the "standard" weight—viz. for a quantity containing 11 parts gold and 1 part alloy, which is the proportion used for English gold coins, whilst in German, French, and American gold coins the proportion is 9 parts gold and 1 part alloy. Any deviations from the standard proportion in England are accounted for by deductions or additions to the weight brought into account, and in the same way in other countries the deviations from absolute fineness are accounted for by deduction, but, as a general rule, bars are not accepted unless they have a certain degree of fineness.

March 14, 1875, whereby 2784 marks are paid for every kilogram of fine gold, and the same is then coined into 2790 marks, thus allowing the mint a profit of 0·215 per cent to meet expenses of coinage. The Reichsbank pays exactly the same rate, and that immediately on ascertaining the weight and fineness, so that the mint is entirely dependent on the bank for the gold bullion it uses. The system in France and Italy, which countries are members of the Latin Union, differs somewhat from that of Germany and England. There gold bullion may be brought to the mints to be coined, and returned in coin of the realm upon completion of the work, usually within a period of ten to thirty days, but less a charge for coinage amounting to 7 francs 44 centimes per kilogram fine. In the United States of America the system is again quite different. Gold bullion is received at any mint or assay office. Of the former there are three, one each at Philadelphia, San Francisco, and New Orleans, and the assay offices are plentifully scattered over the country. The bullion is paid for at once upon ascertaining weight and fineness, generally within two days after deposit, at the rate of $20.67 per fine ounce. If the bullion is not of desired fineness, and requires parting and refining, a charge is made for the operation, and in addition an alloy charge for the necessary amount of copper to bring it to a standard of 900 fine.

With this review of the conditions upon which gold bullion may be deposited, or sold to the principal mints of the world, it will be readily seen that there is little inducement for the actual miner or producer of gold to take his product direct to the mints, and as a matter of fact, with the exception of small quantities at times brought direct to the assay offices of the United States in the western states, the gold received at the mints usually comes from refining companies through the hands of bankers and brokers. The man who possesses gold in a crude state rarely has it at the desired degree of fineness demanded by the mints. He, therefore, except in the United States, must go to a refining company where he usually sells outright at a somewhat lower figure than the mint rate, instead of employing the company to do the work on his account. The refining company turns out the gold in stamped ingots of standard fineness, and again passes over the commodity into the hands of bankers or brokers at a small discount rather than comply with mint regulations and lose interest on capital invested while awaiting the return. In the United States, however, where the return is immediately made, much more gold proportionally is deposited directly by refining companies than by bankers and brokers. However, it matters not through whose hands gold bullion may pass, or what road it may travel, there remains a remarkable economic phenomenon,

not to be found in the case of any other commodity. There is always an open market or recipient, absolutely bound by law to accept this commodity in unlimited quantities at a known, and fixed, mint value or price ; for value and price are here the same, there being no room for the subjective or time elements to enter in except in so far as the national laws of the different countries might be changed. If a man parts with his gold to any one else, or uses it for commercial or industrial purposes rather than take it to the mints, it is because his return is equal to the known mint rate, or because the difference is, in his eyes, equivalent to complying with some of the minor conditions, such as transporting the product to a mint receiving office, or waiting for his money return. Thus also, to whatever use gold may be put, its value can but slightly vary from that stated by law by the principal commercial nations of the world.   S. MCL. L.

GOLD, DISCOVERIES OF.   See PRECIOUS METALS, DISCOVERIES OF.

GOLD, DISTRIBUTION AND PRODUCTION OF. The economic distribution of gold as a medium of exchange is widely different from its geographical distribution as a metal. The United States of America, the United Kingdom, France, Germany, and the western countries of Europe generally, use the largest quantities of gold either for coinage or ornament. The United States are only in part an exception to the statement, as the gold-using states are not the gold-bearing states. Gold is to be found in small quantities in almost every country of the world. In the early ages of the world it probably came mostly from the East,—very likely from the present mines of India : it was next discovered in considerable quantities in South America ; then at the beginning of this century in Siberia, in 1847 in California, and in 1851 in Australia. The rediscovery of the Indian mines, and the opening of those in Queensland, were important factors in the production of recent years, but hardly amount to the addition of a fresh area : British Guiana is in the same category ; the recently-opened goldfields of South Africa added another to the known areas of supply.

In 1891, according to *Statesman's Year Book* (table compiled from U.S.A. mint—for later reports see next page), the yield of the different areas in order of fertility was as follows :

	Tons.	£ Mill.
United States . . .	49·25	6·24
Australia . . .	46·62	5·91
Siberia	35·83	4·54
Africa	21·08	2·67
China	7·91	1·00
	160·69	20·36
From all other sources . .	26·61	3·37

The five areas enumerated now provide about five-sixths of the world's annual consumption of gold. South America, once the leading source of supply, is at present quite a minor area ; the yield from South Africa increases.

Respecting the amount produced in the past, computations have been made by Dr. Soetbeer which are probably as trustworthy as any such figures can be. He places the production of gold "up to 1600" at 750 tons, and up to 1880 at 10,355 tons, and the stock of gold in the world in 1880 as 9500 tons. But Soetbeer's figures give the total production between 1493 (when America had been discovered) and 1600 as over 745 tons, and there must have been a considerable stock previous to this. The following table exhibits the increase of production of gold.

Annual Average.	Tons.	£ Mill.
1493-1520	5·80	·74
1601-1620	8·39	1·06
1701-1720	12·62	1·60
1801-1810	17·50	2·22
1841-1850	53·89	6·83
1851-1855	194·39	24·64
1856-1860	202·80	25·71
1861-1865	182·20	23·10
1866-1870	188·87	23·95
1871-1875	167·98	21·29
1876-1880	169·69	21·51
1881-1885	152·52	19·33
1886-1890	167	21·17
1891-1893	214	27·12
1894	266·5	35·99

The annual averages fluctuate considerably. After 1830, when the Russian supply became important, the production increased nearly 50 per cent. In the ten years after 1840 it increased more than threefold : in the next decade, when California and Australia had been opened up, it had been increased again fourfold. There was a tendency in the supply to fall off steadily from that time for more than thirty years ; but lately it has again been increased, and the output for 1891, over 183 tons, was about equal to that of 1861, and decidedly higher than the average of the four years ending with 1890. As further discoveries are being made in New South Wales, Western Australia, and British Guiana, the supply is not likely to diminish at present. The average annual production since 1848 has probably not been far short of one-tenth of the total production of gold in the preceding 350 years taken together.

Another interesting feature in the production of gold is the comparative fertility of the different areas of supply. Mulhall, taking 500 years to 1880, assigns 21·5 per cent of the total product to Spanish America, 19·7 to the United States, and 17·8 to Australia. But each year alters those proportions, and in 1891 about 27 per cent came from the United States, 25 per cent from Australia, 22 per cent from Russia, over 10 per cent from Africa, as will be seen by the table above.

[The First Report of the Gold and Silver Commission, C. 5099, 1887, quotes Soetbeer's table, and contains the evidence of Mr. Inglis Palgrave and Sir. R. Giffen. The figures for Australia can be found carefully collected in the *Victorian Year-Book* for 1892, pp. 333 *seq.*—Suess, *Zukunft des Goldes* and *Zukunft des Silbers*.]   C. A. H.

GOLD AND SILVER WARE. (See HALL MARKING.)

GOLD CERTIFICATES. Twice in recent history the issue of gold certificates has been authorised in the United States. Power was given to the treasury department under the act of 3rd March 1863. They were discontinued by act of 1st December 1878, but again authorised 12th July 1882. These certificates are issued against deposits of gold in denominations of not less than $20 each, and are designed especially for use as bank reserves, and the settlement of clearing-house balances. The issue of these certificates is suspended whenever the gold in the treasury falls below $100,000,000.

[*Finance Report of the United States* for 1882, p. 171.—Compare Blue Book, *Committee on Indian Currency* (Gairdner's Evidence).—C. F. Dunbar, *Chapters on the Theory and History of Banking*, 1891.]   D. R. D.

GOLD MINING ROYALTIES. (See ROYALTY.)

GOLD NOTES. On account of the popular prejudice in California to paper money of any kind, banks were permitted to be organised in the United States by the act of 12th July 1870, under the national banking law whose issues were to be redeemed in gold coin alone instead of in legal tender which included greenbacks and silver. In all other principal points, however, these institutions were similar to the national banks found throughout the United States. These banks, of which there were never many, were known as gold banks. By the act of 14th February 1880 authority was given to convert these institutions into national banks of the usual form.

[*Finance Report of the United States*, for 1875, p. 219 ; also for 1877, p. 155.]   D. R. D.

GOLD POINTS IN FOREIGN EXCHANGES. The rates of exchange quoted between any two countries are for drafts or bills of exchange, and the price includes, besides the actual equivalent of the standard coin (*a*), some allowance for interest, according to the tenor of the draft, and (*b*) a premium which the seller demands for the economy and superior convenience of his draft, as compared with a remittance in bullion. This premium is greater or less, conversely to the amount of drafts in the market as compared with the demand for them, but it cannot, in any case, rise much above the cost of remitting coin, nor can it at all exceed that amount for any considerable time. The cost of remitting gold between London and Paris is somewhere about one-half per cent, or 4 per mille, Berlin about 5 per mille, and New York about 5 per mille. Therefore by adding or deducting this rate to or from the MINT PAR (*q.v.*), we have a rate which is called the "gold point," or "bullion point," and at which bullion will be remitted one way or the other. The gold points on the London exchange with some of the principal countries are—

London on	Mint Par.	Gold Exports.	Gold Imports.
Paris . .	Fcs. 25·22½	25·12½	25·32½
Berlin . .	Mks. 20·43	20·34	20·52
Amsterdam .	Fl. . 12·10	12·04	12·15
Copenhagen .	Kr. 18·16	18·07	18·23
New York .	$ . . 4·87	4·84	4·90

These are the rates at which bullion remittances become generally profitable, but, as a matter of fact, gold movements begin before these points are reached, as some business houses with special facilities, or undertaking large transactions, find a profit in remitting gold at much closer rates.

In comparing these with current quotations, regard should be had to the other factor (*a*) referred to above—the allowance for interest. On the London exchange, rates, as usually given, are for three months' or ninety days' drafts, the only exchanges quoted "short" being those with Paris, Amsterdam, New York, and Calcutta.

Care must also be taken to distinguish between rates quoted in foreign money and those quoted in sterling. With France, Belgium, Italy, Germany, Austria, Holland, and the Scandinavian Union, exchanges are quoted in foreign money, at so many francs, marks, florins, etc., to the pound sterling ; and, in these cases, the *higher* the quotation the more favourable it is to this country—*i.e.* the greater the amount of foreign money we have to receive. The *lower* gold point is that at which bullion will leave this country. With Spain, Portugal, Russia, India, and China, exchanges are quoted in sterling, at so many pence per dollar, milreis, rouble, or rupee, and the *lower* the quotation the more favourable it is to this country, whilst the *upper* gold point will mark bullion exports.

At some times and places, where a gold standard nominally exists, and the currency consists of inconvertible paper and of subsidiary coinage that is useless for export, the movements of the exchanges are independent of the "gold points," or, it should rather be said that new and fluctuating gold points are set up, governed by the cost of obtaining gold as well as of remitting it.   R. W. B.

GOLD, QUEEN.   See QUEEN GOLD.

GOLDSMITHS ; GOLDSMITHS' NOTES. The date (namely about 1645) at which English goldsmiths extended their operations, from trad-

ing in money and the precious metals to a regular system of private banking, can be approximately fixed through a pamphlet entitled *The Mystery of the Newfashioned Goldsmiths or Bankers discovered* (London. 1676). This pamphlet informs us that the goldsmiths had extended their previous business to lending money and to most of the operations of modern banking, their largest advances being made to the king upon the security of the taxes. The goldsmiths allowed interest to those who placed money with them, and the receipts which they gave for these deposits passed from hand to hand as currency in much the same manner as Bank of England notes do now. That this business soon grew considerably is evident from the testimony of Sir Dudley NORTH in 1680, who, on returning from abroad after many years, was greatly astonished at the new practice of merchants and others making payments by drawing bills on bankers, *i.e.* goldsmiths. Hence it will be seen that the goldsmiths, from the middle of the 17th century onwards, assisted greatly to accustom people to the use of a paper currency. As instances of this it may be cited that the Long Parliament in 1649 agreed to accept Goldsmiths' Hall bills, as well as ready money, in payment for the bishops' lands (Scobell's *Acts*, ii. 86) ; and that in 1696 during the recoinage "all great dealings were transacted by tallies, bank bills, and goldsmiths' notes" (Davenant, *Discourses*, ii. 161). The English goldsmiths of the 17th century in issuing their notes acted on quite a different principle from the continental banks of that date. Most of the continental banks, for example the BANK OF AMSTERDAM (*q.v.*), professed to be merely banks of deposit of coin or bullion, and to hold in this form the full value of the bills issued against these deposits. Our goldsmiths, and the Bank of England following them, purported to give in their bills the equivalent of what they had received, but never pretended to take the deposit for any other purpose than that of trading with it. They did not make their issues square exactly with the deposits of coin and bullion entrusted to them, "but coined their own credit into money." This resulted occasionally in difficulties. The first recorded run on the private banks, or goldsmiths, was in 1667 after the disastrous defeat suffered by the English fleet at the hands of the Dutch at Chatham. Then the stoppage of the exchequer in 1672 seriously affected their credit ; even their honesty was impugned ; and in course of time it was found that paper money issued on the security of a small number of individuals, could not circulate profitably in competition with that of a powerful joint-stock corporation, such as the Bank of England became in spite of the goldsmith's opposition.

[The most interesting information as to the general banking business of goldsmiths is given in the pamphlet of 1676 already mentioned (London, 4to, 8 pp.), which is quoted with additional remarks by Anderson, *Chron. Deduct. of Commerce*, year 1645. Also another pamphlet, *England's Glory in the Great Improvement by Banking and Trade*, London, 1694.—W. Cunningham, *Growth of English Industry and Commerce*, ii. 105, 222, 224.—Thorold Rogers, *First Nine Years of the Bank of England*, pp. 6, 21, 70.—Macaulay, *Hist. of England*, ch. xx.—Davenant, *Discourses on the Public Revenues and Trade of England* (1698), i. 265, and ii. 161.—*Mystery of the New-Fashioned Goldsmiths or Bankers Discovered*, 1676, reprinted in *Quart. Journ. of Economics*, Boston, Jan., 1888.]   H. de B. G.

GOOD (colonial notes) is a term sometimes used in the British colonies for a paper acknowledgment of a debt—something of the nature of an I.O.U. We have met several instances of such acknowledgments being deposited in cases of unauthorised borrowing from funds under the control of the borrower.

But the most distinctive use of the word was to denote government notes in British Guiana: it takes the form "good-for" in the currency history of the Cape Colony. In the case of Berbice in 1800 and 1809 the Court of Policy issued these notes of various amounts in guilders. Similarly in 1806 in Demerara "goods" secured on the colonial revenue were made a legal tender, and those of private persons competed with them in circulation. In the Cape the term "good-for" was confined apparently to the private note which competed with government paper up to the year 1822. Compare French *Bon*, *Bon pour*, etc.

[Chalmers's *History of Currency in the Colonies*, s.v.]   C. A. H.

GOOD DELIVERY. An expression used on the stock exchange. A stock exchange security is not a "good delivery" if it has any defects on its face, *e.g.* mutilation, absence of the proper coupons or of any necessary revenue stamps, irregularity in the number; the name of the owner written on the document when payable only to bearer, etc., and in such a case a purchaser is entitled to refuse acceptance. In cases of dispute the decision of the committee of the stock exchange is conclusive.   E. S.

GOOD-FOR. See GOOD.

GOOD FOR TRADE. "It is good for trade" is a very common popular answer to any condemnation of wasteful consumption or extravagant expenditure. That consumption, whether extravagant or not, of the produce of any particular trade is profitable to the persons actually engaged in that trade is obvious; no one doubts for instance that to break a window is good for the trade of the glaziers. It is hastily inferred from this that extravagant consumption is "good for trade" in general, or profitable to the whole body of producers. But so long as the amount of labour performed and its productiveness remain unchanged, an increased consumption of one sort of produce must be accompanied either by a decreased consumption of another sort of produce or by a decrease of savings. Consequently the expenditure which is "good" for one trade is equally bad for other trades. Whether the extra consumption of one kind of produce is made up for by a less consumption of other kinds or by a decrease of savings makes no difference. Diminished saving is just as "bad" for some trades as diminished consumption is for others; saving is "good" for the trade of all those who produce the kind of commodities which are saved and added to the capital of the country, *e.g.* machinery, factories, railways, ships, and houses. That unusual expenditure in one direction only benefits one set of trades at the expense of others was clearly recognised by many traders after the jubilee rejoicings in 1887, when they found that the extra consumption of the products of other trades was being compensated for by a diminished consumption of the products of their own.

[Comp. Bastiat, *Sophismes Économiques, ce qu'on voit et ce qu'on ne voit pas;* 1. La Vitre cassée.]
                                                  E.C.

GOODS AND CHATTELS. An ambiguous expression like the word EFFECTS (*q.v.*) which, if used in a will, is generally construed as including the testator's whole personal estate unless the context requires a more restricted meaning.   E. S.

GOODS OF THE FIRST ORDER; GOODS OF THE SECOND ORDER. See PRODUCTION, INSTRUMENTS OF.

GOODS, CLASSIFICATION OF.

(1) Material Goods and Personal Goods, p. 229; (2) Durable Goods (Accumulable or Potential) and Transient Goods (Unaccumulable or Actual), p. 229; (3) Consumption Goods and Production Goods, p. 229; (4) Gratuitous Goods (or Natural) and Onerous Goods (or Acquired), p. 229; (5) Appropriable Goods and Unappropriable Goods, p. 229; (6) Transferable Goods and Non-Transferable Goods, p. 230.

The term goods has been used in a very general sense to denote any object of human desire. One of the purposes of a classification of goods is to provide the data for determining a definition of wealth adapted to economic science. But as hardly any of the objects of human pursuit are without some bearing on the science, there is a more important use in classifying them; namely, to bring out the different relations in which these various objects stand to economic activities. For this purpose it is necessary to consider such distinctions as are important in each of the different branches of the science. Accordingly, goods may be classified (1) from a general point of view; (2) from the point of view of production and consumption; (3) from the point of view of distribution and exchange. Under (1) goods may be divided into material and personal, and into durable and transient; under (2) into consumption goods and production goods, and into gratuitous goods and onerous goods ; under (3) into appropriable and un-appropriable, and into transferable and non-transferable.

1. *Material* goods and *personal* goods.

Material goods are those that depend on the properties and positions of material objects, not including human beings (*e.g.* food, climate, shelter provided by houses, transport of commodities). Personal goods consist of (i) attributes of individual persons (*e.g.* strength, knowledge, skill, a good conscience) ; (ii) relations between persons (*e.g.* social organisations, the esteem or trust felt by one person for another) ; and (iii) those benefits conferred by persons on themselves or others which do not involve any palpable change in the properties or positions of material bodies (*e.g.* advice, entertainment, protection, instruction). The act of rendering a utility to a person is called a *service :* a service is material so far as it effects an alteration in material things (*e.g.* cooking of food, cleaning and repairing household goods) ; while a service is personal which creates a personal utility (*e.g.* advice, instruction). The services of domestic servants are partly personal and partly material.

2. *Durable* (accumulable or potential) goods and *transient* (unaccumulable or actual) goods.

Durable goods are those which, being comparatively permanent, are capable of affording utility or a series of utilities at some future time ; while transient goods are the actually realised utilities themselves. Among durable material goods are to be included houses and machines ; and among durable personal goods, abilities and knowledge. Transient material goods would include warmth from fires ; and transient personal goods would include professional advice and hearing of lectures. Durable goods may generally be regarded as the *potential* sources of *actual* or transient goods. But it is obvious that most of the things that are distinguished as transient goods (*e.g.* instruction) may produce more or less *durable* results ; and, on the other hand, that durable goods (*e.g.* coal and food which are destroyed in use) may produce more or less *transient* results.

3. *Consumption* goods and *production* goods.

Man can create or destroy only utilities, not matter. The ultimate object of all economic activity is what may be called the *enjoyment* of utilities. On the other hand, some *sacrifice* of utility in the form of labour or effort is in general a necessary condition for creating utilities. Hence economic science has to take note of two antitheses : viz. (1) between the *destruction* and the *creation* of utilities ; (2) between the *enjoyment* and the *sacrifice* of utility. The terms consumption and production would naturally be used to indicate the former antithesis ; but, as a matter of fact, they have come to be used with more special reference to the latter. In other words, consumption implies *enjoyment*, whether this is or is not attended by the destruction of utility ; and production implies the *sacrifice* of utility, provided this is undergone with the purpose of creating utility. Hence we have the following

important division of goods into consumption goods and production goods. Consumption goods (*i.e.* enjoyment goods) are those which, being in the hands of the person destined to enjoy them, can be directly utilised for enjoyment without further expenditure of labour. Production goods, or auxiliary goods, are the unfinished products or instruments intended to be employed in aid of labour which can only be utilised by further expenditure of labour. According to these definitions, commodities in the hands of dealers, though otherwise completely adapted for direct enjoyment, are to be classed as production goods, because they are not in the hands of those destined to enjoy them, and, moreover, are only to be utilised by the labour of shop-attendants, errand boys, etc. On the other hand, a house of residence, even though occupied by some one other than the proprietor, is to be called a consumption good. Of course any durable consumption good is productive in the sense of affording, from time to time, many utilities ; and, on this account, such durable consumption goods have been called "consumers' capital." But since the utilities afforded by a place of residence, for example, are direct and not indirect, it is called a consumption good, though in order to preserve its capacity for yielding utilities, it may require repairs and cleaning from time to time. Consumption goods are also called *goods of the first order ;* while *goods of the second order* are those used for the direct production of goods of the first order, and so on. These distinctions are, however, not easily applicable (see PRODUCTION, INSTRUMENTS OF).

4. *Gratuitous* (or natural) goods and *onerous* (or acquired) goods.

Goods have also been distinguished according as their capacity to yield utilities is or is not due to human effort. The latter, being gifts of nature, have been called gratuitous ; and the former, being acquired by labour, have been called onerous. Thus Ricardo speaks of "the original and indestructible powers of the soil." But it is obviously not easy to draw the line between what is in this sense original and what is due to labour and industrial organisation. For many purposes it would be more convenient to distinguish as gratuitous those goods which have been handed down to the present industrial generation without effort on their part, *e.g.* permanent properties of the soil and inherited personal aptitudes. But in any case the distinction would be difficult to apply with any exactness.

5. *Appropriable* goods and *unappropriable* goods.

In using the term appropriable, it should be explained that what is appropriated in any case is the *opportunity* of benefiting from goods ; and this opportunity may or may not be secured by legal authority. Appropriation implies some *limitation* of opportunity ; *i.e.* while a single individual or a set of individuals can enjoy the opportunity, others are excluded from it. Possession by an entire political community would, however, not generally be called appropriation. In this sense, such material goods as climate and air, and such personal goods as political and industrial organisations, may be classed as unappropriable. Some appropriable goods (*e.g.* public roads and buildings, rivers and seas, commons, etc.) are actually unappropriated. Hence among appropriable goods we must make a further subdivision into appropriated and unappropriated.

6. *Transferable* goods and *non-transferable* goods.

Appropriable goods have further to be subdivided into *transferable* and *non-transferable*. The means and limits of transferability depend on legal as well as physical conditions. If one person A is in a position to choose whether he shall confer a benefit on B or on C, such a service may be called *transferable*, whether the transference is effected by contract between A and B or between B and C. Non-transferable appropriated goods are either material (*e.g.* opportunities of using public property or natural gifts) or personal (*e.g.* personal attributes, relations of esteem or trust, titles, honours, and other privileges). Transferable appropriated goods are also either material (*e.g.* opportunities of using goods in perpetuity or temporarily) or personal (*e.g.* benefits directly conferred by one man on another).

[Marshall's *Principles of Economics*, 2nd ed. bk. ii. ch. ii. iii. iv.—Sidgwick's *Principles of Political Economy*, bk. i. ch. iii. iv. v. These two works are specially instructive in regard to economic distinctions of goods. In addition should be mentioned the economic works of J. S. Mill, Senior, Hermann, Bastiat, Wagner, and Nicholson.]   w. e. j.

GOODS, ECONOMIC. In English the singular noun Good is usually abstract and psychical; it is usefulness, benefit, or blessing. But by the plural (Goods) is denoted concrete embodiments of usefulness, in short, "commodities" (see COMMODITY), the singular of which word is employed by economists to represent the missing singular of "goods."

As political economy is usually defined by its relation to wealth, and as wealth is defined as a sum of goods, it is clear that the precise definition and the classification of goods are matters of great theoretical importance. The discussions, growing no doubt out of the remarks of Adam Smith on the physiocrats, between Malthus, Ricardo, James Mill, Bailey, Say, and others on the proper line of distinction between productive and unproductive labour, took in later times the form of a debate on the propriety of including "immaterial goods," services, and legal rights among economic goods. The simplest and most intelligible definition of a commodity, a material means, not unlimited in supply, of satisfying human wants, excludes too much; and there is general assent only to the elements of limitation, as it seems obvious that goods of which no "economy" is needed are not economic goods.

To consider this question would be in reality to write a treatise on the whole theory of the fundamental notions of political economy, and it will be enough to refer to the authorities below.

[Marshall, *Principles of Economics*, bk. ii. ch. ii. 1890.—Hermann, F. B. W., *Staatswirthschaftliche Untersuchungen*, 1832, ch. iii.; *Die Güter.*—Schäffle, A., *Mensch und Gut*, 1861.—Wagner, A., *Allgem. Volkswirthschaftslehre, Grundlegung*, 2nd ed., 1879, pp. 12-30.—Menger, Carl, *Volkswirthschaftslehre*, 1871, ch. i. and ii.—Böhm-Bawerk, E., *Rechte und Verhältnisse vom Standpunkte der Volkswirthschaftlichen Güterlehre*, 1881.—Wieser, F., Article "Gut" in the *Handwörterbuch der Staatswissenschaften*.—Say, J. B., *Cours complet d'écon. pol.*, 2nd ed., 1840, pt. i. p. 31, ch. i.; *De nos besoins et de nos biens.*]

                                                  J. B.

GOODWILL,—the expectancy of a continuance, to the advantage of a successor in an established business, of the personal confidence, or of the habit of recurring to the place or premises or to the known business house or firm, on the part of a circle or connection of clients or customers. This expectancy is found to have a marketable value, and may arise from, or be raised in value by, several circumstances, such as the acquisition by the assignee of the sole ownership of the premises in which the old business had been carried on, the assignation to him of existing stipulations in behalf of the vendor, or agreement on the part of the vendor to recommend his successor or to abstain from competition with him. But goodwill in the legal sense, "goodwill without more," or goodwill in the sense of the bankruptcy acts, is restricted to such rights as may pass at law by an assignment of the goodwill without any special stipulation. Under this head will fall the exclusive rights to carry on the old business and to represent that it is the old business which is being carried on, which carry with them the exclusive right to the trade name—if the use of it be not likely to mislead, or be not so used as to mislead the public into a belief that it is the same person who carries on the business or that any of the old members are still in the business—to the trade marks, and any restrictions on others in favour of the business, so long as these are not merely personal, in favour of the original trader. Transfer of the goodwill in the absence of express stipulations leaves the original trader in the same position as any member of the public, free, so long as he does not profess to carry on the old business, to set up a business similar to the one sold, in his own name, where he likes and as he likes, to compete and to solicit old customers publicly or privately, and to represent that he had been a member of the old firm. Goodwill may be voluntarily assigned *inter vivos* as well as bequeathed by will; it is also liable to involuntary alienation upon bankruptcy or insolvency. Where compensation is paid for compulsory purchase of business premises under railway acts and the like, the compensation includes not only the value of the premises, but also as a general rule a sum representing the Goodwill.

[Charles E. Allan, *The Law relating to Good-will*, London, Stevens and Sons, 1889. Compare Schäffle, *Ausschliessende Rechte;* Böhm Bawerk, *Rechte und Verhältnisse.*] A. D.

GOOGE, BARNABY (1540-1594), published *Foure Bookes of Husbandry, collected by M. Conradus Heresbachius, Councellour to the high and mightie Prince, the Duke of Cleve*, etc., newly Englished and encreased by Barnaby Googe, Esq., London, 1577, 4to. This work was in the main a translation of Heresbachius's *Rei Rusticæ libri quatuor*, etc., Colon, 1570, 8vo; Spiræ, 1595, 8vo; Heidelb., 1603, 8vo. Editions of Googe's work were published in 1578, 1586, 1596, 1601, and 1614, and it became the basis of *The Whole Art of Husbandry in foure bookes*, etc., by Captain Gervase Markham, London, 1631, 4to.

[See notice of Googe, *Dictionary of National Biography*, vol. xxii.] W. A. S. H.

GOSSEN, HERMANN HEINRICH (1810-1858), was born at Düren, then a French village. His father and grandfather were government officials, and he followed the same career, with a want of success which is attributed to his predilection for abstract studies. He is described as amiable and unpractical. He retired into private life 1847; occupying himself first with a project of universal insurance, afterwards with his book entitled *Entwickelung der Gesetze des menschlichen Verkehrs und der darausfliessenden Regeln für menschliches Handeln*, which was published at Brunswick in 1854.

This work, which had been generally overlooked even in Germany, and is not mentioned in Roscher's History, was brought to light by Professor Adamson, and an account of it was given by Jevons in the preface to the 2nd edition of his *Theory of Political Economy*. It was extremely rare; there probably did not exist a copy in England except one in the library of the British Museum. It was reprinted at Berlin, Prager, in 1889. The work is an attempt to found economics on a mathematical basis, and the author regarded his services in the reform of the method of the science as similar to those of Copernicus in astronomy. We are told by Jevons that Gossen, who had been entirely unknown to him, had "completely anticipated him as regards the general principles and method of the theory of economics," but had been unfortunate in his development of that theory. J. K. I.

Gossen's book contains two elements of unequal value: a somewhat narrow and pedantic application of utilitarian philosophy to politics and ethics, and a very original formulation of the principle of final utility in economics. He starts from the epicurean or utilitarian first principle, "Man wishes to enjoy his life and makes it the aim of his life to raise the enjoyment of his life to the highest possible degree." Gossen maintains in the spirit of Bentham that the object of all men is to obtain the greatest sum of pleasure; in the spirit of Butler that, because this purpose is universal, it must be the design of the Creator. The true revelation given by the Creator is the command, "Man discover the laws of my creation and act according to those laws."

In obedience to this precept we have to investigate the laws of pleasure. They are two. (1) The magnitude of a pleasure continually diminishes up to the point of satiety, the longer we apply a stimulus or pleasure-giving object of constant quantity without cessation (*wenn wir mit Bereitung des Genusses ununterbrochen fortfahren*). (2) There occurs a similar diminution of the pleasure when we repeat the conditions of a pleasure enjoyed before. The initial magnitude of pleasure is less, and the period of enjoyment up to the moment of satiety is shorter.

These laws of our sentient nature are illustrated by diagrams closely resembling those which Jevons independently constructed, ex-

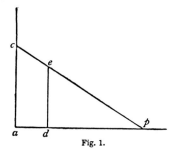

Fig. 1.

cept that Gossen prefers to use the simplest form of "curve," viz. the right line. Thus, in the accompanying figure, time is represented by the abscissa (*e.g. ad*), and the corresponding magnitude of pleasure by the corresponding ordinate (*de*).

The geometrical representation of psychical quantities is defended by the analogy of astronomy, in which science we compute distances of which the direct measurement is impossible. This exaggerated estimate of the mathematical method should be compared with the remarks in the Preface; where Gossen compares his work to that of Copernicus.

Gossen goes on to consider the most advantageous method of employing a given time upon different kinds of enjoyment. He finds that it will be best to leave off each pleasure at a point such that the terminal magnitude of pleasure is the same for each species of enjoyment. This simple principle is worked out by Gossen in considerable detail. Assuming for the sake of illustration the relation between utility and time to be of the simplest, the *linear*, species, he assigns actual numbers, and constructs an imaginary table for the best

employment of a given time (pp. 17-20). He
may seem somewhat deficient in the quality of
mathematical elegance.

To carry out the purpose of our life we
require a knowledge, not only of the laws of
pleasure which have been enunciated, but also
of the outer world in its relation to our happiness (p. 23). From this point of view there is
presented a threefold division of goods (pp. 25-
27). The first class denotes articles ready for
consumption, *e.g.* an apple, or a coat. The
second class denotes materials which require to
be worked up before they take a place in the
first class, *e.g.* wheat and cloth ; also such
articles as a pipe, useless without tobacco, a
stove, without coal. A third class denotes
objects which are altogether of the nature of
means ; such as fuel used for machines, everything used for production which does not subsist
and enure in the finished product.

The law of diminishing utility which was
first enounced with respect to time becomes
applicable to commodities, primarily those of
the first class, and indirectly also those of the
second and third classes—if we take quantity
of commodity as the independent variable or
abscissa, as in the diagram above ; the dependent variable or ordinate being, as before,
magnitude of pleasure.

We have next to take into account the
labour required to produce goods. Gossen's
theory of labour is equivalent to that of Jevons,
but worked out in greater detail. If, in the

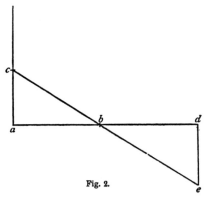

Fig. 2.

accompanying figure (Fig. 2), the abscissa *ad*
represents the time during which force is
uniformly put forth, the ordinates represent
the corresponding utility, beginning with
positive pleasure and descending to the pain of
fatigue. The same figure serves to illustrate
the relation between the quantity produced and
the pleasures or pains of production ; provided
that a constant number of days, or hours, of
work goes to a unit of product. But this
identity is destroyed, and an additional figure
is required when there is a change in what

Gossen calls "skill" (*Geschicklichkeit*) or
productivity of labour (pp. 40, 42, etc.). The
relation between this "skill" and another co-
efficient described as "capacity for work"
(*Arbeitskraft*) forms a nice question of interpretation (cp. pp. 40-42, 48, 53, 58, 64, 73,
108).

The separate representations of the feelings
attending production and consumption are
ingeniously combined by Gossen. He super-
poses on the pleasure of consumption the
pleasure or pain of work by *reversing* the figure
proper to the latter (our Fig. 2) ; laying down
the positive ordinates underneath, not above,
the abscissa. The ordinates of the curve *ce* in
our Fig. 3 (*Gossen*, p. 39) represent as before
pleasure in the way of consumption. The

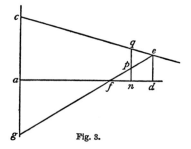

Fig. 3.

ordinates of the curve *ge measured downwards*
now represent the pleasure of labour. Thus *ag*
is the positive pleasure of production at an
initial stage. At the point *f* there is neither
pain nor pleasure. To the objective quantity *an*
corresponds the negative pleasure, the pain of
labour *np*. Hence the total satisfaction derived
from *an* is represented by the figure *gcqp*. This
area is a maximum when the abscissa is *ad*.

This illustration relates primarily to a single
product. But it may be extended to illustrate
the most advantageous distribution of labour
over a variety of employments, the ordinate
representing no longer the utility derived from
a single source, but from a whole set of objects,
in the proportions prescribed by the theory of
final utility.

This theory of economic equilibrium, as we
might call it, is worked out in immense detail
(pp. 40-80). Conclusions tolerably obvious to
common sense are enounced with respect to a
great number of supposed cases ; the enhancement of an existing pleasure (higher pleasure
corresponding to the same amount of means),
the addition of a new pleasure, either requiring
no exertion or derived from labour, a change
in "skill," or in "capacity for work," and so
forth. Gossen illustrates the conclusions by
numerical examples with his usual exhaustiveness.

So far we have investigated the laws according to which the solitary economic man would

regulate his work and pleasures. But in a regime of division of labour there arises the need of exchange. Gossen employs curves of the sort represented in our Fig. 1 in the exposition of a theory of exchange which bears comparison with the constructions of the mathematical economists who have succeeded him. He prettily illustrates the advantages of exchange by the case of two children, one of whom has more bread and butter, the other more milk than he wants (p. 80). Observing that the sum total of utility will vary according to the terms of the exchange, he is led to investigate the arrangement which is productive of "greatest happiness," of which the condition is that the final utility due to the last increment of a commodity should be the same for all persons ; a proportion which is extended so as to apply to the distribution of labour as well as commodities. This utilitarian distribution, according to which "each obtains the amount which he can justly claim," tends to be realised in virtue of the correspondence between private and public interest. This sort of "harmony" has not been described more extravagantly by Bastiat (90-100). The realisation of the true paradise is the removal of hindrances to the free play of self-interest.

Before showing how these hindrances are to be removed, Gossen prefixes several miscellaneous theories, some of which may be noticed in the order in which they occur—not a very lucid order.

The theory of rent is investigated by Gossen in some not very inviting symbols. The effects produced on rent by the addition of a pleasure requiring no exertion, by the increase of "skill," and other changes above adverted to, are formulated with characteristic elaborateness (pp. 103-114).

A consideration of the future value of rent leads to a theory of capitalisation, which has some affinities to those which have been propounded by Jevons and by Professor Marshall (pp. 114-118).

Gossen next inquires what are the independent variables, the determining factors of, as we should say, economic equilibrium. His fourfold division of the ultimate elements deserves attention (pp. 120-121).

The next subject which comes up is the measurement of pleasure. Gossen is as sanguine as Jevons about the possibility of constructing demand - curves. He thinks that the mean results thus obtained might serve as a guide to the individual in his efforts to maximise his own pleasure (p. 127).

Among the miscellaneous remarks which follow may be noticed a distinction between necessaries and luxuries : with a fall in price the total expenditure on a necessary decreases, —on a luxury increases (p. 133 et seq.).

Gossen occupies some pages with "verifica-

tions," among which he places the proposition that rent does not depend on cost of production. There follows an extensive series of commonplaces (p. 148 et seq.) under the head "errors of statesmen and economists."

The "errors" of the moralists are more piquant. Gossen complains that they have disparaged the principle of self-interest. Failing to perceive that "the creation is perfect," they have neglected the motive-power provided by the Creator for his machine. The true religion of the Creator aims at maximising the sum of happiness on the earth. The priests of the true religion are scientific discoverers ; its sacraments physical and chemical experiments. The pedagogues are next arraigned for stereotyping the system of classical education (p. 190).

It remains only to show how to remove the impediments which prevent the law of pleasure being carried out, and earth being turned into a paradise. The "impediments in man himself" are to be removed by a perfect education, of which Gossen prescribes the model. Among artificial or external hindrances is a bad currency, a subject on which Gossen has much to say. He recommends that the state should guarantee the fineness only, not the weight, of the coinage. He disapproves of a legalised rate between gold and silver, speaking with reference to a single state.

Freedom from hindrance does not imply abolition of property (p. 228). But the action of the state must be kept at a minimum. The true church, which is the school, would require no protection.

A system of state-credit or national loanfund (pp. 239-250), and the nationalisation of land (p. 250), are also recommended.

In conclusion (p. 273) Gossen dwells on the benefits to be expected from the adoption of his recommendations : "*Nothing more is wanted to make earth a paradise*" (italicised in the original).

These speculations appear to be, as Jevons says, of inferior merit. Gossen is guilty of a fallacy to which mathematical economists are peculiarly liable : what may be called the "illicit process" from the principle of utility in economics to utilitarianism in the philosophy of conduct. The logical error is aggravated in the case of Gossen by a certain pedantry and want of humour. His strength lay only in the more mechanical portions of the mathematical theory. He was a man of one idea ; but that was an immortal one.

[Preface to the second edition of Jevons's *Theory of Political Economy*, 1879.—*Journal des Économistes*, 4th series, vol. xxx., 1885, p. 68.— *Un Économiste Inconnu*, by Prof. Léon Walras ; containing a biographical notice supplied by Gossen's nephew.] F. Y. E.

GOTHENBURG SYSTEM, THE. Spirits are now sold in Sweden, largely also in Norway and Finland, under the "Gothenburg System." From the beginning of the century, the right of distilling brandy had been so identified with land cultivation that a sort of monopoly of a very deadly kind came into existence. Until 1824 there was "unchecked distillation for use of the household." This turned every peasant's home into a centre for the widest and easiest distribution of a very powerful liquor. The results of this "freedom of a necessary industry" were such as to create alarm in every class. In 1830 the long struggle began which resulted in the famous law of January 1855, by which this free household distillation was practically checked. The minimum quantity to be distilled daily at an authorised still must be 300 kans. (The kan = ·5756 gall.) Legal, medical, clerical officials were prohibited from having any advantageous connection with the manufacture, and to the community was given the right to forbid non-licensed traffic in retail form. No liquor legislation ever had greater or more instant effect. In 1853 between 33,000 and 34,000 distilleries were producing above 35 millions of "kans." In 1855 the stills had been reduced to 3481, with a production of less than 10 millions of kans. Further enactments made debts incurred for brandy not recoverable by law, forbade "drinking on credit," etc. Almost every separate provision of the "Gothenburg System" is here *except one*. Each year's reports from country and town made it clearer that the essential parts of this new legislation could be defeated so long as the sale was controlled by private individuals whose profits depended upon the widest possible distribution of brandy. The Gothenburg System meets this difficulty by giving the entire control into the hands of a company that makes no profit from the sales. In October 1865 the first company began its work. The fact that all gains from liquor sales were taken from the private individual and given to the community enabled the authorities to carry out the previous provisions of the law. Sales on credit or for pawn were stopped. Sales on Sundays and holidays were forbidden, also to youths. Food, and a variety of wholesome drinks upon which the seller *can* make profit, must be on hand. The express motive of this legislation to use the profits for the public good is shown in the erection of reading-rooms and coffee-houses in which latter not even beer is sold. The company is steadily extending these benefits beyond the letter of the law. Legally, spirits may be sold to youths of fifteen. The company has extended the age to eighteen. The hours of closing have been reduced from 10 P.M. to 7 in winter, 8 in summer. It does not use all its licenses, nor allow places of sale to be opened in the new quarters of the town. It

has reduced the strength of the alcohol from 46 to 40 per cent.

A weakness of the system is the temptation of the commune to use the revenues simply for fiscal purposes. Friends and opponents therefore now demand that the profits of the brandy sales should go direct to the government to be used for the objects which are most closely connected with the evils of intemperance. Norway, especially, has recognised this danger, and is showing interesting results. It is, however, conceded that though "brandy is checked, beer and wine go on apace." The spread of beer drinking, especially in the country, is now so serious as to have brought about an agitation for the company control of beer and wine. A leading Norwegian authority, Director Berner, believes that this final step is only a question of time. Though the "Gothenburg System" has been praised far beyond its deserts, the evidence is irresistible that a very distinct social advantage has been won under its influence.

[Reports that have been published since 1885 by Dr. S. Wieselgrin of Stockholm, now general director of prisons, are of great value, as he is one of the few writers upon this much debated subject who speak without passionate prejudices. An entire summary of his opinions may be found in the *Bericht des III. Congresses gegen den Missbrauch geistiger Getränke*, Christiania, Sept. 1890. This report also contains an admirable paper by H. G. Berner, showing the development of this system in Norway. Both articles are followed by a discussion by those who represent friendly and hostile attitudes toward the system. Important matter may also be found (pp. 55, 61, 66, 116, 121, 156, 383) in the bound vol. of the *Internationale Monatschrift zur Bekämpfung der Trinksitten*, 1891. *Erster Jahrgang*, Bremerhafen, C. G. Tienken.—See *Local Option in Norway*, T. M. Wilson, C.E., Bergen, 1890.—Also Dr. Baer, *Der Alkoholismus*, pp. 442 *et seq.*—Dr. Martins, *Handbuch der Trinker und Trunksuchtsfrage*, pp. 387, Gotha.—Dr. Siegfried Wieselgrin's papers are published in German under the title, *Die Entwickelung der Schwedischen Branntwein-Gesetzgebung von 1835-1885*, Emil Strauss, Bonn. —Special *Report* by J. G. Brooks to Massachusetts Govt. 1894.—*Report of Massachusetts Commission* (House Document No. 192, 1894). Obtainable from members of the legislature.—Dr. Gould's *Report on the Gothenburg System*, Department of Labour. Obtainable from the Hon. Carroll D. Wright, Washington D.C.—Articles in *Forum*, December 1892, Mr. Brooks, and March 1894, Dr. Gould.—Article in *Atlantic Monthly*, December 1893, Dr. Gould.—Article in *Arena*, April 1894, Mr. John Koren.—Bishop of Chester, in *North American Review*, May 1894. Article in *Economic Journal* (British Association), June 1894, Mr. Brooks. For a different view of this question, see articles in Jan. and Feb. numbers (1892) of *Internationale Monatschrift.*]   J. G. B.

GOUGE, WILLIAM M. (1796-1863), was born in Philadelphia. He became editor of the

Philadelphia *Gazette* and other journals, and for many years was connected with the treasury department at Washington, and died at Trenton, N.J. He gave special attention to the subject of American money and banking, and his works still remain a principal source of information. He wrote *Short History of paper money and banking in the United States, to which is prefixed an inquiry into the principles of the system, with considerations of its effects on morals and happiness*, Philadelphia, 1833, 2nd ed. 1835, pp. xii., 140, 240. The historical sketch is valuable for the details concerning the organisation of American state banks, and the frauds and abuses associated with their management during a period when there was very lax legislative control. Gouge advised the withdrawal of bank-note issues, and the separation of the fiscal concerns of the government from the banking interest. A portion of this work was republished in England by William Cobbett under the title of *The Curse of Paper Money.* Gouge also wrote *An Inquiry into the expediency of dispensing with Bank Agency and Bank Paper in the fiscal concerns of the United States*, Philadelphia, 1837, pp. 56, in which he advised the establishment of a system of sub-treasury offices; and *The Fiscal History of Texas, embracing an account of its Revenues, Debts, and Currency from the commencement of the Revolution in 1834 to 1851-52, with remarks on American Debts*, Philadelphia, 1852, pp. 327. See also in the *Banker's Magazine*, v. 14, July 1859, "The Banks of the United States," pp. 3-9, in which he still insists upon restricting banks to the work of deposit, transfer, discount, and exchange. While employed in the treasury department under Mr. Woodbury, secretary of the treasury, he compiled several valuable reports.   D. R. D.

GOULD, SIR NATHANIEL (*d.* 1728), merchant of London, was knighted on 14th April 1721. He was a director of the bank of England and member of parliament for New Shoreham, Sussex, from 1700 until his death. He published (1) *An Essay on the Publick Debts of this Kingdom . . . To which is subjoined, An Enquiry into the General Convenience of reducing farther the Interest of our Publick Debts below 4 per cent per annum, in a Letter to a Member of the House of Commons*, London, 1726, 8vo; 2nd ed., 1727; reprinted in 1782, and in Lord Overstone's *Collection of Tracts on the National Debt*, edited by M'Culloch, London, 1857, 8vo. In this pamphlet Gould discussed the sinking fund, showing by the application of the principle of compound interest that it would in course of time more than suffice to pay off the national debt. Gould's work is one of the first in which this argument, which Dr. Price afterwards made famous, is met with. Gould also showed that the debt had been considerably reduced since 1716. His statements

were attacked in *A state of the National Debt as it stood Dec. 24, 1716, with the payments made towards the discharge of it out of the sinking fund, etc., compared with the debt at Michaelmas, 1725* [Attributed to William Pulteney and to Archibald Hutcheson], London, 1727, 4to; reprinted in the Overstone collection; and in *Remarks on a late book, entitled, An Essay, etc., In which the evil tendency of that Book, and the Design of its Author, are fully detected and exposed, etc., in a letter to a Member of the House of Commons*, London, 1727, 8vo. Gould replied to his critics in (2) *A Defence of an Essay on the Publick Debts of this Kingdom, etc.*, London, 1727, 8vo; reprinted in the Overstone collection. The controversy attracted considerable attention, and was alluded to in the House of Commons, 23rd Feb. 1727-28;

[*Treasury Papers*, lxxiv. 11; lxxxv. 116.—Horsfield, *Hist. of Sussex*, vol. ii. appendix, p. 55.—*Catalogue of Knights.—Return of Members of Parliament*, pt. i. 590, 597, 605; pt. ii. 6, 24, 33, 45, 56, 68.]   W. A. S. H.

GOURDE. Standard silver coin of Haytı (divided into 100 cents) of the same weight and fineness as the five-franc piece (see FIVE-FRANC PIECE).   F. E. A.

GOURNAY, JEAN CLAUDE MARIE VINCENT DE (1712-1759), the son of a rich merchant of Saint Malo, was sent by his father to Cadiz in 1729 and remained there until 1744, engaged in trade. But the young man's mind was not wholly absorbed in his business; and according to his *Éloge*, by TURGOT, the fullest account we have of his life, his time| was divided between study and his professional occupations and personal relations. From 1744 to 1746 he travelled in England, Germany, and Holland, carefully noting commercial and naval matters and keeping up a steady correspondence with M. de Maurepas, the French minister of navy. In 1746 his partner died and bequeathed him the whole of his fortune, including the estate of Gournay, from which the title under which he is known is derived. In 1748 Gournay returned definitively to France, purchased in 1749 a *charge* of councillor of commerce, and was appointed in 1751 one of the *intendants* of commerce. Having experienced heavy losses in 1758, he resigned, keeping the honorary title, and died in the following year.

Turgot accompanied him in some of his numerous tours of inspection through France, and sums up the opinions on commerce of his master in the following terms: "M. de Gournay concluded that the only object of the administration should be (1) to give to all branches of commerce that precious liberty . . . which they have lost; (2) to favour industry . . . by promoting the greatest possible competition . . . resulting in the greatest perfection in production and the cheapest price for the buyer; (3) to give at the same time to the latter the greatest possible number of competitors, by opening to the seller all the markets for his produce" (*Éloge*, p. 19, by Turgot, see *Petite Bibliothèque Économique*). "He deemed it impossible that, in commerce left alone, private interest would not be conducive to the general interest" . . . (p. 12). "He was convinced that the money-trade, whose price is the interest paid on money, can only regulate this price with equity . . . by competition and reciprocal liberty" (p. 21). It is with these views, according to Turgot, that Gournay translated the works of Sir J. CHILD and Thomas CULPEPER (Paris, 1754), adding comments which have been lost. Gournay is generally considered as having embodied the "*Laissez nous faire*" of Legendre addressing COLBERT, in the well-known maxim, "*laissez faire, laissez passer*," but Dr. Aug. Oncken in his *Die Maxime Laissez Faire et Laissez Passer* (Berne, 1886, pp. 60-76) ascribes to the Marquis Voyer d'ARGENSON the first half of the formula. Dr. Oncken also refuses to follow DUPONT de Nemours in ascribing to Gournay considerable influence in the development of the physiocratic system (p. 99) and in considering him as a thoroughgoing free trader (p. 109); in fact the *Observations* which are printed along (pp. 72-90) with FORBONNAIS' *Examen des avantages et des désavantages de la Prohibition des Toiles Peintes* (Marseilles, 1755), and which are thought to be written by Gournay himself, though very strong against prohibition, wind up with the proposal of a tax of 10 to 12 per cent on all printed calicoes imported into the kingdom (pp. 87-89). Still it must be allowed that the transition from absolute prohibition to a duty of 12 per cent means something more than "liberal mercantilism" (*Maxime*, p. 109). Excepting his translations, we possess no authentic writings of Gournay. Several are stated to have been written under his direction. This is undoubtedly true of the pp. 254-268 in the first volume of the *Corps d'observations de la Société d'Agriculture de Bretagne* (Rennes, 1760, see note p. 263). Dupont de Nemours is said to have affirmed that the *Considérations sur le Commerce et particulièrement sur les Compagnies, Sociétés, et Maîtrises*, Amsterdam, in 12mo, 1758) were composed by Clicquot Bervache under "the eyes and with the advice of Gournay," and the copy in the Bibliothèque Nationale in Paris bears the MS. note "par De Gournay" in a handwriting of the last century; but M. de Vroil, who inserts a copious analysis of this pamphlet in his *Étude sur Clicquot Bervache* (Paris, 1870), does not support this opinion.　　　　E. Ca.

For Gournay's administrative career see *l'administration du commerce au xviiiᵉ siècle* in app. to Biollay's *Pacte de Famine*. Paris, 1885.

GOVERNMENT, ECONOMIC EFFECTS OF. The economic effects of government on society are extraordinarily complex and elusive. In an organic body it is well-nigh impossible to determine exactly the effect which any one organ exerts upon the others and upon the whole. For all the others react upon it. We may ascribe the progress of wealth or of poverty to the working of government, but we cannot be sure how far the government as well as the economic condition of that society is the result of national characteristics and natural conditions. Every general statement respecting the economic effects of different kinds of government must be regarded merely as a rude approximation. Subject to this caution, it may be said that government affects the economic condition of society chiefly in two ways, the one direct the other indirect. The direct economic influence of government is exerted in legislation, in executive action, in the administration of justice, and in foreign and colonial policy. The indirect economic influence of government is the result of its influence upon the character of the people.

I. *Direct economic influence of Government.*—(1) Legislation. Scarcely any law can be framed which will not by a short or long chain of cause and effect produce some economic modification. But a direct economic influence attaches to legislation upon any of the following topics:

(*a*) The law of property determining the modes in which property may be acquired, the restraints imposed on its alienation, the rules of intestate succession, the limits of testamentary power, the degree to which ownership may be subdivided, the incidents of mortgage, the possible kinds of servitudes, the registration of title, and many other subjects.

(*b*) Commercial law, which regulates the making of contracts, the formation and dissolution of partnerships and joint-stock companies, the procedure in bankruptcy, the peculiarities of bills of lading and negotiable instruments, the rights and liabilities of bankers, the protection of patents, trade marks, and copyrights.

(*c*) The law of procedure, which determines in what manner redress for civil or punishment for criminal wrongs must be sought. Its economic influence will vary as it is more or less conducive to obtaining justice in a reasonable time and at a moderate expense.

(*d*) The criminal law, which, by defending liberty of person and security of property, makes industry and commerce on a large scale possible. Its economic usefulness will depend on its being complete, explicit, and severe enough to deter from crime without being so severe as to awaken general sympathy for criminals.

(*e*) Administrative law, which defines the objects of administration, creates the administrative bodies, and regulates their powers and procedure. Under this head may be placed all the laws which deal with national defence, the army and navy, public health, education, the relief of the poor, and the regulation of industry, whether to protect the producer or to ensure the quality of the product.

(*f*) Financial and fiscal legislation, including all laws determining the standard and denominations of the currency, the incidence of taxation, imposing duties or granting bounties for the encouragement of native industry.

In dealing with the subjects above enumerated the legislator is obliged to consider (1) how much he will bring within the scope of his laws and how much he will leave to individual prudence or virtue; (2) when he is satisfied that legislation is expedient, how much weight should be allowed to purely economic as opposed to moral or political considerations,—in other words, when he should sacrifice the greatest immediate increase of national wealth to promote national security or moral and intellectual progress. The most judicious economists will not maintain that they possess any special knowledge enabling them to give dogmatic answers to these questions. Practical sagacity and political knowledge must determine at any given time the best limit to legislation. Arguments for non-interference based on the natural right of every man to do what he likes, and arguments for interference based on the organic character of the state, do not afford much assistance. The really strong argument for state interference is that co-operation is power, and that the state is the only, or at least the most powerful, co-operative organisation which can be used for certain purposes. The really strong argument against state interference is that it increases the power, in any case enormous, of governments which, under every constitution, monarchic, aristocratic, or popular, are usually composed of very ordinary men, subject to error, to indolence, and to sinister interests.

So, likewise, the choice between the greatest immediate addition to national wealth and some great moral or political gain must be decided, not by the special knowledge of experts, but by broad practical wisdom. But when the legislator wants to ascertain the causes which have resulted in the actual economic condition of society and the extent to which it may be ameliorated by new laws, he may with advantage take counsel of the economist. For such is the complexity of economic phenomena that a new tariff, a new poor-law, or a new regulation of the hours of labour, frequently produces results which its authors never expected and certainly never desired. In order to predict, so far as it is possible, the consequences of economic innovations, special knowledge and habits of scientific analysis are of the utmost value.

(2) *Executive.* —The various forms of administrative organisation and their principal economic effects have been described in another article (see ADMINISTRATION). Here only a few general observations need be added. It is an English tendency to underrate the importance of administration as compared with legislation. For this there are several reasons. Parliament, the assembly which makes laws, is much the noisiest and most conspicuous part of the great machine of government. The administration of national and local affairs has for a long time past been tolerably pure and efficient. Lastly, many things which are elsewhere done by the public administration are here done by private enterprise. Thus we are prevented from realising how much depends on the integrity and efficiency of the administrative body, how terrible may be the consequences where the administrator is inert, corrupt or timid.

(3) *Administration of justice.*—Although the form of the law and the constitution of the courts are settled by the legislature, the quality of the justice actually administered depends on the integrity of the judges, their immunity from intimidation, and their power to enforce their decrees. We hardly realise the importance of the first of these conditions because with us it has been so long fulfilled. But where justice is venal all commercial transactions are affected with uncertainty. There is one law for those who can and will bribe; for those who cannot or will not bribe there is another law. The wrong-doer can escape retribution by dividing his spoil with the judge, and the injured man submits to a loss when he cannot afford to purchase redress. Such a pollution of justice destroys confidence and hope, the mainsprings of industry; and the misery thus engendered may be measured by the eagerness of orientals to find an upright judge. Immunity from intimidation is not less essential than integrity to the righteous dispensation of justice. Judges have at different times been liable to intimidation by powerful individuals —not rare in mediæval England, or by an arbitrary government—as in the reigns of the Stuarts, or by popular agitation, which is the only mode of intimidating that need be feared in western Europe at the present day. In all three cases the result is the same,—the operation of the law is rendered uncertain and the sense of security is deeply wounded. Lastly, there will be little benefit derivable from the integrity or the courage of the courts if they cannot enforce their decrees. Yet this elementary condition of order and economic progress has not been and even now is not universally satisfied in many parts of the civilised world.

(4) *Foreign and Colonial Policy.*—As there is no commonwealth of nations in which each is protected and controlled by an irresistible government, every state must trust to its own strength for the defence of its interests and even of its life. Thus political power is a primary condition of economic development. But nations do not grow into power sleeping. Only by unceasing vigilance, by untiring energy, and

by stubborn fighting courage, can a nation hope to become powerful. War always involves an interruption of industry and a destruction of wealth. But war does not always involve an ultimate economic loss. It may be the only means of securing an economic gain. It has been said that the seven great wars which England waged between 1688 and 1815 left no permanent result except the national debt. It would be far truer to say that the cost of these wars has been returned to England one-hundredfold. They procured for England the free development of her institutions, the supremacy of the seas, the largest share in the carrying trade, a colonial and an Indian empire, —all essential conditions of her economic progress. As founders of English prosperity Wolfe and Clive, Nelson and Wellington, rank with Hargreaves and Arkwright, with Watt and Stephenson. On the other hand, no permanent economic advantage resulted to France from her brilliant victories and European supremacy in the time of the first Napoleon. She sustained grave economic injury in the slaughter of so many of her bravest and most adventurous citizens, and in the violent dislocation of her commerce, and in the false direction given to her energies. Thus there is no simple *a priori* rule for determining the economic effect of a foreign policy. Even if such a rule could be found, it would not be sufficient for our guidance apart from moral and political considerations. Colonial policy likewise has an influence upon national prosperity too extensive to be examined here.

II. *Indirect Economic Influence of Government.*—Whatever strengthens the national character and intelligence is economically beneficial. Therefore a political constitution which tends to develop the intelligence and character of the people tends to make them prosperous. In certain stages of civilisation this benefit is conferred by a powerful autocratic government which represses local feuds, breaks down the barriers of local prejudice, and compels a rude population to orderly industry. In other stages of civilisation the same benefit is derived from a large measure of political liberty. Political liberty is indeed a vague term. It means sometimes freedom from foreign domination, sometimes comparative freedom from interference by the national government, sometimes the possession of a vote in deciding who shall govern, and sometimes the right to take an active personal part in administration. But in any or all of these senses it is a means of prosperity to those who are fit to enjoy it.

Foreign domination involves the transference of a certain amount of wealth from the subject to the sovereign community, whether as mere tribute or in discharge of the cost of government and defence; it often involves considerable interference with the commerce and industry of the subject for the benefit of the sovereign community, and it often depresses energy and intelligence by closing or at least narrowing the possibilities of a great career. These disadvantages, however, may be partly lessened, partly compensated, if the dominant people have much to impart to the conquered, whether in better laws and institutions or in improved mechanical appliances or in general intellectual cultivation. The subjugation of barbarous by civilised nations has been one of the principal means of human improvement.

Personal independence, the freedom of the individual, especially the freedom to associate with other individuals for common ends, is essential to the highest economic development. For that development cannot be attained except by a daring, inventive, and original people. Such a people will not submit to unreasonable and vexatious interference, or if it does, it will lose its most valuable qualities. It may continue to be noted for a plodding industry and a minute thrift, but these virtues are not enough to maintain its pre-eminence. The saying that England has been made by her adventurers will be found more or less true of every great commercial community. But even when personal independence has been too much restricted, the possession of a vote and the imagination that one can change the government whenever one has a mind, mitigate the sense of constraint and the consequent loss of energy. Lastly political freedom in the sense of the right to an active participation in public affairs would be highly stimulating to intelligence and character if men generally availed themselves of it. But this is rarely the case in civilised countries, where business, study, and pleasure absorb the energies of ninety-nine citizens in a hundred. It is a common complaint among ourselves that the composition even of the most important local assemblies tends to become worse rather than better. We cannot here consider how far this complaint is well founded. If such a deterioration were real and long continued, it would reduce self-government to an empty form.

[Adam Smith, *Wealth of Nations*, cp. bks. iv. and v. Mill, *Principles of Political Economy*, bk. v. and on *Liberty* and on *Representative Government*.—Tocqueville, *Democratie en Amérique*, passim.—Stephen, *Liberty, Fraternity, and Equality*.—H. Spencer, *The Man versus the State*.—Ritchie, *Principles of State Interference.*—Jevons, *The State in relation to Labour.*—Montague, *Individual Liberty*.—Dicey, *Law of the Constitution*.—Sidgwick, *Politics* and *Ethics*. —The literature of Free Trade and Protection generally; and the authorities referred to in the articles on ADMINISTRATION; BUREAUCRACY; CENTRALISATION; LAISSEZ-FAIRE.]   F. C. M.

GOVERNMENT REGULATION OF INDUSTRY.

Earlier History, p. 239 ; In the 19th Century, p. 242.

Earlier History.—It will be convenient for the discussion of this topic to divide the survey into three main periods : (1) From the Norman Conquest to the time of Edward I. ; (2) from Edward I. to Elizabeth ; (3) from the days of Elizabeth to the decay of the mercantile system at the close of the 18th century.[1] In the first of these epochs interference with industry on the part of the government was considerably less than in either of the other two ; the regulation of industry was left largely to local and municipal authorities, and that which emanated from the government may be described as of a personal nature, proceeding chiefly from the initiative of the sovereign. In the second period the whole field of national industry is regarded as under the supervision of the government, though much is still left to local municipal or corporate authority. Regulations became national and even international in character, being enacted for a distinctly national purpose ; while in the third period the subordination both of industry and commerce to national purposes and national ends is more and more definitely aimed at. Of course in every period the influence of particular classes, whether landowners, merchants, or manufacturers, must be taken into account, as each class endeavours to modify legislation in accordance with its own particular interests.

I. Before the Norman Conquest, which is here taken as our starting-point, legislation on and interference with industry or commerce were only fragmentary in character. Such regulations as existed were chiefly framed by the king to secure the safety of merchants travelling in his dominions, to promote intercommunication and the proper conduct of trade generally (Cunningham, i. 75, and *Laws of Alfred and Ine*). To suffice for themselves in all industrial pursuits was the aim of the various villages, towns, or districts, though "there is no evidence that the early English villages valued their condition of self-sufficiency so highly as to try to check the development of trade, as had been done by German and Indian communities." Moreover it was perceived, at least by Alfred (*Boethius*, i. c. 17), that the common good depended on the interdependence of the various occupations of industry, and on their harmonious development and working. Royal control consisted chiefly in attempting to secure adequate protection for person and property so that this development of commerce and industry might be efficiently carried on. This royal control, however, became more powerful in many ways with the

[1] For later period, see FACTORY ACTS ; GOVERNMENT REGULATION OF INDUSTRY IN THE 19TH CENTURY.

consolidation of the feudal system in England after the Norman Conquest. That system rested almost entirely on royal authority ; industry and commerce were regulated largely, when regulated at all, by royal decisions. The distinguishing mark of feudalism as regards industry is that royal authority supports local and traditional custom, while that custom left very little opportunity for the development of individual enterprise. Agricultural industry was hampered by the manorial system and collective ownership of land (see MANOR ; AGRICULTURE IN ENGLAND), while prices both of agricultural and manufactured products were regulated by authority, *e.g.* by the ASSIZE OF BREAD AND BEER, which is considerably older than the reign of Henry II., and by the assize of cloth, which, though found in operation in the 13th century, even then refers to the "old assize of the mystery." The development of industry upon anything like a capitalistic basis was interfered with by the system of taxation, which practically discouraged accumulation by the operation of tallages, aids, and fines levied to swell the royal revenue. It should, however, be noted that at this period industry was only affected indirectly by taxation, for the taxes were (i.) not regular, but levied for special occasions of royal need, and (ii.) they fell not on regular incomes derived from industry or trade, or upon industry itself, but on the hoards of wealth accumulated by the rich in whatever walk of life. Also (iii.) in the case of tolls they represented payment given for royal protection. In other matters the whole conduct of industry was subjected to regulations of a local or private character emanating from the gilds (see GILDS and APPRENTICESHIP), or from municipal authority. Almost the only *general* regulation applying to the whole kingdom may be summed up in the arrangement of a uniformity of weights and measures (see ASSIZE OF WEIGHTS AND MEASURES), the assizes of bread, ale, and cloth, and other points in which the king and his court were directly interested as large consumers.

II. The reign of Edward I., inaugurating as it did the system of government, to some small extent at least, by the aid of the representatives of the nation—the first parliament in which all these representatives were summoned together in *one assembly* met in 1295— also inaugurates, as a result of this change in the method of government, a period when the regulation of industry becomes a matter of national and not merely local concern (see Cunningham, *Growth of English Industry and Commerce*, i. 265). It seems to have been the wish of the government of that day that industry should be regulated in the interests of the nation as a whole ; not so much in order to gain national power as to increase the national wealth and to afford plenty to the people.   There seems to have been also a wish to have definiteness and uniformity in prices and in taxation.   In taxation, *e.g.*, fixed customs were levied, the half-mark on each sack of wool and on the *prisa recta* of two tuns on each shipload of wine.   Anything beyond this was regarded as an occasional subsidy for a special purpose.   This taxation interfered, however, to some extent with industry, for, chiefly in order to facilitate the collection of the customs, the export trade was regulated by the "staple" system (see STAPLE).   The export of wool, *e.g.*, was hereby forced into definite channels and allowed only at certain ports by Edwards I. and III., who thus asserted the royal right of controlling trade.   In other points it may be said that the Edwards legislated for industry with a view rather to the interests of the consumer than of anybody else, though Edward III.'s encouragement of Flemish immigration, in 1331 and other years, seems to point to a definite plan of increasing national wealth by promoting new industries ; and his general legislation for the wool trade is a series of attempts to keep up a high price of wool to foreigners—an attempt largely successful, owing to the almost complete monopoly which England possessed in this commodity.   The interference with industry that is marked in the reign of Edward III. by the historically famous First Statute of Labourers (the 25 Ed. III. c. i., A.D. 1351) is strictly in accordance with the spirit of the age in which that statute was enacted.   It was the custom of the time to regulate prices by authority, and this interference on the part of the government did not cause discontent.   Hence parliament was not enforcing a novelty when, in this First Statute of Labourers, and in many subsequent ones, it endeavoured to regulate the price of labour as well as of provisions and cloth.   At the same time it cannot be denied that, owing to the peculiar circumstances of the period succeeding the Black Death (see BLACK DEATH), the legislation in regard to wages of workmen and their right to combine tended to become partisan legislation in the interest of the landowning classes who made the laws.   Still we must be careful to observe that these statutes are in the main a fair attempt to regulate prices and wages *together*, so that one should follow the other. Another important object of all labour legislation from the 25 Edward III. c. 1 and the 12 Richard II. c. 4, was to secure a sufficient amount of labour for agriculture, as being the most important industry in the country, and also as being that in which the landowning legislators were most nearly concerned.   (For a useful summary of the various statutes of labourers, cp. Thorold Rogers, *Economic Interpretation of History*, ch. ii.).   In non-agricultural industries we may notice that in the period from Edward I. to, say, Henry VII.,

government interference becomes more and more marked, as it is more and more needed, owing to the unsatisfactory manner in which the gild system was now beginning to work, and owing to the great development of the manufacturing industries.   In the reign of Richard II. this interference begins to assume the character that afterwards developed into the MERCANTILE SYSTEM (*q.v.*) of Elizabeth and the Stuarts, for it becomes an axiom that commerce and industry are to be regulated with the object of promoting national power through national wealth.   Hence we find numerous statutes framed to encourage native shipping— the 5 Rich. II. st. I. c. 1 may be called our earliest navigation act—to attract bullion into our merchants' hands (5 Rich. II. st. I. c. 2), and to protect native industry against aliens (as by the 33 Hen. VI. c. 5 and the 22 Ed. IV. c. 3).   Now, too, begins more definitely the era of the CORN LAWS (*q.v.*), whereby government tried to encourage arable farming as against the growing practice of sheep-farming for the sake of wool (cp. 12 Rich. II. cc. 3-7), to secure a large agricultural population (7 Hen. IV. c. 17), and to promote corn-growing by allowing the export of English corn (17 Rich. II. c. 7 and 15 Hen. VI. c. 2), and forbidding the import of foreign grain (3 Ed. IV. c. 2 and 23 Hen. VI. c. 5).   In the Tudor period this feeling of a national policy grows stronger, and it is felt that the interest of the individual must be sacrificed to that of the nation, if, by so doing, national power will be increased.   As national power seemed to depend upon the growth (1) of shipping, as a feeder to the navy ; (2) of population, and especially agricultural population, as a feeder to the army ; and (3) of treasure, we naturally find (1) the series of navigation acts continued (*e.g.* 23 Hen. VIII. c. 7, 2 & 3 Ed. VI. c. 19), and (2) the statutes of labourers kept up (*e.g.* 11 Hen. VII. c. 22), and the depopulation of rural districts through sheep-farming or migration to towns severely checked (4 Hen. VII. c. 16 applying to the Isle of Wight).   Also (3) numerous acts were passed to secure a large supply of bullion for this country (cp. Cunningham, *Growth of Eng. Industry and Commerce*, i. 387).   As the gilds were now decaying and their usefulness decreasing, we find the government reducing them more and more under its authority (1 Hen. VII. c. 5) till Somerset, following the policy of Hen. VIII., completed their ruin by confiscating their lands (1 Ed. VI. c. 14, A.D. 1547). At the same time the power of the gilds, especially of those which represented the working classes, being an object of jealousy to the Tudors, the government was by no means loth to interfere with them (cp. also the re-enactment of laws against combinations of workmen by the 2 & 3 Ed. VI. c. 15, and see COMBINATION LAWS).

III. In the Elizabethan code of regulations for industry we find government interference and the desire for the development of national power very strong. So distinctly was this the case that private interests came to be looked upon almost with disfavour, especially in the case of combinations of workmen (see COMBINATION LAWS). Legislation continues much on the old lines in (1) the Navigation Acts of 1 Eliz. c. 13, 5 Eliz. c. 5, the more famous Acts of 1651 and 1660 ; (2) the Corn Laws of 13 Eliz. c. 13, of 15 Charles II. c. 7, encouraging the growth and export of corn, and again by the 35 Eliz. c. 7, which endeavours to force all surplus labour into agriculture, and by all the legislation which followed (see CORN LAWS) ; (3) the protection and encouragement of native manufactures by prohibiting foreign imports (5 Eliz. c. 7) and restricting the export of raw materials that might be worked up at home (as of wool and live sheep, in 8 Eliz. c. 3), while the consumption of native manufactures is to be encouraged, as by the law 13 Eliz. c. 19, providing that men must wear caps of English make. As regards interference with (4) labour and wages, the legislation of Elizabeth has well been termed monumental, and it continued to operate with practically little change till well into the 19th century. The famous Statute of Apprentices of 1563, the 5 Eliz. c. 4 (see APPRENTICESHIP) had for its objects to regulate wages in accordance with prices by assessment, to encourage good service by checking migration from one employer to another, to secure good work by making apprenticeship compulsory—seven years for artisans and longer for husbandry—and to encourage agriculture by making all those who were not otherwise employed serve in husbandry. It was meant to improve rather than to depress the condition of the labourer, and though afterwards much misused by employers, is a curious monument of kindly meant paternal legislation. This act did not apply to new trades that came into existence after 1563, and therefore these were regulated generally by provisions in the patents given to those who started them. In this code of legislation, however, no provision was made for supervising the quality of manufactures, as had been done in previous times (*e.g.* by the aulnager for cloth ; see AULNAGER). Hence we find the state now re-organising companies like the old craft-gilds (cp. Cunningham, as above, ii. 48) or granting to *patentees* rights of search and supervision of particular goods throughout the whole kingdom. This naturally led to monopolies being granted to individuals (see MONOPOLY), and monopolies again came to be a source of revenue to the crown. It must be said, however, in favour of the much-abused monopoly system, so prominent under the Stuarts, that theoretically at least it provided for the government a check upon developments of trade that might prove detrimental to national interests.

The policy of the government in its interferences with industry after the Stuart period, and especially after the revolution of 1688, was to develop the industries of the country in every possible way. In the endeavour to carry out this policy England was only following the example of her continental neighbours, the Dutch and the French, for navigation acts and the protection of native industries were not by any means confined to England. The chief points aimed at by English statesmen of the 18th century were (1) the provision of a sufficient supply of raw material (*e.g.* of wool, and even of woollen yarn, 12 Geo. II. 21), by encouraging imports of such commodities and preventing their export ; (2) the prohibition of the import of finished goods into British markets, while *e.g.* even Indian muslins and calicoes were subjected to strict regulations lest they should interfere with our linen trade (see 11 & 12 Will. III. c. 10); and (3) attempts were made to encourage the consumption of home manufactures, partly by sumptuary laws (*e.g.* by the 18 Geo. II. c. 38, and 21 Geo. II. c. 26, which imposed penalties for wearing French cambric or lawn), and partly by compelling the use of British commodities in certain cases (*e.g.* sail-cloth, 19 Geo. II. c. 27). The woollen cloth trade in particular was most carefully encouraged (see Cunningham, ii. 340), though both in manufactures and in agriculture the policy pursued tended to foster merely class interests. But if certain classes persuaded parliament to legislate in their own private interests, as one class in particular constantly did, parliament still believed that it was doing its best for the country. This was specially the case when the landed interest was the largest in the kingdom and when, as in the 17th and 18th centuries, agriculture was the foremost of our industries. But when the industrial revolution made itself felt in George III.'s reign, and the new manufacturing interests became more dominant, English industry outgrew very quickly the various regulations and restrictions originally intended for its benefit. The ASSIZE OF BREAD AND BEER, for instance, had even in 1709 to be revised (8 Anne, c. 18); the assessment of wages was fast becoming inoperative, and by 1795 seems almost to have been forgotten (Cunningham, ii. 359). In fact "the introduction of machinery brought about the collapse of the industrial system of Elizabeth"—a system of wonderful comprehensiveness that had gathered up the tentative legislation of previous centuries and left its mark, both for good and ill, on that of centuries that followed it.

[Cunningham, *Growth of English Industry and Commerce*, Cambridge, 1892, *passim*, the works of J. E. Thorold Rogers.—Ashley, *Economic History*, i. pt. 2. See also articles in this Dictionary on

APPRENTICESHIP; ASSIZE OF BREAD AND BEER; MERCANTILE SYSTEM; MONOPOLY.]

H. de B. G.

GOVERNMENT REGULATION OF INDUSTRY IN THE 19TH CENTURY. The history of state action in England, during the present century, may be divided into two periods. In the earlier, the legislature was anxious to avoid interference with the economic and industrial action of individuals. In the later period, the legislature has become more and more disposed to regulate their activity. It must not be supposed that either tendency has operated at any one time wholly unchecked by the opposite tendency. The repeal of old and the enactment of new regulations have been, to a large extent, simultaneous. Nevertheless, there has been a marked change in public opinion, and in legislation on industrial questions. This change, being necessarily gradual and irregular, cannot be assigned to any one year. But the repeal of the Corn Laws in 1846 may be regarded as the last great achievement of the policy of LAISSEZ-FAIRE. Since then the policy of state interference has been gaining the ascendency. The circumstances of England, in the beginning of the 19th century, were propitious to the policy of removing all restraints on the economic action of individuals. The improvement of machinery was revolutionising commerce and manufactures. This revolution rendered the ancient system of regulation, dating chiefly from the reign of Elizabeth, totally inapplicable. The attempt to control prices and wages, to ensure a proper training of the workman, or a satisfactory quality of products, became more hopeless than ever. The incessant change and expansion of industry impressed reflective minds as some vast natural phenomenon which could not be guided or controlled. The middle class, which had gained so much in wealth and in political power by the industrial revolution, was instinctively averse to state control. Confident in its talent for business, its energy, and accumulated capital, It felt that, with freedom, it was more than a match for all competitors. The current philosophy fell in with the instinct of business men. It was deeply tinged by the optimism of the 18th century. The economic theory of Adam SMITH, and the legislative theory of BENTHAM, are alike pervaded by a belief in the beneficence of nature or of Providence. Nature or Providence, according to these theories, so orders human life that the endeavour of each to secure his own happiness produces, automatically, the happiness of all. It follows then, that, in almost every case, the state does most for the general welfare by allowing everybody to do the best he can for himself. And thus, in the first half of the 19th century, the economic facts of the time, the instinct of the class which was acquiring political predominance, and the philosophical theories generally received among thinkers and statesmen, all tended to reduce the action of the state within the narrowest possible bounds.

The result was seen in legislation. The apprenticeship and combination laws were repealed. The exclusive privileges of corporate towns were abolished. The poor law, which had been expanded into a system of supplementing wages out of rates, was reformed, and became merely a provision for the destitute. The protective tariff was gradually abolished. But whilst the old forms of state regulation were disappearing, the course of events and of speculation were bringing about a reaction in favour of state interference. For, as the new industrial system developed, it was found to produce evils which individual action could not remedy. These evils led to legislation, for workers in factories, as early as the year 1802 (see FACTORY ACTS). The wage-earning class, which has gradually acquired the largest share of political power, has always felt that its strength lies in combined action—not in individual enterprise—and has usually favoured the principle of state regulation. At the same time, philosophical reflection has taken new forms. The belief in the beneficence of nature has given place to the doctrine of the struggle for existence. This doctrine is incompatible with the notion that the general interest is best secured by everybody's endeavour to promote his own interest. Thus philosophers have become more willing to accept the deliberate regulation of industry by an authority which, at all events, professes to represent the whole community. The reaction towards mediæval ideas, expressed in the high church movement, and in the writings of Carlyle and Ruskin, has also contributed to lessen the value formerly attached to individual responsibility and individual freedom. A third influence, favourable to the extension of state control, may be found in the literature and philosophy of the most civilised continental peoples—especially of the Germans. At the beginning of this century the English people, isolated by its long war with France, and proud of its achievements in that war, had touched the highest point of arrogant self-confidence. Englishmen were inclined to regard all imported theories with suspicion, and, if they related to commerce or industry, with contempt as well. All this has been changed. The material progress of other nations has raised their standing in English eyes. The political and economic pre-eminence of England has been much reduced. Increased facilities for travel and transmission of intelligence have made the Englishman more cosmopolitan. The vast space which the action of government fills in such countries as France or Germany, and the audacious theories which it has generated, have made a deep impression on the English mind.

Lastly, the benevolent despotism which we have established in India, with at least a wonderful apparent success, has re-acted on English political ideas, and has recommended state action to many who would not have been accessible to speculative arguments.

The practical result of the change in public opinion, insensibly produced by all these agencies, is seen in the sweeping legislation of the last forty years. During that time the state has extended its activity in every direction. Following up its first hesitating interference on behalf of children employed in factories, the state has taken steps to secure the safety, health, and comfort of persons engaged in almost every dangerous or unwholesome occupation, whether in mines, in ships, or in factories. It has provided a complete system of gratuitous elementary education. In Wales it has organised secondary education, and everywhere it has begun to promote technical education. It has established an elaborate sanitary administration. It has increased the functions of the post-office, acquired the telegraphs, and re-adjusted the rates charged for the carriage of goods by railways. It has augmented the burthen of taxes, and the number of workmen and officials whom it employs. It has enlarged both the duties and the revenues of local authorities. But all that the state has done is little in comparison with that which it is incessantly called upon to do. It is invited to appropriate the "unearned increment" of the land, or the land itself, at least in towns ; to acquire all mines ; to regulate the hours of labour for all workmen ; to secure to them and their families good lodgings at low rents ; to feed their children whilst at school ; to cater for their amusement ; to provide them with pensions when past work ; to take over one branch of industry after another, as fast as it can find the requisite capital and organise the requisite staff ; in short, to enter upon a course of development which would finally make state action co-extensive with the life of society.

It would be difficult, if not impossible, to attempt an exact estimate of what has hitherto been done in extending the action of the state, or to criticise the proposals for its further extension. Few reasonable men will be disposed to agree with the extreme doctrine of *laissez-faire* inculcated by Mr. Herbert Spencer. They will rather incline to judge each new proposal for state interference upon its merits, testing it especially by means of recorded experience. At the same time they will remember that human nature, whilst capable of gradual modification within certain limits, is, in its main attributes, unchangeable. They will remember that the action of the state is, after all, the action of a number of rather commonplace human beings, and they will be slow to accept any political scheme which puts an enormous strain upon the industry, intelligence, or honesty of those who administer the commonwealth.

[Mill on *Liberty.*—Herbert Spencer, *The Man Versus the State.*—Jevons, *The State in Relation to Labour* (English Citizen Series). — Ritchie, *Principles of State Interference.*—Cunningham, *Growth of English Industry and Commerce in Modern Times.*—Toynbee, *Industrial Revolution.*]

F. C. M.

GRACE, DAYS OF. See DAYS OF GRACE ; BILL OF EXCHANGE, LAW OF.

GRADING. In many markets dealings take place without inspection either of samples or bulk, but upon the basis of certain standard qualities or values, and for this a properly organised system of grading is necessary. Whether the bargains are for consumption or speculation it is equally necessary that sellers and buyers should know exactly what it is they undertake to deliver or receive. In the metal trades the requisite uniformity is obtained by assay. Dealings in bullion on the London market are on the basis of the mint standards. The bars delivered are usually fine, but are reduced to uniformity by calculation on assay. In copper most bargains are in "G. M. B." bars—"good merchantable brands" of about 96 per cent, with allowances for difference in deliveries. In pig-iron there are recognised qualities with different prices for brands of different makers. Raw or thrown silk and wool are capable of containing a considerable amount of moisture, which is not apparent to sight or touch, and which materially affects the value in proportion to weight. It is therefore usual to require a certificate from one of the conditioning houses (see CONDITIONING), as to the proper degree of dryness of every parcel. In mineral oils, quality is tested by special associations, and the certificates of the Petroleum Association in London, and of the United Pipe Line in the United States, are the customary basis of transactions.

In proportion as the articles dealt in are less modified by art, the possibility of bringing them to a fixed basis is diminished, and it becomes necessary to grade them by comparison of their actual condition with some more or less definite standard. Thus the great wheat deals in the States are made in No. 1, 2, or 3 quality, and it is alleged that the arbitrary manner in which a farmer's produce may be graded opens a way to great injustice and fraud. Grading or some means of insuring uniformity of quality is essential in all dealings that are to be settled through a clearing house, as all clearing systems are founded upon the principle that delivery by the first seller is acceptable to the last buyer (see also CLEARING SYSTEM, LONDON ; PRODUCE CLEARING).

R. W. B.

GRADUATED TAXATION

GRADUATED TAXATION, TERM. The term "graduated taxation" is commonly used in contrast to "proportional taxation." Proportional taxation implies the same rate on all amounts of the thing taxed, whether it be property, income, or anything else. Graduated taxation generally means that the rate increases as the amount of property, income, etc., increases. More accurate is the term *progressive taxation*. For in a graduated tax the gradation may be either upward or downward. If the gradation is upward we have progressive taxation; but if the gradation is downward, that is, if the tax rate decreases as the income increases, we have what is technically known as *regressive* taxation, or what the French call upside-down progressive taxation (*progression à rebours*). When the tax rate increases up to a certain point, but remains constant beyond that point, the technical term is *degressive* taxation. That is, the proportional rate is regarded as the normal rate, but on all sums counted downward below this limit the rate diminishes. In one sense it is immaterial whether we call the tax progressive or degressive. But in degressive taxation the proportional rate begins at a comparatively low figure and is considered the normal rate, concessions being made for the smaller amounts; while in progressive taxation the point at which proportion begins is generally put higher up, so that most of the assessments are made at varying rates. The term "graduated taxation" is commonly understood to imply progressive taxation. Strictly speaking the English income tax, with its system of exemptions and abatements below £500, is an example of degressive taxation, and therefore of graduation. But when we speak of the income tax being "graduated," we commonly mean not the present system of degression, but a development of the progressive principle. While graduated taxation therefore technically includes progression, degression, and regression, the term will be here used in the sense of progressive taxation.

Another possible source of confusion must be avoided. If a different rate of tax is levied on different kinds of property or income, we speak not of a graduation but of a differentiation of the tax. But if different rates are levied on inheritances or bequests according to the degree of relationship of the heir or successor, the tax is also called a *graduated* or *progressive* tax. In ordinary cases "graduation" denotes a changed rate for altered amounts; in this case it denotes changed rates for the same amounts going to different persons. In the following discussion the term will be confined to the first and more important case.

History of Graduated Taxation.—The earliest example of graduated taxation is found in Athens. The direct tax (εἰσφορά), as levied by Solon (B.C. 596), was an extraordinary property tax divided into four classes. The graduation was introduced not by changing the legal rate, but by changing the assessable portions of the property. Thus the highest class was assessed at the full valuation; in the second class only five-sixths of the property was assessed; in the third class only five-ninths of the property was assessed; while the lowest class was entirely exempt. When we hear of the tax again in the time of Nausinicus (B.C. 380) the principle of graduation was still observed, although in a slightly modified form. In Rome we have no knowledge of any graduated taxation.

In the middle ages there are several examples, due to the growth of the democratic spirit, especially in the towns. There are but few cases of graduation in the general state taxes. In France the principle of *le fort portant le faible* brought about an application of the graduated scale to the poll and hearth taxes in the 14th century. But the assessors generally inverted the legal principle and made the poor pay higher rates than the rich. Based on these French laws were the English graduated poll taxes of 1379 and 1380, repeated in 1513 and 1641; and the graduated income taxes of 1435 and 1449. In the German empire a progressive property tax was imposed in 1512 in order "that the poor should not be so grievously burdened."

It is chiefly in the mediæval towns that graduated taxation was employed. We have full accounts of its history in Basel and other German towns during the earlier centuries of their existence. But the originally democratic character of the towns was soon modified by aristocratic and feudal influences; and the system soon actually became one of real inequality, pressing more heavily on the poorer classes. We know that this was the case on the continent; and when the history of English local finance comes to be written, it will probably be found to be the case here also. In some places, however, the democratic spirit asserted itself more radically. This is especially true of the Italian republics, whose condition at the period of their great commercial prosperity resembled those of modern cities very closely. The Italian cities, and especially Florence, are the chief examples of graduated taxation in the middle ages.

In Florence at first a general property tax (the ESTIMO, *q.v.*) was employed. In 1427 this was supplanted by the CATASTO (*q.v.*), or tax on the capitalised value of incomes from movables and immovables, which itself gradually gave way to the *decima*, or tenth, a tax on the income from immovables only (see DÉCIMES).

The principle of graduation was first applied to the *catasto* in 1443, under the name of *scala* or scale. One of the chief reasons of its introduction was the evasion of the proportional tax on personal property by the wealthy, and the hope to re-establish the balance in some sort in this way. But the Medici eagerly seized on this course of reasoning, and soon converted the graduated tax into an engine for ruining their wealthy rivals. The rates varied at different times during the 15th century ; some of the more extreme scales were 4 to 33⅓ per cent of the income, and 8 to 50 per cent. The *decima scalata* was one of the causes of Florence's downfall. But it is to be noted that what was begun by the Medici was continued by the democratic government, and that Canestrini, the historian of the tax, expressly tells us that the fault lay not so much in the graduation as in the frequency and burdensomeness of the taxes, and the utter arbitrariness of the whole tax administration. The graduated tax was levied for the last time in 1529.

During the 17th century we hear but little of graduated taxation. In the 18th century we find more frequent examples, until the revolution of 1789 and especially that of 1848 gave the signal for a far more wide-spread application of the principle during the present century.

In 1742 we find a classified income tax in Holland, a progressive income tax (from 1 to 8 per cent) in Prussia. In Geneva the *taxe des grades* of 1789 was levied on a slightly graduated scale. In England Lord North's tax on inhabited houses in 1778 was graduated. This tax was repealed in 1834 ; reimposed without graduation in 1851. Graduation on a degressive plan was introduced into it again in 1890. The French tax on rental values of 1791 was also graduated, as was the United States national tax on dwelling houses in 1798. In Holland, Austria, Baden, and Prussia we find extraordinary property or income taxes levied on the same principle during the first two decades of this century. The graduated principle was also applied in a modified form in Great Britain in the Triple Assessment of 1798 and in the income tax of 1799, the full charge beginning only with incomes of £200 (after 1803, £150).

From about the middle of this century dates a more decided movement toward graduated taxation in the continental countries of Europe, and the last decade or two have witnessed a decided extension of the movement in other parts of the world, including Australia and America. While important examples of graduated taxation are found in the monarchic countries of Europe, the most radical attempts to carry out the principle are found in democracies like those of Switzerland, and Australasia.

In Germany graduation is found both in commonwealth and in local finance. The new Prussian income tax varies from $\frac{8}{10}\frac{2}{0}$ per cent on incomes of 900-1050 marks to 4 per cent on incomes above 100,000 marks. In Prussia, as well as Saxony and other German states, incomes are divided into a large number of classes, and a definite amount of tax is payable for each class. The rate, therefore, varies slightly between the highest and lowest limit of each class. In Baden the system of *Steueranschläge* is followed, according to which only a portion of the actual assessed income is taxable in each class. In the lowest class (500-600 marks) one-fifth of the lowest income is taxable, while the total income is taxable only when it exceeds 30,000 marks. This is the same principle as that of Solon's tax in Athens. In many of the German towns there also exist graduated income taxes, ranging from 1 per cent to 4 or 5 per cent, and in some cases even to 10 or 12 per cent of the income. The municipal income tax, as a general rule, is based on the same assessment and the same principles as the state tax. There is no separate system of graduation.

In Switzerland graduated taxation of property or income exists in some form in sixteen of the twenty-five cantons, while the progressive inheritance tax is found in six cantons, graduated taxation of some kind existing in eighteen out of the twenty-five cantons. In regard to graduated taxation of property or income there are three classes of cantons : (1) Cantons with proportional property tax but graduated income tax, Ticino, St. Gallen, Thurgau, and Oberwalden. The highest rate of the income tax does not here exceed 4 per cent. (2) Cantons with graduated property tax, Geneva and Glarus. (3) Cantons with graduated property and income taxes. Most of the cantons with a property tax levy an income tax on income not derived from property (Baselstadt and Baselland levy it on other incomes also). The graduation is generally much sharper in the income tax than in the property tax, and the rate is in some cases almost 10 per cent.

In so far as the technique of administration is concerned, the cantons may be divided into four classes : (1) Those where different proportions of the assessed income or property are taxable in each class, as in Zürich. (2) Those where the income is capitalised at different rates in each class, as in Solothurn. (3) Those which change the rate for each class, or fix upon a definite sum to be paid by each class. This is true of most cantons. In general a definite rate or sum is charged upon the entire income or property. But a few cantons, like Basel, Zug, Schaffhausen, Aargau, and Vaud, assess the stipulated rate upon each successive increment of the entire amount.

There are many interesting but minor points of difference which it is impracticable to dwell upon here. But the tendency is toward the spread of the principle of graduation and the increase in the scale. The graduated inheritance taxes are found in Bern, Solothurn, Thurgau, Zürich, Uri, and Schaffhausen.

Graduated income taxes are found also in the local taxes of Belgium and Holland, in the national income tax in Holland, and to a certain extent in Denmark and Sweden. In England outside of the degression in the income tax, graduation is found only in the death duties (see DEATH DUTIES ; TAXATION), and in the present INHABITED HOUSE DUTY. In France and Austria the chief instance of graduation is seen in the rental or occupancy tax.

In Australasia we find in most of the colonies graduated inheritance taxes, ranging from 1 per cent to 10 per cent (and in Queensland even to 20 per cent). Here are seen not only the highest graduated inheritance taxes in the world, but also the highest graduated property and income taxes. The most recent act is that of 1891 in New Zealand, which, as lately amended, graduates the land tax from 1d. to 3d. in the pound, according to the value. Graduated property taxes are found also in some of the other colonies.

In the United States the income taxes levied during the civil war were sharply graduated, ranging up to 10 per cent. The income taxes levied by the Confederacy ranged from 5 to 15 per cent, and, in the case of corporate incomes, to 16⅔ per cent. Graduated income taxes were also formerly levied in Virginia. To-day a slightly graduated income tax is still levied in North Carolina. The taxes on corporations are graduated in several of the states, as in Maine (where the excise tax on railways varies from ¼ of 1 per cent to 3¼ per cent of the earnings), Vermont, Wisconsin, Michigan, etc. There is now a strong movement looking toward the adoption of the graduated principle in inheritance taxes, and bills to that effect are pending in several states. In Canada graduated inheritance taxes have recently been introduced in Ontario and Nova Scotia.

Theory of Graduated Taxation.—Graduated taxation has been upheld on three grounds which may be termed, for want of better names, the socialistic, the compensatory, and the economic arguments. The socialistic theory has been advanced, not only by socialists proper, but by economists of repute, like Adolf Wagner, who are opponents of socialism in general, but who propound this particular argument under the name of the socio-political theory. They distinguish between the "fiscal" and the "socio-political" periods in public finance. In the last period, which is now beginning, government must regard it as a duty to bring about a more equitable distribution of wealth, and therefore to interfere with the so-called rights of private property. It is the ethical or social

reasons which justify graduated taxation. This argument may, however, be unconditionally rejected. Although in all fiscal policy there is an undoubtedly social element, this must not be confounded with the socio-political or socialistic element. From the principle that the state may modify its strict fiscal policy by considerations of general national utility to the principle that it is the duty of the state to redress all inequalities of fortune is a long and dangerous step. If the equalising of fortunes were an acknowledged function of government, it would be useless to construct any science of finance. There would be only one simple principle : confiscate the property of the rich and give it to the poor. This argument for graduated taxation is not very strong.

What is called the compensatory argument has been advanced by writers like Royer in France and General Walker in the United States. The latter, *e.g.*, states that differences in wealth are due in no small degree to the failure of the state in its duty of protecting men against violence and fraud ; and that they are in a measure due to the acts of the state itself for a political purpose. Since therefore inequality of wealth is in a measure due to the state's acts of omission or commission, allowance should be made for it in the tax system ; and this can best be done, theoretically at least, through graduated taxation. The objection to this theory is that it furnishes no standard. If graduation is *per se* unequal, it is impossible to correct one inequality by another unless it can be shown that the second will in every respect fit into and counterbalance the first. The test is impracticable.

Similar to this, but of somewhat greater force, is what may be called the "special compensatory" argument. This upholds graduation in some one particular tax, on the ground of its acting as a counterpoise to other taxes. Indirect taxes, *e.g.*, it is claimed, often hit the poor harder than the rich ; hence the regressive indirect taxes must be counterbalanced by progressive direct taxes, like a graduated rental tax, or a graduated income tax, etc. Proportional taxation is still the ideal, but the departure from proportion in one direction must be met by an equal departure in the opposite direction. Some ultra-conservatives, like Leroy-Beaulieu, advocate graduated taxes for this reason.

Arguments for Graduated Taxation.—The most important of these are what may be called the economic arguments. They turn about the general theories as to the basis of taxation. The older doctrine of taxation was that of benefits. Since protection was deemed the chief benefit conferred by government, taxes were regarded as insurance premiums paid for enjoyment of security. Hence, it was argued, taxation should be proportional to the property or income protected. Some writers, however, maintain that the benefits to the individual increase faster than his property or income, since most public expenses are incurred to protect the rich against the poor, and therefore that the rich ought to pay not only absolutely but relatively more. Others have said that certain state expenses confer a proportional benefit on all, but that many kinds of governmental outlay have a special value for the rich. Others confessed that the benefits of state action are theoretically enjoyed by all, but maintained that practically the benefits accrue only to the wealthier classes. Others finally tried to prove mathematically that protection increases faster than property or income. A million pounds belonging to one man is in greater risk of being stolen than the same amount distributed among ten men. Hence the insurance premium ought to be higher. All these writers, arch-individualists as they were, therefore were forced to demand graduated taxation, which other individualists branded as arch-socialism.

These arguments for progressive taxation are not very strong, and if there were space it might easily be argued that if protection or benefit is to be the test of taxation, the scale should be graduated downward not upward. But it is unnecessary to do this, because the whole benefit theory of taxation has almost everywhere been abandoned in favour of the faculty or ability theory. Since individuals do not pay taxes in the ratio of the protection of the state, the arguments, whether of proportion or of graduation, founded on this theory are equally inconclusive. The give-and-take theory of taxation has been replaced by the faculty theory.

According to the faculty or ability theory, every man should contribute to the public burdens according to his ability. But does ability connote a proportional or a graduated tax? Originally taxation of faculty denoted a proportional tax on property, then a proportional tax on income. Already in the 18th century, however, the so-called "clear income" theory was developed, according to which only that part of income which exceeded what was necessary for existence was declared taxable. The minimum of existence was exempted. It is readily seen that if a definite sum is always exempt, the resulting tax would not be strictly proportional, but graduated, as to the whole income, although it would be proportional to a certain excess of income.

The original concession was soon broadened. Not only the satisfaction of absolutely necessary wants but the satisfaction of all wants now became the watchword. In other words, the idea of burden or sacrifice was introduced. Faculty or ability to pay taxes was declared to be measured by that proportion of income the loss of which would impose upon the individual an equal burden or sacrifice with his neighbour. All wants vary from the absolutely pressing wants of mere subsistence to the less urgent wants which can be satisfied by luxuries. The sacrifice involved in giving up a portion of what enables us to satisfy our necessary wants is very different from the sacrifice involved in giving up a portion of what enables us to satisfy our less urgent wants. In order to impose equal sacrifices we must tax the rich not only absolutely, but relatively, more than the poor. That is, the tax must be not proportional but progressive. It is simply an application of the final utility theory of value to taxation.

It may indeed be confessed that this theory does not logically result in any mathematically exact scale of taxation. The imposition of equal sacrifice on all tax-payers must always remain an ideal impossible of actual realisation. Sacrifice bears no absolutely definite relation to amount of commodities. No calculus of pains and pleasures can suffice. Moreover, the sacrifice occasioned by a tax, even if it were absolutely measurable, is only one factor in the problem, and may in individual cases be a minor factor. So that it is utterly impossible to say whether the identical tax on people of identical income will produce the same relative pressure or occasion an equal sacrifice. The attempt to ascertain a mathematical scale of progression must necessarily fail.

Nevertheless graduated taxation may be upheld on the faculty theory. For the elements of faculty are twofold, those connected with acquisition or production, and those connected with outlay or consumption. Now as regards the first set of elements, the possession of large fortunes or large incomes in itself affords the possessor a decided advantage in augmenting his possessions. A rich man may be said to be subject in some sense to the law of increasing returns. The more he has, the easier it is for him to acquire still more. From this point of view faculty may be said to increase faster than fortune or income. This element of taxable capacity would not illogically result in a more than proportional rate of taxation.

On the other hand, the elements of faculty which are connected with outlay or consumption bring us back to the sacrifice theory. Now while the sacrifice theory is not sufficient to make us demand any fixed scale of graduation, it cannot be claimed that it leads necessarily to a fixed proportion. If we never can reach an ideal, there is no good reason why we should not strive to get as close to it as possible. Equality of sacrifice, indeed, we can never attain absolutely or exactly, because of the diversity of individual wants; but it is nevertheless most probable that in the majority of normal and typical cases we shall be getting closer to the desired equality by some departure from proportional taxation. If we take a general view and treat of the average man—and the state can deal only with classes, that is with average men—it seems probable that on the whole less injustice will be done by adopting some form of graduation than by accepting the universal rule of proportion. A strictly proportional rate will make no allowance for the exemption of the minimum of subsistence. It will be a heavier burden on the typical average poor man than on the typical average rich man. It will probably be more severely felt, relatively speaking, by the average man who has only a small surplus above socially necessary expenses, than by the average man who has a proportionally larger surplus.

Hence if we base our doctrine of the equities of taxation on the theory of faculty, both the production and the consumption sides of the theory seem to point to graduated taxation, as at all events lacking in neither logic nor justice.

Arguments against Graduated Taxation.— The arguments against graduated taxation are of two classes—theoretical and practical. In the first class the following are frequently urged:—

1. Graduated taxation is arbitrary and uncertain. This is true in a sense, but it proves too much. For an uncertain rate, if it be in the general direction of justice, is nevertheless preferable to a rate which may be more certain but less equitable. A stability which is unjust is not preferable to an instability which works in the general direction of what is recognised as justice. It is possible that the ostensible certainty of proportion may involve a really greater arbitrariness.

2. Graduated taxation is confiscation, because it must end by swallowing up the whole capital. This objection may be completely obviated by making the graduation itself degressive, so that it would become impossible to reach 100 per cent or any like percentage of large fortunes.

3. Graduated taxation is unprofitable, for the yield will be no greater than with proportional taxation. This, even if true, is no valid objection. For it assumes that the state desires to obtain larger revenues, whereas in reality it desires simply to attain greater justice. If graduation is theoretically more equitable than proportion, the given amount ought to be raised by the first rather than by the second method. If indeed graduation involved a positive loss of revenue, the case would be different. But this has been claimed by no one.

4. Graduated taxation acts as a check to industry and saving. This objection would apply only to such an excessive scale as would swallow up the entire surplus of income—and such a scale has never been known or even proposed. For if the receiver of the larger profits, after paying the graduated tax, is still in possession of a larger net income than his neighbour who with a less product pays relatively less taxes, there is no reason why he should cease to produce or accumulate. He will indeed be less wealthy than before, but his surplus will still be greater than if he stopped production. The objection is applicable to the abuse, not the use, of the principle.

The practical objections to graduated taxation are of greater weight. These are:—

1. Graduated taxation tends to augment fraud. Even under the proportional system property and income taxes in most countries, as actually administered, are honeycombed with fraud. The larger the property or income, the greater the opportunity and inducement to undervalue and conceal. The increase of the rates through graduation is apt to greatly accentuate the tendency. The greater the ostensible equality, the greater the real inequality.

2. Graduated taxation will lead to an exodus of capital. This is true only on the assumption that the system is not a universal but a particular one. If a graduated scale is applied in one town only, or in one province or commonwealth only, the tendency toward migration of capital to a neighbouring town or province will be perceptible. The larger the area of the tax system, the less the inducement to migration. But the tendency is always present although its force has often been exaggerated.

3. Graduated taxation, unless applied to the entire property or income, may work practical injustice. In the English local rates, *e.g.*, holding A may be worth more than holding B, but A may be owned by two persons and B by only one. Or the owner of the smaller holding B may have a hundred other small holdings in other parts of the town or country, while the owner of A has only that one. A higher tax on A, because it is the larger holding, would make the poorer man pay more than the richer man. Graduated taxation of property would here involve absolute injustice. The same would be true of many land taxes, of the property tax as administered in the United States, and of the income taxes in those countries where the assessment is made not on the entire income, but, as in England, separately in different schedules. This objection would not apply to cases of actual general income, or general property, or general inheritance taxes. And it is therefore chiefly in these forms of taxation that the most recent application of the graduated principle has been made. But whenever the tax is of a partial character—and this is frequently the case—graduation would be inadmissible and practically dangerous.

While, therefore, graduated taxation is on the whole defensible as an ideal, and as the expression of the theoretical demand for shaping taxes to the test of individual faculty, it is a matter of considerable difficulty to decide how far, or in what manner, the principle ought to be carried out in practice. Theory itself cannot determine any definite scale of graduation. And considerations of expediency, as well as the uncertainty of the inter-relations between various parts of the entire tax system, should tend to render us cautious in advocating any general application of the principle.

[All the general works on the science of finance discuss this problem. For special studies see Seligman, "The Theory of Progressive Taxation" in *Political Science Quarterly*, vol. viii. No. 2.—more fully, Seligman, *Progressive Taxation in Theory and Practice*, 1894, where a complete bibliography may be found.—Cp. also Sax, "Die Progressivsteuer" in *Zeitschrift für Volkswirthschaft, Socialpolitik und Verwaltung*, 1892; Condorcet, *Sur l'Impôt progressif*, 1792.—Meyer, *Die Principien der gerechten Besteuerung*, 1883.—Neumann, F. J., *Die progressive Einkommensteuer*, 1874.—Scheel, *Die progressive Besteuerung*, in Zeitschrift für die gesammte Staatswissenschaft, vol. 31 (1875).—Vauthier, *De l'Impôt Progressif*, 1851.—Cohen-Stuart, A. J., *Bijdrage tot de Theorie der progressieve Inkomstenbelasting*, 1891.—Bastable, C. F., *Public Finance*, 1892, bk. iii. ch. iii. "The Distribution of Taxation." For the United Kingdom and the alteration in graduation of the death duties made by Sir W. Harcourt's Budget of 1894, see TAXATION.

For Switzerland in particular, see R. H. Inglis Palgrave, "Progressive Taxation as levied in Switzerland," in *Journal of the Royal Statistical Society*, 41-225, 1888).—Foreign Office Report No. 267, Miscellaneous Series, 1892, *Report on the different systems of graduated Taxation in Force in Switzerland.*—"Text of Property Tax of Canton Vaud" in *Quart. Journal of Econ.*, 1887-88.—Cohn, "Income and Property Taxes in Switzerland," *Pol. Sci. Quart.*, 1889.—Schanz, *Die Steuern der Schweiz*, five vols. 1890.—Prof. Greven, "Fiscal Reform in Holland," *The Economic Journal*, 534-540, 1893.]
E. R. A. S.

GRAHAM, SIR JAMES GEORGE ROBERT (1792-1861), was born at Netherby, in Cumberland. He was educated at Westminster and Christ Church, Oxford; and in 1813, as private secretary to the British minister in Sicily, took part in the negotiations with Murat at Naples. After his return to England he entered upon a political career, and was returned for Hull in the whig interest in 1818. He was a close student of political economy, and now translated its principles into practical action on his father's estate. In the civilisation of the borderland and the improvement of agriculture, he did excellent work. Small tenants, who mainly lived by poaching, were replaced by thrifty industrious farmers; the breed of stock was vastly improved; cottages and farm buildings were rebuilt, and drains were introduced, large tracts of marshy land being thereby reclaimed. Under young Graham's guidance,

Netherby farming gained a high reputation among agriculturists. As the result of his studies in political economy, Graham published in 1826 his pamphlet entitled *Corn and Currency*. In this treatise, which gained wide circulation, the writer demonstrated the futility of the efforts made by government to regulate by law the price of money and the price of goods. He also showed that there was an intimate relation between the corn laws and the currency, and his conclusions, as a whole, favoured free trade and free banking. He also took an active part in reforming the system of county finance. Graham succeeded to the baronetcy in 1824, and in 1826 was elected liberal member for Carlisle. In the ensuing year he was returned for Cumberland, and in matters of finance and commercial legislation associated himself with the enlightened policy of Huskisson. Economical reform early attracted his attention, and in 1830 he made his mark in the House of Commons by his motion for the reduction of official salaries, his reputation being further increased by an attack on the salaries received by privy councillors. As an advanced reformer, he was offered by Lord Grey the post of first lord of the admiralty, which he accepted, and was one of the committee of four to whom was entrusted the preparation of the first Reform Bill. While at the admiralty, Graham rendered essential service in reforming the finances of the department. Soon after this, however, he began to recede from his position as a reformer. His last attempt at economical reform was the introduction of a bill for reforming the exchequer office, which was rejected in committee. Graham's abandonment of liberal principles lost him his seat for Cumberland, but he found a refuge at Pembroke. Joining the conservatives, in 1841 he became home secretary under Sir Robert Peel. While retrograde in many matters, Graham cordially supported the free-trade policy of Sir Robert Peel. He expressed his conviction that the duty on imported corn must be abandoned, adding that "the sliding scale would neither slide nor move, and this was its condemnation." Graham supervised the measures adopted for the relief of the Irish famine, and particularly the administration of the poor law. He went out of office with Peel in 1846, and in the succeeding year was returned to the new parliament for Ripon. After the death of Peel in 1850, Graham was the leader of the small but distinguished band of Peelites, and he consistently opposed the tory efforts to restore protection. In 1852 he was elected for Carlisle, and on the formation of Lord Aberdeen's coalition ministry he returned to his old post at the admiralty. He again set himself to the task of securing administrative efficiency and economy. After the fall of the Aberdeen government Graham retained his office in the ministry as reconstituted under Lord Palmerston, but he resigned in February 1855. Graham was haughty in demeanour, and his speeches, though sometimes brilliant, lacked spontaneity ; but he was an able administrator and a model chairman of parliamentary committees.

[Torrens's *Life and Times of Sir James Graham*, 1863.—*The Times*, 26th October 1861.—*Annual Register*, 1861.]

G. B. S.

GRAMONT, SCIPION DE, seigneur de Saint Germain, born in Provence during the 16th century, died, it is believed, in Venice about 1638. He was ordinary secretary of the royal closet under Louis XIII.

His *Denier Royal, traicté curieux de l'Or et de l'Argent* (Paris, 1620) is dedicated to M. de Schonberg, superintendent of the finance of France, and is written to prove that "France is one of the least oppressed (*foulé*) kingdoms of the world, and that the king does not so much burden his people as the general outcry might induce people to suppose" (p. 199). His main position is that "gold and silver, which measure the price of all things, have lost much of their former price and value by the great plenty of them which we now have" (p. 72). "The price of money, although it measures the price of other things, is not itself fixed and stable, but changes, rises and falls according to its plenty or scarcity" (p. 119). "It must be admitted that within the last century more than nine hundred millions of gold and silver have passed through the gate of Spain and entered Europe, spreading as they were attracted by the labour and industry of the different nations" (p. 136). Gramont's conclusion is that if the taxes are nominally higher than in former times, they are not so really, for "as the great quantity of gold and silver . . . has lowered their price, it is necessary that the number (of coins) should compensate (their loss of) value" (p. 262).

Gramont also clearly sees that "debtors have won what their creditors have lost" (p. 125). He, however, clings to the traditional opinion that "money does not take its value from the material out of which it is made, but from its form, which is the mark of the prince, and which could bestow value on any vile and abject matter" (p. 13). This opinion, repeated p. 18, does not agree very well with the rest of his argument.

[See Cossa, *Introduction to the Study of Political Economy* (Eng. Trans., p. 175, ed. 1893).]

E. Ca.

GRAND LIVRE (Fr.). The register of the public debt of France, created under a decree of the 24th August 1793, in 229 articles, by which all the existing debts at that time were consolidated in a five per cent stock. The Great Book was to form the sole and fundamental title of the creditors of the state, and holders of scrip of all public debts—national, provincial, or communal—were required within a given time to produce their claims, the amount of which was inscribed to their credit nominatively and alphabetically. All titles to bearer were suppressed, and the measure facilitated the confiscation of the property of the church and the *emigrés*. Art. 24 of the decree declared that the interest or *rentes* due to the churches were suppressed to the profit of the republic, which would thenceforth provide for the expenses of public worship. Art. 94 ordered the extinction of all sums due to *emigrés* after payment of claims of their creditors. The total amount of the debt consolidated was 2,556,060,000 frs. in capital, and 127,803,000 frs. in *rentes* or interest. A new *Grand Livre* was created in 1797, when two-thirds of the debt were virtually repudiated, holders receiving a fresh inscription of consolidated thirds, the other two-thirds being paid off in assignats or national bonds of fictitious value. After this operation the inscribed debt, further reduced by annullations, amounted to only 40,216,000 frs. in *rentes*. Subsequent borrowings down to the present time have necessitated the opening of other sets of books, but the formula is still retained and loan bills invariably commence with the words, "The minister of finance is authorised to enter on the *Grand Livre* a sum of *rentes* sufficient to produce a capital of," etc. (see RENTE).

T. L.

GRANGERS AND GRANGER LAWS. In 1867 a national secret organisation, known as the Patrons of Husbandry, was formed in the United States. Although its membership was nominally confined to those engaged in agriculture, it grew very rapidly. A local society was called a "grange"—whence the generic term. As granges, these bodies were forbidden by their constitution to engage in political discussions, but were encouraged to advance the interests of farmers along the lines of co-operation, economies in purchases, and an increase in the diversification of crops. In the south and west the Grange movement became active, and established banks, insurance companies, co-operative stores, grain elevators, and warehouses. Although a non-political organisation, it promoted anti-monopoly legislation, particularly against railroads, with a view to lower freight-rates, thus securing as was thought, a freer market for grain. Laws fixing maxima freight and passenger rates were passed in Illinois, Iowa, and Minnesota, popularly known as Granger laws. Although subject to much criticism on the ground that they were unconstitutional, they were sustained by the United States supreme court. The Granger movement declined after 1875, and the granges have retained little influence, save in some sections as social centres in farming villages. (See FARMERS' ORGANISATIONS IN THE U.S.)

[The early history is described by C. F. Adams, Jr., in the *North American Review*, 120 (1875) : 394, and the later history by C. W. Pierson, in the *Popular Science Monthly*, 32 (1887): 199, 368.] D. R. D.

GRANT, JAMES (later part 18th century), entered the service of the East India Company in 1769, was made chief sherishtadar, keeper of records, under the board of revenue of Bengal in 1786, and in 1799 was still in the company's service. He wrote *An Inquiry into the Nature of Zemindary Tenures in the Landed Property of Bengal*, 1790, to show that zemindars were officials, not proprietors of the lands which they held, as payment for their services in collecting dues from the peasants, of the sovereign, the sole landowner. His views, though new at the time, have been accepted in the main.

Grant was an expert in local revenue questions, and wrote an *Historical and Comparative Analysis of the Finances of the Subah of Bengal*,— an *Historical Analysis of the Revenues of the Northern Circars*, and an *Historical Analysis of the Revenue of Bengal* (see Appendix to *Fifth Report of Select Committee of the House of Commons on the affairs of the East India Company*).

[Appendices to 2nd edition of *Zemindary Tenures*, 1791.—*List of the company Civil Servants*, 1799.— *Extracts from Harington's Analysis of the Bengal Regulations.*—Grenville's *British India Analysed.* —M'Culloch's *Literature of Political Economy.*] E. G. P.

GRANT, SIR ROBERT (1779-1838), son of Charles Grant the East Indian Director, was a barrister, a member of parliament in 1826, 1830, and 1831, judge advocate general in 1832, and governor of Bombay in 1834. A man of great and versatile ability, he wrote (1) *The Expediency Maintained of Continuing the System by which the Trade and Government of India are now regulated*, and (2) *A Sketch of the History of the East-Indian Company from its first Formation to the Passing of the Regulating Act of 1773*, both published in 1813 ; and (3) *A View of the System and Merits of the East-India College at Haileybury*, a speech published in 1826. The first of these works is an account of the company's government, and an argument adverse, on political and commercial grounds, to its abolition.

[*Gent. Mag.*, Dec. 1858 (age incorrect).—*Dict. of National Biography.*—*East India Register*, 1835, ii.—*Times*, Oct. 19 and 23, 1838.] E. G. P.

GRAPHICAL OR GRAPHIC METHOD. We have shown in the article on DIAGRAMS how a table of statistical figures may be represented by a curve.

This method of representation, which is much used by engineers and by experimental scientists generally, is now thoroughly established in statistical investigations of economic phenomena.

As was well said by Playfair, the earliest writer to employ this method systematically (who declares his indebtedness to his brother

for its conception), when publishing his first book in 1785, we may compare the clearness of expression thus obtained, as contrasted with the difficulty experienced in grasping the same facts when expressed in a table of figures, with a map of the course of a river. This method gives, as is obvious, a much clearer idea of the country traversed than would be afforded by even the most detailed schedules of the latitude and longitude of places through which it flows.

The accompanying diagram (fig. 1) which was published in the *Times* of 2nd February 1893 shows how the fall in the price of wheat during the year 1892 is represented graphically. A single glance at this curve is sufficient to enable the mind to grasp not only the general fact of a fall in price, but also the varying rapidity of that fall in different months, and the slight temporary checks in its course.

It is clear, on a very slight consideration, that no greater accuracy can be obtained in the graphic representation than is afforded by the tables of figures on which it is based, and indeed the curve is less accurate than the statistical tables, unless it be drawn both on a large scale and with great care.

In spite of this, however, it is likely to prove far more fruitful in directing the attention to the salient features of the phenomena represented than the method of tabulating the results in schedules of figures.

In considering such a curve as that which represents the changes in the price of wheat (fig. 2) during a long period of years, the suggestion is obvious that the repeated rise and fall may be due to the operation of causes varying in intensity in different years, but recurring at regular intervals.

If the intervals between successive maxima or minima were of equal length, this conclusion would be a fair one, and it might be possible to extend the curve hypothetically so as to foretell with some degree of certainty future variations.

Such regularity is not to be found in general, owing probably to the intermingling of the effects of many causes recurring in periods of different duration.

It is possible, however, to eliminate some of the fluctuations by drawing a second curve in the manner shown in fig. 2.

In this figure the heavy line shows the variation of the annual average price of wheat, while the thin line gives the six year averages of the same prices.

If there be any cause recurring at intervals of six years, and in that period producing variations of equal amount evenly distributed on either side of the average, so that its effects, if plotted out by themselves, would give a curve regularly repeated at six-yearly intervals, the process of averaging would entirely eliminate these effects, and would leave a curve showing the effects of all other causes when this one

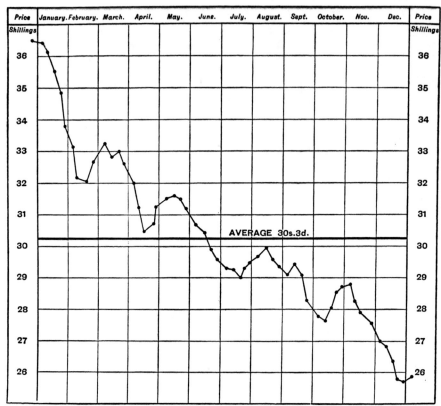

Fig. 1.—Price of wheat per quarter in 1892.

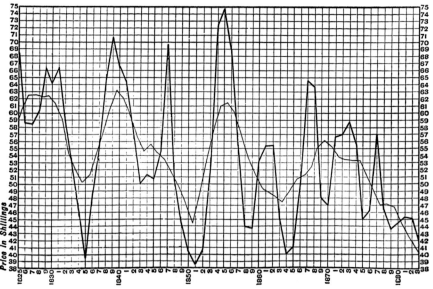

Fig. 2.—Annual and sexennial average price of wheat per quarter, 1825-93.

was omitted. Fluctuations in other periods would be represented on a reduced scale, and those, if there be any, whose period was nearly six years, would be almost completely unrepresented. A three-year or ten-year average would similarly eliminate the effects of other causes repeated at corresponding intervals.

Since the whole variation may be regarded as compounded of variations due to many periodic causes, the repeated application of this device may afford valuable information as to the nature of this complex mixture.

This subject has been carefully investigated by Prof. Poynting, whose paper on the subject in the *Statistical Society's Journal* for March 1884 is most valuable and instructive.

One obvious advantage of this smoothing process is illustrated in the above diagram, where the somewhat violent rise of price in 1847, which was not maintained, and may have been due to extraordinary causes of a temporary nature, is productive of but slight effect in the sexennial average curve, and similarly for the sudden fall in 1870, and for the rise in 1860-62.

The fluctuations of the thin curve are much less irregular than those of the thick line, and suggest a regular variation of longer period. A triennial or decennial average might afford further evidence of such a variation, which is masked in the annual average.

The comparison of two or more curves showing the variations of different phenomena, some-

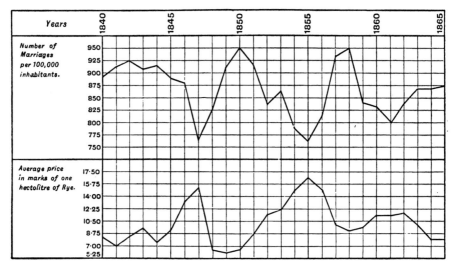

Fig. 3.—Marriage-rate and price of rye in Prussia compared, 1840-65.

times reveals a striking similarity between such variations.

Fig. 3 is a case of such comparison, which is given in Meitzen's work on statistics. In looking at the two curves side by side, it is difficult to avoid the conclusion that in Prussia, during the period 1840-65, the price of so prominent an article of food as rye, regulated in a very powerful measure the possibilities of marriage among the peasants. In other countries, and at other times, the price of food appears to have been but one among several influences of importance, and the agreement between the corresponding curves is in general less marked.

The method of comparison here illustrated has been employed by numerous investigators. Jevons's work on *Commercial Crises and Sun Spots* (in his *Investigations in Currency and Finance*) is one of those best known, and a remarkable agreement is shown between the variations of commercial prosperity and the maxima and minima of spots on the solar surface. Jevons

suggested that the terrestrial weather was affected by these sun spots, and thus, through variations in the harvest, the business world was subject to their influence. It is, perhaps, hardly possible at present either to affirm or deny the truth of the connection, and it is necessary to remark that variations in different phenomena due to entirely unconnected causes may show, for considerable periods, a marked resemblance, which resemblance may be found to entirely disappear in the further history of the facts compared.

Very interesting comparisons between the changes in the prices of wheat, cotton, and silver have also been made, regarding which it should be noticed that, assuming the variations to be similar, the conclusion may be that all are due to causes so connected as to produce effects similar in kind or degree, while, on the other hand, it may be that the variation in one has been the cause of the variations in the others.

In making comparisons between two curves

such as those just referred to, it is desirable to choose such a scale for each that the range of variation is similar in both, otherwise the correspondence may be entirely overlooked. As an example of this we may take the diagram (Fig. 4) given by Prof. Marshall in the jubilee volume of the *Journal of the Statistical Society*, comparing the consumption per head of tea and sugar in the United Kingdom for the years 1860 to 1883. The consumption of sugar is represented in pounds, while that of tea is represented in two curves in pounds and ounces respectively. The comparison of the consumption in pounds would appear to indicate a much more rapid increase in the use of sugar than in that of tea, while the close correspondence between the two rates of increase is evident on comparing the consumption of tea in ounces with that of sugar in pounds.

The method we have illustrated up to the present of representing statistical tables, though that most generally employed for economic purposes, is by no means the only one used. For representing the frequency of winds in different directions, lines may be drawn from a point of such length as to represent, on a scale

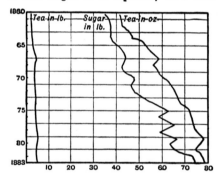

Fig. 4.—Consumption of tea and sugar per head of population in United Kingdom.

agreed on, either the frequency or the intensity of winds from that quarter. The curve which connects the extremities of these lines will express the facts required in a manner hardly possible by such curves as we have used above.

A similar mode of representation may be used to express other facts, as is illustrated in Fig. 5, which is a curve due to M. Janssens, expressing the variations in the death-rate, at Brussels, of children less than a year old and of those less than a month old.

The latter rate is represented by the small inner curve, the former by the outer one. The circle in each case expresses the average for the whole year, and where the curve falls inside it,

the rate is less than the average, while in the blackened part, outside of this circle, we have represented the death-rates in excess of the average. The mode of representing time is

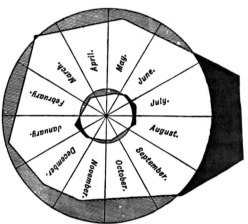

Fig. 5.—Infant mortality in Brussels.

clear from the figure, which shows that the latter part of the summer is that in which the infant mortality of Brussels is highest among children of less than one year old, while the rate exceeds the average among the very young infants both in the winter months and in the middle of summer.

It appears that this method should be especially suitable for the representation of phenomena which recur with some regularity year by year, and should enable the comparison between successive years to be made with much greater ease than is afforded by the curves of the early part of this article.

It is clear that the methods of representation referred to thus far are only adapted to display the simultaneous variations of two quantities, *e.g.* time and price. If it be required to represent the variations of one phenomenon with those of each of two co-existent causes, a surface is the suitable representation, rather than a curve on a plane.

The construction of such surfaces is so difficult that, in general, we are compelled to satisfy ourselves with a series of sections taken parallel to one or other of the three planes of reference.

A very ingenious attempt to represent the changes of economic phenomena, by the use of suitably-shaped figures having three dimensions in space, has recently been made by Dr. Irving Fisher (see STEREOGRAMS). The description of the devices of this writer would require more space than can be given here, and the reader must be referred to the memoir entitled " Mathematical Investigations in the Theory of Value and Prices " in the *Transactions of the Connecticut Academy*, vol. ix., July 1892.

We can only say here that Dr. Fisher has devised a mechanical apparatus for showing how various prices are altered by a change in the supply of purchasing power, or by a change in the conditions of demand or supply of one of the commodities concerned.

Among modes of representing on a plane the shape of a solid figure, besides that of drawing a series of sections, we have the method of employing a graded series of tints or colours, the deepest tints corresponding to the highest parts of the surface or to its lowest parts at choice.

This method is now very commonly employed for the construction of maps. It is easy to see that a plan of a town which shows every street and house will, by the larger or smaller proportion of its surface occupied by lines indicating the presence of houses, reveal at a glance the comparative degree of crowding of dwellings in its different parts, and a reduced copy, so small as not to show the independent tenements, would · still, by the variations in shading, show the varying density of population, so far as the crowding together of dwellings represents that density. The grading of tints shown by such a plan, may be employed for other purposes. Professor Ashley, for example, in his *Economic History*, vol. i. pt. ii. p. 304, employs such a map to show the localities which were more or less extensively occupied by enclosures in the 15th and 16th centuries.

It is obvious that differing tints of the same colour may be replaced by different colours, should such a mode of representation appear more desirable, the significance of each colour being indicated in the margin of the map or diagram.

Another method is to draw contour lines through those points on the plane where the surface, were it constructed, would always stand at the same height above the plane. A series of such contour lines gives a very fairly accurate representation of the shape of the surface. The lines of equal barometric pressure or of equal temperature on weather charts, or the lines where the soundings show equal depth on a chart of a sea or lake, are examples of the mode of representation here referred to.

Charts or maps which show, by any of the methods just named, the statistical variations of the physical or social phenomena of the districts represented, are known as CARTOGRAMS. A simpler though less effective method of indicating such variation, is to place the actual numbers referring to each district in the centre of the space on the map which represents it.

To the comparison of various quantities by drawing squares, circles, triangles, or other figures of such sizes as to be proportional in magnitude to the quantities to be compared, reference has already been made in the article on DIAGRAMS. In regard to these later modes of graphic representation, which are here discussed very briefly inasmuch as their theory is not a matter of difficulty, and in reference to the whole subject, the articles and books quoted may be consulted,

and also, among other writings, the articles "La Statistique Graphique," by M. Levasseur, and "On the Graphic Method of Statistics," by Prof. Marshall, in the jubilee volume of the Statistical Society ;[1] also Marey, *La Méthode Graphique*. Wm. Playfair, *Lineal Arithmetic, a Real Statement of the Finances and Resources of Great Britain*, etc.,—*Lineal Arithmetic or Charts of Commerce and Revenue*.

A. W. F.

GRASLIN, LOUIS FRANÇOIS DE (1727-1790), was from 1757 *Receveur Général des Fermes* in Nantes, where he left behind him the reputation of an enlightened and zealous administrator. His name, in token of public gratitude, has been given to one of the *places* in that town.

Graslin was a steady and consistent opponent of the tenets of the PHYSIOCRATS on the subject of the PRODUIT NET (*q.v.*) and the consequences they deduced from this principle and applied to taxation. His first work, *Sur l'influence de l'impôt indirect sur les biens fonds*, was written in 1767 in answer to a prize question put, under the influence of Turgot, by the *Société Royale d'Agriculture* of Limoges ; the first prize was awarded to M. de PÉRAVY,—who was a follower of the physiocrats in their doctrine on the *produit net*,—and a *mention très honorable* was given to Graslin. Turgot answered by a criticism of Graslin's essay which has been reprinted in the large edition of his *Œuvres* (Paris, 1844, vol. i. p. 439).

Graslin also published his *Essai Analytique sur la Richesse et sur l'Impôt*, Londres, 1767, designed to prove two propositions : "the first, that the produce of land is wealth even when there is no *produit net*, namely when the cost of cultivation is equal to the value of the produce, and the second, that industry, which employs raw material produced by land, is wealth intrinsically, as well as land in its productive capacity" (p. 11). On the subject of taxation he writes : "Not only do the taxes which are improperly called *indirect* [meaning those which are not assessed on the rent of land] not necessarily fall on the landowners, but it is even possible that a tax directly levied on land may be indirectly paid by other contributors" (p. 230). He often quotes the example of Holland, and proclaims the superiority over real and personal taxes of taxes on consumption (p. 303), although he admits that things of first necessity ought never to be taxed (p. 310).

Graslin is by no means a despicable controversialist, but, as was observed by Dupont de Nemours (*Œuvres de Turgot*, i. p. 416, ed. 1844), he spoils his work by "a slight affecta-

[1] For a good recent example see *Return with Diagrams showing the Consumption from 1861 up to the latest date, of Tea, Coffee, Cocoa, and Chicory, of Alcoholic Beverages, and of Tobacco, compared with the increase of population*, 329, Treasury, 1894. See also reference to stereogram in MARRIAGE RATE, also to diagram in MATHEMATICAL METHOD OF POLITICAL ECONOMY.

tion of metaphysics," and his language is often wanting in precision and accuracy.

As Graslin's work preceded the *Wealth of Nations* by nine years, it has been thought that he might have attended the course of lectures delivered by A. Smith in Edinburgh from 1751 to 1754. There is, however, no proof that this had been the case. The fact that his work bears *Londres* on the title-page does not even render it certain that he had ever been in London.

[*Correspondance Contradictoire entre M. Graslin, de l'Académie Économique de Saint Pétersbourg . . . et M. l'Abbé Baudeau, auteur des Éphémérides du Citoyen, sur un des Principes fondamentaux de la Doctrine des Économistes* (London, 1779).]

E. Ca.

GRASWINCKEL, DIRCK, born 1600, studied law, became, 1645, "advocaat-fiscaal der grafelykheids - domeinen in Holland" (advocate-fiscal of the count's domains in Holland), died 1660 at Mechelen (Malines). Besides his political writings he gained great renown by his economical work : *Placaetboek op het stuk van de Leeftocht* (Collections of Edicts on the subject of Food), Leyden, 1651. The 1st part is merely historical, the 2nd, critical ; it deals principally with (*a*) the question of export of corn, whether this should ever be forbidden or not. Government, he says, has a right to forbid it in periods of very high prices and famine, when every country has to take care of itself in the first place ; but in other cases export ought to be free ; (*b*) the question of forestalling. Though dealing in corn is to be permitted, forestalling should not be allowed.

His love for free trade in respect of exports does not prevent him from advocating import duties as a means of raising the price of corn. Like BOISGUILLEBERT, he looks on a high price of corn, although resulting from this cause, as a sign of national well-being. A. F. v. L.

GRATUITOUS UTILITY. Bastiat divides utilities into those which are *gratuitous* and those which are *onerous*, the former being free gifts of nature, while the latter directly or indirectly involve effort in their acquisition (see GOODS, CLASSIFICATION OF). It is assumed that whatever is gratuitous in the above sense is also common to all. This distinction leads up to Bastiat's characteristic doctrine that value is the relation of two services exchanged. Very briefly the argument is as follows. No one will give anything in exchange for that which can be obtained gratuitously by a mere act of appropriation ; hence the phenomenon of exchange-value can arise only in connection with onerous utility. But the recipient of an onerous utility is saved an effort, and when an effort is saved a service is rendered. Hence any exchange of onerous utilities is in effect an exchange of services. This position that the source and measure of value are to be found entirely in the *services* which are embodied

in onerous utilities has, as Cairnes observes in his well-known essay on *Bastiat*, "the unmistakable ring of an axiom of natural justice." "*Services pour services*"—what can be more just ? We have a manifest "economic harmony." Unfortunately the term *service*, as used by Bastiat, is highly ambiguous. There is throughout more or less confusion as to whether services are to be measured by the effort exerted by the man who performs the service, by the effort saved to the purchaser, or by the usefulness of the service ; and this constitutes a fatal flaw in the argument. Another fundamental distinction of Bastiat's—that, namely, between value and wealth—is based upon the distinction between gratuitous and onerous utilities. Gratuitous utilities cannot from their nature possess exchange-value. They are, however, regarded by Bastiat as very important constituents of wealth. The counter theory, which identifies wealth with value, is declared by him to be the glorification of obstacles ; since, if through some revolution in nature those things which are now produced with toil and sacrifice could be obtained gratuitously, they would on this view cease thereby to be wealth. This is not the place in which to discuss the question here raised, which is one of admitted difficulty, particularly in connection with the measurement of wealth (see Sidgwick, *Principles of Political Economy*, bk. i. ch. 3). It may, however, be pointed out that whatever definition of wealth be adopted, political economy has comparatively little concern with gratuitous utilities. To a great extent they do not admit of appropriation, at any rate by individuals ; if appropriated, they are still not made the subject of exchange ; and they are not the produce of human labour. Hence there arise no economic problems relating either to their production or their distribution. But, on the other hand, even if they are technically excluded from wealth, the economist is bound to attach importance to gratuitous utilities whether as factors in the production of onerous utilities or as rendering the production of onerous utilities needless.

[On the subject of this article, see Bastiat's *Harmonies of Political Economy*, translated by P. J. Stirling, 1860.] J. N. K.

GRAUMANN, JOHANN PHILIP (1690-1762), who in the year 1750 became master of the mint of Frederick the Great of Prussia, had formerly been a merchant in Holland, and carried into his official capacity a shrewd, business-like turn of mind. He established the Prussian monetary system, *preussisch Courant*, of coining fourteen instead of twelve thalers out of one mark of pure silver, in order to prevent the outflow of Prussian currency. In his *Versammelte Briefe von dem Gelde, Wechsel und dessen Curs, von der Proportion zwischen Gold und Silber, von dem Pari des Geldes und den Münzwesen verschiedener Voelker, besonders von dem Englischen* (Collected Letters on Money, Bills, and the rate of Exchange, the proportion between Gold and Silver, and the monetary systems of various Nations, chiefly of England), which were published in the year of his death, Graumann displays an unmitigated contempt both for "mere savants" and for "mere masters of the mint," although he uses the learned terminology of the former, even in the simplest questions, and generally has in view the aims of the latter. Graumann points out that it is not by any means a matter of indifference whether the rate of exchange is against or in favour of a nation. He finds only three faults in the English monetary system: the abolition of seigniorage, the prohibition to export English coins, and the over valuation of gold.

[See Roscher, *Gesch. der Nat. Oek. in Deutschland*, p. 420, also Dana Horton, *Sir Isaac Newton and England's Restrictive Policy towards Silver.*]

E. Ca.

GRAUNT, JOHN (1620-1674), statistician, was one of the earliest English writers to perceive the importance of vital statistics, and to deduce therefrom by scientific methods propositions with regard to the social and economic condition of the country. In 1662 he published a pamphlet in 4to (pp. 16 and 85) which immediately attracted much notice and commendation. It was entitled *Natural and Political Observations, mentioned in a Following Index, and made upon the Bills of Mortality*, by John Graunt, citizen of London. *With Reference to the Government, Religion, Trade, Growth, Ayre, Diseases, and the several Changes of the said City.* He tells us (see *First Ep. Ded.*) that he had "reduced several great confused volumes [of the *Bills of Mortality*] into a few perspicuous tables and abridged such observations as naturally flowed from them into a few succinct paragraphs, without any long series of multiloquious deductions." On the publication of his work, which bore on its title-page the modest epigraph: Non me ut miretur turba, laboro, Contentus paucis lectoribus, it was at once recognised that Graunt had opened up a new and fruitful field of investigation, and, at the king's suggestion, he was elected F.R.S. On 30th June 1665 the council of the Royal Society ordered that the book should be printed for the use of its members. Accordingly a third edition (London, 1665, 8vo) and a "fourth impression" (Oxford, 1665, 8vo) were published. Two years after Graunt's death in 1674, Sir William PETTY brought out a new and enlarged edition (London, 1676, 8vo), a fact which may perhaps in some measure account for the mistake of Evelyn, Burnet, and Stoughton, that Petty was the real author of the work. It was reprinted by Birch in 1759. Graunt especially deserves notice as one of the "beginners of an art not yet polish'd, and which time" would "bring

to more perfection" (Davenant). He also published *Observations on the advance of Excise*.

[Graunt's Life, *Dictionary of National Biography.*—The *Assurance Mag.* and *Journal of Inst. of Actuaries* contains a discussion as to the attribution of Graunt's researches to Sir W. Petty. *Vide* articles by Professor de Morgan, and Mr. W. B. Hodge; and by Mr. F. Hendriks *s.v.* Tontines; W. A. Bevan's "Sir W. Petty," *Am. Econ. Assoc.* 1894, review in *Econ. Journal*, March 1895.—Lord Ed. Fitzmaurice, *Life of Sir Wm. Petty*, 1895.]

W. A. S. H.

GRAY, JOHN, LL.D. (18th cent.), assistant private secretary to the Duke of Northumberland in Ireland in 1763-64, wrote *Practical Observations on the Union*, London, 1800, 8vo, and *The Income Tax scrutinised*, London, 1802, 8vo. In the latter, called forth by Pitt's income tax, land is maintained to be the proper object of taxation, and land banks are advocated, with state development of agriculture and the fishing industry.

H. E. E.

GRAY, JOHN (19th cent.) of Galashiels and Edinburgh, author of the *Social System, a Treatise on the Principle of Exchange*, 1831 and 1842; *Remedy for the Distress of Nations*, 1842, and *Money*, 1848. His remedy for distress is a change in the monetary system, founded on the principles that production is the cause of demand and labour is the only measure of value. There is a good deal of useful suggestion with criticisms of contemporary economists and statesmen.

GRAY, SIMON (18th and 19th cents. wrote also under pseudonym of George Purves), of the war office, a writer on economics of great pretensions but less success. He wrote in 1804 his *Happiness of States*, published 1815, including some letters of J. B. SAY (an ed. with additions, 4to, 1819), an attack on the French PHYSIOCRATS and Adam SMITH, whom he misunderstands. It clearly fell flat, for in 1817 he published, under the assumed name of George Purves, *All Classes Productive of National Wealth*, and in 1818, under same name, *The Principles of Population and Production investigated*, the object of both being to advertise the original work, which is constantly quoted and approved. His radical fallacies are the confusion of income with wealth, of the element of price, "chargeability," with productiveness, of expenditure with employment of labour. A few of his statements may serve as examples: "Paper money is the source of new capital, equal to the whole amount in circulation"; "the working classes consume more bread when it is dear than when it is cheap"; a national debt and high taxes enrich a nation; a rapidly increasing population makes future famine unlikely. On the other hand he saw that Adam Smith did not realise the importance of consumption in his scheme of economics, and inveighed against his distinction between productive and unproductive labour.[1]

Gray's other works are: *The Essential Principles of the Wealth of Nations*, etc., 1797, noticed in the

[1] Later economists have endorsed Gray's opinion on this point (see Marshall, *Principles of Economics*, 2nd ed. bk. ii. ch. iii.). Had Gray been less critical and negative, his remarks might have found fuller acceptance in his own time (refer to Cunningham, *Growth of English Industry and Commerce*, ed. 1892, vol. ii. p. 439).

Monthly Review.—Remarks on the Production of Wealth, in a letter to the Rev. T. R. Malthus, 1820—and, under his assumed name, *The Grazier's Ready Reckoner.*—See also Anton Menger, *Das Recht auf den vollen Arbeitsertrag* (2nd ed., 1891).—Roscher, *Pol. Econ.*, trans. Lalor, vol. ii. § 243.

E. G. P.

GREAT TITHES. See TITHES.

GREELEY, HORACE (1811-1872), was born in Amherst, New Hampshire. He was the son of a farmer of limited means ; self-educated, and at an early age apprenticed as a printer, he finally settled in New York, where in 1841 he established the *Tribune*, of which he was the editor until his death. He was an important counsellor in the whig and republican parties, until dissatisfaction with the administration of President Grant led him to join a revolt and to organise the liberal republican party. By this he was nominated for president in 1871. Greeley was an ardent and consistent protectionist ; and no journal did more than the *Tribune* in familiarising the north, and especially the farmer class, with this doctrine. In addition to his editorial work and frequent speeches upon the tariff, mention may be made of an *Introduction*, treating of the present state of the science of political economy and the adaptation of its principles to the condition of our own country, of *Principles of Political Economy*, by William Atkinson, New York, 1843 (Introduction, pp. i.-xv.) ; and of *Essays designed to elucidate the Science of Political Economy, while serving to explain and defend the Policy of Protection to Home Industry, as a System of National Co-operation for the Elevation of Labour*, Boston, 1870, pp. 384. In the latter, political economy is regarded as an art, "the chief end of a true political economy is the conversion of idlers and useless exchangers or traffickers into habitual effective producers of wealth" ; "protection is another name for labour-saving through co-operation." The work is valuable as representing the views of a large part of the more intelligent agricultural population of the northern part of the United States, 1840-1870. See also in *Recollections of a Busy Life*, pp. 528-553, *The Grounds of Protection*. About 1840, Greeley came under the influence of Fourierism ; and the doctrine of "association" was often referred to with favour in the *Tribune*. In 1846 occurred a discussion between Greeley and Henry J. Raymond of the *Courier and Enquirer*, running through twenty-four articles. For an abstract, see *Life of Horace Greeley*, by James Parton, New York, 1855, ch. xvi., *The Tribune and Fourierism*. In 1848-1850 Greeley wrote several articles to show how working men may become their own employers and share in profits ; in 1850 he published *Hints toward Reforms*, New York, composed of eleven lectures and twenty essays, largely devoted to the emancipation of labour.

This phase of his life is referred to in *Recollections of a Busy Life*, by Horace Greeley, New York, 1868, pp. 144-158.

D. R. D.

GREENBACK. This term refers to the legal-tender notes issued by the government of the United States, and so called because the backs of the bills are printed in green ink. They are equivalent to the "legal-tenders" or the treasury notes of the civil war period, as distinguished from the new treasury notes issued under the law of 1890, based upon purchases of silver. There were three issues of greenbacks: Feb. 25, 1862, $150,000,000 ; July 11, 1862, $150,000,000 ; and March 3, 1863, $150,000,000 (£30,000,000 each ; £90,000,000 in all, converting the $ at 5=£1). They were at first issued as a war measure, the government at that time being engaged in suppressing the rebellion in the southern states. Many at the time thought that the issue was unconstitutional, and none of the notes issued previous to the civil war had ever been made legal tender. The supreme court, however, has held that congress has power to impress upon the treasury notes the quality of legal tender not only in times of war but also in times of peace. At the close of the war a portion of the issue was withdrawn, but there was a strong popular opposition to the contraction of the currency, and consequently by the act of March 31, 1878, the treasury department was forbidden to reduce the amount then current in circulation, $346,681,016.

The term "greenback" was also given to a political party which appeared in 1874, and was hostile to the national banks. It opposed the withdrawal of the greenbacks, and in part advocated the payment of the United States debt in greenbacks instead of in gold.

After the early issues the government was obliged to suspend their payment, and the greenbacks circulated at a discount until 1879. For an accurate history of the greenback issues, see *History of United States Notes*, by John Jay Knox.

D. R. D.

GREENLAND COMPANY. During the reign of James I. the whale fisheries first came into notice. After being noted as sources of considerable profit for some time, a period of decay seems to have set in, for in 1693 complaint was made of their fall from their former high position. It was urged that the only available means of revival lay in the formation of a joint-stock company. Accordingly, on 1st October 1693, Sir William Scawen and forty-one others were incorporated as a company of merchants of London trading to Greenland. Their exclusive rights were to cease after the lapse of fourteen years from the date of the incorporation. The enterprise was not a success, and no application was made for the renewal. After the failure of the company various other expedients, as, for instance, bounties to private traders, were employed for the purpose of stimulating the whale fisheries.

[Macpherson, *Annals of Commerce.*—Cunningham, *History of Industry and Commerce*, vol. ii.]

E. C. K. G.

GREG, WILLIAM RATHBONE (1809-1881), born at Manchester, was educated at Bristol under Dr. Lant Carpenter, and at the university of Edinburgh. In 1832 he entered business, from which, however, he retired in 1850. In 1856 he was appointed one of the commissioners of customs, and in 1864 comptroller of the Stationery Office, a position which he held till 1877.

Though Greg's writings contain no positive contributions to economic knowledge, they are full of suggestive criticism and written in a frank easy style. The various subjects of which he treats are canvassed from all points of view, and the theories relative to them explained with the object of discovering the truth or rather the error which they contain. Though he did not deny the advance which had been made in general economic comfort, Greg was more acutely conscious of the difficulties in the way of sound economic and social progress. These he rather overestimates, while on the other hand he underestimates the importance of those economic influences of society which insensibly control the economic individual and modify the evils menaced by a too exclusive devotion to self-interest. His views on Malthusianism deserve mention.

Greg sometimes used the pseudonym of *Cassandra*. His chief writings relating to economic or semi-economic subjects were, *Political Problems of our Age and Country* (1870).—*Enigmas of Life* (1872).—*Rocks Ahead* (1874).—*Mistaken Aims and Attainable Ideals of the Working Classes* (1876).

E. C. K. G.

GRENIERS À SEL. These were established in France in 1342 for levying and collecting the GABELLE (*q.v.*), or tax upon salt. All salt manufactured in France had to be taken to the *grenier* of the province under penalty of confiscation. The *grenier* fixed the producer's price, and sold the salt at a much increased rate to the retail dealers, who were called *regrattiers*. The *grenier* was also a court of justice to decide all disputes arising in connection with the *gabelle*. In the 18th century there were seventeen *greniers à sel*, which were all abolished with the *gabelle* in 1790.

[Clamagéran, *Histoire de l'Impôt en France*.]

R. L.

GRENIERS D'ABONDANCE (France). At all periods of French history it has been the custom to create reserves of the surplus production of corn in years of abundance to meet the deficit in years of scarcity. Such stores were usually formed by the religious communities, but in 1577 a royal ordinance enjoined the local authorities to establish public granaries (*greniers d'abondance*) to hold a minimum of three months' consumption, and authorised them to borrow money at interest for the purpose. No records exist, however, of the extent to which the measure was carried out. Under Louis XV. difficulties appear to have arisen in ensuring a regular supply of bread to the capital, for the government then purchased the great mills and storehouses at Corbeil near Paris to hold 'a permanent reserve of 25,000 sacks of flour.' During the revolutionary period the government had again to intervene in the food supply of Paris by the purchase of 1200 to 1500 sacks of flour daily, which were sold to the bakers at 10 to 15 per cent below their cost price. One effect of that measure was that merchants ceased entirely to send corn to the market, and the bakers became wholly dependent on the government for their supplies; another consequence was that the inhabitants of the region around the capital flocked to Paris to purchase bread. Stringent measures were adopted against the intruders, but bread was nevertheless sold to them secretly, and the consumption in Paris rose from 1500 to 1900 sacks of flour daily. A first step was taken to compel citizens to obtain a card without which bread would not be delivered to them, and this was followed by a decree fixing rations according to the number of the family. M. Thiers describes in his *History of the French Revolution* the scene at the bakeries at the time. A long rope was stretched out from the door to be held by the hand by the people as they waited for their turn; the women would sometimes cut the cord and there was then a rush and a struggle, and armed force had to be called in to restore order. Various other measures were adopted as the necessity for them arose. In 1793 the National Convention ordered the creation of public granaries in each district of Paris, and voted a sum of 100,000,000 livres to stock them. In 1807 Napoleon I. commenced the construction of the immense range of buildings called the *grenier d'abondance* on the south bank of the river at the eastern end of Paris. It covered a space of two acres, and was intended to be six stories high, with mills worked by water power from the Seine in the basement. This magazine was to contain a three months' supply of 180,000 sacks of flour, constantly renewed. The service was, however, never organised, nor was the building ever terminated. Lofts were raised over the ground floor and roofed in, and the whole served for a long time as a warehouse for the stores the bakers were bound to keep as a condition of their privileges, the trade having become a monopoly with the number of shops limited in proportion to the number of inhabitants. The building was burnt during the fighting in Paris on the suppression of the commune, and was not rebuilt. The use for it had ceased, as the trade had been made free in 1863, and all the regulations relating to the compulsory reserves abolished. That the magazine was wilfully destroyed was proved by a document afterwards found in one of the mairies, in which the colonel of one of the insurgent legions reports, "I have set fire to the *grenier d'abondance*." All that now remains of the former restraints on freedom of trade in food supplies are Art. 420 of the Penal Code, which punishes by two months' to two years' imprisonment, and fines of from one to twenty thousand francs, all manœuvres or coalitions to raise or reduce the prices of corn, flour, or bread ; and Art. 30 of the Municipal Law of 1791, which empowers the mayors of communes to fix the prices of bread and meat, while, however, expressly forbidding the regulation of the price of corn or cattle. This law is still applied in many localities, and attempts to revive it at Marseilles in 1893, and more recently at St. Denis, led to strikes of the bakers, who closed their shops for several days rather than submit to it.   T. L.

GRENVILLE, George (1712-1770), was the son of Richard Grenville of Wotton, and his wife Hester, Countess Temple. He was educated at Eton and Christchurch, Oxford, and trained for the bar. Forsaking the law for politics, he was elected M.P. for Buckingham in 1741, and continued to represent that constituency until his death. After holding minor appointments, in 1754 he became treasurer of the navy. In this capacity he effected a useful reform by passing the Navy Bill, which provided for the speedy and punctual payment of seamen's wages. In May 1762 Grenville was appointed secretary of state ; he already held the leadership of the House of Commons. Five months later, however, he was compelled to resign the leadership and the seals, and accepted the post of first lord of the admiralty. He supported Dashwood's unpopular cider tax, on the ground that the profusion with which the late war had been carried on necessitated the imposition of fresh taxes. Grenville became first lord of the treasury and chancellor of the exchequer in April 1763. His fiscal policy precipitated the disastrous war with America, while he lost popularity by the prosecution of John Wilkes. When the famous "No. 45" of the *North Briton* appeared, he caused Wilkes to be arrested under a general warrant. The constitutional struggle which ensued involved ministers in an expenditure of £100,000, besides bringing upon them much odium. In the session of 1764 Grenville brought forward a series of resolutions asserting the right of the imperial legislature to impose taxation on the colonies. The proceeds of these duties were to be paid into the imperial exchequer, and to be applied under the direction of parliament "towards defraying the necessary expenses of defending, protecting, and securing the British colonies and plantations." The Commons also resolved that "it may be proper

to charge certain stamp duties" in America. Grenville allowed a year to elapse before embodying the resolutions in a bill ; but in 1765, in spite of the unanimous protests of the American colonies, the Stamp Act was carried, imposing customs duties upon the importation into the colonies of various foreign products. The act excited such discontent in America that the matter was again forced upon the attention of parliament in 1766. Pitt, in one of his most brilliant speeches, insisted that taxation without representation was illegal, but while he urged the immediate repeal of the tax, he proposed to uphold the dignity of the mother country by asserting the general legislative authority of parliament over the colonies. Grenville defended his ill-fated measure with vigour, but in the end the Stamp Act was repealed, while several of the obnoxious duties imposed in 1764 were withdrawn, and others modified. As Grenville had blundered over the Regency Bill, and was generally distasteful to the king, he was dismissed from the premiership in July 1765. Townshend, the chancellor of the exchequer, having proposed in 1767 to continue the land-tax for one year at 4s. in the £, Grenville carried a motion reducing the tax to 3s., by which the budget sustained a loss of £500,000. It is stated that this was the first occasion since the revolution on which a minister had been defeated upon any financial measure. As the result of his study of economical questions, Grenville wrote in conjunction with William Knox a treatise on *The Present State of the Nation ; particularly with respect to its Trade, Finances, etc. etc., addressed to the King and both Houses of Parliament* (1768). This pamphlet was noticed by A. Smith, *Wealth of Nations*, bk. iv. ch. i., and drew a reply from Burke. Grenville had taken a leading part in the early measures against Wilkes, but being convinced of the futility of a struggle between the House and the electors of Middlesex, he opposed his expulsion from the House of Commons in 1769, in a speech which was the most effective delivered in favour of the constitutional rights of electors. To remedy the evils connected with the trial of election petitions, early in 1770 Grenville introduced his celebrated measure, known as the Grenville Act, which forms "a landmark in parliamentary history" (May's *Constitutional History*). This admirable reforming measure transferred the trial of election petitions from the House at large to a select committee, empowered to examine witnesses upon oath. The act was in the outset passed for one year only, but it was renewed from time to time, and made perpetual in 1774. This act is now repealed, and election petitions referred to judges who report to the house. Grenville attended parliament through the session of 1770, but died on the 20th of November in that year. He was a capable statesman, had a thorough knowledge of the constitution, and exhibited much financial ability ; but he was stern in manner, extremely obstinate, destitute of tact, and governed by a boundless ambition.

[*Parliamentary History.*—*Grenville Papers.*—Walpole's *Memoirs.*—The *Histories* of Stanhope Lecky, and May (Lord Farnborough). —M'Culloch, *Literature of Pol. Econ.*]   G. B. S.

GRENVILLE, WILLIAM WYNDHAM, BARON GRENVILLE (1759-1834) was the youngest son of George Grenville by his wife Elizabeth, daughter of Sir William Wyndham, Bart. He was educated at Eton and Christ Church, Oxford. Elected M.P. for Buckingham in 1782, in the ensuing year he accompanied his brother Earl Temple to Ireland, as private secretary. Appointed paymaster-general in December 1783, he now gave his cousin Pitt valuable aid in the House of Commons. He devoted himself to the study of financial and commercial questions, was made one of the commissioners of the newly-created board of control, and in September 1786 vice-president of the committee of trade. For a few months of 1789 Grenville filled the position of speaker, resigning the office to become home secretary. In March 1790 he became president of the board of control, and in the following November was created Baron Grenville. He had the conduct of the government business in the House of Lords. He was appointed foreign secretary in 1791, in which office he continued for ten years, resigning his seat at the board of control in 1793. Grenville thoroughly carried out Pitt's foreign policy, and rejected all the overtures of the revolutionary government of France. In 1792 he introduced the Alien Act for the registration and supervision of all foreigners in the country, and in 1795 the Treasonable Practices Act and the Seditious Meetings Act. In 1799 he moved the resolutions for the Union with Ireland in a speech occupying four hours, " putting the arguments on strong grounds of detailed political necessity " (Lord Colchester's *Diary*). With regard to his position as a political economist he wrote a letter to Pitt in October 1800, protesting against tampering with the laws of supply and demand, and reminding him that " we in truth formed our opinions on the subject together, and I was not more convinced than you were of the soundness of Adam Smith's principles of political economy till Lord Liverpool lured you from our arms into all the mazes of the old system " (Stanhope's *Life of Pitt*). Grenville was a warm supporter of the Roman Catholic claims, and having drawn up an emancipation scheme which was rejected by the king, he resigned with several other members of the cabinet (February 1801). On the downfall of Addington in 1804, Grenville formed with Fox the Ministry of "All the Talents." In 1807 Grenville carried an act for the abolition of the slave trade, and it received the royal assent the very day ministers went out of office on the Roman Catholic question (25th March 1807). As auditor of the exchequer Grenville refused to issue public money during the incapacity of George III. Parliament was appealed to, and both Houses passed a resolution authorising and commanding the auditor and officers of the exchequer to pay obedience to treasury warrants for the issue of such sums as had been appropriated for the services of the army and navy, as well as money issuable under a vote of credit for £3,000,000. The money was paid, but a protest was entered in the Lords' journals, signed by twenty-one peers, affirming the measure to be unconstitutional, and one that might have been avoided, without injury to the public service, by an address to the Prince of Wales. Grenville strongly opposed the Corn Importation Bill of 1815, and with nine other peers signed a protest drawn up by himself and Lord Wellesley, declaring their opinion that " public prosperity is best promoted by leaving uncontrolled the free currents of national industry " (see Rogers's *Protests of the Lords* and M'Culloch's ed. *Wealth of Nations*, 1853, p. 523, for the protest). Grenville resisted various overtures to take office, as his high sense of honour prevented him from doing so except in a cabinet pledged to deal with Roman Catholic emancipation. His last speech in the House of Lords (21st June 1822) was in support of the Duke of Portland's Roman Catholic Peers Relief Bill. In 1828 Grenville wrote an *Essay on the supposed advantages of a Sinking Fund*, of which only the first part was printed, and privately issued. Grenville died at Dropmore in Buckinghamshire, on 12th January 1834. As a statesman he was distinguished for industry, honesty, and an unusual capacity for business ; and as a speaker he was weighty, lucid, and argumentative.

[*Parliamentary Debates.*—The various *Memoirs* of George III. and George IV.—Sir G. C. Lewis's *Administrations of Great Britain, 1783-1830.*—Lord Colchester's *Diary.*—Yonge's *Life of Lord Liverpool.*—Brougham's *Statesmen of George III.*]
                                    G. B. S.

GRESHAM, SIR THOMAS, *c.* 1519-1579, was the second son of Sir Richard Gresham, merchant ; he was educated at Gonville Hall, Cambridge, apprenticed to his uncle Sir John Gresham, also a merchant, and admitted a member of the Mercers' company in 1543. In 1551 or 1552 he became royal agent or king's factor at Antwerp, in which post he received twenty shillings a day, and which he retained with few intervals during three reigns until 1574, employed in spite of his Protestant views even by Mary. His business was to negotiate royal loans with Flemish merchants, to buy arms and military stores, and to smuggle into England as much bullion as possible. He succeeded in raising the rate of exchange from

16s. to 22s. in the £. and is said to have saved in this way 100,000 marks to the crown and 300,000 to the nation. His operations greatly benefited English trade and credit, though the government could not be induced to pay its debts as punctually as Gresham would have liked. He did not hesitate to remonstrate with and advise Elizabeth and Cecil ; but he was so useful and trustworthy that he was never seriously out of favour, except just after Mary's accession. On Mary's death he advised Elizabeth to restore the base money, to contract little foreign debt, and to keep up her credit, especially with English merchants. Later he taught her how to make use of these English merchants when political troubles in the Netherlands curtailed her foreign resources ; at his suggestion the Merchant Adventurers and Staplers were forced by detention of their fleets to advance money to the state ; but as they obtained interest at 12 per cent instead of the legal maximum of 10, and the interest no longer went abroad, the transaction proved advantageous to all parties and increased Gresham's favour. His journeys to and from Antwerp were very frequent, but in his later years he entrusted most of his public work to his agent, and is not known to have been at Antwerp after 1567. In 1554 he was sent to Spain to procure bullion, a very difficult task in which he was only partially successful ; and in 1559 he was employed as ambassador to the Duchess of Parma, regent of the Netherlands ; it was on this occasion that he was knighted.

In addition to his public services he continued throughout his life to do the work of "the greatest merchant in London." He was, in the language of the day, a banker and goldsmith, with a shop in Lombard Street, as well as a mercer ; but he was a considerable country gentleman besides, with estates, chiefly in Norfolk, where his father held considerable property (see Blomefield, *Norfolk*), and with several country houses besides the house in Bishopsgate which he built and bequeathed to London as Gresham College. He twice entertained Queen Elizabeth as his guest. His wealth was mainly earned by his private business, but he cannot be acquitted of enriching himself at the public expense by at least one dishonourable manœuvre ; and he habitually forwarded his schemes by bribery. The money so gained he applied to public uses, his only son having died young : the foundation of the royal exchange, of Gresham College, and of eight almshouses, and the establishment of the earliest English paper-mills on his estate at Osterley, show the breadth of his interests, his liberality, his charity, his culture, and his commercial enterprise (see EXCHANGE as BOURSE ; GRESHAM'S LAW).

[Burgon, *Life and Times of Sir Thomas Gresham.—Dictionary of National Biography.—Fuller's Worthies, Norfolk*, p. 259.—Holinshed, 1808, iv. 426.—Hall, *Society in the Elizabethan Age*, ch. v. and appendix, for financial character and position.—Fox Bourne, *English Merchants.*—Will of Sir Th. Gresham.]   E. G. P.

GRESHAM'S LAW.   This familiar term was introduced by MacLeod in 1858 (*Elements of Political Economy*), and has since been generally accepted by economists.

It denotes that well-ascertained principle of currency which is forcibly though not quite adequately expressed in the dictum—"bad money drives out good." It has also not infrequently been explained by the statement that where two media of exchange come into circulation together the more valuable will tend to disappear. The principle in its broadest form may be stated as follows :—Where by legal enactment a government assigns the same nominal value to two or more forms of circulatory medium whose intrinsic values differ, payments will always, as far as possible, be made in that medium of which the cost of production is least, and the more valuable medium will tend to disappear from circulation ; in the case where the combined amount in circulation is not sufficient to satisfy the demand for currency, the more valuable medium will simply run to a premium.

This is a principle which obviously has its roots in the ordinary instincts of commercial life, and the cases in which it has asserted itself may be divided into those where (1) of two media intrinsically good, one is by error undervalued ; where (2) it is sought to keep a debased metallic currency in circulation on a par with that of a better metal ; where (3) an inconvertible paper has been made to run by the side of a metallic currency. The reference to paper suggests the observation that the circulation of convertible paper side by side with, and as "the shadow of" gold, is explained by reference to a different principle.

The dictum above quoted appears to have been used first in the proclamation of 1560 respecting the decrial of the base silver coin ; and we know that Sir Thomas Gresham took a prominent part in advising Queen Elizabeth and Cecil on the reform of the currency. (See Burgon's *Life and Times of Sir Thomas Gresham.*)   We do not, however, find the principle stated in his own handwriting.

The actual instances of the operation of the law are numerous, and we shall cite only a few. MacLeod quotes Aristophanes, *Frogs*, as the earliest instance of its recognition. Amongst many in the history of the United Kingdom, besides the prevalence of debased silver which formed the occasion of Gresham's dictum, we may cite the following from Lord Liverpool, referring to the over-valuation of silver prior to the reign of James I.

"It is certain that the rise in the value of

Gold made by James I. in the 2nd and 3rd year of his reign was rendered necessary by the exportation of the Gold. Coin, which had for some time been experienced, and by the very small quantity of it that was then left in circulation. This rise . . . produced a partial and temporary relief . . . but [Stowe] confesses that this plenty of Gold coin did not continue in circulation for any length of time, and that it afterwards began to be exported. It soon became evident that the last-mentioned rise of the value of Gold in the Coins of this Kingdom was not sufficient to make it equal to the relative value of Gold to Silver at the market."

In Mr. Chalmers's recent work on the *History of Colonial Currency*, we have without difficulty noted eighteen instances, and there are many more. In a pamphlet of 1740 on the *Currencies of the British Plantations in America*, we have the following:—" In sundry of our Colonies were enacted laws against passing of light Pieces of Eight. These laws not being put into execution, heavy and light Pieces of Eight passed promiscuously ; and, as it always happens, a bad currency drove away the good currency ; heavy Pieces of Eight were shipped off." And on this Mr. Chalmers comments as follows :— " Imitating the practices familiar to them in England, dishonest persons traded on the desire of the young communities for a metallic currency, by circulating clipped money at the full rate ; and this malpractice was condoned by the Colonies when it was found that the light money was more apt to stay with them than ' broad' pieces." So that throughout the 17th and 18th centuries in the American and West Indian colonies we constantly find a debased currency in possession of the field. Again, when the Treasury tried to introduce sterling into the colonies in 1838, and wrongly valued the dollar for concurrent circulation with the shilling, " by a familiar law, the over-rating of the dollar sufficed to drive out the shillings" which had been shipped from Great Britain.

In the case of the United States we have excellent instances both in the effect of the legislation of 1837 as driving out silver dollars, and in the way in which the inconvertible "greenbacks" formed the chief part of the currency from 1864 to 1879.

[*Elements of Political Economy*, H. D. MacLeod, London, 8vo, 1858, p. 477.—Bi-metallism, id. *ibid.*, 1893. Essay by Dr. Giffen in *Economic Journal*, vol. i. p. 304, explaining common misinterpretation of Gresham's Law.] C. A. H.

GRIFFITH'S VALUATION is the name popularly given to the government valuation of Ireland from Sir R. Griffith under whose directions it was carried out. The first act, passed in 1826 (7 Geo. IV. c. 62), laid down a scale of prices as a basis for valuation, which was by townlands.[1] Subsequent measures, partly

[1] The smallest local division. There were 60,644 townlands in Ireland in 1881.

necessitated by the introduction of the poor law in 1838, amended the original system, but the existing valuation, commencing with Munster in 1848 and ending with Armagh in 1865, was at first carried out under an act of 1846 (9 & 10 Vict. c. 110), and later on under one of 1852 (15 & 16 Vict. c. 63), which last revised the very low scale of prices fixed in 1826 and hitherto retained. The authority of Griffith's valuation—at one time highly esteemed—is now completely discredited not only as a guide for fixing rents, which it was not intended to be, but even as a standard for taxation. The prices assumed by it are not those now existing ; no adequate account is taken of the yield of land, and the different bases of the acts of 1846 and 1852 make the valuation unfair as between the localities affected.

[For origin of system see Seebohm, *Village Comm.*, ch. vii.] C. F. B.

GRIST TAX. See MACINATO.

GROAT. See FOURPENCE.

GROSCHEN (COIN). In German countries the word groschen was originally applied to any large or thick coin. Record exists of gold groschen having been coined as early as the year 1232. The name was, however, more commonly applied to silver coins. The value of the silver groschen varied considerably, as, in addition to there being several kinds of these coins, the weight and fineness of each particular kind was not constant. Their history, in fact, presents a record of more or less continuous debasement, similar to that so frequently met with in tracing the life of coins which have been in use for centuries (*e.g.* crown, denier, groat, livre, penny). The greed or the pecuniary difficulties of successive rulers led to the lowering of the coins either in weight or fineness, until a coin which was, as already mentioned, at one time made of gold, ended its career as one of the smallest silver coins of Germany, with a value of only $\frac{1}{30}$th of a thaler (or approximately 1¼th of a penny).

No indication of the nominal value of groschen is to be found on the older coins, though it is generally placed on the more modern pieces. Silver groschen are not now struck. The following list, however, gives the particulars of those in use in Prussia, Saxony, and Austria during comparatively recent years.

PRUSSIA.

(*Under the Law of 30th September 1821.*)

Silver Coin.	Weight (grammes).	Millesimal Fineness.	Value in German Marks.
Groschen ($\frac{1}{30}$ thaler) . .	2·1924	222·222	0·0877
Half-groschen ($\frac{1}{60}$ thaler) . .	1·0962	222·222	0·0438

(Under the Law of 4th May 1857.)

Silver Coin.	Weight (grammes).	Millesimal Fineness.	Value in German Marks.
Groschen ($\frac{1}{30}$ thaler) . .	2·1959	220	0·0870
Half-groschen ($\frac{1}{60}$ thaler) . .	1·0979	220	0·0435

On the introduction in 1873, under the act of the 9th July of that year, of the imperial German coinage, with the gold mark as the standard of value, the coinage of groschen was discontinued. The new law, however, provided for the coinage of nickel pieces of the nominal value of 10 pfennige (0·1 mark), and these coins, which have taken the place of the old silver pieces, are commonly spoken of as groschen.

SAXONY.
(Under the Law of 20th July 1840.)

Silver Coin.	Weight (grammes).	Millesimal Fineness.	Value in German Marks.
Two new groschen ($\frac{1}{15}$ thaler) .	3·1181	312·500	0·1754
New groschen ($\frac{1}{30}$ thaler) . .	2·1260	229·167	0·0877
Half new groschen ($\frac{1}{60}$ thaler) .	1·0630	229·167	0·0438

(Under the Law of the 19th May 1857.)

Silver Coin.	Weight (grammes).	Millesimal Fineness.	Value in German Marks.
Two new groschen ($\frac{1}{15}$ thaler) .	3·2206	300	0·1739
New groschen ($\frac{1}{30}$ thaler) . .	2·1004	230	0·0870
Half new groschen[1] ($\frac{1}{60}$ thaler) .	1·0502	230	0·0435

Prior to 1840 the groschen represented $\frac{1}{24}$th of a thaler. The coin weighed 1·9856 grammes, and was composed of silver of the millesimal fineness of 368. Its value in modern German marks is equal to 0·1315 mark.

AUSTRIA.
(Under the Convention of 21st September 1753.)

Silver Coin.	Weight (grammes).	Millesimal Fineness.	Value in German Marks.
Kaisergroschen, or 3-kreutzer piece	170·10	343·750	0·1053

No provision was made in the currency law of 29th April 1852 for the coinage of silver groschen ; the smallest Austrian silver coin issued under that law being a ten-kreutzer piece.

[1] The coinage of these pieces was discontinued in 1861, when their place was taken by the copper 5-pfennige piece.

[Friedrich Noback, *Münz, Mass, und Gewichts-buch*, Leipzig, 1879.—*Groschen-Cabinet*, Leipzig, 1749.] F. E. A.

GROSS AND NET. The word "gross" has sometimes been used by economists as a synonym of "total" or "aggregate." J. S. Mill, for instance, often means by "gross produce" total or aggregate produce as opposed to average or *per capita* produce (see, *e.g.*, *Principles*, I. xiii. § 2 *ad fin.*), and by "gross profit" the absolute amount of profits as opposed to the rate of profit (*e.g.*, *Essays on some Unsettled Questions*, etc., p. 92; *Principles*, iv. iii. § 3). Generally, however, "gross" has been used as a correlative of "net"— the net profits, rent, and produce being what is left of the gross profits, rent, and produce after certain deductions have been made. In the case of profits the terms are not properly applicable, since profits are themselves net receipts, *i.e.*, what is left of the gross receipts after all the cost of obtaining them has been deducted. Consequently the term "gross profits" has never attained any precise sense ; it must be variously interpreted according to the context in which it appears. "Gross rent" is the amount of rent paid to the landlord by the tenant, and net rent is the amount left to the landlord after he has paid all expenses of management and repairs (*Wealth of Nations*, II. ii.); "rent" alone usually means in economic works the net rent, while in statistics it means the gross rent. As to the proper application of the terms gross and net produce there was formerly considerable difference of opinion. The PHYSIOCRATS (*q.v.*) held that rent was the only net produce of a country, and looked on profits and wages as merely a part of the necessary expenses of obtaining this net produce. Adam Smith defined "gross revenue" as the whole annual produce, and "net revenue" as what remains of this after deducting the expense of maintaining fixed and circulating capital ; by this definition "net revenue" is made to include the whole of profits, wages, and rent. But Ricardo in his *Principles*, ch. xxvi. "on gross and net revenue," excluded wages from net revenue, apparently on the ground that they consist entirely of necessaries, so that no contributions to the state nor additions to capital can be made from them. James Mill (*Elements*, ch. iv. § 1) adopted the same view in spite of a protest by Malthus (*Political Economy*, 1st ed. pp. 423-425) against it. J. S. Mill (*Essays*, pp. 88, 89) calls it the usual doctrine, and suggests that it should be amended by including in the "net produce" so much of wages as is over and above the smallest amount necessary for maintaining the existing number of workers. Later writers seldom use the terms gross and net produce or revenue, but treat the unqualified "produce" and "revenue" as equivalent to Adam Smith's net revenue. E. C.

GROTIUS, HUGO (Huig van Groot, 1583-

1645), was born at Delft ; at the age of eleven he became a student of the university of Leyden, and early distinguished himself as a classical scholar. At fifteen he entered public life, accompanying an embassy to the French court. On his return he practised law, and was made advocate-general of the FISC for the provinces of Holland and Zeeland in 1607, and pensionary of Rotterdam in 1613. In the religious and political disputes of his country, Grotius supported the party of the "Remonstrants," the party of Arminianism and toleration in religion, and of oligarchic republicanism in politics. In 1618 he was arrested along with J. van Olden Barneveldt, the leader of the Remonstrants, and while the latter was put to death, Grotius was sentenced to imprisonment in a fortress for life. Escaping by the stratagem of his wife, who had him carried out in a chest supposed to contain his books and dirty linen, he crossed the frontier in disguise and made his way to Paris in 1621. He received a pension, nominally at least, of 3000 livres from the King Louis XIII. In 1634 he was appointed Swedish ambassador at the French court. In 1645 he resigned this post and retired to Stockholm ; but dissatisfied with life there, he crossed over to Germany and died at Rostock in the same year. Grotius was distinguished as an historian, a scholar, an elegant writer of Latin verse, and a tolerant theologian who sought to reconcile Catholic and Protestant, and wrote commentaries on the Scriptures in the spirit of scholarship rather than of dogmatic theology. His *De Veritate Christianæ Religionis* was published in 1627 ; his *Annotationes* on the Old and New Testaments between 1641 and 1646. But his greatest fame was won in jurisprudence. Already in 1604 he had written a book *De Jure Prædæ*, which he did not publish, the MS. of which was only discovered in 1868. This work was suggested by his practical experience : he had had to argue for the lawfulness of the capture of a Portuguese galleon by the Dutch East India Company. The short treatise called *Mare Liberum* (printed in 1609) was a chapter of this work : against the Portuguese claim to the eastern waters, he asserted that the ocean was free to all. When disputes about the control of the sea arose afterwards between the Dutch and the English, Selden wrote his *Mare Clausum* (published in 1635) in answer to Grotius. The *De Jure Prædæ* was the germ out of which grew the *De Jure Belli et Pacis*, published at Paris in 1625. Grotius himself tells us that the license which he saw prevailing throughout the Christian world both in the making and in the carrying on of war—it was the time of the Thirty Years' War—was the motive which induced him to undertake his great work (*De Jure Belli*, Proleg. 3, § 28). Parts of the subject he admits had previously been treated of by some of the schoolmen, and by more recent theologians

and lawyers ; but his chief predecessors were, as he says, Albericus Gentilis (*De Jure Belli*, 1589), and Balthazar Ayala (*De Jure et Officiis Bellicis*, 1597). But Grotius may be said to have practically created a new science, "the law of nature and of nations," which in his own lifetime became a subject of academic teaching, and to have written a book on this subject which has attained greater fame than any that has been written on it since. BENTHAM, who attacked the idea of a law of nature, introduced for the law of nations the term "INTERNATIONAL LAW" (*q.v.*). Throughout the 17th and 18th centuries the treatise of Grotius exercised an enormous influence on ethical and legal thought. It came to be less studied only when many of its main principles had been accepted by the more civilised nations, and when the sometimes irrelevant erudition and elaborate citations from ancient authors, which were the fashion of the early 17th century, made it distasteful to a later age. Grotius himself defended his use of the testimonies of philosophers and historians on the ground that they supply evidence of that consent of mankind to which writers on the *jus naturæ* and *jus gentium* were in the habit of appealing ; he admits that his quotations from poets and orators are introduced rather for purposes of ornament. Grotius, while professedly basing his theories on reason and on fact, has still much of the scholastic reverence for authorities— Aristotle, the Bible, the Fathers, the Roman Jurists, the schoolmen themselves ; though he has departed from the scholastic minuteness of argumentation and is saturated with the "classical" learning of the Renaissance. It may be said of Grotius and of his less literary follower Pufendorf that for the Protestant countries of Europe they took the place which the great schoolmen from AQUINAS to Suarez occupied in the Roman Catholic world. When the inevitable reaction against the authority of the name of Grotius began, his critics, such as Paley and Dugald Stewart, forgot that Grotius did not profess to write a complete treatise on ethics and jurisprudence, and that he expressly disclaimed treating the subject of politics. His professed subject is what his title indicates : and the order of the words in the title is also significant,—the phrase, it may be noted, is incidentally used in a passage Grotius quotes from Cicero. But it is only the last part of his third book and the last few chapters of his second that deal strictly with the subjects of international law, *i.e.* with the principles regulating the intercourse of nations in war and in peace. The rest of the work is all intended to lead up to this subject. In bk. i. he treats of the origin of rights and laws in general, discusses the question raised by some Christian writers whether any war is just, deciding that some wars are not contrary to the law of nature or even to the positive divine law. In order to distinguish between public and private war he explains the nature of sovereignty with its different forms and degrees. He then goes on to consider the duty of subjects to superiors, denying the doctrine that the people is everywhere sovereign and that everywhere subjects may be justified in rebelling (see ALTHUSIUS). Grotius qualifies his precept of non-resistance only in cases where the rulers have by the constitution a limited power, or where a legally absolute ruler uses extreme cruelty or practically abdicates (see HOBBES). In bk. ii., in order to discuss all the causes from which war may arise, he examines what things are common, what are property, what is the right of persons over persons, what obligations arise from ownership, what are the rules of royal succession, what rights are obtained by pact or contract, what is the force and interpretation of treaties and of oaths, what is due for damage done, what is the sacredness of ambassadors, the right of burying the dead, and the nature of punishments. Bk. iii. "has for its subject, first, what is lawful in war: and when it has drawn a distinction between what is done with impunity and may even in dealing with foreigners be defended as consistent with justice (*jus externum*) and that which is really free from fault (is in accordance with *jus internum*), it then comes to treat of the kinds of peace and convention in war." It will be obvious even from this brief enumeration of contents, adapted from Grotius's own summary (Proleg. 4, §§ 33-35), that though recognising the distinctions, Grotius has not separated law from ethics nor public from private law.

Of economic questions he does not directly treat. His interest for the economist, apart from his reference to such questions as property, usury, etc., comes mainly from the direct and indirect effect of his conception of the law of nature (see JUS NATURALE). In his use of the term *jus gentium*, Grotius combined the original Roman meaning of it, the customs and principles of right common to different political societies, with a use of the term which was not Roman, as =*jus inter gentes*, the usages recognised as right between independent political societies as quasi-persons, — a confusion of meanings theoretically very misleading, but practically beneficial, since it enabled Grotius to read into questions of international intercourse the humane principles of the Roman *jus gentium* as modified by philosophical ideas about a law of nature.

Grotius, influenced partly by the biblical narrative, partly by classical traditions, and partly by what he had heard of the simple life of barbarous races—such as "certain peoples of America,"—imagined a primitive state in which everything was common. Departure from primitive simplicity and innocence and the growth

of agriculture and other arts made private property necessary. It originated by a certain pact, either express, as by division, or tacit, as by occupation (ii. 2, § 2). "Original acquisition might of old, when the human race could meet together, be made by division: nowadays it is only made by occupation" (ii. 3, § 1). Thus for all practical purposes Grotius follows the Roman jurists in basing the right of property on occupation. The suggestion of the jurist Paulus that property may also arise from the making of new things — an anticipation of LOCKE (*q.v.*), who bases property on labour— Grotius puts aside on the ground that "making" presupposes either previous ownership of the material, or acquisition of it by occupation; otherwise what we make is not ours (ii. 3, § 3). With regard to the ocean, the reason why communism was given up does not exist: it is great enough to suffice for all people (ii. 3, § 3), and moreover it cannot properly be occupied, as lakes or even rivers can, and being largely unknown at the first division of the earth, it could not be divided, and so could only become property now by occupation. So far as small portions of the sea — *e.g.*, bays, estuaries, straits,—can be occupied, they may by the law of nature become the property of nations, and even of individuals, or may be divided between several (ii. 3, § 8); but even such ownership may be contrary to the law of nations—*i.e.* consent or custom (ii. 3, § 10). Thus it was part of the Roman *jus gentium* that the sea was common to all men (*ib.* § 9).

In his chapter "On Contracts" (ii. 12) Grotius does not advance beyond ARISTOTLE (*q.v.*) in his views about value or money, except in so far as he recognises that deferment of payment and other such "accidents capable of being valued" may affect the price (§ 14)—a principle of importance among casuists in regard to the question of interest. Not all monopolies, he holds, are contrary to the law of nature: they may be permitted by a government for a just cause, as in the case of Joseph in Egypt. But a combination to raise prices or prevent by fraud or force the importation of a large quantity of a commodity is wrong (§ 16).

Contrary to the more received opinion, Grotius holds that usury is not forbidden by the law of nature, and points out the fallacies of the usual arguments about the barrenness of money, etc.; but since the divine law forbade Hebrew to lend to Hebrew money on usury, and "since precepts of this sort bind Christians also as being called to a higher pitch of virtue," and since what was a duty towards a fellow-countryman then is for Christians a duty towards all men, usury seems forbidden to Christians by the positive divine law (ii. 12, § 20). But for Grotius, as for the mediæval casuists, there are distinctions between the usury which is forbidden and a taking of interest which is permissible. "Human laws," he says, "which allow something to be covenanted for the use of money, if the rate lie within a due compensation, are not opposed to natural or divine law,—as in Holland it has long been granted to persons in general to require 8 per cent per annum, and to merchants 12 per cent. If they exceed that standard, laws may afford impunity, but they cannot give a right" (*Ibid.* § 22).

[The *De Jure Belli et Pacis* has been edited by Whewell, with an English translation which omits some of the superfluous quotations. 3 vols., Cambr., 1853. The translation was also published separately. There is a careful analysis of the whole work in Hallam's *Introd. to the Literature of Europe*, vol. ii. The accounts of it in Janet's *Histoire de la Science Politique*, in Bluntschli's *Geschichte der neueren Staatswissenschaft*, and in Erdmann's *History of Philosophy* (translated) are much more meagre.—Art. "Grotius" in *Encycl. Brit.* by Mark Pattison.—See also many important references in Maine's *Ancient Law* and *International Law.*—Austin's *Jurisprudence.*—Hall's *International Law*, and in Dr. Bonar's chapter in his *Philosophy and Political Economy.*] D. G. R.

GROUND - ANNUAL (Scotland) a yearly revenue or perpetual annuity payable out of land. (1) In lands originally church lands the superiority or lordship is in many cases in the crown, the vassal holding by tenure direct of the crown at a nominal rent, but paying an annual sum or "ground-annual" to the crown grantee of the revenues of the church lands. (2) In modern practice the building-land speculator, for example, takes land on feu, and, where sub-infeudation is not prohibited at law or by agreement, he sublets to builders at an enhanced Feu - Duty (see FEU) ; but where sub-infeudation is prohibited, he dispones or grants the land to be held not of himself, but of the superior or overlord, subject to a reserved perpetual annual charge or "ground-annual," to be paid to himself his heirs and assignees. This reserved charge, which in its nature is similar to the chief rents frequently affecting freehold land in the North of England, is made a burden affecting the land itself ; and usually the grantee executes a bond, in which he dispones the land back to the granter, but only as a security for the annual payment, for which he also becomes personally liable under the so-called "bond and disposition in security." The documents in the transaction are recorded in the land registers. A. D.

GROUND RENTS. The expression ground rent is generally used in connection with building leases. It is sometimes said or believed that the ground rent represents the yearly value of the ground as distinguished from the value of the building, but this is not necessarily the case. The lessor may prefer to let the land for a lump sum payable at once and to take no rent (a "peppercorn rent"), or a merely nominal annual sum, in which case the ground rent is of course much less than the yearly value of the land. On the other hand annual payments are called ground rents in many cases, in which case they really represent part of the annual value of the building. This arises more especially in the case of "improved ground rents." A builder, having taken a building lease at an annual rent of £10, and having built a house costing £2000, may deal with the property in a great variety of ways. He may assign the lease to an occupying tenant for a price exceeding £2000, the purchaser undertaking to pay the original ground rent ; he may let the house on a short lease for a yearly rent representing the full yearly value, in which case the rent is called the rack rent ; or he may, in consideration of a premium of £2000, grant an underlease for the whole term at an increased ground rent, the increase representing the profit on the transaction. In the last mentioned case the rent is called an "improved ground rent." In order to make the purchase look attractive he may charge a smaller premium than £2000, which will of course necessitate a further increase in the improved ground rent, but in such a case, which in practice occurs pretty frequently, the so-called ground rent partly represents the interest and sinking-fund for the cost of the building, and to that extent exceeds the annual value of the ground. It is sometimes said that ground rents do not pay local rates, but this is a fallacy. The rates are charged on the rack rents, that is to say on the full value, which, of course, includes the ground rent. No doubt the rates are, as a rule, paid by the occupying tenant, but this is generally a condition of the lease, and the tenant, knowing that he has to pay the rates, pays so much less rent (see FINANCE, GENERAL PRINCIPLES OF ; TAXATION).

In the language of auctioneers and others the expression ground rents is frequently used to describe property let on building leases, but this is, of course, inaccurate. The expression "ground landlord" which is often used for the ultimate recipient of ground rents, is also misleading and connected with the popular idea that the lessor owns the land and the lessee the house. During the continuance of the lease the lessor has a merely reversionary interest in the land and the house, the lessee being, subject to the conditions of the lease, their temporary owner. The ownership of the house cannot in any sense be severed from the ownership of the land, and the benefit of an increase in the value of the land in the case of a long lease accrues to the lessee, and not to the lessor, at least not before the expiration of the lease. This fact is also frequently lost sight of when new schemes of taxation are discussed. German writers use the word *Grund-rente* in the sense of economical rent.

[Much interesting information on these subjects

can be found in Mr. C. H. Sargant's books, *Ground Rents and Building Leases*, and *Urban Rating.*— For a different view see B. Costelloe, *Incidence of Taxation* (1893).—*Rep. of Sel. Comm. H. of C. on Town Holdings.*]   E. S.

GROWING CROPS, though not severed from the land, and therefore, strictly speaking, part of the land, are for some purposes looked upon as things not partaking of the nature of real property (see EMBLEMENTS). For the purpose of the Bills of Sale Act (see BILL OF SALE), growing crops, when separately assigned or charged, are deemed to be personal chattels ; but when they are assigned or charged together with any interest in the land on which they grow, they are looked upon as part of the land, and the document embodying the assignment or charge need not be registered as a bill of sale.   E. S.

GROWTH, PROPORTIONATE, may be defined as the increase of a quantity relative to its initial value. For instance the export of coal from England being 23·6 million tons in 1880 and 38·2 million in 1890, the proportionate growth of the export during the period 1880-90 is $(38 \cdot 2 - 23 \cdot 6) \div 23 \cdot 6 = \frac{1}{4}\frac{4}{6}$ or nearly 62 per cent. In general terms, if x_0 be the value of the quantity at the beginning of the period under consideration and x_1 at the end, the proportionate growth during that period is $(x_1 - x_0) \div x_0$. If in a second period the quantity changes from x_1 back to x_0, the proportionate growth downwards, or decrease, is by parity $- (x_1 - x_0) \div x_1$—not the mere negative of the growth upwards, as might seem natural. An attempt to obviate this anomaly is made by Mr. Cooley in "Observations on the Measure of Change" in the *Journal of the American Statistical Association* for March 1893. It may be observed that the difficulty disappears when the growth is *small*.

Proportionate growth may be considered as relative to, or dependent on, some variable other than *time*. Thus the proportionate growth of the demand for a commodity corresponding to a small proportional growth or percentage increment of its price is the measure of Elasticity of Demand (see DEMAND).

The conception of the proportional growth of a quantity being independent of the particular scale or unit employed in measuring the quantity, is particularly appropriate when we want to compare the increase of different things. The ordinary graphic representations of *absolute* growth are not so well suited for this purpose. Thus suppose that, to quote Prof. Marshall, "the consumption per head of tea and sugar in the United Kingdom for the years 1860 to 1883 is represented to the same scale in pounds" in two ordinary curves. "The danger of the popular use of statistical curves is illustrated by the fact that an orator might perhaps carry his audience with him, while he argued that they showed a much more rapid growth of the

consumption of sugar than of tea. But, really, there is very little difference between the two as is seen on comparing 'two curves' in which a pound of sugar is compared against, not a pound, but an ounce of tea" (see GRAPHIC METHOD in connection with Fig. 4).

(Marshall, *Principles of Economics*, bk. iii. ch. iv. p. 160 *et seq.*—*Journal of the Statistical Society*, Jubilee vol. 1885, p. 257 *et seq.*)
                                                   F. Y. E.

GRUNDLER, CHRISTIAN GOTTLOB (latter half of 18th century), merchant in Berlin, author of various treatises on commercial subjects.

Ueber den grossen Nachtheil der Monopolien gegen freye Manufakturen (1787).—*Allgemeine Beiträge zur Handlung* (Berlin, 1788). — *Ueber die Messe zu Frankfurt a. O.* (Berlin, 1807).
                                                   R. H. H.

GUARANTEE. A contract by which one person—called the surety—undertakes to be liable for the debt of another person—called the principal debtor. A contract of this nature must, in accordance with § 4 of the Statute of Frauds, be in writing ; but § 3 of the Mercantile Law Amendment Act provides that it shall not be necessary for the consideration to be set out in writing. This does not, of course, dispense with the necessity of a consideration in all cases where the contract is not made by deed, but the granting or continuing of a loan to the principal debtor is in itself a sufficient consideration to support the promise of the surety.

It is frequently doubtful whether a guarantee is intended to be a continuing one or whether it is merely intended to refer to a special transaction, and the surrounding circumstances may be considered in order to ascertain the intention of the parties (see, for instance, Leathley *v.* Spyer, L. R. 5 C. P. 595). A contract of guarantee must be distinguished from a contract of indemnity, which may be valid though not in writing. The distinction is shown in the well-known case of Birkmyr *v.* Darnell (1 Smith, Leading Cases, 8th ed., p. 326), and expressed in the following words : "If two come to a shop and one buys and the other, to gain him credit, promises the seller : *If he does not pay you, I will*, this is a collateral undertaking, and void without writing by the Statute of Frauds. But if he says : *Let him have the goods, I will be your paymaster*, or *I will see you paid*, this is an undertaking as for himself, and he shall be intended to be the very buyer, and the other to act as but his servant," but it is often very difficult to decide what was the intention of the parties as to these points (see *in re* Hoyle (1893), 1 Ch. 84).

A creditor who is secured by a guarantee must be careful not to alter the terms of his arrangement with the principal debtor without the concurrence of the surety, as a disregard of this rule may have the effect of discharging the surety.

A surety, after having satisfied the creditor, is entitled to an assignment of all securities held by the creditor in respect of such debt, and to use all remedies of the creditor in order to obtain from the principal debtor or any co-surety repayment of the sums expended by him.

[De Colyar, *Law of Guarantees*, 2nd ed., 1885.]
E. S.

GUARANTYISM, a term introduced by WILLIAM ELDER (*q.v.*) to denote the various charitable, savings, and philanthropic agencies organised to promote thrift.

GUARD RENTS, CASTLE-GUARD RENTS. Castle-guard or castle-ward was a form of military service which seems to have been more common in the south and east of England than elsewhere. The tenants, who held lands in virtue of this service, did not follow their lord to war ; their duty was the defence of his castle, where they were obliged to assemble on the approach of an enemy, and remain to assist the regular garrison till the danger was over. In later years this service was compounded for by an annual money payment called castle-guard rent. A long list of guard-rents, in connection with Dover Castle, dated 46 Henry III. is preserved in the *Red Book of the Exchequer*. There is a similar list at the public record office, dating from about 1680. This species of rent is not yet obsolete, for the Earl of Chichester, as owner of Hastings Castle, still receives guard-rents from tenants in the Rape of Hastings.

[C. I. Elton, *The Tenures of Kent*, London, 1867.—*Archæological Review*, i. 57, London, 1888.—*Red Book of the Exchequer*, folios 194 d. and 195.—*Public Record Office Calendars and Indexes*, No. 83.]
A. E. S.

GUARDIANS OF THE POOR. The title and office of guardian appear in Gilbert's Act of 1782 (22 Geo. III. c. 83). Where an incorporation of parishes was formed (see GILBERT'S ACT) the relief of the poor was to be administered by paid guardians, nominated by the justices of the peace, one to represent each of the incorporated parishes. The Poor Law Amendment Act (4 & 5 Will. IV. c. 76) combined parishes into unions for poor-law purposes, and gave the administration of the law to guardians of the poor. Guardians were of two kinds, (1) elected by the several parishes of a union, or by the several divisions of a parish. They were elected annually, or in an increasing number of cases triennially, by owners and occupiers under Sturges Bourne's Act, by which every £50 of rateable value gives a vote up to six ; (2) *ex-officio* guardians, viz. justices of the peace for the particular county, riding, or division, who resided in the respective unions. There were in 1893, 20,687 elected and 7412 *ex-officio* guardians in England and Wales. The quali-

fications, election, and tenure of office have been greatly modified by the Local Government Act of 1894 (56 & 57 Vict. c. 73). Under this act *ex-officio* guardians are abolished. Henceforth every person who represents a parish as guardian will be chosen for three years by the parliamentary and county council electors. The qualification for a guardian is to be an elector or to have resided for twelve months. Sex and marriage are no disqualification. A chairman, vice-chairman, and two members, may be co-opted. The business of guardians in administering the poor law is threefold, viz. (1) to hear and decide applications for relief ; (2) to control the various establishments, workhouses, schools, etc. ; (3) to appoint and control the various officers. The office of guardian is unpaid and voluntary, but one of the most important in the whole range of local government. The effect of a good or bad administration of the poor law is immediately felt over a wide area, and the happiness or misery of thousands depends directly or indirectly upon the action of guardians. Further it is difficult to overstate the importance of the office as a political training.

[Glen, *Poor Law Orders.*—Aschrott, *English Poor Law.*—Nicholls, *History of the Poor Law.*]
L. R. P.

GUARINI, G. B. His claim to recognition lies in the fact that he translated, by direction of Eleanor of Aragon, Duchess of Ferrara, the celebrated work of CARAFA (written originally in Italian between 1469-1482), into Latin, *De regis et boni principis officio*. This translation was printed in 1668 (see Cossa, *Introduction to Political Economy*, translation, p. 158).
A. B.

GUÉRARD, BENJAMIN (1797-1854), a member of the French Institute, rendered invaluable services both to French and Western economic history of the Carolingian period by his able editions of the *Polyptyque* (1836-1844), or census of the Abbot Irminon of Saint Germain des Prés and of the *Polyptyque* of the abbey of Saint Remi in Rheims (1853), and also by his masterly preface (*Prolégomènes*) to the former. In this he explained the condition and status of persons and of land from the time of the invasions of the barbarians to the rise of communal institutions.

[See Dr. Seebohm on "French Peasant Proprietorship under the open field System of Husbandry" in the *Economic Journal*, vol. i. pp. 62-66.]
E. Ca.

GUERRY DE CHAMPNEUF, JACQUES (1788-1852), first a barrister at Poitiers, then public prosecutor, and about 1820 advocate-general of the *Cour Royale*, was in 1824 appointed director of criminal prosecutions and pardons in the ministry of justice, and in this capacity instituted in 1825 the first annual criminal statistics known under the name of *Compte Général de l'Administration de la Justice Criminelle en France*. He lost his post at the revolution of 1830 and returned to the bar ;

but his delicate health and want of leisure never allowed him to publish the results of his juridical and economic studies. E. CA.

GUICCIARDINI, FRANCESCO (1482-1540), was born at Florence, and distinguished himself as an advocate, as a diplomatist, as a civil administrator under pope Leo X. and his two successors, and as lieutenant-general of the papal forces at the defence of Parma. In 1534 he retired to his native city, where he proved a friend to the Medici, and was at the head of the party which brought back Cosmo in 1537.

The fame of Guicciardini will, however, rest on his *History of Italy* from 1492 to 1532. This includes valuable information as to the great trading republics at an interesting epoch. The best edition is that of 1810 by Rosini. A. P. Goddard's translation, London, 1763, is from an incomplete text. R. H.

GUICCIARDINI, LUIGI (1523-1589), nephew of Francesco GUICCIARDINI, the famous historian. He spent a great part of his life in the Netherlands, where he was at first favoured, but afterwards imprisoned by the Duke of Alva.

Among other works, L. Guicciardini published in 1567 his *Descrizione di tutti i Paesi Bassi*, a detailed geographical and topographical account of the Netherlands, showing the condition, resources, and trade of the country. A third edition, revised by the author, was published at Antwerp (Plantin Press) in 1588. R. H.

GUILDER. See FLORIN (Dutch).

GUILDS. For all subjects under this heading—CRAFT GUILDS, FRITH GUILDS, MERCHANT GUILDS, TOWN GUILDS, etc., see GILDS.

GUILDS, SYSTEM IN SPAIN. See GILDS, SYSTEM IN SPAIN.

GUILLARD, ACHILLE (1799-1876), was born at Marsigny (Saone-et-Loire). He was an eminent statistician, and also much devoted to the study of natural science, particularly of botany. The most important economic work by Guillard is his valuable and laborious *Éléments de statistique humaine ou démographie comparée*, 8vo, 1855. A. C. F.

GUILLAUMIN, URBAIN GILBERT (1801-1864), was born at Couleuvre near Moulins, and died at Paris. He was a very intelligent publisher, and in that capacity greatly contributed, through the influence of the many important works which were issued from his house, to extending the knowledge of political economy in France. As a young man he had to suffer much hardship. He came to Paris in 1819, and went into business. In politics he sided with the opposition, and went so far as to become a *Carbonaro* (see CARBONARI). He was a friend of Béranger, and started at first as a political publisher; but becoming acquainted with Adolphe Blanqui, and with Joseph Garnier, he was led to turn his energy towards a speciality which won him great and well-deserved renown. Horace Say, son of Jean Baptiste Say, and father of M. Léon Say, aided him by his advice, and gave him also a pecuniary support which was a strong testimony to the character of both men. Guillaumin's two daughters, of whom the eldest, Félicité, died in 1885 at the age of fifty-six, inherited both his administrative ability and his devotion to economic science. The following are the best known publications of this house:

Dictionnaire du commerce et des marchandises, 1835.—*Dictionnaire de l'économie politique*, 1852. —*Dictionnaire du commerce et de la navigation*.—*Journal des économistes* (monthly), since 1842.—*Annuaire de l'économie politique et de la statistique* (yearly), since 1844.—*Collection des principaux économistes*, 16 vol. large 8vo, 1842.—*Économistes et publicistes contemporains*, 93 vols. 8vo.—*Bibliothèque des sciences morales et politiques*, 64 vols. 18mo, etc. A. C. F.

GUINEA, INTRODUCTION AND RATING OF. Soon after his accession, Charles II. issued a proclamation dated 26th August 1661, under which the older UNITES of James I.—that is to say, those issued prior to 1619, and valued at 22s. (1 lb. troy=£40 : 18 : 4)—were to pass current at 23s. 6d.; and all unites of subsequent dates, which up to this period passed at 20s., were to be valued at 21s. 4d.

The legal weights of these coins and their fine gold contents were as follows:—

Unite or Laurel (Value of), 1604-1661.

Name.	Number of pieces in the lb. troy.	Value of lb. troy by tale. £ s. d.	Legal weight in grains.	Fine gold content in grains.
Unite of 1604, rated at 20s. till 1612 .	$37\frac{1}{5}$	37 4 0	$154\frac{26}{31}$	$141\frac{29}{31}$
Unite of 1604, rated at 22s. from 1612 to 1619 . . .	$37\frac{13}{64}$	40 18 4	$154\frac{418}{491}$	$141\frac{469}{491}$
I. Unite or Laurel of 1619, rated at 20s. till 1661 . .	$40\frac{11}{12}$	40 18 4	$140\frac{380}{491}$	$129\frac{21}{491}$
II. Another Unite or Laurel of 1619 rated at 20s. till 1661 .	41	41 0 0	$140\frac{20}{41}$	$128\frac{32}{41}$

As the standard weight and fineness of these coins were not modified during the reign of Charles I., or during the Commonwealth, it will be seen that the principal coins of crown gold, containing 22 carats gold and 2 carats alloy, were as shown in this table when the proclamation of 1661 above referred to was issued.

When in 1663 steps were taken to amend the coinage by adopting more modern methods of manufacture, new gold coins were ordered to be struck having current values of 100s., 40s., 20s., and 10s. These twenty-shilling pieces were for the most part struck from gold obtained in Guinea and imported by the African Company, from which circumstance they derived their name, and they bore the device of a "little elephant," the stamp of that company. It is hardly necessary to state that gold pieces of the value of 20s. had long been used, having been first struck by Henry VII. in 1489 ; but from the accession of Charles II. the guinea at once took its place as the principal gold coin in this country, a position which it maintained until the great currency reform of 1816.

The weight of the "guinea" being based on that of the second unite of 1619, with a currency value of 21s. 4d., it follows that, as the pound troy produced forty-one of these latter pieces, each twenty-shilling piece weighed 131$\frac{11}{41}$ grains, and the pound of gold was valued at £43 : 14 : 8. In 1670, a fresh indenture directed that the pound should be coined into £44 : 10s.—that is to say, that the weight of each "guinea" should be 129$\frac{35}{89}$th grains, which is identical with the weight of gold of the old standard (994·8) which passed current for 20s., under the indenture made by Charles I. in 1626. Although variations were frequently made in the official rating of the guinea, it may be noted that, in the hundred and fifty years during which it continued to be the principal gold coin of this country, no further change was made in regard either to its weight or its fineness.

During the twenty-five years from 1670 to 1695 the silver currency was gradually reduced, by clipping and other forms of fraud, to such an unsatisfactory state that, although no legal change had been made in the valuation of the guinea, it was impossible for its equivalence to twenty shillings in silver to be maintained ; and in the latter year, in consequence of a memorial received from merchants and others, which showed that the guinea commonly passed for 30s., the House of Commons resolved, on the 15th February 1695, that this coin should not pass above a rating of 28s. Within a fortnight —that is to say, on the 28th February—an act was passed by which the rating was further reduced to 26s. from and after the 25th March 1696 ; and by a later act of the same session it was directed that from the 10th April 1696 the rating should not exceed 22s. The recoinage of silver, which was now being seriously taken in hand, greatly aided the steps taken to regulate the currency of the guinea ; and towards the latter end of 1698, the silver recoinage being then well advanced, a report was presented to the House of Commons by LOCKE and others pointing out that, by fixing its value at 22s., gold was overvalued in this country as compared with Holland, and recommending that the rate should be reduced to 21s. 6d. The House resolved, therefore, "that, under the Act 7 and 8 William III. c. 19, no person is obliged to take guineas at twenty-two shillings apiece," and they were generally received at the lower rate of 21s. 6d. The value thus determined upon was maintained for several years, and, although Sir Isaac NEWTON, in a report to the

Lord High Treasurer in 1711-12, pointed out that "gold is over-valued in England in proportion to silver by at least 9d. or 10d. in a guinea," no action was taken with a view to revise the rating until the 12th August, 1717, when Sir Isaac Newton was directed by the Lords Commissioners of His Majesty's Revenue to lay before them "a state of the gold and silver coin of this Kingdom in weight and fineness, and the value of gold in proportion to silver," etc. In the classic report which he prepared, dated 21st September, 1717, he showed that the intrinsic value of the guinea, as deduced from the ratio of silver to gold in all the principal trading nations of Europe, was about 20s. 8d., so that the legal rating was 10d. in excess of the value of the coin. This over-valuation naturally led to large quantities of the silver currency being withdrawn from circulation ; and the inconveniences thus occasioned were set forth in an address from the House of Commons to the King, who issued a royal proclamation on the 22nd December 1717, forbidding all persons "to utter or receive any of the pieces of gold coin of this kingdom commonly called guineas at any greater or higher rate or value than one and twenty shillings for each guinea." The valuation thus fixed was maintained unaltered throughout the century which elapsed before gold was made the sole standard of value in 1816 ; and it was on this basis that the weight of the present principal gold coin, the sovereign, introduced in the following year, was determined. E. R.

GUINEA TRADE. Englishmen are first known to have traded with Guinea in 1530, for ivory, and not many years later for gold, though the gold from which guineas were coined was first imported by the Royal African Company formed in 1672 (see AFRICAN COMPANIES, EARLY). English trade in negroes began in 1562 ; they were carried to Hispaniola, and there exchanged for goods for the English market ; and ten years later the right of England to share in the Guinea trade was acknowledged by the Portuguese, who frequently hired our ships to carry their slaves to Brazil. It was not until 1662 that the direct English trade in negroes for the supply of the American plantations began. Besides slaves, its staple product, Guinea supplied the merchants with ivory, gum arabic, gum senegal, camwood and other woods, bees' wax, cotton, ostrich feathers, ginger, pepper, rice, and palm oil, in exchange for gunpowder, arms and ammunition, lead and iron goods, brass, copper, tobacco, salt, cocoa, woollen, cotton, and linen goods, bugles, and Bengal goods. In most of these articles trade still continues (see AFRICAN COMPANIES, EARLY).

[Macpherson, *Annals of Commerce.—Gazetteer of the World*, art. "Guinea."—Reclus, *Nouvelle Géographie Universelle*, 1887, tom. 12.—Horton, *The Silver Pound*, 1887.] E. G. P.

HABIT. The economic influence of habit is defined by Prof. H. Sidgwick (*Principles of Pol. Econ.*, bk. ii. ch. xii.), as "the tendency to do as one has done before." This, while it continually presents obstacles "to the adoption of economic improvement," yet on the other hand "has its counterpart in the tendency to expect to be treated as one has hitherto been treated." . . . "Some claims generated in this way have legal validity; as when a right of way is established without express permission of the landowner."

For the economic effect of the tendency to do as others do, see CUSTOM.

HAGEN, KARL HEINRICH (1785-1856), son of a professor of medicine, was born at Königsberg. After studying political science under HOFFMANN, he entered the government service, and in 1811 became professor of political science and political economy (*Staatswissenschaften und Gewerbekunde*) at Königsberg, which appointment he retained till 1894, when he sank into a lingering illness.

Hagen's principal work appears to be the one entitled *Von der Staatslehre und von der Vorbereitung zum Dienste in der Staatsverwaltung*, 1839. Of the seven sections into which this work is divided, the second, fifth, and sixth, entitled respectively Sketch of the Science of Political Economy, the Theory of Finance, and the Study of the Functions of Government (*Cameralwissenschaften*), may be recommended to the economist. The first-mentioned of these has been translated by PRINCE-SMITH, under the title of a *System of Political Economy* (1844). It is enriched with notes derived from Hagen's other writings and from his lectures, and by additions to the text which the author himself contributed. It is divided into several inquiries, of which the third, relating to value, seems the most interesting. From one of the notes to this part (p. 28), it appears that Hagen had made some advance towards the construction of what would now be called a "demand schedule" (Marshall) or DEMAND-CURVE. But the particular formulæ proposed by Hagen are fanciful.

The general conception was employed by him in an interesting attempt to prove the expediency of free trade by mathematical reasoning: *Die Nothwendigkeit der Handelsfreiheit für das Naturaleinkommen mathematisch nachgewiesen*, 1844. The argument appears to be vitiated by not including wages, as well as profits, in the measure of the advantage to the community. It may be worth alluding to the demonstration that, on the assumptions made, a slight degree of protection might produce a slight advantage, which turns into a disadvantage as the tariff is increased. Considerable interest attaches to the criticism of COURNOT's theories of international trade, in a note at the end of the brochure, to which Cournot replies in his *Principes* of 1863. Hagen seems to fall short of Cournot with respect to the assumption above indicated; but to have the advantage in another respect. In estimating the change in the national revenue due to a new import (and *mutatis mutandis* a new export) Hagen takes account of the circumstance that the native labour displaced by the importation is apt to be employed in some other industry. He also professes to take account of the advantage which consumers of the imported commodity derive from a fall in its price. But, like Cournot, he misses the proper conception of CONSUMERS' RENT.

Besides the two works mentioned, Hagen is also the author of some articles in *Beiträge zur Kunde Preussens*, 1803-24; and of the following works: *On Platina Coin* (mentioned without date in the note to the *System of Political Economy* above referred to).—*Observationes œconomico-politicœ in Æschinis dialogum qui Eryxias inscribitur*, 1822. —*Ueber Einrichtung des Creditvereins von Gutsbesitzern im Königreich Bayern*, 1825.—*Aufklärung ueber das Sinken des Werthes des Geldes; aus dem Englischen*, 1839. Of these writings none except the first-named and the works referred to in the text have come under the eye of the present writer. [*Allgemeine Deutsche Biographie.* — Article by Prof. Edgeworth on "International Values," *Economic Journal*, vol. iv. p. 629.] F. Y. E.

HAIA. See FORESTS, MEDIÆVAL.

HAINES, RICHARD (17th century), is said to have been a Sussex gentleman (*Bread for the Poor*, by Philo-Anglicus, 1678, p. 4): he was evidently a royalist in his opinions, and speaks in one place (end of *England's Weal and Prosperity*) as if he were a member of parliament, but his name does not appear in the lists in Cobbett's *Parliamentary History*.

Haines wrote the following pamphlets, all very similar, to advocate his favourite remedies for social and economic evils:

The Prevention of Poverty, or a Discourse of the causes of the Decay of Trade, etc., 1674.— *Proposals for building in every County a Working-Alms-House or Hospital*, 1677 (reprinted in the *Harlean Miscellany*, 1810, vol. viii.)—*New Lords, New Laws, or a discovery of a grand usurpation*, etc., 1674. (Matthew Caffin replied to this pamphlet, *Envy's Bitterness corrected with the Rod of Shame*), 1674.—*Provision for the Poor*, etc., 1678. —*A Model of Government for the Good of the Poor and Wealth of the Nation*, 1678.—*A Method of the Government for such Public Working-Alms-Houses as may be erected in every County for bringing all Idle Hands to Industry*, 1679.—*A Breviat of some Proposals prepared to be offered to the Great Wisdom of the Nation*, 1679.—*England's Weal and prosperity Proposed*, 1681.

His sovereign remedy for decrease of exports and increase of imports, for mendicancy and pauperism, was the erection of great factories, locally governed and established by rates, where the unemployed poor, whom he computed at 200,000, and even criminals, might be set to make linen or woollen cloth, for wages low enough to enable England to undersell foreign goods. The plan is not very carefully thought out ; many of the difficulties which would arise being wholly overlooked. In the second pamphlet he mentions, without explanation, his invention of a plan by which "one man may turn fifty spinning wheels which shall serve a hundred persons to spin with at once ; so that the spinners shall have nothing to do but employ both hands to draw tire from the distaff " ; and also of "an engine by which fifty men may, without striking a stroke, beat as much hemp in one day as a hundred shall do in two days."

E. G. P.

HALE, SIR MATTHEW (1609-1676), a native of Alderley in Gloucestershire, entered at Lincoln's Inn in 1629, and practised success-fully at the bar. Though decidedly royalist in views he took no active part in politics, even during the civil war, and accepted a judgeship from Cromwell in 1653. He represented Gloucestershire in the parliament of 1654, Oxford university in that of 1658, and Gloucestershire again in the convention parliament which restored Charles II. in 1660. The same year he was made lord chief baron, and was knighted, and in 1671 he became lord chief justice. Ill-health induced him to resign this post early in 1676, and he died at the end of the year.

In addition to several legal and scientific and many religious works, Hale wrote *Primitive Origination of Mankind*, 1677, some chapters of which have been published separately as an *Essay on Population*, 1782, but are not very valuable ; *De Successionibus apud Anglos ; The law of Hereditary Descents ;* and *Touching Provision for the Poor*, printed in 1683. In this he summed up existing laws, pointed out their defects, and sug-gested remedies. As the only radical cure for mendicancy and poverty he proposed the establish-ment of workhouses, for which purpose parishes should be grouped in unions ; after their erection by means of the rates they were to become self-supporting — places of industrial education for children and of employment for the poor, especi-ally when other work was scarce.

[*Life and death of Sir Matthew Hale*, by Bishop Burnet, 1682.—Wood's *Athenæ Oxonienses*, 1817, vol. iii.—*Memoirs of the Life, Character, and Writings of Sir Matthew Hale*, by J. B. Williams, 1835.—*Dict. of National Biography* (this gives some of the dates one year later than the other accounts). Campbell, in *Lives of Chief Justices*, dwells at length on Hale's political position.]

E. G. P.

HALE, NATHAN, LL.D. (1784-1863), was born in Westhampton, Mass., graduated at Williams College in 1804, and became a journalist and the editor of the Boston *Advertiser* in 1814. He was among the first to encourage the construction of railways in New England. He wrote *Remarks on the*

Banks and Currency of the New England States, in which an Attempt is made to show the Public Benefits resulting from the System pursued by the Allied Banks of Boston, Boston, 1826, pp. 40, in commendation of the Suffolk bank system. This was a system devised for the more prompt redemption of state bank bills— bills which were often depreciated in value, and regarded with suspicion in localities other than the place of issue. This practice was intro-duced to a limited extent in Boston in 1813, but not fully developed until 1825. The work of assorting and returning the notes to the place of issue was finally undertaken by the Suffolk bank of Boston, from which this policy took its name. It was confined, however, to New England banks, but aided much in giving a sounder banking administration.

He also wrote *The American System ; or the Effects of High Duties on Imports designed for the encouragement of Domestic Industry*, Boston, 1828, pp. 56. He objected to extending the American system of high duties, and questioned the expediency of a warehousing system. It is a strong argument, and is said to have done much to bring about the compromise tariff of 1833.

D. R. D.

HALES, JOHN (16th century), was connected with the well-known Kentish family. He does not appear to have been at any university, but he was a man of wide and varied learning, and founded the grammar school at Coventry. He was clerk of the hanaper in the time of Edward VI. and sat for a time in parliament as member for Preston. The chief economic interest con-nected with him is due to the active part he took in the commission on enclosures in 1548. His elaborate defence of himself and some other papers have been recently printed in full (*Dis-course of Common Weal*, Introduction), and amplify the information in the extracts given by Strype.

Recently good reason has been shown for attri-buting to Hales the well-known *Examination of Complaints* of which W. S. claimed to be the author. Miss Lamond has shown that during his life he was regarded by some people as its author, and has adduced strong reasons from internal evidence in support of this view. Since she published her essay (*English Historical Review*, April 1891), it has received general acceptance. The full evidence, with many biographical details, will be found in her edition of the dialogue published in 1893 under the title *A Discourse of the Common Weal of thys Realm of England*.

If this view be correct it at once appears that Hales was, as an economist, much ahead of con-temporary opinion. His views on the evils of a debased currency, on the balance of trade, on exclusive corporations, and on other subjects are extremely interesting. Hales may well get the credit of having expressed them well and clearly, though there seems to be some reason to believe that he had not thought out these opinions for himself, but was chiefly the mouthpiece of Hugh Latimer (see LATIMER). On the economics of the dialogue, compare the review of the discourse in the *Economic Journal*, December 1893.　　　　W. C.

HALF-CROWN. English coin struck both in gold and silver, concurrently with the gold and silver crown pieces, of the same fineness and of proportionate weight to those coins respectively (see CROWN).　　　　F. E. A.

HALF-IMPERIAL (see IMPERIAL).

HALFPENNY. English coin, struck in silver, copper, and bronze.

Silver Halfpenny :

Reign.	Year.	Weight (grains).	Fineness.	Value.	
				In silver 925 fine, at 5s. 6d. an oz.	In standard silver francs, 900 fine.
				d.	franc.
Edward I. .	1300	11	925	1·512	·146
,,　III.	1344	10	,,	1·375	·133
,,　III.	1351	9	,,	1·237	·120
Henry IV.	1412	7·5	,,	1·031	·099
Edward IV.	1464	6	,,	·825	·080
Henry VIII.	1527	5	,,	·687	·065
Edward VI.	1552	11	,,	1·512	·146
Mary. .	1553	12	,,	1·650	·159
Elizabeth .	1560	4	,,	·550	·053
,,　.	1601	3·75	,,	·516	·049

Copper halfpence were first struck in Charles II.'s reign, and *bronze* halfpence in 1860, on the first adoption of bronze coinage in England. *See* COPPER MONEY (England).　　　　F. E. A.

HALF-SOVEREIGN. English gold coin.

Reign.	Year.	Rating.	Weight (grains).	Fineness.	Value in gold 916·6 fine, at £3:17:10½ an oz.		
		s.			£	s.	d.
Henry VII. .	1485	10	128·00	994·8	1	2	6½
,,　VIII.	1543	,,	100·00	916·6	0	16	3
,,　VIII.	1545	,,	96·00	,,	0	15	7
Edward VI. .	1549	,,	84·625	,,	0	13	8
,,　VI. .	1550	12	120·00	994·8	1	1	1½
,,　VI. .	1551	10	87·25	916·6	0	14	2
Elizabeth .	1558	,,	,,	,,	0	14	2
,,　. .	1601	,,	86·00	,,	0	13	11½
George III. (and subsequently) .	1817	,,	61·63	,,	0	10	0

The value of the current half-sovereign in gold francs, 900 fine, is 12·61 fr. (see POUND STERLING).　　　　F. E. A.

HALIFAX, CHARLES MONTAGUE, Earl of (1661-1715), the distinguished statesman and financier, was educated at Westminster School, and at Trinity College, Cambridge, where he formed a lifelong friendship with Sir Isaac Newton. Entering upon a political career, he signed the invitation to the Prince of Orange, was returned to parliament for Malden, and sat in the convention. Quickly developing a remarkable talent for financial business, he was made, in 1691, one of the commissioners of the treasury, and called to the privy council. In December 1692 he proposed, in the House of Commons, to raise a million sterling by way of a loan. William III. required money for his wars ; the moneyed classes desired sounder investments than bubble companies ; the landed proprietors were hard pressed by the weight of taxation, and some new financial expedient was necessary. Montague's loan bill was consequently accepted, and it passed both Houses without opposition. Thus was laid the foundation of the national debt. "By this memorable law," says Macaulay (*History of England*), "new duties were imposed on beer and other liquors. These duties were to be kept in the exchequer separate from all other receipts, and were to form a fund on the credit of which a million was to be raised by life annuities. As the annuitants dropped off, their annuities were to be divided among the survivors, till the number of survivors was reduced to seven. After that time, whatever fell in was to go to the public. It was therefore certain that the 18th century would be far advanced before the debt would be finally extinguished ; and, in fact, long after King George the Third was on the throne, a few aged men were receiving large incomes from the state in return for a little money which had been advanced to King William on their account when they were children. The rate of interest was to be 10 per cent till the year 1700, and after that year 7 per cent."

By the spring of 1694 it became again absolutely necessary to find some new mode of defraying the war charges. Three years before, William Paterson, an ingenious Scotsman, had propounded a plan for a national bank. The scheme was favourably regarded, but nothing was done. Montague, however, now furthered the plan, and engaged to carry it through the House of Commons, while Michael Godfrey, an upright and opulent merchant, agreed to manage the city. An approving vote was obtained from the committee of ways and means, and Montague introduced a bill whose title gave rise to much comment and sarcasm. "It was indeed not easy to guess that a bill, which purported only to impose a new duty on tonnage for the benefit of such persons as should advance money towards carrying on the war, was really a bill creating the greatest commercial institution that the world had ever seen. The plan was that £1,200,000 should be borrowed by the government on what was then considered as the moderate interest of 8 per cent. In order to induce capitalists to advance the money promptly on terms so favourable to the public, the subscribers were to be incorporated by the name of the Governor and Company of the Bank of England. The corporation was to have no exclusive privilege, and was to be restricted from trading in anything but bills of exchange, bullion, and forfeited pledges" (Macaulay's *England*). In order, however, that the bank should not have the power over the national purse, a clause was inserted in the act which inhibited the bank from advancing money to the crown without the authority of parliament. So popular was the scheme that the whole sum which the new corporation was bound to lend to the state was paid into the exchequer before the first instalment was due, and the Bank of England was successfully launched upon its career.

Montague was now such an acknowledged master of finance that in 1694 he was appointed chancellor of the exchequer. In the ensuing year he carried out his plan for re-coining the money of the kingdom. The new currency was to be of the old standard both in weight and fineness ; all the new pieces were to be milled ; the loss on the clipped pieces was to be borne by the public ; a time was fixed after which no clipped money was to pass, except in payments to the Government ; and a still later time was fixed after which no clipped money was to pass at all. The scheme was carried ; Newton was appointed warden of the mint: and to meet the loss on the coinage a tax on windows was imposed instead of that obnoxious impost the HEARTH-MONEY. In 1696, however, the general distress and monetary confusion throughout the country were such that Montague introduced the system of EXCHEQUER BILLS (q.v.). He had already succeeded in engrafting on Harley's Land Bank Bill a clause which empowered the government to issue negotiable paper, bearing interest at the rate of threepence per day on one hundred pounds. Accordingly, exchequer bills drawn for various amounts from a hundred pounds down to five pounds, were now issued, and rapidly distributed over the kingdom. Montague also projected the scheme for a general fund, which gave rise to the sinking fund, afterwards established by Sir Robert Walpole. He further devised a method to raise the sinking credit of the Bank of England by a second subscription, and his general mortgage plan was warmly welcomed. The authority which the chancellor of the exchequer now wielded in financial matters was unprecedented, and he was publicly thanked by the House of Commons. In 1697 he became premier, but, owing to his vanity and arrogance, his popularity began to wane, and he was obliged to accept the auditorship of the exchequer, and to withdraw from the House of Commons with the title of Baron Halifax. In 1698 he founded a new East India Company, in the interests of greater freedom of trade, and to diminish the power and monopoly of the old company, but both institutions were eventually consolidated in 1708, under the title of " The United Company of Merchants of England trading to the East Indies." The Commons impeached Lord Halifax for breach of trust in 1701, and again in 1703, but the Lords threw out the articles. In 1706 Halifax took a leading part in negotiating the union with Scotland. On the death of Queen Anne he was appointed one of the council of regency, and when George I. took possession of the throne he was created Earl of Halifax, and became first commissioner. Disappointed at not becoming lord high treasurer, he intrigued with the tory leaders, but his schemes and his life ended suddenly on the 19th May 1715.

[Chalmers's *Biographical Dictionary.*—Coxe's *Memoirs of Walpole and Marlborough.*—*Life and Works of the Earl of Halifax*, 1715.—Macaulay's *History of England.*—Thorold Rogers, *First Nine Years of the Bank of England*, 1887.]

G. B. S.

HALL, CHARLES, M.D. (1745 ? - 1825 ?) author of *The Effects of Civilisation in European States*, London, 1805, republished in J. M. Morgan's Phœnix Library, 1850. After a general view of the ills of society, which anticipates Henry George and the later socialists, wherein landed property is stated to be "the basis, source, and substance of all wealth," into which "all must be resolved," it is curious to find the remedies advocated are the abolition of primogeniture and the repression or at least the severe taxation, of "refined manufactures." Hall afterwards, however, suggests a form of state ownership of the land, coupled with individual ownership of the produce. In Morgan's *Hampden in the 19th Century*, London, 1850, Hall is mentioned as having died in the Fleet prison at eighty. "His conversation was particularly animated and intelligent." Hall states that his experience as a doctor led him to consider the sufferings of the poor. He writes from Tavistock. Much stress is laid on the importance of Hall's book, as anticipating the later socialists, by Anton Menger, who, in his *Recht auf den vollen Arbeitsertrag*, 2nd ed., 1891, devotes a section, pp. 57-60, to an analysis of its arguments.

[*Dictionary of National Biography*, vol. xxiv. p. 60.]

H. E. E.

HALL, VAN. See VAN HALL.

HALL-MARKING. Hall-marks are impressions made at a public assay office upon gold and silver wares to indicate the fineness of the metal of which they are composed.

Hall-marking was first introduced in the year 1300, when, at the instigation of the English Gild of Gold and Silver Smiths, the system was enforced by Royal Command, and by the provisions of Stat. 3, cap. 30, of Ed. I. it was necessary to impress upon each piece of plate assayed the effigy of a leopard or a lion's head crowned. This was called the *king's mark*. A second mark, known as the *maker's mark*, was added in 1363 (37 Ed. III., cap. 7) ; and subsequently a third was introduced called the *assayer's mark* or *year letter*, consisting of a letter of an alphabet used for each year ; when one type of letter was exhausted another was adopted. This system of indicating the date is still in use.

The marks used in England in recent times are five in number.

1. The *maker's mark*, the initials of the maker's name.

2. The *standard mark*, or mark to indicate the fineness of the metal.

For gold wares this is as follows :—

For gold 22 carats fine—22 surmounted by a crown.

,,	18	,,	18	,,
,,	15	,,	15 and ·625.	
,,	12	,,	12 and ·5.	
,,	9	,,	9 and ·375.	

For silver wares as follows :—

For silver 11 oz. 2 dwt. fine } or 925 fine—a lion passant.
,,   18 ,, alloy
,, 11 oz.10 ,, fine } or 958·3 fine—Britannia.
,,   10 ,, alloy

3. The mark of the *assay office*.

For London—a leopard's head.
,, Birmingham—an anchor.
,, Sheffield—a crown.
,, Chester—a dagger and three wheat sheaves.
,, Exeter—a castle with three towers.
,, Newcastle—three castles.
,, Edinburgh—a castle.
,, Glasgow—a tree, a fish, and a bell.
,, Dublin—Hibernia.

4. The *year letter* or date mark (described above).

5. The *duty mark*, the head of the reigning sovereign. This mark, which was introduced in 1784, and was continued till the early part of Queen Victoria's reign, is not now used.

Report of Select Committee on Hall-marking with proceedings, evidence, and appendix of acts, etc., 1878 (House of Commons, 328).   F. E. A.

HALLER, KARL LUDWIG VON (1768-1854), born in Bern, entered the State Office (*Staats Kanzlei*) of the republic of Bern at the early age of sixteen, and was wont to congratulate himself on having never attended the lectures of a university, "as he was thus obliged to think for himself." He was sent as secretary on several foreign missions, and after the occupation of Bern by the French republican armies, was admitted into the Austrian civil service. Appointed professor of law in the academy of Bern in 1806, and member of the sovereign council in 1814, he was compelled to resign his professorship in 1817, when he became a Roman Catholic ; up to the year 1830 he chiefly lived in Paris, writing in legitimist papers and living amongst the reactionary society of the French metropolis. After the revolution of 1830, he returned to Switzerland and resided in Soleure, where he died in 1854.

In 1808 he published his *Handbuch der allgemeinen Staatenkunde* which may be considered as the kernel of his large work : *Restauration der Staatswissenschaft oder Theorie des natürlich-geselligen Zustands der Chimäre des künstlich-bürgerlichen entgegengesetzt* (Winterthur, 6 vols., 1820) of which he himself wrote an (incomplete) French translation under the title of *Restauration de la Science Politique ou Théorie de l'État social naturel opposé à la fiction d'un État civil factice* (Lyons, 3 vols., 1830) in which he shows himself a warm admirer of the Middle Ages and an uncompromising opponent of the theory of the social contract and of constitutional government. The heading of the 13th chapter of vol. i. strikes the keynote of his doctrine : *Natürliche Ueberlegenheit ist der Grund aller Herrschaft, Bedürfniss der Grund aller Abhängigkeit und Dienstbarkeit* (Natural Superiority is the Basis of all Sovereignty, Want the Basis of every State of Dependence and Subjection). The domination of the strongest is for him the universal law of nature. He is essentially a writer on political subjects ; but he deals in vol. ii. with economic questions, still always in the light of his mediæval leanings. Ownership in land (ii. pp. 36-60) is a natural institution. The prince ought to live on his private income ; if taxes are needed, they ought to be demanded, but always freely granted. The property and disposal of the proceeds of taxation belong to the prince, if not otherwise specified at the time they were granted. Taxes may be infinitely varied ; a perfect proportional equality is impossible to reach. All have their faults ; the best are those which come nearest to voluntary contributions (pp. 272-354) ; the foundation of charitable, scientific, and literary institutions is the outcome of moral duty ; it has no compulsory and imperative character. It is dangerous to make them completely the prince's affair ; they are often best provided for by private individuals or associations (pp. 359-366).

[For a critical account of Haller, see Mohl, *Geschichte und Litteratur der Staatswissenschaften*, ii. pp. 529-560 and *Zeitschrift für Staatswissenschaft*, Tübingen, 1870, vol. xxvi. pp. 93-105 ; as also Roscher, *Gesch. der Nat. Oek.*, pp. 779-788.]

E. Ca.

HALLEY, EDMUND, LL.D., F.R.S. (1656-1742), the well-known astronomer, author of numerous astronomical and mathematical works, was the inventor of life tables of mortality. He was elected a fellow of the Royal Society in 1678, and became its secretary in 1713 ; was appointed Savilian professor of geometry at Oxford in 1703, and astronomer-royal in 1721. He was the friend of Sir Isaac Newton, in the publication of whose *Principia* he took an important part.

Halley's *Tables of Mortality from Observations made at Breslau*, read before the Royal Society in 1692, and published in the same year in the *Phil. Trans.*, No. 196, though they passed unnoticed at the time, except perhaps in Germany, served as a pattern for future calculators. They have been reprinted in vol. xviii. of the *Assurance Magazine*. "They show the annual movement of a population, the probability of survivorship, the average duration of one or more lives and the money values depending thereon" (*Assurance Magazine*, vol. vi. p. 138). [Walford, *Insurance Cyclopædia.—Dict. of National Biography.—*Graetzer, *E. Halley und Caspar Neumann*, 1883.—Lalande, *Préface Historique aux Tables de Halley*, 1759.—Delisle's *Lettres sur les Tables de Halley*, 1749.—R. Boeckh, *Halley als Statistiker*, 1893.]   E. G. P.

HAMBURG, Bank of. See Banks.

HAMILTON, Alexander (1757-1804), was born in Nevis, West Indies. At the age of fifteen he was sent to New York to be educated. He sided with the colonists in the dispute with the mother country, which was rapidly approaching a crisis, and soon by his activity and vigorous writing attracted the attention of the older leaders. Hamilton was entrusted with responsible positions, and from 1776 to 1781 served as aide-de-camp on Washington's staff. Although occupied with military and political duties, he found time at this period to read widely in history, political economy, and finance. His notebooks and letters display a wonderful comprehension of financial problems, generally to be obtained only by actual experience. In 1781 he entered upon the study of the law, and was appointed continental receiver of taxes for New York. During 1782-1783 he was member of Congress, and wrote a *Report on the Import Duty*, 16th Dec. 1782, works, ed. 1851, vol. ii. 213-223. Hamilton recognised the weakness of the existing form of government, and laboured earnestly to secure the establishment of a strongly centralised government, through the convention of 1787. To secure the adoption of the constitution he co-operated with Madison and Jay in writing the *Federalist*. Upon the establishment of the present form of government in 1789, he was selected, at the age of thirty-two, by President Washington, to take charge of and organise as secretary the treasury department. Rarely has any financier had so many difficult problems presented to him to be solved in so brief a period. Among his many reports the five following are most important: Public Credit, 9th Jan. 1790; National Bank, 13th Dec. 1790; Establishment of a Mint, 28th Jan. 1791; Encouragement and Protection of Manufactures, 5th Dec., 1791; and Public Credit 16th Jan., 1795. These are found in J. C. Hamilton's ed., New York, 1851, vol. iii.; H. C. Lodge's ed., New York, 1885, vol. ii. Finance and Taxation; vol. iii. Finance, Taxation, and Commercial Relations; and in *American State Papers*, vol. i. The first four were issued in a period of less than two years. Besides these reports, Hamilton wrote many others, to be found in the above volumes. All of Hamilton's writings relate to concrete and practical questions of government policy. His state papers are regarded as the ablest issued from the treasury department, showing a remarkable genius in the treatment of finance. As he left, however, no systematic treatise from which his final conclusions may be judged, there has grown up since Hamilton's time a considerable divergence of opinion concerning his real views as to political economy. He differed from R. Morris as to the adoption of a money unit of account for the new coinage, favouring the

dollar instead of the pound or any proportionate part. Although he preferred gold to silver, as more stable, yet, under existing circumstances, he did not regard it wise to contract the quantity of circulating medium, and consequently favoured bi-metallism. In advising the current ratio of one to fifteen, he did not perceive the influence then at work to lower the value of gold, and consequently underestimated silver. He advised a moderate seignorage. He was convinced of the advantages of a "full circulation," and offered this as one of the reasons for the establishment of a national bank. The active capital would be augmented through the operation of credit. This advantage also strengthened his conclusions as to funding the debt. Stock would pass current as specie. Although he favoured bank notes, he opposed treasury notes; his condemnation of the latter was in words often quoted: "The wisdom of the government will be shown in never trusting itself with the use of so seductive and dangerous an experiment. In times of tranquillity it might have no ill consequence, it might even perhaps be managed in a way productive of good, but in great and trying emergencies there is almost a moral certainty of its becoming mischievous. If it should not even be carried so far as to be rendered an absolute bubble, it would at least be likely to be extended to a degree which would occasion an inflated and artificial state of things incompatible with the regular and prosperous course of the political economy." In advising protective tariff duties, Hamilton argued largely from political considerations. He saw the necessity of immediately strengthening the general government. His economic arguments are as follows: Manufacturing establishments not only occasion a positive augmentation of the produce and revenue of the society, but they contribute essentially to render them greater than they could possibly be without such establishments. This follows because it occasions and affords opportunity for the division of labour, an extensive use of machinery, employment to classes, such as women and children, not generally employed, emigration from foreign countries, greater scope for diversity of talents, and securing a more steady demand for the surplus produce of the soil. Hamilton does not state definitely that these considerations should be controlling factors if it were possible to procure from abroad, on good terms, all the fabrics which it may need. He found nowhere a perfect liberty to industry and commerce—expediency, therefore, must be the principle of action for the United States. He did not believe that industry, if left to itself, would flow in the most profitable channel, for custom was a powerful influence. Hamilton was an active federalist, and, in the cabinet, opposed the influence of Jefferson. He resigned 31st

January 1795, and returned to the practice of the law in New York. He still remained an adviser of President Washington, and frequently engaged in political discussions. For two years he held the position of Inspector-General of the army. In 1804 he engaged in a bitter political controversy with Burr, who challenged him, and Hamilton was mortally wounded in the duel fought 11th July 1804.

[For Hamilton's financial administration, see his *Works* referred to, also *Life of Alexander Hamilton* by John T. Morse, jun., Boston, 1876, vol. i. ch. viii.-xi.—*Alexander Hamilton*, by Henry Cabot Lodge, Boston, 1882, ch. v.—For complete bibliography, see *Bibliotheca Hamiltoniana*, by P. L. Ford, New York, 1886.]   D. R. D.

HAMILTON, ROBERT, LL.D. (1743-1829). He studied at Edinburgh, making unusual progress in mathematics under Matthew Stewart, but, though desirous of a literary career, was obliged to enter a bank in order to obtain a knowledge of business, and afterwards to take charge of a paper-mill. In 1769, however, he became rector of the academy at Perth, and in 1779 professor of natural philosophy in Marischal College, Aberdeen. By a private arrangement he taught the mathematical classes instead of his own, and in 1817 obtained the chair of mathematics, which he held until his death.

Besides some mathematical text-books Hamilton wrote an *Introduction to Merchandise*, 1777; three essays on *Peace and War*, 1790, *Government*, and the *Management of the Poor*, 1822; which show enlightened views on economic subjects, *e.g.* bounties, taxes on necessaries, and poor-relief, but a somewhat limited grasp of political matters; and an *Inquiry concerning the Rise and Progress, the Redemption and present State, and the Management of the National Debt of Great Britain and Ireland*, 1813, on which his fame chiefly rests. He was the first not to discover, but successfully to expose, the fallacy underlying Pitt's sinking fund; he proved that "the excess of revenue above expenditure is the only real sinking fund by which public debt can be discharged," and he showed that the existing system was not merely useless, but actually harmful, entailing a high rate of interest and increased cost of management. The *Progress of Society*, 1830, a posthumous publication, treats in simple language of the theories of political economy; the chapters, for example, on value and price are of considerable merit.

[Memoir prefixed to *Progress of Society.*— Chambers's *Biographical Dictionary of Eminent Scotsmen.*—*Dictionary of National Biography.*— M'Culloch, *Literature of Pol. Economy.*]
                                        E. G. P.

HANAPER. An ancient office or department of the chancery, so called from the hamper (*hanaperium*) in which certain records were deposited (cp. PETTY BAG). It was the duty of the clerk of the hanaper to take account of all patents, commissions, and grants under the great seal, and to collect and administer the fees arising from the same. The office was abolished in 1842.

[S. R. Scargill-Bird, *A Guide to the Public Records*,1891.]   A. E. S.

HANCOCK, WILLIAM NEILSON (1820-1888), was the son of Lord Lurgan's land-agent, and was born at Lisburn, county Antrim. He was called to the Irish bar in 1844, was Whately professor of political economy at Dublin University from 1846 to 1851, and professor of jurisprudence and political economy at Queen's College, Belfast, from 1849 to 1853. From 1851 to 1853 he was secretary to the Dublin University Commission, in 1854 to the Endowed Schools of Ireland Commission, and later to several other commissions on Irish subjects. From 1855 to 1866 with a year's interval he was clerk of the custody of papers in matters of idiots and lunatics in the Court of Chancery, and in 1882 he became clerk of the crown and hanaper. He was the chief founder of the Dublin Statistical Society, 1847, and of the Belfast Social Inquiry Society, 1851. Throughout his active life he put forward his economic and social opinions in writing in the form of articles or pamphlets, all marked by knowledge, discernment, and impartiality.

Hancock's works are: *The Tenant-right of Ulster considered economically*, 1845.—*Impediments to the Prosperity of Ireland*, published 1850.—*What are the causes of the Prosperous Agriculture of the Lothians of Scotland?* and, *What are the causes of the distressed state of the Highlands of Scotland?* 1852, all aim at proving, either directly or by comparison with Scotland, that Irish agricultural distress was due not to the race, religion, perversity, or ignorance of the Irish peasant, but to defective land-laws, and mainly to the want of some equivalent to the Ulster tenant-right.—*Three Lectures on the Questions, Should the Principles of Political Economy be disregarded at the present Crisis? and if not, How can they be applied towards the discovery of Measures of Relief?* 1847, discuss the potato famine, deprecating the artificial lowering of prices, and advocating a uniform system of relief in money.—*The Report on the supposed progressive decline of Irish Prosperity*, 1863, brought forward various statistics to disprove such decline, and attributed the increase of emigration to older and deeper-rooted causes than the potato famine.—*The question, Is there really a want of Capital in Ireland?* 1851 (see *Prosperous Agriculture in the Lothians*, p. 16), he answered in the negative.—His *Duties of the Public with regard to Charitable Savings Banks*, 1852, and *The Present State of the Savings Bank Question*, 1855, exposed, by an Irish example, the evils of the existing system, which allowed limited liability and minimised responsibility by dividing it between government and the managers; and advised the abolition of charitable in favour of government or private joint-stock banks.—He also wrote an article on *Local Government and Taxation, Ireland*, 1875, and edited the first two volumes of the *Ancient Laws of Ireland*, 1865.—In some unpublished essays he treated of *The Use of the Doctrine of Laissez-Faire in investigating the Economic Resources of Ireland*, 1847, in which he recommended the alteration of such laws as interfered with economic development; and of *The Workhouse as a mode of Relief for Widows and Orphans*, 1855, in which he advocated the boarding-out system and outdoor relief for these classes of the poor.

[*Memoir* by J. K. Ingram, LL.D., unpublished, read before the Statistical and Social Inquiry Society of Ireland.—*Dublin University Calendar.*—*Belfast Queen's College Calendar.*]   E. G. P.

HANDICRAFT.   See HOME INDUSTRIES.

HANDSAL.   See AUNCEL.

HANSARDS.   One of the English names for merchants of the Hanseatic League, EASTERLINGS being the other. Hansard appears as an English surname in 1254. (Mat. Paris, v. 427).   R. H.

[The honourable connection of the *Hansard* family of printers with the publication of parliamentary debates need not be commented on here.]

HANSE OF LONDON. This hanse, which had no organic connection with the Hanseatic League, was an association for foreign commerce consisting originally of merchants of Flemish towns. It was established for the promotion and security of trade between Flanders and England. It is a well-known fact that Flanders was dependent upon England for her supply of wool; the *Libell of Englishe Policye* says—

By draping of oure wolle in substaunce
Liven her comons, this is her governaunce.

Hence it was natural that a society or league should be formed in Flanders for the protection of her trade with England. As its chief seat or centre of commerce was in London, it was called *hansa Londoniensis;* other names applied to it were *hansa Flandrensis* and "the seventeen towns." Little is known concerning the origin of the association. Though not clearly mentioned before 1240, it seems to have been formed in the second half of the 12th century by seventeen towns of Flanders,—Bruges, Ypres, Lille, Damme, Ardenburg, etc. There is some evidence that a small hanse at Bruges was its original nucleus or starting-point. In the 13th century the number of towns connected with the hanse of London was gradually increased, though the old name, *les dix-sept villes*, was retained. Bourquelot gives a list of fifty-six such towns, many of which were in Hainault and North France,—Ghent, Douai, Arras, Cambrai, Abbeville, St. Omer, Beauvais, Caen, Troyes, Amiens, Rheims, etc.

The hanse of London had the monopoly of commerce with England. Its officers could seize the property of any of their countrymen of Flanders, not belonging to the society, who undertook to trade in England. Besides exercising this monopoly, the hanse protected its members against dishonest dealings; they ceased to have commercial intercourse with any Englishman who had been guilty of fraud in selling wares, or who had acted unjustly toward any one of them. They also traded at the great fairs of Champagne (see FAIRS, MEDIÆVAL); the prosperity of these marts was, in fact, largely dependent upon the hanse of London.

Concerning the organisation of the society, the information furnished by its statutes and by other sources is meagre. Its chief officer, "the count of the hanse," was elected by the merchants of Bruges. He presided over its meetings and courts, and was assisted by the standard-bearer, *scildraca*, who was generally a merchant of Ypres. These two officers also acted as treasurers. The statutes mention, moreover, a clerk, or secretary, and *inventores*, or *arbitri*. The *inventores* were judgment-finders or judges who tried cases falling within the jurisdiction of the hanse; eight of these judicial delegates came from Bruges, four from Ypres, and one or two from each of the other towns of the league.

New members were admitted at Bruges and in England. To gain admittance a person had to pay an entrance fee, the amount of which varied according as the applicant was the son of a member or not. Most artisans and retail dealers were excluded from membership, especially weavers, fullers, shearers, carpenters, shoemakers, wool-beaters, dyers "who dye with their own hands and have blue nails," skinners "who work with their hands," tinkers "who go crying through the streets," cheesemongers, buttermongers, and all who sell by the pound. Such persons could become members only by renouncing their craft or trade, and then, after waiting a year and a day, by paying a high entrance fee. They were, moreover, required to bring a certificate from their town showing that they had been admitted to its *caritas*, or mercantile brotherhood, on payment of the fee required by the municipal authorities. The hanse was evidently made up mainly of wholesale dealers, though some prosperous craftsmen seem to have obtained admission.

There was a close connection between the hanse and the towns to which its merchants belonged. The higher municipal officers had to be members of the society; and before being admitted into the hanse, a person had to join the mercantile gild of his town. Hence the hanse of London may be regarded as a loose municipal league, as well as a society of merchants.

The count of Flanders seems to have exercised no direct supervision or authority over the hanse; but, in some cases, there was probably an appeal from the decisions of its court to a superior commercial tribunal of Flanders consisting of delegates from five important towns. The exact date of its dissolution is shrouded in as much obscurity as that of its creation. It still flourished in 1349. There seem, however, to be no references to it in the second half of the 14th century, and in 1426 the town authorities of Bruges stated that the regulations of the hanse had long been in abeyance. Its period of life thus covered about two hundred years.

[The best account of the hanse of London will be found in Carl Koehne's *Hansgrafenamt*, 1893, pp. 205-245.—See also Bourquelot, *Foires de Champagne*, 1865, vol. i. pp. 134-139.—Varenbergh, *Histoire des Relations diplomatiques entre la Flandre et l'Angleterre*, 1874, pp. 145-155.—Hegel, *Städte und Gilden der germanischen Völker*, 1891, vol. ii. pp. 185-188.—Ashley, *James and Philip van Artevelde*, 1883, pp. 17-20, 141.]　C. Gr.

HANSE TOWNS. The number of towns which belonged for a longer or shorter time to the Hanseatic League is uncertain, as the merchants carefully abstained from furnishing complete details, and the names must be gleaned from records. In documents which mention a considerable number, the classification is geographical. The treaty, for example, with King Magnus in 1372 (*Recesse*, ii. 45), though it omits the Westphalian towns, ranges the others under the headings : *Civitates Maritimæ ; Civitates Livoniæ, Prussiæ, de Mari Australi* (Zuyder Zee), *Zelandiæ, Hollandiæ, Gelriæ* (Guelders). It is usually stated that the towns in the 14th century were divided into three groups or circles (see HANSEATIC LEAGUE, p. 283).

The following list of 115 is founded on one in the *Hansische Geschichtsblätter* for 1871, collated with the Hanseatic map in Prof. Droysen's Historical Atlas and other lists, and the results have also been compared with the names of the towns represented at the various Diets up to 1476. These appear, a few at a time, in the official *Recesse*, and form an absolute test of the right of a town to a place on the roll. Those which are now for the first time added on this authority are marked with an asterisk.

Amsterdam	Elburg	*Kokenhusen
Anklam	Emmerich	Kolberg
*Arnemuiden	*Enkhuizen	Köln a. d. Spree
Arnheim	*Fellin	Königsberg
Aschersleben	Frankfurt a. d. O.	Kulm
*Barth	Gardelegen	Lemgo
Berlin	Gollnow	*Lemsal
Bielefeld	Goslar	Lippstadt
Bolsward	Göttingen	Loitz
Brandenburg	Greifswald	Lübeck
Braunsberg	Grimmen	Lüneburg
Bremen	Groningen	Magdeburg
Breslau	Guben	Middelburg
Briel	Halberstadt	Minden
Brunswick	Halle	Münster
Buxtehude	Hameln	Nordheim
Cologne (Köln	Hamburg	Nymwegen
a. R).	Hamm	Osnabrück
Cracow	Hanover	Osterburg
Danzig	Harderwyk	Osterode
*Demmin	Hasselt	Paderborn
Deventer	Helmstedt	Pernau
Dordrecht	Herford	Quedlinburg
Dorpat	Hildesheim	Reval
Dortmund	*Hindeloopen	Riga
Duisburg	Kampen	Roermonde
Eimbeck	Kiel	Rostock
Elbing	Koesfeld	Rügenwalde

Salzwedel	Tangermünde	Wernigerode
Seehausen	Thiel	Wesel
Soest	Thorn	*Wieringen
Soltbomel	Treptow	*Windau
Stade	Tribsees	Wisby
Stargard	Uelzen	Wismar
Staveren	Unna	*Wolmar
Stendal	Utrecht	Zierixee
Stettin	Venlo	Zutphen
Stolpe	Warburg	Zwolle
Stralsund	*Wenden	

Kneiphof, though only one of the quarters of Königsberg, was separately represented at more than one diet at which a representative of Königsberg was also present. It cannot, however, be included in a list of towns.

Official documents give good reason for believing that the following were also Hanse Towns :

Erfurt	Kalmar	Pritzwalk
Greiffenberg	Kyritz	Werben
Havelberg	Nordhausen	
Höxter	Perleberg	

Many other towns are mentioned in the *Recesse* in a way which shows that they were in some degree connected with the Hansa ; but it is not possible to give a satisfactory list of them.

The *Kontor* towns were :

Bergen	Bruges	London	Novgorod

To these may be added the following, in which the Hansa either had smaller factories or special privileges :

Antwerp	Helsingborg	Roeskilde
Ardenburg	Helsingör	Skanör
Boston	Hull	Stockholm
Bristol	Ipswich	Svendborg
Copenhagen	Kowno	Warberg (Sweden)
Damme	Lisbon	Yarmouth
Dinant	Lynn	York
Falsterbo	Malmö	Ypres
Flensburg	Norwich	
Ghent	Pleskow	

This list could be much extended, but the question of inclusion or exclusion is one of degree, as the league had dealings far and wide.　R. H.

HANSEATIC LEAGUE. An association of German towns which, during the 13th and 14th centuries, secured the entire trade of the countries surrounding the Baltic, exporting their produce to Germany, England, and the marts of western Europe, and carrying back the manufactured goods of the west and the special products of warmer climates.

The word *hansa* is of Mœso-Gothic origin, and denotes an association of a militant character ; it also appears in early documents in the sense of a payment (*Hans. Urk.*, i. No. 33). In 1266 the Hamburg merchants were allowed to have *hansam suam* . . . *per totum regnum* by Henry III. ; but the expression *mercatores de hansa Almaniæ* first occurs as a designation of the famous league in the agreement of June 1282 with the city of London, now in the archives of Lübeck.

Monopoly was the watchword of the Hanseatics from beginning to end of their career ; but while their policy enabled them, in the infancy of the European nations, to amass wealth and gain power, their blind adherence to the same aims and methods in face of the discoveries, new economic views, and developed political life of the 16th century, led to the final destruction of their organisation.

No date can be assigned for the first beginnings of the Hansa. No charter or treaty exists to which historians can point as a foundation statute until the year 1367, though, as the Hansa had at that date become the political arbiter of northern Europe, the deficiency is not due to the absence of strong bonds of association at a much earlier period. There were anomalies in the position of the Hansa. As a power it treated on even terms with princes ; it was also a secret society. On paper it was the obsequious servant of the German emperor ; but, conscious of the weakness of the central authority, then wasting its strength in Italy, the league never condescended to obey the imperial decrees, and indeed was itself a standing contravention of the Golden Bull of 1356, which forbade all such associations. It could raise fleets and armies—one of twelve thousand men is spoken of—and levy large war-contributions, but it never permitted a complete list to be given of the towns which it included. It sufficed that the Hansa should know its own aims and methods, and it was best that its outlying members should not be too surely recognised by those who held them individually in their power. The Hansa assumed an absolute sway over its members, beheading the four burgomasters of Halberstadt in 1425 (*Contin. Chron. Engelhus.*, Leibnitz, ii. p. 84), and almost ruining those towns which, like Brunswick in 1375 (*Recesse*, ii. No. 93), were for a time expelled ; or, like Bremen in 1285 (*Rec.*, i. 34, § 2), unhansed themselves ; yet it had no visible executive.

Some of the earliest traces of that which was destined to become the Hansa are found in England, though in reality the league sprang from two centres of growth—the Cologne trade with England and the Lübeck trade with the Baltic.

The calling of a merchant in the 13th and earlier centuries required physical courage and endurance. Mediæval traders travelled with their goods, and were regarded, in foreign countries, with a jealousy largely due to their persistent attempts to work outside the towns and enter into direct commercial communication with producers, thus carrying away with them the profits which, had they traded under municipal restrictions, would have accrued to the native merchant. This was not only an English feeling ; its counterpart was found abroad, and it was a cardinal point in the policy of the Hansa to enforce far stricter limitations on English merchants on the continent than those which, in spite of the *Carta Mercatoria* of 1303, were imposed on ordinary foreign merchants in England up to the middle of the 14th century. Partnerships between foreign merchants and its own members were absolutely forbidden by the Hansa, and the celibacy to which the

Kontor and factory agents were bound was intended to prevent the growth of family agencies.

Usually a foreign merchant had to pay much higher customs dues than a native. He had to buy, or combine to buy, from rulers the right to travel anywhere, and sell in any market ; and when, as in the case of the Hansa, these privileges were obtained, he became the hated rival of the native trader, who gladly enforced, when possible, the rough justice of reprisal then in vogue. This system is conveniently illustrated by the letter from Stralsund in the *Literæ Cantuarienses* (Rolls Series, iii. 91), and it will be seen that if a previous merchant, from the same place as the trader himself, had proved a defaulter, or his own city or country had ill-treated merchants of the kingdom he was visiting, his goods or his person might be seized in compensation. Again the roads were not infested by ordinary robbers only, for a duke of Brunswick could condescend to plunder merchants so shamelessly as to force the league to vengeance (*Chron. S. Ægid.*, Leibnitz, iii. 598) ; and local magnates exacted so many tolls (see INTERNAL CUSTOMS AND TOLLS) that a Hanseatic merchant, travelling from Thorn to Lemberg, a distance of perhaps 360 miles, was forced to pay tolls sixteen times, the toll per horse amounting to over 31 groats (*Hans. Urk.*, iii. 312).

To these vexations were added the natural perils of the sea and the brutality of pirates and wreckers, for so barbarous were the times that a prince, while agreeing to protect merchants from other plunderers, could stipulate for a share of stranded cargoes for himself.

There must have been heavy profits to induce men to run such risks, and it was but natural that they should seek by combination to make these profits more secure, and obtain comfort and mutual assistance when, as frequently happened, they were compelled to winter far from home. These combinations abroad, among men whose temporary sojourn at a distance in no way impaired their ties of citizenship, led to federations at home between the towns, in which the merchant class was then the controlling element. This was a foregone conclusion, for, during the period of the rise of the Hansa, there was no national commerce in Europe ; towns everywhere dealt with other towns, and merchants having the same aims and methods tended to frequent the same spheres of activity.

Traces have come down from remote times of a great trade in the Baltic before the 11th century. In 975, for example, Otto II. granted a charter to Magdeburg (*Hans. Urk.*, No. 1), which, by referring to the wanderings of German merchants into barbarous countries, clearly alludes to Russia and the North ; and Adam of Bremen, in the 11th century, mentions that the now-vanished city of Julin, or Jumne, was *mercibus omnium Septentrionalium nationum locuples* (Pertz, viii. 312, ll. 15, 22). In Gothland, too, coins of so many Anglo-Saxon kings have been found that the collection made thence is the second best in Europe ; and mingled with these tokens of western trade are coins of the caliphs of more than a thousand different types, testifying to the constant communications with the East by the

Caspian Sea, by the Volga, and the other great rivers of Russia. Gothland, and Wisby its chief town, had thus long been marked out as the central depôt of Baltic produce, and in 1163, but five years after the second foundation of Lübeck, we find a rescript of Henry the Lion (*Lüb. Urk.*, p. 4) respecting the behaviour of the natives and the Lübeckers settled in Gothland ; while in 1199 Germans and Gothlanders were allowed free commercial access to the principality of Novgorod, which stretched in a north-easterly direction along the Baltic and the frontier of Sweden. Their trade was largely in herrings, which, from the beginning of the 12th century up to the middle of the 16th, seldom failed to drive in shoals through the Sound to spawn in the Baltic ; and a hook of land, jutting out from Scania into the Sound, was then the place at which the fish could be best intercepted. There, accordingly, on Danish soil at Skanör and Falsterbo, the Lübeckers had their *vittœ*, or curing establishments, under privileges granted before 1209 by Waldemar II. of Denmark (*Lüb. Urk.*, p. 20). Matthew Paris, however, notes, under the year 1238, that the Gothlanders and Frisians were in the habit of coming each year to Yarmouth to buy herrings (iii. p. 488).

The early Lübeck records contain few traces of other Hanse towns ; but in 1225 there are incidental references to the *Lubecenses, Hamburgenses et ceteri . . . mercatores . . . Daciam frequentare volentes*, to assistance given to certain princes in war, to an agreement with Hamburg in 1226 as to mutual privileges, and to the freedom from tolls granted to men of the Baltic shore in the Lübeck customs tariff (*Lüb. Urk.*, pp. 35-38).

The charter conferring mint privileges and the freedom of the empire on Lübeck in 1226 (*ib.* p. 45) refers to merchants trading thence to England, and frees them from the tolls exacted by Cologne and Thiel ; but the records are strangely reticent, and under the year 1227, when the *Lubecenses* defeated the Danes at Bornhöved (Langebek, i. 122, 286), there is no Lübeck document clearly alluding to the war except an agreement with Riga and the Germans in Livonia not to make a separate peace. In the *Hansisches Urkundenbuch* (i. 232, 303, 345, 650) are documents of 1229 and later dates which seem to presuppose a league, but though the record evidence is not distinct, the existence of a far-reaching bond of union is apparent from public results of most decided character.

In 1249 it is recorded that Eric VI. of Denmark assailed the *Lubicenses in Scania piscantes* (Langebek, i. 123), and that in revenge they burned Copenhagen. Still no mention of other towns is made by the chronicler ; but in 1285 the annalist of the Franciscans of Wisby (Langebek, i. 255) notes that there was war *inter Noricos et Lubycenses ac alias civitates maritimas* which was concluded by the peace of Kalmar ; and the chronicler thus uses the actual official title of the Hansa, whose common

seal bore the legend : *Signum civitatum maritimarum.* His words are interpreted by the record of the arbitration in the *Hansisches Urkundenbuch* (i. 993), and by the *Annales Lubicenses* (Pertz, xvi. 411-429) which mention, under 1285, Lübeck, Wismar, Rostock, Stralsund, Greifswald, Riga, Wisby, and two Netherland towns, Kampen and Staveren, as those concerned.

The same annals show, under the year 1310, an association between Greifswald, Stralsund, Rostock, and Wismar, which Lübeck declined to join (*Hans. Urk.*, ii. No. 175) ; and the northern chronicles (Langebek, vi. 222 ; i. 258) mention the burning of Helsingoër and Skanör by the *civitates stagnales*, or Hanse towns, in 1312, and the siege of Stralsund in 1316. They then proceed to give weary evidence of smouldering warfare up to 1361, when Waldemar III. of Denmark began an attack on the league which really led to its final organisation. At this date the merchants had a very long seaboard open to attack, for they had followed in the wake of the Teutonic knights, and had founded fourteen cities along the Baltic shore as far as Reval and a great factory farther away at Novgorod, so that the time had visibly come for firmly banding together all who had a common aim.

Turning now to the western half of Europe, the Laws of Æthelred (A.D. 978-1016) show the *homines imperatoris* coming to England in their own ships and enjoying special privileges ; and William of Malmesbury, writing before 1142, describes London as being crowded with German merchants (*De Gest. Pont.*, ii. § 1). In 1157, too, there is a charter of Henry II. referring to the *gildhalla* of the Cologne merchants in London, followed by Richard's charter given to the same merchants at Louvain in 1194 (*Hans. Urk.*, i. 14, 40) ; but probably the earliest direct evidence of a western league is furnished by the charter of 1252 granted to the merchants of Cologne, Dortmund, Soest, and Münster *et aliis cum iisdem concordantibus* (*Hans. Urk.*, i. 428). The history of this branch of the Hansa is intimately connected with the history of English commerce (see STEELYARD), though it is certain that the Baltic merchants were also in constant communication with London, Lynn, and the eastern ports. The Cologne or Westphalian association presents, however, few historical features of interest until the eventful year in which, as stated above, the great war with Denmark began. Waldemar III., who had long endeavoured to free his kingdom from foreign influences, struck, in 1361, a treacherous blow at the league by sacking the town of Wisby in time of peace (Langebek, i. 259). At once negotiating an alliance with Norway, the merchants laid a tax on all the exported goods of their league, equipped a fleet, and plundered

Copenhagen. They were besieging Helsingborg when Waldemar, surprising their ships, compelled them to retreat (*Recesse*, i. 374, § 10). Negotiations followed, but the war broke out again, and on the 11th of November 1367, a general council of seventy-seven towns was held in Cologne, at which the *nuncii civitatum de Hanza Theotonica* (*Recesse*, i. 412, 416) drew up the Act of the Cologne Confederation, which was thenceforward regarded as the foundation-statute of the avowed Hanseatic League.

It was to these deputies (Langebek, vi. 228) that king Waldemar addressed his mocking quatrain beginning,

Seuen und Seuentigh Hensen
Hefft seuen und seuentigh Gensen.

But in the year following they had driven Waldemar from Denmark, and the peace of Stralsund was concluded in 1370 during his banishment (*Recesse*, i. 523). By it the Hansa obtained for fifteen years the castles and the bulk of the revenues of Scania, freedom from all tolls in the Sound, and a control over the succession to the Danish crown (*Rec.*, i. 524, l. 33).

This great change in the position of the Hansa was marked by a state visit in 1375 of the emperor Charles IV. to Lübeck as the chief of the confederated towns. He sought political aid in vain from the new power, which had reached its highest level, but he was loaded with gifts instead.

The extant records of the league now begin to assume a different character. The series of minutes of diets begin with those of the Wismar diet about 1260. These early *Recesse* must not, however, be supposed to relate to the league as a whole. No general assembly is known to have taken place before that in 1367, referred to above, and it is certain that small associations of towns sometimes took separate action (Pertz, xvi. 421). The early series of *Recesse* is broken, being not continuous until about 1364; but neither then, nor afterwards do the records reveal any standing council or high officials, though such may have existed, for the chronicle in Langebek (v. 235) states that in 1428 the *communitas urbium* rebelled and created for themselves *novum concilium et senatum*. Another sign of organisation, not connected with the filiation of towns, is observable in the earliest *Recess*, which refers to statutes made for the benefit of all merchants *qui jure Lubicensi gaudent et reguntur*. When they became annual these diets were frequently held at Lübeck, then admittedly the leading city, and one of its burgomasters usually presided.

The correspondence, the treaties, and the *Recesse* themselves disclose the names of the Hanse towns a few at a time (see HANSE TOWNS). It is usually stated that they were divided into three groups, Lübeck leading the Wendish, Pomeranian, and Saxon towns ; Wisby the Gothland and Livonian ; and Cologne the Westphalian ; but a document of 1366 (*Rec.*, i. 381) shows a *terciana Lubecensis*, a *terciana Wisbicensis*, and a *terciana* consisting of Prussian towns. Certainly Cologne formed a fourth *terciana*, so the word cannot be taken in its ordinary sense. The truer classification is perhaps shown by a letter of 1372 (*Rec.*, ii. 45), though it omits Cologne. At a later date Lübeck, Brunswick, Danzig, and Cologne were leaders of regions or circles. For a time Wisby had held a great position in the Baltic, and the dues from the Hanse towns were paid into a common treasury chest there under the care of four aldermen from Wisby, Lübeck, Soest, and Dortmund ; but after the sacking of Wisby in 1361, every sign of leadership passed to Lübeck. In the 14th century Lübeck began to coin gold, twenty shillings of twelve groats each being equal to one easterling pound (see EASTERLINGS), and a large banking business sprang up there, bills of exchange being generally payable at Lübeck or at Bruges.

The lists of towns attending these diets reveal the broad fact that the coast towns from Reval to Middelburg were the really active members of the Hansa, and on them fell the brunt of fighting and negotiation. Even after 1367, Cologne, proudly reluctant to cede precedence to Lübeck, seldom sent representatives, while the rest of the inland towns were almost equally backward. Sometimes the diet, in fixing a place for the next meeting, would require towns to send their deputies to answer complaints ; but often only those of four or five seaports appeared, though at crises the list became much longer.

The business of the diets was varied. Fines were received from recalcitrant members ; letters were written to foreign princes demanding redress for merchants ; questions of peace and war and of alliances had to be decided, war expenses apportioned, old privileges maintained, and others won by negotiation. Laws, too, were made touching commercial conduct, and even the morals of the merchants (*Recesse*, i. 9). Letters on these matters may be read in the Lübeck *Recess* of 1366 (i. 376) ; and it may be remarked that these documents have a special interest in connection with the growth of the LAW MERCHANT (*q.v.*). The trade of the Easterlings was not speculative. Transactions were settled by barter or by cash payments on the transfer of actual commodities, and credit was almost entirely prohibited. Resolute selfishness marks all the acts and writings of the Hansa. It had fixed aims which it pursued untiringly, the chief being to gain absolute control over the Belt and the Sound. The league's desire was that no ship but a Hanseatic ship should pass in or out of the Baltic, or trade anywhere in that sea ; and, broadly speaking, the will of the Hansa prevailed up to the beginning of the 16th century, though the English ADVENTURERS, MERCHANT could not be wholly shut out. So jealously guarded was this region that the early cartographers, who could delineate Africa and show the position of Japan, had to rely on the Ptolemy maps for Europe above N. lat. 53°. This policy of exclusion proved, of course, unendurable to Sweden and Denmark ; and with the latter power, which held the Sound, the Hansa was involved in many wars.

About 115 towns were, at one time or another, included in the Hansa, and the position of a few more is uncertain. It had four great *Kontore* or organised establishments, Novgorod, Bruges, London, and Bergen, and about twenty-eight factories in foreign countries which enjoyed special privileges.

These *comptoirs*, of which the STEELYARD was the most important, differed somewhat according to the nature of the countries in which they were established. The one at Novgorod formed a separate quarter of the town, clustered round a church. Here the merchants lived, as they sought to do everywhere, under their own *Skra* or code of laws (*Lüb. Urk.*, i. p. 700), and maintained a celibate establishment under an elected alderman —a kind of merchant abbot over a commercial monastery, which, like some other early monasteries, had also the characteristics of a fortress. At Bergen about 3000 persons thus lived together in one community, though subdivided according to the towns they represented. By unscrupulous methods they ousted the Norwegians from the whole of the harbour, and even limited the number of Hanse cities which should share the trade. The expenses of these factories were paid mainly by duties on ships; but each town defrayed the cost of the maintenance of its own staff. In all the *Kontor* towns the Hansa had gained great privileges in the way of remission of customs dues. Even as late as the 29th year of Henry VIII., the Hansards were so favoured that, for instance, they exported 33,778 pieces of cloth as against 4608 by other foreign merchants; whereas in 31 Henry VIII., when the latter were allowed to pay "Englische custome" only, the totals were 27,260 for the Hansa, and 24,566 for the others (Cott. MS., Claud. E. vii. *f.* 99).

Notwithstanding fierce quarrels with Denmark, the Hansa obtained thence grain and cattle; and the merchants derived from their own curing establishments on Danish soil in Scania the herrings which they carried to Germany and western Europe. From Sweden the Hansa exported wood, furs, iron, copper, fish, cattle, and corn; importing, among other things, silk stuffs, cotton, hops, salt, spices, and wines. Until the days of Gustavus Vasa, the entire trade of the country was in the hands of the league; and the same may be said of the Russian trade, until the early part of the 16th century, when Ivan the Terrible sacked Novgorod. Even after that, the Hansa sought to revive the monopoly; but the English, the Netherlanders, and the Danes had forced themselves into the Russian trade, and could not be driven out again. While their advantage lasted, the Hansa had exported from Russia furs, leather, wax, honey, tallow, hair, gold, and silver; bringing for Russian use, corn, flour, smoked meats, herrings, beer, wine, Dutch and English cloth, thread, furriery and mercery, copper, zinc, and lead. In Norway, the Hansa had swooped down on the long-established trade of Bergen with Greenland, Iceland, and the Arctic seas, and thrusting aside the natives, had taken to itself, as far as English enterprise allowed, the entire produce of the whale and seal fisheries, the furs, tallow, cod, herrings, and other products of the north. Western and southern Europe formed the opposite pole of the Hanseatic trade, and all the produce of the north and east which was not absorbed in Germany came by sea to Bruges or to London (see STEELYARD). In Bruges, the Hansa merchants met the produce and manufactures of England, Flanders, Spain, Italy, the Levant, and the East, and transacted business with men of all nations. The customs tariff of Bruges in 1380, recorded in the archives of Hamburgh (*Rec.*, ii. 209), shows that the following were the less ordinary articles of commerce which the Easterlings might obtain at Bruges to carry back to the Baltic:—alum, sulphur, tartar, saltpetre, borax, zedoary, saffron, cubebs, rhubarb, tansy; silver, tin, quicksilver, verdigris, vermilion, lapis-lazuli, indigo; almonds, liquorice, caraway, anise, pepper, long pepper, ginger, grains of paradise, cinnamon, nutmegs, cloves, mace, cardamoms, rice, loaf sugar, figs, dates, raisins; Spanish wax, boxwood, frankincense, cotton, and paper. A tariff of 1252 shows swords, shields, armour, copper utensils, boots, cork floats, cloth of many kinds, wood, linen, beer, wine, peltry, and other goods useful in countries like Norway, Sweden, and Russia, which then had absolutely no manufactures of any kind.

Similar information may be obtained from the inventories of the cargoes of two ships, one of which belonged to Thorn. It contained a surprising amount of gold and silver, and some silk (*Hans. Urk.*, iii. 63, 260).

Such was the power of the Hansa, that it compelled all ships, except those bound for England or the Baltic, to stop at Bruges; thus obtaining the chance of being the first buyers of any coveted product. But this prosperity was too great to last. Late in the 15th century, the insolence of the men of Bruges had brought ruin on their own city, and the Hansa, when too late, transferred its factory to Antwerp, only however to find there failure and disappointment.

With France, the league had comparatively little direct dealing. A large part of the French coast was for long periods in English hands; France had, through Marseilles and other southern ports, direct access to the vast trading centres of the Mediterranean; her northern boundaries ran close to the great Flemish towns; and finally, during the 13th and much of the 14th centuries, Amiens, Rheims, Caen, Beauvais, and other towns were included in the HANSE OF LONDON, and had little inducement to join the league.

At Lisbon, the league had a factory through which it obtained Levantine and Oriental goods; but the principal part of the trade with the Italian cities passed overland to Augsburg, Nuremberg, Ulm, and other south German cities which formed a collateral Hansa, and had a factory at Venice.

The great trade with England was mainly concentrated in London; though there were establishments also at Bristol, Ipswich, Yarmouth, Norwich, Hull, and York, and Hanse houses at Boston and Lynn (see Lappenberg's *History of the Steelyard*). Roll No. 268 in the *Miscellanea of the Exchequer* at the Public Record Office, is the account of the customs dues at Lynn for 1286-87, and shows a duty of 6s. 8d. on each sack of wool weighing 2 cwts. Hides and leather were likewise exported. In the roll for 1302, cotton thread, silk, sugar, and spices appear among imports; while cloth, dyed and undyed, was exported by the Easterlings, though there was direct English trade with Norway as well. Of trade with Scotland there are many traces in the *Recesse* and in the Nuremberg *Chronicle.* An interesting letter of invitation to traders from Sir William Wallace, in 1297, is preserved in the archives of Lübeck.

The Hansa did not remain long at the high level of prosperity attained in the second half of the 14th century. The end of the first quarter of the 15th saw the beginning of the decline. The Hansa had grown into a league at a period when Europe generally contained a servile population, no middle class, except in the towns, and few manufactures ; but the feudal and the manorial systems had both collapsed in England ; the new race of tenant farmers had appeared in the country ; and a manufacturing population controlled by craft gilds (see CORPORATIONS OF ARTS AND TRADES ; GILDS), had sprung up in the towns ; meanwhile the nation, unified by parliamentary representation, was fast developing a national policy as regards trade, and awakening to a consciousness of vigour and of resources which it could not allow to be controlled by a selfish company of foreigners.

Changes had also been taking place all over Europe ; even in the Baltic the trade created by the Hansa had been elevating the once simple races. Unseen natural forces, too, were joined against the merchants, and the herrings, which had been perhaps their greatest source of wealth had begun to change their annual course, to the lasting benefit of the Netherlands.

Europe began to see that the Easterlings, or *Ostrelins,* as the French called them, were little more than mere carriers of products, representing neither industrial population nor manufacturing centres. The western and northern nations began to insist on not being excluded any longer from direct trading relations with each other ; yet to threaten the monopoly of the Hansa was still to bring the sword of the confederated cities from its scabbard, and offenders found themselves confronted either by open war, by secretly encouraged raids of pirates, or by the disfavour of sovereigns whom Hanseatic bribes and loans had won over in spite of their better judgment. The once peaceful Hansa now appeared as a tyrant desperately endeavouring to keep up an effete system of privileges and monopolies by threats and violence. The Dutch, once members of the Hansa, had had a fierce war with Lübeck in 1438, and again seceded from the league at the end of the 15th century, boldly coming forward as its commercial opponents. They soon developed such a trade that it was a fleet of no less than 250 sail upon which the Lübeckers fell in 1511 as it was leaving the Baltic ; and when at the opening of the 16th century, Charles V. found himself at the head of an empire with larger interests than those of the Hansa, he wisely favoured the energetic Netherlanders, and looked coldly on the allied cities so threateningly independent of his power.

The discovery of America, and of the new passage to the East Indies round the Cape, had begun to draw trade into other channels ; while the printing press, which quickly found its way to Sweden and Denmark, was undermining a power largely dependent on the ignorance of the nations it traded with. The Hansa, in fact, was bound to give way in the presence of an altered world ; but it declined to do so, and blindly refused to change its ideas and methods.

Within the league, too, there was dissension, and the inland towns began to find that their interests no longer coincided with those of coast towns, whose carrying trade was beginning to slip away.

Reverting, however, to the chronological series of events, the annals show that for many years after the conclusion of the peace of Stralsund, in 1370, the Hansa was in an almost continuous state of warfare. First the piratical *Vitalienbrüder* had to be suppressed (*Recesse,* iv. 279, 330, etc.), a work not ended until 1402 ; then a long and bloody war ensued with Eric the Pomeranian, ruler of the three Scandinavian countries, lasting up to 1435. Five-and-thirty years afterwards the Hansa, at variance since 1452 with the English, was, as Philip de Commines states, at war both with England and France, and came nigh to changing the course of English history by the capture of Edward IV. at sea off Alkmar. The war was concluded by the peace of Utrecht in February 1474, which restored to the Hansards all their privileges in England, and delusively promised reciprocity to the English merchants in the league towns. Cologne had taken the side of England in these quarrels, and had receded from the Hansa, but was re-admitted in 1476 (*Fœdera,* xii. 36).

A war in 1518, between Christian II. of Denmark and Sweden, which enabled the merchants to play once more the part of king-makers, proved disastrous to them ; for Frederick and Gustavus Vasa, to whom they had given thrones, identified themselves with the interests of their newly-gained kingdoms, and with splendid ingratitude determined to break the power of the Hansa. The war which ensued is connected with the spread of Lutheran doctrines, and with the endeavours of Jürgen Wullenweber of Lübeck to gain actual possession of the Sound. He failed, and the outcome of the war in 1534 was the total loss of Scania to the Hansa.

The three Scandinavian nations were now able to trade openly on their own account, while the voyage of Richard Chancellor to Archangel in 1553, and the establishment in England of the RUSSIA COMPANY, turned the flank of the Hanseatic trade with Russia. Other heavy blows, too, now fell on the league. The Czar, Ivan IV., saw that the time was ripe for a descent on Livonia, and no effective resistance being made either by the Teutonic knights or by the Hansa, the country was divided in 1561 between Russia, Sweden, and Poland.

Soon afterwards Lübeck, allying herself with Denmark, entered on a protracted war against Sweden, only ended in 1570. No benefit accrued from these exhausting efforts ; the seizure of Bornholm by the Danes, a serious loss to the league, followed in 1576. A worse event happened when, after a lengthy quarrel with the Hansa respecting its failure to carry out the provisions of the treaty of Utrecht, Queen Elizabeth answered the Emperor Rudolph's expulsion of the Merchant Adventurers in 1597 by closing the Steelyard in February 1598. A naval power that had beaten the Armada, could not be excluded from any sea or from any market ; it was indeed wonderful that the Hansa had maintained its ground so long in face of the MERCANTILIST ideas then dominant in England (see MERCANTILE SYSTEM).

In 1586 the Czar Feodor Ivanovitch restored the factories of Novgorod and Pleskow, but the Swedes and the Poles, no less than the English, Danes, and Netherlanders, interfered with the trade ; and when in 1603 the Czar Boris refused to recognise any Hanseatic town except Lübeck, internal dissensions were added to the difficulties which the Baltic powers threw in the way of the league.

In no quarter of Europe was there any ray of hope for the now obsolete Hansa ; and, when the Thirty Years' War began, dissolution came with it very speedily, and the material prosperity of Germany, the results of the laborious industry of her merchants, was entirely lost.

The last minutes of a diet are of that in 1628, though another was held in 1630 ; and after the peace of Westphalia, in 1648, only Lübeck, Bremen, and Hamburg remained to make an unsuccessful effort to revive the league. A number of deputies met in 1669, but dispersed again without having effected anything. The three great cities, as free cities, were recognised by the treaty of Vienna in 1815, and as free cities and sovereign states now form part of the German Empire.

[Urkundenbuch der Stadt Lübeck, 8 vols., 1843-1889.— Hansische Geschichtsblätter, Leipsic.— Hansische Geschichtsquellen.—Verein für Hansische Geschichte, Lübeck, Hanserecesse, 1256-1476 (quoted as Recesse), 13 vols., 1876-92.—C. Höhlbaum, Hansisches Urkundenbuch, 3 vols.—J. M. Lappenberg, Urkundliche Geschichte des Hansischen Stahlhofes zu London, Hamburg, 1851. —Calendar of State Papers (foreign series).— Langebek, Scriptores Rerum Danicarum, 1786.— Leibnitz, Scriptores Rerum Brunsvicensium.— Pertz, Monumenta Germaniæ Historica.—Rymer, Fœdera, viii.-xii.—A. Krantz, Chronica Regn. Aquilon. 1562.—J. A. Werdenhagen, De Rebuspublicis Hanseaticis, Frankfort, 1641.—Macpherson, Annals of Commerce, 1805.—Sartorius von Waltershausen, Urkundliche Geschichte des Ursprunges der deutschen Hanse, ed. Lappenberg— D. Schäfer, Die Hansestädte und König Waldemar, 1879.—E. Worms, Histoire Commerciale de la Ligue Hanséatique, 1864.—H. Zimmern, The Hansa Towns (The Story of the Nations Series), 1889.—J. de la Gravière, Les Marins du XVe.

siècle, 1879.—Article on "Hanseatic League," R. Lodge, Encyc. Brit., ed. ix.]   R. H.

HANWAY, JONAS (1712-1786), was a merchant and philanthropist. Apprenticed at Lisbon, he began his mercantile life there, but soon returned to London, and in 1743 went to St. Petersburg, where he entered into partnership with an English merchant, and was commissioned by the Russia Company to carry on the attempt begun by John Elton to establish a British trade in wool in Persia and on the Caspian Sea. After more than a year of strenuous effort and perilous adventure he returned to St. Petersburg ; the new trade did not prosper, mainly on account of Elton's behaviour. In 1750 Hanway left Russia and began a life of active benevolence in London, where he was the first man to use an umbrella, a chief promoter of the Marine Society, of the Magdalen Hospital, of plans for benefiting chimney-sweepers, for paving the streets, for reforming the Foundling Hospital, for establishing Sunday schools, and, above all, for preserving the lives of "parish infants," among whom the mortality was then extraordinarily high. In 1762, at the instance of some London citizens, he was appointed a commissioner of the victualling office, in recognition of his public usefulness.

Hanway's writings, seventy-four in number, chiefly occasioned by his philanthropic schemes, are, like his work, miscellaneous and humane. Only the following need be mentioned :—The Essay on Tea, known through Dr. Johnson's review of it.—Historical Account of the British Trade over the Caspian Sea, etc., to which is appended The Revolutions of Persia, a detailed and interesting account of his travels and observations, and Letters on the Importance of the Rising Generation of the labouring part of our fellow-subjects, containing plans for increasing the population by preserving infant life, with some account of the London death-rate and an estimate of the expectation of life at different ages.

[Pugh's Remarkable Occurrences in the Life of Jonas Hanway, Esq., 1787 (abridged in 1798).— Gentleman's Magazine, 1786, p. 812.—Dict. of National Biography.]   E. G. P.

HARCOURT, FRANÇOIS EUGÈNE GABRIEL, Duke of (1786-1865), was from his youth a steady and brilliant champion of liberalism under its different shapes, and the defender of the Greek and Polish national causes. He became a member of the French house of deputies, and of the house of peers (from 1837) ; he was also sent as French ambassador to Madrid (1831), shortly afterwards to Constantinople, and in 1848 to Rome, where he succeeded Rossi. In 1849 he resigned the latter embassy, and lived in retirement on his estates until his death.

In 1846, he accepted the presidency of the Association pour la Liberté des Échanges, with Bastiat as secretary ; his Discours en faveur de la Liberté du Commerce (in the French parliament) were published 1846, in Paris. He insists mainly on the argument that private interests ought never to be privileged at the expense of the general welfare, and that free competition is the only available method to secure this end. E. Ca.

HARD - DOLLAR (or *peso duro*). Old Spanish silver coin.

Year.	Weight.		Fine-ness.	Value.	
	grains.	grammes.		In silver 925 fine at 5s. 6d. an oz.	In standard silver francs 900 fine.
				s. d.	francs.
1707-1728	423·89	27·468	930·50	4 10½	5·68
1728-1772	417·74	27·064	909·72	4 8½	5·47
1772 [1]	,,	,,	902·78	4 8	5·43
1848	405·75	26·291	900·00	4 6½	5·26
1850	402·87	26·105	,,	4 6	5·22
1854-68	400·64	25·960	,,	4 5½	5·19

The subdivisions were all of proportionate weight and fineness until the year 1864, when the escudo (or half-duro) only was of the same fineness, the other fractional coins becoming merely tokens of the fineness of 810, though retaining weights proportionate to the dollar.

In 1868 the coinage of pesetas (francs) was commenced in Spain, and has since been continued. F. E. A.

HARD MONEY. This term is locally applied in the United States to metallic money as distinguished from paper issues. The advocates of hard money are in general opposed to the SOFT MONEY or Greenback party. The term came into frequent use during the political discussions in the decade 1870-80, in favour of the resumption of specie payments. D. R. D.

HARDENBERG, KARL AUGUST, Prinz von (1750-1822), an eminent Prussian statesman, was born at Essenrode in Brunswick-Lüneburg. He belonged to an old Hanoverian family. In 1766 he went to the university of Göttingen, and in 1768 to that of Leipzig,—in the latter making the acquaintance of Goethe. Returning to Göttingen, he there pursued the study of jurisprudence; and in 1770 entered the civil service of Hanover. In the course of some travels in Germany in 1772-73 he stayed for a time in the house of the Freiherr von Stein, father of his future colleague. He conceived an affection for a daughter of the family, but by the influence of his relatives was led to marry, in 1775, a Countess von Reventlow, who by her subsequent conduct ruined his domestic life. During a residence in England in the neighbourhood of Windsor in 1781 he discovered a liaison of his wife with the Prince of Wales which had already created a good deal of public scandal; he quitted, in consequence, the Hanoverian service, and entered, in the following year, that of the Duke of Brunswick. In 1787 he divorced his wife, and married another who seems to have been little more reputable. The Margrave of Ansbach and Bayreuth, who belonged to the house of Hohenzollern, being soon after desirous of

getting rid of his principal ministers, asked the king of Prussia to send him new advisers; and amongst these Hardenberg was appointed. The Margrave, weary of the task of governing, resolved before long to abdicate in favour of Prussia, to which power on his death his territories were to fall; and thus Hardenberg, in 1791, became a Prussian official, and was charged with the entire administration of the two provinces,—which he conducted with great ability. He was employed in 1795 to negotiate with France the treaty of Basel, by which the apparently prudent, but ignoble and ultimately disastrous, neutrality of Prussia was established. From this time his biography is inseparably bound up with the political history of Prussia. He was a member of the supreme finance directory, and during the frequent absences of Haugwitz from Berlin took his place in the conduct of foreign affairs, though the policies of the two ministers were different—Haugwitz favouring subserviency to Napoleon, and Hardenberg advising close relations with Russia and hostility to France. Haugwitz had to resign office in 1806, and was succeeded as foreign minister by Zastrow. The latter retired in February 1807, and after a time Hardenberg took his place, with a kind of dictatorial position. He already saw that a radical reform of the Prussian state was necessary—in fact, a revolution like the French, but one to be effected by peaceful means. At the darkest hour of the reign of Frederick William III. he said, "The question now is of discovering additional resources to save ourselves; later it will be of a thorough regeneration." But he was soon compelled to quit office. Napoleon, finding in him an obstacle to his designs, after the battle of Friedland insisted on his removal, which the king was not in a position to refuse; and accordingly on the eve of the peace of Tilsit he retired to Riga; and Stein, who had been dismissed some months before, was recalled and entrusted, as Hardenberg had been, with a sort of dictatorship. At Riga, whither he was accompanied by Altenstein and Niebuhr, Hardenberg drew up a memoir on the reorganisation of the Prussian state, which is sometimes spoken of, though not very appropriately, as his political testament. In this memorable document he distinctly indicates, and even insists on, all the measures afterwards embodied in what is known as the Stein-Hardenberg legislation (which will be found described in detail in the article on STEIN); and also suggests the abolition of gilds and a movement in the direction of a representative constitution. These measures were, of course, not devised by Hardenberg alone: they were partly the fruit of the matured convictions of the ablest German thinkers, who had converted the great majority of the nation to similar views, and were directly the result

[1] Same as the Mexican dollar.

of the deliberations of the Immediate Commission formed during Hardenberg's tenure of office, of which Altenstein, Schön, Niebuhr, and Stägemann were members. But he cordially adopted the plan—to which he had probably himself largely contributed,—supported it with all the weight of his influence, and loyally urged upon the king the necessity of confiding in Stein as the man most able to deal with the crisis.

When Stein, denounced and proscribed by Napoleon, was forced to leave Prussia, Hardenberg returned to office (June 1810), with the title of chancellor of state; and this position he held to the end of his life. He continued the work of social and economic reform which had been done under the leadership of Stein; indeed, in his agrarian legislation his measures were too radical to receive the approval of Stein, who was less mastered by the modern spirit, and more disposed to preserve and improve old German institutions than to follow what were then called "French models." By his foreign policy, cautious or energetic as circumstances dictated, Hardenberg piloted Prussia successfully through the stormy period which intervened between his return to power and the fall of Napoleon. Because he remained in office during the evil days of 1811-12, he was often accused of acquiescing in the degradation of his country. But he was really all through faithful to Prussia, and his temporary attitude of submission to France seemed to him imposed by the necessities of the situation. He was one of those who signed the peace of Paris in 1814, and on its conclusion was raised to the dignity of prince. He attended the congress of Vienna, and, some years later, those of Aix-la-Chapelle and Verona. He procured from the king, in May 1815, an edict promising the establishment of a system of popular representation; but under the influence of the reaction which prevailed in Germany in 1818 and 1819, this promise was broken, and instead of a states-general, the plan of provincial estates was adopted, which subsisted till 1847. Hardenberg was placed in a false position by continuing to hold the chancellorship when reaction was dominant; and though he was to the last in feeling and principle a reformer, his policy became so indeterminate and ambiguous that when he died, on his return journey from the congress of Verona, Stein declared his disappearance to be a happy event for the Prussian monarchy. But this was a harsh, not to say unjust, judgment, inspired, doubtless, in a great degree by the gross irregularities of the deceased statesman's private life. Be this as it may, Stein and he are indissolubly associated as fellow-workers in a great cause; and, as Ranke has said, whatever weaknesses or sins may be chargeable to Hardenberg, his name is written in imperishable characters on the history of Prussia.

[The materials for Hardenberg's biography used to be drawn from the *Mémoires d'un homme d'état, '92-'15,* which were popularly supposed to be his work. It is now known that this idea was unfounded. His genuine memoirs were edited by Leopold v. Ranke in 1877; they deal, however, only with the years 1804-7. Ranke also published a work of his own, supplementary to the Memoirs, *Denkwürdigkeiten des Staatskanzlers Fürsten von Hardenberg,* 3 vols., 1877. Much information respecting Hardenberg will be found in the late Sir J. Seeley's *Life and Times of Stein,* 3 vols., 1878, which has been largely used in the foregoing sketch.]　　J. K. I.

HARMONIES OF ECONOMICS. The theory that individual interests consciously pursued as such are naturally harmonious was early suggested by many writers, but it was first definitely stated by Henry C. CAREY in America, and Frederic BASTIAT in France, two writers whose works appeared within a year of each other, and whose conflicting claims to originality have never been satisfactorily decided. They sharply antagonise the English school, especially as represented by Ricardo and Malthus. The most important of these conclusions to which exception is taken are thus summed up by Bastiat in his *Harmonies Économiques,* published in 1850.

(1) *The Theory of Value.*—While claiming that value originates in labour, they had agreed in attributing value to natural agents, including land, on which no labour had been expended. These goods, which had cost nothing, were none the less appropriated and made to command for their owners the labour of other men. This Bastiat characterises as "evident injustice."

(2) *The Ricardian Theory of Rent,* according to which the price of the products of the soil is determined by the labour needed to produce them on the least productive soils in cultivation. The excess produced on the more productive soils goes to the landowner as rent and increases in absolute and relative amount as the poorer lands are called into cultivation. The result of this law is stated thus: "Increasing opulence for men of leisure; increasing misery for men of toil; in a word, foreordained inequality."

(3) *The Malthusian Theory of Population.* Population tends to increase more rapidly than subsistence, and this tendency, so disastrous to well-being, can be counteracted only by self-control, which "no one thinks of," or by vice, misery, war, pestilence, famine, etc. The conclusion of this law is stated as "inevitable pauperism."

Against this trio of "evident injustice," "foreordained inequality," and "inevitable pauperism," which together constitute a "theory of discord," Bastiat protests with fervid eloquence rather than with severe logic, or observation of life. He undertakes to prove:
(1) That value is due wholly to labour, or

more exactly to services rendered to one person by another ; (2) that natural agents as such— "the gifts that God had lavished gratis upon his creatures"—are not and cannot be appropriated ; that land values represent only the labour which would be necessary with present methods to bring land from a wild state to its present condition ; (3) that the return to capital increases absolutely but decreases relatively as capital is increased in amount ; (4) that the return to labour increases both relatively and absolutely as capital increases ; (5) that "other things being equal, the increasing density of population is matched by an increasing facility of production."

This "theory of harmony" promises increasing prosperity to all the factors of production on one condition on which Bastiat is never weary of insisting,— namely, *liberty*. Since self-interest, when pursued ever so eagerly, or with ever so great indifference to other men's interests, works good to all, all interference with its action is necessarily detrimental. The state should absolutely limit its function to the maintenance of "justice" (a most ambiguous limitation). Laws restricting the exchange of commodities or otherwise interfering with industrial liberty under pretext of securing harmony of interests are not only destructive to that harmony which can only coexist with liberty, but they are a violation of natural right. This 18th-century argument is one to which Bastiat continually recurs. In logical consistency with his system, he carries the doctrine of *laissez-faire* to its utmost extreme.

Bastiat's proof of the proposition mentioned is peculiar. His one method of argument is that of illustration, a method no doubt legitimate, but usually inadequate and always liable to abuse. Bastiat certainly abused it. It is easy to find cases where value is proportioned closely to labour expended, and a long enumeration has great power over the mind, but when the value of a diamond accidentally picked up is attributed to the labour of appropriation, the argument is strained, to say the least. Still less satisfactory is his treatment of rent. His somewhat piquant imaginary conversations, between a landowner and a would-be purchaser of his products, or his land, completely ignore the fact on which Ricardo's whole theory is based, namely, the unequal productivity of different soils. Disregarding this inequality, Bastiat, as Loria nowadays, asserts that rent is impossible while free land remains. His brilliant language hides his argumentative weakness. While not denying the tendency of population to increase, he sets off against it the constant improvement of production, and assumes that the tendency is innocuous. He thus of course denies the law of diminishing returns, a law which is at best but modified by the facts he adduces. His theory of capital is

in accord with the known tendency of the rate of interest to fall as capital increases, and is little more than a statement of this fact.

Bastiat's optimism is unrivalled in its *naïveté*, and his propositions, even if proved, by no means justify it. Granting that rent is but the payment for services rendered by the land owner "*or his forefathers*," is there no possible "injustice" in a law of unmitigated inheritance complicated by the vicissitudes of conquest, and sharp bargaining ? If capital obtained a relatively smaller share of the product as its amount increases, there still remains the tendency of capital to accumulate in few hands, and thus the relative importance of the *capitalist* may be constantly increasing. The ENTREPRENEUR is ignored by Bastiat, and still more the factor of MONOPOLY, which seems to appear on the scene as naturally as any other factor.

The wide divergence between Bastiat's theory of harmony and the facts of life under every variety of industrial *régime* suggests the fundamental fallacy of his system. It rests upon a false theory of nature. The involuntarily social activities of men are assumed to be natural ; the voluntary activities are artificial and *un*natural. Nature, thus narrowly conceived, is held to be ordained by a beneficent creator ; the artificial, simply because it is contrary to "nature," violates the divine law and natural right, and is pernicious. This was the philosophy of ROUSSEAU and the 18th century.

Henry C. CAREY (in *Harmony of Interests*, published 1849) agrees with Bastiat, if indeed he did not furnish his fundamental propositions. Unlike Bastiat, however, he appreciated the value of arguments from real life ; and while making large use of fanciful illustration, he contributed other arguments of more importance. The chief of these is his argument on rent. Ricardo assumes that men begin cultivation on the best lands, and then descend to the poorer. But Carey tries to prove from history that the opposite has been the case. The evidence adduced is worthy of consideration, though hardly conclusive. Aside from this, however, Carey seems to have overlooked the fact that the chronological order of settlement was an accident of Ricardo's formula, not its essence. When soils of unequal productivity are once in cultivation, the disparity gives rise to rent, whichever was cultivated first.

A more noteworthy result of Carey's observation was his conversion to the theory of PROTECTION. Realising that the agricultural and manufacturing interests are complementary and necessary to each other, he was impressed by the fact that the development of one in the United States, and the other in England, largely destroyed that mutual helpfulness, so great was the barrier of distance and the cost of transportation. American interests plainly required the development of both together. A study of the shifting commercial policy of the United States led him to conclude that a policy of protection was necessary for this. To the promotion of this policy he therefore devoted nearly the whole of his first book, the *Harmony of Interests*. Advocacy of state intervention thus became as pronounced with Carey as that of *laissez-faire* with Bastiat. Thus, while the two agree in rejecting the "theory of discord" of Ricardo and Malthus, and in emphasising the harmony and beneficence of the natural order, Carey freely recognises as belonging to that order forces which Bastiat had denounced as destructive of liberty and so of harmony. Under either form the theory of harmony of interests is optimistic—more so, it will seem to many, than the facts will warrant ; but, as stated by Carey, it at least stands for juster premises, broader recognition of facts, and sounder methods of inquiry, than with Bastiat. Neither writer has had disciples of note, though extensive use has of course been made of their arguments.

[In addition to Bastiat's *Harmonies économiques* and Carey's *Harmony of Interests* already mentioned, may be cited Carey's larger work, *Principles of Social Science;* also criticisms of their theories in Ingram's *History of Political Economy*, Walker's *Land and its Rent*, and especially Böhm-Bawerk's *Capital and Interest*, Smart's translation. Bernard de MANDEVILLE advances the theory that selfish interests advance the public welfare, in his *Fable of the Bees or Private Vices Publick Benefits*, published in 1714. The belief in a harmonious natural order also pervades the writings of Quesnay and the physiocrats generally, as well as those of Adam Smith and Rousseau, underlying their optimism on the one hand, and the doctrine of *laissez-faire* on the other. See also Lassalle's *Bastiat. Schulze von Delitzsch*.]

H. H. P.

HARMONIES OF INDUSTRIES. See HARMONIES OF ECONOMICS.

HARMONISTS. See COMMUNISM.

HARRINGTON, JAMES (1611-1677), an eminent political writer, was the son of Sir Sapcote Harrington of Exton, in Rutlandshire. He studied at Oxford under Chillingworth, and then spent some years on the continent. He was greatly impressed by the flourishing condition of Holland, admiring its commerce, its social developments, and its political liberty. It was here he began his studies in political economy and government ; and he was frequently heard to say that, "before he left England, he knew no more of anarchy, monarchy, aristocracy, democracy, oligarchy, or the like, than as hard words whose signification he found in his dictionary." Although a republican by conviction, Harrington was appointed in 1646 one of the personal attendants of Charles I. That unfortunate monarch delighted in his company, finding him to be very ingenious. "They had often discourses concerning government ; but when they happened to talk of a commonwealth, the King seemed not to endure it" (Wood's *Athenæ Oxonienses*). Harrington became strongly attached to the king, and accompanied him to the scaffold. His execution affected him so much that he retired to his library and his literary pursuits. But to convince his friends that his grief was personal and not political, he produced his *Oceana*. This celebrated work—half romance, half treatise—on political philosophy, was written for the purpose of setting forth the best form of government for a commonwealth. The author's elaboration of his ideal republic was something in the same style as Sir Thomas More's *Utopia*. Harrington's idea was that government should be established upon an equal agrarian basis, rising into the superstructure of three orders—the senate debating and proposing, the people resolving, and the magistracy executing by an equal rotation through the suffrage of the people. The chief political doctrines inculcated in the work are these : the real basis of power is property, especially landed property ; accordingly landed property should be distributed and held in such a way that no one person should derive from it more than a fixed amount of revenue ; the rulers of the commonwealth should be changed every three years, their successors being elected by ballot. The *Oceana* was published in 1656, and excited much controversy. England figured as Oceana, Scotland as Marpesia, Ireland as Panopæa, Henry VII. as Panurgus, Henry VIII. as Corannus, Queen Elizabeth as Partheusa, Cromwell as Megaletor, etc. The work was dedicated to Cromwell, who read it, but characteristically declared that "what he had won by the sword, he would not suffer himself to be scribbled out of."

Harrington not only endeavoured to propagate his republican opinions by writing, but with the same object formed a society of gentlemen called the Rota, who met at Miles's coffee-house, Westminster, and indulged in able and brilliant discussions concerning government and the ordering of the commonwealth. They had a ballot-box, and this being a novel form of voting in England, it attracted great attention. The society continued to meet until General Monk paved the way for the return of Charles II. After the restoration, Harrington lived more privately, but he was still regarded as a dangerous person, who maintained and propagated principles which could never be reconciled with monarchical government. He employed himself now in reducing his politics into short and easy aphorisms methodically digested, and freely communicated his views to all who visited him. While engaged in completing his system, he was arrested at the close of 1661, and committed to the Tower of London for treasonable designs and practices. He suffered a long and severe imprisonment, in the course of which he lost his reason. In his latter years he wrote severely against the Stuarts, especially condemning Charles I., whom he had once strongly admired, for his consummate and obstinate tyranny. He also wrote various essays and papers in defence of his great work. His writings were edited by Toland in 1700, and the *Oceana* was partly reprinted as recently as 1887. Harrington died of palsy at Westminster.

[Chalmers's *Biographical Dictionary.*—Toland's *Life and Works of James Harrington*, 1700.—Birch's edition, 1737.—*Oceana*, as reprinted by Henry Morley, 1887.—Bonar's *Philosophy and Pol. Econ.*, 1893.]   G. B. S.

HARRIS, JOSEPH (1702-1764), said to have begun life as a blacksmith at Talgarth, in Breconshire, his native place, was appointed assay master of the mint in 1748. Besides several works on navigation, trigonometry, optics, and astronomy, he wrote an *Essay on Money and Coins*, in two parts, published in 1757 and 1758. He introduced the first part by an enlightened statement of some leading principles of political economy, still worth reading ; he dwelt particularly on the relation of the minimum standard of subsistence to the cost of production ; and he treated the whole subject of money and of foreign exchanges with singular clearness both of view and of style. He was perfectly free from the mercantile theory of wealth, and not very far from free-trade principles. His monometallism was pronounced, and he doubted whether the existing silver standard could be exchanged for a gold standard. The second part is a vigorous demonstration of the evils which must follow any debasement of the coinage, with an historical account of the variations in the standard before his time.

[*Dict. of National Biography.*—R. Williams, *Dict. of Eminent Welshmen.*—See also references in M'Culloch, *Literature of Political Economy*, and in Jevons's article on Cantillon, *Contemp. Review*, January 1881].   F. G. P.

HARRISON, WILLIAM (1534-1593), clerk in holy orders, is a writer of economic importance through the inclusion in his *Description of England* of many valuable details as to the economic condition of Elizabethan England. Thus he acquaints us with the fact that wine was a home product at that time. In part ii. of the above work he urges that the action of the merchants in procuring the prohibition of foreign bottoms has led to a rise in prices. As this was part of the popular navigation policy, his attack on it shows considerable independence of thought.

In addition to the above work, Harrison left two MSS., one dealing with contemporary weights and measures (1587), the other a chronology.

[Ashley, *Economic History*, vol. i. pt. ii.]   E. C. K. G.

HARTE, REV. WALTER (1709-1774), a friend of Pope, travelling tutor to Lord Chesterfield's son, and vicar of St. Austell and St. Blazey in Cornwall, 1750. Besides miscellaneous essays and poems and an unsuccessful history of Gustavus Adolphus, he wrote two *Essays on Husbandry*, 1764, the first on agriculture in general, the second on the cultivation of lucerne. The former, a literary eulogy of agriculture as the basis and support of all flourishing communities, is rambling and wholly unscientific in its treatment of the subject, but enterprising and suggestive of many foreign, even American and Asiatic, plants and methods which might be introduced into England.

[Chalmers's *Biog. Dict.*; the dates in this account may be corrected by Foster's *Alumni Oxonienses*, 1715-1886.—*Dict. of National Biography.*—*Gent. Mag.* 1774.]   E. G. P.

HARTLIB, SAMUEL (fl. 1630-1660), the friend of Milton and Sir W. Petty, published or edited, sometimes with additions of his own, many valuable works on agriculture and kindred subjects. Amongst these may be mentioned, 1. *A Discourse of Husbandrie used in Brabant and Flanders*, etc. (by Sir Richard Weston), London, 1650, 4to, 2nd ed. ; corrected and enlarged, London, 4to, 1652. When the first edition was published, Hartlib did not know the name of the author. 2. *An Invention of Engines in motion*, etc. (by Cressy Dymock), London, 4to, 1651 ; Reprinted, with a biography of Dymock, in Dirck's *Memoir of Hartlib*. 3. *An Essay for the advancement of husbandry learning ; or propositions for the erecting a College of Husbandry ; and in order thereunto for the taking in of pupils or apprentices. And also friends or fellowes of the same Colledge or Society.* 4. *The Reformed Husbandman ; or a brief Treatise of the errors, defects, and inconveniences of our English Husbandry*, etc., London, 4to, 1651. 5. *Samuel Hartlib, his Legacie ; or an Enlargement of the Discourse of Husbandry used in Brabant and Flanders*, etc., London, 4to, 1651. This work consists of Hartlib's address, Sir Richard Weston's "legacy" to his sons, and "a large letter" to Hartlib (by Cressy Dymock or Robert Child). The third edition (1655) is a much larger work, and has the title *Samuel Hartlib, his Legacy of Husbandry. Wherein are bequeathed to the commonwealth of England, not only Brabant and Flanders, but also many more outlandish and domestick experiments and secrets (of Gabriel Plats and others).* 6. *A designe for Plentie, by an universall planting of Fruit-trees*, etc., London, 4to, 1652. Hartlib did not know the author of this work, which was given to a friend of his by Colonel John Barkstead. 7. *A discoverie for division or setting out of land as to the best form*, etc., 1653. This consists mainly of a letter from Cressy Dymock. 8. *The Compleat Husbandman ; or a discourse of the whole art of Husbandry, both Forraign and Domestick, etc. Unto which is added, A particular discourse of the Naturall History and Husbandry of Ireland.* Two parts, London, 4to, 1659. The second part consists of an appendix to the "Legacie," with the date 1652. 9. *An Essay upon Master W. Potter's Designe ; concerning a Bank of Lands to be erected throughout this commonwealth,* etc., London (*n. d.*) 8vo.

[For an account of Hartlib's life and other publications, see *Dictionary of National Biography.*]

W. A. S. H.

HASSIA, HENRICUS DE. See LANGENSTEIN.

HAWKINS, EDWARD (1780-1867), numismatist and antiquarian, was born at Macclesfield, and educated partly at the grammar school there, partly by private tuition. After being in the Macclesfield bank for a time, he entered into partnership with his father in a bank at Swansea, and together they managed the copper works at Neath Abbey (*Dict. Nat. Biog.*). In 1806 he was elected fellow of the Linnean, in 1821 fellow of the Royal Society, in 1826 fellow of the Society of Antiquaries, and president in 1850 of the Numismatic Society. In 1825 he acted as deputy for Taylor Combe, keeper of antiquities and coins in the British Museum ; upon his death in 1826, Hawkins was appointed to the post, which he occupied until 1861 (*Stat. and Rules of Brit. Mus.*, pp. 41, 43 ; *Medallic Illustrations*, i. vi.). From an early age he had devoted much attention to the study of coins, and amassed a very complete series of English medals, while his collection of English political caricatures was the finest known. Both collections were purchased by the trustees of the British Museum—the medals in 1860, and the prints in 1868 (*Medallic Illustr.*, i. vi.).

Hawkins's most important contributions to numismatic literature, in addition to valuable papers published in the *Transactions* of the Numismatic Society and the Society of Antiquaries, are (1) *The Silver Coins of England* (1841). This, with necessary alterations and additions, has since been edited by his grandson, R. D. Kenyon (1876, 1887), and remains the standard work on the subject. (2) He also collected materials for a work on medals. It was intended to issue this as a Museum publication, but when the portion completed to the close of the reign of William III., was printed and submitted to the trustees in 1852, they declined to pass it, in consequence of the expression of certain political opinions which they considered undesirable in a government publication (*Hansard*, 3rd July 1854 ; *Medall. Illustr.*, i. vi.). After some years the historical notes were, with Hawkins's sanction, revised by his successor, W. S. Vaux, and by Sir A. W. Franks. Further matter, which resulted from inspection of various foreign collections unvisited by Hawkins, led to certain modifications of opinion, and to the addition of many fresh illustrations. The work,

brought down to the death of George II., was eventually edited by Sir A. W. Franks (now keeper of Brit. and Med. Antiquities) ; and by H. A. Grueber (now assistant keeper of coins and medals), as a Museum publication in 1885, under the title of *Medallic Illustrations of the History of Great Britain and Ireland.* (3) *Description of Anglo-Gallic Coins in Brit. Mus.*, begun by Taylor Combe, was completed by Hawkins (1826). In addition to these, Hawkins completed Combe's work in *Description of Ancient Marbles in Brit. Mus.*, v. (1826), and edited parts vii., x. (1839, 1842, 1845). His many valuable memoranda on his collection of prints were purchased by the Museum, and incorporated, after revision, in the *Catalogue of Prints and Drawings in Brit. Mus.*, iii. pt. i. prepared by F. G. Stephens (1877). For the Chetham Society, Hawkins edited *Sir W. Brereton's Travels* (1844), and *The Holy Lyfe and History of Seynt Werburge* (1848).

[See Ward, T. H., *Men of the Reign*, 1885.—*Proc. of Antiq. Soc.*, 23rd April 1868.—*Numismatic Chronicle*, N.S., vii. (1867).—*Athenæum*, 15th June 1867.—Introductions to the various works already mentioned.]

E. A. M.

HAWKINS, SIR JOHN (1719-89). The son of a carpenter, who was afterwards a surveyor, Hawkins was originally brought up to his father's trade, but abandoned it in favour of the law, and became an attorney. He married a Miss Storer, who brought him a large dowry which enabled him to retire from business ; and he became chairman of the Middlesex justices. He was knighted in 1772, in recognition of his services in suppressing the election riots at Brentford in 1768, and the Moorfield riots in 1769. His experience of the bad condition of the roads led him to publish his *Observations on the State of the Highways, and on the Laws for amending them and keeping them in Repair* (Lond., 1763), subjoining to them the draft of a bill consolidating former acts for the maintenance of the highways. The act based on this was so skilfully drawn that for many years it did not require amendment. The treatise takes up the history of various acts of parliament on this head, and shows how they had fallen into disuse, with some remarks on the practical difficulty of legally enforcing the acts in many cases. Hawkins's observations do not apply to turnpike roads, which were in good condition. He also expatiates on the fact that the rich paid proportionately far less than the poor towards the maintenance of the highways. Hawkins had given much attention to music, and also published a *Life and Works of Dr. Johnson* (Lond., 1787), with whom he had been intimate. Boswell, in his *Life of Johnson*, is consistently unjust to Hawkins, who, however, appears to have been a somewhat coarse man. He was buried in Westminster Abbey.

[Chalmers, *Biographical Dictionary* (from information supplied by the family), Lond., 1812-1817.—Boswell, *Life of Johnson*, edited by J. W.

Croker, Lond., 1848.—Sir G. Grove, *Dictionary of Music*, Lond., 1879-88.]　R. H. H.

HAYES, John L, (1813-1887), born in Maine; died in Cambridge, Mass. For the last twenty-five years of his life he was actively identified with the tariff discussions in the United States, particularly defending protective duties in favour of the woollen interests. In 1865 he became secretary of the National Association of Wool Manufacturers, and edited their quarterly publication. He was president of the tariff commission of 1882, and was largely responsible for the report of that body. His writings were voluminous, and for the most part may be found in the several volumes of the *Bulletin* referred to, which is exceedingly valuable as reflecting the protectionist sentiment of the period.

Among his pamphlets may be mentioned *The Fleece and the Loom*, 1866.— *Wools of the United States*, 1872.—*Sheep Industry in the South*, 1878. —*The Farmers' Question*, 1880 ; and various writings on Reciprocity. See " Memoir" by G. B. Stebbins in *Bulletin of Wool Manufacturers*, vol. xviii. p. 97.　D. R. D.

HAYNE, Samuel (fl. 1660-1697), surveyor of customs, was born probably in Devonshire in 1645. For seven years he was clerk assistant to Joseph Ash, collector of the customs of Plymouth and Cornwall. He then became an "adventurer at sea" ; during the Dutch war of 1672, was employed in the prize office and the admiralty ; engaged afterwards in the trade with France ; and in 1680 was appointed riding surveyor of the customs and surveyor for the Navigation Act in Devon and Cornwall.

Hayne published : 1. *An abstract of all the statutes made concerning aliens trading in England. . . . Also, of all the laws made for securing our plantation trade to ourselves, with observations thereon, proving that the Jews (in their practical way of trade at this time) break them all, to the great damage of the king in his customs, etc. . . . Together with the hardships and difficulties the author hath already met with, in his endeavouring to find out and detect the ways and methods they take to effect it*, London, 4to, 1685.　2. *The manifesto of near one hundred and fifty Knights, . . . Merchants and citizens of London, against the Jews now in England. . . .*, London, 1697, fol.　w. a. s. h.

HAYNES, Christopher (fl. 1713), merchant, was apparently engaged in the trade with Spain. During the controversy on the 8th and 9th clauses of the treaty of Utrecht (1713) he contributed " many useful pieces" on that subject to the *British Merchant* (see King, Charles).　w. a. s. h.

HAYNES, John (fl. 1706-1715), wool factor, published : 1. *A view of the present state of the clothing trade in England, with remarks on the causes of . . . its decay, and a scheme of proper remedies for the recovery of it*, etc., London, 1706, 8vo.　2. *Great Britain's glory, or an account of the great number of poor*

employed in the woollen and silk manufacturies ; . . . with the reasons of the decay of these trades, etc., London, 1715, 8vo. (The latter is little more than a new edition of the former ; it is apparently cited by M'Culloch (*Literature of Political Economy*, p. 237), as *Provision for the Poor.*) 3. *Proposals for the more effectual preventing the exportation of wool (n. d.).* He proposed the prohibition of water-carriage of wool, the registration of all wool produced in the country, prosecutions for infringement of the statutes dealing with the wool trade by special commissions appointed for that purpose, and other measures which he thought would prevent the exportation of wool. He is probably identical with the " John Haines" who addressed a memorial to the government in 1702, asking to be appointed " general supervisor " in Hampshire and Dorset for the prevention of the exportation of wool. His request was refused on the ground that the commissioners of customs could not advise the appointment of such an officer, or recommend a person " who had received the censure of the House of Commons on his knees."

[*Treasury Papers*, lxxxii. 26.]　w. a. s. h.

HAXTHAUSEN, August Franz, Freiherr von (1792-1866), was born at Bökendorf in Westphalia. From 1808 to 1813 he studied at the school of mining at Clausthal. He served for some time as a volunteer in the Hanoverian army, and then went to the university of Göttingen to study law. He was there associated with a circle interested in art and poetry, from which proceeded a periodical to which Arnim, Brentano, and the brothers Grimm were contributors ; and occupied himself much in the collection of German popular songs and sagas. In 1819 he returned to his native place, and devoted himself during several years to an earnest study of the agrarian condition of North Germany. He published, in 1829, the results of his researches in relation to the principalities of Paderborn and Corvey. This work attracted the notice of the then crown prince, afterwards King Frederick William IV. ; the author was invited to Berlin, and was entrusted with the mission of examining in the respective localities the agrarian systems of the several Prussian provinces, and communicating the results of his inquiries to the ministry. To give him the necessary influence with the provincial officials, he was made a privy councillor. He travelled for nine years through the Prussian dominions, and collected ample materials for the great work which was projected. He published, however, only one volume, which dealt with the provinces of East and West Prussia (1839). A second volume, relating to Pomerania, was published twenty-two years later by A. Padberg (1861) ; this branch of the subject had been partially handled by Haxthausen in a brief treatise on the formerly Slavic districts of

Germany (1842). An article of his in a German periodical on the Russian ukase of 1842 regulating the contracts between the landlords and peasants in that country, attracted much attention; it was reprinted by the *Allgemeine Zeitung*, the *Débats*, and the *Times*, who all interpreted the signature A. v. H. as being that of Alexander von Humboldt. This article led to Haxthausen's appointment by the Emperor Nicholas to conduct investigations in his dominions similar to those on which he had been employed in Prussia. He travelled extensively in Russia during 1843-44, the king of Prussia continuing his salary during his absence, and so making him independent of the Russian authorities. The fruit of his inquiries appeared in the following publications: —*Studien über die inneren Zustände, das Volksleben, und insbesondere die ländlichen Einrichtungen Russlands* (3 vols. 1847-1852), also published in French with the title *Études sur la situation intérieure, la vie nationale, et les institutions de la Russie* (1848-1853). An English translation by Robert Faris was published in 1856, with the title of *The Russian Empire—Transcaucasia:* this was an account of the family and communal life, and social condition of certain populations between the Black and Caspian Seas (1856); an English translation, by John Edward Taylor, appeared in 1854, before the German original was published. There appeared besides in English, by the same translator, as a kind of supplement to the foregoing, *The Tribes of the Caucasus, with an account of Schamyl and the Murids* (1855). We have also from Haxthausen's pen the following: *De l'abolition par voie législative du partage égal et temporaire des terres dans les communes russes* (1858); and *Die ländliche Verfassung Russlands, ihre Entwickelung und Feststellung in der Gesetzgebung von 1861* (1866). Haxthausen was a member of the United Diet in 1847, and also for a short time a member of the first Prussian chamber. The practical objects which Haxthausen had in view in his treatment of the agrarian condition of North Germany, were the liberation of the soil from the power of capital, and the reform of the constitution of the provincial estates (*Ständische Verfassung*). Roscher regards him as one of the best of the group of conservative writers who at this period treated German economical questions, and who, both as owners of landed property and as state functionaries, understood many things better than the abstract liberal economists. He considers him, in particular, to have thrown new light on the question of the village communities of the middle ages. The same eminent critic speaks highly of his power of accurate observation, as evidenced by his Russian investigations; but remarks that he shows the usual "pseudo-historical" weakness

of reactionaries in recommending the maintenance by the Russians of their *Feldgemeinschaft*, even after the abolition of serfdom, thus confounding the transitory peculiarity of a particular stage of culture with a permanent trait of the national character.

[Lippert in the *Handwörterbuch der Staatswissenschaften*, edited by Conrad and others (vol. iv. 1892).—Reifferscheid in the *Allgemeine Deutsche Biographie* (vol. xi. 1880).—Roscher, *Geschichte der N. O.*, p. 1027.]   J. K. I.

HEARN, WILLIAM EDWARD (1826-1888), born in the county of Cavan, and educated at Trinity College, Dublin, was, after having been professor of Greek at Queen's College, Galway, from 1849 to 1854, appointed in the latter year professor of political economy and other subjects at the university of Melbourne. Later he became a member of the legislative council of Victoria, and took an active part in the affairs of the colony up to his death.

Hearn's principal contribution to economics, the happily-named *Plutology* (1st ed. 1864, 2nd, 1878), is a model of the style which may be called classical. Like Hermann or Ricardo, Hearn holds an intermediate course between the highest abstractions and mere information; neither soaring to mathematical analysis, nor creeping among historical details. As one among many specimens of this method, the chapter on exchange (*Plutology*, ch. xiv.) may be referred to, presenting as it does all the relations of price to utility and cost of production, except those which can hardly be expressed without mathematics. So the chapter on the circumstances which determine the extent of capital may seem to fall short of perfection only by the want of a more quantitatively exact analysis of the influence of DISTANCE IN TIME (*q.v.*) on value. It is justly said by Prof. Marshall: "Hearn's *Plutology* . . . is at once simple and profound: it affords an admirable example of the way in which detailed analysis may be applied to afford a training of a very high order for the young, and to give them an intelligent acquaintance with the economic conditions of life, without forcing upon them any particular solution of those more difficult problems on which they are not yet able to form an independent judgment." Among other high testimonies to the excellence of this work may be cited Jevons's reference, in the "Concluding remarks" of his *Theory*, to "Professor Hearn's views." Hearn wrote several other works, cited below, relating to social science, and was also a frequent contributor to the local press of Melbourne.

The Cassell Prize Essay on the Condition of Ireland, 1851 [In three chapters: (1) investigates the causes of the existing evils; (2) estimates the industrial resources of Ireland; (3) proposes remedies for such distress,—mostly simple legal reforms.]

The Aryan Household, its Structure and its Development: an Introduction to Comparative Jurisprudence, 1879. — The Government of England, its Structure and its Development, 1887.

F. Y. E.

HEARTH-MONEY OR HEARTH-TAX. The earliest such tax in England, "a fumage, or tax of smoke farthings," was levied in Anglo-Saxon times, probably as a customary payment to the king from all hearths but those of the poor.

In 1662 a tax of 2s. was levied on every hearth or stone in all dwelling-houses, except those of the poor who were exempt from church-rate and poor-rate, or fulfilled certain other conditions. In 1689, though the tax produced £170,000 a year, it was repealed on account of its unpopularity : it reached a poorer class than the old subsidies which it had superseded ; it was farmed ; and the inquisitorial visits of the inspectors, or "chimneymen," were deeply resented (see HALIFAX, EARL OF).

[Dowell's Hist. of Taxation and Taxes in England, vols. i., ii., iii.]   E. G. P.

HEATHFIELD, RICHARD (c. 1775-1859), accountant. He proposed a tax of 15 per cent on all property, to pay off the national debt, and endeavoured to explain the advantages which would accrue from this proceeding. The same expedient had been suggested by A. HUTCHESON in 1717, when the debt was only some £50,000,000. The suggestion derives its chief importance from having had the approval of RICARDO, and from having been proposed in parliament by General Palmer in 1832. Heathfield also wrote other tracts embodying the same proposals.

Elements of a Plan for the Liquidation of the Public Debt of the United Kingdom (Lond., 1819), and Further Observations on the Practicability and Expediency of liquidating the Public Debt of the United Kingdom, including some Considerations on Population and the Poor (Lond., 1820).

R. H. H.

HEDGMINT. A word used by Malynes, the existence of which sets before us the frequent manufacture of false money by persons in authority (see POLLARDS and CROKARDS). "If any Hedgmint (for so doe the States of the Vnited Provinces of the Netherlands call the Mints of pettie Lords, which by falsified standards do imitate to coyne the money of other Princes)" . . .

[Malynes, Lex Mercatoria, 1622, p. 489.]

HEDONISM. This term, derived from the Greek hédoné (ἡδονή) = pleasure, is used to describe that philosophy which makes the attainment of pleasure and the avoidance of pain the supreme end of action, —in other words, defines virtue to be that course of conduct which produces the largest sum of happiness. Hedonism is thus the same as epicureanism in the proper sense of that term. Utilitarianism is hedonism modified by the substitution of the

happiness of mankind for the happiness of the individual as the aim of virtuous conduct. Political economy has no necessary connection with either the selfish or the unselfish form of hedonism. Since, however, the one or the other has been very widely accepted in the 18th and 19th centuries, it is natural that many eminent economists should have been hedonists in their moral theories. See MORALITY, SYSTEMS OF, IN RELATION TO POLITICAL ECONOMY and the writers there referred to.   F. C. M.

HEEREN, ARNOLD HERMANN LUDWIG (1760-1842), studied in the university of Göttingen, where he became in 1787 professor of philosophy, and in 1801, of history. As an author, he remained several years uncertain whether to devote himself to philosophy or history ; his first publications were editions of the De Encomiis of the rhetorician Menander, and the Eclogae physicae et ethicae of Stobæus. His most important contributions to historical studies have been collected in his Historische Werke (15 vols. Göttingen, 1821-26), among which ought to be mentioned here vol. vii., Handbuch der Geschichte des Alterthums mit besonderer Rücksicht auf Verfassungen, Handel und Colonien, and vols. viii. and ix. ; Handbuch der Geschichte des Europäischen Stäatensystems und seiner Colonien. But the work which from the moment of its appearance conferred celebrity on his name (vols. x. to xv. of the Historische Werke), and which has been translated into most European languages after having been recast in successive editions, is the Ideen über die Politik, Verkehr und Handel der vornehmsten Völker der alten Welt.

Heeren himself explains his object in the Preface (Vorrede) : "I write neither a history of ancient nations, nor a general history of political systems and trade. . . . My plan is limited, excepting preliminary general views, to isolated pictures of various nations (p. iv. 2nd ed. 1805). I have no hypothesis to found, no favourite tenets to demonstrate, no opponent to overthrow. . . . I state what I have found as I found it ; what is certain as certain ; what is probable as simply probable " (p. vi.).

Heeren may be considered as one of the earliest opponents to what has been called Manchesterthum in Germany. He writes in his chapter Ueber Griechische Staatswirthschaft : "Perhaps the Greeks were not fully aware of the importance of the division of labour, but they were free from the modern school philosophy which would gladly transform nations into mere wealth-producing herds. They felt, of course, that to live, man musť produce ; still it never struck them that man only lives to produce (vol. iii. p. 272). . . . Every high and divine feeling must be trampled down before there is room for such theories as degrade Socrates and Christ to the unproductive (stérile) class (p. 274). . . . It is possible to live happily in Otaheit without regard to the system of Adam Smith" (p. 322).

Nevertheless he had accepted some of the teaching of the new school, especially respecting mercantilism: "Their aim (the Greeks') was not to keep the stock of minted coins inviolate, or to increase it; nothing was heard about the balance of trade, and the resulting high-handed (*gewaltsame*) regulations. They paid taxes, but without the modern object of directing industrial activity by means of the exclusion of this or that class of goods. The export of raw material was not prohibited, manufactures were not favoured at the expense of agriculture. In this sense, industry, commerce, and trade were free" (p. 283).

Heeren's history is perhaps deficient from the standpoint of modern minute criticism of texts, but its fluent and elegant style, its clear statement of facts, and judicial honesty in controversy, account for its former popularity. It has been translated into most European languages (into French in 1830-34, 6 vols. 8vo, and into English: *Historical Researches into the Politics, Intercourse, and Trade of the Principal Nations of Antiquity*, 3 vols. 8vo, Oxford, 1833). [See Notice in M'Culloch's *Literature of Pol. Econ.*, 1845, p. 151.] E. Ca.

HEGEL, G. W. F. (1770-1831), was educated at the Stuttgart gymnasium and Tübingen university. After some years' private tutorship in Switzerland and Frankfurt, and studious leisure in Jena, he became professor in Jena, 1805; for eight years rector of Nürnberg gymnasium, 1808-1816; professor at Heidelberg, 1816; and then at Berlin, 1818, where he remained till his death.

Hegel's leading characteristics are (*a*) his notion of development, and (*b*) his bold and thorough application of it to every phase of life and being. Development is to him a progress through conflict of opposites. Like Heraclitus, he finds that change is the essence of things; and his resemblance to the philosopher of Ephesus is undoubted, however fallacious it may be to find, with Lassalle, an almost complete Hegelian system in the sayings of the ancient philosopher. He finds that not only in our thoughts but in the nature of things, there is a constant process from one extreme to another, and then to a reconciling third, which in its turn becomes an extreme, and finds its own opposite, to be conquered by it and then to lie down with it within the fold of a new third reconciler, the fate of which is in due course the same. But the change is not simply flux and destruction; it is true development. Each third stage is more concrete than the last; each third stage contains in it all that has gone before. Hegel finds this notion most clearly realised in life, and especially in the most concrete forms of human life. Instead of treating law and morality as separate and

separable, he finds these notions to be abstract and false when separated, and to be true and concrete only when viewed together in the family, civil society, and state. Civil society, more particularly, is the domain of what the older economists called "natural liberty," where there is pursuit of private gain obeying laws of which the private persons are unconscious. So far Hegel vindicates to political economy its claim to a realm of its own, civil society. But the limits of it at once appear. Civil society, as it itself grew out of the family, must itself pass into the state, where there is a conscious union of regard for rights with regard for duties, and the public good is deliberately sought. The development of civil society into the state, a development which, in Hegel as in Aristotle, is to be taken logically, not historically, takes place through associations, commercial, professional, and otherwise. Finally the state itself is not an ultimate end; states are individual members of larger groups, and all groups are members of the one humanity. The progress of the human race from generation to generation and age to age is the subject of the philosophy of history; and there is the same relentless process there as in the case of the single society. As Dr. Weryho well expresses it, *mors immortalis* is taken for the law of life.

This idea of development, as a *mors immortalis*, was retained by the Hegelians MARX, Engels, and LASSALLE, when they created the new German socialism. They retained little else, for it became an axiom with them that all that is, is material; and spirit, that was to Hegel not only the roof and crown of things but the very essence of all things, was disowned altogether.

Their materialistic view of history marks a further alteration. Not only is there, to them, no spirit in Hegel's sense; but there is no progress except by changes in economic facts. The state of human societies as regards wealth—and especially the means and modes of producing wealth—is held to determine their condition in respect of all other features, hitherto supposed to be independent. Law, religion, and political institutions are thus supposed to be due to economical causes. This view, recently expounded by Professor Loria with even fewer reservations than by the Germans, would need a separate discussion. It receives no support from Hegel, and cannot be traced to his influence.

Hegel's influence, in fact, on political economy has been much less profound and direct than on philosophy. In no part of his voluminous writings does he give much space to economic discussion; and the keen interest shown by his contemporary Fichte in the condition of the people is absent in Hegel. Yet he deserves mention in the history of political economy, for it was a group of his disciples that first fairly planted the philosophical idea of development in the soil of economics. The Young Hegelians, Marx, Engels, Ruge, taught at Paris, in the *Deutsch-Französische Jahrbücher* (1844), a revolutionary socialism founded on a notion of development derived from Hegel's, though confessedly unlike its parent in many important particulars. Proudhon's attempt to apply Hegelian formulas more literally, in the same direction, was not so skilful, as the controversy between Proudhon and Marx (1846-47) brought out very clearly. No doubt the connection between Hegel's principles and the application of them by this group of his followers did not become closer ; German socialism soon became more economic than philosophical. But the attraction possessed by such a book as Hegel's *Philosophy of Right* for such men as Engels and Marx is a significant fact both for philosophers and economists. (See also LASSALLE, MARX, PROUDHON, RUGE).

Hegel's Works were edited by Marheineke, Schulze, Gans, Hotho, Michelet, Förster, Rosenkranz in 18 vols. (1832-40), to which is to be added a 19th vol. (1887), edited by his son Karl Hegel, and containing his correspondence. [His Life by Rosenkranz was published in 1844. The *Philosophy of Right* is vol. 8 of Works. A summary is given in Bonar's *Philosophy and Political Economy* (1893), bk. iv., ch. iv., "Hegel." Another account, professedly from unpublished MSS. of Hegel, is given by Dr. Georg Mollat, *System der Sittlichkeit von Hegel* (Osterwieck), 1893, and Dr. Mollat has also published Hegel's *Essay on the German Constitution* (1893). For the relation of Marx to Hegel see Bonar *loc. cit.*, and also Barth's *Geschichtsphilosophie Hegels* (Leipzig, 1890), and L. Weryho's *Marx als Philosoph* (Bern and Leipzig, 1894). For the relation of Lassalle to Hegel, see especially Lassalle's *Die Philosophie Heracleitos des Dunkeln*, etc. (1858), and his *Erworbene Rechte* (1861).] J. B.

HEIR. In popular language this expression is generally used for any one who inherits, sometimes also, more especially in the plural form, in the sense of next of kin. The etymological equivalents of the word in the continental languages (*héritier, erede, Erbe*, etc.) are generally used in the sense of the Latin word "*heres*," which designated a person who by reason of his parentage or of a testamentary appointment became the universal successor of a deceased person, and whilst taking over all the predecessor's property, was personally liable for his debts and legacies (unless he had taken advantage of the BENEFICIUM INVENTARII) (*q.v.*). In English technical language the word "heir-at-law" is used for the person to whom freehold property descends in case of INTESTACY (*q.v.*) ; in the case of copyhold property the designation is "customary heir." The words "and his heirs," when added to the name of a

person to whom land is conveyed in fee simple, indicate that he is to take an "estate of inheritance" and not a mere life estate, but they do not in any way prevent him from dealing with the property to the exclusion of his heir-at-law ; the words "and the heirs *of his body*," on the other hand, indicate an estate tail (see ENTAIL).

E. S.

HEIRLOOMS. In the correct use of the term heirlooms are those chattels which by the custom of particular places are attached to an estate of inheritance in land. They are not devisable by will but always descend with the estate. The term is, however, often used to denote chattels that are annexed to an estate of inheritance by the common law or by the terms of a will or settlement.

[Goodeve on *Real Property*, London, 1891.]
J. E. C. M.

HELD, ADOLF VON (1844-1880), a distinguished economist, was born at Würzburg, where his father, Dr. Joseph von Held, was professor of jurisprudence. He pursued the study of political science at his native place, at Munich, and at Berlin. In 1872 he was appointed professor at Bonn, and in 1880 at Berlin ; and in the same year his career, which had so far been one of brilliant promise, was cut short by his death from accidental drowning in the lake of Thun. He had been secretary, and an active member, of the *Verein für Sozialpolitik*. His first publication was *Carey's Socialwissenschaft und das Mercantilsystem*, 1866. Roscher praises his article on Adam Smith in Hildebrand's *Jahrb.*, 1867, as containing one of the most unprejudiced and altogether excellent appreciations of the great Scotchman anywhere produced.

The principal writings of Held were *Die Einkommensteuer*, 1872.—*Die deutsche Arbeiterpresse der Gegenwart*, 1873.—*Sozialismus, Sozialdemokratie und Sozialpolitik*, 1877 (which may be described as a manifesto of the principles and policy of the *Kathedersozialisten*) ; and *Grundriss für Vorlesungen über National-Oekonomie* (2nd edit. 1878). —He left behind him in MS. *Zwei Bücher zur socialen Geschichte Englands*, a portion of a great work, for which he had prepared himself by studies in London during June, July, and August 1875. This highly interesting fragment was edited in 1881 by G. F. Knapp.

[Roscher, *Gesch. der N.O.*, p. 1045.—Lippert in the *Handw. der Staatswissenschaften*.] J. K. I.

Held, though one of the earliest supporters of the *Verein für Sozialpolitik*, founded 1872, and himself a moderate state-socialist, could not refrain from a gibe at "socialists of the chair." Their very name, he said, implied that to become like Bebel and Liebknecht they only wanted courage (see the account of the *Verein* by Prof. Philippovich, *Quart. Journ. of Econ.*, January 1891, p. 228). His *Sociale Geschichte Englands* was certainly one of the causes of the revival in England itself of the study of the history of English industry and the study of the surroundings in which the classical economists produced their works. The first part, containing the industrial and literary history of the fifty-six years from the *Wealth of Nations* to the Reform Bill is of more permanent value than the second which treats of the earlier history of English industry and the growth of modern manufacture. But even in the latter he calls attention to many sources of evidence, especially blue-books, on the condition of the labouring classes, that had been too long neglected by our own countrymen.

In his estimates of writers, statesmen, and popular leaders he is sometimes misled by his bias against Classical Economics, but he has an evident desire to be truthful, and we have always to remember that his book appeared without his final revision.

His theoretical principles were stated in two papers especially. First in his *Rede über die Sociale Frage, gehalten auf der freien kirchlichen Versammlung evangelischer Männer in der Garnisons-Kirche zu Berlin 12ten Oktober 1871* (reprinted, Wiegand, Berlin, 1872). He rejects the abstract method of the classical economists, their undue emphasis on self-interest, their negative view of the state as a mere policeman, their way of opposing self-help and state-help. He admits that we have learned from the socialists to pay due attention to the distribution of wealth. He approves of progressive taxation and interference with the right of bequest.

In his second paper *Ueber den gegenwärtigen Principienstreit in der Nationalökonomie, Preuss. Jahrb., Juli 1872,* he addresses not a popular but a learned audience. He goes a little way into economic history, but deals chiefly with questions of the day. We have, he says, to deal with a new phenomenon—the rise of a school of *Kathedersozialisten* in opposition to *Manchesterthum,* in that very year 1872. Individualism pure and simple has, Held says, no answer to Marx ; and *Kathedersozialismus* is the only safeguard against the "red spectre."

It may be remarked that in this paper as elsewhere Held regards MARX as the teacher and LASSALLE as only the pupil.   J. B.

HELFERICH, JOHANNES A RENATUS VON (1818-1892), was a pupil of F. B. HERMANN, whom he succeeded in the chair of political economy at Munich. Helferich shares with D. G. Mayr the honour of having re-edited Hermann's *Staatswirthschaftliche Untersuchungen.* Helferich was for some forty years one of the editors of the *Tübinger Zeitschrift,* to which from time to time he contributed articles on a variety of subjects ; such as the "Unity of German Currency" (1850), "Sugar-duties" (1852), "The Austrian paper currency" (1855-67), "Éloge of Hermann" (1878). Helferich's principal work on the *Periodic Oscillations of the Precious Metals since the discovery of America to the year 1830* is remarkable on account of its polemic against the Quantity Theory of currency, which the author regards as "*durchaus unrichtig.*" The quantity is but one among the circumstances of supply and demand which govern the value of gold. This value, when once established, is preserved by a certain *vis inertiæ* (p. 38). "The price of goods is dependent on their own value-determination" (*von der eigenen Werthbestimmung abhängig*). The price of goods determines rather than is determined by the quantity of gold (a *sub finem* statement which may perhaps be compared with that made by Mr. Giffen in the *Nineteenth Century* for Nov. 1889). True to his principles, Helferich regards the rise in prices in the period from the discovery of America to 1550 as in the main not due to the influx of gold. He has to admit, indeed, that at a subsequent period quantity is a dominant factor. He made a good use of the historical material available when he wrote. His remarks on the method of measuring the value of money may be read with advantage (see MONEY).

Von den periodischen Schwankungen im Werth der edeln Metalle, von der Entdeckung Amerikas bis zum Jahr 1830. Nürnberg, 1843.—*Zeitschrift für die gesammte Staatswissenschaft,* Tübingen, *passim.* Articles on Taxation, and 'Forstwirthschaft' in Schönberg's *Handbuch.*   F. Y. E.

HELLER. By the provisions of a law passed in August 1892, a gold crown of a hundred hellers has been adopted as the standard of value for Austria-Hungary. This crown, which is money of account, being equal to ·0417 of a pound sterling (or ten pence), the heller is of the value of one tenth of a penny. The coin bearing the name heller is a bronze piece weighing 1·6 grammes. There is also a 2-heller piece in bronze, and 10 and 20 heller pieces made of pure nickel.

Formerly in South Germany four hellers were equal to a kreutzer, and 60 kreutzers to a gulden.
                                                    F. E. A.

HELVETIUS (1715-1771), the son of the first physician of the queen of France ; owed to this high protection the post of farmer-general at the early age of twenty-three. He resigned in 1751, and devoted himself to literary pursuits ; his house had always been a centre of the polite and philosophic society of the time. His principal books are the treatises *De l'Esprit* (1758) and *De l'Homme, de ses facultés intellectuelles et de son éducation* (1776), which was published after his death, and in which he endeavoured to explain the parts of his first book which, after a previous period of brilliant popularity, had given offence in the philosophic circles of Paris.

The main position of Helvetius may be summed up as follows : man is a purely sentient animal only differing from other animals by a higher degree of physical sentiency.[1] Human

---

[1] For the use of this word see Herbert Spencer. "Once more let me emphasise the truth that since a society in its corporate capacity is not *sentient,* and since the sentiency dwells exclusively in its units, the sole reason for subordinating the sentient lives of its units to the unsentient life of the society, is that, etc." (Herbert Spencer, *Justice,* ch. xxix. § 187, ch. entitled, "The Limits of State Duties Concluded").

passions are nothing else but the various modes of manifestation of this physical sentiency, which is the only motor of human actions ; pleasure or pain are their unavoidable results : to pursue the former and to evade the latter is to conform to the only natural law. "He is a virtuous man whose strongest passion is so connected with the general good that for him virtue is in almost every case a matter of necessity." Hence our passions must be, not constrained, but educated : education and consequently legislation are all-powerful, since all men are born with the same physical constitution. To previous bad education and legislation are due the prevailing vices and excessive inequality in the distribution of wealth. Helvetius is thus in some respects a forerunner of modern utilitarianism and hedonism. "This man," Madame du Deffand used to say, "has told everybody's secret."

[See reference to Helvetius in Dugald Stewart, *Lectures on Pol. Econ.*, ed. 1856, vol. ii. p. 390 ; and in Rae, *Life of Adam Smith*, p. 200.]

E. Ca.

HENLEY, WALTER OF (c. 1200 - 1250). The only internal evidence which the treatise of *Husbandry* affords regarding its author is the incidental statement that he had served the office of bailiff. The title of a Cambridge MS. (Univ. Lib. Dd., vii. 6) gives the additional information that he was a knight and subsequently became a Dominican. It appears probable that he flourished in the time of Henry III., and wrote the interesting tract on estate management and the practice of farming which bears his name. It was the best known of several treatises on this subject which were written in England at this time, in Norman French : they are a remarkable group, more especially as there does not seem to be any corresponding literature of the kind at this date in other parts of Christendom. Transcribers were sometimes guilty of making curious confusions among, and rearrangements of these books, but they have been separated out, and translated by Miss Lamond, as Walter of Henley's *Husbandry*, *Seneschaucie*, an anonymous *Husbandry*, and Grosseteste's *Rules*. Walter of Henley's treatise survives in a large number of MSS.,—besides the twenty - one examples enumerated in the Introduction to Royal Historical Society edition, there is a copy in Corpus Christi Library at Cambridge. The book was evidently much used as a handbook, and it was found in many monastic libraries. Several copies of it were made at Christ Church, Canterbury, and one, of a somewhat different text, at St. Augustine's. It held its own as the standard treatise on agriculture till the 16th century, when it was superseded by the work of Sir A. FITZHERBERT, who treated similar topics, but — despite the commonly expressed opinion to the contrary — in all

probability independently. The treatise renders many points of mediæval agriculture clear, *e.g.* the relative expense of cultivation on the THREE FIELD and TWO FIELD system ; the practical hints which it gives, are a great assistance to any one who is anxious to get a clear understanding of the tillage of former days. w. c.

HENRY OF GHENT. See GHENT, HENRY OF.

HERBERT, CLAUDE-JACQUES (1700-1758), farmer-general of the royal mail coaches, mentioned by Adam Smith as a "very faithful, diligent, and laborious collector" of the prices of corn, has sometimes been credited as being the first in date of the advocates of free trade in corn in France. He himself lays no claim to such priority, and in his anonymous *Essai sur la police des grains* (London 1754, Berlin 1755, the London edition is incomplete), he expressly states that the same views had been entertained so far back as 1695 by Boisguillebert in his *Détail de la France*, and, closer to his own time, in 1748 in a *Mémoire sur les Bleds* (*vide* DUPIN). Herbert belongs to the physiocratic school ("All the goods we possess flow from the cultivation of land," p. 2, Berlin edition). His main argument is that free trade in corn will develop the growing of corn. "It is not the obstinate storing of our corn, but its successive and annual production which will feed us. . . . Cultivation is the inexhaustible stock of our supply" (pp. 104 and 105). He rejects, as leading to jobbery, the system of "permissions to export and the erection of store-houses, either by government or by companies." Opposed to import duties, he admits a sort of sliding scale of export duties, which will be "a sufficient counterpoise to keep corn within the kingdom in case of need" (p. 192).

Barbier (*Dict. des Anonymes*) ascribes also to Herbert the authorship of a pamphlet of sixty pages, *Observations sur la Liberté du Commerce des Grains*, which was published the year after his death. The internal evidence renders this rather doubtful. E. Ca.

HEREDITAMENT. An expression used in legal documents for any real property whether consisting of land, buildings, or rights attaching to land (*e.g.* advowsons, rights of common, etc.) The latter are called "incorporeal" hereditaments. E. S.

HEREDITAS, the entire property of a deceased person, to which his universal successor or *heres* succeeded, whether under a will or *ab intestato*. The *heres*, as successor to the deceased, was liable for his debts. E. A. W.

HEREDITY. The persistence of the same character through many generations of a family or a people is a fact often observed and of the utmost importance for economics. The persistence of a peculiar artistic faculty has preserved to some cities, *e.g.* to Lyons, the supremacy in certain manufactures, which, so far as external conditions are concerned, might have flourished equally well in many other places. The persistence of financial skill has made the Jews everywhere the bankers of hostile races and creeds. Persistent energy has made Holland and Lancashire rich; persistent idleness has made Naples and Andalusia poor. The principal causes of this permanence of character are not hard to find. They appear to be four—blood, education, civilisation, and natural environment. As to the first, only physical science can attempt to determine the extent to which physical peculiarities—above all, peculiarities of the brain and the nervous system, are transmitted from one generation to another. Even now there is no agreement among experts as to the mode or extent of such transmission. That it does take place somehow or other few men of common sense will doubt. But it is not only in giving the child a certain physical constitution that the parents' influence on its character and intelligence are so momentous. Education in that larger sense which includes the modelling of feelings, habits, and occupations has always been, and must continue to be, for the most part the work of the father and mother. Although the formal division of castes is unknown in Europe, most occupations are to a great extent hereditary. The child imitates the parent. The parent finds it easier to train his child to his own calling than to any other. To the child the parent imparts much useful knowledge which could not be learnt at school, and many habitual aptitudes indispensable for success in any calling. It thus becomes impossible to compute how much of the child's resemblance to the parent is due to strictly physical causes, how much to subsequent educational influence. Again it is not merely parentage or education, but also inherited civilisation, which contributes to mould the individual on the pattern of his ancestors. An old and deep-rooted civilisation exercises the most penetrating power on all who come within its sphere, whether by birth or by immigration, whether as conquerors or as subjects. Thus successive races of invaders have been permeated by the civilisation of Italy and China, and the older types of thought have endured in spite of infusions of alien blood. Lastly, the effect of natural environment, the conditions of soil, scenery, and above all, climate, tend to maintain physical and moral uniformity through age after age, and favour the illusion that the present inhabitants of a given country are all lineal descendants of those who inhabited it in the earliest period of history. These natural agencies have no doubt contributed much to the assimilation of foreign conquerors by the conquered natives. The joint influence of a peculiar climate and a peculiar civilisation in rendering men subjected to their action like one another and unlike everybody else is well illustrated in the United States of America. The mixed crowd of European immigrants who disembark every year on the shores of the United States are rapidly transformed into the likeness of the older settlers, and their offspring can hardly be distinguished from the offspring of three or four generations of American citizens. But the pure-blooded Yankee who is proud of his descent from the Puritans is a very different man from his English ancestor or cousin. The converse truth is illustrated by the remarkable transformation which many races have undergone when removed to a new home and exposed to new influences. Thus the Jews in their own country were mainly an agricultural and pastoral people; since their dispersion they have lived chiefly in towns and have busied themselves in trading and money-lending. It thus appears that the continuity of national character is the result in varying proportions of unbroken descent by blood, of education, of inherited civilisation, and of unchanged natural conditions. The relative potency of these agencies in any given instance may be roughly conjectured, but can never be exactly determined. Such determination is not, however, necessary for economic purposes. It is enough for economical investigation to know that tribes and nations have certain striking characteristics which may indeed be modified in the long lapse of time or by violent revolutions, but which are in the main permanent. It should, however, be remembered that this permanence is not the same in every stage of civilisation. It is most conspicuous in the earlier, the tribal or at most the national stage. It is less conspicuous in the later, the cosmopolitan stage. Thus in the ancient world the hereditary peculiarities of the Greek and the Jew, the Phœnician and the Roman, the Gaul and the Egyptian, were all strongly marked, whilst they retained their independence, but became somewhat blurred when they were merged in one universal empire. At the present day the different nations of Europe impart to each other their arts, their discoveries, their inventions, their luxuries, and their vices. Each people learns something from its neighbours and abates something of its own peculiarities. But this process of assimilation is in great measure superficial, and leaves the hereditary distinctions of temperament and character almost unchanged.

[F. Galton, *Hereditary Genius; Natural Inheritance.*—E. B. Poulton, *Theories of Heredity.*—Weissmann, *Essays upon Heredity and Kindred Biological Subjects.* — Kindere, *De la Race et de sa part d'influence dans les diverses manifestations de l'activité des peuples.*—Ribot, *Heredity, a Psychological Study of its Phenomena, Laws, Causes, and Consequences.*—J. B. Haycraft, *Darwinism and Race Progress* (1895).]   F. C. M.

HERIOT. When a gesith or thegn received a grant of BOCLAND (*q.v.*) it was customary for the lord to make him a gift of arms and equipment. On the thegn's death this gift was repaid in whole or part from his chattels by the heir, and this repayment, at first customary and then compulsory, is called the heriot. The Norman lawyers confused the heriot with the feudal relief, which was paid by the heir on succeeding to his father's lands. But the two things are perfectly distinct. The relief is directly connected with the tenure of land; until it is paid the estate returns to the overlord, who only grants possession to the heir when the customary payment has been paid. But the heriot has no connection with the land, which passes unconditionally to the heir. It is in fact not so much a charge upon the heir as a payment from the dead man to his lord.

[Stubbs, *Constitutional History*, i. 261.] R. L.

Heriot still survives as a manorial right subsisting on copyhold land in many parts of England, and also in certain places, more particularly in Kent, on freehold land held of a manor. It consists in the right of the lord, on the death of a tenant, and in some cases also on alienation, to seize the best beast, *e.g.* a valuable race-horse, on every tenement held by such tenants. On some manors the best chattel, *e.g.* a diamond necklace, may be taken by the lord. It is frequently difficult to ascertain whether land is subject to heriots or not, as the occasions for making use of the right may only occur at long intervals; and, as the statute of limitations, though it could bar a particular exercise of the right of heriot, could not bar the general right (see Zouche *v.* Dalbiac, L. R. 10 Ex. 172), a continuous non-exercise of the right would, however, tend to extinguish it. The compulsory extinguishment of heriots may, under § 7 of the Copyhold Act 1887, be claimed either by the lord or the tenant, and the compensation payable to the lord is, in such a case, ascertained in the same way as in the case of the enfranchisement of copyhold land.

Heriots, though a picturesque reminder of a past age, have nothing in their favour from an economical point of view. They cause an inconvenience to the tenant out of proportion to the advantage they confer on the lord; their real or assumed existence frequently creates difficulties on the sale of land, and, in many instances, they have caused fruitless and expensive litigation. It would be most desirable for the legislature to fix a period within which compensation for them and similar manorial rights might be claimed by the lords, and to declare that after the lapse of such period all such rights should cease.

[As to the present law relating to heriots, see Elton, *Copyholds*, 2nd edition, 198-210.] E. S.

HERITABLE AND MOVEABLE (Scots Law). Correspond very nearly, with some exceptions, such as teinds or tithes, liferents or estates for life in land, mortgage debts, and others, to real and personal as applied to property in English law, particularly with reference to the respective rights of the heir and the personal representative. In Scots law there are, however, more numerous instances than in English in which property is considered heritable (or real) for one purpose and moveable (or personal) for others: and there are some leading differences of principle, such as that rights in their own nature moveable, but having a tract (or prospective course) of future time, as for example, leases, annuities, and life interests in money, are heritable, and not moveable or personal only.

[For enumerations of heritable and moveable rights, see Bell's *Commentaries*, vol. ii. p. 1, *et seq.*] A. D.

HERITABLE SECURITIES (Scots Law). A generic term, including all forms of real securities, or securities on land or buildings. The most ordinary form in use is a bond and disposition in security, a combination of a personal bond with a redeemable conveyance or mortgage, with power of sale by public auction and of granting an absolute title upon such sale.

[See Craigie's *Digest of Scottish Conveyancing* (*Heritable*).] A. D.

HERMANN, FRIEDRICH BENEDICT WILHELM (1795-1868), one of the most eminent of German economists and statisticians, was born at Dinkelsbühl in Bavaria. He studied at Erlangen and Würzburg. He was afterwards (1821) teacher of mathematics at Erlangen, and (1825) professor of that science in the Polytechnic school of Nuremberg. In 1827 he was appointed extraordinary professor of technology and political economy in the university of Munich. His great work, *Staatswirthschaftliche Untersuchungen* (1832), made his reputation, and procured for him the position of ordinary professor in his university. He was employed by the government as inspector of institutions for technical instruction, and was commissioned to visit, in 1839, the Paris exhibition, of which he published an account (*Die Industrie-Ausstellung zu Paris*). He was also appointed a member of the statistical bureau, and in the capacity of its head he issued, from 1850 to 1867, his contributions to the statistics of Bavaria. He filled from time to time different important posts in the ministries of the interior and of finance. At several conferences of representatives of the German states on taxation, he worked earnestly for the creation of one national system of customs duties. He organised a *Grossdeutsche Partei*, whose motto was "Kein Deutschland ohne Oesterreich." He held that a union without Austria would produce not a lesser Germany, but a larger Prussia. He represented in 1848 the city of Munich in the National Assembly at Frankfort, and voted as a member of the Left Centre. In 1855 he retired from political life, and devoted himself to his professorial duties and to scientific research. He was seized with inflammation of the lungs on 20th November 1868, and, aware of his approaching end, dictated to his son, as long as his strength permitted, the alterations to be introduced into a new edition of his *Untersuchungen*. He died on the 23rd of the same month. [Roscher, *Gesch. der N.O.*, p. 860.—Cossa, *Introd. to the study of P.E.*, English trans., Macmillan, 1893, p. 406.—Kautz, *Nationalökonomie*, ii. p. 633.]   J. K. I.

Hermann in his *Staatswirthschaftliche Untersuchungen* (Munich, 1832, and, enlarged afterwards from his notes, 1870) has left one of the most permanently valuable books on economics in the German language. It covers nearly the whole ground of a text-book, and such a text-book as might have been expected a generation later. Like Schäffle, he says much at the outset on human wants, the notion of "goods," and other psychological aspects of his subject. He lays stress on the distinction of technical from economical, the first relating to the production of certain physical effects by the use of certain physical causes, the second to the disposal of quantities of goods, on the principle of greatest benefit at least sacrifice. He distinguishes the economy of an individual, of a family, and of a larger group. He points out that joint action is not necessarily collective action; a school may be started by the joint action of several fathers for the training of their own several children, but it is not a public or collective institution unless it is created by a union of citizens not specially for themselves but for the general advantage (ed. 1870, p. 95).

His illustrations from education are frequent. As a public man, he took a keen interest in public instruction. He draws also in many other ways on his special knowledge of public affairs in Prussia, and especially in Bavaria. The later edition refers in this connection to his report for the Zollverein's commission on the London Exhibition of 1851 (ed. 1870, p. 214, cp. 426, 466-467). In theory, he is a shrewd and close reasoner. He expressly adopts the abstract method (120, 168, cp. 378). He works out mainly on conservative lines the theory of value, price, demand, etc. He thinks income of consumers is the true wages-fund. He has a wide knowledge even of the minor English and American economists (*e.g.* 203, 259, 266). Some of his distinctions are not perhaps very happy. For example *Nutz-capital*, as distinguished from *Productiv-capital* (221 *seq.*), is on the whole a metaphor, and not to be embraced with the latter under one definition of capital. The distinction, again, of *Hilfstoff* from *Hauptstoff* (320) seems rather technical than economical. But, open him where you will, you find mature wisdom and clear reasoning.

Banfield, in his *Organization of Industry* (1845), acknowledges his debt to Hermann (*e.g.* Preface and pp. 20, 28). But Banfield, who had studied Rau, Von Thünen, and List, had special opportunities in his own travels, official and unofficial, of knowing the Germans. Hermann had little further notice, till Professor Marshall, in his *Principles* (1890), made him full amends for previous English neglect (see esp. p. 106 n., 492, etc.) [see also BANFIELD; GERMAN SCHOOLS].   J. B.

HERRENSCHWAND (—). This writer on political economy has often been mistaken for his brother Johann Friedrich, a Swiss physician, who died in Bern in 1796. He is believed to have been a judge in the Swiss regiments in the French service, and according to the *Nouvelle Biographie Générale* (vol. 24, p. 463) was in 1805 an old man living in Paris. Nothing else is known about him.

He is a turgid and diffuse writer, always professing to set forth the will of the "Creator," or of the "Universe." Blanqui in the bibliography annexed to his *Histoire de l'Économie Politique* (ii. p. 350, ed. 1860) mentions him as a connecting link between Quesnay and Smith. In common with the former, Herrenschwand has a general predilection for agriculture and a state of equilibrium between production and consumption; and in common with the second, he remarks on the beneficial influence of high wages, but his opinions on the evils of foreign trade, and on the usefulness of the accumulation of the precious metals, are quite contrary to their views. His favourite remedy is the multiplication of absolutely independent consumers (*consommateurs indépendants par excellence*), and the increase in their hands of coined precious metals (*Du vrai Gouvernement des Peuples de la Terre*, London and Paris, 1801-1802, p. 89).

His works, although written in French, were published in London; De *l'Économie Politique Moderne. Discours fondamental sur la Population* (London, 1786, and Paris, 1795).—*Discours sur le Crédit Public des Nations de l'Europe* (1786).—*Discours sur la Division des Terres* (1788).—De *l'Économie Politique et Morale de l'Espèce Humaine* (2 vols., 1786).—*Du vrai Principe actif de l'Économie Politique* (1797). Arthur Young, *Travels through France* (2nd ed. vol. i. p. 481), writing on his own studies and those of Sir James Stuart, on the subject of "Population," refers thus to Herrenschwand; "other writers have arisen who have viewed the subject in its right light; and of these none have equalled Mons. Herenschwandt, who in his *Économie Politique Moderne*, 1786; and his *Discours sur la Division des Terres*, 1788, has almost exhausted the subject."   E. CA.

HERRERA, CRISTOBAL PEREZ DE (end of 16th and early 17th century), physician of the royal navy of Spain and of Philip II., wrote several works on the poor, among which may be mentioned his several *Discúrsos del Amparo de los legítimos Pobres* (Discourses on the Protection of the well-conducted Poor), Madrid, 1595, 1598, and 1608. He recommends the erection of special houses (*Albergues*), which are to be supported by the church, the municipal authorities, and private charity; but unlike his predecessor GIGINTA (*q.v.*), he does not in his *Replica* (Reply) to the objections opposed to his discourses, appear to be willing to enforce work on the well-conducted poor, and only considers it as a mode of correction for vagrants and women of bad character; he would even allow the well-conducted poor, whilst inmates of the house, to go out begging on their own account.

More favourable to Herrera's endeavours than to Giginta's, King Philip III. in 1596, ordered, his plan to be executed in fifty towns and rural places; but owing probably to the absence of the test of work suggested by Giginta, its effects were rather favourable to than restrictive of the extension of pauperism.

[Colmeiro, *Historia de la Economia Politica en España* (vol. ii. pp. 29 and 38), *Biblioteca de los Economistas Españoles* (p. 135).—Iglesias, *La Beneficencia en España* (vol. i. p. 257).] E. ca.

HERRIES, JOHN CHARLES (1778-1855), statesman and financier, was the son of a London merchant. In 1798 he entered the public service as junior clerk in the treasury, but was soon promoted to a place in the revenue department, where he so distinguished himself that Pitt employed him to draw up his counter-resolutions against Tierney's financial proposals. He further received the thanks of the prime minister in 1803 for his pamphlet in reply to the financial strictures of Cobbett and Lord Grenville. Herries acted for some time as secretary to Vansittart, and afterwards to Spencer Perceval, and in 1811 he was despatched to Ireland to assist Wellesley-Pole, the Irish chancellor of the exchequer. The same year he was appointed to the arduous office of commissary-in-chief, in which post he did much to cope with the jobbery everywhere prevalent. He had now a great reputation as a political economist, and in 1813, in conjunction with Nathan Meyer Rothschild, he succeeded in carrying out a plan for the collection of French specie for the use of Wellington's army. But owing to the continued dearth of specie in 1815, a large number of 20-franc pieces were, at Herries's suggestion, coined at the mint for the use of the army. The office of commissary-in-chief having been abolished in 1816, Herries retired on a pension; but he was soon appointed to the new office of auditor of the civil list. In 1821 he was appointed one of the commissioners for inquiring into the collection and management of the revenue in Ireland. He was named financial secretary to the treasury in 1823, being returned to parliament during the same year for Harwich. It was under his direction that the consolidation of the customs laws was

effected. When Lord Goderich (Earl of Ripon), became prime minister on the death of Canning, Herries was appointed chancellor of the exchequer at the king's special request. Ministerial complications ensued, the result of which was that Herries left the exchequer and became master of the mint. He served on the finance committee of 1828, and was the first financier to "make the public accounts intelligible." In 1830 he became president of the board of trade, but resigned both his offices when Lord Grey acceded to office. In the session of 1832 Herries made a severe and damaging attack upon the government in connection with the Russian-Dutch loan. He was secretary at war in Peel's ministry of 1834-35. Appointed in 1838 one of the committee on metropolitan improvements, he drew up the greater portion of its second report. He strongly attacked the financial and commercial policy of the Whig government in 1841, but the same year lost his seat in the house. Having retired from Harwich at the dissolution, he unsuccessfully contested Ipswich. He now remained out of parliament for six years. Returned in 1847 for Stamford in the protectionist interest, he strongly opposed the repeal of the navigation laws. In the Derby ministry of 1852 he held the office of president of the board of control, but that ministry was overthrown in December (1852), and in the ensuing year Herries retired altogether from parliamentary life. Herries was not a great statesman or a brilliant speaker, but he acquired the reputation of an able financier and an assiduous public servant.

[E. Herries, *Memoir of the Public Life of J. C. Herries.* — Bulwer, *Life of Lord Palmerston.* — Walpole, *History of England.* — *Annual Register,* 1855. — Art. "Herries, J. C.," *Dictionary of National Biography.*

Herries has recently been appealed to by Mr. W. H. Smith, Mr. Gladstone, and Sir. W. Harcourt, as an authority upon the probability of panic in the event of bimetallism. Mr. Arthur Balfour expressed a very different view of his abilities. "Speech at Bimetallic Conference," London, 1895.] G. B. S.

HEUSCHLING, PHILIPP F. XAVIER THEODORE (1802-1883). An eminent official of the ministry of the interior in Brussels, was a frequent contributor on statistical subjects to the *Journal des Économistes.—La Belgique Judiciaire,—Revue de l'Administration et du Droit Administratif en Belgique. —Bulletin de la Commission de Statistique de Belgique,* etc.

The list of his publications extends over three pages of the Belgian *Bibliographie Nationale* (Brussels, 2 vols. 1888). Among them ought to be mentioned: *Essai sur la Statistique générale de la Belgique* (1838).—*Bibliographie historique de la Statistique en Allemagne* (1845).—*Manuel de Statistique ethnographique universelle* (1847).— *Le Congrès Général de Statistique tenu à Bruxelles en 1853* (Paris, 1853).—*Résumé de la Statistique*

Générale de Belgique de 1841 à 1850 (1853).—
L'Empire de Turquie (1860). He wrote in conjunction with M. Block: *Das Kaiserthum Frankreich und das Königreich Belgien* (Leipzig, 1871),
and collected under the title of *L'Impôt sur
le Revenu* (1873), several of his scattered pamphlets and review articles advocating an income tax
to take the place of indirect taxation and license
duties (*patentes*). He assisted QUETELET (*q.v.*)
in the publication of the *Comptes Rendus des
Travaux de la Commission Centrale de Statistique*,
and Bivort in bringing out the *Annales Législatives
de la Belgique*, and trans. *Princ. of Stat.* of
B. HILDEBRAND (*q.v.*).　　　　　　　　　E. Ca.

HEYSHAM, JOHN, M.D. Edin. (1753-
1834), is best known through his statistical
observations, extending from 1779 to 1787, on
the bills of mortality at Carlisle, in which town
he followed his profession of physician. His
tables include the number of deaths according
to age, sex, and conjugal condition, and are
accompanied by general observations on the
vital statistics of Carlisle, including some
remarks, with statistical illustrations, concerning the value of inoculating for smallpox. His
figures formed the basis of Joshua Milne's
Carlisle Life Table, which from its greater
accuracy very generally superseded the Northampton table previously used, though the
mortality at Carlisle was somewhat lower than
that of England. Heysham took a census of
the town in 1780 and in 1788, and calls attention to the large increase in the number of the
inhabitants, due to manufactories.

An abridgment of *Observations on the Bills of
Mortality in Carlisle 1779-87*, Carlisle, 1797.—
An Account of the Jail Fever at Carlisle in 1781.
Lond., 1782.

[Dr. H. Lonsdale, *Life of John Heysham,
M.D.*, Lond., 1870.—Concerning the Carlisle
Table, see also Joshua Milne, *Treatise on the
Valuation of Annuities*, 2 vols., Lond., 1815, and
C. Walford, *Insurance Cyclopædia*, s.v. *Carlisle
Table of Mortality*, Lond., 1871.]　　R. H. H.

HIDAGE. The earliest tax in English
history, the DANEGELD (*q.v.*), was a tax of
a varying number of shillings on the hide of
land. The original reason for this imposition
was to buy off the Danish invasions under
Ethelred II. But long after this pretext had
disappeared, even after the Norman Conquest,
the danegeld continued to be levied from time
to time under the same name. But after 1163
it disappears from the rolls, and historians have
often supposed that it was never again levied.
But precisely the same charge on land continues
to be made by Henry II. and Richard I. under
the name of hidage, and in the 13th century
as carucage. Hidage therefore is really the
same as danegeld, though it only appears as a
technical term after the latter had fallen into
disuse.　　　　　　　　　　　　　　　R. L.

HIDE. In the original distribution of land
among the English settlers in Britain the

portion allotted to each free man, *i.e.* the homestead with a share in the arable and pasture
lands of the township (see ALOD), was called a
hide. From this use came its later meaning
as a measure of area. By the laws of Edward
the Elder a ceorl who had fully five hides of
land with other qualifications could become a
thegn. But it is impossible to determine the
measurement denoted by a hide in Anglo-Saxon
times, and it is certain that this varied very
much in different localities. After the Norman
Conquest a hide means the same as a carucate,
i.e. the land that can be ploughed by a single
team. This, originally a varying area, is
fixed in the twelfth century at 100 or 120
acres.

[Kemble, *Saxons in England*, i. 88.—*Dialogus
de Scaccario*, i. 17.—E. W. Robertson, *Historical
Essays.*—Stubbs, *Constitutional History*, i. 74.]
　　　　　　　　　　　　　　　　　　　　R. L.

The *hide* or *higid* appears to have meant,
in primitive times, the amount of land
which sufficed for a family; it consisted of
arable land with pasture rights, and has been
generally regarded as the share allotted to each
free warrior (ALOD). Charters quoted by Mr.
Round seem to prove that the hide was an area
of 120 acres.

In Domesday Book the term is used as a
unit of assessment for purposes of calculating
the Danegeld. Like the term *carucato* (properly
160 or 180 acres, see CARUCAGE) it ceases, in
this great record, to be a direct measure of
area; for a large expanse of barren heath, and
a comparatively small but fertile arable holding, might each be rated as a hide. The
principle of *beneficial hidation*, or the favourable rating of certain estates or districts (as *e.g.*
the archiepiscopal land in Surrey) was so far
operative that it is quite impossible to deduce
the area of an estate from the Domesday hides.

HIGGLING of the market is described by
Adam Smith as a process by which "exchangeable value" is adjusted to its measure "quantity
of labour."

"It is often difficult to ascertain the proportion
between two different quantities of labour . . .
it is not easy to find any accurate measure either
of hardship or ingenuity. In exchanging, indeed,
the different productions of different sorts of
labour for one another, some allowance is
commonly made for both. It is adjusted,
however, not by any accurate measure, but
by the higgling and bargaining of the market,
according to that rough equality which, though
not exact, is sufficient for carrying on the
business of common life" (*Wealth of Nations*,
bk. i. ch. v.).

Compare FLEEMING JENKIN: "The higgling
of the market, ascertaining the result of the relative demand and supply in that market, does not
in the long run determine the price of either eggs
or tea; it simply finds out the price which had

been already determined by quite different means" ("Time - Labour System," *Papers, Literary, Scientific*, etc., p. 139). It is possible to accept the writer's account of the *market process* (*Ibid.* p. 123) without contrasting so strongly the determination of price by demand and supply and by cost of production (cp. Prof. Marshall, *Principles*, Preface, p. xi.). Prof. Marshall at the beginning, when treating of the theory of the equilibrium of demand and supply, gives an excellent type of the action of a market (*Ibid.* bk. v. § 2). See also his note on barter at the end of the chapter referred to, and his mathematical note xii. The subject can hardly be apprehended without mathematical conceptions. Thus Mill, in his description of the play of demand and supply (*Pol. Econ.*, bk. iii. ch. ii. § 4), in the absence of the idea of a demand-curve or function, may seem to use the phrases "demand increases," "demand diminishes," loosely. A more distinct idea is thus expressed by Fleeming Jenkin in his *Graphic Representations*. "If every man were openly to write down beforehand exactly what he would sell or buy at each price, the market price might be computed immediately." A similar idea is presented by Prof. Walras (*Éléments d'Économie Pure*, art. 50). In some later passages he has formulated the higgling of the market more elaborately. The present writer, criticising these passages (*Revue d'Économie politique*, Jan. 1891), has maintained that even if the dispositions of all the parties were known beforehand, there could be predicted only the position of equilibrium, not the particular course by which it is reached. Of course special observation may supply the defects of theory. For instance there may be evidence of the incident which Cantillon attributes to the "altercation" of a market, namely the predominant influence of a few buyers or sellers ; "le prix réglé par quelques uns est ordinairement suivi par les autres" (*Essai*, part ii. ch. ii. Des prix des Marchés). Compare Condillac : "Aussitôt que quelques uns seront d'accord sur la proportion à suivre dans leurs échanges les autres prendront cette proportion pour règle" (*Le Commerce et le Gouvernement*, ch. iv. *Des marchés*).

"Higgling" is not always qualified as "of a market." The term may be used in much the same sense as the "art of bargaining" is used by Jevons, with reference to a transaction between two individuals, in the absence of competition (*Theory*, p. 124, 3rd ed.). Thus Professor Marshall, in an important passage relating to the case in which agents of production are held by two monopolists, says that there is "nothing but 'higgling and bargaining'" to settle the proportions in which a certain surplus will be divided between the two (*Principles of Economics*, bk. v. ch. x. end). Moses, in the *Vicar of Wakefield*, did not require a fair for the exercise of the skill

which is thus attributed to him : "He always stands out and higgles and actually tires them till he gets a bargain." F. Y. E.

HIGHWAY RATES. See RATES.

HILDEBRAND, BRUNO (1812 - 1878), a German economist of the historical school who won an enviable reputation among his contemporaries by his scholarly contributions to the science, and especially by a rare administrative power that found its happiest expression in the establishment and editorial management of the *Jahrbücher für Nationalökonomie und Statistik*, was born at Naumburg, a small town on the Saale river, where his father was clerk of the court. In 1836 he began an academic career as privatdocent or lecturer in history at the university of Breslau. Like G. Kries and Carl Knies, however, he soon specialised in political economy. The instructorship developed three years later into an assistant professorship, and in 1841 Hildebrand was made full professor of political science at the university of Marburg. While in this position he represented Marburg in the Paulskirche Conference at Frankfort, and in 1849-50 he sat as representative for the city of Bockenheim in the Hessian parliament. It was in this latter body in September 1850 that Hildebrand moved and carried a motion to refuse the additional grants asked for by the government in the annual budget. A dissolution of the House followed and Hildebrand lost his position as professor at Marburg in consequence of his action. He then went to Switzerland and was made professor of political science, first at Zurich and then at Berne, where he founded the first cantonal statistical bureau. In 1861 he was called to the chair of political economy at the university of Jena, where he remained until his death. It was here that he started the publication of the *Jahrbücher*, which he edited alone until 1873, when Prof. Johann Conrad, a former pupil, became associate editor. Prof. Conrad succeeded to the chief editorship in 1878. In 1864 Hildebrand was made director of the statistical bureau of the United Thuringian States, in which position he published many valuable statistical researches. His chief work, however, was his book entitled "Political Economy of the present and future" *Die Nationalökonomie der Gegenwart und Zukunft*, the first volume of which appeared in 1848. Much material on the industrial condition of labour and manufactures, gathered during a long stay in England in 1846, was utilised in this work. He criticises the different schools from the historical point of view and treats the laws of economic development in modern times ethically and politically. Perhaps his best and severest criticisms are those of Engels, Proudhon, and the theoretical parts of Fried. List's doctrines, although Hildebrand was himself a moderate protectionist. In spite of the fact that this book was welcomed as an important contribution to that stream of literature begun by the historical school, a second volume never appeared, possibly because of disinclination to go further on the same lines, but more probably because of absorption in more practical work.

Hildebrand was a man of great energy and organising power, with a good hold on practical life, and always successful in collecting economic facts from all classes of people. His practical activity occupied itself in the organisation of two small railways in Zurich and Bern, and of a short railway in the Saale valley starting from Jena. He also established several friendly societies in the towns in which he lived. As a university lecturer he was not particularly brilliant, in the form or contents of his lectures ; he usually spoke without notes and in a somewhat disconnected manner, but he laid great stress upon personal work with his students, and his influence on them, especially by way of suggestion and supervision, was peculiarly successful. Criticism and the development of a critical spirit among his students was ever with him a hobby. His chief writings in the order of their appearance are as follows :

Xenophontis et Aristotelis de œconomia publica doctrinœ illustratœ, 2 Teile, Marburg, 1845.—*Die Nationalökonomie der Gegenwart und Zukunft,* I (einziger) Bd. Frankfort a. M. 1848.—*Statistische Mitteilungen über die volkswirthschaftlichen Zustände Kurhessens,* Berlin, 1853.—*Beiträge zur Statistik des Kantons Bern.* Bd. I. 1 Hälfte, Bern, 1860.—*Die Kurhessische Finanzverwaltung,* Kassel, 1860. — *Untersuchungen über die Bevölkerung des alten Italiens* (*Artikel im Neuen Schweizerischen Museum,* 1861.)—*De antiquissimœ agri romani distributionis fide,* Jena, 1862.—*Statistik Thüringens, Mitteilungen des statist. Bureaus Vereinigter Thüringischer Staaten,* 2 Bde, Jena, 1867-78.—*Principes de statistique administrative, enseignés à l' Université de Jéna. Traduit de l'allemand sur les cahiers du professeur et résumés par X. Heuschling,* Brussels and Paris, 1872. [This was an unauthorised translation of a college student's note book which appeared in the *Bulletin de la Commission centrale de statistique,* vol. xii.]

Many valuable articles upon various economic topics in his *Jahrbücher.* S. M'C. L.

HILDRETH, RICHARD (1807-1867), was born in Deerfield, Mass. ; he became a lawyer and editor in Boston, and was the author of a standard history of the United States. He published many works on history and moral and political philosophy, among which is, *The History of Banks, to which is added a Demonstration of the Advantage and Necessity of free Competition in the Business of Banking,* Boston, 1837, pp. 142. Hildreth argued that bank-notes should be subject to the same kind of legislation as bills of exchange. D. R. D.

HILL, SIR ROWLAND (1795-1879), was founder of penny postage in England. In 1819 he established Hazelwood School, near Birmingham, and in 1822 brought out, in conjunction with his brother, Matthew Davenport Hill, a treatise on public education. With the hope that the government might be induced to examine into the home colonies of Holland, which seemed to afford valuable suggestions for our own poor-law administration, he wrote a pamphlet on *Home Colonies* in 1832. In 1835 he was appointed secretary to the commissioners for the colonisation of South Australia, and in that capacity suggested a plan for municipal government which is believed to contain the first scheme ever put forward for proportional representation. In 1837 his pamphlet appeared on *Post Office Reform : its Importance and Practicability,* urging the substitution of a uniform charge—preferably the minimum then in use, one penny—for the complicated system of "rating" then practised. This led to considerable popular agitation, which induced the government to appoint a committee of enquiry in 1838, and to introduce a Penny Postage Bill in 1838, going into effect in 1840. To assist in carrying out the contemplated reforms, Hill was appointed in 1839 to a position in the Treasury. The term for which he was appointed having expired, he was dismissed by the new ministry in 1842 ; and thereupon turned his attention to railway management, as director and then chairman of the Brighton Company (1843-1846). In 1846 a national testimonial was presented to him in recognition of his services in postal reform, together with a subscription of £13,000. In the same year he was appointed to the newly-created office of secretary to the postmaster-general. In 1854 this office was combined in his person with the older office of secretary to the general post office ; and he remained sole secretary till his resignation in 1864. He had been knighted in 1860 ; and on his retirement received a parliamentary grant of £20,000. He was buried in Westminster Abbey.

The principles of the modern postal service are so far-reaching that it may be well to state them in Rowland Hill's own words. His attention, he tells us in his autobiography, was first directed to the subject by his interest in the problems of taxation. He had come to the conclusion that the best tax was that whereof "the productiveness kept pace with the increasing number and prosperity of the nation." "This test brought the tax on the transmission of letters into bad pre-eminence, since during the previous twenty years the revenue derived from the post office . . . had even somewhat diminished." The suggestion, which he attributes to his father, Thomas Wright Hill, that "even for fiscal purposes postage was unwisely high," then occurred to him ; and he "started" upon his work of investigation "with the simple notion that rates must be reduced." "The question to be decided therefore was, how far the total reduction might safely be carried ; and this involved two preliminary inquiries ; first, what would be the probable increase of correspondence consequent upon such or such reduction ; secondly, what would be the augmentation of expense consequent upon such increase." As to the first he concluded from an observation of the cases of several commodities, not only that cheapening was followed by an increase in demand, but that "reduction in price, even if it does not increase the total expenditure on the article, seldom if ever permanently lowers its amount." As to the second, he saw that under the existing system many of the elements of expense "must increase in something like direct proportion to increase in the number of letters." But this he thought by no means necessary ; expense could be effectually reduced by simplicity of operation, and this could be obtained by "reducing the prodigious variety of rates, and adopting means to induce prepayment." "In considering how far the variety of rates might be reduced, I was led to inquire what proportion of postal expense proceeded from the conveyance of letters from town to town, and further how far such expense varied in relation to distance." "I found, first, that the cost of conveying a letter between post-town and post-town was exceedingly small ; secondly, that it had but little relation to distance ; and thirdly, that it depended much upon the number of letters conveyed by the particular mail ; and as the cost per letter would diminish with every increase in number, and such increase would certainly follow reduction of postage, it followed that, if a great reduction could be effected, the cost of conveyance per letter might be deemed absolutely insignificant. Hence I came to the conclusion that the practice of regulating the amount of postage by the distance over which a letter was conveyed . . . had no foundation in principle ; and that consequently the rates of postage should be irrespective of distance. This discovery, as startling to myself as it could be to any one else, was the basis of the plan which has made so great a change in postal affairs" [*The Life of Sir Rowland Hill and the History of Penny Postage*, by Sir Rowland Hill and his nephew G. B. Hill, 1880].

[Bastable, *Finance*, 1892, bk. ii. ch. iii. § 7.]

W. J. A.

HILL - BURTON, JOHN, also known as BURTON, JOHN HILL (1809 - 1881), born at Aberdeen, was educated at Aberdeen university, and after trying in vain to practise at the Edinburgh bar, became a writer for the *Westminster* and *Edinburgh Review*. He helped Sir J. Bowring to edit Bentham's works. His first notable writing, if we except *Benthamiana*, 1843, is his *Life of Hume*, 1846, and *Letters of Eminent Persons to David Hume*, 1849. He edited the autobiography of Carlyle of Inveresk, 1860. His *Biographies of Lord Lovat and Duncan Forbes*, 1847, may be said to have given a foretaste of his *History of Scotland*, 1853, *seq.* which has the signal merits of being faithful to the sources, and thorough, candid, and judicial in the examination of them.

Hill-Burton's chief economical book is *Political and Social Economy, and its Practical Appli-*

cations (Chambers, Edinburgh, 1849). He addresses himself to a supposed need of "the acting and thinking man," to have the true political economy set before him as concretely and as attractively as the false, which was just then, through Louis Blanc and others, neglecting no means of making itself known. He had long hoped to write such a book, and on a larger scale than time now allowed him.

The book deals with applications and illustrations rather than first principles ; and it bears the marks of a time of transition. The writer stands midway between two epochs, and describes both, with no very distinct consciousness that the old political economy like the old régime is giving place to a new. He mentions Mill's *Principles*, 1848, with respect, but in a tone of disappointment (p. 42). He finds Mill's discussion of luxuries, for example, inadequate. On the other hand he himself states the WAGES FUND theory, without any misgivings (p. 54). His first section on production is largely a plea for piecework against time-work. He quotes Thiers against the French socialists on the rights of property (p. 60). His quotation of the remark that there must always be a worst-paid industry (p. 29), does not lead him to any innovations in theory. His allusions to current events, railways, colonies, pauperism, and epidemics, help to make his book at once readable and historically valuable, as enabling us to place ourselves at the point of view of an intelligent English citizen forty-five years ago.

Otherwise it is far inferior in interest to his historical works, and has little or nothing of the charm of his literary masterpiece, *The Book-Hunter*, 1860. It is perhaps not too much to say that he is of most service to economists when he is not writing directly on their subject.

Clear and wise as are the chapters of his *Emigrant's Guide*, 1851, they bear out this statement. Almost at starting he speaks of the colonists as to be ."guided by the eternal laws of political economy, laws as eternal and beneficent as those of the mechanical powers and animal life, laws not easily found, often misconstrued, taxing men's intellects to the utmost, and far more liable than the laws of other sciences to the false direction of prejudice, yet existing in nature beyond doubt," *Em. G.* "Australia, etc.," part i. p. 7.

This is use and wont, and largely obsolete use and wont. There is more character in the description of those who should and those who should not emigrate, the contrasts of national character, the criticisms of Wakefield's plan of emigration (pp. 38 *seq.*), the sudden outburst against the tyranny of proprietors and capitalists (52), the proofs given of the necessity of the interference of the home government (73-88). The statistics of wages in the colonies, and the comments on slave compared with free labour, must also be mentioned (*Em. G.*, part ii.). "South Australia," etc. (pp. 8, 16, 25, 97, 136, 137, etc. America, p. 81, 182, 183).

But Hill-Burton is more at home in his *History of Scotland*, where his economical training often leads him to draw attention to incidents of which an ordinary historian would miss the significance. Such are, for example, his notices in vol. ii. (2nd ed. 1873) of absentee landlords, and the effect, on them, of an act forbidding exportation of goods or money from Scotland during war (1318), p. 306, in vol. iii. of the decreasing wealth of Scotland at the time of the Reformation, pp. 438, 448, of an early instance of a "consul" p. 438, of the currency at the end of the 15th cent., p. 441, of export duties yielding more than import, p. 448. There is no difficulty in adding to this list when we come to the later volumes. The economical element in the questions between England and Scotland when their union was discussed after James I.'s accession (vol. v. 404), and when it was arranged under Queen Anne (vol. viii. 121, 207, etc.), receives adequate though never prolix treatment. The more laboured statement of the latter case in the special *History of Queen Anne* (1880 ed.) pp. 48 *seq.*, does not add much that is important, though there too the historian occasionally uses the eyes and the language of the economist. See esp. vol. iii. pp. 166 *seq.*, on scarcity of money in Ireland *circa* 1705, and iii. 312 on political economy as aided by statistics and "commercial book-keeping."

[*Life* by Mrs. Hill-Burton in *Book Hunter* (large paper ed. 1882). — Blackwood's *Magazine*, September 1881.—*Nat. Dict. of Biog.* (by Richard Garnett).]   J. B.

HIRE is the name given to payments for the use of services or movable things other than money. In the usual economic division of income into rent of land, interest, and wages, net hire, like all other income derived from the possession of property other than land, comes under the head of interest. There is, however, an important characteristic in respect of which hire of things must be classed with rent. In the case of rent and hire, when the borrower returns the loan he returns the thing actually lent, while in the case of interest he only returns a similar thing, not the coins actually lent but similar coins.   E. C.

HIRE AND PURCHASE AGREEMENTS. These agreements (of which the much-advertised purchases "on the three years hire system" are instances) are of interest to economists, as they represent a new form of credit, the application of which seems extending both in England and abroad. They are in reality purchasing agreements which stipulate the payment of the purchase price by instalments, but the purchase does not take effect until the last instalment has been paid, and in the meantime the instalments are dealt with as "rent for the hire and use" of the purchased articles. This enables the vendor to recover the goods in case of non-payment of any of the instalments without having had to go through the formality of registering a BILL OF SALE, and at the same time to retain the instalments previously paid. He is, however, exposed to the risk of the purchaser selling or pledging the goods to a third party who, if acting in good faith and without notice of the vendor's right, is entitled to treat the sale or pledge as valid (Factors Act 1889. § 2 and § 9 : Lee v. Butler [1893] 2 Q. B. 318 ; Helby v. Matthews [1894] 2 Q. B. 262).

There is something to be said in favour of these agreements, as they enable persons of small means to purchase sewing machines or other articles producing income or reducing expenditure, but on the other hand, as they impose no immediate great sacrifice on the purchaser and therefore appear to him much more favourable than they really are, they are frequently used for the purpose of disposing of unmarketable goods or of obtaining excessive prices. The forfeiture of the instalments paid before default also causes great hardship. The abuses of the purchase and hire system seem to be specially felt in Germany, and a government bill on the subject has been drafted.

[For a complete analysis of hire and purchase and other similar transactions and full details as to their use in Germany, see Cohn, *Die volkswirtschaftliche Bedeutung des Abzahlungsgeschäfts.*]
                                          E. S.

HIRING. The contract of hiring (*locatio-conductio*) relates either to things or services. In the case of the hiring of things the hirer is entitled to the possession of the thing for the purpose stipulated, but acquires no property in it. In the case of the hiring of services, the worker is bound to render the service within the time agreed upon, exercising a proper degree of care and diligence on the work.

[Addison on *Contracts*, London, 1892.]
                                          J. E. C. M.

HISTORICAL METHOD. The historical method of economic study is commonly contrasted with the abstract and deductive methods. Such a contrast, however, is to some extent misleading. The study of economics might be concrete without being historical ; and, on the other hand, the historical method may be to some extent deductive. The distinctive feature of the historical method is its recognition of *development* in economic life, and its consequent emphasis on the dynamical, as distinguished from the purely statical elements in industrial and commercial organisation. Such a method of study is generally concrete : for in dealing with a process of growth the interaction of the different elements of social life on one another cannot be overlooked. It is true that a certain amount of abstraction is possible even here. Particular lines of tendency may be traced in the development of industrial life, without any special attention being directed to the special circumstances of different countries or districts, or strata of society, by which the general movement is modified. Such abstraction as this is necessary in a scientific study of any kind. Indeed, even the history of a battle, or any other concrete event, is necessarily abstract, in the sense that it fastens upon certain salient features, and omits what are regarded as unessential details. And this is much more obviously the case when we are endeavouring to trace the history of a great movement, with a view to the discovery of the broad principles by which it is governed. In this sense, then, even the historical method may be said to be to some extent abstract. Still, it may fairly enough be contrasted with the abstract method of economic study, inasmuch as the elements which the historical method omits are merely those that are regarded as too insignificant, or too limited in their sphere, to have any important influence on the concrete process of development as a whole ; whereas, in the abstract method proper, the elements from which abstraction is made are sometimes confessedly of scarcely, if at all, less importance in the concrete life of a country than those to which attention is specially directed. The historical method may, therefore, be described as one particular way in which the concrete study of economics is pursued. It is not, however, the only way. The study of concrete facts at a particular time and place—*e.g.* such facts as those contained in Mr. Charles Booth's *Labour and Life of the People*—cannot properly be said to be an illustration of the historical method, except in so far as these facts are brought into comparison with corresponding facts at other times and places, so as to throw light on the process of historical development. The method of LE PLAY, on the other hand, in dealing with similar matters, is much more distinctly historical. Thus it appears that the method of economic study may be concrete without being definitely historical.

Again, the historical method is not necessarily inductive, in the sense at least in which the inductive method is sharply contrasted with the deductive. No doubt, any valuable historical generalisation must rest on a certain basis of inductive inquiry. But so also must all valuable generalisations with reference to the more statical conditions of human life. But after having, by some process of induction, reached certain general principles, the historical method, no less than the statical, may proceed largely in a deductive way. There may be laws or tendencies of historical development, as well as laws or tendencies operative under particular hypothetical conditions ;[1] and if it is possible to formulate laws of the former kind, their consequences may be worked out deductively, just as the consequences of the latter kind of laws may be traced. The only qualification to this seems to be that laws of the former class are generally more complex in their character than those of the latter class ; and it is more obviously necessary in the case of the former to take account of the particular

circumstances by which their action is modified. Thus on the whole it remains true that the historical method tends to be more inductive than the statical method.

The prominence which has been given to the historical method in recent times is due to a variety of causes, but chiefly to the introduction of that new view of human society which is commonly described as the organic view. The more statical method of study was introduced at a time when the physical and mathematical sciences were predominant, and when human society tended to be thought of as a more or less mechanical system. With the growth of biological science, and especially with the introduction of the theory of development, a new point of view was made possible. Society came to be regarded, not as a mechanical compound of independent elements, but as an organic unity, composed of parts vitally related to one another, and undergoing a continuous process of development. Such writers as Montesquieu, Burke, Hegel, and Comte all contributed, in different ways, to the introduction of this conception ; and wherever it has been introduced, it has made the statical method of study appear inadequate.

Any attempt to balance the importance of the historical method against others would be somewhat beyond the scope of such an article as this. There can be no doubt that some of its advocates have unduly depreciated what they regarded as rival methods. The more statical and the more abstract and the more deductive methods have their own place. The historical method, however, may claim to be the most comprehensive. Other methods have a place within it, rather than it within them. They supply material for it to use and synthesise.

It may be observed, in conclusion, that the adoption of the historical method necessarily brings economics into closer relation to other departments of study than that which belongs to it when it is treated in a more statical way. The influence of political institutions, religion, education, moral principles, etc., cannot be overlooked in dealing with social evolution, even when special emphasis is laid on its industrial side. Economics thus comes to be regarded as a special department of sociology or social philosophy, rather than a strictly independent science. This need not, of course, prevent the recognition of the possibility of making a special study of the industrial side of life, or even of gaining valuable light by confining the attention for a time to that side of life, or to some special aspect of that side. Further, the historical method of study leads us to regard the growth of social life as having reference to an end. A process of development is naturally thought of as a development towards something. The consideration of the ideal form of social order thus comes into prominence, and in this

---

[1] *Cp.* Keynes's *Scope and Method of Political Economy*, pp. 303-304. As an illustration of laws of the former kind, reference may be made to the generalisation of List, in his *Theorie des Nationalen Systems der politischen Oekonomie*, with reference to the stages of economic development through which the nations of the temperate zone pass.

way the study of economic science is brought very closely into relation to ethics.

[For further discussions in connection with this subject, see also ABSTRACT POL. ECC. ; ANALYTICAL METHOD ; A POSTERIORI REASONING ; A PRIORI REASONING ; DEDUCTIVE METHOD ; POL. ECON. AND SCIENCE ; INDUCTIVE METHOD. For a list of books and articles dealing with economic method, see the close of the article on DEDUCTIVE METHOD. The best general treatment of the subject is Keynes's *Scope and Method of Political Economy.* Chaps. iv. and ix. of that work bear especially on the subject of the present article. Bonar's *Philosophy and Political Economy in some of their Historical Relations* will be found useful, though it deals very slightly with the influence of Comte and the development of the historical school. Special reference may also be made to Knies's *Die politische Oekonomie vom geschichtlichen Standpunkte.*—Menger's *Die Irrthümer des Historismus in der deutschen National-ökonomie.*—Mill's *Logic,* bk. v. ch. x. "Of the Inverse Deductive or Historical Method."—Cliffe Leslie's *Essays in Political and Moral Philosophy.* —The article on " Political Economy " by Professor Ingram in the ninth edition of the *Encyclopœdia Britannica.*—Professor Sidgwick's article on "The Historical Method " in *Mind,* old series, vol. xi. No. 2.—Suggestive remarks will also be found in Prof. Sorley's essay on " The Historical Method " (*Essays in Philosophical Criticism,* pp. 102-125)— in Mr. D. G. Ritchie's article "What are Economic Laws" (*Economic Review,* vol. ii. No. 3, pp. 359-377); and in several other recent articles and discussions.] J. S. M.

HISTORICAL SCHOOL OF ECONOMISTS. This is the designation frequently given to a number of writers and teachers, whose work has been marked by certain common traits, and who have exercised an influence tending in general in the same direction. Their teaching, while in large part constructive, has yet been to an equally large extent critical of the methods and results of what is variously described as the " classical," " deductive," or "theoretic " school of economists (see CLASSICAL ECONOMICS ; DEDUCTIVE METHOD). The "classical " school may be said to have remained up to the present dominant in England ; it is strong in Austria and Italy ; and it has included the names best known among the economists of the generation now passing away in France and America. Although, therefore, the historical school is now perhaps on the whole supreme in Germany, has representatives in all other important countries, including England, and is recognised as having done good service to economic science, the value of the movement as a whole cannot but be regarded as still *sub judice.* Moreover, even a colourless description of the movement as a whole would probably lead to misconception, owing to the marked divergencies between its representatives. The present article will, therefore, attempt only to trace the sequence and

affiliation of ideas ; and the reader will refer to separate articles for a fuller account of the personages referred to.

Cliffe LESLIE raised the cry : " Back to Adam Smith." But it can hardly be doubted that Smith's frame of mind was on the whole essentially unhistorical, and that historical narration and inductive reasoning were with him subordinate to a deductive movement of thought. Malthus adduced a wealth of historical information in support of his doctrine of population. But the historical school can hardly be said to have made its appearance until the " orthodox " or " abstract " structure had been completed in England by Ricardo (1817), and there popularised by the Epigoni, and until the facile expositions of J. B. SAY (*Traité,* 1803, *Cours,* 1828) had diffused over the civilised world the principles on which the whole edifice of orthodox theory rested. The immediate literary creator of the historical school was Wilhelm ROSCHER, writing in 1843. Two writers, however, were, in different senses, forerunners of the movement,—Jones and List ; and another, who was contemporary with its beginnings, but exercised no influence on it until a much later stage, was Auguste Comte.

In the midst of the growing success of the Ricardian group, Richard JONES (*Essay on the Distribution of Wealth,* 1831), protested that its conclusions, especially those concerning rent, applied only to a very recent period and a very small area. He urged with excellent soberness the need for historical investigation ; but his plea fell on deaf ears, and the only trace of his influence in economic literature for many years is to be found in J. S. Mill's treatment of peasant tenures. His German contemporary LIST (*National System of Pol. Econ.,* 1841), enormous as was his practical political influence in his own country, must as an economist be regarded as the prophet of a new movement rather than its initiator. His grouping of the economic history of the civilised nations of the temperate zone under five stages was a very rough and ready sketch, and, indeed, inaccurate ; yet it threw into German thought the idea of historical evolution, the fruitful parent of more adequate formulæ.

Meanwhile A. COMTE (*Cours de Philosophie Positive,* 1839-42) was stating the same idea in more philosophical form. To him it seemed that economic phenomena were so intertwined with other social facts that a separate science of them was impossible. The all-inclusive science of society, SOCIOLOGY, he divided into social statics, dealing with facts of co-existence, and social dynamics, dealing with facts of sequence. For social statics the appropriate method was that of direct observation, for dynamics that of comparison,—which could only be effected by means of history. These ideas have of late penetrated into English economic circles through the writings of Dr.

Ingram ; they are familiar to the German economists of to-day. But Comte's writings were altogether unknown to German economists forty years ago ; and the historical school proper, in its earlier phases, was an entirely independent product of German thought.

The decisive word was spoken in the *Grundriss zu Vorlesungen über die Staatswirthschaft nach geschichtlicher Methode* issued by the then young Professor Wilhelm Roscher at Göttingen in 1843. He told his hearers that his teaching would be guided by the historical method, and that he "aimed at reaching for political economy a result somewhat similar to that reached in jurisprudence by the Savigny-Eichhorn method." Thus with Roscher, the new inspiration was the direct result of the effect on contemporary German thought of the arguments of the historical school in jurisprudence. This school had argued that the legal institutions and ideas of a particular period and country were not to be regarded as eternal and necessary, but as the result of a long growth ; and that earlier practices are not so much to be condemned from the modern standpoint as explained in their relation to environing conditions. These ideas were readily transferable to the economic sphere. Hence the historical "method" was, from the first, more than a method with Roscher. It seemed to bring with it, as self-evident, the principle of relativity. This he explained in the well-known and oft-quoted *Preface*. The shape which, in his opinion, political economy ought to assume is indicated in his description of it as the doctrine (*Lehre*) of the laws of development (*Entwickelungsgesetze*) of the national economy (*Volkswirthschaft*). By the side of this phrase, and as equivalent to it, he placed in his later writings what he called the "fine definition" of Von Mangoldt,—"the philosophy of economic history."

Roscher has in recent years been criticised, by some approvingly by others disapprovingly, for his supposed failure to make any effort to reach his own ideal. It is true that his *Grundlagen*, the only volume of his great *System* that has been translated into English, is constructed very much on the old lines, and has been not inaptly described as Mill's *Principles* annotated with citations from the history of economic literature. But this is scientifically the least important of his works. In his *Essays* on particular subjects he was constantly under the influence of the thought of historical movement, though it found unsatisfactory expression in his use of such terms as "higher and lower stages of civilisation," "youth," "maturity," and "old age" ; and he was curiously possessed by the thought that all civilised nations have to run through a like experience. It must be remembered, however, that in spite of his fondness for "*Entwickelung*," Roscher had received

his historical training in an old-fashioned, pre-evolutionary, school. His best work is to be seen in the volumes on *Ackerbau* (Agriculture, 1st ed. 1859 ; 12th ed. 1888), and *Handels- und Gewerbefleiss* (Trade and Industry, 1st ed. 1881 ; 6th ed. 1892), in his *System*. Here he traces the growth and varying shapes of concrete economic institutions,—the bony framework of society ; and these two volumes, when compared with the space given to the same topics in the *Grundriss*, were clearly from the first intended to form the main body of his great treatise. They set an example now generally followed in German universities, but hitherto exercising little influence in other lands. The criticism to which Roscher's *System* is open—and, in their measure, such university courses of instruction also as follow in its footsteps,—is that the separation between the *Grundlagen* and the subsequent parts keeps matters asunder which need to be considered together. It is unsatisfactory, for instance, that the theory of wages and the history of trades unions should each be dealt with in isolation, and that they should be brought into no sort of vital relation with one another.

Soon after the appearance of Roscher's *Grundriss*, the movement to which it gave rise was reinforced by the advent of two other writers, who have since been justly regarded as joint-founders with Roscher of the historical school—Bruno HILDEBRAND, and Karl Knies. Hildebrand's *Nationalökonomie der Gegenwart und Zukunft* (1848) was never completed ; and the first and only volume was chiefly critical. It is from this that the current German criticisms of Adam SMITH have been chiefly drawn. Hildebrand's ultimate object, as declared in his Preface, seems but an echo of Roscher ; it is "to transform political economy into a doctrine (or teaching) of the laws of the economic development of nations." But he held to this conception much more firmly than Roscher did, and expressed it in far more attractive language. Perhaps the best statement of it is presented in the prefatory announcement with which he began the publication of his *Jahrbücher für Nationalökonomie und Statistik* in 1863 : "The economy of nations is, like their language, literature, law, and art, a branch of their civilisation ; like these other branches it moves within certain limits set by natural law ; but within these limits it is a product of freedom and of the labour of the human spirit. Accordingly the science which deals with it is no abstract science, like the natural sciences stating the same law for all relations in time and space, and measuring everything by the same measure. On the contrary, it has for its object to investigate the movement of historical evolution, from stage to stage, alike in the case of individual peoples and in the case of mankind at large, and so to discover the link which the labour of the present generation is to add to the chain of social development. The economic history of civilisation, and with it general political and legal history and statistics, are the only sure foundations whereupon may be erected any useful further construction of economic science. But history must not be the excuse for indifference, or divert men of science from the practical problem of the time. The understanding of the present is most vitally bound up with the understanding of the past ; and he can have no right understanding of history to whom the conditions and needs of his own time are unknown."

Towards the end which he proposed Hildebrand's contribution was twofold. To him is due the distinction between *Natural-, Geld-, und Credit-wirthschaft* (incidentally in his book of 1848 ; elaborately worked out in his *Jahrbuch*, vol. ii. 1864), which has proved so useful a formula in subsequent historical writing ; and the *Jahrbuch* founded by him was the first to furnish a medium for monographs by younger men on economic history.

Professor Knies is undoubtedly a scholar of far deeper philosophic insight than Roscher or Hildebrand. And his work *Die Politische Oekonomie vom Standpuncte der geschichtlichen Methode* (1853) was an elaborate and penetrating criticism of current ideas which even men like Roscher and Hildebrand had handled with scanty discrimination. Thus, as has been well said by Professor Schmoller, his book might almost be called " Prolegomena to a whole scientific epoch." " Whoever," remarks the same writer, " began his economic studies in the decade 1850-1860, knows how deep its influence has been, and how in certain respects it served as a confession of faith to the whole German school."

The thought on which Knies laid most stress was that of the development of economic *opinion* parallel with the development of economic conditions. The idea of the relativity of *doctrine*, already brought forward by Roscher, peculiarly interested him. And, although he encouraged historical study, and was ready to utilise its results, his book probably tended to turn some younger men from pursuing the path opened to them by Roscher and Hildebrand— the search for laws of economic evolution. On the other hand, he had no sympathy with the view which even Roscher had held that the classical doctrine, perhaps in some modified form, could be regarded as an " Allgemeiner Theil," or " Grundlagen," to be studied first. He urged that it rested on conceptions of property, contract, etc., which were themselves the result of history, and which were inextricably bound up with shifting conditions of time and place. That part of the theory which was composed of propositions of absolutely general validity, like the propositions of natural science, would be found to be small indeed.

Until about 1870 the waves of thought flowing by these three writers, Roscher in Leipzig, Hildebrand in Jena, and Knies in Heidelberg, quietly spread over Germany, and took possession of the universities with but little opposition. With divergencies already indicated, the new movement had everywhere the characteristics of insisting—(1) on the relativity of economic theory, (2) on the desirability of the study of economic history—including therein the empirical and statistical observation of the present. Much detail work was done in these latter directions. Outside the country itself, the movement was unknown.

The foundation of the *Verein für Sozialpolitik* at the Eisenach Congress of economists and public men in 1872, gave the signal for an outburst of controversy. Hitherto the professional economists had not made themselves heard in practical politics : now they united in recognising the existence of a " social question," and in invoking the action of the state towards its solution. They thus incurred the enmity of a great many journalists and politicians ; and as most of them were the disciples of Roscher, or Hildebrand, or Knies, the " historical school " became a synonym for the SOCIALISTS OF THE CHAIR. Even among economists themselves, the term was used to shelter all who were in any way dissatisfied with the classical economists and their German followers —to include the " inductive," the " realistic," and the " ethical " within its embrace. Roscher himself in 1874, in his *Geschichte der National-Oekonomik in Deutschland*, seemed to imply that the " realistic," the " historical," and the " ethical " directions were all much the same. But as soon as men of ability, thus for the time brought together in one camp, got beyond the utterance of generalities, divergencies were sure to make themselves felt. Professor Adolph Wagner of Berlin began about 1877, in the *Allgemeine oder Theoretische Volkswirthschaftslehre*, forming the first volume of a great *Lehrbuch*, the construction of a new edifice of economic theory to replace that of the PHYSIOCRATS and Adam SMITH. Professor Gustav Schmoller of Strasburg (since of Berlin) maintained, on the contrary, that the time had not come for such an attempt, and that it should be preceded by a period of empirical, statistical, and historical inquiry. He established a series of *Staats- und sozialwissenschaftliche Forschungen*, wherein, under his guidance, his pupils have published a series of valuable investigations. It was perhaps hardly made sufficiently clear that the generalisations or " laws " at which such historical work was ultimately aiming were not so much laws of coexistence as laws of sequence ; to use Compte's phrase, " dynamic " rather than " static." When the AUSTRIAN SCHOOL (*q.v.*) made itself heard, Professor Schmoller and those who agreed with him lamented—not so much that a fresh resort should be made to abstraction and deduction, and that attention should be concentrated anew by some thinkers on the problem of value—but that this problem should be declared the main problem of economics, and those methods its most appropriate ones. On the other hand it became the practice of those who agreed either with Professor Wagner or Professor Menger to speak of Professor Schmoller as an example of "extreme *Historismus.*" But it is not clear that Professor Schmoller and his disciples have gone beyond the positions assumed by the founders of the school. In his recent article on *Volkswirthschaft, Volkswirthschaftslehre, undmethode* (Conrad's *Handwörterbuch*, 1894), Schmoller writes : "The more inquiry is limited to a particular state of economic affairs, and this is provisionally treated as stable—certainly an allowable methodological device,—the easier it is to grasp the dominant psychical and other causes, to derive therefrom typical forms of organisation, and to explain the elementary and typical economic processes. Whether these are called 'laws' or 'hypothetical truths,' they are, when used with due limitation, the great instruments of knowledge, and the bases of right economic policy." Schmoller goes on, indeed, to say that "they are not ultimate truths. It is necessary to carry through a deeper investigation of the changing causes, and the changing economic forms and processes. This investigation will be threefold—(1) into the shaping of the psychological causes, (2) into the history of economic organisation, (3) into the progress of humanity as a whole." For the first, Schmoller urges a psychological study which shall be wider than the somewhat antiquated balancing of pleasures and pains or utilities ; as to the second, he remarks that the older historical economics pointed to the goal, and recent work in economic history has begun to collect and interpret the necessary material ; and dangerous as the third may be, entering as it does into the fields of the philosophy of history, of teleology, of hopes and prophecies, such bold syntheses will always be necessary to guide us in practical action.

Meanwhile in England, as far back as 1866, Thorold ROGERS had set the example of thorough investigation into the economic life of the past in his *History of Agriculture and Prices in England* (vols. i. and ii., 1866). It was Cliffe LESLIE, however, who first introduced to English thought the ideas which had long been making their way in Germany. In his essay on *The Political Economy of Adam Smith* (1870), Cliffe Leslie criticised the conception then common in England that political economy was a body of necessary and universal truth ; and in that *On the Philosophical Method of Political Economy* (1876), he argued that " the whole economy of every nation is the result of

a long evolution in which there has been both continuity and change, and of which the economical side is only a particular aspect or phase. And the laws of which it is the result must be sought in history and the general laws of society and social evolution." Cliffe Leslie was thus the first to bring together and unite the teaching of Knies and COMTE ; this has been since done more thoroughly, and with a more complete acceptance of Comte's social philosophy by Dr. Ingram in his *History of Political Economy* (in *Ency. Brit.*, 1885 ; separately 1888). Cliffe Leslie's criticism has resulted in a more careful statement of their "postulates," by most English writers since,— as by Bagehot, in *Economic Studies*, 1879. But, as in Germany, so in England, there was urgent need that a beginning should be made in the detailed study and systematic teaching of economic history ; in England it was from Dr. William Cunningham that the impulse was given in this direction, both by his writings (*Growth of English Industry and Commerce*, 1882 ; a new and much larger work under the same title, vol. i. 1890, vol. ii. 1892), and by his academic activity in Cambridge. A little later Arnold TOYNBEE directed the attention of students at Oxford to the "Industrial Revolution of the 18th century" (lectures published in 1884). And interest in the subject has since been stimulated from the historical and legal side by the works of Mr. Seebohm, (*English Village Communities*, 1883 ; *Tribal System*, 1895) ; Professor Maitland (*Select Pleas in Manorial Courts*, 1889) ; and Professor Vinogradoff (*Villainage in England*, 1892) ; from the statistical side by Mr. Charles Booth's *Labour and Life of the People* (1889) ; and from the evolutionary socialistic side by the writings of Mr. Sidney Webb (*History of Trade Unionism*, 1894), and others. It has begun to find a place in the requirements of Oxford and Cambridge examinations ; in America, courses of lectures are regularly delivered upon it in most of the important universities and colleges, usually in connection with departments of economics, but sometimes in connection with departments of history ; and in Harvard a professorial chair has been created with this object. Those who are engaged in this work differ, however, widely from one another in their attitude towards the current English theoretic teaching. The position of the historical school in the three countries, Germany, England, and America, is affected very largely by academic organisation. In Germany there is a recognised distinction between the " Grundlegung " or " Allgemeiner Theil " and other departments of economics. The historical school are in practice to be distinguished from various theoretic schools—(1) by their insistence on the vital importance of a thorough study of economic history *after* the " Grundlegung " ;

(2) by the comparatively small compass into which they would compress the "Grundlegung"; (3) by the comparatively slight attention they would give to the psychology of "value" as a part of the "Grundlegung"; (4) in surrounding the individualist economics of self-interest there stated by general anthropological and historico-philosophical considerations. In England there is no such recognised distinction between the "Grundlegung" and other parts. Indeed, economic teaching in that country seldom includes more than the "Grundlegung." In America, following the example of Harvard, the tendency is to appoint teachers of economic history side by side with teachers of economic theory and finance; to make each "course" independent; and to leave each teacher to define his own relations to economic science as he pleases.

[There is no account of the historical school at all complete; and the student cannot dispense with reference to the actual writings of the leading authors mentioned above. Roscher's *Preface* of 1843 is translated in full in the *Quarterly Journal of Economics*, October 1894.—The best account, though sympathetic, is that of Dr. Ingram in *Hist. of Pol. Econ.*, ch. vi.—Professor Schmoller's essays on *Roscher* and *Knies* (*Zur Litteraturgeschichte der Staats und Socialwissenschaften*, 1888), are brilliant and illuminating surveys of parts of the field.—For a somewhat more partisan presentation of some of the questions at issue than would be suitable here, reference may be made to Ashley, *Econ. Hist.*, i. Preface (1888), and an introductory lecture *On the study of Economic History* in the *Quarterly Journal of Economics*, January 1893. — For a different point of view, see Marshall, *Present Position of Economics* (1885), and Keynes, *Scope and Method of Pol. Econ.* (1891). See also Aug. COMTE; ENGLISH SCHOOL; FRENCH SCHOOL; GERMAN SCHOOLS; HELD; Cliffe LESLIE.]   W. J. A.

HISTORY OF PRICES.   See PRICES.

HITCHCOCK, ROBERT (16th century), of Caversfield, Bucks, served in the Netherlands under Charles V. in 1553.

His chief work, *A Politic Plot for the honour of the Prince* (Lond. 1st Jan. 1580, reprinted in Arber's *English Garner*), was one of the many schemes for the employment of the numerous idle but able-bodied vagrants who caused constant trouble in Elizabeth's reign. Hitchcock proposed that they should be employed as seamen in vessels to be fitted out for the herring and other fisheries, so that the profits which Holland enjoyed from this source might be secured to England. Hitchcock also wrote *The English Army Rations in the time of Queen Elizabeth* (appended to W. Garrard's *The Art of Warre*, 1591), which contains statistics of the victuals necessary for soldiers in garrisons. He quotes from his own experience of the time when he was in charge of 200 pioneers at Berwick in 1551.

[W. Cunningham, *Growth of English Industry and Commerce, Modern Times*, 1893.]   R. H. H.

HOARDING.   When practised by a community, or by large numbers of its members,
hoarding becomes an economic fact worthy of investigation. It may arise from commercial panic, from distrust of existing forms of investment, or from a want of any opportunity of investment. Or it may arise from misgovernment, and the consequent distrust of the holders of power.

In earlier times there was little or no industrial use for capital, except in agriculture or trade; and beyond the limited field of lending on mortgage, or at usury, to those who were oppressed by debt, there was no way of obtaining a return upon capital without entering into active trade. In England, almost up to the close of the 17th century, tradesmen or merchants retiring from business lived literally upon their savings. It is stated that the father of Pope, the poet, having amassed a fortune in trade in London, retired to the country about the time of the Revolution, carrying with him a strong box containing nearly £20,000, out of which he took from time to time whatever was required for household expenses. It was the opinion of writers about the same time, that very large sums were constantly kept hidden in secret places. Probably distrust was largely the cause of some of these cases; and from such or mixed motives these practices continued well into this century, until the growth of our system of banking, and the appreciation of its advantage and safety, together with the increase of joint-stock enterprises, has rendered hoarding no longer necessary. It still continues to be extensively practised in France, partly from the different condition of banking there, and partly from general distrust. The greater part of the war indemnity paid to Germany in 1871 was produced from the hoards of the French peasantry; and the same source supplied a large part of the gold required for the change of standard in Germany a few years later.

The most extensive system of hoarding of which there is any record is that which exists in India, and has been going on there for a very long period. This has undoubtedly arisen from the unscrupulous character of the former rulers of the country, and the habits induced by ages of misgovernment continue to influence the people in their present condition of security, and under their increased opportunities. Both gold and silver, in the form of bullion, of coin, and ornaments are hoarded by the natives of every class. Estimates as to the amount of wealth lying dormant in this way differ very widely, but the population is so numerous, and the habit so universal, that the amount must be very large. Enormous hoards are known to be in the possession of some of the native princes; and from the age of some of the coins contained among these treasures it is evident that the accumulation must have commenced hundreds of years ago.

Among the most civilised communities,

hoarding takes place at times of commercial panic. There is an almost universal distrust, and those who are able to obtain possession of coin or currency store it up, partly to enable them to meet their own impending obligations, and partly out of fear that later on they will not be able to obtain it. Direct evidence of this practice is not usually easy to obtain, but it is clearly indicated by the returns during the panic in London, in 1866. From the 21st March to the 30th May there was a steady decrease in the bullion at the Bank, amounting to £2,578,000 (see DRAIN OF BULLION). Yet at this time the country was gaining gold to much the same extent as usual, the net import during the three months April to June being more than 4 millions. During the same period the notes in circulation increased from 20½ millions to 26 millions, so that there must have been more than 12 millions, in notes and gold, withdrawn and hoarded.

The financial crisis in the United States in 1893 supplies another example, but no direct evidence of the fact is obtainable. The country had an ample supply of currency, not less than 100 millions of dollars (20 millions sterling) having been added thereto during the preceding three years, and their banking facilities were ample, yet there was for a while a perfect currency famine, and firms of the highest standing could scarcely obtain loans upon the most undoubted security.

[See report of Royal Commission on Gold and Silver, vol. i. 1887.—For hoarding in France and Germany: evidence of Mr. W. Fowler.—For hoarding in India: evidence of Sir D. Barbour.—For particulars of hoarding by Maharajah of Burdwan, see ibid. appendix v.—also letter in *Bankers Magazine*, London, 1893, vol. lvi. p. 205.—For currency crisis in U.S., see *Journal Inst. Bankers*, January 1894, vol. xv. pp. 37-42.—Blue book on Indian Currency, 1893.—J. M. Robertson, *The fallacy of Saving*.—Art. on SAVING.] R. W. B.

HOBBES, THOMAS (1588-1679), one of the most distinguished of English philosophers, was born at Malmesbury in Wiltshire, and died at Hardwick, a seat of the Earl of Devonshire. After attending a private school, he became a member of Magdalen Hall, Oxford, and took his B.A. degree in February 1608. Hobbes was recommended to the Earl of Devonshire as a tutor for his eldest son, and thus formed a connection with the great house of Cavendish which lasted to the end of his life, secured him from want, and gave him also the leisure necessary for meditation and study. Afraid that he had given offence by his writings on political philosophy, Hobbes left England at the time of the meeting of the Long Parliament in 1640, and spent eleven years in Paris. Here he made the acquaintance of the prince of Wales, afterwards Charles II. He returned to England in 1651, and from 1653 lived with the Cavendish family. His writings were denounced by some as hostile to liberty and by others as hostile to religion. He was also involved in several scientific controversies ; but he never experienced actual persecution. In the course of his long life, almost entirely devoted to study and to composition, Hobbes wrote many works on a variety of subjects, philosophical, theological, mathematical, physical, and literary. A collected edition of his Latin writings in five, and of his English writings in eleven volumes, was published between 1839 and 1845 by Sir William Molesworth. None of these writings can strictly be termed economical. Ch. xxii. of Hobbes's best-known treatise of political philosophy, *Leviathan* (published 1651), entitled "Of Systems subject, Political and Private," contains, however, some remarks upon the nature and influence of "bodies politic for ordering of trade," *i.e.* those privileged companies which in the 17th century carried on so much of the foreign trade of England. "The end of their incorporating is to make their gain the greater ; which is done in two ways—by sole buying and sole selling, both at home and abroad." Both are gainful to the privileged body because thereby they buy at lower and sell at higher rates. "Of this double monopoly one part is disadvantageous to the people at home, the other to foreigners." But Hobbes thinks that it would be very profitable for a commonwealth if its merchants were bound up into one body to buy in foreign markets, whilst at liberty at home every man to buy and sell at what price he could. For in this way their mutual competition would act only to cheapen the commodities which they sell at home, not to enhance the price of the commodities which they buy abroad. The suggestion is ingenious, although impracticable. The economic doctrine of the *Leviathan* is chiefly contained in ch. xxiv., "Of the Nutrition and Procreation of a Commonwealth." This figurative title is thus explained by the author : "The nutrition of a commonwealth consisted in the plenty and distribution of materials conducing to life ; in concoction or preparation ; and when concocted, in the conveyance of it by convenient conduits to the public use." The materials of nutrition—animal, vegetable, and mineral substances—are the gift of God ; but, as they are partly natural partly foreign, a commonwealth must import that which it lacks "either by exchange or by just war or by labour. For a man's labour also is a commodity exchangeable for benefit as well as any other thing ; and there have been commonwealths that, having no more territory than hath served them for habitation, have, nevertheless, not only maintained but also increased their power, partly by the labour of trading from one place to another, and partly by selling the manufactures whereof the materials were brought in from other places."

The distribution of the materials of nourishment "is the constitution of mine and thine and his ; that is to say in one word propriety (property)." Hobbes is at pains to show that this distribution is entirely the work of the sovereign. This doctrine follows from his general conception of sovereign power as in every sense absolute, and the creator of all social arrangements. But the progress of historical knowledge has rendered his proposition unmeaning. Whilst dealing with distribution, Hobbes makes some very sensible remarks on the impracticability of setting aside any fixed fund or estate to defray the public expenses. It is impossible to prevent sovereign power from falling into extravagant hands ; and besides, "commonwealths can endure no diet," since their expense is not limited by their own will, but by "external accidents and the appetites of their neighbours."

By concoction Hobbes understands "the reducing of all commodities which are not presently consumed, but reserved for nourishment in time to come, to something of equal value, and withal so portable as not to hinder the motion of men from place to place ; to the end a man may have in what place soever such nourishment as the place affordeth. And this is nothing else but gold and silver and money." The natural advantages of gold and silver for this purpose are then explained clearly but incompletely.

Lastly the procreation of a commonwealth is explained as the sending out of plantations or colonies. But nothing is said respecting the economic effects of colonisation.

It may be regretted that a writer of so much analytical power as Hobbes should have bestowed so little attention upon economics. But the explanation is to be found in the circumstances of his time and in the objects of his writings, so far as they deal with political science. The period at which Hobbes published the *Leviathan* was one of political confusion ending in civil war. The original cause of discord was not, as in our time, economic but religious. Men were contending, not for a greater share of the means of material well-being, but for freedom to worship as suited their conscience, and for power to force their mode of worship on those with whose conscience it did not agree. Hobbes endeavoured to extirpate the principle of strife by showing that every species of sovereign is and ought to be absolute, so that resistance to the will of the sovereign, whether prompted by religious zeal or any other motive, is always illogical, immoral, and destructive to society. The real importance of Hobbes's political treatises is to be found not in any occasional remarks upon economic subjects, but in his theory of sovereignty, which was developed by Bentham and the followers of Bentham, and through their writings has passed into current English thought

[Life of Hobbes in the *Dictionary of National Biography*, and the collected edition of Hobbes's *Works, English and Latin*, by Sir William Molesworth, in 16 vols., London, 1839-1845.— Bonar, *Philosophy and Pol. Econ.*, 1893.—Roscher, *Zur Geschichte der Englischen Volkwirthschaftslehre* (1851), pp. 47-53.]   F. C. M.

HOCK, BARON KARL VON (1808-1869). Of Jewish descent, after having studied in the universities of Prague and Vienna, Von Hock entered the financial ministry of Austria and became director of the customs in Trieste and in Vienna. Later on (in 1867) the emperor made him a member of the upper house of the Austrian parliament. His first literary productions were novels, a book on *Descartes and his Opponents* (1835), and another on *Pope Sylvester II. and his Times* (1837), which has been translated into French. When director of the customs in Trieste, he wrote against List's system of national protection (*Der Handel Oesterreichs*, 1844) ; List, who recognised in him a worthy opponent, told him that with the increase of his practical knowledge of trade and industry he would come round to milder economic views, and Von Hock himself confessed in his *Oeffentliche Abgaben und Schulden* (Public Taxes and Debts), 1863, that he had indeed receded from his former unbending free-trading principles. This treatise is described by Professor Ad. Wagner as presenting "in its pregnant conciseness an almost perfect science of finance, and being by far the best on the technique of finance" (*Finanzwiss.* i. 52). Roscher considered that "it provides a fairly (*ziemlich*) complete science for highly cultivated states, although it reads more like the conversation of a highly-gifted and learned man than as a book intended for the use of teachers," but expressly praised Von Hock's "nice distinctions on the incidence and shifting of taxation" (*Gesch. der Nat. Oek. in Deutschland*, p. 1030). According to Professor Bastable, "it is specially good, as might have been expected from the production of a trained official, in its discussion of administrative points" (*Public Finance*, p. 28).

Von Hock also published in 1857 *Die Finanzverwaltung Frankreich's* and in 1867 *Finanzen und Finanzengeschichte der Vereinigten Staaten von Amerika.* In the former, translated into French in 1859, the author has purely descriptive aims ; although he expressly disclaims comparative criticism, he concludes his preface by holding up as a model the German system "with the simplicity of its organisation and the small number of its well-paid and independent officials."   E. CA.

HODGSKIN, THOMAS (19th century), started, with J. Robertson, in 1823, the *Mechanics' Magazine*, and, in 1824, became joint hon. sec. of the London Mechanics' Institute, the predecessor of the present Birkbeck Institute. In 1826 he delivered a course of four lectures on *Popular Political Economy*, published 1827, with numerous additions, mainly of a controversial character.

The main drift of the book is to justify the natural laws which regulate the production of wealth as opposed to the political and social institutions of men. For this purpose the statement of Adam Smith that labour was the *original* producer of all wealth becomes converted into the proposition that "there is no wealth which is not the produce of labour," which carries the inference that private ownership of land is unrighteous. Stress is laid, following J. B. Say, on the influence of knowledge in adding to productive power. Knowledge is developed by the increasing need of it. "Necessity is the mother of invention, and the continual existence of necessity can only be explained by the continual increase of people." Thus, incidentally, the principle of the increase of knowledge, together with that of the division of labour, serves to refute Malthus (see MALTHUS). Hodgskin writes in a highly dogmatic style, *e.g.*: "There is and can be no other rule for determining the relative value of commodities than the quantity of labour required to produce them." "Accumulation of capital, in the present state of society, checks production, and consequently checks the progress of population . . . and of national wealth." The book does not appear to have met with much success, as a promised continuation was never issued.

The importance of Hodgskin lies in the influence of his writings on Karl Marx. [S. and B. Webb, *The History of Trade Unionism*, London, 1894, 8vo, p. 147.—Menger, Anton, *Recht auf den vollen Arbeitsertrag*, 2nd ed., 1891, p. 52 n]. In a letter to Lord Brougham, James Mill writes [Bain's *James Mill*, 1882, p. 363]: "The mad nonsense of our friend Hodgskin, which he has published as a system." In bibliography of *History of Trade Unionism*, an anon. tract, *Labour Defended against the Claims of Capital . . .* by a labourer, 1825, 12mo, is ascribed to Hodgskin [referred to by Böhm-Bawerk, *Capital and Interest*, p. 318, Eng. trans. 1890] ; in Karl Marx's *Capital*, French ed., note on p. 335, another anon. work, *The Natural and Artificial Rights of Property* is further ascribed to him.

[Mention is made of Hodgskin in Goddard's *Life of Birkbeck*, London, 1884.] H. E. E.

HODGSON, JAMES, F.R.S. (1672-1755), mathematician, and an intimate friend of Flamsteed; author of *The Valuation of Annuities upon Lives deduced from the London Bills of Mortality* (Lond., 1747), besides some mathematical and astronomical works. R. H. H.

HODGSON, WILLIAM BALLANTYNE (1815-1880), was born in Edinburgh, where he was educated at the High School, and entered the university at the age of fourteen. After leaving college he devoted himself to lecturing on education, literature, and phrenology, and also to journalism. He was much influenced by George Combe's *Constitution of Man*, which, altogether apart from the phrenology, he considered a most valuable work. In 1839 he

was appointed secretary to the Mechanics Institute, Liverpool, in which he had to control a large number of lectures, and in acknowledgment of his success he was appointed principal. In 1858 he was appointed one of the assistant commissioners to the Newcastle Commission on primary education. In 1870 the Merchant Company of Edinburgh were empowered to use part of their trust funds for the foundation of a chair of political economy in the university of Edinburgh, and Dr. Hodgson was appointed first professor in 1871. The appointment was for seven years only with a right of re-election. The limited tenure—annulled since (1892)—being different from that of all the other Scottish chairs, was such an annoyance that it was with great difficulty he was persuaded to accept re-election in 1878. He held the chair till his death. During his tenure he settled at the beautiful residential estate of Bonaly Tower, near Edinburgh, and here he accumulated a large library, his collection of economic works being presented on his death to the university of Edinburgh. He was twice married, and left by his second wife two sons and two daughters (the elder married to his successor Prof. J. Shield Nicholson).

Dr. Hodgson had a very wide circle of friends and acquaintances, and was a voluminous correspondent with many of the most eminent men of the time in education, literature, politics, and economics. Owing to the demands made upon his time by these and other social requirements, he unfortunately left no work worthy of his reputation. At the time of his death he was engaged on an English dictionary, and part of the materials were used as the basis of a popular work on *Errors in the Use of English* (Edinburgh, 1882), whilst another part of the materials has been incorporated in Dr. Murray's dictionary, now coming out. He wrote in an extremely lucid, attractive, and yet it may be said classical style, and he was an admirable speaker, and one of the best-known conversationalists of the day. In fact, it was by his personal influence mainly that his reputation was established as one of the foremost men in education and economics ; and his literary remains give a very inadequate idea of his vast learning and of his remarkable powers of popularising difficult subjects. He may be described as an orthodox economist, but alike in matter and style to be ranked rather with Adam Smith than Ricardo. He was too widely read in many departments of literature and science to be affected by the narrowness of the traditional ultra-Ricardian school. His contributions to economic literature are reprints of lectures on *Competition* (1870).—*The True Scope of Economic Science* (1870).—*Importance of the Study of Economic Science as a Branch of Education for all Classes* (Royal Institution of Great Britain, 1854, third edition revised, Edinburgh, 1870).—*Economics of the Drink Manufacture* (1874).—*Inaugural Addresses at Edinburgh University* (1871 and 1878).—*Co-operative Congress* (1877).—*The Instruction of the Community, especially the Wage-Earning Classes, in*

Economic Science (Social Science Congress, 1877). He also translated CAVOUR's (*q.v.*) work on Ireland. [J. M. D. Meiklejohn, *Life and Letters of W. B. Hodgson, LL.D.* of *Edinburgh*, 1883.—E. Woodhead, *Student Recollections of Professor Hodgson,* Edinburgh, 1883.—Prof. Nicholson, *Introductory Address at Edinburgh University*, 1881.]
J. S. N.

HOECK, JOHANN DANIEL ALBRECHT (1763-1839), was, during the year 1796, professor of philosophy and cameralistic science at Erlangen.

Previously he had been attached to the civil service, which he re-entered at the expiration of this single year of professorship, and became first a Prussian director of police with the rank of councillor of justice (*Justizrath*) and afterwards a councillor of government (*Regierungsrath*) in the Bavarian service.

Hoeck's works, *Grundlinien der Cameralpraxis* (1819), and *Materialien zur Finanzstatistik der deutschen Bundesstaaten* (1823), are distinguished by an extensive and practical knowledge of his subject, but are deficient in higher scientific qualities.

[*Allgemeine Deutsche Biographie.*]
E. Ca.

HOFACKER, JOHANN DANIEL (1788-1828), doctor and professor at Tübingen. Besides medical publications, he was author of *Ueber die Eigenschaften, welche sich bei Menschen und Thieren von den Eltern auf die Nachkommen vererben, mit besonderer Rücksicht auf die Pferdezucht* (Tübingen, 1828), in which he maintained that in unions where the father is older than the mother, more males than females are born, and *vice versâ*.

[Conrad, *Handwörterbuch der Staatswissenschaften*, s.v., Jena, 1889, etc.]
R. H. H.

HOFFMANN, JOHANN GOTTFRIED (1765-1847), statesman, statistician, and economist, was born at Breslau. He studied at Halle and afterwards at Leipzig. In 1798 he was a teacher in the Collegium Fredericianum at Königsberg. He was entrusted with several public employments through the influence of the President von Auerswald, and showed in all a high order of ability. Hence he was appointed in 1807 to the professorship of practical philosophy and cameral science at Königsberg, and in the following year was made councillor of state. He was made professor of political economy in the university of Berlin at its foundation in 1810. He directed the Prussian bureau of official statistics, which Stein had founded, from 1810 to 1844. He won the confidence of Hardenberg and became his principal adviser. He was at the headquarters of the allies in 1813, and was present at the conclusion of the peace of Paris and at the congress of Vienna, and accompanied Hardenberg on several of his diplomatic missions. After the peace, he held office in the ministry of foreign affairs, and resumed his duties at the university and the statistical board, which had for some time been necessarily suspended. In 1834 he

resigned his professorship owing to failure of sight. He spent his last years in collecting and re-editing his numerous scattered essays and treatises.
J. K. I.

The Prussian statistical bureau was completely remodelled in 1810, and Hoffmann, who may perhaps be considered as the founder of Prussian official statistics, was the first director under the new system. To him is due the radical change in the publication of the statistics of that country, which under his direction were issued as the well-known *Statistische Tabellen*, an official annual publication comprising very miscellaneous statistics. These tables in time became somewhat less comprehensive than at first. Most of Hoffmann's unofficial books were written late in life, after he had retired from office. Some are based on official figures collected by his department, and deal mainly with various aspects of population. His more individual and more strictly economic work is directed chiefly to questions of the freedom of labour and to finance. Generally speaking, his writings show approval of Prussian institutions, as then existing. He was the first who seriously advocated the adoption of the gold standard in Germany.

His most important works are :—*Das Interesse des Menschen und Bürgers bei den bestehenden Zunftverfassungen*, 1803.—*Die Lehre vom Gelde,* [*als Anleitung zu gründlichen Urtheilen über das Steuerwesen, mit besonderer Beziehung auf den Preussischen Staat,*] 1838.—*Die Bevölkerung des Preussischen Staates*, 1839.—*Die Lehre von den Steuern* [*als Anleitung zu gründlichen Urtheilen über das Geldwesen, mit besonderer Beziehung auf den Preussischen Staat,*]1840.—*Die Befugniss zum Gewerbebetriebe* [*zur Berechtigung der Urtheile über Gewerbefreiheit und Gewerbezwang: mit besonderer Rücksicht auf den Preussischen Staat,*] 1841.—*Die Zeichen der Zeit im Deutschen Münzwesen* [*als Zugabe zu der Lehre vom Gelde und mit besonderer Rücksicht auf den Preussischen Staat,*] 1841.—*Das Verhältniss der Staatsgewalt zu den Vorstellungen ihrer Untergebenen*, 1842.— *Sammlung kleiner Schriften staatswirthschaftlichen Inhalts,* 1843.

[R. Böckh, *Die geschichtliche Entwicklung der amtlichen Statistik des preussischen Staats*, Berlin, 1863.—W. Roscher, *Geschichte der National Oekonomik in Deutschland*, München, 1874.]
R. H. H.

HOGENDORP, GYSBERT KAREL VAN (1762-1834), was born at Rotterdam. He first adopted a military career, afterwards studied law under Pestel at Leyden, graduated, and published at the same time an essay, *De æquabili descriptione subsidiorum inter gentes fœderatas.* He was appointed "pensionary" of Rotterdam during the revolutionary period (1795-1813), but he declined all public office and betook himself to trade as a member of the house Gysbert Karel van Hogendorp and Co. In 1813 he stood at the head of the movement against Napoleon, and was a member of the provisional general government. After the return of the House of Orange he was invested with several high offices, but as he could not agree with the king's system of government he resigned them all, retaining only his seat in the second chamber of the states-general (the Dutch House of Commons), where he was almost the sole opposition member. In 1825 he returned to private life, and died 1834.

Hogendorp was in the first place a statesman, in the second an economist, — this is clearly shown by his works ; he never gave a general statement of his principles, which therefore must be gathered from his writings on practical subjects.

In these he principally deals with the questions of taxation, national debts, free-trade, pauperism, and colonies. As to the general principles of taxation he shows himself in many respects a disciple of Adam Smith, like his contemporary GOGEL (*q.v.*) ; from the latter, however, he widely differed, at least in his later period, by his views on the income-tax. In his *Lettres* he proposed such a tax on the basis of a classification of incomes. He approved of free-trade as conducing to national wealth. Government therefore should promote trade and industry only indirectly by good instruction, exhibitions, good roads, canals, etc. Yet he was not opposed to premiums on export, and low duties on the' import of articles taxed at home. He did not regard pauperism as a necessary evil, and disagreed with Malthus's views on population. He early advocated the system of agricultural colonies. His ideas on colonial policy are very remarkable. The best means to promote the development of colonies, he thinks, is to keep political government entirely separate from trading, to let the inhabitants, natives as well as Europeans, obtain property in land, and to prohibit all monopolies.

[His principal economical works are these :— *Gedagten over 's Lands financiën, voorgedragen in Aanmerkingen op het Rapport tot een stelsel van algemeene belastingen, uitgebragt 9 Juli* 1800 (Thought on the Finances of the Country, being Comments on a Report on a System of General Taxation, dated 9th July 1800), Amsterdam, Wed. Doll., 1802.— *Verhandelingen over den Oost-Indischen handel* (Treatise on the East Indian Commerce), *Id.* 1802-3.— *Brieven aan een Participant in de O. I. Compagnie* (Letters to a Shareholder in the East Indian Company), *Id.* 1802-3.— *Missive over het Armenwezen* (Letter on Pauperism), *Id.* 1805.— *Bijdragen tot de huishouding van Staat in het Koningrijk der Nederlanden, verzameld ten dienste der Staten-Generaal* (Essays on the Economic Administration of the Kingdom of Holland, addressed to the States-General), the Hague, 1818-1825. A second edition, edited by the well-known statesman Thorbecke, was published at Zalt-Bommel in 1854.— *Lettres sur la prospérité pub-*

lique, adressées à un Belge dans les années 1828-1830. Amsterdam, Diederich frères. A Dutch translation, 1832.]   A. F. V. L.

HOLDER OF A BILL OF EXCHANGE. The Bills of Exchange Act, 1882, defines a holder of a bill of exchange or promissory note as the "payee and indorsee who is in possession of it or the bearer" ; and further defines a "holder in due course" as a holder "who has taken a bill complete and regular on the face of it under the following conditions : namely (*a*) that he became the holder of it before it was overdue, and without notice that it had previously been dishonoured, if such was the fact ; (*b*) that he took the bill in good faith and for value, and that at the time the bill was negotiated to him he had no notice of any defect in the title of the person who negotiated it" (§ 29). A holder may sue in his own name, and if he is a "holder in due course," a defect of title in any of the prior parties does not affect his right, nor can any right of set-off or counterclaim available against any other party to the bill be exercised against him. If a holder, whose title is defective, obtains payment of the bill the person who pays him in due course is validly discharged (see § 38). If, for instance, a person steals a bill endorsed in blank, and obtains value for it from another person, who has no notice of any irregularity, the purchaser is entitled to payment, being "the holder in due course" ; also if the thief obtains payment from the acceptor, the latter not having had any notice of the theft, he gets a valid discharge, having paid it to the "holder." It should, however, be pointed out that a person holding a bill, the chain of indorsements on which is interrupted by a forged indorsement, according to English law is not a "holder" in any sense, and is not entitled to payment though he gave value for the bill ; also that a payment to a person holding such a bill is not a valid discharge—the only exception being payment in good faith by a banker of a bill payable on demand. English law, in this respect, materially differs from the law of other countries. According to German, Austrian, and Italian law a person, otherwise in the position of a holder in due course, is entitled to sue the acceptor and genuine indorsers though one of the indorsements through which he derives his title is not genuine (German Bill of exchange code, §§ 36, 76, see decision of supreme mercantile court reported Reichsoberhandelsgericht, vol. ii. p. 281 ; Italian Codice di Commercio, §§ 287, 327). French law confers no rights on the holder of such a bill, but declares the drawee discharged if he has paid the holder without having had notice of the loss of the bill (Code de Commerce, §§ 144, 149). As, according to § 72 of the English Act, the validity of an indorsement depends upon the law of the place where it was made, the provisions of foreign law referred to above may frequently become applicable in the case of bills of exchange payable in England, and materially affect the rights of the holders of such bills. E. S.

HOLDINGS OF LAND (FLUCTUATIONS IN SIZE AND THEIR ECONOMIC EFFECTS). During the greater part of our history England has been a country of small agricultural holdings, though of large estates. In all probability there was little change in the distribution of land among the cultivators from Anglo-Saxon times until the 15th century, and it was not until the 18th century was well advanced that large holdings, except for sheep-farming, became common. Seebohm (*English Village Community*, p. 141) gives evidence to show that peasants before the conquest held land in parcels of the same size as those held by their successors under the Normans; a virgate or 30 acres (exclusive of pasture, wood, and waste) may be taken to have been the average, perhaps the normal, holding of the higher class of serf—the *villanus*, while the lower sort, the *bordarius* or *cotarius*, commonly held about 5 acres. Round thinks that pasture was allotted in the proportion of a little more than 3 statute roods to an acre of arable (*Domesday Studies*, 1888, vol. i.). The lord's demesne too, which may generally have comprised from a quarter or a third to a half of the manor (Brodrick, *English Lands and English Landlords*, 1881, p. 8, and Ashley, *Economic Hist.*, i. pt. 2, p. 267) was often let off to free tenants, whose holdings were considerably larger than those of the serfs. Sir H. Ellis's classification (*Introduction to Domesday*, vol. ii. p. 511) gives

Unfree Holders or Serfs.	Free Tenants.
82,609 *bordarii*	10,097 *liberi homines*
1,749 *cosceti*	2,041 ,,
5,054 *cotarii*	*commendati*
108,407 *villani*	23,072 *sochemanni*
369 *radmanni*	
749 *bovarii*	

If it is remembered that about a quarter of the arable land in the country was probably kept in the lords' hands, and that Northumberland, Cumberland, Westmoreland, Durham, and Lancashire, besides Monmouthshire and Wales, were not included in the survey of 1086, a rough idea may be formed of the proportion of the cultivated land of the country held by the different classes of cultivators. In Middlesex alone was any attempt made by the Domesday commissioners to record the size of the holdings as well as the number of holders; elsewhere the villeins were taken, not individually, but by classes.

Little change probably took place in this system before the Black Death of 1349, or even, according to Professor Ashley, before 1450 (*Econ. Hist.*, vol. i. pt. 2, p. 264); and it is very difficult to trace the progress or

estimate the amount of such change as there was. The destruction of something like half the people by the Black Death, the frequent wars, the attractions of growing towns and of an extended trade, must all have helped to thin the rural population; but the central fact is the rapid increase of sheep-farming to meet a growing demand for English wool, and to avoid the expense of arable cultivation when labour was scanty and dear. From this time it is necessary to consider pasture and arable land separately, and the problem becomes more difficult. There is no doubt that the frequent enclosures of the end of the 15th and the first half of the 16th centuries affected both arable and pasture land, and that one result of the agrarian change was to consolidate some small holdings into larger ones; but many of the lands enclosed for sheep-farming were the demesne lands in the hands of the landlords. The legislative attempts to guide or check the change give some indication of its extent; e.g. an act of 4 Hen. VII. forbade farmhouses with 20 acres of arable to be pulled down; an Act of 24 Hen. VIII. ordered the keeping up of all farms from 30 to 50 acres, and an Act of the next year limited sheep-farmers to 2000 sheep, which would mean a legal maximum farm of about 500 acres. (The extent of the enclosures between 1470 and 1600 is roughly estimated with a map in Ashley's *Econ. Hist.*, i. pt. 2). There is abundant contemporary evidence that great numbers of the small farms disappeared, but there is no means of calculating how many remained; or in what proportion the land was divided among landlords cultivating their own demesne, freeholders, leaseholders, and copyholders; or what was the acreage held, collectively or individually, by any of these classes. Nor can the total population during this period be exactly stated. It is reckoned that it amounted to 2,000,000 at the time of the Domesday Survey; in 1377, twenty-eight years after the Black Death had destroyed one-third or perhaps one half of the people, 1,405,602 persons over fourteen years of age paid the poll-tax; in 1574-75 the roll of fighting men numbered 1,172,674.

With the 17th century our information becomes rather more definite, but is founded only upon contemporary estimates, not till the 19th century upon statistics.

Gregory King, writing in 1696 (*Natural and Political Observations and Conclusions*), estimates the numbers of the landed classes as follows:—

160 temporal lords	12,000 gentlemen
26 spiritual ,,	10,000 clergymen
800 baronets	40,000 freeholders
600 knights	140,000 ,,
3000 esquires	150,000 farmers

The whole country population he puts at 4,100,000, the town population at 1,400,000. In the former class leaseholders and copyholders are possibly reckoned together, the freeholders being separately counted, perhaps because they possessed the parliamentary franchise — certainly not because of any superiority in the size of their holdings, for the forty-shilling freeholder need not have possessed much land after the cheapening of silver from the discovery of American mines. As enclosures and other agrarian changes probably took place but slowly during the latter part of the 16th century and throughout the 17th, King's estimate may be taken to hold roughly good for the reign of Elizabeth. But it is not wholly trustworthy; the number of freeholders is generally considered too high (Gneist, *Eng. Const.*, vol. ii. p. 328 ; Toynbee, *Industrial Revolution*), and 150,000 can hardly account for all the non-freeholders who held land. For the copyholders had been numerous on every manor throughout the four centuries following Domesday, and cannot have decreased so fast as King's numbers would imply; and the tenant farmers had been a growing class since most lords of the manor gave up cultivating their demesne in the 14th and 15th centuries.

The annexed table shows the difference between the estimates made by Gregory King and those of Arthur Young about a hundred years later. Unfortunately the first applies to England and Wales, the second to England only.

Authority.	Date.	Population.	Acreage under cultivation.	Holdings.		
Gregory King .	End of 17th century	5,500,000 [1]	{ Arable 11,000,000 Pasture 10,000,000 }	70 Acres and under, 290,000	Over 70 Acres, 4,000
Arthur Young .	End of 18th century	8,675,000	{ Arable 16,000,000 [2] Pasture 16,000,000 }	Farmers, exclusive of those employing no labour, 2,800,000	

During the 18th century the process which converted England from a land of small to a land mainly of large holdings was carried on more quickly. The rise of a moneyed class desiring the political influence which was the monopoly of landowners created a demand for land, and at the same time supplied the capital without which enclosures and the other expensive agricultural improvements of the day could not be carried out. This was the second period of active enclosing, not now, as in the 16th century, mainly for sheep-farming, but for the conversion of the scattered arable strips in the mediæval common fields into separate farms enclosed with hedge or fence. Between 1710 and 1760 334,974 acres were enclosed (Toynbee, 1887, p. 38), and 7,350,577 more were enclosed between 1760 and 1849 (Porter, *Progress of the Nation*, 1851, p. 157). Much of this was of course waste land never before cultivated. Various opinions have been held as to the time and the speed at which the small freeholders disappeared ; some causes for their disappearance are at any rate clear. Dr. Cunningham (*Industry and Commerce*, ii. 478) says " that the pressure of poor-rates was the determining cause which rendered the yeomanry willing to sell, while the high prices of the last year of the [French Revolution] war gave them the opportunity of selling advantageously." It is certain too that the decay of domestic industries after the great mechanical inventions of last century took from the less prosperous of the small farmers their only means of eking out a scanty living. Yet Arthur Young's language often implies the disappearance of many of these small freeholders before his day, and Arbuthnot, writing in 1773, regrets " the loss of that set of men who were called yeomen," though, while protesting, with Dr. Price, against great estates, he cordially approves of large farms (*Inquiry into the Connection between the Present Price of Provisions and the Size of Farms*). It is, however, important to notice that Arbuthnot, in defending large farmers against complaints of their comparative unproductiveness, takes 100 and 300 acres as typical instances of small and large farms respectively. It was in Norfolk, Essex, and on the Wiltshire Downs that Arthur Young, when on his tours, found the largest farms. Of 250 farms described by him in the North the average size was 284⅔ acres.

The 19th century has intensified the changes of the 18th. In 1833 small proprietors were selling even in Kent ; speculation in land during the high war prices had led very generally to borrowing, and, when the unforeseen fall of prices came, to the ruin of many small landowners and the transfer of their land to more wealthy proprietors (*Report of Select Committee on Agriculture*, 1833, pp. x. 195). The first return of the number and size of agricultural holdings was obtained in 1880 ; for the " *New Domesday Book*"—the *Return of Landowners* of 1873 — made no attempt to distinguish between estates and farms. The census, however, of 1851 (see *Encyclopædia Britannica*, 8th edition, art. " England "), carries our statistical information on the point farther back ; but it is probably less exhaustive than later returns, particularly for small holdings.

---

[1] According to Finlaison's calculation for 1700, 5,134,516.

[2] Couling, in 1827, estimated that 25,632,000 acres were cultivated in England about 1801, and 3,117,000 in Wales.

The following table shows the statistics of recent years; it applies throughout to England and Wales. The size of 2558 farms was not stated in 1851.

It is clear that England is not even now wholly cultivated by large farmers, and that small holdings have of late shown a tendency to increase again. But some at any rate of the causes which produced large farming are still active, and some laws and legal customs combine with social and economic conditions (see CULTURE, LARGE AND SMALL ; CONVERSION OF ARABLE INTO PASTURE ; FARMING ;) to make anything like peasant farming difficult in England. The expenses of conveyancing add appreciably to the sum required for purchase, especially in the case of small parcels of land (see Torrens, *Transfer of Land by Registration*, Cobden Club Essays, p. 38, and Kay, *Free Trade in Land*; but for another view, Jevons, *Fortnightly Review*, Mar. 1881). The development of "small culture," such as market-gardening, may be balanced against these adverse conditions, and allotment legislation (see ALLOTMENT) is a sign of reaction against the accumulation of the land in few hands.

The economic effects of the fluctuations in the size of agricultural holdings cannot easily

Date.	Population.	Acreage under cultivation.	Number of occupiers.	100 acres and under.		100 to 300.	300 to 1000.	Over 1000.	Average size of holdings.
1851	17,922,768		225,318	142,358		64,153	15,987	771	Eng. and Wales } 111
1867	(1861) 20,066,224	Arable 13,528,000 Pasture 11,017,000 (round numbers)	390,660						Eng. 68 Wales 47·8
1875	(1871) 22,712,266	Arable 14,605,856 Pasture 12,202,596	470,000	(50 and under) 333,630	(50 to 100) 54,498	63,766	15,633	473	Eng. 57 Wales 47
1880	(1881) 25,974,439	Arable 14,096,176 Pasture 13,267,606	473,638	" 336,149	54,369	66,373	16,241	506	Eng. 59·2 Wales 47
1885	,,	Arable 13,577,235 Pasture 14,122,478	475,140	(¼ acre to 5) 136,425 / (50 and under) 336,571	(5 to 100) 255,083 / (50 to 100) 54,937	67,024	16,035	573	Eng. 59·9 Wales 46·8
1890	(1891) 29,001,018	Arable 13,079,889 Pasture 14,792,439	494,835	(50 and under) 409,422					Eng. and Wales } 56·3

be isolated from the results produced by other factors than mere size ; and there has been no time when contemporary opinion was not divided upon the point. But the best writers have generally agreed as to the value of enclosures, which, from the 16th century at any rate, may be considered as *implying* the amalgamation of small holdings. Fitz-Herbert (*Surveying*) said in 1523 that if an acre of meadow "lie in severalty it is worth half as much again" as if "it lie at large in the common meadows." Tusser in 1557 strongly approved of enclosing not only pasture but arable :

"Good land that is severall, crops may have three,
In champion country it may not so be."

i.e. one-third of the champion land must lie fallow (*Five Hundred Points of Good Husbandry, Somers Tracts*, 1810, ch. 17). Blith, in 1649, alluding to enclosed pasture, speaks of the "disproportion betwixt the profits of one lordship in common, and the next adjoining to it inclosed. The one worth three hundred pounds in common, the other neere a thousand in pasture" (*The English Farmer*, p. 35). Fortrey in 1663 made the same calculation of comparative values. In the 18th century Arbuthnot in 1773 defended large farms against the charge of comparative unproductiveness by arguing that farmers of only 100 acres could not afford to keep the proper number of labourers and of horses, and that an arable farm of 300 acres employed more men than three 100-acre farms. Adam Smith believed that "after small proprietors, rich and great farmers are in all countries the greatest improvers." (*Wealth of Nations*, ed. M'Culloch, p. 76). Arthur Young, while alluding to contemporary complaints against large farms as depopulating and as raising prices, emphasised their connection with the expensive enclosures of his day : "How, in the name of common sense," he asked, "were such improvements to be wrought by little or even moderate farmers ! Can such enclose wastes at a vast expense— cover them with an hundred loads an acre of marle ? . . . No. It is to GREAT FARMERS you owe these" (*Political Arithmetic*, p. 155). Writers of this century are still divided, but perhaps the balance of expert opinion at the present time inclines, for England, to large farms with a moderate sprinkling of very small ones, not for corn or sheep, but for dairying, fruit-growing, and market-gardening.

[For the economic side of the question at the

present day see CULTURE, LARGE AND SMALL; FARMING.—Kebbel, *Agricultural Labourer*, 1893, where the views of various writers are summed up.—Craigie, "Size and Distribution of Agricultural Holdings," in *Journal of Statistical Soc.*, Mar. 1887.—Bear, "State-made Farmers," *Nineteenth Cent.*, April 1891.—Caird, "Agricultural Statistics," *Journal of Stat. Soc.*, Mar. 1869.—Leadam, *Agriculture and the Land Laws*, 1881.—Brodrick, *English Land and English Landlords*, 1881.—Prof. Ashley has paid much attention to enclosures in his *Econ. Hist.*, vol. i. pt. 2.—See also Boutmy, *Constitution d'Angleterre*.—For manorial agriculture Denton's *England in the 15th Century* may be referred to. For the 18th century see Arthur Young's *Tours*, especially *Six Months Tour through the North of England*, vol. iv. pp. 192, 198-267.—F. Forbes, *Improvement of Waste Lands and Dissertation on Great and Small Farms*, 1778. For peasant farming in the Channel Islands, Arnold's *Free Land*, 1880. —Abstracts of many of the Agricultural Statistics are to be found in the *Journal of the Statistical Society*.]

E. G. P.

HOLIDAYS. The term holiday now signifies little more than a day on which no work is done. But the etymology points to the fact that particular days have been reserved from the performance of labour, usually from a religious motive. All religions have set apart certain days for the performance of religious duties. These duties, whether external as in the case of sacrifice, or internal as in the case of prayer and meditation, have always been deemed to require the undivided attention of those who wish to discharge them, and attention cannot be concentrated upon any act without an interval of leisure longer than is needed for its bare performance. The mind must be disconnected, as it were, from ordinary occupation before it can be devoted entirely to religious duties. The feeling of compassion, too, which may be traced in all the religions of civilised men, has tended to multiply occasions of rest and of enjoyment. In all the more primitive religions the rites necessary to express piety and conciliate the higher powers have been so many and complex that the holidays required for worship have also sufficed for rest. Such was the case with the nobler forms of polytheism, as in ancient Greece or Italy. Such also is or was the case with the Latin and Greek churches. Under these circumstances the demand for holidays merely as opportunities of rest does not occur. But in communities professing a simpler form of Christianity, or little influenced by religious feeling, the proportion of time set apart for religious observances is shorter. Strict Protestants have absolutely condemned all secular occupations on Sunday, but, with the reservation of Sundays, have left the whole year for labour. Hence a demand for holidays not of a religious character has been made by modern philanthropists and has been partially conceded, as in this country by Sir John Lubbock's Act creating four bank holidays in each year.

Considered merely on economic grounds, the necessity of a certain number of holidays in every year cannot be denied. It is proved by an overwhelming induction that incessant labour does not yield the largest net product. As productive labour cannot be continued for the whole twenty-four hours, so neither can it be continued for all days in the year. Moreover all reasonable economists will allow that welfare as well as wealth is desirable, and that even the greatest possible production of wealth in a given time would be too dearly bought by degeneration. But no absolute rule can be laid down as to the number of days in the year which should be reserved from industry. In different cases different periods of leisure are determined by difference (1) in national temperament ; (2) in the character of occupations ; (3) in the use generally made of holidays. Thus as regards (1) national temperament, certain races evolve an exceptional amount of energy in a given time, and so require longer periods for the restoration of vital force, whilst others evolve energy more slowly but more continuously, and so require more time to produce the same result. A comparison of the Englishman with the Hindu or Chinaman would probably illustrate this difference. (2) Difference in the character of occupations. Tending the machinery of a modern cotton mill is a more exhausting occupation than guiding a plough, and the occupation of the poet or the discoverer is more exhausting than the care of machinery. Purely intellectual occupations in the case of those who follow them assiduously are carried on more or less involuntarily. Much of the highest and most fruitful thinking may be described as unconscious cerebration. The born lawyer is for ever thinking over cases, the born inventor over mechanical improvements. This kind of labour is therefore not only intense but also difficult for the labourer to arrest. Even prolonged leisure may not give him repose unless accompanied by change of climate, scenery, or society. On the other hand the ploughman's labour ends when the plough stops, the bricklayer's when he has laid the last brick of the day. Thus it may be affirmed that the more intellectual the labour, the longer should be the intervals of rest. (3) the difference in the use generally made of holidays,—a holiday may be spent in a great variety of ways, each with a different economic result. It may be spent (*a*) in mere debauchery, in which case the cost of the holiday is great and the result of the holiday is diminished power of production ; or (*b*) in wholesome pleasure ; or (*c*) in mere vacancy, which, except for the overworked, is comparatively unprofitable ; or (*d*) in religious and domestic quiet, as in the English Sunday at its best, with the result of strengthening and concentrating character. The renewal of energy, the consolidation of character, are all of direct economic value ; and the holiday which contributes in due proportion to all is the best holiday in an economic sense.

It is therefore clear that no rational economist will lay down any absolute rule as to the number of days in each year on which productive labour should be intermitted. He will only say that every class of producer should have as many holidays in the year as are necessary to the highest efficiency, which implies (1) that the faculties are fresh and vigorous, (2) that the habit of industry has not been enfeebled by too many or too long intervals of idleness. These conflicting considerations can be balanced only after an independent experimental inquiry for every calling.

[*Blue Book on Sunday Rest in Various Foreign Countries.* See remarks of Petty and Cantillon on the economic advantages of Protestantism as. wasting fewer days in holidays than Roman Catholicism.]   F. C. M.

HOLLAND, JOHN (d. 1722), the organiser and perhaps the founder of the Bank of Scotland, was a merchant of the STAPLE (Munk, *Roll of Roy. Coll. Phys.*, ii. 92), and connected with the East India Company. This may be gathered from his own words, for he says in reply to a statement that the East India Company's cashiers' notes passed currently in payment for the company's use that he "never saw or knew of such notes, although I was about eight years almost every day conversant in that Business, and for several years since, have had opportunity to know the Affairs and Methods of that Company" (*Discourse*, introduction). Elsewhere he mentions that he was sworn to the English East India Company (*ib.* 13). In 1693 he and several Scotch merchants in London obtained for seven years an exclusive right to manufacture in Scotland "Colchester Baises, and all other sort of Baises, which Baises will consume a great deall of wooll which cannot be otherways profitable" (Acts of Parl. of Scotland, ix. 313). Soon afterwards he and four others made various proposals to William III. for starting a bank and for supplying the government with money, but they came to nothing (*Ruine of the Bank of England*, 4, 5). In 1695, being requested by a Scotch friend to draft a scheme for a bank for Scotland, he with some hesitation did this, and his views were incorporated in the act "for erecting a publick Bank," passed July 1695, which authorised the creation of a bank possessing exclusive banking rights in Scotland for twenty-one years (Acts Parl. of Scotland, ix. 494). This institution differed in kind from any existing banks, for it was the "first instance in the world of a private joint-stock bank, formed by private persons, for the express purpose of making a trade of banking, dependent

on their own private capital and wholly unconnected with the State" ("Banking in Scotland " in Macleod's *Dict. Pol. Econ.*, 124). And to Holland the credit of originating the idea as well as of drafting a workable scheme is in all probability due. Burton (*Hist. Scotland*, viii. 67) regards him as the organiser rather than as the founder of the bank, but gives no definite reason for his opinion. Holland and four of his associates in the baise manufactory—it would be interesting to know whether they were the four above mentioned—were among those empowered to receive the subscriptions, which were quickly taken up. In 1696 he was chosen as the first governor of the bank which he was invited to organise, being at his "own charge and expense," with the prospect of $\frac{1}{10}$ of any profits which might remain after the payment of 12 per cent interest to the subscribers (*Discourse*, 5). He was a gainer by the bargain, and speaks warmly of the justice and generosity which prevented him from losing by his work (*Ruine*, 6). He had to face great difficulties at the outset, for the Scotch knew nothing about banking, and only after some opposition did Holland succeed in obtaining the sanction of the directors to his suggested rules. He was exceedingly anxious that the rate of interest should be kept low, and that every facility should be given to borrowers, but his proposal that the statutable rate (6 per cent) should be reduced to 4 per cent met with much opposition. The African Company, in defiance of the privileges of the bank and with the object of ruining it, almost immediately set up the trade of banking as one of its many departments of work ; but the discretion displayed by Holland and the directors enabled them to tide over the crisis until the collapse of the company left the bank without a rival. Holland, writing in 1715, states that though he had left off business for about twenty years, he could yet spend a good part of his time in doing the business of a bank, and that though living a perfect country life, he spent some time in contriving schemes which might be for the public good (*Ruine*, 6). And from his letters it would seem that his advice was sought in emergencies by the directors of the Bank of Scotland. In 1715 he brought forward a proposal for starting a company which should lend "money on land and for the relief of the poor of the kingdom" (*Directors of the Bank of England*, 6). The rate of interest was not to exceed 4 per cent, and as the possible lowering of the bank rate which might result might be an objection to those interested in the bank, Holland wrote various pamphlets and letters indicating the advantages of a low rate to the nation, and pointing out the ruin which, he considered, must overtake the Bank of England unless it modified its policy. A scheme and rules for the management of a bank in Ireland were also drafted by him and his son

Richard. He died at Brewood Hall, his residence in Staffordshire.

John Holland is known to have written the following pamphlets :—*A Short Discourse on the present temper of the Nation with respect to the Indian and African Company, and of the Bank of Scotland. Also of Mr. Paterson's pretended Fund of Credit* (1696).—*The Ruine of the Bank of England and all Publick-Credit inevitable, and the necessity, in a short time, of stopping the payments upon the several Funds to the Bank, South Sea Company, Lotteries, etc., if the Honourable House of Commons will not themselves be Judges of the means that may be offer'd to prevent it* (1715).—*The Directors of the Bank of England Enemies to the Great Interests of the Kingdom, and also not just to the trust reposed in them by the Adventurers, who chose them to do their best Endeavours, by all honest Means, for the Advantage of the Joint Stock* (1715). — *Some Letters relating to the Bank of Scotland* were published with explanatory remarks in a letter to the Proprietors, by his son Richard Holland in 1723.

[In addition to Holland's own writings, the following may be consulted : Chambers, R., *Domestic Annals of Scotland*, iii. (1861).—Munk, W., *Roll of the Royal College of Physicians*, iii. (1878).—Lawson, W. J., *History of Banking* (1850).—Macleod, H. D., *Dictionary of Pol. Economy* (1863).—Burton, J. H., *Hist. of Scotland*, viii.—*Historical Account of the Establishment, etc., of the Bank of Scotland* (1728).]   E. A. M.

HOLOGRAPH. A term applied to a "deed" or writ written, wholly or in the essential parts, with the granter's own hand. A holograph document, such as a will in the testator's own handwriting, is held in Scots law as well as in French law, and the systems of law derived from French law, to be valid without witnesses. A document may be proved by extrinsic evidence to be a holograph one ; and if it is stated in the body of it to have been written by the granter, the presumption of law is that it is so. But a holograph writing, other than a will or a mercantile document written in the course of trade, does not of itself prove its own date where the date is in dispute or of importance ; this may be proved by other means.   A. D.

HOME INDUSTRIES. This is the older form of industrial occupation, which was gradually, and not without much irritation, superseded by the FACTORY SYSTEM. In contradistinction to the latter, it may be accurately and simply described in the following words, which are taken from the report of the committee of the House of Commons on the woollen manufacture of England, 1806. "In the domestic system, . . . the manufacture is conducted by a multitude of master manufacturers, generally possessing a very small, and scarcely ever any great extent of capital. They buy the wool of the dealer ; and, in their own homes, assisted by their wives and children, and from two or three to six or seven journeymen, they dye it, when dyeing

is necessary, and through all the different stages work it up into undressed cloth."

Up to the time when the factory system began to be practised, all the industries may be said to have been of this nature. The prevailing feature of the system is the existence of the small capitalist, who provides work and livelihood only for himself and a meagre supply of subordinates. This system produced the crafts and GILDS (see also CORPORATIONS of ARTS AND TRADES) of the middle ages ; and the questions of capital and labour to which it gave rise are exemplified in the famous statute of apprentices in our own country (see APPRENTICESHIP, STATUTE OF). It was undermined when the great inventions of last century, and the extension of the principle of division of labour, gave rise to the great organisations of workmen and the concentration of labour power. The savings effected by the large capitalist forced the small capitalists to compete in the only way open to them, viz. by combining their capital and forming one large unit in place of many small ones. Hence the progress of JOINT-STOCK COMPANIES, and the legislation of the present century for facilitating the formation of these. Notwithstanding this process of elimination, there are many scattered survivals of the older system, especially in the textile industries. As an economic system, that of the handicrafts is historically very interesting ; from a social standpoint it contrasts in many ways so favourably with the factory system that many are inclined to regret its decadence and virtual annihilation in England.

[Rogers's *Six Centuries of Work and Wages.*—Ashley's *Economic History.*—Yeats's *Technical History of Commerce.*—Cunningham's *Growth of English Industry and Commerce.*—H. M. Hyndman's *Historical Basis of Socialism.* In Latimer's *Sermons* some interesting facts regarding English home industries in the middle ages may be found. J. L. Green, *The Rural Industries of England*, 1895.—Ad. Smith, "Of Shetland Stockings," *W. of N.*, bk. i. ch. x.]   M. G. D.

HOMESTEAD AND EXEMPTION LAWS OF THE UNITED STATES. *Definition.*—Homestead is the house and land constituting a family residence. In law it is such residence exempt from forced sale.

Provision for the exemption of homesteads from levy for the payment of debts was not made in the common law, but is entirely statutory, being made on grounds of public policy only, because it is not well for the state that a family be deprived of its home : it should be protected against alienation of the home, especially through the improvidence or misfortune of the head of the family. Not only is such legislation modern, but it is even of recent date. The first law on the subject found in America was approved 26th January 1839, in Texas, at that time an independent republic.

At present, out of the forty-four states, four territories, and the district of Columbia, sixteen of the states have constitutional provisions for the exemption of homesteads, and all of them, with the exception of Delaware, Rhode Island, and the district of Columbia, provide for such exemption by statute. All of them exempt a certain amount of personal property, including primarily wearing apparel, furniture, tools, library, cattle, etc. Naturally the details of the laws vary much in the different states. Always the legal possessor of a homestead right must be the head of a family. Usually the owner of the homestead must be living on the property in question,—although in the state of Texas and in some few others the homestead right may be obtained as soon as the property is improved, so that the intent of acquiring a residence thereon is clear. In some states the homestead right is assumed from the fact of the head of a family occupying the property with his family. In other states the property so claimed for exemption must be openly declared at the time the property is made the homestead; and in still others there must be a recorded claim to the homestead in order to give it the right to exemption. The nature of the claim is that of an estate for life, although the wife and children of the owner have also an estate of inheritance, the children's rights lasting until they become of age. In some states, in order to give a clear title to the property if it is sold or mortgaged, the wife must freely sign the deed or the mortgage; and in some cases mention must be specifically made of the fact that by so doing she gives up her homestead rights. This provision has at times been used for fraudulent purposes, the wife signing the mortgage, but not specifically mentioning the homestead. Time and court decisions will, however, remedy such defects. The exemption of the homestead from sale on account of debts is not a complete one. In no case is the homestead claim good as against the state itself on a claim for taxes. Generally the right does not extend to exemption for payment of a debt made to purchase the property itself, nor against a mechanic's lien upon the property, nor to debts already existing when the estate was bought. The amount of the exemption varies greatly in the different states. In Maryland the value of the estate which is exempt, whether real or personal property, is limited to $100 (£20); whereas in Texas, California, North Dakota, South Dakota, and in some of the other states the value of the property exempted may amount to $5000 (£1000). In some of the states the amount of personal property that is exempt from levy is fixed; but the homestead may be a certain lot of ground,—for example, in Minnesota 80 acres or less in the country, or one lot to one half-acre in city or town; and in Kansas 160 acres in country, or 1 acre with improvements in town, regardless of its value. Under this law, if the homestead occupied but one lot of ground in a city, it might be almost palatial in nature and of great value, and still be exempt from levy. In Wisconsin and Iowa equal liberality is shown. In some of the newer states great hardship has often resulted from the fact that creditors could not collect from well-to-do debtors sums due to them, because they had been invested in a homestead. The rule of construction of the homestead and exemption statutes varies in the different states. For example, in Louisiana and Minnesota the construction is strict, the courts holding to the letter of the law; whereas in many of the other states—as, for example, in Michigan—the courts have decided that the construction of the law, on a number of grounds of public policy, should be liberal, and in favour of the owner of the homestead rather than of the creditor.

In the statutes of the federal government the expression Homestead Laws applies to the laws of congress which have provided for the free settlement of the public lands. Under the law of 20th May 1862, "every person who is the head of a family, or who has arrived at the age of twenty-one years, and is a citizen of the United States, or who has filed his declaration of intention to become such, as required by the naturalisation laws, shall be entitled to enter one quarter-section (160 acres) or a less quantity of (certain) unappropriated public lands," and file a homestead claim upon the lands. If he lives upon these lands and makes due improvements for five years, he may receive a clear title to the lands from the United States upon the payment of a small registration fee of 5 or 10 dollars (£1 or £2). If, after he has resided upon the land for three years, he can show that one acre out of every sixteen has been planted with trees, cultivated for not less than two years, and set not over twelve feet apart each way, he may at that time get a patent to his land without waiting for the expiration of the full period of five years. At any time before the expiration of the five years provided by law he may receive his patent upon the payment of the $1.25 (5s.) or the $2.50 (10s.) per acre provided under the regular pre-emption law. It is also provided in this homestead law that no such homestead shall become liable to the satisfaction of any debt contracted prior to the issue of the patent therefor. Under this homestead and pre-emption law nearly all of the free public domain of the United States has been already taken by actual settlers, to the great benefit of the country. To this law has been due, in great part, the immigration of the best of the foreign element now in the United States, as well as the enormous increase in the value of the western lands, and the rapid advance in wealth and culture of the western states.

[The leading authorities on Homestead and Exemption laws in the United States are : Rufus Waples, *The Law of Homestead and Exemption,* 1893 ; Seymour D. 'Thompson, *On Homesteads and Exemptions,* 1878 ; and J. H. Smyth, *Homesteads and Exemptions,* 1875.—A very careful and complete discussion of the subject is found also in Washburn, *On Real Property,* 1887.—Of course the final authority must always be the statutes of the individual states and the legal decisions thereupon.]

The following table contains a very brief digest of the exemptions of real property and personal property in all of the states and territories of the United States, excepting Alaska. The table is modelled after the one prepared for Lalor's *Cyclopedia of Political Science, Political Economy, and of the Political History of the United States,* published in 1883 ; but it has been entirely revised and brought down to date, 1st January 1895.   J. W. J.

STATES.	REAL PROPERTY EXEMPTION.	PERSONAL PROPERTY EXEMPTION.
Alabama	Homestead worth $2000 (£400) 160 acres in country, or one lot in city.	$1000 (£200) of personal property, wearing apparel and other articles.
Arkansas	Homestead to head of family of value of $2500 (£500) 160 acres in country or 1 acre in city, or at least 80 acres in country or one-fourth acre in city regardless of value.	To amount of $200 (£40) and clothing, if unmarried, or $500 (£100) and clothing to heads of families.
California	Homestead worth $5000 (£1000) to head of family, or $1000 (£200) to any person.	$200 (£40) worth of furniture and a multitude of special articles, and life insurance moneys where the annual premium did not exceed $500 (£100).
Colorado	Homestead not over $2000 (£400) in value.	Furniture $100 (£20) stock in trade to amount of $200 (£40) and various articles.
Connecticut	Homestead worth $1000 (£200).	Library, etc., $500 (£100) ; cattle, etc., $300 (£60) and wearing apparel to any person ; to head of family :—many specific articles ; horse, etc., $200 (£40) to physician ; $200 (£40) boat, etc.
Delaware	No real estate exemption.	$75 (£15) tools, etc. ; and books to any person ; to head of family $200 (£40) worth of personal property additional ; in Kent Co. $50 (£10) worth of tools to any person, and $150 (£30) worth of personal property to head of family ; sewing machine.
Florida	160 acres of land in country, or ½ acre and residence in town.	To amount of $1000 (£200).
Georgia	Real estate or personalty to the value of $1600 (£320).	Real estate or personalty to the value of $1600 (£320).
Idaho	Homestead worth $5000 (£1000) to head of family, or $1000 (£200) to any person.	Desks, etc., $200 (£40) ; cabin of miner, etc., $500 (£100) ; life insurance moneys where premium did not exceed $250 (£50) ; library, etc., of physician, attorney, etc. ; many other articles.
Illinois	Residence worth $1000 (£200) to a householder with family.	To any person $100 (£20) personal property ; to head of family, $300 (£60) worth ; to all wearing apparel, etc.
Indiana	To each householder $600 (£120), real or personal, or both.	Property real or personal to the amount of $600 (£120).
Iowa	Homestead to head of family of 40 acres in country or ½ acre in city or town, of the value of at least $500 (£100).	Presses, etc. of newspaper, $1200 (£240) ; household furniture, wearing apparel and many other articles ; life insurance money to a beneficiary to amount of $5000 (£1000).
Kansas	160 acres in country, or 1 acre with improvements in town ; value not limited.	$500 (£100) furniture ; tools, etc. $400 (£80) ; stock, food, etc. $300 (£60) ; and other articles to head of family ; to other person—tools, etc. $400 (£80) and other articles ; pension money for three months.
Kentucky	Land with dwelling to value of $1000 (£200) to a householder.	$100 (£20) furniture, clothing and domestic animals.
Louisiana	Homestead and personal property limited to $2000 (£400).	Homestead and personal property limited to $2000 (£400).

STATES.	REAL PROPERTY EXEMPTION.	PERSONAL PROPERTY EXEMPTION.
Maine	Land and dwelling, value $500 (£100), to a householder.	$50 (£10) furniture, $150 (£30) library, $300 (£60) farm animals, clothing, tools, etc.
Maryland	Real or personal property of value of $100 (£20).	Wearing apparel, books, and many other articles.
Massachusetts	Homestead to value of $800 (£160) to householder having family.	$300 (£60) furniture; tools, etc. $100 (£20); stock, etc. $100 (£20); boat for fishing, $100 (£20); $100 (£20) sewing machine; and many other articles.
Michigan	40 acres in country, or city lot and residence to value of $1500 (£300).	$250 (£50) furniture, $250 (£50) stock in trade, $150 (£30) books, farm animals and minor articles; where judgment is for work, labour or services, not professional, only $500 (£100) worth of personal property is exempt.
Minnesota	Homestead to householder with family, 80 acres in country, or one lot to ½ acre in city or town.	$500 (£100) furniture, etc.; animals, etc.; $300 (£60) tools, etc.; $400 (£80) presses, etc. of newspaper; $2000 (£400) and $400 (£80) worth of stock in trade; and many other articles.
Mississippi	Homestead to householder with family, 160 acres in country, or residence, etc. in city of value of $2000 (£400).	$250 (£50) personal property or specific articles; library, $250 (£50); instruments, etc., $250 (£50); life insurance moneys $10,000 (£2000) to beneficiaries or $5000 (£1000) to executor or administrator for benefit of heirs or next of kin.
Missouri	160 acres, worth $1500 (£300) in country, or buildings in city to value of $1500 (£300) to $3000 (£600).	Furniture $100 (£20), provisions $100 (£20), domestic animals $150 (£30); or in lieu of all specified, $300 (£60) net exemptions.
Montana	Homestead to householder of 160 acres or ¼ acre in city or town, of value of $2500 (£500).	Farming tools, etc., $600 (£120); $100 (£20) books, etc.; cabin of miner with appliances $500 (£100); articles specified.
Nebraska	Homestead not exceeding $2000 (£400) in value.	$500 (£100) exempted when no real estate is owned, and pension money or property purchased or improved with it to value of $2000 (£400).
Nevada	Homestead to head of family to value of $5000 (£1000) in gold coin.	Chairs, etc., $100 (£20); cabin of miner $500 (£100), and $500 (£100) tools, etc., $100 (£20) sewing machine; library, instruments, etc.; many other articles.
New Hampshire	Homestead worth $500 (£100), or so much thereof as does not exceed $500 (£100).	$100 (£20) furniture, $200 (£40) in library, $100 (£20) in tools, $50 (£10) in fuel and provisions, clothing, domestic animals.
New Jersey	Homestead to amount of $1000 (£200) to householder.	To amount of $200 (£40) and clothing.
New York	Homestead to value of $1000 (£200) to householders.	$250 (£50) in furniture, mechanics' tools, instruments, library, etc.
North Carolina	Homestead to value of $1000 (£200) to occupant of an estate.	To value of $500 (£100).
North Dakota	Homestead of value of $5000 (£1000) to head of family.	$100 (£20) books, etc.; wearing apparel; and $1500 (£300) worth of personal property additional.
Ohio	To amount of $1000 (£200) to heads of families only. If homestead sold under prior lien, $500 (£100) paid to widow or heirs.	Clothing, furniture, tools, etc., or $500 (£100) additional exemption if no real estate is owned.
Oregon	Homestead of 160 acres in country or one block in city or town, of value of $1500 (£300), or at least 20 acres in country or one lot in city or town regardless of value.	$300 (£60) in furniture, $100 (£20) clothing, or $50 (£10) for each member of family, $400 (£80) tools, etc.; farm animals.
Pennsylvania	Property, either real or personal, to the value of $300 (£60).	$300 (£60) value of property, either real or personal, besides wearing apparel; where the judgment is for wages of $100 (£20) or less, or board for four weeks or less, no exemption is allowed.

STATES.	REAL PROPERTY EXEMPTION.	PERSONAL PROPERTY EXEMPTION.
Rhode Island	No real estate exemption.	$200 (£40) tools, etc.; $300 (£60) furniture, etc.; books, etc., $300 (£60); many other articles.
South Carolina	Homestead worth $1000 (£200).	$500 (£100) worth of personal property.
South Dakota	Homestead to head of family of 160 acres in country or house and lots in city or 1 acre in city or town, of value of $5000 (£1000).	Books, wearing apparel, etc., to any person; to head of family $750 (£150) additional; to any person $300 (£60) additional; or in lieu thereof:—Books, etc., $200 (£40); $200 (£40) furniture; cattle, waggons, stock, etc., $1250 (£250); library, etc., $300 (£60).
Tennessee	Homestead worth $1000 (£200).	Clothing, furniture, and a long catalogue of miscellaneous articles.
Texas	200 acres with house in country, or lot worth $5000 (£1000), and residence in town, to a family.	Furniture, tools, and many other articles.
Vermont	Homestead worth $500 (£100) to any housekeeper.	Clothing, furniture, farm animals, and sundry stores, $250 (£50) in teams, $200 (£40) professional library, and tool chest of mechanic.
Virginia	$2000 (£400) in real or personal property to head of a family.	Clothing, furniture, library, domestic animals, besides $2000 (£400) real or personal.
Washington	Homestead to householder of value of $1000 (£200).	Wearing apparel; $500 (£100) private library; to householder; $500 (£100) furniture, etc.; cattle, etc., or $200 (£40) personal property; $500 (£100) farming utensils; $500 (£100) tools; $200 (£40) instruments of physician and $500 (£100) library; library of attorney or other professional man $1000 (£200) and $200 (£40) of furniture.
West Virginia	Homestead worth $1000 (£200) to head of a family.	Personal estate not exceeding $200 (£40) in value.
Wisconsin	40 acres with house in country, or house and ¼ acre in town.	$200 (£40) furniture, etc.; $200 (£40) farming utensils; $200 (£40) tools; $1500 (£300) presses, etc. of printer, or where judgment is for wages for services to defendant $400 (£80), many other articles.
Wyoming	Homestead to head of family of value of $1500 (£300).	$150 (£30) wearing apparel; to head of family :— $500 (£100) furniture; and other articles; $300 (£60) tools, etc.; $300 (£60) library, instruments, etc.
TERRITORIES. Arizona	Homestead to head of family of value of $4000 (£800).	Personal property to family of value of $1000 (£200) and other articles.
District of Columbia	No real estate exemption.	Clothing, furniture, etc. to value of $300 (£60); merchants' stock or mechanics' stock or mechanics' tools $200 (£40); family library $400 (£80); and other articles.
New Mexico	Homestead to head of family of value of $1000 (£200).	Wearing apparel, cattle, etc., books, etc., $200 (£40) furniture, and many other articles; to unmarried woman :—$150 (£30) wearing apparel and other articles; instruments, etc., $150 (£30); library of attorney, $500 (£100); many other articles; to head of family not an owner of homestead $500 (£100) real and personal property additional.
Oklahoma	Homestead to head of family of 160 acres and improvements; or 1 acre in city or town; or real or personal property of value of $600 (£120).	Wearing apparel, furniture, and many other articles.
Utah	Homestead to head of family of value of $1000 (£200), $500 (£100) additional for wife, and $250 (£50) additional for each member of family.	$200 (£40) chairs, etc.; $300 (£60) furniture, etc.; $300 (£60) farming utensils; $500 (£100) tools, etc.; instruments, etc.; $500 (£100) cabin of miner and $200 (£40), tools, etc.; many other articles.

HOMOLOGATION (Fr.). Term employed for the formality by which an authority confirms certain acts or conventions between individuals or associations. It is most frequently used in relation to railway tariffs, general or special, which cannot be applied without the homologation in France of the minister of public works. The necessity for it was at first contested by the companies, which argued their absolute right to raise or reduce their rates within the limits fixed by their charters or acts of concession. The government maintained its prerogative of examining the proposed tariffs and imposing its veto by a refusal to homologate, as a measure of public policy, otherwise the established economic system of the country might be frustrated by differential rates in favour of foreign imports, particular merchandise, traders, or localities. The contention of the government prevailed, and all modifications of tariffs are now submitted to the department of public works for homologation.   T. L.

HONOUR (liberty or franchise), a collection of manors, retaining their separate manorial organisation in most respects, even when one central court was held for all. These estates were developments of grants, made by Anglo-Saxon kings, of jurisdiction, with or without land, over large districts, even whole hundreds. None but lords of honours held courts over a district larger than a manor, and even such courts were really aggregations of manor-courts. As local jurisdiction and feudal organisation decayed the great lords might have succeeded in dividing the country among a few large landed proprietors but for the legal checks put upon their jurisdiction (Assize of Clarendon, 9, 11, Stat. of Marlborough), and upon the formation of new manors (Quia Emptores, 1290). Doubtless the caution of the kings helped to keep up the numbers, as well as to keep down the power, of the landed nobility and gentry.

[Stubbs, *Const. Hist.*, 1880, I. 106, 400.—Gneist, *Hist of Eng. Const.*, trans. 1886, p. 148, and ch. xi.—*Magna Carta*, 43.—Digby, *Real Property*, 1876, 52.]   E. G. P.

HONOUR (PAYMENT FOR). Where a bill of exchange has been noted or protested for non-payment, any person may intervene and pay it *supra* protest for the honour of any party liable thereon, or for the honour of the person for whose account the bill is drawn. Payment for honour is known in continental countries as payment by "intervention," a term which expresses its nature as a "negotiorum gestio." It thus constitutes an exception to the general rule of English law that payment by a stranger to the contract is ineffectual to liberate the debtor. Where a bill is paid *supra* protest the person who pays it is thereby subrogated to the rights and duties of the holder as regards the party for whose honour he pays, and all parties liable to that party.

[See § 68 of the Bills of Exchange Act, 1882 ; and Chalmers, *Bills of Exchange*, ed. 4, p. 230.]   M. D. C.

HOOKE, ANDREW (18th century), compared the capital wealth of the country with the amount of the national debt in order to show that the existence of the latter involved no danger to the state. He estimated the growth of capital between 1600 and 1750 by assuming the value of the personal stock to be twenty times as large as the amount of coin in circulation ; to this he added the value of lands and houses ; and thus arrived at a total of a thousand million pounds, or twelve and a half times the amount of the national debt in 1750. Such estimates must always be based on conjecture rather than on knowledge ; and that made by Hooke was distinctly too high. Hooke also suggested a scheme for the discharge of the national debt.

An Essay on the National Debt and National Capital, or the Account truly stated, Debtor and Creditor, London, 1750.

[M. V. D. M. [Monsieur Vivant de Mézagues], *A General View of England from the Year 1600 to 1762 in a Letter to A. M. L. C. D.* Translated from the French, London, 1766.—Sir R. Giffen, in *The Growth of Capital*, London, 1889, p. 90, speaks highly of this publication, which supplies the means for a criticism of that of A. Hooke.]   R. H. H.

HORN, IGNACE EINHORN, also known as Edward Horn (1825-1875), was born at Vag-Ujhély (Hungary) and died at Pesth. Having taken a part in the insurrection of 1849, he was compelled to leave his country and went to Germany, where he published *Hungary before 1848* (in German) in 1851. The publication of this work brought on him a political prosecution. The severe sentence which followed compelled him to take refuge in Belgium, where he published, also in German, his *Statistisches Gemälde des Konigreichs Belgien*, 1853, and *Bevölkerungs-wissenshaftliche Studien aus Belgien*, 1854. In 1855 he established himself at Paris, where he was soon employed as a contributor on the *Journal des Économistes* and on the *Revue Contemporaine* as well as on the *Journal des Debats* and *La Presse*, and also published *Das Kreditwesen in Frankreich*, 1857, *John Law ein finanzgeschichtliche Versuch*, 1858, then *La crise cotonnière et les textiles indigènes* (8vo, 1863) as well as the speech made on his reception into the Institute of Egypt at Alexandria, *Du progrès économique en Égypte*, 1864. In 1866 he published *La Liberté des Banques*. In this work Horn argued against monopoly in banking matters. Horn's essay on Boisguillebert, for which he obtained a prize from the Institute, was published the next year under the title of *L'économie politique avant les physiocrates*, 8vo (these four in French). He also undertook a publication of the greatest value, the *Annuaire international du crédit public*. This was established by Horn with the assistance of other well-known writers in France and elsewhere, but unfortunately it was only continued for the three years 1859, 1860, and 1861.

Horn took an important part during the year 1868 in the economic discussions going on in the public meetings permitted at that time. After this, Horn, who had been naturalised in France, unexpectedly returned to his native country, in which he was appointed to a post of much distinction. It should be added that he was greatly liked by all who knew him ; that all his public occupations never made him a rich man ; and that in the different countries where he took up his temporary abode he was much esteemed. This was particularly the case in France.   A. C. f.

HORNE, ANDREW (d. 1328), an eminent lawyer, legal writer, and chamberlain of London, left two valuable compilations on law and procedure.

Liber Horne (preserved in the Guildhall of London).—*La Somme appelle Mirroir des Justices vel Speculum Justiciariorum*, to which Horne made many important additions, first pub. London, 1642.

[Sir E. Coke, *Prefaces to 9th and 10th Reports*, trans. by G. Wilson, London, 1777.—G. Crabb, *A History of English Law*, London, 1829.]

R. H. H.

HORNECK (also written HORNICK and HŒRNINGK), PHILIPP WILHELM VON (about 1638-1713), a German economist, was born at Mainz. He came at an early age to Vienna with his father, who had been a physician in the Rhineland, and who, having become a convert to Catholicism, was ennobled and made an Austrian imperial councillor. The younger Horneck, about 1690, became private secretary of the prince bishop of Passau, who made him a privy councillor in 1695. His wife was a daughter of J. J. Becher, and he seems to have derived some of his opinions from that economist, whose writings he often quotes. The work by which he is principally known is entitled *Oesterreich über alles, wann es nur will* (1684). It is an attempt to show how by a judicious economic policy the dominions of the House of Hapsburg, whose fortunes were then at a low ebb, might be raised to a higher and more independent position than any other European state. The author seeks to induce his fellow-countrymen to follow the economic methods of France, Holland, and England. The work is based on mercantilist principles ; but, along with much that was erroneous or questionable, it contained many important suggestions for the development of the resources of the empire. It enjoyed a great popularity with the author's contemporaries and several succeeding generations, passed through many editions, and had considerable influence on Austrian policy in the 18th century ; Joseph II., in particular, is said to have attached great weight to it.

[Roscher, *Gesch. der N. O.*, p. 289.]   J. K. I.

HORNER, FRANCIS (1778-1817), born at Edinburgh, and educated at the university there, was called to the Scotch bar in 1800, but, dissatisfied with the law of his native country, removed to London in 1803, and was called to the English bar in 1807. He was appointed, in 1806, a member of the board of commissioners entrusted with the examination of the claims of the creditors of the Nabob of Arcot, but resigned this post in 1809. He entered parliament in 1806, remaining a member, except for one short period, until his early death, at Pisa. As a young man, Horner was remarkably studious, and, after entering parliament, very rapidly came to the front, so that at the time of his death he was one of the foremost of the Whigs, with a constantly-increasing reputation for oratory, sound knowledge, and remarkable integrity, combined with independence. In 1810 he was elected chairman of the Bullion Committee (see BULLION COMMITTEE, REPORT OF). The first part of this is from his pen : it is a concise exposition of the fallacy then generally held by the directors of the Bank of England and others, that the rise in the price of gold was caused by the foreign demand for that metal. Horner rightly attributed it to the over-issue of paper money. Though the resolutions moved by Horner in the House of Commons, in 1811, in favour of the resumption of cash payments, were defeated, and though the bullionists met with no better success in 1816, yet the effects of the Report, and of the controversy which ensued on its publication, were such, that the act for the resumption of specie payments was passed in 1819, following the lines of the recommendations of the committee. As regards other economic questions, Horner opposed the graduated duties on corn, urged the reduction of the peace establishment in 1816, and spoke against the Alien Bills.

Though originating no new theory in political economy, Horner possessed a very complete knowledge of the science—D. Stewart considered him his model pupil—and his critical acumen is well illustrated by his strictures on Adam Smith's deductions concerning the bounty on exported corn (*Edin. Review*, No. ix. pp. 190, etc.), and more particularly on Smith's theory of prices (*Letters, passim*) : there exists also a letter from him to Malthus, attacking the latter's reasoning on the corn question. Apart from the *Report of the Bullion Committee* and *A Short Account of a late Short Administration* (Pitt's), his only writings are essays in the *Edinburgh Review*, of which he was one of the founders. These articles are all noticeable for his thorough knowledge of his subject, this being a characteristic trait in all that he undertook. The most important of these reviews are :—

Thornton's *Inquiry into the Nature and Effects of the Paper Credit of Great Britain* (Oct. 1802). —Canard's *Principes d'Economie politique* (Jan. 1803).—Lord King's *Thoughts on the Restriction of Payments in Specie at the Banks of England and Ireland* (July, 1803). — Miss Williams's *Political and Confidential Correspondence of Louis*

XVI. (Oct. 1803).—*Cursory Observations on the Act for Ascertaining the Bounties, and for Regulating the Exportation and Importation of Corn,* by an M.P. (Oct. 1804).—*Stewart's Short Statement of Facts Relative to the Late Election of a Mathematical Professor in the University of Edinburgh* (Oct. 1805).—*Earl of Selkirk's Observations on the Present State of the Highlands* (Oct. 1805).

[*Memoirs and Correspondence of Francis Horner, M.P.*, edited by L. Horner (1843).—*Edinburgh Review,* clviii. (1843), pp. 261-99.—Lord Cockburn, *Life of Lord Jeffrey* (Edin., 1852).—Lord Brougham, *Statesmen of the Times of George III.*, 2nd series (London, 1839).]   R. H. H.

HORSLEY, W. (1701 ?-1776 ?), published, in 1744, a translation of a French *Treatise on Maritime Affairs*, and an adaptation of Frederick the Great's Anti - Machiavel entitled *Lord Theodore's Political Principles*. In 1746 appeared *The Political History of Europe*, containing a collection of public treaties and a curiously crude historical summary. Horsley is credited, in the British Museum and other catalogues with the *Universal Merchant*, London, 1753,[1] of which the real author was Nicolas MAGENS, written Meggens by Adam Smith in his "Digression Concerning the Variations of Silver," bk. i. *Wealth of Nations*.

Horsley is stated to have translated the work from the German ; he contributed a dedication to Pelham.[2]

[Magens himself in *Further Explanations of some particular subjects contained in the Universal Merchant*, London, 1756, says, "I will add . . . to those, which I ventured to assert in a book upon this and other subjects, published by Mr. Horsley under the too pompous title of the *Universal Merchant.*" The authority for the statement that the book was a translation from the German and the translator Horsley is Sir James Steuart, *Inquiry into the Principles of Political Economy*, vol. ii. p. 158, London, 1767, 4to. Otherwise there would be much to suggest that the book was written in English. For Horsley's connection with Magens, see, further, *Quarterly Journal of Economics*, vol. v. p. 356, *Annual Register*, xix. p. 123.]   H. E. E.

[1] The title is as follows :—*The Universal Merchant,* containing, etc., London. Printed by C. Say, for W. Owen, at Homer's Head, near Temple Bar. MDCCLIII.

[2] To the Right Honourable Henry Pelham, Esq., etc. This Book, calculated for General Use, is with the Greatest Respect, etc., inscribed by William Horsley.

Sir—I have the Greater Pleasure in presenting this Work to your Consideration, as it is the Performance of a Foreigner resident among us who participates with us the Sweets of Liberty, and who gratefully makes us the best Returns in his Power, for the Benefit he receives from the due Execution of equal Laws. . . .

His views, in the reasoning Part, are to establish an universal social maxim. . . .

The Author, after reasoning the Reader into right Notions of Trade, where he falls into many of Mr. Wood's Sentiments, enters into an Enquiry. . . .

His manner of pursuing those Subjects is different from anything I have seen. . . .

—— the Performance in a particular manner claims your patronage, as the Author, though an *Alien* by birth, is a Englishman by Interest. . . .

HOSPITALS. See CHARITY.

HORTON, SAMUEL DANA (1844-1895), a leading American writer upon bimetallism, was born in Pomeroy, Ohio, and died in Washington. He graduated at Harvard University, in arts in 1864, and in law in 1868. After some foreign travel he began the practice of his profession in the Ohio courts, but was diverted from this after a few years to the study of monetary science, by the protracted discussions which preceded the resumption of specie payments by the federal government. As the son of Valentine B. Horton, who as a member of congress in the early part of the civil war secured wide reputation, but also the displeasure of his constituents, by a courageous opposition to paper money inflation, Dana Horton had an inherited interest in questions of currency. From the publication of *Silver and Gold* in 1876 until the end of his life the study of these were his absorbing pursuit. He was a commissioner for the United States in the International Monetary Conferences of 1878 and 1881, and became widely known in Europe and America as an advocate on scientific grounds of international bimetallism. The independent action of the United States in 1878 and 1890 he condemned. "We should offer Europe to take silver as money without stint when she does, but not take a dollar until she does so." Among the impatient or interested advocates of unrestricted silver coinage therefore he did not retain the authority to which his ability and learning entitled him. His researches in the history of the single and double standards of England and France respectively were fruitful and important. He was a frequent speaker and writer of great vigour, originality, and variety of resource, in a style sometimes striking, but often too involved and abstruse to be thoroughly effective.

Omitting many pamphlets, articles, and addresses, the following are the chief of Mr. Horton's publications, valuable for their research and the number of important original documents which they contain —

Silver and Gold, and their relation to the Problem of Resumption (1876, revised in 1877).—*Historical Material for the Study of Monetary Policy*, and *Contributions to the Study of Monetary Policy*, both prepared for the International Conference of 1878, printed with the proceedings of the Conference by the United States government 1879, and including a bibliography of money, and documents to illustrate the monetary history of France, England, and the United States — some here printed for the first time,—*Sir Isaac Newton and England's Prohibitive Tariff upon Silver Money*, being an open letter to Professor Jevons (1881).—*The British Standard of Value*, being an address before section F of the British Association (1885). with an appendix containing hitherto unnoticed reports by Locke and Newton.—*Silver before Congress in 1886*, in the *Quarterly Journal of Economics* (October 1886).—*The Silver Pound* and *England's Monetary Policy since the Restoration, together with the History of the Guinea,* (1887). *Silver in Europe* (1890, revised in 1892). —*The Suspended Rupee and the Policy of Contraction* in the *Economic Journal* (September 1893). [See Obituary by Pres. E. A. Walker in *Economic Journal,* June 1895.]   C. F. D.

HOTCHPOT. It frequently occurs in wills and settlements that power is given to a person to appoint a fund in such shares as he or she shall think fit among the members of a class, *e.g.* the children of a marriage ; in such cases there is generally a direction that if the appointments made by the person to whom the power is given do not exhaust the fund, the unappointed part is to be divided in equal shares among all the members of the class. If nothing further were added injustice might easily result, and for that purpose a clause called the hotchpot clause is generally inserted, providing that no member of the class shall take a share of the unappointed part, without bringing the appointed share into "hotchpot," which means that for the purposes of the division the appointed share must be thrown back into the common fund.   E. S.

HOUGHTON, JOHN, an apothecary and dealer in tea, coffee, and chocolate, was a fellow of the Royal Society and a friend of Halley and other distinguished men of the day. From 1692-1703 he edited a weekly paper called *A Collection for Improvement of Husbandry and Trade,* containing articles on "some matter of public interest in art or science or trade, a price list of corn and some other commodities, from many English market towns, and a number of advertisements" (Rogers, see below). From 17th August 1694 to 17th September 1703 he also kept a weekly register of the price of Bank of England stock, and often of other stock, especially of the East India, the Hudson's Bay, and the African companies ; as well as of the "rate of exchange, especially with Amsterdam." He also drew up *An Account of the Acres and Houses, with the Proportional Tax . . . of each County in England and Wales,* 1693.

[Thorold Rogers, *The First Nine Years of the Bank of England,* Preface. The weekly prices of bank stock are prefixed to this book.—Andrew's *Hist. of Brit. Journalism.*—*Dict. of National Biography.*]   E. G. P.

HOURS OF LABOUR. In strictness, economics are not concerned with the amount of the day which should be given to work. The capacity of the individual for valuable work varies enormously. By stress of facts a political question has arisen in most civilised countries as to the number of hours which the manual labourer should be required to give to his employer each day. The scope of the practical question has thus, whether rightly or not, been distinctly limited.

There are three points of view from which the question may be regarded—(1) that of the dependence of the labourer on his employer ; (2) that of the improvement of the individual life and happiness ; (3) that of the effects on the value of the labour given.

The first two have in turns been uppermost in the minds of those who have advocated the shortening of the hours of labour. The last point of view is one which has only recently attracted real attention in connection with the eight hours movement, though the earlier economists had some notion of it (*vide* J. S. Mill, bk. i.). Yet the most practical method of treating the question of the hours of labour is to establish, if possible, the fact that the work is so much better done on the shorter hours as to make up for the loss of mere time. Professor Thorold Rogers appears to have been the first to suggest this as a practical argument when he held that the excellence of the old masonry and other enduring work of the middle ages was only compatible with the prevalence of short hours. It has recently been asserted by Australian employers that the quality of work has vastly improved with the eight hours day. The most detailed attempt to prove the position is perhaps that of Mr. Rae (*Contemporary Review,* October 1891). It is clear that if the case be made out, the adoption of shorter hours will quickly follow ; and it is obvious that greater leisure ought to be better for the individual workman, and that with a rising standard of life he must become more independent without being less useful.

In Great Britain the attempt to legislate on this subject seems to have been much earlier than on the continent. Putting aside Professor Rogers's theory just noted, and Sir Thomas MORE's proposed 6 hours for the Utopia, we have an act of Elizabeth prescribing a day of 12 hours with 2½ hours' rest, and we know that at the beginning of this century the usual working day was from 11 to 14 hours, and often longer, in the factories. The early factory acts were directed to the relief of young children and women. That of 1802 was the first, limiting the hours for children to 12 a day ; that of 1819 placed the hours for children between the ages of nine and sixteen at 72 per week ; and that of 1825 gave them a Saturday half-holiday. Sir John Hobhouse's act of 1831 reduced the hours for persons under eighteen to 69 per week. The reports of the factory commission (1832-33) took a wider view of the subject. They show that while the working day in many cases at that date ran to 13 hours, it often did not exceed 10 or 11, and was usually 12 to 12½. In Birmingham and Coventry, where the operatives worked, as they now do, chiefly at their own homes, and were independent, the day was usually less than 10 hours, often less than 9. It was about this time that Richard OASTLER and Lord Shaftesbury commenced to advocate a legal maximum of 48 hours per week, which was adopted for children in the regulations for children under thirteen in the act of 1836. The Mines Regulation Act of 1842 was the next step in advance, and after the failure of a ten-hours bill for females in 1844, and of a similar bill for all persons in 1847, the legal day was made 10 hours in 1850. Apart from a certain agitation for further reduction, no advance was made on this till the Factory Act of 1874, which placed the limit at 56½ hours per week. The recent royal commission find that they have now a tendency to approximate to 54 a week. Recent efforts are dealt with in a separate article (EIGHT-HOURS MOVEMENT), but we may mention the Hours of Labour Bill in the session of 1891, and the Shop Hours Acts of 1892, under which no person under eighteen can be employed for more than 75 hours a week in shops.

In the British possessions there is little trace of a history similar to that of the FACTORY ACTS, but as a rule hours of labour are shorter than at home, and Australia is in advance of the whole world in this respect, as the eight hours system has there become thoroughly established since it was first adopted by the stonemasons of Victoria in 1856 (vide art. cit.). In Canada 10 hours is usual, but 9 hours not uncommon. At the Cape 9 hours is the usual length of the working day. In the tropics the style of labour is so different that the mention of any number of hours is hardly a fair criterion. The blue book of the recent royal commission on labour returns them at from 6 to 11 a day in the West Indies, and from 11 to 14 in India.

In most foreign countries there has been a slow growth of agitation in favour of a shorter working day, mostly following in the wake of English experience. Germany has had a special movement arising directly from the efforts of Karl MARX and his school. The United States have had the question settled almost without being raised, owing to the greater independence of labour and the greater profusion of apparent wealth amongst all classes.

In the same district we find different trades working different hours, even in our own country. There seems to be no regular principle determining this. Particular trades have obtained shorter hours by some special agitation often arising out of special events. Where, however, a direct service is rendered to the general public, as in tramcars and restaurants, hours tend to run to greater length.

And different reasons have conspired to bring about the shortening of hours in our own country and the colonies—e.g. in Australia climate was alleged as a factor.

[Hadfield and Gibbins, A Shorter Working Day. —Ricc. dalla Volta, La Riduzione delle ore di lavoro e i sui effetti economici, Florence, 1891.— Webb and Cox, The Eight Hours Day, 1891.— J. G Hobson in Contemporary Review, 1894-95.—

Report of the Royal Commission on Labour— Parl. Paper C. 7421, 1894, p. 12, with the subsidiary reports and evidences especially, C. 6795-xi. f. 1893 (Colonial) and C. 7063, f. 1893-94 (Foreign), which form a very full account with full indexes in separate volumes passim.—First Report of the Factory Commission of 1832.— Schoenhof, Economy of High Wages, Putnams, 1892.—Rae, Eight Hours' Day, 1894.] C. A. H.

HOUSES, TAXES ON. See TAXATION.

HOWARD, JOHN (1727-1790), was the originator of the modern method of dealing with criminals. His career as a reformer dates from his appointment as high sheriff of Bedfordshire in 1773, when, struck with the abuses in the management of gaols, he was led to visit the prisons throughout the kingdom, and afterwards travelled several times over the whole of Europe, devoting his life to the inspection of prisons and hospitals. In his zeal to learn the true facts or to bring relief to prisoners, he never shrank from exposing himself to the infection of gaols, hospitals, and lazarettos ; and ultimately died at Kherson of a fever which was raging there. The facts collected during these journeys were laid by him before the government, and many humane reforms were introduced on his suggestion, the most immediate of which were the two acts of parliament passed in 1774, for the relief of acquitted prisoners in the matter of fees, and for preserving the health of prisoners. He was also successful in introducing reforms in many foreign countries. Among those who most fully recognised his merits was Burke, whose eulogy of Howard, in his speech at Bristol in 1780, is well known. Howard's works include observations on the condition, both administrative and structural, of prisons, hospitals, lazarettos, etc., throughout Europe, together with proposed reforms. In preparing these for the press, he was greatly aided by his friend, Richard PRICE. Howard also paid much attention to the condition of the tenants on his estate at Cardington in Bedfordshire, providing sanitary cottages and schools.

The state of Prisons in England and Wales ; with preliminary observations, and an Account of some Foreign Prisons and Hospitals, Warrington, 1777.—An Account of the Principal Lazarettos in Europe, with various Papers relative to the Plague ; together with further Observations on some Foreign Prisons and Hospitals ; and Additional Remarks on the Present State of those in Great Britain and Ireland, Warrington, 1789. [J. Aikin, A View of the Character and Public Services of the late J. Howard, London, 1792.—W. A. Guy, "John Howard as Statist," Journal of the Statistical Society, vol. 36, and "John Howard's True Place in History" ; ib. vol. 38.—Three Prize Essays, by A. Griffith, A. Rivière, and E. A. Cazalet, in Actes du Congrès Pénitentiaire International (1890), vol. v., St. Petersburg, 1892.] R. H. H.

HOWE, JOHN BADLAM (1813-1882), born in Boston, Mass., died in Indiana.

He was the author of several works on money, as follows : *Monetary and Industrial Fallacies*, Boston, 1878, pp. 248.—*Political Economy of Great Britain, United States, and France, in the use of Money.*—*A New Science of Production and Exchange*, Boston, 1878, pp. 592.—*Monometallism and Bimetallism*, Boston, 1879.—*The Common Sense, the Mathematics, and the Metaphysics of Money*, Boston, 1881, pp. 329. The last of these is a summary of the others. D. R. D.

HOWLETT, JOHN (1731-1800), clerk in holy orders and statistician. Howlett's works merit attention on account of his independence of thought and careful investigation of fact. His researches brought him into considerable opposition to Dr. PRICE (*q.v.*) who—writing in 1779 — concluded that the population of England and Wales must have decreased since the Revolution near a quarter, while Howlett showed that it must have increased. With reference to enclosures, at that time of great consequence, Howlett consistently maintained that they were rendered necessary by the increase in population, and resulted in agricultural improvement.

The nature of Howlett's interests can be gathered from the titles of his works : *An Examination of Dr. Price's Essay on the Population of England and Wales*, 1781.— *An Inquiry into the influence which Enclosures have had upon the Population of England*, 1786. —*An Essay on the Population of Ireland*, 1786. — *Enclosures a cause of improved Agriculture*, 1787. — *The insufficiency of the causes to which the increase of our Poor and the Poor's Rates have been generally ascribed*, 1788. — At the end of Wood's *Account of the Shrewsbury House of Industry*, is a correspondence with Howlett, 1795. — *An Examination of Mr. Pitt's Speech in the House of Commons on 12th February 1796, relative to the condition of the Poor*, 1796.—*Dispersion of the present gloomy apprehensions of late repeatedly suggested by the decline of our Corn Trade*, 1798.—*The Monthly Reviewers reviewed*, 1798. — *An Inquiry concerning the influence of Tithes upon Agriculture*.

[See references in Dugald Stewart, *Lectures on Political Economy*. An article in the *Dictionary of National Biography* by the present writer gives more details with regard to Howlett's private life, etc.] E. C. K. G.

HÜBNER, OTTO (1818-1877), first a merchant, subsequently manager of one of the departments of the Austrian Lloyd Steam Boats Company, made himself prominent as one of the leaders of the German free-trading party. Exiled from Austria after the revolutionary events of 1848, he spent the remainder of his life in Berlin, and supervised, from 1852, the publication of his *Jahrbuch für Volkswirthschaft und Statistik* (Year-book of Public Economy and Statistics), and from 1869 the *Zolltarife aller Länder* (Customs Tariffs of all Countries).

In his book on *Banken* (1854) he maintained that paper currency ought always to be covered by an equal amount in cash. In 1864 he started with success a joint-stock insurance company destined to protect lenders on mortgage against the risks incurred in case of public sales of real estate given in guarantee of loans.

He also wrote a book on the *Finanzlage der Oesterreichischen Monarchie und ihre Hülfsquellen* (Financial Condition and Resources of the Austrian Monarchy) (1849). [See *Allg. Deutsche Biographie*.] E. Ca.

HUC, E., ABBÉ (1813-1860). After having resided in and travelled through China, Tartary, and Thibet during the years 1839-1846, this well-known French missionary published in 1850 his *Souvenirs d'un Voyage dans la Tartarie, au Thibet, et en Chine* (2 vols., 1850) with a sequel *L'Empire Chinois* (2 vols., 1857) ; the latter contains numerous notices and observations on trade, administration, navigation, etc. The fourth chapter of vol. ii. deals almost exclusively with these subjects, and gives some extracts from Chinese writers on the same topics. The same volume (pp. 72-83) presents us with a lively sketch of Wang-nan-Che, a Chinese socialist and harbinger of Mr. Henry George's views on the nationalisation of land, who lived in the 11th century after Christ.

The *Empire Chinois* obtained a prize from the French Academy, and has been translated into English ; the Abbé Huc certainly does not belong to the class of "stupid" missionaries who excited the contempt of Adam Smith. E. Ca.

HUDSON'S BAY COMPANY. After the voyage of adventure and discovery of Captain Newland in 1669, a charter was granted (May 2, 1670) to the adventurers who had taken part in sending out that expedition, constituting them a company with exclusive trading rights in Hudson's Bay and the surrounding district, by the title of *The Governor and Company of Adventurers of England trading into Hudson's Bay*. Though after the revolution the power of exclusive trading based on royal charter came to an end in this and in other instances, the charter of the Hudson's Bay Company was confirmed by act of parliament for seven years ; and the capital possessed by the company, with, in addition, the settlements and forts already founded practically secured it against competition. The company had, however, to endure the direct hostility of the French, who pressed into the territory traversed and worked by the company from Canada. By 1682 the company had five settlements, respectively at Albany River, Hay's Island, Rupert's River, New Severn, and Port Nelson, but with the exception of the last-named, these were all taken by the French in 1686. During the subsequent French war success fluctuated, inclining, however, to the side of the French. By the peace of Utrecht (1713) the forts were restored to the company and reparation promised. This promise does not appear to have been satisfactorily fulfilled.

During the middle of the 18th century the company sustained a severe assault on its powers and privileges, as it was alleged that despite these it had done little or nothing to open up the territories under its control. Its trade was not great. A parliamentary inquiry instituted in 1749 reported at length but no action followed upon it. Over some of the lands the company had acquired definite legal rights, while throughout the whole country it claimed certain privileges.

In 1811 its rights came once more under dispute, and a considerable struggle took place between it and its chief competitor, which ultimately resulted in a coalition against all others. The company still remains and carries on trade, though the purchase of its territory (1868) by the Dominion of Canada deprived it of any remaining claim to any powers beyond those of an ordinary trading company.

[Macpherson, *Annals of Commerce.*—Cunningham, *Growth of Engl. Industry and Commerce*, vol. ii.—Adam Smith, *Wealth of Nations*, bk. v. ch. i., as to the Trade of the Company.]

E. C. K. G.

HUET, FRANÇOIS (1816-1865), the author of *Le règne social du Christianisme* (1853), a liberal Roman Catholic, the representative of what he terms ideal Catholicism, and a social idealist whose theories do not vary much from those of modern "social catholics" in France and Belgium (see CHRISTIANITY AND ECONOMICS). M. de Laveleye's high opinion of this writer's views was fully expressed on p. 137 of the 2nd edition of his *Socialisme Contemporain*. It is to F. Huet and J. S. Mill that De Laveleye dedicated his work on primitive property. Huet is equally opposed to individualism, as being founded on materialism, and to communism as the child of pantheism. He advocates liberal socialism as lying midway between the two extremes, and as resting on a theistic foundation or spiritualistic philosophy. Hence in the second book of his work he treats of "la Société spirituelle," in which the religious interest stands highest, whilst the third book is devoted to "la Société matérielle." In the latter he draws a distinction between "les biens patrimoniaux" and "biens acquis." The latter only was the result of individual labour, and as such can be claimed as private property. The former belong to society as a whole, such as land, etc., the gifts of the earth to which all have an equal right. These should return to the community, as public property, on the death of the present occupier. The first article of Huet's right of inheritance is as follows: Every year a division takes place of the *biens patrimoniaux* released by death. All young people of both sexes aged from fourteen to twenty-five have a share in it, the latter receiving twice the amount of the former. From this it will be seen that the standpoint of the author is that of an advanced Christian Socialist, whose endeavour it is to prove the identity of Christian liberty and the socialistic idea.

[F. Huet, *Le règne social du Christianisme;* cp. an article by G. Kriegmann in *Preussische Jahrbücher*, January 1887.]

M. K.

HUET, PIERRE DANIEL (1630-1721), member of the French academy, and tutor under Bossuet of the son of Louis XIV., directed the publication of the editions *ad usum Delphini* of classical authors, and enjoyed in his time a great celebrity for his erudition, which was rather wide than deep. He wrote several books of religious and philosophical controversy, autobiographical memoirs (in Latin, but since translated into French by M. Nisard), and a *Dissertation on Navigation under Solomon* (1698). Appointed bishop of Soissons in 1685, he had not yet taken possession of his see when he was transferred in 1689 to the bishoprick of Avranches. Shortly afterwards he retired to the abbey of Fontenay near Caen, to devote himself entirely to his learned researches. People wondered why the king had appointed a bishop who had not yet reached the end of his studies.

His *Histoire du Commerce et de la Navigation des Anciens* (1 vol., issued anonymously in 1716, and republished in Lyons in 1763, with the author's name) had been written at the request of Colbert, a long time before it appeared. Commencing at the creation, and including the Persians, Chinese, etc., this book is certainly a rather shallow production, but to be fair, we ought to remember what Huet himself stated in his dedication to Colbert: "Only such an authority as yours could draw me away from the studies which have always engrossed my attention, to direct it towards another so different. . . . No forerunner has opened the road for me, I had no guide to lead me, and no support on which I could lean" (See "Huet," in *Collected Essays*, by Rev. Mark Pattison, Oxford, 1889).

E. Ca.

HUFELAND, GOTTLIEB (1761-1817), a distinguished German economist, was born at Dantzic, studied at Leipzig, Göttingen, and Jena, and became in 1788 extraordinary, and in 1793 ordinary, professor in the university of the last-mentioned place. He passed in 1803 to the high school of Würzburg, and in 1806 to that of Landshut. From 1808 to 1812 he was bürgermeister of his native city, then republican; in the latter year he returned to Landshut, where he resumed his academic occupations, and in 1816 removed to Halle, where in 1817 he died. His principal economic publication—for he also wrote on jurisprudence—was *Neue Grundlegung der Staatswirthschaftskunst durch Prüfung und Berichtigung ihrer Hauptbegriffe*, vol. i., 1807; vol. ii., 1813.

The second volume appeared in a new edition, 1819, with the title *Die Lehre vom Gelde und Geldumlaufe.* His principles were essentially those of Adam Smith, of whom he speaks with warm admiration in the preface to his work; and he did much to extend the knowledge and acceptance of the English economist's doctrine in Germany.

[Roscher, *Gesch. der N.O.*, p. 654.]　J. K. I.

HÜLLMANN, KARL DIETRICH (1765-1846). Appointed professor of history in 1797 at the university of Frankfurt on the Oder, and in 1808 of history and statistics at Königsberg, Hüllmann was sent in 1817 to Bonn, where he was the first rector of the then recently-inaugurated university; for years he acted as the confidential representative of the Prussian government. His literary activity was considerable, as appears from the long list of his historical works.

As an historian, Hüllmann had a decided conservative bias, modified however by the liberal tendencies of the times in which he lived. This appears very clearly from the address to the Germans (*Zuschrift an die Deutschen*), which serves as a preface to the second edition (1830) of his *Geschichte des Ursprungs der Stände in Deutschland* (Origin of the (political) Classes and States in Germany). His best-known work is the *Städtewesen des Mittelalters* (Town Life and Administration in the Middle Ages), 4 vols. Bonn, 1826; "This is still," writes Prof. Ashley in his *Ec. History* (vol. i. pt. ii. p. 5), "the most complete attempt to cover the whole ground of mediæval civic life, and it illustrates the general similarity of conditions all over Western Europe." His other works are *Deutsche Finanzgeschichte des Mittelalters* (1805), giving the history of the mediæval finances of the German empire, not of the various German states, with a supplement on the origin of regal dues (*Ursprung der Regalien in Deutschland*, 1806); *Geschichte der Domänenbenutzung in Deutschland*, 1807 (History of the Management of the State Domains in Germany); *Gesch. des Byzantinischen Handels* (Hist. of Byzantine Commerce), 1808; *Handelsgeschichte der Griechen* (Hist. of Greek Commerce), 1839; he also wrote on the Political Systems of the Ancients (*Staatsrecht des Alterthums*, 1820); the Origin of the Mediæval Ecclesiastical System (*Ursprünge der Kirchenverfassung des Mittelalters*, 1831); the Roman and the Jewish constitutions, etc. E. Ca.

HUMANISM, ITS INFLUENCE ON ECONOMICS. By humanism we mean that tendency of the earlier and later Renaissance which makes the culture of humanity its chief aim, and which in its anthropocentric view of life affects in a marked degree the course of economic theory and practice. As a revolt against the mediæval views of life, being pagan in its origin, it attaches supreme importance to human happiness here below, and puts temporal above spiritual interests. Humanism, in short, as Mr. Symonds defines it, "is an ardent interest in men as men." Hence the beauty of the human form as in classical art, of human virtue according to classical models, and human rights and liberty as conceived of in the republics of antiquity, are its ideals. Accordingly Roscher notes five points of contact between the progress of humanism and that of political economy. (1) As the classical writers represent a high state of civilisation, they raised the general standard of culture and tended to accelerate efforts in the division of labour and the economy of wealth as means thereto; (2) As the higher life of the ancients was mostly developed in the town, so a study of the classics would help in giving force and direction to civic industry of the rising towns towards the close of the middle ages; (3) The patriotism breathing in the classics would stimulate the consciousness of national life and thus encourage the centralising tendencies of "national" economy; (4) The mixed elements of imperialism and democracy reflected in the classical writers would on the other hand foster monarchical absolutism as in the mercantile system, and also its democratic counterpart in the *laissez-faire* doctrine of political economy; (5) The cultivation of the critical spirit of the humanist, which, undermining as it did the foundation of authoritative religion, tended to disparage the spiritualistic ideals of life held up by Christianity in favour of material aims and materialistic pursuits in the place of heavenly felicity. It will be convenient to consider the influence of humanism under these five heads:

1. *Classical culture*, with the revival of learning, brought into prominence the economical doctrines of ARISTOTLE and PLATO, the theory both of state and household economy (πολιτικὴ ἐπιστήμη and οἰκονομία) from which political economy derives its modern appellation. Aristotle's doctrine of wealth (χρηματιστική) and Plato's ideas of the division of labour, and his view of the danger of private property, contain the germs of the science. In a lesser degree this is true of Cicero, Seneca, and Pliny the elder, the first of these, as translator of the *Economics* of Xenophon, being among the earliest economists who show a decided preference for agriculture over manufactures and trade (see Professor Cossa's *Introduzione allo Studio dell' Economia Politica*, 1892, pp. 149 seq.; *ib.* 160-161, English edition 1893; *ib.* 129-140). Not only philosophers and jurists in the 14th century, but humanists such as GERSON, who paid much attention to the theory of value, follow Aristotle (*ib.* 102-105), whilst in the 15th century, when the progress of industry and literary culture were at their height, we find Erasmus platonising in his warnings against overestimating the accumulations of wealth, yet at the same time with Aristotle recognising the importance of commerce, and of money as a means of exchange. Another typical humanist, Ulrich von Hutten, inveighs against luxuries

and monopolies, whilst CAMERARIUS, one of the younger humanists, combated mediæval objections to payments of interest. MORE's *Utopia*, like *The Christian Prince* by Erasmus, bears witness to the influence of classical modes of thought ; the keynote in both is "that the object of nations and governments is the common weal of the whole people."

2. *Civic Industry.*—It was in Italian republics, in cities like Florence for example, that the spirit of the Renaissance found its fullest expression (see CITY, MEDIÆVAL) ; and here, too, the classical ideal of an urban or municipal republic was most closely approached. As the classical modes of industry were reproduced, so here, too, with heightened prosperity and luxurious refinement, we meet the same sharp contrast between rich and poor as of old. There are conflicts between the merchants and the craftsmen : and Savonarola, in one of his sermons, recommends the passing of a law for opening shops and providing work "for the populace now idling in the streets." In estimating the effect of humanistic studies on economic progress there is room for divergency of opinions. Thus, according to Mr. Symonds, "fresh value was given to the desires and aims, enjoyments and activities of man, considered as a noble member of the universal life" (*Revival of Learning*, pp. 46-47). On the other hand Mr. W. S. Lilly, *Nineteenth Century*, p. 5 (Jan. 1893), speaks thus disparagingly of the Renaissance : "It might with far greater truth be called a new birth into servitude. This it was assuredly, both in the political and *economic* order." It has been noticed, too, how in the Germanic towns the energising influence of revived and reformed Christianity, and its consecration of honoured labour, modified the enervating effects of the Renaissance and militated against the classical contempt of handicrafts. We might select as an illustrative instance of this the "city" of London with St. Paul's as the temple of the Renaissance, and the school close by founded by the humanist Dean Colet, with the Royal Exchange founded about the same time in the vicinity of Lombard Street, as bearing the various traces of a contemporary development of commerce, and culture, and religion, under the conjoint influence of the Reformation and Renaissance—an instance showing the truth of M. E. de Laveleye's dictum that "the countries which have embraced the Reformation are decidedly in advance of those which have stopped short at the Renaissance. . . The Renaissance was a return to antiquity, the Reformation a return to the gospel. The gospel being superior to the tradition of antiquity, was sure to yield better fruits" (*Protestantism and Catholicism in their bearing upon the liberty and prosperity of Nations*, p. 32).

3. *Patriotism.*—The pagan view of tribal morality, and its tendency to subordinate the interests of the individual to those of the community, and which as in the neo-paganism of our own time attempts to find in it a kind of substitute for religion, as an antidote against "de-ethicising" influences of scepticism, exercised an important influence on the development of economics in the humanistic era. For the growth of national sentiment stimulated national egoism, and on this is founded the MERCANTILE SYSTEM of political economy. In this respect the effects of the Renaissance were similar to those of the Reformation (see CHRISTIANITY AND ECONOMICS : "Influence of Protestant Thought ").

4. *Imperialism and Democracy.*—The humanists, too, like the reformers, and, it might be added, like the rising towns, had a strong leaning towards royalty and regal protection in the struggle against the common enemy, the rude feudality and barbarian aristocracy of the day. Hence they encouraged royal absolutism. In economics this produced *Colbertism*, or the centralisation of trade and commerce and the establishment of royal monopolies. It also led to the creation of "state romances," or pictures of ideal commonwealths like Fénelon's *Voyage en Salente*, in which an important rôle is assigned to benevolent despotism in the economic management of the state. This is in strict correspondence with the classical conception that the head of the state like the head of the family has the *patria potestas*, hence the idea of patriarchal government as the representative of the state. Royalty, as Guizot puts it, was "la personnification de la souveraineté du droit," just as in imperial Rome the head of the state was "la personnification de l'État, l'héritière de la souveraineté et de la majesté du peuple romain" (*Histoire de la civilisation en Europe*, 6th edition, pp. 221 and 228). Thence were derived the earlier cameralistic and later bureaucratic methods of national economy culminating in the *Ancien Régime*, during which, "en pleine renaissance," to use the words of De Tocqueville, it was the fashion to consider "le droit de travailler comme un privilége que le roi peut vendre" (*Ancien Régime*, p. 154). The reaction against this was the individualism of the revolution, in which the opposite or democratic conception of individual rights finds its expression. "The whole movement of humanity from the Renaissance onward has tended in this direction, *i.e.* the Utopia of a modern world in which all men shall enjoy the same social, political, and intellectual advantages"—in short, "the organisation of society in harmony with democratic principles" (Symonds : *Renaissance in Italy :* I. *Age of the Despots*, p. 30). In the same way Rousseau's demand for a return to nature, where all are free and equal, has been traced to a revival of classical stoicism, and the passionate enthusiasm of French lawyers for "natural law," the *jus*

naturæ of Hobbes and Grotius, on which is founded the theory of the rights of men and the demand for natural liberty extended to commerce and economics. This was adopted by A. Smith from the physiocrats, whose chief dogma is to leave everything to nature and natural laws, and not to interfere with the play of natural forces ; *i.e.* in the language of A. Smith, not to interfere with the obvious and simple system of natural liberty in the economic world. In this demand appeals are made constantly to the "ancients" by revolutionists in their cries for liberty and equality, as the article on political economy written for the *Encyclopædia* by Rousseau "rings with the names of ancient rulers and lawgivers" (see Morley's *Rousseau*, vol. i. 145 and 191 *seq.*), whilst one of the chief promoters of the doctrine of *laissez-faire*, the Marquis D'ARGENSON, looks to the ancient Greek republics as ideal communities where true liberty prevailed. But from this doctrine of "following nature" are derived other doctrines of "classical economy," such as the "natural increase of capital," and the natural right of property," which produced in their turn great inequalities, and led on to the socialistic reaction in favour of collectivism and revolt against the power of "capitalism." The latter leans itself for support on the Roman law of private property, just as government direction of trade and commerce was an imitation of classical Cæsarism. Thus both the idea of individualism in the sense of personal liberty, and the collective individuality of the state, the leading doctrines of abstract and historical methods of political economy respectively, may be traced to the influence of classical conceptions revived by humanistic studies under the twofold aspect of society as a collection of free citizens under the rule of popular sovereignty and a corporate personality with imperial power as the central organ of government, · the two modern autonomies in politics and economics alike having for their object on the one hand the independence of man, and on the other the centralisation of society.

5. *Criticism.*— The critical spirit which humanistic studies and the contemporaneous progress in the natural sciences both in the 15th and 18th centuries called forth was antagonistic to the spiritualistic conceptions of Christianity. The epicureanism of the *Novi Homines* of the Renaissance and the naturalism of the Encyclopædists of the Revolution had for their aim either the culture of human nature, or the use of the newly-discovered forces of nature for the purpose of heightening the "splendid materiality" which captivated all minds then as now. In short, literature, art, and science were all to serve the purpose of terrestrial happiness. The effect of this on political economy as the science of wealth was stimulating. It directed all effort now set free

towards the acquisition of material goods, as, also, it received a special impetus from the contemporaneous liberation of mind, and the growth of commercial enterprise owing to the revolution of prices in consequence of the discovery of America in the 15th, and the revolution of industry by steam and machinery in the 18th centuries. These combined in awakening both the spirit of curiosity and cupidity, the love of learning, and the lust of money as the result of the "outburst of new life, the carnival of liberty and energy." The development of the individual and the progress of society was the superstructure built, or attempted to be erected, on this material basis. Later on the philanthropic or humanitarian as distinguished from the purely humanistic elements of the earlier and later Renaissance are brought into prominence with the characteristic appearance of the "religion of humanity." A corresponding movement in political economy arises which seeks to incorporate it into the science of society, having for its paramount object the evolution of humanity. Henceforth the "economic man" is no longer considered merely in his relation to the community as in classical times, or as the "man as a machine" moved by self-interest and made what he is by the mechanism of natural laws, as in the natural revival of the last century ; but he is now considered as a social unit in his relation to aggregate humanity, pursuing a higher ideal intellectually and morally, *i.e.* the highest development of man and society (see CARLYLE ; CHRISTIAN SOCIALISM ; A. COMTE). [Refer to J. A. Symonds on the *Renaissance in Italy*, cited above.—W. ROSCHER, *Geschichte der Nationaloekonomik in Deutschland* (1874).— H. Eisenhart, *Geschichte der Nationaloekonomik* (1881).—A. Oncken, *Die Maxime laissez-faire et laissez passer, ihr Ursprung, ihr Werden* (1886) ; *Adam Smith in der Culturgeschichte* (1874).—H. von Scheel, *Geschichte der politischen Oekonomie in Handbuch der politischen Oekonomie*, 3rd ed. (1890).—Luigi Brentano, *Die klassische Oekonomie*, Vortrag (1888).]   M. K.

HUMBOLDT, ALEXANDER VON, Baron (1769-1859). Besides his writings on natural sciences, the following works of this celebrated traveller, written in French and published in Paris, are entitled to be noticed from the economic standpoint : *Voyage aux régions équinoxiales du Nouveau Continent* (1807) ; *Essai politique sur la Nouvelle Espagne* (1811) ; and *Essai politique sur l'Ile de Cuba* (1826), as well as *l'Examen Critique de l'Histoire de la Géographie du Nouveau Continent et des Progrès de l'Astronomie Nautique aux XVᵉ et XVIᵉ Siècles* (1834). In 1848, the *Journal des Économistes* published a translation of his historical and statistical *Mémoire sur la Production de l'Or et de l'Argent considérée dans ses Fluctuations* (also printed separately, with a preface by M. Michel Chevalier) which had appeared several years before in a German quarterly review (*Ueber die Schwank-*

ungen der Goldproduktion in Deutsche Viertel-jahrschrift, October 1838). It is interesting to notice that in this mémoire Humboldt predicts that new silver mines will one day be worked in northern America ; he expects the future source of gold supply to be the Altai mountains in Central Asia.   E. Ca.

HUMBOLDT, WILHELM VON (1767-1835), brother of Alexander von Humboldt, the traveller, was descended from a noble family in the Mark of Brandenburg. He was early associated with the celebrated Weimar circle, and much influenced by Goethe and Schiller. One of the foremost scholars of his age, renowned in literature, æsthetics, and the science of language, he fills a large space in the intellectual history of Germany. He ranks among economists by virtue of his work, written when he was still a young man, in 1792, *Ideen zu einem Versuch die Gränzen der Wirksamkeit des Staates zu bestimmen*, not published in full until after his death (by Dr. E. Cauer, Breslau, 1851), in which he pushes to the utmost extreme the limitations of the functions of the state.   J. S. Mill in his book *On Liberty* highly commends this "excellent essay"; but, in fact, it so exaggerates the doctrine of objection to government interference as practically to refute it. The author restricts the action of the state to the preservation of external and internal security, and excludes from it all positive solicitude for the prosperity, nay, even the character and culture, of the nation. The immaturity of the ideas expressed in this essay is obvious. In his zeal for the supremacy of the individual, he proposes that marriage should be terminable at the will of either party, and without any allegation of reasons—a suggestion from which Mill thought it necessary to express his *partial* dissent. The most complete *ad hominem* answer to his doctrines is supplied by his own activity at a later date in the cause of educational reform in Prussia. In 1809, immediately after the retirement of Stein, and when Altenstein was minister, Humboldt returned from Rome, where he had been Prussian representative at the papal court, and was placed at the head of the section of public worship and instruction under Dohna, who had the general control of the department of the interior. In this capacity he devoted himself to the reform of education in the primary schools and high schools and crowned his work by the foundation of the university of Berlin, procuring for it a large public endowment. Afterwards we find him turning his attention to finance and public economy, a study in which he was encouraged by Stein, who recommended to him in particular the writings of FORBONNAIS and GANILH. But his most conspicuous activity in later years was in the fields of politics and diplomacy, into which we cannot here follow him.

[Seeley's *Life and Times of Stein, passim.*— Dove in *Allg. Deutsche Biogr.* — Good account in R. Fester's *Rousseau und die deutsche Geschichtsphilosophie*, 1890, pp. 292-309.]   J. K. I.

HUME, DAVID (1711-76), philosopher, historian, and economist, was born at Edinburgh. He was "seized very early with a passion for literature." After fruitless efforts to apply himself to law and commerce, he paid, in 1734, a three years' visit to France, where he laid down his future plan of life. "To make a very rigid frugality supply my deficiency of fortune . . . and to regard every object as contemptible except the improvement of my talent in literature." In 1738 he published his *Treatise of Human Nature*, which contained, though in bald outline, the substance of the future philosophical writings ; and in 1742 the first series of *Essays Moral and Political*, which was favourably received. After a twelve months' tutorship of Lord Annandale, he was appointed in 1746 secretary to General St. Clair, and in this capacity visited the courts of Vienna and Turin, wearing, according to Lord Charlemont, his uniform "like a grocer of the trained bands." *The Enquiry concerning the Human Understanding*, a recast of the first portion of the *Treatise*, was published in 1748. The years 1749 and 1750 were spent at his old home, Ninewells, in the composition of the *Political Discourses;* "The only work of mine that was successful on the first publication"; and in the recasting of another portion of the *Treatise* into the *Enquiry concerning the Principles of Morals*. "Of all my writings, in my own opinion . . . incomparably the best." In 1752, Hume became librarian to the Faculty of Advocates, and planned the *History of England*, successive portions of which appeared in 1754, 1756, 1759, and 1761. In 1753, he wrote the Essays *On Suicide* and *On the Immortality of the Soul*, which were printed, but promptly suppressed. *The Natural History of Religion* was finished in 1757, but was not published during Hume's life. In 1763 Hume accompanied Lord Hertford to Paris, where his stay was a continuous triumph. Among others who were brought to do him honour, were the future kings, Louis XVI. and Louis XVIII. Returning to England in 1766, he was appointed, in 1767, Under secretary of State, an office he held for a year. In 1769 he returned to Edinburgh, "very opulent." Six years later he was attacked by a mortal disease, and met death with the fortitude and cheerfulness of a philosopher. He appointed his friend Adam Smith his literary executor.

In Hume's own words, he was "a man of mild disposition, of command of temper, of an open, social, and cheerful humour . . . and of great moderation in all my passions." In justice, however, it must be added, that his letters display a less pleasing side of his character, and modify, though they do not reverse, the above verdict. The intemperate extravagance with which everything English is continually condemned, the restless vanity that no praises can satisfy, show the other side to the shield.

It has been asked why the labours of Hume in philosophy came to so sudden an end? "His contributions to metaphysics were written by 1736, when he was five-and-twenty ; his contribution to the philosophy of religion by 1750, when he was thirty-nine ; and after this date, he added nothing." At least two answers may be given, each in itself perhaps sufficient. Hume dearly loved fame, and the *Essays* obtained what had been denied to the *Treatise*. Again, Hume had nothing in him of the martyr's temperament ; he loved to stand well in the thoughts of the great and the respectable ; for this purpose Tory politics were more profitable than heretical philosophy. Be this as it may, it is possible that Hume had already made his full contribution to metaphysics, while the gain to political philosophy has been great. The *History of England* need not detain us ; if it is still read, it is merely on literary grounds. But the two sets of *Essays, Moral and Political*, the later of which was first published under the name of *Political Discourses*, are without doubt κτήματα ἐς ἀεί. The original essays, amidst much ephemeral matter, on *Standard of Taste*, etc. (wherein Bunyan and Addison are compared to a pond and the ocean), contain within them a system of political philosophy. The object of government is the distribution of justice ; "in other words, the support of the twelve judges." There is a "perpetual intestine struggle" between authority and liberty, of which the former must be "acknowledged essential to the very existence of society," while the latter is "its perfection." Parliament, "while, from our very constitution, it must necessarily have as much power as it demands, and can only be confined by itself," is, in fact, restrained by the interest of the individuals composing it, differing from the interest of the body as a whole, inasmuch as they are individually amenable to the influence of the crown. Absolute monarchy is the "true Euthanasia of the British constitution," as being preferable to pure democracy.

In approaching Hume as economist, it must always be remembered that political economy grew out of political philosophy, and that Hume is still in the transition stage. Although he believes in the possibility of a science of economics, and describes its subject-matter, he does not use the term. The economic essays were published (1752) in a volume entitled *Political Discourses*, and the subjects discussed —commerce, refinement in the arts, money, interest, balance of trade, jealousy of trade, taxes, and public credit—are regarded largely from the statesman's standpoint. In his opposition to the views of the mercantilists, upon the BALANCE OF TRADE (*q.v.*), and the precious metals, he had been forestalled by BARBON and Sir Dudley NORTH. His description of wealth recalls the statement in Berkeley's *Querist*, that it consists "of the four elements, and man's labour therein." Even in his theory of interest, Hume had been anticipated by Barbon, and, more recently, by MASSIE. Nevertheless, the lucidity of his style, the subtlety with which the subjects of money and interest, in especial, are treated, and his connection with Adam SMITH, make Hume an important figure in the history of economics.

As an instance of his marvellous acuteness, may be noticed the letter addressed to A. Smith, on the appearance of the *Wealth of Nations*. After cordial congratulations, Hume proceeds at once to seize upon the points most open to criticism. "I cannot think that the rent of farms makes any part of the price of the produce, but that the price is determined altogether by the quantity and demand (*v.* RENT). It appears to me impossible that the king of France can take a seignorage of 8 per cent upon the coinage. Nobody would bring bullion to the mint, it would be all sent to Holland or England" (p. 286 in Rae's *Life of A. Smith*).

In tracing the development of wealth, Hume considers that the advance of agriculture promotes manufactures, by giving rise to superfluous hands. These must either find employment in manufactures or become soldiers. Sometimes the interests of the sovereign and the people are at issue, as to which the choice shall be. As a rule, however, even in the interests of the sovereign, it is well to have a manufacturing class, because they form a reserve fund upon which the state can draw in time of need. "Everything in the world is purchased by labour, and our passions are the only causes of labour." Hence, even avarice and luxury become spurs to industry. "The camp is loaded with a superfluous retinue, but the provisions flow in proportionally larger." MANDEVILLE (*q.v.*) is wrong, and vice, in itself, is never advantageous, but two opposite vices may be more advantageous than one alone. "By banishing *vicious* luxury, without curing sloth or indifference to others, you only diminish industry." Foreign commerce is justified upon similar grounds. "It increases the stock of labour." Imports furnish materials for new manufactures, and exports produce labour in commodities which could not be consumed at home. The acute remark is appended that foreign trade generally precedes refinement in the home manufactures, and gives birth to domestic luxury. In a noteworthy digression, Hume, following LOCKE, asserts strongly the claims of the labouring classes. A too great disproportion of property is a source of weakness. "Every person, if possible, ought to enjoy the fruits of his labour in a full possession of all the necessaries and many of the conveniences of life." The *power of the state* is thereby augmented, in its capacity to bear taxation.

In the *Essay on Money*, the error of those who held that money was more than a commodity is clearly demonstrated, but it is not clear how far Hume always kept himself free from the opposite error of holding it to be less. Money "is none of the wheels of trade ; it is the oil which renders the motion of the wheels more smooth and easy." Men and commodities are the real strength of a community. In a single isolated country, the quantity of money can make no difference, while, in international commerce, the dearness of everything, including labour, which prevails in rich countries, ultimately enables poorer countries to undersell them in neutral markets. "It seems a maxim almost self-evident that the prices of everything depend on the proportion between commodities and money, and that any considerable alteration of either has the same effect, either heightening or lowering the price. Increase the commodities, they become cheaper ; increase the money, they become dearer ; as, on the other hand, a diminution of the former and that of the latter have contrary tendencies." Hence industrial preponderance is continually shifting. Modern improvements in transportation and labour-saving appliances may successfully check this tendency. But if a mere increase in the amount of money is not, in itself, a benefit, how comes it that it does, in fact, seem to promote prosperity? Hume's answer to this question is one of his most important contributions to economics. An increase in the amount of the precious metals is not followed at once by an advance in prices. "Though the high price of commodities be a necessary consequence of the increase of gold and silver, yet it follows not immediately upon that increase." It is only in the interval "between the acquisition of money and the rise of prices that the increasing quantity of gold and silver is favourable to industry" (*v. Money in its relations to Trade and Industry*, by F. A. Walker, London, 1880, pp. 84-87). Hume clearly points out that only circulating money and circulating commodities operate on prices. He does not, however, perhaps fully take into account the rapidity of circulation. Every absolute or relative increase in the amount of money need not produce a corresponding diminution in its value ; the number of trade transactions may increase proportionally. In opposition to Locke and PETTY (*q.v.*), Hume demonstrates that low interest does not arise from plenty of money. High interest arises from a great demand for borrowing ; little riches to supply that demand, and great profits from commerce. Low interest arises from the opposite circumstances. The class of landed proprietors is generally spendthrift, and, when it predominates, borrowers will be numerous, and the rate of interest high. Merchants on the other hand are generally frugal, and an increase of manufactures gives rise to a new lending class, and thereby lowers interest. Low interest and low profits mutually forward each other. It is idle to ask which is cause and which is effect ; they both arise from an extensive commerce. "Interest is the barometer of the state, and its lowness an almost infallible sign of prosperity." Roscher finds in the essay on interest the first clear germ of the important doctrine that "a change in the channels of international trade, which in most countries is the only source of gold and silver, may make the price of the precious metals dearer in one place and cheaper in another, even while the conditions of the production of the mines remain entirely unaltered."

The essays of the *Balance and Jealousy of Trade* contain a clear statement of sound doctrine. "The more is exported of any commodity, the more will be raised at home, of which they themselves will always have the first offer." "I should as soon dread that all our springs and rivers should be exhausted, as that money should abandon a kingdom where there are people and industry." With his habitual caution, however, Hume safeguards himself. He approves of duties on foreign goods, which tend to encourage home manufactures. Still, the only commercial nations which need dread the improvements of their neighbours are such as flourish only by being brokers or carriers. With regard to taxes, the best are such as are levied upon consumption, especially those of luxuries, because these taxes are least felt. Hume denies that all taxes fall ultimately upon the land (see PHYSIOCRATS). If the artisan be taxed, he may be able to pay, by superior industry or by frugality, without raising the price of his labour. Before the spectacle of national indebtedness, Hume's usual optimism fails him. "Why should the case be so different between the public and an individual?" National debts enrich the capital at the expense of the provinces, put the country at the mercy of foreigners, and encourage an idle class of fund-holders. Public stocks are a kind of paper credit, and have all its disadvantages. The taxes, which the interest necessitates, either raise wages, or inflict hardships on the people. "Either the nation must destroy public credit, or public credit will destroy the nation . . . When I see princes and states fighting and quarrelling amidst their debts, funds, and public mortgages, it always brings to my mind a match of cudgel-playing fought in a china-shop." Repudiation would, however, soon be followed by a revival of credit. "Mankind are in all ages caught by the same baits : the same tricks . . . still trepan them. The heights of popularity and patriotism are still the beaten road to power and tyranny,

flattery to treachery, standing armies to arbitrary government, and the glory of God to the temporal interest of the clergy."
[The best edition of Hume's works is in four volumes, edited by T. H. Green and T. H. Grove, 1875, 8vo. The economic essays are in vol. i. of the two volumes of *Essays, Moral, Political, and Literary.*—J. Hill Burton, *Life and Correspondence*, 2 vols., Edinburgh, 1846, 8vo ; and *Letters of Eminent Persons to D. Hume*, Edinburgh, 1849, 8vo, throw light on the economic side of Hume.—The chapter on Hume in J. Bonar's *Philosophy and Political Economy*, London, 1893, 8vo, brings out Hume's position in the history of economics.—Allusions to the essays will be found *passim* in the notes to Roscher's *Principles of Political Economy*, translated from the thirteenth edition by J. Lalor, New York, 1878, 8vo.—Walker's *Money*, New York, 1877, 8vo.—and Gibbs' *Colloquy on the Currency* are among the books which discuss his views on money and interest, London, 8vo.—John Rae, *Life of Adam Smith*, London, 1895, 8vo.—Prof. T. H. Huxley, *Hume*, in John Morley's Men of Letters series.] H. E. E.

HUME, JAMES DEACON (1774-1842), entered the custom house at the age of sixteen. In 1822 he undertook the consolidation of the laws of the customs, which he completed in 1825. In his introduction, Hume states that he was "selected for this service for his supposed practical knowledge of the business of the department, and not for legal knowledge." This consolidation was termed by Huskisson "the perfection of codification." In 1815, according to the Custom Commissioners' Report of 1857, there were 1100 Custom Acts in force. All these, with the additions between 1815 and 1824, were repealed in 1825, by an act in which 443 statutes were enumerated, and the rest repealed by a general definition ; thus sweeping away all the laws of the customs which had accumulated during the space of 550 years, and substituting eleven short plain acts contained in a volume of 411 pages. In 1823 Hume had been appointed controller of the customs, and in 1828 he was promoted to be secretary at the board of trade, a position he held till his resignation in 1840. In 1833 he contributed, under the initials H. B. T., some letters to the *Morning Chronicle*, "on the Corn Laws and on the Rights of the Working Classes," which were republished by him in the following year. He contributed articles in 1836 "on the Corn Laws " and " on the Timber Duties " to the *British and Foreign Quarterly Review*. He gave valuable evidence before the Committee of the House of Commons appointed in 1840 to inquire into the duties levied upon imports. In his evidence he stated that he disliked all treaties, except upon navigation. "I would take what I wanted and leave them (foreign nations) to find the value of our custom." He died in 1842, so that he did not

live to see the final triumph of free trade. But there can be no question that, by the influence he exercised upon the mind and policy of Sir R. Peel, he did much to bring about that triumph. In the words of Sir James Graham, "the history of the board of trade from the time of Mr. Huskisson to the close of Mr. Deacon Hume's services at that board may be considered as the history of Mr. Deacon Hume himself."
Hume published *The Laws of the Customs*, 6 Geo. IV. c. 106-116, with notes, 1825-1832, 6 pts., 8vo.—*The Laws of the Customs*, 3 & 4 Will. IV., 50-60, with notes, 1833-36, 3 pts., 8vo.
[*Life of J. Deacon Hume*, by C. Badham, *Custom Commissioners' Report*, 1857, London, 1859, 8vo.] H. E. E.
M'Culloch, in his *Literature of Political Economy*, speaks somewhat slightingly of Deacon Hume's letters under the signature H. B. T., to the *Morning Chronicle*, which in his view "involve some very questionable and, as we think, wholly untenable positions," p. 80. Tooke, however, in *The History of Prices*, vol. iv. p. 106, speaks in a very different tone of these letters, and shows how accurate an observer Hume was "of events connected with the commerce of the country."

HUME, JOSEPH (1777-1855), was the son of a Montrose ship-master. He studied medicine, became a member of the College of Surgeons of Edinburgh, and in 1797 was appointed assistant-surgeon in the marine service of the East India Company. Later he was transferred to the land service of the company. Applying himself diligently to the study of the native languages and religions, he mastered Hindustani and Persian, and was employed by the administration in political duties. He filled in succession responsible posts in the offices of paymaster and postmaster of the forces, in the prize agencies, and in the commissariat. In 1807 he retired from the service, and returned to England with a fortune of £40,000. Hume now devoted himself to a study of the history and resources of Great Britain, and after visiting the whole of the agricultural and manufacturing centres of the United Kingdom, he spent some time on the continent, increasing his stores of political information.
In 1812 Hume entered parliament for Weymouth, having purchased two elections to the seat. He was at this time, and for a brief period subsequently, a tory. He opposed the Framework Knitters' Bill in the interest of the manufacturers. Upon the dissolution, in the autumn of 1812, the owners of the borough of Weymouth refused to re-elect him, when he took legal proceedings, and recovered a portion of the money he had deposited. While out of parliament he took a prominent part on the central committee of the Lancastrian schools, and closely studied the condition of the working classes, advocating the establishment of savings

banks. He essayed in vain to get elected upon the East India Board, but he was active in exposing abuses, and when the charter of 1793 expired he advocated freedom of trade with India, pointing out that it must result in an enormous expansion of commerce with the East. In 1818 Hume was elected as a liberal for the Border Burghs, and from this period until his death—with the exception of a brief interregnum—he held a seat in parliament, representing in succession the Border Burghs, Aberdeen, Middlesex, Kilkenny, and Montrose. During the whole of his career in the House of Commons he unflinchingly advocated financial and general reforms. He first drew attention to the enormously disproportionate cost of collecting the revenue, and compelled the appointment of a select committee, which reported in his favour. He opposed the scheme for the reduction of the pension charges, and in 1824 obtained a select committee on the combination acts. During the reform debates of 1831 he advocated the extension of representation to the colonies, and three years later he moved for the repeal of the corn laws. In 1835-36 he severely attacked the Orange Society, which was credited with a design to place the Duke of Cumberland on the throne after the death of William IV.

Hume was the sleepless watch-dog of finance, and mainly owing to his efforts the advanced radical party became known as the party of retrenchment. Every item in the returns of the public expenditure was subjected to his severe scrutiny—a task over which he expended much toil and money. He procured the abolition of the sinking fund, and it was he who reintroduced the fourpenny silver coin (see GROAT), which, however, has once more disappeared. He secured the repeal of the combination laws, as well as of those prohibiting the emigration of workmen and the exportation of machinery. He was an advocate of Catholic emancipation, of parliamentary reform, and of the repeal of the test and corporation acts. Hume was one of the trustees of the loan raised for the Greek insurgents, and was charged with jobbery in connection with it; but all that he did was to secure an advantageous liquidation of his holding when the loan was at a discount. He served on more committees of the House of Commons dealing with finance and the public service than any other member. Hume died, 20th February 1855; and Lord Palmerston, in alluding to the event in the House of Commons, observed that it was said of an eminent statesman (Burke) that he "gave up to party what was meant for mankind," whereas "the reverse might be said of Hume, who devoted himself first to his country and then to the general interests of mankind at large." A scholarship in political economy was founded in his memory at University College, London.

[Harris's *Radical Party in Parliament.*—Anderson's *Scottish Nation.*—*Dictionary of National Biography*, art. "Joseph Hume."—*Annual Register*, 1855.—*Gentleman's Magazine*, 1855.—Harriet Martineau's *History of the Thirty Years' Peace.*—Hansard's *Parliamentary Debates.*]
                                                    G. B. S.

HUNDRED. The origin of the administrative division called a hundred in England has given rise to endless discussion among historians. There is no documentary mention of it until the ordinance of Edgar in the 10th century, and hence some have considered it a creation of that king. A tradition, recorded by William of Malmesbury, attributes the formation of hundreds to Alfred. On the other hand, the evidence of Tacitus and the analogy of all other German peoples would lead us to expect the existence of an administrative unit larger than the township and smaller than the tribe or kingdom. Moreover, the ordinance of Edgar does not read at all like the starting of an innovation, but only as regulating the use of an existing institution. Probably the best conclusion is that the English brought over with them the organisation of the hundred, but this name was by no means in universal use till the 10th century. In the western conquests, made after Angles and Saxons became Christian, the organisation may not have been introduced, while it may have fallen into decay in the north and midlands during the Danish wars. The effect of Edgar's ordinance would thus be to revive the hundred system where it had fallen into disuse, to extend it to districts where it had never been introduced, and to definitely fix its uses and arrangements.

The origin of the name hundred is even more obscure than that of the district to which it has been applied. It must at some time have had a numerical significance, such as the settlement of a hundred families or the district which sent a hundred warriors to the host, but it is quite impossible to trace such a meaning in England. The court of the hundred, which met every four weeks, consisted of the freeholders of the district with the parish priests and the reeve and four men from each township. It was the primary court of criminal jurisdiction in Anglo-Saxon times. The hundred was also the basis of military assessment and of the system of mutual responsibility, which in those days served instead of police. The organisation of the hundred was carefully preserved by the Norman kings as a counterpoise to the growth of territorial jurisdiction in the hands of the great barons. But it steadily decayed in the 13th and 14th centuries, and its place was supplied by the rise of the justices of the peace.

[*Essays in Anglo-Saxon Law* (Boston, 1876).—Stubbs, *Select Charters*, pp. 68-70.—Stubbs, *Constitutional History*, i. pp. 96-99.]   R. L.

The geographical division of the counties into hundreds continued, however, and for some purposes is still of practical importance. Thus in several counties the liability of the hundred for the repair of bridges continues, and the county councils have power, under § 3 of the Local Government Act of 1888, to assess and levy hundred rates. Up to the passing of the Riot (Damages) Act, 1886, the inhabitants of a hundred were, under a statute of George IV., liable in certain cases to pay compensation for damage done to property within the area of such hundred in the course of any riotous proceedings (for a modern instance of a claim made under the provisions of the statute in question, see Drake v. Tootitt, 7 Q.B.D. 201 [1881]).

The organisation of the rural police, until a comparatively recent period, also conformed to the division of counties into hundreds. The "high constables," whose office was abolished in 1867, had jurisdiction over their respective hundreds in the same manner as the parish constables over their respective parishes, and the division of counties into hundreds had to be considered in the arrangement of petty sessional divisions (see 10 Geo. IV. c. 46).

In more recent times the areas of the poor-law unions have been found more convenient intermediate units for the purposes of local government, and the rural districts created by the Public Health Act 1875 (see § 9)—the importance of which has been considerably increased by the Local Government Act 1894—are generally coterminous with these areas.

E. S.

HUNDRED ROLLS. In 1274, soon after Edward I.'s return from the Holy Land, special commissioners were appointed to summon juries in the different districts throughout the country in order to inquire into the king's rights, royalties, and prerogatives, and into all frauds and abuses connected therewith, by which the crown suffered loss of revenue. This step had become necessary, for, owing to the encroachments of nobility and clergy during the troubles of the preceding reign, the resources of the crown had been seriously impaired. The results of the inquisitions held on this occasion make up the *Hundred Rolls.* These, therefore, contain particulars of (1) all demesne lands, and of manors which had been alienated from the crown ; (2) tenants in capite and in demesne; (3) losses to the crown through sub-infeudations ; (4) alienations to the church under pretext of FRANKALMOIGN ; (5) wardships and other feudal rights withheld from the crown ; (6) the crown's interest in fee farms, hundreds, wapentakes, and tythings ; (7) *jura regalia,* such as wreck, free-chase, etc. ; (8) illegal and excessive tolls on fairs, and for murage, pontage, etc. ; (9) exactions and oppressions by crown officers ; and (10) unlawful exportations of wool,—the whole forming one of the most valuable records ever compiled. The Hundred Rolls have been printed by the record commissioners in two large folio volumes with an introduction by W. Illingworth.

[Cunningham, *Growth of English Industry and Commerce,* bk. ii. ch. iii., Cambridge, 1890.]

A. E. S.

HUSBAND (AS TO WIFE'S PROPERTY). Husbands who were married before 1883 to wives possessed of property not settled upon them for their separate use, became entitled to extensive rights in respect of such property. All personal property actually in the wife's possession at the time of her marriage became the husband's property ; debts owing to the wife became payable to the husband, if recovered within the wife's lifetime ; if not recovered during the wife's lifetime the husband became entitled to them as administrator of his deceased wife's personal property. In addition to this, if any children were born during the marriage the husband acquired an indefeasible life interest in his wife's real property (he acquired "an estate by the curtesy"). All this has been materially altered by the Married Women's Property Act of 1882. Women who have married since the 1st January 1883 hold all their property as separate property, and the same rule is applied to property acquired after that date by women married before the commencement of the "Married Women's Property Act." A married woman may also dispose of her separate property by will without her husband's concurrence, and the only rights which remain to the husband are the absolute right to the wife's personal estate in case she dies intestate, and a life interest in her real estate in the same event, if there was a child of the marriage.

E. S.

HUSKISSON, WILLIAM (1770-1830), the son of William Huskisson and Elizabeth (*née* Rotton), and educated at schools at Brewood, Albrighton, and Appleby in Leicestershire. In 1783 he was taken to Paris by his uncle Dr. Gem, where he remained for a long time, becoming private secretary to Lord Gower, the English minister, in 1790. On his recall Huskisson returned to England, and in 1793 was appointed to consider the position of the numerous French refugees with regard to the requirements of the Alien Act. In 1795 he became under-secretary for war and colonies, and in the following year entered the House of Commons as member for Morpeth. On Pitt's resignation in 1801 he withdrew from office, only retaining his under-secretaryship for a few weeks after that minister's retirement for the convenience of the incoming secretary. In 1804 he was appointed secretary of the treasury, passed into opposition in 1806, and resumed the position of secretary of the treasury in 1807. In 1810 he resigned with Canning ; in 1814 was appointed chief commissioner of woods and forests, a position which he quitted in 1823 to become president of the board of trade. Having sat in succession for several constituencies, he refrained from seeking re-election at Chichester after his new appointment in order to become one of the representatives of Liverpool. The remaining facts of his official life are few. In 1827 he was appointed colonial secretary, an office resigned in 1828. His death was caused by an accident during the opening of the Liverpool and Manchester railway in 1830.

Throughout his career Huskisson was remarkable for his firm adherence to the principles of sound economic reform. He was a member of the Bullion Committee (see BULLION COMMITTEE, REPORT OF), and in the currency discussion he took an important part in the protest made against an inflated paper currency, both then and in his writings laying down most clearly and vigorously the principles upon which a sound monetary system must be based. During his tenure of office at the board of trade he was responsible for important changes in the economic policy of the country. In the first place he modified the navigation system as affecting the colonies and foreign nations; with regard to the former, introducing changes which permitted direct trade to take place between the colonies and foreign countries in either British ships or those of the foreign nations thus concerned, but reserved the trade between the colonies and England. With regard to the foreign nations he carried a measure in 1825, which enabled the king in council "to place the shipping of any other country on an equal footing with our own, when that country was prepared to grant a similar favour in return." By this act Huskisson prepared the way for the final abolition of the Navigation Act, which, however beneficial in former years, was at the time a serious obstacle to the development of the trade of the country.

In the second place Huskisson began the policy of tariff revision and simplification which was afterwards undertaken by Peel and completed by Mr. Gladstone. This course he entered upon in 1824. His policy was twofold, the removal of the custom duties affecting raw material, and the reduction of the duties imposed on the import of foreign manufactures.

In these instances, as in the other changes of an economic character for which he was responsible—as for instance the repeal of the statutes prohibiting combination in 1825,—Huskisson displayed great moderation and foresight. The changes he made fully answered his anticipations. Too much praise, indeed, cannot be given to Huskisson for the courage he displayed in administrative economics. His knowledge of the details was wide, his grasp of principle firm; and though his speaking was not of the order of high oratory, it was lucid and persuasive, in short of the kind most fitted to the subjects with which he had to deal.

[See especially Huskisson's *Speeches*, 3 vols. —*The Question concerning the Depreciation of our Currency stated and examined*, 1810.—A Paper on the currency 1826 in which he recommends a double standard for this country—silver as well as gold — lately reprinted by the Bimetallic League.]   E. C. K. G.

HUTCHESON, ARCHIBALD (late 17th century to 1740), barrister of the Middle Temple and member for Hastings. He agitated upon the questions of the national debt and the South Sea scheme. Having spoken on the first of these subjects in the last parliament of Anne, in 1714, he laid his proposals for its discharge before George I., and in March 1716, before parliament. He suggested devoting to its payment "so much as shall be sufficient of the estates real and personal of all the inhabitants of Great Britain . . . or by raising of new sinking funds, . . . or by borrowing at lower interest."

He advocated a more frugal expenditure of the public revenue, proposed the abolition of the excise and customs duties, so as to relieve the government of the burden of their collection, and was eager for free and fair elections, frequent parliaments, and the abolition of bribery and corruption.

Hutcheson published :—*A Collection of Treatises relating to the Public Debts and Funds, etc.* ; and also *A Collection . . . relating to the South Sea Stock and Scheme*, London, 1721, fol.—*An Abstract of all the Public Debts remaining due at Michaelmas, 1722, and an Estimate of the Annual Sinking Fund towards the Discharge of the same, etc.*, London, 1723, fol.—*An Abstract of an Account stated by some of the Clerks at the South Sea House, relating to the Estates of the late Directors, etc.*—*The case of Contracts for South Sea Stock in General, etc.* (By A. H.) 1720, fol.—*A Collection of Advertisements, etc. . . . relating to the Last Elections of Westminster and Hastings.* . . . London, 1722, 8vo.— *Copies of some letters . . . from Mr. Hutcheson to the late Earl of Sunderland.* T. Payne, London, 1722, 8vo.—*An Estimate of the Value of South Sea Stock*, 1720, fol.—*Some Computations and Remarks relating to the Money, Subscribers, and the Proprietors of the Public Debts, etc.*, London, 1720.—*A Speech made in the House of Commons, 24th April 1716 (by A. H.)*, 1716, 8vo, 2nd edit. 1722, 8vo.   A. L.

HUTCHESON, FRANCIS (1694-1746). Born in Ireland, but of Scottish descent, Hutcheson was appointed to the chair of moral philosophy in the university of Glasgow in 1727, and was thus a predecessor of Adam Smith. It is chiefly on account of the influence his writings are supposed to have had upon Smith that he is classed as an economist. He was one of the earliest propounders of what is known as the utilitarian doctrine of ethics ; and his teaching in this matter may be regarded as the foundation of the corresponding theory of economics, whose supporters included Smith, Bentham, and James Mill, and in a modified degree J. S. Mill. The following quotation from his inquiry concerning moral good and evil (§ 3) contains the kernel of this doctrine, compressed into remarkably few words. "In equal degrees of happiness expected to proceed from an action, the virtue is in proportion to the number of persons to whom the happiness shall extend." Bentham's often quoted ideal, "the greatest happiness of the greatest number," is to be found in Hutcheson. In his principal work, *A System of Moral Philosophy* (1742), there are many passages which foreshadow the theories subsequently developed by his great successor in the *Wealth of Nations*. Bk. ii. ch. vii. is a discussion on public and private property, the latter of which Hutcheson explains and defends in a manner somewhat different from that commonly employed by modern economists. He also examines the origin of capital, very much as Smith does. Chapters viii. and ix. of the same book are an expansion of the same subject; in the latter he deals with the subjects of contract. He emphasises the sanctity of contracts; but enumerates many limitations to freedom of contract. His style is lucid, and his language frequently quaint and terse. [Bonar's *Philosophy and Political Economy*.] M. G. D.

HUTCHINSON, JOHN HELY (1724-1794), a well-known Irish lawyer and statesman. Upon his marriage with the niece and heiress of Richard Hutchinson, he adopted that name.

He first sat in 1759 as member for Lanesborough, but from 1761-90 for the city of Cork. To quiet his violent opposition, the government made him privy councillor, and for subsequent services he was successively appointed prime serjeant-at-law, alnager, and in 1777 chief secretary of state. In 1774 he also obtained the provostship of Trinity College. In 1785 he accepted a peerage for his wife, who accordingly became Baroness Donoughmore. His greed of money and place won him the title of "ready-money-voter," and it cannot be denied that on more than one occasion he stretched his authority and influence to further his own and family interests.

But apart from this he was an able, if an unpopular, provost, and a clever and far-sighted statesman. Where his private interests were not concerned he followed the promptings of patriotism and public spirit. He was a fearless advocate of independence, of Roman Catholic emancipation, and of free trade; and one of his last votes was in favour of parliamentary reform. Hutchinson is best known to economists as the author of *The Commercial Restraints of Ireland*, a work which originally consisted of a series of letters to the lord lieutenant, Lord Buckinghamshire. It was published anonymously in 1779, but condemned to be burnt by the common hangman for its seditious doctrines. The advocates of free trade, however, gave it high praise.

The author is at pains to discover the causes which had ruined and were still ruining Ireland; and traces it to the selfish, and as he endeavours to show, suicidal, policy of the English parliament of 1699, which absolutely prohibited the exportation of Irish woollen manufactures. Hutchinson, very moderately, points out that, apart from its injustice, this policy was injurious to English interests; that one third of the wealth of Ireland was possessed by England, and that she would receive more than half the benefit of the woollen trade, and even at that price Ireland would obtain some prosperity.

In 1785 he repudiated the accusation of playing into the hands of the government, by his *Letter from the Secretary of State to the Mayor of Cork*, in which he put the case for the Anglo-Irish trade very plainly before his constituents.

He shows that no two countries on the globe are more necessary to the happiness and welfare of each other than these two islands, and advocates a noble equality and reciprocity of commercial tariffs.

The following is a list of his writings: *The Commercial Restraints of Ireland considered*, 1779, 1780, 8vo.—*A Letter . . . to the Mayor of Cork on the Subject of the Bill presented by Mr. Orde, on the 15th Aug. 1785, for effectuating the Intercourse and Commerce between Great Britain and Ireland on . . . Equitable Principles, etc.* Dublin, 1785, 8vo.—*Mr. Hutchinson's Letter to his Constituents at Cork*, 1786, 8vo.—*The Speech of . . . J. H. H. . . . made in the House of Commons on the 26th day of June 1793, on the Resolution . . . respecting the Regulations of the Treasury Board*, Dublin, 1793, 12mo. A. L.

HUYSERS, ARIEN (died in 1806). A Dutch merchant and clerk in the service of the (Dutch) Company of the East Indies. Besides the biography of one of its governors-general, R. de Klerk (Amsterdam, 1787), he published a description of their settlements (*Beschryving der Oost Indische Etablissementen*), Utrecht, 1789, and reprinted in Amsterdam in 1792. [Frederiks en Van den Branden, *Biographisch Woordenboek*, Amsterdam, 1888.] E. CA.

HYPOTHEC (Scots Law). A lien or right existing at law in some particular cases, in favour of a creditor, by way of security over property of his debtor, while that property continues to belong to the debtor and to be in his possession. Examples of this are: the landlord's hypothec for rent, over the crop and stock of his tenant in a pastoral or agricultural holding, this hypothec having now been abolished by the Hypothec Abolition Act, 1880, so far as regards land exceeding two acres in extent; his hypothec over household furniture, etc., in houses, for the rent ; the hypothec of a superior or overlord for the last or current feu-duty or annual payment to him, this hypothec being over the crop and moveable property on the land, and being preferred above the landlord's hypothec for his rent ; the hypothec of seamen over the freight and the ship for their wages ; that of the shipowners against the cargo for freight ; that of freighters over the ship against the shipowners for loss through mismanagement ; and that of ship-repairers over the ship for cost of repairs in a foreign port. The law-agent's right of retainer of documents until paid is also called, in Scotland, his hypothec (see LIEN). A. D.

HYPOTHECA, the right of pledge or mortgage of a thing, constituted by mere agreement without any transfer of possession of the thing to the creditor. It sometimes means the thing thus pledged or mortgaged (see PIGNUS).

E. A. W.

HYPOTHECATION. A general expression for all transactions by which some property is mortgaged or pledged by way of security for a debt. The expression "letter of hypothecation" is frequently used for the document by which goods, the bill of lading relating to which is attached to a bill of exchange, are mortgaged to the holder of the bill, by way of security for the acceptance or payment of the same. As such goods have sometimes to be landed or re-shipped, and during the time before warrants or new bills of lading are issued may be in the possession of the mortgager or his agent, there was a doubt whether the letter of hypothecation did not have the effect of a BILL OF SALE (*q.v.*) and ought to be registered accordingly, but the Bills of Sale Act 1890 has made it clear that the registration of such a document is unnecessary. E. S.

HYPOTHESIS.

(1) The Illustrative Hypothesis, p. 348 ; (2) The Approximate Hypothesis, p. 348 ; (3) The Tentative Hypothesis, p. 349 ; (4) The Explanatory Hypothesis, p. 350 ; (5) The Working Hypothesis, p. 350 ; (6) Relations between the different types of Hypothesis, p. 350.

The word hypothesis is used in science to denote any supposition put forward as a premiss from which deductions are to be drawn. Hypotheses, however, differ in their essential character according to the purposes for which they are constructed and the uses to which they are put. Most of these varieties of application are exemplified in the writings of political economists. It will be convenient to treat the various kinds of hypothesis under different heads, and to give examples under each head of the ways in which hypothesis has been applied in political economy.

(1) *The Illustrative Hypothesis.*—Hypotheses of the first kind are those used in the exposition of complex phenomena. The purpose here is primarily didactic ; the writer having in view the need of familiarising students with the conceptions appropriate to the subject. It is very usual to begin the exposition of any branch of economic study by describing phenomena of a much simpler character than the corresponding phenomena of actual economic life. Simple conditions of a definitely assigned character are laid down for illustration, without any implication that these necessarily accord with reality. Such a use of hypothesis may be called *Illustrative*. One of the best examples of such hypothesis is that used by Professor Nicholson in *Money*, ch. v. § 3. He begins his exposition of general prices by assuming an artificially simplified case in which it is supposed that money consists of counters only of use to effect exchanges, that no exchanges are made without the passing of money from hand to hand at every transaction, and further, that there is a definitely assigned distribution of commodities and of money among a given number of traders. Hypotheses of a similarly illustrative character are used by Mill and Bastable in their expositions of the theory of international values. They begin by assuming that there are but two nations in existence, that these nations trade only in two commodities, and that there are no expenses of carriage, etc., between the nations, or other items of mutual indebtedness, besides exports and imports. We may add that a mathematical treatment of the pure theory of exchange or of distribution necessarily employs simple hypotheses for illustration or exposition, as for example in the works of Cournot and Jevons. Such instances are too numerous to be recounted. Simplifications of this kind, used merely for illustration, and not supposed, at least in their initial form, to accord completely with facts, are necessary for the rigorous exposition of complex phenomena. Sometimes indeed a hypothesis is propounded which does not profess to answer to any possible or probable state of affairs ; as, for example, when an investigation is made of the consequences that would follow from supposing that the amount of coin in circulation is suddenly doubled or halved, or that all the fixed capital of a country is suddenly annihilated. The uses of such hypotheses and the limitations to which they are subject are very instructively treated by Dr. Venn, *Empirical Logic*, ch. xvi. Hypotheses of the illustrative type tend to pass over into hypotheses of a somewhat different kind, to which we may refer under our second head.

(2) *The Approximative Hypothesis.*— Hypotheses made primarily with the purpose of simplifying exposition are often secondarily applied under the supposition that they accord, at least approximately or in the long run, with the nature of the phenomena to be expounded. Indeed the most useful form of the illustrative hypothesis is that in which, after beginning the exposition with the simplest possible description

of conditions, we introduce step by step further conditions till it is believed that all the essential circumstances of the case are included. Nevertheless the point of view of the expository hypothesis is essentially different from that of the hypothesis now to be considered. The propounder of the hypothesis now adopts the position that it expresses a true tendency; that even if the conclusions derived from it do not appear to accord with observation, yet this is only because counteracting agencies have concealed its operation. We are supposed to be dealing, not with fictions, but with abstractions. The use of hypotheses of this kind has been formally justified by Mill, Cairnes, and Bagehot. Undoubtedly the method of hypothesis in this sense is the most fruitful and potent instrument in the hands of the deductive economist. In almost all cases, the risk of error is eliminated if care is taken to express explicitly the precise assumptions employed. In this respect the use of a mathematico-analytic method has a very marked advantage over arithmetical or even diagrammatic expositions; for in the former every assumption must be explicitly formulated, while in the latter we are liable to introduce unnoticed relations between the numbers or points chosen for illustration. An example of errors arising from this source is to be found in the treatment by Ricardo and Mill of the effect on rent of agricultural improvements (Ricardo, *Principles*, ch. ii. § 31; Mill, *Political Economy*, bk. iv. ch. iii. § 4). Hypotheses which profess to represent actually operative tendencies, and are therefore intended to yield results true approximately or in the long run, are often adopted more or less unconsciously. It is in this unconscious employment that their main danger lies. For in such cases the writers have really believed that they were taking into consideration all the essential circumstances of the case, and that the conclusions deduced could be applied in practice to real concrete phenomena. They have often passed unawares from the standpoint of exposition to that of practical application. Hence the use of hypotheses has been sometimes too vehemently attacked by opponents of the deductive school. We may give a few examples of cases in which assumptions have been made more or less consciously and applied perhaps without sufficient qualification to concrete economic facts. Ricardo has been charged with assuming in his theory of value a fixed standard of comfort of the labouring population, or at least a standard determined independently of the play of ordinary economic forces. Again, the same writer and some of his followers have tacitly or explicitly assumed perfect *mobility* of capital and labour in their treatment of distribution and cost of production in domestic trade; while, as regards foreign trade, their theory of international values has been based

on the assumption of the practical *immobility* of capital and labour as between nation and nation. Again, adherents of the wages-fund theory have often based their arguments on the tacit assumption that "the amount of wages that will be paid in any country in (say) a year is fixed absolutely by the amount of capital existing there at the time" (Marshall, *Principles of Economics*, p. 573). Similarly, in maintaining the proposition "Demand for commodities is not demand for labour," Mill in one part of his argument assumes that "the consumer who hires labour postpones the consumption of the fruits of that labour to a later date than he who with an equivalent portion of wealth purchases commodities." One other less important example may be cited from Ricardo, who, in discussing the effect on rent of agricultural improvements, assumes that the demand for corn is absolutely inelastic. As regards many hypotheses that are adopted either as true or as approximately true in application to facts, it should be noticed that their logical character is often likely to elude the reader. For they are sometimes the suppressed premises of an elaborately constructed argument, in which the conclusion which professes to be proved is to all intents and purposes merely a formal or verbal equivalent of the premiss suppressed.

(3) *The Tentative Hypothesis.*—Hypotheses in either of the above forms, illustrative or approximative, are used in the process of deduction, in which the course of the exposition is from the abstract to the concrete. Hypotheses of an apparently opposite type are also used in inductions from specific experience or explanations of concrete phenomena. Here the starting-point is—not some accepted law of nature—but an observed fact. This leads us to consider a third use of hypothesis, where the scientific imagination is called into play, to find some general formula adopted conjecturally which shall connect an empirically observed set of occurrences with a known law of nature. Such a hypothesis is put forward at first merely tentatively, with the clear recognition that it requires verification. The best example that can be cited of such a tentatively adopted hypothesis is. the suggestion of Jevons that the periodicity of commercial crises might be connected with that of the sun-spots. Such a suggestion obviously awaited deductive or inductive verification; and Jevons has shown how, in the course of his investigations, a certain amount of verification was gradually obtained. This case derives a special interest from the fact that Jevons, as a logician, had emphasised the necessity for such tentative guesses in all inductive inquiry. But it would be difficult to find many examples of the inductive hypothesis in its purely tentative stage, because investigators have not as a rule recorded

guesses afterwards found not to accord with facts. Indeed the tentative hypothesis has rather a psychological than a logical interest, as indicating the mental process that must be gone through by an individual whose aim is the discovery of truth and the enlargement of knowledge and insight. Nevertheless, it will not be irrelevant to remark that workers in the field of statistics must have often tentatively brought into comparison two sets of phenomena, such as variations in the price of corn and in the marriage rate, with the view of examining whether the one set of changes can be so harmonised with the other as to suggest causal connection. A very similar investigation is made by Jevons (*Theory of Political Economy*, pp. 167-172), where he adopts a conjectural formula for expressing the relations between the supply and price of wheat in accordance with the estimates known as Gregory King's. This formula has since been amended by Mr. Wicksteed in the *Quarterly Journal of Economics*, April 1889.

(4) *The Explanatory Hypothesis.*—A hypothesis which has been put forward at first tentatively, with a view to future verification or refutation, comes after a time to be adopted as an explanatory theory when it has received some degree of confirmation. Such a theory is spoken of as a hypothesis, because it is not affirmed categorically, but is regarded as a premiss from which conclusions can be deduced which coincide with empirically observed facts or uniformities. The explanatory hypothesis differs from the tentative hypothesis mainly in respect to the point of view from which they are regarded. The latter indicates a stage in the process of *discovery*, the former is concerned with the question of *proof*. For the explanatory hypothesis is a theory regarded as deriving some degree of probability from its accordance with observations of fact. It differs from a law guaranteed by stricter induction in being avowedly subject to more or less doubt. A hypothesis used in explanations falls into one or other of two classes. It may be that the facts put forward as explanatory are not themselves in dispute, but only their causal connection with the phenomena to be explained. Or it may be that the facts put forward as explanatory are themselves open to question, though it is not denied that if true they would be adequate to explain the effect observed. The following are a few examples of hypothesis used in explanation of economic facts. Malthus, observing that the two countries Norway and Sweden closely resembled one another in their general economic conditions, and yet that the average proportional mortality was considerably higher in Sweden than in Norway, inferred that the difference was to be explained by the superior force in Norway of preventive checks to the increase of population due to certain

governmental regulations and national sentiment and customs. Similarly, the difference in the prosperity of two similarly situated countries has been often hypothetically explained as the effect of the maintenance of a policy of free trade or of protection as the case may be. Or again, the fall in the gold-value of silver since 1874 has been explained as effect of the German demonetisation of silver; and the present depression in trade as effect of a scarcity of gold. In Adam Smith many hypothetical explanations of observed facts are to be found. He, for example, suggested that the impossibility of separating the different branches of labour employed in agriculture is the probable reason why improvements in agriculture have not always kept pace with improvements in manufacture. He gave numerous hypothetical explanations of variations in profits, in wages, in riches, etc., gathered from observations extending over large ranges of time and place.

(5) *The Working Hypothesis.*—The expression working hypothesis is in common use, but it seems to bear no universally recognised meaning beyond what is implied by the word hypothesis alone. The word *working* implies that the value attributed to such a hypothesis is due to the expectation that true results can be deduced from it, though in itself it has no claims to be regarded as true or even probable. It is adopted, at a particular stage of scientific investigation, to assist the mind in realising a mass of complex phenomena. In the theory of electricity, the hypothesis of one and that of two fluids are examples of working hypotheses. Similarly, the *social contract* of HOBBES and ROUSSEAU may in the same sense be regarded as a convenient fiction which enables us to understand some of the aspects of social evolution. The working hypothesis, as thus defined, is midway between the illustrative and the explanatory hypothesis. It is not merely illustrative, since it leads to results that agree with experience; but it can hardly be called explanatory, since its use does not depend on any belief in its truth or even its probability.

(6) *Relations between the different types of Hypothesis.*—Though we have hitherto been concerned to bring out the distinctions between different kinds of hypothesis, yet it is equally important to point out the mutual connections between them and to show how they are to be correlated in economic science. The expository hypothesis is derived primarily from generally accepted and comparatively simple laws of nature. It is of value in proportion to the extent to which its results are confirmed by facts directly observed and by uniformities directly generalised from experience. Conversely, the explanatory hypothesis is derived primarily from data of observation; but it is of value in proportion to the degree with which it is confirmed by deductive reasoning from

acknowledged laws of human, social, or physical nature. A complete method, therefore, requires that the processes of induction and deduction should supplement one another, each serving as verification of what is arbitrary or uncertain in the other. The hypothesis used in deduction keeps as closely as possible to the simple laws of human nature known to be actually operative; but, since actual phenomena are due to the composition of many concurrent tendencies, we can never be sure that all these tendencies have been taken into account, or that their comparative force has been correctly estimated. Similarly the hypothesis used in induction keeps as closely as possible to the actual facts of economic life ascertained by direct observation; but, since no mere generalisation is acceptable unless its dependence on fundamental principles of human nature has been exhibited, we must verify any inductively suggested explanation by showing how it may be derived from such fundamental principles. The consilience of deductive and inductive inferences is thus the ultimate criterion by which the value of every sort of hypothesis is to be measured.

[Mill, *Unsettled Questions of Political Economy*, Essay v.—Cairnes, *Logical Method of Political Economy*, *passim*.—Bagehot, *Economic Studies*, Essays i. ii.—Keynes, *Scope and Method of Political Economy*, *passim*, see also DEDUCTIVE METHOD; EXAMPLES; INDUCTIVE METHOD.]

W. E. J.

ICARIA. See CABET, ÉTIENNE; COMMUNISM.

IDDESLEIGH, THE EARL OF (1818-1887), better known as Sir Stafford Northcote, came of an old Devonshire family, and was educated at Eton and Oxford. He was intended for the bar, and in 1841 became private secretary to Mr. Gladstone, whose liberal views on finance and political economy he imbibed. His general political opinions, however, were conservative. In 1845 he accepted a permanent post in the board of trade, and two years later he became legal secretary to the board. During the debates on the navigation laws he published an able pamphlet on the subject which convinced the Duke of Wellington of the necessity and expediency of removing this vestige of the old protective system. In 1851 Mr. Northcote succeeded his grandfather in the baronetcy, and in the following year he rendered signal assistance to the Prince Consort as one of the secretaries of the great exhibition. His labours at this time were so exhausting that his health was seriously impaired, and the first symptoms of that cardiac weakness which afterwards proved fatal were developed. Rest restored his health considerably, and his joint labours with Sir Charles E. Trevelyan in connection with the report on the civil establishments of the crown (1853-54) led eventually to the establishment of the civil service commission, and the throwing open of the civil service generally to public competition.

Sir Stafford Northcote first entered the House of Commons in 1855 as conservative member for Dudley; he sat for Stamford from 1858 to 1866; and for North Devon from 1866 until 1885, when he was raised to the peerage as Earl of Iddesleigh. In 1858 he was appointed financial secretary to the treasury, and when Lord Derby's third administration was formed in 1866, he became president of the board of trade, an office which he exchanged in the following year for that of secretary of state for India. In 1871 he was nominated by Mr. Gladstone one of the special commissioners for the negotiation of the treaty of Washington, which had for its principal object the final settlement of the Alabama claims. The treaty was successfully concluded, and the long and bitter controversy between Great Britain and the United States finally closed. In 1874 Sir Stafford Northcote was appointed chancellor of the exchequer, an office for which he was eminently fitted. He had already published his important work *Twenty Years of Financial Policy: a Summary of the chief financial measures passed between 1842 and 1861; with a Table of Budgets*. In this work—which is one of the best efforts of recent times to record the effects of taxation, including local taxes—the author declared himself a disciple of the financial school of Peel and Gladstone. As chancellor of the exchequer he upheld the doctrines of free trade; and his financial policy included the final extinction of the sugar duties, and a slight increase in the tax on tobacco; the temporary reduction of the income tax to twopence in the pound, the lowest point it had reached from the first imposition of the tax; and the establishment and maintenance of an effective sinking fund, maintained generally by his successors. While out of office, Sir Stafford Northcote acted as chairman of an important parliamentary committee on the income tax, which his report contributed largely to sustain against the attacks of its enemies. From 1876 to 1880 he was leader of the House of Commons, in succession to Lord Beaconsfield. Besides being called upon to deal with parliamentary obstruction as a system, he had to grapple with many critical events, including the Russo-Turkish war, the Berlin treaty, the Zulu war, the Afghan war, etc. From 1880 until 1885 he led the conservative opposition, but a more robust leadership was desired in certain quarters, and he was ultimately elevated to the House of Lords. He became first lord of the treasury in Lord Salisbury's first government, and secretary of state for foreign affairs in the second Salisbury administration ; and was chairman of the Royal Commission on the Depression of Trade and Industry (1885-1886). The principles of Lord Iddesleigh's financial policy were thus defined by himself in a letter to Sir Reginald Welby (1875) : — "1. Prudent, but not deliberately *under* estimates.   2. The habitual retention of a substantial surplus.   3. The retention of the income-tax at a· low fixed rate, not to be disturbed for anything short of a national emergency.   4. The appropriation of a fixed annual sum to the charge for debt.   5. The avoidance of new taxes.   6. As a corollary, the toleration of old ones.   Parliament and the country ought really to make up their minds to deal frankly and courageously with these matters, to eschew sensationalism, and to act on steady principles."

[*Twenty Years of Financial Policy* (1842-1861), by Sir Stafford Northcote, 1862.— *The Times*, Jan. 13, 1887.—*Life, Letters, and Diaries of Sir Stafford Northcote, first Earl of Iddesleigh*, by Andrew Lang, 2 vols., 1890.]   G. B. S.

IDEAL, THE ECONOMIC. However much an economist may protest that political economy is a science, not an art, and that it is no business of his to tell people what they ought to do, he can scarcely help assuming that both they and he have some ideal towards the attainment of which a knowledge of political economy is expected to assist. In English political economy this ideal has usually been considered to be simply the greatest possible creation of wealth. Whether this is a satisfactory ideal or not depends entirely on the way the formula is interpreted.   To make it satisfactory :

(1) "Wealth" must mean average or *per capita* wealth. If it be taken to mean simply aggregate wealth without any regard to the number of persons who have to share that aggregate, this would make the ideal of economic progress "a human ant-hill" (Leroy-Beaulieu, *Répartition des richesses*, p. 126). We no longer believe, with Paley, that "in comparing adjoining periods in the same country, the collective happiness will be nearly in the exact proportion of the numbers, that is, twice the number of inhabitants will produce double the quantity of happiness" (*Moral Philosophy*, bk. vi. ch. xi.). We speak of countries as rich or poor according to the wealth enjoyed by each inhabitant, not according to the wealth of all inhabitants taken collectively.

(2) The creation or "production" of wealth must not be understood in such a way that it is merely equivalent to the accumulation of instruments of production and means of enjoyment. It must mean the creation of income, not the

creation of capital.   Accumulation is only useful in so far as it increases consumable income.   Economists of the school of which M'Culloch was the chief representative were apt to regard the mere heaping up of goods as an end, and men only as the instruments employed in effecting this purpose.

(3) "Wealth" must be taken in its original sense, in which it means material welfare (cp. *Book of Common Prayer*, Prayer for the Queen's Majesty), not in the sense which many definitions have endeavoured to affix to it, of things possessing exchange value. It is a state or condition of human beings, not a number of objects or even objects and services. If wealth were taken merely as things possessing exchange value, and were measured by exchange value, the ideal of the greatest possible creation of wealth would be an extremely unsatisfactory one for two reasons.   (*a*) It would be equally nearly approached whatever the quantity of painful labour expended in producing the wealth ; two communities each with an income of £40 per head would have to be considered as equally near the ideal state even if the one had to work twice as hard as the other to procure that income. (*b*) It would be equally nearly approached however the wealth was distributed ; two communities with equal incomes per head would have to be considered as equally near the ideal state, even if in the one the whole income was distributed without great inequalities, while in the other three-fourths of the whole went to one man.   E. C.

IDEALIST. Like most words which are constantly employed to express praise or blame, the word idealist may be said to have lost all definite meaning.   If we are to speak with philosophical accuracy, all changes, great or small, good or bad, which are effected by human will, are due to idealism.   They are due to the faculty which enables man to conceive as possible and desirable a state of things different from that which actually exists.   In this sense everybody is an idealist.   But in practice it is convenient to reserve that appellation for persons who possess an imaginative faculty beyond the common, especially for those who conceive of society and life as dominated by some one principle which in the actual world can never find perfectly free play.   Men of this type are undoubtedly the most powerful impellers, although not the most skilful executants of moral, political, and economical changes. Their idealism may take the most varied and contradictory shapes, and may be wholesome or pernicious.   The believers in absolutely free competition, the believers in all-pervading state regulation, the believers in universal suffrage, and the believers in philosophical despotism, are alike idealists, although they contradict and vilify one another.   The value of idealism, however, will depend on the intellectual and moral endowment of the idealist, and especially upon his power of comprehending the actual world which he wishes to reform.   F. C. M.

IDEAL MONEY is a term applied to certain species of currency which do not consist of a material thing such as coin, or notes convertible into such things. The principal species of ideal money are — I. Money of Account, and II. Inconvertible Currency.

I. (1) The simplest kind of money of account is that which was employed by the older banks, such as those of Venice and Amsterdam (see BANKS, EARLY EUROPEAN), where the unit was in effect a certain quantity of a standard precious metal. Thus at Venice the ducat banco was equal to 1·2 the standard ducat of the currency. So in the monetary system which was introduced into India on the advice of Sir James Steuart, "an ideal coin was invented by which all rupees might be valued" (Sir W. Hunter, *Rural Bengal*, quoted by Prof. Walker, *Money, sub voce* "Ideal Money," p. 594). Since the unit represents a definite quantity of precious metal, "a money of account of such a character is not properly an ideal money" (Walker, p. 295).

(2) Yet the term is applied not inaptly by Sir James Steuart to a certain money of account proposed by him, of which the unit corresponds to a definite quantity not of one but of two precious metals (*Political Economy*, bk. iii. ch. i. ; and ch. xv.—an obscure passage, as to the interpretation of which see Lauderdale, *Depreciation proved*, p. 70 *et seq.*).

(3) A still more "ideal" money of account would be one referring not to two commodities only but to many, a tabular standard based on an Index Number (see INDEX NUMBERS). As explained in the article on that subject, the unit of such a currency might ideally be conceived as a certain quantity either of utility or of labour.

II. Inconvertible paper-money is in one sense less "ideal" than money of account, in that it consists of a material substance. But in another sense it is less real, since its value, depending on the quantity of the paper-money and the demand for it, does not conform directly to that of objects having INTRINSIC VALUE (*q.v.*) such as the precious metals or commodities in general. The quantity of an inconvertible currency may indeed be regulated so as to be brought into conformity with such standards ; either with the value of bullion as contemplated by the older economists (*e.g.* Mill, *Pol. Econ.*, bk. iii. "On Inconvertible Currency"), or with the index number of recent theory. Some hint of the latter plan may perhaps be gathered from the writers who, during the bank restriction, advocated an "abstract currency," or "ideal money," . . . "not formed of substantial and therefore variable materials" (Gloucester WILSON, and Perceval ELIOT, quoted by Prof. Walker in *Money*). Perhaps they did not deserve the unbounded contempt which was poured on them by orthodox economists, such as CANNING (in the *Quarterly Review*) and PEEL (speech on the Bank Charter Act). But no doubt in the pursuit of the monetary ideal they often wandered into the realms of "nonentity and nonsense" (Canning).   F. Y. E.

IDEOLOGUE. A contemptuous epithet applied by the first Napoleon to the philosophic liberals who kept alive in France the ideas of the 18th century, and assailed the imperial system with literary and social weapons. Napoleon felt the contempt of a man of action for those who merely talked and wrote about politics. His experience of the French Revolution had inspired him with a profound dislike of system-makers and rhetoricians. It must be added that he could not endure frank and independent criticism of his grandiose but immoral and impracticable political schemes, his fatal endeavour to make France the tyrant of Europe, and his reckless continental blockade. Having silenced this criticism in the French parliament and press, he proceeded in 1803 to suppress the department of the moral and political sciences in the Institute, which included such well-known names as Volney, Chénier, Cabanis, and Daunou. They continued the contest with Napoleon in a periodical known as the *Décade philosophique* (see DESTUTT DE TRACY).   F. C. M.

ILLEGAL CONTRACT. Certain contracts are regarded as illegal, *e.g.* where the object of the contract is unlawful, where goods are sold on Sunday, where goods are sold by improper weights or measures. In order to prevent gambling in insurance policies, the insured must always have an interest in the subject-matter insured. Contracts that are in fraud of creditors or of the bankruptcy laws or *contra bonos mores* are not enforceable. Agreements in restraint of trade (see RESTRAINT OF TRADE) are illegal unless the restraint imposed is reasonable as regards both time and space.

[Pollock, *On Contracts*, London, 6th ed., 1894.]
                J. E. C. M.

ILLEGITIMACY. All children born out of wedlock are and remain illegitimate according to English law. The rule of the canon law which enables parents by their subsequent marriage to give the rights of legitimate children to their previous issue, and which is applied in Scotland and most continental countries, has never been introduced into England. English courts would recognise children as legitimate whose parents at the time of their birth and at the time of their subsequent marriage were domiciled in a country in which "legitimatio per subsequens matrimonium" is recognised. Such children could not, however, in any case inherit by descent land situate in England.   E. S.

IMMATERIAL CAPITAL AND IMMA-
TERIAL WEALTH. The word capital has
been made, at one time or another, to include
every concrete good known to economics, many
material and immaterial objects of desire not
usually classed as goods, and even abstract conceptions hardly to be reckoned as objects of
desire. These classifications are considered
under CAPITAL (q.v.). We have here to consider the inclusion of immaterial entities under
capital and wealth.

The commonest of these is "skill." Its inclusion under capital has been due to two
analogies : (1) Skill is productive, and those
who emphasise the productivity of capital
naturally place skill under this head ; (2) skill
is costly. The expense of training a labourer
of a specified grade of skill may be determined
almost as accurately as in the case of a horse.
In productivity and cost therefore skill is
closely analogous to capital.

Against these analogies must be offset certain
contrasts. (1) Skill, like fertility in soil, is
not wholly the result of development. The
cultivated man like the cultivated farm owes
much in the way of productivity to investment,
but the element of natural productivity, however hard to disentangle, cannot be ignored.
A more marked contrast consists in the
disposition of society towards a human creature
as a commodity. A trained labourer is, in an
economic sense, comparable to a machine or
productive commodity having certain qualities
of value ; but for reasons happily beyond the
pale of economics, society draws a deep
distinction between the two (see WAGES).
This distinction is artificial, but its profound
importance cannot be doubted. Skill therefore
resembles capital in being productive and
costly ; it differs from it in standing in a
different relation to exchange and in many
other respects. Convenience is the only just
criterion for determining our classification.

The question therefore arises, What is usage
on this point ? It seems plain that when men
apply the term "capital" to skill they do so in
a purely metaphorical way, and that few things
are more deeply contrasted in men's minds
than labour and capital. The majority of
prominent economists are also opposed to
the inclusion of labour under capital. This
inclusion causes economic questions to be
regarded from an absolutely wrong standpoint, a habit which leads men to speak of
dear labour in the same way in which they
speak of dear coal. To make the similarity
between these the basis of classification is
certain to make men forget that from the
social standpoint these are phenomena of
exactly opposite significance.

Finally, we have to ask whether skill can be
properly called immaterial. Good-will, patents,
and guaranteed industrial privileges generally
are often reckoned as immaterial capital.
When a business pays an income greater than
normal interest on its invested capital, it
acquires an additional value known as good-
will, and roughly equal to the capital which
would produce an equal sum at normal rates.
In the case of many companies this is covered
by an issue of stock. This stock, which becomes indistinguishable from the original issues,
merely capitalises this extra dividend-earning
power of the business. The sale of good-will
is but a clumsier mode of transfer. Good-will,
etc., may properly be called individual capital,
but there is no propriety in calling it immaterial
unless the latter term is extended to all stocks,
mortgages, etc. These have more properly
been called representative goods or capital, i.e.
mere titles to the ownership of other goods,
material or otherwise.

[Schäffle, Ausschliessende Handelsverhältnisse
and Böhm-Bawerk, Recht und Verhältnisse.]

We have still to consider a quite different
theory. Some economists have maintained
that capital does not consist of goods but
of a quality corresponding to an immaterial
essence contained in those goods. Thus
M'Leod speaks of capital as "purchasing
power" or "circulating power," and adds that
it "does not represent commodities in any way
whatever." Kühnast calls it "a complex of
productive, material values." More explicit is
J. B. Clark, who distinguishes between "capital
goods," i.e. goods employed for acquisition or
production, and "capital . . . a permanent
fund of productive wealth, expressible in
money, but not embodied in money." He
adds : "There is a long list of assertions that
are true of capital goods, and that directly
contradict the truth, if they are made concerning true capital, or a permanent productive
fund." It will be observed that he does not
claim that capital is immaterial, and Kühnast
speaks of it as "a complex of productive,
material values," but it seems necessary to
make capital immaterial if we are to distinguish it from goods. Otherwise the distinction
vanishes or reduces itself to a mere difference
in point of view. The last is probably Clark's
meaning.

The first question is as before one of usage.
Clark finds the double concept in popular and
scientific use but unconsciously confused.
Men recognise capital as a permanent fund
expressed in money, while they recognise
capital goods as constantly consumed and
replaced. The distinction, however, is not
certain. Men estimate capital in money,
though it is composed of concrete goods,
because heterogeneous goods have no other fact
in common than value. When for other
purposes people enumerate the items of their
capital in a more exact way, this does not
imply that they are talking of a different

thing. Nor does the fact that capital is spoken of as permanent, while goods are known to be transient, imply anything more fundamental. A herdsman, who buys and sells cattle continually, may say that he keeps a herd of a hundred cattle without implying anything else by the term herd than the shifting aggregate of cattle in his possession. A merchant who speaks of his stock would be surprised to learn that he is talking about something else than the goods in his shop.

The question whether there is utility in such a distinction if established is not easy to discuss. It has found no clear expression in popular speech, and few economists have used it. It is not clear that any important economic truth is dependent upon it or cleared up by it, though such a judgment may be premature. If unnecessary, a distinction so subtle should certainly be abandoned in the interest of simplicity. While it is important to recognise the constant consumption and replacement of capital on the one hand and its position as an aggregate permanency on the other, it is not clear that a redefinition of capital is desirable to that end.

[All important works on economics contain discussions of CAPITAL. See especially Mill, *Principles*, vol. i. bk. i. ch. iv. — Sidgwick, *Principles of Pol. Econ.*, bk. i. ch. v., 2nd ed. 1887.—Marshall, *Principles of Economics*, vol. i. bk. ii. ch. iv., 3rd ed. 1895.—Jevons, *Theory of Pol. Econ.*, ch. vii., 2nd ed. 1879. — Walker, *Political Economy*, pt. ii. ch. iii. 1883. By far the best general survey of the field of literature on this subject is found in Böhm-Bawerk, *Kapital und Kapitalzins*, admirably translated by Smart.]

H. H. P.

IMMATERIAL RIGHTS (see INCORPOREAL PROPERTY).

IMMEUBLES (Fr.) One of the two classes into which property is divided in France. The other is *meubles*. Those terms correspond in a measure to realty and personalty in England. The words immovables and movables do not apply strictly, as there are numerous exceptions on both hands. Properties are *immeubles* by reason of their nature, or the purpose for which they are intended, or on account of the subject-matter with which they are placed in relation (Civil Code, art. 517). The first category comprises land, houses, buildings, crops ungathered, etc. ; the second includes animals attached to the farm, straw and manure, the inmates of rabbit-warrens, pigeon-cots, bee-hives and fish-ponds, implements and utensils for working farms and factories, etc. ; the third, usufructs, right of way and other servitudes on *immeubles*. Art. 528 of the Civil Code classes as *meubles* by their nature properties that may be moved from one place to another, either by their own action, such as animals, or by extraneous force, like inanimate objects ; thus ships are, by art. 531 of the Civil Code, and

art. 190 of the Commercial Code, declared to be *meubles*, they may however be mortgaged under laws of 1874 and 1885, contrary to the provisions of art. 2119 of the Civil Code, which states that no right over *meubles* can be acquired by a *hypothèque* (mortgage) of property remaining in the debtor's possession. The procedure for the execution of judicial seizures differs for the two classes of property.

T. L.

IMMIGRATION. The early history of immigration corresponds to that of COLONIES and EMIGRATION, and reference is made to those articles. By immigration is meant that movement by which persons, on their own responsibility, seek settlement in new countries with the intention of becoming permanent residents there. There is also temporary immigration, as of Italians into France during the harvest season, of French Canadians into the United States during the building season ; but these movements are of local importance and cannot be treated generally. Permanent immigration, on the other hand, is a demographic and economic phenomenon of great importance to new countries such as the United States, Canada, Australia, the Cape colonies, and the republics of South America.

Immigration differs from colonisation inasmuch as the immigrants do not form a new community themselves, but are projected, so to speak, into a state and social organisation already formed, where they undergo a process of absorption and assimilation. When the new country is an independent one (*e.g.* the United States), all political and to a large extent social connection with the country of emigration is broken off. And even where the emigrant seeks a colony of his native country, many of these colonies are in modern times so nearly autonomous that the political and economic influence is much the same as if he had changed his allegiance.

The importance of immigration lies in two directions—namely, in the effect upon the happiness and well-being of the immigrant himself, and in its effect upon the community which receives him. In the history of immigration there have doubtless been frequent abuses, many cases where the immigrant has been deceived by false representations, or has made a mistake, so that he has found himself worse off abroad than he was at home. In many cases he has been unable to cope with the difficulties of the new life, and has either returned home a sadder man or been overwhelmed by adversity. But in the great majority of cases the immigrants have prospered and attained a position of comfort which they would never have reached at home. A more difficult question is the influence of immigration upon the countries which receive the immigrants. In the early history of new countries, additions to the labour-force have always been welcomed as so much aid in the great contest with nature involved in opening up and settling waste tracts of land, in making them accessible by roads and railways, and in carrying on the general work of improvement. Later on, as the community begins to be more self-sufficing, and to feel more self-conscious, questions arise as to the *quantity* and *quality* of the immigration, whether it can be readily assimilated, and whether its character is such as to change the type of civilisation already established and which the community values. This is the modern immigration problem. It can best be studied by the experience of the United States of America, where immigration has been going on for the longest time and on the greatest scale (see art. on EMIGRATION).

Statistics of Immigration to the United States.—Prior to 1820 there was no official record of immigration, but it is estimated that the total number of immigrants from the close of the revolutionary war to 1820 was 250,000. Prior to 1856 the records indicate the arrivals of alien passengers only, but it is estimated that 98 per cent of these were immigrants. The general course of the movement is shown by the following table :

Immigration by Decades.

Decade ending with	Aggregate arrivals.	Annual average.
1830 . . .	143,439	14,343
1840 . . .	599,125	59,912
1850 . . .	1,713,251	171,325
1860 . . .	2,598,214	259,821
1870 . . .	2,314,824	231,482
1880 . . .	2,812,191	281,219
1890 . . .	5,246,613	524,661
Total .	15,427,657	

In the total number from 1820 to 1890 the principal countries are represented as follows :

Germany	.	.	4,504,128
Ireland	.	.	3,481,074
England	.	.	2,430,380
Norway and Sweden	.	925,031
Austria-Hungary	.	434,488
Italy	. . .	388,558
France	. .	366,346
Russia and Poland	.	324,892
Scotland	. .	323,823
China	. . .	290,655
Switzerland	. .	171,269
Denmark	. .	142,517

The proportion from the different countries has varied. During the 40 years from 1821 to 1860 inclusive, over one half of the entire immigration was from England and Ireland, and the greater proportion from Ireland. During the last three decades the proportions have been as follows :

Country.	1861-1870.	1871-1880.	1881-1890.
	Per cent.	Per cent.	Per cent.
England . .	24·54	16·38	12·53
Ireland . .	18·82	15·54	12·49
Germany . .	34·02	25·54	27·70
Austria-Hungary	·34	2·60	6·74
Norway & Sweden	4·72	7·51	10·84
Russia & Poland .	·20	1·86	5·05
Italy . . .	·51	1·98	5·86

Sex.—During the decade 1880-1890, 61·10 per cent of the immigrants were males and 38·90 per cent were females. The proportion varies widely for different nationalities, as is seen by the following table :

Country.	Total.	Males of total.	Females of total.
		Per cent.	Per cent.
Germany . .	1,452,970	57·6	42·4
Ireland . .	655,482	51·0	49·0
England . .	644,680	61·3	38·7
Sweden & Norway	568,362	61·0	39·0
Italy . . .	307,309	79·4	20·6
Russia including Poland	265,088	65·8	34·2
Austria . .	226,038	62·9	37·1
Hungary . .	127,681	73·8	26·2
Scotland . .	149,869	61·6	38·4

Age.—Of the immigrants arriving in the United States during the 10 years from 1881 to 1890, 21·4 per cent were under 15 years of age, 68·1 per cent were from 15 to 40 years, and 10·6 per cent were over 40 years of age. The proportion for the different countries is shown in the following table :

Country.	Under 15 years.	From 15 to 40 years.	Over 40 years.
	Per cent.	Per cent.	Per cent.
Germany . .	26·6	62·2	11·2
Ireland . .	14·1	78·6	7·3
England . .	23·5	65·2	11·3
Sweden & Norway	18·3	73·0	8·7
Italy . . .	15·3	69·2	15·5
Russia . .	24·7	65·9	9·4
Austria . .	22·1	66·3	11·6
Scotland . .	24·2	65·2	10·6
Hungary . .	14·7	74·9	10·4

Occupation.—The statistics show that only 10·35 per cent of the immigrants belong to the professional and skilled artisan classes. The remainder are unskilled labourers, women, children, or without occupation.

Causes.—Immigration varies considerably from year to year. Commercial distress in Europe drives immigrants to America, as after the Irish famine of 1846, and the German dearth of 1853. Bad times in the United States discourage immigration, as during the civil war (in 1861 the immigration sank to 89,724), and the financial panic of 1873, after which the number sank steadily down to 1878, when it was only 138,469. The highest number ever reached was in 1882, a year of great prosperity, when 788,992 immigrants landed in the United States. Aside from this general economic influence, there are two forces in constant operation which tend to keep up a regular stream of immigration. The first of these is the communication between immigrants and their friends at home. Thousands of letters are sent back annually urging their friends and acquaintances to follow them, and hundreds of thousands of dollars are remitted in order to pay the expense. The custom of the steamship companies in selling prepaid tickets greatly facilitates and encourages these efforts. This attractive force remains constant from year to year, although of course it is more active in good times when money is plentiful and places can be found for the new arrivals. A second powerful force in modern times is the activity of the great steamship companies. Enormous steamships sailing regularly every week must be filled. Competition is very keen, and hence each company has thousands of agents scattered through Europe for the purpose of inducing emigration, and thousands of agents scattered through America, selling prepaid tickets on commission. There is thus an artificial stimulation to immigration, inasmuch as the opportunity is given to all sorts of persons and the way made easy. In former times it required considerable energy and some money for a man to emigrate. At the present time it requires but little money and less energy. At various periods foreign governments, especially local authorities, have assisted criminals, paupers, and other undesirable persons to emigrate, but this has now generally ceased owing to protests from the side of the countries receiving the immigrants. So also at various periods new countries have sought to attract immigrants either by paying their passage or by giving them land and the means of settling ; but this has generally ceased as the need for labour has become less pressing. The movement at the present time, therefore, is a purely commercial-industrial one, dependent, on the one hand, on the interests of transportation companies and, on the other hand, upon the supposed economic interests of the individual immigrant. It differs, therefore, from the movement of the last century, in which religious, political, and patriotic motives were more or less involved, and is to be treated principally from the economic standpoint. Immigration to the United States has been affected by the cholera scare of 1892 and the panic of 1893. For the last four years, up to 1894, the figures are as follows :

Year ending June 30th.			
1891	.	.	.	560,319
1892	.	.	.	623,084
1893	.	.	.	502,917
1894	.	.	.	314,467

Such being the facts in regard to immigration we go on to inquire what has been its effect on the population and economic condition of the United States.

Effect on Population.—It would seem that immigration must increase population by the number of immigrants and their descendants ; and as the majority of the immigrants are in the most productive ages of manhood and womanhood, the natural increase of the population must be greatly accelerated. As, however, in the United States there is no complete registration of births and deaths, and as even in such registration as exists no distinction is made between natives and foreigners, we cannot determine what proportion of the present population is due to immigration since 1820. The census of 1890 returned 20,625,542 persons who were either foreign born or who had one or both parents foreign born. This represents approximately the population of foreign descent for two generations. But the immigrants of the earlier years are now represented by grandchildren or by great-grandchildren—that is, by the third and fourth generation, so that the above figure is entirely inadequate. If we should represent the survivors in the third and fourth generation by five millions, we should have the number 25,625,542 as representing the portion of the population due to immigration. A similar result is reached by taking the annual immigration since 1820, and applying to it the rate of natural increase for the whole population. We have no means of knowing, it is true, whether the rate of natural increase is the same for the foreign born as for the native born. It is probably greater, so that our result will be a minimum. Such a calculation gives us for 1890 about 26,000,000 descendants of immigrants, and 29,000,000 descendants of the white colonists.

It is sometimes denied that immigration has had any very decided effect in absolutely increasing the total population of the United States. It is said that the pressure of immigration has retarded the natural increase of the native population, so that the immigrants have simply taken the places which would otherwise have been filled by native-born Americans. The decreasing size of the American family is cited as proof of this tendency. We have no exact statistics upon this point. The census of Massachusetts (1885) showed indeed that the foreign-born women had a larger number of children than the native-born, but that there was a greater mortality among them. The just conclusion seems to be that while immigration is not a clear gain to the population, yet it acts as a powerful stimulus.

A more important result of immigration has been to introduce into the population of the United States great ethnical groups which are separated from each other either by race, by origin, or by parentage. The population of the United States consists now of the four groups shown in the following table :

Population of the United States according to colour, birthplace, and parentage.

Total population .	62,622,250	100·00%
Native White, native parents . .	34,358,348	54·87%
Coloured population .	7,638,360	12·20%
Foreign White . .	9,121,867	14·56%
Native White, foreign parents . .	11,503,675	18·37%

We have here four different elements entering into the population of the United States. The native Americans, that is, the native whites whose parents are native born, number a little over one half of the total population. Upon this native American element is imposed three elements different either in race, or in birthplace, or in parentage. The first is the coloured, 12·2 per cent of the total population, composed principally of negroes. The second element, 14·56 per cent, is composed of white persons born abroad, that is, the survivors of the immigrants. This is the element through which the foreign influence upon the institutions and the people of the United States is exercised. The third element is constituted of native white persons whose parents were foreign born. They may be called the second generation of the immigrants. It is evident that there may be, and probably is, an important difference between these last two classes. The native-born whites of foreign parentage are not to be regarded entirely as foreigners. Born in America, educated in the public schools, learning the English language, they have been subjected to the assimilating influence of American life. These assimilating influences are principally intermarriage, the exercise of political rights, common school education, and social intercourse with the native Americans. It is an important fact that in most of the states the second generation of the immigrants is already more numerous than the first. This indicates that the assimilating influences have a good field in which to work. On the other hand, there are also indications that the assimilating influences have thus far been effective. For otherwise we should certainly find great differences in language, customs, and laws in different portions of the United States, due to the different elements introduced into the population by immigration. The United States would seem to offer in this respect a unique opportunity to study the question of the mixture of races or of nationalities. This, however, is a complicated sociological study into which we cannot enter here.

Economic Effects.—There is no doubt that the rapid development of the material resources of the United States has been greatly aided by immigration. It has furnished the labour-force necessary for the arduous task of opening up a new country, building railways, digging canals, exploiting mines, starting factories, and founding cities. In 1880 nearly 10 per cent of all the persons engaged in agriculture, 25 per cent of those in trade and transportation, and nearly one-third of those employed in manufacturing, mechanical, and mining industries, were of foreign birth. The domestic servants were for the most part females of Irish, German, or Swedish birth. The ordinary craftsmen, such as bakers, butchers, blacksmiths, coopers, masons, plasterers, etc., were largely immigrants or their descendants. The same is true of the employees in cotton, woollen, iron and steel, leather and other factories. A curious fact is that while the immigrants are, upon their arrival, mostly common labourers or agricultural labourers, yet only 23·32 per cent were found employed in agriculture, while 34·89 per cent were employed in mechanical, manufacturing, and mining industry. Doubtless great numbers were employed in the merely mechanical branches of these industries, but the figures show that the unskilled labourer can be readily trained to factory work.

A corresponding fact is that while the immigrants are for the most part from the rural districts of Europe, they congregate after arrival in the larger cities. In 1890, 44·13 per cent of the foreign born were found in cities of 25,000 inhabitants and over. This movement is due partly to the ignorance, inertia, and poverty of many of the immigrants, which retain them in the cities of the east where they land, instead of pushing them forward to the unoccupied lands of the west ; and partly to the modern preference for city rather than country life. It has important economic influence both for the immigrants and the country receiving them. It means a change of occupation and social environment for the immigrant, and an intensification of the movement towards cities which is one of the characteristics of modern civilisation. This movement in America has been accelerated by immigration.

Many attempts have been made to measure the direct economic gain to a country by immigration. There are two items to be considered ; first, the money or capital which the immigrants bring with them ; second, the economic value of the immigrants themselves. The amount of money brought by the immigrants to the United States is not large. For 152,360 immigrants landing at the port of New York during the first six months of 1892, it was returned as $20.09 (£4) *per caput*. This is offset by the large amounts of money sent back to Europe by the immigrants to aid and support their friends or to assist them to emigrate. It has also been suggested that the amount of wealth brought by the immigrants is much less than the *per caput* wealth of the people of the United States, estimated at $1000.00 (£200), so that the average well-being is not increased.

The real economic gain to the United States by immigration consists in the value of the full - grown labour supplied to it by the countries of Europe. Various attempts have been made to estimate this in money. One way is to consider every full-grown immigrant as worth to the United States the cost of his bringing up to the age of fifteen. Estimating that at $1000 (say £200), the 315,054 immigrants in 1890 between the ages of fifteen and forty would represent an enormous sum, $315,054,000. A second method of estimating the economic value of the immigrant is to capitalise his future earnings over and above his future cost of subsistence, according to his probable after-life. This sum will represent the amount of wealth he may be expected to add to the community before he dies. Dr. Wm. Farr estimated the net future value of immigrants from Great Britain on this plan as £175 *per caput*. The money value of an annual immigration of 500,000 souls would be $437,000,000 (say £87,400,000). In fact, as wages are higher, and cost of living not proportionately greater in the States, the real gain would be considerably more.

All these attempts to put a money value on the economic gain by immigration are fallacious. An immigrant is worth the cost of bringing him up only if he becomes an honest, industrious, able-bodied labourer. If he is vicious, idle, or infirm, then he is only a care and a burden to the community that receives him. So, also, there is no real capitalised value of his future earnings unless there is a demand for his labour. Immigration is of economic value to a country if the immigrants can be usefully employed. That is not a matter for statistical computation, but for general observation. The considerations which are of importance from this point of view are as follows :

(*a*) The need of unskilled labour in the new countries is much less pressing than it was forty years ago. This is due partly to the increase of population, partly to the employment of machinery on a grand scale, and partly to the fact that the most productive lands have been occupied. We have the same complaints in regard to lack of employment in new countries as in old. The tendency of the immigrants to congregate in large cities instead of spreading over the country makes the con-

gestion of labour still more acute. Immigration has passed beyond its first phase, where any and every sort of labour force was welcome for the purpose of opening up the country. A sign of this is seen in the general cessation of governmental efforts to stimulate immigration, and the indifference, not to say hostility, with which continued immigration is viewed.

(*b*) The immigration of criminals, paupers, persons diseased in mind or body, and persons unable to support themselves, is a direct economic and social detriment to the community. Since 1882 such persons have been refused admittance to the United States, and, when rejected, the steamship companies that brought them have been obliged to carry them back. Statistics for the United States show that the burden of public and private charity has been greatly increased by the indiscriminate admission of immigrants of all classes. No law of international comity is violated by the refusal to receive these unfortunates. They should be taken care of at home.

(*c*) Immigration sometimes increases the competition in the labour market, and thus lowers wages. It is often denounced by labour organisations on this account. One case is particularly aggravating, viz. when the employers import foreign labourers to take the place of their men who are on a strike. This renders all organisation of labour futile. The law of 1885 in the United States, commonly called the Labour Contract law, forbids the entrance of persons who are already under contract to labour there. But it is extremely difficult to prove the existence of such a contract. Outside of this particular case it does not appear that the ordinary competition due to immigration is felt by the labouring class in a new country where that competition is on the same plane of living.

(*d*) Immigration of masses of men accustomed to a lower standard of living than prevails in the new country may have a disastrous effect on the economic well-being of the community. An example of this is the Chinese immigration into the States. The Chinese are industrious and thrifty ; they, however, are accustomed to live in a way which it is impossible for the American workmen to imitate. They never assimilate with the Americans or adopt western civilisation. Besides the social danger arising from the presence of such an alien element in a new country, there is the economic danger lest the standard of living of the whole labouring class should be brought down to their level. Some of the recent immigration from southern and eastern Europe raises the same question.

Restriction of Immigration.—Legislation in the United States has attempted to meet the dangers noted under the last three heads. The act of 1882 mentioned under (*b*) has been supplemented by the act of 1893, which provides for the exclusion of idiots and insane persons, paupers or persons likely to become a public charge, or suffering from a loathsome or dangerous contagious disease, convicts, polygamists, and contract labourers. The number excluded under the former acts was in 1890, 535, in 1891, 1026, and in 1892, 3732. The contract-labour law of 1885 excludes persons coming under contract to labour. The Chinese exclusion policy adopted in 1882 was made more severe by the act of 1888, which forbade the return to the United States of Chinese labourers who had left there, and by the Geary Act of 1892, compelling the registration of Chinese on pain of deportation. The latter act has not been enforced.

Future Policy in regard to Immigration.— There is no doubt of the political right of a country to restrict or prohibit the immigration of persons whom it considers undesirable. During mediæval times such restrictions were universal. They fell into disuse owing to the increased facilities of communication between countries and the modern spirit of individual liberty. But a state must be sovereign in its own territory, and hence must have the right to exclude persons whose presence it regards as detrimental to its civilisation. In fact, we may say that this is the highest duty of a state, viz. to preserve its standard of civilisation. International comity demands that trade and travel should not be unnecessarily embarrassed, and that prohibitions should be directed against individuals as such and not against nationalities or races, unless the race as a whole proves incapable of assimilation. Numerous political and social effects are connected with immigration which prevent its being treated simply as an economic question. In a democratic country like the United States rapid immigration and easy methods of naturalisation throw political power into the hands of the immigrants, who are often ignorant, unaccustomed to the exercise of political rights, and sometimes venal. The foreign-born males of twenty-one years of age and over constitute 25·67 per cent of all the males of that age. In some of the western states and in many cities they constitute more than one-half. The social effects are felt in the abnormal number of the foreign-born in the poor-houses, asylums, hospitals, and prisons. Their participation in crime is not so disproportioned to their number if we take into consideration that the immigrants are mostly adults. These social effects influence legislation, and in the future the restrictive policy will be more or less severe according as the pressure of immigration is more or less keenly felt by the labouring class, and increase of crime and pauperism, outbreaks of anarchism and other social evils, are attributed by public sentiment to immigration.

Other Countries.—In the British colonies the question of immigration seems to be in almost the same stage as in the United States, only the movement has been smaller and the evils less felt. In Australia we find the same prohibition on Chinese immigration, and the same jealousy of the working-classes in regard to competition in the labour market. The countries of South America welcome immigrants more gladly, but many complaints are heard of the way in which they are treated.

[Besides the Bibliography in Richmond Mayo-Smith, *Emigration and Immigration*, New York and London, 1890, the following recent publications may be mentioned : *Quarterly Reports of the Chief of the Bureau of Statistics*, Treasury Department (No. 2, 1892-93), Washington, 1893 —*Report of the House Committee on Immigration and Naturalisation*, Washington, 1892.—*Correspondence relating to Chinese Immigration into the Australian Colonies*, Parl. Return, 1888.—*Indagini sulla Emigrazione Italiana all' Estero*, Roma, 1890.—Rossi, *Del Patronato degli Emigranti*, Roma, 1893.—Philippovich, "Die Vereinigten Staaten und die Europäische Auswanderung," in Braun's *Archiv für Sozialegesetzgebung*, etc., vol. vi. No. 2, Berlin, 1893.—Report by Burnett and Schloss on *Immigration into America*.]

R. M-S.

IMMORAL CONTRACT. See ILLEGAL CONTRACT.

IMMOVABLES. By "immovables" is primarily meant such things as lands and buildings that cannot be moved. The term is used in a secondary meaning as including rights over immovable things. "The only natural classification of the objects of enjoyment," says Sir Henry Maine (*Ancient Law*, London, 1861, p. 273), "the only classification which corresponds with an essential difference in the subject-matter, is that which divides them into movables and immovables."

[As regards the historical development of the distinction, see Maine's *Ancient Law ;* as to the importance of the distinction in modern law, see Foote's *Private International Jurisprudence*, London, 1890.]

J. E. C. M.

IMPEACHMENT OF WASTE. A tenant for life of an estate—unless expressly declared to be "not impeachable for waste"—is not allowed to do any act, such as cutting down trees or opening mines, that would injure the inheritance. Such acts are called waste (see WASTE), and the tenant is said to be liable or impeachable for waste.

[Goodeve's *Real Property*, London, 1891.]

J. E. C. M.

IMPERIAL. Russian gold coin of the value of ten roubles. Weight, 199·1 grains ; fineness, 900. Value (English standard) £1 : 11 : 9, (French standard) 40 francs. Half-imperials are of the same fineness, and of proportionate weight. Prior to 1886 the half-imperial was 916·6 fine and weighed 101 grains. F. E. A.

IMPORTS AND EXPORTS. Imports and exports are correlative terms ; they denote the organic constituents of that which is known as commerce. Early opinion looked favourably on exports, regarding them as signs of successful trade.

In 1776 Adam Smith published his *Wealth of Nations ;* in 1783 the first reference in parliament was made to that work ; in the same year the younger Pitt became prime minister of England. This period may fairly be taken as the starting-point of the modern history of European trade. The closing years of the 18th century and opening years of the 19th saw almost universal war amongst civilised peoples ; and the war was accompanied by extraordinary efforts to restrict and regulate the trade of the belligerents. It has been said that in the later years of the war Napoleon's chief object was to strike a fatal blow at English trade. The Berlin decree of 1807, and the counter-moves which it called forth, were evidence of the mischief he did to all (see CONTINENTAL SYSTEM). For thirty years, from 1785 to 1815, the trade of Europe was subjected to the double disturbance arising from constant war and from unreasoning interference of all descriptions. The next thirty years (1815-1845) represent a period of rest, and, as far at least as England was concerned, a period of transition. The remaining years of the century to our own time exhibit freetrade England dealing with a world mainly, almost universally, protectionist, and expanding her commerce to a degree of which the tradereformers never dreamed.

A review of foreign legislation during this century shows that in varying degrees protection, sometimes contracting even to prohibition, has everywhere ruled abroad. Commercial treaties and the most favoured nation clause have been a palliative, but have not checked the inveterate evil. The establishment of the German ZOLLVEREIN in 1833 is a leading event in the period, but had little effect on external trade. The United States of America started the theory of absolute commercial independence as early as 1789 ; their consequent efforts at protection have not been uniform ; they rose to their greatest height (before the recent Act) in the tariffs of 1824-28. In 1833 (the Clay tariff), and again in 1846 (the Walker tariff), opposite tendencies prevailed, but since 1860 there has been a gradual tightening of the cords.

The commercial history of Great Britain has been more interesting for this period than that of any other country. The closing years of the 18th century contained the germs of many changes. In 1784 England had parted definitely with her great colonies in the New World, and in 1788 she laid the foundations of Australia. About the same time Ireland was admitted to something like commercial equality ; in 1801 came the union. In 1804 England obtained a lasting footing in South Africa. The East Indian empire was being gradually built up throughout the period ; the Company's East Indian trade being thrown open in 1813, and its China monopoly coming to an end in 1833. Again in 1785 Arkwright's patent was thrown open, and the use of machinery began to spread in the woollen and cotton manufactures. But till past 1820 the national life was weighted with commercial restrictions. "Everything conceivable was taxed," says Rogers. Smuggling was rampant ; the tariff and excise laws were "all but universally disregarded." In 1825 through HUSKISSON (*q.v.*) the first indications of a change came, and the theory of a close colonial trade was broken down. The repeal of the corn laws in 1846, and the freeing of the tariff in 1861, were the final scenes in the commercial emancipation.

The commercial history of the British colonies is more recent. Canada and most of the Australian colonies have tended more and more towards protection. In most of the other colonies the customs tariffs have been sufficiently heavy to operate as some check to trade, but they remain revenue tariffs nevertheless. The discovery of gold in Australia in 1851 gave a special impulse to the trade of those colonies (see COLONIES).

It would have been interesting to compare the gross value of the trade of the world at the end of last century with its value at the present time, but the apparent impossibility of obtaining satisfactory statistics of exports and imports, even of the leading European countries, at so early a date has prevented this attempt. For Great Britain fairly trustworthy figures exist, and the same is true of the United States, and we therefore give tables illustrating the development of the trade of these two leading commercial powers of the world. It is clear that any development of the trade of a single great commercial power is an index of a general development of that magnitude ; as an increase of imports by that power postulates an increase of the exporting power of other parts of the world and *vice versa.* And in the case of Great Britain it can be shown that her trade has always been widely distributed, and that its growth represents a corresponding development of many countries.

At the beginning of the century, Pitt, in the House of Commons, in the course of his resolutions of the 28th July 1801, dealing with the public debt, stated the increase in the exports and imports of Great Britain as follows :

	Imports.	Exports.
Average of six years to 1784	£11,690,829	£8,616,660
" " 1793	18,085,390	14,771,049
For the one year " 1799	29,945,808	24,084,000

The following table however gives a more correct idea of the growth of the foreign trade of the United Kingdom.

Year.	Imports.	Exports.	Population.	Trade per Head.
	£	£		£. s. d.
1786	26,500,000	27,000,000	13,500,000	4 0 0
1800	53,250,000	52,000,000	15,000,000	7 0 0
1815	43,000,000	64,000,000	19,000,000	5 12 6
1830	58,000,000	45,000,000	24,000,000	4 6 0
1845	88,000,000	68,000,000	27,000,000	5 15 0
1860	210,530,873	164,521,351	28,900,000	13 0 0
1875	373,939,577	281,612,323	32,700,000	20 0 0
1890	420,691,997	328,252,118	37,800,000	19 16 3

It may be well to explain that the figures of the earlier years, viz. from 1786 to 1845, are, so far as we know, the first attempt to give some idea of the actual value of exports and imports for those periods. The principles of the calculation are briefly indicated in the last paragraph of this article ; it is enough to say here that the amounts have been calculated with great care and verified in different ways from the most authentic records. The trade between Ireland and Great Britain in 1786, 1800, and 1815 has been excluded, and the foreign trade of Ireland added ; so that those years are on the same basis as the later ones. For figures which can only be approximate we purposely adopt round numbers.

The table justifies the following conclusions—

(1) In the first period, when invention was giving an impulse to industry, the exports and total foreign trade nearly doubled in amount and gave an increase of 75 per cent per head of population.

(2) The volume of foreign trade was practically stationary for the first thirty years of the century, but the amount of exports and imports fluctuated greatly as compared with each other.

(3) The turn for the better was coincident with free trade, and since 1845 the expansion of foreign trade has been continuous. The trade per head in 1860 was two and a quarter times as great as it was in 1845. It was more than half as large again in 1875. Since 1875, judging by the board of trade statistics, the average of the annual imports and exports per head of the population of the United Kingdom has been fairly steady at about £19.

(4) Imports have, as a rule, largely exceeded exports ; the only year in which the exports materially exceeded imports being the year of Waterloo, and this fact agrees remarkably with the statement made by Macgregor that we paid our subsidies to the continent in that war in the goods of British origin for which, in spite of embargoes, there was such a demand on the continent. The theory of the excess of imports will be found fully treated in the article on COMMERCE.

That the trade of the United Kingdom has always been so diversified and widely ramified that its growth is a fair index of expansion in other parts of the world may be gathered from an inspection of the tables of trade with different foreign countries. For the trade of the present day there are the board of trade abstracts. But the same tale is told by an examination of old parliamentary returns. In 1786, for instance, the following countries participated as follows in English trade :

Germany—total trade with England	.	£1,763,952
Holland	,,	,,	.	1,842,057
Russia	,,	,,	.	1,717,604
United States	,,	,,	.	2,443,574

and there was a large trade with our own possessions in Asia and the West Indies.

In 1890 the total trade with the countries above mentioned, which we place here merely for comparison, was as follows :

Germany—total trade with England	£56,589,612
Holland	,,	,,	.	45,245,007
Russia	,,	,,	.	32,597,022
United States	,,	,,	.	143,623,361

The comparison of such figures indicates the general growth of trade in the world.

The following figures exhibit the growth of the imports and exports of the United States within the last half-century.

Year.	Imports.	Exports.	Total per head of pop.
1840	$107,141,519	$132,086,000	$14.05
1848-50 aver. of 3 yrs.	160,331,562	150,563,652	14.34
1858-60 do.	327,885,845	360,518,736	21.54
1868-70 do.	432,578,609	551,544,737	27.67
1878-80 do.	666,966,641	833,229,300	30.07
1888-90 do.	793,558,886	814,880,892	27.40

Mr. Farquhar (*Econom. and Industr. Delusions*) states that the total exports in 1806 and 1807 exceeded $100,000,000, and that this sum was not surpassed till 1834, and he shows that the amount per head of exported merchandise only, excluding specie, rose from $5½ in 1821 to more than $13½ in 1890, having been as high as $17½ *per caput*. This in spite of the unwise commercial policy which Mr. Farquhar seeks to expose. But steady as the progress of trade per head has been, it did little more than double itself between 1840 and 1880, whereas in that period, as we have seen above, British foreign trade was nearly quadrupled. And at the present time the external trade of the States per head of population is not many more dollars than that of Great Britain is pounds sterling.

As a further indication of the growth of trade in the world, we append a table showing the exports and imports of seven chief European countries at intervals during forty years past ; and we have added those of Mexico, Brazil, and Chili, as giving some indication of the development in Central and South America, to which so much European capital has of late years flowed. As far as possible bullion and specie are omitted, but not for Holland, Spain, or the American States; it is impossible to obtain complete uniformity either of years or method of computation from the varying returns which different governments have published; but the average results of the table are sufficiently correct to support general inferences.

IMPORTS.

	1850	1860	1870	1880	1890
	£	£	£	£	£
Austria	16,015,620	23,083,040	36,330,000	50,112,500	50,900,000
Belgium	16,500,000	39,850,000	49,500,000	98,464,000	127,526,400
France	46,309,250	106,290,526	111,259,720	196,300,680	175,932,000
Germany	27,537,292	no return	no return	no return	292,234,500
Holland	24,500,000	38,393,000	49,300,000	60,000,000	108,312,500
Russia	16,000,000	25,900,000	45,500,000	65,000,000	34,673,666
Spain	6,882,493	17,500,000	19,000,000	15,500,000	37,645,517
Mexico	no return	3,000,000	4,695,600	6,000,000	7,230,000
Brazil	7,500,000	13,200,000	19,000,000	25,000,000	23,342,000
Chili	2,800,000	4,990,000	5,200,000	4,550,000	8,850,000

EXPORTS.

	1850	1860	1870	1880	1890
	£	£	£	£	£
Austria	12,337,885	25,680,308	32,950,000	56,350,000	64,280,000
Belgium	16,000,000	35,712,500	49,000,000	85,500,000	117,926,073
France	65,186,500	125,920,000	114,406,280	136,024,560	150,120,000
Germany	26,357,000	no return	no return	no return	246,935,000
Holland	19,687,785	32,603,000	42,200,000	44,500,000	90,627,666
Russia	20,700,000	27,667,000	48,978,000	68,000,000	58,630,666
Spain	4,975,000	11,838,520	12,000,000	17,500,000	37,510,395
Mexico	no return	2,125,000	4,827,000	6,000,000	9,615,300
Brazil	6,826,777	13,700,000	22,500,000	30,900,000	26,500,000
Chili	2,457,250	5,650,000	6,000,000	8,500,000	10,000,000

The figures in the above table under each year are not (except in one or two cases) the actual returns of that year but the mean of two or more years around the year of the decade. It has been impossible, owing to imperfections in all the returns, to take the same years for each decade, or for all the countries in the case of any one decade; but the variations are not material. The sterling amounts for the earlier years are adopted from the old board of trade returns and for the others obtained by conversion at the current rate of exchange.

It will be observed, that the volume of exports in all these countries increased at an even faster rate than those of England. Between 1850 and 1860 in this country exports rather more than doubled themselves, and between 1860 and 1890 they again did the same. But in the latter period those of Belgium and Spain were trebled, those of Holland rose to four and a half times their former amount; and the other countries selected except France increased their output as fast as our own country. Germany in the whole period increased its exports nine-fold. The growth of the imports is in much the same proportion. So that without going into the rate of growth per head of population in each country, allowing for incorrectness of figures and divergence of method in returns, it may safely be inferred that everywhere increase of trade has been considerable. And this increase appears to have been largely independent of the trade policy of each particular country.

We shall now come back to Great Britain and examine the growth of its trade with its own colonies during a century past, and then compare its colonial trade with its foreign trade, as some considerable questions are centred in that comparison.

The following tables show the trade of Great Britain and Ireland with the colonies at three periods. In the year 1815 the germs of the colonial empire of Great Britain as it now exists had been finally established. For 1855 careful returns are available in regard to the colonies; and the new trade policy of Great Britain was well settled. With these years we compare the figures of 1890, as representing the present extent of the trade.

	Imports into United Kingdom.		
	1815	1855	1890
	£	£	£
Channel Islands	97,595	244,501	958,175
Gibraltar	} 199,587	70,621	49,898
Malta		201,075	117,595
North American Colonies	368,873	4,693,065	12,444,489
West Indies and Guiana	8,527,019	5,470,212	2,714,287
British Honduras		492,781	275,293
Australia	nil	4,500,200	29,350,844
Indian Empire		12,668,732	32,668,797
Straits Settlements	} 8,042,292	615,738	5,187,801
Ceylon		1,474,251	3,411,209
Hong-Kong		no figures	1,225,064
Mauritius	141,479	1,723,807	264,900
Cape and Natal	325,045	949,640	6,095,612
West Africa and Gold Coast		283,780	1,075,772
Other Possessions		3,323	321,478
Totals	17,701,890	33,391,726	96,161,214

	Exports from United Kingdom.		
	1815	1855	1890
	£	£	£
Channel Islands	328,581	601,122	919,690
Gibraltar	1,201,142	906,185	896,087
Malta	957,647	702,313	1,126,391
North American Colonies	3,461,742	3,089,170	8,272,743
West Indies and Guiana	7,225,807	1,982,061	3,922,642
British Honduras		173,521	119,150
Australia	40,519	7,221,625	25,470,194
Indian Empire		10,353,475	35,230,114
Straits Settlements		691,299	3,024,655
Ceylon	2,891,416	325,897	964,935
Hong-Kong		no figures	2,741,404
Mauritius		317,945	346,631
Cape and Natal	210,654	836,750	9,803,552
West Africa and Gold Coast	123,188	381,368	941,352
Other Possessions		69,964	742,929
Totals	16,430,496	27,653,235	94,522,469

The figures for 1815 in this return should be somewhat, but not a great deal, higher, as it has been impossible to ascertain and add to them the separate trade of Ireland in that year with the British colonies ; the total, however, would probably not exceed £17,000,000. Both exports and imports came near to doubling themselves between 1815 and 1855, and practically trebled themselves between 1855 and 1890, the rapidity of increase being thus rather greater in the case of colonial than in that of foreign trade. The increase of exports and imports has been extraordinary in the Australian and South African colonies. In the former case the total trade with Great Britain has sprung from £40,000 to a value of nearly £55,000,000 ; in the latter the exports of the United Kingdom have increased over forty-five-fold, the imports from the colony about twenty-fold. The North American colonies send us thirty times as much as at the beginning of the century. There are other points of interest in the table. In 1815 the West Indian trade is seen to be the greater part of the whole ; it is now but one-thirtieth of the aggregate, India taking the first place, with Australia closely following.

With the two columns for 1890 in the last return we will now compare the trade of the United Kingdom in the same year with various foreign countries.

	Imports from.	Exports to.	Total Trade.
	£	£	£
United States . .	97,283,349	46,340,012	143,623,361
France and French ⎱ Possessions ⎰	45,755,056	25,164,403	70,919,459
Germany . . .	26,073,331	30,516,281	56,589,612
Holland and Dutch ⎱ Possessions ⎰	27,123,961	18,121,046	45,245,007
Russia . . .	23,750,968	8,846,054	32,597,022
Belgium . . .	17,383,776	13,594,966	30,978,742
Spain and Spanish ⎱ Possessions ⎰	14,478,349	10,142,298	24,620,647
Sweden and Norway	11,906,345	7,002,269	18,908,614
Italy	3,093,918	8,523,209	11,617,127
South American Republics . .	14,030,691	25,405,648	39,436,339
Other Places . .	46,651,039	40,363,463	87,014,502
Total . .	324,530,783	233,729,649	558,260,432

The table has been so arranged as to show the order of magnitude of our total trade with the United States of America and the chief European countries ; and one thing which is obvious on the face of the two last returns is that the foreign trade of England is far more valuable at the present time than the trade with the British empire. It is well to lay stress on this fact at a moment when Great Britain is often exhorted to let one trade perish so long as she holds the other. The imports from the United States alone are equal to those from the whole of the colonies and India ; though the latter are twice as good customers for our exports as the States. In the various European countries we find a market at least half as valuable again as that of our own possessions. And the sum total of our foreign trade is not far from three times as great as that of our colonial trade. Yet if we

compare the trade per head of population in each case, the comparison is immeasurably in favour of our own possessions. Against this in turn we must remember the heavy debts which our colonies have contracted on the London market. In any case the figures are a sufficient warning as to the inevitable derangement which would result from hasty tampering with the course of our trade.

We will now endeavour to give some idea of the total trade of the world in 1890, and the rate of exports per head in each country, adopting a conventional geographical arrangement.

Country.	Pop. in Millions.	Imports. £	Exports. £	Rate per head of Exports. £ s. d.
EUROPE—				
Un. Kgdom.	37·8	420,691,997	328,252,118	8 15 0
British Pos.	·39	574,195	2,252,942	5 14 0
France . .	38·3	179,480,000	150,120,000	4 0 0
Spain . .	18·0	37,645,517	37,510,395	2 1 4
Portugal .	5·0	10,662,540	7,323,505	1 9 6
Italy . .	30·1	55,095,057	38,904,014	1 6 0
Switzerland .	3·0	40,065,626	29,002,912	9 13 4
Belgium .	6·1	127,526,400	117,926,073	19 10 0
Holland .	4·5	108,312,500	90,627,666	22 10 0
Germ. Emp.	45·2	292,234,500	246,935,000	5 9 0
Aust.-Hung.	41·2	54,514,333	64,280,000	1 10 0
Servia . .	2·2	1,521,790	1,833,622	0 16 4
Roumania .	5·5	14,511,640	11,038,320	2 0 0
Montenegro .	·24	20,000	200,000	0 16 8
Bulgaria .	3·15	3,381,220	2,802,045	0 18 0
Turk. Emp. .	4·82	17,707,288	13,286,478	2 15 0
Greece . .	2·18	4,313,800	3,421,143	1 11 3
Russia . .	95·0	34,673,666	58,630,666	0 12 4
Finland .	2·2	5,040,000	3,600,000	1 11 3
Sweden .	4·78	18,500,000	15,400,000	3 4 6
Norway .	1·98	11,592,155	7,283,140	3 13 0
Denmark .	2·2	17,057,288	18,546,552	8 8 6
		1,458,121,512	1,249,176,591	
ASIA—				
Siberia . .	4·48	1,650,000	1,500,000	0 6 0
Turkish Asia	21·6	4,746,911	4,404,194	0 6 8
Oman . .	1·5	305,120	220,414	0 3 0
Persia . .	9·0	3,500,000	3,500,000	0 8 0
British India	220·5	64,765,418	70,586,570	0 6 6
Afghanistan .	4·0	740,000	675,860	0 3 6
Bhutan .	·03	14,280	14,410	0 9 0
Nepaul . .	2·0	954,000	1,068,400	0 10 6
China . .	402·6	35,775,725	23,576,395	0 1 0
Corea . .	10·0	727,360	546,227	0 1 0
Japan . .	40·0	13,610,000	9,300,000	0 4 6
Siam . .	6·0	2,631,020	3,209,621	0 10 6
BritishE.Ind.	4·63	22,280,252	27,163,872	5 17 0
Dutch do. .	29·76	12,150,000	15,750,000	0 10 6
French do. .	14·2	2,682,000	3,354,000	0 4 8
Spanish do. .	7·12	3,500,000	4,000,000	0 11 3
		170,032,086	168,864,963	
AFRICA—				
Egypt . .	6·87	8,283,329	12,172,988	1 16 0
Tripoli . .	·80	250,000	387,500	0 9 6
Morocco .	5·00	1,793,689	1,632,626	0 6 6
Algeria. .	4·00	10,400,000	10,400,000	2 12 0
Tunis . .	1·5	1,115,000	1,225,000	0 16 0
Liberia. .	1·06	971,259	971,051	0 18 0
Soudan, etc.	10·4	150,000	150,000	0 0 4½
Congo State .	17·	no return	564,500	0 0 9
Brit.W.Africa	1·7	1,602,385	1,709,234	1 0 0
So. Af. Rep.	·68	5,500,000	5,000,000	7 7 0
Orange F. St.	·207	1,000,000	2,000,000	9 19 6
Natal . .	·36	4,417,085	1,379,657	3 16 0
Cape Colony	1·5	10,106,466	10,152,979	6 15 0
Madagascar .	1·5	150,000	150,000	0 2 0
French Pos.	1·2	2,000,000	1,500,000	1 5 0
Mauritius .	·37	1,229,690	2,000,432	5 8 0
		48,968,903	51,395,967	

Country.	Pop. in Millions.	Imports. £	Exports. £	Rate per head of Exports. £ s. d.
AMERICA—				
Greenland .		27,000	20,000	
Canad. Dom.	4·8	24,662,150	19,907,228	4 2 10
Newfoundld.	·202	1,326,845	1,270,770	6 5 9
St. Pierre, etc.		574,000	725,000	
United States	62·6	173,760,000	179,258,175	2 17 0
Brit. W. I.				
and Guiana	1·68	8,977,255	10,009,710	5 19 0
Spanish do. .	2·32	5,000,000	8,350,000	3 12 0
French do. .	·366	2,262,000	2,143,000	5 16 6
Danish do. .	·032	161,500	32,50C	1 0 0
Dutch do. .	·101	450,000	500,000	5 0 0
San Domingo	·65	354,770	310,560	0 9 6
Hayti . .	1·00	3,250,000	2,500,000	2 10 0
Mexico . .	11·39	7,230,400	9,615,300	0 16 10
Nicaragua .	·313	375,475	300,000	0 19 0
Costa Rica .	·238	975,000	1,583,200	6 12 6
Guatemala .	1·482	1,174,745	2,215,544	1 10 0
Honduras .	·432	461,506	461,500	1 0 0
San Salvador	·778	370,000	1,166,000	1 10 0
Brazil . .	14·75	23,342,000	26,500,000	1 16 0
Colombia .	4·5	2,053,200	3,147,300	0 14 0
Venezuela .	2·28	3,344,500	4,004,000	1 18 6
Peru . .	2·62	2,000,000	1,800,000	0 13 0
Ecuador .	1·27	1,431,000	1,394,500	1 2 0
Bolivia . .	1·19	1,200,000	1,800,000	1 10 0
Chili . .	3·2	8,850,000	10,000,000	3 2 6
Uruguay .	·68	6,886,000	6,188,400	9 0 0
Paraguay .	·50	409,840	435,240	0 17 6
Argentina .	4·08	42,800,250	21,000,000	5 3 0
		323,709,436	316,637,947	
AUSTRALASIA				
N. S. Wales .	·751	22,615,004	22,045,937	29 6 8
Victoria .	·S62	22,954,015	13,266,222	15 6 0
Queensland .	·226	5,066,700	8,544,512	37 16 0
S. Australia .	·286	8,262,673	8,827,378	30 17 3
W. Australia	·029	874,447	617,811	21 5 0
Tasmania .	·115	1,897,512	1,486,922	12 18 5
New Zealand	·489	6,260,525	9,811,720	20 1 3
New Guinea .		15,833	8,134	
Fiji . .	·127	206,758	364,532	2 19 0
Hawaii . .	·089	1,392,400	2,604,600	28 18 0
Samoa . .	·036	43,626	20,509	0 11 6
N. Caledon. .				
		532,000	372,000	
		70,121,493	67,970,277	

The materials at command do not admit of this table being perfect. There is a large balance of trade done in the world which is nowhere recorded. Many of the figures are rough averages. The conversion from foreign currencies into sterling admits new error. The varying methods in which returns are compiled is another difficulty. The case of transit trade is yet another, for the same goods may appear under two or three countries. Further, bullion and specie are omitted in most of the European returns, and as a rule are included in all others—but it has been impossible to reduce the returns to a fixed principle in this respect.

Yet with all these drawbacks it may be taken to show roughly that the exports of all the countries of the world amounted to £1,900,000,000 sterling in value in 1890; that 1,250 millions came from Europe, and only about a fourth of that amount, or 317 millions, from the whole of America; that the exports of Great Britain alone are

equal to the whole of those of the American continent (comp. art. on COMMERCE).

Further, we observe that the imports generally exceed the exports; out in a large number of cases, particularly undeveloped countries, this result is not specially prominent. All those imports must be somewhere in the other column of the return as exports, but by the time they appear as imports their money-value has increased by the amount of freight and other charges.

In giving figures to show the comparative producing power of the different populations, we have confined ourselves to the rate per head of exports. The results of these figures are exceedingly interesting. Generally speaking, people in a backward state of civilisation give a low rate of production. Certain of the Australian colonies are at the head of the list, notably Queensland and South Australia, but Hawaii runs them close. Holland and Belgium stand very high, and the comparatively low position taken by Great Britain is remarkable. The United States have a very low rate per head. A little reflection shows that these figures cannot be taken by themselves as an index of a country's prosperity; one country may have an enormous internal trade, to which the exports are no index; another may have a large transit trade. The imports and exports of Malta, as given in the *Statesman's Year-Book*, are an instance of the latter case.

We have hitherto been concerned chiefly with the statistical side of our subject; we have used values as the most convenient form of indicating the wealth involved; comparative value of trade being some index also of comparative volume; although, when we have to do with specific deductions from these figures, there are many cases in which the quantities of commodities and their prices must be examined with care.

There is, however, quite another side of the subject, which is of no little importance, though it cannot here be dealt with at length. The economic lesson of tables of exports and imports—their teaching as to the life and occupation of the people—is one of the most important branches of the study, and one that is usually neglected. This must be shown by tables of the kinds of articles exported. We find in the case of Great Britain a complete change in the nature of its trade during the period under review in this article. Until some years later than 1750 England uniformly exported grain and rough woollen goods; with the closing years of the 18th century she was developing manufactures at home, and her mercantile marine was bringing in tea, sugar, spices, and other tropical produce from her colonies. This was the transition; to-day an examination of her trade-returns presents the picture of a country all but exclusively dependent for her food supply on foreign nations; and exporting her manufactures to every part of the habitable globe. Carrying this economic examination of the returns to those of the colonies, we are struck by the capacity of the British empire to depend entirely on itself in case of need; distance, however, being the great difficulty in the way of a realisation of this imperial independence. No other country in the world, save Holland, stands in anything like the same position as to the imports of the necessaries of life; but the colonial empire of Holland, important as it is, is entirely different in character from that of the United Kingdom. If we turn to the table of the world's trade and treat it similarly, we shall be able to classify the countries of the world according to their production of the necessaries of life, of luxuries, of raw materials, of manufactured goods; and the classification will obviously form a basis for a further sociological examination of the condition of each people.

Another point which may be illustrated by figures of exports and imports is the effect of war on the interchange between nations. War may act in two ways: in checking production and in diverting the course of trade. A great falling off in exports and imports, or a sudden development of trade with a particular country, may equally be the result of a state of hostilities. The trade of the United Kingdom in 1815 and 1855, and the years around these points—the trade of the United States in 1860 and onwards—that of France in 1869-1872, all illustrate the principle.

It remains to consider briefly the value of the available figures representing the trade of various countries. In the length of time for which even approximately accurate figures can be obtained, Great Britain is far ahead of other countries. Probably the United States come next, although we have had great difficulty in tracing any figures at all in the early part of the century. It is a matter of serious doubt how far any set of figures represents what it professes to represent; thus the statement of the trade of the world above given is in the broadest sense provisional, for there are scarcely any countries which make their returns on the same basis. Even the British possessions vary from one another and from the correct system of calculation; they are not even always *bona-fide*. A witness before a recent inter-departmental committee on the subject of the statistical returns of the British empire, admitted that it was at one time a practice in the colony which he represented to cook the returns, so as to accord with the theory that exports should exceed imports. The divergence between official and real values in the figures of British trade prior to 1854 we have already mentioned (see also

DECLARED AND REAL VALUES). The official figures up to that date were founded on valuations of products settled in 1694; these valuations probably held good well into the 18th century; but towards the close of it they had got very far out, and official reports began to recognise this. The inspector-general of imports and exports, after making his official return, would add a computation of the real values. For the adjustment of the imports we have to rely upon general inference from those computations, and upon the fact that in 1854, when the new system was introduced, the real value was found to exceed the official value by $22\frac{3}{4}$ per cent. In regard to the valuation of exports material for adjustment came in during 1798; from which date the declared value of British produce exported is found side by side with the official value; exceeding it by 68 per cent in the first year, and by a diminishing percentage until 1820, when the divergence went the other way, and official value rose from 5 per cent in excess to about 150 per cent at the date when the fictitious official value was finally discarded. It is obvious that any argument based on the official figures was misleading; and we have therefore in this article used all the material at command in adjusting the figures and checking the adjustment, until we obtained figures which, as nearly as it can ever be done, represented the course of the trade of Great Britain prior to 1854. It will, however, be many years before general correctness can be obtained and we can hope to have from every country exports calculated at their value at the port of shipment, and imports representing the value as exports *plus* the value of the freight, insurance, etc., while transit trade is carefully eliminated from importation for consumption. The variant practice as to bullion and specie also needs correction. The separation of these commodities from merchandise is usual in modern statistics and is adopted by the board of trade; it is due to some sort of recognition that they are often in the nature of a transit trade; but the analysis is very imperfect and probably as often wrong as right.

[There is no single work on the study of exports and imports which can be referred to. Sir R. Giffen's essay on the use of import and export statistics, published in the second series of his *Essays on Finance*, is quite the best summary of the theory of the matter.—In Marshall's *Statistics of the British Empire*, 1800-1833, there is a useful introduction to the tables of exports and imports, vitiated by the old fallacy as to official values.—*First Report of the Commissioners of Customs and Appendices* (1857).—The Board of Trade annual *Statistical Abstracts* of the trade of (1) the United Kingdom, and (2) the British possessions.—The similar abstracts of the trade of foreign countries from 1830 to 1860.—Various valuable returns laid before parliament.—The

Statesman's Year - Book and *Annuaire de la Statistique* summarise the returns published by foreign countries.—The *Consular Reports* published annually for Parliament give more detailed but partial information as to foreign countries.—Macpherson's *Annals of British Commerce, passim.*—Pitkin, *Statistics of the United States, New York*, 1817.—Porter's *Progress of the Nation*, 1847, § iii. ch. ix.—M'Culloch, *Account of the British Empire*, vol. ii. pt. iii. ch. v.—List, *System of National Economy* (translated, 1885).—S. Bourne, *Trade Population and Food*, 1880, chs. i., ii., iii., viii., ix., xi. See also COMMERCE and BALANCE OF TRADE.]   C. A. H.

IMPORT DUTIES.

History of Import Duties, p. 367; Incidence of, p. 369; Specific *v. ad valorem*, p. 369; Amount of Duty, p. 369.

History of Import Duties.—A reference to the article on EXPORTS, DUTIES ON, will show that duties on imports, though now so much the more important, were instituted later in time, at any rate in England, than export duties. At first the two were not thought of as distinct forms of taxation: both were merely an impost on the trader. The custom called Scavage, which we find, in the reign of Henry III., levied on all sorts of merchandise brought from beyond seas, was akin to an import duty, and the PRISAGE on wine was practically one taken in kind. But the first real import duties date from 1304, under the name of *parva custuma:* they were levied on foreign merchants only, and in addition to other existing duties, as follows :

Wine, per dolium 2s.
General merchandise, 3d. in the £1 *ad valorem*.

On 20th August 1309 these duties were suspended with a view to seeing whether consumers would gain in the price ; but on 2nd August 1310 they were re-imposed, as "no advantage had ensued either to the king or people." The duty on wine came to be called *tunnage*, and the *ad valorem* duty *poundage* (see TUNNAGE AND POUNDAGE) ; and these under the name of SUBSIDY became a regular part of the financial system of England. In 1548 the duty on wine was 3s. (except for Rhenish), and the poundage 12d. in the £1, or 5 per cent.

The progenitor of the modern tariff rose in the shape of the BOOK OF RATES at a comparatively early period. This book, issued at first by the sole authority of the crown, enumerated the values which were to be assigned to different articles for the purposes of calculating the *ad valorem* duty just referred to. "These values were probably in the earliest instances the current prices of the articles imported." One of these rate-books was "imprinted in 1545." The principle of assessment was laid down ten years later (1555) as "to underrate the most necessary commodities that came into the realm, to draw them hither, and to overrate the superfluous commodities inwards to drive them away."

James I. was not satisfied with this principle, and declared that everything required to be rated higher. He levied a new imposition in addition to the subsidy, thereby complicating the form in which duties were received, and in many cases doubling the revenue which parliament had intended him to derive. This gave rise in 1642 to the issue of a rate-book by the Houses of Parliament only. The book issued in 1662 enumerated 1139 articles inwards, and 212 outwards (see ENUMERATED COMMODITIES).

In the ensuing century it became a growing practice to impose fresh import duties by special acts in special emergencies ; and by 1784 no fewer than 100 new heads of account referable to different funds—*e.g.* aggregate fund, sinking fund, general fund, etc.—had been opened in the customs department, under any or all of which any given article might be liable to duty. An example of this "bewildering and appalling chaos" is given on p. 18 of the First Report of the Customs Commissioners. Merchants hardly knew what they had to pay without expert assistance ; even officers at the outports were sorely puzzled. The whole system hindered trade, and lent itself to smuggling ; so that, in spite of the mercantile theory, which enforced the view that protective import duties were an encouragement to the country's trade, it became felt that the existing system was intolerable. The first step in the direction of reform was made by Pitt's Customs Consolidation Act in 1787. This rated 1200 articles for duty inwards ; of these 300 were rated *ad valorem*. It also provided that all import duties should henceforward be carried to one fund, now known as the Consolidated Fund.

But in the moment that the collection of the import duties was simplified, the idea which assigned to them an important function in enhancing a nation's wealth appears to have gained new strength. For forty years thereafter the followers of ADAM SMITH made no impression on the idea. HUSKISSON, as chancellor of the exchequer in 1825, was the first statesman who showed the possibility of dispensing with a multiplicity of import duties. Sir Robert PEEL, in the tariff of 1841, made the next move ; and with the triumph of the free-trade policy the numbers of articles subjected to duty rapidly diminished, as the following table will show :

Year.	Principal articles.	Subdivisions.	Total number.
1660	490	1140	1630
1787	290	1135	1425
1826	432	848	1280
1841	564	488	1052
1849	233	282	515
1855	153	261	414
1861	19	123	142
1876	10	32	42

At the same time the customs revenue showed no signs of decrease.

In 1855 it amounted to £22,227,570
,, 1860   ,,   ,,   24,391,084
,, 1865   ,,   ,,   22,527,373
,, 1870   ,,   ,,   21,449,843

As a matter of fact there was a considerable expansion due to causes amongst which the progressive simplifications of the tariff had a considerable place. It is calculated that the customs duties remitted between 1855 and 1870 amounted to £14,872,331, and those imposed to £612,915, showing an estimated loss of revenue of £14,259,416, which never took place, as the figures above quoted have shown.

In 1860 there were duties levied on the importation of nineteen articles, in 1890 on ten only, excluding certain minor divisions under "spirits." The subjoined table shows those which had dropped out, and compares the produce for the two dates.

	1860	1890
Sugar, etc., producing	£6,100,288	abolished
Tea	5,444,157	£4,490,506
Coffee	445,999	172,832
Corn, etc.	751,046	abolished
Butter	23,881	do.
Currants	233,897	} 534,831
Raisins	103,196	
Wood	294,134	abolished
Tobacco, etc.	5,674,053	9,061,984
Wine	1,174,103	1,302,160
Spirits	2,413,919	4,681,225
Silk manufactures	16,576	abolished
Other articles	490,515	183,157

The tariff of the United Kingdom, as it stands at the present day, subjects the minimum number of commodities to taxation. It is a tariff of purely revenue duties levied on commodities which are in a great measure luxuries. In the tariffs of import duties of various British colonies we are confronted by considerable divergences, illustrating different phases of history. Those of the older colonies, more particularly the West Indies, have always borne the stamp of the old cumbrous régime; those of the Australian colonies began with a simple levy of *ad valorem* duties on a few imported commodities; but developed, like that of Canada, into an engine for protection. The hand of Canadian legislators has been forced by the proximity of the United States; after an effort in 1867 to work with moderate import duties, the colonial manufacturers overbore the liberal opposition; and the "national" policy of Sir J. Macdonald has, since 1879, been driving the Dominion into stricter forms of protection, chiefly directed against the

United States. The tariff of Canada now fills twenty - seven closely - printed columns of a parliamentary return, and makes a respectable pamphlet by itself. Even Victoria's covers eleven only. The spirit of the new protection has caught all the Australian colonies except New South Wales. Their high duties are directed alike against the mother country and the foreigners. The Cape has been slowly tending to imitate Australia. The Eastern and West Indian colonies, with some exceptions, have tariffs which are in form a survival of the old mercantile system, but their duties are levied simply for revenue purposes, and their rates are rarely excessive. As most of these colonies are under the more immediate control of the crown, there has been a considerable effort made to simplify their tariffs, and remove the duties on food-stuffs and necessaries, but the success has been small; local opinion, particularly in the West Indies, argues that imported food-stuffs are to the negro or coolie a luxury, and that by giving up the duty on such articles, an easily-collected revenue would be lost without one whit improving the condition of the labourer.

India, following the lead of the imperial government, keeps to a small and purely revenue tariff of import duties (see COLONIES; COLONIAL POLICY).

The history of import duties in the European continental countries records a passage from restriction to moderate duties and a reaction to rigid protection. For the import duty is the engine of protection. France, down to 1860, had always adopted a system of jealous exclusion. Macgregor, in 1841, calls the commercial legislation of Spain "the most pernicious and restrictive of all the systems of trading exclusion." The same condemnation was accorded to the other European tariffs except, perhaps, that of the German customs union, which had conferred incalculable benefit on the states included in it by breaking down the barriers of import duties between them, and assigning more moderate duties on the importation of foreign goods. The adoption of free trade by England induced Holland and other countries to modify their import tariffs. The treaty of 1860 with France marked a new era; restriction gave way to duties which, though still protective, were comparatively low. A great increase both in imports and exports was the immediate result. Other nations followed this example, and for some years the import duties of European countries were in practice regulated by treaties in the general interest. Then came the protectionist reaction, which Prof. Bastable dates from the Franco-German war of 1870; war expenditure and national jealousy gave a bias towards a system of heavier duties as between the two rivals; other nations followed with an idea of protecting themselves.

The United States have passed through various stages of doubt; from 1824 to 1875 their import duties were alternately raised and lowered for two or three years at a time; here again the great rise took place in the war period from 1861-65, and subsequent efforts at reduction made no great impression. Since 1883 the tariff has been severely protective, ultimately culminating in the cumbrous McKinley tariff of 1890, which laid crushing duties on all foreign manufactures, though it freed certain commodities which were thought to be required for the home producer.

The South American states, influenced partly by the United States, and partly by European example, levy onerous duties.

To sum up: England stands practically alone in the world as a country with a simple and low tariff; in British colonies the tariffs are usually cumbrous, but fall into two classes, —the one where many import duties are merely the easiest way of getting revenue, the other where those duties are avowedly protective. Of foreign countries it may be said that, at the present day, all except Holland and Belgium which at a considerable interval followed England, have deserted the revenue and adopted the protective tariff.

Incidence of Import Duties.—The popularity of import duties as a source of revenue is usually and probably correctly ascribed to the fact that they are collected without application to any large number of the taxpayers. The question of their incidence has in England been settled for years; the accepted view being that all duties paid by the merchant on importation are added by him to the price of the commodity, and are thus eventually paid by the consumer. It is probable that in early days there was an idea that the foreign merchant paid the tax. But it soon came to be understood that they were at least usually paid by the consumer and not by the merchants; the order of 1309 (see page 367) seems to be clear evidence of this. The proposition that they are actually paid by the merchant himself has been advanced in recent controversies with some of the British colonies, more particularly those in the West Indies, where it is commonly held that an increase of 5 per cent in an *ad valorem* duty cannot be put on the price, but must be borne by the merchant, and, on the other hand, that a remission of duty benefits the merchant only, as price is not affected. This view, however, is difficult to support, and has been contradicted by its advocates in the course of their own arguments. An opposite view was held in the case of these very colonies in 1842 by both the parties to the controversy whether higher import duties were the best means of increasing the inducement to the negro to work (Earl Grey's *Colonial Policy*, vol. i. p. 80 *et seq.*). Again, it has been advanced, chiefly in the

United States, that protective import duties are paid by the foreigner; but this cannot, properly speaking, be true for long, even when the foreigner's market is restricted to the nation which imposes the duty. The foreign producer, if the consumer declines to pay a higher price, may consent to forego for a time a part of his ordinary profits, and in this sense he may "pay the duty"; but eventually he will cease producing; if he is willing to accept a permanently lower rate of profit, this can hardly, in economics, be spoken of as paying the duty. As an illustration we may cite the case of the Bermuda onion-growers, who sent a deputation to New York in 1893, with a view of obtaining concessions in the matter of the import duty on onions. As interesting examples of the operation of certain import duties, we may refer to the old duties on sugar (*v.* M'Culloch, *Taxation*, p. 210), and those on corn (*v.* Leone Levi, *On Taxation*, pp. 77-79).

Specific v. Ad valorem Duties.—The question of specific or rated as against *ad valorem* duties is one that has been vigorously debated, and cannot be considered settled; there are still high practical authorities who state that it costs no greater trouble to collect the latter than the former. The better opinion is, however, that *ad valorem* rates are constantly unfair, and give rise to unnecessary friction between the customs staff and the merchants; Mr. Gladstone, in his budget speech of 1853, adopted this opinion; the customs commissioners in 1857 stated that the labour of their officers had been greatly reduced in consequence of the diminution in the number of *ad valorem* duties. This is equivalent to economy in the cost of collection. The legislation of Great Britain has been based on this opinion; in 1797 there were 300 *ad valorem* duties, in 1842 there were 156, in 1855 they had been reduced to 40: they have now disappeared. In the colonies they remain in full force, though the home government, where it has influence, is gradually obtaining a change to specific rates.

A plan of combining a specific with an *ad valorem* duty on the same commodity has been adopted in the United States, and has spread to Canada. It hampers trade and adds to the labour of collection. Nearly akin to it was the old plan, adopted in England in 1840 and rejected in 1853, of adding a general percentage to all duties. This was till lately a favourite mode of raising additional taxation in many of the British colonies.

Amount of Duty.—It is a question of some nicety whether import duties should be adjusted so as to represent as far as possible a uniform percentage on the value of the commodity. Mr. Gladstone apparently adopted the theory in 1853, and placed the percentage at 10 per cent. But the nature and use of a commodity, and the extent of the demand for it, may render a much higher percentage an equally fair tax. The highest *ad valorem* rate in any British colony upon general merchandise is 25 per cent ; it is usually far lower. Protective tariffs load imports with duties which are usually at least 30 per cent, and the general basis of the McKinley tariff was 50 per cent for all manufactures.

This article would not be complete without reference to drawbacks and the methods of facilitating the collection of duties. DRAWBACKS (*q.v.*) were the original method of relieving a merchant of the payment of part of the import duty when he desired to re-export a duty-paid article. The statute 12 Car. II. c. 4, first admitted this, reimbursing the whole duty in some cases, half in others. In 1788 a fourth of the gross revenue of the customs was returned by way of drawbacks. This system was first modified by permitting the importation of articles merely on a bond for the payment of the duty ; this gave rise to constant fraud, and was the source of much risk and additional labour to the government. The warehousing system, or deposit of commodities in BONDED WAREHOUSES (*q.v.*) until such time as the duty is paid, has almost entirely done away with drawbacks. They still, however, form a common item of account in colonial budgets.

[See sources cited under EXPORTS, DUTIES ON, especially *First Report of Commissioners of Customs*, 1857.—Leone Levi, *On Taxation*, 1860.—Kippax's translation of Ustariz' *Theory etc. of Commerce*, Dublin, 1752.—Macgregor, *Commercial and Financial Legislation of Europe and America*, 1841.—Farquhar, *Economic and Industrial Delusions*, 1891, pp. 54-73.—Bastable, *Commerce of Nations*, chs. vi.-x.—*Returns of Colonial Tariffs*, c6402/91.—Hall, *Hist. of the Customs Revenue of England*.]   C. A. H.

IMPORTS AND EXPORTS, FREEDOM AND RESTRAINT OF. We shall deal with Imports and Exports separately.

Free Imports.—This subject may be considered under two divisions.

(*a*) *General freedom of importation.* This matter may best be studied from the point of view of its converse (see below, IMPORTS, RESTRAINT ON): it is on the whole easier to show the results of moving contrary to natural laws, than to exhibit the working of a natural system. And though the general history of commerce seems to be the history of restriction, yet the natural impulse of commercial man is to exchange his products with others free from let and hindrance.

The leading commercial nations of the middle ages admitted imports free of duty, or at a low duty : and the leading commercial nation of the present day—Great Britain—admits almost all commodities free of duty. The Hanseatic towns, in an age of general exclusion, levied duties ranging from one-half to three-quarters per cent : and Holland for some two centuries, and all through the time of its greatness, kept its ports practically free to the importation of all sorts of merchandise

from all parts of the world. It is somewhat surprising to find that the Turkish empire was the only other European power, till modern times, which kept its ports free for all imports, but the Turkish government spoiled their policy by prohibiting exports ! Early in this century, and before England was converted to free trade, the Argentine republic endeavoured to remove all restrictions on importation ; but it has now fallen under the influence of American example.

At the present time Great Britain and some of her dependencies, notably India, Hong-Kong, and the Straits Settlements, with Holland and Belgium, are the only examples of an importation generally free.

(*b*) *Free importation of special articles.* This is nowadays a usual feature even in countries which are strictly protectionist ; it is usual to admit free of duty various articles which are expected to be of special advantage to the importing nation. These are included in a "free list" (see FREE LIST).   C. A. H.

Free Exports.—As nearly all nations now encourage exportation, not only by refraining from the levy of duties but even by granting bounties, the expediency of leaving export trade generally free may be assumed. The articles on EXPORTS, DUTIES ON, and FREE TRADE will give some idea of the progress of the modern principle, and the cases in which it is still interfered with by duties. It will best be understood by considering the cases of its infraction.

Restraint on Exports.—The idea of prohibiting exports of certain commodities appears to have influenced communities earlier than the attempt to restrain imports. It is based on the idea of preventing—to quote the French statement of it—"all that may contribute to the development of foreign industry."

In the case of England it was first applied in 1261 to the export of wool—the subject of her great original industry. By 8 Eliz. c. 3, and later enactments, severe penalties were imposed on those who exported sheep and wool. But these severe laws failed to attain their end. By 13 & 14 Car. II. 7, hides and leather, by still older statutes, metals, as late as 7 & 8 Will. III. c. 20, instruments of industry, were made the subjects of prohibition. This has all now been reversed for fifty years.

Similar prohibitions, or discouragement of exportation by high duties, were common to most European countries. The French at the end of last century, in the words quoted above, laid down the principle publicly. The Spaniards prohibited the exports of corn up to 1820 : Turkey prohibited all exportation till well on into this century. Greece, on her independence, was more moderate, simply imposing a duty of 6 per cent *ad valorem* on all exports. Sicily, in 1839, had recourse to a monopoly to limit the export of sulphur to a fixed annual amount.

The prohibition of the exportation of precious metals rested on a different shade of the idea, and formed part of the MERCANTILE SYSTEM (*q.v.*), by which they were considered the sole source of wealth to be retained in the country at all hazards.

Prohibition on exportation to an enemy had a somewhat different basis, and still is recognised as perfectly legitimate in the case of munitions of war (see CONTRABAND).

[An excellent summary of the English history will be found in Adam Smith's *Wealth of Nations*, bk. iv. ch. viii.—Art. on BUDGET.—See also Macgregor's *Commercial and Financial Legislation of Europe*, and the works cited under EXPORTS, DUTIES ON.]　　　　C. A. H.

IMPORTS, RESTRAINT ON. This is a subject necessarily interwoven with the history of import duties and the theory of trade. The restriction of importation of foreign goods has, in the history of commerce, taken two forms— (1) absolute prohibition, (2) the imposition of heavy duties. It appears to have had its origin in the desire of keeping all production in the hands of the home-producer ; and so far it is the ancestor of protection which Mill defines as "the prohibition, or the discouragement by heavy duties, of such foreign commodities as are capable of being produced at home": it was used later as a punishment to the foreigner. Its correlative is smuggling : when restriction is at its height, smuggling is rife.

It appears to be true that in modern history England was the first prominent example of a restrictive policy : this policy was carried out rather by the NAVIGATION LAWS (*q.v.*) and by complexity of customs laws than by direct prohibition or through the medium of heavy import duties ; but as late as 1841 Macgregor (*Commercial and Financial Legislation of Europe and America*) could state that English legislation practically prohibited the importation of corn and of foreign sugars and coffee, and up to a recent date this was true of malt.

It was in France, however, that the use of direct prohibition and of the prohibitive duty was first developed. In 1664 Colbert introduced the principle of excluding foreign manufactures by raising the duties on them : the first absolute prohibitions of foreign commodities—woven clothes from India and the East—became law in 1686. The celebrated commercial treaty of 1786 gave a comparatively easy entrance to English manufactures ; but the subsequent wars introduced a complete reversal of this more liberal policy. The episode of the prohibitions based on the Berlin and Milan decrees belongs rather to the story of the war than to ordinary commercial history ; but it illustrated singularly well the futility of restrictions on trade: *viz.* the automatic tendency to defeat their own end. In spite of Napoleon's efforts to exclude English manufactures and thus ruin English commerce, these manu-

factures not only found their way into continental markets, but were brought into France with the connivance of the French ministers: "M. de Talleyrand . . . secretly countenanced the landing of British goods solely for the benefit of France" (Macgregor, work cited, p. 38 note). Prohibition remained a leading feature of the French tariff till the treaty of 1860 with England ; and of late years French legislation has been retrograding in the old direction by imposing heavy protective duties (see IMPORT DUTIES).

In Spain a definite restrictive policy began almost contemporaneously with that of France, and has hardly ever seen any relaxation. The Spanish tariff, besides hampering trade by its complexity, loaded all foreign imports with duties varying from 50 to 100 per cent of value ; and in the middle of the century it contained at least 500 total prohibitions. Holland, after an era of freedom, adopted a few fairly heavy duties in the course of this century, and some actual prohibitions, which were partly political. And, generally, all European nations have been wedded to systems of restraint more or less complete.

The leading modern example of a restrictive policy is the McKinley tariff, which became the law of the United States in 1891 ; it was avowedly a stringent protective tariff, aimed at making the States self-supporting and crushing out foreign competition ; its duties amounted in many cases to 50 per cent of the value of the commodity on arrival, and this was sufficient in some articles to cause a complete transfer of the capital engaged in their production from England to the United States.

The evil effects of a restrictive system are (*a*) its expense to the consumer. Restriction could only be necessary to force a trade out of its natural channel, and that is always expensive. Other bad results appear to be felt more slowly than formerly, for (*b*) smuggling is more easily checked owing to facility of communication ; (*c*) adulteration and counterfeiting are more difficult because of the general prevalence of minute inspection.

In particular cases evils more far-reaching have been traced, and are doubtless still traceable to restriction. Macgregor in 1841 attributed the heavy drudgery of the peasantry and especially the women in France, and the backwardness of cultivation, to dearness of iron consequent on prohibitions of foreign goods. The prohibition of corn has produced evils more patent still. A good illustration of this point occurred a few years back, when the government of Venezuela was forced to suspend its heavy import duties on food-stuffs owing to complete failure of the home crops.

The accepted opinion of economists is that all restraint on commerce is injurious : the whole theory of free trade is built up on that idea. It would hardly be necessary to refer to this, were it not that List and others have argued that restriction at an early period of a nation's history is the source of ultimate wealth ; and the commercial greatness of England has by some been traced to the self-sufficiency produced by past restrictions on foreign trade—that is, to protection in past ages. These reasoners have neglected the fact of England's geographical position and conformation, her comparatively early political freedom, the early invention of machinery, and other factors.

As regards new countries, however, the system has been in some measure justified by the high authority of Mill (bk. v. ch. x. § 1) (see PROTECTION).

There are certain cases in which the importation of special articles is prohibited or restricted on grounds of public safety or morality : obscene books and prints or dangerous explosives are instances which are common to most modern tariffs. The case of foreign reprints of copyright works—which are prohibited from importation into Great Britain and Ireland and also into the colonies unless certain special arrangements have been made for the benefit of the authors (see 5 & 6 Vict. c. 45, § 17 ; 25 & 26 Vict. c. 68, § 10), rests on conventional and quasi-moral grounds.

[Ad. Smith, *W. of N.*, bk. iv. ch. ii. and iii.— For facts see John Macgregor's *Commercial and Financial Legislation of Europe and America*, London, 1841.— See also, for America, Edward Atkinson's *Taxation and Work*, New York, 1892.]

C. A. H.

IMPÔT UNIQUE (or SINGLE TAX). The limited and restricted sense in which this term was used by the physiocratic school is best explained by the following quotations from the writings of Quesnay and his followers. "Taxation ought not to be destructive of nor out of proportion to the total income of the nation ; . . . it must be levied directly on the net return (*produit net*) of land and not on wages, or on the [gross] produce, in which case it would increase the cost of production, be detrimental to trade, and destroy annually a part of the wealth of the nation" (Quesnay, p. 83, ed. Daire, Paris, 1846, p. 332, ed. Oncken). "Men are not at liberty to assess taxation according to their will ; it has an *essential* basis and form settled by the order of nature. . . . Only the portion of crops called the *net product* (meaning after deduction of the outlay made by the agriculturist) should contribute to taxation. . . . Taxation is thus *essentially* a portion of the *net product* of land" (Dupont de Nemours, *Physiocrates*, p. 351, ed. Daire). This system Dupont, in his letters to J. B. Say (p. 405 same ed.), calls a *domanial constitution of finance based on the sharing of returns.* "What is only a portion of a net product can only be taken on a net product ; . . . hence the essential form of the tax consists in taking taxation *directly* where it is present" (Mercier de la Rivière, *Ordre Naturel des Sociétés Politiques*, p. 474, ed. Daire). The Abbé Baudeau considers that a share of six twentieths of the *net product* may be allotted to the representatives of the sovereign (*Intro-*

duction à la Philosophie Économique, p. 760, ed. Daire).

Viewed historically, the idea of the single tax is the result of a reaction against the crushing weight of a vexatious and omnipresent system of taxation. In France, as far back as 1576-1577, the states-general of Blois were asked to consider a motion of one of the members of the *Tiers État* to do away with all the existing taxes, and to establish instead an *impôt unique* described as the "*taille égalée*" (equalised tallage), assessed according to the means of the owner of each dwelling ; it was in fact a kind of proportional hearth-money, from which, however, the nobility and clergy were to be exempted. This proposition was rejected, probably out of mistrust of the court (Clamagéran, *Histoire de l'Impôt*, ii. pp. 217-219). The system recommended by Vauban in his *Dîme Royale* (republished in Daire's *Économistes Financiers du XVIIIe Siècle*, and *Petite Bibliothèque Économique*) is well known, but was rejected by Mirabeau as "absolutely defective because this excellent man, having disregarded the principle that all wealth and income can only be derived from land, makes a muddle of his scheme by introducing an infinite number of double appropriations" (Knies, *Carl Friedrich von Baden's Brieflicher Verkehr mit Mirabeau*, i. p. 37, Heidelberg, 1892). In Italy, BANDINI (*q.v.*) entertained the same notions in his *Discorso Economico* presented in 1739 to the grand duke of Tuscany.

But owing to the unsoundness and iniquity of its financial system, Spain is the country where the single tax theory took the earliest and kept the most persistent hold both of the official and the speculative mind. Eager to defend the founder of its Austrian dynasty against the aspersions of Spanish writers, Mr. Konrad Haebler, in his *Wirtschaftliche Blüte Spaniens im 16. Jahrhundert* (p. 12), ascribes to Charles V. the first idea of a system of taxation based on the establishment of a single and direct tax. During the decay of the Spanish monarchy under the emperor's successors this idea was resumed under different forms: in 1573-75 and 1592-98, the cortes of Madrid proposed a single tax on grist levied when it left the mills, and this system was advocated at different times either by official bodies or private writers down to the middle of the last century. In 1646, Alcázar de Arriaga, in his *Nueva Declaracion de un medio universal para extinguir los tributos en Castilla* (New Declaration of a Universal Plan for Suppression of Taxes), advocated what he denominated the single ALCAVALA, a kind of general income tax of 2 per cent. In 1651 father Bautista DÁVILA proposed a single general and progressive capitation or poll-tax. Centani, however, is more than any one else entitled to be considered as a direct ancestor of the

French physiocrats. In a memorial entitled *Tierras* (Land), and submitted in 1671 to the king of Spain, Centani, taking up an opinion expressed a few years before by Juan de Castro, explicitly asserts that land is the only real wealth (*la tierra es la verdadera y física hacienda*), and insists on the removal of all indirect taxation in favour of a direct and territorial taxation founded on an exact and extensive CADASTRAL SURVEY. About half a century later, the minister ENSENADA gave orders to proceed with this survey in Castile on a plan which had been successfully carried out in Catalonia ; and in 1770, Charles III. decreed the "*única contribucion,*" which was, however, never actually put into force (Colmeiro, *Hist. de la Ec. Polit. en España,* ii. pp. 570-576).

In Baden, the margrave Carl Friedrich, prompted by purely theoretical views, decreed a similar experiment in three villages—Dallingen (district of Pforzheim), Bahlingen, and Theningen (district of Hochberg). Established in the years 1770 and 1771, it by degrees excited the discontent of the population, was gradually abandoned, and came to an end about the beginning of the present century. A good and clear account of this experiment is given in Conrad's *Jahrbücher für Nationaloekonomie u. Statistik,* 1872, vol. xix. (article by Emminghaus, *C. F. von Baden's Physiocratische Verbindungen.* See also Rodolphe Reuss, *Ch. de Butré,* Strasbourg, 1890).

In France, although the physiocratic doctrines always remained confined to theory, their influence may be traced in the steady aversion to indirect taxation of the representative assemblies at the time of the revolution of 1789. But after the space of a very few years, this aversion had to be overcome, for whatever may be its theoretical merits, no system of single taxation could possibly satisfy the ravenous appetites of our modern budget makers.

[In addition to the works mentioned before, see Mirabeau's *Théorie de l'Impôt* (1761), various writings by Turgot collected by Daire in his edition under the heading of *Impôt* (vol. i. pp. 392-434), and Turgot's *Réflexions sur la Formation et la Distribution des Richesses,* in the first volume of *Mélanges* (ed. Daire).—Condillac, *Le Commerce et le Gouvernement* (pp. 355-359), also Cantillon, *Essai sur la nature du Commerce,* 1755 (pp. 55-61, Harvard reprint, 1892).—Saint Péravy, *Mémoire sur les Effets de l'Impôt Indirect* (1768), etc. Among the opponents of the tax are Voltaire, *L'homme aux Quarante Écus.*—Forbonnais, *Principes Économiques* in Daire's *Mélanges* (p. 235 note, and p. 210, notes 1 and 2).—Mably, *Doutes proposées aux Économistes sur l'Ordre Naturel des Sociétés Politiques* (Paris, 1768, pp. 40-44).— GRASLIN (*q.v.*), *Essai Analytique sur la Richesse et sur l'Impôt* (London, 1767).—Rivière, *L'Ami de la Paix ou Réponse à la Théorie de l'Impôt du Marquis de Mirabeau* (1761).—Champalin, *Taxe-Personnelle et Unique* (1789).—Guiraudet, *Erreur des Économistes sur l'Impôt* (1790).

Consult also the valuable article by Dr. Stephan Bauer (*Zur Entstehung der Physiocratie* in Conrad's *Jahrbücher für Nat. Oek. u. Statistik,* Jena, 1890) and Professor A. Oncken (*Zur Geschichte der Physiocratie* in Schmoller's *Jahrbuch für Gesetzgebung,* Leipzig, 1893).] E. CA.

(See EPHÉMÉRIDES ; PHYSIOCRATS ; SINGLE TAX.)

IMPOUND. An expression originally used in respect of distrained cattle only, which were placed into a "pound" by way of security. It is now used generally with respect to any objects which, with some ulterior purpose, are put into a place of security. Thus a judge may order documents to be impounded if he thinks they may furnish material for a criminal prosecution. As to the way in which such documents are to be dealt with, see Rules of the Supreme Court, Order 42, Rule 33A. E. S.

IMPRESSMENT. From the earliest times every free and able-bodied Englishman has been liable to military service, but only for purposes of defence. The service of the primitive FYRD, and of the later militia, was restricted to putting down rebellion and repelling invasion. The sovereign could not lawfully claim the service of the subject for the purpose of manning the fleet, or of forming armies to serve abroad. But voluntary enlistment did not always furnish men enough for these purposes. The Tudors and Stuarts, therefore, had recourse to impressment. Impressment may be defined as an irregular and arbitrary compulsion to serve. It differs from the modern CONSCRIPTION, which is also compulsory, but imposes uniform and definite liabilities either on the whole population or on large classes of the community. In England, sailors were liable to be pressed for naval service (see Alexander JUSTICE), and men of the lower classes generally were liable to be pressed for military service. The impressment of sailors for the navy fell upon so limited a class, and was so convenient as a means of securing the national safety, that in spite of the gross abuses which it involved, it was maintained down to the close of our great naval wars, and never elicited a serious protest either from the courts of law or from parliament. It was otherwise with impressment for military service. The hardships which it involved affected a much greater number of persons, and the military strength which it lent to the crown provoked the jealousy of the friends of constitutional freedom. The impressment of soldiers by Charles I. in the course of his conflict with the Scotch people led to the statutory declaration made in 16 Car. I. c. 28, that no subject ought to be impressed, or compelled, to go out of his country to serve as a soldier except in case of the sudden coming of strange enemies into the kingdom. But parliament regarded impressment as necessary upon occasion, for by this very act it sanctioned the pressing of soldiers to serve in the Irish war. Several acts of parliament in the course of the last century sanctioned the pressing of vagrants, and of idle or disorderly persons. Since 1780 impressment of soldiers has been virtually unknown. Impressment of sailors became unnecessary after the close of the French wars, but has never been declared unlawful. Should voluntary enlistment hereafter fail to supply the needs of the army and navy, recourse will probably be had to some scheme of conscription. The old impressment was inequitable in principle and brutal in execution. Much may be said for the policy of recruiting the army from the least valuable class of citizens. But the pressing of vagrants and disorderly persons would be a feeble resource now that the size of armies has been so much increased.

[See Clode, *Military Forces of the Crown.* — Anson, *Law and Custom of the Constitution.* — Captain Marryat, R.N., *Suggestions for the abolition of the present System of Impressment in the Naval Service,* 1822. — *Edinburgh Review,* Nov. 1814.]   F. C. M.

IMPREST in public accounts denotes an advance to a sub-accountant or individual, usually from an authorised vote, to be accounted for in detail after expenditure.   C. A. H.

IMPRISONMENT FOR DEBT. See DEBT, IMPRISONMENT FOR.

INCOME may be defined as the wealth, measured in money, which is at the disposal of an individual, or a community, per year or other unit of time. This term is not easily freed from ambiguity. Does wealth imply materiality ; as Mill decides in a passage (*Pol. Econ.*, bk. i. ch. iii. § 2) which has been severely criticised by Mr. Cannan with reference to that kind of wealth which constitutes income (*Production and Distribution,* p. 31). The attribute in question may seem to be the only logical ground for a distinction which has been drawn by high authorities: by DUDLEY BAXTER (*National Income,* ch. viii.) between "original earnings," namely, "the productive income from agriculture and manufacture," and the "second-hand income" "paid out of original earnings" ; and by Leone LEVI (*Report of the British Association,* 1881, p. 274), between "income derived from independent sources of production " and an opposite kind including " professional incomes which really constitute the expenditure of other classes." Can "original" and "independent" here mean anything but *material ?* Probably it is best not to take this distinction, and to understand the "aggregate of commodities material and immaterial, including services of all kinds," (Marshall) which have the character of wealth. Among such objects a distinction is drawn between those which commonly fetch a price and those which, though exchangeable, are not commonly exchanged. If a mother hire another woman to watch her baby while she herself works at a factory, the amount of paid services is greater than it would be if the mother attended to her home and the other woman worked in the factory. But the "aggregate of commodities" may well be less. So "no account is commonly taken of the benefit he [a man] derives from the use of his furniture" (Marshall). The distinction between *possibly exchangeable* and *actually exchanged* must be attended to when we compare incomes in widely different states of society in one of which many gifts of nature are free, in another, appropriated. The difference between the "luxuries, conveniences, and necessities" enjoyed by the English labourer, now and in the age of the Tudors, cannot be calculated from the difference in the respective money-incomes.

Next, what is meant by "at disposal," or the term which some would prefer, "net" ? It excludes that portion of incomings which is required to keep up capital, and other outgoings. Are we then to exclude from the income of the labourer the expenditure which is necessary for his efficiency ? This view is taken in a masterly report on the *Common measure of value in direct taxation,* by a committee of the British Association, which included Farr and Jevons and Newmarch (*Report of the British Association* for 1878). They say : " As the horse has to be clothed and stabled, so the productive labourer has to be clothed and housed." But there is this difference, that the cart-horse's food and gear are not "goods of the first order," objects of human consumption.

Again, among outgoings, should we place that portion of earnings which forms compensation for *désagréments ?* If the trade of a butcher "is in most places more profitable than the greater part of common trades " only because it is "an odious business " (Adam Smith), should we say that the real net income of the butcher is the same as that of his neighbour in a common trade ?

The preceding ambiguities are common to individual and social income (which is the sum of the incomes of individuals) ; the following is peculiar to social income : "Is the richness of a nation to be measured by the aggregate money-income of its inhabitants, or by their average income" ? Prof. Marshall, who asks this question, suggests that "a rough notion of the economic strength of a nation . . . may be got by multiplying the aggregate income of its inhabitants by their average income."

It is fortunate that some of these difficulties disappear when the object is only to compare the incomes of different nations, or of the same nation, at different epochs. If the compared incomes are calculated on a uniform though imperfect plan, the ratios between the results are apt to be trustworthy (cp. Nicholson's *Principles of Political Economy,* p. 216) ; provided that account is taken of differences in the value of money. An example of the latter correction is afforded by Sir R. Giffen's estimates of the growth of capital, which are based upon the growth of income.

[The most philosophical treatment of the subject known to the writer is to be found in Prof. Marshall's *Principles* in the chapter on "Income" (bk. ii.), and the sections relating to "National Dividend" (see Index). See also preface to 3rd edition. The statistics in the other works which have been referred to also deserve attention.] F. Y. E.

INCOME TAX IN THE UNITED KINGDOM.

History, p. 375; Scope of the Tax, p. 375; Basis of Charge, p. 376; Exemptions, p. 376; Inequalities, p. 377; Differentiation, p. 377; Graduation, p. 377; Incidence, p. 378; Rate and Yield, p. 378.

History.—It is only within the last century that a general income tax, imposed alike on profits derived from property, from trade and commerce, and from personal exertions, has become a normal method of levying taxation. In England a graduated tax, sometimes called an income tax, was levied in 1435 and again in 1450, but these taxes, as Thorold ROGERS points out, fell short of the scope of a general income-tax, being levied only on those who possessed fixed sources of personal revenues (*Economic Interpretation of History*, p. 130; see also Dowell's *History of Taxation*, vol. i. pp. 112 and 116). In the reign of Henry VIII. taxes levied on earnings were imposed, but unsuccessfully, and from this time until the close of the 18th century no further attempt seems to have been made to levy a general income-tax.

Even under the great strain on our finances caused by the French war, it was with reluctance that W. PITT made, in 1798, the great experiment of imposing a general income-tax, and he only did so after the failure of his attempt to arrive indirectly at the taxation of income by means of his celebrated plan of the TRIPLE ASSESSMENT (*q.v.*). The income-tax imposed by Pitt was repealed on the conclusion of the Treaty of Amiens; but the tax was reimposed within a year by Addington, and remained in force until the end of the war. In 1842 Sir Robert PEEL revived the tax to enable him to introduce fiscal reforms, and to improve the commerce and manufactures of the kingdom. It was intended that the revival should only be temporary, but the tax had now ceased to be a war-tax, and since 1842 it has maintained its place as one of the recognised means of meeting ordinary expenditure. In 1853 the area of the tax, which had previously been confined to Great Britain, was extended to include Ireland.

On one occasion only since 1842 has a serious proposal been made for the immediate repeal of the tax. On the dissolution of parliament in 1874, the prime minister (Mr. Gladstone) in a manifesto to his constituents announced his view that the circumstances of the time rendered it practicable to confer on the country the advantage and relief of the total repeal of the tax, which it had been the "happy fortune" of Mr. Lowe to reduce from 6d. to 3d. But on the re-assembling of parliament, Mr. Gladstone's government found themselves in a minority and resigned. Their successors retained the tax, reducing it however to 2d., the lowest rate at which it has ever stood. If the proposed repeal had been effected, chancellors of the exchequer would have been deprived of the most elastic of taxes, by the aid of which it is always possible to balance a budget; and it is difficult to see how the expenditure of subsequent years could have been met without reviving the tax.

Scope of the Tax.—The Income Tax Acts charge with duty income derived from every source in the United Kingdom, whether the person to whom the income accrues resides in the United Kingdom or abroad; and also income received in the United Kingdom by persons residing in this country from foreign or colonial sources. The duties are ranged under five schedules of charge (16 & 17 Vict. c. 34, § 2) as follows:

Schedule A imposes a duty on the owners of lands and houses in the United Kingdom. *Schedule B* on the occupiers of lands in the United Kingdom. *Schedule C* on annuities, dividends, and interest payable in the United Kingdom on government securities, British, colonial, or foreign. *Schedule D* on annual profits arising to persons residing in the United Kingdom from any kind of property wheresoever situate, or from any profession, trade, employment, or vocation wheresoever carried on; on annual profits arising to persons not resident in the United Kingdom from property situate, or from any profession, trade, employment, or vocation exercised, in the United Kingdom; and on interest of money, annuities, and other annual profits and gains. *Schedule E* on income derived from public offices or employments of profit, and on annuities, pensions, or stipends payable by Her Majesty or out of the public revenue of the United Kingdom. These familiar schedules of charge had their origin in 1803. The tax imposed by Pitt was levied on a general return made by each taxpayer of his income from every source. But in 1803 the present system of charging income-tax upon all property and profit at their first source was introduced, with the twofold object of reducing the temptations to evasion, and of preventing unnecessary disclosure of the amount of the total income of the taxpayers. It is to the adoption of this system that the success which has attended the administration of the English income-tax is mainly due. The duty charged on lands and houses is collected from the occupier, who is empowered, on payment of his rent, to deduct the duty applicable thereto; and the landlord in turn is entitled to deduct a proportionate amount of duty from any ground rent, annuity, rent charge, interest, or other annual sum secured on the property. In like manner the profits derived from a trade or business are assessable in one sum on the company, firm, or person carrying on the concern, and the burden is distributed amongst the persons who are entitled to share in the profits, or to receive dividends, interest, or other annual payments thereout, by deduction of a proportionate amount of duty from each payment. Dividends and interest payable out of untaxed sources, by the agents in England of foreign or colonial governments or companies, are charged in the hands of such agents ; and, wherever practicable, provision is made for the assessment of the tax on distributors of profits, who have no personal interest in escaping payment, instead of on the ultimate recipients. The produce of the tax in 1803 under this system, at the rate of 5 per cent, was almost equal to the produce of the 10 per cent duty levied in 1799 upon the general returns of the individual taxpayers.

Basis of Charge.—Assessments under Schedule A on lands and houses are based in Great Britain on the rack-rental value of the property, subject to the deduction of land tax and certain other public burdens imposed by law on the owners ; in Ireland on the poor-law valuation, subject to reduction in cases where such valuation exceeds the rental value. Until 1894 no allowance was granted in respect of the cost of repairs, insurance, and other expenses incidental to the maintenance of the property in a condition to command its existing rent. But the Finance Act 1894, which equalised the death duties chargeable on realty and personalty, also made provision for the reduction of the income-tax assessment on the gross value of lands and houses under Schedule A by a sum equal in the case of lands to one-eighth, and in the case of houses to one-sixth, of the assessment. Under Schedule B, the farmers' schedule, assessments are also made on the full annual value, but at a lower rate of duty. Dividends and interest chargeable under Schedule C, and the salaries of offices chargeable under Schedule E, are assessed on the actual amount receivable within the year. Under Schedule D assessments are based on an estimate arrived at by taking in some cases, the average profit for the three preceding years, in others, the profits of the preceding or the estimated profits of the current year. Mines are assessable under Schedule A, but according to the rules of Schedule D, on the average profits of the five preceding years, and quarries, ironworks, gasworks, waterworks, railways, etc., on the profits of the year preceding. It is the practice to allow relief at the end of the year when the profits have diminished.

Exemptions.—Of the exemptions from duty granted by the Income Tax Acts, by far the most important are those in favour of persons with small incomes. The extension of these exemptions has been a marked feature of the income-tax legislation of recent years. When Pitt introduced the income-tax in 1799, he exempted persons whose incomes were under £60, and imposed lower rates on incomes under £200. Subsequently, these exemptions were withdrawn entirely in the case of incomes from realised property ; whilst in the case of profits from professions, trades, and offices, the limit of exemption was reduced to £50, and of partial relief to £150. On the revival of the tax by Peel in 1842, exemption was granted to persons whose total incomes from whatever source derived were under £150. This relief was somewhat curtailed in 1853, when Mr. Gladstone introduced an act which exempted incomes under £100, and imposed a reduced rate of duty on incomes between £100 and £150. Ten years later, Mr. Gladstone substituted for the reduced rate on incomes below £150 an abatement of £60 to incomes under £200. In 1872, Mr. Lowe (Lord SHERBROOKE) carried still further the relief of small incomes by granting an abatement of £80 to incomes under £300. In 1876, Sir Stafford Northcote (Lord IDDESLEIGH) exempted incomes under £150 and allowed an abatement of £120 to incomes under £400. And now the Finance Act 1894, introduced by Sir W. Harcourt, exempts incomes which do not exceed £160, and allows an abatement of £160 to incomes not exceeding £400, and of £100 to incomes not exceeding £500. The relief of small incomes is obviously carried to a point far beyond the exemption of the necessary means of subsistence. The statesmen responsible for our finances have defended the relief mainly on the practical ground that it is impossible to levy the tax on the wages of labour ; and to avoid the anomalies which would arise if the tax came into full operation at any given point, it has been thought better to graduate the transition. The relief given has also been defended on the ground that it tends to correct the inequality which arises from the greater proportional pressure of the taxes on articles of consumption on persons with small incomes. The Income Tax Acts also grant exemptions in favour of the buildings of any college or hall in the universities, or of any hospital, public school, or almshouse ; of income legally applicable and applied to charitable purposes ; and of the property and income of registered friendly societies. Savings banks, industrial and provident societies, and the provident funds of trade unions are also entitled to a certain measure of relief. The exemption in favour of payments for life insurance, and of payments to secure deferred annuities, is especially noteworthy. It is of course a partial exemption in favour of savings, and was introduced by Mr. Gladstone in 1853, admittedly as a concession to the general feeling that a man ought to have at any rate the opportunity of investing· his savings without being liable to income - tax upon them (Hansard, vol. 125, p. 1385). The deduction under this head is restricted to a sum not exceeding one-sixth part of the assurer's chargeable income.

Inequalities.—The income - tax has been much criticised, especially in its earlier years, on the ground of its inquisitorial nature and of the alleged inequality of its incidence. Unfortunately an income-tax which entirely ceased to be inquisitorial would in great measure cease to be effective ; but in England this objection has been minimised as far as possible by the assessment of income at its first source in the manner already described. The inequalities of the income tax have been much discussed both in and out of parliament, and the whole subject was thoroughly investigated by the select committees appointed for the purpose in 1851-52 and 1861. One of the main objections formerly alleged against the tax was that no allowance was granted from the assessments upon lands and houses in respect of the portion of the rent which was not available as income, being applied to the maintenance of the property in insurance and repairs. This defect has been remedied by the Finance Act 1894, not indeed by the allowance of the actual outgoings in each individual case, which would involve immense difficulty and friction, but by an all-round deduction calculated to do substantial justice in the great majority of cases. Other objections raised against the scheme of the tax were that it charged savings as well as expenditure ; that it taxed all incomes at the same rate, whether they were permanent or temporary, spontaneous or earned ; and that capital was sometimes taxed as well as income, as in the case of (1) capital given as the consideration for annuities for years or life, which is taxed in the annuity through which it is being repaid with interest, and (2) capital in the course of realisation through the working of mines, which is taxed in the assessment of the entire value of their produce. The committee of 1852 separated without being able to agree in any recommendation, and contented themselves with merely reporting the evidence taken. But the committee of 1861 arrived at the conclusion that no plan had been proposed to them which afforded a basis for a practicable and equitable re-adjustment of the income tax, and that the objections urged against it were objections to its nature and essence rather than to the particular shape which had been given to it.

Differentiation.—In recent years, however, the proposal to impose differential rates of duty under which industrial incomes shall be taxed more lightly than spontaneous incomes has been once more revived. The principle of a differential income tax has received the powerful support of J. S. MILL (*Principles of Political Economy*, bk. v. ch. 2, § 4). Mill would have preferred, if it were possible, to tax only the part of income devoted to expenditure, exempting that which is saved ; on the ground that unless savings are exempted, the contributors are twice taxed on what they save, and only once on what they spend. But he considered that "if no plan can be devised for the exemption of actual savings, sufficiently free from liability to fraud, it is necessary, as the next thing in point of justice, to take into account in assessing the tax what the different classes of contributors ought to save. And there would probably be no other mode of doing this than the rough expedient of two different rates of assessment. There would be great difficulty in taking into account differences of duration between one terminable income and another ; and in the most frequent case, that of incomes dependent on life, differences of age and health would constitute such extreme diversity as it would be impossible to take proper cognisance of." Fawcett (*Manual of Political Economy*, bk. iv. ch. 2) discusses the question at some length. He allows that the income tax ought not to be levied at a uniform rate, if the principle is admitted that each single tax should be so adjusted that every individual should contribute to it in proportion to his ability. He points out, however, that this is impossible in the case of other taxes, and considers that equality of taxation can be best secured, not by botching and patching each single tax, but by contemplating the revenue as a whole. After reviewing some of the obstacles to any attempt to levy the income tax in such a way that each individual should contribute to it in proportion to his means, he adopts the conclusion that the present method of levying the tax cannot with advantage be changed. And this is the view which has been taken by our greatest financial statesmen. Disraeli (Lord Beaconsfield), when he was for the first time chancellor of the exchequer in 1852, unsuccessfully proposed to introduce a differential tax, but he did not afterwards repeat the attempt. On the other hand Pitt, Peel, Gladstone, and others have resisted the introduction of a differential duty. On one of these occasions Mr. Gladstone said (*Hansard*, vol. 169, p. 1838), "Mr. Pitt and Sir R. Peel have both considered this question, and have both left the tax as a uniform income tax, not indeed as the image of perfection in our fiscal system, but as that form on which, as wise, prudent, and practical men, they found it necessary to take their stand."

Graduation.—Another important question in

relation to the income tax is that of graduation. The relief granted to incomes not exceeding £500 constitutes a substantial graduation of the duty in the case of the majority of the persons who fall within the scope of the tax. But in some quarters the opinion is held that the tax should be graduated not only degressively but progressively. The question of progressive taxation has been dealt with elsewhere (see GRADUATED TAXATION). Here it will suffice to mention that there are grave practical difficulties in the way of applying the principle of progression to the income tax. It certainly would not be worth while to abandon the system of assessing income at its source in order to impose higher rates of duty on the larger incomes ; and even if the progressive duties were levied by a separate supplementary assessment, it would be impossible to prevent considerable evasion, and the procedure and penalties necessary to ensure a tolerable degree of accuracy would probably be regarded as very harsh and inquisitorial.

Incidence.—The English income tax is a combination of taxes on rent, profits, and wages, and its incidence is the same as that of separate taxes on those sources of income respectively (see TAXATION, INCIDENCE OF). Bastable (*Public Finance*, p. 436) says : "Taxes on rents, on the higher kinds of wages, or on employers' gains, are not easily shifted. Even in the case of interest, unless the growth of capital is checked, a tax tends to remain on the payer. Therefore speaking broadly we may say that the shifting of an income tax is not to be expected, and in the rare cases where it does happen, is brought about, either by a check in the growth of capital through diminished interest, or by disturbances in the relations of the several industries and trades through its action." And Seligman (*Shifting and Incidence of Taxation*, p. 179) says : "The tax on economic rent and net profits cannot be shifted, so that for all members of the community, except the wage earners, an income tax levied on pure income would indeed tend to stay where it is put. And in so far as the lowest incomes are exempted from the tax, the tendency would also be for the income tax on the labourer to stay where it is put."

Rate and Yield.—The income tax is imposed annually at rates varying according to the financial requirements of the year. The war tax of the early part of the century was levied chiefly at the rate of 2s. in the £. In 1842 the tax was imposed at the rate of 7d. in the £, and so remained for twelve years. It has varied greatly since, touching its highest point (1s. 4d. in 1855 and 1856) during the Crimean War, and its lowest, 2d., in 1874 and 1875. From 1888 to 1892 it stood at 6d., but rose to 7d. in 1893, and 8d. in 1894. The following table gives the rate and yield of the tax at decennial intervals since 1842.

Year.	Rate.	Net produce.	Yield per penny.
1842-43	7d.	5,405,161	772,166
1852-53	7d.	5,670,030	810,004
1862-63	9d.	10,731,673	1,192,408
1872-73	4d.	6,964,353	1,741,088
1882-83	6½d.	12,758,661	1,962,871
1892-93	6d.	13,439,300	2,239,883

[Robinson, *Laws relating to the Income Tax*, 1895.—Dowell's *Income Tax Laws*, 4th ed. 1895. —Ellis's *Income Tax Acts*, 3rd ed. 1893.—*Pratt's Income Tax*, by Ward, 1885.—Dowell's *History of Taxation and Taxes in England*, 2nd ed. 1888.— Cobden, *Speeches, etc.*, 1878. Annual reports of Commissioners of Inland Revenue, especially 1857, 1870, and 1885. Reports of Select Committees on Income Tax 1851-52, and 1861. Hansard's Debates.] F. E. N. B.

INCOME-TAX ON THE CONTINENT OF EUROPE.

Austria, p. 379 ; Bavaria, Wurtemburg, and Mecklenburg, p. 379 ; Germany, Prussia, and North German States, p. 378 ; Holland, p. 379 ; Italy, p. 379 ; Switzerland, p. 379.

Continental writers use the equivalents of the word "income-tax" (Einkommensteuer, impôt sur le revenu, imposta sui redditi) to designate a tax levied on individuals in respect of the whole of their income ; the taxes which are deducted from income as it arises, or levied on the objects from which income is derived, are generally designated by other names (*e.g.* Ertragsteuer). Taxes of the first kind are, as a rule, included by scientific writers among "subjective" taxes, whilst the last-mentioned taxes are called "objective." The rate of income-tax in most continental countries is not adjusted from year to year according to the position of the budget, but is fixed once for all by statute.

Some kind of income-tax exists in Germany, Austria, Switzerland, Italy ; in France the tax called "personnelle mobilière" could not be called income-tax in any sense, and the proposal of a regular income-tax has hitherto been considered too revolutionary to meet with any chance of success.

The principal characteristics of continental income-taxes will appear from the following statement :

1. *Germany.*—The empire has no direct taxes of any kind, but the individual states have income-taxes of some sort. They may be divided into three groups :

(*a*) *Prussia.*—Up to a recent period Prussia had a general income-tax, and certain additional objective taxes, viz. taxes on revenue from land, buildings, and trades. The latter, since the 1st April 1895, have been transferred to the local authorities. The central government now receives a general income-tax, that is, a tax on the whole income of each individual. The tax is progressive, and rises by steps from about $\frac{5}{8}$ per cent to about 4 per cent. In addition to the general income-tax, there is a tax on income from funded property, which is a complementary tax (Ergänzungsteuer) intended to give an advantage to income derived from productive employment. It is levied on the capital value on the whole of each person's real and personal property (not including furniture and movable goods not attached to land, or used as plant for purposes of trade), and is about $\frac{1}{20}$ per cent of the assessed value of the capital which, taking the average return on capital to be 4 per cent, is equal to about $1\frac{1}{4}$ per cent on the income. The Prussian laws relating to income-tax and complementary tax are dated respectively 1891 and 1893; the latter did not come into force until the 1st January 1895.

(*b*) The other *North German States* (excepting *Mecklenburg*) and the *Grand Duchies of Baden* and *Hesse* have a general income-tax, and some additional objective taxes.

(*c*) *Bavaria*, *Wurtemberg*, and *Mecklenburg* have no general subjective income-tax, but a number of objective taxes, viz. taxes on income from land, from buildings, from trades, and from investments. Bavaria has a partial income-tax, intended to affect incomes not coming under the above heads, viz. income from (i) wages below $1\frac{4}{5}$ marks per diem; (ii) professions and farming; (iii) wages above $1\frac{4}{5}$ marks per diem, and salaries. In the first-named class the tax is a fixed amount for each person; in the second class the incomes are sub-divided into categories, each charged with a fixed rate varying from $\frac{1}{3}$ per cent to 1 per cent; in the third class the tax is progressive, the first 1020 marks of each income pay $\frac{1}{3}$ per cent, the next 510 marks $\frac{2}{3}$ per cent, and the rest of the income pays 1 per cent. Wurtemberg has also a similar partial income-tax.

2. *Austria* has a very complicated system. There is no general income-tax. The tax on revenue from land and from Austrian investments is generally deducted at the source. There is no tax on income from foreign investments, and Austrian loans are frequently issued as bearing interest free of income-tax. There is an assessed income-tax on (*a*) income derived from trade, small traders being exempted; (*b*) income derived from professions, salaries, and wages, workmen and domestic servants being exempted; (*c*) income from interest on loans from which the tax is not deducted on payment, and which is not exempted from tax. The tax on income from trades and on interest is 5 per cent, but traders are also subject to an objective tax; the tax on income from professions and salaries is progressive, and rises from 1 per cent to 10 per cent. Additions are made to the regular tax according to the financial requirements of each year, and as they have of late amounted to 100 per cent of the regular tax, the rates seem very high. It appears, however, that the authorities are very lenient in respect of the assessments, and only government officials, whose tax is deducted from their salaries, are the sufferers.

3. *Switzerland*.—In the Swiss cantons there is generally a property-tax, assessed on the capital value of all funded property, but the value in many cases is assigned on the basis of annual income. In addition to this property-tax, most cantons have a supplementary income-tax, which affects income not derived from taxed property. In Basel-stadt and in Basel-land there are general income-taxes in addition to the property-taxes; but in Basel-land, interest derived from invested capital is exempted from income-tax.

4. *Italy*.—All income, except income derived from land, is subject to a general income-tax, which, however, is deducted at the source in respect of dividends and interest on investments, payable in Italy, and salaries. The tax amounts to $13\frac{1}{5}$ per cent, but the various kinds of incomes are differentiated in the following manner: (*a*) income from investments is assessed at the full amount; (*b*) income derived partly from capital and partly from work, such as income derived from industry or trade, is assessed at $\frac{3}{4}$ of the full amount; (*c*) income derived exclusively from work, such as professional income, income derived from salaries or wages, not coming under the next head, is assessed at $\frac{5}{8}$ of the full amount; (*d*) income received in respect of salary by government, provincial, or municipal officials, is assessed at $\frac{1}{2}$ of the full amount. Special rules are applicable to farmers, and there is an elaborate system of exemptions and deductions in respect of smaller incomes.

5. *Holland*.—Recent legislation (1892-93) has introduced a system by which income from funded property is more heavily taxed than other income, though the distinction is not as marked as in Prussia. A property tax is charged on the surplus value of a person's real and personal property over 10,000 florins (property, the value of which does not exceed 13,000 florins, being exempt, and real property not being assessed at its full selling value). This tax rises from $\frac{1}{8}$ per cent to $\frac{1}{5}$ per cent, and —on the basis of an annual return on capital of 4 per cent—is equivalent to a tax on income rising from 1 per cent to 5 per cent; there is also a tax on income not derived from property, which rises from 2 per cent to $3\frac{1}{5}$ per cent (incomes not exceeding 650 florins being exempt).

[See articles "Einkommensteuer," and "Vermögensteuer," in *Handwörterbuch der Staatswissenschaften*, and the works therein referred to; see also Wagner, *Finanzwissenschaft*, vol. ii.—Roscher, *Finanzwissenschaft*.—Meyer, *Deutsches Verwaltungsrecht*.— Bastable. *Public Finance*,

1892.—Greven, "Fiscal Reform in Holland" (*Econ. Journal*, vol. iii. p. 534).]   E. S.

INCOME TAX IN THE UNITED STATES.

An income tax was levied by the act of August 5, 1861, as part of the extraordinary financial legislation to supply revenue for the carrying on of the civil war. Incomes over $800 (£160) were taxed three per cent. The rates were increased by subsequent legislation and incomes under $1000 (£200) exempted. The tax was not levied after 1872. The largest amount collected in one year was in 1866, $72,982,159 (£14,596,432), or about 14 per cent of the net ordinary receipts. The tax was never regarded with favour, though in recent years its re-adoption has been under discussion. An income tax is levied in a few states for local purposes, as in Massachusetts upon all professional incomes above $2000 (£400), and in Pennsylvania upon the incomes of certain businesses.

[For the federal income tax, see *Reports of Commissioners of Internal Revenue*, 1863-1872 ; and for local income taxes, consult index in Ely's *Taxation in American States and Cities*.]   D. R. D.

INCONVERTIBLE CURRENCY (see IDEAL MONEY).

Inconvertible is predicated of paper money for which coin is not obtainable on demand. A paper currency may become inconvertible by a suspension of specie payments, such as the English bank restriction (see BULLION COMMITTEE, REPORT OF) ; or it may be inconvertible from the first, like the French ASSIGNATS. It often purports to be based upon, or to "represent" real wealth,—for instance in Pennsylvania last century there was a paper currency based upon the security of land, "coined land" (Franklin), and in Connecticut taxes were assigned for the redemption of the paper.

The value of an inconvertible paper currency depends upon circumstances common to all kinds of money, namely the quantity and efficiency of the circulation compared with the volume of transactions ; and circumstances peculiar to this kind of money, namely that the supply is not regulated by cost of production, that the demand is limited to a particular country, and varies according as the currency is received by the people with more or less distrust.

From these peculiarities we may judge of the use of an inconvertible currency. The advantage of dispensing with a reserve of precious metal—an advantage which may be very great in time of emergency such as war—is counterbalanced by the danger of depreciation through over-issue. This danger has often proved fatal : *e.g.* the French assignats which were depreciated to nearly $\frac{1}{170}$ (White), or even $\frac{1}{30500}$ (Macleod), of their face value ; and the American "continental currency," which was depreciated to $\frac{1}{1000}$ (Walker). But this danger may be avoided by caution. The notes of the Bank of France were depreciated upon suspension of payment in specie by only two or three per

cent during the revolution of 1848, and scarcely by $1\frac{1}{2}$ per cent during the war of 1870,—differences hardly appreciable in practice.

The value of an inconvertible paper money is liable to fluctuate from the absence of that automatic regulator which the foreign exchanges constitute in the case of convertible paper, and also from variations in popular confidence. A remedy for the evil of fluctuation—as well as that of depreciation—is afforded by the rule that the market price and the mint price of bullion should be the same (see DEPRECIATION). But the remedy may appear imperfect to those who hold that a suspension of payment tends to depreciate not only the value of notes in relation to gold, but also that of gold in relation to commodities—an opinion which has been disputed by Tooke and entertained by Walker (Tooke, *History of Prices*, pt. iii. especially ch. i., and summaries to the other chapters ; Walker, *Money*, ch. xvii.). An ideally more perfect method of regulating an inconvertible paper currency would be to make its value correspond to a TABULAR STANDARD. A paper so regulated would have an advantage in point of stability over the precious metals. But the realisation of this idea is utopian.

[The subject is treated in almost all the general works on political economy and those of which the special subject is money. Mill's chapter on inconvertible currency (*Pol. Econ.*, bk. iii. ch. xiii.) leaves little to be desired except the idea of a standard other than the precious metals for testing the depreciation of paper money. This idea is supplied by Professor F. A. Walker in his *Money*, together with much interesting historical matter and numerous references (see also INFLATION).]   F. Y. E.

INCORPORATION OF COMPANIES.

Companies may be "incorporated" (invested with the rights of corporate bodies) by special act of parliament, by royal charter, or under the Companies Acts. The first-named method of incorporation is usually adopted in the case of railway, canal, and similar companies : the second has become exceptional, the incorporation under the companies acts being now most frequently resorted to. The Companies Act 1862, § 18, provides that upon the registration of the memorandum and—where necessary—of the articles of association, the registrar of joint-stock companies is to issue a certificate of incorporation, and that thereupon a company is to become capable of exercising all the functions of an incorporated company. As the memorandum and articles are complete on being signed by seven members, whose holding may be restricted to a merely nominal amount, it will be seen that the incorporation of a company does not in any way prove that it has any substantial existence, and bills have from time to time been submitted to parliament by which it was endeavoured to impose more stringent conditions on the incorporation of companies. None of these bills have as yet found favour with the legislature.   E. S.

INCORPOREAL PROPERTY. The legal distinction between things corporeal and incorporeal first appears in the Roman system. "Corporeal things are those which by their constitution admit of being handled, such as land, a man, clothing, gold, silver, and in a word numberless other things. Incorporeal things are those which cannot be touched, such as those which have only a legal existence, like an inheritance, a usufruct, or obligations however contracted" (*Institutes of Justinian*, bk. ii. pt. ii.). An inheritance in Roman law, it must be remembered, meant the sum total of the proprietary rights and liabilities of a person deceased. This legal distinction was itself derived from a philosophical distinction made by the Stoics between objects of sense and objects of the intelligence. But it involves a confusion of thought. For it is clear that the corporeal things of Roman law are the objects of rights and liabilities, whilst the incorporeal things are rights or liabilities themselves. In the English law of real property the distinction between things corporeal and incorporeal is used in a still more arbitrary way. Lands and houses are said to be corporeal hereditaments. A reversion, a remainder, rights of common, rent charges, and advowsons are said to be incorporeal hereditaments. Under the rules of the common law different modes of transfer were applicable to corporeal and to incorporeal hereditaments respectively. For the transfer of corporeal property a delivery actual or symbolic was necessary. It was said to *lie in livery*. Incorporeal property was supposed not to admit of delivery. It was therefore transferred by means of a writing and was said to *lie in grant*. This practical difference was, however, abolished by the act 8 & 9 Vict. c. 106. The distinction between corporeal and incorporeal hereditaments has no rational foundation. The corporeal hereditaments are objects of rights; the incorporeal hereditaments are peculiar species of rights. A right in possession is just as incorporeal as a right in reversion, whilst the object of the right, say a house, is equally corporeal in either case.

The distinction between things corporeal and things incorporeal may, however, be used in a more rational way. If by proprietary rights we understand rights available against all the world as opposed to rights only available against particular persons and capable of pecuniary valuation, we find that some proprietary rights have definite material objects corresponding to them, whilst other proprietary rights have no such object. Thus to the right of ownership always corresponds a particular horse, house, book, etc. But nothing of the sort corresponds to a copyright or patent right. He who has the copyright in a book has merely the right to prevent

any other person from publishing it. He who has taken out a patent for an invention has simply the right to prevent any other person from applying the invention. It is not the control over the material object, the manuscript or the model,—for that the owner already possesses to the fullest extent, it is the forbearance of others from certain actions which make a copyright or patent right valuable, and which may be said to be the object of either right. The same reflection applies to the right in a trademark.

The importance of rights of this class would hardly be recognised except in a high stage of economic and legal development. In so far as their recognition secures an adequate reward to the creative faculties of man, it is a potent means of economic progress. But the distinction between things corporeal and things incorporeal as hitherto drawn in legal systems is of little value for jurisprudence and of no consequence for economics.

[Moyle, *Institutes of Justinian*.—Williams, *Law of Real Property*.—Holland, *Jurisprudence*. See also IMMATERIAL CAPITAL.]   F. C. M.

INCREASING RETURNS. From the time when DIMINISHING RETURNS (*q.v.*) to agricultural industry first began to attract attention it was held that the returns to manufacturing industry increase with the increase of the absolute amount of labour employed. The contrast between agriculture and manufactures in this respect was pointed out by Malthus (*Nature and Progress of Rent*, 1815, p. 45), West (*Application of Capital to Land*, p. 7), and M'Culloch (*Political Economy*, 1st ed. pp. 277-278). It was elaborated by Senior (*Political Economy*, 8vo ed. pp. 81-86) and J. S. Mill (*Principles*, bk. iv. ch. ii. §§ 1-3). The tendency of later writers has been rather to soften the contrast ; they insist upon the fact that up to a certain point agriculture gives increasing returns and that manufactures are subject to diminishing returns inasmuch as they require both raw materials and space (Marshall, *Economics of Industry*, 1879, pp. 21-26, 89-90). In *Principles*, vol. i. bk. iv. ch. xiii. § 3, Prof. Marshall says, "While the part which nature plays in production conforms to the law of diminishing return, the part which man plays conforms to the law of increasing return."

[An interesting review of the various standpoints from which the laws of increasing and diminishing returns have been laid down will be found in J. R. Commons, *The Distribution of Wealth*, 1893. See also J. H. Hollander in *Quart. Journ. of Ecs.*, January 1895.]   E. C.

INCREMENT, THE UNEARNED. 1. *What is meant by the Unearned Increment.*—Although the germ of the idea may be traced in the *Wealth of Nations*, and is distinctly seen in Ricardo's *Principles*, the term "unearned increment" was first invented by J. S. Mill. By "unearned increment" is meant that increase in the value of anything subject to a natural monopoly which is due not to the expenditure of capital, labour, or skill by the proprietor, but to the general progress of society resulting in an increased demand for that thing. An unearned increment may thus arise upon any kind of property of which the supply cannot be increased, e.g. the pictures of a dead artist. But the only kind of property usually considered with reference to the unearned increment is land. For land is the most important thing subject to a natural monopoly. Land is essential to the human race, as affording them room for their habitation, food to maintain life, and the raw material for all their industry. The extent of land available is also limited. True, the limit is not absolute. Much of the surface of the globe lies as yet unused and even unexplored. Even in civilised and populous countries there is always some land allowed to lie waste or far less improved than it might be. But the land not yet used or improved is land which, on account of position, or climate, or infertility, or some other disadvantage, is comparatively inconvenient. Mankind resort first to the land which is, under all the circumstances, most convenient to them. This land is so far limited that with the progress of society and the recourse had to less favoured land, economic rent makes its appearance. Economic rent, a thing quite distinct from rent in the ordinary sense, represents an unearned increment. But even if all the land belonging to a community were equally suitable for every purpose, its value would rise with the progress of the community and there would result an unearned increment.

The growth of the unearned increment in a progressive society is not uniform or uninterrupted. In the case of arable land, the unearned increment may be reduced or even annihilated by such causes as agricultural improvements or better means of communication which open up new sources of supply. Thus over a great part of rural England at the present day the rent actually obtainable represents a very moderate return on the capital which the landlords or their predecessors in title have expended on the improvement of the land and the buildings. Economic rent and unearned increment have not merely ceased to grow but have for the time being disappeared. Similar fluctuations may occur with reference to property in mines. Setting aside the depreciation resulting from progressive exhaustion, mines usually tend to become more and more valuable as society advances in prosperity. The increased demand for minerals and the improvement of means of transport bring an unearned increment to the mine-owner. But in this case also, the progress of society may open up new sources of supply and lessen the value of the old. Thus

the working of silver mines in Europe has been made unprofitable by the competition of far richer mines in America and Australia. Here therefore economic rent and unearned increment have been annihilated. The most striking illustration of the unearned increment is afforded by land which derives its value from situations, such as the building sites in or near great cities. The advantage of situation is a monopoly of the strictest kind. It cannot be communicated to land which does not naturally possess it. It is so valuable that wealthy individuals or corporations will pay almost any price to obtain it. The shopkeeper who desires the custom of the rich must have premises in a fashionable street. The millionaire who desires the pleasures of good society must have a mansion in a fashionable quarter. A great bank must have its principal office in a central part of the capital. A great warehouse must be situated conveniently with respect to docks or railway stations. Many persons are obliged to live close to the place where they do their work, and there is a great deal of work which can be performed only in places possessing a peculiar advantage of situation. Owing to these and similar circumstances the competition for good sites in a great city is extraordinarily keen. Within recent years land in the city of London has been known to sell at the rate of £150,000 per acre, or higher, whilst excellent arable land within thirty miles of London has been sold for considerably less than £10 an acre. The whole difference between these prices may be regarded as an unearned increment (see BETTERMENT).

2. *The Unearned Increment as a subject of Taxation.*—With the progress of democratic ideas and of the desire to impose taxation as far as possible upon property, it was natural that proposals should be made for transferring to the state the unearned increment, which is the result not of the exertions of proprietors, but of the general growth of society. Such proposals differ chiefly as they are more or less far-reaching. They may be distinguished into three classes accordingly as they (1) contemplate the transfer of the ownership of land from private persons to the state, or (2) whilst contemplating the continuance of private property in land, would involve the appropriation of the unearned increment by the state, or (3) provide for such appropriation only in the case of unearned increment arising from special causes.

3. *Criticism of these Proposals.*—(1) Proposals of the first class are sometimes extended to every species of landed property, and sometimes are restricted to certain species on which the unearned increment happens to be unusually large, such as mines or building sites in cities and towns. When they extend to all kinds of land they amount to schemes for what is termed land nationalization, a subject too extensive

to be properly discussed here (see LAND, NATIONALIZATION OF). Shortly it may be said that such proposals have the appearance of a certain logical completeness, but would involve enormous practical unfairness in execution. Proposals for the transfer of particular kinds of landed property from private individuals to the state may be less difficult to carry out although less logical in theory. Upon the foundation of a colony it may be practicable to retain as a public patrimony land possessing special advantages of situation or of mineral wealth. But in any old country where private property in land of all kinds has been fully established for many centuries, schemes for the acquisition of urban land by municipal bodies, or of mines by the state, are not likely to be carried out. If fair compensation were given the operation would be perilous, for the public authority would have incurred the fixed charge of an immense debt in return for a property which might at any moment suffer depreciation through a decline of national prosperity. If no compensation or nominal compensation were given, the confiscation of the land in question would involve such an attack on rights of property as would amount to a revolution. In this case it is unlikely that private ownership of other sorts of land could survive.

(2) Proposals of the second class would not involve the abolition of private property in land. They are directed to the taxation of landowners to the extent of the unearned increment. J. S. Mill proposed and Mr. Dawson and other writers have repeated the suggestion that all the land in the United Kingdom should be subjected to a periodic official valuation and that the state should take for itself any increase in value which could not be shown to be due to the labour and capital of the proprietors. Schemes of this kind are not open to the moral or political objections which may be made to all schemes of confiscation. But their execution would involve serious difficulties. If Mill's proposal were applied to agricultural land, it would be found almost impossible to say how much of a growth in value was due to the general progress of society and how much to improvements effected by the proprietors. If the state were to call periodically for their accounts and to allow them the current rate of interest on the capital shown to have been spent in improvements, it would discourage all the most intelligent and useful improvers. For the return upon agricultural improvements is not really uniform. Some never repay their cost ; others are highly profitable. It may also be urged that if the state is to deprive landowners by special enactment of increase of wealth due to the progress of society, the state should also guarantee them against loss of wealth due, not to their own default, but to changes in economic conditions.

(3) Schemes which provide for the appropriation by the state of unearned increment arising from certain special causes only must be considered each on its own merits. One of the most familiar schemes of this kind is known as Betterment (see BETTERMENT). Its object is to secure for municipal authorities the whole or part of the increase in value accruing to town property from the execution of improvements at the public expense.

4. *Conclusion.*—In conclusion, it may be said that no practicable scheme for securing the unearned increment on land to the state has yet been devised. Further it may be doubted whether the subject is of really momentous consequence. It is true that in Great Britain during the past hundred years, and still more in new countries such as the United States, the unearned increment on certain kinds of landed property has been prodigious and has resulted in vast private fortunes. It is natural therefore that reformers should find in the appropriation of the unearned increment a substitute for every other kind of taxation, and should debate upon the good which the national and local authorities might have done with this vast revenue which nobody would have missed. A sceptic might reply that a great revenue which is raised without being felt is usually spent in the most foolish and mischievous manner, as may be seen by the use which our American kinsmen have made of the resources derived from their stringent tariff. But further, it may be urged that the state has an indefinite power of taxation, and that under a democracy, which is the most costly of all forms of government, taxation is always becoming heavier, and is more and more thrown upon property, especially, where land-owners are few, upon landed property. Under these circumstances, it is certain that the national and municipal authorities will in future draw an ample revenue from landed property whether or no any unearned increment has accrued thereon. Lastly, it may be said that the interest taken in the subject of the unearned increment in this country is due to the comparatively small number of landed proprietors amongst whom that increment has been shared. In a country of small proprietors the subject would be too invidious and would be abandoned to theoretical writers.[1]

[See Adam Smith, *Wealth of Nations*, bk. v. ch. ii.—Ricardo, *Principles of Political Economy of Taxation*, ch. x.—Mill, *Principles of Political*

---

[1] The " unearned increment " on land has been referred to throughout this article, as the examples which economic writers have taken have been practically without exception drawn from that particular class of property. The doctrine is, however, theoretically as applicable to every other description of property—for example, to shares in trading companies. Such shares have been known to have risen in price from £1 to £40 in a short space of time. Would the £39 in this case be " unearned increment " ?

Economy, bk. v.—and *Papers on Land Tenure in Dissertations and Discussions*, vol. iv.—Cobden's later speeches.—Dawson, *The Unearned Increment*. Many references to the subject are scattered through the extensive literature relating to RENT.] F. C. M.

INCREMENTUM or CREMENTUM, a term used in mediæval accounts. To understand its exact meaning requires some knowledge of the manner in which a statement of receipt and expenditure was drawn up in the middle ages. The simplest way to explain it will be to take a particular example. Suppose we consider the form of a bailiff's yearly account of the estate under his management. First comes the *onus* or charge beginning " This accountant is charged with," or " This accountant renders account of so much for so and so," mentioning all the items of the year's income : then follows the expenditure account, beginning " of which (money) so much (is expended) in so and so," mentioning all the items of expenditure. At the end, or in the case of the Pipe Rolls at the beginning, is the amount of money handed over by the accountant, and finally the statement *debet* or *quietus est* or *habet de superplus* with the sum owed by him to the estate or by the estate to him, as the case might be. The difference between this and a modern statement of receipt and expenditure is not apparent on the face of it. Consider, however, one typical item, the rental account for instance. On the charge side will be simply : " Rents—so much," without any particulars. On the expenditure side, before the sums spent in repairs etc. will be a number of entries such as " so much for rent unpaid for such and such a house because unlet," or " because its rent has been reduced by that amount," or " because it is in ruins." In fact the charge is the whole rental of the estate as ascertained by a survey made at some time, it might be years before the bailiff entered into office, any diminution of rental being accounted for as a modern bailiff would account for expenditure. Any increase in this rental, owing to new sources of revenue being developed since a survey was made, was called *Incrementum*, and was either accounted for under a separate sub-heading or added to the amount of the charge year by year. This system was carried out to a great extent in all mediæval accounts, the tendency being, whenever possible, to charge the accountant with a definite sum, which did not vary from year to year, and to consider any fluctuations as distinct items of revenue or expenditure under the names of *incrementum* and *allocutiones* or *acquietantiæ*. One of the principal fiscal provisions of Magna Charta, as issued in 1215, was, that the counties should be kept at their old ferms *absque ullo incremento* (see FARM OF THE COUNTIES, PIPE ROLLS).

[Madox, *History of the Exchequer*, London, 1769.]   A. E. S.

INDEMNITÉ (Fr.). Besides the ordinary acceptation of the word indemnity as compensation for damage by individuals or prejudice caused by acts of the authority in the general interest, it is employed in France to designate the payment received by persons exercising public functions unpaid. The indemnity of senators and deputies is fixed by the electoral laws of 1875 at fr. 9000 (£360) a year. If they already exercise an office paid by the state their salary is suspended while they sit in parliament, unless the salary is greater than the indemnity, in which case they receive the difference. The law declares expressly that the functions of municipal councillors are gratuitous, the only exception being the right of the council to allow a sum of money to the mayor to uphold the dignity of his office ; but the Paris municipal councillors, taking advantage of the distinction made between salary and indemnity, have for some years past voted themselves annually an indemnity, first of fr. 4000 (£160) each, afterwards increased to fr. 6000 (£240) for their personal expenses. The illegality of the vote is incontestable, but the government has so far tolerated the infraction of the law.   T. L.

INDEMNITY. A promise whereby one person undertakes to indemnify (to hold harmless) another against a liability undertaken on behalf of indemnifying party. An indemnity must be distinguished from a GUARANTEE (*q.v.*). If a person is entitled to indemnity against a liability he may, when sued in respect of such liability, serve a "third party notice" on the indemnifying party, who will thereupon become bound by the judgment, unless he becomes a party to the action and disputes his liability.   E. S.

INDENTURE. A deed under seal, if made between two or more parties, is called an "indenture"; if it is the deed of one party only, a "deed poll." The first-mentioned name came to be used as deeds executed by several parties were generally copied out twice on the same parchment, which was then separated by an indented division.   E. S.

INDEX NUMBERS are used to indicate changes in the value of money. The objects for which this measurement is undertaken are thus well stated by Sir R. Giffen (Second Report of the committee appointed for the purpose of investigating the best method of ascertaining and measuring variations in the value of the monetary standard. Report of the British Association, 1888) :—(1) The fixation of rents or other deferred payments extending over long periods of time, for which it has been desired to obtain a currency of a more stable sort than money is supposed to be. (2) To enable comparisons to be made between the value of money incomes in different places, which is often an object of great practical interest : not only individuals contemplating residential changes, but also governments and other large spending bodies, spending money in widely distant places, having to consider this question. (3) To enable historians and other students making comparisons between past and present to give an approximate meaning to the money expressions which they deal with, and say roughly what a given fine, or payment, or amount of national revenue or expenditure in a past age would mean in modern language. To which some would add : (4) To afford a measure of the extent to which trade and industry have been injuriously affected by a variation in prices ; and of the correction which it would be desirable to apply to the currency.

An index number is constructed by combining several items, each of which is a ratio between the price of a certain article at a particular date under consideration (*e.g.* last year or month) and the price of the same article at a period taken as base or standard (*e.g.* 1867-77, in the index number constructed by Mr. Sauerbeck, *Journal of the Statistical Society*, 1886 and 1893). These ratios are generally expressed as percentages. *E.g.* the percentage for *flour* in 1885, as given by Mr. Sauerbeck, is 63 ; meaning that the price of flour in 1885 is to the average price of the same article in 1867-77 as 63 : 100. The term index number is sometimes applied (*e.g.* by Mr. Sauerbeck, *op. cit.*) to each of these items, as well as to their combination.

The percentages are usually compounded by taking an AVERAGE of them. But a result of equal generality may be obtained by taking their sum. One of the best-known index numbers, that of the *Economist*, is thus constructed. Twenty-two articles having been selected, the price of each article at the current date compared with its price at the standard period (1845-50) is expressed as a percentage ; and the sum of these percentages is put as the index number. Thus the *Economist* index number for the year 1873 is 2947 ; such a sum is easily reduced to the form of an average by simple division (*e.g.* 2947 ÷ 22 = 134). Accordingly in what follows it will be sufficient to consider the latter form only.

The construction of an index number presents the following problems : (*a*) What are the commodities of which the prices are to be taken ? (*b*) How are the prices to be ascertained ? (*c*) How are the ratios between the prices of each article at the current and the standard dates to be combined ?

The answers to these questions vary according to the purpose in hand (above, pp. 384-5). As appropriate to the first purpose, a standard of deferred payments, two methods present themselves, viz. to arrange that the debtor should pay, the creditor receive, either (1) the same quantity of goods and services, the same amount

of utility, so to speak ; or (2) the product of the same quantity of labour—or more exactly effort and sacrifice.

Of these methods the former has been more generally accepted. It is adopted for instance by the British Association Committee already referred to, as *par excellence* the measure of the change in the value of the monetary standard. The former method is indeed more practicable, perhaps more intelligible. However, in favour of the latter there are some weighty considerations and authorities. It seems to be the nearest possible approach to Ricardo's conception of a commodity invariable in value, "which at all times requires the same sacrifice of toil and labour to produce it" (*Principles*, iii. ch. xx., "On Value and Riches," cp. Mill, bk. iii. ch. xv., "On a Measure of Value"). "A standard," says Mr. Leonard Courtney, "should be something which as far as possible involves the same labour and the same sacrifice in obtaining it" (*Nineteenth Century*, March 1893). Prof. Marshall, in his evidence before the royal commission on gold and silver, says, speaking of appreciation of gold : "When it is used as denoting a rise in the real value of gold, I then regard it as measured by the diminution in the power which gold has of purchasing labour of all kinds—that is, not only manual labour, but the labour of business men and all others engaged in industry of any kind" (Question 9625).

If the first method is adopted, the answers to the questions above set are as follows : (*a*) The commodities of which the prices are to be taken should be articles of consumption rather than materials and implements. Payments for personal services should be included, but not wages in general. (*b*) Retail prices should be used. (*c*) The proper combination of the ratios is an average of the kind technically called *weighted* (see AVERAGE). The general principle according to which the weights are to be assigned is that they should represent the importance of each commodity to the consumer. But this idea may be embodied in different plans.

1. One plan is to assign as the weight of each percentage, or ratio between prices, the value of the corresponding commodity at the initial or standard period. According to this plan the index number is the ratio between these two values : the quantities initially consumed at the prices of the current date, and the same quantities at the standard prices. This method is exemplified by Sir R. Giffen's estimate of the change in the value of money between 1873 (and 1883) and *earlier* years, in his report on prices of exports and imports, 1885, table v.

2. Another plan is to assign, as the relative importance of each percentage, its value at the particular epoch, the current year. This plan is adopted by Mr. Palgrave in his memorandum

on *Currency and Standard of Value* . . . in the third report of the royal commission on depression of trade and industry, table xxvii.

3. According to another plan, the index number is the ratio between the following two values: the quantities consumed at the current date at the current prices, and the same quantities at standard prices. This plan is adopted by Mr. Sauerbeck (*Journ. Stat. Soc.*, 1886, p. 595).

4. Or, instead of taking either the initial quantities or those of the current date, a mean between the two may be taken. This is the plan adopted by the British Association Committee. They estimate "the average national expenditure on each class of article at present and for the last few years"; and put for the relative importance of each commodity a round number corresponding to that estimate. Thus the estimated expenditure per annum on *wheat* is £60,000,000, and on *meat* £100,000,000: that is respectively 6·5 per cent, and 11 per cent of the sum of the corresponding estimates for all the commodities utilised by the committee. As convenient approximations, the weights five and ten are recommended by the committee.

If the index number based on labour (see above, p. 385), rather than on consumption, is adopted as the standard for deferred payments, it would be proper by analogy to take as the measure of appreciation or depreciation the change in the pecuniary remuneration of a certain set of services, namely all, or the principal, which are rendered in the course of production throughout the community during a year, either at the initial or the current epoch; or some expression intermediate between the two specified. But it may be doubted whether the statistics requisite for this method are available.

With regard to the second and third of the purposes above enumerated, the determination of the comparative value of money at distant places and remote times—one or other of the two methods indicated would seem to be theoretically proper.

For the fourth purpose, the regulation of currency, the proper construction of the index number would seem to be as follows: (*a*) The "articles" of which the prices are taken into account should be both commodities and services; (*b*) both wholesale and retail prices should be used; (*c*) the relative importance of each article should be proportioned to the demand upon the currency which it makes. But here as in other parts of the subject theory halts a little, and statistics lag far behind theory.

Considering the theoretical doubts and statistical difficulties which attend the determination of *weights* proper to each purpose, there is much to be said in favour of assigning equal relative importance to all the items; especially if care is taken to include many articles such as *corn*,

cotton, etc., which for any of the purposes which may be contemplated must be of first-rate importance. Such is the character of some of the principal index numbers which have been constructed—those of the *Economist*, of Jevons, of Soetbeer, and of Mr. Sauerbeck.

In the construction of such an index number the use of the arithmetic mean is not imperative. Jevons employs the geometric mean. His reasons for preferring it are not very clear (the "Variation of Prices," *Currency and Finance*, p. 120). A more intelligible explanation is given by Prof. Westergaard (*Wahrscheinlichkeitslehre*) —the geometric mean alone presents a certain consistency between its results, which may be thus indicated. Taking any three dates, x, y, z, put the symbol $\left(\dfrac{y}{x}\right)$ to denote the index number for the date y referred to the date x as standard; with similar interpretations for $\left(\dfrac{z}{x}\right)$ and $\left(\dfrac{z}{y}\right)$. Then $\left(\dfrac{y}{x}\right) \times \left(\dfrac{z}{y}\right) = \left(\dfrac{z}{x}\right)$, as it *ought* by analogy with perfect measurements in other sciences, if the geometric mean be used, but not if any other mean be employed. The geometric mean has also the advantage of being less liable than the ordinary average to be unduly affected by extremely high prices (*Report of the British Association*, 1887, p. 283). The great objection to the geometric mean is its cumbrousness.

There is another kind of mean which has some of the advantages of the geometric, and is free from its essential disadvantage; namely, the median (see AVERAGE), which is formed by arranging the items in the order of magnitude, and taking as the mean that figure which has as many of the items above as below it. For instance the median of the forty-five percentages on which Mr. Sauerbeck's index number is based was, for 1892, 66; while the arithmetic mean was 68. It is difficult to see why the latter result is preferable to the former; if what is required is an *index* of the change in general prices, not specially referred to any particular purpose, such as of securing a constant benefit to a legatee.

The perplexity of a choice between such a variety of methods is much reduced by the two following considerations. *First*, beggars cannot be choosers. The paucity of statistical data (see the report drawn up by Sir R. Giffen in the *Report of the British Association* for 1888, p. 183) restricts the operation. Thus for the purpose of index numbers based on consumption (above, p. 385) retail prices are theoretically appropriate; but "practically it is found that only the prices of leading commodities, capable of being dealt with in large wholesale markets, can be made use of" (Giffen, *loc. cit.*). *Second*, the difference between the results of different methods is likely to be less than at first sight appears. For instance, the probable difference between the index number constructed by the British Association committee, and six others which have been proposed by high authorities—supposing the different methods to be applied to the same data, viz. the prices of twenty-one articles specified by the Committee may thus be expressed. The discrepancy which is as likely as not to occur between the committee's and other results is from 2 to 2·5 per cent. The discrepancy which is very unlikely to occur is from 8 to 11 per cent (*Report of the British Association* for 1888, p. 217). In fact, the index number for the year 1885, as determined from the same data by seven different methods, proved to be 70, 70·6, 73, 69, 72, 72, 69·5 (*ibid.* p. 211).

The practical outcome of these two considerations is thus well expressed by Giffen (*loc. cit.* p. 184), "The articles as to which records of prices are obtainable being themselves only a portion of the whole, nearly as good a final result may apparently be arrived at by a selection without bias, according to no better principle than accessibility of record, as by a careful attention to weighting. . . . Practically the committee would recommend the use of a weighted index number of some kind, as, on the whole, commanding more confidence. . . . A weighted index number, in one aspect, is almost an unnecessary precaution to secure accuracy, though, on the whole, the committee recommend it."

[Airy, G., *Memoirs of the Astronomical Society*, xxviii. (refers to a physical problem which has considerable analogy to the determination of the changes in the value of money with respect to things in general ; namely, the determination of the motion of the solar system in space—relative to the stars in general).—Bela Foldes, W., *Jahrb. f. Nat. Oekon.*, 1882 ; *Statistische Monatsschrift* (Vienna), 1881 (refers to changes in the value of Austrian inconvertible currency).—Bourne, S., *Journal of the Statistical Society*, 1879 (exemplifies the principle of *weight*).—Cross, W., *Standard Pound v. Pound Sterling*, (1856) (proposes a change in the standard *per saltum*, as often as the index number changes to the extent of say 3 per cent).—Drobisch, M., *Bericht. Kön. Sachs. Gesell. Wissenschaft* (Leipzig), 1871 ; *Jahrb. f. Nat. Oekon.*, 1871 (suggests ingenious methods of combination).—Edgeworth, F. Y., "Memoranda on the best methods of ascertaining and measuring variations in the value of the monetary standard" (*Report of the British Association* for 1887, 1888, 1889), (a voluminous disquisition, of which the above article may be regarded as an abridgement). —Forsell, H., *Guldbristen* (Stockholm, 1886), translated into English (interesting as showing the different results which can be brought out when different articles are selected). — Giffen, Sir R., *Parliamentary Reports*, 1881-85 ; *Essays in Finance ; Report of the British Association* for 1888, p. 181 *et seq.* (very masterly).—Jevons, *Currency and Finance* (quite classical).—Laspeyres, *Jahrb.*

f. Nat. Oekon., 1864, 1871 ; *Zeitschrift für die Gesammte Staatswissenschaft*, 1872 (constructs important index numbers for various classes of goods).—Lehr, J., *Statistik der Preise*, 1885 (proposes a cumbrous but theoretically interesting scheme).—Lowe, Joseph, *Present State of England*, 1833 (one of the fathers of this school of writers).—Marshall, *Contemporary Review*, 1887 (offers very valuable suggestions for the construction of an index number based on consumption).—Nicholson, J. S., *Journal of the Statistical Society*, 1887 (recommends an index number based on the change in the monetary value of property or capital).—Nitti, *La Misura delle Variazioni di Valore* (contains some subtle criticism and many useful references).—Palgrave, R. H. I., *Third Report on Depression of Trade* [Appendix B.], (constructs an important weighted index number, and discusses other forms). — Shuckburgh, Sir George, *Phil. Trans.*, 1798, part i. (perhaps the earliest attempt to construct an index number).—Poulett Scrope, *Political Economy* (1833) (proposes an index number under the name of a *Tabular Standard*). —Sauerbeck, A., *Journal of the Statistical Society*, 1886, and 1893 (constructs an important index number based on the prices of forty-five articles) ; *Economic Journal*, June and September 1895 (replies to objections against their index numbers by Mr. N. G. Pierson and Mr. Sauerbeck).—Scharling, W., *Jahrb. f. Nat. Oekon.*, 1886 (throws some doubt on the apparent change in the purchasing power of money).—Sidgwick, H., *Political Economy*, bk. i. ch. ii. (states different methods of constructing an index number based on consumption).—Soetbeer, *Materialien zur Währungsfrage*, 1886, brought up to date in the *Jahrbücher f. Nat. Oekon.*, 1892 (one of the most important contributions to theory and practice).—Walker, *Money and Trade*, and *Political Economy Appendix* (regards the use of a tabular standard as limited).—Walras, *Théorie de la Monnaie*, 1886 (proposes to regulate currency by means of a proper index number).—United States report on retail prices by the Senate Committee on Finance, 1892 (an interesting verification of the principle that simple and "weighted" averages are not likely to differ very much).] F. Y. E.

INDIFFERENCE, LAW OF, a designation applied by Jevons to the following fundamental proposition : "In the same open market, at any one moment, there cannot be two prices for the same kind of article."

This proposition, which is at the foundation of a large part of economic science, itself rests on certain ulterior grounds : namely, certain conditions of a perfect market. One is that monopolies should not exist, or at least should not exert that power in virtue of which a proprietor of a theatre, in Germany for instance, can make a different charge for the admission of soldiers and civilians, of men and women. The indivisibility of the articles dealt in appears to be another circumstance which may counteract the law of indifference in some kinds of market, where price is not regulated by cost of production.

[Jevons, *Theory of Exchange*, 2nd ed. p. 99 (statement of the law).—Walker, *Pol. Econ.*, art. 132 (a restatement).—Mill, *Pol. Econ.*, bk. ii. ch. iv. § 3 (imperfections of actual markets).—Edgeworth, *Mathematical Psychics*, pp. 19, 46 (possible exceptions to the law of indifference).]

F. Y. E.

INDIRECT TAXATION, in the ordinary English use, is that which is "demanded from one person in the expectation and intention that he shall indemnify himself at the expense of another" (Mill, *Principles*, bk. v. ch. iii. § i.), *i.e.* it comprises taxes on commodities levied from producers or dealers.

The administrative application of the term, at least on the continent, is wider. "Indirect taxation is levied on the occurrence of a fact, act, or exchange ; it does not require lists of contributions regularly or periodically established" (Leroy-Beaulieu, *Science des Finances*, t. i. p. 225, cp. Wagner, *Finanzwissenschaft*, vol. ii. p. 239). It therefore covers taxes on successions and gifts as well as the stamp and registration duties.

According to the PHYSIOCRATS (*q.v.*) all taxes, except that levied on the *produit net*, were indirect, since they were necessarily shifted to it (see DIRECT TAXATION and TAXATION).

[A. Wagner, *Finanzwissenschaft*, vol. ii. pp. 239-247.]

C. F. B.

The passage from Mill quoted above includes, among the class "Indirect," such taxes as—

"the excise or customs. The producer or importer of a commodity is called upon to pay a tax on it, not with the intention to levy a peculiar contribution upon him, but to tax through him the consumers of the commodity, from whom it is supposed that he will recover the amount by means of an advance in price" (Mill, *Principles*, bk. v. ch. iii. § i.).

Mill's definitions of direct and indirect taxes make the difference to turn upon the mode of incidence, a division probably originally suggested by the theory of the PHYSIOCRATS (*q.v.*) that all taxes being paid ultimately out of the "net produce" of land, it would be better to impose a single tax charged *directly* on the landowners than to assess the fund *indirectly* by other taxes. But, as Sidgwick (*Principles of Political Economy*, bk. iii. ch. viii. § 8) says—

"we can only partially succeed in making the burden of 'direct' or 'indirect' taxes fall where we desire ; the burden is liable to be transferred to other persons when it is intended to remain where it is first imposed ; and, on the other hand, when it is intended to be transferred, the process of transference is liable to be tardy and incomplete."

Thus—

"In the common parlance the distinction between direct and indirect taxes is practically relegated to the mind of the legislator. What he proposes should be borne by the original payer is called a direct tax, what he intends to be borne by some one else than the original tax-payer is called indirect. Unfortunately the intention of the legislator is not equivalent to the actual result. We must either revise our nomenclature, or declare the present distinction without much value" (Seligman, *On the Shifting and Incidence of Taxation*, 1892, p. 183).

A distribution of taxes subject to change with every new theory of incidence must necessarily, whatever may be its value in economy, be almost useless for administrative purposes. Hence Bastable states that—

"practical financiers have adopted a different basis of distinction, and regard those taxes as direct which are levied on permanent and recurring occasions, whilst charges on occasional and particular events are placed under the category of indirect taxation" (*Public Finance*, ed. 1892, p. 251).

Under this method the income tax is direct, and the excise and customs indirect, as in Mill's definitions, but the death duties from direct become indirect. This classification, which is based on the possibility or otherwise of having a list of tax-payers (*rôle nominatif*) is that adopted in France. P. Leroy-Beaulieu objects to it as empirical, and confounding things which ought to be distinguished. He would define a tax as direct if it was intended to charge the tax-payer immediately and proportionally to his fortune or revenue, and as indirect if otherwise (*Science des Finances*, 1892, vol. ii. 225). Wagner (*Finanzwissenschaft*, 1890, vol. ii. 237-247) gives a full account of the controversy with respect to terminology. He favours a definition based on incidence.

Ely urges that—

"the nature of the economic goods on which the tax is laid should be made decisive in separating taxes on things, other taxes being grouped about these" (*Taxation in American States and Cities*, p. 76).

He therefore would define indirect taxes as—

"taxes on articles of consumption, or on commodities . . . and also taxes levied on occasion of certain transactions, as the payment of money by check, or the recording of deeds or mortgages" (p. 69).

Bastable, desirous of retaining the broad line of division that the old meaning of "direct" and "indirect" gave, observes that—

"if we take the terms, not as giving a complete classification of taxes, but as marking the presence or absence of a certain characteristic, they may be employed with advantage, but rather to suggest reasons for discrimination than to definitely settle results."

He starts, then,

"with the conception of direct taxes as those levied immediately on the subject, and therefore embracing taxes on income and property, or on their component parts, in opposition to duties on commodities and on exchange, where there is a shifting of the burden from the immediate payer to the subject which justifies the name of indirect," and proceeds to consider the merits and defects of each class. On the borderland between direct and indirect taxes he places taxes on transfers, on contracts, on communication and transport, and in short the numerous charges on acts (p. 318-19).

In favour of direct taxation may be urged facility and small cost of collection, combined with definiteness of yield, whilst against it are the unpopularity of the collector's demand for payment, the difficulty of taxing directly the poorer members of society, and the inelasticity of certain forms of charge, e.g. on lands and houses, the assessment of which is usually of necessity fixed for some years. Indirect taxation is more costly to collect, and more variable in its yield, owing to the power of increasing or diminishing consumption of taxed commodities at will, but it is hardly felt at the time of payment, is available for reaching the poorer classes, and in times of prosperity is automatically expansive. Its special drawback is the danger of loss through the disturbance of industry, particularly by excise interference with freedom of manufacture. (For the point of view of a finance minister, see Hansard, [162] 583-585.)

"Modern governments favour indirect taxes. . . . In France their amount represents four or five times that of direct taxes; in Italy, about double, in Belgium nearly triple, and in England triple also . . ." (René Stourm, *Dict. d'Économie Politique*, 1892, art. " Impôt "). See also the table derived from Leroy-Beaulieu, Bastable, p. 286. In Germany the imperial taxes are all indirect, but the states derive a large proportion of their revenue from direct taxes. (See DIRECT TAXATION. COST OF COLLECTION OF TAXES. TAXATION.)   F. A.

INDIRECT UTILITY. A distinction has been drawn between direct and indirect utility. "Direct utility," Jevons says (*Theory of Political Economy*, ch. iii.), "attaches to a thing like food, which we can actually apply to satisfy our wants. But things which have no direct utility may be the means of procuring us such by exchange, and they may therefore be said to have indirect utility."

Jevons refers, in connection with this, to the following passage in Garnier, *Traité d'Économie Politique*, 6th ed. ch. i. § iii. : " Utility is direct or indirect. It is direct in the case of things the immediate application of which satisfies our wants ; a loaf of bread possesses this utility for a man suffering from hunger. It is indirect in the case of things which are only the means whereby we can procure what is necessary to satisfy those wants, which they cannot themselves satisfy. For instance, a man possesses two pieces of bread : with one he satisfies his hunger ; this is an example of direct utility : urged by thirst, he exchanges the other for something to drink ; this is an example of indirect utility.

" Utility which is no longer direct acquires the quality of being interchangeable, and becomes also *Value* " (see UTILITY).

INDIVIDUALISM. This term was applied by J. S. Mill (*Socialism*, p. 114) to that system of industrial organisation in which all initiative is due to private individuals, and all organisation to their voluntary agreement. Under such a system the functions of the state are restricted to the maintenance of order, including the defence of the country, the enforcement of contracts, and in general to supplying the conditions necessary to the working of voluntary action. The natural antithesis to individualism is COLLECTIVISM or we may say SOCIALISM, a system under which industry is directly organised by the state, which owns all means of production and manages all processes by appointed officers.

In its extreme form individualism would deny to the state industrial activities of every sort, even the construction of roads, bridges, and harbours, and the coinage of money. Going still farther, it is discovered that the so-called repressive functions of the state are mostly industrial. Lawsuits are a species of compulsory arbitration of disputes, including industrial ones. The punishment of theft is the repression of a personal activity known to be pernicious. A few have been found who disapprove even of these functions of the state and urge their entire abolition. They are properly known as anarchists or disbelievers in any government, and they represent the utmost range of individualism. In the following discussion it will be understood that only a qualified individualism is intended, that is to say, such a compromise with the opposite principle as has been represented by the most individualistic of modern states.

The essential features of individualism are, (1) private property in capital, to which are added almost of necessity the rights of bequest and inheritance, thus permitting transfer and accumulation. (2) Competition, a rivalry between individuals in the acquisition of wealth, a struggle for existence in which the fittest survive.

It is evident that both these principles have advantages and disadvantages for society. In entering a field where controversy has been violent, only a brief enumeration of admitted tendencies is appropriate. Among the advantages of individualism should first be mentioned the enormous incentive it furnishes to the accumulation of property and so indirectly to the production of wealth. Tasks are undertaken in hope of unusual personal advantage which would not be undertaken by a man receiving a moderate and fixed reward not influenced by special achievements. It is plain that a considerable class of persons are thus induced to exert to the utmost faculties which would otherwise lie dormant. Further, the control of funds of capital by individuals enables them to develop ideas of great value to society, but ideas which society would not value until so developed. Thus it is claimed that individualism not only excites ingenuity but gives it scope, and utilises it in a way that socialism would not so obviously do. Finally, quite apart from all material advantages there should be noted the intellectual qualities which individualism develops—shrewdness, penetration, aggressiveness, and independence. These characterise in a high degree the foremost members of an advanced individualistic society.

Certain disadvantages are, however, equally obvious. The principle of natural selection seems to be abnormally active in a vigorous individualistic society. If great incentives are furnished to certain men, their number is increasingly small. The hope of accumulation becomes a forlorn hope to most men in a highly organised individualistic society, and they suffer from a dearth of incentives destructive even of the simplest economic virtues. Thus the impetus given to production by individual incentives is partly neutralised by the deterioration or arrested development of the masses of the productive population from whom these incentives are increasingly withheld. It is further neutralised by the fact that the control of capital means also privilege in consumption. If men of wealth are merely capitalists, and consume moderately, the only danger arising from their disproportionate ownership is that of excessive formation of capital, but to this danger we must add that of occasional spendthrift consumption, alike detrimental and irritating to society. The tendency of capital to accumulate in the most competent hands has also its counterpart in the chances of inheritance, which often give it to those who are incompetent.

The more conspicuous disadvantage of individualism is the waste involved in competition. Its cost in active antagonisms and divided efforts is enormous, and has been frequently discussed. Finally, the intellectual qualities developed by individualism are more or less balanced by the ethical weakness which it involves. Individualism is avowedly egoistic. Competition has often seemed ruthlessly to eliminate ethical sentiment. At the best it threatens its existence.

It is impossible to weigh the merits and demerits of individualism without a fuller consideration of socialism than present data will allow. Suffice it to say that its disadvantages have been felt so seriously as to lead many countries of late to modify the system by increasing the industrial functions of the state.

The experiences of corporate industry cannot well be discussed here, but it is plain that such a system is not individualistic, and that the principles of management are such as government is familiar with, and might conceivably use with an efficiency proportioned to the excellence of its own organisation. In this respect corporate industry resembles socialism as well as in the further respect that competition and its attendant waste are frequently eliminated, though the benefit that might result has not always inured to society.

The existing industrial system is in many respects a mixture of socialism and individualism and is doubtless destined to remain so, though in what proportion the two will ultimately combine it is impossible to predict. No scheme of complete socialism has been proposed which provides at all adequately for the utilisation of human originality for the ends of progress, or appreciates the value to society of a leisured class. On the other hand it is alleged that the best individualistic systems have largely squandered and perverted originality and developed a leisured class which has not risen to the level of its duties. The modern tendency of society to limit individualism is doubtless due to deeper ethical considerations, the development of which is one of the most remarkable features of the day.

[Any standard work on political economy is an analysis of the individualistic system. Ely, *Outlines of Economics*, analyses the present mixed system as such. Mill discusses the difficulties of collective or state industry. The weakness of individualism is stated with great force by socialist writers, best of all perhaps in Edward Bellamy's socialist romance, *Looking Backward*. Defence and counter criticism are to be found in the works of opponents of socialism, *e.g.* Rae, *Contemporary Socialism*, and Graham, *Socialism new and old*. See also Montague, *Individual Liberty*.— Nicholson, *Principles of Political Economy*, vol. i. ch. xv.—Donisthorpe, *Individualism.*—Walker, " Mr. Bellamy," etc., *Atlantic Monthly*, Feb. 1890.—E. Richter, *Zukunftsbilder*, 1892.]

H. H. P.

INDORSEMENT. See BILL OF EXCHANGE.

INDUCTIVE METHOD. There is some ambiguity in the use of this expression. Sometimes it is used with reference to any inquiry in which results are arrived at by the study of concrete facts. The following passage from Prof. R. M. Smith, *Science Economic Discussion*, p. 111, illustrates this acceptation of the term. " Finally, we may ask, what can the inductive method do when it faces some great economic problem which affects the whole community and civilisation itself? Such a problem is the labour problem. What is the condition of the labouring class? Has that condition deteriorated or improved? The inductive method has not shrunk from attempting to find an answer to even such questions as these. Thorold Rogers has laboriously traced the condition of the English labourer during the last six centuries, for the purpose of answering this question historically. Giffen has attempted, by statistics, to show that the condition of the labouring class has materially improved during the last fifty years." Dr. Keynes, on the other hand, objects to this use of the term (*Scope and Method of Political Economy*, p. 192, note) on the ground that "what is naturally understood by induction and the inductive method is a process of reasoning whereby, on the strength of particular instances, a general law is established." From this point of view, the instances given by Prof. Smith would rather be regarded as illustrating the statistical or realistic or concrete method of economic inquiry. It seems clear, however, that when an inductive method is spoken of it is not usually restricted to a method by which general laws are ascertained. Thus, Prof. Sidgwick says (*Scope and Method of Economic Science*, p. 33) that "even as regards the present condition of industry in the more advanced countries, to which the theory of modern economic science primarily relates, there is, I conceive, no dispute as to the need of what is called a 'realistic' or 'inductive' method—*i.e.* as to the need of accurately ascertaining particular facts when we are inquiring into the particular causes of particular values, or of the shares of particular economic classes at any given place and time." Here the inductive method is identified with the realistic, and is not conceived as necessarily concerned with the ascertainment of general laws, but only of particular causes at a particular place and time. The discussion of the correct use of the term induction must evidently be left to writers on inductive logic ; but it may be permissible to remark here that Mill's influence has perhaps tended to narrow the use of the term in a way that is neither conformable to popular usage nor convenient for scientific purposes.[1] At any rate, when we speak of the inductive method with reference to political economy, it seems best to understand it as meaning any method by which results of scientific value are obtained which are not directly deducible from principles already known. If the term is thus understood, Mill's inductive methods represent only a small part of inductive investigation ; and the instances given by Profs. Sidgwick and Smith, so far as the results to which they refer are regarded as having scientific value, are correctly taken as illustrations of induction. It seems necessary to say that the results must have scientific value ; for probably no one would regard mere economic history or mere statistics as illustrating the inductive method, or any other method, except in so far as they supply

results that are capable of throwing light on economic tendencies. Even Mill would no doubt have been willing to describe the instances given by Prof. Smith as "subsidiary to induction" ; and perhaps it is simplest to regard processes subsidiary to induction as being themselves inductive in their nature.

Assuming, then, that induction and deduction are to be understood in such a sense that between them they exhaust all the methods by which economic truths of any scientific value are ascertained, we have next to ask, What is the importance of the inductive method in economic research ? This subject has been already to a considerable extent discussed in the article on DEDUCTIVE METHOD, and it is not necessary to add much to what is there said. The classical economists, led by Ricardo, are certainly chargeable with having comparatively neglected the inductive method. There are, however, some certain grounds on which their action may be defended. It may be said, on the one hand, that the facts to be dealt with by the economist are too complicated, and too little amenable to experimental treatment, to be suitable for the application of the inductive method. For this reason it may be urged that the observation of economic facts is seldom of any scientific value, except by way of verifying or correcting the results of deductive reasoning. This is no doubt largely true. A purely inductive investigation would be a long one ; and the practical importance of some economic truths naturally renders us impatient of slow processes. Also, it is no doubt true that the economist has seldom the power of modifying his facts experimentally, so as to facilitate investigation. The importance of the latter point, however, may be exaggerated. The absence of experiment is partly compensated by the natural enterprise of human nature, on the one hand, and, on the other hand, by the possibility of forecasting results. The former fact gives rise to what is sometimes described as "unintentional experiment." This is perhaps an inaccurate expression ;[1] but it is certainly true that the natural enterprise of human nature renders experiment less necessary in such a subject as economics than it is in the case of objects that are comparatively inert or that are difficult to observe under varying conditions. The power of placing ourselves imaginatively in different circumstances, and considering what the result would be,[2] is also a condition that renders actual experiment relatively unnecessary. It may be urged, however, on the other hand, that the latter circumstance

---

[1] It is probable that the somewhat narrow view which Mill took of the aim and scope of induction is largely responsible for his low estimate of the value of the inductive method in economics. See his *Essays on some Unsettled Questions of Political Economy*, Essay V., and *System of Logic*, bk. vi. ch. ix.

[1] See Keynes's *Scope and Method of Political Economy*, p. 169, note.
[2] This is what Cairnes describes (*Logical Method of Political Economy*, pp. 90-94) as "an inferior substitute" for experiment, or as "experiment conducted mentally." Cp. also Keynes's *Scope and Method of Political Economy*, p. 172, note.

to a great extent renders the inductive method itself unnecessary. "In order to know, *e.g.*," says Cairnes (*Logical Method of Political Economy*, p. 88), "why a farmer engages in the production of corn, why he cultivates his land up to a certain point, and why he does not cultivate it farther, it is not necessary that we should derive our knowledge from a series of generalisations proceeding upward from the statistics of corn and cultivation to the mental feelings which stimulate the farmer, on the one hand, and, on the other, to the physical qualities of the soil on which the productiveness of that industry depends. It is not necessary to do this—to resort to this circuitous process—for this reason, that we have, or may have if we choose to turn our attention to the subject, direct knowledge of those causes in our consciousness of what passes in our own minds, and in the information which our senses convey, or at least are capable of conveying, to us of external parts. Every one who embarks in any industrial pursuit is conscious of the motives which actuate him in doing so," etc. It is unnecessary, then, in such cases as these, to resort to the inductive method of inquiry, because the chief causes involved are known to us either by direct personal experience, or by sympathetic imagination, or by the instrumentality of language. But this is only partly true. In complicated cases it is difficult to disentangle motives—even our own,—and to estimate to what extent different considerations have weight in our conduct. And this is especially difficult when we have to compare the actions of men in different times and nations. In such cases an inductive method of investigation seems to be indispensable.

Summing up, then, we may describe the place of the inductive method in economics in this way. On the one hand, it is the method by which the premises of the deductive method are secured, and by which its results are verified. On the other hand, it is the method by which important facts are ascertained to which the deductive method cannot as yet be applied. The importance of carefully ascertaining the premises that ought to be adopted in deductive reasoning was very much overlooked by the earlier economists. They seemed frequently to get their premises out of the air without any preliminary investigation. Similarly, they tended to be rather remiss in the verification of their results. But perhaps their chief error lay in the tendency to overlook the importance of those elements in economic life to which the method of deductive inquiry is not at present applicable—*e.g.* to the study of consumption, and to the investigation of special economic forces,—as, for instance, that of custom—operative at particular times and places. Their errors in these respects have been well emphasised by the historical school. It is perhaps worth

noting that Carlyle also, in his less scientific way, brought out the importance of inductive inquiry. In chap. ii. of his essay on "Chartism" he suggests a number of statistical inquiries with respect to the condition of the working classes, which would form the basis for a line of inductive investigations. It must be confessed, however, that inquiries of this kind have not as yet furnished us with much definite light either on economic tendencies or on methods of practical reform. But there is every reason to hope that they will be more fruitful in the future. And if the results of the deductive method have hitherto been more imposing, they have probably also been more misleading. The careful inquiries set on foot by such writers as LE PLAY or Mr. Charles Booth can hardly fail in the end to be both light-bearing and fruit-bearing. This is especially the case when such inquiries are conducted in accordance with the principles of the HISTORICAL METHOD. In economics, as in other sciences that deal with life, the genetic method combines, to a large extent, the advantages both of deduction and of induction. [Further information with regard to the inductive method will be found in most systematic treatises on political economy, as well as in works on inductive logic.—Wagner's *Lehr- und Handbuch der politischen Oekonomie* is specially instructive (3rd edition, 1892, pp. 194-225).—Dilthey's *Einleitung in die Geisteswissenschaften* may be found suggestive.—Reference may also be made to the various works mentioned at the end of the article on DEDUCTIVE METHOD (see also HISTORICAL METHOD ; STATISTICS, etc.).]   J. S. M.

INDUSTRIAL COLONIES. The proposal to found industrial colonies owes its origin to two causes. *First*, the real or supposed existence of a class whose poverty or destitution results from want of employment, whether the cause of that want be incompetence, vice, the state of production, or overpopulation. *Secondly*, a tendency on the part of population to flock into the towns, swelling the numbers of the above class. Hence, the object of such colonies may be said to be twofold, to prevent unemployed labourers from drifting into a state of vagabondage, and to raise the vagabond class to industrious independence.

Historically, we find these causes playing a part in Greek colonisation, which was closely bound up in the population question, and in those Roman settlements which represent an attempt to solve the agrarian difficulty. In modern times several experiments have been made. In Holland the scheme of planting out the unemployed population of towns in the country dates from 1818, and has taken two forms. (1) The semi-penal colonies of Veenhuizen and Ommerschans, which are supported and controlled by the state, and to which vagrants are sent by order of the magistrate. (2) The colonies founded and maintained by charitable societies at Frederiksoord and

Willelmsoord, in which the destitute are settled and trained in habits of industry by a carefully graduated system of charity and self-interest. In Germany, since 1882, charitable societies have adopted the system of industrial colonies as a means of reclaiming the vagrant class by giving them an opportunity of steady work and of self-improvement.

The introduction of the system into this country would be to carry out the spirit of the Elizabethan poor-law, which directed the overseers to set the able-bodied poor to work. But the difficulty of organising any such employment has been found insuperable. The parish farm, the "roundsman" system, were both of them attempts to remedy destitution by "finding work," that is by paying out of the rates for work which does not pay in itself. "Every device for relieving the poor by means of employment must prove illusory in the end, excepting where it is connected with the development of fresh resources for the remuneration of industry."

[H. Mills, *Poverty and the State*, 1887.—*Essays on the Principles of Charitable Institutions*, 1834. —*Charity Organisation Review*, Jan. 1888. Holland, *Poor Law Conferences* (W. Midland), 1887. —Blue book on *Methods of Employing the Unemployed* (Bd. of Trade, Labour Department, 1893, for complete bibliography).—*Labour Colonies*, Mavor, 1892.—"General" W. Booth, *Darkest England Social Scheme*, 1892, for working of his farm colony.]   L. R. P.

INDUSTRIAL COLONIES (BELGIUM). The present agricultural beneficent colonies of Belgium are the survivors of six state provincial *Dépôts de Mendicité* and two state-aided colonies of the private *Société de Bienfaisance* all existing in 1831. The two latter are extinct, and three of the former are closed. There remain—(1) a *dépôt* at Bruges for women and girls above eighteen ; (2) an agricultural school at Reckheim for pauper lads aged fifteen to eighteen ; and (3) the agricultural colony at Hoogstraeten, to which have been added the old Dutch colonies of Merxplas and Wortel, taken over by the Belgian government in 1870 at a cost of 800,000 francs (about £32,000). The colonies are under the control of the department of justice. They comprise (a) a non-able-bodied colony, Hoogstraeten, extent 270 acres, accommodation 1300 ; (b) an able-bodied colony, Merxplas, 180 acres, accommodation 3600 ; and (c) working ground, Wortel, for the latter, 1410 acres. The total stock comprises about 40 horses, 320 cattle, 140 pigs, and 230 sheep. The area is thus allocated, viz.—arable and pasture 910 acres, heath 245, roads 320, buildings and gardens 74, with some fir-wood and uncultivated. The staff consists of 76 persons, besides farm-servants, master-millers, bakers, gardeners, and foremen, and about 140 soldiers. In October 1890 the total population, excluding staff, was 4000, of

whom 2800 were able-bodied. The daily cost per head was about 65 centimes for an able-bodied, and 85 for an infirm person (about 6½d. and 8½d.). The inmates are all adult male vagrants and mendicants sentenced by police courts. They are classified according to ability and character, the classes being kept quite separate. The buildings were erected by colonist labour. The work comprises plaiting, spinning, metal lattice-work, embankment, scavenging, farm and garden work, forestry, brick and tile making, building, carpentry, joinery, etc., and necessary domestic labour. It is allotted according to classes. The colonists are allowed to earn money, of which two-thirds are paid to them on discharge : the earnings vary from 15 to 18 centimes *per diem* (about 1½d. to 1¾d.). It is a leading principle that all trades shall be encouraged, and many skilled tradesmen are among the staff. The presence of many good colonist workmen is accounted for by drink, according to the officials. The products of the work are partly taken by government and partly sold outside.

Recidivism is the rule : in December 1890, only 247 out of 4213 colonists were there for the first time. The general conduct is said to be good. The punishments are cells, or transfer to a lower class. The sanitation is good. The labour of the colonists does not nearly pay for cost of maintenance. No precise accounts were, however, obtainable in 1890. The colonies appeared to be excellently managed : the question of cost and of reformatory success being the two chief points open to doubt.

[H. G. Willink, article in *Charity Organisation Review*, Jan. 1891, "Agric. Ben. Col. of Belgium." —George Nicholls, *Report on the Condition of the Labouring Classes, etc. in Holland and Belgium*, May, 1838.—Mavor, *Labour Colonies*, Board of Trade Labour Department ; *Blue Book on Employment of Unemployed*, 1893].   H. G. W.

INDUSTRIAL COLONIES (GERMANY). The *Arbeiter Kolonie* has three distinctive features. It grew out of the conviction that for the treatment of the defective classes employment in the open air was advantageous. It was founded by a religious body as "a work of free compassion." It was established on the principle that work should be provided for the unemployed instead of other forms of relief. The farm or colony system had in 1834 been adopted by Dr. Wichern at the *Rauhe Haus*, Hamburg. This institution, originating in a home for boys, became afterwards a settlement of homes, including a training home for a brotherhood of men to be engaged in the work of practical charity. Out of this movement sprang the *Innere* Mission (1849). One of its branches was at Bielefeld, where in 1866 a colony for epileptics was opened. In 1872 Dr. von Bodelschwingh was placed in charge of this colony. In 1882 he applied the colony system to the problems of vagrancy and bought an estate at Wilhelmsdorf near Bielefeld for the purpose of employing vagrants on the reclamation of the land. He argued that on this method half the cost of the vagrants' maintenance would be met, many would be deterred from vagrancy, a check would be put on indiscriminate almsgiving, and those who remained in the colony three or four months would learn the new trade of working on the land, and might "return to the life of a citizen." There are now 26 colonies, 3 Roman Catholic, the rest Protestant. Two are in towns; the rest are farm colonies. All are under the supervision of the *Centralvorstand deutscher Arbeiter-Kolonien.* In connection with them are lodging-houses (*Herbergen zur Heimat*) 426 in number, where the wayfarer or vagrant can obtain food and lodging at low rates; and, in many instances, relief stations (*Verpflegungsstationen*), where he can obtain relief in return for a task of work. Of these there are about 1900. These lodgings and stations are placed at intervals along the main routes. By German law vagrancy is a punishable offence. The wayfarer in self-justification may produce a way ticket (*Wanderschein*), which is checked as he passes from place to place, and by which he is obliged to travel according to a certain route. Arrived at the "colony" the police make inquiries about him. He is set to work. After fourteen days he receives, in addition to his maintenance, 2¼d. to 3¼d. a day. If he wants clothes he is supplied with them. The price is stopped out of his wages, though he often leaves before his payments are complete. Any able-bodied man wishing to work is admitted. Habitual drunkards are excluded. Dismissal is the only form of punishment. The "colonies" were established and are supported by grants from state and local authorities and by subscriptions. Their produce is chiefly consumed within the colonies. On the statistics of the colonies the works of Dr. Berthold, the most important writer on the subject, give the fullest information. There are about 8000 persons admitted in the year. The vagrants in Germany have been estimated at 150,000. Of these more than half are in the prime of life, 25 to 45. About 79 per cent represent themselves as single. About 76 per cent have been in prison. About 44 per cent are unskilled or partially skilled labourers. About half have been in the "colonies" more than once. Many return to them frequently. In the winter the "colonies" are full to overflowing. In 1890 about 3500, in 1891 nearly 2000, were turned away. The pressure lasts during the winter. About 64 per cent leave of their own wish: about 19 per cent —a decreasing number—obtain situations. As to results: prosecutions for vagrancy have decreased from 23,093 (1880) to 13,583 (1890). The colonists are kindly treated and work fairly well. Employers are disinclined to take men

from the "colonies." Many who find situations do not keep them. Better-class men think it a reproach to enter them. As a cure for these evils, Dr. Cronemeyer proposes a combination of the "industrial colonies" with "home colonies" (see below) for the industrious and reformatory, or penal colonies for those who require more strict supervision or punishment. Dr. von Bodelschwingh proposes (1) larger establishments in the towns to equalise the pressure; (2) a system of asylums for the incapable and crippled; (3) temporary colonies in bad years. Professor J. Mavor (Report, Labour Department of Board of Trade, C. 7182 (1893)) has dealt very carefully with the economic questions of the colonies. He says: "It is because the colonist is non-efficient that he does not compete with the labour market." But if this be so, a chief aim of the system, when established (see above), is not fulfilled. Next the supply of winter board and lodging should have the effect of reducing the relatively higher wages of unskilled labour in summer trades. Lastly, although the numbers concerned are relatively small, yet the minimum subsistence wage fixed by the colony for the purpose of inducing men to seek outside employment, may tend to some extent to become the maximum wage for low-grade labour in the district (p. 285). A home colony has been established at Bremerhaven. Colonists are there at first lodged in barracks, then in family cottages. There are twelve families. At this colony there is a considerable deficit, made good chiefly by voluntary contributions.

In the colony for epileptics at Bielefeld are about 1100 patients, under the care of Westphalian deaconesses and brotherhood. Adults and children are admitted, and may remain even when the epilepsy has terminated in imbecility or insanity. Admission is chiefly by payment on a graduated scale of charges. About 75 per cent of the patients are of the lower classes. They live in houses dotted about in the neighbourhood. Each house is under separate supervision, under the charge of a house father or mother. At different houses are different workshops. The colony with its church, etc., forms a society within itself. Expenditure about £31,000, of which about £1200 from patients' payments; the rest, grants from local authorities and contributions.

The test of a system for dealing with vagrancy is whether it assists those whom it relieves to return as soon as possible to self-supporting work in the open labour market. There is probably in all modern communities a substratum of vagrancy which cannot be removed. In times of industrial pressure this is increased by recruits from the ranks of inferior and usually unskilled workmen, who are the first to be discharged when fewer hands are employed. A good system would offer the minimum attraction to these to become permanent vagrants. There are two methods of relief : (1) to employ and to endeavour to reform character or improve capacity ; (2) to relieve under conditions of wholesome deterrence. The former is the German system. But the statistics do not seem to show that much is accomplished by way of reform. The latter is the English method ; it makes no direct attempt to reform, but relies on the applicant preferring to gain his own livelihood to accepting relief on unattractive conditions. The result may be tested in two ways. Is the number of vagrants supported in winter large as compared with those supported in summer ? If so, the system is used as a means of partial dependence by the habitual vagrant. Next, is vagrancy on the increase ? In Germany the winter and summer number of the colonists varies widely. In England the winter and summer numbers of vagrants relieved by the poor-law vary comparatively little, except in a year of exceptional industrial pressure. Next the claimants for relief at the colonies increase yearly, though it may possibly be argued that the supply of necessary accommodation in Germany has not yet been brought to a level with the requirements, and hence a continual increase for the present may be expected. This contention apart—it would seem that the system draws the vagrant into dependence instead of preventing or reforming his vagrancy. In England, vagrancy seems to fall and rise quickly according to the industrial state of the country. If this be so, it is probably due in part to the fact that the German system is one of relief by employment, with no deterrent conditions. The work is taken as a payment for relief given. It is not laborious and yet it seems to justify the request for relief. A large number therefore take it without dislike or scruple. And as this process goes on, the better-class men become reluctant to apply ; and the worse in a manner appropriate the institution to their own purposes. The latter part of this criticism may be applied to the English system ; but now in many parts of England separate accommodation, with cleanliness, decency, and freedom from intercourse with others, is afforded to vagrants, so that the self-respecting man can, if he wishes, keep to himself.

[For other colonies in Germany and elsewhere see *The Epileptic and the Crippled* (Charity Organisation Series).—For bibliography, see Professor Mavor's *Report*, p. 431. The following are selected : *Die Arbeiter-Kolonie :* monthly organ of the *Centralvorstand*, Bielefeld.—G. Berthold, *Die Entwickelung der deutschen Arbeiter-Kolonien, 1885-86*, Leipzig, 1887.—*Die Weiterentwickelung, u.s.w. 1886-87*, Berlin, 1889.—*Statistik, 1887-89*, Berlin, 1891.—*Die Deutschen Arbeiter-Kolonien, 1889-91*, Berlin, 1893.—E. Cronemeyer, *Eine Zuflucht der Elenden*, Bremerhaven, 1893. — *Die Herbergen zur Heimat und mit ihnen verbundenen Verpflegungsstationen im Jahre 1891*, Bielefeld, 1892.—*Deutscher Herbergsverein Jahresbericht 1893*, Bielefeld, 1894.—C. von Massow, *Die Natural-Verpflegungsstationen und die Nothwendigkeit ihrer Reform als Voraussetzung ihres Fortbestehens*, Bielefeld, 1887.—*Statistik der Verpflegungsstationen*, 1890. Count Rumford in Bavaria (1789) founded industrial colonies.]

C. S. L.

INDUSTRIAL COLONIES (HOLLAND). There are two classes of colonies, the free colonies belonging to a charitable society, and the beggar colonies belonging to the state.

The original free colonies were founded in 1818 by a private society, *Maatschappij van Weldadigheid*, which was promoted by General van den Bosch, and was composed of a number of supporting districts, each entitled to have in the colonies as many families as it had contributed capital sums of 1700 guilders (say £140 each) ; and the district was liable for outfit, travelling, furniture, and incidental expenses. The idea of the founders of the society was that pauperism might, to a large extent, be prevented by providing agricultural training and employment for able-bodied, deserving, destitute persons.

By Dec. 1821, 121,000 guilders (say £10,000) had been thus collected, and 300,000 guilders (£25,000) borrowed : the number of buildings was 500 ; total population 2100. The colonies comprised about 3000 acres, chiefly heath-land, near Steenwijk, Drenthe, purchased at from 22s. to 30s. per acre. A quantity of land was afterwards bought at Wateren, but sold in 1859. The colonists were divided into 3 classes, viz. (*a*) families, (*b*) boarders, (*c*) orphans. Heads of families began as "labourers," with the prospect of rising to be "free farmers." Besides farming, the chief work was weaving, the products being sold to government. Colonists' earnings, over a certain sum, belonged to the society. In 1820 the society founded the beggar colony of Ommerschans in Overijssel, 1900 acres being granted by government ; and soon afterwards another at Veenhuizen in Drenthe, 2380 acres being purchased. There were three main classes of colonists (*a*) persons committed for begging ; (*b*) voluntary inmates ; (*c*) old soldiers. By 1827 the population of Ommerschans and Veenhuizen together amounted to 4518, including officials.

The principal authority on the early history of both the free and beggar colonies is a report by Count Arrivabene embodied in a pamphlet by Nassau Senior, 1835. Mr. Senior himself considered failure inevitable.

During the next quarter of a century the colonies struggled on under increasing difficulties, caused partly by general bad management, partly by the hopeless insolvency of the beggar colonies. The society was repeatedly helped by the state, but matters grew worse until, in 1859, the government took over the beggar colony, excusing at the same time all moneys due to the state, and paying off also all the private debts of the society.

The authority for this period is Sir John M'Neill's report, 1853, in which he unreservedly condemns both kinds of colony, the free colony because it did not foster self-reliance, the beggar colony because of its expense. Since 1859 the free colonies have been more carefully managed, though the main lines are unchanged, and they have not much altered in size. Much of the land is now comprised in six large farms managed by the society—manufactures have been established, a forestry department has been organised. Colonists keep all their earnings ; piece-work has largely supplemented time-work ; and there are now more "free farmers" than "labourers." Still on an average not more than six fresh families are admitted annually ; and the colonies are not self-supporting.

The beggar colonies have been gradually concentrated at Veenhuizen. In 1888 the population of Ommerschans was 400, with about 40 officials, and of Veenhuizen about 2020. Nine-tenths were persons under sentence for begging. The colonists are employed on agriculture and simple handicrafts. In 1886 only about one-third of all the expenses, amounting altogether to about 665,000 guilders (say £55,400), was met by the colonists' labour. Such labour is said to be very inefficient. The system is not deterrent, about two-thirds of the beggar inmates having been at the colony at least twice before.

For an account of both kinds of colony in the present day see Mr. Willink's articles written in 1888. He considers that the free colonies, good as their work may be, do not annually deal with enough fresh cases to furnish a solution of the problem of the indigent poor, however beneficial they may be to their limited number of inmates : and that the beggar colonies are not successful either as a deterrent, or from an economical point of view.

[Nassau Senior, *Statement of the Provision for the Poor, etc., in America and Europe* (Fellowes, 1835).—Mary Hennell, *An Outline of various Social Systems* (Longmans, 1844). — George Nicholls, *Report on Condition of Labouring Classes, etc., in Holland and Belgium*, May 1838.—Article in *Quarterly Review*, Dec. 1835.—Eighth Annual Report of the Board of Supervision for the Relief of the Poor (Scotland), containing Report by Sir J. M'Neill, 1853.—Herbert V. Mills, *Poverty and the State*, 1886.—W. Tallack, article in *Public Opinion*, 1st Oct. 1886, and article in *Leisure Hour*, Feb. 1887.—H. G. Willink, *Dutch Home Labour Colonies*, 1889.—Mavor, *Labour Colonies.*—Board of Trade Labour Department Blue Book on *Employment of Unemployed*, 1893. Labour Commission—Foreign Reports.] H. G. W.

INDUSTRIAL EDUCATION in England is not, as in France, Germany, and other countries, entirely a government concern. Apart from the government science and art department which has its headquarters at S. Kensington and at the School of Mines in Jermyn Street, in connection with which evening classes and examinations are held throughout the country, industrial education in England is—quite characteristically—almost entirely promoted by charitable endowment and by local or private enterprise. By far the most important and recognised factor in its promotion is the City and Gilds of London Institute which not only provides, but subsidises other establishments which are providing sound technical instruction, and encourages in the principal industrial centres of Great Britain the formation of evening classes for workmen and foremen. The Clothworkers' Company are also working in the same direction, and the other great livery companies of London are being pressed to expend a portion of their wealth in furthering the same object.

The universities of Oxford and Cambridge, London and Manchester, and the university Colleges of London and elsewhere, are giving great attention to science and art as applied to industry. But what is even more important, the local school boards and municipal councils of the country are taking up the matter with a keen interest.

Elementary technical education both for girls and boys has now for many years been introduced into the curriculum of the elementary day schools. Evening classes, usually in connection with the government science and art department, are held ; and continuation schools are being provided in the higher-grade schools instituted in the larger industrial centres. The royal commissioners in their last report (1885) on technical education, deplore that England is singularly lacking in continuation schools of this kind ; but an effort is being made to supply this want, especially in Manchester and other industrial centres.

Bristol and Birmingham are paying great attention to the subject of primary and secondary technical education. In Liverpool the school board have, by the introduction of elementary technical instruction, attempted to connect the primary with the secondary schools. In Manchester, besides the higher-grade schools before mentioned, there are several technical schools for artisans. Oldham has a school of science and art with evening classes adapted for the technical instruction of young men engaged in the various mechanical and textile works of the neighbourhood, particularly machine construction and the manufacture of cotton.

Of secondary technical schools and colleges the most important and best endowed is the Finsbury Technical College, established in 1883 by the City and Gilds of London Institute, as a model trade school for instructing artisans. Only second to this are Firth College, Sheffield, and University College, Nottingham ; which both receive grants from the Institute. These colleges are furnished with workshops and laboratories and possess every appliance for the illustration and application of industrial methods in carpentry, building, engineering, chemistry, dyeing, art designing, carriage building, metal plate work, and many other branches of trade and industry.

In special weaving and dyeing schools the commissioners found England very deficient as compared with France and Germany, but they bestowed unqualified praise on the Yorkshire weaving schools of Leeds, Bradford, and Keighley, all which are largely supported by grants from the Clothworkers' Company. The Leeds school was erected by the company at a cost of £15,000. There is also a fine weaving school at Glasgow.

Many other institutions, such as the London Polytechnic, the Royal Engineering College at Cooper's Hill, the Royal Naval College, Greenwich—especially adapted for the study of shipbuilding—and the Crystal Palace School of practical engineering—exist, where instruction is given in every branch of trade and industry. As specimens of private voluntary enterprise in this direction mention must be made of Messrs. Mather and Platt's workshop school at Salford, maintained at their own charge for the technical education of their own workers. At Cambridge the commissioners were particularly struck by the mechanical workshops, instituted by Professor J. Stuart, to enable the sons of manufacturers and others to combine with university training instruction of a kind immediately practicable to their calling. The special feature of the Allan Glen's Institution at Glasgow is workshop instruction. Ireland appears to be somewhat deficient in evening classes for artisans, but in the reformatory and industrial schools of the religious brotherhoods and sisterhoods, boys are instructed in a variety of trades, and in every department of farming and gardening. Also many of the Irish national schools have school-farms attached. In addition to this, the Grocers' Company support a school of agriculture at Templemole ; there is also the Albert National Agricultural Training Institution at Glasnevin, with three farms attached, and there is the Munster Dairy School.

Ireland is more advanced in this branch of instruction than England. The English government, except by the S. Kensington examinations, has done little or nothing to promote agricultural education. The few schools that exist are self-supporting. The Royal Agricultural Society of England, and the Highland and Agricultural Society of Scotland, encourage this branch of study by acting as examining bodies. The Scottish society makes a special branch of forestry, with drainage, fencing, bridge building, and the chemical knowledge of soil properties.

Among the agricultural establishments in England, the Royal Agricultural College of Cirencester, organised by the Farmers' Club, holds the first place. The college farm consists of 500 acres devoted to arable, pasture, and dairy farming ; and it also possesses botanic gardens. Excursions are made by senior students to the neighbouring farms and herds. In 1880 the Downton Agricultural College, Wilts, was opened on somewhat similar lines.

Agriculture is also included in the curriculum of the county schools. Some years ago an attempt to open a British Dairy School failed, but the effort is illustrative of a felt want of some such institution.

Perhaps the most interesting and instructive institution for the analytic and scientific study of farming and agriculture is the private experimental station at Rothamsted, established by Sir J. B. Lawes. Minute investigations and comparisons of soils, manures, crops, and pasture are made. Experiments in stock feeding and stock breeding are carried on upon a most extensive and elaborate scale.

In conclusion the commissioners found that although the British government has almost entirely neglected the technical education of agriculturists, it has made an effort by its examinations to spread a book knowledge of agriculture.

[*Report of the Royal Commission on Technical Education*, 1885.]   A. L.

INDUSTRIAL EDUCATION IN THE UNITED STATES. Education with special reference to the economic life of the people is being promoted in the United States in three different ways : (1) A general introduction of what is termed manual training in the public school system of the large cities ; (2) in the establishment of trade schools ; (3) in the founding and endowment of higher technical schools and colleges which include a specialised education for the direction of manufacturing, mining, and agricultural industries. With regard to the first experiment, manual training, it is to be observed that it is not artisan education. It " signifies instruction in tool work as an educational discipline." This training, if grafted upon the public school system, is generally taken in connection with the high school studies, and consists in exercises in drawing, modelling, and wood-working, with sewing and cooking for girls. In some of the larger schools which have private endowments, as at Chicago and St. Louis, the course of study embraces pattern-making, foundry-work, forging, and machine shop-work. Manual training as an educational method is largely the growth of the past ten years. There is no uniformity in these schools in the different parts of the country, and some of them are so far developed that they may be regarded as "schools of apprenticeship," though the brief courses pursued in them seem wholly inadequate for the mastery of any trade."

Of the trade schools, there are as yet but few. The best known and most successful is that established by Col. Auchmuty at New York. Here instruction for fees is given in bricklaying, plastering, plumbing, carpentry, house, sign, and fresco painting, stone-cutting, blacksmithing, tailoring, and printing. A few large manufacturing establishments and railroads have specialised schools for instruction in particular artisan work; and training of this character is being incorporated into the discipline of the better reformatory institutions for youth and men, as at the Elmira Reformatory. All these distinctively serve as apprenticeship schools.

Institutions of the third class include—(a) agricultural colleges founded since 1860, for the most part under endowments of the national government, and generally attached to a state university for its administration; and (b) institutes of technology for the special education of engineers, architects, and chemists. Colleges and state universities have also very generally introduced similar training into their curricula.

[See *Eighth Annual Report of the United States Commissioner of Labour, 1892.—Industrial Education*, Washington, 1893, pp. 707. This contains a valuable bibliography of twenty pages, relating to the subject of technical training in the United States and Europe.]   D. R. D.

INDUSTRIAL PARTNERSHIP. This term is generally used of a system of industry under which the employer is so far in partnership with the employed that he accords to them a share in the profits which are realised (see PROFIT-SHARING). It has been more widely adopted abroad than in England, and it has there been applied to a variety of industries. The term is sometimes also employed of a system by which the actual workmen take upon themselves all the responsibilities of management, and endeavour to eliminate the employer entirely, and secure for their own advantage the whole of his profits. But this latter system is more usually called co-operative production (see CO-OPERATION) and the term "industrial partnership" confined to the system which was first mentioned. This system possesses advantages over that of co-operative production, because the workmen enjoy the benefit of a share in the profits, and the stimulus of an interest in the success of the undertaking, without ceasing to avail themselves of the advantage of the experienced and interested management of the employer (see EMPLOYERS AND EMPLOYED). It has been asserted that the system leads to an increase in wages by the addition of the share of profits which is distributed without occasioning any encroachment on the gains of the employer. It has been affirmed that this is the case because the workmen are rendered more careful in the avoidance of waste, are less disposed to listlessness or idleness, and require less constant and watchful superintendence. The system has been applied with three main varieties of method.

The share of profits is sometimes given wholly in cash, sometimes it is set aside or invested in order to secure a provision for the old age or sickness or death of the workman, and sometimes it is treated partly in the first, and partly in the second manner. The difficulties of adopting and working the system may be said to consist partly in the possible inconvenience of a wish on the part of the men to interfere in the details of management, partly in their probable disinclination to share in losses as well as in profits, and partly in the absence in some trades of an opportunity for making a fresh addition to profits through the avoidance of waste or of idleness. Its advantages are summed up in the feeling of joint interest in the success of the concern which it tends to create between masters and men. The system is perhaps best known in connection with the successful trial of it made by the Parisian house-painter, M. LECLAIRE (*q.v.*).

[The system of profit-sharing, or industrial partnership, is thoroughly examined, and the instances of its application recorded and investigated in detail, in N. P. Gilman's *Profit Sharing between Employer and Employee*. A shorter account is given in Sedley Taylor's *Profit Sharing*; and notices of the system are contained in Babbage's *Economy of Machinery and Manufactures*, under the heading "A new system of manufacture"; in J. S. Mill's *Political Economy*, bk. iv. ch. vii. § 5; Fawcett's *Manual of Political Economy*, bk. ii. ch. x.; Jevons, *State in Relation to Labour*, ch. vi., and *Methods of Social Reform*, p. 122; and Cairnes's *Essays in Political Economy*, No. v.; cp. Robert, *La Participation aux bénéfices*; also Schloss, *Methods of Industrial Remuneration*; and B. Potter, *The Co-operative Movement*, for criticism of the system (see CITÉ OUVRIÈRE; FAMILISTÈRE; GODIN).]   L. L. P.

INDUSTRIAL RÉGIME is a phrase which only now appears to be in process of crystallisation into a definite use in economic language; and we can hardly define it satisfactorily without sketching the history of the term so far as we can trace it. In 1821 St. Simon wrote his treatise *Du système industriel*: he did not, so far as we can discover, use the phrase under discussion; but he and his followers used *l'industrialisme* to indicate at one time generally the modern industrial organisation, at another time the particular industrial organisation which they advocated. Probably through Comte the idea passed into the works of Herbert Spencer, who distinctly opposes modern "industrialism" to mediæval "militarism," and uses the phrase "militant régime" but not its implied opposite (*Data of Ethics*, ch. viii., etc.).

Apparently the actual phrase is quite modern, and Sir R. Giffen seems to have been one of the first who adopted it; he includes, under the general term "industrial régime," all those phenomena which go to make up the economic stage : in other words, "the sum of the chief features in the industrial organisation of a country like England." But the particular organisation of industry in England differs not merely in degree, but to some extent also in kind, from that of many other civilised communities ; and this fact leaves the meaning above attached to the phrase indefinite. Out of this arises an application of the term "industrial régime" to particular forms of industrial organisation—e.g. "competition as opposed to socialism"—the system of large tenures as opposed to peasant properties. Here the term becomes even more vague. We should hesitate to deny to the most strictly socialistic régime the title to be called industrial, especially when the phrase now in question had its birth in a communistic writing.

Clearly the simplest signification to affix to it would be that of the industrial organisation of any country, however rude, as opposed to mere nomad and marauding existence. In this case the industrial régime of any country will be the sum of its industrial features, and will vary with the state of economic development. C. A. H.

INDUSTRIAL REVOLUTION, THE. At the close of the last, and the opening of the present century a change, or rather a series of changes, passed over the agricultural and manufacturing industry of England, which has been aptly described by the name of the Industrial Revolution. The changes which then took place were of considerable magnitude, and the conditions of industry, both in manufactures and in agriculture, may without any great extravagance be said to have been revolutionised. Until this time the general character of industry in England presented nearly the same features as those which it had exhibited during the greater part of the middle ages ; and from that time the commencement of our modern system of industry dates. AGRICULTURE IN ENGLAND (q.v.) and manufactures alike were then generally prosecuted on what we should term primitive and unsystematic methods. Men were raising complaints that half the land of the country was waste. The size of the farms was small, and the method of cultivation unscientific. In many parts of the country there were still open unenclosed fields ; in nearly all there was an absence of any proper system of rotation of crops, and of turnips and artificial grasses. Quarrels were continually arising about the rights of pasture on the common meadows, and about the boundaries of the many scattered minute parcels of land of which an individual's holding was made up.

Nor was the position, or character, of manufacturing industry different. It was carried on, with few exceptions, by craftsmen working with their own hands in their own homes (see DOMESTIC SYSTEM OF INDUSTRY), although even then there were exceptions, for some capitalist employers existed, and some factories had been built by the middle of the eighteenth century. The mechanical appliances and tools which the craftsmen used were generally of a simple and rude description, and the number of persons working under their direction was small. The apprentices (see APPRENTICESHIP), limited in number and term of service, and the JOURNEYMEN (q.v.), with their wages fixed, in theory if not in practice, by the magistrates, lived in the house, and ate at the table, of the master-craftsman. Employment, such as it was, was regular ; fashions varied slowly and slightly ; and men produced in the main, though not exclusively, for a market which was close at hand. They were intimately acquainted with the conditions of that market, and the state of the roads was such that intercourse and trade with distant towns were rendered difficult. The workman who ventured to move from one town to another was not merely liable to be sent back to his original abode under the law of settlement (see SETTLEMENT ; POOR LAW), stigmatised by Adam Smith (Wealth of Nations, bk. i. ch. x.) as an "evident violation of natural liberty and justice," for fear that he might eventually come upon the rates in his new dwelling-place, but he might also be excluded from employment by the restrictive privileges of some exclusive trade corporation which were, in Adam Smith's words, a "plain violation" of that "most sacred and inviolable property which every man has in his own labour." The goods which the craftsmen made were often taken to the halls of the different corporations to be stamped as genuine. The woollen industry was now, as it had been for a long time previously, the staple industry of the country, and was carried on at Norwich, and in the west of England, and the west Riding of Yorkshire. The iron industry, which was prosecuted in Sussex, where the iron was still smelted by charcoal in small furnaces blown by leathern bellows worked by oxen, was said to be gradually dying out ; and the cotton industry was so insignificant as to be mentioned but incidentally, by Adam Smith, who lived on the very eve of the industrial revolution, and himself, perhaps, assisted in affording a shelter within the walls of Glasgow University to James Watt, the inventor of the steam-engine, seeking protection from the exclusive tyranny of the local corporation of hammermen, who had refused to allow him to practise his trade. Adam Smith declared that there had been only three inventions of note in the cotton industry for the space of three centuries. Banking was as yet in its infancy, and the Bank of England did not issue notes of a lower denomination than £20. The external commerce of the country was hampered by a number of vexatious restrictions, and duties on imports and bounties on exports abounded, while the colonies were regarded as a field for the commercial monopoly of the mother country. Such was the general condition of affairs before the changes which introduced the modern industrial system. Those changes were bewildering in their magnitude, and, to some extent also, in the rapidity with which they were effected. Agriculture underwent a transformation, the chief part of which, however, seems to have been accomplished in the earlier half or two-thirds of the 18th century. Large farms began to take the place of small farms. The inclosure of the open field was actively prosecuted, and sometimes injustice was done to the rights of the smaller commoners. Scientific cultivation was substituted, in a more or less considerable degree, in different parts of the country, for primitive methods. Bakewell improved the breed of cattle. Townsend—"Turnip Townsend" as he was nicknamed—introduced the cultivation of turnips. Coke at a later time devised an improved system of rotation of crops. But in manufacturing industry the changes were more revolutionary, and they occurred in the latter part of the century. Four great inventions were made in the cotton industry—that of the spinning-jenny by Hargreaves; that of the water-frame by Arkwright; that of the mule by Crompton; and the most considerable and important, in its consequences to the old handicraft occupations, of all, that of the power-loom by Cartwright. This last invention dealt a fatal blow to the fortunes of the old hand-loom weavers, and their distress has furnished a stock illustration of the temporary misery which may be occasioned by the introduction of machinery, at any rate to those workmen the labour of whose hands it supersedes. But other industries besides that of the manufacture of cotton were affected by the changes of the times. The smelting of iron by coal was introduced by Roebuck, and the decaying iron industry revived, and abandoned the charcoal forests of Sussex for the coal seams of the north and the Midlands. Canals, such as the Grand Trunk connecting the Trent with the Mersey, and the Grand Junction, which afforded the means of communication between London and the chief towns of the Midlands, were constructed under the direction of the inventive genius of Brindley, and the roads of the country were improved under that of Telford. Mills were erected on the banks of rivers in order that use might be made of the water-power which was there available to drive the new machinery, and then came the most wonderful and important discovery of all—that of the steam-engine, to be followed in its turn by the railway. All these changes gave a great stimulus to the production of wealth and the growth of population. They kindled a spirit of eager and restless enterprise, which was sometimes inclined to be reckless of injury occasioned to human life and health, and to give little consideration to the wrench to human affections which was not infrequently the consequence, direct or indirect, of the changes. For trade passed from quiet villages to noisy towns; from the home of the handicraftsman to the factory of the employer; from the master, who lived together with his apprentices and journeymen, and was in general "so joined together" with them in "sentiment" and "love that they did not wish to be separated if they could help it," to the employer who had hundreds of "hands" working under him, whose very faces he might not himself know. Division and subdivision of labour (see DIVISION OF LABOUR), organisation and localisation of industry, were carried out on a scale, and to an extent, unknown before. Master-merchants and wholesale dealers arose. Manufacturers began to produce for distant and fluctuating markets, and to crowd into, and dismiss from, their factories, as the changing demands of varying trade required, multitudes of men, women, and children. There seems to be reason for believing that something like a regular system of transporting children from London to the new manufacturing districts of the country was in operation; and there is unfortunately no doubt that the greed of parents joined with the eagerness of employers to increase the number and intensify the labour of the young apprentices in the factories. Population was stimulated by the lax administration of the poor law, and by the numerous chances of earning a livelihood which presented themselves; and also, so to say, torn up by the roots from its old abodes, while the industrial world was pervaded by restless movement. The workmen were forbidden by law to combine with a view to the regulation of trade, but, under the guise of friendly societies, they formed themselves into TRADES UNIONS (q.v.), and attempted in certain trades to restore the old system, by which the number of apprentices was limited, and the magistrates determined the rates of wages. They failed ultimately in this endeavour; but they did not cease to maintain, under circumstances of difficulty, their unions; and the state, by its FACTORY ACTS (q.v.), placed restrictions of increasing rigour and comprehensiveness on the employment of women and children. The industrial revolution was undoubtedly a time of great distress, which was intensified by the existence of CORN LAWS (q.v.) preventing the importation of food from abroad to make up for the scarcity occasioned by bad harvests at home and by the depression of trade which followed the close of the great war. The financial demands of the war combined with the opportunity afforded to England to supply the commercial wants of the continental nations, in whose country, and by whose soldiers the war was chiefly prosecuted, to stimulate increased production ; and the brilliant series of inventions which were made towards the close of the last century, permitted the stimulus to be effective. The pressing need of the time seemed to be that of increased production ; and the nation was less inclined to regard those permanent interests, which might have been consulted by greater consideration for the health and the education of the young, than to promote the obvious and immediate interests of the moment. The industrial revolution may be said to cover the period embraced by the writings of the three great older economists, ADAM SMITH, MALTHUS, and RICARDO (q.v.). The first lived on the eve of the revolution, amid the relics of the routine and regulation of a former era. The second lived in the midst of the revolution, and his writing reflected the gloom and despair of the time. The third lived towards the end of the revolution, and the assumption of a pervading competition, which is the basis of his reasoning, was not a wholly inaccurate representation of the actual state of affairs.

[For an account of the industrial revolution the student should consult Toynbee's *Industrial Revolution*, Miss Martineau's *History of the Peace*, and, for the evils of the old factory system, Karl Marx's *Capital*, which is, however, obviously biassed.—For the struggle of the old trade unions, Brentano on *Gilds*, and Howell's *Conflicts of Capital and Labour*, are of use ; and, for an account of the changes in agriculture, reference should be made to Prothero's *Pioneers and Progress of English Farming*, ch. iv.—Held, *Sociale Geschichte Englands*.—For much general information, Tooke and Newmarch, *History of Prices*, 6 vols. ; cp. also W. Cooke Taylor on the *Modern Factory System*.—S. and B. Webb on *The History of Trade Unionism*.]   L. L. P.

INDUSTRIES, LARGE AND SMALL. One of the most marked tendencies of modern times in industrial matters is to increase the scale on which commerce and manufacture are conducted. The DOMESTIC SYSTEM OF INDUSTRY (q.v.) has given place to the FACTORY SYSTEM (q.v.) ; smaller factories have made way for larger establishments which really comprise several factories beneath one roof—for not merely are there separate rooms devoted to distinct operations, but there are sets of rooms so devoted— private ventures have been superseded by public COMPANIES (q.v.) controlling greater masses of capital, and employing greater numbers of workers ; and various SYNDICATES (q.v.) and TRUSTS (q.v.) and other kinds of combinations have been formed. The use of steam as a motive power has probably contributed to this tendency to concentration of industry in large establishments, for it can only be generated in one spot and distributed over a small area. But there are other advantages possessed by the system of production on a large over that on a small scale, which have assisted the movement, and these would not cease to be opera-

tive, were steam replaced by some fresh motive power, such as electricity, which could be generated at a common centre and distributed by wires over a comparatively large area. These advantages may be classified under three heads : (1) *Economies of management.*—A large undertaking permits of a more systematic organisation, and a more thorough application of the principle of the DIVISION OF LABOUR (q.v.). It allows of a better arrangement of buildings and of mechanical appliances. It affords the opportunity for the experimental trial of new machinery, to the expense of which a smaller undertaking would be unequal. In all these ways it tends to economy, and in other ways also it effects a direct saving. "One high chimney can make a draught for a large furnace as well as for a small one ; one door-keeper can admit five hundred men as easily as fifty." The different clerks, stokers, and mechanics can be kept more fully employed on their own special work in a large than in a small undertaking ; and the employer at the head of a large establishment is able to devote his time and his thoughts more exclusively to the general direction and superintendence of the business. (2) *Economies of purchase.* —A large undertaking can generally buy what it requires on more advantageous terms than those enjoyed by a smaller undertaking. It can employ well-paid and trustworthy agents. It can draw its supplies from a wider area. It can obtain greater facilities for transport. It can buy in larger quantities, and can afford experimental purchases of machinery and materials. (3) *Economies of sale.*—Somewhat similar advantages belong to the larger undertaking in the matter of selling as in that of buying. It can push its wares by advertising and employing commercial travellers. It can secure the cheaper and more expeditious and efficient transport of these wares to their ultimate destination. It can ascertain the condition of remote markets. It can offer a more abundant variety of patterns and styles. It can perhaps inspire greater confidence in its customers. The advantages thus possessed by large over small undertakings are very great ; and to them must be added the consideration that there are some enterprises the magnitude of which is such that they could not be successfully accomplished without the resources of capital commanded by a large trading company. The system of limited liability (see LIMITED LIABILITY ACTS) has permitted of the formation of these companies with comparative ease ; and Professor Marshall has said (*Economics of Industry*, original edition, bk. i. ch. viii.) that "there does not seem to be any limit to the amount of wealth which a single trading company can profitably manage in a business which can be managed by routine, and does not require the bold enterprise and prompt decision of a single mind." But there are, on the other hand, advantages which belong to small, and are not possessed by large, undertakings; and there are departments of industrial activity to which the system of production on a large scale has as yet been applied only in exceptional cases. Smaller subsidiary industries are continually springing up to supply some of the wants of the larger; and AGRICULTURE (q.v.) is, at present at any rate, following at a gradual pace in the steps of manufacture. The introduction of mechanical appliances is indeed advancing, and the larger farmer may possess an advantage over the smaller in the matter of the economical use of these appliances, and of his farm-buildings and materials and implements. He may, too, possess greater scientific knowledge, he may display more vigorous enterprise, he may command more abundant capital, and adopt a better rotation of crops. But, with all these unquestionable advantages, it is still the case that agriculture permits of less systematic organisation than manufacture, and of a less thorough application of the principle of the division of labour. The labourers must be scattered over the country, and they cannot be concentrated in masses as they are in the manufacturing centres. Their work varies with the seasons, and they cannot devote their entire energies to some small department of a great industry. And, again, the business of superintendence, and the advantage of unremitting personal watchfulness and close personal interest, are more obvious and important in agriculture than they are in most branches of manufacture. It is in this matter of superintendence and of personal interest that the small master enjoys a superiority over the large, and that the private venturer has a resource and a stimulus which can hardly be possessed, and are rarely exhibited, by the salaried officials of a public company. In industries, then, which demand the incessant vigilance of personal interest, and do not possess a market large enough to render profitable the thorough application of the principle of the division of labour, the system of production on a small scale has, even in manufacture, advantages over production on a large scale (see EMPLOYERS AND EMPLOYED).

[J. S. Mill, *Political Economy*, bk. i. ch. ix., and Marshall's *Principles of Economics*, bk. iv. ch. xi.]   L. L. P.

INDUSTRY, CAPTAINS OF. This title has been sometimes given to the employers of modern industry. They have been regarded as the leaders of an industrial army, which is under their command, obeys their orders, and depends to a very large extent for success or failure on their judgment and enterprise. They have in a sense to determine on the plan of action, to organise its means, and to superintend its execution. The employer of older times

was a craftsman who lived and worked together with a small number of apprentices and journeymen (see DOMESTIC SYSTEM OF INDUSTRY), and produced his goods, frequently to order, and generally for a steady unchanging market close at hand. Now production is carried on in anticipation of demand, goods are made according to varying fashions of divers materials brought from remote countries, and they are sold at a distance from their place of production and often on credit. The scale on which business is habitually conducted has largely increased (see TRADE), and the number of persons working under an employer has grown together with the size of his factory. The difficulty and importance of the labour of management have undergone a corresponding extension, and the employer has become the most prominent and responsible personage in the world of industry. His authority is despotic, and his power for good or for evil immense. And, just as an army follows the directions, and depends on the generalship, of the commander, so the industrial army obeys the orders and relies on the ability and discretion of the employer, the captain of industry. It is this idea of leadership which has suggested the metaphor, together with the conception of the modern world of industry as the scene of the eager unceasing competition of rival armies of producers.

[For the function of the employer the books mentioned in the articles on EMPLOYERS AND EMPLOYED; EMPLOYING CLASS; and ENTREPRENEUR, should be consulted.]   L. L. P.

INDUSTRY, ORGANISATION OF. The organisation of industry, unlike most forms of organisation outside the purely physical world, is not in any great measure due to the conscious endeavour of individuals; it rather grows out of the acts of people for their own ends. It thus contrasts with the organisation of labour (see TRADES UNIONS), and any other combination of the same class (as FARMERS' ORGANISATIONS, U.S., q.v.); for such organisations are deliberately formed for special purposes,—generally the defence of classes, interests, or industries, —and have definite aims in view. It is claimed by socialists and collectivists that under a socialist régime this organisation would be carried on with a particular aim—the development of the talent and energy of the whole community; that it would be controlled and regulated by the wisdom of the great body of the people; and that it would, therefore, apart from the special economic effects in distribution of wealth and labour, be more successful than it is at present, when it is dependent on the interests or caprices of individuals. On the other hand, it is maintained that under a system of individual freedom the energies of each are, by force of nature, driven into those channels in which they will be of most use; and that the machinery by which industry has come to be regulated, though not the result of a definite scheme, is the consequence of principles of human nature which must always in the long run produce the most satisfactory organisation for the community, because ability and capacity are attracted to their proper channels. Whatever view is taken, it is certain that without organisation of one kind or another industry would now be useless and impossible ; and the existing organisation is so deeply rooted that it would be difficult to do more than amend it in detail. It is part of the industrial life of every civilised nation.

The earliest phase, historically, of this organisation is what is called division of employments ; and the earliest division of employments, like the origin of capital, is lost in the past. We find in some of the oldest records, however, that people are mentioned as engaged in certain specified employments. In the Pentateuch artificers in brass are named ; and dyeing and weaving we read about as recognised occupations. There was also, at a very early period, a division between rural and urban forms of industry. The dynasty of Pharaohs, who befriended the Israelites, are understood to have been a race of shepherd princes or chiefs who were ultimately driven out by the later dynasty who held the kingdom in the time of Moses. The curious episode of the purchase and storage of grain by Joseph could only have occurred in a state of society where the town and the country had diverse industries and interests. The progress of industry among the Greeks and the Romans is not easy to trace : that the division of employments attained to a greater degree among them than with the eastern races is certain, but further than this it cannot be said that any organisation is traceable.[1] The division of employments was also retarded greatly by the use of slaves. The localisation of industry, with which we are now so familiar, is found only in its earliest form, where absolutely necessary ;—as where precious metals were discovered, or a natural harbour existed, and a port created to serve the surrounding country. What in modern times forms one of the most important features in the organisation of industry—the massing the people engaged in the same employment or manufacture together in certain towns and districts, apart from natural or geographical causes, is a much later development. This phenomenon in the progress of industry is far more common in the present century than it has ever been before ; it is, in fact, one of the predominant characteristics of the age we live in, though it is still capable of further development, if the same forces that have acted in the past continue to act in the

future. This great change is the result of the new physical forces which have come into operation ; steam, electricity, and rapid means of carriage and communication.

In mediæval times, the organisation of industry was attempted to be carried out on a set plan in a far greater degree than in modern times. The whole series of associations, international, national, and local—as the HANSE towns, the STAPLE towns, the merchant and craft GILDS—were attempts made to organise industry through combination for the benefit of the whole association, and through it of each individual member. The unions in separate trades, existing when the means of communication was poor, and distance in space an almost insuperable barrier to the promotion of common interests, frequently caused a subsidiary localisation to take place, the remains of which are seen in the nomenclature of certain districts and streets in the large towns. In the city of London, the names of some streets still indicate the occupations of former occupiers. Prof. Ashley (*Economic History and Theory*, vol. i. p. 96) gives instances which could be multiplied readily in almost every city of considerable size and antiquity.

These localisations were not the result of the convenience to an individual of being in the neighbourhood of those in his own trade, an object which we are used now to see attracting men, but were part of a determined effort to produce an offensive and defensive union for the preservation and furtherance of class interests. If the trade was threatened, either by imposts of the government or by foreign competition, from other towns usually, or by defections from its own ranks, it was necessary to act in unison ; and to do this, the trade must be capable of being called together at the shortest notice. Again, if any member was threatened with injustice as an individual, it was important that all the trade should be ready to defend him, if need be, without delay. It is probable that this congregation of trades led by gradual steps to the modern form of grouping, by which industries become localised. In a great number of instances an industry becomes fixed in certain localities by some geographical or geological advantage. The mouth of a large river is naturally used for dock-yards and ship-building ; the more easily coal can be conveyed, the more likelihood is there that such a trade will flourish. Of course the presence of coal-fields fixes the locality of a mining industry ; and the neighbourhood of coal-fields assists in the rise of industries which constantly require a great quantity of fuel, such as iron and steel manufacture. In a greater number of cases, however, there is no determining cause of the kind we have mentioned, and the prevalence of a trade in any particular town or district is probably due to the indi-

[1] (See *Manufacturing Arts in Ancient Times*, by James Napier, London, 1874, for an interesting account of early localised industries.)

vidual enterprise of some one man. In this country, as in others, we have many examples of such apparently haphazard localisation. There is no reason in nature why china should be made in Dresden ; nor why glass-blowing should be predominant in Venice, and carpet-making in Brussels. The lace manufacture in Nottingham, the former silk industry at Coventry, the shoe trade of Northampton, are all familiar instances of the same phenomenon. The origin of these particular local trades and others like them is interesting, but of no scientific value. What is of importance about them is the consequence that we have capital of the same class and labour of the same kind drawn together, with the result that the former, even where it is fixed or specialised, becomes more transferable and easier to realise, while the latter loses much of its natural immobility. The general wage in a trade is much more accurately known where the trade is largely confined to one district than where it is scattered over the country ; and thus the remuneration of agricultural labourers, who belong to a trade in which localisation is impossible and organisation singularly difficult to obtain, has always exhibited a very marked divergence in different parts of the country, while the wages of coal-miners remain approximately the same in all different coalfields. From year to year the farm-labourer in Wiltshire goes on taking 30 per cent lower wages than the man who is doing the same kind of work in Yorkshire ; but if a rise in wages is obtained by miners in one district, even of a small amount, those in the other districts immediately endeavour, through their unions,—and often successfully, —to obtain a like advance in their own rates.

The features of the modern organisation of industry which are the most striking and the most important are the specialisation of capital and of labour, and the interdependence of trades. The occurrence of these phenomena have, no doubt, led many thinkers of this century to discuss the question whether, when one group of labourers or capitalists depends so greatly on others over which they have no direct control, it is not possible and advisable to place the whole industry of the nation under some central authority ; so that, as socialists say, it may be guided by reason for the common benefit, instead of by chance and caprice for the advantage of certain individuals. The cause of this mutual dependence is really, in one or other of its many forms, the tendency which Adam Smith named the DIVISION OF LABOUR. If we take any manufactured article, not of an elementary kind, we find that a perfect multitude of people have combined to produce it and bring it into the market where we find it ; often the difficulty, in fact, is to find some class of labourers who have not had a hand in the business. Take such a commonplace thing

as a lead-pencil, costing a penny. In the making it, of course, the miners who dug the metal and the hewers who cut the cedar have been employed, besides the workers in the pencil factory who cut each into its proper shape. Then there are the men who compounded the mixture of glue used in cementing the pieces of wood together, and holding the lead fast. But this does not nearly exhaust all the labour concerned in the product. Machinery was required to dig for the lead, and coals were needed to keep in action the engines that drove the machinery. Coal-miners, smelters, iron-moulders, mechanical engineers had all a part, therefore, in the construction of the pencil ; and not only they, but all the persons engaged in the industries necessary to feed the businesses of coal-mining, smelting, etc. Ships brought the wood of which the pencil was made, railways carried the lead ; and, apart from all these, agriculture was required to produce the food which kept in life the various workers employed in all these industries. It would be impossible to apportion the part performed by each different class of labourers in the product, in the example given ; but it serves to show the entire dependence of one industry on another, under the present system ; and the means by which anything affecting in a permanent or serious degree one branch of trade is certain to exercise economic consequences on many others. It is this which embodies the real organisation of industry in modern times. It is the consequence, as the above illustration shows, of the manifold specialisation of labour and capital. It is probably to this phase of modern life, more than to any other, that we owe the growth of economics as a science ; and it is in the fuller consideration of the mutual dependence of various forms of capital and labour on one another—what is called the social aspect of industry—that further developments of the science in all likelihood are to be looked for.

[Rogers, *Six Centuries of Work and Wages.*— Maine, *Village Communities.* — Ashley, *Economic History and Theory.* Also the *Report of the Royal Commission on the Depression of Trade.*]

M. G. D.

INFANTS. The civil law distinguishes two stages of infancy, the one previous and the one subsequent to the attainment of puberty. The distinction has been retained in many continental countries and also in Scotland, but English law recognises one stage of infancy only, viz. the whole time before the age of twenty-one. Infants are subjected to various disabilities (as to which see DISABILITIES OF INFANTS), and their persons as well as their property are frequently placed under the care of a guardian. This is always the case on the death of an infant's father. Before 1886 the testamentary guardian appointed by the father was not in any way subject to the mother's control, but the Guardianship of Infants Act 1886 provides that on the death of the father the mother is to be the guardian either alone or jointly with any guardian appointed by the father. The mother may also by deed or will appoint any person to be guardian of her infant children after the death of herself and the father. Infants are but rarely placed under the guardianship of a third person during the father's lifetime, and the only procedure available for that purpose is an application to the Chancery division of the High Court ; the court will not, however, interfere with the father's authority except on very strong grounds, as for instance habitual cruelty or immorality. Modern statutes have in various ways extended the legal rules for the protection of infants. Thus it is provided by the Prevention of Cruelty to Children Act 1889, that any person over sixteen years of age, who, having the custody of a boy under the age of fourteen years or of a girl under the age of sixteen years, wilfully ill-treats or neglects such boy or girl, shall be liable to a fine or two years' imprisonment with or without hard labour. The same statute also imposes punishments for causing children to beg or to be in any street or in any premises licensed for the sale of intoxicating liquor, "whether under the pretence of singing, playing, performing, offering anything for sale, or otherwise." It also authorises any petty-sessional court to order that a child may be taken out of the custody of any person convicted or committed for trial for the ill-treatment or neglect of such child. Another danger to which infants of more mature age are frequently exposed has been provided against by the Betting and Loans (Infants) Act of 1892, which makes it a misdemeanour to send circulars to infants inviting them to bet or to borrow money.

[As to the legal position of infants, and the duties and rights of guardians, see Simpson, *The Law of Infants*, 2nd ed., by E. J. Elgood.—Eversley, *The Law of Domestic Relations*.]   E. S.

INFLATION
Great Britain, 1797-1819, p. 405; United States, 1862-1879, p. 406.

GREAT BRITAIN. The examples employed for illustration are that of Great Britain in the years 1797-1819, and that of the United States in 1862-79.

Many more might be cited, but these are sufficient to show the main results of an excessive supply of paper money not redeemable in specie. While "money itself is a mere contrivance for facilitating exchanges which does not affect the laws of value," of itself, an excess of the paper money in circulation issued by official fiat, and without any reference to the cost of production of the precious metals represented by it, must inevitably influence prices. The theory on the subject is explained by Professor Walker (*Money*, ch. xiv.-xvii.) with great clearness, and with copious illustrations.

Specie payments in Great Britain were suspended by order in council, 26th February 1797, owing to a run on the Bank of England. The Bank Restriction Act was passed in that year. The resumption of specie payments on the gold basis, established by the act of 1816, was directed by Sir Robert Peel's Act of 1819, and completed in 1821 and 1822. The Bank of England resumed payments in specie on 20th August 1819.

The effect was well described by Ricardo. "From 1797 to 1819 we had no standard whatever by which to regulate the quantity or value of our money. Its quantity and its value depended entirely on the Bank of England, the directors of which establishment, however desirous they might have been to act with fairness and justice to the public, avowed that they were guided in their issues by principles which, it is no longer disputed, exposed the country to the greatest embarrassment. Accordingly, we find that the currency varied in value considerably during the period of twenty-two years when there was no other rule for regulating its quantity and value but the will of the Bank" (Ricardo's Works, 2nd ed., 1852 ; London, *On Protection to Agriculture*, § 5, p. 467).

The effect of the restriction of cash payments, and the divergence produced between the value of gold and of the paper currency, is broadly shown by the following Table, derived from Mushet.[1]

Market Price of Gold, Value of Currency and Depreciation of Value of Currency in England, 1800-1821.

Year.	Average market price of gold per. oz. from February 1800-1821.			Average per cent of the value of the currency at the market price of gold.			Average percentage depreciation of value of the currency.
	£	s.	d.	£	s.	d.	
1800	3	17	10½		Par.		Par.
1801	4	5	0	91	12	4	8·4
1802	4	4	0	92	14	2	7·3
1803[1]	4	0	0	97	6	10	2·6
1804	4	0	0	97	6	10	2·6
1805	4	0	0	97	6	10	2·6
1806	4	0	0	97	6	10	2·6
1807	4	0	0	97	6	10	2·6
1808	4	0	0	97	6	10	2·6
1809	4	0	0	97	6	10	2·6
1810	4	10	0	86	10	6	13·5
1811	4	4	6	92	3	2	7·8
1812	4	15	6	79	5	3	20·7
1813	5	1	0	77	2	0	22·9
1814	5	4	0	74	17	6	25·1
1815	4	13	6	83	5	9	16·7
1816	4	13	6	83	5	9	16·7
1817	4	0	0	97	6	10	2·6
1818	4	0	0	97	6	10	2·6
1819	4	1	6	95	11	0	4·5
1820	3	19	11	97	8	0	2·6
1821	3	17	10½		Par.		Par.

[1] By the evidence of Mr. Abraham Goldsmid before

In considering this table the further question remains : Does the premium on gold, in a country having inconvertible paper, fairly measure the full depreciation in respect to purchasing commodities ? Professor Walker considers (*Money*, p. 388) that the power of the paper was "much further diminished than its power to purchase gold."

The fluctuations in prices for the period (1797-1819) as chronicled by Tooke, *History of Prices*, vol. i. pp. 210-373, vol. ii. pp. 1-6, and 387-420, are illustrated by the following figures.[1]

Year.	Prices per quarter, Winchester measure. Mean price for the year.	Butter (Waterford), per cwt.		Tea (Congou), per lb.		Timber (Memel Fir), per load.	
	s. d.	s.	s.	s. d.	s. d.	£ s.	£ s.
1797	62 0	85	88	2 10	4 5	2 15	..
1798	54 0	60	63	3 0	3 9	2 10	3 0
1799	75 8	78	82	2 5	2 7	3 8	3 10
1800	127 0	85	90	2 10	3 7	5 10	5 15
1801	128 6	115	117	3 4	3 6	5 15	6 0
1802	67 3	65	70	3 0	3 9	3 12	3 14
1803	60 0	85	94	2 8	3 8	5 5	6 5
1804	69 6	75	80	2 8	3 3	3 15	4 0
1805	88 0	68	70	3 1	3 6	3 15	4 0
1806	88 0	96	100	2 11	3 8	3 10	3 15
1807	78 0	108	110	2 10	3 9	4 0	5 0
1808	85 3	100	105	3 2	3 8	6 10	7 0
1809	106 0	82	84	3 0	3 7	14 0	14 10
1810	112 0	90	95	3 1	3 10	8 10	9 10
1811	108 0	115	118	2 11	3 6	10 0	11 10
1812	118 0	110	118	3 2	3 8	9 10	10 0
1813	120 0	84	90	2 11	3 7	5 10	7 0
1814	85 0	138	140	3 5	3 10	7 5	7 15
1815	76 0	111	116	3 2	3 7	5 0	5 10
1816	82 0	62	68	2 6	3 6	3 5	3 15
1817	116 0	93	94	2 9	3 5	2 10	2 15
1818	98 0	130	134	2 11	3 7	3 5	3 10
1819	78 0	74	78	2 10	3 6	3 10	3 15

The general effect is perhaps more clearly shown by Jevons's table of prices in his chapter on the Depreciation of Gold (*Investigations in Currency and Finance*, p. 155).

Year.	Average ratio of prices to the prices of the year 1849 (1849 = 100).
1789	133
1799	202
1809	245
1819	175
1829	124
1839	144
1849	100

Jevons (*Investigations in Currency and Finance*, ch. iii. heading p. 119) warns us (pp. 130-131) against attributing every rise in

the Bullion Committee 1810, the market price of gold was stated to be £4 per ounce from 1803 to 1809. *Third Report of Royal Commission on Depression of Trade and Industry*, Appendix B. Memorandum of Standard of value. R. H. Inglis Palgrave, p. 314.

[1] Tooke's *History of Prices*, vol. ii. pp. 389, 408, 416, and 417. London, 1838.

prices to the influence of the monetary circulation ; but while he regards that Tooke was "partly and only partly right" in holding this view, he considers that "we must assign some part of the elevation of prices" to the manner in which the precious metals were driven out of circulation by the use of paper. It is difficult to estimate with absolute accuracy the effect of over-issues of irredeemable paper on prices. The price of some articles of consumption appears to have been more largely influenced by this cause than that of others, during the period between 1797 and 1819. Again, the effect of alterations in the amount of the currency on prices is more marked at some periods than at others, according as banking facilities are largely used or otherwise. But the table which Jevons himself has compiled leaves no doubt that the inflation resulting from the over-issues of paper currency during the period of bank restriction in Great Britain must have been very great, and that it must have largely exceeded the difference between the value of gold and that of the currency indicated in Mushet's tables quoted above.

UNITED STATES (1862 - 1879). The period of inconvertible paper money in the United States from 1862 to 1879 is often referred to as the inflationist period. Strictly speaking, "inflation" took place in the United States at other times, markedly in 1815-18 and in 1834-39,—both these being connected with bad banking legislation,—and again in 1854-57, when there was a very simple case of inflation and crisis, not complicated in essentials by currency derangement. But the period 1862-1879, as the one in which the features of "currency inflation" were most marked, will be the one dealt with here.

The issues of paper money began under great financial stress in the course of the civil war, in February 1862, when a first batch of 150 millions of dollars (30 millions sterling) was put out ; two more of the same amount followed in July 1862 and March 1863, making a total issue of 450 millions (90 millions sterling) of United States notes or "greenbacks." In addition there were put forth in 1863 and 1864 considerable amounts, the maximum being about 200 millions (40 millions sterling) of interest-bearing legal tender notes, which inflated the currency still further. The result was a rapid disappearance of specie in 1862, and a sharp rise in prices in 1862-65. With the close of the civil war in 1865, the administration—and especially Mr. M'Culloch, the secretary of the treasury,—set to work at once to contract the paper issues, and succeeded without much difficulty in getting rid of the interest-bearing notes referred to. A beginning was also made in contracting the United States notes proper. But in April 1866 congress passed a resolution restricting the pace at which the notes should be paid off; for six months no more than 10 millions of dollars (2 millions sterling) of notes should be withdrawn, and thereafter no more than 4 millions (£800,000) a month. This resolution marks the beginning of the struggle between the inflationists and the advocates of resumption; for the paper issues had been made solely under financial stress in the civil war, and had in no quarter been originally regarded as advisable or likely to endure. The inevitable hardships of contraction and falling prices caused the inflationist movement. The inflationists urged the permanent retention or increase of the inconvertible paper money, the most extreme wing demanding the issue of enough paper to pay off the whole funded debt—over 2000 million dollars (400 millions sterling); the most moderate asking only that the volume of paper be left unchanged, so that the country might "grow up" to it. From 1866 to 1879 the contest was carried on with varying fortune in congress and before the public. In 1868 the inflationists gained a point by the passage of an act forbidding further contraction and leaving the volume of the United States notes at the point where it then stood—356 millions (71 millions sterling). In the height of the panic of 1873 the then secretary of the treasury, Mr. Richardson, put forth some notes previously retired, under questionable legal authority. This became the occasion for a bill, passed by both houses of congress in 1874, providing for an increase of the paper issues to 400 millions (80 millions sterling). The bill marked the height of the inflationist movement; it was vetoed by President Grant, who thus dealt the movement a heavy blow. A compromise bill was then passed, in 1874, fixing the volume of United States notes at 382 millions (76½ millions sterling). Next year (1875) the end of the struggle was brought in sight by the passage of the Resumption Act, which provided for resumption of specie payment in 1879. A gradual decline in the volume of paper was to take place *pari passu* with an expected enlargement of the volume of national bank notes. But this decline was again stopped by an act passed in 1878, which virtually fixed the amount of United States notes at the point then reached —$346,681,016 (69⅓ millions sterling). At that they have remained to the present time (1895). Resumption was successfully accomplished at the date fixed (January 1, 1879); and therewith the movement for paper money inflation came to an end. The demand for an increase in the currency after 1879 took another direction in the agitation for the free coinage of silver or the issue of currency based on silver purchases. [There is no good history of the monetary policy

of the United States since 1860. Some accounts of it are in Bolles, *Financial History of the United States*, Philadelphia, 1886, vol. iii.; J. K. Upton, *Money in Politics*, Boston, 1885. The texts of the various legislative measures are accurately collected in Dunbar, *Laws of the United States on Currency, Finance, and Banking*, Boston, 1891.]
F. W. T.

INGOT. Metal cast in a mould of a size and shape convenient for handling. The word, which is derived from the wedge- or tongue-shaped ingots used by the Romans (*lingo*, to lick with a tongue, Fr., *lingot*), is seldom used in connection with other than the precious metals, though such a cast block of any metal may properly be called an ingot. The shape of the ingots of the precious metals now in use in this country, though varying to some extent, generally approximates to that of an ordinary brick made with slightly sloping sides. In the London bullion market these pieces of metal pass by the name of "bars."

In China transactions in bullion are carried on by means of shoe-shaped ingots, known as "Sycee" silver; while in Japan ingots of copper are cast, under water, into canvas receptacles, the shape of the resultant mass being that of a shallow dish or saucer.

Gold ingots sent by the Bank of England to the Mint for coinage are of an average weight of 400 ounces troy. They are of two kinds— "coarse" and "fine." The latter are not, however, composed of metal which is absolutely pure, but have a mean millesimal fineness of 999, while the coarse bars contain on an average 897 parts of fine gold in 1000. Prior to 1889 the mean weight of such ingots was 200 ounces troy, but in consequence of changes in the practice of the bullion market, their weight was then doubled.

The silver ingots purchased by the Royal Mint for coinage are of an average weight of 1100 ounces troy, and an average millesimal fineness of 995·8.
F. E. A.

INHABITED HOUSE DUTY, a tax on inhabited houses calculated by reference to their annual value and payable by the occupier, was first imposed in Great Britain in 1778, the idea being derived from the *Wealth of Nations* (bk. v. ch. ii. part ii. art. i.). Originally the rates were 6d. in the £ for houses worth £5 and below £50 per annum, and 1s. in the £ for those worth £50 or more. The tax was continued at various rates, the highest being 2s. 10d., till its repeal in 1834. This tax, rather than the more objectionable window tax, was selected for repeal on the ground that the great houses, such as Chatsworth, etc., being charged much more highly, relatively, to the window tax than to the house tax owing to the difficulty of ascertaining their annual value to let, the repeal of the window tax would benefit more particularly the richer classes. The annual produce of the tax at the date of the repeal was about £1,200,000.

This selection was ultimately allowed to be a mistake; in 1851 the policy of 1834 was reversed, the window tax repealed, and the inhabited house duty re-imposed with certain alterations. The rates were 6d. for shops, public - houses, and farm - houses, and 9d. for dwelling-houses. From 1851 the tax has held its place in our fiscal system, modifications having been made from time to time with a view, more particularly, to afford relief in respect of business premises. In 1890 graduation was re-introduced, to the extent of charging the duty at lower rates as respects houses of small annual value. The present rates are :

On shops, public - houses, hotels, inns, coffee-houses, farm-houses, lodging-houses, of the annual value of
    £20 and not exceeding £40—2d. in the £
    exceeding £40   ,,   £60—4d.   ,,
    exceeding £60 . . . . 6d.   ,,
On private houses, clubs, and business premises other than shops (unless exempt) of a similar annual value, 3d. 6d. or 9d. in the £ as the case may be.

The principal exemptions are:—houses below £20 of annual value; houses belonging to Her Majesty or any of the royal family; public offices; hospitals; charity schools; poor-houses; houses or tenements occupied solely for business or professional purposes (a caretaker allowed); artisans' dwellings. The tax is under the administration of the commissioners of inland revenue, and the chief enactments concerning it are:—14 & 15 Vict. c. 36 ; 43 Geo. III. c. 161 ; 48 Geo. III. c. 55 (Sch. B) ; 41 & 42 Vict. c. 15, § 13 ; 53 & 54 Vict. c. 8, §§ 25 and 26 ; 54 & 55 Vict. c. 25, § 4. It does not extend to Ireland.

In 1892-93 the yield of the tax was £1,411,510. The following table shows the number and annual value of the houses charged in 1891-92.

		Number.	Annual value.
2d.	Shops or warehouses	249,283	£12,476,571
4d.	Beer-houses	85,850	6,293,157
or	Farmhouses	31,110	767,575
6d.	Lodging-houses	13,887	835,794
9d.	Dwelling-houses	889,635	45,119,664

[Dowell's *History of Taxation and Taxes in England*, vol. iii. p. 178.—Dowell's *House Tax Laws*, 1893.—36th *Report of Commissioners of Inland Revenue*, pp. 27-31.—See for various motions in Parliament, Hansard, (123), 903, (197), 1802, (200), 1374, (280), 90, (285), 224, (335), 436. See ASSESSMENT ; TAXATION.]   F. A.

INHERITANCE, ESTATE OF. An estate in land extending beyond the duration of one or more lives is called an "estate of inheritance." Such an estate must be either an estate "in fee simple, which in popular language is described as absolute ownership," or an estate tail (see ENTAIL).   E. S.

INHIBITION (Scots law). An order against contracting any debt which may become a burden or charge on heritable property (realty) or which may give rise to process issuing against the realty of the party inhibited, to the prejudice of the complainer. It takes effect as of course by registration, in the General Register of Inhibitions in Edinburgh, of a summons containing a "warrant for inhibition," duly issued and served. The inhibition is personal to the debtor, and applies only to realty vested or in expectancy at its date, and to voluntary obligations undertaken after its date. The effect of an inhibition, standing alone, is merely to deter purchasers; but it may be followed by an "adjudication," by which the creditor may be adjudged a preference over other creditors whose claims originated after the inhibition. There is also an inhibition by a husband against his wife—obtained by a bill to the Court, issued as of course without reason assigned, and registered in the General Register of Inhibitions,—by which it is notified to the public that the wife's agency has been cancelled, except in regard to necessaries for which it may be proved that the husband has not otherwise made provision.   A. D.

INLAND NAVIGATION. See CANALS.

INOFFICIOSUM TESTAMENTUM is the term used in Roman law to signify a will which may be set aside because it violates the duty of natural affection existing between certain near relations, as when a parent, without proper cause, leaves less than the legal share (*portio legitima*) to a child, or a child leaves less to a parent (see LEGITIM).   E. A. W.

INSCRIBED STOCK. A SECURITY (*q.v.*) is called "inscribed" to distinguish it from a security which passes from hand to hand by delivery. A register is kept, where in the case of English or government loans or in the case of shares in an English company, transfer of ownership can be made. Registration or inscription is found suitable to English habits and ideas. On the continent and in America there is a prejudice against anything which publishes the ownership of securities, and bonds or shares to bearer are there preferred. As to the risk of forged transfers of inscribed securities see FORGED TRANSFER.   A. E.

INSCRIPTION MARITIME (FRANCE)—the system of recruitment for the navy organised by a law of the year iv. of the first republic (1796). All men who have made two over-sea voyages on a state or merchant vessel, or have served eighteen months at sea, or been two years engaged in fishing, are inscribed on the maritime register, and may be called for service in the fleet from the age of eighteen to fifty. The period of obligatory service is from twenty to twenty-seven years of age, after which the *inscrits* pass into the reserve and are only liable to service in case of war, and in the order of the classes to which they belong, those most recently liberated being taken first. From the ages of eighteen to twenty the young men may, on demand, anticipate the time for commencing the period of obligatory service. Since 1874 engineers and stokers on steamers are comprised in the maritime inscription. The *inscrits* enjoy many privileges ; they have a monopoly of the fishing in French waters, and may alone obtain concessions of parts of the shore or banks of tidal rivers and salt-water pools, for taking or breeding fish ; they are not liable to any other public service ; and have a right to a pension at the age of fifty, after twenty-five years' service in any kind of navigation, which pension is continued, but reduced, to their widows and orphans. A contribution of 3 per cent of their wages, whether earned on state or merchant ships, is, however, made to the pension fund, called the *Caisse des Invalides de la Marine*. During the period of obligatory service the men may obtain furloughs for service on merchant or shipping vessels. The number of men belonging to the maritime inscription serving in the fleet is about 24,000, forming about two-thirds of the crews, the remainder are volunteers or men drawn in the ordinary military conscriptions to serve as marines, not enjoying the privileges of the *inscrits*, and having no right to a pension although liable to military service to the age of forty-six (cp. IMPRESSMENT).

[" Rapport adressé au Ministre de la Marine au nom de la Commission chargée de l'étude des questions se rattachant au régime de l'inscription maritime," *Journal Officiel*, 12 Decembre 1890.]
T. L.

INSOLVENCY. See BANKRUPTCY LAW AND ADMINISTRATION.

INSPIRATIONISTS. See AMANA SOCIETY.

INSTALMENT. When the payment of any sum of money, instead of being effected altogether on one date, is to be divided into several parts to be effected on certain successive dates it is called a payment by instalments.   A. E.

INSTITORIA ACTIO is an action of Roman law maintainable against the owner of a business on account of a contract entered into with the superintendent or manager (*institor*). The manager himself, as party to the contract, was liable to an action on the contract he had made, as well as his master—Roman law, owing principally to the frequent employment of slaves in commercial transactions, not fully recognising the principle of contractual agency, which is essential to modern commerce.   E. A. W.

INSTRUMENT, NEGOTIABLE. A negotiable instrument differs from an ordinary contract or instrument, securing the payment of money, in three respects :

(1) It is assignable by virtue of the usage of trade, whereas a contract or "thing in action" is not ordinarily assignable at common law. A negotiable instrument purporting to be payable to bearer may be assigned by mere delivery ; or if purporting to be payable to order, then by indorsement completed by delivery.

(2) The consideration for its issue or transfer is presumed until the contrary is proved.

(3) If it gets into the hands of a holder for value without notice, he holds it free from any defects of title which would have vitiated it in the hands of any previous holder.

The term "negotiable instrument" is usually confined to the original and typical negotiable instruments, namely, bills of exchange, promissory notes, and cheques ; and the term "negotiable security" is applied to the negotiable bonds and scrip which in recent years have become so common in the money market. For the most part these instruments would be governed by the same considerations as promissory notes payable on demand. For revenue purposes, however, they are subject to special stamp regulations (see also COMMERCIAL INSTRUMENT).

[Chalmers, *Bills of Exchange*, 4th edition, pp. 312-327.]   M. D. C.

INSURANCE

History, p. 409 ; Life, Theory of, p. 410 ; Law and Practice of Life, p. 416 ; Marine, p. 418 ; Mutual, p. 419 ; State (Germany), p. 419.

INSURANCE, HISTORY. There appear to have been two forms of contract akin to insurance known to the ancients. The first is mentioned by A. Böckh (*Public Economy of Athens*). He states that "the idea of an institution for the insurance of slaves first occurred to Antigenes of Rhodes" (in the time of Alexander the Great, 356-323 B.C.), "who undertook, for a yearly contribution of eight drachmas for each slave that was in the army, to make good his price, as estimated by the owner at the time of elopement." Bottomry (see BOTTOMRY, LOAN ON) was also known to the Greeks. Among the Romans, the earliest mentioned transaction of this nature is the contract, noticed by Livy, made after the battle of Cannæ, for the supply of stores to the Roman government, the contractors stipulating that the state should bear all losses which might arise from the enemies' attacks, or from storms. But with the barbarian invasion, and consequent cessation of commerce, all such practices fell into disuse. The origin of modern insurance is obscure. Instances of some form of insurance are found amongst various nations in early mediæval times, but there appears to be no direct connection between them and the methods now adopted. The first form of mediæval insurance was undoubtedly marine, the system being afterwards extended to other objects.

Many countries or towns have claimed to be the birthplace of *marine* insurance, particularly Barcelona, Wisby, and Bruges ; but it appears really to have originated among the commercial cities of Italy, the earliest mention referring to Florence (14th century). It may even have been practised in the 13th century: an unedited Pisan document (the *Breve Portus Calleritani*, 1318) is supposed to refer to insurance at Cagliari. *Chambers of Insurance* were established at an early date on the continent, notably at Barcelona and Bruges. The period of its introduction into England is equally obscure ; in the earliest statute on the subject (1601), it is stated that it "hathe been tyme out of mynde an usage amongst merchantes." Bacon quotes it as a usual practice in 1558.

The insurance on a ship and its cargo representing usually too large a sum for a single individual, it is divided amongst several underwriters, each of whom guarantees such a fraction of the risk as he thinks proper. By far the greater portion of marine insurance in this country is done at Lloyd's, now a corporation, but formerly simply a meeting-place for underwriters. This institution originated in the coffee-houses established in London towards the end of the 17th century, one of which, owned by Edward Lloyd (first mentioned in 1688), became the resort of marine insurers, and ultimately all their underwriting was done there ; as the business grew larger, it was removed to the Royal Exchange in 1774. Two companies, the "London" and the "Royal Exchange" Assurance Corporations, obtained in 1720 a charter with a monopoly, as companies, of marine insurance business. No other company was formed until 1824, when Rothschild obtained the repeal of this exclusive charter, and founded the "Alliance" Insurance Company. The companies did not interfere much with individual underwriting. The amount of marine property insured in 1810, according to estimates made at the time of the Royal Commission, was about £160,000,000, of which some £130,000,000 was underwritten at Lloyd's.

The first *fire* insurance office in London was set up after the Great Fire, in 1667, by N. BARBON (*q.v.*), although schemes had been suggested in 1635, 1638, and 1660. But fire insurance almost certainly existed earlier on the continent. Part of the functions of fire insurance companies was to extinguish fires ; this was undertaken in their own interests, and all the important companies in London maintained fire brigades until 1866, when they were taken over by the Metropolitan Board of Works. Fire engines were first introduced into London from Holland in 1633. Barbon's method was individual underwriting : the first joint-stock association was founded in 1681 "at the back of the Royal Exchange." The oldest existing office is the "Hand in Hand," which dates from 1696. The growth of fire

insurance business can be best judged from the following table :

Year.	Value of Property insured.
1783	£135,000,000
1800	200,000,000
1840	645,000,000
1860	1,000,000,000
1868	1,430,000,000

These values are the amounts on which duty was paid ; as this was abolished in 1869, statistics of fire insurance since 1868 are only officially given of such offices as undertake also life business. Life insurance offices are compelled to make an annual return to the Board of Trade. The *Finance Chronicle*, however, gives the premiums received by fifty-four British offices in 1894 as nearly £19,000,000, and the claims paid as £13,000,000.

[C. Walford, *Insurance Cyclopædia*, 1871-80. —F. Hendriks, "Contributions to the History of Insurance," in *Assurance Magazine*, vol. ii., 1852. —F. Martin, *History of Lloyd's and of Marine Insurance in Great Britain*, 1876.—W. Gow, *Marine Insurance*, 1895].   R. H. H.

INSURANCE, LIFE, THEORY OF. The object of insurance is to spread the burden of losses, which to the individual would be crushing, over a large body of insured, and so render that burden easy to bear. This object is effected by collecting from each of the insured a sum, called a premium, proportioned to the risk to be insured against ; and out of the fund so formed, those of the insured who have experienced loss from the contingencies covered by the insurance, are indemnified.

Materials are not available for ascertaining accurately the extent to which life assurance is practised in the United Kingdom. All active companies are required by the Life Assurance Companies Act 1870 to make periodical returns to the board of trade, but these returns do not distinguish between home and foreign business, and they are not made up by the different companies to a uniform date. The last available figures (board of trade, 1894) show that at their then latest periodical valuations, British companies were liable under their life policies to the amount of £628,070,176 ; that in their respective last financial years they received in premiums £22,790,349 ; and that at the dates of the last balance sheets the invested funds, accumulated entirely out of premiums, and exclusive of share capital, amounted to £194,175,429. Assurances on lives insured by British offices, and resident in the colonies and abroad, are included in these aggregates, but on the other hand assurances granted by colonial and foreign companies on lives resident in the United Kingdom are excluded. These sources of error are in opposite directions, and the figures may be taken roughly to represent the amount of life assurance existing at the present day on the lives of persons resident in the British Isles.

From the magnitude of the totals it is manifest how important to the community is a sound system of life insurance, and the object of the present article is to explain, as briefly and as simply as possible, the scientific principles on which the business is conducted, and which experience has shown to be safe and trustworthy.

In early days life policies were granted only for short terms, generally for a year, or less; the earliest, of which full particulars have been preserved, was made on 15th June 1583, for £383 : 6 : 8 on the life of Wm. Gybbons for one year, the premium being at the rate of £8 per cent. No record seems to remain of the age of the life assured, probably that was a detail not thought of at the time. This policy was underwritten by thirteen private individuals, after the manner of marine insurances at Lloyd's in the present day.

About the year 1650, societies for the assurance of lives began to be formed. The principle on which they were worked was, that each surviving member had to pay a fixed contribution in respect of each death ; so that the amount receivable by the representatives of a deceased member varied according to the numbers in the society at the time of his death, and the contributions of the members varied according to the number of deaths which occurred in any particular year. No attempt was made to graduate the contributions of members according to their respective ages. In 1705 the "Amicable Society" was formed. Its system at first was to charge each member an annual premium of £6 : 4s., besides certain annual dues, and to divide among the representatives of the members who might happen to die in any particular year the amount received in premiums in that year to the extent of £5 per contributing member, so that in a year in which there happened to be few deaths, the share in respect of each death would be large ; and in the event of many deaths, small. At first no limit of age was imposed, but soon it was found that an influx of an undue proportion of old lives would reduce the death money inconveniently, and in 1707 the regulation was passed that members on admission must be between twelve and forty-five years of age. For a century this rule remained in force, and it was not until 1807 that a table of premiums was adopted graduated strictly according to age.

The weakness of the early assurance societies was that with the growing age of the members the death rate increased and the claims became onerous, so that either the contributions demanded from the members had to be augmented, or the amounts paid on death reduced.

The societies formed on this unsound basis all succumbed to the inevitable strain, except the Amicable, which, taught by experience, altered its constitution ; but in 1762 the Equitable Society was formed on the principle which is now recognised to be the only sound one ; and it still carries on business as one of the most successful financial institutions of the country.

Life insurance differs from other descriptions of insurance in that the risk to be insured against is constantly increasing with the duration of the contracts. That the rate of human mortality increases with the age was dimly known at a very early period, the Romans at the commencement of the Christian era valuing annuities charged on estates by a table giving values large for young lives, and constantly diminishing with advancing age. There seem, however, to have been no efforts made to estimate the true rates of mortality until 1671, when John de Witt, Grand Pensionary of Holland, presented a report, not published until long afterwards, on the subject, to the states-general ; and it was not until 1693 that the first real mortality table was formed, by E. HALLEY, Astronomer-Royal of England, and published that year in the *Philosophical Transactions*. It was based on observations made on births and funerals in the city of Breslau.

When the Equitable Society was started in 1762, it employed for the calculation of its premiums a mortality table constructed from the London bills of mortality. This showed heavy rates of mortality, beyond those which the subsequent experience of the society proved really to prevail, and in 1781 the Northampton table was adopted which, however, still showed an excessive death-rate.

A mortality table tells us how many persons out of a given number born, or starting from a given age, survive to each subsequent age ; and consequently it also shows how many out of the given number at the commencement die in each year of their age. The number with which the table commences is called the *radix* of the table. It is usual to arrange the table in columns, the first column containing the age attained, the second the number who attain that age, and the third the number who die between that age and the next higher age. The age is usually denoted by x, or one of the other letters at the end of the alphabet. The number who attain age x is denoted by the symbol l_x, and the number who die between ages x and $x+1$ by the symbol d_x. The following is an illustration of a mortality table. It is the early portion of the H^M *Healthy Males* table formed by the institute of actuaries from the experience of twenty British life offices. It will be observed that the commencing age is ten years, and the radix is 100,000. The radix is a purely arbitrary quantity, chosen only for the sake of convenience—

Age.	l_x.	d_x.
10	100,000	490
11	99,510	397
12	99,113	329
13	98,784	288
14	98,496	272
15	98,224	282
16	97,942	318
17	97,624	379
18	97,245	466
19	96,779	556
20	96,223	609
21	95,614	643
22	94,971	650
23	94,321	638
24	93,683	622
25	93,061	617

The mortality table affords the means of calculating the probabilities of life and of death. Thus, there being l_x persons alive aged x, of whom l_{x+t} survive to age $(x+t)$, there are, out of l_x chances altogether, l_{x+t} chances of any one of the l_x persons surviving to age $(x+t)$. Therefore the probability of a person aged x surviving to age $x+t$ is $l_{x+t} \div l_x$. This probability is denoted by the symbol $_tp_x$, or when $t=1$, simply by p_x. In a similar way, as $l_x - l_{x+t}$ persons, out of l_x living at age x, die before reaching age $(x+t)$, the probability of dying between ages x and $(x+t)$ is $(l_x - l_{x+t}) \div l_x$, which $= 1 - _tp_x$.

In financial transactions involving life contingencies, the operation of interest must be taken into account, because the premium has to be paid by the assured at the commencement of the contract, and the sum assured is not paid until the close; consequently the office keeps the premium invested in the interim, and secures interest on it. If by i we denote the interest in a year on £1, or more generally on 1 unit of value, whether that unit be a pound, a franc, or a dollar, etc., then 1 invested at the beginning of a year will amount to $(1+i)$ at the close. This is called the *amount* of 1 in a year. Similarly if any other sum S be invested for a year, it will produce Si in interest, and at the end of the year will amount to S$(1+i)$. The original unit, 1, having amounted to $(1+i)$ in a year, if that amount be again invested, it will amount at the end of the second year to $(1+i) \times (1+i)$ or $(1+i)^2$, which is the amount of 1 at compound interest in two years. Proceeding thus, we find that the amount of 1 in three years is $(1+i)^3$, and generally the amount of 1 in t years is $(1+i)^t$.

Seeing that $(1+i)^t$ is the amount of 1 in t years, it follows that 1 is the present value of $(1+i)^t$, to be received at the end of t years; and, by simple proportion, the *present value* of 1 to be received at the end of t years is $1 \div (1+i)^t$ or $(1+i)^{-t}$. This present value is usually denoted by the symbol v^t. Thus, the present value of 1 due at the end of one year is v, where $v = 1 \div (1+i)$ and $(1+i) = 1 \div v$.

Suppose it were desired to provide an endowment of £100 for a child now aged fourteen on his attaining age twenty-one, what premium should be paid down, assuming interest at 3 per cent? It will be well to solve the problem first in general symbols. If there be l_x persons aged x, we shall have l_{x+t} surviving at age $(x+t)$. Therefore, if an endowment of 1 is to be secured to each of them at age $(x+t)$, the sum of l_{x+t} must be provided at the end of t years. For that purpose, $v^t l_{x+t}$ paid down now and invested will suffice; and as there are l_x persons who must each pay his proportion, the sum to be paid by each is $v^t \cdot \dfrac{l_{x+t}}{l_x}$ or $v^t {}_tp_x$. This is called the present value of, or the single premium for, the endowment. Thus, the present value of the endowment is the sum to be received, discounted down to the present time, and multiplied by the probability of receiving it. Taking up now the numerical example: by the specimen mortality table given above, there are 98,496 children aged fourteen, of whom 95,614 will attain the age of twenty-one; hence, if each of the survivors is to receive £100, the sum of £9,561,400 will have to be provided at the end of seven years. At 3 per cent interest the present value of 1 to be received in seven years is ·8130915, and the present value of £9,561,400 is £7,774,293. There being 98,496 children, the sum to be paid down now in respect of each is £78·930, or £78 : 18 : 7, which is the present value of, or the single premium for, the endowment of £100. Or, looking at the matter in another way: the probability of a child aged fourteen attaining the age of twenty-one is 95,614 ÷ 98,496 or ·97073; and the value of 1 to be received certainly at the end of seven years is ·8130915. Therefore the value of 1 to be received conditionally on a child aged fourteen surviving until aged twenty-one is ·97073 × ·8130915 or ·78930, and the value of £100 so to be received is £78·930 as before.

It should be noted that in speaking of the present value of an endowment we assume a sufficient number of endowments to allow of the law of average asserting itself. If there were only one endowment, and the child happened to survive, the sum paid at the commencement would not amount to the sum to be provided. In the case of the above example it would amount to only £97·073, and the £100 could not be paid in full. On the other hand, should the child happen to die, there would, at the end of the term, be the sum of £97·073 in hand without a claimant. It is only when there are a sufficient number of lives to obviate accidental fluctuations that the figures work out properly. The same observation applies to every kind of contingent benefit.

An annuity is an annual payment to be made either for a fixed term of years, or during the existence of a given life, or of a given combination of lives. In the former case the annuity is called an annuity-certain, and, in the latter, a life annuity, or simply an annuity. According to the elementary principles already discussed, the present value of the first payment of an annuity-certain of 1 per annum is v; that of the second payment v^2, and so on. If the annuity be for n years its value is denoted by $a_n >$, the angle round the suffix showing that no contingency is involved. We therefore have the value of an annuity-certain

$$a_n >, \times = v + v^2 + v^3 + \ldots \text{ etc. } \ldots + v^n.$$

The series is a geometrical progression, and by the usual formula for summing such a series, the sum is $v\dfrac{1-v^n}{1-v}$, from which, remembering that

$v = \dfrac{1}{1+i}$, we have $a_n >, = \dfrac{1-v^n}{i}$.

It will readily be seen that a life annuity consists of a series of endowments, and by the formula we have already obtained for the value of an endowment, we have, writing a_x for the value of the life annuity where the age of the nominee is x,

$$a_x = \frac{1}{l_x}(v l_{x+1} + v^2 l_{x+2} + v^3 l_{x+3} + \text{ etc.})$$

There is no way of summing this series except by actual addition. Here each number in the column of l_x is multiplied by a power of v, the index of the power having no reference to the age of the life, but only to the length of time which must elapse before a particular payment of the annuity is to take place. If, therefore, we have calculated by the formula the value of an annuity on a life aged x, all the multiplications and additions must be done over again if we are called upon to calculate the value of an annuity on a life of any other age, and the work becomes tedious and lengthy. In early days the labour was abbreviated by employing a simple relation which exists between the value of an annuity on a given life, and that of an annuity on a life one year older. At the end of the first year the life, if he survive, will be entitled to a payment of 1, and he will also be in possession of an annuity for the remainder of his life, the value of which will then be a_{x+1}. He will, therefore, at the end of a year be in possession of cash and of an annuity together worth $1 + a_{x+1}$. The value of this at the beginning of the year is $v(1 + a_{x+1})$, and the chance of receiving it is p_x. Therefore the actual present value is $v p_x (1 + a_{x+1})$ which is a_x. Therefore, commencing at the oldest age in the mortality table, at which the value of the annuity is zero, and working backwards year by year, a complete table of annuity values can be formed, and it is about as easy to calculate the complete table as to calculate the value of an annuity at the youngest age.

If, however, we look again at the series representing the value of the life annuity, we shall easily introduce a modification which will enable us, by a simple division, to calculate the value of an annuity on a life of any age we please. The value of the annuity is represented by a fraction, and if we multiply both numerator and denominator by the same quantity, we do not alter its value. Let us then multiply by v^x, and we have

$$a_x = \frac{1}{v^x l_x}(v^{x+1} l_{x+1} + v^{x+2} l_{x+2} + v^{x+3} l_{x+3} + \text{ etc.})$$

where each value of l is multiplied by a power of v, the index of which is the same as the suffix of that particular l. If now we write D_x for $v^x l_x$, we have

$$a_x = \frac{D_{x+1} + D_{x+2} + D_{x+3} + \text{ etc.} +}{D_x}$$

Let us now write the successive values of D in a column, and sum that column from the bottom upwards, and place in an adjoining column against each age the sum of the column D from

the age one year older to the end of the table, and let us denote that sum by the symbol N, that is

$$N_x = D_{x+1} + D_{x+2} + D_{x+3} + \text{ etc.} +$$

We then have two columns, the relation of which to each other is such that

$$a_x = \frac{N_x}{D_x}$$

Such columns are called commutation columns, and the principles on which they are constructed have been extended and applied to many other kinds of benefits besides annuities. They will be found in all collections of actuarial tables.

One great advantage of commutation columns is, that by means of them the values of temporary and of deferred benefits can be calculated with great facility. Thus, if the annuity is to run for only t years, all the payments after t years must be left out of account, and it is easily seen that the value of the temporary annuity is $\dfrac{N_x - N_{x+t}}{D_x}$. If, on the other hand, nothing is to be paid for the first t years, then the value of the deferred annuity is $\dfrac{N_{x+t}}{D_x}$.

The endowment and the annuity already considered are benefits receivable if a nominee survive, but the same principles hold if the benefit be receivable at death. What is the present value of, or single premium for, an assurance payable at the end of the year of the death of a person aged x? Assuming l_x persons of that age, each to be assured, d_x will die in the first year, and the sum d_x will have to be provided at the end of the year, and the present value of that sum is $v d_x$. Similarly, the sum d_{x+1} will have to be provided at the end of the second year— its present value is $v^2 d_{x+1}$—and so on for future years. The value of all the l_x assurances is therefore

$$v d_x + v^2 d_{x+1} + v^3 d_{x+2} + \text{ etc.},$$

and the value of each of them is therefore the sum of that series divided by l_x. By multiplying each of the terms of the series, and also the denominator, by v^x, the value of the fraction is not changed, while a column is thereby formed for assurances similar to the D column already described for annuities. The function $v^{x+1} d_x$ has the symbol C_x assigned to it, and

$$M_x = C_x + C_{x+1} + C_{x+2} + \text{ etc.},$$

so that if we write A_x for the single premium for the assurance, we have

$$A_x = \frac{M_x}{D_x}$$

We have thus obtained by independent processes direct from the mortality table, the respective values of the annuity and the assurance; but these two functions are closely related, and, having the value of one, we can at once assign the value of the other. The annuity consists of a payment of 1 to be made at the end of each year which the nominee completes; and the assurance consists of a payment of 1 to be made at the end of that year on which the nominee enters but does not complete, namely the year in which he dies. Therefore the value of the assurance is the difference between the values of two annuities, the one payable at the end of each year on which the nominee enters, and the other payable at the end of each year which he completes. Now $v(1 + a_x)$ is evidently the value of the first of the annuities, and a_x is the value of the second ; and we have

$$A_x = v(1 + a_x) - a_x$$

This equation is quite independent of the rate of mortality ; it depends solely on the rate of interest, and was skilfully used by the late William Orchard in preparing his celebrated *Conversion Tables*. By means of these tables the value of the assurance and also the annual premium for the assurance, can at once, and without calculation, be found from the value of the annuity.

We have found the single premium for the assurance, but it is not often in practice that a single premium is convenient. To find the annual premium we may look on A_x as the purchase money of an annuity, the first payment of which is to be made at once, because it is customary with assurance offices to make the annual premiums payable at the commencement, and not at the end of each year. Since $1 + a_x$ is the purchase money of such an annuity of 1 per annum, unity will purchase $\dfrac{1}{1 + a_x}$ per annum, and A_x will purchase $\dfrac{A_x}{1 + a_x}$ per annum, which is therefore the annual premium corresponding to the single premium A_x. Using the symbol P_x for the annual premium, we therefore have

$$P_x = \frac{A_x}{1 + a_x}.$$

In former days the single and annual premiums used in practice were those given by the formulas above discussed, but the rate of mortality shown by the mortality tables then in use was much in excess of that actually prevailing, and the rate of interest employed in the calculations was below that which could be secured on safe investments. It therefore follows that the formulas gave rates in excess of those theoretically necessary, and left a margin for expenses and contingencies. The Equitable Society found that margin so great that large surpluses resulted, and these were distributed as bonuses among the policy-holders. In later years, however, when the true rates of mortality were better known, it became the custom, with a majority of offices, to calculate the single and annual premiums by mortality tables closely representing the real facts, and to employ practical rates of interest. Under these circumstances it was therefore necessary to add to the mathematical premium deduced from the mortality table a margin called "loading," to cover the expenses of the business, to provide against contingencies, and to create a fund out of which the policy-holders might obtain bonuses, because the practice of the Equitable in dividing the surplus amongst its members had become very popular, and other societies, in order to compete successfully, had to follow the same course.

We have discussed so far only assurances for the whole of life, and it is not our purpose to go into further detail. By similar processes, more or less complicated according to the nature of the contingencies to be covered, premiums may be calculated for all kinds of risks, but those wishing to investigate the question further should consult the text-books mentioned lower down.

We have already remarked that life assurance differs from assurance of other descriptions in that the risk to be insured against constantly increases with the duration of the contracts. It will be observed that the formula given above for the annual premium provides for a uniform premium payable throughout life. It follows from this that in the earlier years the assured pays an excess beyond that required for the risk, while in later years the risk is greater than the premiums received. Therefore, if the insurance society is to remain solvent, the surplus premiums of earlier years must be religiously husbanded and accumulated at interest, so as to provide for the deficiency when the lives assured become advanced in age. In other forms of insurance all that is necessary in the way of reserves is a sufficient proportion of the premium for the unexpired risk of the year, and a reserve fund to cover accidental fluctuations. With life assurance, however, the case is different. The unexpired risks of the year must be provided for, and also a guarantee should exist to provide against accidental fluctuations ; but over and above these two reasons for providing a reserve, there is the increasing rate of mortality, which necessitates large accumulations. In fact, the so-called reserves of life assurance companies are, for the most part, not in the nature of reserves as usually understood ; that is, they are not surplus funds to guard against contingencies, but merely accumulations of excess of premiums received when the risk is small, and laid by against the time when the risk will become great ; and they are just as much required for the purpose of solvency, and apart altogether from fluctuations, as the premiums themselves. This being a very important principle, in fact the fundamental principle underlying life assurance, it may be useful to give a numerical illustration of its operation. In an ordinary mortality table the rate of mortality increases but slowly for many years, and to base our illustration on it would involve very lengthy calculations. It is better, therefore, to take an exaggerated example, the principle remaining the same. Let a society be supposed to exist consisting of fifty-five persons, and let the rate of mortality be such that one of these will die in the first year, two in the second, three in the third, and so on, until ten die in the tenth year, when all the members of the society will have passed away. Let it be arranged that each of these members be assured for £100 by an annual premium payable throughout the duration of the contract. What will the premium be, and what will be the working of the fund ? Of course, in practice, interest would be secured on the investment, but for the present purpose it is a needless complication, and we may leave it out of account. By assuming interest the figures would be slightly altered, but the principle guiding them would not be changed.

Were the rate of mortality to remain constant as at the commencement, we should have one person in fifty-five die in each year, and therefore the premiums to insure £100 for a year would be $\frac{100}{55}$, or £1 : 16 : 5 nearly. Seeing, however, that in the second year two out of fifty-four die, and in the third year three out of fifty-two, etc., it is manifest that this initial premium would be too small, and if in each year the premium collected were to be equivalent to the risk incurred, the premium would be an increasing one, in the second year $\frac{200}{54}$, or £3 : 14 : 1 nearly, in the third year $\frac{300}{52}$, or £5 : 15 : 5 nearly, until in the tenth year it reached 100 per cent, and there would be no assurance at all. It will be found, however, that if fifty-five persons pay a premium in the first year, fifty-four in the second, fifty-two in the third, and so on, the total number of premiums to be paid throughout the ten years will be 385 ; and, there being fifty-five claims of £100 each to be paid, an easy calculation brings us to 14·2857, being $\frac{1}{7}$ of £100, or £14 : 5 : 9 nearly, as the uniform annual premium to be paid by each member who enters on a year, that £100 may be paid to the representative of each on death.

The following table shows the working of the fund. The first column gives the year, the second the number of members who commence the year, that is the number of premiums to be paid for that year ; the third the number of deaths in the year, that is the number of claims to be paid ; the fourth the amount of premiums to be received at the commencement of each year, the fifth the amount to be paid in claims in that year, and the sixth the accumulated funds at the end of each year.

(1) Year.	(2) Members at commencement of year.	(3) Deaths in year.	(4) Premiums paid for year.	(5) Claims paid in year.	(6) Funds at end of year.
1	55	1	785·71	100	685·71
2	54	2	771·43	200	1257·14
3	52	3	742·86	300	1700·00
4	49	4	700·00	400	2000·00
5	45	5	642·86	500	2142·86
6	40	6	571·43	600	2114·29
7	34	7	485·71	700	1900·00
8	27	8	385·71	800	1485·71
9	19	9	271·43	900	857·14
10	10	10	142·86	1000	000·00

It will be noticed that the uniform premium, sometimes called the "level premium," of £14 : 5 : 9 per cent is, at the beginning, much in excess of £1 : 16 : 5, the premium for that year's risk, sometimes called the "natural premium," whereas, after a short time, the natural premium becomes much heavier than the level premium. Our hypothetical fund increases until the fifth year, when it attains its maximum, and then it is gradually drawn on to meet the excess of claims, until at the end of ten years, when all the members have died, the funds have entirely disappeared. This illustrates the purpose for which life assurance funds are created. If a life office were to close its doors to new business its funds would increase for many years, remaining for a short time at the maximum figure, and then would begin to be drawn upon, the drafts rapidly increasing in amount, until at last, with the death of the last life assured, the funds would be entirely exhausted.

It is assumed in the calculations of the level premium that the contract will remain in force for the whole duration of the life of the assured, that the assured will pay the premium regularly year by year, that the office will reserve and invest the difference between the premiums received and the amount actually necessitated by the risk incurred, and that on the death of the life assured the claim will be met. It often happens, however, that after a time the policy is no longer required, and in justice to the policy-holder a portion, at any rate, of the excess of premiums he has contributed should be returned to him. This is the surrender-value of the policy. In early days surrender-values were not granted, and the insurance offices reaped large profits from this source. For many years now, however, it has been the custom to grant liberal surrender-values, and this source of profit is a thing of the past. It is not usual to pay back the whole of the reserve value. The company has no option in respect of the continuance of the contract. If the policy-holder tenders the premium the company must receive it, and it is only on the motion of the policy-holder that the contract can be terminated. Manifestly he will be guided by his own interests in deciding whether to continue or surrender, and it is only fair to the other members, who elect to adhere to the bargain, that a portion of the reserve value should be kept in hand. It is, however, a matter of opinion what is a fair and proper allowance to make for cancelled policies, and the practice of the offices differs within moderate limits in this respect. Nevertheless, at the present day, all companies make a substantial allowance.

We have seen above that, for the purpose of solvency, a life company must retain large funds in hand. Were merely the mathematical or net premiums charged, and were it certain that the rate of mortality shown in the mortality table would accurately correspond with the actual event, the accumulations of the company would be exactly the amount of reserve required ; but companies charge loaded premiums, and therefore the accumulations in a well-managed office are greater than the necessities of the case demand. It is, therefore, the custom to make periodical valuations. These are of too complicated a character to be discussed here, but briefly we may say that the object is to ascertain how much of the invested funds consists of the excess of premiums which must be set aside to provide for future risks, and how much is real surplus. When the surplus is ascertained, it may be divided according to the constitution of the company, and hence arise the bonuses to policy-holders, which are almost a universal feature of life assurance as carried on in the United Kingdom. The valuation shows what surplus cash is in hand. If the whole of that be allotted as a bonus to increase the sum assured, it is manifest that when the lives are young the same amount of cash will give a larger reversionary addition than when the lives become more advanced in age. Some offices adopt this course, and give a reversionary bonus which decreases as the policy grows older. This, however, is not a system which is very popular with the public, who do not understand the reasons for a decreasing bonus. With many offices, therefore, it is the practice, in the early days of the policy, not to divide the whole of the surplus that policy has created, but to retain part of it in hand, so that, later on, when the life has become older, there may be no necessity for reducing the periodical reversionary additions. Hence has arisen the custom of making the valuation of the office at a much lower rate of interest than that which will probably be realised, and here again we have an illustration of the effects of the operation of the law of increasing mortality. Did the mortality not increase with the age, the reversionary bonus would not cost more with the lapse of time, and there would be no need for making these specially great reserves. It thus appears that, in order fully to understand the finance of life assurance, an intimate knowledge of the complicated principles on which it is based is requisite. Space, however, forbids us from entering further upon this most interesting and important question here, but these brief explanations will suffice to show that knowledge and discretion are required to judge wisely of our insurance companies. They differ in essential principles from all other financial institutions, and must be measured by a completely different standard.

[Here only a few of the more important English works on life assurance can be mentioned. For further information consult catalogues of libraries of Institute of Actuaries in London, and of Faculty of Actuaries in Edinburgh.]

J. Graunt (q.v.) was one of the first English writers; A. Demoivre (q.v.) expounded in his *Treatise of Annuities on Lives* (1725) his famous "Hypothesis for the Law of Human Mortality," which, before trustworthy mortality tables existed, was much used in calculating life contingencies. Dr. Richard Price published (1st ed. 1771) *Observations on Reversionary Payments*, containing the Northampton Table of Mortality, for many years employed by insurance offices in calculating their premiums and reserves, which, even at the present day, has not been entirely abandoned. Francis Baily published *Doctrine of Life Annuities and Assurances* (1810); and Joshua Milne, *Treatise on the Valuation of Annuities and Assurances on Lives*, etc. (1815). This latter work contained the Carlisle Mortality Table, the first constructed on correct principles, and which immediately came into very general use. In 1825 Griffith Davies published a tract explaining the nature and use of commutation columns, and a few years later, after his death, his uncompleted *Treatise on Annuities* was published by his executors without date. Also in 1825 Benjamin Gompertz published in the *Philosophical Transactions* his remarkable exponential formula for the law of mortality, which was extended and improved many years later by William M. Makeham in the pages of the *Journal of the Institute of Actuaries*. David Jones's work on the *Value of Annuities*, etc., appeared in 1844, until recently the principal text-book on the subject; and in 1849 Peter Gray published his *Tables and Formulæ*, an important volume, dealing principally with the construction of life assurance tables. Lastly, in 1887, the Institute of Actuaries issued its official *Text-Book* on life contingencies, by George King.

[Since the establishment in 1848 of the Institute of Actuaries, its journal has been the medium of publication of all important contributions to the science of life contingencies. The first number was issued in 1851, and it has appeared quarterly, with unfailing regularity, ever since. Many useful papers will also be found in the *Transactions of the Actuarial Society of Edinburgh*, commenced in 1863.]   G. K.

INSURANCE, Life, Law and Practice of. The contract of life insurance is a contract under which, subject to the payment of an annual premium by the insured, the insurer undertakes on the death of the insured or some other specified person to pay a certain sum of money to the representative of the insured or, as the case may be, to the insured himself. Unlike the contract of fire or marine insurance, it is not a contract of indemnity in the strict sense, but the person who originally insures must, by virtue of 14 Geo. III. c. 48, have an insurable interest in the life of the person on whose death the payment is promised, and Lord Ellenborough in the well-known case of Godsall v. Boldero (2 Smith, Leading Cases) held that such interest must continue up to the time of the claims becoming due; but insurance companies, as a matter of practice, did not take advantage of this doctrine, which was subsequently overruled by the unanimous decision of the court of Exchequer Chamber in Dalby v. India and London Life Assurance Company (2 Smith, Leading Cases). According to the doctrine now governing the subject, the existence of an interest at the time of the insurance is sufficient. The question as to the nature of the interest which is required to make a life insurance effective has been frequently before the courts. A creditor has an insurable interest in his debtor's life; a tenant holding a lease terminable at the end of a life has an insurable interest in such life, and every man is deemed to have an unlimited insurable interest in his or his wife's, and every woman in her or her husband's life. A parent cannot insure the life of a child without having a pecuniary interest in the child's life, but a child's burial expenses may be insured. It is very doubtful whether insurances of this class should be permitted, the temptation to crime resulting being so great. The interest in a life policy may be assigned to a purchaser or donee, and it is provided by the Policies of Assurance Act 1867, that this may be done either by indorsement on the policy or by a separate instrument, but an assignment is not effective for all purposes until a written notice of its date and purport has been given to the insurance company.

As a general rule the proceeds of a policy on the life of the insured, unless assigned during his lifetime, form part of his estate and are therefore subject to the payment of his debts. It is, however, possible since the date of the Married Women's Property Act of 1882 to take out a policy for the benefit of the wife or husband of the insured or of her or of his children, by which means the person for whose benefit the insurance has been effected takes the insurance money without any deduction in respect of debts unless the creditors of the originator of the policy can prove that his object was to defeat their claims, in which case they are entitled to the payment of a sum equal to the aggregate sum of the premiums paid in respect of the policy.

An insurance policy becomes void if the insured life is terminated by virtue of a judicial sentence (Amicable Assurance Society v. Bolland (Fauntleroy's Case), 4 Bligh, N. S. 194) and probably also if the life of the insured is terminated by his own act (see Horn v. Anglo-Australian Life Assurance Company, 30 ; Law Journal (Chancery, 511) if he was of sound mind at the time of committing suicide. It is, however, usual to insert express conditions in the policy, so as to provide against events of the nature described, and which in most cases save the rights of assignees for value. Mrs. Maybrick's case raised the question whether a policy taken out by a husband for the benefit of his wife becomes void if the wife kills the husband. It was held that in such a case the trust in favour of the wife must fail, but that the policy is not avoided, and forms part of the husband's estate (Cleaver v. Mutual Association [1892], 1 Q. B., 147).

It is frequently stated in the forms of proposal for life insurance that certain statements to be made by the person whose life is to be insured referring to his health or to the nature of his occupation or possible changes of residence, are to form the basis of the contract between the insured and the insurance company. In such a case the untruth of any such statement invalidates the policy (Hambrough v. Mutual Company, Weekly Notes, 1895, p. 18). Insurance companies have, however, frequently begun to restrict the conditions as much as possible so as to make their policies practically indefeasible.

The competition between insurance companies has also produced a great many variations in the scheme of assurance intended to attract customers. It is usual from time to time to grant additions to the sums insured, dependent upon the profits of the company as ascertained on the taking of the periodical valuations. Persons who are willing to forfeit the chance of such bonuses can insure at lower premiums ; or the ordinary premium is paid at the commencement, and a reduction corresponding to the bonus is made whenever bonuses are declared. Some companies also accept reduced premiums at the commencement, so as to attract persons with small but increasing incomes. Persons who do not like to be burdened with the payment of the premiums during the whole of their life may also, by paying a higher premium at the beginning, secure a certain sum on death by the payment of a limited number of premiums. Thus a person aged 25 may insure the payment of £100 on his death by making 10 annual payments of £4 : 7s., or 15 of £3 : 4 : 6, or 20 of £2 : 13 : 8, or 25 of £2 : 7 ; 6.[1] A person who is desirous of terminating his payments need not forfeit his policy if he has paid the premiums during a certain number of years (2 or 3 years as a general rule), but he may, on giving notice in proper time, receive an immediate cash payment which is called the "surrender value," or he may receive a "fully-paid policy" for a sum payable at his death. Insurance companies do not generally state the surrender values beforehand, but they frequently guarantee a minimum surrender value, e.g. one third of the total premiums paid, and as a rule, pay much higher sums than the guaranteed minima. Thus one company, in the case of a person entered at the age of 30, now allows for a policy for £100, the annual premium being £2 : 9 : 4, the sum of £4 : 3s. after 5 years ; £8 : 19s. after 10 years ; £21 : 7s. after 20 years; £36 : 17s. after 30 years ; £53 : 12s. after 40 years. The same company guarantees fully-paid policies for an amount equal to the aggregate of the premiums paid. Policies are also frequently granted for securing sums payable at certain ages or on death, if the insured dies before reaching the age. These assurances which are called endowment assurances are useful for several purposes. Thus, a father who wishes to secure a certain sum for the advancement of a child in life, may do so by paying a corresponding annual sum. In the event of the child's death before attaining 21, the company retains the premiums, but it may also be arranged that the premiums are to be returned, in which case they are of course higher. Thus, an annual premium of £3 : 1 : 8 paid from the birth of the child, will secure the payment of £100 on such child attaining the age of 21 ; but if the return of the premiums on death is stipulated for, the premium is raised to £3 : 10 : 4 annually. Another purpose for which endowment insurances are taken out is to provide for retirement from a profitable occupation at a certain age. It is possible for a person 30 years old to secure the payment of £100 on reaching 60 years, by paying an annual sum of £3 : 7 : 6 ; if the payment is to be made on attaining 65 years, the premium is reduced to £2 : 19 : 6.

[1] The figures here given are taken from the tables of various insurance companies, and each case of course applies to the company only from whose tables they have been taken, but they illustrate the general principle.

In case of death before attaining the age in question, the £100 are paid in either case. It is also possible to secure an annual sum payable from a certain age during life by paying an annual premium up to the time of reaching that age. Thus a person aged 30, by paying an annual sum of £2 : 1 : 7, may secure an annuity of £10 payable from the time of his reaching the age of 60 during his life ; and if the annuity is to commence when the insured reaches 65 the premium is reduced to £1 : 8s.

The ordinary annuity business of an insurance company enables a person, by paying a lump sum, to secure a yearly income during life, either immediately or from some later date, —this is called a deferred annuity. This annuity business is in reality the exact opposite of the life insurance business ; a person insuring his life deprives himself of income in order to increase his estate on his death, whilst an annuitant reduces his estate on his death in order to increase his income. The annuity business is also a sort of protection to insurance companies inasmuch as a miscalculation in the tables of mortality which would produce a loss in one department would produce a corresponding gain in the other. Insurance companies have also provided means for facilitating the payment of estate duties. These duties being payable before probate can be granted, cannot, in the first instance, be paid out of the estate of the deceased ; the difficulty is overcome by the insurance company, in return for an annual premium, undertaking to pay estate duty up to a certain amount, which amount is paid direct to the revenue authorities, and can therefore be paid without risk to the company, although the authority of the personal representatives has not as yet been definitely confirmed by probate. There are many other ways in which insurance companies have tried to meet the various contingencies and risks of pecuniary loss which may occur, and new methods are constantly invented to do this in a more efficient and economical way.

The solidity and solvency of insurance companies generally, notwithstanding the complicated nature of their transactions, supply a most convincing testimonial, not only to the prudence and capability of the persons concerned in their management, but also to the truth of the doctrine of probabilities which is the basis of their operations. There is, however, one danger which recent events have made more serious, although it does not seem to have been generally recognised as yet. This is the diminution in the rate of interest in all first-class investments, which of course must materially affect the income whilst not decreasing their expenditure. This makes it all the more necessary to provide some means by which the public can be assured of the solvency of insurance companies. The advertisements which make a large parade of the total sum of the invested funds ought not to be taken for more than what they are worth, their sufficiency depends entirely on the extent of the liabilities, as to which no idea can be formed by anybody except practised experts, and the public cannot attach any importance to statements not certified by such experts. The Life Assurance Companies Acts, 1870-1872, have recognised this want, and provided that every insurance company must, at intervals of at least five years, obtain actuarial reports as to their financial position, and prepare statements as to their life assurance and annuity business on the basis of such report, which report and statement must be submitted to the board of trade. It is also provided that a separate account should be kept of all receipts in respect of life assurance and annuities, and that all such receipts should be carried to a separate fund, which is to be as absolutely the security of the life policy-holders and annuitants as though it belonged to a separate company carrying on no other business except life insurance and annuity business. It is also required that revenue accounts and balance-sheets containing a number of prescribed details should be prepared annually and deposited with the board of trade. These balance-sheets must contain a detailed list of the investments under prescribed heads. Insurance companies must also, on starting business, deposit a sum of £20,000, which sum may not be withdrawn until the insurance fund has reached £40,000. Means are thus provided for the public to form their own opinion, but as the least prudent companies are generally the most active in touting for business, occasional losses cannot be prevented, though up to the present they have been comparatively rare.

[See arts. on ANNUITY ; TONTINES. For law of life insurance : see Bunyon, *Law of Life Insurance*, 3rd ed., 1892.—Crawley, *Law of Life Insurance*, 1882.—Porter, *Law of Insurance*, 2nd ed., 1887.]

E. S.

INSURANCE, MARINE. Marine insurance may be defined as a contract whereby the insurer, in consideration of a premium, undertakes to indemnify the assured, in manner and to the extent thereby agreed, against losses caused by perils incidental to marine navigation. The informal note of the contract, which is drawn up when it is entered into, is called the "slip." The formal instrument, which is afterwards drawn up from the slip, is called a "marine policy." The liability of the insurer under his contract is called, as also in the case of other insurance, the "risk."

Though marine insurance is essentially a contract of indemnity, it is not a formally perfect indemnity, because, for example, in the case of a valued policy, the sum recoverable may exceed the real loss, while, in the case of an unvalued policy, the sum recoverable may fall short of the real loss, as the amount of the loss is then estimated according to certain arbitrary rules. But this depends rather on inveterate adherence to certain traditional forms of policy than on the nature of the contract itself ; for the parties may make any stipulation they please.

The peculiar incidents of marine insurance all flow logically from its character as a contract of indemnity. In the first place it is a contract *uberrimæ fidei.* Hence each party must spontaneously disclose to the other all facts relating to the adventure which are not within the actual or presumed knowledge of the other party. In the second place the assured must have a pecuniary interest in the subject-matter insured, otherwise insurance would degenerate from a contract of indemnity into a mere gaming contract. Thirdly, when the insurer pays on the footing of a total loss, the right of subrogation accrues to him, that is to say, he acquires all rights and remedies of the assured in respect to anything that may remain of the subject-matter insured. Moreover, if the assured elects to treat a constructive total loss as an actual total loss, he can only do so by giving notice of abandonment to the insurer, if there be anything of value to abandon. Fourthly, if the subject matter insured has never been imperilled, or if for any other reason, not due to the fault of the assured, the risk has never attached, the assured is entitled to a return of the premium.

[Arnould on *Marine Insurance,* 6th ed., and M'Arthur on *Marine Insurance,* 2nd ed. See AVERAGE (MARITIME) ; BOTTOMRY, LOAN ON.]

M. D. C.

INSURANCE, MUTUAL. Life and fire insurance are sometimes carried on by companies formed on a mutual principle. Marine insurance, ordinarily and in its origin, is a contract whereby one person, in consideration of a premium, undertakes to indemnify another person against the losses incidental to marine navigation. But a custom has sprung up in modern times whereby associations of ship-owners become their own insurers. The members of the association mutually guarantee each other against marine losses. If the members number more than twenty, they must register under the Companies Acts in order to constitute a legal body. The individual guarantees take the place of the premium, and the details of the contract are of course subject to the rules and regulations of the particular association. Subject to these qualifications a contract of mutual insurance is on the same legal footing as an ordinary contract of insurance with an underwriter or insurance company (see *Arnould on Marine Insurance,* ed. 6, p. 152). M. D. C.

INSURANCE, STATE (GERMANY).—*History.* The compulsory state insurance of Germany grew naturally out of philosophic conceptions of the state that date from the early years of this century. In the voluminous discussion which preceded the sickness and accident laws, in imperial rescripts, in several of Prince Bismarck's speeches, in the *Begründung* of the accident law, we find the idea constantly repeated that the state has wide and various, as well as definite and positive, Christian duties, especially toward the weaker members of society. No one doubts LASSALLE'S influence in shaping much social legislation in Germany. He has told us what he owes to two books of FICHTE, one written in 1796, the other in 1800. SISMONDI'S work published in 1819 is frequently quoted by those who acted most powerfully upon the preliminary discussion out of which the laws sprang. Sismondi returned from a journey among French manufacturing centres with the same feelings that made Karl Marlo a socialist. Sismondi wrote, "Nous regardons le gouvernement comme devant être le protecteur du faible contre le fort," etc. When Prof. Winkelblech (Karl Marlo) came back from his journey, he not only wrote passionately in this same spirit, but he conceived and clearly expressed the thought of a remedy in universal compulsory insurance. In his *Organisation der Arbeit* (probably written before 1850), vol. ii. p. 328 *et seq.,* he maintains, in a criticism of the liberal school, that no remedy for social evils is adequate save obligatory insurance. Dr. Schaeffle, who is often called the father of this system, was influenced directly and powerfully by Winkelblech.

Even before the Franco-Prussian war the thought which was later elaborated in *Der Korporation-Hülfskassenzwang* appears to have occurred to Schaeffle. Both the theory of the state and the theory of compulsory insurance were therefore waiting upon occasion before the legislation came. After the founding of the *Verein für Socialpolitik* in 1872, the idea of the insurance scheme was kept before the public mind, especially through writings of Wagner, Schmoller, and other *Kathedersocialisten.* Feb. 12, 1879, came the first imperial word from the throne. Another followed in Feb. 1881, and in Nov. of the same year the imperial message was sent forth. From 1874 the extraordinary growth of the social democracy had also influenced many of the conservatives to seek a remedy in compulsory insurance. To this end an agitation was begun in the Reichstag 1878. The ministry of 1879 announced "the government accepts the theory that the working man who has become incapacitated through age or in consequence of his work should not be a burden upon the public," etc. The two attempts upon the emperor's life in 1878, while they led to strong repressive measures against the socialists, gave rise also to positive reforms. At the opening of the Reichstag in 1879 the emperor referred directly to the anti-socialist law, adding an earnest wish that the house would co-operate in a series of positive social reforms initiated by the state. This historic relation to socialism is of signal importance in any attempt to appreciate or criticise this legislation.

Insurance against Sickness.—The first law (against sickness) passed by a powerful majority June 15, 1883. Sick funds or associations already centuries old were taken as a basis. These older *Knappschaftskassen* were even compulsory among Prussian miners as early as 1854. The law of 1883 makes this compulsion universal. To give elasticity and freedom seven forms of associations are established.

(1) Local sick fund, managed by townships for different branches of trade. (2) Factory funds. (3) Building funds. (4) Mining funds. (5) Trade or gild funds. (6) Free funds that may be managed with greater independence, being only obliged to do at least as much for the labourer as the law prescribes. (7) Communal fund, including those who do not fall under either of the above funds. Both payments and receipts under these seven associations differ in details. The law does not fix any weekly amounts, it is left to each insurance office to fix them, see § 20 of the law. Generally the sick receive relief during 13 weeks— (1) for medical treatment, including medicines and appliances, (2) in case of complete disability, at least one half the average wage of the place in which he works. As a precaution the pay begins on the third day of sickness. The sick may be taken to a hospital and half his wage given to those dependent upon him. (3) An amount at death for burial expenses equal to twenty days' wage. (4) Women at time of childbirth are supported during three weeks. This insurance is supposed to represent a money value very nearly ⅔ the average wage. The labourer himself pays ⅔ and the employer ⅓ of the amount, although, as in the old age and invalidity law, many employers pay both contributions, thus adding directly to the wage. Recent statistics show nearly 8,000,000 insured, and more than 100,000,000 marks go yearly to sick relief alone. It is estimated that the employer pays 3·69 marks *per insured;* the employed, 10·09 marks; that the relief averages 11·77; the management and costs, 0·81 marks; and the funds, 9·72. Sickness averages 15·7 days at an expense of 32·41 marks. The relief per 100 insured (sick persons), male 37·4 marks, female 31·8, total 36·3. Relief per 100 marks for sick pay, 47·91 ; doctor, 19·97 ; medicine, 16·04 ; hospital, 10·49 ; burial, 4·28 ; childbed, 1·31.

The law against *Accidents* passed 6th July 1884, came into operation 1st October 1885. Several amendments extend the principle practically to the entire wage-earning class, a part of this amount to the injured and to his survivors. Both sick and accident laws will eventually

insure nearly 17,000,000 of people. The proposed extension of the law to widows, orphans, and house industry will come into effect as early as practicable. Even if the sickness is caused by accident, the sick fund must bear the burden until the beginning of the fourteenth week. This throws a large proportion of lesser hurts wholly on to the sick funds. Help is rendered under the accident law even if the accident is caused by sheer negligence of the labourer. Wilful self-injury alone is excepted. The responsibility of insuring the labourer is wholly with the employer. The simple fact that one is a wage-earner alone constitutes one a member of an insurance society. Small officials with salary below 2000 marks (£100) yearly are included. The pecuniary burden also is thrown wholly on the employers. The principle of *le risque professionnel* is fully accepted, it being supposed that employers, under such definite responsibility, would guard against accident costs for which they alone have to pay.[1] The management is through trade associations of employers with mutual liability. Premiums are based upon wages, and are determined yearly by estimates of wage or salary during the previous year, and also upon the extent and kind of risk to which the given trade subjects the labourer. Elaborate schedules of danger are used to determine the risks in the different industries. From the end of the thirteenth week of incapacity the injured receives (paid through the post office) while absent from work, two-thirds his usual wage. If only partly incapacitated medical attendance is supplied, and in case of death, a sum equal to twenty times the daily wage goes to the family for funeral expenses, and an annuity to the widow ; one-fifth of the husband's earnings to each child till the fifteenth year, 15 per cent of such earnings, or one-fifth, if the child is motherless. The entire annuity may in no case exceed three-fifths of the father's earnings. A board of arbitration composed of employers and representatives decide disputed questions, the imperial insurance bureau in all cases having final judgment. This higher commission is composed of three permanent members including the chairman. These are appointed from proposals of the Bundesrath, by the emperor, and hold office for life. Four non-permanent members are chosen by the Bundesrath, two by the trade associations, and

[1] Of the delicate question of personal responsibility for accidents, it should be said that an employer who causes an accident, even by negligence, is liable to the injured for an *excess* of the award above what the law gives. They must be responsible to the trade association, or sick fund, which pays in first instance, for the *full* amount. Other persons are liable for the whole damage. The various charitable unions have still the same duties as before, though their expenses may be paid by the trade association. So that compensation for industrial injuries becomes a certainty. The certainty is of a nature that has almost wholly done away with the constant litigation under the employers' liability law of 1871, and is considered in this respect throughout Germany an improvement of first importance.

two by representatives of the workmen. The non-permanent members hold office four years. The imperial bureau can command books, witnesses, correspondence, and all documents necessary to the decision of any question in dispute. The expenses of this bureau are borne by the empire. Its accounts are laid yearly before the Reichstag. In 1890 there were 64 industrial trade associations, and 48 agricultural associations. These include 390,622 trades classed as industrial, with 4,843,621 separate agricultural interests, 4,926,672 and 8,088,698 persons are included in these respective interests, *i.e.* above 5,000,000 of businesses (Betriebe) with more than 12,000,000 of insured persons. The entire outgo of these associations exceeds 36,000,000 marks with reserve funds of 55,000,000. The law was extended to the carrying traffic in May 1885. Here the empire or the state has direct control instead of the trade association. The extension of the law (15th March 1886) to military officers and soldiers has rather to do with pension than insurance legislation. May 5, 1886, the law was applied to agriculture and forestry, in which the work is of such uniform character that the institutions could conform to state, provincial, or county lines. Calculations are not here made upon the wages of the injured but upon an average rate of agricultural wages. Direct taxes like the land tax may be made the basis of assessment. The building and marine accident law passed in 1887. The most important change here is that, in the "deep building"[1] a single trade association for the empire was formed, and the method by assessment gave place to a charge on capital[2] (Umlageverfahren durch Kapitaldeckungsverfahren). To estimate results properly, it should be seen that the lighter accidents—nearly 90 per cent—come under the sick law. [The labourers really contribute to the *accident* fund *inversely* to the employers' contribution to the *sick* fund, *i.e.* the labourers bear 11 per cent of the accident burdens while the employers bear 33⅓ per cent of the sick-fund burdens. These facts gave the basis for common representation upon the arbitration of both employer and employed.] The cost per accident is about 200 marks. Compensation per 100 marks 68·66 marks to the injured, 21·35 to survivors, 8·61 for cure, 1·38 for burial. In 1890 the employers paid, per person insured, 2·98 marks, expenses of compensation, 1·40, management, 0·40, funds, 5·52. It is significant that the

---

[1] "Tiefbau" is the building of bridges etc. as distinguished from houses "hochbau."
[2] The expression "charge on capital" requires some explanation. The difference between "Umlageverfahren" and "Kapitaldeckungsverfahren" is this:—According to the first-named system assessments are made in each year to cover the losses of the previous year. According to the second system (which is the ordinary insurance system), fixed premiums are paid out of which reserve funds are formed for the payment of losses.

most skilled physicians are more and more called for all serious cases. This is unquestionably setting a higher standard of health restoration both in cities and country. Fifty-six of the sixty-four trade associations have already adopted measures of *prevention* against accidents. It has been found that the best skill and elaborate preventive methods pay in the long run.

The last law—invalidity and old age—dates from 22nd June 1889. It was early conceived to be necessary for the completion of the scheme, The two previous laws passed with strong majorities, the last with a small hesitating one. Its first distinction from the other laws is that it applies not to any special business or branches of any trade, but to the whole mass of the "working population," so long as wages do not reach £100 yearly. At least 12,000,000 of workers will fall under this form of insurance. Beginning with the sixteenth year, men and women are classified according to their wages in four different classes.

Class 1, up to 350 marks yearly, for which 14 pfennigs are paid weekly.
Class 2, up to 550 marks yearly, for which 20 pfennigs are paid weekly.
Class 3, up to 850 marks yearly, for which 24 pfennigs are paid weekly.
Class 4, above 850 marks yearly, for which 30 pfennigs are paid weekly.

As payments are not made when the insured is out of work (unless from free choice) only forty-seven weeks are "paying time" in the year. This allows for sickness and idle time. The contributions during the year (forty-seven weeks) would thus amount to—

3s. 3½d. for class 1st.
4s. 8½d. „ „ 2nd.
5s. 7½d. „ „ 3rd.
7s. „ „ 4th.

These payments are made half by employers, half by the labourers, the state adding to each paid annuity a yearly subsidy of 50 marks. The annuity is due at the completion of the seventieth year. It is distinctly the purpose of this law to give only enough to guard the insured against actual suffering. It is paid, however, even if the insured is earning full wages. Thirty years of contribution (47 × 30 = 1410 weeks) give claim to the pension. If no time is lost, twenty-seven years suffice to secure the annuity. No separate contributions are necessary for the old-age pension, as this is covered by the invalid insurance claims. If one who is drawing old-age pension secures invalid pension, the former is discontinued. All who have contributed five years, and are permanently disabled, receive the invalid pension at whatever age the disability falls. If an accident disable him, he draws invalid pension, only in case he does not fall under the accident law. "Invalidism," under the third law, is supposed to cover only permanent disablement. This disability is defined as unfitness to earn one-fourth the usual wage. If thereafter the labourer becomes able to earn more than this sum, his payments may be in part or wholly withdrawn. It is estimated that ten times as many persons will draw invalid pensions as those that draw old-age pensions. It is expected that eventually a sum of 250,000,000 of marks yearly will go alone for invalid pensions. The annuities from incapacity are reckoned on a basis of sixty marks, increasing in proportion to the contribution.

Class (1) 350 marks   2 pfgs. (8¼ pfngs. = 1d.)
  ,, (2) 550 ,,   6 ,,
  ,, (3) 850 ,,   9 ,,
  ,, (4) 850+,,   13 ,,

One who had for example made 100 payments in class (1), or 100 × 2 pfg. = 200 pfgs. ; 150 payments in class (2), or 150 × 6 pfg. = 900 pfgs. ; 50 payments in class (3), or 50 × 9 pfg. = 450 pfgs. ; 300 payments in class (4), 300 × 13 pfg. = 3900 pfgs.

Here the insured who had paid during the 600 weeks would receive 2·00 + 9·00 + 4·50 + 39·00 = m. 54·50. The state adds 50 m. The minimum basal annuity is 60 m. If he had had 40 weeks' sickness and served 10 weeks of military duty, for which time the state pays, we have the following result to add to the above 600 weeks' payment in the four classes.

		Marks
1. By the state	. . . .	50·00
2. Basal annuity	. . . .	60·00
3. Affixed stamps in the 4 classes during 600 weeks	. . .	54·50
40 weeks' sickness 40 × 6 [1]	. .	2·40
Military service 10 × 6 .	. .	0·60
		167·50

This amount (167·50 marks) represents the invalid pension, which may at any time, and in any case, be reckoned simply as above shown.

To secure the old-age pension, contributions must have been made thirty years (30 × 47). As this would have caused great injustice to those approaching the seventieth year, it was decided to give the pension earlier to those who, at the time the law took effect, had passed the fortieth year of age. One, for example, who had in 1891 reached the age of forty-seven, would have, instead of 30 × 47, only 23 × 47 weeks to contribute, i.e. his years for contributing would be lessened by as many as he had already passed the fortieth year. One who was nearly seventy would have only to show that he had worked regularly 141 weeks before the law came into effect in 1891.

Here the 1st wage class has a pension of 4 pfg.
  ,,   2nd   ,,   ,,   6 ,,
  ,,   3rd   ,,   ,,   8 ,,
  .,,   4th   ,,   ,,   10 ,,

If a man completing his seventieth year has

[1] Time of sickness and military service is reckoned as in second class, i.e. 6 pfgs.

paid during 1800 weeks (500 in 1st class, 400 in 3rd class, 900 in 4th class), and had been sick 50 weeks, and served 40 weeks as soldier (or 90 weeks under 2nd class), his account would stand as follows :—

    900 in IV. Class
    400 ,, III. ,,
     90 ,, II. ,,
     20 ,, I. ,,

    1410 weeks.

or the exact number of weeks the law demands. As only 1410 are required, 480 of the 500 in 1st class are omitted.

We have thus—

				Marks
(1) State payment				= 50·00
(2) 900 ,,	IV. class at 10 pfg.			= 90·00
(3) 400 ,,	III. ,,	8 ,,		= 32·00
(4) 90 ,,	II. ,,	6 ,,		= 5·40
(5) 20 ,,	I. ,,	4 ,,		= 0·80
				178·20

as the pension.

In case of any sickness so serious as to make permanent disability probable, the insurance authorities may secure such extra medical attention as they see fit, though the insured can make no such claim. The payments are made .in stamps, to be had at every post office. The stamps are affixed to a card containing fifty-two spaces. The cost of the stamps is 14, 20, 24, and 30 pfg., according to the wages received. These payments are made by the master, who is supposed to deduct one half the sum from the weekly wage. As a fact it is more and more common for the employer to pay the whole for the more personal service, as. the deduction is found to create dissatisfaction, especially with the servant class. In Baden the "sticking," which has caused so much unpleasantness in Germany, is done by the officials. The employer pays, to an official who calls at the door, a lump sum. When the card is filled, a record of it is made at the office, and a new one issued, so marked as to show where the previous card may be found. To women who marry half the sum of their actual contribution is restored without interest, and to the widows and dependants of men who die before receiving the pension, provided contributions have been made for at least five years. The actual burden to the state of paying for time of military service, and for its officials, is estimated at 8,000,000 marks yearly. This does not include the extra burden upon the post office, nor the vast service that is rendered without compensation. It is claimed that the costs have not thus far risen above the estimates. In 1891, 132,917 claims for old-age pensions were allowed costing 16·63 millions of marks ; 6·65 millions fell to the government's share. The average pension was 125·08 marks.

The advantages to the labourers are said to be far greater than any which private companies could give, as the insured get the state subsidy and the contributions of employers without cost to themselves. After five years of contributions, the yearly invalidity pension is five and a half times greater than all the contributions of the insured. In the first year (1891) 132,917 annuities were given (15,306,754 marks), and nearly 100,000,000 marks received for stamps.

When the "stability stage," *Beharrungs-zustand,* is reached, about 1,500,000 persons, in a population of 50,000,000, will receive benefits equal to 330,000,000 marks annuities (£16,500,000). The three laws together will eventually distribute annually about 500,000,000 marks (£25,000,000).

[See *Special Report Commissioner of Labour,* U.S.A., 1894, by John Graham Brooks. Two Bills which are intended to effect the compulsory insurance of the great bulk of the wage-earning classes of Switzerland against sickness and accident have been lately issued, Sept. 1895.] J. G. B.

INSURANCE AGAINST SICKNESS. See INSURANCE, STATE.

INSURANCE THEORY IN TAXATION. See TAXATION.

INTEGRAL AND DIFFERENTIAL CAL-CULUS. The integral calculus provides a method of great importance in all branches of science which require the aid of mathematics, enabling us to deal satisfactorily with variable quantities, such as are far beyond the reach of the ordinary methods of arithmetic and algebra. Its object is to provide a means of adding together quantities which are so small as to be individually imperceptible, but so numerous that their sum is a perceptible quantity. This can only be done in one class of cases, where the quantities are the small increments by which a variable quantity increases from moment to moment. The method of procedure is to compare the small increments of an unknown quantity with small increments of a quantity upon which the changes of the first quantity depend. The change resulting from the united effect of these small increments can then be deduced from the known quantity by the process of *integration,* which is, as its name implies, the fundamental operation of the calculus, thus :—Let x and y be two variable quantities, which are not independent, so that if x varies y must vary also. Let x change to $x + \Delta x$ (where Δx denotes a small increase in the value of x) and y in consequence changes to $y + \Delta y$; then the increase of y is to the increase of x in the ratio $\Delta y : \Delta x$. Now the differential calculus tells us that when Δy and Δx are sufficiently diminished, the fraction $\Delta y/\Delta x$ approaches a definite limit which can always be found, and is denoted by the expression dy/dx: this expression is called the differential coefficient of y with respect to x, and the finding of it is the fundamental operation of the differential calculus. If, then, we know the ratio L of a small increment of an unknown quantity y to the corresponding increment of a known quantity x, in the notation of the differential calculus $dy/dx = \mathrm{L}$. In the notation of the integral calculus $\int_{x_0}^{x_1} \mathrm{L}\, dx$ measures the amount by which Y has increased while x has changed from x_0 to x_1 ; x_0 and x_1 are called the limits of the integral. Suppose we know the value of y, say b, corresponding to any particular value, say a, of x, then $y = b + \int_a^x \mathrm{L}\, dx$ gives the general value of y in terms of x. The symbol $\int$ was originally an S standing for sum ; $\int \mathrm{L}\, dx$ meant the sum of the quantities obtained by multiplying the increments of x by the variable quantity L.

The differential calculus provides a method of comparing quantities which are so small as to be individually imperceptible, but bear to each other a finite ratio. *Differentiation* is the process of finding this ratio when the small quantities are the increments by which two quantities, whose variations are mutually dependent, increase from moment to moment. Suppose the magnitude of a variable quantity y depends upon that of another variable x: then y is called a function of x. If x be increased by a small quantity Δx, y will be increased correspondingly by a small quantity Δy. The fraction $\Delta y/\Delta x$, as Δx is continually diminished, approaches a certain definite limit denoted by dy/dx and called the differential coefficient of y with respect to x. Of course the quantity dy/dx is a function of x, so that it can be treated in the same way as y has been : the expression $d(dy/dx)/dx$ or d^2y/dx^2 is called the second differential coefficient of y with respect to x. This process may be continued *ad infinitum.* It is as an introduction to the higher branches of mathematics that the differential calculus is valuable ; while it can very seldom be employed alone for the direct elucidation of a problem, without it, higher mathematics could not be employed at all.

The following example is taken from Marshall's *Principles of Economics,* vol. i. appendix note 1. Let h be a pleasure of which the probability is p, and which will occur if at all at a time distant t : let r be the rate of interest per unit, which must be added to present pleasures before comparing them to future, and let $\mathrm{R} = 1 + r$; then the present value of the pleasure is $ph \, \mathrm{R}^{-t}$. If ω be the probability that a person will derive an element of happiness Δh, from the possession of say a piano in the element of time Δt, then the present value of the piano to him is $\int^t \omega \mathrm{R} \dfrac{dh}{dt}\, dt$. If we are to include all the happiness that results from the event at whatever distance of time, we must make the upper limit of the integral infinity. The same appendix contains many examples of the use of the calculus in economic reasoning.

[The ordinary text books in use are those of Todhunter, Williamson, and Edwards, on the *Differential*, and Todhunter and Williamson on the *Integral* calculus.—Greenhill, *Differential and Integral Calculus*, gives a very rapid insight into the methods and capabilities of the calculus, but is very difficult.—Wicksteed, *Alphabet of Economic Science.*]   A. E. S.

INTENSIVE CULTIVATION means the cultivation of the soil by agriculturists who use artificial means to increase its natural fertility. It is the only practicable method of cultivating a fixed plot of land, and it is the opposite of the "extensive" cultivation of nomad farmers who "arva per annos mutant et superest ager," Tacitus, *Germ.* 26 (comp. Horace, *O.*, III. xxiv. 14; Caesar, *B. G.*, iv. 1; Marshall's abstract of the reports to the Board of Agriculture, Midlands, p. 17), or where each, like the Yorkshire farmer a century ago, "every year . . . ploughs up a fresh part of his sheepwalk to take a crop or two, and then lets it lie fifteen or twenty years" (A. Young's *Northern Tour*, ii. 14). Pastoral methods leaven unscientific agriculture. The application of science, at first to prevent exhaustion of the soil, characterises non-nomad or intensive agriculture. This expression accordingly means scientific cultivation.

Scientific cultivation includes—(1) the rotation of crops on a double, triple, or quadruple system. The double system is described in Virgil's *Georgics*, i. 73, and in A. Young's *Political Essays*, p. 153. The latter writes (1772), "It is in some parts of England, and in many of France, the practice to divide a farm into two parts; half every year sown with wheat and the other half fallow." This double or convertible system only differs in degree from that of the Yorkshire farmer referred to. The triple system was introduced into England in Henry III.'s reign, the quadruple by Lord Townshend last century (Prothero's *Pioneers and Progress of English Farming*, pp. 4, 42). (2) Drainage had its first scientific English exponent in 1649, its latest in 1834 (*ib.* pp. 97, 249). (3) Spade husbandry was advocated by Sir H. Platte, "author of *Adam's Arts Revived*" ("*Compleat Husbandman*," S. Hartlib, p. 6), in 1601. (4) As for manuring, marling, and liming, the first was an incident of mediæval villein tenures, the last two are devices of peculiarly English origin (Fitzherbert's *Book of Husbandry*, ed. Skeat, p. 134; cp. Sir R. Weston's "We have lime and marl of which they know not the use," *Brabant Husbandry*, p. 4). (5) Bones were introduced in 1772, and their use soon made general by Coke of Holkham. (6) Nitrates date from 1839; then came guano; then machinery. Discoveries have ceased since 1851, according

to Sir J. Caird (Ward's *Reign of Queen Victoria*, vol. ii.). As for results, Sir J. Lawes's experiments at Rothamsted, annually detailed in the *Royal Agricultural Journal*, show how wheat can be grown for fifty consecutive years (cp. Prout's *Profitable Clay-farming*), and that properly-dressed grass-land yields two or three times as much as undressed grass-land (Caird's *Landed Interest*, pp. 24 and 39), agricultural thus in its turn reacting on and leavening pastoral methods.

Political economists base upon intensive cultivation—(1) a justification of property in land. These processes, they say, "alter" land, make the useless useful, and increase land qualitatively if not quantitatively, thus making it like any other commodity (Mill's *Pol. Econ.*, ii. 2, 5; Laveleye's *Primitive Property*). (2) Or they argue for security to the capitalist-cultivator: thus improving-leases of twenty-one years were recommended by Sir R. Weston in the 17th, Lord Townshend and Mr. Coke in the 18th century, and now by Sir J. Caird on these grounds. (3) Those who advocate peasant proprietorship as the best stimulus for intensive cultivation, quote A. Young's "the magic of property turns sand to gold"; "give a man secure possession of a bleak rock and he will turn it into a garden; give him a nine years' lease of a garden and he will convert it into a desert" (*Travels in France, 1787, 30th July, 7th November*)—remarks elicited from a partizan witness by the effects of peasant proprietorship in Flanders. (4) Intensive cultivation doubtless illustrates the law of diminishing or limited returns (see J. H. Hollander, The Concept of Marginal Rent, *Quart. Jour. of Econs.* Jan. 1895; S. N. Patten's *Premisses of Pol. Econ.*, ch. vi.; and Sidgwick's *Pol. Econ.*, bk. ii. ch. vii., note); and the principle of specialising growth to soil illustrates an opposite tendency (Carey's *Principles of Social Science*, i. 106, 107; cp. Mill's *Pol. Econ.*, bk. i. ch. xii. 3). The first should not therefore be pursued to the exclusion of the second principle—this is probably the meaning of Mr. Prothero's "Agriculture cannot hold its own by intension against extension" (p. 123). Sir J. Caird, however, discusses a case in which reliance would and could be placed on the first as a temporary substitute for the second principle, viz. supposing war cut us off from foreign supplies (*Landed Interest*, pp. 19 and 20).

                                                J. D. R.

INTERCURSUS MAGNUS, or (Treaty of) Great Intercourse, was the name given by contemporaries to the treaty of 1496 between Henry VII. and the Archduke Philip, re-establishing trading relations between England and the Netherlands. It indicates no fundamental change of policy on either side, and did little more than restore earlier conditions and customs. The joy with which it was received, and the designation given to it, are to be explained by the fact that, owing to the support given to Perkin Warbeck by the Duchess Margaret, trade between the two countries had been suspended for two years. To the English weavers the market for their cloth furnished by the Netherlands was already valuable, while the Netherlands needed English wool and the privilege of fishing in English waters, so that the suspension of intercourse caused great distress on both sides.

[Schanz, *Englische Handelspolitik* (1881), ch. i. —The text of the *Tractatus Pacis et Intercursus Burgundiæ* is in Rymer, *Fœdera* (2nd ed. 1727), xii. 578 *seq.*] W. J. A.

INTERCURSUS MALUS, or (Treaty of) Evil Intercourse, was the name given by the Netherlanders to the treaty of 1506 between Henry VII. and the Archduke Philip, by which trade was re-established between England and the Netherlands on more favourable terms for the former, after a temporary suspension due to political complications.

In future English merchants were to be allowed to sell their cloth in the Netherlands in both large and small quantities, and no penalties were to be imposed upon the purchasers. The carrying out of this treaty would have seriously affected the woollen manufactures of the Netherlands, and the Archduke had probably only been compelled to accept it by the tempest which cast him upon the English shores. The treaty was never confirmed ; and, although a new treaty was signed in 1507, Henry was obliged to abandon his claim so far as it concerned English cloth.

[Schanz, *Englische Handelspolitik* (1881), ch. i.—The text of the treaty is in Rymer, *Fœdera* (2nd ed. 1727), xiii. 132.] W. J. A.

INTERDICT (Scots law term). Equivalent to prohibitory injunction. A. D.

INTERDICTIO AQUÆ ET IGNIS, the ordinary form of Roman banishment under the republican constitution of the Roman state. It was carried into effect by a decree of the people being passed declaring a person to be in exile, and prohibiting every one from supplying him with fire and water so as to prevent his return. Fire and water were the symbols of religious purity, —to deprive a citizen of these was to cut him off from all communion with the state, and so to free it from the contamination of his guilt. Such banishment was accompanied by loss of citizenship.

[Smith's *Dict. of Antiq.*, *s.v.*] E. A. W.

INTERDICTION. There is a procedure in the law of all countries by which persons suffering from certain diseases or propensities (weakness of intellect, insanity, idiocy, etc.) may be subjected to all or some of the incapacities to which infants are subjected under the general law. This procedure, in Scotland as well as in French-speaking countries, is called "inter-diction." The Italian term is "Interdizione"; in German-speaking countries the term "Entmündigung" is used. The same or a similar procedure may, in Scotland as well as in all continental countries, be also used in the case of persons of wasteful or extravagant disposition, if their relatives have reason to fear that they would, if unchecked, waste their property. The disabilities which may be attached to prodigals are not, however, identical in all cases with the disabilities to which persons of unsound mind are subjected. Thus in France prodigals are not subject to "interdiction" in the ordinary sense, but they may be prohibited from entering into certain transactions without the concurrence of a person appointed by the court, who is called "conseil judiciaire" (see Code Civil, art. 513), and a similar rule applies to all interdicted persons in Scotland, there being a special procedure for persons of unsound mind in the strict sense. In Scotland there is also a "voluntary interdiction," which enables a person to protect himself from his own weakness of intellect or facility of disposition.

The fact that England and the countries deriving their law from England do not recognise the right of any person to prevent the extravagance of a relative by judicial proceedings, is closely connected with the other fact that the law of the same countries allows persons to dispose of the whole of their property by gifts *inter vivos* or by will without considering their issue or other relatives, whilst in Scotland, as well as in continental countries, the wife or husband and the descendants, at least, are entitled to a certain portion of the property, which cannot be taken away by gift or will. According to the view of Scots and continental law, the head of a family is more in the position of a trustee than of an absolute owner ; in England this is not so as a matter of law, but the universal use of family settlements shows that, after all, the Scots and continental law is in accordance with the natural disposition of man-kind. E. S.

INTERDICTION (Scots law). Restraint directed against extravagant management of real estate by persons liable to be imposed upon may be by a voluntary bond not to do anything which may affect heritable estate without the consent of persons named in the bond, called "interdictors." Or it may be judicial, imposed by authority of the Court of Session, sometimes at the instance of near relatives, occasionally at its own hand. The interdiction is published by being registered in the General Register of Inhibitions, Edinburgh ; and it then operates to render voidable any dealings with the realty only, except such as shall have been effected with the consent of the interdictors, or such as may be onerous (for adequate consideration) or rational (reasonable). The person interdicted may even himself raise au action to have his improper transaction annulled.   A. D.

INTERDICTUM was a formal order of a Roman magistrate commanding the party to whom it was addressed to do or abstain from doing something. In many ways it corresponds to the interdict of Scots law, and to some extent to the injunction of English law.

[*Gaius*, iv. f. 139, 140 ; *Institutes of Justinian*, 4, 15, § 8.]   E. A. W.

INTERESSE TERMINI. The interest that a tenant at common law has in a lease granted to him before he enters on the premises. A lease at common law is regarded before entry as a contract only ; after entry the tenant takes an interest in the land.

[Goodeve's *Real Property*, London, 1891.]
                                        J. E. C. M.

INTEREST.

Theory of, p. 426 ; Interest and Usury, p. 429.

THEORY OF. Interest is the name given to that which is paid for the use of a loan. This payment often includes elements of a nature different from that which is strictly called interest. If there be any probability that the loan will not be repaid, the borrower will be compelled to add something to his offer in order to induce the lender to risk his capital. Often, too, what goes under the name of interest includes the allowances which must be made for the maintenance of the full value of capital subject to wear and tear. These allowances for depreciation and risk being made, and duly subtracted from the *gross interest*, there remains the *net interest*, the pure payment for the use of the loan apart from contingent risks, etc.

It is not proposed here to review the various theories which have been advanced to account for the existence of interest. For a review of these in detail the reader may be referred to E. von Böhm-Bawerk's *Geschichte und Kritik der Kapitalzins-Theorien* (translated under title *Capital and Interest*, by Professor W. Smart), where they are one by one examined for the purpose of showing that they are unsatisfactory, preparatory to the enunciation of Professor von Böhm-Bawerk's own theory. We shall merely give here the principal heads of the classification adopted in *Capital and Interest*. These are as follows :

Productivity theories. Interest is the price of the productive services of capital. Malthus, J. B. Say, Von Thünen, Carey, and Leroy-Beaulieu are named as some of the chief exponents of this group of theories.

Use theories. Interest is the price paid for the use of productive capital. The line of division between this and the former group seems far from clear. J. B. Say is named as the founder of the theory, which has been elaborated by German writers in the main, among whom Hermann, Mangoldt,

Schäffle, Knies, and Menger are some of the chief names mentioned.

Abstinence theories. Interest is the payment made for abstaining from unproductive use of wealth. The leading exponents of this theory named are Senior, Cairnes, and Cherbuliez.

Labour theories. Interest is the wage of the capitalist's labour, which, in some statements, means the labour which created the capital. The chief exponents of these theories are James Mill, Courcelle-Seneuil, Rodbertus, and Schäffle.

Exploitation theories. Interest arises from the exploitation from the labourer of the wealth which he alone produces. Rodbertus and Marx are the leading supporters of these theories. Besides these principal groups, Turgot's fructification theory, a group denoted *colourless* theories, including, among leading writers, Ricardo, Torrens, M'Culloch, M'Leod, and Rau, and a number of minor, or composite, systems, represented by Molinari, Roscher, Cossa, Jevons, Hoffmann, J. S. Mill, and Henry George among others, are dealt with more briefly.

In rendering an account of interest, we have to account for two phenomena. The first is that it should be necessary to guarantee to lenders not merely the repayment of the principal of the loan, but of a further sum. The second, that borrowers should be willing to pay such additional sums, or, to put the same matter otherwise, that they should prefer to borrow and to repay a sum greater than that borrowed, rather than to abstain from borrowing at all.

It may be said that lenders ask for interest because they know it can be obtained, and that they simply take all they can get. While this is true, it is also true generally that if the payment obtainable by way of (net) interest be increased or decreased owing to any cause whatever, the disposition of lenders to make advances responds to such changes of the conditions of loans ; and the amount of capital available to borrowers depends on the terms they are able to offer. In regard to the other side of the question, it is not sufficient to urge that sheer necessity for ready capital accounts sufficiently for the offer of a premium in order to obtain it. This may be quite enough when we consider the case of a spendthrift, or that of an individual who finds himself unexpectedly called upon to meet demands beyond his means, but it does not suffice to account for the deliberate borrowing by merchants and manufacturers for the purpose of extending their business operations, borrowing which they would clearly avoid if it did not promise to yield them a profit over and above the sum paid by way of interest on their loans.

Böhm-Bawerk in his account of the matter dwells on the fact that immediate enjoyment is preferred to a remote though certain enjoyment, precisely equal in all other respects, or, to use more general terms, that present goods are worth more than future goods of equal amount. He deduces the result that the repayment with interest, at the end of the period of the loan, is a payment of a value precisely equal to that borrowed ; that, to use an illustration, if the rate of interest be 5 per cent, £105, a year hence, has precisely the same value now as £100 in hand.

To take into account the difference in valuation of present and future goods is doubtless essential in our problem, and it has long been recognised that this is the case. It is, however, hardly sufficient of itself for the complete solution of the problem, and some of the contentions urged in the theories which Professor von Böhm-Bawerk rejects need to be given a place even co-ordinate with that assigned to the substitute which is offered.

In stating the theory, it is necessary to insist on one point, namely, that we are considering the rate of interest on current loans and current investments, that is to say, the rate of *net* interest on present investments either in new or old enterprises. The fact that old investments return to the investors rates either greater or less than the rate actually paid on current loans is discounted by the changes in price of the shares in such enterprises.

We have, in addition to accounting for the willingness of borrowers to pay interest, and for the unwillingness of lenders to make loans without interest, to attempt to render some account of the influences determining the actual rate of interest.

Let us first consider the borrower's side of the question, and consider, not the case of a borrower forced to obtain ready money to meet his engagements, but of a borrower who can choose whether he will borrow or not, and is influenced by the prospect of realising profit or loss on the transaction.

The use of capital in industry, as has been so often pointed out by writers on economics, enables the producer to adopt indirect methods of production in place of direct processes, and these are adopted because, though the product is, by their means, obtained only after considerable delay, its amount is largely increased as compared with what is obtained by processes yielding a more immediate return. From the increased product, besides the wages of labour and the reward of the entrepreneur and the rent of any land used in the process, the capital itself must be replaced, a due allowance be made for the risk involved of complete or partial loss, and we have then left, in general, a sum available for payment of interest. We may conveniently refer to this as the net yield of capital. It is the net amount by which the product is increased through the adoption of the indirect in place of the direct process of production. It must be clear that this net yield is not likely to be identical in all the different avenues open for the investment of capital. In some it will be greater, in some less. Those investments which promise the greater net returns will be sought after in preference to those which can offer only the less. A borrower who is in possession of an opportunity for using capital thus productively will be deterred from increasing his borrowings if the expected returns be less than he must pay for the loan, but stimulated to increase his borrowings in the opposite case.

If we suppose that the amount of capital which can be borrowed is limited, we may also assume that the richer fields for investment are first occupied, and that gradually the poorer opportunities are utilised as far as the capital available will permit. This tacitly assumes that the amount of capital available is limited independently of the rate of return offered. In this case then, the investments would proceed till the available capital was exhausted and the rate of expected net return on the poorest investment actually made would be the rate of interest obtainable on loans, if we suppose all the capital lent at the same rate, for this poorest investment would not be made on our hypothesis if the rate to be paid were greater than the rate which it is anticipated will be earned.

Since the amount of capital offering for investment is not fixed, but varies with the expected return, the above investigation requires some modification. We have indicated, however, the nature of such change as must be made. If, for precision, we assume the market rate to be 3 per cent per annum, we may conclude, from the point of view here taken, that those who can offer a *net* return of 3 per cent or more are all able to obtain the capital they can employ at this rate, while those opportunities for investment which promise any smaller return cannot be developed so long as the lending rate does not fall.

In thus expressing the conditions of the equilibrium rate, we have partially anticipated the other side of the question, the lender's position. The explanation of interest as the reward of abstinence on the part of the lender has been the subject of a great deal of ridicule at various times, and the notion that the lending of large sums by millionaires involves a degree of painful abstinence proportioned exactly to the magnitude of the sum lent is, indeed, calculated to provoke ridicule (see especially Lassalle's *Herr Bastiat Schulze-Delitzsch*). Professor Marshall has preferred to substitute the word *waiting* for the word *abstinence*, and to speak of interest as the reward of waiting, so as to avoid the association of ideas which suggests inevitably that abstinence involves self-denial, even to a painful degree.

It is certainly true that the amount of capital which can be borrowed depends in general on the (net) rate which can be offered in payment. The owner of goods, or of the means of obtaining goods, which can be used in production may be conceived as having the choice of entering on production himself, of lending to another, or of obtaining and consuming unproductively the value of the wealth which is at his disposal. Whether he will do the one or the other is largely determined by the rate obtainable by lending, or by employing capital himself. The satisfaction afforded by present consumption is balanced against the satisfaction to be obtained by the opportunity of increased command of the means of satisfaction obtainable by postponing consumption. Doubtless very large sums might be lent if the return obtainable were far less than even at present. The supply of loanable capital might be large even if interest were zero, but, on the other hand, as the rate rises, the supply undoubtedly increases. If, again, for the sake of precision, we assume that 3 per cent per annum is the actual rate, most of the capital actually lent would probably be lent if the rate were below 3 per cent, but not the whole. The last additions to the supply, tempted out by the last increment in the rate payable, may not unfairly be supposed to be lent under circumstances where the actual interest obtained, or bargained for, is regarded as the equivalent of the postponement of consumption, and not more than that equivalent.

The actual rate being 3 per cent, those who are willing to lend find investments for all the capital on which they are content to take interest at 3 per cent or less, while capital which they are unwilling to lend at rates not greater than 3 per cent remains unlent.

The case of interest may, therefore, be said to be comparable with the ordinary cases of equilibrium of demand and supply, the equilibrium rate being such that lenders willing to take that rate or less find investment for their capital at that rate itself, while opportunities for utilising capital in production so as to obtain a return equal to, or greater than that rate, are utilised.

In the case of capital actually invested and not transferable from an unprofitable to a profitable employment, the actual yield affects the valuation of the capital, this valuation being such as would, at the current rate of interest, produce the net yield obtained. Thus the valuation of capital sunk in productive or unproductive enterprises may be vastly greater or much less than its value when the investment actually took place. Such changes in valuation are only capable of producing an indirect effect on current rates of interest, and that mainly by influencing estimates of future returns to new investments.

Changes in the level of interest may be due to causes affecting either the demand for or the supply of loanable capital. Scientific discoveries and useful inventions extend the field for profitable investment, and, by affording more abundant opportunity of realising large returns, tend to raise the rate of interest. Changes in the influences which affect the accumulation of capital or the willingness of lenders to accept a return of given amount, such as changes in the estimate of the future in comparison with the present, tend to increase or decrease the supply of capital offering at every rate possible, that is to say, tend to cause equilibrium to be established at higher or lower rates as the changes are in the direction of limiting or of increasing the supply.

The influence of changes in the value of money, inasmuch as such changes affect the actual return obtained from investments, and cause it to be different from the nominal return, is of importance in modifying the market price of loans. Further, readiness of realisation is of great importance to many investors, and a lower rate of interest is often accepted when it is of importance to be able to recover the value of the capital invested without loss of time and with a minimum of cost. These circumstances find their place in the general theory, modifying some of its details, but without altering the broad outlines which are sketched above.

[The remarks which conclude the article on "Capital" apply equally here. Böhm-Bawerk's references to the writers whom he criticises may be consulted in seeking the views of particular writers, those writers whose theories are, in their main outlines, similar, being treated together so far as possible, and footnotes indicating the parts of their writings where their theories may be sought. In particular, reference may be made to Roscher's *Political Economy*, bk. iii. ch. iv., to Marshall's *Principles*, bk. vi. ch. vi. (2nd ed.), to Common's *Distribution of Wealth*, and to bk. ii. ch. vi. of Sidgwick's *Principles of Political Economy*. See also Cliffe Leslie's essay on the *History and Future of Interest and Profit*, and the interesting discussion in Wieser's *Natural Value*, bk. iv. and ch. xi. bk. v.

Besides the treatment of interest in systematic treatises, a considerable amount of valuable discussion of many points in the theory has taken place in various periodical publications. A sketch of Böhm-Bawerk's theory was given in the *Quarterly Journal of Economics*, April 1889, and the issue of the English translation of his treatises provoked a lively discussion in that Journal, in which Professor Walker joined in July 1892, in a sense unfavourable to the Austrian writer. This continued till the end of 1893, and has been revived by the appearance of the first instalment of Böhm-Bawerk's reply to his critics in January 1895. Among articles in German periodicals, an appreciative notice of Böhm-Bawerk's work by Knut Wicksell in *Jahrbücher für Nationalökonomie und Statistik*, may be mentioned. The *Political Science Quarterly* and the *Annals of the American Academy of Political and Social Science* have also contained occasional articles on the subject which was being debated in the Harvard *Journal*. In a contribution to the *Annals* in November 1893, Professor Arthur T. Hadley seeks a justification of interest on the ground that it affords the best available method of effecting a proper selection of employers. Among discussions of the objections to interest on moral grounds, Prof. H. S. Foxwell's article on "The Social Aspect of Banking" in the *Journal of the Institute of Bankers*, February 1886, may be referred to. Prof. Smart's article, "The New Theory of Interest" in the *Economic Journal*, December 1891, gives a brief account of Böhm-Bawerk's theory, convenient for those who do not desire to read his works themselves.] A. W. F.

INTEREST AND USURY. "Interest," as distinguished from "usury," the older name, now always employed in an objectionable sense, is usually taken as meaning a moderate, in opposition to an excessive, return exacted by a creditor for the loan of capital. This connotation has a certain historical justification. The word "interest" (*interesse*) really refers to the compensation which under the Roman law was due from the debtor who had made default. The measure of compensation was *id quod interest*, the difference between the creditor's position in consequence of the debtor's laches and the position which might reasonably have been anticipated as the direct consequence of the debtor's fulfilment of his obligation. From this idea of compensation has come that of profit on the loan of money, for which the Latin technical term was *fœnus* or *usura*. The evil significance of this term arose from the fact that, despite the laws limiting interest, the most exorbitant rates were charged by aristocratic Roman money-lenders to provincials (Cic. *ad Att.* v. 21, § 11). In primitive societies the return of a payment, whether in money or kind, for the loan of capital, using this word in its widest sense (cp. Levit. xxv. 36, Deut. xxiii. 19), appears to have been sometimes an unknown, always a repugnant practice. This repugnance is to be accounted for by the fact that in early stages of civilisation loans are employed, not as capital, for profitable production, but for consumption, and are consequently needed, as a rule, by persons in want. To exact not only a return for the commodity consumed or for the money spent, but something more besides, appears to be to take advantage of a neighbour's necessities. Tacitus observes of the Germans that both interest and usury were unknown among them : "Fœnus agitare et in usuras extendere ignotum" (*Germ.* 26).

Where the practice of lending on interest prevailed in early societies we naturally find high rates, and as a consequence the existence of a class of debtors who in default of payment, whether of principal or interest, have been adjudged slaves to work off the debt. Caesar (*B. G.* iv.) tells us that Orgetorix had a great number of debtors in his service, and after the Germans had been brought into contact with Roman civilisation, they followed the Roman law of reducing debtors to slavery when insolvent. This was probably the mischief against which the Mosaic law guarded by its prohibition to the Jews to lend upon usury except to strangers (Deut. xxiii. 20), a prohibition authoritatively interpreted by a Sanhedrim of seventy Jewish doctors in 1807 to include interest in any sense. That the Mosaic injunction was not observed appears from Nehem. v. 7 foll., which recounts a restitution to Jewish debtors of the lands on which money had been advanced by Jews at the rate of 1 per cent per month (Salvador, *Histoire des Institutions de Moise*, iii. c. 6).

The practice of enslaving the insolvent debtor, common alike to ancient Egypt (Diod. i. 79), Greece, and Rome, was abolished at Athens by the *Seisachtheia* of Solon (B.C. 594) which, according to some ancient writers, included a reduction of the rate of interest, stated by Plutarch to have been about 16 per cent (Plut. *Solon*, 13). In the opinion of Mommsen no restriction was put by it upon interest. At Corcyra, in the 2nd and 3rd centuries B.C., loans on good security commanded 24 per cent, while the common rate at Athens in the time of the orators was 12 to 18 per cent. These high rates, so far as they are not to be attributed to the risk run by the creditor, are partly due to the dearth of capital, partly, as Roscher has pointed out (*Ansichten der Volkswirthschaft*, i. 18), to the cheapness of labour, the rate of interest being determined by the returns to capital which in slave states absorbs all that is produced except the barest minimum of subsistence. But such high rates are exceedingly oppressive to agriculturists, whose fortunes are always precarious. It was principally for the benefit of this class that the *Seisachtheia* of Solon was passed, and it was from the same class that the characteristic words for interest both in Greek and Latin (τόκος, *fœnus*) were borrowed. Interest was "produce." Upon this turned the logomachic argument of Aristotle against interest, that coin could not breed, and that, therefore, money derived from the loan of money was unnatural (*Polit.* I. x. 4, 5). This point of view, though it arose out of a coincidence of terminology, for centuries dominated European thought. Aristotle, in fact, was seeking justification for the general sentiment against those who lent money on interest. But that he tolerated interest appears from a passage in the *Ethics* (IV. i. 40) in which he ranks among those who ply illiberal trades "lenders of small sums at high interest," *i.e.* in the common acceptance of the word, usurers. So with Plato, who is generally represented as altogether condemning interest. It is true that he forbids the payment of interest in his ideal state, but in the same passage (*Laws*, v. 742) he also forbids repayment of capital, and these prohibitions must be interpreted not as of general import, but in conjunction with his desire to exclude private possession of wealth. In another passage of the same work (xi. 921 c) he expressly enjoins the payment of an obole per drachma monthly by way of interest, *i.e.* 200 per cent per annum, in case of wilful neglect to pay, after the lapse of a twelvemonth, for goods received. It must be remembered that the Greek sentiment against money-lenders was not confined to that class, the literature from Homer to Aristotle treating with scarcely less disdain the callings of the merchant and the manufacturer.

The ancient law of Rome allowed interest ; which, as usual in agricultural communities, reached an exorbitant height. As at Athens, so in the early history of Rome, popular suffering necessitated a readjustment of debts. The law of the Twelve Tables (B.C. 451-450) first, according to Tacitus (*Ann.* VI. xvi. 3), limited the rate to $\frac{1}{12}$th part of the capital, *uncia, unciarium fœnus*.[1] The hatred in which money-lenders were held is visible in the provision mentioned by Cato (*De Re Rustica* procem.), that they were condemned for transgression of the law to twice as high a penalty as the thief. In B.C. 347 interest was fixed at 5 per cent : in B.C. 342 it was abolished altogether by the Lex Genucia. But the nobility controlled the civil procedure through the prætorship, and as the law did not bind any but Roman citizens, the evasion was practised of issuing loans in the names of Latins and allies (Livy, xxxv. 7). By the Lex Sempronia (B.C. 194) this mode of evasion was suppressed. Although the prohibition of interest long remained law, it was found impracticable. The consequence probably was, according to the opinion of Montesquieu and Adam Smith, a rise in the rate of interest to compensate the creditor for increased risk, and accordingly, during the economic crisis of B.C. 89, which followed the Social War and the Asiatic troubles, prosecutions of creditors by dishonest debtors took place. These were eventually put an end to in the following year by the Lex Unciaria of the consuls Sulla and Rufus, which fixed the rate of interest at 12 per cent per ann. This rate was known as *centesima usura*, *i.e.* $\frac{1}{100}$th part of the capital per month. By a decree of the senate

[1] *Fœnus unciarium* $\frac{1}{12}$th or 8⅓ per cent for the *lunar* year, therefore 10 per cent for the *solar—usura centesimæ*, 1 per cent per month, 12 per cent per annum. Ramsay, *Roman Antiquities*, p. 420.

in B.C. 50 this became the legal limit throughout the Roman provinces.

The dislike felt by the Romans to the exaction of interest showed itself in the remedies granted by the law against the debtor. While in the case of a sum of money lent (*pecunia certa credita*) the creditor could enslave the person of his debtor for the unpaid principal, he had only a civil remedy against his property for the interest. Creditors accordingly hit upon the device of bringing claims for interest under the form of actions for money lent, and thereby enforcing the judicial enslavement of the debtor (*addictio*). This legal artifice was put an end to by the Lex Pœtelia in B.C. 325, which further allowed a debtor in temporary difficulties to surrender his property. But as regarded the really insolvent, the old law remained in its severity, so far as the principal of the debt was concerned. It is to the credit of Julius Cæsar that by the *Lex Julia de bonis cedendis*, he revolutionised the law of Rome and laid the foundation of all modern systems of bankruptcy by allowing the debtor to formally cede his estate and enter upon a "new financial existence, in which he could only be sued on account of claims proceeding from the earlier period and not protected in the liquidation, if he could pay them without renewed financial ruin" (Mommsen, *Hist. Rome* bk. v. ch. xi.). Such remained substantially the state of the law until the time of Justinian (A.D. 533). Justinian fixed new rates of interest. Whereas in the case of *fœnus nauticum* or bottomry, there had been no limit, he reduced it to a maximum of 12 per cent per annum. Compound interest was not allowed, nor could any claim for arrears of interest be made for a larger amount than the amount of the principal debt. The new rates were adjusted to a classification of ranks, presumably constructed upon the basis of a hypothetical ability to pay interest. While the maximum payable by merchants and business men was 8 per cent, that for persons not in business was 6 per cent, while distinguished personages, *illustres*, and agriculturists, ranked together as capable of paying 4 per cent. This classification probably suggested the later doctrine of the canonists, that all questions involving profits or interest must be considered relatively to the class of society concerned. All mediæval legislation regarded the suitable maintenance of rank as essential to the welfare of society (see SUMPTUARY LAWS). The Roman law also laid the foundation of two other doctrines which became corner-stones of the canonists' teaching. It has been seen that even Plato allowed a penal interest of 200 per cent in cases where a debtor had wilfully neglected, after a year's delay, to discharge his obligation. Such delay was technically known in Roman law as *mora*, and even in cases where interest was not otherwise payable, as in *fideicommissa*, it became due upon proof of mora, subject to the discretion of the judge (*Dig.* lib. 19, tit. 1, 49, 1). The fact that the rate of interest due for mora was determinable by the rate locally current, suggests that the ground of the adjudication was that the creditor had been prevented dealing profitably with his money in the interval, which is the doctrine of LUCRUM CESSANS, as expounded by the canonists. Further, by the Roman law mora with its penalties was incurred by the debtor for any consequential loss to the creditor. This became the canonical doctrine of DAMNUM EMERGENS (*q.v.*).

The early ecclesiastical history of interest has already been given (CANON LAW). In England it was forbidden by two northern synods in 787. Before the Conquest, canonical and secular provisions were placed side by side in the compilations of the Anglo-Saxon kings. William the Conqueror, by his separation of the work of the bishops' courts from the work of the sheriffs' courts, paved the way for the study and application of canonical principles, which took place in the 12th century. The real founder of the study of mediæval canon law in England was Theobald, Archbishop of Canterbury (1139-61). Its codification began in the reign of Henry III. To this age belong the constitutions of Richard Poore, Bishop of Salisbury, 1217-28, which forbid the taking of the produce of a pledge after the principal sum has been received from it *deductis expensis*. A contemporary canonist, one of the very few English authors on the subject, was Thomas Chabham (or Chobham, fl. 1230), who wrote eight books, *De Casibus et Pœnitentiis*. He was also the author of *Casus aliquot de pignoribus et in quibus latet Usura*. Both these treatises are in MS. in the British Museum. He defines usury as *incrementum fenoris abusu cris crediti*, a definition which embraces interest. But it is remarkable that when William Lyndewode collected the constitutions of the Church of England in the reign of Henry V., a collection which formed the canon law of the realm, scarcely any mention of usury occurs. Possibly this was a concession to the claims of the lay lawyers to take cognisance of the practice of exacting interest as an offence against the common law (see ENGLISH EARLY ECONOMIC HISTORY). In 1364 Edward III. empowered the city of London to issue an *ordinatio contra usurarios*. But parliament complained of the practice of usury in 1390, and a more explicit *declaratio usuræ* was issued by the mayor of London. This defined the offence of usury to consist in the lending "gold or silver to receive gain thereby, or a promise for certain without risk" (CANON LAW). There is much to show that these condemnations of usury were prompted by hostility to the Italian financiers who practised the taking of interest in transactions effected by bills of exchange. Repeated

complaints of this were made by the Commons, the belief being general that by means of bills of exchange the kingdom was depleted of the precious metals. · This is expressed in the *Libelle of Englyshe Polycye* (1436). With the cessation of the Wars of the Roses a marked development of credit set in, and though the charging of interest on bills of exchange was still subject to ecclesiastical and popular reprobation, we learn from Pauli's *Three Memorials* that a class of native exchangers had sprung up in England. Upon the accession of Henry VII. a reaction took place. The control of policy was in the hands of John Morton, Archbishop of Canterbury, chancellor, and afterwards cardinal. Morton was a canonist, who had been a leading counsel in the ecclesiastical courts, and on the opening of parliament in 1487 delivered a speech condemning the practice of usury and unlawful exchange, that is, exchange in which interest was reckoned. (See DRY EXCHANGE ; and MORTON'S FORK). In the same session an act, which bears marks of ecclesiastical influence, was passed against both. The act condemned under the term "new chevesaunce" the loan of money at fixed interest to begin from a certain date. The "Acte agaynst exchaunges and rechaunges" specially struck at accommodation bills. The "Acte agaynst usury and unlawfull bargaynes" (3 Hen. VII. c. 5) gives examples of the way in which the ecclesiastical laws against usury were evaded. Sometimes the form of a sale was gone through, the object sold being an obligation, and the advance for a less sum than the obligation acknowledged being taken in exchange, a system which continued down to the time of Jeremy Bentham, and is described by him. Sometimes a pledge, as a horse, was delivered up, of which the creditor enjoyed the use without setting it off, as he was bound by canonical law to do, *pro tanto* against the principal. Sometimes the device of sale and resale was resorted to. This was the fictitious sale of goods to the borrower on credit, and their repurchase at a less sum of ready money paid by the lender. The sum booked against the borrower included both capital and interest, while the goods remained in the lender's hands. Sometimes a bill of DRY EXCHANGE (*q.v.*) was drawn. Sometimes a gratuity was promised by way of interest. All these evasions were in use on the continent, and had been condemned at numerous synods both there and in England. The offence under the act of 1487, of demanding a fixed percentage, was based on the old canonical doctrine that no claim for interest arose except in the case of DAMNUM EMERGENS, and perhaps also in that of LUCRUM CESSANS, and that these could not be estimated beforehand (CANON LAW). In this respect England, by the act of 1487, fell behind the contemporary doctrine and practice of the continent. The act proved a failure, in the opinion of the framers of its successor, owing to the unskilfulness of the drafting. In 1495 Morton again addressed parliament upon the evil, and introduced a fresh "acte agaynst Usurye" (11 Hen. VII. c. 8). This repealed the act of 1487. Under the new act the stipulation for interest at the time of the making of a loan was the offence. But a clause "savyng laufull penalties for nonpayment of money lent," by allowing the fixing of *pœna conventionalis*, or *usura punitoria* (CANON LAW), opened a wide loophole for evasion. Sale and resale were defined as illegal when the borrower was at the time *in necessite*. Mortgages in which the creditor should not account for mesne profits were condemned, there being no "aventure" attached to the loan to justify the creditor in receiving them as interest. From this time the law remained unchanged for fifty years. Nevertheless the practice of taking forbidden interest continued, as may be gathered from contemporary popular writers. To some extent it was condoned by being included specifically or implicitly in the general pardons issued from time to time by Henry VIII. The customary rate of interest at this period was 10 per cent upon good security. After the assumption by Henry VIII. of ecclesiastical supremacy in 1544, "all offences of usurie and corrupt bargaynes" were excepted (35 Hen. VIII. c. 18) from the general pardon ; but in the following year, for the first time in the history of England, the demand of a fixed rate of interest was made legal by 37 Hen. VIII. c. 9, which repealed the act of 1495. The maximum was to be 10 per cent per annum. By a clause intended to cover some of the canonical justifications of a contract for the payment of interest, opportunities were afforded for the evasion of this maximum. The importance of the act is that it was a clear breach with the canon law, which recognised no quantitative distinction between usury and interest. It is upon the distinction created by this act that our modern conception of the two rests. The act caused lively remonstrances on religious grounds. The reforming party, as a rule, followed LUTHER (*q.v.*) in his earlier view of the sinfulness of interest. In 1552 Northumberland, who posed as an extremist in religious matters, passed a bill through the Lords "against usurie," which became law (5 & 6 Ed. VI. c. 20). This was a drastic prohibition of interest in any shape or form, a clean sweep being made of all the canonical exceptions justifying interest. Probably the customs of London based on the canon law were maintained, as having received regal confirmation. Attempts were made in the following year, without success, to mitigate the severity of the new act. It is doubtful whether the government of Mary permitted the enforcement of a law repugnant to the ecclesiastics as a defiance of the canon

law, especially as the chancellorship was in the hands of Gardiner, bishop of Winchester, and afterwards of Heath, archbishop of York. In 1558 Mary herself offered the city of London dispensation from the penalties of taking usury if they would advance her a sum of money at 12 per cent interest. But the act of 1552 remained unrepealed until 1571, when Elizabeth re-established the rate of 10 per cent (13 Eliz. c. 8).

With the Reformation the canonist doctrine naturally came up for review. The general trend of the opinion of reformers, and this was shared by Luther in his later years, was that interest was tolerable as a concession to human frailty. This argument was adopted by Bacon. But CALVIN and Dumoulin, better known as MOLINÆUS, a French jurist, were not satisfied with a negative protest against the intolerant prohibitions of ecclesiastical dogma. They re-opened the whole question *ab initio*. In a letter to Œkolampadius, Calvin boldly questions the Aristotelian logomachy on which the patristic and scholastic position was so largely based. Money, he argued, was not fruitful ; but neither was a house, which, it was admitted, could lawfully be let for profit. He pointed out that the concessions made by the canonists in fact involved a license to take interest, and that the persistence in a verbal prohibition was "puerorum instar ludere cum Deo." But he adopted, as matter of Christian discipline, the rule that interest should not be demanded of men in urgent need, and as matter of state discipline, that the legal rate should not be exceeded. Molinæus (*Tractatus Contractuum et Usurarum*, 1546) founded his justification on the Roman law that there is inherently involved in a loan an *interesse*, whether in the shape of "lucrum cessans" or of "damnum emergens." This justification of interest, which brought upon Molinæus the censures of the church, naturally found favour in the great mercantile and Protestant community of Holland. Grotius, while assenting to Molinæus's criticism of ARISTOTLE, nevertheless hesitated to explain away the language of Scripture which had been for so many ages accepted as prohibitory (*De Jure Pacis ac Belli*, II. xii.). This step was taken by SALMASIUS in 1638 when professor at Leyden, who in fact popularised the arguments advanced by Molinæus.

In England the prohibition of 1552 having proved a failure, Elizabeth in 1571 re-established the rate of 10 per cent. In 1624 the rate was reduced to 8 per cent. The principle being practically conceded, discussion ranged about the question of a legal rate. The wealth of Holland towards the end of the 17th century being accompanied by a low rate of interest, led to the conclusion formulated by Sir Josiah Child in his new *Discourse of Trade*, first published in 1668, that the relation of the two was that of effect and cause, and that prosperity might be secured for this country by a reduction of the legal rate of interest to 4 per cent (Child). But this opinion was combated by other contemporary writers. Of these the best known is Sir William Petty, who in 1682 published a treatise under the title *Quantulumcunque*, condemning altogether laws regulating the rate of interest. LOCKE is generally taken to have written in the same sense; but though the arguments in his tract, *Considerations of the lowering of Interest and raising the Value of Money*, tend in this direction, he expressly adduces two reasons why there should be a law to regulate interest. His first is that there may be a rule of practice for courts of law in assessing debts and damages. Such a rule of practice prevails at the present day. His second reason is that thoughtless borrowers, "young men and those in want, might not too easily be exposed to extortion and oppression," a line of thought afterwards adopted by Adam Smith.

In the meanwhile the new doctrines made but slow headway in Roman Catholic countries. It is true that successive refinements of the canonists in deference to the advancing exigencies of commercial life had left nothing but the husk of the prohibition remaining. But a defence of interest upon its own footing, following the lines of Calvin and Salmasius, was too venturesome an assault on the position so long maintained by the church. Even as late as the reign of Louis XIV., interest on commercial debts was forbidden, with an exception in favour of the flourishing industrial city of Lyons ; nor did interest become legal until the revolution. In England, opinion had so far passed over to the opposite camp that Adam Smith, writing in 1776, assumed interest as necessary to production in providing the capitalist with an incentive to productive expenditure. About the same time in France, Pothier, a French jurist, and the celebrated TURGOT resumed the ancient controversy as to the justification of interest.

The occasion which produced Turgot's essay on *Les Prêts d'Argent* was a commercial crisis in Angoulême in 1769. A feature of this crisis was an excessive number of accommodation bills upon advances to borrowers for purposes of unproductive consumption. Notwithstanding that the legal rate of interest in France was at this time 4 per cent, there were, as Adam Smith tells us, "several very safe and easy methods of evading the law." The bankrupt borrowers, unable to obtain further advances, followed the example set by Richard II. of England, and combined to prosecute their creditors under the usury laws. Turgot, at that time intendant of Limoges, procured the removal of the cases from the local courts to the council of state, and drew up for its guidance a memorandum, "Sur les Prêts d'Argent," in defence of interest. In this

treatise, which was not published till some years later, he first establishes the necessity of interest for commercial and industrial purposes ; he then refutes the arguments of the schoolmen ; he inquires into the historical causes which have rendered money-lenders odious ; and concludes by demanding that the taking of interest should be legalised and the rate left to be settled between borrower and lender. Like Adam Smith, he adopted the standpoint of individualism, that a man has a right to do what he will with his own, and that, on the whole, this liberty is most conducive to the general well-being. Turgot also addressed himself to the arguments advanced by Pothier and his school upon legal grounds. Their contention was that in a contract which is not gratuitous, equity demands an equality in the values exchanged. One party should not give more than he has received, nor the other receive more than he has given. This maxim of equity is violated when the lender receives back more than the capital. The argument was, as Pothier admitted, a reproduction of that of the *res fungibiles* of Aquinas (see AQUINAS ; FUNGIBLES). Turgot's reply is first, that equality of values depends on the opinion of the two contracting parties as to the degree to which the objects exchanged will satisfy their demand ; secondly, in this following Molinæus, he challenges the fundamental position upon which the prohibition of interest had been based, viz. that a loan is a transfer of property, and that an owner of property (the transferee) cannot be called upon to pay for the use of that which is his own. "Misérable équivoque encore," replies Turgot, "il est vrai que l'emprunteur devient propriétaire de l'argent considéré physiquement comme une certaine quantité de métal. Mais est il vraiment propriétaire de la valeur de cet argent ? Non, sans doute, puisque cette valeur ne lui est confiée que pour un tems et pour la rendre a l'échéance" (*Mémoire*, § 27). Turgot's memoir saved the money-lenders of Angoulême, and so far effected a change of public opinion in France that at the Revolution the national assembly declared all loans on interest legal. The work of Turgot in France was finally done for England by Jeremy BENTHAM (*q.v.*) in his celebrated "Letters in defence of Usury." In these he finally disposed of those pleas for legal maximum rates based on the assumed necessity of protecting the simple and discouraging the prodigal, which had been accepted by Locke and Adam Smith. In England the whole of the acts against usury, dating from that of 1545, were repealed in 1854. For the list of them see the schedule to 17 & 18 Vict. c. 90. In Denmark they were repealed in 1855 ; in Spain in 1856 ; in Sardinia, Holland, Norway, and Geneva in 1857 ; in Saxony and Sweden in

1864 ; in Belgium in 1865 ; and in Prussia and the North German Confederation in 1867.

A new act against usury was, however, introduced for the whole of Germany in 1880, and amended and extended in 1893. It is now a criminal offence to obtain a profit by taking advantage of the necessitous condition or inexperience of any person in reference to loans or other transactions, "exceeding the usual rate of interest in such a way that the profit seems out of proportion to the service rendered," and all transactions of this nature are null and void ; it is also a criminal offence to "trade as a usurer."

Professor Foxwell, while avoiding any justification of the claim to interest upon abstract, moral, or metaphysical grounds, and anticipating the possibility of the arrival of a time when the tendency of interest to a minimum may result in a natural compulsion upon the capitalist to pay a "negative interest" to the banker who undertakes the care and management of his capital, justifies interest upon the practical ground that it is necessary in the existing state of society as an inducement to the capitalist to save. It is interest which "brings about economic equilibrium" between the demand for capital, of which the function is to give labour more effective power and continuity, and its accumulation.

The tendency of profits, including in this term the bare interest upon capital, to a minimum, has been discussed at length by J. S. Mill. Mill assumes that there is "some particular rate of profit which is the lowest that will induce the people of that country and time to accumulate savings and to employ those savings productively." This rate is determined by (1) "the strength of the effective desire of accumulation"; (2) "the degree of security of capital engaged in industrial occupations." These two determinants interact and grow in force with the progress of civilisation. In a country where population is increasing, capital becomes increasingly applied to agricultural industry, which progressively yields less (see DIMINISHING RETURNS), a law which conditions the whole rate of profit. Where population is not increasing, the competition for labour causes a rise of wages, with the same result. The counteragents to the tendency are therefore the loss of capital in commercial crises and unsound investments ; inventions, cheapening articles of common consumption, and thereby reducing the cost of labour ; and importation of food from abroad.

It is to be observed that Professor Foxwell's view that there is no absolute minimum is more probable than that of Mill, who underestimated the force of the tradition of accumulation. Hence, Böhm-Bawerk throws modern theories into three classes. The first of these, to which he gives the name the "naïve produc-

tivity" theory, attributes the production of interest to capital, which in the distribution of the product only claims that of which it was originally the source. The second, which he calls the "socialist exploitation theory," regards interest as the appropriation of that which is due to labour, out of which it sprang, labour being the sole source and measure of value. The third view is intermediate. While accepting the first view of capital as being in conjunction with nature and labour a source of production, it dwells upon the importance of exchange values in determining the amount which can be appropriated by the capitalist. While the first two theories confine their attention to interest as a problem of production, "the interest problem in its last resort is a problem of value" (Böhm-Bawerk, *Capital and Interest*, trans. by Smart, Macmillan, 1890 ; *Conclusion*, p. 423).

While Adam Smith accepted interest as an economic fact without endeavouring to justify it on analytical grounds, he indirectly furnished a basis for a revisal of the whole question of its justification. In discussing the sources of wealth, Adam Smith, while he frequently mentions land and capital, leant to the doctrine that wealth was exclusively derived from labour. This position was borrowed from Locke, who lays down that labour "put the difference of value on everything" (*Civil Government*, bk. ii. ch. v. § 40). Ricardo, like Adam Smith, without elevating the proposition into a system, adopts the general idea. As to this, see Professor Marshall's note on Ricardo's theory of production in relation to value (*Principles of Economics*, bk. vi. ch. vi.). From this it was an easy transition to the view of the modern socialists, that interest is abstracted—wrongfully abstracted—from labour. The connecting link between the two views is the French economist SISMONDI in his *Nouveaux Principes d'Économie Politique*, first published in 1819. Sismondi escapes the logical conclusion of the theory by ascribing the right to interest to the original labour which forms capital. The scientific socialists, however, claiming to rest their teaching upon Adam Smith and Ricardo, regard the returns to capital, whether called by the name of profit or interest, as a fraud upon the labourer to which hunger compels him to submit.

Of this school PROUDHON was the earliest distinguished representative in France ; in Germany, RODBERTUS-JAGETZOW and Karl MARX. According to Rodbertus, interest—profit and rent alike—rests on two grounds, one economic, the other legal. The economic ground lies in the fact that since the introduction of division of labour the labourers produce more than they require to support themselves in life, and so allow them to continue their labour, and thus others are also able to live upon the product. The legal ground is the existence of private property in land and capital, and Marx reproduces the same idea. In the view of the anti-socialist economists, these conclusions are only arrived at by divorcing propositions of Adam SMITH and RICARDO from their context and ignoring the fact that capital is in itself productive and belongs to the capitalist as the reward of abstinence from its expenditure. The economists who earliest insisted on the first of these characteristics of capital were J. B. SAY and Lord LAUDERDALE, while N. W. SENIOR, formerly professor of political economy at Oxford, is the founder of the abstinence theory (CAPITAL). Eclectic economists, such as Roscher, include both these elements.

The American economist, Mr. F. A. Walker, turns the point of the old Aristotelian and canonical objections to interest by insisting that in actual fact, exemplified by cases in which no coin passes, as well as in theory, interest is paid for the use of the objects for the acquisition of which credit is given or money lent. He leans to the modern view that in the states of society in which prohibitions of interest originate, there may have been justification for them, and they probably exercised some effect. These conclusions he applies to similar conditions in modern communities, as for instance, in extensive regions of the United States, where agriculture is prosperous, where industry has made some progress, yet where the community still remains mainly non-commercial. But he agrees that in highly commercial countries "usury" laws become purely mischievous.

Recent English economists, such as Mr. Sidgwick, show the natural English tendency, exemplified in Adam Smith and Ricardo, to abandon discussion of the metaphysical justification of interest, and accepting it as an ultimate fact, to confine themselves to analysing the economic laws by which its rate is determined.

The general conclusions of economists as to the determinants of the rate of interest may be summarised as follows. In civilised communities a general level of "net" interest tends to establish itself, the differences between rates being for the most part due to differences in the risk of the investment. That on the whole, in such communities, small command less interest than large amounts of capital owing to the difficulties of collection and the irregularity of withdrawal. Of this savings banks are an example. The mere increase of capital does not lower the rate of interest (Hume, *Essay on Interest*; Ricardo, *Principles*, ch. xxi.), which is determined, on the analogy of Ricardo's theory of rent, by the competition of borrowers and its least productive employment. Hence, as a community increases in civilisation, and capital has to be employed on less fertile lands and less productive investments, the return to capital tends to decline ; in other words, interest falls. Influences which counteract this tendency are the acquisition by a nation of fresh land or a cheapening of the means of subsistence by the abolition of protective duties; the conversion of circulating into fixed capital (see CAPITAL); the destruction of capital by war, and the emigration of capital.

Within the limits of the Roman Catholic communion the principle has constantly been upheld that to accept usury is sinful. This was laid down by Bossuet in his *Traité de l'usure*, and repeated by Benedict XIV. in the encyclical on usury of 1745 intituled *Vix pervenit*. But

when the era of the reformation opened up the whole question, the energy of the canonists was devoted not to fortifying the old positions, but to emptying the principle of its application. Concessions were at first made in those directions in which the severity of the prohibition had from early times been mitigated. Rent-charges upon land, and their purchase and sale, had been canonically legal since 1425, subject to the charge being really attached to land or fixed property yielding actual returns. But in 1452 a bull of Nicholas V. had permitted the inhabitants of the kingdoms of Aragon and Sicily to enter into contracts for the payment of interest on loans based on personal credit (*census personalis*). Against the principle of this concession a reaction took place under Pius V., who, by a bull *Cum onus* in 1568, reverted to the old limitations. But the concession of Nicholas V. had already done its work. The Jesuit casuists, solicitous to adapt the church to contemporary exigencies, discovered a number of reasons for disregarding the new bull. It required, they affirmed, to be invested with authority by promulgation and acceptance in the several countries of Europe. Others, as Liguori, maintained that it only prohibited such loans where fraud was present. Though Benedict XIV. lent his sanction to the condemnation of the *census personalis*, the system continued to flourish even in Rome itself. Another concession which opened the door to the ruin of the whole system was that known by the name of the *contractus trinus* (see ECK, Johann). This, as its name imports, was a combination of three contracts. The first of these, which laid the foundation for the others, was the contract of partnership in risk of profit or loss (*societas*) which had always been allowed. The two subsidiary contracts were contracts of assurance. By the surrender of a part of his expected profit the capitalist could insure himself against loss of capital ; by the surrender of a further part he could insure a fixed return (*venditio lucri incerti pro lucro certo*). Now regarded together, and as between the same parties, these three contracts represented an advance of money at a fixed rate of interest. As such they were before the 16th century canonically illegal, though each taken by itself, where the parties were different, was legal even though in respect of the same transaction. Convenience suggested that all these contracts should be made between the same parties, and commerce naturally adopted this plan. As usual in the history of interest, it remained for the theologians to find a justification for the *fait accompli*. This was accomplished by Eck and Major early in the 16th century. But, as in the case of the *census personalis*, so in this, the Catholic reaction at first, by the bull *Detestabiles* of Sixtus V. in 1583, condemned the *contractus trinus* as usurious and illegal. The new school of casuists, on the other hand, took up the position that the condemnation only applied to cases where usurious practice was potent. Finally, as in the *census personalis*, commercial convenience smothered the protests of doctrine.

In short, by the 17th century the condemnation of usury had been gradually extruded till it had no application outside loans pure and simple. And even in this sphere the concession which had then firmly established itself of allowing the LUCRUM CESSANS and DAMNUM EMERGENS to be calculated beforehand at a fixed rate per cent, left little more than a mere husk of doctrine. The question came up for review before the Roman curia in 1740. The city of Verona raised a loan at 4 per cent, and justified its proceeding by a discourse published by an eminent lawyer, Scipio MAFFEI. The pope, Benedict XIV., issued a special commission to cardinals, prelates, and theologians, to restate the doctrine of usury according to the most recent view. Of this commission the outcome was the encyclical *Vix pervenit* issued in 1745. The old doctrine was reaffirmed, and returns of interest upon loans condemned, except in cases where the claim to interest rested upon some other title than merely that of money lent, or could be justified by the conformity of the contract to one of those forms recognised by the church as legitimate. But the discussion by theologians was not silenced. At last in 1822 an event happened which again compelled the Roman curia to deal with the subject practically. A female penitent at Lyons was refused absolution for receiving legal interest from invested property. She appealed to Rome, and the holy office decided against the confessor, provided the penitent expressed willingness to submit to the judgment of the church. But no formal decision on such cases followed, and in 1838 a general notice was issued to confessors no longer to importune penitents on account of being in receipt of interest. For all practical purposes the doctrine, while it remains intact, has ceased to exist.

[Boeckh's *Public Economy of Athens.*—Grote's *History of Greece.*—Mommsen's *History of Rome*, 2 vols., London, 1868, 1875.—W. A. Hunter's *Roman Law*, London, 1885. As to the prohibition of interest by the canon law, and its peculiar influence in the development of the LAW MERCHANT, see Endemann, *Handbuch des Handelsrechts*, i. pp. 13-14, 19-20.—Goldschmidt, *Universal geschichte des Handelsrechts*, pp. 137-172. For the scholastic doctrine, Endemann's *Studien*. For the revolt against scholasticism, Child's *New Discourse of Trade* (1690).—Locke's *Essay on Civil Government.*—Hume's *Essay on Interest.*—Turgot's *Les Prêts d'Argent.*—Bentham's *Defence of Usury*, Works, vol. iii. Edinburgh, 1843. For the new socialist doctrine, Rodbertus, *Socialökonomische Ansichten*, Jena, 1882.—Böhm-Bawerk on *Capital and Interest* (translated by Smart), London, 1890. On the rate of interest, see J. S. Mill's *Political Economy*, bk. iv. ch. iv.—Professor Foxwell in *Journal of Institute of Bankers*, vii. (1886).—Von Wieser, *National Value*, edited by W. Smart, 1892. —Distinction from discount, Supino, *Saggio de lo Sconto* (1892). All books on the general principles of political economy treat of the subject.] I. S. L.

INTERLOPERS were persons who, not being members of the companies chartered by the crown, nor having a license from them, traded on their own account to the countries to which the companies had the sole trade. Throughout their existence, the companies suffered much from the competition of these outsiders. The relations between them therefore have an important bearing on economic development, particularly on the growth of free trade. It would be impossible here to give a full account of those relations during the latter half of the 16th and 17th century. But a few instances from the history of the trading companies, and a summary of the arguments for and against the claims of the outsiders, will show the nature of the questions at issue. In 1604, the "free traders" nearly succeeded in breaking up the monopoly of the companies, especially the Merchant Adventurers and the Russia Company. Two bills directed mainly against these associations—(1) "for all merchants to have free liberty of trade into all countries" ; (2) "for enlargement of trade for his majesty's subjects into foreign countries," passed the Commons "with great consent and applause of the House (as being for the exceeding benefit of all the land), scarce forty voices dissenting," but they were rejected by the Lords. Complaints of the monopoly of the Merchant Adventurers were again made to the House of Commons by the merchants and clothiers of Exeter and other parts of the west of England in 1638, 1643, and 1645. The ordinance of 1643, regulating the company, appears to have been a concession to the outsiders, and under the Commonwealth and Protectorate there appears to have been a movement of opinion in their favour. A committee for trade, appointed by the common council of London, reported to the council for trade in 1651, that they found the Staplers "unnecessary and disadvantageous," and the discussions in the council in 1656 show strong opposition to the claims of the Merchant Adventurers. Interlopers were a source of difficulty to the Russia Company throughout its career, and important concessions were made to them in 1654. Similar difficulties were experienced by the Levant or TURKEY Company (q.v.), the EASTLAND Company, and the EAST INDIA Company. The history of the last-mentioned company supplies several important cases. In 1604, James I. granted to Sir Edward Michelborne and his associates a license "to discover the countries of Cathaia, China, Japan, Corea, and Cambaia, and the islands and countries thereto adjoining, and to trade with the people there, notwithstanding any grant or charter to the contrary." Michelborne greatly injured the East India Company, but in 1607 they decided to drop their suit against him in the Admiralty. In 1637, Charles I. granted a license to Sir William Courten and others, to trade to Goa, Malabar, and China; his association, or the Assada Merchants, as they were called, competed with the East India Company for many years. In 1650-51, on the recommendation of the council of state, a union was effected between the company, the Assada Merchants, and a third body, the Merchant Adventurers, trading to the Indies, which became the basis of a united joint stock. But three years later, the last two petitioned the council of state for an open trade. The interlopers achieved a temporary success, and for three years the company, the Assada Merchants, and the Merchant Adventurers, as well as numerous private traders, competed with each other, with the result that the East India trade was completely disorganised, and Cromwell was forced to renew the charter of the company. The leading case on the claims of the companies against the interlopers is *The East India Company* v. *Sandys* (1684). It was argued at great length before Lord Chief Justice Jefferies, Holloway and Walcot, by Holt (afterwards lord chief justice), Finch (afterwards Earl of Nottingham), and Sawyer, for the plaintiff; and Treby (afterwards lord chief justice), Pollexfen (afterwards lord chief justice), and Williams for the defendant. Judgment was given for the plaintiff, and Sandys' ship and goods were confiscated.

It will now be convenient to summarise the arguments for and against the interlopers. There were two distinct questions at issue: 1. Did the creation of such companies as have been noticed fall within the limits of the royal prerogative? 2. Could they, under cover of their charters, pretend to an exclusive trade? On the first, opinion was by no means unanimous, some people contending that parliament alone could impose the restrictions on trade which the very existence of a company involved. Additional force was given to this argument, when the companies made the royal grant the pretext for excluding all others from the trade. The outsiders answered the second question in the negative. It was contended that the king could create corporations for carrying on a trade, but he could not restrain others from exercising that trade; such restraint was restraint of a common right; it appropriated to one or a few what others might lawfully use before the grant was made. A charter conferring such exclusive privileges was therefore void. The East India Company, which was a joint-stock company, came, it was said, within the provisos of the statute of monopolies,

at any rate, after the expiration of their first charter, though the same objection could not perhaps be urged against the regulated companies. Many statutes were quoted in defence of the claim for free trade; on more general grounds it was held that the right to trade was "a right, natural and human," and a charter against natural and civil right was void. On the other hand, a distinction was drawn between inland and foreign trade, and it was maintained that by common law subjects had no absolute right to pursue the latter, which presupposed treaties or leagues of amity concluded by the king of England with foreign powers; that no statute had ever given a general liberty of trade to Englishmen to or with all nations, and that the special statutes dealing with particular nations or particular commodities were not declaratory, but introduced a new law. The distinction between joint stock and regulated companies was held to be of no weight, because it did not touch the question of right, whether a company could or could not have a grant of an exclusive trade. On the ground of expediency, the case for the companies against the interlopers was strong. The men to whom the first charters had been granted were frequently the first discoverers of the trade, and it seemed only fair that they should enjoy a monopoly to reimburse them for their outlay. Their position was analogous to that of the patentee of a new invention, whose claim to a monopoly for a limited period was universally conceded. The companies also were put to great expense for the maintenance of official establishments and factories, for negotiating treaties, for costly presents, and for other objects. It was unfair that interlopers should step in and reap the fruits of their enterprise, without undertaking any of their arduous and expensive duties. They would naturally be able to undersell the companies in the home markets, and the trade would ultimately be destroyed. It was also maintained that experience was in favour of the company organisation, for the trade could not be carried on successfully by any other means. To those arguments the interlopers had an effective reply. Considerations of expediency did not effect the right to an exclusive trade, and it was that which they called in question. To urge expediency in defence of the companies was to set up convenience, or the pretence of convenience, against law; and such an argument might be as effectively used against the companies as in their favour. It might, for example, be urged by the Assada Merchants, as a reason for suppressing the East India Company. There was no objection to the grant of a monopoly for fourteen years to the first discoverers of a trade, but it should then determine. Besides, most of the trades monopolised by the companies had been carried on by private traders, or associations of private traders, before the grant of exclusive charters. Those who claimed liberty of trade were willing to bear their full proportion of necessary charges, nor did they wish to dissolve any company. On the contrary, a joint stock was, as a rule, necessary for distant trades. They merely claimed that people should be free to form companies or not, as the conditions of the trade should determine, and that no one company should enjoy a monopoly (see COMPANIES). W. A. S. H.

INTERNAL CUSTOMS AND TOLLS. It has sometimes been asserted of taxes that they supply nations with more causes of grief than of well-being. Whether this sweeping assertion is generally true or not, it is certainly confirmed by experience in respect to internal tolls and customs. France, the earliest unified of western continental powers, affords us a striking example of their mischievous operation, which may serve as an illustration of the inconvenience and injury they cause to the trade of a country.

As appears by one of their names, *droit de haut passage*, French customs are, during the feudal ages, difficult to separate from tolls proper. From 1360 they were called *imposition* or *traite foraine*, and as the provinces had preserved their own special constitutions, several of them, such as Picardy, Artois, Anjou, Poitou, Berry, Auvergne, Languedoc, etc., successively adopted them, the duties being collected by a body of officials called *masters of the ports*, but with various tariffs and under different names—*tablier* at La Rochelle, *prévôté* in Nantes, *comptable et convoi* in Bordeaux, *coûtume de Bayonne*, *trépas de la Loire*, *traite foraine* in Anjou, etc. The most vexatious of these customs were those of Lyons and Valence (formerly of Vienne), which commanded the passage of the Rhône, and through which *all* goods, whether foreign or home-made, on their way to or from southern France, were compulsorily and unmercifully obliged to pass. The former amounted to 5 per cent, the latter to 3 per cent, and Forbonnais mentions four cases in which it had to be paid twice ; not including the tolls levied by private individuals, he reckons that thirteen different duties were exacted between Lyons and Arles, a distance of 150 miles (*Recherches sur les Finances de la France*, i. pp. 358, 359). The same author quotes the bitter complaints made against the customs of Valence by a deputy of Lyons at the states of Dauphiné in 1600 : "These customs are a rock and a cause of shipwreck. They are hatched and grow like crocodiles. . . . The terrified merchants fly from this passage as if it were a cut-throat place (*un coupe-gorge*) . . . and if caught, only recover their liberty when the officers have rummaged their bales to the bottom and their purses also " (*Recherches*, i. pp. 40, 41). The eloquence of the worthy

member for Lyons was lost, for these customs continued until 1790.

On the Loire, where Forbonnais enumerates 28 tolls, the oppression was quite as vexatious, and Louis XIV., under the direction of Colbert, uses in the preamble of the edict of 1664 language quite as strong as had been heard sixty years before in the states of Dauphiné. "We have ascertained," are the royal words, "that under different names such a diversity of these [duties and tolls] have been set up that we have been filled with astonishment at the institution of so many levies and impositions, sufficient to disgust our subjects from continuing their trade. . . . The merchants cannot possibly have a sufficient knowledge of them, still less their factors and carriers, who are constrained to rely on the good faith of the managing clerks, often doubtful" (P. Clément, Colbert's *Letters and Instructions*, vol. ii. pt. ii. pp. 787-796).

In this edict, Colbert endeavoured to alleviate and unify the chaotic system bequeathed by past ages, but the *Pays d'États*, who in contrast with the *Pays d'Election* enjoyed the privilege of voting and assessing their taxes, steadfastly resisted ; the minister was obliged to submit, and France had to be divided into three regions.

1st. Twelve provinces, mostly round Paris and between the Somme and the Loire, in which the internal customs were abolished ; they were called *les cinq Grosses Fermes* on account of the system of farming their taxes (see FARMING OF TAXES).

2nd. The so-called *provinces étrangères* (Britanny, Auvergne, southern France, the Franche Comté, and Flanders), which maintained their interior lines of customs.

3rd. The provinces *traitées comme pays étranger* (considered as foreign) Alsace, Lorraine, Toul, Metz, Verdun, and the seaports Marseilles, Dunkirk, Bayonne, and Lorient, which enjoyed the envied privileges of being free ports.

The enlightened views of Colbert thus only became law in the central parts of the kingdom ; everywhere else he met with a stubborn resistance prompted by a perhaps justified fear of royal encroachments, by local jealousies, and also by surviving notions on the means of securing plenty, which had been dominant in the middle ages.

The system of tolls proper (*tonlieux* and *péages*) on travellers and goods by land or by water covered with an inextricable net the whole of the kingdom. Imposed by force and under the penalty of confiscation by nobles (*rouage* or *rotaticum*, *cauciage* and *carragium* on carts, *pulverage* on flocks of sheep, *pontage* or *pontaticum* on bridges, *rivage* or *ripaticum* and *mutaticum* on barges and their cargoes, etc.), and by townships (*carragium*, *portage*, and *barrage*), they were an object of unceasing complaint. Several ordinances of Louis IX., Charles VII., Louis XI. and Francis I. attempted to put limits to these extortionate demands : new *péages* were prohibited and it was decreed that the existing ones must be sanctioned by deed or immemorial possession. An ordinance of 1561 ordered that the nobles who levied tolls were to keep the roads in repair, and another of 1663 declared that tolls might only be collected under authority of the king. The *Assemblée de Commerce*, summoned in 1700 by Louis XIV., petitioned for the suppression under compensation of all private tolls, and about 1200 were suppressed in 1724, but thousands of them still survived on the eve of the French revolution. "A barge laden with wine from Languedoc, sailing up the Rhône and proceeding to Paris by canals and the Loire, has to pay from thirty-five to forty various duties and tolls, exclusive of the tolls on the Rhône and the entry in Paris, in fifteen or sixteen different places . . . which makes the journey a fortnight longer than if all were paid at once in one same *bureau*" (from MS. in the *Archives Nationales* quoted by Taine —*Ancien Régime*, p. 471). In his *Finances de l'Ancien Régime* (i. 473), M. Stourm relates the history of a Paris commissary of police sent on an official mission to buy wine in the south, and convey it in person to Paris, so as to ascertain experimentally what were the fiscal incidents of the journey. From Roanne to Melun, about 240 miles, he had to pay 16 *péages seigneuriaux*, 7 *octrois*, without reimbursement on leaving the place, and the customs duty according to the tariff of the *Cinq Grosses Fermes* already mentioned. The honest commissary in despair did not proceed farther than Melun. Well might Necker exclaim in his *Administration des Finances*: "These laws are so confused that scarcely one man or two out of each generation succeeds in mastering them completely"(p. 473). He introduced a bill for the abolition of internal tolls and customs before the *Assemblée des Notables* in 1787, but this reform was only voted in 1790 by the national assembly considering that "these divers duties had made the different parts of the state foreign to each other."

From that day, the restoration of internal customs has never been attempted in France, although what might be called municipal customs still exist under the name of OCTROI (*q.v.*). As to the roads, the revolutionary government first tried a system of voluntary *corvées* inspired "by the generous fire which animates our free and republican souls," but as this generous fire turned out to be totally wanting, the directory, in 1797, set up turnpikes (*barrières*) on the highways : the tariff for a four-wheeled cart with two horses amounted to 80 centimes (8d.) and to 1·20 fr. (say 1s.) for spring-carriages, per 15 miles. But this imitation of the English turnpikes was not successful, and in 1806 the then minister of finance, GAUDIN (*q.v.*), had to give it up and to confess that "it excited frequent brawls,

constant complaints, and that it only yielded 16,000,000 of francs, against an expenditure varying from 30,000,000 to 35,000,000" (*Notice sur les Finances*). Thus, in France at least, practical experience contradicts Adam Smith's opinions that carriages and lighters might "easily" pay for "the maintenance of public works exactly in proportion to the wear and tear which they occasion of them" (*Wealth of Nations*, bk. v. pt. iii. ch. i.). Moreover, on the roads, the expense of the collections of the turnpike dues absorbed 23 per cent of the proceeds. On rivers and canals, although it was an easier task to collect them at the sluices, where barges and lighters are necessarily detained, navigation is also free since 1880 ; the levying of tolls by companies or corporations who have executed public works, is quite exceptional, and must in each case be conceded by a special law. The prevailing feeling looks on the construction and repairing of roads and canals as a public service, which ought to be covered by the public revenue ; however, for the latter, there were in 1889 some unavailing attempts to cause the French parliament to reconsider the question. A tax of 10 per cent on travellers' fares in public vehicles has existed since 1797 ; similar taxes are laid on fares and freight by rail, but these receipts have no specific allocation to the repair of roads and are included in the total revenue of the state.

Germany has, naturally owing to its state of political division, been one of the countries where the system of internal customs and tolls has received the most excessive extension. Vainly did successive diets declare that such unauthorised tolls had no legal existence ; the petty princes and sovereigns persisted, and at length succeeded in obtaining the legal recognition of their prerogatives. Sometimes the different provinces of one particular state were fenced round with tolls, for instance in Prussia, where the Great Elector Frederick William (1620 - 1688) having introduced a system of excise varying from province to province, compensatory excise-duties (*Ergänzungsaccise*) had to be paid on the passage from one province into another. After the peace of 1815, Prussia initiated the movement of reform of German internal customs, which culminated in the conclusion of the ZOLLVEREIN (*q.v.*) and of internal tolls on the transport of goods and travellers. On the Oder about thirty provincial tolls were suppressed, numerous communal and private tolls were redeemed, and on canals the dues were henceforward calculated on the capacity of the barges and lighters, without having any longer regard to the nature of their cargoes. The same policy of simplification was from 1838 applied to roads and highways ; still down to 1867 such dues as *Pflaster-, Brücken-, Damm-, Fahr - gelder* (pavement, bridge, dyke, passage tolls) were levied, besides the *Chausséegeld*, which was only abolished in 1874. (Article *Binnenzölle* in Conrad's *Handwörterbuch der Staatswissenschaften*, Jena, 1889-1890). In the states of southern Germany their suppression had taken place earlier : Bavaria and Würtemberg, 1828, Baden, 1831.

[For Germany, see Hüllmann, *Deutsche Finanzgesch. des Mittelalters*, 1805.—Falke, *Gesch. des deutschen Zollwesens*, 1869 ; and Roscher, *Gesch. der Nat. Oek.*, p. 950. For France, besides the already-mentioned works, the articles " Douanes," "Droits," " Péages," in the *Encyclopédie Méthodique*.—Renauldon, *Traité historique et pratique des droits seigneuriaux* (Paris, 1765). — Moreau de Beaumont, *Mémoires sur les Impositions de la France* (1785). — Clamageran, *Histoire de l'Impôt en France* (1867-76).—Vignon, *Études historiques sur l'Administration des Voies Publiques en France avant 1790* (Paris, 1862), and the articles "Canaux de Navigation," "Douane," "Péage," "Routes et Chemins," and "Voies de Communication" in Guillaumin's (old) *Dictionnaire d'Économie Politique*.]　E. CA.

INTERNAL REVENUE TAXES IN THE UNITED STATES. In the United States this term is applied to federal taxes imposed upon domestic manufactures, trade, or income. It does not include revenue derived from sales of public lands, postal revenues, or patent fees. Internal revenue duties have been imposed at three different periods: 1791-1802 ; 1813-1817 ; and 1862 until the present time (1893). During the first period taxes were levied upon distilled spirits (1791), carriages, licenses for retailing wines and liquors, snuff, refining sugar, auction sales (1794), stamped papers (1797), and a direct tax of $2,000,000 (£400,000) (1798). The first of these duties was very unpopular in certain sections of the country, not only on account of the special burdens which were imposed upon farmers, who were the distillers of the period, but also because it was regarded as a British tax, hostile to American freedom. Opposition gave rise to the whisky rebellion in the western part of Pennsylvania. The republican party under the leadership of Jefferson was pledged to the repeal of the existing internal revenue duties ; and with their succeeding to power, this was done in 1802. The necessities of war revived these taxes in the second period, and a similar reason occasioned their imposition at the beginning of the civil war. In the last period they were sweeping in their embrace ; and, owing to the urgency of the times and general ignorance of the incidence of such taxes, there was frequent change and no system. The first of these measures was the act of July 1, 1862, which imposed specific and *ad valorem* duties upon manufactures, licenses upon occupations, a general income tax, and a tax upon gross receipts of transportation companies. The system was further extended by the act of June 30, 1864 ; and it was estimated by Mr. David

A. Wells that between eight and fifteen per cent of the value of the finished product was collected by the treasury department. So productive indeed were these taxes that from 1864 until 1868 they exceeded the customs revenues. With the close of the war many of the internal revenue duties were reduced or repealed, until taxes were imposed only upon the manufacture and selling of distilled liquors, fermented liquors, tobacco and cigars, and oleomargarine.

During the first period, 1792 - 1801, the internal revenue duties varied from 5 to 9 per cent of the net ordinary receipts ; in the second period, they constituted about 13 per cent ; and since 1862 they have been one of the principal props of financial support, furnishing in recent years about 40 per cent of the net receipts. As the country has become accustomed to the taxes, and they are favourably regarded by many as desirable sumptuary regulations, it does not appear probable that they will be removed in the near future.

[For the early period see H. C. Adams, "Taxation in the U.S. 1789-1816," in *Johns Hopkins Studies*, vol. ii. ; and for the period of the civil war, *Reports of the Special Commissioner of Revenue* (D. A. Wells) for the years 1866-68 ; also annual *Reports of the Commissioner of Internal Revenue* (published without Tables in the *Finance Reports*).]　D. R. D.

INTERNATIONAL. See INTERNATIONAL WORKING MEN'S ASSOCIATION.

INTERNATIONAL COINAGE. The idea of having one and the same measure of values for all civilised nations received a strong impetus from the great exhibition in London of 1851. The difficulty then experienced in comparing the prices of similar exhibits from different countries and the values of the exhibits of one country as against those of another, led to the discussion of the possibility of establishing an international standard ; the question came up at various meetings of the international statistical congress. In December 1865 France, Belgium, Italy, and Switzerland made the convention by which the currency of the Latin Union was established. In 1867 the conference at the Paris exhibition invited wider consideration of the idea thus adopted. Two delegates from Great Britain attended this conference, which recommended that a uniform gold standard be adopted by civilised countries with coins of $\frac{1}{10}$ fineness ; and that the gold coins thereafter struck by countries the parties to the convention should be multiples of five francs. About the same time several countries had been making some move in the direction of assimilating their coinage to that of their neighbours.

The royal commission of 1868, which arose out of the Paris conference, marks for Great Britain the most important epoch in the history of the idea. That commission examined some of the leading economic thinkers of the day, such as Bagehot, Jevons, and Newmarch, of whom the latter was almost alone in being very lukewarm about the matter ; the principle of an international coinage was warmly espoused by several witnesses. The commission summed up the evidence as tending to show—

1. That time would be saved to all traders in calculations and comparing foreign price-lists.

2. That small traders would be relieved from a disadvantage which at present they suffered in their inability to keep a staff conversant with foreign price-lists, etc.

3. That commercial travellers would be much aided in pushing their wares.

But the commission very rightly pointed out that these advantages, even if not exaggerated, would only be obtained by complete uniformity of weights and measures as well as coins. As regards coins it stated the absolute necessity of some sort of international mints so as to assure each country that the international coins did correspond in intrinsic value with their denomination ; it pointed out the necessity of a uniform charge for mintage ; and after discussing the various possibilities as to the choice of a coin for a common standard, concluded that a measure which would cause so much disturbance of existing contracts, and was after all only a partial measure, could not be lightly entered into ; and they reported distinctly against any suggestion that Great Britain should merely adopt a gold coin of the value of 25 francs instead of the sovereign.

Here the matter rested so far as Great Britain was concerned for thirteen years. But the conference of 1867 is thought to have borne fruit in the adoption of a gold standard by Germany in 1871, and the alteration of other national currencies. When in 1882 delegates on behalf of the British Indian and imperial governments attended another conference at Paris upon the question, the idea had taken a new turn ; in 1867 the general opinion of the parties who met in conference had favoured a single gold standard ; now the United States, as well as some other countries, had declared for a double standard. The possibility of agreement on an international currency was farther off than ever.

The system generally supported by advocates of change as the best to be adopted is a decimal system (see DECIMAL SYSTEM), and to some extent the movement in favour of an international measure of value became mixed up with the movement in favour of international weights and measures. Even if the principle of the decimal system be admitted, we have still to face the difficulty of electing between the two chief decimal systems of the world—those of the United States and of the Latin Union. And there is at least a question whether the mere theoretic convenience of the decimal system

should weigh against other considerations, e.g. that of keeping in currency the most generally known coin of the world. The Commission of 1868 on that ground suggested that the sovereign was best adapted for an international standard —but they did not consider whether it should be redivided on a decimal system ; this is of course a matter of pure convention.

The general objections to a change which falls with different weight on different countries are chiefly (1) the necessity of revising all contracts ; (2) the expense attendant on re-coinage. They will be found well stated in the late Mr. Newmarch's evidence before the commission of 1868. We are assuming that subsidiary coins will follow the standard, and that thus one class of difficulties will disappear.

There is, however, one important point touched on by Mr. Goschen in his evidence before the same commission—viz. whether making a "coin" a universal measure will not be to substitute a token for the commodity known as gold.

The idea of an international coinage is not impossible, though at present impracticable. In the 15th and 16th centuries the Spanish dollar and Portuguese Johannes became for all practical purposes international coins, and at the present time the English sovereign comes almost as near to that ideal as the Spanish dollar did.

[The publications of the International Association for obtaining a uniform decimal system, etc., etc., especially a *Concise Narrative* by Leone Levi, 1867.—The report of the Royal Commission of 1868 in *P. P.* of 1868, vol. xxvii.—The reports of the delegates to the International Monetary Conference 1882 in *P. P.* of 1882, vol. liii.]

C. A. H.

INTERNATIONAL LAW.

I. INTRODUCTION.—International Law may be defined as *the rules which determine the conduct of the general body of civilised states in their dealings with one another.* Some writers regard it as deduced from principles of natural justice implanted by the Creator in the human breast (Vattel, Wheaton, Hautefeuille), while others look upon it as a body of precepts drawn from the practice of states, and resting for their validity upon express or tacit consent (Hall, Stephen). The latter view is in accord with the facts of history. Modern international law is derived from usage, some of it extending back to remote antiquity, but most being the growth of the last three centuries. Rules have been adopted partly because they were convenient and partly because they were deemed just and merciful. The law of nations is ultimately shaped by the public opinion of the civilised world.

II. THE LAWS OF PEACE. 1. *Independence.* — Every fully sovereign state possesses the right of managing all its affairs without interference from other states. This is called the right of independence. It is conditioned by an obligation to respect the corresponding rights of other members of the family of nations. Mutual intercourse is as impossible among states without mutual concession as it is among individuals. Political communities, like Egypt and Bulgaria, which are not allowed entire freedom of action in external affairs, cannot be regarded as fully sovereign and independent ; but a state which submits temporarily to restrictions imposed by treaty is not held to have forfeited thereby its title to independence. Intervention takes place when a state interferes by force or threat of force in the internal affairs of another state, or in questions arising between two or more states. Such action trenches upon independence, and is therefore to be looked upon with grave suspicion. Each case must be judged on its own merits. Publicists differ widely as to what are lawful grounds of intervention. It is best to restrict intervention to cases where the duty of self-preservation overrides the obligation of respecting a neighbour's freedom of action. Undoubtedly a state may intervene to ward off a direct and pressing danger to its own safety or its highest national interests.

2. *Property.* — Modern international law assumes that sovereignty is territorial (Maine, *Ancient Law*, ch. iv.). States possess arsenals, museums, hospitals, munitions of war and similar objects ; but their territorial possessions are by far the more important. Their dominion extends not only over the land within their boundaries and all the rivers and lakes enclosed therein, but also over the sea to the distance of three miles from low-water mark along their shores, and over the narrow bays and gulfs indenting their coast. The best rule with regard to inlets is that, if the line drawn from headland to headland across the entrance is less than ten miles in length, they are territorial waters, if more, they are a part of the open sea. In the former case the marine league is measured from the imaginary line across the opening, in the latter from the shore around the bay. The ten-mile rule has not, however, been adopted universally in practice, like the three-mile limit. The open ocean is free from territorial dominion. Its use is common to all, and none have exclusive rights within it. The old claims to dominion over large portions of it have become obsolete, the last relic of them having disappeared when the arbitrators of Paris decided, in 1893, against

the claim of the United States to exercise jurisdiction in Behring Sea for the purpose of preventing vessels of other nations from catching seals therein. There is a right of innocent passage through natural territorial waters when the channel connecting two portions of the high seas runs through them. All vessels at peace with the territorial power possess it ; and it has been secured as regards the artificial channel of the Suez Canal by the convention of 1888, which neutralised that water-way. Fisheries in territorial waters are reserved for subjects of the local sovereign ; fisheries in the high seas are open to all. But these simple rules are often modified by treaty stipulations. If a river flows through more countries than one, it is now the custom for them to grant reciprocal rights of navigation. If a river flows between two countries, the territory of each extends to an imaginary line drawn along the middle channel (*Thalweg*).

3. *Jurisdiction.* — Jurisdiction is in the main territorial ; but states have a personal jurisdiction over their own subjects wherever they may be, though it cannot be enforced if the territorial jurisdiction of any other power conflicts with it. Each state exercises authority over all persons and things within its territory, with some few exceptions. Questions of jurisdiction assume an international aspect when two states put forth conflicting claims with regard to the same individual. Thus a person born in one country and naturalised in another, may be regarded by each as its citizen ; and, if he returns to the country of his birth, it may possibly deal with him in a way that causes the country of his naturalisation to interfere for his protection. England in 1870 recognised the naturalisation of her subjects abroad as depriving them of their British citizenship ; and, with regard to her naturalised subjects, she protects them abroad except in the country of their birth, but there she will not interfere on their behalf unless by its law they have ceased to be its subjects. This rule avoids all trouble ; but countries which, like the United States, claim to protect their naturalised subjects wherever they may be, meet with constant difficulties in the matter of compulsory military service. Latterly these have been avoided by treaty stipulations whereby the obligation is not to be enforced unless the person concerned had actually come under it before he left his native land. Citizens of one country domiciled in another must pay all state and local dues, but they cannot be compelled to serve in the army. Real property is for all purposes under the local law ; but if personal property is situated in one country and its owner is domiciled in another, the *lex domicilii* (see DOMICIL) prevails with regard to it. A state's jurisdiction extends to all ships, except foreign men-of-war, in its territorial waters, to

all its own ships on the high seas, and to all pirates seized by its vessels. Some states follow France in declining to exercise authority over foreign merchantmen in their ports, when only the interior order and discipline of the ship are concerned. In such cases the law of the country to which the ship belongs is applied. Foreign sovereigns visiting a country in an official capacity, and the resident diplomatic agents of foreign powers, are exceptions to the rule that a state's jurisdiction extends to all persons and things within its territory. Their persons and property are inviolable. They are exempt from ordinary legal processes, and even in cases of grave misbehaviour all that can be done is to escort them out of the country. Land forces of foreign states may not enter the territory without permission ; but when in it they are under the authority of their own officers. Foreign ships of war enter friendly ports without special permission. While there they are exempt from the local jurisdiction in most matters, but are bound to observe port and health regulations, and also neutrality regulations should their country be a belligerent. They may give asylum in extreme cases to political refugees and fugitive slaves, but not to ordinary criminals. The local authorities have no right to effect arrests on board. Western states have obtained by treaty for their subjects in oriental countries under native rule exemption from the local jurisdiction, and subjection instead to consular courts of their own nationality or mixed tribunals. Most civilised powers are now bound by extradition treaties to surrender to one another criminals, who, having committed a grave offence in the territory of one state, succeed in escaping to another. Political offenders are usually excepted from these stipulations.

4. *Equality.*—The doctrine of equality means that the rights and obligations of each independent state are the same, not that all are equal in influence. Since outward forms are the signs of equality or the reverse, the rules of etiquette between states are treated of under this head. Some of them regulate precedence at court ceremonials, others are concerned with diplomatic rank and the order of the signatures to international documents, while a third class deal with salutes by foreign war-vessels visiting a port and salutes between vessels at sea.

5. *Diplomacy.*—Diplomatic intercourse is now carried on by means of agents accrdeited by each state to its neighbours, and permanently resident at their capitals. These agents are divided into four classes : (1) ambassadors, and papal legates or nuncios ; (2) envoys and ministers plenipotentiary accredited to sovereigns ; (3) ministers resident accredited to sovereigns ; (4) chargés d'affaires accredited to ministers of foreign affairs. The classes rank in the order given ; but within each class precedence is determined by length of residence at the court to which its members are accredited. A state may refuse to receive a given individual as the diplomatic agent of another state if he is one of its own subjects, or personally obnoxious to its sovereign, or openly hostile to it or its institutions ; and it may ask for the recall of a diplomatic agent, and even dismiss him, if in its opinion he has seriously misconducted himself. Such rejections are consistent with friendliness between the powers concerned, but a refusal to continue diplomatic intercourse at all is a sign of rupture and generally the prelude of war. Diplomatic ministers possess large immunities. In all matters governed by the *lex domicilii* their residence abroad is held to be a residence in their own country. Their persons are inviolable. They are free from legal processes. Their official residence may not be entered, except in extreme cases, by the local authorities, nor may their papers be seized. The members of their suite who are in the diplomatic service are free in most matters from the local jurisdiction ; and their wives and children, and even their servants, share their immunities to a considerable, though not very precisely determined, degree.

III. THE LAWS OF WAR. 1. *Preliminary Points.*—War is a contest carried on by public force between states, or between states and communities having, with regard to the contest, the rights of states. Private wars have been abolished in civilised countries. All wars are now public, in that they are carried on by governmental authority. There are various ways of obtaining redress by force, which are held to fall short of war, though they differ from it only in the intention of the parties. They are reprisals, EMBARGO (*q.v.*), and pacific blockade (see BLOCKADE). The first involves the destruction or seizure by one state of property belonging to another in the territory of the latter or on the high seas. The second is used when the aggrieved state seizes all the ships of the offending nation found in its ports. The third is like an ordinary blockade except that the ships of third powers cannot be captured. No formal DECLARATION OF WAR is necessary. The moment war begins the public armed forces on both sides are free to act, private individuals are obliged to refrain from pacific intercourse with enemy subjects, and some treaties with the enemy are abrogated, while others, such as extradition treaties, are suspended. When a province or colony revolts from the mother-country, other powers may without offence accord it recognition of belligerency, if it carries on war in civilised fashion, possesses a regular government and a fairly well-defined territory, and if the interests of the recognising state demand that it should fix the *status* of the revolted community. Such recognition grants all the rights and obligations conferred on lawful belligerents.

2. *Enemy Persons.*—Enemy subjects found within a state's territory at the outbreak of war are allowed to remain on condition that they live quietly and peacefully and give no information or assistance to their own state. A right to expel them exists; but it is rarely used, the action of the French government of national defence in expelling Germans from the department of the Seine in 1870, being the only instance in modern times. The population of the enemy's country is divided into combatants and non-combatants. With regard to the former, quarter is given when asked for, prisoners are cared for, and, if possible, exchanged, the sick and wounded are well treated and the practice of slaughtering the defenders of a fortress taken by assault has died out. With regard to the latter, they are to be protected from personal insult and injury; but, when they reside in territory in the enemy's occupation, they may be compelled to perform for him any service not distinctly military, and must give no aid or information to their own side. Women and children are sometimes allowed to leave places about to be bombarded.

3. *Enemy Property on Land.*—Real property situated in the state and possessed by enemy subjects is not confiscated or sequestrated, nor is personal property unless the proper authorities order seizure. The outbreak of war renders such property confiscable, but does not *ipso facto* confiscate it. Debts due from subjects of one belligerent to subjects of the other cannot be collected during the war, but the right to demand them revives at the conclusion of peace. Debts due from a belligerent state to subjects of the enemy are not confiscable. Movables taken in war on land are called "booty." They should be sold and the proceeds divided among all concerned according to a regular plan. If booty is recaptured before the captors have held it for twenty-four hours, or before they have brought it within their lines, it reverts to the original owners. When an invader holds a portion of his enemy's country in firm possession, he is said to occupy it. In that case he may use immovables belonging to the invaded state, and, though he may not alienate them, he may appropriate the rents and profits derived from them, unless they are devoted to the support of religion, charity, or education. State movables may be appropriated and alienated, except legal documents, state papers, works of art, and scientific instruments. Neither private immovables nor the profits arising from them may be confiscated, but military necessity justifies their destruction. Private movables are unconfiscable unless of immediate use in war. Requisitions may be levied on occupied districts, which are thereby compelled to furnish articles needed for the daily consumption of the invaders. The taxes are paid into their military chest, and sometimes further sums are exacted under the name of contributions (see ENEMY GOODS).

4. *Enemy Property at Sea.*—Maritime capture can be carried on in the territorial waters of either belligerent and on the high seas. Private as well as public property may be captured; but vessels exclusively engaged in works of exploration, discovery, or humanity, vessels engaged in coast fisheries, and vessels driven by stress of weather into their adversary's ports, are usually exempt from seizure. Moreover, in recent wars merchant vessels of one belligerent found in the ports of the other at the outbreak of war have been allowed a reasonable time to depart, and cargoes of works of art have been restored to enemy owners. And further, enemy goods not contraband laden on board neutral vessels are free from capture under the Declaration of Paris of 1856 (see article on that subject). With the exceptions just given, enemy ships, and enemy goods on enemy ships, are good prize. Belligerent cruisers have a right to stop and overhaul all merchantmen on the high seas in order to discover whether they are liable to capture. Prize Courts are established by belligerents to try the validity of captures made by their cruisers; and it is the duty of captors to bring every prize in for adjudication. But extreme necessity is held to justify the destruction at sea of vessels taken from the enemy. If captured property is recaptured, it is restored under certain conditions to its original owners. Great Britain restores if the recapture is made during the same war.

5. *Agents and Instruments of Warfare.*—Regular soldiers and sailors are legitimate combatants; but guerilla troops and levies *en masse* are held lawful only when they can be easily distinguished from non-combatants and respect the laws of war in their operations. Savage or half-civilised troops, regularly embodied and drilled, and led by civilised officers, are employed by many states. Privateers are forbidden by the Declaration of Paris; but the question of the legality of a volunteer navy, raised by Germany in 1870, has not been definitely settled. The crews of merchant ships may not fight except to resist an attack upon their own vessel. Assassination, the poisoning of food and water, and the use of poisoned weapons and of explosive bullets below 14 oz. in weight, are forbidden. Devastation of an enemy's territory is deemed lawful only when justified by overwhelming military necessity. Stratagems which involve breaches of faith are condemned.

IV. THE LAW OF NEUTRALITY. 1. *The Nature of Neutrality.*—Neutrality is the condition of those states which in time of war take no part in the contest, but continue pacific intercourse with the belligerents. Neutral governments must give no assistance to either belligerent and preserve perfect impartiality between them. Neutralised states are those which, like Belgium and Switzerland, are obliged, as a condition of·having their national existence respected and defended by other states, to abstain from warfare except in the strictest self-defence. Provinces have been neutralised, and also persons and things, such as those concerned with the care of the sick and wounded, which have been protected by the Geneva Convention of 1864. The Suez Canal was neutralised by a great international treaty in 1888.

2. *Rights and Obligations as between Belligerent and Neutral States.*—A belligerent state may not carry on hostilities within neutral territory, or use it as a base of operations, or recruit in it, or obtain supplies of arms or warlike stores for its cruisers in neutral ports and waters. Its vessels must obey reasonable regulations made by any neutral as to the length of their stay in its ports, the admission or exclusion of their prizes, and the amount of coal they may take in. If its troops are driven across a neutral frontier they must submit to being disarmed and interned. A neutral state is bound not to give armed assistance to either belligerent, nor to permit belligerent troops to march through its territory, nor to sell ships or arms to belligerents, nor to lend money to either of them, nor to allow them, or its own subjects for them, to levy troops, or fit out armed expeditions within its dominions or increase the armament or fighting crew of any vessel of war in its waters. It must restrain its subjects from engaging in the military service of belligerents within its territory or accepting letters of marque from them; and it lies under a vaguely-defined obligation to prevent the original departure from its territory of vessels built and fitted out therein for the naval service of either belligerent. The Geneva arbitration of 1872 has not cleared up this point.

3. *Ordinary Maritime Capture.*—The old rule that governed cases of maritime capture uncomplicated by special circumstances of character, destination or control, was that enemies' goods were prize, even if found on neutral ships, and neutral goods were not prize, even if found on board enemies' ships. Attempts began in the 17th century to substitute for it the rule that enemies' goods in neutral ships were not prize, and with this was joined the rule that neutral goods on enemies' ships were prize. The Declaration of Paris adopted the portion of the opposing rules most favourable to neutrals, and decreed that enemies' goods, except contraband of war, should be free under the neutral flag; and neutral goods, with the same exception, should be free under the enemies' flag (see DECLARATION OF PARIS). Neutral goods on board a belligerent cruiser are liable to capture, and they would probably be adjudged good prize if found on an armed enemy merchantman. Resistance by neutral merchantmen to belligerent search renders both ship and cargo good prize. In the absence of special agreement neutrals cannot avoid belligerent search by sending their merchantmen to sea under the convoy of their ships of war. Neutral vessels under belligerent convoy are good prize.

4. *Contraband Trade.*—Belligerents have a right of capturing on the way to the enemy such goods as are directly necessary to the conduct of his hostilities, even though they are carried in neutral vessels. The goods are called "contraband of war" (see CONTRABAND); and the offence of the neutral consists not in selling them, but in carrying them. A belligerent destination is essential; and if a merely colourable neutral destination is interposed between the port of departure and the real termination of the voyage, the doctrine of continuous voyages applies, and the goods are condemned as contraband. Articles useful primarily and ordinarily for warlike purposes, such as arms and ammunition, and the machinery for making them, are always contraband. Articles useful primarily and ordinarily for peaceful purposes, such as books, music and furniture, are never contraband. With regard to articles useful for warlike and peaceful purposes indifferently, technically termed articles *ancipitis usus*, such as clothing, food and coal, there is great difference of opinion. British and American courts and jurists favour the doctrine of occasional contraband, which makes them good prize or not according to such circumstances as the nature of the port to which they are going, the special character of the goods themselves, and the special needs of the enemy. Continental opinion inclines strongly to a restriction of the list of contraband goods, and as a rule rejects the doctrine of occasional contraband, though in 1884 France endeavoured to regard food (rice) as contraband in the course of her operations against China. The British doctrine is strongly based in reason and authority, but there can be no doubt that our courts and statesmen have sometimes given it an undue extension. The usual penalty for carrying contraband is confiscation of the contraband goods, but the whole cargo is confiscated if the proportion of contraband goods to innocent goods is large, and both belong to the same owner. The vessel also is confiscated if it is owned by the owner of the contraband goods, or if any fraudulent device, such as showing false papers, is used to avoid capture.

5. *Blockade.*—Belligerents have the right to capture neutral merchant vessels attempting to enter or leave the enemy's ports, if they are able to maintain a ship of war or a squadron in such a position that any attempt at ingress or egress is eminently dangerous. But they cannot

obtain this right by merely proclaiming a port or a coast-line blockaded, and supporting the proclamation by no force at all or by an entirely inadequate one. Such attempts are called paper blockades. When the Declaration of Paris asserted that a blockade to be binding must be effective, it did but declare an undoubted principle of international law. Military or strategic blockades are those which are carried on with a view to the ultimate reduction of the place blockaded. Commercial blockades are those carried on with the object of weakening the enemy by cutting off his external trade. They are certainly lawful; but there is a growing feeling against them caused by the fact that with modern facilities of land communication they will in most cases cripple neutral trade without inflicting serious injury upon the belligerent subjected to them. When a state establishes a blockade, it generally sends a diplomatic notification thereof to neutral governments. The British school of publicists hold this to be equivalent to notification to neutral ship-masters, but the French school require a warning to be given direct to the neutral ship-master on his first approach to the blockaded port. Thus notification has little or no effect in French practice; whereas English prize law varies considerably according to its presence or absence. The doctrine of continuous voyages applies to BLOCKADE (q.v.) as well as to CONTRABAND (q.v.). The offence or breach of blockade attaches the moment the blockade-runner leaves its own waters, and is not deposited till the end of the return voyage. The usual penalty is confiscation of ship and cargo; but, if they belong to different persons and the owner of the cargo did not know that the port of destination was blockaded, the ship alone is confiscated.

6. *Unneutral Service.*—Neutral individuals are forbidden to perform certain services for a belligerent, such as transmitting signals or messages for warlike purposes, carrying military or naval despatches, or carrying persons in the military, naval or civil service of the belligerent government. These are not matters of contraband trade. They amount to entering the service of the belligerent, though to a limited degree and for a temporary purpose. It is sometimes difficult to draw the line between what is allowed and what is forbidden in these matters. For instance it has been decided that to carry men returning from abroad to perform military duties in a belligerent army was not unneutral service, because the men were unarmed and unorganised and travelled as ordinary passengers, though cases of arms were in the hold of the vessel which took them. But it has also been decided that to carry shipwrecked officers and men of a belligerent navy home to their own country was unneutral service, because they were organised and the vessel was specially

hired by their government to transport them. The two important tests are the knowledge of the master of the vessel, and the character of the contract he enters into. If he knows that he is signalling or carrying persons useful in war for a belligerent, and especially if in addition he has made a special contract with an agent of the belligerent government, he will not, if captured, escape the penalty of the confiscation of his ship. Usages are growing up in favour of the exemption of duly certified and sealed mailbags from belligerent search; but at present they have not crystallised into law. Exemption has been granted in recent wars as a matter of comity.

[Acollas, *Droit de la Guerre.*—Bar, *Private International Law,* Gillespie's translation.—Bernard, *Neutrality of Great Britain during the American Civil War.*—Calvo, *Droit International.*—Cushing, *Treaty of Washington.*—De Martens, *Guide Diplomatique.*—Foelix, *Traité du Droit International Privé.*—Hall, *International Law.*—Halleck, *International Law,* Baker's ed.—Hautefeuille, *Des Droits et des Devoirs des Nations Neutres,* vol. i.—Heffter, *Droit International,* pp. 269 *et seq.*—Lawrence, *International Law.*—Maine, *International Law.*—Manning, *Law of Nations,* bk. iv. chs. vii. and viii.—Nys, *Guerre Maritime,* ch. iii.—Ortolan, *Diplomatie de la Mer.*—Piggott, *Exterritoriality.*—Phillimore, *Commentaries.*—Story, *Conflict of Laws.*—Twiss, *Law of Nations.*—Wharton, *Conflict of Laws.*—Wheaton, *International Law,* Dana's ed. pt. ii.

See the works of Hall, Manning, Maine, Ortolan, Halleck, Phillimore, Calvo, Heffter, Hautefeuille, Nys, and the others cited in the body of this article. See also Bluntschli, *Droit International Codifié.*—Wharton, *Digest of the International Law of the United States.*—Kent, *Commentaries.*—Woolsey, *International Law.*—Creasy, *First Platform of International Law.*—Fiore, *Nouveau Droit International Publique.* — Pommeroy, *International Law in time of peace.*—Hertslet, *Map of Europe by Treaty;* and the publications of the *Institut de Droit International;* arts. ANGARIE, DROIT D'; AUBAINE, DROIT D'.]   T. J. L.

INTERNATIONAL LAW, PRIVATE.

I. INTRODUCTION.—Many more or less complex cases are brought before courts of law, so connected with different countries that it becomes a question of what country the law ought to be applied to them. The department of law which answers that question is called private international law, or the CONFLICT OF LAWS (q.v.). Its basis is sometimes said to be international comity, as if it was only through comity that a court ever applies a foreign law. But this is not so. Suppose, for example, that the heirship to an estate in England depends on the validity of a marriage which took place in Scotland. The English court is impelled by much more than comity to apply Scotch law, and not English, to the question whether that marriage could be valid without the presence of a clergyman or a registrar. The selection of a law is itself matter of legal principle, which ought to lead to the same selection being made in all countries. And to a great extent that result is attained, but in many cases the selection is so difficult that neither all countries, nor all judges and authors in the same country, are agreed on it. The subject is eminently one which lies *inter apices juris*. As may be seen from the example just given, the questions dealt with in it arise not only between independent states, as France and Italy, but also between different parts of the same state possessing distinct systems of law, as England and Scotland. And the principles, and the solutions to which they lead, are the same for both cases, so far as circumstances permit.

II. DOMICILE AND NATIONALITY.—Domicile and political nationality occur so frequently among the circumstances determining the selection of a law that the careful examination of those two characteristics, with a view to the classification of persons by them, is considered to be a branch of private international law. Domicile is divided into that of origin and that of choice (see DOMICIL). Without going into all the distinctions necessary in practice, the former is the domicile which a person derives at his birth, usually from his father, and the latter is that which a person of full age establishes for himself by fixing his residence within a certain jurisdiction, with a sufficient character of permanence. There is on the continent of Europe a wide and growing tendency to substitute political nationality, as a determining element in the selection of a law where a person is concerned, for domicile, which is the older criterion. English judges have not followed that movement, and, even where it prevails, no test but domicile can be applied to distinguish persons who, within the same independent state, belong to parts possessing distinct systems of law, as Englishmen from Scotchmen, Austrians from Hungarians, or men of New York from Pennsylvanians. The law which belongs to a person, and the jurisdiction to which he is subject, either on the ground of his domicile or on that of his nationality, are called his personal law and jurisdiction. That term, for the purposes of the English courts, means the law or jurisdiction of the domicile, even although the person in question is of British nationality, but has a non-British domicile. In certain other countries—France, for instance,—the personal law or jurisdiction is taken to be that of the nationality, subject to the necessity of using domicile in order to distinguish persons of, say, British nationality into Englishmen, Scotchmen, South Africans, or others.

III. CAPACITY. — This may be absolute or relative. The question whether a person is of the age required by law to make a will, marry, or conclude any other contract, is one of absolute capacity ; that of whether two persons are incapable of marrying one another on the ground of consanguinity or affinity is one of relative capacity. Both kinds of capacity have usually been referred on the continent of Europe to the personal law, and in England also the capacity to make a will has always been referred to the law of the testator's domicile. But in England formerly the capacity, whether absolute or relative, for marriage or any other contract, was referred to the law of the place where it was entered into, the *lex loci contractus celebrati ;* and so it still is in the United States. Now, however, Lord Westbury, Lord Justice Cotton, and Lord Halsbury, have pronounced that capacity depends entirely on the law of the domicile.

IV. MINORS AND LUNATICS. — The guardians and curators, whether of the person or of the estate, appointed for a minor or a lunatic by the jurisdiction which claims him on the ground either of his nationality or his domicile, can exercise their functions in England, both as to his person and as to his movable property. But the English court also has jurisdiction, and can appoint guardians or committees, though it will only do so in aid of the foreign jurisdiction, so long as the appointees of the latter are not abusing their powers.

V. MARRIAGE AND DIVORCE.—The validity of a marriage, as regards the form of its celebration, like that of any other contract, is universally held to be governed by the law of the place of celebration. We have seen the rules as to the capacity of the parties.[1] Divorce has been granted in England when the husband, whether petitioner or respondent, is resident here, though his residence may not amount to domicile ; but the English court shows a strong tendency not to recognise the divorce of persons domiciled in England, when decreed by a foreign court on the ground of mere residence, and since the decision in *Le Mesurier* v. *Le Mesurier*, June 1895, it is probable that in future it will only be granted in England to persons domiciled here. The place where a marriage was contracted is immaterial in a suit for divorce, and the grounds for decreeing divorce can only be those which are admitted by the law of the country in which the court sits, the *lex fori*.

VI. PROPERTY AND WILLS.—Property is divided into movable and immovable, terms which are equivalent to our personal and real estate, except that terms of years in land are immovable property though personal estate in England. This line of demarcation between movables and immovables is recognised for the purposes of private international law even in England.

A distinction must be drawn between questions affecting a particular piece of property, movable or immovable, and those affecting the entirety of a person's property, or of the movable part of it, on the occasion of his marriage or death. The former class of questions, as, for instance, the form and effect of a conveyance of land, or the

---

1 One consequence of those rules is that a man domiciled in England gains nothing by going through the form of marriage with his deceased wife's sister, even in a European country where such marriages are allowed to its own subjects. The relative capacity being generally tested in Europe by the personal law, it will not be a marriage even where the form is gone through, unless the parties have previously naturalised themselves there, or transferred their domicile to that country, which would be incompatible with the intention of returning to live in England.

conditions necessary for passing the property in a lot of deal planks, are decided by the law of the country where the piece of property is, the *lex situs*. As to the latter class of questions, the oldest rule, still maintained in England, determined the rights which husband and wife take in one another's movables on marriage by the law of their domicile, which is necessarily that of the husband, and determined the beneficial succession to the movables of a testator or intestate by the law of his last domicile, but left similar questions for immovables to the *lex situs*. Now, however, there is a growing tendency on the continent to consider that the whole mass of a person's property, immovable as well as movable, ought to be dealt with on his marriage or death as a unit, in accordance with his personal law.

What has been said as to the beneficial succession to movables on death being governed by the law of the deceased's last domicile (or nationality) applies, as a general rule, to distribution on intestacy and to the validity of wills in matters of substance, such as the proportion of his property of which a testator can dispose, or the extent to which he may tie up his property. The formal validity of a will, as with respect to the number of witnesses, or to its being notarial or holograph, has usually been referred on the continent, in common with the forms of contracts and acts in general, to the law of the place where it is made, the *lex loci actus*. But the old English practice required that a will of movables should be made also in the form of the domicile, so that both in this case and in that of contracts it took the peculiar line of determining both formal and substantial validity by the same law, though with this difference, that in contracts the rule for the capacity was taken from that for the form, the law of the place of contract, while in wills the rule for the form was taken from that for the substance, the law of the domicile. But now, by Lord Kingsdown's act, a will of personal estate will be held in the United Kingdom to have been well made if it follows the form either of the testator's last domicile, or of the country in which he was domiciled when it was made ; or, if he was a British subject, that of the place where it was made ; or, if such British subject made it out of the United Kingdom, the form required in that part of the British dominions in which he had his domicile of origin.

VII. CONTRACTS AND TORTS.—The validity of a contract in point of form is determined by the law of the place where it was made, except that foreign stamps are not required in England on bills of exchange. In other contracts it is agreed that foreign stamps, which are necessary to their validity where made, cannot be dispensed with ; but that principle is frittered away in England by a doctrine that a contract may be valid although, for want of a stamp, no available obligation arises from it.

The intrinsic validity and the effects of a contract are determined by the law of that country with which the contract has the most real connection, especially by the law of the country to which the parties looked as that in which it was to be fulfilled.

In order that an act may be sued on in England as a TORT, it must be a tortious one both by the law of the country where it was done and by English law.

VIII. LIMITATION OF ACTIONS.—No part of private international law presents more difference of doctrine between authors, or more difference of practice between different countries, and between different periods in the same country, than this. In England it is settled that the time of limitation is always the English one, and within that time actions are entertained on contracts or tortious acts, though barred by the law of the country to which the contract properly belonged or where the act was done, and after that time are not entertained, though the obligation from the contract or tort is in full vigour in that country.

IX. BANKRUPTCY.—There has always been a considerable body of opinion in favour of bringing all the assets and all the liabilities of a bankrupt into one focus at his domicile, but this has been resisted not only, as in the somewhat parallel cases of marriage and death, by the theoretical objection to comprising immovable assets in the principle, but also by the practical convenience which is often found in having concurrent bankruptcies in the different countries where the debtor has carried on business, instead of sending all the creditors to his domicile, from which they may be very remote. In England every one is subject to be adjudicated bankrupt who is domiciled here, or within the last year has ordinarily resided or had a dwelling-house or place of business here ; that he has been made bankrupt elsewhere does not prevent his being adjudicated one here, if it seems expedient to the court that this should be done ; the syndics, or other administrators appointed in a bankruptcy in the debtor's domicile, can sweep his movable property in England within their administration, so long as there is no concurrent bankruptcy against him here ; an English creditor must hand over to the trustees in an English bankruptcy any payment which, after its commencement, and not by virtue of any security given prior to its commencement, he has obtained out of the bankrupt's movables in a non-British country ; and a discharge under the bankrupt law of a foreign country will only relieve the debtor, in England, from contracts governed as to their effects by the law of the same country, and from torts committed in it.

X. FOREIGN JUDGMENTS.—A foreign judgment, for a sum of money, can be sued on in England when the court which pronounced it was competent by reason of the defendant's being either a subject of that country by nationality, or domiciled in it, or resident in it in a sense looser than that which is needed for domicile but such as is generally sufficient for jurisdiction. All these are grounds of competence having reference to the defendant's person, and are admitted as such everywhere. Where the competence of the foreign court was founded on the circumstance that the obligation sued on had special reference to that country, there is no equally general acceptance of definite rules for jurisdiction, and the English court will not now admit an action on the foreign judgment. In any case where the competence of the foreign court is admitted and the action entertained, the foreign judgment will be allowed the force of *res judicata*, that is to say, the defendant will not be allowed to dispute it, for alleged error either of fact or of law. The courts of many countries entertain actions not resting on any of the grounds of competence above mentioned. In France, for instance, a Frenchman can sue, although both the defendant and the obligation may have no connection with France. But the judgments in such actions will not be enforced in any other country than that in which they are pronounced. The grounds above mentioned are the only ones of what may be called international competence.

XI. PROCEDURE.—This is always governed by the *lex fori;* that is to say, every court follows its own procedure, and no other, whether in rules of evidence or in any other particular.

XII. THE METHOD OF AMENDMENT.—We must warn the reader that our limits have only allowed us to present a selection of important points, and to treat them especially with reference to the rules prevailing in England, and in a very general way even with reference to those rules. We hope, however, that enough has been said to show how desirable it is that the subject should be settled on a uniform basis for all countries, and how hopeless it is that such a result should be attained except by international agreement. Doctrinal discussion has been at work for seven centuries, with no further result than we have seen. Governments have therefore been at last impelled to take up the subject, and in September 1893 the delegates of fourteen countries met at the Hague, on the invitation of the Netherlands, in a conference on the codification of private international law. In June 1894 the conference reassembled, the delegates of sixteen countries taking part, and a portion of the work, amounting to fifty-nine articles, has been drafted and submitted to the respective governments. It is much to be regretted that the British government declined the invitation to the conference (see CONFLICT OF LAWS).

[The following are a few of the principal works. England : Westlake, *Private International Law*, 3rd ed., 1890. — Foote, *Foreign and Domestic Law*, 2nd ed., 1890.—Dicey, *Law of Domicil*, 1879.—United States: Wharton, *Conflict of Laws*, 2nd ed., 1881.—Story, *Conflict of Laws*, often re-edited : Continent of Europe: von Bar, translated from German into English, by Gillespie, 2nd ed., 1892.—Laine, 1888.—Asser, translated from Dutch into French by Rivier, 1884.—*Revue de Droit International et de Législation Comparée*, Brussels, from 1869.—*Journal du Droit International Privé et de la Jurisprudence Comparée*, Paris, from 1874.]   J. W.

INTERNATIONAL SECURITIES. A certain number of stocks and shares are dealt in indiscriminately : on the London market, on the Paris bourse, on the exchanges of Germany or Austria, on those of Holland, and even in New York. The ability of holders to realise in any of these markets, or in that one out of several which may happen to be the best for his purpose, puts such stocks into a different category from those which depend upon a single local and limited market. To give instances, the bonds of the French or Italian governments are dealt in freely on most of the European exchanges, and of Italian bonds it might be said that the best market is almost anywhere outside Italy. The *locale* of market for specific government bonds changes from time to time. Thus, since Russia grew, or was thought to have grown inimical to England, Russian bonds were gradually realised here and sent to Germany or Holland or France ; and, whereas Germany was the chief market for Russian securities, after London had lost taste for Russian stocks, France afterwards stepped in and by degrees relieved German holders of a large portion of the Russian sterling bonds which had been bought in Berlin, Frankfort, and on other stock markets of Germany. The shares and bonds of the South Austrian Railway Company (formerly Lombardo-Venetian) were at one time a favourite medium of remittance between markets, these being realisable not only in Vienna, but just as freely in Berlin or Paris or London. Of late years certain American railroad shares have taken the rank and distinctive features of international securities, and bankers have been heard to declare that they would rather advance money upon American railroad shares which carried no dividend, and which might be thought intrinsically valueless, but which could be realised in almost any great market of the world at a pinch, than lock up money in British Colonial stocks for which the market was confined to London, and was not always a free market even on the London stock exchange. A large part of the remittances between countries is now conducted by means of the purchase and sale by *arbitrage* dealers of these international securities. Nothing can be more prompt than the execution of an order by telegraph to buy or sell in Paris securities which were sold or bought against those operations in London, for example. These arbitrage dealings have a strong influence on the exchanges. Thus, suppose money is scarce in London and plentiful in Paris, the scarcity here naturally induces holders of French or other bonds to realise. The pressure to sell in this market reduces the price in London below the equivalent on the Paris bourse. Instantly the arbitrage dealer sees his opportunity, buys here—in the cheaper market, that is—and sells in Paris, which is contemporaneously the dearer market. The French exchange on London thereupon tends to rise, and cash drifts hither if the operations described are sufficiently large and numerous (see ARBITRAGE).   A. E.

INTERNATIONAL TRADE. A term used to describe commercial dealings between different countries, as opposed to those taking place within a single country or region. The separation between foreign and domestic trade, due originally to the importance attributed to the former in the MERCANTILE SYSTEM (*q.v.*), has been retained on scientific grounds. There is not such facility for moving labour and capital from country to country as would equalise wages and profits, while the effect of cost of carriage and other obstacles to exchange is very prominent. The ordinary theory of exchange therefore failing to completely interpret the facts, a special explanation is needed, the outlines of which are :—

The difficulty of moving labour and capital is regarded as the cause of the peculiar features of foreign trade. "A nation in the economic sense is a group of producers within which labour and capital freely circulate" (Bagehot), while they do not easily pass outside it. This relative immobility, sometimes regarded (e.g. by J. S. Mill) as the result of distance solely, seems more correctly conceived by Cairnes as the product of all the forces—"viz. geographical distance, differences in institutions, language, religion, and social customs"—which separate the economic groups called "nations." As labour and capital cannot move freely from country to country, normal international values will not depend on cost of production, the existence of industrial competition being requisite for the full operation of that regulator. Nevertheless exchanges between countries will be advantageous owing to (1) diversities in natural resources, and (2) the existence of special industrial aptitudes, the result of social development. Though cost will not determine value, it will not be without effect on the course of trade. "The existence of international trade" depends on "a difference in the comparative as contradistinguished from the absolute cost of producing the commodities exchanged" (Cairnes). If, e.g., England gives France coal in exchange for wine, the cost of producing coal as compared with wine must be less in the former than in the latter country.

It is conceivable that both coal and wine may be more cheaply produced in France, but the advantage being greater in the case of wine, it is profitable to obtain coal by means of exchange ; thus a difference in comparative cost of producing commodities will suffice to create a trade in them, unless (a) the hindrances to exchange be such as to absorb the gain, or (b) other countries offer more favourable terms. Cost of production, so far as it is operative within the trading countries (see COMPETITION AND CUSTOM) acts as a limiting force on foreign trade. Within the bounds set by comparative cost exchanges are mainly governed by the strength of reciprocal demand (see INTERNATIONAL VALUE).

The benefit of international as of all exchange lies in the increased enjoyments of the exchangers and therefore in the goods received, i.e. the only direct advantage of foreign commerce consists in the imports (Mill). Exports are merely the price or consideration paid for what is obtained by these means, a proposition which follows from and illustrates Adam Smith's maxim, "Consumption is the sole end and purpose of all production . . . a maxim so perfectly self-evident that it would be absurd to attempt to prove it."

The general gain of foreign trade can be further divided into, (1) the obtaining of articles which could not be produced at home ; (2) the cheapening of goods which could be so produced but at greater cost ; (3) the more efficient distribution of industrial forces and consequent larger production by the extension of "the territorial division of labour" (Torrens), the last chiefly found in the case of manufactures.

Possible evil results should in theoretical discussion be noted, viz. (1) specialisation of industry, of which foreign trade is but one form, increases the chance of so-called over- (really mis-) production. It is more difficult to gauge the amount of product required in a widely extended market ; and such disturbances as wars and failure of crops may produce serious effects. (2) The extension of international exchange may intensify the action of the "law of diminishing returns." In the case of a food-exporting country increased foreign trade is equivalent to an increase of population. When the product is an exhaustible one (e.g. English coal or Peruvian guano), the evil is more apparent (cp. Jevons, Coal Question, pp. 370 seq.). See MINES AND MINERALS, EXHAUSTION OF.

In interpreting the facts of international trade, valuable assistance is afforded by the proposition that "gold and silver having been chosen for the general medium of circulation, they are by the competition of commerce distributed in such proportions amongst the different countries of the world as to accommodate themselves to the natural traffic which would take place if no such metals existed and the trade between countries were purely a trade of barter" (Ricardo). Its truth is shown by considering that any other distribution would be unstable, as either export or import of bullion would be necessary ; it is in fact a special case of the general law that relative prices must be adjusted to relative values.

Until this proposition was formulated "the theory of foreign trade was," as Mill justly remarks, "an unintelligible chaos." By its aid the problems of international trade and values are freed from a complicating element. The precious metals can be regarded as simply an instrument for facilitating exchanges ; normal values are not altered by their fluctuations (see MONEY), which only affect prices. Monetary changes, like any other trade disturbance, may be followed by temporary movements, which however do not invalidate the general principles.

The actual working of international trade is carried on by means of the FOREIGN EXCHANGES, (q.v.) supplemented by telegraphic facilities and the modern developments of BANKING (q.v.), but as in the case of money these agencies alter no essential feature. The fundamental conditions of exchange hold good alike under a "barter," "money," or "credit economy."

The above outlined theory furnishes a logical basis for the practical rule of FREE TRADE (q.v.). "To those who accept the economic theory of international trade, no further proof of the essential soundness of this fundamental principle of commercial policy is needed" (Cairnes, cp. Cherbuliez, t. 2, p. 55), though particular theoretical exceptions may be suggested (cp. Mill, *Principles*, bk. v. ch. 10, § 1; Sidgwick, bk. iii. ch. 5). It may also be usefully employed in discussing the effect of taxation on imports and exports (cp. Mill, *Essays* and *Principles*, bk. v. ch. 4, § 6).

The theory of international trade first stated by Ricardo, more elaborately developed by Mill and Cairnes, may be regarded as the recognised English doctrine, though there are some dissentients (*e.g.* Mr. M'Leod), and even those who do not reject the theory, sometimes, with Prof. Sidgwick, minimise its importance. On the continent it has not met with much acceptance, being either ignored or controverted. The principal objections may be grouped as : (1) international does not differ from domestic trade, and therefore needs no special explanation ; (2) the assumptions made are incorrect, so that the conclusions do not interpret the facts (COURNOT, q.v.); (3) though logically correct, they have no application to the complications of actual trade (Lexis). Some continental writers have however given admirable expositions, especially A. E. Cherbuliez.

[Ricardo, *Principles of Political Economy and Taxation* (1817), ch. vii.—Torrens, *Economists refuted* (1808) ; ib. *External Corn Trade*, 1st ed. (1815).—J. S. Mill, *Essays on some Unsettled Questions of Pol. Econ.*, pp. 1-46 (1844) ; *Principles*, bk. iii. ch. 17-22 inclusive.—Cairnes, *Leading Principles*, pt. iii. (1874).—A. E. Cherbuliez, *Précis de la Science Économique* (Paris, 1862) t. i. pp. 335-391.—Mangoldt, *Grundriss* (2nd ed. 1871) pp. 97 *seq.* 203 *seq.*—Most English text-books contain statements of the theory (*e.g.* Fawcett, Walker, MacVane, Andrews).—See also Bastable, *Theory of International Trade* (1887).—Beaujon, *Handel en Handelspolitiek* (Harlem, 1888).—For criticism, see A. Cournot, *Théorie des Richesses* (1863), livre iii. ch. 6.—Lexis, art. "Handel" in Schönberg's *Handbuch der Politischen Oekonomie* (2nd Au.) bk. ii. pp. 753-758. Also references under INTERNATIONAL VALUE, THEORY OF.] C. F. B.

INTERNATIONAL VALUE, THEORY OF. The problem of international *value*, as distinct from that of international *trade*, deals with the question, "On what principle is the increase of wealth which results" from foreign trade "shared amongst the nations which co-operate in producing it ?" Or, since the division of gain depends on the ratio of exchange, "What causes determine the proportions in which trading nations exchange their products" (Cairnes). Its solution depends on an application of the fundamental principle of supply and demand.

Under INTERNATIONAL TRADE (q.v.), it appeared that the terms of exchange must lie between limits fixed by the relative costs of producing the exchanged goods in the trading countries. Thus if the production of 10 yards of cotton yarn or of silk requires a given cost in France, while 20 yards of cotton-yarn can be produced in England at the cost of 10 yards of silk, the exchange of English cotton-yarn for French silk may be profitably carried on at any ratio between 10 yards silk : 10 yards cotton-yarn, and 10 yards silk : 20 yards cotton-yarn. Less than the former France will not take, more than the latter England will not give. Within these bounds the rate of exchange will depend primarily on the comparative strength of demand. Should the English demand for silk be keen, while that of France for cotton-yarn is feeble, the terms of exchange will probably approach to 10 yards silk for 20 yards cotton-yarn, the precise ratio being so fixed as to equalise the reciprocal demand for the exchanged commodities : *e.g.* if, at the ratio 10 yards silk : 19 yards cotton-yarn, England takes just 100,000 yards silk and France 190,000 yards cotton, the "equation of international demand" (J. S. Mill) will be attained, and so long as the conditions are unchanged the ratio will be stable. An increased demand on the part of either country will tend to alter the terms to its disadvantage—suppose that France needs more than 190,000 yards of cotton she will have to offer say 10 yards silk for 18 yards cotton, and the amounts exchanged may be 110,000 yards silk for 198,000 yards cotton-yarn, which will again equalise reciprocal demand.

In the simple case supposed the equation of demand is not determinate ; "several different rates . . . may all equally fulfil the conditions. . . . It is conceivable that they might be equally satisfied by every numerical rate which could be supposed" (J. S. Mill). This theoretical indeterminateness may be removed by taking into account for each country "the capital which it has to spare from the production of domestic commodities for its own consumption" (Mill), or by remembering that as the demand on each side is that of a whole country, it will not be likely—as Cairnes points out (*Leading Principles*, 1st ed. p. 103) in the similar case of reciprocal demand between non-competing groups—to be easily altered.

Hindrances to exchange, such as cost of carriage, unnoticed in the preceding remarks, reduce its advantage and cause a divergence of values in the trading countries. In the absence of impediments, values must be the same in both, but cost of transport and all similar items will raise the value of each commodity in the importing country, so that, *e.g.*, silk will be dearer in England and cotton-yarn in France. The division of this charge will depend on the readjustment of demand which the change in values will probably produce, and, as there is no precise law for the variations of demand, any change in the amount of hindrances to exchange, will be likely to alter the terms already established, and therefore the proportion of gain derived ; " but no absolute rule can be laid down for the division of the cost any more than for the division of the advantage, and it does not follow that in whatever ratio the one is divided the other will be divided in the same " (Mill).

In practice countries will generally trade not in *two* but in many commodities. "Those articles in which the difference in comparative cost is greatest will first enter into international commerce ; " but as obstacles to traffic are reduced additional commodities will be exchanged—" a movement which tends to extend until no goods remain whose transfer would give an advantage to either of the parties " (Mangoldt). The extension of trade makes value more stable, and tends to bring about a fairer division of gain, *e.g.* the French demand for cotton-yarn may be feeble while that of England for silk is strong, but the addition of iron and coal to English exports will act on the total French demand and improve the position of England.

Commerce moreover is not limited to two nations. Most staples are produced in more than one country, and are traded in by many. The consequence is a further limitation on the possible fluctuations of value. To the small French demand for cotton a German one may be added, and the advantage of France in the exchange of silk may be reduced by the competition of Italy as a producer of that article. Commodities the subjects of foreign commerce have their values fixed in the market of the world, local deviations being the result of particular hindrances to trade. International values lie "in the region of the most complicated questions which political economy affords " (Mill), and can only be elucidated by use of the principle that "trade among any number of countries, and in any number of commodities, must take place on the same essential principles as trade between two countries and in two commodities " (*ib.*) (cp. Jevons, *Theory*, 2nd ed. p. 124).

International prices have to be carefully distinguished from international values. Prices tend to adjust themselves to values (see INTERNATIONAL TRADE) by the alterations in distribution of the precious metals. Price—the value of money—is a special case of the value problem. The precious metals have their international value fixed by the same conditions as those obtaining in the case of other commodities. "The countries whose exportable productions are most in demand abroad and contain greatest value in smallest bulk, which are nearest to the mines, and which have least demand for foreign productions, are those in which money will be of lowest value " (Mill), this lower value

being the result of increased quantity. The theory of international value due in its main features to J. S. Mill has been severely criticised by Cournot and in England by Prof. Sidgwick, who regards "the division of the double cost of carriage which trade involves between the two sets of commodities" as "the question which a special theory of international values has to answer." On the continent it has been neglected by most text-book writers. According to M. Block, "*Les économistes du continent ont bien fait de laisser 'la théorie de la valeur internationale' de l'autre côté de la Manche*" (*Science Économique*, ii. p. 172). Cherbuliez, Mangoldt, and Beaujon are, however, exceptions. The prevailing view in England and the United States may perhaps be summed up in Jevons's judgment of Mill's theory as being " always ingenious and . . . nearly always true " (*Theory*, 154).

[See references under INTERNATIONAL TRADE. Special for international value are J. S. Mill, bk. iii. ch. 18-19.—Cairnes, *Leading Principles*, pt. iii. ch. 3.—Sidgwick, bk. ii. ch. 3.—F. Y. Edgeworth, "The Theory of International Values," in *Economic Journal*, vol. iv.—Mangoldt, *Grundriss, Anmerkung*, ii.—Beaujon, *Hoofstukk*, 3.—Bastable, ch. 3. See also Torrens, *The Budget* (1842), and criticism in *Edinburgh Review*, July 1843 (by Senior).]   C. F. B.

INTERNATIONAL WORKING MEN'S ASSOCIATION, THE. This association, which came to be generally known by the abbreviated title of "The International," was founded in 1864. Its origin was very different from its ultimate development. It was suggested by some representatives of English working men in an address presented to some French workmen who had come over on the instance of the Third Napoleon to visit the London exhibition of 1862. It was suggested as a means of interchange of thought and opinion on the solution of the labour problem, among other economic questions affecting the welfare and condition of society. It was suggested as a means of creating an union of interest and feeling between the working men of different countries. It had apparently in its origin no definitely socialistic aims, it even held that the socialist schemes, which had been professedly put forward as solutions of the labour problem, were idle chimeras and magnificent dreams. But, as soon as the suggestion took practical shape, the committee which was formed requested Karl MARX (*q.v.*), the author of *Das Kapital*, to draw up the programme and to prepare the statutes of the association. He impressed upon it from the outset the stamp of his own socialistic views ; and, although throughout its history he never held any higher office than that of corresponding secretary for Germany, he seems to have exercised a predominant influence over its deliberations and acts. The statutes, which were adopted at the congress held at Geneva in 1866, declared, in the characteristic language of modern scientific SOCIALISM (*q.v.*) that the "economic subjection of the labourer to the possessor of the means of production is the first cause of his political, moral, and material servitude, and that the emancipation of labour is consequently the great aim to which every political movement ought to be subordinated." This phrase of the "emancipation of labour" was conveniently ambiguous, and was interpreted differently by the working-men members of different countries. The English trade-unionists saw in it far less than the Russian nihilist BAKOUNIN (*q.v.*), who merged his more violent "Alliance of Socialist Democracy" in the larger organisation of the International; but for some years a working basis of agreement was found by cherishing a distant ideal of a revolutionary nature at the same time as immediate practical ends of so comparatively moderate a character as free education, gratuitous justice, and a normal working day of eight hours, were sought to be accomplished. The association held periodical congresses in various towns, and gained a footing in different countries. In Belgium it had as many as eight federations of associations, and several journals; in Holland it possessed a branch in almost every town in 1869, and in Spain its organisation extended throughout the length and breadth of the country and comprised a membership of more than 300,000. It did not spread in Norway or Sweden, nor yet in Switzerland, although its congresses were not unfrequently held in the last-mentioned country. It exercised, M. de Laveleye observes, little real influence in Germany or in England, but in the latter country it obtained the nominal adhesion of 30,000 trades-unionists represented at the Trades Union Congress of 1867. From the first there were discordant elements in the association, and after the revolution of the COMMUNE OF PARIS, which followed the Franco-German war, and met with the approval of the leaders of the International, the English members dropped off. At the first congress, which was subsequently held, at the Hague in 1872, the association broke up into two rival factions on the questions of the nature of the political constitution of the society of the future, and of the means by which that new society was to be substituted for the present *régime.* The centralist democratic socialists, led by Marx, were in favour of centralised authority, the anarchic socialists, led by Bakounin (see NIHILISM), disliked central government and favoured the old communal system. The former advocated legal and peaceful organisation, and a gradual though inevitable evolution from the old order to the new; the latter urged revolution. Bakounin was expelled from the association; and for a time two

separate organisations maintained a lingering existence and then died away. The connection of the English trades unions with the International had never been very close, although the first president was Odger, a noted unionist leader, and the first secretary, Cremer, another unionist leader of repute. There can indeed be little doubt that generally the International possessed far less power in reality than that with which it was commonly credited. But it certainly inspired wide-spread alarm. It was joined for a short time by the Italian Mazzini. It was suspected of being the real author of the Paris Commune. It has been the subject of a parallel between itself as the Red and the Roman Catholic church as the Black International. Its first manifesto concluded with the words "Proletarians of all countries, unite," and from its outset it aroused the repressive hostility of the governments of France, Italy, Austria, and Spain.

[J. Rae's *Contemporary Socialism*, chs. ii. and iv.—De Laveleye's *Le Socialisme Contemporain*, ch. x.—Hyndman's *Historical Basis of Socialism in England*, ch. xii.—Labour Comm., *Foreign Reports* on Germany, should be consulted. See also *Le Devenir Social*, June 1895. *En mémoire du manifeste du parti Communiste*, by A. Labriola.]   L. L. P.

INTERPLEADER. Where a person is under liability for any debt or goods in respect of which he expects to be sued by two or more parties making adverse claims thereto, he may bring the adverse claimants before the court, or compel one of them to relinquish his claim by a mode of procedure called "interpleader." The same mode of procedure is available for a sheriff or sheriff's officer taking goods in execution which are claimed by a third party.

E. S.

INTERRUPTION OF PRESCRIPTION. See PRESCRIPTION.

INTERSTATE COMMERCE LAW (U.S.A.). The constitution of the United States, while leaving to the authorities of the several states the right and duty of controlling the operations of common carriers, reserves to congress the right to regulate commerce between the states. When the constitution was framed, this provision was chiefly intended to prevent the individual states from erecting custom-houses on their borders, or in any wise taxing the business which should originate in other parts of the union. But as time went on it began to have an important bearing on railway regulation. For the through or "interstate" traffic tended to increase in volume faster than the local or state traffic, until, in 1886, it furnished from three-quarters to nine-tenths of the business and the revenue of many leading lines. Under these circumstances, local legislation which could only affect a small part of the traffic of such lines was obviously of little use ; more especially since fairness in railroad rates is a relative matter, and the justice of a local charge depends not alone on conditions affecting that shipment by itself, but also on the scale of charges adopted for through traffic on the same line.

The United States courts did all that they could to meet this difficulty ; but there was a clamour for legislation which should settle the principles to be applied more definitely and speedily than the courts were likely to do if left to themselves. The first attempts to secure such legislation were made in 1873 ; but it was not until 1878 that a systematic and continuous agitation of the subject was begun, which finally led to the passage of the Interstate Commerce Act nine years later. In 1878, Mr. Reagan of Texas, formerly postmaster-general of the confederate states, introduced a bill providing for the adoption of equal mileage rates on all the railroads of the country. Such a proposal was obviously impracticable, and was successfully resisted by the railroads. In subsequent years Mr. Reagan introduced a succession of bills, each a little more moderate than its predecessor, but all endeavouring to subject the railroads to somewhat arbitrary regulations which would have interfered with the successful conduct of their business.

The division on these Reagan bills was based not on party, but on locality. They found their chief support in the south and west, where there are many shippers and few shareholders ; while they were opposed in the central and eastern states, where the railroad capital of the country is chiefly owned. These bills also commanded much stronger support in the House of Representatives than in the Senate, because the latter body is largely composed of men who are themselves property-owners on a considerable scale, and understand the fatuity of laws aimed to restrict investors' profits in any radical fashion.

Down to 1885 the moderate party was strong enough to defeat all legislation. But it had become obvious by this time that the public demanded the enactment of a law of some sort, and that it was futile to resist such a demand much longer. Accordingly the United States Senate appointed a special committee under the chairmanship of Mr. Cullom of Illinois to investigate the situation and draft a bill.

Their report was made in 1886 ; their bill provided that all traffic of any given kind was to be charged the same rates under substantially similar circumstances and conditions ; that is, that personal preferences of every kind were to be declared illegal. It further prohibited the worse sort of local preferences by providing that through traffic should not be given a lower aggregate rate than the traffic to and from intermediate points. It made provision for certain exceptions to this rule by appointing a commission which should have discretionary power to suspend its operation in certain specific cases.

Only on the first of these points was the report of the Senate committee satisfactory to the advocates of the Reagan bill. In the matter of local preferences, they wished to secure something much more nearly approaching equal mileage rates. The establishment of a commission with power to make exceptions seemed to them likely to make the whole law nugatory, and they were therefore opposed to its creation. On the other hand they were extremely anxious to prohibit divisions of traffic or earnings, known in America as Pools. They feared that if competition could be restricted by these agencies, the railroads would comply with the law by raising their through rates instead of lowering their local rates.

The views of Mr. Cullom prevailed in the Senate, those of Mr. Reagan in the House. Early in 1887 a compromise was finally adopted, prohibiting pools, creating an interstate commerce commission, and wording the section with regard to local discriminations or preferences so ambiguously as to leave grave doubts as to what it actually meant. This compromise bill became law February 4, 1887, and constitutes what is known as the Interstate Commerce Act.

The ambiguity of the section concerning local discrimination placed upon the interstate commerce commission the somewhat unforeseen duty of making a provisional interpretation of its doubtful points. This interpretation, popularly known as the Louisville and Nashville decision, was made in so able a manner as to command universal respect, and was reported and quoted exactly as if it were a judicial opinion. This led to a demand for similar opinions on the part of the commission on other points connected with the operation of the law. The commission was composed entirely of lawyers, and this work of interpretation was perhaps more congenial to them than some of the other duties contemplated by the Act. This became their important work, which they did in person, while other functions were relegated to subordinates. At first their success was phenomenal. Their decisions were marked by moderation and good sense, and bade fair to create, with unexampled ease, a large body of transportation law. But the commission, as was perhaps natural, undertook a little more than it was likely to be able to carry out under the most favourable circumstances ; while the retirement of Mr. Walker and the illness of Judge Cooley deprived it of the services of its two most active members. It was drawn into an attitude of hostility to the courts in certain questions of jurisdiction ; and hence the influence of the commission is not so great as it seemed likely to be a few years ago.

With regard to the benefit derived from the operation of the law, there is considerable difference of opinion. It is generally thought that there are much fewer discriminations or preferences than there were when the act was passed, and that those which continue to exist are of a less glaring character. There is more publicity both of rates and of accounts than before the passage of the act. On the other hand the clause prohibiting pools has proved decidedly harmful. It has combined with several other causes to produce a good deal of depression in American railroad profits ; it has more than once put responsible railroad men at the mercy of irresponsible ones ; and it has prevented the development of far-sighted schemes of railroad policy which would do as much good to the shippers as to the companies. At present the prohibition is pretty generally evaded ; but efforts to secure its repeal have thus far been unsuccessful (see also RAILWAYS).

A. T. H.

INTESTACY (ENGLAND). In the case of a person dying without having left any directions as to the disposal of his property answering the requirements of a valid will, or having left a will the directions of which do not deal with the whole of his property, there is said to be an "intestacy." In most countries the devolution of property as to which a person dies intestate does not depend on the nature of the property ; but in England a distinction is drawn between real and personal property—real property going generally to one person, called the "heir-at-law," and personal property being generally divided among several persons, collectively called "the next-of-kin," subject in both cases to any rights a surviving husband or wife may be entitled to. The rules for ascertaining the heir-at-law and the next-of-kin in a given case are too complicated to be stated here. It is sufficient to mention that if an intestate dies leaving several sons and daughters, his real estate goes to his eldest son and his personal estate is divided among all the children, the issue standing in a deceased parent's or ancestor's place. If he leaves daughters only they all take the real estate as COPARCENERS (q.v.). The preference of the eldest son and his issue in the case of real estate, when spoken of in political pamphlets, is generally described as the "rule of" PRIMOGENITURE. The importance of the rule and its injustice have often been exaggerated ; but although the attacks against the rule have to a certain extent subsided, there is no doubt that the time when the devolution of real property will be made equal to the devolution of personalty cannot be far distant. It should be pointed out that the general rules as to the descent of real property are in some places displaced by local custom (see BOROUGH ENGLISH ; GAVELKIND) ; as to personalty, all such special customs have been abolished by the "Act for the Uniform Administration of the estates of Intestates" passed in 1857. The rights of the surviving husband or wife of an intestate are not of much practical importance as regards realty (see HUSBAND, AS TO WIFE'S PROPERTY ; DOWER) ; the personal estate of an intestate wife goes to the husband, whether there be children or not ; on the other hand the widow of an intestate receives one third of his personal estate, if there is any issue, and one half if no issue survives. It is further provided by the Intestates' Estates Act 1890 that the real and personal estate of any man dying intestate, and leaving a widow but no issue, shall, if of a net value not exceeding £500, belong to the widow absolutely and exclusively, and also that in case the net value exceeds £500, the widow shall have a charge upon the whole estate for £500.

Real property situated in England descends, according to English law, without any regard to the domicile of the owner (see DOMICILE) ; the devolution of personal property on the other hand is regulated by the law of the intestate's domicile without any regard to the local situation of the property (see also ADMINISTRATION, LETTERS OF ; ADMINISTRATOR).

E. S.

INTIERI, BARTOLOMEO (1677-1757), was a Florentine ecclesiastic. He founded the chair of political economy at Naples in 1754—the first in Europe—under the title of a professorship of commerce and mechanics. He attached three conditions—(1) that the teaching should be entirely in Italian—this was contrary to the custom of the time, all scientific teaching being then in Latin ; and was intended to obtain a wider circle of students. (2) That GENOVESI (q.v.) should be the first professor. (3) That after his death no ecclesiastic should be appointed to the chair.

Intieri is supposed to have assisted in suggesting to GALIANI (q.v.) the principles on which his work was founded (Ingram, History of Pol. Ec., p. 72). His influence over economics was therefore considerable, though he left no original work of his own.

A. B.

INTRINSIC VALUE is attributed to an article when it (1) is not "spontaneously supplied by nature," but "requires labour to obtain it" ; and (2) is "useful for other purposes than being employed as money" (Fawcett, Manual, bk. iii. ch. v.). Or one only of these attributes may form the definition ; the term thus coinciding with "real value," which sometimes means the quantity of labour required for the production of an article (Ricardo, Principles, ch. xx. and passim), and sometimes "the amount of necessaries, comforts, and luxuries of life" that it will purchase (Marshall, Principles, p. 666).

The term, in one of these senses, is often employed in monetary theory. For instance,

Ricardo, "Gold and silver, like other commodities, have an intrinsic value" (*High Price of Bullion*, par. '1) ; and Fawcett, "the substance chosen as money should possess an intrinsic value."

There is no objection to this terminology, if it does not suggest the misconception that all value is intrinsic, that inconvertible paper-money cannot possibly act as a medium of exchange and common *denominator*. The erroneousness of this view is well shown by Professor Walker (*Money*, ch. i. and xiii.). To avoid the suggestion of error, it might be better to speak with Senior of "intrinsic causes of value" (*Pol. Econ.*, p. 16); and to follow those who assert that "nothing can have an intrinsic value" (BARBON); "it is a contradiction in terms" (Macleod, *Credit*, ch. ii. §§ 17-18).

But when we use the term in this sense—or want of sense—we incur the danger which often attends correction of popular phraseology ; namely, that some important property may be lost sight of. If, with Jevons, we regard value as a mere ratio of exchange (*Theory*, ch. iv.), let us take care, with Jevons, to remember that "there is a close connection" between value in this sense, and "esteem" or "final degree of utility" (*loc. cit.*). The relation between value in exchange and the other attribute of "intrinsic value," viz. cost of production, is not less likely to be lost sight of. The author of *A Critical Dissertation on Value*, S. BAILEY, may be instanced as one who incurred these dangers when he maintained that value is nothing positive or intrinsic, but merely a relation in which two commodities stand to each other. Locke uses the phrase in a sense which may be gathered from the subjoined passages :—"The raising of one species of your coin beyond its intrinsic value is done by coining any one species with less silver in it than is required by that value it bears in your money." "Silver which makes the intrinsic value of money." (See Locke's *Considerations of the Lowering of Interest*.)   F. Y. E.

INVECTA ET ILLATA. The right of hypothec, which came to be of general application in Roman law, was first established by the prætor in case of a tenant-farmer agreeing with his landlord that the farming stock brought into his holding (*invecta et illata*) should become security for his rent. According to Roman law, movable property of a tenant put into a town-house warehouse, and (*invecta et illata*) under a contract of letting and hiring, was hypothecated to the landlord by operation of law without any agreement to that effect.   E. A. W.

INVENTORY DUTIES. See DEATH DUTIES.

INVESTMENT. The investment of money by an individual means either some form of lending the money at interest, or its exchange for property from which a profit, rent, or income of any kind is expected, whether this property is already in existence or is being produced by those to whom the money is paid. The money invested may be either on the one hand the proceeds of the repayment of a loan, or of a sale of property, or on the other hand an amount saved from income. In the first case the investment, or more properly the reinvestment of the money, is simply the completion of an exchange of one sort of property for another : when, for example, a man sells a house and buys with the proceeds a share of a ship, he has merely exchanged the house for the share of the ship. The amount of money which can be invested or reinvested in this way is only limited by the extent to which exchanges of property take place ; the more property is bought and sold the more money there will be to invest or reinvest. But the amount of money which can be invested from savings is a strictly limited quantity. It obviously cannot exceed the amount saved, and it must also, unless useless hoards are accumulated, always come up to that amount. There is an impression that savings may lie in a country "idle" or uninvested, but in a country like England this is never the case. If it be inquired where the accumulation of idle savings or uninvested money is to be found, the invariable answer is "In the banks." But if the balance-sheets of the banks be examined it will be seen that, after accounting for the amounts in transit between one bank and another, almost the whole of the "money" in their possession has already either been lent at interest, or spent in the purchase of securities. The term "money" in this case is merely applied to a figure representing the number of pounds the banks' various investments are taken to be worth. Even the balance which a bank holds at the Bank of England, and which to the bank which keeps it there is really "idle money," may be and frequently is lent out again by the Bank of England itself. The comparatively small quantity of money remaining is as necessary and useful to the banks as the small quantity which an individual carries in his pocket is to him, and though apparently at rest has been well described as the most "hard-worked" money in the country.

The savings and the new investments of the world are in short identical. They are the additions made to the accumulated wealth of the world, the new railways, roads, houses, mills, canals, and such like things, and the improvements effected in the old ones. When it is said that £200,000,000 a year is saved by a community what is meant is that £200,000,000 worth of its annual produce is not consumed but is added to its accumulated wealth or capital.

Though the amount the community adds to its capital depends on the amount saved by individuals, the individuals who save do not in all cases settle in what form the additions to the capital shall appear. When a man lends his savings without stipulating how they shall be employed, or lets them "lie" at a bank, he practically delegates the decision of this question to the borrower, or the banker. Similarly, when he buys already-existing property, he virtually delegates the decision to some one who, having sold existing property, invests the proceeds in new property. What the new capital of a community shall consist of thus comes to be settled to a great extent by a special class of financiers, promoters, and speculators.

E. C.

The investment of capital by an individual in an undertaking already existing is only a transfer of the command of currency from one person to another. It makes no diminution in the floating cash in the banks, but places the command of a portion of it in one hand instead of in another. Where banking is fully developed, it does not even momentarily diminish available currency. The transfer as a rule is carried out by cheque, and the only effect upon currency is in the extent to which bankers may think it desirable to increase their cash holdings in times of more active demand. In the case of the investment of floating capital in a new undertaking, as in the construction of works not immediately productive, there is a diminution of the immediate purchasing power of the community. It diminishes by so much the amount of consumable or exchangeable goods that can be produced. If the country be previously producing enough only for its own support, it must now import to supply some part of its requirements. If it had already imported, it must now import more. The immediate effect upon the money market is, that the exchanges become unfavourable, and bullion must be exported.

If investments be made in a foreign undertaking, whether a new one or one already in existence and under foreign ownership, the effect is the same. It diminishes the immediate power of taking goods from abroad, substituting therefor an increased power in the future. But the capital is, nevertheless, really locked up, and great danger may arise from this fact being disguised by credit issues. The financial crisis of 1846-47, and some others of equal importance, have been ascribed to the too rapid conversion of floating capital into fixed capital. It would give, perhaps, a more exact view of the condition of these times to describe them as resulting from the undue expansion of credit founded upon the fixed capital invested. R. W. B.

INVOICE. A statement giving particulars of goods forwarded by a trader to a customer, and of their cost, and of the charges concerning the same. Some foreign countries require invoices to be legalised by their consuls, or verified by declarations as to their accuracy.

The omission of the prescribed formalities may cause the custom-house authorities at the port of destination to forbid the importation.

E. S.

INVREA, FABIO, a Piedmontese marquis. The book he wrote, though little known, deserves notice for the able development of the theory of wealth which it contains.

Discorsi sulla pubblica ricchezza, ossia sopra di quanto la costituisce, sulla di lei origine, aumento e ripartizione (Genova), 1846.—Referred to in the *Bibliografia dei Trattati e compendii d'Econ. politica scritti da italiani dal 1765 al 1891*, by Prof. Cossa. A. B.

I.O.U. An acknowledgment of indebtedness worded as follows: To A.B.—I.O.U. [I owe you] £10—signed C.D. If such a document contains a promise to pay, it should be stamped as a promissory note. E. S.

IRISH CURRENCY. This term at the beginning of the present century denoted a money of account different from that in use in England. It disappears with the act of 1825, which finally assimilated the currency of Ireland to that of Great Britain.

The English denominations of money came early into use in Ireland. The value and the rating of coins were both tampered with on occasion, alike by the sovereign, and, apparently, by the Irish parliament; and throughout the variations in the intrinsic value of the English coinage, the Irish coins appear to have remained always less valuable. The records of receipts of revenue between Henry VIII. and James I. give amounts both in English and Irish currency, the latter being accounted less valuable by one-third, so that the amounts of English are three-fourths of the amounts in Irish currency. In fact there existed exactly the state of things described in the article on COLONIES (especially sections on Currency).

By a proclamation of James II. when a fugitive in Ireland (25th March 1689), the guinea is rated at £1 : 4s. Irish, and the shilling at 13d. Irish. This seems to be the first establishment of the ratio afterwards more particularly associated with the term "Irish currency"; and it is therefore incorrect to date that ratio from W. WOOD's halfpence (1725), as Mr. Culley does in his evidence cited at foot. This ratio, which subsisted through the 18th century, gave a difference of $8\frac{1}{3}$ per cent on amounts of English converted into Irish money. All transactions between the two kingdoms were adjusted on this basis, and this inconvenience tended to enhance the premium on bills of exchange which between 1812 and 1815 had risen to 10 per cent; so that £118 : 6 : 8 Irish money was required to pay a debt of £100 in England. After the union this became more and more intolerable; the first important measure in alleviation was that of 1817 which authorised the transfer of government and certain other funds between the kingdoms at the so-called *par* of 8⅓ per cent. The anomaly was abolished by the act of 1825 (6 Geo. IV. c. 79), which assimilated the currency in all parts of the United Kingdom, and enacted that contracts entered into previous to the date of the act should be satisfied by a payment in English currency of ¹³⁄₁₃ of the amount expressed to be owing in Irish currency. The copper tokens of Ireland were called in under the same act.

[*House of Commons Papers*, 1868-69, vol. xxxv. pt. 2, p. 379. Evidence of Mr. Culley before the Commission on International Coinage, 1867-68.—Kelly's *Cambist*, 1831, pp. 401-403.]   C. A. H.

IRISH LAND LAWS. See LAND LEGIS-LATION, IRISH.

IRON AND STEEL AS MONEY. Little doubt exists as to the extensive use of iron as money in very ancient times (probably in the period from 1000 to 600 B.C.), though, on account of the rapidity with which that metal rusts, no specimens now exist, and their exact form is therefore uncertain. Probably, however, they resembled in shape the small ingots which are found in use at the present day in Central Africa.

Experiments were made at the Royal Mint, London, in the year 1884, with a view to dis-cover what would be the rate of wear of steel coins. The average wear after 26 hours' friction was ·0032 grammes of soft steel and ·0029 grammes of hard steel coins. When soft and hard steel coins were subjected to friction to-gether, the soft coins lost, after 52 hours' friction, ·0077 grammes, and the hard coins only ·0042 grammes. The amount of metal lost, even in the case of the hardened steel, approximates closely to the loss sustained by standard gold and silver coins, when subjected to the same process.   F. E. A.

IRREGULARITY OF EMPLOYMENT is more a social than an economic question, and it is one which the earlier economists hardly noticed. It has of late years been thoroughly recognised as an evil requiring careful investiga-tion. The board of trade is now carrying out inquiries which it is hoped will throw consider-able light on this subject. The Americans have also been paying much attention to it, but without particular success. At present, there-fore, no series of well-observed facts exists to support generalisations on the subject.

Inconstancy of employment, as Professor Marshall terms it, is one of the chief conditions which presents itself for consideration in con-nection with the mass of unemployed in all countries. It may in this connection be viewed either as a result or a cause. Some men are so inefficient, so lazy, or disinclined for regular work, that they prevent themselves from being regularly employed. And in dealing with questions of irregularity of employment, it is of primary necessity to decide whether the case in point is such a result or no. It is only when it is a cause of distress arising outside the worker himself that its consideration falls within the proper sphere of economics. Here it is closely connected with the problem of the "unemployed."

The causes of irregularity in employment are :

(1) Essential conditions of the occupation—the work of the painter and mason are liable to be interrupted in certain states of the weather—the effect of a season on the demand for certain goods. Thus furriers are much harder at work in the autumn ; and it is in evidence before the labour commission (C. 6708, III. 1892, p. 44) that in the confectionery trade the girls are often out of work from December, when the Christmas demand is over, up till February.

(2) Accidental circumstances which indirectly produce irregularity :

(*a*) The use of machinery. Of itself the use of machinery might be quite regular in effect, but constant labour - saving improvements tend to displace labour. The tendency of employers to produce in excess of the current demand is not strictly attributable to machinery, as suggested in evidence before the Labour Commission (C. 7063, I. 1893).

(*b*) Fluctuation of trade, produced by causes perhaps too complicated to classify roughly, but arising from the competition : (*a*) of home manufacturers, (*β*) of foreign countries. Thus "foreign tariffs" were cited before the labour commission as a cause of irregularity in employ-ment : and the fall in prices was suggested as having that effect in the course of the enquiries of the Gold and Silver Commission, and that on Depression in Trade (1886).

The above heads probably include all the causes at work, but the analysis is not perfect. "Influx into towns," by which is meant over-competi-tion of hands for any given work, has been cited as another cause, but this really only describes one of the conditions arising in part out of irregular employment ; though doubtless the condition reacts so as to make matters worse.

DOCK LABOUR (*q.v.*) presents probably the worst instance of irregular employment, certainly the most prominent at the present time. It is in evidence before the labour commission that the average number of months for which the labourers were at work was seven ; the rest of the year they used to "hang about the gates and starve":—the evil is the irregularity of employment reducing the average wage to 10s. a week ; some only get 5s. ; some are out of work for months" (C. 6708, II. 1892, pp. 9 and 12). On the other hand one witness of great experience (Mr. Hill) contended that this state of things was the fault of the men. At the time of the late dock strike attention was directed to the importance of regulating the labour, and something has been done in this direction.

As above stated, the problem whether it is possible to counteract irregularity in employment has only recently come up for solution. Professor Marshall doubts if the evil which "rightly attracts public attention" is greater than it was in past ages.

The palliatives or remedies hitherto suggested are practically but three, which require consideration in detail.

(i) It is contended that the remuneration or wages of an irregular employment tend to be proportionately higher than those which are more regular. Professor Marshall lays this down, (*Econ. of Ind.*, 1881, vol. i. p. 537), and instances the medical man.

(ii) The eight hours day is relied on by several witnesses before the labour commission for making employment more regular. No one, however, has explained how this effect will be manifested. It cannot of itself affect the irregularity arising out of the use of machinery or fluctuations of trade; and as it will tend to increase the productiveness of the labour employed, it will not immediately stop over-competition by opening avenues for the unemployed. Yet if it is allowed to come naturally, and as the result of experience, it will combine with other causes to operate in the direction of greater regularity.

(iii) Organisation of all labour as far as possible into permanent services with some security of tenure for the individual seems the most hopeful solution. The most prosperous employés as a body at the present day are those of the great railway companies, and next to them those of some large firms where a reciprocal feeling exists between masters and men, resulting in permanence of engagement accompanied by provisions for sickness and old age. The elimination of daily competition is the first step to the better regulation of labour. At the same time there should be ample power to dismiss bad and incompetent men. This has always been the difficulty in the organised system, and is precisely the point where the trades-union system is apt to break down.

Finally, it has been suggested as an advantage in irregular forms of employment, that there are periods of leisure. But when these are prolonged, there is a danger of anxiety as to the future which more than compensates for enforced idleness. Leisure to be valuable should be accompanied by regular employment.

[Professor Foxwell, *Irregularity of Employment and Fluctuations of Prices.*—Marshall, *Economics of Industry*, vol. i. pp. 537-38, 736-37.—Reports of Labour Commission, *passim*, especially Tom Mann's evidence in C. 7063 (1893), vol. i., and Sidney Webb's in *id.* vol. ii. See Evidence of Select Committee on Unemployed, 1895 ; and G. H. Duckworth in *Econ. Journal*, March 1896.]

C. A. H.

IRRITANCY (Scots law). Forfeiture of lease or of tenancy in FEU through some neglect or contravention. This may arise by force of law, or under the terms of the contract. Irritancies arising by force of law—such as loss of a feu through non-payment of the feu-duty for two years—are purgeable at any time before judgment by payment or restitution or fulfilment of the condition. An irritancy arising from agreement can, in general, not be so purged.

[Rankine, *On Leases*, 461.] A. D.

ISELIN, ISAAK (1728-1782), a Swiss physiocrat. He belonged to an old business family of Bâle, and passed the greater part of his life in his native city, where, after vain attempts to obtain a professorship at the university, he was elected, in 1756, secretary to the council (secretary of state). In this position he displayed great literary capacity, occupying himself at first with philosophical and historical subjects, but labouring entirely during the last ten years of his life (1772-1782), under the banners of the physiocrats. To the older pre-physiocratic period belong his works : *Patriotische und Philosophische Träume eines Menschenfreundes* (Patriotic and Philosophic Dreams of a Philanthropist), 1755, and *Geschichte der Menschheit* (History of Mankind), 1762. Both compositions show little originality. The second named exhibits a rather arbitrary reading of history, somewhat in the sense of the later *Esquisse* of CONDORCET. The change to the doctrines of the physiocrats is first obvious in the *Versuch über die gesellige Ordnung* (Essay on Social Order), 1772, where it is said in the preface that an "able man" (was it Schlettwein ?) had some time before directed him to the study of the French economists. But the instruction seemed obscure to him, and "the fervour with which some defenders of these truths extolled the discoveries of their teachers seemed to me to be charlatanry rather than that honourable zeal for the truth which animates noble minds." Afterwards, by good fortune, the EPHÉMÉRIDES DU CITOYEN (*q.v.*) came into his hands, after reading which, QUESNAY became in his eyes "what NEWTON is in the eyes of a mathematician." The new standpoint comes to light, fully matured, in the work which appeared four years later :—*Träume eines Menschenfreundes.* (Dreams of a Philanthropist), 1776. This book is by no means a second edition of the work published in 1755, as is generally supposed, and as might have been conjectured from the kindred title, but quite a new work. He expresses himself thus on the subject, in the preface : "What I put into print twenty years ago under the title of *Patriotische und Philosophische Träume eines Menschenfreundes*—(Patriotic and Philosophic Dreams of a Philanthropist), and what I now publish entitled *Träume eines Menschenfreundes* (Dreams of a Philanthropist), although they agree in design, are nevertheless two quite different things. Those were merely sentiments of a young man, to give a new edition of which would be quite needless, and which may fairly be allowed to sink into oblivion." Iselin thus publicly retracted his old ideas in favour of the authors who had adopted Quesnay's teaching, as the Marquis of Mirabeau, Baudeau, Comte d'Albon, and others. Commencing from the same year, 1776, Iselin published a monthly journal in German, dedicated to the propaganda of the doctrines of the economists ; this bore the title, borrowed from the French organ of the school, *Ephemeriden der Menschheit* (Ephémérides of Mankind, or Library of Moral Philosophy and Politics). This soon gained a great reputation in German-speaking countries, and numbered among its contributors many of the most prominent economic authors of Germany. After the death of Iselin, which took place in 1782, it was carried on under the editorship of G. W. Becker, professor at the "Adeligen Gymnasium" in Dresden. For the rest, Iselin did not in all points agree with the "eminent Quesnay." He would have allowed the IMPÔT UNIQUE to be assessed progressively instead of proportionately ; and if indeed he occasionally says with Mirabeau that the best corn law is *none*, yet elsewhere again he defends the public granaries condemned by Quesnay. How unhistorically, besides, Iselin reasoned, regardless of his former historical studies, is shown in the passages in his *Träume* (Dreams) where he maintains that only "chance and caprice have produced the difference between one people and another people," and when he then concludes that "everywhere likewise the laws must be the same, what is just in China must necessarily also be so at San Marino." Human institutions have corrupted the natural order, and Iselin concludes his *Träume* (Dreams) with an ideal constitution, by means of which "instructive fiction" he tries to reconcile the republicanism of his Swiss fatherland with the enlightened despotism recommended by Quesnay. Finally, Iselin proves himself to be a true son of his generation, anticipating the complete salvation of mankind in the *education* of the people. This caused Basedow, the German apostle of education, to appear to him, with Quesnay, the person most worthy of emulation.

[A. v. Miaskowski, *Isaak Iselin*, Basle, 1875.—W. Roscher, *Geschichte der National-ökonomik in Deutschland*, 1874.] A. O.

ISNARD, ACHILLE NICOLAS, born in Paris, died in 1802 or 1803. He published, anonymously, in 1781, a *Traité des Richesses* (London and Lausanne, 2 vols., 8vo), and in 1801 his *Considérations théoriques sur les Caisses d'amortissement de la Dette Publique* (Paris, 1801). The former is directed against the theory of the *produit net* and of the single tax of Quesnay ; Isnard does not mention Adam Smith, although generally concurring with the latter's views on the origin of wealth, the effects of protection, and of the accumulation of gold and silver, etc. Isnard, who was an engineer, has frequently recourse to mathematical symbols, although he does not venture farther than equations of the first degree and simple problems in the rule of three. As having done this, he is mentioned by Jevons in his *Theory of Political Economy*, 2nd ed. 1879, appendix i. p. 301. E. Ca.

ISOLA, FRANCESCO (first half of 19th century), Italian economist, is mentioned by A. Graziani in his *Idee economiche degli scrittori Emiliani e Romagnoli sino al 1848*, etc., Modena 1893, pp. 156-7. He was appointed, by the papal government, a member of the committee for the reform of the commercial code, and found in the materials thus provided the basis of his treatise on political economy. Isola was a protectionist, for though nominally a supporter of free-trade, he admits many exceptions to this principle. He proposes to prohibit the import of such articles as would injure the sale of similar home products ; and also to limit the goods imported, fearing a general excess of production. He also discusses general values, considering that these originate in the demands of consumers, and in the scarcity of the goods themselves. He considers that with respect to money it is its intrinsic value as a commodity which, together with rapidity of circulation, forms the total purchasing power of the circulating medium, and determines the quantity of goods a market may require. He wrote also on interest and taxation, recommending that this should fall on superfluous wealth, and recommending indirect taxation.

Istituzioni di Commercio e di Economia civile, Roma, 1811. A. B.

ITALIAN SCHOOL OF ECONOMISTS.

Introduction, p. 460; The Early Phase, p. 461; Superficial and Optimistic Phase, p. 465; Scientific Phase, p. 466.

No one now, we imagine, would agree with Augustin Thierry, in characterising political economy as "cette science bourgeoise surgie dans les villes d'Italie," nor would conscientious scholarship ever entitle Italy to take the earliest place chronologically in economic research. Nevertheless it is beyond question that the early development of commercial wealth in mediæval Italy, the vigorous industries and economic inter-relations of her republican cities, attracted Italian thinkers early to the study of political economy. Italy can boast of a prominent position in the history of the science from the remotest times.

Italian economic thought, when traced from its first sources down to the present day, shows in its evolution, though chequered by many irregularities, three well-marked stages, corresponding to certain analogous conditions of the social evolution of the country. There is at first a roughly-developed, almost archaic phase of economic inquiry, the product of *patriarchal* economic relations ; to this succeeds the *super-*

ITALIAN SCHOOL OF ECONOMISTS 461

ficial and optimistic phase of the science, the product of the *small industry* system, when wealth was still scanty and distributed fairly equally ; finally there is the *scientific* phase, developing with the expansion of capital. The first phase extends from the middle of the 13th to the end of the 18th century ; the second carries us on to 1870 ; the third, initiated about 1870, is developing beneath our eyes, and may not yet have attained its maturity.

1. *The Early Phase.*—Economic thought in Italy seizes at the outset on the more obvious forms of social life, and advances gradually to investigation of the less obvious phenomena. Thus every phase of economic science is distinguished from its preceding phase by the deeper nature of its inquiries. The few early writers of Italy who touch on economic questions, put forward only external points, and, instead of analysing them closely, confine themselves to praise or criticism from a purely theological standpoint. The first advance in more thorough-going inquiry is found in the writings of political thinkers who are only concerned to trace the outlines of economic conditions in so far as these subserve their theories on legislation and administration. Hence when writers enter for the first time on the field of genuine economics, they turn to the most obvious and external economic subject, namely to currency ; and a rich and varied literature rises and flourishes round that subject. Greater depth is attained in analysis of inland and foreign trade and its regulation. Thence the way is opened up to the investigation of value ; the first treatises dealing with the more external manifestations, secondary forms, or market values, without bringing out the inner *nexus* connecting value with distribution of wealth. Not till the termination of the early phase do we come across some passing observations on the production and distribution of wealth ; but these embody no definite doctrine.

One of the first Italians in the 13th century to reflect on economic facts was St. Thomas AQUINAS, who set himself to oppose usury,— both by authority of the Bible, popes, and councils, and on the principle that time belongs to God and may not be sold. He also wrote learned treatises on monetary and fiscal politics, with acute remarks on the nature of wealth. The theological standpoint is no less dominant in the 14th century, when both Paolino Minorita (1315) and Egidio Colonna (1247-1316) wrote. The former treats of the management of landed estates, of the family, and the citizen ; the latter, of taxes. In the 15th century theological economics were developed in the writings of St. ANTONINUS, archbishop of Florence (1389-1455), and of St. Bernardino of Siena, who wrote in the first half of the 14th century. They reach the real gist of the theory of the circulation and distribution of

wealth from the basis of theological morality, though they too have their say against usury. In the 15th, 16th, and 17th centuries the disquisitions of theologians become more interesting and practical, stimulated by the new phenomena of deposit and loan banks of the Monti di Pietà (see MONTS DE PIÉTÉ) and the public revenue derived therefrom. The banks, defended by some theologians, were assailed chiefly by the Augustinians. The Monti di Pietà were condemned by the Augustinian Nicolò Barianno and the Dominican Tommaso DE VIO, but defended by the Franciscan Da Busto and others. Even the mechanism of bills of exchange became at that epoch the subject of subtle polemics among theological writers, some of whom, like Fathers Bernardo GIUSTINIANI and Ortensio Capellone, attacked profit derived from exchange operations, while others, like Fathers Antonio di San Salvatore and Basilio Alemanni, defended it.

Meanwhile a more discriminating and scientific tendency began gradually to replace older scholastic and religious views ; attention was paid to reasons of state and the practice of good government. Some timid manifestations of this tendency had not indeed been wanting at remoter epochs. In the 14th century Petrarch, in his book *De republica optime administranda*, expatiated on justice and moderation in imposts and on the abuses of farmers of taxes. Andrea de Isernia too, the Neapolitan legist, expressed some remarkable opinions as to the extent to which domain land might be alienated, and on farming of taxes. In the following century this scientific tendency makes a greater advance through the writings of Giovanni Gioviano PONTANO, Benedetto Cotrugli, and especially Diomede CARAFA, who in his work *De regis et boni principis officio* gives expression to ideas, new in part, on the utility of commerce and on the harmony between incomes and public expenditure, on the convenience of farming taxes, and on the assessment of taxes. The 16th century can boast of still greater progress in the same direction made by men like Matteo PALMIERI, Francesco GUICCIARDINI, and Nicolò Machiavelli. The first occupied himself largely with political economy, advocating proportional taxation. The second frequently introduces economics into his historical writings, and with great skill traces the contrast between *proportional* and *graduated taxation*. The third insists on the economic necessity of good government, recommends that to ensure prosperity to industry the state should guarantee the security of property and grant bounties to the most skilled and capable producers ; he also maintains, like MONTESQUIEU later, that countries are populous in virtue of the goodness and mildness of their respective governments ; and, finally, anticipates MALTHUS in affirming that there is a limit to the powers of production of the soil which checks the indefinite increase of the human race (see in particular bk. ii. of the *Storie Fiorentine*, chs. i. and ii. ; also the discourses on the first *Decade* of Livy, bk. ii. chs. iii. and v.). Even with greater force than Machiavelli, Giovanni BOTERO had held this argument in his work *Ragione di Stato, con tre libri delle cause della grandezza e magnificenza delle città* (three books dealing with the causes of the greatness and magnificence of cities) (1589), in which he insists, from the political standpoint, on the necessity of providing an equilibrium between the increase of population and that of subsistence, and urges the foundation of colonies as a remedy for an excess of the former. Botero moreover has some remarkable observations, inspired it is true in part by BODIN, on government monopolies and on the restraints placed on commercial liberty.

The evidence of the advance amongst Italian thinkers in the direction of abandoning the general and abstract considerations so dear to the ancient writers for a thorough investigation of their social mechanism, is seen in the very numerous contemporary treatises on currency. The deplorable state of the Italian monetary system, the continual debasement of coin by different rulers, and the great variety of coins current in the different states of the peninsula, to the great detriment of trade, could not fail to engage the attention of economists, and it is no marvel if, as GANILH said, Italy was always famous for the worst currency and the best writings on currency. First of these in order of time is the *Discorso sopra le monete e della vera proporzione fra l'oro e l'argento*, 1582, by Gaspare SCARUFFI, who was first to propose the international unification of monetary systems and universal, or at least European, bimetallism with a ratio (corresponding to that in force in his day) of 1 to 12. After Scaruffi, DAVANZATI (1588) published two short treatises, remarkable for elegance of style, one on coinage, in which he maintains that the expenses of mintage should be borne by the state, the other on exchanges. Unlike other writers, *e.g.* BROGGIA, who exaggerated the importance of money as facilitating hoarding, Davanzati does not lose sight of money as an instrument of circulation, comparing it to the circulation of the blood, which, if congested at any point produces atrophy and dropsy, whence he concludes that an equal distribution of money should be brought about in all parts of Italy. Geminiano MONTANARI (1633-1687) opposes the sweating of the coinage by rulers, and lays down useful precepts on the methods of regulating judiciously the circulation, with suggestive remarks on money. Still more distinguished and less remote from the actual focus of the science are the works of GALIANI on currency (1750),—free from most of the prejudices of mercantilism,—of PAGNINI, *Sul giusto prezzo delle cose* (On the fair price of Commodities) 1751, which contains profound reflections on the different characteristics of the circulating medium in ancient and modern economy, and the excellent *Osservazioni sopra il prezzo legale delle monete* (Observations on the legal price of Money)

by Pompeo NERI the Florentine (1751). But all these writers who investigate currency from the standpoint of the mint and the state rather than from that of the economist, are excelled by Antonio SERRA of Cosenza, who in his *Breve trattato delle cause che possono fare abbondare li regni d'oro e d'argento* (Short treatise on the causes which can lead to abundance of Gold and Silver) (1613), sets forth lucidly a theory of money in relation to international trade, admirably elucidating the mechanism of exchange and showing that a favourable exchange, believed by his contemporaries to be effected by sovereign decree, is the natural result of excess of exports over imports, and that therefore the only way for a nation to secure and maintain it is by promoting industry and encouraging enterprise, and not, as MUN said later, by imposing custom-duties on manufactured imports ; especially, maintains Serra, by developing manufactures, inasmuch as these have an indefinite possibility of increase, while agricultural commodities follow the law of DIMINISHING RETURNS. A remarkable forecast this of the famous law expounded later in England by WEST, RICARDO, MALTHUS, and J. S. MILL. Not less praiseworthy is the vehemence with which Serra opposes the debasing and sweating of the coinage,—the very mode, on the other hand, occurring to M. Antonio DE SANCTIS as the best for remedying the fall in exchange and the crises in the kingdom of Naples. To the list of writers on currency we may add the names of Domenico and Luigi DIODATI, of TURBOLO, and of Romeo BOCCHI (1621), who treated with ability of payments and compensations. There are other writings called forth by the establishment of banks at Venice and Genoa, but unimportant as regards theory.

The analysis of currency naturally led Italian economists on to study the kindred, perhaps deeper, subject of international trade. They discussed various systems referring to the economic conditions of the day. The difficulty of importing foreign corn through defective transport, together with the increase of population which began to press on demand, induced economists, *e.g.* SEGNI (1602), and TAPIA (1638), to favour the system of *annona* (stores), called the *Sistema Annonario*, or system of providing food, and of corn stores (GRENIERS D'ABONDANCE), intended to ensure the country abundance of food by stopping exports. These arrangements, which were urged on by the complaints of agriculture, stifled the improvements in transport, which would have rendered the importation of grain possible ; meanwhile the increase in population made this necessary. The discussion thus aroused gave rise early to controversy, and led to the institution of the MERCANTILE SYSTEM, which, while allowing the free importation of raw produce, lays prohibitive duties on the import of manufactures, seeking to develop national manufactures while sanctioning the introduction of cheap foreign corn. Mercantilism in its primitive form was defended by BELLONI (1750), an author commended by Sir James STEUART—

Belloni recommended that export of money should be prohibited. This doctrine was fully expounded by Antonio GENOVESI (1765), unquestionably the most illustrious of Italian mercantilists, who popularised the system among southern writers, whilst the negative side of mercantilism, free trade in corn, found a brilliant apostle in the Abbé Galiani (1770).

Mercantilism was bound to meet immediate opposition ; the serious injuries which it inflicts on landowners—ever uneasy and influential—and the fiscal burdens which it inflicts on trade, could not fail to favour the growth of an opposite view, termed by Cossa *Agrarian protectionism*. This, inspired by the landed interest, desired to lay heavy duties on import of grain, and insisted on free export of manufactured goods. Its most noteworthy representatives are PASCOLI (1733) and BANDINI (1775). Economists everywhere in Italy have remained loyal to the doctrine of restriction of trade, more in the form of mercantilism than of agrarian protection, and this even when the theory of free trade had matured in France and England. Even the influence of theories of the physiocrats, so evident in BECCARIA and VERRI, did not remove this predilection. The solitary luminous exception in this as in other respects is afforded by ORTES, who, proceeding on different principles from those of the physiocrats, and, as we shall see, positively original, concludes in favour of absolute freedom of foreign trade.

Nevertheless many Italian economists of this first period were in favour of free inland trade, either combating the abuses of trading corporations—GENOVESI, VERRI (1771), and BECCARIA (1769) ; or calling for their total suppression—VASCO (1794), FABBRONI (1778), and GIANNI.

Much less valuable is Italian economic opinion on finance. There is throughout a predilection for taxes on land, due much less to the influence of the physiocrats than to the distinctly agricultural character of Italy in past centuries, and the almost entire absence of manufactures. To the taxes on land which Botero, Bandini, and FILANGIERI (1780) advocated as the only source of revenue, Genovesi proposed to add the poll-tax ; Verri, duties on exports of raw produce, and imports of manufactured goods ; Ammirato (1594) excise - duties ; BROGGIA (1743), beside taxes on land and manufactured goods, advises a tax of the tenth of all capital producing interest, with moderate customs and an excise on provisions. But none of these writers has the remotest idea of the possibility of a tax on profits, which holds so large a place in the system of RICARDO,—a remarkable fact, as showing how slightly capital, and the returns from it, had as yet been developed. Filangieri's proposal for extraordinary revenue deserves to be commemorated. He recommended the

institution of a fund for the use of the more deserving and enterprising citizens, who were to be bound to repay the advances which had been made them when called on to do so by the state. There are also interesting discussions by writers on finance on the exemption from taxation of the nobility and clergy, which the most eminent —such as Genovesi, Bandini, Fra Paolo Sarpi— vigorously condemned.

These empirical studies, which discussed only practical questions, were soon followed, partly owing to the foundation of chairs of political economy at Naples (1754), Palermo, Milan, and Modena, by deeper researches extending into theory, which began, though imperfectly, to take the form of a pure science. In this connection the discussions on the theory of value are important : these were principally connected by our best economists with analyses of the theory of "money," and are distinguished by acumen and insight. In the Italian view of the theory of value, two absolutely distinct phases appear ; in the former, represented by Davanzati, Montanari, Pagnini, Genovesi, and Paoletti (1772), the element of " cost " is absolutely excluded, and "value" is represented as governed wholly by "utility " ; in the latter, expounded by Galiani, Beccaria, Fabbroni, value on the contrary is based on "cost of production." [1] The cause of this development of theory was a corresponding advance in the economic mechanism of society in Italy. In the first period the non-existence of free competition between producers, or else the restrictions which limited it, rendered it impossible to determine "value" by the factor of "cost," and inevitable that it should be determined by the factor of "utility." In the second period, when competition between producers was unchecked, "value" naturally tended to become commensurate with "cost of production." Nevertheless, even at a more advanced stage of their inquiries, Italian economists of that epoch always confine themselves to the more superficial and unimportant aspects of the question of value, dwelling especially on market value, and are not able to analyse the elements of the cost of production, oscillating (like VANDERLINT and STEUART) in perpetual ambiguity between labour and wages. This is not wonderful considering how childish were the ideas of the economists, even of the highest repute, respecting production and distribution of wealth, which nevertheless are the data essential for resolving cost of production into its constituent elements. Only the very best Italian economists of the 18th century possessed any notion of the theory

[1] The position of Ortes is eclectic. Originally he deduces value from demand and supply, but afterwards he measures it by the quantity and quality of the labour employed in production and transport, and thereby explains the greater value of the commodities in the metropolis and the greater quantity of money which circulates there.

of capital, while their views on production were meagre and vague. The observations of Beccaria on division of labour are always quoted. "Everybody proves by experience," he says, "that the constant application of hands and wits to the same kind of work and product renders the same easier, better, and more fruitful than would be the result did every one make by himself merely what is necessary to himself ; whence it comes that some pasture cattle, some card wool, others spin it, some grow corn, others make bread, raiment, tools for the agriculturists and labourers, causing growth and concatenation of arts and a division of them so as to serve common and private utility among all classes and conditions." (*Elem. di Ec. Pubblica*, pt. i. ch. i.).

Here we get, it is true, the social division of labour, but nothing about its technical division, or specialisation within the same industry, an exact idea of which Adam Smith was to set forth in so masterly a manner seven years later. Yet these observations by Beccaria, and those of Verri, that in production man does not create, but confines his operations to collecting and separating material already existing, with some considerations by the same author on the influence of climate on efficiency of labour, are all that is worth gleaning from the works of the earlier Italian economists on the subject of production.

Nor do their writings on the distribution of wealth take any higher rank ; inasmuch as they have not attained to an exact definition of income, wages, profits, and rent of land. Botero's view, that population is limited by subsistence, is restated by Beccaria, and more clearly still by Ricci (1787), but these writers treat the subject only in a superficial manner, and not in such a way as to entitle them, as some would have it, to be regarded as precursors of MALTHUS. Of more frequent occurrence in the writings of the economists of this epoch, *e.g.* CARACCIOLI (1784), PAOLETTI, Beccaria, whose remarks on wages are termed "classic" by the Russian writer Wernardski, is the assertion that high prices of provisions, and the rise in money wages which ensues, are injurious to industry,—an assertion which, put forward contemporaneously in England by a series of economists, and repeated by Smith, is the logical consequence of the theory which reckons wages among the elements of the cost and of the value of the product. One marked characteristic of the Italian economists of this period is the absolute eclecticism with which they perpetually oscillate between the mercantilists and the physiocrats, and strive to reconcile the deductions from both. Besides this it is well to note the lofty and humane principles inspiring their remarks on economic relations, contrasting favourably with those of their French and English contemporaries,— their sympathetic interest in the fate of the producer—which they consider more important than the exigencies

of production—their courageous denunciation of the wretchedness of the peasants, their thoroughgoing predilection for small farming, and finally their eloquent pleading that the legislator should intervene to mitigate economic inequality and injustice,—in these matters they sound the prelude to what is now known as socialism of the chair (see SOCIALISTS OF THE CHAIR). This tone is common to all the economists of the peninsula, and not, as some hold, peculiar to central and northern Italy, since it is equally shown in the works of the southern Genovesi, Galiani, Filangieri, and Broggia, and in those of the northern Beccaria, Vasco, and Verri, and again among the Tuscans, Bandini, and Paoletti. All our economists of whatever school concern themselves not only, like Adam Smith, with the *wealth of nations*, but also, and as much, with the *public weal*, for which the very titles of their works are the proof, namely those of Vasco, Paoletti, Palmieri, MURATORI, etc.—a significant difference, attesting the ethical and philanthropic character of economic science in Italy. This character is possibly due in part to the fact that some of our economists, like Ortes, Paoletti, Bandini, Galiani, Ammirato, Vasco, Genovesi, and Pascoli, have been ecclesiastics ; others, like Beccaria, Verri, Scaruffi, D'Arco, Carraccioli, are nobles ; while few only, like Davanzati, Broggia, Belloni, have been merchants or bankers. Nevertheless the generous and noble expressions to which we have referred, and which deservedly attract so much sympathy to our economists of this epoch, do not rise from the narrow limits of sentimental literature nor do they show any profound reflection on the laws of economics.

One amongst them, however, does not deserve this criticism, and rises far above his contemporaries. This is the Venetian monk Giammaria Ortes, one of the greatest economists of the 18th century.[1]

---

[1] *The opinions of G. Ortes.*—G. Ortes was unquestionably the most original thinker among all Italian economists. In his *Economia Nazionale* (1774), his *Riflessioni sulla Popolazione* (1790), and in some of his minor writings, he develops a complete system of economic science. The fundamental notion from which he starts is, that a given population cannot consume, and therefore cannot produce, more than a limited quantity of goods, and that this quantity is just such as to require for its production not more than the labour of one-half of the given population. Hence he deduces the opinion that a man cannot increase his own wealth without reducing to a corresponding extent the wealth of another man ; in other words, that the increase of individual wealth involves a correlative increase of misery. From the principle that one-half the population suffices for social production, Ortes, anticipating modern socialism, deduces the hopeless case of a relatively excessive population, due not to a positive excess of population above the means of subsistence, but to the impossibility of increasing consumption, and *therefore* social production, beyond a certain point. In this deduction Ortes manifests a logical acumen far superior to that of SISMONDI. The latter, whose influence on MALTHUS and RICARDO was considerable, also starting from the limitation of social consumption, admits the necessity of the introduction of machinery to meet the relative excess of population.

The last remark of our note on the opinions of Ortes, indeed, applies more or less to all Italian political economy of the early period. The leading features of the social economy which succeeded the abolition of serfage in Italy were for a long period the breaking up of capital, the growth of metayage, the continuance of small industry,—in other words they presented a stunted form of capitalism crossed and complicated by numerous relations of personal service between labourer and proprietor, the relics of feudalism. This network of economic relations created a scientific literature in which it was reflected. No sound theory of distribution could be formulated in a country where the phenomena of distribution had not assumed a distinct and fixed character, nor had those glaring contrasts to which a social economy

Ortes, however, in his *Riflessioni sulla Popolazione*, published fourteen years after his principal work, admits, in partial divergence from what he had there laid down, that a population might possibly outrun its means of subsistence—an emergency which is in contradiction to the axiom, that *wealth is a constant function of population*, since it implies that, up to a certain point, wealth increases at a lower ratio than population. Finally, from the fact that the unemployed can only live at the expense of the employers (*i.e.* those who have property), Ortes deduces the principle that *real income is equal to each*, because those who have property have to distribute all the returns which are in excess of what they consume beween the workers and the unemployed. These quaint doctrines, which MARX very ably made use of to support his own, betray constantly the backward state of the science, exaggerating the importance of consumption and attributing to this factor, which only influences the surface of things, phenomena which have their roots deep down in the organism of production. Still more defective are the investigations of Ortes on capital and profit. Defining capital as the sum of the means of subsistence necessary to the worker, he does not take into account capital sunk in machinery, raw material, etc. While he recognises the economic justice of interest on capital, he declares it to be a thing which, properly considered, is entirely anomalous, for the reason, that capital lent at interest yields a return to the lender and a wage for the workers, but nothing to the borrowing ENTREPRENEUR, who hence will have either to go to the wall or to steal from his creditor. This observation is obviously erroneous, because capital does produce, besides interest and wages, the reward of the *entrepreneur*. But these doctrines appear less strange when viewed in relation to the economic conditions of the time. The principle of fixity in production is a faithful image of the economic positions of the expiring Venetian republic, in which there was no progress in production, and every industry was languid. The hopeless case of an unemployed class was true enough of a country in which the accumulation of capital was feeble, and shackled by the countless fetters of antiquated methods of production. The definition of capital given by Ortes fits an epoch when capital in its technical shape is almost non-existent. And the same idea of real income being equal for every man may be considered a tolerably correct expression of the relations of feudal economy, which, in placing the strength of the property-holder in the number of his followers, broke up his returns between a large number of clients, and ultimately reduced to the same figure the consumption of himself and of his dependants. The disconsolate fatalism of Ortes which sees no remedy whatever for the economic evils of the day, and the only palliative in the endowment of monasteries to relieve the wretchedness of the poor—which restricted thus the scope of economics to the mitigation of human misery,—all this distinctly and completely reflects the state of decay under which Italy was groaning. Hence in reading at this day the works of Ortes there is still profit, not in the nebulous musings of a recluse, but in the theorising of a genius over an age now buried. [See also art. on ORTES.]

gives rise, in which capital is more fully developed, had a fair field to display themselves. Hence, all that Italian economists of past centuries have written on distribution is collectively of very small value. But while they were excluded, through the defects in the existing economic position, from the possibility of investigating the deep-lying social relations, they set themselves eagerly to examine those more patent economic relations the growth of which, being independent of that of more fundamental relations, had opportunity to display itself even in Italy. Hence, the considerable body of writings on currency, which are the best part of Italian economic literature, as well as on commerce, usury, and taxation ; while the investigations on value, which occur frequently at this epoch, are confined to analyses, more or less effective, of wants, utility, competition, or monopoly, but which do not in the least account for the influences determining the part played by value in the deepest relations of capital and profit and in the technical organism of production. Certain it is that the closer we approach our own times, the more frequently do we find among Italian economists good examples of a profound analysis of the economic structure of society, as in the works of ORTES, GALIANI, BECCARIA, VERRI, GENOVESI, and PAGNINI (*q.v.*). But, generally, throughout this epoch, and even among these, we look in vain for that fine economic sense which distinguishes their English contemporaries so conspicuously.

2. *Superficial and optimistic phase.*—With the close of the 18th century, capital had begun to develop its influences in Italy to a degree hitherto unknown. It seemed therefore that the causes of the slow advances of economic theory were ceasing to operate, and that the era of scientific economics in Italy was to begin. But there were weighty reasons which influenced capitalistic economy and kept it backward. The most powerful of those was the want of political union ; this involved a close network of inland custom-duties, which stifled economic progress and the growth of capital. Hence, the absence of farming and industry on any large scale and the scanty use of machinery. This absence of production on a large scale is certain to react on theory and to produce a school of superficial and optimistic political economy. The inferiority of the work of most of the writers of this epoch is, therefore, not surprising, nor that the few original thinkers should gradually drift from tedious superficiality to optimistic doctrines. During this epoch no important contributions were made to the theory of the distribution of wealth, or to the analysis of property, while there is no lack of suggestive investigation into such secondary matters as currency, trade, and taxation.

The period 1800-1848, is for Italian economics an inglorious time of depression and decadence, yet it was distinguished by the monumental collection of classical Italian economists, formed by Baron Custodi, *Scrittori Classici Italiani di Economia Politica*, forty-three volumes, 8vo, Milan, 1802-16. The importation of Smith's doctrines, instead of acting as a stimulus to reflection, only evoked a number of second-rate compilations. There are but one or two writers of this period who stand out from the general level of inferiority by their able investigations into some special problems. Amongst these is Melchiore Gioja (1767-1829), the advocate of large landed estates and industrial protection, remarkable rather for some important observations on the division of labour, which were praised by Babbage, than for his indefatigable collecting of statistics, and his infelicitous attacks upon Smith and Say. There was also Gian-Domenico Romagnosi (1761-1825), a masterly critic of free trade, who showed his concurrence with the ethical view now upheld in Germany, and who combated the population theories of Malthus though not without committing serious blunders ; Luigi Molinari Valeriani (1758-1828), author of deep, careful investigations into "market value"; Francesco Fuoco (died 1841), who expounded the Ricardian theory of rent, and is noted for the pre-eminence he assigns to the distribution of wealth over its production ; Carlo Cattaneo (1801-1869), a defender of free trade and a critic of the system of List (1789-1846) ; Pellegrino Rossi (1787-1848), who lectured on political economy, expounding English economics, and criticised the Code Napoléon from the economic standpoint ; Antonio Scialoja (1817-1877), who published *Principles of Social Economy*, toning down the theories of the English school ; finally Camillo Cavour (1810-1861), distinguished for his admirable writings on the corn trade, the Irish question, and his speeches on economic and financial subjects. All these writers inherited an ethical standard in economics which up to 1848 characterised the Italian school of economists ; and all, however they may differ in the systems they uphold, hold most pronounced opinions on the moral functions of the state and its social duties towards the classes who possess no property.

Towards 1850 a distinct awakening succeeds to these indecisive writings of unsystematic writers, proceeding from the optimistic school and its head, Francesco Ferrara.[1]

[1] F. Ferrara, born 1810, of Sicilian origin, professor at the university of Turin, and subsequently deputy and minister of finance, is unquestionably the most talented Italian economist of this period. Ferrara has written no comprehensive work, but has expounded his ideas not only in a course of able lectures, but also in a series of *Introductions* to the numerous volumes of the *Biblioteca dell' Economista* which he edited, and which contain translations of leading foreign economic works. In these introductions, which combine the attractions of a brilliant style, a method of teaching of vast range and marvellously elaborated, there is found not only a series

3. *Scientific Phase.*—The conditions of the time favoured the abandonment of optimistic doctrines for objective and positive inquiry. Under the regime of political unity the obstacles of criticisms, biographies, and bibliographies, but also Ferrara's own theories, forming a symmetric and usually concordant whole. These take their rise from the theory of value, which he declares to be the mother-idea of the science, and develops with much originality save where he adheres closely to the doctrines of Carey. Like him, Ferrara opposes Ricardo's theory of value and that of J. B. Say, to land himself in the formula of *cost of reproduction*. This theory, which he carefully develops, seems to Ferrara to be alone capable of summing up and unifying all economic phenomena, inasmuch as it explains value as well in the case of production which may be indefinitely increased as in the case in which increase takes place under augmented difficulty, and also in monopolies. However, to include these last within the circle of his theory, he is compelled to have recourse to a subtle distinction between *physical* and *economic* reproduction, and maintains that the value of the monopolised products is given by the cost, not of the physical reproduction, which is impossible, but of the *economic* reproduction, *i.e.* by the cost of the products which would be obtained instead of the monopolised products.

In this way Ferrara believed he had subsumed the true heads of value under a single law, overcoming the Ricardian theory which is forced to postulate two laws for competition and monopoly respectively. But further, he held that cost of reproduction ought to explain and measure by the same standard all the relations of the distribution of wealth. Hence, Ferrara argues, rent, profit, wages, are only so many instances of the law of cost of reproduction. To rent in particular, on which English science has left the indelible stamp of its strong hand, Ferrara devotes his best energies ; strengthening himself by his theory of value, he attacks the doctrine of Ricardo and reconstructs the rent of the landowner as the natural and legitimate reward of capital and labour. Here, however, Carey inspires and directs Ferrara, who, if he does not distinctly grant that cultivation proceeds from sterile to fertile soils, admits that economic progress renders the cultivation of fresh soil more productive than those previously taken in hand, thus ensuring an advantage to the land latest brought into cultivation over the first. The owners of the later land cultivated derive in consequence a surplus rent, or surplus over ordinary profit, due to the superior methods they have designed and carried out. Hence rent results, not from increasing cost of production, but from decreasing cost of reproduction, and involves neither usurpation nor injustice. Further, since the same theory is to explain all economic phenomena, profit is measured by the cost of reproduction of capital, wages by the cost of reproduction of labour ; which means that ultimately demand and supply of capital produce profit, demand and supply of labour produce wages.

In his minor works, the *Prefazioni* and the *Lezioni*, Ferrara sought to apply his favourite theory to certain practical questions, using pure science to throw light on the economic facts of which he was an eye-witness. Among these writings are the exhaustive articles on "Banks" and on "Inconvertible Paper Currency" (Corso Forzoso), abounding in admirable remarks on the circulating medium in Italy (see Assignat; Bullion Committee, Report of; Forced Currency; Inconvertible Currency): others on the banks of Venice and on taxation of flour, which Ferrara defends with partial inconsistency in view of his free-trade theories. It is not wonderful that so extraordinary and gifted a writer should have created a flourishing school attracting into his orbit the best intellects of the peninsula. Minghetti, in a well-known work remarkable for brilliancy of style (*Della economia pubblica e delle sue attinenze colla morale e col diritto*, 1858), accepted and supplemented Ferrara's theory ; Reymond in his *Études sur l'Economie sociale et internationale* (1860-61), further confirmed it ; Antonio Ciccone, Angelo Marescotti, Giovanni Bruno, Todde, and others commented on it in their treatises. During a long period, Ferrara occupied a solitary and preponderating position in Italian economic literature, due rather to his marvellous ability than to the soundness of his doctrines. Italian intelligence has extricated itself from the spell of the illustrious theoriser ; his system has gradually been abandoned.

to the establishment of a social economy based on capital became slowly removed. The distressing phenomena of a critical period of social evolution in Italy were attracting investigation. Statistical research, directed by the hand of Bodio, revealed the vitiated character of the system by which wealth was distributed, the encroachments of the *latifundia*, the spread of short leases ; and important publications showed that the actual state of the rural classes was as degraded as it well could be. Sonnino, Villari, Franchetti, Mme. White Mario, Lombroso, Stivanello, Mortara,—all these illustrated the condition of the agricultural classes in a series of memorable monographs, while the exhaustive work of the agrarian commission contributed ample materials invested with official authority. In those reports Emilio MORPURGO drew in the dark hues of truth the deplorable wretchedness of the agricultural classes in Venetia. And the reports of JACINI, Angeloni, Branca, Tanari, and Damiani showed that Italy had reached her lowest level of misery, inasmuch as from provinces mutually dissimilar there was heard but one wail and the selfsame moan.

A new habit of research and criticism informed economic thought from end to end of the peninsula, and a legion of clever and ardent youths flung themselves into the open field of social inquiry. Theirs is the merit that Italy occupies a position in the political economy of to-day on a level with more advanced countries ; theirs is the merit that she has entered on the scientific phase.

Even in the preceding generation Italian writers were not wanting who set themselves to study economic relations with impartial criticism e.g. Girolamo Boccardo, who in his *Trattato teorico-pratico di Economia Politica* (1853), still the delight of the Italian student—defended and repolished the exact theories of Ricardo. It was, however, especially in the field of technical and specific inquiry that scientific economics was to prevail. Among the first indications of this tendency was the book by Baer, *L'avere et l'imposta* (1872), praised by J. Stuart Mill,— the *Logica delle Imposte* (1867), written by Pescatore, a calm and impartial study of public finance ; and Jacini's work, *La Proprietà fondiaria e le Popolazioni agricole in Lombardia* (1854), a good example of positive analysis. But the real initiator of the scientific method is undoubtedly Angelo Messedaglia. A distinguished physicist and mathematician, Messedaglia appeared least of any one inclined to examine the burning questions of economics, his turn of mind inclining him rather to more special and calm studies. Therefore he launched into a series of investigations into population, public loans, currency, taxes on real property, in which he sought to secure not the triumph of a school, but to lay bare and differentiate the most intimate connections of economic

phenomena in a number of monographs written with conscientious and exact precision.

In his book *Della Teoria della Popolazione, principalmente sotto l'Aspetto del Metodo* (1858), unfortunately unfinished, Messedaglia puts forward an emendation of the Malthusian theory, namely, that the two progressions of subsistence and population cannot proceed as mutually isolated and independent. The latter is strictly limited by the former, which gives a different result from that reached by Malthus. For, given the former rate, two, three, four, five . . . and the latter, two, four, eight . . . it is evident that in the latter the second term will be suddenly reduced to three by the limit of subsistence killing off the surplus. Hence the successive doubling of population can only start from three, raising numbers in the third turn no higher than six. This again, colliding with a sum of subsistence equal to four, becomes reduced to four, and this by the given rate gives eight. Hence the real progression for population is two, four, six, eight, ten . . . *i.e.* an arithmetical progression with a constant difference double that of the rate of subsistence. Equally important are Messedaglia's further developments of the population theory, the statistics moreover of which, and the methods of handling them, he has expounded and criticised with great acumen in a solid work on the *Vita Media* (average of life). In his book on public loans, Messedaglia discusses the different questions connected with raising public loans, and in his recent work on currency, the history of money and prices, and the controversy on the legal standard. Finally his report *Sulla Perequazione Fondiaria* (1884) gives a history of the Cadastre (see CADASTRAL SURVEY) from the earliest times, and of the character of the surveys of land, and the taxes based on them in widely-separated and contrasted countries and states. The works of Messedaglia are in some points open to criticism, especially for their eclecticism and the indefiniteness of his results, but his labours will leave an enduring mark on Italian economic thought.

Messedaglia's strictly scientific method, which he employed on technical subjects extraneous to social controversies, has been applied by other and well-known economists to the most burning questions concerning the distribution of wealth. Among these Emilio Nazzani should be mentioned, who, while the prevailing school was yet seeking to draw a veil over the more painful phenomena of our economic system, courageously examined the laws of rent (1872), profit (1877), and wages (1880), developing and amplifying the theories of Ricardo. The writings of Nazzani mark a new starting-point in Italian political economy, leading it to reject optimistic fallacies and to initiate a vigorous criticism of the relations of production. However, neither he nor the other Italian economists of the same school have adopted the extreme conclusions of their doctrines, but have laboured rather to qualify them by every possible means. Thus Nazzani seeks to soften the asperities of the Ricardian theory of rent, and the teaching of the English school; nevertheless he has laid the foundations of solid inquiry into the laws of distribution.

Again Fedele Lampertico influenced the economic revival in Italy by reproducing English and German theories in a lengthy treatise (1874, etc.); while Luigi Luzzatti, eloquent opponent of the exaggerations of *laissez faire*, has ably dealt with treaties of commerce, tariffs, currency, and credit, both in his writings and parliamentary life.

But the chief honour of the peaceful revolution whence scientific economics in Italy have sprung belongs unquestionably to Luigi Cossa; he has not only contributed a noteworthy and original essay on the limits of production, and diffused and championed in Italy the theories of the English school, harmonising them with those of Germany (which have also been popularised in Italy by Cusumano), France, and Holland, in which he is extremely well read; but he has also by teaching, by prizes, and instructive writings stimulated the economic studies of young Italy, creating around him a compact phalanx of able and diligent disciples.

A testimony to the awakening power of such masters may be seen in the numerous publications of youthful Italian economists, all educated in the new and progressive tendencies and agreed in the search for truth, however else they may differ. Of those cultivating exact science are Buzzetti, who has dealt with internal values and agricultural contracts,—Ricca-Salerno, who has dealt with capital, public loans, and wages,—Graziani, with machinery and wages,—Alessio, Bertini, Valenti, and Tangorra, with the theory of value,—Manara and Masè-Dari, who have examined rent,—Supino, capital and its transformations,—Majorana, economic laws,—and many others besides. While these economists are mainly deductive in treatment, others complement abstract research by a judicious application of the historic method. Among these, Cognetti de Martiis has written on primitive forms of economic evolution and the origin of socialism, —Toniolo on the factors of the economic power of medieval Florence, and the relation of scholasticism to humanism. Other writers apply sociology to political economy, like Vanni, an eminent philosopher, and Nitti, author of the book on *Catholic Socialism*, in their works on population. Ugo Rabbeno, who follows the inductive method, has treated of co-operation, its laws, and development in Italy and England, with great talent, and also has written a work on the phases of American protectionism. Equally skilled in statistical method, and more decided partisans of the socialism of the chair, are Carlo F. Ferraris, author of a book on labour insurance in Italy, and Augusto Mortara, who, in his work *I Doveri della Proprietà fondiaria e la questione sociale*, suggests state intervention in the tenure of land on behalf of the labourers.

Meanwhile there is no falling off in more strictly technical publications, as on credit, trade, and finance. First among these should be noticed Maffeo Pantaleoni's *Teoria della Traslazione dei Tributi*, skilfully explaining the shifting incidence of taxation. This book, not to mention others by the same author (*v.* works named later), shows how great has been the progress of scientific investigation in Italy. We may mention the labours of MAGLIANI, to whom we owe the most thorough critique of bimetallism, of Ferraris, Stringher, Piperno, G. Luzzatti, De Viti, Loria, Benini, Lorini, in monetary questions to which modern Italian economists, like their earlier brethren, and unhappily for the same reasons, have given much attention. Thus on banks we have works by Boccardo, De Jehannis, the *Storia delle Banche* by Rota, and the *Principii di Scienza bancaria* by Rota and by Ferraris. On rural economy there are the writings of Bertagnolli (*v. Authorities*), and others of equally high quality, by Bianchi, Emilio Cossa, and Sartori. On subjects of applied economics mention should be made of the labours of Graziani (*Teoria delle Operazioni di Borsa*), of Supino in his essay on discount, and especially in his *Navigazione dal Punto di Vista economico*, in which he discusses questions of freight, cost of navigation, and generally the economy of maritime enterprise. The writings of Montemartini and Della Bona on crises are also worth note, of A. Rossi and Benini, both protectionists, on the balance of trade, of Dalla Volta on industrial combination and forms of wages, of De Viti, Salandra, Alessio, Zorli, Graziani, and Puviani on financial questions. Here, too, quite apart from the subjects of the day, mention must be made of the bibliographical series published by a group of writers, Alberti, Montanari, Cusumano, Ricca-Salerno, Fornari, Sinigaglia, Loria, Errera, Gobbi, Supino, Conigliani, Graziani, Balletti, De Viti, Bertolini, under the editorship of Cossa.

The acclamation which in recent years greeted the rise of the AUSTRIAN SCHOOL (*q.v.*) could not fail to excite a fascination on Italian minds. The natural consequence has been a multitude of commentators on the theories of JEVONS, Menger, Böhm-Bawerk, Sax, and Wieser. For instance, Graziani accepts their theory of value in his *Storia critica della teoria del valore in Italia*, and so in part does Pantaleoni in his *Principii di Economia pura*, and Alessio in his essay on value, already mentioned. Again Sax's theories on finance are reproduced in the *Manuale di Scienza delle Finanze* of Ricca-Salerno, and accepted, with certain modifications, by Conigliani in his *Teoria degli Effetti economici delle Imposte*, by Graziani (*Di alcune questioni intorno alla Natura e agli Effetti economici delle Imposte*, 1889; and *Natura economica delle Imposte sulle Successioni*, 1890), and by Mazzola (*I Dati scientifici della Finanza pubblica*, 1887).

Economic study has received a vigorous impulse in Italy through the *Giornale degli Economisti*, an able review, edited by eminent writers with the collaboration of the best intellects in the kingdom. It courageously opposes protection, both agrarian and industrial, which has come to the front of recent years in Italy, to the great injury of national economy, and bestows a keen and conscientious criticism on the monetary and bank policy of the Italian government.

The work of certain other writers does not come under any of the preceding categories. Among these are economists who are free-traders and optimists, such as Berardi, De Johannis, Martello, Dalla Volta, Bertolini, Todde, Pinna-Ferrà, Pareto, etc., whose organ is *L'Economista*, and a rising knot of authors occupied with socialist theses,—defended with moderation and learning by Napoleone Colajanni in *Socialismo e Sociologia criminale*,—and of which the leading organ is *La Critica sociale*, ably edited by Filippo Turati.

Finally there are some Italian economists whose line of thought diverges from all the foregoing. These see in the analysis of the relations of real property a key by the aid of which they seek to penetrate the yet unsolved problems of the distribution of wealth ; following this method they have reached a number of results in the theories of value, currency, profit, interest, rent, population, and the interpretation of economic and political history. The system was set forth for the first time by Achille Loria in *La Rendita fondiaria e la sua Elisione naturale*, 1879 ; and *Analisi della Proprietà capitalista*, 1889 ; and applied to sociology by him in *Les Bases économiques de la Constitution sociale*, 2nd éd., Paris, 1893. It starts from an analysis of the economic influences exerted by the presence, or absence, of free land, not like WAKEFIELD, to deduce how new countries should be organised, and still less to mourn with Von THÜNEN over the distribution of wealth obtaining in old countries, but to trace out the organic laws and structure of the capitalistic economy. Amongst Loria's analyses we may mention that which reduces value to *complex labour*, complementing Ricardo's theory ; his analysis of money, in which he traces the origin of money, completes Mill's doctrine of international values, and corrects FULLARTON's theory on *hoards ;* his analysis of the distinction between *technical capital* and *wage capital ;* his distinction between distribution of wealth, *i.e.* distribution of the produce between wages and income,—and re-distribution of wealth, *i.e.*, distribution of income between earnings of the undertaker (*entrepreneur*), interest on capital, rent of land and taxes ; the amount of the bank reserve ; the theory of the systematic excess of population ; the comparative analysis of the economic development of the American and Australian colonies, and of Europe, showing how the economic relations existing in ancient Europe are reproduced in modern colonies. This system, which has been called "the landed property system of political economy," now counts amongst its partial or thoroughgoing adherents Rabbeno, Nitti, E. Cossa, Garlanda, A. Mortara, Masè-Dari, Flora Sartori, Bianchi, Supino, De Marinis, Coletti, Petrone, and others.

[Recent works are :—Alberti, *Le corporazioni d'arti e mestieri negli antichi economisti italiani*, Milano, 1888.—Alessio, *Saggio sul sistema tributario in Italia*, Torino, 1883-87 ; *Studii sulla teoria del valore nel cambio interno*, Torino, 1890.—Baer, *L'avere e l'imposta*, Torino, 1872.—Balletti, *Gasparo Scaruffi e la questione monetaria nel secolo XVI*, Modena, 1882.—Benini, *Le basi di una nuova teoria della circolazione*, Cremona, 1887. —Bertagnolli, *La colonia parziaria*, Firenze, 1877 ; *Vicende dell' agricoltura in Italia*, Firenze, 1881 ; *L'economia dell' agricoltura*, Roma, 1886. —Boccardo, *Trattato teorico-pratico di economia*

politica, Torino, 1853.—Buzzetti, *Sull' indole Economica dei contratti agrari*, Milano, 1874 ; *Teoria del Commercio internazionale*, Milano, 1877. —Cattaneo, *Scritti di economia publica*, Genova, 1887-88.—Cavour, *Opere politico-economiche*, Napoli, 1860.—Ciccone, *Principii di economia sociale*, Napoli, 1866-68.—Cognetti de Martiis, *Le forme primitive dell' evoluzione economica*, Torino, 1881 ; *Socialismo antico*, Torino, 1889.— Colajanni, *Socialismo e sociologia criminale*, Catania, 1884-89.—Conigliani, *Teoria degli effetti economici delle imposte*, Milano, 1890.—Cossa, E., *Primi elementi di economia agraria*, Milano, 1890. —Cossa, Luigi, *Introduzione allo studio dell' economia politica*, 3a edizione, Milano, 1892 ; *Saggi di economia politica*, Milano, 1878 ; *Primi elementi di economia politica*, 9a ed., Milano, 1891 ; *Id. id. di scienza delle finanze*, 6a ed., Milano, 1892.—Cusumano, *Le scuole economiche della Germania*, Napoli, 1875 ; *Dell' economia politica nel medio evo*, Bologna, 1876 ; *La teoria del commercio dei grani in Italia*, Bologna, 1877. —Dorado Montero, *El positivismo en la ciencia juridica y social italiana*, ii., Madrid, 1891.— Ferrara, *Prefazioni alle Serie I. e II. della Biblioteca dell' Economista*, Torino, 1850-70 ; *Memorie di Statistica*, Roma, 1890.—Ferraris, C. F., *Saggi di economia statistica, etc.*, Torino, 1880 ; *L'assicurazione degli operai, etc.*, Roma, 1888; *Principii di Scienza Bancaria*, Milano, 1892 ; *Moneta e corso forzoso*, Milano, 1879.—Fornari, *Delle teorie economiche nelle provincie Napoletane*, Milano, 1882-88.—Fuoco, *Saggi economici*, Pisa, 1825-27. Melchiore Gioja, *Nuovo Prospetto delle scienze economiche*, Milano, 1815-17.—Graziani, *Di alcune questioni intorno alla natura ed agli effetti economici delle imposte*, Siena, 1889 ; *Natura economica delle imposte sulle successioni*, Siena, 1890 ; *Teoria delle operazioni di borsa*, Siena, 1890 ; *Storia critica della teoria del valore in Italia*, Milano, 1889 ; *Le idee economiche degli scrittori emiliani e romagnoli sino al 1848*, Modena, 1893 ; *Studii sulla teoria economica delle macchine*, Torino, 1891 ; *Di alcune questioni relative alla dottrina del salario*, Torino, 1893.—Gobbi, *La concorrenza estera e gli antichi economisti italiani*, Milano, 1884 ; *L'economia politica negli scrittori italiani del secolo XVI.-XVII.*, Milano, 1889.—Lampertico, *Giammaria Ortes e la scienza economica al suo tempo*, Venezia, 1865 ; *Economia dei popoli e degli stati*. Milano, 1874-84.—Loria, A, *La rendita fondiaria e la sua elisione naturale*, Milano, 1879 ; *Analisi della proprietà capitalista*, Torino, 1889 ; *Les bases économiques de la constitution sociale*, Paris, 1893 ; *La teoria del valore negli economisti italiani*, Bologna, 1882 ; *Studii sul valore della moneta*, Torino, 1891.—Lorini, *La questione della valuta nell' Austria-Ungheria*, Torino, 1893.—Luzzatti, *L'inchiesta industriale ed i trattati di Commercio*, Milano, 1878.—Magliani, *La questione monetaria*, Roma, 1872 e ss. (in the Nuova Antologia.)— Majorana, *Le leggi naturali dell' economia politica*, Roma, 1890.—Manara, *Concetto e genesi della rendita fondiaria, suoi correttivi e sua naturale elisione*, Roma, 1882.—Masè-Dari, *L. A. Muratori, come economista*, Bologna, 1893 ; *Della influenza della coltivazione intensiva sulla rendita fondiaria*, Torino, 1888.—Mazzola, *L'assicurazione degli operai in Germania*, Roma, 1886 ; *I dati scientifici della finanza pubblica*, Roma, 1890.—Messedaglia, *Dei prestiti pubblici e del miglior sistema di consolidazione*, Milano, 1850 ; *Della teoria della popolazione principalmente sotto l'aspetto del metodo*, Verona, 1858 ; *La moneta e il sistema monetario in generale*, *La storia e la statistica dei metalli preziosi*, Roma, 1881-83 ; *Relazione sul Titolo I. del progetto di legge sull' imposta fondiaria*, Roma, 1884.—Minghetti, *Dell' economia pubblica e delle sue attinenze colla morale e col diritto*, Firenze, 1858 ; *Opuscoli letterarii ed economici*, Firenze, 1872.—Morpurgo, *Saggi economici e statistici sul Veneto*, Padova, 1868 ; *I contadini nel Veneto*, in the *Atti dell' inchiesta agraria*, Roma, 1882.—Mortara, Augusto, *I doveri della proprietà fondiaria e la questione sociale*, 2a ede., Roma, 1885.—Nazzani, *Saggi di economia politica* Milano, 1881 ; *Sunto di economia politica*, 4a ed., Milano, 1881.—Nitti, *Le popolazione ed il sistema sociale*, Torino, 1894 ; *Il socialismo cattolico*, Torino, 2a ed., 1891.—Pantaleoni, M., *Teoria della traslazione dei tributi*, Roma, 1882 ; *Teoria della pressione tributaria*, Roma, 1887 ; *Dell' ammontare probabile della ricchezza privata in Italia*, Roma, 1885 ; *Principii di Economia pura*, Firenze, 1889.—Pecchio, *Storia dell' Economia pubblica in Italia*, 2a ed. Lugano, 1832.—Pescatore, Matteo, *La logica delle imposte*, Torino, 1867.—Perrone, *La Terra nella odierna economia capitalistica*, Roma, 1893.—Puviani, *Alcune questioni intorno all' imposta sui fabbricati*, Bologna, 1890.—Rabbeno, Ugo, *La cooperazione in Inghilterra*, Milano, 1885 ; *La cooperazione in Italia*, Milano, 1886 ; *Le Società cooperative di produzione*, Milano, 1889 ; *Protezionismo americano*, Milano, 1893 ; *Raccolta degli economisti toscani*, Firenze, 1847-49.—Reymond, *Études sur l'économie sociale et internationale*, Turin, 1860-61.—Ricca-Salerno, *Saggio sulla teoria del capitale*, Milano, 1877 ; *Teoria generale dei prestiti publici*, Milano, 1879 ; *Del salario e delle sue leggi*, Padova, 1878 ; *Storia delle dottrine finanziarie in Italia*, Roma, 1881 ; *Manuale di Scienza delle Finanze*, Firenze, 1888.—Romagnosi, *Collezione degli articoli d'economia politica e statistica*, Firenze, 1835, Valenti, *Le*

idee economiche di G. D. Romagnosi, Roma, 1891.—Rossi, Pellegrino, *Cours d'Économie politique*, Bruxelles, 1852.—Rota, *Storia delle banche*, Milano, 1874 ; *Principii di scienza bancaria*, 2a ed. Milano, 1885.—Scialoja, *I principii dell' economia sociale*, Napoli, 1848 ; *Scrittori classici italiani d'economia politica*, Milano, 1803-16, Custodi collection, 43 vols.—Strugher, *Della estinzione del corso forzoso negli stati Uniti*, Roma, 1879.—Supino, *La scienza economica in Italia dalla seconda metà del secolo XVI. alla prima del XVII.*, Torino, 1888 ; *Il saggio dello sconto*, Torino, 1892 ; *La navigazione dal punto di vista economico*, Roma, 1890 ; *Teoria della trasformazione dei capitali*, Torino, 1891.—Tangorra, *La teoria economica del costo di produzione*, Roma, 1893.—Todde, *Note sull' economia politica*, Cagliari, 1885.—Toniolo, *Dei remoti fattori della potenza economica di Firenze*, Milano, 1882.—Valenti, *La teoria del valore*, Roma, 1890.—Valeriani, Molinari, *Saggio di Erotemi, ecc.*, Bologna, 1825-28.— Vanni, *Studii sulla teoria sociologica della popolazione*, Città di Castello, 1886.—Viti, De, *Moneta e prezzi*, Città di Castello, 1884.—Wernardsky, *Kritiko-istoritcheskoe islidowanie obi italianskoi politiko-economitcheskoi literature*, Moscow, 1849.—Zorli, *Diritto tributario italiano*, Brisighella, 1892.]   ACH. L.

IVERNOIS, SIR FRANCIS D' (1757-1842). A French émigré, was knighted by George III. He returned to France in 1814.

His principal works were : *Tableau historique et politique des pertes que la révolution et la guerre ont causées au peuple français dans sa population, son agriculture, ses colonies, ses manufactures et son commerce*, London, 1799. A work in form too much resembling a party pamphlet, but many of its reflections are valuable ; and *Sur la Mortalité proportionelle de quelques populations considerée comme mesure de leur aisance et civilisation*, Genève, 1832.

[The *Nouvelle Biographie générale*, Paris, 1858, vol. xxv., contains a full notice of him, and lists of works. See also Coquelin and Guillaumin's *Dictionnaire de l'économie politique*, Paris, 1852-1853.]   H. E. E.

JACINI, COUNT STEFANO (1837-1891) belonged to a Lombard family of Casalbuttano. He studied in Switzerland, then at Milan by order of the Austrian government, lastly in Germany. In his youth he travelled through Europe and the East. He then applied himself again to study, and published *La proprietà fondiaria e la popolazione agricola in Lombardia*, Milano, 1854 ; 3rd ed., 1857. During a famine in the Valtellina, invited by Maximilian of Austria, then governor of Lombardy, he wrote *Le condizioni economiche della Valtellina*. Mr. Gladstone translated this pamphlet into English to show how intolerable the Austrian rule was in Italy. In 1860 Jacini became minister for agriculture and commerce, Cavour, whom he had supplied with information as

to the relations of Austria to Lombardy and Venetia, being Premier.

He gave a strong impulse to the execution of the St. Gothard tunnel. His report to Parliament on that occasion, 25th February 1866, is a good example of his positive method, stating ascertained facts which had been made thoroughly known through a public inquiry. After being appointed a Senator he published several political writings, "Sulle opere pubbliche in Italia nei loro rapporti con lo Stato.—Sulle condizioni della cosa pubblica in Italia dopo il 1866." His positive method made a deep impression on the nation when the Italian parliament, 15th March 1877, ordered an inquiry into agriculture and the position of agriculturists (*Inchiesta Agraria*). The result of this inquiry was published in 15 volumes 4to, 1881-1885, Rome (Tip. del Senato) with a preface by Jacini, vol. i. containing an explanation of its aim and a statement at the end *Relazione Finale* (vol. xv.) collecting its conclusions which, according to his own words, applied the experimental method to the study of Italy as an agricultural nation. Jacini did not rely on theory, his works show great clearness of observation, he sided with free trade, just when the protective system was cherished by the supporters of agricultural interests. A rich landowner himself, he supported the principle that property is a social necessity if it were only to preserve and to increase agricultural wealth, its defence lies in the service it renders to society. A. B.

JACOB, WILLIAM, F.R.S. (1762?-1851), merchant in London, was appointed in 1822 to the comptrollership of corn returns, which post he retained during twenty years. He was commissioned by the Government in 1825 and 1827 to report on the condition of agriculture in some of the states of northern Europe ; the results of his observations are contained in two *Reports* which contain valuable information and very full statistics of the state of land and the agricultural produce of those countries at that period. On the suggestion of Huskisson he undertook an inquiry into the production and consumption of the precious metals. This work shows great research, but is defective, which may be attributed partly, for the more recent periods, to the insufficient historical information available then. But, as regards earlier times, Jacob appears to have put together more information than any one previously, and his conclusions concerning the subsequent and middle ages are quoted as authoritative by many recent writers on the subject, as by Walker in *Money*.

An historical Inquiry into the Production and Consumption of the Precious Metals, 2 vols., London, 1831.—*Report on the Trade in Foreign Corn, and on the Agriculture of the North of Europe. . . . To which is added an Appendix of Official documents. Averages of Prices*, etc., London, 1826.— "A Report . . . respecting the Agriculture and the Trade in Corn in some of the Continental States of Northern Europe," in the *Pamphleteer*, xxix., 1828, and several other pamphlets on agriculture. R. H. H.

JACTUS NAVIS LEVANDI GRATIA (General Average). When a ship and its cargo are in peril of the sea, and the master of the ship orders a sacrifice of property to be made for the purpose of avoiding the danger, such as that of throwing cargo overboard to lighten the ship, the loss thus arising has to be shared in common between the ship-owner and owners of cargo, *i.e.* among all those who benefit by its having been made. This provision of Roman law was derived from the maritime law of the Rhodians ; hence it is called *lex Rhodia de jactu* (see AVERAGE, MARITIME). E. A. W.

JAKOB, LUDWIG HEINRICH VON (1759-1827), a distinguished economist, was born at Wettin. He studied at Merseburg and Halle, and in 1791 became professor of philosophy at the latter place, where he strove to popularise the doctrines of Kant. He lectured also with great success on political economy. The Russian government invited him to fill the chair of economic science at Kharkow, and the suppression of the university of Halle in 1806 induced him to accept the offer. He speedily learned Russian and lectured in that language on political science. He was favoured by the minister Speransky, and in 1809 was called to St. Petersburg as member of an important finance commission. On the re-establishment of the university of Halle, he returned to Germany and resumed his professorial work. The Russian government on his retirement ennobled him and granted him a pension. He was a voluminous writer on philosophical subjects in the earlier part of his career.

Jakob's principal economic publications were : *Theorie und Praxis in der Staatswirthschaft*, 1801; *Ueber die Arbeitleibeigner und freier Bauern in Russland*, 1815 ; *Grundsätze der Nationaloekonomie, oder Theorie des Nationalreichthums*, 1805 (3rd enlarged edition, 1825); *Die Staatswissenschaft theoretisch und praktisch dargestellt und erläutert*, 1821. He closely followed Adam Smith, whilst at the same time seeking to place in a clearer light the fundamental conceptions of the science. He translated into German (1807) the treatise of J. B. Say and (1803) Thornton's *Paper Credit of Great Britain*. J. K. I.

JANNET, CLAUDIO (1844-94), after having graduated as doctor of law at Aix in Provence, and as doctor of political sciences at Louvain, practised some time at the bar in Aix. Having been introduced to LE PLAY, he became the most brilliant of his disciples and fellow-labourers, and following his method, made a personal inquiry into the state of the populations of Dauphiné and Provence.

Jannet wrote in 1867 an essay on the *Lex Voconia*, and after having published in 1873 his *Institutions Sociales et le Droit Civil à Sparte*, he returned from a journey in America with his *États Unis Contemporains*—pub. 1876,—a critical examination of the institutions, moral conditions, and ideas prevalent in the great republic after the war of secession ; this book, which in thirteen years went through four editions, established the reputation of Jannet as an acute observer, although he certainly did not see American democracy in the same favourable light as De Tocqueville forty years before. However, in his last edition (1889), he is glad to testify that "the political condition of the United States has considerably improved" (see his monographs in the *Ouvriers des deux mondes, e.g.* "Un Metayer de Texas.")

Having been elected the first professor of political economy at the Catholic Institute of Paris, Jannet occupied this chair until the time of his death. According to one who knew him well, he aimed "at following the method of observation and keeping to the exact study of facts, so as to give economic science a solid foundation, and at illustrating it by judicious historical descriptions of the past and comparative information derived from both continents, breathing into the whole the spirit of elevated moral thought." This object he successfully attained, both in his academic lectures and in the two large works published during this period : *Le Socialisme d'État et la Réforme Sociale*, 1889, and *Le Capital, la Spéculation et la Finance au XIXe Siècle*, 1892. Jannet probably was the most scholarly and certainly one of the best and most widely informed of the French economists of his generation ; with a marked Roman Catholic and conservative bias, his standpoint is the standpoint of unrestricted economic liberty combined with a due acknowledgment of the relativity of economic phenomena and deep religious and moral convictions. To socialistic schemes of reform, whatever might be their origin, he was firmly opposed ; although he admitted that the rise of *Kathedersocialismus* was the natural outflow of the past history of Germany, he would not admit that a socialistic legislation could achieve its supposed ends even in Germany. Denying thus to the state any right of interference with questions of production, distribution, and consumption, he however, recommended in case of need a liberal policy of *subventions*, to be provided as well by the masters (*patronage*) as by communal and corporation funds. In common with LE PLAY, he consistently strove to obtain the reform of the French law of bequest, and to restore the power of paternal authority on this point as a remedy against rural depopulation and the demoralisation of the wealthy classes of society. Jannet was a frequent contributor to the leading French periodicals, such as the *Réforme Sociale*, the *Économiste Français*, the *Correspondant*, the *Revue des Deux Mondes*, and the *Polybiblion* (see BEQUEST, POWER OF).   E. Ca.

JANSSEN, SIR THEODORE (d. 1748), director of the SOUTH SEA COMPANY, contributed several articles on the trade between Great Britain and France to the *British Merchant*, edited by Charles KING (*q.v.*), during the controversy on the commercial treaty with France in 1713. Of the papers afterwards republished as the *British Merchant*, 3 vols. 8vo, London, 1721 and 1743, Janssen was the author of *General Maxims in Trade, particularly applied to the Commerce between Great Britain and France*, reprinted in the *Somers Tracts*, 4to, 1752, vol. iv. ; 4to, 1809, vol. xiii. After giving a short summary of the principles of the MERCANTILE SYSTEM (*q.v.*) in the form of "maxims in trade assented to by everybody," he discusses the various branches of English commerce which would be affected by the proposed treaty with France, and concludes that "the high duties are the only fence we have left against an inundation of French commodities upon us," and that if the treaty were carried into effect "our capital stock of gold and silver would be diminished." The treatise has no scientific value, but it is a good illustration of the mercantile system in its most unreasonable form. It appealed to the prejudices of the

merchants, whose vigorous opposition to the treaty secured its rejection.

[For further particulars of Janssen's career *vide Dictionary of National Biography*.]   W. A. S. H.

JARROLD, THOMAS (1770-1853), a physician, born in Essex, and educated at Aberdeen, practising first at Stockport, then at Manchester, was the author of *Dissertations on Man, Philosophical, Physiological, and Political, in answer to Mr. Malthus's Essay on the Principle of Population*, 1806.

He thinks Malthus has not sufficiently noticed that increase of food depends on human action (29-30) ; also there is no proof that, where discomforts are great, increase of population is slow, and *mutatis mutandis* (16, 17). Vice, for example drunkenness, is not only sometimes a check, but sometimes a cause of population (38 *seq.*). Dr. Jarrold draws on his medical experience, and this gives his book a character of its own. "During three years, I have attended with considerable care to the diseases of the poor of the town of Stockport, and in that period have not seen fewer than 5000 sick persons who then were or had been employed in manufacturing cotton" (60). He thinks the factory children (200 in number) were healthier than those of other occupations, though factory work is that "to which the eyes of the public are directed with the most watchful jealousy." If there were more of his own experiences and less of his criticisms, which are seldom well-founded, the book would have been of greater value. His paradox, that "an unsound constitution in a civilised country most commonly proves prolific" (305), has found supporters in our own days ; but is hardly a demonstrable any more than a comfortable doctrine. Few will agree with him now in condemning Malthus for finding "an analogy in principle" between the vegetable, animal, and human kingdoms in respect of increase (329), or in regarding Malthus as destitute of due faith in Providence (327 *seq.* cp. 364). If the book in its main arguments has a family likeness to many other refutations of Malthus, it is at least superior to most of them in moderation of tone.

His other writings were — *Letter to Samuel Whitbread, M.P., on the Poor Laws*, 1807.— *Anthropologia or Dissertations on the Form and Colour of Man* (Stockport), 1808.—A paper on National Character in *Transactions of Manchester Literary and Philosophical Society*, 1811.—*Instinct and Reason philosophically investigated with a view to ascertain the Principles of the Science of Education* (Manchester), 1836.—*Education of the People*, Part I. (Manchester), 1847.   J. B.

JARVIS, EDWARD (1803-1884), born in Concord, Massachusetts ; lived in Boston. He was educated as a physician, and devoted much attention to vital statistics. He edited the vital statistics of the United States census of 1860, published in vol. iv. of the census of that year ; and contributed many papers to periodicals and societies on subjects relating to the increase of the population.

Among these may be mentioned *The Increase of Human Life*, and *Infant Mortality*, Boston, 1873.

He was the second president of the American Statistical Association, serving from 1852 until his death.   D. R. D.

JENKIN, HENRY CHARLES FLEEMING (1833-1885), an eminent electrician, and professor of engineering at the university of Edinburgh, deserves notice here as having contributed to political economy some very original papers of the highest theoretical importance and of considerable practical interest.

In a paper on "Trade Unions," in *North British Review*, 1868, Jenkin refutes the belief that unions cannot be economically beneficial to their members, by a masterly analysis of the law of demand and supply. He represents the relation between price and demand by a *function*: $D = f\left(\frac{1}{x}\right)$; or, more elaborately, $D = f\left(A + \frac{1}{x}\right)$; where x is the price, and A is an unknown constant; so that the decrease of x, or increase of $\frac{1}{x}$, corresponds to what has since been called an "extension" of demand, the increase of A to a "rise" (see COURNOT). Similarly, the equation $S = F(B + x)$ expresses the relation between price and supply. The equation $F(B + x) = f\left(A + \frac{1}{x}\right)$ determines the price x. Descending to practical details, the writer discusses, in the light of first-hand knowledge, the policy of trade unions with respect to piece-work, over-time, and other arrangements. Much weight attaches to his advice as to the rights and limitations of combination.

In the paper on *The Graphic Representation of the laws of Supply and Demand, and their application to Labour*, 1868, resuming his mathematical analysis, he continues to show "how much the value of all things depends on simple mental phenomena, and not on laws having mere quantity of materials for their subject." He constructs a demand curve and a supply curve virtually identical with Cournot's constructions. "In a given market, at a given time, the market price of the commodity will be that at which the supply and demand curves cut." Jenkin calls this the *first* law of demand and supply. Attention should be called to the statement (*Papers*, p. 86) that "the law only comes into operation where buyers and sellers can approximately estimate whether at a given price the quantity wanted or the quantity for sale is the greater." The *second* law formulates the effect on price of an increase of the "whole supply," or of the "whole purchase fund." The *third* law is: "In the long run the price of the manufactured article is chiefly determined by the cost of its production, and the quantity manufactured . . . by the demand at that price." Here "cost of" production is no one fixed cost, constant for all quantities"; and the first and third laws seem to differ only as "*short periods from long.*" In applying these laws, Jenkin conceives the action

of a combination as modifying the supply curve. "The legitimate action of trade unions is to enable the labourer to set a reserve price on his merchandise." . . . "The power of bargaining, or, in other words, of reserving some of the goods for sale, may lower the supply curve.". . He employs largely the conception of the "cost of production of a labourer"; from which he deduces just conclusions as to the importance of a high standard of life.

The paper on the *Incidence of Taxes*, 1871, opens with a brilliant exposition of the principle now known as CONSUMER'S RENT. Jenkin had re-discovered not only the general theory which Dupuit first propounded, but also the particular approximation by which Dupuit made it applicable (DUPUIT, *Papers*, p. 114). The effect of a tax on price is represented by Jenkin in much the same way as it had been by Cournot. In conclusion, he discusses two particular taxes —on houses and on rent; employing in the treatment of the latter subject a supply curve of a very peculiar construction.

The *Time-labour System* is a proposed new form of contract between men and masters. Men are to be engaged for a long period—say, six months,—each man is liable to dismissal, but the master engages to receive as substitute any competent workman, at the same wages, for the unexpired period. Also, each man is free to throw up his employment on condition of finding a competent substitute. The object is to correct the characteristic imperfection of the labour market—namely, that a master cannot take on a few additional men at an advance of wages without raising wages all round.

In the paper entitled *Is one man's gain another man's loss?* Jenkin enhances some elementary principles of economics by the physical metaphor of a "closed circuit," round which money travels in one direction, goods in another. "If we imagine all our closed barter circuits drawn as lines from man to man, with arrowheads to show which way the goods travelled, every man [in an imaginary isolated community of workers] would have as many lines coming into him as went out."

The papers described here are published—some for the first time—in *Papers Literary, Scientific*, etc., London, 1888, 2 vols. 8vo, edited by Sidney Colvin and J. A. Ewing, with a memoir by Robert Louis Stevenson in his most charming style.   F. Y. E.

JENNINGS, RICHARD (flourished in the middle of the 19th century), of Trinity College, Cambridge, will be remembered as one of those who in Jevons's words first "clearly appreciated the nature and importance of the law of utility." In his *Elements of Political Economy*, conformably to the definition of the subject as the relation between human nature and exchangeable objects, Jennings begins with psychology and physiology. He distinguishes two kinds of commodities — *primary* and *secondary:* the former exciting nerves of common sensation, *e.g.* the sensation of warmth or cold, and that which follows the satisfaction of hunger ; the latter exciting nerves of special sensation, sight, hearing, smell, etc. —roughly corresponding to necessaries and luxuries. The difference between these classes is that "necessaries may confer their full amount of satisfaction in the absence of luxuries ; while luxuries cannot be enjoyed by those who want the necessaries of life." Another difference is that "the satisfaction which is derived from objects which affect the special senses is less dependent on quantity." Here reference is made to what is now called the LAW OF DIMINISHING UTILITY, thus formulated by Jennings. "With respect to all commodities our feelings show that the degrees of satisfaction do not proceed *pari passu* with the quantities consumed—they do not advance equally with each instalment of the commodity offered to the senses and then suddenly stop— but diminish gradually until they ultimately disappear " (p. 98). The law of increasing disutility is stated with corresponding clearness (p. 120). That its operation is more marked in the case of bodily than that of mental labour is an important observation. There is much more psychology, but of a less original character. In the second book, Jennings applies his principles to the phenomena of exchange. He anticipates that economic theories "may be expressed in figures " . . . "exhibited in the formulæ, and analysed by the different methods of algebra and fluxions." He looks also for rather drastic applications of the new political economy. Thus one of his proposals is that a considerable share of the property of proprietors dying without leaving near relations should revert to the state.

A similar vein of suggestion is found in Jennings' later work, *Social Delusions* . . . Convinced that, "in determining the incidence of taxation, the condition of women is an object worthy of attention," the author proposes to tax the employment of men in domestic service and in shops, in order to make room for women in those callings (p. 115). The proposal that we should select our statesmen by a sort of examination in the theory of value shows a certain want of humour. A similar criticism applies to much of the tirade against fallacies. The second work does not form an advance upon the first.

Natural Elements of Political Economy, 1855. —*Social Delusions concerning Wealth and Want*, 1856.

[*Athenæum*, 1856, p. 898.— *Westminster Review*, July 1856.—Jevons, *Theory of Political Economy*, ch. iii. p. 59, 2nd ed.—Cairnes, *Character and Logical Method of Political Economy*, pp. 56, 110, 224.] F. Y. E.

JENYNS, SOAME (1704-1787), poet and miscellaneous writer, sat in parliament from 1742 till 1780, and was a lord commissioner of the board of trade and plantations, from 1755, until it was merged with another department in 1782.

Jenyns' economic writings, probably owing to his official position, attracted attention at the time beyond their deserts. His views on economic questions are generally unsound, and he is not consistent ; he imputes the high price of provisions, about 1767, to the national debt, and to the increase of individual wealth, which increase he also attributes in part to the national debt. These opinions are only noteworthy inasmuch as they are an instance of the mistakes made by contemporary observers, even when well placed for observation, in recording the events which passed under their eyes. He maintained the right of the home government to tax the American colonies at will. Of his writings, which have been collected by his biographer, Cole, into four volumes (1790), those dealing with economic questions are—

Thoughts on the Causes and Consequences of the present High Price of Provisions (1767).— *The Objections to the Taxation of our American Colonies by the Legislature of Great Britain briefly considered* (1765).—*Thoughts on a Parliamentary Reform* (1784).—*Thoughts on the National Debt* (first printed in Cole's edition, 1790).

[*Biographical Memoir*, prefixed to C. N. Cole's edition of Soame Jenyns' works, 1790.—Chalmers's *Biographical Dictionary.*—R. Anderson, *Complete Collection of the Poets of Great Britain*, vol. xi. 1794, p. 983.] R. H. H.

JETONS DE PRESENCE (Fr.) are the form in which attendance fees are paid in France to directors or members of committees in public companies or societies when the functions are presumed or declared to be honorary. Some companies give a *jeton de presence*, usually ten francs, to shareholders who attend the annual meetings. The *jetons* are generally silver medals specially coined, bearing the name of the company, and which may be exchanged for their nominal value in cash. Rich directors frequently keep them to use as counters for card-playing at home.

[*Dictionnaire des Finances*, ii. 450, 1894.] T. L.

JETSAM AND FLOTSAM. See FLOTSAM AND JETSAM.

JEVONS, WILLIAM STANLEY (1835-1882), one of the greatest English economists of the 19th century, was born at Liverpool. His father, Thomas Jevons, was in the iron trade, and interested in all the new engineering schemes of his time. His mother, Mary Ann Jevons, was the eldest daughter of William Roscoe, the author of the *Life of Lorenzo de Medici*, a man of much learning and refinement. Her mind had been cultivated by constant companionship with her father and by the intellectual society which she enjoyed under his roof. She was a person of considerable poetical talent and strong religious feeling. W. S. Jevons, the ninth child of these parents,—with other relations of much education and ability,—was thus early brought under influences which assisted to develop his mind and character. His mother encouraged her children in their love of drawing and music. She "carefully fostered," W. S. Jevons wrote, "a liking for botany, giving me a small microscope and many books, which I yet have. Strange as it may seem, I now believe that botany and the natural system, by exercising discrimination of kinds, is the best of logical exercises. What I may do in logic is perhaps derived from that early attention to botany."

Early in 1846 Jevons was sent to the Mechanics' Institute High School, Liverpool, of which Dr. W. B. Hodgson, afterwards professor of political economy in Edinburgh, was then head-master. In 1850 he entered University College School, London, and in 1852 matriculated at the University of London, with honours both in chemistry and botany. Meanwhile the means of earning a livelihood had to be sought, and Professors Williamson and Graham, who had observed his great ability and power of work in the college laboratory, recommended his appointment as assayer to the new mint at Sydney. Further study in other directions had now to be checked. He studied assaying at the Paris mint, and in 1854, when not yet nineteen, sailed for Sydney. He remained five years in Australia, filling his post at the mint with skill and success. The study of meteorology attracted him strongly, and he devoted himself to it with his wonted thoroughness. His interest in later life in recording the periodicity of the "sun-spot" disturbances and the connection between these and changes in the seasons, the price of corn, and commercial crises, was doubtless quickened by these investigations. During this period, political economy also appears to have attracted his attention.

His position at Sydney was an honourable one. The income was considerable, the more creditable to him because attained at so early an age, and the more important because he was now entirely dependent on his own exertions. But an ardent desire for further opportunities of mental improvement overcame all other considerations. "Another year's regular hard study," he wrote to his sister Lucy (Mrs. John Hutton) in 1858, "especially at my increased age, will be invaluable, and its loss would be regretted to the end of my life." He returned to England in 1859, re-entered University College, took the B.A. degree 1860, the Ricardo scholarship the same year, the M.A. with a gold medal 1863. He was, 1866, appointed professor of logic and mental and moral philosophy and Cobden lecturer on political economy in the Owens College, Manchester, posts which he held till 1875, when the strain of increasing work, coupled with somewhat failing health, compelled him unwillingly to resign. In the same year, 1875, he was elected professor of political economy in University College, London, a post which he retained till 1880.

Jevons was elected Fellow of the Royal Society in 1872. He married, in 1867, Harriet Ann, third daughter of Mr. J. E. Taylor of Manchester, founder and proprietor of the *Manchester Guardian* paper. His marriage was an eminently happy one. His love for music was a constant solace. He had constructed himself a very well-toned organ for his house, and was an unusually accomplished musician.

Though reserved in character, he was a very pleasant companion and extremely instructive in conversation. One who had the advantage of knowing him, and frequently experienced the help which his powerful mind brought to the solution of any economic problem, remarked of his conversation, "It was more like talking with an early Greek philosopher, if one can realise what that would have been, than with one of our contemporaries."

Perhaps the most remarkable feature in his life was his early and unswerving conviction that he was destined to do some great work, his entire devotion of himself to preparation for it, and afterwards his unhesitating renunciation of anything, however tempting, that seemed to stand in the way of it. Thus in 1851, when he was sixteen, he writes, "I began to think that I could and ought to do more than others,"—in 1857 when twenty-two, that he has "one wish, or one *intention*, viz. to be a *powerful good* in the world,"—in 1863, when twenty-seven, and saddened by want of immediate success on his return from Sydney, he still sees a hope in his "capacity of seeing the sameness and difference of things, which if history and . . . experienced men are to be believed, is a rare and valuable kind of power." His subsequent career was the carrying out of these convictions. He could let nothing draw him aside from the endeavour to carry out his scientific career to the utmost limit of his capabilities.

While it is primarily as an economist that Jevons claims attention in the *Dictionary of Political Economy*, his researches as a logician and a student of scientific method cannot be ignored. Indeed it will be convenient to begin with an examination of the *Principles of Science*, in which Jevons sums up and applies the results of his long and severe researches in logic. He bases his system upon the generally received axioms that "whatever is is," that "a thing cannot both be and not be," and that "a thing must either be or not be." But to these he adds the principle of "the Substitution of Similars," that is to say, the axiom that whatever is true of A is true of everything that cannot be distinguished from A in the relation contemplated. Thus if B is identical with A then B may be substituted for A in any assertion that has been shown to be true of A. The next and crucial step is to bring every proposition into the form of the assertion of an identity. Thus the proposition "men are mortal" becomes in Jevons's system "man" is the same as "mortal man." Therefore if anything can be said of "man" the same can be said of "mortal man," and if "man" can be predicated of any subject, "mortal man" can be predicated of the same subject. Now whatever may be thought of the psychological principle that a proposition *is* the assertion of an identity, it is unquestionable that it logically *involves* such an identity. Jevons can therefore throw his propositions into a form which at once admits of the application of the principle of the "substitution of similars." Let us take the two propositions (1) "Cæsar" is the same as "the man Cæsar"; (2) "man" is the same as "mortal man." Now (2) enables us to substitute "mortal man" for "man" in (1), and we have "Cæsar" is the same as "the mortal man Cæsar"; or symbolically putting A for Cæsar, B for man, and C for mortal, we have (1) A is the same as AB, (2) B is the same as BC, whence by substitution A is the same as ABC. It is now possible to elaborate a system in which every proposition shall be convertible, and to found upon it a symbolical manipulation of terms, with its appropriate algebra, that constitutes an indefinite advance upon the "Barbara, Celarent, etc." of Petrus Hispanus. Having reduced deductive reasoning to a mechanical process, Jevons found no insuperable difficulty in constructing a syllogising machine; but he regarded this triumph as possessing little practical though considerable theoretical significance. From his reconstruction of deductive reasoning Jevons goes on to contend that induction is an inverse process entirely dependent upon the laws of deduction for its validity. The next step is to show that mathematics is but a special application of logic, and that the mathematical equation is subject to precisely the same laws as the logical identity, the apparent difference being due to the universal presence in the equation of certain limiting conditions which are not assumed unless expressly stated in the logical identity. The doctrine of chances is now developed in immediate dependence upon the law of "substitution of similars"; for the root principle of the doctrine of chances is that inasmuch as belief ought to depend upon the distribution of our knowledge and ignorance, therefore we should believe the same about one event as we believe about another, our knowledge or ignorance of which is the same. The doctrine of chances in its turn is made the basis of the whole system of scientific investigation and induction, in the development of which Jevons's genius finds a thoroughly congenial field, and in which the scope of his scientific reading becomes manifest.

We will pass from this treatise on method to a collection of writings on currency and finance, which forms an almost ideal application of the "principles of science" to a group of problems of equal complexity and importance. The volume contains papers written at every period of Jevons's literary life, and, as Professor Foxwell remarks in his preface, it is not till they are read together that the impressive unity of conception, firmness of grasp, and tenacity of scientific purpose which they reveal can be adequately felt. With equal patience and sagacity Jevons separates out the sæcular from the periodic variations in the phenomena of price, discount, pressure on reserves, frequency of bankruptcies, and so forth. His elaborate logarithmic and other tabulations are models of sound method and laborious research illuminated by theory, not likely soon to be superseded. His brilliant attempt to bring the periodicity of commercial fluctuations into connection with that great physical period which is indicated, for instance, by the changes in the aspect of the sun-spots and the electrical condition of the earth, if not conclusively successful, is suggestive of the highest range of physico-economic law which we are ever likely to attain. From his examination of the actual phenomena of the currency, Jevons proceeds to the discussion of questions of monetary policy, both domestic and international. He deals with such questions as the possibility of an international coinage, the principles of note-issue, the best means of maintaining the standard weight of coins, and of securing (by the institution of a compound unit of value) an assured stability in the standard of deferred payments. On the now burning question of bimetallism, Jevons's position, though perfectly unequivocal, is almost certain to be misunderstood by those who know it only at second hand. He fully recognises the serious nature of the evils deplored by bimetallists, and the theoretical possibility of maintaining a fixed ratio between gold and silver by international agreement; but the precarious nature of such an agreement, and the danger of sudden disturbance to existing obligations, appeared to him to be fatal objections. Thus bimetallists and monometallists alike appeal, with perfect sincerity and justice, to the authority of Jevons at one point or another of the argument, and it may be confidently asserted that when the controversy is waged within the lines laid down by Jevons, the era of scientific discussion will have definitely begun, and a decision on scientific grounds will not be far distant.

In addition to his studies in finance, Jevons treated a great variety of questions relating to state control and management. On the broad principle of state socialism and individualism Jevons was without prejudices. His determining principle was purely Benthamite. "Will a measure increase the sum of happiness?" was the only question which he would admit as ultimately relevant. But the evidence upon which we must rely for an answer is often ambiguous, always in large part indirect, and generally conjectural. Hence the necessity of extreme caution in arriving at conclusions, together with a considerable degree of boldness in hazarding experiments. Our only guides are experience and analogy; and wherever experience seems to contradict analogy, as will often be the case, our rule must be to analyse more carefully and so correct the analogy, instead of ignoring or denying the experience. Following these principles, Jevons collected a vast mass of information on social questions, and analysed it so scrupulously that his work is almost equally valuable when experience has confirmed and when it has contradicted his anticipations. In examining questions of state action, Jevons very carefully distinguishes between state *control* of private enterprise and state *management* of enterprise. With reference to the former, we can only say that there is a presumption against interference, in so far as unimpeded freedom must be held to be a source of happiness, and therefore any restriction of freedom an evil. But this presumption must yield in innumerable instances to the demonstrated fact that greater happiness has resulted from control. A conspicuous instance is furnished by the FACTORY ACTS, and Jevons would gradually extend their principle so as to prohibit altogether the employment of child-bearing women in factories. The conditions under which state management, as distinct from state control, is likely to be advantageous, were submitted by Jevons to a rigorous analysis, which ought to be the starting-point of all discussions of the subject. The conditions he held to be favourable to state management are as follows : (1) where numberless wide-spread operations can only be efficiently connected, united, and co-ordinated in a single all-extensive government system ; (2) where the operations possess an invariable routine-like character ; (3) where they are performed under the public eye or for the service of individuals who will immediately detect and expose any failure or laxity ; (4) where there is but little capital expenditure, so that each year's revenue and expense account shall represent with sufficient accuracy the real commercial conditions of the department. An exhaustive examination of the facts, with reference to these criteria, led Jevons to pronounce in favour of the state management of telegraphs and telephones, and the establishment of a parcel post, none of them accomplished facts when he wrote ; but against the state management of railways, which however should be strictly controlled in the interests of the community. It may be mentioned that Jevons had a strong dislike and suspicion of trade unions, based on grounds of economic theory. But he looked for their gradual transformation into co-operative societies, and would leave them absolutely free. On similar grounds he placed small hope in methods of arbitration and conciliation, trusting rather to the free play of competition. It should be noticed in connection with labour questions that Jevons never lost sight of the vital distinction, so generally overlooked, between the horizontal cleavage of the industrial community into various grades of skilled and unskilled labour, managers, capitalists, landowners, and so forth, and the vertical cleavage into the agri-

cultural interest, the coal interest, the iron interest, etc. Through neglect of this distinction a class movement and a trade movement may easily be confounded. Jevons had a profound faith in the future of industrial partnerships—a faith that survived rude shocks, for he frankly owned that English experience was against him, and that French experience is always unsafe ground for reasoning by analogy to England.

The mass of work already reviewed is great ; but we have still to notice the treatise by which Jevons's place in the history of economic theory will ultimately be determined. In his *Theory of Political Economy* he attempts nothing less than the reconstruction of the science of economics as the calculus of human satisfactions. Production derives its whole significance from consumption ; that is to say, from the satisfactions to which it ministers ; and the significance of any special unit of product is due to the increment of satisfaction which it is capable of producing. Hence the scale of equivalence of any two commodities is determined by the scale of equivalence of the increments of satisfaction which they are capable of producing. Exchange value then is determined by incremental efficiency as a producer of satisfaction. But this incremental significance is not absolutely fixed. It depends on the amount of the commodity already possessed or enjoyed by the individual or the community whose satisfaction we are considering. Thus we obtain the formula that if $F(x)$ represents the whole significance, or value in use, of a commodity to its possessor, then $F'(x)$ will represent the significance of an increment of it to him, or in other words, will be the gauge of its exchange value (see DEGREE OF UTILITY and FINAL DEGREE OF UTILITY). Should the incremental efficiency, and so the exchange value of the product of a given combination of productive efforts be greater when such efforts are turned into one channel than when they are turned into another, this fact will determine the course they will actually take. The more significant product will therefore be increased in quantity, and the less significant decreased. Hence the incremental significance of the former will decline, and that of the latter will rise, until there is equilibrium. There will now be equivalence between the relative expenditures of productive effort and the relative values of the product ; though it will not be the cost of production that has determined the value of the products, but the (anticipated) value of the products that has determined the direction of productive effort. These principles, together with the "law of indifference"—in reality a new application of the "substitution of similars"—enable Jevons to throw the theory of exchange into the form of systems of equations. From this we must inevitably proceed to the theory of distribution.

Value had long been recognised as the cause and not the effect of rent. Jevons declared it to be the cause and not the effect of wages also. Hence the theory of distribution must be built up afresh, taking as the starting-point the significance of the product to the consumer. Jevons has left much for his followers to do in working out this theory. The form of his equations is open to just criticism. He seems hardly to have realised the full consequences of his method. But none the less his *Theory of Political Economy* has succeeded in its aim. When all its implications have been worked out the science will be reconstituted. On the questions of priority and originality, cp. arts. on COURNOT; GOSSEN; and the works of Walras and Menger.

In addition to the above, Jevons wrote a considerable number of technical and miscellaneous essays on scientific and social subjects, an industrial treatise, *The Coal Question*, dealing with the possible exhaustion of our coal mines, which had a powerful influence in initiating the serious attempt to pay off the national debt, and a number of more or less elementary and popular books on logic, monetary science, problems of state management and control, and political economy.

In reviewing the whole work of this bold and patient thinker, it is impossible not to regard his death,—in the plenitude of his powers, and in the midst of works which promised to equal anything he had yet done in significance,—as one of the heaviest losses that science has suffered in our generation.

A full bibliography of Jevons's works appears in Appendix B to his *Letters and Journal*, 1886, edited by his wife, which contains a classified list of his principal works, with the dates of their first issue or collection. *Primer of Logic*, 1876. — *Elementary Lessons in Logic*, 1870. — *Pure Logic and other Minor Works* (collected), 1890. — *Principles of Science*, 2 vols., 1874.— *Studies in Deductive Logic*, 1880. — *The Coal Question*, 1865. — *The State in Relation to Labour*, 1882.—*Methods of Social Reform* (collected), 1883.—*Money*, 1875.—*Investigations in Currency and Finance* (collected), 1884.—*Primer of Political Economy*, 1876.—*Theory of Political Economy*, 1871.—*Principles of Economics*, a fragment.—"Fall in Gold," 1863, in *Investigations*, —Art. on "Cantillon."—*Contemp. Review*, Jan. 1881.—Art. on "Bimetallism," *Contemp. Review*, May 1881.   P. H. W.

JEWS, ECONOMIC POSITION AND INFLUENCE OF, IN ENGLAND. The Jews lived in mediæval England for rather more than two hundred years, from shortly after the Norman conquest till 1290. During the whole of that time they were without any share in the national or municipal life of the country ; and, as far as our knowledge goes, no large section of them followed, except for the sixteen years from 1274 to 1290. any occupation except that of dealers in money. But their relations to the king, and to the various orders of the nation, underwent considerable changes during their residence, and their history is divided into three clearly-defined periods.

I. (From the Conquest to 1194.) The first body of Jews came to England from Rouen shortly after the Conquest, at the invitation, it is said, of William the Conqueror. They were no doubt the first in a position of dependence on the royal favour and protection, for there was no feudal or customary law to which they could appeal. From William Rufus, Henry I., Stephen, and Henry II., they met with support and encouragement. By the two Henrys especially they were upheld in the possession of a body of privileges which allowed them to go where they pleased throughout England, to buy or receive in pledge whatever was brought to them, except things of the church, to settle in any town where they chose, free alike from the payment of local tolls and taxes, and from the jurisdiction of the local courts, and finally, to hold land in pledge or fee. They enjoyed the royal favour because they helped to fill the royal exchequer. The earliest extant pipe roll contains entries of fines and amercements of the Jews, and of payments rendered by them to the king in return for help received from him in the recovery of money that they had lent on interest. We have very little information as to the amount of their annual contribution to the exchequer, during the earlier part of this period ; but in the latter half of the 12th century, when the royal income was about £35,000, the Jews cannot have paid less than £3000 a year. And besides this, they helped the king by making advances to him, to be repaid when the collection of the FARM of the counties should provide him with a fresh stock of ready money.

The wealth that enabled them to provide so considerable a proportion of the royal income, was drawn from the proceeds of the business that they carried on, men and women alike, singly and in firms, as the only great money-lenders in the kingdom. Barons who were impoverished by war, crusading, litigation, or extravagance, and religious houses which had suffered from bad management, the claims of hospitality, or the expense of new buildings, had no way of raising ready money except by pledging to the Jews some of their lands or other possessions. Hence they spread throughout the country, and their communities became large, rich, and numerous. They were recognised as being the "royal usurers," and, as such, entitled to take up their position in towns which might otherwise have been closed to them. For, although they had friendly relations with some Christians, they were generally regarded with superstitious dislike, and on various occasions the charge of murdering or mutilating Christian children was brought against them, and widely believed to be true. But there was no great demonstration of the general dislike in which they were held till 1189. In that and the following years fierce popular attacks were made on them in London, York, Colchester, Norwich, Lynn, Stamford, Bury St. Edmunds, and Lincoln. The loss to the royal exchequer that ensued, and the evident possibility of a recurrence of the massacre, suggested to Richard I. the necessity of still further securing the safety of the Jews, and of the revenue that they yielded. He therefore introduced, in place of the old informal protection, a thorough organisation of the Jewry as a branch of the royal administration. The Jews were henceforth bound to register all their debts, pledges, mortgages, lands, houses, and rents ; and were allowed to enter into no contracts, except in certain towns, which were selected by the king for the purpose, and in each of which was maintained a staff of lawyers, registrars, and custodians, for the purpose of witnessing and enrolling every bond to which a Jew was a party, and of preserving in sealed chests an indented portion or "chirograph" of each. Moreover, special justices or proctors were appointed to settle all disputes between Jews and Christians.

II. (From 1194 to 1274.) Richard's organisation of the Jewry was introduced in 1194, and from that year to the end of their residence in England, the Jews occupied the position of complete subordination to the king, which it marked out for them. Their dependence on the king, and on him alone for protection, their absolute want of all legal rights to life or property, and the obligation imposed on them of rendering to the royal officers an account of all their possessions, and of transacting all their business under supervision, made it impossible for them to escape any burden that they might be called on to bear. And their masters showed them little mercy. Sometimes the king made a free grant to a favoured subject of land on which a Jewish mortgagee had claims, sometimes he cancelled the obligation of a Christian debtor to a Jewish creditor. But the royal attacks were often made on a much larger scale. John, in 1210, plundered the Jews, and reduced them to such a state of need that "they prowled about the city like dogs" (*Chronicles of Lanercost*, p. 7). Henry III. exacted from them a third of their property in 1230, another third in 1239, 20,000 marks in 1241, 60,000 marks in 1246, and great sums, of which the amount is not stated, in 1243, 1244, 1250, 1252, 1254, and 1255. So unsparing were the royal demands that in 1210 many of the Jews left the country, and in 1254, and again in 1255, their chief representatives entreated Henry III. to give the whole community permission to do so. But the request was refused.

It was during the reign of John and the first forty years of the reign of Henry III. that the Jews yielded the greatest revenue to the royal treasury. It has been calculated that the annual average tallage alone amounted at one time in the 13th century to £5000 (*Papers of the Anglo-Jewish Historical Exhibition*, p. 195) ; and, besides this, their escheats, fines, amercements, reliefs, and fees of all kind must have made up a large sum.

Nevertheless, profitable as they were, the royal power could neither protect them completely against plunder, nor maintain them in possession of all the unpopular privileges that made them rich. Their right of settling wherever they wished in England was gradually taken from them, owing no doubt to the dislike with which, on account of their immunity from local jurisdiction and taxation, their foreign origin, their religion, and their occupation, they were regarded by the towns. Special decrees of expulsion were obtained against them by Bury St. Edmunds, Leicester, Newcastle, Wycombe, Southampton, Berkhampstead, Newbury, and Derby, at various times between 1190 and 1263 ; and in 1245 a general order was issued by the king that henceforward no Jew was, except with the royal permission, to settle in a town where Jews had not formerly been in the habit of dwelling. This restriction must have seriously affected their power of acquiring the wealth that they needed to meet the royal demands. And they were exposed also to more direct attack in the towns. The Jewry of London was plundered by a riotous crowd in 1204, that of Norwich in 1234, and those of Oxford and Bristol later on.

Far more serious, however, than the enmity of the towns was that of the barons. In the constitutional struggle that preceded the civil war, the whole baronial party saw its efforts after reform thwarted because the king, when supplies were refused, could fall back on the Jewry ; and the Great Council attempted, apparently with little effect, to secure a share in the management of the Jewish revenue. But the lesser barons had, in addition, personal grievances of their own to avenge. Many of them had had to mortgage to the Jews lands which had then passed by sale into the possession either of greater barons (*Petition of the Barons*, § 25, in Stubb's *Select Charters*, etc., pp. 385-386), or of religious bodies (cp. Burton, *Chronica Monasterii de Melsa*, Rolls series, *passim*), and were thus irretrievably lost to their former owners. And the same thing might happen to any land that was pledged to a Jew. Hence, during the civil war, the barons lost no opportunity of attacking the Jewries and destroying the deeds in which debts were recorded. Between 1262 and 1268, the Jewries of London, Worcester, Cambridge, Winchester, Canterbury, Exeter, Northampton, and Lincoln were sacked ; some by De Montfort, some by his sons and adherents, some by the freebooters who after his death represented his party.

On the restoration of tranquillity, the king's son, Edward, the patron of the cause of the "knights bachelors," could not but take up the work of restoring to its former knightly holders such of the land of England as had passed into the possession of the Jews. An attempt of this kind, indeed, was in thorough harmony with Edward's lifelong policy of trying to rescue the feudal organisation from the confusion into which it had begun to fall, in consequence of the transference of land from holders who could render military service to such as, like religious corporations and Jews, were unable to do so. Henry III. had already safeguarded the royal estates by forbidding the tenants on them to pledge their land to the Jews (*Norfolk Antiquarian Miscellany*, i. 328); but on other estates there was no legal check on such alienation. Jews could be "seised" of lands, and some of them were recognised holders of portions of knights' fees. Edward determined to defend the land of all feudal holders in the same way as the royal demesne was defended. The loss that would be caused to the royal income by the imposition of the necessary restrictions on Jewish transactions was less serious now than it would have been earlier in the reign, for the exactions of Henry III. and the attacks of the barons had impoverished the Jews ; and it was compensated by a political gain, since a policy of the kind accorded with the prejudices of the knightly class at the same time as it protected the feudal organisation to the king's advantage. The church also, like the baronage, had its lands encumbered with obligations to the Jews, and was eager to welcome restrictive measures. The consequence of this combination of forces was that, in 1269, a statute was passed enacting that from that time forth no land should be pledged to a Jew as security for the repayment of money, and cancelling some of the agreements to that effect that had already been entered into ; and in 1270 it was followed by a second statute which made it unlawful for Jews to acquire English land, not only by way of pledge, but even by purchase, and which ordered that all land in the possession of Jews was to be restored to its original Christian owners.

These measures made Jewish usury on a large scale practically impossible in the future ; for they forbade Jews to remain in possession of the only widely distributed commodity that could serve as a security for advances. Four years later, an even more severe measure to the same effect was called forth by the action of the church. In 1274, the council of Lyons, in accordance with the doctrine of the sinfulness of usury that had been held by Christian teachers since the time of the early fathers (see AQUINAS), ordained that communities, corpora-

tions, and individuals should no longer permit foreign usurers to live on their lands. Edward, in obedience to the decree, issued a statute ordering that henceforth no Jew should practise usury in England, and that all who had pledges deposited with them should, after receiving repayment of the money that had been advanced on them, return them to their owners before the following Easter. Permission was granted to the Jews to practise merchandise or live by their labour ; but they were to be confined henceforth to the king's towns and were not to be in scot or lot with their fellow-inhabitants, but were to be tallaged by the king separately as his serfs.

III. (1274-90.) The conditions imposed on the Jews by Edward's statute made it impossible for any great number of them to enter on a new calling ; since the prohibition which forbade them to be in scot and lot with the other inhabitants of the towns where they lived excluded them from citizenship, and therefore in most cases from membership of the gild-merchant and of such craft-gilds as were in existence at the time. Thus it was impossible for them, except under crushing disadvantages, to carry on a trade or handicraft in a town (see CORPORATIONS OF ARTS AND TRADES ; GILDS). If they were to follow any mercantile pursuit at all, their choice was limited to those trades for which membership of a municipal or trade organisation was not necessary. The only such pursuit to which the energies and capital of a large number of men could be suddenly transferred was the wholesale trade in corn, wool, and other agricultural produce, which was carried on by capitalists who seem to have been in the habit of making advances of money to the producer as prepayment for the yield of a yet ungrown harvest. Jews had long had some slight share in trade of this kind ; and many of them now took to it on the publication of Edward's statute. But it was open only to those who had command of a fair amount of capital available for speedy transference. There were many English Jews of humble means, of whom, when usury was still allowed, some had begun to keep pawnshops, while others had lent money in small sums to meet the demand caused by the growing tendency towards the commutation of services and rents in kind for payments of money ; and these had no resource except to become household servants and day-labourers, if they could find employers, or else to carry on in secret their former dealings. Thus the severe conditions of Edward's statute led to dishonesty; some Jews continued to practise usury, and others were convicted of clipping the coin. Edward attempted to mitigate the difficulties that his first measure had caused, by issuing an amended statute which allowed usury in a modified form. But the attempt never had a fair trial. The church, alarmed at the influence that the Jewish faith and rites exercised on Christian heretics, and on conforming Catholics as well, had attempted during the 13th century to restrict the intercourse between believers and Jews ; and in 1286, Honorius IV., dissatisfied with the efforts made by the English bishops to enforce the canonical decrees on the subject, issued a special bull to the Archbishops of Canterbury and York and their suffragans, in which he begged them with the greatest urgency to use every possible means by which the intercourse might be lessened (Baronii, *Annales Ecclesiastici*, sub anno). If such advice was to be carried out, it was impossible for the Jews to work their way into trades and handicrafts ; and usury being now forbidden, the bull was therefore practically an appeal for the expulsion of the Jews. A king of Edward's piety could not disregard the wishes of the pope.

But there were two causes which rendered it now an easy sacrifice for a king of England to give up the Jews. First, they had lost immensely in wealth during the period from the outbreak of the civil war till 1290. Their tallage alone at one period of the 13th century had, as has been said above, amounted to £5000 annually ; but in 1271, the annual value of the Jewry was estimated by the king at only 2000 marks (Rymer, *Fœdera*, i. 489) ; and the records of the reign of Edward I., show that in some years the contribution of the Jews was only a few hundred pounds (Public Record Office, *Exchequer of Receipt, Jews' Rolls*). Secondly, there had grown up in their place a new set of royally - favoured money - lenders, the Italian merchants, who were the greatest financial and commercial power in Europe, and whose vast resources were always at Edward's service in time of need.

Edward therefore could yield speedy obedience to the desire of the pope. He was in Gascony when the bull reached England, but before his return he expelled the Jews of the province ; and in 1290, a year after his return, he issued a decree, ordering all Jews under pain of death to leave England. The whole community, numbering 16,000, departed from the country in the same year. They were allowed to take away their movable property with them, but their debts and houses fell into the hands of the king.

For two centuries the decree forbidding Jews to live in England was, in all probability, completely effective. The one known fact to the contrary is, that in 1410, a French Jew, a physician, was allowed to come to England, to remain here for two years, and during that time to practise his profession in any part of the realm (Rymer's *Fœdera*, 2nd ed., viii. 667). But in 1492, when the great expulsion of the Jews of Spain took place, some of the refugees sought a home in England. They were not money-lenders, like the mediæval Jews who had been expelled from England, but merchants engaged in foreign trade. The little community thus founded has continued to exist and to grow till the present day. For two centuries it was not recognised by the law, but in 1656, a commission appointed by Cromwell to consider the legality of the presence of Jews in England, reported that "the Jews deserving it may be admitted into this nation to trade and traffic and dwell amongst us as Providence shall give occasion." From that time, the Jews were recognised as English subjects, not distinguished in the eyes of the law from other Englishmen, except by certain political and other disabilities, nearly all of which attached equally to Roman Catholics, and have now been removed. Perhaps the only one remaining is their ineligibility to the office of Lord Chancellor.

[An admirable and almost complete bibliography of the subject is given by J. Jacobs and L. Woolf, *Bibliotheca Anglo - Judaica*, London, 1888, 8vo, pp. xiii-xix, and 1-35. The most comprehensive histories and collections of documents are :—J. Jacobs, *The Jews of Angevin England*, London, 1893.—S. Goldschmidt, *Geschichte der Juden in England, XI. und XII. Jahrhundert*, Berlin, 1886.—D. B. Tovey, *Anglia Judaica*, Oxford, 1738.—W. Prynne, *A Short Demurrer against the Jews' long-discontinued Remitter into England*, London, 1656.—A Gentleman of Lincoln's Inn (P. Carteret Webb), *The Question whether a Jew, born within the British Dominions, was before the making the late Act of Parliament, a Person capable by Law to purchase and hold Lands to him and his Heirs, fully stated and considered*. London, 1753. — J. E. Blunt, *History of the Establishment and Residence of the Jews in England*, London, 1830. See also *Transactions of the Jewish Historical Society of England*, 1895.— *Papers read at the Anglo-Jewish Historical Exhibition*, 1888.—Articles by B. L. Abrahams, on the expulsion of the Jews from England, in *Jewish Quarterly Review*, vol. vii., Nos. 25, 26, 27.]

B. L. A.

JEWS, EXCHEQUER OF THE. It has been mentioned in the preceding article that in 1194 there were appointed by Richard I. special officers for the affairs of the Jews, viz.—local staffs of clerks and registrars to supervise Jewish business in those towns where it was allowed to be transacted, and to keep counterparts of Jewish bonds, and in addition proctors or judges to deal with cases in which Jews were concerned. The local officers remained, during the residence of the Jews in England, in the position to which they were originally appointed. But the proctors acquired powers and duties which made them, like the barons of the exchequer, the heads of a judicial and administrative system. In the 13th century, they were known no longer as "proctors," but sometimes as "Justiciars deputed to the charge of the Jews" (*Justiciarii ad custodiam Judæorum assignati*), sometimes as "guardians of the Jews" (*custodes Judæorum*);

sometimes, with reference to the fact that they presided over the exchequer chamber set apart for Jewish revenue and accounts, as "Justiciars of the Exchequer of the Jewry" (*Justiciarii ad Scaccarium Judaismi*).

In their judicial capacity they tried nearly all the Jews that were charged with any offence for which a non-Jew would have had to appear before one of the king's ordinary justices; they also decided civil suits between Jew and Jew, and between Jew and Christian. At the king's order they could set aside, or modify, contracts to which Jews were parties. But arbitrary action of this kind was exceptional; as a rule they administered the special system of law that had grown up, partly from the recognition of Jewish custom, and partly from the action of kings who issued charters, writs, and statutes defining the duties, position, and privileges of Jews. The only other officers who had jurisdiction over Jews in England were the constables of certain royal castles, the chancellor of the university of Oxford, and the judges who were sometimes exceptionally appointed to try heinous charges such as those of child murder and of clipping the coin.

In their fiscal capacity the justices of the Jews were the responsible custodians of the Exchequer Chamber of the Jews (*Scaccarium Judaismi*), its great seal, its chests, and its accounts. They had to see that all the claims which the king had against Jews, or which arose out of transactions in which Jews were concerned, should be presented and enforced. For this purpose they provided the sheriff of each county with *extractæ*, or lists of the sums which he was expected to collect as Jewish revenue (*de summonitione scaccarii judaismi*): and, in order that they might have at their disposal the necessary information, they kept records of the king's claims on Jews and their debtors; they heard declarations concerning, and gave their sanction to, changes which were to take place in the ownership of Jewish property, as for example when a Jew having received payment of a debt, gave up his claim on the debtor; they made arrangements for the management and transference of property that came into the king's hands on account of Jewish claims. But, important as were their duties in connection with the Jewish revenue, they did not receive any money except from the barons of the exchequer. The sheriffs, or any other officers who might on special occasions be appointed to make collections from the Jews paid in their money to the great exchequer; thence, except when it went direct to the king's wardrobe, it was transferred to the Exchequer of the Jews; and the justices of the Jews were responsible for having it ready for use by the king when he needed it. As it was collected for the most part in silver, they were sometimes ordered to exchange it for gold, so that it might be in a form more convenient for the king's use. They had to present periodically to the barons of the exchequer an account of their receipts and disbursements.

Nor were their functions wholly judicial and fiscal. Besides interpreting as judges the special acts relating to the Jews, they were responsible as executive officers for their carrying out. At various times they were ordered to see that regulative and restrictive enactments issued by Henry III. and Edward I. were duly observed; they kept lists of all foreign Jews who arrived in England, and they and the king alone had the power to allow a Jew to change his residence from one town to another. In order that they might be able to discharge their executive functions, they were invested with a general authority over the king's "bailiffs and faithful subjects" which enabled them on the one hand to order the seizure of the person, family, and goods of any Jew who failed to pay what he owed the king, and on the other hand to transfer to a Jew the lands pledged as security by a defaulting debtor.

Their status was that of officers of the exchequer, subordinate to the treasurer and barons, by whom they were inducted into office. Thus they enjoyed all the privileges and dignity that belonged to those who were *e gremio scaccarii*: and on the other hand, the barons could, as superior officers, overrule their proceedings, punish them, suspend or expel them from office, and discharge any of their duties. Thus we find the barons conducting scrutinies of the chests containing the deeds of the Jews, taking part in the assessment and enforcement of their tallage, sanctioning the release of their debtors, deciding their disputes, and giving directions for the apportionment of their estates; although all these duties naturally belonged to the justices appointed especially for Jewish affairs. This imperfect distribution of duties is not surprising in a branch of the administration which, while it lasted, was dependent to an exceptional degree on the will of the sovereign, and which ceased to exist before it could, like other branches of the administration, be reorganised by the genius of Edward I.

It remains to be added that the justices of the Jews appear to have varied in number at different times from two to five, and were, in the 13th century at any rate, without exception Christians; whereas their subordinate staff, made up of clerks, escheators, bailiffs, presbyter, and keepers of records, regularly included both Jews and Christians. (See KING'S CATTLE.)

[W. Prynne, *A short Demurrer against the Jews' long-discontinued Remitter into England*, London, 1656.—T. Madox, *The History, and Antiquities of the Exchequer of the Kings of England*, ch. vii.— *Papers read at the Anglo-Jewish Historical Exhibition*, London, 1888, pp. 136-230.—J. Jacobs, *Jews of Angevin England*, 1893.] B. L. A.

JEWS, Houses for Converted. During the residence of the Jews in England before 1290, three institutions were founded, at the royal expense, for the reception, maintenance, and education of converts from Judaism to Christianity. The first, founded by Henry II., was at Bristol ; the second, founded by Henry III. in 1232, was in New Street, London, at the southern end of the present Chancery Lane ; the third, founded by the same king, probably somewhat later in his reign, was at Oxford. No doubt the two kings were both impelled by the same feeling to found these houses, viz. by the hope that their obedience to the teaching of the church, which bade all Christians help in the conversion of the Jews, would be regarded by the spiritual power as a set-off against the fact that they encouraged Jews to dwell in their kingdom, and shared in the profits of their usury.

Concerning the Houses at Oxford and Bristol, we have no information except as to the authorities which were responsible for their management, the one at Oxford being, as may be conjectured with absolute confidence, under the direction of the Dominican Friars, and the one at Bristol being, as we know from documentary evidence, under the joint direction of the Fraternity of Calenders, the mayor of the town, and the monastery of St. Augustine.

On the other hand the official documents relating to the *Domus Conversorum* of London are numerous, and supply us with information concerning its history over a period which begins with its foundation and does not end till more than three centuries after the expulsion of the Jews from England by Edward I.

At the time of the foundation of the House in 1232, Henry III. made lavish provision for its support. He gave the ground on which it was built, he bore the expenses of building, and made an annual grant of 700 marks from the exchequer as a provision for its officers and inmates until some special source of revenue should have been set aside for the purpose. Three years later he granted to the House, no doubt in substitution for the annual payment from the exchequer, certain lands and tenements in London, and also such other property in London as should from time to time be escheated. His intention was, according to the account of his contemporary Matthew Paris, that the life of the inmates should resemble that of members of a religious order. The buildings were planned so as to give accommodation similar to that of a monastery ; and the converts were to live according to a "rule," a word that was often used to describe the ordinances of a monastic order, and were to regard the *Domus* as a lifelong home where they might dwell without the need of servile labour or the practice of usury, and might study the Christian law under competent teachers.

The attempt to maintain the religious character of the house was kept up during the pre-expulsion period. There were always a clerical warden, and two or more resident clerics besides, who were charged with the duty of instructing the inmates and celebrating religious services on their behalf. Indeed, Edward I., in his endeavour to encourage the converts in the study and practice of Christianity, went so far as to command that the warden should in the appointment of chaplains, give the preference to such converted Jews as should show themselves to be fit for the post.

The supply of money for the support of the house was less constant, and was affected by the fluctuations in the king's Jewish revenue. Throughout the reign of Henry III. the early endowments were undisturbed and provided a sufficient income. But Edward I., who was heavily in debt at his accession, seems to have resumed possession of the lands and houses which his father had set aside for the support of the converts. In 1280, however, he granted them, in addition to an annual payment from the exchequer, the deodand, the yield of the poll-tax of 3d. a head levied on the Jews, a half of the property of any Jew who should become converted to Christianity, and all the property belonging to Jews that, on account of the misdoings of its owners, or for any other reason, should fall into the king's hands. All these sources yielded, as we know from the still extant accounts rendered by the keeper of the house from 1280 to 1286, an average income of only £108, and did not rise in any year higher than £150. Even this small amount was not to be depended on, as the annual grant of 80 marks from the exchequer was, in 1285, reduced to 40 marks, and was in some years withheld altogether. In 1290 the converts presented a petition bitterly complaining of their poverty, and Edward, into whose hands some Jewish property had fallen at the expulsion, answered the petition in 1292 by promising a grant from the exchequer to begin at £202 : 0 : 4 yearly, and to be reduced, whenever any convert then in the house should die, by the amount of the saving that would thus be effected. The greater part of the grant was spent in the payment of the allowance made to the converts, each of the forty-four men receiving tenpence weekly, and each of the fifty-three women eightpence. The rest of the money went to pay the salaries of the warden, chaplains, and clerk, and the cost of repairs of the building. By 1308 the inmates were reduced to seventeen men and seventeen women, and the annual grant to £120. The exchequer still neglected to issue the money regularly, and the converts frequently complained that their pay was years in arrears and that they were half-starved. Nevertheless new inmates, foreigners of course, entered the house from time to time, the latest date at which their presence can be traced being 1610.

The office of warden of the House, which was annexed by Edward III. to that of keeper of the rolls, was, down to the time of Lord Lyndhurst, filled by the masters of the rolls who lived, by virtue of their position, in the house that was built on the site of the original *Domus*.

[The printed matter that has been consulted for the purpose of the above article is contained in Rymer's *Fœdera.—The Rolls of Parliament.*— Madox's *History of the Exchequer.—Calendar of Patent Rolls from 1281 to 1292.*—Devon's *Issues of the Exchequer* (Record Commission).—Matthew Paris, *Chronica Majora.*—Toulmin Smith, *English Gilds.*—Anthony Wood, *History and Antiquities of Oxford.*—W. J. Hardy, in *Leisure Hour* for November 1892, on "A bit of old London." In addition, there have been used the Manuscript Calendar, in the possession of the Public Record Office, describing the documents concerning the *Domus Conversorum* that are preserved there, and the accounts of the *Domus* from the eighth to the fifteenth years of Edward I., which are in the Public Record Office and belong to the series "Q. R. Exchequer, Jews." See also *Bibliotheca Anglo-Judaica* (by J. Jacobs and L. Wolf) published in connection with the Anglo-Jewish Historical Exhibition.]   B. L. A.

JOBARD, JEAN BAPTISTE AMBROISE-MARCELIN (1792-1861). A Frenchman by birth, he was sent as surveyor in the Netherlands during the French dominion, and was naturalised after the events of 1815. He soon afterwards started a large lithographic establishment in Brussels, which was ruined by the revolution of 1830, then took to journalism, and was appointed in 1841 director of the Belgian *Musée de l'Industrie*. In this capacity he started the *Bulletin* of the *Musée*.

Jobard had always been passionately interested in technology, social reform, and patents and copyright. Being himself an inventor and a strenuous upholder of the maintenance of copyright, he published, in order to defend his views, besides numerous pamphlets on this question, his *Nouvelle Économie Sociale ou Monautopole industriel, artistique, commercial, et littéraire*, Paris, 1844; and later on his *Organon de la Propriété Intellectuelle*, Paris and Brussels, 1851. This gives the substance of the former work in a condensed form.

His claim in favour of unlimited copyright was criticised by M. Coquelin in the old *Dictionnaire d'Économie Politique*, vol. i., article *Brevets d'Invention*, but has been upheld since by M. de Molinari in the *Journal des Économistes*, xxx., p. 177. He also wrote a *Rapport sur l'Exposition de l'Industrie française en 1839* (2 vols., Brussels and Paris, 1841-42); several *Voyages Industriels* through different countries; and in 1849 a notice on *Brevets de Priorité* (patents for priority), written with the assistance of leading Belgian manufacturers.

[*Biographie Nationale de Belgique*, vol. x. pp. 494-499.]   E. Ca.

JOBBER. On the stock exchange a jobber was originally regarded as a kind of professional speculator, but, by degrees, the term has come to be applied to the professional dealers who stand on the stock exchange and "make a market" for the special securities to which they give attention. The verb "to job" probably proceeded originally from the practice by speculators of buying small quantities or "jobbets" of stock or shares. The national debt would be too large a morsel for anybody to buy or sell, but it is within the powers of any capitalist to job to a small extent in consols. For a description of the jobber in his later phase we may refer back to the heading DEALER.   A. E.

JOE (see JOHANNES), was a nickname derived from *Johannes*, but applied in the West Indies and American colonies throughout the 18th century to the *Double Johannes* or *Dobra*. A "broad joe" was of course a perfect dobra, as opposed to the clipped and sweated specimens which rapidly became common.   C. A. H.

JOHANNES, familiarly spelt *Joannese* by English contemporaries, was the Portuguese gold coin which was first minted in 1722 to take the place of the MOIDORE series of coins. It took its name from the reigning king, John V. It represented 6400 reis or a half-dobra, and in weight half a Portuguese *onça* of gold of twenty-two carats fine.

Its interest to the English is due to the prominent position which it occupied down to 1800 in the currency systems of the West Indian colonies, then the most important of our possessions. But there and in America, by a very natural error, the coin was known as the "half-joe," and the term "joe" was reserved for the full dobra—a coin rather on a par with the doubloon of Spain. The uniform fineness which led to the "joe's" rapid popularity, also encouraged the sweating and clipping of which they were the victims, as well as a considerable manufacture of counterfeit "joes" in Birmingham about the end of the last century. In 1821 a change was made in their value, and in 1835 they were displaced in Portugal, the loss of Brazil having affected the demand for Portuguese gold.

The value of the joannese in English money, in 1831, is given as 35s. 11·98d., and that of the half-joannese (which is not the half-joe, as above explained) at 17s. 11·56d. [Kelly's *Cambist*, *passim*, and Chalmers's *Colonial Currency*, p. 396; Eckfeldt and Dubois, *Manual of Gold and Silver Coins*.]   C. A. H.

JOHNSON, SAMUEL (1709-1784). The great lexicographer occupies an interesting place in the history of economics in England. His formal contributions to the subject were few; indeed it may be said that the preface to Rolt's *Dictionary of Commerce* (1761) and his *Considerations on Commerce* (1766) were all that he wrote on the subject. But his opinions were freely expressed in conversation, and reflect an interesting phase of thought. A man of strong common sense, he had read LOCKE (*Life*, iv. p. 105), PETTY (*ib.* i. p. 440) and many other classical English writers ; he may be regarded on the whole as putting forth the views of the ordinary educated Englishmen of the time preceding the publication of the *Wealth of Nations*. He fills this position more distinctly, as he was not carried away by the burst of enthusiasm which followed the appearance of Adam Smith's book. His general attitude on the subject of commerce is summed up in his own words, "As to mere wealth, that is to say, money, it is clear that one nation or one individual cannot increase its store but by making another poorer ; but trade procures what is more valuable, the reciprocation of the peculiar advantages of different countries" (ii. p. 430, also p. 98). But though inclined to regard traders as engaged in trying to make their gains at the expense of each other, he distinguished their occupation from gambling on account of its indirect effects (ii. p. 176), and held English merchants in high repute (i. p. 491 n.).

He was also a shrewd observer, and Boswell has put on record many of his remarks on topics of interest. He saw the advantages which accrue from the intervention of middlemen (see MIDDLEMAN, ii. p. 426). He expressed the strongest opinions in regard to the American planters, and may be regarded as one of the precursors of the anti-slavery agitation (ii. p. 27), but he was not a sentimental philanthropist in English affairs, and deprecated the raising of wages of day-labourers as more likely to induce idleness than to raise the standard of comfort (iv. p. 176). He made some interesting remarks on the increase of population, and called attention to the positive checks to its growth (ii. p. 101) ; but his most valuable suggestions arose from his observations in the Hebrides, on the transition which he there noted from a natural to a moneyed economy (iii. p. 262), and on the effects of this change on social institutions ; natural economy has so entirely passed away in the nations which the economist studies most closely, that his remarks upon it possess a special interest.

[*Life of Johnson*, and *Journal of Tour*, ed. by Dr. G. Birkbeck Hill, to which ed. the pages cited refer. The editor's app. to vol. ii. shows Johnson's views on the slave-trade. For A. Smith's opinion of him see John Rae, *Life of A. Smith*. For Johnson's on A. Smith, see Boswell's *Life*. Johnson's pamphlet, *Taxation no Tyranny*, etc., 1775, scarcely deals with economics.]　　　W. C.

JOINT DEBTORS. When several persons are jointly liable to the same debt or demand, each is liable for the whole debt, but they must, as a rule, be sued together during their joint lives, and a voluntary release to one of them will discharge them all. In the case of an order of discharge in bankruptcy, however,

persons who are jointly bound with the discharged bankrupt remain liable (Bankruptcy Act 1883, § 30 [4]). If one of several joint contractors interrupts the operation of the Statute of Limitations (see LIMITATION, STAT. OF), by a written acknowledgment of the debt, the other debtors do not lose the benefit of the statute, but he can be sued alone (9 Geo. IV. c. 14, §§ 1 and 2).

The above-mentioned rule that joint debtors must generally be sued together, and that the voluntary release of one discharges them all, constitutes one of the differences between joint liability and "joint and several liability," but the most characteristic difference consists in the fact that the estate of one of several joint debtors is discharged by his death, if any of the co-debtors survive, whilst the estate of a person jointly and severally liable remains liable after his death.

The contractual liabilities of a partnership are in England and Ireland joint liabilities, but the estate of a deceased partner is liable for debts and obligations incurred whilst he was a partner, subject however to the prior payment of his private debts (Partnership Act 1890, § 9). For wrongful acts or omissions partners are, on the other hand, liable jointly and severally (*ib.* §§ 10-12). In Scotland partners are liable jointly and severally for all debts of the partnership (*ib.* §§ 9-12).　　E. S.

JOINT PRODUCTION — JOINT PRODUCTS. When two or more things are produced by one and the same process, so that the expenses of producing them all together are not greater than the expenses of producing one of them alone would be, then those things are called *joint products*: for example, beef and hides, wheat and straw.

The value of joint—as of single—products is determined by two conditions relating to final and total utility. (1) That the last increment of the producer's outlay should just be compensated by the sum of the prices of the last increments of the products. (2) That the "net advantages" accruing to the producer should be as great as in any other occupation open to him. The value of joint products is regarded by Mill as a[1] "peculiar case," apparently because it varies with the demand for the products ; whereas in general he supposes cost of production, and accordingly value, to be unaffected "although the demand should be doubled, trebled, or quadrupled," (Ricardo, ch. xxx.). But with the wider conception of cost of production varying with the quantity produced (Sidgwick, *Pol. Econ.*, bk. ii. ch. 2, § 7 ; Marshall, *Principles, passim*), this difference between single and joint products disappears.

It is pointed out by Prof. Marshall that the definition of joint products is seldom so

---

[1] Jevons, *Theory, Pol. Econ.*, 3rd ed. ch. v., points out: "These cases . . . form the general rule," etc.

perfectly realised but that one may be increased without increasing the others. The product then is no longer "joint" with respect to its *marginal* expense.

[Mill, *Pol. Econ.*, bk. iii. ch. xvi.—Marshall, *Principles*, 2nd ed., bk. v. ch. vi. § 5.—Sidgwick, *Pol. Econ.*, bk. ii. ch. ii. § 10.]   F. Y. E.

JOINT FAMILY is, according to Hindoo law, a family union of persons, and their wives, descended through males from a common male ancestor, or supposed to be so descended, having a continuous existence like a corporation with its property in common. There is no definite limit to the number of persons who may be members of such a family, or to the closeness of their relationship to one another. Descendants through males from a common male ancestor are presumed to be united in this way. "The strength of the presumption," it has been laid down, "varies in every case. The presumption of union is stronger in the case of brothers than in the case of cousins, and the further you go from the founder of the family, the presumption becomes weaker and weaker." The family remains joint until partition, when each member of the family who has a right to an individual share of the joint estate is in the position of becoming founder of a new joint family. As long as the family is joint and undivided no member of it has any right to a particular portion of the joint property. The proceeds of it belong to the common purse, and are dealt with according to family arrangement; the fact that a person has acquired property for the family does not give him any advantage in respect of the enjoyment of the family property; the most that can be claimed as a legal right by a member of a joint family, so long as it is joint, is maintenance. Whatever is acquired by a member of a joint family belongs to his family not to himself, but to this rule exceptions have been allowed from an early time. Thus, according to the laws of Manu, "property acquired by learning belongs solely to him to whom it was given, likewise the gift of a friend, a present received on marriage, or with the honey mixture"; and again, "what one brother may acquire by his labour without using the patrimony, that acquisition made solely by his own effort he shall not share, unless by his own will, with his brother." The question whether property acquired by a person in commerce can be claimed by his family, or whether it belongs to himself, as having been made *solely* by his own effort, is a frequent subject of litigation in India; the result in many cases, owing to the presumption in favour of joint property, causes great hardship to individual acquirers. The administration of the joint family property is vested in a manager chosen by the family, who is generally the eldest male of the eldest line, he being a competent person. The manager acts as agent of the family within the scope of his powers, not as owner of the family property, like the head of a patriarchal family, from which the joint family is in many cases derived. Important acts relating to the family property require the concurrence of those members of the family who are interested in a partition. There is a great difference between the two schools of Hindoo lawyers, the Mitacshara and Dayabhaga, as to the position of those members of the family who can claim a share by partition. According to the Dayabhaga teaching, which prevails in Bengal, the members of the family are owners of their undivided shares, and the sons take no interest whatever in the family property in the lifetime of their father. According to the Mitacshara, on the other hand, the son immediately on his birth becomes one of the co-owners, and the co-owners hold the family property not as individuals, but as a corporation; no single member having any ownership in it whatever. Thus the share of a co-owner in Bengal is treated as individual property, which may be alienated by him, and made liable for his debts; whilst under the Mitacshara a co-owner has, strictly speaking, nothing which his creditors can seize or which he can alienate. But this strict view of the Mitacshara joint ownership is giving way in some parts of India, and an approach is being made towards individual ownership. There is, of course, no inheritance in a Mitacshara joint family. Any member of a family who is a co-sharer may, according to both schools, claim a partition.

The typical Hindoo joint family is joint in food, worship, and estate, *i.e.* it has a common meal in the common homestead, common religious rites, and common property. The joint family organisation exists with more or less difference of detail in many countries, as in Armenia, Russia, and among the Southern Slaves. It has not been confined to peoples of Aryan origin, as has sometimes been supposed.

[Mayne, *Hindoo Law and Usage*, ch. viii.—De Laveleye, *Primitive Property*, ch. xiii.-xvi.—Maine, *Early Law and Custom*, ch. viii.]   E. A. W.

JOINT OWNERSHIP. Property may be held by several persons as tenants-in-common, or as joint tenants. In the former case the share of a deceased tenant is part of his estate, in the latter it accrues to the surviving joint-tenants or tenant.   E. S.

JOINT-STOCK COMPANIES. Joint-stock companies are divided into incorporated and unincorporated COMPANIES (*q.v.*), but the latter have ceased to be of any practicable importance. Companies belonging to the first-named description are incorporated by royal charter, or by a special act of parliament, or by registration under the Companies Act. The constitution of companies incorporated by royal charter depends entirely on the provisions of the charter in each case. It is not unusual to provide in such charters that the members of a company are liable for the debts of the company for an amount exceeding the amount of their respective shares. Railway, canal, dock, and waterwork companies carrying on business in the United Kingdom are always incorporated by special act, but they generally adopt the provisions of the Companies Clauses Act 1845, and are.therefore to a great extent governed by uniform regulations. These regulations differ in several material respects from those governing the third class of companies—companies incorporated by registration. Thus, whilst the Companies Acts leave it to the articles of each company to determine the constitution of the managing body, the Companies Clauses Act contains explicit directions as to the appointment, rotation, powers, and proceedings of directors (§§ 81-100). The Companies Acts, with the exception of the act of 1879, which only applies to *banking* companies formed or transformed into limited companies after its date, do not prescribe a compulsory audit of the accounts ; on the other hand companies governed by the Companies Clauses Act must have their accounts audited in accordance with the provisions of that statute (§§ 101-108). There is no power either under the Companies Clauses Act or under the Companies Acts to pay dividends out of capital, but whilst a company registered under the last-named statutes is absolutely incapable of sanctioning such payments, the special act of a railway, canal, dock, or waterwork company may authorise them, and the payment of unearned dividends at a fixed rate during the construction of the undertaking is sometimes provided for in this manner. (As to the difference between the debenture-stocks issued by the two respective classes of companies, see DEBENTURE STOCK.)

The most numerous class of joint-stock companies consists of those formed under the Companies Acts. These acts, the principal of which is the Companies Act of 1862, are occasionally referred to as the Limited Liability Acts, an expression which is somewhat misleading, inasmuch as companies with limited liability were in existence for a considerable time before 1862, and the Companies Acts moreover deal with unlimited, as well as with limited companies. Limited companies are subdivided into companies limited by shares and companies limited by guarantee ; unlimited companies into such as have a fixed capital, and so-called "mutual companies," which have no fixed capital. The new companies registered since the passing of the Companies Act of 1862 and up to the 31st December 1892 consisted of—

39,911 Companies limited by shares.
950 Companies limited by guarantee.
134 Unlimited Companies with a fixed capital.
318 Mutual Companies.

41,313

In 1892 the newly-registered companies consisted of—

2279 Companies limited by shares.
73 Companies limited by guarantee.
3 Unlimited Companies with a fixed capital.
5 Mutual Companies.

2360

It will be seen that the unlimited companies with a fixed capital form only a very small part of the whole number. The mutual companies and those limited by guarantee are somewhat more numerous, but hardly any of the companies registered in either way are trading companies in the strict sense. The usual form of association adopted by trading companies not being railway, canal, dock, or waterwork companies, carrying on business in England, is that of companies limited by shares.

One of the most striking features of the law of the Companies Acts is the complete absence of any restrictive conditions in respect of the formation of companies. On the Continent, companies are, as a rule, not incorporated until the whole of the capital has been subscribed (as to Germany, see *Handelsgesetzbuch*, § 209, d, e ; as to France, *Loi sur les sociétés*, 24th July 1867, § 24 ; as to Belgium, *Loi sur les sociétés*, 18th May 1873, § 29 ; as to Italy, *Codice di Commercio*, § 131) and until a certain portion of it has been paid up (in Germany, 25 per cent, *l.c.* § 210 ; in France, 25 per cent, *l.c.* § 24 and § 1 ; in Belgium, 5 per cent, *l.c.* §§ 29, 31 ; in Italy 30 per cent, *l.c.* § 131). There are also in the law of most continental countries various provisions for securing an inquiry—at the outset—into the circumstances of the promotion of every company. Thus, for instance, in Germany it is the first duty of the directors of a newly-formed company to issue a special report on these matters, and if any of the directors have taken part in the promotion or sold any property of the company, another report must be issued by independent auditors (*l.c.* § 209), and it is also provided that any purchases of property for a sum exceeding one-tenth of the capital of a company made within two years from the incorporation of the company must be approved by the shareholders in general meeting (*l.c.* § 213 f.). No similar precautions exist in English law. A limited company is incorporated as soon as the MEMORANDUM OF ASSOCIATION (*q.v.*) is filed at the office of the registrar of joint-stock companies, and this can be done before any shares, excepting the seven shares to be subscribed for by the persons who sign the memorandum, have been disposed of. The publicity of transactions, by which shares are allotted as fully paid in exchange for property or services, is, in some measure, provided for by § 25 of the act of 1867, which requires such shares to be paid for in cash, unless previously to the issue of the shares the contract according to which they are to be allotted is filed with the registrar ; but no machinery is supplied by the law to secure an independent valuation of the assets sold by the promoters of the company. The Provision of Companies Act 1867, § 38, which requires certain particulars about contracts to be referred to in any prospectus offering shares, has not proved of much practical advantage, and it is frequently evaded by the insertion of a "waiver clause" into the forms of application for shares.

The principle of "laissez-faire" also pervades the rules as to the management of companies and the keeping of accounts. A company excluding table A by its articles (see ARTICLES OF ASSOCIATION) is almost entirely unfettered in these respects ; it may leave the entire management in the hands of one person for life, and though a meeting of the shareholders must be held annually (Companies Act 1862, § 49) it is not necessary, in the absence of directions in the articles, to submit any accounts to the shareholders at any such meeting. The foreign codes have elaborate rules on these points and also on the valuation of assets, and the formation of reserve funds (see as to directors and managers of companies in Germany *l.c.* § 209 f., §§ 224-235 ; in France, *l.c.* §§ 22, 26, 40, 44 ; in Belgium, *l.c.* §§ 43-49 ; in Italy, *l.c.* §§ 139-142, 147-152. As to the confirmation of accounts by general meetings in Germany, *l.c.* §§ 239, 239 b [185 c] ; in France, *l.c.* §§ 32, 34 ; in Belgium, *l.c.* §§ 27, 35 ; in Italy, *l.c.* § 154. As to the valuation of assets and formation of reserve funds in Germany, *l.c.* § 239 b [185 a, 185 b] ; in France, *l.c.* §§ 34, 36 ; in Belgium, *l.c.* §§ 62-65 ; in Italy, *l.c.* §§ 176, 182). British company law does not require the assets to be valued periodically, and it is even unnecessary —in the absence of any special regulations in the articles—to provide for the depreciation of wasting property (see Lee *v.* Neuchatel Asphalte Company, 41 Chancery Division 1 ; Bolton *v.* Natal Land Company [1892], 2 Chancery 124 ; Verner *v.* General Trust [1894], 2 Chancery 239) ; dividends cannot be paid except out of profits, but in ascertaining the profits for that purpose, it is not necessary to take into account any decrease, however serious, in the value of a company's property.

Directors, in England as elsewhere, are liable for fraud and for any acts done by them in excess of their powers (see DIRECTORS, LEGAL DUTY OF) but whilst on the Continent they can be made responsible for losses caused by ordinary negligence (see as to Germany, *l.c.* § 241 [2] ; as to France, *l.c.* § 44 ; as to Belgium, *l.c.* § 51, 52 ; as to Italy, §§ 147-149), British directors are safe from all claims as long as they keep within their powers and are not acting for

their personal advantage (see Lord Hatherley's remarks in Turquand *v.* Marshall, 4 Chancery Appeals, on p. 386 : "However ridiculous and absurd their conduct might seem, it was the misfortune of the company that they chose such unwise directors "). As mentioned above, the Companies Acts do not—except in certain specified cases—require the accounts to be submitted to a periodical independent audit. In France, Belgium, and Italy independent auditors (*commissaires, sindaci*) ; must be appointed by the shareholders (see as to France, *l.c.* §§ 32-34 ; as to Belgium, *l.c.* §§ 47, 48, 54, 58 ; as to Italy *l.c.* §§ 183-184). Their duties include the inspection of the accounts and securities during the whole of the year for which they are elected, and they may convene general meetings of the shareholders in case of necessity. Another peculiarity of British—as distinguished from foreign—companies is their power to issue debentures, the holders of which in case of a winding-up may take possession of the whole undertaking (see DEBENTURE). This may produce great hardship to ordinary creditors. No doubt the law requires debentures to be registered in the "register of mortgages and charges" kept by the issuing company (Companies Act, 1862, § 43), but the omission to register— though it imposes a penalty on the directors— does not render the debentures invalid (Wright *v.* Horton, 12 Appeal Cases, 371) ; moreover, the register—if existent—may be inspected by *actual* creditors only and not by *intending* creditors ; and it is therefore impossible, before giving credit to a company, to ascertain whether the whole of its assets have not been pledged to debenture holders.

In one way, shareholders in British companies are better protected than those in foreign companies. On the continent the officers of a company have unlimited powers to bind the company, while in England engagements entered into beyond the powers defined by the memorandum and articles are of no effect (see ULTRA VIRES, DOCTRINE OF).

The question as to the relative advantages of the respective tendencies of British and continental company law is not easily answered. There is no doubt that the great majority of the more important companies in the United Kingdom have hitherto been managed honestly and prudently : gross instances of fraud and recklessness occur from time to time, but it is by no means certain whether, under the stringent regulations of continental law, such occurrences are less frequent.

The law should allow full scope to the great variety of objects for which companies are created, as inelastic rules as to the conditions of incorporation and internal organisation may stifle legitimate enterprise. This has been shown in Germany, where the stringency of the provisions enacted in 1884 has—already in

1892—made it necessary to introduce a new kind of mercantile associations, *Gesellschaften mit beschränkter Haftung* (Partnerships with Limited Liability), which are not subject to the restrictions of company law.

The chief fault of English company law is the unsatisfactory nature of the rules as to the liabilities of directors. As the law stands, a director who does not take any active part in the proceedings of the board is almost free from responsibility (see for instance "Cullerne *v.* London and Suburban Building Society," 25 Queen's Bench Division, 485), and the frequent practice of directors, of leaving everything in the hands of one or two "active" colleagues is actually encouraged by the decisions of the courts.

The habitual disinclination of shareholders to ascertain whether unusually high dividends have been earned in a legitimate way is a frequent cause of disaster, which cannot, however, be dealt with by legislation.

The disasters of the "Liberator group," and of a number of so-called "trust companies," have, in recent times, attracted the attention of the public to the deficiencies of English company law, which are also pointed out in a very interesting report issued by the board of trade, pursuant to § 29 of the Winding-up Act, 1890 (Third Annual Report, 1894, pp. 305); new legislation is recommended in the same for the purpose of securing the following among other objects. (1) The compliance with definite requirements as to subscription and payment of capital ; (2) the disclosure of fuller information in prospectuses ; (3) the securing of a substantial interest in the company on the part of its first subscribers ; (4) the prevention of fraud by the sale of insolvent undertakings ; (5) the limitation of borrowing and mortgaging powers and fuller disclosure of mortgages ; (6) more efficient audit and fuller publication of balance sheets, etc. A departmental committee, consisting of Lord Davey as chairman, and a number of theoretical and practical experts in company law, has recently considered a draft which will embody some of these proposals.

There are many details in respect of which improvements could, no doubt, be effected, but nothing will alter the fact that companies in their present form, like many other contrivances due to the modern spirit of invention, have, while enlarging the sphere and increasing the intensity of human activity, also produced risks and dangers which were formerly unknown.

[As to the law of joint-stock companies incorporated under special acts, see Hodges on *Railways;* Brown and Theobald on *Railways.* As to the law of companies incorporated under the Companies Acts, see Lindley on *Company Law ;* Buckley on *The Companies Acts.* A more popular exposition is contained in Hamilton : *A Manual of Company Law for the use of Directors and Promoters.*

Statistics relating to companies registered under the Companies Acts are contained in the annual returns of the registrar of joint-stock companies ; see also the articles on COMPANIES.] E. S.

JOINT TENANCY. Where two or more persons have an estate given to them as joint tenants, they hold it jointly, so that on the death of one, the whole estate belongs to the survivors or survivor ; whilst if the estate or property is given to them as "tenants in common," the share of a deceased tenant goes to his heir in the case of real property, and to his personal representative in the case of personal property. Trustees are usually made joint tenants.

[Goodeve's *Real Property*, London, 1891.]
J. E. C. M.

JOINTURE. A jointure was an estate in freehold land given to a wife to take effect on the death of her husband, so called because in former days the estate was given in joint tenancy or jointure to both husband and wife. In modern times, provision is made for the wife by charging the lands of the husband with the payment of a yearly sum.

[Goodeve's *Real Property*, London, 1891.]
J. E. C. M.

JONES, DAVID (1806-1854), Actuary of the Universal Life Assurance Office. Very favourably held in estimation as the author of a book *On the Value of Annuities and Reversionary Payments*, with numerous tables. To which is appended a treatise on "Probability," by Sir William Lubbock, Bart., F.R.S., and J. E. Drinkwater Bethune, A.M., 2 vols., 8vo, London, 1844, published by the Society for the Diffusion of Useful Knowledge (pp. xxx. and 1136, with 64 pages comprising the treatise referred to). This work, which has become scarce, continues to be appreciated as one of the most useful guides, from a practical point of view, for the solution of the many problems that require accurate solution in the business of life assurances and annuities. The former are included in Jones's work under the designation of reversionary payments.

A translation into German appeared in 1859, at Hanover. Jones, David, *Leibrenten und Lebens-Versicherungen*, Deutsch bearbeitet und mit Tabellen versehen von K. Hattendorf. F. H.

JONES, ERNEST CHARLES (1819-1869), poet, novelist, and politician, was brought up to the bar, but attached himself in 1846, at first as a follower of Feargus O'Connor, to the Chartist movement, of which he was a prominent advocate. Gradually, however, as the importance of the Chartist movement decreased, he became more identified with the extreme radicals. In 1848, he was sentenced to two years' imprisonment, with a fine, for seditious speeches. He was on the staff of the *Northern Star*, the Chartist organ, and afterwards edited *Notes to the People*. He was a brilliant and impressive democratic orator, but his statements are exaggerated.

His writings on economic or political subjects, apart from articles in the organs above mentioned, are all reprints of lectures, and include — *Evenings with the People*, 1856-57.—*Labour and Capital*, 1867.—*Democracy vindicated—a Reply to Professor Blackie*, 1867.

[R. G. Gammage, *History of the Chartist Movement*, 1854 (this author is very severe on Jones, with whom he was constantly at strife).—*The Times*, 27th January, etc., 1869.]　　R. H. H.

JONES, RICHARD (1790-1855), son of an eminent solicitor, was born at Tunbridge Wells. At the age of twenty-two he entered Cambridge, where the society of Herschel, Whewell, and other future savants is said to have fostered in him the love of positive inductive knowledge. After leaving Cambridge he took orders, and was curate for several years in Kent and Sussex. Meanwhile he was composing his first and principal work, *An Essay on the Distribution of Wealth, and on the Sources of Taxation*, of which the first division, or "book," on rent, —not destined to have a sequel—was published in 1831. Soon afterwards Jones was appointed professor of political economy in the newly-established King's College, London ; where he delivered an introductory lecture in 1833. From King's College he was transferred to Haileybury, as the successor of Malthus. He occupied the chair of political economy and history at Haileybury for several years ; but his academic pursuits, and the completion of his projected work, were interrupted by the active part which he took in the commutation of tithes. He showed great practical ability as tithe commissioner, an office which he held till 1851. He was afterwards a charity commissioner.

The rôle of Jones in political economy was like that of Bacon in physical science : to preach the importance of experience, and the danger of hasty generalisation.

"If we wish to make ourselves acquainted with the economy and arrangements by which the different nations of the earth produce or distribute their revenues, I really know of but one way to attain our object, and that is to look and see" ("Introductory lecture at King's College," *Literary Remains*, p. 569).

"To complete the knowledge really and securely attainable . . . will still require the patient and assiduous observation and labour of many minds. . . . During this process the too hasty erection of whole systems, a frail thirst for the premature exhibition of commanding generalities, will probably continue to be the sources of error most to be guarded against" (Preface to *Essay on Distribution of Wealth*, p. 39).

Aristotle's method was not more objectionable to Bacon than Ricardo's was to Jones.

"Mr. Ricardo was a man of talent, and he produced a system very ingeniously combined of purely hypothetical truths ; which, however, a single comprehensive glance at the world, as it actually exists, is sufficient to show to be utterly inconsistent with the past and present condition of mankind (*ib.* p. 7)."

Like Bacon, Jones did not illustrate his new method by any very remarkable discoveries. The following are specimens. Jones contends that the Ricardian theory of rent does not apply to the payments made to the owners of the soil over the greater part of the world. He disputes what is now called the law of diminishing returns, " the opinion that the powers of agricultural capital necessarily decrease as the quantity employed increases " (*Essay*, p. 197) ; regarding it as invalidated by "improvements in the arts of production" (*ib.* p. 199). He denies that a fall in the rate of profits is always attended with a diminution of savings (*Literary Remains*, p. 371). All these propositions are admitted by moderate followers of Ricardo, by J. S. Mill for example. However, against some of the narrower Epigoni, some of Jones's strictures (*e.g.*, *Essay*, p. 182) may be justified.

Accordingly it may be regretted that Jones's criticisms were not more favourably received by his contemporaries—M'Culloch, for instance, hardly thinks him worth notice (*Literature of Political Economy*). For the reaction against over-generalisation, if headed by Jones, would have come sooner, and would have been more moderate, inasmuch as Jones did not abjure the use of deductive reasoning within certain limits, *e.g.* with respect to farmers'—as distinguished from peasants'—rents.

Thus his demonstration of the propositions that the rise of rents from the employment of any given quantity of auxiliary capital will be less than that which would take place from the employment of an equal amount of capital in the maintenance of additional labour (*Essay*, p. 225), and that "a rise in the relative value of raw produce . . . will always be followed by a decrease of the share of the producing classes . . . and by a corresponding rise in the produce rents of the landlords" (*ib.* p. 245) is highly abstract.

His formula that the interests of the landlords are indissolubly connected with those of their tenantry and the community at large is just as liable to misconstruction as the converse Ricardian paradox which he combats. In short, as Gibbon said of a more important protest, "we shall rather be surprised by the timidity, than scandalised by the freedom," of the reformer.

A similar moderation characterises Jones's contributions to economic history, of which the best specimen is the "Essay on Primitive Political Economy," forming an article in the *Edinburgh Review* for April 1847 (reprinted in the *Literary Remains*, p. 291). The writer looks at past events in the light of modern theory. He has not reached that pitch of culture from which all the truths of political economy appear only "relative" to the circumstances of the age. He roundly takes our ancestors to task for their "delusions" (*ibid.*), and, in terms calculated to shock the delicate historical sense of the present day, exhibits "the errors and wanderings of our forefathers" (Introductory Lecture, *Literary Remains*, p. 541). He presented clear general views, such as the distinction between the "balance of bargain," and the "balance of trade," without parading obscure authorities. He was a philosophic historian, and not a mere chronicler. He deserves to be regarded as the founder of the English historical school.

An Essay on the Distribution of Wealth, and on the Sources of Taxation, pt. i., Rent [no more published], 1831.—An introductory lecture on Political Economy, delivered at King's College, with a syllabus of a course of lectures on the Wages of Labour (reprinted in *Literary Remains*), 1833.—A few remarks on the proposed commutation of tithes, with suggestions of some additional facilities, 1833.—Remarks on the manner in which tithes should be assessed to the poor's rate under the existing law, with a protest against the change which will be produced in that law by a bill introduced into the House of Commons by Mr. Shaw Lefevre, 1838.—[The impression of a "full man" which Jones's writings convey is confirmed by the genial picture of his personality which Miss Edgeworth gives in her (unpublished) memoirs (vol. iii. p. 55): "Such crowds of ideas as he poured forth, uttering so rapidly as to keep one quite on the stretch not to miss any of the good things."]—A very unfavourable review, in which the hand of M'Culloch may be traced, in the *Edinburgh Review* for 1831 (vol. liv.), disputes many of Jones's facts as well as all his theory. Whewell, in his Preface to the *Literary Remains*, makes a rejoinder.—A letter to the Right Honourable Sir Robt. Peel on the bill introduced into Parliament by the Attorney-General to exempt all persons from being assessed as inhabitants to parochial rates, 1840.—Textbook of lectures on the Political Economy of nations, delivered at the East India College, Haileybury, 1852 [republished among the *Literary Remains*].—*Literary Remains*, consisting of lectures and tracts on Political Economy. Edited with a prefatory notice by the Rev. William Whewell, D.D.   F. Y. E.

JOURDAN, ALFRED (1825-1892), dean of the faculty of law at Aix in Provence, and professor of political economy at Aix and Marseilles, was also a frequent contributor to the *Revue d'Économie Politique*.

Besides several writings on law, Jourdan published a *Cours Analytique d'Économie Politique*, eds. 1882, 1890.—*Du Rôle de l'État dans l'Ordre Économique ou Économie Politique et Socialisme*, 1882. "The law of the historical development of the economic mission of the state is to abstain more and more from direct *tutela*, such as technical regulations, but to contribute more and more towards the improvement and increase of the social machinery put at the

disposal of emancipated human industry," p. 395. He also wrote *Des Rapports entre le Droit et l'Économie Politique ou Philosophie Comparée du Droit et de l'Économie Politique*, 1888. "Both sciences are based on the same primordial facts; the instinct of social aggregation and human liberty. Political economy traces the motive principle—the necessity of satisfying human wants with the smallest possible amount of exertion; but it is only directly concerned with material interests; whilst law has a more extended territory. For both, progress has always been realised through liberty, namely, the removal of certain trammels." The author's conclusion is : "Ethics and economics stand, as sciences, in the same relation to the science of law as natural philosophy and chemistry to the science of mechanics." The two latter works were rewarded with a prize by the French Academy of Political and Moral Sciences.   E. Ca.

JOURNEY (*Mint*). A word used in the Mint to represent a certain weight of gold or silver coin, originally supposed to represent a day's work, and which had to be delivered by the coiners at the end of each "journée" or day. A "journey-weight" of gold is 180 oz. troy, and of silver 720 oz. troy.   F. E. A.

JOURNEYMAN, a term originally denoting a labourer working by the day (*journée*), came in England to be applied, before the end of the middle ages, to all craftsmen working for hire, as distinguished, on the one side, from the "masters," "craft-holders," or "shop-holders" who employed them, and, on the other, from the apprentices. In the 14th century, however, the journeyman was also commonly distinguished from the "serving-man," "valet," or "yeoman," who was engaged for a considerably longer period. We may perhaps see in the supersession of these other terms by "journeyman," an indication that with the growth of industry it became increasingly exceptional to contract for a long period of service. Such a contract, it must be added, would become less advantageous to the employer when once the system of apprenticeship had been definitely established, and he had thus secured a permanent working force of another kind, and it would also naturally tend to disappear before the extension of the practice of piece-work.

In the picture commonly drawn by modern writers of the mediæval "gild-system" in its best period, the position of journeyman is represented as the normal intervening stage between apprenticeship and mastership,—a stage out of which the industrious and skilful journeyman could easily rise after a few years. This picture is perhaps true of some industries —in certain localities—in particular periods; and it has served as a useful standard of comparison wherewith to contrast what have been supposed to be earlier and later conditions. But it is difficult to reconcile with the historical evidence. Even as late as the 14th and 15th centuries apprenticeship was only slowly coming to be a necessary prerequisite of hired labour; and, when it had, full membership of the craft, with the right to set up as an independent master, was already restricted in such a way as to be beyond the reach of the average journeyman. The relation of the journeymen to the GILDS or "crafts" is still somewhat obscure and varied probably from place to place. They were subject to the control of the gild, and their wages were regulated by its officers: in some few cases they appear as taking part in the making of ordinances and even in the election of officers. But as a rule, and certainly towards the end of the 15th century, the masters were alone regarded as in any real sense members or "combrethren" of the craft company.

So long as apprenticeship was enforced, the name of "journeymen" or "free journeymen" continued to be used for those who had served seven years to any art or craft under a lawful "master." It is still in common use in some industries still organised in small shops—*e.g.* that of the bakers; and in others which, like the hatters, have only recently passed into the factory stage, and retain the tradition of earlier conditions.

[The literature of the subject will be found under CORPORATIONS OF ARTS AND TRADES, GILDS, and elsewhere. For a recent summary see Ashley, *Economic History*, part ii. (1893), § 34.—Mrs. Green, *Town Life in the Fifteenth Century* (1894), vol. ii. chs. iv. v., takes up a position which, if hardly supported by sufficient evidence and not altogether clear, is independent and suggestive. The most convenient collection of material will be found in H. T. Riley, *Memorials of London*, 1868.]

W. J. A.

JOURNEYMEN'S SOCIETIES. As soon as there grew up a class of journeymen who realised that they were likely to remain in that position for many years, if not all their lives, and, therefore, that they had class interests to defend, distinct from, or opposed to those of the masters, separate societies of journeymen began to make their appearance. In accordance with the tendency of the later middle ages towards the formation of religious gilds, such societies would seem to have been usually, at first, of a religious character, as is indicated by the names "fraternity," "brotherhood," "confrèrie," and "Bruderschaft." Although in some cases this may have been caused by a desire to avoid condemnation by the public authorities, there is no reason to believe that the journeymen were not moved by the same motives as led other classes to form religious associations. Yet these fraternities would naturally tend to concern themselves with the other interests of their members; and the mere fact of association would lend strength to the journeymen in their negotiations with the masters. The "confrèries" of "compagnons" were a prominent feature in the industrial life of France in the 15th century; their later history still awaits investigation. In Germany "Gesellenverbände" of various kinds were numerous in the 15th century; in some industries they were to be found as late as the present century; and they were the occasion of a long series of imperial and territorial decrees. In England they played a much less important part, partly because industry here was less developed, partly because of the absence of the rule concerning a period of travel, to which may be largely attributed their rapid spread on the continent. Evidence has, however, already been found of their existence in the following London crafts at the dates here stated :—the saddlers, 1383-1396; cordwainers, 1387; tailors, 1413-1696; blacksmiths, 1435; carpenters, 1468; drapers, 1493-1522; ironmongers, 1497-1590; founders, 1508-1579; fishmongers, 1512; clothworkers, 16th century; armourers, 1589; and in the following provincial towns :—Coventry, the weavers, before 1450; Exeter, the tailors, before 1512; Oxford, the shoemakers, 1512; Bristol, the tailors, 1570; and with the further publication of municipal records other instances will doubtless be found. So far as we can judge from our scanty evidence, they seem to have begun as voluntary combinations, in the teeth of the masters and the civic authorities, and to have commonly had among their objects the increase of wages. They were met by strong measures of repression, to which possibly some succumbed, but in many cases they were recognised after a time, sometimes as the result of a formal compromise, and ultimately they sank into a position altogether subordinate to the companies of masters, and became convenient to the latter as a machinery for relieving poor journeymen. Their organisation resembled in general character that of the masters' companies, with periodical assemblies, wardens, contributions, and common-box.

[Our most consecutive information concerns the association among the tailors of London, which under the names of the "fraternity of yeomen," or "valets," "the yeomen fellowship," and, from 1569 onwards, "the bachelors' Company" survived till 1661, when it was suppressed by the Merchant Taylors' Company. Here the development was complicated by the gradual separation between the Merchant Taylors' Company and the industry from which it derived its name. The evidence will be found in C. M. Clode, *Memorials of the Merchant Taylors' Company* (1875), and *Early History of the Merchant Taylors' Company* (1888). But more instructive is the "Ordinance granted by the worshipful masters and wardens, with all the whole company of the craft of blacksmiths of London, to the servants of the said craft" in 1434, which is evidently of the nature of a compact between two bodies, and contains conditions curiously resembling modern trades union policy. It is printed by Mr Coote in *Trans. London and Middlesex Archæol. Soc.* (1874), iv. And almost equally interesting is the indenture between the shoemakers and their journeymen in Oxford (1512), when the struggle seems to have turned upon the possession of "the box of the journeymen"; this is given in *Records of Oxford* (1880). An attempt is made to present and estimate the value of the information at present accessible in Ashley, *Economic History*, vol. i. pt. ii. (1893), § 35. See however the recent criticism by S. and B. Webb, in *The Hist. of Trade Unionism* (1894), ch. i. For Germany, see G. Schanz, *Gesellenverbände* (1877), and for France, Levasseur, *Histoire des classes Ouvrières*, vols. i. and ii. (1859).] w. j. a.

JOVELLANOS, GASPAR MELCHIOR DE (1744-1811), had a most chequered existence. He was originally public prosecutor in Seville, then in high favour at the court of Madrid, where he became a member of the *Sociedad Económica* and of the *Academia de Historia*; but he fell into disgrace after the accession of Charles IV., was exiled to Gijon, his native place, then recalled to the court and appointed a minister, to be imprisoned again in 1801, first in a convent and then in a fortress in the Balearic islands. Released at the time of the French invasion, he rejected the offers of Napoleon, was made a member of the *Junta Central* of government, and took a leading part in the debates on the Spanish constitution put forward in Cadiz.

On his tombstone in Gijon he is described as having been "a magistrate, a minister, a father of his country, a man of letters, an orator, a poet, a jurisconsult, a philosopher, an economist, —always distinguished, often eminent."

His works, exclusive of his *Memoirs*, which have been printed separately in Paris (1825), have been republished in Rivadeneyra's *Biblioteca de Autores Españoles* (Madrid, 2 vols. 1858-59); the economic writings are to be found in vol. ii. The most important are the *Informe á la Junta General de Comercio sobre la Libertad de las Artes* (1785) (Report on the liberty of the crafts), and the *Informe de la Sociedad Económica al Real Consejo de Castilla sobre el expediente de la Ley Agraria* (1794) (Report on Agrarian Reform). In both, Jovellanos starts from extremely liberal principles, but sometimes restricts them in their final application. Thus, he is strongly opposed to the existing *gremios* or craft-gilds, charging them with oppressing the artisans (p. 37) and inability to adjust supply to demand (p. 38), but although proposing their abolition, he demands a "general immatriculation (enrolment) of all persons connected with a craft, whether as masters, artisans, or apprentices," in order to submit them to the guidance of "*sindicos*" belonging to the craft, but appointed by the local authorities. No free association of people belonging to a craft is to be allowed (p. 41). In his *Informe sobre la Ley Agraria*, Jovellanos inveighs against the existence of *baldíos* (waste-lands), *tierras concejiles* (communal property), and *mayorazgos* (entails), against the extent of land owned in

clerical mortmain, and against the privileges of the MESTA granted to the owners of the migrating flocks. He advocates the inclosure of common fields, and proposes to legalise the sale of all such land to the peasants in their vicinity. He urges that more roads and canals should be constructed as well as more works of irrigation. Internal trade in corn should be free, but "in our present situation, free export of corn, either absolute or restrained according to prices, is not necessary and would not be useful" (p. 116). Even the import of corn is only to be allowed temporarily, and should be suspended in years of acknowledged abundance. E. CA.

JOYCE, JEREMIAH (1763 - 1816), was a Unitarian minister, and tutor to the sons of Lord Stanhope. Early in 1794, he was imprisoned on a charge of high treason, but at the end of six months released without trial. He remained, until his death, secretary of the Unitarian Society and minister of the Unitarian Chapel at Hampstead. In 1797, he published an analysis or rather abridgment of Adam Smith's *Wealth of Nations*. His annotations are not numerous, but have an interest as reflecting affairs of his day. They refer chiefly to Smith's proposals for obtaining a revenue from the taxation of the colonies,—among which "America," writes Joyce, "the grand, principal resource, is *now* entirely and for ever out of the question" (p. 290). Among other things he notices Pitt's proposal to "double the turnpike tolls . . . seizing upon one half of them for the exigencies of the State" (p. 232).

Joyce's publications are very numerous; those that are connected with political economy are— *A complete Analysis . . . of . . . Adam Smith's . . . Wealth of Nations*, 1797, 8vo, 1821, 12mo, 1877, etc., 8vo.—*The Arithmetic of Real Life and Business*, 1809. A. L.

JUDGMENT. A judgment is the decision of the court on one of the main subjects of an action brought before it. A judgment need not necessarily put an end to the action, as it may only deal with part of the claim or not finally adjudge on any part of the claim. If a defendant in an action fails to appear or to plead in accordance with the prescribed rules, judgment "by default" may be obtained against him. In actions in which unliquidated damages are claimed, a defendant is in such a case ordered to pay "the damages to be assessed." This is called an "interlocutory judgment," because a further step, viz. the assessment of the damages, must be taken before the rights of the parties are finally adjusted. In the Chancery Division of the High Court a judgment frequently directs certain inquiries to be made, or certain accounts to be taken. This is done before the chief clerk in chambers, who subsequently issues a certificate as to the result; the action is then brought before the court "on further consideration," and if no further inquiries are necessary, directions are given for a final judgment declaring the rights of the parties.

A final judgment materially alters the mutual rights of the parties. It enables a successful party to issue execution against the property, and in case of need against the person, of the party whom it affects (see ATTACHMENT; ELEGIT; FIERI FACIAS). If it directs the payment of money it creates a debt more easily enforced, and in most cases less easily barred by the Statute of Limitations (see LIMITATION, STATUTES OF) than the claim in respect of which the action was brought. As between the parties and their successors in title the subject matter of the litigation cannot, after the lapse of the period allowed for an appeal, or after an unsuccessful appeal, be contested again. The latter rule is generally expressed by saying that a judgment creates an "estoppel inter partes," or that the case has become "res judicata."

The Judgments Extension Act of 1868, and the Inferior Courts Judgments Extension Act 1882, render judgments obtained in England, Scotland, and Ireland effectual in any other part of the United Kingdom. The judgments of foreign courts cannot be enforced in England without a fresh action in an English court, but the judgment in such an action must be in favour of the plaintiff unless the defendant can prove that the foreign judgment was obtained by fraud; that the court in which it was obtained had no jurisdiction; or that it violates a vital principle of English public policy. E. S.

JUDGMENT DEBTOR. A person to whom directions have been given by a JUDGMENT (q.v.) to pay a sum of money to another person. E. S.

JUDICIAL FACTOR (Scotland). An administrator appointed to an estate by the Court of Session, in the exercise of its equity jurisdiction "ex nobili officio of the court."

Factors may be factors loco tutoris on children's estates, or loco absentis, as where an owner is absent; curators bonis, as where the owner has become incapable of managing his own affairs, or upon failure of trustees, or where trustees have been removed on suspicion of misconduct, or generally where there is a risk of the property perishing or being injured or going to waste. The appointment is made upon petition; and the nominee of the petitioner is, if suitable, usually appointed; but the court may recall the appointment, as on his insolvency.

The sheriffs of the counties may appoint judicial factors to estates of not more than £100 a year, all told. Judicial factors are under the supervision and general superintendence of the Accountant of Court. This officer sees that they give due security, and that the funds are properly lodged in bank. He audits their accounts once a year, makes any such requisitions or orders on them as he considers necessary, and reports any failure or misconduct to the Court or, if necessary, to the Lord Advocate

for prosecution. He gets information from the banks as to balances, etc., and is the official custodier of bank receipts and vouchers. He makes an annual report of all the estates under his superintendence. The court does not interfere unless the accountant makes an application to it, or unless leave is required to grant abatements of rent, to sink funds in an annuity, or the like. The judicial factor is paid for his time and trouble by a commission, fixed by the Accountant. Under the Judicial Factors Act 1889, § 13, the appointment of a judicial factor has the full force and effect of an assignment or transfer, duly executed, of all property situated or invested in any part of the British dominions, and belonging to or forming part of the estate under his charge; and all debts must be paid or assignments or transfers executed accordingly.   A. D.

JUDICIAL RENT, see LAND LEGISLATION, IRISH.

JUNG STILLING, JOHANN HEINRICH (1740-1817). The surname Stilling was derived from the pietist congregation, Die Stillen im Lande, the "quiet country people" to which his family belonged. Jung was essentially a self-made man; up to the age of twenty, his time was divided between teaching in village schools and tailoring; through self-exertion and the assistance of friends, he was enabled to study in the university of Strasburg, where he obtained the degree of doctor of medicine; later on he lectured on cameralistic sciences at Kaiserslautern and Marburg, but this did not prevent his attaining a wide celebrity as an operator for cataract. Jung Stilling made a strong personal impression on Goethe (see Wahrheit und Dichtung, bk. ix.); during the last twenty years of his life he gave himself entirely up to mystic literature.

As an economic writer, Jung belongs to the philanthropical and eclectic school, with strong absolutistic leanings which flourished in Germany during the second half of the 18th century under the influence of Sonnenfels, and of his theory of the largest possible population. On this last principle, he goes to the extreme of claiming the protection of the police for pregnant unmarried girls, even against their own parents. Land, in his opinion, might be subdivided to the minimum sufficient to supply the subsistence of a family. Jung was opposed to craft monopolies (Gilds), but favourable to the craft system,—this he wants made compulsory: "craft examinations are necessary in order to prevent the manufacturing of rubbish." In matters of national finance he has a predilection for state domains and royal dues. He appears to have learned very little from Adam Smith, but is most of all swayed by his strong religious feelings: nations whose practice is based on purely commercial principles would soon come to destruction; and exclusively selfish commercial aims are as much to be reprobated in nations as in individuals. Excise-duties have the great disadvantage of being borne by the weakest party in buying and selling.

Jung Stilling's best-known economic works are the *Staatspolizeiwissenschaft* (1788); the *Lehrbuch der Finanzwissenschaft* (1789); and the *Grundlehre der Staatswissenschaft* (1792).

[See Roscher, *Gesch. der Nat. Oek. in Deutschland*, pp. 552-555; and *Allgem. Deutsche Biographie*.]   E. Ca.

JURANDE. This was the name of the elected board which managed the affairs of a trade-gild or corporation in France. Its chief functions were to maintain the interests of the gild, to regulate the terms of admission and the length of apprenticeship, and to issue *lettres de maîtrise* to those who were qualified for full membership. The advantages and disadvantages of these close corporations were the same in France as in England. They gave some security for good workmanship, but they raised the price of most of the commodities which passed through their hands. At last Turgot succeeded in 1776 in extorting from Louis XVI. an edict for their suppression. It is a curious illustration of Adam Smith's close connection with the French economists that the preamble to this edict contains many of the arguments which he advanced in the same year against trade corporations (*W. of N.*, bk. i. ch. x.). Turgot's reform was not lasting. The system of *jurandes* and *maîtrises* was revived after his fall; but they were finally abolished in 1791.   R. L.

JURISDICTION. The jurisdiction of English courts does not extend beyond England; in certain cases, however, leave may be given to serve defendants out of the jurisdiction with writs or notice of writs. If the service is properly effected in such a case, judgment may be obtained against a foreign defendant, but such a judgment could not be enforced abroad, except under the sanction of a foreign court.

[Piggott, *Service out of the Jurisdiction*.]
                                                 E. S.

JURISDICTION, SCOTCH. In Scotland jurisdiction is not, in principle, assumed, except upon certain established grounds. The general rule is that the "pursuer" must follow the defender's domicile. The domicile, which is considered sufficient to found jurisdiction against the defender, may be his domicile of succession, that which would regulate his status and the succession to his property. But, by custom, forty days' residence in Scotland is held to imply an intention of remaining in the country, and consequently, any person, who has been more than forty days in Scotland, may be cited to appear as a defender, on the strength of that circumstance alone, until the implication is rebutted by his having been forty days absent from the territory of the court. When this has occurred, or when he is not in Scotland at all, jurisdiction over him, if it exists, must be founded upon some other ground; if it can be, he may be cited in his absence. Among grounds which give the court jurisdiction, may be mentioned the subject matter

of the action being a question relating to realty in Scotland. The ownership of real property in Scotland is held to give the Scotch courts jurisdiction over the owner, in respect of all matters except status, so that, if he be resident abroad, he can be cited as an absent person at the office of the keeper of edictal citations, Edinburgh, and the action goes on against him. Where the cause of action, whether contract or delict, has arisen within Scotland, then, if along with this the defender have been personally cited in Scotland, the court has jurisdiction. Again, if a foreigner sue in a Scottish court, he is bound to answer any counter claim which has relation to the same matter, or any set-off fairly set against his own suit or claim. And if a stranger have moveable property in Scotland, the fund or effects due or belonging to him, if substantial, and not merely elusory (though this limiting condition does not appear to be very operative), may, after the fashion introduced in Holland in the 16th century, be attached at the suit of the pursuer, by an *arrestum jurisdictionis fundandæ causâ*, which is only loosed on security being found to appear and defend. The effect of this arrestment is to found jurisdiction, except in cases of status, or actions of declarator of rights, or of reduction of writings, but the jurisdiction fails upon the death of the defender. The judgment which may be pronounced is not limited to the value of the article arrested. With the exception of judgments in absence in actions in which jurisdiction has been founded by the last-mentioned means, all judgments of the Court of Session for debt, damages, or expenses may be enforced in England or Ireland, on registering them within twelve months in the books of the high court in England, or of the common pleas in Ireland; after such registration they have the force of judgments of those courts respectively, this power being reciprocal between the three countries.

In Scotch civil cases, but not in criminal, the House of Lords has appellate jurisdiction in respect of all final judgments, and also of interlocutory judgments in which there has been a division of opinion among the judges of the court, or as to which the court has granted leave to appeal.

[Rankine's *Erskine's Principles of the Law of Scotland*.]   A. D.

JURISDICTION OF STATE. See INTERNATIONAL LAW.

JUROS (*Spanish term*). Ferdinand and Isabella, and later on the Spanish kings of the house of Austria, were wont to raise money by accepting private loans from their subjects at varying rates of interest, the payment of this and the reimbursement of the capital being assigned on the general revenue. It was specified that the indentures could be held by right of inheritance (*por juro de heredad*), whence the name. These *juros* were a cause of frightful financial mismanagement, especially when at the time of compulsory reductions of interest, those held by the inquisition or ecclesiastical corporations were declared to be privileged. The unprivileged or *Seculares*, as they were called, very often were sold at a ruinous discount to holders of privileged stock, so that the liabilities of the royal treasuries derived no advantage from these iniquitous proceedings.

[See the article "Juros" in Canga Argüelles, *Diccionario de Hacienda* (London, 1826) ; ch. vi. of Konrad Haebler's *Wirtschaftliche Blüte Spaniens* (Berlin, 1888) ; and Colmeiro, *Historia de la Economia Política en España*, ii. pp. 578-581.]

E. Ca.

JURY (ENGLAND). Before the Conquest, one of the means by which an alleged offender was brought to justice was by accusing him in the sheriffs' tourn, the criminal side of the old county court. He was accused by a kind of committee of twelve from among the suitors of the court (public officials, lords of lands, and, from each township, the parish priest, the reeve, and four men), or by a private accuser ; or else in the hundred court, by the reeve and four men of the township.

The suitors were properly the judges ; and the accused was cleared either by ordeal or by compurgation, *i.e.* witnesses swore that his oath of innocence was true. After the Conquest, he was accused before the justices by the oath of "the body of the country and the lawful knights of the county" ; he might clear himself by ordeal, though even then he might have to suffer banishment ; but speaking generally, the accusation was equivalent to conviction, because the twelve accusers spoke from their own local knowledge. This was the origin of the present grand jury in England, which consists of such a number, usually twenty-three, of good and lawful men of the county, usually county magistrates, as may supply the necessary twelve accusers. In the course of time the element of local knowledge became less effective, and the ordeal was practically abolished after the Lateran council of 1216, so that there was no means of testing the truth of the accusation ; and hence the custom arose of remitting the matter to an inquest. An inquest was a Norman mode of obtaining information for the use of the justices by referring the matter of fact in dispute to persons possessed of the requisite local knowledge. If the persons so referred to testified to the truth of a fact, it was held as proved ; but it must be proved by their own oaths. They themselves were the witnesses ; and if they knew nothing of the matter, they could not testify. This kind of inquest by a jury of twelve was, after the great assize of Henry II., the regular mode of ascertaining facts relating to rights in land and the like, these being matters well known to the neighbourhood, the vicinity (*vicinetum*) or "venue." If some testified on one side and others on the other, additional witnesses were added until there were twelve in favour of one side or the other ; then the inquiry stopped, and the finding of the twelve was their "truth-telling" or *veredictum* or verdict. The jurors, being witnesses, could be individually examined by the justices.

The next stage was that the jurors, in order to prepare their sworn report, collected information in their own way. Persons possessed of particular information were called in to testify : the jurors, on being satisfied that they spoke the truth, on the ground of personal acquaintance with their credibility, adopted their information, and themselves "dared to swear" to it. They thus prepared themselves to give sworn answers to questions as to specific facts ; and by the middle of the 15th century they had arrived at a practice of giving general verdicts on the whole matter. The procedure was thus one based on the jurors' personal knowledge, and was one adapted to small neighbourhoods.

In criminal cases the accusers are now represented by the grand jury, who, as it were, from their own local knowledge of the venue, inform the judges what crimes have been committed within their district. They obtain this knowledge by hearing enough evidence to show that there is a *primâ facie* case in support of the indictment or of the presentment by the coroner's jury. If they are satisfied of this, they endorse the bill of indictment "True bill," and it then becomes an indictment, a sworn accusation by the grand jury ; if not, they endorse it "No true bill," and the prisoner is discharged, but can be indicted again. The modern equivalent of the inquest is the jury in civil cases, the petty jury in criminal cases, while the name is retained in the coroner's inquest. In the two former cases the jury consists of twelve jurors whose verdict must be unanimous ; in the last it consists of twelve or more, of whom a majority not less than twelve must concur in the verdict. Juries have a right to return any verdict without being subject to being punished at the will of the court. It is only in rare cases that the element of personal knowledge on the part of jurymen now comes into play ; in general it is assumed that they have none.

The right to have a civil case tried by a jury is now absolute only in actions of slander, libel, false imprisonment, malicious prosecution, seduction, and breach of promise of marriage. In other actions, trial by jury can only be had on an order of the court, but this, in common-law actions, is never refused if either party applies for it. A special jury can always be had, on proper notice, at the risk, as to the extra expense, of the applicant. When a juryman is withdrawn by the parties with a view to a settlement, or when he falls ill or dies, or when agreement seems hopeless, the jury is discharged, and the case, if it is to go on, must be re-tried before a new jury.

[Stephen, *Hist. of the Criminal Law of England.*—Stubbs, *Constit. Hist.*]

A. D.

JURY (SCOTLAND). The early history of the jury in Scotland is much the same as in England. In criminal cases there is no grand jury ; the jury consists of fifteen persons, of whom five must be special jurors ; and the verdict is given by a majority. The forms of verdict in use are "guilty," "not guilty," and "not proven." The last operates as a bar to any fresh trial on the same charge : it has the same effect as a plea of *autrefois acquit* in England. It is understood, and is intended by juries, to mean that the jury are not satisfied as to the innocence of the prisoner, but think the crown authorities have not proved his guilt. It seems, however, that this is a comparatively recent interpretation of the verdict, and that "not proven" formerly differed from "not guilty" only in referring to the charge instead of to the person; the converse verdict being either "proven" or "guilty."

Jurors in Scotland must have £5 a year from land, or personal property over £200 in value: special jurors must have £8 : 6 : 8 from land, occupy a £30 house or possess personal property over £1000 in value. Each party has five challenges, of which not more than two can be challenges of special jurymen. The verdict is delivered by the foreman or "chancellor" *viva voce* unless a written verdict is directed, and he must say whether the verdict is unanimous or by a majority.

In civil cases, trial by inquest was anciently the usual form; but the ecclesiastical courts assumed a much larger jurisdiction in early Scotland than in England; and the session of James I. and the daily council of James IV. superseded jury trials to a still further extent; so that after the institution of the Court of Session, jury trial in civil cases had practically fallen into disuse except in respect of inquests, which the sheriffs of counties were directed by the Scottish chancery to hold, in reference to the ascertainment of heirs, the finding persons to be lunatic, the delimitation of the widow's third in lands, and the partition of property among heirs-portioners. In 1815, however, it was thought by parliament that trial by jury ought to be made more use of in civil cases in Scotland; and a new court, the jury court, was established, to ascertain facts on remit from the other courts. In 1831, this court was, however, absorbed in the Court of Session, which takes jury trials when required. The cases appropriate to jury trials are, to summarise them roughly, actions arising from alleged wrong-doing, where damages and costs are alone sued for, actions against innkeepers, carriers, etc., actions on insurance policies, some shipping cases, and the annulling of deeds and contracts as having been obtained by coercion, etc. But in practice, litigants are found to prefer trials before a judge without a jury. In jury trials issues are usually adjusted and placed, in print, in the hands of the jurymen, so that they may answer the precise questions put to them. Jury trials take place before the Court of Session in Edinburgh, or before the sheriffs in the county towns; sometimes on circuit. Either party may move for a special jury. The verdict must be unanimous, or, after three hours, by a majority; while in case of equal division the jury is discharged after six hours. The parties may agree to take a special verdict at any time; and, in the course of the trial, a juror may be withdrawn.

[Bell's *Dictionary of the Law of Scotland.*— Mackay's *Practice of the Court of Session.*— Macdonald's *Criminal Law of Scotland*,—50 & 51 Vict. c. 35.]   A. D.

JUS AD REM: JUS IN RE. Barbarisms purporting to be derived from the Roman law, but which first appeared in the *Brachylogus* and passed into secular jurisprudence from the canon law.

A *jus ad rem* is a right, relating to a thing, enforceable by an action *in personam; e.g.* a right on the part of A to make B deliver up a specific chattel. A *jus in re* is an absolute right to a thing, enforceable by an action *in rem;* the right which an owner has in his own property. A *jus ad rem* is based on an obligation, and is good as against the party bound; a *jus in re* is good as against the world.   A. D.

JUS NATURÆ, as understood by the PHYSIOCRATS, is the right which a man has to do that which is beneficial or advantageous to himself. This right he can only make use of by conforming himself to the order of nature and obeying natural laws.

Up to the middle of the 18th century the question of man's natural rights had been much neglected by philosophers, though LOCKE speaks of it (Bonar, *Philos. and Pol. Econ.*, p. 98), and QUESNAY's views, though not original as regards their subordinate propositions, amounted in the sum to an expansion of the ideas of mankind with respect to the due order of society. Personal liberty and proprietorship of the results of his labour are man's primary rights. These would be destroyed if it were not the duty of all men to abstain from invading them. Hence rights and duties are reciprocal and interdependent. But duties are burdens, and therefore in a sense evils. They exist only to exclude greater evils, and so their existence must depend upon their utility. For subsistence, property is requisite, and this implies inequalities among men, as the ability to acquire is not uniform. Again, for food-production the first essential is land, which is best cultivated when it is a permanent possession, and property in land is therefore desirable. Finally, as all men are not willing to respect rights and duties, means for their protection must be provided, and this provision is Government; but government should have no other mission than the protection of the rights of liberty and property, and legislation should be mainly the enunciation of such natural laws as are best calculated to preserve the social order (see GOVERNMENT, ECON. EFFECTS OF).

[F. Quesnay, *Le Droit Naturel* in *Physiocrates*, E. Daire, Paris, 1846.—G. Schelle, *Du Pont de Nemours*, 1888.—J. Bonar, *Philos. and Pol. Econ.* (1893), p. 135 *seq.*]   R. H.

JUS NATURALE, JUS GENTIUM, JUS DIVINUM, JUS HUMANUM. In these phrases the term *Jus* is used not in its sense of a particular "right," but in its sense of "principle of right" = *droit, diritto, Recht*. There is no proper English equivalent for it, as the use of "Law" is apt to cause confusion with the meaning of "law" = *lex, loi, legge, Gesetz, i.e.* a definite statute or judicially-enforced custom. Thus English readers may need to be reminded that international "law," a use of the term "law" to which Austin objects, is in other languages not *lex*, but *jus, droit international, Völkerrecht*, etc.

ARISTOTLE had recognised a distinction between "natural" justice (τὸ φυσικὸν δίκαιον =jus naturale), which is the same at all times and in all places, and "conventional" justice, τὸ νομικὸν δίκαιον, which depends on institution and may therefore vary (Eth. Nic. v. 7, § 1). The Roman jurists distinguished the jus civile of Rome or of any particular state from the jus gentium or principles of right commonly recognised among the various nations and tribes known to them, the principles according to which "equity" was administered by the prætors in cases where aliens were concerned. When the Romans came to be influenced by Greek, especially Stoic, philosophy, jus naturale came to be used (e.g. by Cicero) as an equivalent but more philosophical term for this jus gentium. [Maine's view about the jus gentium in his Ancient Law is corrected in part by H. Nettleship in Journal of Philology, vol. xiii. p. 169, seq.] Philosophical associations tended to introduce into the conception of "natural law" the ideas of simplicity and of perfection, and thus the notion came to serve the cause of legal reform. One jurist, Ulpian, attempted to distinguish the jus naturale from the jus gentium : jus naturale he defined as that which nature teaches to all animals, e.g. the bringing up of offspring, jus gentium as that which is common to the whole human race. In accordance with this distinction, slavery is said to exist jure gentium, having arisen out of capture in war ; but "by the law of nature all men were born free" (Justinian, Inst. i. 2). Later writers tend to regard jus naturale or lex naturalis as distinct from jus gentium, but not simply on the ground taken by Ulpian. The law of nature is to them not merely, as to the older Roman lawyers, a common element amid the diversities of human institutions, but that portion of the "eternal law" or system of divine government in which man as a rational creature can always and everywhere, though in varying degrees, participate, (THOMAS AQUINAS, Summa, 1a 2ae, qu. 93. art. 2) : whereas the jus gentium, containing much that is due to tacit or express agreement, is rather counted as part of positive human law, jus humanum, the other part being jus civile, the law of this or that particular state. This had been the view of Isidore of Seville (d. 636 A.D.). His Sententiæ were a main channel through which scraps of ancient learning passed to the mediæval world. Thomas Aquinas accepts the view of Isidore about the subdivision of human law, but holds that all human law is derived from the law of nature, as conclusions from premisses ; so that the jus gentium is in a sense natural to man, though distinguishable from the law of nature, especially from that which is common to all animals (1a 2ae, qu. 95, art. 4). Suarez (De legibus, ii. 17 and 19), laying still less stress on Ulpian's distinction, agrees on the whole with Aquinas. From these authorities apparently is derived the view of GROTIUS (q.v.), who rejects the opinion of Ulpian as of little use (i. 1, § 11), but regards the jus gentium as properly a division of instituted human law, jus voluntarium humanum, being the product of tacit or express agreements among nations (Jus gentium, it should be noted, is coming to mean jus inter gentes), whereas the jus naturale in the strict sense consists of principles which can be deduced by reason from the primary necessities of man's rational and social nature. But on this subject there is much division of opinion, and even those who adopt the distinction do not always consistently separate the jus gentium from the jus naturale. PUFENDORF (De Jure Naturæ et Gentium, ii. 3, § 22) follows Hobbes (De Cive, c. xiv. 5, 4) in dividing natural law into the natural law of individuals and of states—jus gentium now meaning quite definitely "international law." Pufendorf denies that there is any positive "law of nations" apart from either the law of nature or the civil law of particular states. Barbeyrac, Grotius's commentator, makes the same criticism. Later writers on the law of nations seem mostly to agree in recognising two elements in the jus gentium, one derived from "nature" or reason, the other from the actual usage of the more civilised nations : thus we can distinguish a jus gentium naturale and a jus gentium positivum or voluntarium (see Wheaton's International Law, pt. i. ch. i.). This view seems to recognise the element of truth in the conflicting theories.

The law of nature is, by Thomas Aquinas and his followers, regarded as immutable even by the will of God, though it may be added to by the positive law of both God and man. The positive law of God, jus voluntarium, positivum, or divinum, is the law of God as specially revealed to mankind at large, or to any particular portion of mankind. The law of nature might, as coming also from God, "the author of the rational nature of man," be called jus divinum; but among Christian theologians that term is generally given to the jus positivum divinum. In regard to the positive divine law of the New Testament, a distinction is always recognised by Catholic theologians between "precepts" binding on all men and "counsels of perfection." It may be noted that the schoolmen generally speak of lex naturalis, lex divina, etc., rather than of jus, probably because they are thinking of God as legislator. Grotius (I. i. § 10) holds that the jus naturale would exist and be binding even if we were to suppose that there was no God, an attempt to separate jurisprudence from theology which he does not consistently follow out : this Pufendorf (II. 3 § 19) will not allow, holding that the obligation of natural law is from God.

In these theories we have the source not only of the modern German theories of *Naturrecht*, but of these doctrines about "natural liberty," "natural rights," etc. which play so large a part in the politics and economics of the 18th century and even of our own time. It should be noted that in all the more careful writers on the law of nature, that law is supposed to deal not only with what may be supposed to be a "state of nature" apart from human institution, but also with circumstances created by institutions. Thus the rights of private property as they now exist in any particular country are only rights by natural law in the sense that they may not be contrary to natural law, which allows the right to acquire property ; but when once such rights have been introduced or defined by positive human law, obligations to respect property-rights are created which are obligations of natural law apart from positive institution. Pufendorf would not regard such obligations as belonging to natural law in the strictest sense, but only "reductively" (II. 3, § 21), and Thomas Aquinas carefully distinguishes the senses in which anything may be said to be according to the law of nature (1a 2ae, qu. 95, art. 5). Such careful distinctions are not always observed by those who have used the phraseology of natural rights in later times, especially in practical controversies (see INTERNATIONAL LAW ; LAW).

[Besides Maine, *Ancient Law* (1st ed. 1861) and the other works referred to in the article, may be named Moritz Voigt, *Das jus naturale, aequum et bonum und jus gentium der Römer*, 4 vols., Leipzig, 1856-75.—J. Bonar, *Philosophy and Political Economy*, 1893, bk. ii.—D. G. Ritchie, *Natural Rights*, 1895, ch. ii.—Lorimer, *Institutes of Law* (1st ed. 1872, 2nd ed. 1880) is an application of the German theory of *Naturrecht*.]

D. G. R.

JUS RELICTÆ (Scots Law). The widow's share of the free movable property, other than personal bonds bearing interest, of a predeceasing husband ; one third if he have left children, one half if none. This share is reckoned after the predeceasing husband's personal obligations have been provided for : hence the widow may have both *jus relictæ* and a right to demand performance of the provisions of a settlement, unless she have, either explicitly or by inevitable implication, and with full knowledge of her legal rights, given up her *jus relictæ*. This widow's right takes precedence of any will made by the predeceasing husband, and vests in her by mere operation of law ; and it can be enforced against the husband's executor. By the Scotch Married Women's Property Act of 1881, § 6, a surviving husband is given an analogous right over the estate of the predeceasing wife.

A. D.

JUS STILLICIDII. See SERVITUDE.
JUST PRICE. See JUSTUM PRETIUM.
JUSTA CAUSA. According to Roman law a delivery of property in order to operate as a conveyance by delivery (*traditio*) must be accompanied by a legal act, such as a contract of sale or exchange, showing an intention to transfer the right of property in it. The term for a legal act of this nature is *justa causa traditionis*.

E. A. W.

JUSTI, JOHANN HEINRICH GOTTLOB VON (1720-1771), a German economist, was born at Brücken in Thuringia. He studied jurisprudence at Wittenberg, and afterwards—having served meantime in the Prussian army—at Jena and Leipzig. He was then for some time in the service of the Duchess of Sachsen-Eisenach. He was made, apparently in 1750, professor of the cameral sciences in the newly-founded Ritter-Akademie (Theresianum) at Vienna, and is by some accused of having changed for the time his religious profession in order to obtain this appointment. The outline of economic doctrine which he prepared with a view to his lectures was warmly approved by the then minister Haugwitz, and he was employed in various commissions by the government. In 1753 he quitted the Austrian service, and at Erfurt and Leipzig engaged in various literary undertakings for a livelihood. In 1755 he settled at Göttingen as member of the council of mines and commissioner of police. In 1757 he went to Copenhagen, and, coming thence to Berlin, was made director of mines and superintendent of glass and steel works. He was, however, frequently in collision with his colleagues and subordinates, and was finally disgraced in consequence of a deficit in his accounts, due apparently not to fraudulent design, but to his improvident household management and singularly unsystematic mode of life. He died a prisoner in the fortress of Küstrin.

Justi was a man of remarkable gifts and indefatigable industry. His importance in the history of political economy arises from the fact that he was the first German systematic writer on the science. In his earlier publications he stands on the basis of the mercantilist doctrine, but in his later works he was influenced by the encyclopædists and tended towards views similar to those of the physiocratic school. His principal economic writings were: *Staatswirthschaft oder systematische Abhandlung aller ökonomischen- und Cameralwissenschaften*, 1755, dedicated to the Empress Maria Theresa, of whose political practice his work is the theoretical counterpart ; *Entdeckte Ursuchen von dem verderbten Münzwesen*, 1755, in which he denounced the debasement of the currency by the King of Prussia and the Duke of Würtemberg ; *Grundsätze der Polizeiwissenschaft*, 1756, a treatise on administration, a branch of theory of which L. von Stein declares him to have been the father, but which he unduly extended so as to make it include the subjects of the circulation of money and public credit ; in this treatise occurs his well-known dictum that a state cannot have too many inhabitants ; *Abhandlung von den Steuern und Aufgaben*, 1762, in which he proposed to substitute for excise duties a tax on the net profits of traders ; and *System des Finanzwesens*, 1766, dedicated to Frederick the Great ; this was the first systematic work in German on the subject of finance ; it gives, says Cossa, the rational classification of public expenses, and contains a good account of sources of revenue, but an insufficient treatment of public loans. In the spirit of the mercantilists, he regards taxes as "bridles" to be used by a government in directing the industry of producers into the lines most advantageous to the whole community. A number of his minor pieces on economics were published collectively in two vols. in 1760-61, and another series in three parts (1761-64), in which the most remarkable is *Von der Finanzverwaltung des Postwesens*, in which he objects to the monopoly possessed by the state post-office, and condemns the practice of making the post, in any great degree, a source of public income.

[Inama in *Allg. Deutsche Biogr.*—Lippert in *Handb. der Staatswissenschaften.*—Roscher, *Gesch. der N.O.*, p. 444.—Cossa, *Introd. allo studio dell' E.P.*, p. 259. See, too, Hasbach's *Untersuchungen über Adam Smith*, 1891, pp. 224-25, 229. Best account in G. Marchet, *Studien über die Ueberwaltungslehre in Deutschland*, 1885.—Seligman, *Taxation*, 1895.] J. K. I.

JUSTICE or JUSTICIARE is a word frequently used by Madox in his description of the collection of a scutage. When a tenant *in capite* was unable to make his tenants pay the amounts due from them, he was in the habit of obtaining the permission of the court of exchequer to *justiciare tenentes suos*, meaning thereby, to distrain on their goods, and, if necessary, to call in the aid of the sheriff to enable him to do so. (*See* KNIGHT'S SERVICE.)

[Madox, *History of the Exchequer*, London, 1769.] A. E. S.

JUSTICE, ALEXANDER (c. early 18th century), besides his work *A general treatise of the Dominion and Laws of the Sea*, ancient and modern (especially French and English), together with a proposal to abolish *Pressing for the Navy*, 1705, which includes information on marine insurance, also wrote a *General Treatise of Monies and Exchanges* : *In which those of all Trading Nations are particularly described and considered. With an Account of all the Foreign Banks and different Species and Denominations of Monies . . . and of the Method and Practice of Foreign and Domestic Exchanges* (1707), a merchants' handbook of English and foreign coinage, banks, mercantile bills and notes, weights and measures, and exchanges. In the dedication, speaking of exchange, he says, "some years' experience I have had myself in that way of business," and the work is entirely that of a practical man, never touching the theoretical side of his subject.

[See Thorold Rogers, *First Nine Years of the Bank of England*, 1887, pp. 37, 42.] E. G. P.

JUSTICE SEAT. See FORESTS, MEDIÆVAL.

JUSTUM PRETIUM, "just price." The doctrine of "just price"—that there was for every article at a particular time a just price, for which alone it should be sold—played a great part in the economic teaching of the mediæval church, and had great influence upon the action of the public authorities. The stress which the great schoolmen, beginning with Peter Lombard, laid upon it from the 12th century onwards, must be explained not only by the growth of trade, but also by the revived study of the Roman law, which had laid down that every man had a natural right to overreach another ; against this teaching the doctrine of the church must be regarded as a conscious protest. It was formulated systematically in the *Summa Theologica* of AQUINAS, who was followed by most subsequent writers. But although Aquinas and the other schoolmen felt no difficulty in proving that it was not allowable in conscience, whatever might be the rule of civil law, to sell a thing for more than it was worth, they seldom gave much attention to the question what constituted just price. It is probable, however, that what some of them definitely stated, for instance LANGENSTEIN— viz. that a man could determine for himself the just price of the wares he had to sell by simply reckoning what he needed in order to suitably support himself in his rank in life— was assumed as a matter of course by Aquinas and other writers. The whole scholastic and canonist view of society rested on the idea of *status ;* and this particular doctrine was only applicable so long as every class directly or indirectly engaged in production had a recognised standard of living. And even then difficulties were presented by wares like corn, the supply of which depended upon the seasons. Here it was impossible not to allow that the price must vary ; but it was attempted to remove as far as possible all opportunity for the arbitrary exercise of the individual will, by insisting that the whole local supply should be laid before the whole body of purchasers in the open market. This was to a large extent the motive which guided legislation in the matter of forestalling, etc.

Knies and others have remarked that what the doctrine of just price aimed at may be described as a *normal* price, in accordance with *cost of production*, instead of a fluctuating price dependent upon the chances of the market. This is an accurate description, if it be understood that cost of production was to be determined by a fixed standard of living on the part of the producers, and was not to include any element of *interest*. Perhaps the contrast between mediæval and modern ideas of value is best expressed by saying that to us value is usually something subjective, consisting of the mental determination of seller and buyer, while to the schoolmen it was in a sense objective, something intrinsically bound up with the commodity itself.

[W. Endemann, *Studien in der romanisch-* | *kanonistischen Wirthschafts- u. Rechtslehre*, vol. ii. (1883), v.—Ashley, *Economic History* (pt. i. 1888, pt. ii. 1893), §§ 16, 64.] w. j. a.

KACORAWNS, a money current in Guinea and Benin "which is *gold* drawn out into *wier*, and cut afterwards into small pieces for all triviall commodities." No minted coin appears to have been employed at this period (*circa* 1650) in these countries, the payment being made in gold and by weight.

[Lewes Roberts, *The Merchant's Mappe of Commerce*, London, 1638.]

KANE, SIR ROBERT JOHN (1809 - 1890), was an Irish scientist and statistician. In 1843 he delivered a course of lectures in Dublin, which in the following year he published under the title of *The Industrial Resources of Ireland* (2nd ed., Dublin 1845, 8vo). His object was, he tells us, " to obtain materials for the discussion of the problem . . . what field of *work* does Ireland really present ? " After describing the geological strata of Ireland, the lie of the coal and other mineral beds, her water power, agriculture, linen trade, and her excellent internal communication by means of navigable rivers, lakes, canals, and railways, he compares the low average cost of unskilled labour with the dearness and scarcity of skilled labour, and in conclusion insists that Ireland will never become rich by waiting idly for English capital to come to her : she must, the author points out, create a capital for herself, always remembering that "labour is capital : intellect is capital."

In 1846 Kane was knighted, and the same year was appointed director of the Museum of Irish Industry, for the foundation of which he had successfully agitated. In 1873 he was made a commissioner of national education, and, in 1877, elected president of the Royal Irish Academy. In 1880 he became vice-chancellor of the newly created Royal University of Ireland.

He published *The Large and Small Farm Question Considered*, 1844, in which he advocated the formation of small farms in Ireland.—*Address delivered at the Public Distribution of Prizes . . . by Sir John R. Kane*, Cork, Queen's College, 1850, 8vo. — *Elements of Practical Pharmacy*, Dublin, 1831, 12mo. — *Elements of Chemistry, Illustrated*, Dublin, 1846, 8vo ; 2nd ed. 1849, 8vo.—*The Queen's University in Ireland and the Queen's Colleges ; Their Progress and Present State*, Dublin, 1856, 8vo.—*The Irish Watering Places*, 1845, 8vo. A. L.

KANT, IMMANUEL (1724-1804). Kant was born and bred at Königsberg, East Prussia ; and, except the few years when he was private tutor a few miles off, the whole of his life was spent in his native town. From 1755 to 1770 he gave lectures at the university on mathematics, philosophy, and theology, becoming professor of philosophy 1770, and doing the work of the chair till 1797. His *Critique of Pure Reason* appeared in 1781 ; *Critique of Judgment*, 1790 ; *Doctrine of Right, and Doctrine of Virtue* (*Metaphysic of Ethics*), 1797. His complete works fill eight stout octavo volumes in Hartenstein's newer edition (1867 *seq.*, Leipzig).

Kant is to modern philosophy what Adam Smith is to modern economics. Professor Oncken has even tried to show an agreement between them in general principles of philosophy (*Smith und Kant*, Leipzig, 1877). They agree, he says, in reintroducing teleology alongside of mechanism in the world. They both, he says, distinguish between the world of spirit and the world of sense, Adam Smith's *Moral Sentiments* being supposed to deal specially with the spiritual world, his *Wealth of Nations* with the sensible. Kant's dualism, however, was not merely of two aspects or elements of the same world : he conceived man to be member, at the same time, of two entirely different worlds. As the recipient of impressions from the senses man is strictly under physical law ; his very motives, as sensible, are part of the world-wide chain of causes and effects. He is a phenomenon among phenomena. But as a moral being he is a law to himself and an end to himself, a cause but not an effect. He is a noumenon, a member of the intelligible as distinguished from the sensible world. It is impossible to find any conception closely approaching this in Adam Smith, though we may grant to Professor Oncken that the two philosophers both conceive religion to represent duty as divine commandment. Their agreement reaches farther in the neutral sphere of political philosophy. Kant conceives civil society as existing to secure not the happiness of its members, which depends on themselves, but their freedom. It is founded on an original contract, not as a fact of history, but as a logical postulate. All give up their original license under the law of nature, in order to get real liberty by a political union. This liberty is the end of all laws ; the first principle of law or right is : " So act that your freedom shall not interfere with another man's freedom." Force may be used to secure this. Kant's view of the powers of the state approached absolutism, though he had also a weak side for the French revolution, and allowed that when men are ripe for it, a republic is the best form of government.

Originally, which means no more than in abstraction from civil society, all land was in common—Kant does not say all things were—

and private ownership is founded on the social contract, and therefore, in a sense, on a common ownership. The state secures private rights, and in return may tax private owners. The state may impress citizens as soldiers, because the state makes it possible for these citizens to come into the world at all, and thus in a sense creates them, and has the ownership and disposal of them.

Kant's state is essentially regulative rather than constructive or socialistic. The notion of contract is stretched by him very far, to include, for example, marriage. It is under the head of contract that he lays down most of his economic propositions, which are not very profound. He does not, like Locke, base property on labour ; he defines money as the means of exchanging one man's industry with another's, but labour plays, on the whole, a minor part in his notion of economical arrangements. Silver seems to him the best money ; and he finds an analogy between money, as a means of exchanging goods, and books, as a means of exchanging ideas. He quotes the *Wealth of Nations*, rather loosely, and speaks in praise of commerce and trade. Though the commercial spirit seems, like the aristocratic, unsocial, it will one day, he thinks, lead to the fulfilment of his fond hope of a permanent peace among the nations. In his *Anthropology* (1798) he gives his estimate of the nations as they were then. The French, he says, have given the world the language of conversation, the English the language of trade. The difference of national character appears even in the way in which, for example, a rich man is described. In English, "he is worth a million" ; in Dutch, "he commands a million" ; in French, "he possesses a million." In Kant's essay on the "Aufklärung" or *Illumination* (1784), and on Herder's *Philosophy of History* (1785), he gives his view of what was even then called evolution. It is, he says, essentially a notion of metaphysics, and not of physical science ; but it is not therefore the less but the more trustworthy.

Kant's followers were often economists (see GERMAN SCHOOL), but he needs mention in a history of political economy chiefly because his philosophy begat that of FICHTE and HEGEL, which determined the character of modern German socialism.

[The best English account of Kant's whole philosophy is by Edward Caird, Master of Balliol, *The Critical Philosophy of Immanuel Kant* (Maclehose, Glasgow, 2 vols., 1889). The literature on Kant, both in English and in German, is very large. For the economical passages in his writings, compare Bonar's *Philosophy and Political Economy* (Sonnenschein, 1893).] J. B.

KARL FRIEDRICH (1728-1811), at first margrave, then (1803) elector, and finally (1806) grand duke of Baden, was born at Carlsruhe. Succeeding his grandfather before he was ten years old, he finished his studies, and visited France, Italy, England, and Holland before returning to Carlsruhe. His regime was tolerant and enlightened, and he attracted many residents to his state. He preserved his dominions from the evils suffered by others during the Seven Years' War, and made great sacrifices to maintain peace with revolutionary France. He excluded the *emigrés* from Baden, and remained faithful to the fortunes of Napoleon, by whose aid he greatly enlarged his possessions. His *Abrégé des Principes de l'Économie Politique* appeared in the *Éphémérides du Citoyen*, Paris, 1772, with a preface by Dupont de Nemours. It was dedicated to the Marquis de MIRABEAU, for whom the author had a profound admiration. He was the most important German convert won by the physiocrats. His book is of little scientific value and contains nothing original, but it produced a considerable effect at the time of its appearance, and has still a certain historical interest as proceeding from the chief of a State.[1]

[See C. Knies, *Carl Friedrichs von Baden brieflicher Verkehr mit Mirabeau und Du Pont* (Heidelberg, 1892).—Review of this in *Econ. Jour.*, vol. iii. 1892.] J. K. I.

KAY-SHUTTLEWORTH, SIR JAMES PHILLIPS (1804-1877), the founder of the modern national school system. He studied medicine at Edinburgh, where he took his M.D. in 1827. Both as student and practitioner at Manchester, he devoted much time to the housing and sanitary condition of the poor. The cholera outbreak in 1832 confirmed many of his conclusions, and resulted in the publication of his pamphlet on *The Moral and Physical Condition of the Working Classes employed in the Cotton Manufacture in Manchester* (London 1832, 8vo). In 1831, he published an anonymous *Letter to the people of Lancashire concerning the future representation of the Commercial Interest.* He was an ardent advocate for parliamentary reform and the repeal of the corn laws. In 1834 he was chosen to introduce the new poor law locally, and next year became assistant poor-law commissioner. In 1841 the government published his reports on the training of pauper children. The subject of national education became henceforth the study of his life ; and in 1839 he was appointed secretary to a committee of privy council, nominated to dispose of public money voted for purposes of national education. This same year—with the help of a friend—he established the first training college for teachers at Battersea. During the cotton famine of 1861-65, Kay-Shuttleworth—who had been created a baronet under this name in 1849— worked vigorously to relieve, without pauperising, the poor. In 1863, he was high sheriff

---

[1] Refer to his experiment on *Impôt Unique*, and to account of this by Emminghaus mentioned *s.v.* IMPÔT UNIQUE.

of Lancashire, and in 1870 received the honorary degree of D.C.L. from the university of Oxford.

His numerous writings on educational and social questions are chiefly collected in the following volumes :—*Public Education as affected by the Minutes of the Committee of Privy Council*, 1846-52, London, 1853, 8vo. — *Four Periods of Public Education as reviewed in 1832, 1839, 1846, and 1862*, London, 1863, 8vo. — *Thoughts and Suggestions on Certain Social Problems*, etc. . . . London, 1873, 8vo. — *The Results of the Education Act*, Fortnightly Review, May 1876. **A. L.**

KELLEY, WILLIAM D. (1814-1890), born in Philadelphia, practised law, served as judge from 1846 until 1856 ; in 1854 abandoned the democratic party and became a republican and protectionist. In 1861 he entered Congress and served until his death. He was thoroughly identified with the cause of protection, serving for many years on the committee of ways and means, and for a portion of his term as its chairman. His loyalty to the protective system was unwavering, and is well expressed in a speech made 25th March 1870, which also illustrates the views of many of his party.

"Protection cheapens commodities ; the internal revenue system is expensive and inquisitorial and should be abolished at the earliest possible day ; free trade means low wages and a limited market for grain ; protective duties are not a tax ; protection stimulates immigration ; skilled workmen are the most valuable commodity we can import."

He was earnest in his advocacy of legal tender treasury notes, convertible into securities, the interest of which should be payable in the same currency. In his support of legal tenders he opposed the extension of the national banking system. At the close of the civil war he opposed the contraction of the currency, and made a speech in favour of what he termed an inexportable currency. He also supported the silver legislation of 1878.

[His opinions are typical of a considerable group within his own party, and thus stand in economic history for more than an individual expression. They may be found expressed in *Speeches, Addresses, and Letters on Industrial and Financial Questions*, Philadelphia, 1872, pp. xxx. 514.] **D. R. D.**

KELLOGG, EDWARD (1790-1858), born in Norwalk, Conn., engaged in business in New York, and died there. His interest in economic questions was aroused by the crisis of 1837, for which various causes were assigned by different investigators. He came to the conclusion that commercial disturbances and economic evils in general were due to a lack of credit facilities. He consequently proposed a national currency to be based upon actual property or land security to be loaned to individuals at a uniform rate of interest and therefore of uniform value in all parts of the country. Through this agency

wealth would be more fairly distributed, as labour would not be subject to capital.

This thesis is developed at length in *Currency, the Evil and Remedy*, by Godek Gardwell, N.Y., 1844.—*Labour and Other Capital, the Rights of each Secured*, N.Y., 1849, pp. 298 ; and in a revised edition of the latter, entitled *A New Monetary System the only Means of securing the Rights of Labour and Property*, N.Y., 1861, pp. 366. **D. R. D.**

KELP, RENT OF, instanced by Adam Smith (*W. of N.*, ed. M'Culloch, p. 66) to prove that rent may be exacted for land never improved by human industry. Kelp-burning was practised in Ireland long before it was begun, towards the middle of the 18th century, on the western coasts and islands of Scotland. Estates hitherto valueless brought in large kelp-rents to their owners ; but since changes in chemical processes have greatly diminished the demand for kelp, many of the shores on which it was gathered below high water-mark have ceased to produce rent. In 1845 nearly one-third of the rental of one parish in the Orkneys was being paid for kelp, at the rate of two guineas per ton, a great decrease from earlier rates ; in another parish the decrease was from £20 or £15 a ton to £5. As late as 1827 the landlords of a parish in Sanday island were estimated to receive a kelp-rent of £4320, or £9 a ton. On the chief estate in South Uist reductions in the price of kelp reduced the rental by more than two-thirds. When the price was high £20 a ton was an ordinary rent, and even in 1830 the net kelp-rent of the western islands of Scotland was £20,000, of North Uist alone £7000.

The manufacture still continues on the Irish coasts, though at lowered prices, ranging at present from £1 to £5 a ton according to quality and time of year.

Arthur Young (*Tour in Ireland*, 1780) gives several instances of rent paid by kelp shores ; in Galway, he says, "the shore is let with the land against it, and is what the people pay their rent by" (p. 231) ; in Sligo he mentions an estate the coast of which let for £100 a year for making kelp (p. 215). But he gives few figures.

[*Statistical Account of Scotland*, 1845, vol. xiv., xv.—*Penny Encyclopædia*, 1839, art. "Kelp."—Brewster's *Edinburgh Encyclopædia*, 1830, art. "Scotland."—Private information from Ireland. —*Times*, 12th November 1890.] **E. G. P.**

KEMPER, JEROMMO DE BOSCH (1808-1876), son of Joan Melchior Kemper, born at Amsterdam, studied law at Leyden, 1825-1830. He became a famous criminalist, and from 1834-1852 was public prosecutor. In 1852 he was appointed professor at the university of Amsterdam. For a short time he was also a member of the states - general. He rendered great services to the study of statistics by founding the Dutch Statistical Society. His principal works on economical subjects are :—*Geschiedkundig onderzœk naar de Armoede in ons vader-*

*land, hare oorzaken, en de middelen, die tot
hare vermindering zouden kunnen worden
aangewend* (Historical Inquiry into Pauperism
in our Country ; its Causes and the Means to
diminish it), Haarlem : Erven Loosjes, 1851.
*Handleiding tot de kennis van de wetenschap
der samenleving* (Treatise on Social Science),
Amsterdam, 1863.

Kemper belonged to the historical school.
His works give evidence of enormous reading
on a variety of subjects.   His method is
eclectic.   He advocated scientifically and politically the *"juste milieu"*; but his principles are
somewhat vague.

His treatise on social science is a very
important work, full of learning ; it is an
introduction to his political history of Holland,
and his system of Dutch public law.

A. F. v. L.

KERNETTY was one of the items in the
revenue of the petty princes of Ireland, as
distinguished from the monarch.   It was a
land tax of 3s. 4d. per acre on ploughed land,
and was devoted to the maintenance of the
prince's mansion house.   C. A. H.

KERSSEBOOM, WILLEM (1691 - 1771), a
Dutch actuary, and an able representative of
those economic students who followed the
method of inquiry styled political arithmetic
(see ARITHMETIC, POLITICAL), was brought into
notice through his books written between the
years 1737-1742. He was an official in the financial administration of the province of Holland,
which at that time possessed sovereignty ; and
having to superintend the government contracts
relating to annuities, was led to calculate one
of the earliest tables of mortality and survival.
On these tables, calculated by means of direct
observation, he bestowed a vast amount of
labour.   They served as the basis for the
valuation of life annuities, in those days an
important source of revenue to the Province,
and won him a well-merited reputation as an
actuary.

He endeavoured to calculate also the number
of the population by applying his tables of survival to the number of the births. This ingenious
estimate, made at a time when exact statistics
of the population were yet unheard of, would
have secured his reputation, had the number
of births on which he based the whole calculation been correct.   This, however, was not in
the least the case, the number of births being
only a rather rough estimate.   The value of
these books as statistics is therefore not equal
to their ingenuity.

[On Kersseboom, see X. Heuschling, *Bull. de la
Comm. Centr. de Stat. de la Belgique*, tome vii.
p. 397 ; Dr. A. Beaujon, *Jubilee volume of the Paris
Stat. Soc.*, 1866. p. 66 ; John, *History of Statistics*,
i. p. 227 *et seq.* ; also article in *Handwörterbuch
der Staatswissenschaften*.]   C. A. V. S.

KEYS, QUEEN'S (Scots Law).   That part

of a warrant which authorises a messenger-at-
arms to break locks, in order to get at a debtor
or his goods.   A. D.

KHRAN.   The standard of value and the
money of account in Persia.   A silver coin 890
fine, weighing 71 grains.   Value : English
standard (925 fine at 5s. 6d. an oz.) 9¼d. ;
French standard (silver francs 900 fine), ·91
franc.   F. E. A.

The exchange value of the khran has fallen
greatly since 1865, owing as much to uncertainty
as to its intrinsic value as to the fall in the gold
price of silver.   C. A. H.

KIND, PAYMENTS IN.   The payment of
rent, wages, and other dues in commodities
other than money, usually in agricultural
produce—known in England as payment "in
kind"—was, in early society and in mediæval
times, but part of a condition of things to
which HILDEBRAND (*q.v.*), and many German
economists and historians following him, have
given the name "Natural-wirthschaft."   In
this "natural," as opposed to a "money,"
"economy," the distribution of wealth, so far
as it took place at all outside the family, was
effected by equivalencies of land, services, and
commodities, especially of grain, without the
intervention of money : feudalism has been not
inaptly described as but a peculiar form of
"natural economy."   In the earliest economic
stages, payment in kind may be looked upon
as an outcome of the method of barter which
prevailed in all exchanges ; but long after
barter had disappeared in all ordinary buying
and selling, the periodical dues of serfs and
even of other tenants continued to be paid,
partially at least, in kind.   Over large parts
of Europe the practice has survived to the
present day in the shape of MÉTAYER tenure
(*q.v.*).   In industry, the payment of wages
partly in commodities was among the earliest
evils complained of upon the rise of the
domestic manufacture, and gave rise to legislation in England as early as 3 Hen. VIII.
The TRUCK SYSTEM (*q.v.*), as it was called,
continued to exist in spite of renewed legislative
prohibition, and became even more widespread
upon the advent of the "great industry."
The act of 1 & 2 William IV. c. 37 went
far to destroy it, but it lingered on for some
time, here and there, in various forms.

[Bruno Hildebrand's distinction between *Natural*- and *Geld-wirthschaft* is referred to in his
Nationalökonomie der Gegenwart und Zukunft
(1848), and worked out at length in an article in
his *Jahrbücher für N.O.*, vol. ii. (1864).   For the
English Middle Ages see Ashley, *Econ. Hist.*, i.
pt. 1, § 6 ; for the German, K. W. Nitzsch,
Gesch. d. deutschen Volkes (2nd ed. 1892), *passim*.
Adam Smith, following the physiocrats, regarded
the metayer tenure as altogether unsatisfactory,
and declared that rents in kind and rents in
service were "always more hurtful to the tenant
than beneficial to the landlord" (*W. of N.*, bk. v.

ch. ii. art. 1). J. S. Mill, however, took up its defence, so far as Italy was concerned, and "regretted that a state of rural well-being . . . should be put to hazard by an attempt to introduce . . . a system of money-rents and capi-talist farmers" (*Principles of Political Economy*, bk. ii. ch. viii. § 4). Of the truck system a brief account is given by Brentano, in Schönberg's *Handbuch d. P. Œ.* (1882), i. 971. Adam Smith held that "the law which obliged the masters in several different trades to pay their workmen in money and not in goods" was "quite just and equitable." The truck method has been commonly, and no doubt justly in the main, condemned as a means of undue control by masters over their men. Yet some among the thorough-going Radicals objected to the legislation of 1831, and maintained that "such state interference in freedom of contract" was "always mischievous" (see *Frederick Hill, an Autobiography*, 1893, p. 76).]   W. J. A.

KING, CHARLES (fl. 1713), chamberkeeper to the treasury, merchant of London, was the editor and joint author of the *British Merchant*, a periodical published in opposition to the government, in 1713-14, during the controversy on the 8th and 9th clauses of the Treaty of Utrecht. These clauses provided (1) that all subjects of Queen Anne and the king of France should enjoy the same commercial privileges as the most favoured nation ; (2) that, on the part of England, the duties on French goods should not be greater than the duties on those of any other country, and all prohibitive laws passed since 1664 should be repealed ; (3) that, on the part of France, English goods should be rated according to the tariff of 1664, and all laws contrary to that tariff should be repealed. The approach to freedom of trade implied in these clauses aroused the opposition of the commercial classes, and when Defoe defended the government proposals in the *Mercator*, the *British Merchant*, under the editorship of Charles King, was published in order to counteract his influence. In addition to King, the writers who contributed articles were, Henry Martin, "who had the greatest hand in them," Sir Charles Cooke, Sir Theodore Janssen, James Milner, Nathaniel Toriano, Joshua Gee, Christopher Haynes, David Martin, and others. The agitation was successful, and the obnoxious clauses were abandoned. In 1721, King collected the papers and republished them with the title *The British Merchant ; or, Commerce Preserv'd*, 3 vols. 8vo. By the order of the Earl of Sunderland when he was first lord of the treasury, a copy of this work was sent to every parliamentary borough for the use of the inhabitants.

[For a notice of King, see *Dictionary of National Biography*.]   W. A. S. H.

KING, GREGORY (1648-1712), was perhaps the ablest of the small group of 17th century writers who laid the foundations of statistical investigation in England. His work, *Natural and Political Observations upon the state and condition of England*, 1696, was for that period a remarkable achievement, and there is much in it of permanent value and interest. Only certain sections of it, however, published in Charles Davenant's *Essay upon the Probable Methods of making a people gainers in the Ballance of Trade*, etc., London, 1699, 8vo, were accessible to King's contemporaries. In 1802 George Chalmers appended large selections from it to his *Estimate of the Comparative Strength of Great Britain*, etc., London, 8vo ; 2nd edition, 1804, 8vo. Chalmers also published a complete edition with the title, *Natural and Political Observations and Conclusions upon the state and condition of England*, 1696, by Gregory King, Esq., Lancaster Herald. *To which is prefixed, A Life of the Author*, etc. A new edition, London, 1810, 8vo.

In this work, King states that "the ensuing treatise depends chiefly upon the knowledge of the true number of the people in England, and such other circumstances relating thereunto, as have been collected from the assessments on marriages, births, and burials, parish reports, and other public accounts." Section i. deals with the population. Taking as the basis of his calculations the returns from the hearth tax, on Lady Day, 1690, King reckons that there were 1,319,215 houses on that day. He allows an increase of 1000 per annum, and subtracts 1 in 36 or 37, which he estimates were improperly included in the hearth-tax returns. He thus calculates that in 1696 there were about 1,300,000 inhabited houses. He then calculates the "number of souls" per house from "the said assessments on marriages, births, and burials in several parts of the kingdom" to be $5\frac{1}{2}$ in London, within the walls ; $4\frac{1}{2}$ full for the six parishes without the walls ; $4\frac{1}{4}$ almost for the rest of the bills of mortality ; $4\frac{1}{3}$ "at a medium" for cities and market towns ; and 4 "at a medium" for villages and hamlets ; he adds 104,460 for omissions in the assessments ; 80,000 "transitory people and vagrants" ; and reaches a total of about 5,500,000. In section ii. he discusses "the proportion of England, in acres and people, to France, and Holland to Europe, and to the world in general ; with a calculation of the number of the people now in the world" ; in section iii. " the several distinctions of the people, as to males and females, married and unmarried, children, servants, and sojourners." Using the same authorities, he calculates that in London and the district covered by the bills of mortality there were 10 males to 13 females ; in cities and market towns, 8 to 9 ; and in villages and hamlets, 100 to 99. In section iv. he discusses "the several ages of the people"; in section v. "the origination and increase of the people of England"; and concludes (1) "that although each marriage in London produces fewer people than in the country, yet London in general . . . is more prolific than the other great towns; and the great towns than the country; (2) that·if the people of London of all ages were as long-lived as those in the country, London would increase in people much faster *pro ratâ* than the country"; and (3) that the principal checks in London on the growth of population were immorality, luxury, and intemperance, "greater intenseness to business," "unhealth-fulness of coal and smoke," and a relatively greater disparity of age between husbands and wives. On the last point he gives some observations based upon the Lichfield registers. In section vi. he deals with "the annual income and expense of the nation as it stood in anno 1688"; giving his famous "Scheme" printed by Davenant, and the quantity of silver and gold in England, France, and Holland, in Europe, and "the world in general"; in section vii. "the several sorts of land in England, with the value and product thereof." In his estimate of the "yearly consumption of flesh," he calculates that there were 1,280,000 persons who by reason of their poverty did not contribute to church or poor, and consequently eat not flesh above 2 days in 7, and 1,020,000 who received alms and consequently eat not flesh above once a week." His estimate of the influence on the price of corn, if a defect of one-tenth, two-tenths, be in the harvest, was adopted by many subsequent writers.[1] Sections viii. to xiii. are taken up with calculations of revenue, the probable yield of certain taxes proposed by him, a comparison of the state of England, France, and Holland, etc. There are also appended to Chalmers's edition of King's work "A scheme of the inhabitants of the city of Gloucester," and "A computation of the endowed hospitals and alms houses in England."

[Full particulars of King's life and a list of his heraldic and other works are given in the *Dictionary of National Biography*.] W. A. S. H.

KING, PETER, Lord (1776-1833), collaterally related to the philosopher Locke, is perhaps best remembered by economists in connection with the instructions which he issued in 1811 to his tenantry requiring them to pay their rents in gold, or in notes sufficient by the purchase of

[1] This estimate, sometimes known as "Gregory King's Law," is set out in full in the art. on CH. DAVENANT. It supposes that a defect in the harvest may raise the price of corn in the following proportions:—

Defect.		Above the Common Rate.
1 tenth		3 tenths
2 tenths		8 ,,
3 ,,	raises the price	1·6 ,,
4 ,,		2·8 ,,
5 ,,		4·5 ,,

gold "to secure the payment of the real intrinsic value of the sum stipulated." King thus practically asserted the fact of the *depreciation* of the Monetary Standard (see BULLION COM., Report of); the theory had been stated in his *Thoughts on the Effects of the Bank Restriction;* 1st. ed., 1803, 2nd ed., 1804, under title, *Thoughts on the Restriction of Payments in Specie at the Banks of England and Ireland.* In this classical tract King lays down two tests of depreciation, the market price of bullion and the state of the exchanges ("King's Law," Macleod, *Theory of Banking*). It should be observed that the depreciation which King attributed to the bank-notes was understood by him in a wider sense than what has been called DEPRECIATION *proper* — diminution in the value of the paper relatively to gold. Thus, he assumes in his *Thoughts* (1803) that the bullion has not become dear but the paper cheap (Lord Fortescue's edition, p. 76). And in the speech justifying the letter to his tenantry (1811), he maintains that "the gold itself, compared with the best standard of value, has in all probability become much cheaper and more abundant" (*ibid.* pp. 240-244). The contrary is affirmed by Mill (*Pol. Econ.*, bk. iii. ch. xiii. § 6), following Tooke (*History of Prices*, pt. i.). The "great city job," as King called the bank restriction, was not the only object of his attack; he also directed a brilliant tract and several speeches in parliament against the "grand land job," the corn laws.

[Lord King wrote the *Life of Locke;* his tracts and speeches relating to bank restriction, corn laws, and other economic subjects, are collected in the *Selection from the Speeches and Writings of the Late Lord King* by Earl Fortescue, 1844. There is an appreciative review of the *Thoughts* by Horner in the second volume of the *Edinburgh Review*. See also Ricardo's *Letters to Malthus*, pp. 148, 150.] F. Y. E.

KING'S CATTLE (*i.e.* chattels) was a term applied to the Jews in early English history, because they or their estates were reckoned a part of the king's revenue, or rather a source of his revenue, taxable at will. The profits of the levies on them were sometimes farmed out (see JEWS, EXCHEQUER OF THE). C. A. H.

KING'S PEACE. At a time when private feud was prevalent in England, there were certain places and occasions which were specially under the protection of the king. To disturb the peace at such places and on such occasions was an offence against the king's peace. The king's peace was analogous to the peace of every household, which it was an offence to disturb, or to the peace of the church, which, however, soon came into the province of the king's peace, but it was a graver offence to disturb the king's peace than to disturb any other person's peace. Gradually the king's peace came to be extended beyond the small number of places which it protected originally. Thus it is provided in the laws of William the Conqueror that violence on one of the four great public roads (Watling Street, Erming Street, Fosse, Hykenild) is a breach of the king's peace ; and gradually the king's peace came to be extended over the whole kingdom. The officers appointed to keep order, and prevent and punish criminal offences were, therefore, called "custodians of the peace," subsequently "justices of the peace," and the words "against the peace of our Sovereign Lady the Queen" still occur in indictments for criminal offences.

[Sir F. Pollock, The King's Peace, *Law Quart. Rev.*, vol. i.—Pollock and Maitland, *Hist. of Eng. Law.*] R. S.

KINGSLEY, CHARLES (1819-1875), born at Holne vicarage, Devonshire, was son of the Rev. Charles Kingsley, who held the living of Barnack in Northamptonshire, 1824-1830, and was then at Clovelly, 1830-1836, until presented to St. Luke's, Chelsea, 1836-1860. To these surroundings in the fen country and the Devonshire village many of the influences moulding C. Kingsley's tastes may be traced. In 1831 he was sent to a school at Clifton, where he witnessed the Bristol riots of the same year, which, he said later, were his first lesson in social science. In 1836 he became a student of King's College, London, and in 1838 he entered Magdalene College, Cambridge. He threw himself with great eagerness into the many interests of the place, pursuing his studies in an erratic fashion, which prevented him from attaining the highest distinctions in his examinations. In July 1842 he was ordained to the curacy of Eversley, Hampshire, a place with which he was, with the exception of a very short interval, connected until his death, as he was presented to the living in 1844. In 1845 he was appointed a canon of Middleham. In addition to his pastoral work during these and the following years, Kingsley was engaged in writing, in teaching, and in studying social questions as they came under his own observation as a country clergyman, and as they were thought out by F. D. MAURICE, with whom an acquaintanceship, begun in 1844, soon ripened into friendship. In 1848 he accepted the professorship of English literature and composition at Queen's College, Harley St., of which Maurice was then president, but resigned on account of ill-health in the following year. Maurice's influence over Kingsley was unbounded, and on many points the latter claimed to be but the interpreter and populariser of his friend's views. Taking as active a part as his residence and work in the country permitted during the Chartist movement of 1848, Kingsley worked with J. M. Ludlow, Thos. Hughes, and others who, under the guidance of Maurice, advocated reform rather than revolution as the right method for the regeneration of society. He and the other

Christian Socialists (see CHRISTIAN SOCIALISM) urged the adoption of Christian principles, as supplying the soundest basis for the socialistic views then coming to the front, while they promoted the cause of co-operation, as the best cure for the evils produced under the competitive system, by starting co-operative associations, and by pressing for parliamentary action in sanitary and other matters affecting the welfare of the working classes.

Kingsley's literary gifts were freely employed in various ways to point out grievances, to suggest remedies, and to give wholesome advice to labourers as well as to employers. Under the name of "Parson Lot" he contributed various articles to *Politics for the People*, a paper of which seventeen numbers were published ; and to the *Christian Socialist*, a journal which was issued between Nov. 1850 and June 1851 ; while a pamphlet entitled *Cheap Clothes and Nasty*, 1850, appeared under the same pseudonym. To this period also belong his earliest novels, which aimed at spreading the same truths in a different form and to a larger circle. Thus *Yeast*, which appeared in *Fraser's Magazine*, 1848, raised social questions as they affected the rural population ; while *Alton Locke*, 1850, described the condition of artisans in large towns. For the fearless expression of his views at this time Kingsley was frequently attacked with great bitterness, although his opinions were by no means extreme ; his aim, as a reformer, was to awaken men to a sense of their duties and responsibilities, rather than to advocate measures which would deprive them of their privileges. In later life he displayed tory rather than radical tendencies, and as early as 1857, though dwelling in *Two Years Ago* on the necessity for sanitary reforms, there is a change in his attitude, induced by his own more prosperous circumstances and by the improvements which, in various ways, had resulted from the efforts of the Christian Socialists and others. His novel *Hypatia*, 1853, presents an earlier condition of society which had to face problems in some respects similar to those of his own day, while *Westward Ho !*, 1855, a story of Elizabethan times, marks his aversion to those Romish practices which seemed likely to be more widely spread as the result of the Tractarian movement. This same feeling is also reflected in his one drama, *The Saint's Tragedy*, which, though primarily describing mediæval conditions, clearly indicates his views upon current social and religious movements. In 1859 Kingsley was appointed chaplain in ordinary to the queen, and held the regius professorship of modern history at Cambridge, 1860-1869. In 1869 he was also appointed a canon of Chester, and in 1873 was preferred to a canonry at Westminster. This he retained until his death.

Kingsley was not only a conscientious parish priest, a favoured court preacher, an ardent social and sanitary reformer, a widely-read novelist, and a university professor, but also a keen sportsman, a zealous naturalist, and a poet of no mean order. The versatility and wide range of his interests led him to undertake work in many fields, while it hindered the attainment of the highest place in any one direction; but it doubtless contributed to the widespread influence he has exercised over many different types of persons. To his teaching and example must be attributed no small share in the awakening of that increased earnestness in facing social problems which characterises the present generation.

Kingsley's works have been collected in thirty-six volumes, and include, in addition to the novels already mentioned, many volumes of children's books, sermons, lectures on history, on social and sanitary matters, on scientific matters.

[*Charles Kingsley: His Letters and Memories of his Life*, by his wife, 1877. — Hughes, T., *Memoir* in preface to *Alton Locke*, 1876.—*Life of F. D. Maurice*, by his son. — Kaufmann, M., *Charles Kingsley, Novelist and Social Reformer*.]

E. A. M.

KITE. The term "kite" serves to denote accommodation bills, when used systematically for the purpose of "raising the wind," or obtaining capital by pure credit for trading or speculation. Such transactions are frequently carried on in duplicate form, as when A draws upon B and obtains advances thereon under discount, and B draws upon A for the same purpose and to a corresponding amount. "Kiteing" has also been carried on, particularly in the United States, for obtaining the use of money even for one or two days by cross deposit of cheques for similar amounts in different banks, so as to obtain fictitious credit (see also ACCOMMODATION BILL). R. W. B.

KLOCK, KASPAR, also Glock and Glocke (1583-1655), studied law at Marburg and Cologne, and was successively one of the magistrates of Bremen and chancellor of the bishops of Minden and of the counts of Stolberg. He published collections of judicial decrees, which went through several editions, and two treatises on finance : the *Tractatus nomico-politicus de contributionibus in Romano-Germanico Imperio aliisque regnis ut plurimum usitatis* (Bremen, 1634); and the *Tractatus juridico-politico-polemico-historicus de Aerario* (1651 and 1671); "two unending, discursive, encyclopedic works, where economic, juridical, financial dissertations run along mingled up and with political, historical, and other digressions" (Ad. Wagner, *Finanzwissenschaft*, i. 33). A thorough mercantilist, most of his views are quite in keeping with mediæval practice, e.g. his strong partiality for fines and *amerciaments* levied on criminals, because of all taxes, "quae ad coercenda scelera imperantur," are "omnium justissima, utilissima et sanctissima." He is not, as many of his contemporaries, opposed to the extension of noble estates (*Rittergüter*), but is no friend of property in mortmain belonging to the church, and would see it entirely devoted to charitable and educational endowments.

He does not share the common admiration for the Dutch system of excise, which spread during the second half of the century ; and, except in cases of urgent necessity, rejects taxation of bread and meat. His leading principle is that "all taxes ought to be proportioned to the wealth (*secundum facultatem patrimonii*) of those on whom they are imposed. Nothing but injustice can result from a want of proportion between the burden and the strength of those who are required to bear it."

[Roscher, *Gesch. der Nat. Oek. in Deutschland*, pp. 210-217.] E. Ca.

KNIGHTHOOD, DISTRAINT OF. In the 12th century the holder of twenty librates of land (v. KNIGHT'S FEE) was expected to furnish a fully-armed warrior to serve for forty days in the year. In the reign of Henry III. all tenants-in-chief holding such an estate were compelled by writs issued to the sheriff to take up knighthood. Edward I. in 1278 showed his disregard of tenure by a writ enforcing knighthood upon all holders of land worth £20 a year, whether tenants-in-chief or not. Towards the end of his reign the qualification was raised to £40 a year, at which it remained. The penalty for not obeying the writ for distraint of knighthood was a fine, and such writs became in the future merely a method of raising money. The practice of issuing such writs became more and more rare, until it was revived in 1629 by Charles I., and they were strictly enforced during his eleven years of arbitrary government. The distraint of knighthood, with the other relics of the feudal system, was abolished at the restoration. R. L.

KNIGHT'S FEE. The Norman conquest introduced into England the tenure of land on military service, which is so prominent a characteristic of feudalism. At first the amount of service was not defined, but by the time of Henry II., the unit of assessment in the case of land held by military tenure was the *feodum militis* or knight's fee. This was not a fixed area of land, like the five hides which had been the qualification for thegnship (see HIDE), but was measured by the annual income derived from land. Land worth £20 a year was compelled to furnish a fully-equipped warrior to serve for forty days in the year. The extent of a knight's fee varied from two and a half to six hides. This measure was naturally the basis of SCUTAGE (see p. 510), which was a money payment in lieu of service in foreign wars. Lands held in socage were not measured by knight's fees but by hides.

[Stubbs, *Constitutional History*, i. 261-265.] R. L.

KNIGHT'S SERVICE.

Origin, p. 508; Description of fee, p. 509; Personal Service, p. 510; Scutage, p. 510; Economic Aspects of Knight's Service, p. 510.

ORIGIN. Tenure by knight's service (*servicium militare*) is a feudal tenure by free and uncertain service. Free or honourable service consisted in attending the feudal lord to war as opposed to base service, for example, ploughing his land. It is called uncertain because it was performed when demanded by the lord, and was not fixed in amount like the certain service of ploughing for a stated number of days or of paying rent. In the returns to the Inquest of 1166 concerning knights' fees, quoted from the Black Book of the Exchequer by Mr. Round in the *English Historical Review*, there are instances of very early enfeoffment. For example, William de Colecherche holds by military service "de antiquo tenemento a conquestu Anglie." The holdings in Domesday are expressed in hides, not in knights' fees, but the survey was taken for the purpose of levying geld which was always assessed on the hide. The Ely History tells us that, in 1072, William I. ordered the abbots and bishops of all England to furnish to the army the forces due from them for an expedition against Malcolm, King of Scotland (*debita militæ obsequiae transmitti*): and that William II., at the beginning of his reign, exacted with harshness the *debitum servitium* imposed by his father on the churches. Long before the Conquest there was a tendency in England, from the allodial system of holding land independently and performing services as a member of the community, to the feudal system of holding by service due to a personal lord. From Alfred's time the consent of the witan to grants of bocland grew less important and the distinction between folcland and king's land less marked, so that each estate given by the king became looked upon as a grant entailing personal service to him. By the laws of Cnut (c. 77), even when estates of bocland were cut out of folcland, this land, if forfeited for cowardice in battle, became, not folcland again, but king's land. The thegn, two of whose qualifications were that he "had fully five hides of his own land" and "special duty in the king's hall," owed personal military service at his own expense, and the right of summoning the thegns belonged to the king. All this reminds us of the feudal tenant and his relation to his lord; the thegn has but to acknowledge that the five hides which give him his position are not "his own," but are held of his lord the king by the service already attached to them. Thegnage continued to exist in the north of England for centuries after the conquest. The northern thegns paid fines in commutation of personal service in Normandy in John's reign; and under the Tudors, their successors still owed military service against the Scotch for fifteen days in the year. In all these ways the English were approaching feudalism before they became the subjects of the feudal lord of Normandy.

DESCRIPTION OF THE KNIGHT'S FEE (*feodum militare*). This was the unit of assessment of the service due from a feudal tenant. A tenant-in-chief was enfeoffed by the service of furnishing to the king's army so many fully-equipped knights, this number being his *servitium debitum*. The formation of knights' fees was a gradual result of this arrangement between the king and the tenant-in-chief; for on the latter rested the responsibility of fulfilling his *servitium debitum*, and the means by which this was effected concerned only himself and the knights by whom this *servitium* was made up. Many early instances of subinfeudation, that is, of dividing the lands of a tenant into "fees" each of which furnished a knight, are found in church-lands. One reason of this is that it was a greater advantage to churchmen than to lay barons to have the fulfilment of their military service assured. The *servitium debitum*, however, did not take the place of the English military organisation. As the aid and trial by battle did not displace the geld and moot, so the *fyrd* or duty of every free man to serve, not by homage to a lord, but as a member of the community, existed side by side with knights' service. In 1138, the *fyrd* called together by the northern clergy and nobility, with Archbishop Thurstan at their head, won the battle of the Standard, and again in 1173 a Scotch invasion was repulsed by the fyrd of Yorkshire. The fyrd was re-modelled in 1181 by the Assize of Arms, which ordered every free man to bear arms. The holder of a knight's fee was to have a breast-plate, a helmet, a shield and a spear, and he who owed the service of more knights than he had enfeoffed, was to provide the same arms for these (c. 1). The Assize of Arms was enforced by Henry III. in 1252. The Statute of Winchester (1285) connected the fyrd very closely with the keeping of the peace, and directed that a view of armour should be held twice yearly (c. 6). The knight's fee usually contained an amount of land worth yearly £20, and as the value of land was not uniform, the size of a knight's fee was not everywhere the same. The normal size of a fee was four hides, each hide containing 120 acres; the five hides, which occur frequently as knights' fees, may once have been the holdings of Saxon thegns. The number of knights' fees created in England by William I. is given by Ordericus Vitalis as 60,000. Mediæval writers, however, often used 60,000 to mean simply a large number, and Stephen de Segrave, justiciary under Henry III., reduces it to 32,000. But the scutage raised under Henry II. was far too small to represent so many fees; and Alexander Swereford, compiler of the Red Book of the Exchequer, writes in 1230 of this number as "absurd and amazing," as he well might, for it would have left no English land to be held otherwise than by military service. Modern historians, have, like Swereford, put small faith in these large numbers, and Mr. Round shows that the whole body of knights, from both the church and lay fiefs, "can scarcely have exceeded, if indeed it reached, 5000."

PERSONAL SERVICE.—Though personal service could be afterwards commuted for a fine, it was at first an essential condition of feudal tenure. The personal relationship of the feudal tenant to his lord could not be expressed more forcibly than in the oath of homage. He who, in return for his land, gave his services to his lord in the emphatic words "Ego devenio homo vester" was naturally expected to attend him in person to war, and to risk his own life in his service. Churchmen were, of course, exempt from personal service, though they held their lands from the reign of William I. as baronies, but the *servitium debitum* was due from them as from the lay barons, and quite as rigorously exacted. Under the Norman kings, feudal tenants followed the king across the sea, and foreign service was not refused until the loss of Normandy in John's reign. From this time, frequent fines "ne transfretent" appear in the Pipe Rolls to escape service abroad, and in 1297 the earls refused to go to Flanders, because, as they very clearly told the king, there was no precedent for it—"videtur toti communitati quod ibi non debent aliquod servitium facere ; quia nec ipsi nec predecessores sui seu progenitores unquam fecerunt servitium in terra illa." In the charter of the same year, Edward I. pardons all knights who had not obeyed his summons to Flanders ; he is careful, however, to mention "rancorem nostrum et malam voluntatem" which they have thus incurred (c. 5). From Richard I.'s time, tenants sometimes paid fines to send substitutes to the army instead of obeying the summons in person. The recognised term of service for a knight was forty days in the year, and, if the duration of service would exceed this time, the king's summons was expressed in the language of a request rather than of a demand. Edward I., in his writs for continued service in the Welsh war in 1277, uses the words "affectuose rogamus," and he has to satisfy the cautiousness of the barons by promising that the lengthened term of service shall not be a precedent. In 1157, Henry II. directed that every three knights should equip one of their number for three times the term of service, and this was also done by Richard I. and John, the latter ordering nine knights to provide a tenth with 2s. a day. This reminds us of the old use in Berkshire, where, according to Domesday, holders of one hide, instead of serving themselves, paid each 4s. to send a fully-equipped warrior for every five hides (i. 56).

SCUTAGE.—Scutage was a tax levied on the knight's fee, on the hide like the English gelds. The *Dialogus de Scaccario* says that it was so called because it was paid by those who owed the service of the shield (*quia nomina scutorum solvitur*) (i. 9). The name first appears on the Pipe Roll of 1156, when Henry II. wanted supplies wherewith to carry on his war in opposition to his brother Geoffrey's claims on Anjou. The rate was 20s. on a fee, and it was only levied on church lands. The Great Scutage was levied in 1159 for the war in defence of Eleanor's claim on Toulouse. It was assessed not only on church lands, but on other fees both in Normandy and England, as a commutation for personal service: the rate in England was two marks, and in Normandy sixty Angevin shillings or fifteen English. From this time the word was generally used to mean a payment in place of military service, but, unlike the English *fyrdwite*, which was a fine incurred by neglect of the fyrd, the *Dialogus* tells us that scutage was levied because the king preferred to expose mercenaries rather than his own subjects to the chances of war (i. 9). Tenants-in-chief obtained writs from the marshal "pro habendo scutagio suo," empowering them to levy scutage on their under-tenants, and they might enforce payment by distress, or procure a writ to the sheriff for that purpose. Before 1166, the scutage paid to the king was only on fees formed before Henry I.'s death (*de veteri*), but after the Inquest of that year it was levied also on new fees (*de novo*), thus cutting off the profits of those lords who had enfeoffed more knights than their *servitium debitum* required. The rate of scutage under Henry II. varied from one mark to 20s. There were three scutages in Richard I.'s reign for the wars in Wales and Normandy, and under John, who increased other taxes also, the rate was raised to two marks and scutage taken almost yearly. Magna Carta provided that it should only be levied by consent of parliament (c. 12) and by the charter of 1217 it was to be taken as in the time of Henry II. (c. 44). But Henry III. "scutagium per totam Angliam sibi fecit extorqueri," and the rate in his reign was as high as three marks. Scutage became of less importance under Edward I. ; after 8 Edward II. it was sometimes levied when the king went to war in person, until Richard II. remitted it on the occasion of his fruitless expedition to Scotland in 1385. It was abolished by statute 12 Car. II. (c. 24), 1661.

ECONOMIC ASPECTS OF KNIGHT'S SERVICE.— The feudal system was not without importance as a means of increasing the revenue. There were seven "feudal incidents" connected with knight's service by which this was effected.

1. *Aids* were at first benevolences granted from a feudal tenant to his lord when there was special need for them, "de gracia et non de jure," but the three chief aids early become recognised claims of the lord on his dependant (see AID, AUXILIUM).

2. *Relief* so called because it "incertam et caducam hereditatem relevebat," was a fine paid to the lord by the heir on succeeding to a feudal tenure. The *Dialogus* gives 100s. as the fixed amount for a knight's fee in Henry II.'s reign, but says that the relief of a barony is still settled in each case by the king (ii. 10). Magna Carta determined the relief of a barony at 100s. "per antiquum relevium" (c. 2).

3. *Primer Seisin* was the king's right to one year's profit of the lands of a tenant-in-chief if the heir was of age.

4. *Wardship.*—The lord was entitled to the wardship of the heir until he was twenty-one and of an heiress until she was fourteen years of age (raised to sixteen by Stat. of Westm. c. 22) without accounting for the profits of the estate.

5. *Marriage.*—If a feudal ward refused a suitable marriage he forfeited to his guardian the value of the marriage ; that is, the sum which a jury assessed, or which would have been paid to the guardian for the marriage. If after a suitable marriage had been offered, he married without the guardian's consent, he forfeited double value—but the double value was not exacted in the case of heiresses.

6. *Fines for Alienation* were payable if a tenant alienated the land without the lord's consent. These are only found from tenants-in-chief.

7. *Escheat* was the reversion of the fief to the lord, and took place if the tenant left no heirs of his blood or was guilty of treason or felony.

The feudal incidents gave room for much oppression, for nearly every important occurrence in the tenant's life could be made an occasion for enriching his lord. All the charters and reforms issued from time to time, not before they were urgently needed by the people, were chiefly directed against the severities of feudalism. The Inquest of Sheriffs, in 1170, shows how easily Knight's Service could lead to abuses. The king had been abroad for four years, and this inquest was to inquire into the proceedings of the sheriffs and bailiffs during his absence. By the statute of *Quia Emptores* in 1290, any free man could sell the whole or part of his holding to be held by the buyer immediately of the same lord and by the same services as formerly. Before this, if a feudal tenant alienated part of his land he had still to answer to his lord for the rents and services due from the whole, and became himself the lord of the purchaser. Subinfeudation had been carried so far (we find holdings of $\frac{1}{100}$ and $\frac{1}{200}$ of a knight's fee) that the feudal dues had to be paid in some cases to many under-tenants before they reached the lord, whose profits were thus diminished : the statute of 1290 gave him a direct claim on the actual holder of his land, and it also improved the condition of the latter by removing the small owners whose lordship had been oppressive. It did not, however,

apply to tenants-in-chief, who could not alienate their land until 1 Edward III., and then only by a license for which they paid a third of the yearly value of the land. Besides the three recognised aids, the under-tenants often paid their lord's debts to the Jews, and, though they are sometimes said to do so "pro bona voluntate," such very good will as this was probably only produced by the oppressions of feudalism. By Magna Carta no scutage or aids were to be taken without the consent of parliament except the three lawful aids, and these only in reasonable amounts (c. 12) and, as in Henry I.'s charter, it is expressly set forth that these reforms shall affect the under-tenants (c. 15). Further, all tenants-in-chief are to be summoned to parliament with forty days' notice before any other aid is levied (c. 14)—so carefully had experience taught the barons to guard their rights and their money against their feudal lord the king. The aid in 1168, for the marriage of Henry II.'s daughter Maud to the Duke of Saxony, the first occasion of a levy on the new enfeoffment, was at the rate of one mark on the fee ; for Richard I.'s ransom in 1193, the aid was 20s. on the fee, but so large a sum was needed (£100,000) that a tax was also levied on land not held by military service ; the aid granted by parliament to marry Henry III.'s sister Isabel to the Emperor was at the rate of two marks. But the amounts were not fixed until 1275, when the statute of Westminster directed that the rate should be 20s. on the fee, and that the aid should not be demanded until the son to be knighted was fifteen, or the daughter to be married seven years of age (c. 36): there could obviously be no settled rate for the aid for ransom. Edward III. levied an aid of 40s. on the fee, but without the consent of the commons, for knighting the Black Prince, in 1346. Scutage, the burden of which fell chiefly on the under-tenants, was an important contribution of feudalism to the exchequer, especially from the abolition of Danegeld in 1163 until its restriction by Magna Carta : and in Henry III.'s reign, money began to be raised by distraint for knighthood. Measures for this purpose were first taken in 1224, and in 1274 an inquiry was made into their enforcement by the sheriffs. The yearly value of land, the possessor of which had to receive knighthood or pay a fine, varied from £15 to £40, and in 1285 was as high as £100, but the normal sum was £20, the accepted value of a knight's fee. In 1278, Edward I. made knighthood obligatory on all who owned twenty librates of land, whether holding by military service or not. This measure not only increased the revenue by the fines it brought in, but also tended to break down the distinctions between the military and other tenants. The disorders and confusions of the Wars of the Roses had the same tendency, but the feudal rents and services continued to be felt as oppressions until military tenures were finally abolished by Charles II. in the year after the restoration (Statute 12 Chas. II. c. 24).

[Blackstone, *Commentaries*, bk. ii. (1809).— Stubbs, *Select Charters* (1870); *Const. Hist.* (1880). —Freeman, *History of the Norman Conquest* (1867).—Gneist, H. R. von, *History of the English Constitution*, translated by P. A. Ashworth (1891). —Madox, *History of the Exchequer* (1769).— Hearne, *Liber Niger Scaccarii* (1728).—Norgate, K., *England under the Angevin Kings* (1887).— Pollock, F., *The Land Laws* (1887).—Round, J. H., *The Introduction of Knight-Service into England* (*Eng. Hist. Review*, July, Oct. 1891 ; Jan. 1892). —Maitland, F. W., *Northumbrian Tenures* (*Eng.. Hist. Review*, Oct. 1890).—Hall, H., *An Unknown Charter of Liberties* (*Eng. Hist. Review*, April 1894).—Oman, C. W., *The Art of War in the Middle Ages* (1885) ; *Testa de Nevill* (*Record Commission*, 1807) ; *Pipe Rolls, temp.* Henry II., John, Ric. I., Henry III. ; *Parliamentary Writs* I. (*Record Commission*, 1827).]   M. T. M.

KNIGHTS OF LABOUR. See TRADES UNIONS, U.S.A.

KNOX, JOHN J. (1828-1892), was born in New York. After engaging in private banking he entered the service of the treasury department of the United States government in 1862 ; in 1867 became deputy-collector of the currency ; and, in 1872, comptroller. The latter position he held until 1884, when he resigned and was chosen president of a national bank in New York city. He was an earnest advocate of monometallism ; and favoured the continuance of the national banking system through the establishment of a safety fund.

J. J. Knox's twelve reports as comptroller of the currency contain valuable historical material relating to state and national banks. Among these reports those of 1875 and 1876 are the most important. In 1884 he published *United States Notes* (published New York ; reprint, London) a history of the issues of paper currency by the government.   D. R. D.

KOPECK. One hundredth of the Russian rouble ; a copper token coin.

Silver coins : 50 and 25 kopecks ; 900 fine, weight 154·32 and 77·16 grains. Value (English standard), 1s. 8½d. and 10¼d. ; (French standard) 2 and 1 franc. Also token silver coins, 500 fine, of the nominal value of 20, 15, 10, and 5 kopecks, as well as token copper coins of 2, ½, and ¼ kopecks.   F. E. A.

KOPS, J. L. DE BRUYN (1822-1887), was born at Haarlem. He studied law at Leyden, 1840-47, was an advocate at Haarlem 1851, functionary at the department of finances at the Hague 1864, professor at the polytechnical school at Delft 1868, member of the second chamber of the states-general till his death.

He was one of the founders, and for some time president, of the statistical society of Holland, for years editor of its statistical year-book, and afterwards also of its statistical abstract (1881-83). In 1852 he founded the periodical, *De Economist*, and remained its editor till his death.

His economical works are : *Grondbeginselen der Staathuishoudkunde* (Principles of Political Economy), Leyden, 1850.—*Handelscijfers : overzicht van den In-uit-en doorvoer der Nederlandsche handelsartikelen in elk der Jaren 1846-1855* (Statistics of Trade. Summary of the Import and Transit of Dutch articles of Trade in each of the years 1846-1855), Amsterdam, 1857. His essays, treating of a variety of subjects, however, mostly appeared in *De Economist*. In general he belonged to the school of Bastiat ; as to taxation he was an opponent of excise duties, especially of local ones such as the OCTROI. At a later period he eagerly combated the duty on sugar. His chief merit is that he contributed greatly to popularising political economy by his simple and intelligible style ; his work, *The Principles of Political Economy*, was for some time the most generally used text-book in Holland.   A. F. V. L.

KOSEGARTEN, WILHELM (1792-1868), began life as a barrister in Hamburg, but was appointed in 1839 *docent* at the university of Bonn, and in 1855 extraordinary professor of political sciences at Graetz. In his *Betrachtungen über die Veräusserlichkeit und Theilbarkeit des Landbesitzes* published in 1842, he evinces a predilection most entirely opposed to the spirit of his time for mediæval forms of payment in kind or in labour, though, according to Roscher, he successfully dispels some of the delusive fallacies of the extreme advocates of the subdivision of land. His deep-rooted aversion to what a certain German school calls *Manchesterthum* and reactionary feelings are still more conspicuously displayed in his *Geschichtliche und systematische Uebersicht der Nat. Oekonomie*, Vienna, 1856 ; for him, a system based on self-interest and avarice must unavoidably lead to the pauperisation of the masses. He expresses a similar bitter hatred for free competition, manufactures, railways, machinery, schemes of universal money, weights and measures, etc., and a corresponding admiration for legislation against usury and the engrossing of corn, and in favour of state industries, etc. Constitutionalism also comes in for its share of reprobation, because in the actual state of conflict between capital and labour, it is impossible for the owners of property to represent the bulk of the nation.

[Roscher, *Gesch. der Nat. Oek. in Deutschland*, p. 1025.]   E. CA.

KRAN. See KHRAN.

KRAUS, CHRISTIAN JAKOB (1753-1807), a distinguished German economist, was born at Osterode in East Prussia. In 1770 he went as a student to the university of Königsberg, where he was in intimate relations with Kant, von Auerswald, and Hamann, and where he became, in 1781, professor of practical philosophy and cameral science—a position which he held till his death. In later life he abandoned most of Kant's views to which he had been attached, devoted himself altogether to economics, and lectured on agriculture, manufactures, trade, and finance. He translated in 1790 the political portion of Hume's *Essays*. He was an ardent admirer of the *Wealth of Nations*, which he was the first to make known and interpret to his fellow-countrymen. Adam Müller called him a "mere echo" of Smith; he was at least his earnest disciple. In 1797 he wrote : "For the last six years, and latterly without any concealment, I have not only expanded the only true, great, noble, and beneficent system" (by which he meant Adam Smith's) . . . "but have succeeded in possessing some excellent heads with it" . . . ; and again in 1796, "Scheffner has a perfect right to say that the world has never yet seen a more important book than that of Adam Smith; assuredly, since the time of the New Testament, no work has had more beneficial effects than this will have, if it should be more widely diffused and more deeply impressed upon the minds of all who have to do with public affairs" (Seeley's *Life of Stein*, i. 409). Von Schön says —"Kraus was my great teacher ; he mastered me entirely, and I followed him without reserve." "It was from Kraus," adds Professor Seeley, "that he (Schön) gained that idea of the connection of national wealth with industrial liberty, which was to be embodied partly by his exertions in the emancipating edict of Stein's ministry" (i. 375). Kraus died at Königsberg, 25th August 1807. He published little except lecture programmes ; his chief influence was exerted through his oral teaching. Von Auerswald, Herbart, Süvern, and Hüllmann edited (1808-1819) his *Vermischte Schriften* in eight vols., with a biography by J. Voigt ; and his *Staatswirthschaft* was published by V. Auerswald (1808-1811), and reprinted at Breslau in 1837. He advocates in these writings the removal of monopolies and restrictions on trade, the free division and alienation of landed property, and the abolition of the system of gilds.

[See J. Kautz, *Theorie und Geschichte der National Oekonomik*, ii. 621.—Roscher, *Geschichte der deutschen Nat. Oek.*, 608.—*Handwörterbuch der Staatswissenschaften*, iv. 72.]   J. K. I.

KREUTZER. One hundredth of the Austrian florin ; a copper token coin.

There are also silver token coins of the nominal value of 20 and 10 kreutzers, and copper ½-kreutzer pieces. In the coinage which existed all over south Germany down to 1876 the kreutzer was the sixtieth part of the florin. Since the introduction, in 1892, of the new crown currency, the coinage of kreutzers has been discontinued. The crown, which is equal in value to half a florin, is divided into 100 hellers. The new heller being, therefore, of the value of half a kreutzer.   F. E. A.

KRIES, KARL GUSTAV (1815 - 1858), appointed in 1844 extraordinary professor of political sciences in Breslau, resigned his chair in 1850, and was elected a member of the Prussian house of deputies. During a journey in England, he entered into connection with the Irvingites, and became subsequently a deacon of an "apostolical" congregation in Berlin, his religious feelings giving a tinge to his opinions on the treatment of the poor, a subject which he had personally investigated in England and on which he wrote a posthumously published book, entitled *Die Englische Armenpflege* (1863). During his Silesian professorship, he had already examined the state of the spinners and weavers of that province (*Ueber die Verhältnisse der Spinner und Weber in Schlesien*, 1845), and had written still earlier a history of taxation in Silesia under the Austrian rule (*Historische Entwickelung der Steuerverfassung in Schlesien*, 1842). In a review of John Stuart Mill in Rau's *Archiv* (new series, x. 378), he utters sentiments which have since widely prevailed in Germany. "The most important task of political economy is to show how the relation of man to inanimate things, how his sentient nature, is and must be the basis and spur to his mental and moral development. Just now it ought to explain how different is an emulation tempered by considerations of justice, equity, and of the well-being of our fellow-citizens from a headlong competition only caring about self-interest."

[See Roscher, *Geschichte der Nat. Oekonomik in Deutschland*, p. 1043.]   E. Ca.

KRÖNCKE, KLAUS (1771-1843), a Hessian privy councillor and inspector of the Rhine, published his theories almost exclusively in the shape of algebraical formulæ. In his *Steuerwesen nach seiner Natur und seinen Wirkungen untersucht* (1804), and in his *Anleitung zur Regulirung der Steuer* (1810), he recommends for agricultural countries a single and direct tax on persons and not on things, apportioned by the fiscal authorities according to the physical and mental productive capabilities and actual faculties, whether corporal or incorporal, of each taxpayer, professional incomes being rated lower than life interests. He proposed to abolish all indirect taxes, but he would allow the taxes on industrial incomes to be adjusted so as to exert an educational influence on the national industry. "If out of ten, even only one of such attempts succeeds, the gain ought to be considered."

[Roscher, *Gesch. der Nat. Oek. in Deutschland*, p. 664.]   E. Ca.

KRUG, JOHANN LEOPOLD (1770-1843). A graduate of theology in Halle, he gave up in 1799 the ecclesiastical career in order to devote himself to statistical researches, for which he had always felt inclined, and having attracted the attention of the king of Prussia by a pamphlet on the *Serfdom* (*Leibeigenschaft*) *of the Prussian Peasantry*, he obtained in 1800 the appointment of privy *Registrator*, which gave him access to state archives. Later on, he organised the Prussian statistical board. His *Betrachtungen über den Nat. Reichthum des preussischen Staats* (1805) are described by Roscher as one of the first attempts towards a comprehensive statistical work. His other books are: *Ideen zu einer staatswissenschaftlichen Statistik* (1807); *Abriss der Staatsoekonomie* (1808); *Geschichte der Staatswissenschaftlichen Gesetzgebung im preuss. Staate* (1808); *Geschichte der Preussischen Staatsschulden*, which, written in 1823, was only published in 1861, a long time after the author's death, on account of some disagreement with the Prussian censorship. His acquaintance with early times is rather inadequate. Krug's opinion that all indirect and personal taxation is ultimately borne by land, and his rejection of such taxes, allows him to be numbered amongst the last followers of the physiocrats.

The favourite object of his studies was assistance to the poor. Opposed to workhouses and obligatory assistance, he recommends the principle of insurance (*Die Armenassecuranz*, 1810).

[Roscher, *Gesch. der Nat. Oek. in Deutschland*, p. 497, and his life by Inama in the *Allgemeine Deutsche Biographie*.] E. Ca.

KURICKE, REIN (17th century), a German author,—

Wrote, in 1667, a treatise entitled *Jus Maritimum Hanseaticum* (Gottingen), and also *Diatriba de Assecurationibus* (Hamburg, 1667). The *Jus Maritimum* was reprinted by Heineccius and included in his *Fasciculus Scriptorum de Jure Nautico et Maritimo*, Halle, 1740. According to PARDESSUS, (*q.v.*), the *Jus Maritimum* is simply the Latin translation with a commentary of the Lubeck *recess* (or ordinance) of 1614, which became the maritime law of all the cities belonging to the Hanseatic league. Pardessus himself gives its original German text with a French translation (*Collection des Lois Maritimes*, vol. ii. pp. 528-558); in his opinion, Kuricke's long and learned commentary might usefully be reduced to a few pages (see LAW MERCHANT). E. Ca.

LABORDE, ALEXANDRE, Comte de (1774-1842), was born at Paris and died in the same city. This author, the son of a well-known banker to the court who perished in 1794 on the revolutionary scaffold, and the father of a distinguished archæologist, is known from an economic point of view by his work, *De l'esprit d'association dans tous les intérêts de la communauté* (1818, 8vo ; 2nd ed. 1821, two vols. 8vo ; 3rd ed. 1834, 8vo).

It would appear from what Laborde has written that he must have heard Adam Smith and J. B. Say spoken of ; but this is about all he appears to have known of them. We must, however, recognise in this author an unaffected, honest, and unprejudiced mind. He lays weight on the importance of labour and of the value of liberty in economic matters. A. C. f.

[The work, *De l'esprit d'Association*, develops the advantages to a community of the spirit of association in all its branches : Industrial association to assist production ; military association to secure possession ; the advantages of credit associations ; benevolent, scientific, literary associations, etc. It is interesting as marking the ideas of association current at the time before protection was advocated so strongly as has been the case since—before, on the other hand, socialism and communism were as prominent as they are now. *Dictionnaire de l'Economie Politique*, ed. Coquelin et Guillaumin.]

LABOULAYE, EDOUARD RÉNÉ LEFEBVRE (1811-1883), was born and died at Paris. He was perhaps rather an enlightened and deter-

mined liberal than an economist ; but well read as he was in moral and political science, in history, and in law, as well as in political economy, he exercised a powerful and happy influence on the political fortunes of his country. A brilliant speaker, he knew how to impart a serious and instructive tone to his works, which were many in number and varied in character, without injury to their style. Like Alexis de Tocqueville, whom he greatly admired, he was a strong partisan of decentralisation.

Laboulaye wrote *L'État et ses Limites*, 1863, the title of which sufficiently indicates the object of the work. In *Paris en Amérique* he displayed a humorous spirit which emphasises the difference between American and European manners and customs. *La Liberté religieuse*, 1850 ; *Le parti liberal*, 1863 ; *L'histoire des États-Unis depuis les premiers essais de colonisation jusqu'à l'adoption de la constitution fédérale* (1620-1789), etc., are, as well as his *Études morales et politiques*, works from which an economic spirit is never absent, though the inculcation of political economy is not their first object. By direct statement and indirect allusion he was an enthusiastic and eloquent populariser of the science. His high-minded and loyal character was held in the highest esteem both by his opponents and his friends. He translated, or it may rather be said paraphrased, the works of Franklin and Channing.

Laboulaye was a deputy to the national assembly, and afterwards a senator for life. He occupied from 1848 onwards the chair of comparative legislation (*Legislation Comparée*) at the college of France.

Curiously enough, Laboulaye, who so well appreciated the better side of the American institutions, never crossed the Atlantic.

A. C. F.

LABOULINIÈRE, PIERRE (beginning of the 19th century), was a sub-prefect in France and Italy under the first French empire.

Laboulinière used the practical knowledge he had acquired in this capacity to write the following works:—(1) *Plan d'une statistique générale pour le Piémont* (1803) ; (2) *De l'influence d'une grande révolution sur l'agriculture, le commerce, et les arts* (1808) ; and (3) *De la disette et de la surabondance en France ; des moyens de prévenir l'une en mettant l'autre à profit et d'empêcher les trop grandes variations dans le prix des grains*, 1821. Laboulinière recommended a system of *réserves à domicile* (home-stores). In years of plenty associations were to be formed, protected, and helped by the state, and local authorities were to buy corn at the market price, with the proviso that the farmer was to keep it in store until the next year of scarcity, when it was to be sold. The farmer, who had been paid in cash at the time of the purchase, was to get either a share of the profit or an indemnity proportionate to the length of time during which the corn had been stored in his granaries.

E. CA.

LABOUR. In everyday life we speak of the labour either of man or of domesticated animals (see *Wealth of Nations*, ed. M'Culloch, supp. note i.). The earlier economists too, as a rule, sought merely to interpret popular language. "The *Wealth of Nations* contains scarcely a definition" (Senior, *Pol. Econ.*, p. 5). Adam Smith in general restricts the term labour to *human* exertion, while speaking, on occasion, of "labouring cattle" (*Wealth of Nations*, bk. ii. ch. i.). He, however, departs from popular usage when he asserts that in agriculture "Nature labours along with man" (bk. ii. ch. v.). But M'Culloch, insisting on the absence of any fundamental distinction between the operations of domesticated animals, of machinery, and of nature, defines labour as including each : "any sort of action or operation, whether performed by man, the lower animals, machinery, or natural agents, that tends to bring about any desirable result" (*loc. cit.* cp. J. B. Say, *Cours Complet d'Économie Politique Pratique*, 1828-30, pt. i. ch. ix. pp. 239-40, also *Traité d'Économie Politique*, 2nd ed., 1814, bk. i. ch. vii. pp. 52-53. See Senior's criticism, *Pol. Econ.*, ed. 1872, p. 57). If, however, this be the logical outcome of popular usage, the line of thought it indicates is from the economic standpoint irrelevant. In the department of production man stands forth as, with more or less success, subjugating the rest of nature, a task in which his labour is certainly more efficient in proportion as he utilises, rather than combats, nature's forces. It is, doubtless, also more efficient the more he is aided by the capitalised labour of the past, whether that be realised in

domesticated animals or inanimate machinery. Nevertheless, in the department of distribution the contrast between labour and capital is of fundamental importance. Both these distinctions M'Culloch's definition tends to obscure. Confusion in the subject matter is the natural sequence of such a wide interpretation of the term labour, just as on the other hand confusion ensues when, on the strength of an analogy indicated by Adam Smith (*W. of N.*, bk. ii. ch. i.), but valid only for certain purposes and within certain limits (see LABOUR, SKILLED). CAPITAL is made, as by Say (*Cours Complet*, pt. i. pp. 284-285, 316) and M'Culloch (*Principles*, 5th ed. pp. 294-295), to include, for general purposes, the labour power or even the person of the labourer (cp. Böhm-Bawerk, *Positive Theory of Capital*, trans. Wm. Smart, 1891, pp. 50-54). Hence most economists, to adapt the term labour to scientific use, have restricted its signification (cp. Sidgwick, *Principles*, 2nd ed. p. 51).

Again, the era of machinery, with its substitution of intelligence for strength (Marshall, *Economics*, vol. i. bk. iv. ch. ix.), has widened the popular conception of labour; still, physical exertion is the paramount idea. Scientific analysis, however, has resulted in including mental exertion also. From the economic standpoint the cabinet minister, or the *entrepreneur*, labours no less than the navvy. Hence particular discussions necessitate qualifying epithets, *e.g. unskilled* labour, or labour *of management*. At the same time, it appears that the extension of the conception adopted by Courcelle-Seneuil and others, and implied in the phrase "labour of saving" (*travail d'épargne*), is a departure from the ideas and language of everyday life, accompanied by no corresponding gain for the purposes of science (cp. Böhm-Bawerk on "Labour Theories" of the origin of interest, in *Capital and Interest*, Eng. trans., 1890, bk. v. p. 300 *seq.*).

Economists are, however, at one with popular usage in regarding labour as, on the whole, irksome exertion, or such as would not be undergone but for the stimulus of some ulterior aim, *e.g.* the desire to provide for present or future needs, or, it may be, to avoid the lash. (On the comparative inefficiency of the latter stimulus, see Cairnes, *The Slave Power*, 2nd ed., 1863, p. 44 *seq.*). J. B. Say's definition, "action suivie, dirigée vers un but" (*Traité*, 2nd ed., vol. ii. p. 476), is simple but too comprehensive ; since, as Senior points out, it covers "a walk taken for the purposes of health, and even the exertions of an agreeable converser" (appendix i. to Whately's *Logic*, ed. 1855, p. 233). And, as the same author elsewhere remarks, "Ordinary language does not allow us to consider those undergoing labour who exert themselves for the mere purpose of amusement" (*Pol. Econ.*, ed. 1872, p. 57). High authorities, it is true, have regarded labour as essentially disagreeable (see J. S. Mill, *Principles*, bk. i. ch. i. § i.). Jevons, however, while emphasising the painfulness of labour, admits that, when the irksomeness of beginning is over, the worker, entering into the spirit of his work, finds in it for a time an excess of pleasure ; and only when he begins to grow weary does the UTILITY (*q.v.*) of labour itself again approach zero, after which the irksomeness increases, till the labourer desists when the disutility of labour equals the utility of the reward (*Theory of Pol. Econ.*, ch. v.). Labour, it thus appears, though in general a DISCOMMODITY (*q.v.*), is not universally painful (cp. Sidgwick, *Principles*, 2nd ed. pp. 37-38, 58 n.).

To sum up, labour is effort, bodily or mental, put forth by human beings, not exclusively for the sake of the pleasure immediately associated therewith, but, partly or wholly, with a view to the attainment of some ulterior object (cp. Jevons, *Theory*, 2nd ed. p. 183 ; Marshall, *Economics*, 2nd ed. bk. ii. ch. iii. § 2).

Senior (in appendix i. to Whately's *Logic*, ed. 1855, p. 233) asserts that "the word Labour signifies both the *act* of labouring and the *result* of that act" (see M'Culloch's criticism, that the phrase "accumulated labour" is "merely a compendious, though inaccurate, mode of signifying the accumulated products or results of labour"—*Wealth of Nations*, M'Culloch's ed. p. 435 n.). We certainly do consider labour with reference either to its internal or its external aspect,—to the mental and physical expenditure or to its productivity. The one is in no sense a measure of the other. Indeed, it is doubtful whether exact quantitative treatment is in either case possible (see *Wealth of Nations*, bk. i. ch. v. ; Jevons, *Theory*, 2nd ed. 124-125, 221. ; Sidgwick, *Principles*, 58 n., 92). At all events, economists have usually restricted themselves to an analysis of the determining elements of (1) intensive "quantity of labour" (see Nicholson, *Effects of Machinery on Wages* (1892), pp. 11-12, 26, 45 *seq.*, 77 *seq.*), or (2) efficiency. The latter includes, *firstly*, the causes which influence individual efficiency (see Walker, *Wages Question*, pt. i. ch. iii. ; Sidgwick, *Principles*, 2nd ed. bk. i. ch. iv. §§ 4, 5), *secondly*, the nature of the organisation of labour (see Marshall, *Economics*, vol. i. bk. iv. ch. viii. to xiii. ; Sidgwick, *Principles*, bk. i. ch. iv. §§ 6-8. See also DIVISION OF LABOUR ; EFFICIENCY OF LABOUR ; INDUSTRY, ORGANISATION OF).

Man's labour cannot produce matter but only utilities (see PRODUCTIVE LABOUR). Even thus, however, its *rôle*, as LOCKE (*q.v.*) shows, is sufficiently important. The American Indians, though they have a fruitful soil, "yet, for want of improving it by labour, have not one-hundredth part of the conveniences we enjoy ; and the king of a large and fruitful territory there feeds,

lodges, and is clad worse than a day labourer in England" (*Civil Government*, bk. ii. § 41.— cp. *Wealth of Nations*, bk. i. end of ch. i.). Indeed, to the labour of appropriation alone is due much that is commonly attributed to the bounty of nature (see CAPITAL, cp. Locke, *Civil Government*, bk. ii. §§ 40-43). "Labour was the first price, the original purchase money that was paid for all things" (*Wealth of Nations*, bk. i. ch. v. cp. introd. p. 1). It is, at any rate, evident that the aggregate of labour involved in the production of any commodity includes much more than that immediately concerned. To form the "strange catalogue" (Locke, *Civil Government*, bk. ii. § 43), a practically infinite regress of acts must be taken into account, many of which, however, since they enter into the final act of production in merely infinitesimal quantities, may, in practice, be neglected (cp. J. S. Mill, *Principles*, bk. i. ch. ii. § 1). For certain, though not for all purposes, the labour indirectly involved may be treated as condensed in the material and immaterial capital immediately employed (see Ricardo, *Principles*, ch. i. §§ 3, 4 ;—Böhm-Bawerk, *Capital and Interest*, trans. Wm. Smart, 1890, pp. 97-102, 297-300 ; and bk. vi., especially p. 375 *seq.*—Wieser, *Natural Value*, trans. C. A. Malloch, 1893, bk. v. ch. ix. x.).

[An exhaustive treatment of such a fundamental conception as labour would involve a discussion of many of the most vexed questions in economics. See COMFORT, STANDARD OF ; POPULATION ; PROPERTY ; SOCIALISM ; VALUE ; VALUE, STANDARD OF ; WAGES ; and authorities cited in text.

The subject is admirably treated in Prof. J. S. Nicholson's *Principles of Pol. Econ.*, vol. i., 1893, bk. i. ch. v.]   A. B. C.

LABOUR AND CAPITAL. The employment of these two terms as the antitheses of one another has for long been a commonplace of popular discussion. Disputes between capital and labour, the interests of capital, and the claims of labour, are topics familiar to every student of journalistic and periodical literature. Nor is it until the last few years that any serious doubt has been thrown in economic treatises upon the reality and appropriateness of the antithesis. The prominence, which has lately been given in those treatises to the functions of the employer in the production of wealth, and to his share in its distribution, has tended to substitute a new antithesis, for, on the one hand, trade disputes, it is seen, arise between employers and employed rather than between capitalists as such and labourers as such, and, on the other, if there be an antithesis between capital and labour, the employers, as such, may claim a place together with the employed in the ranks of labour. A group of writers, among the more distinguished of whom have been Bagehot in our own country, and General Walker in the United States of America, have shown that the employer is the moving and the guiding spirit of modern industry, organised, as it is, on the grand scale; and that he may, with the remarkable development of the banking and bill-broking system which has obtained in England and America, own but a fraction of the capital employed in his business. Accordingly capitalists may furnish him with capital, and labourers may offer to him their labour; and, if either of these two parties has a quarrel with the other, they only fight from behind the back of the employer, who has to bear the real brunt of the conflict. From this point of view, undoubtedly, the disputes, which occupy so prominent a place in popular discussion, are misnamed disputes between capital and labour, and should more properly be called disputes between EMPLOYERS AND EMPLOYED (q.v.). Again, recent writers on economics in England, like Professors Marshall and Sidgwick, have exhibited a disposition to consider the earnings of employers as belonging to the same genus as the wages of labourers; and although they may, making allowance for the human element involved, consider that both are determined by the same general principles as those which apply to the remuneration of capital, they have unquestionably tended to shift the antithesis from the position it has occupied in ordinary speech. For, if there be a real opposition between capital and labour, then the second member of the antithesis will include, on the arrangement of their treatises followed by these recent writers, a class which popular phraseology would certainly assign to the first. This alteration, despite the important developments of economic thought with which it is connected, and of consequences of no small pertinence to the validity of the arguments commonly employed in the discussions which have centred about the antithesis, has scarcely as yet established itself firmly even in scientific speech, and for the most part the phrase is used in its old familiar sense. It is in this sense that Mr. G. Howell, describing the history of Trade Unions, calls his book, *Conflicts of Capital and Labour.* It is in this sense that the late Mr. W. T. Thornton entitled his well-known treatise, *The Claims of Labour.* And it was largely in this sense also that Karl Marx gave the designation of *Das Kapital* to his epoch-making book; while it is certainly in this sense that many, if not most, of his numerous disciples, less acute in their economic analysis and less competent in their employment of subtle dialectic than their master, have been led into perverse interpretations of the constitution of industrial society. No doubt the employment of the term in this sense has given rise to serious misapprehension which might have been corrected by a more scientific analysis. But the employment is so stereotyped that Mr. Mallock, in a recent book on *Labour and the Popular Welfare,* is compelled to have recourse again and again to the familiar contrast, although he discerns clearly enough the fallacies it has occasioned.

It may be asked whether the antithesis between labour and capital is a reality; and the scientific answer states that it is both real and unreal. So far as the production of wealth is concerned, employers and employed are co-operating partners, and so, indeed, are labour and capital. In modern industrial society either of the two partners requires the services of the other. Nor are they merely necessary to one another, but it is their true interest that they should both be as efficient as possible. The more efficient they are, the larger will be the total amount of wealth produced; and the wealth so produced determines the absolute size of their shares in its distribution. It is the true interest, therefore, of the employers that the employed should earn sufficient wages to maintain them in the utmost efficiency of body, mind, and character; and it is the true interest of the employed that the earnings of the employer should be adequate to induce him to put forth his utmost powers in the organisation and development of his business. And similarly capital, requiring labour to co-operate with it in the production of wealth, needs as efficient labour as possible; and labour cannot dispense, without suffering for it, with capital of adequate quantity and quality. But neither efficient labour nor adequate capital will be forthcoming if it be discouraged by the smallness of its reward. So far, therefore, as the production of wealth is concerned, the interests of the two parties are harmonious, and the antithesis is unreal and misleading. But, given the production of wealth, the antithesis is strictly applicable to the distribution of the wealth so produced. Here employers and employed, and similarly capital and labour, find their interests conflict; for, the larger the share of the one party, the smaller must inevitably be the share of the other. When the older economists maintained that wages could not rise save at the expense of profits, just as when they insisted on the inelastic character of the wages-fund, they were possessed by the conception of a law of diminishing returns contracting the area of profitable employment of capital, and they did not keep continually present to their minds the possibility of increased production. Later inquiry has shown that an increase of wages, and also a diminution of the hours of the working-day, may be accompanied, if it only result in greater efficiency and a larger output, by no decrease—sometimes even by an increase—in the profits of employers and the earnings of capital. But, when once the amount of production is fixed, the possibilities of contests, bitter and protracted, over the distribution become imminent. So far, then, as the production of wealth is concerned, the antithesis between labour and capital,—whether we interpret the phrase in the familiar sense, which would be more scientifically expressed as an antithesis between employers and employed, or whether we use labour and capital in the wider signification of agents in the production of wealth (including employers under the head of labour)—is so far unreal; but, so far as the distribution of wealth is concerned, it is as pertinent as it is real. The scientific observer must here content himself with the sage, if ambiguous, counsel that neither party will act well or wisely for its permanent interests if it pushes any advantage it may happen to possess in the distribution of wealth so far as to affect prejudicially its production. It will then commit the error, celebrated in fable, of "slaying the goose which laid the golden eggs." But the application of this wise caution to practice is beset with so much difficulty that it may serve to restrain excess rather than to offer positive guidance. The combatants may be usefully reminded of their necessary dependence on one another, but they will not on that account be disposed to forget the inevitable opposition of their interests. Labour and capital will continue to be opposed in popular parlance; and the scientific student will be compelled to allow that the opposition has a basis in reason. The antithesis, therefore, whether the terms be used in a narrower or wider sense, cannot be said to be unreal. But it must be added that it has undoubtedly been responsible for no little amount of error. Partly this error has arisen from the particular expression given to the antithesis, and partly from mistaken ideas which have lain beneath it. Unquestionably the advocates of the claims of labour have frequently forgotten to consider the effects of the measures they support upon the production of wealth, and to remember that their constituents are equally interested with their opponents in increasing, or at least maintaining undiminished, that production. The idea of "making work by abstaining from work" is as delusive as it is attractive and popular, but it ignores the fact that production is the only source of distribution. Undoubtedly, too, it is possible that a strike may drive away a trade from a town, a district, or a country, and that the ultimate gain of a dispute may never be sufficient to compensate for the temporary loss. And, again, employers have not been always too ready to recognise the serious mischief of underpaid or degraded labour; and the history of the factory laws affords a warning, by no means unneeded, that employers—as indeed also parents and the nation at large—may at times of pressure sacrifice the permanent welfare of a country to its apparent immediate needs. Such errors as these connect themselves with an excessive emphasis laid upon the antithesis between labour and capital. Others arise from defective analysis, which the more scientific expression of the antithesis has done something to correct. The ardent hopes which were formed of the disappearance of industrial disputes with the inauguration of a system of co-operative production, connect themselves with such a faulty analysis. On the one hand, the importance of the part played by the employer, and the difficulty of discovering any effective substitute for him in co-operative management, have been slurred by the setting of capital in antithesis to labour; for it would then seem that it is only the acquisition of capital by labourers which is needed to remove that antithesis. On the other hand, a more deeply rooted fallacy lies beneath. For the antithesis is not so much between the abstractions capital and labour as it is between the concrete realities capitalists and labourers. The abstractions admit of reconciliation, but such reconciliation does not remove difficulties, which, so long as the main elements of human nature remain unaltered, must arise between men and women, capitalists and labourers. It is the individuals, and not the groups only, which are liable to quarrel, and, by setting up an antithesis between the groups as such, we are only too likely to forget the failings of the individuals who compose them. This subtle influence, which seems to attach to an abstraction, is probably responsible for another fallacy which may be noticed. It is a favourite practice with writers of a socialistic tendency, while laying immense stress on the mischievous nature of capital and the capitalistic system, and emphasising its inherent hostility to the interests of labour, to withdraw at the same time its pretended title to a useful place in the industrial economy by maintaining its original identity with labour. Out of labour it has come; and to labour its wrongful gains rightfully belong. If machinery be used in the production of wealth, it is in its origin the product of labour, and capital as such makes no contribution to that production. This reasoning, which occupies a prominent position on the pages of most socialistic treatises, is generally accompanied by a tendency to ignore, or to minimise, the functions of the employer; and in this respect it may be attributed to the faulty analysis which the altered statement of the antithesis between capital and labour has served to correct. But, as a matter of fact, while professing to insist on the antithesis, it endeavours in reality to remove its foundation. For, if capital be in its source and origin but labour, why should the two terms be opposed? The true answer is that the development of a phenomenon may be different from its origin, and may work such a change as to make it at once unreal and inaccurate to resolve the phenomenon into its primary source. In the modern world what is known as capital is so distinct from what is known as labour that to explain the functions of the one by those of the other is to confuse and not to enlighten. It is a distortion of language and a misrepresentation of fact to argue that capital fulfils no function of its own in the production of wealth because it may ultimately have found its source in labour. The question is, what is it now, and not what it may have been a generation or more ago. The contention of the Austrian school of economists represented by Böhm-Bawerk, who regards capital as being essentially an exchange of present goods for future goods, is rarely more convincing than when its dialectic is employed in refuting that of Marx. One of the strongest reasons for the necessity of organisation to protect the interests of labour in the form of trade unions is that capital can afford to wait for the future, while labour, isolated and unorganised, cannot hold out for a reserve price, but must seek employment in the present. In this sense, then, there is a real antithesis, and it is an antithesis, not between employers (as such) and employed, but between capital and labour.

[Besides the books mentioned in the text the student may be referred to those under ARBITRATION; CONCILIATION, BOARDS OF; EMPLOYERS AND EMPLOYED; STRIKES; and TRADES UNIONS. The particular passages which should be studied in the books mentioned in the text are Walker, *Wages Question*, chs. i., xiii., xiv., and xv.— Bagehot, *Economic Studies*, pp. 52 and 53.— Sidgwick, *Principles of Political Economy*, bk. ii. chs. i., viii., and ix.—Marshall, *Principles of Economics*, bk. iv. chs. vi. and xii. ; bk. vi. chs. i., ii., vi., vii., and viii.—Howell, *Conflicts of Capital and Labour*, ch. iv.—Böhm-Bawerk, *The Positive Theory of Capital* (Smart's translation), bk. ii. chs. i. and ii.—*Capital and Interest* (Smart's translation), bk. vi.—Cp. also Nicholson's *Principles of Political Economy*, bk. i. chs. v. and vi., for definitions of labour and capital.] L. L. P.

LABOUR DEPARTMENT. The development of the English labour department may be briefly traced as follows. In 1886 the board of trade was charged with the duty of supplementing, correcting, and systematising the statistics relating to labour, which had hitherto been only incidentally furnished in official reports. Mr. John Burnett, the general secretary of the Amalgamated Society of Engineers, was, accordingly, appointed to the newly-created post of "labour correspondent," and, with his assistance, the commercial department of the board of trade proceeded to draw up several volumes of wages statistics and to issue annual reports on trade unions and strikes. The services of experts also began to be engaged to furnish the board of trade with reports on special topics of industrial interest from time to time. In 1893 the staff engaged in this work was enlarged, quartered in a separate office, and

placed under the immediate control of a new official called the "commissioner for labour," and the labour department, thus equipped, undertook the task of preparing for monthly issue a journal called *The Labour Gazette*, in addition to the annual and other reports above mentioned. But, in acquiring its present quasi-independent position, the department has remained subject to the general supervision of the controller-general of the commercial, labour, and statistical departments of the board of trade, is not represented in parliament by a special ministerial chief, and discharges no administrative function whatever. Thus, the inspection of factories, chemical works, and mines is performed by the home office ; the care of emigrants, seamen, and railway servants is entrusted to other departments of the board of trade ; the protection of the accumulated capital of the working classes is a task devolving upon the registry of friendly societies ; the superintendence of the action of local authorities as regards education, sanitation, and poor relief is divided between the education office and the local government board ; while the post office, the war office, and the admiralty, and several other departments are large employers of labour. All these functions are discharged quite independently of the labour department of the board of trade.

Nor does that department, in its turn, monopolise the duty of preparing labour statistics,— a duty which is to a very large extent performed by the above-mentioned administrative departments in the course of their ordinary reports, while the task of preparing a decennial census of the occupations of the people is assigned to the general register office. Nevertheless, the labour department is doing a large amount of very useful statistical work.

The principal publications of the labour department from 1886 to the end of the parliamentary session of 1894 are as follows: "Six Annual Reports on Trade Unions" (*Parl. Papers*, c. 5104 of 1887 ; c. 5505 of 1888 ; c. 5808 of 1889 ; c. 6475 of 1890 ; c. 6990 of 1893-94, and c. 7436 of 1894).—"Five Annual Reports on Strikes and Lockouts" (*Parl. Papers*, c. 5809 of 1889 ; c. 6176 of 1890 ; c. 6476 of 1890-91 ; c. 6890 of 1893-94, and 7403 of 1894). —"Returns of Wages Published between 1830 and 1886" (*Parl. Papers*, c. 5172 of 1887).— "Return of Wages Paid in the Principal Textile Trades" (*Parl. Papers*, c. 5807 of 1889).—"Return of Wages Paid in the Minor Textile Trades" (*Parl. Papers*, c. 6161 of 1890).—"Return of Wages Paid in Mines and Quarries" (*Parl. Papers*, c. 6455 of 1890-91).—"Return of Wages Paid to the Police and to Persons Employed on Roads and at Gas and Water Works" (*Parl. Papers*, c. 6715 of 1892).—"Report on Wages of Manual Labour" (*Parl. Papers*, c. 6889 of 1893-94).—"Report on Sweating in the East End of London" (*Parl. Papers*, c. 331 of 1887).—"Report on Rates of Wages in Belgium" (*Parl. Papers*, c. 5269 of 1888).

—"Report on Sweating in Leeds" (*Parl. Papers*, c. 5513 of 1888).—"Report on the Condition of Nail Makers and Small Chain Makers" (*House of Commons Papers*, 385 of 1888).—"Returns of Expenditure by Working Men" (*Parl. Papers*, c. 5861 of 1889).—"Report on Profit-Sharing" (*Parl. Papers*, c. 6267 of 1890-91).—"Report on Wages and the Cost of Production" (*Parl. Papers*, c. 6535 of 1890-91).—"Two Reports on Alien Immigration from Europe to the United States of America" (*Parl. Papers*, c. 7113 of 1893-94).—"Report on Agencies and Methods for Dealing with the Unemployed" (*Parl. Papers*, c. 7182 of 1893-94).—"Two Reports on the Volume and Effects of Recent Immigration from Eastern Europe into the United Kingdom" (*Parl. Papers*, c. 7406 of 1894).—"Report on Profit-Sharing" (*Parl. Papers*, c. 7458 of 1894).—"Report on the Fishing Apprenticeship System" (*Parl. Papers* c. 7576 of 1894); and the *Labour Gazette*, London, May 1893, and monthly.

There are similar departments in the Dominion of Canada, the United States, Germany, and France. The United States and France publish a *Bulletin du Travail* monthly like our *Labour Gazette* (see BUREAU OF LABOUR, and BUREAU OF LABOUR IN THE UNITED STATES). T. G. S.

LABOUR EXCHANGE.

I. The Proposal, p. 520; II. The Scheme, p. 520; III. Labour Exchange Notes, p. 521; IV. The Principles on which Labour Notes were based, p. 522.

This term is sometimes used loosely as the equivalent of labour registry (see also BOURSE DU TRAVAIL). Accurately and historically it applies to a class of institutions which found much theoretical favour amongst early co-operators and the associates of Robert OWEN'S propaganda. Numerous labour exchanges, marts, and banks flourished in England in 1832, 1833, and 1834 for the direct exchange of the products of labour according to the amount of labour expended in making them, without the intervention of money or the expenses of the ordinary machinery of distribution. Their fundamental principle was the doctrine that labour is the source of all wealth, and labour-cost the true measure of value : the operation of this principle was considered to be interfered with and distorted by the intervention of money, a monopolised and limited commodity, as a medium and essential of exchange. The exchanges met a popular requirement, and, had the constant efforts of the more clear-headed among their directors been successful in maintaining a strict commercial system of valuation, might have been long-lived. But the labour-value theory, and the conventional rating of all labour at sixpence an hour for purposes of valuation in exchange, or for labour notes, defeated these efforts. The valuation of the price of materials was also a constant difficulty. Sharp tradesmen took labour-notes in their shops, and picked out the goods in the exchanges that were saleable at a profit on their "labour value." This process accelerated the accumulation of

stocks so that no one cared to take at the price of sixpence per hour for the time of their makers : the "labour-note" became depreciated *pari passu* with this depreciation of the security on which it rested ; its depreciation enabled traders who took it to skim the deposits still closer, until the goods in stock, and the labour-note, had fallen to a commercial value below that which the workman of average skill could earn in the ordinary labour market in the time represented by their price, and the exchanges one by one collapsed, after furnishing a very interesting illustration to the history of theories of value.

[*The Crisis*, 1832-34.—Holyoake, *History of Co-operation.* — Noyes, *American Socialisms; Gazette of Labour Exchanges*, 1833-34.—B. Jones, *Co-operative Production* (1894), ch. viii.—*Labour Exchanges.—The Birmingham Labour Exchange Gazette.—Gazette of the Exchange Bazaars.*] S. O.

The history of this movement may be best brought under four heads : I. *The Proposal.* II. *The Scheme.* III. *Labour Exchange Notes.* IV. *The Principles on which Labour Exchanges were based.*

I. *The Proposal.* In 1820 R. Owen wrote that there were three stages in the history of exchange : (1) barter, which admitted "the only equitable principle of exchange," which was to exchange "the supposed value of labour in one article against the amount of labour contained in any other article" (" Report to County of Lanark," *Autobiography*, ii. 278). As wealth increased, barter became impossible, and (2) artificial exchange, or exchange through some medium with a value of its own, introduced the commercial stage, which forgot "the natural standard of labour." But the increase of wealth was superseding the use of the gold and silver standard, and had partly done so during the suspension of cash payments between 1797 and 1819 (*ib.* p. 266). (3) The third stage began when exchange would be "equitable" as in the first stage, and by means of a medium, as in the second stage. The new medium, in order to reflect without deflecting the "natural standard of value," should not possess a value of its own. What was it to be ? England had solved the question in 1797 by making the new medium bank notes. The new medium was to be paper. This plan only differed from its realisation in suggesting a day-unit for an hour-unit. In 1823 he recommended "notes representing any number of "days' labour or part of a day's labour" (*Reports of Meetings in Dublin*, p. 127). "Equitable labour exchange" applies therefore to barter as well as to exchange by labour notes.

II. *The Scheme. The First Scheme* (1827-30) is often attributed to Josiah WARREN, who after assisting in the disastrous communistic experiment of OWEN at New Harmony (1825-27 ; for Owen's plan, see below) became an individualist. No account is obtainable of Warren's first experiment (*c.* 1828) at Cincinnati ; but the New Harmony experiment (1842) is thus described by Macdonald : the purchaser paid *in cash* wholesale prices plus 5 per cent for general expenses and added a promise to labour for, say, the hour during which the

INTEGRITY

EQUITABLE LABOR EXCHANGE

INSTITUTION

TRUTH.

FOR THE INDUSTRIOUS CLASSES

To the STOREKEEPER of the EXCHANGE

TWO HOURS by Out of

GRAY'S INN ROAD, LONDON. ESTABLISHED 1832.

TWO

No 3879

INDUSTRY

storekeeper attended to him ; he then valued his promise in kind (or in cash ?) and redeemed it accordingly (Noyes, pp. 96, 97). We do not read of the storekeeper buying with labour-notes but with cash, and in 1852 Warren said it was his rule that what was bought with cash must be sold for cash (*Equitable Commerce* by Josiah Warren, pp. 85, 91, 92, 109, etc.). The labour notes were merely a medium for paying store servants for their trouble in kind. The only interest of the scheme is that it was a co-operative store. Warren had ulterior views no doubt, but these were to be carried out by corn-notes (*see below*). In England, at that date "co-operative society" meant what we should now call a club whose members subscribed 1s. a week or so to a "community fund," or a fund for starting an Owenite "village" in which producers should produce all that they wanted and so turn communists ; "trading associations" meant co-operative stores in the modern sense based on this community fund. "Union exchange" meant co-operative stores bought from co-operative producers. In August 1827 Dr. King grafted on "The London Co-operative Society" at 36 Red Lion Square, a "union exchange" (*Co-operative Magazine*, ii. 421), which Lovett called "The First London Co-operative Trading Association." During September, Owen, then on a flying visit to England, saw Dr. King and induced him to divide the community fund amongst the members each month. In announcing this change (1st December 1827), Dr. King wrote of his scheme as a scheme for "exchanging labour," which meant buying and selling at cost price, and as leading to everything Owen ever contemplated (*ib.* ii. 548). It is hard to see how the Owenite ideal of economical self-sufficiency could be obtained by a group of townsmen if they gave up the plan of a permanent community fund. But there was one other possible method, alliance with other groups of co-operative producers. This method was probably present to Dr. King's mind.

Again on 1st October 1827 the Brighton co-operators, whose prophet was Dr. King, proposed a similar exchange union with labour-notes or "notes for the value of so much labour "as is brought in" (*ib.* p. 511). Meanwhile the example of London and Brighton spread through the kingdom, and we come to *the second scheme* (1829-34), whose *differentia* is the alliance of co-operative societies, in the modern sense, through labour-notes. On 13th January 1830, "The British Association for promoting Co-operative Knowledge" officially proclaimed the federal idea (London, *Co-operative Magazine*, p. 28), the idea of forming what 'the *Quarterly Review* of November 1829 (p. 373) called "a bazaar of co-operative shops." Owen, who had permanently returned to England in the previous August, inspired, but did not head the new departure. On 28th April 1832, the *Crisis* advertised an "exchange bazaar" in New Road, Marylebone, then the headquarters of the British Association, "on an equitable time valuation," under the signatures of Dr. King and Macpherson. According to Lovett (*Life*, p. 47), this meant labour-notes.[1] Owen, his hand being thus forced

by his disciples, then published his full scheme (*Crisis*, 16th June 1833), with draft labour-notes (*ib.* 30th June), and rules (*ib.* 30th June and 8th September). Owen's "Institution "—as the headquarters of his "Association of the Industrious Classes, founded 1831" were called — was at Bromley's Bazaar, Gray's Inn Road. It had been a club for ventilating unpopular religious views, but was now quickly adapted to its new purpose. Deposits began 3rd September ; exchanges, 17th September, and a branch office was opened 8th December in Blackfriars. The maximum deposits in the Bromley Bazaar reached 38,772 hours in one week, and after a month the branch office recorded 32,759 hours' deposits, 16,621 hours' exchanges (*Crisis*, ii. 7) ; Holyoake writes £ for hours). The "institution" merged in the Blackfriars branch from January to May 1833, when it migrated to 14 Charlotte Street, Fitzroy Square, whence it formed a Birmingham branch which opened on 29th July and 12th August 1833 for deposits and exchanges respectively. This "institution" was by far the most important federal centre of the new movement, but while it invited non-members as well as members to deal with it, co-operative societies usually kept their organisations distinct from it. Owen had undertaken to absorb into it every trade, benefit, and co-operative society in the kingdom (*Crisis*, 14th April 1833), a year later it abandoned federalism on industrial lines (*Crisis*, 7th June 1834).

Meanwhile co-operative societies had been swept into the stream mainly by Owen. Pare (Owen's son-in-law) and Dr. King turned their clubs, "trading associations," and "union exchanges" into "equitable exchanges," federated throughout the length and breadth of the land, and in a year or two were nearly all engulphed (Booth says "all but four," *Robert Owen*, p. 154, but see *Working Men Co-operators* by Acland and Jones, p. 23).

III. *Labour Exchange Notes.* "This little and apparently insignificant instrument would bring prosperity to all,"—so said Owen of the *first* of the notes represented here (*Crisis*, 2nd October 1832), which bears date fifteen days after the Bromley bazaar stores were opened for Exchange. The example published in Lloyd Jones's *Life of Owen*, 2nd ed., 1895, p. 240, is marked "Birmingham Branch," has no reference to an eight hours' day (as the one given here has), but has the same pattern. "The sun of truth" recalls the titles of two Owenite newspapers, the daily and weekly *True Sun.* The beehive commemorates one of Owen's favourite fables (*Crisis*, ii. 40). The scales of justice adorn, also, J. Warren's corn-note of 1852. The note is in form a bill of exchange, and in substance a deposit-receipt, and therefore, unlike the I.O.U.'s devised by Warren, precluded credit. It was transferable in name and fact, but not in law. The *second* and *third* of these notes were obviously issued by the "London Co-operative Trading Association," and the word "central" indicates that they too were federating. There is no trace of notes actually issued by this or any other co-operative society before April 1832. E. Nash, the secretary of Owen's central association, whose name appears on the first note, often warned people against

---

[1] The commission charged was 8½ per cent = to 1d. in 1s.

notes issued by non-affiliated societies which worked on slightly different lines (*Crisis*, i. 143); perhaps this society was referred to. On 14th April 1833, "extensive premises in Red Lion Square, lately the Labour Exchange and Institution for the Working Classes," were advertised for sale; these premises were apparently referred to. *The third note* marks the point where the labour-standard degenerates into or emerges from the money standard. Owen's first draft-note (*Crisis*, 20th June 1832) also stated that "the price of labour is 6d. an hour"; but the rules explain that this superscription only meant that materials were valued thus; Warren's notes, which he suggested for general use, were as follows:—

Cost the Limit of Price.	Seven Hours	Not transferable	7-12 pounds.	
(Figure of Justice) Justice	Due to Jacob Smith SEVEN HOURS' LABOR. In House Rent or SEVEN-TWELVE POUNDS of CORN.			Labor for labor.

Warren's circulating medium, which he forbade to circulate, in effect substituted corn for labour, just as this third note substitutes corn or labour as the standard of value. This note is practically a bill of exchange; only a technicality of English law prevents it being regarded as such.
[Noyes, *American Socialisms.*—Benjamin Jones, *Co-operative Production* (1894), ch. viii. Labour Exchanges. For corn notes, see House of Commons' discussion, 11th and 12th June, 1822, and passages from Adam Smith and Locke cited by Western in support, and criticised by Ricardo.]   J. D. R.

IV. *The Principles on which they were based.* As the ASSIGNATS (*q.v.*) were a paper currency based upon land, so Robert OWEN proposed in 1820, and his societies tried to carry out in 1832, a currency based upon labour. His labour notes were warrants issued on the strength of an hour's labour, and entitling the holder to goods from the store of the issuing exchange "to the value of one hour." Articles were to be exchanged at cost price, cost being assumed to be simply the labour spent on them. For the sake of bridging over the transition from the old currency to the new, labour was valued at 6d. an hour. Thus at the labour bank in the Gothic Hall, Marylebone, those who deposited goods at the stores were paid in labour-notes according to the value of the goods as so estimated.

For several months there was every sign of success, and some hundreds of London tradesmen agreed to take the notes in payment from their customers. The prosperity of the co-operative exchanges caused the rise of spurious rival institutions which soon forfeited the public confidence, and in the course of the year brought themselves to their models to a common ruin.

In any case no permanent prosperity could have been expected. Beginning with the error of treating all value as a matter of cost and all cost as labour, the promoters of the scheme were, besides, not equal to the task of distinguishing between the hour's labour of the skilled and industrious and the hour's labour of the unskilled

or the idle. To discriminate accurately by having regard to length of training and to the ease or difficulty of the labour attested by the note would have complicated a scheme of which the most vaunted merit was its simplicity. Owen himself, too, was conscious that, especially at first, the ways and even the language of ordinary business must be preserved. But his followers, with few exceptions, were without discretion, and imposition was easy. Men brought goods that were unsaleable in the ordinary market, turned them into labour-notes, and with these notes drew useful and saleable articles from the stores. If careful valuation had been made for them by a common pawn-broker, the exchange societies might, at a small expense of dignity, have purchased a longer lease of life.

The idea of a labour note was in Owen's mind as early as 1820. In the Report to the County of Lanark, 1820 (*Life*, vol. ii. 267 *seq.*, he says that "the natural standard of value is in principle human labour," "the average of human labour or power may be ascertained; and, as it forms the essence of all wealth, its value in every article of produce may also be ascertained, and its exchangeable value with all other values fixed accordingly, the whole to be permanent for a given period. Human labour would thus acquire its natural or intrinsic value" (see VALUE, MEASURE OF).

Owen continues (*ib.* p. 278), "To make labour the standard of value it is necessary to ascertain the amount of it in all articles to be bought and sold. This is in fact already accomplished, and is denoted by what in commerce is technically termed the 'prime cost,' or the net value of the whole labour contained in any article of value the material contained in or consumed by the manufacture of the article forming a part of the whole labour." "The genuine principle of barter was to exchange the supposed prime cost of, or value of labour in, one article against the prime cost of, or amount of labour in, one article, against the prime cost of, or amount of labour contained in any other article. This is the only equitable principle of exchange," and it may be secured without sacrifice of modern improvements (p. 279), "by permitting the exchange to be made through a convenient medium to represent this value." He goes on (p. 304): "A paper representative of the value of labour manufactured on the principle of the new notes of the Bank of England will serve for every purpose of their [the association's] domestic commerce or exchanges and will be issued only for intrinsic value received and in store."

It must be said that these notes cannot fairly be compared with ordinary bank notes; they were not issued for profit or on a calculation of probable demands for payment, but simply to effect the exchange of two supposed equivalents both actually existing at the time of exchange. Over-issue was impossible, for the goods might be said to go with the notes, as with bills of lading. In theory they were always convertible. If depreciation occurred, it was because of the spread of disbelief in the possibility of carrying out the conditions of the scheme, not from the nature of the case owing to an issue beyond the needs of the public.

[A. Held, *Sociale Geschichte Englands* (1881), i. 366-372.—Anton Menger, *Recht auf den vollen Arbeitsertrag*, 2nd ed. 1891, pp. 59, 94, cp. also pp. 89, 90, for the *Arbeitsgeld* of Rodbertus, and *passim* for parallels from later socialistic writers, with whom the idea became very popular.— The idea occurs in W. Herbert's pamphlet on *Harmony*, 1825, p. 32 ; and W. Thompson's *Distribution of Wealth*, 1824, p. 524.—G. J. Holyoake, *History of Co-operation* (1875), vol. i. ch.

viii.—Benjamin Jones, *Co-operative Production* (1894), ch. viii. (the best short account).

Among the original authorities are the *Crisis* (organ of the co-operative societies), the Life of Lovett the chartist, and the Place Collection in the British Museum.]   J. B.

Other "labour notes" besides these, appear to have existed. The following is a description of a proof of one which is preserved in a collection made by Francis PLACE, in four volumes of his, Owen's, and similar authors' writings ranging from 1817 to 1832 on *Labour Questions and Political Economy*.

Removed from the Gothic Hall to
No. 17 Hertford Street, Tottenham Court Road.

INDEPENDENT

EXCHANGE

Here is a view
of a Gothic Hall
4 stories high
with 7 windows
in front (copper plate)

BAZAAR

The true standard
of Value, is Labour

The Equitable
reward of Labour
is Equal Labour

No. 48

No. 48

Deliver to the Bearer, Goods
to the Value of 10 hours labour

Ten

(blank
not signed)

} Managers

At foot of the example from which this description is taken, is written, it is believed in Place's own handwriting—*discontinued*.

The "Gothic Hall" referred to, or rather depicted on the labour note described above, was in the New Road, Marylebone. It is described in an octavo page, broadside, in one of the four volumes collected by Place. The broadside says "Labour Exchange was begotten in the years 1827 and 1828,[1] but was not born until the month of April 1832, when it came into existence in the New Road, Marylebone, where it continued for some time to grow and thrive, and promised in due time to become a full grown man. But unfortunately, in the month of September of the same year, it was placed at nurse . . . in Gray's Inn Road. . . . After undergoing about four months' ignorant, experimental torture, it died, much lamented by all its real friends . . ." (Broadside is signed W. K., Charlotte Street, Portland Place, June 1835).

LABOUR IN PRISONS. See PRISON LABOUR.

LABOUR IN RELATION TO THE LAW. Under this heading it is proposed to sketch the general nature of the legal relations subsisting between wage-paid manual labourers and their employers.

Formerly, the law would not permit a workman to practise a skilled trade unless he had served a regular apprenticeship ; and, in some

industries, the ancient system of master, journeyman, and apprentice still survives. But, since the final repeal of the Statute of Apprenticeship (5 Eliz. c. 4) in 1814, it has been deprived of its legal sanction, and, in the larger industries, is rapidly becoming obsolete (see APPRENTICESHIP ; APPRENTICESHIP, STATUTE OF).

At the present day, the nature of the legal relations between employer and workman, depending, as it does, so largely on the terms of the contract of service, varies very considerably. In the average case, however, the workmen employed in the larger and better paid industries are engaged for about a fortnight, although the contract is understood to be renewed at the end of that time, unless one or other of the parties shall have given a stipulated length of notice to terminate it. Every such contract is enforceable at law, so as to render liable to damages the employer ceasing to employ, or the workman ceasing to work without giving the stipulated notice, but not so as to enable any court to compel specific performance, or grant an injunction against a contemplated breach of the agreement. A workman leaving his employment voluntarily and without notice, cannot recover wages for the uncompleted period of service in the course of which he leaves. When summarily dismissed for no fault of his own, he can recover the full wages that would have become payable if he had received

[1] First published and recommended in No. 1 and 11 of the *Union Exchange Gazette*, and afterwards continued through the columns of the *Weekly Free Press* newspaper.

the proper notice ; but, if he has been guilty of misconduct, he can only recover the wages, of which, at the date of his dismissal, payment is actually due. The types of misconduct that will justify the summary dismissal of a workman are : (*a*) dishonesty ; (*b*) disobedience to lawful and reasonable orders ; (*c*) habitual neglect in the discharge of ordinary duties ; (*d*) drunkenness, or gross immoral conduct ; and (*e*) incompetence ; but, if a workman be ordered to do anything outside the sphere of the particular duties which he has expressly or by implication undertaken to discharge, he is not guilty of "disobedience to a reasonable order" in refusing to comply.

An employer can recover damages from any person who has succeeded in persuading his workmen to break their contracts with him, or in keeping them away from their work by force. He also has a right of action against any person who has employed his workmen after receiving notice of their previous engagement to work for him. He can recover from the workmen themselves the wages which their breach of contract has enabled them to earn elsewhere, and can even claim from the person who has wrongfully employed but not paid them, a sum equivalent to the value of their services. Finally, he can recover damages from any person who, by using or threatening to use violence, has deterred workmen from entering upon or renewing contracts to work for him, while any agreement that he may have made not to employ a particular workman or class of workmen is "in restraint of trade," and not enforceable against him.

Conversely, a workman can recover damages from any person who has succeeded in persuading his employer to break his contract with him, and he can even sue any person who, by threatening or using violence, has deterred him from entering upon or renewing a contract of service. Indeed, whatever may be said of an employer's freedom to choose his workmen may also be said of a workman's freedom to choose his employer.

The contract between employer and workman almost always includes a definite agreement as to wages, and from the sum agreed upon no deduction that is in contravention of the Truck Acts may be made (see TRUCK ACTS). If the wages are made payable "by the piece," the employer, being under agreement to pay them at specified periods, and not to terminate the contract without giving a stipulated length of notice, is bound to find employment for the workman between the date of the notice and the date of the termination of the contract.

An undertaking is implied on the part of the workman to conform to the general rules of discipline prevailing in the employer's service, and, so far as relates to the employer's responsibility for his workmen's personal safety, there is implied, on his part, an obligation to use due diligence to associate them with competent mates and superiors.

On leaving his employer's service, a workman cannot demand any testimonial of character. Testimonials given to him by former employers, however, are his property, although any person subsequently employing him may impair their value by writing an adverse opinion on the same paper. These "character-notes" are "privileged," and may, therefore, contain defamatory statements without exposing the writer to an action for libel. But proof of malice will destroy the privilege, and, whereas wilful falsehood proves the presence of malice, truthfulness does not prove its absence. A workman writing or uttering a false character of himself is guilty of forgery.

By the following statutes, the legal relation of employer and workman has been further defined.

The Preferential Payments in Bankruptcy Act 1888.—By this act, workmen are given priority over certain other classes of creditors in respect of the wages due to them from a bankrupt employer. Similar provisions are contained in the Companies Acts 1862 and 1867, in respect of the wages due from a company in process of winding up.

The Wages Attachment Abolition Act 1870.— This act forbids judges and magistrates to make orders for the attachment of workmen's wages.

The Truck Acts 1831 and 1887.—These acts compel employers to pay their workmen's wages in coin and in full (see TRUCK ACTS).

The Payment of Wages in Public Houses Prohibition Act 1883.—This act is, in its object, analogous to the Truck Acts.

The Employers' Liability Act 1880.—This act amends the common law of negligence as applied to the conduct of employers and workmen *inter se*, by making every employer liable, in certain specified classes of cases, for the personal injuries caused to his subordinate workmen by the carelessness of their foremen (see EMPLOYERS' LIABILITY ACT).

The Factory Acts 1878-95.— The primary object of these acts is to regulate the conditions of labour in manufacturing establishments where "protected persons" (*i.e.* women, young persons, and children) are employed ; but some of their provisions bear directly upon the employment of adult males. Among other statutes regulating the employment of protected persons, the Agricultural Gangs Act 1867 ; the Children Dangerous Performances Act 1879 ; the Prevention of Cruelty to, and Protection of Children Act 1872 ; and the Shop Hours Acts 1892 and 1895, may here be noticed (see FACTORY ACTS).

The Trade Union Acts 1871, and 1876, *and the Trade Union (Provident Funds) Act* 1893.— These acts have rendered the property of the associations, formed by employers and workmen for the protection of their respective interests, legitimate objects of trusts, notwithstanding that their purposes may be "in restraint of trade" ; and they have exempted from income tax the portions of a trade union's funds that are set apart for provident benefits. But they have not given trade unions the legal *status* of corporations, or enabled them to sue and be sued in the courts (see TRADES UNIONS).

The Conspiracy and Protection of Property Act 1875.—This act regulates the conduct of strikes. It provides that no combination to do any act in furtherance of a trade dispute shall be indictable as a conspiracy, unless the contemplated act would be criminal if done by one individual ; but it renders liable to fine or imprisonment any person who, with a view to compelling another person to do or abstain from doing any act which the latter has a legal right to abstain from doing or to do, uses or threatens to use violence towards him, persistently follows him about, hides his tools, or, except for the purpose of communicating information, besets his residence or place of work (see STRIKES and COMBINATION LAWS).

The Employers and Workmen Act 1875.—This act confers and enlarges certain jurisdictions as to disputes between employers and workmen. It enables county courts, and, in some cases, courts of summary jurisdiction—(*a*) to adjust and set off claims, whether for wages, damages, or otherwise ; (*b*) to rescind contracts of service on such terms as may be just ; and (*c*) with the plaintiff's consent to accept security from the defendant for the performance of so much of his contract as is unperformed, in lieu of damages. The Arbitration (Masters and Workmen) Acts 1824 to 1872, also make provision for settling disputes between employers and workmen ; but they are, and always have been, entirely inoperative.

In addition to these statutes, there is a large mass of legislation regulating the conditions of employment in particular industries. Of this the following acts are among the most important examples. The Alkali Works Regulation Acts 1881 and 1892 ; the Canal Boats Acts 1877 to 1884 ; the Coal Mines Regulation Act 1887, and the Coal Mines (Check Weigher) Act 1894 ; the Cotton Cloth Factories Act 1889 ; the Hosiery Manufacture (Wages) Act 1874 ; the Merchant Shipping Act 1894 ; the Metalliferous Mines Regulation Acts 1872 and 1875 ; the Metropolitan Public Carriages Act 1869 ; the Quarries Act 1894 ; the Railway Regulation Act 1893 ; and the White Lead Factories and Bakehouses Act 1883.

[See Jevons, *The State in relation to Labour.*— Rumsey, *Legal Handbook for Employers and Employed.*] T. G. S.

LABOUR, MOBILITY OF. By the "mobility of labour" is meant the degree of facility with which, in response to any inducement, labourers move from one employment or place to another. For, the labour being inseparable from the labourer, "the mobility of labour and the mobility of the labourer are convertible terms" (Marshall, *Principles*, vol. i. 2nd ed., bk. vi. ch. iv. § 5).

The movement of progressive societies from status to contract (cp. Maine, *Ancient Law*, p. 170) has necessarily involved a corresponding increase in the mobility of labour. In the old VILLAGE COMMUNITIES (*q.v.*), and even now in the stationary civilisations of the East, the workers' position is, with a few "safety valves"

(Bagehot, *Economic Studies*, p. 35), fixed by the rigid rule of CUSTOM (*q.v.*) (see also CASTE ; FRICTION IN ECON.). Under the feudal system (see FEUDALISM), it was scarcely less rigidly fixed by "inherited and forced, rather than free, contracts" (Cunningham, *Growth of English Industry*, vol. i. (1890), p. 129, cp. *ib.* p. 5). But in modern western nations there is, to a considerable extent, freedom of movement,—most pronounced of all in the United States, the country which has broken most completely with the traditions of the ancient world. Under the modern industrial *régime*, however, so large in number, so incalculable in their operation, are the variable causes that affect the demand for the produce of any given industry or locality, and so quick the response of capital to the call of higher interest, that there is a continual tendency to disturb the relation subsisting between the supply of and the demand for labour. And, since perfect mobility is the attribute only of that mythical being, the ECONOMIC MAN (*q.v.*), labour is, during the process of readjustment, in some cases at a scarcity value, while in others its remuneration is much below the natural level (cp. Sidgwick, *Principles*, 2nd ed., bk. ii. ch. xi. § 7).

With reference to movement from employment to employment, altogether apart from impediments to mobility in its every aspect arising from legal restrictions and combinations of labourers (see APPRENTICESHIP ; APPRENTICESHIP, STATUTE OF ; CORPORATIONS OF ARTS AND TRADES ; GILDS ; TRADES UNIONS), the tendency under free competition to equality in the net advantages of different employments "in the same neighbourhood" insisted on by Adam Smith (*W. of N.*, bk. i. ch. x., beginning), is now seen to be subject to greater qualification than he was disposed to admit (see Sidgwick, *Principles*, pp. 192-193, 317-323 ; Walker, *Wages Question* (1886), p. 192 *seq.*). J. S. Mill speaks of the industrial society of his day as distinguishable into four grades, between which the mobility of labour was practically non-existent (*Principles*, bk. ii. ch. xiv. § 2 ; cp. Cairnes, *Leading Principles of Pol. Econ.* (1874), pp. 69-73). But the subsequent course of social evolution has, as Mill foresaw (*loc. cit.*), greatly loosened the bonds of custom and tradition (cp. Marshall, *Principles*, bk. iv. ch. vi. § 7). At present the chief obstacles to this "vertical movement" (Marshall) are, directly or indirectly, traceable to the unequal distribution of wealth. It is this that keeps the higher forms of labour at a "monopoly" (Mill, *loc. cit.*), or rather "scarcity" (Sidgwick, *loc. cit.*) value. The lower the grade of labour, the less able and the less willing, on the average, are parents to "sacrifice themselves for the sake of their children" (Marshall, *Principles*, bk. vi. ch. iv. § 2 ; cp. bk. iv. ch. vi. § 7), and this obstacle is only diminished, not removed, by the growth of morality and enlightenment, and by state-aided education. But in opposing the "horizontal movement" (Marshall), *i.e.* from one employment to another in the same grade, this cause is important only in so far as it tends to perpetuate the sway of custom, ignorance, and inertia over the poorer classes. The chief hindrance to such movement seems rather to be this, that all save the lowest forms of labour involve on the part of the workman a certain amount of technical skill and training, which is rendered useless by a change of occupation. In this connection, however, Prof. Marshall notes that the increasing use of complex machinery, calling as it does for judgment and general intelligence, rather than mere manual dexterity, tends, while accompanied by increasing subdivision of labour, to replace the former well-nigh insurmountable barriers between different employments by "thin lines of division," which are easily passed on the appearance of any considerable and lasting inducement (cp. *Principles*, bk. iv. ch. vi. § 2 ; ch. ix. §§ 3, 4, 5 ; bk. vi. ch. v. § 3).

As regards movement between different localities, that poverty and ignorance are not the only impediments in the way of such migration is clear, since "the increased facilities of locomotion, and the extended knowledge possessed by the working classes as to the conditions of life in parts outside their immediate localities," have not, within the last quarter of a century, materially increased the "migration within the borders of England and Wales" (*Census* (1891) *General Report*, p. 61).[1] It still, then, "appears evidently from experience that man is, of all sorts of luggage, the most difficult to be transported" (*Wealth of Nations*, M'Culloch's ed., p. 34). Historic legal restrictions apart (see SETTLEMENT, POOR LAW), we have here to reckon not only with the influence of marriage and the existence of family life, but also with the labourer's natural attachment to early friends and the scenes of childhood, including a feeling of reluctance, half unconscious it may be, to forsake the vicinity of the green churchyard where his forefathers sleep. In opposing the transfer of labour from one country to another, the combined influence of these motives is *à priori* more powerful ; and there are frequently in this case additional drawbacks, such as difference of climate, geographical distance, and peculiarities of national character in respect of language, religion, political institutions, and modes of

life (cp. Cairnes, *Leading Principles*, pt. iii. ch. i. § 2). It is this relatively greater immobility of labour, as between different nations, that is generally held to necessitate a special theory of INTERNATIONAL TRADE (*q.v.*) (see EMIGRATION).

[In addition to the references in the text, see Cliffe Leslie, *Essays in Political and Moral Philosophy* (1879), Essays xii. xxiv. — Marshall, *Principles of Economics*, vol. i., 2nd ed. bk. iv. ch. xii. §§ 6-12 ; bk. vi. ch. iii. § 2 (reply to Cliffe Leslie), ch. iv. §§ 2-5, ch. v. §§ 1-3.—Nicholson, *Effects of Machinery on Wages* (1892), ch. i. *passim*, ch. v., also pp. 70, · 129 - 130. — Walker, *Wages Question*, chs. x. xi. xviii. On legal restrictions, gild regulations, etc., see *Wealth of Nations*, bk. i. ch. x. pt. ii.—Brentano, *History and Development of Gilds and Trade Unions.*— C. Gross, *The Gild Merchant* (1890). — Sir G. Nicholls, *History of the English Poor Laws* (1854). On international mobility, see above, vol. i. p. 761, col. 1, par. 2.—Ricardo, *Principles*, ed. Gonner (1891), p. 117.—J. S. Mill, *Principles*, bk. iii. ch. xvii. § 1.—Cliffe Leslie, in *Fortnightly Review*, xxv. p. 942 (June 1879).—Bastable, *Theory of International Trade*, 1887, ch. i.—Edgeworth, in *Economic Journal*, vol. iv. p. 35 (March 1894).— *Census* (1891), *General Report*, pp. 5 - 6, 83-84, 126.]

A. B. C.

LABOUR NOTES. See LABOUR EXCHANGE ; OWEN, ROBERT.

LABOUR ORGANISATION. See INDUSTRY, ORGANISATION OF ; TRADES UNIONS.

LABOUR, PRODUCTIVE. See PRODUCTIVE LABOUR.

LABOUR RENT. See RENT, LABOUR.

LABOUR, SKILLED. The wealth of a nation in any given environment depends chiefly on "the skill, dexterity, and judgment with which its labour is generally applied" (*Wealth of Nations*, p. 1) ; or, in other words, the greater his skill the more successful, *ceteris paribus*, is man in turning the rest of nature, animate or inanimate, to the satisfaction of his wants (see EFFICIENCY OF LABOUR). But, while there are as many kinds and qualities of skill as there are varieties of mind, skill of some sort is inseparable from even the rudest forms of LABOUR (*q.v.*) (cp. Duke of Argyll, *Unseen Foundations of Society*, 1893, p. 78). There is thus no clear-cut distinction between skilled and unskilled labour. The case illustrates well the principle of continuity, the difference being in degree rather than in kind (cp. Marshall, *Principles of Economics*, 2nd ed. p. 104, Pref. p. xiii.). The distinction, moreover, such as it is, must vary from age to age and from country to country. Thus all English, and still more all American, labour is skilled in comparison with that of more backward races ; and to our mediæval ancestors much of what we now regard as rude or unskilled would have seemed skilled labour ; just as much of the so-called skilled labour of to-day, *e.g.* that of the copying clerk, may be

---

[1] The *Report* (p. 61) states that the native population shows "stationary habits of a very decided character." The percentage of "stationary natives" (*i.e.* natives of England and Wales enumerated in their native counties) was 74·04 in 1871, 75·19 in 1881, 74·86 in 1891, proportions practically identical. It is, however, noted that "the counties that retain the largest proportion of their natives are, as might be expected, those which offer the best chances of remunerative occupation."

the unskilled of future generations (cp. Marshall, *Principles*, pp. 730-732). These, however, are familiar difficulties in the way of economic classification and definition (cp. Sidgwick, *Principles of Pol. Econ.*, 2nd ed. p. 50).

What then is implied in the phrase "skilled labour" as ordinarily understood? Clearly general intelligence, foresight, energy, and honesty are qualities which, depending as they do largely on inherited race character, and on early environment and training, constitute the raw material of all industrial skill whatever— a material, too, of very various qualities in different races and individuals (cp. F. A. Walker, *Pol. Econ.*, 2nd ed. pp. 51-53). The phrase, however, as commonly used, seems to imply, in addition to this, the possession of a certain amount of technical skill—of ability specialised in some particular direction, whether it be of the faculties required in business management or for the professional work of lawyers, physicians, accountants, and such like, or the manual dexterity, the quickness of hand and eye, the technique of particular industries. Skilled labour, then, may be taken as labour differentiated, by training and experience, to such an extent that its transference to other occupations would involve, *ceteris paribus*, an appreciable industrial loss, as contradistinguished from the general mass of rude or unskilled labour, the transference of which from one occupation to another would, in this respect, involve no great sacrifice of labour power (see LABOUR, MOBILITY OF).

This acquired skill of the labourer is by Adam Smith included in the "fixed capital" of the society (see CAPITAL). It may, he says, in a noteworthy passage, "be considered in the same light as a machine or instrument of trade which facilitates and abridges labour, and which, though it costs a certain expense, repays that expense with a profit" (*Wealth of Nations*, M'Culloch's ed. p. 122). And the analogy is striking though incomplete; the motives which determine the supply of material capital do influence to a certain extent the supply of that personal capital which we term industrial skill. But the theory of EXCHANGE (*q.v.*) does not exhaust the problem of DISTRIBUTION (*q.v.*). A man's industrial skill, though partly the reward of his own effort and sacrifice, is also in great part due to the effort and sacrifice of his parents on his behalf. He who sows, acts in the full consciousness that the harvest, on its material side at least, will in all probability be reaped by another. And this fact alone—independently of the longer duration of the working life of man compared with that of a machine, and the consequently greater difficulty of forecasting future earnings (cp. Marshall, *Principles*, bk. vi. ch. v. §§ 1, 2)—suffices to differentiate to a certain extent the production of skill from that of material capital. For "the investment

of capital in the rearing and early training of the workers of England is limited by the resources of the parents in the various grades of society, by their power of forecasting the future, and by their willingness to sacrifice themselves for the sake of their children" (*ibid.* bk. vi. ch. iv. § 2).

There is, however, no question that industrial development is steadily raising the ratio of skilled to unskilled labour (cp. Nicholson, *Principles of Pol. Econ.*, vol. i. 1893, p. 120). On the one hand, the growing comfort, morality, enlightenment, and forethought of the mass of the people, and a keener appreciation on the part of governments of the importance of industrial forces in determining national strength, and of the consequent urgent need of education, combine to rapidly increase the supply of trained abilities (see Marshall, *Principles*, bk. iv. ch. vi.); while on the other, the progress of science and its practical application to industrial processes, accompanied as it is by the growth of a world-wide interdependence of industry, is probably associated with an increase no less rapid in the demand for industrial skill (see DIVISION OF LABOUR; LOCALISATION OF INDUSTRY).

Machine production being specially characteristic of the present industrial era, the portion of this problem which has received most attention is the effect of machinery on skill. In the matter of the introduction of machinery, as so often in economic questions, it is necessary to carefully distinguish between the immediate and the ultimate effects of the change. The former, as experience shows, are, from the standpoint of the labourer at least, pernicious. Machinery, when introduced, depreciates the value of the labourer's only capital—his skill; for unskilled labourers, including women and children, can by its aid accomplish the task which formerly demanded the highly specialised skill and judgment of the artisan; and the amount of hardship thus occasioned will be greater the more sudden the change and the less the mobility of the displaced labour (cp. Nicholson, *Effects of Machinery on Wages*, 1892, pp. 43-44). But this is only the transitional aspect of the problem, which remains to be contemplated from the point of view of social statics (*ibid.* pp. 55-56, 83 *seq.*). Machinery once generally adopted—is the result an increase in the ratio of skilled to unskilled labour, or is the net effect the reverse of this? That the invention, manufacture, management, and repair of machinery, and the organisation and other functions consequent on the *régime* of machine production, yearly demand higher and higher forms of skill, is a truth implied in the universal recognition of the growing importance of technical education (see EDUCATION). And that this highly skilled labour is itself a steadily increasing proportion of the whole seems probable. In favour of this view, see Marshall, *Principles*, bk. iv. ch. ix. §§ 3-6 ; Nicholson, *Effects of Machinery*, pp. 82-92 ; Giffen, *Essays in Finance*, 2nd series, 1887, Essays, ix. x. xi., cp. also *Census 1891, General Report*, p. 57 etc. Against it see Hobson, *Evolution of Modern Capitalism*, 1894, pp. 252-254. So far, therefore, the tendency of machinery would seem to be, as Professor Marshall insists, to increase the proportion of labour engaged in occupations which are at once more interesting, more intellectual, and call into play the higher forms of skill (*loc. cit.*).

A more debatable point is the influence of machinery on the skill of the machine tender—the ordinary factory hand. On the one side it is maintained that machinery, while increasing man's power over nature, and narrowing the field for muscular exertion and mere manual skill, tends at the same time to lessen the monotony of labour, and to correspondingly increase the scope for the operation of the higher mental faculties, which, too, the worker is better able to develop since his labour is less exhausting (cp. Marshall, *Principles*, bk. iv. ch. ix.). On the other side it is held that, except as regards a few industries such as watchmaking, this view is much too optimistic ; that, in general, under the system of minute division of labour which accompanies the use of complex machinery — partly cause and partly consequence,—the factory hand is not properly trained to understand as a whole the operation of which his work is but a fraction (see APPRENTICESHIP) ; that, in consequence, his labour is monotonous and affords no scope for mental activity ; that the habit of conforming to the automatic movements of the machine tends to dwarf the mind ; and that, in so far as machinery lessens the need for muscular exertion and manual skill, it tends to diminish within the factory the differences in skill, reducing all to one low level (see Hobson, *Evolution of Capitalism*, ch. ix. §§ 1, 4, 5). That there is a stratum of truth in this latter or more pessimistic view need not be doubted. But it may be noted (1) that it is doubtful how far it can be reconciled with the continued preference of masters for piecework, or the increasing differences in the wages of workmen (cp. Nicholson, *Effects of Machinery*, 87-88,— Hobson, *Evolution of Capitalism*, 258-259) ; (2) that, as its logical outcome, we should expect to find machinery cutting wedge-like into industrial society—elevating, educating, intellectualising its few masters, degrading and brutalising its many slaves. This, it is true, was apparently the experience of Great Britain in the earlier part of this century ; but the degradation of labour which then ensued was not, as experience shows, a necessary concomitant of machine production, but simply a feature of the industrial chaos which intervened between the old system of regulation and the new—between the shelving of the Statute of Apprenticeship and the gradual substitution of factory legislation (see APPRENTICESHIP, STATUTE OF ; FACTORY ACTS). And, at the present time, the mental, no less than the physical and moral, degradation of labour is most pronounced in those occupations in which division of labour and the use of machinery are least conspicuous (cp. Nicholson, *Principles*, p. 120) ; while, as a rule, the least educative parts of factory labour are performed by those who have risen to it from even less skilled occupations (Marshall, *Principles*, p. 323). On the whole, therefore, it would seem that the effect of machinery on the skill of the machine tender will depend chiefly on the environment in which it works—on the minds with which it comes into contact. As Professor Nicholson says : "Machinery of itself does not tend to develop the mind as the sea and the mountains do, but still it does not necessarily involve deterioration of general mental ability" (*Effects of Machinery*, 80-81). It will educate only those who are prepared for it. Under its sway, general ability is, as Professor Marshall notes, becoming a relatively more important factor of industrial skill (*Principles*, pp. 265, 313-323, 607). Hence, that the worker may reap whatever benefit may be in his work, a sound general education, including a training in elementary science, is the great desideratum of the age of machinery.

But, whatever be the direct influence of machinery on the skill of the factory hand, there can be no question that the modern industrial *régime*—at once the cause and the consequence of machinery—with its large towns, interdependence of industries, and increasing complexity of life, calls for much more skill and greater intellectual activity than formerly on the part of the average citizen. The very forces, moreover, which are thus lengthening the period of tutelage, are at the same time providing the means of support during that period (cp. Giffen, *Essays in Finance*, 2nd series, 1887, p. 374, etc.) ; and the state prohibition of the labour of children (see CHILDREN'S LABOUR) is thus in accordance with the trend of industrial evolution.

[In addition to the authorities cited in the text, see Prof. W. Cunningham, *Growth of English Industry and Commerce*, vol. i. 1890, pp. 313-314 (on Craft Gilds).— C. Babbage, *Economy of Machinery and Manufactures*, 1832.—R. W. Cooke Taylor, *The Modern Factory System*, 1891. —G. Schulze-Gävernitz, *Der Grossbetrieb*, Leipzig, 1892.—A "Memorandum on the state of the skilled-labour Market" appears in the monthly issue of the *Board of Trade Journal*.] A. B. C.

LABOUR STATUTES originated in an attempt to remedy by legislation the dearness and scarcity of labour which followed the great pestilence of 1349. The first great statute of labourers (23 Ed. III. st. 2) which served as the basis of nearly all subsequent legislation, ordained that able-bodied labourers of either sex "within the age of threescore years of age . . . not exercising any craft of his own whereof he may live, nor proper land about whose tillage he may himself occupy, and not serving any other," should serve any one who needed his services, and this for such wages and livery as was accustomed to be given in that neighbourhood in the twentieth year of the reign.

The penalty for refusing to work, for departing from work without license, or before the term agreed upon, or for giving alms to "valiant" beggars who refused to labour, was imprisonment. The same enactment was also applied to the labour and wages of artificers; and sellers of victuals were forbidden under heavy penalty to ask more than a reasonable price. Owing to the ineffectiveness of this statute it was re-enacted in the twenty-fifth year (st. 2, c. 1, 2) with more precise definition as to agricultural and artisan wages, which were still to remain at the standard of the twentieth year, and none for festival days (see also 4 Hen. IV. c. 14). Labourers were to serve by the year instead of by the day, and were not to leave their town if they could obtain work there. The punishment for infringement of this statute was a heavy fine, the stocks, or imprisonment of forty days for the first, and a quarter of a year for the second offence, at the discretion of the justices. The fines from the labourers were to go either to the party sueing, or if none would sue, they were to be in aid of the town's contribution to the Fifteenth (see FIFTEENTHS and TENTHS). Labourers fleeing from one county to another were to be sent to their county gaol, and this ordinance was to be observed in London as well as in all the boroughs of the land (see also 31 Ed. III. i. c. 7).

In the thirty-fourth year the penalty of imprisonment was substituted for that of fine or ransom. All alliances of workmen were to be unlawful and void; and all such leaving their service for another place were to be outlawed, imprisoned, and burnt in the forehead with an iron F in token of falsity. But this pain of burning was not to be put in execution unless by the advice of the justices.

In the thirty-sixth year the fines of artificers and labourers were to be levied to the use of the Commons. This statute was again revived in the forty-second year of Edward III., and confirmed in 2 Richard II. (1, c. 8) (repealed 5 Eliz. c. 4). By the statute 12 Rich. II. c. 3—*For the regulation of servants, labourers, beggars, and vagabonds* (repealed 21 Jac. I. c. 28; see also general words, 5 Eliz. c. 4), it was enacted that any such wandering from their place of employment without sealed letters or testimonial explaining the cause of his going and the time of his return, should be put in the stocks till he could find surety for his return. Severe penalties were imposed on the forgers of such letters, and on such as received labourers wandering without them. By this statute artificers not otherwise employed were compelled to work as husbandmen. This was confirmed by the statute of the following year (13 Rich. II.), which further ordained that the justices in quarter sessions should assess the rate of labourers' wages. By 4 Hen. IV. c. 14, labourers were not to be hired by the week, nor to take hire for holy days nor Evens of feasts. Statute 7 Hen. IV. c. 17 confirmed that of 25 Ed. III. and 12 Rich. II., concerning labourers, and further enacted that by reason of the continued scarcity of "servants of husbandry," no one who had not rent to the value of at least 20s. a year might apprentice his or her child to any craft or mystery, but only to such labour as the said parent used (in part repealed by 8 Hen. VI. 11; 12 Hen. VII. 1; and entirely by the operation of 5 Eliz. 4, § 2).

But, inasmuch as servants and labourers continued to "flee from county to county, to the great damage of gentlemen and others to whom they serve," it was decided by the 2 Hen. V. (st. 1, c. 4) that all previous labour statutes should be firmly holden and put in due execution; and as all the legislation of this period was in the landowner's interest, it is not surprising to learn that in the fourth year of the same reign the penalty for excessive wages (12 Rich. II. c. 4) was to be imposed on the taker only (expired 6 Geo. I. 11).

In the next reign, however, the justices received power to proceed against masters as well as servants, and were again empowered to regulate wages and prices (2 Hen. VI. c. 18). A similar enactment was made in the sixth, and confirmed in the eighth year, until in the 23rd Hen. VI. c. 12, we get an act for fixing servants' wages, which provided that servants of husbandry proposing to engage with a new master, must first give warning to the old, otherwise the new covenant is void, and the said servant compelled to serve his first master for a year. In this statute the wages of every kind of labourer and artificer were assigned, whether with or without food and clothing. No man was to be excused "to serve by the year upon the pain to be justified as a vagabond."

By the 11th Hen. VII. c. 22, wages were once more fixed, and in addition the hours of work and of meals for labourers were particularly defined. Notwithstanding the social and economic changes that had taken place, wages were kept rigidly at their former rate, and the bailiff alone received a rise from his former 23s. 8d. (23 Hen. VI.) to 26s. 8d. per annum. During the summer half year the labourer was to work from 5 A.M. till 7 or 8 P.M., with half an hour allowed for breakfast, and an hour and a half for dinner and a mid-day sleep. In the winter term he was to work from sun-rise to sunset. Deductions were to be made from his weekly wages for hours misspent; and a labourer assaulting his overseer could be imprisoned at the king's will. Next year, however (12 Hen. VII. c. 3), the first portion of this statute, that referring to wages, was re-pealed, and this fact, taken in connection with the subsequent repeal (4 Hen. VIII. c. 5) of the penalties on masters who gave excessive wages, might seem to point to a freer competition of capitalists for the services of labour, had it not been almost immediately followed by the string-ent enactments of 6 Hen. VIII. (c. 3) reviving in all its rigidity the wage standard of 23 Hen. VI. c. 12. The London artisans, however, by representing the additional charges to which they were subject, obtained (7 Hen. VIII.) exemption from this statute. From the frequency with which these labour statutes were re-enacted and proclaimed, we may deduce their practical in-efficiency to remedy the economic evil. But the evil itself was changing. The landowners, de-spairing of effectual legislative remedies, set about helping themselves. Sheep-rearing was found to pay better than corn-growing, and required far fewer working hands. The population had in the meantime increased, so that gradually it be-came not so much the grievance of masters who could not obtain labourers as that of labourers who were obliged to wander in search of masters. A great amount of really pressing poverty, as well as of crime and vagabondage, was the result of this state of things, and Edward VI.'s first parliament found it necessary to deal with the matter. This statute (1 Ed. VI. c. 3), for *the punishment of vagabonds and the relief of poor and impotent persons*, may be called our first poor-law. It was of a terribly harsh and repressive nature. Infant beggars might be taken as apprentices or servants—the males till twenty-four, the females till twenty years of age—and those running away from such service were to become *slaves*[1] for their remaining years of service, and might be punished with chains or otherwise. Masters might let or sell the services of such a slave or child. Slaves or slave children wounding or conspiring against their masters were to become *slaves for life*. Vagabonds were to be branded with the letter V and sent to their native parish. They might be worked on the road in gangs, with rings of iron round their necks, and could be sold by the city or borough which owned them. Im-

potent beggars, however, were to be provided for by their native parish. It seems, however, to have proved impossible to execute this barbarous statute, and in the 3rd and 4th Ed. VI. it was repealed, and the 22 Hen. VIII. was revived in its stead. In addition to this a more careful provision was made for the poor and impotent. The mayors of towns were to remove the sick and poor to their proper parishes, and the aged poor able to work were to be employed. Lepers and bedridden persons were allowed to beg by their proctors. Pauper children above five years of age might still be taken into service without consent of their parents, but there is no mention of chains or slavery. And, further, there is a protective clause by which the justices might discharge such children from the service of a bad master.

Elizabeth began her reign by a sanguine *Act touching divers orders for artificers, labourers, servants of husbandry, and apprentices*. This, after lamenting the inefficiency of the existing laws as to wages and hiring, which could not "conveniently, without the great greefe and burden of the poor labourer and hired man, be put in execution," repealed them so far as related to hiring and wages. The statute then goes on to decree concerning compellable service in husbandry, concerning the testimonial to be carried by wandering servants, the regulation of hours of labour, the annual assessment of wages by the justices of the peace "according to the plentie or scarcitie of the time," the penalties for giving or receiving higher wages than those so fixed, and so on, very much—for all its claims to originality—on the lines of former legislation. The last portion of it dealt exclusively with the regulations for the taking of apprentices, who were to be bound for a term of not less than seven years, and none might follow any trade or mystery to which he had not been bound apprentice for the legal term (*vide infra* 17 Geo. III. c. 33, and repealed 35 Geo. III. c. 124). But the comparative leniency of this pauper legislation proving ineffective to check the prevailing pest of rogues, vagabonds, and sturdy beggars who swarmed all over the country, recourse was, in the fourteenth year, once more had to the extremest rigour. The former statutes (22 Hen. VIII., 3 & 4 Ed. VI., and 5 Eliz.) were repealed. Persons above the age of four-teen taken begging were to be imprisoned; beggars convicted of "vagabondage" were to be "grievously whipped," and burnt through the right ear, unless some honest person of the value of £5 would take him into his or her service for a year; and the beggar quit-ting such service was to be whipped as above. Beggars offending a second time were to be deemed felons, and a third time, as felons without benefit of clergy. Hereupon follows a strict and detailed list of such as were to

---

[1] *Servi*, trans. *slaves* in Record Comm. ed. *Statutes of the Realm*. The word might be rendered *Bondmen*, yet the *Servi* had all the badges of actual slavery.

be deemed vagabonds, among which were students of Oxford and Cambridge begging without license, and play-actors who had no acknowledged patrons. Provision was to be made for the poor and impotent, and their parishes taxed for their maintenance.

The 39th Eliz. explained and revived this statute ; and it was reinforced by 1 Jas. I., and heavy penalties were imposed upon those who gave less than the appointed wages.

In the 14th Charles II. c. 12, elaborate provisions were laid down for the organisation of the parish workhouses, and for the apprehension of sturdy beggars and vagabonds, who were to be compelled to work in houses of correction. Nothing, however, was herein attempted as to the assessment of wages or in respect of amelioration of the labourer's condition, although from this time onwards we meet with no more labour statutes of the harsh mediæval type. The legislature is either content, as in the present instance, to continue and pass on the work of former governments, or simply to repeal what was becoming inconvenient and obsolete.

This statute of 14 Chas. II. was renewed at various periods by 1 Jas. II. c. 17 ; 3 Will. & Mary, c. 11 ; 4 Will. & Mary, c. 24 ; 11 Will. III., c. 13 ; 6 Anne, c. 34 ; and, finally, made perpetual by 12 Anne, c. 18. A timidity no doubt engendered by centuries of repressive legislation restrained the labourer from seeking work far afield. To remedy this was passed, in 8 & 9 Will. III., *an act for supplying some defects in the laws for the relief of the poor of this kingdom.* This—recognising that many labourers became chargeable to their parish "merely for want of work," "who would, in any other place where sufficient employment is to be had, maintain themselves and families," and who, by reason of the difficulty of leaving their own parish, do not dare to settle elsewhere, "though their labour is wanted in many other places where the increase of manufactures would employ more hands"—enacted that labourers might change their parish, carrying with them a certificate from the place they left, and to which they were liable to be again removed in the event of their becoming chargeable.

An act, in the 22nd year of George II., providing for the more effectual preventing of frauds and abuses by persons employed in various manufactories, and for preventing combinations of workmen, and so, apparently, largely in the interest of the masters, yet also provided "for the better payment of their wages." The necessities of the improved industries also contributed to the slow emancipation of labour, for in 17 Geo. III. c. 33, we get *an act to allow master dyers within the counties of Middlesex, Essex, Surrey, and Kent, to employ journeymen in their trade who have not served apprentice thereto.* This was in contravention of 5 Eliz., which prohibited the use of certain trades to any persons who had not been apprenticed thereto for seven years at least. Similarly the hat makers, in the 55th chap. of the same act, petition for the repeal of the 5th and 8th Eliz. The 33rd Geo. III. c. 40, repealed 5 Eliz. 4, § 15, whereby justices in quarter sessions were to assess wages ; the 35th Geo. III. c. 124 also repealed in favour of the wool-combers, 5 Eliz. concerning apprentices, and the statute of the 54th year c. 96 repealed for ever paragraph 31 of 5 Eliz. c. 4.

[FACTORY ACTS ; POOR LAWS ; SERVUS ; TRADES UNIONS ; WAGES ; J. Thorold Rogers, *Hist. of Prices.*—Cunningham, *Hist. of Industry and Commerce.*—F. D. Longe, *An Inquiry into the Law of Strikes,* 1860.—Jevons, *State in Relation to Labour.* —Howell, *Handy Book of the Labour Laws.*]

A. L.

LABOUR, UNPRODUCTIVE. See PRODUCTIVE LABOUR.

LABOURERS, LAW OF. See LABOUR STATUTES.

LACHES. Delay in prosecuting a right. The doctrine is laid down in the following words by Lord Camden in Smith *v.* Clay :— "A court of equity has always refused its aid to stale demands, where the party has slept upon his rights for a great length of time. Nothing can call forth this court into activity but conscience, good faith, and reasonable diligence." The doctrine is applied where a plaintiff is setting up an equitable title to land, where a plaintiff is seeking specific performance, and in other cases.

[Story's *Equity Jurisprudence,* London, 1892, gives the English and American authorities.—See also Snell's *Equity,* London, 1894, and Fry on *Specific Performance,* London, 1892.] J. E. C. M.

LACROIX, EMERIC DE (in Latin CRUCEUS), born c. 1590 in Paris. Very little is known about his life, except that he published an edition of Statius and two Latin poems on Henry IV. and Louis XIII.

His *Nouveau Cynée ou Discours des Occasions et Moyens d'establir une paix générale et la liberté du Commerce par tout le monde,* Paris, 1623, shows that its author was greatly in advance of his times. To secure a perpetual peace, he recommends the institution in Venice of a permanent congress, consisting of the ambassadors of the principal sovereigns of the world, to be entrusted with the mission of settling all international quarrels by arbitration. Peace being thus secured, he urges sovereigns to repress every kind of oppression on the part of their officials, and insists on the necessity of abolishing the sale and purchase of offices. Justice should be valued higher than military courage ; merchants should be honoured as being more useful than "nobles, priests, and magistrates." . . . "It is reasonable to levy small taxes on imports and exports, but this must be done with the utmost moderation, especially for commodities which cannot be dispensed with, such as corn, wine, salt, meat, fish, wool, and leather, so that merchants may enjoy greater freedom and the inhabitants obtain them cheaper." Lacroix denies that there exists any reason "to make a distinction between the foreign and the native merchant : the conditions of trade must be equal everywhere," and he enlarges on the happiness of men who are allowed "to come and go freely, to be connected with each other without any scruple about their native country, as if the whole of the earth were, what it really is, the common city of all." He also argues for uniform coinage, weights and measures, and universal education by the state.

Lacroix was aware that his contemporaries were not ready to accept his plans, and concludes in a calm but despondent tone : "All I can do is to express these wishes and humble remonstrances, which will probably not be heeded. Still I desire to submit this testimony to posterity. If it turns out to be useless, I shall take refuge in patience."

E. Ca.

LADING, BILL OF. See BILL OF LADING.

LÆNLAND. As large estates grew up in Anglo-Saxon times, the practice developed of letting outlying portions to tenants, who cultivated but did not own the land. The rent paid for such lands might be in money, in kind, or in labour, and was sometimes a combination of all three. Some writers draw a distinction between "unbooked lænland," in which the conditions of tenure were vague and arbitrary, and terminated with the tenant's life, and "booked lænland," where the conditions were definitely laid down in writing, and the agreement might be for several terms of life. The whole subject of Anglo-Saxon tenures is so obscure, and the authorities are so scanty and of such doubtful authenticity, that it is not safe to lay down too distinct dogmas.

[*Essays in Anglo-Saxon Law* (Boston, 1876).— Kemble, *Saxons in England*, vol. i.—Kemble, *Codex Diplomaticus ævi Saxonici*.]   R. L.

LA FARELLE, FRANÇOIS FELIX (1810-1872), born at Anduze, has been reproached as regretting that the ancient corporations, with their system of masters and journeymen, no longer existed, and as desiring to see the re-establishment of similar organisations. There has been a little exaggeration in this. La Farelle recognised clearly and described the defects in the organisation of labour in the 18th century throughout the whole of Europe. His work is moderate in tone. How distinctly events have moved may be seen by comparing the law of 11th March 1884 on syndicates in France with the regulations of the decree of 14th and 17th June 1791, which says (art. 2): "Citizens of the same rank or profession, contractors, those who keep open shops, workmen and journeymen of any trade whatsoever, may not, when they meet, name for themselves either presidents or secretaries or syndics, they may not keep minutes, pass resolutions or deliberate, or lay down regulations for the benefit of their supposed common interests."

La Farelle proposed to distribute officially through the agency of administrative authority all merchants, artisans, and workmen of the industrial classes and professions either in societies or in different localities. They were to be free, doubtless, either to join or to leave ; the arrangement was not obligatory, it was only, at least in the towns, designed to correct through competition the faults inherent in all associations of this character. "People of the same trade seldom meet together," says Adam Smith, "even for merriment and diversion, but the conversation ends in a conspiracy against the public, or in some contrivance to raise prices." Competition alone can remedy this serious inconvenience ; now the organisations of La Farelle, entirely open as they were in reference to those outside, and as he planned them absolutely free, did not allow competition, at all events in the same town. Many of the defects of the mediæval corporations would thus have been re-established.

In studying his period the works of La Farelle are still both useful and instructive. La Farelle wrote many works on workhouses and reformatories ; we need only mention of these the *Progrès social au profit des classes populaires non indigentes*, 1839, 2 vols. in 8vo, which won the Montyon prize in 1840, and *Plan d'une réorganisation disciplinaire des classes industrielles de France*, preceded and followed by historical dissertations on human labour in ancient and modern times, 1842, 8vo, 2nd ed. 1847, 8vo. These two books form practically one, the first giving the plan which was ably developed in the second.

A. C. f.

LAFFEMAS, BARTHÉLÉMY DE (1545-1612). First a gentleman of the chamber of Henry IV. of France, he became general controller of trade. He published several tracts on the advantages which would accrue to France from mulberry-tree plantations and the breeding of silkworms, and others on commercial questions, which he viewed from the strictest stand-point of mercantilism.

Among the latter may be mentioned the *Sources des abus et monopoles glissés sur le peuple de France*, and the *Trésors et richesses pour mettre l'état en splendeur* (1598),in which he advocates, amongst other regulations, the establishment of a uniform system of weights and measures for the whole kingdom, and his *Discours d'une liberté générale et vie heureuse pour le peuple* (Discourse on a general liberty and happy life for the people), 1601.

[Pigeonneau, *Hist. du commerce de la France* (1889), vol. ii. pp. 272-278.]   E. Ca.

LAFFEMAS, ISAAC DE, SIEUR DE, son of Barthélémy de LAFFEMAS (*q.v.*), civil lieutenant of Paris and subsequently member of the council of state, wrote a *Histoire du Commerce de France* (1606), in which he follows his father's footsteps and insists on the usefulness of acclimatising the breeding of silkworms and of prohibiting the introduction of foreign silks.   E. Ca.

LAFFITTE, JACQUES (1767-1844), born at Bayonne, died at Paris, was an honest man in all senses of the word. It is of him that Cormenîn said, "his private life was a living sermon." Unfortunately his too optimistic faith that everything was for the best, and perhaps a touch of vanity in his disposition, blinded him to the faults of others, and he weakly allowed himself, particularly towards the end of his life, to be imposed upon by unscrupulous persons. Hence reverses occurred which injured the reputation to which he had so high a claim. Unusually gifted as he was with the qualities which lead to success in banking business, he came to Paris, and, a little before 1789, entered the banking-house of M. Perregaux. His qualities both of heart and head made him welcome to the chief, whose son-in-law and successor he afterwards became. From this time he began to accumulate a fortune which became considerable. He was a regent of the Bank of France at the time when those events took place which led to the fall of the first empire. At this period of difficulty (6th April 1814) he was appointed provisional governor of the Bank of France. In this capacity he proposed a reform, which, had it been adopted, would have considerably improved the government of that institution. At that time the state governed, and the shareholders superintended it. Laffitte wished to appoint the directors of the Bank of France from among the shareholders, the state to be nothing more than the inspector or controller of the operations on behalf of the public interest. This useful improvement, however, was prevented by the nomination, on the 6th April 1820, of Gaudin, Duc de GAËTA, as the governor.

In 1815 Laffitte was appointed to the chamber of representatives, and from that time onwards he continually was a member of the legislative assemblies. Liberal by temperament, he freely supported a constitutional government. Hence, under the restoration he was on the side of the opposition, where he filled an important position. Loyal and cautious, he courageously braved the risk of losing his popularity by upholding measures which he considered important to the prosperity of the country, such, for instance, as the plan for the conversion of the public debt introduced in 1825 by his political adversary, M. de Villèle. Besides this, Laffitte greatly assisted in bringing about the revolution of 1830. Louis Philippe, it may even be said, owed his crown to him. The king thought he paid him sufficiently by appointing him for some months, from 2nd November 1830 to 3rd March 1831, minister of finance. Unfortunately for Laffitte, the severe crisis which broke over the country at this moment struck his bank, weakened by acts of rare generosity. The man who, during the six years he was governor of the Bank of France, had refused to accept the salary, £2400 a year, attached to that office, who had been alternately the guardian of the valuables of Louis XVIII. fleeing to Ghent, of Napoleon when he left France after Waterloo, of the Orleans family when in difficulties ; the man who, in 1814, opened a subscription for a loan to carry on the war, putting his own name down for £12,000, but was alone in this ; who, in 1815, advanced £80,000 to feed the army compelled to retire to the other side of the Loire, and at many other times assisted the country when in financial necessity, had to turn to the Bank of France and to the king himself to meet a claim for £600,000. Laffitte completely shielded his creditors from loss, but the support of the government of 1830 was but sparingly granted him. The gratitude of the citizen king did not blind him to his own interests. Laffitte must have reflected sadly on the want of gratitude in the public and the politicians of the time. In 1837, when seventy,—an age when men of a different stamp of character seek retirement from work,—he re-entered business life and established the Bank of Commerce and Industry, *Caisse du commerce et de l'industrie*, which was wrecked by the revolution of 1848.

He died in 1844, and was spared the knowledge of this further trouble ; little as he had been appreciated in his lifetime, his funeral showed that the public was not quite indifferent to his memory.

The works which Jacques Laffitte left behind him were on financial subjects of the day. The most important is the one in which he courageously took up the question of the conversion of the public funds. *Réflexions sur la réduction de la Rente et sur l'état du crédit*, 1824, a publication which passed through several editions. A. C. F.

LAGRANGE, JOSEPH LOUIS (1736-1813). Born in Turin, but of French descent, this celebrated mathematician resided in France after the death of Frederick II., who had appointed him director of the Berlin academy. He enjoyed the steady protection of Louis XVI. and of the Emperor Napoleon.

In his *Essai d'Arithmétique Politique sur les premiers besoins de la France*, printed in 1791 by order of the *Assemblée Constituante*, Lagrange takes as the standard of the wealth of a nation the proportions between its vegetable food reduced to terms of corn and its animal food represented by butcher's meat. By three parallel estimates—grounded on the alimentary allowance of soldiers, the consumption of the towns which made returns of the quantities of food introduced, and the average annual produce of arable land and pastures—he computes that for the army the proportion between both kinds of food was as 7 to 2, for Paris 21 to 10, and for the whole of France only 15 to 2. He comes to the general conclusion that France in his days produced enough corn for its consumption, but only about half the quantity of butcher's meat which would have been requisite to put each inhabitant's allowance on the same proportion as the allowance of a common soldier.

Lagrange's *Essai* will be found in the *Collection des Principaux Économistes* (ed. Daire), vol. xiv. ; *Mélanges*, pp. 608, 614.   E. Ca.

LAING, SAMUEL (1780-1868), was the author of *Notes of a Traveller*, in which the social and political condition of many European countries is commented upon. The *petite culture* of Belgium and its system of *pauper colonies* is described accurately and carefully (see *Brit. and Foreign Rev.*, vol. xvi. (1844) p. 586 ; and *Dublin Univ. Mag.*, vol. xix. 1842, p. 579).

In 1836 Laing published his *Journal of a Residence in Norway during the years 1834, 1835, and 1836, made with a view to enquire into the moral and political economy of that Country, and the condition of its Inhabitants*, London, 8vo. The high praise he here bestowed upon the Norwegian method of land tenure contrasts sharply with his subsequent attack on the system of peasant proprietorship in his *Comments on the Social and Political State of the European Peoples* (1848-49), and caused J. S. Mill to remark (*Principles of Pol. Econ.*, bk. ii. ch. vi. § 3) upon his inconsistency.

Other publications were :

Preussen . . . in seiner politischen Entwickelung . . . dargestellt durch B. Constant und S. L. 1844, 8vo.—*Address to the Electors of Scotland*, Edinburgh, 1833, 8vo.—*Notes of a Traveller, on the Social and Political State of France, Prussia, Switzerland, Italy, and other parts of Europe during the present century*, London, 1842, 8vo ; 2nd series, 1850, 8vo ; 3rd series, 1852.—*A Tour in Sweden in 1838*, London, 1839.—*Observations on the State of Denmark and Duchies of Sleswick and Holstein in 1851*, demy 8vo, 1852.—*Observations on the Social and Political State of European People in 1848-49*, demy 8vo, 1850.   A. L.

LAISSEZ-FAIRE, LAISSEZ-PASSER, HIS-TORY OF THE MAXIM. Gournay is still generally credited with being the inventor of this phrase, and this apparently on the authority of his friend Turgot, who, however, in his *Éloge de Gournay*, simply says : "It ought to be added that the . . . system of M. de Gournay is remarkable in this respect, that . . . in all times and everywhere the desire of trade has been concentrated in these two words, *liberty* and *protection*, and most of all liberty. The remark of M. Le Gendre to M. Colbert is well known : "*laissez nous faire*" (Turgot, *Petite Bibl. Econ.*, p. 40, "*Il faut dire encore*," etc.). This supposed agreement of the views of Gournay with the observation of Le Gendre has been translated by Dupont de Nemours into the positive statement : "From his (Gournay's) profound observation of facts he had drawn the celebrated axiom, *laissez-faire, laissez-passer* " (*Œuvres de Turgot*, ed. Daire, i. p. 258) ; and has been followed by most of the writers on economic literature down to M. G. Schelle, Dupont's last biographer (*Dupont de Nemours et l'École Physiocratique*, Paris, 1888, p. 19).

In *Die Maxime Laissez Faire et Laissez Passer*

(Bern, 1886), Prof. August Oncken has thoroughly sifted and examined all available evidence on this subject, and comes to conclusions which may be definitively accepted, although he has not completely succeeded in identifying Le Gendre. The latter appears to have been François LEGENDRE, the writer of an arithmetical treatise entitled *L'Arithmétique en sa Perfection selon l'usage des Financiers, Banquiers et Marchands*, which went through nine editions between 1657 and 1687. Prof. Oncken has not been able to find out on what occasion the above reply was made to Colbert, but is inclined to believe that it must have been about 1680.

Still Legendre was a merchant and not a political writer ; his answer was probably unpremeditated, and was wanting in the distinction of literary fame. In the writings of his contemporary, BOISGUILLEBERT (*q.v.*), we meet, however, sentences which are closely allied to Legendre's utterance, such as : *Il n'y avait qu'à laisser faire la nature et la liberté* (*Factum de la France*, p. 286, ed. Daire), and, *Ainsi dans le Commerce de la Vie, elle* (nature) *a mis un tel ordre que pourvu qu'on laisse faire*, etc. (*ibid.* p. 280).

The worthy Norman magistrate, Boisguillebert, would thus have been the first to use with a scientific purpose, if not the actual first half of the maxim, at least language approaching to it. After him we must come down to the Marquis d'ARGENSON, in order to find a distinct and clear enunciation of the same principle conveyed still more pointedly in the essay to which he gave the title of *Pour gouverner mieux, il faudrait gouverner moins* (In order to govern better, we ought to govern less) (*Journal et Mémoires du Marquis d'Argenson*, 1858, vol. v.). Here he emphatically declares that *Laissez faire, telle devrait être la devise de toute puissance publique* (*Laissez faire* ought to be the motto of every public authority), p. 364. The same line of reasoning is consistently followed, and similar expressions are used, in his *Pensées sur la Réformation de l'État* and in sundry contributions to the *Journal Économique*, the authorship of which has been brought home to D'Argenson (Oncken, *Die Maxime Laissez faire*, pp. 66-80). Neither Quesnay nor Adam Smith uses the expression, but it is printed several times in the EPHÉMÉRIDES DU CITOYEN, and now in its complete form (*laissez-faire, laissez-passer*), and constantly put into the mouth of Gournay (see the quotations in Oncken, pp. 86-89). MIRABEAU, MERCIER-LA RIVIÈRE, and LETROSNE in their works give vent to the same theory, but under the parallel French or Italian form : *Le monde va de lui-même* or *Il mondo va da se* (The world goes by itself) (Oncken, pp. 84, 85). From what precedes, we may, it seems, safely conclude that if Gournay is not the actual inventor of the maxim, he put it into circulation through his conversations, after having contributed its second half.

Although the PHYSIOCRATS had numerous contemporary adherents in Germany, the latter do not appear to have adopted the expression, unless the maxim of ISELIN (born at Basle 1728), *Lasset der Natur ihren Gang* (Let nature have her course), in his " Ephemerids of the human kind " (*Eph. der Menschheit*), be considered as an attempt towards a translation (Oncken, p. 127).

In England, J. Stuart Mill employed the actual French words *laisser faire* (but in the infinitive, not the imperative mood) in the table of contents of his *Principles of Political Economy*, as a heading to § 7 of ch. xi.   E. Ca.

LAISSEZ-FAIRE IN ENGLAND.

Theory, p. 535 ; Legislation, p. 537.

Theory.—Laissez-faire has never been preached as an absolute dogma by any English economist, though every English economist has recognised its value in connection with certain philosophic or juristic ideas and in relation to certain definite facts. MANDEVILLE was more a philosopher than an economist ; and, like Franklin, he probably advocated bounties quite as much as freedom from restraint, but his language is vague (*Fable of the Bees, or Private Vices and Public Benefits*, 1714 ; ed. 1772, ii. 142). The "private vices" which figure in his title consist mainly of "avarice," which he, in common with D. HUME (*Works*, ed. Grose and Green, iii. 610) and A. SMITH (*Moral Sentiments*, pt. iv. ch. i.) used to designate the desire for gain, or the economic sense (cp. Franklin's use of "to cheat," *Works*, ed. 1882, ii. 376). His "public benefits" involved such fallacies as these : "The real pleasures of all men are worldly and sensual " (ii. 118), and "Extravagance is good for trade " (*passim*). Still his writings first familiarised people with the idea that economic activity, by whatever bad names it might be called, was a far more legitimate ideal of statesmanship than the still blank perfection of the utopians. At the same time the philosophic doctrine of "the social contract" tended to reduce the functions of government to a minimum. A. Smith went to work in a very different spirit, as the chapters of the *Wealth of Nations* on the "Sovereign or Commonwealth" sufficiently show. Completing what Dudley NORTH, D. HUME, and others had begun, he exposed the unwisdom of definite instances of state intervention, such as the mercantile system, protection, apprenticeship, corporation, combination, and settlement laws. And his exposure was made at the psychological moment. He wrote that "the statesman who should attempt to direct people in what manner they ought to employ their capitals, would assume an authority which could be trusted not only to no single person,

but to no senate or council whatever " (*Wealth of Nations*, 4, 2), of a society innocent of the factory system. Factory inspectors would have been an anachronism in his day. Where he pleaded for "natural liberty " every living contemporary fact echoed his plea : thus his attack on "the colonial system" was published in the year of the declaration of independence (1776), and while inveighing against monopolists, he sheltered James Watt from the persecution of the "Hammermen." And he grounded his plea on an old-world belief in the pre-established harmony between selfish impulses and the aims of society, meeting the objection that "natural liberty " led to an unjust distribution of wealth by the reply that wealth was not happiness (*Moral Sentiments*). In the next generation (1817) RICARDO's language created, although it did not justify (Marshall's *Principles*, 553), the fallacy that unrestricted competition was the best and only principle regulating the distribution of wealth—a fallacy which Mill dissipated in 1848 by showing that it confused a hypothesis or at best a tendency with a natural law. Similarly Sir J. Bowring represented the current inferences drawn from BENTHAM's writings when he wrote in his Introduction (p. 77), that "the preservation of security is *all* that political economy looks to from the legislature, security for wealth created, security for the exercise of ingenuity and industry in creating more, security for enforcing the performance of contracts." Yet Bentham arrogated to government (1) coinage and the restriction on the issue of notes adopted in principle in 1844 ; (2) the duty *e.g.* of improving communication where profit was certain, but it was uncertain who would profit (*Manual of Political Economy*, ch. iii. § 2, note) ; (3) the duty of providing information by registries of births, tenures, etc. ; (4) of promoting education and health—thus CHADWICK, the father of English sanitary legislation, was Bentham's disciple. Indeed it cannot be said that Bentham's rule that government must "stand out of the sunshine " of industry (*ib.* ch. i.) was subject to the sole reservation that government must fix "the mechanism of exchange in order that the forces of society may act freely," unless mechanism and exchange are used in a wide sense. Meanwhile the most visible results of Bentham's and Ricardo's influence were the abolition of combination and usury laws, and of those poor-law regulations which had made it people's interest to add to poverty. A new generation passed. FREE TRADE sealed the triumph of the policy of "adding wings by striking off fetters " ; and men forgot that the champion of free trade who wrote, "Wherever the deductions of political economy lead I am prepared to follow " (Morley's *Cobden*, 2, 97), wished to forbid the supply of money when demanded by the biggest customer in the money market, for reasons which many people thought sentimental, but which he thought involved the first principles of morality (*ib.* 69 n.). Darwin's *Origin of Species* (1859) was suggested by the work of an economist, MALTHUS, and furnished a wider basis for blind belief in competition than that which economists claimed. A Benthamite might argue that the state should define "tenancy" as a right of property including the right to game, compensation for improvements, etc., just as it defines "mortgage" as a right of property including the right to redeem ; but students of Maine's *Ancient Law* (1861) stigmatised such definitions as a retrograde substitution of status for contract. H. Spencer blended references to the old poor-law with his curious identification of Maine's new principle with A. COMTE'S old principle of industrialism ousting militarism (*Contemporary*, xl. 512, 513, etc.). His conception of the duty of the state towards industry is practically that expressed by Sir J. Bowring (*v.s.*) ; and since 1853 (*Essays*, ed. 1891, vol. iii. pp. 229-471 ; *Man versus The State*, 1884 ; Introduction to T. Mackay's *Plea for Liberty*, 1891) he has unceasingly urged that "positively-regulative" acts are either (like the Licensing and Banking Acts) gratuitous and ineffectual blunders, or else (like the Adulteration of Food and Metropolitan Building Acts) blunders intended to counteract, but actually intensifying, the evils arising from its "negatively - regulative" shortcomings. Professor Huxley's phrase "administrative nihilism" describes his wishes if not his practical views. Further expression was given to these intellectual tendencies in R. LOWE'S speeches against land reform in Ireland (Hansard, 183, p. 1078 ; 190, pp. 1483, 1493, etc.) and in Bonamy PRICE'S application of "the principles of *abstract* political economy to the people and circumstances of Ireland exactly as if he had been proposing to legislate for the inhabitants of Saturn and Jupiter" (Gladstone's speech, April 7, 1881). The first note of revolt against this new tendency was sounded in 1862 by Cliffe LESLIE who was as much influenced by Maine as J. S. MILL was by Austin or RICARDO by BENTHAM ; but he had seized his master's concrete method instead of misappropriating his results (*Essays in Political Economy*, Nos. 1, 3, and 15). CAIRNES was at this very time proving the failure of competition to act freely in regard to retail trade or where there were "non - competing groups" ; and supported in the *Fortnightly* for January 1870 a proposal which anticipated that very Irish land law of 1881 which, according to a misquotation of Mr. Gladstone's speech, banished political economy to Saturn and Jupiter (*Essays in Pol. Econ.*, p. 203). In the same year his address on political economy

and *laissez-faire* relegated the latter to the rank of a fairly sound maxim (*ib.* 232). BAGEHOT laid down (1876) the principle that political economy established conclusions only applicable to exceptional and artificial conditions of society such as obtained in certain industries existing in England at that date (*Fortnightly*, xix. 218, 226, etc.). JEVONS wrote in 1876 that it was all very well for industry to ask the state to stand out of its sunshine, but what if it was already an industry which stood in the sunshine of other industries ? (*ib.* xx. 629), and suggested the extension of the Artisans' Dwellings Act 1881 (*ib.* 630). He had already declared that experience might, but "no abstract principle can, guide us in determining what kinds of industrial enterprise the state should undertake and what it should not," and urged in 1867 the state monopoly of telegraphs established in 1868 (*Manchester Statistical Society Trans.*, April 1867, p. 9). Walker's *Wages* (1876) emphasised the truth, mixed with fallacies in THORNTON'S book on *Labour*, 1869, that the conditions of fighting between employers and employees are unequal, the former fighting for profit, the latter for life, and that the labourer brings himself into the market, this same self being the object for which, as well as a means by which, wealth is produced. The modern view that self-interest acts with infinitely varying degrees of force in different cases is enlarged upon in Sidgwick's *Principles*, bk. iii. (1883), and TOYNBEE'S *Industrial Revolution*, (1884) ; the latter writer holds "that between men who are unequal in material wealth there can be no freedom of contract" (p. 216), and is also dominated by the idea expounded in Professor Green's *Free Contract* (*Writings*, iii. 365) that personal and patriotic considerations enter with peculiar force into labour and land questions, and that negative is only the handmaid of positive freedom. These writers all agree in their general direction, but differ in their application of their principles. For instance, Jevons wrote that "an eight hours *bill* is in no way an illegitimate object to keep in view" (Lecture on the *Trades Unionists' Political Association*, 1868) ; Fawcett only approved of this movement for shortening hours of work provided that it repudiated state intervention (Hans. 219, p. 1421). Again Cliffe Leslie attacks, Jevons and Bagehot defend, the use of the expression "Law" to describe the operation of competition. All, however, unite first in condemning legislation to determine wages, though all would not approve of Fawcett's simile "we might as well think of regulating the tides by act of parliament" (*ib.*). And, secondly, all condemn the regulations, which have the force of law, for restricting production and making unnecessary work, which have in so many cases been adopted by

TRADES UNIONS, and which seem copied from mediæval legislation or guild rules. Thirdly, all agree that where wages are compulsorily raised, *e.g.* by a strike, this means either that "the operation of economic conditions" is being, in Cairnes's phrase, "accelerated," or that the consumer is being taxed, a process which is protection, and therefore open to those arguments against protection which no English economist has renounced (Cairnes, *Leading Principles*, pt. 2, ch. 3, etc.). Strike leaders used to justify their action on the former ground, or, as they put it, on the ground that profits were too high ; the leaders of the coal strike of 1893 adopted the latter grounds. It cannot, therefore, be said that the adverse criticisms formerly passed by economists on the intervention by political bodies in industries are out of date ; these adverse criticisms or *laissez-faire* arguments first made economists a force in the state, and they are as valid now as when they were first used. On the other hand economists realise that negations are only a part of their message, and the easiest part to understand and to translate into practice. Indeed, it is probably the only part in which their science can be treated as an art, and they can have recourse to the imperative mood. "Trade never so well freed, and all tariffs settled or abolished, and supply and demand in full operation, we have merely cleared the ground for doing" (*Past and Present*, p. 159). Hitherto they have, like J. D. HUME, opposed ; or, like Mill and Fawcett, partly opposed and partly apologised ; or, like Cobden, have not voted, where constructive industrial legislation, *e.g.* the FACTORY ACTS, was concerned. The later economists have adopted a different tone, but have only displayed the unanimity which we expect from historians or philosophers, not that which we require from people entitled to apply their ideas to real life (see GOVERNMENT REGULATION OF INDUSTRY).

J. D. R.

Legislation.—Recent laws interfering with free industry may be classed under three heads :—

First, there are the laws gradually extending principles laid down in earlier legislation, such as—

(*a*) The laws relating to town life. These laws were first consolidated by the Towns' Improvement Clauses Act 1847, and The Public Health Act 1848 ; the latter is now superseded by The Public Health Act 1875. Amending acts and local acts are also numerous. Consolidated laws relating to London were first made in 1844, and lastly in 1891. All these laws are lineally descended from the act passed for rebuilding London after the great fire (19 Car. II. c. 3), which contained provisions for paving and drainage, for the height and materials of houses, for prohibiting "noisome trades," for compulsorily taking land in order to widen streets, and for enforcing all this by means of commissioners, surveyors, and summary judicial proceedings. One of the acts amending the parent act contained power to pull down dangerous dwelling-houses at the cost of the owner (33 Geo. II. c. 30, § 26). The modern versions of these provisions extend the definition of " dangerous dwelling-houses " so as to include the danger arising from over-crowding, living in cellars, etc., and extend the scope of the sanitary provisions to populous places or even the country (Public Health Act 1872), and powers are given to destroy food exposed for sale and unfit for food. (i) A singular offshoot of the law against dangerous dwellings is the series of Housing of Working Classes Acts consolidated and amended in 1890 (53 & 54 Vict. c. 70). Under this act, where unhealthy or obstructive areas or dwellings are pulled down, the local authority can buy the site and erect and manage labourers' dwellings.[1] The power to buy land and erect labourers' dwellings was borrowed from the Labouring Classes' Lodging Houses Act 1851 (§§ 35 *et seq.*), which had up till then remained almost a dead letter. The provisions in this behalf contained in a previous act (The Artisans' and Labourers' Dwellings Improvement Act 1875) took away with the left what they gave with the right hand. So that the act of 1890 is a substantially new public act. (ii) Still more singular is the development of the law against unhealthy food. It united itself with the act against the "adulteration of bread" (6 & 7 Will. IV. c. 37) which replaced the Assize of Bread Acts (51 Hen. III. to 55 Geo. III. c. 99), and the result of the union was the 6th section of The Sale of Food and Drugs Act 1875, which makes a person criminally responsible who sells "to the prejudice of the purchaser any article of food or any drug which is not of the nature, substance, and quality of the article demanded by such purchaser," § 6, except in a few cases. Public analysts assist in the detection of offenders. (iii) Municipalities can erect, buy, and manage baths and wash-houses since 1846[1] (9 & 10 Vict. c. 74). The local government board superintend the administration of all these acts.

(*b*) Shipping laws, including the wage-law of sailors, were first consolidated in 1854 (17 & 18 Vict. c. 104). The chief innovation of this law was that it gave the board of trade wide powers of supervision and control over the construction and safety of ships, over the grant of certificates to captains, and over the mode of paying wages, etc. The Passengers Act 1855 contained provisions as to the number and accommodation of passengers ; and the Merchant Shipping Amendment Act 1871, as to the draught of the ship when loaded ; these provisions, which have been gradually added

[1] Here a public body directly competes with private industries.

to, may be regarded as corollaries from the provisions as to "safety" in pt. iv. of the act of 1854. But § 168 of the last consolidating act (The Merchant Shipping Act 1894) borrows from 43 & 44 Vict. c. 16 a principle which finds no parallel in earlier acts, although it was foreshadowed by Lord Stowell's argument that no contractual freedom obtains between master and man (1 Haggard's Adm. Rep. 355). It enacts that the court can rescind unjust and substitute just terms in the contract between master and man ; that is to say, the court can settle the amount of wages.[1]

(c) The prohibition to pay wages in kind, which dates from the middle ages, was for the first time extended to agricultural labourers, for certain purposes, and other labourers by the Truck Amendment Act 1887 (see TRUCK SYSTEM).

(d) The General Post Office, which acquired its monopoly of carrying letters by 12 Car. II. c. 35, acquired a telegraph monopoly under 31 & 32 Vict. c. 110. Its issue of postal orders (under 3 & 4 Vict. c. 96, § 38), and its savings banks (24 & 25 Vict. c. 14), imply an assumption on its part of the rôle of poor man's banker, and represent a new departure.[2]

Secondly, there are the laws directly arising out of new inventions which have changed the face of society.

Thus (a) railways had to create their lines by means of compulsory purchases (see Lands Clauses Consolidation Act 1845), and they subjected themselves, in return, to certain disabilities (see Railway Clauses Consolidation Act 1845), the chief disability being that of having to run cheap trains, and of having their maximum rates fixed and, in case their concern was a success, revised from time to time by government (7 & 8 Vict. c. 85).[1] The authorities exercising jurisdiction over these matters are under the Railway and Canal Traffic Acts 1888 to 1894, partly the board of trade and partly the railway and canal commissioners. It is easy to see how a maximum rate might in many cases mean the same thing as the actual rate. Thus bye-laws under the Town Police Clauses Act 1847, and the provisions of the Metropolitan Stage and Hackney Carriages Act 1853, perhaps suggested by railway law, fixed the actual fare for cabs.[1] It is also to be noted that the provision for penny-a-mile fares in the act of 1844 (7 & 8 Vict. c. 85, § 6) has developed into The Cheap Trains Act 1883, under which the board of trade and railway commissioners have to be satisfied of the accommodation provided at this rate, and of the adequacy of provision for cheap workmen's trains. The limits within which they exercise their discretion are not defined.[1]

[1] Here the state regulates prices.
[2] Here the state directly competes with private industries.

(b) The rise and progress of the FACTORY ACTS (1802-1895) is traced elsewhere.

Thirdly, there are laws dictated by a new social policy with regard to old social conditions.

(a) The Elementary Education Act 1870 authorised the use of compulsion to make parents send their children to school. The compulsory clauses have been more and more enforced, especially under the Amending Act of 1880.

(b) Commissioners appointed by government have since The Land Law (Ireland) Act 1881 fixed the rents of Irish tenants, and since the Crofters' Holdings (Scotland) Act 1886 of Scotch "crofters."[1] The Irish act was extended to lessees by the Land Law (Ireland) Act 1887.

(c) The Allotment Acts 1832-1882 enabled local authorities to hold, hire, and enclose land for the purpose of letting it to industrious cottagers. These acts were chiefly if not exclusively applied for the purpose of restoring to the poor land taken from the poor under Inclosure Acts (see *e.g.* 8 & 9 Vict. c. 118, § 73). The Allotment Acts of 1887 & 1892 and sections 9 & 10 of the Local Government Act 1894, go further and enable local authorities to take land compulsorily for the purpose of allotments. Historically these laws grew out of pauper legislation (59 Geo. III. c. 12 ; 1 & 2 Will. IV. c. 42), logically they are the expression of new agrarian ideas to which there is no analogy since the Tudor and early Stuart policy of "laying land to houses" for the benefit of small tenants and labourers (see *e.g.* G. Roberts' *Social History*, 1856, p. 184).

(d) Compulsory terms are often read into certain contracts which pass property. Thus it is provided by 17th century judge-made law that a mortgagor cannot contract away his power of redeeming. The agricultural tenant *qua* agricultural tenant, can kill ground game under The Ground Game Act 1880, and has compensation for improvements under the Agricultural Holdings Act 1883. The tenant-right of Irish tenants includes under the land act of 1870 compensation for disturbance, and under that of 1881 fixity of tenure and free sale. Under the Merchant Shipping Acts 1854-94, the sailor's contract for wages involves a lien on the ship. The Employer's Liability Bill, which passed the House of Commons in 1893, gave workmen compensation for accidents on the false analogy of this principle, by compulsorily inserting an implied term in the contract between employer and employee. It has always been a moot point where the law of contract ends and the law of property begins. In all the above cases, except perhaps the last, the sphere of the latter was enlarged at the expense of that of the former. The judiciary or legislature held in these cases that certain contracts shall be construed as necessarily involving the transference of certain rights of property. How far this means may be used to favour new schemes of social policy is one of the historical problems of our time (see LABOUR IN RELATION TO THE LAW ; LABOUR STATUTES).   J. D. R.

LAISSEZ-FAIRE (from American point of view). In treating the subject of *laissez-faire*, the earlier writers on economics in the United States follow the general lines laid down by their English contemporaries. For the most part they accept *laissez-faire* as an economic maxim, though they are by no means in agreement concerning the limits of its application as a fixed rule of practical statesmanship. The great point of controversy lay in its pertinency to the system of protection practised by the federal government, and upon this the principal American economists are divided. The " orthodox school " have displayed their deference to the classical English economists by going in many instances to an even greater extreme of claiming for all economic laws the force of unbending laws of nature. Thus Amasa WALKER (*Science of Wealth*, p. 110) maintains that so far as the state urges the claims of its own safety, in justification of interference with industry, "the principles of economic science must be silent," but that this interference is rarely, if ever, necessary, and that it cannot be too often repeated that individuals only need to be " let alone." A. L. Perry (*Political Economy*, p. 96) speaks of the natural laws of production as " inexorable " in their operation, and as taking their revenge without pity whenever custom or legislation thwarts them. In his later *Introduction to Political Economy*, p. 153, he asserts that it would be nothing less than " presumptuous " for certain men to set up at will barriers to trade and then to undertake to defend these barriers as an economical blessing to the world. William G. Sumner, in the fifth of his *Lectures on the History of Protection in the United States*, repeats that we are living here " under immutable and inexorable laws of social organisation," which we can neither avoid nor evade, and which avenge themselves when we try to escape their operation. Simon Newcomb ranges himself with the " orthodox school," but is more moderate in his views. His *Principles of Political Economy* (p. 444 *et seq.*) distinguish between *laissez-faire* as a principle and as a policy. He enumerates certain non-economic limitations to its practical application ; he further distinguishes between what he terms the " let-alone " principle and the " keep-out " principle, the former claiming that the government should not stop the citizen, the latter that it should not act itself. A review of the criticisms urged against the " let-alone " principle leads Newcomb to the conclusion that it cannot be regarded as a neces-

sary and universal truth, but that the exceptions adduced are insufficient to prove the principle entirely invalid. In a later essay (*Science Economic Discussions*, p. 64) Newcomb tones down his contention for *laissez-faire*: " The school of non-interference claims that, as a general rule, these [economic] ends are best attained by giving the adult individual the widest liberty within the limits prescribed by considerations of health and morality."

The AMERICAN SCHOOL of early economists deny the universal applicability of *laissez-faire*, but they, too, are not at one with each other. Henry C. CAREY, the apostle of the protective system, regards *laissez-faire* as the goal in which that system is to end (cp. *Social Science*, iii. p. 442). His works would lead us to infer that the doctrine of *laissez-faire* is disastrous in its operation only when applied in a community in which industrial development is still to be accomplished (*ibid.* p. 516). Among his followers, Horace GREELEY (*Essays*, p. 129) simply refuses in so many words to accept the doctrine, which he proceeds to demolish with the adjectives "fallacious, pestilent, and utterly mistaken," while E. Peshine SMITH (*Manual of Political Economy*), and Robert E. Thompson (*Political Economy*), uphold the protective system as an exception to *laissez-faire*, as a condition of greater economic freedom yet to come. Francis BOWEN, likewise of the school of Carey, professes faith in the "let-alone" principle, whose limitations, he says (*American Political Economy*, p. 18), are nearly as obvious as the principle itself ; and which is in no way infringed by the maintenance of a protective tariff (*ibid.* p. 21).

President Francis A. Walker holds aloof from both these " schools," though inclining slightly to the one first discussed. With reference to *laissez-faire* he agrees substantially with Cairnes and Jevons, whom he quotes with approval in his *Political Economy*, but adheres to the policy so far as to insist (p. 416) that freedom is the rule and restraint the exception. While the necessity of making exceptions to the rule of freedom of individual action has been completely established, those who make these are bound to show cause for every such act of interference ; their case is to be made good against a powerful presumption in favour of liberty—the condition which has the promise not only of that which now is, but also of that which is to come (*ibid.* p. 464).

The real revolt against *laissez-faire* appears with the rise of the " new school "of American economists comprising the younger writers more or less influenced by German thought. This group, under the leadership of Richard T. Ely, was active in forming the American Economic Association in 1885 to protest against the all-sufficiency of *laissez-faire*. Ely had but shortly before asserted (*Past and Present*, p. 23) that *laissez-faire* "never held at any time in any country, and no maxim ever made a more complete fiasco when the attempt was seriously made to apply it in the state." The first paragraph of the declaration of principles which he proposed for the newly-formed association concluded with these words : "We hold that the doctrine of *laissez-faire* is unsafe in politics and unsound in morals, and that it suggests an inadequate explanation of the relation between the state and the citizens." The discussion upon this subject disclosed the fact that while there were grave objections on the part of many present to taking a decided stand on the question of state interference, the trend of opinion was substantially in harmony with the declaration formulated by Dr. Ely. As finally accepted, however, the first paragraph reads : "We regard the state as an agency whose positive assistance is one of the indispensable conditions of human progress," while an appended note announces that it was proposed and adopted as a general indication of the views and purposes of those who founded the association, but was not to be regarded as binding on individual members. The general views of the "new school" also find expression in an exhaustive arraignment of the *laissez-faire* doctrine by Henry C. Adams, a leading member, entitled *The Relation of the State to Industrial Action*, and republished by the American Economic Association. Adams follows closely the analytical methods of Cairnes. He restates the doctrine in the form of a syllogism, and denies its logical basis ; but he refuses to stop with Cairnes at destroying its claims as a working rule of economics, and supplies its place with a newly-formulated principle of state interference. He contends that it becomes the duty of the state to interfere in industrial relations, (1) to determine the plane of competitive action ; (2) to realise for society the benefits of monopoly ; and (3) to restore social harmony by extending the functions of the state. From this position, namely, of fixing a field where the rule of interference is to be recognised, toward which many of the younger economists seemed to incline a few years ago, a reaction has set in in very recent times—a reaction in which the attitude of President Walker is finding favour with the greater number of economic students in the United States. J. Lawrence Laughlin (*Journal of Political Economy*, I. No. 1) maintains that "the once-called 'new school'" is losing its authority in the American Economic Association, but this has been strenuously denied. The general drift of economic opinion, as indicated in the current writings of members of the association, however, appears to be against the exercise of state interference in every case where the preponderance of evidence is not clearly in favour of its expediency and beneficence.

The applications of the maxim of *laissez-faire*

may be conveniently discussed with reference to the violations of the rule of non-interference by the federal, state, and municipal governments. (1) The legislation of the federal government has never conformed to the doctrine of *laissez-faire*. The very first revenue law enacted in 1789 professes in its preamble to afford protection to American industries, and this purpose has never been absent from the tariff, whether proposed by one political party or the other ; while the author of the latest Wilson tariff law acknowledges that it is a protective measure. An outright bounty on sugar has been the culmination of the protective policy. The United States held stock in each of the two United States banks. It furnished funds for the first experiments with the electric telegraph, and encouraged the building of railroads by the grant of land subsidies and even by the loan of money. It suppresses note issues by state and private banks, and interferes to prevent the sale of food products under false names (as oleomargarine). (2) The state governments have been no less active in participating in industrial undertakings. They have built railroads, subscribed to the stock of railway corporations, and given them aid by donations of land and money. They have later stepped in to limit the abuses of private railroad management, in some instances ending in the statutory prescription of maximum rates of charges for the transportation of passengers and freight. They at one time quite generally entered into the banking business. Factory legislation of all kinds has found its way on to the statute-books of different states, while a few states have established limits upon the hours of daily labour. (3) American municipalities, when duly authorised thereto, have not hesitated to overstep the bounds prescribed by *laissez-faire*. Their activity lies largely in the field of so-called "monopolies of service." In 1890, nine cities owned and operated gas-works ; out of 2037 water-works plants, 877 were under public management ; about 150 cities and towns operated electric lighting plants ; one street railway was conducted by a municipal administrative board. At the same time many other cities shared in the profits of these quasi-public enterprises. The activity of American municipalities in this field appears to be on the increase.

[Amasa Walker, *Science of Wealth*, N. Y., 1866.—A. L. Perry, *Political Economy*, N. Y., 1883 ; *Introduction to Political Economy*, 1883.—William Graham Sumner, *Lectures on the History of Protection in the United States*, N. Y., 1884.—Simon Newcomb, *Principles of Political Economy*, N. Y., 1886.—H. C. Carey, *Social Science*, Phila., 1877.—Horace Greeley, *Essays designed to elucidate the Science of Political Economy*, Phila., 1869. — E. Peshine Smith, *Manual of Political Economy*, Phila., 1877.—Robert E. Thompson, *Political Economy*, Phila., 1882.—Francis Bowen, *American Political Economy*, N. Y., 1870.—Francis A. Walker, *Political Economy*, N. Y., 1883.—Richard T. Ely, *Past and Present of Political Economy*, Balto., 1884.—Henry C. Adams, *Relation of the State to Industrial Action*, Balto., 1886.— C. F. Dunbar, "Reaction in Political Economy," in *Quarterly Journal of Economics*, Boston, Oct. 1886.—J.

Lawrence Laughlin on "Political Economy in the United States," in *Journal of Political Economy*, Chicago, I., No. 1, 1893.—*Science Economic Discussion*, N. Y., 1886.—*Report of the Organisation of the American Economic Association*, Balto., 1886.]
V. R.

LA JONCHÈRE, DE. See DE LA JONCHÈRE.

LAKH or **LAC** is a Hindustani word meaning 10,000, commonly used in Indian finance in computing rupees.
C. A. H.

LALOR, JOHN (1814-1856), was a writer on social questions. He graduated at Trinity College, Dublin, in 1837. As an assistant poor-law commissioner he collected much valuable information, but in 1836 he left Ireland for London, where he became one of the editors of the *Morning Chronicle*. About 1844 he also became editor of a Unitarian weekly paper, *The Enquirer*, to which he contributed papers on social questions, such as the Factory Bill, Ireland, and Education.

Lalor's last work was *Money and Morals: a Book for the Times* (London, 1852). The problem here discussed is what will become of the ten millions of new gold which, "within a comparatively short period," says Lalor (p. 103), have come into England. The author thinks that instead of coming into the currency the influx will quicken trade, especially in Lancashire (p. 110), encourage rash speculation, and effect a rise not only in manufacturing, but also in agricultural incomes. In short, it will exist as capital (p. 124). In the second part of the work Lalor advocates "the adoption of a financial policy, which, though perfectly consistent with free trade in the food of the people, is not consistent with the exaggerated maxim of leaving the whole direction of industry to private interest" (p. 125). As a precaution against the *laissez-faire* principle, he suggests the expenditure of excess capital in agricultural or colonising loans, in the improvement of town dwellings, sanitation, and the water-supply. The position of England among the nations, and the national defences, are next discussed, while in part iii. the author passes on to consider the remedy for the social evils with which England is threatened. After discussing the respective prescriptions of Auguste COMTE and T. CARLYLE, Lalor insists that practical Christianity can be the only effectual cure for the diseased body politic. A portion of the book was in 1864 reprinted as *England among the Nations*.
A. L.

LA LUZERNE, CÉSAR-GUILLAUME DE (1738-1821), termed by Lecky "an eminently wise and high-minded statesman," entered the church and became Bishop of Langres at the age of thirty-two. In 1789 he endeavoured to stem the democratic torrent by proposing the establishment of a second chamber, and, when this proposal was rejected, the addition of 600 members to the representatives of the nobles and clergy. Unable to influence events, he retired to his diocese, and afterwards emigrated to Switzerland, whence, however, he returned on the accession to power of Napoleon. After

the restoration he was made a peer of France, and in 1817 a cardinal.

Among numerous other works he wrote *Dissertations sur le prêt du commerce*, Dijon, 1823, 8vo, 3 vols. ; a voluminous treatise on the lawfulness, from the stand-point of the Roman Catholic Church, of taking interest for money (see INTEREST AND USURY).

[*Dictionnaire des Parlementaires Français*, Paris, 1891, vol. iv.—*Nouvelle Biographie Générale*, Paris, 1860, vol. xxix.—*Introduction to the Study of Political Economy*, by L. Cossa, Eng. trans., London, 1893, 8vo, p. 162.]
H. E. E.

LA MARE, DE. See DE LA MARE.

LAMBE, SAMUEL (fl. 1657), merchant, published *Seasonable Observations humbly offered to his Highness the Lord Protector*, London, 1657, fol., in which he suggested the establishment of a bank at London. His scheme was, that governors should be chosen from the trading companies, that the bank should "let out imaginary money on credit at 2½ or 3 per cent at most," and receive deposits withdrawable on demand, that all "bills of exchange" should be received and paid into the bank, and that the profits should go "to the good men who manage the bank." The bank was also to supply another subordinate one "with stock to let out any sum under £5 or £10 at reasonable rates upon pawns or other security." Lambe's proposals were referred to a committee of the East India Company for their consideration on 30th Dec. 1657. His work also contains useful information on the Navigation Act, the competition between England and Holland, and other subjects.
W. A. S. H.

LAMBIN DE SAINT FÉLIX. See LOTTIN, A. P.

LAMMAS-LANDS, LAMMAS-MEADOWS, were open-field arable and pasture lands, held in severalty and enclosed during the growing of the corn and hay crops respectively, but open during the rest of the year to all who had rights of common upon them. They were thus commonable, not common, lands. Under the old open-field system of agriculture such common rights might be upon the whole a convenience to the inhabitants, but the introduction of roots made rights of winter pasture intolerably wasteful ; as late, however, as 1844, lands subject to these rights were still abundant in England, though there were few or none in Wales.

Lawyers generally distinguish "lammas" from "shack" lands by the fact that the former were commonable to other inhabitants besides those having severalty rights on the land. But Nasse (*Feldgemeinschaft*, p. 3) denies this distinction, which he thinks a mere local detail. The classes of commoners varied locally : they were "sometimes the inhabitants of the parish ; sometimes a class of inhabitants, as the freemen of the neighbouring town, or even the householders; and perhaps more generally the owners or occupiers of ancient tenements within the parish, usually termed tofts" (G. W. Cooke, *Acts for facilitating the Inclosure of Commons in England and Wales*, 1850). The usual time for the resumption of common rights was Lammas-day, 12th August[1] (the old 1st August) for arable lands, and 6th July (the old Midsummer) for meadows. Commonable meadows were probably called lammas-meadows by analogy, as it is rare to find them opened as late as Lammas-day. In some cases the common rights lasted till November, in some till the middle of February. The fixed dates for opening, especially Lammas-day, gave rise to difficulties which were met in various ways. About Nottingham, when the customary day arrived, according to a witness before the select committee in 1844, "the population issue out, destroy the fences, tear down the gates, and commit a great many other lawless acts, which they certainly have a right to do." These Nottingham lands were used for recreation, not for pasture. In other places things were managed better. On the lands of St. John, Hackney, on 26th July 1692, the "proprietors of the commonable lands" were "allowed ten days to carry off their crops on account of the wett"; and there is a similar entry in 1763 (Garnier, *English Landed Interest*, 1892, p. 202). Scriven (*Law of Copyholds*, 6th edition, p. 310) cites a case where the beginning and end of the season were regulated by bye-laws made by the tenants of the manor; and an act of 13 Geo. III. c. 81, § 7, enacted that three-fourths in number and value of the occupiers of open- and common-field lands might agree in a meeting to postpone the opening for a reasonable time. Later enclosures have left few traces of these commonable lands.

[See evidence of Messrs. Blamire, W. Keen, T. Hawkesley, T. S. Woolley, R. F. Graham, and H. Chawter before Select Committee on Inclosures, 1844.—J. Williams, *Rights of Common.*—Elton, *Treatise on Commons and Waste Lands.*—Woolrych, *Rights of Common.*—Vinogradoff, *Villainage in England.*—Maine, *Village Communities*, Lecture iii.—Marshall, *Rural Economy*, of various counties. —For similar French custom, see Seebohm, "French Peasant Proprietorship," *Econ. Jour.*, 1891.]

E. G. P.

LAMOND, ELIZABETH (1860-1891), was the eldest daughter of William Lamond, advocate at the Scotch bar. She had hoped to devote herself to teaching, and she was engaged in this work at St. Andrews before entering Girton College, Cambridge, where she obtained honours in history (1885-1887). After a few months of

[1] The new style was introduced throughout the British dominions in 1752, by omitting eleven nominal days after 2nd Sept., and dating the next day 14th Sept. instead of the third.

teaching at Winchester her health gave way and she was forced to occupy herself with literary work. In 1890 she edited for the Royal Historical Society four unpublished treatises in Norman French, *Walter of Henley, Seneschaucie*, the anonymous *Husbandry*, and Grosseteste's *Rules*. The translation and glossary gave proof of her scholarly feeling and accurate knowledge. In the course of researches connected with this work, she discovered that the well-known dialogue, published by W. S. in 1581, had been composed some years earlier, and in a convincing article in the *English Historical Review* in April 1891, gave good grounds for believing that it had been really written in 1549, that John HALES was the author, and that Coventry was the place of writing. She was not able to complete the edition of the *Discourse on the Common Weal of this Realm of England*, on which she was engaged at the time of her death; but a posthumous publication contains the result of her researches. *Walter of Henley*, Longmans. —*Discourse of Common Weal*, Camb. Univ. Press. See also a review of the latter work in *Economic Journal*, December 1893.   W. C.

LAMPREDI, GIOVANNI MARIA (18th century), professor of public law in the university of Pisa, and author of *Del Commercio dei popoli neutrali in tempo di guerra*, Milan, 1831, 12mo.

This work, which according to M'Culloch (*Lit. of Pol. Econ.*, p. 127) is well reasoned and of considerable authority, was twice translated into French, first by Jos. Accarias de Serionne (La Haye, 1793, 2 vols. 8vo), and again by Peuchet (Paris, 1802). The latter, in his preface, remarks that Lampredi has on the whole treated his subject impartially, but with a strong bias in favour of neutral goods passing free.

Other publications of Lampredi are:—*Del governo civile degli antichi Toscani e delle cause della lor decadenza, discorso*, Lucca, 1760, 4to.—J. M. L. . . . *de licentia in hostem liber singularis, in quo S. Cocceii sententia de infinita licentia in hostem . . . confutatur*, Florence, 1761, 8vo.—*Saggio sopra la filosofia degli antichi Etruschi, dissertazione istorico-critica*, Firenze, 1756, 4to.   A. L.

LAND. Primitive custom recognises certain rights in and over land: the "right of the first clearer" to regard the land which he cultivates as his own family holding (Baden Powell, *Systems of Land Tenure in British India*, i. 221); the right of a chief or freeman to a share in the territory which he helps to defend against outsiders; the right of a chief to levy tribute from those who hold land under his protection. There is at this stage no ownership in the modern sense of the term; the powers of the individual are controlled by family rights and local custom. Common ownership, it should be noted, is not a mark of social equality, but rather of inequality ; it grows out of the combination of members of a ruling family to maintain their landlord-right, or of members of a subject community who can only live and pay their tribute by adopting co-operative methods of husbandry. When the state comes into existence the family loses some of its importance ; the individual chief or house-father is not merely the administrator of a common inheritance ; he is *dominus* or owner of his land ; it is a thing *in patrimonio*, to be disposed of by will or settlement, a thing *in commercio*, which he can sell or mortgage. *Dominium*, absolute ownership, is the basis of the Roman law of ownership and possession. The system had great economic advantages, but the small cultivating owner could not hold his own under the stress of competition ; the tendency was towards the formation of LATI-FUNDIA (*q.v.*), large estates cultivated by slaves. The Teutonic chiefs who founded their kingdoms on the ruins of the empire admired the precision of Roman law ; but they retained the primitive belief in the tribal or national organisation of society. The king as leader of the nation was lord paramount over all lands, and claimed service and allegiance from their owners ; he was not in direct relation with the peasantry, except on his own estates, but he protected them, so far as he had power, against the oppression of their immediate lords. England is a typical example of feudal monarchy ; the state, represented by parliament and the king's judges, broke down the rights of the great lords, and gave freedom of disposition to all owners of land. In 1285 the lords obtained an act to maintain the strict rule of entail ; but the courts did not favour "perpetuities," *i.e.* arrangements for tying up property for indefinitely long periods ; the statute was evaded, and the owner in fee tail was enabled to exercise all the rights of an owner in fee simple. Military tenures were finally abolished in 1661. The services of SOCAGE tenants (ordinary freeholders) were commuted for fixed sums of money ; with the change in the value of money these annual payments became of no importance and were bought up or forgotten. Copyhold tenure, where it survives, still operates to curtail the freedom of disposition enjoyed by the owner of land ; but the Copyhold Acts, passed between 1841 and 1887, provide a variety of forms whereby copyhold lands may be enfranchised or turned into freehold (see the Copyhold Act 1894). The Real Property Commission of 1830 marks a turning-point in the history of our land laws ; the suggestions of the commissioners were embodied in a long series of reforming statutes. Forms of settlement and conveyance have been simplified, and extensive powers of disposition have been given to limited owners, *i.e.* to persons having a life

estate or other limited interest in land. Under the Settled Land Act of 1882 a tenant for life may sell a family estate ; the purchase money is treated as capital to be invested, and remains subject to the trusts of the settlement. In many points the law of real property has been assimilated to the rules which govern the devolution and disposition of personal property. Legislation has not destroyed the sentiment which leads an owner of land to add to his estates and to transmit the inheritance undivided to his eldest son ; the practice of re-settling family estates in each generation still prevails among the great landlords. There has been of late years a marked reaction against the liberal doctrine of absolute ownership and free contract. The Agricultural Holdings Act of 1883 is based on the assumption that a tenant-farmer is not in a position to contract freely with his landlord, and must therefore be protected by the state. The Irish Land Acts of 1870 and 1881 had gone farther in the same direction ; they introduced a kind of dual ownership in land, and attempts have since been made to restore the rule of individual ownership by assisting the tenant to purchase his landlord's interest. In Scotland, the crofters of the highlands and islands have obtained legislation of a similar character. In England, there has not been as yet any urgent demand for judicial rents or schemes of land purchase ; farmers are fairly content with the Agricultural Holdings Act, and labourers with the acts which facilitate the acquisition of allotments and small holdings. Socialist ideas in regard to land have begun to influence the popular mind. Sir Henry Maine pointed to the rapid settlement of North America as an example of what can be done under a system of individual ownership ; Mr. Henry George uses the United States as an example of the evils caused by permitting large tracts of land to be held and disposed of by private owners. Mr. George would "nationalise" the land by taxing it up to its annual value ; and in England various plans have been proposed for intercepting what is called the "unearned increment" in the value of land (see BETTERMENT). If the legislature succeeds in creating a large body of small owners, there will probably be a reaction in favour of absolute ownership ; for this reason the more logical among Mr. George's disciples oppose the measures which have for their object the multiplication of peasant proprietors.

Laws requiring the registration of all titles to land are advocated on the ground that they help to simplify transfers. They have worked well in new countries, but great difficulties are encountered in applying such laws to an old country where titles are already complicated. In England the acts permitting or requiring registration have not been successful.

[Fustel de Coulanges, *Origin of Property in Land* (Eng. trans. by M. Ashley).—Baden Powell, *Systems of Land Tenure in British India*.—Cobden Club, *Systems of Land Tenure in different Countries*.—Shaw Lefevre, *Agrarian Tenures*.]

T. R.

In connection with Land the following articles occur in the Dictionary :— Agricultural Community ; Agricultural Holdings Acts ; Agricultural Systems ; Agriculture in England ; Allotments ; Arable Land, Conversion of, into Pasture ; Commons ; Corvée ; Cottiers ; Culture, Large and Small ; Depopulation ; Depression, Agricultural ; Domesday Book ; Emigration ; Enclosures ; Enfranchisement of Land ; Entail ; Farming ; Feudalism ; Forests, Mediæval ; Forests, Economic Aspects of ; Gangs, Agricultural ; Holdings, Large and Small ; Impôt Unique ; Land ; Land Companies ; Land, Domaine Congéable ; Landgafol ; Land, Law Relating to ; Land Legislation, Irish ; Land, Nationalisation of ; Lands, Public, of the United States ; Land Registration ; Land System in the American Colonies ; Land Tax ; Land Tenures ; Land Banks, Schemes of, in England ; Landes-Creditkassen ; Majorat ; Manor ; Métayage ; Métayer, in West Indies ; Minorat ; Open Fields ; Peasant Proprietors ; Primogeniture ; Rent ; Rent Charge ; Rent of Land ; Serf ; Services, Predial and Military ; Settled Land.

LAND COMPANIES may, as a result of practical experience, be divided into two classes : one consisting of those which are concerned with the exploitation of large blocks of land, chiefly abroad ; the other of those which deal rather with the financing of owners and occupiers of land and the realisation of their produce.

(1) Companies which take up blocks of land may be again subdivided into two classes, consisting respectively of—

(*a*) Those whose primary object is colonisation. A notable example of these, both from its own history and its close connection with Edward Gibbon WAKEFIELD, was the old New Zealand Company of 1825, which became in 1838 the New Zealand Colonisation Company, and in 1839 the New Zealand Land Company. To a large extent this company, by taking up lands and allotting them to settlers, was the parent of colonisation in New Zealand. It was a type of a regular system of which there were other examples about the same period of English history. In later times (1884), the Methuen settlement in South Africa, which turned out a failure, was a company of this kind, and the more recent Bechuanaland Concessions Company, now merged in the London and Pretoria Financial Agency, had a similar object in taking up and re-selling large areas of farm land.

(*b*) Those companies whose primary object is the use of the land for mining, timbercutting, etc., and more rarely for actual cultivation. This is the more popular class at the present time ; and of late years many large

concessions of land all over the world have been given for these purposes both by civilised and savage states. The Bechuanaland Land and Exploration Company, the Mexican Concessions Company, the Pahang Concessions Company, are instances which have been recently before the public. Such companies are too often of a speculative character, and too apt to rely upon making profits by parting with portions of their territory to other companies.

The British South Africa Company is a notable instance of a company combining both functions [cp. COLONIES, GOVERNMENT OF, BY COMPANIES].

(2) "Land mortgage and financial agencies" is the general term adopted in the share lists for companies of our second class, but their titles vary ; for instance we have the Anglo-African Land, Mortgage, and Investment Company, the Auckland Agricultural Company, the British Land and Mortgage Company of America, and others all devoted to the same class of business. There are at least fifty companies with a paid-up capital of over £20,000,000 enumerated in the stock exchange lists primarily connected with the land. One "deals with real estate," another is designed "to lend on first mortgages in the States and Canada," another is to work certain estates with a view to resale ; others deal in products as well as land. But all have the general scope above indicated (see also MORTGAGE BANKS).

C. A. H.

LAND, DOMAINE CONGÉABLE (literally ejectable domain, also called *tenure covenancière* or holding by covenant). This form of tenancy, peculiar to Celtic Brittany, which has not yet disappeared, seems to have been introduced during the last centuries of the middle ages ; a law of the 6th of August 1791 suppressed the feudal incidents which had gradually been annexed to it, but allowed the principle on which it is based to continue. The position of landlord and tenant is as follows : with respect to third parties, the tenant enjoys all the rights of a freeholder ; with respect to his landlord, he is only bound to pay a fixed rent, which in former times was generally very low. In modern times the practice of nine years' leases has prevailed, the leases being renewable on the payment of a fixed sum of money called *commission* or *nouveauté*. The landlord has only the ownership of the ground (*fonds*), the tenant owns the buildings and enclosures which he has erected, the trees he has planted, even the one-year-old furze which grows on waste land : hence the distinction between the *foncier* and the *superficiaire* or *domanier*. The former may always serve on the latter a notice to leave (*congément*), but in that case he is obliged to pay him a full compensation according to a detailed valuation for the buildings, plantations, crops, enclosures, improvements, etc. Owing to the heavy expenses entailed by a *congément*, this system led to the stability of the tenantry and the most efficient cultivation consistent with the nature of the land and the agricultural knowledge of the period ; it is, in fact, a thorough application of tenant right.

The general predilection for the ordinary farm system, and in other cases the passion of the French peasantry for the investment of their savings in land, have exerted an unfavourable influence on the maintenance of this kind of tenancies ; still at the end of the second empire it was computed that about one-third of the territory of Brittany was held under these terms.

[Duseigneur, *Histoire du Domaine Congéable* in his *Études sur l'Histoire du Finistère* (pp. 355-414), Brest, 1878.—Baudrillart, *Les Populations Agricoles de la France, Normandie et Bretagne* (pp. 387-395), Paris, 1885.—Paul Henry, *Une vieille Coutume Bretonne : Le Domaine Congéable*, Angers, 1894.] E. Ca.

LANDGAFOL, a customary rent paid to the lord of the manor by his tenants, distinct from other customary payments due to him on special occasions. The distinction grew clearer with the process of commuting services and payments in kind for money (see GAFOL).

[Vinogradoff, *Villainage in England*.—Round, *Domesday Studies*, vol. i. p. 133.—*Domesday of St. Paul's*, Archdeacon Hale's note, p. lxix.] E. G. P.

LAND, LAW RELATING TO. The law of property is chiefly concerned (1) to define the nature of the rights which are recognised in objects of property, and (2) to define the modes in which such rights may be acquired, transferred, or extinguished. With respect both to the rights of which it is the object and to the acquisition, transfer, or extinction of such rights, land differs from every other object of property. Land is immovable, imperishable, and wide in extent. It is a prime necessary of life, and furnishes the raw material of all wealth. It admits of being used in innumerable ways. It has been a basis of political power and social consideration. It is susceptible of what Bentham terms "a value of affection," as distinct from market value in a higher degree than any other object of common use. At the same time it is limited in quantity, and although it can be rendered more productive by the expenditure of capital and labour, the returns from this expenditure fall off after a certain point has been reached, and at a remoter point become inappreciable. As compared with other forms of wealth, land is, in the long run and in most countries, the most generally and the most ardently coveted. Under these circumstances it is natural that the law relating to land should be complex, and should differ much in different times and places.

The right of property in land admits of subdivision in various ways. The state is everywhere supposed to have certain rights over the land which are indispensable for the safety and welfare of the public. These rights are sometimes termed its EMINENT DOMAIN. A familiar instance is afforded by the claim of the state when it thinks expedient to purchase or to enable others to purchase land which the owner is not disposed to sell. The Roman lawyers held that though there might be full ownership in the soil of Italy, there could be only a possessory right in the soil of the provinces which was, strictly speaking, vested in the Roman people or in their representative the emperor. The chief practical indication of this difference was the land-tax, which was paid by the provinces, but not by Italy. In eastern countries the proprietary right of the sovereign is so large and vaguely defined that it is difficult to say how far the subject can ever be deemed a proprietor. But the subdivision of proprietary rights over land with which we are most familiar has resulted from the feudal conceptions of tenure and of particular estates in land (see FEUDALISM ; MANOR).

According to the rigorous feudal theory, the sovereign alone has property in the land, and no subject can be more than a tenant. But every tenant may give himself sub-tenants, and they may repeat the process indefinitely. Thus the land would come to support an ascending hierarchy of tenants closing in the king as lord paramount. Each would have rights that could not be lawfully infringed, and duties that could not be lawfully discarded. Each would be protected by law, and still more by custom, against the rest. The king, who had the loftiest theoretic claim, would probably derive the least practical advantage from the land. It would be difficult, were the doctrine of tenure carried to its logical conclusion, to say who, if any, of the persons interested in the land could be termed its proprietor. But the process of subdividing interests in the land is carried still further by the help of the doctrine of estates in land. For each person in the ascending scale which we have described might have his interest in the land either for life, or to himself and the heirs of his body, or to himself and his heirs generally. He might have an estate for life, or an estate tail, or an estate in fee simple. If his estate were only for life he would be unable to devise it by will, or to give anybody rights in the land lasting beyond his own decease. Nay, more, his power of using and enjoying the land would be restricted in the interest of those who were to come after him. If his estate were an estate in tail or in fee simple his powers of alienation and enjoyment would be more extensive. Under feudal law, in brief, not only may proprietary rights be divided between lord and vassal, but they may also be divided between tenant in possession and tenant in remainder (see art. ENTAIL). A man who has the largest estate possible in land, in English law a tenant in fee simple, can thus carve out of his own interest a number of lesser estates to take effect after his death, so as to control its devolution for many years. The natural wish of landowners to exert this power to the utmost has given rise to *family settlements*, and the endeavour of the judges to restrict the practice of settlement in the public interest has given rise to the rules against *perpetuities*. The decay of the manorial system produced a distinct form of imperfect ownership of land, known in England as copyhold tenure, which was once widely extended in western Europe, but was abolished on the Continent by the French Revolution, and is gradually disappearing in England by the operation of the acts for the enfranchisement of copyholds.

The tenures of which we have hitherto spoken are distinctly feudal in origin, and have either been abolished, as in France, or have been rendered almost unmeaning as in England. In England, successive statutes, framed without any regard to symmetry, have removed almost all the inconveniences attaching to the feudal law of real property, and have left hardly anything of feudalism save names and forms. The relation of landlord and tenant has nothing feudal about it. Indeed, the strictly feudal law regarded a lease as unworthy of its attention, as may be seen by the fact that leaseholds are regarded not as *real* but as *personal* property. The practice of letting land for a money rent has been recognised by all civilised legal systems. It does not involve a division of ownership, but it may assume forms which are tantamount to such division. Thus, by the Roman contract of EMPHYTEUSIS the tenant acquired the land in perpetuity, subject to the obligation of paying rent. The Irish tenant, whose rent can be altered only at intervals of fifteen years, and then only by the decision of a court, has an interest in the land which often exceeds in market value the interest of the landlord. Such a tenant can hardly help regarding himself as at least part proprietor. Political, economical, and social forces are constantly operating on the legal relations of the classes living on the land, and may turn a nominal tenant into a virtual owner, as they have turned nominal owners into virtual serfs. Even when it is easy to ascertain the proprietor of a piece of land, his right of property may be limited by rights over that land vested in other persons. Such rights are described in Roman legal language as *jura in re aliena*. They are of two kinds. Some are valuable in themselves, whilst others are valuable only as security for a debt due from the owner of the land. Rights of the first class, known in Roman law as *servitudes*, and in English law as *easements*, and

profits-à-prendre, are exemplified in the right of way across another's land, in the right not to have ancient lights darkened by the erection of new buildings, and in rights of common which include the right of grazing cattle, the right of digging gravel, the right of cutting turf and firewood, and so forth. Rights of this class may be enjoyed by a man as proprietor of certain land, and are then said in English law to be *appendant* or *appurtenant*, or they may be enjoyed by him irrespective of any such property, and are then said to be *in gross*. A similar distinction was expressed in Roman law by calling some servitudes *prædial* (Lat. *prædium*, an estate) and others *personal*. It is worthy of note that the Roman lawyers regarded a right of usufruct in land, the nearest equivalent of the English estate for life, not as a form of property, but as a personal servitude. The second class of rights enjoyed with reference to the land of another includes such as form a security for debt. As land, whilst highly valuable, can neither be removed nor concealed, it has always been the favourite security for money lent, and the law of *mortgage* forms an important chapter in the law of land. In the primitive mortgage the debtor conveys the land to the creditor subject to a condition that it shall be reconveyed to himself when he repays what he has borrowed. Should he fail to pay punctually he will lose his land, although its value may far exceed the amount of the debt. The injustice of such a transaction led to the invention of improved forms of mortgage. The *hypotheca* of later Roman law was a contrivance by which the mortgaged land was left in the ownership and possession of the debtor whilst the creditor obtained the right of realising his debt out of it in case of default in payment. The modern English mortgage, the result of the correction of the common law by courts of equity, resembles the *hypotheca* in its practical working, although it retains the form of a conveyance.

The modes of acquiring, transferring, and extinguishing rights of property are in the main similar for land and for other objects of value. Land which has no owner—there is none such in England—may be acquired by the first occupant or by the owner of other land to which it accedes, as where a field is enlarged by alluvial deposit. The course of years (see LAPSE OF TIME; PRESCRIPTION) may extinguish an old and create a new proprietary right. Sale, gift, exchange, and succession, testamentary or intestate, transfer rights of property in land as in other things. But a peculiar form is often required for transactions affecting interests on land. Land cannot be passed from hand to hand like a movable. It is peculiarly necessary, therefore, to provide evidence of transfer. In primitive times, when writing was either unknown or little used, this object was attained by requiring for every transfer of land certain solemn- forms which might impress the memory, not merely of the parties, but also of the community or at least of the neighbours. Such was the primitive Roman *mancipation*, a formal sale in the presence of five witnesses and of a man who held the balance used to weigh the uncoined money of the early Italian society. Such, too, was the old English ceremony of *livery of seisin*, the symbolical delivery of land by the seller to the purchaser. But where the art of writing has been generally diffused, written documents are found more convenient to execute and more effectual in preserving an exact record of what has been done. In England at the present day a deed is the recognised form for conveyances, leases, mortgages, and so forth. But where manifold interests have been created in reference to one piece of land, such documents are apt to be lengthy, and where dealings in land are frequent they accumulate to an inconvenient extent. Hence the advantage of a further reform, the registration of title (see LAND REGISTRATION). An efficient system of registration ensures a complete, concise, and authentic record of all transactions affecting land, and thus promotes the abbreviation of legal documents and the reduction of legal charges. England is one of the few civilised countries which does not possess an effective registry of title to land.

Passing from the outline of the law relating to land to the suggestions which have been made for its improvement, we have to remember that every plan of reform is to be judged in relation at once to the existing circumstances and to the object which it is designed to accomplish. The object of an agrarian reformer may be either to improve the condition of tenants on the land of another, or to multiply proprietors, or to put an end to private property in land and vest it either in the sovereign or in municipal authorities. The first of these objects is sought by measures securing to the tenant compensation for the improvements which he has made (see AGRICULTURAL HOLDINGS ACTS), or fixity of tenure at a fair rent and freedom to sell the interest on the land which such fixity creates (see F's, THE THREE ; and LAND LEGISLATION, IRISH). The second object, that of multiplying proprietors, may be obtained by various expedients, such as (1) the establishment of a system of free alienation and registration of title so as to encourage sales and to make the sale of small parcels of land expeditious and cheap, or (2) making advances of public money to tenants, especially to such tenants as already enjoy fixity of tenure, in order that they may buy out their landlords and become full proprietors, or (3) enabling lessees of house property to compel the lessors to sell the reversion, and thus enlarging leaseholds into

freeholds, what is commonly known as lease-hold enfranchisement, or (4) enforcing the partition of landed estate among the children of a deceased owner, on the principle adopted by the *Code Napoléon*. It may be said that there is a real affinity between reforms of the first and of the second class. Measures tending to secure to tenants the advantages known as the Three F's find their natural complement in measures tending to turn tenants into full proprietors. For what is virtually a divided ownership can hardly be permanent in a society not governed by immemorial custom. The charms of property are most strongly felt by him who is absolute proprietor. Reforms of the third class, reforms which aim at the abolition of private property in land, are advocated on totally different grounds, and imply a totally different economic theory. To this class belong proposals for the "nationalisation" of land, *i.e.* the transfer to the state of all private rights of landed property, and proposals for the "municipalisation" of land in towns, *i.e.* the transfer to the municipal authority of all private rights to land within its jurisdiction. Those who advocate changes of this nature differ on the question of giving or refusing compensation to evicted owners. But they agree on the more fundamental point of allowing no private person to be more than a tenant. Far more restricted in scope, and resting in some measure on narrower arguments, is the proposal to give municipal authorities the advantage of what is known as betterment (see BETTERMENT), in other words, to give them the power of charging the expense of municipal improvements upon the owners of land which is increased in value by such improvements.

[Holland, *Jurisprudence.*—Poste, *Institutes of Gaius.*—Moyle, *Institutes of Justinian.*—Pollock and Maitland, *History of English Law.*—Digby, *History of the Law of Real Property.*—Blackstone, *Commentaries*, vol. ii.—Edwards, *Law of Real Property.*—Williams, *Principles of the Law of Real Property.*—Goodeve, *Modern Law of Real Property.*—Pollock, *The Land Laws* (English Citizen Series) ; (comp. SASINE ; SEISIN).]

F. C. M.

LAND LEGISLATION, IRISH. The history of modern legislation with regard to land in Ireland is full of economic interest. The agrarian troubles of Ireland have arisen from many causes, the most important of which are, perhaps, the following : (1) The forcible dispossession of the original proprietors by foreign conquerors. The first English conquest of Ireland, effected under the Plantagenets, did not lead to chronic agrarian strife, because the Anglo-Norman barons adapted themselves to Irish ways and became Irish chiefs. But the three subsequent English conquests by Elizabeth, by Cromwell, and by William III., led to the confiscation of much the greater part of the land of Ireland, and established a new class of landowners closely connected with England and severed by religion from the peasantry. In parts of the north of Ireland not only the native chiefs but the native cultivators had been ousted to make room for English or Scotch settlers, and here the new landlords and tenants lived on tolerably good terms. But elsewhere the owners and the cultivators were too generally enemies, or at least aliens, to one another.

(2) The defects of the new agrarian system introduced by conquest. The English conquerors naturally introduced into Ireland the agrarian system to which they were accustomed at home. But they omitted one thing essential to its proper working. Since agriculture became a progressive art in England all great agricultural improvements have been made by the landlord. They would not have been made by the tenant who has no legal fixity of tenure. In Ireland the making of agricultural improvements was commonly left to the tenant. He was generally too poor to execute them properly, and he had no security for compensation when he had made them. For he had no legal fixity of tenure, and with the growth of population was exposed to a severe competition for holdings. In Ulster and in some districts elsewhere custom protected the tenant against arbitrary eviction or the appropriation of his improvements by the landlord. Under this custom, known as the ULSTER TENANT-RIGHT, the tenant could sell his interest in the holding to his successor. Where this custom prevailed, agriculture as a rule flourished. Elsewhere it was very backward.

(3) The normal balance of occupations was never attained in Ireland. Agriculture, especially in the south and west, was almost the only resource of the population. Ireland is not well adapted for manufacturing industry, and such industries as the English and Scotch settlers had brought with them were too often crushed or hampered by the misdirected legislation of the English parliament in the 18th century. Commerce and manufactures, which would have drawn off the surplus population, and furnished new capital for the improvement of the land, were thus reduced to the narrowest limits.

(4) The evils arising from these causes were intensified by the introduction of the potato, which in the 18th century became the staple food of the Irish peasant. This cheap and abundant food enabled a poor and prolific people to multiply at a rate hitherto unknown in old countries. In 1741 Ireland may perhaps have contained two million inhabitants. In 1841 it contained upwards of eight millions. The majority of these eight millions were sunk in extreme poverty. The land was subdivided to an extent incompatible with its proper cul-

tivation or the well-being of the cultivator. Competition raised the rent of land in many cases beyond the amount that could be extracted from the soil. It necessarily followed that hundreds of thousands of tenants were hopelessly in arrear with their rent and exposed at every moment to eviction. Under these circumstances the proprietors themselves could not be prosperous. They had too generally adopted the careless, sociable, and extravagant habits of the native gentry whom they had displaced. They were in many instances hopelessly sunk in debt or burdened with family encumbrances, and quite unable to face the expenditure necessary to put their affairs into decent order. Such was the agrarian condition of Ireland when the potato blight of 1846 and 1847 brought about, first, a terrible famine; secondly, a great mortality from epidemics; and lastly, an immense emigration to the New World. In a short time Ireland lost one-third of her population. About the same time the repeal of the corn laws deprived the Irish farmer of his advantage in the best market of Europe. The potato blight and the repeal of the corn laws led to a wide extension of pasturage and to evictions of tenants. These in turn added fuel to the agrarian discontent which has always been smouldering in Ireland. Then it was generally felt that something must be done. But the public opinion of England and the sentiment of the Irish peasants were not in accord. The ruling passion of the Irish as of the French peasant is to become proprietor of his holding. This passion, however, could not be gratified without the breaking up of great estates, which involved sacrifices on the part of Irish landowners, and was distasteful to the English landed interest. Failing full property in his holding, the Irish tenant desired fixity of tenure, which most landowners were unwilling to concede. The economic ideas then predominant in England were opposed to any interference with the free play of competition, and the determination of rent by the higgling of the market. Thus the progress of Irish agrarian reform was slow. It falls into three stages.

I. An attempt to get rid of embarrassed landowners, and to replace them with new men of energy and capital.

II. A gradual concession to the Irish demand for what are known as the Three F's—(see F's, THE THREE), fair rent, fixity of tenure, and freedom of sale.

III. An attempt still in progress to turn the tenant into a proprietor by advances of public money for the purpose of enabling him to buy his farm.

I. The Encumbered Estates Acts.—

The first of these is the act 11 & 12 Vict. c. 48, 1848, to facilitate the sale of encumbered estates in Ireland. It was followed by the act 12 & 13 Vict. c. 77, 1849. This provided that the owner of an encumbered estate or an encumbrancer might apply to the commission established by the act for an order to have the land sold notwithstanding any restrictions of settlement. The commission was empowered to authorise a sale, if the charges on the estate amounted to one-half of the income thereof, and to pay off encumbrances out of the proceeds, handing over the balance to the owner or to other persons interested in the land. This act has been amended by subsequent statutes. The jurisdiction of the commission was transferred by the act 21 & 22 Vict. c. 72, 1858, to the landed estates court, which still exists as a branch of the supreme court of judicature in Dublin, and still performs its original function. The immediate success of the act was striking. Vast quantities of land were transferred from insolvent to solvent proprietors. But it did little towards assuaging agrarian discontent. The new landlords had no hold upon popular sentiment. They were much stricter men of business than their predecessors. They were on the whole more unpopular than the old landlords. Improvements in most cases were still made by the tenant, and the tenant was still without security. Thus the agrarian difficulty remained formidable.

II. The concession of fair rent, fixity of tenure, and freedom of sale.

The first change in this direction was made by the act 33 & 34 Vict. c. 46, the Landlord and Tenant (Ireland) Act 1870, of Mr. Gladstone's first administration. This act (1) gave the force of law to the Ulster custom and to similar customs existing in other parts of Ireland ; (2) granted in cases of eviction not coming within such customs a compensation for disturbance, graduated so as to be most liberal in the case of the smallest farms, but limited in any case to a sum not exceeding £250 ; and (3) granted compensation for improvements made by the tenant, the presumption being that all improvements were made by the tenant or by his predecessor in title. Some of its other provisions, intended to assist tenants in the purchase of their holdings, will be noticed hereafter.

A much more extensive change was made by 44 & 45 Vict. c. 49, the Land Law (Ireland) Act 1881, of Mr. Gladstone's second administration. This act extended to all agricultural tenancies not under lease the benefit of the Three F's—fair rent, fixity of tenure, and free sale. The fair rent may be determined either by recourse to the land courts established under the act, or by agreement between landlord and tenant. An agreement filed in the court acquires the same force as a decision of the court. The rent thus ascertained cannot be altered during a statutory period of fifteen years, and so long as it is paid the tenant cannot be evicted. Nothing is said in the act as to the principles on which the fair rent is to be determined, except that no rent is to be charged for improvements made by the tenant or his predecessors in title. Under certain conditions specified in the act the tenant may sell his interest in the holding. A tenant of the rateable value of £150 or upwards was allowed to contract himself out of the act. The court referred to in the act was to be either the civil bill court of the county or the Irish land commission. The land commission was to consist of three persons, one of whom must have practised at the bar for ten years, and obtained the rank of a judge of the supreme court. The commission has full power to determine all questions of law or fact and to make rules of procedure. But the business of determining rents is almost entirely performed by the assistant commissioners.

The act of 1881 was amended by the act 50 & 51 Vict. c. 33, the Land Law (Ireland) Act 1887, which extends its provisions to leaseholders, and allows a temporary reduction in judicial rents fixed before 1st January 1886, to meet the fall in prices between 1881 and 1887. The importance of this act will be understood when we remember that out of 600,000 cultivating tenants in Ireland about 150,000 are leaseholders. The acts of 1881 and 1887 together have made an agrarian revolution in Ireland. Without professing to affect the landlord's proprietary right, they have rendered him practically little more than an annuitant. Under the provisions of these acts rents have been reduced upon an average from 20 to 25 per cent. The interest of the tenant now frequently sells for more than the interest of the landlord. Moreover, the ascertaining of rent, whether by judicial decision or by agreement outside the court, is a process which takes time. It will hardly be completed for the whole of Ireland before the period of fifteen years has elapsed, when it will have to begin afresh. Thus the idea of a further alleviation of his burthens is constantly kept before the tenant. When to these circumstances we add the general tendency of modern feeling about landed property, we shall see that the landlord has no security for the retention of the proprietary interest left to him, and that the acts above-named form only one stage in the Irish agrarian revolution.

III. The conversion of the tenant into a proprietor by advances of public money for the purpose of enabling him to buy his farm.

For many years past a few discerning men had seen that the Irish tenants, once set in motion, would never rest until they had become proprietors. J. S. MILL exaggerated, perhaps, the advantages of peasant proprietorship, but he was the first English economist to refute the doctrine that the peasant proprietor was necessarily poverty-stricken and thriftless. His advocacy of peasant proprietorship was continued by other writers, and found willing listeners in the political party most hostile to the landed interest. John BRIGHT was perhaps the first public man of mark to advocate the conversion of Irish tenant farmers into proprietors. When the Irish Church was disestablished by the act 32 & 33 Vict. c. 42, 1869, he procured the insertion of clauses which gave the tenants of church lands an opportunity of purchase. One-fourth of the purchase-money was to be paid down, and the remaining three-fourths with interest at 4 per cent might be paid in sixty-four half-yearly instalments. Several thousand tenants took advantage of these clauses. The Landlord and Tenant Act of 1870, and the Land Act of 1881, contained provisions intended to promote purchase by tenants. The greater part or the whole of the purchase-money was to be advanced by the state and repaid in thirty-five annual instalments of 5 per cent. But very few purchases were effected under these provisions. By the act 48 & 49 Vict. c. 73, the Purchase of Land (Ireland) Act 1885, commonly known as Lord Ashbourne's Act, much more liberal assistance was granted to tenants desirous of purchasing. The whole purchase-money was to be advanced by the state and to be repaid in forty-nine annual instalments of 4 per cent. A sum of £5,000,000 was made available for the purposes of the act, and three years later £5,000,000 more was advanced for the same purpose. The success of these acts is shown by the fact that the whole sum of £10,000,000 has already been issued to tenants purchasing their farms. The annual instalments have hitherto been paid with great regularity. The last important act relating to this subject is the Purchase of Land (Ireland) Act 1891, 54 & 55 Vict. c. 48. Under this act the landlord may be paid in government stock. The total amount of government stock which may be created for this purpose is limited by the provision that the annual charge for interest and sinking fund is not to exceed the amount annually granted from the treasury to local authorities in Ireland. Very elaborate precautions have been taken to ensure the treasury against loss, and these precautions have to some extent deterred Irish farmers from availing themselves of the act. Special provisions have been inserted for the benefit of tenants with small holdings and of congested districts. Although it is too soon for any decisive judgment on the merits of the last land purchase act, it is certain that these acts alone offer any honest and peaceable solution of the agrarian problem in Ireland. The complicated mechanism of the Land Act of 1881 can hardly be permanent, and the ascertainment of rent by courts acting without definite principles and liable to external pressure, must always be an unsatisfactory process. The judicial rent may serve as a basis for the calculation of the selling value, but has no stability in itself. The landlord must be in constant alarm for what is left to him, and the tenant in constant unrest until he has acquired all.

The remedial acts above referred to are long and intricate, and cannot be fully understood without a long preliminary study. The ultimate causes of Irish agrarian disturbance are well explained in Lecky's *History of Ireland in the Eighteenth Century*. Its progress can be followed in a vast mass of parliamentary papers, the most important being the Report of the Devon Commission appointed by Sir Robert Peel in his second administration. The Report was presented in 1845. [The literature of the subject is bulky, but in great part obsolete, owing to recent legal and economical changes. The following are a few of the more useful publications :—J. S. Mill, *Chapters and Speeches on the Irish Land Question* (reprinted from *Principles of Political Economy*, and Hansard's *Debates*).—W. O'Connor Morris, *Land System of Ireland* (Oxford Essays, 1856).—*Letters on the Land Question in Ireland* (reprinted from the *Times* in 1870).—*Land System of Ireland* (reprinted from *Law Quarterly Review*, 1888).—J. Boyd Kinnear, *Ireland*.—M. Longfield, *Tenure of Land in Ireland* (Cobden Club Essays, Systems of Land Tenure in various countries).—W. E. Montgomery, *History of Land Tenure in Ireland*.—Right Hon. G. Shaw-Lefevre, *Agrarian Tenures*.—*The Irish Peasant, a Sociological Study*, anonymous, published by Swan, Sonnenschein, and Co.—Cliffe Leslie, *Land Systems*.]   F. C. M.

LAND, NATIONALISATION OF.   This term is used to denote the extinction of all private proprietary rights in land and the vesting of all landed property in the state. The extinction of private property in land is one of the objects contemplated by systematic socialists who desire to give the state exclusive control over all the means of production, and to restrict private property to property in wages. But the "nationalisation" of land has also been advocated by persons who are not systematic socialists, and who are not averse to the continuance of private ownership of capital. Such persons justify their proposals on the ground that private property in land is peculiarly indefensible. Land, they argue, is not the product of human industry or ingenuity, but the free gift of nature. At the same time the value of land is increased, without any effort on the part of landowners, by the growth of population, by the accumulation of capital, by every advance in civilisation. Land, they argue, yields an unearned increment (see INCREMENT, THE UNEARNED), and this increment is intercepted by landowners who are thus enriched by the labour and parsimony of others, and levy a tax on human improvement. The wage-earner, it is alleged, rarely earns more than a scanty subsistence, and the interest on capital declines as the mass of capital increases. The whole surplus accumulations of progressive communities, it is inferred, go to enrich an unproductive class. The state, they conclude, should evict all landowners, with or without compensation, and become for the future the sole landlord. In this way the unearned increment would be secured for the common good. The field of industry would be indefinitely enlarged, the production of wealth enormously increased, and its distribution so much improved that poverty would disappear and well-being become universal.

Put in this form the argument in favour of the "nationalisation" of land is an argument for the transference of the unearned increment to the state. The theoretical basis of "nationalisation" is to be found in the writings of RICARDO and of J. S. MILL. RENT Ricardo defines as "that portion of the produce of the earth which is paid to the landlord for the use of the original and indestructible powers of the soil." If this were so, rent would afford a revenue to the landlord without the landlord rendering any service in the production of wealth. Ricardo was aware, indeed, that rent in this sense is something different from rent in the popular sense, which includes remuneration to the landlord for capital expended by him upon the land. Ricardo knew that he was defining not rent commonly so-called, but that which has since been described as *economic* rent. But the popular writers and orators, such as Mr. Henry George, who have caught at his definition, have either forgotten or ignored his qualifying statements. Again, the increase of rent in Ricardo's sense of that term is due to the circumstance that the land cannot be increased in quantity, and so forms the subject of a monopoly. With the growth of population and of riches the demand for land becomes more intense, and the landowner is enabled to charge a higher price for "the use of the original and indestructible powers of the soil." The rise of rent, Ricardo says, is a symptom, but it is "never a cause of wealth." Mill, following upon Ricardo, described the rise of rent resulting from the general progress of society as the "unearned increment." He argued that as it was due to the exertions of the whole community, it should for the future go not to the proprietors of land, but to the state. Here again the advocates of "nationalisation" carry an economic theory to its extreme consequences, and propose to transfer to the state not merely all future but also all past increments of this description.

In reality we cannot be too careful how we apply abstract definitions to concrete affairs. It is undoubtedly possible to discover forms of landed property, such as mines or sites adapted for building, which may sometimes yield a large and increasing revenue without any effort or expense on the part of the proprietor. But with agricultural land the case is far different. There it is difficult to prove the existence, and impossible to measure the amount, of the unearned increment. In this country, at all events, land has been rendered fit for cultivation at a great expense to the proprietors. The rent which they now receive often represents an inadequate return upon capital which they or their predecessors have sunk even in the buildings necessary for the proper cultivation of the soil, to say nothing of improvements effected in the soil itself. In other cases it may represent an adequate return, but no more. But in these cases we cannot determine, except for a very recent period, how much has been spent in improving the land, and therefore cannot discriminate accurately between the unearned increment and the return on capital. Thus even where an unearned increment exists, any attempt to appropriate it to the state would be illusory.

Mill proposed to leave landowners in the enjoyment of whatever unearned increment should have accrued down to a given date, and to take by way of taxation only such unearned increment as should arise subsequently. But this proposal, far more equitable as it is, would not meet the wishes of those who advocate nationalisation of the land. In an old community like the United Kingdom it would leave the bulk of rent in the receipt of private individuals. Any serious decline of prosperity would deprive the state of all advantage from such taxation. If, for example, the legislature had followed Mill's suggestion, and had fixed on 1st January 1850 as the date of appropriation, it would now receive nothing from the agricultural land of the United Kingdom.

The "nationalisation" of land, therefore, would not be confined to the unearned increment. It would extend to the whole value of the land. The land might be "nationalised" either by a formal abrogation of all private rights of property or by levying on all landowners a tax equal to the rack-rent of their estates. In either case a question arises as to what compensation, if any, should be given to the evicted owners. If "nationalisation" is to deprive landowners of all return for the capital which they or their predecessors in title have expended on the improvement of their land, it would be a confiscation of the most violent and unequal kind. We may go further, and say that open and peaceable enjoyment for an indefinite time under the sanction of law and received morality constitutes a very strong claim to compensation for the loss of the unearned increment itself. "Nationalisation" of land, effected without compensation, or with merely nominal and delusive compensation, is open to the objections based on law, morals, and public policy which can be brought against the abolition of all private property whatsoever, and to the additional objection of making one class a victim to all other classes. If effected with substantial compensation, the "nationalisation" of land becomes far less lucrative to the state, and may sometimes end in actual loss.

But let us suppose "nationalisation" of land to have been carried out on such terms of equitable compensation to evicted owners as left the state a considerable margin of revenue. Even this margin would be further curtailed by the force of circumstances. (1) In so far as the former owners were impoverished by the change, their contributions to the imperial and municipal revenues and to public charities would be diminished. (2) A great quantity of land is held by corporations ecclesiastical, municipal, educational, and charitable, rendering a variety of public services which must be provided for in other ways when the corporate estates have been confiscated. (3) A costly public department with an immense staff would have to be instituted for the dispatch of agrarian business. (4) All the permanent improvements which in England have been executed by landowners must henceforwards be executed either by the state or by its tenants. If the state is to execute these improvements, we know from recorded experience of public works that they will always be costly, and very often prove unremunerative. All the capital required must be borrowed by the state, and a heavy charge for interest and sinking fund will be placed on the newly-acquired revenue from the land. If improvements are to be executed by the tenants, they must be tempted to improve by the concession of fixity of tenure at a fair rent.

The necessity of such fixity of tenure has been fully proved by the experience of Asiatic countries. There the first condition of prosperity has been the restriction of the claims made upon the cultivator by his landlord the state. A bad oriental government lays waste the country by taking from the cultivator everything it can. A good oriental government makes well-being possible by granting the cultivator a moderate assessment fixed for a term of years. With every prolongation of the term, and with every alleviation of the assessment, agriculture improves and the community becomes richer. The comparative well-being of the people of British India is due chiefly to the circumstance that the government has reduced its demand on the farmer to what is virtually not a rent, but a moderate land-tax.

The same necessity for fixity of tenure where the state owns the land will be more apparent when we consider to what a degree the amelioration of the soil of Europe in the past has been a labour of love inspired by the sense of ownership. Capital has been lavished on the land, not always to the advantage of the owner, but almost always to the advantage of the commonwealth. The land has been the French peasant's bank and the English squire's hobby. Nor is it only money that the fond proprietor puts into the soil; he puts his mind into it also. He knows better than any other man its wants and its capabilities. He takes care that the work done upon it is done thoroughly. This vigilant affection is possible only to the man who has either full property, or an interest resembling full property in the soil.

If therefore the state is to be landlord, its tenants must have fixity of tenure on favourable terms. Once the tenants have gained this point they are part proprietors for all practical purposes, although not so described in books of law. Their interest in the land, as the experience of Ireland shows, may often sell for more than the interest of their landlord. Nor is this all. As the history of copyhold tenure and the history of Ireland in recent years have proved, the man who has become a part-proprietor never rests until he has become an exclusive proprietor. If part-proprietors are numerous they are almost certain to succeed in achieving this object.

It seems likely, therefore, that the additional revenue which would result from the "nationalisation" of land would neither be large nor permanent. It certainly would not enable the state to discard other sources of revenue. It might for a few years produce a revenue of some magnitude. But every party which could not otherwise obtain a majority would promise in turn to lessen the burthens of the rural voter. Sometimes it would be compelled to fulfil its promises, and then its opponents would be reduced to make promises still more liberal. At last the ownership of land by the state would become a mockery, and the ultimate result of "nationalisation" would have been the transfer of the land from one set of proprietors to another. In this case nothing would have been gained, at least nothing which could not have been gained far more cheaply. The state already possesses a power of taxation limited only by considerations of prudence or of justice, considerations which under any conceivable scheme must limit its exactions from the soil. Yet in England there are, at the present time, hundreds of thousands of acres which, after supplying a humble and precarious livelihood to the farmer and labourer, and discharging the rates and taxes, yield but a nominal rental to the landlord. A comparatively small increase of local and imperial taxation would virtually oust the owners of such land, and leave the cultivators hardly wherewithal to keep themselves. What more could be effected by "nationalisation" in any form?

The plan of "nationalisation," as distinct from complete socialism, has hardly attracted attention outside the United States, the United Kingdom, and some of our colonies. It has found favour only where the exceptional economic progress of the last hundred years has added surprisingly to the value of certain kinds of land, and this additional value has been shared among a comparatively small number of owners. In a stationary country there is no such growth in value, and in a country where proprietors are numerous such growth as there is excites little jealousy.

[Ricardo, *Principles of Political Economy and Taxation.*—Mill, *Principles of Political Economy.*—Henry George, *Progress and Poverty.*—Moffat, *Mr. Henry George, the Orthodox* (a criticism of the last-mentioned work).—Marshall, *Principles of Economics.* — Seligman, *Shifting and Incidence of Taxation.* — Nicholson, *Principles of Political Economy;* the literature of socialism generally, as the fundamental principles of land nationalisation are the common property of socialist writers. See arts. on P. E. DOVE and W. SPENCE.] F. C. M.

Some further reference to Henry George's *Progress and Poverty* in relation to his proposal for the nationalisation of land is advisable here. To make this point clear, it is necessary to go back to Mr. George's theory on wages. He argues that "wages depend upon the margin of production, or upon the produce which labour can obtain as the highest point of natural productiveness open to it without the payment of rent." From this standpoint Mr. George examines in his fifth book "the primary cause of recurring paroxysms of industrial depression," and the causes of "the persistence of poverty amid advancing wealth," and arrives at the conclusion that these spring from the existence of private property in land. As Mr. George considers this not only unjust, but the cause of the evils existing in modern society, he would give no compensation to the owners, but he would give security for improvements. He would "appropriate rent by taxation." This taxation might be crushing. Mr. George states, in one place "the monopolist in agricultural land would be taxed as much as though his land were covered with houses and barns, with crops, and with stock." In another, the taxes would "fall as heavily upon unimproved as upon improved land." By adopting this plan Mr. George anticipates a removal of many of the inequalities of wealth, but he thinks that wages would rise, that the general rate of interest would rise also, that universal prosperity would follow. It is curious, though somewhat sad, to observe the various directions in which different thinkers believe they have found a universal remedy against pauperism. The endeavour reminds the reader of the search for the philosopher's stone in the middle ages. The investigation is ever fruitless, but ever attractive to the speculative mind.

This reference is to the first statement of Mr. George's opinions. In a later edition he considers that "private property in land always has, and always must, as development proceeds, lead to the enslavement of the labouring class." The principle Mr. George advances would be equally valid against the existence of any property at all, and, however the inequality of wealth may menace civilisation, the destruction of all wealth would be fatal to human progress.

LAND, PUBLIC, OF THE UNITED STATES. The total amount of public lands owned by the government of the United States has varied greatly at different times, owing to extensive acquisitions on the one hand and sales and gifts on the other. In the course of its existence the government has possessed in its own name 2,708,388 square miles; and the largest amount owned at any one time was in 1848, amounting to 1,890,013 square miles. The public domain has its origin (1) in cessions made by the different states originally forming the union, many of which gave up large tracts of western lands; (2) by purchases or treaty cessions, as Louisiana in 1803, Florida, 1819, purchase from Texas in 1850, the Gadsden purchase in 1853, Alaska in 1867, and the Oregon cessions; (3) by the Mexican war. As settlers' rights had already been acquired within the territories annexed, it by no means followed that all the land thus brought under the American flag was part of the public domain. From the outset it has been the policy of the government to be liberal in its grants of land. Lands have been disposed of in four different ways: (1) by grants to individuals; (2) grants to states; (3) grants for internal improvements either to states or corporations; (4) sales. No attempt has been made to secure any substantial revenue from the public lands, and, when sold, but a nominal price as a rule has been charged. The total receipts from public lands from 1798 until 1893 were 283,000,000 dollars. A much larger sum, however, has been expended in the extinction of Indian titles, purchase-money for annexations, and for surveys. The economic advantages to the nation cannot be measured by the receipts entering into the budget accounts, as nearly three-fourths of the lands have been given away to soldiers as bounties, to assist corporations in the construction of railways through sparsely-settled regions, and indirectly to promote immigration through gifts to actual settlers under the Homestead Act of 1862. Generous grants have also been made to individual states for the establishment of productive funds for common-school and university education. Only very rarely has the revenue from public lands constituted an important element in the treasury receipts. The largest amounts received from this source were in 1835 and 1836, $14·7 and $24·8 millions, or about 40 and 50 per cent respectively of the total net receipts in those years. The sales at that period were exceptional, due in part to the construction of canals and railways, and the extension of banking credits. Under the Homestead Act of 1862 a citizen, or an alien who has filed a declaration of intention to become a citizen, may enter upon not more than 160 acres of unappropriated public land

and may acquire title in five years. In 1892 there were 567,000,000 acres of public lands left, of which one-half was unsurveyed. A large part is known to be arid, and can be utilised only after large public expenditures.

It is difficult to estimate the economic effects of the public land policy of the United States. It is impossible to do more than note its relation to the rapid growth of the population, especially west of the Mississippi ; its influence upon rents in the east and older districts ; and the mitigation of the evils arising from a too rapid congestion of population in large cities, by furnishing an immediate and attractive outlet for industrial activities.

[See Richmond Mayo-Smith in *Emigration and Immigration* (New York, 1890), p. 56 : " When trade became unprofitable a man could take to agriculture. Our public land has been our great safety-valve, relieving the pressure of economic distress and failure."—*Annual Reports of the Commissioner of the Public Land Office.*—Thomas Donaldson, *Public Domain,* Pub. Doc. Washington, 1884.—A. B. Hart, "Disposition of the Public Lands," *Quarterly Journal of Economics,* 1 (1887), 169.—W. C. Ford, in Lalor's *Encyclopedia of Pol. Sci.,* 3, 460-478.]   D. R. D.

LAND PURCHASE ACT. See LAND LEGISLATION, IRISH.

LAND REGISTRATION. Land is by far the most important article of commerce. Owing to its physical peculiarities it is the subject of more varied rights and interests than any other commodity. Owing to those peculiarities, also, it does not admit of being held in the same close and constant physical possession as do most movable objects. It is thus at once peculiarly important and peculiarly difficult for those who enter into transactions with respect to land, who buy or who advance money upon land, to be certain that the person with whom they are dealing has a title to that land. Where no special legislation has been devised for their assistance, intending purchasers or mortgagees must conduct for themselves and at their own risk an inquiry into the title of the intending seller or mortgagor. This inquiry may be troublesome and expensive, and does not always yield a certain result. Moreover it must be repeated as often as any fresh transaction with reference to the land is begun. Such is still the case in England. A history of the title to the land extending formerly to sixty and now to forty years, has to be made out before any prudent person will buy the land or advance money upon the land. But a special legislation may render dealings with land less cumbrous and more secure. The titles to all the land within the limits of the state may be ascertained and recorded once for all by a public agency. All subsequent transactions affecting the land may be similarly ascertained and recorded. It will then be possible, by referring to these records, to determine what persons are at any moment interested in any piece of land either as owners or as incumbrancers. No further inquiry as to title will be necessary. The past history of the title will be of no practical consequence. Such is the case in the great majority of civilised states at the present day.

In France a system of registration of deeds has existed since the reign of Napoleon I. In every arrondissement, a subdivision comparable to our poor-law union, there is a registry office. Sales and mortgages of land must be registered there, or they will not be valid as against subsequent dealings with the land. The register is public. A lease need not be registered, but in case of litigation the tribunals will not take cognisance of it without registration. The registration fee on a purchase amounts to 5 per cent. For a mortgage it varies from £1 : 5s. to £1 : 15s. For a lease it varies from 1 to $\frac{1}{4}$ per cent on the net amount accruing from the lease. In Prussia the system of registration is at least as cheap and expeditious. In all cases of alienation, proprietary rights are acquired by an act of conveyance followed by registration. The conveyance consists simply of two verbal declarations at the local registry office. The registered proprietor declares his assent to the registration of the purchase, and the purchaser declares that he demands such registration. Mortgages are created in a similar manner, and a certificate of charge upon the land is negotiable. The expenses of sale and of mortgage are adjusted on very low sliding scales. Thus where land is sold for £150 the fees amount only to 12s. The time required is in ordinary cases under an hour. A somewhat similar system was established in South Australia by the late Sir Robert Torrens, and proved so successful that it has been adopted by all the Australian colonies and by New Zealand. The speed and economy both of first registration and of registering all subsequent dealings with the land are most remarkable. The registry does not give an indefeasible, but only a guaranteed title. Experience shows that the guarantee hardly ever has to be made good.

The advantages of registration have not escaped the notice of English legislators. The registration of deeds relating to land as distinct from registration of title has long been known in England. As early as the 27th year of Henry VIII. the Statute of Enrolments required all bargains and sales of freehold land to be made by deed and enrolled within six months at Westminster or in the county where the land was situated. But this act was eluded by a technical contrivance which cannot be fully explained here. Under the Commonwealth bills for the registration of dealings with land were brought into parliament, but none of them became law. In 1669 a committee of the House of Lords reported that the uncertainty of title was one cause of the depreciation of land, and recommended as a remedy a system of registration. In the reign of Anne separate registries of deeds were established for the county of Middlesex and for the East and West Ridings of York. In the reign of George II. a similar registry was instituted for the North Riding. A registry of deeds has long been established in Scotland and in Ireland, and is highly valued in those countries. A bill for a general system of registration was introduced in 1758, but was not passed. The subject then dropped for a long time.

In 1830 and again in 1857 royal commissions reported in favour of the registration of title, and their opinion was made more impressive by the practical success of systems of registration in other countries. The first act for the registration of titles in England, known as the act to facilitate the proof of title to and the conveyance of real estate (25 & 26 Vict. c. 53), was passed in 1862 by the efforts of Lord Westbury, then chancellor. Under this act an office of land registry was established in London. Registration of title was to be voluntary. No title was to be registered unless it were such as a court of equity would consider to be a good marketable title. Once registered the title became indefeasible. The registrar was to deliver a land certificate to the person registered as having title to the land, and the deposit or endorsement of the certificate was to be effectual as a sale or mortgage of the land. This act may be said to have been a failure from the beginning. Only a few hundred titles have been registered under it. The making out of a title for registration was found to involve a far heavier expenditure of time and money than was needed to make out a title sufficient for an ordinary conveyance. In one instance the office took two years and five months to make the preliminary inquiries, and only once did it accomplish this task in less than five months. The average amount of the registration fees appears to have been about £50, and this is said to have been only one-third of the total expense incurred by owners registering. Even when the title had been duly registered, subsequent dealings with the land were not made cheaper or more expeditious. A royal commission, which reported in 1870, came to the conclusion that the act had failed because the conditions which it imposed were too rigorous. It required the person registering to show a marketable title. It required boundaries to be defined and partial interests in the land to be recorded. Accordingly in 1875 Lord Cairns, then lord chancellor, procured the passing of the Land Transfer Act (38 & 39 Vict. c. 87). Under this act any person might be registered as the proprietor of land if he could satisfy the registrar that he was *primâ facie* entitled to it

in fee, and that there was possession in the same right. In this case the registration did not prejudice the enforcement of any adverse estate, right, or interest, but the lapse of time would perfect the registered title. If application were made for an absolute title, and on examination it appeared that the title could be made out only for a limited period or subject to certain exceptions, the registrar might except from the effect of registration any estate, right, or interest arising before a specified date, and register the title not as absolute, but as "qualified." In this case also lapse of time would perfect the title. It was hoped by these expedients to lessen the expense of registration, and thus encourage the public to register. But this act failed as completely as its predecessor. In 1879 a select committee of the House of Commons appointed to consider what steps could be taken to simplify title and to facilitate the transfer of land, reported as follows :—

"Various causes have been assigned for the reluctance of landowners and mortgagees to avail themselves of the act. Its unpopularity has been ascribed (1) to the absence of any power to remove from the register a title which has once been placed upon it ; (2) to the disinclination of solicitors to recommend to their clients a course of dealing with their property which may tend eventually if not immediately to curtail their own profits ; (3) to the general distrust of all projects of land registration, inspired by the break-down of Lord Westbury's act ; and (4) to the indisposition, both of the public and the legal profession, to familiarise themselves with a new system, and to run the risk of an experiment which involves so great a departure from established usage."

The committee, whilst admitting that there might be some force in these contentions, did not think them sufficient to account for the failure of the act of 1875. They considered that the difficulty of tracing the title to freeholds, and the complexity of the interests which can be created in English land, were the gravest obstacles to its success. Mr. Brickdale, in his pamphlet on the *Registration of Title to Land*, takes a different view. He argues that the registration of title will succeed only where it is easier to prove a title to the satisfaction of the registrar than to the satisfaction of an ordinary purchaser. But this cannot be the case where registration gives an indefeasible title, for there exhaustive evidence must be required if the risk of doing injustice to the true owner is to be avoided. He argues from the experience of the Australian colonies that registration should give not an indefeasible, but a guaranteed title, in other words, a right to compensation where the person registering himself as owner *bona fide* turns out not to be the owner. Experience has shown that the cases in which compensation has to be given are very few, and that ample funds for the purpose can be raised by imposing a small fee upon all persons who register. Mr. Morris, in his essay on the *Registration of Title*, proposes to dispense with proof of title altogether. He would have registration commence in every case with the next dealing with the fee simple after the passing of a Registration Act. The vendor and purchaser, or their respective solicitors, would appear before the registrar and make statutory declarations, the vendor that he believed himself to be entitled to sell, the purchaser that he had in fact purchased. The purchaser would then be registered as having merely a possessory title which time would ripen into full ownership. Both Mr. Brickdale and Mr. Morris hold that direct compulsion to register is unnecessary and undesirable, although Mr. Morris would give all registered transactions legal priority over unregistered.

In 1888 a further attempt to improve the existing system of registration was made by the Land Charges and Registration Act (51 & 52 Vict. c. 51). A bill for compulsory registration was introduced in 1895 with the support of the late and the present chancellor, but was subsequently dropped. Under its provisions a merely possessory title might be placed on the register.

It seems clear that no system of registration will ever be voluntarily accepted by landowners unless it results in an immediate as well as in an ultimate saving of time, trouble, and expense. But if it can be made to effect this immediate saving it will be readily used without at all events direct compulsion. The present time is propitious for a reform of our abortive system. The principal obstacle to a large traffic in small parcels of land lies in the cost and trouble of transfer. Owing to the difficulty of transfer the bulk of the people look upon land as a luxury which they are not likely ever to acquire, and in this age all such luxuries excite envy and hatred. Vast schemes of confiscation which would be hooted down in France or Prussia are sometimes propounded in England. The only remedy is the augmentation of the number of landed proprietors, and the best means of bringing about this augmentation is to facilitate dealings in land by an efficient system of registration.

[See text of the acts above referred to.—Reports of the Land Transfer Commission appointed 1868 and of the select committee on Land Titles and Transfer appointed 1878.—R. Torrens, *Essay on Transfer of Land by Registration of Title.—Land Transfer*, a review of the subject published by order of the Bar Committee, 1886.—F. Brickdale, *Registration of Title to Land.—* R. B. Morris, *Registration of Titles*, 1886, and *Summary of the Law of Land and Mortgage Registration*, 1895, and the valuable lists of authorities in both works. —Say and Chailley, *Nouveau Dictionnaire d'Economie Politique*, s.v. *Cadastre*. Art. on CADASTRAL SURVEY.]   F. C. M.

LANDSETTUS, one of the many appella-tions for the peasant landholders on a mediæval manor, chiefly found in the eastern counties.

[Vinogradoff, *Villainage in England.*]

E. G. P.

LAND SYSTEM IN THE AMERICAN COLONIES. The agrarian policy of the various American colonies was largely dependent upon the character and instincts of the different groups of settlers. In the division of the soil, better even than in the forms of government, were expressed the political and social ideas of these settlers, and as these ideas varied, so did the methods of land-distribution and the forms of land-tenure. Such variations may be ascribed in part to hereditary inclinations, to the influence of habit and previous environment, and to the political ideas that had stimulated the colonists to leave England for America ; in part to climate and staple products, the influence of which, though important, is likely to be exaggerated. The fitness of a territory for a given staple, cultivable only on a large scale, will militate against small holdings ; while a land confined by sea and mountain, and broken by frequent ranges of hills, will not be favourable to large plantations.

The title to all lands in America claimed by virtue of discovery and occupation was vested in the Crown. The king was as absolute a sovereign of these territories as of his ancestral demesne. He disposed of them freely, and conveyed to the grantees, by letters patent, such powers as seemed to him good. Such patents were issued to petitioners, conveying to them rights in the soil and the power of free disposal of it. Lands granted in this way were held by the petitioners in free and common SOCAGE, which was the normal and typical free tenure, that is, tenure by fealty and fixed services. The most common of the latter was the payment of rent. This form of tenure was embodied in all the early charters, though the form of the rent varied. In the charter to Raleigh in 1584, to the Virginia Company of London in 1609 and 1611-1612, to the New England Company in 1620, to the Massachusetts Bay Company in 1629 and 1691, to the Governor and Company of Connecticut in 1662, and to the Governor and Company of Rhode Island and Providence Plantations in 1663, the service took the form of a payment of one-fifth of all the gold and silver. This had, however, rather the character of a reservation than a rent. The grant to Lord Baltimore in 1632 exacted, in addition to the reservation of one-fifth of all the gold and silver, an annual payment of two Indian arrows to the king at Windsor ; the grant to Gorges in 1639, one quarter of wheat ; the grant to the Duke of York in 1664, forty beaver skins ; the grants to the proprietaries of Carolina in 1663 and 1665, twenty marks ; and the grant to Penn in 1681, two beaver skins. It is not surprising that so free a tenure should have been conceded when we realise how burdensome a military tenure would have been to settlers engaged in such distant and hazardous undertakings, how willing the Stuart kings were to offer every encouragement to these colonists, and how strong was the opinion in England—note the action of parliament in 1610—that all feudal dues and incidents should be abolished.

The patentees, whether single proprietaries, groups of proprietaries, or joint-stock companies, made subgrants to those who would co-operate directly in bringing about settlement. Such grantees might be organised as joint-stock companies, as was the case with the Massachusetts Bay Company. This company, a patentee of the New England Company, although receiving a charter directly from the king, distributed lands under certain prescribed rules to individuals and to land-communities, who had power to subdivide the land further among *bona fide* settlers. Or such grantees might be a number of proprietaries, as in the case of New Jersey, where the proprietaries received their title by a conveyance from the Duke of York — himself a patentee of Charles II.,— and having erected a frame of government, gave the governor and council of the new province the power to distribute lands to individuals, but retained in their own hands the privilege of granting town-patents. In the majority of cases, however, the first patentees, whether a single proprietary, as in Pennsylvania, Maryland, and New York, a chartered company, as in Connecticut and Rhode Island, or a group of proprietaries, as in Carolina, conveyed title, either directly or through the governor or deputy-governor, to those who were to be the final owners of the soil, if individuals, or to those to whom was entrusted the task of further division among themselves, if members of a land-community.

The methods according to which lands were distributed differed in detail, but in general were much the same everywhere. The scheme of division based on the share-right, that is, the right of each shareholder to a certain amount of the newly-discovered territory, and to a share in the profits of the venture, was the outcome of the joint-stock system. In Massachusetts Bay there was allowed to each subscriber of £50, 200 acres; in New Jersey to every armed freeman who shared in the settlement, 150 acres; in Maryland to each adventurer bringing over ten additional persons, 1000 and later 2000 acres; in Carolina, in 1669, to each free-born individual over sixteen, 150 acres. This system was easily extended by the grant of additional acres for each new settler transported to the colonies, for each man-servant or woman-servant possessed, for each apprentice or indentured servant, or for each member of a family, especially children.

Such methods are inevitable when land is plentiful and a rapid increase of population desired. In addition to these grants of fixed amounts extensive grants were made to individuals who were of rank in the colony, or had performed meritorious service. Lastly, grants were made to communities of settlers who desired to establish towns. In Connecticut and Rhode Island the last two forms of distribution were the only ones employed. In Pennsylvania, in the laying out of a town, grants were made to " first purchasers " according to a fixed agreement at the rate of ten acres to every 500 purchased. Any attempt at systematic distribution seems to have been given up at an early date in Pennsylvania. The proprietary and the land-office acting in his absence seem to have disposed of the territory at their own will and pleasure.

Lands thus granted were in the northern colonies generally held in FEE (*q.v.*). In Massachusetts Bay there were a few instances of grants for life or for rent. In the other colonies a small QUIT-RENT was demanded. This was in New Jersey and Carolina a half-penny to the acre; in Pennsylvania for the " first purchasers," one shilling, though later the rent dropped to one penny or half-penny an acre. In Maryland the quit-rent was first paid in kind, four hundred pounds of wheat; later the amount was diminished, and money sterling substituted for the wheat rental. In Virginia a rental of one shilling, to be paid after seven years in agricultural commodities, was imposed; this, after 1688, was paid in tobacco at the rate of one penny per pound. In South Carolina it was a penny per acre before 1694, after that date one shilling sterling per one hundred acres until 1731, when the old rate was restored. All such rentals, of course, lapsed with the independence of the colonies, and all landed property became alodial freeholds (see ALOD).

In none of the charters issued were the rights of the Indians, the native occupiers of the soil, recognised. The Crown claimed absolute and positive sovereignty. Nevertheless, the opinion was held very generally by the colonists and by others that the natives should not be dispossessed of their property without some compensation. Extreme views, however, were held on both sides. Cotton Mather said it was unnecessary to recognise the Indian claims at all, and later lawyers denied that the Indian deed created a title, holding that it was no more than a quit-claim, the fee being in the king. On the other hand, Roger Williams and the New Jersey squatters claimed that titles based on Indian purchase were alone worthy of consideration. In nearly every case, however, the colonists purchased their lands of the Indians for small amounts of merchandise, and protected the natives in the fields and hunting-grounds reserved for them. Cases of hard treatment and actual dishonesty were fortunately not common. Titles that rested on Indian deeds only had to receive the sanction of the local courts or of the colonial assemblies, while some of the colonies were obliged to forbid unlicensed purchasing entirely, because of the confusion caused by it. Massachusetts Bay forbade it in 1633, Rhode Island in 1643, Maryland in 1649, Connecticut in 1663. Virginia discouraged sale by the Indians of their lands, but in New Jersey the number of titles that rested on Indian deeds only was so large as to lead to serious dispute followed by riots in 1749. Reservations and even towns were set apart for the Indians by many of the colonies, but, inasmuch as the Indian question was an ever-recurring one, a considerable mass of legislation was called into existence in settling it. The eastern Indians, yearly decreasing in number, continued to occupy their reservations till long after the revolution. To-day a few half-breeds still linger in the territory of the original colonies, but the lands owned by them are very small in extent.

After this general view of the land system in the American colonies, a more detailed examination of the Virginian and New England system is necessary. By the charter of 1609 the Treasurer, Council, and General Association of Adventurers in England were authorised to divide the soil of Virginia according to such methods as they might prescribe, employing the governor and council in Virginia as ministerial agents. The requirement to send all patents to England for confirmation involved so much delay as to retard seriously the growth of the colony, and with the recall of the letters-patent in 1624, the power fell into the hands of the royal governor acting for the Crown. There were three grounds upon which a grant might be issued : First, the purchase of a "bill of adventure," by which the purchaser of a single share at £12 : 10s. was entitled to 100 acres in the first division of the soil, and 100 acres in addition when the first plantation was seated. The purchasers of bills before 1625 were exempt from quit-rent. Of the original subscribers it is estimated that about two-thirds, either in person or through agents, took up their lands, while one-third sold their rights to others. By means of extensive purchasing of shares on the part of private associations, engrossing of lands began on a large scale ; but after 1624 the associations were unable to maintain their position, and, with the dissolution of the company, these lands fell into the hands of private individuals. The second ground was the performance of some meritorious service. The recipients were generally officers of the state, clergymen, physicians, and others. To these the company, and after-

wards the Crown, gave large portions of land, in the form either of shares or, after 1624, of money. Special grants were made to the governors who became in time the agents of the Crown in dispensing like favours to those of lesser rank. To those who guarded the frontiers every inducement was offered, and large quantities of land situated along the border were patented to single individuals or groups of men. The third ground was the head-right, that is to say, any shareholder or other person who transported an emigrant to the colony was allowed fifty acres. The object of this was to increase the population, and to promote individual ownership in the soil. This method of distributing land became very much more common after 1624. Abuses crept in, and on many pretexts it became possible to obtain land without having transported a single emigrant. This abuse was connived at because of the feeling in Virginia that a simpler method of acquiring title should be adopted. The economic growth of the colony demanded the abolition of such expensive methods, and those who were desirous of bringing new land into tillage did not wish to be hampered by unnecessary burdens. Thus it took Virginia over fifty years to reach that policy of land-distribution which the New England colonists had been employing since the beginning of the settlement. The size of the portions allotted in Virginia increased with the growth of the colony. From 1634 to 1650, though the largest grant was for 3500 acres, the average area of soil acquired did not exceed 446 acres. From 1651 to 1700 the average size of the patents was 674 acres, though individual patents ran as high as 20,000 acres. The only conditions attached to such grants were, first, that the land be seated, that is, that a small house or cabin be erected upon it, and a portion of the soil tilled ; secondly, the payment of quit-rent to the amount of 1s. per 50 acres after seven years had passed, reckoning from 1618, the date of the adoption of the law. Settlers were exceedingly remiss in the payment of this rental, as was the case in all the colonies where it existed, for they did not like it, and sought by every means to evade it. Failure to fulfil these conditions, particularly the first, caused such land to escheat to the Crown, as did also lands of intestates who died without heirs. There existed, in consequence, at various times in Virginia large amounts of forfeited territory, for which new patents were constantly granted.

Thus it will be seen that Virginia was a land of large individual holdings, and it will also be noticed that these holdings tended to become larger. This was due to the nature of the colonists, the character of the country, and the conditions of agriculture. There scarcely existed the small land-communities, through whose agrarian activity and methods of subdivision a system of small freeholds was introduced. For these we must look to New England, and must follow the process of land-distribution one step farther.

In addition to the gifts to individuals, the colonial authorities of Massachusetts Bay, Connecticut, and Rhode Island made grants of territory to groups of men bound together by ties of blood, religion, and common political ideas. These groups or companies were organised on a joint-stock basis for the purpose of purchasing the land necessary for the establishment of a town. To these men the purchase of the lands of the Indians was a duty higher even than that of obtaining a title from the Crown. For this purpose a common fund was raised, to which all those who were to join in the undertaking subscribed. After a grant had been obtained from the colony the land was purchased. It was then divided slowly, as need required, the share of each being chiefly determined by his contribution to the common fund. This share was called the "purchase right," and was generally, though not always, expressed in pounds. The "purchase right," while corresponding in a sense to the "bill of adventure," nevertheless differed in two particulars. First, the amount of land given was determined not only by the amount of money subscribed, but also by the size and importance of the family of the subscriber. A "purchase right" was therefore in part a family holding. Secondly, the "purchase right" was not a certain amount of land taken up all in one piece, as was the land taken up under a Virginia patent, but it was a bundle of separate shares situated in many parts of the village territory, and a right to the enjoyment of privileges common to all. In the earlier days the "purchase right" included a right to a homestead, a right in every important division of land, a right to use all lands left common for pasturing sheep and cattle, a right in all woods for the masting of swine and gathering of timber, and a right to share in whatever resources the town possessed, such as fisheries, vineyards, mines, etc. This definition of the "purchase right" shows that in dividing their lands the New England proprietors had before them two objects. First, equity, which was to be obtained by making the divisions as equal as possible. Engrossing of lands was thus prevented. Secondly, such an increase of population as would bring about a rapid cultivation and improvement of the soil. Both of these objects were to be attained by a system of small and scattered holdings only. The system of this kind with which the colonists were familiar was that of the English village community, and therefore the plantations of New England reproduced that system as nearly as possible. The lands were divided

into long and narrow fields, called variously tiers, furlongs, shots, squadrons, and quarters. These were subdivided into lots ranging from one acre to forty or more in size. Adjacent to these fields, which formed the chief arable land of the community, were meadows, divided in severalty, yet thrown open, like the LAMMAS LANDS (q.v.) of old England, after haying-time. There were also the common pastures for sheep and cattle, and the outlying waste and wilderness. The "purchase right" gave to the holder scattered lots in the majority of fields, in this respect corresponding to the YARDLAND of the English VILLEIN; it also included sub-rights in all common lands and undertakings. The common rights in New England differed from those in some parts of old England, notably at Ashton and Cote (Giles, History of Bampton, p. 76), in that they were probably appendant to the homestead only and never to the person. The rights in undivided lands could, however, be retained by persons living outside the town, though even this was denied by some of the colonial lawyers, who asserted that such rights were appendant to the homestead only. Inasmuch as the commons in some of the towns were not divided into severalty until the end of the 18th century, there arose frequent disputes between the towns and the descendants and assigns of the old proprietors regarding the ownership of these lands.

Thus it will be seen that while in Virginia the soil was divided into large plantations varying from 200 to 20,000 acres in size, in New England it was divided into petty holdings as small as one acre or even half an acre in size. In Virginia a quit-rent was demanded; in New England the land was held in full ownership, limited only by certain liabilities to forfeiture in case of alienation or removal. As the colonies became better established, and the economic condition changed, all these restrictions on full ownership were removed. This had been done in New England by the middle of the 18th century, while in the other colonies all proprietary rights, manorial obligations, quit-rents, forms of primogeniture, entail and intestacy escheat, were abolished in 1776. The form of freehold tenure, thus defined by the different state laws and constitutions for the settled and cultivated lands, was extended by the ordinance of 1787 to the unoccupied lands of the nation. These lands, by the peace of Paris in 1783, had ceased to be Crown lands, and, after the state cessions of 1785 to 1790, had been taken in trust by the government of the United States for the benefit of the whole people.

[No systematic, compact account of the land system in all the American colonies has as yet been written, nor can a satisfactory knowledge of it be obtained from the material thus far printed.

Histories of the United States pass over the subject almost entirely. Much information can be obtained from town and colonial records and from local and state histories. The charter regulations can be found in Poore's *Charters and Constitutions*, Washington, 1878. There is a small amount of information in Winsor's *Narrative and Critical History*, vols. iii. and v. The only systematic attempt to investigate the subject will be found in the *Johns Hopkins Studies in History and Political Science*, as follows : vol. i., "The Germanic Origin of New England Towns," "Parish Institutions of Maryland," "Old Maryland Manors " ; vol. iii., " Virginia Local Institutions," " Maryland Local Institutions " ; vol. iv., "Dutch Village Communities on the Hudson River," "Pennsylvania Boroughs," "History of the Land Question of the United States " (this work is of importance for the period after 1776 only), "The Land System of the New England Colonies " ; vol. vii., "The River Towns of Connecticut ; vol. xiii., "Government of the Colony of South Carolina." See also Howard, *Local Constitutional History of the United States*, Baltimore, 1889. — Sargeant, *Land Laws of Pennsylvania.*—Brown, *Genesis of the United States*, Boston, 1891.— Weeden, *Economic and Social History of New England*, Boston, 1890. —Bruce, *The Economic History of Virginia in the Seventeenth Century*, New York, 1895 ; and an article in the *Zeitschrift für Sozial und Wirthschaftsgeschichte*, vol. ii., entitled, " Die Stadt in Neu-England, ihr Ursprung und ihre agrarische Grundlage."]   C. M. A.

LAND TAX. The origin of the existing land tax in England is usually referred to the year 1692, when the valuation was made on which the quotas subsequently fixed were based. In that year parliament, discontinuing the system in force during the civil war and the Commonwealth, under which a specified sum was raised from each county and from certain towns by the MONTHLY ASSESSMENTS, directed by the act 4 W. & M. c. 1, the levy of a definite rate of 4s. in the pound—the same as for a SUBSIDY on land in Tudor times—on the true yearly value of all personal estate, offices, lands, tenements, and hereditaments in England, Wales, and Berwick-on-Tweed. Adopting in the main the machinery used in raising the monthly assessments, the act provided for a valuation of the subjects of charge by parochial assessors to be appointed by the commissioners named for putting the act in execution.

The yield of the tax as thus levied (£1,922,712) fell short of what was anticipated, owing doubtless to incorrect returns, and year by year it showed such a tendency to decrease that, in 1697, parliament found it desirable to revert to the system of granting a definite total sum to be paid in specified amounts charged in the act upon counties and certain named towns. A total sum of £1,484,015 : 1 : 11¾, as for a rate of 3s. in the pound, was granted, and the commissioners were directed to set down the several proportions which, *in their judgment*, ought to be charged upon every hundred or other division towards raising the amount charged on the whole county or town. In every hundred or division the particular sum required was to be levied, first, by a rate of 3s. in the pound on the assumed income from goods, merchandise, and personal property—every £100 in value being considered to represent an income of £6—and on income from offices ; and *the residue of the sum* by a pound rate on the annual value of real estate. In the following year, 1698, a similar total sum was granted, but on account of the difficulties that had been experienced in apportioning the amounts fixed for the counties and towns among the various hundreds or divisions, the act making the grant, 10 W. III. c. 9, directed that each hundred or division should contribute the same proportion that it had paid under the assessment for 1692, the year when a new valuation was made.

The tax thus originally intended to bear in the first instance on personal estate and offices was subsequently, when personal property— though always by law primarily chargeable— had in practice almost entirely slipped out of assessment, described as an "aid by a land tax," or, in fiscal expression, "the annual land tax." It was granted in the same form, but at rates varying between 4s. and 1s. according to the exigencies of the times, for the next hundred years, the proportions for the hundreds and divisions remaining as fixed by the valuation of 1692. That valuation was very unequal even at its first establishment, and the lapse of years necessarily made it more so. Complaints of inequality were therefore frequent, but as, with the growth of the towns and the improvements in agriculture, the tax had become in most districts light compared with the nominal charge of 4s. or less per pound annually imposed, there was no general demand for a revision.

In November 1797 the usual act (38 Geo. III. c. 5) was passed granting the land tax (£1,989,673 : 7 : 10¼ for England, Wales, and Berwick-on-Tweed, as for a rate of 4s. in the £) for the service of the following year, and on 2nd April 1798 Pitt produced his plan for the redemption of the tax, which was brought into operation by the act 38 Geo. III. c. 60. Pitt's object was to diminish the pressure of the funded debt in the market by causing the absorption of a large amount of stock ; and to effect this so much of the land tax as by the act for 1798 was charged on the several counties and towns in respect of lands, tenements, and hereditaments was made perpetual, subject to redemption. Redemption was to be effected by transferring to the commissioners for the reduction of the national debt for cancellation so much 3 per cent stock (2¾ per cent stock substituted by 52 & 53 Vict. c. 42-59) as would yield a dividend exceeding the land tax to be redeemed by one-tenth part. This amount of stock consideration was reduced in 1853 by 17½ per cent. As the result of redemption, the property became exonerated from land tax, provision being made, however, that in certain circumstances the charge should be kept on foot for the benefit of the redemptioner. The amount of tax redeemed in the years 1798 and 1799, when stock stood at an average of 56, and the price payable represented 20¾ years' purchase of the charge, was, for England and Scotland, £435,888, nearly a quarter of the whole charge, but in after years the progress of redemption became slow. The total amount redeemed in England up to 31st March 1893 was £858,000, leaving about £999,000 as the land tax now payable.

This sum, subject of course to future redemptions, is required to be raised by an annual assessment at an equal pound rate not exceeding 4s.[1] on all the unexonerated lands, tenements, and hereditaments within the areas charged with separate quotas. It may here be mentioned that, as respects the period between 1697 and 1798, the quotas fixed for each hundred or division were required by law to be assessed *equally* within every parish or place within the hundred or division, although in practice effect was not always given to this requirement. But in the important case of *Regina v.* Land Tax Commissioners for Tower division, it was decided by the Court of Queen's Bench in 1853 (2 E. and B. 694) that the act 38 Geo. III. c. 60 fixed, as from 1798, *a separate quota for each parish or place*, and that there was no power to equalise the quotas payable by the several parishes or places within any division. At the present time many of the quotas have been altogether redeemed, and in the parishes or places liable to assessment the rates charged vary between a fraction of 1d. and a little under 3s. in the £. The net amount of the fixed quotas is paid over as part of the inland revenue, any surplus unavoidably raised being applicable to the remuneration of the assessor and the redemption of the quota for the particular parish or place. The tenant of the property is the person required by law to pay the tax, but in the absence of agreement to the contrary he is entitled to deduct the amount out of his rent. There are certain exemptions for hospitals and colleges.

As before stated, personal property, originally placed in the forefront of the tax, gradually slipped out of assessment. In 1798 the remaining charge was found to amount to a little over £5000, and this charge was continued by Pitt in the various districts subject to it till 1833, when it was repealed. That

[1] Proposed, 1896, to be reduced to 1s.

part of the old land tax which was collected from offices, and which amounted in 1798 to about £126,000, was also then continued as a separate annual grant, finally disappearing in 1876, except as regards certain salaries charged on public revenue.

Under the act 38 Geo. III. c. 5, Scotland was charged with a separate sum of £47,954 : 1 : 2, which was subsequently made perpetual, subject to redemption. The amount now remaining unredeemed is about £34,000, and the apportioned quotas are in some districts raised by a small rate on lands, houses, and trade, and in others are paid out of the common good. There is no land tax in Ireland.

The generally accepted view of the incidence of the existing land tax in England is well expressed by Giffen, *Essays in Finance*, 1st series, p. 242 :— "As a fixed charge upon land for generations, it is now past all controversy a rent-charge. In many instances it has long since been redeemed, the property having subsequently changed hands ; in others, inheritors of property have acquired it under the burden, and have calculated their income minus the tax, while purchasers, in buying, invariably allow for it. To reduce (abolish ?) it now would be to present the landowners of England with a capital sum of nearly £30,000,000. Their estates, relieved of the burden, would become at once so much more valuable, and if they did not sell, they would pocket an additional income which they never inherited or paid for."

[Dowell's *History of Taxation and Taxes*, 2nd ed. vol. iii. bk. ii. ch. i.—Bourdin's *Land Tax.*—1st, 13th, and 28th Reports of Commissioners of Inland Revenue (see Taxation).]   F. A.

LAND TENURES (or Landlord and Tenant in the United Kingdom). The relation of landlord and tenant springs out of a contract by which the proprietor of land lets it on hire for use by some other person. Under this contract the proprietor is entitled to payment for the use of the land,—a rent whether in kind or in money, and the tenant acquires certain possessory rights in the land available against third parties as well as against the proprietor. Experience has shown that as a rule the proprietors of large estates can make more out of their land by thus letting it for hire than by dealing with it in other ways. The high cultivation of the land involves an expenditure of capital to which the proprietor may be unequal, it also requires special knowledge which the proprietor may not possess, and close personal supervision which he may not be able to give. Hence proprietors are naturally led to devolve on other men who have the requisite knowledge and capital the business of utilising the land, and in order to obtain their assistance concede to them at least for a time exclusive rights of possession and enjoyment. Unlike the bailiff or caretaker, who is a mere living instrument of the proprietor, the tenant is the legal occupant of a given parcel of land, and can exclude the interference of the proprietor himself.

On the other hand, the landlord has very generally possessed special means of recovering his rent from a tenant who has fallen into arrear. The ordinary creditor has not, in the absence of express agreement, any mortgage on his debtor's property. But Roman law gave the landlord a HYPOTHECA or implied mortgage on the tenant's stock, so that he could satisfy his claim out of it in preference to other creditors. English law allows the landlord the extrajudicial remedy of distraint. Without going into court he can distrain on the goods and chattels found on the farm for which rent is due. He is entitled to sell the goods thus seized, and to satisfy his claim out of the proceeds of the sale. By the AGRICULTURAL HOLDINGS ACT of 1883, the landlord is prevented from distraining for more than a year's rent, and from taking by way of distraint machinery or live-stock which, although found upon the farm, belongs to a third party.

It follows almost inevitably from the independence of a tenant, as compared with a labourer, that he should supply part of the capital required for the cultivation of his holding. He must at least find his own tools, and keep himself alive until the first crop sown by him becomes marketable. This seems to be all the capital required by that class of metayers who receive from their landlords the whole of the stock for their farms (see MÉTAYAGE). But usually the tenant supplies much more than this small capital. He may supply the whole of the stock. Or, besides supplying the stock, he may spend a considerable sum in keeping the land fit for cultivation, and this expenditure will increase rapidly as INTENSIVE CULTIVATION (q.v.) becomes general. Finally, he may defray the expense not merely of keeping the land in order, but also of what are termed permanent improvements, such as drainage and farm buildings,—this last case is practically unknown in England.

In so far as the tenant's capital is spent on the lasting improvement of the land, he has a moral and may have a legal claim to compensation.

In considering the relation of landlord and tenant we have to take account of three things: the mode of fixing the rent, the duration of the lease, and the compensation to be paid for tenant's improvements.

1. *The Rent.*—The rent to be paid by the tenant may be fixed in various ways. It may be fixed by competition, the landlord offering a vacant farm for the highest rent obtainable. This method is commonly adopted in England. But in England, though most farms are let from year to year, it has been the general practice of good landlords to allow a satisfactory tenant to remain in possession, practically in perpetuity. Again the rent may be merely nominal, but coupled with the obligation to pay a large fine whenever the lease is renewed.

This is the principle of the beneficial lease formerly common in England, especially on the estates of corporate bodies, but now fallen into desuetude. Again the rent may be fixed at a certain proportion of the gross or net produce of the holding, as in the metayer tenure. In all these cases the rent is determined by the agreement of the parties. In other cases the rent may be customary. Long lapse of time may have rendered it unalterable, in spite of changes in the value of money or an increase in the demand for farms. Again the rent may be judicial—fixed periodically by a court on an estimate of what a man of average capacity can fairly pay for a given piece of land. But judicial determination of rent only takes place when there is a dispute between a tenant in possession and his landlord as to what rent should be paid.

Each of these modes of determining rent has its peculiar advantages and disadvantages. The fixing of rent by competition works very well in a country like England, where there are many other industries beside agriculture, and where, as farming is carried on, the competition for holdings is limited to men of some capital and special training. Under these conditions it gives landlords every motive for spending pains and money on their land so as to enhance its letting value, whilst it stimulates the tenants to farm the land effectively, or in default admits abler men to carry on the work of cultivation. But where the needful conditions do not exist, where agriculture is almost the only industry, where competition for land is fierce and irrational, where landlords are often not improvers and frequently are absentees, the system of competitive rents does not promote good farming and excites much ill feeling. In Ireland the competition for land in many cases induced the offer of a rent which could never be paid, and assisted in multiplying a miserable and lawless rural population. The system of beneficial leases seems more indulgent to the tenant, but it destroys the landlord's interest in improving his land. When it was in common use in England, the lands let on beneficial lease compared generally very unfavourably with the lands let at a rack-rent. The method of fixing the rent at a proportion of the produce has the advantage of roughly adjusting the tenant's payments to his means, and reducing the rent in an easy automatic manner when agriculture becomes less profitable. It has the further advantage of making the landlord as it were a partner with the tenant, and of interesting him directly in the improvement of the land. Where rent has been fixed by custom the landlord has no interest in the improvement of the land, and the progress of agriculture depends wholly on the skill, capital, and industry of the tenant who is secure of any surplus which he can extract from his farm. But custom operates chiefly in poor communities where agriculture is not progressive. The judicial determination of rent assures to the tenant in possession a full return for all improvements made by him, but it also secures him against the competition of abler men who might do better with the land, and hence removes incitement to improvements. It has no benefits for a new tenant who comes in after paying a full competitive price for his predecessor's tenant-right, for the interest on the sum so paid when added to the judicial rent will often equal and sometimes even exceed a full rack-rent. Under this system the landlord's control over his land and sense of enjoyment in it are so much reduced, that he is apt to do nothing more for the improvement of his estate and to sink into a mere annuitant. The periodic determination of the rent causes recurring friction, and the constitution and procedure of the court become the playthings of political parties. The system of judicial rents, probably, can hardly be more than exceptional and temporary.

2. *The Duration of the Lease.*—This may vary from one year to a practical perpetuity. An agricultural tenant must occupy the land at least for a year in order to derive any return from his labour. For this reason the English courts have caught at any pretext for turning a mere tenancy at will into a tenancy from year to year. Through the operation of the Agricultural Holdings Act a tenancy by the year virtually secures the enjoyment of the land for two years. But much more important, as mentioned before, is the custom of all good landlords not to disturb a satisfactory tenant. There are many instances in England of a farm let nominally from year to year which has remained in the hands of the same family for several generations. Leases for a term of years are common in England and much more frequent in Scotland and Ireland. The Settled Land Act 1882, empowers every tenant for life to grant agricultural leases for a term of twenty-one years. The lessee for a term of years has evidently a strong incentive to industry in the earlier years, but he is apt to relax his efforts during the later years of his term. Yet the large farms of Scotland, the best of their class in the world, have usually been held for a short term of years. Leases for long terms are not unknown in the United Kingdom, and the Roman contract of EMPHYTEUSIS was practically a lease for ever. The tenant could never be disturbed, provided he paid his rent and did not lay waste the holding. Where the rent has been fixed by custom, the tenant has a virtual lease for ever. Where the rent is determined judicially, it must be reassessed at moderate intervals. In Ireland the interval was fixed by the Land Act of 1881 at fifteen years, but a bill has been introduced this year (1895) for reducing it to ten years. As a general rule, it may be laid down that where landlords have the means and the will to improve the land, leases for moderate terms will suffice to ensure high farming, but where landlords are not in the habit of making improvements leases for longer terms are desirable. Tenancies from year to year are compatible with high farming only where custom gives an additional security to the tenant.

3. *Compensation for Tenant's Improvements.*— The general rule is that the property in the soil includes everything which is affixed to, or embodied in, the soil. If a tenant gives up possession, therefore, he loses any right to his improvements. But as this is inequitable to him and injurious to agriculture he ought to receive compensation. Again, if he is to be compensated for his improvements he should be obliged to obtain the landlord's consent for making them, as otherwise he might compel the landlord to reimburse him for reckless and fanciful expenditure. Compensation may be either direct or indirect, customary or legal. If the tenant has a lease for a term of years at a low rent he may be regarded as receiving indirect compensation for the improvements which he has executed. If he pays a competitive rent, compensation must be direct and must be paid him on quitting the farm. In England custom has generally thrown on the landlord the burthen of making the most durable and costly improvements, and has sometimes given compensation to out-going tenants for improvements which they had made. But it was found necessary to supplement custom by legislation (see AGRICULTURAL HOLDINGS ACTS). Where the tenant enjoys fixity of tenure at a judicial rent no special legislation is needed to ensure compensation for his improvements.

The relation of landlord and tenant in the East, particularly in India, differs greatly from that in western Europe. A few words only can be given to it here. Baden-Powell's great work on *Systems of Land Tenure and Land Revenue in British India*, contains much information. Baden-Powell appears to have proved that neither Mohammedan nor Hindu jurists had a clear conception of property in land, and in consequence the several interests of the different classes who live on the land have never been defined with the legal precision customary in Europe. The relations subsisting between those whom we should call landlords and tenants differ in different provinces. It has been the policy of the government to recognise the claims of actual occupants, and to give them what might be called a tenant-right. This is said to have been the intention even of Lord Cornwallis and of those who assisted him in the permanent settlement of Bengal, although it was not carried out till many years afterwards. But the subject of Indian tenures is too extensive and too intricate to be discussed within the limits of this article. To illustrate European institutions by Indian parallels, though always attractive and sometimes useful, is generally unsafe.

The relation of landlord and tenant in the case of mines or of buildings presents certain peculiar features, for which see MINES ; ROYALTIES.

[Williams, *Principles of the Law of Real Property*. — Woodfall, *Law of Landlord and Tenant.*—The works referred to in the articles on the Three F's (see F'S, THE THREE, and LAND LEGISLATION, Irish) ; the acts referred to above. —Mill, *Principles of Political Economy*, bk. ii. —Marshall, *Principles of Economics.*— Nicholson, *Principles of Political Economy.*—Brodrick, *English Land and English Landlords.*—*Systems of Land Tenure in Various Countries* (Cobden Club), 3rd ed., 1876.]   F. C. M.

LAND BANKS, SCHEMES OF, IN ENGLAND, 1695-96. A rival banking scheme to that of the Bank of England. The idea of it was first broached by Hugh CHAMBERLEN who, in November 1690, issued from his house in Essex Street the first draft in his "proposal to make England rich and happy." In the session of 1693 he brought the proposal before the Scottish parliament, and in the month of July it was examined by a committee. In this form of his scheme Chamberlen proposed, against a conveyance of an estate for 150 years, to create bills to the value of 100 years' rental, 40 years' rental to be advanced on loan and rental to the landowner, 30 years' rental to form the capital of a joint-stock for the benefit of subscribers, 10 years' rental to be advanced to government as a loan, and remainder for working expenses. The scheme not passing the Scotch parliament, it was brought before the English parliament in December 1693, but slightly altered. Subscribers were to convey £150 rental for 150 years to secure a loan of £100 per annum for 100 years, and in addition to exchange £1000 in gold or silver for the intended company's bills, thus £400 in allotment, £300 at end of first year, £200 at end of second year, and £100 at end of third year. For this he would receive in the company's bills £1000 down, £1100 at end of first year, £1200 at end of second year, £1300 at end of third year, and £1400 at end of fourth year. Of the £10,000 loan created, therefore, the conveyor got £6000, another £3000 was to form a joint-trading stock, the remainder was for government loan and working expenses.

The scheme was taken up by the tories out of rivalry to the whig Bank of England (see Kennet, and Burnet, "a new ballad of the land bank, or credit restored," published c. 1696, in which Harley and Foley are especially mentioned), and a huge scheme was launched by which the land bank undertook to raise a loan of £2,564,000 for William's government. The scheme received the sanction of parliament in April 1696, after bitter opposition from the Bank of England. By the act 7 & 8 Will. III. c. 31, the duties on salt, glass, etc., and tobacco pipes were appropriated to form a fund to raise £179,480 per annum, being interest on the proposed loan. By the act the subscription was to be closed before 1st August 1696, and half the loan was to be subscribed before the incorporation of the company. The bank was further to lend £500,000 on land securities.

The deed declaring the constitution of the "Office of land credit" was sealed 10th August 1695, but not enrolled in chancery till 15th July 1696. The provision on the first draft of the scheme as to the exchange of £1000 in gold was omitted and other details altered.

Before parliamentary assent to the scheme the subscription had been opened on the 25th October 1695. It met with no response, was closed, and again opened on the 18th November with like effect, and a third advertisement was tried on the 20th December. The 6th number of the "monthly account" of the bank, issued 7th January 169$\frac{5}{6}$, says that since the 25th October £40,000 had been lent out on land security. This must be looked upon as distinct from the institution established by the act of April 1696.

Subscriptions for the latter were to open 25th May 1696, and the first meeting of subscribers was called 8th June. From the first it proved a total failure. Kennet says the scheme did not produce a penny, and was a serious blow to credit generally (see Macaulay).

Chamberlen in 1700 and 1705 again brought his schemes before the Scotch parliament, but in vain.

RIVAL SCHEMES.—1. That of John BRISCOE, presented to parliament in 1694. Offered to subscribers bills to the value of $\frac{3}{4}$ of the estate settled, at £3 : 0 : 10 per cent interest. Coupled with this were proposals for raising £1,000,000 for government aid. Not receiving the sanction of parliament Briscoe opened his subscription without it (11th June 1695). By the 13th July 1695 estates to the rental of £29,460 were subscribed, by 27th July £51,438, by 3rd August £60,270, by 2nd December over £200,000, the estates being drawn from almost every county of England and Wales. According to Briscoe's assertion, also, of the million loan £650,000 was subscribed. There is no further evidence as to the progress of the project.

2. A scheme drafted in a tract undated and unsigned, entitled "An account of the office for transferring and discounting land bills" at Hercules Pillar, Fleet Street, near Temple Bar. Owners of land to draw $\frac{3}{4}$ value of estate conveyed, in bills discountable at 1 per cent 6 months after the registration of the estates. To provide a fund for discounting, the manager to be empowered to call in 10 per cent or more of the value of all the estates registered.

3. An anonymous "Proposal for erecting a general bank which may be fitly called the Land Bank of England" 1695.

4. Nicholas BARBON is said to have founded a land bank, which on the 15th August 1695 was going on successfully (Luttrell's "relation"). On the following 4th February 169$\frac{5}{6}$ this coalesced with Briscoe's bank.

5. Thomas Dalby, "Propositions for general land banks," an undated pamphlet signed as above (of 1695 almost certainly). He proposes two alternative schemes—(1) funds not to exceed $\frac{1}{4}$ of rental of lands engaged, (2) land banks secured by a parliamentary fund of which he gives a sample scheme.

6. John ASGILL, who was accused of plagiarism of Briscoe's ideas, proposed an anonymous scheme in tract entitled "To the knights, citizens, and burgesses in parliament assembled, a short scheme or proposal for a National Land Bank." Landowners to subscribe £4,000,000, $\frac{1}{4}$ of this to be government loan and the fund of the bank. Landowners to have $\frac{3}{4}$ value of estate advanced, viz. on £100 rental £1200 in money at £3 : 0 : 10 per cent. (This is apparently Briscoe's.)

[Thorold Rogers, *First Nine Years of the Bank of England*].

W. A. S.

LANDES-CREDITKASSEN. Government mortgage banks established in some parts of Germany, chiefly for the purpose of assisting peasant proprietors (see MORTGAGE BANKS).

E. S.

LANDING-WAITER is the name which, in the customs departments of the United Kingdom and the colonies, denotes the officer who receives and checks imported goods at the place of landing. The rules of the department in Queen Elizabeth's reign show that the *waiter* was the officer who superintended importation, as distinguished from the *searcher* who looked after exports—who "waited on" the lighters which brought the goods to the pier. Later the term became *land-waiter* and then *landing-waiter*.

[See *First Report of Commissioners of Customs*, 1857.] C. A. H.

LANGE, FRIEDRICH ALBERT (1828-1875), was born at Wald near Solingen in the district of Düsseldorf. He was son of Dr. J. P. Lange, well known as a theologian and a professor at Bonn. His father was called to Zürich, and the boy's early youth was spent there. He went to Bonn to study philology and philosophy; after teaching for some time at Cologne, he returned to Bonn as *privat-docent*. From 1858-62 he was master in the gymnasium at Duisburg, but resigned this position when the government forbade teachers to take a part in political agitation. His deep interest in the social and economic questions of the time led him to engage in several journalistic enterprises, always showing himself a decided adversary of reaction. After a residence of some years at Winterthur in Switzerland, he became, in 1870, professor of inductive philosophy at Zürich, and in 1872 accepted an invitation from the minister Falk to fill the chair of philosophy at Marburg. His health began to fail, but he continued to work energetically, lecturing and writing, till the end came. Personally, he appears to have been a man of singularly pure and elevated character, with high moral ideals, and filled with zeal for the advancement, and especially the enlightenment, of the working classes.

Lange is most widely known by his *Geschichte des Materialismus*, 1866 (afterwards remodelled and largely rewritten), which was translated into English by E. C. Thomas, 1877-81. His principal economic work is *Die Arbeiterfrage in ihrer Bedeutung für Gegenwart und Zukunft beleuchtet*, 1865, republished in 1870 with considerable changes, especially with a larger element of theoretical discussion. It is this work which has led to the position assigned him as one of the scientific socialists. His socialism is of a peculiar type, making him an interesting, but also a somewhat perplexing figure. He is repelled by the pervading egoism of the existing system of society, and looks forward to a better organisation, but does not adopt any of the dominant popular creeds of his day. Accepting the proposition that competition tends to force wages down to a minimum, he yet does not wish to abolish the wage system. He does not admit Marx's theory of value, nor does he approve his project of expropriation. He holds the *Konsum* and *Vorschuss-vereine* of Schulze-Delitzsch to be an altogether insufficient solution of the social problem, but rejects also the productive associations of Lassalle, except for agricultural exploitation. Malthus he regards as an immature forerunner of Darwin, and refuses to explain human development by the struggle for existence which prevails amongst the lower animal races ; indeed, as he pointedly says, the contemporary labour movement is in its essence a "struggle against the struggle for existence." He is more critical than constructive, and represents a transitional and indeterminate stage of sociological opinion.

Besides his *Arbeiterfrage*, Lange published the following economic writings : — *Jedermann Hauseigenthümer*, 1865, intended to naturalise in Germany the system of the English building societies ; and *J. S. Mill's Ansichten über die sociale Frage und die angebliche Umwälzung der Socialwissenschaft durch Carey*, 1866, "the best general estimate of Mill as an economist."—Bonar, *Philosophy and Pol. Econ.*, 1893.

[Weinkauff in *Allg. Deutsche Biogr.* ; Lippert in *Handw. der Staatswissenschaften*.] J. K. I.

LANGENSTEIN, HENRY OF (1325-1397), also called HENRICUS DE HASSIA from his native country in Germany. He was some time lecturer and vice-chancellor of the university of Paris, and from 1383 to 1397, the year of his death, professor in Vienna, where he was invited by the archduke Albert III. of Austria, founder of the faculty of theology in the high school of Vienna. Langenstein's *Tractatus de contractibus et de origine censum* is inserted in Joh. Gerson's *Tractatus diversi* (vol. iv. fol. 185-253), Cologne, 1484.

Langenstein is a staunch upholder of the mediæval canonistic views. By means of taxes, the temporal powers should maintain the *justum pretium*, taking, however, into account local considerations, the condition of men, and the disposition of the times. A few discreet elders (*discreti senes*) have to compute, after a careful examination, what each man actually wants according to his *status*, for *status* is more exacting than nature. Every commercial transaction must be based on the *equality of quantities*. He extends the prohibition of usury to the Jews, but would allow them to apply themselves to crafts, trade, and agriculture.

The purchase of rent-charges, very prevalent in Germany during the middle ages, as it allows men to live in idleness, is sinful, exceptin; as a way to provide for one's old age or as a remuneration of services rendered to the church or state. He also objects to the redemption of rents on the basis of a return of 12½ per 100 as dishonest.

[Roscher, *Gesch. der Nat. Oek. in Deutschland*, pp. 18-21, and Brants, *Les Théories Économiques aux XIII.ᵉ et XIV.ᵉ Siècles* (Louvain, 1895), pp. 71, 81, 119, 175, and 201.] E. CA.

LAPSE OF TIME AS CREATING OR EXTINGUISHING RIGHTS. In most legal systems the mere lapse of time has been allowed some effect in creating or extinguishing rights. This principle has taken two forms—acquisition by prescription, and limitation of actions (see LIMITATION, STATUTES OF;

PRESCRIPTION). Prescription plays a more important part in Roman than in English law. Under the early civil law land might be acquired by two years', and movables by one year's uninterrupted possession. By the law of Justinian, ten years' uninterrupted possession gave property in land, if the person against whom the possessor claimed lived in the same province. But if he lived in another province, and, therefore, was less able to protect his rights, twenty years' uninterrupted possession was needed to turn the possessor into an owner. Three years' uninterrupted possession was necessary in the case of movables. But in all cases something more than the mere lapse of time was needed to transfer ownership. The possessor must have acted *bonâ fide*, believing himself to be entitled to the thing possessed, and his possession must have had its origin in some act which, if performed by the true owner, would have given him a legal title to the property, *e.g.* gift, sale, exchange, bequest. The later Roman law, however, recognised that mere uninterrupted possession for a very long period might by itself confer ownership. In English law prescription was not recognised as a means of acquiring property, except in the case of EASEMENT or SERVITUDE, *e.g.* right of way, right of water, right of ancient lights. Even here it was necessary to show enjoyment from time immemorial, *i.e.* from the first year of Richard I., although, where this could not be done, evidence of enjoyment for a long time past was admitted as proof of a lost grant of the right in question. Finally, the Prescription Act 1832 (2 & 3 Will. IV. c. 71) put the matter on a rational footing, by recognising the right of a person who had enjoyed the easement for a specified time—forty years in the case of a right of way, or twenty in the case of a right of light. The enjoyment must not have been merely by permission, nor by force, nor by stealth. By the limitation of actions is meant the loss of a right to sue which is not exercised within a given time. This principle was recognised in the later Roman law, but is much more prominent in English law. Thus at the present day every species of civil action, except an action against a fraudulent trustee, must be brought within a limited time. An action for the recovery of land must be brought within twelve years of the time when the right of action accrued. An action for breach of a simple contract must be brought within six years ; an action for breach of a contract under seal within twenty years. Actions for TORT (*i.e.* civil injury) must be brought within the time fixed by statute in each case. It will be noticed that the limitation of actions does not, like prescription, transfer a right of property from one person to another. It only takes away from the aggrieved person the most effectual means of asserting his right. Thus if A owes B a debt for which B cannot sue because he has let the time slip by, and if A for any reason afterwards pays B a sum of money without mentioning the purpose to which it is to be applied, B can apply the money to payment of the time-barred debt. But it has been provided by statute that when the right to bring an action for the recovery of land has been lost by lapse of time, the title to the land shall also be extinguished. The lapse of time for the purpose either of prescription or of limitation of actions is always interrupted by any acknowledgment of the right of the party, against whom time is running, made by the other party.

The principle which underlies both prescription and limitation of actions has been keenly discussed by jurists. Some have argued that the loss of rights by lapse of time is a just penalty upon the person who neglects to enforce them, whilst others have laid stress upon the hardship of disturbing a long-continued possession, which is generally innocent, and others upon the public interest in limiting litigation. Litigation is at best a costly and uncertain remedy for wrong. But the longer the time which has elapsed since the right of action accrued, the greater becomes the expense and the smaller the chance of finding out the truth. He who does not set about asserting his right of property or obtaining redress for his wrongs within a reasonable time probably suffers little in losing his remedy.

The principle of prescription has a political as well as a merely legal application. History contains many instances of wholesale violence and injustice, revolutions, conquests, and confiscations which dispossess not a few individuals, but whole multitudes in order to enrich a crowd of new possessors. But when these changes have received the sanction of time, a statesman, however much he may deplore them, will not attempt to undo them by any sweeping act of restitution.

Catastrophes such as the Norman Conquest of England, or the English Conquest of Ireland, or the French Revolution, cannot be undone. Even if the old possessors of the land or their descendants had all their title-deeds in order, restitution could not be made except as the result of a prolonged civil strife. The new settlement has become the basis of innumerable transactions and is interwoven with immense interests. Remedial legislation for the social evils which it has generated may be most necessary. But such legislation must be based on the principle that no private person is responsible for the public crimes of a past generation. So far as there is any responsibility for those crimes, it rests upon the whole community, which is therefore bound to bear the burthen of whatever compensation to the victims or to their descendants may be thought just or necessary.

[Holland, *Jurisprudence.* — Markby, *Elements of Law.*—Moyle, *Institutes of Justinian.*—Gale on *Easements.*—Darby and Bosanquet, *Statutes of Limitations.*] F. C. M.

LARGE AND SMALL TRADE. See TRADE.

LA RIVIÉRE, MERCIER DE. See MERCIER DE LA RIVIÈRE.

LA ROCHEFOUCAULD LIANCOURT, ALEXANDRE FRÉDÉRIC, Duc de (1747-1827). Before the French Revolution he lived on his estates, where he busied himself with agriculture, was elected in 1789 a member of the national assembly, fled to the United States during the Reign of Terror, and published on his return the result of his observations in his *Voyage aux États unis d'Amérique fait en 1793-1798* (Paris, 8 vols. 1800).

He was one of those who attended the dinners of the *Économistes* at the home of the Marquis de MIRABEAU, and always took a zealous and active interest in questions of public and private charity. He published a condensed translation of Eden's *History of the Poor,* for the *Recueil de Mémoires sur les Établissements d'humanité* of DUQUESNOY (*q.v.*) (vol. vii., Paris, 1799-1804). His other publications are *Finances et crédit* (1789).—*Notice sur l'Impôt territorial en Angleterre* (1790 and 1804).—*Plan du comité pour l'extinction de la mendicité présenté à l'Assemblée Nationale* and *Travail du comité de mendicité* (both 1790).—*Les Prisons de Philadelphie* (1796 and 1819).—*Notes sur la législation anglaise des chemins* (1801) and a *Statistique Industrielle du Canton de Creil* (Senlis, 1826). A letter of his to Adam Smith is given by Dugald Stewart (see *Cat. of A. Smith's Library,* Macmillans, 1894). A. Smith's reply will be found in *Econ. Journ.,* March 1896. E. Ca.

LA ROCHEFOUCAULD LIANCOURT, FRÉDÉRIC GAETAN, Marquis de (1779-1850). He was the son of the Duke of La Rochefoucauld who lived 1747-1827, and a member of the French house of deputies during the reigns of the restored Bourbons and of King Louis Philippe. He wrote almost exclusively on subjects connected with prison administration.

Mémoires sur les Finances de la France en 1816.—Examen de la Théorie et la Pratique du système Pénitentiaire, and as a sequel *Conséquences du Système Pénitentiaire* (1842).—*Examen du Projet de Loi de la Réforme des Prisons* (1844).—*De la Mortalité Cellulaire* (1844). E. ca.

LARRUGA, EUGENIO DE (about the middle of the last century), born in Saragossa, was placed by King Charles III. at the head of the government departments of the mines, the mint, trade and manufactures. He published, with the financial assistance of the king, his *Memorias políticas y económicas sobre los frutos, comercio, fábricas y minas de España* (Madrid, 45 vols., 1785-1800), a most copious source of documentary information on the economic policy followed in Spain from the reign of Philip II. to the author's own time. In his *Discurso Proemial* (preface), Larruga puts forward his own views as a steadfast opponent

to the interfering and meddlesome spirit which animated Spanish princes and statesmen since the accession of the House of Austria ; he lays great stress on the necessity of basing economic reasoning on accurate and extensive knowledge of facts. E. ca.

LASSALLE, FERDINAND (1825-1864), born at Breslau, the most conspicuous amongst the founders of the social democratic party in Germany. An able and brilliant man, he earned notoriety at an early age in connection with a social scandal, was conspicuous for his energy as an agitator and the vigour of his defence in repeated political prosecutions, and was killed at thirty-nine in a duel. His speculative activity, which was considerable, was devoted rather to general social philosophy and constitutional jurisprudence than to abstract economics, in which his views coincide generally with those of RODBERTUS or MARX, and have little originality. His earliest controversial pamphlet (1849) is his defence on his trial for incitement to resist the unconstitutional collection of taxes. In 1857 he published a treatise *Die Philosophie Herakleitos dargestellt,* reflecting the Hegelianism which underlay his own political philosophy. In 1859, *Franz von Sickingen,* a drama of the Peasant Revolt, indicated an approach to a less ideal attitude towards the social problems of his own generation, and a pamphlet on *The Italian War* further emphasised his growing absorption in the German revolutionary movement. Writings on constitutional and social philosophy followed, including the important *System of Acquired Rights* (*Das System der erworbenen Rechte.* Brockhaus, Leipzig, 1861). In 1862 he plunged deeper into burning economic and industrial questions in his *Working Men's Programme.* In this and in repeated similar utterances he combated the individualist philosophy, and the "laissez faire" political doctrine which the "Manchester school" had founded on abstract economics, asserting, against their "policeman's idea" of the state, the organic conception of the state as "the unity of individuals in an ethical whole," . . . furnishing individuals with an indefinite variety of "means for attaining a degree of culture, power, and freedom that would be to every one of them as individuals absolutely unattainable." He insisted that "by an iron and inexorable law . . . under the domination of supply and demand, the average wages of labour remain always reduced to the bare subsistence which, according to the standard of living of a nation, is necessary for maintenance and reproduction," that the preaching of "self-help" was idle in the face of the efficiency of consolidated capital, and produced only "the repulsive caricature of working men with working men's means and employers' minds," and that the only avenue towards freedom for the wage-earning class lay through the application of its political power to the employment of the credit of the state in furnishing capital for productive enterprises to be carried on by democratic associations of workers. s. o.

In February 1863 Lassalle was invited by the Central Leipzig Committee to summon a general congress of the working men of Germany to meet in that city for the purpose of preparing a programme of labour agitation. He published an *Open Letter of Reply*, in which he dwelt on what he called the iron or " brazen law" (*chernes Gesetz*) of wages, already laid down by Turgot and Ricardo, but which he stated in an exaggerated form — namely, that the remuneration of the labourer can never differ much from the minimum regarded in any state of society as necessary for the maintenance of his life and the continuation of his family. Hence he infers that the workman is entirely excluded from the benefits of the growing productivity of labour which accompanies the progress of civilisation. To improve his position he must get rid of the *entrepreneur*, and become himself a capitalist. And, to this end, productive associations of workmen must be founded, and the government must supply them with the capital, or credit, necessary for their operations.

In the same year Lassalle opened a correspondence with Rodbertus, hoping to win his co-operation ; but, though their ultimate aims were similar, no argument could convince Rodbertus that the plan of productive associations with state credit would do any real good, nor any importunity induce him to admit that the socialists should be a political as well as an economic party.

In 1864 Lassalle published his *Herr Bastiat-Schulze von Delitzsch, der ökonomische Julian*, a clever but somewhat coarse production, in which he attacked Schulze-Delitzsch, an honourable and useful man, for the principles he had borrowed from Bastiat, and denounced his system of co-operation as an utterly insufficient solution of the labour problem, expounding at the same time his own views and vindicating his practical proposals. In this book, which had for second title *Capital and Labour*, occurs the celebrated passage in which he ridicules the "abstinence" theory of profit in what Böhm - Bawerk calls " his tumultuously eloquent, but absurdly rhetorical way." "The profit of capital," he says, "is the wage of abstinence ! Happy, even priceless expression ! The ascetic millionaires of Europe ! Like Indian penitents or pillar saints they stand : on one leg, each on his column, with straining arms and pendulous body, and pallid looks, holding a plate towards the people to collect the wages of their abstinence. In their midst, towering up above all his fellows as head penitent and ascetic, the Baron Rothschild ! This is the condition of society ! How could I ever so much misunderstand it !" (See Böhm - Bawerk's *Capital and Interest*, Eng. tr. by W. Smart, p. 277.)

Lassalle's principles have not continued to find favour with the German social democrats ; they have been supplanted by those of Karl Marx, who is now the undisputed oracle of the party. These two writers are in several respects contrasted. Lassalle was patriotic in his sentiments ; at the time of the Italian war he had called on Prussia to take the opportunity of breaking with Austria and establishing German unity ; "gross-Deutschland *moins les dynasties*" was his programme. Marx was cosmopolitan, and inspired the German socialists with the international idea. Lassalle was idealistic, and appealed to social justice. By Marx the necessity and nature of the predicted revolution were founded on the laws of the material development of society, as he conceived them. Lassalle was a believer in the ability and duty of the state to interfere for the protection of the working class against capital, and to introduce the new era which he regarded as about to open. Marx rejected the help of the existing state, and looked for a direct transformation through democratic force of the whole organisation of society.

Lassalle is said to have shown himself an original thinker by his work in the field of jurisprudence, but he is certainly not such in economics. He derived his principles, with eclectic freedom, from the English economists, from Louis Blanc, or from Rodbertus and Marx ; the last, indeed, asserted that all the general theoretical propositions in his works had been borrowed from his (Marx's) published writings, and that he had not always understood them aright.

It was as an agitator that Lassalle was really great ; of the names *Denker* and *Kämpfer* written on his tomb, he deserves the latter much more than the former. He created the German labour movement, and gave to it in its early days much of his own fire and energy. He also stimulated the growth of state socialism ; it is thought by some that he influenced in this direction the views of Bismarck, who admired his talents and enjoyed his conversation. All must admit that he rendered at least one permanent service—that of fixing the attention and interest of all classes of the population on what is known as the social question. There was much that was unsound alike in his intellectual and moral character ; he was more showy than solid, inordinately vain and arrogant, and somewhat theatrical in his public manifestations, and had little self-control or moral scruple ; but he was true to the cause he took in hand, and fearless in its advocacy ; and his action on his followers, though misleading, was not degrading.

[The best edition of his collected writings is that begun in 1892 by E. Bernstein. His letters to Rodbertus have been separately published, with a preface by Prof. Wagner. One of the best biographies of him is that by G. Brandes, a Dane, which has been translated into German—*F. Lassalle, ein litterarisches Charakter-bild*, 1877 ; 2nd ed. 1879. English readers will find a full and trustworthy account of him and of his political activity in *German Socialism and Ferdinand Lassalle*, by W. H. Dawson, 1888. Mr. George Meredith's *Tragic Comedians* is founded on the story of Lassalle's life, and a short biography of him is prefixed to the novel in the edition of 1892.

In the present sketch Diehl's article in the *Handwörterbuch der Staatswissenschaften* and Plener's in the *Allgemeine Deutsche Biographie* have also been consulted, and the former largely used. See also Bonar's *Philos. and Pol. Econ.*, 1893.—Rae, *Contemporary Socialism*.] J. K. I.

LASTRI, MARCO (18th century). A Tuscan abbé and writer. For students of economic and statistical sciences his researches on the population of Florence are important as an early collection of statistics. Lastri worked through the baptismal registers of San Giovanni, Florence, and collected a long list of baptisms (1451-1774) from which, by calculating the proportion between births and population, he endeavoured to estimate the population of the commune of Florence. The researches of Lastri, which are based on sound statistical information, and permeated with a good knowledge of the literature of the subject, were continued by Zuccagni Orlandini down to the present century, when, in 1818, a system of civil registration was introduced into Tuscany and a regular census commenced.

Ricerche sull' antica e moderna popolazione di Firenze, per mezzo dei registri del battistero di San Giovanni, dal 1451 al 1774.—Florence, Cambiagi, 1785.

[Salvioni, *La Statistica storica*, in the *Rassegna Nazionale*, Florence, 1885.] U. R.

LATHES (of Kent), a very old division of the county, perhaps representing shires existing at the time of the heptarchic kingdom of Kent. The six lathes or "lests" found in Domesday do not quite correspond with the five modern districts of the same name. Three or more hundreds go to make a lathe, which, like the riding of Yorkshire and Lincolnshire, and unlike the rape of Sussex, was a judicial division, with a court higher in dignity and power than that of the hundred, lower than that of the county. The name of lath is found also applied to a court held for the management of Romney Marsh.

[Stubbs, *Const. Hist.*, i. 100.—Ellis, *Introd. to Domesday*, i. 178.—Hasted, *Hist. of Kent*, i. cxiii. For Romney Marsh, see Hasted, iii. 535.—Palgrave, *English Commonwealth*, p. 101.] E. G. P.

LATIFUNDIUM, a word used by Pliny and a few other classical authors to denote a large landed property, estate, or farm. It is not to be confused with the *latus fundus* of the *gromatici* (see TERRITORIUM). The effects produced by the proprietorship of large extents of the soil of Italy falling into a few hands are discussed by J. E. T. Rogers in his *Industrial and Commercial Hist. of Eng.*, p. 248, but the same subject is far more satisfactorily dealt with by Dr. Cunningham in his *Growth of English Industry*. Neither author has, however, given any measure of the excess to which this system had run under the Roman Empire, although the former quotes the well-known passage in Pliny's *Natural History*, xviii. 7 : *Verumque*

confitentibus latifundia perdidere Italiam, jam vero et provincias. Sex domini semissem Africæ possidebant cum interfecit eos Nero princeps.

Pliny here asserts that six persons owned half of the province of Africa—the modern Tunis—meaning, no doubt, the part known as Zeugitana, a region so fertile that its plains furnished Rome with its principal supply of grain. There may be exaggeration in the passage, but, roughly estimating Zeugitana at 8000 square miles, and assuming that an unusual proportion was waste, we find that each owner must have possessed some hundreds of square miles of corn-producing land. This would seem scarcely credible were it not for Seneca's words : *amnes magni, magnarumque gentium termini, usque ad ostium a fonte vestri sunt. Hoc quoque parum est nisi latifundiis vestris maria cinxistis.*

These words, though somewhat rhetorical, show that *latifundium* is, in truth, a term which belongs to geography rather than to land-surveying. Such tracts were cultivated by organisations controlling large bodies of men, originally slaves, later either slaves or serfs. The disadvantages of slave labour are shown in Pliny's words, *coli rura ab ergastulis pessimum est.* Whatever opinions may be held as to the relative merits of large and small farming generally, there can be no doubt that cultivation on the scale of the *latifundia*, by so notoriously inefficient a means as slave labour, must have been wasteful in the extreme.

This bad system, which prevailed in Italy as well as in the provinces, grew up, as Dr. Cunningham states, through the dying out, under the pressure of many wars, of "the old type of Roman citizen, who cultivated his own land and also fought in the armies of the republic." "Some," he adds, "were killed off, and many more were utterly impoverished, so that the old system of proprietary cultivation was superseded by the *latifundia* cultivated by dependants." It thus appears probable that when Pliny charges the system with ruining Italy, he points no less at the wastefulness of the slackened cultivation, which the surveillance of a single master could never render energetic, than at the loss of a sturdy race of free peasants who tilled the soil and defended their native country. The Licinian Rogations of 367 B.C., by limiting estates and insisting on the partial use of *free* labour, show how early these bad effects were felt.

The growth of this vast greed of land is described by Mommsen (vol. ii. pp. 397, 398, and vol. iii. pp. 427, 428). He treats specially of the *latifundia* in the second part of his *History of the Provinces*, pp. 333-334.

[Pliny, *Hist. Nat.*, xviii. 4, 7.—Seneca, *Epist.*, 88, 89.—Th. Mommsen, *Hist. of Rome*, translated by Dickson, Lond., 1868.—Fustel de Coulanges, *La Gaule Romaine.*] R. H.

LATIMER. HUGH (1472-1555). Latimer lived at a most interesting period in English history. The son of a yeoman, he rose to take a prominent position in his university (Cambridge) and the church, and he had ample opportunity of observing the changes which were going on in every rank of society and in many parts of the country. His views on economic as on other subjects are contained in his *Sermons*, and are either introduced by way of illustration, or are covered with fervid rhetoric like that of the Hebrew prophets denouncing the evils of their day. It was in this spirit that he attacked the progress of ENCLOSURES, and the proceedings of landlords who enhanced their rents. But his remarks on the coinage show that he understood the evils of a debased currency much more clearly than some of the professed financiers of his time, and that he was by no means a mere rhetorician, but a man who had thought carefully on the topics on which he spoke so forcibly. In this view, there seems to be considerable probability in the opinion put forward by Miss LAMOND, in her edition of the *Discourse of the Common Weal of this Realm of England*, that Latimer is the original of the doctor in that dialogue, and that the views expressed by Pandotheus may be attributed to him. His justification of competition is the only point in which the doctor goes beyond Latimer's known views, but this is not really inconsistent with the bishop's opinions so far as known.

[*Sermons* (Parker Society).—*Discourse of Common Weal of Realm of England*. Introduction, xxi.]

w. c.

LATIN UNION (amounts in francs converted as 25 = £1). This name designates the monetary union organised in 1865 between France, Belgium, Italy, Switzerland, and (1868) Greece. Its originators and many of its leaders have continually had in view a greater international union that would eventually include the leading powers of Europe and accomplish some of the advantages that a uniform monetary system would bring. With these propagandist ends in view it may be questioned whether the name was well chosen, and whether the term "Latin" has not been the means of keeping out other nations than those of the Latin peoples. At all events, in the twenty-six years since Greece joined there have been no new members admitted. The union exists for purposes of maintaining a uniform and interchangeable coinage circulation among the five states which compose it, according to its treaty stipulations and the regulations adopted by its various conferences. Its basis is the French monetary system as established by the law of 7 Germinal An XI. (1803), with the franc composed of five grammes of silver nine-tenths fine as its unit. Subsequent treaties have altered the theoretical importance of this original decision, and have modified the real basis considerably.

In the four countries that organised the union there existed already for many years a similar coinage system, patterned more or less after the French system, and providing for full legal-tender gold and silver coins. Though no formal agreement existed, the coins of one of these countries circulated freely in the others. During the period immediately following the great gold discoveries in California and Australia, gold came freely to the mints which had a bimetallic basis. Public opinion feared a deluge of gold. A tendency to hoard silver and to underestimate gold made itself felt. Gold fell slightly in value. Silver coins began to disappear, especially the five-franc pieces, and a dearth of small change in silver coins, which were also full value silver and not token coins, was manifest. Some measure to protect silver was necessary. Switzerland was the first to act. By law of 31st January 1860 made the five-franc piece instead of the franc her monetary unit, and reduced all smaller silver coins to token coins by making them $\frac{800}{1000}$ fine. Italy, by law of 24th August 1862, took a similar course, except that she reduced the fineness of only the franc, fifty centimes and twenty centimes pieces to $\frac{835}{1000}$ fine. Finally a French law of 24th May 1864 reduced the half-franc and twenty centimes pieces to $\frac{835}{1000}$. Belgium alone maintained the old $\frac{9}{10}$ standard for all her silver coins, and of course she suffered most from the changes that were taking place. She therefore was the first to propose a remedy, though the time was ripe in other countries also, because three different standards of fineness for the small coins existed, and they did not circulate freely in all four countries as of old; commerce felt the strain; bankers' premiums became a disturbing element. Moreover, a kilogram of silver ($\frac{9}{10}$ fine) was now worth 200 francs (£8) in Belgium, 185·55 francs (£7 : 8 : 5¼) in France and Italy, and only 177·77 francs (£7 : 2 : 2½) in Switzerland. Belgium proposed that delegates from all the four countries having the franc for their basis should meet in Paris to discuss some measure for united action. The other three governments accepted, and the conference thus called ended its labours by signing the first Latin Union Treaty on 23rd December 1865. Ratifications were exchanged at Paris, 19th July 1866, and it went into effect 1st August 1866.

The treaty only affected gold and silver money, and in general provided as follows: (1) for coinage of gold $\frac{9}{10}$ fine in coins of the denominations of 100, 50, 20, 10, 5 francs with specified weight for each, proportional to 1·61290 grammes for the five-franc gold piece; (2) for coinage of following silver coins, the five-franc piece $\frac{9}{10}$ fine, 25 grammes in weight; pieces of 2, 1, ½, ¼ francs based on one gramme of silver for the twenty centimes piece, $\frac{835}{1000}$ fine. The legal tolerance and size was also prescribed for each coin. All token coins not made according to these regulations were ordered to be withdrawn from circulation before 1st January 1869, except the Swiss two- and one-franc pieces coined in conformity to the law of 31st January 1860. All gold coins and the silver five-franc pieces were made legal tender in the public treasuries of all the states of the union so long as the effigies originally stamped on them had not disappeared, nor their weight been reduced by wear below ½ per cent for the gold coins, and 1 per cent for tolerance of the silver coins after deducting legal tolerance. The small silver coins were made legal tender for payments not exceeding fifty francs within the state in which they were coined, and were to be received without limit by the public treasuries of the state that coined them when presented by its citizens. The same coins must be accepted by the public treasuries of other states in payments not exceeding one hundred francs. The token coins were to be redeemed at any time at their nominal value, in gold or silver five-franc pieces, by the issuing state, when presented in amounts not less than one hundred francs by another state or by private parties, and this clause to continue in force for a period of two years after expiration of treaty. The total amount of subsidiary coins (2, 1, ½, ¼ franc) issued by any state shall not exceed a sum equal to six francs per inhabitant. This sum, estimated not according to actual, but probable population at date of expiration of treaty, was fixed at 239,000,000 (£9,560,000) francs for France, 141,000,000 (£5,640,000) for Italy,[1] 32,000,000 (£1,280,000) for Belgium, and 17,000,000 (£680,000) for Switzerland; these figures to include the coins already issued by France under law of 1864, estimated at 16,000,000 (£640,000); by Italy under law of 1862, estimated at 100,000,000 (£4,000,000); by Switzerland under law of 1860, estimated at 10,500,000 (£420,000). The states agreed to furnish each other annually full information respecting their coinage and monetary condition. Any state might enter the union thus formed by simply accepting the gold and silver coinage system provided for in the treaty. The treaty was made to run for a period of fifteen years, and if notice for its termination was not given by any contracting state one year before the expiration of this term, it would continue in force for a further period of fifteen years, and so on from period to period of fifteen years each. Greece notified the union in 1868 of her adherence to the terms of the treaty, but she was not able to coin money at once, and did not, in fact, become a member of the union until 1876. The extraordinary events in Italy in

1866, and in France in 1870-71, causing a forced circulation of paper money for a time, interfered somewhat with the satisfactory development of the union. Of greater moment, however, was the change that soon took place in the value of silver. In the two years following 1866 the five-franc piece was an over-valued coin, and almost disappeared from circulation. In 1867, however, eighteen states, assembled in international conference at Paris, expressed themselves in favour of a single gold standard, and the great rush for gold commenced. Holland and Germany began to unload great quantities of silver on the Latin union, thus withdrawing its gold until general alarm was felt. Especially in Switzerland did this remelting and exchange process take place. The coinage of all four states, however, showed abnormal increase in output of five-franc pieces in the year 1873. Preliminary preventive measures were taken by France and Belgium independently of the union, and a new conference was called, which assembled in January 1874. At this conference Belgium reported that her coinage of five-franc pieces since 1866 had amounted to 463,000,000 francs (£18,520,000), of which 111,000,000 (£4,440,000) were coined in the year 1873; France had a total of about 400,000,000 (£16,000,000), and in 1873 had coined 154,000,000 (£6,160,000); Italy in a total of 160,000,000 (£6,400,000) for past five years, 42,000,000 (£1,680,000) in 1873. Belgium had already suspended coinage of five-franc pieces by law of 18th December 1873; France had limited it by ministerial decree (1873), first to 280,000 francs (£11,200) a day, and then to 150,000 francs (£6000); Italy had lowered her tariff in order to make coinage of five-franc pieces less profitable. A general proposal, therefore, to sanction these acts and for the future to limit the coinage of five-franc pieces met with universal favour. A new treaty, dated 31st January 1874, provided that coinage of five-franc pieces for the year 1874 should not exceed 120,000,000 francs (£4,800,000) divided as follows : France, 60,000,000 (£2,400,000); Italy, 40,000,000 (£1,600,000); Belgium, 12,000,000 (£480,000); Switzerland, 8,000,000 (£320,000); these figures to include the outstanding " bons de monnaie " (mint certificates for bullion not yet coined), amounting to 40,000,000 francs (£1,600,000) for France, Belgium, and Italy. Switzerland declined to coin any at all. Italy was accorded some special privileges on account of large silver reserve in bars held by her national bank, which wished to profit by coining it at once before the price of silver experienced a further fall, and also for the recoinage of a large number of old Bourbon silver coins which the Italian government was withdrawing from circulation. The new treaty put a restriction on the right of admission of new parties to the union, making it conditional on consent of all contracting

[1] After the war of 1866, when the territory of the kingdom of Italy was enlarged, this quota was raised to 156,000,000 francs (£6,240,000) by an Italian law of 1868, which was later approved by the other states of the union.

parties. The Bank of France and the National Bank of Belgium had closed their doors to the five-franc pieces, and the new treaty expressed the desire that they, as well as the public treasuries, should accept them. They agreed in letters to their respective governments to do so for one year. A better arrangement was adopted whereby statistics and information concerning the monetary circulation in the states of the union could be obtained, as the clause to this effect in the treaty of 1865 had remained a dead letter. France now assumed the presidency of the union for purposes of publication of such information. It was further agreed to hold annual conferences at Paris.

The situation in January 1875, when the third conference met, was much the same. Silver had continued to fall in price, and the product increased. Switzerland favoured further limitation of coinage. France and Belgium preferred to continue the arrangement adopted for the year 1874, which was done, the banks of France and Belgium continuing their agreement also. However, in compliance with Italy's request for more latitude in her recoinage, and in order to keep all states on the same footing, each state was authorised to coin one-fourth more than its quota for 1874. Italy was granted some further favours in that she was permitted to put in circulation the 20,000,000 (£800,000) reserve already coined under agreement of 1874 and held by her national bank. Switzerland again voluntarily renounced a possible profit by refusing to coin at all. The wisdom of her course is shown by her better position in possible case of dissolution of the union as regards the liquidation clause which was later adopted.

The conference of 1876 decided to return to the old 120 millions (£4,800,000) limit adopted in 1874, and of this sum Greece was allowed a disproportional share, amounting to 12 millions (£480,000), to enable her to fall in line with the system of the union. The banks renewed their obligation.

In 1877 a still more radical change was accomplished without a conference by diplomatic correspondence, the contracting parties agreeing to entirely suspend the coinage of five-franc pieces. The outlook was not a hopeful one, and not until November 1878 did the states assemble in a new conference, to consider the knotty problems that presented themselves. The condition of the silver market was appalling; the relation of the two metals had undergone a greater change since the commencement of the union than had occurred for centuries. Paper money, for which the union made no provision, was a source of trouble in several of the states. The date for the expiration of the treaty was near at hand. Therefore the conference of 1878 decided to regulate silver coinage for the year 1879, and then to adopt a new treaty, to go into effect in 1880. As for 1879, Belgium, Greece, France, and Switzerland agreed to coin no five-franc pieces, but Italy insisted on being allowed a quota of twenty million francs, in order to issue new coins with head of her new king; this was granted, and all five states then agreed to issue no " bons de monnaie " during the year. The chief features of the new treaty were—(1) the suspension of coinage of five-franc pieces, until, by unanimous consent of the contracting parties, it should be resumed ; (2) a slight change in the apportionment of subsidiary coinage, still maintaining the six franc per inhabitant basis ; (3) a special clause respecting paper circulation in Italy, by which the Italian government agreed to annul all notes for less amounts than five francs, and the other states agreed to collect and return to Italy all her minor coins in their territory ; (4) special provision for the carrying out of Article 8 of treaty, providing for return of Italian coins, in which France was to be the banker from whom Italy was to redeem the same ; (5) the new treaty was to remain in force for six years (to 1st January 1886), but if no notice has been given one year in advance, it is to continue from year to year, in all events to remain in force one year after notice of its termination has been given. A liquidation clause was discussed, providing that, in case of dissolution, each state would redeem in gold its five-franc pieces held by the other states. This did not meet with much favour, and no action was taken until 1885. Switzerland and Italy wished foreign coins to be made legal tender in France and Belgium, not merely in public treasuries, but also for individuals, as had long been the case in their territories, but France refused. The banks of France and Belgium, however, renewed their obligation for the whole period of the new treaty. In the next few years Switzerland had so large a part of her coinage in foreign silver that she desired some agreement on the question of what would be done in case of dissolution. She, therefore, in 1884, gave notice that she wished to terminate the treaty at date of its expiration, but was willing to consider proposals for a new one. A conference met at Paris, 20th July 1885, and 6th November signed a new treaty, which Belgium did not adhere to until a month later (12th December). No great change was made in arrangements adopted in 1878, except as regards the important liquidation clause, which caused the Belgian delegates to leave the conference. This clause provided that each state, in case of dissolution of the union, shall redeem from every other state of the union its five-franc pieces in five-franc pieces of the state presenting them, or in gold or convertible paper. Special provisions were made as follows : — France shall pay Switzerland all in gold, or in Swiss five-franc pieces, her gold payment, however, not to exceed 60,000,000 francs (£2,400,000). Italy's maximum payment in gold or Swiss five-franc pieces to Switzerland shall be 20,000,000 francs (£800,000), and her maximum paper obligation 30,000,000 francs (£1,200,000). Switzerland had coined little silver, and thus received the most favourable conditions in the liquidation clause. Between France and Italy it was agreed that the maximum of balance to be settled by either party should be 200,000,000 francs (£8,000,000). In the special agreement, by which Belgium adhered to the treaty, it was provided that she should redeem only one-half of her five-franc pieces held by France, but that in order that France might dispose of the remainder in commerce, Belgium agreed not to alter her monetary system within five years of date of dissolution without being prepared to redeem the other half of her five-franc pieces in gold, and, furthermore, she guaranteed to pay in gold for all over 200,000,000 francs (£8,000,000) of the total balance held by France. The maximum payment by Belgium to Switzerland was fixed at 6,000,000 francs (£240,000), but in case a balance remained, the same agreement, not to change monetary system, held good as towards Switzerland. The banks of France and Belgium again agreed to receive all five-franc pieces during the period of new treaty. The new treaty was made to run for six years, until 1st January 1891, and then from year to year, in the same manner as provided in the treaty of 1880. This treaty is still in force (1896), and the chief question that has come up in the intervening period has had to do with the continual flow of Italian small silver into Switzerland and France, and the consequent dearth of change in Italy, owing to the disarranged financial condition of that country. So great was this dearth of small change in the summer of 1893, that private firms were compelled to issue credit coupons to meet their needs, and in many cases postage stamps were used as money. A conference was called in October 1893 to partially revise the treaty of 1885. The Italian subsidiary coinage question was the sole object of discussion, and an agreement was signed by which the other states are to withdraw from circulation all Italian coins of the denominations of 2, 1, ½, and ¼ francs within four months after exchange of ratifications, and to receive the same no more in their public treasuries. The coins thus withdrawn are to be held in 500,000 franc (£20,000) lots at the disposition of the Italian government, bearing interest at 2½ per cent from the day that notice has been sent to Italy that the coins are at her disposal. The interest shall be 3½ per cent from tenth day after coins are sent until day of cash payment, and in no case shall this delay exceed three months. One-half of the value of such holdings shall be redeemed in gold pieces, in denominations of 40 francs or over, and the balance in government paper. France was charged with the executive management of details of this operation. The Italian government agreed to redeem a minimum of 45,000,000 (£1,800,000) during the first four months after ratification of agreement, and a minimum of 35,000,000 (£1,400,000) every three months afterwards until the whole sum is redeemed. After Italy has taken back all her small money she ceases to be obliged to receive in her public treasuries the subsidiary coins of other states of the union, according to terms of Act 7 of treaty of 1885, and may take measures to prevent her coins leaving her territory, as may the other states take prohibitory measures against their entrance into their own.

Looking back over the history of the Latin Union, no one will deny that it has played an important rôle in the monetary affairs of Europe, far as this rôle may be from the bright dreams of many of its founders and warmest supporters. It has not only fixed the monetary policy of five great nations, and thus affected the interests of 75,000,000 people, but has also influenced the monetary systems of Roumania, the South American States of Colombia, Ecuador, Venezuela, Peru, and Chili, Spain, Austria-Hungary, and Finland, all of which at one time or other had the same system, or issued coins that would circulate in the union, thus raising the population affected to at least 150,000,000. If external forces have been too strong for the union, and it has in self-defence been compelled to restrict its bimetallic principle, this fact has not been due in any way to an unfriendly attitude towards silver, as the record of its coinage will testify. From 1866 to 1894 the total coinage of gold has been a little over three billion francs (£120,000,000), and that of silver ($\frac{9}{10}$ fine) in five-franc pieces, one billion and a half (£60,000,000). It has been said that several of the states of the union would prefer to be free again if it were not for fear of the difficulties of liquidation in case of dissolution. Though occasional proposals for dissolution have been brought up in one or two parliaments, this desire does not in any way meet with general approval in any one of the countries concerned. The advantages of international interchange of money are too great for any country of the union to wish to do away with them. In its most troubled periods the difficult problems that the union has had to meet have always been satisfactorily adjusted, and the most serious of these have had to do with more or less unwarranted suspicion of the future.

Somewhat similar experiments in international monetary unions may be profitably studied by comparing the history of the Austrian-German monetary union founded in 1857 between Austria and the states of the German ZOLLVEREIN, and the Scandinavian union organised in 1875 between Denmark, Norway, and Sweden, and still in force.

[*Procès-Verbaux des conférences de l'union latine*, Livres jaunes, 1874-94.—*Systèmes monétaires des différents pays*, 1 fascicule. Paris, Imp. nationale, 1888. —Fauchille, "L'union monétaire latine." *Annales de l'école libre des sciences politiques*, October 1886.—Van der Rest, *L'union monétaire latine, son origine et ses phases diverses*, Revue de Droit international, vol. xiii. Brussels, 1881, pp. 5-21 and 268-280.—Bamberger, *Die Schicksale des lateinischen Münzbundes*, Berlin, 1885. Translated into French by R. G. Levy, "Le métal-argent à la fin du xix.⁰ siècle," Paris, 1894.— *Report from Select Committee on depreciation of Silver*, 1876. Appendix, pp. 84, 85, 92-99.—De Parieu, *L'union monétaire de la France*, etc., Revue contemporaine, October 1866.—Serrigny, *Observations critiques sur la convention monétaire du 23 décembre 1865*, Revue critique de législation et de jurisprudence, vol. xxxiv. 1869.—*Report, Gold and Silver Comm.*, 1886.] S. M'C. L.

LAUDERDALE, EIGHTH EARL OF (1759-1830). James Maitland, afterwards Earl of Lauderdale, entered parliament in 1780. He was appointed, in December 1787, one of the managers of Warren Hastings' impeachment. He succeeded to his Scotch peerage in 1789, and in the following year was elected a representative Scotch peer. As a politician he boxed the political compass. One of the founders of the "Friends of the People," he lived to oppose the Reform Bill of 1832. In private life he is described as violent tempered, shrewd, and eccentric. The same capricious character marked his literary work.

In 1804 he published an *Inquiry into the nature and origin of Public Wealth and into the means and causes of its Increase*, Edinburgh, 8vo (trans. into French by E. Lagentie de Lavaïsse, Paris, 1808), 2nd edition, greatly enlarged, 1819, 8vo, wherein—after an acute criticism of the view that labour affords an unvarying standard of value—a theory of value, as depending upon the interaction of demand and scarcity, and the influence of the distribution of wealth upon the direction which labour **takes**, is very clearly brought out. In his enforcement of the truth of Bacon's dictum, that money like muck is no good unless it be spread, he supplied considerations to some extent lacking in *Wealth of Nations* (see DISTRIBUTION); but the usefulness of the book is marred by captious criticisms of the principle of DIVISION OF LABOUR (*q.v.*), and by eccentric views on finance, which found further expression in *Three letters to the Duke of Wellington . . . wherein the nature and tendency of a Sinking Fund is investigated, and the fallacy of the reasoning by which it has been recommended explained*, London, 1829, 8vo. Saving and spending are the bad and good genii of Lauderdale's economy, and he maintains, with the utmost gravity, that a great extra expenditure is the most fertile means of increasing public wealth, and a sinking fund the most active means of diminishing it. In treating of the sources of wealth Lauderdale claims for capital a place by the side of land and labour. Capital produces a profit, either from its supplanting a portion of labour which would otherwise be performed by the hand of man, or from its performing a portion of labour which is beyond the reach of the personal exertion of man to accomplish. To Lauderdale belongs the credit of having been the first to put forward a connected theory on the nature of profit, in the form of a theory, and not of scattered observations. See Böhm-Bawerk, *Capital and Interest*, Engl. trans., London, 1890, 8vo, bk. ii. ch. iii.—"The indirect productivity theories." Lauderdale's importance in the history of economics lies, not in his conclusions, but in the fact that he was the first in England to consider systematically the fundamental conceptions on which the science is based. In this respect alone he is in advance of Adam Smith. (In this connection, see Bagehot's *Economic Studies*, "Adam Smith and our modern economy.") Among numerous other pamphlets and published speeches, he wrote *The depreciation of the Paper Currency of Great Britain proved*, London, 1812, 8vo, and *Further Considerations on the State of the Currency*, etc., Edinburgh, 1813, 8vo. The Journal of the House of Lords contains eighty-six protests under his signature. He was one of the earliest to allow that capital is in itself productive, and is the result of abstinence.

[*Dictionary of National Biography*, vol. xxxv. p. 355.—*Introduction to the study of Political Economy*, by L. Cossa, trans. by L. Dyer, London, 1893.] H. E. E.

LAUREL, ENGLISH COIN. See GUINEA, INTRODUCTION AND RATING OF.

LAVELEYE, ÉMILE DE (1822-1892), born at Bruges, died at Liège, was a remarkable thinker, and his writings were brilliant in style. Unfortunately for his fame, being not only an economist but also a philologist, an historian, a student of law, a politician, and a moralist, he was scarcely able to fathom the depths of all the subjects he undertook. Absolutely sincere in mind, he allowed himself some inconsistencies of expression which he rolly admitted. At one time he frankly acknowledged himself a "socialist of the chair"; but towards the end of his life the disquieting spectacle of the progress of socialism appeared to draw him nearer to those whom earlier he had stigmatised as "orthodox economists."

His principal economic writings are—*Le Marché Monétaire et ses crises depuis cinquante ans*, 8vo, in which he announced himself in favour of the unity and monopoly of banks of issue. *Le socialisme contemporain*, 8vo, 1881; with essay on luxury, etc. (several editions have been published), in which he examined critically the doctrines of Rodbertus, Karl Marx, Ferdinand Lassalle, etc.; and *De la propriété et de ses formes primitives*, 8vo, 1873. He maintained that property was a civil institution, agreeing in this with John Stuart Mill. His last work was *Eléments d'économie politique*, 12mo, 1882, a text-book on the elements of the science. In monetary questions De Laveleye was a partisan of a double standard, and produced many works supporting bimetallism. He contributed to several periodicals of the day, among others to the *Revue trimestrielle*, to the *Libre recherche*, to the *Revue des deux Mondes*, and to this Dictionary the article on COMMUNE. All men of science admired his sincerity, the boldness with which he championed new ideas, his modesty, and his absolute truthfulness. These qualities gave his works an attractive power which won him many readers. The obituary notice of Emile de Laveleye, written by his pupil and successor in the chair of political economy at Liège, Professor Ernest Mahaim, in the *Economic Journal*, vol. ii., speaks of "the governing idea of his life as being found in the supremacy of justice. He was persuaded that the human race was marching toward an ideal of justice, an image of God, to which ultimately it would attain. He had faith in the boundless progress of mankind, and in the solidarity of all men ; and he discerned in the future a society of love, peace, and justice, bringing universal happiness. Emile de Laveleye is a great figure in the century that is passing away."

Professor Mahaim describes de Laveleye as an academic socialist. He believed in the frequent necessity of state intervention to secure the triumph of the common interest over particularist egoism. His criticism, in the *Contemporary Review*, of Mr. Herbert Spencer's *The Man versus the State*, disclosed how far he repudiated the "orthodox" credo. ". . . He often sent articles to English newspapers, amongst others to the *Times* and *Pall Mall Gazette*. . . . He had a great affection for England ; of its language he had perfect mastery ; and on its soil he counted many of the most distinguished politicians among his friends."   A. C. F.

LAVERGNE, LOUIS GABRIEL LÉONCE GUIL-HAUD DE (1809-1880), was born at Bergerac, and died at Versailles. Rural economy was his special study, and in 1850 he was appointed professor in this subject at the recently-founded *Institut Agronomique*. The suppression of this higher-grade school in 1852 closed his class. It should here be mentioned that at the re-establishment of the *Institut Agronomique* in 1876 he was replaced in the chair of rural economy ; but on this occasion illness broke off a course of lectures which were well attended and highly appreciated. Before 1848 he held several administrative positions, and represented the division of Lombez in 1846 as a deputy. The revolution of 1848 brought him some leisure, which he employed in the study of political economy, applying himself to agriculture, the subject in which his interests lay. In 1871 he was elected deputy for the department of La Creuse. In December 1875 he was appointed a life senator. Originally a constitutional monarchist, he courageously and unreservedly joined the republicans as soon as he ceased to believe in the possibility of the restoration of the monarchy. During the closing years of his life he declared himself in favour of the establishment of an import duty on grain. He considered that this duty would have countervailed the taxes imposed in France as compared with the countries whence the corn was imported. He sincerely believed that in doing this he did not derogate from those views on commercial liberty which he had always expressed, and appealed in

support of this opinion to the part he had taken in the campaign in favour of free-trade at the end of the reign of Louis Philippe.

In 1854 he produced his first important work, the *Essai sur l'Économie rurale de l'Angleterre, de l'Ecosse, et de l'Irlande*, 18mo. This work, which has reached its fourth edition, won for him admission to the Institute (Academy of Moral and Political Science). He collected, under the title *L'Agriculture et la population*, a series of articles which had appeared (1855-57) in the *Revue des deux Mondes*. The first edition appeared 1857, the second edition 1860-61, 18mo. In 1860 he sent to the press *Économie rurale de la France depuis 1789*, 4to, which has attained three editions. In the same year (1860) he published *Les Voyages d'Arthur Young en France de 1787 à 1789*, 2 vols., and *En Italie et en Espagne en 1787 et 1789*, 18mo. This work also appeared in 8vo, preceded by an introduction. The translations were made by M. H. T. Lesage, one of his old pupils at the *Institut Agronomique*. In 1863 he produced *Les assemblées provinciales sous Louis XVI.*, 8vo, a work which was highly thought of by Guizot. In the following year (1864) he published in the *Revue des deux Mondes* an article entitled, "Le Banque de France et les banques départementales," in which he declared himself in favour of local banks. Finally, in 1870, he published in Guillaumin's collection of contemporary economists and authors, *Les Économistes français du XVIII.ᵉ Siècle*, 8vo. The appreciation of all these works has considerably increased since it became known how conscientious the author's investigations were, and how careful he was that every statement he made should be strictly accurate.   A. C. F.

[The brilliancy of Lavergne's writings, the clearness of his style, his impartiality, and the correctness of his judgments, have been fully appreciated in the notice in the *Nouveau Dict. d'Écon. Pol.*, ed. Say et Chailley.]

LAVOISIER, ANTOÎNE LAURENT (1743-1794), was born at Paris ; his occupation as a farmer-general brought him to the revolutionary scaffold in the same city. "The Republic has need neither of *savants* nor of chemists," was the brutal and disreputable reply of Fouquier-Tinville, the public prosecutor, when an effort was made to explain to him the irreparable loss science would suffer through Lavoisier's death.

Endowed with very rare qualities of mind, Lavoisier excelled in all that he attempted. At once a financier, a farmer-general, a deputy, and a highly-placed official, his discoveries as a scientific man have immortalised his name ; but the time needed to complete his economic works was not granted him. Thus his work *De la richesse terri-toriale de la France*, remains unfinished—even a great part of that which once existed has disappeared. That portion of it which research has been able to recover is published in the first volume of *Mélanges d'économie politique* (1847), in the collection of Guillaumin, which also contains a fragment on *Les consommations de la ville de Paris*, and an *Essai d'arithmétique politique*. Count Roederer considered that the celebrated geometrician Lagrange, the intimate friend of Lavoisier, might have been the author of this.

A. C. F.

LAW. The influence of law on the economic well-being and trade of a country is dealt with under separate headings, of which the most important are enumerated here: *e.g.* Agency, Law of ; Allowance System ; Angarie, Droit d' ; Arbitration ; Arrangement, Deed of ; Articles of Apprenticeship ; Articles of Association ; Bankruptcy, Law and Administration ; Bequest, Power of ; Bill of Exchange, Law of ; Canon Law ; Civil Law ; Code Napoléon ; Combination Laws ; Commandite, Société en ; Companies, English and Scotch Law ; Conflict of Laws, Foreign, Domestic ; Conspiracy, Common-Law, Doctrine of ; Contract, Law of ; Copyright ; Corn Laws ; Courts of Law, England, Ireland, Scotland ; Descent of Property ; Domicil or Domicile ; Entail, Law of ; Factor, English Law ; Factor, Scots Law ; Factor's Acts ; Factory Acts ; Factory Laws in the United States ; Foreign Law in English Courts ; Foreign Traders and their Rights, History of ; Frauds, the Statute of ; Fraudulent Conveyance ; Fraudulent Preference ; Freehold, Legal ; Game Laws ; Gilbert's Act ; Government, Economic Effects of ; Government Regulation of Industry ; Grangers and Granger Laws ; Hire and Purchase Agreements ; Homestead and Exemption Laws of the United States ; Illegal Contract ; Interest and Usury ; International Law ; Intestacy ; Joint Stock Companies ; Labour Statutes ; Land, Law relating to ; Land Legislation, Irish ; Law Merchant ; Legislation, Elizabethan ; Lex Loci Contractus : Lien ; Limitation, Statutes of ; Liquor Laws ; Local Option ; Moratory Law ; Mortgage ; Negotiable Instruments ; Onerous Property ; Partnership ; Poor Law ; Poynings Law ; Pre-emption ; Primogeniture ; Principal and Agent ; Property ; Restriction on Labour ; Roman Law ; Settlement (Poor Law) ; Trades Unions ; Truck. The laws of political economy will be found described under their respective subjects.

LAW, JOHN (1671-1729), of Lauriston, was the son of James Law, an Edinburgh goldsmith. Condemned to death for killing Edward Wilson in a duel in London in 1694, the sentence was commuted for imprisonment, but an appeal being brought by one of Wilson's relatives, Law fled to Amsterdam, where he is said to have closely studied the operations of the bank (see BANKS, EARLY EUROPEAN). A pamphlet entitled *Proposals and Reasons for constituting a council of trade for Scotland* (1701) is sometimes attributed to him, but it appears to have been written by William PATERSON (*q.v.*), founder of the Bank of England (Saxe Bannister's *Life and Writings of Paterson*). In 1705 he submitted to the Parliament of Scotland a scheme for the establishment of a national bank, on lines indicated roughly in his pamphlet published the same year, *Money and Trade considered, with a proposal for supplying the nation with money*, Edinburgh, 4to ; 2nd edit. London, 1720, 8vo ; Glasgow, 1750, 8vo ; Somers' *Tracts*, London, 1809, 4to, vol. 13. His scheme, however, was rejected, partly through Paterson's influence. During the next few years he made frequent overtures to various European governments to undertake some of his financial projects. His proposal for a bank in France was submitted to the council on October 24, 1715, but though it received the support of the Duke of Orleans, it was rejected in the form suggested, owing to the influence of the Duc de Noailles. On May 20, 1716, letters-patent were issued to Law and his associates for the establishment of a Banque Générale. The capital of the bank was divided into 1200 shares of 5000 livres each, payable in four instalments, one-fourth part in specie, and three-fourths in state notes. Each shareholder had one vote for every five shares he held, and the bank regulations were to be decided upon by a general meeting of the shareholders. The bank was authorised to issue notes payable at sight and to the bearer, to discount bills, and to receive money on deposit. It was stipulated on Law's notes that they should be payable in coin of the same standard and weight as on the day of issue, a provision of great importance in the fluctuating state of the French currency. On April 10, 1717, Law's notes were ordered to be received in payment of taxes. Law now embarked on his famous scheme of colonisation, known as the Mississippi scheme. His *Compagnie de la Louisiane ou d'Occident* was incorporated in August 1717. It absorbed the company founded by Antoine Crozat in 1712, and also the Compagnie du Canada. The rights conferred upon the company extended over the territory drained by the Mississippi, the Ohio, and the Missouri. The directorate consisted of Law and six others. In August 1718 the company acquired the monopoly of tobacco for a payment of 4,020,000 livres. In December of the same year, the Banque Générale was converted into the Banque Royale, and its notes guaranteed by the king. The change was effected by the government purchase of the 1200 shares of which the capital of the bank had been formed. On these shares only the first fourth had been paid, 375 livres in specie, and 1125 livres in paper whose value was not more than the 400 livres at the current rate. The purchase was made at par and in silver. In 1719 the Compagnie d'Occident absorbed the Compagnie des Indes Orientales and the Compagnie de la Chine, taking the name of the Compagnie des Indes. It absorbed also the Compagnie d'Afrique and the Compagnie du Sénégal. In the same year the company obtained the control of the mint, undertook the payment of the national debt, and received the farm of the revenues. The bank and the company thus had complete control of the colonial trade of France, its currency, banking, and fiscal system. Speculation in the shares of the company and the bank reached a height unparalleled even in England in connection with the South Sea Bubble. Law introduced reforms, reduced taxation, promoted agriculture, industry, and in some directions encouraged free trade. It was confidently predicted that English trade both in the East and West Indies would be ruined. On 5th January 1720 Law became controller-general of the finances, and on 23rd February 1720 the Compagnie des Indes was united to the Banque Royale. But the reaction had already set in, and once the confidence of the public was disturbed, the downfall of Law's system was speedy and certain. Violent measures were resorted to in order to stop the drain of specie which began as soon as speculators exchanged the paper money for coin. The crisis was precipitated by the decree of 21st May 1720, gradually reducing the value of the bank-note to one-half. Panic followed ; the decree was rescinded a week later, but the bank suspended cash payments. Law was soon after obliged to leave France ; he died at Venice.

[There is a whole literature of books, etc., relating to Law and his "System." Refer to the histories of Lacretelle, Lemontey, Martin, Michelet, Voltaire, Louis Blanc, etc., and the following works :—Pierre Bonnassieux, *Les Grandes Compagnies de Commerce.* —P. A. Cochut, *The Financier Law : his Scheme and his Times.*—A. Macf. Davis, *An Historical Study of Law's System,* reprinted from the *Quarterly Journal of Economics* for April 1887.—Duhautchamps, *Histoire du Système des Finances pendant les années 1719 et 1720.*—Forbonnais, *Vue générale du Système de M. Law,* in his *Recherches et Considérations sur les Finances en France.*—J. Heymann, *Law und sein System.*—Jobez, *Une préface au Socialisme, ou le Système de Law et la chasse aux Capitalistes.*—Levasseur, *Recherches historiques sur le système de Law.*—Nicholson, *Treatise on Money,* and *Essays on present Monetary Problems.*—Pereire, *Enquête sur la Banque de France.*—Saint-Simon, *Mémoires.*—Thiers, " Hist. de Law " in *Revue Progressive,* 1826.—Vuitry, *Désordre des Finances et les excès de la spéculation.*—J. P. Wood, *Sketch of the Life and Projects of John Law of Lauriston.*— For Law's works, see *Œuvres de Jean Law,* Paris, 1790.—E. Daire, *Économistes Financiers du xviiie siecle.*—*Tafereel der Dwaasheid* [1] (Picture of Folly), 1720 (see TAFEREEL.)]

[See Life, *Dict. of Nat. Biog.* ; arts. on DUTOT ; MELON ; SYSTÈME.] W. A. S. H.

LAW MERCHANT means the law applicable to merchants as such and to mercantile transactions. " Mercantile transactions " mean buying in order to resell, and a " merchant " is one who makes a profession of these transactions. Generally speaking, the sphere of law merchant

¹ A remarkable collection of prints and pamphlets relating to Mississippi Scheme and Dutch East India Co.

is coextensive with what economists call EXCHANGE ; but transactions with regard to land are usually excluded, and in France even land-jobbing is so ; and although petty traders are as a rule included, it required in England a judicial decision, and in Leipzig (1682) a struggle, to include them ; and the German and Spanish codes still exclude trading artisans. Productive industries ancillary to exchange, though excluded by early writers like STRACCA and SCACCIA, are now always included in its scope, e.g. the construction of ships for traffic, and the manufacture of raw materials (French " Code de Commerce," art. 632, 633 ; German do., 271-275 ; Italian do., 3 ; Spanish do., 325): and it extends to important " distributive " questions,—thus, the wage-law of sailors (assigned in England to the Admiralty Division of the High Court), the bankruptcy of traders (of which our judge in bankruptcy—who is sometimes a judge of the Chancery, sometimes of the Queen's Bench Division—takes cognisance), and of companies (over which a special judge, usually the judge in bankruptcy, has jurisdiction), the relationship of partners (between whom our Chancery Division takes accounts), of factors and principals, assurers and assured (who usually come before our Queen's Bench Division), form substantial chapters of English books on Lex Mercatoria, like those of MALYNES (1622) and Beawes (1751), and of every commercial code. If " law merchant " does not fit exactly into any one of the three departments of political economy, neither does it quite conform to any one legal conception. Most law merchant may be regarded as a particular application of the general idea of contract, yet Malynes', Beawes', or Jacob's (1718) " Lex Mercatoria " combine the instruction contained in Tate's *Modern Cambist* or Inglis on *Book - keeping,* with what we should call legal instruction ; and the continental codes of commerce and the English Merchant-Shipping Acts still make book-keeping a statutory duty ; and further " bills of exchange," which at first blush look like the merest contracts, are overladen with minute arbitrary rules which the most ingenious jurist could not have deduced from the idea of contract. The truth is that " law merchant " was a body of rules laid down by merchants for regulating their conduct one with another. Economical definitions of exchange and juristic definitions of contract are derived from these rules, not *vice versa.* In all the great matters relating to commerce, legislators have copied, not dictated. The copying of merchant rules into the statute book, though literal, has not been without effect. On the one hand, mischievous rules, like those relating to apprenticeship, combination, and monopoly, might have lived for ever had they not as state laws been exposed to the search-lights of a fiercer criticism ;

on the other hand, good rules have been expressed in scientific language, and being thus expressed, have spread their influence over other walks of life. "Law merchant" has been by this means one of the chief incentives to progress. Its mode of action has been two-fold ; it has either contributed directly to the main stream, or it has run in a bed of its own making.

The first mode of action is the rule in ancient Rome and modern England. Thus the idea of agency was at first represented in Roman law by two actions only, that of "traders" ("institores" or "negotiatores") and of "ship-ping merchants" ("exercitores") ; later in the day these two actions were generalised, and the contract of agency was admitted as valid. And here is an instance of incorporation without generalisation. The "laws of the Visigoths" (xi. iii. 2), which were the western substitute for Justinian's Digest, enacted that transmarine "negotiatores" should carry their own judge with them, a custom followed by mediæval merchants, who were invariably accompanied by some travelling judge called "consule sul mare," "Hansgraf," "Kurt," etc. Some mercantile usages, however, existed side by side of the codes, like dialects by the side of civilised speech, e.g. the Rhodian sea-laws, which date back to classic Greece, and the principles of Sociétés en Commandite (see COMMANDITE, SOCIÉTÉ EN), which anticipate the latest com-pany law (Silberschmidt's Die Commenda, etc., 1884). But this collateral existence of law merchant is a rare feature in Roman law.

Conversely during the middle ages, as upon the continent to-day, exclusion is the rule, incorporation the exception. "The grandeur and historical significance of the mediæval merchant is that he created his own law out of his own needs and his own views," writes Goldschmidt. This creative task was twofold. He had to create his own courts and his own jurisprudence.

(i) MEDIÆVAL COURTS were territorial, so that the traveller or merchant, the terms were once almost synonymous, had to carry his judge with him, or special courts had to be invented for him—just as there were special courts for ecclesiastics—or else he was beyond the pale of law. Mercantile courts may be divided, according to their constitution, into four kinds.

First, there was the gild type, whose most conspicuous development was witnessed in the Italian town. There, during the late 12th and 13th centuries, the system of having a special judge was borrowed by merchants at home from merchants abroad, and the "consule sul mare" became "consule del mare" ; and at the same time the demo-cratic and federalising tendencies of Italian institutions invested his character with a new importance. At that time gild, if "arte" may be so construed, federated with gild and formed some "curia mercatorum" or "curia maris" under the presidency of a consul, usually elected by those whose names were on the gild-register (matricola). Early in the 14th century and onwards, codes of customs, sometimes called "statuta," sometimes "consue-tudines," were drawn up within the gild in order to define the functions which its officials exercised. In the early "codes of the mer-chants" ("brevia mercatorum") these functions are mainly administrative ; the judicial element is meagre ; but in administering the famous "Consolat del mar" of Barcelona (circa 1370), which had grown out of earlier Italian and Spanish codes, and soon became a general maritime code for the western Mediterranean, the "consul of the sea" was administering one of the civilised codes of the world. The Pisan "consul of the sea" was, during the 13th and 14th centuries, the judge who administered the sea-codes of Pisa, which were the most highly developed sea-codes prior to the "consolat," and included matters in any way connected with the sea (Schaube, p. 140). But Pisans who were not members of the sea-gild could, if they chose, demur to his jurisdiction (p. 141). Whatever he was practically he was not at this date theoretically the commercial judge of Pisa. Barcelona rounded off the work which Pisa had just failed to complete. There, the town was a stronger power behind the gild than in Italy, and during the 14th century it had appointed the sea-consul. And behind the town stood the king of Aragon, who gave the sea-consul of Barcelona exclusive and compulsory juris-diction since 1347 in maritime, and since 1401 in all mercantile matters ("omnes causas civiles provenientes ex quibuscunque actibus mercan-tilibus ubicunque in terra et in mari," Schaube, p. 254). This was the first court of its kind ; and the example of Barcelona was followed in Montpellier (1463) and even Paris (1563), where the "curia maris" and "consul maris" had had an indigenous origin under the respective titles "Métier de l'eau," "Prévôt des marchands de l'eau." The courts of "the aldermen of the merchant" or "the merchant" in the foreign factories of the Hanseatic League, though interesting as an incident in the history of the consulate, played no part in the evolution of the commercial court.

The "fair-courts" of France, which are con-nected with the Italian institution of federated merchant gilds (see MEDIÆVAL FAIRS), only ripened into permanent commercial courts of some definite district in 1669 (Troyes), and Leipzig (1682) was the first instance of a similar development in Germany. They were general in England under the name PIEPOWDER (q.v.) courts ; but in the more important centres were, in and after 1353, overshadowed by the courts of the STAPLE (*q.v.*). These sat for the purpose of administering "law merchant" instead of "common law," and were composed of "the mayor of the staple" (who was annually re-eligible by "the commonalty" of local merchants), at least two "constables" (elected by the "commonalty" of local merchants), and two assessors (elected by "the merchants strangers"); officials of the city where and when they sat had to enforce their orders (27 Edward III. stat. ii. c. 21-24). A few years later (36 Edward III. stat. i. c. 7) their jurisdiction was limited, in the case of English merchants, to "pleas touching merchandise, and surety of merchandise between merchants." The mediæval "fair-courts" of France and Germany had practically the same constitution as the "staple courts"; and the modern French commercial courts are similarly composed of "président," at least two "juges" and "suppléants," all elected by the "commercial notables" (see NOTABLES COMMERÇANTS) of a district; and the decisions of these courts are enforced by the ordinary courts. The courts of the staple vanished with the staple in the 16th and 17th centuries, and at the same date piepowder courts fell into disuse. For two or three centuries they fashioned and administered the unwritten "law merchant" as it was understood in England.

Secondly, there was the municipal type, which flourished most in Germany. Thus Nürnberg became a "free city of the empire," where justice was dispensed by a nominee of the imperial representative ("Schultheiss") jointly with nominees of the town council ("Schöffen"). In 1313 the "Schultheiss" was subordinated to the Schöffen for the purposes of trade-disputes ("statuta de rebus venalibus"). After 1497 other town-law followed in the wake of trade-law, and the "Schultheiss" was nominated by the town council. In 1508 trade-law ("Kaufmannshandel") was again separated from the mass of town-law; appeal to the imperial tribunal being disallowed in trade disputes. Meanwhile, Lübeck and Hamburg, which had had a somewhat similar history, celebrated their freedom by adopting almost identical "water-law" in 1270 and 1299. This town-law was the chief nucleus of the law of the Hanseatic league. What is not an adaptation of Lübeck town-law in "Dat Hogheste Water-Recht" (or as it is miscalled "The Wisbuy Ordinances") is a translation of "The Rolls of Oléron and Judgments of the Sea"; and "Dat Hogheste Water-Recht" was, it is believed, the code of the league until the league's commercial "recesses" (1369 to 1614) superseded, or (far more usually) re-enacted it. These "recesses" are still more essentially town-law; they were issued exclusively by deputies

of the towns; they were inspired by Lübeck, the capital city of the league; and the only domestic judiciary referred to in them is "the council of the town," or simply "the town"; and that, although some of these towns contained a "shipowners' company" with "aldermen" (Recess 1591 art. 18 and 19). Yet the first sea courts of first instance are those of Hamburg (1623) and Lübeck (1655), neither of which developed into commercial courts until long after the latter were an accomplished fact in Nürnberg. It was not sea-law nor any court for sea-law which led to the institution of commercial courts in Germany, but "bourse" law and specifically "bank" law. In 1560 Nürnberg erected a bourse ("Herrenmarkt"); and as in London, Frankfurt, and elsewhere, its president ("Markts-Vorsteher") assumed disciplinary power over the brokers and factors connected with it. In 1621 the bank was started, and the "Markts-Vorsteher," together with five merchant deputies, were given exclusive cognisance of banking disputes which in 1624 were identified with mercantile disputes. Things, however, requiring "altiorem indaginem," or the examination of witnesses upon oath, were withheld from this tribunal until 1697, in which year it added to its old title "bank-court," a new title borrowed from the court of the fair at Botzen, namely, "mercantile court." Silberschmidt has conclusively traced the critical changes of 1621, and 1624, and 1697, if not of 1508, to an Italian origin. The mercantile court of Nürnberg was the first of its kind in Germany. In England, as in Nürnberg down to 1560, the town courts, in the absence of piepowder and staple courts, dispensed law merchant from the 12th and 13th centuries and onwards. The towns often represented the merchants politically; thus, when Edward I. wanted a tax on "merchandise" he got together deputies from forty-two towns (Stubbs' *Select Charters*, A.D. 1303). GILD MERCHANT is the most important economic attribute of town life; sometimes as at Preston it is the town (Hegel, i. p. 94). An elected judiciary is one of the commonest privileges of the earliest town charters. The towns are in the first instance called on to administer "law merchant" to foreign merchants under the "carta mercatoria" (Rymer's *Fœdera*, ii. 2, 747), and the Ipswich town-court set apart special days for administering "the law pypowdrous in time of fair and marine," "the law of merchandise and law of the sea" (*Black Book of the Admiralty*, ed. Travers Twiss, ii. p. 21-25). London, perhaps, had a separate court, "the court of the hustings," for mercantile matters (Hegel, i. 60); if so, it soon became a general civil court. No gild court ever exercised any important judicial duties in England (Gross, i. 113); so there was nothing to prevent English town courts from becoming fountains of law merchant like Lübeck or Nürnberg ; and perhaps if Marquardus instead of Lord Coke had been our 17th century jurist, we should learn that this was the case, but we have no proof of it. English town-courts, like the stannary courts for tinners in Cornwall, played a silent part in the growth of "law merchant."

Thirdly, there were central national courts. An appeal lay from the English staple courts to the chancellor (27 Edw. III. st. ii. c. 24), from the French fair courts at Troyes to the "parlement" at Paris. And there were national courts of first instance. The Arragonese code of 1266 ("Siete Partidas") mentions deputy admirals with judicial authority appointed by the king. In England the admiral was in the 14th century instructed by the king and council to appoint deputies "discreet in the ancient customs of the sea," "to exercise exclusive jurisdiction over maritime affairs" (*Black Book*, i. p. 3, 69), and to take the Rolls of Oléron as law. These deputies are the precursors of the modern judges of the admiralty division of the high court, who, however, lost their jurisdiction over maritime contracts before Lord Coke's time (2 Gallison's Reports, 398). The history of the French admiralty ran on similar lines down to 1790 ; the famous "Ordonnance de la Marine" 1681, which, along with the "Ordonnance de Commerce" of 1673, is the basis of the code of 1807, gave the deputy admiral (since 1554 called "admiralty judge") cognisance of maritime contracts ; in 1790 this power was taken from him, and was shortly afterwards vested in the tribunals of commerce.

Fourthly, we find voluntary arbitrative bodies. A commercial college was in 1485 established at Antwerp for this purpose. In England the arbitration of "grave and discreet merchants" blossomed into the short-lived and impotent insurance court of 1601 (see 43 Eliz. c. 12) ; and stockbrokers and underwriters, before being admitted, agree to submit their mutual differences to their respective committees ; agreements of this kind were first made binding in England in the case of "merchants and traders" only, in 1698 (9 & 10 Will. III. c. 15), as in France where at the present day these agreements are only valid if commercial. With these exceptions the control of the English exchange, in the city sense, over its members remains what it was in Frankfurt and Nürnberg at the close of the 16th century. Arbitration is the root of all law ; and the peculiarly lay constitution of the Austrian "Wechsel - Gerichte" or bill of exchange courts of 1717, and of the modern French commercial courts, somewhat ostentatiously proclaim this origin for law merchant.

To sum up this section—the commercial courts arose in consequence of some branches of commercial law—sea-law or bourse-law—breaking away from the other branches of civil law. The branch that broke away was at the time growing very quickly ; while the other branches were hardly growing at all.

(ii) MEDIÆVAL JURISPRUDENCE included such feudal barbarities as "ordeal of battle" and "compurgation," and took its tone from ecclesiastical prejudices which denounced the taking of interest upon capital, and whose spokesman, St. Chrysostom, wrote, "No Christian ought to trade, or if he did, he ought to be cast out of the Church" (Goldschmidt, p. 139). If then mercantile morality crystallised into laws, it might be expected that these laws would be animated by a very different spirit from that of the prevalent system of law. The characteristics of "law merchant" may be summed up under the following heads :

(*a*) It is non-national. It is part of the instinct of merchants to seek for points of agreement instead of difference with one another. How uncritical this instinct was may be illustrated by the odd details which pass from one code to another. Thus the 53rd chapter of the Consulat prescribes, as a scale for assessing damages, a compromise between that in Roman law and Oléron law. Pardessus regards this compromise as unique (II. 21), yet the very thing recurs in the "Coutumes d'Amsterdam," etc. (art. 33-34). The 54th chapter of the Consulat, in describing jettison, puts a speech into the captain's mouth ; this Thucydidean expedient is taken from the corresponding article (8) in the "Rolls of Oléron." Indeed, borrowing was so reckless that none knew whence they borrowed. Frenchmen claimed the "Rolls of Oléron" as French, Flemings as Flemish, Swedes as Swedish, Englishmen as English. The Consulat has been disputed property between Spain, Italy, and the south of France. In the 17th century the process is more deliberate, but is still non-national ; thus the opinions ("parere") of the "Markts-Vorsteher" in some German town circulated in other towns in Germany and Italy with an authority which recalls that of the "responsa prudentum." Even national unity which, in the 16th century, severed the wider unity which had prevailed for commercial purposes, has in modern times substituted a wider for a narrower unit ; thus it made the code of commerce of 1861 into a German code in reality as well as in name, and it turned the Sardinian code of commerce of 1842 into the first Italian code of 1865. And national supplemented by international agencies have quite recently produced what is almost an international code for preventing collision at sea (Phillimore's *International Law*, vol. iv. ch. 41), and for copyright. The Roman dream of an universal law has never wholly faded away. Indeed, jurists, forgetting that modern law is a new creation and not a reminiscence, have often overrated the influence of this dream upon the men of the market-place. The above-cited instances have nothing to do with Rome ; they are caused by infection not heredity.

(b) A common attribute of mercantile jurisprudence is that its procedure is milder against the person and stricter and quicker against the property of the delinquent. The making of contracts by part payment has passed from law merchant into general law (Pollock and Maitland's *History of English Law*, 1895, ii. 207, cp. Pertile, 4, 474). English land was first made liable for debts under "The Statute of Merchants," 1285, "The Statute of the Staple," 1353, and the statutes relating to deceased traders only (1807-33) ; and English bankruptcy from 1571 to 1861 applied only to persons who "used the trade of merchandise," "sought their living by buying and selling," and the like. Diderot's definition of bankruptcy : "Faillite est lorsque un marchand ou négociant se trouve hors d'état de remplir les engagements qu'il a pris relativement à son commerce ou négoce," still holds true of France, Italy, and every Romance nation. The lien of shipowners and bankers on what is consigned to them *quâ* bankers and shipowners is Roman, but is also rediscovered in the fair courts and sea courts of the middle ages ; and other special liens have been admitted into modern law. Code of Comm., Fr., 306-8 ; Ital., 508 ; Germ., 409 ; Span., 665, as to shipowners and to mercantile agents,—in Germany every trader has a lien against traders in respect of trade transactions —(Co. Comm., 313). As for speed, which is generally the excuse for detaching commercial from other actions, in ancient Athens commercial causes (ἐμπορικαὶ δίκαι) had to be despatched in a month, and a month is the average delay in deciding an action entered on Mr. Justice Matthew's recently instituted "Commercial Cause List."

(c) The fundamental characteristics of sale, contract, and status differ in mercantile and other civil law. A purchaser of goods in "open market" (see MARKET OVERT), including a London shop, has in England a good title against all the world, and if you add "unless the real owner restore his purchase money to the purchaser" and leave out the word "London," you have French, Italian, and Spanish law (Co. Civ., Fr., 2280 ; It., 709 ; Sp., 1955, 464 ; cp. Co. Comm., Germ., 306-8). This law is mediæval, not Roman, and contradicts the general civil law of modern Europe. A sale or pledge by mercantile agents not authorised to sell or pledge passes a good title to the goods under the English FACTORS' ACTS (1823-77, re-enacted 1889), which only generalise a mediæval and modern maritime law, and COMMERCIAL INSTRU-

MENTS (*q.v.*) when "negotiable," which means assignable at "law merchant," pass a similarly good title ; moreover, contracts embodied in them were assignable long before other contracts. It is a maxim of "law merchant" that a contract binds whether written or not ; and this is allowed in most commercial codes (Fr., 17 ; Germ., 317, 34, etc. ; It., 44 ; Co. Civ., Fr., 1341 ; It., 1341), and is enforced by extra-legal sanction on the London stock exchange (*Rules of the Stock Exchange*, Stutfield and Cautley, 1893, p. 39) : and merchants obtained the concession that the consideration for a guarantee need not be in writing ("Mercantile Law Amendment Act," 1856, § 4), but otherwise in this matter civil have prevailed over commercial principles in England as in the last Spanish code (Co. Comm., 51 ; Civ., 1280). Passing to special contracts, in France and Spain the guarantee of a bill of exchange, in Germany and Italy every commercial guarantee, and in England every guarantee, enables the creditors to proceed directly against the guarantor ; except in these cases, the creditor, as in later Roman law, must first proceed against the principal debtor (Co. Comm., Fr., 142 ; Germ., 281 ; It., 40 ; Sp., 487 ; Civ., Fr., 2021 ; Sp., 1137). Everywhere we find common carriers and common innkeepers liable for loss of or damage to goods entrusted to them, unless *vis major*, or intrinsic defect, cause the loss or damage (Smith's *Leading Cases*, 9th ed., 236, Co. Comm., Fr., 97-98-103 ; It., 400 ; Sp., 361 ; Germ., 395 ; Co. Civ., Fr., 1784 ; It., 1631 ; Sp., 1602, as to carriers ; contrast, Co. Civ., Fr., 1789 ; It., 1636 ; Sp., 1182-83, etc.) ; or, as in Italy, Spain, and England, accident ; an enactment which is Roman as well as mediæval. Where formalities are insisted on by the commercial code but not under the civil law, it is usually because a new entity is created ;—thus partnerships and joint-stock companies, if commercial, are registered (Co. Comm., Fr., 42 ; Germ., 86, 151, 176, 210 ; It., 90 ; Sp., 16-17), except in England, however, companies, and under the rules of the stock exchange (39) stock exchange partnerships, are registered ; or it is because a new status is conferred, *e.g.* on infant traders or married women. The status of married women has been hardly affected by Roman law, but is the result of secular conflicts between mercantile canon and feudal law, of which we see traces in the present law of nations. Before 1882, married women, if trading in "London," had "by custom," *i.e.* law merchant, in the city courts complete capacity, and if trading else-where with their husbands' consent, had capacity to contract, sell, and pledge, so far as their trade property was concerned ; since 1882 the partition dividing traders from non-traders is broken down. Similarly, married

women trading with their husbands' consent
have in Germany and Italy complete capacity,
in France and Spain capacity to contract, sell,
and pledge, so far as their trade property
is concerned ; (Commercial Codes, Germ., 7-9 ;
It., 14 ; Fr., 5 ; Sp., 6, 10 ; contrast, Civil
Codes, Fr., 217-226 ; It., 134-5 ; Sp., 59, 60,
1263) ; and this law came from mediæval
town law or gild law (Pertile, iii. 243 ; Goldschmidt, p. 221, n. 117). Briefly, law
merchant dismisses pedantic distinctions of
outward form, of the personality of contracting
parties, of title and of sex, in order that it may
carry ideas of sale and contract to their last
conclusions ; and discusses the responsibility of
married women and "infants" as it discussed
that of the stranger on a broad human basis.

This section may be summed up thus :
mercantile law was far better and is still somewhat in advance of other civil law. That will
explain what is described above as the breaking
away of the commercial branch from the other
branches of civil law. But an interesting
question arises—which was the trunk ? On
the one hand the arrangement of the French
codes and the language of English judges
assume that the civil law is primary and the
commercial code is secondary ; that the latter
is an offshoot and variation of the former.
If history had begun with Justinian's codes,
this view would be right ; but Justinian's
codes were the last result of centuries of competition between civil and prætorian law, the
latter being in the main law merchant ; and
besides history to a large extent started its
course again in the middle ages. On the other
hand, the new Italian, the new Spanish, the
new Portuguese (1888), and the German commercial codes, erect "law merchant" into a self-
centred body of law, like criminal law ; and
mediæval history is on the side of this view ;
law merchant was built up in courts of its
own ; these courts were invented at a time
when mercantile law had little or nothing to
learn from other contemporary civil law, and
the latter had everything to learn from the
former. Perhaps the question is incapable of
solution, as we should first have to determine
the origin of our ideas of contract and civil
responsibility ; it will be enough for our
purpose to state that these ideas first attained
clear expression in connection with mercantile
transactions ; and in modern Europe long after
mercantile transactions had been relegated to
autonomous mercantile courts.

[A. Lattes, *Il diritto commerciale nella Legislazione statutaria delle città Italiane*, 1882-83 ;
Studii di diritto statutario, 1887 (Italian and
mediæval).—Pertile, *Storia del diritto Italiano*,
1891-95.—A. Schaube, *Das Konsulat des Meeres
in Pisa*, 1888, in Schmoller's *Staats und socialwissenschaftliche Forschungen*, vol. 8 (includes
Italy, Spain, and Western Mediterranean).—W.

Silberschmidt, *Die Enstehung des deutschen
Handelsgerichts*, 1894 (includes Austria, and sum-
marises the whole history).—L. Goldschmidt,
Handbuch des Handelsrechts, vol. i., 1891
(ancient and mediæval ; a mine of learning).
Refer also to C. Hegel, *Städte und Gilden der
Germanischen Völker in Mittelalter*, 1891 (in-
cludes Scandinavian countries, North France,
Paris, and Belgium). — C. Gross, *The Gild
Merchant* (1890) (British). —Stracca, *Tractatus
de Mercatura seu Mercatore*, 1553.—Marquardus,
*Tractatus politico-juridicus mercatorum et commer-
ciorum singularis*, 1662, and works of MALYNES,
Beawes, and Jacob mentioned in the article
COMMERCIAL LAW. The references to ancient
and mediæval maritimes codes are from Pardessus,
*Collection de lois maritimes antérieures au
XVIII⁰ siècle*, 1828-45.]   J. D. R.

LAWS OF POLITICAL ECONOMY—
EXAMPLES.

Law of Constant Return, p. 582 ; Costs, p. 582 ; Demand,
p. 582 ; Derived Demand, p. 582 ; Diminishing Returns,
p. 583; Diminishing Utility, p. 583; Increasing Returns,
p. 583 ; Indifference, p. 583 ; Satiable Wants, p. 583 ;
Subordination of Wants, p. 583 ; Substitution, p. 584 ;
Supply, p. 584.

LAW OF CONSTANT RETURN. — In general,
the increase of the scale on which an industry
is carried on is accompanied by a change in
the proportionate cost of its product ; but when
the increased difficulties of extractive industry
(see DIMINISHING RETURNS) are set off against
the economies arising from improved organisation in manufacture (see INCREASING RETURNS)
we may find an exact balance struck, and an
increased produce obtained by labour and sacrifice increased just in proportion. In such a
case, the law of *constant returns* is said to hold.

LAW OF COSTS.—This is one of the names
under which the well-known statement, that exchange value tends to an equality with cost of
production, is referred to (see COST OF PRODUC-
TION).

LAW OF DEMAND.—This law is practically
as follows. In every case, the more of a thing
is offered for sale in a market the lower is the
price at which it will find purchasers, or, in
other words, the demand price for each unit
diminishes with every increase in the amount
offered (see article DEMAND). (Marshall.
Principles of Economics.)

LAW OF DERIVED DEMAND.—When a commodity is such that there exists no independent
demand for it, the demand for the goods, in
the production of which it is associated with a
number of others, serves to determine a law of
derived demand for the commodity in question.
The aggregate of the prices at which the appropriate supplies of the other things, which
are associated with it in the production of the
goods, will be forthcoming, being subtracted
from the price at which the corresponding
quantity of those goods can find purchasers,
the remainder is the limit of the demand price
for a given amount of the said commodity.

LAW OF DIMINISHING RETURNS.—If one, or more, of the industrial agents, the co-operation of which is necessary for the production of any commodity, be increased, the others remaining unaltered, the amount of the product will generally be increased. If the increase of product be in a less proportion than the increase of the industrial agents considered, we express the fact by saying that in this case the product obeys the law of diminishing returns.

The usual definitions found in economic treatises combine a statement of the law with the assertion of its applicability to the case when increased capital and labour are expended on the same land. As the law is of far wider application, its statement, free from the reference to the particular case of land, seems to the writer to be desirable.

[For the limitations connected with the use of the law in the case of land, see DIMINISHING RETURNS.]

LAW OF DIMINISHING UTILITY.—The facts of human nature on which the law of demand is based are expressed in the law of diminishing utility. Professor Marshall states it thus:—"The Total Utility (that is, the total pleasure-affording power) of a commodity to a person increases with every increment of his stock of it, but does not increase so fast as his stock increases. If his stock of it increases at a uniform rate, the pleasure derived from it increases at a diminishing rate." A few lines later this is abbreviated, and at the same time expressed more precisely as follows:—"The marginal utility of a commodity to any one diminishes with every increase in the amount of it he already has."

Some of the few exceptions to the law as stated in this form, and mentioned in Professor Marshall's footnote, are excluded by the wording adopted by Jevons, viz.:—

"The degree of utility varies with the quantity of commodity, and ultimately decreases as that quantity increases."

The expressions "degree of utility" and "marginal utility" are used to signify the same thing, and these latter statements make it clear beyond any possible doubt that it is not the *total* utility but the *marginal* utility which diminishes. (For a full explanation of these phrases, see DEGREE OF UTILITY.)

LAW OF INCREASING RETURNS. — When, under the circumstances supposed above (see "Law of Diminishing Returns"), the increase of product is in greater proportion than the increase of the industrial agents concerned, the *Law of Increasing Returns* is said to be in operation.

The improved organisation of manufacturing industries which is possible when the scale of production is enlarged, causes the law to be applicable to them in general. Further, if the increase of numbers among a people be not accompanied by conditions leading to a decrease of the average of individual strength and energy, their collective efficiency will increase in greater proportion than their numbers, that is, the law of increasing returns will apply to the national industry at large (see also INCREASING RETURNS).

LAW OF INDIFFERENCE.—This is the name applied to the law that "In the same open market, at any one moment, there cannot be two prices for the same kind of article." This is a particular case of the law of substitution (see below), and the case of which the truth is most obvious, since the substituted commodity is similar in every respect to that which it replaces. It must be added that the hypothesis in dependence on which this law is formulated is that the dealers in the market considered are in possession of sufficient knowledge of what is taking place, and are sufficiently active in pursuit of their own interest, to lead them to refuse to pay to any person more than would be demanded at the same time and in the same place, by any other for articles precisely similar to those purchased (see INDIFFERENCE, LAW OF).

LAW OF SATIABLE WANTS.—This title is used by Professor Marshall as an alternative to that of the law of diminishing utility. The form of statement of this latter law, which Jevons quotes from Richard Jennings (see Jevons, *Theory*, p. 56), throws that feature of it into prominence which leads to the use of the title now under consideration. It is as follows:—"With respect to all commodities, our feelings show that the degrees of satisfaction do not proceed *pari passu* with the quantities consumed; they do not advance equally with each instalment of the commodity offered to the senses and then suddenly stop; but diminish gradually until they ultimately disappear, and further instalments can produce no further satisfaction." We need not proceed further with the quotation, which would merely yield us another expression of the law of diminishing utility at length. The concluding phrase of the passage quoted embodies the idea of "satiable wants."

LAW OF THE SUBORDINATION OF WANTS.—The same fact is expressed somewhat differently and, in some respects, more in accordance with actual experience, by Banfield, thus:—"The satisfaction of every lower want . . . creates a desire of a higher character." In commenting on this Jevons corrects and explains it as meaning "permits the higher want to manifest itself."

It would, perhaps, be more correct to say that the lower wants are not *absolutely* satisfied, but that, when their satisfaction has proceeded to a certain point, the desire to satisfy higher wants is more urgent than the desire to afford increased satisfaction to the lower wants. While noting, however, that frequently the power of affording satisfaction by increasing the consumption of a given commodity is not exhausted when such increase ceases, and consumption of an entirely different nature substituted, it is not asserted that instances do not occur, and that frequently, in which, to use the words of Jennings, "further instalments can produce no further satisfaction." The statement of Banfield may be expressed differently, as, for instance, by Senior, who writes :—"It is obvious that our desires do not aim so much at quantity as at diversity." This is referred to by Jevons as Senior's so-called "law of variety." The further explanations which Senior gives are just the expression of the law of diminishing utility already seen to be practically identical with the law under consideration.

LAW OF SUBSTITUTION.—When there is more than one method of producing a given result, the least costly method available will be selected. If there be more than one of which the cost, taking all the circumstances into account, is the same, it will be a matter of indifference which is employed of these equally costly methods, but any less costly method which can be substituted will tend to displace the others.

The practical carrying out of such substitution as is referred to will depend, clearly, not only on its feasibility, but also on the knowledge of business men that such substitution is possible and would decrease the cost of production. A limitation of this nature might be expressed in the enunciation of the law if desired.

LAW OF SUPPLY.—The law of costs is practically identical with that now under consideration. For the limitations and explanations necessary, see SUPPLY. A. W. F.

For Law of Distribution, see DISTRIBUTION, LAW OF ; Law of Population, see MALTHUS, REV. T. R. ; POPULATION ; Law of Wages (Iron), see LASSALLE ; MARX, KARL ; WAGES. See also Article on DEMAND ; DIMINISHING RETURNS ; INCREASING RETURNS.

LAWS OF POLITICAL ECONOMY, GENERAL PRINCIPLES.

The observation of natural phenomena reveals many instances where two sets of facts are seen to accompany one another or of which the one is observed to follow the other in invariable connection. When such coincidences have been noted, they are frequently placed on record in a statement of the form : "The events A and B will always be found to occur together." A statement of this kind expresses in a general form the result of such experience as has fallen to the lot of the propounder of this "law" or "rule." A wider and more prolonged experience may show that the apparent connection is, after all. no more than a coincidence, or series of coincidences, and that there is no invariable link binding the observed events inseparably together ; while, on the other hand, the closer observation of each event, which is naturally aroused by the apparent connection, may show that the generalisation rests on sound foundations, and that human experience presents no instance where the "rule" does not hold.

Sometimes the statement goes further and takes the form "The event A always produces, as its result, the event B." This is more than a mere statement of a definite sequence in time of the events, and implies a causal connection between them. Equally with the form of statement previously mentioned, the test of experience alone can suffice to establish confidence in the truth of such a rule as this. In some branches of science, the process of testing the truth of the hypothetical "law" suggested by the study and comparison of recorded facts, can be pursued by means of experiments all the details of which are under the control of the experimenter. If the statement be found, not only to agree with all recorded experience in the past, but to agree also with the experience obtained by conducting experiments and making observations directed to the special end of testing the truth of this particular allegation, confidence in its truth becomes firmly established, and what was alleged previously in a hesitating and tentative manner as a probable statement of general application may be referred to as a fully determined "law." The term is properly used in precisely the same sense in economic science as in physical science, and a "law" of political economy must be regarded in somewhat the same light as, for instance, Kepler's laws of planetary motion. It is a generalisation from past experience which is found to agree with all that is known, and to satisfy all tests, up to the present, which can be applied to determine its validity.

In every science, what may be called derivative laws are obtained, by combining the results of the rules which direct observation has established. These may be enunciated in the form of extremely simple "principles," the truth of which is established by the consideration that, only if these principles be accepted can observed results be accounted for ; or they may be of a complex nature, obtained by the process of uniting the effects of many causes and thus obtaining the complex effect of a complex cause.

Some frequently quoted laws of political economy are of this nature, and much misunderstanding has resulted from an almost universal habit of omitting, in the enumeration of the causes supposed to be in action, some which are of extreme importance, but the absence of which is so unlikely that it is not contemplated or even recognised as possible. This causes little confusion with minds trained in this class of investigation, but is the source of serious error and of much distrust of economic theory in the popular mind. Too often, even those who might be expected to have in mind the limitations in view of which a given effect may be expected to follow a given cause, have wholly overlooked such of these limitations as were considered to be so obvious as not to need explicit enumeration, and have consequently been led to results inconsistent equally with the rigid application of theoretical knowledge and with facts then or subsequently observed.

In economics the process of inductive demonstration of a general principle is often peculiarly difficult. The conduct of experiments specially devised to avoid the complications arising from the interaction of many causes is difficult if not impossible. The most that can be done is to obtain as many different combinations of causes as possible, so as to trace the common element in the varying combination of results with as much precision as can be attained. Similarly, when it is sought to apply our knowledge to predict the result of any proposed arrangements, the modifying effect of surrounding circumstances must not be left out of account, for, though each cause produces its own effect, the composite result may be quite other than is indicated, while attention is confined to a single cause with its appropriate effect.

It will be seen, therefore, that economic laws are not in any sense absolute statements. They relate to assumed conditions of society, and do not profess to do more than give certain clues to the probable result of any set of causes when those conditions are entirely changed. The reason of this is that though the laws which are known may be quite sufficient to unravel the complications of the changed conditions so far as the *kind* of result is concerned, the lack of precision as to *quantitative* relations between causes and effects which characterises most economic laws often renders it impossible to predict in detail the outcome of untried combinations. Within wide limits, however, the laws which are generalisations from past and present experience may render invaluable help in the prediction of the result of any hypothetical set of conditions in the future. Too much care cannot be taken to remember that we often state the laws without anything like a complete enumeration of the conditions in connection with which we always contemplate their operation. Further, to quote the words of Professor Marshall, "The laws of economics are statements of tendencies expressed in the indicative mood, and not ethical precepts in the imperative."—*Principles*, Pref. to 1st ed.

In addition to the laws which refer to human societies and to the influence of the human mind on the relations between things and persons, there are some statements of the result of observation of physical nature which are also frequently made use of in economic investigations, and are also generally regarded as laws of political economy. In the definitions which follow, an example of this class is found in the law of decreasing returns.

In conclusion, we may say that, being convinced by observation, though perhaps not wholly by observation, that the events of the industrial world manifest order in their mutual relations, we seek to determine, as far as possible, what is the nature of that order. The results, expressed in words, constitute the "laws" to which we have been referring.

[See Cairnes, *Leading Principles*, etc. ; *Character and Logical Method*, etc.—Huxley, *The Progress of Science* (in Method and Results).—Jevons, *The Principles of Science.*—Keynes, *Scope and Method*, etc.—Mach, *Science of Mechanics.*— Marshall, *Principles of Economics.*—Mill, *Logic.*—Ritchie, *What are Economic Laws?* (in Darwin and Hegel). —Whewell, *Philosophy of Discovery.*— Bonar, *Philosophy and Political Economy.*]   A. W. F.

For other articles connected with this heading see ECONOMIC LAW; GRESHAM'S LAW; LAW OF DIMINISHING RETURNS, see DIMINISHING RETURNS ; LAW OF INCREASING RETURNS, see INCREASING RETURNS ; LAW OF INDIFFERENCE, see INDIFFERENCE, LAW OF ; SURPLUS, LAW OF.

LAWFUL HOURS. The state in some cases prescribes the time within which a trade may be carried on, or the number of hours per day, or per week, a class of persons may be employed. By the Licensing Acts, 1872-74, intoxicating liquors are only permitted to be sold during certain hours of the day. By the Factory and Workshop Act, 1878, the period of employment of young persons and women, in textile and non-textile factories, is to be between 6 A.M. and 6 P.M., or between 7 A.M. and 7 P.M. ; but in the trades specified in Schedule III. pt. i., the period may be between 8 A.M. and 9 P.M. On Saturdays when work commences at 6 A.M., if not less than one hour is given for meals, manufacturing processes must cease, in textile factories, at 1 P.M., and all other work at 1.30 P.M., in non-textile factories all work must cease at 2 P.M. (see FACTORY ACTS). The act also contains special provisions relating to children, and to holidays. Under the Coal Mines Regulation Act boys between twelve and sixteen cannot be employed under ground for more than fifty-four hours per week, nor more than ten hours in any one day. Restrictions have also been imposed on the hours of boys, girls, and women working above ground. Premises licensed for the sale of intoxicating liquors in London, are to be closed on Saturdays from midnight until 1 o'clock on Sunday, and from 11 o'clock until 5 on Monday morning, and on other days from 12.30 midnight until 5 A.M. In towns outside London they are to be closed from 11 P.M. on Saturday until 12.30 P.M. on Sunday, on Sunday afternoons, and from 10 P.M. on Sunday until 6 A.M. on Monday ; on other days they are to be closed from 11 P.M. until 6 A.M. the following morning. In the country they are to be closed from 10 P.M. on Saturday until 12.30 P.M. on Sunday, and from 10 P.M. on Sunday until 6 A.M. on Monday ; on other days they are to be closed from 10 P.M. until 6 A.M. the following morning. By the Factory and Workshop Act, 1895, restrictions are placed on the employment of young persons and women over time, and the employment of young persons at night, and the hours of work in laundries.

[Redgrave's *Factory and Workshop Acts*, 1878-1891, London, 1893.—Von Plener's *Factory Legislation*, London, 1873.—Pease's *Coal Mines Regulation Act*, London, 1888.—Paterson's *Licensing Acts*, London, 1892.] J. E. C. M.

LAWSON, JAMES ANTHONY (1817-1887). From 1840-1845 Whately professor of political economy at Trinity College, Dublin ; was appointed solicitor-general in 1861 ; and in 1865 attorney-general for Ireland. He represented Portarlington in parliament 1865-1868, when he was made fourth justice of common pleas ; in 1882 he was transferred to the Queen's bench.

During his occupation of the professorial chair at Trinity, Lawson delivered *Lectures on Political Economy* (London, Dublin, printed 1844, 8vo) in which he defined the subject as that "science which treats of the nature, and production of value, and the laws which regulate the distribution of wealth among the different orders of the community."

After vindicating the science from the charge of inattention to facts, he pointed out (lecture ii.) that a high state of civilisation implied inter-dependence, whether of states or individuals. In his third lecture he maintained Archbishop Whately's position against the Malthusians, and disputed the theory that population increases in geometrical progression as against the arithmetical ratio of the food supply.

He then went on to expose the fallacies of the mercantile system (lecture iv.), and (v.) the error of classing "consumption" as productive or unproductive. In an appendix to this series he attacked Colonel Torrens's defence of the expediency of "retaliation."

In 1855 Lawson addressed the Dublin Young Men's Christian Association on the *Duties and Obligations involved in Mercantile Relations*, advocating the economic necessity and expediency of commercial probity, and deprecating the criminality of speculation and improvidence.

[*Dictionary of National Biography*.] A. L.

Lawson was the first secretary, and was afterwards (1858 and 1870-72) president of the Dublin Statistical Society. He contributed to its transactions, besides a presidential address, papers on the connection between statistics and political economy, on the comparative advantages of direct and indirect taxation, on the over-population fallacy, on commercial panics, and on the patent laws. He was also (1849 and 1851) Barrington lecturer on political economy to the same society.

LAY DAYS. The contract entered into by a shipowner and the hirer of a ship usually contains a stipulation that the goods will be taken out of the ship within a certain number of days after her arrival. These days are called lay days. After the time has expired, the hirer, or party liable, is as a rule bound by the contract to pay a certain sum for every additional day taken for unloading (see DEMURRAGE).

J. E. C. M.

LEAKE, STEPHEN MARTIN (1702-1773), Garter King at Arms, writer on English coins. His father was Captain Martin, adopted by Admiral Sir John Leake as his heir, Leake having married Martin's wife's sister. Stephen Martin Leake held many public posts, and was Fellow of the Society of Antiquaries when about five-and-twenty. He had a life-long connection with the College of Arms, and wrote several essays (unpublished) on matters of heraldry. His chief work is *Nummi Britannici Historia ; or, an Historical Account of English Money, from the Conquest to the Uniting of the Two Kingdoms by King James I., and of Great Britain to the Present Time*. The first edition was published in 1726, 8vo, pp. 144. The second edition, considerably enlarged and virtually rewritten, appeared in 1745 (8vo, pp. 428), and was re-issued by the publishers in 1793 : all published in London. Leake designed this work "for the use and benefit of the curious collector." It is a kind of chronological descriptive handbook to English coins, the first of its kind, taking the coinage reign by reign, with full descriptions, and with a few illustrative plates. M'Culloch, *Lit. Pol. Econ.*, p. 162, speaks of it as "this valuable treatise." Ruding, *Annals of the Coinage*, 1840, pp. viii., ix., considers that "as far as it goes it has great merit, but the plan is too much contracted . . . and is founded chiefly on the authority of printed books, instead of original records."

[Noble, *A History of the College of Arms and the Lives of all the Kings, Heralds, and Pursuivants*, etc., 1804, pp. 408-414, also on pp. 380, 383, 385, 394. — *Dictionary of National Biography*, art. "Leake, S. M."] E. D.

LEASE. A document under seal under which the use of any land or buildings is granted for a definite number of years, or for a period measured by the duration of any life or lives being in existence at the time when the lease is made. The person who grants the use of the land is called the lessor, the person to whom it is granted the lessee. A lease generally contains a number of covenants respectively to be performed by the lessor and by the lessee. The lessor's principal covenant is the covenant "for quiet enjoyment." The lessee's covenants, with the exception of the covenant to pay rent, vary according to the nature of the lease. In a building lease they generally include a covenant to build a house of a certain value and nature on the demised land ; and in most leases of houses the lessee undertakes to keep the premises in good repair. An agricultural lessee, as a general rule, enters into covenants as to the system of cultivation and the nature of the crops, and also as to keeping up flocks and preserving trees ; and the lessee of mines promises to work them effectually. Leases mostly contain a proviso for re-entry in case of non-observance of any of the covenants, but the law, to a certain extent, protects lessees against an unfair use of this right (see ENTRY, RIGHT OF). Protection is now also given to agricultural lessees in respect of fixtures and unexhausted improvements (see AGRICULTURAL HOLDINGS ACTS ; and as to agricultural leases in Ireland see LAND LEGISLATION, IRISH).

A lease is a very good illustration of the fact that the same legal form may be used for a number of transactions which, viewed in their economical aspect, have hardly anything in common. In the case of an ordinary building lease the lessee is for all practical purposes the owner of the property, and during the currency of the lease reaps the benefit of all improvements and increases in value ; whilst in the case of a short-dated lease at rack-rent all changes in the value of the property affect the lessor to a much greater extent than the lessee.

In the case of a building lease the owner, on the expiration of the lease, enters into possession of his land and of a valuable addition to it ; in the case of ordinary leases at rack-rents the property remains, as much as possible, in the same state ; but in the case of a mining lease the subject-matter of the lease, viz. the minerals, is entirely taken away by the lessee. In the first-named case the principal advantage derived by the landlord is the addition to his property ; in the second case his entire gain consists in the rent ; in the third case there is generally a fixed rent, and in addition a royalty proportionate to the output. All these circumstances ought to be considered in schemes of taxation affecting the relations of landlords and tenants.

[As to the law relating to leases see Foa, *Relationship of Landlord and Tenant*, 1891.— Woodfall, *Law of Landlord and Tenant*, 15th ed. 1893.]   E. S.

LEASEHOLD PROPERTY. Property held under a LEASE (*q.v.*). If the lease is for a term of years, however long, the lessee's interest is in the nature of personal as opposed to real property (see CHATTEL). Leaseholds let for a term of years of at least three hundred years, of which at least two hundred years are unexpired, not being subject to any rent having a money value, and not liable to be determined for condition broken, may now be converted into freeholds by the lessee without the concurrence of the lessor's successor in title.

[Conveyancing Act 1881, § 65 ; Conveyancing Act 1882, § 11.]   E. S.

LEAST SQUARES, METHOD OF, is a rule for obtaining the best average result from a given set of observations. Suppose, for instance, that it is sought to ascertain the quantity of coin circulating in a country ; and that by different modes of procedure, each purporting to be equally valid, there have been obtained several values for the sought quantity, say $x_1, x_2, x_3,$ . . . x_n ; the best result is in general obtained by determining x so that the sum of squares $(x-x_1)^2+(x-x_2)^2+ \ . \ . \ . \ +(x-x_n)^2$ should be a *minimum*. This value of x proves to be $(x_1+x_2+ \ . \ . \ . \ +x_n) \div n$, the arithmetic mean (see AVERAGE) ; so that in this case the method of least squares coincides with ordinary practice. It has a more distinctive character in cases where the data are more complicated. Suppose that each *datum* purported to be, not the value of the circulation, but of some quantity depending on the circulation and one or more *other* unknown quantities ; as in the case of the statistics relating to the rupee circulation which Mr. F. C. Harrison has discussed in the *Economic Journal* (Dec. 1891). As argued by the present writer (*ibid.* March 1892), if we regard the circulation as possibly increasing during the years under observation, we should have *twelve* equations for two unknown quantities, viz. the-circulation-of-1890 and the yearly-rate-of-increase. Put x for the logarithm of the first quantity and y for that of the second ; then from observations relating to successive years we obtain twelve equations of the form $x - ny - a = o$; where n specifies the year under observation, and a is a numerical datum. Call the left-hand members of these equations respectively $X_1,$ $X_2,$ etc., $X_{12}.$ The best value of x (and y) is obtained by determining x and y so that the sum of squares $X_1^2 + X_2^2 + $ etc. $+ X_{12}^2$ should be a *minimum*.

In the examples above given the average sought has been an objective thing, not, as more commonly in statistics relating to social phenomena, a *type* (see AVERAGE). But there is no reason why the method of least squares should not be employed to determine averages of the latter class. However, the data from which types are elicited are seldom of the complicated sort above instanced. Accordingly the rôle of the method of least squares in the social sciences appears to be inconsiderable.

A voluminous catalogue of writings relating to the method of least squares has been compiled by Mr. Mansfield Merriman. His own text-book on the subject is remarkably clear and simple. It should be remarked that he appears to take for granted the prevalence of the Law of Error. Whereas it has been held by some mathematicians that the method of least squares is applicable even where that law does not prevail (see ERROR, LAW OF).   F. Y. E.

LEBER, C. (1780-1859), was a head clerk in the French ministry of the interior.

He published the *Collection des meilleurs Dissertations, notices, et Traités Particuliers relatifs* à l'*Histoire de France* (Paris, 1838, 20 vols.), and an *Essai sur l'Appréciation de la fortune privée au Moyen Age* (2nd ed., 1847), which first appeared in the 1st volume of the *Mémoires des Savants Étrangers*, printed by authority of the French Academy of Inscriptions. This "essay" was long considered as an authority on the subject of prices in France during the middle ages, and comprises sundry tables of prices, official salaries, etc., with the corresponding modern figures. The latter may be usefully compared with similar tables published by M. d'Avenel in the *Revue des Deux Mondes*, 15th June 1892, pp. 795 and 803, and in the latter's great work, *Histoire Économique de la Propriété, des Salaires*, etc., 1894.   E. Ca.

LEBLANC, FRANÇOIS (died 1698), a French numismatist, born in Dauphiny. Being a man of fortune, he took up the study of coins and medals, and formed a fine collection. In 1688 he travelled in Italy, and on his return published his *Traité historique des Monnoyes de France depuis le commencement de la Monarchie jusqu'à present*, Paris, 1690. This volume treats only of the regal coins, and contains numerous plates. A second, twice as long, which describes the seigneurial coinage, has never been printed. From the reign of Philippe le Bel the printed work is founded on the registers of the *Cour des Monnaies*, and contains elaborate tables giving the value of the mark of gold and of silver year by year, together with the value and degree of fineness of the *gros*, *blancs*, *testons*, and other coins, with the same chronological exactitude. In 1689 the author had published, at Paris, his *Dissertation sur quelques monnoyes de Charlemagne, Louis le Débonnaire, Lothaire et ses successeurs, frappées dans Rome*. This was reprinted with the larger work in the Amsterdam edition of 1692.   R. H.

[Cantillon, *Essai* (Boston reprint 1892), p. 137 refers to Leblanc, *Traité des monnoyes*, Paris, 1692 (1711, 1714, 1723). This work is described by H. Higgs, Harvard *Journal of Economics*, vol. vi., p. 437, as "a practical little book on the working of a mint."]

LECLAIRE, EDMÉ-JEAN (1801-1872), the founder of French PROFIT-SHARING, was the son of a village shoemaker. On leaving school he knew, at most, how to read and write, and never mastered the mysteries of spelling. At seventeen he migrated to Paris, and was apprenticed to a house-painter. Nine years later he set up in business by himself, and from the first prospered greatly. The idea of profit-sharing was first suggested to him by a M. Frégier in 1835, who, however, afterwards refused to believe in its feasibility. It was not till 1842 that Leclaire felt himself able to put the idea into practice. He informed his workmen of his intention of dividing among a certain number of them, afterwards termed the *noyau*, kernel, or *élite*, 50 per cent of the annual profits after deducting 5 per cent for interest on capital, and £240 for salary of management. At first

the men looked on the proposal with suspicion, but when, as the result of the first year's working, he threw on the table a bag of gold, and proceeded to divide among forty participants sums amounting to over £11 each, the object lesson proved convincing. The sums received varied according to the amount of the yearly wage. In the following years, both the amount distributed and the number of participants steadily increased. In 1838 he had established a mutual aid society, which was reconstituted in 1853, and henceforth maintained altogether out of the annual profits, instead of by the members' own contributions. In 1864, though not without some opposition, retiring pensions were substituted for the right to future division of the funds of the mutual aid society, and it was made a perpetual sleeping partner, *commanditaire*, in the firm of "Leclaire & Cie." In the following year Leclaire retired from active management over the business, to Herblay, near Paris, where he endeavoured, with little success, to interest the country people in profit-sharing. In 1869 a formal deed was drawn up, setting out the manner in which profits were to be divided between the managing partners, the regular staff, and the mutual aid society. Two years after, Leclaire, taking to heart the taunt of a socialist workman, "Your house is nothing but a box of little masters who 'exploit' the others," threw open the benefits of participation to all workmen employed. In 1872, on the day following the distribution of £2000 among 600 men, as the annual bonus, Leclaire died, but the work of his life still lives in the firm that bears his name, and in the seventy firms which practise the system in Paris alone. He had himself always advocated profit-sharing on business lines. He left behind him a fortune of £48,000, and always maintained that had he followed the beaten track he could not have succeeded as well, even by sharp practices. Though his motives were in reality lofty, he carefully refrained from putting them forward. In the presence of death, he wrote that he was "the humble disciple of Him who has told us to do unto others as we would wish them to do unto us"; but such had not been his usual note. According to the present constitution of the firm, the capital is £32,000, £16,000 being provided by the mutual aid society, and £16,000 by the managing directors, in unequal shares. To enable men without capital to be partners, it is provided that the out-going partner may not withdraw his capital until it has been replaced out of the sums accruing to his successor as share in profits. In fact, one of the present partners has risen from the ranks. In the case of the death or resignation of one of them, his successor is elected by the "noyau," who are themselves admitted by the "comité de conciliation," consisting of the partners, and eight other members, five workmen, and three clerks, or foremen. Of the net profits, 25 per cent go to the managing partners, 25 per cent to the mutual aid society, and 50 per cent·are distributed among the employees in cash. This 50 per cent is divided by the whole amount of wages and salaries paid during the year, to obtain the ratio of bonus to wages. Each man's earnings are then multiplied by this percentage to find the sum due to him. The ratio of bonus to wages averaged during a series of years over 20 per cent. Wages have always been paid at the highest rate current in the trade. In 1892 there were 936 participants. The mutual aid society has a capital of more than £110,840. It had, in 1893, 230 members. It provides, besides ordinary benefits, a pension of £60 to those over fifty who have worked for the firm twenty years, half of which is continued to the widow for life ; and a lump sum of £40, payable to the family at the man's death. In addition, all employees, whether members of the society or not, can claim, if disabled while in the firm's employ, a full retiring pension, and in any case are entitled after reaching the age of fifty to one of £40, with £20 for widow.

[*Biographie d'un homme utile*, par ·Charles Robert, Paris, 1878.—*Profit Sharing between Capital and Labour*, by Sedley Taylor (pp. 1-25), London, 1884.—Reference to the principle, Mill, *Principles of Political Economy*, vol. ii., Appendix. —*A brief Sketch of the Maison Leclaire*, by Mary Hart, London, 1882.—*La Participation aux bénéfices*, par C. V. Boehmert, trad. par A. Trombert, Paris, 1888, 8vo, pp. 245-263.—*Profit-Sharing*, by N. P. Gilman, Cambridge, Mass., 1889, 8vo, pp. 66-105.—*Patrons et Ouvriers de Paris*, Paris, 1880, 8vo, pp. 127-134—See also the ann. vol. ; commencing 1879 ; *Bulletin de la Participation aux bénéfices*.—Accounts of his progress by Leclaire, particularly *Compte rendu . . . sur les resultats de Paris*, 1865. The latest information is in the preface to an account of *Réunion solennelle pour l'inauguration de la rue Jean Leclaire*, Paris, 1894 (see also PROFIT-SHARING).] H. E. E.

LEET COURT. Without entering upon the difficult questions of the origin and development of the leet, of its relation to the sheriff's tourn and view of frankpledge on the one side, and to the court baron on the other, it must suffice here to describe it in its economic aspect. It enforced, and in part originated, numerous economic and social regulations which are now either considered unnecessary or committed to specialised local and central bodies. Besides some criminal offences which were presentable at the leet, but punishable at the next gaol delivery, the charge to the jury included various smaller crimes, such as the use of false weights and measures and breach of the peace ; some police work, such as view of frankpledge ; some manorial matters, such as the breaking of boundaries and hedges, the pursuit of villeins, the treatment of stray beasts ; some unneighbourly acts, such as eavesdropping ; and a great many regulations on social and economic subjects. Of these some were sanitary : waters were not to be corrupted, nuisances of various kinds were forbidden, diseased cattle were to be removed from commons, stale fish and meat were not to be sold. Others were directed towards the repair of highways, the practice of archery, the preservation of fish and game ; and a considerable number of restrictions were placed on economic liberty, some of which would now be regarded as intolerable. For instance, apparel was to be minutely suited to the rank of the wearer, and the quality of French and Gascon wines to the rank of the consumer ; the ASSIZE OF BREAD AND BEER was enforced, prices of victuals were fixed, and middlemen were expected not to make more than 5 per cent profit on their sales ; trees were to be felled, and tanning was to be carried on, according to fixed rules ; millers must not take excessive toll, one grain in twenty or in twenty-four being considered enough ; forestalling was forbidden ; certain trades were not to be united ; and labourers were not to "conspire" to obtain shorter hours or increased pay.

These courts, which existed, though at first often without the name of leet, on very many manors, ranked as royal courts of record. They can still be traced in some places, but since the 16th century the growth of the commission of the peace has nearly destroyed them.

[For historical position of the leet, see Maitland's *Select Pleas in Manorial Courts*, Introd., with note A on meaning of the word.—For business of the court, see Kitchin's *Jurisdictions*, 1651.— Scriven's *Copyholds*.—Harland's *Manchester Court Leet Records* (Chetham Soc.).—Wilkinson's *The Manner and Forme how to keep a Court Leete*, 1620. —See also Stubbs, *Const. Hist.*—Garnier, *English Landed Interest*, pp. 364-379.—Pollock and Maitland, *History of England*.] E. G. P.

LEFÈVRE DE BEAUVRAY, PIERRE (1724-1790), was an advocate in the parliament of Paris.

He published in 1769 and 1770 (Paris and Amsterdam) his *Dictionnaire social et patriotique ou Précis raisonné des connaissances relatives à l'économie morale civile, et politique*, reprinted in 1774 under the title of *Dictionnaire de recherches historiques et philosophiques*. E. Ca.

LEGACY. A legacy is a gift made by will of a portion of a person's personal estate. A legacy always implies (*a*) that the gift is made by a will, and (*b*) that it is to take effect out of the personal and not out of the real estate. Where a testator desires to make his real estate liable for a legacy, he charges its payment on such estate. A legatee can claim his legacy only after the payment of the testator's debts, as the law prefers the claim of a creditor to that of a legatee. If after payment of debts there are not sufficient assets to pay all the legacies, the position of the legatees depends on the nature of the legacy.

1. If a legacy be *general, i.c.* if it does not refer to any specific thing, it is liable to be reduced in proportion to the deficiency of assets.

2. If a legacy is *specific, i.e.* if it is of a specific thing, the legatee is entitled to such thing unless the testator has parted with it in his lifetime.

3. If a legacy is *demonstrative, i.e.* if it is in its nature general, but a specific fund has been mentioned out of which it is to be paid, it is not affected by the alienation of such fund during the testator's lifetime, and it is not liable to be reduced until the fund out of which it is payable is exhausted.

[Snell's *Equity*, London, 1894.—Williams on *Executors and Administrators*, London, 1893.—The rule of perpetuities applies to legacies, *i.e.* the corpus cannot be rendered inalienable for a longer period than a life or a series of lives in being at the date of the testator's death and twenty-one years afterwards. A legacy for superstitious uses is void (Goodeve, *Personal Property*, London, 1892). As regards the limitation of the power of bequeathing legacies, see Mill's *Pol. Econ.*, bk. v. ch. ix.; and Bentham's Works, edited by Bowring, Edinburgh, 1843, vol. ii. (see BEQUEST, POWER OF; DEATH DUTIES)].

J. E. C. M.

LEGACY DUTIES. See DEATH DUTIES.

LEGAL TENDER. The phrase "legal tender," in its primary acceptation, denotes a valid offer of payment of a debt; in its secondary and derivative sense, that which can be validly offered—that particular species of money which, in the absence of special agreement to the contrary, creditors are by law bound to accept in payment of debts. Where the mode of payment has been clearly laid down in the original CONTRACT, governments have, save in the case of some particular species of contracts (see TRUCK ACTS), in general restricted themselves to enforcing when necessary the contract thus made. But, to avert the evils incident to uncertainty in the interpretation of contracts, it has usually been found necessary to give a precise definition of what will, in the absence of agreement to the contrary, constitute a legal tender of payment of a debt.

What money is legal tender? In this country the current coin of the realm is legal tender—gold for payment of any amount, silver for a payment not exceeding forty shillings, bronze for a payment not exceeding one shilling (33 Vict. c. 10, § 4). Bank of England notes, payable to bearer on demand, are, except at the bank itself or its branches, legal tender for all sums above five pounds, so long as the bank continues to pay on demand its notes in legal coin (3 & 4 Will. IV. c. 98, § 6). Bank of England notes, however, are not legal tender in Scotland or Ireland; nor are the notes of the English country banks, or of the Scotch and Irish banks, legal tender anywhere. But a tender of payment in money other than legal tender (*e.g.* country bank notes, or a

cheque, or silver coin for a debt exceeding 40s.) will, if otherwise valid, be sufficient, unless objected to on that account.

In the United States of America, U.S. gold coins are (1895) legal tender for any sum; as also the U.S. silver dollar, except in the case of agreement to the contrary. The smaller silver coins are legal tender for a sum not exceeding ten dollars (say £2). For the extent to which United States notes are legal tender see BANK NOTE (U.S.A.). See also BIMETALLISM; CIRCULATING MEDIUM; CONVERTIBILITY OF BANK NOTES; COLONIES, CURRENCY IN; CURRENCY; DEBASEMENT OF COIN, HIST. OF; INCONVERTIBLE CURRENCY.

Supposing the *quality* of the tender unobjectionable, *what constitutes a legal tender of it?* By English law the debtor must produce and offer—unless the creditor clearly dispense with production—to the creditor, or to one who is presumably his authorised agent and does not disclaim authority, the sum due, at the proper time and place, and so that the creditor or his agent can examine and count the money. The tender must be unconditional, *e.g.* it must not involve an admission by the creditor that no more is due, or that it itself is not due. A tender by one of several joint debtors, or to one of several joint creditors, is valid as tender by, or to, all. Tender of more than is due is valid, but not if change is required and the creditor objects to give it. Tender of a part of an entire debt is not valid, and there can be legal tender of one of several distinct debts only if the debt be specified on account of which the tender is made.

[See Jevons, *Money and the Mechanism of Exchange*, 8th ed. 1887.—F. A. Walker, *Money*, 1878.—Smith's *Mercantile Law*, 10th ed. 1890, pp. 667 *seq.*—Benjamin, *On Sales*, 4th ed. 1888, pp. 714 *seq.*]

A. B. C.

LEGATUM, in Roman law, is a bequest to a person by will of a formal kind, charged by the testator on the universal successor, *heres*, to whom he leaves his entire property. The *legatarius* or legatee, the object of the testator's bounty, being only a particular successor, does not, like the *heres*, incur any liability for the testator's debts. The form of the *legatum*, which is not that of request, but of command, distinguishes it from the FIDEICOMMISSUM (*q.v.*).

E. A. W.

LEGISLATION (ELIZABETHAN). More than one hundred statutes, dealing with the social and economic questions of the reign of Elizabeth, were passed between 1558 and 1601. If we add to these the numerous private acts of a similar character and the public acts which had only an indirect relation to economic affairs, we have to contemplate a legislative achievement which for permanent and far-reaching results is without parallel in the history of England. It is impossible within the limits of an article to give a complete analysis of these statutes, still less to trace in detail the results of their operation. Whether we regard the remarkable unity of purpose with which they are pervaded, the skill with which they make use of the social and political influences of the time, or the expedition with which they were framed, criticised, amended, and passed into law, they are of the greatest importance in the economic development of the country. To understand their full significance they should be considered in their mutual relations to one another. They represent a deliberate and, on the whole, a successful attempt to grapple with the problems of the reign of Elizabeth on the principles of the MERCANTILE SYSTEM (*q.v.*). They are, in fact, the embodiment of that system at its best, before it had degenerated into a mere chaotic mass of tariff regulations for the protection of the interests of small groups of merchants and manufacturers. In spite of the economic errors which it was difficult if not impossible to avoid in that age, the acts for the encouragement of agriculture and navigation, the statute of apprenticeship, and the acts dealing with pauperism, are, in relation to the political theories and social structure of the 16th century, worthy of the admiration with which they have been regarded. A list of the acts passed in a single year, the fifth of Elizabeth (1562-1563), will give some idea of the activity of the Elizabethan parliaments. There were acts (1) " for the mayntenance and increase of tillage " (c. 2) ; (2) " for the reliefe of the poor " (c. 3) ; (3) " touching dyvers orders for artificers, laborers, servantes of husbandrye, and apprentises "—APPRENTICESHIP, STATUTE OF (*q.v.*) (c. 4) ; (4) " touching certayne politique constitutions made for the maintenance of the navye "—NAVIGATION LAWS (*q.v.*) (c. 5) ; (5) " agaynste suche as shall sell any ware for appareill without readye moneye " (c. 6) ; (6) " for thadvoyding of dyvers forreyne wares made by handye craftsmen beyonde the seas " (c. 7) ; (7) " touching tanners, couriours, shoemakers, and other artyficers occupying the cutting of leather " (c. 8) ; (8) to revive 21 Hen. VIII., " touching servantes embeaselyng theyre maysters gooddes " (c. 10) ; (9) " agaynst clyppyng, washing, rounding, or fylyng of coynes " (c. 11) ; (10) " touching badgers of corne and droves of cattell to be lycensed " (c. 12) ; (11) to continue 2 & 3 Ph. and M. " for the amending of highe wayes " (c. 13) ; (12) " for the punishement of vagabondes callyng themselfes Egiptians " (c. 20) ; (13) " for the punishment of unlawfull taking of fishe, deare, or hawkes " (c. 21) ; (14) " agaynste the caryeing of sheepskins, etc., over the sea, not being staple wares " (c. 22). Of the more important of these acts, the statute of apprenticeship was not further amended during the reign of Elizabeth, though its operation was indirectly affected

by the changes which took place in the poor - law (14 Eliz. c. 5 ; 18 Eliz. c. 3 ; 35 Eliz. c. 4 ; 39 Eliz. cc. 3, 4, 5 ; 43 Eliz. c. 2). For subsequent legislation in continuation or amendment of the act for the maintenance of tillage, reference should be made to 13 Eliz. c. 13 ; 31 Eliz. c. 7, 39 Eliz. cc. 1, 2, and some clauses of the Navigation Acts (1 Eliz. c. 13 ; 13 Eliz. c. 11 ; 23 Eliz. c. 7 ; 39 Eliz. c. 10) have an important bearing on the same subject. Other statutes which should be noticed are those making felony the exportation of leather, tallow, and raw hides (1 Eliz. c. 10), for the incorporation of merchant adventurers for the discovery of new trades (8 Eliz. c. 17), and " agaynst usurie " (13 Eliz. c. 8). The principles of this legislation were not new. The ordinance (1349) and the statute of labourers (1351) may be said to have contained the germ of subsequent legislation on the regulation of wages and pauperism. Navigation acts had been passed in the reign of Richard II. But there are seldom entirely new departures in economic legislation. It is the sagacity with which old laws were repealed, modified, or extended to new problems which distinguishes the reign of Elizabeth as a great constructive age. The bills which became law were only a small proportion of those actually considered by parliament or the committee appointed for that purpose. Statutes were framed and got through both Houses with great expedition, but not hastily or without careful consideration. The development of the poor-law well illustrates the procedure in regard to all the economic legislation of this period. The interest in the subject was so great in 1571 that there was a debate on the first reading of a measure introduced into the House of Commons. This bill was rejected or allowed to drop in the Lords, and a second bill introduced in that House on 12th May 1572. It passed the final stage on 4th June, although during the interval there had been considerable disagreement between the two Houses, and conferences had been necessary. In 1597, when the poor-law for practical purposes reached its final state, one committee had no fewer than eleven bills under consideration, all relating to pauperism. Sometimes there took place a lively debate in a full House, as in the case of the Usury Act of 1571. But as a rule the work was done by committees consisting of Bacon, Cecil, Raleigh, and other well-known men, who met day after day until the legislation was put into shape. An account of the administration of the Elizabeth acts would involve the economic history of England until the early part of the 19th century. W. A. S. H.

LE GENDRE, FRANÇOIS (17th century), was the author of *l'Arithmétique en sa perfection mise en pratique selon l'usage des Financiers, Banquiers, et Marchands*, which went through ten editions from 1646 to 1691, and was even reprinted in 1806 and 1813.

Le Gendre is thought by Professor Oncken to be probably the French merchant who, according to the *Mémoires Historiques* of de la Houssaye (1731), answered Colbert : "*Laissez nous faire*," when consulted by the minister, with some other leading merchants, as to the best method for the improvement of trade. De la Houssaye puts the reply in the mouth of an Orleans merchant named Hazon. See Arts. on LAISSEZ-FAIRE.

[August Oncken, *Die Maxime Laissez-faire*, Bern, 1886, pp. 22-38.]　　　　　E. CA.

LEGITIM. A term in Scots law. It signifies the right of succession of children to the personal estate of their father to the extent of one-third. This right vests in them at their father's death, and is indefeasible by his will. It may, however, be expressly renounced by any child, or discharged by special provision.
　　　　　M. G. D.

LEGOYT, ALFRED (1815-1885). Legoyt, an eminent French civil servant, statistician, and economist, began life as a lawyer, but soon entered the public service in the office of the ministry of the interior. In 1839 he already occupied the posts of *Chef de Bureau de l'administration générale*, and of *Secrétaire de la Commission Permanente des Archives*. In 1852 he succeeded MOREAU DE JONNÈS as *Directeur du Bureau de la Statistique Générale de la France*, which post he held until an advanced age. He accomplished much useful work in his department, including the establish-ment of the extensive system of agricultural and industrial statistics which exist in France.

Among his later works may be mentioned his essay on *Les Forces Matérielles de l'Empire Allemand*, published in 1877, and his remarkable monograph on *Suicide*, published in 1881.
　　　　　W. H.

LE HARDY DE BEAULIEU, CHARLES, (1816-1871), was born at Uccle near Brussels and died at Mons. He was one of the most scientific popularisers of economics of his time.

His remarks, "The intervention of the state in all branches of human activity is suitable in the infancy of societies : . . . The system of liberty characterises manhood," show a man deeply liberal in mind. He showed himself clearly the disciple of Adam Smith, of J. B. Say, of Bastiat, of Dunoyer, and of M. Gustave de Molinari. He was a very able mining engineer, but becoming blind at the age of forty-two, he devoted himself exclusively to moral and political science. A free trader by conviction, he laboured for the cause of commercial liberty in Belgium.

The chief of De Beaulieu's economic writings are, *Du Salaire*, 1st ed. 1858-59 ; 2nd ed. 1862, 8vo ; *Traité élementaire d'économie politique*, 1861, 8vo ; *La Propriété et sa rente*, 1862, 8vo.　A. C. f.

LEIB, JOHANN GEORG (beginning of the 18th century), was one of the numerous German authors whom the contemporary methods of the French administration filled with admiration ; according to his opinion, everything "which belongs to *Oeconomia regia* was perfectly well understood in France."

In his principal work, *Von Verbesserung Land und Leuten*, Leipzig and Frankfort, 1780, Leib describes the leading object of statesmanship— "to keep money in the country and invite in money from its neighbours." He divides the population into the sustentative (*nahrhafte*) classes, comprising artisans, peasants, and merchants, and the unsustentative (*nichtnahrhafte*) classes ; still, even peasants are only producers in so far as their productiveness conforms to the above leading principle.

[Roscher, *Gesch. der Nat. Oek. in Deutschland*, p. 302.]　　　　　E. CA.

LEIBNIZ (LEIBNITZ), BARON GOTTFRIED WILHELM VON (1646-1716), was too universal in genius and sympathies not to devote time and energy to the consideration of economic problems. In his correspondence he claimed to have studied them, and especially those connected with currency, even to the extent of studying mines and metallurgy, "as much as any one," and to have accumulated much material on this subject. He held that "political economy was by far the greatest part of political science " (Dutens, v. 214 *et seq.*), and urged that economic knowledge, "for lack of which Germany was perishing," should to a greater extent be imparted in education (v. 175 *et seq.*). But beyond the weight of his influence and counsels applied where his position as philosopher and statesman gave opportunity, and a few judgments on economic matters scattered amongst his political monographs and his letters, he has left no contribution to economic thought, but room instead for regret that a scholar so eminently fitted, as Roscher has remarked, by his philosophic breadth of vision, his mathematical and judicial perspicacity, and his sympathetic interest in, and sagacious judgments respecting, the actual condition and course of affairs, to have been a great economist, should not have anticipated Adam Smith by a century. The task of gleaning from his writings the scattered judgments alluded to has been efficiently carried out in Roscher's *Geschichte der Nationaloekonomik* (cp. xvii. pp. 329 *et seq.*), and may here be summarised. Leibniz formulated the sources of wealth by saying that "the strength of a country lies *in terra, rebus, hominibus*" (iv. 531), but especially *in hominum numero* (iv. 502) ; in connection with which latter statement we find him estimating the population of Prussia by multiplying the annual number of births by thirty. He would not admit opposing interests in trade and agriculture, but saw only an economic harmony which taxation should be so adjusted as not to disturb. Agriculture was to commerce and manufactures as the root and trunk of a tree to the branches (v. 577). Elaboration of matter involves waste. A nation exporting raw material only to reimport it when made up is as a man who consents to buy of a thief a horse identical with the one of which he has been robbed, because of this sole difference that it has lost its tail (Onno Klopp, *Die Werke von Leibniz*, Hanover, 1864, i. 140). He warmly praised Locke's writings on currency, but held that our restoration of the coinage in 1696 was too costly, if magnanimous. He held it was no use to establish a sound currency without also establishing a *tarif raisonnable* of the prices of commodities, else we get into the circle of measuring money by money (Dutens, vi. 250). The regulation of the currency could only be effectively carried out by international agreement (233-266). He approved of interest (v. 480), but mostly hoarded his own capital, and he had a mathematician's weakness for lotteries (v. 533).

Leibniz' works are in several collections, not one complete. *Opera*, ed. G. G. Dutens (Geneva, 1768, 6 vols. 4to.); German ed. by Pertz and Gerhardt (19 vols., 1873-90), and by O. Klopp (11 vols., 1862-84), and one in French, by Foucher de Careil, 1859, etc., to which the pages quoted refer.) C. A. F.

LEMONNIER, CHARLES (b. 1808). A French advocate, in early youth a fervent disciple of ST. SIMON (*q.v.*), a selected edition of whose works he edited in 1859. He practised at the Bordeaux bar.

In 1843 he published *Commentaire sur les principales polices d'assurance maritime usitées en France (Paris, Bordeaux, Marseilles, Le Havre, Nantes, Rouen, Dunkerque, Bayonne)*, Paris, 8vo, 2 vols., a work of recognised authority. Lemonnier was one of the founders of "la ligue internationale de la paix et de la liberté," and a regular contributor to its journal, *Les États unis d'Europe.— Les bases d'une organisation fédérale de l'Europe*, appeared in its pages. *La question sociale*, Paris, 1871, 8vo, is a reprint of an address delivered at a meeting of the League at Lausanne. Political economy, being a branch of morals, is founded, like the latter, on the independence and liberty of the individual. Following ROUSSEAU and LOCKE, Lemonnier maintains that the foundation of the social contract is property; at the same time great alterations in the law are needed, to secure its proper diffusion.

[Introduction to *Les États unis d'Europe*, Paris, 1872, 16mo, by V. Poupin.] H. E. E.

LENDA or LEZDA, inland custom duties paid by merchants in Aragon. The *lenda maritima* was equivalent to our modern customs. E. CA.

LENZI, DOMENICO (14th century). A Florentine; among many writers on economic subjects, of that period, Lenzi, a corn chandler, is noted for a history of the prices of provisions, and of the complaints of the frequenters of the Mercato Vecchio, Florence,

against the officials who levied the tax on provisions. He also initiated ideas of greater freedom in trade.

Specchio umano o Diario di Domenico Lenzi (1320-1335), pub. with illust. by P. V. Fineschi, ent. *Storia compendiata di alcune carestie edovizie di grano, occorse in Firenze*, Florence, Viviani, 1767. [See G. Toniolo, *Scolastica ed umanismo nelle dottrine economiche al tempo del rinascimento in Toscana*, Pisa, Nistri, 1887.] U. R.

LÉONCE DE LAVERGNE (Louis Gabriel Léonce Guilhard de). See LAVERGNE, L. G. L. G. DE.

LE PLAY, PIERRE GUILLAUME FRÉDÉRIC (1806-1882), though not, in many respects, to be classed among strict economists, exercised a profound influence upon economic study by the originality of his work and the strength of his following. The son of a custom-house officer, he was born at La Rivière Saint-Sauveur, a village near Honfleur, was educated at the *École Polytechnique* in Paris, where he distinguished himself in mathematics and natural science, and, on passing out of the school, entered the service of the state as a mining engineer, in which capacity he showed great energy and powers of observation. In 1832 he was appointed co-editor of the *Annales des Mines*, in 1834 head of the newly-formed permanent committee of mining statistics, and in 1840 professor of metallurgy at the school of mines. He systematically spent his long vacations in foreign travel, closely observing not only the nature of the soils and their mineral deposits, but also the peoples who dwelt upon them, and the works, especially of steel, iron, copper, etc., in which they were employed. He commenced these voyages in 1829 by a visit of seven months to Germany, Belgium, and Holland; and subsequently extended his travels to England, Spain, Denmark, Sweden and Norway, Austria, Hungary, Italy, Switzerland, Russia, and the west of Asia, returning to England, e.g., as often as seven times. The early fruits of these studies are *Observations sur le mouvement commercial des principales substances minérales entre la France et les puissances étrangères, pendant les douze dernières années, et particulièrement pendant les années, 1829-31 (published in the Annales des Mines, 1832); Observations sur l'histoire naturelle et la richesse minérale de l'Espagne*, 8vo, 1834 (at the request of the Spanish government); *Vues générales sur la statistique, suivies d'un aperçu d'une statistique générale de la France*, 1840; and *Descriptions des procédés métallurgiques employés dans le pays de Galles pour la fabrication du cuivre, et recherches sur l'état actuel et sur l'avenir probable de la production et du commerce de ce métal*, 496 pp., 8vo, 1840. In 1851 he was sent by the government to London to report upon the cutlery and steel instruments exhibited at the great exhibition, and in 1855 was entrusted with the arrangement and classification of products at the Paris exhibition, of which he became commissioner-general. He held the same post on behalf of France at the London exhibition of 1862, and at the French exhibition of 1867 ; and was created counsellor of state in 1855, and senator in 1867, in recognition of these services. After the senate fell with the empire in 1870 he did not seek to re-enter Parliament, but devoted the remaining twelve years of his life to the propagation of his views upon social peace and the reconciliation of material progress with industrial harmony. In the course of the travels already referred to, Le Play had minutely studied the lives and economic circumstances of some 300 families, considered by local authorities to be fairly typical of their class, and had noted a multitude of facts with regard to them in the hope that comparison and induction would disclose the factors upon which the well-being of families really depends. A selection of thirty-six of the most valuable and complete of these family monographs constituted his great work, *Les Ouvriers Européens* (1st edition, a luxurious folio printed at the Imprimerie Nationale, 1855 ; 2nd edition enlarged, 6 vols., 8vo, 1877-79). The core of each monograph is an elaborate budget of the yearly receipts and expenses of the family, each item figuring separately with its quantity and average price. Capital is also taken into account, and inventories with prices are given of every article possessed by the family, while income or consumption in kind is carefully accounted for, and every accessory portion of revenue is rigidly traced to its precise source. The budgets thus framed are the most technically exact and complete which have yet appeared, and must serve as models for all further studies of this kind. Grouped round the budget are numerous classified details which influence or explain the budget itself, such as the composition of the family in age, sex, number ; history of the family ; morals and hygiene ; nature of employment ; means of existence ; mode of existence, number and nature of meals, kind of dwelling, furniture, clothing, recreation ; and excursuses upon large general questions or small particular details incidentally suggested by the budget. The academy rewarded the book on its appearance with the Monthyon prize of statistics. In 1856 Le Play founded the *Société internationale des études pratiques d'Économie Sociale* to pursue these studies in different countries. The society received and has retained the support of a great number of persons, including the most eminent of French economists, and still publishes every three months a family monograph in its series *Les Ouvriers des deux mondes*. In 1881 the society commenced the publication of an economic journal, *La Réforme Sociale* (still flourishing,

published fortnightly), which is read also by the two or three thousand members of the *Unions de la Paix Sociale*, or small local clubs, founded in 1872, to study and apply the methods of Le Play. The members of the *Société d'Economie Sociale* also meet periodically for discussions, banquets, etc.

The facts tabulated in the family budgets, while highly valuable, suggestive, and even inspiring, have not yet yielded any economic generalisations. On this side the study is merely objective, not inductive. The principal conclusions arrived at by Le Play himself bear rather upon the morals than the economics of industry. They are, *e.g.*, the duty of the employer to promote with paternal care (*patronage*), yet unobtrusively, the material comfort and moral well-being of his employés and their families, and not to content himself with a cash-nexus ; the importance of preserving the family as a cohesive element in society, and, to this end, the advantage of free power of testation (see BEQUEST, POWER OF) ; the duty of the state to protect the weak and injured, and to provide, as in England, a remedy for seduction by an action for damages ; the advisability of maintaining local and flexible customs rather than imposing from above general and inflexible regulations ; and the advantages of perquisites and privileges as a sauce to wages. Such considerations, notwithstanding their importance, belong chiefly to the domain of the statesman rather than the economist. The careful studies of fact made and recorded by the school of Le Play, in their monographs and their journal, are of great value to economists ; but Le Play himself rated theory too low to impose any dogma of theory upon his followers, and economists of varied shades of thought are thus enabled to unite among his following in spite of their divergencies of view.

The *Ouvriers Européens* was a collection of facts. *La Réforme Sociale* (2 vols., 8vo, 1864, 7th ed. 3 vols., 18mo, 1887) is the sequel of conclusions mainly moral. The other chief works of Le Play are *L'Organisation du Travail*, 1870 (an American translation by G. Emerson, Philadelphia, 1872 ; and a Spanish translation, 1894) ; *L'Organisation de la famille*, 1872 ; *La Constitution de l'Angleterre* (in collaboration with M. Delaire), 1875 ; *La constitution essentielle de l'humanité*, 1880.

Le Play had evidently no scientific training in economic theory. His grievances against Adam Smith and Malthus, for example, are largely imaginary, and would have been dispelled by personal acquaintance with their works. His ambition to achieve for social science the success which observation, classification, and comparison had rendered to natural science, can hardly be said to have been achieved ; but his mineralogical knowledge, joined to natural sagacity and penetration, aid him to throw into strong relief the influence of environment and "outside" circumstances upon the fate of industries and of individuals, while his close study of the family shows clearly the modifications which pure theory, on a hypothesis of perfectly "fluid" individuals, must admit before it corresponds to the facts of real life. His division of the stages of civilisation into three groups according as the family is patriarchal or stable (with community of goods), a *famille-souche* or family stock (with primogeniture and younger branches), or, lastly, unstable (with forced partition, as in France), belongs rather to sociology than to economics, and is not invulnerable to criticism. It was indeed partly from schism on this point, partly from other motives, that a small dissident group of Le Play's disciples has been formed, who claim to develop rather than stereotype his method. Their journal is *La Science Sociale*. The *Société d'Économie Sociale* has branches in almost all countries. The most active and vigorous is that of Belgium.

"The school of Le Play," says Professor Gide, "seeks to re-establish social peace by authority in a threefold form : that of the father in the family, the master in the factory, the church in the state, with the condition of reciprocal duties on the part of these social authorities" (*Prin. d'Écon. Pol.*, 4th ed. 1894, p. 35) ; and he points out that it has departed from the traditional optimism of the economists, classical and socialist, in France. This definition of their principles is not entirely accepted by Le Play's followers, who contend that devotion to social duty and moral responsibility rather than authority are the true watchwords of the school.

[See FRENCH SCHOOL ; CHRISTIANITY AND ECONOMICS ; (ROMAN CATHOLIC SCHOOL) ; article on "Le Play" by Henry Higgs, in *Harvard Quarterly Journal of Economics*, June 1890.— "Les cent monographies de famille comparées" . . . by Cheysson and Tocqué in *Bulletin de l'Institut International de Statistique*, 1893.— "Workmen's Budgets," by Henry Higgs, *Journal Royal Stat. Soc.*, June 1894.—F. Auburtin, "Le Play," in *Guillaumin's Petite Bibliothèque Économique*, 1893.—Ch. de Ribbe, *Le Play d'après sa correspondance*, 1883.—C. Jannet, in *Quatre écoles d'économie sociale*, Geneva, 1890.—P. de Rousiers, "Le Play and Social Science" (*Annals of American Academy*, 1894).] H. H.

LEPTA (modern Greek coin). The equivalent of the French centime (see CENT ; CENTESIMI).

LEROUX, PIERRE (1797-1871), born and died at Paris, was a philosopher rather than a socialist. After hard but desultory studies he became a printer, and in 1824 established *Le Globe*, which periodical he devoted in 1831 to St. Simonism.

A few months after, he, with Bazard, separated himself utterly from his coreligionists, who met in the Rue Monsigny, on the occasion of the publication of Enfantin's views on, or rather against, marriage. Leroux then became chief editor of the *Revue Encyclopédique* ; established in 1819 and abandoned in 1833, sixty-two volumes, two being tables. In 1838 he started, with Jean Reynaud, *L'Encyclopédie nouvelle*, a monumental work never completed through lack of funds ; eight volumes only appeared, 1838-41, in small quarto.

Having been appointed a member of the constituent assembly in June 1848, he was implicated in the proceedings resulting from the attempt of 15th May against that body, but it was soon seen that he had been calumniated. He was again elected in 1849 to the legislative assembly. When the *coup d'état* of December 1851 occurred, he was exiled and lived out of France until his return at the end of the last empire. He died at Paris during the commune, and was honoured by a public funeral, being looked upon rather as the head of the socialist school than as a theosophist.

As a philosopher, Leroux opposed the ideas of the eclectic school as exemplified by Cousin and Henry Jouffroy, and substituted pantheism slightly tinged with materialism. He also believed in the transmigration of souls, a doctrine incompatible with individuality. Man is only part of a whole, proceeding thence at birth to return thither at death, and to leave it again, but on a higher level, —a progress repeated incessantly and eternally in the past and in the future. Again, with Pythagoras, he accepted the power of number. The "triad," or group of three, played an important part in the development of his philosophico-socialist ideas. Man is sensation, or sentiment, or intellect. He may be, and sometimes is, all three at once, but one of these tendencies predominates in him. The union of three individualities, one possessing sensibility (imagination), another sentiment (the heart), the third knowledge (reason), as the predominating quality is indispensable for the realisation of progress. Social harmony results from this triad, which Pierre Leroux discovers in God—as power, love, intelligence ; in the family—as father, mother, and child ; in the nation—city, commune, state ; in the people—citizen, partner, functionary ; in the motto of the French republic —Liberty, Equality, and Fraternity (perhaps author of it) ; in production—capital, labour, land, etc., etc. Pierre Leroux discovers it everywhere, attributing to it a secret power, recalling the astrologers of the middle ages. The reasoned proof of this pretended law must not be asked of Pierre Leroux ; he takes little pains to demonstrate it—he asserts and prophesies at random. Besides this, though he never betrayed pontifical tendencies like Enfantin and Auguste Comte, he proposed to establish a religion. His socialism was entirely speculative. He neither sought to enthrall by brute force nor to inveigle people to his ideas. Thoroughly sincere in his errors, but convinced that he was right, he set forth his doctrines with warmth, with an eloquence often marred by wilful exaggerations, by intentional repetitions wearisome to the reader.

He was an ardent partisan of equality not only in public but in private life. He approved meals in common. Individuality according to him is an evil, collective action alone promotes the welfare of humanity. The state holding the instruments of production in its own hands is to distribute work according to the capabilities of every man, to divide the results according to the necessities of every man. Property, through inequality, is the scapegoat charged with all the sins of this world. He thus reaches a collectivism and even a communism which anarchists would consider rather reactionary nowadays. However, he preserves the family and unreservedly asserts the existence of God. But he denounces Malthus and his disciples at least as vigorously as Proudhon did.

There is nothing new in the economic ideas of Pierre Leroux, except his intemperate declamations against society, embodied in a great mass of quotations generally warped from their right meaning by change of surroundings, but showing the extent of his reading, ill directed as it was. Pierre Leroux, with his great intelligence, could, by methodical and close study, have produced useful and durable works. He preferred the easier road of half-knowledge and substituted sophisms for science, thus flattering the ignorance of the masses and obtaining some popularity, though without having aimed at it.

Pierre Leroux was sincere and did not deserve the epithets of quack and mountebank which Proudhon less than any one else had the right to apply to him. He lived simply, even for a workman of his condition. His private life won the esteem of all who knew him.

Leroux wrote much ; the following are his principal works :—*De l'humanité*, 2 vols. 8vo, 1st ed. 1840, 2nd ed. 1845 (contains an article in the *Revue des deux mondes* of 15th February 1836 on "Le Bonheur").—*De l'Egalité*, 1st ed. 1838, 2nd ed. 1848, 8vo, composed of articles which appeared in the *Encyclopédie nouvelle*.—*De la ploutocratie ou du gouvernement des riches*, 16mo, 1848, an article which appeared in 1843 in the *Revue indépendante*, a monthly republican publication established by Mme. Georges Sand in Nov. 1841, in opposition to the *Revue des deux mondes*, the monarchical periodical of that time. The *Revue indépendante* ceased to appear 24th February 1848, and forms 39 vols. 8vo).—*D'une religion nationale ou du culte*, 1844.—*Malthus et les économistes, ou y aura-t-il toujours des pauvres*, 1849 ; articles which appeared in 1846 in the *Revue Sociale*, a monthly periodical started by Pierre Leroux in October 1845, with this sub-title, *Ou solution pacifique du problème du prolétariat*. It ceased to appear in 1847.—*Discours sur la situation actuelle de la société et de l'ésprit humain ;* one vol. 8vo, in 1841, in two vols. 12mo, 1847,—a reproduction of several articles published before 1841.—*Le carrosse de M. Aguado*, a fragment, 8vo, 1848.—*Du christianisme et de son origine démocratique*, 12mo, 1848, an extract from the *Encyclopédie nouvelle.*—*Projet d'une constitution démocratique et sociale*, 8vo, 1848.—*La grève de Samarez*, a philosophic poem, Paris, 1864, unfinished, only three parts appeared.
A. c. f.

LESLIE, THOMAS EDWARD CLIFFE (1825 ?-1882), was born in the county of Wexford, Ireland. The year of his birth is commonly said to have been 1827, and that date appears on his monument at Belfast; but according to the matriculation book of Trinity College, it was 1825. He was the son of an Anglican clergyman. After receiving some instruction in the classics from his father, he was sent to King William's College in the Isle of Man. In 1842 he entered the university of Dublin. It is worthy of notice that John E. CAIRNES, William E. HEARN, author of *Plutology* and *The Aryan Household*, and Richard H. WALSH, afterwards professor of political economy at Dublin, and author of a work on *Metallic Currency*, were in the same class with Leslie. He obtained a scholarship in Trinity College, a distinction then to be won only by classical knowledge, and graduated as senior moderator in logics and ethics in 1847. He was called to the bar in 1848 ; but in 1853, ceasing to seek practice, became professor of political economy and jurisprudence in Queen's College, Belfast, continuing, however, to reside in London. He now devoted himself altogether to economic and social studies, and during the following years wrote many articles in different periodicals on questions of the day. He travelled on the Continent in his holidays, and studied personally the economic condition of France, Belgium, and Germany, especially of the rural population in those countries. The writings founded on these observations attracted much attention, and excited the admiration of J. S. MILL ; a good specimen of them is supplied by the essay on Auvergne. In the course of these tours he made the acquaintance of some distinguished men—amongst them, of L. de LAVERGNE and E. de LAVELEYE ; to the memory of the former of these he paid a warm tribute in an obituary notice in the *Fortnightly Review* for February 1881 ; and with the latter he continued in relations of cordial intimacy to the close of his life.

In 1870 he published *Land Systems and Industrial Economy of Ireland, England, and Continental Countries ;* and two essays of his appeared in volumes issued under the auspices of the Cobden Club, one on the *Land System of France*, 2nd ed., 1870, a defence of peasant proprietorship ; and the other on *Financial Reform*, 2nd ed., 1871, a criticism of the system of indirect taxation. In 1879 he collected a number of his scattered papers under the title of *Essays in Political and Moral Philosophy*. A second edition of this volume has appeared since his death, in which some of the essays have been omitted ; and others, written after 1879, have been included. Those who would either understand the character of his mind, or conceive aright his systematic views on political economy, must study both these volumes. He had now arrived at the fulness of his powers ; he had matured his opinions, and extended his experience and knowledge in various directions. It was natural to expect from him something designed on a larger scale than anything he had yet produced. He was known to have been long engaged in preparing an economic and legal history of England. But the manuscript was, unfortunately, lost in some unexplained way during a tour in France, and the book was never rewritten. The article on the "History and Future of Profit" in *Fort. Review*, Nov. 1881, "is believed to have been in substance and form an extract from it." The papers he left behind contained many notes, references, and isolated passages, intended beyond doubt as materials towards this work, but nothing was found sufficiently complete or coherent to be given to the world. He had suffered for years from a painful malady, recurring at uncertain intervals, which often made intellectual exertion impossible ; so that, whilst some perhaps thought he might have done more, those who knew him wondered that he was able to do so much. He sank under one of the attacks of this disease during a visit to Belfast on professorial duty.

Leslie has treated several special subjects, such as PRICES, WAGES, the DISTRIBUTION OF THE PRECIOUS METALS, and the Irish agrarian question, with great ability. But the eminent service which secures to him a permanent place in the history of social science was that of having founded the English historical school of political economy. He was the first of our fellow-countrymen to lay down and defend the philosophical principles on which the HISTORICAL METHOD rests. This he did to some extent in earlier writings ; but what may be called his decisive manifesto on the subject was an essay which appeared in the Dublin university periodical, *Hermathena* (vol. iv. 1876), followed up by an article entitled "Political Economy and Sociology," in the *Fortnightly Review* for January 1879.

He has himself mentioned that the first influence which inclined him in this historical direction was that of Sir Henry Maine, whose lectures he had attended as a law student. Maine had represented existing juristic institutions as the result of a long evolution, and Leslie was thus led to apply the same method to the economic phenomena of society. At a later period he became acquainted with Roscher's *Geschichte der National-Oekonomie in Deutschland*, and gave an account of it in the *Fortnightly Review ;* and he also mentions with marked commendation Knies's well-known treatise on economic method. He was, however, by no means a mere copyist of these works, but approached the whole subject from an independent point of view of his own, though well acquainted with the general line taken by Roscher and other German economists. He was also much influenced by the *Philosophie Positive* of Auguste Comte, of whose "prodigious genius" he speaks in one of his essays,

though he did not accept the social polity or the religious system of that great thinker. But, after allowing for all these influences, there remain in the way in which he presents, vindicates, illustrates, and applies the method, such freshness and originality as show it to have been, in the form in which he conceived it, a genuine product of independent thought. Most of what he has left us is fragmentary, but it has a value far more than corresponding to its quantity. His labours, though they have largely modified contemporary opinion, have not yet by any means produced their entire effect, or fully received the recognition they deserve ; it may be safely predicted that, with the progress of general sociology, they will be more and more highly appreciated, and he will be seen to have taken a leading part in a great work of scientific reform.

[*Encycl. Brit.*, 9th ed.—*Handw. der Staatswissenschaften.* The present article, like the two here cited, is largely founded on personal knowledge.] J. K. I.

LETROSNE (or LETRÔNE) GUILLAUME FRANÇOIS (1728-80), born at Orleans, died at Paris, began life as a writer on legal subjects and a pupil of the well-known Pothier. At first "natural rights" and the "rights of man" entirely absorbed his intellectual activity, but in 1764 he was attracted by Quesnay and became one of his followers.

Till 1777 Letrosne did not write more than articles for the *Journal de l'agriculture, du commerce, et des finances,* and pamphlets. His most important economic work is *De l'ordre social, ouvrage suivi d'un traité élémentaire sur la valeur, l'argent, la circulation, l'industrie, le commerce intérieur et extérieur,* 2 vols. 8vo, 1777. The first volume, a course of lectures on social order ; the second contains a treatise with the special title "De l'interêt social par rapport à la valeur, à la circulation, à l'industrie, et au commerce intérieur et extérieur." This section is reprinted in the collection of Guillaumin (*Physiocrats*, 1846). This work is praiseworthy,—the style is more simple and clear than is usual among the physiocrats. Though Letrosne possessed the *lumen siccum,* he never attained the reputation of Mercier de la Rivière ; but his book, *De l'administration provinciale et de la réforme de l'impôt,* followed by a *Dissertation sur la féodalité,* 1779, is still frequently quoted. It is a ponderous volume, scientific in tone, which, from the point of view of the financier, had the advantage of appearing four years before the work of Necker on the administration of the financial affairs of France ; and from the point of view of the politician, of appearing ten years before the celebrated night of 5th August 1789. A. C. f.

Eugène Daire, in the short notice of Letrosne in the *Collection des Principaux Economistes*, remarks of tome ii. of the second section of the work mentioned above, *De l'interêt social par rapport à la valeur,* etc., "that it treats the economic questions with which it deals with a depth of view which it is impossible not to recognise."

The school of the physiocrats had complete confidence in the continuity of material progress and in its influence on the welfare of individuals. "No one can live without the aid of his fellows ; the labour of others helps us ; the transformations of matter, the improvements in transport ; the improvements of the land, all inventions past and present, whether near or at a distance, all are useful to us."

The paragraph at the conclusion of Letrosne's book expresses these opinions with force and fulness. "I have shown in this work what is the origin of value and its influence on the revenues and the prosperity of a nation. I have marked out the functions of money, the source and the effect of circulation. I have described the nature of the results of industry and commerce, their usefulness in relation to our wants, but their absolute sterility in relation to the increase of our wealth.

"From these truths I have deduced the *unity of social interests and its conformity with the laws of justice*. . . . The philosophers . . . never cease to tell us that it is necessary to encourage cultivation. We must support industry and look on them as two sisters. Without doubt they are two sisters ; but one an elder sister who supports the younger, and the elder sister has never sought for exclusive privilege nor for advantage, nor for bounty against her younger sister. Industry has to be supported, but this should not be by injuring either directly or indirectly the cultivation of the land which supports it. It is not through the leaves, it is through the roots that the tree grows ; the leaves adorn it, and even contribute to its growth, but it is the roots which supply the sap which they employ."

LETTER OF ADMINISTRATION. See ADMINISTRATION, LETTERS OF.

LETTER OF ALLOTMENT. A subscriber to a new company, or to an issue of shares, bonds, or public securities, receives, in reply to his application, a letter, properly signed, in which is stated the amount, if any, allotted to him or her. It is usual, on this letter, to specify the amounts payable, and the dates on which they respectively fall due. The letter also contains a receipt for the amount already received from the subscriber.

We would here register a firm protest against the way in which allotments are sometimes made. All applicants are naturally supposed to be on the same footing ; but even great houses, never suspected of legal dishonesty, have been known to allot good things to favourite friends, and comparatively bad things to the general public. It is a question if law ought not to be brought to the assistance of public opinion.   A. E.

LETTER OF APPLICATION. When an issue of shares, bonds, or other securities is offered to the public, those who apply do so in the terms laid down and on the form provided by the PROSPECTUS (*q.v.*). The form is usually a mere request for the allotment of a specified quantity of the issue, the subscriber enclosing a cheque for the sum stipulated—usually 5 per cent or more of the amount applied for—without which his application will not be entertained.   A. E.

LETTER OF CREDIT. See CREDIT, LETTER OF.

LETTERS PATENT. See PATENTS.

LEÜ (Roumanian coin). The equivalent of the French franc (see FRANC).

LEV (Bulgarian coin). The equivalent of the French franc (see FRANC).

LEVANT COMPANY. See TURKEY COMPANY.

LEVANT DOLLAR. See DOLLAR, MARIA THERESA.

LEVANTINE THALER. See DOLLAR, MARIA THERESA.

LEVI, LEONE (1821 - 88), economist and statistician, born at Ancona of Jewish parents, in later life became a Christian and a devoted member of the Presbyterian Church. Trained to a commercial career, he went to Liverpool in 1844, to extend his brother's business as commission-agent and merchant. He became naturalised, and acquiring the English language, soon established a connection. After the crisis of 1847, however, the business failed, and he obtained employment in a mercantile house in Liverpool. In 1849 he advocated, in letters to the *Liverpool Albion*, the establishment of representative chambers of commerce, and of permanent tribunals of commerce, constituted of a legally-trained judge, with mercantile assessors. These letters formed the basis of two pamphlets, —*Chambers and Tribunals of Commerce, and proposed General Chamber of Commerce in Liverpool* (1849), and *The State of the Law of Arbitrament, and proposed Tribunal of Commerce*(1850). The Liverpool chamber of commerce was immediately established, with Levi as honorary secretary ; similar institutions followed at Leeds, Bradford, Hull, and other centres of industry, and finally in London. As secretary to the Liverpool chamber, Levi acquired through official channels "exact information about foreign chambers of commerce, and the laws applying to commercial transactions in their respective countries." The result was a synopsis of the commercial law of Christendom which might serve as a step towards an international code of commerce. He interested the Prince Consort and other influential personages, and further expounded the scheme in lectures delivered in the chief cities and towns of the kingdom. In 1852 he wrote *Commercial Law : its Principles and Administration ; or, the Mercantile Law of Great Britain compared with the Codes and Laws of Commerce of the following Mercantile Countries* (fifty-nine being enumerated), *and the Institutes of Justinian*. The publication became an international event, and gold medals and prizes were showered on the compiler. At Levi's suggestion, a congress was held in November 1852, to discuss practical measures for harmonising the laws of the three kingdoms.

As the result of a royal commission of inquiry, the Mercantile Law Amendment Acts of 1856 were passed, which removed some of the more conspicuous discrepancies between English, Scotch, and Irish law. The commission likewise examined into the expediency of introducing the principle of trading with limited liability into the law of partnership, but to Levi's disappointment reported against the proposal. In 1853 Levi gave evidence before a parliamentary committee in favour of the collection of agricultural statistics, but nothing of importance in this direction was done until thirteen years later. In 1855 he read a paper before the Law Amendment Society, *On Judicial Statistics*, and drafted a bill on the subject which Brougham introduced in the Lords but afterwards withdrew.

Levi was appointed, in 1852, to the newly-constituted chair of commercial law at King's College, London. He removed to the metropolis, and was called to the bar at Lincoln's Inn in 1859. He long and ably discharged the duties of his ill-remunerated professorship. A free-trader by conviction, and not content with arguing against protection on abstract grounds, he collected a large mass of statistics of a practical character. His communications to the meetings of the British Association, and his letters to the *Times* on commercial and financial subjects, gave him a high reputation as a statistician. He was a frequent contributor to the journals of the Statistical Society, and represented the society at foreign congresses. In 1861 he received from the university of Tübingen the degree of doctor of economical and political science. He was honorary secretary of the metric committee of the British Association, and of the international association for promoting one uniform system of weights, measures, and coins. In 1887 Levi visited Italy as a delegate from the Statistical Society to the congress of European statisticians held at Rome. He also visited his native town of Ancona, where he founded, in connection with the technical institute, a free scientific library and a lectureship on the laws of commerce in relation to science and moral international laws.

The following is a list of the most important of Levi's works :—In 1854 he published his *Manual of the Mercantile Law of Great Britain and Ireland*. In support of his views on international arbitration he published *The Law of Nature and Nations as affected by Divine Law*, 1855 ; *Peace the Handmaid of Commerce, with Remarks on the Eastern Crisis*, 1876 ; *War and its consequences, Economical, Commercial, Financial, and Moral, with Proposals for the Establishment of a Court of International Reference and Arbitration*, 1881 ; and *International Law, with Materials for a Code of International Law*, 1887. He also wrote *Annals of British Legislation, being a classified and Analysed Summary of Public Bills, Statutes, Accounts, and Papers, Reports of Committees and of Commissioners, and of Sessional Papers generally of the Houses of Lords and Commons, together with Accounts of Commercial Legislation, Tariffs, and Facts relating to Foreign Countries*, 1856-65. The fourteen volumes of this work were afterwards expanded into eighteen under the title of *Annals of British Legislation*, being a digest of the parliamentary blue-books to 1868.

To the condition, wages, and savings of the working classes Levi paid special attention—see reference to this in his papers on Changes in Average Wages, etc., by A. L. Bowley, *Journal of Statistical Society*, June 1895. Among the reports and pamphlets which Levi wrote on those topics are *Wages and Earnings of the Working Classes, with some Facts illustrative of their Economic Condition, from Authentic and Official Sources*, in a report to Mr. Michael T. Bass, M.P., 1867. *Estimate of the amount of Taxation falling on the Working Classes of the United Kingdom*, a report to Mr. M. T. Bass, M.P., 1873. *Work and Pay, or Principles of Industrial Economy ;* two courses of lectures delivered to working men in King's College, London, with the report of the committee of the British Association on combinations of labourers and capitalists, 1877. *The Economic Condition of Fishermen*, 1883, being a paper read at a conference at the International Fisheries Exhibition.—*Wages and Earnings of the Working Classes*, a Report to Sir Arthur Bass, 1885.

Levi's most important work was his *History of British Commerce and of the Economic Progress of the British Nation*, 1763-1870, published 1872, second edition 1880, with graphic tables, and a continuation down to 1878. The history embraced the researches of a lifetime, and became a standard work of acknowledged value. In addition to the above, the author published many separate lectures on economic or commercial subjects. He likewise edited treatises on the metric system of weights and measures.

[*Journal of the Royal Statistical Society*, vol. li.—*Men of the Time*, 12th ed.—*Dictionary of National Biography*, vol. xxx. ; and the various works of Levi, together with an autobiographical fragment, *The Story of my Life*, privately printed in 1888.] G. B. S.

LEWIS, SIR GEORGE CORNEWALL (1806-1863), was an eminent scholar, author, and statesman.

In 1830, together with J. S. MILL, he attended Austin's lectures on jurisprudence at London University, and, as the first fruit of his studies in this line, there appeared, in 1832, his well-known and suggestive *Remarks on the Use and Abuse of some Political Terms*, an attempt "to illustrate the various uses of the principal terms belonging to political science," undertaken "with the view of affording to political speculation the assistance to be derived from a technical vocabulary" (p. 1).

In 1833 Lewis was appointed assistant-commissioner on the Irish Poor Inquiry Commission, and was shortly afterwards directed to make a particular inquiry into the condition of the poorer Irish resident in the United Kingdom. See his report in appendix to *First Report of Irish Poor Inquiry Commissioners* (*Parl. Papers*, 1836,

xxiv. 427-642), also his *Remarks on the Third Report of the Irish Poor Inquiry Commissioners* (London, 1837). Again in 1834 he was included in the commission to inquire into the state of church property and church affairs generally in Ireland. The facts that came to his knowledge, and the conclusions he arrived at on the Irish problem, are clearly set forth in his *Local Disturbances in Ireland and the Irish Church Question* (London, 1836), in which, *inter alia*, he advocates the introduction of an efficient workhouse system (cp. *Letters*, pp. 47-50, 83-85, 189-191). In January 1839 he succeeded his father, Sir Thomas Frankland Lewis, as one of the three principal poor-law commissioners, and held this difficult post till the commission was dissolved and reconstituted in 1847 (cp. *Letters*, pp. 102, 103, 149-151).

In 1847 Lewis entered parliament, and in Lord John Russell's first administration he held office, first as secretary to the board of control (1847-48), then as under-secretary to the home office (1848-50), and finally as financial secretary to the treasury (1850-52). While at the home office he endeavoured, though without success, to carry bills—(1) abolishing turnpike trusts and placing highways under a mixed county board ; (2) amending the law of parochial assessment (*Letters*, pp. 204, 205, 220, 223). Defeated in the general election in 1852, he re-entered parliament in 1855, and shortly afterwards, on the invitation of Lord Palmerston, he reluctantly accepted office as chancellor of the exchequer. To him it fell to meet the financial drain of the Crimean war ; and this, in his war budget of 1855 and his transition budget of 1856, he accomplished with a considerable measure of success. Of the total war expenditure, amounting to about seventy millions (see Buxton, *Finance and Politics*, vol. i. p. 155 n.), more than half was contributed by immediate taxation. While he borrowed, he at the same time imposed taxes sufficient, if maintained, to extinguish within a limited period the additional debt ; and that this was not effected is to be ascribed mainly to the fact that his statesmanlike proposal, in his budget of 1857, to maintain taxation on a modified war footing till 1860, was only partially adopted. It was on the occasion of introducing the budget of 1857 that Lewis startled friends and opponents by protesting against the principle of simplicity in taxation advocated by Adam Smith (*Wealth of Nations*, M'Culloch's ed., pp. 397-400), and subsequently adopted with striking success as the guiding principle in the fiscal legislation of HUSKISSON, PEEL, and Gladstone. As against this he commended the doctrine of Arthur Young, that taxation should bear "lightly on an infinite number of points, heavily on none" (quoted by Northcote, *Twenty Years of Financial Policy*, p. 309). In November 1857, owing to the existence of an acute commercial crisis, the Bank Charter Act was suspended on Lewis's recommendation (see BANK NOTE ; CRISES). To cover this action he obtained the passing of an Indemnity Act in the following month, and at the same time a select committee was appointed to inquire into the working of the Bank Acts.

Lewis was not a great speaker ; he lacked the oratorical impulse. But he was at once a quiet, unpretentious scholar of great and varied learning, and a statesman of high principles and reliable judgment ; a plain man who could not be ambiguous, and who never mixed, as BAGEHOT puts it (*Biog. Studies*, pp. 208, 209), the diagnosis with the prescription, whose character was marked by a straightforward simplicity, untiring industry, great regard for facts, and a born love of truth. His knowledge was as accurate as it was varied ; his conversation itself had "the flavour of exact thought" (*ib.* p. 245). His writings, which cover a vast variety of subjects, and in most of which the influence of Austin's method and teaching is apparent, have suffered somewhat in popularity from their weight of learning. They would probably have been more influential had they been less exhaustive. Those most interesting from the economic stand-point are his works on philosophical and practical politics.

Remarks on the Use and Abuse of some Political Terms, London, 1832 ; new ed. with notes and appendix by Sir R. K. Wilson, Oxford, 1877.—*An Essay on the Government of Dependencies*, London, 1841 ; new ed. by C. P. Lucas, Oxford, 1891.—*An Essay on the Influence of Authority in Matters of Opinion*, London, 1849 ; 2nd ed., London, 1875. —*A Treatise on the Methods of Observation and Reasoning in Politics*, London, 1852, 2 vols. This great "organon for the use of the political inquirer" is, as its author anticipated, little read (cp. *Letters*, pp. 208, 219-220). Besides remarks on the relations between politics, ethics, and economics, it contains discussions on political terms, on the relations between history and theory, on the science, art, and practice of politics, on political induction, the province of experiment, prediction in politics, political ideals, etc., all more or less interesting to the economist (cp. Bagehot, *Biog. Studies*, pp. 238, 239).—*The Financial Statement, 1857, Speech of the Chancellor of the Exchequer in Committee of Supply*, London, 1857.—*Speech on the Introduction of the Bill for the better Government of India*, London, 1858.—*Speeches on Moving the Army Estimates in Committee of Supply in March 1862*, London, 1862.—*Letters of Sir G. C. Lewis to various Friends*, ed. by Sir Gilbert F. Lewis, London, 1870.

[Bagehot's *Biographical Studies*, ed. by R. H. Hutton, 1881, pp. 206-46, 330-33.—*Economic Studies*, 1880, pp. 58, 59, 78.—Walpole's *History of England*, 1880-86, vols. iii. iv. v.—Greville, *Memoirs*, ed. 1888, vols. vii. viii.—Sir S. H. Northcote, *Twenty Years of Financial Policy*, 1862, pp. 264-334, 343-347.—Buxton, *Finance and Politics*, 1888, vol. i. pp. 153-65.—*Dict. of Nat. Biog.*, vol. xxxiii., art. "Lewis, Sir G. C." The bibliography contains a full list of Lewis's contributions to the *Edinburgh Review*, some on economic questions. — *Encyclop. Brit.* vol. xiv.]

A. B. C.

LEWIS, MATTHEW or MARK (latter part of 17th century), writer of school-books and of pamphlets describing various schemes for bringing in the millennium by the substitution of credit for money (see MURRAY, Robert). Lewis apparently anticipated Murray by several years in the proposal to establish storehouses for dead stock on a kind of pawnbroking basis, upon which stock bills of credit were to be issued. Its worth may be estimated from the following example : "Suppose a silk man hath one thousand pounds, he buys silk with it, pawns it in the office for £800 ; this he lays out [on credit ?] again in silk, and pawns that for £700, and so downward. By the help of these banks he lays in four or five thousand pounds' worth of commodities with one thousand pounds." By these methods all the unemployed are to be set to work, and "the running cash of the nation . . . increased it may be a hundredfold, answerable to the credit issued out." The *Proposals* . . . *how this Tax of £160,000*, etc., gives a brief account of a bank established by the "Signiors of Venice not many years since," by which a £100 bill of credit became worth £120 in specie. Nothing, Lewis contended, would be easier than to start such a bank at home, by raising a local land-tax and issuing credit upon it. This idea he developed in the following year in his *Large Model of a Bank*, and in a separate summary of the same : "Whoever can create such a fund that may give out such bills of exchange (or credit current) that shall be always answered with money when demanded, he doth in effect create so much money." His proposed bills are virtually cheques, drawn *not* on cash but on credit only. The one noticeable suggestion in his proposals (*Short Model*) is that by which the "precinct" in which a local branch of his bank is established is to make good all the acts of this branch in case of local loss or defalcation, a principle which bears some resemblance to the unlimited local liability basis of the German and Italian agricultural banks of the present day.

He wrote : *Proposals to Increase Trade, and to Advance His Majesties Revenue, without any hazard or charge to any body, and with apparent profit to every body*, 1677, 12mo, pp. 16.—*Proposals to the King and Parliament how this Tax of £160,000 per moneth may be raised, by a Monethly Tax for one Year, without any Charge to any particular person, and with great advantage to the whole Nation*, 1677, 8vo, pp. 7.—*Proposals to the King and Parliament, or a Large Model of a Bank ; shewing how a Fund of a Bank may be made without much charge, or any hazard, that may give out Bills of Credit to a vast extent, that all Europe will accept of, rather than Mony*, etc., 1678, 8vo, pp. 42.—*A Short Model of a Bank, shewing how a Bank may be erected . . . with apparent profit to every body, except Thieves, Brokers, and Griping Usurers*, etc., n. d. 8vo, pp. 6. [M'Culloch, *Lit. Pol. Econ.*, pp. 157-159.—H. D. Macleod, *Banking*, ch. ix.] E. D.

LEX LOCI CONTRACTUS. The law of the place in which a contract is made generally governs the rules as to its performance, unless a contrary intention appears from the facts of the case. In many cases, however, the law of the place in which the contract is to be performed (*lex loci solutionis*) must be deemed to be applicable, and, if the contract applies to real property, the law of the place in which the property is situate (*lex situs*). The formal requirements are generally determined by the law of the place where the contract is made, and the conditions as to the contractual capacity of the parties depend upon the law of their respective domiciles.

[As to the English opinions on these matters, see Westlake, *Private International Law ;* as to the views of continental writers, see Von Bar, *Internationales Privatrecht,* 2 vols., 2nd ed., 1889.] E. S.

LEX MERCATORIA (see LAW MERCHANT).

LEYMARIE, ACHILLE (1812-1861), a French historian and economist.

Author of a *Histoire du Limousin,* 2 vols. (1845) and of a *Histoire des Paysans en France* (2 vols. 1856). In this work he almost exclusively deals with the legal status of the French peasantry from the Roman Conquest to the French Revolution, principally to the 17th century ; their purely economic life, activities, etc., are not investigated. E. CA.

LIABILITY, LIMITED. Trading with limited liability was sanctioned under the well-known maxim of Roman law, "Si quid universitati debetur singulis non debetur nec quod debet universitas singuli debent" (D. 3, 4, 7, § 1). The members of a corporation were not liable for the corporation debts. Corporate rights, however, were rarely granted in ancient Rome for trade purposes ; Justinian's *Digest* mentions as principal instances of trading partnerships with corporate rights those "vectigalium publicarum . . . vel aurifodinarum vel argentifodinarum"; "pistorum . . . et naviculariorum" (D. 3, 4, 1 pr.). During the middle ages partnerships in which one partner was liable for a fixed sum only, known by the name of "commenda"—whence the modern "commandite,"—is derived (see COMMANDITE, SOCIÉTÉ EN), were a favourite form of association. Trading companies with many characteristics of modern limited companies appear in Italy from the 12th century downward. The most powerful of these was the Genoese "Società delle compere e dei banchi di S. Giorgio" existed 1407 1816 (see BANKS, EARLY EUROPEAN). The discoveries of the 16th century gave a fresh stimulus to corporate enterprise, and led to the formation of new companies with limited liability throughout Europe, among which the EAST INDIA COMPANY (*q.v.*) was the most prominent.

The legislation of the present century, which culminated in the English Companies' Act 1862, made it possible to obtain corporate rights by mere registration and without the necessity of a Royal Charter or special Act. This led to an enormous expansion of limited liability enterprise in this country (as to the economical effects of this expansion, see COMPANIES, INCREASE OF). The bulk of this enterprise is no doubt carried on by companies in the usual sense of the word, but limited liability has also penetrated into private partnerships (see PARTNERSHIP).

[Salkowski, *Inst. des Röm, Privatr.*—Goldschmidt, *Universalgesch. des H. R.*—Silberschmidt, *Die Commenda.*—Primker, *Die Aktiengesellschaft* in Endemann's *Handbuch,* vol. i.—Lindley, *Company Law.*]
E. S.

LIABILITIES ON SHARES. The liabilities on shares in companies vary according to the nature of the company and the special circumstances under which the shares are held. In companies with unlimited liability each shareholder is, in case of a winding up, liable to contribute without limit ; in companies incorporated by charter the liability is determined by the terms of the charter, in many cases each shareholder in the event of a winding up is liable to contribute a sum equal to the amount of his holding in addition to the amounts, if any, remaining unpaid on his own shares. In companies limited by shares a shareholder who has paid up the nominal amount of his holding in cash is not liable for any further amount, unless the company issues bank-notes, in which case the shareholders are liable in the same way as if the company were registered as an unlimited company (see Companies Act 1879, § 6). This rule is of practical importance in the case of companies registered in England, but having branch establishments in foreign countries. If the shares are not fully paid the shareholders are liable for the amounts remaining unpaid ; and in the case of a winding up former shareholders are also liable, unless they have ceased to be shareholders for more than a year before the announcement of the winding up ; but their liability is restricted to debts incurred during the time of their membership, and they cannot be called upon for any contribution, unless the amount recoverable from the existing shareholders is insufficient to meet the debts owing by the company.

The Companies' Act of 1879, which was passed in order to enable unlimited companies to adopt limited liability—the failure of the City of Glasgow Bank and the consequent ruin of many of its shareholders having caused much misgiving among shareholders in banks generally—has introduced the principle of "reserve liability," viz. a liability which can be enforced in the case of a winding up only. Many of the large joint-stock banks had been established with unlimited liability, and had thereby been enabled to trade with a comparatively small capital. The act of 1879 enabled them to register as limited companies, and to increase their capital, on condition that the increased capital was not to be called up, except for the purpose of a winding up. This facility has been made use of to a very large extent, and the credit of the companies in question has, if anything, improved, as it has been generally thought that many wealthy and careful capitalists who had refused to subject themselves to an unlimited risk, do not object to a definite though considerable liability and become shareholders in the re-constructed banks. Reserve liability may also be introduced by any limited company in respect of any part of its uncalled capital (Companies Act 1879, § 5). Mr. Justice Vaughan Williams in his appendix to the report of the Board of Trade Committee, on Company Law Reform, recommends that a compulsory reserve of this nature should in future be attached to uncalled capital generally (see Report, c. 7779, p. xxiii.)

The original allottee and any subsequent holder with notice of shares credited as fully paid, in consideration of property transferred to a company, is liable to pay up the full amount unless an agreement relating to the issue of such shares was at the time registered at the registry of joint-stock companies (Companies Act 1867, § 25). Persons selling property to companies in exchange for fully paid up shares are frequently not aware of this rule, which in this way causes some hardship, but is on the whole useful.

[Lindley, *On Companies,* 5th ed., 1891.—Buckley, *On the Companies Acts,* 6th ed., 1891.—Palmer, *Shareholders' Legal Companion,* 15th ed., 1895.]
E. S.

LI. See CASH.

LIARD. A copper coin worth three DENIERS or the quarter of a SOU. It was first coined under Louis XI. The most probable derivation of the word, which is very uncertain, is from the name of a family in Dauphiné, where it was first used. The liard continued to be a coin in ordinary circulation till the time of Louis Philippe. R. L.

LIBER HOMO. A man who is personally free, as opposed to *servus,* a slave, and also, though in a far less marked way, to *villanus,* as is exemplified by the Domesday entry : *liber homo . . . qui modo effectus est unus de villanis.* The laws of Ina draw a wide distinction between the free man and the *theow,* fixing no wergild for the slaying of the latter. In Domesday the expression *liber homo* is very comprehensive, covering even tenants *in capite,* and in one instance a thegn is strangely recorded as *liber homo teinnus.* Geographically, however, the survey limits the class in a singular way to three of the Danish counties, for 9935 out of the total of 10,097 *liberi homines* are concentrated in Norfolk, Suffolk, and Essex, as are also, with practically no exception, the 2041 *liberi homines commendati,* freemen voluntarily placing themselves under the protection of powerful barons and paying for the privilege. The unfree classes in the survey, the *servi, bordarii, coscets,* and *cotarii,* and the *villani,* who represent the ceorls in a more or less degraded form and have as a body only a qualified sort of freedom, amount to 222,485. Various unsatisfactory theories have been started to account for the practical absence of *liberi homines* from thirty-one of the English counties ; but it is at least a curious coincidence that the bulk of them appear in the second volume of Domesday, which includes only Norfolk, Suffolk, and Essex, and is a digest of the original returns made on a slightly different plan from the first volume. Vinogradoff (p. 132), remarks that the conquest had cast free and unfree peasantry together into the one mould of villenage, while Bishop Stubbs adds that the Norman knight practically declined to recognise the minute distinctions of Anglo-Saxon dependence, and it is very probable that those who summarised the original returns for the first volume of the survey may have interpreted their instructions in a way adverse to claims of freedom. For further facts bearing upon this point, see LIBERE TENENTES.

A *liber homo* in possession of land was not bound to be in a tithing ; his wergild was usually 200s. ; his ordeal was by hot iron ; but on the other hand he sometimes paid MERCHET. If he held land in villenage his status was not affected — indeed there are cases in Domesday of knights who so held — but he could have no action at law against the lord for recovering or defending an unfree holding. Sir H. Ellis shows that the vavassors who appear in the Suffolk part of the survey were reckoned in among the *liberi homines*, and the class certainly holds the inferior thegns and the allodial tenants. It was of course recruited by manumissions, intentional and otherwise, for the *nativus* of Norman times, as Bishop Stubbs remarks, who could obtain admission into a merchant-gild in a town, and was unclaimed by his lord for a year and a day, became a freeman. The church favoured the liberation of the peasantry, and manorial usages caused the growth of a class of customary tenants, predecessors of the copyholders of a later day, who crept by degrees into the position of freemen, the process being favoured by the tendency to commute labour services for fixed rents. Free land—land, that is, which provided rent not labour—was a continuous influence favouring an alteration in the personal status of its holders. The gradual rise of the peasantry to the absolutely free condition they reached in the days of Elizabeth and James I. is ably sketched in Hallam's *Middle Ages*, c. viii. pt. 3.

[Ellis, *Introd. to Domesday*, i. 54, 55 ; ii. 488. —Kelham, *Domesday Book illustrated*, 1787.— Stubbs, *Constit. Hist.*, i. 417, 428.—Vinogradoff, *Villainage in England*, 1892.—Seebohm, *English Village Community*.] R. H.

LIBERE TENENTES. Free tenants or holders of portions of demesne land scattered over the open fields of a manor among the acres held in villenage. The expression *libere tenens* denotes primarily economic condition, a free tenure mainly by fixed money payment as opposed to the tenure of the *villanus*, which

comprised base services—that is week-work, tallage often of uncertain amount, the payment of MERCHET and fines on sales of cattle ; but a *libere tenens* was generally also a LIBER HOMO (*q.v.*), and was thus usually opposed in status to the unfree *nativus* or *rusticus*, who in his economic aspect was termed *villanus*. Between these two classes there were grades of peasantry, *free socmen*, *molmen*, and *censuarii*, who seem to have been more or less free in status. The difficulty of classification is further increased by the fact that villeins sometimes held free land, and by cases in which *libere tenentes*, as in the Ely survey of 1277, paid merchet and tallage, and attended boon-works with their labourers. On the other hand, the *Extenta Manerii* of 4 Edw. I. in the *Statutes of the Realm*, only recognises *libere* or *liberi tenentes*, *custumarii*, and *cotters*.

There is only a doubtful trace of the term in Domesday (Kelham, p. 255, *libere tenuerunt*), but there are some *liberi tenentes* on a manor in the fragment of a Domesday of St. Paul's. There were none on this manor at the time of the great survey, though there were then twenty-four *villani*. In 1181 there were eighteen *libere tenentes*, and in 1222 there were thirty-four.

In the lists of manorial tenants in the more complete of the returns called the HUNDRED ROLLS, about 1279, the *libere tenentes* emerge as a large class clearly divided from *villani*, though the same man is sometimes seen to be included in the list of tenants in villenage, and in the roll of freeholders. That this did not affect his free status is, however, apparent from records as well as from Bracton's statement that the fact of holding a villein tenement does not make a free man a villein.

The directions in the *Extenta Manerii* for taking the extents of manors are virtually the same as those in *Fleta*, which prescribe an inquiry *de libere tenentibus ;* how many of them are within and without the manor ; the nature and tenure of their lands, whether by socage, military service, fee-farm, etc. ; which hold by charter ; what rents they pay ; whether they do suit at the lord's court ; and what accrues to the lord at their death. These heads of inquiry render evident the legal position of the *libere tenentes*. As regards economic position, the contrast is between the *libere tenens* and the *villanus*, the free man on land which chiefly pays rent, and the man more or less unfree on land which provides labour.

[Bracton, i. p. 192, Rolls ed.—*Fleta*, ii. c. 71. —*Rotuli Hundredorum*, Record Commission.— Ellis, *Introduction to Domesday*, i. pp. 63-66, 237 n.—Seebohm, *English Village Community*, 1884, pp. 33, 54, 86-89.—F. W. Maitland, *Select Pleas in Manorial Courts*, pp. 60-73.—Vinogradoff, *Villainage in England*, 1892, pp. 202, 203, 443.] R. H.

LIBERTUS, a freedman, *i.e.* a person who

has been manumitted from the legal state of slavery. A master who manumitted a slave became the *patronus* of his freedman, and had, as such, certain rights in respect of him and his property. Freedmen were subject to some legal incapacities.

[Smith, *Dict. of Antiquities.* (*Jus trium liberorum et Lex J. P. Poppæa.*)]   E. A. W.

LICENSES FOR SALE OF GOODS, ETC. See TAXATION.

LICENSES, HISTORY OF. Licenses played a large part in the financial system of the English monarchy. From the 14th to the 16th centuries there was no department of civil life in which a dispensation from obligations, whether of customary or statute law, could not be obtained by the purchase of a license. Some of these were issued upon the theory that the subject matter was within the prerogative of the king as king (see the statute *De Prerogativa Regis*, in "Statutes of the Realm," i. 226). Such were those exempting from customs dues, the control of the ports being part of the royal functions. Others, such as licenses to enfeoff, not uncommon in early times, were granted by the king as feudal over-lord. The Rolls of Parliament exhibit their astonishing variety. As to land, licenses were granted for mortmain, for cutting wood by the lord of a manor within a royal chase, for dealing with reversions of land held in chief of the king, for enclosing and fortifying towns, for enclosing cemeteries, for alienating lands held of the king, for building castles, for enclosing parks or woods, for constructing conduits, and for founding chantries or religious houses. If a grant were made of a market or fair, the right could not be transferred by the grantee without the king's license. In this matter the system was adopted by the grantees themselves; no merchant, for example, being allowed to trade at the fair at Winchester without a license from the bishop. Wardships being within the prerogative, marriage of a ward of the king without license was an offence. A license was requisite to enable lords or commons to leave parliament; to send the precious metals out of the kingdom; to transact business by bills of exchange; to leave the realm; to carry arms in Wales, or cross-bows and guns in England. But those licenses which were the most profitable, and which occasioned incessant disputes, were licenses remitting customs, and those permitting export or import contrary to the tenor of statutes or of proclamation.

The principal licenses for export were those granted to wool merchants. With the exception of north-country wools, the entire export was directed by statute to the staple of Calais (see STAPLE). The object of this was to provide, by the duties levied at the staple, for the maintenance of the garrison, the mint, the fortifications, and the civil administration of Calais and its dependencies. But it was frequently worth the while of merchants to pay a high price to the king on condition of being allowed to export staple goods elsewhere than to the staple; for the staplers, straining their opportunities as monopolists, were accustomed to extort so high a price for wools as to leave a large profit to an exporting merchant whose goods had only been subject to the cost of the license to avoid their exactions. To the king the transaction furnished the advantage of ready money and independence of parliamentary control; while the nation in the long run had to supply the deficit created in the resources of Calais. These licenses were, therefore, repeatedly declared illegal by parliament, but persisted in by successive sovereigns. Other licenses of a similar character were those for the export of sheep and horses, of corn, cheese, and butter, when these were restrained either by statute or by proclamation. A comparison of the licenses granted for the import of wine, during the reign of Henry VIII., seems to point to the conclusion that the grants were regulated, not by the price of wine, but by the fluctuations in the revenue. The *Domestic State Papers* confirm this view, for the recipients were frequently officials of the royal household or tradesmen who had supplied goods to the king, and who were by this means satisfied of their debt.

While from the point of view of the modern constitutionalist, licenses of exemption from statutes were clearly illegal where those statutes expressly prohibited them, the contrary was held by the subservient judges of Henry VII. The growing independence of the Commons in time suppressed the system, but the question of the dispensing power and of its limits was not finally settled till the revolution of 1688 (see TAXATION).   I. S. L.

LICENSES (Continental war). One of the clearest rules of International Law is that war puts an end to all commercial intercourse between the subjects of the belligerent states. Moreover the commerce of neutrals with the powers at war is subject to many restraints. But it is within the competence of either of the hostile governments to remove or suspend any of the restrictions imposed upon commerce by the laws of war; and when this is done, the relaxation takes the form of *licenses to trade*. Such licenses are *express* or *implied*. The latter, as being of comparatively slight importance, may be dismissed in a few words. An *implied license* to trade is given when the commander of a force in the enemy's country issues a proclamation inviting the inhabitants to bring provisions and other commodities into his camp for sale. *Express licenses* are either *general* or *special*. The former occur when permission is granted to whole classes of people to trade in particular articles or at particular places; the latter are granted to particular firms and individuals, and authorise them to carry on a commerce described in the documents they receive and limited by the conditions expressed therein. The best example of a general license on a large scale is found in the permission granted to British subjects at the beginning of the Crimean war, by Order in Council of 15th April 1854, to trade with all unblockaded Russian ports in articles not contraband of war (see Halleck, *International Law*, Baker's ed., ii. 156 note). The Emperor Napoleon III. gave similar permission to French subjects, and the Russian government allowed free ingress to English and French goods, the property of English or French citizens, if brought in neutral vessels. These grants made such inroads on the ordinary rule of non-intercourse that no special licenses were required during the war ; and so strong have commercial interests become during the present century, that in all probability similar permissions will be issued at the beginning of future wars between great trading nations, unless indeed private property at sea, not being contraband or destined for a blockaded port, is exempt altogether from belligerent capture, as it was in the war of 1866, between Austria on the one side and Prussia and Italy on the other. Considerations such as these make an examination of the law of special licenses less important now than it would have been at the beginning of the present century. And it must be noted that the practically universal adoption of the rule that the neutral flag covers enemies' goods, unless they are contraband of war, has operated as a general permission to all neutrals to engage in many kinds of trade that were forbidden them by the older practice of nations. Thus the importance of licenses has been still further diminished. Nevertheless they played so prominent a part in the great continental war with revolutionary and imperial France, that it is necessary to describe both the circumstances which led to their issue in enormous numbers, and the rules of law with regard to them which were enforced by the prize courts of the period, and are still referred to as authoritative in treatises on international law (see DECLARATION OF PARIS).

The prohibitions and restraints by which both England and France endeavoured to injure one another through interference with the commerce of neutrals, culminated in the Milan and Berlin Decrees of Napoleon I., and the retaliatory British ORDERS IN COUNCIL. The net result of these deplorable measures was that from the close of the year 1807 each of the two powers claimed the right to confiscate all ships, with some exceptions in favour of neutrals, that traded with the ports of the other or its allies. In addition Great Britain denounced the penalty of seizure and condemnation against vessels which carried a French *certificate of origin*, in testimony that their

cargoes did not consist of British goods, and France declared that she would regard as good prize any vessel which touched at any English port, paid any tax to the English government, or submitted to the search of an English cruiser. These maritime measures were backed up on land by the CONTINENTAL SYSTEM (*q.v.*), which Napoleon developed out of the theories and tentative efforts of the Jacobinical leaders. He believed that it was possible to ruin England by excluding her manufactured goods and colonial produce from the continent of Europe. Wherever the arms or the diplomacy of France prevailed, the ports were closed against British commerce, and British goods found within the territory were destroyed. An enormous rise in the price of such commodities was the result, and a vast system of smuggling immediately arose. The attempt to put it down by espionage and military violence had no little effect in rousing the most apathetic populations to resist French domination. Bourrienne describes in his *Memoirs* how the possession of a little sugar from an English West-India island was held to be a crime of the deepest dye, and punished with terrible severity. But British colonial produce and British manufactured goods found their way into the continent of Europe in spite of all that French officers could do under the strictest rules of military occupation. Hamburgh became a centre of a contraband trade with northern Germany, and Bourrienne gives an amusing account of some of the devices which were discovered and stopped. On one occasion an extraordinary increase in the number of funerals attracted attention, and on the hearses being searched they were found to be full of English sugar. Yet so impossible was it to do without supplies which could come only from English commerce, that Napoleon's generals were sometimes obliged to trade surreptitiously with England in order to meet the needs of the forces under their command. Great Britain, too, felt the consequences of the dislocation of trade caused by the violence of the belligerents, though she did not suffer to the same extent as her adversaries. The parliamentary debates of the period are full of the complaints of harassed interests and ruined merchants. On both sides circumstances were too strong for rulers. They were compelled to mitigate the severity of their restrictions by the grant of licenses to trade. These were issued in enormous numbers, chiefly to their own subjects, but sometimes to neutrals. The prize courts of the belligerent powers were constantly employed in deciding cases connected with them ; and thus an elaborate law of licenses grew up. It will not be necessary to do more than give its main outlines, because in all probability much of its detail will never be wanted again.

The grant of a license is an act of sovereignty, and must therefore emanate from the central authority of the state, the law of each country deciding what department of its government has the right to issue such permissions. The only exception to this rule is to be found in the right possessed by all military or naval commanders, and all governors of occupied places, to give licenses to trade within the limits of their own commands. A state may, however, accept and ratify licenses given by subordinate authorities, in which case they acquire, by the fact of recognition, the validity they did not possess in their own nature. Licenses may be granted to enemies, to neutrals, or to subjects. Their effect is to remove all personal disabilities due to the war, in so far as such removal is necessary for the due conduct of the trade allowed by the license. Thus an enemy subject may sue and be sued in the courts of the country in respect of all matters connected with the transactions for which permission has been given, though the rules of International Law allow the subjects of one belligerent no standing in the courts of the other. But it must be noted that the possession of a license from one belligerent affords no protection against the warlike force of the other. Unless he, too, has allowed the trade in question, he may consider the possession of a permit from his enemy as in itself ground for capture and condemnation. The trade must be conducted according to the terms of the license reasonably and equitably construed. A small excess in the quantity of the goods allowed will not vitiate the license, but a material change in their quality will cause the forfeiture of vessel and cargo. A license cannot be transferred unless it is made negotiable by express words ; but it may be used by the agent of those on whose behalf it was granted, provided that he is named in its clauses. The employment of two or more small vessels instead of one large one will be allowed, but the use of an enemy ship instead of a neutral ship will be regarded as fatal. A license to send goods to a particular port covers the return voyage in ballast, and will even protect both ship and cargo if it was impossible to deliver the goods at the destination named. Stress of weather and other unavoidable causes will excuse delay in the termination of a voyage, but it must always be commenced at the time stated in the license.

[The literature of this subject is very voluminous. C. Robinson's *Admiralty Reports* give many of the British cases, and others will be found in the *Admiralty Reports* of Dodson and Edwards. Hautefeuille discusses licenses in the continental war from an ultra-French point of view, in his *Droits et Devoirs des Nations Neutres, Discours Préliminaire*. A vigorous presentation of an English view, almost equally biassed, will be found in the famous work, *War in Disguise, or the*

Frauds of the Neutral Flags. The law of the matter is summarised in Halleck's *International Law*, ch. xxx. ; Wheaton's *International Law* (Dana's ed.), §§ 408-410, and note 198 ; Hall's *International Law*, § 196 ; Lawrence's *International Law*, § 235. An article by Rose in the *Historical Review* for October 1893, on "Napoleon and English Commerce," gives a clear and concise account of the continental system and its results.]

T. J. L.

LIEN (derived from the French word *lien* [Lat. *ligamen*] = tie) is the right to retain goods until payment of a debt due by the owner of the goods. It differs from a right of pawn or pledge inasmuch as it does not give a power of sale to the person retaining the goods. By the common law every one has a lien on articles delivered to him to work on for the amount of the value of such work. This is called a specific lien. Other liens are created by special agreement or usage of trade ; these as a rule are general liens, that is to say, they authorise the detention of goods in respect of debts not specifically incurred in relation to the goods. Bankers', brokers', and innkeepers' liens belong to this category.

[Smith, *Mercantile Law*, 10th ed. 1890.—Coote, *On Mortgages*, 5th ed. 1881 or 1884.] E. S.

LIFE INSURANCE. See INSURANCE.

LIFE TABLES. See INSURANCE.

LIGHT GOLD AND SILVER COIN, WITHDRAWAL OF, FROM CIRCULATION IN THE UNITED KINGDOM AND COLONIES.

United Kingdom.—Gold Coin. From 1816, when the present gold currency was introduced, until 1842, the law of the United Kingdom as to withdrawing light gold coin from circulation required every person receiving a sovereign below the least current weight (122·5 grs.) to cut and return it to the tenderer, the latter having no alternative but to suffer whatever loss the deficiency in the weight involved. This law remained practically inoperative. To carry it out would have required every person receiving either a sovereign or half-sovereign to possess a delicate balance with which to test the weight of the coin. The Bank of England and some Government Offices were the only places where the law was not ignored ; great care, therefore, was taken by the public to prevent light gold coins from falling into the hands of the only institutions where it was liable to be cut. Full-weight pieces were also carefully selected for export and for melting for industrial purposes. Hence the gold currency became more and more exclusively composed of worn pieces. On 8th June 1842 a Treasury minute was issued directing that a letter should be addressed to the Bank of England, "requesting them to give public notice of their readiness to receive gold coin not being of the weight at which such coin is authorised by law to be current, at the rate of £3 : 17 : 10½ per ounce, and to transmit the same, when received, to the Mint, for recoinage." From this date till 14th March 1845, a considerable recoinage of light gold coin was undertaken by the Mint, the coin received from the Bank of England being of 2,860,282 ozs. in weight, and £11,137,223 in value.

During this recoinage the law that the loss arising from the lightness of the coins was chargeable to the last holder was strictly enforced. Much inconvenience was caused to the public by the endeavours of shopkeepers and others, who had to pay gold coin into their banking accounts in the ordinary course of business, to transfer this loss from their own to their customers' shoulders. Persons with no accurate means of testing the weight of a coin would calculate its value in some rough way, and decline to receive the same, except at a reduction of 6d. or even 1s. from its nominal value, though the actual deficiency in weight did not perhaps justify a deduction of more than half the amount thus estimated.

From 1845 to 1870 the Bank of England received light gold coin from the public at £3 : 17 : 6½ per oz., the deduction of 4d. from the "Mint price" being made to cover the expense of the assay, of melting the coin into bars, and of sending these to the Mint. The mint at that time declined to receive gold for coinage except in bars.

On 1st August 1870 the regulations of the Mint were altered so as to permit it to receive light gold coins, in parcels of not less than £100, for re-coinage. The same *weight* of gold was returned to the importer, coined at the rate of £3 : 17 : 10½ per ounce, *free of charge*. The bank, being thus relieved from the necessity of melting worn coin into bars, raised its price for the coins to £3 : 17 : 9 per ounce, or only 1½d. less than the Mint price. The Mint required the importer of light gold coin to give two days' notice, and to wait an indefinite time for the coin to be re-struck and returned. On the other hand the Bank of England paid for the coin on its receipt, and the public, in practice, found it more profitable to accept at once the Bank's slightly lower price, than to incur the uncertainty connected with dealing directly with the Mint. This system remained in force from 1870 to 1889, during which time £21,421,697 in light gold coin was recoined at the Mint, the whole being received through the Bank of England.

In 1889 an Act of Parliament was passed directing the withdrawal of all gold coins issued before the present reign, at the expense of the State (see DEMONETISATION). This was the first time Parliament recognised the duty of the State to relieve the last holder of a light gold coin from the cost of defraying the loss on its withdrawal. This principle was re-affirmed by the Coinage Act, 1891 (54 & 55 Vict. c. 72), which provides that all light gold coins except those fraudulently dealt with shall be exchanged at full nominal value. Section 1 (sub-sect. 3) defines a greater deficiency in weight than three grains per piece as *primâ facie* evidence of illegal treatment.

By 31st December 1895, when this act had been in operation for three years and nine months, a very considerable improvement had been effected in the gold currency circulating in the United Kingdom, which, generally speaking, had been placed in a satisfactory condition. The following amounts of light sovereigns and half-sovereigns had been withdrawn from circulation :—

To 31st December 1895.	Amount withdrawn.	Loss through deficiency of weight.
Sovereigns .	£17,274,000	£189,715
Half-sovereigns	11,226,000	263,861
	£28,500,000	£453,576

Sterling-using Colonies.—Gold Coin. In Cape Colony, Natal, and Fiji, Colonies in which the Coinage Act 1870 is in force, the law is the same as in the United Kingdom. No special arrangements exist in the remaining sterling-using Colonies for the renewal of the gold coinage. In 1890, however, when pre-Victorian gold coins were demonetised, the Sydney and Melbourne branch Mints were authorised to exchange such pieces at full nominal value, and there can be little doubt that a similar arrangement would be made in the event of the re-coinage of gold which is now in progress being brought to a close. For the present, it is open to colonists to export light gold coin to this country, for presentation at the Bank of England for exchange.

United Kingdom.—Silver Coin. The silver currency of the United Kingdom consists of token-coins, on the issue of which a profit accrues to the State. On the withdrawal of these coins, therefore, a loss is necessarily incurred. In England and Wales new silver coin is issued to the public, and worn silver coin withdrawn from circulation through the medium of the Bank of England. The Bank of Scotland and the Bank of Ireland perform the same service in Scotland and Ireland respectively.

Sterling-using Colonies.—Silver Coin. Worn silver coin circulating in colonies is collected by the Colonial Governments and shipped to London for exchange at its full nominal value. In addition to the loss on its recoinage, the Home Government bears the expense of the freight of such coin from the various colonies to London.

Loss on withdrawal of worn Silver Coin. The total amount of worn silver coin, from both the United Kingdom and the Colonies, exchanged at the Royal Mint at its full nominal value, the loss on which has been defrayed by the British government, has, from 1861 to 1895 inclusive, been as follows :—

	Worn silver coin.	Loss.
1861-70	£1,131,900	£156,110
1871-80	2,580,090	314,124
1881-90	2,653,522	324,866
1891	203,465	24,258
1892	227,216	25,942
1893	294,113	31,589
1894	389,778	40,966
1895	443,993	47,947

Colonies in which sterling currency is not used bear the loss which arises from the wear of the coins in circulation, but at the same time, whatever seignorage accrues on the issue of the subsidiary pieces is an addition to the colonial revenue.

The imperial bronze coinage, first issued in 1860, is as yet subject to no conditions as to withdrawal from circulation when worn.

[See *Annual Reports of the Deputy Master of the Mint.*]   F. E. A.

LIMIT OF CREDIT. See CREDIT.

LIMITATION, STATUTES OF. "Time is a power the influence of which the human mind cannot resist; what has existed for a long time seems fixed and unchangeable, for the very reason that it has existed so long; it would be a public evil if this belief were allowed to result in disappointment" (Windscheid, *Pandekten*, i. § 101). The principle thus stated by one of the most eminent modern writers on law has been recognised in all countries and at all times. The lapse of time in all legal systems creates rights and extinguishes rights, or at least the power to enforce them. In the earlier Roman law *usucapio*, the acquisition of property by long enjoyment, was distinguished from *praescriptio*, the barring of the remedy for the enforcement of a right in consequence of lapse of time; but the two principles gradually became merged together, though in some systems of law they are still distinguished by different names (*e.g. Ersitzung* and *Verjährung* in German). In England the object of law, as established by the Statutes of Limitations, is not so much to create possessory titles—although this result in most cases is obtained incidentally—as to bar the remedy of persons who, through ignorance or neglect, have failed to exercise their rights for a considerable period. The length of the period depends on the subject matter of the right. The right to recover chattels, rights arising under simple contracts, and rights to claim damages for wrongful actions, are, as a general rule, all barred after the lapse of six years, but damages for assault and other similar torts cannot be recovered after the lapse of four years, and a person slandered by spoken words loses his remedy if he allows two years to elapse without making use of his remedy. Time does not run against infants or lunatics; they may respectively bring their actions within six years after attaining full age or recovering their sanity; absence beyond seas on the part of the plaintiff is no longer a ground for depriving a defendant of his right to rely on the statute, but if the defendant is absent from the United Kingdom the operation of the statute is interrupted. A written acknowledgment of a debt or any payment of principal or interest from which the existence of the debt can be clearly inferred is also sufficient to prevent it from becoming barred (21 Jac. I. c. 16; 19 & 20 Vict. c. 97, §§ 9-15; 4 & 5 Anne, c. 16).

Rights arising under sealed contracts are not barred before the expiration of twenty years, and with respect to these rights there are rules, similar to those mentioned above, as to the interruption of the operation of the statute by acknowledgment or by the fact that the creditor is an infant or a lunatic (3 & 4 Will. IV. c. 42).

The right to recover land must be exercised within twelve years from the time that the right accrues, unless the person entitled is under the disability of infancy or insanity; but even in the event of disability the lapse of thirty years is sufficient to take away the right to recover. It should, however, be pointed out that, even irrespectively of the possibility of disability, a person having been in possession of land for a period exceeding twelve years is not thereby made secure against interruption. If, for instance, a person having a life interest in land purports to sell the fee simple, the purchaser and any subsequent purchaser may be ejected within six years from the time at which the person entitled after the expiration of the life interest becomes entitled in possession. Thus, if the tenant for life is twenty-one at the time of his fraudulent sale, and dies at the age of ninety-one, seventy-five years of undisturbed possession may not suffice to prevent an ejectment (3 & 4 Will. IV. c. 27; 37 & 38 Vict. c. 57).

The statutes of limitation are not applicable to equitable rights, excepting equitable interests in land, but the courts of equity have, except in the cases of trust and fraud, adopted rules analogous to those of the statutes in question. As regards trusts, the former law was that no lapse of time prevented beneficiaries from recovering damages against trustees for breaches of trust,—however innocent, *e.g.* unauthorised investments; but since 1888 trustees, unless they have been guilty of fraud, or appropriated trust property for their own benefit, are entitled to plead lapse of time (Trustee Act, 1888, § 8), and directors of companies, who were formerly held to come under the same rules as trustees in respect of the statutes of limitation, are entitled, as well as trustees proper, to avail themselves of the benefit of this innovation (*re* Land Allotment Company [1894] 1 Chancery 616). There are special rules as to the limitation of proceedings directed against the crown, and of penal actions to which it is unnecessary to refer in detail.

Speaking generally, the statutes of limitation bar the remedy but do not destroy the right, but as regards real property the effect of the lapse of time is a divesting of title or a transference of title to somebody else (see Dawkins *v.* Lord Penrhyn, 4 Appeal Cases, 51).

[Darby and Bosanquet, *Statutes of Limitation*, 2nd edition, 1893.]   E. S.

LIMITED COMPANIES. See JOINT-STOCK COMPANIES.

LIMITED LIABILITY ACTS. See LIABILITY, LIMITED.

LINGUET, SIMON NICOLAS HENRI (1736-

1794), a clever French barrister, historian, and journalist, threw himself into the midst of the political and philosophical controversies of his time, under the impulse of an innate and quarrelsome love of contradiction. Although he took good care to remain quiet during the Reign of Terror, he perished on the scaffold.

Linguet assailed the Physiocrats in his *Réponse aux docteurs modernes . . . avec la réfutation du système des philosophes économistes* (London, 1771). In his pamphlet on bread and corn, *Du Pain et du Blé*, London, 1774, reprinted in 1789 under the title *Du Commerce des Grains, édition augmentée d'une Lettre sur le mérite politique et physique du pain et du blé* (On the corn trade, with a letter on the physical and political properties of bread and corn) he wages war against the consumption of bread, which he calls a slow poison. He was also opposed to the cultivation of potatoes, which might acquire the fearful qualities of corn.

His following works may also be mentioned : *Annales politiques, civiles et littéraires du XVIIIe Siècle*, London, 1777-1792, xix. vols.—*La Dîme Royale avec des réflexions sur la contrebande*, 1764, reprinted under the title of *L'Impôt territorial*, 1787. — *Traité des Canaux navigables*, 1769.—*Réflexions des Six Corps de la Ville de Paris sur la suppression des Jurandes*, 1776 (Reflections of the Six Parisian Corporations on the Abolition of Crafts).

[Cruppi, *Un Avocat-journaliste au XVIIIe Siècle, Linguet*, Paris, 1895.] E. Ca.

The attack on Montesquieu made by Linguet in *La Théorie des lois civiles* (1767), provoked a reply from the abbé MORELLET in *La Théorie du paradoxe*, which Linguet, always prepared for controversy, answered in *La Théorie du libelle, ou l'art de calomnier avec fruit.*

LIPS, ALEXANDER (1779-1838), was a professor of political and economic sciences in the university of Marburg, who at the same time superintended the management of his own estate of Marlofstein, where he founded an agricultural school.

Professor Roscher calls him a queer fellow (*ein wunderlicher Kauz*) and in fact, the proposal brought forward in his *Universal Peace* (*der allgemeine Friede*), 1814, to abolish the hitherto military foundation of nobility, and to give it a basis purely according to population, is rather startling ; the titles to be conferred were to be in strict proportion to the number of people sustained by each new nobleman. Lips is thus one of the last representatives of the *populationistic* school, which was so powerful in Germany in pre-Malthusian days. Lips was most active in insisting on the necessity of spreading agricultural education, of breaking up entails, and of abandoning fallows and the three-field system for intensive modes of cultivation and the breeding of cattle.

But his attention was not monopolised by the improvement of cultivation, and although favourable to free trade as a principle, he considers protection to be indispensable to infant industries. In this respect, he is a harbinger of LIST.

Lips was a copious writer on topics of the day. He published, 1813, a *Staatswissenschaftslehre oder Encyclopädie und Methodologie der Staatswissenschaft*, in which the state is presented as the rightful interpreter of human reason ; his main economic work is : *Deutschland's Oekonomie, ein Versuch zur Lösung der Frage, wie kann Deutschland zu lohnendem Ackerbau, blühender Industrie und wirksamem Handel gelangen ?* (Germany's economy ; an attempt to solve the question how Germany can secure a remunerative agriculture, flourishing manufactures, and an effective trade), 1830.

[Roscher, *Gesch. der Nat. Oek. in Deutschland*, pp. 992-993.] E. Ca.

LIQUID ASSETS are cash, and such other parts of a banker's assets as can be instantly converted into cash. A banker's assets are generally divided under the following heads :

1. Cash.	4. Bills of Exchange.
2. Money at Call.	5. Loans and Advances.
3. Government Securities.	6. Premises.

Of these the first three are usually reckoned as liquid assets, but cash alone is really liquid, whilst all the others are so in more or less degree. It is necessary to observe, too, that their degrees of fluidity will depend upon the extent to which they might be required to be converted, and the conditions under which the operation would have to be performed. In times of prosperity and confidence, securities of a miscellaneous character can generally be promptly turned into cash, but there are other times when consols alone are saleable. Another consideration arises with regard to "money at call." As an asset in the balance sheet of a single bank it is only second to actual cash, but in the aggregate, as appearing in the accounts of all the banks in a city, it has quite a different character. It is money lent to brokers against bills of exchange and other securities, and each broker relies on his being able to repay his debt to one bank by obtaining an advance from another. Thus the reduction of money at call in the accounts of one bank means the increase of the same item with another. Hence it might be that at a time of panic the liquid character of the whole asset would disappear, and it would be no more liquid than the bills or securities against which it had been lent. Ultimately, the fluidity of these assets depends largely upon the conditions under which legal tender notes are issued. Bills of exchange, though not usually reckoned as liquid, have some advantages of their own in this respect. They really represent floating capital, *i.e.* capital shortly replaceable by the results of its investment, and are therefore always gradually liquidating themselves. R. W. B.

[G. Rae, *The Country Banker*, 1886, and later editions.—R. H. Inglis Palgrave, *Notes on Banking*, 1873.—*Bankers' Magazine*, London, *passim*.]

LIQUIDATED DAMAGES. Where the parties to a contract agree that a fixed sum will be paid as damages for its breach in case a breach occurs. The object of such an arrangement is to secure the due performance of the contract and to avoid the necessity of resorting to a court in case of breach in order to have the amount of damages ascertained. The courts of equity disregarded the arrangement of the parties and introduced a distinction between liquidated damages and penalties. Where the primary intention of the parties was that if the particular act was not done, the fixed sum was payable, such sum was regarded as liquidated damages ; but where the primary intention was to secure the doing of some act and the fixed sum was merely the machinery for securing that the act would be done, such sum was then regarded as a penalty, and the court, instead of ordering such sum to be paid, might award a reasonable compensation. The courts of common law did not recognise the distinction, but the result of the 8 & 9 Will. III. c. 2, § 8, was that where the court held the sum fixed to be in the nature of a penalty, the actual damage suffered only could be recovered ; but if it was not a penalty, the amount agreed was payable.

[Mayne on *Damages*, London, 1894.—Story's *Equity Jurisprudence*, London, 1892.—White and Tudor's *Leading Cases in Equity*, London, 1895, for a summary of the principles on which the courts proceed in determining whether a fixed sum is a penalty or not.]   J. E. C. M.

LIQUIDATION. The term "liquidation" is usually applied to the dissolution or winding up of a company incorporated by Act of Parliament in the manner prescribed by such act. An unincorporated company can be dissolved under the articles prescribed by its deed of settlement or by a court where the business cannot be carried on as intended, and a company incorporated by charter may be dissolved in the manner therein provided. But where a company is incorporated by act of parliament it cannot, without the assent of the legislature, be dissolved at the will of its members ; and as a corporation is distinct from the persons composing it, the death or lunacy or bankruptcy of a member does not affect the existence of the body corporate. Acts of parliament were passed from time to time to give courts of bankruptcy jurisdiction over incorporated trading companies and to enable such courts to apply the assets to the payment of debts. Jurisdiction was also given to the Court of Chancery to compel members of a bankrupt company to contribute to the discharge of the company's debts where the assets were insufficient to pay the creditors in full. The drawbacks of these acts were: (1) that notwithstanding the winding up of a company the creditors might take proceedings against any shareholder for the full amount of his debt ; (2) the creditors had to proceed against the company in bankruptcy, and frequently there arose a conflict between the courts of equity and of bankruptcy ; (3) the shareholders could not initiate proceedings to dissolve the company ; and (4) the expense of taking proceedings was very great. Between 1856 and 1858 some of these defects were removed, and at length in 1862 the Companies Act 1862 (25 & 26 Vict. 289) was passed to consolidate and improve the law. Under this act three modes were provided for winding up a company : (1) compulsorily, *i.e.* by the court ; (2) voluntarily, *i.e.* by the shareholders without the intervention of the court ; and (3) voluntarily but subject to the provision of the court.

When a company resolves to go into liquidation or is ordered to be wound up, a person is appointed liquidator whose duty it is to collect all the assets, to pay all debts, and to distribute any surplus amongst the shareholders—due provision being made for the payment of all costs. When the affairs of the company are finally wound up, the court makes an order dissolving the company, and notice of this order is given to the registrar of joint stock companies, who makes a minute in his books to the effect that the company is dissolved.

In 1875 an important step was taken by the legislature with the object of assimilating the law of winding up to the law of bankruptcy. The Judicature Act 1875 (38 & 39 Vict. c.77) provided that as far as the rights of secured and unsecured creditors, and as to the debts and liability proveable, and as to the valuation of annuities, etc., the same rules should prevail on winding up as in bankruptcy. In 1890 a further step was taken by the Companies (winding up) Act 1890 (53 & 54 Vict. c. 63), which was passed for the object of introducing into the winding up of companies the same procedure as that which prevailed in bankruptcy, and of subjecting the administrative acts of liquidators to the control of a government department. It was alleged that under the system, which allowed the petitioning creditor to practically nominate the liquidator, the assets were wasted in unnecessary costs whilst the liquidation was unnecessarily prolonged (see Debate in House of Commons, 28 Feb. 1890). Under the act of 1890, the official receiver in bankruptcy is the official liquidator of companies ; inquiries are of necessity instituted as regards the manner in which the affairs of the company have been carried on ; whilst the board of trade is charged with the duty of seeing that the liquidator faithfully performs his duties.

The effects and the advantages of an official administration in the case of liquidation of companies are discussed in the reports of the board of trade under section 29 of the Companies (winding up) Act 1890, published in 1893 and 1894, and in the Report, published in 1893, of the Inter-Departmental Committee appointed to inquire into limits of the action of the board of trade as regards the liquidation of companies.

J. E. C. M.

LIQUIDATOR (a) PROVISIONAL (b) OFFICIAL. (a) Previous to 1891 the court at any time after the presentation of a petition for winding up might appoint a provisional liquidator, though it was not usual to do so until the hearing of the petition. The object of the appointment was to protect the assets of the company ; the order of appointment always stating what he was to do. Under the Companies Act of 1890 the only person who can now act as provisional liquidator is the official receiver. Upon the making of an order to wind up a company he becomes *ex-officio* provisional liquidator, but may be appointed as such if necessary at any time after the presentation of a petition.

(b) When no other person is appointed liquidator in a compulsory winding up, the official receiver becomes liquidator ; in a voluntary winding up the shareholders appoint their own liquidator. A liquidator acts subject to the control of the committee of inspection, of the shareholders, and of the board of trade and of the court. With the consent of the committee he can carry on the business of the company and bring or defend actions, and compromise all claims. But he can without such consent sell the property of the company, collect assets, and distribute dividends. The directions of the shareholders override any directions of the committee. In matters of administration, the liquidator is controlled by the board of trade, and as far as his legal powers are concerned he is subject to the control of the courts.

J. E. C. M.

LIQUOR LAWS. British legislation for the regulation of the sale of intoxicating liquors practically begins with 9 Geo. IV., and has been subject to modifications and extensions, down to the present time. In some respects legislation is more advanced in the British colonies and in certain portions of the United States than it is in the mother-country. In Great Britain Sunday closing is partial, whereas it is very general in the colonies ; while the principle of LOCAL OPTION (*q.v.*) has obtained in many colonies, and even total prohibition in certain districts of America. Great improvements were made in the licensing laws by the acts of 1872 and 1874, though they contain only a part of the statute law with regard to licensing. It has been remarked that a more thorough reform of the laws would have been effected by an act repealing all existing statutes and re-enacting their provisions in a codified form. As matters stand, it is difficult to grasp in full scope and detail the spirit of the numerous existing enactments. The Act of 1872 introduced by Henry Austin Bruce, home secretary, afterwards Lord Aberdare, is the principal act. It does not apply to Scotland, however, and only partially to Ireland. Severe penalties are imposed by the act on the illicit sale of liquor, on drunkenness in any public place or highway, upon permitting drunkenness or gambling, or the harbouring of prostitutes on licensed premises, upon harbouring constables on such premises during their hours of duty, and upon bribing or attempting to bribe them. The act further fixed the hours of closing, but empowered the local authority to grant exemptions from them when the convenience of many persons engaged in lawful business so required. Any licensed person, on a third conviction for offences against the act, is to forfeit his licence, and to be disqualified for five years, and his premises for two years, from receiving another ; but a conviction more than five years old is not to be taken into account for the purpose of increasing any penalty. In every district a register of licences is to be kept showing particulars of all convictions, etc., which shall be open to inspection by any ratepayer, holder of a licence, or owner of licensed premises. A licensing committee of not less than three members is appointed annually by the justices in counties and boroughs. In boroughs, however, licences must be confirmed by the body of justices who would, but for the act, have been authorised to grant licences. An annual value is fixed by the act for all licensed premises according to their situation. Penalties under the act are recoverable by summary conviction, subject to an appeal to quarter sessions. No justice can take part in administering the act who has any beneficial interest in the manufacture or sale of intoxicating liquors. The act of 1874 modified that of 1872 as regards the hours of closing and other points, many of the modifications being of a mitigatory character. The statutes relating to the drink traffic embrace provisions with regard to the grant of licences, the qualifications of premises for a licence, the powers of licensing authorities, the transfer and removal of licences, protection of owners, the conduct and closing of premises, offences against public order, legal proceedings, refreshment houses, liabilities of innkeepers, brewers' licences, and various minor details touching the traffic. The public revenue is largely fed by the excise duties and licences. Pitt first produced a general scheme of excise in 1784, and this was embodied in the Consolidation Act of 1826, which forms the basis of the existing law. The malt duty was abolished in 1880, but brewers and distillers must still take out an excise licence, and pay duty on everything manufactured. A licence is also necessary to wholesale or retail dealers in beer, spirits, or wine. By the Local Government Act of 1888 the duties on retailers' licences are transferred to the county councils. An act of 1830 allowed beer licences to be taken out without application to the magistrates, but later acts brought all beer-houses and refreshment-houses under their control. Special sessions are held once a year under the General Licensing Act of 1828, for the grant and renewal of licences, and at more frequent intervals for dealing with applications for transfers. The Wine and Beer-house Act of 1869 defines the regulations with regard to licences for the sale of drink to be consumed off the premises. In Scotland, the Home Drummond Act of 1828 regulates the general licensing arrangements, but the Forbes MacKenzie Act of 1853 (amended in 1862 and 1867) provided a new form of magistrates' certificate, which prohibited the sale of liquor between 11 P.M. in large towns, or 10 P.M. in the country, and 8 A.M., and during the whole of Sunday. The Irish licensing laws are similar to those of England, but with some modifications in favour of the publican. An act of 1874 introduced six-day licences, and in 1878 another act enforced total closing on Sunday, except as regards the five largest towns. The liquor regulations prevailing in the colonies are very diverse. New Zealand possesses elective licensing committees, but no new licences can be granted until the ratepayers have been appealed to by a poll. Victoria enjoys the principle of local option, combined with compensation; in Queensland all houses may be closed in any locality by a majority of two-thirds of the ratepayers, while a bare majority can limit the number of licences and prevent the issue of fresh ones; and in New South Wales there is a form of local option which consists in making representations to the licensing magistrates as to the number and increase of licences. In South Africa stringent legislation exists against the sale of intoxicants to the natives, but there are frequent complaints that it is not sufficiently enforced. As regards the whites, the laws are lax and inefficient. Legislation in the crown colonies on the drink traffic is also very varied, local option being occasionally met with. Sunday closing and the prohibition of the sale of drink to minors are regulations in many of these colonies. The imperial parliament has periodically discussed the liquor question as affecting India and Ceylon. It has frequently been asserted—though the Indian government has denied the charge—that the Indian authorities have endeavoured to stimulate the sale of drink among the natives for the purpose of improving the revenue, and a similar charge has been made against the colonial government of Ceylon. Whatever cause may be responsible for the result, the sale of drink in India has admittedly increased of recent years, and parliament will no doubt shortly be called upon to legislate on this matter. Canada has a local option law

known as the Scott Act (1878), under which localities can close, by a majority of votes, all licensed premises without compensation; but when public opinion changes in any district the suppression may be reversed. Then, there are other restrictive laws which apply to special provinces. Speaking generally, restrictive laws prevail in some form throughout the whole of the Dominion, while in the North-West Territories there is total prohibition. Throughout the larger portion of Canada and the states of the American Union, as well as in some of the Australasian colonies, two important provisions prevail, under one of which the relatives of any person who comes to his death through intoxicating liquor may sue the seller for damages; while under the other the relatives of intemperate persons may notify the sellers of drink not to supply it to such persons, and magistrates may also notify habitual drunkards to whom drink cannot be sold. This latter power is now being adopted in many colonial liquor acts, either in a severe or in a modified form. In many states of the American Union prohibitive legislation, as the Maine liquor law, obtains, and, in others where this is not the case, the high-licence system is adopted, which keeps down the number of objectionable drinking saloons. Alike in Great Britain and the colonies the public sentiment is being moved in favour of legislation which shall strike still further at the growth of the liquor traffic, by restricting both the liberty of consumption and the number of those engaged in the trade (see GOTHENBURG SYSTEM; LOCAL OPTION).

[35 & 36 Vict. c. 94, and 37 & 38 Vict. c. 49.—Spofford's *American Almanac, Statistical, Financial, Political*, 1879-84.—*Chambers's Encyclopædia*, new ed. vol. vi.—*Hazell's Annual*, 1894.—Dewar's *Liquor Laws for Scotland.*—Stone's *Justices' Manual.*]

G. B. S.

LIRA (Italian coin). The equivalent of the French franc (see FRANC).

LIST, FRIEDRICH (1789-1846), was the son of a respectable tanner at Reutlingen. Not liking his father's business, he became a clerk in the public service. He continued a diligent course of self-culture, and already in 1816 had risen to the post of ministerial under-secretary. The king of Würtemberg, being desirous of calming popular effervescence in his State by liberal concessions, made Von Mangenheim his chief minister. List warmly supported the reform movement, and was appointed in 1817 professor of economics and "Staatspraxis" in the university of Tübingen. On the fall of the minister, List, having acted as adviser of the recently-founded society of trade and manufactures, which aimed at the abolition of internal duties as an impediment to commerce, was obliged in 1819 to resign his professorship. He was elected a member of the Würtemberg chamber, and worked earnestly for an extension of self-government, for the introduction of jury-trial and publicity of proceedings in criminal cases, for the sale of the domains, and other reforms. He was in consequence expelled from the chamber and condemned to a ten months' imprisonment, from which he was released on promising to quit the country. He then emigrated to America, where he remained from 1825 to 1832, was successful as a journalist and as a speculator in coal and railways, and acquired favour with the Pennsylvanian manufacturers by his *Outlines of American Political Economy*, 1827, which contained a defence of protective duties. After having been employed on a mission to Paris, he became in 1832 United States' consul, first at Leipzig, and afterwards for Baden. On his settlement in Germany he devoted himself to the advocacy of a railway system for that country, to which, at the time, many interests and prejudices were opposed; and really gave a powerful impulse to its construction. He threw himself somewhat later into the agitation for a ZOLLVEREIN, and contributed greatly to its success by his ardour and eloquence. With this practical movement his name must always be closely associated, and through it, with the history of Germany. He was personally ill-supported by the public, and had to struggle with financial difficulties; and, bodily disease and suffering being added, he sank under the burden, and died by his own hand 30th November 1846.

Germany owes List a great debt of gratitude for the services he rendered in the promotion of her material prosperity. When residing in America, he said that his own country always lay in the background of his plans, and on his return he worked in her interest with extraordinary zeal and assiduity. As an author, he is known chiefly by his *Das Nationale System der Politischen Oekonomie*, of which the first and only published volume, dealing with INTERNATIONAL TRADE, appeared in 1841 (7th ed., by Eheberg, 1883). In this work he is much indebted to A. MÜLLER, a deeper thinker than himself, some of whose best thoughts are reproduced in it, though in a less abstract and more practical form. Like that writer, he takes up a position in some respects strongly antagonistic to Adam SMITH, who, in his opinion, kept private interests too exclusively in view, and, when he ceased to be individualistic, became cosmopolitan. The *national* idea is predominant in List. Between the individual and humanity —he says—stands the nation, a collective and continuous existence, possessing a deep-seated unity founded on a thousand bonds of feeling and interest—with a descent, a language, a literature, a history of its own, and laws, institutions and economic aptitudes peculiar to itself. To its permanent well-being, on which depends the ultimate highest good of all its members, the immediate interests of individuals, which do

not always further it, should be strictly subordinated. The really important object is not the present creation of exchange values, but the development of the productive powers of the nation. The requirements of different nations must be met in different ways, depending partly on their respective characteristics, but chiefly on the degree of development which they have attained. All communities—at least those of the temperate zones—after emerging from the hunter and pastoral systems of life, pass through three successive economic stages: (1) that of agriculture; (2) that of agriculture united with manufactures; and (3) that of combined agriculture, manufactures, and commerce. The last of these forms of national economy, as it is the product of a higher grade of evolution, so also is greatly superior to the others in its reflex influence on civilisation. It marks the full maturity of a society; and it is the function of government to facilitate by suitable economic measures the natural movement of the community towards this highest stage. In the purely agricultural period, free trade with richer and more cultivated societies is the right policy as tending most to the advancement of the national culture. And it becomes so again when the productive powers of the nation have been fully developed. But in the intermediate stage a gradually introduced protective system is the proper resource for training and maturing the industrial capacities of a people, which, in its absence, could not hold their ground in the home market against the competition of more advanced communities. Thus the protective system ought not to be a permanent order of things, but temporary and provisional only. It is, in fact, a means of industrial education carried on at the expense of the nation, and ought to cease with the necessity for it. According to List, England alone in his time had reached the highest stage, and France was approaching it. For England free trade was the right policy. When Germany under, and by means of, protection, should have completed her industrial education, and so enabled herself to overcome the obstacles to her success in the markets of the world presented by the already-acquired superiority of other countries, free trade ought to become *her* policy also. And the adoption of that system by all nations under like conditions would realise the economic ideal and mark the consummation of general well-being. This theory, though stated too absolutely and thus requiring modification, seems certainly to contain some elements of truth. List, besides criticising effectually weak points in the systems of his predecessors, did much towards introducing the relative historical spirit into economic studies, and emphasising the political—and in some degree also the moral—considerations which often enter into the solution of industrial problems. His writings referring for the most part, directly or indirectly, to questions of the day, had a powerful effect in Germany by interesting the middle classes in economic doctrines and making those doctrines subjects of general discussion.

Apart from his errors of principle, and the materialistic tinge which—though he would have repudiated the charge — undoubtedly colours his ideas, his chief faults are a tendency to exaggeration, the product in part of his eager temperament and exuberant rhetoric, his habit of unduly depreciating the economists whose views he controverted, and looseness and want of system in his exposition of scientific principles. He had the art, however, of catching the popular ear ; and indeed it is impossible not to be attracted by the freshness, the vigour, and the tone of profound conviction, which characterise his writings, as well as by his ardent patriotism, and his intense belief in the great future which awaited his country. The success of his principal book, though aided by the harmony of its doctrines with the contemporary circumstances and aspirations of Germany, was not exclusively due to this, but was the merited reward of its contributions to economic thought.

Besides the publications above-mentioned, List wrote much in the public journals of his time in favour of the creation of a railway system and the establishment of the ZOLLVEREIN, and founded, in 1833 and 1843 respectively, special organs for the advocacy of these objects. He also contributed a series of articles to the *Staats-Lexicon* of Rotteck and Welcker. Amongst his minor pieces may be mentioned, *Das Nationale Transport-system* (1838). —*Die Ackerverfassung, die Zwergwirthschaft und die Auswanderung,* 1842, in which he advocated the 'grande culture,' and *Die politisch-ökonomische National-einheit der Deutschen* (1846). There is a collected, though not complete, edition of List's writings by Häusser (3 vols., 1850), which contains also a biographical memoir of him. His principal work has been translated in America by G. A. Matile, with preface by S. Colwell (1856), and in England by S. Sampson Lloyd (1885).

[Leser in *Allg. Deutsche Biogr.*—Eheberg in *Handw. der Staatswissenschaften.*—Roscher, *Gesch. der N. O.,* p. 970.—Kautz, *Die gesch. Entwickelung der N. O.,* p. 670.]   J. K. I.

LITERARY PROPERTY. See COPYRIGHT.

LITTLE GOES. A species of lottery declared unlawful by 42 Geo. III. c. 119.

[Wharton, *Law Lexicon, sub voce.*]

LITH, JOHANN WILHELM VON DER (1709-1775), belongs to the numerous class of German writers and statesmen who, during the last century, considered most questions of administration and finance from the standpoint of what they called *populosity, i.e.* the development of population. This prepossession, natural in a country which had been depopulated by the havoc of religious and political wars, was pushed by them to an undue exaggeration, shared by the German princes anxious to strengthen their

military power. For instance, these writers mostly advocated the excise system because excise duties are paid without compulsion, and do not excite the population to emigrate.

These and parallel opinions are maintained by Von der Lith in his *Politische Betrachtungen von verschiedenen Arten der Steuern* (Political Considerations on different kinds of Taxation), 1751, and in his *Neue vollständige erwiesene Abhandlung von denen Steuern und deren vorthéilhafter Einrichtung in einem Lande nach den Grundsätzen einer wahren, die Verbesserung der Macht eines Regenten und die Glückseligkeit seiner Unterthanen wirkenden Staatskunst* (A new and complete Exposition of a beneficent System of Taxation on the principles of a true statecraft which furthers the power of a ruler and the happiness of his Subjects), 1766.—Roscher, *Gesch. der Nat. Oek. in Deutschland,* p. 425, describes the latter book, although dry and heavy, as showing a solid knowledge of German and foreign financial institutions and literature.   E. CA.

LIVERY. The term "livery," meaning at first an allowance (*liberatio*) in food and clothing to the servants of great mediæval households, soon came to be restricted to the gift of clothing, and then to the clothing itself. It became common in England in the 14th century for the great lords to clothe their retainers in a uniform, and to give "livery of company" also to their friends and dependants, a practice which greatly increased the tendencies of the time towards baronial lawlessness and faction. Accordingly it was restricted by a long series of statutes, beginning in the reign of Richard II. ; though it was not until the accession of Henry VII. that the government was strong enough to enforce them.

[Dr. Stubbs, *Const. Hist.,* iii. § 471, was the first to lay stress upon the custom of livery as "an important element among the disruptive tendencies of the later middle ages." The well-known story of Henry VII. and the Earl of Oxford is told by Lord Bacon in his *Life* of that king (see, for another sense of the term, LAND, LAW RELATING TO ; SEISIN).]   W. J. A.

LIVERYMEN. The wearing of a uniform LIVERY (*q.v.*) was not peculiar to baronial retinues ; it was common upon festive or ceremonial occasions with the members of fraternities of various kinds—including the fraternities of crafts. In a petition of 1389, the Commons prayed not only that the liveries of lords should be restricted, but also that no livery should be given "under colour of gild or fraternity," and "that no craft should give livery to any." In 1406, however, the statute concerning liveries expressly exempted "gilds and fraternities, and also the people of misteries that be founded and ordained to a good intent and purpose." At this time probably every member of the companies of crafts wore the livery from time to time ; but before the end of the century it had in London become a mark of a certain superiority of some members over others—a change due perhaps to the increasing costliness of the attire, and the unwillingness of ordinary freemen to lose the time necessary for attending pageants. Among the drapers in 1493 there were 114 "of the craft in the clothing," 115 "of the brotherhood out of the clothing," and 60 in the bachelors' company. By about the middle of the 16th century the "livery" constituted in most of the crafts a higher grade to which the more substantial freemen were admitted by the court of assistants, upon the payment of heavy fees. In the smaller companies it would seem that the "livery" at first included all or almost all the employers, in the greater only the more substantial ; but during the next century the companies began to lose their close connection with the industrial occupations from which they had arisen. An act of common council in 15 Edward IV., ordering the heads of the companies to come to elections "with the honest men of their misteries in their best liveries," led to the liverymen obtaining an exclusive right to vote both for the chief civic magistrates and, until 1835, for the members of parliament for the city ; the gathering of the liverymen of the companies for the former purpose is known as the "common hall." The social position of liverymen during the last two hundred years is sufficiently indicated by the act of the court of aldermen in 1697, "that no person shall be allowed to take upon himself the clothing of any of the twelve companies unless he have an estate of £1000, of the inferior companies unless he have an estate of £500." At present, with about 10,000 ordinary freemen, there are some 7300 liverymen in the several companies ; of these about 1500 constitute the courts of assistants (see also COMPANIES, CITY OF LONDON).

[The early history of the "livery" will be found in Ashley, *Economic History*, i. pt. ii. pp. 125-132. The present position of the livery in the various companies may be best studied in the *Report of H.M. Livery Companies' Commission* (1884), which is conveniently summarised in the *Introduction* to Mr. W. Carew Hazlitt's *Livery Companies* (1892), where also will be found some indications as to the peculiar privileges and burdens of liverymen.]   W. J. A.

LIVERY COMPANIES. This term for those "companies" in London which have grown out of the old fellowships of crafts, and the LIVERYMEN (*q.v.*) of which had an exclusive right to the civic franchise, would seem to have come into use in the 18th or early 19th century, probably with the appearance of "companies" of another sort from which they needed to be distinguished. William Herbert, the librarian to the Corporation of London, entitled his book *The History of the twelve great Livery Companies* (1834), and the royal commission

of inquiry appointed in 1880 was designated the "Livery Companies' Commission." But it does not seem that any clear distinction has been drawn by competent authority between "livery" companies and those other companies —of which several survived until quite recently —which had a somewhat similar origin (see COMPANIES, CITY OF LONDON).   W. J. A.

LIVERPOOL, CHARLES JENKINSON, first Earl of (1727-1808), was born at Winchester, of an old Oxfordshire family. After a distinguished career at Oxford, he began to prepare for public life. In March 1761 he was appointed by Bute an under secretary of state, entered the House of Commons, and filled various minor offices until 1772, when he was appointed vice-treasurer of Ireland, and a privy councillor. Three years later he purchased from Fox the valuable patent place of clerk of the pells in Ireland, and became master of the mint. In 1778 he was appointed secretary at war under Lord North, and was supposed to possess almost unbounded influence over the king and the prime minister. Pitt, whose commercial and financial policy he warmly admired, appointed him a member of the board of trade in 1783. Jenkinson had a large share in framing the commercial treaty between Great Britain and America of 1784, and he also assisted to establish the South Sea fishery. In 1786 he was created Baron Hawkesbury, and was appointed chancellor of the duchy of Lancaster and president of the committee of council for the affairs of trade and plantations. He was created Earl of Liverpool in 1796.

Lord Liverpool's speeches in the House of Peers were almost entirely confined to economic and financial questions. In 1797 he defended the constitution and conduct of the committee appointed to report on the suspension of cash payments ; and the following year spoke in defence of the Assessed Taxes Bill, by which an income tax of 10 per cent was imposed on incomes above £200.

Lord Liverpool wrote *A Discourse on the Conduct of the Government of Great Britain in Respect to Neutral Nations*, published 1758, 2nd ed. 1794 ; (this tract, which is described by M'Culloch, *Lit. Pol. Econ.*, as being "learned, moderate, and able," supports the view that "neutrals are not to be allowed to carry on a trade during war from which they had been excluded during peace,") and *A Dissertation on the Establishment of a National and Constitutional Force in England independent of a Standing Army*, 1756.

In 1785 appeared, in 3 vols., his *Collection of all Treaties of Peace, Alliance, and Commerce between Great Britain and other Powers, from the Treaty of Munster in 1648 to the Treaties signed at Paris in 1783*.

In 1805 Lord Liverpool addressed his well-known letter to the king (George III.), published as *A Treatise on the Coins of the Realm*, 1805, reprinted 1846, and in 1880 by the Bank of England, which "comprises . . . a greater amount of information respecting the coins of the kingdom, and a more comprehensive and elaborate expositiou of the principles on which the coinage should be conducted, than is perhaps to be met with in any other publication " (M'Culloch, *Lit. Pol. Econ.*).

This work was originally written, with the cooperation of George Chalmers, as a draft report for a conference of the privy council in 1798, appointed to enquire into the state of the coins, etc., and it had great influence in the adoption of the gold standard in 1816. (See second Earl of LIVERPOOL.)

[Yonge's *Life of the Second Earl of Liverpool.*— Stanhope's *Life of Pitt.*—*Annual Register*, 1808. —And *Dictionary of National Biography*, vol. xxix.]
G. B. S.

LIVERPOOL, ROBERT BANKS JENKINSON, second Earl of (1770-1828), educated at Charterhouse and Christ Church, Oxford, entered parliament in 1790. Appointed in 1794 to the India board, he became, five years later, master of the mint. When his father was raised to an earldom he was known as Lord Hawkesbury. He was a close student of political economy and finance ; in 1796 he maintained that the commercial condition of Great Britain—notwithstanding the pressure of the great war—was more prosperous than at any antecedent period, and regretted that the system of appropriating a million annually to the extinction of the national debt had not been adopted at the close of the previous war in 1748, as the burden would have since been lifted from the shoulders of the nation. Hence it was natural that he should regard the sinking fund established by Pitt as "unquestionably the greatest measure ever produced by the ingenuity or wisdom of man," and gave his adhesion to the financial axiom that the supplies, or a considerable portion of them, should be raised within the year.

As foreign secretary he negotiated the Treaty of Amiens in 1801. Two years later he was raised to the Upper House as Baron Hawkesbury during his father's lifetime. In 1808 he became Earl of Liverpool on the death of his father. In 1810 the bullion committee of the House of Commons reported on the depreciation in the currency. Lord King and other large landowners refused to receive their rents except in gold ; and guineas were extensively bought at from twenty-three to twenty-seven shillings, by agents of the government, to remit to the Peninsula. Lord Stanhope introduced a bill in the House of Lords to make it illegal for any person to give more money for guineas, half-guineas, etc., than their lawful value. Lord Liverpool at first opposed this bill, but subsequently assisted in carrying it through.

During the same session he supported Mr. Vansittart's bill on the sinking fund, which repealed the act of 1802, but adhered to Mr. Pitt's original measure of 1792. Lord Liverpool also supported Mr. Vansittart's celebrated reso-lutions, in opposition to those of Mr. Horner, which advocated a return to cash payments. One of Vansittart's resolutions affirmed that bank-notes were equal to gold despite the fact that £100 of notes could only purchase £86 : 10 : 6 of gold. Party feeling alone can account for the support Vansittart received.

In 1812 Lord Liverpool came into power at the head of a purely Tory ministry, the first ten years of which witnessed much reactionary movement on the continent and at home, the mismanagement of the national finances, the increase in the duty on foreign corn, and the adoption of coercive measures for dealing with discontent in England. All these things were charged to the incapacity of the government. Personally, Lord Liverpool was a free trader, and regarded the corn law of 1815 merely as an experiment. When Huskisson and Canning joined the ministry, he began to liberalise the tariff, and desired to retain a portion of the property tax, a measure which would have greatly favoured the working classes. But opposed by Whigs and Tories alike, it was defeated in the Commons. In spite of its reactionary policy on certain national questions, and much vacillation of opinion, Lord Liverpool's ministry may be regarded as the pioneer administration of free trade.

Besides those already mentioned, the following are the principal financial events of Lord Liverpool's ministry. In 1816 he carried the measure entitled " An Act to provide for a New Silver Coinage, and to regulate the currency of the Gold and Silver coin of this Realm " ; which established the gold standard in this country and made silver token money (coined at the rate of sixty-six shillings to the owner instead of sixty-two) the standard rate, and limited to forty shillings as legal tender. The effect of this act has been severely criticised, and it was commented on by W. HUSKISSON (*q.v.*) at the time. In 1818 he carried a proposal fixing the ensuing year as the time for the resumption of cash payments. He cordially supported Peel's bill to regulate the employment of children in factories. In 1819 reduction in taxation was followed by various measures in the direction of free trade ; and in 1820 the premier expounded his liberal ideas on the subject of foreign commerce, but showed that our laws with respect to agricultural produce alone threw an insurmountable obstacle in the way of complete freedom of trade. The sinking fund was a blunder which has never been defended ; but Liverpool's general policy with regard to the currency and commercial panics during the early years of George IV.'s reign has been both warmly eulogised and objected to as the cause of much financial trouble.

In 1821 the bill for the resumption of cash payments was carried through both Houses, and in defending the substitution of gold for £1 notes, to the extent of six or seven millions, Lord Liverpool also vindicated the measures taken to establish an efficient sinking fund, to the amount of five millions. He expressed himself as opposed in principle to legislation which favoured or burdened one industry more than another, and had approved, on its own merits, a system of unrestricted trade ; though he admitted that a country which had so long followed an opposite policy could not easily abandon it. But in 1826 he avowed that neither the corn law of 1815, nor that of 1822, was applicable to existing circumstances of prevalent distress and industrial depression. He declared himself individually responsible for the ministerial proposal to confer on the administration a discretionary power to permit a limited importation of corn ; and this power was shortly afterwards exercised. In fact the premier's opinions were moving so rapidly in the direction of an amelioration of the corn laws, that he prepared a measure of relaxation which was introduced in the new parliament, though illness prevented him from personally conducting the measure.

The severe money panic in England at the close of 1825 led to the stoppage of a great number of banks, while the whole circulation of the country was practically paralysed. Government at once resolved to issue one- and two-pound Bank of England notes to relieve the country, and an extraordinary coinage of sovereigns was ordered. In the session of 1826 the Small Note Bill was passed, which provided for the suppression of notes under £5. By a further measure the law of 1708 was repealed, and banks with any number of partners were allowed to be established beyond sixty-five miles from London, while the Bank of England was permitted to establish branches to be carried on by its agents.

[*Memoirs of the Public Life and Administration of the Earl of Liverpool*, 1827.—*Life of the Second Earl of Liverpool*, by C. D. Yonge, 3 vols. 1868.—Kebbel's *History of Toryism*, 1886.—*Dictionary of National Biography*, vol. xxix.—*Annual Register*, 1828.]   G. B. S.

LIVING WAGE. This expression is generally confused with the cognate "minimum wage," *e.g.* the lowest rate paid on a sliding-scale arrangement, which may be defined as the claim of labour to a definite low daily or weekly wage, without any guarantee of the permanent employment which would make it a wage sufficient to live on. It came to the front during the great coal strike of 1893. But it is impossible to limit the claim of a living wage to any section of workers,—by whom, indeed, it might be attainable given strict combination, limitation of numbers, and maintenance of price,—and the expression seems likely to take root as the claim of labour generally to a preference share in the total product of industry.

Plausible as the catchword seems, on examination it does little more than suggest questions. Is any preference share really possible—say that the guarantee of a living raised the sluice-gates of population? Suppose the claim granted, is the "living" in question mere physical subsistence or life at a conventional level? and is it a "family wage" or an "individual" one? If Great Britain's estimated income, divided by

its population, gives some £36 per head, what kind of living wage does that income provide even on the footing of an equal distribution? Would the national income be maintained and increase if it were thus distributed? How far may the "living" of capital be reduced without reducing the national dividend and so reducing the living wage? Unless industrial efficiency increase proportionally with the living wage, how could our free-trade country compete with others? All the same, has labour not a better claim to a preference in the national dividend than any other factor? If equal distribution would give so small a sum per head, what kind of living does the present distribution afford to the masses?

The expression gives at least one valuable reminder. Giffen (*Essays in Finance*, second series, 1886, p. 463), comparing wages in 1883 with wages fifty years before, has calculated that the income of the manual labour classes per head has increased on the average much more than 100 per cent. Taking this with the fact that wealth in Great Britain seems to increase more than twice as fast as population, it is obviously possible that the standard of living should steadily rise ; and it is right that average industry should claim a wage rising in correspondence — always remembering that a real rise in wage may be expressed in low prices, and that changes in currency may even disguise an increase of wage in lower money figures. But the dislocations seemingly inevitable in any system of competitive industry make any guarantee of a living wage by individual employers impossible, and throw doubt on the possibility of its being guaranteed under any imaginable organisation of human society.

[Giffen, *The Growth of Capital*, 1889.—Smart, *Studies in Economics*, 1895.—Marshall, *Elements*, ch. xii. § 16, cp. STANDARD OF COMFORT.]   w. s.

LIVRE. Of the many notable features in the financial history of France none is more remarkable than the complete distinction between money of account and the money in actual circulation. The distinction was neither unique nor original, but in no country was it so sharply drawn as in France from the 10th to the 18th century. The origin of the money of account is traced by all authorities to a capitulary of Charles the Great, which ordered that the pound of silver (*libra argenti*) should be divided into 20 *solidi*, and each SOLIDUS (*q.v.*) into 12 *denarii* (see DENARIUS). From this time the terms of commercial transactions, whether sales or contracts extending over a period of time, were expressed in *livres*, SOUS, and DENIERS. These always retained the same proportion to each other, 12 *deniers* to the *sou*, and 20 *sous* to the *livre*. In Frankish times all three terms may have denoted actual coins, but under the Capet kings these disappeared from circulation. In the 11th century the MARK, containing 4608 grains, took the place of the *livre* or pound as the ordinary measure for the weight of bullion. From this time the *livre* ceased to connote any idea of weight, as it had already of coin, and thus the separation of the money of account was completed. In later times the names reappear, *e.g.* the *sou d'or* and the *denier d'or*, but the existence of these coins was very short-lived, and they had no connection whatever with the *sou* and the *denier* as terms of account. An infinite variety of coins were issued from time to time, such as the *agnel* or *mouton d'or* and the *gros* and *petits tournois* under Saint Louis, the *écus d'or* and the *blancs* of the Valois kings, the *louis d'or* and the *louis d'argent* of the Bourbons, etc. But the value of all these coins was expressed in the money of account, *i.e.* in *livres*, *sous*, and *deniers*.

The break-up of the Karolingian empire put an end to the monetary centralisation which Charles the Great had established. In *Francia Occidentalis*, which became France, the great vassals claimed and obtained the right of private coinage in their own domain. What is more extraordinary is that the money of account became localised as well as the circulating coins. Thus we hear of *livres*, *sous*, and *deniers* with local designations, *e.g.* Parisis, Tournois, Manceaux, Poitevins, Toulousains, Angevins, etc. The Capet kings, originally dukes of Paris, naturally adopted the *livre parisis* of their own domain. As time went on the power of the crown developed steadily at the expense of feudal privileges. Saint Louis ordered that the royal money should circulate everywhere side by side with that of the lords, and forbade the latter to imitate the king's coin. This policy, steadily pursued by his successors, resulted in the recognition of a single currency for the whole of France, and the local money, where it survived, was restricted to small copper coins with a very small area of circulation. But during the process of centralisation, one of the local monies of account came to be adopted by the crown. The *livre tournois* had come into general use in southern France, and when Languedoc was annexed to the royal domain, its method of reckoning was retained side by side with that of Paris. From this time we have two alternative monies of account, the *livre sou* and *denier parisis*, and the *livre sou* and *denier tournois*. The former money was always valued a fourth higher than the latter. A *livre parisis* equalled 20 *sous parisis* and 25 *sous tournois*. Thus when a mark of silver was valued at 2 *livres parisis*, it would at the same time be equivalent to 2½ *livres tournois*. This double system lasted till the reign of Louis XIV., who abolished the *livre parisis* and retained only the *livre tournois* and its divisions, which had long been the money of account in ordinary use.

Although the proportion between the *livre*, the *sou*, and the *denier* remained unaltered from the time of Charles the Great to the Revolution, their actual intrinsic value was subject to constant change, almost invariably in the direction of depreciation. It would take too long to trace the variations in the value of the *livre*, which have been treated with equal learning and acuteness by several French writers. A few salient facts must suffice. The exact weight of Charles the Great's *libra argenti* has been disputed, and the amount of silver it contained has been variously estimated as equal to 86 francs 97 centimes, or to 78 francs 20 centimes of modern money. Of course its purchasing power was infinitely greater, but it is simpler and safer to measure only intrinsic value in silver. Under Louis IX. (1226-1272) the *livre* was equivalent to only about 18 francs. By the 18th century it had fallen to practically 1 franc, and at times to about 80 centimes.

This steady depreciation of the money of account was primarily due to the fact that the coinage was in the hands of the king, who considered that he had a right to make a profit or SEIGNIORAGE on the process. It is obvious that the distinction between money of account and actual money offered to the French kings exceptional temptations and opportunities for debasement. In other countries, where no such distinction existed, the king could only debase by re-coining the metals either with less weight or with a larger admixture of alloy. In France the king could employ this method if he chose, but he could also have recourse to a simpler expedient. When the crown ordered the issue of coins, it was necessary not only to fix their proportion to the mark of gold or of silver, but also to settle their value in terms of the money of account. This latter value was not always expressed on the face of the coin, and therefore it was perfectly easy for a king to depreciate the *livre* by a new edict giving a greater nominal value to the same coin. The royal methods may be illustrated by two actual facts from the history of Philip IV., who is pilloried both in contemporary chronicles and in history as the *faux-monnayeur*. When he came to the throne he found a silver coin in circulation, called the *gros tournois*, issued by his grandfather, Louis IX. Fifty-eight of these coins were made from the mark of silver, and the value of each was 1 *sou*, or the twentieth part of a *livre*. Among the new coins struck by Philip was a *petit tournois*, of which 116 were made from the mark, and which should therefore have been worth 6 *deniers*, or just half the *gros* of Louis IX. Instead of this, the edict fixed its value at 7½ *deniers*. As the new piece could not have circulated side by side with the older coinage, a new ordinance raised the *gros tournois* from 1 *sou* to 15 *deniers*, without making any change whatever in the coin itself. The result of these two changes was to reduce the intrinsic value of the *livre tournois* from about 18 modern francs to about 14 francs 40 centimes. It is needless to insist upon the damage that must have been done to trade by such changes as these serve to illustrate, and history is full of the indignation which they excited. There was one obvious remedy for these abuses, viz. to fix bargains by weight of silver, so that the debtor should in the end pay to the creditor as many marks as he had received. This expedient was frequently attempted, but was as often prohibited as being an attack upon the royal prerogative. With the old monarchy fell the monetary system which it had at once misused and upheld. The constituent assembly introduced the modern arrangement by which the mint is simply a business organisation for affixing a stamp to the precious metals, and charges nothing beyond the expense of the process, except in the case of coins whose legal tender is limited. This change was completed by the law of the 17th Germinal of the year xi. (28th March 1803), which fixed the franc at 5 grammes of silver with a fineness of nine-tenths. It is true that the law of 14th July 1866 lowered the intrinsic value of the franc and limited its legal tender. But by that time events had occurred which practically established a gold standard in France, confirmed by the law of 1875, closing the mint to the free coinage of silver. The change of standard makes no difference to the fact of the disappearance in France of that distinction between the money of account and the coin in circulation of which the *livre* is the most prominent illustration.

[See Ducange, *Glossarium*, s.v. "Moneta."— Le Blanc, *Traité historique des monnaies de France.*—Vuitry, *Études sur le régime financier de la France.*—P. Clément, *Jacques Cœur et Charles VII.*] R. L.

LIVRE DE RAISON, THE, was, in the language of the old French law, the ledger into which every banker and merchant was obliged to enter his receipts and expenditure. But in southern France and especially in Provence, the term included family-books (*livres de famille*) in which the head of the family used to put down genealogical details and miscellaneous notices, for instance of political events, famines, etc., which happened to strike his mind; the information yielded is often invaluable for the student of economic history.

[Attention was first called to the *Livres de Raison* by M. Charles de Ribbe, a friend and disciple of Le Play, in his *Famille au 16me Siècle* (1867). Since then many have been published, some of them going so far back as the 14th century; a bibliography on the subject occupies 52 pages in M. Tamizey de Larroque's *Livre de Raison de la Famille de Fontainemarie* (Agen, 1890). See also Ch. de Ribbe, *Le Play d'après sa Correspondance* (1884), pp. 127-139.] E. CA.

LIVRET (Fr.), the little book workmen in France were formerly required to hold under a law of 1st December 1803. It was delivered by the mayor of the place of domicile, and served to contain the date of entering and leaving the service of each employer, and had to be presented for the *visa* of the mayor, or commissary of police of the district, on each change of employment or residence. Masters were forbidden to make any other entry, either favourable or unfavourable, concerning the conduct or qualifications of the workman, but, if the man owed money for wages advanced, the debt could be noted on the *livret*, and the next employer became liable for a sum not exceeding thirty francs, which he could recover by a deduction of 10 per cent from the workman's pay. The *livret* served as a passport in the interior, and workmen travelling without one were liable to be arrested as vagrants. *Livrets* were abolished by a special law of 2nd July 1890, but by the same law masters are compelled to give, if demanded, a certificate containing exclusively the date of entry and leaving, and the kind of work on which the man was employed. *Livrets* were at one time imposed by decree on domestics of both sexes, but the rule was rarely observed. T. L.

LLOYD'S. The name of the association by which UNDERWRITING business is mainly carried on in London. The meeting of merchants who, in 1688, habitually used the coffee-house of Edward Lloyd in Tower Street, and which afterwards migrated to his coffee-house in Lombard Street, gradually developed into the powerful institution incorporated by the act of 1871, with "all the rights and privileges of a corporation sanctioned by parliament." According to this act of incorporation the three main objects for which the society exists are—first, the carrying out of the business of marine insurance; secondly, the protection of the interests of the members of the association; and thirdly, the collection, publication, and diffusion of intelligence and information with respect to shipping."

The association is managed by a committee appointed by the members. Of these the "underwriting" members deposit security for the fulfilment of their engagements. The business is conducted in a very simple manner through brokers who write down the name of the ship, the master, the circumstances of the voyage, and the amount to be insured. Each underwriter who agrees to join subscribes his name and the sum he takes.

The immense development of the shipping business of this country in recent years (see FREIGHT) has been followed by a very large increase in the business of marine insurance, of which a great part is carried on at Lloyd's (see INSURANCE, MARINE).

LLOYD'S BONDS. Instruments under seal invented by a parliamentary draftsman, whose name was Horace Lloyd, issued by companies acknowledging indebtedness for a specified sum, and containing a covenant to pay that sum with interest on a specified day. They were at one time much used by railway companies for the payment of contractors, who thereby acquired a security which they could realise, or on which they could raise money. They could be issued in respect of an existing debt only, and not for the purpose of borrowing in excess of borrowing powers. As it is now usual for railway companies to obtain extensive power for the issue of debentures or debenture stock, the name of Lloyd's bonds is no longer seen except in legal text-books.

[Tarrant, *Lloyd's Bonds*, 1867.] E. S.

LOAN (MUTUUM), CANONIST DEFINITION OF. The arguments by which the canonist doctrine of usury were supported, rested, for the most part, on a particular conception of "lending," *mutuatio*, derived from the Roman law. The Roman lawyers had defined *mutuum* (as distinguished from *commodatum*) as involving a transference from one person to another, of the ownership (*dominium*, as distinguished from USUS), in the thing lent. From this definition the canonists deduced the conclusions (1) that the lender could not justly receive gain (*lucrum*) from the use of a thing that no longer belonged to him, and (2) that the burden of risk was transferred, passed to the borrower with the ownership, the lender being also, as a rule, secured against risk by holding a pledge or in some other way. Hence, *e converso*, when risk was shared (as in various forms of partnership, SOCIETAS), it was concluded that ownership had not passed; that there was therefore no *mutuum;* and that accordingly the prohibition of usury did not apply. (See MUTUUM.)

[The very name was derived, according to the Roman lawyers, from the change of ownership, The explanation, "mutuum appellatum est, quia quod ita tibi a me datum est, ex meo tuum fit," is given in almost identical terms in Gaius iii. 90, Paulus in *Dig.*, xii. 2, 2, and in Justinian *Instit.* xiv. Ignorance of the juristic distinctions of the middle ages frequently blunts the edge of modern criticism of the usury doctrine. They are given in a conveniently brief form in Miles Mosse, *Arraignment of Usury*, 1595 : " *Lending* maketh a translation of the propertie ; *letting* doth onely make an alienation of the use. . . . *Lending* is the translation of the dominion of a thing for no price ; *selling* is the alienating of a thing for a set price to be paid. . . . In *lending* I looke for mine owne againe ; in *exchanging* I looke for some other thing in lue of mine owne," etc. See also Ashley, *Economic History*, vol. i. pt. i. p. 152; pt. ii. pp. 419, 454; Böhm-Bawerk, *Capital and Interest*, p. 22 ; F. X. Funk, *Zins und Wucher*, pp. 170 *seq*.] W. J. A.

LOANS, FORCED. From a very early date English kings found it necessary to meet extraordinary expenses by borrowing on the security of future revenue. For a long time loans were chiefly raised from foreigners, such as the Jews ; and after their expulsion in 1290, from firms of Italian bankers. The growth of wealth in the 15th century rendered it possible to raise large sums from native lenders, and the simultaneous revival of the royal power rendered it almost impossible to refuse the demands of the commissioners acting under authority of a privy seal. Under Edward IV. and the Tudors the exaction of compulsory loans from wealthy subjects became a frequent and almost regular expedient of the crown. Elizabeth, we are told, was extremely careful to repay these sums by a stipulated time, but her predecessors were by no means so punctilious. Twice in the reign of Henry VIII., in 1529 and 1544, parliament practically converted these loans into BENEVOLENCES (*q.v.*) by formally releasing the king from the obligation of repayment. That these exactions met with so little resistance was due partly to the formidable powers of the Star Chamber, and partly to the general popularity of the government. The mass of the people saw no reason to resent burdens which fell almost exclusively upon the wealthy. Things had completely changed when Charles I. and Buckingham endeavoured to raise the famous loan of 1627 for an unpopular war with France. No such general exaction had ever been attempted by the Tudors. The sum to be paid was five subsidies (see SUBSIDY), and every man rated in the subsidy books was to contribute in proportion to his rating. If any one refused, he was to be bound over to answer for contempt before the privy council. Considering the extreme doubtfulness of repayment, the demand was practically an attempt to levy a general subsidy without the authority of parliament. The terror inspired by the Star Chamber induced most people to pay rather than risk the penalties for refusal. But many prominent men, including Hampden, Eliot, and Wentworth, declined to comply with an illegal demand, and to contribute to an enterprise of which they disapproved. Seventy-six of the recusants were committed to prison on a special warrant of the king. But the failure of Buckingham's expedition led to increased resistance and forced Charles to summon his third parliament in 1628. This assembly drew up the Petition of Right, which demanded "that no man hereafter be compelled to make or yield any gift, loan, benevolence, tax, or such-like charge, without common consent by act of parliament." From this time the illegality of forced loans has been unquestioned.

[Hallam, *Constitutional History of England.*— Gardiner, *History of England*, vol. v.] R. L.

LOANS, LOCAL. See LOCAL GOVERNMENT.

LOANS, PUBLIC.

METHOD OF RAISING. Government loans are either internal or external. The special characteristic of an *internal loan* is that it is payable, interest and principal, within the country issuing it. A foreign holder of such a loan stands on the same legal footing as a citizen; but occasionally, and not as a matter of right, special arrangements have been made by foreign governments for the payment of coupons abroad, for the convenience of foreign holders, through an agent. Such an arrangement might, of course, cease at any moment.

An *external loan* is raised in part, or entirely, abroad, and its principal and interest are payable abroad as well as at home. Most countries have issued loans of both kinds. The means by which loans of either class are issued are:

A. Public issue:
  (1) By tenders at (or above) a *minimum* price per cent.
  (2) By tenders at a fixed price per cent.
B. By direct sale to a banking or financial house, which house sells again to the public when and how it pleases. In this case the first purchaser is said to take the loan "firm," and when retailing the loan to the public he may, of course, invite tenders either at a *minimum* or at a fixed price.

The selection of the mode of issuing the loan depends on circumstances. Countries whose financial position is good go direct to the public, merely paying a bank, or a financial house, a commission for the use of their premises and staff, if they do not issue through a bank of their own. French loans are issued through the bank of France, but when France was financially paralysed by the events of 1870-71 she raised a large loan through a great Anglo-American house. The British government makes issues through the Bank of England, the United States through its treasury; countries of less than the highest credit issue their loans through finance houses, with whom the loans are said to be "domiciled."

If the loan is issued at a *minimum* price, the competition for it among investors takes the form of the offer of prices above the *minimum*; if at a fixed price the competition takes the form of applications in excess of the amount really wanted. In the former case allotments are made on the principle of giving a certain percentage of the amount tendered for at a certain price, and giving all tenders above that price in full. The price will, of course, depend on the extent of the tenders. Sometimes a "syndicate" applies for more than the whole loan, and only gets a small proportion because it has not offered as much as the general public, but usually syndicates hit on a figure at which they get nearly all they wish for.

If tenders are made at a fixed price, the method usually followed in the case of foreign loans, the *nominal* amount of the tenders is sometimes enormous, but many of the largest applicants would be very sorry to be taken at their word. French government loans and the issues of the Crédit Foncier have been applied for thirty or forty times over. The plan of the issuers in such cases is to allot to all small tenders in full, and the balance of the loan, after this is done, is divided *pro rata* among the larger applicants, whose tenders are assumed to be, and probably are, more or less speculative.

It does not come within the scope of this article to discuss the purposes for which public loans are issued, but it is not out of place to observe that when a finance house takes a loan "firm," this operation *may* mean that it has already lent the government money in some form or other, by an advance on treasury bills, for instance. When this is the case there is often a very considerable difference between the price the government obtains for the loan and that at which the finance house sells it to the public. In the past some very remarkable transactions of this kind have taken place, particulars of which will be found in the report of the House of Commons committee on loans to foreign states, 1875. The difference in price may be justified, for the money lent in the first instance may have tided the borrowing state over a period of difficulty and enabled it to improve its credit to such an extent that the price asked at a subsequent date is justified. In all such cases the character and position of the house which issues the loan is the real guarantee for its soundness, and intending subscribers to a loan cannot be too careful in considering the history, especially the recent history, of the house whose name they will have to rely on.

Conversion Loans.—Of late years loans of this class have been numerous, owing to the amount of capital seeking investment having increased much more rapidly than the volume of securities available for this purpose. All the great states of the world and many minor countries have taken advantage of this condition of things to convert their debts from a higher to a lower rate of interest. The method adopted is usually to announce a new issue at the lower rate, to which the holders of the older issues have the right to subscribe in bond on specified terms. If they do not wish to do this they are paid off at par with the money subscribed to the new loan by the public. Sometimes such a conversion fails, through nearly all the old holders refusing to send in their bonds and the public subscribing nothing, the government having over-estimated its credit. On several occasions the credit of the government has been amply good enough to justify the operation, but its *right* to carry it out has been questioned by holders of the older loans, on the ground of the wording of the bond, which, it is contended, does not permit redemption before a certain date. The contention of the government, in such cases, usually is that the words relating to redemption mean that the loan must be redeemed at the date mentioned *at the latest.* The conversion of the Egyptian preference loan, in 1888, led to disputes of this kind, and more recently, in 1894, the conversion of the Turkish tribute loans caused a similar discussion. It is probable that these precedents will reduce the readiness of the public to subscribe to loans in future, except at slightly lower prices, unless a specific engagement is entered into that the loan will not be redeemed or converted before a certain date.

Form of Documents of Ownership.—Loans are either registered as stock or are issued in the form of bonds to bearer, with a sheet of coupons attached representing the amounts of interest due half yearly (or quarterly). This last is the form in which the majority of external loans are issued, as such bonds are more widely marketable than registered stock. They are liable to be stolen, however, while certificates of registered stock are of no use *per se* to any one but the rightful owner.

Underwriting.—This term is used to denote an agreement entered into with an issuing house by capitalists who bind themselves to take part of a loan to be issued by such house at a certain price, in case the public do not subscribe for it. The majority of loans of any magnitude are thus "underwritten." The consideration for the service rendered is paid in the form of a commission. If the loan is sold to the public, the underwriters merely pocket their commissions, but if not they have to take up their quotas. In times of speculative activity many people of inadequate means make money in this way, but eventually some of them get caught, the speculative fever of the public having diminished. Many of the embarrassments which followed the financial collapse of November 1890 were due to incautious underwriting.

Issue of loans above or under par.—The decision as to the price at which a loan shall be issued is dictated by various circumstances. In the case of governments whose credit is only moderately good, the usual practice is to sell the loan at less than par, in order to make it more attractive, for a cautious investor who has made up his mind to choose one of two loans at different rates of interest, but yielding the same rate on the capital invested, will almost invariably take that which is under par. Governments in good credit, on the other

hand, usually ask at least par for their issues, though this rule is not invariable, as it has, in some cases, been considered worth while issuing at a discount in order to establish a loan at a low rate of interest in the market. The most remarkable instance of this was the persistent issue by the British government of 3 per cents, which, until within the last few years, were usually under par. On the whole the policy has been justified by results, but in most cases unless the discount is moderate the creation of debt, which is only partly represented by the actual receipt of cash, is of doubtful wisdom, the better plan being to borrow at par at a higher rate of interest for a moderate term of years, which enables the country to take advantage of any improvement in its credit by refunding at a lower rate when the old loan matures.   W. H.

LOCAL FINANCE is becoming, with the growth of local administrative activity, a subject of increasing importance. The aggregate receipts of the local authorities of England and Wales for 1892-93, excluding receipts from loans, amounted to £55,549,402.

The principal items were :

Public Rates . . .	£30,201,903
Imperial Contributions . . .	9,042,637
Tolls, dues, and duties . . .	3,338,355
Receipts from real and funded property	1,616,263
Sales of property . . .	264,981
Fines, fees, penalties and licences ; including £80,562 school fees .	658,268
Revenue from waterworks . .	2,723,303
do. gasworks . .	4,333,589
do. markets, cemeteries, burial grounds, sewage farms, baths and wash-houses, libraries, fire - brigades, lunatic - asylums, hospitals, tramways, slaughter-houses, and harbours, piers, and docks ; *excluding* receipts entered as rates, tolls and dues, etc. .	1,096,032
Repayments in respect of private improvement works . . .	926,517

The sum entered as public rates is rather more than half the total. These rates, which constitute, strictly speaking, nearly the whole of local taxation, are levied upon the occupiers of real property ; the sum payable by each occupier being in proportion to the annual value of the lands, premises, etc. occupied. The poor law provides for the assessment and collection of the poor-rate ; and with this rate several others, *e.g.* the county council, rural district council, and parish council rates, are collected. The general district and other rates separately collected, are based on the poor-law valuation. There is, however, a reduced assessment of agricultural land, railways, etc. to certain urban charges, and it is suggested that the system should be generally modified in another direction by the levy of special rates for town improvements upon the persons primarily benefited. Financially speaking, the areas of the separate local authorities are independent ; but the metropolis occupies an anomalous position — it is an aggregation of authorities whose financial independence of each other is modified by the presence of a common poor fund and an equalisation of rates fund.

The poor rate valuation of England and Wales at Lady Day 1892 was £157,722,913 ; of the metropolis alone £33,370,826. The sums raised as rates represent for England and Wales an average rate of 3s. 10·0d., or 20s. 7d. per head of the population. The average for the metropolis, however, is 5s. 1·2d. or £1 : 19 : 11 per head ; for the provinces, 3s. 5·9d. or 17s. 3d. per head. The rates show an increase in ten years of 21·1 per cent, a rate of growth about five times greater than that of taxation for imperial purposes. In considering further the geographical distribution of the burden, it will be found that the increase is almost entirely confined to urban districts. In the decade in question the rates rose in the metropolis 35·0 per cent ; while those levied by urban sanitary authorities rose 37 per cent. The rates levied by extra-metropolitan poor-law, and rural highway, authorities, show a decrease. In addition to local taxation, £9,042,637 was received during the year from imperial taxation, and distributed thus :

County Councils	£3,149,197
Poor Law Authorities . . .	1,609,350
School Boards	2,319,251
Municipal Corporations . . .	1,047,092
Other Authorities	1,149,608
	9,274,498
Deduct amounts remaining undistributed the previous year. .	1,438,761
	7,835,737
Add like amounts this year . .	1,206,900
Total . . .	£9,042,637

£6,439,508 of the above represented the produce of certain imperial taxes permanently granted to the local authorities ; and therefore was not a charge of annual supply, but belonged rather to the category of charges on the CONSOLIDATED FUND. The expenditure of the surplus from this sum, after meeting the charges for certain services, is within the discretion of the grantees.

The aggregate local expenditure, excluding expenditure out of loans, was £56,170,115. The principal items were :

Relief of the poor, including salaries, but excluding pauper lunatics .	£7,184,158
Pauper lunatics	1,766,932
Police	4,696,864
Education, including expenditure of school boards, school attendance committees, reformatories, and industrial schools, and expenditure upon technical and intermediate education	5,425,341
Highways, street improvements, and turnpike roads . . .	7,247,853
Gasworks	3,480,925
Public lighting	1,045,230
Waterworks	1,010,008
Sewerage and sewage disposal works	1,223,836

Markets and fairs	£324,383
Cemeteries and burial grounds .	301,603
Fire brigades	255,802
Parks, pleasure grounds, etc. . .	346,139
Public libraries and museums .	285,334
Baths, wash-houses, etc. . .	209,844
Bridges and ferries . . .	177,249
Hospitals	313,344
Harbours, piers, docks, and quays .	1,370,402
Land drainage, embankment, and river conservancy	281,364
Other public works and purposes .	3,598,746
Private improvement works . .	766,218
Payment in respect of loans raised for all the purposes mentioned .	11,909,913
Salaries, establishment, legal and parliamentary expenses not charged to particular undertakings . .	2,464,050

The numerous and increasing duties imposed by parliament upon the local, especially the urban authorities, involves an expenditure which has in the past steadily grown, and which there is reason to believe will continue to increase in the future. Economies must therefore chiefly be administrative. Some supplementary means there are : for example, the making of an annual financial statement or budget by the county councils is compulsory ; and the audit of accounts by the central authorities is general, the auditor disallowing any item of account which is contrary to law. Municipal corporations and metropolitan parishes, however, elect their own auditors, and form an important exception. In several instances the rate in the £ which may be levied is limited. It may also be noted that a considerable part of the outlay of urban authorities is upon undertakings of an industrial nature, and that the more important of these usually return a profit.

Scotland.—The receipts of local authorities, exclusive of loans, are returned for 1892-93 as follows :

Rates, including water-rates, £338,551	£3,779,525
Tolls, dues, fees, fines and rents .	1,111,275
Imperial contributions . . .	1,356,619
Other receipts	1,302,705
	£7,550,124

The rateable value was £24,180,483, and the rates as above averaged 3s. 1½d. in the £, or 18s. 6d. per head of population. The expenditure is returned as follows :

By parochial boards :	
Poor expenditure . . .	£863,956
Other do.	137,278
School boards	1,691,071
Burgh authorities	3,375,435
County councils	947,939
Heritors for ecclesiastical purposes .	42,398
Harbour authorities . . .	1,050,127
District fishery boards . . .	11,627
	£8,119,831

Rates to the amount of £1,496,868 fell upon owners, and £2,282,657 upon occupiers.

Ireland.—Local receipts for 1894 were :

Rates on real property . . .	£2,963,956
Tolls, fees, stamps and dues . .	490,557
Other Receipts	294,909
Imperial contributions . . .	331,928
	4,081,350

The chief items of expenditure were :

By grand juries for roads, bridges, lunatic asylums, etc. }	1,407,397
By harbour authorities . . .	403,003
By guardians on poor relief, etc. .	1,297,530
By town authorities for sewers, town-improvements, paving, cleaning, and lighting streets, etc. }	978,438
By town authorities for water supply	204,669

The rateable value was £14,187,538.

[Local taxation returns (England and Wales)—(Scotland)—(Ireland).—Reports of the local government board.—Return : *Local Taxation*, 10th April 1893 (168 of 1893).—*Report on Local Taxation*, Scotland (C. 7575 of 1895).—Wright and Hobhouse, *Local Government and Local Taxation*, 2nd ed., London, 1894.—G. H. Blunden, *Local Taxation and Finance*, London, 1895. For earlier dates: G. J. Goschen, *Reports and Speeches on Local Taxation*, London, 1872.—R. H. Inglis Palgrave, *The Local Taxation of Great Britain and Ireland*, London, 1871.—Danby P. Fry, *The Local Taxes of the United Kingdom*, London, 1846. Also see C. F. Bastable, *Public Finance*, c. vii., London, 2nd ed. 1895.—H. Fawcett, *Manual of Political Economy*, London, 1883.—W. H. Smith, *Relation between Local and Central Taxation*, Econ. *Journal*, June 1895.]

w. h. s.

LOCAL GOVERNMENT. The term "local government," often used somewhat vaguely, is best confined to denote the structure and operations of those smaller bodies which are needed to supplement the action of the central authority. Employed in this sense, it has to be distinguished from federalism, and from the government of COLONIES and dependencies. The organs comprised under the designation "local government" are completely subordinate to the central legislature, but have received a delegated power for their special functions. Owing to the greater size of modern states, this process of delegation, scarcely required in the classical city state (πόλις), has been largely carried out, and is likely to increase in importance. In many cases local legislative or executive powers mark the earlier existence of complete independence, which has disappeared under the gradual CENTRALISATION that has been so prominent a feature in European history. But quite apart from these survivals there has been deliberate and conscious creation of local institutions in most of the chief modern states, and even where older formations have been preserved, they are rather adapted to meet new ends than simply retained as relics of a past condition, as conspicuous examples the English legislation of 1888 and 1894 may be mentioned. Amongst the reasons for assigning part of the public functions to local bodies, the primary one is the desire to entrust special interests to the persons chiefly concerned. It is on this ground that most of the work of municipal corporations and the similar rural councils has been regulated. The care of roads, the disposal of sewage, lighting and water supply, are obviously matters of greater interest to the inhabitants of each town or district than to the nation at large. It is but just that the cost of particular services should fall on those who benefit by them, and that they should have the direction and management of such works. Another class of duties that may advantageously be assigned to local governing agencies, is that on which rigid and minute supervision is likely to be beneficial. Thus, the management of the English poor law is probably more effective than it would be if placed directly under a centralised authority. Local administrators, from their acquaintance with the particular circumstances, can form a sounder judgment on matters of detail than the best organised central department.

Again, it is often desirable to secure diversity rather than uniformity : the same general function has to be discharged in different ways according to the varying needs of different communities. Special conditions and habits have to be taken into account, and met by suitable arrangements. The concession of liberty to the several localities is the natural and most effective way for attaining this object. Legislation and administrative action proceeding from a local source will not fail to bear the impress of the conditions and special needs of the area for which it was intended. Moreover, room is given for the trial of experiments, and for discovering by the test of experience the merits of several competing methods. The best modes of relieving indigence, or of regulating the drink traffic, are most likely to be discovered by the adoption of different plans by local authorities, leading ultimately to general imitation of the successful ones (cp. Jevons, *Methods of Social Reform*, pp. 266-270).

In constitutional countries a further reason for the diffusion of local government is the promotion of the public education of the citizens, a work in which "local administrative institutions are the chief instrument" (J. S. Mill, *Representative Government*, ch. xv.). Great Britain and the United States afford examples of the high value of the political training obtained by the exercise of "self-government," as opposed to the bureaucratic system resulting from CENTRALISATION (see BUREAUCRACY).

The extent to which this process of devolution can conveniently be carried is limited by the need for attending to the general interests of the nation. All matters of national concern belong *prima facie* to the central power. General legislation, the national defences, and the more important administrative works are of this class. There is, besides, in many cases, an advantage in the existence of a uniform system, constructed on a single pattern, and directed from a common centre. The higher standard of intelligence and better technical skill at the command of the State is an additional reason for entrusting tasks that specially require these qualities to it, rather than to the smaller divisions.

Though profoundly influenced by historical conditions and by the accidents of recent politics, the division of tasks between central and local government very largely conforms to the principles stated above. Between the different sets of local authorities the same guiding rules are also applicable. "As the county is to the nation, so is the parish to the county," seems to be an approximately correct proportion. The areas of local government, and the subdivisions admissible, are to be determined on these grounds. One peculiarity of local government deserves special mention, viz. the predominantly economic character of its work. Indeed, it is possible to trace a resemblance between the private company and the MUNICIPALITY or COMMUNE. This feature leads to the belief that in the local governing body it is desirable to represent, not persons merely, but the various economic interests. Equal voting power, without reference to the condition and interests of the voter, is a more than questionable arrangement. This becomes very prominent in LOCAL FINANCE. One class of persons determines expenditure, and therefore necessarily the amount of taxation or local debt. Another class has to bear the burden, perhaps without compensating benefit.

In the execution of its allotted work the local authority may err by excess or defect. It may seek to unduly enlarge its functions, and trench on the field reserved for the State, or infringe the rights of individuals ; so on the other hand it may fail to discharge its duties, and thus injuriously affect the welfare of the community or some section of it. Undue interference with property or excessive taxation may be given as examples of the former, neglect of sanitary precautions, inadequate or inefficient poor - law administration of the latter error. It is obvious that in a limited area special interests can more readily acquire power, and unpopular persons or groups are more open to oppression.· Remedies for such evils are to be found partly in the cultivation of public spirit and the sense of responsibility ; but where this fails it is necessary to protect those aggrieved, either by allowing them to seek redress from a court, or by application to a department of the central government, like the Local Government Board in England. The

power of the state has, however, to be exercised in many cases in which no individual appears as complainant. The needs of modern society have led to the establishment of a system of inspection and control, limited, however, in its action, and chiefly dealing with poor - law administration (see LOCAL FINANCE). The advantages of centralised and of local government are to a great extent combined by the method of supervision applied by the central government to local activity.

A grave problem in local government is the assignment of suitable divisions. Poor-relief, education, sanitary administration, the maintenance of roads, etc., would appear to be distinct duties calling for the creation of as many separate agencies. Simplicity and uniformity in plan are, however, very desirable. The principle "that in each local circumscription there should be but one elected body for all local business " (Mill, *Representative Government*) is generally sound. English legislation has gone too far in the multiplication of local authorities with intersecting boundaries. In this respect the French system exhibits a marked contrast. The natural opposition between "town" and "country" makes a special form of local government necessary for the former, assuming, in such cases as London, a great complexity. Finally, separate administration is desirable for certain economic matters, such as a DOCK, and a harbour, and arterial drainage, where the chief interest appertains to the class of traders or landowners rather than the community at large. Deviations from the general plan of subdivision should always be justified by some special necessity.

[In addition to the various works on local government mentioned under LOCAL FINANCE, the following may be referred to : J. S. Mill, *Representative Government*, ch. xv., London, 1861.—S. Amos, *The Science of Politics*, ch. vii., London, 1883.—H. Sidgwick, *The Elements of Politics*, ch. xxv., London, 1891.—*Local Government and Taxation in the United Kingdom*, Cobden Club, 1882.—Jenks, *An Outline of English Local Government*, London, 1894.—Albert Shaw, *Municipal Government on the Continent of Europe*, 1896 ; *Do. in Great Britain.*]   C. F. B.

LOCAL GOVERNMENT IN THE UNITED STATES.

The form of local government in the United States is prescribed by the constitution and laws of each of the several states, each state having thus its own system. However, three general types may be distinguished : the town system, found especially in the New England states ; the county system, found especially in the southern states ; and the mixed township-county system, found in the central and north-western states.

In New England, the early settlers had mostly come from English towns, were members

2 S

of the same religious congregation, and there was among them no sharp line of division into social classes. The necessity of co-operation in much of their work, the danger of attack from hostile Indians, the fact that they had come to America for religious freedom and wished to worship together, kept them grouped into small settlements. It was but natural that their government, partly from tradition, especially from the pressure of local conditions, should be in form a pure democracy, though doubtless men of ability and means had great influence. The form exists to-day.

Regularly, at least once a year, and as much oftener as is needed to carry on well the town business, a town meeting is called by the town officers, the purpose of the meeting being stated in the call. Every grown man who is a voter is entitled to attend, and in the smaller towns the attendance is generally large, though the fine formerly imposed for non-attendance has been abolished.

At this meeting a presiding officer—the moderator—is chosen, and the town clerk acts as secretary. Each voter is entitled to make any motion relating to town business, and to speak. Here all questions relating to town improvements—roads, school-houses, drains, are discussed and acted upon; needed taxes are levied; general regulations regarding town matters, e.g. the running at large of cattle, the muzzling of dogs, are made; the reports, made in detail, of the town officers, and their recommendations and estimates for the ensuing year, are heard and acted upon; new officers are elected.

The officers are "selectmen" from three to nine in number, who have the general oversight and management of affairs not otherwise assigned; the town clerk, who keeps the records and registers; the treasurer; assessors who estimate the value of property for purposes of taxation; a tax collector; constables to keep the peace, serve legal papers for the local courts, etc.; a school committee; overseers of the poor; and various other officers as needed, and as suits the pleasure of the meeting. Usually there is a pound master to impound stray cattle, a path master to care for the local roads, sometimes a measurer of wood, sealers of weights and measures, fence-viewers, and others. These officers carry out the will of the town as expressed at the meeting, or as they have been given discretionary power. Within their province they are supreme, no county or state authority having right of control unless by securing a change in the law.

In New England, the county has almost no governmental functions, serving chiefly as a judicial district for certain courts of record; though in some states county officers, usually a board of commissioners, lay out roads connecting different towns, issue certain county licenses,

see to the maintenance of county buildings, and care for some few other matters that concern several towns in common. It is noticeable that of late years the importance of the county in New England is increasing. In the main, however, the state is a group of towns.

The early settlers in Virginia, a typical southern state, had received their grants of land as individuals, not as congregations. Many of the estates were large; the county was well supplied with streams, so that access to them was easy. The chief crop was tobacco, for the production of which unskilled labourers working under overseers are fitted. In consequence, negro slaves were soon introduced, and the "poor whites" who were compelled to perform manual labour lost social standing. An aristocratic type of society soon developed. Instead of town meetings, for which the settlement in large plantations at a distance from each other, as well as the type of society, were ill-adapted, a representative parish system developed. The twelve vestrymen, in whose hands most of the local governmental functions were placed, were at first elected by the people; but soon they were granted or took the power of filling vacancies in their own number, and thus established their aristocracy. The minister presided at meetings, and had power of appointment of certain officers; the vestrymen appointed the churchwardens, apportioned parish taxes, acted as overseers of the poor.

Many of the functions exercised in New England by the town were here left to the county. The county was smaller generally than in New England. It was also the judicial district; but the court, besides judicial functions, had generally in the south administrative duties as well. It superintended the repair and construction of roads and bridges, dividing the county into highway districts and appointing local road surveyors. It estimated and assessed and collected the county taxes, cared for county buildings, etc. In later years, especially since the war of the rebellion, the courts have been confined more closely to judicial work, though in North Carolina, Tennessee, and elsewhere they still retain much administrative power, the sheriff, for example, collecting taxes, to the levying of which the judges must consent. In most of the southern states the chief administrative duties are given to a board of commissioners elected by the people, together with generally a county treasurer, auditor, superintendent of education, superintendent of the poor, superintendent of roads, etc. In many of the states the county is divided now into school districts which are in good part self-governing; in some, town government has been introduced. The tendency is clearly toward the adoption of some form of town government.

As the central and western states were settled, the forms of local government adopted were naturally modelled after those of the states from which most of the settlers had come ; but as the population was mixed, the advantages of both plans were seen as well as their weaknesses, and the result has been a mixed form, sometimes called the township-county form. Even those of the older states, situate between New England and the south, e.g. New York and Pennsylvania, have a mixed form. In nearly all cases the predominance of the town plan shows that the early settlers were chiefly from New England or from states settled first by New Englanders— for example, Michigan, Wisconsin, Illinois, while the predominance of the county idea is found in those settled chiefly by southerners, e.g. Indiana, or by the middle states having a mixed form of local government. Illinois furnishes an odd example of a state in which a compromise was made leaving to each county a choice between the two systems. At first the southern counties chose the county system, the northern counties the town system ; but of late years the town system has been adopted in about four-fifths of the counties.

In the main we find two types of the mixed system. In one, e.g. in Michigan, the town has a town meeting, as in New England, with similar powers ; but instead of a board of selectmen a set of town officers, each with a special function, is chosen, though the supervisor, clerk; and justice of the peace serve as a town board to audit accounts and perform a few other minor duties. The supervisor of each town, however, represents his town in a county board of supervisors that has wide powers. It provides for erection of county buildings, prescribes the form of county records, procures supplies for county officers, levies taxes, settles claims against the county, equalises taxes among the different towns, sets off and organises towns and gives them their names, alters and lays out main roads, and builds bridges, or grants subsidies to small towns to aid them in similar work, and performs many other duties that relate to territory larger than the town. The chief characteristic is the representation of the towns in the board.

In most of the states with the mixed town-county system there is no town meeting, but the town officers are elected to perform independently, under the statute, their duties. Sometimes there are many officers, sometimes, as in Indiana, the one township trustee has great power and performs many functions. In these states the towns are not represented in the county board ; but the board, usually of three commissioners, is elected directly by the people, sometimes, as in Indiana, each one particularly representing a special district of the county in which he is resident, though chosen on a general ticket. The powers of the board of commissioners are substantially the same as those of the board of supervisors already described.

The counties have also the usual officers needed for so much administrative and judicial work : clerk, treasurer, registrar of deeds, auditor, sometimes assessor, superintendent of schools, surveyor, superintendent of the poor, sheriff, prosecuting attorney, county judge, judge of probate or county administrator, coroners, the names of whose offices explain their duties. One should also mention in connection with local government in rural districts the villages that have an organisation in many ways resembling that of cities (see MUNICIPALITY—UNITED STATES OF AMERICA). In many states, under general statute, a village of some 250 or 300 inhabitants and upwards, by special vote of the residents, may be organised into a corporate body independent in its local affairs of the town in which it is situated. It elects a president and small council with power to pass ordinances, to levy taxes for local improvements, sewerage, lighting, fire protection, etc., appoint officers to keep the peace and perform other needed functions.

As regards the relations of the local governments to the state, they are all under the constitution and statutes, so that by general laws the legislature may often materially modify their forms, and the county and town officers are often made to serve as state officers in duties for which they are suited by their position, e.g. collection of taxes, serving process for state courts, etc. Thus the government is a well-co-ordinated system throughout, with, generally speaking, no conflicting authorities.

[Howard, *Local Constitutional History of the United States.—Johns Hopkins University Studies in History and Political Science.—*Bryce, *American Commonwealth.—*Fiske, *Civil Government in the United States.—*The statutes of the several states.]

J. W. J.

LOCAL OPTION is a phrase recently brought into general use, which, perhaps, had its origin in a letter written by Mr. Gladstone in 1868, in which, dealing with the question of the Permissive Bill, he said that he was disposed to "let in the principle of local option wherever it is found satisfactory." This principle is wider in its scope than that of the old permissive measure, which, if carried, would have permitted the ratepayers from time to time to decide either entirely to prohibit or to leave alone the liquor traffic within their district, whether parish, burgh, or other local area. Local option is applied to such legislation as would enable a majority of the ratepayers of any district either to maintain unchanged, to increase, diminish, or wholly suppress, the houses for the sale of intoxicating liquors. As to the method of exercising these powers, it might be periodically, either by a plebiscite or through a board of representatives elected for the purpose by the ratepayers. The difficulty as regards legislation lies in the great number of vested interests, as well as in the limitless variety of opinion as to the precise amount of restriction to be employed. Thorough defenders of the existing liquor traffic system in its entirety, however, are few in number. On the other hand, the GOTHENBURG SYSTEM (*q.v.*)—by which municipalities would take over liquor shops and manage them in the interests of the community—has not met with much support in Great Britain ; nor has the American high-licence system any considerable body of supporters. At the same time, efforts have been made to restrict the publican's trade. The provisions in Bruce's act of 1872 led the way in this direction.

Local option was first brought formally before parliament in March 1879 by Sir Wilfrid Lawson, but his motion was rejected by a majority of 88. In March 1880 the proposal was defeated by a majority of 114, but three months later, in the new parliament, it was carried by 29. Nothing, however, of a practical nature came of the vote. Another motion was carried in 1881 by a majority of 42, and yet a third one in 1883 by 87. Other important questions intervened to prevent legislation, but it is almost universally admitted that something must be done to give localities practical control over licences. Among various forms of local option put forward, it may be noted that the United Kingdom Alliance desires a power of direct veto, by which the electors of any place might, if they so pleased, veto the issue of all licences for the sale of liquor, and thus prevent the sale of strong drink. One of the great difficulties in the way of practical action has been that of deciding what should constitute a "locality," who should be the constituents, and what should be the necessary majority for abolition. Compensation to those engaged in the trade is another moot point round which controversy has fiercely raged.

In 1892 the number of licensed victuallers in England and Wales was 73,480 ; beer-house keepers with licences for consumption on the premises, 31,092 ; and for consumption off the premises, 12,580 ; being a total of 117,152 public-houses and beer-shops, or one to every 250 of the population ; an increase over previous figures. This did not include wine-licences for refreshment-houses, or the wine and spirit licences for consumption off the premises. During 1892 the expenditure of the United Kingdom on spirits, wines, and beer amounted to £140,866,262, which gave a yearly average of £3 : 13 : 11 for each man, woman, and child, or £18 : 9 : 7 for each family of five persons. These figures exhibited a slight decrease as compared with 1891, when the total expenditure was £141,220,675 ; the average expenditure per head, £3 : 15s. ; and the expenditure per family of five persons, £18 : 15s. While the total drink bill for 1892, however,

exhibited a reduction of £353,413, as compared with 1891, the total amount for 1891 exhibited the large net increase of £1,725,205 as compared with 1890 (*Parliamentary Returns* and Hoyle's *Statistics*). Convinced of the necessity for coping with this gigantic traffic, the government has on several occasions initiated legislation, but so far its efforts have proved abortive. In 1890 it proposed to arm the county councils with powers which would have enabled them to reduce the number of public-houses ; the compensation scheme put forward, however, was so vigorously attacked that the government was compelled to abandon its proposals. Again, in 1893, Sir William Harcourt introduced into the House of Commons a bill to establish the control of the liquor-traffic by a popular vote operating through the direct veto, called the Direct Veto Bill, or the Liquor Traffic (Local Control) Bill. It was advanced through its first stages, but the exigencies of public business, and the difficulties it encountered, compelled its withdrawal. The bill was again introduced in the session of 1894, but it did not get beyond its first reading. Sir William Harcourt brought it forward for the third time in 1895, but it was dropped on the overthrow of the Government of which he was Chancellor of the Exchequer. Though the question of local option is in legislative abeyance, its propagandists are urgently pressing forward their views by means of the platform and the press (see LIQUOR LAWS).

[*Chambers's Encyclopædia*, new ed. vol. vi.— Reid's *Temperance Cyclopædia*.—*Hazell's Annual*, 1894.—Rae's *Handbook of Temperance History*.— *The Alliance News* ; and *Local Option*, by Messrs. Caine, Hoyle, and Dawson Burns.]   G. B. S.

LOCAL TAXATION. See LOCAL FINANCE.

LOCALISATION OF INDUSTRY. By localisation of industry is meant the concentration of different industries in different localities, a phenomenon in its international aspect aptly described in TORRENS's phrase, "territorial division of labour" (*The Economists Refuted*, 1808, p. 14, quoted by Bastable, *International Trade*, 1887, p. 20). For the economic principle underlying DIVISION OF LABOUR (*q.v.*) finds its fullest expression in this specialisation of particular localities to particular industries— this arrangement of productional activities with special reference to the diverse aptitudes, capacities, and resources of different peoples and places (cp. Cairnes, *Leading Principles of Pol. Econ.*, 1874, pt. iii. ch. i. § i.).

The influence of the special industrial tendencies of different races is naturally most conspicuous as between widely divergent civilisations. But, generally speaking, in the industrial as in other spheres of human activity "nationalities are not disappearing but increasingly developing and characterising themselves" (Flint, *Philosophy of History*,

1893, pp. 26-27). *National character* is thus a factor of increasing importance in determining the distribution of the world's industry. It is seen in greatest relief when, as in the case of the Dutch, it triumphs over circumstances seemingly the most adverse. Nevertheless, man's LABOUR (*q.v.*) is more productive in proportion, not as he combats, but as he utilises nature's forces—a truth to which the Anglo-Saxon race itself in its colonising character has done ample homage. And Dutch history, closely interrogated, merely shows, not that physical conditions are unimportant, but that many of the obstacles to industrial development thence arising are relative to the intelligence, energy, and enterprise brought to bear on them. At any given stage in the progress of CIVILISATION (*q.v.*), *physical conditions* have thus, independently of their bearing on character (cp. Marshall, *Principles*, bk. i. ch. ii. §§ 1, 3), an important influence on the localisation of industries, both as between different countries and between different localities in the same country. Under a competitive *régime* commodities tend to be produced "not only by the fittest men but in the fittest places" (Bastable, *Commerce of Nations*, 1892, p. 16). 1. Apart from its influence on the energy of man and the durability of his work, the *climate* of a place determines the nature of its vegetable and animal products, and, therefore, to a certain extent, of its industry. Hence the great trades of the world take place naturally between countries differing widely from each other in climatic conditions. "By means of glasses, hot-beds, and hot-walls," says Adam Smith, "very good grapes can be raised in Scotland, and very good wine, too, can be made of them, at about thirty times the expense for which at least equally good can be brought from foreign countries" (*Wealth of Nations*, M'Culloch's ed. p. 200). 2. *The geographical position* and *water communications* of a country are also important factors in determining its industrial *rôle*. The situation of Britain as regards the great COMMERCIAL ROUTES (*q.v.*), her abounding natural harbours and navigable rivers, have immensely aided in establishing her commercial supremacy. Such advantages, however, are in some degree relative to the economic environment of a particular epoch. "Britain has been in turn a great corn-growing, wool-growing, and coal-producing island; and the changes from one employment to another have been due, not so much to climatic or physical changes, as to the relations of trade in which its inhabitants have stood to other peoples" (Cunningham, *Growth of English Industry*, vol. i. pp. 12-13). 3. *The geological formation* of a country not only affects its superficial features and water supply, but determines the character of the soil and, thus, the nature and quality of the vegetation it supports, as well as the abundance or scarcity of its mineral wealth. These, however, are conditions which do not remain constant under the hand of man (*v.* Sidgwick, *Principles*, 2nd ed. pp. 94-95).

Within the same country, those elements of economic friction which impede COMMERCE (*q.v.*) and specialisation as between different countries—*e.g.* national prejudice, legislative restraints, differences in language or currency, in custom or law, risk in transport, etc.—are, in modern times, either altogether absent or present only in a modified degree. Here, therefore, the influence of physical causes is naturally more conspicuous. The commercial prosperity of cities like Liverpool and Glasgow, Clyde shipbuilding, Sheffield cutlery, the "lead pencils" of Keswick, even the pottery of Staffordshire, are typical of the influence of natural environment (cp. Marshall, *Principles*, pp. 327-328). But there are many examples of localised industries which cannot be thus accounted for, having had their origin in the now oft-forgotten social, political, and other conditions of a bygone age. Such is the order of things in countries where custom and tradition are still dominant. In England itself, up to the time of the INDUSTRIAL REVOLUTION (*q.v.*) the settlements of foreign artisans, made under Plantagenet and Tudor direction, supplied in the main the key to the localisation of English manufactures (cp. Marshall, *Principles*, p. 328 ; Nicholson, *Principles*, vol. i. pp. 114-115). Even now, when each locality has to justify its claim at the bar of the keenest competition, cases of this sort are numerous. Some, like the silk weaving of Spitalfields in London, are slowly dying, but others continue to thrive. Indeed, an industry, once firmly established in any place, is often more than compensated for any chance inferiority in respect of physical endowment by the cumulative effect of its *acquired* advantages over would-be rivals, in the matter of (1) business connection based on its established reputation ; the commodities of a town or district may win a name for themselves just like those of a single firm, and this is as much a source of income, and of industrial strength, to the inhabitants, as his professional reputation to the lawyer or physician (cp. Sidgwick, *Principles*, p. 84) ; (2) perfected organisation, with facilities for drawing on abundant supplies of the different varieties of skilled labour (*v.* LABOUR, SKILLED) and of specialised machinery ; which, in turn, is closely connected with (3) adequate support from the neighbourhood of (*a*) supplementary industries, which permit of economy of skill, and, by affording scope for the labour of some members of a family, tend to cheapen the labour of the others without lowering their standard of living (*v.* COMFORT, STANDARD OF), (*b*) subsidiary industries supplying the requisite tools and machinery, and furnishing the means of conveyance and communication (cp. Marshall, *Principles*, p. 330 *seq.* ; Sidgwick, *Principles*, p. 372). The locality, however, if it is to retain possession, "must be the first to adapt itself to any new conditions" (Nicholson, *Principles*, vol. i. pp. 116-117). The increasing super-session of hand-made by machine-made lace is steadily concentrating this industry in Nottinghamshire and Derbyshire, at the expense of other English counties, notably Northampton-shire (*Census 1891, General Report*, p. 50). Possibly the most magnificent example at once of cumulative strength and of delicacy of opera-tion is found in the history of the varied influ-ences which have made, and maintain, London the world's "clearing house" (see CLEARING SYSTEM) (cp. Bagehot, *Lombard Street*, pp. 32-35 and ch. iii. ; Goschen, *For. Exch.*, 5th ed. pp. 32-37). A powerful localised industry, moreover, while attracting supplementary and auxiliary industries, tends to outbid, and thus repel, industries competing with it for labour or elbow-room (cp. Sidgwick, *Principles*, p. 377). Glasgow, Liverpool, Hull, even Leeds and Manchester are becoming specialised for purely commercial purposes, while the pressure of ground-rent drives the manufactures into the surrounding districts. Owing to this "sub-stitution of business premises for houses" the population of Central London has declined nearly 14 per cent in thirty years (*Census, 1891, General Report*, pp. 14-15). But, to resume, even within the same country the physical conditions of a particular time are clearly not all-powerful in determining the localisation of industries. The face of every old-inhabited country is dotted over with the evidences of a time when not only were the physical conditions, as already noted, other than they now are, but man's power of dealing with them was less than it now is, and, in the eco-nomic sense of the term at least (*v.* Bastable, *Theory of International Trade*, ch. i.), the present "nation" was not—"the Norwich merchant who visited London" being "as much of a foreigner there as the man from Bruges or Rouen" (Cunningham, *Growth of English Industry*, vol. i. p. 175).

It is worthy of note, as affecting localisation, that the progress of the industrial arts is per-petually changing the economic import of physical conditions. While charcoal was used in Britain for smelting—as even now in Sweden —and the blast furnaces were worked by water, the iron works were located where timber and water-power were most readily available. But, since coal came into use as fuel, and steam-power was introduced, this industry has become definitely localised in the districts of the north and west, where coal and iron are found together (*v.* Cunningham, *Growth of English Industry*, vol. ii. p. 461, 462). Similarly, the woollen manufacture, which early in the 18th cen-

tury was widely distributed over England —flourishing chiefly where the raw material was plentiful—has, since the introduction of machinery, become concentrated in the north where power and mechanism are at hand (cp. Hobson, *Evolution of Capitalism*, pp. 26-28). Specialisation, too, implies organisation for EXCHANGE (*q.v.*) and it is in the removal of the barriers—physical, political, and social— which obstruct commercial intercourse that the progress of civilisation has, perhaps, most con-spicuously affected the localisation of industries. If we take the history of England as typical, then the contrast is sufficiently striking between the 9th century, with its simple, all but self-sufficing, groups existing in mutually mistrust-ful isolation, and the complex, highly special-ised, industrial organism of the 19th, with its security-based credit organisation, its world-wide connections and sympathies. Naturally, the advance has sometimes been more marked in one of its aspects, sometimes in another. From the 13th century onwards the influ-ence of political and social consolidation is especially notable. As the authority of the central government grew, national life and organisation more and more superseded local or municipal feeling and regulations. "That there should be similar laws, similar customs, similar taxes, similar conditions of business throughout the length and breadth of the land was," says Professor Cunningham, "a very great gain for purposes of internal trade" (*Growth of English Industry*, vol. i. p. 244). But to trace the various steps of the advance is the province of industrial history. Produc-tion is no longer carried on with a view to local or even national requirements in the first place, with the merely incidental exchange of a surplus. This extension of the MARKET (*q.v.*) permits of greater specialisation, and, as a consequence, many of the industries which flourished in England when the area of COMPETITION (*q.v.*) was more restricted are now leaving her. Such *e.g.* is the case with certain branches of agri-culture and of mining, glove-making, and the manufacture of straw-plait, of linen, and of silk (see *Census 1891, General Report*, pp. 43-57). Thus, evolution of the social as of the physical organism shows us alike "differentiation" and "integration," a greater subdivision of functions between its separate parts—a greater specialisa-tion—on the one hand, and, on the other, a more intimate connection—a greater interde-pendence (cp. H. Spencer, *Principles of Sociology*, vol. i. 2nd ed. pt. ii.—Marshall, *Principles*, bk. iv. ch. viii. § 1).

[The increasing prominence of localisation in the industrial world is reflected in works on the general theory of *Economics*. The subject is admirably treated, from slightly different standpoints, by Prof. A. Marshall, *Principles of Economics*, vol. i. 2nd ed. 1891, bk. iv. ch. x.—Prof. J. S. Nicholson,

Principles of Political Economy, vol. i. 1893, pp. 114-117, 129, 130.—Prof. H. Sidgwick, *Principles of Political Economy*, 2nd ed., 1887, pp. 371-373, 376, 377.—See also G. Schulze-Gävernitz, *Der Grossbetrieb*, Leipzig, 1892.—R. W. Cooke Taylor, *The Modern Factory System*, 1891.—J. A. Hobson, *Evolution of Modern Capitalism*, 1894, ch. ii., ch. iii. § 10, ch. iv.—Leonard H. Courtney, "The Migration of Centres of Industrial Energy" in *Fortnightly Review*, Dec. 1878, vol. xxiv. N.S.—Duke of Argyll, *Unseen Foundations of Society*, 1893, ch. xvi.—J. E. Thorold Rogers, *Six Centuries of Work and Wages*, 1886, pp. 46-47, also chs. iv. v.—Adam Smith, *Wealth of Nations*, bk. iii. ch. iii.—*Harvard Quart. Journ. Econ.*, Ap. 1896.—L. A. Ross, *The Location of Industries.*—W. Cunningham, *Growth of English Industry and Commerce*, vol. i. 1890, vol. ii. 1892, *passim.*—The sections on "Trade and Industry" in *Social England*, ed. H. D. Traill, in course of publication, vols. i. ii., 1893-94.—G. G. Chisholm, *Handbook of Commercial Geography*, 1889.]   A. B. C.

LOCK-OUT. This term is contrasted with the term Strike in cases of industrial dispute. A strike is the weapon of the employed, while a lock-out is that of the employers. The masters close their works after a certain day if the men will not accede to their terms, whereas in the case of a strike the men cease from work after a certain day if the masters will not grant their demands. In strictness the term *lock-out* should, no doubt, be employed when the act leading to the dispute originates with the masters, and the term *strike* when the men are the aggressive party; but in practice it is difficult in many instances to determine which party really provoked the quarrel, and either may seek to fasten the responsibility on the other. In this case the term lock-out may be applied by the men to the dispute, while the masters may employ the term strike. Supposing, for example, that the masters give notice of a reduction of wages and the men decline to accede to it, they would still often be described as "striking," whereas the original motion would have come from the masters. Or, again, supposing that the men give notice of an appeal for an advance, and the masters say that rather than accede to the request they will close their works, it is very probable that the newspapers would report that the masters had locked the men out. In conclusion, therefore, it may be said that the use of the terms is not in practice strictly defined, but that the term *strike* is probably more common than that of *lock-out*.

[For books to be consulted see article on STRIKES.]   L. L. P.

LOCKE, JOHN (1632-1704), the philosopher, was born at Wrington in Somerset. His father was a country attorney and small landed proprietor, who served on the Parliamentarian side in the civil war, which lasted through Locke's boyhood. Locke was educated at Westminster school, 1646-1652, and at Christ Church, Oxford, where he matriculated as a "Student" in 1652, took his B.A. in 1656 *N.S.*, and his M.A. in 1658. He held various college offices between 1660 and 1665. In 1665 he went as secretary to Sir Walter Vane on an embassy to the elector of Brandenburg at Cleve. In 1666 he received a royal dispensation, allowing him to retain his studentship at Christ Church without taking holy orders, and studied medicine, but did not take his M.B. till 1675 *N.S.*, and never took his M.D. In 1666 he made the acquaintance of Lord Ashley, afterwards first Earl of Shaftesbury, at Oxford, and in the following year took up his residence with the Ashley family in London as physician and confidential adviser,—though he continued to reside at Oxford from time to time. He acted as tutor to Anthony Ashley, second Earl, negotiated his marriage with Lady Dorothy Manners, and assisted as accoucheur at the birth of the third Lord Shaftesbury (the philosopher), whose education he afterwards superintended. His connection with Lord Ashley brought him into active connection with public affairs. It was probably for Lord Ashley that he wrote an *Essay concerning Toleration*, first published in Mr. Fox Bourne's *Life*, which contains the ideas afterwards developed in his famous *Letters on Toleration* published 1689-1706. Ashley was one of the "lords proprietors" of the colony of Carolina, and *The Fundamental Constitutions of Carolina*, published among Locke's *Works* in 1720, were probably drafted by Locke, though it is only the articles on religion that reflect his own views to any extent. In 1668 Locke was elected a Fellow of the Royal Society, but seems to have preferred the less formal discussions of a small circle of friends. Through one of these discussions, probably about 1670-1671, he first came upon the project afterwards elaborated in his *Essay concerning the Human Understanding*. In his medical pursuits Locke enjoyed the friendship and shared the ideas of Sydenham. In 1672 he made a short tour in France, in the suite of the Countess of Northumberland. When Ashley was made Earl of Shaftesbury and Lord High Chancellor in 1672, Locke became his "secretary of presentations." In October 1673 he became secretary to the council of trade and foreign plantations, which office he retained till 12th March 167⅘, but he never apparently received his salary of £500. From November 1675 to April 1679 Locke was abroad in France, chiefly at Montpellier, mainly for the sake of his health. During part of the time he had charge of a pupil. When he returned to London, Shaftesbury was again in power and office, as President of the Council, and Locke seems to have been occupied in political service for him. During the brief Oxford parliament of March 1681, Locke again occupied his rooms at Christ Church. After

Shaftesbury's arrest in July 1681, Locke's movements and frequent absences from Oxford were clearly regarded with suspicion by political opponents, though there is no evidence that he was directly engaged in the plots for making the Duke of Monmouth king. He left Oxford in the summer of 1683, and after a short visit to Somerset went to Holland where Shaftesbury had died in January 168¾. On 16th November 1684 the dean and chapter of Christ Church, in obedience to peremptory orders from the king —in which Locke was accused of "factious and disloyal behaviour"—deprived Locke of his studentship. Locke's residence in Holland gave him opportunity for literary work. His *Essay concerning the Human Understanding* was written there, and probably the greater part of his *Treatise of Civil Government.* Locke enjoyed the friendship of Limborch, professor of theology among the "Remonstrants" (Arminians), and of Le Clerc. To the former was addressed his *Epistola de Tolerantia*, not published till 1689, when it was almost at once translated into English by William Popple. In Le Clerc's *Bibliothèque Universelle*, one of the earliest literary and scientific periodicals, Locke published his plan for keeping a common-place book (*Methode Nouvelle de dresser des Recueils*) — his first publication, 1686, and an abstract of his *Essay*, January 168¾. In February 168⅚, Locke returned to England with the Princess Mary and Lady Mordaunt. Through Lord Mordaunt, afterwards Earl of Peterborough, he was offered the post of ambassador to the Elector of Brandenburg and afterwards that of ambassador to Vienna, but declined both on the ground of bad health. He was made commissioner of appeals, and seems to have retained this small office till his death. There is a tradition that Locke himself negotiated the Toleration Act (1689), which, however, fell far short of his views. Unable to endure the smoke and fogs of London, Locke made an arrangement to live at Oates in the parish of High Laver, in Essex —the manor-house of Sir Francis Masham, whose wife was a daughter of Dr. Ralph Cudworth, the Cambridge "Platonist": and, except for occasional residence in London, Oates was Locke's home till his death in 1704.

The *Essay concerning the Human Understanding* and the *Two Treatises of Civil Government* and a *Second Letter on Toleration* were all published in London in 1690. In 1692 he published, anonymously, a tract entitled *Some Considerations on the Lowering of Interest and Raising the Value of Money in a Letter sent to a Member of Parliament:* the date of the dedication is 7th November 1691. The "Member of Parliament" was Sir John Somers, who Locke says had put him "upon looking out his old papers concerning the reducing of interest to 4 per cent, which had so long lain by forgotten." The date of these "old papers" must be 1672,

when the exchequer was closed. In this tract of 1692 Locke controverts the view of Sir Josiah Child, that the rate of interest could be fixed at a low rate, say 4 per cent, by law. Locke, though ready to approve of a legal rate of 6 per cent, argues that "generally speaking" the price of the hire of money cannot be fixed by law; and that any attempt to fix the rate of interest below "the true and natural value" can only harass trade and is sure to be defeated by the devices of expert traders. Locke argued against Sir Josiah Child, *Observations concerning Trade* (1668 reprinted 1690) that the example of Holland did not prove that a low rate of interest fixed by law was the cause of national wealth ; for in Holland there was no law limiting the rate of interest at all, and the low rate of interest was owing to the abundance of ready money. In the second portion of the treatise, Locke exposes the fallacy in the notion of "raising our coin," *i.e.* depreciating the currency. In 1692 Locke published a *Third Letter for Toleration :* and in 1693 *Some Thoughts concerning Education*, dedicated to his Somersetshire friend Edward Clarke, with whom he had corresponded when in Holland about the education of his children. A second edition of the *Essay*, with alterations and additions, appeared in 1694 ; and a third edition, which is only a reprint of the second, in 1695. A fourth, with alterations and additions, was published in 1699—dated 1700.

In 1694 Locke became one of the original proprietors of the Bank of England. In the spring of 1695 Locke took a leading part in bringing about the repeal of the Licensing Act, thus securing the principle under which what is called the liberty of the press exists in this country, viz. that every one may publish what he chooses in writing as in speech, without previous licence, but that he must be answerable for it afterwards. Locke is said to have drawn up the paper of reasons expressing the dissent of the Commons from the Lords' amendment, which reintroduced the statute ; and, as Locke's friend Edward Clarke was the leading manager on the part of the Commons in the conference with the Lords, the statement is extremely probable. In the same year Locke was able to render another great service to his country. He drew up for the use of the lords justices, who were governing England during the absence of King William on the continent, and who included among them Locke's friends Lord Somers and the Earl of Pembroke, two pamphlets on the currency question : (1) *Some Observations on a Printed Paper entitled, For Encouraging the Coining Silver Money in England, and after for keeping it here* (this pamphlet, now lost, was an answer to Locke's treatise of 1692) ; and (2) *Further Considerations concerning Raising the Value of Money.* In these, resuming and enforcing the arguments of his tract of 1692, he combats the proposal of William LOWNDES (*q.v.*), secretary to the treasury, who wished to raise the nominal value of the coins, making the crown-piece 6s. 3d., and so on in proportion, depreciating the whole currency to the extent of one-fifth. "An ounce of standard silver can never be worth an ounce and a quarter of standard silver. Nor can it ever rise or fall in respect of itself." The resolutions which were introduced into the House of Commons by Charles Montague—afterwards Lord HALIFAX,—and carried there, embodied Locke's opinions. The old standard value of silver coins was to be retained *both* as to weight and fineness. In this year (1695) also Locke published his *Essay on the Reasonableness of Christianity as delivered in the Scriptures*, which was followed by *A Vindication of the Reasonableness*, etc., and *A second Vindication* in 1697, in answer to the attacks of John Edwards, who accused him of heresy. The years from 1697 to 1699 were to some extent occupied by Locke's controversy with Stillingfleet, bishop of Worcester, on questions arising out of the *Essay concerning the Human Understanding*. But during these years Locke was also performing, so far as his health would permit, important public functions. From May 1696 to June 1700 he was one of the salaried commissioners in the council of trade and plantations, a revival of the body of which he had been secretary in 1673, and which was the predecessor of both the colonial office and the board of trade of the present day. The commissioners had also to consider questions affecting the condition of the poor. Locke, though in bad health and unable to stay in London, except in summer and autumn, was the most diligent member of the board, and had the most influence in it. His resignation in 1700, owing to increasing infirmity, was reluctantly accepted by the king. Among other duties we find that Locke was specially commissioned "to draw up a scheme of some method of determining differences between merchants by referees that might be decisive without appeal." In 1697 Locke's report on the means of discouraging the Irish woollen industry, and, by way of compensation, encouraging the Irish linen industry, was the report selected from among others and approved by the other commissioners. It is dominated by protectionist principles. In the same year another report of Locke's was adopted—on the employment of the idle or necessitous poor. Special features of Locke's proposals are industrial schools for children, with free meals as a substitute for a money allowance to parents with many children ; and equalisation of poor-rates in each city or town, instead of separate rates for each parish.

During the last four years of his life, in his retirement at Oates, Locke was chiefly occupied with a commentary, published 1705-1707 (after his death), on some of the Epistles of St. Paul. A little treatise *Of the Conduct of the Understanding*, intended for an additional chapter in his *Essay*, never received his final revision, and was published among his posthumous works. His last literary effort was a *Fourth Letter for Toleration*, unfinished. He died 28th October 1704.

This sketch of Locke's life, and enumeration of his writings, will have sufficiently illustrated his extraordinary versatility. His *Essay concerning the Human Understanding* makes an epoch in the history of philosophy. He introduced the method, which became prevalent in England and France during the following century, of treating philosophical questions from the standpoint of psychology. Locke's cautious but unsystematic account of the origin and nature of knowledge was developed by Condillac and others into a thoroughgoing materialistic sensationalism, and by Hume into complete philosophical scepticism. By Voltaire and others Locke was regarded as the initiator of common-sense rationalism in opposition to the authority of both ecclesiastical and philosophical dogmatism. Similarly, by his plea for the simplification and diminution of doctrines in religion, Locke became the forerunner of the "Deism" of the 18th century. His writings on toleration did much to advance the cause of liberty of thought on the continent as well as in England. Locke indeed exempts Roman Catholics and Atheists from his tolerance, but on political, not religious, grounds. The Roman Catholic is to be excluded, not because of his belief, or the forms of his worship, but because he is the subject of a foreign potentate ; the atheist, because he cannot be a good citizen. But Locke's principle of regarding religious belief as a matter with which the civil magistrate should not interfere became one of the watchwords of "liberalism." His *Treatise of Civil Government* was a philosophical defence of the principles of the revolution of 1688, and its contents came to be accepted as the true exposition of the Whig creed. Its leading ideas, that civil society is based upon a compact for the defence of the rights of liberty and property, and that a people may rebel against rulers who are no longer true to the trust reposed in them, and may change the form of their government—are the same as those formulated by ROUSSEAU in his *Contrat Social*, though Rousseau's logic is more relentless and his language less cautious. The very phrases of Locke's *Treatise*, as well as its ideas, are echoed in the American Declaration of Independence. In practical politics, Locke was the confidant of Shaftesbury in his anti-absolutist policy ; he was, it would seem, directly concerned in the negotiations which led to William of Orange coming over to England ; he helped the passing of the Tolera-

tion Act—an instalment at least of liberty ; he
succeeded, where Milton had failed, in bringing
about the abolition of a literary censorship ; he
was a main instrument in giving the country a
sound currency. As an educational reformer he
was the advocate of many principles that have
since been accepted. Amid all these claims to
be remembered, it is often forgotten that Locke
was a reformer also in medicine, and apparently a practical physician of no mean skill.

Locke's contributions to economic theory are
to be found in the tracts on money which have
been mentioned above, and in certain passages
of his *Treatises of Civil Government.* The first
treatise is a criticism of Sir Robert Filmer's
Patriarcha, written about 1642, but not
published until 1680, twenty-seven years after
the author's death. Filmer had used the origin
of government in the patriarchal family as an
argument for absolute monarchy. Locke, in
order to refute Filmer's absolutist theories,
denies the historical connection between the
patriarchal family and civil government. Civil
government, Locke argues in the *Second* and
more important *Treatise,* results from a compact by which mankind, originally free, equal,
and independent, pass from the state of nature
into the civil or political state. This original
state of nature is not, however, as on the theory
of HOBBES, a state of war of all against all, but
has a "law of nature" to govern it. By the law
of nature man already possesses rights of person
and property ; and it is for the better securing
of these natural rights that government is instituted, and when a government fails to fulfil
the purposes for which it was instituted, a
change of government, though not to be lightly
undertaken, is justified. Locke probably
derived his conception of the law of nature
largely from GROTIUS and perhaps also from
Grotius's follower PUFENDORF, whose *De Jure
Naturæ et Gentium* was published in 1672. The
only previous writer on political theory on whom
Locke expressly bases any of his opinions is
"the judicious Hooker"—an authority acceptable to the ecclesiastical party, against whose
political theories he had to argue. It is
characteristic of Locke's unsystematic method
of philosophising, that in his political treatise
he makes use of that idea of a law of nature
(see JUS NATURALE), which belongs to the
same type of thinking that he attacked in his
polemic against "innate ideas" in the *Essay.*
Locke's own language about the supposed
"state of nature" is studiously moderate, but
he undoubtedly prepared the way for that
idealisation of the state of nature which we
find in Pope's *Essay on Man* ("The state of
nature was the reign of God," etc.,) and in
Rousseau's *Discourse on Inequality* (1754). The
use of the idea of "nature" by the PHYSIO-
CRATS (*q.v.*) and by Adam Smith may also be
traced to Locke's influence.

In treating of the subject of property, Locke,
it should be observed, is primarily concerned
to refute the idea of Filmer that kings have by
descent from Adam (presumably according to
the English custom of primogeniture !) dominion
over all the creatures (see i. ch. 4). "God
hath given the world to men in common. . . .
Yet every man has a property in his own person.
. . . The labour of his body and the work of
his hands we may say are properly his. Whatsoever, then, he removes out of the state that
nature hath provided and left it in, he hath
mixed his labour with, and joined to it something that is his own, and thereby makes it
his property" (ii. ch. 5, §§ 26, 27). This
theory, which bases property on labour, and
which may have influenced but must not be
confused with Adam Smith's basing of *Wealth*
on labour (*Wealth of Nations,* Introduction), is
applied by Locke only to the state of nature.
In any given country, the property rights of
individuals depend upon the law of the land,
i.e. on compact (*ibid.* § 35. Cp. Grotius's
theory) : and thus, though the individual is by
nature free to choose what society he will join
himself to, he has to submit to the laws about
property in any commonwealth of which he
becomes or remains a member (ii. ch. 6, § 73).
There seems some inconsistency between this
acceptance of "consent" as the basis of actual
property rights and the theory that government
exists for the purpose of defending the natural
right of property. Locke would doubtless have
solved the contradiction by passing, as he constantly does, from the phraseology of the "law
of nature" to utilitarian considerations. Locke
is only concerned to prove the advantage of
fixed and determinate laws, which may be
changed for the "common good," against
arbitrary government. His theory of property
might be made a premiss for anarchical conclusions : he himself does not apply it in any such
way. He fully recognises that "where there
is no law, there is no freedom" (ii. ch. 6, § 57).
The economic doctrines of Locke's three tracts
on money have already been referred to. In
his views about interest and about the currency
Locke is in harmony with subsequent economic
theory. On the other hand he was still completely under the influence of the MERCANTILE
SYSTEM, maintaining incidentally, while discussing the other two questions, that the commercial prosperity of a country is to be measured
by the excess of its exports over its imports.

                                                    D. G. R.

LOCKE ON CURRENCY.—Locke had always a
good eye for economical facts ; we read in his
Journal, for example, how the expenses of the
Languedoc canal were met (*Life of Locke* (1829),
pp. 53, 55, cp. 272), and how salt was prepared
and taxed at Picais (*ib.* p. 61), how the peasants
in the Bordeaux country lived, and what wages
they got (*ib.* p. 76), what was the mortality of

Paris as compared with that of London (*ib.* 80). His remarks on the comforts of the poorest civilised man as compared with the savage (*ib.* 84-86), are probably the original source of a well-known passage in Adam Smith (*Wealth of Nations*, i. end of ch. i.). His derivation of property from labour was, as he stated it, an original and suggestive idea, even if open to many criticisms; and his political philosophy has had its influence on political economy.

But his best-known economical writings are on currency. His biographer, Lord King, was himself an economist with decided views on the currency (see KING), and he describes Locke's proceedings in this regard with much feeling (*Life of Locke* (1829), p. 240 *seq.*). Before Montague and Somers carried out in 1695 their great reform of the English currency, they had taken Newton and Locke into their counsels. Locke had thought deeply on these matters for twenty years, he tells us, before his pamphlet *Some Considerations of the consequences of the lowering of Interest, and raising the value of Money* (written 1690, published 1691), and that pamphlet was but a new expression of long-formed views. The "Considerations" were drawn out against those who desired to reduce interest to 4 per cent by act of parliament; Locke says that interest will be high when "money"—and he is not always careful to distinguish metal money from loans—is scarce, and parliament cannot make it plentiful, though it can multiply perjury amongst borrowers and lenders, and obstruct trade by bad laws. As for the attempt to keep gold and silver within the country, he says it is an attempt "to hedge-in the cuckoo." He recognises the need of an adequate amount of metal currency in nations having any trade at all; it will be in proportion not simply to the trade but to the "quickness of circulation." "The very same shilling may pay twenty men in twenty days." The nature of the transactions must be considered, and also the habits and necessities of the parties concerned. Money will go further if there are many small payments at short intervals, rather than a few large payments at long intervals. He calculates that "it cannot be imagined that less than a hundredth part of the labourer's yearly wages, one eighth part of the landlord's yearly revenue, and one fortieth part of the broker's yearly returns in ready money, can be enough to move the several wheels of trade, and, how much the ready cash of any country is short of this proportion, so much must the trade be impaired and hindered for want of money" (*Considerations*, Works, vol. ii. p. 15, ed. 1740). The value of money is subject to the same variations as the value of other "consumable commodities." The quantity of ready money compared with the "vent" or the number, of buyers and sellers, determines the value of money

(p. 16); and the vent and value depends on the necessity or usefulness of the articles.

The foregoing will be a sufficient sample of Locke's manner. The treatise, though nominally on the currency, is to a large extent a general discourse on the general principles of economics. There is even a hint of the doctrine of rent. "Were all the land in Romney marsh, acre for acre, equally good, that it did constantly produce the same quantity of equally good hay or grass, one as another, the vent of it, under that consideration, being of an equal worth, would be capable of being regulated by law," etc. (*ib.* p. 18). Locke refuses to consider the consumers as worthy of special account : "There are so few consumers," he says (p. 16), "who are not either labourers, brokers, or landlords." It is the labourers he most favours, tracing as he does all value as well as property to labour. His explanation of interest by the analogy of rent has been well said, by Dr. Böhm Bawerk, rather to discredit rent than to vindicate interest ; "the unequal distribution brings you a tenant for your land, and the same unequal distribution of money brings me a tenant for my money" (p. 19). The one is as lawful as the other ; but there is no more than an analogy ; rent does not cause interest or interest rent, they vary differently (pp. 20, 21). On the other hand Locke is physiocratic ; he thinks that all taxes fall eventually on the landholder (p. 31). In this treatise and in the appended short observations on a printed paper entitled, "For encouraging the coining silver money in England," Locke maintains boldly what is known as the QUANTITY THEORY of the currency, and he makes little or no distinction between demand for the metal money and demand for loans. He also (p. 33), not very logically, defends a legal rate of interest though refusing to fix it below current rates. As to the coinage, he prefers the new milled silver to the old hammered, but thinks that both will leave us speedily if our seignorage remains nominal, and especially if our foreign balance is against us (pp. 46, 47). The raising of the denomination or the increase of alloy he considers as debasement and fraud (pp. 43, 44). In respect of the standard, he is a silver monometallist, but, with his easy-going inconsistency, would have gold still coined, since, as a matter of fact, it is there and used among us.

"The effect indeed and ill consequence of raising either of these two metals in respect of the other is more easily observed and sooner found in raising gold than silver coin, because your accounts being kept and your reckonings all made in pounds, shillings, and pence, which are denominations of silver coins or numbers of them, if gold be made current at a rate above the free and market value of those two metals, every one will easily perceive the inconvenience. But there being a law for it, you cannot refuse the gold in payment for so much. And all the money or bullion people will carry beyond sea from you will be in silver ; and the money or bullion brought in will be in gold. And just the same will happen when your silver is raised and gold debased in respect of one another, beyond their true and natural proportion (natural proportion or value I call that respective rate they find anywhere without the prescription of law). For their silver will be that which is brought in, and gold will be carried out, and that still with loss to the kingdom answerable to the over-value set by the law. Only, as soon as the mischief is felt, people will (do what you can) raise the gold to its natural value " (p. 51).

" Money is the measure of commerce and of the rate of everything, and therefore ' ought to be kept (as all other measures) as steady and invariable as may be.' But this cannot be if your money be made of two metals whose proportion and consequently whose price constantly varies in respect of one another. Silver for many reasons is the fittest of all metals to be this measure, and therefore generally made use of for money. But then it is very unfit and inconvenient that gold or any other metal should be made current legal money at a standing settled rate. This is to set a rate upon the varying value of things by law, which cannot justly be done " (p. 51). " What then (will you be ready to say) would you have gold kept out of England? Or, being here, would you have it useless to trade, and must there be no money made of it? I answer, quite the contrary. 'Tis fit the kingdom should make use of the treasure it has. 'Tis necessary your gold should be coined and have the king's stamp upon it, to secure men in receiving it that there is so much gold in each piece. But 'tis not necessary that it should have a fixed value set on it by public authority ; 'tis not convenient that it should, in its varying proportion, have a settled price. Let gold, as other commodities, find its own rate. And when by the king's image and inscription it carries with it a public assurance of its weight and fineness, the gold money so coined will never fail to pass at the known market rates, as readily as any other species of your money " (p. 52). " There being no two things in nature whose proportion and use does not vary, 'tis impossible to set a standing regular price between them. The growing plenty or scarcity of either in the market (whereby I mean the ordinary places where they are to be had in traffic), or the real use or changing fashion of the place, bringing either of them more into demand than formerly, presently varies the respective value of any two things. You will as fruitlessly endeavour to keep two different things steady at the same price one with another as to keep two things in an equilibrium

where their varying weights depend on different causes. Put a piece of sponge in one scale and an exact counterpoise of silver in the other ; you will be mightily mistaken if you imagine that because they are to-day equal they shall always remain so. The weight of the sponge varying with every change of moisture in the air, the silver in the opposite scale will sometimes rise and sometimes fall. This is just the state of silver and gold in regard of their mutual value " (*ib.*). " It is the interest of every country that all the current money of it should be of one and the same metal, that the several species should be all of the same alloy and none of a baser mixture, and that the standard once thus settled should be inviolably and immutably kept to perpetuity. For, whenever that is altered, upon what pretence soever, the public will lose by it " (52, 53).

When the government were known to be resolved on the reform of the coinage, William LOWNDES, secretary to the treasury, published his *Report concerning an Essay for the amendment of the silver coins* (dated Sept. 1695) and Locke was invited by Lord Somers, and challenged by Lowndes himself, to answer it. This he did in *Further Considerations concerning the raising the value of money, wherein Mr. Lowndes' arguments for it in his late report concerning " An Essay," etc., are particularly examined* (1695). The reasoning of this second pamphlet is substantially that of the first. There is the same faint tinge of mercantilism—" The other case wherein our money comes to be melted down is a losing trade, or, which is the same thing in other words, an over-great consumption of foreign commodities " (p. 82).—But the cogency of the reply is beyond dispute. There is no doubt that the government were wise in getting rid of the clipped money instead of levelling down the rest to the value of the clipped (see MERCANTILE SYSTEM ; RECOINAGES ; also HALIFAX, EARL OF (Chas. Montague); and NEWTON).

In 1696 Locke was made a member of the Council of Trade (*Life*, p. 143). His correspondent Molyneux writes to him from Dublin about the proposed bill for the encouragement of the linen manufacture in Ireland (Oct. 4, 1697, *Works*, vol. iii. 591): " I am apt to think that you will have the consideration and modelling thereof at your committee of trade." Locke is one of the economists who have been able to apply their principles to practical politics during their own lifetime. The influence of his political and educational writings has been considered elsewhere. Their bearing on economics, though indirect, is very important, and the same may be said of his general philosophy.

[Locke finds a place in all the chief histories of political economy. Roscher's account is perhaps the most full (*Zur Geschichte der Englischen*

Volkswirthschaftslehre (1851), pp. 93-106). Dr. Lippert's notice of him, in the *Handwörterbuch der Staatswissenschaften*, contains good references to literature. His theory of interest is criticised in Dr. Böhm Bawerk's *Geschichte und Kritik der Zinstheorieen* (1884), pp. 51, 52. Dr. Zuckerkandl examines his "quantity theory" of the currency in his book *Zur Theorie des Preises* (1889), pp. 137-141. For other remarks on this part of Locke's work, see H. D. M'Leod, *Bimetallism* (1894), pp. 25-34.—Miklashevsky, *Money* (Moscow, 1895), pp. 271-274. When Professor Ingram, *Hist. of Pol. Econ.* (1888), p. 54, finds fault with Locke for in any degree connecting lowered interest with gold discoveries, it is fair to remember the argument urged by Cliffe Leslie in his last published paper (*Fortnightly Review*, 1881), in favour of a connection.]   J. B.

[Locke's *Complete Works* were published 1714, 1722, etc. ; and in nine vols., London, 1853. The *Treatise of Civil Government* has been reprinted in Morley's *Universal Library*, 1884, and bk. ii. also in Cassell's *National Library*, 1889. Many previously unpublished papers of Locke's appeared first in Lord King's *Life of Locke*, 1829), (reprinted in Bohn's Series, 1858) ; Mr. Fox Bourne's *Life of Locke*, 2 vols., 1876, contains the fullest account of the man and his writings, published and unpublished. Shorter accounts are T. Fowler, *Locke*, English Men of Letters Series, 1880, and A. C. Fraser, *Locke*, Philosophical Classics for English Readers, 1890. Locke's economic theories are discussed in Dr. Bonar's *Philosophy and Political Economy* (1893). See BARBON ; ENGLISH SCHOOL ; INTEREST ; LOWNDES.]

LOCOMOTION, TAXES ON. See TAXATION.

LOCRÉ, JEAN GUILLAUME, BARON DE ROISEY (1758-1840), a French jurisconsult, was appointed secretary to Napoleon's council of state in 1800.

His principal works are :

Législation Française, ou recueil des lois, des règlements d'administration, et des arréts généraux basés sur la Constitution, Paris, 1801-4 ; only the first volume was published.—*Procès-verbaux du conseil d'état*, etc., Paris, an 12 de la république, 4to.—*Esprit du Code Napoléon*, etc., Paris, 1807, 8vo, 6 vols. (incomplete), only deals with first book of Code.—*Esprit du code de commerce*, 2nd ed., Paris, 1829, 8vo, 4 vols.—*Esprit du code de procédure civile*, etc., Paris, 1816, 8vo, 5 vols.—*Discussions sur la liberté de la Presse, la Censure*, etc., Paris, 1819, 8vo.—*Législation civile, commerciale et criminelle de la France*, Paris, 1827-1832, 31 vols. 8vo.

[*Nouvelle Biographie Générale*, Paris, 1860, vol. xxxi.]   H. E. E.

LODLAND, a name sometimes given to land whose tenant was bound "to carry loads or possibly to load waggons," this being one of the various forms of compulsory manorial service.

[Vinogradoff, *Villainage in England.—Domesday of St. Paul's*, 1222, p. 49, with Archdeacon Hale's note, p. lxxvii.]   E. G. P.

LOGIC AND POLITICAL ECONOMY. There is a certain alliance between the different

sciences usually classed as "moral." In fact, in the earliest efforts at systematic thinking, the different departments of philosophic speculation were not clearly separated, and the more practical problems of ethical and social science were always treated along with purely theoretical questions. But there is perhaps a special reason for considering the connections between political economy and logic. For, of all the moral sciences, political economy has reached the highest degree of systematisation, and yet there remains considerable controversy as to the true logical method appropriate to the science. Hence it is not surprising that the same men have shown interest in the two subjects. This has been especially the case with English writers, of whom WHATELY, MILL, and JEVONS are the most notable. Though Whately's *Lectures on Political Economy* have not made the impression that their marked ability might seem to have warranted, yet any student of his logic must be struck with the ingenuity and aptness with which he enforces the formal doctrines of logic by illustrations of arguments, definitions, and fallacies taken from economic discussions. But, in England, the two writers who have in modern times exerted the greatest influence on economic studies—J. S. Mill and W. S. Jevons—have also been the two most noted contributors to logical theory. Mill narrates in his autobiography (pp. 157-166) his dissatisfaction with those methods of treating social and political questions that were current in his time, and records his prolonged attempts to discover the true method. This led him to work at the logic of the moral sciences, the results of which form the last book of his logic. One of the causes that induced him to search for the most appropriate logical method for political and social investigations was the controversy between James Mill and Macaulay, arising out of the former's *Essay on Government*. The method advocated by Macaulay was purely empirical, and was named by J. S. Mill the "chemical method," because, in his view, it was specially appropriate to such a science as chemistry, in which scarcely any laws were known connecting the properties of compounds with those of the elements of which they are composed. The method of James Mill's essay was, on the other hand, abstract and deductive, the final conclusions being derived from a small number of definitely-assigned postulates, in the deductions from which no allowance was made for causes mutually counteracting or modifying one another : and this J. S. Mill called the "geometrical method." He urged, on the one hand, that it was futile to apply comparative observation and experiment to the complex facts of social life, and, on the other hand, that a science like geometry, which excludes all time-relations and the interference of causes, was not the type on which sociology should be moulded. He, therefore, looked to mathematical physics as the supreme science that applies a deductive method to phenomena of causation. In his view the principle of the composition of causes underlay the entire procedure of physics. The same principle seemed to him applicable to the various forces at work in shaping the characters of societies and of individuals. But, in his search for distinctions of method, J. S. Mill went farther and, taking a hint from Comte, distinguished the *indirect* from the *direct* application of this form of the deductive method. In the direct method, the investigator, starting from general tendencies expressed in abstract form, proceeds to combine the laws of these tendencies in order to deduce conclusions of successively increasing complexity. In the indirect method, he begins with the data of specific observation, and formulates empirical uniformities which have to be subsequently confirmed or modified by deduction from simple laws acting under known conditions. For political economy J. S. Mill seems to have held that the *direct* deductive method was adequate, but that the indirect method was required for moral and social science in general. In his own economic writings J. S. Mill broke loose still further from the influence of his immediate predecessors —BENTHAM, RICARDO, and James MILL—and reintroduced into political economy a good many of the historical characteristics so prominent in Adam SMITH.

In the case of Jevons we can similarly trace how the course of logical speculation may bear fruit in economic study. Jevons's own account of the general character of scientific method was very closely allied to Mill's special account of the DEDUCTIVE METHOD. He differed, however, from Mill, not only in his conception of the fundamental principles underlying scientific methods, but also in the view that a combination of deduction with induction was required in every science, and not only in the concrete human sciences. Jevons maintained with greater clearness than Mill the thoroughgoing *antithesis* between formal and empirical canons of inference, and at the same time urged the necessity of their *synthesis* in every scientific investigation.

On the formal side Jevons showed a bias towards mathematical modes of thought and expression, and this bias is indicated both in his logical schemes and in his most important contributions to economic theory. On the empirical side, Jevons was strongly impressed with the problematic character of all generalisation from experience ; and his conception of the function of hypothesis is illustrated by the conjectural explanation he suggested of the periodicity of commercial crises as connected with that of the sun-spots. But what specially characterised Jevons's view of logical method was the prominence he attached to the combination of formal and empirical principles through the inverse application of the theory of probability. And this conception no doubt inspired his highly suggestive and valuable statistical researches into variations of prices, periods of commercial crises, etc.

[Apart from the above examples of writers equally devoted to logic and to political economy, the connection between the study of the two subjects is more definitely brought out by reference to works on the method of political economy which well-known economists have published, such as : Malthus, *The Definitions of Political Economy.* —Cairnes, *The Character and Logical Method of Political Economy.* — Neumann, " Grundbegriffe der Volkswirthschaftslehre," in Schönberg's *Handbuch.* — Menger, *Untersuchungen über die Methode der Staats - wissenschaften.* — Keynes, *Scope and Method of Political Economy.*—Sidgwick, *Principles,* and *Scope and Method of Economic Science* (address to Brit. Assoc.).— Marshall, *Present Position of Economics* (inaugural address at Cambridge). From such works as these we can appreciate the importance of combining with technical knowledge of the specialities of economic science, a habit of detached thought on the general forms of reasoning.]   W. E. J.

LOMBARDS. From the time of Henry III. (1216-1272) to that of Edward III. (1327-1377) companies of Lombard merchants were bankers and money-lenders to the kings of England, and also traded largely in the wool of English monasteries, especially from Cistercian houses. Intercourse with Rome, and the collection of the Pope's taxes, brought to England many Italians, who not only acted as agents of the Pope, but often made loans to the people to enable them to meet the papal demands. And Italian merchants at Rome advanced money in the reign of John to agents of religious houses, and to ambassadors with letters of credit from the king. The enormous cost of the crusades (see CRUSADES, ECONOMIC EFFECTS OF), enabled money-lenders to charge a high rate of interest (Close Roll, 32 Henry III., shows that the Jews charged 45 per cent.) ; the censure of the Church and the general opinion respecting usury gave the Jews and Lombards a monopoly. The Jews were protected by the king ; the Lombards, to evade the charge of usury, granted gratuitous loans to which was added a sum, nominally the cost of repeatedly sending for payment if the debt was overdue. In 1235, however, Roger, bishop of London, excommunicated them for practising usury, and ordered them to leave his diocese, but he was summoned to Rome in consequence, and the Lombards continued to trade in London, where they built for themselves "nobilissima palatia." Matthew Paris, who speaks of them as "usuarii Transalpini quos Caursinos appellamus," says that the bishops dared not interfere with them because they called themselves merchants of the Pope, and that the citizens dared not speak ill of them because they were protected by certain great men, "quorum ut dicitur pecuniam ad multiplicandum seminabant Templo Romanæ Curiæ"; but they were so hated as usurers and deceivers of the poor, that, had it not been for their costly mansions in London, hardly one would have stayed in England. Henry III., whose resources were exhausted by the demands of the Pope, pledged his gold and silver plate to Siennese merchants for £550. Lucca merchants sent money from England to Prince Edward in Palestine. The customs, fixed in 1275, were frequently assigned to the company of the Frescobaldi of Florence, who also became keepers of the Exchange and farmers of the New Custom imposed on aliens in 1303. Edward II. paid of his father's debts to the Frescobaldi £56,500, to the Bellardi £1800, to the Bardi £4600, and ordered the barons of the Exchequer to hear suits of the Frescobaldi for debt and to levy their debts as those of the King. In 1309, he granted the citizenship of London, to John Vanne, a merchant of Lucca, with exemption from the duties and taxes which citizenship implied. In 1312, the King writes to the Pope, asking that the Frescobaldi, who have left England for the Roman Court without accounting for the profits of the customs, may be arrested and sent back, but he promises that they shall not forfeit life or limb. The same year the discontent of the people led to the abolition of the New Custom which was resumed in 16 Edward III.; aliens were forbidden to receive customs, and the Frescobaldi were to be arrested until they rendered account. The Lombards, taking advantage of Edward III.'s need of money in the French war, and knowing his resources, charged a high rate of interest and grew very cautious in exacting security. Thus, in 1339, the King writes from Antwerp that he has with great difficulty contracted a loan, falling deeply into usury ("incidentes graviter in usurias"), and that no fees are to be paid to ministers of the Crown until his return, but all money due to the Exchequer is to be sent to him, save only that needed for defence against the Scotch and the sums owing to the Bardi and Peruzzi; four days later he enters into a bond with a merchant of Lucca, by which the Earls of Derby, Nottingham, Salisbury, and Suffolk promise that, if the debt is overdue, they will not cross the sea to England without permission of the great money-lender. But, in January 1345, despite their caution, the Bardi and Peruzzi became bankrupt, Edward III. owing to the former 900,000 gold florins, and to the latter 600,000. The firms had borrowed to lend to him, and when he failed to pay they lost credit, and the failure of other banking-houses followed. Lombards continued to trade in England and to negotiate bills of exchange.

In 1361, Walter de Barde was appointed master of the mint at the Tower, and in 1364 of that at Calais. As the English cloth trade developed and less wool was exported, the Lombards imported made goods into England until this was prohibited in the interests of home manufacture. Some of the Frescobaldi and Anthony Cavallari, a merchant of Lucca, were employed by Henry VIII., and frequently appear as the King's debtors, but not as his creditors. After the fall of the great Lombard houses, Englishmen became the king's bankers in their place; this, with the more favourable conditions of commerce, contributed in the 14th and 15th centuries to the rise of English merchants.

[Bond, E. A. "Loans supplied by Italian Merchants to the Kings of England," Archæologia, xxviii., 234 (1840).—Cunningham, The Growth of English Industry and Commerce (1890).—Stubbs, Constitutional History, ii. (1880).—Hall, History of the Custom Revenue (1885).—Madox, History and Antiquities of the Exchequer (1711).—Ashley, Introduction to English Econ. History and Theory (1892).—Rymer's Fœdera, ii. iii.—State Papers, Henry VIII., Foreign and Domestic, i. ii.]. M. T. M.

LOMBARD LOAN, a name used on the continent for loans on stock-exchange securities.

[See Meier Rothschild, Handbuch der Handels-wissenschaften (1880), vol. i. ch. vii., pp. 527-528, Das Lombardgeschaft.] E. S.

LOMBARD STREET, a synonym for the London money market.

[Cp. Bagehot, Lombard Street.]

LOMÉNIE, LOUIS DE (1815-1878), a French Academician; known by his works on French society in second half of the 18th century, and especially by his book on the Mirabeau family:

Les Mirabeau, vols. i. and ii. 1879; vols. iii. iv. and v. 1889-1891; the three last volumes left unfinished, and continued by the author's son, M. Ch. de Loménie, deal with the great orator of the French Revolution. Having obtained access to a mass of unpublished papers and letters written by the Marquis de MIRABEAU (q.v.), the economist, and his brother—a brave and shrewd naval officer, generally known under the name of the Bailli de Mirabeau, from his rank in the Order of Malta, commemorated by Carlyle, French Revolution as "the worthy uncle,"—M. de Loménie, determined "to attempt, with the necessary documents in hand, the revision of the sentence passed upon the marquis by posterity" (vol. i. p. 349), alluding to the unpopularity which became the latter's lot after his family squabbles and high-handed proceedings against his disgraceful wife and no less disgraceful children. In his impartial, interesting, and pleasantly-written book, M. de Loménie has successfully performed the task he undertook. The marquis certainly entertained and acted on early ideas as to the extent of his patria potestas and conjugal authority, but he was a respectable and high-minded man, a title to which the future member of the Assemblée Constituante had no claim whatever.

Of the abrupt conversion of the marquis to the

doctrines of QUESNAY (*q.v.*), and his life-long rather idolatrous devotion to the doctor's memory, the second volume gives many details, most of which have since been reproduced in the literature on the subject. Economists will regret that the correspondence between the marquis and his brother, the naval officer who sneered at the reformer Quesnay's post of physician to the king's mistress, was too voluminous to be given in full, instead of extracts only being published (vol. ii. pp. 213-217). E. Ca.

LOMÉNIE DE BRIENNE, ETIENNE CHARLES, COMTE DE BRIENNE (1727-1794):

Was brought up as a priest, became archbishop of Toulon, and in that capacity had a seat in the states of Languedoc. He gave his name to the Canal de Brienne, and became a member of the assembly of notables summoned by CALONNE at Versailles, 22nd February 1787. The public finances were in grave disorder. He vehemently opposed the plans proposed by Calonne, became president of the newly-appointed council of finance in April, and prime minister in August, of the same year (1787). "He had been pronounced by Hume to be the only man in France capable of restoring the greatness of the kingdom" (Rae, *Life of A. Smith*) but he "did much to precipitate the Revolution by his incapacity." The measures by which he proposed to rectify the public finances—a rearrangement of the tax of the VINGTIÈME, and a loan—were rejected by the parliament, and in August 1788 he was dismissed from office to make place for NECKER. The times were turbulent. The treasury was empty. The wealth of the country was in the hands of the privileged classes, and they were exempt from taxation. Thus the government was without resources. It would have required a more powerful grasp than that of Loménie de Brienne to restore order. Though subservient to the revolutionary authorities, he could not escape. He was arrested as a " suspect " during the Reign of Terror, and died in prison.

[Droz, *Histoire de Louis XVI.,—Nouveau Dictionnaire d'Économie Politique*, Paris, 1892.]

LONGFIELD, MOUNTIFORT (1802-1884), Irish judge, was the first professor of political economy at Trinity College, Dublin. A very learned real property lawyer, he was appointed one of the three commissioners under the Incumbered Estates Act 1849; and in 1858, when the landed estates court was set on foot, he became a judge of that court.

Longfield's *Lectures on Political Economy*, delivered in 1833, Dublin, 1834, 8vo, deal mainly with the distribution of wealth, and endeavour to show that the only order in which a correct analysis of the sources of revenue can be carried on is—(1) rent, (2) profits, (3) wages. From this analysis Longfield considers that the logical deduction flows that it is "impossible to *regulate wages generally* either by combinations of workmen or by legislative enactments." "The expense of supporting the labourer in that style which he has been accustomed to consider indispensable to his decent subsistence, has no effect in regulating the price of his labour." He criticises Adam Smith's

statement that labour is the measure of VALUE (*q.v.*), and has some acute observations on the probable effects of a low rate of profit. The object of *Four Lectures on the Poor Law*, Dublin, 1834, 8vo, is to bring out the distinction between the two kinds of poor law, the one which aims at improving, by its means, the condition of the labouring classes, and the other, which only concerns itself with bare relief for the destitute. It was just because Longfield realised the evils attached to the former that he was in favour of the enactment of the latter, for fear that at some future time the two should be pressed forward together. The best known of Longfield's writings is the essay he contributed on "Irish Land Tenure" to a volume of *Cobden Club Essays*, London, 1870, 8vo. He also published, 1835, *Three lectures on Commerce, and one on Absenteeism.*

Longfield was second president (succeeding Archbishop Whately) of the Statistical Society of Dublin. He published in its Transactions, besides presidential addresses, papers on the limits of state interference with the distribution of wealth ; on the legal impediments to the transfer of land ; on banking, and a proposal for an act to issue law debentures in connection with sales in the landed estates court.

[*Dictionary of National Biography*, vol. xxxiv.] H. E. E.

LORD, ELEAZAR (1788-1871), wrote:

Extracts from a letter on National Currency addressed to the Secretary of the Treasury, Nov. 1861 (New York, 1864, 8vo) ; also *Six letters on the necessity and practicability of a national Currency* (New York, 1863, 8vo), in which he treated of (1) The necessity and measures requisite to the institution of a uniform national currency ; (2) the resumption of specie payments by the state banks, and a new trial of the old system. In 1834 he published an *Essay on Credit, Currency and Banking*, where in nine chapters he treats of the use of credit, a metallic currency, the principles and regulations of the currency, the present banking system and its proposed modifications, bank capitals, the regulations of banking, and a national bank. A. L.

LOTTERIES, CONTINENT OF EUROPE (francs converted as 25 = £1 ; marks as 20 = £1 ; Austrian florins as 10 = £1). The first lottery with prizes in money is recorded at Florence in 1530. Lotteries with prizes in goods are stated to have taken place earlier. This form of gambling extended itself in a very short time throughout Italy, nearly all the large Italian towns appearing to have established one or other of these descriptions of lottery by the second half of the 16th century. The form in which it became most popular later on, and which is still in use in several countries, took its origin from a political act at Genoa. At the elections to the great council five names out of ninety had to be drawn every year in that city, and betting began to be carried on on these names ; this led to the formal "lotto" or "number" lottery, in which the names were replaced by numbers. The player chooses in this system one or more from all the numbers (ninety), five of which are drawn out as winners ; the prizes he may get are widely different according to his having divined one (simplum), two (ambo), three (terno), four (quaterno), or five (quinterno) of these numbers. It can be played for any sum upwards beyond a certain minimum. The winnings consist in a multiplication of the stake ; they are, however, always more or less smaller than the sum which had to be paid according to the mathematical probability of the especial number combinations. There are

$$e.g. \ \frac{90 \times 89}{1 \times 2} = 4005 \text{ ambos in } 90 \ ; \ \frac{5 \times 4}{1 \times 2} = 10 \text{ of}$$

which being drawn in the five winning numbers the mathematical chance is $= \frac{10}{4005} = \frac{1}{401}$. The prizes, however, paid by the states for the "ambo"-gain are only two hundred and forty times (Austria-Hungary) or two hundred and seventy times (Italy) the stake. The chance for a

"terno" is $\frac{90 \times 89 \times 88}{1 \times 2 \times 3} = 117 \times 780 ; \frac{5 \times 4 \times 3}{1 \times 2 \times 3} =$

$10 ; \frac{10}{117 \times 780} = \frac{1}{117 \times 78}$. Stakes pay only a sum of four thousand eight hundred times (Austria-Hungary) or five thousand four hundred times (Italy) the stakes. At the end of the 17th and in the 18th century the lotto became exceedingly popular. It was introduced in Vienna (1752), in Berlin (1763), and in twenty-nine other German towns, also in France, Spain, and Belgium. The states perceiving the great profit which was to be made by such an undertaking, established a lottery monopoly nearly everywhere, and always either managed the play themselves or had it managed by farmers, who had to pay a large yearly rent. Soon, however, the moral and economic dangers of the play, which were overlooked at the commencement, became obvious, and the "lotto" scheme was vehemently attacked. To quiet their consciences, governments very often combined the play with charitable purposes. In Spain the expenses of the town hospitals and of other useful institutions were borne by the profit of the lottery. From the year 1777 the farmer of the lottery monopoly at Vienna was obliged to provide a dowry for five young girls, whose names were drawn together with the numbers of the lottery.

As, however, the bad influence of the system became more and more perceptible, lotteries being only games of chance, the aggregate number of players in which are sure to lose a part of their venture, the beginning of the 19th century proved very unfavourable for the lotto. It was replaced in 1810 throughout the greater part of Germany, and a few years later in Spain, by other forms of lottery ; and, according to the example of England—where lotteries were not allowed after 1826, one sanctioned by mistake, temp. William IV. (see LOTTERIES, ENGLISH), was cancelled—all state lotteries were abolished in

France (1836), in Belgium (1830), and Sweden (1841). The number lottery exists at the present day in Italy, Austria, and Hungary only.

Another chief form of lotteries, the "Class" or "Dutch" lottery, was originated in Holland at the beginning of the 16th century, nearly at the same time as the first money lotteries were played at Florence and in some other Italian towns. In this system, a certain sum is divided amongst a certain number of lots of various sizes (whole, half, and quarter lots) which are drawn in different "series" or "classes." There were always a few large and a great many smaller prizes, the amount of both augmenting with every "class," and the largest winnings being played at the last class. To induce people to play on all the series, States do not allow playing for a later class, unless lots have been played, or at least paid for, on all the series that had been previously drawn. For every lottery, two of which are instituted every year, 160,000 lots called stammlöse are issued, which are played in seven parts called classes or series. Now the price of the lots is the same, about 40 marks (£2) including the tax for every class, though the amount of the winnings augment with the series, 8000 prizes being played in the first, 10,000 in the second, 12,000 in the third, and 65,000 in the last class. Besides this the value of the prizes also greatly increases with the later classes. The smallest prize is 65 marks (£3 : 5s.) in the first, 105 marks (£5 : 5s.) in the second, 155 marks (£7 : 15s.), and 210 marks (£10 : 10s.) in the 4th ; the largest 30,000 marks (£1500) in the first, 45,000 marks (£2250) in the second, 60,000 marks (£3000) in the third, and 600,000 marks (£30,000) in the fourth. It would therefore not be natural for any one to play on any but the last class had not the following system been put into force. A lot may be purchased for the price of 40 marks for every class, but this is only the case if the lot is bought at the beginning of the lottery for all the classes at the same time. If any one desires to buy a lot for the second class after the first has been played, he must pay the price for both classes (80 marks) ; after the second class is played the price is 120 marks, and after the third 160 marks. It would seem, therefore, as if every one who wants to play on the later classes ought to buy the lot for all the classes as well. This, however, is not quite the case. If a lot is drawn, the winner gets besides his prize a lot without charge, called freilos, for the next class. And as 30,000 lots are drawn in the three first classes, there is a good chance of saving the stake for the following classes and to play on the whole lottery for 40 marks (£2). This possibility is lost, of course, if the lot is bought for all the classes at once. The "class" lottery was introduced with some changes into England

and to the northern part of Germany, but did not attain the popularity of the "lotto" until the first half of the 19th century, when it took the place of the latter in many countries. It was abolished in England in 1816, and soon after in France, Belgium, Sweden, together with the lotto, as mentioned before. There is a "class lottery" at the present day, in the greater number of the German states (Prussia, Saxony, Hamburg, Brunswick, etc.), and in Spain, Denmark, Holland, and Servia.

After these two lottery schemes had been long in use, a third form, the "interest" lottery, was introduced in close connection with the growing want of credit of the states. To be able to get cheap credit the states combined some of their loans with a lottery of this description : the interest paid to the creditors of the state was a much lower one than the market interest of the country, but the bond-holders also shared in a lottery at the same time. The prizes were supplied by the state with one part of the profits, which accrued to it by paying less interest for the loan than it would have paid for the same sum had it not been combined with the lottery.

The great moral and economic mischief caused by lotteries is generally acknowledged. But the influence of the three state lottery systems which we have described is not equally mischievous. There is no doubt that the "number" lottery is the most dangerous. The very small stakes and the enormous winnings that may possibly be obtained, induce the poorest classes (working people, maidservants) to try their fortune, and very often this leads to a "systematical" play, thus absorbing continually a very large part of the income of many poor families. The great variety of the combinations of the numbers excites the imagination, and favours superstition, the interpretation of dreams (dream-books), as well as many swindles. All these evils are very seriously felt both in Italy and Austria-Hungary, where the "lotto" system still exists. The greater cost of the lots of the "class lottery" excludes most people to whom gambling might prove the most dangerous. Besides this the "class lottery" is in some countries, especially in Prussia, regulated in a manner so as to limit the play to the smallest possible circle. The selling of lots is confined to the "Einnehmers" (receivers), appointed by the "state lottery management" from the ranks of comparatively rich merchants, and even so they are very much checked as to the freedom of their transactions by minute restrictions. They have to pay down a deposit of 12,000 m. (£600). Most of the tickets are taken by "well-to-do" people, working people take them comparatively seldom—to an extent, it is estimated, of from 8 to 18 per cent of the whole. The whole class of women servants who play very wildly in Italy, Austria, and Hungary,

hardly play at all in Germany. There is the less to be said against the "interest" lottery, because in the worst case the loss here only extends to one part of the interest, the capital always remaining assured for the bondholder.

The profit made by the states through the lottery is considerable. In the budget-year (1894) the gain of Prussia made through the lottery was 9,753,500 marks (£487,675), being 5 per cent of the public revenue; that of Saxony 5,200,000 marks (£260,000), 3 per cent; of Brunswick 1,240,000 marks (£62,000), 10·25 per cent; of Austria 7,486,720 florins (£748,672), 1·22 per cent; of Hungary 2,739,500 florins (£273,950), 0·6 per cent; of Spain 24,000,000 pesetas (£960,000), 2·5 per cent; of Italy 25,000,000 lire (£1,000,000), 2·8 per cent. In these countries, and especially in the smaller ones, the play is universal, and reaches enormous dimensions; in Brunswick, for instance, lots are reckoned to cost every year 60 marks (£3) per head of the public; in Schwerin 17·28 marks; in Hamburg 31·68 marks. The institution, when carried on by the state, is an attraction to many who would not think of gambling under other circumstances. It is not true that, as defenders of the lottery systems (Marcinowsky) have often said, "the rage for gambling" is sure to seek other opportunities when the opportunity of the lottery is taken away. Many facts prove the contrary. In France there was in 1837, the year after the abolition of lotteries, 525,000 francs (£21,000) more money deposited in the savings banks than the year before. In the same way a great increase of the deposits was stated in Bavaria after the lottery had been brought to an end (1861). At Brussels one year after its abolition there were 7837 fewer objects pawned and 3609 more pawns redeemed. All experience in countries where state lotteries have ceased, pleads for their abolition.

Beside the state lotteries, private lotteries occupy a large field in some countries, principally Germany, Austria - Hungary, Italy, Holland, Belgium, and France. They may be divided into two chief forms. (1) Lottery loans, managed after the example of the state interest lottery, with a long duration (generally seventy to eighty years), with series of drawings, the nominal value of the lots being generally paid back successively. (2) Ordinary lotteries (occasion lotteries) with a single drawing, sometimes with prizes in kind. The most common of the first sort of the private lotteries are the great city lottery loans. There are fifteen of these with a nominal value of 2,405,423,460 francs (£96,216,938) in existence at the present time in France; fifteen in Belgium and Holland, 510,416,820 francs (£20,416,673); 8 in Germany, 155,190,000 marks (£7,759,500); 8 in Austria, 263,266,300 florins (£26,326,630); 7 in Italy, 69,317,500 lire (£2,772,700). Some lotteries for charitable purposes, as, for instance, the well-known "red" and "white cross" lotteries, and the great lottery loans of some large banks, principally mortgage banks, are issued in the same manner.

As to the ordinary or "occasion" lotteries, they are arranged for the most different objects. From 1885 to 1893, for instance, 5771 of these have been permitted in Germany, amounting to a nominal value of 140,880,500 marks (£7,044,025), that is, 15,653,390 marks (£782,669) per year, 3020 of which were for charitable, 1652 for agricultural, 270 for art, 276 for church building, 223 for various other purposes. These lotteries need not be condemned if arranged in a manner that only those people should participate in them who take some interest in the purpose of the play, as for instance, the picture lotteries at the great art exhibitions. But in many hundreds of them it is only the dazzling prizes that attract players from all classes, who are rarely conscious of the very small chance of winning, and do not care the least about the object of the lottery.

In the last few years, new laws (*Loossperrgesetze*) have been enacted in Germany and Austria-Hungary, prohibiting the introduction of foreign lotteries and the arrangement of new lotteries, unless authorised by special act of parliament. Some of the minor occasion lotteries can be allowed by government license. It is therefore very probable that there will be, in a short time, a considerable decrease in these countries in which they were until now the most favoured, when the great lottery loans will be brought to an end and new ones will not be allowed.

[Heckel, "Lotterie und Lotteriebesteuerung," in the *Handwörterbuch der Staatswissenschaften.*— Roscher, *System der Volkswirthschaft*, Stuttgart, 1886, iv. § 30.—L. v. Stein, *Lehrbuch der Finanzwissenschaft*, Leipzig, 1885, ii. p. 345.—Marcinowsky, *Lotteriewesen im Königreich Preussen*, Berlin, 1892.—Block, "Lotterie" in the *Dictionnaire de l'Administration.*—Endemann, *Beiträge zür Geschichte der Lotterie und zum heutigen Lotterierecht*, etc., Bonn, 1882.—Lasson, *Lotterie und Volkswirthschaft*, Berlin, 1894.—Leroy-Beaulieu, *Traité de la science des Finances*, Paris, 1883, p. 341.—Roscher, *Von dem verderblichen Einfluss der Lotterie auf den Staat*, Leipzig. 1795.— Bastable, *Public Finance*, 2nd ed. pp. 221-222.— comp. Adam Smith, *Wealth of Nations*, bk. i. ch. x. "That the chance of gain is naturally overvalued, we may learn from the universal success of lotteries."]

G. B.

LOTTERIES, ENGLISH. The first state lottery in England was announced in 1567 to provide funds for the repair of harbours and fortifications. It was officially described as a very rich lottery-general of money, "plate, and certain sorts of merchandises." The greatest prize consisted of £3000 in cash, and the value of £2000 in plate, tapestry, and other fabrics.

The prizes were displayed at the house of Dericke, the queen's goldsmith, in Cheapside, and a woodcut was appended to the proclamation depicting a large show of plate ; but the 400,000 lots were not quickly sold, as the drawing, according to Stow, did not begin until 11th January 1569. It was carried on day and night, until 6th May, in a building erected at the west door of St. Paul's. The lots cost 10s. each, but could be subdivided. The queen issued a second proclamation, and the lord mayor made an appeal to the people, while the Earls of Pembroke and Leicester, and Sir W. Cecil, wrote, on 30th August 1568, to urge the merchant adventurers to promote the lottery ; but the people were distrustful, and the lots remained on hand until Elizabeth characteristically sent scolding missives to the justices of Kent and several other counties, and menacingly appointed an agent to report to her "the former doings of the principal men of every parish" with respect to the scheme. A copy of the original broadside still exists. For this and other interesting details as to this early lottery, see the 7th *Report of the Historical MSS. Com.*, App. pp. 619 b-621 b.

No lottery followed in the next year. The one for armour, mentioned by Stow, was certainly under royal consideration in 1585, as appears from a letter from the lord mayor to Walsingham, but the queen does not seem to have ventured on a third experiment.

Stow gives, under the year 1612, an account of "a liberall lottery" which James I. granted for the colonies in Virginia. Sixty thousand blanks were cast out on this occasion, as the lots were not fully taken up, but the prizes were not reduced. This is referred to in the *Domestic State Papers* for 1611-18, p. 120, which also mention, p. 130, a proposal for a private lottery, about this date, which was rejected by the lord mayor. The king's council, on 22nd February 1615, recommended another project for a Virginia lottery. A lottery is said to have been held in 1619 at Reading, and licence was given, in 1627, to Michael Parker, and another to raise money by a lottery to carry out the scheme for an aqueduct from springs at Hoddesdon to London. A fresh licence was given to Parker in 1631, and the matter seems to have been taken in hand by George Gage, and much money collected, which, about 1637, still remained on deposit, though the undertaking had failed.

A fresh project appears in the *State Papers* in 1640, when a "standing lottery" was sanctioned, "like that granted to the Virginia company."

Puritanism seems to have permitted the committee for lands in Ireland to hold a lottery at Grocers' Hall in 1653, but the *State Papers* from 1649 to 1659 are silent on the subject. In 1660, however, the mayor of Norwich complained of the "puppet-shows and lotteries" which came with the king's licence and sign-manual, and injured the trade of the town.

A lottery was also granted in 1660 for the ransom of English slaves from the Mediterranean pirates. A private one was asked for in the same year, and licence for a game called *l'oca di Catalonia*, which, as afterwards appears from the *State Papers*, was really a lottery, was granted to F. Corbet, a groom of the queen's privy chamber.

In 1661 a lottery for the fisheries was allowed, and in August 1663 (*8th Rep. Hist. MSS. Com.*, 539) there are traces of the famous Royal Oak lottery. A letter of 1664 (*Dom. S. Papers*, pp. 454-455) shows that the *Oca di Catalonia* was changed into the "Royal Oak."[1]

On 27th January 1664 a royal declaration annulled the former grant to Corbet, who had transferred his rights to Sir A. des Marces and another, who were allowed thenceforwards "the sole exercise of lotteries, for the benefit of the Royal Fishing Company."

This "Royal Oak" seems, from letters among the *State Papers*, to have been carried on in the provinces by travelling agents who obtained the permission of mayors to stay for a specified number of days.

At an uncertain date, but about 1664, Thomas Killigrew obtained a licence to begin when the fishing company's licence, for two remaining years, should have run out. In 1665, however, the company tried for a monopoly of lotteries in England, and, in 1666, for one in Scotland for seven years. They seem to have succeeded, as in February 1667 there is a petition for permission to succeed the royal fishing company in the "sole licence of holding lotteries in his majesty's dominions," which request was granted for three years.

This patent monopoly lasted to the end of the century, the Royal Oak having been excepted from the operation of 10 & 11 Will. III. c. 17, which prohibited all other lotteries.

The government, however, from 1709 to 1825, acted shamelessly in raising large sums annually by lotteries in which the prizes were terminable or perpetual annuities. Contractors took up

the tickets and sent itinerant salesmen through the country, who sold fractions of the £10 shares. Minor evils sprang up, as might have been expected, which had to be checked by the acts 19 Geo. III. c. 21, and 42 Geo. III. c. 119, and by Perceval's Act, 1806, which limited the drawings to one day.

In 1736 an act was passed for building Westminster Bridge by means of a lottery of 125,000 tickets at £5 each. This succeeded, and in 1774 the brothers Adam disposed of their property in the Adelphi, by permission of parliament, in a lottery of 110 prizes.

Towards the end of the century lotteries passed into the hands of the chancellors of the exchequer, and an average profit of nearly £350,000 was made for the public purse. Some benefit came from the evil, for the British Museum was aided; but public opinion at last demanded the abolition of the system, which was effected by 4 Geo. IV. c. 60, and the last lottery was drawn in October 1826. Private lotteries had been forbidden by 12 Geo. II. c. 28, and later statutes.

By a strange blunder, lotteries for the improvement of Glasgow were sanctioned by 1 & 2 Will. IV. c. 8, but they were suppressed by 4 & 5 Will. IV. c. 37. The last lottery of which the public has heard was Dethier's twelfth-cake lottery, which was stopped on 27th December 1860. Art unions were legalised by 9 & 10 Vict. c. 48.

[The tragedy as well as the buffoonery of these evil institutions will be found portrayed in Hone's *Everyday Book*, ii. pp. 1404-1535, while the Appendices to the 4th, 5th, 7th, and 8th *Reports of the Hist. MSS. Com.* contribute new and authentic details. See also *Brit. Mus. Additional MSS.*, Nos. 4458 (36), 5755 (1), 5801 (p. 460), 32,711 *f.* 521, 32,975 *f.* 428, and *Lansdowne MSS.*, 660 *f.* 120, 1215 *f.* 234.

Calendar of State Papers, domestic series, from 1547 to 1667.—J. Ashton, *English Lotteries*, 1893. —Dawson Turner's *Collection of Lottery Bills*, in the Brit. Museum, see "Lotteries" in the great catalogue.—*Encycl. Britannica*, art. "Lotteries." — Beckmann, *Inventions*, ed. Bohn, 1846, ii. pp. 414-429.]
R. H.

LOTTIN, ANTOINE PROSPER (1739-1812), was a Parisian bookseller.

He published under the pseudonym of Lambin de Saint Félix an *Essai sur la Mendicité* (Amsterdam, 1779) ; and, under the pseudonym of M. de Saint Haippy, a *Discours sur ce sujet: Le luxe corrompt les mœurs et détruit les empires*, Amsterdam and Paris, 1784.
E. CA.

LOTTO (see LOTTERIES, CONTINENT OF EUROPE).

LOTZ, JOHANN FRIEDRICH EUSEBIUS (1771-1838), a distinguished German economist, was born at Sonnefeld, then in the duchy of Sachsen-Hildburghausen, now belonging to Saxe-Coburg. He studied law at Jena, and held successively several official appointments in his native duchy.

---

[1] In Catalan Spanish the current term for goose is *oca*. The game of oca does not appear to be played in Spain nowadays, unless it be as a children's game ; but it is thus described in the *Diccionario Enciclopedico Hispano-Americano*, Barcelona, Montaner and Simon, vol. xiv. p. 43, 1887 and onwards. "Oca—a game which consists in a series of sixty-three divisions arranged in a spiral ellipse painted on a board or card-board. These divisions represent different objects ; every ninth number, counting from No. 1, represents a goose or "oca," and others represent rivers, wells, bridges, ships, or other objects at hazard. The game is played with two dice, and according as the numbers on them come out the game goes on." It would appear probable that the original name of the game may have been *Oca de Cataluna*, and under that name have passed into France, and into England. The game of goose appears to have been well-known in England. Goldsmith in the *Deserted Village* mentions

"The pictures plac'd for ornament and use,
The twelve good rules, the royal game of goose."

In 1819 the university of Bonn offered him the professorship of public law and state economy, which, however, he declined. In 1824 he became privy councillor in the service of Saxe-Coburg, and died at Coburg.

His most important writings were *Revision der Grundbegriffe der National-Oekonomie*, 4 vols., 1811-14, which, though prolix and excessively abstract, is yet, on account of the author's able analysis of fundamental conceptions, such as those of value and price, strongly recommended by Roscher to the careful study of all young economists ; and *Handbuch der Staatswissenschaften*, 3 vols., 1820, 2nd ed. 1837, which, though a useful work, is much inferior to the preceding. Lotz was one of those who did most to make the doctrines of the *Wealth of Nations* known in Germany. Allowing for some physiocratic leanings, he belongs essentially to the school of Smith, though differing from him on special points ; thus, not labour, in his view, but the creative powers of nature, and of the human intellect, are the great factors in the work of production ; he regards Smith as having attended too exclusively to value in exchange, as distinguished from value in use ; and he considers his praise of parsimony as too unconditional. He was an earnest reformer, though sometimes misled by a tendency to doctrinaire exaggeration. He treats political economy as a mere theory of enlightened self-interest. As a free-trader he goes even further than Smith, repudiating all intervention of the State in economic life. He chose for the motto of his *Revision* the words : "Ubi libertas, ibi divitiæ," and proclaimed as the one service he desired to render, that of assisting in the removal of the fetters which impeded industry. Perhaps his most serious error is the assertion of the unproductiveness of capital, which, though he was as far as possible from being a socialist, favours socialistic views ; regarding this doctrine, however, he appears to contradict himself. His greatest general defect as a thinker is his want of historical sense, with which are connected the too absolute form which he gives to many of his theorems, and the practice of denouncing, as simply erroneous or perverted, ideas and institutions which ought to be treated as the natural fruit of the earlier stages of social evolution.

[Schumann in *Allgemeine Deutsche Biographie*, vol. xix. 1884.—Lippert in *Handwörterbuch der Staatswissenschaften*, vol. iv. 1892.—Roscher, *Geschichte der N.O.*, p. 655 *seq.*]   J. K. I.

LOUIS, DOMINIQUE, Baron (1755-1837), born at Toul and died at Bry-sur-Marne, was minister of finance during many troublous times, as shown by the dates when he held the post—1st April 1814-20th May 1815 (first invasion) ; 9th July-26th September 1815 (second invasion) ; 30th December 1818-18th May 1819 (liquidation of an intense crisis) ; 30th July-1st November 1830 (Revolution) ; finally 13th March 1831-10th October 1832 (the ministry of Casimir Perier). On each occasion he showed a practical mind and a rare fertility of resource. Originally an abbé, he left his country when

the Revolution broke out. On his return under the consulate, he rose, through the intervention of his friend MOLLIEN, to high positions under government, and was appointed to the council of state, in which office he exhibited great energy. He maintained that a government which possessed the power to fulfil its engagements should unhesitatingly do so, and on one occasion answered Napoleon "a government must pay all it owes even for its follies." Appointed minister of finance at the fall of the empire, he re-established order and restored confidence. Though a supporter of free trade, he did not propose to sweep away all customs duties. When placed again at the head of the treasury, after the fall of the government of the 100 days, he did his best to overcome the innumerable difficulties which arose from the position of affairs.

Resolute but not overbearing, Louis respected the privileges of parliament in matters of public finance. When the *Chambre Introuvable*[1] opposed his broader views he resigned office, which he resumed in 1818 and established the small "*grand-livres*"—a decentralisation of the administration of the consolidated debt to the advantage of the departments. The formation of the retrograde Cabinet of Decazes caused Louis to leave the treasury 19th November 1819. When the revolution of 1830 broke out, the new government recalled him to his post. Here he maintained his high reputation, and after he had for the fourth time left the treasury when the ministry of Jacques Laffitte was formed, he was summoned to it again when Casimir Perier came into power. This was his fifth and last tenure of office. He retired at the age of seventy-seven.

Baron Louis always showed his respect for economic doctrine, and particularly for the famous maxims of Adam Smith on taxation. One of his best known sayings was "Give me a good policy and I will give you good finance."   A. C. F.

LOUIS D'OR, HISTORY OF. This gold coin was first struck in 1640 under Louis XIII., from whom it received its name. Its original value was ten livres : on one side was the head and name of the king, on the other four fleurs-de-lis with the legend, *Christus regnat, vincit, imperat*. The value of the louis d'or was subject to constant variations. Under Louis XIV. it was raised to twenty livres, and at one time to twenty-four. Under Louis XV. the value rose to thirty and even to thirty-six livres. Since the introduction of decimal coinage in 1795, the chief gold coin in France has been the piece of twenty francs. This was usually called a louis d'or after the Restoration and under Louis Philippe. During the second empire it was called a napoleon, but the term louis has survived to the present day in occasional use.   R. L.

[1] The *Chambre Introuvable*, elected October 1815, was named thus because Louis XVIII. found it so reactionary in opinion as to be "more royalist than the King," hence it was dissolved in September 1816.

LOUIS D'OR. French gold coin issued during the reigns of Louis XIII.-XVI.

List of Coins known under the title "Louis d'Or."

Reign.	Denomination.	Weight.	Fineness.	Value in gold 916·6 fine at £3:17:10½ per oz.		
		gr.		£	s.	d.
Louis XIII. (1610) .	Louis . .	6·692	906	0	16	6¾
	Louis . . .	6·692	904	0	16	6¼
	Louis . . .	6·692	901	0	16	5½
Louis XIV. (1643) .	Louis au Soleil .	8·127	902	1	0	0¼
Louis XV. (1715) .	Louis . . .	8·127	902	1	0	0¼
	Louis de Noailles	12·163	902	1	9	11½
	Louis à la Croix .	9·774	904	1	4	1½
	Louis à la Croix .	9·774	892	1	3	9½
	Louis Mirletons .	6·480	896	0	15	10¼
	Louis . . .	8·127	896	0	19	10¾
Louis XVI. (1774) .	Louis . . .	8·127	896	0	19	10¾
	Louis . . .	7·649	900	0	18	9½
	Louis Constitutionel . .	7·649	902	0	18	10¼

[P. Bonneville, *Traité des Monnaies d'Or et d'Argent*, Paris, 1806.] F. E. A.

LOWE, Joseph (early 19th century), wrote: *An Inquiry into the State of the British West Indies* (London, 1807, 8vo) a broad-minded and sympathetic plea for the West India planter. The author advocates a generous colonial policy, and scouts the notion that England has suffered by the loss of America or the Irish union. In a series of five chapters he points out the value of the West Indies as a market for English manufactures, lays stress on the depreciation of sugar, which has caused the emigration of negroes and planters; and proposes, among various other remedies, either the reduction of the duty on that article, or the abolition of the monopoly (see also *Edinburgh Review*, vol. xi. 145). Jevons observes that the idea of the just standard of value described by G. P. Scrope—see his pamphlet, *An Examination of the Bank Charter Question*, etc., 1833, also referred to as a tabular standard in Scrope's *Principles of Pol. Ec.*, 1833, ch. xvi.,—may have been suggested by the ingenious work of Joseph Lowe: *The Present State of England in regard to Agriculture, Trade, and Finance* (London, 1822, 8vo). In his 7th chapter, the author supports Mr. Simon Gray's as opposed to Malthus's theories of population, and maintains that the increase of our population "is replete with considerations equally satisfactory" in regard to "external" as "internal affairs, the stability of our finances, the reduction of the more injurious portion of our taxes" (see p. 245). Jevons adds that a second edition of this book appeared in 1823; and it was also reprinted (in German) in Leipzig the same year and in New York in 1824.

A. L.

LOWE, Robt. See Sherbrooke, Viscount.

LOWNDES, William (1652-1724), secretary to the treasury, was appointed to that office in 1695. With a view to the recoinage of 1696, he was requested to undertake an investigation into the state of the currency, the results of which were published with the title, *A Report containing an Essay for the Amendment of the Silver Coins*, London, 1695, 8vo. In this important work, while he repudiated any measure which would have the character of debasing the currency, he suggested, as a necessary measure for placing it upon a satisfactory basis, that all denominations of the silver coin should be raised 25 per cent. Lowndes had carefully examined the records of the mint and other documents, and he ably defended his position with historical arguments based upon these materials. He also maintained that the price of silver had risen to 6s. 5d. *an oz.*, and that if the measure he proposed were adopted, persons who melted down the coin would have "less profit by fourteen pence half-penny in the crown." Further arguments he used in support of his scheme were that it would encourage the bringing of bullion to the mint to be coined, and would make the coinage "more in tale, more commensurate to the general need thereof." To meet the objection that people would lose 20 per cent on contracts already made, he maintained the scarcity of silver. He computed the amount of "weighty money" hoarded up at £1,600,000. The most famous of the replies to Lowndes' *Essay* was written by John Locke (*q.v.*), and was entitled *Further Considerations concerning the raising the value of money, wherein Mr. Lowndes' arguments for it in his late report concerning "An Essay," etc., are particularly examined.* While the opposition accepted the views urged by Lowndes, Montagu and the government adopted those of Locke, and the recoinage on the old standard was carried on Dec. 10, 1698, in the House of Commons, by 225 to 114. In addition to the part he took in the currency controversy of 1695-96, Lowndes was instrumental in bringing about an amalgamation between the Old and New East India companies. He died in 1724. While replying to Lowndes' *Essay*, Locke paid a high tribute to his ability. "He is a man known so able in the post he is in, to which the business of money peculiarly belongs; and has shewed himself so learned in the records and matters of the mint, and so exact in calculations and combinations of numbers relating to our coin, either already in use or designed by him, that I think I should have troubled the publick no more on this subject had not he himself engaged me in it; and brought it to that pass, that either I must be thought to renounce my own opinion or must publickly oppose his" (Preface to *Further Considerations*, etc.).

[A full account of Lowndes' life is given in the *Dictionary of National Biography*. For a discussion of the relative merits of the views of

Lowndes, Locke, and the other disputants in the currency controversy of 1695-96, and their historical importance, see LOCKE ; RECOINAGES.]

W. A. S. H.

LOYD, SAMUEL JONES (1796-1883), OVERSTONE, BARON, a banker, was the son of a Welsh dissenting minister, who became a partner in Jones, Loyd and Co., a Manchester banking firm, afterwards merged in the London and Westminster Bank. Born to great wealth and an influential business connection, Loyd made the fullest use of his opportunities. He was in the House of Commons from 1816 to 1823, but his importance, politically, lay in the influence which he exercised over successive cabinets and chancellors of the exchequer. Already in 1832 we find him a recognised authority on finance.

The evidence he gave before the committee of the House of Commons on renewing the charter of the Bank of England, was directed (1) against the multiplication of issues of paper money, and in favour of (2) a single bank of issue, (3) a regular publication of accounts, including bullion, and (4) the repeal of the usury laws (see INTEREST). (Preface to 1858 publication of evidence given before 1857 House of Commons Committee upon Bank Charter Act of 1844). In 1840 he had given similar evidence before another committee, when he urged the separation of the departments of the Bank of England. This plan had been supported by the bank directors, Mr. J. H. Palmer and Mr. G. W. Norman, who also gave evidence before the same committee (see BANK NOTE). The Bank Charter Act of 1844 followed mainly upon the lines he had set out, and its provisions were defended by him before committees of the House of Commons in 1848 and 1857. In 1844 he had succeeded his father as partner in the bank, and in 1850 he was made Baron Overstone. He was of course not infallible. His distrust of the joint-stock system of banking (see Bagehot's *Lombard Street*, ch. ix.) was unfounded. On his general currency theory, the opinion of economists is much divided (see CURRENCY DOCTRINE). The disadvantages of the bank act of 1844 are now fully recognised, and various attempts at improvement have been made. Some also will condemn his opposition to the DECIMAL SYSTEM (*q.v.*) ; but he combined with a complete mastery of the details of banking an active interest in the theoretic side of financial questions, and a singular lucidity in their illustration. He was, moreover, through a long life, the strenuous opponent of all schemes of inconvertible paper. Lord Overstone enabled M'Culloch to edit a collection of *Scarce and valuable Tracts* on (1) *The National Debt and Sinking Fund*, by Harley, Gould Pulteney, Walpole, Hume, Price, Hamilton, and others, London, 1857, 8vo ; (2) *Paper Currency and Banking*, by Hume, Wallace, Thornton, Ricardo, Blake, Huskisson, and others, 1857; (3) *Commerce* by Evelyn, Defoe, Richardson, Tucker, Temple, and others, 1859.—In 1858 M'Culloch edited a volume by Lord Overstone of *Tracts and other publications on Metallic and Paper Currency*, 8vo.—This contains (1) *Reflection on causes and consequences of pressure of money market*, 1837. (2) *Remarks . . . on the condition of issues of the Bank of England and of the country issues during 1839-1840* ; (3) *Letters to J. B. Smith, Esq.*, 1840; (4) *Thoughts on separation of Departments of Bank of England*, 1840 ; (5) *The Petition of Merchants . . . or Bank Charter Act with comments on each clause*, 1847 ; (6) *Letters to Times on same, and on state of Currency in 1855 ;* (7) Extracts from evidence before committee of House of Commons on banks of issue ; and (8) *Extracts from Evidence on commercial distress.*

[*Times*, Nov. 19th, 1883,—*Dict. of National Biography*, vol. xxxiv., and works referred to.]

H. E. E.

LUBBOCK, SIR JOHN WILLIAM (1803-1865), was educated at Eton and Cambridge, and early in life joined the banking and mercantile firms of Lubbock, Forster, and Co., and Lubbock and Co., of which his father, the second baronet of his name, was the head. Business and scientific inquiry, particularly astronomy, the theory of the tides, and mathematics, were his chief occupations. Perhaps the work on *Probability* (1838-1844), written jointly with Mr. Drinkwater Bethune, is the one by which Sir J. W. Lubbock is best known. It was the earliest, and, its size considered, the best of the modern English introductions to the subject. The book was anonymous, but by an extraordinary error of the binder the second edition was lettered on the outside as " De Morgan on Probabilities." Sir J. W. Lubbock did not discover the mistake for years, De Morgan very properly disclaimed it, but naturally did not think it was for him to do more. The business in which Sir J. W. Lubbock was engaged supplied a curious "illustration of the way in which the doctrine of probability applies in every subject. It is a paper contributed by Sir J. W. Lubbock on the clearing of the London bankers. By observation it was ascertained that the daily differences at the clearing house, the money actually wanted to balance the demands of those who are to receive and those who are to pay, is only, one day with another, £29,000. To meet daily contingencies, the banks keep in the Bank of England balances which amount to from two to three millions. Sir J. W. Lubbock recommends that the clearing balance should be paid out of a common fund, which would put the banks so far in the position of being one concern, and would enable them to employ a large part of the sums they must now leave idle. The goodness of the advice is manifest."

Sir J. W. Lubbock's researches in the lunar and planetary theories date from 1832 ; his separate work *On the Theory of the Moon and on the Perturbations of the Planets* was published, the principal portion 1834-1838, with supplementary parts up to 1850. His investigations on the tides and on the heat of vapours and on refraction, 1840, showed high scientific power. Those on the tides did valuable service for navigation, and some of the tables he devised are believed to be still in use. He contributed nearly a hundred memoirs to the publications of the Royal and other scientific societies, and took an active part in the formation of the British Association. But perhaps the most striking achievement of Sir J. W. Lubbock's life was the vigour with which he maintained scientific study together with devotion to business.

Sir J. W. Lubbock was treasurer and vice-president of the Royal Society, 1830-35 and 1838-1845. He wrote a pamphlet *On Currency*, published anonymously in 1840, and also many anonymous scientific articles besides seventy or eighty memoirs in his own name: for the full list of these see the Royal Society's catalogue of scientific memoirs, 1870, p. 105, and for further particulars see obituary notice in the president's address, 1866.

LUCAS, CHARLES JEAN MARIE (1803-1889) a member of the institute of France and inspector of prisons:

He wrote in 1829 an essay on usury *De l'usure considérée dans ses rapports avec l'Économie Politique*, but from the beginning almost entirely devoted his activity to questions of penitentiary reform.—*Du Système pénitentiaire et de la Peine de Mort*, Paris, 1827.—*Du Système Pénitentiaire en Europe et aux États Unis*, 1828-1830. — *La Question Pénitentiaire en Europe et aux États Unis*, 1844. — *Observations sur l'Établissement de la Déportation*, 1853.—*La Peine de Mort et l'Unification pénale à l'occasion du Code Pénal Italien*, 1874.—*L'École Pénale Italienne*, 1877.— *De l'État anormal en France des crimes capitaux*, 1885. He also wrote *Le Droit de légitime Défense dans la Pénalité et dans la Guerre*, 1873, and *La Conférence de Bruxelles sur les lois et coûtumes de la Guerre*, 1874.　　　　　　　　　E. Ca.

LUCK. The husbandman and the merchant are properly represented by Horace as suppliants of fortune. For every *entrepreneur* is an " adventurer," exposed to the whole chapter of accidents which have been indicated under the head of CONJUNCTUR.

The entrepreneur who had produced a commodity, or acquired skill and position, or connection, does not obtain in each particular case a remuneration proportioned to the efforts and sacrifices which he has undergone. Rather his advantage is governed by the law of RENT. And yet it is not a true rent. For the properties which yield it are not "original" (Ricardo), but acquired; and there is a correspondence between the cost of acquiring these properties and their quasi-rent (Marshall); discernible in the long run, though obscured by the action of chance in individual cases. An industry cannot continue unless the prospects of success in it are sufficiently brilliant to elicit the efforts and sacrifices which it costs to embark upon it. The question, how the attractiveness of a business is affected by its riskiness, has been discussed under the head ALEATORY.

An average or "normal" correspondence between cost and value being recognised by theory; how large, in fact, are the fortuitous divergences on either side of this position of equilibrium? A gloomy answer to this question is supplied by Prof. Wagner in a passage referred to under CONJUNCTUR. "It is not," he concludes, "personal merit, or one's own fault; it is *not* work, or thrift, or foresight; not idleness or extravagance, or improvidence, but chance (*Conjunctur*) which is the decisive factor in determining the fate of most economic interests." (Compare J. S. Mill, *Chapters on Socialism. Fortnightly Review*, 1879, p. 226). Some of the numerous authorities, cited by Prof. Wagner, countenance the opinion that trade and industry are continually becoming more aleatory. On the other hand, Schäffle holds (*Aussch. Verhält.*, p. 35) that the sphere of chance becomes smaller as that of intelligence becomes larger. The remark is specially true of those calamities which physical science can guard against. But credit-waves and price fluctuations, changeable fashions and migratory customers, new inventions rendering old plant unsaleable, are elements of chance which do not seem to diminish with the progress of intelligence.

Civilisation certainly brings one remedy to insecurity, insurance. The principle is not confined to insurance offices; "when a great company, or even a great merchant, has twenty or thirty ships at sea, they may, as it were, insure one another" (*Wealth of Nations*, bk. i. ch. x.). Antonio having had " an argosy bound to Tripolis, another to the Indies, . . . a third at Mexico, a fourth for England, and other ventures," Bassanio might well ask with surprise: "Have all his ventures failed? What! not one hit!" This sort of insurance is connected by Prof. J. B. Clark with the philosophy of utility in an important article in the *Quarterly Journal of Economics*, 1893. (Cp. art. by John Haynes, *Risk as an Economic Factor, ibid.*, 1895).

Co-operation, also, in the modern form of a combination or concert between producer and consumer, should be mentioned as a corrective of the aleatory element in trade. Socialism offers more drastic remedies—themselves perhaps somewhat aleatory. This much certainly may be demanded of governments, that they should not aggravate insecurity by fitful taxation and unstable currency.　　　F. Y. E.

LUCRUM CESSANS, *i.e.* the gain to one person that is hindered by the non-return by another of a loan at the appointed time was recognised as justifying a claim for compensation or "interest," in the early sense of that term, even by some canonists and schoolmen contemporary with AQUINAS, though he himself refused to admit it, and in the 15th century it was very generally accepted by the best theologians. They could argue with some force that the increase of opportunities for reasonably safe investment destroyed the force of Aquinas's argument that damage done could be more readily measured than opportunities missed (see DAMNUM EMERGENS).

[With the Roman lawyers "interest" was the measure of compensation in breach of contract, and this included "lucrum"; see Puchta, *Instit.* (9th ed.), § 260; Windscheid, *Pandektenr.* (7th ed.), § 258. But the term, "lucrum cessans," seems to date from Accursius (d. 1260).—Endemann, *Studien in der romanisch-kanonistischen wirthschafts- und Rechtslehre*, ch. viii., §§ 1, 4; Ashley, *Econ. Hist.*, i. pt. ii. § 65.] W. J. A.

LUDDITES. The riots of 1816, which resulted in the breaking of many knitting frames in Nottingham and the neighbourhood, were deliberately and carefully organised. Those who engaged in them were known as "Luddites," a word derived, it is said, from the name of a half-witted lad, Ned Lud, who (1779) broke a frame under considerable provocation. The condition of the framework knitters was very miserable; the trade was habitually overstocked with apprentices, and there were large numbers of skilled hands, among whom, when trade was bad, a small amount of employment was spread. The riots appear to have been directed as acts of vengeance on certain unpopular masters. The organisation was secret, and in the then state of the law, apart from overt acts of violence, was criminal; those who took part in the operations were bound by oaths, and there appears to have been a close connection between the Luddite riots and the outbreak about the same date of the Shearmen in Yorkshire. Economically, however, the grievances of the two were very different; the framework knitters broke up machinery which had been used with but little alteration for two hundred years; the operations of the Shearmen were directed against the substitution of machine for hand labour in the finishing of cloth. Besides the accounts in the *Annual Register*, the curious may consult Mrs. Linnæus Banks' *Bond Slaves*, an historical novel, founded on personal reminiscences and private information regarding these struggles.

["*Swing*,"—Cobbett, *Letter to the Luddites*.]
W. C.

LUDER, AUGUST FERDINAND (1760-1819) was born at Bielefeld, studied at Göttingen, became professor of history at the Brunswick Carolinum 1786, Hofrath in Brunswick 1797, professor of philosophy in the university of Göttingen 1810, and in 1817 honorary professor at Jena, where he died. He was one of the group of economists who were the first to diffuse in Germany a knowledge of the principles of Adam Smith, Kraus and Sartorius being the others. He began his literary career with publications on geography and statistics, and in his principal work on economics, *National-*

industrie und Staatswirthschaft, which Roscher calls a paraphrase of Smith's system, he seeks to illustrate the doctrines of the *Wealth of Nations* by means of geography and books of travel. In his *Nationalökonomie oder Volkswirthschaftslehre*, which appeared in 1820 after the author's death, he still follows Smith. He holds that all history speaks in favour of free competition, and maintains—in this going beyond his master—that the interest of the individual can *never* be at variance with that of society at large. He claims to have been the first to reform politics and the historical sciences by developing the influence of industry on intellectual and moral culture, but surely some acknowledgment of Hume was here called for.

Besides his economic writings, and many translations of French, English, and Dutch books on the condition and resources of different countries, Lüder published two works—*Kritik der Statistik und Politik*, 1812, and *Kritische Geschichte der Statistik*, 1817—the object of which was to show the worthlessness, and even the misleading tendency of political theory and statistics, studies to which he had himself devoted much time and labour. He points to the many calculations and predictions of political speculators which had been falsified by the events of his own time; and he succeeds in exposing the superficiality, narrowness of view, and especially the materialistic one-sidedness with which statisticians were often chargeable. But he falls into extravagance in his censures, and carries his scepticism to such a length as would make trustworthy history impossible, because perfect accuracy is unattainable. It may be, however, as some have thought, that even his exaggerations were useful as representing a necessary reaction against the unduly high estimate of statistics entertained by some of his predecessors and contemporaries.

[Leser in *Allg. Deutsche Biogr.*—Stammhammer in *Handw. der Staatswissenschaften.*—Roscher, *Gesch. der N. O.*, p. 619.] J. K. I.

LUDEWIG, JOHANN PETER (1670-1743), a professor of law in the university of Halle, and steady admirer of King Frederick William I. of Prussia.

He principally lectured on German legal and economic history, and published *Germania Princeps* (1702), and in 1709 an Introduction to the monetary history of Germany during the Middle Ages,—*Einleitung zum deutschen Münzwesen mitlerer Zeiten.*—But his most noteworthy work is his *Panegyricus* (1727), written on the occasion of the foundation by Frederick William of a chair of economy, policy, and cameralistic in the university of Halle, emphasising the fact that a sound economic policy is the real basis of military power; the ascendency of Rome in old times, and of France under Henry IV. and Louis XIV., he ascribes to the wise economic policy of their rulers. All their qualities are found gathered in the person of "our anointed Salomo." Quite naturally Ludewig has nothing but words of blame for historians, who only care about wars, and neglect "great deeds performed at home."

[Roscher, *Gesch. der Nat. Oek. in Deutschland*, pp. 356-359.]   E. CA.

LUNACY, LAW OF. The economic position of the persons and the property of those whose absence of mental power incapacitates them from taking charge of their own affairs, has in England been the subject of numerous statutes during the last sixty years, which, in so far as they remained in force, were all consolidated by the Lunacy Act 1890, amended in respect of some minor details by the Lunacy Act 1891. There can be no doubt that the legislation on the subject has produced excellent results, and that the detention of persons falsely alleged to be of unsound mind or the infliction of inhuman treatment on those who are detained as lunatics, could now but rarely occur. The law as it stands secures (*a*) a competent supervising body having jurisdiction in all matters concerning persons of unsound mind ; (*b*) appropriate establishments for the reception of lunatics ; (*c*) an efficient investigation of the condition of the patient prior to his reception as a lunatic ; (*d*) humane treatment during detention and ample opportunities to be discharged on recovery ; (*e*) the protection of the property of persons who are unable to manage their own affairs.

(*a*) *Lunacy Authorities.*—The principal control in lunacy matters is exercised by the lunacy commissioners—a government department consisting of four unpaid, three paid legal, and three paid medical commissioners, one of the unpaid commissioners being the chairman, and of a legally-trained secretary. They have to supervise and inspect all establishments in which lunatics are received, and to see that all the regulations for the welfare of the inmates are properly carried out. They investigate complaints made by persons detained as lunatics, and have wide powers as to directing the discharge of any patients. The jurisdiction as to inquisitions and the management of the property of lunatics is exercised by the Lord Chancellor and the Lord Justices of Appeal, but most of their functions are now delegated to the two Masters in Lunacy, who must be barristers of at least ten years' standing. There are also legal and medical chancery visitors, whose duty is to visit the persons who are found lunatics by inquisition (see below).

(*b*) *Establishments for the Reception of Lunatics.*

A lunatic may be detained in one of the following ways :—(1) in an asylum or workhouse, (2) in a registered hospital, (3) in a licensed house, (4) as a single patient. Asylums principally used for pauper patients are provided by counties or boroughs ; but they may also receive private patients against payment. A pauper patient may also be detained in a workhouse on a certificate by the medical officer that it is not necessary to remove him to an asylum, and that the accommodation in the workhouse is sufficient ; and the county or borough authorities may also send pauper lunatics to hospitals or licensed houses.

An asylum is under the supervision of a visiting committee appointed by the county council or borough council to the jurisdiction of which it belongs. The unions to which the pauper inmates are chargeable have to pay a weekly sum in respect of each patient, the amount of which is fixed by the visiting committee, and may be altered from time to time so as to ensure as far as possible that the receipts cover the expenses, including the salaries of officers and attendants.

Registered hospitals are charitable establishments generally intended for the reception of patients of small means not being paupers, who are admitted free of charge or against a small annual payment ; but in many of these establishments there is a separate department for persons paying at a higher rate. Prior to the registration of a hospital the regulations must be approved by the Home Secretary ; and it is the duty of the commissioners to see that the regulations are properly carried out. It is a criminal offence for the superintendent of a hospital to receive more patients than the certificate of registration allows. The accounts of hospitals, in so far as they do not come under the jurisdiction of the charity commissioners, must be submitted to the commissioners in lunacy.

Licensed houses are private establishments for the reception of lunatics. The licensees whose licence is dated prior to the Lunacy Act of 1889 enjoy a practical monopoly, as no new licences are granted except to them or their successors in business. The licensing jurisdiction in the metropolis and its immediate neighbourhood is exercised by the commissioners in lunacy ; in all other places the licences are granted by the justices of the county or borough in which the house for which the licence is required is situated. A licence states the number of patients it authorises ; its duration is left in the discretion of the licensing authority, but must not exceed thirteen months, and it may at any time be revoked by the Lord Chancellor on the recommendation of the licensing authority. The commissioners in lunacy may, with the sanction of the Home Secretary, make regulations for the government of any licensed house. In each county or borough in which the justices are the licensing authority they must appoint at least three of their number and also a medical practitioner to act as visitors of licensed houses within the county or borough.

Single patients received in unlicensed houses are in various ways subject to the control of the commissioners in lunacy.

The average number of patients resident during 1892 in the various establishments described above was as follows :—

	Males.	Females.	Total.
County and borough asylums	25,403	31,135	56,538
Registered hospitals . .	1,007	1,354	2,361
Licensed houses . . .	1,787	2,333	4,120
Single patients . . .	190	250	440
There were also :—			
In naval and military hospitals	237	6	243
,, criminal asylums . .	480	159	639
,, idiot establishments . .	1,209	585	1,794
	30,313	35,822	66,135

(*c*) *Detention of Lunatics.*—It is a criminal

offence to receive or detain a lunatic against payment unless the fact of his being of unsound mind has been established in one of the prescribed ways.

When persons have considerable property it is usual to have an inquisition with or without a jury, and if the judge or master in lunacy or the jury find that the patient "is of unsound mind and incapable of managing himself or his affairs," he is placed under the care of a "committee of the person," for which office a near relative is generally chosen. A "lunatic so found by inquisition" may be detained in any establishment for the reception of lunatics or as a single patient, but in all other cases a "reception order" is required. A reception order is either made on petition or on summary process by a justice of the peace, the latter method being adopted in the case of paupers or lunatics wandering at large, and the former in all other cases, and is never made unless two medical practitioners certify independently of each other that the patient is of unsound mind. A reception order is not valid beyond a certain period, unless a report be made by the medical attendant to the effect that the patient is still of unsound mind. It is also necessary for the medical attendant, whenever a new private patient is received, to send a special report to the commissioners in lunacy, and the patient is thereupon visited ; and if in such visit it appears that the detention is improper, the commissioners may order his discharge.

In cases of imminent danger patients may be detained for seven days on an urgency order accompanied by one medical certificate. Inquisitions have lately become very rare, and most patients are now detained under reception orders.

(d) *Treatment of Lunatics.*—The proper treatment of persons of unsound mind is provided for in various ways, particularly by the compulsory visits which must be paid to all establishments in which lunatics are kept by the commissioners, and, as regards lunatics coming under their jurisdiction, also by the chancery visitors, visitors of licensed houses, and asylum visiting committees. It is also provided that every hospital and licensed house may at any time, by day or night, be visited by any one or more of the commissioners in lunacy. There are also various provisions for ensuring the right of every person detained as a lunatic to communicate with the lunacy authorities and to receive visits from his friends ; for securing regular medical attendance ; for regulating the use of mechanical means of restraint ; and for facilitating the discharge of patients after recovery. The commissioners in lunacy publish annual reports about their visits and other matters coming to the notice of their department.

(e) *Property of Lunatics.*—The property of lunatics so found is placed under the care of a "committee of the estate," who may be the same person as the "committee of the person" (see above). It is now also possible to obtain powers of management as to the property of persons of unsound mind not being lunatics so found by inquisition. The committees and other persons who manage the property of lunatics are under

the control of the lunacy judges and of the masters in lunacy (see above).

[The Lunacy Acts 1890 and 1891 ; see also the Reports of the Select Committees appointed to inquire as to the Treatment of Lunatics, dated 1859, 1860, 1877, 1878. As to the state of the law prior to 1845 see Dr. Forbes Winslow's edition of the act of 1845 ; see also INTERDICTION.]

E. S.

LUNDINARIUM or Mondayland, a name often found in manorial records for the small plots of land held by cotters, the lowest class of villeins, who were bound to work for their lord only on one day in the week, generally Monday.

[Vinogradoff, *Villainage in England*, 1892, pp. 153 note, 256, with references to cartularies of Christchurch Canterbury, and of Gloucester.]

E. G. P.

LUNETTI, VITTORIO (17th century) ; born at Naples, of Genoese descent. He wrote on the commercial side of political economy, and carried on the discussion on the serious state of affairs—economical, monetary, and financial—in the kingdom of Naples—a discussion in which De Santis, Serra, Biblia, and Turbolo had taken part. To meet the exceptional scarcity of coin and the high rate of exchange then ruling in Naples, he proposed to establish a fixed equitable rate of exchange and to forbid the export of coin. He desired to abolish customs and duties and to leave imports and exports free, but at the same time would restrict the privilege of trade in grain to the government. His writings as a whole, compared with those of his predecessor, Antonio SERRA, are not of first-rate importance. Serra had previously discussed, with considerable acumen, the question of international payments, advocating free export of money and free exchange.

Lunetti's works are : *Politica mercantile : degli espedienti et arbitrii per publica utilità*, etc., Naples, 1630.—*Ristretto dei tesori di tanti utili ed incredibili avanzi che si avra con la esecutione della Regia Tavola nella fedelissima città di Napoli*, Naples, 1660.

[For Lunetti, see L. Cossa, *An Introduction to the Study of Pol. Econ.*, translated by Dyer, Macmillan, 1893.—U. Gobbi, *L' economia politica negli scrittori italiani del secolo XVI.-XVII.*, Milan, 1889, pp. 318-326. — T. Fornari, *Delle teorie economiche nelle provincie Napolitane*, Milan, 1882, vol. i. pp. 293-301.]

U. R.

LUPO, GIAMBATTISTA (16th century). A scholastic theologian of San Gemignano, Tuscany, who wrote a Latin work on usury in which he discusses that question, expounding the traditional reasons for its prohibition and the exceptions rendering it permissible. Lupo differentiates between the various forms of usury, and examines various contracts—especially those of exchange, to show at what point they cease to be lawful and become usurious ; he maintains that, when in doubt, the judges are not to assume usury. In Lupo's comments on the scholastic theory of just price (see JUSTUM PRETIUM), which contain some of the germs of the present theories of value, he divides just price into "naturale" and "legitimum."— Natural price is that which usually prevails in the place and time where a contract is made ; it depends on the conditions of place, time, and custom of the contractor, on the quantity of goods and money, buyers and sellers, etc. "Tantum valet res, quantum vendi potest." The law of demand and supply is evidently referred to here. Lupo further says that legitimate price is fixed by the law of a prince or of those in like authority. Whoever fixes it must consider the intensity of the need, the copious supply or scarcity of the article and of the labour employed in its production, the disagreeableness of the business, the changes for better or worse in the goods, etc. Finally legitimate price must be based on natural price. Lupo divides "just price" into maximum, medium, and minimum.

Lupo wrote : *De usuris et commerciis illicitis*, Venetiis, apud Giuntas, 1577.

[See Gobbi, *L' economia politica negli scrittori italiani del secolo XVI.-XVII.*, Milan, Hoepli, 1889.—Montanari, *Contributo alla storia della teoria del valore negli scrittori italiani*, Milan, Hoepli, 1889.]   U. R.

LUSHBOROUGHS, OR LUSSHEBOURNES, were imitated English pennies, or sterlings, coined abroad, to be distinguished from crocards, pollards, and other prohibited coins, which were genuine foreign coins, but imported into England in the 13th century as being of less weight and value than the English sterlings. In most instances even lusshebournes need not be regarded as counterfeit coins ; though the reverse was always more or less closely copied from the English sterling, the obverse usually bore an honest legend, the real name of the prince who issued them, and of the town where they were minted. More often than not, however, the portrait followed the type used by one or other of the English kings, chiefly the three Edwards, but the portrait itself was not seldom absent and replaced by some local symbol. The cross of the reverse was never omitted, and was generally accompanied by the pellets of the English type, though in the place of these it is not uncommon to find letters, or trefoils, roses, birds, or other ornaments, and occasionally the angles of the cross are left unfilled. It is the reverse by which these foreign coins are identified. They were generally of less value than the English original.

These "counterfeit sterlings" had a wide circulation. Public and private interests were alike served. An international currency, even imperfect, was advantageous to trade, and lords and bishops found the advantage of coining money which was acceptable beyond the narrow limits of their domains. As that money which had the

best credit was most likely to be imitated, and as much of the trade of the Low Countries was with England, the English sterling naturally became the type of the foreign imitations. The Low Countries were the chief centre of trade, and the chief issuers of sterlings, the circulation of which was favoured by the political alliance of the Flemings with the first and third Edwards. The sterlings of Hainault, Namur, Cambrai, and the Flemish provinces proper must especially be regarded as a *bonâ-fide* coinage, but the case is different with Luxemburg, where real counterfeits were issued, and from which the English appellation for these foreign sterlings was derived. Luxemburg, or the corruptions lusshebourne and lushborough, became a popular name for all imitated or false coins. The sterling type reached Luxemburg towards the close of the 13th century through Brabant, and some were issued by the Count Henry, afterwards the emperor Henry VII. His son, John the Blind, 1309-1346, minted false sterlings of inferior value, with the name, or some misspelt approach to the name, of the English king, or with some other alteration of the legend with intent to deceive.

Not many foreign sterlings were struck after the third quarter of the 14th century, but they continued in circulation altogether for more than two centuries in spite of the attempts made in England during Edward III.'s reign to stop their introduction. English merchants made their profit out of the importation of them. In 1346 lusshebournes were worth only 8s. a pound, or even less. An ordinance forbade their introduction under heavy penalties, yet the next year several merchants were put to death or fined for bringing them in. The Statute of Treasons, 1352, made the introduction of lucynburghs treason, yet Langland in his *Piers Ploughman*, written about 1362, and Chaucer in the *Canterbury Tales* (Monk's Prologue), written after 1386, both use lusshebourne as a word familiarly known.

The following are the principal places at which foreign sterlings were minted :

Brabant, Bonn, Bremen, Cambrai, Cologne, Flanders, Hainault, Holland, Liège, Lorraine, Louvain, Luxemburg, Maestricht, Mainz, Metz, Namur, Strasburg, Treves, Utrecht. Chantard gives plates of coins minted at forty-two other places, chiefly German and Flemish, besides the English issues of Aquitaine and Calais, and a few specimens from more distant parts of Europe,—Aragon, Castile, Majorca, Norway, Portugal, and Sweden. [The fullest account is given by Chantard, *Imitations des Monnaies au Type Esterlin*, 1871, —See also Snelling, "View of Counterfeit Sterlings," in his *Miscellaneous Views*, 1769.—Ducange, *Glossarium.*—Knyghton, *Chronicle*, an. 1347.— Ruding's *Annals*, i. 22.—*Numismatic Chronicle*, 1st. ser. vi. p. 76, 1844.—Pike's *Hist. of Crime*, i. 267, with ref. to *Controlment Roll*, m. 66. Yorkshire, for case of prosecution.]   E. G. P.

LUTHER, Martin (1483-1546), the German reformer, is an interesting figure in economic history, both because he gave forcible expression to a large body of contemporary opinion, and also because he exercised a distinct influence on the action and thought of his time. A trained theologian, he was conversant with the economic teaching of the fathers, the greater schoolmen, and the earliest canonists : a man of warm sympathies, he had a keen sense of social evils around him, and was ready to apply the lessons of the church with but little regard to practical difficulties : a peasant's son, he looked with peculiar distrust upon the trading class, and regarded the great centres of commerce as but little better than "robber-towns." He shared in all the popular notions of his time ; attributed the rise in prices to monopoly and the new great trading companies ; thought that the import of foreign wares, like English cloth, was robbing the land of its gold and silver, and would soon leave it penniless ; and held that men who were ready to work ought to marry young, and leave it to God to provide for their offspring. In economic thought his influence was probably felt most strongly in relation to usury. Like others among the reformers, he helped to bring about a temporary reaction towards the severer doctrine of earlier centuries ; he expressed himself in more sweeping terms than the theologians of the previous generation, and, in particular, expressed his disapproval of certain views with regard to INTEREST, in its narrower and original sense, and "rent charges" (Rentenkauf), which were already coming to be widely accepted. It is not unlikely that the example of the protestant divines contributed to bring about the similar temporary reaction in the Roman Catholic Church during the "counter-reformation." His influence in another direction may be praised with less qualification. He pointed the way to the establishment of a wise system of poor-relief, based on the three principles that mendicancy should be prohibited, that each town should be responsible for its own poor, and that there should be proper investigation by the parson and other qualified persons. In his constitutional and social views Luther was intensely conservative ; he regarded the PEASANT'S REVOLT as likely to produce anarchy, and he had no scruple in urging the princes to resort to severe methods of repression.[1]

[Luther's most important writings in this regard are, *Der Grosse und Kleine Sermon von Wucher* (1519), *An den christlichen Adel deutscher Nation von des christlichen Standes Besserung* (1520), *Ordnung eines gemeinen Kastens* (1523), *Von Kaufshandlung und Wucher* (1524), *An die Pfarrherrn, wider den Wucher zu predigen* (1540). For an abstract of his utterances, with typical

specimens, see H. Wiskemann, *Darstellung der in Deutschland zur Zeit der Reformation herrschenden nationalökonomischen Ansichten* (1861), which needs, however, to be supplemented by the references scattered through G. Schmoller's *Zur Geschichte der nationalökonomischen Ansichten in Deutschland während der Reformationsperiode* (1861). Neither of these writers, indeed, sufficiently indicates Luther's relation to the previous teaching of the church.] W. J. A.

LUXURY is defined as the consumption of commodities which are not necessaries (*Wealth of Nations*, bk. v. ch. ii. art. iv.). "By necessaries I understand," says Adam Smith (*loc. cit.*), "not only the commodities which are indispensably necessary for the support of life, but whatever the custom of the country renders it indecent for creditable people, even of the lowest order, to be without. A linen shirt, for example, is, strictly speaking, not a necessary of life. . . . But, in the present times, through the greater part of Europe a creditable day-labourer would be ashamed to appear in public without a linen shirt." A more precise definition of luxury is derivable from Prof. Marshall's use of the term "necessary." "The income of any class in the ranks of industry is below its *necessary* level when any increase in their income would, in the course of time, produce a more than proportionate increase in their efficiency" (*Principles*, bk. ii. ch. iv.). Whether a particular article is necessary, in either sense, depends upon habits and climate. A definition of luxury irrespective of those circumstances is unattainable. However, the description given by Butel-Dumont "jouissances superflues" is sufficiently accurate for the expression of the principal economic theories on the subject.

Modern economists, unlike ancient philosophers, do not denounce luxury. Hume maintains that "the increase and consumption of all the commodities which serve to the ornament and pleasure of life are advantageous to society ; because at the same time that they multiply those innocent gratifications to individuals they are a kind of storehouse of labour which, in the exigencies of state, may be turned to the public service" (*Essays*, pt. ii., Essay 1-2 *Of Refinement in the Arts*, and compare Essay 1, *Of Commerce*). M'Culloch dignifies as productive any gratification, however trivial,—*e.g.* "blowing soap-bubbles"—to attain which a person is stimulated to work. J. S. Mill looks rather to the educational effect of luxury. "To civilise a savage he must be inspired with new wants and desires, even if not of a very elevated kind, provided that their gratification can be a motive to steady and regular bodily and mental exertion" (*Pol. Econ.*, bk. i. ch. vii. § 3). "The opening of a foreign trade . . . sometimes works a sort of industrial revolution . . . inducing those who were satisfied with scanty comforts and little work to work harder

---

[1] Luther "anticipated A. Smith's proposition that labour is the measure of value."—Cliffe Leslie, *Fortnightly Review*, July 1875.

for the gratification of their new tastes, and even to save and accumulate capital for the still more complete satisfaction of those tastes at a future time" (*Ibid.*, bk. iii. ch. xvii. § 5). Moreover, a "stock of labour" employed in manufacturing luxuries may supply men (Hume, *loc. cit.*), or at least money, for the maintenance of fleets and armies. It has been said that Napoleon was crushed by the English manufacturers. In case of famine, too, labour usually employed in procuring luxuries may be diverted to the production of necessaries ; directly, or in exchange for exported manufactures. Another sort of provision against a national disaster is constituted by luxury in the form of precious ornaments (cp. Adam Smith, bk. ii. ch. iii., concerning expenditure on "durable commodities"). Luxury not only remedies an occasional deficiency in the food supply of a people, but also prevents population increasing in excess of subsistence, by forming a standard of comfort below which prudence forbids to populate (Senior, *Lectures on Population*, J. S. Mill, *passim*, and other classical economists). So various are the benefits of luxury. So truly does Voltaire say of modern society : "Le superflu, chose très nécessaire."

Because economists do not follow the ascetic moralists in denouncing luxury, they do not therefore follow MANDEVILLE in applauding "the unmixed prodigality of voluptuous and heedless men" (*Fable of the Bees*, remark *k*). The celebrated dictum, "Private vices public benefits," is plausible only when applied to the extravagance of a particular class. The question is whether the expenditure of the "unnecessary" wealth of the upper classes is more beneficial to the working class than other ways of dealing with that wealth : which are principally—destroying it, investing it, giving it away.

Pace Fawcett (*Manual*, bk. i. ch. iv. p. 23, 4th ed.), destroying wealth is worse than giving it to workmen in exchange for some service, however futile. Investment tends (*a*) to increase the amount of fixed capital, or more generally to diminish the amount of waiting between effort and fruition ; (*b*) to increase the remuneration of labour. The first tendency (*a*) can hardly be other than beneficial, the saving in question being by hypothesis confined to a particular class of society. This seems to be the principal lesson to be derived from Mill's discussion of the question (*Pol. Econ.*, bk. i. ch. v. §§ 5 and 8). The second tendency (*b*) the offer of better terms to the working class may have various results. (1) It may lead merely to the increase of population ; which all would not regard as beneficial. (2) It may lead merely to an increase of idleness. "At one time," says the hero of Miss Edgeworth's *Ennui*, "I had a mind to raise the wages of labour, but Mr. Macleod said, it might be doubted whether

the people would not work less when they could with less work have money enough to support them." (3) Increased wages may be expended on luxuries which may possibly be less liberal than the luxuries foregone by the wealthy. (4) The result may be to increase efficiency and to further increase' wages ; the expenditure of the capitalist class being restricted to necessaries. Altogether, considering the diversity and remoteness of these deductions, it may be doubted whether economic reasoning much strengthens the motives to saving which ordinary prudence supplies to the wealthy classes. Lastly, Dives might give away part of what he now spends on himself. It is difficult to believe that rational benevolence cannot discover a better way of employing money than to spend half a guinea on a dish of green peas (Hill's *Boswell*, p. 56 and cp. note). When Dr. Johnson asked, "Has it not gone to the *industrious* poor, whom it is better to support than the *idle* poor," he forgot that the industrious poor would be equally employed in making things to be given away as in making objects of luxury. As Hume says (*Essays*, pt. ii. 2), "that labour which at present is employed only in producing a slender gratification to one man would relieve the necessitous and bestow satisfaction on hundreds." On the other hand, charity often defeats its own end ; and the disinterested resignation of luxuries must be preached with caution. To resign all luxury is a rule of conduct which cannot justly be prescribed for one class only, and which becomes absurd when applied universally. This absurdity is happily illustrated by Miss M. Benson, *Capital, Labour, and Trade*, ch. iii. "The end of it would seem to be an immense population working all their days, living on the bare necessaries of life,"—like ants.

The old and noxious fallacy that the extravagance of the rich is necessary for the employment of the poor is now nearly extirpated. But there is some appearance in contemporary socialist literature of an opposite misconception. It seems to be held that production on a large scale is not possible unless the masses are large consumers, beyond what is necessary for efficiency—for otherwise the proposition is a truism. The most intelligible argument in favour of this thesis is that the unsteadiness of the demand which a wealthy class has for whimsical luxuries is apt to discourage production.

The attempt to restrain luxury by SUMPTUARY LAWS, or to utilise it by TAXATION will be treated elsewhere.

[Mandeville, *Fable of the Bees.*—Cantillon, bk. i.—Berkeley, *Querist.*—Melon, *Essai Politique sur le Commerce.*—Hume, *Essays*, pt. ii. Essays 1 and 2.—Voltaire, *Le Mondain, Défense du Mondain ou l' Apologie du luxe.*—Butel-Dumont, *Théorie du luxe, ou traité dans lequel on entre-*

prend d'établir que le luxe est un ressort non-seulement utile, mais même indispensablement nécessaire à la prosperité des États. —Steuart, *Principles of Political Economy,* bk. ii. ch. 20.— Ferguson, *Essay on Civil Society,* pt. vi. § 2.— Say, *Cours Complet,* vols. 1 and 2 *passim.*—Rau, *Ueber den Luxus* and *Lehrbuch.*—Roscher, *Ueber den Luxus* and *Volkswirtschaft,* etc.—Mangoldt, Article on "Luxus" in Bluntschli, *Staatswörterbuch,* vol. vi.—H. Sidgwick, "Luxury" article in the *International Journal of Ethics,* October 1894.—Baudrillart, *Histoire du luxe.*—M'Culloch, *Principles,* pt. iv. On Consumption.—J. S. Mill, *Pol. Econ.,* bk. iv. ch. vi.—De Laveleye, "Le luxe" in *Socialisme Contemporain.*—Gunton, *Wealth and Progress,* pt. i. ch. 2.—Sidgwick, *Princ. of Pol. Econ.,* bk. iii. ch. ix. § 5.—Locke, *Considerations on the Lowering of Interest,* mentions the preference people have for things because of their dearness.] **F. Y. E.**

LUZAC, ELIE (1723-1796), born at Noordwyk, studied law at Leyden, became a bookseller and publisher, and, after having graduated in 1759, also a lawyer; he wrote many juridico-philosophical works, and translated Montesquieu's *Esprit des Loix.*

His economical work is entitled *Holland's Rijkdom* (Holland's wealth), and is a translation of a French work, *Commerce de la Hollande, par Accarias de Sérionne* (Londres, 1778), but greatly amended and completed. A German translation of the French edition by Beuzler appeared 1778, two of the Dutch editions by Engelbrecht (Greifswold, 1788), and by LUDER (Leipzig).

The work contains an historical exposition of the growth and decline of the Dutch trade from the middle ages to the author's time, followed by an inquiry into the causes of its decline and the means of restoration. Under the first—excluding moral and political causes—he mentions the levying of high taxes on necessary victuals as causing high wages, and in consequence high prices, and the importation of East Indian articles which could be obtained at home. As efficient means of redress he considers the establishment of a limited free port; taxes principally on articles of luxury; the granting of privileges of various kinds to manufacturers and their workmen with a view to lowering prices, etc. The historical part of the book is by far the most interesting.

A. F. V. L.

MABLY, GABRIEL BONNOT, ABBÉ DE (1709-1785), elder brother of Condillac, born at Grenoble, died at Paris, was a communist in theory, but he neither aimed at being the leader of a school nor expected to put his ideas into practice. In character he was upright, never trifling with his duty. At first it seemed that he was destined to take orders,—he was educated by the Jesuits at Lyons and afterwards at their seminary of St. Sulpice in Paris. But early in life he entered on a secular career and became the secretary of his uncle, Cardinal de Tencin, then minister of state. The Cardinal seems to have been singularly incapable, for it was the duty of Mably to draw up even his simplest notes. In this position Mably was so highly thought of that he was charged with important diplomatic missions; thus in 1743 he was sent to Prussia to conclude a secret treaty against Austria; and in 1746 he drew up the instructions for the plenipotentiaries who were engaged at the Congress of Breda. But he soon came to a disagreement with Cardinal de Tencin, and in a cause which was entirely to his honour. The Cardinal wished to disannul a protestant marriage. Mably opposed this energetically. "I wish to act as a cardinal," his uncle said to him; "act as a statesman," replied Mably, who left him and a settled career for authorship.

In his first work, *Parallèle des Romains et des Français par rapport au gouvernement,* 1740, 2 vols. 12mo, Mably by no means appeared as the communist leveller he afterwards became. In it he extolled absolute monarchy, regarding men as incapable of governing themselves; and he was warm in praise of luxury. This phase of thought did not last long. In 1748 he produced the 1st ed. of *Le Droit public de l'Europe fondé sur les Traités,* 2 vols. 12mo (the 3rd edition in 1764 was continued to the treaty of Paris, 1763, in 3 vols.), in this, after having approved negro slavery in the colonies, he began to show the extent of existing social inequalities. In 1763, he published *Les Entretiens de Phocion sur le rapport de la morale avec la Politique traduits du Grec de Nicoclès,* 12mo. This travesty, as it may almost be called—the best of his writings in style, and a happy example of rhetorical exaggeration—eulogises the institutions of Lycurgus, and marks the author as a member of the school of J. J. Rousseau. It is a step towards those socialistic ideas which caused Mably to be placed among the forerunners of communism, though of itself it would not have been a sufficient basis for the reputation which later years have awarded him. In 1768, Mably addressed to the economists, in the person of Mercier de la Rivière, his *Doutes proposés aux philosophes économistes sur l'ordre naturel et essentiel des sociétés politiques,* 12mo. This publication embodied an attack on landed property. "It is property which introduced indolence and sloth into the world . . . I see, from the moment that property in land was established, inequality in fortunes begin; are not clashing and conflicting interests the necessary result of inequality in fortune,—all the vices of riches, the vices of poverty, the impoverishment of mind, the corruption of habits, etc. . . . ? Property has peopled the earth only with brigands and thieves. The greater the effort we make to return to equality, the nearer we shall be to happiness." Personal property alone found favour with him. In 1776, in his work, "*De la législation ou principes des Loix*, 2 vols. 12mo, and in the work *Des Droits et des Devoirs des Citoyens*, which only appeared after his death, he supported the system of community in goods. He feared, however, that property would not allow itself to be abolished as easily as he wished. Plato had said 2000 years before, "This would be too much to ask of men born and brought up as they are now." Like Plato, Mably exclaimed, "The evil at the present time is too inveterate to allow us to hope for a cure." And he admits as transitory methods of improvement—better land laws, limitation of fortunes, a Spartan education, sumptuary laws, the abolition of the right of bequest, the interdiction of trade, and the abasement of arts and industries. He proscribed neither family life nor religion ; he even wished for an established religion and selected the Catholic religion. He maintained it was necessary that the state should be intolerant. Instead of a centralised state he wished for a federation ; and to promote this, he published in 1784 his *Observations sur le gouvernement et les lois des États-unis d'Amérique*, 12mo, in which he prophesied the fall of that country, if it continued to give to commerce and industry the pre-eminence which has since been the basis of its prosperity. As has been seen, Mably took, though in error, a step beyond J. J. Rousseau. The latter preached equality and a return to what he called the state of nature. Mably demanded, as the means for realising this ideal, a community of goods without inquiring, as Cabet did later, into the details of the means of bringing it about. And yet in the following passage of his book, *Le Droit public de l'Europe fondé sur les traités*, vol. ii. pp. 417-418; 3rd edition, 1764, Mably had given proof of a power of intuition which ought to have saved him from the mistakes just described. "What would cause a singular revolution in Europe would be if America shook off the yoke of Spain in order to govern itself by its own laws. No doubt the rebels, with a view to interesting Europeans in their fate and preventing them from supplying help to their opponents at the court of Madrid, would be willing to open to them all their ports and to lavish their wealth on them, but this event would only give a transitory prosperity to our avarice. The Americans will soon possess our arts and manufactures, their land will soon bear our fruits ; and in consequence, as they will have no longer any need of our merchandise or our produce, Europe will gradually fall into the same state of indigence she was in four centuries ago." The complete works of Mably were published after his death in 1789, 12 vols. 8vo ; in 1793, 26 vols. 12mo ; in 1794, 15 vols. 8vo ; finally in 1797, 12 vols. 8vo. His posthumous works appeared in two editions, 1790-91, 4 vols. 12mo ; 1797, 3 vols. 8vo. A. C. f.

[See Sudre, *Histoire du Communisme.*]

MACADAM, John Loudon (1756-1836), invented the "macadamised" system of road-making, which effected "the greatest improvement in the means of inland communication subsequent to the introduction of canals and before the great extension of railways" (Waller's *Imperial Dictionary of Universal Biography*, art. Macadam). It was while acting as road trustee in his native county of Ayrshire that Macadam's attention was drawn to the condition of highways. In 1811 he laid the result of his investigations before parliament. In 1815, as surveyor-general of the Bristol roads, he so successfully applied his methods that in 1823 parliament granted him £10,000 in return for his expenses in the public service.

Macadam published *A Practical Essay on the Scientific Repair and Preservation of Public Roads*, London, 1819.—*Remarks on the Present System of Road-making*, 5th edit., 1822 ; 9th edit., 1827 (Longmans).—*Observations on the Management of Trusts for the Care of Turnpike Roads*, London, 1825. A. L.

The use of stones of uniform size broken into angular pieces, which have a tendency to lock together into a hard and compact mass, was the prominent feature of the system carried out by Macadam—"Such a size as you can comfortably put into your mouth," was his rule with his workmen (see also Life, *Dict. Nat. Biog.*). The economic advantages of improved methods of communication are almost incalculable (see Canals ; Communication, Means of ; Transport, Cost of).

MACANAZ, Melchior de (born about the end of the 17th century), became *Intendente general* of Aragon, and on behalf of King Philip V. carried on negotiations in Paris with the papal nuncio for the repression of the abuses existing in the Spanish church. He defended the prerogatives of the crown with such acrimony that he roused the permanent hatred of the Spanish clerical party, and was obliged to cross the French frontier. On his return to Spain some years later he was apprehended and confined in the castle of Segovia, where he remained till the accession of Charles III. He did not survive his liberation many years.

The most noteworthy economic writings of Macanaz are the *Auxilios para bien gobernar una Monarquía Catolica* (Helps for the Right Government of a Catholic Monarchy), published separately after his death in 1789, and also included in the *Semanario Erudito* of Valladares (Madrid, 1788, vol. v.) ; the *Avisos Políticos, Máximas prudentes y Remedios universales*, presented to King Ferdinand VI., and his *Representacion expresando los notorios males que causa la despoblacion de España* (Representation on the Notorious Evils Caused by the Depopulation of Spain). Many of his writings have not been printed.

Macanaz is a warm follower of Colbert (see *Auxilios*, pp. 233-236, 243, 287-289, vol. v. of *Semanario Erudito*). He also lays down some of the principles on which the assessment of taxes should be based. Adam Smith later insisted on similar rules : taxes "must be . . . adjusted to the means of the subjects (p. 290) . . . the raising them must not weigh heavily on the taxpayers" (p. 292). At the same time, he rejects all taxes whatever on food (bread, meat, wine, and salt), and recommends the establishment of an official and exact return of the means of each individual subject, on which a tax of 10 per cent, including all kind of taxes on eatables, might be assessed (pp. 290-291). E. Ca.

M'CULLOCH, JOHN RAMSAY (1789-1864), statistician and economist, born at Whithorn in Wigtownshire, studied in Edinburgh, and entered the office of a Writer to the Signet there.

He soon abandoned the law, and devoted himself to the study of economics. His first publication (1816) was *An Essay on a Reduction of the Interest of the National Debt*, in which he sought to prove that such reduction was the only possible means of relieving the distresses of the commercial and agricultural interests; while it was also a just measure, and one founded on the surest principles of political economy. For ten years (1817-1827), M'Culloch contributed the economic articles to the *Scotsman*, and for two years (1818-1819) he was editor of that journal. In 1818 he wrote an article in the *Edinburgh Review* on Ricardo's *Principles of Political Economy*, and for nearly twenty years after that he contributed almost all the economic articles to the *Review*.[1] Proceeding to London in 1820, he formed classes for the study of political economy, and in 1824 delivered the Ricardo lectures. The materials in these lectures were afterwards expanded into an article on political economy for the supplement to the *Encyclopædia Britannica*, and they were also substantially utilised in a separate publication entitled *A Discourse on the Rise, Progress, peculiar Objects, and Importance of Political Economy*, 1824-1825. Subsequently M'Culloch published a still more extended and formal treatise on *The Principles of Political Economy ; with a Sketch of the Rise and Progress of the Science*, 1825. Between 1830 and 1886 six other editions of this work appeared in London and Edinburgh.

M'Culloch was examined before the parliamentary committee on the state of Ireland in 1825, when "he argued that absenteeism could not materially injure that country, because rent was ordinarily remitted through the medium of bills of exchange drawn against exports." This theory was trenchantly attacked in *Blackwood's Magazine* (vols. xix. and xxiv.). In 1828 he was appointed to the new but unendowed chair of political economy in University College, London, which he resigned in 1832. M'Culloch published, in 1826, an *Essay on the Circumstances which determine the Rate of Wages and the Condition of the Labouring Classes*. This was perhaps his most distinctively original work, but the famous "wages fund theory" which he propounded, and which was very largely accepted for at least a generation, was ultimately abandoned by the best economic authorities. A *Treatise on the Principles, Practice, and History of Commerce*, which M'Culloch contributed to the *Library of Useful Knowledge*, 1831, was remarkable as an early exposition and defence of the principles of free trade. It was followed in 1832 by M'Culloch's important statistical work, *A Dictionary, Practical, Theoretical, and Historical, of Commerce and Commercial Navigation*. This comprehensive publication embodied the researches of twenty years. It was succeeded in 1837 by *A Statistical Account of the British Empire*, undertaken by M'Culloch, with the aid of a body of

specialists, for the Society for the Diffusion of Useful Knowledge.

In 1838 M'Culloch was appointed comptroller of Her Majesty's stationery office, a post which he held until his death. He did not relax his economic studies after his appointment to the comptrollership, but published in 1841 his *Geographical, Statistical, and Historical Dictionary*, which contained brief descriptions of the various countries, places, and principal natural objects in the world. In 1845 appeared his *Treatise on the Principles and Practical Influence of Taxation and the Funding System;* and during the same year he published his *Literature of Political Economy*, "a classified catalogue of select publications in the different departments of that science, together with historical, critical, and bibliographical notices," a work of great use to the economic student. The results of M'Culloch's inquiries into the influence of primogeniture, entails, compulsory partition, etc. over the public interests, appeared in his *Treatise on the Succession to Property vacant by Death*, issued in 1848 ; and a work of his on *Economical Policy*, containing treatises and essays on various subjects, and memoirs of Quesnay, Adam Smith, and Ricardo—was published five years later. He edited in 1856 for the Political Economy Club,—of which he was one of the original members—a *Select Collection of Valuable Tracts on Money*, by Vaughan, Cotton, Petty, Lowndes, Newton, and others. In 1856 he edited *Early English Tracts on Commerce*, by Mun, Roberts, North, and others : for Lord Overstone, in 1857, *Tracts on the National Debt and the Sinking Fund*, by Harley, Gould, Pulteney, Walpole, Hume, Price, and others :—in 1857, *Tracts on Paper Currency and Banking*, by Hume, Wallace, Thornton, Ricardo, Blake, Huskisson, and others ;—in 1859 pamphlets on *Commerce*, by Evelyn, Defoe, Richardson, Tucker, Temple, and others ;—in 1859, *Economical Tracts*, by Defoe, Elking, Franklin, Turgot, Anderson, Schomberg, Townsend, Burke, Bell, and others. He also collected Lord Overstone's *Tracts and other Publications on Metallic and Paper Currency*, 1857, and his *Evidence before the Select Committee of the House of Commons of 1857 on Bank Acts*. In 1860 he contributed to the *Encyclopædia Britannica* (8th edition) the article on *Taxation*, which was separately reprinted the same year.

In addition to the works specified above M'Culloch wrote a great number of minor pamphlets, tracts, and articles on subjects connected with political economy. He edited A. SMITH's *Wealth of Nations* with copious notes, etc. (1828, 2nd ed. 1838, 3rd ed. 1863), and also the works of RICARDO, with a life of the author (1846, 2nd ed. 1852). M'Culloch was no original thinker, but a close student and follower of Smith and Ricardo, whose principles he expounded, and he assisted in the dissemination of the ideas on economic questions which prevailed at the beginning of the 19th century, and furthered useful legislation with regard to them. His treatment of these questions was little marked by breadth or elevation ; this and his habit of dogmatism tended to alienate many from the science of which he was, at the time. one of the prominent exponents. Until the

---

[1] For a list of these, see *Notes and Queries*, 5th October 1878.

rise of Mill, his *Principles* had a considerable vogue among English and European students of political economy. His description of his own Library, *A Catalogue of Books the property of a Political Economist* (privately printed, London, 1st ed. 1856, 2nd with adds. 1862), and the critical notices of the books it contains, are evidence of the extent of his studies.

[*Annual Register*, 1864; "Men of the Reign," *Scotsman*, Nov. 12, 13, 1864.—*Dictionary of National Biography*, vol. xxxv.—Bain's *Life of James Mill.*—*Chambers's Encyclopædia*, vol. vi.; Quaritch, *Dictionary of English Book-Collectors*, pt. vi., Feb. 1895, gives, along with life, portrait and facsimile of letters.] G. B. S.

MACE. A denomination of the Chinese money of account, but not a coin. 100 cash = 1 mace (*see* CASH). F. E. A.

M'FARLAN, JOHN (fl. end of 18th century), clergyman and philanthropist, was one of the ministers of the Canongate, Edinburgh. When he published *An Inquiry concerning the Poor*, Edinburgh, 1782, 8vo, he had been for fifteen years connected with almost every charitable foundation in Edinburgh. The *Inquiry* treats of the causes of poverty, and the different methods employed to provide for the poor, and then proceeds to suggest reforms, of which the more important are, an improved police, efficient voluntary managers, and paid inspectors, and the building of houses of correction in every parish. The book is dedicated to Lord Kames, to whose suggestions it is owed much. H. E. E.

MACGREGOR, JOHN (1797-1857), was a native of Scotland, eldest son of David Macgregor of Stornoway. He emigrated to Canada early in the century, became a member of the house of assembly of Prince Edward's Island, and later travelled through North America, returning to England in 1828. He was a friend of J. Deacon HUME of the board of trade, and with him projected a vast work on the statistics of the British empire, which was never undertaken : he occupied his time, however, with other works on history and statistics. In 1840 he succeeded Hume as joint secretary at the board of trade, but resigned in 1847. Macgregor expressed his views with vigour alike in his writings and in evidence before several committees of the houses of parliament. His views were favourable to free trade, and his evidence before the committee of 1840 was considered a severe blow to protection. The general tendency of his opinions was strongly utilitarian.

Of his more purely economic or statistical works, the chief were :—*The Resources and Statistics of Nations*, London, 1835, 8vo.—*Commercial and Financial Legislation of Europe and America*, London, 1841, 8vo.—*The Preference Interests or the miscalled Protective Duties shown to be Public Oppression*, 1841.—*Financial Reform*, 1849.

[See *Dictionary of National Biography*.]
C. A. H.

MACHAULT D'ARNOUVILLE, JEAN BAPTISTE (1701-1794), one of those few ministers of Louis XV. who were both honourable and able. He never aimed at becoming a financier, and was master of appeals when D'Argenson, who had divined his ability, procured his appointment as commissary of the treasury at Valenciennes, from which he was subsequently promoted, without his knowledge, to the office of controller-general in place of Philibert Orry, a functionary who was a faithful slave to the ideas of Cardinal Fleury. Machault was raised to power at a difficult time. For four years Europe had been in confusion through the war of the Austrian succession. France was the preponderating force in the struggle, and though she obtained military success, her financial affairs felt the disastrous effects. Cardinal Fleury was dead, and with him the system of economy which, though blamed by some, had at least the advantage of easing the shoulders of the taxpayers. The era of senseless prodigality and the costly reign of recognised mistresses began. Madame de Pompadour was the first of these. Machault had to meet this order of things, and to deal with the most urgent claims. The commencement of his ministry (1745-48) was entirely given up to shifts of all kinds which there is no need to detail. The Treaty of Aix-la-Chapelle (1748) gave peace to Europe, and made the state of affairs more bearable. Machault profited by this to establish reforms in taxes and in the management of the national debt. Instead of the tax of the tenth, a war tax not paid by all classes, he established the tax of the twentieth (VINGTIÈME *q.v.*), a permanent and general contribution. The nobility and clergy were called on to pay it like the rest of the population. The produce of the twentieth was employed to maintain a sinking-fund, intended to lighten the weight of the national debt. Machault then introduced liberal measures which reanimated business, and showed for a moment a glimpse of prosperity and abundance. His reforms excited unanimous opposition among the privileged classes. The clergy bestirred themselves to such effect that they were exempted from paying the tax on condition of making a donation. The *Pays d'états* (see INTERNAL CUSTOMS AND TOLLS) obtained the same exemption by a trifling contribution. These checks and others of the same class determined Machault to resign the controllership (1754), and he passed to the admiralty, to which his great administrative ability enabled him to render valuable services. A court intrigue was the cause of his definitely giving up the admiralty and at the same time the keepership of the seals which he had held since 1750. In 1757 he returned to private life, which he only left to die in prison. The reforms he had instituted did not last, and the foundations he had laid were broken up as soon as he retired from office.

[M. Marion, *Machault d'Arnouville: étude sur l'histoire du contrôle général des finances de 1749 à 1754*, Paris, 1891, 8vo.]   A. C. F.

MACINATO, or grist tax, in Italy. The idea of taxing the grinding of cereals is of old date in Italy. In Sicily a tax of this description existed in the middle ages ; probably the Arabs introduced it. Such a tax certainly existed as a right of the crown under the Normans (1168).

The tax was in force at Florence in 1288,— at Milan in 1333 ; and it was rearranged, suppressed, and reimposed several times. Towards 1650 the grist tax became general nearly all over Italy—imposed with minute care in Florence, Sicily, Piedmont, and the Venetian republic. In Tuscany a law of Cosimo I. (7th Oct. 1552) graduated the grist tax from $3\frac{4}{7}$ *soldi* down to $1\frac{4}{7}$ *soldi* for every *staio* (a measure of the period), according to the various species of cereals, and comprised every grain, from corn to maize, barley, beans, etc.

This tax was levied throughout Tuscany, but with a higher tariff in Florence.

Introduced only for three years, to raise the funds for war, it gave such satisfactory results that it was continued 126 years without interruption, and gradually brought to perfection in technical details. In 1675 the government farmed the tax out till the 1st of June 1678, when it was suppressed and a personal tax substituted for it. Only in some districts the taxation of flour was continued in an OCTROI at the town-gates, till, with the progress of free-trade principles, this duty also disappeared in Tuscany.

In Sicily the grist tax was universal when parliament regulated it in 1565. This charged the collection of the tax on the local governments—the central government dividing it amongst the towns and rural districts, and avoiding direct contact with the taxpayers.

As, however, a great deal of clandestine grinding was carried on, the government made contracts with the landlords or their tenants, to commute for a fixed annual charge the liberty of grinding the corn necessary for themselves and their dependents. In this way a distinction between the civic and the rural gristing tax was introduced.

In Sicily the grist tax did not answer so well as in Tuscany. It was modified several times and temporarily suspended on several occasions as on the revolution of 1648, against the viceroy. In 1843, by a decree of the 22nd July 1842, the government took the grist tax directly into its hands, except for Palermo and Messina, and leased it out for six years. Every mill was put under the control of an official who weighed the quantity ground. The revolution of 1848 suspended the tax, but it was re-imposed, with a lower tariff, by the revolutionary government itself, and continued

by the Bourbons, as soon as they returned. In 1860, Garibaldi, as Dictator, abolished the tax, 19th May 1860, and Sicily has never again been subject to it.

In Piedmont the grist tax was first introduced in 1577, as a duty due to the ducal mills of Fossano ; in 1614, Carlo Emanuele I. extended it to the whole of his dominions to provide for his army, but he substituted a capitation tax for it the next year.

In 1616 the grist tax was reintroduced, unsuccessfully leased out in 1619, abolished in 1621, re-established in 1622. A hearth tax (*fuocaggio*), was substituted for it in 1635. The grist tax was re-introduced in 1691, but it was transformed into a direct tax on mills. In the next year a capitation tax was substituted, which in 1701 again gave way to the grist tax, definitively abolished in 1713 by Victor Amedeo.

In the Venetian republic, the grist tax was introduced in the beginning of the 16th century, and continued till the downfall of the republic.

In the remainder of Italy the history of the *macinato* is uniform. Everywhere it seemed indispensable : at Milan, at Parma, in Genoa, in the papal states. Only in Naples the grist tax seems to have been generally a communal tax or local government tax, and not connected with the central government. With similar traditions it was quite natural that the Italian government, when the budget deficit increased to 400 millions of lire (16 millions sterling), and made it necessary to find a tax with a broad basis and a rapid effect, should have fallen back on the grist tax.

Nevertheless the chamber of deputies did not immediately accept it, from repugnance to a tax which had been very odious in ancient times, and which could by a very small variation of the tariff be transformed into an instrument of great fiscal pressure.

Sella proposed it, 13th Dec. 1865, and parliament would not even consider his bill. His successor, Scialoja, re-introduced it, 26th January 1866, and the financial committee of the chamber rejected it.

After the war of 1866 Scialoja re-introduced, 16th January 1867, a grist tax, and again was beaten. His successor, Depretis, re-introduced the same bill as Scialoja had done, 11th June 1867. The chamber appointed a special commission of eighteen members to consider the bill, and this commission re-introduced it with modifications 21st April 1868. But the chamber rejected the proposals of its commission, inviting it to study the proposition over again, and a second report was presented 30th May 1868. On the 7th July 1868 the bill passed the chamber and became law 1st January 1869. The system adopted consisted in applying an instrument in the mills which registered the revolutions of the millstone or those of the cylinders and taxed the miller in accordance, giving him the right to charge every customer a fixed rate, according to the weight of the cereals ground, viz. 2 lire for every hundred kilogr. of corn; 1 lira for maize and barley; 1.20 lire for oats and 0.50 for other cereals. As the instruments which ought to have been applied were at first not ready in sufficient number, much arbitrary taxation took place, and provoked riots, in repressing which blood was shed. The tax gave, immediately after the first year, extraordinary results, as the following figures prove:

Year.				Lire.
1869	.	.	.	17,582,410
1870	.	.	.	26,957,284
1871	.	.	.	44,585,709
1872	.	.	.	59,109,999
1873	.	.	.	64,347,323
1874	.	.	.	68,879,570
1875	.	.	.	76,642,310
1876	.	.	.	82,521,093
1878	.	.	.	83,139,767

After 1878 the tax began to be partially reduced. The tax was abolished completely in 1884. The results for the four years after 1878 were:

Year.			Lire.
1879	.	.	. 75,485,305
1880	.	.	. 56,627,279
1881	.	.	. 57,617,701
1882	.	.	. 51,607,695

In 1874, the methods for applying the tax reached their greatest perfection by the invention of a new instrument which weighed the corn which was being ground, instead of counting the revolutions of the millstone.

In 1876, however, a new political party came into power, and sought popularity by reducing the macinato provisionally and voting for its abolition in 1879. The proposal was rejected at the time, but this vote was the primary cause of the financial troubles Italy soon after experienced (see MAGLIANI). The tax was abolished completely in 1884.   M. P.

MACLEAN, J. H., Scotch advocate, was the author of *Remarks on Fiar Prices and Produce Rents*, Edinburgh, 1825, 8vo. By FIARS PRICES are meant, the prices of the various kinds of grain, as determined by juries summoned by the sheriffs for the purpose. The juries, which consist of experts, meet in February and March, and, having examined witnesses and returns of sales, specify in their verdict the average prices of the different descriptions of grain in the county during the preceding year; and the sums, stipulated to be paid in lieu of grain, etc., are determined by the results of their verdicts. They appear to have been struck as early as the end of the 16th or beginning of the 17th century.

[Adam Smith, *Wealth of Nations*, bk. i., ch. xi.—M'Culloch's *Literature of Political Economy*, p. 196.]   H. E. E.

M'LENNAN, JOHN F. (1827-1881) anthropologist, contributed the article on "Law," to the *Encyclopædia Britannica*, 8th ed. In 1865 he published *Primitive Marriage*, wherein the very curious and widespread custom of marriage by capture was first carefully considered. Promiscuity, with complete absence of the sense of kinship, kinship through female only, polyandry with its modifications, leading in turn to kinship through the father;—these, according to M'Lennan, represent the successive stages of social progress. In the course of his argument, he was brought into conflict with the theories of Sir Henry Maine. *The Patriarchal Theory*, edited and completed by his brother, and published in 1885, contains a more detailed criticism of Maine's position. *Studies in Ancient History*, published in 1876, contained a reprint of *Primitive Marriage*, together with other essays.

The most important of the other writings of M'Lennan were articles on Totemism in the *Fortnightly Review*, N.S., vols. vi. and vii. Although the services of M'Lennan as a pioneer have been generally recognised, his conclusions have not, as a rule, found favour with subsequent writers, e.g. Herbert Spencer, *Principles of Sociology*, vol. i. ch. iv.-vi.—C. N. Starcke, *The Primitive Family*, London, 1889, 8vo (International Science Series).—and E. Westermarck, *The History of Human Marriage*, ch. iv.-vi., xiv. and xxii., London, 1891, 8vo. See, however, W. Robertson Smith, *Kinship and Marriage in Early Arabia*, Cambridge, 1885, 8vo, who finds striking confirmation to the general soundness of his construction "in the field of Semitic facts." Sir H. S. Maine, *Early Law and Custom.*—A. Lang, *Custom and Myth*.

[*Dictionary of National Biography*, vol. xxxv. p. 210.]   H. E. E.

MACNAB, HENRY GREY (1762-1823) M.D., social reformer, was a pupil of the philosopher Reid at Glasgow university, where he afterwards held an appointment. In 1786 he published a *Plan of Reform in the mode of Instruction practised in English Schools*, Glasgow, 4to. In *A Letter addressed to John Whitemore, Esq.*, *M.P.*, London, 1801, 4to, on the subject of the London coal supply, he incidentally states that he had lived his whole life in a coal mining country, and had had many opportunities of investing in mining speculations, but had always avoided them on the ground that the average profits did not compensate for the capital required and the attendant risks. At the time of the rupture of the Treaty of Amiens, Macnab, being in France, was detained as a hostage. He was, however, allowed to pursue the practice of medicine and the study of social questions. At the close of the war he preferred to remain in France.

In 1818 he published *Analysis and Analogy recommended as the means of rendering Experience useful in Education*, Paris, 4to, a not very lucid treatise on a difficult subject. Macnab took great interest in the experiments of Robert OWEN (*q.v.*), and in 1819 published *The new views of Mr. Owen impartially examined*, London, 8vo. The sympathy shown by the Duke of Kent to Owen may have been due to the influence of Macnab, who had been appointed the Duke's physician. In his last work *Observations on the Political, Moral, and Religious State of the World*, London, 1820, 4to, he seems, to some extent, to have anticipated the theories of Froebel.

[*Gentleman's Magazine*, 1823, i. p. 378.—Alger's *Englishmen in the French Revolution*, London, 1893.—*Biographie Universelle*, vol. lxxii. *supplément*, p. 654.—*Dictionary of National Biography*, vol. xxxv.] H. E. E.

MACPHERSON, DAVID (1746-1816) historian, was the son of an Edinburgh tailor and clothier. He started in life as a land surveyor. About 1790 he settled in London, and henceforth devoted himself to authorship. Macpherson edited Andrew Wyntoun's *Orygynal Cronykil of Scotland*, 1795, 4to, 2 vols. In 1796 he published *Geographical illustrations of Scottish History*, 4to. His chief work was *Annals of Commerce, fisheries, and navigation*, London, 1805, 4to, 4 vols. The first vol. deals with the earliest accounts, up to the discovery of America, and for this Macpherson is solely responsible. In the second and part of the third volumes, dealing with the period from 1492 to 1760, he merely edits and alters the *History of Commerce* by Adam ANDERSON (*q.v.*). The last volume carries the history down to the meeting of parliament, after the union with Ireland. The book displays much labour and research, and has been generally accepted as a leading authority on the subjects dealt with, especially in the later years chronicled. In 1812 appeared a *History of European Commerce with India*, London, 4to, wherein he opposes the views of Adam Smith on the subject of the East India Company. Macpherson was for some time one of the deputy-keepers of the public records.

[*The Historians of Scotland*, edited by D. Laing, vol. ix. pp. xxxvii.-xlix.—*Dictionary of National Biography*, vol. xxxv. p. 258.] H. E. E.

MACUTA, a native African word, appears to have been originally simply a method of counting in certain parts of West Africa; a macuta being composed of ten units. Montesquieu, *De l'esprit des Lois*, livre xxii. ch. viii., describes the *macute* as "un signe des valeurs sans monnoie; c'est un signe purement idéal." Thence it became a money of account. The Portuguese at Angola adopted it as a denomination in their local coinage, making it equal to 50 reis. The Sierra Leone Company in like manner, from 1791 to 1805, made it the basis of their monetary system, striking a dollar of 10 macutas, equal in weight, but not in fineness, to the Spanish dollar; they also struck a small silver coin to represent the macuta or 10 cents, but these appear to have had but a small circulation.

[Chalmers, *Colonial Currency*, p. 208.] C. A. H.

MADDISON, SIR RALPH (1571?-1655?)

was knighted in 1603 by James I., by whom he was frequently employed in commercial affairs. In 1640 he protested against the proposed debasement of the coinage, and, during the Commonwealth, appears to have held office at the mint.

He was the author of *England's Looking in and out*, London, 1640, 8vo, reprinted in 1641. The second chapter contains a statement of the theory of the BALANCE OF TRADE (*q.v.*). The book was reissued in 1655, under the new title of *Great Britain's Remembrancer, looking in and out*, London, 8vo, with new chapters on the establishment of a bank, a council for the affairs of the mint, and free ports.

[*Dictionary of National Biography*, vol. xxxv. p. 297.] H. E. E.

MADISON, JAMES (1751-1836), the eldest son of a Virginian planter, entered public life in 1776 as a delegate to the Virginia convention, which framed the state constitution. He was a member of the first assembly, and in 1780 was elected delegate to the Continental Congress. In 1787 Madison again became a member of congress, and took a leading part in the Philadelphia Convention of that year, which framed the present American Constitution. He was elected to the new congress in 1789, and continued a member until 1797. From 1801 to 1809, during the two terms of Jefferson's presidency, Madison was secretary of state, and from 1809 to 1817 president. His claim to be the "father of the constitution" is based on the grounds, that the Annapolis Convention of 1786, from which the Philadelphia Convention took its rise, was proposed by him; that the "Virginia plan," out of which the constitution was evolved, was mainly his; and, lastly, that it was owing to him that the Virginia Convention adopted the new constitution. His subsequent public career opens out more controversial matter. By a curious irony of fate, the denouncer of "faction" (see *Federalist*, No. x.) became himself, with more or less reason, counted among the factious.

It is as one of the authors of the *Federalist* that Madison will be best remembered. These papers, written in support of the new constitution in 1787 and 1788, have taken rank among classics. That they should have issued through the medium of newspapers speaks very highly for the intelligence of the public thus addressed. Of the eighty-five papers, fourteen were undoubtedly by Madison, and three others were almost certainly the joint work of him and Hamilton. On the question of the authorship of Nos. xlix., lviii., lxii. and lxiii. there has been much controversy. In forming a judgment, internal evidence does not help, as the style is throughout uniform, grave, sonorous, based it would seem on Addison in his more serious mood. The Nos. xxxvii.-xlviii. contain a masterly general view of the powers conferred by the new constitution.

[*The Federalist*, edited by Henry Cabot Lodge, London, 1888, 8vo, the editions are numerous, but the above is an excellent one, in one volume. —W. C. Rives, *Life and Times of James Madison*, Boston, 1859, 8vo. — Sydney H. Gay, *James Madison* (in American Statesmen Series), Boston, 1889, 8vo.]   H. E. E.

MADOX, THOMAS (1666-1727) studied law and was admitted to the Middle Temple. He was a clerk in the lord treasurer's remembrancer's office, and afterwards in the augmentation office. In 1714 he was appointed historiographer royal. He died without issue at Arlesey in Bedfordshire. In 1702 his *Formulare Anglicanum, or a Collection of Ancient Charters* was published. His most important work, *The History and Antiquities of the Exchequer of the Kings of England to the end of the Reign of Edward the Second*, appeared in 1711 (2nd edition, 1769). He says that it is not only a history of the exchequer, "but likewise an apparatus towards a history of the ancient law of England." This was followed by his *Firma Burgi, or an Historical Essay concerning the Cities, Towns, and Buroughs of England*, 1726 ; and *Baronia Anglica*, 1736 (reissued in 1741). He also intended to write a feudal history of England. The materials collected by him for the works which he prepared for publication, and for others which he projected, are now in the British Museum, comprising ninety-four volumes of notes and transcripts. Madox had a high conception of his duty as an historian. He says that "writing of history is in some sort a religious act, and ought to be undertaken with purity and rectitude of mind." He is generally cautious in his statements, and always tries to confirm them "by proper vouchers." His vouchers are copious extracts from the pipe rolls, the memoranda of the exchequer, and from other ancient records. "The public records," he says, "are the foundation (*sic*) which sustain the whole fabrick of this history [of the exchequer], a foundation solid and unshaken." This foundation was laid so broad and strong in both the *History of the Exchequer* and the *Firma Burgi* that they will long continue to be of great value to students of economic, legal, and constitutional history.

                                                        C. Gr.

MAFFEI, SCIPIONE (1675-1755). Was born in Verona and studied literature. He fought in the Bavarian army at the battle of Donawerth. In 1710, he, with the assistance of others, started the *Giornale dei letterati*. He travelled a great deal in Europe.

In his work, *Dell' impiego del danaro* (3 vols., Verona, 1774), he deals in a striking manner, though without much novelty in argument, with the question of interest, and endeavours to reconcile the church doctrine hostile to usury with the varying requirements of commerce, maintaining that to receive compensation for the loan of money is opposed neither to morality nor to the Gospel. This book of Maffei's aroused against its author much angry feeling and recrimination. It pro-

voked the censure of Ballerini and Concina, and drew from Benedict XIV. the encyclical letter "Vix pervenit" (1745). Ultimately it caused the author's banishment by the Venetian government.

[G. Maffei, *Storia della letteratura italiana*, Milan, 1834.—Giuliari, *Bibliografia Maffeiana*, in the *Propugnatore*, vol. xviii., Bologna, 1885.— Cossa, *Introduction to the Study of Political Economy*, London, 1893.]   U. R.

MAGENS or MAGEN, called by Adam Smith MEGGENS, by Steuart, MEGENS, and in *Dictionnaire de l'économie politique*, Paris, 1853, MAGENDS, Nicholas (d. 1764), a German merchant, was for many years resident in England, and gained a great reputation in commercial matters.

He was the author of the *Universal Merchant*, London, 1753, and its *Postscript*, 1756, which were translated by W. HORSLEY (*q.v.*). The titles of later German editions are given in C. J. Kayser's *Index Locupletissimus librorum*, Leipzig, 1834, etc., 4to, 4th part, as *Der allgem. Kaufmann Worinnen das Theoretische u. Praktische der Handlung enthalten ist*, Berlin, 1762, 4to, and *Beitrag zu allgem. Kaufmann od. Traktat von d. Handlung u. d. Vortheilen die aus d. Reduction des Geld-Interesse entspringen, nebst einen Traktat wider den Wucher: aus d. Engl. übers u., als ein 2 theil des allgem. Kaufmann zu gebrauchen*, Potsdam, 1763 - 64. The author, after a general treatise on trade and on wealth, by which is meant not merely gold and silver, the common medium of trade, but a preeminence of industry, manufactures, and commerce, enters into an enquiry concerning bullion, after which he considers the nature, operation, and effects of banks in general and in particular. The treatise concludes with "a further illustration of the business of exchange from the tables of Sir Isaac Newton, with remarks and additions."

In the British Museum Catalogue the only works under the name of Magens are *Versuch über Assecuranzen, Havereyen und Bodmereyen insgemein*, etc., Hamburg, 1753, 4to, and a translation, *Essay on Insurances, to which are annexed some brief hints to Merchants and Insurers concerning risks to which navigation is exposed in time of War*, etc., London, 1755, 4to. The author gives as his reason for publishing, the want of any treatise in English on maritime and mercantile insurance. The translation is so much increased and amended as to make a new work. It is chiefly devoted to foreign views. "Those persons advance too much who insist that all insurances made in Great Britain on the shipping and products of foreign countries are beneficial to this nation" (Pref., p. 5). After introductory remarks on insurance, general averages, etc., the rest of the first volume is devoted to leading cases. The second volume is taken up with a collection of ordinances and laws of various dates.

[*An Inquiry into the Principles of Political Economy*, vol. 2, pp. 158-9 by Sir James Steuart, London, 1767, 4to.—*Quarterly Journal of Economics*, vol. 5, p. 356.—*Gentlemen's Magazine*, vol. xxxiv.]   H. E. E.

MAGLIANI, AGOSTINO (1825-1891). An Italian economist and financier ; born in Saurino, in the Neapolitan provinces. He studied law. Originally an official under the Neapolitan government, which he defended in a pamphlet published in 1857, he entered, after 1860, the service of the kingdom of Italy. In a short time he was appointed senator, and then a councillor of the court of cassation. He was minister of finance of the kingdom of Italy three times, and on the last occasion he held this post for ten consecutive years, 1879-1889.

Magliani wrote with ability, and in a bright and elegant style, on economical and financial matters, and was also an impressive parliamentary orator, well acquainted with the theory of finance, and a most able financier in practice. His most important measures were the abolition of the forced currency (1883), and of the duties on the grinding of cereals (1884) (see MACINATO), and the law effecting the organisation and readjustment of the land-tax (1886).

He was a powerful financier, of great breadth of view, confident in the future of his country. The time has perhaps not yet come for judging the full effects of his work ; but this has left deep traces on Italian finance and the economic condition of the country.

Magliani won much praise, but he incurred also, more especially in his latter years, bitter reproaches for the weakness by which he first countenanced lavish expenditure and then wasted the resources of his financial capacity in devising temporary remedies, and the system of finance under which Italy still trembles on the verge of disaster.

Amongst Magliani's economical and financial works may be noted :

La quistione monetaria, 1874. Numerous articles in the *Nuova Antologia*, Rome, amongst them ; *Sistemazione delle imposte dirette.—L' azione economica dello stato.—La Finanza e la libertà politica.—Le imposte locali ed i comuni.*

Amongst his numerous financial speeches published in the Italian parliamentary records, we cite as the most important :

Abolizione graduale della tassa sulla macinazione del grano (The Gradual Abolition of Duty on the Grinding of Grain) (in the senate, 1880).— *Sul provvedimenti finanziarii* (in the chamber of deputies, 1882), and the financial statements made in the chamber in 1882, 1888, etc.   U. R.

MAITLAND, JAMES. See LAUDERDALE, EIGHTH EARL OF.

MAIZIÈRES, PHILIPPE DE, also MEZIÈRES (1312-1405), a French knight who was sometime chancellor of Lusignan, the French king of Cyprus, and made war against the Saracens. About 1370 he entered the service of king Charles V. of France, and was some years in charge of the education of the dauphin, the future Charles VI.

Maizières retired in 1379 to a convent in Paris, where he wrote his *Songe adressant au Blanc Faucon à Bec et Pieds Dorés*, 1389, the White Falcon being in fact the king of France in person. The author in the capacity of a pilgrim (the book is sometimes called the *Songe du Pèlerin*), leads *Vérité* through the countries he had himself visited in his travels, and points out the abuses and disorders he has noticed and the remedies which he suggests. One of the grievances is usury as practised by the Jews, and the remedial scheme of Maizières may be shortly summarised as follows : The king ought to constitute an initial fund derived from the proceeds of aids (taxes) and domains, and entrusted to the management of honest and pious men, who were to lend these monies to the poor people of each diocese or manor, *châtellenie*, on good security or pledge, "namely, which is to be worth more than the money they have received." At the end of the year, the debtors would "repurchase," without usury, the objects given in pawn, but in token of gratitude they would offer "freely" a tithe or one-tenth, to be converted to the increase of the sum originally given by the king. Still Maizières appears to have been suspicious about the punctual payment of these free offerings, for he elsewhere advises the States General, "in order to lay down all scruples, to determine, by mutual agreement with the Church, the amount of the alms to be offered to God, this agreement to be published as a law or good custom approved by the *Cour Royale*." In Maizières' plan we meet all the features of the charitable *Montes Pietatis* (see MONTS DE PIÉTÉ), which were first founded in Italy about eighty years later, and were then under the influence of the Franciscans imitated from the Italian state *montes*, whose object had been purely financial.

[Professor Victor Brants, *Philippe de Maizières et son projet de Banque Populaire* (a short tract of 16 pages, Louvain, 1880), and the same writer's *Théories Économiques aux XIIIᵉ et XIVᵉ Siècles* (pp. 159-162), Louvain, 1895.]
E. Ca.

MAJESTAS. The *crimen majestatis*, or *læsœ majestatis*, is the *crimen* of treason, *i.e.* the charge or the crime of injuring, or attempting to injure, in various ways, the sovereign power and greatness (*majestas*) of the Roman people, or of its representative, the emperor. (See Smith's *Dict. of Antiquities, s.v.*).   E. A. W.

MAJOR, JOHN (?1469-?1549), was one of the most distinguished of the later schoolmen, and a leader of the nominalist party. A Scot by birth, he became famous as a professor of theology at Paris, and then spent the last eighteen years of his life as provost of the college of St. Salvator at St. Andrews. In his *Commentaries on the Sentences*, published about 1516, he touched current economic discussion in several points. His opinion that a community might properly restrain the liberty of public begging was of great assistance to those in Catholic countries who sought to introduce reforms in the relief of the poor. On the other hand, his opinion that the "triple contract," *contractus trinus*, defended by ECK (*q.v.*), was not usurious, was overborne for the time by the Catholic counter-reformation.

[CANON LAW. See for estimates of Major's position as a theologian, T. G. Law in *The Scottish Review*, April 1892 ; and the *Life* prefixed to Major's *History of Greater Britain* (Scottish Hist. Soc., 1892), by H. T. W. Mackay. For his economic opinions, see Ashley, *Econ. Hist.*, i. pt. ii. pp. 340-341, 443-446.]   W. J. A.

MAJORAT, the French and German term (in Spanish *Mayorazgo*) for an entailed real estate annexed to a title of nobility and descending by right of PRIMOGENITURE (*major natu*). Abolished in France at the time of the French Revolution, majorats were re-established in 1806 by Napoleon under two forms : the *majorat de propre mouvement* founded by the head of the state with a grant of real estate as a reward for distinguished services, and the *majorat sur demande*, by which heads of families were legally authorised to settle thus their previously acquired real property. After the Bourbon Restoration none but owners of *majorats* could be summoned to the House of Peers. After 1830, when the peerage ceased to be hereditary, the creation of new *majorats* was prohibited, and the existing *majorats sur demande* were restricted to two *degrees* or lives. Since 1848, the whole subject is controlled by articles 896 and 1048 of the *Code Civil ;* these enact that *substitutions,*—entails of property,— either real or personal, are only valid for one life, and in favour of grandchildren, or of children of the brothers and sisters of the Donor ; with the further limitations that this concession only applies to such portion of his property as the testator, if he has children, is allowed to bequeath (see BEQUEST, POWER OF). In Germany, the foundation of *majorates* is still allowed by law and such entailed property is included under the general judicial name of *Familienfideicommisse*. Personal as well as real property may be settled thus, but generally only when the value exceeds a minimum which varies in each particular state. In Prussia a settlement of personal property cannot be less than a money capital of 30,000 marks (say £1500), and a real estate thus disposed of must at least yield a net income of 7500 marks or £375. In other respects, the conditions required also vary between one state and another ; for instance in Prussia the real estates must be rural estates, *Landgüter*, houses being excluded. The general principle is that the settled estate must be important enough to uphold the prosperity of the family, which consequently is endowed by law with a permanent right of control.

In the eastern provinces of Prussia 1975 estates covering 1,408,860 hectares (3,522,150 acres), of land, or 6·20 per cent of the whole territorial area are thus owned mostly by princely and noble families. This proportion of the total territory is larger than it is in Cis-Leithan Austria, where it only reaches 4·1 per cent, covering 880 estates. This description of limited ownership is, in fact, only met with in the districts where feudal influences and traditions have maintained their former ascendency. Of the above-mentioned East Prussian estates 197, or 92 per cent, have an area larger than 1000 hectares (2500 acres). More than 300 estates have been settled thus since the end of the first half of the present century ; however, it ought not to be forgotten that the larger portion of *Familienfideicommisse* (see FIDEICOMMISSUM) established during this century were formerly held by feudal tenures, which have disappeared. Of the estates larger in extent than 1000 hectares (2500 acres), 43·4 per cent are farmed, 34·2 managed by stewards and only 22·4 *administrirt*, *i.e.* personally managed, by the holder himself.

This survival of aristocratic tenure of land is not always considered as invariably advantageous, and fears have often been expressed that it may lead to an excessive concentration of landed property in the hands of a few families, and, when the owner for the time being is heavily in debt, to an inferior system of cultivation. It is also pointed out that this concentration leading to the extension of the LATIFUNDIUM (*q.v.*) is especially to be deprecated in a country where the population is rapidly increasing, and where an increasing proportion of the inhabitants may thus be cut off from the possession of land.

To conclude, the German *Anerbe* and *Hofrecht* in its modern form, to a certain extent founded on the same principle as the American HOMESTEAD AND EXEMPTION LAWS, is intended to protect small peasant ownership against the risk of division, but it is not enacted that the *Hof*, the family dwelling *with* land, shall be inherited by the eldest heir. In some districts it is transmitted by MINORAT, in others recourse is had to ballot or even to drawing by lot, whenever the owner has not exercised his right to appoint the heir expectant among his natural and legal heirs. The former has always to indemnify the latter to the amount of their shares of the inherited privileged property.

[See *Majorat* in Holtzendorff, *Encyclopædie des Rechts* (Leipzig, 1870), and *Fideicommisse* in Conrad's *Handwörterbuch der Staatswissenschaften.*]   E. CA.

MAKER (of Promissory Note). A promissory note is a signed unconditional promise in writing to pay a certain sum to, or to the order of, a specified person, or to bearer. The person who makes the promise is called the maker of the note. Sometimes he is spoken of as the "drawer," but he must be distinguished from the drawer of a bill of exchange. The drawer of a bill is only liable if the drawee or acceptor dishonours it. The position of the maker of a note is analogous to that of the acceptor of a bill. He is the principal debtor on the instrument. He undertakes "to pay it according to its tenour," and is "precluded from denying to a holder in due course the existence of the payee and his then capacity to indorse."

[Bills of Exchange Act, 1882, §§ 88, 89.]   M. D. C.

MAKING-UP (on the stock exchange). Twice every month a general settlement takes place in the stock exchange, when accounts are made up in all stocks and shares other than those in the consols department, in which the settlement takes place only once a month. A settlement is prolonged over three days. On the first day attention is given to the making-up of accounts. For speculators, this is a very important matter. It is then that they discover the exact amount of "differences," to be paid or received, on running accounts. A speculator has, say, an account open for the rise in a certain stock which he has bought at 80; the stock, at the time of making-up, is 81, and the gross difference due to him is 1 per cent of the amount bought. The real difference is less by the broker's charges. If the stock has fallen to 79, he has to pay a difference of 1 per cent in addition to the broker's charges. On the making-up day, accounts are also carried over, if it be found possible to renew bargains, till the succeeding settlement, when a Contango or a BACKWARDATION (*q.v.*) is charged for the accommodation. Speculators inquire keenly about the state of markets on making-up day, indications being obtainable of the extent and strength or weakness of the speculative account open. As a rule, but not invariably, the account is unwieldy when the contangoes are high, and strong when those charges are low.   A. E.

MALA FIDES. See FIDES, BONA, MALA.

MALATOLTA, MALETOUTE, MALTOLTE. The origin of CUSTOMS DUTIES (*q.v.*) in England is wrapped in great obscurity. Probably they arose from an early royal right of PRISAGE and PRE-EMPTION, which developed into PURVEYANCE in the case of domestic produce, and into customs in the case of exports and imports. Originally the charges at the ports were arbitrary and uncertain, but they were gradually limited and fixed by custom. Any charge over and above the customary dues was called *mala tolta*, or evil tax. Thus in art. 41 of *Magna Carta*, merchants are granted freedom to enter and quit the kingdom *sine omnibus malis toltis*. In 1275 the first parliamentary grant of customs is made to the crown, namely half a mark on the sack of wool and on three hundred wool fells, and a mark on the last of leather, and these export duties came to be known as the *magna sive antiqua custuma*. From this time the word maltolte acquires a definite and technical meaning, viz. an additional charge of forty shillings on the sack of wool levied by the arbitrary authority of the king. In this sense it is expressly prohibited in clause vii. of the new articles added to the charter in the great confirmation of 1297. From this time any exceptional charge upon wool, over and above the recognised customs, can only be made by authority of parliament: in other words the *mala tolta* becomes the SUBSIDY (*q.v.*).

[Stubbs, *Select Charters.*—Hall, *The Customs-Revenue of England.*]   R. L.

MALCHUS, KARL AUGUST VON (1770-1840), was minister of the kingdom of Westphalia in the times of Napoleon, and later on minister of finance of the kingdom of Wurtemberg.

He wrote, besides minor works, the *Organismus der Behörden* (organisation of state officials), 1821; the *Politik der inneren Staatsverwaltung* (Policy of the interior administration of the State), 1823; a *Statistik und Staaten Kunde* (The science of Descriptive Statistics), 1826, and his *Handbuch der Finanzwissenschaft und Finanzverwaltung* (Handbook of the science and administration of Finance) 1830, the latter dedicated to the King of Prussia. Roscher considers him as having been a trustworthy official, but deficient in systematisation, range of ideas, and historical knowledge, still trustworthy for information on contemporary institutions and statistics (*Gesch. der Nat. Oek. in Deutschland*, pp. 741-749). He also published in 1838 a survey of the regulations adopted by saving banks throughout Europe, *Die Sparkassen in Europa.*   E. Ca.

MALEBRANCHE, NICOLAS (1638-1715), a priest of the Roman Catholic church, and a member of the oratory at Paris, was one of the ablest of the followers of Des Cartes, while his ascetic training held him back from being an absolute adherent of his philosophy. Though not himself a direct contributor to economic theory, Malebranche is of interest to the students of economics; his works form a good example of the influence which those whose philosophic thought is deep, but general, may exercise over that special study; he is considered to have inspired QUESNAY and his pupil (Victor) MIRABEAU with their ultimate postulate of an order of nature, as "the principle and basis of natural rights and natural law" (Mirabeau, *loc. cit. infra*). Quesnay devoted himself during his youth to the study of Malebranche's writings, and Mirabeau quotes the whole of the second chapter of the *Traité de Morale* in the preface to the *Philosophie rurale* (1763), as giving an ideal exposition of "order" as "the central and rallying point of true wisdom." It should be noted, however, that whereas by "order," Mirabeau means the course of "the physical laws of nature," observation of, and obedience to, which is man's "sole and worthy guide"; and apart from which he only "begets abstract and general ideas, and is lost in the crowd of the phantoms of his imagination," he would, had he studied the first chapter, have seen that a recluse like Malebranche virtually took the opposite view. The latter distinguishes "order" from "nature," calling it "l'ordre immuable," knowable only to reason, its subjective counterpart, when sense and imagination are shut out; and to follow which alone is virtue, while to follow nature is sometimes to "wound order." He rejects the stoic identification of following God with following nature, and merely allows, that, "although the order of nature is not precisely our law, and submission to it is in no way a virtue, it must be observed that one has often to take account of it," *i.e.* when "the immutable order" requires it. Malebranche's order is not the moral order, if positive morality be meant. "Morality changes according to countries and times." It was rather an ideal order, or order of "abstract ethics," viewed as part of the divine plan of the universe, in which spirit was considered almost to the exclusion of anything so transient and uninteresting as matter.

[*Traité de Morale* (1684, 1697, 1707), ed. H. Joly, Paris, 1882.—Cossa, *Introd. to the Study of Political Economy*, London, 1893, p. 266.—Mirabeau, V., *Philosophie rurale*, Paris, 1763.—*Nouv. Dict. de l'Economie politique*, art. "Quesnay." —Bonar, *Philosophy and Pol. Econ.*, 1893, p. 145. See especially Hasbach *On Malebranche's Influence on Quesnay and the Physiocrats.*]   C. A. F.

MALESHERBES, Chrétien Guillaume de Lamoignon de (1721-1794), was, under Louis XV., president of the court of Aids and director of the *Librairie* (office of the Censorship, and for licensing the printing of books), evinced a most liberal spirit in these functions, and was exiled from Paris when, in the last years of this reign, the courts of justice were dissolved by authority of the king. Under Louis XVI., Malesherbes was recalled, made a minister at the same time as his friend Turgot (*q.v.*), 1774, and again in 1787; he defended the king during his trial before the national convention. He perished on the scaffold.

Malesherbes, who was a member both of the Paris academy of sciences and of the French academy, has written a great number of memorials and notices on various subjects; only a few of these have been printed. The following should be noticed here: The *Mémoire sur les Moyens d'accélérer l'Économie Rurale en France*, 1790— read before the Royal Society of Agriculture; it insists that the society should establish branches in the provincial towns, so as to be a board of correspondence and of diffusion of useful theoretical and experimental knowledge both for scientific men and resident professional agriculturists—and the *Idées d'un Agriculteur patriote sur le défrichement des terres incultes*, 1791. Waste lands are generally dry and meagre; to bring them under cultivation requires either heavy investments of money, which capitalists are unwilling to supply, or a very strict economy in their working which can only be expected if the labourer himself works for his own profit. The best solution of the problem would be to let such lands to tenants according to the system of *Domaine congéable* (see Land Tenures) used in Brittany.
        E. Ca.

MALESTROIT, Seigneur de—(second half of 16th century) member of the royal council of France, and comptroller of the mint (*du fait des monnoies*), was the author of *Les Paradoxes sur le fait des Monnoies* (Paris, 1566).

Malestroit would be quite forgotten if his book had not called forth the celebrated *Réponse* and

Discours . . . pour réponse aux paradoxes du sieur de Malestroit, by Bodin (*q.v.*). Malestroit maintained that prices had not risen in France for three centuries, goods being always exchanged for the same quantities of gold or silver, the standard of the coins having been lowered in the same proportion as the prices had *apparently* risen. "The metals being the true and just criteria of the high or low prices of things," this lowering would have been harmless for the subjects of the French monarchy if their rebellious temper had not led them to refuse the coins at the value imposed by the lawful will of the sovereign. In fact, Malestroit adheres to the doctrine of some Canonists respecting *valor impositus* and *valor extrinsecus*, and considers coins as purely representative signs of value, destitute of any intrinsic value of their own (see Canon Law).

[Baudrillart, *Jean Bodin et son temps*, 1853, pp. 168-169; see also Malynes.]   E. Ca.

MALLET, Jean-Roland (d. 1736), head of the finance department of Louis XIV., under the controller-general Desmarets, by whose orders he wrote :—

Comptes rendus de l'administration des finances du royaume de France pendant les onze dernières années du règne de Henri IV., le règne de Louis XIII., et soixante-cinq années du règne de Louis XIV., avec des recherches sur l'origine des impôts sur les revenus et dépenses de nos rois, depuis Philippe le Bel jusqu'à Louis XIV., et différents mémoires sur le numéraire et sa valeur sous les trois règnes ci-dessus. Paris, 1720. Reprinted by Necker with pref. and introd., 1789.   A. L.

MALLET, Sir Louis (1823-90), grandson of Mallet du Pan, and son of John Lewis Mallet, who was placed by Pitt in the audit office about 1800, entered the same office in 1839, and in 1847 the board of trade. In 1860 he was appointed an assistant commissioner for drawing up the tariff under the treaty of commerce with France. He was made a member of the council of India in 1872. In 1875 he became permanent under secretary of state for India and had a leading share in the reconstruction of the customs tariff. He was a bimetallist.

His articles and pamphlets were collected by his son and published in one vol., *Free Exchange* (1891), which represents a complete statement of the Cobden principles.   H. R. T.

MALLET DU PAN, Jacques (1749-1800), born near Geneva, died in England, collaborated with Linguet in his *Annales*, to which he published a supplementary series *Mémoires historiques, politiques et littéraires* (1779-82). He went to Paris in 1784 and contributed to the *Mercure de France*, in which his account of the debates of the assembly in the early revolutionary period is very valuable. He also edited *Journal historique et politique de Genève* (Paris, 1784-88). He came to England in 1798, where he made many friends and founded the *Mercure Britannique* (1798-1800).

Besides some economic contributions to the above-mentioned periodicals, Mallet du Pan added notes to the translation from the English of *Remarques sur le tarif du Traité de commerce conclu entre la France et l'Angleterre* (Paris, 1788, 8vo).

H. R. T.

MALLET, P. H. (1730-1807), a professor at Geneva, wrote *De la ligue Hanséatique*, Genève, 1805, 8vo., which only claims to be a résumé and not a history.

H. E. E.

MALON, BENOÎT (1841-1893). Born in a village of central France, he made his way to Paris as a workman, and from 1866, the year of his affiliation to the INTERNATIONAL, took an active part in most of the strikes and republican manifestations during the later years of the empire. A member of the COMMUNE (*q.v.*) of Paris, 1871, Malon escaped after its suppression, to Geneva, and studied the works of the leading sociologists and economists. Of these, J. Stuart Mill appears to have been his favourite author. He then began to write on social subjects ; in this he was indefatigable ; and, returning to France, founded the *Revue Socialiste*, of which he was editor. This publication is the organ of the so-called French scientific socialists.

As stated in his last book *Le Socialisme Intégral* (1892), Malon's views may be summarised as follows. He agreed with MARX that the working class is at the present time the victim of a financial and industrial capitalism, founded through an abuse in the appropriation of part of the produce of labour. He demurs to Marx's statement that in its course the whole history of mankind has always been determined by purely economic and materialistic causes ; he asserts that idealistic motives have also often inspired great historical movements. Consequently for him, socialistic reforms, to be complete, must be "integral," in other words give satisfaction to "all the sentimental and moral forces which reside in the human soul." His ultimate aim is the socialisation of all the agents of production. This would produce a state of social organisation where "the means of production will be in common, the produce distributed according to justice, and consumption remain free." Deprecating violence, Malon urges as a transitional measure the immediate resumption by the state of banks, railways, mines, and quarries, and the municipalisation of gas and water companies, tramways, and even cabs, as well as the foundation of a ministry of labour and an eight hours bill. For a self-taught man, the extent of Malon's reading was really considerable, though his inquiries into the conditions of life during the middle ages strike the reader by want of insight. This is no doubt due to his passionate antagonism to the Church.

Besides the *Socialisme Intégral*, Malon published *l'Internationale, son histoire et ses principes* (1872).—*Spartacus* (1873).—*l'Histoire critique de l'Économie Politique* (1876).—*l'Histoire du Socialisme* (5 vols. 1882-85)—a French translation of Lassalle's *Arbeit und Capital*, and of Schaeffle's *Quintessenz des Socialismus*, and contributed numberless articles to socialistic reviews and newspapers.

E. Ca.

MALOUET, PIERRE-VICTOR, Baron (1740-1814), was a distinguished naval and colonial administrator, the minister and friend of Louis XVI. In 1763 he entered the Admiralty, and was sent to Rochefort, where he superintended the embarkation of the expedition for colonising Guiana. He was sub-commissioner and intendant at San Domingo from 1767 to 1774, and it was here that he prepared the materials for his subsequent work on colonial administration. He came under the notice of M. de Sartines, who entrusted him with the examination of the projects submitted for the colonisation of Guiana. Malouet, now naval commissary-general, obtained the adoption of his own views, and was sent to Cayenne charged with their execution. In 1779 he was recalled, but his schemes were carried out by the engineer Guisan, to whom he had explained them.

In 1780, after negotiating a loan of £6,000,000 from the Genoese, he was appointed naval intendant at Toulon ; an office he retained for eight years. In 1789 he was elected deputy for Riom. He continued to be a firm adherent of the Bourbon cause, and an admirer of the British constitution. In 1792 he was obliged to seek refuge in England. In 1801 his advice was courted as to the best way of reorganising the French navy. He was appointed naval commissary-general, and in 1803 was sent to superintend the new arsenal at Antwerp. Here he remained for six years, directing the immense naval undertakings and co-operating in the measures which obliged the English to withdraw from Walcheren. In 1810 he was nominated counsellor of state, but in 1812 his independent expression of opinion caused him to be exiled from Paris. In 1814 he was once more entrusted with the administration of the navy, but he died before he could complete the work.

Malouet wrote :—*Mémoire sur l'esclavage des nègres*, Paris et Neufchâtel, 1788, 8vo.—*Lettres à ses commettants*, 1789, 8vo.—*Mémoires sur l'administration de la marine et des colonies*, 1789, 8vo.—*Opinion sur les mesures proposées par MM. de Mirabeau et de Lameth, relativement à la sûreté intérieure et extérieure du royaume*, 1789, 8vo.—*Collection de ses opinions à l'assemblée nationale*, Paris, 1791-92, 3 vols. 8vo.—*Défense de Louis XVI.*, 1792, 8vo.—*Examen de cette question : Quel sera pour les colonies de l'Amérique le resultat de la révolution française, de la guerre qui en est la suite, et de la paix qui doit la terminer?* Paris, 2nd ed., 1796, 8vo (1st ed., London).—*Lettre à un membre du parlement sur l'intérêt de l'Europe au salut des colonies de l'Amérique*, 1797, 8vo.—*Collection de mémoires et correspondances officielles sur l'administration des colonies et notamment sur la Guiane française et hollandaise*, Paris, an X. (1802), 5 vol. 8vo, avec cartes et plans.—*Considérations historiques sur l'empire de l'armée chez les anciens et les modernes*, Anvers, 1810, 8vo.

A. L.

MALT SILVER is defined by Jacob under the name of *malt-scot* as money paid for making malt. *Scot* is **A.S.** *sceat*=money. In the custumal of Meopham, Kent, it occurs in the form of *malt-gavel*, and in the rental of Eastry in the same county as *malt-rent* and *malt-penny*. Those who owed service to the lord of the manor were obliged to use the village mill or pay a fine. Prof. Thorold Rogers, in *Agriculture and Prices in England*, gives the prices paid for the manorial service of making malt for several years between 1270 and 1400, chiefly from the south-eastern counties. These prices vary from 1d. a quarter in 1270 to 6d. in 1361, and 2d. in 1380. The mill being the franchise of the lord, he paid no fixed price for the service, and hence the variation in payments. Malt silver, which is money paid by, not to, the tenant, if connected with this service of making malt, means the fine paid to the lord for exemption therefrom. The word silver, however, in compound words has generally the meaning of toll, and malt silver or scot was more probably the fine paid by tenants for liberty to make their own malt.

[Jacob's *Law Dictionary.* — Somner, W., *Treatise of Gavelkind* (1660).—Thorold Rogers, *The History of Agriculture and Prices in England*, i. ii. (1866).]   M. T. M.

MALT TAX. See Taxation.

MALTHUS, Thomas Robert (1766-1834). The name appears variously in parochial registers, but the form Malthus is as old as the 15th century, and the two branches of the family, the Yorkshire and the Berkshire, can be traced from that date. The economist belongs to the Berkshire branch, to which also most probably belonged Francis Malthus, the author of a book in French and in English on *Military Fireworks* (1629, etc.), and Thomas, the publisher and printer (end of 17th century). The great-grandfather of the economist was Daniel Malthus, Queen Anne's apothecary, and the friend of Sydenham the physician, after whom he named his only son Sydenham. The son of Sydenham Malthus, Daniel, father of the economist, was a man of considerable attainments. He corresponded with Voltaire, and was the literary executor of Rousseau. On his little estate, the Rookery, near Dorking in Surrey, his second son, Thomas Robert, was born. Thomas Robert was educated first under the Rev. Richard Graves at Claverton, near Bath, and then under Gilbert Wakefield in his private school at Nottingham. In 1785 he went to Jesus College, Cambridge, where he took his degree (B.A.), and was ninth wrangler, in 1788. He became fellow of his college in 1797. In all his early life Malthus was brought into close contact with the supporters of radical not to say revolutionary views; and his father was a zealous partisan of the new doctrines. Yet the son, when he first thought of authorship in 1797, and wrote the *Crisis*, a political pamphlet never published, was a cautious and

moderate whig, as he remained all his life. He took orders and a curacy at Albury, whither his father had removed in 1787. Godwin's *Enquirer* (1797) was naturally a topic of conversation between father and son ; their discussion "started a general question of the future improvement of society ; and the author at first sat down with an intention of merely stating his thoughts to his friend, upon paper, in a clearer manner than he thought he could do in conversation. But, as the subject opened upon him, some ideas occurred which he did not recollect to have met with before " (Preface to Essay, 1798), and he accordingly wrote and published a book called *An Essay on the Principle of Population as it affects the Future Improvement of Society, with remarks on the Speculations of Mr. Godwin, M. Condorcet, and other Writers.*

In his preface (dated 7th June 1798) the then anonymous author says he has " read some of the speculations on the future improvement of society in a temper very different from a wish to find them visionary," but he sees "great and unconquerable difficulties " in the way of human improvement (p. 7). The power of population is indefinitely greater than the power in the earth to produce subsistence for man (p. 13). This proposition depends on the two "postulata" : i. "That food is necessary to the existence of man ; ii. that the passion between the sexes is necessary, and will remain nearly in its present state" (p. 11). "Population, when unchecked, increases in a geometrical ratio. Subsistence increases only in an arithmetical ratio " (p. 14) ; but, "by that law of our nature which makes food necessary, the effects of those two unequal powers must be kept equal" (p. 14). Writers like Adam Smith, Hume, and especially Wallace (p. 8), have seen this before ; but they have not shown the way in which the levelling must take place. There is a constant check on population from the difficulty of subsistence. It is no difficulty peculiar to man. The race of plants and the race of animals experience it ; nature scatters the seeds of life profusely, but is sparing in the nourishment necessary for the rearing of them ; the results are waste of seed, sickness, and premature death. Among mankind the effects are misery and vice—the former certain, the latter probable (pp. 15, 16). In no place and at no time "has the power of population been left to exert itself with perfect freedom " (p. 19). The manners have never been so pure and simple or the food so abundant that no check has existed to early marriages "among the lower classes from a fear of not providing well for their families, or among the higher classes from a fear of lowering their condition in life" (pp. 18, 19). Yet in all societies the instinct is so strong that there is "a constant effort towards an increase of population. This effort as constantly tends to subject the lower classes of society to distress, and to prevent any great permanent amelioration of their condition" (p. 29). It results in oscillations between comparative comfort and distress—the distress caused by the increase of population due to previous comfort, and the comfort caused by the thinning down of the previous excess of population (pp. 29-31). This phenomenon is veiled by the difference between nominal and real wages, and it is subject to many other "interrupting causes" in modern times. But the general principles remain true of all states of mankind, the savage and barbarian (ch. iii.), and the European (ch. iv.), including England. Where the positive check, repressing an increase already begun, is not traceable (p. 71), there is the preventive, which "operates in some degree through all the ranks of society in England" (p. 63). Even the lowest classes have a love of independence and fear of letting their families sink in the scale of comfort. "The parish law of England, it must be confessed, is a system of all others the most calculated gradually to weaken this sentiment" (p. 68). The poor laws "tend to depress the general condition of the poor"—(1st) by tending to increase population without increasing food; (2nd) by diminishing the share of the industrious (pp. 83, 84). They have contributed to raise the price of provisions, and lower the real price of labour (p. 86). Mr. Pitt's Poor Bill (then under discussion, 1797-98) has the defect mentioned ; it tends to increase population without increasing the food (p. 94; cp. p. 134).

That these checks are the true causes of the slow increase of population in Europe is shown, Malthus thinks, by the comparatively rapid increase that follows the removal of them. In a new colony, as in America, there is much room and food, and the "knowledge and industry of an old state operate on the fertile unappropriated land of a new one" (p. 137). "Throughout all the northern colonies the population was found to double itself in twenty-five years" (p. 105), in some even in fifteen (p. 106), while the settlements first colonised increased slowly or came to a standstill (p. 107). WALLACE and CONDORCET are both wrong in supposing that the difficulty of an "overcharged population" can only occur in a very remote future (p. 142 seq.). It has always been felt, and is felt now (cp. p. 153). Condorcet's plan for providing every one with a comfortable provision for a family would only lead to a greater increase of population (p. 150). Condorcet's idea of the "organic perfectibility" of the race, including the indefinite lengthening of life, is not founded on scientific argument, that is to say, on observed facts (pp. 157, 158). By attention to breed, and condemning all the bad specimens to celibacy, no doubt "a certain

degree of improvement similar to that among animals might take place among men" (p. 170). Otherwise the increase in longevity would only give greater weight to the "argument of population" (p. 171). GODWIN's system of equality, to be produced by reason and conviction, "wears much more the promise of permanence than any change effected and maintained by force" (p. 174). But Godwin dreams that all can live in the midst of plenty and share alike in the bounties of nature (p. 178), all causes of misery and vice being removed, reason governing instead of passion (p. 180 seq.), useless luxuries being abandoned unanimously, and "the spirit of benevolence, guided by impartial justice, dividing the produce among all the members of the society according to their wants" (p. 182). Such a society would tend even more than a new colony to favour population, especially as Godwin would abolish the form of marriage ; and, in spite of the increased production due to a better distribution of property, there would be such a growth of numbers that the new equality would disappear, and the old struggle, as well as the old inequality, would come back (pp. 180-190, cp. pp. 194-198). A cause of distress is at work here which cannot be traced to human institutions, but is due to human nature itself (p. 191); and Godwin's "society without government" would feel the force of it as much as the present societies with governments. It would be found necessary in Godwin's society to put some check on population, and the most natural and obvious would be "to make every man provide for his own children" (p. 199). "And thus it appears that a society constituted according to the most beautiful form that imagination can conceive, with benevolence for its moving principle instead of self-love, and with every evil disposition in all its members corrected by reason and not force, would, from the inevitable laws of nature and not from any original depravity of man, in a very short period degenerate into a society constructed upon a plan not essentially different from that which prevails in every known state at present, I mean a society divided into a class of proprietors and a class of labourers, and with self-love for the mainspring of the great machine" (pp. 206-207).

But the same argument which proves that Godwin's society would collapse if founded, serves also to prove that it never could be founded at all (p. 210 seq.). The passion between the sexes shows no tendency whatever to disappear, and we have no reason to believe with Godwin that in the future it will be the obedient servant of cool intellect. It is also a passion perfectly in harmony with the nature of man, and in no wise an evil in itself (pp. 211-216).

After disposing of Godwin's attempts to prove the indefinite physical improvement and longevity of man (ch. xii.), Malthus finds fault with the abstract character of his reasoning (ch. xiii.), and points out how subordinate is the part played by mere reasoning in the affairs of life. The later discussions in the *Essay* (*e.g.* ch. xiv. on "Perfectibility," etc.) add nothing essential to the main arguments, though there are remarks on wages, wealth, and capital of importance in view of his general economic doctrines (*e.g.* ch. xvi. 321 ; ch. xvii.). After telling us how Dr. Price had unwittingly been the means of convincing him of the truth of his new views on the ratios of increase, Malthus concludes his book with a brief statement of his own philosophical view of the world. The world is to man a state of trial ; without the wants of the body, and the difficulty he finds in supplying them, his intellect would not be developed. The law "that population should increase much faster than food" (p. 361) is calculated to produce exactly the strong stimulus that was needed for intellectual activity as well as for industry of any kind. In the same way moral evil seems necessary to the creation of moral excellence (ch. xix.).

The *Essay* of 1798 was anonymous, but it made a great sensation, and its author was soon known. Godwin and he met in London in August 1798, and a correspondence followed, of which something is given in Godwin's *Life* (ch. i. p. 321). The arguments of Godwin and others made some impression ; and in thinking of a new edition the "author of the essay" revised his work not only by the aid of travels of his own in 1799 and 1802, but in the light of abundant criticism poured upon him from all sides. *An Investigation of the Cause of the present High Price of Provisions* (1800) contained a promise to make the *Essay* bear more directly on present society, as well as to illustrate its principle "from the best authenticated accounts we have of the state of other countries" than England. Accordingly in 1803 Malthus published under his own name the stout quarto that embodies his mature views on his subject (*An Essay on the Principle of Population, or a view of its past and present effects on Human Happiness,* a new edition, very much enlarged). Besides hearing of vice and misery, we now hear of moral restraint as a check on population. "Of the preventive checks, that which is not followed by irregular gratifications may properly be termed moral restraint" (2nd ed., p. 11). The author confesses in his preface that he had taken too gloomy a view of human nature in his first essay. Accordingly, in this second, an allowance is made throughout for the influence of moral restraint. In the fourth book there are two chapters entirely devoted to this subject. He recommends a "virtuous celibacy," a "prudential restraint," a "period of delayed gratification," the result of which, if generally adopted, would be (he thinks) that "all squalid poverty would be removed from society, or at least be confined to a very few who had fallen into misfortunes against which no prudence or foresight could provide" (p. 495). Whatever may be thought of the possibility of the general observance of such a rule of conduct, there is no doubt that Malthus sincerely believed that the chastity he recommended "has the most real and solid foundation in nature and reason, being apparently the only virtuous mean of avoiding the vice and misery which result from the principle of population" (*ib.* p. 496).

Apart from this introduction of moral restraint, the principles of the first essay remain unaltered. But the application is different. Instead of very general illustrations, there are now detailed descriptions of typical savage, barbarian, and civilised countries, drawn from a wide range of authorities. These occupy more than half of the book. The utopias of Godwin and Condorcet are dismissed in three short chapters (pp. 354-386), after which emigration and the poor laws are discussed, and the author slides into what may be called economics proper, the relations of wealth to wages, of commerce to agriculture, and the effects of bounties on corn. Various aspects of the principle of population, especially its bearings on charity and on civil liberty, are then considered. With all its qualifications of the theory of the first edition, this second gave much offence by some indiscreet phrases and illustrations. The solemn contrast of the matron and the maiden lady, to the advantage of the latter, occurs in the second edition, pp. 549-550; and disappeared afterwards. The famous passage, describing "nature's mighty feast" and the uninvited guests, occurs there too, in connection with civil liberty (bk. iv. ch. vi. p. 531). It involves a denial of the *right* to support, in the strict sense of the word *right;* and, though it occurs only in this edition of the Essay, Malthus never abandoned the position maintained in it. He considered that our poor laws, in conceding the right, were "attempting to reverse the laws of nature." Hence his proposal that public notice should be given that no child born of any marriage taking place after a year from the said notice, and no illegitimate child born two years from said notice, should be entitled to parish relief,—also that the clergy when conducting the marriage service should call the attention of the husband to his obligation to support his own children and the wrongfulness of his marrying without a fair prospect of being able to support them (bk. iv ch. vii. p. 538). He does not approve of the prohibition of marriage by the state even where there is no such prospect ; it is enough to leave foolish men to the "punishment provided by the laws of nature" (p. 539).

There was much opposition to the views of

the essay. Many of the replies to it are largely rhetorical and do not concern us here. Malthus disposed of his critics very temperately in the successive appendices to his various editions. The substantial soundness of his main positions is not disputed by economists now, and his influence on the study of statistics is admittedly great. The effect of his essay and other works on general economic speculation will be considered below.

But the essay seems fairly open to the following comments.

1. The necessity of food and the necessity of the instinct of sex, his two postulates, are not equally absolute.

2. The growth of population and the increase of food are not well illustrated by a mathematical formula (geometrical and arithmetical ratio) which suggests greater exactness than the case allows.

3. The expression " tendency " is not applicable to the growth of population in the same sense as to the increase of food. Malthus admits this, but not perhaps with sufficient prominence and frequency.

4. The periods of the doubling of population and of the doubling of food are stated too absolutely, in so far as the idea is sometimes conveyed that, without respect of climate, race, and country, the periods will be nearly the same for all human beings, if only the moral, political, and social conditions are identical.

5. Malthus often speaks as if population must always increase up to the limits of the food as soon as these are sufficient to secure the standard of living (cp. Tract on Rent, p. 8). But such an instance as France shows that the standard may be secured and yet no increase take place. Hence it is not evident now, whatever it was in his days, that all countries feel the pressure of population, except in the sense that all either exercise preventive checks or suffer from the positive.

6. The argument of the biologists, expounded by Mr. Herbert Spencer, would show that possibly in the future the intellectual energies of man may grow at the expense of the sensual. The basis of this argument, however, is not very firm (see POPULATION).

7. Malthus proposed late marriages as a remedy for over-population; the neo-Malthusians, admitting the full force of his general argument, propose as a remedy early marriages with restriction of family (see BRADLAUGH ; James MILL ; PLACE). The name Malthusian in its widest sense is applied to all who recognise the existence and the need of any checks on population.

The first achievement of Malthus was the exposition of the theory of population ; and his name has been associated so closely with this theory that, like Darwin's, it has added a new adjective to the language of civilised peoples.

His second achievement was his contribution to the economic doctrine of rent.

When the East India Company resolved in 1805 to found a College at Haileybury (Hertford) for the preparation of their cadets, they made Malthus their first professor of history and political economy, and he began his duties at the opening of the college in 1807, continuing till his death in 1834. He twice appeared in print in defence of his college against the criticisms of Lord Grenville and others. He lived at Haileybury very contentedly and industriously, and was blessed with good physical health all his life. The pamphlet on the Nature and Progress of Rent (1815) contains the substance of lectures delivered at Haileybury (see " Advertisement," or preface, of the pamphlet). Malthus had intended to keep these notes till he could include them with others in a regular treatise on political economy ; but the agitation on corn duties, which was then at its height and had already drawn from him one pamphlet, induced him to follow it up by this other. In the first (Observations on the Effects of the Corn Laws, 1814) he had stated the arguments for and against protection of agriculture, holding the balance between the two opinions, but hinting that the political dependence caused by a free trade was a serious evil, and that agriculture was more important than manufacture. In a third pamphlet (Grounds of an Opinion on the Policy of Restricting the Importation of Foreign Corn, 1815), he plainly advocated a temporary protection, to keep up prices in order to keep up high farming. Between the two others came the tract on Rent, of much more consequence than either. " The rent of land," he says, " is that portion of the value of the whole produce which remains to the owner of the land after all the outgoings belonging to its cultivation, of whatever kind, have been paid, including the profits of the capital employed, estimated according to the usual and ordinary rate of the profits of agricultural stock at the time being." This is the point towards which actual rents are constantly gravitating ; and the immediate cause of rent is the excess of price above cost of production. How is such excess possible ? It is not due, as SAY and BUCHANAN think, to the monopoly of property, though the idea is sometimes countenanced by Adam SMITH, but to three causes: (1) that the soil yields more than enough to support the cultivator ; (2) that the food and materials thus procured cause an increase of population in proportion to them ; and (3) that the fertile lands are comparatively scarce, (p. 8, cp. p. 10). Hence the paradox that "the cause of the high price of the necessaries of life above the cost of production is to be found in their abundance rather than their scarcity " (p. 13). In the case of real monopolies like choice vineyards, the supply does not raise up its own demand. It is otherwise with agriculture, where a lessened fertility diminishes the demand by diminishing the population. On the other hand, where fertile lands are to be had in abundance, as in the earlier periods of society or in the colonies (p. 17), the result is high wages and profits, but little or no rent. But the diversities of soil make their effect felt as time goes on. "The accumulation of capital beyond the means of employing it on land of the greatest natural fertility and the greatest advantage of situation must necessarily lower profits, while the tendency of population to increase beyond the means of subsistence must, after a time, lower the wages of labour" (p. 17). The cost of production will thus fall; but the value of the product will rise, and its rise creates an excess which is rent (p. 18). "The separation of rents as a kind of fixture upon lands of a certain quality is a law as invariable as the action of the principle of gravity." Rents are thus due not to human artifice but to the laws of nature (p. 20).

The rise and fall of rents are governed by the four causes of the diminution of cost of production—(1) accumulation of capital and consequent fall of profits; (2) increase of population and consequent fall of wages; (3) agricultural improvements and consequent diminution in the number of hands needed; (4) increase in the price from increased demand, especially in a manufacturing nation, and consequent lowering in the *proportion* of cost to price (p. 22). But these causes need not act together (p. 26, cp. p. 34).

The general principle is true that "rents naturally rise as the difference between the price of produce and the cost of the instruments of production increases" (p. 27). It is also true that "a progressive rise of rents seems to be necessarily connected with the progressive cultivation of new land and the progressive improvement of the old," while "a fall of rents is as necessarily connected with the throwing of inferior land out of cultivation and the continued deterioration of the land of a superior quality" (p. 32). It follows also that "the price of produce in every progressive country must be just about equal to the cost of production on land of the poorest quality actually in use, or to the cost of raising additional produce on old land, which yields only the usual returns of agricultural stock with little or no rent" (p. 35, p. 36). "Corn, in reference to the quantity actually produced, is sold at its necessary price like manufactures" (p. 39). It is as with machinery in manufactures; when improvements are introduced but not carried out universally, the employers of the improved machines will reap surplus profits (cp. p. 55 note), the manufactured article being demanded in greater quantities than the improved machines can supply, and the price being accordingly fixed by the cost of producing the article by means of the old fashioned ones (cp. pp. 37-39, 41, 45).

The Law of DIMINISHING RETURNS was thus clearly formulated in this tract on rent. Though logically implied in the theory of population, it was not expressly stated in the essay of 1798; there are hints of it (especially p. 46 for extensive cultivation, pp. 90 and 107 note for intensive, cp. 186-188). The 2nd edition of the essay (1803) is somewhat clearer on the subject (p. 5 for intensive, p. 7 extensive, cp. the comment on ANDERSON, p. 472). The essay did not contain the author's mature views on rent till its 5th edition (1817). These views appear also, as might be expected, in the *Political Economy* (1820 and 1836). They were very little affected by the long correspondence of Malthus with Ricardo on the subject, still less by the public criticisms of the latter and of M'Culloch, Torrens, and many others. The view of Malthus that agricultural improvements raised rents has on the whole been justified by experience rather than Ricardo's to the contrary effect.

The bearing of the law of population on wages is so close that this subject occupied the thoughts of Malthus from the first. He observes (Essay, 1798, p. 35), that "the want of freedom in the market of labour, which occurs more or less in all communities, either from parish laws or the more general cause of the facility of combination among the rich, and its difficulty among the poor, operates to prevent the price of labour from rising at the natural period, and keeps it down some time longer, perhaps till a year of scarcity, when the clamour is too loud and the necessity too apparent to be resisted." "It must have risen long before, but from an unjust conspiracy" of the rich (*ib.* p. 36). He starts therefore with no class prejudices in favour of the employer; but his "principle of population" compels him to believe that "no possible form of society could prevent the almost constant action of misery upon a great part of mankind if in a state of inequality, and upon all if all were equal" (p. 36). Even though an English labourer does not marry without reflection, or at the earliest possible age, he does so soon enough and improvidently enough to find his children more sickly than those of the richer classes. The healthiness of a country life is proverbial; yet "the lads who drive ploughs are very rarely seen with any appearance of calves to their legs" (p. 73). Combination itself, which, he allows, might quite possibly secure a shorter day's labour (of 6 or 7 hours) to the labourers without prejudice to production (p. 298, cp. p. 301), would hardly stand against the necessities of the poorest. "Those that had large families would naturally be desirous of exchanging two hours more of their labour for an ampler quantity of subsistence," and it would be "a violation of the first and most sacred property that a man possesses to attempt by positive institutions to interfere with his command over his own labour" (p. 299).

Real wages ("the comforts of the labouring poor") depend on the "funds destined for the maintenance of labour and will be very exactly in proportion to the rapidity of this increase" (p. 305), but Adam Smith was wrong in supposing that whatever increases "the revenue or stock of a society" increases these funds. It is not so unless the additional revenue is convertible into a proportional quantity of food ; and this last is true in agriculture but not in manufacture (p. 306 seq.).

A rise of wages caused by an extension of manufacture will be merely nominal if there is no proportional increase of provisions (p. 307), for then the price of provisions will rise and the real wages remain as they were before. Importation can never in a large country like ours be sufficiently great to prevent this (p. 311). Hence Malthus thinks Dr. PRICE might have plausibly supported his view of the depopulation of England by arguing that the increased trade and manufacture created no new supplies of food, and therefore provided for no increased numbers (pp. 312, 313). In this respect Malthus is physiocratic (p. 327) ; and, in the first essay at least, he supposes wages to be close to the physical necessaries of life, and the most important of these to be bread. He is consistently physiocratic too in reckoning manufacture unproductive to society in comparison with agriculture (p. 333), though often very remarkably productive to individuals (p. 334). In later works he makes much more ample allowance for the difference between a high and a low standard of living, as affecting wages and population.

His maturer views of wages were developed with constant reference to the rival theories of RICARDO. Malthus refused to consider mere necessaries "the natural price of labour" ; that is a "most unnatural" price, for it implies a stationary society and standard of comforts. The true definition of natural wages is "that price which in the actual circumstances of the society is necessary to occasion an average supply of labourers, sufficient to meet the average demand" (Pol. Econ., 1820, p. 247). The market rate is sometimes above and sometimes below this point. The resources of the country and the demand for labour may increase ; and then the rate of wages goes up, and the habits of the people will be probably so affected that a higher standard of comfort will be adopted ; or they may stand

still or decrease, and the rate go down and the standard of comfort be lowered. A high standard of comfort is the effect as well as the cause of high wages (ib. pp. 248-249, 256-257). The standard is now so complex that happily wages do not depend wholly on the price of corn (Pol. Econ., 1820, p. 291). By high and low wages Malthus does not mean, like Ricardo, a high or low proportion to profits, but a greater or a less command of the comforts of life (ib. pp. 91, 326, 327, 214 n. etc.).

The relation of wages to capital (defined as "that particular portion" of material wealth, "which is destined to be employed with a view to profit," Pol. Econ., 1820, p. 293) is not regarded as one of simple dependence ; the demand for labour depends not only on capital but on revenue (pp. 248, 261, 301 n.). Here as elsewhere Malthus objects to the Ricardian neglect of "demand" and exclusive attention to "supply." Nevertheless he allows that the proportion which capital, whether fixed or circulating (p. 261) bears to labour has a very important influence both on wages and profits (pp. 301, 302). He did not formulate the theory of a WAGES FUND ; but he was to some extent the cause of it (see especially Pol. Econ., 1820, pp. 301 seq., a good example of the abstract or deductive method). He even states that "if the market were comparatively understocked with labour, the landlords and capitalists would be obliged to give a larger share of the produce to each workman. Every effort to ameliorate the lot of the poor generally, that has not this tendency, is perfectly futile and childish. It is quite obvious, therefore, that the knowledge and prudence of the poor themselves are absolutely the only means by which any improvement in their condition can be effected. They are really the arbiters of their own destiny ; and what others can do for them is like the dust of the balance compared with what they can do for themselves" (p. 306).

But profits do not depend, as Ricardo supposes, purely on the cost of obtaining the labourer's necessaries, any more than the value in exchange of commodities generally depends wholly on their cost in labour. Ricardo takes demand as constant, and explains all values by the cost of their supply (pp. 308-11, etc. ; but see RICARDO).

Malthus differed from what he called the new school of political economy (see Quarterly Review, January 1824), meaning Ricardo and his followers M'Culloch and James Mill, in regard to their three main principles. The first was that the natural or normal value, in exchange, of a commodity is determined by its cost, and that its cost means labour. The second, that demand affects values very little or not at all. The third, that profits are determined not by competition of capitalists but by the fertility of the least fertile land which it is worth while to cultivate. Thus in value profits play so small a part that they may be neglected. Malthus questions all three of these propositions. Cost, or as he prefers to say, the "conditions of supply," includes a reference to demand and supply; "natural prices" are "regulated by the ordinary and average relation of the demand to the supply" instead of their extraordinary and accidental relations (*Political Economy*, 1820, p. 84). Profits also must enter into the conditions; and the "varying quickness of their returns" is of importance in the determination of prices (*ib.* p. 88, cp. *Tract on Value*, p. 12 n.). "The articles which were of a nature to require a long preparation would be comparatively very scarce, and would have a great exchangeable value in proportion to the quantity of labour which had actually been employed upon them, and on the capital necessary to their production" (*ib.* p. 89). The varying proportions of fixed capital entering into different commodities were recognised by Ricardo himself as requiring a qualification of his principle (*ib.* p. 90, see RICARDO).

Malthus attached great importance to the search after a measure of value; and the lukewarmness, as well as scepticism, of Ricardo on the subject is partly explained by the fact that Ricardo had not a "historical mind." Malthus was anxious to have a key to the interpretation of economic history, especially the statistics of prices and wages in past times, and particularly since 1790. In his *Political Economy* (1820) he thought that a mean between corn and labour was the measure he desired (pp. 132, 133), except for corn itself, of which the best measure was the labour commanded. In his tract on the *Measure of Value* (1823) he confesses that he was wrong (p. 23 n.) and that "labour alone is the true measure." He quotes Ricardo's dictum "in all countries and at all times profits depend on the quantity of labour requisite to provide necessaries for the labourers on that land or with that capital which yields no rent," only to deduce from it the constant value of labour (*Value*, p. 29 n.); and thinks that if the value of labour be constant, labour is capable of being used as a measure of all other values (cp. pp. 30, 31). "The labour worked up in a commodity could not in many cases be ascertained without considerable difficulty; but the labour which it will command is always open and palpable" (p. 54 n.). This was Adam Smith's doctrine, though he was not always consistent. Malthus may be more consistent, but he was hardly more successful in the practical application of labour as a measure of value. Ricardo's attitude of suspense and scepticism seems justified. In our own time Professor Marshall (Gold and Silver Commission, evidence, December 1887, final report, pp. 1, 3) uses labour as a

measure of the value of gold, but does not put it forward as a universal measure.

It was obvious, of course, that the precious metals had no constant value; and the question of the changes in the value of gold and silver was pressed on the attention of all economists at the epoch of the great war. The fluctuations of general prices from the war and of corn from the seasons were complicated by variations due to the state of the currency, and especially the suspension of cash payments authorized in 1797 and continued till 1821. An economist who had lived through the first two decades of the new century would necessarily be expected to have an opinion about the cause of the high price of food in 1800, about the effect of the CONTINENTAL SYSTEM 1806-12, about the disappearance of guineas in those times, about the Bullion Committee 1810 (see BULLION COMMITTEE, REPORT OF), and about a "general glut" after the war.

From the end of 1808 the foreign exchanges had become very unfavourable to this country, and the bullion committee reported in 1810 that this low state of the continental exchanges, together with the high price of bullion, measured in notes, was caused by "an excess in the paper circulation," due originally to the suspension of cash payments. Malthus and Ricardo agreed with this conclusion, but differed about the general relation of currency to the exchanges. Ricardo considered that "the exportation of the coin is caused by its cheapness, and is not the effect but the cause of an unfavourable balance" (*Works*, p. 268). Malthus thinks, on the contrary, that the unfavourable balance might be due to purely commercial causes, of which the exportation of gold and silver would be only the effect. A view very like Ricardo's has been maintained by Professor Marshall before the Gold and Silver Commission (*Evidence*, final report, December 1887 and January 1888, pp. 11, 48-50); but economists have not yet reached unanimity on the subject.

In regard to the apparent general glut that followed the war, it was the view of Malthus (see *Political Economy*, 1820) that a general over-production had really occurred, and was the explanation of general low prices; a certain amount of luxurious living was, he thought, really good for trade. Consumption must keep pace with production; in England in his day the latter seemed to him to have outstripped the former. J. B. Say (*Lettres à M. Malthus*, 1820), Ricardo, and James Mill were no doubt right in pointing out that general could not mean universal, for supply involves demand. But they were wrong in leaving the impression that particular cases of over-production could never be numerous enough to cause any wide distress; and it seems fair to say that the theory of population can bear to be applied on the one side or the other with equal plausibility.

The theory of population remained after all the greatest achievement of Malthus ; and this notice of him may be fitly concluded by some account of his applications of it to the poor law.

"To remedy the frequent distresses of the common people," he wrote in 1798, "the poor laws of England have been instituted ; but it is to be feared that though they may have alleviated a little the intensity of individual misfortune, they have spread the general evil over a much larger surface." He adds that it is often remarked with surprise that, notwithstanding the immense sum, nearly three millions, that is annually collected for the poor in England, there is still so much distress among them. "Some think that the money is embezzled, others that the church wardens and overseers consume the greater part of it in dinners. All agree that somehow or other it must be very ill managed" (*Essay*, p. 74). But, if there were a rate of 18s. in the £1 instead of 4s., the case would not be materially different. If wages were from 1s. 6d. a day made up to 5s., the labourers, it might be said, could then eat meat every day. But the transference of 3s. 6d. to every labourer would not increase the stock of meat, but by increasing the number of buyers would simply raise the price. If it caused more cattle-rearing, there would be less corn-growing, and corn would rise (pp. 75, 76). "When subsistence is scarce in proportion to the number of people, it is of little consequence whether the lowest members of the society possess 1s. 6d. or 5s. They must at all events be reduced to live upon the hardest fare and in the smallest quantity." Moreover, there would on the first receipt of the additional wages be less inclination for work and a greater impulse to an increase of numbers (pp. 76, 77). "I cannot by means of money raise a poor man and enable him to live much better than he did before without proportionably depressing others in the same class" (p. 79). The poor laws tend to increase population without increasing the food, and they decrease the share of the industrious poor for the benefit of the pauper (pp. 83, 84). They diminish both the power and the will to save among the common people (p. 87). It is good for society that dependent poverty should be held disgraceful (p. 85). The very possibility of falling back upon parish relief removes a strong motive for providence and for avoidance of the ale-house (pp. 88, 89). In order to give an assistance to some which is a doubtful blessing to them, we subject the whole of our people to "a set of grating, inconvenient, and tyrannical laws totally inconsistent with the genuine spirit of the constitution" (p. 92) namely, the laws of settle-

ment. It is not good to "force population" as Pitt's bill of 1796 seemed to do. There is no real gain to the public from the resulting low wages (p. 134, cp. p. 94).

Such was the strain of reasoning in the first essay ; and it recurs in the later writings. The tract on the high price of provisions (1800) contends that the high price is mainly due not to over-issues of the country banks but to the attempt of the poor-law authorities to increase the allowances in aid of wages, so as to overtake the price of corn,—an attempt which caused the poor to compete with the rich in raising the price still further. The dealers were not at fault ; by keeping their supplies till prices were highest they furnished supplies when they were most needful ; and, after all, the high price has been a real benefit conferred on us for once by the poor laws. So many more of our fellow-citizens have been made by it to feel the effects of the scarcity and economise, that the stock of food has gone farther than it would otherwise have done, the farmers have been encouraged to add to the supply by extended cultivation, and the merchants by importation (*High Price*, pp. 19, 20). That at such a time, too, it would be impossible to leave the poor simply to shift for themselves, he does not expressly concede till the 3rd ed. of his essay (1806, vol. ii. p. 169). Otherwise the tract of 1800 may be said to have been incorporated in the essay without change. The remarks on the part played by the issues of the country banks are expanded. Coming first as an effect of the rising prices, the issues became in their turn a cause of them (see 2nd ed. pp. 402-403 ; 7th, p. 299 ; *High Price*, pp. 23-24).

In the 2nd ed. (1803) of the essay, and all the later ones, the poor laws take a much larger place than before. More stress is laid on the impossibility of their requirements. He had said (1st ed. pp. 98, 99) : "We tell the common people that, if they will submit to a code of tyrannical regulations, they shall never be in want. They do submit to these regulations. They perform their part of the contract ; but we do not, nay cannot, perform ours ; and thus the poor sacrifice the valuable blessing of liberty and receive nothing that can be called an equivalent in return." In the 2nd ed. (bk. iii. ch. vi.), he shows this in detail of the promise to find work, quoting DEFOE and EDEN. He quotes HANWAY and HOWLETT to show the great mortality of parish children, whose protection (be it remembered) was the object of the first FACTORY ACT (1802), and concludes "that the poor laws have destroyed many more lives than they have preserved" (p. 416). Moreover, though marriage is encouraged by the poor laws, it is hindered by the deficiency of cottages and the reluctance of the land-holders to build new ones (bk. iii. ch. vi. 3rd ed. vol. ii. p. 182).

The proposal of Malthus for the abolition of the poor laws has been already mentioned. He would rely on private charity, and he sees (2nd ed. p. 540) that "the only difficulty would be to restrain the hand of benevolence from assisting those in distress in so liberal a manner as to encourage indolence and want of foresight in others" (*ib.*). He is stern in allowing the sins of the parents to be visited on the children (p. 543). The parish support of deserted children multiplies the desertions (p. 541). What we ought to encourage is family affection and the self-reliance and responsibility of the head of the family. To force a man to marry, however, as is done by some parishes after a case of seduction, is to add evil to evil (p. 542).

If the poor laws were removed, the English people would show, even more strongly than before, their "spirit of industry and foresight." Without the general prevalence of the "strong desire of bettering their own condition" the poor laws would have ruined them in time past (pp. 545-546). But Malthus recognised that abolition must be gradual. "I should be sorry to see any legislative regulation founded on the plan I have proposed till the higher and middle classes of society were generally convinced of its necessity, and till the poor themselves could be made to understand that they had purchased their right to a provision by law, by too great and extensive a sacrifice of their liberty and happiness" (*Letter to Whitbread*, 1807, pp. 6, 7). One valuable preparation would be popular education, especially if it included among its subjects political economy (*Essay*, bk. iv. ch. ix.). Malthus is at all times unwilling " to push general principles too far " (2nd ed. p. 418), and he is patriotic and statesmanlike. Though he sent nothing to the press that is not connected either with political economy or with his college, he was a man of wide reading, varied tastes, and not simply a man of one idea. He was genial and hospitable, and made no private enemies. Sydney Smith, Harriet Martineau, and Mackintosh are loud in his praise. Thomas Love Peacock who satirises his views in *Melincourt* (1818) treats " Mr. Fax " with a good-nature and respect entirely withheld from M'Culloch (" MacQuedy ") in *Crotchet Castle* (1831). The popular notion of his person was for a long time even more inaccurate than of his writings. "No economist of the first rank has been so utterly misrepresented" (Prof. Nicholson, *Pol. Econ.*, i. p. 175, 1893). He was not without honour, however, in his lifetime. He was Fellow of the Royal Society, and of the Royal Society of Literature, a foreign member of the Institut, and of the Berlin Academy of Sciences. He helped to found the Political Economy Club and the Statistical Society. His book on *Population* was translated into nearly all European languages, and has probably received more refutations than any other economical work whatsoever.

The Crisis, 1797 (not published). — *Essay on Population* (see above), 1798, 8vo (anonymous). — *An Investigation of the Cause of the Present High Price of Provisions*, 1800, 8vo (anonymous). — *An Essay on the Principle of Population, or a View of its Past and Present Effects on Human Happiness, with an Inquiry into our Prospects respecting the Future Removal or Mitigation of the Evils which it occasions*, by T. R. Malthus, 4to, 1803. — The same, 3rd ed. in 2 vols. 8vo, 1806, including an appendix containing replies to critics. The appendix was also printed separately in 4to, 1806. — *A Letter to Samuel Whitbread, Esq., M.P., on his proposed Bill for the Amendment of the Poor Laws*, 8vo, 1807 (March). — *Essay on Population*, 4th ed. in 2 vols. 8vo, 1807 (same as 3rd). — Review of Newenham's Inquiry into the Population of Ireland, Dudley on Commutation of Tithes, and a Sketch of the State of Ireland, *Edinburgh Review*, July 1808. — Review of Mushet, Blake, Huskisson, Ricardo, Bosanquet, on the Depreciation of paper currency, *Edinburgh Review*, February 1811. — *Letter to Lord Grenville on the East India Co.'s Establishment for the Education of their Civil Servants*, 1813. — *Observations on the Effects of the Corn Laws and of a Rise or Fall in the Price of Corn on the Agriculture and General Wealth of the Country*, 1814 (3rd ed. 1815). — *An Inquiry into the Nature and Progress of Rent and the Principles by which it is regulated* (February), 1815. — *The Grounds of an Opinion on the Policy of Restricting the Importation of Foreign Corn, intended as an Appendix to Observations on the Corn Laws* (February), 1815. — *Statements respecting the East India College, with an Appeal to Facts in Refutation of the Charges lately brought against it in the Court of Proprietors* (January), 1817, a reply to Joseph Hume and Randle Jackson; a skilful defence of Haileybury College. — *Essay on Population*, 5th ed. in 3 vols. 8vo (January), 1817, the additions being also, as before, printed separately, under the title " Additions to the 4th and former editions of an *Essay on the Principle of Population*," 1817 (preface dated 7th June). — *Principles of Political Economy considered with a view to their Practical Application* (April), 1820 (Preface dated 1st December 1819. — Review of Godwin's Inquiry concerning the Power of Increase in the numbers of Mankind, *Edinburgh Review*, July 1821 (authorship not certain). — *The Measure of Value stated and illustrated with an Application of it to the Alterations in the Value of the English Currency since 1790* (April), 1823. — Review of Thomas Tooke's Thoughts and Details on the High and Low Prices of the Last Thirty Years, *Quarterly Review*, April 1823. — Review of the Essay (by M'Culloch) on Political Economy in the Supplement to the 4th, 5th, and 6th editions of the *Encyclopædia Britannica*, *Quarterly Review*, January 1824. — Article on Population in above, Supplement, 1824. — Paper contributed to the *Transactions of the Royal Society of Literature*: " On the Measure of the Conditions necessary to the Supply of Commodities " (4th May), 1825. — *Essay on Population*, 6th ed.

2 vols. 8vo, 1826 ("Advertisement" dated 2nd January), the last ed. published in the author's lifetime.—Evidence before Select Committee of House of Commons on Emigration, *Third Report*, pp. 311-327 (5th May), 1827.—*Definitions in Political Economy preceded by an Inquiry into the rules which ought to guide Political Economists in the Definition and Use of their Terms, with Remarks on the Deviation from these rules in their writings*, post 8vo, 1827. (A criticism of Adam Smith, J. B. Say, Ricardo, James Mill, M'Culloch, and Samuel Bailey. The later ed. by Cazenove is garbled.—Paper contributed to the *Trans. of the Roy. Soc. of Literature:* "On the Meaning which is most usually and most correctly attached to the term Value of Commodities" (7th Nov.), 1827.—*Letters to Professor W. N. Senior on the Subject of his Lectures on Population* (letters dated 23rd and 31st March), printed with said lectures 1829. —*A Summary View of the Principle of Population*, containing the gist of article on "Population" in Supp. to *Ency. Brit.*, 1830.—*Principles of Political Economy considered with a view to their Practical Application*, 2nd ed. with considerable adds. from author's own MS., and original memoir (by Otter, Bishop of Chichester), 1836.—There may still be in existence—(1) The Crisis; (2) The letters to Ricardo corresponding to the series mentioned below;[1] (3) Notes of his lectures at Haileybury. He had thoughts of converting one course at least (on Adam Smith) into a book (see Ricardo's *Letters*, p. 56). One set of student's notes (taken *c.* 1830) exists, but adds little to our knowledge of Malthus. A 7th ed. of the *Essay* was published by Reeves and Turner (1872), and a new ed. with biography, etc., Ward and Lock, 1890, ed. G. T. Bettany. Parallel chapters from 1st and 2nd eds. of the *Essay* are given in Macmillan's Economic Classics (ed. Prof. W. J. Ashley), *Malthus*, 1895.

[A good portrait is given with the art. Malthus in *Dict. de l'Écon. Pol.*, 1852; those in the *Petite Bibliothèque Economique*, 1889, and Dr. Drysdale's *Life of Malthus*, 1889, are inferior.—Bonar (J.), *Malthus and his Work*, 1885; *Philosophy and Political Economy* (1893).—Bagehot, W., *Economical Studies*, 1880.—Cannan, E., *Theories of Production and Distribution, 1776-1848* (1893).—Cairnes, J. E., *Logical Method of Pol. Economy*, 2nd. ed. (1875).—Comte, Charles, *La Vie et les Travaux de Malthus* (Acad. des Sciences morales et politiques, 28 Dec. 1836).—"Hans Ferdy" (A. Meyerhof), *Beschränkung der Kinderzahl*, 1894.—Held, A., *Zwei Bücher zur sozialen Geschichte Englands*, 1881.—Hollander, J. H., "Concept of Marginal Rent" (*Quart. Jour. of Econ.*, Jan. 1895).—Garnier, Joseph, *Du Principe de la Population* (1857).—John, Prof. V., *Die Jüngste Entwickelung der Bevölkerungs theorie* (Intern. Congress of Demography), (Vienna), 1887.—Keynes, J. N., *Scope and Method of Pol. Econ.* (1891).—Kautsky, K., *Einflusz der Volksvermehrung auf den Fortschritt.*—Lebrecht, V., *Il Malthusismo ei Problemi Sociali* (1893).—Leser, Prof. E., *Untersuchungen zur Geschichte der National-ökonomie*,

1881.—*Malthus Drei Schriften über Getreidezölle* (1896).—Mill, J. S., *Pol. Econ.*, 1848, and *Autobiography*, 1873.—Payne, J. O., *History of the Family of Malthus* (1890).—Soetbeer, Heinrich, *Stellung der Sozialisten zur Malthusischen Bevölkerungslehre* (1886).—Ricardo, *Works, passim*, and *Letters of Ricardo to Malthus*, 1810-23 (1887). —Smissaert, H. B., *Overzicht der Bevolkingsleer van Malthus*, 1879. (A good analysis of the whole essay).—Toynbee, A., *Industrial Revolution*, 1884. —Patten, Prof. S. N., *Malthus and Ricardo*, 1889. See also the French and German dictionaries. Malthus is noticed in almost every general treatise on political economy.] J. B.

MALTHUSIANISM. See MALTHUS.

MALYNES, GERARD DE (early 17th century), merchant, was born at Antwerp of English parentage. About 1586 he was a commissioner of trade in the low countries. He came to London and was frequently consulted on commercial questions by the privy council in the reigns of Elizabeth and James I. He was an assay master at the mint. With William Cockayne he obtained a patent to supply farthings, April 1613, but in a petition addressed from the Fleet prison, complained six years later that he had been ruined by being paid in his own coins. Among his projects was one for a system of state pawnbroking. He was called upon by the standing commission on trade for evidence on the state of the coinage, and published the following pamphlets in course of a controversy with Ed. MISSELDEN (*q.v.*).

The Maintenance of Free Trade according to the essential parts of traffique, namely, commodities, moneys, and exchange of moneys by bills of exchanges for other countries, or an answer to a Treatise of Free Trade, or the meanes to make trade flourish, lately published [by Ed. Misselden], London, 1622, 12mo.—Commodities are the body, money the soul, and exchange the faculty of the soul. "All the causes of the decay of trade are almost all of them comprised in one, which is the want of money" (p. 104).—*The Centre of the Circle of Commerce: Or a Refutation of a Treatise entitled the Circle of Commerce or the Balance of Trade*, also directed against Misselden, appeared in 1623, 4to. His chief point is that his opponent did not consider the "predominant part of trade," "viz. the mistery of exchanges," "showing his maine scope to be, to have the moneys of the realme inhaunced, and the foreine coyne to be currant at an equall value."

By far the most remarkable work of Malynes was—*A Treatise of the Canker of England's Commonwealth, divided into three parts; wherein the author, imitating the rule of good phisitions, first, declareth the disease; secondarily, sheweth the efficient cause thereof; lastly, a remedy for the same*, Lond., 1601, 16mo. In this publication Malynes argues that the disease is the decrease of our wealth by (1) transportation of money or bullion; (2) selling our home commodities too cheap; (3) buying foreign commodities too dear. All this results in the overbalancing of our exports by our imports ; and the cause of this overbalance Malynes shows to be the abuse of the money exchange between England and other countries. He insists that "gain is the cause of exportation of our monies," as the result of which home prices fall and foreign prices rise. After giving a description of the foreign exchanges, the author proposes as remedy : (1) the exchange for all places to be kept at a certain price ; (2) higher customs to be placed on imports and paid by the foreigner ; (3) the transport of bullion to be prohibited. His leading idea was that public authority alone could fix the terms of exchange and even the value of money, quite irrespective of the cost of the precious metals. He strongly urged the bullionist policy.

Saint George for England, Allegorically Described (R. Field, Lond., 1601, 8vo), is an account of the social evils in the state. "This dragon," Malynes says, in his preface to the reader, "is 'foenus politicum,' his two wings are 'usura palliata' and 'usura explicata,' and 'his taile unconstant cambium.' The virgin is the king's treasure. The champion S. George is the king's authority."

He also published *England's View in the Unmasking of two Paradoxes* (by De Malestroict) ; *with a replication unto the answer of Maister J. Bodine* (Lond., 1603, 12mo).—*Lex Mercatoria,* a compendious collection containing the sea laws of Edward III., the Hanse sea laws, and certain books treating of merchants' accounts and the law merchant (Lond., 1622, fol. ; 1629, fol. ; 1636-51, fol. ; 1653, 1655, 1656, 1660, fol. ; 1686, fol.).— *The Commonwealth of Bees, represented by Mr. G. Malynes by way of a digression in his great book called Lex Mercatoria,* 1655, 4to.

[See ENGLISH EARLY ECONOMIC HISTORY).— *Dict. of Nat. Biogr.,* vol. xxxvi., pp. 9-11.]

A. L.

MANAGEMENT, PAYMENT FOR. See EARNINGS OF MANAGEMENT.

MANCHESTER SCHOOL, THE. The group of ideas comprehended in the term "Manchester school" has for its centre and source the doctrine of free trade derived from Adam SMITH. The illustrious Scotchman, indeed, declared that to expect that the doctrine would ever become a practice in the United Kingdom was as absurd as to expect the establishment of a Utopia. The principal ground of his scepticism was the political power of the protected interests—of manufacturers chiefly, who, he said, were formidable to the government, and who, upon occasion, were accustomed to overawe the legislature. The course of events has shown that, in England at all events, the power of the monopolists has not been so insurmountable an obstacle to the progress of free trade as Adam Smith anticipated. This fact is traceable to the influence of the Manchester school. The *Wealth of Nations* was published in 1776, and its teachings were apparently unheeded for many years.

But the leaven was silently working, and before the end of the century it had taken possession of the mind of Mr. Pitt, whose policy during his prime ministry, from 1783 to 1801, was visibly influenced by the book, which he read diligently. To it may be ascribed, with some confidence, the portion of the Act of Union with Ireland (1800) providing for the abolition in 1820 of all customs duties between Great Britain and Ireland. In the latter year the policy of free trade was for the first time boldly advocated, as the basis of a comprehensive fiscal reform, in the famous petition to parliament of the merchants of London, drawn by Thomas Tooke (see MERCHANTS' PETITION). This was almost immediately followed by a similar petition from the chamber of commerce of Edinburgh. The presentation of these documents led to the appointment of a select committee of the House of Commons, and its report, published on 18th June 1820, was in harmony with the argument and prayer of the petitions. The investigations and conclusions of the committee were not entirely abortive, for they were the cause of the tariff reforms initiated in 1825 by HUSKISSON, who, with Mr. Gladstone, the father of the Right Hon. W. E. Gladstone, had shared in its labours. Meanwhile one retrograde step had been taken. In 1819 the provision for the complete liberation of trade between Great Britain and Ireland was abandoned by an act extending the then existing customs arrangements for a further period of twenty years, but reducing the duties by one-fourth at the end of every five years.

In 1820 the Manchester chamber of commerce was founded, or rather reconstituted, for it had previously existed under the title of the Commercial Society, established in 1794, the minutes of which are still preserved. One of the first acts of the new body was to protest against this backward step "as an infraction of the act of union, and an unnecessary continuance of restrictions highly injurious to both countries." The protest, which was put forward by deputation to government and by petition to parliament, was, after some delay, successful. Thenceforward opinions in favour of the abandonment of protection gained a permanent hold upon the minds of leading merchants and manufacturers in Manchester, and found expression almost every year at the chamber of commerce. In particular, import duties on foreign grain were the subject of strong condemnation, on the ground that they raised the cost of food and restricted trade with foreign countries. Towards the close of 1838 the agitation culminated in a broad and emphatic denunciation by the chamber of the policy of protection, Richard COBDEN taking the leading part in this act. Immediately afterwards the ANTI-CORN LAW LEAGUE (*q.v.*) was founded, and it was not dissolved until its object was accomplished in 1846. The vigour and the variety of resource and method by which the work of the League was carried on, as well as the educational effect of its constant demonstration of the soundness of the principle of free trade, gained for the League world-wide attention. Thenceforward the doctrine of free trade became associated with the birthplace and home of the body which had made it a living force in national politics.

The name " Manchester school " did not originate with the League. It was bestowed from without, and has had an extensive recognition in Germany, where it has acquired a meaning wider than the speeches and writings of its exponents warrant, although undoubtedly the main ground upon which the policy of free trade was advocated impelled them to take up a distinct position on other questions besides that which was the main object of their efforts. LAISSEZ-FAIRE was in general their guiding maxim, but not without regard to other controlling principles. Among these separate questions the most prominent were war, colonial policy, and factory legislation.

From the idea of free interchange of the products of industry to that of international peace, the transition of thought is natural and obvious. When therefore the leaders of the Manchester school had secured legislative acceptance of the principle of free trade, they turned their attention to other obstacles to its progress. One of these they found in international jealousies and mistrust, which they ascribed partly to mutual ignorance, and partly to the practice of maintaining large armaments. These, they said, produced two evils. They laid heavy burdens on industry in the shape of excessive taxation, and they discouraged trade by preventing the growth of commercial confidence, and by furnishing an excuse for upholding the system of protection abroad. Peace, non-intervention in foreign political affairs, and reduction of warlike expenditure were consequently among their watchwords. But Cobden did not seek these objects merely because he thought they would promote material prosperity. Peace was rather the end, and free trade the road to it. Speaking on one occasion in 1850, he said, " Do not suppose that I advocated free trade merely because it would give us a little more occupation in this or that pursuit. No ; I believed free trade would have the tendency to unite mankind in the bonds of peace, and it was that more than any economic consideration which actuated me in the struggle for free trade." Their earnest advocacy of peace and non-intervention when speaking on questions of public policy, and their undisguised sympathy with the peace society, led to the misconception, somewhat widely entertained, that Richard COBDEN and John BRIGHT, the chief apostles of the Manchester school, were in favour of " peace at any price." Both of them, however, took pains to repudiate the doctrine of non-resistance—Cobden frequently, and Bright on at least one occasion. At Wrexham, in October 1858, Cobden said, " I have not, as you have observed, pleaded that this country should remain without adequate and scientific means of defence. I acknowledge it to be the

duty of your statesmen, acting upon the known opinions and principles of ninety-nine of every hundred persons in the country, at all times, with all possible moderation, but with all possible efficiency, to take steps which shall preserve order within and on the confines of your kingdom."

It was a part of the teaching of the Manchester school, that the relations between the colonies and the mother country should be radically altered. Its exponents contended that the heavy charge then imposed upon the home treasury as a contribution towards the expenses of administration and defence of the colonies should be abolished, and that the preferential treatment at British custom houses of certain colonial productions should be discontinued. Both these changes have long since been made, but the advocacy of them fifty years ago formed the basis of a charge that the Manchester school desired to sever the political connection of the country with the colonies. This charge also was explicitly denied. Mr. Cobden declared in 1849, in answer to it, that he wished to retain them, " not by the sword, but by their affections," and in justification of his objection to the maintenance of forces there at the expense of the British exchequer, he affirmed that the colonists were more lightly taxed than the home population, and were well able to bear the cost of their own defence.

The attitude of the school towards factory legislation cannot be described as in all respects friendly. Of the practice of forbidding by law the employment in labour of the young its exponents usually approved, but they were, as a rule, opposed to all interference with the liberty of grown persons (see FACTORY ACTS). In 1836 Mr. Cobden wrote, for the information of the electors of Stockport, respecting the protection of young persons from excessive labour, " I will not argue the matter for a moment with political economy. It is a question for the medical and not the economical profession. . . . Nor does it require the aid of science to inform us that the tender germ of childhood is unfitted for that period of labour which even persons of mature age shrink from as excessive. In my opinion—and I hope to see the day when such a feeling is universal—no child ought to be put to work in a cotton mill at all so early as at the age of thirteen years ; and after that the hours should be moderate, and the labour light, until such time as the human frame is rendered by nature capable of enduring the fatigues of adult labour. Had I been in the House of Commons during the last session of Parliament, I should have opposed with all my might Mr. Poulett Thomson's measure for postponing the operation of the clause for restricting the hours of infant labour." The point of these observations, so far as they bear upon the general question of factory legislation, is that the man who may be regarded as, before all others, the exponent of the doctrines of the Manchester school, here emphatically declares that economic considerations are subordinate where considerations of humanity are in conflict with them. *Laisser faire* was therefore not an invariable tenet of the school.

The educational work of the Anti-Corn Law League, its struggles and its triumph, made a deep impression upon the minds of economists and statesmen in foreign countries, especially in Germany, France, and Italy. When, therefore, in 1846 and 1847, Mr. Cobden visited several of the European capitals, he was received as the hero of a beneficent revolution, and the principles of the Manchester school were proclaimed as a kind of gospel. Hardly any practical result in the shape of legislation abroad was realised, but the opinions and the hopes of economic thinkers with regard to the prospects of free trade, especially of those who had already been influenced by the teachings of the PHYSIOCRATS and of Adam Smith, were greatly strengthened. But the influence of the Manchester school has not remained extensive, except perhaps in Holland (see DUTCH SCHOOL). It is still strong amongst a comparatively small number of able writers and statesmen in France, who, however, have little force in practical politics. In Germany it has been largely extinguished by the teachings of the historical and socialist schools. At the hands of their exponents it has received severe and sometimes ill-founded criticism. Schönberg has attributed to the Manchester school, as its fundamental base, the doctrine that selfishness is the most energetic and the sole legitimate economic motive, and that its free expansion can alone establish the best economic condition. There can be no doubt that individualism, with a minimum of restraint, was constantly proclaimed or implied in the speeches and writings of Cobden and Bright. It must be remembered, however, that they were confronted by an actual condition in which a long course of interference with individual freedom of commerce and industry had produced formidable evils which naturally evoked reaction in observant and energetic minds.

A survey of the work of the Manchester school presents two prominent facts of essential importance. The first is that its leaders made no attempt to write systematic treatises of economics, nor even to expound methodically a particular set of economic ideas. They were men of action rather than students, although they were both. Thoroughly imbued with the teachings of Adam Smith, they saw in the legislation, and in the ruling economic maxims of their time, a state of things extensively opposed to the principles of their master. And fortune had given them a practical as well as a theoretical interest in labouring to make these principles a living and successful force in politics. The second fact is that their sphere of employment was not the study nor the lecture-room, but the popular platform, the floor of Parliament, the newspaper, and the pamphlet. Denunciation of their opponents, appeals to sectional interests, and various other weapons of popular controversy, as well as connected argument and methodical reasoning, were frequently brought into their service. The task they had undertaken was not only to convert a nation but to overthrow powerful interests whose supremacy seemed to Adam Smith invincible. Vehemence and passion were therefore not seldom displayed, with the inevitable result that the motives of their opponents were sometimes unjustly represented, and occasionally what was simply ignorance in high places was described as a kind of malevolence. These faults were perhaps inseparable from an enterprise eminently one of political warfare, quickened by the sight of widespread suffering, due largely to bad laws. They have also, however, inevitably perhaps given ground for unfavourable judgments upon the Manchester school, and for some misapprehension as to its doctrines and aims. In the light of history, however, the results of its labours are allowed to be in the highest degree beneficent, and the published speeches and writings of Cobden and Bright may fairly take rank as classical. For apart from what is of historical or temporary interest, they deal with principles of abiding importance. Moreover, the "unadorned eloquence" and homely persuasiveness of Cobden's utterances, not less than the surpassing beauty frequently found in those of Bright, give them a permanent value.

Much of their work and of their teaching has stood the test of time, even if further progress has not been made. Free trade holds still, theoretically and practically, an unassailable position in the United Kingdom. Elsewhere it has gained little ground, mainly because no means have yet been found in protectionist countries of overcoming those dominant interests which induced Adam Smith to despair of the triumph of free trade even in England. Non-interference in foreign affairs, and the avoidance of entangling political alliances have, to a large extent, been accepted as the basis of foreign policy. The financial independence of the colonies has become a fact. On the other hand, warlike expenditure and the cost of government have increased enormously at home and abroad. The functions of government too have grown at the expense of individualism. In these respects the march of events has gone mainly in opposition to the doctrines of the Manchester school. Its exponents were indeed strongly in favour of the maintenance and spread of popular instruction under the control of public authority, and of the extension of local administration. They would, however, have opposed much of that interference with trading operations, of which the Merchandise Marks Act is a type. The school is gone, although its work remains. But both its work and much of its teaching have taken a firm hold of the organisation and the mind of the British nation. See A. J. Balfour's Essay on Cobden and the Manchester School, published in *Essays and Addresses*, Edinburgh, 1893.

[Archibald Prentice, *History of the Anti-Corn Law League*, 2 vols., 1853.—Henry Dunckley, *The Charter of the Nations*, 1854.—Henry Ashworth, *Cobden and the League*, 1876.—*Annual Reports of the Manchester Chamber of Commerce*, 1820-1846.—Richard Cobden, *Speeches*, edited by John Bright and James E. Thorold Rogers, 2 vols., 1870.—John Bright, *Speeches*, edited by James E. Thorold Rogers, 2 vols., 1868.—John Morley, *Life of Richard Cobden*, 2 vols., 1881.—Dr. Gustav Cohn, *A History of Political Economy*, translated by Dr. Joseph A. Hill, Philadelphia, 1894.—J. E. Cairnes, "Political Economy and Laissez-faire," in *Essays in Political Economy*, 1873.] E. H.

MANCINI, CELSO (died 1612), a philosopher and politician, was born in Ravenna, the exact date not known. He taught moral philosophy at the university of Ferrara, and was made a bishop by Clement VIII. His principal work is *De Juribus principatum*, Libri novem, Romæ, 1596. The fifth book contains economic and financial matter of considerable merit. Mancini displays sound ideas on exchange and the theory of money. He distinguishes between the two duties of the state in reference to money, the care required for its maintenance, and the determination of its value, which both must correspond to the relations of the market. Mancini maintains the exclusive right of a prince to coin money—but he denies his right to debase it. Agreeing in this with other political writers of his day, Mancini regards it as the duty of a prince to maintain abundance in his dominions, exercising a paternal influence over them. The most important part of the fifth book is on finance, especially taxation. He enumerates the different taxes adopted in his day and proposes a rational classification of them, establishing the fundamental rules of finance, as the relation between taxes and the amount of public expenditure, and the proportion they should bear to the wealth of the citizens. Mancini's arguments throw considerable light on the subject of taxes, and indicate the first outlines of a doctrine which was developed much later ; he also discusses tithes.

[See Gobbi, *L'economia politica in Italia negli scrittori italiani del secolo XVI-XVII*, Milan, 1889.—Supino, *La scienza economica in Italia nei secoli XVI-XVII*, Turin, 1888.—Rava, *Celso Mancini, filosofo e politico del secolo, XVI*, Bologna, 1888.—Graziani, *Le idee economiche degli scrittori emiliani e romagnoli*, Modena, 1893. — Ricca-Salerno, *Storia delle dottrine finanziarie in Italia*, Rome, 1880.] U. R.

MANCIPATIO, according to Gaius (I. 119, Poste's translation), is an imaginary sale which is only within the competence of Roman citizens, and consists in the following process :—In the presence of not fewer than five witnesses, citizens of Rome above the age of puberty, and another person of the same condition who holds a bronze balance in his hands and is called the balance-holder, the alienee, holding a bronze ingot in his hands, pronounces the following words : "This man I claim as belonging to me by right quiritary, and be he (or, he is) purchased to me by this ingot and this scale of bronze." He then strikes the scale with the ingot, which he delivers to the transferor by way of purchase money. Gaius adds (I. 122), "The reason of using a bronze ingot and a weighing scale is the fact that bronze was the only metal used in the ancient currency, which consisted of pieces called the as, the double as, the half as, the quarter as ;

and that gold and silver were not used as media of exchange, as appears by the law of the Twelve Tables ; and the value of the pieces was not measured by number but by weight."

In early Roman law *mancipatio* was an actual sale of property ; but in course of time it became merely a form of transfer, the money (*œs, rausdusculum*) paid to the transferor by the transferee being a merely fictitious payment. When conveyance by delivery was established, *mancipation*, or cession in court, was still necessary for transferring legal ownership in *res mancipi—i.e.* land in Italy, rural servitudes, slaves, fourfooted beasts of draught and burden. "The list of *res mancipi* thus comprises the principal appendages, movable and immovable, of an old Italian farm" (Sohm, *Institutes of Roman Law*, trans. by Leddie, p. 230).

Mancipatio was used for the purpose of transferring family rights over persons as well as rights of property. It was also a means of making a will, established by the law of the Twelve Tables. E. A. W.

MANCUS, a denomination used in Anglo-Saxon times and till the 12th century ; almost certainly not a coin but only money of account, equivalent to a weight of 675 grains troy of silver, to thirty pennies or six shillings in value. [Ruding (*Annals of the Coinage of Great Britain*, ed. 1840, pp. 103, 111) thinks that an Italian gold coin of this name may have been imported into England, but used only for a short time. The mancus was reckoned in either silver or gold.— Eccleston, *Introduction to English Antiquities*.] E. G. P.

MANDAT (Fr.). An order or authorisation to pay a sum of money. The term is employed in French administrative departments, the *mandat* being signed by the director, or by the treasury, or the receivers-general of taxes, in which case it is called a *mandat du trésor*.

The MANDAT DE CHANGE, now obsolete, was an imperfect letter of exchange, which by custom the drawee was not bound to accept, and which was not protested in default of acceptation. There was no special legislation with regard to the *mandat de change* as for letters of exchange, and more recently for the cheque, now substituted for the *mandat*.

MANDAT DE POSTE, a post office order.

MANDATS TERRITORIAUX were a paper money during the revolutionary period. ASSIGNATS having become valueless in 1795, the material of which they were made was destroyed publicly with some ceremony. The government was shortly again embarrassed for money, and, by a law of the 18th May 1796, ordered the issues of 2,400,000,000 of francs of *mandats territoriaux* secured on national or confiscated property, the sale of which was decreed at twenty times the revenue it produced. The public had, however, no confidence in this new paper, and on the first day of its issue it lost 82 per cent of its value, 100 francs in mandats being exchanged for 18 francs in coin. In less than a year the mandats had become so much depreciated that they were abolished as a legal tender, although they continued to be received for a short time in payment of arrears of taxes.

MANDAT, a proxy ; its effects are described in articles 1984 to 2010 of the civil code.   T. L.

MANDATUM, a contract, binding by mere agreement between the parties, whereby one of them, "*mandator*," gives, and the other, "*mandatarius*," undertakes to perform, a commission without any payment being promised for its execution.   Each party may revoke the contract at pleasure, but the mandatary is liable, if by so doing he causes loss to the mandator. The mandatary can claim compensation for necessary outlay in the execution of his commission.   E. A. W.

MANDEVILLE, BERNARD DE (1670 ?— 1731), satirist, was born in Holland, where he practised as a physician.   Of his life, after his settlement in England, little is known.   After producing several works of an ephemeral character, Mandeville became suddenly famous as the author of the *Fable of the Bees, or Private Vices Publick Benefits*.   The poem had been published as early as 1705, under the title of the *Grumbling Hive*, in a sixpenny pamphlet, and had apparently not attracted much notice. In 1714, it appeared, 12mo, under its new title with numerous notes.   A second edition followed in 1715, with additional notes, and an essay on "Charity and Charity Schools."   Mandeville may be right in his surmise that the powerful interests attacked in the latter essay may have drawn attention to the *Fable*.   In any case, the 1723 edition was presented as a nuisance by the grand jury of Middlesex, and the work denounced by writer after writer.   New editions followed in quick succession, until in 1806 it had reached its eleventh.   The vogue appears, henceforth, to have waned, and the *Fable of the Bees* is now more often alluded to than read.   The merits of Mandeville lie rather in a style often singularly powerful for the pen of a foreigner, in poignant hints, scattered in the byways of the book, *e.g.* the passage in which he anticipates the modern view that hospitals should be as much schools of medicine as places of cure, and in his remorseless exposure of the seamy side of human nature rather than in his central paradox.   So far from private vices being, in themselves, or, "by the dextrous management of a skilful politician," public virtues, it can be clearly demonstrated that every private vice involves a direct public waste to the community.   In discussing the subject, Dr. Johnson quoted the words of Sir Thomas Browne, "Do devils lie ?   No, or hell would

not subsist."   Vice is, in its essence, anti-social, and on this "the truth, the whole truth, and nothing but the truth" is contained in Plato's *Republic.*   The most reasonable statement of the case is contained in a passage, wherein Mandeville says, "Those who can enlarge their views . . . may in a hundred places see good spring up, and pullulate from evil as naturally as chickens do from eggs " ; but the evil which is inchoate good is different from vice.   Mandeville's imposing structure of moral paradox rests for its basis on an economic fallacy.   The proposition, that private vices are public benefits, is the ethical equivalent to the economic delusions that spending, of necessity, benefits the community, and saving injures it ; that luxury, as a matter of course, is good for trade, that it is "prudent to relieve the wants of the poor, but folly to cure them " ; that "ignorance is a necessary ingredient in the mixture of society " ; that the aim of the legislature should be to keep labour cheap ; and, lastly, that the yearly imports should never exceed the exports. Experience, no less than theory, has abundantly shown the falseness of all these notions. It must be remembered that Mandeville lived before the growth of the modern industrial system (see INDUSTRIAL RÉGIME).   A society wherein the steady demand of the working classes themselves should afford the best custom to manufactures ; wherein the capricious and fluctuating requirements of luxury could be regarded as an evil, however inevitable : wherein trade pre-eminence should largely depend upon the technical education of the workers, and high wages by no means of necessity spell low profits ; wherein the main of imports should be to supply the raw produce of manufacture, and to feed the producers at the cheapest rate, —such a society was not dreamt of in Mandeville's philosophy.

In the essay on "a search into the nature of society," added in the 1723 edition, Mandeville contends with much force that it is the power of the evils which surround them which drives men to be sociable.   In a second part to the *Fable*, published in 1728, 2nd ed. London, 1733, 8vo, he endeavours, in six dialogues, to show up the real character of human virtue and the meanness of the motives of which it is the outcome.   *An Inquiry into the origin of Honour*, 8vo, appeared in 1732.

[*Dictionary of National Biography*, vol. xxxvi., article by Mr. Leslie Stephen contains the few facts known as to his life.

The more notable of Mandeville's critics were— Bishop Berkeley, in *Alciphron*, dialogue 2, wherein Lysicles is Mandeville, 2nd vol. of *The works of George Berkeley*, 4 vols., London, 1871, 8vo.— Adam Smith, *Theory of Moral Sentiments*, pt. vii. § 2, an unfavourable opinion both from the economic and ethical points of view.— W. Law, whose *Remarks, etc.* were republished in 1844, with a characteristic introduction by F. D.

Maurice. — Hutcheson, *Inquiry into the original of our ideas of Beauty and Morals*, 1726. See also Leslie Stephen, *English Thought in the 18th Century*, 1876, 2 vols., 8vo, ch. ix. § 34-44 and ff. "Mandeville, by attempting to resolve all virtue into selfishness, stimulated the efforts towards a scientific explanation of the phenomena." **H. E. E.**

MANGOLDT, HANS KARL EMIL VON (1824-1868), was born at Dresden and studied law and political science at Leipzig, Geneva, and Tübingen. In 1848 he was employed by the Saxon minister of foreign affairs ; and the department of the interior entrusted to him, in the same year, the preparation of a history of the industries of that state. But in June 1850 a reactionary *coup d'état* was carried out by the government of Von Beust, and Mangoldt sent in his resignation, stating his reasons for the step. He not only thus lost his official position, but in consequence of the act was often afterwards pursued by the enmity of the minister. Having further studied economics at Leipzig, he undertook in 1852 the editing of the *Weimar Gazette*, which however he soon resigned, again on the ground of political convictions. In 1855, by the publication of his principal work, *Lehre von Unternehmergewinn*, he established his scientific reputation, and in 1858 became extraordinary professor of political economy in the university of Göttingen, in which capacity he visited the London Industrial Exhibition of 1862 at the cost of the Hanoverian government. He was appointed in the same year to the chair of political and cameral sciences at Freiburg ; and, after a visit to the Paris exposition of 1867, he fell into ill health and died at Wiesbaden.

In 1863 Mangoldt published *Grundriss der Volkswirthschaftslehre*, which Cossa thinks one of the best existing compendiums of the science ; a 2nd ed. appeared in 1871. In 1868, he began in the *Bibliothek der gesammten Handelswissenschaften* a treatise on political economy, which he did not live to finish. He also contributed a number of articles to Bluntschli and Brater's *Staatswörterbuch*, amongst which are estimates of Colbert, Carey, Bastiat, and Mill.

Mangoldt's special importance in the history of economics is due to his having been the first, with a partial exception in favour of Hufeland, to submit what is now called "the earnings of management" to a thorough investigation. He was, in essentials, a follower of Adam Smith, but, says Adolf Wagner, "kept himself free from the one-sided views of the radical Manchester school" which exaggerated or perverted the doctrines of the great Scotsman. Roscher describes him as a somewhat dry writer, but possessing a sagacious and penetrating intellect ; he particularly admires his definition of the science of economics as "the philosophy of the history of (practical) economy," and approves his saying that an economic fact is not scientifically explained till the inductive and deductive explanations of it coincide.

[Leser in *Allg. Deutsche Biogr.*—Schmidt in *Handw. der Staatswissenschaften.*—Cossa, *Introd. Pol. Ec.*, London, 1893 ; Roscher, *Gesch. der N. O.*, p. 1039. See also GERMAN SCHOOL.]

J. K. I.

MANIFEST is the British term for one of the most important of a ship's papers, which sets forth (manifests) the particulars of the cargo. To the customs department, especially where most articles are dutiable, as in many British colonies, it is an essential document ; all ships making an entry in such ports are required to furnish a duplicate of the manifest, and by it the duties are checked. **C. A. H.**

MANLEY, THOMAS, was one of a number of 17th-century agitators for the better regulation of English trade and commerce. He was anxious for a strictly protective foreign policy, and in 1677 published his *Discourse*, showing that the export of wool is destructive to this country. He advocated the prohibition of unprofitable imports, such as foreign wines, "brandies and baubles," and actually proposed the revival of the ancient sumptuary laws — with a view to encourage the English woollen manufacture which, in the face of foreign competition, was obviously declining.

Manley fell into the error of wishing to promote the interests of the manufacturers at the consumers' expense.

In 1669 Manley published his *Usury at 6 per Cent Examined*, in which he opposed the liberal theories of Sir Thomas Culpeper, and J. C. (Sir Josiah Child), who had advocated the cheapening of money. Manley was anxious to keep up a high rate of interest, from a fallacious notion that it was advantageous to trade.

Manley's works are : *A Discourse shewing that the export of wool is destructive to this kingdom, wherein is also shewed the absolute necessity of promoting our woollen manufacture, and moderating the importation of some commodities and prohibiting others, with some easie expedients tending thereunto.* Licensed 8th March 1676, London, printed, 1677.—*Usury at 6 per cent examined and found unjustly charged by Sir Thos. Culpeper and J. C., with many crimes and oppressions whereof 'tis altogether innocent. Wherein is shewed the necessity of retrenching our luxury and vain consumption of foreign commodities imported by English money ; also the reducing the wages of servants, labourers, and workmen of all sorts, which raiseth the value of our manufactures 15 and 20 per cent dearer than our neighbours do afford them by reason of their cheap wages ; wherein is likewise hinted some of the many mischiefs that will ensue upon retrenching usury ; humbly presented to the High Court of Parliament now sitting*, London, 1669.

A. L.

MANOR, THE (Historical). The starting-point in the economic history of the early and middle ages is the manor, and in consequence, a knowledge of the character and transformation of its constituent parts is essential to an understanding of the progress of agrarian and industrial life. In origin the manor is probably connected with the tribe. Although scholars are not agreed as to the stages of manorial development, yet the tendency of current investigation is to associate it with certain economic processes which accompanied the transition from tribal to territorial life. Those who are unwilling to give up entirely the older views of Von Maurer, Kemble, and Maine see between the tribal and the manorial stages a distinct transitional form distinguished from the tribe by its territorial basis, from the manor by the freedom of its members, and from both by the extent of its self-government (Vinogradoff in *English Historical Review*, July 1893, p. 542). Others, more radical in their rejection of the old theory, deny the existence of such a stage, and connect the manorial directly with the tribal stage by an unbroken chain of rank, wealth, serfdom, and private property.

When historical information begins, the landed estate is found to exist with many of the features of the fully-developed manor. The earliest evidence is, however, inconclusive, owing to its meagreness and to the uncertainty regarding the dates of the first praedial documents, the custumals of Hysseburne and Dyddenham. In Anglo-Saxon times the manorial unit is rather economic than legal, and although the seignorial element was fully developed in that period, nevertheless the fully feudalised estate does not appear even in the *Rectitudines Singularum Personarum*, the chief pre-Norman document. Economic life had become manorialised but not feudalised. There existed, on the one hand, the manor house with its court, and the lord's demesne, under the *gerêfa*, or reeve, at this time the sole officer in control; on the other, the agricultural community with the dependent tenantry, the meadows, pastures, commons, and waste.

The manorial unit was therefore composed of two essential parts, one the seignorial, distinct from the point of view of jurisdiction and taxation; the other the vill or township, a unit in matters of service and labour. Seignorial rights, in part traceable to royal grants, are in greater part the result of causes both tribal and military. The measure of the Roman influence in creating such rights is as yet indeterminate. Although there is no express mention of such rights in the early charters, yet there is reason to believe that the right to hold a court of one's tenants and the right to exact fines arising from the judgment of such court is older than the first express grant of *sake* and *soke* in the charter of Cnut of the year 1020. The powers exercised in such a court were purely civil. Criminal and penal jurisdiction was probably of a later date, and originated in an express grant from the king. The determination of this question regarding seignorial rights is important; for the manorial court represents the close unity between the lord and the vill quite as much as does the open field system, inasmuch as the court was the meeting of the village community with the lord or the gerêfa as the presiding judge. It was a single court exercising police duties and certain criminal functions according to the terms of the charter by which jurisdictional powers were conferred. The second constituent element was the agricultural community, of which the lord was a part as his demesne lay largely in the open fields, and was subject to the rules that regulated the cultivation of those fields. The tenantry were of two classes; first, the *gebûras*, each of whom held in addition to his house and outfit of oxen a yardland normally of thirty acres, scattered in acre and half-acre strips throughout the open fields; secondly, the *cotsetlas*—in origin probably of the 9th or 10th century—each of whom had a cot and five acres of land scattered like those of the gebûras. The cotsetlas rendered no GAFOL—payment in money, produce, and work—and had no outfit of oxen. The *geneâtas*, if a separate class, could not have been numerous, and may have been of the nature of riding-men. Their identity is problematical. The obligations of the tenantry were divided into three groups; the gafol, the regular work upon the demesne, known as WEEK-WORK, and the PRECARIUM or special work in ploughing time and harvest. These services were originally personal, but afterwards became attached to the land. The main interest of the estate was agricultural. Cattle were kept for draught animals, cows for their calves, their beef, and their milk, sheep for their mutton and fleece. Nearly all necessities were supplied by the estate itself. Artisan work, largely that of slaves, was subordinate to the agricultural needs, and furthered mainly the agricultural economy. Yet, with all its isolation, each estate had some communication with the outside world. Surplus produce was sold for money or exchanged for metals and salt. The stage was one of self-sufficing economy, a stage in which the seignorial and the agricultural elements became so firmly bound together as to require the forces of centuries to disintegrate them. Yet the two parts were quite separate, the lord and the manor-court standing above the gafol-payers and exercising authority over them. In this sense the gafol-payers were in a position of dependence, a servile community under the gerêfa, who with the four best men attended the hundred and shire-moots. If such representations be incident to Anglo-Saxon times it witnesses to the legal position of the townsmen as being folk-free. The gebûr and cotsetla were "frigean men," though freedom was purely a relative quantity. In the 13th century, when the place of the reeve and four men in the county and hundred courts can be traced in the evidence of the extents, it is clear that they were in the majority of cases VILLEINS. At that time reeveship was a mark of servile status.

In the general organisation of the manor, we find no change in Domesday book. The *villani* are the gebûras, the *cottarii* and *bordarii* the cotsetlas. The amount of land held is practically the same, a virgate to the villein, a portion normally five acres to the cottar. Although the Norman Conquest increased but little the number of manors, yet it rendered them more powerful, by giving them a distinctly feudal character. Its feudalising influence tended to define the social status of the villeins, to place the free and the unfree in a common classification, and to prevent villeinage from lapsing into slavery. The manorial system became more complex, the feudal lord was the centre of many manorial units, each complete in itself, and a duplication of offices thus became necessary. The seneschal, as deputy of the lord, presided at the courts, audited accounts, conducted sworn inquests and extents. The bailiff managed the demesne, and collected rents and dues. But the reeve and bydel still continued to serve in subordinate capacities, and on smaller manors still remained the sole officers in charge under the lord. From the agricultural standpoint, manorial enterprise during this period was still collective rather than individual, and in consequence expansion and change took place very slowly.

But the breaking down of the cumbersome system of labour rents tended to increase the number of social groups upon the manor. In this respect the post-Domesday estate is exceedingly complex. LIBERE TENENTES, including those holding by military and free service, whose earlier existence has been denied because of their omission in Domesday, now appear. Below the freeholders are to be found many groups of those holding by base tenure, arranged in classes, not necessarily exclusive of each other, but indicative of dwelling, status, service, or holding. Of the first class are the villani, of the second the *nativi*, of the third the *consuetudinarii, custumarii, akermani, carucarii,* of the fourth the *hidarii, virgatarii, ferendelli,* and the more local classes, *landsettagii* in north Norfolk, *tenentes Honilond, tenentes Forlonda, tenentes Penilond* at Gloucester Abbey, etc. As the result of commutation MOLMEN began to appear who, by paying rent, were freed from work, thus in service, though not in status, approaching the free tenantry. *Gavelmanni* and *censuarii* may represent a line of rent-paying tenants, who, though living in villeinage, had never been bound to labour services. *Lundinarii, cotlandarii, cotarii, coterelli,* as successors of the old cotsetlas, had as a rule no part in the common arable, and were inferior to the villeins, and sometimes served under them.

Judicially there is no reason to believe in an extensive increase of curial functions. It is uncertain what is to be understood by *manerium* in Domesday, and there is little evidence of the smaller jurisdiction of manors in the reign of Henry I.

Three processes were taking place which were to destroy eventually the compactness and unity of the village and manorial group. Such disintegration was the inevitable outcome of the opening of markets, roads, and lines of communication with the continent, the growth of commerce, the political centralisation within the kingdom itself, and above all the increasing dominance of industry over agriculture. Re-arrangements in state and society led to re-arrangements in the manorial organisation. The first process, commutation, tended to free the individual from bondage to the lord and the land, and to break down an archaic relationship, which has its historical justification in having been an economic necessity in an age of decentralisation. The second, the increase of separate plots, farms, leases, and enclosures, destroyed the open field system, and the old forms of agriculture. The third, the absorption of manorial rights of justice by the royal courts, led to the gradual withdrawal of all real power from the manorial courts. To these may be added the growth of hired labour, the increase of exchange, and the consolidation of holdings, wherein the single acre strips begin to get united into larger strips, while still preserving the open field system.

Commutation began very early. The later system of money rents cannot be said, however, to have grown in every instance out of a system of labour services. It is quite possible to see in such payments an unbroken continuity of rent-paying tenants from Anglo-Saxon times. Money payments were made by the gebûr as a part of his obligation to the lord. In Domesday book the value of works performed is estimated in money, and on post-Domesday manors this became a regular part of the bailiff's accounts. While labour-rents were expressed in money-values for convenience in estimating the profit or loss of the manor, a few of the villeins who formerly did work began to pay money, as in the case of the molmen who still remained technically villeins. An examination of early mediæval evidence would probably show many cases of commutation where manorial conditions made this possible. The 13th and 14th centuries show a steady increase in this transformation; which was inevitable from the pressure of external economic forces. Payments in kind, and in labour service, rapidly gave way to payments in cash. On later manors it would seem that the lord preferred the old custom of labour-rents; and bailiffs' accounts of this period furnish instances of a reckoning in works, while the payment was actually made in money. It would seem to have taken a long time for commutation to have become an established fact. But the obligations of barons and holders *in capite* to pay scutage (though but two were levied after 1306), aids and hidage, the inconveniences of festivals and the changes of weather, the simplifying of manorial accounts, and the necessity of paying in cash for goods purchased off the estate, made the change unavoidable, even though it was resisted by the manorial lords. Such resistance was in part due to conservatism, in part to the fear of giving bondmen the standing of free men, and in part to the uncertainty of obtaining hired labour. The change was effected earlier on the royal demesne than on the ecclesiastical estates. The emancipation of the bondmen, due to the influence of the royal courts of justice, the winning of privileges by the chartered towns, and the teachings of Protestantism, went steadily on by the side of the commutation movement. It was not, however, until the days of Elizabeth that villeinage began to approach its end. At that time public opinion turned against the institution ; the last case of bondage was pleaded in 1618, and, though a few cases of servitude lingered on, it shortly became extinct.

With the growth of commutation went also the transformation of the farm, and the rise of the wage-system. Where, as in the case of the chapter of St. Paul's, a general assessment of a certain amount of produce for the benefit of the chapter was made upon all the manorial estates of a lord, each estate was put under the charge of a *firmarius*, who acted toward that estate *in loco domini*, retaining for himself all received over and above the assessment. The *firmarius* was sometimes one of the residentiary canons, as at St. Paul's, sometimes the bailiff or steward, sometimes the village itself. The inconvenience of transportation, and the growth of money payments within the village, soon necessitated a single cash payment, though for a time it was optional for the lord to receive either produce or money. Rentals became very common after the 13th century.

The payment of wages began as a commutation of labour either during special seasons of the year or for special classes of work. Week-work was probably the first labour to be commuted, and *precariæ* probably were the last. Hired labourers were in the first instances the old villeins. In the 13th century labourers engaged in threshing, winnowing, mowing, and harvesting were paid a regular wage, as also were those engaged in special duties, as the swine-herd, sheep-herd, and others, who in earlier times received perquisites or exemption from certain duties. Many of these were doubtless freeholders, and the custom first began upon the lord's demesne. The use of hired labour increased in the period preceding the Black Death, but that event struck it a severe blow. The increase of leases and sheep farms was an unavoidable result of the scarcity of labour. But, as the population recovered itself, commutation made it necessary and possible for the lord to hire labourers, and in the 15th century such labour was generally paid by piece-work. By 1450 there existed on every manor, besides the freeholders and customary tenants, a small body of labourers who were largely dependent on wages, though they supported themselves from the produce of small plots of land as well. But the class of wage-receivers was not confined to those resident on the estate. Itinerant artisans, serving sometimes two or three villages, sometimes a number of manors, passed from place to place paid by the day because unattached to a holding. It is probable, however, that some manors still retained their own smiths, wrights, shoemakers, etc.

The changes which altered the agrarian condition of England made the dissolution of the village community most evident. The manor house and the lord's demesne, the freehold plots, the lands in villeinage, the meadows, pastures, commons and waste were parts of one organic whole. But when a profit-gaining economy took the place of the old self-sufficing economy ; when a stage of industry took the place of a stage of agriculture, to be in turn supplanted by an era of commerce and trade ; when a convertible husbandry followed by rotation of crops took the place of the open-field system, then this agrarian unit dissolved. The earliest change in the primitive order was the introduction of the cottar holdings in Anglo-Saxon times, and of the freeholdings later. After the conquest, portions of demesne fell into the hands of rent-payers, and small holders and irregular plots increased. The earliest innovations took place on the demesne lands, which, as directly under the charge of the bailiff, were let out or enclosed for pasture. There is reason for thinking that by the 15th century the lords had succeeded in partially withdrawing their portions from the open fields. The process of inclosing lands not merely for sheep-rearing, but for more economical husbandry, began with the demesne, the freeholder's plots, and the common. The enclosure of the common fields, and the eviction of tenants which began in the 15th century, is the most important phase of the new movement, and some doubt exists regarding the security or insecurity of villein tenure. The evictors were lords of manors, *firmarii*, and the customary tenants themselves ; the evicted were doubtless *nativi*, holders *ad voluntatem* on the lord's demesne and waste, and customary tenants holding in the open fields. Evictions cannot have been limited to any special class. Freehold evictions are occasionally recorded, though this was clearly illegal (see Leadam, *Inquisition of 1517*, p. 189). On the whole, security of tenure for the customary tenants, and later the copyholders, seems assured, although it would be rash to offer a final opinion until a thorough examination has been made of manorial court rolls. Enclosures of demesne, meadow, and pasture, important as they were in transforming the appearance of the old manor, were not so vital to the mediæval economy as were the enclosures of the open fields. These struck at the root of the old system, and when complete, the agrarian individuality of the manor was destroyed. The minute subdivisions of the old virgate system had already begun to give way to the union of strips whenever possible, and the two processes continued side by side through the 18th century. The enclosure of the common fields was at its height in the latter part of the 15th century, and again from 1760 to 1844, when nearly 4000 acts were passed (see ENCLOSURES). These acts were the result of new economic conditions due to rotation of crops, the demand for food from manufacturing towns, and the increase of capital. England could not afford to retain the open field system; it was too uneconomical. Its place was filled by a system of consolidated farms, large capitalists, and division of labour. Traces of the old order can be seen not infrequently to-day, as near Manchester, in Gloucestershire at Upton, at Stogoursey near Bridgewater.

If commutation and enclosure affected chiefly the agricultural element of the manor, the loss of rights of justice affected the seignorial element. Under Henry III., so extensive were the assumptions of REGALIA by the lords, and so effective were their encroachments upon the jurisdiction of the king's justices, that the period preceding the reign of Edward I. may be considered as the era of greatest manorial jurisdiction. This led to an inquiry by king Edward into the seignorial warrant for such privileges, the important results of which were the return known as the HUNDRED ROLLS, the Statute of Gloucester of 1278, the writ Quo Warranto, and a general limitation of the franchises, although the forfeited privileges were often restored for a sum of money. The end of the 13th century marks, therefore, the beginning of the decay of the larger jurisdiction of the manorial courts. They lost in large part the exercise of high justice, and by interpretation of the Statute of Gloucester actions in civil cases were limited to forty shillings. The courts became local, possessing a mixed civil and criminal jurisdiction of a limited character. The presentment was made by the full court, or by the body of selected jurors, and the law of the court was mainly the custom of the manor. Through the 13th and 14th centuries there seems to be no evidence to show that there was more than one court upon the manor, or more than one way of constituting that court. In time, however, a distinction began to be made between cases that affected free men and those that affected unfree men, and the court baron, the court of the free tenants, and the customary court, the court of the villeins, made their appearance. Much earlier, however, many lords had begun to exercise a royal franchise in the view of FRANKPLEDGE twice a year; occasionally oftener. This was the beginning of the court leet, a name which appears toward the end of the 13th century. The correct title of this court was, however, always, *Visus franciplegii*.[1] The court baron and the customary courts were lord's courts and existed on all manors. The court leet was the king's court, and existed only on such manors as had the view of frankpledge. In the former the suitors were the judges, in the latter the lord or his steward. With the decay of villeinage the customary court ceased to be held, while the officers and functions of the court leet steadily increased by statute. The court baron and the court leet became the only local courts (except the *curia militum*) in the 15th century. The former concerned itself with tenures, admittances, rents, trespasses, civil actions of forty shillings, waifs and strays, etc.; the latter took the view of frankpledge, preserved the ASSIZE OF BREAD AND BEER, judged breaches of the peace, regulated commons, fences, nuisances, etc. But the intricacies of their own cumbersome machinery led to a rapid cessation of their activity. Their judicial power in civil cases was nearly gone by the time of Henry VIII., and there seems to have been a period between this time and the rise of the justice boards, established by many towns and parishes for their own needs, when many of the lesser cases were not taken up at all. Still, on some manors, with the increase of duties under new statutes, the activity of the courts continued. Though they met with regularity, yet the cases with which they concerned themselves grew fewer and fewer, until by the beginning of the 18th century the court leet had practically fallen into disuse. Its functions have been absorbed by municipal authorities, local boards, sanitary authorities, etc.

[The literature of the manor is so extensive that it will be possible to indicate here only the representative works upon the subject. Palgrave, Kemble, Freeman, Stubbs, Maine, Green, and others have discussed the origin and earlier history from the older point of view. For more recent opinions, see Seebohm's *English Village Community*, 1883.—Ashley, *Economic History*, pt. i. ch. i. 1888.—Earle, Introduction to *Land Charters and Other Saxonic Documents*, 1888.—Andrews, *Old English Manor*, 1892. For the mediæval and later history see Nasse, *Agricultural Community*

---

[1] = View of frankpledge. See Stubbs, *Constit. Hist. of England*, i. 88, 108; ii. 434.

of the Middle Ages, 1871.—Thorold Rogers, *History of Agriculture and Prices; Work and Wages.* — Scrope, *History of the Manor and Ancient Barony of Castle Combe*, 1852.—Scrutton, *Commons and Common Fields; Land in Fetters.*—Prothero, *The Pioneers and Progress of English Farming*, 1888.—Vinogradoff, *Villainage in England*, 1892.—Ashley, *Economic History*, pt. ii. ch. iv. 1893.—Cunningham, Introduction to *Walter of Henley* (edited by Miss Lamond for R. Hist. Soc., 1890).—*Growth of English Industry and Commerce*, 1890, 1892.—Leadam, "The Last Case of Bondage in England," *Law Quarterly Rev.*, vol. ix. p. 348.—Cheyney, *Enclosures of the Sixteenth Century*, 1895.—*A Discourse of the Common Weal of this realm of England* (edited by Miss Lamond), 1893.

The controversy regarding the security or insecurity of villein tenure will be found in Ashley, *Economic History*, pt. ii. ch. iv. ; "The Character of Villain Tenure," *Engl. Hist. Rev.*, April 1893, pp. 294-297.—Leadam, "Inquisition of 1517" in *Transactions of R. Hist. Soc.* (N.S.) vol. vi. pp. 167-314 ; vol. vii. pp. 127-292 ; vol. viii. pp. 251-331, "The security of Copyholders in the Fifteenth and Sixteenth Centuries," *Engl. Hist. Rev.*, Oct. 1893, pp. 684-696 ; "Villeinage in England," *Pol. Sc. Quart.*, Dec. 1893, pp. 653-676. The history of manorial jurisdiction has never been fully treated. See, however, Pollock and Maitland, *History of English Law*, 1895.—Liebermann, *Über die Leges Edwardi Confessoris*, 1896.—Maitland, Introduction to *Select Pleas in Manorial and Other Seignorial Courts* (Selden Society, 1888).—Stephen, *History of the Criminal Law of England*, vol. i. 1883.—Blakesley, "Manorial Jurisdiction," *Law Quart. Rev.*, vol. v. p. 113.—Lambard, *Eirenarcha*, 1614.—Kitchin, *Le Court Leete et Court Baron*, 1623.—Wilkinson, *Treatise . . . with . . . method for keeping of a Court Leet, Court Baron, and Hundred Court*, 1628.—*Durham Halmote Rolls* (Surtees Soc.).—*Manchester Court Leet Records*, 12 vols. For a graphic representation of the open field system, see *Sixteen Old Maps of Properties in Oxfordshire*, Clarendon Press, 1888. Also articles named in text and AID ; KNIGHT'S SERVICE (SCUTAGE).]

C. M. A.

MANORIAL ACCOUNTS. See COURT ROLLS.

MANORIAL EXTENTS. See MANOR.

MANSFIELD, WILLIAM MURRAY, FIRST EARL OF (1705-1793), lord chief justice of England from 1756-1788, and leader of the tory party which opposed the great Pitt. Murray was called to the bar in 1731. In 1742, he entered parliament as member for Boroughbridge, and was created solicitor-general. In 1754 he became leader of the House of Commons, and attorney-general. In 1756 he was created a peer by the title of Baron Mansfield of Mansfield, Notts, and made chief justice of the King's Bench, an office which he held for over thirty years, until obliged to resign through bodily infirmity. During his long occupation of the bench, Lord Mansfield was busied in

reforming many abuses of procedure, and was noted for his prompt and admirable judgments.

Mr. Justice Buller, in delivering an important judgment, observed that Lord Mansfield might be called "the founder of the commercial law of this country." In this sense his influence over business transactions has been long enduring.

A. L.

MANSUS (MANSUM), generally the chief mansion, manor house, hall, or court of a lord ; but the word has several shades of meaning, including *farm*. Brompton (Twysden's *Decem Scriptores*, 913, 12) uses it for the house of a chieftain ; Richard of Hexham writes of a *mansum* in Carlisle granted to his monastery, and of a *mansum* elsewhere, for use for the herring-fishery ; Matthew Paris mentions a *mansus* suitable for a vicar of a church, in fact, a manse. It is used in other cases (Ramsey, *Cartul.* i. 284-5) in which it implies a house with land around it inhabited by a husbandman. For the word as a measure of land, see Stubbs, *Constit. Hist.*, i. 83, n. 2 (1880).

R. H.

MANTELLIER, PHILIPPE (1811-1884), a French judge and antiquary :—

Published first in the *Mémoires de la Société Archéologique d'Orléans* and later on separately, his *Histoire de la Communauté des Marchands fréquentant la rivière de Loire*, Orléans, 1863 and 1869, and his *Mémoire sur la valeur des principales Denrées et Marchandises, qui se vendaient ou se consommaient en la ville d'Orléans au cours des 14e-18e siècles*, Orléans, 1862.

E. CA.

MANUFACTURE. As in the cognate instance of the word factory (see FACTORY SYSTEM), a remarkable transformation has occurred in both the popular and technical meanings of the word manufacture. Originally this term signified hand labour, as its derivation indicates, but now more generally machine labour—exercised in the production of a saleable commodity. In the opinion of some authorities, indeed, this transformation has been complete. "Manufacture," says Dr. Ure (*Philosophy of Manufacture*, bk. i.), "is a word which in the vicissitudes of language has come to signify the *reverse* of its intrinsic meaning, for . . . the most perfect manufacture is that which dispenses entirely with hand labour." This statement seems rather too uncompromising in view of well-known facts. It was not quite correct to say then, and it is certainly not correct to say now, that either in technical or popular parlance manufacture invariably connotes the idea of machinery. It may be that factory legislation has shown a tendency in that direction, but it is also a tendency at issue with some among its own express enactments. Thus the Factory Acts Extension Act 1867 contained a definition of "manufacturing process" as "any *manual labour* exercised by way of trade or for purposes of gain in or incidental to the making of any article " ; and this conception is continued throughout subsequent acts without any further qualification. A distinction, indeed, is also made in them between *making* and *manufacturing*, which might appear to give some colour to the above presumption : commodities being held in a general way to be made or manufactured according as to whether the productive act is performed in a factory or workshop—that is to say, by hand only or with the assistance of other motive power ; but from this general implication a considerable number of purely manual industries were nevertheless excepted from the first and made factory industries by law. Still less is Dr. Ure's definition acceptable to popular usage. In ordinary conversation it is commonly the comparative size of producing establishments which decides whether they shall be styled manufactories, and, more properly, the circumstance of whether the industries pursued there are carried on by means of congregated and divided labour. Mr. BABBAGE (*Economy of Machinery and Manufactures*, ch. xiii.) makes the distinction here under discussion in something like that way. "A considerable difference exists," he says, "between the terms *making* and *manufacturing*. The former refers to the production of a small, the latter to that of a large number of individuals " ; and in fact it is difficult, in view of the rapid changes in productive methods together with the vagaries of statutory treatment, to ignore the element of magnitude as one necessary criterion of any sound working definition. Some novel and interesting views on this subject are propounded by Marx (*Capital*, pt. iv.). The organisation of manufacture, he contends, "has two fundamental forms—" that in which the manufactured article "results from the mere mechanical fitting together of partial products made independently," and where it " owes its completed shape to a series of connected processes and manipulations." He passes these two forms under review, naming them respectively heterogeneous and serial manufacture, and raising some nice distinctions between them, but to no great practical result. He is content to find, finally, in the division of labour " the distinguishing principle of manufacture" ; and this, with some accretions born of modern mechanical methods of production, is probably as near to a specific idea of the nature of the process as, in the absence of a more authoritative definition of it, we can attain.

[Dr. Ure, *Philosophy of Manufactures*, Bohn's ed.. 1861.—Charles Babbage, *Economy of Machinery and Manufactures*, 1846.—Karl Marx, *Capital*, English translation, 1887.—R. W. Cooke-Taylor, *Introduction to a History of the Factory System*, 1886, ch. i.—George Jarvis Notcutt, *The Factory and Workshop Acts*, 2nd ed., 1879.] R. W. C. T.

MANUMISSION. The act of freeing a slave or serf. A term adopted from Roman law. In the early Roman republic this could only be accomplished by a solemn public act in one of three ways : (1) *per vindictum*, a ceremony before the prætor ; (2) *per censum*, *i.e.*, the enrolment of the slave's name on the quinquennial census of Roman citizens ; (3) by testament ; the slave becoming in each case a Roman citizen. Later, slaves were freed more simply, but with restrictions on the number freed ; and freedmen were not admitted to full citizenship. Justinian however abolished these restrictions and made all freedmen citizens. In England, at the time of the Norman Conquest, the act of manumitting a serf was a symbolical one. The lord led his villein before the sheriff in a full meeting of the country or to some other public place such as a church, and there declared his intention of setting him free, invested him with the freeman's arms, the sword and spear, pointed to the roads lying open to him in all directions, and the ceremony was complete. In later times manumission was effected either directly by charter or indirectly by a collusive action at law, in which the serf was, with his lord's consent, made to occupy a position which could only be occupied by a free man.

[Du Cange, *Glossarium mediæ et infimæ Latinitatis.*—Pollock and Maitland, *History of English Law*, Cambridge, 1895.—Hunter, *Roman Law.*]

A. E. S.

MANUOPERATIONES(MANOPERA). These form one of the three great classes of service anciently due from manorial tenants to their lords, the others being *araturæ* and *averagia*, ploughings and carryings. The *manopera* were rendered in actual labour, principally of a purely agricultural character, and are frequently described in cartularies under the terms *operationes*, *hand-dainæ*, *day-werke* or *week-work*. These were in a special way a mark of servile status, but like other indications of that kind, cannot be absolutely trusted without clear confirmatory evidence. In the 13th-century manorial extents, in the Ramsey cartulary, many instances of day-labour occur, with values of the service attached. In one case the labour of a man for five days in the week, on unspecified and therefore probably miscellaneous, services from 1st August to 29th September, is reckoned to be worth four shillings to the monastery, about a penny a day. In a case in the Gloucester cartulary, iii. 54, the valuation is only one half-penny a day.

[Vinogradoff, *Villainage in England*, pp. 287, 288.—Seebohm, *English Village Community*, 2nd ed., p. 79.—Ramsey Cartul., Rolls Series.]

R. H.

MANZONI, ALEXANDER (1784-1873), the celebrated Italian poet and novelist.

Between 1821 and 1823 he wrote the work which entitles him to notice in these pages,

—*I promessi Sposi* (The betrothed Lovers), a romance. The story is based on an elaborate study of the social conditions of the people of Lombardy in the 17th century, of interest to the economic student. Manzoni was a fervent patriot.

He lived quite retired from the world. In 1834 he published his *Osservazioni sulla morale Cattolica*, a defence of his religion against the attack made by Sismondi in the 127th chapter of his *Italian Republics*. In 1842 appeared Manzoni's *Storia della colonna infame*, an historic appendix to the description of the Plague of 1630, which forms the most interesting episode in his *Promessi Sposi*.

In 1860, Manzoni was nominated a senator of the kingdom of Sardinia.

I promessi Sposi, storia Milanese del secolo xvii., Paris, 1827, 3 vols. 12mo. The best French translation is that of Rey-Dusseuil, Paris, 1828, 5 vols., 12mo, 1841, 12mo. English trans., the Minerva Library, ed. by G. T. Bettany, 1889.
[See Cossa on the success with which Manzoni maintained that the study of economics was not incompatible with sound moral principle.—Cossa, *Introduction to the Study of Pol. Econ.*, p. 107, Eng. trans., London, 1893.]   A. L.

MARACHIO, MASSIMO (18th century), a Venetian ; one of the later absolute defenders of trade corporations. In 1789, the academy of agriculture, arts, and commerce of Verona offered a prize on the then much debated question : Is it advisable or not to allow trades to be united in corporations with power of control and privileges ; what are the advantages and disadvantages of this ?

Marachio sent in an essay, full of mistakes and prejudice, inspired with ideas of a most exclusive character, in defence of the corporations. He complains of certain abuses in them, but on the whole considers them excellent ; arguing in their defence against the many writers who opposed their privileges. He advocates minute division of trades, and attributes the faults of the system entirely to human weakness.

Istituto di tenere in corpi le arti riguardato nelle sue teorie e nelle sue forme, Venice, 1794.
[G. Alberti, *Le corporazioni d'arti e mestieri e la libertà del commercio negli antichi economisti italiani*, Milan, 1888.]   U. R.

MARC. See MEASURES AND WEIGHTS.

MARCET, MRS. JANE (1769-1858), was the daughter of Francis Haldimand, a Swiss merchant resident in London. She married in 1799 Dr. Alexander Marcet, a physician of distinction, and published in 1806 *Conversations on Chemistry*, a book for beginners which had an enormous success. This was followed by *Conversations on Political Economy, in which the Elements of that Science are familiarly explained* in 1816, and by numerous other works, among which *John Hopkins' Notions on Political Economy*, 1833, and *Rich and Poor*, 1851,

relate to the subject of this dictionary. The first edition of the *Conversations on Political Economy* is of some importance to the historian of economic theory, as it shows what were the accepted doctrines just before Ricardo's *Principles* appeared. J. B. SAY remarks that it "presents very good principles in a very pleasant form" (*Traité*, 8vo ed. p. 42 n.), and RICARDO uses a phrase which implies that it generally keeps "on neutral ground" (*Letters*, ed. Bonar, p. 133). In regard to the theory of rent it shows how much of Ricardo's work was already done by the discussions in which he had taken part about the corn law. In regard to profits, it appears rather to halt between the Smithian and the Ricardian view. The rate of wages, it says plainly, "depends upon the proportion which capital bears to the labouring part of the population of the country" (p. 117). It contains J. S. MILL's first fundamental proposition respecting capital, almost in the same words—"industry is limited by the extent of capital" (p. 153). A second edition was called for very soon (Ricardo's *Letters*, ed. Bonar, p. 132), and published in 1817, and a seventh was reached by 1839. Though the fact does not appear to be recognised or stated in any case except that of Miss MARTINEAU (*Autobiography*, vol. i. p. 138), it is probable that the work exercised considerable influence on the economic theory of the middle of the 19th century by helping to form the first impressions of young economists. The other two economic works are of less importance. The fact that they were intended, in part at any rate, for the use of the working class, shows a significant change of opinion, inasmuch as in the *Conversations* the principal interlocutor gives a ready adhesion to the exclamation of her pupil, "Surely you would not teach political economy to the labouring classes, Mrs. B. ?" The tendency of *Rich and Poor* is sufficiently indicated by the following passage from the preface : "These dialogues contain a few of the first principles of political economy, and are intended for the use of children, whether rich or poor. No portion of that science is more important to the lower classes, as it teaches them that the rich are their friends, not their foes."

[*Dict. Nat. Biog.* and works cited in text.]
                                        E. C.

MARESCOTTI, ANGELO (1815-1892). Born in Lugo in Romagna, Italy. He first studied medicine, which he practised until 1848, he then took part in the wars of Italian independence, and was entrusted with important political duties in 1859. Afterwards he became a deputy and finally senator of the kingdom of Italy. He was appointed professor of political economy at the university of Bologna, of which chair he held for many years. "Italy," wrote Minghetti, " owes her thanks to Romagnosi and Marescotti for making her first aware of that harmony between the elements of law and economics which we find so well sustained by German economists."

Marescotti wrote many economic works, often brusque in style. Amongst them we note the following :—

Discorsi sulla economia sociale (4 vols.), 1856.— *Le finanze e gli organismi finanziarii*, 1867.—*Conferenze sull' economia studiata col metodo positivo*, 1878.—*I fenomeni economici e le loro cause*, 1880. —*La legislazione sociale e la questione economica*, 1886.—*L'economia sociale e l'esperienza*, 1888.

U. R.

MARGIN (in monetary transactions). On a security the difference between the amount advanced against goods or securities and their market value. In the practice of banking this ranges from 10 to 25 per cent according to the nature of the pledge, and the usual range of fluctuations in its value. Should the security become depreciated, the margin has to be kept up by an additional deposit. Speculation "upon margins" or "upon cover" is conducted upon the deposit of a certain amount of cash, usually 5 or 10 per cent of the value of the purchase, the transaction being closed immediately the cover has "run off." Business of this sort in relation to stocks or shares is usually conducted by brokers outside the stock exchange ; and for speculation "upon margins" in produce of different kinds special institutions exist, as the Produce Clearing House in London ; and similar organisations in other cities (see CLEARING SYSTEM). R. W. B.

MARGIN (in economics) denotes a limit fixing the position of economic equilibrium. If, in mathematical language, the advantage of the economic man is regarded as a function of several variables, those values of the variables for which the value of the function is a maximum, are margins. There are thus as many margins as there are variable economic quantities. They may be classified under the heads (I.) production, and (II.) consumption.

I. Producers being divided into (A) the owners of AGENTS OF PRODUCTION, of three species, and (B) the ENTREPRENEUR ; we have a corresponding classification of margins.

A. (1) There is the "final" or marginal disutility of labour. "Labour will be carried on until the increment of utility from any of the employments just balances the increment of pain" (Jevons's *Theory of Political Economy*, ch. v. p. 201, 2nd. ed.). It is argued by Prof. Patten (*Dynamical Political Economy*) that in a prosperous society where amusements are open to the labourer, and the choice between work and rest is not his only one, he will not work on up to the limit of marginal disutility; "disutility" implying positive pain, not merely diminution of pleasure. It seems best to define with Prof. Marshall "the discommodity of labour" as what "may arise from bodily or mental fatigue, or from its being

carried on in unhealthy surroundings, or with unwelcome associates, or from its occupying time that is wanted for pastime, or for social and intellectual pursuits" (*Principles of Economics*, 3rd ed. bk. iv. ch. 1, § 2). (2) There is also for the capitalist a margin of investment ; a point at which he will decline to forego present consumption for the sake of the "discounted pleasures" of the future (Marshall, *Principles*, bk. v. ch. iv. § 1 *et passim*). (3) The landlord's offer of his agent of production is not limited by a margin on the supposition that he has no other use for the land. But where he has a choice between letting the land and using it for his own pleasure or profit, there may be a margin limiting the amount.

B. The outlay of the entrepreneur on each factor is similarly pushed up to a margin. There will be (1) a "marginal shepherd" (Marshall), and (2) a marginal "dose" of capital. The idea of a marginal increment of land (3) is less familiar, but is discernible in the case of a manufacturer hesitating whether he will rent an additional site for a new building, or add a new story to an old building (Marshall, *Principles*, bk. v. ch. viii. § 6). The older writers employ the idea if not the term with reference not to the quantity, but the quality of the land rented (Ricardo, *Pol. Econ.*, ch. ii. ; Mill, *Pol. Econ.*, bk. iv. ch. iii. § 5). The "margin of cultivation" denotes the lowest quality of land which is just worth the farmer's while to cultivate "below which the cultivation of land cannot descend" (Fawcett, *Manual*, bk. ii. ch. iii.).

The entrepreneur's products are sold either to other entrepreneurs, whose purchases have been already considered under the head of capital, or (II.) to consumers who extend their outlay on each commodity up to a certain margin. The margin of consumption is defined by the condition that in every branch of a consumer's expenditure, the "last" increment of money—that pound, or penny, about the application of which he hesitates—will procure the same amount of utility, called "marginal" or "final." Of course the marginal utility procured by a unit of money may differ for different consumers, and for the same consumers at different times.

Margin thus conceived as a point of maximum advantage is correlative to that quantity which it is sought to maximise ; sometimes called a RENT or Surplus.

[The subject is treated by almost all mathematical economists, and by those who employ more or less clear mathematical conceptions without explicit symbols. Jevons's exposition of "final" utility in his *Theory of Pol. Ec.* forms an admirable introduction to the subject. The fullest and most accurate exposition of the different kinds of margin and their relations is to be found in Prof. Marshall's *Princ. of Econ.* A clear and simple statement, unencumbered by mathematical phraseology, is given by Prof. J. B. Clark in his paper on the *Three Rents*. A similar praise is deserved by the writings of the Austrian school, so far as the general principle is not obscured by their peculiar doctrines of "pseudo-marginal" utility, "imputed" value, and other "casuistical complications." The marginal value of money is treated by Prof. V. Pareto and Signor Barone in the course of a series of articles in the *Giornale degli Economisti*, which are summarised in the *Economic Journal* for March 1895. The unit in which marginal utility is to be measured is considered by Dr. Irving Fisher in his *Mathematical Investigation*. He has exhibited the analogies between economic margin and physical equilibrium. See also *The Alphabet of Economic Science*, 1888, by Wicksteed, who first used the phrase "marginal" instead of "final utility," and FINAL DEGREE OF UTILITY.]   F. Y. E.

MARGINAL LABOUR. See MARGIN.

MARGINAL UTILITY. See FINAL DEGREE OF UTILITY and MARGIN.

MARIANA, JUAN DE (1536-1623). This celebrated Jesuit father, best known by his *Historia de España* and his apology of tyrannicide in his treatise *De Rege et Regis Institutione*, lectured during his youth on theology in Rome and in Sicily, and on the doctrines of St. Thomas Aquinas for five years at the university of Paris. At the end of an absence of fifteen years he returned to Spain and settled in Toledo, where he resided until his death. The publication of his treatise *De Monetæ Mutatione*, which he himself translated into Spanish, brought him into trouble, and he was confined for a year in a convent in Madrid. Some bold strictures on the government of the Society of Jesus, to which he belonged, entitled *Discursus de Erroribus qui in formâ gubernationis Societatis Jesu occurrunt*, found among his papers, did not, of course, mend matters with the influential authorities at the Spanish court.

In 1609, at the date when Mariana wrote his treatise *On the Alteration of Money*, the Duke of Lerma was flooding Castile with masses of debased small coins (*vellon*), a practice which, under the influence of the so-called *arbitristas*, or financial schemers, did not abate until the accession of the Bourbon dynasty. Charles V. and Philip II., although not irreproachable, had been far more cautious in this respect than their successors. Mariana fearlessly maintained that "the king, having no right to tax his subjects without their consent," had no right to lower the weight or the quality of the coinage without their acquiescence. "Two things are certain : the king enjoys the prerogative to alter the outward form of the coins, provided he does not make them worse than they were before ; . . . secondly, in case of necessity —as, for instance, during a war—he may be allowed to lower the coinage under two conditions —the first that this be done for a short time not exceeding the period of necessity ; the second that, the necessity being over, due damages be granted to the people who have suffered (ch. iii.)." But, "money having two values—one intrinsic and natural which depends on the purity and

weight of the metal, to which may be added the cost of the coinage, which is worth something ; and a second value, which may be called legal and extrinsic, fixed by the prince, . . . the real use of money — what has always been done in well-managed states—is secured when these two values are exactly adjusted (ch. iv.)." The following chapters give historical details on the Spanish mint.

Three chapters of the *De Rege* are also devoted to economic subjects : taxation, the means of subsistence, and the poor ; here also Mariana evinces his strong spirit of justice, as when he opposes taxation of necessaries, but his views on foreign imports, the cultivation of corn, etc., are mainly those of his contemporaries.

The tract on money was printed at Cologne in 1609, and the *De Rege* at Toledo in 1599 and Frankfort in 1611. Both are published (in Spanish) in the *Obras de Mariana* in the *Coleccion de Autores Españoles* of Rivadeneyra (2 vols., Madrid, 1854).

[Dr. Contzen, in his *Geschichte der volkwirtschaftlichen Literatur im Mittelalter* (1872), deals almost exclusively with the treatise *De Rege*, of which he gives a summary analysis (pp. 207-222). —See also the article "Mariana" in Bayle's *Dictionnaire Historique*.—Hallam, *Literary History of Europe*, ii. pp. 142-144 (edit. 1872).—Colmeiro, *Historia de la Economia Politica en España*, ii. pp. 476-484.]   E. Ca.

MARINE INSURANCE. See INSURANCE, MARINE.

MARITAGIUM. Usually *maritagium* means the feudal right of a guardian to give in marriage his ward, whether male or female, though the word often means the dowry or estate which passes to the husband with the lady. At other times it is used in the sense of *valor maritagii*, the sum the guardian could get for the match by sale. It is asserted that in the reign of Henry III. a sum of 10,000 marks was paid on one occasion. On the other hand in the Pipe Roll of 5 Hen. II., p. 65, there is a payment of 5 marks. An interesting case which illustrates the subject, and supplies original documents, may be found in the *Chronicon Petroburgense*, Camden Society, 1849, pp. 61, 62, and 72-77.

[Ducange, *Glossarium mediæ et infimæ Latinitatis* (Henschel and Favre).— Hallam, *Middle Ages*, c. 2, pt. 1.]   R. H.

MARITIMA ANGLIÆ is defined by Cowell as the revenue accruing to the king from his rights over the sea. It included such items as wreck and fish royal, the latter being all whales and sturgeon cast upon the seashore. This revenue was originally accounted for by the sheriff of each county, but in later times was entrusted to the admiral (see DROITS OF ADMIRALTY).

[Cowell, *Interpreter*.— Blackstone, *Commentaries*.]   A. E. S.

MARK (English money). The Anglo-Saxon mark, as well as the half-mark, was money of account only, in value 13s. 4d., reckoned in either gold or silver as equivalent to 3600 grs. troy of silver. Its value early in the 10th century was estimated at 100 pennies, but in the 12th and afterwards the mark was worth 160 pennies. It was a denomination probably of Danish origin, and is first found in 878.

[Eccleston, *Introd. to English Antiquities*.—Ellis, *Introd. to Domesday*, i. 164.] E. G. P.

MARK (GERMAN). In 1873 the gold mark, of 100 pfennige, was adopted as the standard of value, and as the money of account, of the new German Empire.

The mark consists of ·3982 grammes (6·146 grains) of gold 900 fine, and is equal to English standard gold of the value of 11·747 pence.

There is no standard coin of less value than five marks, the metallic currency consisting of the following pieces:

COINS OF THE GERMAN EMPIRE.

Standard Coins, Gold.

Denomination.	Weight.		Fineness.	Value.	
	Grms.	Grains.		In gold 916·6 fine at £3:17:10½ per oz.	In gold francs.
				s. d.	francs.
Twenty marks	7·965	122·923	900	19 6¾	24·69
Ten marks .	3·982	61·461	900	9 9¼	12·35
Five marks .	1·991	30·730	900	4 10¾	6·17

Subsidiary Coins, Silver.

Denomination.	Weight.		Fineness.	Value.	
	Grms.	Grains.		In silver at 5s. 6d. an oz.	In silver francs.
				s. d.	
Five marks . .	27·777	428·697	900	4 9¼	5·55
Two marks . .	11·111	171·478	900	1 10¾	2·22
Mark . . .	5·555	85·739	900	0 11½	1·11
Fifty pfennige .	2·777	42·869	900	0 5¾	·55
Twenty pfennige	1·111	17·148	900	0 2¼	·22

In addition to the above gold and silver coins there are nickel pieces of the nominal value of 20, 10, and 5 pfennige, and copper pieces of 2 pfennige and 1 pfennig.

The valuation at which the subsidiary silver coins are current bears practically the same ratio to that of the gold pieces as in the case of British coin; the value of the standard gold mark exceeding that of the silver mark piece, when reckoned at 5s. 6d. an oz. troy, to the extent only of ·27d.

The total amount of German imperial coin issued since its introduction in 1873 to the 31st December 1894 is given below. The coins have been manufactured at the mints of Berlin, Munich, Dresden (now Muldene Hütte), Stuttgart, Carlsruhe, Hamburg, Hanover, Frankfort, and Darmstadt. The three last-named mints are, however, at present closed.

IMPERIAL GERMAN COINAGE, 1873-1894.

	Marks.	£
Gold	2,895,073,075	141,915,346
Silver	488,535,775	23,947,832
Nickel	52,431,360	2,570,165
Bronze	12,660,744	620,625
Total . . .	3,448,700,954	169,053,968

F. E. A.

MARK SYSTEM, THE, is the term customarily used to designate the social and agrarian organisation of society which, it has been believed, preceded the manorial and feudal systems, and formed the basis upon which those systems rested (see FEUDALISM; MANOR). The unit of this system is the mark, a region greater or less in extent, independent, isolated, and occupied by a group of self-governing cultivators, politically free, who held and cultivated land in common with periodical distribution of the arable. The essential characteristics of the mark system are, therefore, personal freedom, self-government, and communal ownership of land.

The mark theory has occupied so important a place in modern historical and economic discussion that a brief résumé of the circumstances of its origin and development is necessary. The theory did not spring full grown upon the world; that portion of the theory which relates to the freedom and the social status of the primitive marksman has a long history behind it. *A priori* reasoning has tended at all times to give to man at the beginning of his economic and political development certain natural rights. Independent of and preceding any theory of the mark, these accepted teachings regarding primitive man were based upon the ancient philosophy, the Bible, and the *jus naturale* that entered into the mediæval thought at the time of the re-invigoration of the Roman law. This idea of original freedom was present in the dogmas of the church, and was vaguely and speculatively held by the philosophers of the 18th century. Through the teaching of Rousseau it became a political power, while it entered the economic system through the speculations of the PHYSIOCRATS. From the same source there sprang the cardinal doctrine of the romantic school, namely, the freedom of the natural man; and the whole theory became more definite when it was used as a political weapon against reactionism in France and Germany, and for reform in England by the liberal school. This school in its analysis of the fundamental rights of man brought into being the imposing figure of the primitive Teuton, thus localising the theory. Grimm and others, as the result of their studies in Germanic origins and philology, believed that the primitive Germans lived in groups, the members of which were united by ties of blood and religion. When this point was reached the agrarian element only was needed to complete the theory.

In the period from 1840 to 1850 certain historical students, Olufsen, Haxthausen, and Haussen, began to investigate the subject of the village communities of Denmark and lower Germany ; and in 1854, after years of penetrating and exhaustive study, von Maurer published the results of his researches in the same field. In consequence of these investigations and of the conclusions drawn from them, the group, *sibbe* or *sept*, of Grimm and his fellow scholars became a part of the primitive social unit, the village community, with its open fields, communal land-holding, and co-operative agriculture. In the meantime in England, Kemble, representing the new historical interest in Anglo-Saxon institutions, the desire for precedent in the reform agitation of the period from 1832 to 1846, and, under the stimulus of German romanticism, the spirit of German historical investigation, had presented, five years before von Maurer's work appeared, a similar theory for England. His theory, however, was characterised by vagueness and by absence of detail. To him the original settlement was based on possession of land only, and the smallest and simplest of the divisions was the mark. The word mark, as used by Kemble, connoted :— first, the forests and wastes beyond the arable, that is, the boundary land that separated the possessions of one community from those of another ; secondly, the whole district occupied by the community ; and finally the community itself, a group of families or households, settled on the plot enclosed by the boundary. The original basis of Teutonic society was, he thought, this community, a voluntary association of freemen, originally united by ties of blood—a relation, however, that in the process of time tended to give way to territorial and political interests. This group, zealously excluding others, developed and carried on a system of cultivation for the good of all its members. Various marks covering England, existing in independence and isolation, seised of full power and authority to regulate their own affairs, differed greatly in size, powers, and customs. Each possessed a court, and exercised supreme jurisdiction. Kemble was indebted for the first idea of the mark to the writings of Zeuss and Grimm, and he found evidential support for it in the occurrence in Beowulf and the charters of the words *mearcmôt, mearcbeorh, mearclond*, and furthermore in patronymics, and on these he laid great stress. He represented the marks as "great family unions comprising households of various degrees of wealth, rank, and authority ; some in direct descent from the common ancestors, or from the hero of the particular tribe, others more distantly connected, through the natural result of increasing population ; some admitted into communion by marriage, others by adoption, others even by emancipation, but all recognising a brotherhood, a kinmanship, or sibsceaft ; all standing together as one unit in respect of other similar communities ; all governed by the same judges, and led by the same captains ; all sharing in the same religious rites, and all known to themselves and their neighbours by one general name" (*Saxons in England*, vol. i. pp. 56-57).

Beyond the evidence above mentioned, Kemble brought forward nothing to support his view. But von Maurer in Germany did what Kemble had not done, he gave the minutest detail of the social and agrarian life, and supported it with what seemed to be indisputable evidence, namely, the customs of the 11th and 12th centuries, which he considered the survivals of an earlier age, and the occasional statements in earlier documents, which he interpreted in the light of the mark theory. In 1869 Nasse strengthened the theory by further English evidence, drawn from the laws and charters. But he, taking the existence of the mark for granted, concerned himself chiefly with the agrarian aspects ; and, although he recognised the presence of free peasant proprietors and found traces of communalism, he hardly touched the questions of freedom and communal ownership.

It was left for Sir Henry Maine and Emile de LAVELEYE to extend and to give greater currency to the conclusions already reached. In 1871 Maine, in his *Village Communities in the East and West*, both summarised the views thus far presented by Maurer, Nasse, Landau, Gessner, Haxthausen, and others, and widened the field of investigation by evidence collected in India. Here he saw, not survivals of primitive life, but actual communities, living types of the western mark. The Indian village community became of great importance, and Maine threw out suggestions for further investigation in calling attention to the village communities of America and to the house communities of the South Slavonians. This phase of the subject found expression and elaborate extension in Laveleye's *De la propriété et de ses formes primitives*, 1877, in which was gathered evidence from almost every part of the globe to show the universality of the mark system and of its analogues. When this point had been reached historical scholars very generally accepted the theory. Maine readily transformed the mark into the manor through the extension of Kemble's idea regarding the first marksman ; and Freeman and others, following further suggestions of Kemble, and conceiving of history as a continuous development, brought forward the theory that the mark was the germ whence had evolved the life of the state, the protoplasmic cell, containing within itself, as it were, the laws of its own growth.

But in a theory based so largely upon subjective foundations a reaction was inevitable. As historical criticism became keener the evidence appeared more and more insufficient and incohesive ; with the change of political ideals, the question came to be recognised as strictly historical ; exaggerations due to over-enthusiasm underwent correction, and gradually the problem was reduced to its proper proportions. The mark as drawn by Kemble and von Maurer is not at present supported by any historical scholars. The attack, as thus far completed, has destroyed the idealism of the primitive mark ; it has disproved the exaggerated freedom of the Teuton, and the existence of the first marksman and the court of the mark ; it has denied the Kemble-Maurer interpretation of the word *mearc* itself, and has thrown doubt upon the supposed symmetry of the primitive land system ; it has made prominent the tribal character of early Teutonic life, and has questioned the independence and self-conscious-ness of the primitive folk ; it has removed from the support of the theory the evidence from America, Russia, and Switzerland, and, through the work of Baden-Powell on *The Land Systems of British India*, it has struck a heavy blow at the accuracy of the evidence derived from the east ; and, finally, it has demonstrated that except for a judicious use of the comparative method, the evidence for each country must be interpreted by itself.

The movement against the mark theory was practically begun by Seebohm in 1883 and by Fustel de Coulanges in various writings from 1886 to 1890. By them the two most essential characteristics, freedom and communal owner-ship, were categorically denied, and a theory of primitive serfdom and private property was substituted. This has given rise to a new school, which, denying the existence of the free village community, has connected manorial institutions directly with the tribal, has recognised a predominant influence of Roman custom, has set up the manor as the prevailing type of local life and has declared the mass of the population to have been originally in serfdom.

A large body of the more conservative historians still advocate, however, a modifi-cation of the old doctrine, and believe that Seebohm, Fustel de Coulanges, and their followers are too extreme in their views. The best representatives of this school, Vinogradoff, Round, Glasson, and Flach, are willing to admit the presence of private property, inequality, and in a measure serfdom, but assert the existence of a free village community stage differing from the tribal system on the one hand and the manorial on the other. Although recognising, at a later time, the coexistence of the village community and the manor, they would still preserve the essential characteristics of the mark system without its exaggerations.

[Brentano, *Volkswirthschaftslehre*, 1893.—V. Maurer, *Einleitung zur Geschichte der Mark, Hof, Dorf, und Stadtverfassung*, 1854.—Kemble, *Saxons in England*, 1849, new ed. 1876.—Nasse, *Ueber die mittelalterliche Feldgemeinschaft und die Einhegungen des sechszehnten Jahrhunderts in England*, 1869, transl. 1871.—Maine, *Village Communities in the East and West*, 1871.—Laveleye, *De la propriété et de ses formes primitives*, 1877, new ed. 1891.—Seebohm, *The English Village Community*, 1883 ; *Tribal System in Wales*, 1895.—Fustel de Coulanges, *Recherches sur quelques problèmes d'histoire*, 1886 ; *Le problème des origines de la propriété foncière*, 1889 ; *L'Alleu et le domaine feodal*, 1890.—Glasson, *Histoire du droit et des institutiones de la France ; Les communaux*.—Vinogradoff, *Villain-age in England*, 1892.—Andrews, *Old English Manor*, 1892.—Flach, *Origines de l'ancienne France*, 1893.—"Village Communities in Spain," *Quarterly Review*, October 1895.] C. M. A.

MARKED CHEQUE. In London, after the clearing house closes, the bankers send round and present at the various offices any cheques that have been shut out of the clearing, a cashier being in waiting at each bank to "mark" or "answer" the cheques. Marked cheques are payable in the first clearing of the next day, and cannot be refused for any reason. In some places it is the practice of bankers to mark cheques drawn upon them by writing across the face "Good for £   ," the marking being officially signed. A cheque so marked is avail-able for completing important transactions, thus avoiding the risk and trouble of carrying cash.

In the United States, and particularly in New York, the practice of marking, or "certifying," cheques has been carried to very great lengths. Certified cheques are largely used in daily busi-ness, especially by brokers, and the certification is given, in many cases, against securities, or even only on the credit of the drawer. By the National Bank Acts, banks organised under that system are prohibited from certifying cheques for amounts beyond that which the drawer has at his credit at the time, but banks organised under the laws of the state of New York are subject to no restrictions in the matter. By judicial decisions the certification of a cheque is an acceptance, and renders the bank liable indefinitely as to time of presentment.

[For extent of the practice in New York, see *Report, Comptroller of Currency*, Washington, 1882 ; also *Journal of Inst. of Bankers*, vol. iii. p. 400 ; and vol. v. p. 278.] R. W. B.

MARKET AS PLACE OF SALE. Deter-minate areas and times for intercourse between buyers and sellers were a necessity of trade before communication and transportation were facilitated by the inventions of the present century ; and, even now, for the sale of some commodities, such as live stock and dairy pro-duce, they are but slowly losing their practical importance, in spite of the modern middleman and shopkeeper.

In the middle ages the right to carry on trade, or to permit it to be carried on, at a particular time and place, was called, like the place itself, a *market* (Fr. *marché;* Ger. *Markt*); and this term included in its widest sense both the weekly or semi-weekly market, lasting but a few hours, and the more considerable annual mart, lasting several days, known as a fair (Fr. *foire;* G. *Messe, Jahrmarkt*). Coke lays it down that "every fair is a market, but every market is not a fair." The term *market* was, however, more commonly reserved for the smaller and more frequent assembly (Ger. *Wochenmarkt*); and these alone will be considered here (see FAIRS AND MARKETS; MEDIEVAL FAIRS).

In England, during the later middle ages, not only did every borough possess a market, but also the lords of most considerable and of many inconsiderable villages; and the right to demand toll thereat was a valuable franchise. From an early date the right to establish a market was held to belong exclusively to the crown; and no market could be defended in the courts save upon the ground of such a grant or of immemorial prescription. In the 10th century an attempt seems to have been made by repeated decrees of the witan to limit all sales to "ports" or market-towns, a measure closely connected with the insistence upon the witness of "credible" men to every transaction. But this policy was either defeated or abandoned, for the number of markets in the rural manors evidently began to increase about this time. The Domesday Survey records some fifty markets or fraction of markets (*i.e.* rights to receive fractions of the profits), and it registers many complaints as to the setting up of markets without authority and the exaction of undue tolls. The pecuniary advantages derived from the possession of a market were, however, so large that every considerable magnate sought to obtain a grant from the crown, and many did not scruple to set up markets without waiting for permission. The chief obstacle to their success lay in the vested interests of markets already established. Before making a grant it was usual to inquire, on a writ *ad quod damnum*, whether it would be prejudicial to existing rights. When a market was established without a grant some neighbouring lord or borough was pretty sure to bring a suit against the new rival on account of the "nuisance" or "damage" he occasioned. The rule laid down by Bracton is that a market becomes a nuisance if set up within six miles and two-thirds of one already existing, on the ground that sellers could travel on foot that distance, sell their wares, and return within the compass of a day. The illegal assumption of market rights was probably put an end to by the *Quo Warranto* inquiries of Edward I. Grants of market privileges were

made in the 13th century in more than 3000 instances, in the 14th in more than 1500. By that time the country was pretty well supplied with such facilities for trade; so that in the first 82 years of the 15th century only some 100 grants are to be found. By the first statute of Westminster (3 Ed. I. c. 31), the king was empowered to take into his own hand the franchises of markets where outrageous tolls were demanded. Markets were commonly held during the earlier centuries in churchyards and on Sundays. The former custom was prohibited by the statute of Winchester (13 Ed. I.); the latter was abandoned in many places early in the 13th century, as a result of the moving sermons of Eustace de Flay, and was finally prohibited by 27 Henry VI. c. 5. It was in the markets and by the market officers that the men of the middle ages sought to introduce and maintain their simple-minded ideals of trade. All the rules with regard to Forestalling (see FORESTALLERS AND REGRATORS) aimed at bringing consumer and producer as nearly as possible face to face in the open market. Yet while restrictive in some respects, in others market intercourse led to a relaxation of previous restraints. Thus during the period of the dominance of the merchant gild it was common to suspend on market days, in whole or in part, the regulations limiting freedom of trade on the part of non-members. And the same tendency is illustrated by the growth in England and abroad of the rule of MARKET OVERT, by which a *bona fide* sale, made on the market day and at the place assigned for the market, transfers the legal property of the thing sold to the vendee, so that his title is good against all save the king, however defective that of the vendor may be (see also MANOR).

[The English material for the history of fairs and markets is conveniently brought together in the Report by Messrs. Elton and Costelloe for the *Royal Commission on Market Rights*, vol. i. (1889). It has a large appendix of documents, a calendar of grants from 1 John to 22 Ed. IV., lists of fairs in 1792 and 1888, and a list of general and local acts of parliament. See also the chapter on "The Town Market" in Mrs. Green's *Town Life*, vol. ii. (1894). In many English and continental towns a stone cross was erected in the centre of the market place in the later middle ages. For a description of the farmers' wives and daughters sitting with their butter and eggs on the steps of the cross "until a certain hour in the afternoon, after which, if all their goods were not disposed of, they took them unwillingly to the shops and sold them at a lower price," see Mrs. Gaskell's novel of *Sylvia's Lovers*, ch. ii. These market-crosses were often "polygonal buildings with an open archway on each of the sides, and vaulted within, large enough to afford shelter to a considerable number of persons; of these good examples remain at Malmesbury, Salisbury, Chichester, Glastonbury, etc." (Parker, *Concise Glossary of Architecture, s.v.* "Cross"). In more recent times market halls have been generally erected by municipalities, though the market women can by no means always be induced to pay for the privilege of shelter.

There has of late been an animated discussion among German scholars as to the part played by the market in the growth of the municipal constitution. A summary of the evidence and arguments on one side will be found in L. Goldschmidt, *Universalgeschichte des Handelsrechts* (vol. i. of his *Handbuch des H.*, 1891), pp. 126 *scq.*, who goes so far as to say "The town tribunal is originally and essentially the market tribunal, the town itself a market, the town peace a market peace." For the keenest criticism of this view, see G. von Below, *Der Ursprung der deutschen Stadtverfassung* (1892).]   W. J. A.

MARKET (on the stock exchange). The stock exchange is a remarkable case of development of the original meaning of a "market." Within the stock exchange the consol market, the home railway market, the foreign stock market, the American market, the miscellaneous market, the mining market, with its off-shoot the "Kaffir" market for South African shares, —each is spoken of as an assemblage of dealers standing ready to buy or sell the various stocks and shares indicated by the titles of their respective markets. Outside the stock exchange a market is not so regarded. A person wishing to buy or sell sends in his broker to inquire as to "the state of the market" in consols, or American shares, or mining shares, as the case may be. The broker goes to the dealers, knowing exactly where to find his men, and gets their quotations of price and tendency, and, what is important, he has the opportunity to examine the prices "marked"— on a board provided for the purpose—at which previous business had been done. Thus it is possible to get at once the record of price and the personal opinions of competitive dealers, both being elements of a market. Further, the quotations of price which the dealer gives are not simply an expression of opinion ; if he quotes a price for a given amount of stock or quantity of shares, he must deal. For example, if the dealer quotes 90 to 90¼ for a specified quantity of Italian bonds of £100 each, he must take them at £90, or sell them at £90 : 5s. Nothing could be a more definite quotation, a more exact reflection of the actual state of the market. There is little possibility of picking up stock cheaply, as a connoisseur could pick up a fine old Italian violin from some ignorant villager ; on the other hand, there is little risk of fraud upon an ignorant seller. The member of the stock exchange who attempted to cheat an outside seller, or his broker, would be subject to the severest censure from the committee for general purposes (see EXCHANGE, STOCK), and would be sent to Coventry by the more scrupulous of his colleagues. Nothing, then, could be a more

complete instance of a market than is given by the stock exchange. We get records or markings, the opinion of a concourse of dealers, competition, and a check upon dishonest dealing. [For defin. of market, Jevons's *Theory of Pol. Econ.*, ch. iv. ; *Theory of Exchange*. Also Cournot, *Recherches, etc.*, 1838, p. 55 n.—Giffen, *Stock Ex. Speculation*. See Art. HIGGLING OF THE MARKET.]
                                                        A. E.

MARKET OVERT. The law of market overt constitutes a fitful and illogical application to English law of the French maxim "en fait de meubles, possession vaut titre." The general rule in England is that no one by transferring goods to another can give a better title than he himself possesses. But when a person in good faith buys goods in "open market" and according to the usages of the market, he acquires a good title to them, in spite of any want of title in the seller. The rule only applies to ancient, and not to modern statutory markets. All sales by shopkeepers in the city of London, when the goods themselves are in the shop, are by custom sales in market overt, but the custom does not extend beyond the city limits. Hence if a stolen watch be sold in Fleet Street, the buyer may get a good title to it, while he gets no title to it if he buys it in the Strand. Wholesale mercantile transactions, it may be noted, are to a great extent protected by the Factors Act, 1889. [Benjamin *on Sales*, ed. 4, p. 9, and the *Reports of the Markets and Fairs Royal Commission*, 1888.]   M. D. C.

MARKET VALUE. See VALUE.

MARKETS AND FAIRS. See FAIRS AND MARKETS.

MARKKA (Finland). The metallic currency of Finland consists of the following coins (imperial decree of 8th November 1865):

Denomination.	Weight grammes.	Millesimal Fineness.	Intrinsic Value.	
			English Standard. Gold : £3:17:10½ per oz., 916·6 fine. Silver : 5s. 6d. per oz., 925 fine.	French Standard. Gold francs, 900 fine. Silver francs, 900 fine.
Gold—			s. d.	francs.
20 markka	6·452	900	15 : 10½	20
10 „	3·226	900	7 : 11	10
Silver—				
2 markka	10·365	868	1 : 8½	1·99
markka	5·182	868	10½	·99
50 penni[1]	2·549	750	4½	·42
25 „	1·274	750	2	·21

There are also copper coins of the nominal value of 10, 5, and 1 penni.

The standard gold markka (not a coin) is the

[1] The piece of money which, reckoned in French standard silver francs, is only worth ·42 franc, is in reality a token coin passing as the half of a *gold* standard markka.

equivalent of the gold franc as well as of the Russian quarter rouble, the penni being of the same nominal value therefore as the French centime.   F. E. A.

MARLO. KARL. This was the pseudonym under which Karl Georg WINKELBLECH (1810-1865) published his economic writings. Winkelblech was born at Ensheim, near Mainz, studied physics and chemistry at Giessen—the latter under Liebig—became *privat-docent* at Marburg in 1837, and in 1843 was appointed professor of chemistry in the higher trade-school at Cassel. In early life he showed strong literary tastes, carrying about with him habitually a volume of Goethe, Schiller, or Lessing. The impulse which made him an economist came from a German workman whom he met during a journey in Sweden undertaken for technical objects. This casual companion drew so vivid a picture of the sufferings of the class to which he belonged that Winkelblech resolved to devote for the future his most earnest studies to the condition of the workers, rather than, as previously, to the instruments and processes of industry.

His principal work, which remained unfinished at his death, is *Untersuchungen über die Organisation der Arbeit, oder System der Weltökonomie*, 3 vols., 1850-59. It produced little effect in Germany, perhaps—as Lippert suggests—in consequence of the social discouragement and apathy then prevailing. It was highly praised by Schäffle in his *Kapitalismus und Socialismus* (1870), and the attention thus drawn to it led to the publication, in 1884-86, of a posthumous second edition, enlarged and containing a biographical sketch of the author.

The book opens with a history and criticism of the progressive life of the most important civilised nations—France, England, the United States of America, and Germany, and a study of their comparative ripeness for what he regards as a necessary transformation of the basis on which their economic systems rest. The tendency of modern changes in the industrial sphere had been to abolish the smaller capitalists, and to create a great mass of *prolétaires*, who can never hope to attain social independence, and whose wages will never suffice for much more than to sustain their lives. Employment, too, has become uncertain, and the increased division of labour has made work monotonous and uninteresting. The working classes do not enjoy any true domestic life; wives and mothers spend their days in factories, and cannot superintend their families; and morality suffers from the employment of the younger women in manufactures. The physical condition of these classes is deplorable, their dwellings are overcrowded, their food is insufficient, and drunkenness, improvidence, and a spirit of revolt are the necessary results of their entire position. The modern *prolétaire* is the successor of the ancient slave and the mediæval serf; and it may be doubted whether he is more advantageously situated than those who had at least an assured existence. This is, it will be seen, the picture habitually drawn by the socialists,

in which the dark side of our industrial life alone appears. But it is real enough in many of its features to make us ask anxiously for the remedies which the author suggests.

According to his view of economic history, there have successively prevailed two different ideas of right, which he calls the Pagan and the Christian respectively. Under the reign of the former it was regarded as natural and legitimate that the masses should be sacrificed to ensure enjoyment and splendour to the few; whilst the Christian idea asserts the equality of all, and requires that each member of the community should have a share of the produce of the social labour proportional to his useful participation in the work. The former principle, to which he gives the name of *Monopolismus*, is represented by ancient slavery,—and its later modifications, serfdom and forced labour,—and continued to reign down to the French Revolution. The Christian principle, though accepted by the general conscience, has as yet only partially influenced practice; privileges, monopolies, and gambling speculation still exist, sometimes in aggravated forms. Two efforts have been made to realise the new principle—Liberalism, aiming at universal liberty, and Communism, aspiring after a *régime* of equality. But both these systems are one-sided and erroneous. Liberalism, based on the merely negative idea of unlimited competition, after demolishing the old privileges, has become the parent of plutocracy, whilst communism, distributing products according to wants, not services, and so weakening the motives to exertion, would infallibly beget indolence. These opposing systems he sought to reconcile, and to unite true liberty with true equality by the establishment of a *panpolismus*, the aim of which would be to raise to the highest attainable level the self-development and legitimate life-enjoyment of all the members of the community. Under this *régime* the obligation to labour will be universal, every one will have a right of access to the means of production, and will be supplied with work, and each will obtain for his personal use the entire amount of his contribution to the common stock. The state will take into its hands not only railways and roads, postal communication, water-supply, banks, and educational institutions, but also forestry, mining, fisheries, and trade—so far as it has to do with such raw products or manufactures as are fitted for exhibition and sale in warehouses. Under private management will be agriculture, cattle-rearing, and trade and transport in the narrower sense; but these occupations will be carried on not by independent speculators, but by guilds or industrial societies (*Zünfte*), organised by the state. Existing capitals in the possession of individuals at the instalment of the new system will not be interfered with; but its operation will prevent their subsequent increase. The instruments of production will be common property, but the instruments of enjoyment—the fruits of industry—will be the property of individuals. Foreign competition will be limited by protective duties. Winkelblech admits that his own, like every other social plan, must fail, if provision is not made against an undue multiplication of the workers. "Whoever," he says, "promises to the people to rescue them from wretchedness without setting himself against over-population, excites expectation which can never be realised, and should be looked upon as a dangerous demagogue." Adopting the theory of MALTHUS, Winkelblech regards the practical safeguards proposed by its author as altogether insufficient. Agreeing with him in advocating the suppression of a state provision for the destitute, he would go farther, and would enforce by law the abstinence from marriage in certain cases, which his predecessor only contemplated recommending as a moral duty. He would make it obligatory upon every member of his societary system to contribute to an assurance fund against the consequences of age, sickness, or misfortune, and for the maintenance of the widow and orphans he might leave at his death. No one should be permitted to marry until he could show that he had sufficient means to guarantee his payments to such a fund, and additions should be made to this "marriage capital" according to the number of his children. Such individual cases of distress as might continue to exist under the new order of things would be left to be dealt with by private beneficence.

ROSCHER speaks of Winkelblech as one of the most solid (gründlich), moderate, and conscientious of the socialists, and he appears to deserve that description. He took no part in political agitation, but maintained throughout the attitude of a thinker. His denunciations of the existing economic system were dictated, not by class-hatred but by genuine sympathy with the working people. But he expected too much from his new social order, even if it were possible to establish it. As Cossa remarks, whilst he saw clearly the difficulties which every form of socialism has to encounter in its almost certain results of insufficient production, excessive consumption, and the stimulus to an indefinite increase of population, he had at the same time a very undue degree of confidence in the precautions he suggests against those dangers.

[Lippert in *Handw. der Staatswissenschaften.*— Roscher, *Gesch. der N. O.*, p. 1021—Cossa, *Introd. to the Study of P. E.*, p. 539.—Rae, *Contemporary Socialism*, ch. ii.—W. H. Dawson, *German Socialism*, p. 48.] J. K. I.

MARMONTEL, JEAN FRANÇOIS (1723-1799), a distinguished 18th-century prose and verse writer.

Voltaire encouraged him to produce plays for the stage, and by the favour of Madame de Pompadour, he was appointed clerk of public buildings. In 1763 he entered the Academy, to which he became Perpetual Secretary. He was a member both of the electoral assembly of 1789 and of 1797, but was degraded for his moderation. His connection with political economy lies mainly but not entirely in the fact of the emotional interest the perusal of his *Mémoires* excited in the mind of J. S. Mill, at a very critical stage of that writer's career. His *Mémoires* have allusions to QUESNAY and other matter of economic interest.

[Mill's *Autobiography*, p. 140, ascribing to the experiences of this period "marked effects on my opinions and character"; also see Cossa,

Introd. to the Study of Pol. Econ., translated by L. Dyer, London, 1893, p. 331.—Marmontel's *Works* in 32 volumes, were published in 1787, 8vo.] A. L.

MAROGNA, CONTE GIAN GIUSEPPE (18th century), born in Verona; wrote on trade corporations for the prize competition offered for this subject by the academy of Verona, 1789 (see MARACHIO).

Marogna holds an intermediate place between the advocates of free labour and the supporters of old restrictions; he shows the disadvantages of some of the trade corporations, and suggests their partial abolition. Desiring to promote the improvement of manufactures, he suggested the uniting in trade corporations only those crafts which required skill and intelligence, leaving the rest free, and suppressing the corporations of merchants and dealers. For these latter, rather than for those of artizans, he fears the injurious effect of monopoly. Though Marogna advocates abolishing the corporations of merchants, he does not support free trade, but, on the contrary, recommends state interference in determining prices.

Sul governo delle arti-ragionamento, Verona, Moroni, 1792. [G. Alberti, *Le corporazioni d'arti e mestieri, e la libertà del commercio negli antichi economisti italiani*, Milan, 1889.] U. R.

MARPERGER, PAUL JACOB (1656-1730), was originally a merchant, before he entered the Danish and the Prussian civil services. At the time of his death he was an aulic and commercial councillor in Dresden.

Until the middle of the last century Marperger enjoyed a great reputation in Germany as being "perhaps the most distinguished supporter of cameralistic science," and "almost the only German author on trade." He was an inexhaustible writer on commercial subjects; his book on Banks (1716) is best known. Roscher is very severe on Marperger, and considers him as having simply diluted anterior publications and added to them some very trite moral sentiments (*Gesch. der. Nat. Oek.*, pp. 301-302). E. CA.

MARQUE, LETTERS OF. This term is derived from the mediæval Latin word *marcha*, a frontier, a letter of marque being a licence granted by a sovereign to a subject who has sustained wrong and been denied justice in a foreign state, to cross the frontiers and execute reprisals, that is, recover his property or seize an equivalent by way of compensation. Hence the full phrase is "letters of marque and reprisal." The fundamental idea, which was borrowed from the Roman law, was that nations formed a *societas* or partnership, with the customary incident of unlimited mutual liability. So far as the individuals were concerned upon whom such reprisals were taken, it was argued by the mediæval civilians that they could obtain indemnity from their countrymen, members of the same "societas"; whilst between them and the foreigner no such tie existed. Letters of marque were granted by John and Edward III. The earliest case mentioned by Ducange is in a charter granted by James, king of Aragon, in 1326. In the black book of the Admiralty, I. 385, is a complaint laid by a merchant of Danzig in 1409 against Henry IV.'s step-son, John, Duke of Brittany, and his subjects for the plunder of his ship. He was granted letters patent to seize Breton ships and goods in Irish waters to the amount of his loss, "nomine distruccionis vocate marquæ." The peculiarity of this case is that the grantee was an alien who claimed as being in amity with England. In 1416 a statute was passed reciting the wrongs and injuries sustained by English subjects at sea, and empowering the lord chancellor, where justice was denied to letters of request, to grant letters of marque (4 Hen. V. st. 2, c. 7). Such letters were not regarded as a breach of the peace. They were issued not only on behalf of individuals but of particular towns, as in 1487 by the emperor on behalf of Cologne against Scotland (Macph. I. 707). The feeling grew up in the 15th century that they were incompatible with treaties of peace, and Henry VII. remonstrated at their issue against the English by Ferdinand and Isabella in 1488. (*S. P.*, Sp. 17, p. 4 ; 21, p. 12 ; 34, p. 22, etc.). But numerous instances occur during the reign of Henry VIII. in which this practice continued. (*S. P.*, Dom. Hen. VIII. III. 2224. Acts Priv. Counc., I. 107, 108, etc.).

A limitation was, however, introduced into treaties, ·as into that between England and France on 7th August 1514, binding the sovereigns on either side only to issue "letters of reprisals, marque, or counter-marque" against principal delinquents and then only in case of denial of justice. (Rym. *Foed.* Hague ed. VI. i. 65). An example of such letters is given in Molloy, I. 46, dated 17 Car. II. Such letters of marque are now disused, and the term "letters of marque" is applied to commissions issued in time of war by the lords of the admiralty in conformity with various acts of parliament to owners of merchant vessels, called privateers, allowing them to capture ships of the enemy and to divide the prizes, which would otherwise belong to the crown. During the Crimean War the allied powers issued no letters of marque. By the Declaration of the Conference of Paris in 1856 privateering was abolished so far as the contracting powers were concerned. These were Great Britain, France, Austria, Russia, Prussia, Sardinia, and Turkey. Spain, Mexico, Venezuela, and the United States have refused assent to this agreement.

[Ducange. *Glossar.*—Molloy, *De Jure Maritimo*, 1769. — Blackstone, *Commentaries.* — Halleck, *International Law*, London, 1893.]   I. S. L.

MARRIAGE (FEUDAL SYSTEM). The lords of tenants by knight's service had the right

of bestowing in marriage their female wards while under age. This right, which was probably of gradual growth, makes its appearance as settled law about the 11th century. Its operation was soon extended, and a gift by the king, of a widow, in marriage, and her lands, is recorded in Domesday (Ellis, i. 337). It was required that the match should be, as Blackstone says, without "disparagement or inequality," and that the king's license should be given. This was to avoid marriages to the king's enemies. The right was afterwards extended to the case of male wards. If the infant refused to obey, he or she forfeited the value of the marriage, that is the sum actual or assessed which the guardian could have received for it. Marriage without the guardian's consent entailed a double forfeit. The right was only valuable in the case of the children of tenants by knight's service, for though, as Littleton states, it was in a sense also an incident of socage tenure, the *valor maritagii* did not in that case belong to the guardian—who was not an overlord, but was the person nearest of kin to the ward who was not in the line of inheritance. The MERCHET, or fine, for permission to manorial tenants of the villein class, and sometimes even to the freeholders, to marry was a minor source of revenue to the lord ; but it was totally different in origin from the feudal right. Henry I. by his charter of 1101 declared the right abolished, but his decree was inoperative in this respect. It reveals incidentally that widows as well as children of the king's barons, and *homines* were, as stated above, liable to the oppression, and that the barons claimed the same right over their own tenants by knight's service. The *Rotuli de dominabus et pueris et puellis de donatione regis*, drawn up in the 31st year of Henry II., gives a list of widows, their ages, children, and lands, thus showing the system in full operation. A special condition as to heirs, and the abolition of the right over widows, was granted by Magna Charta, but the sale of wards is recognised by the statute of Merton (20 Hen. III. c. 6), and the Hundred Rolls (*temp.* Edw. I.) include a return as to marriages and wardships. The whole system became intolerably oppressive in the 16th and 17th centuries, and was finally abolished by statute, 12 Car. II. c. 24. A vast bulk of original documents respecting wards and minors down to the time of the act exists in the Public Record Office (see MARITAGIUM and WARDS).

[*Fleta*, bk. i. c. 13 ; bk. iii. c. 11.—*Bracton*, ii. pp. 2-46 (Rolls ed.).—S. Grimaldi, *Rotuli de dominabus*, 1830, p. 4.—Spelman, *Feuds and Tenures*, cap. xv.—Blackstone, *Comment.* bk. ii. c. 5.—Hallam, *Middle Ages*, c. ii. pt. i.—Ellis, *Introduction to Domesday*, i. 337, 338.—Stubbs, *Select Charters*, 1881, pp. 100, 101, 297, 298.— Maitland, *Select Pleas in Manorial Courts*, p. 24, etc.—Scargill-Bird, *Guide to the Public Records*, 1891, pp. 113-117, 336-338.]   R. H.

MARRIAGE-RATE may be defined as the ratio between the number of persons belonging to a certain population who marry in a year, or other unit of time, and the number of the population. This is the sense in which the term is used in the English registrar-general's tables. In other countries the number of marriages, not of persons married, is often used as the numerator of the fraction which forms the marriage-rate. It has been proposed to use for the denominator not the entire population, but only the marriageable part of it. Some international statistics of this " specific " marriage-rate are given by Bertillon in his masterly discussion of " Matrimonialité," in the *Annales de Démographie Internationale*, vol. i. p. 20.

The definition of marriage-rate presents a difficulty which has been met in the case of other rates, viz. that the population cannot be supposed constant during so long a period as a year. This difficulty might be serious if the population were very small, especially in a peculiar case mentioned by Prof. Westergaard, (in the *Revue d'Économie Politique* for May-June, 1891, p. 443), where the occurrence of a marriage tends to diminish·the population under consideration, namely, the persons belonging to a certain occupation, which is usually abandoned on marriage.

The marriage-rate acts through the birth-rate on the increase of population. How indirect is this action appears by observing that in countries which have a particularly small natural increase, *e.g.* France and Massachusetts ('16 and ·65 per cent respectively, for the period 1865-1883, while the average for Europe is 1·06), the marriage-rate is either not particularly small (in France ·78 marriages per 100 living compared with ·83 for Europe), or even particularly large (in Massachusetts ·94 marriages per 100 living). For the number of the children to a marriage is particularly low in these countries (Marshall, *Principles of Economics*, note to ch. iv. bk. iv.).

Among the causes of variations in the marriage-rate, vicissitudes in material prosperity are prominent. Dr. Farr, surveying the ups and downs of the marriage-rate in England for nearly forty years, assigns an external cause for each fluctuation, now the influx of Australian gold in the year of the great exhibition, now a commercial panic, or the Crimean, or even the Abyssinian war. A similar explanation is attempted by Dr. Bertillon in the publication above referred to. The price of the principal article of food is a main factor under this head ; especially where the population is poor and near the brink of subsistence. The connection between the price of grain and the frequency of marriage is apparent in the statistics of Sweden and other continental countries[1] (cp. Sir Rawson

[1] See diagram, *Marriage-rate and price of rye in Prussia compared*, in art. on GRAPHIC METHOD.

Rawson, *Statistical Journal*, 1885, Quetelet, *loc. cit.* and most of the general treatises on statistics). In more advanced countries commercial crises and the state of international trade have at least as much effect as variations in the price of wheat on the marriage-rate. In England a fall in the marriage-rate has often been accompanied by a fall in the price of wheat (Dr. Ogle, *Journal of the Statistical Society*, vol. liii. (1890), p. 258). "The statistics even seem to suggest," says Prof. Marshall, "that this is not a casual coincidence," and he suggests an interesting explanation of the paradox (*Principles of Economics*, bk. iv. ch. 4, § 7).

It may happen that though wealth increases, yet the standard of comfort increasing more quickly, the marriage-rate declines. This may be in part the explanation of the decline in marriage-rate which has occurred in recent years in many civilised countries [see Sir Rawson Rawson's *International Statistics*, p. 521, also *Movimento dello Stato Civile : Confronti Internazionali*, 1865-83, Tavola I. *bis* ; and *Bulletin de l'Institut International de Statistique*, Table I., *bis*].

As another cause of variation in marriage-rates may be mentioned the different proportions of persons at each age in different populations. The manner in which the frequency of marriage varies with age is strikingly shown by a *stereogram* due to the Italian Statistical Museum, of which there is a copy in the rooms of the London Royal Statistical Society, an explanation in the society's jubilee volume, 1885, p. 247, and a criticism in the Journal for March 1894 (cp. Quetelet, *Physique Sociale*, vol. i. p. 275 and context).

Difference of season is also a cause of variation of marriage-rates, referred to periods shorter than a year. The deterrent influence of Lent is marked in Roman Catholic countries. A minimum in the month of March is matched in the adjacent months by maximum—or at least large—numbers of marriages displaced, as it were, from their natural position. On this head Quetelet well says : " Les lois naturelles ne sont point totalement effacées sans doute, mais il est difficile de saisir leurs effets au milieu des lois religieuses et des habitudes civiles." (*Physique Sociale*, vol. i. p. 261.)

The delicacy with which marriage-rates thus respond to the action of assignable causes is not inconsistent with the peculiar constancy which has been attributed to these statistics. The oscillations are not only precise, but also minute as compared with other coefficients in vital statistics—in particular with death-rates. This contrast is well shown by the diagram in Dr. Longstaff's *Studies in Statistics*, which presents the variation of the two rates from year to year in England. That of the two rates the one which depends more upon human volition should be the steadier is a circumstance deserving the attention which it has received from Quetelet (*loc. cit.*) and others. It may be ranked with the stability of the numbers of suicides as one of the wonders of moral statistics. It is not unreasonably used as proof that the reign of law extends over the domain of volition. (Cp. Mill, *Principles of Logic*, bk. vi. ch. ii.— Venn, *Logic of Chance*.)

[In addition to the works cited in this article the general treatises referred to in the article on DEATH-RATE should be consulted.]   F. Y. E.

MARRIAGE SETTLEMENT (also called ante-nuptial settlement), a settlement made, in contemplation of marriage, of funds respectively contributed by the intending husband and wife or their respective relatives or friends. The usual trusts of such settlements are : to pay the income of the husband's fund to the husband for life and the income of the wife's fund to the wife for life ; after the death of either of them to pay the whole income to the survivor for life or until remarriage ; after such death or remarriage to divide the fund among the children or issue of the marriage in such shares as the husband and wife or the survivor shall have appointed, and in default of appointment among the children of the marriage who shall attain the age of 21 years or, being daughters, marry under that age.

A marriage settlement, not being considered a voluntary settlement, is not defeasible in the settlor's bankruptcy.

One of the reasons which brought marriage settlements into general use, viz. the extensive rights which the law gave to a husband over his wife's property, has been removed by the Married Women's Property Act 1882 and the amending Acts, but the custom to have marriage settlements has remained unchanged.

No doubt the desire on the part of the friends of persons who are about to marry to secure an adequate and indefeasible provision for the intending husband and wife and their children is justifiable, but the practice of settling property, on marriage or otherwise, cannot, on the whole, be considered advantageous to the community. In the first place it diverts a considerable amount of capital from trade and industrial enterprise, and creates an artificial demand for so-called trustees' securities—thereby unduly increasing the facilities for borrowing of a special class of companies and public bodies. But its principal disadvantage is the fact that the persons concerned—knowing that in any event they can rely on a comfortable income—are less inclined to resist any temptation leading them to extravagance or recklessness. A system which allows a large number of persons to enjoy every comfort and luxury while their creditors must be satisfied with a small dividend on their claims, should not be encouraged by the law. If it were made illegal to impose any restraints on anticipated dealings with income, a great part of the mischief would be avoided. As the law stands, restraints on anticipation in express terms are invalid, except in the case of married women, but the ingenuity of draftsmen has overcome this difficulty by the insertion of clauses in many settlements declaring that the income is to be forfeited on any attempted alienation or on bankruptcy, and that on such forfeiture it is to be applied by the trustees for the benefit of the person to whom it originally belonged in his or her family. In this way the enjoyment of the income is virtually retained, and it is only the creditors who suffer by the forfeiture.

Marriage settlements like other settlements have always been subject to succession duty, and, when the interest of any successor exceeded £10,000, to Mr. Goschen's estate duty, of 1 per cent, and now they are subject to Sir William Harcourt's graduated estate duty.   E. S.

MARRIED WOMEN IN FACTORIES. See FEMALE LABOUR.

MARSHALL, WILLIAM (1745-1818), was one of the few really noteworthy English writers on agriculture ; to the student of agrarian development his works are probably quite as valuable as those of his contemporary and rival Arthur YOUNG, though their style and arrangement prevented their obtaining the same popularity. He came of farmer stock in the North Riding, and began his long series of agricultural experiments, and of treatises describing them, in 1774. His most important works fall into two groups. First come the twelve volumes in six pairs, describing the *Rural Economy* of Norfolk (1787), Yorkshire (1788), Gloucestershire (1789), the Midland Counties (1790), the West of England (1796), and the Southern Counties (1798), respectively. In these he carried out the *Plan* he had submitted to the Society of Arts in 1780 ; that is to say, he resided for a year or more, sometimes acting as agent or manager of estates, in one district after another, "minutely registering the provincial practice." Some time before, "in a journey of four or five hundred miles through the central parts of the Island, I experienced the inutility of a *transient view*,"—a thrust at the contemporary *Tours* of Arthur Young. The new Board of Agriculture and its secretary, Young, found in him an indefatigable critic ; and the *Reports* or *Surveys* drawn up under its authority occasioned a second series of volumes from Marshall's pen. To show how much better he could arrange the material, he drew up in five volumes *A Review and Complete Account of the Reports to the Board of Agriculture* for the Northern (1808), Western (1810), Eastern (1811), Midland (1815), and Southern and Peninsular (1817) "departments," respectively. In 1808 he retired to an estate he had purchased on the vale of Cleveland, and died there, while busy upon the construction of a building at Pickering for his proposed rural institute or college of agriculture.

[A list of his other works will be found in John Donaldson's *Agricultural Biography* (1854). Perhaps the most important of them are *Minutes of Agriculture, made on a farm of 300 acres of various soils, near Croydon, Surrey* (1778).—*Planting and Rural Ornament* (1796).—*On the Appropriation and Enclosure of commonable and intermixed lands* (1801).—*A Treatise on the Landed Property of England* (1806).]   W. J. A.

MARTIN, FREDERICK (1830-1883), started in 1864 that useful publication *The Statesman's Year Book*, and edited it until the December of 1882.

Among his works are :—*Commercial Handbook of France*, London, 1867, 8vo.—*The History of Lloyd's and of Marine Insurance*, London, 1870, 8vo.

[*Dictionary of National Biography*, vol. xxxvi., p. 275.]   H. E. E.

MARTIN, ROBERT MONTGOMERY (1803-1868), historical writer and statistician, is said to have been born at Tyrone, Ireland. He studied medicine, but apparently never practised. In 1820 he visited Ceylon, and thence travelled to the Cape of Good Hope, Australia, and India. From 1831, when he completed his *History of the British Colonies*, to 1844, he lived in England, taking a great interest in colonial trade questions, and devoting an untiring energy to the compilation of statistics. He gave evidence before the committee on the China trade. In 1844, he was appointed treasurer of Hong-Kong, but did not succeed in that capacity. Soon returning to England, he gave himself up once more to statistical research.

His chief works, apart from his *History of the Colonies*, were :—*Ireland before and since the Union*, 1844.—*Political, Commercial, and Financial Condition of the Anglo-Eastern Empire*, London, 1832.—*Analysis of the Parliamentary Evidence on the China trade*, 1832.—*Ireland as it was, and ought to be*, 1833.—*Poor law of Ireland*, 1833.—*Taxation of the British Empire*, 1834.—*Statistics of the British Colonies*, 1839.—*Monetary System of British India*, 1841. In 1848 he republished his two works on Ireland under the title *Ireland as it Was, Is, and Ought to Be*, in order to show that "no greater evil could befall Ireland than a disunion of the solemn legislative compact of 1801." [*Dictionary of National Biography*.]   C. A. H.

MARTINEAU, HARRIET (1802-1876), became first famous through the publication of *Illustrations of Political Economy*, 18 vols. in 9, London, 1832-34, 16mo ; the form of which was suggested by Mrs. Marcet's *Conversations on Political Economy*. In the curious autobiographical notice left behind for the *Daily News*, she wrote, "The original idea of exhibiting the great laws of society by a series of pictures of selected social action was a fortunate one ; and her tales initiated a multitude of

minds into the conception of what political economy is, and of how it concerns everybody living in society. Beyond this there is no merit of a high order in the work. It did not pretend to offer discoveries or elucidations of prior discoveries. It popularised in a fresh form some doctrines and many truths long before made public by others." Difficult as it may be to a generation which has been taught that *les dénoûments ne sont pas des conclusions* to credit it, the success of these tales was extraordinary. Within a few years their circulation reached to 10,000. Cabinet ministers, newspaper editors, and politicians appear to have vied for the privilege of having their proposals supported by the stories. A further series, *Poor Laws and Paupers illustrated*, 4 vols. in 2, London, 1833-34, 16mo, was undertaken at the suggestion of Lord Brougham. *Illustrations of Taxation*, 2 pts. 1834, 12mo, completed this branch of Miss Martineau's work. In her *History of the Thirty Years' Peace, 1815-1846*, 1849, 8vo, 2 vols., however, and in her *British Rule in India*, London, 1857, 8vo, considerable attention is given to the economic aspects of history. Her views on economic questions underwent great alterations. At first a "strict Benthamite," and adherent of the classical political economy, her American experiences considerably modified her views on the subject of property. She was led to expect further changes "which will probably work out in time a totally new social state," wherein the ideals of R. OWEN (*q.v.*) would to some extent be fulfilled. Her breach with the old orthodox political economy was no doubt widened by the positivist influences under which she came.

[*Harriet Martineau's Autobiography, with Memorial by M. W. Chapman*, 3 vols. 1877, 8vo.—*Dictionary of National Biography*, vol. xxxvi. p. 309.]   H. E. E.

MARTINEZ DE LA MATA, FRANCISCO (middle of the 17th century). The author describes himself as a brother of the order of penitents and servant of the afflicted poor, on the title of his *Memoriales ó Discursos en razon del remedio de la despoblacion, pobreza y esterilidad de España*, which were published about 1650, and reprinted by CAMPOMANES (*q.v.*) in his *Apéndice á la Educacion Popular*, vol. i., Madrid, 1775. Some extracts will also be found in SEMPERE's *Biblioteca Ec. Politica*, vol. iii., Madrid, 1804. Martinez de la Mata is a fervent representative of the later form of mercantilism : "Kingdoms and republics flourish by the manufacturing and traffick of the produce of industry, tillage, and breeding ; these reciprocally assist each other, but the *principal* nerve is manufactures (*artes*), which increase the population. . . . Labourers only bring into existence the fruits of the soil and leave them in the state in which nature supplies them ; as long as they remain thus their value is low, but this multiplies even a hundredfold when they are handed over to manufacturers," p. 3.

"France, Genoa, Venice, Florence, Holland, and England, have grown rich through the permission given to the subjects of Spain to consume their merchandise. . . . This is how they became deluged with gold and silver," p. 7.

He gives the list of the crafts (*gremios*) which had disappeared, p. 31; complains of the introduction of 120,000 foreigners, p. 130; describes, with many particulars, the professions which the latter had acquired, pp. 134 *seq.*; and gives details on the decline of some branches of industry, such as gloves in Ocaña, p. 252, and hosiery in Toledo, p. 261.

[Colmeiro, *Biblioteca de Economistas Españoles,* p. 115.]   E. CA.

MARULLI, VICENZO (18th century), a Neapolitan; one of the many Italian writers who in the 18th and beginning of the 19th century wrote on charity organisation then engrossing the attention of governments, and the labours of the studious. Marulli's work, like others, owed its origin to the inquiry made by the Neapolitan government in 1802, as to "the best means of maintaining and employing the poor of the kingdom of Naples and in the houses of correction." Marulli objects to begging, and would suppress it; he advises poor relief being carefully regulated in order that poverty may not be increased by it. He advocates establishing asylums, hospitals, etc., and especially a good organisation of public charity in order to avoid the disadvantages and incitement to idleness often arising from indiscriminate private charity. Begging can only be strictly forbidden when well-organised systems of charitable relief are established to meet the wants of the poor.

Ragionamento sulla mendicità, Naples, Stamperia Simoniana, 1804.

[Fornari, *Delle teorie economiche nelle provincie napoletane,* vol. ii., Milan, 1888.]   U. R.

MARX, HEINRICH KARL (1818-1883), distinguished as a socialistic theorist and agitator, was born at Trier. His father, who with his family passed in 1824 from Judaism to Protestantism, was a legal official. After receiving instruction at the gymnasium of his native place, Marx studied from the year 1835, first jurisprudence, then philosophy, at Bonn and Berlin. He settled at Bonn with the view of becoming a docent in the university. But his friend Bruno Bauer's difficulties with the government, arising from his theological views, convinced Marx that he too would find it difficult to maintain an academic position under Prussian rule. He and Bauer began, in 1842, at Cologne, the publication of the *Rheinische Zeitung* in the interest of the radical opposition. Towards the end of the same year Marx undertook the management of the journal, and removed from Bonn to Cologne. The govern-

ment forbade the continuance of the paper from 1st January 1843; and Marx, accompanied by Arnold RUGE, now went to Paris, having first married a young German lady to whom he had been for years betrothed. He and Ruge entered on a joint journalistic enterprise, which, however, speedily came to an end, partly from a difference of principles between the two associates. Ruge attached himself to the Hegelian philosophy and political radicalism; Marx studied economics, and through the influence of French writers, notably PROUDHON, became a socialist. In 1844 began the relation between Marx and F. Engels, which terminated only with the death of the former. Marx took part in producing a weekly journal published in Paris with the title *Vorwärts,* which covered with ridicule the absolutism and sham constitutionalism of the German princes. The Prussian government applied to the Guizot ministry for the expulsion of Marx from France, which was granted; and accordingly, at the beginning of 1848, he removed to Brussels, where he was joined by Engels. The two friends prepared, January 1848, the manifesto of the communist party at the request of a secret propagandist league; many German editions of this document have since appeared, and it has been translated into most of the European languages. The February revolution having broken out, Marx was expelled from Belgium, and at the invitation of the provisional government of the French republic, returned to Paris. He went to Cologne in the same year, and set on foot the *Neue Rheinische Zeitung;* among the contributors to this journal was LASSALLE. After having been twice before the courts of law for advising resistance to the government, Marx was expelled from Prussia. Retiring to France, he was forced to quit that country also, and fixed his permanent residence in London. During the following years he wrote much on current politics, and was the English correspondent of the *New York Times.* The first-fruits of his long-continued economic studies appeared in his *Zur Kritik der politischen Oekonomie,* pt. i., 1859. But, finding himself not yet in a condition to develop the consequences of his fundamental principles, he discontinued this work, and, returning to his studies, embodied his views finally in *Das Kapital,* of which the first book was published 1867, the second was edited after the death of the author by Engels 1885. The third part appeared in 1894.

In 1864 the INTERNATIONAL Association was founded, and Marx early took a leading part in its proceedings. His plan of a body of statutes and his inaugural address were preferred to those of Mazzini, which were put in competition with them; and thus he became the chief of the organisation, and wrote all the documents issued by the general council. The watchword of the party now became "Proletariate of all countries, unite." The fall of the French commune made the maintenance of the International in Europe impossible ; the anarchists created internal discussions in the body ; and the general council was transferred to New York. Marx now devoted himself diligently to the extensive studies required for the completion of his treatise, learning—it is said—with a view to this, the Old Slavonic, Russian, and Servian languages ; he continued, however, to exercise great influence by correspondence and personal interviews with the socialist leaders in different countries. But his failing health increasingly impeded his work ; and after the loss of his wife and of his eldest daughter, he died, sitting in his arm-chair. He was buried in Highgate cemetery.

The characteristic features of Marx's system are his view of the nature of capitalistic production, and his materialistic theory of history. According to him labour alone creates value, and the value of a commodity is measured by the quantity of labour which is socially, i.e. normally, necessary for its production. In existing society, the instruments of production are in comparatively few private hands. The other members of the community have nothing but their labour-power to sell. This is bought by the capitalist ; but, even when he pays its market-price, he does not pay its full value ; he appropriates to himself a portion of the product of the workman's labour, the whole of which ought to go to the workman ; and what is so appropriated, called by Marx the surplus-value (Mehrwerth), is the source of the capitalist's income. A value equivalent to the workman's subsistence, or, in other words, to the wages actually paid him, would be produced in a small number of hours ; but he is forced to work longer for those wages, and the product of this additional work, the surplus-value, goes into the capitalist's pocket, though he has no right to it. Hence, the effort of the capitalist to lengthen the working day, and of the workman to shorten it ; and in this struggle, so long as it is a purely economic one, the weaker—the workman—goes to the wall. When the capital embarked in a successful enterprise is increased, the surplus-value, as a whole, is enhanced ; and, as the productivity of labour rises with the progress of society, and as the workman's subsistence is thus supplied by a shorter labour-time, again the surplus-value is increased. Accordingly the tendency of the industrial world is to the development of industry on the great scale, and to the ever greater use of machinery ; and the increased division of labour, thus rendered possible, leads to the employment of women and children in manufactures—a new exploitation of the working-classes for the advantage of the capitalist, which also depresses the wages of men. An intense war of competition goes on between different capitalists, and, whilst there is perfect organisation within the individual factory, there is anarchy in social industry, regarded as a whole, which results in periodically recurring crises. The changing

proportions of "constant" and "variable" capital, i.e. of the permanent instruments of production on the one hand, and labour-power on the other, leads to fluctuations in the movement of population ; and the result is the creation of a disposable industrial "reserve-army," on which capital can call to meet any special demand ; and the existence of this class makes those who are actually employed more dependent and more willing to submit to the dictation of the capitalist. All this had been said in substance by other socialists ; but Marx here introduces what appears to be a new conception of his own. The capitalist system, he says, contains within it the seeds of its own destruction. The concentration of vast enterprises in the hands of a few magnates, the centralisation of the means of production in modern industrial establishments, and the associated form which labour takes in these establishments, will make it easy, when the due time arrives, for the state, once subjected to the political control of the proletariate, to step into the place of the capitalist. Those who have been hitherto the expropriators of the workmen will now themselves be forcibly expropriated ; all private will be transformed into collective enterprises, and the instruments of production will be used by the whole of society on a definite plan for its common ends.

The new social system thus to be arrived at is the last stage of a historical progress which Marx conceives as follows:—He adopts the view of Hegel (not peculiar, however, to that philosopher or his school) that the life of society is one of ceaseless change, the ideas and institutions of each period having only a rotative and temporary raison d'être, and necessarily giving place in due time to others which succeed as members of an ordered series. Marx holds—here diverging from his master—that the determining factor of these changes is purely material. The fundamental and causal element of the social evolution is economic. All other social forms—the legal, literary, religious, —in fact the entire civilisation of an epoch, is the outcome of its economic constitution—of the contemporary modes of production and exchange. The political state of a country at any period reflects the economic requirements of the class then dominating production ; and thus all history, subsequent to the primitive community of land-ownership, is a picture of the successive wars of classes. In each period are developed under the ruling class new productive powers which ultimately become irreconcilable with the existing forms of production ; and the class which represents these forces, and through them rises into importance, struggles with and overcomes that previously supreme. The constitution of society is changed, and a new order introduced. Thus feudalism was vanquished by the insurgent bourgeoisie ; and the bourgeoisie in its turn will be overthrown by the class it now plunders and oppresses—the proletariat. This will be brought about not by any moral triumph of ideas of justice, but by a historical necessity inherent in the existing conditions and movement of industrial life. The long-continued series of social struggles will then be closed ; class wars will be brought to an end by the disappearance of classes.

The adherents of Marx's doctrine speak of it as "scientific socialism," in contrast with the "utopian socialism" which in various shapes preceded it. This is certainly unjust, especially to RODBERTUS : if there be such a thing as scientific socialism, Rodbertus is entitled to be regarded as its founder. But, however this may be, Marx's work represents the now-prevalent form of socialism. *Das Kapital* has become, we are told, "the Bible of the social democrats." But it can only be a storehouse of facts and arguments for the leaders; it must be "caviare to the general." An English socialist has described Marx's style as "singularly brilliant"; but that is not the ordinary estimate. Roscher speaks of his "schwerfällig abstracte und doch unpräcise Ausdrucksweise," and Cossa characterises it as "stile sempre oscuro e talvolta inintelligibile."

Das Kapital has been translated into English by S. Moore and E. Aveling. Marx's friend Fr. Engels published in 1878 (2nd ed. 1886) *Herrn Eugen Dühring's Umwälzung der Wissenschaft;* and three chapters of this book were arranged as a pamphlet and translated into French by Marx's son-in-law Paul Lafargue (1880), with the title, *Socialisme utopique et Socialisme scientifique*. A good English version of this tract, bearing the same title, has been published (1892) by E. Aveling, and may be recommended as giving a clear and vigorous statement of the main lines of Marx's doctrine. The most remarkable of Marx's minor publications are the following :—*Einleitung zur Kritik der Hegelschen Rechtsphilosophie*, and *Zur Judenfrage*, 1843, in the former of which appear germs of thought which he afterwards more fully developed, especially his materialistic theory of history ; *Die Heilige Familie*, 1845, written in conjunction with Engels in opposition to the philosophic views of Bruno Bauer ; *Misère de la Philosophie*, 1847, in which he keenly criticised the *Philosophie de la Misère* of Proudhon, who had at one time much influenced his opinions, and in which the essential features of Marx's general economic system are already distinctly visible ; *Discours sur la question du Libre Échange*, 1848 ; and *Der achtzehnte Brumaire des Louis Bonaparte*, a commentary on the history of the *Coup-d'État*, inspired by fierce indignation against L. Napoleon, and admiring sympathy with the insurgents of June 1848. [For Marx's biography see art. on him by Fr. Engels in *Handw. der Staatswissenschaften*. Criticisms on his theories will be found in the same work, art. *Sozialismus und Kommunismus*, by Adler ; in E. de Laveleye's *Socialisme Contemporain* (English trans. by Goddard Orpen), ch. iv. ; Rae's *Contemporary Socialism*, ch. iii. ; Bonar's *Philosophy and Political Economy*, bk. v. ch. i. ; and the preface by Vilfredo Pareto to a series of extracts from *Das Kapital* published in the *Petite Bibliothèque Economique*. For the chief difficulty in the theory of surplus value and Marx's own way out of it, see Engel's Preface to *Kapital*, vol. iii., 1894, and the article on it by F. Butlin in *Econ. Journal*, 1895.] J. K. I.

MASERES, FRANCIS (1731-1824), mathematician and social reformer, was called to the bar in 1758. During the years 1766-69 he was attorney-general of Quebec. In 1773 he was appointed cursitor baron of the exchequer, a post he held till his death. He is said to have refused an increase of salary, but his private means were large. In 1774 he became a bencher of the Inner Temple, and is among the old benchers immortalised by *Elia*.

Maseres was the author of a *Proposal for establishing Life Annuities in Parishes*, London, 1772. A bill, embodying his scheme, passed the House of Commons in the session of 1772, but was thrown out by the lords. He defended it, in *Considerations on the Bill for enabling Parishes to grant Life Annuities*, London, 1773, 8vo, and again in his magnum opus, *The Principles of the doctrine of Life Annuities familiarly explained*, London, 1783, 4to. Its provisions, which enabled parishes to grant life annuities, and to invest the moneys received in the 3 per cent bank annuities in their own names, are worth noting, inasmuch as some politicians are advocating a solution of the Old-Age Pension question, by leaving to localities a large discretion in the initiation of various schemes. It is but fair, however, to say that Maseres did not believe that the life annuities he proposed would be bought by "day-labourers in husbandry, who are hardly able to save anything out of their wages."

The Principles, etc. is a volume of over seven hundred pages, but the great bulk of this is taken up with applications and illustrations. The actual principles are contained in the first ninety pages. Maseres made use of the tables of KERSSEBOOM and DEPARCIEUX, as given in the appendix of De Moivre's *Treatise on the Valuation of Annuities*. Maseres was also the author of numerous mathematical treatises, of pamphlets on subjects connected with North America, and of translations from the French. He also edited a great number of reprints of historical works.

[*Dictionary of National Biography*, vol. xxxvi. p. 407.] H. E. E.

MASLOV (19th century), a Russian economist, was the author of *Systems of Economics*, 1820 ; mentioned in Cossa's *Introduction to the Study of Political Economy*, p. 452 (trans. by L. Dyer, London, 1893) as belonging "to the domain of the history of economic literature." H. E. E.

MASSELIN, JEAN (died in 1500), was a canon of Rouen after 1468 and *orator* of the Norman clergy. Elected by the *bailliage* (bailiwick) of Rouen as its representative in the states general of 1484, he left a journal of their proceedings (*Diarium Statuum Generalium Franciæ*), and was himself on several occasions their spokesman, insisting with a firmness tempered by moderation on the necessity of financial reform.

The *Diarium* of Masselin was published 1835 (text and translation) in the *Collection des Documents Inédits pour l'Histoire de France*. E. Ca.

MASSIE, JOSEPH (d. 1784), economist and pamphleteer. He occupies an important position in the economic history of the 18th century, as a critic of the views of LOCKE and Sir Wm.

PETTY, and as having anticipated certain economic points more generally known in connection with the names of HUME and Adam SMITH. He wrote with insight on the causes of social and industrial evils, *e.g.* begging, prostitution, and theft ; and foresaw what a noxious and plentiful crop of ills was springing up for a later generation to deal with, through sentimental philanthropy, the unreformed poor-law, and the herding of deserted and pauper children in barrack "homes." Above all, considering the epoch, he is noteworthy as having been one of the earliest advocates of the systematic study of economic and commercial matters upon a wide and well-verified basis of statistics and history, by applying to economics the inductive method of the Baconian philosophy. His extant works are mainly fiscal, dealing with monetary problems, various branches of trade, and questions of taxation (*v. infra*, Nos. 1-7, 10-12, and 14-25) ; some of these are quite short, and such as might now be published in the reviews, or even in the daily papers.

The most important of his works are five in number—the *Essay on the Governing Causes of the Natural Rate of Interest* (No. 1), *Calculations of Taxes* (No. 3), the *Plan for the Establishment of Charity-Houses* (No. 8), the *Knowledge of Commerce as a National Concern* (No. 16), and *Observations relating to the Coin of Great Britain* (No. 17).

In the *Natural Rate of Interest*, Massie criticises what he gathers to be the opinion of Locke, that the rate of interest at any given time depends on the proportion which the quantity of money in a country bears to the debts of its inhabitants to one another, and to its trade ; that the profits of trade are instrumental in raising interest ; and that the proportion which money bears to trade not only governs interest, but the profits of trade as well ; while to Sir Wm. Petty, the rate of interest depended upon the quantity of money alone. Massie, on the other hand, who may or may not have been acquainted with Nicholas BARBON'S *Discourse of Trade* (1690), of which there seems to have been no copy among the fifteen hundred economic books and pamphlets which Massie collected at great outlay of time and money, and who anticipated Hume's published opinion on the same line of thought by two years, believed the governing causes to be (1) natural necessity ; (2) liberty ; (3) the preservation of men's private rights ; (4) public security. He therefore concludes that the natural rate of interest is governed " by the profits of trade to particulars " ; that the profits of trade are governed by the proportion which the number of traders bears to the quantity of trade ; and that the number of traders in turn is governed by the necessity of trade, and the encouragement with which it meets.

In *Calculations of Taxes*, Massie pours mild ridicule on the " ingenious men " who had evolved the proportion of taxation to incomes out of their inner consciousness. No calculations could be valid unless based on the following data : (1) the number of people in the nation ; (2) the pecuniary amount of their incomes or needful expenses ; (3) the rise in prices both of commodities and of labour, which is caused by taxation ; (4) the total sum paid annually in taxation throughout the whole kingdom. At the time Massie wrote the last item alone of these data was verifiable in the ordinary way. In order to arrive at some approximate idea of the proportionate amount of taxation contributed by individuals, he works out thirty typical cases, each containing such an annual balance-sheet as might naturally be worked out by each of thirty different heads of families in receipt of thirty different incomes, from a wealthy nobleman with a rent-roll of £20,000 a year to a rural labourer on 5s. a week.

The *Plan for the Establishment of Charity-Houses* and the other essays on social reform in the same volume are not only among the most interesting of Massie's writings in themselves, but are valuable on account of three positions which he there lays down, viz. (1) that the Elizabethan poor-law was a *causa causans* of evils which it was intended to cure ; (2) that the removal of multitudes of people from "our natural and fixed basis, land, to the artificial and fluctuating basis, trade," is fraught with grave social and industrial evils ; and (3) that the problem of prostitution is really not so much moral as economic. The remedies which Massie proposed were the equalisation of poor-rates in different localities, and the abolition of the settlement clauses of the poor-law ; the union of parishes to support a workhouse ; the entire separation of the honest and respectable poor from the loafer, the casual, and the " suspect," the three latter to be punished and put to hard labour in quite separate but neighbouring establishments, while the taint of pauperism was not to be attached to the former ; the teaching of new trades to the honest and respectable poor, and the careful selection of new trades so as to avoid increasing the keenness of competition among persons already provided with suitable employment elsewhere ; the establishment of charity-houses or " preservatories " for unemployed, deserted, or destitute women and girls, where they would be quite safe, and free from workhouse taint, and which would serve both as labour-bureaux and as training schools in newer industries. Massie laid great stress on national care for working women and girls, partly for the sake of the next generation ; partly because competition for work, being within much narrower limits, is keener for women who stand alone than for men ; partly from humanity, because they cannot resist brute force ; and partly because a ruined woman almost inevitably becomes a social danger. In return for the national service rendered by women in every rank of life Massie held that the nation, and particularly London, should protect them from being driven to evil courses by economic distress, by means of a penny rate levied on all houses in the metropolis on the basis of the poor-rate assessment, in addition to voluntary contributions. Other contributory causes of 18th-century lack of employment Massie held to be the decline of the woollen trade, the enclosure of commons and waste lands, and the growing practice of letting *e.g.* 500 acres to one farmer rather than 50 acres to each ten farmers.

The *Representation concerning the Knowledge of Commerce as a National Concern* is a plea (1) for such organised national collection and systematic storage of economic and commercial facts as is now provided for, to a limited but increasing extent, by the various departments of the Board of Trade ; (2) for the compilation of adequate outlines of commercial history—Massie here incidentally mentions that though he had spent twelve years in collecting some 1500 tracts, treatises, pamphlets, etc., on economic subjects, he yet found it impossible to compile satisfactory outlines of the history of any one British industry ; and (3) for the recognition of economics as a branch of liberal education and learning, to be dealt with by persons of wide knowledge, trained intelligence, and impartial soundness of judgment, who would discover " fixed principles " instead of trying to further personal commercial interests.

Observations relating to the Coin of Great Britain criticises Locke's views on money, and contains Massie's own suggestions as to remedying the then scarcity of silver and the over-valuation of gold, and a reprint of Sir Wm. Petty's *Quantulumcunque*. In Massie's opinion the main thesis, which Locke had failed to *prove*, was that " money cannot be raised above its intrinsic value, or, in other words, be made to pass current for more than the gold and silver in it is really worth as bullion " ; that an artificial over-valuation cannot be maintained, and that the only effect of such attempt is to cause a proportionate rise in prices. "The proper remedy for the present scarcity of silver money is reducing the current rates of guineas, and of other gold coins, which have long passed for more shillings and pence than the gold contained within them in bullion, when compared with the value of silver in bullion."

Massie's lesser works contain shrewd remarks apropos of *inter alia* the habitual fleecing of the British consumer by the West Indian sugarplanters ; the fatuity of imposing a new cyder-tax just when the woollen trade showed a tendency to migrate from the cyder counties into beer-drinking Yorkshire ; the raising of extra means to carry on the war (1757) by the commercially harmless plan of laying a tax on bachelors and childless widowers ; and the view that the North American colonies were a distinct hindrance rather than an advantage to British trade.

Massie wrote and published at London, usually, if not always, at his own expense, the following works :

(1) *Essay on the Governing Causes of the Natural Rate of Interest,* 1750, 8vo.—(2) *Observations upon Mr. Fauquier's Essay on Ways and Means for raising Money to support the present War,* 1756, 8vo.—(3) *Calculations of Taxes for a Family of each Rank, Degree or Class : for one year,* 1756, 8vo.—(4) *A Letter to Bourchier Cleeve, Esq. ; concerning His Calculations of Taxes,* 1757, 8vo.—(5) *Considerations on the Leather Trade of Great Britain,* 1757, 8vo.—(6) *Ways and Means for Raising the Extraordinary Supplies to carry on the War for Seven Years,* etc., 1757, 8vo.—(7) *Reasons humbly offered against Laying any further British Duties on wrought silks of the manufacture of Italy, the Kingdom of Naples and* Sicily, or Holland, 1758, 4to.—(8) *A Plan for the Establishment of Charity-Houses for Exposed or Deserted Women and Girls, and for Penitent Prostitutes ; Observations concerning the Foundling-Hospital, Shewing the Ill Consequences of giving Public Support thereto ; Considerations relating to the Poor and the Poor's-Laws of England ; also A New System of Policy, most humbly proposed, for Relieving, Employing, and Ordering the Poor of England ;* and *Forms of the principal Accounts necessary to be kept for those Purposes,* 1758, 4to.— (9) *Orders appointed by His Majestie (King Charles I.) to be straitly observed, for the Preventing and Remedying of the Dearth of Graine and Victuall* (a reprint), 1758, 8vo.—(10) *A Proposal for making a Saving to the Public of Many Thousand Pounds a Year in the Charge of Maintaining His Majesty's Marine Forces,* 1758, 4to.—(11) *Calculations and Observations relating to an Additional Duty upon Sugar,* 1759, s. sh. fol.—(12) *A State of the British Sugar-Colony Trade ; shewing, that an Additional Duty of Twelve Shillings per 112 Pounds Weight may be laid upon Brown or Muscovado Sugar,* 1759, 4to.—(13) *Farther Observations concerning the Foundling-Hospital,* 1759, 4to.—(14) *A Computation of the Money that hath been exorbitantly Raised upon the People of Great Britain by the Sugar-Planters, in One Year, from January 1759 to January 1760,* 1760, s. sh. fol.—(15) *To the Printer of the Gazetteer. A list of the various classes of people employed in . . . the Woollen Manufactory ; A State of the Exports to and Imports from the British Sugar-colonies ; Facts . . . relating to the new Malt Tax,* etc., etc., 1760, obl. fol.—(16) *A Representation concerning the Knowledge of Commerce as a National Concern,* 1760, 4to.—(17) *Observations relating to the Coin of Great Britain . . . whereunto is annexed, Sir William Petty's Quantulumcunque concerning Money,* 1760, 4to.—(18) *Reasons humbly offered against laying any farther Tax upon Malt or Beer,* 1760, s. sh. fol.—(19) *General Propositions relating to Colonies,* 1761, s. sh. 4to.—(20) *Brief Observations concerning the Management of the War, and the Means to prevent the Ruin of Great Britain,* 2nd ed., 1761, 4to.—(21) *An Historical Account of the Naval Power of France, from its first Foundation to the present Time, with a State of the English Fisheries at Newfoundland for 150 Years past . . . to which is added, a Narrative of the Proceedings of the French at Newfoundland, from the Reign of King Charles the first to the Reign of Queen Anne . . . First printed in the Year 1712, and now reprinted for general Information,* 1762, 4to.—(22) *Observations relating to British and Spanish Proceedings . . . to which is added a Proposal for replacing the New Taxes on Malt and Beer,* 1762, 4to.—(23) *Observations on the new Cyder-Tax, so far as the same may affect our Woollen Manufactures, Newfoundland Fisheries,* etc., 1764, fol. and 4to.—(24) *Brief Observations and Calculations on the present high Prices of Provisions,* 1765, s. sh. fol.—(25) *The Proposal, commonly called Sir Matthew Decker's Scheme, for one general Tax upon Houses, laid open,* etc., date uncertain, but probably in or shortly after 1757.—(26) Papers of ephemeral political interest.—(27) MS. catalogue of Massie's

collection of economic books, pamphlets, etc., dated 29th November 1764, Lansdowne MS. 1049 in British Museum.

[Roscher, *Political Economy*, vol. i. p. 150, tr. Lalor, New York, 1878.—Dr. W. Cunningham, *Growth of English Industry and Commerce*, vol. ii., see index ; and in *Economic Journal*, 1891, p. 81.—L. Cossa, *Introduction to the Study of Pol. Econ.*, tr. L. Dyer, 1893, pp. 224, 243.—M'Culloch *Lit. Pol. Econ.*, pp. 251, 330-31.—For date of death, *Gentleman's Magazine*, 1784, pt. ii. p. 876.]

E .D.

MASTER AND SERVANT. The early history of the relation of master and servant in England is that of a gradual transition from a relation of status to one of contract. In Anglo-Saxon times there were two classes of workers, the *ceorls* and the *theows*, whose condition differed somewhat. The ceorls were in a condition intermediate between slavery and freedom, corresponding to that allowed by a conquering race to friendly natives of an invaded country : they had a certain choice of masters ; they could hold land ; they sometimes had slaves of their own ; they had certain rights in the township lands ; they might acquire property, might purchase their freedom and might even become thanes. The theows were real slaves, as if they represented conquered hostile natives (*nativi*): they were not allowed to leave the land ; they had no remedies against violence on the part of their master, and an injury done to them was a wrong done to the master ; and they were, in fact, frequently sold abroad. The number of these slaves was increased by constant wars and by the practice of selling oneself to buy food or to pay a weregeld or to maintain a privilege of asylum. On the other hand, slavery tended to disappear under the influence of the church, which encouraged manumission ; but at the same time the ceorls probably tended to become worse off. After the conquest, the condition of the actual slaves seems to have become better, while that of the ceorls and the Saxon masters was depressed ; so that we find them mostly grouped as different varieties of one class of serfs or villeins. As time went on, the lot of the villein, though painted by Bracton in 1289 in miserable colours from the legal point of view, seems to have undergone substantial amelioration : various modes of becoming a freeman became available, such as becoming a member of a gild in a privileged town and remaining in that town for a year and a day, escaping as runaways and not being followed up, being emancipated in order that they might be engaged as soldiers, and so forth ; and in particular, he who had entered into a contract with his lord was considered as a freeman, and such contracts became very frequent, for the indefinite villeinage services were largely commuted for fixed money payments. Thus we find villeins holding land in

their own right and employing labourers ; so that except locally, in particular manors, the grievous incidents of villeinage (*see* VILLEINAGE) as described by Bracton seem, as Professor Thorold Rogers has pointed out, to have died out by the end of the 13th century, at any rate in their extreme form. The tendency to loosen the bonds of villeinage through neglect on the part of the lords, or through commutation of indefinite services for definite money rents, was at the same time somewhat neutralised by a tendency to read into the institution of villeinage the doctrines of SERVITUS (*q.v.*) of the Roman law ; but the burden of proof came to rest on the lord asserting a claim, for much land had come to be held under villeinage tenure by persons whose status was that of freemen ; and in the meantime the presumption of law was in favour of freedom, so that no seizure could be effected of any person alleged to be a villein. Thus things went on until the year 1349. In the meantime a great class of free labourers or craftsmen had sprung up in the towns ; united in GILDS (*q.v.*) they were free as against the world, but were much restricted by the bye-laws of the gilds, which themselves restricted the individual liberty of non-members as far as they could, through prescription or custom, assert the right of doing so. In 1349 came the great plague, which thinned the ranks of labourers and raised the rate of wages. This was felt by the employers of the day to be a great evil ; the old rights of villeinage were reasserted, and various attempts were made to enforce them. From the middle of the 13th to the middle of the 14th century the struggle lasted. The villeins resisted being interfered with, by litigation, by force, by rebellion, by ignoring the Ordinance of 1349 and the confirming statute of 1351 which attempted to regulate wages ; and on the other hand, passports for travelling, poll-taxes, attempted exclusion from apprenticeship, investigation of pedigrees, and the like, were set in force ; but the upshot was a practical defeat of the lords, for we find no averment in Jack Cade's rebellion of 1450 that the exactions of the lords were a grievance. By the time of Edward VI. and Elizabeth, villeins in gross—that is, persons whose personal status was that of villeinage—had almost died out ; villeins regardant—that is, persons holding under villeinage tenure, and who might possibly be freemen—became merged in the copyholders ; and the last reference to villeinage occurs in a law-suit of the year 1618, in which it was pleaded. Simultaneous with the decadence of the villeinage system was the growth of free labour ; but its grievance was the want of work. The population grew much more rapidly than the means of support ; and though many became attached to the manor-houses as " idle serving men " whose wages were nominal but who were fed and lodged, there were still many reduced to vagrancy. This feature of English life first becomes extremely prominent during the reign of Henry VIII., and it was thought fit to enact the most severe laws against vagrancy or wandering in search of employment, from the place of settlement, without licence to do so. The attempt to suppress vagrancy was combined (5 Eliz. c. 4) with an attempt to regulate wages and to keep craftsmen under control : apprenticeship was enforced ; craftsmen must render service in their craft when called upon, and that at rates to be fixed by the justices at Easter sessions ; and refusal to do so was enforceable by imprisonment. As regards workmen, the policy of the act of Elizabeth was the policy of English law until 1867 : breach of contract of service remained until that year an offence punishable by imprisonment ; and a long series of acts extended the principle to particular cases and made it, after the Union, apply to Scotland. Any able-bodied person not having any visible means of livelihood could, at law, be put to service ; but a large part of the original act had long fallen into abeyance, for the justices had long ceased to assess wages at sessions. Overlapping these acts were the series of FACTORY ACTS from 1802 onwards, and the Merchant Shipping Acts ; and in 1867 the contract of service was finally reduced to the same condition as any other contract, and breach of it made punishable, except in particular instances, only by damages, while combination was no longer illegal as a means of keeping up or raising wages, and the restrictions on the emigration of workmen were removed. The relation of master and servant is thus now a question of contract : but Mr. Macdonell points out in *Master and Servant* that there are still some points in respect to which the maxims of English law seem to a greater or less extent to have been founded on the relation of status. These are : that a master is justified in committing an assault in defence of his servant, or a servant of his master ; that possession by the servant is possession by the master, and that the master is liable for his servants' acts, apparently to an extent beyond that traceable to mere agency ; that an action lies for enticing away or harbouring a servant ; that the master has, in theory, a right of correcting his servant, though this is now probably not the law ; and that in many cases somewhat outside the domain of mere agency, acquisitions by the servant are acquisitions for the master. Besides this, the older ideas seem to cling to the word "servant," so that it is very difficult to frame a definition of it, applicable to all cases, from those of a Carriers Act to an action by a father for loss of his daughter's services by seduction of her. Mr. Macdonell suggests the following : —" One who for a consideration agrees to work subject to the orders of another."

[An excellent historical summary, with full references, is given in Macdonell's *Master and Servant;* which, with Smith's *Master and Servant,* and Eversley's *Law of the Domestic Relations,* may also be consulted for the law. For the Scots law, see Fraser's *Master and Servant.*—See Vinogradoff, *Villainage in England.*—Broom, *Constitutional Law* (Somersett's case and the notes upon it). See MANOR.]   A. D.

MASTERS' ASSOCIATIONS. Some of these societies aim at providing the benefits of insurance and trade protection for their members, without any special reference to their relations with their work-people, while others have been formed for the express purpose of joint resistance when individual employers have found themselves too weak to cope with the growing strength of the men's trade unions. The majority, however, may be considered to have both objects in view. There are at present about 100 of these masters' associations in existence, about a quarter of the total number being connected with the building trade. Being "temporary or permanent combinations for regulating the relations between workmen and masters, or masters and masters," they are trade unions within the meaning of the trade union acts. Very few of them, however, are registered under those statutes (see TRADES UNIONS).   T. G. S.

MASTROFINI, MARCO (19th century), born at Monte Compatri near Rome. He became an abbé, and is best known to economists through his book on usury, *Le usure* (Rome, 1831), which was well received, republished several times, and gave rise to much discussion. Though Mastrofini lived in this century, his opinions entitle him to be ranked among the canonists. His book in fact revives the old disputes as to the lawfulness of interest (see CANON LAW).

Mastrofini analyses the question of usury, taking it primarily from the standpoint of the ecclesiastic and of the moralist, rather than from that of the political economist. He argues from a desire to reconcile the doctrine of the church with the requirements of economics, and with a somewhat ostentatious display of learning in support of a theory, already broached by other writers, that the prohibition of the canonists referred not to interest received on money, but to usury in its more modern sense, that is to say, to exorbitant interest. He therefore asserts that a moderate compensation for the loan of capital is theologically permissible. He further maintains that the church prohibition had reference only to poor debtors. But while we may appreciate Mastrofini's endeavours to legalise, from a theological point of view, a fact which is rooted in the public economy of the world, we must recognise that his assertions are historically incorrect, and not based on a thoughtful interpretation of those on whose testimony he relies.

[Cossa, *Introduction to the Study of Political Economy,* London, 1893.—Graziani, *Le idee eco-*

nomiche degli scrittori emiliani e romagnoli, etc., Modena, 1893, p. 164, and others.] U. R.

MATERIAL PROPERTY. See PROPERTY.

MATERIAL SERVICES. See PERSONAL SERVICES ; SERVICES.

MATHEMATICAL METHOD IN POLITICAL ECONOMY. The idea of applying mathematics to human affairs may appear at first sight an absurdity worthy of Swift's Laputa. Yet there is one department of social science which by general consent has proved amenable to mathematical reasoning—STATISTICS. The operations not only of arithmetic, but also of the higher calculus, are applicable to statistics (see ERROR, LAW OF, and PROBABILITY). What has long been admitted with respect to the average results of human action has within the last half-century been claimed for the general laws of political economy. The latter, indeed, unlike the former, do not usually present numerical constants ; but they possess the essential condition for the application of mathematics : constancy of *quantitative*—though not necessarily numerical—relations. Such, for example, is the character of the law of DIMINISHING RETURNS (*q.v.*) : that an increase in the capital and labour applied to land is (tends to be) attended with a less than proportionate increase in produce. The language of FUNCTIONS is well adapted to express such relations. When, as in the example given, and frequently in economics (see Marshall, *Principles*, preface, p. xiv.), the relation is between *increments* of quantities, the differential calculus is appropriate. In the simpler cases the geometrical representations of functions and their differentials may with advantage be employed (cp. CURVES and FUNCTIONS).

Among the branches of the economic calculus *simultaneous equations* are conspicuous. Given several quantitative—though not in general numerical—relations between several variable quantities, the economist needs to know whether the quantities are to be regarded as *determinate*, or not. A beautiful example of numerous prices determined by numerous conditions of supply and demand is presented by Prof. Marshall in his "bird's-eye view of the problems of joint demand, composite demand, joint supply, and composite supply " (*Principles*, Mathematical Appendix, note xxi.). "However complex the problem may become, we can see that it is theoretically determinate " (*Ibid.*, cp. Preface, p. xv.). When we have to do with only *two* conditions, two *curves* may be advantageously employed instead of two *equations* (see CURVES and FUNCTIONS).

The mathematical operations which have been mentioned, and others—in particular the integral calculus, are all contained in the calculus of *maxima* and *minima*, or, as it is called, *of variations ;* which seems to comprehend all the higher problems of abstract economics

For instance, Prof. Marshall, after writing out a number of equations " representing the causes that govern the investment of capital and effort in any undertaking," adds, " they may all be regarded as mathematically contained in the statement that H − V [the net advantages] is to be made a maximum " (*Principles*, Mathematical Appendix, note xiv.). It was profoundly said by Malthus, " Many of the questions both in morals and politics seem to be of the nature of the problems *de maximis et minimis* in fluxions." The analogy between economics and mechanics in this respect is well indicated by Dr. Irving Fisher in his masterly *Mathematical Investigations*.

The property of dealing with quantities not expressible in numbers, which is characteristic of mathematical economics, is not to be regarded as a degrading peculiarity. It is quite familiar and allowed in ordinary mathematics. For instance, if one side of a plane triangle is greater than another, the angle opposite the greater side is greater than the angle opposite the less side (*Euclid*, Book I.). Quantitative statements almost as loose as those employed in abstract economics occur in the less perfectly conquered portions of mathematical physics, with respect to the distances of the fixed stars, for instance (see Sir Robert Ball, *Story of the Heavens*, ch. xxi.) ; *e.g.* before 1853 it was only known that "the distance of 61 Cygni could not be *more* than sixty billions of miles." It is really less than forty billions.

The instance of astronomy suggests a secondary or indirect use of mathematical method in economics, which physical science has outgrown. As the dawn of the Newtonian, or even of the Copernican, theory put to flight the vain shadows of astrology, so the mere statement of an economic problem in a mathematical form may correct fallacies. Attention is directed to the data which would be required for a scientific solution of the problem. Variable quantities expressed in symbols are less liable to be treated as constant. This sort of advantage is obtained by formulating the relation between quantity of precious metal in circulation and the general level of prices, as Sir John Lubbock (senior) has done in his pamphlet *On Currency* (anonymous, 1840). Thus the mathematical method contributes to that negative or dialectic use of theory which consists in meeting fallacious arguments on their own ground of abstract reasoning (see some remarks on this use of theory by Prof. Simon Newcomb in the June number of the *Quarterly Journal of Economics*, 1893 ; and compare Prof. Edgeworth, *Economic Journal*, vol. i. p. 627). The mathematical method is useful in clearing away the rubbish which obstructs the foundation of economic science, as well as in affording a plan for the more regular part of the structure.

The modest claims here made for the mathematical method of political economy may be illustrated by comparing it with the literary or classical method in the treatment of some of the higher problems of the science.   The fundamental principle of supply and demand has been stated by J. S. Mill with much precision in ordinary language (*Pol. Econ.*, bk. iii. ch. 2, §§ 4, 5, and, better, review of Thornton, *Dissertations*, vol. iv.).   But he is not very happy in indicating the distinction between a rise of price which is due to a diminution of supply—the dispositions of the buyers, the DEMAND CURVES remaining constant—and the rise of price which is due to a displacement of the demand curve.   He appears not to perceive that the position of equilibrium between supply and demand is *determinate*, even where it is not *unique*—a conception supplied by equations with multiple roots or curves intersecting in several points.   The want of this conception seems to involve even Mill's treatment of the subject in obscurity (*Pol. Econ.*, bk. iii. ch. 18, § 6).

The use of simultaneous equations or intersecting curves facilitates the comprehension of the "fundamental symmetry" (Marshall) between the forces of demand and supply; the littérateurs lose themselves in wordy disputes as to which of the two factors "regulates" or "determines" value.

The disturbance of the conditions of supply by a tax or bounty, or other impediment or aid, gives rise to problems too complicated for the unaided intellect to deal with.   Prof. Marshall, employing the mathematical theory of CONSUMERS' RENT, reaches the conclusion that it might *theoretically* be advantageous to tax commodities obeying the law of decreasing returns in order with the proceeds to give bounty to commodities following the opposite law (*Principles*, bk. v. ch. xii. § 6).   The want of the theory of consumer's rent renders obscure Mill's treatment of the "gain" which a country may draw to itself by taxing exports or imports (*Pol. Econ.*, bk. v. ch. 4, § 6 ; cp. bk. iii. ch. 18, § 5).   This matter is much more clearly expressed by the curves of Messrs. Auspitz and Lieben (*Untersuchungen*, Art. 81).

The preceding examples presuppose free competition ; the following relate to monopoly.   The relation between the rates and the traffic of a railway is shown with remarkable clearness by the aid of a diagram in the appendix to Prof. Hadley's *Railroad Transportation*.   By means of elaborate curves Prof. Marshall shows that a government having regard to the interest of the consuming public, as well as to its revenue, may fix a much lower price than a monopolist actuated by mere self-interest.   The taxation of monopolies presents problems which require the mathematical method initiated by COURNOT.   His reasoning convinces of error the following statement made by Mill (bk. v. ch. 4, 6) and others : " A tax on rare and high-priced wines

will fall only on the owners of the vineyard," for " when the article is a strict monopoly . . . the price cannot be further raised to compensate for the tax."   Cournot obtains by mathematical reasoning the remarkable theorem that in cases where there is a joint demand for articles monopolised by different individuals, the purchaser is apt to come off worse than if he had dealt with a single monopolist.   This case is more important than at first sight appears (see Marshall, *Principles*, bk. v. ch. x. § 4).

Under the head of monopoly may be placed the case of two individuals or corporate units dealing with each other.   The indeterminateness of the bargain in this case is perhaps best contemplated by the aid of diagrams (see on this case article on EXCHANGE, VALUE IN, and references there given).

These examples, which might be multiplied, seem to prove the usefulness of the mathematical method.   But the estimate would be imperfect without taking into account the abuses and defects to which the method is liable.   One of these is common to every *organon*—especially new ones—liability to be overrated.   As Prof. Marshall says, " When the actual conditions of particular problems have not been studied, such [mathematical] knowledge is little better than a derrick for sinking oil-wells where there are no oil-bearing strata."   Again, the mathematical method is a machinery, the use of which is very liable to be overbalanced by the cost to others than the maker of acquiring it.   Not only is mathematics a foreign language " to the general "; but even to mathematicians a new notation is an unknown dialect which it may not repay to learn.   As Prof. Marshall says, " It seems doubtful whether any one spends his time well in reading lengthy translations of economic doctrines into mathematics that have not been made by himself."

This estimate of the uses and dangers of mathematical method may be confirmed by reference to the works in the subjoined list ; which does not pretend to be exhaustive.

[Auspitz, R., und Lieben R., *Untersuchungen über die Theorie des Preises*.—Cournot, A., *Recherches sur les Principes Mathématiques de la Théorie des Richesses*, 1838.—Dupuit, E. T., *De la mesure de l'Utilité des Travaux Publics*, Annales des Ponts et Chaussées, 2e serie, 1844 ; *De l'influence des Péages*. . . .Ibid. 1849.—Edgeworth, F. Y., *Mathematical Psychics*, 1881 ; Presidential Address to Section F of the British Association 1889.—Gossen, H. H., *Entwickelung der Gesetze des menschlichen Verkehrs*, 1855, new ed. 1889.—Jenkin, Fleeming, *Graphic Representation of Laws of Supply and Demand*, and other papers, collected in *Papers, literary, scientific*, etc., 1887.—Jevons, W. Stanley, *Theory of Political Economy*, 2nd ed. 1878, 3rd ed. 1888.—Keynes, J. N., *Scope and Method of Political Economy*. — Launhardt, W., *Mathematische Begründung der Volkwirthschaftslehre* 1885.—Marshall, Alfred, *Principles of Economics*

2nd ed. 1892.—Pantaleoni, M., *Principii di Economia Pura.*—Pareto Vilfredo, Articles in the *Giornale degli Economisti* (1892 and 1893, summarised in the *Economic Journal* for March 1895, p. 113).—Walras, Léon, *Éléments d'Économie Politique pure*, 2nd ed., and other writings.—Wicksteed, P. H., *Alphabet of Economic Science.*—A list of mathematico-economic books is given in the first appendix to Jevons's *Theory.* F. Y. E.

MATHIAS DE SAINT JEAN, JEAN EON (1600-1681), known as *Frère procureur général* of the Carmelite friars in France, pub. under the name of "an inhabitant of Nantes," *Le Commerce Honorable ou Considérations politiques contenant les motifs de nécessité, d'honneur et de profit qui se trouvent à former des Compagnies de toutes personnes pour l'Entretien du Négoce de Mer en France*, Nantes, 1646.

As shown by the title, this book initiates the policy followed later by Colbert when he encouraged the foundation of the great trading companies with both Indies, the Levant, and Senegal. Mathias has a general and a special object. His general object is to demonstrate the natural usefulness and legitimacy of international trade and navigation, "which afford the most convenient and easy means granted by God to establish a perfect and universal society amongst the nations of the earth" (p. 133), an argument on which Mathias extensively dilates with great warmth and insight. His special object is to prove that French navigation being in a condition of utter decay, which he ascribes to the national want of enterprise, to depreciation of trade as a profession, and to the keenness of foreign competition, the securest way to emerge from this state of stagnation is to establish powerful trading and maritime companies, the shares of which ought to be subscribed by the French *noblesse;* this, he maintains, can be done without any fear or danger of a loss of status on their part. He also gives detailed statistical information on the imports effected in French ports by foreign bottoms, and calculates the profits which foreigners derive from these imports.

As to the practical legislation recommended, Mathias is not very consistent with his premises on the inherent usefulness of international trade. In his opinion the exclusion of foreign flags and strict reciprocity of custom-house duties would be insufficient to restore prosperity to French trade, and he advocates the return to the "just and wise by-laws" (p. 61), against foreign merchants which compelled them to take up their abode in the house of a known merchant,[1] and to offer their wares for sale at once. But he did not allow them to act as agents of foreign commercial houses. E. Ca.

MATTIA (DI), NICOLA (18th century). Mattia, in reply to the inquiry made in 1802 by the Neapolitan government as to the best means of maintaining the poor (see MARULLI), says that charity can be but a temporary remedy in doing this which can only be secured by placing poor citizens in a position to supply their wants by their own work. The real remedy for begging and vagrancy is to eliminate the causes of the evil by encouraging the sources of wealth. Charitable assistance should be temporary, and only given to those incapable of work. Almshouses even should be temporary, because the hope of finding an asylum in them encourages idleness. Vagrancy should be remedied by cultivating the uncultivated land in the kingdom of Naples, and thus forming a civilised and industrious nation. Mattia proposes the establishment of houses of correction and the assigning to them of waste land for cultivation.

Riflessioni su l'impiego dei poveri e dei vagabondi, e sul modo di estirparli dalla società civile, relativamente al Regno di Napoli, Naples, 1805. [See Fornari, *Delle teorie economiche nelle provincie napoletane*, vol. ii., Milan, 1888.] U. R.

MATRICULATION TAX. See FINANCE, GERMANY.

MATURITY OF BONDS. A bond, or debenture, usually matures after a given time, and is then presentable for redemption to the issuing state or corporation like a matured bill. Sometimes a bond is "drawn" by lot, and is then redeemable at par, or at some specified price, and those who possess bonds, subject to such drawings, should ask their banker or broker to make proper inquiry from time to time. A. E.

MAUGHAM, ROBERT (d. 1862), co-founder with Bryan Holme of the Incorporated Law Society, and its first secretary. Maugham was an active promoter of the interests of the legal profession, and wrote several legal textbooks and handbooks. His chief work, from the economic standpoint, is his *Treatise on the Principles of the Usury Laws*, in which, taking as a motto Shakespeare's "Borrowing dulls the edge of husbandry," he briefly traces the history of the statutory regulation of interest on loans, adversely criticises the proposal made in the early years of this century to repeal the usury laws which fixed the maximum rate of interest at 5 per cent, and contends that, while the laws may occasionally press hardly on individuals, it is essentially desirable, in the interest of the nation generally and on general principles of public utility, that there should be some legal restriction upon the rate of interest demanded. Further, he maintains that there are excellent reasons, given in detail, why there should be some distinction in the law between dealing in money and dealing in other species of property. He criticises Bentham's *Defence of Usury* closely and in detail, and also examines the criticism of Lord Redesdale's views by Sir W. D. Evans, quotes from Grotius, Pufendorf, Vattel, Paley, Bacon, Blackstone, and Adam Smith, and refers also to the Jewish regulations, which were political rather than ethical. Maugham also wrote a treatise on the

---

[1] See for similar English custom, MERCHANTS, ALIEN.

law of copyright, giving a brief historical view, and examining the library tax, piracy, transfer, principles of the laws, the then state of copyright law, with extensive citation of cases, precedents, etc.

A Treatise on the Principles of the Usury Laws; with Disquisitions on the Arguments adduced against them by Mr. Bentham and other writers, and a Review of Authorities in their Favor, London, 1824, 8vo, pp. 81.—*A Treatise on the Laws of Literary Property, comprising the Statutes and Cases relating to Books, Manuscripts, Lectures; Dramatic and Musical Compositions; Engravings, Sculpture, Maps, etc. Including the Piracy and Transfer of Copyright; with a Historical View, and Disquisitions on the Principles and Effect of the Laws,* London, 1828, 8vo, pp. 261.

[*Solicitor's Journal and Reporter,* vi. pp. 699, and 727.—*Dictionary of National Biography,* art. "Maugham, Robert."]　　　　　E. D.

MAUNDY MONEY. The royal alms, known as "Her Majesty's Royal Maundy," are distributed annually by the Lord High Almoner on Maundy Thursday, on behalf of the Queen. They consist of various cash payments made to persons of both sexes over sixty years of age, who are in necessitous circumstances, and who have at one time given employment to others and paid rates and taxes.

One of the maundy gifts is a payment, made in silver coins, of the value of as many pence as the years of the reigning sovereign's age, to a like number of persons of both sexes. In the present year (1896), therefore, seventy-seven men and seventy-seven women will receive the sum of 6s. 5d. apiece. The money is paid entirely in silver coins of the nominal value of 1d., 2d., 3d., and 4d. respectively, and it is to these small silver pieces, which are struck specially at the Royal Mint for the purpose, that the title "Maundy Money" is applied. These coins bear on the obverse the effigy of Her Majesty, with the usual inscription, "Victoria Dei Gratia: Britt: Regina: F. D. ; and on the reverse the figure "1," "2," "3," or "4," surrounded by a wreath of oak and laurel leaves, and surmounted by the royal crown. The edges of the coins are not milled, and the threepences, therefore, are identical with the coins of that denomination struck for general circulation. Collectors of coins frequently purchase the maundy monies from the original recipients, at enhanced prices, and with the exception of the threepences, a few of which may occasionally find their way into circulation, maundy coins do not pass into general use. The first coinage of small silver pieces intended solely for distribution on Maundy Thursday was struck in 1663. Prior to that date silver pence had been struck for general circulation, and the coins which formed part of the maundy alms were such as were to be found in the ordinary currency of the country.

The title Maundy, applied to the Thursday before Easter, is derived from "dies mandati"—the day of the mandate—as, on the day before Good Friday, Christ, after washing the disciples' feet, gave his new commandment, "That ye love one another" (John xiii. 34). Hence arose the custom of washing the feet of the poor by royal and other distinguished persons. This ceremony, which was accompanied by doles of food and clothing, can be traced back to the 4th century. James II. was the last king of England who washed the feet of the recipients of the maundy doles, but the custom is still occasionally observed in Austria and other European countries. The baskets from which the "mandate bread" was given away became known as "maunds."

At the ceremony of washing the feet of the poor, it was an ancient custom of the kings and queens of England to present one or two of the most necessitous with a gown from the royal wardrobe. This gift was, however, subsequently redeemed by a money payment supposed to represent the value of the garment.

As no provision was made to ensure the suitability of the maundy gifts to the various requirements of the poor persons, somewhat rough bartering among the recipients frequently took place, and, with a view to check these practices, the various doles were from time to time substituted by money payments, the last of the gifts in kind to survive being that of clothing for the men, which was distributed so recently as the year 1881. It having been found, however, that in most instances the men parted with the goods for less than their original cost, a sum of £2 : 5s. per head is now given instead of clothing. Thus the maundy alms are at the present time composed entirely of cash payments, amounting in all to about £5. The total sum is made up as follows: (1) The gift of pence per year of the sovereign's age, which is handed to the selected persons in a white leather purse ; (2) sums of £1 : 10s. in lieu of provisions, and £1 in lieu of the gown formerly given by the sovereign, inclosed in a red leather purse ; and (3) a further gift of 35s. to the women, or 45s. to the men in lieu of clothing, this last gift being inclosed in a paper packet.

The ceremony of the distribution of the maundy alms, which is of much interest, took place in the Chapel Royal, Whitehall, from 1714 to 1890, but since the latter date, the chapel having been closed, the gifts are distributed in Westminster Abbey.　　F. E. A.

MAURICE, JOHN FREDERIC DENISON (1805-1872), is noticed here for his connection with the Christian socialists (see CHRISTIAN SOCIALISM). We must remember, however, his protest against the "attempt to treat a human being as composed of two entities, one called religious, the other secular." As early as 1836 he expressed his conviction that "political economy is not the foundation of morals or politics, but must have these for its foundation or be worth nothing." For many years he brooded over social questions. As chaplain at Guy's Hospital, we find him regretting his own helplessness. In 1840 and again in 1842 weighty letters from Mr. Daniel Macmillan, on the divorce of the Church and the leaders of the working classes, addressed to Archdeacon Hare, and forwarded to Maurice, gave much food for thought. In 1844 he made acquaintance with C. KINGSLEY and was appointed in 1846 chaplain at Lincoln's Inn. In the same year Mr. Ludlow suggested to him a scheme for bringing the leisure and good feeling of the Inns of Court to bear upon the destitution and vice of the neighbourhood. In 1848 he became editor of *Politics for the People*, a weekly publication, which only lived through seventeen numbers. The first number, on 6th May, contained a characteristic article by him on "Fraternity." In December of the same year the Bible readings were begun, from which sprang the meetings with working-men, held at Maurice's house during 1849. These meetings bore fruit in the starting of a Tailors' Co-operative Association. Maurice had appeared, at times, somewhat lacking in enterprise ; he had a natural distrust of the spasmodic energy of the "go ahead." In advocating co-operation, he did not commit himself to any specific social plan. He remained throughout true to the conviction that the fundamental fallacy lay in "assuming that lands, goods, money, or labour are the basis of society, whereas human relations not only should, but do, lie beneath." In November 1850 appeared the first number of the *Christian Socialist*. By socialism Maurice meant "the acknowledgment of brotherhood in heart, and fellowship in work." The name suggested a struggle with unsocial Christians and un-Christian socialists. Years afterwards he justified its use on similar grounds. Yet above all he dreaded the formation of a new party with himself as leader. He protested against elaborate machinery, and held that to build associations upon decrees of a central board, was to build upon the sand. He saw clearly the danger of weakening moral influence by intermeddling with commercial details, and recognised in the Working-Men's College, founded in 1854, a more excellent way of serving co-operation. The following passage, written in 1849, and repeated almost verbatim in 1868, represents his economic faith. "The state, I think, cannot be communist ; never will be ; never ought to be. It is by nature and laws conservative of individual rights, individual possessions. . . . But the church, I hold, is communist in principle ; conservative of individual rights and property only by accident. . . . The union of church and state . . . is precisely that which should

accomplish the fusion of the principles of communism and property." It is noteworthy how closely this view resembles that of the CANON LAW (*q.v.*) towards private property. Nothing is easier than to criticise the Christian socialists : that the co-operative societies started by them mostly failed, while those started by the hard-headed workmen of the north (see CO-OPERATION) succeeded, was only what was to be expected. Yet even the direct results were not without importance, since the act of 1852, which legalised the position of such societies, was mainly their work. It is, however, to the indirect results that we must chiefly look. If the whole attitude of the working-class leaders towards religion and culture has been revolutionised, if the church of England, in its relations with the English people, has felt the breath of a new spirit, it is to the Christian socialists, and above all to Maurice, that the result is in large measure due. When he died there was a burst of popular grief such as had not been, it was said, since the death of the Duke of Wellington. Mystic, subtle, as he might be, working men understood him, because he understood them and their requirements—that a message for them to grasp must be something other and more living than mere opinions.

Of his forty-eight published volumes, not one is directly concerned with economic questions, and yet of all of them it may be said, as of his preaching at Lincoln's Inn, that whatever turn they take, they bring one's thoughts to the present day. As a good example of his manner may be cited the Lecture on masters and servants, in *Social Morality*, London, 1869, 8vo.

[For his attitude towards social questions see the correspondence in his life, edited by his son, Frederic Maurice, London, 1884, 8vo, 2 vols., and Charles Kingsley's Life, edited by Mrs. Kingsley, London, 1877, 8vo, 2 vols.—Art. by Prof. John on "Genossenschaftsbewegung" in *Zeitschrift für Volkswirthschaft* (Wien, band iii. heft iii. October 1894).—Art. by Thos. Hughes in *Econ. Review*, April 1891.]   H. E. E.

MAUVILLON, JAKOB (1743-1794), an eminent German economist of the school of the PHYSIOCRATS, was born at Leipzig, the son of a Frenchman settled there as teacher of languages. He studied the science of engineering, and in 1771 entered the Carolinum at Cassel as teacher of military architecture ; here the title of captain was conferred on him in 1778. In 1784 he was called to the Carolinum at Brunswick as teacher of politics and military tactics ; here he attained the rank of lieutenant-colonel. His literary career began with translating French and English works and treatises into German, particularly the *Histoire philosophique et politique des établissements et du commerce des Européens dans les deux Indes*, by RAYNAL (Hanover, 1774-78). His conversion to the doctrines of the physiocrats was brought about by translating Turgot's *Réflexions sur la formation et la distribution des richesses*. This appeared at Lemgo in 1775, under the title of *Untersuchungen über die Natur und den Ursprung der Reichthümer und ihrer Vertheilung unter den verschiedenen Gliedern der bürgerlichen Gesellschaft* (Enquiries into the nature and origin of Riches, and their distribution among the various members of Society). He came forward as a convinced adherent of the new doctrine in the *Sammlung von Aufsätzen über Gegenstände aus der Staatskunst, Staatswirthschaft und neuesten Staatengeschichte* (Collection of Essays on matters of Politics, Political Economy, and the most recent State-History), 1st vol. 1776, 2nd vol. 1777. Besides a number of economic treatises by foreign authors, including TUCKER's *Four Tracts*, the work also contains an exhaustive essay by Mauvillon himself:—*Von der öffentlichen und privaten Ueppigkeit und den wahren Mitteln ihr zu steuern, nach den Grundsätzen der neueren französischen Physiokraten* (On Public and Private Luxury (*Luxe*), and the true means of checking it, according to the principles of the later French Physiocrats). This essay is remarkable, that in it for the first time, evidently borrowed from the French compilation "Physiocratie," by Du PONT (1768), the expression "physiocratic system" was employed for Quesnay's doctrine, and "Physiocratists" for his followers.[1] Mauvillon dedicated the book to C. W. Dohm, his colleague, at that time professor of cameralistic science at the Carolinum at Cassel, whose antagonism to the "physiocratic system" he knew, and whom he, in the dedication, invited to a rejoinder. Thence a literary conflict arose round the "physiocratic system," in which there took part, besides Dohm, who answered in a treatise published in the Deutsches Museum, *Kurze Darstellung des physiocratischen Systems* (Short explanation of the Physiocratic System) (1778), a large number of other political authors. (On this conflict, see article GERMAN SCHOOL OF POLITICAL ECONOMY.) In 1780, Mauvillon published a rejoinder, *Physiokratische Briefe an den Herrn Professor Dohm* (Physiocratic Letters to Professor Dohm). This is his principal work in economics.

Mauvillon is described by W. Roscher as intellectually the most important of the German physiocrats. That, however, is saying too much, since this position is undoubtedly due to SCHLETTWEIN (*q.v.*). Mauvillon acknowledges in the *Physiocratische*

Briefe (Physiocratic Letters) themselves, that he has read but little of original physiocratic compositions. "There may thus perhaps be many things in my essays that are not entirely physiocratic, or that have not been said, or have been expressed differently, by the French economists. All that I desire is, that what I have said should be proved to be true. But if a name is needed, call it *Mauvillonish*" (p. 202). This "Mauvillonish" idea apparently causes him, in the treatise on "Luxury," to arrange the three social classes in such a manner that the landed gentry form a member of the productive class ; but on the other hand besides the sterile unproductive class is made a special *salaried* class, composed of public officials, clergy, artists, and so forth. Mauvillon shares the full enthusiasm of the French physiocrats for their opinions. Quesnay's system is not to him like any other, that has advantages and disadvantages, but it is the only true system ; it must, like virtue, be the best under all circumstances.—The co-operation of Mauvillon, in the work published by Count H. G. Mirabeau : *De la Monarchie Prussienne sous Frédéric le grand*, 1788, is well known. Mauvillon also published this work, some years afterwards, in German, under the title of *Von der Preussischen Monarchie unter Friedrich dem Grossen unter Leitung des Grafen von Mirabeau abgefasst und in deutsche Uebersetzung herausgegeben von J. Mauvillon Herzogt Braunschweigischen Oberstlieutenant* (On the Prussian Monarchy under Frederick the Great. Composed under the direction of Count Mirabeau, and published in German translation by J. Mauvillon, Lieutenant-Colonel of the Duchy of Brunswick), 1793. In the preface he describes his own share of the work as follows :—"Count Mirabeau really did not write this work, and the calumnious rage of his enemies and mine has compelled me to make this known. Only a few additions in the first and last books, and in the article on silk manufactures are by him. But to him, nevertheless, is mainly due the honour of the book, for he had conceived the idea of it, instilled it into me, gave me the means of accomplishing it, directed my work, and improved it very much after it left my hands." Mirabeau's *Lettres à un de ses amis en Allemagne, écrites durant les années 1786-90*, Brunswick, 1792, were addressed to Mauvillon, who published a German translation of them that same year.

Mauvillon also wrote several works on military science and history which, as remote from economic subjects, need not be noticed here.

[E. Leser, art. "Mauvillon" in the *Allgemeine Deutsche Biographie.*—W. Roscher, *Geschichte der Nationalokonomie in Deutschland* (History of National Economics in Germany).—Coquelin and Guillaumin, *Dictionnaire de l'Économie Politique*, art. "Mauvillon."]   A. O.

[1] Du Pont has generally been regarded in economic literature as the originator of the expression "Physiocracy." In my edition of the *Oeuvres de Quesnay*, (Frankfurt A. M., 1888), I have, at p. 696 note, shown that this expression occurs half a year before the publication of Du Pont's work, in the *Ephémérides du Citoyen*, and indeed in an essay by the Abbé Baudeau. As Quesnay had, as editor, assisted in arranging the title-page of the *Physiocracy*, in which his writings are collected, I believed the authorship of the word belonged to Quesnay, and all the more because Du Pont himself had never claimed it.   A. O.

MAXIMUM. See REVOLUTION, FRENCH.

MAXIMUM SATISFACTION is the object towards which the economic man strives ; the MARGIN, which constitutes economic equilibrium. A great part of economic theory may be regarded as a statement of the conditions of maximum satisfaction (cp. Marshall's *Principles*, mathematical appendix, note xiv.). Thus the theory of market price—that the demand at that price should equal the supply at it (Mill, bk. iii. ch. 2)—may be deduced as the condition of the price for which the satisfaction of the buyers and sellers should be a maximum.

It is understood that this maximum is subject, or—as the mathematicians say, *relative* —to certain limitations. Thus, in a market, it is assumed that property passes only by exchange. It is not denied that an equalisation of property would—abstracting ulterior consequences—be productive of a greater sum total of utility than is produced by the play of the market under a regime of unequal property (Sidgwick's *Pol. Econ.*, bk. iii. ch. vii. ; Jevons's *Theory*, 2nd ed. p. 153 ; Marshall's *Principles*, bk. v. ch. xii.).

It should be understood also that the *maximum* value of a function (see FUNCTIONS) is not necessarily the greatest possible value, but only the greatest of all values in the neighbourhood —a peak, but not the summit. There may be more *maxima* than one ; and one *maximum* may be greater than another (Marshall, *loc. cit.* note). Accordingly, while it is true that any disturbance by which trade is shifted from an equilibrium to a neighbouring position, causes a diminution in the sum total of utility, it is also true that a disturbance, by which trade is shifted to the neighbourhood of a new equilibrium, may cause an increase in the sum total of utility. The latter kind of change is apt to occur when, by a stimulus to increased production, the advantages of production on a large scale are secured. Now it is quite conceivable that such a stimulus should be given by governmental interposition. Thus, while it is right to hold with Messrs. Auspitz and Lieben (*Theorie der Preise*, p. 425) and the classical economists, that a bounty causes a diminution in the sum total of utility, the organisation of industry being supposed unchanged ; it is also right to hold with Professor Marshall that bounty, by bringing about a re-organisation of industry, may cause an increase in the sum total of utility.

Altogether, the doctrine that maximum satisfaction, or the greatest general good, is attained by exchange free from government intervention, is theoretically true in a much narrower sense than has been supposed by many publicists, and even by some theoretical economists. Its validity as a handy rule for practice is not denied.

[There is implied in the preceding argument a certain conception, which it is impossible here to express fully, concerning the modification of the law of supply—or SUPPLY-CURVES — which is involved in a re-organisation of industry, consequent on an enlarged scale of production. The view expressed on this subject by Mr. H. Cunynghame in the *Economic Journal* for March 1892 is in the main accepted by Prof. Edgeworth. His own view is expressed in the *Economic Journal*, vol. iv. p. 436. In his *Mathematical Psychics*, he has pointed out analogies between the principle of maximum utility in economics and the principle of maximum energy in physics.] F. Y. E.

MAYOR, the annually-elected chief magistrate of a corporate town in England.

At the date of Domesday Book towns were governed by a *præpositus*, or reeve, and in many the payments due from the inhabitants to the king had been commuted for a fixed annual amount, the *firma burgi*, but there was, as yet, no municipal organisation unless the claims of London, set forth in the *Statement* addressed by the corporation to the city of London commission (1893), are historically valid. Under Henry I., however, London obtained by charter the election of its own sheriff, perhaps in place of the portreeve, and, in 1191, the citizens extorted the recognition of the *communa* they had long been trying to gain. This implied complete municipal self-government under a mayor, to the exclusion of all royal officers except the judges ; but the *communa* must not be confounded with the merchant gild, from which it is essentially distinct in idea, though Glanville, in one passage, seems to treat the two as convertible terms. Indeed, it cannot be proved that London ever had a *gilda mercatoria*.

Henry Fitz-Alwyn, the first mayor of London, showed, in the affair of William Fitz-Osbert, that a corporation was not, in any modern sense, the champion of liberty ; and in the year 1200, by purchasing a charter for the abolition of the ancient weavers' gild, the new municipality manifested a determination to control, without a rival, the trade and manufactures of the city.

The mayoralty of London is typical of the office in all other places, the charters of provincial towns frequently containing direct references to the customs of London as a standard. Some towns were allowed to have mayors at an early date—Leicester, for example, in 1208, but Norwich had no mayor until 1402. The *Liber de Antiquis Legibus* assigns the date 1189 for Fitz-Alwyn's mayoralty, but not being a contemporary authority, its evidence must yield to that of Richard of Devizes and Benedict of Peterborough, who fix the year 1191 for the *communa*. Fitz-Alwyn held the office for life, and, in 1215, two years after his death, the king granted to the city the right of electing the mayor annually ; but many of the subsequent mayors served for four or more years.

The customs of London were confirmed by

the 13th article of Magna Charta, and the high position of the mayor is shown by the fact that the *major de Lundoniis* was one of the twenty-five barons charged with carrying out the provisions of the charter.

A mediæval mayor played an active part in regulating the trade of his town. All questions arising from contracts between merchants, and all matters relating to apprentices, came before him, and he enforced the assize of measures, and the ASSIZE OF BREAD AND BEER. Wine, also, was tested by his authority, and the price of it might be fixed by his directions. All matters, too, relating to breaches of the regulations of the craft gilds were determined by him, and he thus gained a controlling influence over manufactures.

But more direct methods were not wanting, by which the mayor, with the advice, of course, of his council, settled matters which would now be left to the free bargaining of the parties concerned, and the *Liber Albus* of London may be consulted to show (pp. 289, 711, 712) that there was no hesitation about fixing the prices of meat, poultry, and fish, or the wages of carpenters, masons, and other workmen within the city, while on p. 418 of the same record may be read a document which is nothing less than a commercial treaty with Amiens and other towns.

An excellent idea of the position of a mayor in a provincial manufacturing town may be obtained from Blomefield's *History of Norfolk* (Norwich volume).

The history of the London mayoralty, from the reign of John, is the history of London itself, for which vast materials may be found in the records already quoted, and in the *Statutes of the Realm*. The mayor of London is supposed to have been first styled *Lord Mayor* in 1354, when the fourth charter of Edward III. gave him the honour of having gold or silver maces. He is summoned to sit and sign with the privy council the proclamation of a new sovereign. The mayor of Dublin, first appointed in 1409, was styled Lord Mayor by Charles II. in 1665, and the mayor of York has also for some time been entitled to the same special dignity, which recently was also conferred on the mayors of Belfast, Birmingham, Liverpool, and Manchester.

Mayors are now elected under the Municipal Corporations Act of 1882, 45 & 46 Vict. c. 50, from among "the aldermen, or councillors, or persons qualified to be such," on the 9th of November in each year, but the lord mayor of London is elected by the liverymen from the number of aldermen, the city of London not coming under the provisions of the above-mentioned statute. The chief functions of a modern mayor are to preside over the meetings of the council, to act as a justice of the peace for the borough, to act as returning officer

at parliamentary and municipal elections, and to revise, with the aid of two assessors, the burgess lists when the borough is not represented in parliament.

[A. Pulling, *Laws, Customs, etc., of London*, 1854.—W. Maitland, *Hist. of London*, 1756.—Stubbs, *Constit. Hist.* and *Select Charters.*—James Thompson, *Essay on Eng. Municipal Hist.*, 1867.—H. A. Merewether, *Hist. of Boroughs*, London, 1835.—*Liber de Antiquis Legibus*, Camden Soc., 1846.—*Liber Albus (Munimenta Gildhallæ Londoniensis*, Rolls series).]   R. H.

MEAN is generally used in the same sense as AVERAGE. Some statisticians restrict the term to that species of average which is the centre of a group fulfilling the Law of Error (see ERROR, LAW OF).   F. Y. E.

MEAN AFTERLIFETIME. This word was proposed by Dr. W. FARR (*q.v.*) to express what is often called the EXPECTATION OF LIFE, *i.e.* the calculated length of time that persons, in the aggregate, live. "The idea intended to be expressed by 'expectation of life' is the mean time which a number of persons at any moment of age will live after that moment : it is the French *vie moyenne*. And this technical idea is strictly and shortly expressed by *after-lifetime*, a pure English word, formed on the same analogy as *afterlife*." W. Farr, *Vital Statistics*, p. 478.

MEAN, ARITHMETICAL. See AVERAGE.

MEAN PRICES. See PRICES.

MEANS, METHOD OF. The method of means or averages is mainly directed to two purposes : (1) to ascertain an objective quantity, such as the stature of a certain man, by taking the mean of several fallible observations ; (2) to find a so-called "subjective mean," such as the stature of the "mean man" (Quetelet) which may represent or typify the members of a species. Of these problems the latter kind is more frequent in the statistics with which political economy is concerned.

[See AVERAGE, and the references given under that head.]   F. Y. E.

MEASURE OF VALUE. See STANDARD.

MEASURES AND WEIGHTS. The measures and weights here dealt with are those which were in use in this country during the five centuries after the Norman conquest. At the beginning of that period the various systems were beginning to emerge from a state of chaos, at the end they were, except for scientific definition, almost the same as now. During this time the units, which were destined to survive, were standardised ; statute after statute was promulgated, ordering standards to be kept in various places for reference, and officers were appointed to examine and condemn false weights and measures. The immediate object of these acts was mainly fiscal, namely the prevention of the frauds on the customs revenue which were perpetrated by skilfully varying the size of the customary measures. As an instance of this fraud may be quoted the chaldron of sea-coal which grew enormously in size through the imposition of a duty on each chaldron landed.

Some commodities were sold by number, and here it must be remembered that our ancestors counted by the score, not the hundred, the latter not meaning necessarily 5 score, but 5 score and 8, 5 score and 12, or 6 score, according to the locality and the nature of the articles enumerated. A thousand being 10 hundreds, might be and sometimes was 1200. A dicker was 10, a dozen generally 12, but a dozen of iron was 6 pieces; a bind of eels 10 sticks of 25 each; a bind of skins 30 timbres of 10 each; a hundred of garlics 15 ropes of 15 each; but a hundred of most things was 6 score, of horse shoes 5 score; a cade of red herrings was 6 hundreds, each of 6 score; a last of herrings 20 thousands.

Linear and area measures have not altered much since the 13th century. The table contained in *De admensuratione terræ* printed among the *Statutes of the Realm* as of uncertain date, but probably compiled about A.D. 1300, is, except for the omission of the land chains, exactly the same as our modern long measure and area measure. At the time of the compilation of Domesday Book, however, and for a considerable time after, the area of the acre seems to have varied locally, but the acre, rod, and furlong, although originally independent units, were already definitely related to each other; the length of the ordinary field in the direction of the furrows being a furlong, a field a rod wide was called a rod or rood and four roods made an acre. The yard at this time was not looked upon as a subdivision of the furlong, but was merely a cloth measure. The Roman measures—the mile, and the foot with its subdivisions, were unknown; the measure for long distances was the leuca of 12 quarentines or furlongs, which, however, in Domesday book was only used for measuring woodland. The two other Domesday units of land measurements, the HIDE and the carucate (see CARUCAGE), have long puzzled antiquaries. The hide seems to have been a unit for the assessment of taxation, not a true measure, although a hundred years later in the *Dialogus de Scaccario* it was stated to be 100 acres. The carucate was as much land as required one plough team, the bovate or oxgang being the share attributed to each beast, an eighth of a carucate if eight oxen made a team. These two units soon lost their meaning and became obsolete, the carucate first, the hide after. The first recorded attempt at standardising was that of Henry I. who ordered that the *ulna* or yard, hence called *ulna regis*, should be as long as his own arm. His example was followed by Richard I. and John, who caused standard yards to be made of

iron. This yard was not the cloth yard, which does not seem to have been legally determined till the 14th century. Of miscellaneous measures of length and area may be mentioned—the solanda or double hide; solium, about 120 acres; virga or customary yard; tey, toise, or fathom of two yards.

The standard weight from the conquest till the time of Henry VIII. was troy weight. The troy pound seems to have been an arbitrary standard, although attempts were made to base it upon the weight of a grain of corn, by defining the pennyweight as the weight of 24 grains of wheat, and when it was found that this was not true, altering the number to 32. An old weight called the auncel was abolished by the statute of 25 Edward III. Although the legal pound was the troy pound, the merchants of the 15th century seem to have preferred a pound of 16 ounces; this pound was finally legalised by the act 24 Henry VIII. c. 3, where it is called *haber de payes;* it had already superseded the troy pound for most practical purposes. The most important table of weights in the middle ages was the wool weight.

7 lb. = 1 clove or nail, sometimes called great pound.	13 stone = 1 pocket or sarpler.
14 lb. = 1 stone.	16 stone = 1 pack.
2 stone = 1 tod.	26 stone = 1 sack.
12 stone = 1 wey.	12 sacks = 1 last.

A load varied from 168 to 175 stone. Although this was the table ultimately established by law, it was actually subject to great local variations. The clove or nail was often 8 lb. The stone varied locally from 7 lb. to 20 lb., and a long string of statutes did not succeed in making it uniform. The same remark applies to the sack. A weight called *pondus* was sometimes used and seems to have been about 20 lb.

For butter—

$$3 \text{ lb.} = 1 \text{ quart.}$$
$$2 \text{ quarts} = 1 \text{ pottle.}$$
$$7 \text{ or } 8 \text{ lb.} = 1 \text{ clove.}$$
$$14 \text{ lb.} = 1 \text{ pot.}$$
$$56 \text{ lb.} = 1 \text{ firkin.}$$
$$112 \text{ lb.} = 1 \text{ kilderkin.}$$

The stone or petra of lead was 14 lb.
5 stone made a pig, pes, formel, fodmael or fontinellus.
30 pigs made a charrus, carecta, or plaustrata, which weight, however, seems not to have been distinguished from the fother of 19 hundreds of 108 lb. each.
The following were the most common miscellaneous weights.
The bundle or garb of steel contained 30 pieces, and 25 pieces made a hundred of 108 lb., the bundle was also used for vetches, etc.
Mark of gold or silver = $\frac{2}{3}$ of a troy pound.
Quintal of iron contained from 96 lb. to 120 lb.
Seem or sum of glass was 20 stone of 5 lb. each.
Wey of cheese was by statute 224 lb., but varied locally from 168 lb., *i.e.* 6 quarters, to 300 lb.

Wey of barley, malt, or tallow was 6 quarters or 108 lb.

Wey of salt, 25 quarters.

The table of corn measures which can be drawn up from 14th century accounts is identical with that now in use. There was, however, in use till the reign of Edward III. a bushel of 9 gallons (or 2145 oz.), which only became obsolete after being declared illegal by numerous statutes. The first attempt to combine weights and measures into one system seems to have been made by the act of 12 Henry VII. c. 5 which declared that the gallon of wheat was to contain 8 lb. troy. There were a great number of customary dry measures; the following list omits those of which the name only is known.

Boll = 6 bushels.

Butt of salmon = 84 gallons.

Cade of tar = 12 gallons.

Celdra or chaldron of sea-coal or oats = 4½ quarters, but the coal chaldron varied considerably at different dates.

Cipha or sieve = about 5 quarters.

Coomb of east coast or ring of Huntingdonshire = ½ quarter.

Crannock (Irish) of oats = 16 bushels.

Last = 80 bushels of corn or 12 barrels of fish.

Load, seem, or sum = 6 or 8 bushels, or 12 trugg, but a sum of oats was 24 trugg or 2 quarters.

Mitta or met of salt = 2 bushels.

Pottle of butter = 2 quarts (v.s. under weights).

Strike = ⅛ quarter.

Windle of nuts, a Cumberland measure, was a bushel.

A measure called "water-measure" was in use in the 15th century containing 5 pecks; it was originally legalised for use on board ship, and continued to be used for fruit till modern times.

The liquid measures did not become important till the development of the wine trade in the 14th and 15th centuries, when a great number of strange measures were introduced from abroad. The barrel was a very variable quantity, almost every liquid having a different standard. The following wine measures were defined by statutes 2 Henry VI. c. 14, Richard III. c. 13, and 23 Henry VIII., viz.: tun, 252 gallons; pipe or butt of Malmsey, 126; tertian or puncheon, 84; hogshead, 63; tierce, 41; barrel, 31½; and runlet, 18⅓ gallons.

It must be remembered that, in dealing with any set of mediæval accounts, the equivalent of the various weights and measures given above must only be used as a rough approximation, to be verified or corrected by collating a number of accounts of the same place and date.

[Thorold Rogers, *History of Agriculture and Prices*, Oxford, 1866-1887.—Martin, *Record Interpreter*, London, 1892. — Halliwell, *Dictionary, Archaic and Provincial*, London, 1847.—Donisthorpe, *Measures*, London, 1895. — Round, *Domesday Studies*, London, 1888.—Ellis, *General Introduction to Domesday Book*, London, 1833.]

A. E. S.

MECHANICS OF INDUSTRY.   Just as all the physical sciences have their basis in the general principles of the abstract science of statical mechanics—the same primary laws of motion governing phenomena, whether of solids, liquids, or gases—so, according to JEVONS, does the structure of economic science, in all its branches, rest on an abstract theory of political economy, which concerns itself only with general laws, simple in nature, and deeply grounded in the constitution of man and the outer world, and which he designates "the mechanics of self-interest and utility" (*Theory of Political Economy*, 2nd ed. 1879, pref. xvii.-xviii., p. 23; art. on "The Future of Political Economy" in *Fortnightly Review*, November 1876, vol. xx. N.S., pp. 624-626). This, he says, "is entirely based on a calculus of pleasure and pain" (*Theory*, p. 25; cp. pref. vii.). For just as the theory of statics rests on "the equality of indefinitely small amounts of energy," so here economic phenomena are "explained by the consideration of indefinitely small amounts of pleasure and pain" (*ib. loc. cit.*); and the laws of exchange-value "are found to resemble the laws of equilibrium of a lever as determined by the principle of virtual velocities" (*ib. loc. cit.*, also ch. iv., see EQUILIBRIUM). Similarly, in the work of Professor Marshall (*Principles of Economics*, vol. i. 2nd ed. 1891), in which VALUE (*q.v.*) is recognised as the central idea in economics, the whole structure is at once seen to rest on the balancing of indefinitely small increments of utility against the corresponding increments of disutility (see DISCOMMODITY; FINAL DEGREE OF UTILITY). Still the theory of UTILITY, which results from the conception of "a calculus of pleasure and pain," is, as Dr. Keynes insists, rightly to be regarded as an essential premiss rather than as an integral portion of economic science (cp. *Scope and Method of Political Economy*, 1891, p. 88 n.).   A. B. C.

Dr. Irving Fisher in his *Mathematical Investigations in the Theory of Value and Prices*, has a good chapter on "Mechanical Analogies." Of these the most essential appears to be the analogy between mechanical equilibrium considered as a position of maximum energy, "where the impelling and resisting forces along each axis will be equal," and economic equilibrium considered as a position of maximum TOTAL UTILITY, "where the marginal utility and marginal disutility along each axis [each branch of production or consumption] will be equal." So in Prof. Edgeworth's *Mathematical Psychics*, pt. i. § 2, there is considered the analogy between the first principles of economics and "those principles of maximum energy which are among the highest generalisations of physics, and in virtue of which mathematical reasoning is applicable to physical phenomena quite as complex as human life." Professor Marshall too has indicated that all the conditions of economic equilibrium may be comprehended in the one condition that the total utility or net advantages should be a maximum (*Principles of Economics*, Mathematical Appendix, 2nd ed., note xiv.). But in his third edition (*ibid.* note xiii.) he appears to shrink from the wider applications of this principle to "every field of economics." . . . "Such discussions have their place, but not in a treatise like the present."

MEDIA ANATA, a tax of 50 per cent on the amount of their salary, which, from the time of Philip IV., was levied on all Spanish officials during the first year of their appointment. E. CA.

MEDIÆVAL FAIRS. The great continental fairs are one of the prominent characteristics of mediæval mercantile life, and the part they took in the development of international commerce and mercantile law is of conspicuous importance. Their origin must be ascribed to the great religious festivals which attracted large numbers of people to certain places at fixed periods, and therefore created exceptional opportunities for mercantile intercourse ; this explains their names ("fair" and "foire"—derived from "ferial" ; "messe" = "mass"), and also the special protection which was given to their frequenters. The records of some of them, as, for instance, the fair of St. Denis in Paris, go back to the 7th century, but the time of their fullest development is reached in the 12th century, when the six fairs of the Champagne country were successively held at Provins, Troyes, Bar, and Lagny, at periods extending over the whole year, and were frequented by merchants coming from France, Italy, Spain, Savoy, and Switzerland, Flanders and Brabant, England and Germany. These merchants enjoyed numerous privileges ; they were under the protection of the counts of Champagne, not only while they were taking part in the fair, but also on their way to the same, and on their homeward journey (*conductus nundinarum*), which, at a time when the plundering of traders was a regular source of income for the noble inhabitants of the castles near which their roads passed, was a considerable advantage, and they could not be arrested for debts previously incurred. On the other hand, claims arising from debts incurred at the fair were specially privileged both as regards procedure and priority.

A special "fair" tribunal was established, which had exclusive jurisdiction in respect of all transactions entered into at the fair, and in the case of persons returning to their houses without paying their debts, had power to issue a writ requiring the court of the place in which the defaulter was resident, to proceed against him. If such requisition was not complied with, the city or country to which the court belonged was placed under "interdict," which involved an exclusion of all its citizens from the privileges of the fair.

Being the great international meeting-places, these fairs offered exceptional opportunities for all money-changing transactions ; and on the other hand, the coins issued in Champagne were largely used for international payments ; hence the expression "troy" weight = weight of Troyes.

Promissory notes and bills of exchange payable at the fairs were convenient remittances in all mercantile countries, and the bankers who frequented the fairs seem to have established a regular system of clearing among themselves. Thus it was that not only through the interchange of goods, but also through personal contact, a feeling of community of interests was established among traders of all nations which could not fail to have a civilising influence in all countries. A uniformity of prices and mercantile customs was established to the great advantage of the general public, and the facility for the enforcement of debts and mercantile engagements generally by means of the extensive powers of a central tribunal, fostered trade by diminishing its risks.

Through local causes, the fairs of the Champagne began to decay in the middle of the 14th century, and some time afterwards those of Lyons began to assume an increased importance, which reached its climax in the 17th century. At the same time the fairs in Germany, especially the one at Frankfort-on-the-Main, began to develop, without however at any time attaining the international importance of the French ones. The Leipzig fair obtained pre-eminence in the 18th, and had great importance throughout the present century, but it has now ceased to exercise any material influence. The great fair of Nijni Novgorod in Russia is likewise failing.

[The information given above is mostly derived from Goldschmidt, *Universalgeschichte des Handelsrechts*, a book full of interesting economical information. See also the numerous authorities quoted by Goldschmidt, especially :—Bourquelot, *Études sur les foires de Champagne ;* see also Dr. Rathgen's article : *Märkte und Messen* in Conrad's *Handwörterbuch*, and the authorities mentioned therein ; article "Foire" by Turgot, in *Encyclopédie* of Diderot and D'Alembert ; see also MARKET.]
E. S.

MEDICI, THE. Though Florence was long shut out from unrestricted access to the sea, her trade and industry early exceeded those of towns such as Pisa and Lucca, which had the command of ports. The feudal aristocracy was overthrown by the industrial classes ; the nobles were compelled to live within the walls and to submit to republican rule ; and their repeated attempts to recover their former ascendency never succeeded for any length of time. The commonwealth rested essentially on commerce and the arts. The population, for political as for other purposes, was regimented in trade gilds ; associations of this kind had long existed, but they received their definitive organisation only in the latter part of the 13th century. Their number, after several changes, was fixed at twenty-one—seven greater and fourteen lesser. The most important industries were represented by the greater gilds, especially by the cloth-weavers, or Calimala,[1] the silk-weavers, and the money-changers. The wools of Italy were coarse, from the neglected condition of pasturage, as of agriculture generally ; and the cloth-weavers imported wool from France, Flanders, Spain, and Portugal, England, and Scotland. The manufacturers of the Calimala were forbidden by statute to deal in home-made cloths ; they imported the foreign fabrics made from the finer wools of Flanders, Holland, and Brabant ; these they dyed and dressed, and then sold, at first in Italy and the East, and at a later period in France and England, and even in the countries from which, in the undressed state, they had been brought. Many of these manufacturers were members of distinguished families whose names often recur in the history of Florence. The silk-weavers were already numerous in the early part of the 13th century, and rose to greater importance when the cloth manufacture declined in consequence of the growth of the corresponding crafts amongst the Flemish, French, and English, which sought to exclude the Italian wares. But money-changing was the business which was the chief source of the wealth of the city. The origin of bills of exchange, placed in 1199, has been attributed to the Florentines ; the commerce of Florence at least greatly extended their use. Banking was more flourishing there than in any other centre at the opening of the 13th century. In that century the Florentines had monetary dealings with Henry III. of England, and conducted the financial affairs of the holy see, which they long continued to manage to their great profit. Notwithstanding several reverses, arising from the action of the French and English sovereigns, the Florentine banks were numerous and powerful at the beginning of the 15th century. The Medici, the Bardi, the Acciajuoli, the Buonacorsi, and other great Florentine houses, had agents or branch establishments in London, Bruges, Paris, Lyons, Avignon, and Marseilles, besides those at Rome, Genoa, and Naples. In 1422 seventy-two exchange houses and tables are said to have existed at

Florence in the *Mercato Nuovo* or its vicinity. The Florentine merchants of the period were notable, not merely for ability as men of business, but for personal dignity, public spirit, munificence, and patronage of art, to a degree not equalled by those of any other country ; and of this combination of qualities several of the Medici presented eminent examples.

The Medici family first appears about the end of the 12th century. Giovanni de' Medici was a leader of an armed expedition of Florentines in 1251, and another member of the family took part in the expulsion of Walter de Brienne in 1342. They put themselves at the head of the *popolani grassi*, or superior trading classes, composing the greater gilds, who wrested the supremacy from the nobles in 1344. But the founders of the greatness of the family were Salvestro, and Giovanni surnamed di Bicci. Salvestro, who was gonfalonier in 1378, led a popular movement against the tyranny and proscriptions of the Albizzi. His son Veri was averse to public life, and devoted himself to commerce, which had already enriched the family. The defence of popular interests against the aristocracy became the hereditary policy of the Medici, and was effectively maintained by Giovanni di Bicci, who belonged to a different branch from Salvestro. Born in 1360, he inherited great wealth from his father Averardo, which he increased by his own ability, diligence, and prudence. In the register of property, 1427-1430, for purposes of taxation, Giovanni was second in the list of contributors. He had business relations, not only with the other Italian states, but with France and Flanders. All the great monetary affairs of Italy were transacted by him, notably those of Pope John XXIII. He expended largely from his private resources on public objects. As a politician his efforts were steadily directed to appeasing the enmities of classes and maintaining the internal peace of the republic. Giovanni's eldest son was Cosmo (1389-1464). He followed in the footsteps of his father. As a merchant he was skilful and successful. He had banks in all the countries of the west and was ruler of the European money-market. The agents who conducted his foreign speculations shared his prosperity ; and hence, as Machiavelli informs us, originated many enormous fortunes in the hands of Florentines, as in the cases of the Tornabuoni, the Benci, the Portinari, and the Sassetti. His great profits from banking, trade, and farming, added to his inherited property, enabled him to spend large sums in the erection of churches and convents, as well as on his own household and social expenses, which latter, however, he restricted within prudent limits, thus avoiding public prejudice. The loans which he made to the state and to private citizens established his popularity, and, after his temporary fall and brief exile, were amongst the solid foundations of the power which he retained without interruption to the end of his life. He guided his political party amidst great difficulties with consummate skill, and conciliated opinion by his uniform courtesy

---

[1] "The term seems to have been taken from the name of the street in which the guild is situated. The street led to a house of ill-fame ; hence the name *Callis Malus*, in the sense of *l'ia Mala*, evil road or lane."—*Villari*.

and his freedom from ostentation. Though practically the supreme director of the state, he assumed the manners rather of the first citizen of Florence than of its dictator. He did much for the furtherance of learning and art ; and, on the whole, well deserved the title of *Pater Patriæ*, which by public decree was inscribed above his tomb.

Some members of the liberal school of the present century, who habitually exalted what they vaguely called liberty above good government, have spoken in a hostile, or at least a grudging, spirit, of the early Medici, because, from circumstances much less dependent on their personal efforts than on the condition of Florence in their times, the administration of the state came into their hands. But Voltaire has justly said that there never was a family whose power rested on more legitimate grounds, and it would be difficult to find, in the period to which he belonged, a nobler type than that of Cosmo.

His son Piero (1416-1469) was an excellent and highly esteemed citizen, but much inferior to his father in political acuteness and practical sagacity ; and his grandson Lorenzo "the Magnificent" (1448 - 1492), though a brilliant and imposing figure, did‧ not approach at all so nearly as Cosmo to the ideal of the chief of an industrial republic. As the Medici took more and more upon them the character of princes, they "forgot to be merchants." Their agents often neglected or mismanaged their affairs ; and the commercial wealth of the family became completely dilapidated. Piero is thought to have seriously injured their political influence by demanding back loans which his father had made to many private persons—a proceeding which led to the insolvency of a number of merchants. But the failing resources of the Medici were largely supplemented out of the revenues of the state ; and the republic, by diminishing the interest on the public debt and by other expedients, as Hallam says, "screened their bankruptcy by its own."

The later Medici cannot be followed here ; they were no longer engaged in commerce, and in their political action did not rise above the other Italian rulers of their times.

[Machiavelli, *History of Florence.*—Guicciardini, *History of Florence.*—A. von Reumont, *Lorenzo de' Medici,* English translation by R. Harrison, 1876.—Pasquale Villari, *Two First Centuries of Florentine History,* English translation by Linda Villari, 1894.] J. K. I.

MEDINA, FRAY JUAN DE (lived towards the middle of the 16th century), was a Benedictine monk, and became the abbot of the monastery of this order in Salamanca. On the occasion of the regulations proposed by the government of Castile against the swarms of professional beggars who infested the country, a Dominican monk, fray Domingo de Soto, in his *Deliberatio in causa Pauperum* (Salamanca, 1545), had maintained their natural right to beg, and to pass from poor and destitute regions to other and richer parts of the monarchy. In his treatise entitled *De la órden que en algunos*

pueblos de España se ha puesto en la limosna para el remedio de los verdaderos pobres (On the Regulation of Almsgiving for the Remedy of the Real Poor), also printed in Salamanca in 1545, by the same printer and reprinted in Valladolid in 1757 under the new title of *La Caridad discreta con los Mendigos,* Medina asserts the right and the obligation of the local authorities to provide for the wants of their own and honest poor, and to expel, without mercy, all shameless and able-bodied beggars strangers to the locality. "Justice must temper mercy, and almsgiving must be dealt with in an unambiguous way."

[The debate between the two reverend antagonists is very clearly summarised by Don Manuel Colmeiro in his *Hist. Ec. de España,* vol. ii. pp. 34-36.]
E. ca.

MEDIUM OF EXCHANGE. See MONEY.

MEDJIDIE. Two Turkish coins bear the name Medjidie (after the Sultan Abdul Medjid) ; the gold medjidie, or Turkish pound, and the silver 20-piastre piece. The gold medjidie, of 100 piastres, is a coin weighing 111‧359 grains of gold of the millesimal fineness of 916‧6, and is equivalent in sterling value to 18s. 0¾d. or to 22‧78 francs of French standard gold, $\frac{9}{10}$ fine. The silver medjidie is a token coin weighing 371 grains, with a millesimal fineness of 830. F. E. A.

MEEK, Sir JAMES (1778-1856), was appointed in 1830 comptroller of the victualling and transport services at the admiralty. In 1841 he visited various foreign ports and cities to collect information as to the cost and supply of agricultural produce, etc. His report, which was printed by order of the House of Commons (*Parliamentary Papers,* House of Commons, 1842, vol. xl. No. 7), contained a mass of information, arranged in a tabulated form. It was of much service to Sir R. Peel in the preparation of his free-trade measure of 1846.

[*Dictionary of National Biography,* vol. xxxvii. p. 209.] II. E. E.

MEES, WILLEM CORNELIS (1813-85), was born at Rotterdam. He studied law at Utrecht, 1830-38, practised as a lawyer at Rotterdam (1838-47), where in 1843 he was also appointed secretary of the chamber of commerce. In 1849 he became secretary of the Netherland Bank, and 1863 president, which post he continued to hold until his death. Before he took his degree he wrote *Proeve eener Geschiedenis van het Bankwezen in Nederland* (History of the Banking System in Netherland), Rotterdam, 1838. His academical dissertation was entitled : *De vi mutatae monetae in solutionem pecuniae debitae.*

He also wrote the following works on economics :—*De Werkinrichtingen voor Armen uit een staathuishoudkundig oogpunt beschouwd* (The Workhouses for the Poor, from an Economic Point of View), 1844 ; *Het Muntwezen van Nederlandsch Indië* (The Currency System of Dutch India), Amsterdam, 1851 ; *Overzecht van enige Hoofdstukken der Staathuishoudkunde* (Leading Chapters of Political Economy), Amsterdam, 1866. Of several speeches delivered in the Royal Academy of Sciences, the following are the most remarkable :—(*a*) *De Muntstandaard in verband met de pogingen tot invoering van eenheid van Munt* (The Standard of Currency, in Relation to the Efforts to Institute Unity of Currency) ; (*b*) *Opmerkingen omtrent gelijke verdeeling van Belasting* (Remarks on an Equal Division of Taxes) ; (*c*) *Poging tot verduidelijking van eenige begrippen in de Staathuishoudkunde* (An Attempt to give General Information on Political Economy).

Mees was essentially a man of science, and a very correct thinker on economical subjects. He generally agreed with the doctrines of Ricardo and Malthus. Intellectual and moral development was considered the best means for improving society. His *Chapters* is a very remarkable book, tending especially to set forth the connection between the rate of interest and the rate of wages, and the bearing of both on prices. The *History of Banking* is very complete.[1] He was a bimetallist by conviction ; he advocated this system not only in his writings, but also at the Paris monetary conferences of 1867-68 as a delegate of the Dutch government. It may be claimed for him that he was one of the first who sought to place the doctrines of bimetallism on a scientific basis. As secretary and president of the Netherland Bank he gained great reputation ; his management of that institution was greatly admired, and he largely contributed to its extension and improvement.   A. F. v. L.

MEETING, COMPANY. The Companies Act 1862 makes it obligatory for every company incorporated under its provisions (§ 49) to hold once at the least in every year a general meeting, and minutes of all resolutions and proceedings at any general meeting must be entered in books provided for that purpose (§ 67). It is usual to provide in the articles for one general meeting to be held at a certain period of each year, and to call such meeting the "ordinary" general meeting of the company, power being given to the directors and also to a certain number of shareholders to cause "extraordinary" meetings to be convened for special purposes. (See Table A., art. 29-34.) E. S.

MELANCHTHON, PHILIP (1497-1560), like LUTHER (*q.v.*) and the other Reformers, dealt freely and at length with the economic topics of the time in his sermons and other writings. In his general attitude, as we might expect, he resembled Luther ; but his less passionate temperament, and his more scholastic learning

show themselves in several matters. Especially was this the case in regard to the burning question of usury (see INTEREST AND USURY). He follows the later canonists in approving of each of the three methods, and these in their most liberal form, by which a profitable investment was sought for capital,—the purchase of rent charges (*Census, Zinskauf*), partnership, and "interest" in its earlier sense. In the case of the last, while abiding by the old principles that the lender must lose a real opportunity of profit to have a just claim for recompense, and that the compensation must be reasonable, he took the decisive step of distinctly maintaining that compensation could justly be bargained for to run from the moment of the loan, and not simply on account of "MORA," or delay in repayment after an appointed time. See also NAVARRUS.

[Citations from his *Dissertatio de Contractibus,* and other works will be found in H. Wiskemann, *Darstellung* (1861), etc., and in G. Schmoller, *Zur Geschichte,* etc. (1861).—For an account in English see Ashley, *Economic History,* i. pt. ii. p. 457.]

                                                        W. J. A.

MELON, JEAN FRANÇOIS (16—-1738), born at Tulle, died at Paris. Originally practising as a lawyer at Bordeaux, he became in 1712 the paid secretary of a literary society, and then was appointed to the financial council established at Paris on the death of Louis XIV. He was then employed by D'Argenson and appointed inspector-general of *fermes* at Bordeaux. Afterwards he became the secretary of John Law, with whom he remained until the *Système* ceased to exist. Thence he passed into the service of the regent. At the death of the Duke of Orleans (1723) he returned to private life.

These successive occupations show a variety of ability which explains the welcome given by Melon's contemporaries to his *Essai politique sur le Commerce* (editions in 1734, 1736, 1742, 1761), and the influence he exercised in his time. The writings of Melon influenced DUTOT (1738), and the writings of the latter gave the tone to PARIS DUVERNEY (1740). The "inside" account of the *système* of J. Law, which Melon gives, is important. He favoured slavery in the colonies, the mercantile system, and the balance of commerce; but he did not support a protective system as at present understood, and was aware that the interest of the consumer precedes that of the producer. He shows a mind which might have been favourably influenced by Quesnay and Adam Smith, had he lived half a century later.

Guillaumin's collection (*Économistes Financiers du XVIIIᵉ siècle,* 1843) contains his *Essai politique sur le Commerce* as well as the *Réflexions politiques sur les Finances et le Commerce.*

[See reference to Melon—Hume, *Essays,* No. I., *on Commerce*—as to occupations of population in France, and in note Q, in which Melon's opinions are criticised. Turgot thought Melon eclipsed by Montesquieu and others, including Quesnay. *Œuvres,* ed. Daire, v. ii.]   A. C. f.

---

[1] It clears up much on the history of the Netherlands Bank, misunderstood by A. Smith.

MEMORANDUM OF ASSOCIATION.

Certain particulars respecting a company to be formed under the Companies Acts must be embodied in a document signed by at least seven members of the company, which document is called the memorandum of association. In the case of a company limited by shares, the required particulars are (1) the name of the proposed company ; (2) a statement as to whether the registered office of the company is in England, Scotland, or Ireland ; (3) the objects for which the company is to be established ; (4) a declaration that the liability of the members is to be limited ; (5) the amount of capital, and the number of shares into which it is to be divided. The directions as to the rights and, duties of shareholders and directors, and as to the manner in which business is to be carried on, are generally given by a separate instrument, the name of which is "articles of association," but which, in the case of a company limited by shares and willing to abide by the regulations laid down by "Table A" (in the schedule to the act of 1862), is not required. A great difference between the memorandum and articles arises from the fact that the latter can at any time be altered by special resolutions, whilst the former cannot be altered even by the unanimous vote of the shareholders, except subject to certain conditions and restrictions. Before 1890 the only alternative which was permissible was an increase of the capital of a company limited by shares, but the Companies (Memorandum of Association) Act, 1890, provides that, subject to the consent of the court, and to the compliance with certain formalities, alterations, as regards the objects of the company, may be made if it appears that they are required in order to enable the company (a) to carry on its business more economically or more efficiently ; (b) to attain its main purpose by new or improved means ; (c) to enlarge or change the local area of its operations ; (d) to carry on some business which may conveniently be combined with the former business ; (e) to restrict or abandon any of the objects specified in the memorandum.

If any alterations are required which cannot be effected in the above-mentioned manner, a reconstruction of the company becomes necessary.

[Buckley, *Law and Pract. under the Comp. Acts*, etc., 1888.]   E. S.

MENDICITY.

Mendicity differs in character in different countries and at various times, but it everywhere embodies two ideas, viz. living at the cost of others, and wandering from place to place in search of the means of subsistence. In ancient Greece the mendicant was a familiar figure, he was tolerated if not encouraged, as witness the combat between Odysseus and Irus, for the post of "gaberlunzie" in Ithaca. In Rome mendicancy was common and was not forbidden by law, though in the later days of the empire repressive measures were adopted. The early days of Christianity were marked by an absence of the mendicant class, but it soon began to grow, and the laws of Justinian on the subject were necessitated by the halo of sanctity with which the church at times surrounded the beggar. In this country, the attitude of the ruling power towards mendicancy has varied greatly. The 14th century saw a series of acts passed, each more stringent than the last, on this subject. Sturdy beggars were to be put in the stocks, sent to gaol, and generally treated as a public nuisance, and with great wisdom the act of 1349 punished with imprisonment those who gave to such. But the law was almost powerless in the face of the encouragement which the beggar found at the religious houses throughout the country, and in the countless forms of indiscriminate charity. There is ground for thinking that mendicancy flourished during the 15th century, and it was only towards the middle and end of the 16th that measures against it were enforced, possibly in part owing to the sounder teaching of the reformers on the subject. Then we find Southampton ordering that beggars should have their hair cut, and parliament decreeing punishment in a progressive scale of severity. Whipping, branding, cutting off the gristle of the ear, even death, were the penalties assigned ; whilst a loophole, so to say, was given by the provision which empowered the granting of licenses to beg. Lastly, in 1576 it was enacted that houses of correction should be provided in which the unemployed, who were generally vagrants, should be set to work. The end of the century saw a considerable abatement of the evil. From 1601 onwards the treatment of mendicancy has been a part of the general poor-law system of England. But the "rogue and vagabond" is the despair of the framers of acts for the relief of the poor, and dealing with settlement. Thus a consolidating act of 1713 lays it down that any person wandering about the country on any one of a long list of pretences is to be summarily arrested and removed to his settlement, or if he have none, to be dealt with by the poor-law authorities of the parish in which he is apprehended, but previously he may be flogged or set to hard labour, or committed for seven years to the custody of any person who will undertake to set him to work in Great Britain or the colonies. By the act of 1744 even women are to be flogged for vagrancy, and as late as 1824 flogging is retained as the appropriate punishment for "incorrigible rogues."

Under the new poor law of 1834 the vagrant was not distinguished from the ordinary pauper. Admission to a workhouse was a right enjoyed by all the destitute alike, with a corresponding freedom of discharge. Hence the vagrant found in the workhouse a convenient and cheap resting place. This led to the provision of 1842, by which the guardians were empowered to prescribe a task of work to be done before he quitted the workhouse, and punishment in the case of neglect to do it. By the act of 1871 he was to be detained till 11 o'clock, and if he reappeared at the same workhouse twice during a month, he was liable to detention till 9 A.M. on the third day after his admission. Special provision is now made for him in the way of accommodation and diet.

But the question of mendicancy is not one which can be solved by act of parliament. The legislature may provide for the treatment of "casuals," and make begging a crime, but such preventive measures will only be effective so far as they are supported by public opinion. The ordinary man feels compunction in "giving a beggar in charge," he has a certain sympathy with him, he lends a willing ear to his sad tale, he shirks the trouble of inquiry, he too often believes him. And so long as the demand for beggars in this shape continues, so long will the supply be forthcoming. Mendicancy takes many forms: the travelling hawker, duly furnished with a police license, the wandering musician, are in reality mendicants, for the sums they receive are out of all proportion to the services they render. The life of the mendicant has attractions of its own, as shown by the character of Edie Ochiltree in Scott's *Antiquary*, and the disinclination of mendicants to accept an offer of regular employment. Attempts to provide such employment are not wanting, they are seen in the work of the Salvation Army and the labour homes of the Church Army. In the same spirit philanthropists in Holland and Germany have founded INDUSTRIAL COLONIES (*q.v.*) in which vagrants may be gradually trained in the ways of regular and civilised living.

[For early and mediæval mendicancy, W. J. Ashley, *Economic History*, vol. i. pt. 2, ch. v., where a list of authorities is given.—English mendicancy is treated by C. J. Ribton James, *History of Vagrants*.—The attitude of the legislature may be followed in Nicholls, *History of the Poor Law*, and Aschrott, *The English Poor Law System*.]   L. R. P.

MENGOTTI, FRANCESCO (1749-1830). An economist and statistician, born near Feltre (Belluno). He was appointed in 1806 president of the general administration of finance in the Venetian provinces, and afterwards held the same post at Ancona; he was a senator in the first kingdom of Italy. When the Austrians returned into Italy, Mengotti became a councillor of the Venetian government, and vice-president of the board of taxation in Milan, where he died.

His best-known work is on *Commerce*, called by him "Colbertism" from Colbert. This was a prize subject, set in 1791, by the "Accademia dei Georgofili" at Florence, and the prize was adjudged to Mengotti's paper. In this essay the writer endeavours to reconcile the MERCANTILE SYSTEM and the doctrines of the PHYSIOCRATS. He advocates free competition, and suggests the measures necessary for the adoption of free exchange. He, however, commits the error of attributing the origin of mercantilism to Colbert, who, while he frequently experimented in and applied its methods in France, was not its inventor. Mengotti's style is pleasing; his work had great success, and went through several editions.

Mengotti also wrote an essay (1787) on the commerce of the Romans, which obtained a prize at the Academy of Inscriptions in Paris. In this work the author maintains the theory that the Romans did not understand the importance of trade, that they thought only of enriching themselves with the spoils of every nation, and that their sole commerce was that of transporting into Italy all the riches of the countries they had conquered. Finally, Mengotti wrote a work on treasuries and public loans.

Del commercio dei Romani dalla prima guerra punica a Costantino, dissertazione, 1787. — *Il Colbertismo, dissertazione*, Florence, 1792.—*Se sia piu saggio il sistema degli antichi di avere un tesoro ovvero quello dei moderni di fare degli imprestiti per sovvenire di pubblici bisogni*, 1828.
[Lod. Bianchini, *Della scienza del ben vivere sociale*, Palermo, 1845, pp. 279, 280.—Pecchio, *Storia dell' economia pubblica*, Turin, 1852, pp. 209-213.—Cossa, *Introduction to the Study of Political Economy*, London, 1893.—F. Facen, *Mengotti e le sue opere* (1875, nella Rivista Veneta).]   U. R.

MENIER, ÉMILE JUSTIN (1826-1881), a great French chocolate manufacturer and a member of the house of deputies.

Author of: *Théorie et Applications de l'Impôt sur le Capital*, 1874; *L'Avenir Économique*, 2 vols., 1875 and 1879; *La Réforme Fiscale;* and *Les Travaux de Paris par l'Impôt sur le Capital;* —made himself prominent as an indefatigable advocate of the taxation of fixed capital, and the immunity of circulating capital from all taxes.
                                        E. Ca.

MENSARIUS. In a general sense *mensarius* (cp. *trapezita* in Plautus) means a banker or a money-changer, and if it was not originally the precise equivalent of *argentarius* (see ARGENTARII) it probably became so in the closing days of the Roman republic, for Suetonius (*Augustus*, 2 and 4) in one passage applies the term *argentarius* to the grandfather of Augustus, and in another describes him in the same sentence as *nummularius* and *mensarius*, two words which Festus shows are equivalent by explaining one by the other. But these words may conceivably have denoted different aspects of his business. Livy (vii. 21) supplies a safer clue in the passage: *quinqueviris creatis, quos mensarios ab dispensatione pecuniæ appellarunt;* and again, (xxvi. 36) *argentum, æs signatum, ad triumviros mensarios referamus*. From these words it appears probable that *mensarii* were bankers in an especially public sense, and controlled the payments and loans made from public money ; but the matter is one upon which opposite views have been held by scholars.

[Smith, *Dict. of Greek and Roman Antiquities.* —Mommsen, *Hist. of Rome,* 1894, ii. pp. 86, 343, iii. 83.—Deloumie, *Les Manieurs d'argent à Rome.*]

R. H.

MERCANTILE SYSTEM. By the mercantile system we mean the economic policy of Europe from the break-up of the mediæval organisation of industry and commerce to the dominance of the system of LAISSEZ-FAIRE (*q.v.*). Strictly speaking, there is only one country, viz. England, in which the mercantile system can be studied in all its phases. In other European countries the growth of the system of *laissez-faire* has been arrested, or a revival of mercantilism has taken place, from various causes, such as the creation of the German empire, and increased military expenditure. It is conceivable also that even so far as England is concerned there might be some return to mercantilist principles if a definite attempt were made to carry into effect a scheme of imperial federation. The object of the mercantile system was the creation of an industrial and commercial state in which, by encouragement or restraint imposed by the sovereign authority, private and sectional interests should be made to promote national strength and independence. Writers of the mercantilist school regarded political economy as a branch of the science of statesmanship, and, unlike the early advocates of *laissez-faire,* held that private interests did not necessarily, or even usually, coincide with the interests of the community. There are many points of resemblance between the mercantile system and state socialism (see SOCIALISM). An organised industrial and commercial state is an ideal common to both, and many of the measures adopted under the former would no doubt re-appear if any considerable approach to the latter took place. But they differ in the ultimate end proposed. The object of the one was national self-sufficiency ; of the other, it is the improvement of the lot of the wage-earners. The mercantile system involved regulation and control by the central authority, but not necessarily the imposition of protective duties. Thomas MUN (*q.v.*), its principal English exponent, admits cases in which free importation or exportation is desirable, and many of the early writers regard with great approval the "lowness of customs" imposed by the Dutch republic. Whether, on the principles of the mercantile system, a duty should be imposed or not, would depend upon the relation of the industry or trade concerned to the general economy of the nation. But in effecting their objects mercantilist statesmen did, as a matter of fact, find it necessary to invent a very elabo-rate system of DISCRIMINATING DUTIES (*q.v.*), and so long as the principles of the mercantile system were accepted, any considerable approach to freedom of trade was impossible. Adam SMITH makes the theory of the BALANCE OF TRADE (*q.v.*), as elaborated in MUN'S *England's Treasure by Foreign Trade* (1664), the central doctrine of the mercantile system. He represents that most of the restraints and pro-hibitions of that system were the result of its teaching, or of ideas to which Mun gave expression. But in the light of modern his-torical research it can scarcely be maintained that the mercantile system was merely the outcome of a failure to distinguish between wealth and money. Mun's work, all of which was written before 1628, though not pub-lished until 1664, taken together with the pamphlets of Edward MISSELDEN and other writers, no doubt gave to the mercantile system something in the nature of a theoretical eco-nomic basis, but the system was "established" long before the controversy on the balance of trade and the bullion policy of the EAST INDIA COMPANY. The NAVIGATION LAWS, the CORN LAWS, the acts for the encouragement of tillage, the statute of apprenticeship, the Elizabethan poor law, and other great measures which con-stitute the mercantile system (see APPRENTICE-SHIP, STATUTE OF ; LEGISLATION, ELIZA-BETHAN), cannot be traced to the influence of any group of economic writers. They were the result of the efforts of statesmen so to direct the economic forces of their time as to create a strong and independent State. In Adam Smith's time the conditions which had really inspired the old regulations had practically disappeared. He made the mercantile system seem ridiculous by showing that it was based upon a mere popular fallacy. Apparently unconscious of the gulf between the 16th or the 17th century and his own time, he attacked the mercantilists because they had not fulfilled objects they had never had in view. His chapters are admirably designed for the demoli-tion of an already undermined and tottering system of political economy, but they do not convey a true impression of the real character and aims of his opponents. His defence of the Navigation Act of the Long Parliament, and his distinction between productive and unproduc-tive labour and consumption, transferred to the sphere of practical statesmanship, would afford a complete justification of the mercantile system. It is impossible, within the narrow limits of an article, to give even a sketch of the rise, progress, and decay of the mercantile system, or to estimate its results. Only a brief indica-tion of the general lines of development can be attempted. The influence of the system at any time depends upon a variety of circumstances, —the wealth of the country, the state of industry and commerce, the nature and the extent of foreign trade, the degree of political consolidation, the strength of the sentiment of nationalism, the power of the central authority and its relation to local or municipal bodies. Some of the earlier phases of the movement can be usefully studied in the commercial and industrial policy of James I. of Aragon. In the case of Barcelona, as in that of England, mercantilism succeeded a policy of free trade. In England the efforts of Edward I. to bring the industry and commerce of the country under the control of the government, and Edward III.'s free trade policy, were followed by a mercantilist regime. During the 15th century the development of the system can be traced in the struggles and rivalries of the staplers, a mixed body of English merchants and foreigners, the Hanse merchants, and the merchant adventurers, and the trade regulations of Edward IV. (see ADVENTURERS, MERCHANTS; HANSE OF LONDON; STAPLE; etc.). By the end of the century the general features of the mercantile system are well defined.

The general character of the economic problems which English statesmen had to grapple with in the 16th century has been indicated in a former article (see ENGLISH EARLY ECONOMIC HISTORY). The result was the mercantile system as embodied in the legislation of Elizabeth (see LEGISLATION, ELIZABETHAN); the organisation of the trading companies (see TRADE, FOREIGN REGULATION OF); and the NAVIGATION LAWS (*q.v.*). An instructive parallel may be drawn between the economic policy of England at this period and that of France, Sweden, and other European countries. Henri IV. "dressed a new plan of the French monarchy; and though his great designs were intercepted by an immature death, and also by a succeeding minority, yet the great Cardinal Richelieu resumed it again. He first taught France that the *fleur de luces* could flourish at sea as well as on land, and adorned the sterns of his new-built ships with this prophetic inscription, ' *Florent quoque lilia ponto* '" (Sir Philip Medows). But it was not only in this direction, but in his general policy, that he acted in accordance with the principles of the mercantile system; while Cardinal Richelieu was still more active in the same direction. The history of the system during the 17th century is practically the history of the internal measures, and the trade and diplomatic relations of England, France, Holland, and Sweden. Cromwell in England, and Colbert in France, are generally regarded as typical mercantilist statesmen. But this is scarcely true of Cromwell, Strafford approaching much nearer the ideal. In the time of the Commonwealth and protectorate, unmistakable signs can be discovered of the break-up of mercantilism, and the approach of a period of *laissez-faire*, particularly in relation

to the trading companies, the poor law, and certain industrial statutes; and by the end of the 17th century the decay of pure mercantilism was very marked. It is curious to notice how closely in this respect France and England kept pace with each other. The causes of the decay of the mercantile system have already been briefly indicated (see ENGLISH EARLY ECONOMIC HISTORY; FREE TRADE, EARLY HISTORY OF). It is necessary to observe, however, that economic policy was in certain directions in advance of economic theory. That nations should pass through a mercantilist "stage" seems inevitable. In the economic policy of the Great Elector, Frederick William (reigned 1640-1688), and Frederick the Great (reigned 1740-1786), features similar to those of England at an earlier date can be discerned. Though the theory of the balance of trade has disappeared, the policy of regulating industry and commerce with a view to national interests as distinct from those of the consumer is still prevalent throughout Europe and in the colonies. It cannot be said, therefore, that the mercantile system, in some of its essential characteristics, has by any means disappeared.

[Schmoller, *Mercantile System*, trans. by W. J. Ashley. Macmillan.]   W. A. S. H.

MERCANTILISM. See MERCANTILE SYSTEM.

MERCERS. The early history of this craft is obscure. They seem to have been originally traders in small wares, and " mercer " and " merchant " were frequently used interchangeably. But the term soon came to be restricted to dealers in what is now called haberdashery; and during the 15th century silks and velvets became their main articles of trade.

In London the mercers rose to importance during the reign of Edward III. Like some other misteries, their first formal association was probably in the form of a religious fraternity; and such a "fraternity of mercers" is mentioned as early as 1321. In 1365 they contributed more than all, save three other London misteries, to the expenses of carrying on the war in France; in 1377, like eight other misteries, they elected six members of the common council. It was not, however, until 1393 that the men of the mistery of mercery of the city of London secured by the payment of a heavy fine letters patent from Richard II., licensing them " to have a perpetual community" with power to elect four wardens to regulate the craft. The reason assigned for the license shows not only that the community was still largely of a religious character, but also that the mercers of that date were no longer content to deal in goods imported by others, but were themselves beginning to engage in foreign trade. It sets forth that " several men of the mistery often by misfortunes of the sea and other unfortunate casualties had been impoverished . . . wherefore the men of the mistery desired to ordain some certitude for the sustentation of such poor, as well as of a chaplain to celebrate divine offices." Among the most successful of the great merchants of the mercers' company was Sir Richard WHITTINGTON (lord mayor in 1398, 1407, and 1420), who appointed it by his will (1421) trustee of his college, almshouse, and other charities. The company had already, in 1393, received permission to hold lands to a certain value in mortmain ; by letters patent in 1424 it was expressly given the right to have a common seal, and to sue and be sued as a corporate person. It was from among the mercers that the organisation of Merchant Adventurers (see ADVENTURERS, MERCHANTS), arose early in the 15th century ; · and the two bodies long remained closely connected. So rapidly did the wealth of the mercers and their corporate dignity increase that during the second half of the 15th century the mercers' company was frequently placed first among the London misteries on ceremonial occasions, and this precedence was definitely confirmed to it by an order of the court of aldermen in 4 Henry VIII. In 1511 and subsequent years, Dean Colet, the son of a mercer, made the company trustee for his newly-founded school at St. Paul's, and granted to it considerable estates for the purpose. It built for itself a hall and chapel during 1517-52. During the later Tudor reigns the company grew in wealth and importance ; it shared in the reputation of its member Sir Thomas GRESHAM ; and it contributed largely towards the provision of troops, the storing of the city granaries, and other public purposes. Its position in the economic history of the 17th century is rendered sufficiently evident by the facts that it was in Mercers' Hall that the Council of Trade held its meetings in 1660, that there the earliest operations of the Bank of England took place in 1694, and that there subscriptions were received for the United East India Company in 1698. By this time, however, the company had come to be dissociated from the occupation whose name it bore. The loss of its buildings in the great fire of 1666 seriously embarrassed its finances : to pay off its debts it engaged, in 1698, in a most unprofitable scheme of granting annuities, from the disastrous effects of which it was only enabled to recover by means of a lottery authorised by 4 George III. During the present century its income has been enormously increased by the falling-in of building-leases in London. The annual revenue in 1879-80 was £82,758 (corporate, £47,341 ; trust, £35,417) ; and the livery in 1892 numbered 185.

There arose mercers' companies during the 15th, 16th, and 17th centuries in most other important English towns. The statute of apprentices (5 Eliz. c. 4) placed the craft of the mercer next after that of the "merchant trafficking into any parts beyond the sea" in the list of those occupations for apprenticeship to which a larger than the ordinary property qualification was necessary on the part of the parents. In the curious unions of incongruous crafts which were effected in the 16th and still more in the 17th century, it was frequently the mercers who gave their name to the chief craft organisation in the town. The main purpose of these later organisations was to enforce the law of apprenticeship, and to exclude strangers from the industry and trade of the several towns.

[For the London Company, see W. Herbert, *History of the Twelve Great Livery Companies* (1834), vol. i., and W. C. Hazlitt, *The Livery Companies of the City of London* (1892).—For other English towns a list of references will be found in C. Gross, *Gild Merchant* (1890), i. 129 *n*. 1 ; 139 *n*. 2.—*The Laws of the Mercers Company of Lichfield* of 1623, transcribed by Mr. W. H. Russell, are printed in the *Trans. of the R. Hist. Soc.*, N. S., vii. (1893).] W. J. A.

MERCHANDIZE, MARKS ON. See TRADE MARKS.

MERCHANTABLENESS, IMPLIED WARRANTY OF. According to the civil law which is followed in many continental countries the seller of a thing is held to guarantee the buyer against any latent defect in it. But the general rule of English law is *caveat emptor*. The buyer is entitled to have the article he contracted for, but its quality and condition must be the subject of express stipulation. In modern times the tendency is to narrow the rule of *caveat emptor*, and a notable exception engrafted in it is the implied warranty of merchantableness. When goods are bought by description from a manufacturer or dealer, and the buyer has no opportunity of inspecting them before purchase, the law implies a warranty or condition that they shall be merchantable, that is to say, that they shall be reasonably fit for the purposes for which such goods are ordinarily used.

[Benjamin on *Sales*, 2nd ed. p. 549.—Chalmers, *Sale of Goods Act*, 2nd ed. p. 29.] M. D. C.

MERCHANT ADVENTURERS. See ADVENTURERS, MERCHANTS.

MERCHANT LAW. See LAW MERCHANT.

MERCHANTS, STATUTE OF. See LAW MERCHANT.

MERCHANTS, STAPLE. See STAPLE.

MERCHANTS.

Merchants, History of English, p. 729 ; Merchants, Alien, p. 731.

MERCHANTS, HISTORY OF ENGLISH. Before the conquest, as long after, the merchant united several functions which subsequently became differentiated. He was the owner, whether individually or as a partner with others (CANON LAW ; PARTNERSHIP, CANONIST THEORY OF), both of the goods transported and of the vessel in which they were carried. "I enter *my* ship with *my* merchandise and sell *my* things," says the merchant in Archbishop Ælfric's *Colloquium.* On the other side, the merchant vendor of ready-made articles was at first indistinguishable from the artisan, who was eligible to the gild merchant (see GILDS). The merchant shipowner was necessarily a man of considerable wealth, and by a law of Ina of the 8th century, every merchant who had made three voyages was "thaneworthy," even though by birth a serf. The enumeration, in the dialogue above referred to, of the articles imported, points to a southern trade for the most part. "What do you bring to us?" the English merchant is asked. He replies: "Skins, silks, costly gems, and gold, various garments, pigments, wine, oil, ivory and orichalcus, copper and tin, silver, glass, and such like." The metallic imports, excepting gold, were probably the fruit of a coasting trade with Cornwall; the skins from Scandinavia.

The Norman conquest and the military ideas which then became dominant repressed mercantile activity. Internally trade was hampered by local privileges and tolls; at the ports by excessive duties. But in the middle of the 13th century the creation of the STAPLE showed the importance which the kings were beginning to attach to the export of wool to the low countries, where it was manufactured into cloth, large quantities of which were imported into England. About the same time began the endless disputes between the kings and the corporation of London as to the rights of alien merchants, showing the influence which the English mercantile class was beginning to assert. To the same period belongs the statute of merchants (see LAW MERCHANT). The great development of this class dates, however, from a century later, and was due to a concurrence of various causes. The first was the successful rivalry of the staplers with the Italian exporters of wool, who were privileged to ship wool without paying staple dues, and who in return supplied the kings, especially Edward III., with money for the necessities of state. The second was the expulsion of the Jews (see JEWS, ECONOMIC POSITION AND INFLUENCE OF) in 1290, which had set free their hoarded wealth. Thirdly, the dissolution of the order of the Temple in 1308 (see TEMPLARS) set free large accumulations of capital during the twenty-six years which elapsed before the bulk of the Templars' property, though by no means all of it, was transferred from the crown to the Knights Hospitallers. Fourthly, the northern coal-trade and the manufacture and export of cloth, specially stimulated by the invitation of Flemish artisans to this country by Edward III., created the first wealthy class of manufacturers and the first wealthy class of exporters of finished goods. This class, represented in both branches by the Canynges of Bristol,

sprang up with extraordinary rapidity, aided by the favouring circumstances already enumerated. Its rise suggested to Edward III. a means of disembarrassing himself of his Italian creditors, whose resources he had seriously drained, and whom he felt himself wholly unable to repay. In 1338 he made a proposal to the English merchants of the pre-emption of the 30,000 sacks of wool granted him as a subsidy. After pressure put upon them by the king and council, and by the Commons, a group of English speculators appears to have contracted for the wool upon conditions which, it may be inferred, were prejudicial to the Italians, who were in the same year generally arrested throughout the kingdom. In 1342 the merchants met in London, as a sort of sub-estate of the realm, and granted Edward III. a subsidy of 40s. a sack without consent of parliament. In requital they were gratified, in 1343, by the statutory raising of the price of wool, a policy possible to a country which enjoyed a monopoly. Two years later the king's creditors—the Bardi and Peruzzi—failed, and the English speculators assumed the title of "The King's Merchants," together with the financial functions which had for a time enriched their Italian rivals. They farmed the CUSTOM, large latitude being allowed to their impositions. They favoured the export of their own wools, and placed impediments in the way of those of their competitors. They farmed the SUBSIDIES (*q.v.*), buying the wools cheap and selling them, as the Commons complained in 1348, at a profit of 60 per cent. They acquired vast wealth as royal exchangers (see EXCHANGER, ROYAL) and as masters of the MINT, in which last capacity they were accused, in 1351, of malpractices with the coinage. They contracted for PURVEYANCE—buying provisions at nominal prices in the king's name, and reselling them at large profits,—for provisioning garrisons, and for raising troops, whose number and quality did not always tally with the muster roll. To this period belongs the rise of the great London trading companies, such as the pepperers or grocers, and drapers, and of the great capitalists, of whom the De la Poles and Whittington are the most notable. It is to be observed that Richard de la Pole, who belongs to a generation earlier, built up his fortune at the beginning of the reign of Edward III. by such contracts with the crown, while Whittington lent money on the security of subsidies. In 1406 to the merchants was entrusted the keeping of the sea, and one of their number, Nicholas Blackburn, was made admiral of the fleet.

After the Wars of the Roses the financial organisation of the kingdom was more complete, and transactions between the crown and its subjects were conducted through the agency of the two great mercantile societies of the staple and the merchant adventurers (see

ADVENTURERS, MERCHANTS; STAPLE), with one or both of which bodies eminent merchants, such as the Greshams, were as a rule associated. The internal tranquillity which followed upon the accession of Henry VII. was naturally advantageous to this class, and when public opinion became stirred, in the close of the 15th century, against the practice of inclosure, the "merchants, clothiers, and others," were attacked as engrossers of land and evictors. Even Thomas Cromwell, himself sprung from their ranks, contemplated an act in 1535, "That no merchant shall purchase more than £40 lands by the year." A bill to this effect, limiting the sum to £50, was actually introduced into parliament in 1559. These are evidences of the opulence of the class who, emulating the example of the De la Poles, extended their influence by aristocratic or, in the case of the Boleyns, even royal alliances.

During the decay of the staple under Henry VIII., and after its ruin on the capture of Calais under Mary, English mercantile enterprise availed itself of the new discoveries. The Thornes of Bristol made their way to the New World; Hawkins of Plymouth to Guinea and Brazil; Hore of London founded a colony in Newfoundland. These expeditions led to the formation of such trading companies as the RUSSIA; the TURKEY (see GUINEA TRADE); and the EAST INDIA and the VIRGINIA companies (see notices of these COMPANIES). It was through connection with these companies that the best known among the merchant princes of the 17th century gained their fortunes, such as Sir Thomas Smythe, Dudley NORTH, Sir Josiah CHILD, and Edward Colston of Bristol. The closing of the exchequer by Charles II. (see EXCHEQUER, CLOSING OF) was an influential factor in determining the sympathies of the mercantile class towards the revolution, and it was to them that the foundation and success of the bank of England, a mainstay of William III.'s government, was due. The general diffusion of wealth during the last century, due to the development of manufacturing industry, caused the disappearance of the line of demarcation which down to that time had distinguished the merchants from other classes.

To sum up. The great age of English merchants was the 14th century, when they were enriched partly through extension of trade, but more especially through financial business with the crown. The second period of prosperity, associated with the staple and the merchant adventurers, lasted from the conclusion of the Wars of the Roses till towards the close of the reign of Henry VIII. The third began with the exploitation of the new discoveries by the great trading companies, and lasted till the Civil War. The fourth was due to the extension of trade with America and India during the close of the reign of Charles II. After this time great fortunes were amassed by the development of internal trade, the term merchant reverting to its ancient signification, and no longer necessarily bearing a connotation of foreign adventure.

[Stubbs, *Const. Hist. Eng.*, vol. ii.—Schanz, *Englische Handelspolitik*, 1881, 2 bde.—*Trans. Roy. Hist. Soc.*, 1895.—H. R. Fox Bourne, *English Merchants*, 2 vols., 1866.—J. W. Burgon, *Life of Sir T. Gresham*, 2 vols., 1839.—W. S. Lindsay, *Hist. of Merchant Shipping*, 4 vols., 1874.—State Papers, Domestic, Hen. VIII.—Sir F. Palgrave, *The Merchant and the Friar*, 1837.] I. S. L.

MERCHANTS, ALIEN. Under the Anglo-Saxon kings and for two centuries after the conquest, the attitude of the English people and government towards aliens trading in this country was, as might be expected from the backward condition of our civilisation, one of suspicion and hostility. Safe conduct was at first granted to individuals, then to nationalities, as to the subjects of the emperor by Ethelred II. The reign of John was marked by an unprecedented liberality of treatment. Upon his accession John issued circular letters to his officials at the ports forbidding the oppression of alien merchants in the matter of tolls, and ordering that they should enjoy the same security as English merchants in their respective countries. Similar provisions were embodied in §§ 41, 42 of Magna Carta. These gave rise to long contention as to the meaning of the phrase *sine omnibus malis toltis* (see MALATOLTA), from which foreign traders were to be exempt, and which was eventually decided to include all duties not voted by parliament. With regard to the stipulation for freedom of trade, the interests of the chartered towns were opposed to those of the crown and aristocracy. London from the first led the opposition to aliens, and on this account supported the barons against Henry III., during whose reign extensive immigrations took place. The alien merchants, on the other hand, learnt to associate themselves in nationalities or cities and to conclude private treaties, promising reciprocity for such trading privileges as the citizens were disposed to concede to them. Such an arrangement was entered into with London by the merchants of Amiens, Corby, and Nesle in 1237. In 1267 the HANSE (see arts. on subject) established a factory in London, and soon afterwards the English a similar one in Danzig. But the normal policy of London was one of petty persecution of aliens. With the accession of Edward I. the system of reciprocity between towns was replaced by the control of the central government. Edward seized the city's charters and extended the trading privileges of the aliens. Upon the restoration of the privileges of London in 1298 a renewal of former repressive ordinances against foreigners took place. In 1303 Edward issued the Carta Mercatoria in favour of foreign merchants. This is one of the most notable documents of English history. It had a national scope. It guaranteed personal safety to all foreign merchants. It allowed them to import all kinds of wares ; to sell wholesale both to freemen of towns and to strangers, and to sell retail to all both spices and mercery. Authorities in towns and markets were to be attentive to their complaints and to administer justice according to the LAW MERCHANT. Alien merchants were entitled to demand mixed juries in trials between aliens and Englishmen, and a judge was specially appointed to take cognisance of cases in which they were concerned. They in return were to pay additional customs. All that was left of the exclusive privileges hitherto so jealously insisted upon by the towns was the retail trade. In 1311, under the feeble government of Edward II., the Londoners, with the assistance of the barons, procured a repeal of the articles of this charter as to residence and retail trading, and restricted the stay of foreign merchants to forty days. Although in 1322 Edward II. felt strong enough to restore the charter, a reaction in favour of the city set in with the accession of Edward III. The restrictions upon aliens' freedom of trade were renewed. The necessary consequence was a rise of prices, which led to the re-establishment of the aliens in their privileges. This was followed by a series of acts protecting aliens against unjust arrest for the debts of others, allowing them to make sales on board their ships, affording them an interval after the outbreak of war for the removal of their goods, accepting their own declarations as the basis of payment of customs, and exempting them from the exactions of royal purveyors. But the opposition of the city was persistent, and the tide again turned at the end of Edward III.'s reign. While Richard II.'s policy was wavering, Henry IV. cultivated the good-will of the city by large concessions, so that in 1406 the clothworkers and merchants of the country complained of exclusion from direct dealings with the foreigner. A relaxation was then made, allowing wholesale dealing between English and foreign merchants everywhere. Subject to this provision, the ascendency of the city was definitely established. The high water mark of protection against alien merchants was an act of 1439 (18 Hen. VI. c. 4). By this act trade among foreign merchants was prohibited ; hosts were to be appointed with whom they should lodge, and who should supervise their contracts : a stay limited to eight months was allowed for the transaction of business, and goods were to be taken out in exchange for those imported, the object of which was to check an alleged depletion of gold. The effect of this rigorous act was to drive the foreign merchants from places where it was enforced

into the country, where they embarked in the trade of export of wool. By an act of 1465, directed against the Italians, who were foremost in this business, executory contracts for the purchase of wool were forbidden (4 Ed. IV. c. 4). But foreign merchants profited from the struggle between the rival houses of York and Lancaster. The Italians generally supported the Lancastrians, and received concessions in the way of customs dues from Henry IV. Edward IV. leaned on the Hanse (see HANSE TOWNS), and in return for their aid in his restoration in 1471 concluded with them the Treaty of Utrecht (1475), conceding to them extensive privileges in England. With the object of gaining the favour of the commercial classes, Richard III. pursued the anti-Italian policy of his brother. The act of 1485 "touchinge the Marchauntes of Italy" (1 Ric. III. c. 9) restored many of the restrictions of the act of 1439 which had expired, but its effects were probably more felt in the country than in the towns, which protected themselves in their privileges by the sedulous enforcement of their customs. This perhaps accounts for the fact that Henry VII. ventured, immediately after his accession, to repeal the portions of Richard's act which affected Italian merchants (1 Hen. VII. c. 10), which he would scarcely have done had London been vitally interested in their maintenance. Possibly the Italians, who, as we know from the *Libelle of Englyshe Polycye*, were notorious for their skill in bribing the official classes, took advantage of Henry's financial difficulties and rendered a pecuniary equivalent for the restoration of their privileges. The country gentry also would favour concessions facilitating the operations of profitable customers. But three years later Henry revived the act of 1465 against executory purchases of wool (4 Hen. VII. c. 11). This act expired in 1499, and an interval of comparatively free trade followed accompanied by numerous immigrations and consequent dissatisfaction in London and other large towns. In 1514 the trading companies of the whole kingdom joined in a remonstrance to the king, and petitioned for a revival with increased stringency of the act of 1439. This petition proving ineffective, it was followed three years later by the riot long after known as "evil May day," directed, however, principally against foreign handicraftsmen. In 1523 the exclusive trading privileges of the city of London were invaded by an act permitting country clothiers to deal directly with foreign merchants (14 & 15 Hen. VIII. c. 1). Discontent was also expressed, as it had been by the parliaments of Edward IV. and Henry VII., at the exemptions from aliens' customs duties obtained by means of letters of naturalisation. In 1530 parliament laid down the principle that naturalised aliens should continue in future to pay aliens' dues (22 Hen. VIII. c.

8), which involved a large protective difference in favour of the English merchant. But a notable reversal of policy was effected by Cromwell in 1539, when by an exercise of high prerogative alien merchants were for a fixed period of seven years placed, as far as customs duties were concerned, upon the same level as Englishmen. Pursuing the same policy, while bidding for popular support by discouraging alien handicraftsmen, Cromwell, as Henry a century earlier, favoured alien merchants by suspending in their favour the execution of the act "concerning strangers" of 1540 (32 Hen. VIII. c. 16). This act revived that of 1483 (1 Ric. III. c. 9), which limited to eight months the time allowed to foreign merchants within which to dispose of their wares. But it was only enforced for the purpose of recruiting the treasury with the fees paid upon naturalisation. Upon the expiration of the proclaimed period in 1547, a return was made to the policy of differential duties on exports which were finally abolished by an act of 1672 (25 Car. II. c. 6). A collection of documents has been printed by Schanz, ranging from 1485 to the reign of Elizabeth, which set out the grievances of alien merchants. These may be classed under three heads—complaints against English commercial law, such as the navigation acts ; against the customs, and against officials, whether of the crown or of the towns, especially of London. Among the first class of grievances were the prohibition to buy what were known as STAPLE wares except through the middleman, the stapler, and those forbidding the export of manufactures in an unfinished state, or of raw material, except at the cost of an expensive licence. It was also disadvantageous to the foreign importer to be compelled to take English goods in exchange, burdened with the enormous profits of the staplers, rather than to ship tin and hides from the warehouses of the Hanse. To enforce this regulation a vexatious system of demanding surety had been devised (5 Hen. IV. c. 9 ; 4 Ed. IV. c. 6). Against "Customers"[1] there were many complaints. An act of 1487 (3 Hen. VII. c. 7) provided that merchandise should be entered in the customers' books in the name of the true owner. This, until repealed by 1 Hen. VIII. c. 5, furnished numerous pretexts for confiscation. In 1530 an attempt was made to revive a statute of 1381, forbidding foreign merchants to transact business by letters of exchange without a royal licence. This was done to check the decline in English exports. The measure, opposed by GRESHAM, was only maintained *in terrorem*, a common policy of this period. Liberty of exchange was granted by proclamation in 1538.

Numerous complaints arose out of the multi-

tudinous petty exactions levied under the pretext of local customs and tolls upon foreign merchants. Some four-and-twenty of these are enumerated. In the roadstead, at the port of unlading, in the market-places of the towns, upon lading the return cargo, upon clearing, upon entering at the customs, whether outwards or inwards, excuses were found for these demands. As English merchants, especially citizens of London and other chartered towns, were exempt from many of them, besides enjoying the advantage of differential customs, they were not unpopular in England, so far as they increased the protection enjoyed by native subjects. It was affirmed on the one side and denied on the other that these exactions had been multiplied during the first half of the 16th century. It is significant that the grievance of "going to host" had disappeared, that invention having been found to result in surreptitious partnerships between the foreign merchants and their hosts, in which they had secured the advantages intended to be reserved to Englishmen (cp. the "act for the trewe payment of the kinges customes," 1 Hen. VIII. c. 5). Resident alien merchants were made to contribute to the subsidies, a line of distinction being generally drawn by the subsidy acts between aliens in possession of property up to a certain value and those in receipt of wages. The history of the relations of the English government to alien merchants during the 16th century shows the growing enterprise of English merchants and their dissatisfaction at the privileges enjoyed by favoured corporations, like the Hanse, or by individuals wealthy enough to purchase royal letters of licence (see LICENSES). With this national feeling the Tudor governments gradually associated themselves. With the disestablishment of the Hanse, begun under Edward VI. and practically completed under Elizabeth, the exceptional position of alien merchants in this country came to an end.

[Schanz, *Englische Handelspolitik*, Leipzig, 1881, 2 vols.—Ochenkowski, *Englands wirthschaftliche Entwickelung*, Jena, 1879.—R. Jones, *Pol. Econ.*, ed. 1859, pp. 309-315.—Ashley, *Economic History*, etc., pt. i. 1888, pt. ii. 1892. *Statutes of the Realm.*]   I. S. L.

MERCHANTS' PETITION OF 1820, THE. A very able document, drawn up by T. TOOKE (*q.v.*), subscribed by all the most eminent merchants in London, and presented to the House of Commons in 1820 by Mr. Alexander Baring. The contents of its fifteen paragraphs may be thus summarised.

The end of foreign commerce is to import what can be best produced abroad, and to export, in payment, what can be best produced at home. This end can only be attained where there is freedom from restraint. The maxim, "to buy in the cheapest and to sell in the dearest market," applies to international

---

[1] Officers of customs, H. Hall, *Customs Rev. of England*.

transactions. Unhappily, a very different policy has prevailed, and "jealousy and hostility" have taken the place of "mutual benefit" and "harmony." The fallacy of the protectionists consists in supposing that imports from abroad tend to discourage home products, whereas they actively stimulate such industries as are in fact suitable to the importing country. This follows from the rule that exports must, in the long run, pay for imports. Protection seldom benefits the protected, and never to the extent of the loss occasioned to others. When once the road of protection is travelled, there is no halting, until all foreign commerce whatsoever is destroyed; indeed England might, with as good reason, demand protection against Scotland, or Scotland against England, and the different counties of each country against each other.

An inquiry would probably show a connection between a protective policy and the distress prevalent. A declaration in favour of free trade would carry weight abroad, where protectionists can point to the authority and example of England, and would tend to counteract the commercial hostility of foreign nations. Although a policy of RECIPROCITY (q.v.) may be defended, in particular cases, on diplomatic grounds, "it does not follow that we shall maintain our restrictions in cases where the desired concessions cannot be obtained. Our restrictions would not be the less prejudicial . . . because other governments persisted in preserving impolitic regulations." In any case "the recognition of a sound principle or standard" may be expected to have a salutary influence on other states. The petition does not complain of duties collected for purely revenue purposes. "It is against every restrictive regulation of trade, not essential to the revenue, against all duties merely protective from foreign competition, and the excess of such duties as are partly for the purpose of revenue, and partly for that of protection" that its prayer is addressed.

The language, as to reciprocity, quoted above, is noteworthy, as it is often said that the case for free trade rested on the expectation that other nations would follow England's example. It is related that the second Lord LIVERPOOL (q.v.), after reading the petition, expressed his hearty agreement with every word of it. Some time had to pass before free trade was seriously considered. The petition, however, was "the originating impulse to the movement, which, by progressive steps, had led to the final establishment of the principles therein enunciated."

[Tooke's *History of Prices*, vol. v. p. 396; and vol. vi., London, 1838-57, 8vo: app. 1, pp. 331-344, where the petition itself is printed in full, with Mr. Tooke's account of the circumstances in which it originated.—Smith's *Wealth of Nations*, edited

by M'Culloch, 4th edition, note xv., Edinburgh, 1850, 8vo.—Nassau Senior's *Three Lectures on the transmission of the Precious Metals, and the mercantile theory of Wealth* (delivered at Oxford in 1827), London, 1830, 8vo.]   H. E. E.

MERCHET was the payment due from a villein tenant on a manor to his lord for leave to give his daughter or his sister in marriage. With the exception of an uncertain tenure, it was probably the most constant mark of serfdom, yet cannot be considered as an absolute test, as it was neither universal among holders who were certainly villeins, nor entirely absent from SOCMEN on ancient demesne. Occasionally, it seems, the payment was only due if the marriage would remove the woman from the manor or the hundred to which she belonged.

[Bracton's *Note-Book*, ed. Maitland, 1887, cases 395, 753.—Ducange, *Glossarium.*—Vinogradoff, *Villainage in England.*]   E. G. P.

MERCIER (*alias* LEMERCIER) DE LA RIVIÈRE, PAUL PIERRE (1720-1794), was a member of the parliament from 1747 to 1759, where his attractive but determined character, his high integrity and loyalty, made him respected. In 1757 he was appointed steward of the island of Martinique, and discharged his duties there with great disinterestedness and fertility of resource. He even devoted his personal credit, and when necessary his own money, to the public service. He reaped nothing but ingratitude from this at first. The Duc de Choiseul, then minister for the navy and foreign affairs, took umbrage at his applying the principles of free trade to the colonies which he governed in complete opposition to the colonial system in force at that time. He was recalled; but he had anticipated this and returned to France by order of his doctor, July 1764.

On his retirement to private life he wrote and published, in 1767, *L'Ordre Naturel et Essentiel des Sociétés Politiques* (1 vol. 4to, or 2 vols. 12mo), a work which made such a sensation in his time that some of his contemporaries placed it, not only on a level with, but even above *L'Esprit des lois*. This book, apart from its physiocratic errors and inordinate overpraise of absolute power (the author suggests the despotism of China as an ideal model), contains some fine passages which were obscured by the tone of exaggeration in it. It explains the ideas of the PHYSIOCRATS. Their economic opinions, which are very simple, may be summed up thus: there is only one industry which gives a net product capable of increasing social wealth —this is agriculture. Other industries can only produce an equivalent to the amount employed in them. In one word, agriculture alone is really productive. Hence, taxation is in the end always borne by agriculture, and to avoid useless and costly repercussion of taxation it would be better to have a single tax—the IMPÔT UNIQUE. Adam Smith, who was in a position to judge this book impartially, says (*W. of N.*, bk. iv. ch. ix.) that it contains "the most distinct and best connected account of this doctrine," that of the

ÉCONOMISTES (q.v.). The Empress Catherine II. invited Mercier de la Rivière to St. Petersburg. According to her account of the matter, by his pretentiousness and want of tact, he made himself ridiculous there. He returned, according to the Czarina, dismissed, but largely rewarded by her. This had little in common with the disinterestedness he had shown at Martinique. Mercier, according to his own statement, refused the position and pension he was offered, only taking what had been agreed on when he left France. This seems nearer the truth. Catherine sneered at him ; ''He believed,'' she wrote to Voltaire, ''that we walked on all fours and he came charitably to set us on our hind legs.''

Mercier de la Rivière wrote many works, but only those on political economy are quoted here. L'intérêt général de l'état ou la liberté du commerce des blés, 1770, 12mo.—Procès pendant au tribunal du public ; lettre sur les économistes (undated, probably 1787). Du Pont (de Nemours) has cleverly summed up L'ordre naturel in De l'origine et des progrés d'une science nouvelle. This, as well as the work of which it is an abridged version, is printed in Guillaumin's collection (Physiocrates, 1846).

[For the less-known events of the life of this author see the notice read in 1858 at the Académie des Sciences morales et politiques, by M. Felix Joubleau. See also account in L. de Lavergne, Les économistes français du XVIIIe siècle.]

A. C. f.

MERCIER, Louis Sébastien (1740-1814), a Parisian barrister, journalist, and member of the convention during the revolutionary period, —was a most copious and voluminous writer ; and it is impossible to give here a complete list of his writings.

His best-known work is the Tableau de Paris (12 vols., Amsterdam, 1783-1788), which, notwithstanding its desultory and declamatory form, is valuable evidence of the moral and physical aspect of Paris on the eve of the revolution ; it is full of life and keen observations. In 1792 he published a pamphlet, Réflexions d'un Patriote sur les Assignats, les craintes d'une banqueroute Nationale, etc., intended to demonstrate that the fears concerning an impending national bankruptcy were unfounded. One of the first in date of his works is L'An 2440, rêve s'il en fût jamais (1771, reprinted 1800); it is the dream of a disciple of Voltaire and Rousseau, but free from any tendency towards a communistic reform of society. E. Ca.

MEREDITH, Sir William (1724 - 1790), Whig politician, succeeded to the baronetcy in 1752. In 1765 he was appointed a civil lord of the admiralty. Horace Walpole describes him as inflexibly serious but of no great head, a judgment which his Historical Remarks on the Taxation of Free States, London, 1778, 4to, belie. In this work, in the form of letters to a friend, Meredith points the moral of the folly of attempting to tax the American colonists, by the examples of Carthage, Rome, Sparta, and Athens.

[Dictionary of National Biography, vol. xxxvii. p. 271.] H. E. E.

MERELLO, Michele (17th century). An economist who wrote on the deposit banks established in Italy in the '16th century. He describes the establishment of the historic bank of St. George, Genoa (see BANKING), founded to consolidate and provide for the redemption of the debts of that republic by uniting the creditors in a single institution and allowing them the proceeds of certain taxes for a certain number of years. The unification of these creditors was called compera. Merello, who objected to taxes, praises this system because the cession made by the state was for a certain number of years only and did not entail a perpetual burden on the citizen.

Della guerra fatta dai francesi . . . con una breve dichiarazione dell' istituzione della compera di San Giorgio, Genoa, 1607.

[Gobbi, L'economia politica negli scrittori italiani del secolo XVI.-XVII., Milan, 1889.—Ricca-Salerno, Storia delle dottrine finanziarie in Italia, Rome, 1880.] U. R.

MERENDA, Antonio (17th century), was professor of civil law at the university of Pavia, and author of a treatise on exchange. The important changes in economics had weakened the old doctrines, and admitted the lawfulness of profits made from productive employment of money. Merenda protested in the name of CANON LAW (q.v.) against the comparatively liberal opinions of many writers of his day ; who, though they proclaimed the most absolute respect for the principle that loans should be gratuitous, in practice sacrificed the enforcement of this doctrine, leaving openings for evasion. Merenda opposes any reconciliation between ecclesiastical precepts and the requirements of common life. He does not deny that LUCRUM CESSANS (q.v.) supplies a lawful motive for demanding compensation, but he requires such absolute and complete proof, almost impossible ever to obtain, that the efficacy of this principle is effectually annulled. Merenda does not doubt the lawfulness of a true and real exchange, but he adds that it becomes unlawful as soon as the suspicion arises that payment is to be made in a different place from that fixed in the contract. Merenda, distinguishing loans from exchange, and contrasting gratuitous loans with onerous exchange, is opposed to those forms of exchange which conceal usury (see INTEREST and USURY), and criticised those authors who, by defending the means adopted by traders, regarded them as lawful. He also opposed fairs where usurious exchanges were effected.

De cambio nundinali Tractatus, Pavia, 1645.

[Cossa, An Introduction to the study of Political Economy, trans., London, 1893. — Gobbi, L'economia politica negli scrittori italiani dei secoli XVI.-XVII., Milan, 1889.—Graziani, Le idee economiche degli scrittori emiliani e romagnoli, Modena, 1893.] U. R.

MERGER. The term merger signifies the ending of a legal right by its absorption into a higher right of the same kind. Thus when a lessee purchases the property let to him, his rights as a tenant merge in his more extensive rights as a proprietor. When a man entitled to a servitude or an easement over his neighbour's land (e.g. a right of way) buys that land, his servitude or easement is similarly merged. Again, a simple contract is merged in a subsequent contract under seal, if made between the same parties and dealing with the same subject-matter. For a contract under seal confers more extensive rights than a simple contract does. Thus, a simple contract must be sued upon within six years of making. A contract under seal can be sued upon at any time within twenty years of making.   F. C. M.

MERIVALE, HERMAN (1806 - 1874), was trained at Oxford, where he took a first in classics, and was elected fellow of Balliol, 1832. Recognised by his contemporaries as "one of the two best educated men in his university generation" (Dr. Vaughan, Funeral Sermon at the Temple Church, Feb. 1874), he maintained this position during life, for, according to an obituary notice in the *Economist*, he was "one of the most acute and best read political economists of his time." In 1837 he was elected to the newly-instituted chair of political economy at Oxford. In his preliminary lecture the professor distinguished between political economy the science and political economy the art, defending the science from the attacks of those who have looked to it as to a sort of philosopher's stone which would turn everything it touched into gold. Its object, he maintained, was *not to create but to prove ;* and he utterly repudiated the idea that political economy was based on a degrading estimate of human nature.

He then considered the principles on which colonisation should be conducted, as connected with emigration, employment of labour, the disposal of public lands, and the system of E. G. WAKEFIELD (*q.v.*). His eighth lecture exposes the fallacy of the colonial system then in vogue. He pointed out that "altho' under certain conditions . . . a country might gain by the possession of an artificially monopolised market for its manufactured commodities, yet in actual practice such gain is found to be wholly illusory."

The publication of these lectures led to his employment under government ; he became under-secretary of state in two of the most important departments of government for the long period of twenty - six years — from 1847 until his death in 1874.

The late Lord Lytton wrote, in his copy of Merivale's *Historical Studies :* " The author is one of the most remarkable men I have ever met. The main characteristic of his intellect is massiveness—and it is the massiveness of gold . . . he belongs to the very highest order of mind in my time and country. I can compare him to no other of less calibre than Macaulay . . . Macaulay is the finer artist, and Merivale the more original thinker."

Five Lectures on the Principles of a Legislative Provision for the Poor in Ireland, 1838. —*Lectures on Colonisation and the Colonies,* 1st ed., 1838 ; 2nd ed., 1861.   A. L.

MERTON, THE STATUTE (OR PROVISIONS) OF, 20 Hen. III. (1235-36), contains several chapters, but that of most economic importance is c. 4, which is what is commonly understood when the "Statute of Merton" is referred to. "Whereas," it runs, "many magnates of England, who have infeoffed their knights and free tenants of small tenements in their great manors, have complained that they cannot make their profit (*commodum*) of the residue of their manors, as well as of the wastes, woods, and pastures . . . it is provided that whenever such feoffees do bring an assize of novel disseisin for their common of pasture, and it is acknowledged before the justices that they have as much pasture as suffice to their tenements, and that they have free ingress and regress from their tenement into the pasture, then let them be content therewith." If it is proved that they have not sufficient pasture, they shall recover their seisin, and the disseisors shall be amerced and pay damages ; if they have, then "let the others make their lawful profit of the residue."

[The statute is printed in *Statutes of the Realm* (1810), i. p. 1. The comments of Bracton, with a translation and some observations thereon, will be found in Digby, *Hist. of the Law of Real Property* (4th ed. 1892), pp. 190-208. It will be observed that the statute guaranteed only the rights of free tenants. Lord Chancellor Herschell has recently declared in the House of Lords that "the Statute of Merton has been practically obsolete for centuries, and it is only in comparatively recent times that it has been revived and again put in force," and that "the means of trying the right of the lord to enclose is a process which is not only obsolete, but which has ceased to exist." *Times* Report, 28th July 1893.]   W. J. A.

MESNIL MARIGNY, JULES DU (1810-1885). His *Économie Politique devenue science exacte* (Political Economy made an Exact Science, Paris, 4 ed. from 1859 to 1883) is principally written to confute J. B. Say's theory of exchanges, and to maintain that "the benefits which two nations reap from mutual exchanges of the same value may be very unequal." This leads to the assertion that "each nation must have its own political economy appropriated to its physical conditions and to its national character."

The avowed scope of his *Histoire de l'Économie Politique des Anciens Peuples de l'Inde, de l'Egypte, de la Judée et de la Grèce* (Paris, 3 vols., 1878, 3rd ed.) is to prove "in an irrefutable way, and by a great number of instances, that the system of protecting national manufactures . . . was very often followed in antiquity." E. ca.

MESSANCE, M. (18th century), an eminent statistician, revenue officer at S. Etienne-en-Forez in the reign of Louis XV. In 1759 he became under secretary to M. de la Michodière, intendant of Auvergne, and in this capacity he continued the statistical investigations instituted by his chief, with a view to disproving the theory of the author of *L'ami des hommes*, the Marquis de MIRABEAU, as to the decline of population in France. In 1763 he presented the result in book form to the intendant, who insisted on its being printed in Messance's name [*Nouvelles Recherches*, p. 5].

In 1775 Messance sent a table of mortality, which he had prepared, to Voltaire, who in a humorous reply commented on its accuracy and utility. Messance's two works on population were issued at an interval of twenty-two years ; in the second of these he refers to Necker's *Administration des Finances*, and Adam Smith's *Wealth of Nations*, both which publications had preceded it. His works are entitled :

Recherches sur la population des généralités d'Auvergne, de Lyon, de Rouen, et de quelques provinces et villes du royaume, avec réflections sur la valeur du blé, tant en France qu'en Angleterre, depuis 1674, jusqu'en 1764, Paris, Durand, 1766, 4to.—*Nouvelles recherches sur la population de la France avec des remarques importantes sur divers objets d'administration*, Lyon, 1788, 4to. [*Dictionnaire de l'Économie politique*, p. 158.] See also references in *Wealth of Nations*, bk. i. chs. viii. and xi., where A. Smith speaks in high terms of the investigations which Messance had made (cp. Levasseur, *La population française*).

A. L.

MESSOR, an officer found on large estates, whose duty was to superintend the harvest on the manor, and in some cases to collect fines due to the lord from his tenantry. Under the manorial agricultural system there was an official, either elected or appointed, for almost every separate function. [Vinogradoff, *Villainage in England*.] E. G. P.

MESSUAGE (Low Lat. *Mesuagium*), a dwelling, means properly a dwelling-house with the land belonging to it, but is often used for a garden, stable, or any kind of domestic building. [Cowel, *Interpreter*, London, 1727.] A. E. S.

MESTA. "The *mesta*"—writes, towards the very end of the last century, M. de Bourgoing, a French diplomatist, who had a long experience of Spain,—"the *mesta* is a company of powerful sheep-owners, rich monasteries, Spanish grandees, wealthy individuals, who have succeeded in feeding their (migrating) flocks at the expense of the public during all the seasons of the year, and in obtaining unconsidered legal enactments to sanction a state of things which has been at first prompted by necessity "

(*Tableau de l'Espagne*, vol. i. pp. 75-123, edit. 1807. The two first editions of 1789 and 1797 are anonymous). This necessity resulted from natural circumstances—the difference of climate between the cold mountains of northern and the warm plains of southern Spain, and from historical conditions—the existence, during the centuries of warfare between the Moors and the Christians, of an extensive debateable land, exposed to armed incursions and destitute of the security which is the primary requisite of agricultural cultivation. In 1200 king Alonso VIII. of Castile first granted the itinerant cattle herds the privilege of grazing on all waste and open lands, but subject to the obligation to compensate the owners for all damage to inclosed fields, vines, gardens, standing crops, etc. This privilege, gradually enlarged and confirmed under subsequent reigns, led to most abusive encroachments, especially under the growing influence of the *Honrado Concejo de la Mesta* or Honorable Association of the Cattle-owners. The exact date of its foundation is unknown, but it certainly goes back very far into the middle ages. About 1500, Ferdinand and Isabella, being in want of money, listened to the solicitations of the *Concejo de la Mesta* and gave it an official status by appointing a president and calling to that post a minister and member of the royal council. In 1511, the ordinances and laws concerning the *mesta* were by royal command collected by Palacios Rubios, a celebrated jurisconsult of the time, approved and promulgated. The privileges thus confirmed may be epitomised as follows :

1. The right of pasture on all open lands, which led to constant and successful interference of the *mesta* against all attempts of inclosing or even putting under tillage hitherto unbroken land. Their pretensions were formally recognised by a law of 1633, forbidding the plantation of new vines and the ploughing of previously uncleared land.

2. The obligation to keep open at all times *cañadas* or broad tracks for the free and unimpeded passage of the cattle, which were to be able to move "grazing." No inclosures were tolerated on either side of the *cañada*, and the flocks unmercifully invaded the neighbouring gardens and fields.

3. The exemption from several taxes and tolls, which indirectly led to new burdens imposed on the already overburdened tillers of the soil.

An official census of 1480 puts down at 2,694,032 the heads of cattle, which in 1477 had migrated through the passes of Castile ; another account of 1563 gives the following numbers : 2,303,027 sheep and goats, 14,127 oxen, and 25,215 pigs. In 1724, USTARITZ (*q.v.*) computes the number of migrating sheep at 4,000,000 (which figure is confirmed by an official census of 1746), with a much higher estimate for settled and permanent flocks.

The devastations caused by the wandering flocks of the *mesta* have been the main cause of the ruin of Spanish agriculture. This frightful oppression lasted until the end of the last century, and only receded before the strenuous endeavours of the enlightened statesmen of the time, Florida-Blanca, Rodriguez de Campomanes, and most of all JOVELLANOS (*q.v.*).

[A substantial historical account of the *mesta*, and of the Spanish literature on the subject, is to be found in chs. xxxiv. and lxiv. of Colmeiro's *Historia de la Economia Política en España*. See also Bonwick's *Romance of the Wool Trade* (1887).—Haebler's *Wirtschaftliche Blüte Spaniens im 16 Jahrhundert* (Berlin, 1888).—Goury du Roslan's *Essai sur l'Histoire Économique de l'Espagne* (Paris, 1888).—Cos Garayon's articles on *La Mesta* in the *Revista de España* (vols. ix. and x.).—M. Ansiaux, "Hist. de la Décadence économique de l'Espagne," in *Révue d'Écon. Pol.*, 1893-94.—The leading legislative enactments have been collected in the 3rd book of the *Nueva Recopilacion de las Leyes de España*.] E. CA.

METALS, PRECIOUS. See GOLD ; PRECIOUS METALS, Discoveries of ; SILVER.

MÉTAYAGE ; MÉTAYER, called in legal phraseology *colonat partiaire*—an expression taken from Roman law—refers to a cultivator who pays his rent in kind : it is a particular method of *fermage* or farming land. *Métayage* differs from *fermage* in that the rent, instead of being paid in *money* and *fixed* throughout the whole period of the lease, is paid *in kind*, and consequently *varies* with the yield itself ; a portion of the yield, usually the half, being set aside for this purpose.

This arrangement is very usual in certain countries, as in Italy, Portugal, the countries bordering on the Danube, in Russia, and also in France. In France, out of 33 million hectares cultivated (nearly 82,000,000 acres), $4\frac{1}{2}$ millions (11,000,000 acres)—14 per cent—are managed on the *métayer system*, 27 per cent under the usual arrangements for farming ; the remainder, 59 per cent, being cultivated by the proprietors themselves. In Italy, out of less than 11 million hectares cultivated (27 million acres), $5\frac{1}{2}$ millions, or 50 per cent, are managed on the *métayer* system.

Métayage appears to have been much more in use formerly than at present. Arthur Young, at the time of the revolution, estimated the land cultivated on this system in France to be $\frac{7}{8}$ or 87 per cent of the whole. From this continued decrease it might be concluded that *métayage* is an antiquated institution, condemned sooner or later to disappear.

It is true that *métayage* seems better adapted to poor districts, and that it may be in time superseded by *fermage*, that is by money rents, or by the proprietor cultivating his own land himself, in proportion as the district becomes richer and the cultivation better, that is, more intensive. The *fermier*, in fact, is always a capitalist, and even, more generally in England, a fairly large capitalist, while the *métayer* generally has no capital, and possesses nothing but his labour and some agricultural implements of little value. He tills the ground himself and avoids everything connected with an expensive mode of cultivation, what is called in France *la culture intensive*, for what good would there be in his spending, for instance, £100 more a year to increase the raw product by £200 ? He would only get the half of this product (£100), and in consequence would not gain a penny. On the other hand the owner himself hardly cares to invest a large capital in working the farm, for the dividing by half the addition to the raw product arising from the employment of this capital, would be too disadvantageous to him.[1]

However, if *métayage* appears inferior to *fermage* from an economic, it is superior to it from a moral point of view. And this superiority has been sufficient to maintain the institution in many countries, and even now rallies round it more supporters perhaps than formerly. This moral superiority springs from the following causes :

(1) While *fermage* establishes enmity between the owner and the *métayer*, *métayage* establishes a unity of interests between them. Both share alike in good and bad fortune ; there is a real association between them, and it is one of the oldest and most admirable forms of PROFIT SHARING which those who see in co-operation the solution of all social difficulties should regard with favour.

(2) The *métayer* is never straitened by the mode of payment, because he pays in kind. He only gives the proprietor what the earth itself gives—nothing, if it yields nothing—much if it yields generously. He never has to pay the landlord anything out of his pocket. On the other hand the *fermier* is always compelled to provide the money even when the land yields him nothing, is often straitened, and comes to regard the proprietor as an oppressor, a kind of tax-collector.

(3) The *métayer* is guaranteed against injurious exploitation to which the *fermiers* so often find themselves exposed through competition among themselves, which sometimes raises the rent to an exorbitant amount (rack rent). *Métayage*, by its customary fixing the division of the product into halves, wards off completely the influence of competition on price, quenches all controversy as to the amount of the rent, and does not permit the proprietor to monopolise all the profit (FAIR RENTS, *q.v.*).

(4) *Métayage* gives better assurance of a long duration of lease than *fermage*. In *fermage*, as a matter of fact, the owner is always seeking for a new *fermier* who will pay him a higher

[1] This may be modified by a certain standard of farming being required by the *usages locaux*.

rent than the former tenant. But in the métayer system, what is the good of a change of métayer, since the rent is the same whoever be the tenant? The owner has no reason for dismissing his tenant, or at least none but personal reasons. There are métayer farms which remain constantly in the same family, passing from father to son, as in the Limousin is stated to have been the case for 300 years.

(5) Finally in métayage the owner necessarily takes much more interest in the cultivation of the land and the success of the harvest—since his share depends on it—than in fermage, as in this case he receives his rent in money whatever occurs. Hence intercourse is more intimate and even familiar between the owner and the métayer.

For all these reasons the métayer system may be considered as an element of social peace and capable of solving in certain cases the agrarian question.

Moreover, the contract according to the métayer system can be modified according to the circumstances, and thus lends itself better to the exigencies of an improved culture. For example there might be a system of métayage in which the métayer would provide more or less considerable capital. This is the case in the south of France, and assists the planting of some large vineyards there. The proprietor merely provides the ground; the métayer, the "vine-dresser" as he is termed, plants this at his own expense, employing considerable capital, and the vintage is divided between them after the 5th or the 7th year. A system of métayage might also exist in which the landowner would advance the capital, stipulating for the payment of a moderate interest, and this might assist a solution of the problem of agricultural progress. In a word the time-honoured system of métayage might be re-instituted in different ways and adapted to new requirements, while still keeping those essential characteristics which are its great recommendation, namely that it forms an "association of gains and losses" as defined in the old French law.

[Jean Cruveilhier, Étude sur le Métayage, Paris, 1894.—H. Higgs, "Métayage in Western France," Economic Journal, March 1894.— Du Maroussem, "Métayers du Confolentais," Ouvriers des Deux Mondes, 1890.—Vladimir Pappafava, "Étude sur le colonage partiaire," Bulletin de la Société de Législation Comparée, June 1885.—Discussion à la Société d'économie politique de Paris sur le métayage : compte rendu dans le Journal des Économistes, April 1891.—A. Smith, W. of N., bk. iii. ch. ii.—J. S. Mill, Pol. Econ.—Jas. Caird, Report on India, 1880, p. 6.— Consult also La Loi française du 18 juillet 1889 sur le bail à colonat partiaire.]   C. G.

MÉTAYER, in West Indies. The métayer system of cultivation has an interesting example in some of the West Indian colonies— notably Grenada, St. Vincent, and Tobago, where it is also termed "métairie" or "métayage." It was introduced for the purposes of sugar cultivation when these islands were under French rule, and has subsisted to this day. Up to 1887 or 1888 there had been very little friction between the owners and métayers, but about that time certain judgments of the then chief justice of Trinidad and Tobago caused a stir in the latter island, and in 1889 a committee investigated the whole question of relations of the two parties to the contract. The contract had originally been, as a rule, a parol agreement; there had recently been a tendency to employ written agreements, and in 1888 the legislature of Tobago had proposed to regulate the contract by local ordinance.

The agreements between landowner and métayer vary considerably in their details, but their usual outline is as follows :

(a) The landowner—
  (1) provides land for sugar cultivation,
  (2) at crop time gives the use of mill and machinery, carts and mules, or one of these, and also provides certain skilled hands for manufacture.

(b) The métayer undertakes—
  (1) to cultivate the land to the best of his ability,
  (2) to keep the roads across or around his land in good repair,
  (3) to give his labour on other parts of the estate at a fixed rate for certain days in each month,
  (4) to resign to the landowner half the sugar made from his land, besides a considerable proportion of the molasses.

The proportions with which the produce is divided are not always the same ; but a fairly even division is the basis of the arrangement.

The system has never been the economic success which one might have hoped ; the sugar was usually roughly manufactured, and owners complained that their mills and boilers were often damaged. But it has been useful where, as in Tobago, there has been great dearth of floating capital to pay the wages of labour.   C. A. H.

METHOD OF POLITICAL ECONOMY.

(a) Scope of Economics, p. 739; (b) Economics and General Sociology, p. 741 ; (c) Divisions of the Science, p. 741 ; (d) Formal Economics, p. 741 ; (e) Narrative Economics, p. 742 ; (f) Constructive Economics, p. 743 ; (g) Inductive Methods, p. 744 ; (h) Deductive Methods, p. 746 ; (i) Criticism and Combination of Methods, p. 747.

(a) Scope of Economics.—Before treating of the various methods applicable to economic investigation, a brief examination of the scope of political economy is necessary. It is almost universally agreed that economics deals with wealth, or, more precisely, with those human activities the end of which is the appropriation of wealth. But admitting this common standpoint, there are yet two different directions in which economic study may proceed. The science may aim at merely ascertaining facts or at directly regulating conduct—its propositions may be couched either in the indicative or in the imperative mood. On the former view economics is called a positive or theoretical science, on the latter a regulative or practical science. But, whichever of these two views is taken, a further distinction must be made according as the propositions of the science have an abstract and general or a concrete and special application. The precepts of regulative economics, and the uniformities of positive economics, cannot be immediately applied to the guidance of conduct or the interpretation of phenomena. For every rule must be modified in consideration of the peculiar conditions of the society and epoch to which it has to be applied ; and the recognition of the single pursuit of wealth must be qualified by consideration of other ends and motives. Thus the precepts laid down by the regulative science may be either *general, i.e.* applicable to all societies, or *special, i.e.* having reference to the particular conditions of a given society. And again they may be either *abstract, i.e.* restricted to the consideration of a single end, such as the maximising of production, or the equalising of distribution ; or *concrete, i.e.* prescribing a due co-ordination and subordination of different human ends. Similarly, the facts described by positive economics may be either of *general* applicability to all societies, or may take account of the peculiarities of *special* social institutions and forms of civilisation. And again they may treat of men in an *abstract* form, so far as they pursue wealth alone ; or in a more *concrete* form, as subject to various influences that conflict with the pursuit of wealth.

Although the distinction between precepts and facts—between a regulative and a positive science—has been maintained as essential, especially by British economists from SENIOR onwards, yet there are some grounds for merging the two aspects in a single treatment. In the first place, a precept may always be expressed as a conditional uniformity—" If such conduct is adopted, such a result will follow," *e.g.* if pauperism is encouraged, the average wages of the working man will be lowered. The reader may then be left to his own judgment to decide whether the result in question or its avoidance is desirable. Secondly, in many cases there is practical unanimity in regard to the desirability of certain ends. Other things being equal, greater wealth, or the more equal distribution of wealth, may be assumed as a desirable result. Agreement as to the end in view is more particularly obvious in technical problems, such as

banking, currency, state finance, and taxation. In the third place, it may be urged that the aims of individuals as well as governments are determined by their ethical ideals ; and that therefore it is impossible, or at least undesirable, to separate the actual from the moral aspect of human pursuits. For these reasons it may be maintained that the distinction between the positive and the regulative sides of economic study is less fundamental than that between its abstract and its concrete aspect. In the actual course of discussions on method, it has been often supposed that the positive treatment of the science will necessarily assume an abstract character, and that the regulative treatment must assume a concrete character. For those writers who have aimed at regulating conduct in the interests of a given society have naturally recognised the need of examining its complex conditions ; and those who are only concerned with theorising on economic phenomena have naturally tended to treat in isolation the single pursuit of wealth. In the latest development of the controversy, it has been acknowledged by the more impartial writers on both sides that there is room for work in all fields. The ultimate aim of economic investigations is, no doubt, practical, *i.e.* to guide conduct in the actual conditions of affairs. For this purpose we must understand the operation of causes in the society in which we move. But, further, we require a general estimate of the comparative values of different ends of human pursuit. And, in order to understand the particular facts of any one individual society, we need the guiding principles of general theory. The propositions of economics expressed in their most accurate form will be doubly conditional, thus : " Given such or such a constitution of society, if such or such measures are taken, such or such a group of effects will follow." Of the effects produced some will be desirable, others undesirable. To determine whether the balance is towards the good or the evil, some reference to ethical considerations is necessary. Again the results to be anticipated from any course of action depend on the nature of the society for which the measures are proposed. Complexity of conditions and complexity of effects have thus to be taken into account. As a basis of practical economics we need, on the one hand, a general theory of the action of industrial forces ; and, on the other hand, an ethical survey of the value of human ends. The former is a necessary preliminary for the explanation of the concrete facts of society, and the latter for the discovery of right rules of conduct appropriate to these concrete facts. It follows, then, that a *science* of economic causes and effects must precede the *art* of political economy ; and that this art is related to the science in the same way as any branch of applied knowledge is related to the corresponding theoretical knowledge.

(b) *Economics and General Sociology.* — Although the name political economy is still preserved, the science, as now understood, is not strictly *political : i.e.* it is not confined to relations between the government and the governed, but deals primarily with the industrial activities of individual men. On the other hand, the science does not deal with individuals, *quâ* individuals. It is not, therefore, in any sense a branch of psychology. Even when it discusses the utility of objects of desire, and the sacrifice incurred in procuring them, it only measures utility and sacrifice, not subjectively, but as embodied in objective form. Hence the subject matter of economics gives it a place among the social, rather than the political or the psychological, sciences. Being admittedly a social science, the question has arisen as to its relations with other social sciences, and its position relatively to general sociology. Some writers, under the influence of COMTE, have maintained that economics cannot be profitably treated at all as an independent branch of study. They hold that there is such an intimate consensus amongst all the causes and effects of social life, that it is impossible to isolate any one group of phenomena—such as the industrial—and to treat this apart from the others. On this view economic facts cannot be explained without taking into account all concurrent causes, and rules for economic guidance cannot be formulated without taking into account all concurrent effects. All thinkers allow that no one group of

social phenomena is completely isolated from another. But, in answer to the extreme Comtist view, it is urged that there are certain kinds of effects which are predominantly due to a single kind of cause, and that there are certain kinds of causes which produce a single predominantly-important kind of effect. So far as this is true, the explanation of economic phenomena and the regulation of economic conduct may be treated independently of other sides of social life. Science has never been advanced except by specialisation. A distinction may, however, be made between two parts of economic doctrine. When the economist attempts to trace the general forms of transformation which economic phenomena present in the course of development, and to make broad comparisons between one society and another, it is true that economic phenomena cannot usefully be treated apart from the influences of religious, moral, intellectual, and political conditions. But when tracing the modes in which industrial forces operate under given social conditions, he need not enter into a scientific analysis of these conditions, and, assuming them to be relatively staple, he need not analyse the slow and gradual changes which they undergo. In brief, even though the theory of economic *evolution* may properly be subsumed and absorbed under the general science of social evolution, yet the doctrine of what may be called the statics and dynamics of industrial forces is rightly treated in entire independence of other branches of social science.

(c) *Divisions of Economic Science.*

Positive Economics

Descriptive				Constructive			
Formal		Narrative		Inductive		Deductive	
Definitions	Divisions	Chronological	Comparative	Pure	Mixed	Pure	Mixed

Putting aside the ethical function of criticising economic ideals, and regarding rules of conduct as properly expressed in the form of conditional statements assigning the connection between measures and their consequences, we may confine attention to economics as a *positive* science that deals with relations of fact. So regarded it falls into two main divisions, which may be called respectively *descriptive* and *constructive*. The former branch describes the conceptions and facts with which the science deals ; and the latter establishes laws and uniformities. Descriptive economics again divides into a *formal* and *narrative* branch ; of which the former analyses and classifies the conceptions needed for understanding the science in its widest applications, and the latter investigates historically and comparatively the various forms of economic life exhibited by different communities and at different epochs. Constructive economics, again, adopts a method

which is either predominantly inductive or predominantly deductive ; and under each head we must recognise a mixed method in which induction is modified by deduction, or deduction modified by induction. The above table will serve to show the scheme of the chief departments of economic science.[1]

(d) *Formal-Descriptive Economics.*—It must be acknowledged at once that the various departments of economics cannot be treated altogether independently of one another. The descriptions of economic phenomena must be regarded as in the first place provisional, and

[1] See also arts. on ABSTRACT POL. ECON. ; ANALYTICAL METHOD ; A POSTERIORI REASONING ; A PRIORI REASONING ; DEDUCTIVE METHOD ; EXPERIMENTAL METHODS IN ECONOMICS ; GRAPHIC METHOD ; HISTORICAL METHOD ; HYPOTHESIS ; INDUCTIVE METHOD ; LEAST SQUARES, METHOD OF ; LOGIC AND POL. ECON. ; MATHEMATICAL METHOD IN POL. ECON. ; MEANS, METHOD OF ; OBSERVATION (as distinct from Experiment) ; STATISTICAL METHOD ; SYNTHESIS ; SYNTHETIC METHOD.

the form that they ultimately assume is necessarily dependent on theory. However, a general survey of ideas and facts must precede any investigation into the uniformities and dependencies among economic phenomena. In the formal-descriptive branch a provisional understanding is supplied of such general conceptions as those of wealth, capital, labour, appropriation, exchange, barter, money, and of the various subdivisions into which these conceptions fall. This branch of investigation involves the logical process of *definition* and *division*. Some writers are impatient of discussions of this purely formal character. Questions of definition are regarded as trivial, on the ground that they lead to merely verbal controversies. Definitions are, however, necessary mainly to prevent the confusion so prevalent between controversies about words and controversies about matters of fact or theory. Economics, in particular, has to borrow words from common speech, and common speech is ambiguous ; hence, in default of a clearly assigned connotation, the economist is liable to introduce into his own writings confusion, misunderstanding, or inconsistency. Many disputes, for example, about capital have arisen from the failure to observe that different persons understand the term in different senses : and this applies to professed economists as well as to the ordinary man. The problem of definition gives rise to several difficulties. (1) Most of the terms employed, though in current use they cover a fairly understood range of application, are yet without any precise connotation. Definition therefore requires at the outset an *inductive* process of analysis and comparison to discover the characteristics common to all the various applications of the term. Often, however, a term is used so loosely that any possible definition will lead to a modification of its generally recognised scope in the direction either of expansion or of restriction. Nevertheless, the ordinarily understood range of a term in common use ought to be attended to ; and it not infrequently turns out that the inductive investigation of popular usage will disclose important points of agreement or difference between classes of phenomena that would probably be overlooked if a more *a priori* mode of definition were adopted. (2) But, secondly, the process of defining a term is further complicated by the fact that some proposition into which the term enters is assumed to be true. For example, in the definition of capital it will be assumed that capital is a form of wealth which co-operates with other independent factors in the production of wealth. The definition of capital from this point of view provides an answer to the question " What other factor besides the raw materials supplied by nature and the efforts of human beings contributes to the production of wealth, and how far can this factor be conceived as independent

of the others ?" Or the definition of capital may implicitly answer the question " What is the nature of the service to the community and of the sacrifice to the individual which secures the payment of interest ?" (3) Again, definitions involve a classification of economic phenomena, and so necessitate consideration whether the resulting classes are mutually exclusive and collectively exhaustive. Now the question of exclusiveness and exhaustiveness cannot be answered on merely logical grounds, but requires an investigation into matters of fact. Indeed the results of any such investigation may vary with variations in the stage of society considered. Hence even definitions partake of the character of relativity ascribed to all economic formulæ. (4) But more important than any other consideration is the question of framing a classification that will subserve the purposes of scientific investigation. Our definitions should lead to the formation of classes of which *universal* propositions of the greatest number and importance can be asserted, and between which the most impressive differences subsist. This latter aim is difficult to achieve because of the continuity of economic phenomena, *i.e.* the fact that different classes imperceptibly merge into one another leading often to limiting cases. The recognition of this principle of continuity is perhaps the most important characteristic of modern economic theory. (5) Definitions have finally to be completed by the construction of a nomenclature and terminology, in which a compromise has to be made between the claims of technical precision and convenience on the one hand, and of current phraseology and intelligibility on the other.

(*e*) *Narrative Economics.*— In narrative or historical economics are included not only accounts of past events in chronological order, but also comparisons between different societies, whether contemporaneous or not. Here we deal with particular facts ascertained by specific experience. In contrast with the *formal* branch of descriptive economics, the historical deals with actual phenomena having a definite position in time and space, and is thus concrete and circumstantial. But even the narrator must *select* his facts, and use his judgment as to what is of importance in reference to the particular species of phenomena which circumscribes his narrative. Again, no mere record of isolated events can be of service to science. The grouping of facts—whether as simultaneous or as successive—must be guided by assumptions of causal connection. In the first place, then, economic history cannot be comprehensible or instructive without a previous survey of the special conceptions systematised by formal economics. But this is not all. As formal economics requires reference to facts in order to procure appropriateness to its conceptions, so history requires reference to ideas in order to secure coherence and systematisation in its presentation of facts. History is unavoidably coloured by the writer's theories of causal relations. Narrative economics, which occupies a middle position between formal and constructive economics, looking backwards, leads to modifications of the conceptions formulated by formal economics, and, looking forwards, becomes itself subject to modifications from constructive economics. One very important division of narrative economics is *Economic Statistics*. Although the range and implication of the term statistics appear to be very variously understood, yet we may at any rate regard statistics in the first instance as merely a descriptive-narrative department, dealing specially with numerical or quantitative results. The arrangement of such results in a coherent and instructive form requires not only logical and mathematical knowledge of a technical kind, but also special economic acquaintance with the action of industrial forces. The mere descriptive function of statistics is of course subordinate to its function of suggesting or verifying uniformities of cause and effect.

The importance to the economist of a wide knowledge of the various forms of economic institutions and habits that have actually appeared at different times and places, cannot be exaggerated. Some would hold that this historical knowledge is no part of economic science proper ; others, that it practically exhausts the whole of the science. Since, however, it is one of the functions of history to criticise theory, and one of the functions of theory to criticise history, it would seem that acquaintance with particular facts and understanding of general laws are so intimately bound up, that there is as much need to protest against the exclusion of history from theory as against the exclusion of theory from history. The historian of industry requires training in economic reasoning, and the economic reasoner requires constant appeal to concrete facts. On these grounds narrative economics should be included as an introductory though necessary part of the whole of economic science.

(*f*) *Constructive Economics.*—The central aim of the science of political economy is the discovery and establishment of general truths relating to industrial life. The uniformities investigated may be divided on several different principles. Perhaps the most important distinction is that previously alluded to between *laws of industrial development* and *laws of the statics and dynamics of industrial forces*. The former department is a branch of the science of social evolution :— the science which traces regularity in the tendencies according to which one stage of society is in the course of time supplanted by another. This study necessarily regards man and society as in some sense organised wholes ; *i.e.* it recognises all sides of human and social nature as co-operating towards

some end consciously or unconsciously pursued. Not only are comparisons instituted between different stages of the same developing community, but also between any different communities that offer examples of different stages of development. On the other hand, the interactions between industrial forces present problems of an entirely different kind. Here the general condition of the society to which the investigation relates is accepted as a *datum*, not accounted for as a result of development. Hence in this treatment, no elaborate analysis of the various sides of social life is necessary. Whether it be the play of competition or the *vis inertiæ* of habit and custom, whether it be legalised serfdom or *laisser faire* that is assumed as the dominant characteristic of the society, either hypothesis is taken merely as a starting point for further investigations. Associated with this distinction of scientific aim is the distinction of scientific method. There is a natural alliance between laws of development and an inductive method based exclusively on experience ; and a similar alliance between laws of interaction and a deductive method based mainly on calculation. Nevertheless there have been not a few writers who have treated evolution by highly *a priori* methods, while there have been many writers working with a fixed background of social conditions who have used the method of specific experience. In short, we have no right to identify the theorems of evolution with the inductive method, nor the theorems of dynamics with the deductive method. There is another distinction, viz. that between *abstract* and *concrete* economics which is liable to be identified with the distinction between the deductive and the inductive methods. By an abstract treatment of economic problems, is meant one in which the forces in operation are fictitiously simplified for purposes of investigation or exposition. The deductive method necessarily *begins* with an abstract treatment ; but, in its complete form, qualifying conditions are gradually introduced which render the treatment approximately truthful to the real complexity of human life. The inductive method, on the other hand, begins with the complexities of actual economic conditions ; but as it mounts up to higher and higher laws its statements become more and more general and, therefore, in a sense abstract. Pure induction starts with concrete detailed instances as its data, or premises, and works up from these to uniformities of increasing simplicity. Pure deduction starts with abstract elementary principles as its data or premises, and works down from these to uniformities of increasing complexity. The former passes from statements of greater to those of less circumstantiality ; the latter from statements of less to those of greater circumstantiality. Symbolically from such premises as "*ab* is *pq*, *ac* is *pr, bc* is *qr"*; induction infers that *"a* is *p, b* is *q, c* is *r"*; while deduction infers the former from the latter. But no known writer has ever confined himself to the method either of pure induction or of pure deduction. There are two ways in which the methods of induction and deduction mutually co-operate in science; firstly, either method may be used to confirm or refute the *conclusions* of the other; and secondly, either method may be used to control or determine the *premisses* of the other. As to the former point, the term *verification* is usually given to an *a posteriori* confirmation of a deductively inferred result; and the term *explanation* to an *a priori* confirmation of an inductively inferred result. Whether the treatment of a question is to be called inductive or deductive depends on the preponderance of intellectual labour involved. If this be chiefly devoted to the collection, description, and comparison of facts, the method would be characterised as inductive; if to the consideration of alternative possibilities, the calculation of forces in combination, and the tracing out of chains of effects on general principles, then the method would be characterised as deductive. In induction the writer relies mainly on the number and variety of the instances cited, and on the degree of circumstantiality with which each case can be described in both its quantitative and its qualitative aspects. But here the results cannot be safely applied except within a narrow range of experience. Hence the need of *a priori* confirmation, which will often determine the limits of applicability of the empirically obtained uniformity. In deduction, the writer relies on exactness in the statement of postulates, exhaustiveness in the survey of alternative possibilities, and thoroughness in the tracing out of a chain of effects dependent on any postulated change. But here the result must be regarded as expressing only a *tendency* which may or may not be realised in the actual complexities of life. Hence the need for an *a posteriori* confirmation, which will transform the statement of a mere tendency into one of realised fact. It should be specially noted that the confirmation by one method of a result reached by the other does not usually amount to an independent establishment of it. For the examples brought forward to confirm an *a priori* deduction may often be few and incompletely analysed; and the principles adduced in confirmation of an *a posteriori* induction may often be indeterminate and incompletely synthesised. A method is to be characterised as inductive or as deductive, according as the form in which *facts are analysed*, or that in which *principles are synthesised*, is the more logically cogent. We next examine how either method is used in regulating the *premisses* of the other method. The premisses of the deductive argument are conclusions derived from observation, which may be either of a very general kind, or of a more special kind applicable to a given state of society and dependent on scientific analysis of economic phenomena. Such premisses refer either to the action of single isolated forces, and thus supply major premisses or principles; or else to the particular conditions of the society under consideration, and thus afford minor premisses. Somewhat in the same way as induction supplies premisses for deduction, so the results of deduction determine the form assumed by the premisses of the inductive process. For in order to bring facts together to any purpose, it is necessary to know in general outline the agency of economic forces. The relation of cause and effect does not involve merely or necessarily contiguity in space and time. Hence the collector of facts needs the guidance of theory in order that his analytical descriptions may include all that is relevant and exclude all that is irrelevant.

(*g*) *Inductive Methods.*—The inductive method rests on a collection, analysis, and comparison of concrete instances, with the view of discovering, within the range of observation, uniformities that may be extended beyond that range. The instances are collected as they agree or differ in respect to some one circumstance, which it is sought to connect causally with some other circumstance. There are thus two fundamental methods of induction, that of *agreement* and that of *difference*. Each of these methods assumes several subordinate forms, and these varieties of form may be combined so as to increase the cogency of any inference. In the method of difference, we infer with respect to some circumstance in which the compared instances *differ* from one another; in the method of agreement, with respect to some circumstance in which the compared instances *agree* with one another. In the method of difference it is essential that the instances compared shall *agree* with one another as closely as possible in all circumstances not known to be irrelevant; in the method of agreement, that they shall *differ* from one another as far as possible in all such circumstances. Expressing the methods symbolically, in comparing instances AB and AC, when the conclusion relates to A, we are employing the method of agreement, when to B or C, the method of difference. For example, if we compare two countries resembling one another only in the fact that both have adopted a policy of free trade [A], and infer that their prosperity is due to this policy, we are employing the method of agreement. If we compare two countries differing from one another only in the fact that one has adopted free trade [B] and the other protection [C], and infer that the superior or inferior prosperity of one is due to this difference of policy, we are employing the method of difference. It should be pointed out that the functions of the two methods are not precisely identical. The method of difference proves—not that the differential circumstance would in *all* cases be efficient—but only when conjoined with the accompanying circumstances of the case. By this method alone it is impossible to discover how many of these accompanying circumstances were part-agents in producing the effect observed. It is therefore impossible to determine the range over which the causal relation may be extended. In order to *generalise* with respect to any one circumstance, we require the method of *agreement*, by which all other circumstances are shown to be irrelevant. Thus, if we can find a sufficiently varied group of strikingly prosperous communities, agreeing with one another only in the adoption of FREE TRADE, we have evidence that free trade *under any circumstances* will lead to prosperity. Causal connection in any single instance can only be proved by the method of difference, while a generalisation or uniformity can only be established by the method of agreement. The latter method determines, within certain limits of probability, the range over which we may extend any causal connection otherwise established. The explanation of this contrast is as follows : The law of causation tells us that *total agreement* between the causes operative in two instances would ensure *total agreement* between their effects ; and conversely. Hence, if there is a *partial difference* between the effects in two instances, there must always be at least a *partial difference* between the causes ; and conversely. This principle is that upon which the method of difference rests. On the other hand, it is not in general true that a *partial agreement* between the effects manifested in two instances would ensure even a *partial agreement* between their causes ; and conversely. The method of agreement is, therefore, not absolutely reliable, since it depends on a principle which is not universally and without qualification valid. The two methods of agreement and of difference are necessary to supplement one another ; the latter being required to establish *causal* connection in a single instance and the former to establish *uniformity* of connection.

Since, however, we can seldom fulfil the requirements of either of the two methods, we must practically have recourse to the *joint method*. Here we collect two sets of instances —one circumstance that is present in every instance of the first set being absent, or otherwise modified, in every instance of the second set. The more closely any pair of instances taken from the two sets agree, the more nearly we approach the requirements of the method of difference ; and the more the instances in each set vary among themselves, the more nearly we approach the requirements of the method of agreement.

So far, in analysing the above methods,

reference has been made to circumstances as simply *present or absent*. But the most important applications of induction are—not to mere *qualitative* agreement or difference—but to *quantitative* agreement or difference. Precisely the same methods apply to quantitative variations as to qualitative presence or absence, except that instead of taking only *two* instances, or two *sets* of instances of presence and absence respectively, we take any number of instances, or any number of *sets* of instances, in each of which a different magnitude of the variable quantity is presented. This method is called the *method of concomitant variations*. If the instances taken agree in all respects except in the magnitude of the variable quantity, the method is a mere extension of the *method of difference*. But the case in which instances are arranged in *groups*, according to the magnitude of the quantity present, is an extension of the *joint method*. This, in fact, constitutes the *complete method of pure induction*. Instances are arranged in separate heads, according to the various modifications of which some phenomenon is susceptible. Instances under each head, agreeing in some particular modification, are chosen which shall *differ* as far as possible as regards other accompanying circumstances ; while instances under different heads are chosen which shall *agree* as closely as possible in regard to all other accompanying circumstances. When, from such a group of instances it is found that one variable quantity remains constant whenever another is constant, and differs when the other differs, we have the highest, purely empirical, ground for inferring causal connection between the two quantities.

The complete method of pure induction not only assigns causal connection between two phenomena on the ground of the concomitance of their quantitative variations, but it further determines the *law* according to which the variations in the one phenomenon follow variations in the other. Thus, if the method could be applied to economic data, not only would it establish a causal relation, say, between the price of corn and the marriage-rate, but it would determine the one quantity as a *function* of the other. Similarly, in connecting the price of corn with the amount supplied. To elicit, from a number of arithmetical data, the most probable law of variation involves special mathematical and logical canons, for which the articles on STATISTICS ; LEAST SQUARES, METHOD OF ; AVERAGE, etc., should be consulted.

Theoretically, the chief difficulty of applying pure inductive methods to economic phenomena is owing to the *composition of causes*. An effect in the economic world is invariably due—not to one kind of cause—but to the co-operation and interaction of a number of different causes, which all contribute to determine the actual phase or degree manifested in the effect. Hence, by mere observation, it is impossible to detect the underlying agreement in different instances of the effect of any one cause,—the effect due to this one cause being modified through inter-mixture with the effects due to others. Instances compared according to the method of difference are not, however, in the same way vitiated by the action of the composition of causes. If the force operative in two instances, otherwise similar, differs in kind or intensity in the two instances, then any observable difference in the effect may be ascribed to this difference in the cause, although other forces may be operating in conjunction with that observed. A special variety of the method of difference applied to cases of composition of causes, is called the *method of residues*. This method is partly of an *a priori* and deductive character. It applies to cases in which the effects of all but one of the causes in operation are known, both as regards number and magnitude. If then, the actually produced effect is compared with that which would have been produced by the composition of the causes whose effects are known, the difference will determine the amount due to the cause in question. A simple example in economics of the method of residues is supplied by examining the rates of exchange of foreign bills. If the rate of discount current at the time is known on *a priori* or independent grounds, then a comparison between the exchange and the rate of discount will determine how much of the effect is to be put down to the temporary inequality of mutual indebtedness between the countries.

(*h*) *Deductive Methods.*—The character of the results reached by the deductive method will depend mainly upon the nature of the data or postulates which are assumed as premisses. It would not be possible to enumerate all the assumptions that have been made by different economists and for different purposes, but there are some half dozen which may be taken as typical and almost universally applied. Of these six data, two belong to each of the divisions, physical, psychological, and social. (1) The two physical or natural laws presupposed are the law of DIMINISHING RETURNS, which arises from the necessity of having recourse to inferior agents of production, or to their use under less advantageous circumstances ; and the law of INCREASING RETURNS which results from the increased possibilities of industrial organisation under extension of supply. Both these laws represent *tendencies* ascertained by ordinary observation, which work in opposite directions. Hence more exact knowledge as to the magnitude of the forces in particular circumstances has to be supplied by further detailed observation. (2) The two psychological data are general expressions of the nature of DEMAND and of SUPPLY, so far as these depend on the characters of individuals. The law of demand

is to the effect that the utility afforded by any increment of any kind of desired object diminishes with increase of the amount possessed: the law of supply is to the effect that every one tries to procure material well-being with the least possible sacrifice. These assumptions are common to almost all economic reasonings of a deductive type, though they are not always explicitly formulated. Here, as in the case of the physical presuppositions, further detailed observation is required to determine the precise degree in which these psychological forces act under any circumstances. In particular, the law of supply requires to be made more definite by an estimate of the influences of habit, inertia, ignorance, or custom, which materially affect its application. (3) The two sociological data relate to the conditions of freedom and restraint under which the economic activities of a community take place. Speaking generally, it is assumed on the one hand that individual action is controlled by certain legalised institutions with regard to property, and, on the other hand, that individuals are free to act according to their own will within certain limits. A similar remark applies here, as before, namely that the precise degree of freedom or of restraint, operative under any circumstances, has to be determined by specific observation. In analysing the postulates of deductive economics, reference is generally made to *competition ;* but under this term a good many ambiguities are concealed. Competition is sometimes used to exclude any form of combination ; but abstract economics does not exclude any form of combination which individuals may find it to their interest to enter into. Again, competition sometimes implies merely legislative freedom for every one to act for his own interest ; but at other times it implies that equal remunerations are secured for equal services. Now this latter depends on the *effectiveness*, not on the mere *freedom*, of competition. Again, freedom of competition may imply the absence — not merely of governmental interference—but also of all sentiments, habits, or dispositions which might check the active pursuit on the part of every one of his own interests. There is a distinction between the restraints imposed by the social and legal environments and those due to psychological and individual character. Now, with respect to all these and similar presuppositions of deductive economics, considerable difference of opinion has arisen as to their validity or import. Some writers hold that they are of universal application, though, of course, requiring further determination by specific observations of particular communities (cp. Jevons, "The Future of Political Economy," *Fortnightly Review*, vol. xxvi. p. 625). Others hold that they express tendencies only which are liable to be counteracted by various forces of a secondary kind (cp. Mill, Cairnes, etc.). Others, again, hold that the postulates of economics relate to societies within a narrowly limited range, viz. those which have reached the most highly developed and complicated form of industrial organisation (cp. Bagehot, *Economic Studies*, pp. 19, 20). Lastly, some have held that the premisses of deductive economics are absolute fictions, applicable to no society of individuals that has existed or ever could exist (cp. F. Harrison, Cliffe Leslie). The truth is that, without further modification, few of the conclusions of deductive economics can be applied to the explanation or regulation of concrete circumstances ; but that the method is necessary for controlling and guiding inductive observation. Moreover, the different postulates of deductive economics have different values in relation to different classes of phenomena. In some cases many more qualifications are needed than in others. These qualifications suggested by inductive observation can often be introduced into the deductive process itself. But, in any case, the limits of validity of deductively reached results must be examined by comparisons with experience ; and in this consists the importance of deduction, checked, tested, and confirmed by induction.

(*i*) *Criticism and Combination of Methods.* In political economy *induction* alone is inadequate for the following reasons : (1) There is hardly any scope for experiment, whereby the effect of a single cause coming suddenly into operation in the midst of an unchanging environment could be observed. (2) The cause of any effect consists always of a conjunction of a large and intricate number of conditions which cannot be measured or empirically observed in separation. (3) The effects produced are often at first inappreciable ; and cannot in any case be looked for until long after the first introduction of the cause. (4) Hence the effects are continually liable to be modified and interfered with by other co-operating or conflicting agencies, which come into operation after the special cause under investigation. On the other hand, *deduction* alone is inadequate for the following reasons : (1) The data or first principles of the science cannot be ascertained with quantitative exactness. (2) The character of the objects to which the science applies is liable to fundamental changes, so that there is no permanent basis upon which calculation can rely. (3) Even in a stationary society, the kind and degree of qualifying circumstances that modify the results cannot be known *a priori.* (4) No principle is known, like the parallelogram of forces in physics, according to which the effects of various forces in combination can be calculated.

In face of these obstacles to cogent inference by either the inductive or the deductive method, the fact that so much has been written in political economy which professes to employ one or other of these methods requires explanation. The answer is to be found in the consideration that much of what has been written comes rather under the *descriptive* than under the *constructive* head. Much of what is called deductive economics concerns itself with the preliminary process of clearing up misconceptions and presenting alternative possibilities in an exhaustively systematic form. So far as inferences have been worked out, they have merely made explicit what is involved in the postulates assumed at the outset, by carrying them to their inevitable consequences. This work of clearing up ideas, in so complicated a subject as that of the interaction of industrial forces, is so difficult, that no amount of care and trouble is thrown away in attempting to execute it efficiently. On the other hand, much of so-called *inductive* economics is concerned with the process of enlarging one's views of the varied forms in which economic life has been manifested from time to time, and of presenting problems from experience for theory to solve. So far as inference has been here introduced, it has consisted mainly in propounding a mere *suggestion* that, where agreements or differences have been observed, there is probably some causal connection which theory is required to explain. Such work is also extremely useful. What can alone be called *constructive* economics —involving genuine inference from the known or postulated to the unknown—has actually involved the co-operation of deduction and induction. Here, again, there is room for workers of opposite tastes and abilities, for we may still distinguish a method that is predominantly inductive but aided by deduction from one that is predominantly deductive but aided by induction. In the former, the facts of history are collected and prepared in the light of general theory, and an explanation of their connections is sought for on universal *a priori* principles. In the latter, the principles assumed are chosen on the ground of general conformity with experience, and a verification of the conclusions inferred is sought for in specific experience. So far as inductive generalisation fails to receive confirmation from indubitable general principles, it is led inductively to examine its facts more comprehensively. And so far as deductive calculation fails to receive confirmation from indubitable particular experiences, it is led deductively to apply its principles more concretely. Thus each method may learn from the results of the other without losing its own distinguishing characteristics.

[The English works in which the subject has been exhaustively treated are J. N. Keynes, *Scope and Method of Political Economy,* and J. E. Cairnes, *Character and Logical Method of Political Economy.* But almost all systematic writers on political economy have dealt more or less incidentally with the question of method. Without pro-

fessing to supply an exhaustive bibliography, the following important works may be mentioned :—
W. J. Ashley, *English Economic History and Theory.*—W. Bagehot, *Economic Studies.*—M. Block, *La Science Economique.*—A. E. Cherbuliez, *Précis de la Science Économique.*—G. Cohn, *Grundlegung der Nationalökonomie.*—L. Cossa, *Guide to the Study of Political Economy.*—C. F. Dunbar, "Reaction in Political Economy" (*Quarterly Journal of Economics*, October 1886).—B. Hildebrand, "Die gegenwärtige Aufgabe der Wissenschaft der Nationalökonomie" (article in *Jahrbücher für Nationalökonomie und Statistik*, vol. i., 1863).—J. K. Ingram, *History of Political Economy.*—W. S. Jevons, "The Future of Political Economy" (*Fortnightly Review*, November 1876), and *The Theory of Political Economy.*—K. Knies, *Die politische Oekonomie vom Standpunkte der geschichtlichen Methode.*—T. E. Cliffe Leslie, *Essays in Political and Moral Philosophy.*—F. List, *The National System of Political Economy.*—T. R. Malthus, *Definitions in Political Economy.*—(Also J. Bonar, *Malthus and his Work*).—A. Marshall, *Principles of Economics; Present Position of Economics.*—C. Menger, *Untersuchungen über die Methode der socialwissenschaften und der politischen Oekonomie insbesondere*, and *Die Irrthümer des Historismus in der deutschen Nationalökonomie.*—J. S. Mill, *Essays on some unsettled questions of Political Economy*, and *Logic*, bk. vi.—W. Roscher, *Principles of Political Economy.*—E. Sax, *Wesen und Aufgaben der Nationalökonomie.*—H. von Scheel, "Die politische Oekonomie als Wissenschaft" (Schönberg's *Handbuch*, vol. i.).—G. Schmoller, *Zur Litteraturgeschichte der Staats und Sozialwissenschaften.*—G. Schönberg, "Die Volkswirthschaft" (Schönberg's *Handbuch*, vol. i.).—N. W. Senior, *Political Economy*, and *Introductory Lectures before the University of Oxford.*—H. Sidgwick, *Principles of Political Economy*, and *Scope and Method of Political Economy.*—C. Supino, *Il método induttivo nell' economia politica.*—"Science Economic Discussion" (*The Science Company*, New York, 1886).—A. Wagner, "Grundlagen der Volkswirthschaft" (*Handbuch der politischen Oekonomie*, vol. i.).]   W. E. J.

METHUEN TREATY. Portugal had been closely allied with England since the marriage of Charles II. with Catharine of Braganza (1661) and the recognition of Portuguese independence (1668) to which English arms and diplomacy had essentially contributed. But when the great question of the Spanish succession was raised in 1700, Pedro I. of Portugal was induced by France to acknowledge the Bourbon claimant, Philip V. It was a notable success for the Grand Alliance when, in 1703, Portugal deserted the Bourbon cause and joined in the war as a partisan of the Archduke Charles. In the negotiations which led to this change of sides a prominent part was taken by John Methuen, the English envoy at Lisbon. Methuen now seized the opportunity to secure commercial advantages for England by reopening the Portuguese market to English wool, which had been excluded from that country since 1680 in the hope of encouraging native agriculture and manufactures. On 27th December 1703, he succeeded in concluding the brief but famous treaty which has immortalised his name. It consists of two simple and straightforward articles : British woollen manufactures are to be admitted into Portugal on the same terms as before the prohibition, provided that Portuguese wines shall pay in Great Britain a duty one-third less than that charged upon wines from France. For more than seventy years this treaty was consistently observed, with the result that the cultivation of the vine was vastly extended in Portugal, and that in England port superseded burgundy as the ordinary wine drunk by the gentry. The treaty was regarded as specially advantageous to England, because a large portion of our exports were paid for in the gold which Portugal derived from Brazil. Hence the mercantilists reckoned that the balance of our trade with Portugal was more favourable than that of trade with any other country. This contention led Adam Smith to make a special attack upon the Methuen Treaty, which he condemned on three grounds : (1) British capital could have found more advantageous employments than the Portuguese trade into which it was artificially attracted ; (2) we gave differential advantages to Portuguese wines, while Portugal promised none to English woollens ; (3) England was forced to undertake the burdensome task of defending a very weak ally against Spain and France. It is undoubtedly true that the disadvantage at which French wines were placed in the British market contributed to strengthen and prolong the hostile feelings between France and England during the 18th century.

The first blow to the Methuen Treaty was dealt by the great Portuguese minister, Pombal. The market for British goods was restricted by sumptuary laws and by the systematic protection of native industry. In 1767 it was reckoned that our exports to Portugal had fallen from £1,500,000 to £735,000, and that the balance of the precious metals had sunk to £105,000. The dissatisfaction thus created facilitated Pitt's negotiations with France, and art. 6 of the famous commercial treaty of 1786 stipulated that "the wines of France, imported directly from that country, shall pay no higher duties in Great Britain than those now paid by the wines of Portugal." This was a virtual abrogation of the Methuen Treaty, but the subsequent outbreak of the long wars with the French republic and empire prevented the new agreement from being fully carried out. During the war, Portuguese wines paid 9s. 1d. a gallon and French wines 13s. 9d., and thus port retained its ascendency over burgundy and claret during the early part of the present century. In 1825 the duties were reduced, but the same proportion was retained, and it was not till 1832 that Lord Althorpe, as chancellor of the exchequer, carried the equalisation of duties upon foreign wines at 5s. 6d. per gallon. In 1836 Portugal formally released England from the obligations of the Methuen Treaty.[1]

[Adam Smith, *Wealth of Nations*, bk. iv. ch. 6.—Macpherson, *Annals of Commerce*, vol. ii. —Leone Levi, *History of British Commerce*.]

R. L.

METRIC SYSTEM—ENGLAND. The action of England in respect to the metric system of weights and measures has been characterised by precisely the same slowness and vacillation as has been described under the heading of DECIMAL SYSTEM in relation to coinage. Had it not been taken up, with more or less of zeal and perseverance, by various private individuals in the last hundred years, no English government or its executive would have so much as given it a thought. Space compels us to do no more than briefly refer to what has been done during the second half of the current century. Entirely through private agitation, and mainly through that of the Metric Association, founded in London by some few leading men of science and business, a parliamentary committee was named in 1862 for the consideration of suggested reforms in our system of weights and measures. They recommended, with unanimity, a cautious but steady introduction of the metric system, and its legalisation, but not compulsorily until sanctioned by the general conviction of the public, and that a department of the board of trade should undertake the care and verification of the standards under the new system, and spread the knowledge of it in government departments and among the people, and use it alongside the present system in levying customs duties and in government contracts. It was also to be made one of the subjects for examination in competitions for entering the civil service. The *gramme* was to be used as a weight for foreign letters and books at the post-office. The metric system was to be taught in all schools receiving grants of public money. The recommendation of the International Statistical Congress, as to its use in our public statistics, was adopted ; this was that its use should be allowed in private parliamentary bills, and metric and imperial measures exclusively used until the former came to be generally adopted. A bill was introduced into parliament to make the chief of these recom-

1 Contemporary opinion differed as to the effect of the inpost.
" Firm and erect the Caledonian stood,
  Good was his mutton and his claret good.
' Let him drink port,' the English statesman cried.
  He drank the poison and his spirit died."
Contra :—
" Drink the port ; the claret's dear, Erskine, Erskine.
Ye'll get fou on't. never fear, my jo Erskine."

mendations compulsory at a date to be fixed, say at end of three or more years. In committee the government objected to the compulsory provision, and substituted a permissive bill which was agreed to, and became the "Metric Act" of 1864. In 1868 a bill, afterwards abandoned, was brought in to introduce the metric system by compulsion, after a period to be inserted by government. In 1871 a bill with the same object was introduced, but Mr. J. B. Smith, then member for Stockport, who had long laboured with the Metric Association in discussing and arranging the terms of this bill, was defeated on a second reading by a majority of five. In the last quarter of the century, mainly arising from the decease of some of the most active and influential members of the Metric Association, and partly from the few survivors being tired of the apathy of the general public on this question, there arose a certain positive retrogression in the interest taken in it. At the present date (1895) a new body, under the revived name of the Decimal Association, has again taken it up, and a parliamentary committee, after resuming the task of taking evidence, has reported almost unanimously in favour of legalising the metric weights and measures immediately, and of making their use obligatory at the end of two years, with provision for teaching the system in the meanwhile in every public school as a necessary and integral part of arithmetic. It would be a welcome sign of progress, if, in the public advantages expected to accrue from the recently elected strong government and executive, these recommendations be allowed to bear fruit in the shape of a complete reform. This ought, however, in our opinion, to be extended also to coinage, as if so important a step in the commercial and daily life, and in the education of the people, be once taken, it should not be in a piecemeal, but in a complete manner. The precedents of other European countries should be kept in view. They have not feared the change, but, greatly to their advantage, have successfully carried it through.   F. H.

METRIC SYSTEM (FRANCE, etc.), the system of weights and measures established in France by the law of 18 germinal, year III. (17th March 1795), and since adopted by a great number of other countries. The idea of a scientific basis for a standard from which all weights and measures could be derived had been put forward a century earlier by the astronomer Picard. The unit he proposed for his standard was the length of a pendulum, beating one second at the sea-level at forty-five degrees of latitude. No uniform system of weights and measures then existed in France, and although the *toise*, and the *livre*, were common expressions, the length of the one, and the weight of the other varied in the different provinces, and even between towns of the same province. A general reform of the various systems was one of the desiderata contained in several of the "cahiers" submitted to the *États Généraux* which preceded the revolution of 1789, and the subject was taken up by the constituent assembly on a proposal by Talleyrand. By a royal decree of the 8th of May 1790, the king of England was to be invited to appoint a commission of savants to meet one of French academicians, and determine the length of the pendulum, as proposed by Picard. Political events prevented the execution of this project, but the French academy of sciences named a committee formed of Borda, Lagrange, Laplace, Monge, and Condorcet, to carry out the work. That body, however, set aside Picard's plan of the length of a pendulum as the basis of the new system, as well as a proposal to take a fraction of the length of the equator, and adopted as the initial measure, to be called the mètre, the ten millionth part of a quarter of the terrestrial meridian, with decimal multiples and divisions. There, however, remained to determine the length of the quadrants. Many savants had, during the century, taken measurements of parts of the meridian, but the results differed considerably. Picard fixed the length of the degree at 57,060 toises of six feet. Some astronomers put the degree as high as 57,422 toises, others as low as 56,750. Fresh surveys were ordered, and Delambre and Méchain were charged in 1792 to measure the arc of the meridian between Dunkirk and Mont Jouy near Barcelona. Those limits were selected as being at about equal distances, the one from the north pole, the other from the equator, each extremity being at the sea level. The result of their labours, which spread over a period of seven years, was to fix the distance from the poles to the equator at 5,130,740 toises, a ten millionth part of which was taken as the standard mètre. The length of the degree according to their calculation was 57,008 toises, differing but slightly from the 57,060 toises obtained by Picard more than a century earlier. A committee of weights and measures was then appointed to complete the work, by composing a system of weights and measures based on the metre, with decimal multiples and divisions. To indicate the multiples the Greek prefixes, *deca* ten, *hecto* a hundred, *kilo* a thousand, and *myria* ten thousand, were adopted ; and for the divisions, the Latin, *deci* a tenth, *centi* a hundredth, *milli* a thousandth. A *décamètre* is consequently a lineal measure of ten mètres, a *décimètre* a tenth of a mètre, a *kilomètre*, the ordinary measure of road distances, one thousand mètres, a *millimètre* a thousandth of a mètre. Other measures and weights are derived from the mètre. For surface measurement the unity is the square of a mètre on each side ; with the multiples square décamètre, having sides of ten mètres, and the divisions of a square decimètre, or sides of one-

tenth of a mètre, etc. For land measurement, the square décamètre, containing 100 square mètres, is called an *are*, and 100 ares, or 10,000 square mètres, an *hectare*. For solids the principal measure is the cubic metre of a square mètre on each of the six faces, the same bulk of water forming the ton weight of liquids. The *litre* is a thousandth part of the ton, or a measure having a tenth of a mètre, or ten centimètres on each face. The weight unit is also derived from the measurement of liquids, a cubic centimètre, or cube of one hundredth of a mètre on each face of distilled water, at the temperature of greatest density, forming the *gramme ;* a thousand grammes make the *kilogramme*, or French double pound, which is the principal commercial unity of weight. The division of the mètre and the gramme into one thousandth parts, the *millimètre* and the *milligramme*, permits calculations of great nicety, and those weights and measures are now commonly employed in the sciences and industrial arts in countries which have not adopted the metric system generally.

Comparative tables of the English equivalents of the French weights and measures are to be found in most books of arithmetic and works of reference, and it will suffice here to state that the mètre is 39·370 inches, or 1·093 yards ; the litre, 61·027 cubic inches, or 1·760 pints ; the hectolitre, 2·751 bushels ; the gramme, 15·432 grains ; the kilogramme, 32·150 ounces troy, or 2·204 pounds avoirdupois ; the square mètre, 10·764 square feet ; the hectolitre, dry measure, 2·751 bushels ; the kilolitre, or ton measurement 35·316 cubic feet. Conversely the English inch is 0·025 metres ; the yard, 0·914 mètres ; the mile, 1609·31 mètres ; the square yard, 0·836 square mètres ; the acre, 0·404 hectares ; the pint, 0·567 litres ; the gallon, 4·543 litres ; the bushel, 36·347 litres ; the grain, 6·479 centigrammes ; the ounce avoirdupois, 28·349 grammes ; the pound, 453·592 grammes ; the cwt., 50·802 kilogrammes. In the above equivalents decimal figures beyond three in number are omitted.

The metric system was definitely constituted by a law of the 10th December 1799, and became compulsory from November 1801, but did not apply to the currency. The famous law of the 7th Germinal year xi. (28th March 1803), however, established the monetary system on its present bases, the weight of the coin being fixed in grammes with decimal subdivisions of the franc into decimes and centimes, or tenths and hundredths of the franc. The new system had to contend with old habits and prejudice. The population continued to employ old names adapted to divisions of the new weights and measures, such as a foot of a third of the mètre, an *aune* or ell of 1·20 mètres, a pound of 500 grammes, an *arpent* or acre of two-fifths of an hectare, etc., and those infractions of the law were tolerated by successive governments until a law was passed in 1837, interdicting, from the 1st January 1840, under severe penalties, the use of any other weights and measures than those of the metric system. The principal exceptions to the use of the metric or decimal system in France, are in the divisions of time, and the measurement of angles, for which the old numeration is preserved, and all attempts to bring those quantities into concordance with the system have been abandoned. Absolute perfection is difficult, and the original idea of taking for the standard a certain and incontestable lineal measure has not been completely realised. Since the first mètre was cast in platinum, and deposited at the archives in an iron safe, secured with four locks, other measurements of the meridian have been taken, and have proved that the real length of the quadrant is 5,131,180 toises, or 440 more than obtained by Delambre and Mechain. The latter of those savants is said to have himself discovered an error in his calculations, but did not dare to reveal it for fear of raising doubts on all the work of the commission. The mètre has remained as first established, in spite of that imperfection.

An international convention met in Paris in 1875, and decided on the formation of a permanent bureau of metric weights and measures. The countries represented were France, Belgium, Italy, Spain, Portugal, Sweden and Norway, Germany, Austria, Switzerland, Denmark, Russia, Turkey, the United States of America, Argentina, Peru, and Venezuela. England did not send any delegate, but gave her adhesion in 1884, and some other states, including Japan, have since joined in. The international bureau is established in a government building, in the park of St. Cloud, with a permanent staff charged to make and provide prototypes of the mètre and the kilogramme, the expense being borne in common. Besides the original mètre, preserved at the Paris archives, exact reproductions are also deposited at the Observatory, and the Conservatoire des Arts et Metiers. The international prototypes are made of 90 parts of platinum, and 10 of iridium, and have a length of 102 centimetres, the mètre being marked by indented lines at one centimètre from each end. Most of the states above named have adopted entirely the metric system, others, including England, have legalised it, while a third class of states have decimal monies, weights, and measures, not concording with the metric system, but which are a step towards it, and will facilitate a future adhesion to it. The merits of the system as a whole are so universally admitted that they do not require to be demonstrated.

[P. Leyssenne, Traité d'Arithmétique.—Larousse, Grand Dictionnaire du xix⁰. Siècle (s.v.)—Duvergier, Collection des Lois et Décrets depuis 1788.]

T. L.

METROPOLIS, MANAGEMENT OF (see also COMPANIES, CITY OF LONDON). For purposes of local government London is divided into two distinct areas, the City of London—formerly the City and County of London—and the modern administrative County of London. The former comprises the area within the old city walls, and some districts lying immediately without, in all some 671 acres, about one square mile, with a population (1891) of 301,384, and by night 37,705. The corporation of City of London consists of the lord mayor, the two city sheriffs, the court of aldermen, and the court of common council. The elective bodies are the liverymen and the ratepayers. The LIVERY are the freemen of the city companies or gilds, which are now (1893) 76 in number, and have 8807 members, who are entitled to vote in common hall. The ratings are 11,280 in number, giving 29,337 municipal voters, the total assessment being £4,153,930. The aldermen, 26 in number—one for each ward,—are chosen by the ratepayers, and hold office for life. The alderman for the ward of Bridge Without is not elected by the ratepayers of that ward, but the seat, when vacant, is taken, generally by seniority, by one of the other aldermen, whose ward immediately elects a fresh representative. The ratepayers also elect common councilmen, varying from 4 to 16 for each ward, and amounting in all to 206, who hold office for one year only, the elections taking place annually on St. Thomas's Day. The lord mayor, who must previously have served the office of sheriff, is chosen annually, on the 29th September, by the court of aldermen, from two members of their own body selected on the same day by the liverymen in common hall. Both the selection of the livery and the choice of the aldermen usually fall upon the next in seniority. The two sheriffs are also elected by the livery. From the time of Henry I. the livery possessed the right to elect both the city sheriff and the sheriff of Middlesex, but by the Local Government Act of 1888 the last-named right was withdrawn, and the citizens now elect two sheriffs for the city.

The corporation has complete and exclusive powers of local government throughout its own area. It maintains and controls its own police, and administers justice at the Guild Hall and Mansion House. It appoints judges to hold courts of assize for criminal cases at the Old Bailey—the aldermen being justices of that court, and throughout the city, and having, besides, special powers enabling any of them to do alone any act which in any other place requires the presence of two justices of the peace. The court of aldermen holds licensing sessions for the city. It also appoints judges for the trial of civil causes in the City of London Court, and the Mayor's

Court, the latter having exclusive jurisdiction in a variety of causes arising out of city customs, and also in causes in equity, if arising entirely within the city. The court of aldermen holds separate meetings for its special duties, but for administrative purposes the aldermen sit in common council with the councillors, and have equal powers.

The Administrative County of London comprises urban and suburban districts outside the city boundaries, extending for some nine or ten miles on every side. It extends over some 117 square miles, and contains an area of 74,771 acres, not including the city, with a population (1891) of 4,194,413. This area was formerly without any joint or corporate administration, its local government being entirely in the hands of the vestries of the different parishes, but by the Metropolis Local Management Act of 1855 the metropolitan board of works was established, with powers for drainage, sewerage, lighting, cleaning, and general improvements. By the Local Government Act of 1888 this body was superseded by the London county council, with extended powers of government over the same area under the title of the Administrative County of London. This body consists primarily of 118 councillors, who are elected by the electors of the parliamentary boroughs in the metropolis, including the city, the number of councillors for each division being double the number of members it returns to parliament. The councillors at their first meeting elect a number of aldermen, not exceeding in all one-sixth of their own number. From this enlarged body they elect a chairman, a paid deputy, and a vice-chairman. All the members of the council sit together, and have equal powers. The councillors hold office for three years, and retire all together. The aldermen hold office for six years, nine or ten of them retiring every three years. At present (1895) there are 118 councillors, not including the chairman, and 19 aldermen.

The funds of the council are raised by levies upon the different parishes and districts within its area, all parishes paying an equal rate per £1. The rateable value (April 1895) is £34,225,532. By the Equalisation of Rates Act 1894, a rate of 3d. in the pound may be made half yearly to form an equalisation fund, which is to be distributed among the parishes on the basis of population. It has also power to raise money by loan, and the gross debt amounts (1895) to £34,858,656, including £12,205,129 in loans to different vestries and school boards.

For judicial purposes the London county council has power to direct, with the approval of the home secretary, the holding of quarter sessions for the county of London, and has the right to petition the crown to appoint a chairman therefor. The chairman of the

county council is a justice of the peace *ex officio.*

The sheriff of the county of London is appointed by the crown in the same way as the sheriffs of Middlesex and other counties.

For general criminal jurisdiction the county of London is in the district of the Central Criminal Court: a district comprising 269,140 acres, say 420 square miles including the city, with a population (1891) of 5,260,680. The Central Criminal Court holds quarter sessions and sessions every month. For police jurisdiction the county of London is comprised, by act of 1829, in the Metropolitan Police District, which extends over a radius of 15 miles from Charing Cross, and covers 442,750 acres, or 692 square miles, not including the city, having a population (1891) of 5,596,101. The metropolitan police are under the direct control of parliament, acting through a commissioner appointed by the home secretary. One-half of the cost of police is voted by parliament, and the other half is raised by precept upon the different parishes according to rateable value.

For educational purposes it is administered by the London school board, established under the Elementary Education Act 1870, whose district is the same as that of the London county council. This board has 58 members who are elected every three years by the ratepayers, women being entitled to vote, and eligible as members. The Chairman of the board is appointed by the members, but not necessarily selected from among themselves.

Many important matters relating to the health of the metropolis, such as fever and smallpox hospitals, and the care of imbeciles, are under the control of the metropolitan asylums board, one-third of whose members are nominated by the Local government board, the remainder being elected by the various bodies of poor-law guardians.

Matters relating to the port of London and the river Thames are in the hands of the city corporation as port sanitary authority, and the Thames conservancy. This body consists of 38 members, of whom 8 are nominated by the corporation, and a like number by the London county council.

The lieutenancy of London is in a commission named by the crown under the privy seal, and under Act of 1673, and consisting of the members and chief officers of the corporation, but not all of the councillors, and other merchants and bankers of the city who are recommended by the lord mayor. The court of lieutenants has the same powers with regard to the reserve forces as the lords lieutenant of the counties. A Royal Commission was appointed (1893) "to consider the proper conditions under which an amalgamation of the City and County of London could take place, and to make specific and practical proposals for the purpose." The Commission included one member of the City Corporation, but the Commission declining to receive evidence as to the desirability of amalgamation, as well as its practicability, the Corporation retired from the inquiry in November 1893. A report was presented in September 1894, but up to the end of 1895 the matter had proceeded no further. R. W. B.

METZ NOBLAT. See DE METZ-NOBLAT.

MEUBLES. See IMMEUBLES.

MEYNIEU, MADAME MARY (died in 1877) ; an Englishwoman by birth, married to a Frenchman. She became a widow after fifty years of wedded life, but continued to live in France. Highly cultivated and accomplished, she was one of the few women who have written on political economy, and she was highly successful in popularising the science.

Her principal works are : *Eléments d'économie politique*, a statement in a series of dialogues between a teacher and pupil for the use of the primary normal schools, Paris, 1839, 8vo.— *Histoire du paupérisme anglais*, 1841, 8vo.
A. C. f.

MÉZAGUES, VIVANT DE (18th century), believed to be the author of a "letter" on the general condition of England, under the initials M. V. D. M., is stated by his translator to have been at the head of the finances of France (c. 1754-60). The object of the "letter" is to show that the wealth and trade of England were not greater than those of France. With this view the author examines into the balance of trade between England and other countries (including Ireland), the national income and debt, exchanges, imports and exports of bullion, war expenditure, etc. He concludes that England, after having been a gainer by her trade during the 17th century, was in 1761 a loser from a monetary point of view. He supports his argument by statistics from official and the best private estimates, and carefully considers objections. He calculates that the "territorial income" of England about 1760 was £20,000,000 sterling ; also that from two-fifths to a third of the national debt was held by foreigners.

Bilan général et raisonné de l'Angleterre, depuis 1600 jusqu'à la fin de 1761; ou Lettre à M. L. C. D. sur le produit des terres et du commerce de l'Angleterre, par M. V. D. M., 1762 ; translated into English under the title *A general view of England respecting its policy, trade, commerce, taxes, debts, produce of land, colonies, manners, etc.*, *argumentatively stated from the year 1600 to 1762, in a letter to M. L. C. D. by M. V. D. M.*, London, 1766. [See Andrew HOOKE.]

[Coquelin and Guillaumin, *Dictionnaire de l'Économie politique*, Paris, 1854.—R. Giffen, *Growth of Capital*, London, 1889.] R. H. H.

MICHAELIS, OTTO (1826-1890), was successively a journalist, a member of the Prussian chamber of deputies, of the imperial *Reichstag*, and a councillor of the German chancery. He was one of the most steadfast and brilliant representatives of the German free-trading party ; when Prince Bismarck's leanings towards a protective policy became notorious, he resigned his office in the imperial chancery, but was placed at the head of the board of the *Invalidenfonds*. He was with Julius FAUCHER (*q.v.*) one of the founders of the *Vierteljahrschrift* and an honorary member of the Cobden Club.

After having published a book against the state monopoly of railways (*Das Monopol der Eisenbahnen* 1861), Michaelis later on showed himself willing to make concessions on this subject ; his *Volkswirthschaftliche Schriften*, 2 vols., 1857, which deal with the management of railways, the commercial crisis of 1857, commercial speculations, public loans and banking, and his contributions to the *Vierteljahrschrift*, deserve to be noticed. In his chapter on value (*Das Kapitel vom Werthe*), which first came out in the same periodical, he states that the notion of value is purely subjective, and springs from the efforts to be made in order to get possession of a thing, leaving aside the further purpose of exchange. He was a strong opponent of a fiduciary circulation of bank-notes. E. ca.

MICHEL, FRANCISQUE (1809-1887), editor of the first volume of the Gascon Rolls (*Rôles Gascons*) in the *Collection des Documents Inédits*, of municipal records of Bordeaux, etc. His writings, chiefly on antiquarian subjects, are numerous.

His *Histoire du Commerce et de la Navigation de Bordeaux* (2 vols., Bordeaux, 1867-68), entirely based on local and on national (English and French) records, is highly esteemed and full of information on the intercourse between Bordeaux and England during the period of English dominion.
E. CA.

MIDDLEMAN. A "middleman," in the broadest sense, is one through whose hands goods pass from one trader to another or to a consumer. Owing to the inaccurate habits of thought prevalent respecting economics, the term has acquired a dyslogistic meaning in consequence of the considerable profits which are frequently made by the persons or corporations included under it. The middleman is supposed in some mysterious and blameworthy manner to have insinuated himself between the producer and the consumer, taking an exorbitant profit from both, and various wild schemes have from time to time been devised for "eliminating the middleman" who is figured by half-educated people as a person with no real *raison d'être*, since he performs no useful function. This idea is, in the main, absurd, but like more widely spread opinions it is based on a truth. To get rid of *all* intermediate agencies between producer and consumer is a dream which even the most rabid assailant of the middleman would admit to be impossible of realisation, but there is no doubt that in certain cases middlemen continue to obtain business long after the economic justification for their existence has ceased. To do what has always been the custom is easier than to strike out a new path, and for this reason people follow the old ways in their daily business unless a very great advantage can be shown to result from a change.

CO-OPERATION as applied to DISTRIBUTION is a device, and a very effective device, for getting rid of a number of middlemen. Various attempts have been made to "bring producer and consumer together," especially in the case of agricultural produce, the profits of the salesman, in the case of meat especially, being supposed to be excessive. They probably are in many cases; for though retail tradesmen are fierce competitors one with another in large towns, their competition does not take the form of cutting down prices to any serious extent, and in small towns a practical monopoly of the supply of such articles as meat often exists. Moreover, the strong demand arising from the wants of the big towns, especially London, tends to keep up prices, for the London salesman would be quick to take advantage of any unusual cheapness. It is, however, difficult to avoid the conclusion that middlemen are essential to nearly all businesses involving movements of commodities over considerable distances, and as there is competition even among them, their profits cannot be more, on the average, than the services rendered justify, though occasionally an excessive profit may be made for a time. W. H.

MIDDLE PRICE. Dealers on the stock exchange, when asked the price of a given security, sometimes say, "87 middle," or some other middle price, at which they are not prepared to deal, but which is half way between the prices which buyers offer and sellers are prepared to accept. A middle price is therefore not a formal QUOTATION (*q.v.*), although transactions are sometimes based on it (see also MARGIN). A. E.

MIL. The 1000th part of a monetary unit. It is perhaps more frequently applied to the United States dollar than to any other coin. The smallest United States coin issued appears to be a copper half-cent, of which $ 39,926.11 coined by the mint of Philadelphia were stated to be outstanding in 1894. These half-cents each $= 2\frac{1}{2}$ mils. The value of the mil is about $\frac{1}{4}$ of 1 farthing.

[*Report of the Director of the United States Mint*, 1894. The mil was proposed as the smallest coin of the DECIMAL SYSTEM (*q.v.*) Some comments on the use of the mil will be found in Bagehot, *A Universal Money*, pp. 45-62, 2nd ed. 1889.]

MILL. A mill is properly "an engine or machine for grinding or comminuting any substance" (Webster), and is an implement

of great antiquity, its rudimentary form being preserved in the quern or hand-mill from time immemorial used for grinding corn, and occasionally to be met with still in remote places. At what period in the history of ancient civilisation mills of a larger construction began to be used is uncertain; but a persistent tradition, founded on a remark of Strabo's, points to the first water-driven corn mill as having been in use near the palace of Mithridates, in Asia Minor, who died 63 B.C. Such mills were introduced into Britain by the Romans, and were common throughout Europe during the middle ages. Gradually they were applied to other purposes, to grinding colours, crushing oil, and sawing stone and timber. Later still a use was found for them in connection with metal manufacture; as an alternative to hammering by hand; and in textile manufacture, in the special process of *fulling*,[1] or pounding cloth. At the time of the introduction of the modern FACTORY SYSTEM their utility was extended in a variety of directions; and about the same time that astonishing series of mechanical inventions commenced which resulted in the possibility of *spinning*, and at length of *weaving*, by machinery. The places where these operations were performed seem to have been called at first mills or factories indifferently, partly, we may judge, because of the extension of their utilities in these directions, partly because many old mills—corn mills and fulling mills— were then turned into factories. The earlier factory acts, accordingly, made no distinction between these terms, and the original technical signification of the former seemed in some danger of being lost in this connection. Subsequently the term mill was dropped, except in certain specific relations which are defined, as *mill-gearing*, *iron mill*, but a survival of this confusion of nomenclature may still be noted in the factory districts, where that part of a textile manufactory where spinning is carried on is often spoken of as distinctively the mill, whilst the part where weaving is performed is called the factory, with obvious reference to those earlier meanings.

[John Beckman, *History of Inventions*, articles "Corn Mills," "Saw Mills" (Bohn's edition).— R. W. Cooke-Taylor, *Introduction to a History of the Factory System*, ch. i.] R. W. C. T.

---

[1] "The operation of *fulling* bore a sufficiently near resemblance to the earlier and proper processes of mill work, not to appear utterly foreign from the older conception of a mill, and was in fact sometimes called 'milling,' in obvious accord with this view. Soon, however, the term began to include other processes more remote. In 1551 complaint is made to parliament of the establishment of 'gigge mills'—contrivances, that is, for raising a *pile* or *nap* on cloth, a process, therefore, wherein little trace of the original meaning of the word 'mill' remains; and at length *winding*, *spinning*, and a variety of operations dealing with the treatment of fibrous material are found spoken of as performed in mills; operations wherein the original technical signification is altogether lost" (Cooke-Taylor, *Introduction to History of Factory System*, p. 11).

MILL, JAMES (1773-1836) was born in the village of Northwater Bridge, Forfarshire. His father was a shoemaker. His early years were exempted from the drudgery of manual labour by the discerning partiality of his mother. He was sent to the university of Edinburgh at the age of seventeen, and having completed the usual studies, became licensed as a preacher. But abandoning this career, Mill went to London in 1802, and supported himself by literature. He married in 1806, and in course of time had a family of nine children—"conduct than which nothing could be more opposed," as his son says, "to the opinions which, at least at a later period of his life, he strenuously upheld." Struggling and burdened as he was, he had the energy to compose a great book, *The History of India*. The publication of this work in 1818 led to Mill's obtaining a lucrative appointment in the India office. His position in the office continued to rise in dignity and emolument up to his death.

Mill's earliest work was economic, *An Essay on the Impolicy of a Bounty on the Exportation of Grain and on the Principles which ought to regulate the Commerce of Grain*, 1804 ; a rare pamphlet which, from M'Culloch's notice of it, seems to have referred to the restrictions on the trade between England and Ireland. In 1807 he wrote *Commerce defended : an Answer to the Arguments by which Mr. Spence, Mr. Cobbett, and others, have attempted to prove that Commerce is not a source of National Wealth*, which led to his acquaintance with Ricardo. The advantages of the territorial division of labour are well expounded ; but the following view of the gain by international exchange appears less orthodox : "Whenever a cargo of goods of any sort is exported, and a cargo of other goods bought with the proceeds of the former is imported, whatever the goods imported exceed in value [*i.e.* money-value, as the context shows] the goods exported beyond the expense of importation is so much clear gain to the country." In 1808, reviewing Thomas Smith, "Money and Exchange" in the *Edinburgh Review*, Mill asserts the principle that money is a commodity, and thus describes its uses. "First we go to market with money. Secondly, we account by means of it. . . . Abstract ideas or ideal standards are of no use in going to market," or for any other purpose. Some years later (1816-23) Mill contributed several articles to the supplement to the *Encyclopædia Britannica* (1823), of which the most famous, criticised by Macaulay, *Edinburgh Review*, 1829, is that on *Government*. The articles in the Supplement which most deserve notice here are on *Banks of Savings, Beggars, Benefit Societies*, and *Colonies ;* containing strong assertions of the Malthusian doctrine (see especially p. 246 of *Supplement*, vol. i.). The article on *Economists*

treats only of the political principles of the French school.

Much of the matter contained in the writings which have been referred to is presented in a summary form in Mill's masterpiece, *Elements of Political Economy*. This composition originated in 1819, as J. S. Mill tells us, in instructions given to him by his father in the course of their daily walks. The abstracts of these lessons, prepared by the son, served the father as notes from which to write his book, which was published in 1821. A second edition—considerably altered—appeared in 1824 ; a third in 1826. Several of the alterations in the third edition were founded on criticisms made by J. S. Mill and his friends. Although the book, in J. S. Mill's words, "has now for some time finished its work," it is still interesting as a type of the classical political economy (J. S. Mill's *Autobiography*, p. 121). The capable author proposing "to compose a schoolbook of political economy" (Preface) "an epitome of the science" (ch. iii. § 10), and professing "to have made no discovery" (Preface), is naturally regarded as the interpreter of his contemporaries, especially of Ricardo his intimate friend (cp. Prof. Ashley on the *Rehabilitation of Ricardo, Economic Journal*, vol. i. pp. 478-479). Admirable as the work is, considered as a summary representation of received theories, there are two features of the original which seem to be exaggerated in the miniature picture (1). With M'Culloch, James Mill represents value as depending wholly on quantity of labour (cp. M'Culloch, *Principles of Political Economy*, pt. iii. § 1). He explains away the part played by *waiting* (as we should now say). "If the wine which is put in the cellar is increased in value one-tenth by being kept a year, one-tenth more of labour may be correctly considered as having been expended upon it." . . . "How then can it [time] create value ? Time is a mere abstract term. It is a word, a sound" (*Elements*, 2nd ed. p. 97-99). This view is criticised with just severity by S. BAILEY (*Critical Dissertation on Value*). (2) The theory of population as presented by James Mill appears particularly dismal ; owing partly to his very precarious "proof that capital has a less tendency than population to increase rapidly" (*Elements*, ch. ii. § 2, art. 3), partly to his not taking sufficient account of improvement in the arts of production. "The grand practical problem, therefore, is to find the means of limiting births." A more original feature is the proposal to tax additions to rent—J. S. Mill's "unearned increment."

Upon the whole political economy, as treated by James Mill, may afford one of the advantages which he claims for the science in the dialogue entitled "Whether Political Economy is useful" (*London Review*, 1836) namely, contemplative pleasure. Even Dr. Ingram allows to the *Elements* "the character of a work of art." But Mill's work does not afford another advantage which he claims for political economy in the same dialogue, namely, a "comprehensive commanding view" such as that by which a general is enabled to realise his practical purpose. James Mill's work in political economy, as in politics, seems to be vitiated by the excessive use of deductive reasoning—what his son calls the geometrical method (*Logic*, bk. vi. ch. viii.). His principal services to political economy were indirect—to have instigated Ricardo to write (see J. S. Mill's *Autobiography*) and to have been the father and the teacher of J. S. Mill.

[*Life*, by Professor Bain, 1882.—*J. S. Mill*, by Professor Bain (full of references).—MacVey Napier, *Correspondence*.— J. S. Mill's *Autobiography*.—Mrs. Grote's *Personal Life of George Grote*, pp. 21-25. See an exposition of fallacies on rent tithes, and containing an examination of Mr. Ricardo's theory of rent, viz. the doctrine of the impossibility of a general glut and other propositions of the modern school. . . . Being in the form of a review of the third edition of Mr. Mill's *Elements of Political Economy*, by Perronet Thompson. —*History of Theories of Production and Distribution*, by E. Cannan.]   F. Y. E.

MILL, JOHN STUART.

Early Works, p. 756 ; *Essays on some Unsettled Questions of Pol. Ec.*, p. 756 ; *Principles of Political Economy*, p. 757 ; Other Works, p. 763.

JOHN STUART MILL (1806-1873), was the eldest son of JAMES MILL, by whom he was educated. The teacher was exacting, the pupil precocious ; and John, at a marvellously early age, attained proficiency in all the principal branches of learning, particularly the speculative sciences. At the age of thirteen he received from his father peripatetic lectures on political economy ; and it must have been about the same period that, in his own words, "Mr. Ricardo invited me to his house and to walk with him in order to converse upon the subject" (*Autobiography*, p. 54). At the age of sixteen he wrote in the *Traveller* in defence of Ricardo and James Mill, his first appearance in print. He contributed frequently to the *Westminster Review*, which was started in 1824, thirteen articles, he says (*ibid.* p. 97), of which only some are specified by him. Those on the game laws, the law of libel, and the corn laws, attest the versatility and precociousness of the writer. Among the "reviews of books of political economy," which he speaks of having written, may probably be placed the review of the *Critical Dissertation on Value* (by S. BAILEY) in the fifth number of the *Westminster* (Jan. 1826). The relation of cost of production to value is, according to the writer, like the relation of the pendulum to a the movement of a clock—a regulator, not

a cause. "Demand is the cause of value." The issue between the author of the *Dissertation* and James Mill as to the influence of DISTANCE IN TIME on value is avoided.

Other youthful essays were published in the *Parliamentary History and Review*, the first two numbers of which relating to the sessions 1825 and 1826 are to be found in the Bodleian. The first contains—beside the article on the *Catholic Association*, acknowledged by Mill (*Autobiography*, p. 118)—some remarks on combination and combination laws (*Review*, for 1825, p. 730), which may perhaps be attributed to Mill. The theory that "the rate of wages must in the long run depend on the relation between the capital of a country and its population," is employed to prove the impossibility of raising general wages by combination. The second number contains an article headed *Paper Currency — Commercial Distress*, justly referred to in the *Autobiography* (*loc. cit.*), as an "elaborate essay." The remarks on theory and experience (*Review*, for 1826, pp. 654-659), and on the "double standard" (*Hist.*, p. 659) are characteristic. This essay and that on the Reciprocity principle in Commerce are described by Mill (in his *Autobiography*) as "original thinking." They were not, however, included by him among the articles which he has republished in his *Dissertations and Discussions*. Among ephemeral writings which have not been reprinted may be noticed the *Notes on Newspapers* in the *Monthly Repository* of 1834. They evince that rare union of qualities which he himself has characterised as "practicality" and devotion to "large generalisations" (*Autobiography*, p. 190). Referring to the then burning question of trades unions, he maintains that workmen cannot keep up the rate of wages by combination, but that they ought not to be prevented from learning this by experience (*Monthly Repository*, 1834, pp. 247, 366, 435).

Meanwhile the young philosopher had cultivated his dialectic powers by taking part in debating societies, formed largely but not exclusively of the followers of Bentham. The picked band which used to meet in the morning in Grote's house "brought out new views of some topics of abstract political economy." To this origin Mill refers the first and fourth of the essays, which are contained in the *Essays on some Unsettled Questions of Pol. Econ.* . . . These *Essays* were written in 1829 and 1830, but (with the exception of the fifth, which appeared in the *Westminster Review*) they did not find a publisher till 1844. The *Essays* deserve to be studied as anticipating, and sometimes transcending, the *Political Economy*.

Of the first essay the substance, and in large part the very words have been embodied in the great chapter in the *Political Economy* on "International Values" (bk. iii. ch. xix.), and in the important section which deals with protection (*ibid.* bk. v. ch. iv. § 6). With this should be read the passages in the preface to the *Essays*, which expresses the opinion that the relaxation of non-protective duties beyond what may be required by the interest of the revenue should in general be made contingent upon the adoption of some corresponding degree of freedom of trade by the nation from which the commodities are imported. In the second essay the influence of consumption upon production is stated more fully than in the passages of the *Political Economy* which are below (p. 758) referred to as corrective of a wrong interpretation of the doctrine "Demand for commodities is not a demand for labour." In the third essay there is obtained a definition of wealth as consisting of "permanent sources of enjoyment," and a corresponding definition of productive labour, more philosophical perhaps than the definitions which in deference to popular opinion have been adopted in the *Political Economy* (bk. i. ch. 3). The fourth essay explains and corrects Ricardo's doctrine that "profits depend upon wages ; rising as wages fall and falling as wages rise." The justice of the correction will be evident if we regard "wages" as paid in a money of which the unit is a product of a constant quantity of labour (Ricardo, *Pol. Econ.*, ch. 1, § 6). But this monetary standard is not quite perfect, and the Ricardian proposition is not quite true, unless we use "labour" as short for "effort and sacrifice," and take account of variations in the quantity of *abstinence* or waiting which is required for the production of a unit of the standard (cp. *Memorandum on variations in the value of the Monetary Standard*, Report of the British Association, 1889, § vii.) This refinement is reproduced in the *Political Economy* (bk. iii. ch. xxvi. § 3, but not in the corresponding passage bk. ii. ch. xv. § 7). In the fifth essay the not very epigrammatic definition of *Political Economy* agrees with that which is adopted in the "Preliminary Remarks" of the *Political Economy*. Discussing the method of the science, Mill holds the balance between abstract reasoning and observation. The *a priori* method is the only certain or scientific mode of investigation. But he who does not "sift and scrutinise the details of every specific experiment must rest contented to take no share in practical politics, to have no opinion, or to hold it with extreme modesty," on the applications of his doctrines. There is a most weighty caution against the "danger of *overlooking* something." The only remedy is to place oneself at the point of view of an opponent, and either to discern what he sees or thinks he sees, or make out clearly that it is an optical delusion. A beautiful example of this procedure is afforded in the second of the *Essays*, where Mill points out that the descrip-

tions which have been given of OVER-PRODUCTION are applicable to a commercial crisis.

The method of political economy was further elucidated in the *Logic* published in 1843. His dominant idea is thus expressed : "I always regarded the methods of physical sciences as the proper models for political" (*Autobiography*, p. 165 ; cp. *ibid.* p. 160).

The combination of *a priori* reasoning from general propositions with specific verification, the direct deductive method, which has proved so successful in mathematical physics is prescribed for political economy (*Logic*, bk. vi. ch. ix.). It is a question whether this view was, or could consistently be, retained by Mill, when he began to doubt the universality of the principle of self-interest, which he once had regarded as the foundation of economic reasoning (*Essays*, p. 138), when under the influence (see also A. COMTE) of the St. Simonians "his eyes were opened to the very limited and temporary value of the old political economy" (*Autobiography*, p. 166), and when, under a more intimate influence, he looked forward to a time when "it will no longer either be, or be thought to be, impossible for human beings to exert themselves strenuously in procuring benefits which are not to be exclusively their own" (*ibid.* p. 230 *et seq.* ; cp. on the ultimate premisses of Political Economy, Marshall, *Principles of Economics*, bk. i. ch. v. § 5).

Thus prepared, Mill began his treatise on *Political Economy* in 1845, and finished it in 1847 with marvellous celerity. An analysis of this classical work may be useful.

J. S. Mill's *Principles of Political Economy*, for a work that has been so much read, has been but little commented on. To remedy, in however slight a degree, this deficiency is the design of the following paragraphs.

The preliminary remarks contain a sketch of the progress and a description of the object of political economy. The definition of wealth as "all useful or agreeable things which possess exchangeable value," leaving in uncertainty the question "whether immaterial products are to be considered wealth," should be compared with the discussion of this question in Mill's *Unsettled Questions* (Essay 5), and in one of the chapters of his *Political Economy* (bk. i. ch. iii. § 3). In his earlier view, the "skill and the energy and perseverance of the artisans of a country are reckoned part of its wealth, no less than their tools and machinery" (*ibid.*) ; but in the later treatise the term is applied only to "what is called material wealth."

The first inquiry about wealth relates to its cause. "The requisites of production are two : labour and appropriate natural objects" (bk. i. ch. i. § 1, par. 1). These are the "primary and universal requisites" (bk. i. ch. i. § 1, par. 1). But since "there is another requisite, without which no productive operations beyond the rude and scanty beginnings of primitive industry are possible" (bk. i. ch. iv. § 1, par. 1), we may say that "the essential requisites of production are three : labour, capital, and natural agents" (bk. i. ch. x. § 1, par. 3 ; cp. AGENTS OF PRODUCTION).

A "general survey" (ch. vii., first sentence), of the requisites of production, occupies the first six chapters. The "conceit . . . that nature lends more assistance to human endeavours in agriculture than in manufactures," is refuted in the first chapter. In the first section of the second chapter it is shown how "an article fitted for some human use" (an article of the "first order," as it is now the fashion to say)—such as bread—is produced, partly by labour employed directly about the thing itself—such as that of the baker—and partly by the indirect labours of the reaper, the ploughman, the ploughmaker, who all "ultimately derive the remuneration of their labour from the bread or its price." This important passage is referred to at a more advanced stage, as setting forth the "component elements of cost of production" (bk. iii. ch. iv. § 1). The modes in which labour is indirectly instrumental to the production of a thing are analysed in the remainder of the second chapter ; the term "indirect," it may be observed, sometimes importing simply the relation of means to end (§ 1, § 3, par. 1) ; sometimes, as in the case of savants (§ 8, last par.), that "the material fruits, though the results, are seldom the direct purposes of the pursuits of the savants, nor is their remuneration in general derived from the increased production which may be caused incidentally . . . by their discoveries" (cp. § 7, par. 1).

Capital is defined as the physical requisites of production which are the products of labour (ch. iv. § 1, par. 12 ; cp. ch. x. § 1, par. 3). The term admits of nice divisions which are traced in the fourth chapter. The "fundamental propositions respecting capital" which form the fifth chapter, may be described without much exaggeration in Prof. Nicholson's words, as "a strange combination of axiom and paradox, of error exposed and truth suppressed, of practical wisdom and unreal hypothesis" (Nicholson's Principles, bk. i. ch. vi. § 7). More than one of the propositions at least "expresses his [Mill's] meaning badly" ; as Prof. Marshall says (Principles of Economics, note to bk. vi. ch. ii.).

The proposition which has most "exercised the ingenuity of all subsequent writers" (Nicholson), is the fourth, that "demand for commodities is not demand for labour." The following is a contribution to the interpretation of this locus vexatissimus.

Mill does not mean to deny that consumption is the motive to production. The fact that desire evokes labour is constantly present to

him (see Preliminary Remarks, two passages in the middle, pp. 13, 19, ed. 1878, bk. i. ch. vii. § 3 ; bk. i. ch. viii. § 2, last par. ; bk. i. ch. xiii. §§ 1 and 3 ; bk. iii. ch. xvii. § 5, and cp. Unsettled Questions, Essay 2). He may be credited with making two assertions, one correct and one not so. The true lesson to be derived from the passage is that capitalisation is apt to be increased by the postponement of the consumption (Marshall, loc. cit.). But it is erroneously implied that "to spend money on the direct hire of labour is more beneficial than to spend it on hiring commodities" (Marshall). Ceteris paribus it comes to much the same whether a rich individual spends his money on "velvet" (Mill's favourite instance), or in payment of workmen to roll the "velvet green" (Ruskin). The most serious refutation of this error is that which forms the appendix to bk. iv. of Prof. Simon Newcomb's Political Economy. The great difficulties which Mill's doctrine presents may further be illustrated by the parallel passage in Fawcett's Political Economy, and by the explanations of the doctrine which are offered by Prof. Sidgwick (Pol. Econ.), Prof. Laughlin (Edition of Mill), Mr. Herbert Thompson (Theory of Wages), and others.

After the general survey of the requisites of production (bk. i. ch. vii. § 1), we "advance to the second great question in political economy, on what the degree of productiveness of these agents depends" (ibid.). Among causes of superior productiveness (chs. vii. viii.) a prominent place is given to combination of labour, or co-operation, including division of labour as a species. Most of the advantages attending division of labour are enumerated in the chapter on co-operation. One advantage described by Jevons as the "multiplication of services" in cases where "nearly the same time and labour are required to perform the same operation on a larger or on a smaller scale" (Whateley, Lectures on Political Economy, lecture 6), is postponed by Mill to the chapter on "production on a large and on a small scale" (bk. i. ch. viii.). Two important cases of production on a large scale are presented by joint-stock companies (ibid. § 2), and the grande culture in agriculture (§ 4). The distinction which Mill draws between gross and net produce per acre (ibid.) is vital.

Having considered the means by which the efficacy of the agents of production is promoted (bk. i. ch. x. § 1, par. 1), we proceed to consider the "law of the increase of production" with respect to each of the agents (ibid. par. 4). The term "law" applied to the rough generalisations which alone are possible on these subjects is open to criticism (cp. Sidgwick, Pol. Econ., bk. i. ch. vi.).

"The increase of labour is the increase of mankind, of population ;" the theory of which is here opened (ch. x.).

The law of the increase of capital (ch. xi.) involves the "effective desire of accumulation," which has been considered in the article on DISTANCE IN TIME AS AN ELEMENT OF VALUE. The "law of the increase of production from land" (ch. xii.) is what is now called the *law of diminishing returns.* The relation of this law to that of *increasing returns* is thus well expressed by Mill (*ibid.* last par.): "All natural agents which are limited in quantity are not only limited in their ultimate productive power, but, long before that power is stretched to the utmost, they yield to any additional demands on progressively harder terms. This law may, however, be suspended or temporarily controlled by whatever adds to the general power of mankind over nature, and especially by any extension of their knowledge, and their consequent command of the properties and powers of natural agents." The "consequences of the foregoing laws," the dangers of over-population, are set forth in a concluding chapter (bk. i. ch. xiii.). Of Mill's gloomy views on this subject, Prof. Nicholson has said, "surely in the whole range of social philosophy it would be difficult to discover a more striking instance of the overbearing influence of a dominant idea"—considering that Mill himself has given "what is probably the most complete account yet published of the modes in which this law of diminishing returns may be counteracted" (Nicholson, *Principles*, bk. i. ch. x. § 4).

"The principles which have been set forth in the first part of this treatise (bk. i.), are in certain respects strongly distinguished from those on the consideration of which we are now about to enter. The laws and conditions of the production of wealth partake of the character of physical truths." But the distribution of wealth which forms the subject of the second book, is "a matter of human institution solely." "Society can subject the distribution of wealth to whatever rules it thinks best" (bk. ii. ch. i. § 1, cp. *Autobiography*, p. 246). The distinction thus drawn is objected to by Prof. Nicholson (*Principles*, bk. ii. ch. i.) and others, *e.g.* Mr. J. H. Levy, *Outcome of Individualism*, p. 16. But there is surely a very intelligible difference, in degree at least, between the two classes of "laws."

Considering the different modes of distributing the produce of land and labour, Mill compares the institution of private property with communism and socialism, and suggests that "the decision will probably depend mainly on one consideration, viz. which of the two systems is consistent with the greatest amount of liberty and spontaneity" (bk. ii. ch. i. § 3). The following weighty sentence condenses much that Mill has taught in his book on *Liberty*—"it is yet to be ascertained whether the communistic scheme would be consistent with that multiform

development of human nature, those manifold unlikenesses, that diversity of tastes and talents and variety of intellectual points of view which not only form a great part of the interest of human life, but, by bringing intellects into stimulating collision, and by presenting to each innumerable notions that he would not have conceived of himself, are the mainspring of mental and moral progression" (*Pol. Econ.*, bk. ii. ch. i. § 3 end).

Before condemning private property we must consider it not as it is, but as it might be in its best form (*ibid.* penultimate par., cp. L. H. Courtney, "Difficulties of Socialism," *Economic Journal*, vol. i.); which implies the "guarantee to individuals of the fruits of their own labour and abstinence," but "not of the fruits of the labour and abstinence of others transmitted to them without any merit or exertion of their own" (*ibid.*); not unlimited power of bequest, nor unrestricted property in land, nor any proprietary rights in abuses (ch. ii.).

"Private property being assumed as a fact" (ch. iii. § 1, par. 1); we go on to consider the distribution of produce between the three classes "whose concurrence, or at least whose permission, is requisite to production," viz. landowners, capitalists, and labourers—not necessarily different persons (ch. iii.).

"Under the rule of individual property the division of the produce is the result of two determining agencies, competition and custom" (ch. iv.). The cautions with respect to the imperfect degree in which "the natural effect of unimpeded competition" is realised (*ibid.* § 3), may be read with other passages relating to method; such as bk. iii. ch. i. § 5 (guarding against "improper applications of the abstract principles of political economy") bk. ii. ch. xvi. § 4; "the truths of political economy are truths only in the rough"—bk. iii. ch. iv. § 6 (on the danger of "sweeping expressions").

Mill's attempt in the later chapters of the second book to deduce the action of competition on distribution before he has formulated the law of supply and demand which governs that action, is open to grave objection (Marshall, *loc. cit.*).

Mill's recognition of the empirical or historical method is abundantly illustrated by the chapters on *Peasant Proprietorship and Métayers* (bk. ii. chs. vi. vii. viii.), which teem with evidence; out of which, the extracts from Sismondi, Michelet, and Arthur Young may be selected as of permanent interest.

From métayers Mill proceeds to cottiers (ch. ix.), with especial reference to Ireland; and argues that, almost alone among mankind, the cottier is in this condition that "he can scarcely be either better or worse off by any act of his own." The "means of abolishing cottier tenancy," proposed by Mill, have partly passed into legislation. The principle of judicial rents is thus sanctioned : "rent paid by a capitalist who farms for profit, and not for bread, may safely be abandoned to competition ; rent paid by labourers cannot, unless the labourers were in a state of civilisation and improvement which labourers have nowhere yet reached, and cannot easily reach under such a tenure."

It might be difficult to answer the question —why upon the same principle the bargain between employers and labourers should not be sheltered from competition. One answer is afforded by the wage-fund theory, which is stated at the beginning of the chapter on wages (bk. ii. ch. xi.). It was subsequently renounced by Mill (see below, p. 763). But that theory, though left standing in the latest editions of the *Political Economy*, was recanted by Mill in his review of Thornton ; when, as Prof. Marshall thinks, "he took to himself blame for confusions of thought of which it is not certain that he had been guilty" (*Principles of Economics*, note at the end of ch. ii. bk. vi.).

The overthrow of the wage-fund theory does not involve the fall of Mill's practical conclusions concerning wages. They are at best strengthened and heightened by that theory (see *e.g.* ch. i. § 6, penultimate par., ch. xii. § 1, pt. iii.). But it is rather on the theory of population set forth in the first book that Mill grounds his rejection of "popular remedies for low wages" (ch. xii.), and his own prescription which is, that the overcrowding of the labour market is to be prevented by "a due regulation of the numbers of families" (ch. xiii.).

Among accessory recommendations should be noticed Mill's preference for an heroic measure, "a sudden and very great improvement in the condition of the poor" (ch. xii. § 4, pt. iv. ; ch. xi. § 2, last par. ; ch. xiii. § 3, par. 1, § 4, par. 3). "Small means do not merely produce small effects, they produce no effect at all" (ch. xiii. § 4, par. 3).

The chapter on differences of wages (bk. ii. ch. xiv.), in different employments, corrects Adam Smith's classical exposition of the subject. The theory of non-competing groups, commonly ascribed to Cairnes, is implied in § 2 (as pointed out in Prof. Marshall's article in *Fortnightly Review*, 1874). The short passage on the wages of women (§ 5 and end of § 4), has been little improved on.

The chapter on profits is free from certain errors which have been attributed to the classical economy. The function of superintendence is recognised (§ 1). Absolute equality of profits is not postulated. "That equal capitals give equal profits, as a general maxim of trade, would be as false as that equal age or size gives equal bodily strength ; or that equal reading or experience gives equal knowledge. The effect depends as much upon twenty other things as upon the single cause specified." Cliffe Leslie

himself could say no more (§ 4). In the last section of the chapter, the definition of "cost of labour" demands attention (cp. bk. iii. ch. xxv.), and *Unsettled Questions* referred to above, p. 756.

The chapter on rent (bk. ii. ch. xvi.), taken with the subsequent chapter on *Rent in Relation to Value* (bk. iii. ch. v.), forms a luminous statement of the Ricardian theory. Yet notwithstanding his apparent clearness, Mill is really "a little inconsistent," as Prof. Marshall has said (*Economic Journal*, vol. iii. p. 86), on the fundamental question whether rent enters into the cost of production when there does not exist a no-rent margin of land. The affirmative is distinctly asserted (bk. iii. ch. v. § 2, par. 3) ; and elsewhere (bk. ii. ch. ii. § 2, par. 1), it is implied that there is an essential distinction between "countries fully occupied," and those which are not. Whereas the distinction appears to be unessential in an earlier passage (bk. ii. ch. xvi. § 4). Rent is said to be an "element of cost of production," under peasant production (bk. iii. ch. vi. § 2).

At length, at the beginning of bk. iii., the theory of value is introduced. Mill's definition of the "value or exchange value of a thing" as its general power of purchasing, the command which its possession gives over purchasable commodities in general" (bk. iii. ch. i. § 2), suggests something deeper than a mere ratio (see EXCHANGE, VALUE IN).

Mill's threefold classification of valuables (ch. ii. § 2 ; cp. DIFFICULTY OF ATTAINMENT) has been criticised as omitting the category of things which are produced in greater quantities at a less cost. Moreover the first class "things of which it is physically impossible to increase the quantity beyond certain narrow limits," of which the characteristic is that "the value depends on the demand and the supply," is defined in terms too narrow to include all the objects which possess that attribute, viz. labour and articles of foreign trade (bk. iii. ch. ii. § 5, last par.), and loanable capital (bk. iii. ch. xxiii. § 1).

The general theory of demand and supply seems to be stated by Mill as clearly as is possible without the aid of mathematical apparatus (bk. iii. ch. ii. §§ 3 and 4). Distinct intimations of the phenomenon which would now be described as the greater or less elasticity of the demand curve are to be found (bk. iii. ch. ii. § 4, par. 1 ; *ibid.* ch. xviii. § 8, referring to "extensibility of demand ").

The third and fourth chapters of the third chapter are concerned with "necessary" (ch. iii. § 1) value, that which depends on *cost* of production. The different senses in which Mill uses cost may be distinguished by observing that the term is applied sometimes (1) to the efforts and sacrifices attending production, sometimes (2) to the pecuniary equivalent of the same (the "expenses" of production in Prof. Marshall's phrase) ; and that the expenditure, whether in the way of labour or of money, may relate either (*a*) to the finished commodity, or (*b*) to the workman's part therein, exclusive of the capitalist's (and entrepreneur's) effort and sacrifice or the (pecuniary remuneration thereof). For instance, 2 (*a*) must be understood when it is said that "Profits as well as wages enter into the cost of production which determines the value of produce " (bk. iii. ch. iv. § 4, par. 1). The following are instances of (*b*): bk. ii. ch. xv. § 7 ; bk. iii. ch. iii. § 1, par. 1, ch. iv. § 1. In connection with international trade *cost* is used in sense 1 (bk. iii. ch. xviii. § 9).

The theory of value having been summed up (bk. iii. ch. vi.) ; the second volume enters on the subject of money. The functions of money described by Jevons as a "measure of value " a "medium of exchange" and "a standard for deferred payments," are in other words stated in the first chapter of the second vol. (bk. iii. ch. vii. §§ 1, 2). The relation between demand and supply and cost of production is made particularly clear in the case of money (bk. iii. chs. viii. and ix.). The "quantity-theory" of money and its limits could not be better stated than in the proof which is given of the antithetical statements : "That an increase of the quantity of money raises prices, and a diminution lowers them, is the most elementary proposition in the theory of currency, and without it we should have no key to any of the others " (bk. iii. ch. viii. § 4) : "That the value of the circulating medium . . . is in the inverse ratio of the quantity " is to be received with "qualifications which, under a complex system of credit like that existing in England, render the proposition an extremely incorrect expression of the fact " (ch. viii. end). However, objection has justly been taken to the statement that, "the natural and average prices of commodities are not affected by credit" (ch. xii. § 1, par. 1).

The chapters on a "double standard" and "on a measure of value " (chs. x. xv.), may be selected as bearing on questions of great interest at present. In the former, Mill does not consider *international* bi-metallism. In the latter, he seems to contemplate two of the principal methods of measuring a change in the value of money : viz. the labour and the consumption standard (see INDEX NUMBERS). With reference to Mill's disparaging remarks on "the necessary indefiniteness of the idea of general exchange value " (ch. xv. § 1), Prof. Sidgwick has pointed out (*Pol. Econ.*, bk. i. ch. ii. § 3) that Mill himself has employed some such conception in the passage where he maintains that during the last five years of the French war "the value of the standard itself was very considerably raised" (Mill, *Pol. Econ.*, bk. iii. ch. xiii. § 7).

The chapter on "some peculiar cases of value " is of peculiar interest as showing Mill's conception of the relation between "cost of production " and "a law of value anterior to cost of production, and, more fundamental, the law of demand and supply" ; which "when cost of production fails to be applicable . . . steps in to supply the vacancy " (bk. iii. ch. xvi. § 1).

The antecedent law of supply again "steps in " in the theory of international values (ch. xviii. § 1). The great chapter on this subject may be divided into two parts, the original draft (§§ 1-5) and the additions suggested by "intelligent criticisms," chiefly Thornton's (§ 6 *et seq.*). The first part deals mainly with two problems (1) the case of a trade being established—a "barrier " (Cournot) being removed—between two countries (§§ 2-3), and (2) the case of an already established trade being facilitated by an improvement in the process of manufacture of an export. In the latter case benefit does not necessarily accrue to the country in which the improvement has taken place (§ 5). In both cases it may be objected that benefit is estimated by an improper measure, that of exchange-value (see *Theory of International Values*, pt. i., by Prof. Edgeworth, *Economic Journal*, vol. iv. pp. 35, 424, 606).

Of the second part of the chapter (§§ 6-9) it is well said by a high authority on international trade : "Nothing is gained by the laborious and confusing discussion " (Bastable, *International Trade*, p. 29). The introduction justifying the addition is particularly objectionable. "It is conceivable that the conditions might be equally satisfied by every numerical rate which could be supposed " (§ 6, last par.). "The equation of international trade" would thus be a very odd sort of equation !

Reinforced by the principles of international trade, Mill returns to the theory of money (chs. xix.-xxii.). He continues the subject of international trade in the chapter on "the competition of different countries in the same market" (criticised in part iii. of Prof. Edgeworth's theory of international trade, *Economic Journal*, vol. iv.).

It is impossible here to notice in detail the many detached topics which are treated in bk. iii. The "rate of interest " (ch. xxiii.) has already been referred to as a case of demand and supply, rather than "necessary" value which depends on cost of production. In the immediately following chapter, by a not very obvious transition, the rival theories respecting the influence of bank issues on prices—the so-called currency theory and banking principle —are discussed with moderation (see Walker, *Money.*—Cp. FULLARTON).

The Dynamics of Political Economy (bk. iv. ch. i. § 1) is the subject of the next book. It is attempted to compound the counteracting tendencies which we now call the law of decreasing and the law of increasing returns ; though Mill will not allow that "even in manufactures increased cheapness follows increased production by anything amounting to a law" (*ibid.* ch. ii. § 2). Considering the three factors of industrial progress, capital, increase of population, and improvements in production, Mill inquires how the increase of one or more of these affects wages, profits, and rent (*ibid.* ch. iii.). For example, one case is : Capital increasing, population and the arts of production stationary. In this case wages will rise, profits will fall, rent will rise if the labourers consume more, or more costly, food (*ibid.* § 2). The case of arts of production progressive, capital and population stationary, presents most difficulty (*ibid.* § 4). *Primâ facie* wages would rise, profits would be unaffected, rent would fall. The Ricardian paradox that landlords may be injured by agricultural improvements is supported by reasoning which, as pointed out by Prof. Marshall (*Principles of Economics*, note to bk. vi. ch. ix.), is deficient in generality. Attention should be called to the generalisation contained in the following passage : "It is quite in accordance with common notions to suppose that if, by the increased productiveness of land less land were required for cultivation, its value, like that of other articles for which the demand had diminished, would fall" (bk. iv. ch. iii. § 4). Here a problem of distribution is treated simply as one of value ; and indeed throughout the chapter there is, as Professor Marshall has pointed out (*Principles of Economics*, note to ch. iii. bk. vi.), "scarcely any trace of those confusions in his discussion of the theory of distribution" which disfigure the second book.

The chapters (chs. iv. and v.) on the "tendency of profits to a minimum," are important as bearing on the question : How far is it safe for the working classes to press on the gains of the saving classes (see Cairnes, *Leading Principles*, bk. ii. and cp. Marshall, *Economics of Industry*, 2nd ed. bk. ii.).

The chapter on the stationary state (ch. vi.) is particularly characteristic of the author. Of an increase of population he says, "even if innocuous, I confess I see very little reason for desiring it."

The last chapter of the fourth book "on the probable futurity of the labouring classes," enjoys the distinction of being "entirely due," according to a statement in the *Autobiography*, to Mrs. Mill. Her hand is perhaps to be traced in the delicately ironical description of what may be called the aristocratic theory of the relation between the great and the labouring poor—"a theory also applied to the relation between men and women" (ch. vii. § 1). The principal hope which the Mills hold out for the futurity of the labouring classes is productive co-operation—a hope which does not seem at present in the way of being fulfilled. There are many now who disagree with the favourable estimate of *competition*, which concludes the chapter. "If the slopsellers and others of their class have lowered the wages of tailors, and some other artisans, by making them an affair of competition instead of custom, so much the better in the end."

The fifth book treats of *government ;* the functions of which are described with a freedom which might not have been expected from the son of James Mill ; "the admitted functions . . . embrace a much wider field than can easily be included within the ring-fence of any restrictive definition." As explained in the first chapter (par. 2, § 3), the "necessary" and acknowledged functions (1) are first considered (chs. ii.-ix.) ; then (2) "optional" interferences of government (*a*) grounded on erroneous theories (ch. x.) ; (*b*) really advisable (ch. xi.). Of the chapters relating to the "necessary" functions, five (chs. ii.-vi.) are devoted to taxation. In the chapter on the general principles of taxation, "equality of sacrifice" is assumed as the first principle (ch. ii. § 2). In applying this principle to progressive taxation, Mill employs considerations which would now be connected with the doctrine of "final utility" (ch. ii. § 3, par. 2). (See FINAL DEGREE OF UTILITY.) That doctrine had been asserted by him more explicitly in an earlier passage : "the difference to the happiness of the possessor between a moderate independence and five times as much, is insignificant when weighed against the enjoyment that might be given . . . by some other disposal of the four-fifths" (bk. ii. ch. ii. § 4, last par.). The incidence of various taxes is discussed by Mill with Ricardian rigour (bk. v. chs. iii.-vi.) ; and other ordinary functions of government are considered as to their economical effects (chs. viii., ix.).

Of "optional" interferences grounded on erroneous theories (ch. x.), protection is first discussed in a splendid and candid section, in the course of which occurs the often quoted passage, in which protecting duties are said to be defensible "on mere principles of political economy, when they are imposed temporarily (especially in a young and rising nation), in hopes of nationalising a foreign industry, in itself perfectly suitable to the circumstances of the country." Another *locus classicus* in this chapter is the section on *combination*.

In the last chapter it is maintained that LAISSEZ-FAIRE is the general rule ; but liable to large exceptions. Among these one of the most striking is the admission that upon certain assumptions the legal limitation of the hours of work might be advisable. A still more stringent governmental interference — transcending the proposals even of socialists—is put forward in a former chapter : to restrict the numbers of population by law (bk. ii. ch. xiii. § 2).

It will be understood that what has been attempted here is not to construct a table of contents magnified in a uniform proportion, but to select some leading topics and characteristic passages which may assist the student to comprehend Mill's system.

The *Political Economy* was revised in successive editions, but not much altered. Some of the changes in the second edition (1849) were favourable to socialism, one of the additions to the third edition (1852) is probably not an improvement, namely the sections 6-8 in the chapter on " International Values " (bk. iii. ch. xviii., cp. Bastable, *International Trade*, p. 29).

Some modifications of the doctrines stated in the *Political Economy* are to be found in Mill's later writings. In a review of Thornton in the *Fortnightly Review*, 1869, republished in the *Dissertations and Discussions* (vol. iv.), Mill recants the wage-fund theory. He did not, however, in his latest editions, withdraw the passages in chapter xi. of the second work. He seems to have regarded the correction as "not yet ripe for incorporation in a general treatise on political economy" (preface to eighth edition). In three posthumous articles on socialism published in the *Fortnightly Review*, 1879, Mill perhaps states the case against existing institutions more forcibly than in the *Political Economy*. However, he exposes the exaggerations of socialists with respect to the remuneration of capital and business power. He looks, not for a total renovation of society, but for such a modification of the idea of property as will make the institution work better than at present.

The rest of the acts and writings of J. S. Mill should occupy much space in a complete biography. But for the present purpose they need only be briefly referred so far as they contain applications and completions of his economic doctrines. In his *Liberty*, he continues the discussion of the limits of governmental interference, cp. *Pol. Econ.*, bk. v. In his *Subjection of Women* (1869), he advocates a cause in favour of which he had already stated what may be called the economic arguments (*Pol. Econ.*, bk. ii. ch. xiii. § 2, ch. xiv. § 5). The appropriation by the state of the "unearned increment" of land was agitated by Mill in papers and speeches which are collected in the fourth volume of the *Dissertations and Discussions*. With respect to this proposal it is forcibly urged by Thorold Rogers that "if, more than twenty years ago, Mr. Mill's scheme had passed into the region of practical politics, the purchase [of the land by the state] would have been disastrous . . . to the people of the United Kingdom" (*Economic Interpretation of History*, p. 515). The creation of a peasant proprietary, which Mill had proposed so far back as 1846 in the *Morning Chronicle* (see *Autobiography*, p. 235, and *Pol. Econ.*, appendix to vol. i.) was advocated in his pamphlet on *England and Ireland* (1868). Many of the causes which have been mentioned were promoted by Mill during his parliamentary career (1866 - 68). Among the measures which he advocated in parliament, the proposal to create a municipal government for the metropolis and to pay off the national debt are also of economic interest.

It would be impossible here to enumerate all the points at which Mill brought economic theory to bear upon practical politics. Like Adam Smith, he "associates the principles with their applications " (preface to first edition of *Pol. Econ.*). He treats political economy "not as a thing by itself, but as a fragment of a greater whole " . . . "for practical purposes inseparably intertwined with many other branches of social philosophy." The breadth of view required for this wider treatment of the science was obtained by his pre-eminence in general philosophy. In this respect also he, and he alone, is comparable to Adam Smith.

Among the circumstances which influenced Mill's intellectual life, must be mentioned his connexion with the India Office ; where he was constantly occupied for thirty-five years, down to 1858, when the government of India was transferred to the crown. He himself has attributed a salutary influence to this official work. He has also acknowledged a large debt of inspiration to his wife, formerly Mrs. Taylor, whom he married in 1851. He ascribes to her, not the abstract parts of his political economy, but some of the socialistic elements; in particular, the chapter in the fourth book on the futurity of the labouring classes. Her influence did not cease with her death (1858). "I bought a cottage as close as possible to the place where she is buried, and there her daughter . . . and I live constantly during a great part of the year. My objects in life are solely those which were hers ; my pursuits and occupations those in which she shared or sympathised."—*Autobiography*. Thus cherishing her memory as a religion, Mill lived at Avignon up to the year 1873, when he succumbed to a local endemic disease.

[The chief original source of information as to the facts and feelings of Mill's life is his *Autobiography*. It is supplemented by Prof. Bain's *J. S. Mill*. See also *John Stuart Mill*, by W. L. Courtney. Among the few works, or parts of works, which are directed systematically to the criticism of Mill's *Political Economy* may be mentioned : Marshall's *Principles of Economics*, passages relating to Mill, in particular the note at the end of bk. vi. ch. ii. ; also article in *Fortnightly Review*, "On Mr. Mill's Theory of Value," 1876. —E. Cannan's *History of the Theories of Production and Distribution.*—J. Bonar, *Philosophy and Political Economy*, chapter on J. S. Mill.—Nicholson, *Principles of Political Economy.*—F. A. Lange, *Mills Ansichten über die soziale Frage*, etc., Duisburg, 1865.—Prof. J. Laughlin has published an abridged and annotated edition of Mill's *Political Economy.*] F. Y. E.

MILLAR, JOHN (1735-1801), historian, was called to the Scotch bar in 1760, and in the following year accepted the appointment of professor of law in the university of Glasgow, which post he held till his death. His lectures, which were extempore, attracted many students. In politics, Millar was an advanced whig, although opposed to universal suffrage. He strongly sympathised with the American colonists, and regarded the success of Pitt in 1784 as a fatal blow to the English constitution ; even the excesses of the French revolution did not cause him to agree with Burke. Millar wrote *An historical view of the English Government, etc.*, London, 1787, 4to, 3rd ed., 1803, 8vo, 4 vols., which was designed as a counterblast to Hume. Only two volumes of the work were published in Millar's lifetime, and the last consists of essays which were intended to be worked up into the narrative. Those on the advances of manufacture and commerce, and the effect of that advance upon the morals of the people, are still of interest. Following Adam SMITH (*q.v.*), Millar recognises that "mercantile people are the best judges of their own interests." Millar's other work, *On the Origin of the distinction of Ranks*, London, 1771, 4to, 4th ed., Edinburgh, 1806, 8vo, containing a study of primitive society, is remarkable for its anticipation of the views of more recent writers. The prescience of his views on gynæcocracy, or that stage of social development wherein, through kinship counting from the mother, the position of woman is most important, is borne witness to by J. F. Maclennan, in his *Studies in Ancient History*, London, 1876, 8vo, p. 420. Millar is still under the sway of 18th century notions, such as that of the "simplicity" of savage races, and he wrote before the dawn, as it were, of the new science of anthropology. That, under these circumstances, he should have accomplished what he did, is much to his credit. It should be added that he was the valued friend of Adam Smith and David Hume.

[Memoir by John Craig prefixed to 1806 ed. of *Origin*, etc. as above. *Dictionary of National Biography*, vol. xxxvii.] H. E. E.

MILLES, THOMAS (between about 1550 and 1630), Customer[1] of Sandwich, was the author, among other works, of the following :

The Customers Replie, or Second Apologie. That is to say, An Aunswer to a confused Treatise of Publicke Commerce, printed and dispersed at Middlebourghe and London, in favour of the private Society of Merchants-Adventurers. By a more serious Discourse of Exchange in Merchandise, and Merchandising Exchange. Written for understanding Readers onely, in favour of all loyall Merchants, and for the advancing of Traffick in England, London, 1604, 4to. A note by the author shows to what decision he had

arrived : "That Merchandising Exchange is that Laborinth of Errors & private Practise, whereby (though Kings weare Crownes & seem absolutely to raigne) particuler Bankers, private Societies of Merchants, & covetous persons (whose End is Private gayne) are able to suspend their Counsailes & controle their Pollicies . . . thus making Kings to be Subiects, and Vassalles to be Kings " . . . —therefore it is in the interest of Kings themselves to "relieve & maintaine . . . free-borne Traffick . . . and English Traffick."—*The Customers Apologie, the body whereof is to be read more at large in the Thesaurario Bodleyano Oxonii, and heere only abridged, paraphrased, and fitted into the written Table or Epitome of all his other Workes, touching trafficke and customers*, n.d. or place of publication, with manuscript notes.— *An Abstract, almost verbatim (with some necessarie Additions) of the Customer's Apologie, written eighteen yeares ago, to shew their distresses in the Out-Ports, as well through want of Maintenance and Meanes to beare out their Service ; as Countenance and Credit in regard of others.*—A third abridgment, n.d., no title-page.— *The Customers Alphabet and Primer, conteining Their Creede or Beliefe in the true Doctrine of Christian Religion, Their Ten Commandementes*, etc., etc., 1608.—*An Out-Port-Customers Accompt, of all his Receipts*, . . . n.d.

[*Dict. Nat. Biog.*, art. "Milles, Thomas."] E. D.

MILLONES Y CIENTOS, duties levied in Castile on the consumption of meat, oil, wine, vinegar, ice, sugar, dried grapes, and tallow candles ; first granted temporarily by the *Cortes*, they came to be continued every six years, and lasted to this century. Their operation was very vexatious and so irregular that, according to a memorial presented in 1646 by Alcazar de Arriaza, a pound of meat, which was sold at that time for 22 *maravedis* in Aranjuez, cost 46 in Ocaña, a few miles off.

[Canga Argüelles, *Diccionario de Hacienda* (London, 1826).—Colmeiro, *Historia de la Economía Política en España*, vol. ii. pp. 542 and 550.] E. ca.

MILNE, JOSHUA (1776-1851), was appointed actuary to the Sun Life Assurance Society in 1810.

He published, in 1815, *A Treatise on the valuation of Annuities and Assurances on Lives and Survivorships*, London, 1815, 8vo. The Carlisle Table contained in this work, which was founded on the published observations and private correspondence of Dr. HEYSHAM of Carlisle, started a new era in life assurance. Though its results were slightly more favourable, the Carlisle Table does not differ greatly from the English Tables, which are based on the observation of thirty years, and on materials drawn from the whole of England. *The Life of Dr. Heysham*, by Dr. Lonsdale, London, 1870, contains Milne's correspondence on the subject. Milne wrote the articles in the *Encyclopædia Britannica*, 4th ed., on "Annuities," "Bills of Mortality," and "Law of Mortality" ; the last of which was reprinted as Appendix G. 3 of *Report*

---

[1] The receiver of Customs duties. Dowell, *Hist. of Taxation and Taxes in Eng.*, 2nd. ed., vol. i. p. 171.

from the Select Committee of the House of Commons on the Laws respecting Friendly Societies, 1827. He also gave evidence before this committee. He is quoted by Malthus in the latter's art. on Population, *Encyc. Brit.* (1824) see Bonar's *Malthus*, 1885, p. 72.

[*Dictionary of National Biography*, vol. xxxviii. p. 8.] H. E. E.

MILNER, JAMES (d. 1721), merchant of London, contributed articles on trade between England and Portugal to the *British Merchant*, during the controversy on the 8th and 9th clauses of the Treaty of Utrecht (1713), (see KING, CHARLES). He also published *Three Letters to the South Sea Company and the Bank*, etc. London, 1720, 8vo.

[For further notice of Milner's life see *Dictionary of National Biography*.] W. A. S. H.

MILREIS (PORTUGUESE). The money of account in Portugal is the reis. Gold is the standard of value, the milreis, or 1000 reis, being the smallest coin of that metal. The larger gold coins, pieces of 2000, 5000, and 10,000 reis, are proportionate to the milreis in weight, and identical in fineness. The milreis weighs 27·37 grains, is composed of gold of the millesimal fineness of 900, and is equivalent in sterling to 4s. 4¼d., and in gold francs, 900 fine, to 5·6 francs. F. E. A.

MINE, COST BOOK PRINCIPLE. See COST BOOK.

MINES. Down to the year 1688 all mines in England yielding gold or silver belonged to the crown. It was a common practice for the kings of the 14th and 15th centuries to grant charters to adventurers to enter upon private lands to search for mines. These included lead, tin, and copper mines, each of which contained silver or gold in small quantities, for the doctrine, as affirmed by the court of exchequer chamber in 1568, was that "be the quantity of it ever so small, yet the king shall have the whole of the base metal." The rights of the lords of the soil were so far respected that the mining charters contained clauses forbidding mining under houses or castles, sometimes also under arable lands and meadows, without their licence. A double royalty was imposed, one to be paid to the king, a second, somewhat less in amount, to the landlords. A lease of copper mines by Edward IV. reserves a royalty of one-eighth to the king and one-ninth to the lords of the soil ; a lease of lead mines by the same king reserves one-sixteenth to the landlords and one-twelfth to the king. Pursuant to the general commercial and industrial policy of the middle ages, the inhabitants of mining districts in England were incorporated in district bodies invested with exceptional rights. The most notable instance of these corporations is that of the Stannaries or tin mines of Devon and Cornwall (STANNARIES). Analogous powers were given to the mining law

court of the foresters of Dean, which passed rules for the working of the mines and provided for the settlement of disputes among those enfranchised of the forest. The lead miners of Derbyshire in the same way enjoyed the right of a great Court Barmoot. In these exceptional districts the crown retains those paramount rights which were once probably universal, and the customs have been defined by modern acts of parliament (14 & 15 Vict. c. 94. High Peak, 15 & 16 Vict. c. 163. Low Peak, 1 Vict. c. 43 ; 24 & 25 Vict. c. 40 ; 34 & 35 Vict. c. 85, Forest of Dean, etc.). Miners under royal charters were also commonly free from being impleaded in the king's courts saving for life, limb, or land. They enjoyed the rights of chartered towns, being quit of tolls and tallages.

In 1568 an attempt was made to confine the rights of the crown to mines worked for the precious metals, and to exclude them from those mines in which the precious metals were a secondary incident. But the ancient principle was reaffirmed, three justices dissenting. In 1688 a momentous revolution was effected by parliament. By 1 Will. & M., c. 30, it was enacted that "noe mine of copper, tin, iron, or lead shall hereafter be adjudged, reputed, or taken to be a Royall Mine although gold or silver may be extracted out of the same." By this clause an immense property was transferred from the nation to the landowners. By an act of 1693 (5 Will. & M., c. 6) a modification was introduced in favour of the crown. While the subject may under this act work his base metals at will, the crown has the right of pre-emption of the ore at such prices as would represent its fair value in the absence of royal metals. Those prices were fixed by the act, and having now become obsolete, the crown's rights are not, in fact, exercised. But the royal prerogative, in the case of a mine worked for gold, was affirmed by the court of appeal in 1891 in the case of the Att. Gen. *v.* Morgan. Alum mines were occasionally claimed by the crown, and in the reign of James I. all the judges held that the crown could grant licenses for working saltpetre for gunpowder in any lands of the subject, for the defence of the realm, though the owners of the land were also left at liberty to mine upon their own account.

Owing to the scarcity of the precious metals felt towards the close of the middle ages, constant efforts were made by the English kings themselves to discover them in this country. The science of mining being very imperfect, foreigners were frequently brought in from abroad, as appears from the mining patents granted by Edward IV. and Henry VIII. Wolsey took a particular interest in the development of mining industry. Under Edward VI. endeavours were made to discover and work mines in Ireland, but these proved a failure. Metallurgy was so little understood that under Mary a commission was appointed to learn the art of refining from a German adventurer. In the time of Elizabeth mining engineers were still largely German. The rights of the crown naturally checked mining enterprise until the act of 1693, from which it received a great impetus.

Coal mining was practised in the north of England and the south of Scotland from very early times, and the leasehold system with royalties was common in the 14th century. A frequent practice with corporations was to limit the quantity of coal to be worked per diem in order, doubtless, to prevent exhaustion of the supply, it being a prevalent opinion that the coal mines could only be worked near the surface. In 1610 Sir George Selby informed parliament that twenty-one years would exhaust those of Newcastle. This stimulated invention for draining mines in order to work the lower levels, from which developed the whole art of modern coal mining.

Until the present century, except in the case of royal mines, there may be said to have existed no general statutory regulations for the working, management, and inspection of mines, nor for the security of those employed. By 5 & 6 Vict. it was forbidden to employ females underground after 1st March 1843. The employment of boys under ten was also forbidden. The inspection of coal mines by government was undertaken in 1850 by 13 & 14 Vict. c. 100, which empowered the appointment of inspectors. Analogous provisions were enacted for metalliferous mines in 1872 (35 & 36 Vict. c. 77). This act raised the age for the employment of boys to twelve, after the example of the Mines' Regulation Act of 1860 (23 & 24 Vict. c. 151). There is a natural parallelism in the legislation affecting the two classes of mines, that for coal mines being distinguished by the special precautions ordered by the legislature with the object of preventing explosions, etc. Common features are the prohibition of the payment of wages in public-houses; notice to inspectors in case of explosions, accidents, and loss of life; rules as to the opening and working of new shafts; and codes of offences in the nature of contravention of the rules for the safe working of the mines approved by the secretary of state. The principal acts now in force are, for the regulation of coal mines that of 1887 (50 & 51 Vict. c. 58), and for the regulation of metalliferous mines that of 1872 (35 & 36 Vict. c. 77).

[Plowden's Commentaries, The Case of Mines.— —T. Houghton, The Orders and Rules of the Court of St. Briavells, London, 1687.—The Compleat Miner, London, 1688.—Sir John Pettus, Fodinæ Regales, London, 1670; also A Collection of Scarce and Valuable Treatises upon Metals, Mines, and Minerals, trans. from the Spanish of Albaro Alonzo Barba, director of the mines at Potosi, 2nd ed. (Hodges, London), 1740, with diagrams. —R. L. Galloway, Hist. of Coal Mining in Great Britain, London, 1882.—Att. Gen. v. Morgan, L.R.C.D. (C.A.), 1891, i. 432.—W. Bainbridge,

Law of Mines and Minerals, 5th ed., London, 1878, ed. by A. Brown.— Report of Mining Royalties Commission.—C. Le Neve Foster, Mines and Minerals. First Annual General Report upon the Mineral Industry of the United Kingdom of Great Britain and Ireland for the year 1894, 1895.]
I. S. L.

MINES AND MINERALS, EXHAUSTION OF. While this circumstance sometimes brings about the impoverishment of the district where it occurs, the following causes make it difficult to obtain precise information on the subject—(1) more careful search, better means of communication, and improved methods of working have tended to increase the supply from districts which were becoming exhausted: (2) the general growth of population masks the effects of a local decline, and the latter may be prevented, where mines are failing, by the development of other industries. This sometimes is exemplified in the mines. Dolcoath, by deepening the workings, was transformed from a copper mine to one producing tin. The great open working at Carclaze, though its tin is now almost valueless, is continued for china clay. (3) Mines and quarries in ancient times were frequently worked by slave or convict labour, an example followed more recently by Spain in America and by Russia in Asia. A settlement of this type adds little to the prosperity of the immediate neighbourhood, and the effects of its disappearance are comparatively unimportant. (4) In districts where labour is free, the settlements at first are hardly more than camps; log-huts or shanties being the nearest approach to permanent buildings. In case of a speedy failure, the horde disperses like birds of prey from a consumed carcase, and leaves hardly more trace of its presence. (5) If, however, the undertaking is prosperous, the camp is gradually changed into a city; and the instances of this are at present so young that, as yet, they are in the full tide of success. In these cases the effects of the exhaustion of the mineral wealth of a district are still in the future. The harvest is still being reaped; few fields have yet been absolutely cleared. Instances must mainly be sought in localities comparatively unimportant; but exhaustion is only a question of time, and such investigations as those of Jevons on The Coal Question[1] remind the economist of the necessary limitations of the nature of this part of our wealth.

Precious Metals.—Much might be said as to the effects produced on the more civilised part of the world by the arrest—from the decline of Rome till about the 9th century—of any serious efforts to obtain fresh supplies of gold

[1] "A little reflection will show that coal is almost the sole necessary basis of our material power . . . England's manufacturing and commercial greatness, at least, is at stake in this question, nor can we be sure that material decay may not involve us in moral and intellectual retrogression."—Jevons, Coal Question, Introd.

and silver,—commodities liable to considerable waste from wear and the purposes to which they are applied ; but this is beside the question now considered. Moreover, if a want once seemed likely to occur, owing to the exhaustion of Spain and other *el dorados* of the old world, it has been more than remedied since the discovery of America by the constant opening up of new fields in that and other parts of the globe.

In remote parts of Egypt and the regions about the eastern Mediterranean, places may be found, now deserted, in which formerly the search for gold was actively prosecuted, but no instance is more striking than that of the *Ruined Cities of Mashonaland*, described by Mr. Bent. Here, at various localities between the Zambesi and the Limpopo, often almost buried by vegetation, ruins are found of fortified towns, the walls of which, built of granite blocks, are sometimes 12 to 15 feet thick. Their inhabitants evidently had settled among an unfriendly people to work the district for its gold—they disappeared perhaps as late as the 9th century, and a higher was replaced by a lower type of civilisation, if that term is applicable to the natives of Mashonaland. Again, for a time at least, Mexico supplied an object-lesson in the same kind. Here, during the civil wars from 1810 to 1824, many important silver mines were abandoned, the population dwindled, that of Potosi falling at this period from 130,000 to 9000, and the indirect loss even to agriculturalists was very great. Similar effects have been noted in Columbia, Chili, and Peru from like causes. The Laurium mines, till lately, afforded another example ; worked in classic times they were afterwards abandoned, and ruins marked the sites of places once flourishing. Since 1870 they have been reopened, and even the old slags are being smelted over again. America and Australia have afforded instances of the mushroom growth of settlements, followed by no less rapid desertion. In 1857 there was a rush to the Frazer river (Columbia), followed in 1863 by an exodus of from 15,000 to 20,000 people to Nevada.

Other Metals.—Copper mines were worked in the Sinaitic peninsula about Sarabit-el-Khadim by the ancient Egyptians, where ruins and tablets indicate the presence of a considerable colony ; now the region is deserted. Many ruined buildings in Cornwall mark the sites of mines, especially of tin, exhausted or disused. The decline in population in parts of that county has been very marked.

The following tabular statement, drawn up from the census reports of 1881 and 1891, will show how seriously the population of some of the parishes in the mining districts of Cornwall, has been affected, the decline in one case amounting roughly to 25 per cent ; the larger towns, as might be expected, having suffered least.

Parish.	1881.	1891.
Breage	3017	2751
Callington	1925	1888
Helston	3432	3198
Kea	2470	2103
Liskeard	4053	3984
St. Agnes	4630	4249
St. Cleer	2865	2124
St. Ives	6445	6094
St. Just	6409	6119
Wendron	4584	4250

The same may be said of other spots in Derbyshire, Devonshire, Wales, etc., though the population as a whole has increased.

The Weald of Sussex was once the seat of important iron-works ; the last furnace, at Ashburnham, was extinguished in 1828 (Woodward, *Geology of England and Wales*, pp. 357, 361). The woods often conceal abandoned mines and heaps of slag.

Coal, petroleum, etc.—In Britain the mines of coal, often with associated ironstone, in parts of Staffordshire and Shropshire are beginning to show signs of exhaustion, with the same result. But these industries are so modern, comparatively speaking, that probably almost a century must elapse before marked effects are produced. In various parts of the United States, particular localities have become thronged and prosperous by the discovery of mineral oil, and have been deserted owing to its unexpected exhaustion, but the causes already named have restricted the area affected and prevented any remarkable consequences.

Ornamental minerals and rocks.—The turquoise mines of Sinai, like those of copper, were once busy and are now deserted. In the days of the Pharaohs and under the dominion of Rome, the quarries of Egypt were in full activity. Those for granite and the neighbouring ruins near the first cataract have been often described. Yet more striking are those at Jebel Dokhan, from which the red porphyry, so largely exported to Italy, was obtained. These lie at a height of 3650 feet above high water mark, nearly 100 miles from the Nile and on the eastern side of the watershed between it and the Red Sea. The remains of several Roman stations are passed on the route from Kuneh. From the chief quarry a road " led down to an ancient town with workshops." Hence a path went to an old town in the valley, and beyond are the ruins of a Roman temple. In fact deserted quarries are not rare in the mountainous country between the Nile and the Red Sea (*Brit. Assoc. Rep.*, 1887, p. 802). From Algeria and Tunis marbles were exported in large quantities by the Romans ; the quarries were deserted, the district was sparsely inhabited, till a few years since, when some of them were again opened (*Brit. Assoc. Rep.*, 1885, p. 1028). The white marble of Thasos was in great request in the age of Hadrian, and was worked at much earlier dates. The remains of a quay constructed round the headland, the tombs and other ruins of a town and two villages at least, "all in former days thriving on the quarrying and export of marble," indicate the "former position of a commercial centre, dating for centuries before the Christian era, and leaving traces of having continued in prosperity down well into the period of the eastern empire" (*Brit. Assoc. Rep.*, 1887, p. 200). We cannot, owing to the circumstances already mentioned, point to any striking instance of a country ruined by the exhaustion of its mineral wealth, but notwithstanding this the lesson is plain. The mineral store of each district and of the whole earth is practically limited in quantity, be it gold, or any other metal, be it coal or any fuel. The formation of a fresh supply is a process so slow that, for all practical purposes, it may be excluded from consideration. The waste also of the precious minerals is considerable ; the wear and tear of the more homely is large ; the destruction of combustibles is complete. Hence the store, sooner or later, must be exhausted, now in this country, now in that. In agriculture, provided manures can be obtained, the land seems never to lose its productive power ; the mine or quarry, once worked out, has played its part for good in the economy of the earth, and the ill which it has done "lives after it." Metallurgical processes are attended with drawbacks even at the time, but though, when the minerals are no longer obtained, noxious fumes are no more emitted to devastate the neighbourhood, the waste heaps of rubbish or slag still remain, whereon no useful herb can grow and only a forest can spring up after long years. In some districts also the general ruin of the surface, the choked beds of rivers, and large tracts of fertile meadows buried beneath barren gravels, are the heritage bequeathed by the miner. The decline and fall of the nation whose prosperity has depended solely on its mineral wealth, will be not less appalling than that of imperial Rome.   T. G. B.

MINING ROYALTIES. See ROYALTIES.

MINGHETTI, MARCO (1818-1886). A statistician and political economist born at Bologna. In 1848, when Pope Pius IX. appeared to espouse Italian nationality, Minghetti became a member of the pontifical council of state, and minister in the first liberal secular ministry of Pius IX. But when the pope set himself against the war of independence, Minghetti resigned office and joined the camp of Charles Albert. He fought at Custozza and Goito, and later on was a colleague of Count Cavour at the Paris congress of 1857. He then became, under Cavour, general secretary of foreign affairs, secretary of the interior in 1859, minister of the interior in 1860, and ambassador. After having greatly assisted in the formation of united Italy, he became president of the council of the kingdom in 1863, and again from 1873 to 1876. An able financier, he applied himself primarily during his ministry to restore Italian finance, and when he left office the budget was balanced.

Minghetti was an eloquent and incisive speaker, a man of the broadest culture, a man of letters, and an historian. He is well known by economists for several works, but chiefly for his book on the relation between economics, ethics, and justice. In this work, ably and clearly written, moderate in opinion, and giving evidence of sound culture, Minghetti based economic science on ethics and law, anticipating, to a certain extent, the modifications which were afterwards applied to the English classical school—placing himself on an intermediate ground between this school and the new theories, principally developed in Germany. While too moderate a man to ally himself with the "socialists of the chair," Minghetti attaches more importance to the phenomena of the distribution of wealth than to those of production, and this basis of his eventually formed one of the canons of the new doctrines. This order of ideas inspired various social laws of which he became a promoter, for example, the law on children's labour, on emigration, on pensions, etc.

Originality and depth of research are perhaps wanting in the writings of Minghetti on economics, but on subjects more his own he was one of the most far-seeing and deep thinkers, and one of the purest and most elegant writers of modern Italy.

Dell' economia pubblica e delle sue attinenze colla morale e col diritto, Florence, 1852, 2nd ed. 1868.—*Opuscoli letterari ed economici*, Florence, 1872.—*Miei Ricordi*, Turin, 1889-90 (posthumous publication, unfinished.

[Vapereau, *Dictionnaire universel des contemporains*, Paris, 5th ed., 1880.—Cossa, *Introduction to the Study of Political Economy*, trans., London, 1893.—Graziani, *Le idee economiche degli scrittori emiliani e romaguoli*, etc., Modena, 1893, p. 179-185, and others.]   U. R.

MINIMUM (Rate of Discount). The rate known as the "bank rate" is settled every Thursday at the weekly meeting of the bank directors, and published when the meeting is over. It was formerly the minimum rate current not only in the bank discount office, but in the market generally. This lasted as long as the resources of the Bank of England formed the greater part of the capital in the money market, or even later, whilst the bank remained the largest single influence therein. But now, although the deposits of the bank have increased, those in the hands of the other banks have grown in far greater proportion, and the competitive effect of this outside capital is increased by the fact that it is mostly in the hands of a small group of large and powerful banks, instead of being wielded by a large number of banks each individually small. The result of this change has been to bring the rate of discount in the open market, for long periods together, down much below the bank rate ; the bank directors being supposed, in fixing their rate, to have regard not only to the amount of capital they have to employ, but also to the state of the circulation and the condition of the foreign exchanges. On the other hand, it has been strenuously contended by the late Mr. Thomson Hankey, and some other prominent directors of the bank, that the bank's policy should be governed by the ordinary considerations relating to their banking business only.

As a fact the directors have never reduced the official rate below 2 per cent, notwithstanding that in recent years the open market has frequently stood for months together at, or about, 1 per cent. It is understood that the bank minimum now only regulates its relations with the outside market, and that its own customers obtain accommodation at the rates charged by other banks. The bank rate still governs, at a distance, rates charged or allowed in some cases upon advances or deposits. R. W. B.

MINIMUM OF SUBSISTENCE, THE. The doctrine that the labourer cannot permanently earn more than the minimum of subsistence, that is, enough to keep him and his wife and children alive, has often been ascribed to political economists as a body. It has been used to prove at one time the inutility of any attempt to raise wages, and at another time the injustice of the existing order of society. This doctrine, however, has not been universally taught by political economists, and is not borne out by facts. It is connected with the doctrine of the wage fund, and the mode in which it has grown up will best appear from a brief survey of the course of speculation on the subject of wages.

For this purpose we need not go back further than the French Économistes of the last century. TURGOT (e.g.) declared that the labourer could not in the long run gain more than a bare subsistence, probably basing this assertion on the experience of his own time and country. The bulk of the labouring population of France had been reduced by fiscal and social abuses to a bare subsistence—sometimes even to less, seeing that many died of hunger in bad seasons. In Great Britain at the same time the condition of the labouring class was incomparably better. We find accordingly that Adam Smith does not agree with Turgot on this point (cp. Rae, *Life of Adam Smith*, pp. 220-222). "There are certain circumstances," he writes, "which sometimes give the labourers an advantage, and enable them to raise their wages considerably above this rate," namely, "the lowest which is consistent with common humanity" (*Wealth of Nations*, bk. i. ch. viii.). He then proceeds to inquire what circumstances have this beneficial effect. He concludes that "the liberal reward of labour, as it is the necessary effect, so it is the natural symptom of increas-

ing national wealth. The scanty maintenance of the labouring poor, on the other hand, is the natural symptom that things are at a stand, and their starving condition that they are going fast backwards" (*ib.*).

The next economists to be considered with reference to the minimum of subsistence are MALTHUS and RICARDO. "Malthus," Dr. Bonar says, "without knowing it, was certainly the father of the theory of a wages fund" (Bonar, *Malthus and his Work*, ed. 1885, p. 270). He was deeply impressed with the poverty resulting from an unlimited increase of population, and he seems to have thought that only prudential self-restraint could raise the labourer's income above the minimum that could keep him alive. Ricardo expressed himself on this subject in a way which seems at first sight to coincide with Turgot's assertion. "The natural price of labour is that price which is necessary to enable the labourers one with another to subsist and to perpetuate their race without either increase or diminution" (Ricardo, *Principles of Political Economy*, ch. v.). But he qualifies this proposition by others which have been too commonly disregarded. "It is not to be understood that the natural price of labour estimated even in food and necessaries is absolutely fixed and constant. It varies at different times in the same country and very materially differs in different countries. It essentially depends on the habits and customs of the people." He adds—"The friends of humanity cannot but wish that in all countries the labouring classes should have a taste for comforts and enjoyments, and that they should be stimulated by all legal means in their exertions to procure them." Ricardo thought that real wages might increase with the increase of capital, but he thought that after the period at which all fertile land had been taken up, real wages would tend to fall. Thenceforward rent would grow at the expense of wages and of profits. Some of his expressions would suggest also that the only way in which the labourers could permanently improve their condition was by restricting their number. Whoever may have originated the doctrine of the wages fund, J. S. MILL was the first to formulate it clearly and precisely. From his conception of the WAGES FUND it followed that the labourers' wages must sink to the minimum of subsistence unless the number of labourers were severely kept down. Mill therefore denounced large families with extraordinary violence. Although he afterwards admitted the incorrectness of his views respecting the wages fund, he never completely recast his theory of wages. LASSALLE and later socialist writers eagerly adopted the conceptions of a fixed wages fund and a minimum of subsistence for the labourer as helpful in proving that under the existing order of society the labourer must always be miserable, and that therefore the existing order of society is inhuman. For similar reasons these conceptions have been employed by Mr. George and by others who wish to abolish private property in land. But, since Mill and Lassalle wrote, the whole subject of wages has been reconsidered in the light of experience, and the doctrine of the minimum of subsistence has been seriously shaken. It has been found that countries in which wages are high can compete successfully with countries in which wages are low, and that real wages may be raised without labour becoming really more costly. The explanation of those facts is twofold. In the first place the wages which just keep a man alive are not enough to keep him efficient. It is a true economy to pay the labourer such wages as will maintain him in full vigour of mind and body. In the second place ill-paid labour is wasteful and dear ; it is labour uneconomical to employ. Every rise of wages stimulates the employer to improve his methods of organisation and his mechanical contrivances. Thus it is that within certain limits to be determined only by experience the rise of wages does not necessarily involve loss to the employer. If therefore the labourers are organised, they can apply pressure sufficient to keep wages much above the minimum of subsistence. Natural wages, if so objectionable a term is still to be used, should denote those wages which are really—not apparently—the most economical to pay.

Again the old theory of the wages fund must be modified. General Walker repudiates the wages-fund theory altogether. He holds that wages are paid out of the product of labour, and can be increased indefinitely so long as that product continues to increase (Walker, *Political Economy*, pt. v. ch. vi.). Another American economist, Mr. Gunton, goes further and says that wages are determined by the cost of production of labour, in other words, by the standard of living among the labourers. There is not space here to examine these recent theories. But the doctrine that the remuneration of the labourer tends to dwindle to the minimum on which he can support life may be considered obsolete.

[See article on F. Lassalle (for Iron Law).— Turgot, *Sur la Formation et Distribution des Richesses*, § vi.—Adam Smith, *Wealth of Nations*, bk. i. ch. viii.—Malthus, *Essay on Population—Political Economy.*—Ricardo, *Principles of Political Economy and Taxation*, ch. v.—M'Culloch, *Principles of Political Economy.*—Senior, *Political Economy.*—Mill, *Principles of Political Economy*, bk. ii. chs. 11, 12, 13.—Walker, *The Wages Question.*—Marshall, *Principles of Economics*, bk. vii. especially chs. 2 and 3.—Nicholson, *Principles of Political Economy*, bk. ii. ch. 10.—Schoenhof, *The Economy of High Wages.*—Gunton, *Wealth and Progress.*]　　　　　　　　F. C. M.

MINIMUM WAGE. See LIVING WAGE.

MINORAT is nowadays an institution peculiar to Germany and German Austria, according to which *Bauerngüter*, which may be defined as entailed peasant holdings, are inherited by the youngest male heir in the nearest degree of relationship ; in former times it existed in French Brittany under the name of *Droit du Juveigneur* [1] (see BOROUGH ENGLISH). In contradistinction, entailed estates belonging to noble families descend, in Germany, by MAJORAT (*q.v.*), and even for *Bauerngüter*, the rule of *minorat* is far from being universally followed. Where it prevails it is considered that at the time of his father's death, the eldest children will probably be able to provide for themselves and be independent. But, under other aspects, *minorat* is subject to adverse criticism : there is often a long uncertainty before it is known who will be the heir of the holding, and the latter frequently is only placed in the way of being productive after the actual owner is already incapacitated by old age. Moreover, another unfavourable circumstance is that the heir is too often still a minor when the holding descends to him.

[Holtzendorff, *Rechtslexicon*, ii. 128 ; and Roscher, *Nationalökonomik des Ackerbaues*, § 92, pp. 328-333, ed. 1888.]　　　　　　　E. Ca.

MINT (Latin *Moneta*, a name of Juno, in whose temple money was coined in Rome, hence mint, coined money, Anglo-Saxon *mynet*). As the right to issue coin belongs, in modern societies, exclusively to the sovereign power (Hale, Coke, Blackstone), it follows that a Mint cannot legally issue the coins of the country in which it is situated except under the directions of the sovereign or other central authority. In Anglo-Saxon times a large number of mints were established throughout this country under the control of MONEYERS,—officials responsible for the integrity of the coinage. Since the Norman conquest it appears to have been a common practice, even as recently as the 17th century, to establish a temporary Mint where the sovereign happened to reside, and it was not till after the great recoinage of silver at the end of that century (see under Sir Isaac NEWTON) that all coinage operations were concentrated, so far as England and Ireland are concerned, in the Tower of London. The Dublin Mint was closed in 1696. The Edinburgh Mint, first erected in 1574, was not finally abolished until 1815.

Early in the present century, in 1811, the Mint was removed from the inconvenient premises which it occupied in the Tower to the present site on Tower Hill, and in 1850 the complete control of all its operations passed into the hands of the government.

The primary duty of a Mint, namely the conversion of bullion into coin, naturally entails other duties connected with the precious metals.

[1] From *juventor*, taken as comparative of *juventa.*

Thus the hall-marking of plate, and the refining, melting, and casting of gold and silver into commercial bars, are undertaken by certain foreign Mints, but in this country the work of the Department may be grouped under the four following heads :

1. *The coinage of gold presented by private holders for that purpose.*

Under § 8 of the Coinage Act 1870 (33 Vict. c. 10), "any person" is entitled to bring gold bullion to the Mint and, subject to certain specified stipulations, "such bullion shall be assayed and coined, and delivered out to such person without any charge for such assay or coinage, or for waste in coinage" (see FREE COINAGE). Any alloying metal required is also supplied without charge, and a provision of the Coinage Act 1816 (56 Geo. III. c. 68), is re-enacted to the effect that out of every twenty troy pounds weight of standard gold bullion there shall be produced 934 sovereigns and one half-sovereign. This corresponds to the troy ounce being valued at £3 : 17 : 10½ (see GUINEA, INTROD. AND RATING OF). Since the Bank Charter Act 1844 (7 & 8 Vict. c. 32), all persons are, under § 4, "entitled to demand, from the Issue Department of the Bank of England, notes in exchange for gold bullion at the rate of £3 : 17 : 9 per ounce of standard gold," subject to the metal being melted and assayed by persons approved by the bank at the expense of the owner. It will thus be seen that there is a difference of only 1½d. per ounce in the two rates, and experience has shown that the delay necessary for coinage operations leads holders of bullion to take advantage of the Bank Charter Act, and obtain payment at once rather than incur this delay. Thus it happens that, as concerns the gold currency, the Mint in this country deals exclusively with the Bank of England ; it should be added that coins which are no longer legal tender, in consequence of their having been reduced in weight by wear below their least current weight, are received for recoinage through the same channel.

2. *The coinage and issue of token silver and bronze pieces as they are required, from bullion purchased on account of the Government.*

The arrangements in force for the issue and maintenance of subsidiary coins are essentially different in character, primarily in consequence of the fact that, whereas these are merely tokens and, therefore, only legal tender to a limited extent, gold coins are intrinsically worth their face-value and of unlimited legal tender.

In connection with the silver currency, however, it is interesting to note that § 9 of the Coinage Act 1816 directed that from a date to be fixed by royal proclamation "any person or persons, native or foreigner," might bring silver coin, plate, or bullion to be converted into coin at the rate of sixty-six shillings per troy pound, sixty-two shillings being returned to the importer and four retained by the Mint to meet the cost of assaying, loss, and coinage. No such proclamation was ever issued, and this section remained a dead letter therefore until the Act was repealed in 1870. Under the provisions of the Act passed in that year, whenever token coins are required to be struck, the requisite silver and bronze bullion is purchased in the market with sums advanced for the purpose out of the Consolidated Fund, and, on issuing this coin at its full nominal value, the Master of the Mint pays the proceeds into the exchequer under two heads:—(*a*) Repayments of advances for the purchase of bullion ; and (*b*) SEIGNORAGE (*q.v.*), or, as now defined in practice, the excess of the circulating value of the coin above the purchase price of the metal used in its manufacture.

Worn silver coin is received by the Mint at its nominal value, and all expenses connected with the supply of Imperial token coins to Colonies, and their renewal, are also borne by the Department.

3. *Execution of coinages required by British Colonies and Dependencies.*

Subject to the requirements of the Imperial currency being met, the Royal Mint undertakes the execution of any coinages required by Colonies at fixed charges which are calculated to cover the actual cost of the work performed. The requisite bullion having been delivered at the Mint by the colonial agent, is converted into coin and shipped to the colony at the expense of that colony, all profit in respect of seignorage of course falling into the colonial exchequer. If from any cause the Department is not in a position to undertake such a coinage, the work is usually performed, under government control, by a private firm in Birmingham.

4. *Manufacture of naval, military, and other medals, and miscellaneous duties.*

The manufacture of medals forms an important subsidiary branch of the work of most Mints. In this country they are struck on behalf of the several departments—the War Office, Admiralty, and India Office, as well as for the Royal and several other learned societies. No special reference is here necessary, however, to this branch of work, or to the miscellaneous other duties performed by the Mint, such as the verification of the standard of plate hall-marked at certain assay offices, independent examination of coin issued from Indian, Australian, and, occasionally, certain foreign Mints, etc.

Some allusion should be made to the branch Mints established at Sydney and Melbourne by orders in council passed in 1853 and 1869 respectively. Immediately after the early discoveries of gold in Australia, the question of establishing local Mints for coining the precious metal, and thus facilitating its use in commerce, was raised in several of the colonies. New South Wales was the first to obtain the necessary authority, and, although the question of establishing another branch in Victoria was frequently raised, it was not actually opened until 1872. When first issued the Sydney coins were not intended to circulate in the United Kingdom, but application was soon made by the colony for this concession to be granted, and in 1862 the question was considered by a select committee of the House of Commons. As a result of this committee's report, acts were passed in 1863 and 1866, under which Royal Proclamations were issued in the latter year declaring Sydney coins to be legal tender in the United Kingdom and in specified colonies. Similarly the coins to be struck at Melbourne were legalised in 1869. Since 1871 the coins of both Mints have been identical in design with those of the Royal Mint in London, being distinguished only by the mint-marks S and M respectively. The current expenses of the branch Mints are met out of permanent annual appropriations made by the local legislatures, of £15,000 in the case of Sydney, and £20,000 in that of Melbourne, all revenue being paid into the local treasuries. Unlike the Royal Mint, they impose a coinage charge which amounted to 1 per cent, or nearly 9½d. per standard ounce, in 1855, but has for many years been reduced to 1½d. ; it is evident, however, from the published returns that the present rates do not cover the expenses. No token coins are struck, the issue of silver and bronze coin being confined to the Mint in England. In view of the recent gold discoveries in Western Australia, steps are now (1895) being taken to erect a third Australian branch Mint at Perth.

[Ruding's *Annals of the Coinage.* — *Encyclopædia Britannica*, 9th edition, article "Mint."— For early English mints see "The English Currency under Edward I.," by C. G. Crump and A. Hughes (*Economic Journal*, vol. v., 1895).—Chalmers's *Currency in the British Colonies.*—Annual Reports of the Deputy-Master of the Mint.—Annual Reports of the Director of the United States Mint. —*Report of Select Committee on the Royal Mint*, 1837 (R. 465).—*Report of Commission on the Royal Mint*, 1849 (c. 1026).—*Report of the Royal Commission on International Coinage*, 1868 (R. 4073).]   E. R.

MINT, UNITED STATES. The mint of the United States was established, under the act of 2nd April 1792, in Philadelphia. In 1873 its administration was made a bureau of the treasury department under a director. In 1835 branch mints were established at Charlotte, N.C., at Dahlonega, Ga., and New Orleans ; in 1852 at San Francisco ; in 1862 at Denver ; in 1863 at Carson, Nev. Coinage, however, has been suspended at Denver, Charlotte, and New Orleans. According to the act of establishment, the unit of account was the DOLLAR divided into tenths or DIMES, hundredths or CENTS, and thousandths or MILS. Foreign gold and silver coins passed current at certain established rates, until by act of 21st February 1857 they ceased to be legal tender. By the act of 1792 a gold dollar (see DOLLAR, UNITED STATES) was to contain 24·75 grains of pure gold, and the silver dollar (see DOLLAR, UNITED STATES) 371·25 grains of pure silver, the relative value of the two metals being 15 to 1. There was free coinage of both metals, and no charge save that in case of immediate payment in coin, a deduction of one-half per cent from the weight of the pure gold or silver was made. The gold coins authorised were the EAGLE $10 (= £2:1:1), the half eagle, and the quarter eagle. The fineness was 916⅔ parts gold per 1000 (¹¹⁄₁₂th fine). The silver coins authorised were the dollar, 416 grains in weight, the half dollar, quarter dime, and half dime—all being proportional parts of the dollar in weight, and in fineness 892·43 parts in the 1000. There was no change in the weight or fineness until, by the act of 28th June 1834, the relative value was changed to 1 : 16·002 by reducing the amount of pure gold in the dollar to 23·20 grains, and increasing the fineness of the coins to 0·899·225. Again by the act of 18th January 1837 the fineness was raised to 0·900, which changed the pure gold in the dollar to 23·22 grains.

In 1837 the weight of the silver dollar was fixed at 412½ grains. The fineness of silver coins was also fixed at ·900. The next important change was by the act of 21st February 1853, when free coinage of silver pieces of less than one dollar in value were closed, the fractional parts of the dollar made subsidiary, and the weights reduced, the half dollar weighing 192 grains. The coinage of the double eagle $20 (= £4 : 2 : 2½), and the one dollar, gold, was authorised 3rd March 1849, and the three dollar, gold, 21st February 1853. The coinage of the two latter was discontinued in 1890. The coinage of a three cent piece was also provided for by act of 3rd March 1851. By act of 12th February 1873 the coinage of the silver dollar, half dime, and three cent piece was discontinued, and the weight of the subsidiary coin slightly raised, that of the half dollar to 192·9 grains.

The act of 28th February 1878 (BLAND ACT) restored the coinage of the standard silver dollar, though not free, and provided for the purchase at the market price by the government of silver bullion at from $2,000,000 (say £400,000) to $4,000,000 (say £800,000) per month, and its coinage. This policy was again changed by the act of 14th July 1890, which authorised the monthly purchase of 4,500,000 ounces of silver, or so much thereof as might be offered at the market price, not exceeding $1·00 for 371¼ grains of pure silver, and the issue in payment of treasury notes redeemable on demand in coin. It was also provided that so much silver should be coined as might be necessary to redeem the treasury notes issued in payment for the silver. In accordance with this a limited amount was coined until 1893, when the act of 1st November repealed the purchasing clause.

By the act of 12th February 1873, individuals had the right to deposit silver bullion for coinage into trade dollars (see DOLLAR, TRADE); this was discontinued 3rd March 1887. For a brief period a twenty cent silver piece was struck, and in 1892, 5,000,000 silver half dollars, known as Columbian half dollars, were struck, and also 40,000 quarters.

By the act of 2nd April 1792 the coinage of a copper one cent and a half cent of 264 and 132 grains respectively was authorised. The weight of the cent was afterwards reduced to 208 and then to 168 grains. Copper coinage was discontinued in 1857, and in its place was minted a nickel one cent coin, 72 grains in weight, and consisting of 88 per cent copper and 12 per cent nickel. A further change in this coin was made, 22nd April 1864, by reducing the weight to 48 grains, and changing the composition to 95 per cent copper and 5 per cent tin and zinc. A two cent piece was also authorised, discontinued in 1873. Between 1865 and 1890 a three cent piece was authorised; and 16th March 1866 a five cent coin, popularly known as a nickel, 75 per cent copper and 25 per cent nickel, was authorised.

The total coinage of all the mints until 30th June 1893 has been as follows:

Gold.		
Double eagles, 1850-93	$1,145,463,340	(£229,092,668)
Eagles, 1793 - 1804, 1838-93 . . .	$217,694,120	(£43,538,824)
Half eagles, 1793-1893	$199,533,635	(£39,906,727)
Three dollars, 1854-89	$1,619,376	(£323,875)
Quarter eagles, 1796-1808 ; 1821-93 .	$28,595,567·50	(£5,709,113)
Dollars, 1849-89 .	$19,499,337	(£3,899,867)
Silver		
Trade dollars, 1873-83	$35,965,924	(£7,193,184)
Dollars, 1793 - 1805 ; 1836-73 ; 1878-93	$427,363,688	(£85,472,737)
Half dollars, 1793-1893	$127,149,056·50	(£25,429,811)
Quarter dollars, 1793-1893 . . .	$44,901,449	(£8,980,289)
Twenty cents, 1875-78	271,000	(£54,200)
Dimes, 1793-1893 .	$28,115,898·90	(£5,623,179)
Half dimes, 1793-1805 ; 1829-73 .	$4,480,219	(£896,043)
Three cents, 1851-1873 . . .	$1,282,087	(£256,417)
Minor Coinage.		
Five cents . .	$12,971,127·40	(£2,594,225)
Three cents . .	$941,348·48	(£188,269)
Two cents . .	$912,020·00	(£182,404)
Cents . . .	$10,666,775·08	(£2,133,355)
Half cents . .	$39,926·11	(£7,985)
Total—Gold . .	$1,612,405,375·50	(£322,481,075)
Silver .	$669,929,323·90	(£133,985,864)
Minor .	$25,531,198·07	(£5,106,239)
Grand Total . .	$2,307,865,896·57	(£461,573,179)

Of this total amount nearly one-half has been minted at Philadelphia, and nearly as much in San Francisco.

As indicated by foregoing statements, there has been a large seignorage on silver coinage, and up to 1st Nov. 1893 there had been paid into the treasury of the United States on this account $74,262,970·99 (£14,852,594).

From the standpoint of administrative finance, the bureau of the mint is an important office. In the fiscal year ending 30th June 1893 the expenditures were $1,020,590·30 (£204,118), of which $210,500·08 (£42,100) was for salaries, and $636,135·61 (£127,227) for wages. The income was $2,765,869·86 (£553,173), of which $164,638·11 (£32,927) were from charges for parting and refining bullion, and the larger part of the remainder from seignorage. In 1873 the charge for making gold coins was reduced to one-fifth of one per cent, and in 1875 entirely abolished, save that the depositor pays for the copper used in alloying the gold.

The legal limit of tolerance in fineness of gold coins is 0·001, and of silver coins 0·003. Each year there is an annual trial of coins by an independent commission appointed by the president. [A valuable summary of the legislation in regard to coinage may be found in the *Twenty-first Annual Report of the Director of the Mint*, 1893, pp. 83-94. See also H. R. Linderman, *Money and Legal Tender*, New York, 1879.—W. A. Shaw, *The History of Currency*, pp. 246-266.]

D. R. D.

MINT PAR OF EXCHANGE. The equivalent, in terms of one coinage, of the quantity of pure metal contained in another standard coin, both being of the same metal, and taken at mintage weights. The sovereign contains 113·001597 grains or 7·322379 grammes of fine gold, and the following are its equivalents in the coins of other gold-standard countries. The value in pence of the unit of each country is also given.

£1=				
France, and Latin Union . . }	fcs.	25·221	. franc	= 9·515d.
Denmark and Scandinavian Union }	kr.	18·159	. krone	= 13·216d.
Germany . . .	mks.	20·429	. mark	= 11·747d.
Holland . . .	fl.	12·107	. florin	= 19·823d.
Austria . . .	fl.	10·088	. florin	= 23·789d.
Austria .	New fl.	12·009	. florin	= 19·985d.
Portugal . .	mil.	4·504	. milreis	= 53·284d.
Brazil . .	mil.	8·901	. milreis	= 26·934d.
United States .	$	4·867	. dollar	= 49·316d.
Argentina . .	$	5·044	. peso	= 47·578d.
Uruguay . .	$	4·705	. peso	= 51·003d.
Chili . .	$	5·335	. peso	= 44·985d.
Chili .	New $	13·213d.	. peso	= 18·163d.

The par given above for France serves also for the other countries of the Latin Union—Belgium, Switzerland, Italy, and Greece ; francs being altered for Italy into *lire*, and for Greece into *drachmas*. It serves also for Spain with francs altered into *pesetas*, though quotations are usually made in pence per dollar, or piastre, of five pesetas. The par given for Denmark serves also for Sweden and Norway.

Mint pars are given above for Spain, Italy, Portugal, Brazil, Argentina, and Chili, although at present (1895) their actual exchanges are in terms of more or less inconvertible paper money.

R. W. B.

MINT PRICE OF BULLION. With free and open mints that which is frequently called the mint price is the equivalent in terms of coin. By the Coinage Act (33 Vict. c. 10, § 8), any person may bring gold bullion to the mint, and receive the same again, assayed and coined, without charge, provided the bullion be of such character as not to require refining. The sovereign weighs 123·27447 grains of standard gold, i.e. $\frac{11}{12}$ fine, and, therefore, for every ounce of gold bullion of equal fineness that is brought in, the importer will receive back in coin, $£\frac{480}{123·27447} = 3·89375$ or £3 : 17 : $10\frac{1}{2}$. The importer will of course have to wait his turn, and also whilst his parcel of gold is being coined ; and, in order to avoid this, one of the conditions imposed in the charter of the Bank of England is that it shall always purchase bar gold, by payment in its own notes, at the rate of £3 : 17 : 9 per oz. standard. The difference is about equal to twenty days' interest at 3 per cent.

Where a charge is made for coinage, it may perhaps be said that there is a mint price. The following are the coinage terms in some principal countries with open mints :—

GOLD.

Great Britain	.	no charge.
United States	.	no charge.
France	.	about $\frac{1}{4}$ per cent.
Germany	.	about $\frac{1}{4}$ per cent.
Holland	.	from $\frac{3}{10}$ to $\frac{6}{10}$ of 1 per cent.

SILVER.

British India	.	$2\frac{1}{10}$ per cent.[1]
Mexico	.	5 per cent.
Japan	.	1 per cent.

Where the mint is closed against either metal and purchases are made for coinage on government account, the mint price is necessarily the same as the market price.   R. W. B.

MINTAGE, FREE. The power of free mintage of gold was granted to any one who brought standard gold and silver to the English mint by the act of 1666 (18 Chas. II. c. 5), which, commencing with the statement "whereas it is obvious that the plenty of current coins of gold and silver of this kingdom is of great advantage to trade and commerce," in order to encourage this "plenty," enacted that "plate or bullion of gold or silver should be assayed, melted down, and coined with all convenient speed, without any defalcation, diminution, or charge for assaying, coinage, or waste in bullion." This act, as will be perceived, established free mintage for both gold and silver in this country. With respect to silver, the act of 1798-1799 (38 Geo. III. c. 59), prohibited further silver coinage, and the statute of 1816 (56 Geo. III. c. 68), which established the coinage of silver money on its present basis,

[1] Closed since June 1893.

practically restricted free coinage to gold bullion only. This act was repealed, but was re-enacted in substance by the coinage act of 1870. The gold bullion coined in England is practically all received through the Bank of England, which makes a charge of $1\frac{1}{2}$d. per ounce for delivering gold coin without delay in exchange for the bullion. Similar enactments, with slightly different rates of charges, are in force in France, Germany, the United States, and the other principal countries of the world.

[*Report of International Monetary Conference.* Paris, 1878, with Appendix by Mr. Dana Horton. —W. A. Shaw, *The History of the Currency, 1252 to 1894.*]

MIR is the modern survival of the ancient free Russian village community. In its conditions of land tenure, it resembles the eastern and western mark system. Both probably came from a common Aryan origin. As now constituted, each village has its *Mir* or popular assembly administered by an "elder." The *Mir* itself, however, performs the periodical assessments and distribution of the common land, which is cultivated on the "three-field system" by the whole community working together. After harvest, the fields are common pasture. Owing to the encroachments of neighbouring large proprietors, the communities seem to have lost their ancient rights of common woods and pastures. When required, these are now rented from the neighbouring landowner. Each household may, by repaying the sum advanced by the state for its acquisition, become the private owner of land ; and this, says Mr. Kovalevsky, "unless communistic doctrines come to the rescue, threatens the *Mir* with extinction."

[M. Kovalevsky, *Mod. Customs and Ancient Laws of Russia,* 1889-1890, pp. 69-119.—See also Haxthausen, *De l'abolition . . . du partage égal et temporaire des terres dans les communes russes,* Paris, 1858, 8vo.— *les institutions rurales de la Russie,* 3 vols., Hanover, 1847-1853, 8vo.—Laveleye (Émile de, Baron), *Les Communautés de famille et de village* (Extrait de la *Rev. d'Écon. Pol.,* pp. 19, Bar le Duc (1888), 8vo).—*Primitive Property,* Lond. (Camb. printed), 1878, 8vo.—Maine (Sir H.), *Village Communities in the East and West,* Lond., 1871, 8vo, 3rd ed., 1876, 8vo.—Mackenzie Wallace, *Russia.*—Maurer (G. Ludwig von), *Einleitung zur Geschichte der Mark—Hof-Dorf-und Stadt-Verfassung, und der öffentlichen Gewalt,* München, 1854, 8vo. That the *Mir* system works badly, see Duke of Argyll, *Unseen Foundations of Society,* 1893, pp. 572-573.]   A. L.

MIRABEAU, VICTOR RIQUETTI, marquis de (1715-1789), sometimes described by his pseudonym as *L'Ami des Hommes,* or distinguished from his son, the Comte de MIRABEAU, by the names of Mirabeau *père,* Mirabeau *ainé,* the elder Mirabeau, or the marquis of Mirabeau.

He was born at Perthuis in Provence, where his ancestors, the Riquetis, had settled in the 13th century after being driven out of Italy. In his youth he served as an officer in the army, and was decorated for his bravery in the Bavarian campaign. In 1737 he succeeded to his father's title and estates, and quitted the army, soon afterwards embarking upon the studies of rural and political economy, in pursuit of which he exhibited unwearied energy for half a century. He came early in life under the influence of the views of CANTILLON, but subsequently became an enthusiastic adherent of QUESNAY and one of the leaders of the PHYSIOCRATS. Quesnay indeed was the quasi-sacred founder of the sect, and originator of its creed, but Mirabeau was the militant chief of the school ; and, after Quesnay's death in 1774, he became its acknowledged head. The history of his domestic severities, his protracted quarrels and fifteen years of lawsuits with his wife, and his rigour towards his children, which drew down upon him the jibe that he was at once *l'ami des hommes et l'ennemi de sa femme et de ses enfants*, show us that, like Rousseau, he was sometimes unable to harmonise the sourness of his conduct with the sweetness of his counsels. But they also make more than ever remarkable the amazing activity with which he found time to carry out numerous hardy and unremunerative agricultural experiments, to act as the social centre of the ÉCONOMISTES (*q.v.*) at his Tuesday receptions, and to produce a crop of propagandist literature in books, in newspapers, in letters, and in lectures, almost unequalled in volume and in vigour ; while his tenderness for his mother and his affection for his brother, the bailli de Mirabeau, with whom he exchanged upwards of four thousand lengthy letters equally devoted and didactic, prove—what is otherwise abundantly clear—that his family troubles would not have arisen without the gravest faults on the side of his wife and his sons.

Educated, as he says, in a mountain chateau by "a tutor at thirty crowns," and quitting college at the age of thirteen, the marquis of Mirabeau owed his erudition chiefly to his own application and assiduous study. In 1747 he wrote an (unpublished) *Testament politique* for the guidance of his son, as yet unborn ; and inspired by ambition for the aggrandisement of his family, urged the future enemy of aristocratic privilege to defend his order against encroachments of the royal power ! The reactionary tone of this document is little in keeping with his later views. He continued to ruminate upon the art of government : "12 principles laid down in 12 lines, and graven in the head of the prince or his minister would," he thought, in 1749, "if strictly carried out in detail, correct all the abuses of society and bring back the age of

Solomon." A friend of VAUVENARGUES, an admirer of MONTESQUIEU, and presenting in himself, as De TOCQUEVILLE has observed, the spectacle of a feudal character invaded by democratic ideas, he was already given to philosophise upon statesmanship, and wrote a *Système politique de la France*, which remains in manuscript. But it was in 1750 that he published anonymously his first treatise, the *Mémoire concernant l'utilité des États provinciaux*, 12mo, Rome ;[1] a plea for a measure of decentralisation and local self-government, considered by Lavergne to be the most substantial of his voluminous economic and political works, and at first attributed by a judge so competent as D'ARGENSON to Montesquieu himself. Contrasting the systems of the *pays d'élection*, where the repartition of taxes was effected from above by the authority of the intendant, a royal officer, and the *pays d'état*, where the repartition rested upon the local and mutual decision of the taxpayers, he concluded strongly in favour of the latter as more equitable and more profitable to the treasury, and recommended the general establishment of local assemblies adopting its best features. His views contributed largely to the creation of such bodies in 1787 ; but they were swept away with the monarchy before they could take root. (For *pays d'élection* and *pays d'état* see INTERNAL CUSTOMS AND TOLLS.)

In some manner not yet accounted for, Mirabeau had obtained, and for many years retained, possession of the unpublished manuscript of Cantillon's *Essai sur la Nature du Commerce en général*, when the rightful owner recovered the *Essai* and caused it to be printed and published in 1755. The manuscript had made a deep impression on Mirabeau. At one time he seems to have intended to modify and publish it as his own. Subsequently he proceeded to write a running commentary upon the *Essai*, and it is the work thus commenced which appeared, subsequently to the publication of Cantillon's manuscript, under the title of *L'Ami des Hommes, ou Traité de la population*, in three parts, with the imprint à Avignon, 1756, 4to and 12mo. This remarkable treatise created the greatest sensation throughout the whole of Europe. It is said to have gone through forty editions, and was translated into several languages. Its anonymous author, soon discovered, became the idol of the day, and was generally referred to by the sobriquet which he had chosen for the title of his book. The meridional vivacity of his style, his wit, his naïve egotism, his piquant irony and frequent paradox gave him a great literary vogue, and led some of his readers to compare him to MONTAIGNE ; while the importance of his subject and the ability of his views, in

1 "Rome" was a false imprint. The book was really published in France.

turn original, daring, and profound, earned for him the more durable attention of those who cared rather for the matter than the style. The prodigal luxuriance of his ideas, unconnected by any firm and consistent grasp of principle, makes his book comparable to a pathless tract of tangled jungle, and renders it impossible to summarise it succinctly. But its leading assertions are the following : Population is the source of wealth, and the means of subsistence are the measure of population. Agriculture is the great source of subsistence. A large population is desirable ; and to this end the encouragement of agriculture is the means. "Men multiply like rats in a barn if they have the means of subsistence." Luxury, idleness, and public debts are to be reprobated. The very rich are "like pikes in a pond." The influx from country to town should be counteracted and absenteeism should cease. Religious toleration, free trade—internal and external,—a more equal distribution of wealth, a diminution and more equitable partition of the burdens of taxation, are among the *desiderata* for the economic improvement of the country ; and a ministry of agriculture should be created for its encouragement and support, to keep pace with the aid which science can render to agriculture, and to favour the development of canals, modes of communication, drainage, etc. The peasant is everywhere to be held in honour, and the king's ideal should be to be a *roi pasteur*. The hardihood of the author may be sufficiently indicated by two quotations. In his preface he personifies "la voix de l'humanité qui réclame ses droits" ; and in his conclusion he apostrophises the king in favour of that class of his subjects which is "the most useful of all, those who see beneath them nothing but their nurse and yours—mother-earth ; who stoop unceasingly beneath the weight of the most toilsome labours ; who bless you every day and ask nothing from you but peace and protection. It is with their sweat and (you know it not !) their very blood that you gratify that heap of useless men who keep saying that the greatness of a prince consists in the value, and above all, the number, of favours he divides among his courtiers, nobility, and companions. I have seen a tax-gathering bailiff cut off the wrist of a poor woman who clung to her saucepan, the last utensil of her household, which she was defending from distraint. What would you have said, great Prince ?" etc.—Evidently some of the qualities of the younger Mirabeau were inherited from his father.

After reading L'Ami des Hommes, QUESNAY, who agreed with many of the author's opinions, desired to make his acquaintance, and Mirabeau has left a graphic account of their interview, in which Quesnay persuaded him that wealth is the source of population, not population the source of wealth. Mirabeau now became the fervent admirer of Quesnay, and between them they founded the school of the physiocrats. As Madame de Pompadour's medical attendant, Quesnay was unable to quit his post at Versailles day or night. His position at the court also imposed upon him some delicacy and reserve in openly criticising the government. The tempestuous marquis supplied in himself more than enough of initiative, energy, courage, and resource. The deference which he always exhibited to Quesnay enabled the latter to hold him somewhat in check by frequent correspondence, reading his proofs, chastening his style, and amending his views. But the impetuosity of Mirabeau was not to be wholly curbed ; and he remained to the last perhaps the most independent member of "the sect."

In 1758 appeared a continuation of *L'Ami des Hommes* (pt. 4, no imprint ; 4to and 12mo), in which the hand of Quesnay is plainly visible. It consists of a *Dialogue entre le Surintendant d'O. et L. D. H.*, a reprint of the *Mémoire sur les États provinciaux*, with a reply to objections which had been published against it, and a series of, separately paged, *Questions intéressantes sur la Population, l'Agriculture, et le commerce proposées aux Académies et autres sociétés sçavantes des Provinces*, asking for local information upon agricultural conditions, and also suggesting some general considerations somewhat in the style of Berkeley's *Querist*. These questions, the reader is informed, are not by the author of the *Mémoire sur les États provinciaux*. In 1760 appeared the fifth and sixth parts, without publisher's name or place of publication,—the whole forming three quarto or six 12mo volumes. The fifth part contains the essay written for the prize of the Berne Agricultural Society in 1759 on the reasons why Switzerland should prefer to grow corn. This is followed by extracts from the first six books of an English work, translated from Hale's *Complete Body of Husbandry*. The sixth part (no separate title page) is made up of a *Réponse à l'Essai sur les Ponts et Chaussées, La Voierie, et les Corvées*, and by the *Tableau Oeconomique avec des explications*. Mirabeau had already denounced the CORVÉE in his *Mémoire*, and he now replies to a supporter of them. His "explanation" of Quesnay's *Tableau* involves some manipulation of the original in order to make it comprehensible to himself and to others. But it is doubtful whether Mirabeau with his small capacity for consecutive reasoning ever fully understood the harder-headed Quesnay any more than he had rightly understood Cantillon.

The same year which terminated the *Ami des Hommes* saw the publication of a *Théorie de l'Impôt*, (1760, 4to and 12mo, no imprint), a work of considerable ability which seemed likely to create an almost equal stir. No one could doubt who was the author. "Seigneur," he begins, in the tones already noticed of exhortation and of hardly-veiled menace, "Seigneur! you have twenty millions of subjects, more or less, all with a little money and almost all capable of rendering you such service as you require; and yet you can no longer obtain service without money nor money to pay for service. In plain language, your people hold back from you without knowing it, for they are still well-disposed to your person even though they be not to the agents of your authority." And he puts into the mouth of the king the soliloquy that his position as the head of his people is justified only so long as, and only because, he costs them less than he is worth to them. If, as the author asserts on his first page, "nous sommes en un siècle mol et craintif," he shows clearly enough that he is himself not lacking in temerity. He was, for his boldness, imprisoned (16th December 1760) in the chateau of Vincennes. The king was furious against him; but ultimately yielded to Madame de Pompadour and Mirabeau's friends, and allowed him to be liberated on Christmas eve, with orders to reside at his property at Bignon, and not in Paris. For two and a half years the physiocrats held silence in the press, and taught by word of mouth. In 1763 Mirabeau made a convert of DUPONT DE NEMOURS, who, writing in 1769 of the Théorie de l'Impôt, says, "This sublime work has to my knowledge been multiplied by eighteen editions." It is not, as might be supposed, a mere plea for the IMPÔT UNIQUE. It proposes a reorganisation of financial administrative machinery, the abolition of the Fermes (see FARMER-GENERAL), a reduction in the taxation upon salt, with the object of increasing the total yield, and a special tax upon tobacco farms. The DOMAINE, the post, and the MINT were to be further sources of revenue. Many just and valuable remarks on taxation are scattered throughout the volume, and entitle the author to rank as one of the earliest important writers on the subject. In 1763 appeared his Philosophie rurale, Amsterdam (Paris), 4to, "the best, or the least bad," says DAIRE, "of all his works." It is the most complete and compact account of his physiocratic views, for which the reader is referred to the article PHYSIOCRATS, and owed a good deal to Quesnay, by whom, Dupont states, the whole of the seventh chapter was written.

Mirabeau received the grand cross of Wasa from Gustavus III. of Sweden on the foundation of the order, and counted among his other notable admirers and correspondents, Leopold, grand-duke of Tuscany, afterwards Emperor of Austria, Stanislas-Augustus, king of Poland, and KARL FRIEDRICH, grand-duke of Baden. The dauphin boasted that he knew L'Ami des Hommes by heart; but, when it was proposed to place the Éphémérides under his protection, though Quesnay, Dupont, and TURGOT agreed to the plan with its prospect of shelter from too rigid censorship, and though the dauphin had himself approved of the terms of the proposed dedication, Mirabeau refused to be a party to the project, and threatened to withdraw if it were adopted. His threat, which prevailed, indicates his dominant influence in the party and his independence of his colleagues. As has already been indicated in the course of this article, Mirabeau was one of the first to perceive an important principle of POPULATION, and to express a belief in what has since been called the elasticity of the exchequer; but his chief economic importance lies in his powerful support of physiocracy.

The limits of this article admit of little more than an enumeration of his other principal works. According to M. de LOMÉNIE (q.v.) he left forty volumes, besides several unpublished writings. His popularity waned after the lawsuits which followed upon his quarrel with and separation from his wife in 1757, the odium which he incurred from the stern measures he adopted to repress his profligate and spendthrift son by imprisoning him at Vincennes and elsewhere, under lettres de cachet, and the success of the latter in unjustly inflaming the public mind against an Ami des hommes, whom he painted as a demon of harshness and inhumanity. It could hardly fail to lend colour to prejudice that the writer who declaimed so vigorously against absenteeism was hardly ever present in his own property, that, much as he disapproved of public debts, he incurred with fatal facility an increasing burden of private loans, that for an expert in rural philosophy his agricultural experience was singularly unfortunate, and that having denounced lettres de cachet in his writings he employed them against his own household in profusion. He died 13th July 1789, the day before the storming of the Bastille.

His later writings often appeared anonymously and in foreign countries, by the care of his friends. Such are Les Devoirs, Milan, 1770, 8vo, seen through the press by the Marquis de Longo, professor of political economy at Milan. (Men should receive economic instruction as a guide to conduct. And so elementary education should be compulsory, and free where the recipient cannot afford to pay). —Entretien d'un jeune Prince avec son gouverneur par L. D. H., Publié par M. G. . . . (l'abbé Grivel), Paris, 1785, 4 vols. 8vo and 12mo.—Hommes à célébrer pour avoir bien mérité de l'humanité par leurs écrits sur l'Économie politique. Ouvrage publié par P. Boscovitch, ami de l'auteur, Bassano, 2 vols. 8vo.—Mirabeau was one of the principal writers in the ÉPHÉMÉRIDES du citoyen (1765 to 1768), and the Journal de l'agriculture, du commerce, et des finances (1764 to 1774).—Among his other works may be mentioned Réponse du correspondant à son banquier, 1759, 4to (a reply to FORBONNAIS).—*Éléments de philosophie rurale*, La Haye, 1767, 12mo (an abridgment of the *Philosophie rurale*).—*Lettre sur le commerce des grains*, Amsterdam and Paris, 1768, 12mo.—*Les Économiques par L. D. H. dédiées au grand-duc de Toscane.* Amsterdam and Paris, 1769-72, 2 vols. 4to or 4 vols. 12mo.—*Lettres d'un ingénieur de province à un intendant des ponts et chaussées, pour servir de suite à l'Ami des Hommes,* Avignon, 1770, 12mo.—*Lettres Économiques,* Amsterdam, 1770, 12mo.—*La Science, ou les Droits et les Devoirs de l'homme, par L. D. H.,* Lausanne, 1774, 12mo. — *Lettre sur la législation par L. D. H.,* Berne, 1775, 3 vols. 12mo.—*Supplément à la théorie de l'impôt,* La Haye, 1776.—*Éducation civile d'un prince par L. D. H.,* Doulac, 1788, 8vo.—*Rêve d'un goutteux, ou le Principal,* (end of 1788) an 8vo pamphlet, his hopes of the Constituent Assembly about to meet.

[See *Mémoires . . . de Mirabeau écrits par Lui-même, par son Père, son Oncle, et son Fils Adoptif* (Lucas de Montigny), Paris, 1834-35, 8 vols. 8vo. —Mirabeau *fils, Lettres écrites du donjon de Vincennes . . . recueillies par P. Manuel,* 4me ed., Paris 1803, 8 vols. 12mo.—L. de Loménie, *Les Mirabeau,* Paris, 1879-91, 5 vols. 8vo (M. de Loménie has rehabilitated the private character of the elder Mirabeau by a careful examination of the facts which explain and in great measure excuse his severity towards his wife and children. He has convicted M. de Montigny of prejudice and misrepresentation, and has made clear the admiration which in his latest years the younger Mirabeau expressed for his father).—E. Daire, *Les Physiocrates,* Paris, 1846, 2 vols. 8vo.— L. de Lavergne, *Les économistes français du xviii⁰ siècle,* Paris, 1870.— C. Knies, *Brieflicher Verkehr Karl Friedrichs von Baden mit Mirabeau und Du Pont,* Heidelberg, 1892, 2 vols. 8vo.—A. Stern, *Das Leben Mirabeaus.* Berlin, 1889, 2 vols. 8vo.—A. Oncken, *Der ältere Mirabeau und die oekonomische Gesellschaft in Bern,* Berne, 1886.—G. Schelle, *Du Pont de Nemours et l'École physiocratique,* Paris, 1888.— Strecheisen-Moulton, *J. J. Rousseau, ses Amis et ses ennemis,* Paris, 1865, 2 vols. 8vo.—Grimblot, *Souvenirs du Baron Gleichen,* 1868.—S. Bauer in Conrad's *Jahrbücher,* Bd. 1, H. 2, NF. 145.— Henry Higgs in *Economic Journal,* i. 262, iii. 354. —Unpublished manuscripts in the Archives Nationales, Paris.]   H. H.

MIRABEAU, HONORÉ GABRIEL RIQUETTI, Comte de (1749-1791), born at Bignon near Nemours, and died in Paris.

A son of the Marquis of MIRABEAU (*q.v.*), the many wild incidents of his stormy life and the extraordinary force of his character caused him to occupy a very different position in general history from his father. The political career of the son is bounded by little more than two years (1789-1791), but during them he won an immense though an evanescent influence, and seemed for a moment as if he would have swayed the whole course of the revolution. "One can say that, had Mirabeau lived, the history of France and of the world had been different," Carlyle, *French Revolution* (chapter on "Mirabeau"). Here, however, we are concerned only with his economic reputation, which was far inferior to that of his father.

Though not a dogmatic economist, he employed his wonderful eloquence on subjects distinctly economic in character. Setting aside his dissolute youth and certain works regrettable for his reputation, and willingly omitting his acrid political writings, his pamphlets on *La Caisse d'escompte, la Banque Saint-Charles, la Compagnie des eaux,* and even his *Dénonciation de l'agiotage,* though they are polemical in character and directed against individuals and particular interests, and his speeches at the national assembly deserve attention, peculiarly the *Discours contre la banqueroute* (26th September 1789). The speeches and opinions of Mirabeau were published by Barthe in 1820, 3 vols. 8vo, and more recently by M. A. Vermorel, 5 vols. 12mo, in the *Bibliothèque Nationale.*   A. C. f.

[See also LOMÉNIE, LOUIS DE.]

MIRO, VICENZO DE (18th century), was regent of the supreme council of Italy. Charles VI. emperor of Germany and archduke of Austria, appointed him president of the commission of 1718, summoned to organise a new census for the state of Milan. This census was celebrated in the history of taxation. The object of the system proposed was to remedy the inequalities of the ESTIMO (*q.v.*) fixed in 1548, and to establish a fair proportion between the payments of the contributors.

The commission presided over by Miro fixed the basis of the taxation, proposed the regulations required, and almost completed the whole work. Miro remained in office until 1731. The labours of the commission were interrupted by the war in 1733. The work was resumed in 1749 by a second commission, under the presidency of POMPEO NERI (*q.v.*). This was dissolved in 1758. A government commission rearranged the CATASTO (*q.v.*) in 1760.

[Carlo Lupi, *Storia dei principii delle massime e delle regole seguite nella formazione del catasto prediale introdotto nello stato di Milano l' anno 1760.* Milan, 1825.]   U. R.

MISSELDEN, EDWARD (early 17th century). was deputy-governor of the merchant adventurers company at Delft between 1623 and 1633, and negotiated a private treaty with the Dutch and the East India Company, who employed him from 1624 to 1628 in their negotiations about the Amboyna outrages. He had various missions on behalf of the merchant adventurers. The appointment of the standing commission on trade in 1622 give rise to his—

Free Trade, or the Means to make Trade flourish; wherein the causes of the decay of trade in this kingdom are discussed, and the remedies also to remove the same are represented (Lond., 1622, 8vo, reprinted in 1651). The author points out (I.) the causes of the want of money here, which are (*a*) the value of English coins. These are current at a higher rate in Holland, whither the money is attracted. (*b*) The excessive consumption of foreign commodities. (*c*) The want of an East India stock here. (II.) The causes of the foreign want of money, which are (*a*) the recent wars ; (*b*) the trades maintained out of Christendom with ready money. The causes of the decay of trade are found by Misselden to be the scarcity of money and the want of the East India stock, also usury and heavy lawsuits. The fish trade is decayed by the encroachments of strangers on our coasts. The disturbances in the cloth trade, the ill-making and false-sealing of cloths, are also blamed. The export of wool and wool-fells is a grievance ; and the author censures the merchants adventurers for their heavy impositions on English cloths. Ch. iii. deals with monopoly ; and ch. iv. with the want of government in trade. The remedies proposed by Misselden are to make foreign coins current at equal value with our own, and so keep the money in the realm ; to reform excessive consumption of foreign commodities by allowing only certain imports, say of the tobacco grown in Virginia or the Bermudas only. Merchant ships ought, he says, to go in fleets together for safety. The remedy for usury he finds to be the plentiful circulation of money and bills of exchange, and he advocates the total uprooting of monopolies. MALYNES (q.v.) attacked Misselden as overlooking "the predominant part of trade"—viz. the mistery of exchange. The latter replied in *The Circle of Commerce: Or the Balance of Trade, in defence of Free Trade, opposed to Malynes Little Fish and his Great Whale, and poized against them in the scale; wherein also exchanges in general are considered,* J. Dawson for N. Bourne, Lond., 1623, 4to.   A. L.

[*Dict. of Nat. Biogr.*, xxxviii. pp. 51-2.]

MISTERY (or MYSTERYE ; MYSTERY is a form dating from the 17th century), was a common designation in the later middle ages for a body of persons engaged in a particular branch of manufacture or trade, not in their capacity as individuals but as an organised group. It has no etymological connection with μυστήριον ; and its association with that which is "mysterious" belongs to an age when its original meaning was forgotten. It is derived from the Latin *ministerium*, through the mediæval form *misteria;* and it was used precisely in the same way as the French forms *mistere, mestrer, mestier,* and *métier.* Its introduction into England was probably due to the use of French in official documents ; and the native English term, which was used side by side and interchangeably with it, was *Craft.*   W. J. A.

MOFFAT, ROBERT SCOTT (19th century): The author of *The Economy of Consumption: An Omitted Chapter in Political Economy* (1878), in which Mill's theory of capital, his doctrine that there cannot be a general over-production of commodities, and other approved tenets and authors, are subjected to a hostile criticism. The practical outcome of the work is to recommend as "the true policy of the labourer" what is called a time-policy —that is, the limitation of the hours of the work, rather than of the rate of the wages. A portion of the work relating to this policy is reprinted as a separate book, entitled, *The Principle of a Time-Policy, being an Exposition of a Method of Settling Disputes between Employers and Labourers in*

regard to Time and Wages by a simple process of Mercantile Barter, without recourse to Strikes or Locks-Out (1878). In the preface some reviews of the preceding work, one of them by Cliffe Leslie, all of them exceedingly unfavourable, are quoted at some length and rebutted. The author further enforces his principle in a letter to Lord Justice Bramwell on the *Regulation of Production.* He also wrote *Henry George the Orthodox.*
          F. Y. E.

MOHEAU. This statistical writer of the 18th century scarcely received at the time the due acknowledgment of his deserts. Even his book *Recherches et Considerations sur la Population de la France,* was attributed by Lalande, in the *Journal des Savants,* to Montyon, who (see Meitzen, *History of Statistics*) assisted in the work. The first portion of the *Recherches* contains statistical tables, the second is devoted to the analysis of various causes likely to influence population.

The dedication "*à un roi*" is dated 1774, and the permission to print it, 1777 (*Dict. de l'économie Politique,* art. "Moheau.")

Moheau's work was published in Paris, Montard, 1778 ; 2 books of 280 and 160 pp. in 1 vol. 8vo.
[M'Culloch, *Literature of Pol. Econ.,* p. 264, speaks highly of it, moreover recommending his book as a model for similar work.]   A. L.

MOHL, ROBERT VON (1799-1875) was successively professor of political science in the universities of Tübingen and of Heidelberg, an official in Wurtemberg, the minister of justice of Germany under the government of the Frankfort parliament of 1848, and the representative of Baden at Frankfort and Munich (1861-1871). At his death he was a member of the German Reichstag representing an electoral district of Baden.

His literary activity was considerable, his subjects being public and administrative law. His two principal works are the *Polizeiwissenschaft* (3rd ed. 1832-34, 1844-45, and 1866) and the *Geschichte und Litteratur der Staatswissenschaften* (1855-58). Mohl does not take the word *Polizei* in its present restricted sense of repressive justice, but in the wider sense of internal and administrative state-policy, as it was often understood by old German and French writers. According to his own definition, the *Polizeiwissenschaft* is "the systematically ordered science, which explains the principles on which the state ought to interpose to protect its citizens against overpowerful external hindrances," but his book only deals with the principles of the science in the *Rechtstaat,* or legal state, by which he means the state "where the collective life of the nation is so ordered that each individual member is helped and assisted towards the utmost possible free and many-sided display and utilisation of his individual energies." In the *Rechtstaat,* the scope of the state is thus mainly negative, although many not purely negative interferences may be sanctioned on motives of expediency and in new cases. For instance, Mohl would not be adverse, in cases of over-population, to compulsory emigration enjoined according to a lottery arranged much on the same basis as the military conscription in force on the continent. For all this, on the whole and in principle, the views of Mohl are those of a liberal statesman.

Mohl's *Geschichte und Litteratur der Staatswissenschaften*, is not written on the ordinary plan of a continuous history of development, but under the form of bibliographical monographs. It is a real monument of both historical and critical learning. It only deals with modern states after the end of the middle ages.

[Cohn, *Hist. of Pol. Econ.*] E. Ca.

MOHUR. The Indian government mohur is a token gold coin nominally representing the sum of 15 standard silver rupees. It weighs 180 grains (the same weight as the silver rupee), and is composed of gold of the millesimal fineness of 916·6. Its intrinsic value in sterling is £1 : 9 : 2¼ (⅓ fine), whereas the gold value of 15 silver rupees, at the present low price of silver (1895), is little more than 16s. The gold coins of India are, however, in practice bought and sold as bullion.

Besides the mohur there are gold pieces of the nominal value of 10 and 5 rupees ; these smaller coins being proportionate in weight to the mohur, and of the same fineness. Prior to 1835 mohurs of slightly different values were issued in the three presidencies. The Madras mohur was of the same weight and fineness as the present coin ; that struck in Bombay weighed 179 grains of gold 920 fine ; while that issued at Calcutta was, from 1818 onwards, of the weight of 204·7 grains, 916·6 fine, and from 1793 to 1818 had been of the weight of 190·894 grains, 995·7 fine.

[R. Chalmers, *A History of Currency in the British Colonies*, 1893.] F. E. A.

MOHUR, HISTORY OF. A gold coin of northern India (Persian *muhr* "a seal"). Like the silver RUPEE, the gold mohur probably represents the old Indian weight of 100 *ratis* (seeds of *Abrus Precatorius*), or about 175 grains, and dates back perhaps to Vedic times. Its weight has fluctuated with the endeavour to maintain a ratio between silver and gold. Thus, in the 14th century the weight of the mohur was raised to about 200 grains, but gradually reverted to the ancient type. In 1766 the East India Company struck for Bengal a mohur, which for the first time was declared to be a legal tender of payment, as the equivalent of 14 sicca rupees ; its gross weight was 179·67 grains, 833·33 fine, containing 149·72 grains of fine gold. In 1769 the Bengal coin was increased in gross weight to, 190·773 grains of *sequin* fineness, containing 190·1 grains of fine gold, which was to be legal tender for 16 sicca rupees. In 1818, when the fineness was reduced to eleven-twelfths in accordance with the Company's principle of 1806 (see *infra*), the gross weight of the Bengal 16 rupee mohur was raised to 204·7 grains,

making the fine weight 187·6 grains. In Bombay the mohur was not legal tender, but was approximately the equivalent of 15 Bombay rupees. From 1774 its gross weight was 179 grains, the millesimal fineness being 953 in 1774, and 920 from 1800 to 1833, with the result that the fine content of the "old" mohur was 170 grains as against 164·7 grains for the newer coin dating from 1800. Lastly, in 1818 the Company struck a mohur for Madras, which was to be a legal tender to government alone at 15 rupees. The following principles, which were embodied in the Madras coin of 1818, were laid down by the Company in 1806 : "Although we are fully satisfied of the propriety of the silver rupee being the principal measure of value and the money of account, yet we are by no means desirous of checking the circulation of gold, but of establishing a gold coin on a principle fitted for general use. This coin, in our opinion, should be called a gold rupee, and be made of the same standard as the silver rupee, viz. 180 troy grains gross weight, and 165 troy grains fine gold." In 1835 by Act XVII. the Company, in striking one uniform coinage for the whole of its dominions, and in establishing the Madras mohur as the type for the new Company's mohur, enacted that "no gold coin shall henceforward be a legal tender of payment in any of the territories of the East India Company." The same principles were observed as regards the government mohur by Act XIII. of 1862, when the Company's rule came to an end, and again by section 12 of the India Coinage Act, 1870. The weight and fineness of the coin have not been changed since 1818.

[Bengal, *Regulations of the East India Company*, Nos. xxxv. of 1793, xlv. of 1803, xiv. of 1818 ;—India Office records.—Sir James Steuart's *Principles of money applied to the present state of the coin of Bengal*, 1772.—Yule, *Hobson-Jobson, Gloss. of Indian Terms used in English*, 1886, pp. 438-39.] R. C.

MOIDORE (PORTUGUESE). The Moeda de Ouro (or gold money) was a Portuguese coin issued from about the year 1640 to the year 1732. It was of the millesimal fineness of 916·6 and weighed 83 grains, being, therefore, of the sterling value of 13s. 5½d. A double Moeda de Ouro was also issued, and it is to this coin, which had a world-wide circulation, that the name "moidore" is usually applied. F. E. A.

The coin known by this name, also called the Lisbonnine, was reckoned equal to 10 crusados or 4000 reis ; in 1688 Peter II. raised its rating to 4800 reis. Its uniform goodness, fineness, and weight, soon made it a favourite coin both in Europe and in the British colonies. Early in the 18th century, for instance, it was the chief coin current in Ireland, and had established itself in the West Indies, more particularly at Barbados.

In Ireland it had appeared before the close of the 17th century, coming in, as Sir Isaac Newton tells us, in course of trade ; rated at 28s. it was over-valued, and drove out silver and other gold, so that at the beginning of the 18th century, according to a contemporary writer, they were "reduced to moydores, the most inconvenient coin of all others in our present circumstances." Before the rating was reduced the coin had also spread over into, and become common in, the West of England.

In Barbados, whither it came about 1705, it passed for 35s. till 1715, and afterwards at 37s. 6d. And, although Mr. Chalmers calls it comparatively unimportant in the West Indies as compared with Spanish gold, in Barbados for many years the moidore was the usual coin named in local advertisements, and was clearly the most prominent coin in the island.

In spite of not being struck after 1732, it long remained in circulation, and only gradually gave way to its successor the JOHANNES (*q.v.*). The popular rating of the coin in English money was 27s., based on Sir Isaac Newton's rating in 1717, when he distinguishes between doppia moeda "new coined" 26s. 10¾d., doppia moeda "as they come to England," 26s. 9 $\frac{1}{10}$d.

[Kelly's *Cambist*, 1831.—Eckfeldt and Dubois, *Manual of Gold and Silver Coins*, Philadelphia, 1851.—Chalmers, *Colonial Currency*, p. 396.]

C. A. H.

MOLESWORTH, SIR WILLIAM (1810-1855), eighth baronet, was educated in Germany ; he afterwards went to Cambridge, whence he was expelled for challenging his tutor. He completed his studies at the university of Edinburgh. Molesworth was M.P. for East Cornwall from 1832 to 1837, following generally the lead of Grote, to whom he had been introduced by C. Buller. In 1835 he founded the *London Review*, which, after a few numbers, first by itself, and then of joint life with the *Westminster Review*, was finally, in 1837, absorbed in the latter. Molesworth's most noteworthy contributions are stated to have been "On the Orange Conspiracy," and "On the policy of the Radical Party in Parliament," (*London and Westminster Review*, April 1836 and January 1837). From 1837 to 1841 he represented Leeds in parliament. In the former year he obtained a committee of the House to inquire into the system of TRANSPORTATION (*q.v.*), and wrote the report, which strongly recommended its discontinuance. The four years 1841-45, during which he had no seat in the House, were mainly devoted to editing the works of HOBBES (*q.v.*). He returned to parliament in 1845 as member for Southwark, which seat he held till his death. From this time he chiefly applied himself to questions connected with the colonies. He strongly advocated the granting to them of complete self-government, and supported the views on colonisation of E. Gibbon WAKEFIELD (*q.v.*). There appears to have been considerable satisfaction in the colonies, when, after being first commissioner of works in Lord Aberdeen's government in 1853, Molesworth was made by Lord Palmerston, in 1855, secretary of state for the colonies. His period of office was too short for him to fulfil such expectations, but it may be noted that an act of his, in appointing a Canadian to the governorship of the Windward Islands, pointed the way to a method of consolidating the empire which is, at length, being followed. Molesworth was not a man of much originality of mind, nor a great orator or debater. He only spoke after laborious preparation, and his speeches, many of which were published, were of the nature of essays. He deserves notice as the first of the radicals to attain cabinet rank, though the peculiar kind of philosophic radicalism to which he adhered found little favour, on some grounds, with other members of the party.

[Molesworth's only literary work except articles in reviews, none of which were republished, and speeches, was an edition, in 17 volumes, of the *Works Latin and English of T. Hobbes*, London, 1839-46, 8vo.—See *Notices of the late Sir W. Molesworth* (privately printed), London, 1857, 8vo.—The *Dictionary of National Biography*, vol. xxxviii. notice by Mr. Leslie Stephen, which refers to *Philosophic Radicals of 1837* (privately printed) by Mrs. Grote, London, 1866.]

H. E. E.

MOLINA, LUDOVICUS (1535-1600), a distinguished Jesuit theologian of the 16th century, was a Spaniard by birth, and taught at Coimbra and Evora in Portugal. He was the author, among other works, of a treatise *De Justitia et Jure* (1593-1600), which dealt at considerable length with usury and the relation between business practices and moral theology (see INTEREST AND USURY). It was reprinted more than once, after his death, and exercised considerable influence on the subsequent development of economic thought.

[W. Endemann, *Studien in der romanisch-kanonistischen Wirthschafts- und Rechtslehre* (i., 1874, ii., 1883), treats him as a signal example of that method of argumentation which, in his opinion, finally took away all practical force from the earlier canonist doctrine, see especially, i. 385, ii. 118, 249 ; cp. Ashley, *Econ. Hist.*, i. pt. ii. 452.]

W. J. A.

MOLINÆUS, CAROLUS, the Latinised name of Dumoulin, Charles (1500-1566), a distinguished jurist of Paris, was the author of *Extricatio Labyrinthi de eo quod interest*, and *Tractatus contractuum et usurarum redituumque pecunia constitutorum* (both in 1546), and of some other pamphlets on the problem of usury. In these, especially in the *Tractatus*, he criticised the canonist doctrine with a freedom which aroused a storm of condemnation. He was forced to leave France, and his book was condemned to be burnt and put on the *Index*. In 1553 he accepted a professorship at Tübingen, and soon afterwards became a member of the council of the Duke of Würtemberg.

The opposition he encountered is not to be attributed to his practical conclusions, which scarcely went beyond those of some contemporary canonists of high authority, such as NAVARRUS (*q.v.*). Like them Molinæus approved of a regulation of interest by authority, and condemned uncharitable dealings. What seems to have distinguished him was his attack on the theory of usury itself,—his denial that all payment for the use of money was forbidden by holy writ, and bad in itself. The point at issue might seem to be a purely verbal and technical one : whether gain could be contracted for in consideration of a "loan" (MUTUUM) *eo nomine*. According to the current definition of the canonists, *mutuum* involved so complete a transference of property, that payment for the *use* became inconceivable. But what was really involved was the whole conception of usury, which the Roman Catholic Church was not disposed to abandon, and has not abandoned to the present.

[Endemann, *Studien*, i. p. 62.—Böhm-Bawerk, *Capital and Interest* (Eng. trans.), p. 29.—Ashley, *Econ. Hist.*, pt. ii. p. 454.]   W. J. A.

MOLLIEN, FRANÇOIS NICOLAS, Comte, (1758-1850) born at Rouen and died at Paris, was one of the ablest administrators of finance during the first empire. He began at the age of sixteen in the office of the FARMERS-GENERAL, which he left in 1791 for cotton-spinning in the environs of Evreux (Eure). In 1799 the first consul summoned him back to office, and entrusted him with the administration of the sinking fund, then just instituted. Mollien discharged the duties of his office with the most absolute honesty and with great ability, order, and punctuality. The emperor, who highly appreciated these qualities, appointed him, 27th January 1806, minister of the treasury in the place of Barbé-Marbois, who had been unable to defend himself against the insidious manœuvres of Ouvrard. Mollien held this post during the empire and the *cent jours*. From 1801 to 1815 the treasury was separated from the department of finance, strictly so called, and constituted a separate department. Under the restoration and the government of July, Mollien accepted no public office, though he was twice offered the administration of finance in the early part of the reign of Louis XVIII., but in 1819 he was made a peer and in this quality sat in the Luxemburg until 1848.

In many pamphlets on subjects of the day (1818), in parliamentary reports and some scattered notes, Mollien produced work of great value. He began to write, after 1817, his *Mémoirs d'un ministre du trésor public*, 1780-1815, 4 vols. 8vo,

1845. In 1837 a first, but very imperfect, edition was published. This remarkable work has never been on sale, and copies of it are very rare. The absorbing personality of Napoleon I. did not allow Mollien's talents their full value ; but his memoirs exhibit the solidity of his intellect, the sincerity of his statements, and the breadth of judgment which he applied to the incidents passing under his eyes, and to the events on which it is to be regretted that he had not a greater influence. Mollien was a man of strong character, and notwithstanding his devotion to Napoleon, who in his eyes represented France from 1800 to 1815, he maintained the right of expressing his opinions freely and his independence. At the council of state before 1806, and as minister of the treasury, he had often to oppose the ideas of Napoleon, who, however, was never displeased with him. He even sought his conversation and invited his criticism. Napoleon was not displeased with the boldness of Mollien, who after his conversations with the head of the state reproduced the whole of them in his memoirs. This gives that book its great importance. It is known that Mollien's father, a leading merchant, put the *Wealth of Nations* into the hands of his son as soon as the translation of Germain Garnier was published. The reading of this early fixed Mollien's views on the great truths of economics, as the perusal of his memoirs proves.

[See W. Bagehot's *Econ. Studies* (ed. 1880, p. 2), and his reference to Napoleon's phrase *Ce bon Mollien qui me donne des francs pendant que les autres ne me donnent que des idées*.—Also Cl. Jannet in *Le Capital, la spéculation et la Finance au XIXᵉ siècle* (1892).]   A. C. f.

MOLMEN were a class of manorial tenants defined by Vinogradoff (*Villainage in England*) as "rent-paying tenants who may be bound to some extra work, but who are very definitely distinguished from the 'Custumarii,' the great mass of tenants who render labour services." He regards them as standing below the freeholders, but as having risen from real serfdom by getting their tenure fixed and their services commuted, drawing this distinction between *mal* (a Danish word = rent) and GAFOL, that the former was a commuted, the latter an original money payment. If this view is correct—and the matter can hardly be regarded as settled—the chief interest of molmen and of their holdings, "molland," is the illustration they afford at an early period of the process by which the villeins in general afterwards became free. The word is of fairly frequent occurrence, especially at the time of Edward I.

[*English Hist. Review*, articles by Elton and Vinogradoff, July 1886, Round, January 1887, Stevenson, April 1887. For law of dower and female inheritance among molmen and for some differences between "mollond" and "werklond," see Archdeacon Hale, *Domesday of St. Paul's*.]   E. G. P.

MOLSTER, JOHANNES ADRIAAN (1827-1889).

A Dutch lawyer and writer of essays on public subjects in reviews, was the author of a *Geschiedenis der Staathuishoudkunde* (Amsterdam, 1857), a history of political economy, interesting for the information given in it on Dutch economic literature.   E. Ca.

MONCADA, SANCHO DE (beginning of the 17th century) lectured on theology in the university of Toledo, and published, in 1619, eight *Discursos* on various economic subjects, which were the uncompromising expression of the prohibitive tendencies then prevalent in Spain, and, consequently, obtained a wide celebrity among his countrymen. They were republished at Madrid in 1746 under the title *Restauracion Política de España*. Moncada does not admit for a moment that the wars abroad, the system of laws, the excessive number of idle persons, the debasement of the currency, etc., could fairly be looked upon as responsible for the depressed state of Spain : "the misfortune of Spain flows from the trade with foreigners, who carry away our raw material and our silver," p. 9, ed. 1746. His only remedy is the prohibition of exports of raw materials and precious metals, and of the imports of manufactured articles, enforced by the penalty of death pronounced against smuggling, and the delivering to the Inquisition of all persons accused of exporting money, "as this money is going to assist the enemies of the church," p. 40 of the 1st Discourse, *Riqueza Firme de España*. Still Moncada is aware that the influx of American gold and silver, had brought about the general rise of prices, which had put Spanish industry at a disadvantage in its competition with foreign countries, where the rise of prices was proceeding more slowly, *Disc. on España con Moneda*, p. 54.

Moncada concludes by demanding the erection of a special university for political science in Madrid, and the institution of lectures on the same subject in the provincial universities. These lectures are to be delivered in the vernacular language, not in Latin, pp. 147-159.

[Colmeiro, *Hist. de la Ec. Pol. en España*, ii., pp. 333-334.]   E. Ca.

MONDAYLAND. See LUNDINARIUM.

MONEDA FORERA, a poll tax levied first every seven and then every five years, by the kings of Castile, and paid as an acknowledgment of their royal prerogative. In time of financial distress the *Cortes* often granted at once three, five, or more *monedas*.   E. Ca.

MONEDA, PEDIDOS, or SERVICIOS (*Peita* or *Pecha* in Aragon), are the names given to the extraordinary subsidies voted by the *Cortes* of Castile. They were apportioned, but in a very irregular way, amongst the inhabitants according to their presumed means ; it was considered by some towns a valuable privilege to be exempted from them by their *fueros* or charters. It was officially admitted that "they yielded little and

left the fields untilled"; still many of them became permanent, under the name of *servicios ordinarios*. Noblemen and the clergy were exempted from the *servicios ordinarios*.

[Canga Arguelles, *Diccionario de la Hacienda* (London, 1826).]   E. Ca.

MONEDAGE, a general tax levied in Aragon on all movable and real property. Knights were the only persons exempted from *monedage*.
                                                  E. Ca.

MONETARY CONFERENCES (INTERNATIONAL). Four times in recent history the leading powers of the western world have met together by diplomatic arrangement to confer on monetary problems. These four great conferences, known as International Monetary Conferences, *par excellence*, were held at Paris in 1867, 1878, 1881, and the fourth in 1892 at Brussels. International conferences on monetary questions are, however, not restricted to these. The German states before the foundation of the empire, Germany and Austria, the Scandinavian kingdoms, the papal states, and the countries of the LATIN UNION, have held many monetary conferences of an international character, but only the four great conferences, in each of which over twelve countries were represented, are included in the scope of this article.

France and the countries of the Latin union enjoyed the privilege of a certain reciprocity in monetary policy, and the benefits of a common monetary unit many years before the formation of the Latin union in December 1865. The men who were instrumental in bringing about the union entertained bright dreams of the possibility of an international union of much greater dimensions, and of the establishment of an international money based on a common unit of value and standard of weight and !fineness. The success attending French efforts in outlining the policy of the Latin union led her government to undertake the greater task of relieving the commerce of the world of the difficulties and inconveniences of international exchange. Hence France sent out invitations to all the powers to join her in a conference to this end to be held in Paris, June 17th, 1867. Previously France had, through diplomatic correspondence, submitted copies of the Latin union treaty to the powers, and called special attention to the clause whereby other states might be admitted, and asked at the same time for a statement and discussion of the objection that any state might have to becoming a party to this compact. The idea at the basis of the conference called was in reality the extension of the treaty of 1865, though the invitations stated that "the commissioners will assemble without any programme arranged in anticipation—(and)—the conference proposed has not otherwise any immediate object than to call out an interchange of views and discussion of principles ; in a word to seek for the bases of ulterior negotiations."

Representatives of eighteen of the principal countries of Europe, and the United States of America, assembled under the presidency of the French minister of foreign affairs, and subsequently under that of the vice-president of the conference, the distinguished writer on money, M. de PARIEU, who at that time was vice-president of the French Council of State. Eight sessions in all were held, and the whole discussion centred in the question of uniformity of coinage. Few signs were visible of the "battle of the standards," "the future of silver," "bimetallism," etc., and similar questions which have been the all-absorbing topics of subsequent conferences. Following the order of topics arranged by an international committee, able and dignified discussion was given to all difficulties which might arise from any attempt to unify the coinage of different nations. The U.S. expressed itself willing to coin a gold dollar and its multiples, equal in weight and fineness to 25 frs., and urged France to issue a coin of this value, and England to reduce the sovereign to the value of 25 frs., and change its fineness from $\frac{11}{12}$ to $\frac{9}{10}$ fine. The cost and difficulty of re-coinage was thoroughly discussed, and the commissioners soon gave up any idea that may have been entertained of applying uniformity to any other than gold coins of which there seemed to be a relative scarcity, but which the majority of the countries seemed determined to introduce as soon as possible.

The first decision reached by the conference was that the cost to the several nations of adapting their coinage systems to some known and existing system would be less than in the case of the adoption of an entirely new system, and that under existing circumstances the Latin union treaty of 1865 offered the best basis for a general agreement. Secondly, gold was declared to be the only standard suited to international money ; Prussia, the most important silver-standard country represented at the conference, voted also for gold, it being agreed that some time might be necessary in which a transitional silver or double standard would obtain in silver-standard countries. The Netherlands was the only country to vote against the gold standard. It is interesting to note that Mr. Ruggles, the representative of the United States, declared emphatically that the United States had the gold standard, though the double standard existed legislatively but had been virtually abolished in practice. A scarcity of gold was, however, feared, and a resolution was adopted to the effect that "in countries that have had the silver standard up to this time, as well as in those of the double standard, that the relation between the value of gold and silver should not be established at a rate too low to permit the serious introduction of gold." It is significant

that Prussia voted "no" on this resolution, and the United States refused to vote.

Additional dignity and importance was attached to the conference by the Emperor of France deputing Prince Jerome Napoleon to preside over the sessions after the fourth session, and the fact that the Prince emphasised in strong language the chief aim of the conference and the hope that practical results in the shape of international diplomatic treaties on the subject would be accomplished. So positive a statement rather frightened the English delegates, and Sir Rivers Wilson reminded the president of the purely deliberative character of the proceedings according to the terms of the invitation, and further declared that England would occupy a very independent position with respect to changing her system of monetary units, weights, and standard to conform to any continental system.

The question of desirable fineness was readily settled at $\frac{9}{10}$ standard, and a unanimous vote declared that "there should be types with a common denominator for weights in gold coins of identical fineness." The five-franc piece was adopted as the common denominator, although a larger unit (e.g. ten francs), met with some favour in the discussion, and England and Sweden voted against the five-franc piece. It was further agreed that gold coins, with the common denominator of five francs, should have legal circulation in the states mutually bound by the monetary treaties. The twenty-five franc piece was added to the list of coins, though the fifteen franc piece, intended to harmonise with existing coinage in Holland and in South Germany, was rejected by a close vote.

With this the labours of the conference practically ended. The delegates supposed that they had found the basis of a fixed and fundamental international system of money in adopting the gold standard, coins of equal weight and fineness, and divided according to the decimal system with the five-franc piece as a unit. Such understanding applied only to gold coins : each state was to remain free to coin silver for change in any way it pleased.

France agreed to assume responsibility for re-convening the conference if further negotiation was necessary after replies had been received from the various governments upon receipt of the proceedings of the present one; an answer was requested on or before 15th February 1868. England favoured a much longer period of delay, and several other countries preferred some extension of the time to permit the question involved being discussed in their respective legislatures. The conference adjourned with buoyant hopes of success on 6th July 1867, but the results of its labours never met with a sufficiently successful response on the part of the powers to warrant a re-convening of the conference.

Certainly no more praiseworthy, prudent, and intelligent effort to bring about uniform coinage has ever been made, but it merely demonstrated that any such uniformity among nations, differing widely in habits and customs, cannot be secured at one blow, but must come, if ever, as the result of a very gradual evolutionary process.

The second international monetary conference was called by the United States of America in pursuance of an act of congress dated 28th February 1878, which directed the President to invite the governments of Europe to join in a "conference to adopt a common ratio between gold and silver for the purpose of establishing internationally the use of bimetallic money, and securing fixity of relative value between those two metals." Faith in international bimetallism as a remedy for monetary evils had gained ground since 1867. The silver production of the U.S. had attained immense proportions, and had secured as an industry great political influence in congress. The U.S. silver commission had made an elaborate report in 1876. Germany was well established on a gold basis, and German silver had disturbed the market and threatened greater depreciation. Some form of international bimetallism seemed feasible, and the question of ratio, it was thought, was the great obstacle which a conference might settle. The conference met in Paris, 16th August 1878. Twelve countries were represented. Germany alone of the great powers declined to participate.

The United States submitted two propositions: —(1) "It is the opinion of this assembly that it is not to be desired that silver should be excluded from free coinage in Europe and the United States of America. On the contrary, the assembly believe that it is desirable that the unrestricted coinage of silver, and its use as money of unlimited legal tender, should be retained where they exist, and, as far as practicable, restored where they have ceased to exist." (2) "The use of both gold and silver as unlimited legal tender money may be safely adopted: first, by equalising them at a relation to be fixed by international agreement; and secondly, by granting to each metal at the relation fixed equal terms of coinage, making no discrimination between them."

These propositions were discussed at great length, and much documentary evidence was presented, from several countries, bearing on their coinage and their attitude towards silver. The collective answers of the European powers, with the exception of Italy, to the propositions of the United States were presented at the seventh and last session, 29th August, in the following form:— "The delegates of the European states represented in the conference, having maturely considered the proposals of the representatives of the United States, recognise (1) that it is necessary to maintain in the world the monetary functions of silver as well as those of gold, but that the selection for use of one or the other of the two metals, or of

both simultaneously, should be governed by the special position of each state or group of states. (2) That the question of the restriction of the coinage of silver should equally be left to the discretion of each state or group of states, according to the particular circumstances in which they may find themselves placed; and the more so, in that the disturbance produced during the recent years in the silver market has variously affected the monetary situation of the several countries. (3) That the differences of opinion which have appeared, and the fact that even some of the states which have the double standard find it impossible to enter into a mutual engagement with regard to the free coinage of silver, exclude the discussion of the adoption of a common ratio between the two metals." The delegates of the United States, in replying to these answers, stated that they had come to the conference expressly to enter into a mutual engagement for the free coinage of silver, and that the failure of attaining any practical results did not rest with them. The Italian delegates maintained that the conference "in systematically avoiding to pronounce itself upon the possibility or impossibility of a fixed relation, to be established by way of international treaty, between coins of gold and silver, leaves its task unfinished." They further claimed that the French ratio could be maintained by France, England, and the United States.

The third international monetary conference was convened by joint action of the French and American governments, "to examine and adopt, for the purpose of submitting the same to the governments represented, a plan and a system for the establishment of the use of gold and silver as bi-metallic money according to a settled relative value between those metals." The conference met at Paris in July 1881, and held thirteen sessions.

Nineteen countries were represented. At the close the following declaration was made in the name of the French and American governments:—"(1) That the depreciation and great fluctuations in the value of silver relatively to gold are injurious to commerce and to the general prosperity, and the establishment of a fixed ratio of value between them would produce the most important benefits to the commerce of the world. (2) That a bi-metallic convention entered into by an important group of states for the free coinage of both silver and gold at a fixed ratio and with full legal-tender faculty, would cause and maintain a stability in the relative value of the two metals suitable to the interests and requirements of commerce. (3) That a convention which should include England, France, Germany, and the United States, with the concurrence of other states, which this combination would assure, would be adequate to produce and maintain throughout the commercial world the relation between the two metals that such convention should adopt. (4) That any ratio now, or lately, in use by any commercial nation, if so adopted, could be maintained, but that the adoption of the ratio $15\frac{1}{2}$ to 1 would accomplish the object with less disturbance to existing monetary systems than any other ratio."

This declaration met with outspoken opposition especially from Mr. Forsell of Sweden, who said that it was better to acknowledge at once that bimetallism had collapsed, and that the resolutions of the European delegates at the conference of 1878 should be re-affirmed. The conference adjourned to 12th April 1882, to give time for further instructions from the several governments and scope to diplomatic negotiations, but was never reconvened.

At the international exhibition of 1889 at Paris, an attempt was made to organise a monetary conference. A number of sessions were held and many eminent persons took part. The report of the discussions can be found in the general reports of the exhibition. This conference, however, is rarely mentioned as one of the international conferences, because no official importance was attached to its proceedings, and its delegates were not appointed directly by their respective governments for this purpose.

The fourth international conference was called by the United States "for the purpose of conferring as to what measure, if any, can be taken to increase the use of silver as money in the currency systems of nations." It met at Brussels, 22nd November 1892, and held ten sessions, adjourning 20th December to meet 30th May 1893. Twenty countries were represented. As the United States called the conference, it was expected that the American government would have some definite plan to present for securing the end in view—an increase in the use of silver. The instructions to the American delegates were extremely vague, simply saying that they should do all in their power to "bring about a stable relation between gold and silver . . . (and) to secure, if possible, an agreement among the chief commercial countries of the world looking to international bimetallism . . . (and) failing to secure international bimetallism . . . to secure some action upon the part of European countries looking to a large use of silver as currency, in order to put an end to the further depreciation of that metal." After some delay at the beginning of the conference, the representatives of other countries refusing to express any opinions until the United States presented a plan, the following general declaration was made on the part of the United States delegation :

1. That the re-establishment and maintenance of a fixed parity between gold and silver, and the continued use of both as coined money of full debt-paying power, would be productive of important benefits to the world.

2. That these ends can be accomplished by removing the legal restrictions which now exist on the coinage of silver into full legal tender-money, and restoring by international agreement the parity of value between the metals which existed prior to 1873 at such ratio as may be decided upon by this conference.

3. That the essential provisions of such an international agreement should be

   1. Unrestricted coinage of both gold and silver into money of full debt-paying power.

   2. Fixing the ratio in coinage between the two metals.

   3. Establishing a uniform charge (if any) to the public for the manufacture of gold and silver coins.

The discussion of this programme, which was so general and contained nothing but a re-statement of the old bimetallic position, soon proved futile and destined to come to nought. The American delegates said that the complications arising from their ignorance of the public law of the different European countries made it impossible for them to outline a more detailed scheme except after much discussion on the part of the conference. They called attention to a plan which had been proposed at the conference of 1881 by M. Moritz Levy to withdraw gold coins and notes of less value than 20 francs, and that of Adolph Soetbeer which was published in the *Hamburgische Börsenhalle* for 23rd August 1892, and in the *Neue Freie Presse*, Vienna, 20th September 1892, shortly prior to Dr. Soetbeer's death. Dr. Soetbeer proposed :

1. The acknowledgment of a fixed weight of pure gold as a universal basis for currency.

2. Recoining all gold and issuing no gold coins of less than 5·8065 grammes of pure gold (= 20 francs or $3.96) at mint charges of 2 per thousand (= $\frac{1}{5}$ of 1 per cent) and agreement to withdraw from circulation all smaller gold coins within a period of ten years.

3. Issue of gold certificates for gold deposits in amounts, or multiples, of 500 grammes of pure gold, upon actual deposits of coin.

4. Retirement of all paper money representing less than the value of 5·8065 grammes pure gold and to issue no more.

5. Retirement within fifteen years of all silver coins current with a value of more than 10 per cent of the fixed minimum gold coin, and coining major silver coins to be receivable for all public dues by the country issuing them, to any amount, at the ratio of 20 to 1 ; to be legal tender to thrice the amount of lowest gold coin ; coinage only on government account.

6. Subsidiary silver coins to be issued as each country may determine.

7. Silver certificates to be issued only against actual deposits of major silver coins, in denominations of half the smallest gold coin or any multiple.

8. Mutual reports of laws and operations to be exchanged annually.

9. Withdrawal from compact only upon one year's notice.

These two propositions, together with that of Baron Alfred de Rothschild, for the establishment of a union of the governments represented, into a syndicate which should guarantee the purchase of £5,000,000 sterling worth of silver annually for five years, provided the price did not go up beyond 43 pence per ounce standard, and also provided the United States government continued its purchases of 54,000,000 of ounces yearly, received the chief share of attention at the conference. Suggestions, looking to the withdrawal from circulation of small notes and small gold coins in order to force more silver into use and the issue of silver certificates on bars, and schemes requiring privileged banks of issue to hold silver as well as gold reserves, had been made at the conference of 1881 but had attracted little attention. The discussion of such measures, looking to the increased use of silver, but maintaining strictly the gold standard, was the characteristic feature of the Brussels conference. The plans already mentioned, as well as others made by M. Tietgen, Sir Wm. Houldsworth, M. Allard, M. de Foville, M. Forsell, M. M. Levi, and M. Sainctelette, were referred to a special committee of twelve, which made two reports, in one of which the plan of M. Moritz Levy was favourably recommended. The president of the conference declared that he found it impossible to keep the ensuing discussion to the subject before the conference, namely, the report of the committee ; it would expand in all cases to a discussion of the general principles of bimetallism. It was therefore agreed that the simple proposition of the United States, respecting bimetallism, be taken up. Long discourses followed ; that of Senator Jones of the United States, which covers 100 folio pages of the *Procès-verbaux*, going into the greatest detail. A few sessions of aimless general discussion sufficed to show that no agreement could be reached between the advocates of the single and double standard. The usual statements that the other countries must wait for England to take the initiative in a bimetallic union were made, and the usual device, adjournment for further advice from the several governments, was followed. The conference adjourned, to meet 30th May 1893, but was never re-convened. The debates of this last conference were less original and of less value than those of any of the preceding ones. The questions discussed had become firmly rooted in the politics of the various countries, and the discussion was consequently less free and untrammelled. The specific propositions for temporary, if not permanent, relief of generally admitted congested monetary symptoms, which to some extent distinguished the Brussels conference from its predecessors, can hardly be said to have received the discussion and adequate consideration they deserved, so intense was the feeling on the general bimetallic controversy.

Since the adjournment of the Brussels conference the parliaments of England and Germany were both compelled by strong political pressure to pass resolutions (House of Commons, Res. 26th February 1895, German Reichstag, Res. 16th February 1895) favouring another conference, and the congress of the United States, just previous to its recent adjournment, passed a resolution (3rd March 1895) providing for the appointment of delegates should a new conference be called. Later (July 1895), all interested parties were looking to the chancellor of the German empire to take the initiative in calling another conference, but he did not relish the responsibility, being disinclined to take action until forced to do so by the agrarian-bimetallic party in Germany. On 17th March 1896, the House of Commons agreed to a resolution urging on "the

Government the advisability of doing all in their power to secure by international agreement a stable monetary par of exchange between gold and silver." No immediate action however appears likely to follow.

[The official proceedings of the various conferences have been published in the French language under the general title *Conférence Monétaire Internationale*, Procès-verbaux. The dates of these publications are as follows :
(1) *Pub. of the Ministère des affaires étrangères*, Paris, Impr. imp., 1867.—(2) Ditto, Paris, Impr. nat., 1878.—(3) Ditto, 2 vols. *a.* Sessions 1 to 8, avril-mai, 1881. Paris, Impr. nat., 1881, p. 341 ; *b.* Sessions 9 to 13, juin-juillet, 1881, p. 226, Paris, 1881.—(4) *Conférence Monétaire Internationale*, 1892, Procès-verbaux. Bruxelles, 1892, p. 424.

These official reports have been translated into the various European languages by the various governments that participated. For English translations, see the following :
" Report of the Master of the Mint and Mr. Rivers Wilson on the Inter. Mon. Conf. held in Paris, June 1867." London, March 1868.—"Diplomatic Correspondence" (U. S. Cong. Pub.), 2nd Sess. 40th Cong., vol. i. 1867-68, pp. 295-380. (Contains the diplom. cor. of the American government, the report of the U.S. commissioners, and the full text of conference of 1867.)—International Monetary Conference, 1878. Washington, Govt. Printing Office, 1879. Sen. Exec. Doc., No. 58, 45th Cong., 3rd Sess., p. 910. (A huge volume containing English translation of proceedings and several hundred pages of historical material, collected by S. Dana Horton, bearing on monetary treaties and the monetary question in general.) Proceedings of the International Monetary Conference, 1881 (April, May, June, and July). Washington, 1877, p. 558. H. R. Misc. Doc. 396, pt. 3, 49th Cong. 1 Sess. Proceedings of the Brussels Monetary Conference. Washington, 1893, Govt. Printing Office.

For summaries of the proceedings and brief discussion of the work of the several conferences, see *Coinage Laws of the United States*, 1792-1894, 4th ed., Washington, 1894, p. 847. Also *Monetary Systems of the World*, by M. L. Muhleman, pp. 170-176, New York, 1895. (Not always free from slight errors in statement of facts).]

S. M'C. L.

MONEY. The term "money" is applied to any commodity, whatever its substance or its form, which, whether by law or by convention, becomes the common medium of exchange in any community. The difficulties of BARTER or TRUCK, that is of direct exchange, are so great that subdivision of labour and diversification of industry can be carried but a very little way under such a system. Tribes in no very advanced stage feel the need of a common medium of exchange ; hence, the history of money is almost co-extensive with the history of mankind beyond the purely savage state. Oxen were used as money among the Greeks of the Homeric period. Sheep served the Italians at a later period, as the common medium of exchange. After the abandonment of Britain by the Romans, we find the inhabitants, in the scarcity of coin, returning to the use of "living money," especially in Scotland and Wales. "It is very possible," says Sir Henry Maine, "that kine were first exclusively valued for their flesh and milk ; but it is clear that, in very early times, a distinct and special importance belonged to them as the instrument or medium of exchange." Cattle and sheep may be a good money or an inconvenient money, according to the circumstances of the community. In a pastoral state they present many advantages. They carry themselves, and thus avoid one of the objections to the employment of grain. The opportunities for grazing which everywhere exist, and the familiarity of all persons with guarding and tending animals, reduce the trouble and risk of using them. On the other hand, cattle and sheep have two serious drawbacks as money. The first is, that each animal represents too large an expenditure of labour to answer in small purchases. Even calves and lambs scarcely meet the requirements of "change." The second drawback is, want of uniformity in quality. Even in a picked herd or flock there is great room for choice. If goods are sold for cattle or sheep, the buyers will pay in the smallest and lankiest specimens to be found. This was the experience of the Massachusetts colony so long as cattle were received in payment of taxes. If such disadvantages attend the use of "living money" even in a pastoral state, the cost of keeping them and the risk and trouble which attend their nurture and custody in any highly civilised state are so great as absolutely to preclude their use. Of the cereals, wheat, corn, and rye have extensively fulfilled this office. These and other grains have two important qualifications for such use: (1) the being in universal request for consumption as food : and (2) in allowing almost indefinite subdivision. But they are subject to two serious drawbacks : (1) in the great weight of a quantity which represents a day's labour ; and (2) through their liability to deterioration from rust, insects, excessive moisture, undue heating, or the mere passage of time.

The literature of travel is full of stories regarding the rice money of the Coromandel shore, the cacao money of the aboriginal Mexicans, the oil money of the Ionian islands, the rock-salt money of Abyssinia, the wampum money of the early New Englanders, the tobacco money of Maryland and Virginia in the same period, the tea money of the Russian fairs, the date money of the African oases, the beaver and sealskin money of many northern countries, and a host of other commodities adopted, in one place or another, for meeting the requirements of a common medium of exchange. One great class of substances have a peculiar importance in the history of money, from the earliest times and amid a wide circle of nations. The metals, especially seven of them, have been found to possess in a high degree the material properties required. Iron, lead, tin, and copper, one or another, early became the money of most of the countries whose history is known. The money of Lacedæmon was of iron ; and this metal, at least until recent times,. served the inhabitants of Senegambia ; Sweden, when impoverished by the wars of Charles XII., went back to the use of COPPER MONEY (q.v.). Lead was extensively employed in exchange by the early Romans and the early English ; and is still given and taken in Burmah in small payments. Tin was used by the Mexicans as money, even after silver and gold were known. It was long so employed in Sweden ; and more recently served in that capacity among the Chinese, along the shores of the Malay peninsula, and in Prince of Wales' Island. Of the four metals named, however, copper has the greatest importance in the history of money. From its higher cost of production it superseded iron when that metal came, in the development of mining industry, to possess a value for its bulk unsuited to the uses of exchange ; while yet silver was too precious for the ordinary transactions of daily life. During the silver famine of the middle ages, copper came back to be the principal money of the people of Europe. The employment of copper in a diminishing degree has continued in Europe and America nearly down to our own day ; but this metal, or recently the closely allied bronze, has now sunk in all civilised states to the rank of "token-money," or change. Over no small part of the world, however, it is still an important element in the monetary circulation. We have now to speak of a fifth metal. Between 1828 and 1845 the emperor of Russia sought to bring platinum into use as a money metal ; but the effort failed, owing to the extreme difficulty of rendering that metal from ingots into coin, and from coin into ingots, as the exigencies of exchange might require.

Of all the metals, two have enjoyed a pre-eminence in the history of money which has given them the name of the PRECIOUS METALS. Not that they are the most costly. Several are more valuable even than gold ; but this is true only of metals found in extremely limited quantity, like iridium or venadium, far below the requirements of a general medium of exchange. Of the two precious metals, silver was first used as money. We read of it in early Hebrew history. It was long coined by the Greeks and Romans, while gold remained merely treasure, devoted to regal and sacerdotal uses. The extreme beauty of silver, with its numerous applications to the economy of, life, make it an object of admiration and desire among people of all degrees of social advancement. Easily fusible, highly ductile, nearly imperishable, silver would have filled our utmost conception of a money-metal did not the earth yield one transcendent product, in comparison with which even silver fades from desire. "The compendious value of gold," to use Mr. Jacob's expression, allowing a vast amount of purchasing power to be concentrated for conveyance or concealment in little bulk ; its durability, its fusibility, ductility, and malleability, properties of the highest importance for the purposes of coinage and circulation, and its numerous uses in the industrial and decorative arts,—all these combine to make it chief of money-metals.

The foregoing are among the articles which have served the world in one stage or another of social advancement, as the common medium of exchange. It is of the essence of money that all persons who have anything to sell shall take it as a matter of course. The extensive use of an article in exchange does not necessarily make it money. Those transactions, however numerous and important, may be nothing but acts of barter. So long as men take an article in exchange, having any great degree of uncertainty as to their finding a person who will take it from them ; so long as men accept it with the feeling that it is something which they are buying, and which they will have to sell over again, something for which they must needs hunt up a purchaser, that article is not money. Anything to be money must have acceptability so nearly universal that practically every person who has any product or service to dispose of will freely take it, in preference to seeking, at the time, the specific products or services which he may require from others, since he is fully assured that with this thing, money, he can, at times and in form and in amount to suit his immediate necessities, obtain what he shall desire. Each person, thus, whatever his place in the industrial order, accepts money without reference either to his own need to consume any of the particular article so used, or to the character or the credit of the person who offers it. When he has anything to sell, he takes money from any man, because he knows that any other man will take it from him whenever he wishes in his turn to buy. If an article reaches this degree of acceptability, it becomes money, no matter what it is made of or why people want it. The carved pebbles formerly used by the Ethiopians, the wampum which circulated in the 17th century between the New England colonists and the natives, the glass beads used along the Arabian Gulf, the shells and red feathers employed throughout the isles of the Indian Ocean, were all money, though capable of serving no purpose but that of ornament and decoration.

We have thus far spoken of the principal, the characteristic function of money, namely, that of the common medium of exchange. This is the distinguishing office of money. Whatever does this is money. But incidentally, money performs another important service to exchange, namely, by furnishing a price-list, or price-current, of all articles in the market. Since these are, by turns, exchanged for money, each is expressed in terms of money ; and, in consequence, all can at once and readily be compared among themselves as to value. The value of any article in terms of money is called its PRICE. The foregoing office of money has been termed by economists generally that of a measure of value ; but that term is not descriptive, and has proved highly misleading. A better statement would be that money in this connection fulfils the office of the common denominator in exchange, or denominator of values (see DENOMINATOR, COMMON). The numerators consist of the prices of the several articles in the market ; and, inasmuch as the denominator is common to all, these can readily be compared among themselves. Some economists have made the mistake of speaking of this as an independent, and even as the principal office of money. Thus, Mr. Mill says that "the first and most obvious" of the inconveniences of doing without money would be "the want of a common measure of values" : and Prof. Francis Bowen says, "We can do without money as a medium of exchange, and can even barter commodities for other commodities without the use of any medium. But we cannot do without money as a common standard or measure of value." Even Prof. Jevons writes as if one article might serve as a medium of exchange, while another might serve as a measure of value, in the same community. But it ought to be perfectly evident on a moment's reflection that it is only by, and through, an article being used as the common medium of exchange, that we obtain the prices which make up the price-list or price-current. Consequently, if we did without money as the medium of exchange, we should perforce have to do without it as the denominator of values. Having thus seen the two ways in which money, even in societies but a little advanced industrially and commercially, facilitates exchange, allowing the division of labour to be carried out to its economic maximum, time and place considered, we are prepared to make a better statement than that yet offered regarding the primitive function of money ; and we say that money serves as the common medium of exchange : (a) dispensing with "the double coincidence of wants and of possessions," to use the phrase of

Prof. Jevons, which is involved in direct exchange ; (*b*) furnishing a price-current of all commodities in the market.

Regarding the philosophy of money in its uses thus far described, there is practically no difference of opinion among economists of standing. The value of money is admitted by all to be governed by the operation of the ordinary law of demand and supply. There being—in any community, at any time, according to the state of the arts and according to the extent to which the division of labour has been carried,—an economic need or demand for a certain amount of money-work to be done, in carrying commodities from producers to consumers, the quantity of the money-thing which is available to do that work will determine its value. If shells constitute the money of a community living by the sea, then, if there be much exchanging to be done, that is, if there be a large demand for shells to effect exchanges, and if shells be scarce, each shell will have a high value. Prices will be correspondingly low, that is, a large amount of commodities will sell for but few shells. If the supply of shells be suddenly increased, as by a great storm bringing them up on to the shore, the value of shells will fall ; that is, prices will rise. The relation of the value of primitive money to cost of production is, with a single exception to be hereafter noted, the same as in the case of any commodity not used as money. If the cost of production of that which serves as money is diminished, as by improvements in an art or by the discovery of new resources in nature, the supply will be increased, and its value will fall in consequence, that is, prices will rise. If the cost of production of that which serves as money is increased, as by the exhaustion of natural resources, its supply will fall off ; its value, demand remaining constant, will be enhanced, that is, prices will fall. The exception above referred to is that noted by Mr. Mill, namely, that, while a prospective increase or decrease of supply, in the case of any commodity not used as money, generally results in its price falling or rising without awaiting the marketing of the new supply, the value of money only changes—demand being all along assumed constant—with the actual changes of supply, inasmuch as prices are the result of real exchanges of commodities for money.

Having thus stated the law of primitive money, let us now proceed to observe the action of money in societies industrially and commercially advanced, and into which credit enters. In such societies, goods are not always exchanged for money at the time ; an equivalent is not always or perhaps habitually given on the spot. Future payment is often stipulated for ; and a new money-function appears, that of the standard of deferred payments. We are

thus able to give a full and final definition of money, namely, that it is that which serves (1) as the common medium of exchange, (*a*) dispensing with the double coincidence of wants and of possessions involved in barter ; (*b*) furnishing a price-current of all the commodities in the market. (2) As the standard of deferred payments. To put it in another form, money is that which passes freely from hand to hand, in full payment for goods, in final discharge of indebtedness, being accepted equally without reference to the character or credit of the person tendering it, and without the intention on the part of the person receiving it himself, to consume or enjoy, or otherwise use it than by passing it on, sooner or later, in exchange.

The introduction of credit into the commercial and industrial society, devolving upon money the additional function of a standard of deferred payments, has hindered the unanimous concurrence of economists as to what money exactly is, and as to what money exactly does. The use of credit instruments, the introduction of bills of exchange, drafts, and cheques, and the accumulation of deposits in banks, introduce an element into the philosophy of money which it is difficult to resolve to the satisfaction of all thinkers and writers. Some insist on regarding every form and instrument of credit as a part of the monetary circulation ; some on treating bills of exchange and bank deposits, at any rate, in this way ; others, still, regard bank deposits, at the least, as money, since cheques are freely drawn on these for the discharge of indebtedness. Lord Overstone (see Jones LOYD) may be regarded as the leader of the school of writers who classify bank deposits as money. Prof. Sidgwick holds the same view, and would alter the definition given above by substituting the words "from owner to owner," in place of the words "from hand to hand." A great deal is to be said on either side of this question, and there is no present reason to suppose that a general agreement on the subject can be reached. The writer contents himself with presenting his own reasons for holding that credit instruments generally, viz. bank accounts, bills of exchange, and cheques drawn on deposits in bank, should be excluded from the category of money.

These reasons are as follows :—Let us revert for a moment to the primitive condition of industry and trade, before credit has been introduced. Money serves here as the general medium of exchange ; yet barter may in many instances be resorted to. These acts of direct exchange reduce, to that extent, the field for the operation of money. They diminish, by just so much, the money work to be done, and by consequence, the demand for money. But no one looks on them as a part of the money supply ; no one regards acts of barter as in any sense constituting a use of money. In an advanced industrial and commercial state, credit limits the field for the operation of money, as barter did in a primitive state. The mutual cancellation of indebtedness, which the introduction of credit effects through the use of book accounts, bank deposits, etc., withdraws a certain, it may be a vast, body of exchange transactions from the field in which money operates ; but within that field, thus reduced, money does its work in precisely the same way, and as completely under the ordinary law of supply and demand (see DEMAND ; SUPPLY AND DEMAND) as, in the primitive state, money did its work within the field of exchanges which had been diminished by barter. After all that credit can do in the mutual cancellation of indebtedness, there still remains, in the community most highly advanced, even where banking has been carried to its utmost limits, a vast volume of transactions which must be effected by the use of money. The sufficient proof that these must be effected by the use of money is found in the fact that they are so effected, for money would not be used, since its use involves expense, unless this were economically necessary. Money being thus necessarily employed over a vast field of exchange transactions, after all the efficiency of credit is exhausted, the value of money within that field is determined precisely as it was determined before credit was introduced. There being a certain quantity of the money-work to be done, the quantity of the money-thing available to do that work fixes its value. If there be more of it, its value will fall and prices will rise. If there be less of it, its value will rise and prices will fall. The exchange transactions which, in the result, are cancelled by the use of credit, simply diminish by so much the field in which money would otherwise operate. In this respect they correspond exactly to acts of barter in primitive communities. It is true that if the quantity of money be diminished and its value in consequence rises, there will be an economic effort to expand the range of the mutual cancellation of indebtedness, since, as was said, the use of money always involves a certain expense ; while, if the quantity of money be increased, there will be a tendency to relax efforts to secure the widest possible cancellation of indebtedness, and in consequence, a larger body of exchange transactions will involve the use of money. But it remains true that, however the field in which money operates may be broadened or narrowed by such a cause, it is that field which determines the amount of money-work to be done, that is, the demand for money ; while the supply of money will be in nowise affected except as its higher or lower value at the time may stimulate or retard its production.

But it may be asked, if bills of exchange and bank deposits are not to be treated as money, shall bank notes be so regarded ? We may answer, " Yes." Bank notes do the money-work and are therefore the money-thing. When issued by institutions of undoubted solvency, they pass freely from hand to hand, in full payment for goods, in final discharge of indebtedness, leaving no trace of their course, such as cheques and bills of exchange do through successive endorsements. They are accepted without reference to the character or the credit of the person who offers them, except solely as the bad character of that person might require more scrutiny to ascertain that the notes were genuine. His mind satisfied on that point, whoever has sold goods receives the notes of solvent banks precisely as he would receive gold or silver coin, even though the man offering them were a well-known rogue. Bank notes are, therefore, in every sense, money. Bills of exchange and bank deposits are merely instruments for the mutual cancellation of indebtedness, and are not money.

We have thus passed through the entire extent of the functions of money, dwelling long enough upon each to be able to see what money is and what money does. In order to anticipate objections and to resolve doubtful cases, it is, however, desirable to speak more at length of each of these functions by turns. And, first, of the medium of exchange, that is, of money as dispensing with the double coincidence of wants and of possessions, implied in barter. It will be observed that every use of money involves a double transaction. Instead of commodities being exchanged directly for each other, each in its turn is sold for money ; and the commodity desired is purchased with that money. There are, thus, two transactions in place of one ; but, as the acceptance of money is universal and a matter of course, those two transactions involve less, probably far less, possibly almost indefinitely less, effort than would direct-exchange, where it is essential to find some one who not only wants what you have, but has what you want. In order to secure and maintain the universal acceptability of money, it is, in primitive societies, necessary that the article adopted for this use shall be some material thing, having intrinsic properties which make it an object of general desire for its own sake. When, however, we advance to contemplate highly civilised societies, we find them sometimes using as money an article whose value depends entirely on convention or law. Bank notes are not things useful in themselves ; while the difference between a bank note for five, and a bank note for ten pounds exists only in the substitution of one arbitrary symbol for another. Mutual confidence or legal authority entering, it ceases to be essential, however desirable it may continue to be, that the article used as money shall be something having useful properties. The savage builds his canoe of materials every part of which will float of itself; the civilised man constructs his ship out of materials every part of which by itself would sink to the bottom. The difference between savage money and civilised money is not less remarkable. It is universal confidence or universal respect for law which enables modern societies to substitute for that "material equivalent or recompense,"—to use the phrase of M. CHEVALIER—which is the characteristic of all primitive moneys, a money of mere convention, like bank notes or government paper. Yet for the same reason the possibility of a serious catastrophe always attaches to such money. If confidence fails, if the *fiat* of government is carried beyond the limits of obedience, the acceptability of the money may gradually or abruptly cease (see FIAT MONEY); and an industrial and commercial system which has been built up on the basis of such a monetary circulation may be shattered or brought to ruin. A view of these evil possibilities attending all money into which credit enters, or to which mutual confidence is essential, has caused many excellent writers, especially in America, to deny the name money to anything which is not a "material equivalent or recompense," and especially to government issues. These writers make the mistake of saying that government paper is not money, when they really mean to say that it is bad money. Now, wholly in addition to the distinction between money and not-money, we have the distinction between good money and bad money. Anything is money which does the money-work, even though it does this with less of convenience and with more of danger than would some other thing. During the paper-money period of the United States, namely, from 1863 to 1879, "greenbacks" unquestionably performed all the offices of money. They circulated with the utmost freedom; they were cheerfully and even eagerly received; men worked for them or gave goods for them, without challenge or question; they furnished a "price current" as clear and intelligible as ever did gold in such use; they were, with the single exception of the distant and isolated communities on the Pacific coast, the standard of deferred payments universally employed. Therefore, greenbacks were money. At the same time, being in excess, they inflated prices, excited to speculation, kept industry and trade in a state of agitation, and caused a continual transfer of wealth from the productive to the speculative classes. They were, therefore, bad money.

Money of mere convention has liability to two evils. The first is, that not being a "material equivalent or recompense," it is subject to be issued in excess. Especially is this true of paper put out directly by the government. Not the wants of trade, but the exigencies of the treasury, are apt to determine the amount of issues; and whenever such issues take place in excess of the wants of trade, they almost inevitably go from bad to worse. Prices become inflated, speculation sets in, and there is often both a popular and a fiscal demand for still larger issues, to sustain the inflated prices (see ASSIGNAT; BULLION COMMITTEE, REPORT OF; INCONVERTIBLE CURRENCY). Yet there are historical instances of such money being issued and maintained without excess, or, at any rate, marked excess, through the exceptional prudence and moral courage of legislators or fiscal authorities. On the other hand, as in France after the war of 1870, the natural or material forms of money cannot be increased arbitrarily. Being products of labour, they can only be increased by the application of corresponding amounts of labour to their production. They have in this a safeguard against excess which is lacking in all moneys of mere convention. The second evil liability of money of convention arises from the fact that the force of such convention has its territorial limits, whether those of a small community or those of a large state. Owing its acceptance to convention within those limits, any local excess cannot be reduced by exportation. Such money has no natural drainage. Wherever it is poured out, it makes a swamp. On the other hand, the material forms of money are subject to exportation to communities which have no respect for local convention other than their own, but which have personal or social wants that may be satisfied by the intrinsic properties of these articles. The exportability of money reaches its highest point in the case of gold and silver. The demand for these metals being universal, any local excess anywhere is at once drained off; and each community retains only so much as is required to keep its own prices on a level, cost of transportation being taken into account, with prices in the countries with which it trades. The beneficial influence of this on commerce, and in the second degree upon production, cannot be over-estimated. It is, indeed, almost essential to the maintenance of the vast system of modern production. During the paper-money period of the United States already referred to, prices, owing to the non-exportability of the GREENBACK, were out of all relation to the general prices of commerce. The exporter sold his goods for gold, and then sold the gold for whatever it would bring at the time, in the local money. Trade, and in consequence, production, became highly speculative, with the most mischievous results to the industry of the country, not to speak of grave social and political evils.

But, even in cases where, through exceptional prudence and courage on the part of the government, paper is not issued in excess, very considerable evils may yet be produced by the use of such money. During the suspension of specie payments by the Bank of France, from 1871 to 1877, the premium on gold was, by the remarkable sagacity of the directors, kept at a very low figure, almost vanishing at every favourable turn of trade. Yet even this was not without momentous consequences to the commerce of that country. In his valuable work, *Lombard Street*, published at about the close of that period, Mr. Bagehot remarked :— "The note of the Bank of France has not, indeed, been depreciated enough to disorder ordinary transactions. But any depreciation, however small, even the liability to depreciation without its reality, is enough to disorder exchange transactions. They are calculated to such an extent of fineness, that the change of a decimal may be fatal, and may turn a profit into a loss. Accordingly, London has become the sole great settling house of exchange transactions in Europe, instead of being, as formerly, one of two."

Let us now consider the second function of money, that of the common denominator of values. There is no other point on which writers on money are so generally in error as here. The cause of that error is largely found in a vicious terminology. Having begun by calling money, in this relation, the measure of value, they seem to have felt themselves bound to show that money does measure values. Thus, Prof. Francis Bowen writes : "A measure must be homogeneous with the thing measured. As that which measures length or capacity must itself possess length or capacity, so that which measures value must have value in itself, or intrinsic value." . . . Prof. Thorold Rogers says : "We need some common measure of value as we need measures of length and capacity." And Mr. Mill, as referred to above, mentions among the first and most obvious wants of exchange that of " a common measure for values of different sorts." From this notion, that money measures values, has come the dictum, common to most economists, that a money of mere convention, not having INTRINSIC VALUE (*q.v.*), not being "a material recompense or equivalent," cannot perform this function, whatever it may do as the universal medium of exchange. It would appear that all this confusion has arisen from the use of a misleading term. If we read further in the works of these writers, we find that the function they are really treating of is merely that of a common denominator in exchange. Now, it is not essentially the office of a denominator in exchange to measure values ; but only to express them, as measured. If we contemplate money of pure convention—for example, mere pieces of paper curiously engraved—and if we assume for such money a general acceptability, such as money of this kind has frequently

possessed, and possesses to-day in many countries, a moment's reflection will show that, by being actually exchanged against these pieces of paper, all commodities in the market become measured as to their value, without regard to the cost of production of the money itself. If all producers desire these pieces of paper, and desire them very much, no matter for what reason, then all commodities which have a high cost of production, and are in corresponding demand, will exchange for many pieces of the paper, or otherwise the supply of such commodities would rapidly fall off ; while commodities having a low cost of production will exchange for few pieces of paper, since, otherwise, the supply of such commodities would rapidly increase, which would at once bring down their price. In this way, that is, by the efforts of all producers to bring to market those commodities which will command the greatest number of these pieces of paper for a given expenditure of time and labour, all the commodities in the market will be differentiated as to value, exactly as if the money consisted of gold or silver. With a money of gold or silver the effort of each producer to bring to market the commodities which, for a given expenditure of time and labour, will command the greatest number of coins of a certain denomination, differentiates all commodities in the market as to value, without reference to the cost of production of the coins themselves. The action in the case of money of mere convention is identical ; and the results are just as exact. By the mere fact of being exchanged for any kind of money, each commodity takes its place on the price-current, high up or low down, according to the demand for it, and according to the ease or difficulty with which it can be brought to market—that is, according to demand and supply. It is this conception of the function of money as a common denominator of values, which underlies the discussion of IDEAL MONEY by Sir James STEUART and Messrs. F. Percival ELIOT and Gloucester WILSON. These writers were far nearer the truth than their critics. Probably the history of philosophy furnishes no instance of an equally mischievous result from the use of a false terminology, with that which has followed the phrase, "measure of value," in its application to money.

Let us now speak of the remaining function of money, that of a standard of deferred payments. The emergence of this function, consequent on the development of the credit-system, lays on that which shall be used as money a requirement altogether additional to those made upon it in a state of society where all commodities are paid for at the time of delivery. In the earlier state, it would not matter much, if at all, should the article used fluctuate widely and rapidly as to its own cost of production or its own conditions of supply. But when credit is given—that is, when payments are deferred,—it becomes at once of · vast, if not supreme, importance that money shall remain reasonably stable in value, from time to time. It is here that money of mere convention displays its greatest weakness, since its quantity can be arbitrarily increased to any extent. Yet in this respect those forms of money which have "intrinsic value," which constitute "a material equivalent or recompense," fall far short of what is to be desired. Even gold and silver, which, owing to their practical indestructibility, remain highly stable in value from year to year, yet fluctuate enormously from age to age. The story of the spasmodic and often intermittent production of the precious metals has been told in other parts of this work (see GOLD AS STANDARD). So tremendous have been the consequent fluctuations in value that it has frequently been proposed to substitute CORN RENTS, in contracts for considerable terms of years ; and, in a vast number of instances, rents, annuities, etc., have actually been stipulated for in bushels of wheat. The cereals, while they fluctuate far more than gold or silver from year to year, have been more stable, at least until a very recent date, through long periods of time. Even these, however, fall so far short of supplying all the conditions of a good standard of deferred payments, that it has been by many writers proposed to create a TABULAR STANDARD, or multiple tender, the nature and office of which will be found described under the title INDEX NUMBERS.

Another point which requires consideration in the philosophy of money is the effect of corruption or debasement of the coin—assuming, now, metal money to be in use—upon the value of money. There are two cases : (1) where corruption or debasement is universal, all coins being alike diminished as to weight, or impaired as to fineness ; (2) where the coin has been irregularly corrupted or debased. In the latter situation, it is usual for writers on money to say that the principle known as GRESHAM'S LAW will at once begin to operate. This law, or theorem, which derives its name from Sir Thomas GRESHAM, the founder of the Royal Exchange of London, is, as commonly stated, that bad money invariably drives out good money. Thus expressed, the theorem is incorrect. Bad money will only drive out good money when the sum of the two is in excess of the wants of trade ; that is, in excess of the amount which is necessary to keep prices in the community on a level, cost of transportation being taken into account, with prices in the communities with which it trades. So long as bad money and good money together only make up the amount which is needed, neither will drive the other out. RICARDO correctly states the principle in his reply to C. BOSANQUET : "It is a mistaken theory to suppose that guineas of 5 dwt. 8 gr. cannot circulate with guineas of 5 dwt., or less. As they might be in such limited quantity, that both one and the other might actually pass in currency for a value equal to 5 dwt. 10 gr., there would be no temptation to withdraw either from circulation. There would be a real profit in retaining them." It is only when the total amount of money comes to be in excess of the wants of trade, that exportation or melting of the coin begins. In such a situation, Gresham's law operates with almost absolute certainty. · The exporter, or the manufacturer of gold or silver plate, selects for his purposes the coins of fullest weight or of the highest purity, thus withdrawing them from the circulation, whose average quality is in consequence reduced. This, however, goes on only so fast and so far as the total amount of money is in excess. Should the introduction of abraded or debased coin continue, all the better coins would, in time, be exported or sent to the melting pot.

In the second case of corruption or debasement of the coin, viz. where such corruption or debasement affects the whole body of coins, the effect upon the value of money constitutes one of the most difficult questions in the philosophy of this subject. The ·writer believes that the truth in this matter is wholly on the side of Ricardo. No matter to what extent the corruption or debasement has proceeded, coins will still pass for their full denominative value, provided only the amount issued be not excessive. Ricardo failed, probably from inadvertence, to affix a single proviso which is essential to the correctness of this statement, viz. that popular knowledge of the corruption of the coin should not create a popular indisposition to use the coin. If this were to take place, it would cause an extension of the field of barter or of the operations of credit. Such an extension of the field of barter on the one hand, and of the operations of credit on the other, would of itself constitute a reduction in the demand for coin, which would necessarily reduce its value, that is, raise prices. Ricardo is unquestionably right in saying that there are numerous historical instances of a coinage largely abraded or debased, circulating without a corresponding reduction, if not indeed without any reduction at all, from its proper denominative value. The purchasing power of money being determined wholly by the relations of demand and supply, government can, by limiting the supply, in a very large degree control the value of money. Ricardo even goes so far as to regard paper money as money upon which the SEIGNIORAGE (q.v.) is 100 per cent. But, while it is thus in the power of government, by controlling the supply, largely to influence the value of paper money, the economist who has a reasonable reference to the nature of political forces can never give his approval to paper money not instantly and unconditionally convertible into coin of full value. As Alexander HAMILTON says, "paper emissions are of a nature so liable to abuse, and it may even be affirmed so certain to be abused, that the wisdom of government will be shown in never trusting itself with the use of so seductive and dangerous an expedient."

It has been said that money, while it has value, has not price, the latter term being reserved to express the value of other things in terms of money. This is true, so long as one article only is used as money. Let us, however, take the case of a community in which both gold and silver are used in this relation. Since gold and silver have separate sources of supply, and have also, in some measure, independent causes of demand, as e.g. for use in the arts, then we shall have a gold-price of silver, and a silver-price of gold. This is the situation which BI-METALLISM (q.v.) contemplates; and it is the effort of that system to extinguish all preference for either of these metals, at a ratio agreed upon, and fixed by law,—e.g. 15½ of silver to one of gold, as under the French law of 1803,—so that the gold-price of silver and the silver-price of gold shall remain constant.

[The literature of money is almost measureless. A complete bibliography would form a considerable volume. The first important writer on money was ARISTOTLE; and there is no stronger proof of the greatness of this early philosopher than that his conception of the money function still influences scientific thought. As European society emerged from the monetary confusion and disorders consequent on the silver famine of the middle ages, Nicole ORESME, moved by the abuses of the French coin, published in 1360 his treatise on money, a work which, after being long lost to the world, was, about 1862, discovered by the eminent German economist, ROSCHER, of Leipzig, and has since been put out by M. WOLOWSKI, in the original Latin text, with an introduction and a French translation. No work expresses more strikingly the pernicious effects of that morbus numericus, which wrought such misery among the people and caused such weakness in the governments of Europe, and which had afflicted France with special virulence. Oresme's treatment of the principles of coinage and seigniorage is characterised by great precision. At the beginning of the 16th century, the astronomer COPERNICUS addressed to the king of Poland his treatise Monetæ Cudendæ Ratio, which deals with the then universal evil of the corruption and debasement of coin. But it was Italy which made the largest of the earlier contributions to the philosophy of the subject. Mr. Stephen COLWELL remarks that this country was long noted for the worst money and the best writers on money. The coin of Italy was sunk into an abyss of discredit while BECCARIA and VERRI were expounding the true laws of monetary circulation, and the works of SCARUFFI and NERI were manuals for the mints of the continent. Among the early English writers on money, say from 1682 to 1717, the most distinguished names are those of Sir Wm. PETTY, Dudley NORTH, John LOCKE, William LOWNDES, John LAW, and Sir Isaac NEWTON. In 1730 SWIFT published his Drapier's Letters, concerning Wood's brass halfpence, more notable as an example of satire and invective than as a contribution to the theory of money. Shortly before the publication of Adam SMITH's Wealth of Nations, Sir James STEUART's Enquiry into the Principles of Political Economy dealt at length with the problem of money; and the same writer, acting for the East India Company, in 1772 wrote his treatise on the

coin of Bengal. HARRIS's essay upon money and coins (1757), belonging to this period, contains matter of historical interest. Adam SMITH's great work (1776) did not add much to the philosophy of money. His compatriot and contemporary, David HUME, on the other hand, though in brief compass, made a contribution of no little value. The suspension of specie payments by the bank in 1797, and the long controversy which followed the bullion report of 1810, gave rise to an immense volume of literature, much of it of permanent value. The tracts and other publications of Lord KING, Sir Francis BARING, R. TORRENS, BOSANQUET, Boyd, MUSHET, Hill, VANSITTART, Fonblanque, General Craufurd, Lord LAUDERDALE, William BLAKE, Arthur YOUNG, William HUSKISSON, Francis HORNER, David RICARDO, and Henry THORNTON, are deserving the attention of every student of monetary science. The giants of this controversy were the last four. Ricardo's tracts on money perhaps occupy the highest single place in the literature of the subject. Lord LIVERPOOL's treatise on the Coins of the Realm (1805) derives its chief interest from its relation to the demonetisation of silver by the English government, in 1816. Thomas and Matthias ATTWOOD were the champions of FIAT MONEY. Following the resumption of specie payments, in 1819, there came within a few years Sir Walter Scott's letters on the currency of Scotland (Malachi Malagrowther); Sir James GRAHAM's Coin and Currency; Sir Henry PARNELL's Observations on Paper Money, Banking, and Overtrading; SENIOR's Cost of Obtaining Money; JACOB's Inquiry into the Production and Consumption of the Precious Metals; and, greatest of all, Thomas TOOKE's Inquiry into the Currency Principle, 1844. Tooke assumed and strongly fortified the positions regarding the operation and influence of paper money, which he afterwards assaulted with such distinguished ability in his History of Prices. Belonging to the next period, that, namely, between 1832 and the time of the Australia and California gold discoveries, are Poulett SCROPE's Examination, etc., FULLARTON's valuable work on The Regulation of Currencies, and James WILSON's Capital, Currency, and Banking. Most of the economic interest of this period centred in the action of parliament regarding the Bank of England; and the report on the bank charter, in 1833, from the secret committee; and the first and second reports of the select committee upon banks of issue, 1840 and 1841, are among the most valuable blue books issued since the bullion report of 1810. Peel's act of 1844, regulating the privilege of issue, gave rise to an enormous literature. Chief among the disputants were Thomas Tooke, Lord Overstone (Samuel Jones LOYD), Colonel TORRENS, George Warde NORMAN, James W. GILBART. The chapters regarding money in Mr. Mill's great work on political economy are among the most important contributions of this time to the theory of that subject. The Californian and Australian discoveries, about 1850, produced several works of marked value, particularly William NEWMARCH's New Supplies of Gold, and J. E. CAIRNES's Essays on the Gold Question. Maclaren's History of the Currency may be mentioned. The demonetisation of silver by Germany, following the American Civil War, produced a controversial literature rarely equalled. The same period has also witnessed the publication of some important constructive works, pre-eminently Mr. BAGEHOT's Lombard St., Prof. JEVONS's Money and the Mechanism of Exchange, and Mr. Goschen's Foreign Exchanges. Mr. Ernest SEYD published several pamphlets in favour of bi-metallism early in the course of the controversy; Mr. H. Hucks Gibbs (now Lord Aldenham), Prof. H. S. Foxwell, and Prof. J. Shield Nicholson have led in the recent discussion on the same side; while Sir Robert Giffen and Lord Farrer have upheld monometalism. The report of the commons committee of 1876, on the depreciation of silver, is of great importance.

In the United States, money or "currency" (Mr. M'Leod calls this word "a mischievous Yankeeism") has always been a favourite theme. Pelatiah WEBSTER's Nature and Operation of Money (1792) is interesting and valuable. Prof. W. G. Sumner's History of American Currency presents much information. Accounts of the paper money issues of the several colonies have been written by FELT, PHILLIPS, Brownson, and others; and of the revolutionary paper money by J. W. Shuckers. The works of Alexander HAMILTON, Albert GALLATIN, and Daniel WEBSTER, contain much that is of value in the theory of money. Messrs. Condy Raguet and Wm. M.

Gouge were among the passionate opponents of bank money. Prof. George TUCKER's *Money and Banks* is a work of merit. Stephen Colwell's *Ways and Means of Payment* contains much useful information. The theory of bank money is treated with great fulness in Prof. Amasa WALKER's *Science of Wealth*. The "inflation period," 1862 to 1879, brought on extended discussions of inconvertible paper money, in which the leading participants were Henry C. CAREY and H. C. Baird on the FIAT MONEY side; and David A. Wells and W. G. Sumner on the HARD MONEY side. Mr. John J. KNOX's work, *United States Notes*, furnishes the most accurate account existing of the national issue of paper money. H. R. Linderman's *Money and Legal Tender* is a useful manual. Francis A. Walker's large treatise on money was published in 1878; and his smaller work, *Money, Trade, and Industry*, in 1879. Mr. S. Dana HORTON is easily the most learned of the writers in favour of bi-metallism (see his *Silver Pound and Silver in Europe*); Prof. J. Laurence Laughlin's *Bi-metallism in the United States* is strongly monometallist in its bearings.

In France, the treatise of M. CHEVALIER, *La Monnaie*, the third volume of his "Cours d'Économie Politique," has held a pre-eminent place. During the first flood of the new gold, Chevalier wrote a work on the *Probable Fall in the Value of Gold*, which was translated into English by Richard COBDEN. The proceedings of the *Enquête Monétaire* of 1870 are of great interest. Courcelle-SENEUIL's *Opérations de Banque* is a leading work. Léon FAUCHER's small treatise on the *Production of the Precious Metals* is a work of merit. Louis WOLOWSKI's writings on money in general, and particularly those in favour of bi-metallism, hold a high rank. The most energetic advocate of bi-metallism is M. Cernuschi, whose special antagonist for many years was M. Feer-Herzog of Switzerland. M. Esquirol de Parieu and M. Levasseur take the monometallist side. F. Lenormant's essay upon the money of ancient nations is of permanent value. The reports of the conference of the Latin union (France, Switzerland, Italy, and Belgium), and those of the international MONETARY CONFERENCES of 1867, 1878, 1881, and 1892, are of great value. Other writers on money who should be mentioned in any bibliography, however short, are Emile de LAVELEYE of Belgium, Prof. Léon Walras of Lausanne, Vrolik and MEES of Holland, and N. P. van den Berg of Batavia, now Governor of the Bank of Holland. William ROSCHER's treatise on money (translated into French by Wolowski), and Knies' *Das Geld* are perhaps the most important German works on this subject. Philip Geyer's *Theorie und Praxis des Zettelbankwesens* may also be mentioned. Bamberger's *Reichsgeld* and other writings are among the ablest extant upon the mono-metallic side. A. SOETBEER's investigations into the production of the precious metals are of high value. Prof. Miklashewsky, *Study of the chief positions of the classical theory in regard to the question of money* (Moscow), 1895. Leroy-Beaulieu, *Écon. Pol.*, 1896, vol. iii.]   F. A. W.

MONEY AND PRICES. See PRICES.

MONEY (QUANTITY-THEORY). See the QUANTITY-THEORY OF MONEY.

MONEY OF ACCOUNT. The "money of account," or the terms in which values are recorded, is, in modern monetary systems, generally the same as the standard of value of the country in which the accounts are kept; the metallic and note currency being reckoned in the same measure, while values less than that of the standard are expressed decimally. Thus, in the states of the "Latin Monetary Union" (France, Belgium, Italy, Switzerland, and Greece) accounts are kept in francs, in Germany in marks, in Scandinavia in crowns, and so forth. The money of account in Great Britain presents a slight variation from that of the majority of modern states from the fact that, although large sums are recorded in pounds, values smaller than that of the standard are expressed in shillings, pence,

and farthings, instead of in decimal parts of a pound.

Though, from the point of view of simplifying and facilitating commercial transactions, it is desirable that the money of account should be identical with the standard of value, this is by no means a condition essential to the practical working of a monetary system. Neither is it necessary that the terms in which values are accounted should be represented by an actual coin in the circulation of the country. In England, for instance, when the shilling was the money of account, there were many years during which the only coins in use were silver pence, while at the same time the standard of value was a pound troy of silver of the millesimal fineness of 925.

Similar, and more recent examples of complex systems of currency and account are to be met with. Several such instances occurring in the early history of the British colonies are recorded by Mr. Chalmers in his *History of Currency in the British Colonies*, 1893, an interesting case being that of the Leeward Islands. In the 17th and 18th centuries the standard of value in this colony was a commodity known as "Muscovado sugar"; this article being also the principal medium of exchange. Accounts were, however, kept in sterling terms, and we learn that, by an Act passed in the year 1700, ratings of commodities in sterling, for purposes of account, were fixed as follows:

12s. 6d. current money for every 100 lbs. of Muscovado
2s.   ,,   ,,   1   ,, Indico
9d.   ,,   ,,   1   ,, Cotton wool ginn'd.
1½d.   ,,   ,,   1   ,, Tobacco or ginger.

In Newfoundland, until so recently as 1887, when an Act consolidating and amending the currency legislation of the colony was passed, a money of account known as "Halifax currency" was in use. The ratings of coin in circulation under this system of account were fixed by an Act of the Assembly of the island passed in 1845, and were as follows:

	£	s.	d.	
Doubloon	3	16	9¾	currency
Sovereign	1	4	0	,,
Crown		6	0	,,
Dollar		5	0	,,
Shilling		1	2¾	,,

[See also IDEAL MONEY.]   F. E. A.

MONEY MARKET. A term applied to an organisation which has always existed in a more or less developed form in countries where wealth has had time to accumulate. Only its modern characteristics can be dealt with here, and the examination thereof must be confined to London, the largest and most highly organised example of the species.

The London money market consists of—(*a*) the Bank of England; (*b*) the joint-stock banks; and (*c*) one or two powerful private banks, the discount houses and bill brokers; (*d*) the large mercantile houses who have money to lend from time to time ; and (e) the Stock Exchange. As a rule the term "the market" is employed to denote classes (b) and (c) alone, the Bank being regarded as outside "the market," meaning the market for bills, while (d) and (e) are similarly excluded because their operations are of an intermittent character, and in the case of (e) are, as a rule, "all one way," the Stock Exchange being more of a customer for dealers in money than a dealer in money itself. There are, however, certain wealthy stock exchange firms who are really dealers in money, and not infrequently lend their surplus balances in Lombard Street. The great merchant houses are often very large lenders, through their possessing temporary control of considerable sums of money derived from loans, subscriptions to loans, remittances from foreign governments, and in other ways ; and, on the other hand, they often take money out of the market by discounting bills or selling stock. They are, therefore, like the Stock Exchange, too closely allied to "the market" in the narrow sense of the term to be omitted from the list of elements making up the real market.

(a) The Bank of England.—Twenty years or more ago the Bank was an integral part of the London money market, possessing a power which it has not now. Formerly it had considerable influence on the discount rate, being a considerable holder of bills, but for many years past it has ceased to compete for bills with the great joint-stock banks, two of which have so large a share of this class of business that they practically control the discount rate on any day on which they are both buyers, or both "hold off" from the market. The Bank rate of discount has ceased to be any indication of the real discount rate in London, except very occasionally. This is not a satisfactory state of things, as the loss of control over the discount rate has involved the loss of power to influence the foreign exchanges, a power which is needed by the Bank in order to enable it to protect its reserve, which is the sole cash reserve of all the banks in the United Kingdom. The Bank has never explicitly admitted its responsibility for the reserve, but it does admit it implicitly. On the other hand, the banks ostensibly deny that they have any responsibility in the matter, but there is good reason for believing that they recognise it in practice, and will help the Bank to maintain a proper reserve should the course of events again place it in danger.

(b) The great joint-stock banks possess enormous power in the money market, owing to the magnitude of their deposits. The National Provincial Bank of England and the London and County Bank together hold over £70,000,000 of deposits, and the London and Westminster and Lloyd's, the latter a country bank with an important office in London, hold about £50,000,000 more. The National Provincial and the London and County are the largest buyers and holders of bills in the market, and, as already observed, the rate of discount for the day usually depends on their operations. The banks meet from time to time to arrange what rate shall be allowed on deposits.

(c) The discount houses and bill brokers are also large buyers of bills, but they are not such "firm" holders of them as the banks. The smaller brokers, indeed, hold very few bills, though their turnover is often large, since they act as intermediaries between the great banks and the holders, as creators of bills. Strictly speaking they are not competitors for bills, but they provide the machinery by means of which the banks compete for them. The larger brokers and the discount houses are competitors of the banks, and hold considerable amounts of bills, which, however, they are quite ready to "turn out" at a profit, while banks, in nearly all cases, hold the bills until maturity. The bill brokers and discount houses work largely with money borrowed at call and short notice (seven or fourteen days). They publish the rates they are prepared to allow from time to time, which are usually in harmony with the terms offered to depositors by the banks, but they change their scale more frequently than the banks. Their meetings are of a more or less informal character, and changes are rarely made by any individual house alone, even when strong views as to the expediency of the proposed movement are taken by it. The brokers have a large area to borrow from. They obtain most of what they use from banks, but are also in close touch with the stock exchange money brokers, lending to them and taking money from them on consols and other high-class securities ; and they have the Bank of England to rely upon in the last resort, though recourse to that institution is surrounded with restrictions, regarding the policy of which much difference of opinion exists.

The working of the Money Market.—Under normal conditions the London money market works very smoothly. Bills to a very large amount fall due every day and are paid ; the "money" is reinvested in other bills, or if these cannot be secured on satisfactory terms, the "money" is lent in the short loan market on bills or stock, for periods which may vary from one day to a fortnight ; or the "money" may be employed on the stock exchange either as a monthly loan on consols or until the "next account," which usually means about a fortnight. One great bank almost invariably reinvests money obtained from the payment of bills falling due daily in other bills, but most banks allow themselves a certain latitude in this respect, and the bill brokers have many more bills in their cases at some times than at others, though they always try to keep up a certain average. In normal times all money in the hands of the market is lent up to the last penny, at some rate, by about 4 P.M. if possible. If nothing else can be done with it, it is lent "for the night," often at a rate which seems hardly worth accepting. Recently the Bank announced that it would not receive applications after 2.30 P.M. The high price at the present time (1896) of all the best investments, including bills, and the low prices of commodities and slackness of trade, have, for some years past, made money redundant in the market, except for brief periods. There has been no disposition to invest capital for long periods, or to "lock it up" in industrial occupations. All who possess or have the control of loanable capital prefer, at such times, to keep it in a form as easily convertible into cash as possible, in order that when an opportunity occurs for profitable investment, advantage may at once be taken of it. When a revival of trade has begun, and the prices of commodities have risen, a change takes place in the attitude of the controllers of wealth. They find that more money is wanted to do a given amount of business than before, and that there is more business to do. The surplus money disappears from the market, and lenders have less difficulty in "placing" such surplus balances as they have on hand. When once this process has begun, it usually leads to a state of things the exact opposite of that we have been discussing; not only is all available money eagerly borrowed, but credit is stretched to the utmost. A great deal is invariably lent to the wrong people and on wrong securities, and finally a collapse of a more or less serious character occurs in credit. At such times the only quarter whence loans can be obtained is the Bank of England, as all other institutions have employed their resources to the utmost. On two occasions prior to 1866 the pressure on the bank was so great that the chancellor of the exchequer had to allow the bank to suspend the act of 1844, which restricts the note issue (see PEEL, Sir R.). The way in which the lock-up of capital in unsaleable securities, or securities on which loans cannot be obtained, comes into existence, may be very different at different times (see articles on CRISES).

The "money," or more properly the "loanable capital" with which the money market deals, is of a peculiar kind. It may be defined as wealth in its least specialised form, a form it can only assume in a very rich country, where all the specialised forms of wealth, but more particularly those which are easily exchangeable for other kinds of wealth, such as gold and high class securities, are very plentiful. All countries which have developed the modern form of civilisation possess a certain amount of "money-market money," but in all but a few

it is of small amount. The supply of it in this country is enormous, but not unlimited, as events have more than once shown. Credit is based on this almost impalpable form of wealth, and when it has been exhausted by an excessive granting of credit, the fabric of credit breaks up. In the London money market, the organisation by which, to use a physiological analogy, non-specialised wealth is "secreted" and accumulated, is more effective than in any other at present known. This is owing to the fact that savings are almost universally deposited in banks, and that we possess a "one reserve system," as Bagehot called it, whereby the Bank of England has become the sole depository of the reserves of the banks of the United Kingdom. The system is not without disadvantages, but it is highly economical, and it appears likely to continue.

[J. S. Mill, *Political Economy*, bk. iii., *passim*, but especially chs. ii. and xii.—Bagehot, *Lombard Street.*—Goschen, *Foreign Exchanges.*—H. Sidgwick, *Principles of Political Economy*, bk. ii. chs. iv. v.—Palgrave, *Bank Rate in England, France, and Germany.*—George Clare, *A Money Market Primer and Key to the Exchanges.*]

W. H.

MONEY BILL (in Parliament). A "money bill" is a bill which seeks either to impose taxation or to allocate public moneys to some particular purpose. By constitutional usage such bills must originate in the House of Commons on the initiation of the government of the day. The resolution overthrowing the introduction of the bill must be passed in committee of the whole House (standing order 58). The House of Lords may reject, but cannot amend a money bill.

Where a bill is not a money bill, but incidentally involves the grant of public money, the grant must be passed by a committee of the whole house, and adopted on report before the clause which deals with the grant can be considered in committee on the bill.

The object of these provisions is, first to preserve the control of the elective branch of the legislature over all matters of supply, and secondly, to safeguard the public purse from unexpected attacks on it by private members.

[Anson, *Law and Custom of the Constitution*, vol. i. pp. 252-257.] M. D. C.

MONEYS TO BE PROVIDED BY PARLIAMENT. This is a technical phrase used in drafting acts of parliament. When the expenditure of public money is authorised, and it is intended that the expenditure shall not be charged on the permanent consolidated fund, but shall be voted annually in committee of supply, the act provides that the expenditure in question shall be defrayed "out of moneys to be provided by parliament." M. D. C.

MONEYERS may be called the manufacturers of coin, every mint having one or more in charge of it, with, except perhaps in the earliest periods, subordinate workers under them. After Norman times they were no longer the sole officers of the London mint, but were assisted on the one hand and checked on the other by a growing staff of officials with separate duties. From the first, the responsibility of their office was recognised by the laws regarding them, and especially by the heavy penalties, such as the loss of a hand, which were enacted not only against false moneyers who counterfeited the coin, but against the authorised moneyers if guilty of any offence in the exercise of their office. The practice, found as early as the Anglo-Saxon period, of stamping on the coin, usually on the reverse, the name of the moneyer from whose mint it was issued, was probably intended as a check on irregularities, the more necessary on account of the large number of mints existing in the country.

In early days, when almost all public work was done locally, the mints were most numerous, as is known chiefly from the fact that from the reign of Athelstan (925-940) the name of the town of issue was commonly added to that of the moneyer. He ordered indeed that there should be a moneyer in every burgh, but it is not likely that this law was more than an extension of an already prevalent custom. In London, Canterbury, and Winchester there were at this time eight, seven, and six moneyers respectively. At one time or another there have been more than sixty royal mints in England, three in Wales, and one in Scotland, besides seven episcopal and two monastic mints in England ; and this is exclusive of a considerable number of places for which the possession of mints and moneyers has been claimed on doubtful grounds. After Henry III. died 1272, the number of mints greatly declined, and the moneyers' names no longer appeared on the coins ; and after Edward VI. died 1553, the mint in the Tower was almost the only one ever used in England except by Charles I. and during the recoinage under William III.

Moneyers seem to have held a position in regard to the king between that of a tenant-in-chief and a Jew, with special liabilities and special protection. They were obliged, if the king visited their town, to coin as much silver as he pleased ; they paid relief direct to the king, and he was their heir if they died intestate ; they paid an annual rent to the king and a sum of money on every renewal of the coinage for the new dies sent them from the London mint ; the moneyers of London were excepted from the privilege granted by Henry II. to the other citizens of not pleading outside the city except in suits with foreigners. On the other hand they received some compensation for their disabilities ; they sometimes enjoyed the right of *sac* and *soc* (see SOCAGE), they were sometimes exempted from TALLAGE, and they sometimes

lived in a rent-free house. No doubt their business was profitable and was worth the certain payments and the possible penalties.

To preserve the uniformity of the coinage all moneyers had to use the dies supplied from London ; even the two archbishops, who in early Anglo-Saxon days had put their own names and effigies on their coins, were obliged after Athelstan to use the royal dies, and later to pay an annual rent to the master of the mint ; but they took the profits and at one time were allowed to distinguish their coins by some special mark. After Henry VIII. archiepiscopal coining ceased.

In the 17th century the moneyers of London were paid according to the bullion coined, not by a fixed salary, and their duties are described as follows in the *Report of a Select Committee* of 8th April 1697 ; "The moneyers draw, cut out, size, blanch, edge, and coin those bars (prepared by the workers) into monies, sissel and brokage back to the masters, by weight ; these live in the country, attend the mint whenever called, take apprentices, and form themselves into a government, by electing one of them to be their Provost."

[Athelstan's Laws in Wilkins's *Leges Anglo-Saxonicæ*, 59.—Ellis, *Introd. to Domesday*, i. 174-177.—Ruding, *Annals of the Coinage*, pref. and ii. 135, etc. and appendix, p. 465.—Madox, *Hist. of Exchequer*, especially for tallage paid by moneyers.—Cunningham, *English Industry and Commerce*, vol. i.] E. G. P.

MONOMETALLISM. This term is applied to designate a monetary system in which the standard of value consists of one metal, whether of silver as now in Japan, and formerly in Germany, or of gold. Such a system, based upon gold, is found in England to-day. The silver and bronze coins circulating are token currencies, do not contain as much metal as their face-value represents, are regulated in their issue, and limited in their character of legal tender to small amounts—in the case of bronze to 1s., and in that of silver to £2. Gold alone, in the form of coin or of paper convertible into gold on demand, is legal tender without restriction in the payment of debt ; and gold alone in the form of bullion is receivable to any amount at the mint, or by the Bank of England as the agent of the mint, and exchangeable for legal tender of the realm. Although, therefore the current media of exchange may consist of bronze and silver for small payments, and of notes and various credit-instruments, such as cheques and bills of exchange, for large payments, and gold may be actually employed in domestic transactions only for payments of intermediate amounts, yet the standard of value is gold alone ; for the notes are convertible into gold on demand, and the various credit-instruments are promises to pay, which, according to the regulations of legal tender, can in the last resort be made only in gold, or in paper convertible into gold on demand. The superstructure of CREDIT (*q.v.*) rests on the foundation of "cash" in the Bank of England; and "cash" consists of gold or paper convertible into gold.

This monometallic system was introduced into England on the resumption of cash payments after the period of the Bank Restriction. The system prevailing before had been one in which silver had formed the unit of account, but gold had been rated to it. Since the abolition of seigniorage charges in 1666, with the exception of a brief interval during the recoinage under William the Third, when the importation of gold guineas was prohibited for a few months to allow of the successful accomplishment of the necessary operations, and, at a later time, of the suspension of the free coinage of silver in 1798, the mint was freely open to the unrestricted coinage of both silver and gold, and both metals were indifferently regarded as unlimited legal tender in the payment of debt. In 1774 the tender of silver by tale was indeed restricted to £25, but it was apparently allowed to be tendered by weight without restriction. Between the recoinage under Elizabeth and that under William the Third, the silver remained unaltered in intrinsic value, but the gold was changed some four times. At the time of the later recoinage the current gold coin was the guinea, which nominally passed at twenty shillings. Owing to a deteriorated condition, due partly to wear and tear, partly to deliberate clipping and sweating, and partly to constant exportation of the heavier and better coins, the silver—of which the unit of account was the pound, but the coins actually current were for lower denominations—fell in value so rapidly that the guinea rose to thirty shillings. The question then presented itself, whether the silver should be reinstated in its former position, or the change in its value recognised and stereotyped in the new coinage. It was determined to restore the Elizabethan standard, and by successive stages the rating of the guinea was reduced. But, both before and after the recoinage, the silver was under-rated and the gold over-rated, in comparison with the rating which prevailed in other countries, and the increasing production of gold in the 18th century gave an added force to the natural consequences of this act. In accordance with the operation of GRESHAM'S LAW (*q.v.*) the over-rated metal found its way to the mint in increasing quantities, and the under-rated metal left the country; and, when a new recoinage was effected in 1774, the gold had taken the preponderant place in the currency, and its deteriorated condition demanded the chief notice, while the restriction mentioned

above of the legal tender of silver by tale to sums of less than £25 seems to have been due to the existence of a large quantity of light silver which had taken the place of the heavier coins sent abroad. The recoinage was followed in 1798 by the suspension of the free coinage of silver; and, at the resumption of cash payments, gold was formally adopted as the standard, a heavy seigniorage was charged on the coinage of silver, its reception at the mint was definitely stated to be no longer free, and its character of legal tender was limited to sums no greater than £2. These changes were carried into effect by the younger Lord LIVERPOOL, but were in general agreement with the principles advocated by his father in the well-known *Treatise on the Coins of the Realm.* In some respects, indeed, they appear to have gone beyond the alterations recommended in that treatise, especially with regard to the seigniorage on silver. The elder Lord LIVERPOOL does not seem to have contemplated a charge exceeding the cost of coinage, which is technically known as BRASSAGE (*q.v.*), but it is probable that the heavier charge was prompted by a desire to meet the inevitable expense attendant on the resumption of cash payments.

The history, which has been given in brief, of the original adoption of the monometallic gold standard in England, has acquired considerable importance in recent discussions on the merits of the system. It is urged by critics of monometallism that its introduction was accidental, that it conflicted, not only with previous practice, but also in reality, though not in appearance, with the theory of the older monetary authorities, and that it was made without a full appreciation of its possible results. On the other hand, the supporters of the system maintain that the Legislature merely endorsed by its sanction the informal and spontaneous choice of the people, that great inconvenience had arisen from the previous system, that the chief monetary reformers had repeatedly urged the adoption of the principles on which monometallism was founded, and that it was deliberately introduced to secure advantages which subsequent experience has shown to be inherent in it. These different views appear sharply antagonistic; but the difference turns to a considerable extent on the particular interpretation placed on certain words and actions, which admit of different meanings. There seems, for instance, little doubt that before the resumption of cash payments the currency had become preponderantly gold, and that a change in that direction had been evident throughout the 18th century. It is contended that this change was due, not to the deliberate preference of the people, but to an accident occasioned by over-rating of the gold and under-rating of the silver; and it is urged that, at the time of the suspension of the free coinage of the latter metal, the conditions of production were altering in such a way that, had there been no such suspension, the currency would have become preponderantly silver. In a similar way different interpretations have been put on language used by PETTY and LOCKE, by NEWTON and by Adam SMITH (*q.v.*). They speak of one metal as the only possible "standard"; "one metal," says Locke, "alone can be the money of account and contract"; but the reformers of William the Third in thus speaking seem to have had especially before them the desirability of maintaining the Elizabethan standard for the silver pound, and they were fully aware that the gold was rated to it. They recognised a system under which both metals were freely received at the mint, and were indifferently legal tender in the payment of debt. They expressly urged the desirability of making the English rating accord with that prevailing abroad; and it was because their advice was followed imperfectly that the currency became preponderantly gold. Nor can there be doubt that the depletion of the silver was a real inconvenience; and that it was met successfully by the provisions for token coinage made at the introduction of the gold standard.

For the purpose of a convenient *internal* currency, regarded from the point of view of the media of exchange, such a monometallic system as that introduced into England at the beginning of the century possesses certain advantages. But the standard so formed is exposed, without any such compensatory action as is found in BIMETALLISM (*q.v.*), to the fluctuations in value of a single metal, whether these fluctuations be due to changes in production, or to alterations in the monetary policy of other countries, such as have characterised the last twenty years. It secures, it is true, a sufficient supply of convenient coins in the shape of tokens for small payments, and effectually prevents their exportation to other countries. Under the older forms of bimetallism, in which it was common for both the standard metals to be turned into coin, disadvantage attached to the use of the cheaper metal, silver, for large payments, as the coins required to settle a transaction of considerable amount were, either individually, or in the total mass, of great bulk, and the definite substitution under the monometallic system of the more valuable metal, gold, obviated this inconvenience. The comparative lightness of the English sovereign and the heaviness and cumbrous size of the French five-franc piece furnish examples of this difference. But now in a country like England coins are chiefly used in domestic trade, either as small change, or as a reserve against the issue of paper and as a basis for the superstructure of credit; and the more recent proposals for bimetallism contemplate the continuance of silver and bronze as token currencies for small denominations, of gold for purposes of change in larger dealings, and of paper money and credit instruments for negotiating still greater payments. In bimetallism, as thus conceived, the two metals would replace the one, in the main, if not exclusively, as a reserve against the issue of paper, and as a basis for the superstructure of credit. They would be freely receivable at the bank in exchange for legal tender, and they would indifferently form the basis of it. So far as the *domestic* trade of the country was concerned, it might, it is contended, be carried on as it is at present under our monometallic system.

With regard to *international* transactions, which would thus be chiefly affected by the adoption of bimetallism or monometallism, opposing arguments have been advanced by the supporters of either system. The use of a single standard is considered to attract business, at any rate of a financial nature, to the country where it is established, because every one knows precisely the mode in which he will be called upon to discharge his obligations to others, or will find that others meet their obligations to him. In London, for instance, it is contended, you are now always paid in gold, and pay in gold. Under a bimetallic system you might be paid in gold or silver, at the option of the debtor; and you yourself might pay in either metal as you preferred. This possibility, it is maintained, would not merely give rise to the inconvenience of being compelled on occasions to deal in international transactions with a bulkier instead of a lighter metal, but it would generate an uncertainty which would tend to drive away the business now attracted to London by the plain and recognised interpretation given there to monetary bargains.

On the other hand, monometallism, unless universally based on the same metal, fails to provide a par of international exchange. At present western nations appear, unless the tendencies of national policy are reversed by international action, to be likely to adopt by successive stages a gold standard.[1] The example of England was followed by Germany at the conclusion of the Franco-German War, and Holland and the Scandinavian States imitated the action of Germany. The United States returned to specie payments on a gold basis after the civil war; in 1873, the Latin Union suspended the free coinage of silver, and adopted what has been distinguished as a limping or halting bimetallism, and the Austro-Hungarian Empire is now engaged in establishing gold monometallism. But in the East, China and Japan, and indeed a large part of the whole world, are on a silver monometallic basis, and are likely to remain so. It should be added, that some writers think that, were it possible, silver alone would form a better standard for the world than gold. Experience has shown that it is more stable in value; and high authority (*e.g.* that of Ricardo), can be cited in its favour.

To these arguments monometallists answer that the difficulties of exchange between gold and silver-using countries have been exaggerated. There are, in short, they contend, no circumstances which would warrant the serious step of changing a monetary system, recommended not merely by its intrinsic merits—its simplicity and its convenience, and its freedom from international entanglement—but also by familiarity due to long establishment. A change in such a system would occasion a panic, or at least create confusion; and on negative and on positive grounds alike it is maintained that monometallism is the better system. Such contentions are not of course admitted by bimetallists (see BIMETALLISM); but they are confidently advanced.

[For the literature of the subject see the references under BIMETALLISM. For the history of the introduction of gold monometallism into England, Mr. R. H. Inglis Palgrave's Memorandum contained in the *Third Report of the Depression of Trade Commission* should be consulted, also Mr. Dana Horton's writings, especially his *Silver Pound*, Mr. W. A. Shaw's *History of Currency*, and Lord Aldenham's *Colloquy on Currency*. Lord Liverpool's *Treatise on the Coins of the Realm* shows what considerations had weight with the authors of the change; and the reports of the debates in parliament at the time of the resumption of cash payments should be consulted. The evidence before the *Gold and Silver Commission*, together with the final report of the Commission, supplies an authoritative account of the arguments advanced by supporters and opponents of monometallism; and the evidence given before the *Commission on Agriculture* by Sir Robert Giffen and Lord Farrer, and by Professor Foxwell and Mr. Everett, should be referred to for a more recent statement of the case. The *Report of the Brussels International Monetary Conference* should also be consulted. Sir Robert Giffen's *Case against Bimetallism* on the one side, and Professor Nicholson's *Money and Monetary Problems* (especially the essays at the end), on the other, contain discussions of various important aspects of the question. Professor Taussig's *Silver Situation in the United States*; M. de Boissevain's *The Monetary Question*; Mr. E. Helm's *Joint Standard*, and Professor Foxwell's articles and pamphlets should also be studied, and the publications of the Gold Standard Defence Association and of the Bimetallic League, which are authoritative, although avowedly controversial. Jevons's *Investigations in Currency and Finance*, and also his *Money and the Mechanism of Exchange*; General Walker's *Money* and also his *Money, Trade, and Industry*, and Professor Sidgwick's *Principles of Political Economy*, may be consulted for a more general and theoretical treatment of the question.]   L. L. P.

MONOPOLIES. The issue of letters patent, granting the recipients the exclusive right of dealing in particular commodities or pursuing a particular trade, began long before the time of the Tudors, but it was only under them that monopolies began to be a serious abuse, and it was not till near the end of Elizabeth's reign that they became a real grievance. The subject came under discussion in parliament in 1601, when Mr. Laurence Hide on 20th November brought in a bill entitled "An Act for the explanation of the Common Law in certain cases of Letters Patent." The list of monopolies read on this occasion included such things as salt, currants, iron, playing cards, carriage of leather, ashes, bottles, vinegar, coals, etc. The salt monopoly is said to have raised the price from 16d. to 14s. or 15s. a bushel. Discussion on this occasion was stopped by a message from the queen, who promised to revoke all objectionable patents and grant no more. James I. on his accession issued a proclamation suspending all existing monopolies till the council should decide that they were not prejudicial to his subjects, but before the end of his reign they were being granted as freely as they had been by his predecessor. Matters were brought to a crisis by the action of the Purveyors (see PURVEYANCE), of whom Giles Mompesson (afterwards Sir Giles) was the most notorious. He originated a scheme by which the licensing of inns and ale-houses, then as now, under the justices, should be subject to the approval of two commissioners, himself and another, appointed by letters patent. The enormous bribes and fees exacted by these commissioners enraged the people, already excited about the general question of monoplies; the matter was taken up in parliament in the spring of 1621, Mompesson fled to the continent, and on the 31st March the monopoly bill passed the Commons, the three most obnoxious patents, those for inns, gold wire, and concealed lands, having meanwhile been cancelled by proclamation. In 1624 the monopoly bill passed the Lords. By it all monopolies, except the protection of inventions for twenty-one years, were declared illegal, the decision in any case being put into the hands of the judges. The exemption from its action of corporations, an exemption made on behalf of the great trading companies, the Levant Company and the like, was destined to give trouble in the next reign. In 1631 a company was formed and obtained a patent for making soap of English materials. In the following year it was invested with power to condemn all bad soap, thus obtaining a practical monopoly. A great quarrel ensued between the company and private manufacturers, which lasted several years and was of great political importance. In 1634 similar companies obtained monopolies for salt, shipping of coal, malt, and starch, and others were formed in succeeding years till 1639, when most of the patents were revoked by proclamation. Then followed the civil war which put an end to the question of monopolies as it did to so many other vexed questions of royal prerogative.

[See *The Great Case of Monopolies*, and Lord Coke's remarks on it. — Hallam, *Constitutional History of England.*—Prothero, *Statutes and Constitutional Documents*, Cambridge, 1894.—Hume, *History of England.*—Gardiner, *History of England*, London, 1888.]   A. E. S.

MONOPOLIES IN THE UNITED STATES. In the United States, aside from copyright and trade marks, there are no legal monopolies of consequence excepting the patent right. The patent right secures to the owner and his assigns the monopoly of the manufacture and sale of the patented article for seventeen years.

In certain isolated cases the state itself has owned and managed, either directly or by lease, certain industries, as, for example, the salt industry in the state of New York until the year 1894 ; but such cases are so rare that they are not worthy of detailed consideration.

The so-called " natural monopolies," meaning thereby the railroads, telegraphs, telephones, waterworks, gas and electric lighting plants, etc., in the United States, are ordinarily in private hands, under the more or less careful supervision of the state authorities. At the beginning of the era of railroad building there was no thought on the part of the citizens of a necessity for restricting railroads in their privileges ; and in earlier years what laws were passed were either directly for the encouragement of the railroads, by means of grants of lands or guarantees of loans, or else they were general laws permitting any responsible corporation to undertake the building of a railroad in whatever locality it thought desirable, the power of EMINENT DOMAIN for compulsory purchase of private lands being granted freely. Within a few years later, however, especially after the smaller roads first built began to combine into longer through routes, the necessity of some restriction made itself felt. At first in New Hampshire, and soon afterwards in certain other states, temporary commissions were appointed to investigate the causes of accidents, and to recommend or, if necessary, prescribe certain regulations to prevent similar misfortunes in the future. In the years from 1850 to 1870, however, the roads had become so powerful and had made their influence so strongly felt through their discriminations in rates between different localities and especially, as it was thought by the farming classes, through their exorbitant freight rates, that much hostile feeling was aroused. In the states of Illinois, Wisconsin, and Iowa especially, laws were passed prescribing strictly the rates of traffic, as well as restricting the freedom of administration in many other ways. These somewhat arbitrary laws were found to be so stringent that it was necessary to repeal some of them within two years. But the feeling against the railroads still existed, and careful control of them was attempted in other ways. In the eastern states, following the lead of Massachusetts, railroad commissions were appointed, with powers of investigating in detail the business of the roads, with the duty of advising the railroad managers, and with instructions to report annually to the legislature the conditions found, but with no power to enforce their decisions ; it being hoped that the pressure of public opinion would be sufficient to secure just action on the part of the roads. In several other states, following the lead of Illinois, commissions were appointed with power not merely to advise the roads but to prescribe specific rates for freight and passenger traffic, to insist that sufficient facilities for handling traffic be provided, to make classifications of freight and passenger traffic, to regulate connections between trains, etc., and, through the courts, to enforce their decisions.

This method of control by the legislatures has spread from state to state until at present twenty-two states have railroad commissions for the control of the traffic that is carried on within the state.

Inasmuch, however, as a large part of the traffic is interstate, and inasmuch as under the United States constitution interstate commerce is under the control of the United States, it was found necessary to establish in 1887 the interstate commerce commission, a board consisting of five members appointed by the President, whose duty it should be to have the oversight of interstate commerce as the state commissions have of commerce within the separate states (see INTERSTATE COMMERCE LAW, U.S.A.). The powers of the commission are in the main those given to the commission of the state of Illinois. Under certain general rules laid down by the statute, the commission is empowered to prescribe reasonable rates, to take cognisance in a judicial way of complaints made of violation of the law, and to make rulings regarding them, the power of enforcement, however, being in the hands of the United States courts.

While, as yet, neither the state commissions nor the interstate commerce commission have been able to prevent all abuses, the law being frequently evaded, especially as regards discrimination in rates between different shippers, it is nevertheless true that these abuses, under the careful oversight of the commissions, are becoming rapidly less. The commissions are greatly extending their power, they are acting harmoniously one with the other, and there can be little question that they will be able in the future gradually to assume a more strict control of the railroads than has been the case heretofore.

In the United States the telegraphs are in the hands of private corporations. Earlier there were many competing companies, most of which, however, were gradually absorbed by the more powerful ones, until at present (1895) only two of consequence remain : the Western Union Telegraph Company, which controls from 85 to 90 per cent of the lines throughout the country, and the Postal Telegraph Company which controls the remainder.

Within the municipalities it is customary for the waterworks to be owned and managed by the municipality, though there are of course very many exceptions. Until within a very few years the gasworks were all owned by private corporations, but recently several cities —some twelve or fifteen—have obtained control of their gas and electric lighting plants. The only large city, however, which owns its own gasworks is Philadelphia. The tendency at present is clearly toward public ownership and management of the lighting facilities in the cities. The telephones in the United States are owned entirely by private corporations, most of them by the Bell Telephone Company, though, since the expiration of some of its patents within the last year, several rival companies have been started.

Of chief significance, however, in the United States are those monopolies which may be called capitalistic monopolies, the industries that become monopolies simply through the advantages that come from the use of large capital. The first great monopoly of this class was the Standard Oil Company, which, through a process of rapid growth through ten or fifteen years, with the advantages of lower freight rates on the railroads than its rivals could secure, finally, in 1882, was organised into the Standard Oil Trust, a combination that was able to control 85 per cent of the total output of refined petroleum in the country. For many years the business of the trust was confined entirely to the refining industry, the petroleum fields and raw petroleum being in the hands of other companies ; but of late years one of the largest and most important of the petroleum fields has fallen into the hands of the Standard Company. The other most important capitalistic monopolies are the American Sugar Refining Company (Sugar Trust), the Distilling and Cattle Feeding Company (Whisky Trust) ; with several other large ones, especially the combinations controlling cotton-seed oil, linseed oil, white lead, dressed meat, cordage, and tobacco. In very many other industries, however, the leading manufacturers and dealers have formed combinations so that over large stretches of territory they have been able to hold almost a complete monopoly, some of the latest books on the subject giving, of the names simply of monopolies, lists that fill eight pages closely printed, and contain the names of some hundreds of distinct monopolistic establishments.

The word trust, as applied to monopolies in the United States, describes simply a form of business organisation. It is really a partnership of corporations. The plan was first devised by the Standard Oil Company, and was afterwards adopted by many others. It consisted, briefly, of an organisation made by a surrender on the part of the stockholders of the different corporations entering into the trust, of their separate shares of stock, to a board of trustees, the trustees holding from the individual stockholders an irrevocable power of attorney. In return the trustees issued trust certificates which represented an equitable share in the combined properties. The business of all the corporations was then managed in unison by the trustees, and the profits of all, being pooled, were distributed among the certificate holders in proportion to their holdings. In this way the interests of the different corporations were made common, the management was made harmonious, and no member, corporation or individual, had it within his power to withdraw from the organisation, as had been done earlier by members of some of the tentative pools that had been organised to prevent competition. Owing to hostile legislation against trusts, many of them have been put back into the corporation form by issuing to each trust-certificate holder a corresponding amount of capital stock in the new corporation, giving him an undivided interest in all establishments represented.

The causes of these industrial monopolies are clearly to be found in the modern form of industrial organisation, in which immense amounts of capital are required. Competition between such great establishments becomes so fierce that often ruin threatens all the rival establishments unless some form of agreement between them is reached. In many instances they have been aided by the railroads, which gave them preferential freight rates, sometimes the tariff laws have helped them.

The results of these monopolies are in part beneficial to society, in part dangerous. (1) A great saving to society is effected by working the best plants in the combination to their full capacity, and stopping the others entirely. (2) All the production in any one line is put under the management of the leading experts in the country. (3) A great organisation with branches in different parts of the country, by supplying its customers from the nearest establishments, is able to save much in transportation, especially in the case of bulky articles. (4) A very large establishment is able to save much in the way of side products that in a small establishment must be wasted. (5) A very great establishment can often afford to keep in its employ inventors and experts whose sole business it is to devise new and improved methods of production. (6) Through these savings it is possible for the monopolies, while still making a good profit, to lower prices to consumers. A careful study of their influence on prices within the last few years in the United States, however, shows that, while their prices might have been lowered, the monopolies preferred rather to increase their profits, so that the prices have been somewhat higher than formerly under the system of free competition. It has been impossible, however, for the prices to be kept much above the level of competitive prices, on account of the new rivals that were thus called into the field. In the case of the sugar monopoly, for example, the higher prices demanded soon after the organisation of the Sugar Trust, within two years called several powerful rivals into the field, which forced prices down to competitive rates again for some two years, when, these rivals combining with the original trust, it thus obtained control of more than 90 per cent of the refining plants in the country, and again put the prices above competitive rates. Under monopoly, prices are doubtless somewhat steadier than under a system of free competition, but when changes are made in price, they are likely to be made with less warning and to be greater in extent than under a competitive system.

One of the greatest evils in connection with the trusts has been the speculation in their stocks by the managers. Nearly all of the most important of these capitalistic monopolies have been thus dishonestly managed. Again, there is a tendency, on account of the certain market and sure profits, for the managers of monopolies to become less enterprising, inventive, careful in business methods, than those with competitors, though as yet this tendency has not been strongly manifested in the United States. The fact that a much smaller proportion of the men engaged in business in the country are placed upon their own individual responsibility under the monopoly system, will beyond question have a powerful effect upon social conditions and business habits. Beyond doubt too the fact that these large enterprises were likely to be attacked by legislators, and that they also have desired important legislation, at times, in their own interest, has led often to corruption of legislatures and courts.

The danger to the public from these organisations has been so keenly felt that congress and no fewer than eighteen states have passed laws declaring them illegal, and prescribing heavy penalties for their promotion. Several court decisions also declare them illegal under the common law. Nevertheless, under some form they still continue. They are so clearly a product of present industrial conditions and methods that they can hardly be suppressed. Beyond question, the wisest way to deal with them is to control them by inspection and publicity, and possibly by some control over unreasonable prices, as there is in Canada. A commission like a railroad commission could probably control them sufficiently. Their possibilities for good are too many to make it desirable to destroy them.

[*Report of the Committee on Manufactures of the House of Representatives*, 50th Congress, No. 4165. —*New York Senate Report on Trusts*, 1888.— *Report of Canadian Legislature on Trusts and Combinations*, 1888.—W. W. Cook, *Trusts; Corporation Problem; Stock and Stockholders; and Corporation Law*, ch. xxix.—Beach, *On Private Corporations*, ch. xli. The last two authorities give bibliographies.—Stimson, *American Statute Law*, vol. ii.—*The Economic Journal*, March 1892. —*Political Science Quarterly*, March, September, December 1888 ; June 1889 ; September 1894.— *Atlantic Monthly*, March 1881.—S. C. T. Dodd. *Combinations, their Uses and Abuses.*—H. D. Lloyd, *Wealth against Commonwealth.*—Ernst von Halle, *Trusts, or Industrial Combinations in the United States.*]   J. W. J.

MONOPOLY means literally sale by one man ; but the term is extended to denote either sale, or purchase (*e.g.* of labour), by either one man or a group acting as one man (*e.g.* a trade union). The definition thus enlarged is usually, or should properly, be limited by the condition that the monopolist deals, not with another monopolist, but with parties who compete against each other. Thus Ricardo (*Political Economy*, ch. vii.): "Commodities are only at a monopoly price . . . when the competition is wholly on one side . . . amongst the buyers." And this limitation is reasonable ; for value in "isolated exchange" (Böhm-Bawerk) is not determined by the same laws as in "one-sided competition" (*id.*). Such is the definition here adopted ; to the exclusion of a wider sense sanctioned by authority, according to which monopoly exists wherever the number of sellers is not reduced to one, but restricted to a class. It is in this sense that Adam Smith speaks of "the monopoly of the colonial trade," and Cairnes and Professor Bastable, of a country having the monopoly of an article, although the traders in the privileged country are not supposed to be in combination. So Mill treats of the "natural monopoly in favour of skilled labourers" (*Pol. Econ.*, bk. ii. ch. xiv. § 2, § 3, par. 1, ch. xv. § 3, last par.) ; and, in another connection, considers the case of the "sharers in the monopoly" being "numerous" (bk. v. ch. x. § 4). Senior, observing that competition is not free where the concurrence of "an appropriated natural agent" is required, describes the proprietor of such agent as a monopolist. According to him, all landlords are monopolists (*Political Economy*, p. 105) ; Schäffle designates as *Monopol Verhältnisse*, those advantages which he has treated of as "ausschliessende Verhältnisse." But according to the view here taken, *Monopoly* does not include RENT and quasi rent.

Monopoly in the sense here adopted plays a greater part in modern economics than has been assigned to it in the classical treatises. Witness the spread of trade unionism, the growth of combination in the new form of trusts, the prevalence of joint-stock companies, particularly railway companies. Mr. Baker estimates that the yearly earnings of all "transportation lines" in the United States, are about one-tenth of the total value of all the year's products. The sphere of monopoly is also being enlarged by the growth of municipal and governmental industries.

The determination of value under monopoly is not so simple as might be supposed from some expressions of classical writers. Thus Adam Smith says: "The price of a monopoly is upon any occasion the highest which can be got" (*Wealth of Nations*, bk. i. ch. vii.); and Ricardo "when a commodity is at a monopoly price, it is at the very highest price at which the consumers are willing to purchase it" (*Political Economy*, ch. vii.). These propositions are true theoretically, upon the hypothesis that the monopolist makes a separate bargain with each buyer. But in practice he must often find a uniform price for all, or at least a whole class of purchasers. The simplest case is where one price is made for the whole market, and the article monopolised is supplied without cost, *e.g.* the water of a "mineral spring" (Cournot). The price is determined by the condition that price × the amount demanded at that price—the product of an ordinate and co-ordinate of the DEMAND CURVES—should be a maximum. The case is less simple, the representation less elegant, when cost of production is incurred by the monopolist, and when he fixes different prices for the same articles sold to different classes (*e.g.* theatre tickets to soldiers and to citizens), or for different articles which have in part JOINT PRODUCTS; such as the carriage of different classes of goods on a railway, the permanent expenses of which are paid out of the rates indiscriminately. The only general principle is to charge on each article "what the traffic will bear."

So far, we have supposed only one monopolist. But when there are two monopolists controlling respectively two factors of production, *e.g.* gas and water power, for which there is a joint demand, the determination of value is more difficult (Marshall, *Principles*, bk. v. ch. x.), the oppression of the consumer is likely to be greater (Cournot, *Principes*, ch. ix.).

There are several circumstances which prevent monopoly prices from rising to the full height determined by the preceding theory. The monopolist, for the sake of his own future custom, will not exact the uttermost farthing. Thus American railway companies nurse infant

cities, and have even "discriminated" in favour of individuals who are likely to be good customers. Again, the monopolist will refrain from provoking competition by excessive prices. He may be influenced, too, by a regard for public opinion, and even a concern for the interests of the consumer. The last feeling may especially be expected where the monopoly is held by government. In this case, the surplus which the monopolist seeks to maximise will not be simply his own net revenue, but some mean between that surplus and CONSUMERS' RENT, which Prof. Marshall calls *Compromise Benefit* (*Principles*, v. ch. xiii.).

In general, prices under monopoly are higher than they would have been under competition, *other things being equal*. But other things are not equal, for the expenses of production are apt to be less under monopoly, owing (1) to the advantages of production on a large scale; (2) the avoidance of waste incident to competition. Four or five tobacconists in America spend annually in advertising against each other some 3,000,000 dollars (say £600,000), of which two-thirds at least could be saved by combination (Jenks). The balance of forces tending to raise and to lower prices, seems to be against the consumer in the case of some trusts which Prof. Jenks has examined. Even if the price of whisky, or refined sugar, has fallen, it has not fallen as much as might have been expected in view of the fall in the price of the raw material. Nor is the consumer much benefited by the alleged greater steadiness of monopoly prices. The variations in the price of whisky became, after the formation of the trust, less frequent, but more violent.

The injury to consumers is fairly well evidenced. The injustice to producers is even more clearly evident. Mr. Baker estimates that out of 18,000,000 American workers, some 5,500,000 derive benefit from monopolies; that is, about one-third are benefited at the expense of two-thirds. The greater part of the extra gains are concentrated in the hands of a much smaller minority. The high rate of profits enjoyed by trusts may be another evidence of inequitable gains, which it is difficult to obtain owing to the practice of watering stock.

One remedy for these evils is fortunately of comparatively easy application, where the monopoly is a corporation, namely publicity.

[For the definition of monopoly, consult Sidgwick, *Political Economy*, bk. ii. ch. x.; Senior, *Political Economy*, p. 103; and the *Nouveau Dictionnaire de l'Économie Politique*, with the references there given. As to the prevalence of monopoly at present, Foxwell "Monopoles" in the *Revue d'Économie Politique* for 1889; *Parliamentary Papers*, Foreign Office miscellaneous series, No. 174, 1890, c. 5826, 32, Report on Trusts; C. W. Baker, *Monopolies and the People*. On the value of monopolised articles, Cournot, *Principes Mathematiques*; Marshall, *Principles*, bk. v. ch. xiii.; Auspitz and Lieben, *Theorie der Preise*, 72-75, and other mathematical economists; Hadley, on *Railway Transportation*, and other works relating to railway rates. On the good and evil of modern monopolies, Foxwell and Baker as before; also J. W. Jenks in *Economic Journal*, March 1892; *Political Science Quarterly*, September 1894; Andrews, in *Quarterly Journal of Economics*, January 1889. The most forcible denunciation of monopoly is to be found in classical chapters of the *Wealth of Nations*, bk. iv. ch. vii. pt. iii., and ch. viii.; also bk. v. ch. i. Cp. Mill, *Political Economy*, bk. v. ch. x. § 4.] F. Y. E.

(See EXCHANGE, VALUE IN; PATENT LAWS.)

MONROE DOCTRINE, the name given to a celebrated declaration of policy made by President Monroe on behalf of the United States. It arose out of two separate complications. The first was the design of the Holy Alliance[1] to give assistance to Spain in her attempts to reduce her revolted South American colonies to submission; and the second was the series of differences between the United States, Great Britain, and Russia with regard to territorial dominion and boundary lines in the north-western parts of North America. Great Britain was strongly opposed to the Holy Alliance, and CANNING, who was then secretary of state for foreign affairs, informed the American government of its intentions, and proposed a joint declaration, setting forth that the two countries were determined to prevent the intervention of any foreign power in the struggle between Spain and her colonies. This project fell through; but it was known that the two English-speaking peoples were prepared to act in concert. Their determination to assist each other in keeping the Holy Alliance out of South and Central America was not affected by their differences with regard to the other matter dealt with by the doctrine under review. Under these circumstances, on 2nd December 1823, President Monroe, in his annual message to congress, declared, *first*, that "the American continents, by the free and independent condition which they have assumed and maintain, are henceforth not to be considered as subjects for future colonisation by any European powers"; and *secondly*, that "we [the United States] should consider any attempt on their [the European powers'] part to extend their system to any portion of this hemisphere as dangerous to our peace and safety. With the existing colonies or dependencies of any European power we have not interfered and shall not interfere. But with the governments who have declared their independence and maintained it, and whose independence we have, on great consideration and on just principles, acknowledged, we could not view any interposition for the purpose of oppressing them, or controlling in any other manner their destiny, by any European power,

[1] Formed by Alexander I., emperor of Russia, in 1815; in conjunction with Francis I., emperor of Austria; and Frederick William III., king of Prussia.

in any other light than as the manifestation of an unfriendly disposition towards the United States."

These declarations have become a sort of sacred text, and they have shared the fate of other sacred texts in being overloaded with a mass of comments. And, as is usually the case, the commentators may be divided into two classes, those who seek to extend and those who seek to restrict the meaning of the original. The first part of the Monroe doctrine has been taken to forbid the acquisition of any further dominion on the North American continent by European powers (message of President Polk, 2nd December 1845); while the second part was held to justify even a strongly-worded protest against the confederation of the Canadian provinces (resolution of the House of Representatives, 27th March 1867). On the other hand, Mr. R. H. Dana, in his edition of Wheaton's *International Law*, sums up an elaborate examination of the whole subject by the statements that the declaration against colonisation referred only to the acquisition of sovereign title by new and original occupation, and the declaration against European interposition in the affairs of American states was meant to do no more than forbid the extension to the American continent of the system whereby the great powers exercise control over European affairs.

We need not discuss the statement that the American continent is closed against future colonisation. Whatever may have been the case in 1823, it is certain that in 1896 there is no part of the New World which does not belong to a civilised state. Territory in it may, therefore, be acquired by cession or conquest, but not by occupation in that technical sense which signifies the taking and keeping possession of what was at the time of seizure the property of no recognised subject of INTERNATIONAL LAW. The existence of boundary questions does not militate against this view. They presuppose that the districts in dispute are under the rule of some civilised power, the only difficulty being to apportion them among rival claimants.

The really important part of the Monroe doctrine is the assertion of the principle that the state-system of Europe must not be extended to America. Washington, in his farewell address, bequeathed to his countrymen the policy of keeping clear of European entanglements. They accepted the legacy, and soon showed a strong disposition to add to it the corollary that Europe must refrain from meddling in Transatlantic affairs. The circumstances already mentioned brought this clause of their political creed to the front, and it has remained ever since a cardinal principle of the external policy of the United States. Statesmen have differed as to how far it should be carried, but none have been found to deny it. Successive administrations have acted upon it with more or less of vigour, and the American people support it with practical unanimity. Like most other doctrines the Monroe doctrine has grown with the process of assertion and definition. It has been subject both to healthy development and to unhealthy growth. If we want to know what it is held to cover at any particular time, we must refer to the words and deeds of the American statesmen of that time rather than to the intentions and designs of President Monroe or Mr. John Quincy Adams, his secretary of state. There can be no doubt that in its name the United States would object to the acquisition of fresh territory on the American continent by any European states, whatever were the means employed for obtaining it ; and quite recently President Cleveland has argued that it justifies his intervention in the boundary dispute between Great Britain and Venezuela. The United States do, in fact, occupy a position of pre-eminence in the New World very similar to the position of the six great powers in Europe, though they have kept themselves free from pledges to other American states to assist them against European attacks ; and they define and defend their hegemony by reference to the Monroe doctrine. That doctrine is not international law ; but it is a cardinal principle of American policy, which other powers must take into account if they wish to keep on good terms with the great Transatlantic republic. Indications have not been wanting that the doctrine may develop an economic side, which would in practice tend towards a commercial union of American states.

[Wharton, *International Law Digest*, §§ 57-68. —Dana, note on the "Monroe Doctrine," in his ed. of Wheaton's *International Law*. — Lawrence, *Principles of International Law*, § 136.—*American History Leaflets*, No. 4. President Monroe's message of 1823, containing the statement of the Monroe doctrine, is given in full, in No. 56 of the *Old South Leaflets*, recently published by the directors of the Old South Studies in History, Old South Meeting House, Boston, Mass.]. T. J. L.

MONTAIGNE, MICHEL DE (1533-1592). Although, in his rambling way, the author of the *Essays* touched on innumerable topics, he rather cautiously avoided social and political questions.

"We owe submission and obedience to all kings, for this is due to their office, but we only owe our esteem and affection to their virtues" (bk. i. ch. 3). Having satisfied his conscience with this restriction, Montaigne, who lived in the midst of the havoc of religious and civil wars, invariably repeats that he is "disgusted with novelty, whatever may be its features" (bk. i. ch. 22).

He had come to the conclusion that "the profit of one man is the loss of another" (bk. i. ch. 21), and expressly mentions the merchant as

an illustration. On sumptuary laws, he is more enlightened ; he considers them as going against their object, as good examples derived from kings and great people would be much more effective (bk. i. ch. 43). Some hints on the desirableness of instituting municipal offices of information, and on the usefulness of keeping detailed and accurate family journals and account books (bk. i. ch. 34), are probably the only remaining utterances of Montaigne which ought to be noticed here.

E. Ca.

MONTANARI, GEMINIANO (1633-1687). Born at Modena, Italy. An able mathematician and astronomer, he was mathematical professor for fourteen years at the university of Bologna, and afterwards professor of astronomy and meteorology at the university of Padua, in which city he died. To students of economics he is known by his two works on coins, written about 1680, and published seventy years later by Argelati in his collection of works on coins, and afterwards reproduced in the collection of CUSTODI. These works possess much merit notwithstanding the evident traces of the influence of BODIN—an influence greatly felt by all thinkers at that period.

Fluent and animated in style, Montanari freely criticises the mistaken views held in his day on the coinage question, and the injurious effect of alterations in coins, and the raising their nominal value ; and points out the rules which should be observed in coining money at the mints. His investigations on money necessarily lead him to an examination of the question of value. He combats the idea of an invariable relation of the value between gold and silver asserted by Bodin and SCARUFFI. He reduces the laws of value to the element of scarcity —understanding scarcity not as absolute, but relative to the extent of the demand.

In his researches, says Graziani, Montanari succeeds in explaining all the general phenomena of value, though without thoroughly understanding the intricate and difficult subject—the value of money.

Breve trattato del valore delle monete in tutti gli stati, 1680.—*La zecca in consulta di stato, trattato mercantile*, etc. 1687. Republished by Custodi in his collection of Italian classical economists, under the title of *Delle monete, trattato mercantile*.

[Cossa, *Introduction to the Study of Political Economy*, London, 1893.—Bianchini, *Della scienza del ben vivere sociale*, Palermo, 1845, p. 170.—Graziani, *Le idee economiche degli economisti emiliani e romagnoli*, Modena, 1893, pp. 45-48.] U. R.

MONTAZGO, called *carnerage* in Aragon, a toll levied by Spanish kings on migrating flocks of cattle at certain passes in the mountains. It was suppressed in 1758.

[Canga Argüelles, *Diccionario de Hacienda* (London, 1826). See also MESTA.] E. Ca.

MONTCHRÉTIEN, ANTOYNE DE (c. 1576-1621), a Huguenot, a second-rate poet, and a hard-ware manufacturer, dedicated in 1615 to the king (Louis XIII.), and the queen-mother, his *Traicté de l'Œconomie Politique*. This seems to be the first work ever issued under that title; and the use of the phrase is undoubtedly significant. But there is absolutely no ground for the assertion, maintained by some enthusiastic French writers, and notably by his latest editor, M. Funck-Brentano, that Montchrétien was the creator of political economy, or even that he was in any way a considerable economist. There is hardly a single argument or proposal in the book that is not borrowed from earlier writers; the passages which have been most praised for the trade policy they advocate are taken almost verbatim from BODIN. The book is really nothing but a thick mercantilist pamphlet; its style is grandiloquent and long-winded, and full of repetitions; and it is only valuable for the miscellaneous information it gives as to contemporary conditions of industry and trade in France.

The *Traicté* has been edited with a long introduction by M. Funck-Brentano (Paris, 1889); and its unoriginal character demonstrated in the *Eng. Hist. Rev.*, vi. (1891), 779. W. J. A.

MONTESQUIEU, CHARLES DE SECONDAT BARON DE LA BRÈDE ET DE MONTESQUIEU (1689-1755), born and died at La Brède near Bordeaux. One of the ablest thinkers of the 18th century, he may be considered rather a student of political science than of political economy alone, a science which in his time scarcely existed, at least not as a distinct branch of study. Following on some works in which he asserted more than he could prove, Montesquieu wrote in 1721 his *Lettres Persanes*, which for a time were all the fashion, and seven years later (1728) opened to him the doors of the French academy. This book, keen and witty criticism as it was of the men of his time, would not, however, have secured to the author that widening renown which his name has attained.

The works which have immortalised the name of Montesquieu are the two following: the first, critical and historical, is entitled *Considérations sur les causes de la grandeur des Romains et de leur décadence*, 1734; the link it possesses with economic science is through politics, as in the passage, "It is not fortune (in our time we should say chance) which rules the world. . . . There are general causes — moral or physical — which operate in each kingdom, which raise, preserve, or ruin it; every accidental occurrence is subordinate to these causes; and if the chance of a battle, that is to say a particular cause, ruins a state, this takes place because there was a general cause which led to the destruction of the state by a single battle. In short the principal force induces all particular accidents," ch. xviii. Again, the universality of immaterial laws is asserted thus: "As men at all times have had the same passions, though the occasions which produce great changes are different, the causes are always the same" (ch. i.).

The second book, *De l'Esprit des Lois*, 1748, on a much larger scale than the first, was written throughout in the same exact and concise style

peculiar to the author, and had been under preparation for some time (1728-1748), the latter year being the time of its appearance. The reputation of this masterpiece has increased with time; but it was warmly welcomed even on its first appearance.

Madame du Deffand said with a sneer, that it was "de l'esprit sur les lois." Voltaire appreciated it more highly when he wrote "the human race had lost its title-deeds; M. de Montesquieu has found them and returned them." The fact is, that though the work may have grown antiquated both in form and through the advance made in moral and political science during a century and a half, it attains in many passages a marvellous elevation, which excites first astonishment and then admiration. The remarks on the influence of climate on national character and economic condition, bks. xiv.-xvi., are among Montesquieu's most characteristic points. Some passages on economic questions may be selected, in which the author is indisputably in advance of his age. Thus in bk. xx. ch. ii. "The natural result of commerce is peace. Two nations trading with each other make themselves reciprocally dependent. If it is to the interest of one to buy, it is to the interest of the other to sell, and all unions are founded on mutual necessities." Bk. xx. ch. ix., "it is commerce which sets the right value on commodities, and which establishes true relations between them." In the countries in which loans of money at interest are not regarded favourably by the law, "the lender takes on himself the risk of breaking the law," and "the rate of interest increases in proportion to the risk of the loan not being paid." "Continence is naturally linked with the expansion of the race," bk. xxiii. ch. ii., written a century before Malthus, he appears to anticipate some of that writer's conclusions. Montesquieu was in favour of direct taxation of individuals, not a taxation in proportion to their wealth, but a taxation in proportion to the surplus remaining after the satisfaction of their ordinary wants. In short, he proposed to divide the citizens, as at Athens, into classes, according to the condition of the individuals. No doubt there were economic subjects on which he too readily adopted the mistakes of his time. He supported the sale of offices; he inclined to the mercantile system; he had no clear idea of the economic position of money, though he said, and rightly, "that the use of money by a nation was one indication of civilisation," bk. xviii. ch. xv. He preached also the equalisation of individual property, sympathising too much with the spirit of Lycurgus in this. It was the influence of this spirit which caused him to regard a long-continued period of national security as leading to corruption and decadence. He would willingly have consented to give up the use of money to attain the ideal of government realised by the Jesuits in Paraguay. Though he could not free himself from some of the economic errors of his time, Montesquieu showed often, and on points of the highest importance, the superiority of his judgment. In these cases he was much in advance of his contemporaries. It should not be forgotten that his book *L'esprit des lois* appeared ten years before the *Tableau Économique* of Quesnay, and twenty-eight years before the reforms of Turgot and the publication of the *Wealth of Nations*. This great thinker dominated his own age and often anticipated the economic ideas of the future.

[See references to Montesquieu in A. Smith, *W. of N.*, bk. i. ch. x., as to effect of law on rates of interest ; bk. v. ch. i., as to education and morals among the Greeks. — Hume, *Essays*, No. XI., on "Populousness of Ancient Nations," and in note T.]   A. C. f.

MONTHLY ASSESSMENTS were a tax first levied by the long parliament during the civil war, continued throughout the commonwealth, and occasionally used under Charles II. and William III. They were an improvement upon the old SUBSIDIES, being more evenly assessed rather than more productive. A sum, based upon the highest produce of a subsidy, was fixed, and proportionately assessed upon both real and personal property by local commissioners for each county ; it was levied upon occupiers, to be by them deducted from their rent. Church lands and goods were included, and it was the establishment of this as permanent which occasioned the cession by the clergy in convocation of their taxing powers in return for the right of voting at parliamentary elections. The tax varied from £35,000 to £120,000 a month, and was generally levied for three or more months in succession, a proportionate sum being also sometimes obtained from Scotland and Ireland. After 1690-91, the year of the highest sum ever raised by this tax, monthly assessments gave way to a new form of property-tax.

[Dowell's *Hist. of Taxation*, vols. ii. iii.—For details of assessment in 1660 see Sinclair, *Public Revenue*, i. 304, note.]   E. G. P.

MONTHS, FOURTHS OF. In any analysis of the returns of the Clearing House, reference is frequently made to the "Fourths of the Month." The origin of this is found in the fact that a custom exists in many branches of trade to date the bills drawn on their debtors on the first day of the month. These bills become, according to the English mercantile law, by the operation of the DAYS OF GRACE (*q.v.*), payable on the fourth of the month in which they fall due. Hence a larger number of purely commercial transactions, as a rule, pass through the Clearing House on the fourth of the month than on any other day, and the amount of the returns is regarded as a proof of activity or slackness in trade. This observation refers, as stated, to the "purely commercial transactions" ; those on stock exchange account days, and consol settling days, largely exceed the "fourths of the months," but it is only the latter which are under notice here.

The table which follows shows the amounts paid on the "fourths of the month," since the commencement of the publication of the clearing house returns in 1868, to the present time. The totals of the annual clearings are likewise added, and columns of proportional figures. By these the progress of the transactions of the "fourths of the month," relatively to the total transactions, can be easily traced. It will be observed by comparing column three with columns four and six, that the amount of business done on the "fourths of the month" has not kept 'its own relatively to the total transactions. This corresponds to the known fact that fewer bills of exchange are now drawn in proportion to business done than used formerly to be the case. At the same time the "fourths of the month" are still important, and the amount of business done on those days is carefully watched and noted by those engaged in business.

London Clearing House Returns, 1868-1895.

The following table gives the particulars as divided between the amounts received on the Fourths of the Month and the total ; columns of proportionate figures have been added which show the proportion which each of these heads bears to the total transactions of each year, and also the difference between the amounts in each year and in the year 1868, the earliest to which the statement extends.

1	2	3	4	5	6
Year.	Clearings on Fourths of the Month.	Proportion of amount in each year to 1868. 1868=100.	Proportion of Fourths of the Month to total.	Total Clearing for the Years.	Proportion of amount in each year to 1868. 1868=100.
	£	100	%	£	100
1868	155,068,000	100	4.5	3,425,185,000	100
1869	169,729,000	110	4.7	3,626,396,000	106
1870	176,137,000	114	4.5	3,914,220,000	114
1871	211,095,000	136	4.4	4,826,034,000	141
1872	256,899,000	166	4.3	5,916,452,000	172
1873	272,156,000	175	4.5	6,070,948,000	177
1874	265,427,000	171	4.5	5,936,772,000	173
1875	245,810,000	159	4.4	5,685,793,000	166
1876	225,936,000	146	4.5	4,963,480,000	145
1877	232,630,000	150	4.6	5,042,383,000	147
1878	217,753,000	141	4.4	4,992,398,000	146
1879	213,348,000	138	4.3	4,885,937,000	143
1880	236,809,000	153	4.1	5,794,238,000	169
1881	253,133,000	163	3.9	6,357,059,000	185
1882	238,150,000	153	3.8	6,221,206,000	181
1883	239,080,000	154	4.0	5,929,404,000	173
1884	242,659,000	157	4.2	5,798,555,000	169
1885	221,873,000	143	4.0	5,511,071,000	161
1886	215,519,000	139	3.7	5,901,925,000	172
1887	256,469,000	165	4.2	6,077,097,000	177
1888	272,091,000	175	3.9	6,942,172,000	203
1889	290,711,000	187	3.8	7,618,766,000	223
1890	289,107,000	186	3.7	7,801,048,000	228
1891	264,501,000	170	3.8	6,847,506,000	200
1892	260,422,000	168	4.0	6,481,562,000	190
1893	268,084,000	173	4.1	6,478,013,000	189
1894	261,547,000	168	4.1	6,337,222,000	185
1895	283,610,000	182	3.7	7,592,886,000	222

MONTS DE PIÉTÉ. Early in their history several small Italian states exacted from their citizens forced loans, on which interest was paid ;

the sums of money thus raised formed what was called a *mons*, or heap. The name of *montes pietatis* is derived from this ; the second word distinguishes these from the earlier founded *montes coacti*, and is given to the charitable funds for granting loans on the security of pawned articles, which were established in Italy towards the middle of the 15th century (Orvieto, 1463, Perugia, with papal authority, 1467, Viterbo, 1472, etc.). The Franciscans were their warmest advocates, and various spiritual and temporal privileges were granted to the contributors to this pious purpose ; but as they proved inadequate to attract the necessary funds, several *montes* began to accept deposits at a moderate rate of interest. This, and the levying a small percentage to cover working expenses, gave rise to a fierce controversy between the Franciscans on the one side and the Dominicans on the other, the latter maintaining that the system was based on usury (see CANON LAW). However, in 1515, the Lateran council and the pope, Leo X., sanctioned the right to levy a moderate interest, provided the object were not to realise a private gain. Thenceforward the Italian *monti di pietà*, mostly under ecclesiastical management, enjoyed the steady protection of the popes, though some of them, especially the *mons* in Rome, assumed much of the character of a bank, and became owners of considerable property.

In Spain, notwithstanding the national religious devotion, and the rapid success of these institutions in the Spanish Netherlands, the first *monte de piedad* was not founded till the beginning of the 18th century under Philip V., the first king of the Bourbon dynasty. They now exist under government supervision in the most important towns. The *montes de piedad* are to be distinguished from the numerous *montes pios*, which like the *montes granatici* in Italy, supplied corn, wine, and agricultural produce generally, to the population during periods of scarcity or at seed-time.

North of the Alps, the *monts de piété* found at their first introduction a congenial soil in the Netherlands, where the pawning business had until then been monopolised by Italian money dealers, whose authorised rate of interest varied from 20 to 55 per cent, and who, in the popular Flemish language, have left their name (*Lombaard*) to the *monts de piété*, although a designation literally translated from the French (*Berg van Barmhertigheid*) has taken its place in modern times. They were first introduced in 1618 by Wenceslas Cœberger under archduke Albert, and soon were in operation in all the principal towns. Placed under the control of a general superintendent, they rather combined the characteristics of banking and of charitable establishments, lending at from 15 to 18 per cent. In modern Belgium the managing officers are appointed by the communal authorities, and

the funds supplied primarily by the *Bureaux de Bienfaisance* (poor boards), secondarily by the municipality itself.

In Germany, the civic authorities had, from the commencement of the 14th century, established banks on their own account in some of the imperial towns, Frankfurt 1402, Nuremberg 1598 ; these banks cleared the way for the adoption of *Pfandhäuser* on the Italian model. The first of these was founded in 1591 at Augsburg and still exists. This example was soon followed in Nuremberg, Ulm, and later in Hamburg (1650). A great number of these establishments, often of a municipal, sometimes of a private character, were started during the 18th century. Owing to the federal constitution of the German empire and the legislative powers of the individual states, state, municipal, and private *Leih* and *Pfandhäuser* co-exist at the present day ; the Berlin *Leihhaus*, for instance, is a royal institution. The ruling principle may be stated thus : private *Pfandhäuser* must be licensed, and are submitted to control by the local authorities, but the licence cannot be withheld on other grounds than personal unworthiness, or the absence of the need for such an establishment. The authorities of each state may require its foundation, wherever the want is felt. Generally speaking, the same system of licensing prevails in Austria.

In France, notwithstanding some ineffectual attempts under Louis XIII. and Louis XIV. it was long before the *Monts de Piété* were naturalised. After 1577 one was installed in Avignon, which city was papal territory until the French Revolution. In 1777 a royal patent was granted to the managers of the hospitals to set up a house for loans on movable pledges in Paris ; they lent at 10 per cent *per annum*, and from 1777 to 1789 the yearly totals of their loans amounted on an average to about 8,000,000 sterling. The National Assembly decreed the liberty of the profession, and during the troubled period of the first republic the most frightful abuses ensued. In 1797 the Directory appointed five *administrateurs* of respectability to re-open the *Mont de Piété*, which had been closed in 1795, and to start it anew with their own capital, amounting to £20,000. The rate of 3 per cent per month at which they advanced money was gratefully hailed by crowds of needy borrowers. Through the confidence they inspired, the *administrateurs* were able to raise money on lenient terms, and gradually to bring down the rate of interest on their own loans to 12 per cent per annum. In 1804 Napoleon paid off their shares, and the Paris *Mont de Piété* became a public institution enjoying a monopoly for this kind of transactions. Until 1840 twenty-four *commissionnaires* acted as intermediate agents between the population of distant quarters and the *Mont de Piété* itself, but they were then suppressed, and branch establishments organised in their place. Similar institutions are now to be found in all the chief towns of France ; under a law of 1851, they must be authorised by the municipal council and managed by a paid director assisted by a board, whose unpaid members are appointed by the prefect and presided over by the *Maire*. The surplus of receipts over expenses, after a proper deduction for forming the necessary capital, must be paid over to hospitals or other charitable institutions, according to the decision of the prefect. The *Monts de Piété* are entitled to accept donations and legacies.

The contracting a loan is authenticated by a document called *reconnaissance ;* the value of the article pledged is ascertained under the joint responsibility of official *commissaires priseurs ;* and as *reconnaissances* are transferable, this way of proceeding has given rise to a rather unpleasant traffic based on the lowness of the estimates (see the *Économiste Français*, August 1890, p. 133). At the end of the stipulated term, generally one year, the articles must be redeemed or the engagement renewed ; if these formalities are not gone through, they are sold by public auction, the borrowers having three years to claim the eventual surplus resulting from the sale. Any borrower may require the sale of the articles he has deposited at the end of three months. The Paris *Mont de Piété*, whose operations exceed those of the forty-one provincial *Monts de Piété* (say about £1,400,000 against £1,000,000 a year), grants advances, since the beginning of 1894, on securities such as shares, debentures, national stock, etc. It accepts deposits at from 2 to 3 per cent, and charges 7 per cent (commission included) on its loans.

Many objections have been made to *Monts de Piété*. It has been said that they put on the same footing the spendthrift, the prostitute and the deserving head of a family, and that they deprive the borrower of the use of the pawned articles, whilst the owner of a mortgaged property keeps its management in his hands and is thus enabled to earn the monies required for payment of interest and repayment of principal. Still it cannot be doubted that they afford means of assisting small tradesmen and working people during temporary embarrassment and that now as at the end of the last century there is a great deal of truth in Turgot's opinion (in his *Mémoire sur les Prêts d'Argent*), that "the poor man is happy to find the assistance he wants without being exposed to any other risk than the loss of his pledge." (See CANON LAW ; PAWNBROKING.)

[Endemann, *Studien in der Romanisch kanonistischen Wirthschafts- und Rechts-Lehre*, pp. 460-471, Berlin, 1874, 1883. — Iglesias, *Beneficencia en España*, pp. 399-403. — De Decker, *Les Monts de Piété en Belgique*, Brussels, 1844. — Blaize, *Les Monts de Piété*, Paris, 1856. — Neumann, *Gesch. des Wuchers in Deutschland.* — E. Duval, *Manuel de Législation des Monts de Piété*, Coulommiers, 1886 ; and *Le Mont de Piété de Paris*, Imprimerie Nationale, 1881, and the articles *Leihhäuser* and

Pfandleihgeschäfte in Conrad's *Handwörterbuch der Staatswissenschaften*, Jena, 1892.]   E. ca.

MONTYON, ANTOINE ROBERT AUGET, Baron de (1733-1820), was born and died in Paris. Montyon was known chiefly by the establishment of his "prix de vertu," and also by the Montyon *prix de Statistique* founded in his honour, and won, among others, by LE PLAY.

He left two works, still often read, though they contain much rubbish mixed only with a little that is good. These are : *Quelle influence ont les diverses espèces d'impôts sur la moralité, l'activité, et l'industrie des peuples*, 8vo, 1808, reprinted in 1848 in Guillaumin's collection (*Mélanges d'économie politique*, t. ii.), and *Particularités et observations sur les ministres des finances de France les plus célèbres de 1690 à 1791*, 1812, 8vo. In the first of these works, Montyon writes rather as a philanthropist than an economist or a financier. He desired that taxation should inculcate morality, should favour marriage, be heavy on those who remained single, and hinder luxury. In the second, he extolled Necker, and declares that Turgot had done nothing important for the prosperity of France. He showed his firmness of character when he chose rather to forfeit his position as commissioner than to acquiesce in the violation of the irremovability of the magistrates committed in 1771, by the chancellor N. de Maupeou, the protégé of Mme. Du Barry.   A. C. f.

MONYPENNY, DAVID, author of a work on the *Poor Laws* "a work of considerable authority," M'Culloch (*Lit. of Pol. Econ.*, p. 298).

He wrote : *The claims of the Established Church of Scotland on the country . . . in the present Crisis. . . .* 2nd ed., Edinburgh, (1838 ?), 8vo.—*Proposed Alterations of the Scottish Poor Laws . . . considered and commented on.* Edinburgh, 1840, 8vo.—*Remarks on the Poor Laws and on the Method of Providing for the Poor in Scotland*, 1st ed., 1834, 8vo, 2nd ed., with additions, 1836, 8vo.   A. L.

MOORE, ADAM (fl. 1650) was author of *Bread for the Poor and Advancement of the English Nation promised by enclosure of the Wastes and Common Grounds of England*, London, 1653, 8vo. Moore lays stress on the effect of adjacent commons in engendering idleness, with its consequence, penury. Commons being divided into "uplandish" and "marish," their respective merits as breeding and feeding places for horses, cattle, and sheep, and as providing fuel, are dealt with. The conclusion is that one-fourth part of the commons, when improved, will be worth as much as the former whole. Assuming that there are two million acres of such wastes in England and Wales, the enclosure of one-fourth of these will maintain an additional 750,000 of population. Moore proposes a "grand committee" for each county to settle private claims. The poor cottagers are to be protected by the portions allotted to them being held in free SOCAGE for ever, under a small yearly rent. The value of their holdings would be thus raised from about 3d. to £40 or £50 (see ENCLOSURES).

[The merits of the tract have been perhaps overrated by M'Culloch, *Literature of Political Economy*, but its value as historical evidence is undeniable.] H. E. E.

MORA. A party to an obligation who fails to perform what is due from him when he has received notice from the other party demanding performance, *interpellatio*, is, according to the terminology of Roman law, *in mora—mora debitoris*. From the time of its occurrence he is bound to put the party who makes the claim in an equally favourable position, as if performance had been made without any default. So he must pay interest from that date, though he may not previously have been liable to do so ; and he becomes liable for all loss or damage attributable to accident, as well as to negligence, where he holds the property of another as bailee. So too, if the thing to be delivered falls in value after *mora* has set in, he must pay the highest value the thing has reached since that occurrence, unless he can prove that the party to whom he should have made delivery of the thing would not have disposed of it.

In some cases actual notice of the claim is not necessary to constitute *mora*, as when a future time of payment is fixed by the contract, according to the maxim, *Dies interpellat pro homine*. A party who is entitled to performance may be in *mora—mora creditoris*—on his side. This happens if he refuses to accept performance, when performance is duly tendered to him. The effect of this is, not to discharge the obligation, but to make him liable for all loss to the other party, which is a consequence of his not having accepted performance.

E. A. W.

MORAL RESTRAINT. See MALTHUS.

MORALITY, SYSTEMS OF, IN RELATION TO POLITICAL ECONOMY. The relation of morals to economics is often misunderstood. Political economy is, properly speaking, a science rather than an art. It aims in the first instance at the explanation of a certain class of facts, the facts, namely, of the production and distribution of wealth. The special knowledge of economic facts possessed by the economist may enable him to give valuable advice on economic questions, but this, strictly speaking, is not his business. His business is to explain, not to exhort. It is therefore beside the mark to speak of economists, as such, preaching a low morality or rejecting morality altogether. There is, however, a real relation between economics and moral science. For the facts with which political economy is concerned are in great measure facts of human conduct, and all human conduct is included in the field of moral inquiry. Hence a twofold connection between morals and economics. For

in the first place the economist cannot explain the action of human beings with reference to wealth, unless he has a theory of human nature, and a theory of human nature must include a theory of morals. The theory of morals of an economist need not be original or peculiar ; it may not even be very clearly conceived ; but a theory of morals he must have. The economist's theory of human nature and of morals will affect his account of the motives which unfit men for exertion, of the uses of competition, of the effects of the institution of private property, the influence of slavery or of personal freedom, of the economic bearing of different forms of religious belief or political constitution, of the result of different occupations on the economic capacity of man, of the economic results of the growth of population, the subdivision of land, the increase of luxury and countless other phenomena which come within the purview of his science. Thus the Greek theory that complete leisure is necessary to the perfect life, led Aristotle to hold that there must exist a class of producers themselves incapable of that life, but making it possible for those who were more gifted. Aristotle concluded therefore that the institution of slavery which he found in existence was a necessary condition of the highest civilisation. The mediæval doctrine that it was sinful to take interest for money, tended to prevent any exhaustive inquiry into the nature and uses of capital. The modern doctrine that comfort is an aid to virtue, and an abundance of means a help towards a good life, has led speculative minds to devote much more attention to the processes of production and distribution, and to take a much more complacent view of lives spent chiefly in the acquisition of wealth. How differently different minds will interpret the same economic facts may be seen by comparing Adam Smith with Ruskin. To Adam Smith happiness, that is the greatest amount of pleasure and the least amount of pain, was the only rational end of action ; he approved of personal freedom and competition as means to this end. To him, therefore, modern society appears to be in a constant state of improvement. Ruskin does not allow that happiness in this sense is the end of action. He maintains that subordination and co-operation are the true means of obtaining the highest good. He therefore regards as indications of decay much that Adam Smith regards as indications of improvement. In no science, least of all in the sciences which deal with man in society, can there be such a thing as pure passive observation. The scientific intellect always brings as much as it finds, and unconsciously imposes its forms of thought on the object which it studies. What we are and whither we are going nobody can fully tell ; and each man's version of human character and destiny is tinged with the colour of his own mind.

The charge of a low morality so often brought against the classical economists rests partly, no doubt, on the misconception of supposing that they approved of everything which they recorded, but it also rests partly on the fact that they accepted the current moral theories of their time. These theories were various forms of what is known as HEDONISM (Gk. ἡδονη, pleasure). Locke and his successors were supposed to have shown that the soul is a mere sentient subject. If this be so, good must mean pleasure, and evil pain. The rational end of action must be the greatest amount of pleasure with the least amount of pain. This moral doctrine took two principal forms, one egoistic, the other philanthropic. According to the egoistic or Epicurean version the individual can seek only his own happiness ; according to the philanthropic or utilitarian version he can seek and should seek the happiness of all. The link between the two theories is supplied through the social instinct, by gratifying which man secures at once his own happiness and that of his fellows. The utilitarian doctrine, first outlined by Hume, and afterwards elaborated by Bentham, seems to have been the theory of morals accepted by Adam Smith, by Malthus, and by most of their immediate disciples, French and English. But the philosophic and practical shortcomings, even of this enlarged hedonism, were severely exposed in the philosophical reaction of the 19th century. With all its kindliness and common sense the favourite moral theory of the older economists appeared defective both in depth and in elevation. They were accused of explaining social phenomena by the help of a low conception of human nature. The charge was grossly exaggerated, but it was not altogether destitute of foundation. Later economists frequently seem to have no definite theory of human nature, good or bad.

In the second place the economist has to take account of the various theories of morals which have found acceptance in different ages and countries. It is true that the mass of mankind never formulate a theory of conduct. Men act upon instinct, but the instinct implies a doctrine, and this doctrine is made explicit by the accredited teachers of the day, philosophers, priests, or men of letters. Did space allow, it would be easy to show how different has been the influence upon the production and distribution of wealth exercised by the classical, the mediæval, and the modern ideals of conduct. But the subject would require many volumes for its elucidation. The position taken by economists with reference to morality and systems of morals is to be understood rather by the general tenor of their writings than by reference to particular passages.

It is the utilitarian spirit, not the utilitarian dogmas, which so many of the older economists adopted.

[The reader may consult, Locke, *Essay on the Human Understanding.*—Hume, *Treatise on Human Nature.*—Bonar, *Philosophy and Political Economy.*—Ashley, *Economic History of England,* bk. ii.—Adam Smith, *Wealth of Nations*—Sidgwick, *Principles of Political Economy,* bk. iii. chs. vi. and vii.—Marshall, *Principles of Economics,* vol. i. (3rd ed.) bk. i. ch. v.—Keynes, *Scope and Method of Political Economy,* ch. ii.—Ruskin, *Unto this Last.*—Wagner, *Nationalökonomie.*—Mackenzie, *Social Philosophy.*]   F. C. M.

MORATORY LAW. A moratory law is a law passed in times of emergency, postponing for a specified time the due date of bills of exchange and other obligations. The delay or period of grace accorded by the law is sometimes, though not perhaps correctly, spoken of as a "moratorium." During the Franco-German war of 1870-71 moratory laws were several times passed by the French government. Their international effect was discussed at length and their validity upheld in the case of *Rouquette v. Overmann* (1875) L.R., 10 Q.B. 525. It is of the essence of a moratory law that it should be enacted to meet some special political or commercial emergency. For example the Bank Holidays Act 1871, which makes all bills maturing on a bank holiday payable on the succeeding day, could not properly be described as a moratory law, because it is a permanent enactment. (See also MORA.)   M. D. C.

MORCELLEMENT. This French term, literally "parcelling," is specially used to express the division of land among small peasant proprietors. Those French writers who believe that this division has been pushed to a dangerous extent, also frequently employ the expressions *émiettement* (reducing into crumbs) or "pulverisation" (in German *Zwergwirthschaft*).

It is applied both to cultivation and to ownership of land. In the former sense, much naturally depends on the kind of cultivation peculiar to the region, as corn or the vine, and to the opportunities for the sale of produce —as garden cultivation near large towns. Leaving for the moment this aspect of the question, and dealing exclusively with the *morcellement* of ownership, we notice first that it is a mistake to suppose that the existing division of land in France is entirely due, as is often stated, to the operations of the *Code Civil* (articles 815-842), enacting that the children of a deceased landowner are entitled to claim shares of his property equal in value and in kind. As known by all readers of Arthur Young, the number of peasant proprietors in France was large before the French Revolution, the principle of the present laws of succession being then in force for the property of commoners. In a paper read in 1889 before the

International Institute of Statistics, and published in the *Bulletin du Comité des Travaux Historiques et Scientifiques* of the ministry of public instruction for 1890, pp. 98-116, a French statistician, M. Gimel, computed the number of taxed landowners, before the French revolution, consequently excluding the privileged *noblesse*, at four millions. The fact is that the abolition of entails, the confiscation and sale by auction of the *nationalised* estates, and the extension of the equal division of successions, combined to give a powerful impulse to an already existing tendency.

To ascertain the present number of landowners in France, the number of *cotes* or individual "extracts" from the communal rolls of direct taxation on real property has first to be taken ; then as the same man often owns land in different *communes*, it is calculated that the number of *cotes* is about twice that of the number of actual proprietors. M. de Foville, the best authority on this subject, estimates the number of owners of real property in France at the following dates as follows :

Before the Revolution.	.	4 millions.
About 1825	. . .	6½ ,,
About 1850	. . .	7 ,,
In 1875	. . . .	8 ,,
In 1890	. . . .	from 7½ to 8 millions.

According to the decennial *Enquête* of 1882, out of the total number, 4,835,000 are rural landowners, of whom 3½ millions personally cultivate their own land.

In the agricultural *Enquête* of 1884, a classification based on the extent of land individually owned was included and carefully carried out ; it shows the following proportional percentages for very small, small, medium-sized, and large properties.

Land.	Number of *cotes*.	Occupied Area.
	per cent	per cent.
Under 2 hectares (5 acres) . .	74·09	10·53
From 2 to 6 hectares (5 to 15 acres)	15·47	15·26
From 6 to 50 hectares (15 to 125 acres)	9·58	38·94
From 50 to 200 hectares (125 to 500 acres)	0·74	19·04
Above 200 hectares (500 acres) .	0·12	16·23

The number of 10,426,328 *cotes* or "extracts" covering an area of 5,211,456 hectares or 13 millions of acres, is given for the very small properties under 5 acres. This shows that in France small and even diminutive peasant proprietorship certainly exists to a considerable extent. Still it is intermingled with a far larger proportion, in area, of medium-sized and large ownership, and it cannot consequently be maintained that as a rule the land is in a state of "pulverisation." In fact, the majority of these Lilliputian holdings are cottages with gardens annexed ; and it will

not be foreign to the present subject to state that a recent official inquiry on house property, 1887-1890, has shown that out of a total of 8,914,500 houses and dwellings, 4,969,200 were wholly and 491,100 partially occupied by their owners. There are 36,000 *communes* in all, and it is impossible to find a single house or cottage let to a stranger in more than 2000 of these.

The French legal system of inheritance has found opponents both among the friends and the enemies of small peasant-proprietorship. Among the former must be reckoned LE PLAY and his disciples, who contend that this system defeats itself when the hereditament is too small to be conveniently divided, as, in that case, the property is offered for sale and bought up by investors with capital or rich neighbours, who add their purchases to their own estates. As a remedy, they propose the introduction of the American HOMESTEAD AND EXEMPTION LAWS (*q.v.*). The mere abrogation of the article of the *Code* which enjoins compulsory division in shares of the same *kind*, would probably be more favourably accepted by public opinion. Another objection, which is directed against the *petite propriété* itself, maintains that it leads to neo-Malthusianism amongst French peasants ; the *petite propriété*, however, exists on a large scale at the present time in Belgium and in many parts of Germany ; both these are countries where the population is increasing rapidly ; consequently rural neo-Malthusianism in France cannot be exclusively or even mainly ascribed to the division of land. Besides, in France itself the departments, where population is stationary or decreasing, are not invariably those where the average size of ownership in land is the smallest.

In former time, it used also to be alleged against the *petite propriété* that it is comparatively less productive than the larger estates owned or farmed by men familiar with the art of scientific cultivation, and in possession of considerable capital. In France this objection is no longer heard much of, as most people believe that the greater energy of the small freeholder amply compensates any inferiority in this respect. This greater energy finds full scope for its exertions in several branches of culture, as vine-growing and market-gardening, to which the soil and climate of France are peculiarly congenial, and which accordingly have spread and prospered there. Moreover, this objection also applies rather to extreme division of cultivation than to extreme division of ownership, and loses much of its weight in practice, because small landowners often farm land belonging to other people and make up thus a fair-sized occupation. However, it cannot be denied that the division of cultivation arising from an excessive separation of property has in many instances and for a long time caused waste, but, where this was or is the case, the remedy is readily available by mutual exchanges, and by what has been called *commussation* or *remembrements*: From 1860-1890, M. Gorce, a surveyor in Nancy, has thus been empowered by syndicated groups of landowners to redistribute their lands and fields, and has carried out this operation in twenty-five communes of the department of Meurthe and Moselle with such success that the average increment of value of the land thus redistributed has been valued at 500 francs per hectare, or £8 per acre. On the other side of the Rhine, and also in Germany and in Austria, a legal sanction has been granted to *commassation*, and the decision of a majority made binding for the whole local body of landowners ; it is stated that two millions of separate and widely dispersed hectares, five millions of acres, have thus been consolidated into groups of connected areas.

Last and by no means least important, it is generally felt on the continent that the existence of a numerous class of very small but independent peasant proprietors is one of the safest bulwarks against the disintegrating influences at work in large closely-peopled centres.

[The standard work on the subject is M. de Foville's *Morcellement*, Paris, 1885. The same author wrote the article " Morcellement " in the *Nouveau Dictionnaire d'Économie Politique*, 1892. All French writers on agriculture from Olivier de Serres downwards, and the physiocrats and economists of the last century, have more or less examined the question. Roscher has, according to his method, carefully stated the arguments *pro* and *contra* in his *Nat. Oekonomik des Ackerbaues* (12th ed. 1888, bk. ii. chs. 4 and 11), and concludes in favour of a state of equilibrium based on a judicious mixture of large, middling, and small holdings. For the special modern French literature see Morel de Vindé, *Considérations sur le Morcellement*, 1826.—Faucher, *État et tendances de la petite propriété en France*, 1836.—H. Passy, *Essai sur la division des héritages*, 1838.—Piogey, *Du Morcellement du Sol en France*, 1857.—Legoyt, *Du Morcellement de la propriété en France et en Europe*, 1865.—Bretagne, *Étude sur le cadastre et les abornements généraux*, Nancy, 1870.—Gimel, *Division de la propriété dans le département du Nord*, Lille, 1877.—*La division de la Propriété*, 1883.—*Mémoire sur la Division de la Propriété avant et après* 1789, 1889.—Lavergne, *Économie rurale de la France.*]   E. CA.

MORE. SIR THOMAS (*c.* 1478-1535), was born in Milk Street, Cheapside, in 1478 (Seebohm's *Oxford Reformers*, Appendix C.), or about 1480 (C. More's *Life of Sir Thomas More*, which was published in 1627 according to Lewis and Singer, in 1631 according to Hunter). After being educated under Nicholas Holt, and living as page in Archbishop Morton's household, and learning Greek as well as Latin in Oxford—probably at Christ Church (C. More), Thomas joined Lincoln's Inn 1496 ; was called to the bar. made reader at Furnival's Inn, and under-sheriff of the City of London (1502-1519). In

1505 he married Jane Colte, by whom he had a daughter Margaret, afterwards wife of William Roper his biographer, and two other daughters and one son. As burgess of parliament he defeated Henry VII.'s demand for an aid on the marriage of his daughter (1504), which offence cost his father imprisonment and £100 fine, and drove the offender from the highway of his profession into the quiet bye-paths of historical and literary compositions (*e.g. Historia Richardi III. ; Epigrammata*, etc.). Under Henry VIII. he returned to the law, and as counsel for the pope beat the king in a case of forfeiture which came before the Star Chamber ; which service the defeated litigant rewarded with knighthood, a mastership of requests, and a privy councillorship (Roper's *Life of More*, written about 1557, pub. 1626). About 1521 he was made under treasurer, and in 1523 speaker. As speaker, he defeated Cardinal Wolsey's tyrannous attempt to compel the Commons to discuss in his presence the grant of a subsidy (Roper, confirmed by Hall's *Chronicle*, p. 656; Brewer's *Hist. of Henry VIII.*, 469, misleading) ; yet the king at this time was a constant though not over-welcome visitor at Chelsea, and Sir Thomas was made chancellor of the Duchy of Lancaster (1526-32). In 1529 he was ambassador to Cambray in order to conclude a league between Francis I., Charles V., and Henry VIII. Henry used at this time to urge Sir Thomas to declare against the papal dispensation which legalised his marriage with his sister-in-law Queen Katherine, and Sir Thomas replied by pointing out authorities opposed to the king's contention (*e.g.* St. Augustine), and by pleading inability to offer an opinion of his own in the matter. On 25th October, Wolsey having fallen, Sir Thomas was made lord chancellor. It was as lord chancellor that Sir Thomas had to inform both houses of parliament of replies from the universities of Oxford, Cambridge, Bologna, etc., declaring the king's marriage void (Gairdner's *Letters and Papers of the Reign of Henry VIII.*, vol. v. No. 171) ; and he discharged this irksome task without adding views of his own, but resigned soon afterwards (16th May 1532), and retired on £100 a year. The clergy subscribed £5000 to reward him for his theological polemics (*e.g. Responsio ad Lutherum*, 1523), but he would not accept a penny from them. Then his persecution began, first for bribery as lord chancellor, then for complicity with Elizabeth Barton, attainted of high treason by 25 Henry VIII. c. 12. Both charges broke down, the first ludicrously, the second ominously, More remarking "quod differtur non aufertur." For the king's " Act of Matrimony and Succession " was even then being passed (25 Henry VIII. c. 22), and section ix. of the act (confirmed by 26 Henry VIII. c. 2) made it misprision of treason not to swear "to defend all the contents of the act and of every part of it," and the act, besides regulating the succession, which More offered to swear to (*English Works*, ed. Rastell, 1557, p. 1428), declared Henry VIII.'s marriage with Katherine null. Sir Thomas would not swear what he did not believe, and went to the Tower (April 1534), and was deprived of his estates in November (26 Henry VIII. c. 23), (*Archæologia*, xxvii. ; p. 369, *Froude*, ii. 242 misleading). The same parliament of November 1534 enacted that the king should be and have the title of Supreme Head of the Church (cap. i.), and that it was high treason to contrive to deprive him of any of his titles (cap. xiii.). Rich's perjured testimony (which Froude alone believes) brought More within the scope of these two last mentioned enactments. He was tried for high treason on this last charge (1st July) and executed (7th July). Stapleton's *Tres Thomæ* (1589), and perhaps Hall's *Chronicle*, represent More as an ultramontane protagonist, whereas he was an advocate of præmunire (Roper, ed. Singer, 1822, p. 66); Mr. Froude (*Hist. of England*, ii. 395), citing a story of Roper's p. 73) as mistold by C. More (whom he miscalls Sir Thomas's grandson), suggests that More had spoken seditiously against Anne Boleyn, a suggestion never made at the time. Roper, followed by Rev. T. E. Bridgett in his *Life and Writings of More* (1891), says that More refused "an oath of supremacy" which never existed : Lord Campbell (*Lives of the Chancellors*, i. 564), ignoring 25 Henry VIII. c. 22, declares that More's commitment to the Tower was illegal. All these statements and suggestions are erroneous ; Sir James Mackintosh's *Life of More* (1831), as supplemented by the actual Indictment and Lady More's Petition (printed in 1838 in *Archæologia*, xxvii. 370) contain the only true and full account.

The character of Sir T. More, as drawn by his trusty biographer Roper (whom Stapleton and C. More only echo and add to) is a classic picture of a perfect gentleman. His even and Socratic temper was never ruffled. The stories about More's cruelties to Protestants, which arose fifty years after his death, and have been lately revived by Froude and the *Dictionary of National Biography* (1894), may be dismissed as fabulous (Bridgett, ch. xiv.). Erasmus was his friend since 1497 (Ep. 14), (Froude, *Erasmus*, pp. 43, 111, etc.), and his description of the Chelsea home, which all the children and eleven grandchildren shared, illustrates the domestic virtue of Sir Thomas as vividly as Roper's picture of the lord chancellor kneeling before his father the judge in the judge's court, and asking a blessing before going to his day's task. So strong and so gentle, so bright and so unworldly, so good a son, and father, and citizen, this saintly lawyer, this incorruptible courtier, this humorous ascetic, this Roman Catholic who died for freedom of conscience at the hands of those who vaunted themselves its champions, strikes our imagination by his singularity as much as he touches our hearts by his simplicity.

More's only famous book is his *Utopia* published in Latin (1516), and translated into German (1524), Italian (1548), French (1550), and lastly by Robynson into English (1551). It begins by arguing, as Lord Campbell says, like Romilly or Mackintosh against indiscriminate severity in the punishment *e.g.* of theft when economical conditions caused theft. Those economical conditions were twofold—(1) the quantity of men "having no craft"

as More styles them, and including priests, servingmen (our unproductive workers), gentlemen and noblemen, valiant and sturdy beggars, and most women (our unproductive consumers). (2) Men were being driven into theft by the turning of ploughland into sheep-runs and the consequent clearances. He thought this second tendency could be checked by penal statutes, and that penal statutes were stronger than the economic motive which in those days was called avarice ; in this he erred in company with Latimer, Hales, and every writer of the time except W. Stafford (see Cunningham's *Growth of English Industry and Commerce*, 252, 268); the first evil he thought would be palliated by a law prescribing a maximum of wealth, but only cured by doing as in Utopia. Book 2 describes the island of Utopia (οὐ τόπος or εὖ τόπος, bad Greek for "Nowhere" or "Good Place") which is communistic. In Utopia all produce, except the very learned, who have a licence not to produce ; and each producer alternates farm industry with some civic industry like building. As none are idle none are overworked, the normal working day being six hours, not nine hours, as a misprint copied from Robynson's 2nd edition of 1556 (where it is corrected in MS.) into Dr. Arber's, and the Camelot, Kelmscott, and other reprints indicates. Criminals work like *servi pœnæ* on the degraded but necessary tasks of killing animals for food, hunting, and scavengering. These are the only slaves in Utopia. Each has his task to do, and plenty of leisure and pleasure ; and the criminal code, which does not apply to beliefs—as "it is no man's power to believe what he list"—is short and plain, so that criminals are fewer than in European commonwealths, which are "nothing but a certain conspiracy of rich men procuring their own commodities under the name and title of the commonwealth." The same rulers punish crime and prescribe tasks ; but the latter is their main duty,—the former is easily and soon done. As Prof. Cliffe Leslie remarks, the economics of production always presuppose certain assumptions as to the consumer, a truth which was seen more clearly in the 16th century than by A. Smith and his successors. In More the productive machinery is simplified by assuming perfect and unchanging simplicity of taste in the consumer. Luxuries do not exist ; and only implements of iron, which is held in high esteem, and earthenware are in common use. The (elected) king sets an example of sobriety to his subjects, and unlike the pretentious rulers of Bacon's New Atlantis—a book founded on *Utopia*—lives like a common citizen. Children are allowed to wear what we miscall "precious stones," but grown-up people spurn these baubles. Gold and silver, which are imported in exchange for the export of surplus products, and which for centuries afterwards were commonly deemed synonyms for wealth, are used in Utopia to fetter criminals or are formed into domestic utensils which shall be nameless, or in case of war are paid to foreign mercenaries. This is the only use for money by dwellers in Utopia ; for, somewhat like Fichte in *The Closed Commercial State*, he makes the members of the nations barter with one another, and the nation carry on foreign trade by means of money, thus inverting the usual modern view. Exchange scarcely occasions any difficulty in such a simple state. Each district sends up to the capital statistics of supplies, which are then distributed by the state so as to make each district equal ; and the district feeds, clothes, and houses its members. The capital stores up a reserve of supplies sufficient to tide over two years in case of emergency, or exports the residue in return for I.O.U.'s which are only realised when some purpose to which gold and silver are put in Utopia has to be fulfilled. The means of existence are always enough and more than enough for the population, whose numbers are kept down. It was the tendency in those times to think that numbers meant strength (Ingram's *History of Pol. Ec.*, p. 37). But in Utopia no town has more than 6000 families, and no family has more than sixteen members over thirteen years of age, for the families live patriarchally like More. Similarly with the farms. An excess over the prescribed limits means emigration, and emigration may mean war, for this sort of war is lawful. The other details of Utopia scarcely belong to political economy—the glass windows, the garden to each house (a suggestion expanded in Lytton's *Coming Race*, Bebel's *Position of Women*, and Morris's *News from Nowhere* into the identification of town and country), the priests, who are "of exceeding holiness and therefore few," always married, and sometimes female ; the artificially-hatched chickens which run after the men who hatched them; the absence of leagues and lawyers; the common dining-rooms in each street; the houses changed by lot every ten years and so on, somewhat as RUNDALE tenure. But the central conceptions are economic. He anticipates Sir Wm. PETTY in perceiving that wealth is the offspring of labour, and is still more modern in identifying it with necessaries, and he sees that necessaries imply a composite conception, *i.e.*, of what people ought to and do as a fact accept as such. Again the organisation of those who produce wealth with a view to its production with the least possible effort to the producer, and to the avoidance of waste, stamps the work as economical in its plan. His task is of course made easier by the ideal outline to the book; and by the assumption that communism will work. But it must be borne in mind that the ideal outline is filled in with practical details; he for instance alone amongst modern Utopians grapples with the crucial question of punishment; and secondly, unlike his model PLATO and his follower CAMPANELLA his communism is not pursued into family relationships, and those who complain that communism supplies no adequate incentive to work will find this objection raised by More at the end of book i., and the absence of an answer to it adverted to at the end of book ii. So far from being dogmatic, the conclusion of the matter is a note of interrogation. He ends and we end all but convinced. The book belongs more to literature than to science, and uses the actual only to decorate the ideal world. Like his life, the first part of his book grows out of the problems, and hardly rises above the ideas, of his age; the second part vividly reflects his character and takes us back to Plato, but also forward into the 19th century. It belongs to every age.

[J. Bonar, *Philosophy and Political Economy* (1893), pp. 62-67, 69, 290.—*Die Geschichte des Socialismus*, edited by Bernstein and Kautsky, b. 1, th. 2, absch. 4 (vol. i. pp. 448 *et seq.*).—Diodato Lioy, *The Philosophy of Right*, translated by W. Hastie (1891), vol. i. pp. 262 *et seq.—The Dialogues of Plato*, translated by B. Jowett, 3rd ed. (1892), vol. iii. pp. ccxvii.-ccxxxi.—H. Morley's reprint of *Utopia*, Bacon's *New Atlantis*, and Campanella's *City of the Sun*, etc., entitled *Ideal Commonwealths* (1885). — *Voyage en Icarie*, by CABET (*q.v.*) (1840), which is an expansion of More's *Utopia*, but modifies several details, *e.g.* expulsion and not slavery is the penalty of idleness. The Nauvoo community formed in Illinois (1849) on the model of Cabet's book, was shifted to the banks of the Nodaway, Iowa (1860), and split into two parts (1879); the only prosperous part (Icaria-Speranza in California), consisted of fifty-two persons, but gradually reintroduced private property in 1883-84, and expired soon after. The other part was dying in 1883. Still, this is the most successful non-religious experiment in communism.— Dr. Albert Shaw, *Icaria* (1884), pp. 123, 147.— Dr. H. Lux, *Étienne Cabet und der Ikarische Communismus* (1894), p. 266.—For More's views on money cp. A. Smith, *Wealth of Nations*, iv. i., para. 4.]   J. D. R.

MOREAU, CÉSAR (1791-1829):
French vice-consul in London, the founder of the *Société française de Statistique Universelle*, published numerous statistical works on French and English navigation in modern times enumerated in the (old) *Dictionnaire d'Économie Politique* and in Guérard, *France Littéraire*, 1834, vol. vi. p. 294.   E. Ca.

MOREAU DE BEAUMONT, J. L. (1715-1785).
Successively councillor in the Paris parliament, master of requests and *Intendant des Finances*, was author of *Mémoires concernant les Impositions et Droits en Europe*, 4 vols. 4to, 1768-69, 2ᵉ éd., avec des Suppléments, 5 vols. 4to, 1787. The second and third volumes deal with France; in the preface of vol. i. the author expresses the opinion that in France uniformity of taxation "could alone put an end to the evils which were experienced, but that it is easier to see and feel the ills than to apply the remedy." Moreau's *Mémoires* (published anonymously) are mainly descriptive and con-

sidered to be authoritative on the subject as far as France is concerned.

[The reference to this work in A. Smith's letter to Mr. Sinclair, printed in Bonar's *Catalogue of the Library of A. Smith* (Macmillan, 1894), shows the writer's appreciation of it. A. Smith describes himself as having "frequent occasion to consult the book himself, both in the course of his private studies and in the business of his present employment (as Commissioner of Customs), and is therefore not very willing to let it go out of Edinburgh." He obtained it "by the particular favour of Mr. Turgot, the late Controller-General of the Finances. I have heard but of three other copies in Great Britain. . . . If any accident should happen to my book, the loss is perfectly irreparable." There are several quotations from Moreau de Beaumont in the *Wealth of Nations* referring principally to taxation in other nations of Europe. The use Adam Smith made of the book is a good illustration of his method of study and investigation, and the pains he took to master every detail of his subject. See also Stourm, *Dict. Hist. des Finances*, 1895, p. 25, who complains of the undue importance given to secondary matter. Cunningham, *Econ. Jour.*, No. 1, vol. i., maintains that A. Smith's canons of taxation were largely derived from Moreau de Beaumont.]   E. Ca.

MOREAU DE JONNÈS, ALEXANDRE (1778-1870), born at Rennes, died at Paris. A distinguished statistician, left many works important in their time, but now out of date. He volunteered as a soldier when fourteen years of age, was a prisoner in England from 1809 to 1815, and after the conclusion of peace devoted himself to statistics.

Thiers, minister of commerce, in 1834 appointed Moreau head of his statistical department, which through the periodical reports issued by him soon became one of the most important branches of the office. He continued this duty till 1852. Under his direction twelve huge quarto volumes were published in 1837 at the beginning of the second inquiry, which work, or at least the plan of it, may be considered as his. Besides this official collection, and not including his labours on physical science, the following works of his may be mentioned :—

Le commerce au XIXe siècle, 2 vols. 8vo, 1827. — *Statistique de l'Espagne*, 8vo, 1834.—*Statistique de la Grande Bretagne et de l'Irlande*, 2 vols. 8vo, 1838.—*Recherches statistiques sur l'esclavage colonial et sur les moyens de le supprimer*, 8vo, 1841.—*Éléments du Statistique*, 8vo, 1st ed. 1847, 2nd ed. 1876.—*Statistique de l'agriculture de la France*, 8vo, 1848.—*Statistique des peuples de l'antiquité*, 4 vols. 8vo, 1871.—*La France avant ses premiers habitans*, 16mo, 1876. — *Statistique de l'industrie de la France*, 16mo, 1876.   A. C. f.

MOREL VINDÉ, CHARLES GILBERT, Vicomte de (1759-1842), a peer of France and member of the academy of science and royal society of agriculture, was a frequent writer on economic and agricultural subjects.

Considérations sur le morcellement de la pro-

priété territoriale en France, 8vo, 1826.—*Sur la théorie de la population*, 2nd ed. 8vo, 1829. [A complete list of his works will be found under his name in Quérard, *La France Littéraire au 18ᵐᵉ et au 19ᵐᵉ siècle*, Paris, 1834.]　E. Ca.

MORELLET, ABBÉ ANDRÉ (1727-1819), born at Lyons and died at Paris. Though an economist, he was not a physiocrat, inclining rather to the opinions of Gournay than to those of Quesnay, though always respectful to the latter.

He was by conviction a persistent partisan of freedom in economic matters, though he wrote no dogmatic work, but was constantly engaged in polemics attacking monopolies and privileges with arguments derived from practice. Hardships marked his youth. His father, a stationer in a small way, treated him with severity. There were thirteen brothers and sisters in the family. He early left his home and joined the Jesuits, from whom he received his first education. Persevering work and a bright intellect gained him admittance to the Société de Sorbonne, a private society endowed for the gratuitous reception of the deserving, no preference being shown to people of fortune or rank. He there became acquainted with many who afterwards became famous, the most illustrious of whom was Turgot. Like Adam Smith he had charge of the education of a young man of a wealthy family, to whose care he devoted ten years, five being at the Collège de Plessis. He raised both the standing and the numbers of that institution through his knowledge of the men of mark at that time, including a few foreigners, principally Italians.

Morellet discovered in a library at Rome a book on the legal practice of the church, written by an inquisitor of the 14th century. He made extracts from it, the outcome of which was the *Manuel des inquisiteurs*, which, in his time (1762), made a great stir. Voltaire was delighted with the book, and thenceforward held Abbé Morellet in high esteem, and amused himself by calling him Abbé *Mords-les*, because of his sarcastic and incisive style.

Morellet's first economic work was *Réfléxions sur les avantages de la libre fabrication et de l'usage des toiles peintes en France*, 12mo, 1758. The object was to secure freedom for the industry referred to in the interior of the country. Morellet did not go so far as to ask for free import of foreign goods. Probably he stopped lest he should alienate the *Compagnie des Indes*, with whom he was not yet prepared to quarrel. In the narrow limits of his *Mémoire* he gained a complete success. He introduced into France the most important work of BECCARIA by a translation still in common use. Its appearance two years after the publication of the work itself (*Dei Delitti e delle Pene*) assisted in abolishing torture in France, partially in 1780, and completely nine years after.

Morellet's great triumph was the suspension of the privileges of the *Compagnie des Indes*, on 13th August 1769, in consequence of his *Mémoire sur*

la situation actuelle de la Compagnie des Indes, Juin 1769. Necker, at that time only a clerk in a Swiss bank, took up the defence of the company in the form of a reply to Morellet.

The conflict with privileged commercial companies recommenced on the renewal of the monopoly of the Indian trade, to the advantage, if indeed it can be said to the advantage, of a new company in 1785. The impetuous Abbé wrote again in 1787, and re-edited the *Mémoires relatifs à la discussion du privilège de la Compagnie des Indes*, besides publishing a reply to Abbé d'Espagnac, the well-known stock-jobber of the 18th century.

The same year in which he was drawn into the controversy with the Indian company he published the *Prospectus d'un nouveau dictionnaire du commerce*, 8vo, a dictionary upon which he worked twenty years and then gave up. Peuchet profited by his work in his *Dictionnaire universel de géographie commerçante*, 5 vols. 4to, 1799-1800 (years vii.-viii.).

The translation by DIDEROT into French of the *Dialoghi sul commercio dei grani* of Abbé GALIANI (*q.v.*), appeared in 1770. Morellet quickly took up his pen in the cause of freedom in the export trade. Unfortunately, error was more attractive than the plain truth, and with the public the Neapolitan Abbé had more success than his French fellow-economist. Morellet again took up arms for the same cause, this time against a writer whose celebrity was yet only dawning, though he had already crossed swords with him. Necker, in *La législation et le commerce des grains*, 8vo, 1775, argued against free trade. In an analysis of this work published in 8vo, 1775, Morellet showed all its weak points from the economic side. Again this time the victory was against Morellet.

The Revolution now commenced. It may well be believed that the Abbé did not lay down his pen, but with the exception of a refutation of a book on, or rather against, property, 1792, by the Girondin Brissot, who, anticipating Proudhon by half a century, held the opinion that property was robbery (*la propriété c'est le vol*), the works of Morellet at this time were political and literary. He died at the commencement of the restoration, aged ninety-two, not of old age, but by an accident. He was still in full possession of his mental faculties. Morellet's translation into French of the *Wealth of Nations*, though apparently carefully made, was never printed, see John Rae, *Life of Adam Smith*, 1895, p. 359. He mentions in his *Mémoires* that he met Adam Smith in Paris, and discussed free trade, banking, etc. with him, and that A. Smith spoke French very badly.
[Lavergne, *Les Économistes du xviiiᵉ siècle*.]
　　　　A. C. f.

MORELLY. Nothing certain is known of Morelly's life, except that he was born at Vitry-le-François, and was a teacher there. His works would have been as little known as he was, had it not been for the socialists who have extolled the communistic opinions they contain.

The first : *Le Prince, les délices du cœur, ou Traité des qualités d'un grand roi et système d'un sage gouvernement*, 1751, 2 vols. 12mo, is entirely political, and describes in its different parts the duties of an absolute monarch.

The second : *Naufrage des îles flottantes ou la Basiliade de Pilpaï ; poème héroïque traduit de l'indien*, 1753, 12mo, is a story in which the author declaims on the return to the state of nature in opposition to the state of civilisation. In his next work the author speaks modestly of this poem "as new in its subject as in the construction in which truth is reclothed in all the graces of epic poetry."

The third and last is : *Le Code de la nature ou le véritable esprit de ses lois, de tout temps négligé, méconnu*, 1758 and 1760, 12mo. This book, wrongly attributed to Diderot, is written in a dogmatic form. Property is abolished except in the case of things for personal use. The state supplies work and living to all, the first according to talents, strength, and age, the second according to needs. Inconsistently, like many communists, he is in favour of family life and marriage. Fourier has borrowed a great deal from Morelly.   A. C. f.

MORGAN, AUGUSTUS DE (1806-1871), born at Madura, Madras, was the son of Colonel De Morgan and descended on his mother's side from James Dodson the mathematician. In 1823 he entered Trinity College, Cambridge, and came out as fourth wrangler in 1827. He was the first occupant of the chair of mathematics at University College, London, and held it for more than thirty years.

In 1838 De Morgan published his *Mathematical Treatise on the Theory of Probabilities*, and, subsequently, an *Essay* on the same subject, with especial reference to their *Application to Life Contingencies and Insurance Offices*. In 1847 appeared his *Formal Logic*, while from 1841 till shortly before his death he was closely occupied with the question of a *Decimal Coinage*.[1]

He proposed to make the change a very gradual one, by introducing *the royal*, a tenth of a sovereign, our florin, with its half and

---

[1] De Morgan bestowed a vast amount of unrewarded time and trouble on the propaganda of views in favour of a reform of the English system of money to a decimal system of currency and notation. He laboured incessantly with this view by giving evidence before parliamentary committees, in lectures to various scientific bodies, and in the Decimal Association (vide article DECIMAL SYSTEM). The particular method he advocated was the "pound and mil" scheme, retaining our pound sterling and subdividing it into 1000 instead of, as at present, 960 farthings. De Morgan may be fairly said to have been, taken all round, one of the best appreciated and esteemed men of his position in the past generation. In tuition and in literary matters, his versatile aid and almost boundless store of information were liberally given. Painstaking and minute research was his strong point. He had lost the sight of one eye in infancy. The strain upon the remaining eye, involved by his constant industry in accumulating stores of knowledge, must have been severe. The writer once had occasion, in a letter to him, to mention one of the Bernoulli family of mathematicians of the last century, and spelt the name wrongly, that is with two i's, Bernouilli. "Oh," replied De Morgan, "you have deeply offended me. Pray always keep in mind the personal interest I take in one-eyed philosophers."   F. H.

quarter, our shilling and sixpence. He then proposed to get the decimal part of this *royal* in the *groat*, a coin worth about 2½d., the tenth part of which would be approximately a *farthing*.   A. L.

MORGAN, WILLIAM (1750-1833), nephew of Dr. PRICE (*q.v.*), whose works he edited with a memoir, occupied, as actuary to the Equitable Insurance Society (1775-1830), a leading place among the pioneers of life insurance. The aim of Morgan's financial pamphlets was to show that the war expenditure had added so enormously to the national debt that "if the same unexampled dissipation of the public treasure be continued much longer, it must inevitably terminate in bankruptcy and ruin."

His works include :—*The doctrine of annuities and assurances on lives and survivorships stated and explained*, London, 1779, 8vo.—*A Review of Dr. Price's writings on the subject of the finances of this Kingdom*, London, 1792, 8vo.—*Supplement* to above, London, 1795, 8vo.—*Facts respecting the expense of the War*, 4th ed. London, 1796, 8vo. —*An appeal to the people of Great Britain on the present alarming state of the Public Finances*, 3rd ed. London, 1797, 8vo.—*A comparative view of the Public Finances from the beginning to the close of the late Administration*, 3rd ed. London, 1801, 8vo.—*Supplement* to above, London, 1803, 8vo.— *A view of the rise and progress of the Equitable Society*, London, 1828, 8vo.

[For Morgan's actuarial work consult Walford's *Insurance Cyclopædia*, vol. ii. pp. 596-622, and vol. iii. pp. 5-7, for biographical details, *Dictionary of National Biography*, vol. xxxix. p. 40, and authorities there given.]   H. E. E.

MORHOF, DANIEL GEORG (1639-1691). In his *Polyhistor* (published 1688) Morhof deplores that economics, which are nearly connected with political science, have been left to the care of *illiterati* and have not undergone a thorough scientific investigation, although they are the foundation of the well-being of the whole state. The means by which domestic wealth is increased and preserved ought to be closely examined, for "the preservation of economic wealth through a clever management is the basis of the entire science of economics and chrematistics." He recommends his readers to consult the books written by travellers, and is a great admirer of the internal administration of France.

[Roscher, *Gesch. der Nat. Oek. in Deutschland*, pp. 328-329.]   E. Ca.

MORPURGO, EMILIO (1836-1889), born in Padua, an able economic writer. He took part in politics, was a deputy, general secretary of public instruction, and devoted to practical problems in Italian economics, finance, and instruction. He also occupied himself with science and instruction, and filled, with much distinction, for many years, the chair of statistics in Padua. Amongst his practical works, his *Report on the Condition of the Peasants and Agriculture in the Venetian Provinces*, made on the occasion of the agrarian inquiry, takes a high place. This work is a model of its kind for method, for accuracy, and the ideas embodied.

Morpurgo studied the practical problems of finance and the organisation of technical instruction in Italy. His scientific activity was chiefly applied to statistics, on which subject he has left deep traces by his remarkable studies of demographic, financial, and moral statistics, and also in his historical and theoretical researches. His most important work in this branch of study is a volume on statistics and moral sciences, in which he collects and states the principal results of modern statistical research. We note among Morpurgo's writings: *La statistica e le scienze morali*, Florence, 1872.—*L'istruzione tecnica in Italia*, Rome, 1874.—*La finanza*, Rome, 1876.—*Le condizioni dei contadini e le condizioni della proprietà e dell' economia agraria nel Veneto*, in the "Atti dell' Inchiesta Agraria," vol. iv., fasc° 1 and 2, Rome, 1882-83.   U. R.

MORRIS, CORBYN (d. 1779), writer on fiscal subjects, held various posts in the public service in Scotland and in England, and was an upholder of the mercantile theory. He attracted attention by a pamphlet entitled *A Letter from a Bystander to a Member of Parliament*, in which he examines the economic basis of the crown. This letter provoked a sharp controversy in print : replies and counter-replies embody "much curious discussion and information with respect to taxation and the expenditure of the public revenue for a lengthened period" (M'Culloch, *Lit. Pol. Econ.*, p. 328). Morris also urged the impolicy of England's insuring the ships of a nation (*i.e.* France) with which she was at war : his papers on this subject carefully examine the arguments on the other side, and hypothetical problems are worked out in detail. In his *Essay* on Insurance, the author candidly states that in working out the subject he started not from ascertained facts but from reflections of his own, and that these last did not accord with the views of "a very ingenious and worthy merchant" to whom he had communicated them. The reader is to expect "no information concerning what are the present customs . . . but . . . an endeavour to establish the just maxims . . . upon a fair open footing of reason and equity." He adds that in working out insurance problems he soon found, as was not unnatural in a Cambridge man, that "without the aid of some higher calculations," *i.e.* of mathematics, "all must be left unsettled and loose, and bounded by general guesses." Hence his problems are stated and worked quite on mathematical lines. In 1751 he published some vital statistics concerning London, and a little later urged the establishment of a national registry-general of the population, and of the annual proportion of births to deaths. His statistical work on London was reprinted and brought nearly up to date in 1759. The scarcity

of silver coin in England at that time also attracted Morris's attention, and by working out the respective values of existing gold and silver coin as bullion, he arrived at the conclusion that silver was scarce in England because the existing proportion of pure gold to pure silver was as $1 : 15\frac{2 \cdot 2 \cdot 2 \cdot 2}{13 \cdot 8 \cdot 8 \cdot 5}$, whereas in the other chief trading countries of Europe it was as $1 : 14\frac{1}{2}$; and that there was consequently a temptation to export silver abroad, the gross profit upon 100 lbs. troy weight of gold being some $40\frac{1}{2}$ per cent. The remedy, in Morris's eyes, was to alter the English ratio of gold to silver to the continental figures. His plan for account-keeping on landed estates grew out of his own need of something better than his steward's rather haphazard method of checking rents, etc.

The following works seem all to have been published in London :

A Letter from a Bystander to a Member of Parliament, wherein is examined what Necessity there is for the Maintenance of a large regular Land-force in this Island, etc., London, 1741-42, 8vo.—*An Essay towards illustrating the Science of Insurance, wherein it is attempted to fix, by precise Calculation, several important Maxims upon this Subject*, etc., 1747, 8vo, pp. xv. 61.—*An Essay towards deciding the Important Question whether it be a National Advantage to Britain to Insure the Ships of her Enemies ; addressed to the Rt. Hon. Henry Pelham*, 1747, 8vo, pp. 50 ; the impolicy and illegality of the practice are clearly shown ; 2nd edit. 1758, pp. x. 34.—*Observations of the Past Growth . . . of the City of London*, 1751, fol.—Ditto reprinted, and with statistics to the end of 1757, 1759, 4to.—*A Letter balancing the Causes of the present Scarcity of our Silver Coin, and the Means of immediate Remedy, and future Prevention of this Evil*, 1757, 8vo, pp. 20.—*A Plan for Arranging and Balancing the Accounts of Landed Estates*, 1759, fol. pp. 39.
[M'Culloch, *Lit. Pol. Econ.*, pp. 243, 272, 327.—*Dict. Nat. Biog.*, art. "Morris, Corbyn."]
                                                  E. D.

MORSTADT, EDUARD (1792-1850), professor at the university of Heidelberg, lectured on economics, finance, and law, and founded, in 1834, a monthly paper, *Der Nationalökonom*, of which he remained the editor until the end of the following year.

Morstadt published a German translation of Say's *Cours d'Économie Politique*, with an introduction in which he defines political economy : "a science whose real object must not be to dictate oracles to her high priests when sitting under their nocturnal lamp, but is to become the confidant of princes, the teacher of nations, and the interpreter of universal history." A supporter of free trade and an opponent of restrictive legislation of labour, he was very fond of delivering himself of curious economic definitions (see under his name, Prof. Conrad's *Handw. der Staatswiss.*, iv. p. 1230), and of editing other writers' works with critical notes ; on the occasion of such an edition

of Klüber's *Public Law of the German Confederation*, he was most unmercifully handled by Robert
von Mohl, his colleague and former contributor.
His own contributions to the *Nationalökonom.* are
all very short ; his analysis of the three possible
courses of action which a government is able to
follow with regard to population, is given in the
already mentioned article of Professor Conrad's
Handwörterbuch. E. Ca.

MORTGAGE (= *dead pledge* — as distinguished from *vif gage* = living pledge, *i.e.* a
pledge taken into the creditor's possession and
producing income which gradually pays off the
debt) is the name of a security given by a debtor
on property remaining in his possession—the
hypotheca of Roman Law—and thus differing
from a security on property handed over to the
creditor, which is described by the name of
"pawn" or "pledge," the *pignus* of Roman
law. In the case of a "legal mortgage" the
legal ownership is expressed to be conveyed to
the creditor, on condition that on repayment of
the debt before a certain date, it is to be reconveyed to the debtor, but, owing to the influence
of the equitable doctrines introduced by the
Court of Chancery, the debtor's right to redeem
—generally called the EQUITY OF REDEMPTION
—continues, although the date for repayment
has elapsed and cannot be taken away except
by an order of the court (called a FORECLOSURE
order) which is not made absolute for some time.
In the event of the mortgagor not complying
with the conditions of the mortgage there are
other remedies open to the mortgagor besides
foreclosure. He may, unless the mortgage deed
contains any stipulations to the contrary, sell
the property, or have a receiver of the rents and
profits appointed, or he may enter into possession, and he may also enforce the debtor's
personal liability to pay the mortgage debt.
Mortgages of land and houses occur most
frequently, but mortgages of debts, reversionary
interests, life policies, and other "choses in
action" are also very common. Mortgages of
chattels being deemed bills of sale (see BILL OF
SALE), are void if they are intended to secure
a debt of less than £30, and must in other
cases conform to the statutory rules as regards
form and registration.
An "equitable" mortgage is a transaction
which in certain events entitles the mortgagee
to the execution of a legal mortgage, and
practically entitles him to all the remedies open
to a legal mortgagee. There is, however, this
difference, that a "legal" mortgagee having no
notice of a prior charge at the time of lending
the money, has the first right on the security,
whilst the priorities between "equitable" in-
cumbrances depend entirely on the order in
which the respective advances were made. The
most common instance of an equitable mortgage
is a mortgage by "deposit of title deeds" which
is deemed to be an agreement on the part of

the mortgagor to execute a legal mortgage
whenever called upon to do so.
A "submortgage" is the mortgage of a mortgage debt and of the securities relating to the
same ; a "contributory" mortgage is a mortgage by several mortgagees, each being entitled
to an aliquot share of the mortgage deed.
[As to Mortgages by Companies, see DEBENTURE.
Coote, on *Mortgages.*—Fisher, on *Mortgages.*—
Cavanagh, *Money Securities.*] E. S.

MORTGAGE BANKS. Banks and other
public institutions whose only business it is
to lend money on mortgage, are much more
common on the continent than in England—
Germany being the country in which they have
attained the greatest importance. They may
be divided into three classes : (1) Mutual associations of landowners (*Landschaften, Kredit-
vereine,* etc.) ; (2) Mortgage institutions administered by government, or provincial or
other local authorities (*Landes Kreditkassen,
Provinzialbanken,* etc.) ; (3) Ordinary joint-
stock banks.
The first landowners' association was established
in Silesia by Frederick the Great, soon after the
end of the seven years' war (1756-1763), which
caused much distress in that province. The large
landowners of the province were compelled to
join it, and they were all jointly and severally
liable for the mortgage bonds (*Pfandbrief*) issued
by the association. Every member was entitled
to raise loans on mortgage up to a certain amount,
the borrower receiving mortgage bonds instead of
money. It was, however, easy to dispose of their
bonds, as owing to the excellent security which
they gave to the holders they soon became
a favourite investment.
No profit was to be made on the transactions
of the association, the interest on the mortgages
being only slightly higher than the interest on
the bonds, so as to allow for expenses of management. The supreme control of the association
was exercised by a government commissioner—
generally by the governor of the province.
The success of the Silesian association soon led
to the formation of other similar ones in other
Prussian provinces, and, in course of time, associations of peasant proprietors were founded in some
places on analogous principles. There are now
nineteen such associations in Prussia, among
which the one for the province of Schleswig
Holstein, founded in 1882, is the youngest, and
there are four in other parts of Germany. Outside of Germany they exist in Austria-Hungary,
and, in a modified form, in the rural parts of the
canton of Zurich (*Garantiegenossenschaften*).
(2) The above-mentioned associations are mainly
adapted for loans to large landowners, whose joint
credit is sufficient to enable them to issue their
bonds at a relatively low rate of interest ; the
peasant proprietors' associations do not have the
same advantages, and are only available in limited
areas. For this reason the intervention of government and local authorities was generally felt as
a necessity, more especially in those parts of
Germany where it is customary for one son to

take over the father's property, and to pay a money compensation to his brothers and sisters for their share in the estate. The first impulse to the institution of state establishments for the purpose of granting loans to landowners was given by the legislation for the compulsory enfranchisement of land subject to manorial rights, which in most parts of Germany, though initiated at the beginning of the present century, did not become effective till about 1850. In order to facilitate the payment of compensation to the lords of manors, loans were granted by the state governments or provincial governments on the security of the enfranchised land, and this led to the establishment of a regular system of government mortgage banks. Such banks exist in many parts of Prussia and other parts of Germany, and the total amount advanced by them in 1889 amounted to about 418,000,000 marks (21,000,000 sterling). Most of the loans granted by these institutions are repayable by yearly instalments. A curious combination of government and private agency exists in Mannheim, where the *Rheinische Hypothekenbank*—an ordinary joint-stock bank,— has a separate department for loans on agricultural property, which by virtue of a convention with the government of the grand-duchy of Baden must be carried on without profit, and is under government supervision. Government banks also exist in Austria and Russia.

In the United Kingdom advances by public authorities on the security of land occur in various manners. The advances under the Purchase of Land (Ireland) Act, 1891, etc. (see LAND LEGISLATION, IRISH), are made for purposes similar to those for which the German state loan institutions were originally established ; the public works' loan commissioners are entitled to advance money on the security of land for the purpose of constructing dwellings for the working classes (Housing of Working Classes Act, 1890, § 67), and the provisions of the Small Holdings Act, 1892, under which county councils are empowered on the sale of any small holdings to allow part of the purchase money to be paid by instalments, and in the meantime to be charged on the land, also require to be mentioned in this connection.

Special facilities have been given in continental countries as well as in the United Kingdom for loans in respect of the improvement and drainage of land. In Germany, special banks (*Landesculturrentenbanken*) were instituted either as government establishments, as in Saxony, Bavaria, and Hesse, or under the provincial authorities. Loans granted for these purposes are in most cases specially secured and are repayable by fixed instalments.

In England and Scotland advances may be made out of public funds with the sanction of the board of agriculture, and are secured by terminable rent-charges by means of which the capital is paid off in twenty-two years. Such rent-charges may be created notwithstanding any settlements or entails (see the Public Money Drainage Act, 1846, and the amending acts). Similar powers are given to the commissioners of public works in Ireland by the Landed Property Improvement (Ireland) Acts.

(3) The authorities and institutions mentioned under the two first heads make their advances for public purposes and not with any view of profit, but there are numerous establishments, partly competing with them, and partly supplementing them, which are in a position to make advances on terms not less advantageous than they, and yet are able to pay dividends to their shareholders. The first mortgage bank was established in Stockholm in 1668, but its example does not seem to have been followed at the time ; 1835 a *Caisse hypothécaire* was formed in Brussels, but the first institution formed on the modern system (viz. that of a share company issuing debentures for an amount corresponding to the amount of the mortgages held by it) was the *Crédit foncier de France*, founded in 1852 under government supervision. In Germany a number of banks on the same system were formed after 1860 : the Bavarian Mortgage Bank was founded in 1834, but did not begin to issue debentures till much later. The capital of these banks at the beginning of 1891 amounted to 332 million marks (£16½ million), and the debentures issued by them to over 3000 million (£150 million). Their 3½ per cent debentures are generally quoted over par. There are also such mortgage banks in Austria - Hungary, Switzerland, and Italy. In the latter country a new privileged institution was founded in 1890 (*Istituto italiano di credito fondiario*). The Argentine mortgage banks, and more especially the provincial ones, are but too well known in this country.

In the United Kingdom it had been expected that the Mortgage Debenture Act of 1865, and the Mortgage Debenture (Amendment) Act of 1870 (28 & 29 Vict. c. 78 ; 33 & 34 Vict. c. 20) might assist landowners, and on the other hand provide sound investments for capitalists ; but the result was very disappointing. The acts provide that the securities upon which debentures issued under their authority may be founded are to belong to certain special descriptions, and are to be deposited and registered in the office of land registry, and to be accompanied by a statutory declaration of a surveyor as to the value of the mortgaged properties, and contain other safeguards in favour of the debenture holders, but the precautions imposed have not proved very effective, and the only important company which availed itself of the provisions of the acts in question was recently compelled to go into liquidation. The question as to the economical advantages and disadvantages of the various forms of mortgage banks cannot well be discussed in general terms, as the answer depends on the local circumstances, of which there is an infinite variety. The great danger of special facilities for mortgaging land arises in times of inflation, when they multiply the opportunities for reckless gambling ; on the other hand it is an advantage that there should be special financial institutions for the purpose of making advances on real property, as it is clearly not within the province of ordinary banks to lock up any substantial part of their funds in such advances.

Where there are numerous small holders, the intervention of the public authorities is almost a necessity, as it would not pay establishments carrying on business on strictly commercial principles to lend small sums except on very onerous terms.

[As to continental mortgage banks, see Buchenberger, *Agrarwesen und Agrarpolitik*, ii. 97-190.—Hecht, *Die Staatlichen und provinziellen Bodenkreditinstitute in Deutschland;* and the same author's articles, "Landschaften," and "Hypothekenaktienbanken," in *Handwörterbuch der Staatswissenschaften*.]   E. S.

MORTGAGE BOND. Bonds issued by a railway or other corporation are sometimes secured by the mortgage of some particular assets or assigned property. American railroad companies have floated a great number of mortgage bonds on the London market, besides some income bonds. The latter are practically preference capital ; they are not secured by mortgage, and the interest for each year is payable out of the income of that year only.   A. E.

MORTGAGE DEBENTURE. A debenture secured by a mortgage of property. The use of the word does not, however, in itself give any rights to the holder, and may therefore in many cases be misleading (see DEBENTURE).
            E. S.

MORTGAGEE. A creditor secured by a MORTGAGE (*q.v.*) of property.   E. S.

MORTGAGES, REGISTRATION OF. The compulsory registration of mortgages in a public register is much more universal than the registration of land or deeds affecting land generally (as to which see LAND REGISTRATION). Thus in many places mortgages of land are not effective unless registered, although there is no similar requirement as regards transfers of property (*e.g.* the Argentine Republic). The reason for this must be sought in the fact that the publicity of mortgages is desirable not only for the purpose of avoiding disputes as to title, but also for the purpose of preventing people from obtaining credit by the apparent ownership of property, which in reality is not available for their general creditors. As in England, mortgages may be effected not only of land, but also of movable property, a special safeguard was required in respect of the latter, and this explains the reason of the statutes requiring the registration of a BILL OF SALE (*q.v.*), which, however, exclude the bills of sale of limited companies. The latter are required to keep a register of all their mortgages, but as the validity of the mortgages does not depend on the compliance with that rule, it fails to fulfil the object for which it was introduced (see JOINT-STOCK COMPANIES). The law in this respect, and the law as to the registration of mortgages in England generally, will probably be changed at no distant date.

[On the whole subject of registration, see R. Burnet Morris, *A Summary of the Law of Land and Mortgage Registration*, 1895.]   E. S.

MORTGAGOR. A debtor who charges property by way of MORTGAGE (*q.v.*).   E. S.

MORTIMER, THOMAS (1730-1810), a voluminous author and compiler, the merits of whose work cannot quite be taken at his own valuation, was appointed in 1762 English vice-consul to the Austrian Netherlands, with the promise, according to his own statement of the reversion of the consulate. The story of his wrongs is told at length in the *Remarks on the case of T. Mortimer*, 2nd ed., London, 1770, 8vo. In 1765 he translated Necker's work *On the Administration of the finances of France*, 3 vols., 8vo. Mortimer's most important work, the *Elements of Commerce, Politics, and Finance*, 4to, in three treatises on these important subjects, designed as a supplement to the education of British youth after they quit the public universities or private academies, appeared in 1772. On the BALANCE OF TRADE (*q.v.*), Mortimer claims to have originated the theory that it depends on the amount of the total commerce carried on to all quarters of the world. The portion on finance, while strenuously combating "idle notions of refunding the capital" of the national debt, contains some acute criticism of Dr. Price's views on a SINKING FUND (*q.v.*). In an advertisement, prefixed to a reprint of the book in 1780, Mortimer roundly accused Adam Smith of having plagiarised from him, and claims that the *Elements* had helped to put a stop to fictitious insurances at Lloyds, and had suggested to Lord North the taxing of certain luxuries, and to Lord Beauchamp his bill for the prevention of arrests for debt for sums under £10. The *Elements* exhausted Mortimer's attempts at original work ; for the rest of his life he was busy with work for the booksellers. In his old age he complained to Isaac Disraeli of the hardships of his position.

Among Mortimer's other works were : *Every man his own Broker, or a Guide to Exchange Alley*, London, 1761, 12mo, 13th ed., 1801.—*The Universal Director*, London, 1763, 8vo.—*Dictionary of Trade and Commerce*, 2 vols., London, 1766, 4to.—*Student's Pocket Dictionary*, London, 1777, 12mo.—*General Commercial Dictionary*, London, 1810, 8vo.—*A Grammar illustrating the Principles of Trade and Commerce*, London, 1810, 12mo.—*Nefarious practice of Stock-jobbing unveiled*, London, 1810, 8vo.

[*European Magazine*, vol. xxxv.—*Dictionary of National Biography*, vol. xxxix.—M'Culloch's *Literature of Political Economy*, pp. 52, 53.]
            H. E. E.

MORTMAIN. Under the feudal system the lord who had a corporation for tenant was under considerable disadvantages. His tenant could not die, could not marry, be a minor, or commit a felony : thus a great part of the lord's profits were taken away. In addition to this, the great religious corporations, such as the templars, held royal charters granting them further immunities. The matter was made worse by a practice which grew up during the 12th century: a tenant would alienate his land to a monastery and be received back as a tenant of the monastery, thus depriving his original feudal lord of his rights. This last process was declared illegal by the great charter of 1217. A clause of the abortive provisions of Westminster, A.D. 1259, which was re-enacted in the statute De Viris Religiosis, generally known as the Statute of Mortmain, in 1279, made all alienations to the church illegal, whether made in FRANKALMOIGN or otherwise, without the lord's consent. According to later statutes an inquisition, *ad quod damnum*, had to be held, and it was only after this inquisition had shown that neither the king nor any one else would suffer loss thereby, that an alienation to the church was allowed. Apparently it was not till near the end of the 14th century that it was discovered that any corporation was as bad a tenant as the church; for it was not till the statute of 15 Richard II., A.D. 1391, that alienation to any corporate body was subjected to the same laws as alienation to the church.

[*Statutes of the Realm.*—Pollock and Maitland, *History of English Law*, Cambridge, 1895.]

A. E. S.

MORTON'S FORK.[1] This was a dilemma devised by Bishop Morton, chancellor under Henry VII., afterwards cardinal and archbishop of Canterbury, to swell the contributions to a Benevolence (see BENEVOLENCES), levied for a proposed war with France (1491). A clause was inserted in the instructions to the commissioners: "That if they met with any that were sparing, they should tell them that they must needs have, because they laid up; and if they were spenders, they must needs have, because it was seen in their port and manner of living."

[Bacon, *History of the Reign of King Henry VII.* (ed. Lumby), p. 93.]

R. L.

MOS (custom). "Jus quod moribus constitutum est" is customary law, which is opposed to "lex" statute law (see Smith's *Dict. of Antiquities*, art. Jus).

E. A. W.

MÖSER, JUSTUS (1720-1794) was born at Osnabrück, where his father held a high legal office. He studied at Jena and Göttingen from 1740 to 1742, and, afterwards practising as an advocate in his native place, won the esteem and confidence of his fellow-citizens, which he retained in several important public positions which he filled.

ROSCHER, who declares *him*, and not Hugo or Schlosser, to have been the father of the historical school of law—a judgment which is, however, not generally accepted,—pronounces him also the greatest German political economist of the 18th century, and this on the ground of his possession of the following

[1] Morton's connection with this dilemma has been controverted. Bacon, *History of King Henry VII.*, speaks of it as "a tradition."

qualities:—(1) his open sense, equally for the higher social facts and for the homely every-day life of communities; (2) his thorough acquaintance with, and warm feeling towards, the people, in both senses of that word—the lower classes, and the nation at large; and (3) his mastery of HISTORICAL METHOD. He has not put forward any *system* of political economy, but his very numerous writings abound in original economic ideas, scattered through them, as Goethe says, like gold nuggets and gold grains. He shows himself to us as a soundhearted, healthy-minded man, somewhat wayward and paradoxical in his mental habits, and "old world" in his views. He is opposed to the "liberal-rationalistic" school of Adam SMITH, dislikes the highly developed division of labour, objects to generalising and centralising tendencies, and looks with admiration and affection on many institutions of the feudal period. It was well that justice should be done to the merits of that age, but, in showing that the principles and practice of the past suited the contemporary social environment, he is sometimes led, like most lovers of antiquity, to represent them as adapted to the present, when they are really and necessarily obsolete and incapable of revival.

How strongly Möser impressed Goethe, and what an influence he had upon his youth, may be seen in bk. xiii. of the *Wahrheit und Dichtung*. His principal work, which takes rank as a German classic, is his *Patriotische Fantasieen*, 3 pts., 1774-1778, a series of short essays, which in many respects remind the reader of Franklin.

[Wegele in *Allg. Deutsche Biogr.*—Schmidt in *Handw. der Staatswissenschaften.*—Roscher, *Gesch. der N. O.*, p. 500.—Cohn, *Hist. of Pol. Econ.* (see arts. on CAMERALISTIC SCIENCE; GERMAN SCHOOL).]

J. K. I.

MOSER, FRIEDRICH KARL VON (1723-1798), after having studied law at Jena, and been some time engaged in tuition, successively entered into the civil service of several German princes, but roused a vindictive animosity against himself by his bold denunciations of the official exactions committed in the small German states. His outspokenness led to his being sentenced in 1780, by the faculty of law in Frankfurt-on-the-Oder, to six years' imprisonment in a fortress, and a fine of 20,000 florins. He however, succeeded in evading actual imprisonment.

He was a frequent and fragmentary writer on diplomacy and public law, but is best known by his book *Der Herr und der Diener, geschildert mit patriotischer Freiheit* (The Master and the Servant depicted with patriotic Freedom), 1759, in which he declares that "times are near when the choice will not be between good and bad, but between bad and worse," and professes to be ashamed to be a German, when he thinks "what kind of men most of the heirs presumptive will be."

Although he manfully struggles against the narrow and selfish *Particularismus* of the German princes, he is not a follower of the French philosophers, but finds in St. Paul's remarks in the *Epistle to the Romans* on the powers that be, a right exposition of the duties of the subject ; he praises Mirabeau the elder, but denies that there only exists one model of a good government. His own leanings are in favour of the state of things anterior to the Thirty Years' War.
[Roscher, *Gesch. der Nat. Oek. in Deutschland*, pp. 529-532.—Bluntschli, *Gesch. des allg. Staatsrechts*, pp. 404-413.]　　　　　　　　　E. ca.

MOSER, JOHANN JACOB (1701-1785), had as chequered an existence as his son Friedrich von MOSER (*q.v.*). A man of great classical attainments, he was successively a lawyer, a university professor at Tubingen and Frankfurt-on-the-Oder, a member of the government of Wurtemberg and other German states, and founded an academy for political science in Hanau. His unguarded language in defence of the rights of the *Landstände* of Wurtemberg against their domineering duke got him into trouble, and he was imprisoned for six years (1758-1764).
He wrote about 400 volumes and pamphlets, and is considered as the founder of the science of German public law. He published a *Bibliothek von oekonomischen und Cameral Polizei-schriften* (Ulm, 1758), and some dissertations on economic questions ; in his autobiography, he states that for a long time, cameralistics and the science of interior state policy had been his favourite studies. Roscher expressly mentions his *Grundsätze einer vernünftigen Regierungskunst nach der jetzigen Denkungsart* . . . *verständiger Regenten* (Principles of a rational art of Government according to the opinions and practice of intelligent Rulers), 1753, in which Moser designs to demonstrate that trade, the interior state policy, etc., form "a connected and systematic whole." As announced by its title, this book is an exposition of what was done in well ruled states of these times (England and France being often put up as examples), but abstains from doctrinal investigations of what ought to be. Although Moser had some quarrels with Friedrich Wilhelm I. of Prussia, he derives a good number of the "principles" he recommends from this king's policy.
[Roscher, *Gesch. der Nat. Oek. in Deutschland*, pp. 441-443.—R. von Mohl, *Literatur der Staatswissenschaften*, ii. pp. 401-412.—Bluntschli, *Allgem. Staatsrecht*, 2nd ed. p. 402.]　　E. ca.

MOSSE OR MOSES, MILES (fl. 1580-1614), divine, was the author of *The Arraignment and Conviction of Usury*, London, 1595, which may be taken as a representative statement of the more liberal church view of usury (see INTEREST AND USURY) at the close of the 16th century. Mosse distinguishes between the sin of usury and usury itself.
[Ashley's *Economic History*, vol. i. pt. 2, p. 469, London, 1893, 8vo.—*Dictionary of National Biography*, vol. xxxix. p. 184.]　　　H. E. E.

MOST FAVOURED NATION CLAUSE. This is inserted in many commercial treaties. It binds each of the contracting powers to give to the other in certain matters the same treatment which it gives or may hereafter give to the nation which receives from it the most favourable terms in respect of those matters. The nature of such stipulations will be understood from the following example, taken from a convention on trade-marks concluded between Great Britain and the United States in 1878.— "The citizens of each of the contracting parties shall have, in the dominions and possessions of the other, the same rights as belong to native subjects or citizens, or as are now granted or may hereafter be granted to the subjects and citizens of the most favoured nation, in everything relating to trade-marks and trade-labels." The concession here is strictly limited as to its subject matter ; but in many cases the most favoured nation clause is made general in its terms, and covers all matters of trade and navigation. When such large expressions are used it sometimes happens that a state finds itself called upon to grant to a distant or unfriendly power, or even to a keen commercial rival, privileges it has given for valuable consideration to a friend and neighbour. Nations who have adopted protectionist theories of international trade are likely to find themselves in this predicament more often than those who are content to let commerce take its course without attempting to control it in their own interests by constant higgling with other powers. The inconvenience of having to give to one set of foreigners concessions for which a valuable equivalent has been extorted from another set has been avoided by means of the doctrine that the most favoured nation clause applies only to concessions which are gratuitous, and does not entitle the party which claims under it to privileges which some other state has gained by giving corresponding privileges in return, unless the claimant also is content to offer a fair consideration for them. It can hardly be said that this is a rule of international law ; but it has been adopted in such a large number of cases that a state which acts upon it cannot be accused of bad faith.
English commercial treaties containing a most favoured nation clause will be found in Hertslet's *Treaties*. The view of the meaning of the clause enunciated above is explained and defended in Wharton's *International Law Digest* (§ 134).　　　　　　　　T. J. L.

MOTIVES, MEASURABLE. A term suggested by Professor Marshall as offering one way of marking off the sphere of economics from that of other social investigations. Motives are measurable so far as they can be relied on to produce constant effects which can be quantitatively estimated. Again measurable motives can be balanced one against another, as when we estimate the amount of sacrifice a person is willing to undergo in order to procure a given utility. Here the sacrifice and utility have both to be expressed in objective form before they can be economically measured. This is possible only when objects of desire or aversion can be freely transferred by contract between individual and individual. It is because economics deals primarily with such objects that the science has assumed a greater precision and exactness than any other social science. This characteristic has made it possible to examine economic phenomena by abstract, deductive, and, even to some extent, mathematical methods. W. E. J.

MOVABLES. Things which from their nature are capable of being moved from one place to another. The classification of things into movables and immovables is the only classification that corresponds with an essential difference in the subject matter. A leading distinction between movable and immovable property· is that as to the latter the rules of inheritance follow the *lex situs*, while as to the former they follow the *lex domicilii*. The *lex situs* decides whether an article is a movable or not.

[Sir Henry Maine in *Ancient Law*, London, 1880, traces the gradual development of the distinction in Roman law.] J. E. C. M.

MÜLLER, ADAM HEINRICH (1779-1829), was born at Berlin. In his nineteenth year he went to the university of Göttingen, where he at first occupied himself with theology, and then became a student of jurisprudence, in which he was a pupil of Hugo. He afterwards sought to complete his education by the private study of the natural sciences, which he had previously neglected. He early formed a close intimacy with Friedrich GENTZ, his elder by fifteen years ; and this connection exercised an important influence both on his material circumstances and his mental development in after life. The two men differed widely in character and in their fundamental principles, but agreed, at least in their later period, in their practical political aims, and the friendship between them was brought to an end only by Müller's death. The relations of the latter with the Junker party, and his co-operation with them in their opposition to HARDENBERG'S reforms, made any public employment in Prussia impossible for him. In 1805 he was in Vienna, where he became a convert to Roman Catholicism, and, through Gentz, was brought into relations with Metternich, to whom he was useful in the preparation of state papers. He spent the years 1806-1809 in Dresden, being occupied in the political education of Prince Bernhard of Saxe-Weimar. In 1813 he entered the Austrian service, and in 1815 accompanied the allies to Paris ; he was ennobled by the emperor in 1820. In 1827 he settled a second time in Vienna, and was employed in the state chancellery. He was one of the principal literary instruments of the reaction, and took part, as Gentz's assistant, in framing the Carlsbad resolutions.

He was a man of remarkable powers and of great versatility, a born orator, and distinguished as a writer, not only on politics and economics, but on literature and æsthetics. As Gentz said of him : " He impresses us with a sense of his superiority even when we believe him to be on a wrong path." His principal work is his *Elemente der Staatskunst* (1809), which contains the substance of a course of lectures which he delivered at Dresden before a number of statesmen and diplomatists. He was, along with Gentz and HALLER, a member of the school of politicians and economists in Germany, which has been called the romantic, as harmonising in spirit with the literary school of Tieck, Schlegel, and Novalis, and looking back with admiration and regret to the church and state of mediæval times. In political economy he represents a reaction against the doctrines of Adam SMITH, whom, whilst he highly commends him in certain respects, he censures as presenting a one-sidedly material and individualistic conception of society, and as being too exclusively English in his views. Müller's leading idea is that of the organic unity and continuity of the state and of social institutions in general—a principle for which he may have been in part indebted to BURKE, whose *Reflections* were translated by Gentz. The economy of a society, he holds, is something more than the sum of the private economies of its members ; the individual must always be regarded in relation and subordination to the community. The capital of a country is not material only ; its language and culture, its character and experience, its laws and constitution, are true portions of the national wealth. The state is not merely a mechanism for the maintenance of order and the administration of justice ; it represents all the physical and spiritual possessions and requirements of the nation, and ought to bind together the whole inner and outer life of the people into a harmonious and energetic unity. Not merely should it study present production and immediate gain, but keep before it the increase of productive power and the development of civilisation in the future, and preserve for coming generations their entire inheritance, intellectual, moral, and economic. Müller considers Smith's theory of the division of labour defective in not sufficiently emphasising the dependence of such division on capital—on the labours and acquisitions of the past—and sets beside it, by way of correction and completion, a theory of the national combination of labour as no less important, though little more than indicated by Smith. The practical system of Smith might suit England sufficiently well, because the spiritual and material life of the people rested on a firm basis of traditional sentiments and old institutions reaching back to the middle ages, which continued to keep alive national self-consciousness and knit together the several social classes in a healthy union. But the ends thus spontaneously attained must, in continental countries, be affected by governmental action steadily maintaining the national idea and systematically developing the productive powers and general energies of the nation. In the economic sphere, he defends a policy of restrictions on importation as one means towards this development.

Müller's strength lies in breadth and comprehensiveness ; his defect in want of definiteness of conception and expression. Notwithstanding his eminent ability, he does not seem to have exercised much influence on the thought of his own time or of the succeeding period. His project of a Roman Catholic revival, and his retrograde attitude in politics, doubtless created a prejudice against his general philosophical views ; but it ought always to be remembered that his doctrines, though favouring the reaction, were not dictated by self-interest ; throughout his career he advocated principles essentially identical, and, in supporting Metternich's policy, he believed himself to be serving the highest interests of Germany and of Europe. Some of his higher tendencies, freed from much of their alloy, are reproduced in the writings of the historical school of German economists (comp. GERMAN SCHOOL).

Among the publications of Müller less important than the *Elemente der Staatskunst*, the following may be enumerated : *Die Theorie der Staatshaushaltung und ihre Fortschritte in Deutschland und England seit Adam Smith*, 1812.—*Versuch einer neuen Theorie des Geldes*, 1816.— *Vermischte Schriften über Staat Philosophie und Kunst*, (2 vols., 2nd ed., Vienna, 1817)—and *Von der Nothwendigkeit einer theologischen Grundlage der gesammten Staatswissenschaften und der Staatswirthschaft insbesondere*, 1819.

[Mischler in *Allg. Deutsche Biogr.*—Lippert in *Handw. der Staatswissenschaften.*—Roscher, *Gesch. der N.O.*, p. 763.—Kautz, *Die Gesch. Entwickelung der Nat.-O.*, p. 659.—Cossa, *Introd. allo Studio dell' E.P.*, p. 320.—Cohn, *Nat. Oek.*, i. p. 12.]

J. K. I.

MULTIPLICATION OF SERVICES is a term employed by Jevons (*Scientific Primer*) to denote that one of the advantages attending *Division of Labour* which arises when "nearly the same time and labour are required to perform the same operation on a larger or on a smaller scale"—in the words of WHATELY, who seems first to have pointed out this advantage (*Lectures on Political Economy*, vi.). Thus, "if a messenger is going to carry a letter to the post-office, he can as readily carry a score" (Jevons, *loc. cit.*). This advantage is connected with production on a large scale, under which head it is treated by Mill (*Pol. Econ.*, bk. i. ch. 9).

"Multiplication of copies" (Jevons, *loc. cit.*)

is a particular but important case. When once type has been set up, additional copies can be printed without much additional expense. A similar advantage is afforded by the use of "interchangeable parts" (Marshall) in machinery.

F. Y. E.

MUN, THOMAS (1571-1641), the best-known writer on the mercantile system, was son of John Mun, mercer, of London. As a member of the committee of the East India Company, and of the standing commission on trade (appointed in 1622, reappointed in 1625) "he was in his time famous amongst merchants and well known to most men of business, for his general experience in affairs, and notable insight into trade" (*England's Treasure by Foreign Trade*, John Mun's epistle dedicatory to Thomas, Earl of Southampton). In 1621 he published, in defence of the East India Company, *A Discourse of Trade from England into the East Indies*, reprinted in the same year, in Purchas's *Pilgrims* (1625), and in *Early English Tracts on Commerce*, London, 8vo, 1856. He is, however, best known by his posthumous work, *England's Treasure by Foreign Trade, or The Balance of our Foreign Trade is the Rule of our Treasure*, London, 8vo, 1664, republished in 1669, 1698, 1700 (in Lewis Roberts' *Mappe of Commerce*), 1713, 1755, 1856 (*Early Tracts on Commerce*), and 1895 (*Economic Classics*, edited by W. J. Ashley). There are two well-known allusions to this work in Adam Smith's *Wealth of Nations*, bk. iv. ch. i., in the first of which Smith quotes the concluding paragraph of the fourth chapter : "If we only behold the actions of the husbandman in the seed-time," etc. ; and in the second, states that "the title of Mun's book . . . became a fundamental maxim in the political economy, not of England only, but of all other commercial countries."

The importance of Mun's work in the development of economic theory in England has been pointed out (ENGLISH EARLY ECON. HIST., vol. i. pp. 722 *seq.*, 730). The date of its composition and its publication are of considerable interest. It was published twenty-three years after Mun's death, by his son John, who states in the epistle dedicatory that it was left to him "in the nature of a legacy" by his father. But it appears to consist of several short papers, some of which were written about 1622, and all before 1628. Whether the final form and arrangement of the treatise is due to Mun himself or his son John, there is nothing to show. Ch. i., on "the qualities which are required in a perfect merchant of foreign trade," probably formed part of the "former discourse," to which he alludes in his address to his son, in which he proposed to teach him "how to love and serve his country, by instructing him in the duties and proceedings of sundry vocations." The opening sentence, the marked difference of style between this chapter and the rest of the treatise, and other circumstances, point to this conclusion. In ch. ii., on "the means to enrich the kingdom," etc., and ch. iii. on "the particular ways and means to increase the exportation of our commodities," etc., he follows the order indicated in the address to his son. The following chapters are taken up with (1) the discussion of the advantages of the exportation of bullion ; (2) replies to various arguments employed by MALYNES and MISSELDEN, in their controversy of 1622-23, and to the advocates of the debasement of the currency ; (3) the fuller discussion of points briefly touched upon in ch. iii.; and (4) the method of calculating the balance of trade. Chs. iv. to vii. correspond almost verbatim to the *Petition and Remonstrance of the Governor and Company of Merchants of London trading to the East Indies*, which was drafted by Mun, and presented to the House of Commons in October 1628. This portion of *England's Treasure* may have been the rough draft of the *petition*. The differences between the two at any rate point to the fact that the latter was based upon the former. Chs. viii. to xv. are entirely taken up with the discussion of various arguments urged by Misselden and Malynes, and the advocates of the debasement of the currency. He objects to Misselden's contention that the want of money was due to the undervaluation of silver (*Free Trade, or The Means to make Trade flourish*, 1622), no less than Malynes's theory of the foreign exchanges (*The Maintenance of Free Trade*, 1622 ; *Lex Mercatoria*, 1622, etc.). He devotes the whole of ch. xiv. to a discussion of the "admirable facts" attributed to the bankers by Malynes, whom he accuses of "disguising his own knowledge with sophistry to further some private ends by hurting the public good," *i.e.* by re-establishing the office of royal exchanger. In his first pamphlet, Misselden had been anything but friendly to Mun's views on the East India Company ; but his second pamphlet, *The Circle of Commerce*, etc., 1623, gives unmistakable evidence of Mun's influence. Ch. xv. of *England's Treasure* appears to be mainly a reply to Malynes's *Canker of England's Commonwealth*. Chs. xvi.-xviii., "on Revenue, etc.," must have been written not later than the early years of the reign of Charles I. ; while ch. xix., in which Mun discusses the fishing trade, and quotes from the Dutch proclamation of 19th July 1624, was put into shape not very long subsequent to that date. The last two chapters deal with "the order and means whereby we may draw up the balance of our foreign trade," and "the conclusion upon all that hath been said concerning the exportation or importation of treasure." There appears to be no allusion throughout the treatise to any event later than

1624. No part of the work can have been written later than 1628, when the Petition and Remonstrance was presented to parliament, and most of it belongs probably to the years 1622-1625. The inquiry after the restoration into the desirability of legalising the exportation of bullion, followed by the act of 1663 (15 Car. II. c. 7), probably suggested the publication of Mun's work.

[A full account of Mun's life is given in the *Dictionary of National Biography*. For other points in his work see ENGLISH EARLY ECONOMIC HISTORY and ENGLISH SCHOOL OF POLITICAL ECONOMY, vol. i. pp. 719-737 (refs. to EXCHANGER, etc.), and the authorities quoted there. See MERCANTILE SYSTEM.]   W. A. S. H.

MUNICIPALITY.

Roman, p. 829 ; Mediæval, p. 830 ; Modern, p. 831 ; Municipal Government in Belgium, p. 831 ; in France, p. 832 ; in Italy, p. 834 ; in Prussia, p. 834 ; in United States of America, p. 837.

THE term municipality is ambiguous. Sometimes it signifies a town which is treated as a distinct unit for purposes of administration and sometimes the administrative authority in such a town. In another article (see ADMINISTRATION), it has been shown that in a large community it is impossible to concentrate the whole business of executive government at one spot, and that the centres of administration must be multiplied. It has also been shown that most governments have not merely spread their official administrators over the whole territory, but have enlisted private citizens in such portions of administrative work as immediately affect a particular neighbourhood. A certain degree of decentralisation and of local self-government is necessary to the proper administration of a great civilised state. Towns and cities have naturally obtained the largest share of these privileges, and for a long time throughout the greater part of Europe local self-government meant municipal self-government.

Roman Municipalities.—The earliest available instance of municipal self-government on a grand scale is afforded by the Roman power. Whilst the Romans established a universal empire, they never quite abandoned the antique idea that the city is the normal political community. Under the Roman emperors the Mediterranean world was divided into thousands of urban communities. Each city possessed a more or less extensive territory, and within this territory certain powers of self-government were exercised by those who possessed the franchise of that city. As the whole empire, or at least all its civilised portions, were thus divided into urban districts, no antithesis arose between urban and rural authorities. It was as though every English county were administered by those who possessed burgess rights in the county town, but it must be added that residence was not in antiquity a necessary condition of obtaining such rights. The Roman municipal system was unquestionably a boon to the countries in which it was established ; it served to keep alive the local patriotism, the interest in public business, and the spirit of public munificence so apt to dwindle among the subjects of a despotic monarchy. Magnificent remains scattered over most of the countries of the Mediterranean still show how nobly the municipal authorities of the Roman towns provided for the health, the convenience, the education, and the amusement of the burgesses. It is true that municipal extravagance and mismanagement were also common. Those defects afforded an excuse for the interference of the central government, and by degrees the Roman municipalities became practically powerless. Finally the barbarian conquests wrought such havoc in the Roman municipal system that it is doubtful how far any connection can be traced between it and the municipal system of the middle ages which next claims attention.

Mediæval Municipalities.—When the era of barbarian inroads finally closed in the tenth century, and the revival of civilisation brought prosperity again to towns, a new period of municipal development began. In this period municipal life is strongly contrasted with rural life. Feudalism laid its closest grasp on the rural districts, where a hierarchy of petty princes reigned one above another, and the lowest class of the population were in an almost servile condition. Important towns generally succeeded in placing themselves under the immediate protection of the sovereign or of a feudal magnate of the highest class, and all the inhabitants of such towns were personally free. Thus in the towns there was a scope for ambition and a security for hoarded wealth unknown in the country districts. In this period also municipal self-government frequently grew into something like political independence. None of the municipal towns of the Roman empire could have hoped to resist the will of the Roman emperor. But the municipalities of the middle ages had only to deal with feudal monarchs, whose real power was often as little as their titles were pompous. In the mediæval system of warfare, the means of attack were so much inferior to the means of defence that it was extremely difficult to reduce a large walled city, defended by a numerous and enthusiastic people. The burgess militia, however inferior to regular troops, were often more than a match for the arrogant and undisciplined knighthood. The most superficial readers of mediæval history know how the burghers of Milan stood a siege by the Emperor Frederick Barbarossa, and how the burghers of Ghent more than once faced the chivalry of France in the open field. Thus the great municipal towns of Italy became practic-

ally sovereign states, and the great municipal towns of Germany and Flanders became hardly less than sovereign. Lastly, the municipal organisation of mediæval towns was to a large extent industrial. There is no room here to discuss the history of the merchant and craft gilds or their relation to the government of the towns in which they arose. Nor is it safe to lay down any general law of development with reference to the constitutions of mediæval municipalities. In a majority of cases, perhaps, the result was the absorption of power by an urban aristocracy of commerce and industry, as opposed to the feudal aristocracy of land-owners in the country districts. Under these circumstances it was natural that mediæval burghers should be prone to fierce internal dissensions, and to an exclusive local patriotism, not merely hating the feudal lords and contemning the peasantry, but intensely jealous of the power and prosperity of any town but their own, a fatal weakness which was fully exemplified in the history of Flanders, and of Italy. At the same time the services rendered to civilisation by the mediæval municipalities were incalculable. At a time when the bulk of the country population in central and western Europe were little better than beasts of burthen, the municipal towns were sanctuaries of industry, art, and learning. Their wealth was such as under the conditions of the time might seem incredible, were it not yet attested by the splendour of their churches, of their municipal buildings, and even of their private mansions. But the condition of their freedom and power was the continuance of semi-barbarism without the walls. When feudal anarchy had been suppressed in the country districts, monarchs no longer needed the support of privileged towns. When the invention of gunpowder had transformed the art of war, town walls were no longer impregnable, and the burgher militia became useless against professional soldiers. The exclusive jealous spirit which set town against town, and class against class, made impossible all resistance to a centralised despotism. From the close of the 15th century onwards, the central government everywhere gained rapidly upon municipal independence.

In England the history of municipal development was somewhat different. Self-government by the free inhabitants prevailed there in rural as well as in urban neighbourhoods, and the representatives of the towns took part in the county courts. Again the towns were relatively far less important in England than in Italy, Germany, or even France, for mediæval England was an agricultural and pastoral, rather than an industrial or commercial country. Thirdly England attained national unity and a powerful government at a comparatively early time. Lastly, the old free institutions were never overthrown in England as elsewhere. Owing to all these causes municipal towns in England never occupied so distinct or so conspicuous a place, whilst they escaped such a complete enslavement as befell municipal towns on the continent of Europe.

Modern Municipalities.—The third period of municipal development, which may be termed the modern period, may be dated from the French revolution. That revolution, and the revolutions which followed it, have converted the despotic monarchies of central and western Europe into governments more or less popular. The same desire for self-government which prompted this change led to a demand for reformed municipal constitutions. In England reform came more naturally as the feeling of local independence and the interest in local affairs had never quite died out. In the United States vigorous municipal institutions existed even prior to the separation from the mother country. This new municipal life differs from the municipal life· of the middle ages in several weighty respects. The long-continued pressure of the central government, and the changes wrought by modern civilisation, have lessened the contrast between town and country. Municipal self-government has been very generally extended with some modifications to the rural districts of this and of other countries. Again, the modern municipal town cannot aspire to political independence. Military power is now centred in the hands of the national government to an extent never paralleled save under the Roman emperors. Lastly, the exclusive spirit which formerly parted town from town, and the ruling class of each town from the rest of the citizens, has practically disappeared. Modern municipal self-government is democratic, and the only dangers which threaten its future are those incidental to democracy, such as the withdrawal of sensitive and high-minded men from public life, the too ready reception accorded to demagogues, and the popular fallacy that too much money cannot be raised in rates or spent in wages. Several cities of the United States have afforded the most alarming examples of robbery and corruption. It is not reassuring to learn that a common remedy for these evils is to appoint some eminent citizen as a dictator, for this is an acknowledgment that municipal institutions have no power of self-purification. In Germany it is a not infrequent practice for the municipality to entrust the administration to a professional expert. In France, and especially in Paris, municipal profusion is conspicuous. Similar tendencies are not unknown in England. What functions should be entrusted to a municipal body is a large and complex question which cannot be solved without wide experience. Watching, lighting, sanitary control, and the execution of public improvements, are clearly

within its province. Much may be said in favour of entrusting to it the provision of such articles of general use and necessity as are already subjects of a virtual monopoly, *e.g.* the supply of gas and water. But there is nothing to justify the belief that the municipality should be sole landlord or sole capitalist in the town. There is no reason to suppose that a town council is fit to manufacture cotton goods or ship plates. The supply of men fit for municipal office is small ; the time which they can give to public affairs is limited ; and under the conditions of modern life much alteration in either respect is not likely to be made. The tendency to ask of municipal bodies more than they can possibly perform is the most serious danger which threatens municipal self-government in modern Europe.

[Smith, *Dictionary of Greek and Roman Antiquities.*— Hegel, *Geschichte der Italienischen Städteverfassung.*—Villari, *History of Florence.*—Perrens, *Histoire de Florence.*—Sismondi, *République Italiennes.*—Luchaire, *Les Communes Françaises.*—Zeller, *Histoire d'Allemagne.*—Gross, *The Gild Merchant.*—Alice S. Green, *Town Life in the Fifteenth Century.*—Cunningham, *Growth of English Industry and Commerce.*—Ashley, *Economic History of England,* and the general histories of England, France, Spain, and Germany.]

F. C. M.

MUNICIPAL GOVERNMENT IN ENGLAND. See CORPORATION, MUNICIPAL ; METROPOLIS ; MUNICIPALITY.

MUNICIPAL GOVERNMENT IN BELGIUM. The words *municipalité, municipal* are not used by the Belgian constitution or laws on the subject ; the words *commune, communal* have alone a legal standing.

Under the Dutch rule of the beginning of this century, a distinction was maintained between the administration of the towns and what was called the "flat country" (*le plat pays*) ; the communal law of the 30th March 1836 submitted the whole of the territory to a uniform communal legislation.

According to the constitution, the communal councils must be directly elected by the electoral body ; their power extends over all subjects of communal interests, the central government having only the right to declare void any resolution in contradiction with the general interest, and their sessions and accounts must be kept open to publicity. These general principles laid down in the constitution of 1831, have been further developed by the already-mentioned law of 1836 which is still in force, except, as we shall presently see, for the mode of election of the councillors.

The number of councillors varies from seven to thirty-one according to the figure of the population ; no restriction is laid on their meetings ; they meet whenever it is expedient for the transaction of communal business, the *bourgmestre* (mayor) occupying by right the chair. Their right to impose local taxes to supply the financial wants of the *commune* is far more extended than in France and in Italy, and in fact, almost unlimited.

The *bourgmestre*, who is at once the agent of the king and the head of the *commune*, is nominated by the king, who possesses the right of selecting him even outside the communal council, a royal prerogative which remains practically dormant. With the *échevins* (aldermen, from the Flemish *schepen*, in mediæval Latin *scabini*) formerly nominated by the king, now elected by the council, the *bourgmestre* forms the *collège échevinal*, or executive committee entrusted with the daily local administration, but in matters of *état civil* (public registration of births, marriages, and deaths) and of police, the *bourgmestre* has a distinct and individual authority of his own and is personally responsible for public order.

The king cannot dissolve a communal council, though he may cancel any resolution, illegal or opposed to the general good. The *députation permanente* of the provincial council is also entrusted with some powers of control on certain specified subjects, but, on the whole, Belgium is one of the countries on the continent where local autonomy and independence is most extended, and most solidly founded on an almost uninterrupted transmission of traditions and customs tracing their origin to the flourishing period of Ghent, Bruges, Ypres, etc., during the last centuries of the middle ages.

A quite recent law (May 1895) has considerably enlarged the communal electoral body. Every Belgian citizen aged thirty and having three years' residence is now entitled to one vote. He may acquire from one to three extra votes, if he is married, in possession of certain degrees or diplomas, put down on the rolls of direct taxation for a certain *minimum* amount, or if he proves that he is in receipt of a certain income.

[For a general historical sketch of the communal government during the middle ages see Professor Van der Kindere, *Le Siècle des Artevelde*, Brussels, 1879, and Alphonse Wauters, *Les Libertés Communales, Essai sur leur Origine et leurs premiers développements*, Brussels, 1878. Several collections (*Recueils des Ordonnances, des anciennes coutumes de la Belgique, coutumes de Flandre, du Brabant*, etc.) have since 1850 been published by official authority.

For tho more purely legal aspect see Charles Faider, *Études sur les Constitutions Nationales* (1842), and *Coup d'Œil historique sur les institutions provinciales et communales en Belgique* (1834). —For present times De Brouckère et Tielemans, *Répertoire du Droit Administratif de Belgique* (8 vols., 1834-56 unfinished).—De Fooz, *Le Droit Administratif Belge* (1866). — Leemans, *Des Impositions Communales en Belgique* (1866).—Giron, *Essai sur le Droit Communal en Belgique* (1862). —Bivort, *Commentaires sur la Loi Communale de Belgique*, 9th ed. (1882) ; and Giron, *Le Droit Administratif de la Belgique*, 3rd ed. (1885).]

E. CA.

MUNICIPAL GOVERNMENT IN FRANCE.

The *commune* is the ultimate territorial and administrative unit of France ; this name is now equally applied to the towns and the rural parishes (*paroisses*) which used to be kept distinct before the French Revolution. At the time of the latter, the *Assemblée Constituante* recognised the legal existence of about 44,000 *communes* for continental France ; the present number slightly exceeds 36,000, about one-half of which have a population inferior to 500 inhabitants. It is generally considered that a further reduction of this number by means of the consolidation of neighbouring diminutive rural *communes* would be desirable.

Excepting Paris and, to some extent, Lyons, all French *communes* are regulated by the law of the 5th of April 1884 on municipal organisation, which has repealed or modified the former legislation of 1837 and 1855 ; according to the preliminary report presented to the chamber of deputies, it was intended to be "a reform most favourable to the extension of communal freedom." The following summary will show that space still remains for further extension, and that, with the exception of their everyday business, French municipal authorities are only allowed to move under the *tutela* of the central government and its official delegates, the *préfet* and the *sous-préfet*.

"The municipal body of each *commune* is composed of the municipal council, the *maire* and one or several *adjoints* (or deputies of the *maire*)." Such is the text of article 1 of the law. The minimum number of municipal councillors is 10 for *communes* under 500 inhabitants, and progressively rises with the population to a maximum of 54. The *maire* and *adjoints* are elected from their own body by the municipal councillors, themselves directly elected by all male inhabitants above twenty-one, settled in the *commune* or resident there six months and not in actual receipt of relief from the *Bureau de Bienfaisance*. Non-resident voters are admitted on their demand, if their names are on the list of taxpayers, but nobody is allowed to vote in more than one *commune*. All male inhabitants, paupers of course excluded, or taxpayers above twenty-five years of age are qualified to be elected, but the number of non-resident councillors must not exceed one-fourth of the total number of councillors. Several classes of state or municipal officials, such as the public schoolmaster and priests, cannot be elected.

Municipal councils are elected for four years ; they may, in case of urgency, be suspended for one month by the *préfet* of the department, but the President of the Republic is alone empowered to dissolve them and his decree must state the motives of the dissolution. He then appoints a provisional delegation of 3 to 7 members entrusted with the management of urgent affairs ; a new election must take place within two months.

The *maire* and municipal councillors can draw no salary, but the reimbursement of actual expenses is permissive, and the *maires* of large towns sometimes are awarded what are called *frais de représentation*—expenses for receptions and entertainments, etc.

Municipal councils have four annual ordinary sessions, three of a fortnight and one for the debates on the budget which may last six weeks. The *préfet* and *sous-préfet* may summon them for an extraordinary convocation, so also may the *maire* who is further obliged to summon the council whenever required to do so by a majority, specifying the object of its request. In this case he must inform the *préfet*, and only the specified questions can be discussed.

The *maire* is legally the chairman, except when his own administrative accounts are examined. As a rule, the meetings of the council are open to the public, and an extract from the journals must be stuck up at the door of the town hall within the week. Every inhabitant or taxpayer is entitled to claim the perusal of the journals, municipal budget, and accounts, etc.

The specific functions of the council as enumerated by article 61 of the law are—

(*a*) to regulate by its resolutions the business of the *commune*.

(*b*) to give its advice when required by law or by the superior authorities.

(*c*) to protest if necessary against the *quota* of apportioned taxes assessed on the *commune*.

(*d*) to express wishes (*vœux*) on all subjects of local interest.

(*e*) to draw up the list from which the prefectoral authority nominates the assessors for the apportionment of certain taxes. An extract of all resolutions is to be sent within a week to the *sous-préfet* by the *maire;* if these exceed the range of the legal attributions of the council they are legally void and are declared so by the *préfet*. Political wishes fall under this description ; still the delegates of all the municipal councils make up the bulk of the electoral body for the French Senate. Every taxpayer and any person having an interest at stake, is also entitled to sue for a declaration of nullity of a resolution within a fortnight. The council of state is the supreme jurisdiction for all suits of this kind.

French *communes* are legally capable to own property, both movable and real, constituting either their public domains, *e.g.* schools, hospitals, streets, libraries, churchyards, etc. or their private domains, *e.g.* houses, arable land, fields, woods, consolidated state funds. Houses and land may be sold, rented, and farmed, but the terms of these transactions must be approved by the superior authorities,

even for leases, when they exceed eighteen years. The same approval is necessary for all resolutions on rights of commons, on acceptance of legacies and donations, if hampered with charges or conditions, or giving rise to opposition from the family of the testator or donor ; for the communal budget, the vote of supplementary supplies ; the raising of extraordinary taxes or contracting of loans, if their principal exceeds a certain proportion. The foundation or suppression of fairs must also be sanctioned by the *préfet*. Even resolutions, which do not require his sanction, only become executory one month after they have been notified to him.

The council is not allowed to publish proclamations or to enter into correspondence with other municipal councils, unless in a few specified cases and always under the prefectoral supervision. No *commune* can appear in court without being authorised by the *préfecture*.

The budget of each *commune* is proposed by the *maire*, voted by the municipal council, and sanctioned by the *préfet* ; whenever the communal income exceeds 3,000,000 of francs (£120,000), the final approbation of the President of the Republic is requisite. Certain items of expenditure are compulsory ; let us mention as such the registration of births, marriages, and deaths ; the repairs of communal buildings and public churches—for the latter in case of insufficiency of the means at the disposal of the *conseil de fabrique* (vestry)—the communal share in the expenses concerning public instruction ; the keeping in order of cemeteries and communal roads ; the salaries of specified communal functionaries, etc. The *commune* must also provide for the expenses of its police, notwithstanding the fact that in towns of more than 40,000 inhabitants, the personal regulation of the force belongs to the President of the Republic. Thus, although the *maire* is nominally the head of the municipal police, his immediate subordinates, the *commissaires* of police, are in fact the agents of the prefectoral administration. It must not be forgotten that the *maire* himself is at the same time the elected representative of the *commune* and the local agent of the central government ; until the end of the second empire, he was appointed by government, which has kept the right to dismiss him.

In one respect the communal councils are subject to the permanent control of local taxpayers. Article 123 of the law empowers any one of these to initiate at his own risk, and with the agreement of the *conseil de préfecture*, "the lawsuits which he considers to belong to the *commune*, and which the council having been invited to discuss has refused or neglected to prosecute." The resulting judicial decision binds the *commune*.

From this slight sketch it will appear that,

compared with other countries, the French municipal authorities are confined within rather narrow official trammels. French political parties clamour for decentralisation as long as they remain in opposition, but too often drop these views when actually in power.

[See *les Controverses sur la Décentralisation administrative* in the *Revue Politique et Parlementaire* (April and May 1895), by Léon Aucoc, the highest authority on the subject.

French urban municipalities and *communes* have a double origin ; in southern France they were generally survivals or revivals of Roman Municipia ; in the north they arose during the 12th century from the revolts of the *bourgeoisie* against their feudal lords. For this movement see Augustin Thierry, *Lettres sur l'Histoire de France* and *Essai sur la Formation et les Progrès du Tiers État.*—Guizot, *Cours de l'Histoire de la Civilisation en France*, and numerous monographs such as Prou, *Coutumes de Lorris aux XIIe et XIIIe Siècles* (1884).—Giry, *Établissements de Rouen* (1883).—Bonvalot, *Le Tiers État d'après la Charte de Beaumont* (1884), etc. The French kings favoured the *communes* in their struggles against their *Seigneurs* (see Giry, *Documents pour les relations de la Royauté avec les Villes au XIIe et au XIIIe Siècles*, 1885). Two centuries later we find them quarrelling with the towns on their privilege of exemption from taxation. The towns had to submit to the royal power. For the period extending hence to modern times, see de la Poix de Fréminville, *Traité Général du Gouvernement des communautés des villes, bourgs, villages et paroisses* (1760).—Boileau, *Recueil de Règlements concernant la Municipalité* (1785).—Raynouard, *Histoire du Droit Municipal en France* (1829), and Béchard, *Histoire du Droit Municipal au Moyen Age et dans les Temps Modernes* (1875).

For the present times, see Pascaud, *De l'Organisation Municipale et Communale en Europe, aux États Unis et en France* (1877).—H. de Ferron, *Institutions municipales et provinciales comparées* (1884), and the great work (in 8 vols.) of A. Batbie, *Traité théorique et pratique du Droit Public et Administratif* (1885). —Yves Guyot, "Municipality of Paris," *Contemporary Review*, 1883.]

E. Ca.

MUNICIPAL GOVERNMENT IN ITALY.

The law of the 20th March 1865 is still in all essential points the great charter of Italian municipal organisation. On four of these points it is modelled on the Belgian legislation : thus the *sindaco* (or mayor) is nominated by the king who can also remove him ; the qualification of a voter is based on the annual payment of one or another direct tax with a *minimum* varying from 5 to 25 lire (say 4s. to £1) according to the population ; moreover, owners of university degrees, civil and military officials, professors, bearers of an Italian order, etc. are electors by right, and unlettered citizens cannot vote ; in financial matters and questions of communal property, the control over the resolutions of the communal council rather belongs to the *deputazione provinciale*

(permanent delegation of the provincial council) than to the prefect ; and, fourthly, the *giunta municipale* comprising the *sindaco* and from two to ten *assessori*—the latter elected by the members of the *consiglio comunale* among their own members—have corporate existence recognised by law, like the Belgian *collège échevinal.* In other points the example of France was followed. Thus communal councils have two ordinary annual sittings, not exceeding thirty days each, unless a prolongation be granted by the provincial deputation ; for extraordinary sessions they must be summoned by the prefect, acting either *ex officio*, or on the petition of the *giunta*, or of one-third of the councillors, and in these extraordinary sessions resolutions can only be taken on questions specified beforehand. In the interval between the sittings, the *giunta* represents the communal council, to which it is accountable. In all deliberations concerning the budget, the prefect has always the right to be heard. He, as well as the communal councils themselves, may appeal to the king against any decision taken by the provincial deputation in its controlling capacity.

[Several papers on Italian Municipal Administration have appeared in the *Bulletin de la Société de Législation Comparée*, 1877, pp. 97-126 ; 1881, pp. 266-307 and 325-344 ; 1882, pp. 413-430.]

E. Ca.

MUNICIPAL GOVERNMENT IN PRUSSIA.

The year 1808 marks the beginning of a new era in the history of the Prussian administrative system, and especially in the form of municipal government. The social and political condition of the country immediately after the Thirty Years' War demanded radical changes, if it was to maintain its individuality amongst the civilised nations. The cities, after having attained, during the second half of the middle ages, a large measure of local independence and general prosperity, gradually lapsed into a condition of state tutelage. The 17th and 18th centuries found them stripped of every vestige of municipal authority and self-government. They had become *close corporations*, whose officials were appointed through, and dependent upon, state patronage. The complete disruption of the country through the crushing defeats inflicted by Napoleon in 1806 and 1807 made this organic weakness so apparent to the leading statesmen of the time that positive steps towards reform were immediately taken. The group of laws known as the *Stein-Hardenbergsche Gesetzgebung* forms the first and most important chapter in the series of administrative reforms of which the legislation of 1872 and 1876 marks the closing step.

To Stein is due the Municipal Corporations Act of November 19th, 1808, which is still the basis of municipal government in Prussia. In the acts of 1831, 1850, and 1853, which latter is at present in force, modifications in a conservative spirit were introduced tending towards a somewhat stricter control of municipal action by the central government.[1]

The general characteristics of municipal government in Prussia find such distinct expression in the organisation of the administration of Berlin that the description of the latter gives an adequate idea of the general system.

The general city administration of Berlin is in the hands of an Executive Board or *Magistrat;* a Municipal Council ; and a series of *Deputations* or committees, the nature of which we shall have occasion to examine.

The *Executive Board (Magistrat).*[2]— This board occupies a twofold position. It is entrusted with the execution of purely city affairs, and is also the representative of the state for the exercise of the more general or state functions. In the former of these capacities it is responsible to the municipal council, in the latter to the central government.[3] It is composed of a chief-mayor, vice-mayor, and thirty-two aldermen. Of these thirty-four offices, seventeen are professional in character, and therefore paid ; the remaining seventeen unsalaried or honorary, to which every citizen is eligible. Acceptance of the unsalaried offices is obligatory. All members of the executive board are elected by the city council, the salaried members for a period of twelve, the unsalaried for six years. All are re-eligible, and the salaried offices are practically life positions.

The mayor is the presiding officer of this board, and has the legal right to veto its decisions.[4] Where the board and the mayor are in actual conflict the ultimate decision is placed in the hands of the supreme administrative court (*Oberverwaltungsgericht*). It is necessary to examine briefly the method of settling these disputes, as this illustrates one of

[1] It is important to note that the Prussian system makes very clear distinction between urban and rural communities, and that the laws applying to each are entirely different. In this respect it differs entirely from the French system of local government, where no such distinction is made, the same form of local government applying there to both urban and rural communities.

[2] The salaries of the most important offices in the city government are as follows :
In the executive board the minimum compensation of paid members is 7000 marks. These salaries are increased from year to year in proportion to the term of service.
The highest salary of a regular member of the executive board is at present 11,600 marks.
The mayor receives 30,000 marks.
The vice-mayor 18,000 marks.
The salaries of chiefs of departments range from 3000 to 6000 marks. A few, such as the superintendent of the city insane asylum, receive as much as 9000 marks.
Members of the town council receive no compensation.

[3] It is to be noted that the government of Berlin is representative of the municipal system in the seven eastern provinces of Prussia. In the western provinces a system more closely resembling the system of the French *communes* is to be found.

[4] Very few instances of the exercise of the right have occurred, so that it is almost looked upon as non-existent. It has nevertheless given the mayor a very strong influence, moral if not legal, in determining the policy of the board.

the leading features of the Prussian administration. The question of the jurisdiction of the administrative courts and the semi-judicial bodies, which has acquired such importance since the reforms of 1872, 1876, and 1883, is exceedingly complicated. They are intended to settle such administrative disputes as may arise between the citizen and the public administration and between the various organs of the local or general administration. In cases where such differences have arisen between the executive board and the municipal council, the general rule is an appeal to the district committee[1] as administrative court of the first instance, and to the supreme administrative court for final decision. Berlin offers an exception to this general rule, for in cases of such differences the supreme administrative court acts as first and final resort.

The vice-mayor acts as substitute to the mayor in the details of his administrative duties. The remaining fifteen salaried members of the executive board are as follows :—two corporation counsel, two school councillors, two city architects, a city treasurer, and eight additional members. It is characteristic of the Prussian system that the incumbents for these salaried offices are chosen from all parts of the kingdom. The office of mayor in the larger towns is a purely professional one. Men who have gained a reputation as efficient administrators in the smaller cities are called to fill the important offices in more important centres. The choice of the city council for both salaried and non-salaried members of the executive board requires the approval of the provincial government. This apparently far-reaching restriction on local self-government is, as a general rule, a mere matter of form. It is to this executive board that the great bulk of the general city administration falls. In addition to its executive functions it may be regarded as constituting a part, at least, of the legislative branch of the city government, inasmuch as all decisions of the municipal council require the approval of the executive board. That this combination of executive and legislative powers makes the executive board by far the most important of the organs of the city administration is evident. In cases where the city council and the executive board come into conflict the supreme administrative court decides, upon the appeal of either body.

The detailed control and general administrative supervision of the various municipal departments is exercised by the committees, or *deputations* already mentioned. We have here one of the peculiar characteristics of the

[1] This committee is composed of the district president, two members appointed by the king, and four citizens elected by the provincial committee. Although Berlin has such a committee, it does not exercise the same extensive functions as in other parts of the kingdom ; its constitution is also somewhat different.

Berlin administrative system. It is an attempt to bring about a personal union between the executive and legislative branches of the city government and the general body of citizens. These committees are made up of city councilmen and private citizens, elected by the city council, to whom the executive board adds a number of its members. One of the latter acts as presiding officer. The exact proportion of representation from the various bodies is determined by municipal ordinance. There are at present the following *deputations :*—on taxation and military affairs, poor-law administration, streets and public buildings, street cleaning, schools, city property, parks, pensions, fuel, stationery, public health, statistics, street lighting, water-works, savings-banks, gymnastics, and industrial schools. The heads of the various municipal departments are, for the most part, experts entrusted with the executive policy of their particular department, and are responsible to these deputations for their financial and administrative methods.

The Municipal Council.—The leading feature of the Prussian Municipal Corporations Act is the absence of any minute and detailed grant of power, either to the city as a whole or to the municipal council in particular. On the one hand, its competency is limited by the general sphere of municipal action, and, on the other by the powers expressly and exclusively vested in the executive board. Not only is it charged—in connection, as a rule, with the executive board—with the financial and general administrative legislation, but it also exercises a strong control over the purely executive acts of the city administration. This is done through a series of standing committees entrusted with the examination of the accounts, contracts, and other acts of the various departments. It is, however, important to note that the executive branch is not compelled to carry out the will of the city council, unless this meets with its approval. In order that this conflict may be avoided as far as possible, the executive board has the right, and, upon the demand of the city council, may be required, to send representatives to the meetings of the council. The city council is elected by the tax-payers through what is known as the *three-class* system, adopted in 1849 for state elections, and soon after incorporated in the Municipal Corporations Act. The tax-payers are, for purposes of electing members of the municipal council, grouped into three classes, according to the amount of direct taxes paid by each. The first class comprises those among the most heavily-taxed inhabitants whose total contribution is one-third of the aggregate. They elect one-third of the city councillors. The next group, paying an equal amount, *i.e.* another third of the total sum, elect the same number. The remaining qualified voters elect the final

third of the total number of city councillors. It is evident that, according to this system, the wealth of the community really determines the character of the municipal council. Thus in 1887, with 3849 voters of the first class, 17,730 of the second, and 192,274 of the third, a comparatively small percentage of the population of Berlin exercised the controlling voice in the election of its council.

To the general rule of local self-government in the various municipal departments, there is one important exception, which is, however, not peculiar to Berlin, but characteristic of all the large Prussian cities. In all the smaller communities, the mayor is entrusted with the police administration. In cities the population of which exceeds 10,000, the minister of the interior has the power to place an official appointed by and responsible to him at the head of the police service. He is known as the president of police (*polizei-präsident*). He has charge of the department of public safety in the narrower sense of the term. The other branches of the police service, *i.e.* such as are not immediately concerned with the preservation of peace and order, like the health, trade, and building police, remain a part of the city administration proper.

The cost of the police service is paid out of the state treasury, but the city is required to contribute 2½ marks per capita of population. This represents hardly one-third the entire cost.[1]

To sum up the general characteristics of the Prussian system, we find in the first place a strong tendency towards decentralisation, in order directly to interest a large body of citizens in the work of public administration. In the various deputations, poor-law commissioners, ward provosts, and the like, nearly 10,000 of Berlin's citizens are devoting some of their best energies to the city's welfare.

The city council, while possessing important legislative functions, exercises an important control over the acts of the executive board. The position of the latter both as executive branch of the city government and upper chamber of the legislative branch, gives it the preponderating influence in determining the general policy of the city administration. The unique position occupied by the *deputations* is another of the distinguishing features of the Prussian municipal system. And finally, the fact that at the head of the several municipal departments, and determining their executive policy, we find a series of experts who are devoting their undivided attention to the gradual development of their particular departments, is of the utmost importance in explaining the admirable methods pursued on the more technical sides of municipal action.

[1] Although Berlin pays 2½ marks per capita, the smaller cities pay a much smaller sum. The per capita contribution is graded according to population.

Through this happy combination of individual responsibility and popular control, the administration of Berlin has reached a degree of efficiency to which perhaps no other of the great cities of the world can offer a parallel.

[Gneist, R. von, The Government of Berlin, Contemporary Review, 1884. — Leidig, Preussisches Stadt.—Pollard, James, Berlin : A Study in Municipal Government, London, 1893, Blackwood and Sons. — Rowe, L. S., Die Gemeindefinanzen von Berlin und Paris, Jena, 1893, Gustav Fischer. —Schoen, Paul, Die Organization der städtischen Verwaltung in Preussen.—Hirth's Annalen des Deutschen Reichs, 1891, Nos. 9, 10, and 11.— Steffenhagen, Städtische Verwaltung und Verfassung in Preussen, Berlin, 1887.—Shaw, Albert, Municipal Government in Continental Europe, New York, 1895.] L. S. R.

MUNICIPAL GOVERNMENT IN UNITED STATES OF AMERICA (PENNSYLVANIA, PHILADELPHIA). In considering the question of municipal government in the United States, it is necessary to bear in mind the distinction between the American and the continental ideas of the municipality. In the former the municipality is the creature of the legislature, with clearly and minutely defined powers, which form the absolute limits to its action. No general sphere of municipal action, within the limits of which it may exercise its own discretion without the menace of interference on the part of the state legislature, is recognised. On the European continent we find a much broader view prevailing. The law distinctly recognises a field of municipal action, with which the central government can in no wise, or at least only in extreme cases, interfere. The continual interference of the state legislature in municipal affairs has been one of the characteristic features of municipal development in the United States. The large cities have been the greatest sufferers in this respect, and their history and present condition cannot be understood without a distinct recognition of this fact.

The municipal system of the state of Pennsylvania recognises two kinds of municipal corporations ;—boroughs and cities. The former is, in general, an incorporated township or portion of a township or townships, with less than 10,000 inhabitants. The cities are for purposes of government divided into three distinct classes.[1] The effect of this division upon the question of state interference in municipal affairs we shall have occasion to examine when treating of the municipal provisions in the state constitution. The three classes above mentioned are as follows :

1. Those containing a population of 600,000 or over.
2. Those with less than 600,000 but exceeding 100,000.
3. Those with less than 100,000.

[1] Act, 8th May 1889, Pa. Laws, p. 135, 1. Act held to be constitutional, see Wheeler v. Phila. 77, Pa. 347.

While the differences in the form of government of these various classes of cities are important, the existing organisation of the city of Philadelphia is sufficiently typical to give a general idea of municipal organisation in Pennsylvania. The main differences relate to the number, power, and duties of officers.

In order to understand Philadelphia's present form of government, which only dates from 1887, it is necessary to contrast it with its predecessor. The period of "close corporate" existence, which form had been modelled by Penn in his charter of 1701, after English models, came to an end in 1789, when a modern municipal corporation was created. The history of the city's administration from this period down to its reorganisation in 1887, shows that it was impossible to obtain efficient government with a decentralised system, so long as the attitude of the citizens towards their municipalities remained what it was. The mayor, who was originally a member of councils, soon ceased to be so. The mode of his election also underwent radical changes. At first he was elected by the aldermen ; this plan was followed by a system of election by councils ; and it was not until 1839 that election by the people was introduced. Nor did the extent of his power remain the same. The period immediately succeeding the introduction of popular election of the mayor marks the greatest change in this respect. Up to that time the mayor had full power of appointment. He was now stripped of this. This was but the beginning of a movement which ended in the degradation of the office of mayor to little more than head of the police system. It received no definite check until the new charter of 1885 came into effect in 1887. The extensive power of appointment, as well as other less important functions, were gradually absorbed by city councils, which during the period under consideration had also undergone a change of organisation. In 1796 the legislative branch of the city government became bicameral ; being divided into common and select councils. "They inherited the powers of which the mayor had been shorn, which gave to the local legislature a twofold character ; combining within itself both executive and legislative functions." Its methods were that of government by standing committees. A long chapter of the very worst abuses followed, due to the entire lack of an adequate fixing of responsibility in municipal affairs. In 1854 the consolidation of the surrounding suburban districts with the old " city " took place. No changes in the methods of government were effected however, so that Philadelphia continued to suffer from an inefficient, extravagant, and corrupt administration, of which the history of the Gas Trust, so well described by Mr. Bryce in his American Commonwealth, is but one instance. The agitation for a change in the form of government extends over a series of years, and after one defeat in the state legislature, the act for the "Government of Cities of the First Class" known as the Bullitt Bill, was passed in 1885, and came into effect on the first of April 1887.

The fundamental principles upon which this act is based are those which have found expression in almost all the attempts at the reform of city government in the United States within recent years. It is an attempt to definitely fix responsibility by greatly increasing the power of the mayor; giving to him all the powers of an executive, and taking from the councils as far as possible their executive functions.

The legal position of the American municipality in the state makes it necessary, in order to comprehend the city organisation in all its bearings, to examine the state constitutions, which generally contain provisions which may be regarded as complementary to the municipal corporation acts.

In this sense the Pennsylvania state constitution of 1873 served to pave the way for the radical reforms introduced by the act of 1885. It was hoped that a provision effectually prohibiting special and local legislation would be inserted. As a matter of fact we find such a clause in the state constitution,[1] but owing to the very liberal interpretation of the court as to the power of the legislature to divide the cities into classes, the object intended has not been attained, at any rate as regards Philadelphia. Philadelphia is the only city of the first class in the commonwealth, so that general legislation for cities of the first class is in reality special legislation as regards Philadelphia. A further provision of the state constitution which is of importance in the municipal system deals with the question of city indebtedness prohibiting a county, city, borough, or township from maintaining a debt in excess of seven per centum of the assessed valuation of the taxable property therein contained. But even this provision has shown itself of but little importance. It is only necessary for the city to increase the valuation of its taxable property, which in some cases has been done to the extent of 1000 per cent, in order to make the "seven per cent" extremely elastic. Furthermore the county, the city, the general school district, and the ward school district, have each the same power, so that in one city the actual indebtedness might be 28 per cent and still remain in absolute conformity with the legal provisions. The conditions are somewhat different in Phila-

delphia, where the city and county are co-extensive. Another important clause of the state constitutions is aimed to abolish one of the very worst forms of encroachment upon local self-government, viz., the practice of the state legislature to establish special state commissions entrusted with the execution of municipal improvements and the disbursement of the city revenue. Section 20 of Article iii. provides that "The General Assembly shall not delegate to any special commission, private corporation, or association, any power to make, supervise, or interfere with any municipal improvement money, property, or effects, whether held in trust or otherwise, or to levy taxes, or perform any municipal function whatever." Six further provisions are intended to protect the cities against state legislation on the one hand and local short-sightedness on the other. They may be classified as follows:

1st. Forbidding the state legislature to authorise any local body—be it county, city, borough, township, or other incorporated district—to become a stockholder in any corporation or association, or to lend its credit to such bodies.[1]

2nd. That no such local body shall be authorised to increase its indebtedness by an amount exceeding by two per cent the statutory seven per cent of the assessed property valuation without the consent of the electors at a public election.[2]

3rd. The state government is absolutely forbidden to assume the indebtedness of any local bodies unless such debt be incurred in the suppression of domestic insurrection or to repel invasion.[3]

4th. Upon contracting a debt every local body is required to provide for the annual collection of a tax, in order to meet the payment of interest and the liquidation of the principal within thirty years.[4]

5th. No municipal commission may incur any liability except "in pursuance of an appropriation made therefor by the municipal government."[5]

6th. Every city is required to create a sinking fund which "shall be inviolably pledged for the payment of its funded debt."[6]

With these restrictions and limitations in mind—which at the same time illustrate the American method of dealing with municipalities, —we are prepared to examine the actual provisions of the act of 1st June 1885, which created for the city of Philadelphia in many respects, a new form of government, or at least introduced into it new principles. As we have already seen, the greatest change introduced

---

[1] Act iii. § 7. "The General Assembly shall not pass any local or special laws, authorising the creation, extension, or impairing of liens; regulating the affairs of counties, cities, townships, wards, boroughs, or school districts; authorising the laying out, opening, altering, or maintaining of roads," etc.

[1] Constitution of Pennsylvania, Art. ix. § 7.
[2] Ibid., Art. ix. § 8.
[3] Ibid., Art. ix. § 9.
[4] Ibid., Art. ix. § 10.
[5] Ibid., Art. xv. § 2.
[6] Ibid., Art. xv. § 3.

into the form of city government was in the position of the mayor.[1] It is difficult to understand how the city fared so well under the old *régime*. The city departments were in no way co-ordinated. No unity of purpose and action was possible : continued rivalry and jealousy hampered any general movement for more economical and efficient government ; and responsibility was so divided as to make it practically impossible to definitely fix it upon any one person or even one set of persons. This the new city charter has attempted to remedy through greatly increasing the power of the mayor. He is now the real executive of the city government, so that responsibility for the administration is centred in him. This principle was not, however, carried as far as the original framers of the bill had intended. Instead of placing in his hands the appointment of the heads of all the executive departments, as the theory of full responsibility would require, he was only given the appointment, with and by the consent of select councils, of the three most important of these—viz. the director of the department of public safety, the director of the department of public works, and the president and directors of the board of charities and corrections. Through the provision for a department of public safety the mayor has been relieved of what was formerly his main function—*i.e.* the police administration. Through his power of appointment and dismissal, he still retains the general control of this department. He is furthermore required to see that the ordinances of the city and the laws of the state are executed and enforced, to communicate to councils annually a statement of the finances and general condition of the affairs of the city, to recommend to councils all such measures as he shall deem expedient, to call special meetings of councils when required by public necessity, and "to perform such duties as may be prescribed by law or ordinance ; and he shall be responsible for the good order and efficient government of the city." In order to make the latter provision effective he is given additional far-reaching powers. He convenes the heads of departments for consultation and advice, and calls upon them

[1] The salaries of the more important officials in the city government are as follows :

The Mayor receives	$12,000
Director of Department of Public Safety	10,000
Director of Department of Public Works	10,000
City Comptroller	8,000
City Solicitor	10,000
Receiver of Taxes	10,000
City Treasurer	10,000
Three City Commissioners, each	5,000
Recorder of Deeds	10,000
Registrar of Wills, fees and	5,000
Sheriff	15,000

The last six offices are distinctively county and not municipal offices, but as the city and county of Philadelphia are co-extensive in area, all salaries mentioned above are paid out of a common fund.

for reports ; he is *ex officio* a member of all municipal boards, and has the power to dismiss any officer appointed by him. He may disapprove of any item of appropriation bills ; whereas formerly he was limited to accepting or rejecting the budget *in toto* as voted by the councils. Whenever he thinks proper he may appoint three persons to examine the accounts of any city department, trust officer, or employee. The mayor is elected by the people for a term of four years, and is not re-eligible for the next succeeding term. He must be twenty-five years of age, and have been a citizen and an inhabitant of the state five years and an inhabitant of the city for the same period previous to his election. Besides the three executive departments already mentioned—of two of which the mayor appoints the heads, and, in the case of the department of charities and corrections, the president and directors,—the charter provides for six further departments, making a total of nine,—viz. the department of receiver of taxes, the department of city treasurer, the department of city controller, the department of law, the department of education, and the sinking fund commission. Of these, it is readily seen that the departments of public safety and public works, of which the mayor appoints the directors, are the most important. Under the former the entire police administration is placed, including the health police, which is under the supervision of a board of health composed of five members appointed by the mayor, with the consent of select council, for a term of three years. Of this board the director of public safety is *ex officio* the president. The building police is in the hands of a board of building inspectors composed of three members appointed by the director of the department of public safety. The department of public works—whose director is also appointed by the mayor, with the consent of select council, for a term of four years —includes the management of the water- and gas-works owned by the city and the distribution of the same ; the grading, paving, repairing of the public highways ; the construction and repair of public buildings, with the exception of those used for educational or police purposes, bridges, parks, etc.; surveys, engineering, sewerage, drainage ; and "all matters in any way relating to or affecting the highways, footways, wharves, and docks of the city." One of the exceptions to the general control of this department, and at the same time characteristic of American methods of municipal government, is the existence of the public building commission, which was created by act of the state legislature in 1870 for the erection of public buildings in Philadelphia. This commission is retained and assured independent existence by the new charter.

The third department, wherein the mayor

exercises wide powers of appointment, is that of charities and corrections, which is under the charge of a president and four directors. It has the management of charities, almshouses, hospitals, houses of correction, and like institutions. The power given to the mayor over the six remaining departments is neither so direct nor efficient, inasmuch as he exercises no power of appointment in their general constitution.

The department of receiver of taxes is in charge of a receiver of taxes who is elected by the people every three years. All officers in any way connected with the receipt and collection of city taxes, licences or fees, are under his direction and control.[1] The department of city treasurer is under the direction of a city treasurer who is also elected for a term of three years. He receives the moneys of all the other departments, and pays all warrants duly issued and countersigned. An important provision of the present charter, intended to correct many former abuses, is that "all the moneys . . . of the city received by any officer or agent thereof, shall be deposited daily in the city treasury."[2]

The most important of the financial departments is that of city controller, at whose head is placed an official elected for three years, and known as the "city controller." His functions are numerous, complicated, and upon their proper discharge depends, to a very great extent, the honest and efficient financial administration of the city. He is charged with the inspection, revision, and auditing of the accounts of the several departments and trusts. No warrant may be paid by the city treasurer unless countersigned by him. He has the financial control of the appropriations made by councils, and is personally responsible for any disbursements in excess of such appropriations. He has furthermore very important duties with regard to contracts. The department of law, which has charge of all the legal business of the city as well as the preparation of all contracts, has at its head a "city solicitor," elected for a term of three years. The sinking fund commission, created in 1857, and composed of the mayor, city controller, and a citizen elected by councils, has the management of the sinking fund for the payment of the city debt. The "department of education," which is under the management of a board of 37 members appointed by the court of common pleas, has

general control of the educational system of the city.

We have now before us the executive branch of the city government, viz. the mayor and the various executive departments, the three most important of which are directly dependent upon his choice for their executive heads. In this way the old departmental conflicts have been avoided, as the heads of these departments stand to the mayor somewhat in the same relation as the cabinet to the president of the United States. The position of mayor of Philadelphia has thus been raised to one of high honour and dignity, and it is hoped in this way to attract the very best of its citizens to the office.

Another very characteristic feature of the present city organisation is the position occupied by the legislative branch of the city administration, which comprises a common and a select council. The upper branch or select council is composed of 37 members, one being elected in each ward for a term of three years. The lower branch, or common councils, have 123 members elected in the several wards ; the basis of representation being one member for every 2000 taxable voters of the ward. Councilmen must be residents of the wards from which they are elected. Each branch elects its own president, and these in turn appoint the 20 standing committees of councils. The committees consist of 12 members each, 6 from the lower and 6 from the upper chamber. The presidents are members of the standing committees.

Previous to the adoption of the present charter, the inferior position occupied by the mayor found its complement in the almost unlimited power of councils. To correct the abuses growing out of the exercise of executive functions by the legislative branch was one of the main objects the new charter had in view. It aims at restricting councils to legislative, to the exclusion of executive functions. All ordinances directing or interfering with the exercise of the executive functions of the mayor, departments, boards, or heads or officers thereof, are prohibited. Councils are furthermore deprived of all power of appointment, though the appointment of all officers drawing salaries from the city treasury requires the consent of select councils. Still this principle of relieving councils of executive functions has hardly been consistently carried out, for as regards certain city functions, especially the public highways, public sewers, and the like, councils still exercise distinctively executive functions.

Inasmuch as the city of Philadelphia is coterminous with the county, the duties of certain county officers form a portion of the sum total of the administrative work of the city. These are the county judges, pro-

[1] Two departments which seem naturally to fall within this one department have been expressly excluded by the present charter, viz. the board of revision of taxes, and the board of city trusts. The former is composed of three members appointed by the court of common pleas ; the latter of fifteen members, viz. the mayor, president of the two branches of councils, and twelve citizens appointed by the supreme court, the district court, and the court of common pleas.
[2] Act, 1st June 1885, Art. vi.

thonotary, registrar of wills, recorder of deeds, clerk of quarter sessions, district attorney, coroner, and city commissioner. It has also been decided by the courts that the city treasurer and controller are to be regarded as county as well as city officers. These officers are all elected by the people at the fall election, whereas the election for municipal offices takes place in the early part of the year. To this rule the prothonotary forms an exception, as he is appointed by the board of judges.

In conclusion it may be said that the changes introduced by the charter of 1885, while hardly realising to the full extent the sound theories of government which the framers had in mind, still mark a great step in advance in the American municipal system. More recently Brooklyn has realised still more fully the principle of executive responsibility centred in the mayor and the restriction of the city councils to purely legislative functions. It is curious to note that while the principle of concentration of power is making itself so distinctly felt in American cities, some of the most efficient continental municipalities have been clearly tending towards a division of executive authority amongst a great number of bodies—committees and the like. It remains to be seen whether the American system which aims to give to the mayor a position of such great importance and authority, will be able to withstand the strain which the rapidly increasing sphere of municipal activity will necessarily place upon it.

[Allinson and Penrose, "Philadelphia, 1682-1887," *Johns Hopkins University Studies*, extra vol. ii.—Dillon, John F., *Law of Municipal Corporations*, 4th ed., 1890; Little, Brown, and Co., Boston.—Goodnow, F. J., *Comparative Administrative Law*, 2 vols., Putnams, N.Y., 1894. —Gould, E. R. L., *Local Government in Pennsylvania*, 1st series, *Johns Hopkins University Studies*, No. III.—Howard, *Local Constitutional History of the United States*, *Johns Hopkins University Studies*.]   L. S. R.

MUÑOZ, ANTONIO, is the *nom-de-plume* under which D. Enrique RAMOS (second half of 18th century) published his *Discurso sobre la Economía Política* (Madrid, 1769). His predilection for agriculture displays some leanings towards physiocracy; according to D. Manuel Colmeiro (*Bibl. de Economistas Españoles*) his opinions on cultivation, population, taxation, and trade show discrimination and a sound knowledge of theory.

It was once thought that MUÑOZ was a pseudonym of CAMPOMANES (*q.v.*), but this opinion has been abandoned.   E. Ca.

MÜNSTER, SEBASTIAN (1489-1552), was originally a Franciscan monk, then a teacher at the universities of Heidelberg and Basle.

He wrote in 1540 a German, and in 1550 a Latin, edition of his *Cosmographia Universalis*, which remained a standard book until the 17th century

was already far advanced. Roscher (*Gesch. der Nat. Oek.*, p. 96), describes it as a collective work remarkable for its encyclopædic aims, the accuracy of its information on foreign countries, and the real insight it displays into the economic condition of the latter.   E. Ca.

MURATORI, LUDOVICO ANTONIO (1672-1750), born at Vignola (Modena), a great man in Italian history and literature. His life, first in Milan, then in Modena, was given to study. He was a priest, and the author of many writings, among which the most noteworthy are: *Antiquitates italicæ medii ævi*, Milan, 1738-1743; *Rerum italicarum Scriptores*, Milan, 1723-1738 (xxvii. vols.); and *Annali d' Italia*, Milan, 1744-1749. Recently the importance of Muratori in economics has been recognised. Many of his writings touch upon economics, in the numerous investigations they contain on the economic conditions of mediæval civilisation, the condition of industry, trade, agriculture, and colonisation.

From the point of view of theory, Muratori's ideas on economics are neither original nor profound. He does not understand the nature and character of the laws of value, and, above all, he falls into the grosser errors of mercantilism regarding money and commerce. He confuses the nature and economic use of money, and advises a prince, in order to make his country prosperous, to do all in his power to get as much money as possible into the country and let as little as possible go out. As regards commerce, he combats the prohibition of import of foreign goods, high import duties, and privileges granted to producers in a country to promote its industries. He also advises restrictive measures in the interior. Though failing to understand thoroughly the deeper phenomena of economics, Muratori's mind, better suited to the analysis of historical facts than to economic deductions, succeeds most in researches relating to economic and financial policy, grasping firmly the relations between civil and political institutions and social conditions. Thus Muratori points out the baneful effect of very large holdings, of entails, and of committing properties to trustees. He studied taxation, and went deeply into the question of charity. In his writings on charity he ascribed much importance to benevolent works carried on by the prince of a country to provide for the happiness of his subjects, and studied, from a practical point of view, the organisation of charitable institutions to enable them to attain the object desired. For economists, Muratori's most important works are: *Della carità cristiana* Modena, 1723. — *Rudimenti di filosofia morale*, Modena (undated, probably about 1735).—*Trattato della pubblica felicità*, Modena, 1749.

[On Muratori as a literary man and historian there is an entire library. On Muratori as an economist, see E. Masè Dari, *L. A. Muratori, come economista*, Bologna, 1893. — A. Graziani, *Le idee economiche degli scrittori Emiliani e Romagnoli*, Modena, 1893.]   U. R.

MURDRUM. This term was applied in Norman times to any secret murder, when the criminal could not be discovered. William I. found it necessary to prevent the assassination of his Norman followers by special penalties. It was accordingly enacted that if the body of a murdered man were found and the murderer was unknown, either it must be proved that the dead man was an Englishman, or else a heavy fine was imposed upon the hundred in which the body was discovered. This is sometimes called the law of Englishry. In course of time the term *murdrum* was extended from the offence to the fine levied on the district. By the time of Henry II. the distinction between Norman and Englishman had become so obscured by intermarriage that the law could no longer be enforced in the old sense. The only class that remained distinctly English was that of the villeins, and therefore the *murdrum* was not exacted unless it could be proved that the dead man was a villein. As the motive which had led to the law had now disappeared, the penalty soon became obsolete. [*Dialogus de Scaccario,* i. c. x.]   R. L.

MURRAY, ROBERT (b. 1635), writer on trade, banking, and national revenue. His *Proposal for the Advancement of Trade* started from the position that as the circulation of money was stagnant and depressed trade, the circulation should be increased by using credit instead of money : storehouses on a kind of public pawnbroking basis were to be provided, in which traders were to deposit their "dead stock" at 6 per cent. per annum, and credit notes were to be issued on these goods at $\frac{2}{3}$ or $\frac{3}{4}$ of their then market value. Murray assumes that there will always be a steady market value for "dead stock" when convenient to the proprietor to sell. This assumption vitiates most of his economic suggestions. The *Proposal for the Better Securing our Wooll against Exportation* is based on a protectionist policy, and is a plea to revive and enforce the laws of the staples. All the unemployed are to be set to work, on a credit basis, in growing and working up wool, the object being to find a market by underselling and beating the foreign merchants out of the field. The *Proposal for a National Bank* was inspired by the basis, on public security and under public control, of the Bank of Amsterdam. Murray wished to see a similar bank established in the city of London, "so constituted that no little private sinister ends can possibly be advanced to the public detriment,"—he had failed to grasp the importance of the Bank of England established in the previous year (1694). Murray's bank was to be established on securities in land "or any other valuable securities or depositums" ; it was to supply a public need, to remit money at safe and reasonable rates by means of cheques, and to discount bank, foreign, and inland bills. The *Reasons . . for Translating the Duty of Excise from Mault-Drinks to Mault*—a

change which Murray considered would affect no one but the "consumptioner,"—is only worthy of notice owing to the plea for Free Trade towards the end. The government is asked to "take off all customs for import and export, except of such goods where the duty laid is intended to amount to a prohibition ; this may make England become a free port, the great and good effects of which are too many and too obvious to stand in need to be repeated. This alone . . . will effectually secure our African and East India trade from any whatsoever competitors." In the *Proposal for . . . Advancing to the Crown any Fixed Sum,* etc. he suggests that the state shall issue bills of credit upon Tallies of Pro, struck upon a fund to be formed by settling some branch of the royal revenue to be charged by act of parliament with an annual payment for a limited term, *e.g.* £400,000 for eleven years, or £200,000 for twenty-two years, the bills to range in value from £5 to £100, and to be accepted as legal tender in trade, etc.

The following works were, so far as stated, all published in London :—

A Proposal for the Advancement of Trade upon such Principles as must Necessarily Enforce it, 1676, fol. pp. 7.—*Composition Credit, or a Bank of Credit made Current by Common Consent in London, more Useful than money,* 1682.—*Account of the Constitution and Security of a General Bank of Credit,* 1683.—*A Proposal for a National Bank, consisting of Land, or any other valuable Securities or Depositums ; with a Grand Cash for Returns of Money, etc. . . . the whole to be under the Care, Inspection, Trust, and Controul of the Publick Authority, and Legal Magistracy,* 1695, sm. 4to, pp. 4 and 8.—*A Proposal for the Better Securing our Wooll against Exportation, by Working up, and Manufacturing the same. With the Method and Manner of Setting and Keeping the Poor in Constant and Full Employment. . . . Under the Government of such of the Principal Nobility and Gentry . . . who are willing to undertake so Good and Pious a Work,* n.d. (? 1695), sm. 4to, pp. 4.—*A Proposal for the more Easie Advancing to the Crown any Fixed Sum of Mony, to carry on the War against France ; And Payment of the Debts Contracted thereby,* n.d. but probably 1696.—*Reasons Humbly Offer'd to the Honble. House of Commons, for Translating the Duty of Excise from Mault-Drinks to Mault ; whereby may be Advanced to the Crown above Twenty Millions, for Carrying on the War against France,* n.d. sm. 4to, pp. 4 (another edition with slightly different wording).—*An Advertisement for the more easy and speedy collecting of Debts,* n.d.

[M'Culloch, *Lit. Pol. Econ.,* p. 159.—*Dictionary of National Biography,* art. "Murray, Robert."] (See also CHAMBERLEN, HUGH ; LAW, JOHN ; LEWIS, M.)   E. D.

MURRAY, WILLIAM. See MANSFIELD, FIRST EARL OF.

MUSCOVY CO. See RUSSIA CO.

MUSHET, ROBERT (1782-1828), entered the royal mint about 1804. He became a recognised authority on the currency question, (see BULLION COMMITTEE, REPORT OF), and gave evidence before the committees of the Houses of Lords and Commons which sat in 1819, on the resumption of cash payments.

His works comprise *An enquiry into the effect produced on the national currency and rates of exchange by the Bank Restriction Bill*, 3rd ed. corrected and enlarged, London, 1811, 8vo, in this a seignorage of 10 per cent on the silver coin is recommended, and an arrangement for the management of the silver currency.—*Tables exhibiting the gain and loss to the fund-holders arising from the fluctuations in the value of the Currency from 1800 to 1821*, 2nd ed. corrected, London, 1821, 8vo, the best history of the variations between the value of the gold coin and the paper in circulation at this period.—*An attempt to explain the effect of the issues of Bank of England upon its own interests, public credit, and county banks*, London, 1826, 8vo.

[*Dictionary of National Biography*, vol. xxxix. p. 430.—See also Ricardo, *Letters to M'Culloch*, ed. by Hollander, American Econ. Association, vol. x. pp. 111-113, 1895. Ricardo criticised the *Tables* and Mushet incorporated his suggestions in 2nd ed. 1821.—*Reports from, and evidence taken before, the Committees of the Houses of Lords and Commons on the expediency of the Bank of England resuming Cash Payments*, 1819.] H. E. E.

MUTUAL INSURANCE. See INSURANCE, MUTUAL.

MUTUUM is one of the *real* contracts of Roman law. It is a contract of loan which is created by the lender delivering to the borrower a thing of an exchangeable kind, "*res fungibilis*" (see FUNGIBLES), such as money, so as to make the borrower owner of it, on the express or implied understanding that an equal quantity of the same kind of thing is to be returned. The lender cannot claim interest on the loan unless he makes a special contract distinct from the *mutuum*, entitling him to do so. It is distinguished from COMMODATUM, where the actual thing lent is the thing to be returned (see also LOAN, CANONIST DEFINITION OF). E. A. W.

END OF VOL. II

LIST OF CONTRIBUTORS

TO THE PRESENT AND PREVIOUS VOLUME.

INITIALS.	NAMES.
B. L. A.	B. LIONEL ABRAHAMS, India Office.
C. M. A.	Professor CHARLES M. ANDREWS, Bryn Mawr College, U.S.A.
F. A.	FREDERICK ATTERBURY, Secretaries' Office, Inland Revenue.
F. E. A.	F. E. ALLUM, Royal Mint, Tower Hill.
W. J. A.	W. J. ASHLEY, M.A., Professor of Economic History in Harvard University.
A. B.	Professor ANGELO BERTOLINI, Bari, Italy.
A. E. B.	A. E. BATEMAN, Board of Trade.
C. F. B.	C. F. BASTABLE, LL.D., Professor of Political Economy in Trinity College, Dublin.
E. E. N. B.	E. E. N. BOWER, Assistant Secretary, Inland Revenue.
E. W. B	EDWARD W. BRABROOK, Chief Registrar of Friendly Societies.
G. B.	GYULA BECK DE MADARAS, Doctor Juris, University of Budapest.
J. B.	J. BONAR, M.A., LL.D., Civil Service Commission.
J. G. B.	JOHN GRAHAM BROOKS, Cambridge, Mass., U.S.A.
R. C. B.	R. C. BEAZLEY.
R. W. B.	R. W. BARNETT.
S. B.	STEPHAN BAUER, Doctor Juris, University, Vienna ; Handelskammer, Brünn, Austria.
S. BO.	STEPHEN BOURNE, F.S.S.
S. C. B.	SYDNEY C. BUXTON, M.P.
T. G. B.	Rev. T. G. BONNEY, D.Sc., F.R.S., Professor of Geology and Mineralogy, University of London.
A. C.	Rev. A. CALDECOTT, M.A., Fellow of St. John's College, Cambridge.
A. C. f.	A. COURTOIS, fils, Secrétaire Perpétuel de la Société d'Economie Politique de Paris.
A. B. C.	A. B. CLARK, M.A.

INITIALS.	NAMES.
A. K. C.	A. K. CONNELL, M.A., New College Oxford.
C. E. C.	CLARA E. COLLET, M.A.
C. G. C.	C. G. CRUMP, Public Record Office.
E. C.	EDWIN CANNAN, M.A., Balliol College, Oxford.
E. Ca.	E. CASTELOT, Correspondent of the British Economic Association, Paris.
G. C.	GEORGE CLARE.
J. B. C.	J. B. CLARK, Ph.D., Professor of Political Economy, Amherst College, Amherst, Mass.
M. D. C	His Honour Judge M. D. CHALMERS, Member of the Council of H.M.'s Secretary of State for India.
P. G. C.	Major P. G. CRAIGIE, Board of Agriculture.
R. C.	ROBERT CHALMERS, Treasury.
W. C.	Rev. Professor W. CUNNINGHAM, D.D., Fellow of Trinity College, Cambridge.
W. J. C.	W. J. CORBETT, M.A., Fellow of King's College, Cambridge.
A. D.	Dr. A. DANIELL, Advocate, Edinburgh.
C. F. D.	C. F. DUNBAR, LL.D., Professor of Political Economy in Harvard University.
D. R. D.	D. R. DEWEY, Ph.L.D., Professor, Massachusetts Institute of Technology, Boston, Mass.
E. D.	E. DIXON, Girton Coll., Cambridge.
M. G. D.	MARK G. DAVIDSON, Advocate, Edinburgh.
T. W. R. D.	T. W. RHYS DAVIDS, LL.D., Ph.D., Professor of Pali and Buddhist Literature in University College, London.
A. E.	A. ELLIS.
F. Y. E.	F. Y. EDGEWORTH, M.A., D.C.L., Professor of Political Economy in the University of Oxford.

INITIALS.	NAMES.
H. E. E.	HUGH E. EGERTON, M.A., Oxon. ; Barrister-at-Law.
R. T. E.	R. T. ELY, Director of the School of Economics, Political Science, and History, and Professor of Political Economy in the University of Wisconsin.
T. H. E.	T. H. ELLIOTT, Secretary, Board of Agriculture.
A. de F.	A. DE FOVILLE, Directeur de l'Admn. des Monnaies de France, Membre de l'Institut, Paris.
A. W. F.	A. W. FLUX, M.A., Fellow of St. John's College, Cambridge, Owens College, Manchester
C. A. F.	CAROLINE A. FOLEY, M.A. (Mrs. T. W. Rhys Davids).
S. N. F.	STEPHEN N. FOX, B.A.
W. F.	WILLIAM FOWLER, LL.B.
C. G.	C. GIDE, Professeur d'Économie Politique à la Faculté de Droit de Montpellier, France.
C. Gr.	Dr. CHAS. GROSS, A.M., Inst. in History in Harvard University, Cambridge, Mass.
E. C. K. G.	E. C. K. GONNER, M.A., Professor of Political Economy in the University College, Liverpool.
E. O. G.	E. O. GREENING.
F. H. G.	F. H. GIDDINGS, M.A., Professor of Sociology in Columbia University, New York City.
H. de B. G.	Rev. H. de B. GIBBINS, Head Master, Liverpool College.
H. B. G.	H. B. GREVEN, Professor of Political Economy in the University of Leyden, Holland.
J. G.	JOHN GLOVER, F.S.S.
A. H.	A. HUGHES, Public Record Office.
A. T. H.	A. T. HADLEY, Professor of Political Economy in Yale University, New Haven, Connecticut, U.S.A.
C. A. H.	C. A. HARRIS, Chr. Coll., Cambridge, Colonial Office.
E. H.	ELIJAH HELM, Manchester.
F. H.	F. HENDRIKS, F.S.S., F.I.A.
G. H. H.	G. H. HUNT, Treasury.
H. H.	HENRY HIGGS, LL.B., Secretary's Department, General Post Office.
H. Ha.	HUBERT HALL, Public Record Office.
R. H.	RICHARD HOWLETT, F.S.A. Civil Service Commission.
R. H. H.	REGINALD H. HOOKER, Agricultural Department.
W. H.	WYNNARD HOOPER.

INITIALS.	NAMES.
W. A. S. H.	W. A. S. HEWINS, M.A., Pembroke College, Oxford ; Director of the London School of Economic and Political Science.
J. K. I.	J. K. INGRAM, LL.D., Senior Lecturer in Trinity College, Dublin.
J. W. B. I.	J. W. BRODIE INNES.
E. J.	E. JOHNSTONE.
J. W. J.	J. W. JENKS, Ph.D., Professor of Political Science, Cornell University, U.S.A.
W. E. J.	W. E. JOHNSON, M.A., King's College, Cambridge.
G. K.	GEORGE KING, Vice-President of the Institute of Actuaries, and Chairman of the Life Offices Association.
J. B. K.	JOHN BOYD KINNEAR, Barrister-at-Law, Lincoln's Inn.
J. N. K.	J. N. KEYNES, M.A., D.Sc., late Fellow of Pembroke College, Cambridge.
M. K.	Rev. M. KAUFMANN, M.A.
A. L.	ALICE LAW, Girton College, Cambridge.
Ach. L.	ACHILLE LORIA, Professor of Political Economy at the University of Padua ; Correspondent of the British Economic Association.
A. F. V. L.	A. F. V. LEYDEN, Doctor of Law, Holland.
C. S. L.	C. S. LOCH, B.A.
E. L.	EMANUEL LESER, Ph.D., Professor of Political Economy in the University of Heidelberg.
E. de L.	Professor E. DE LAVELEYE, Liège.
G. B. L.	G. B. LONGSTAFF, M.A., M.D.
I. S. L.	I. S. LEADAM, M.A., formerly Fellow of Brasenose College, Oxford.
R. L.	R. LODGE, M.A., Professor of History in the University of Glasgow.
S. M. L.	STANLEY M. LEATHES, M.A., Fellow of Trinity College, Cambridge.
S. M'C. L.	Dr. S. M'C. LINDSAY, Assistant Professor of Sociology, University of Pennsylvania, U.S.A.
T. L.	T. LONGHURST, Hon. Secy., British Chamber of Commerce, Paris.
T. J. L.	Rev. T. J. LAWRENCE, M.A., LL.D., Rector of Girton ; Lecturer in Maritime Law at the Royal Naval College, Greenwich.
W. L.	WALTER LUPTON.

INITIALS.	NAMES.
A. C. M.	A. C. MILLER, M.A., Professor, University of Chicago.
E. M.	EWING MATHIESON.
E. A. M.	ELLEN A. M'ARTHUR, Vice-Mistress and Lecturer of Girton College, Cambridge.
F. C. M.	F. C. MONTAGUE, M.A., sometime Fellow of Oriel College, Oxford, Professor of History in University College, London.
F. W. M.	F. W. MAITLAND, LL.D., Professor of the Laws of England in the University of Cambridge.
J. M.	Professor JAMES MAVOR, University of Toronto.
J. E. C. M.	J. E. C. MUNRO, LL.D., Lincoln's Inn.
J. S. M.	J. S. MACKENZIE, Professor of Philosophy, University College, Cardiff.
M. T. M.	MARY TRICE MARTIN.
R. M.-S.	RICHMOND MAYO-SMITH, Ph.D., Professor, Columbia University, New York City.
S. M.	SAMUEL MONTAGU, M.P.
J. N.	J. NISBET.
J. S. N.	J. S. NICHOLSON, M.A., D.Sc., Professor of Political Economy in the University of Edinburgh.
V. N.	VAUGHAN NASH.
A. O.	Professor A. ONCKEN, University of Berne.
E. B. O.	E. B. OSBORN, M.A.
S. O.	SYDNEY OLIVIER, B.A.
E. G. P.	ELEANOR G. POWELL, Somerville College, Oxford.
F. P.	Sir FREDERICK POLLOCK, Bart., M.A., Professor of Jurisprudence in the University of Oxford.
G. H. P.	G. H. POWNALL.
G. R. P.	G. R. PARKIN.
H. H. P.	H. H. POWERS, Ph.D., Professor of Economics, Leland Stanford Jr. University, California.
J. P.	J. PEIRSON, F.C.A.
J. R. P.	J. R. PAGET, M.A., Temple.
L. L. P.	L. L. PRICE, M.A., Oriel College, Oxford.
L. R. P.	Rev. L. R. PHELPS, M.A., Fellow of Oriel College, Oxford.
M. P.	Signor M. PANTALEONI, Rome.
R. E. P.	R. E. PROTHERO, M.A., late Fellow of All Souls College, Oxford.
R. L. P.	R. L. POOLE, M.A., Jesus College, Oxford.
W. P.	Rev. WILLIAM PATRICK, D.D.

INITIALS.	NAMES.
D. G. R.	D. G. RITCHIE, M.A., Professor of Logic and Metaphysics, University of St. Andrews, N.B.
E. R.	E. RIGG, Royal Mint, Tower Hill.
G. R.	Professor G. ROSSI, Office of the Treasury, Rome.
J. R.	JOHN RAE, M.A.
J. D. R.	J. D. ROGERS, M.A., B.C.L., Barrister-at-Law, formerly Stowell Fellow of University College, London.
J. E. T. R.	Professor J. E. THOROLD ROGERS, M.A., sometime Professor of Political Economy in the University of Oxford.
L. S. R.	Dr. LEO S. ROWE, Philadelphia.
T. R.	T. RALEIGH, M.A., Fellow of All Souls College, Oxford.
U. R.	UGO RABBENO, Professor of Political Economy at the University of Modena.
V. R.	VICTOR ROSEWATER, Ph.D., Columbia.
W. R.-A.	Professor W. ROBERTS-AUSTEN, F.R.S., Royal Mint, Tower Hill.
A. E. S.	A. E. STAMP, M.A., Public Record Office.
C. A. V. S.	Dr. C. A. VERRIJN STUART, Secretary of the Central Commission of Statistics, The Hague, Holland.
E. S.	E. SCHUSTER (Doctor Juris, University, Munich), Lincoln's Inn.
E. R. A. S.	Professor E. R. A. SELIGMAN, Ph.D., Columbia University, New York City.
F. E. S.	F. E. STEELE.
G. B. S.	G. BARNETT SMITH.
G. F. S.	GUSTAV F. STEFFEN.
H. S.	HENRY SIDGWICK, Litt.D., Professor of Moral Philosophy in the University of Cambridge.
H. M. S.	H. MORSE STEPHENS, M.A., late of Balliol College, Oxford.
J. S.	JOHN SMITH, Board of Trade.
T. G. S.	T. G. SPYERS, B.A., late Demy of Magdalen College, Oxford, Barrister-at-Law, Inner Temple.
W. S.	WILLIAM SMART, M.A., Lecturer on Political Economy, Queen Margaret College, Glasgow.
W. A. S.	W. A. SHAW, Public Record Office.
W. H. S.	W. H. SMITH, Royal Court of Justice.
F. W. T.	Professor F. W. TAUSSIG, LL.B., Ph.D., Harvard University.
H. R. T.	H. R. TEDDER.
R. W. C. T.	R. W. COOKE TAYLOR, H.M. Superintending Inspector of Factories and Workshops.

INITIALS.	NAMES.
N. P. V. de B.	Dr. N. P. VAN DEN BERG, Governor of the Bank of Holland, Amsterdam.
B. E. W.	B. E. WALKER, Toronto, Canada.
E. W.	E. WATERHOUSE, B.A.
E. A. W.	E. A. WHITTUCK, M.A., Oriel College, Oxford.
F. A. W.	General F. A. WALKER, President of the Massachusetts Institute of Technology, Boston, Mass., U.S.A.
G. W.	GRAHAM WALLAS, M.A.
H. G. W.	HENRY GEORGE WILLINK.
H. L. W.	HENRY LEE WARNER, M.A., late Fellow of St. John's College, Cambridge.
J. W.	J. WESTLAKE, Q.C.
P. W.	PAUL WATERHOUSE, M.A., A.R.I.B.A., Balliol College, Oxford.
P. H. W.	Rev. P. H. WICKSTEED, M.A.
S. W.	SPENSER WILKINSON, M.A., late of Merton College, Oxford.

The EDITOR takes the responsibility of the unsigned Articles.

Printed by R. & R. CLARK, LIMITED, *Edinburgh.*

CPSIA information can be obtained at www.ICGtesting.com
Printed in the USA
LVOW12s0025200215

427592LV00002B/91/P